Russia, U   & Bela

a Lonely Planet travel survival kit

John Noble
Andrew Humphreys
Richard Nebeský
Nick Selby
George Wesely
John King

Russia, Ukraine & Belarus

1st edition

Published by
Lonely Planet Publications
Head Office: PO Box 617, Hawthorn, Vic 3122, Australia
Branches: 155 Filbert St, Suite 251, Oakland, CA 94607, USA
                    10 Barley Mow Passage, Chiswick, London W4 4PH, UK
                    71 bis rue du Cardinal Lemoine, 75005 Paris, France

Printed by
Colorcraft Ltd, Hong Kong

Photographs by

Andrew Humphreys	John King
Richard Nebesky	John Noble
Nick Selby	Robert Strauss
George Wesely	Roger Hayne

Front cover: Church of the Intercession on the Nerl, Boglyubovo (John Noble)

First Published
January 1996
Reprinted with August 1996 Update supplement

Although the authors and publisher have tried to make the information as accurate as possible, they accept no responsibility for any loss, injury or inconvenience sustained by any person using this book.

National Library of Australia Cataloguing in Publication Data

Russia, Ukraine & Belarus.

    1st ed.
    Includes index.
    ISBN 0 86442 320 9.

    1. Russia (Federation) – Guidebooks. 2. Ukraine –
    Guidebooks. 3. Belarus – Guidebooks. I. Noble,
    John, 1951 Oct. 11 – . (Series: Lonely Planet travel
    survival kit).

914.7

text & maps © Lonely Planet 1996
photos © photographers as indicated 1996
climate charts compiled from information supplied by Patrick J Tyson, © Patrick J Tyson, 1996

John Noble

John comes from the valley of the River Ribble in northern England and finds the culture shock of Russia greater than any other country he has visited. That's probably why he keeps going back there. He worked on several Lonely Planet guides in three continents before taking on, with John King, the gargantuan *USSR – a travel survival kit* project in 1989. When that book was finally, irrevocably being printed 2½ years later, the country it was about decided to abolish itself. John took a long, deep breath, then returned to the ex-USSR to write Lonely Planet's *Baltic States* guide, followed by parts of this book, which he coordinated, and *Central Asia*. He now lives in that favourite New Russians' holiday spot, southern Spain, along with his wife Susan Forsyth (also an experienced ex-USSR traveller) and children Isabella and Jack, who have yet to sample life beyond the Zapadny Bug.

Andrew Humphreys

Born in England, Andrew stayed around just long enough to complete his studies in architecture before relocating to Egypt. He stayed there for three years, documenting Islamic monuments and working for the country's largest English-language magazine, *Cairo Today*. In 1991, he took a circuitous sweep via Jamaica to land in newly independent Estonia, where he began working for the *Tallinn City Paper* before co-founding a new publication, *The Baltic Outlook*. Whilst living in Estonia, Andrew updated the Baltic chapters of Lonely Planet's *Scandinavian & Baltic Europe on a shoestring*. With the last vestiges of his Siberian suntan now fading, Andrew is currently completing his 'post-Soviet trilogy', co-authoring the upcoming *Central Asia – a travel survival kit*.

Richard Nebesky

Richard was born in Prague but left with his family after the Soviet-led invasion in 1968 and came to Australia. With a BA in politics and history, he took to the road, and has travelled, skied and worked in Europe, Asia, North America and Africa. He joined Lonely

Planet in 1987, and since then he has been co-author of LP's *Eastern* and *Central Europe* phrasebooks, *Prague city guide* and *Czech & Slovak Republics* guide, and has helped to update *Australia*, *Indonesia* and *Thailand*. For this book, Richard updated and expanded the Volga Region and Caucasus chapters and the Voronezh and Ramon sections of Western European Russia.

Nick Selby

Nick was born and raised in New York City. He worked for five years as a sound engineer, but after 3½ years in a two-metre-by-two-metre cubicle mixing music for an American soap opera, be decided that anything – *anything* – would be a step up. In 1990 he took a job as a morning DJ at Warsaw's first privately owned radio station, Radio Zet, and soon afterwards did a stint as a creative director at a multinational advertising agency there (a post from which he was unceremoniously sacked). With another American expat, he set up Fresh Air Publications Russia in St Petersburg, and in 1992 he wrote *The Visitor's Guide to the New Saint Petersburg*. Since travelling around Asia and all too little of Australia in 1993, he now spends his time travelling and writing with Corinna, his wife.

George Wesely

George was raised in California amid the rich traditions of a Ukrainian family. He studied architecture in both Copenhagen and Budapest, mingling his education with extensive travel jaunts with his wife Lori. After eventually receiving the degree of Master of Architecture from UC Berkeley in 1993, he moved to Prague, where he lived and worked for a year before researching and writing the Ukraine and Belarus sections of this book. He currently lives in San Francisco and between travels works in the profession of architecture.

John King

John grew up in the USA, destined for the academic life, but in a rash moment in 1984 he took off to China for a year, teaching

English and travelling. Since then he has squeezed out a living as a travel writer and photographer, encouraged by his wife, Julia Wilkinson, who does the same. Together they split their time at 'home' between south-west England and remoter parts of Hong Kong. John is author of LP's *Karakoram Highway – a travel survival kit*, co-author of *Prague* and *Czech & Slovak Republics*, and is at present hard at work on the forthcoming LP guide to *Central Asia*. As co-author, with John Noble, of the original LP *USSR* guide, John laid many of the foundations upon which this book was built.

From the Authors

John Noble John would like to thank everyone who helped him gather information along the way – especially Carl Dwyer, Natalia Glukhova, Sergey Kurgin and Kostya, Tom Hochman, Jan Passoff, Colin Richardson, Olga Rybakova, Neil Taylor, and all those readers of *USSR – a travel survival kit* who wrote in with tips; Andrew, George, Nick and Richard for their enthusiasm, dedication and stamina; Lonely Planet's London office for passing on all those faxes and e-mails; the team in Melbourne (too many to mention individually) for their heroic efforts in managing to keep this sprawling project on schedule; and not least the Great Bear itself – 'Once it gets its claws into you...'

Andrew Humphreys Blessings to John Noble for laying much of the groundwork in Kaliningrad and to John King for breaking the ice in Siberia. Thank you also to the 'without whom brigade': Jan Passoff of the Travellers Guest House in Moscow; Michael Spectre of the New York Times; Rashit Yahin in Severobaikalsk; Yuri Nimerovsky and Angus Mackay in Irkutsk; Nadia Storozh and Sveta Musatova in Khabarovsk; Marko Arolinna, Helen Melnikova and Jeff Bond in Vladivostok; Dennis Kirichenko in Petropavlovsk. However, the heights of my gratitude are reserved for Gädi Farfour, my companion on the tracks for much of the research. And if the quality of information seems to taper a little in the Far East, that's because Gädi had gone home.

Richard Nebesky Richard would like to thank John Noble, all the Lonely Planet staff who worked on the guide, and the following people who helped him along the way in Russia: Natasha Pechyonkina, Oleg Gavrilov and his colleagues, Larisa A Shramkova, Nonna B Kerkis and Jan Passof.

Nick Selby Many thanks to John Noble and Richard Nebesky, Elena Vvedenskaya, Regina Shoykut, Steven Caron (twice), Angela Wilson, Bernard Goldstein, Eugene Patron, Nancy, John & Ben, Ann-Sofie and Lars Gyllenhaal and Peder Axenstein, Valyery Berlin, Lloyd Donaldson, Christy Wyatt, Eric Johnson, Melanie Morningstar, Petri and the staff at the Helsinki Eurohostel, Scott Wayne and the WTO, Tom Brosnahan, Dr Madelaine Stein, Shannon Farley, the Harvard Russian Research Center and the Weidener Library, the AAASS, REI Adventure Travel, Merilee at the Boston Youth Hostel, Eric Johnson and Internews Moscow, Reiner, Sabine, Anja and Gino, and most important, Corinna. Thanks also to Suzanne Brammerloh at Peter TIPS, and to Margaret Phillips and Eriko Kojima, two intrepid travellers who took the Valaam Overland challenge and passed with flying colours! Finally, big thanks to the staff at the UK and Australian offices of LP.

George Wesely Special thanks to Debra Friedman for her kind hospitality in Kiev, as well as to Oksana Shubovich, Todd and the rest of the Kiev gang; to Bill Pridemore and Liz Soller for a fine evening in Kharkiv; to William Boggs and Anne Zollner for their kindness in Odessa; to Shannon Matthews for good insight in Ivano-Frankivsk; to Chris 'the Juggler' Sly, Heather Balaam and the rest of the Minsk contingency for their fun and games; and finally to Luis Bravo, Ian McGonagle and all of the Prague companions for providing a safe refuge. Above all, thanks to my wife Lori for her invaluable companionship, research, guidance, love and support.

Thanks are also due to those travellers who took the time and trouble to write to us about their experiences in the former USSR; they are listed at the end of the book.

From the Publisher
This book was edited by Nick Tapp, Brigitte Barta, Miriam Cannell, Jane Fitzpatrick, Janet Austin, Lindsay Brown, Steve Townshend, Paul Smitz, Kristin Odijk, Steve Womersley and Diana Saad. Sally Steward and Louise Callan helped with the language section, and Alison White, Jane Marks, Adrienne Costanzo, Anne Mulvaney, Suzi Petkovski and Carolyn Hubbard did additional proofing and map-checking. Richard Nebesky keyed in most of the Cyrillic script, and Kolya Cowall (Russian), Zina Sinitsky and Sophia Kats (Ukrainian), and Steve Elkanovich (Belarusian) proofed and assisted with Cyrillic languages. Special thanks to Dan Levin for creating and managing the Cyrillic font. Andrew Tudor coordinated the mapping, design, illustration and layout of the book with assistance from Jacqui Saunders, Chris Klep, Tamsin Wilson, Margaret Jung, Jane Hart, Louise Keppie and Trudi Canavan, who variously drew maps and illustrations. Peter Morris drew the cartoons. Kerrie Williams did the index.

Warning & Request
Things change – prices go up, schedules change, good places go bad and bad places go bankrupt – nothing stays the same. So if you find things better or worse, recently opened or long since closed, please write and tell us and help make the next edition better.

Your letters will be used to help update future editions and, where possible, important changes will also be included in an Update section in reprints.

We greatly appreciate all information that is sent to us by travellers. Back at Lonely Planet we employ a hard-working readers' letters team to sort through the many letters we receive. The best ones will be rewarded with a free copy of the next edition or another Lonely Planet guide if you prefer. We give away lots of books, but, unfortunately, not every letter/postcard receives one.

Contents

THE RUSSIAN FAR EAST 828

UKRAINE

FACTS ABOUT UKRAINE 873

FACTS FOR THE VISITOR 901

GETTING THERE & AWAY 929

GETTING AROUND..937

KIEV 944

CENTRAL UKRAINE..979

WESTERN UKRAINE...989

Map Legend

BOUNDARIES

.... International Boundary
.... Regional Boundary

ROUTES

.... Freeway
.... Highway
.... Major Road
.... Unsealed Road or Track
.... City Road
.... City Street
.... Railway
.... Underground Railway
.... Tram
.... Walking Track
.... Walking Tour
.... Ferry Route
.... Cable Car or Chairlift

AREA FEATURES

.... Parks
.... Built-Up Area
.... Pedestrian Mall
.... Market
.... Cemetery
.... Forest
.... Glacier, Ice Cap
.... Mountain Ranges

HYDROGRAPHIC FEATURES

.... Coastline
.... River, Creek
.... Intermittent River or Creek
.... Rapids, Waterfalls
.... Lake, Intermittent Lake
.... Canal
.... Swamp

SYMBOLS

✪ CAPITAL	.... National Capital	
◉ Capital	.... Regional Capital	
CITY	.... Major City	
● City	.... City	
● Town	.... Town	
● Village	.... Village	
▼	.... Place to Stay, Place to Eat	
☕	.... Cafe, Pub or Bar	
✉ ☎	.... Post Office, Telephone	
❶ $	.... Tourist Information, Bank	
☻ Ⓟ	.... Transport, Parking	
🏛 ⌂	.... Museum, Youth Hostel	
⌐⌐ ⚑	Caravan Park, Camping Ground	
✝ ✝	.... Church, Cathedral	
☪ ✡	.... Mosque, Synagogue	
⌸ ⌸	Buddhist Temple, Hindu Temple	
✛ ★	.... Hospital, Police Station	

.... Embassy, Petrol Station
.... Airport, Airfield
.... Metro Station, Swimming Pool
.... Shopping Centre, Gardens
.... Winery or Vineyard, Zoo
.... One Way Street, Route Number
.... Stately Home, Monument
.... Castle, Tomb
.... Cave, Hut or Chalet
.... Mountain or Hill, Lookout
.... Lighthouse, Shipwreck
.... Pass, Spring
.... Beach, Surf Beach
.... Archaeological Site or Ruins
.... Ancient or City Wall
.... Cliff or Escarpment, Tunnel
.... Railway Station

Note: not all symbols displayed above appear in this book

Introduction

Russia, Ukraine and Belarus, the three core republics of the old Soviet Union, were the ones that finally killed off the USSR with their Minsk Declaration of December 1991, which proclaimed that the Soviet Union no longer existed and set up instead a much looser grouping of fully independent nations, the Commonwealth of Independent States (CIS). Since then the three neighbours have followed separate paths, all struggling to find their feet as independent countries, with Ukraine often at loggerheads with Russia, but Belarus forging closer ties with its big neighbour once an initial surge of nationalist energy had been spent.

The three countries have many differences but also much in common. Their peoples form the three branches of the Eastern Slav group, with a shared heritage which goes back to the Kievan Rus state founded in the 9th century. Their languages are distinct but closely related. Most of Ukraine and Belarus were part of the Russian Empire for over a century before they became founding members of the USSR in 1922. Today, all three countries are going through similar upheavals as they try to adapt to massive change – from cogs in the Soviet machine to separate nations with, to varying extents, free-market economies. Old certainties and systems of work, beliefs, state support, law and order, ethnic relations, transport, and more, have evaporated. New hardship, uncertainty and conflict – between regions, religions, ethnic groups – have arisen as a result. The level of crime has increased. But gradually, patchily, something new is emerging, symbolised by the lines of private-enterprise kiosks along city streets, selling anything from vodka and Marlboro cigarettes to socks and soap. A few traders have made huge personal fortunes. Beggars have also appeared, but fears of starvation have receded. The majority of the three countries' many ethnic groups seem to have decided that cohabiting is better than seceding or fighting. It's fascinating to witness this transformation.

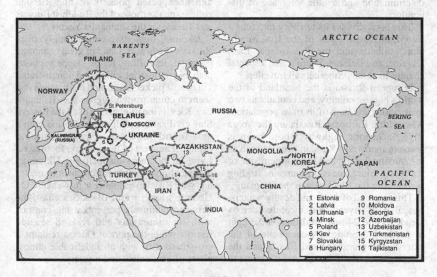

1 Estonia	9 Romania
2 Latvia	10 Moldova
3 Lithuania	11 Georgia
4 Minsk	12 Azerbaijan
5 Poland	13 Uzbekistan
6 Kiev	14 Turkmenistan
7 Slovakia	15 Kyrgyzstan
8 Hungary	16 Tajikistan

The territory the three countries cover stretches almost halfway round the globe, across 11 time zones. At the same moment as potato farmers in Belarus climb down from their tractors after a day's work, reindeer herders in Kamchatka, in Russia's Far East, may be rousing their herds for the next day's grazing. As well as endless tracts of forest, steppe and plain, these countries contain great variety of landscape – as well as of people, culture and fauna.

This whole canvas is now spread open as never before for travellers. Gone are Soviet-era restrictions on movement and much of the clogging red tape. Despite stories in Western media about economic collapse, ethnic strife, escalating crime and deathtrap aircraft, travel in Russia, Ukraine and Belarus is no more daunting than in most of the rest of the world. True, trains are slow, flying potentially hazardous, and the older hotels often dilapidated. But a new wave of finer hotels, good restaurants and private tourist services is rippling out from the major cities. Costs can be tailored to almost any budget. To explore these countries, all you need are a sense of curiosity and, when appropriate, a sensible caution, a spot of determination and a little tolerance of discomfort.

This book divides its territory into four – European Russia (west of the Ural Mountains); Siberia and the Russian Far East; Ukraine; and Belarus. There's also a special chapter for Trans-Siberian rail travellers.

European Russia is the heartland of the world's biggest country, and contains its two major cities and four-fifths of its population. Also within European Russia are the Volga River, a historic highway whose basin is home to many non-Russian peoples such as the Muslim Tatars; and the northern side of the spectacular Caucasus mountains striding across from the Black Sea to the Caspian.

This is a land of snow and deadly winters, but also of rivers that meander across meadows and 24-hour midsummer daylight in northern latitudes. A composite of the extravagant glories of old Russia and the drab legacies of the Soviet era, it's home to the mysteries of the Orthodox Church, to rusting industrial cities and millions of people who still work the land, and to the 'New Russians', the generation making the most of the anything-goes post-Soviet era. Its people, in the words of one of their own proverbs, 'love to suffer', yet they also love to party and can be disarmingly warm-hearted and hospitable.

From Russia's European heartland the old tsarist empire spread out to absorb hundreds of neighbouring peoples – across Siberia to the Pacific, westward into Ukraine and Belarus, and south to other areas now again independent of Russia, the Transcaucasus and Central Asia.

Siberia, for generations a place of snowbound exile for people the rulers in Moscow or St Petersburg didn't like, today has its share of industrial development and cities, but remains mostly untamed and empty of people. Famed among travellers as the reason for the world's longest train ride, it's also dotted with some of the globe's major natural wonders – the exquisite Altay Mountains; serene Lake Baikal, the world's deepest and, some say, most beautiful lake; the volcanoes and geysers of Kamchatka – and unexpected pockets of non-Russian culture such as those of the Buddhist Buryats and Tuvans or the shamanist Yakuts.

Ukraine, now emerging strongly from Russia's shadow, is a land of great economic potential. Its rolling, fertile steppe supports both big industrial cities and innumerable villages of picket fences and duck ponds that seem to come from a bygone age. Its major city, Kiev, is the mother city of all the Eastern Slav civilisations, full of history and with a new-found importance as the national capital. The west of the country, focused on Lviv, is the most distinctively Ukrainian region, almost Central European in character and with Russian influence at its weakest. On Ukraine's long, warm Black Sea coast, the Crimean peninsula presents a big contrast with its mountains and relaxed seaside resorts, while the port of Odessa remains a crossroads city with an indefinable atmosphere of excitement and mystery.

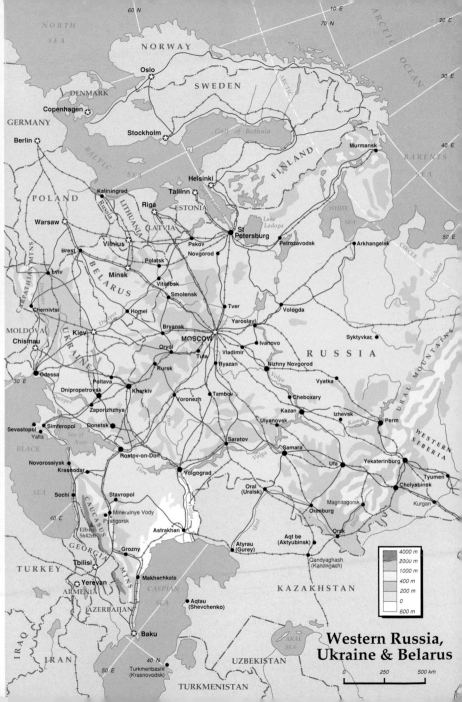

Western Russia,
Ukraine & Belarus

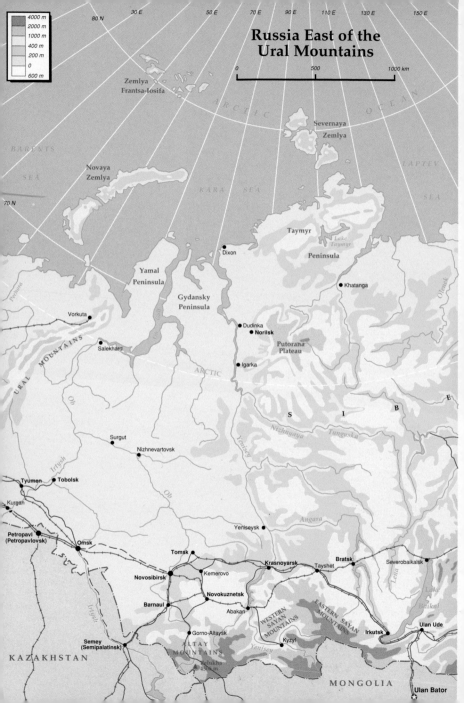

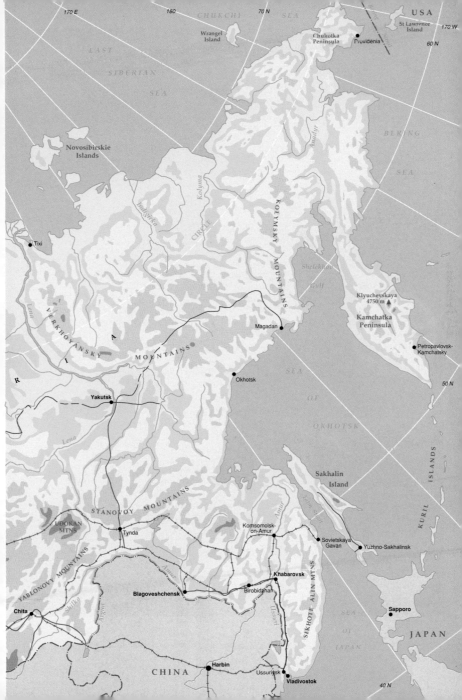

Church of the Resurrection, St Petersburg

Belarus is a flat, in-between land, its people the victims of centuries of wars between Russians, Poles, Germans, Lithuanians and others. Born for the first time as an independent state in 1991, it's hardly a mainstream tourist attraction, but it can surprise those who take time to explore it. Its modern capital, Minsk, is an increasingly cosmopolitan city, while other cities such as Hrodna and Polatsk preserve the imprint of the past, and the countryside has a haunting, old-fashioned beauty.

The opening up of this whole Eastern Slavic realm emphasises perhaps more than anything its differences from the outside world. The unique landscapes, ways of life and histories here constantly surprise and challenge the outsider. What an American ambassador to Moscow once said of the Soviet Union remains true of Russia, Ukraine and Belarus: 'There are no experts...only varying degrees of ignorance'. The ignorance may, on the surface, be less now, but, however you get here and whatever you do, you can be sure these places won't be quite what you expect.

Place Names in Russia, Ukraine & Belarus

Many towns and cities in Ukraine and Belarus are now officially called by their local names instead of by the Russian versions that were current in Soviet times. Thus for example, in Ukraine, Lvov has become Lviv; in Belarus, Grodno is now Hrodna. You'll find such places referred to by their local names in the Ukraine and Belarus chapters of this book. Russians, however, still mainly use the Russian names, so where these places are mentioned in the Russian chapters of this book, you'll find the Russian names in brackets to assist in understanding timetables, signposts and so on.

In addition, some places have dropped Soviet-era names completely and reverted to their older titles: for example, the Russian cities known in Soviet times as Sverdlovsk and Gorky are now again Yekaterinburg and Nizhny Novgorod. We use the new names but you'll find mention of the old ones too.

· An Alternative Place Names appendix is at the back of the book. ■

EUROPEAN RUSSIA

Facts about European Russia

European Russia – Russia west of the Ural Mountains – comprises only a quarter of Russia but is still bigger than any other European country. With four-fifths of Russia's population, it's very much the country's hub. It is a land of much variety, stretching from the frozen tundra which borders the Arctic Ocean to the peaks of the Caucasus, Europe's highest mountains, 3000 km south. Between these extremes lie Russia's two greatest cities and much more.

Virtually all this huge canvas, of which only pockets were truly open to foreigners during the Soviet years and much of which is still little known to the outside world, can now be explored by anyone who wants to do so.

Russia's most vital cities are Moscow, in the country's historic heartland at the centre of European Russia, and St Petersburg, established less than 300 years ago on the Gulf of Finland as Russia's gateway to Europe. In these two places tsars reigned and the world's greatest communist state was born, Russia's unique architecture flowered, and the mysteries of the Russian Orthodox Church flourished and flourish again today. Here too, the fruits of all the country's modern changes are at their greatest – as any traveller can experience in hotels, shops and restaurants or while sampling the nightlife. Within a few hundred km of these cities are dozens of smaller places where you can witness together the country's historic grandeur, the beauty of its gentle countryside and the perennial, bitter hardness of Russian life.

To the north lie tracts of forest, lakes, marshes and tundra – a vast new world for hikers, skiers and campers. As well, the north is dotted with intriguing human enclaves such as the Arctic ports of Murmansk and Arkhangelsk, Kizhi Island with its extraordinary assemblage of old wooden architecture, remnants of Gulag labour camps, and the venerable churches and monasteries of Vologda and elsewhere.

East from Moscow, then south, flows the Volga River. The Volga is one of Russia's historic highways and links many cities of both ancient and modern importance – among them Yaroslavl, Nizhny Novgorod, Kazan, Volgograd (once Stalingrad) and Astrakhan – along its course to the Caspian Sea. Numerous ethnic minorities, whose religious beliefs range from Islam to Buddhism to animism, live in or near the Volga basin, reminders of European Russia's proximity to Asia.

European Russia's other great waterway, the Don River, flows south from near Moscow to enter the Sea of Azov, an offshoot of the Black Sea, near Rostov-on-Don. Between the two rivers begins European Russia's steppe, part of the great, rolling grasslands – now largely given over to agriculture – which stretch all the way across the northern hemisphere from Mongolia to Hungary.

The steppe gives way on European Russia's southern fringe to the Caucasus Mountains. Stretching between the Black and Caspian seas, the Caucasus is a range of spectacular beauty and home to an incredible jigsaw of ethnic groups. Many of these groups were not conquered by Russia until the 19th century; today some are tragically mired in bloody conflicts with each other or with Russia.

Where the Caucasus Mountains meet the Black Sea, Russia even has a coastal riviera, to which its people flock for summer holidays.

Though the practicalities of travel outside the main cities may demand some patience and persistence, Russia never fails to surprise, not least with its people's bizarre combination of gloom and high spirits, rudeness and warm hospitality, secrecy and openness. In the end you'll have shed your own shaft of light on the place that Winston Churchill characterised as 'a riddle wrapped in a mystery inside an enigma'.

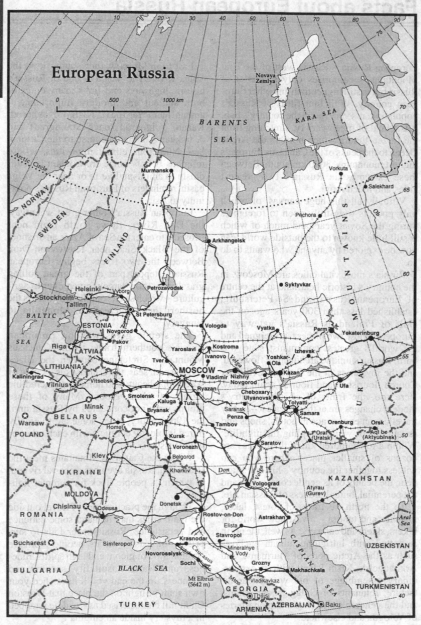

European Russia

HISTORY
Early History

European Russia's earliest known people inhabited the basin of the Don River about 20,000 BC. By 2000 BC a basic agriculture, relying on hardy cereals, had penetrated from the Danube region as far east as the Moscow area and the southern Ural Mountains. At about the same time, peoples in Ukraine and southern areas of European Russia domesticated the horse and developed a nomadic, pastoral lifestyle.

While central and northern European Russia remained a complete backwater for almost 3000 years, the south was subject to a succession of invasions by nomads from the east. The first written records, by the 5th century BC Greek historian Herodotus, concern a people called the Scythians, who probably originated in the Altay region of Siberia and Mongolia and were feared for their riding and battle skills. The Scythians spread as far west as southern Russia and Ukraine by the 7th century BC. Their empire, which stretched south as far as Egypt, ended with the arrival of another people from the east, the Sarmatians, in the 3rd century BC.

The Sarmatians were followed in the 4th century AD by the Huns, also from the Altay region, then by the Huns' relations the Avars, then by the Khazars, a grouping of Turkic and Iranian tribes from the Caucasus, who occupied the lower Volga and Don basins and the steppes to the east and west between the 7th and 10th centuries. The crafty and talented Khazars brought stability and religious tolerance to areas under their control. Their capital was Itil, near the mouth of the Volga. In the 9th century they converted to Judaism. By the 10th century they had mostly settled down to farming and trade.

The Slavs

The migrants who were to give Russia its predominant character, however, were the Slavs. There is some disagreement about where the Slavs originated, but in the first few centuries AD they expanded rapidly to the east, west and south from the vicinity of present-day northern Ukraine and southern Belarus. The Eastern Slavs were the ancestors of the Russians; they were still spreading eastward across the central Russian woodland belt in the 9th century. From the Western Slavs came the Poles, Czechs, Slovaks and others. The Southern Slavs became the Serbs, Croats, Slovenes and Bulgarians.

The Slavs' conversion to Christianity in the 9th and 10th centuries was accompanied by the introduction of an alphabet devised by Cyril, a Greek missionary (now St Cyril), and simplified a few decades later by a fellow missionary, Methodius. The forerunner of Cyrillic, it was based on the Greek alphabet, with a dozen or so additional characters. The Bible was translated into the Southern Slav dialect. This became known as Church Slavonic and is the language of the Russian Orthodox Church's liturgy to this day.

Vikings & Kievan Rus

The crucial factor in the creation of the first Russian state was the potential for trade along river routes across Eastern Slavic areas – between the Baltic and Black seas and, to a lesser extent, between the Baltic and the Volga. Vikings from Scandinavia, called Varyagi (Varangians) by the Slavs, had been nosing east from the Baltic since the 6th century AD, trading and raiding for furs, slaves and amber, and coming into conflict with the Khazars and with Constantinople (Istanbul), the eastern centre of Christianity, as they went. To secure their hold on the trade routes, the Vikings made themselves masters of settlements in key areas – places such as Novgorod, Smolensk and Kiev. Though by no means united themselves, they managed to create a loose confederation of city states in the Eastern Slavic areas. The founding of Novgorod in 862 by Rurik of Jutland is traditionally taken as the birth of the Russian state. Rurik's successor, Oleg, became Kiev's ruler two decades later, and the Rurikid dynasty, though soon Slavicised, maintained its hold to produce the dominant rulers in Eastern Slavic areas until the end of the 16th century.

The name Rus may have been that of the dominant Kievan Viking clan. In later years the term Russian or Great Russian came to be used for Eastern Slavs in the north, while those to the south or west were identified as Ukrainians or Belarusians.

Prince Svyatoslav made Kiev the dominant regional power by campaigning against quarrelling Varangian princes and dealing the Khazars a series of fatal blows. After his death, his son Vladimir made further conquests, and persuaded the Patriarch of Constantinople to establish an episcopal see – a Church 'branch' – in Kiev in 988, marking the birth of the Russian Orthodox Church. He also introduced the beginnings of a feudal structure to replace clan allegiances, though some principalities – including Novgorod, Pskov and Vyatka (north of Kazan) – were ruled democratically by popular assemblies or *veches*.

Kiev's supremacy was broken by new invaders from the east – first the Pechenegs, then the Polovtsy, who sacked Kiev in 1093 – and by the effects of the European crusades from the late 11th century onwards, which broke the Arab hold on southern Europe and the Mediterranean, reviving west-east trade routes and making Rus a commercial backwater.

Novgorod & Rostov-Suzdal

The northern Rus principalities began breaking from Kiev after about 1050. The merchants of Novgorod joined the emerging Hanseatic League, a federation of city-states that controlled Baltic and North Sea trade. Novgorod became the League's gateway to the lands east and south-east.

As Kiev declined, the Russian population shifted northwards and the fertile Rostov-Suzdal region north-east of Moscow began to be developed. Vladimir Monomakh of Kiev founded the town of Vladimir there in 1108 and gave the Rostov-Suzdal principality to his son Yury Dolgoruky, who is credited with founding the little settlement of Moscow in 1147. Rostov-Suzdal grew so rich and strong that Yury's son Andrey Bogolyubov sacked Kiev in 1169 and moved

the court to Vladimir. The Church's headquarters remained in Kiev until 1300. Rostov-Suzdal began to gear up for a challenge to the hold on the Volga-Urals region of the Bulgars. The Bulgars were a people who had originated further east several centuries before and had since converted to Islam. Their capital, Bolgar, was near modern Kazan, on the Volga.

Tatars & the Golden Horde

It's hard to overstate the fear instilled by the Tatars, the name used by Slavs for the mostly Mongolian invaders who suddenly thundered out of Asia in the 13th century. Within 30 years these horsemen built the largest land empire the world has ever seen, slaughtering as many as a quarter of their new subjects in the process.

This was the work of a Mongolian warlord called Temuchin (1167-1227), from south of Lake Baikal, who by 1206 had forged a powerful tribal alliance centred at Karakorum in present-day Mongolia, and named himself Jenghiz Khan (Great Ruler).

After his armies overran north China and Korea they turned west through Central Asia, Afghanistan, Iran, the Caucasus and into the plains between the Volga and Don rivers. There they met the armies of the Russian princes and thrashed them at the Battle of Kalka River in 1223. This push was cut short by the death of Jenghiz Khan, but his grandson Batu Khan returned in 1236 to finish the job, laying waste Bolgar and Rostov-Suzdal and annihilating most of the other Russian principalities, including Kiev, within four years. Novgorod was saved only by spring floods which prevented the invaders from crossing the marshes around the city.

Batu and his successors ruled the Golden Horde – one of the khanates into which the empire of Jenghiz had broken – from Saray on the Volga (near modern Volgograd). The Horde's control over its subjects was indirect: though it raided them in traditional fashion if they grew uppity, it mainly used local princes to keep order, provide soldiers and collect taxes.

Rulers of Russia – Rurik to Yeltsin

Following is a list of the major rulers of Russia or the Soviet Union. In line with common usage, rulers' names before 1700 are directly transliterated, but are Anglicised from Peter the Great until 1917, and transliterated after that – thus Vasily not Basil, Mikhail not Michael, Alexey not Alexis; but Peter not Pyotr, Catherine not Yekaterina etc.

Ivan the Terrible was the first ruler to have himself formally called tsar. Peter the Great began using emperor, though tsar remained in use. In this book we use empress for a female ruler; a tsar's wife who does not become ruler is a tsarina. A tsar's son is a tsarevich and his daughter a tsarevna. ■

Rurik of Novgorod	862-82	Peter I & Ivan V	1689-96
Oleg of Kiev	882-912	Peter I (the Great)	1696-1725
Svyatoslav	962-72	Catherine I	1725-27
Vladimir I	980-1015	Peter II	1727-30
Yaroslav the Wise	1019-54	Anna	1730-40
Vladimir II Monomakh	1113-25	Elizabeth	1741-61
Yury Dolgoruky	1149-57	Peter III	1761-62
Andrey Bogolyubov	1157-74	Catherine II (the Great)	1762-96
Alexandr Nevsky	1252-63	Paul	1796-1801
Daniil of Moscow	1276-1303	Alexander I	1801-25
Ivan I (Kalita)	1325-40	Nicholas I	1825-55
Dmitry Donskoy	1359-89	Alexander II	1855-81
Ivan III (the Great)	1462-1505	Alexander III	1881-94
Vasily III	1505-33	Nicholas II	1894-1917
Yelena (Regent)	1533-47	Alexandr Kerensky	1917
Ivan IV (the Terrible)	1547-84	Vladimir Lenin	1917-24
Fyodor I	1584-98	Iosif Stalin	1929-53
Boris Godunov	1598-1605	Nikita Khrushchev	1957-64
False Dmitry	1605-06	Leonid Brezhnev	1964-82
Vasily Shuysky	1606-10	Yury Andropov	1982-84
Mikhail Romanov	1613-45	Konstantin Chernenko	1984-85
Alexey	1645-76	Mikhail Gorbachev	1985-91
Fyodor III	1676-82	Boris Yeltsin	1991-
Peter I & Ivan V (Regent: Sofia)	1682-89		

Alexandr Nevsky & the Rise of Moscow

One such 'collaborator' was Alexandr Nevsky, Prince of Novgorod, a Russian hero (and later a saint of the Russian Church) for resistance to invaders from the west – German crusaders and Swedes. His victory in 1240 over the Swedes on the Neva River, near present-day St Petersburg, earned him his nickname, Nevsky. Batu Khan put him on the throne as Grand Prince of Vladimir.

Nevsky and his successors acted as intermediaries between the Tatars and other Russian princes. By shrewd diplomacy the princes of Moscow obtained and hung on to the title of Grand Prince from the early 14th century while other princes resumed their feuding. The Church provided spiritual backing to Moscow by moving there from Vladimir in the 1320s, and was in turn favoured with exemption from Tatar taxation.

But Moscow proved to be the Tatars' nemesis. With a new-found Russian confidence, Grand Prince Dmitry put Moscow at the head of a coalition of princes and took on the Tatars, defeating them in a great battle at Kulikovo on the Don River in 1380. For this he became Dmitry Donskoy (which means 'of the Don') and was canonised after his death.

The Tatars crushed this uprising in a three-year campaign but their days were numbered. Weakened by internal dissension, they fell at the end of the 14th century to the Turkic Empire of Timur (Tamerlane), which was based in Samarkand. Yet the Russians, themselves divided as usual, remained Tatar vassals until 1480.

Moscow vs Lithuania

Moscow – or Muscovy, as its expanding lands came to be known – was champion of the Russian cause after Kulikovo, though it had rivals, especially Novgorod and Tver. More ominous was the rise of the Grand Duchy of Lithuania, which had started to expand into old Kievan Rus lands in the 14th century. At first just a headache for Moscow, it became a threat in 1386 when the Lithuanian ruler Jogaila married the Polish queen Jadwiga and became King of Poland, thus joining two of Europe's most powerful states.

With Jogaila's coronation as Wladyslaw II of Poland, the previously pagan Lithuanian ruling class embraced Catholicism. The Russian Church portrayed the struggle against Lithuania as one against the Pope in Rome. After Constantinople, centre of the Greek Orthodox Church, was taken by the Turks in 1453, the metropolitan or head of the Russian Church declared Moscow the 'third Rome', the true heir of Christianity.

Meanwhile, with the death of Dmitry Donskoy's son in 1425, Muscovy suffered a dynastic war. The old Rurikids got the upper hand – ironically, with Lithuanian and Tatar help – but it was only with Ivan III's forceful reign from 1462 to 1505 that the other principalities ceased to oppose Muscovy.

Ivan III (the Great)

Ivan III brought most of the Great Russian principalities to heel. Novgorod was first, in 1478, as it was no longer able to rely on the Tatars as a diversion. Two years later a Russian army faced the Tatars at the Ugra River south-west of Moscow. Though they parted without a fight, after that Ivan simply stopped paying tribute to the Golden Horde.

Tver fell to Moscow in 1485, far-flung Vyatka in 1489. Pskov and Ryazan, the only states still independent at the end of Ivan's reign, were mopped up by his successor, Vasily III. Lithuania and Poland, however, remained thorns in Russia's side.

Servants & Serfs

When Ivan III took Novgorod he installed a governor, exiled the city's influential families and ejected the Hanseatic merchants, closing Russia's 'window on the West' for two centuries. The exiles were replaced with Ivan's administrators, who got temporary title to confiscated lands for good performance.

This new approach to land tenure, called *pomestie* (estate), characterised Ivan's rule. Previously, the greater nobles *(boyars)* had held land under a system of patrimony *(votchina)* which gave them unlimited control and inheritance rights over their lands and the people on them. The freedom to shift allegiance to other princes had given them political clout too. Now, with few alternative princes left, the boyars' influence declined in favour of the new landholding civil servants.

This increased central control spread to the lower levels of society with the growth of serfdom. Before the 1500s, peasants could work for themselves after meeting their masters' needs, and could even change jobs during the two weeks around St George's Day in November. These rights were less frequently bestowed by the new masters, who lacked the old sense of obligation, and peasants became a permanent fixture on the land.

The Cossacks

The word 'Cossack', from the Turkic *kazak*, meaning free man or horseman, was first applied to residual Tatar groups and later to serfs, paupers and drop-outs who started fleeing south from Russia, Poland and Lithuania in the 15th century. They organised themselves into self-governing communities in the Don basin, on the Dnipro (Dnepr) River in Ukraine, and in western Kazakhstan. Those in a given region, eg the Don Cossacks, were not just a tribe; its men constituted an army *(voysko)*, within which each village-regiment *(stanitsa)* elected a leader *(ataman)*.

Mindful of their skill as fighters, the Russian government treated the Cossacks carefully, offering autonomy in return for military service. Cossacks were the wedge that opened Siberia in the 17th century. By the 19th century there were a dozen Cossack armies from Ukraine to the Far East.

But they still raised hell when things didn't suit them. Three big peasant uprisings in the Volga-Don region – in 1670, 1707 and 1773 – were Cossack-led. After 1917 the Bolsheviks abolished all Cossack institutions (though some cavalry units were revived in WW II).

Ivan IV (the Terrible)

Vasily III's son, Ivan IV, took the throne in 1533 at age three, with his mother as regent. After 13 years of court intrigues he had himself crowned 'Tsar of all the Russias'.

Ivan IV, 'Tsar of all the Russias', whose behaviour after the death of his first wife, Anastasia, earned him the title 'the Terrible'

The word 'tsar', from the Latin *caesar*, had previously been used only for a Great Khan or for the Emperor of Constantinople.

Ivan IV's marriage to Anastasia, who was from the Romanov boyar family, was a happy one – unlike the five that followed her death in 1560, which was a turning point in his life. Believing her to have been poisoned, he instituted a reign of terror that earned him the sobriquet *grozny* (literally 'awesome' but in this case translated as 'Terrible') and nearly destroyed all his earlier good works. In a fit of rage he even killed his eldest son and heir, Ivan.

His subsequent career was indeed terrible, though he was admired for upholding Russian interests and tradition. During his active reign (1547-84) Russia defeated the surviving Tatar khanates of Kazan and Astrakhan, thus acquiring the whole Volga region and a chunk of Caspian Sea coast and opening the way to Siberia. His campaign against the Crimean Tatars, however, nearly ended with the loss of Moscow.

Ivan's interest in the West and his obsession with reaching the Baltic Sea foreshadowed Peter the Great, but he failed to break through and only antagonised the Lithuanians, Poles and Swedes, setting the stage for the Time of Troubles. His growing paranoia led to a savage attack on Novgorod, which finally snuffed out that city's golden age.

Boris Godunov & the Time of Troubles

When Ivan died of poisoning in 1584, rule passed to his second son, the hopeless Fyodor I, who at least had the sense to leave government to his brother-in-law, Boris Godunov, a skilled 'prime minister' who repaired much of Ivan's damage. Fyodor died childless in 1598, ending the 700-year Rurikid dynasty, and Boris ruled as tsar for seven more years.

Then a Polish-backed Catholic pretender arrived on the scene claiming to be Dmitry, another son of Ivan the Terrible, who had died in obscure circumstances (murdered on Boris Godunov's orders, some said). This 'False Dmitry' gathered a huge ragtag army as he advanced on Moscow. Boris Godunov conveniently died, his son was lynched and the boyars acclaimed the pretender tsar.

Thus began the Time of Troubles, or Smuta (1606-13), a spell of anarchy, dynastic chaos and foreign invasions. At its heart was a struggle between feudal landholders (the boyars) and central government (the tsar). The False Dmitry was murdered in a popular revolt and succeeded by Vasily Shuysky (1606-10), another puppet of the boyars. A second False Dmitry (who claimed to be both the previous Dmitrys) challenged Shuysky, Swedish and Polish invaders fought each other over claims to the Russian throne, Shuysky was dethroned by the boyars and the Poles occupied Moscow from 1610 to 1612.

Eventually a popular army, rallied by the Church and supported by Cossack mercenaries, removed the Poles. In 1613 a Zemsky Sobor, or Assembly of the Land, with representatives of the political classes of the day, elected 16-year-old Mikhail Romanov tsar, the first of a new dynasty that was to rule until 1917.

Russia in the 17th Century

Though the first three Romanov rulers – Mikhail (1613-45), Alexey (1645-76) and Fyodor III (1676-82) – provided continuity and stability, there were also big changes that foretold the downfall of 'old' Russia.

Acquisitions The 17th century saw a huge growth in Russian lands. The 'opening' of Siberia, begun by the Stroganov merchant family and Cossack mercenaries under Ataman Yermak Timofeevich, remains one of history's biggest and most explosive territorial expansions.

Additionally, when Cossacks in Ukraine appealed for help against the Poles, Tsar Alexey couldn't resist their pleas, and in 1667 Smolensk, Kiev and lands east of the Dnepr came under Russian control.

Serfdom Authority in the countryside had collapsed during the Time of Troubles. Thousands of peasants fled to Cossack areas or to Siberia, where serfdom was unknown. Landlords, in despair, found support from the government. The peasants' right to move freely was abolished in 1646. In 1675 they lost all rights to the land and, in a uniquely Russian version of serfdom, could be sold separately from the estates they worked. They were, in effect, slaves.

In 1670-71 Cossacks, runaway serfs and adventurers joined in a huge uprising in the Volga-Don region, led by the Cossack Stepan (Stenka) Razin. Razin's army of 200,000 seized the entire lower Volga basin before he was captured and killed. He remains a folk hero today.

The Church Internal conflicts transformed the Church into a friend of authority, distrusted as much as the government was. In the mid-17th century, Patriarch Nikon tried to bring rituals and texts into line with the 'pure' Greek Orthodox Church, horrifying those attached to traditional Russian forms.

The result was a bitter schism between Nikon's New Believers and Old Believers who, under government persecution, formed a widespread, occasionally fanatical religious underground. In the end Nikon himself was sacked by Tsar Alexey over the issue of Church authority in the newly acquired Ukrainian territories, while Old Believers survive to this day.

Peter the Great

Peter I, known as 'the Great' for his commanding 2.24-metre frame and equally commanding victory over the Swedes, dragged Russia kicking and screaming into Europe, made it a major world power and insulted all his administrators and soldiers by shaving off their beards.

Born to Tsar Alexey's second wife in 1672, Peter spent much of his youth in royal residences in the countryside, organising his playmates into military regiments. Energetic, inquisitive and comfortable in any circle, he often visited Moscow's European district to learn about the West. Dutch and British ship captains in Arkhangelsk gave him navigation lessons on the White Sea.

When Fyodor III died in 1682, Peter became tsar, along with his feeble-minded half-brother Ivan V, under the regency of Ivan's ambitious sister, Sofia. She had the support of a leading statesman of the day, Prince Vasily Golitsyn. The boyars, annoyed by Golitsyn's institution of a stringent ranking system, schemed successfully to have Sofia sent to a monastery in 1689 and replaced as regent by Peter's unambitious mother.

Few doubted that Peter was the true monarch, and when he became sole ruler, after his mother's death in 1694 and Ivan's in 1696, he embarked on a modernisation campaign, symbolised by his fact-finding mission to Europe in 1697-98 – he was the first Muscovite ruler ever to go there. Historical literature abounds with tales of his spirited visits to hospitals, workshops and trading houses, his stint as a ship's carpenter in Amsterdam and his hiring of some 1000 experts for service in Russia.

He was also busy negotiating alliances. In 1695 he had sent Russia's first navy down the Don River and captured the Black Sea port of Azov from the Crimean Tatars, vassals of the Ottoman Turks. His European allies weren't interested in the Turks but shared his concern about the Swedes, who held most of the Baltic coast and had penetrated deep into Europe.

Peter's alliance with Poland and Denmark led to the Great Northern War against Sweden (1700-21), the focal point of his career. The rout of Charles XII's forces at the Battle of Poltava (1709) heralded Russia's power and the collapse of the Swedish Empire. The Treaty of Nystadt (1721) gave Peter control of the Gulf of Finland and the eastern shores of the Baltic Sea. In the midst of this (1707), he put down another peasant rebellion, led by the Don Cossack Kondraty Bulavin.

On land taken from the Swedes, Peter founded a new city, which he named St Petersburg after his patron saint. In 1712 he made it the capital, symbol of a new, Europe-facing Russia.

Peter's Legacy Peter succeeded in mobilising Russian resources to compete on equal terms with the West – a startling achievement. His territorial gains were small, but the strategic Baltic territories also added ethnic variety, including a new upper class of German traders and administrators who formed the backbone of Russia's commercial and military expansion.

Peter was also to have the last word on the authority of the Church. When it resisted his reforms he simply blocked the appointment of a new patriarch, put bishops under a government department and in effect became head of the Church himself.

Vast sums were needed to build St Petersburg, pay a growing civil service, modernise the army and launch naval and commercial fleets. But money was scarce in an economy based on serf labour, so Peter slapped taxes on everything from coffins to beards, including an infamous 'Soul Tax' on all lower-class adult males. The lot of serfs worsened, as they bore the main tax burden.

But even the upper classes had to chip in: aristocrats could either serve in the army or

Peter the Great, who worked as a ship's carpenter in Amsterdam before he became tsar

the civil service, or lose their titles and land. Birth counted for little, as state servants were subject to Peter's Table of Ranks, a performance-based ladder of promotion with the upper grades conferring hereditary nobility. Some aristocrats lost all they had, while capable state employees of humble origin, and even foreigners, became Russian nobles.

Peter died in 1725 without naming a successor, and the matter was again decided by intrigue and force. If it hadn't been for a government structure built on the Table of Ranks and a professional bureaucracy with a vested interest in its preservation, Peter's reforms might well have died with him.

After Peter

For 37 years after Peter's death, Russia suffered ineffectual rulers. Day-to-day administration was handled by a governing body called the Supreme Privy Council, staffed by many of Peter's leading administrators. Dominated by the Dolgoruky and Golitsyn boyar families, the council elected Peter's niece Anna of Courland (a small principality in present-day Latvia) to the throne, with a contract stating that the council had the final say in policy decisions. Anna ended this experiment in constitutional monarchy by disbanding the council.

Anna ruled from 1730 to 1740, appointing a Baltic German baron, Ernst Johann von Bühren, to handle affairs of state. His name was Russified to Biron, but his heavy-handed, corrupt style came to symbolise the German influence on the royal family that had begun with Peter the Great.

During the reign of Peter's daughter, Elizabeth (1741-61), German influence waned and restrictions on the nobility were loosened. Some aristocrats began to dabble in manufacture and trade.

Catherine II (the Great)

Daughter of a German prince, Catherine came to Russia at the age of 15 to marry Empress Elizabeth's heir-apparent, her nephew Peter III. Intelligent and ambitious, Catherine learned Russian, embraced the Orthodox Church and devoured the writings

Catherine II (the Great)

of European political philosophers. This was the time of the Enlightenment, when talk of human rights, social contracts and the separation of powers abounded.

Catherine later said of Peter III, 'I believe the Crown of Russia attracted me more than his person'. Six months after he ascended the throne she had him overthrown in a palace coup led by her current lover (it has been said that she had more lovers than the average serf had hot dinners), and he was murdered shortly afterwards.

Enlightened Despotism Catherine embarked on a programme of reforms, though she made it clear that she had no intention of limiting her own authority. She drafted a new legal code, limited the use of torture and supported religious tolerance. But any ideas she might have had of improving the lot of serfs went overboard with the rebellion of 1773-74, led by the Don Cossack Yemelyan Pugachev.

Pugachev claimed he was Peter III. His rebellion, which spread from the Urals to the Caspian Sea and along the Volga, was Russia's most violent peasant uprising. Hundreds of thousands responded to his promises to end serfdom and taxation, but were beaten by famine and government armies. Pugachev was executed and Catherine put an end to Cossack autonomy.

In the cultural sphere, Catherine increased the number of schools and colleges and expanded publishing. Her vast collection of paintings forms the core of the present-day Hermitage collection. A critical elite gradually developed, alienated from most uneducated Russians but also increasingly at odds with central authority – a 'split personality' common among future Russian radicals.

Territorial Gains Catherine's reign saw major expansion at the expense of the weakened Ottoman Turks and Poles, engineered by her 'prime minister' and foremost lover, Grigory Potyomkin. War with the Turks began in 1768, peaked with the naval victory at Çeşme (Chesma) and ended with a 1774 treaty giving Russia control of the north coast of the Black Sea, freedom of shipping through the Dardanelles to the Mediterranean and 'protectorship' of Christian interests in the Ottoman Empire – a pretext for later incursions into the Balkans. Crimea was annexed in 1783.

Poland had spent the previous century collapsing into semi-independent units with a figurehead king in Warsaw. Catherine manipulated events with divide-and-rule tactics and even had a former lover, Stanislas Poniatowski, installed as king. Austria and Prussia proposed sharing Poland among the three powers, and in 1772, 1793 and 1795 the country was carved up, ceasing to exist as an independent state until 1918. Eastern Poland and the Grand Duchy of Lithuania – roughly, present-day Lithuania, Belarus and western Ukraine – came under Russian rule.

Alexander I
When Catherine died in 1796 the throne passed to her son, Paul I. An old-school autocrat, he antagonised the gentry with attempts to reimpose compulsory state service, and was killed in a coup in 1801. His son and successor, Alexander I, Catherine's favourite grandson, who had been trained by the best European tutors, kicked off his reign with several reforms, including an expansion of the school system that brought education

within reach of the lower middle classes. But he was soon preoccupied with the wars against Napoleon which were to dominate his career.

After Napoleon defeated him at Austerlitz, north of Vienna, in 1805 and then at Friedland, near modern Kaliningrad, Alexander began to negotiate. The Treaty of Tilsit (1807) left Napoleon in charge as Emperor of the West and Alexander as Emperor of the East, united (in theory) against England.

1812 & Aftermath The alliance lasted only until 1810, when Russia resumed trade with England. A furious Napoleon decided to crush the tsar with his Grand Army of 700,000, the largest force the world had ever seen for a single military operation.

The vastly outnumbered Russian forces retreated across their own countryside through the summer of 1812, scorching the earth in an attempt to deny the French sustenance and fighting some successful rearguard actions. Napoleon set his sights on Moscow, the symbolic heart of Russia. In September, with the lack of provisions beginning to bite on the French, the Russian general Mikhail Kutuzov finally decided to turn and fight at Borodino, 130 km from Moscow. The battle was extremely bloody, but inconclusive, with the Russians withdrawing in good order.

Before the month was out, Napoleon entered a deserted Moscow; the same day, the city began to burn down around him (whether by Russian or French hand, or by accident, has never been established). Alexander ignored his overtures to negotiate. With winter coming and his supply lines overstretched, Napoleon ordered a retreat – he was unable to do anything else. His troops starved and were picked off by Russian partisans. Only one in 20 made it back to the relative safety of Poland, and the Russians pursued them all the way to Paris.

At the Congress of Vienna, where the victors met in 1814-15 to establish a new order after Napoleon's final defeat, Alexander championed the cause of the old monarchies. His legacies were a hazy Christian fellowship of European kings, called the Holy Alliance, and a system of pacts to guard against future Napoleons – or any revolutionary change.

More Territorial Gains Meanwhile the Russian Empire was inching outwards. Russian merchants had arrived in Alaska in 1784 and established a solid trading community. Russian ships dropped anchor in San Francisco Bay in 1806. The kingdom of Georgia united with Russia in 1801. After a war with Sweden in 1807-09, Alexander became Grand Duke of Finland. Russia argued with Turkey over the Danube principalities of Bessarabia (essentially, modern Moldova) and Wallachia (now in Romania), taking Bessarabia in 1812. Persia ceded northern Azerbaijan a year later and Yerevan (in Armenia) in 1828.

Decembrists
Alexander died in 1825 without leaving a clear heir, sparking the usual crisis. His reform-minded brother Constantine, married to a Pole and living happily in Warsaw, had no interest in the throne.

Officers who had brought back liberal ideas from Paris in 1815 preferred Constantine to Alexander's youngest brother, the militaristic Nicholas, who was due to be crowned on 26 December 1825. Their rally in St Petersburg was squashed by troops loyal to Nicholas; several of these so-called Decembrists (Dekabristy) were executed and over 100 – mostly aristocrats and officers – were sent into Siberian exile.

This was the tsarist elite's first cry for change. Officers, intellectuals and children of the clergy formed secret societies. Many looked to the American and French revolutions for inspiration. Others drifted towards the typically Russian solution of anarchism – which would in the future be represented by gurus such as Mikhail Bakunin and Pyotr Kropotkin, who loathed all authority and upheld the virtues of the village commune.

Political debate revealed two trends: 'Westernisers' wanted to rebuild Russia on European lines; 'Slavophiles', generally Orthodox, believed the tsarist tradition could be revitalised with the old idea of the Zemsky Sobor consultative assembly.

Nicholas I
The reign of Nicholas I (1825-55) was a time of stagnation and repression under a tsar who put his faith in his army. The social revolutions that shook Europe in 1830 and 1848 passed Russia by.

There were positive developments, however. The economy grew, and grain exports increased after Britain removed its tariffs. Nicholas detested serfdom, if only because he detested the serf-owning class. Peasants on state lands, nearly half the total, were given title to their land and, in effect, freed.

In foreign policy, Nicholas' meddling in the Balkans was eventually to destroy Russian credibility in Europe. Bad diplomacy led to the Crimean War of 1854-56 against Ottoman Turkey, Britain and France, who declared war after Russian troops marched into the Ottoman provinces of Moldavia and Wallachia – ostensibly to protect Christian communities there. An Anglo-French-Turkish force besieged the Russian naval headquarters at Sevastopol, at the tip of the Crimea. Inept command on both sides resulted in a bloody, stalemated war.

Alexander II & Alexander III
The 'Great Reforms' Nicholas died in 1855. His son, Alexander II, saw the Crimean War stirring up discontent within Russia and accepted peace on unfavourable terms. The war had revealed the backwardness behind the post-1812 imperial glory, and the time for reform had come.

The serfs were freed in 1861. Of the land they had worked, roughly a third was kept by established landholders. The rest went to village communes, which assigned it to the individual ex-serfs in return for 'redemption payments' to compensate former landholders – a system that pleased nobody.

The abolition of serfdom opened the way for a market economy, capitalism and an industrial revolution. Railroads and factories were built, and cities expanded as peasants left the land. Foreign investment in Russia mushroomed during the 1880s and 1890s. But nothing was done to modernise farming, and very little to help the peasants. By 1914, 85% of the population was still rural, but their lot had barely improved in half a century.

Revolutionary Movements The reforms raised hopes that were not satisfied. The tsar refused to set up a representative assembly for all of Russia. Peasants were angry at having to pay for land they considered theirs by right. Radical students, known as *narodniki* or Populists, took to the countryside in the 1870s to rouse the peasants, but the students and the peasants proved to be worlds apart and the campaign failed.

Other Populists saw more value in cultivating revolution among the growing urban working class, or proletariat, while yet others turned to terrorism: one secret society, the People's Will, blew up Alexander II in 1881.

Not all opponents to tsarism were radical revolutionaries. Some moderates, well off and with much to lose from a revolution, called themselves liberals and advocated constitutional reform along Western European lines, with universal suffrage and a national parliament *(duma)*.

The terrorist groups were genuinely surprised that there was no uprising after Alexander II's assassination. Most were rounded up and executed or exiled, and the reign of his son Alexander III was marked by repression of revolutionaries and liberals alike.

Discontent was sometimes directed at Jews and took the form of violent mass attacks, or pogroms. At their height in the 1880s, these were often fanned by the authorities to unload social tension onto a convenient scapegoat. Tending towards intellectual and commercial professions, Jews were hated as shopkeepers and industrialists by the lower classes and as political radicals by the authorities.

Territorial Expansion During the reigns of Alexander II (1855-81) and Alexander III (1881-94), Central Asia (modern Kazakhstan, Uzbekistan, Turkmenistan, Kyrgyzstan and Tajikistan) came fully under Russian control. In the east, Russia acquired a long strip of Pacific coast from China and built the port of Vladivostok, but sold the 'worthless' Alaskan territories to the USA in 1867 for just US$7.2 million.

Marxism

Many revolutionaries fled abroad. Two who went to Switzerland, Georgy Plekhanov and Pavel Axelrod, became converted to Marxism and founded the Russian Social Democratic Party in 1883. As Marxists they believed that Russia was passing through a capitalist phase on its way to socialism, and that the urban proletariat was the only class with revolutionary potential.

One of their converts was young, upper middle-class Vladimir Ulyanov, better known by his later pseudonym, Lenin. In 1895 he took charge of Russia's first Marxist cell in St Petersburg, which earned him three years of Siberian exile. On his release in 1899 he went to Europe, where he remained (except for a few secret visits) until 1917, rising to joint leadership of the Party with Plekhanov.

Social democrats in Europe were being elected to parliaments and developing Marxism into 'parliamentary socialism', improving the lot of workers through legislation. The question of what to do in Russia, where there was no parliament, only an active secret police, came to a head at a meeting of the Socialist International movement in London in 1903.

Among Russian socialists, Lenin stood for violent overthrow of the government by a small, committed, well-organised Party, while Plekhanov stood for mass membership and cooperation with other political forces. Lenin won the vote through clever manoeuvring, and his faction came to be known as the Bolsheviks, or majority people; Plekhanov's faction became the Mensheviks, or minority people. The

Mensheviks actually outnumbered the Bolsheviks in the Party, but Lenin clung to the name, for obvious reasons. The two factions coexisted until 1912, when the Bolsheviks set up their own party.

Back at home, in 1900 the Populist movement became the Social Revolutionary Party, the main revolutionary force in rural Russia. Liberal politicians formed the Union of Liberation in 1903, and this soon became the Constitutional Democrats (Kadets).

Russo-Japanese War

Nicholas II, who succeeded his father, Alexander III, in 1894, was a weak man who commanded less respect than his father, but was equally opposed to representative government.

The first serious blow to his position was a humiliating defeat by Japan. Though in 1875 Russia and Japan had managed to agree on who should have Sakhalin Island (Russia) and who should get the Kuril Islands (Japan), by the turn of the century they were at odds over their respective 'spheres of influence' – Russia's in Manchuria, Japan's in Korea. As in the Crimea 50 years before, poor diplomacy led to war. In 1904 Japan attacked the Russian naval base at Port Arthur (Dalian) in China.

Defeat followed defeat for Russia on land and sea. The ultimate disaster came in May 1905, when the entire Baltic fleet, which had sailed halfway around the world to relieve Port Arthur, was sunk in the Tsushima Straits off Japan.

Revolution of 1905

In Russia, unrest became widespread after the fall of Port Arthur. On 9 January 1905, a priest named Georgy Gapon led a crowd of 200,000 workers – men, women and children – to the Winter Palace in St Petersburg to petition the tsar for better working conditions. Singing 'God save the Tsar', they were met by imperial guards, who opened fire and killed several hundred. This was 'Bloody Sunday'.

After the Tsushima Straits debacle the country broke into anarchy, with wild strikes, pogroms, mutinies and killings of landowners and industrialists. Social democrat activists formed *soviets* in St Petersburg and Moscow. These workers' councils, with representatives chosen by acclaim, proved remarkably successful: the St Petersburg Soviet, led by Mensheviks under Leon Trotsky, declared a general strike which brought the country to a standstill in October.

The tsar gave in and promised a duma (parliament). General elections in April 1906 gave it a leftist majority and it demanded further reforms. The tsar disbanded it. New elections in 1907 pushed the duma further to the left. It was again disbanded and a new electoral law, limiting the vote to the upper classes and ethnic Russians, ensured that the third and fourth dumas were more cooperative with the tsar, who continued to choose the prime minister and cabinet.

The capable prime minister, Pyotr Stolypin, abolished the hated redemption payments in the countryside. Enterprising peasants were now able to acquire decent parcels of land, which could be worked efficiently; this led to the creation of a new class of 'big farmers', or *kulaks*, and to a series of good harvests. It also made it easier for peasants to leave their villages, providing a mobile labour force for industry. Radical activists lost their following.

But Stolypin was assassinated in 1911, and the tsarist regime again lost touch with the people. Nicholas became a puppet of his strong-willed, eccentric wife, Alexandra, who herself fell under the spell of a sinister Siberian peasant named Rasputin. Rasputin was killed by court nobles in December 1916.

WW I

Russia's involvement with the Balkans made it a main actor in the world war that began there in 1914. The war was badly managed from the start. Heavy defeats in Prussia were followed in 1915 by German advances deep into Russia itself. By the time the Germans halted, to concentrate on trench warfare in France, an estimated two million Russian troops had been killed and Germany controlled Poland and much of the Baltic coast, Belarus and Ukraine.

The tsar responded to protests by disbanding the duma and assuming personal command in the field, where he couldn't make much headway. At home, the disorganised government failed to introduce rationing, and in February 1917 in Petrograd (the new, less 'German' name for St Petersburg), discontent in the food queues turned to riots. Soldiers and police mutinied, refusing to fire on demonstrators. A new Petrograd Soviet of Workers' & Soldiers' Deputies was formed on the 1905 model, and more sprang up elsewhere. The reconvened duma ignored an order to disband itself and set up a committee to assume government.

Now there were two alternative power bases in the capital. The soviet was a rallying and debating point for factory workers and soldiers; the duma committee attracted the educated and commercial elite. In February the two reached agreement on a provisional government which would demand the tsar's abdication. The tsar tried to return to Petrograd but was blocked by his own troops. On 1 March he abdicated.

Bolshevik Revolution of 1917
The provisional government announced general elections for November, and continued the war despite a collapse of discipline in the army and popular demands for peace. On 3 April Lenin and other exiled Bolsheviks returned to Petrograd via Scandinavia in a sealed railway carriage provided by the German army. Though well and truly in the minority in the soviets, the Bolsheviks were organised and committed. They won many over with a demand for immediate 'peace, land and bread', and believed the soviets should seize power at once. But a series of violent mass demonstrations in July (the 'July Days'), inspired by the Bolsheviks, was in the end not fully backed by them and was quelled. Lenin fled to Finland, and Alexandr Kerensky, a moderate Social Revolutionary, became prime minister.

In September the Russian military chief of staff, General Kornilov, sent cavalry to Petrograd to crush the soviets. Kerensky turned to the left for support against this insubordination, even courting the Bolsheviks, and the counter-revolution was defeated. After this, public opinion massively favoured the Bolsheviks, who quickly took control of the Petrograd Soviet (chaired by Trotsky, who had joined them) and, by extension, all the soviets in the land. Lenin decided it was time to seize power, and returned from Finland in October.

During the night of 24-25 October 1917, Bolshevik workers and soldiers in Petrograd seized government buildings and communication centres, and arrested the provisional government, which was meeting in the Winter Palace. (Kerensky managed to escape, eventually dying in the USA in 1970.) Within hours, an All-Russian Congress of Soviets, meeting in Petrograd, made the soviets the ruling councils in Russia, headed by a 'parliament' called the Soviet Central Executive Committee. A Council of People's Commissars became the government, headed by Lenin, with Trotsky as commissar for foreign affairs and the Georgian Iosif Stalin as commissar for nationalities.

Local soviets elsewhere in Russia seized power relatively easily, but the coup in Moscow took six days of fighting. The general elections scheduled for November could not be stopped, however. More than half Russia's male population voted. Roughly 55% chose Kerensky's rural Socialist party and only 25% voted for the Bolsheviks – so, when the new assembly met in January, the Bolsheviks disbanded it after its first day in session.

Civil War
The soviet government wasted no time introducing sweeping measures. It redistributed land to those who worked it, signed an armistice with the Germans in December 1917 and set up the Cheka, a secret police force; Trotsky, now military commissar, founded the Red Army in January 1918. In March the

Bolshevik Party renamed itself the Communist Party and moved the capital to Moscow.

In March 1918, the Treaty of Brest-Litovsk surrendered Poland, the Baltic provinces, Ukraine, Finland and Transcaucasia to Germany and its allies, enabling the Soviet regime to concentrate on internal enemies. These were becoming numerous in the countryside because of food requisitions by armed trade-union detachments.

In July the former tsar and his family, who had been interned for months, were killed by their communist guards in Yekaterinburg. Two months later, the Cheka began a systematic programme of arrests, torture and executions.

Those hostile to the Bolsheviks, collectively termed 'Whites', had developed strongholds in the south and east of the country. But they lacked unity, as they ranged from tsarist stalwarts to landlord-killing Social Revolutionaries (who were opposed to the Brest-Litovsk treaty), from Finnish partisans to Japanese troops. The Bolsheviks had the advantage of controlling the heart of Russia, including its war industry and communications. Full-scale civil war broke out in early 1918 and lasted almost three years. The main centres of opposition to the Bolsheviks were:

- In the south, tsarist and liberal sympathisers under generals Kornilov and Denikin, plus Cossacks clamouring for autonomy.
- Ukraine, which was under German control until November 1918, and then occupied variously by nationalists, the army of newly independent Poland, and Denikin's troops.
- Admiral Kolchak's government of 'all Russia' in Omsk, Siberia, which was supported by 40,000 Czech prisoners of war, the most formidable fighting force the Red Army had to deal with.
- The Baltic provinces and Finland, which waged successful wars of independence.
- British, French, US and Japanese troops who made mischief round the periphery. The Japanese were the biggest threat as they established themselves in large tracts of the Far East, but they eventually pulled out in 1922.
- Uprisings by peasants, as a result of famine in 1920-21; and by sailors at the Kronstadt naval base near Petrograd in 1921, against soviet monopoly of power. These sailors had been

among the first supporters of the revolution, but the Cheka executed them in their thousands.

By 1921, the Communist Party had firmly established one-party rule, thanks to the Red Army and the Cheka, which continued to eliminate opponents. Some escaped, joining an estimated 1.5 million citizens in exile.

'War Communism'

During the Civil War, a system called 'War Communism' subjected every aspect of society to the aim of victory. This meant sweeping nationalisations in all economic sectors and strict administrative control by the soviet government, which in turn was controlled by the Communist Party.

The Party itself was restructured to reflect Lenin's creed of 'Democratic Centralism', which held that Party decisions should be obeyed all the way down the line. A new political bureau, the Politburo, was created for Party decision-making, and a new secretariat supervised Party appointments, ensuring that only loyal members were given responsibility (Stalin became Party general secretary in 1922).

War Communism was also a form of social engineering to create a classless society. To some extent it worked, in that many 'class enemies' were eliminated by execution or exile, but the economic consequences were disastrous: forced food requisitions and hostility towards the larger, more efficient farmers, combined with drought and a breakdown of infrastructure, led to the enormous famine of 1920-21, when between four and five million people died.

The New Economic Policy

Lenin suggested a strategic compromise with capitalism. The New Economic Policy, or NEP, was adopted by the 10th Party Congress in 1921 and remained in force until 1927. The state continued to own the 'commanding heights' of the economy – large-scale industry, banks, transport – but allowed private enterprise to re-emerge. Farm output improved as the kulaks consolidated their holdings and employed landless peasants as wage earners. Farm surplus was sold to the cities in return for industrial products, giving rise to a new class of traders and small-scale industrialists called 'Nepmen'. In the state sectors, wages were allowed to reflect effort as professional managers replaced Party administrators. By the late 1920s, agricultural and industrial production had reached prewar levels.

But the political tide was set the other way. At the 1921 Party congress, Lenin outlawed debate within the Party as 'factionalism' and launched the first systematic purge among Party members. The Cheka was reorganised as the GPU in 1922, with much greater powers to operate outside the law; for the time being it limited its activities to targeting political opponents. The Union of Soviet Socialist Republics, a federation of theoretically independent Soviet Socialist Republics (SSRs), was established in 1922. The initial members were the Russian, Ukrainian, Belarusian and Transcaucasian SSRs. By 1940 the number had reached 11 with the splitting of the Transcaucasian SSR into Georgian, Armenian and Azerbaijani SSRs and the addition of five Central Asian republics.

Stalin vs Trotsky

In May 1922, Lenin suffered the first of a series of paralysing strokes that removed him from effective control of the Party and government. He died aged 54 in January 1924. His embalmed remains were put on display in Moscow, Petrograd became Leningrad in his honour, and a personality cult was built around him – all orchestrated by Stalin.

Lenin had failed to name a successor, although he expressed a low opinion of 'too rude' Stalin. The charismatic Trotsky, hero of the Civil War and second only to Lenin as an architect of the revolution, wanted collectivisation of agriculture – an extension of War Communism – and worldwide revolution. He attacked Party 'bureaucrats' who wished to concentrate on socialism in the Soviet Union. But even before Lenin's death,

the powers that mattered in the Party and soviets had backed a three-man leadership of Zinoviev, Kamenev and Stalin, in which Stalin already pulled the strings. As Party general secretary, he controlled all appointments and had installed his supporters

Lenin's statue still adorns many Russian cities

wherever it mattered. His influence grew with a recruiting drive that doubled Party membership to over a million.

Trotsky and his diminishing group of supporters were expelled from the Party in 1927. In 1929 he went into exile, ending up in Mexico, where an agent of Stalin wielding an icepick finished him off in 1940.

Five Year Plans & Farm Collectivisation

With Trotsky out of the way, Stalin took up Trotsky's farm collectivisation idea as part of a grand plan to turn the USSR into an industrial power. The first Five Year Plan, launched in 1929, called for a quadrupling of output by heavy industry, such as power stations, mines, steelworks and railways. Agriculture was to be collectivised to get the peasants to fulfil production quotas, which would feed the growing cities and provide food exports to pay for imported heavy machinery.

The forced collectivisation of agriculture destroyed the country's peasantry (who were still 80% of the population) as a class and as a way of life. Farmers were required to pool their land and resources into collective farms (*kolkhozy*), usually consisting of about 75 households and dozens of sq km in area, which became their collective property in return for compulsory quotas of produce. Kolkhozy covered two-thirds of all farmland, supported by a network of Machine Tractor Stations which dispensed machinery and advice (political or otherwise). Another farm organisation was the *sovkhoz*, a state-owned business for large-scale farming of single crops by paid staff.

Farmers who resisted – and most kulaks did, especially in Ukraine and the Volga and Don regions, which had the biggest grain surpluses – were killed or deported to labour camps in their millions. Farmers slaughtered their animals rather than hand them over, leading to the loss of half the national livestock. A drought and continued grain requisitions led to famine in the same three regions in 1932-33, in which a further six million or more people died. Some say Stalin deliberately orchestrated this to wipe out

opposition. An estimated 20 million country people left for the cities by 1939, by which time virtually all those left were 'collectivised'.

In heavy industry, if not in consumer goods, the first two Five Year Plans produced faster growth than any Western country ever showed. By 1939 only the USA and Germany had higher industrial output.

The Gulag & Purges

Many of these new mines and factories were in Central Asia or the resource-rich, but thinly populated, region of Siberia. A key labour force was provided by the network of concentration camps – now referred to as the Gulag, from **G**lavny **U**pravlenie **Lag**erey (Main Administration for Camps) – which stretched from the north of European Russia through Siberia and Central Asia to the Far East.

Many of the early camp inmates were farmers caught up in the collectivisation, but in the 1930s the terror shifted to Party members and other influential people not enthusiastic enough about Stalin. In 1934 Sergey Kirov, the popular Leningrad Party secretary and Stalin's second-in-command, who favoured alleviating the lot of the peasants and producing more consumer goods for urban workers, was murdered by an agent of the secret police (now called the NKVD).

This launched the biggest series of purges yet. That year 100,000 Party members, intellectuals and 'enemies of the people' disappeared or were executed in Leningrad alone. In 1936 the former Party leaders Zinoviev and Kamenev made absurd public confessions, admitting to murdering Kirov and plotting to kill Stalin, and were executed.

This was the first of the Moscow show trials, whose charges ranged from murder plots and capitalist sympathies to Trotskyist conspiracies. The biggest was staged in 1938 against 17 leading Bolsheviks, including the Party theoretician Bukharin. Throughout 1937 and 1938 the NKVD's 'black raven' vans continued quietly to take victims from their homes at night; most were never heard of again. In the non-Russian republics of the

USSR, virtually the whole Party apparatus was eliminated for 'bourgeois nationalism'. The ghastly business clawed its way into all sectors and levels of society – even 400 of the Red Army's 700 generals were shot. Its victims are thought to have totalled 8.5 million.

The Gulag population grew from 30,000 in 1928 to eight million in 1938. Prisoners were underfed, mistreated and literally worked to death; the average life expectancy was about two years, and 90% of inmates didn't come out alive. The Gulag continued well after WW II, and Boris Yeltsin announced the release of Russia's 'last 10' political prisoners from a camp near Perm in 1992.

The German-Soviet Pact

In 1939 the UK and France tried to persuade Stalin to join them in declaring war on Germany if it should invade Poland. They were coolly received. If the Germans were to walk into Poland they would be on the Soviet border, not far from Minsk, and ready, if the USSR was hostile, to roll on Moscow. Stalin needed time to prepare his country for war, and saw a deal with the Germans as a route to territorial gains in Poland.

On 23 August 1939, the Soviet and German foreign ministers, Molotov and Ribbentrop, stunned the world by signing a nonaggression pact. A secret protocol stated that any future rearrangement would divide Poland between them; Germany would have a free hand in Lithuania, and the Soviet Union in Estonia, Latvia, Finland and Bessarabia, which had been lost to Romania in 1918.

Germany invaded Poland on 1 September; the UK and France declared war on Germany on 3 September. Stalin traded the Polish provinces of Warsaw and Lublin with Hitler for most of Lithuania, and the Red Army marched into the newly acquired territories less than three weeks later. The Soviet gains in Poland, many of which were areas inhabited by non-Polish speakers and had been under Russian control before WW I, were quickly incorporated into the Belarusian and

Ukrainian republics of the USSR. The Baltic states were made republics of the USSR in 1940 (along with Moldavia, they brought the total of SSRs up to its final number of 15). But the Finns offered fierce resistance, fighting the Red Army to a standstill.

The Great Patriotic War

When Hitler put his secret plans for an invasion of the Soviet Union into effect as 'Operation Barbarossa' on 22 June 1941, the Soviet Union was not completely unprepared for war. The second and third Five Year Plans had given priority to arms industries, the army budget had increased 40-fold between 1933 and 1940, and universal military service had been introduced in 1939. But the disorganised Red Army was no match for the German war machine, which advanced on three fronts. Within four months the Germans had overrun Minsk and Smolensk and were just outside Moscow; they had marched through the Baltic states and laid siege to Leningrad; and had captured Kiev and most of Ukraine. Only an early, severe winter halted the advance.

The Soviet commander, General Zhukov, used the winter to push the Germans back from Moscow. Leningrad held out – and continued to do so for 2¼ years, during which over half a million of its civilians died, mainly from hunger. In 1942 Hitler ordered a new southern offensive towards the Caucasus oilfields, which got bogged down in the battle for Stalingrad (now Volgograd). Well aware of the symbolism of a city named after the Great Leader, both Hitler and Stalin ordered that there be no retreat.

The Germans, with insecure supply lines along a front that stretched more than 1600 km from north to south, also faced scorched earth and guerrilla warfare. Their atrocities against the population stiffened resistance. Stalin appealed to old-fashioned patriotism and eased restrictions on the Church, ensuring that the whole country rallied to the cause with incredible endurance. Military goods supplied by the Allies through the northern ports of Murmansk and Arkhangelsk were invaluable in the early days of the war. All

Soviet military industry was packed up, moved east of the Urals, and worked by women and Gulag labour.

The Soviet forces slowly gained the upper hand at Stalingrad, and on 2 February 1943 Field Marshal von Paulus surrendered what was left of the encircled German Sixth Army. It was the turning point of the war. The Red Army drove the Germans out of most of the Soviet Union by the end of the year and reached Berlin in April 1945.

The USSR had borne the brunt of the war. Its total losses, civilian and military, may never be known, but they probably reached at least 26 million. Recent estimates by some Western historians have put the figure as high as 40 million, or one-quarter of the Soviet Union's population – an astonishing statistic. The battle for Stalingrad alone cost an estimated one million Soviet troops, more than the combined US casualties in all theatres of the war, and the Smolensk-Moscow campaign of 1941 took the lives of 1.5 million.

The Red Army's successes meant that the US and British leaders, Roosevelt and Churchill, had to observe Stalin's wishes in the postwar settlement. At Tehran (November 1943) and Yalta (February 1945), the three agreed each to govern the areas they liberated until free elections could be held.

Soviet troops liberating Eastern Europe propped up local communist movements, which formed 'action committees' that either manipulated the elections or simply seized power when election results were unfavourable.

Postwar Stalinism

Control over Eastern Europe, and a postwar modernisation of industry with the aid of German factories and engineers seized as war booty, made the Soviet Union one of the two major world powers. The development of a Soviet atomic bomb as early as September 1949 demonstrated industry's new power. But the first postwar Five Year Plan was military and strategic (more heavy industry); consumer goods and agriculture remained low priorities.

A Cold War was shaping up between the communist and capitalist worlds, and in the USSR the new demon became 'cosmopolitanism' – warm feelings towards the West. The first victims were the estimated two million Soviet citizens repatriated by the Allies in 1945 and 1946. Some were former prisoners of war or forced labourers taken by the Germans; others were refugees or people who had taken the chance of war to escape the USSR. There were even prewar fugitives. They were sent straight to the Gulag in case their stay abroad had contaminated them. Party and government purges continued as Stalin's reign came to resemble that of Ivan the Terrible, with unpredictable, often shattering decisions.

The Cold War

In 1947 US President Harry Truman initiated a policy of 'containment' of Soviet influence within its 1947 limits. The US, British and French forces occupying western zones of Germany unified their areas. The Soviet troops in eastern Germany retaliated by blockading western Berlin, controlled by the Western powers, in 1948; it had to be supplied from the air for a year. This led to the long-term division of Germany. In 1949 the North Atlantic Treaty Organization (NATO) was set up to protect Western Europe against invasion. The Soviet Union replied with a series of military alliances which led to the Warsaw Pact in 1955.

The Khrushchev Era

Stalin died, allegedly of a stroke, in 1953. An estimated 20 million people had died in his purges, forced famines and labour camps, yet he had become something of a god in his own lifetime. Even inmates in the Gulag camps wept. Churchill commented that when Stalin took Russia on, it only had the wooden plough, but he left it with nuclear weapons.

Power passed to a combined leadership of five Politburo members. One, Lavrenty Beria, the head of the NKVD, was secretly tried and shot (and the NKVD was reorganised as the KGB, the Committee for

State Security, which was to remain firmly under Party control). In 1954 another, Nikita Khrushchev, a pragmatic Ukrainian who had helped carry out 1930s purges, launched the Virgin Lands campaign, bringing vast tracts of Kazakhstan and Central Asia under cultivation. A series of good harvests did his reputation no harm.

During the 20th Party congress in 1956, Khrushchev made a famous 'secret speech' about crimes committed under Stalin. It was the beginning of de-Stalinisation, marked by the release of some Gulag prisoners and a thaw in the political and intellectual climate. The congress also approved peaceful coexistence between communist and non-communist regimes. The Soviet Union, Khrushchev argued, would soon triumph over the 'imperialists' by economic means. Despite the setback of the 1956 Hungarian rebellion, which was put down by Soviet troops, in 1957 he emerged the unchallenged leader of the USSR.

In October 1957, the world listened to radio 'blips' from the first space satellite, Sputnik 1, and in 1961 Yury Gagarin became the first person in space. The Soviet Union seemed to be going places. But foreign crises undermined Khrushchev. In 1961 Berlin was divided by the Wall to stop an exodus from eastern Germany. In 1962, on the pretext of supplying the USSR's Caribbean ally Cuba with defensive weapons, Khrushchev stationed medium-range missiles with nuclear capability on the US doorstep. After some tense calling of bluff that brought the world to the brink of nuclear war, he withdrew the missiles.

A rift opened between the Soviet Union and China, itself now on the road to superpower status. The two competed for the allegiance of newly independent Third World nations and came into conflict over areas in Central Asia and the Far East that had been conquered by the tsars.

At home, the agricultural sector performed poorly and Khrushchev upset Party colleagues by decentralising economic decision-making. After a disastrous harvest in 1963 forced the Soviet Union to buy wheat from Canada, the Party's Central Committee relieved Khrushchev of his posts in 1964, because of 'advanced age and poor health'.

The Brezhnev Reaction

The new 'collective' leadership of Leonid Brezhnev (first secretary) and Alexey Kosygin (premier) soon devolved into a one-man show under the highly conservative Brezhnev. Stalin was once again portrayed as a national hero and Khrushchev's administrative reforms were rolled back. Economic stagnation was the predictable result, despite the exploitation of huge Siberian oil and gas reserves. But despite increased repression, the 'dissident' movement grew, along with *samizdat* (underground publishing). Prison terms and forced labour did not seem to have the desired effect, and in 1972 the KGB chief, Yury Andropov, introduced new measures that included forced emigration and the use of psychiatric institutions.

The growing government and Party elite, known as the *nomenklatura* ('list of nominees'), enjoyed lavish lifestyles, with access to goods that were unavailable to the average citizen. So did military leaders and some approved engineers and artists. But the ponderous, overcentralised economy, with its suffocating bureaucracy, was providing fewer and fewer improvements in general living standards. Incentive and initiative were dead; corruption began to spread in the Party and a cynical malaise began to spread through society.

Repression extended to countries under the Soviet wing. The 1968 Prague Spring, when new Czechoslovak Party leader Alexander Dubček promised 'Socialism with a human face', was crushed by Soviet troops. The invasion was later defended by the 'Brezhnev Doctrine' that the Soviet Union had the right to defend its interests among countries that fell within its sphere of influence. In 1979 Afghanistan would be one such country. Relations with China fell to an all-time low with border clashes in 1969. The military build-up between the two countries was only toned down in the late 1980s.

Ironically, the Brezhnev era also included

the easing of superpower tensions, known as détente. US President Richard Nixon visited Moscow and the two superpowers signed the first Strategic Arms Limitation Talks (SALT) treaty, restricting the number of nuclear ballistic weapons.

Andropov & Chernenko

Brezhnev was rarely seen in public after his health declined in 1979. Before he died in 1982, he came to symbolise the lifeless state of affairs in the country. The average age of Politburo members was 69.

Brezhnev's successor, the former KGB chief Yury Andropov, replaced some officials with young technocrats and began campaigns against alcoholism (which was costing the economy dearly) and corruption. He also clamped down on dissidents and increased defence spending, while the economy continued to decline.

Andropov died in February 1984, only 14 months after coming to power. The geriatric generation tried to cling to power by choosing the frail, 72-year-old Konstantin Chernenko as his successor. But Chernenko had only a year to live.

Gorbachev

Glasnost Mikhail Gorbachev, a 54-year-old Andropov protégé from Stavropol on Russia's southern steppes, was waiting to step up as general secretary. Articulate and energetic, he understood that the Soviet economy badly needed sparking back into life, and soon departed radically from the policies of his predecessors with greater openness at home and abroad. He launched an immediate turnover in the Politburo, bureaucracy and military, replacing many of the Brezhnevite 'old guard' with his own, younger supporters, and he clamped down vigorously on alcohol abuse. 'Acceleration' in the economy, and *glasnost* (openness), first manifested in press criticism of poor economic management and past Party failings, were his initial slogans. The aim was to spur the dangerously stagnant economy by encouraging some management initiative,

rewarding efficiency and letting bad practices be criticised.

Foreign Affairs In foreign policy, Gorbachev discontinued the isolationist, confrontational and economically costly policies of his predecessors. Most of the world was delighted to find an active intelligence at the helm in the Soviet Union. The constructive Georgian Eduard Shevardnadze replaced the dour Andrey Gromyko as foreign minister. At his first meeting with US President Ronald Reagan in Geneva in 1985, Gorbachev suggested a 50% cut in long-range nuclear weapons. By 1987 the two superpowers had agreed to remove all medium-range missiles from Europe; other significant cuts in arms and troop numbers followed. The 'new thinking' also put an end, in 1988-89, to the Soviet Union's 'Vietnam', the now-unpopular Afghan war. Relations with China improved too.

Perestroika At home, Gorbachev soon found that he could not expect a programme of limited reform to proceed smoothly and that he had some hard choices to make. The Chornobyl (Chernobyl) nuclear disaster in April 1986 led to one step along this road. Gorbachev announced there would be greater openness in reporting embarrassing things such as disasters; it had taken the authorities 18 days to admit the extent of the disaster at the power station in Ukraine, and even when they did, it was in a heavily expurgated form.

The anti-alcohol campaign won little but unpopularity and caused huge growth in illegal distilling. Before long it was abandoned.

But above all it was becoming clear that no leader who relied on the Party could survive as a reformer. Many Party officials, with their privileged positions and (in some cases) opportunities for corruption, were a hindrance to, not a force for, change. In the economy *perestroika* (restructuring) became the new slogan. This meant limited private enterprise and private property, not unlike

Lenin's NEP, plus further efforts to push decision-making and responsibility out towards the grass roots. New laws were enacted in both these fields in 1988, but their application met resistance from the centralised bureaucracy.

Glasnost was supposed to tie in with perestroika as a way to encourage new ideas and counter the Brezhnev legacy of cynicism. The release at the end of 1986 of a famous dissident, Nobel Peace Prize-winner Andrey Sakharov, from internal exile in Nizhny Novgorod was the start of a general freeing of political prisoners. Religions were allowed to operate more and more freely.

Political Reform In 1988 Gorbachev appealed over the Party's head to the people by announcing a new 'parliament', the Congress of People's Deputies, with two-thirds of its members to be elected directly by the people, thus reducing the power of the bureaucracy and Party. The elections were held and the congress convened, to outspoken debate and national fascination, in 1989. Though dominated by Party apparatchiks, the parliament also contained outspoken critics of the government such as Sakharov.

End of the Empire Gorbachev sprung repeated surprises, including sudden purges of difficult opponents, but the forces unleashed by his opening up of society grew impossible to control. From 1988 onwards, the reduced threat of repression and the experience of electing even semirepresentative assemblies spurred a growing clamour for independence in the Soviet satellite states in Eastern Europe, then in the USSR's Baltic republics, then Moldavia, then the Transcaucasian republics. The Eastern European countries threw off their Soviet puppet regimes one by one in the autumn of 1989. The Berlin Wall fell on 9 November. The Brezhnev Doctrine, Gorbachev's spokesperson said, had given way to the 'Sinatra Doctrine' – letting them do it *their* way. The formal reunification of Germany on 3 October 1990 marked the effective end of the Cold War.

In 1990 the three Baltic republics of the USSR also declared (or, as they would have it, reaffirmed) their independence – an independence which for the time being remained more theoretical than real. Before long, most other Soviet republics either followed suit or declared 'sovereignty' – the precedence of their own laws over the Soviet Union's. Gorbachev's proposal for an ill-defined new federal system, to hold the Soviet Union together, won few friends.

The Rise of Yeltsin Also in 1990, the populist reformer Boris Yeltsin won the chairmanship of the parliament of the giant Russian Republic, which had three-quarters of the USSR's area and more than half its population. Soon after coming to power, Gorbachev had promoted Yeltsin to head the Communist Party in Moscow, but had then dumped him in 1987-88 in the face of opposition to his reforms there from the Party old guard. Yeltsin had already by that time declared perestroika a failure, and these events produced a lasting personal enmity between the two men. Gorbachev struggled increasingly from then on to hold together the radical reformers and the conservative old guard in the Party.

Once chosen as chairman of the Russian parliament, Yeltsin proceeded to taunt and jockey for power with Gorbachev. He seemed already to have concluded that real change was impossible not only under the Communist Party but also within a centrally controlled Soviet Union, the members of which were in any case showing severe centrifugal tendencies. Yeltsin resigned from the Communist Party and his parliament proclaimed the sovereignty of the Russian Republic.

At street level, organised crime and black-marketeering boomed, profiting from a slackening of the law-and-order system, and preying on many of the fledgling private businesses by running protection rackets.

In early 1990 Gorbachev persuaded the Communist Party to vote away its own constitutional monopoly on power, and parliament chose him for the newly created post of executive president, which further distanced the organs of government from the Party. But these events made little difference to the crisis into which the USSR was sliding.

Economic Collapse & Old-Guard Reaction

Gorbachev's economic reforms, while wounding the old centralised command system badly enough to prevent it reaching even Brezhnevite levels of efficiency, were not profound enough to yield a healthy private sector or a sound, decentralised state sector. The old system was crippled but had not been replaced.

Prices went up, supplies of goods went down, people got angry. Some wanted all-out capitalism immediately; others wanted to go back to the suddenly rosy old days. Gorbachev tried to steer a middle course to prevent a showdown between the radical reformers and the conservatives in the Party and the armed forces – a tack which achieved nothing and pleased no-one.

Much of the record 1990 harvest was left to rot in fields and warehouses because the Party could no longer mobilise the machinery and hands to bring it in, while private enterprise was not yet advanced enough to do so. When Gorbachev, still trying to keep a balance, backed down in September 1990 from implementing the radical '500 Day Plan' – to shift to a fully fledged market economy within 500 days – many saw it as submission to the growing displeasure of the old guard, and the loss of his last chance to save reform.

His Nobel Peace Prize, awarded in the bleak winter of 1990-91, when fuel and food were disappearing from many shops, left the average Soviet citizen literally cold. The army, the security forces and the Party hardliners called with growing confidence for the restoration of law and order to save the country. Foreign minister Shevardnadze, long one of Gorbachev's staunchest partners but now under constant old-guard sniping for 'losing Eastern Europe', resigned in December 1990, warning of impending hardline dictatorship.

Fall of the Soviet Union

By spring 1991 Gorbachev appeared increasingly weak, directionless and under the old guard's thumb, with his popularity at an all-time low. Boris Yeltsin, committed to ending communist power and resigned to letting the republics – many of which now demanded full independence – go their own way, was already arguably more powerful than Gorbachev. In June Yeltsin was voted president of the Russian Republic in the country's first-ever direct presidential elections. Yeltsin demanded devolution of power from the Soviet Union to the republics, and banned Communist Party cells from government offices and workplaces in Russia. Gorbachev won some respite by fashioning a new union treaty, transferring greater power to the republics, which was to be signed on 20 August.

The Coup Matters were taken out of Gorbachev's hands, however, on 18 August, when a delegation from the 'Committee for the State of Emergency in the USSR' arrived at the Crimean dacha where he was taking a holiday and demanded that he declare a state of emergency and transfer power to the vice-president, Gennady Yanaev. Gorbachev refused and was put under house arrest. The old-guard coup had begun.

The eight-person State of Emergency Committee, which included Gorbachev's defence minister (Dmitry Yazov), his prime minister (Valentin Pavlov), his interior minister (Boris Pugo) and his KGB chief (Vladimir Kryuchkov), as well as Yanaev, planned to restore the Communist Party and the Soviet Union to their former status. On 19 August tanks appeared on Moscow's streets and it was announced that Yanaev had assumed the president's powers. But things didn't go according to the plot. Boris Yeltsin escaped arrest and went to the Moscow 'White House', seat of the Russian parliament, to rally opposition. Crowds gathered at the White House, persuaded some of the tank crews to switch sides, and started to build barricades. Yeltsin climbed on a tank to declare the coup illegal and call for a general strike. Troops ordered to storm the White House refused to do so.

The following day huge crowds opposed to the coup gathered in Moscow and Leningrad. The leaders of Ukraine and Kazakhstan rejected the coup. Estonia declared full independence from the Soviet Union. Coup leaders started to quit or fall ill. On 21 August the tanks withdrew; the coup leaders fled and – with the exception of Pugo, who shot himself – were arrested.

Demolition Gorbachev flew back to Moscow on 22 August, but his time was up. The old-style Soviet Union and the Communist Party were already suffering the consequences of their humiliation in the failed coup. Yeltsin had announced that all state property in the Russian Republic was under the control of Russia, not the Soviet Union. On 23 August he banned the Communist Party in Russia. Gorbachev resigned as the USSR Party's leader the following day, ordering that its property be transferred to the Soviet parliament.

Latvia had followed Estonia by declaring independence on 21 August (Lithuania had already done so back in March 1990). Most of the other republics of the USSR followed suit. International, and finally Soviet, recognition of the Baltic states' independence followed by early September.

Gorbachev embarked on a last-ditch bid to save the Soviet Union with proposals for a looser union of independent states. In September the Soviet parliament abolished the centralised Soviet state, vesting power in three temporary governing bodies until a new union treaty could be signed. But Yeltsin was steadily transferring control over everything that mattered in Russia from Soviet hands into Russian ones. On 8 December Yeltsin and the leaders of Ukraine and Belarus, meeting near Brest in Belarus, announced that the USSR no longer existed. They proclaimed a new Commonwealth of Independent States (CIS), a vague alliance of fully independent states with no central authority. Russia kicked the Soviet government out of the Kremlin on 19 December.

Two days later, at a meeting in Almaty, Kazakhstan, eight more republics joined the CIS, and the USSR was pronounced finally dead. (The only absentees among the 15 republics of the USSR were the three Baltic states and Georgia. Georgia joined the CIS later.)

Gorbachev, a president without a country, formally resigned on 25 December, the day the white, blue and red Russian flag replaced the Soviet red flag over the Kremlin.

Russia under Yeltsin
Economic Reform & Regional Tensions
Yeltsin was quick to announce plans to move to a free-market economy in Russia. Changes included the phasing out of state subsidies, freeing of prices, reduction in government spending, and privatisation of state businesses, housing, land and agriculture. In November 1991 Yeltsin had appointed a reforming government to carry this out. He himself was given the jobs of prime minister and defence minister, as well as president, as an emergency measure.

With the economy already in chaos, and the 1991 harvest the lowest in years because the distribution system had broken down, some local regions of Russia started hoarding scarce foodstuffs or declaring autonomy and control over their own economic resources. All the 20 nominally autonomous ethnic regions scattered across Russia, some of them rich in resources vital to the Russian economy, declared themselves autonomous republics, leading to fears that Russia might disintegrate as the USSR had just done. These worries were eventually defused, however, by a 1992 federative treaty between the central government and the republics; by a new constitution in 1993, which handed the other regions increased rights; and by changes in the tax system (see the later Government section for more information).

Conflict with the Old Guard The Russian parliament, although it had supported Yeltsin against the coup in 1991, could not tolerate the fast pace of his economic reforms, the weakening of Russian power which stemmed from his demolition of the Soviet Union, his arms-reduction agreements with the USA and his need for Western economic aid. Elected in 1990 under Gorbachev-era voting rules, the parliament was dominated by communists and Russian nationalists, both opposed to the course things were taking.

By as early as April 1991, Yeltsin's ministers were complaining that their reforms were being stymied by contradictory legislation from the parliament. As the austerity caused by economic reform continued to bite – though there was more in the shops, ordinary people could buy less – Yeltsin's popularity began to fall and his opponents in parliament launched a series of increasingly serious challenges to his position. Another complaint was a steady rise in organised crime, which was to some extent the result of the opening up of the economy – though corruption in the bureaucracy, which was now deeply mixed up in embezzling and smuggling state property, even oil, went back at least as far as the Brezhnev era.

Yeltsin was forced to sacrifice key ministers such as Yegor Gaidar, architect of the economic reforms, and to compromise on the pace of reform. In December 1992 parliament chose Viktor Chernomyrdin, an oil and gas-industry apparatchik, as prime minister to replace Gaidar. It continued to issue resolutions contradicting Yeltsin's presidential decrees, leaving overall policy heading nowhere. Though the president had strong executive powers, Russia's confused, much-amended, Soviet-era constitution failed to make clear the division of powers between president and parliament. The leaders of parliament's opposition to Yeltsin were its chairman Ruslan Khasbulatov and Yeltsin's own vice-president Alexandr Rutskoi, both men who had backed him against the 1991 coup.

In April 1993 a national referendum gave Yeltsin a big vote of confidence, both in his presidency and in his economic reform policies. But the National Salvation Front, an aggressive communist-nationalist group with strong links to parliament, continued to stir trouble, including May Day riots in Moscow which left 600 people injured. Yeltsin started moves towards framing a new constitution which would kill off the existing parliament and define more clearly the roles of president and legislature.

White House Showdown Finally, with neither party having demonstrable constitutional right on its side, matters came down to a trial of strength. In September 1993 parliament convened with plans to remove many of the president's powers. Yeltsin 'dissolved' the parliament, which in turn 'stripped' Yeltsin of all his powers. Yeltsin sent troops to blockade the White House, ordering the members to leave it by 4 October. Many did, but on 2 and 3 October the National Salvation Front attempted an insurrection, overwhelming the troops around the White House and attacking Moscow's Ostankino TV centre, where 62 people died. Though Yeltsin enjoyed only patchy support from the armed forces, next morning loyal tanks and troops stormed the White House, leaving at least 70 dead. Rutskoi and Khasbulatov were arrested. Yeltsin's use of force won him few friends.

1993 Elections Elections to a new form of parliament were held in December 1993. The name of the more influential lower house, the State Duma, consciously echoed that of tsarist Russia's parliaments. The inaptly named Liberal Democratic Party, led by the neofascist Vladimir Zhirinovsky, won a sizeable chunk of seats, though not enough to dominate the Duma, which was split between Communists (whose party had been relegalised in 1992), nationalists and reformers. Zhirinovsky blamed Jews and foreigners for Russia's troubles, courted Saddam Hussein and had advocated, among other things, executing gangsters and resurrecting the Russian empire by annexing most of the old Soviet Union and even portions of Poland, Finland and Alaska. The size of his vote was interpreted more as a protest against falling living standards and rising crime than as a positive endorsement of his views.

At the same time as the elections, a national referendum gave the go-ahead to a new Yeltsin-drafted constitution, which gave the president a clear upper hand over parliament. The constitution also enshrines the rights to free trade and competition, private ownership of land and property, freedom of conscience, and free movement in and out of Russia, and bans censorship, torture and the establishment of any official ideology. A few months later it was found that electoral officials had fraudulently manipulated the referendum returns to achieve the 50% turnout needed for the vote to be considered valid, but by then no-one seemed to be interested in taking up cudgels over the issue.

In one of its more noteworthy actions, in February 1994 the Duma declared an amnesty for the coup plotters of 1991 and Yeltsin's parliamentary opponents of 1993. Rutskoi and Khasbulatov were freed from prison. (The 1991 gang had been freed in 1992 and their treason trial in 1993 had fizzled out.)

The new cabinet picked by Chernomyrdin (still prime minister) after the elections left out any leading economic reformers, but the pragmatic and increasingly influential Chernomyrdin turned out to be more of a reformer and less of an old-guard hack than many had expected. The year 1994 saw some benefits of economic reform take hold in a few big cities, notably Moscow and St Petersburg (the name to which Leningrad had reverted in 1991), where a market economy was taking root and an enterprise culture was developing among the younger generations.

The Mafia In the country at large, progress was slower and Yeltsin, increasingly perceived as indecisive and dictatorial, sank lower and lower in popular esteem, with two years of his presidential term (until 1996) still to run.

The big problem preoccupying everybody was crime and corruption. The 'Mafia' – a broad term encompassing the many thousands of corrupt officials (including some Yeltsin-era appointees), business people,

financiers and police, as well as small and big-time gangsters – had spread into every corner and level of society. Yeltsin had described them as a 'threat to Russia's strategic interests and national security' in 1993. By 1994 about one in 5000 Russians was being murdered each year, about twice as many as in the USA and about 10 times more than in Britain. Politicians, industrialists, financiers, even TV stars were among the victims of contract killings (for which the normal price was reportedly US$2000 a corpse). One of Yeltsin's advisers reported in 1994: 'every, repeat every, owner of a shop or kiosk pays a racketeer'. The FBI opened an office in Moscow to help fight international organised crime and drug trafficking, in which Russia was a rising 'star'.

Gangsters had not only profited from economic liberalisation through being some of the few people with capital to invest, but also hindered it by scaring off potential entrepreneurs. No-one was able to do a thing about it, least of all Yeltsin, despite some blustery pronouncements. With the problem reaching such high levels of society, the only possible solution seemed to many to be an all-out war on crime – a prospect which raised the spectres of suspended civil rights and a deepening of Yeltsin's dictatorial tendencies.

War in Chechnya Foreign policy reflected the growing mood of conservative nationalism at home. Russia was concentrating on making most of the former Soviet Union into its 'sphere of influence'. While the need for a buffer zone between Russia and the outside world was one reason for this, the millions of ethnic Russians living in the former Soviet republics, many of them already moving to Russia as political tides turned against them, were also a concern. Russian troops had intervened in fighting in Georgia, Moldova and Tajikistan with the aim of strengthening Russia's hand in those regions, and by early 1995 Russian forces were stationed in varying numbers in all the other former republics except Estonia and Lithuania.

But the Russian military's most significant adventure since the Afghan War was a disaster. This was the war in Chechnya, intended to bring to heel this Muslim republic of around one million people in the Caucasus, which had declared independence from Russia in 1991. Chechnya, prone to internal conflicts and noted as the homeland of many of the most powerful and violent gangsters in Russia (some of whom had staged Russia's biggest bank fraud when they defrauded the Russian central bank of US\$325 million in 1992), also sat across the routes of the pipelines which bring oil from the Caspian Sea to Russia. Its leader, Jokar Dudaev, seemed to enjoy taunting Moscow and flouting its laws.

Attempts to negotiate a settlement or have Dudaev deposed had got nowhere by November 1994. Yeltsin, perhaps hoping to cash in on the nationalist mood in Russia, ordered his army and air force into Chechnya for what was meant to be a quick operation to restore Russian control. But the Chechens, whose fighting tradition goes back to 19th-century wars against imperial Russian forces, fought bitterly. Their resistance was also fuelled by an anti-Russian resentment stemming from 1943-45, when the Chechens were among six peoples from the Caucasus region deported en masse to Central Asia for alleged collaboration with the invading Germans (the surviving Chechens were allowed back in the 1950s).

By April 1995 at least 25,000 people, mostly civilians, were dead, and the Russians had only just gained full control of the Chechen capital, Grozny, which had been reduced to rubble by bombing, shelling and house-to-house fighting. Some 300,000 or more people had fled their homes, Dudaev was still holding out in southern Chechnya, and guerrilla warfare looked likely to go on for some time.

GEOGRAPHY
European Russia dwarfs all other European countries in size but still makes up only a quarter of the 17 million sq km area of Russia, which is the world's biggest country. The border between Europe and Asia runs down the west side of the Ural Mountains, 1300 km east of Moscow.

Cities and towns are concentrated chiefly across the middle half of European Russia, thinning out in the frozen north and the southern steppe.

Boundaries
In the north, European Russia faces the Arctic Kara and Barents seas and the White Sea (an inlet of the Barents Sea), and has a short border with Norway and a longer one with Finland. The Novaya Zemlya and Zemlya Frantsa-Iosifa island groups, the latter stretching to the edge of the permanent Arctic icecap, are also part of European Russia. South of Finland, Russia opens on the Gulf of Finland, an inlet of the Baltic Sea. St Petersburg stands at the east end of this gulf. In the west and south-west, Russia borders Estonia, Latvia, Belarus and Ukraine. The small Kaliningrad region of Russia lies disconnected from the rest of the country, between Lithuania, Poland and the Baltic Sea. East of Ukraine, stretches of Russian coast on the Sea of Azov, an inlet of the Black Sea, and on the Black Sea itself, intervene before Russia's borders with Georgia and Azerbaijan in the Caucasus mountains. East of the Caucasus, Russia faces the Caspian Sea, and north of the Caspian its border with Kazakhstan runs up to the Urals.

Topography
Most of the country is flat. The Urals rise no higher than 1900 metres. The plains to their west are never more than 500 metres high, averaging just 170 metres. Only in the Caucasus, marching across between the Black and Caspian seas on European Russia's southern fringe, are major elevations reached. Here, just on the Russian side of the border with Georgia, stands 5642-metre Elbrus, Europe's highest peak.

Rivers & Lakes
Hundreds of rivers snake across the plains. The biggest is the 3690-km Volga, Europe's longest river and until the 20th century one

of Russia's major highways. The Volga rises north-west of Moscow, then flows eastward for about half its length before turning south at Kazan and emptying into the Caspian Sea near Astrakhan. Long stretches of the river are now reservoirs for hydroelectric purposes. The Volga also has the biggest drainage basin (1.38 million sq km) of any European river. The next-longest rivers are the 1870-km Don, which rises south of Moscow and flows south into the Sea of Azov, and the 1810-km Pechora, which flows from the Urals to the Barents Sea.

With all these 'highests' and 'longests', you might bet on Europe's biggest lake being in Russia, too. In fact it contains the two biggest, both north-east of St Petersburg: Lake Ladoga (18,390 sq km) and Lake Onega (9600 sq km).

CLIMATE

The central fact of the Russian climate, which has a deep effect on the national psyche, is its long, dark, very cold winters, whose severity is explained by the fact that so much of the country is so far north and so far from the open sea. (See Appendix III at the back of the book for climate charts.)

Moscow & St Petersburg

The two main cities are both warm from about mid-May to early September (see charts in Appendix II at the back of the book). Summer days in these northern latitudes are long – so long that at midsummer in St Petersburg there's no real darkness. Autumn is brief, and by the end of November Moscow is frozen most of the time. Serious snow arrives in December and stays till late March/early April. St Petersburg, beside an arm of the Baltic Sea, is a few degrees milder than Moscow in winter but in midwinter is reduced to about five hours of murky light a day. Spring arrives fast with a great thaw, a month or so long, in March and April, and people go a touch crazy. Thousands of extra cars emerge from winter storage onto city streets.

The South

South of Moscow the inland climate is similar to that in Moscow, though perhaps a few degrees warmer in summer. The Black Sea coast is mild – it rarely freezes, and from mid-May to early September temperatures typically reach between 20°C and 27°C. Coastal waters of the Black Sea itself are usually in the low 20s from June to September.

The North

Up north, as you'd expect, it gets even colder than in Moscow. Arkhangelsk, despite being on the coast, averages around 5°C below Moscow's temperatures, and inland it's even more bitter. Murmansk, which benefits from the dying eddies of the Gulf Stream, is a bit warmer, and its port is ice-free all year round – but here, 200 km inside the Arctic Circle, there's permanent darkness in December and January.

Rainfall

July and August, the warmest months, are also the wettest months in most places, with as many as one rainy day in three. But only the Caucasus receives really serious precipitation. The area between Moscow and St Petersburg is marginally wetter than most of the rest of European Russia, but still gets only half as much rain in a year as New York, and even receives less than Rome. The lower Volga, from around Saratov, is a bit drier.

FLORA, FAUNA & ENVIRONMENT

European Russia's natural vegetation falls into several east-west bands. Northernmost is the tundra, which covers the northern 150 km or so of mainland and southern Novaya Zemlya. (Northern Novaya Zemlya and Zemlya Frantsa-Iosifa are mostly ice-covered.) Delicate lichens, mosses, grasses, flowers and a few low shrubs and trees grow in the tundra on the permafrost, a frozen bog hundreds of metres deep. Seals, walruses and polar bears live on or near the coasts; lemmings, polar foxes, wolves and (sometimes domesticated) reindeer live inland.

Next is the *taiga*, the northern pine, fir,

spruce and larch forest, which stretches from the Arctic Circle to the latitudes of St Petersburg and Yaroslavl. The vast stretches of forest and tundra across the country serve as a major carbon sink, which helps to minimise the release of carbon compounds that contribute to global warming. The taiga shelters elk, some reindeer, wolves, brown bears (also native to the mixed forest further south), beaver, lynx, foxes and many smaller furry animals.

Further south, stretching in the west from around St Petersburg almost to Ukraine, is a band of mixed forest roughly 500 km wide, in which broad-leaved species (predominantly birch) steadily replace conifers as you move south. Deer, wolves, lynx and foxes are among its fauna. Moscow lies in this belt.

From the latitudes of Voronezh and Saratov down into the Kuban area north of the Caucasus stretches the steppe (from *stepi*, meaning plain), the flat or gently rolling band of low grassland, mostly treeless except along river banks, which runs intermittently all the way from Mongolia to Hungary. Since much of the steppe is on humus-rich *chyornozyom* (black earth), superb for grain growing, most of it is cultivated and no longer in its natural state. Fauna of the steppe are mostly small, but herds of the small saiga (a type of antelope), an ancient animal which once grazed all the way from Britain to Alaska, still roam the more arid steppe regions around the northern Caspian Sea. These areas are being desertified because of the huge herds of sheep grazed on them. The delta through which the Volga River enters the Caspian is, in contrast to the surrounding area, very rich in plant and wildlife. Huge carpets of the pink or white Caspian lotus flower spread across the waters in summer, many millions of birds of over 200 species frequent the delta, and wild boar and 30 other mammals roam the land.

The steppe gives way to alpine regions in the Caucasus, a botanist's wonderland with 6000 highly varied plant species and glorious wild flowers in summer. Fauna of the Caucasus include the tur (a mountain goat),

the bezoar (wild goat), the endangered mouflon (mountain sheep), the chamois (an antelope), the brown bear and the reintroduced European bison. The lammergeier (bearded vulture), the endangered griffon vulture, the imperial eagle, the peregrine falcon, the goshawk and the snowcock are among the Caucasus' most spectacular birds. Both types of vulture will occasionally attack a live tur.

Conservation

Russian wildlife has always been hunted – for furs as much as for meat – and some species are now also threatened by pollution. Official 'Red Books' list endangered and now supposedly protected species of animal and plant life.

State Nature Reserves Many of the former USSR's 160 state nature reserves (*zapovedniki*), ranging in size up to several thousand sq km, are in European Russia. These are areas set aside to protect fauna and flora, often habitats of endangered or unique species, where controls are very strict. There's also a class of *zakazniki*, areas where protection is limited to specific species or seasons.

These reserves are important for several reasons, and they are the source of some of the best news coming out of Russia today. Unlike most other developing countries, Russia has both an extensive and strictly policed network of reserves, and the educational and scientific infrastructure necessary to support it. In terms of size and geographic representation, this network is virtually unsurpassed. The biological diversity of Russia is better documented than that in most Western countries. And the dedication of the scientists and others who act as guardians of Russia's wilds is truly astounding.

But, as with reserves in developing countries, the entire network is in danger of collapse due to a shortage of funds. Governmental agencies, along with the scientific community and other, nongovernmental organisations, are working to raise money to support the network. Some reserves are open to visitors but you usually can't roam freely. Information on some reserves and how to visit them is included in regional sections of this book. A visit to one of the reserves is usually a fascinating experience, and is a boon to the reserves and the people who work on them – your money goes a very long way here.

These reserves have certainly helped the cause of many animals that might otherwise have been in danger, among them the brown bear and polar bear. One notable success story is that of the European bison, Europe's largest mammal, whose world population of 48 in 1927 was all in captivity. Thanks to breeding programmes at reserves like Prioxko-Terrasny, south of Moscow, and Belavezhskaja Pushcha, which straddles the Belarus-Poland border, these bison have been returned to the wild in places like the Caucasus; there are now over 3000 in Russia and the rest of Europe.

Pollution

As you'll notice every time you breathe on a city street or gaze across an urban skyline, environmental cleanliness has not ranked high among the priorities of Russia's rulers. In the Soviet period, Russia suffered from having a bureaucracy with a penchant for massive projects, which didn't worry about these projects' side effects or admit its mistakes – or even, as the 1986 Chornobyl (Chernobyl) disaster in Ukraine most famously showed, tell people when their lives were in danger. Environmental awareness has increased since the late Soviet period, but in these economically desperate times the emphasis has been on exploiting all available resources. A lot of aged industrial plant, which even when new took little care of its wastes, still operates. In 1992 Russian government scientists calculated that 15% of the country was 'ecologically unsafe' for people. In that year it was also reported that the average 40-year-old would have consumed 28 kg of toxic chemicals in food grown in the former USSR.

Notable Soviet-induced environmental disasters of European Russia include:

- up to 2.7 million people still living in areas of Russia affected by the Chornobyl disaster (mostly in the west around Bryansk); 400,000 of them are in areas from which it is recognised they should be moved; there are increased rates of cancer and heart problems among these people;
- at least 120 underground and atmospheric nuclear tests on the Arctic Novaya Zemlya islands, and abnormally high cancer rates among the local Nentsy people and their reindeer herds;
- Russia's nuclear power stations are widely regarded as accidents waiting to happen, though its 11 RBMK Chornobyl-type reactors (four near St Petersburg, three near Smolensk, and four near Kursk) have all been modified to correct the design defect that led to the Chornobyl disaster; more safety incidents are reported at the supposedly safer VVR-type reactors;
- desertification of the Kalmyk Steppe areas around the northern Caspian Sea because of overgrazing by sheep;
- erosion of fertile black-earth steppe lands because of excessive cultivation;
- severe pollution of the Volga by industrial waste, sewage, pesticides and fertilisers; and a chain of hydro-electric dams along the river, blocking fish spawning routes and slowing the current, which encourages fish parasites (it now takes water 18 months to flow from Rybinsk to Volgograd, instead of the one month it used to);
- all main rivers, including the Volga, Don, Kama, Kuban and Oka, have 10 to 100 times the permitted viral and bacterial levels;
- chronic overfishing of the Arctic Barents Sea, pollution of both the Baltic and Black seas (though the ex-Soviet states are not the only or even the major culprits in either case), and the near extermination of life in the Sea of Azov from overfishing, salination and industrial pollution;
- many cities with excessive toxins in their air.

GOVERNMENT

Russia is governed by an executive president and a two-house legislature or parliament. This system was ushered in by the new constitution of 1993. The previous constitution, which failed to separate clearly the powers of president and parliament, was to a large extent to blame for the 1993 White House shoot-out. The new system is an improvement in this respect but still leaves room for potential conflict, since both the president and the parliament can (and do) make laws.

The parliament has an upper house, the Federation Council, and a lower house, the

State Duma, and is chosen by national elections every two years – though some members have been campaigning for a longer term. The Federation Council has, among other things, most of the responsibility for legislation on the relationship between the central government and the regions; the State Duma oversees economic legislation. The exact make-up of the two houses is still evolving; at the time of writing the Federation Council has two members from each of Russia's regions, territories and republics, giving a total of 178 members. The State Duma has 450 members, half of them elected in first-past-the-post contests in local constituencies, and half on a national basis by a proportional representation system in which voters merely name party preferences.

The president, elected in direct, universal-suffrage elections, serves a four-year term. (Boris Yeltsin was elected in 1991 under an earlier constitution which gave him a five-year term.) Defence, security and foreign policy are largely in the president's hands, and a number of special powers give the president a constitutional upper hand over parliament. The president can:

- issue decrees which have the force of law;
- nominate the prime minister – and disband the State Duma and call new elections if it rejects the president's nominee(s) three times;
- select the cabinet in consultation with the prime minister;
- veto legislation (and the veto can only be over-ridden by a two-thirds majority in both houses of parliament);
- declare a state of emergency and temporarily curb some civil rights.

Several key government ministries and committees report directly to the president, not the prime minister – among them, those for defence, the interior, foreign affairs, espionage, TV and radio.

Republics & Regions

Russia is officially known as the Russian Federation, a name which acknowledges the existence of 21 semiautonomous republics within it. The rest of Russia is divided into 68 regions (*oblasti*) and territories (*krai*). About two-thirds of the republics, regions and territories are in European Russia; the rest fall east of the Urals.

The republics exist as a result of the old Soviet system of nominally autonomous republics for many minority ethnic groups. In Soviet times those autonomous republics that lay surrounded by, or next to, Russia were grouped with it in a 'federation' which made up the USSR's Russian Republic. After the collapse of the Soviet Union, all these republics declared varying degrees of autonomy from Russia, the most extreme being Chechnya, in the Caucasus, which unilaterally declared full independence. At the same time, even some of the regions – especially those rich in resources – began to pass laws that conflicted with Moscow's, and to declare 'economic sovereignty' and other types of autonomy, leading to fears that Russia itself might crack up as the USSR had done.

In 1992 President Yeltsin struck a deal with all but two of the then 20 republics, which gave them 'sovereignty' and control over their own natural resources and foreign policy. This pacified most of the republics. (One of the absentees, Tatarstan on the Volga, came more or less into line later; the other, Chechnya, having spun off a separate new republic, Ingushetia, in the meantime, became an international talking-point when it was invaded by Russian forces in 1994.) But the republics' sovereignty, which in theory permitted them to stop paying taxes to Moscow, provoked jealousy in some of the regions and territories, which said they, too, wanted to be republics.

The 1993 constitution awarded regions and territories much the same status as republics and declared that federal laws always took precedence over local ones. By 1994, with the notable exception of Chechnya, republican and regional rebelliousness was on the wane, deflated also by a fairer division of tax revenue between the centre and the regions.

ECONOMY

Russia is a country of astonishing resources. Russian economics is the attempt to avoid an equally astonishing failure to capitalise on those resources. Since 1991 Russia's rulers have been trying to introduce capitalism as the way to reach this goal. Their progress has been steady, though often impeded, and their results mixed.

Legacy of the Past

The centralised, state-run 'command economy' of the Soviet era, based on large single-product units with priority on military and heavy industrial development, turned a nation of peasants into a superpower and the world's number two industrial giant. But by the 1980s this system, with its industrial plant getting out of date and few incentives for the workers other than corruption, was becoming less and less efficient. Gorbachev's attempts at reform disrupted the planned economy but were not drastic enough to develop a workable substitute.

Market Reform & Industry

The new government of independent Russia in 1991 was strongly pro-market and aimed for a quick transition to capitalism. But the economy it had to start with was a shambles. The food distribution system and trade with other ex-Soviet republics had more or less collapsed, and there was a huge budget deficit. The reformers' first task was to make enough food available to stave off starvation. This they did by removing state controls on most prices – goods reappeared in the shops at much higher prices but trading, rather than hoarding, became worthwhile again. The reformers were heavily criticised for the increased prices of basic foodstuffs – setting the tone for years of struggle with those who tried to salvage some aspects of the old system. This led to a stop-go path for economic reform.

One of the main battles was over military and heavy industry. There was an 80% cut in military procurement spending in 1992, and

further cuts after that. This helped to spark conservative resistance to cuts in other government spending on industry. Inefficient, 'rust-bucket' factories – some producing goods they could not sell, others not even producing anything – were kept open with government subsidies as the old bureaucracy fought to prop up the sources of its privileges. The printing of money needed for this kept inflation very high, with prices multiplying about 25 times in 1992 and 10 times in 1993. By 1995 inflation was down to about 150% a year. The rouble fell from around 50 to the US dollar in mid-1991 to around 4500 by mid-1995.

Gradually, however, government spending was reined in and subsidies were drastically reduced. This and other effects of the old system's collapse led to a steady fall in total output of 15% to 20% a year in the early 1990s. By 1994 output was less than half what it had been in 1990. Inter-enterprise debts reached crisis levels, amounting by late 1994 to US$57 billion. Workers could not be paid and factories halted production. Fraud and embezzlement of resources on a vast scale have reduced not only the profitability of enterprises but also the government's tax income.

Though far more goods are now available in Russia and private commerce flourishes in the bigger cities, Russian industry is all too rarely the beneficiary as many of the goods are imported. Nearly all sectors of industry were still in trouble by early 1995, though overall prospects were certainly brighter than four years previously.

Privatisation

Privatisation proceeded steadily and by 1994 around 100,000 of the 180,000 state businesses had been sold off – with, inevitably, a measure of corruption among those in charge of the process. Shops and small factories were sold first, bigger factories later. By the end of 1993 the private sector already employed an estimated 42% of the workforce and produced 35% to 40% of national output. More than 40 million Russians are now shareholders. But in 1994 more than

600 products were still being made by monopolies, many of which the government could not allow to close for fear of disrupting supply to their customers.

Western Aid & Investment
Russia has continued to need large-scale Western loans to help meet its budget deficits, which the cost of the 1994-95 Chechen war only worsened. Western investment in Russia, which the reformers hoped would be a major source of capital, has been badly scared off by political instability, high taxes, and a highly complicated, often contradictory legal framework.

Living Standards
Market reforms have created a sizeable class of wealthy and comfortably off Russians – in many cases thanks to criminal or semilegal activities. At the other end of the scale are the inevitable victims. Unemployment, officially nonexistent in Soviet times, was officially about 2% by the end of 1994, though in reality it was probably 10% or more. Many workers on lengthy unpaid leave from dead-end factories were not counted in the official figures.

In US dollar terms, average monthly wages rose from US$10 in early 1992 to US$85 in 1994.

Agriculture
One important area where change was particularly slow was the countryside. Though grain harvests recovered from the 1991 levels, which were the lowest in years, agriculture continued to eat up big government subsidies. Only in October 1993 did a presidential decree, which allowed land to be bought and sold freely, open the way to decollectivisation of Russia's 26,700 state and collective farms, where 27 million people live. The 200,000 private farms which had come into existence were still mostly tiny, short of money and often victimised by local officials.

POPULATION & PEOPLE
Some 117 million of Russia's 150 million

people live in European Russia. Three-quarters of European Russia's people live in towns and cities, the most densely populated areas being around Moscow (population nine million) and St Petersburg (five million), and the areas stretching east of Moscow as far as Kazan and Samara, and south to Voronezh and Saratov. The biggest cities after Moscow and St Petersburg, all with populations of one to 1.5 million, are Nizhny Novgorod, Samara, Kazan, Perm, Ufa, Rostov-on-Don and Volgograd.

About 80% of European Russia's people are Russians. The rest belong to dozens of smaller ethnic groups, all with their own languages and cultural traditions (in varying degrees of life), and varied religions. Their complex distribution has been shaped by war and migration over many thousands of years. Among them are not only Ukrainians, Belarusians, Georgians and others from former Soviet republics, but also many groups whose chief homeland is within Russia. Most of the major groups among the latter have their own republics within Russia, some of which – notably Chechnya and Tatarstan – have proved resistant to incorporation in the new Russia since 1991 (see Government). Many of these groups are, however, minorities even within their republics.

More information on minority peoples can be found in the regional chapters.

Middle Volga Minorities
The region east of Moscow, around the middle section of the Volga River and its tributaries, contains the biggest ethnic minorities, though they're still outnumbered about three to one in the region by Russians. The system of republics in this region stems from Soviet attempts to limit the influence of the Tatars, historical rivals of the Russians.

The region's, and European Russia's, biggest minority are the Tatars themselves, who are descended from the Mongol-Tatar armies of Jenghiz Khan and his successors and from earlier Hunnic, Turkic and Finno-Ugric settlers on the middle Volga. The Tatars are mostly Muslim, and some 1.8

million of them form nearly half the population of the Tatarstan republic, whose capital is Kazan, on the Volga. Tatarstan, rich in oil and with an important truck-building industry, bargained hard over its political connection with the rest of Russia following a 1992 referendum in favour of 'sovereignty' for Tatarstan. With about 2.5 million more Tatars in nearby republics and regions, even a 1920s proposal for a larger Tatarstan republic encompassing several of these was resuscitated. A million or so Tatars live in other parts of European Russia, and a further million or so elsewhere in the former USSR.

Two other important groups in the middle Volga region are the Chuvash (1.8 million) and the Bashkirs (1.5 million). The Chuvash, descendants of the pre-Mongol-Tatar settlers in the region, are Orthodox Christian and form a majority in Chuvashia (capital: Cheboxary). The Bashkirs are a partly Turkic people, nominally Muslim, about half of whom live in the Bashkortostan republic (capital: Ufa). Here, however, they are outnumbered both by Russians and by Tatars.

The other four major groups of the region are Finno-Ugric peoples, descendants of its earliest known inhabitants, and distant relatives of the Estonians, Hungarians and Finns: the 1.2 million Orthodox or Muslim Mordvins, a quarter of whom live in Mordovia (capital: Saransk); the 800,000 Udmurts or Votyaks, predominantly Orthodox, two-thirds of them living in Udmurtia (capital: Izhevsk); the 700,000 Mari or Cheremys, with an animist/shamanist religion, nearly half of them in Mary-El (capital: Yoshkar-Ola); and the 350,000 Komi, Orthodox, mostly in the Komi Republic (capital: Syktyvkar).

Of all these groups only the Tatars and the Chuvash are not outnumbered in their own republics by Russians.

Northern Minorities

About 140,000 members of another Finno-Ugric people, the Karelians, live in European Russia. Some 80,000 of them form 10% of the population of the Karelia republic north of St Petersburg. More Karelians live across the border in Finland.

Just 1900 or so Saami (Lapps), another Finno-Ugric people spread over both Russia and Scandinavia, live in the far north-west.

Southern Minorities

The northern Caucasus, which is in Russia, is a real ethnic jigsaw of at least 19 local nationalities. Several of them have been involved in ethnic conflicts in recent years, some of which stem from Stalinist gerrymandering of their territories. Resentments were also fuelled by Stalin's deportation of four entire Caucasus peoples – the Chechens, Ingush, Balkars and Karachay – to Central Asia in 1943-45, allegedly for collaboration with the German invaders. Those who hadn't died were allowed to return in the 1950s.

The Chechens, a Muslim people almost one million strong, are renowned for their fierce nationalism. This prompted Chechnya to declare independence from Russia in 1991 and, four years later, led to a savage war, in which Russia attempted to regain control of Chechnya.

The biggest of the other groups are the 600,000 Avars, mostly in Dagestan, descendants of a people related to the Huns who came from China or Mongolia around 1500 years ago; the mainly Christian Ossetians, probably descended from a group of Sarmatians pushed into the Caucasus around 400 AD, over 300,000 of whom form a majority in North Ossetia, where they have been involved in bitter violence with the neighbouring Ingush; the 390,000 Muslim Kabarda, mostly in the Kabarda-Balkar republic; about 300,000 Dargin in Dagestan; and approximately 240,000 Muslim Lezgians, speaking 20 or more different languages, also in Dagestan.

Cossacks

The Cossacks, particularly in places north of the Caucasus such as Krasnodar, Stavropol and Novocherkassk, have been reasserting their identity. After the Bolshevik revolution the Cossacks, who had mostly sided with the Whites in the Civil War, suffered massacres, deportations and victimisation and were not recognised as a separate ethnic group. They were registered under other nationalities, usually Russian or Ukrainian. Cossacks are trying to revive their military traditions and have strong Russian nationalist tendencies, merging into xenophobia and anti-Semitism. In 1920 there were about four million Cossacks, but it's difficult to estimate the number of Cossacks today.

Jews
From about one million Jews in Russia in 1989, some 700,000 remained by late 1993. Most are in urban European Russia, but there's also a small, conservative community of 19,000 'Mountain Jews' in the Caucasus. Rising anti-Semitism in Russia, as well as a relaxation of exit rules since the mid-1980s, contributed to an exodus to Israel, Germany, the USA and elsewhere.

After Kiev's destruction of the Judaic Khazar Empire, Russia had few Jews until the 1772-95 partitions of Poland brought in half a million, who were confined by law to the occupied lands – roughly, present-day Ukraine, Belarus, Lithuania and eastern Poland, the so-called Pale of Settlement. The notion of a 'Jewish problem' grew in the 19th century, exploding in the 1880s into pogroms and massive emigration to Western Europe and the USA.

On top of Soviet antireligious policies, Stalin devoted himself after WW II to the destruction of Jewish cultural life, shutting schools, theatres and publishing houses. An attempt to set up a Jewish Autonomous Region in the Far East was a flop. The denial of Jewish applications for emigration in the early 1980s gave rise to the issue of 'refuseniks'. With its new religious freedoms, glasnost also brought an upsurge in grass-roots anti-Semitism, and emigration grew to a flood.

Germans
In 1992 Russia and Germany signed an agreement to restore the ethnic German republic on the Volga, south and east of Saratov, in a bid to stem the rapid flow of ethnic Germans from Russia to Germany, though it is doubtful whether the agreement will be carried out. Many Germans had settled in this and other Russian regions in the 18th century. The republic was abolished by Stalin. In 1992 the former Soviet Union officially had two million ethnic Germans, and in reality probably more, though the majority of these were in Kazakhstan, Central Asia and Siberia, largely as a result of Stalinist deportations.

Russian Returnees
Well over 20 million Russians live outside Russia in other former republics of the USSR. The greatest numbers in 1989 were in Ukraine (11.4 million), Kazakhstan (6.2 million), Uzbekistan (1.7 million) and Belarus (1.3 million). Russians also formed 20% or more of the population in three smaller republics – Estonia, Latvia and Kyrgyzstan. These numbers are now all reduced as many Russians, some of whose families have been settled outside Russia for generations, have moved to Russia to escape wars, discrimination or just anti-Russian sentiment in the newly independent states. Some have come as refugees from fighting, others as 'economic migrants'. An estimated 2.5 million had moved to Russia by 1995, and there were fears that millions more would follow if conditions for Russians in the other republics did not improve.

ARTS & CULTURE
Information & Tickets
Practical information on how to find out what's on and get tickets for concerts, theatres, sports events etc is given under Entertainment in the Facts for the Visitor chapter that follows and in city chapters.

Literature & Drama
19th Century The poet Alexandr Pushkin (1799-1837) is revered as the father of Russian literature. Almost every step he took – and he travelled *very* widely around tsarist Russia – is marked by a monument or museum. *Yevgeny Onegin*, a verse novel, was his major work.

The first, and probably shortest, important Russian novel, *A Hero of Our Time* by Mikhail Lermontov (1814-41), makes a great travelling companion in the Caucasus, where it's set. Its cynical antihero, Pechorin, is an indirect comment on the climate of the times. Pushkin and Lermontov launched a long tradition of conflict between writers and the state, and both died in duels widely perceived as set up by the authorities. The satirical *The Government Inspector* by Nikolai Gogol (1809-52), who also wrote the novel *Dead Souls*, was the first major Russian play.

Ivan Turgenev (1818-83) was the first of the three great novelists of the second half of the 19th century. Bazarov, hero of his *Fathers and Sons*, became a symbol for the antitsarist nihilist movement. *The Possessed* by Fyodor Dostoevsky (1821-81) is both a satire of provincial society and an analysis of political violence. Like his other great works – *Crime and Punishment*, set in the St Petersburg slums, *The Idiot* and *The Brothers Karamazov* – it combines profound treatment of questions of morality and faith with deep psychological probing. *War and Peace* by Lev Tolstoy (1828-1910) is a panorama of Russia during the Napoleonic Wars. It's a pinnacle of world literature but it won't leave you much time for seeing today's Russia if you read it while you're there. On a slightly smaller scale, *Anna Karenina* is the tragedy of a woman who violates the rigid sexual code of her time.

Chekhov & Gorky The plays of Anton Chekhov (1860-1904) – *The Seagull, Three Sisters, The Cherry Orchard, Uncle Vanya* – look tragicomically at the angst of the provincial middle class in the stagnating late 19th century. They owed much of their early success to 'realist' productions at the Moscow Art Theatre by Konstantin Stanislavsky, which aimed to show life as it really was. Maxim Gorky (1868-1936) painted a graphic picture of urban poverty and brutality from the same era in his autobiographical *My Childhood* and in the play *The Lower Depths*.

Revolutionary Period The Futurist poets who emerged as the revolution approached used shock tactics – slang, eroticism, abrupt switches of tack – to stir people out of complacency. Though many supported the revolution, their lives often ended in tragedy. Vladimir Mayakovsky (1893-1930), almost the revolution's official bard for a long time, committed suicide; Anna Akhmatova (1888-1966) was persecuted into silence for most of her later life; Osip Mandelstam (1892-1938) died in a Stalinist transit camp near Vladivostok. Akhmatova's and Mandelstam's lives are painfully recorded by Nadezhda Mandelstam in her autobiographical *Hope Against Hope*.

Boris Pasternak (1890-1960) was another persecuted Futurist poet, best known in the West for his novel *Dr Zhivago*. Less of an outcast was Alexandra Kollontay (1872-1952), a senior Party figure and feminist, renowned for commenting that sex was like scratching yourself – it relieved an itch. Her novels include *A Great Love*, based on Lenin's affair with Inessa Armand, and *Love of Worker Bees*.

Soviet Era In 1932 the Party officially demanded Socialist Realism from art and literature. This meant 'concrete representation of reality in its revolutionary development...in accordance with...ideological training of the workers in the spirit of Socialism'. Writers had to convey the Party's messages – and please Stalin.

Mikhail Sholokhov (born 1905), with his sagas of revolution and war among the Don Cossacks, *And Quiet Flows the Don* and *The Don Flows Home to the Sea*, was one of the few decent writers to win approval. *The Master and Margarita* by the great satirist Mikhail Bulgakov (1891-1940) was banned for ages. It's a wacky comic novel with a serious twist, in which the Devil turns up in Moscow to cause all manner of anarchy and make idiots of the system and its lackeys.

The Khrushchev thaw saw the emergence of poets like Yevgeny Yevtushenko and Andrey Voznesensky (both born in 1933), who managed to remain on the right side of the authorities, and the novelist Alexandr Solzhenitsyn (born 1918), who didn't. *One Day in the Life of Ivan Denisovich*, a short tale of Gulag life, was published in the USSR in 1962, but Solzhenitsyn fell foul of the Brezhnev clampdown and was exiled in 1974. He went to the USA and finally returned to Russia in 1994. His *Cancer Ward* and *The First Circle*, both written before his departure, are powerful accounts of the 1930s, but *The Gulag Archipelago* is his major work. One Russian said of it to us: 'You read this book, *then* you come to this country'. Through interviews and the testimony of hundreds of Gulag prisoners, Solzhenitsyn brings to light some of the most heinous prison conditions the world has ever known, in a style so familiar that you're enveloped in the stories before you're quite aware of it.

Glasnost brought forth a flood of writing previously suppressed. Two of the chief new talents to emerge since then are Viktor Yerofeev, whose erotic novel *Russian Beauty* has been translated into 27 languages, and Tatyana Tolstaya, whose *On the Golden Porch*, a collection of stories about big souls in little Moscow flats, made her an international name when published in the West in 1989.

Drama began to come in from the cold at Moscow's Taganka Theatre, where Yury Lyubimov staged some famously provocative productions in the 1970s. Lyubimov was sacked in 1984, but then came glasnost and a burst of new subjects, treatments and theatres.

Ballet

Russian ballet grew out of dance schools set up in 18th-century St Petersburg and Moscow. Though the dancers were initially of low status (in Moscow they came from an orphanage), their performances were patronised by the tsars. In the 19th century, French and Italian teachers and dancers brought new techniques, and ballet developed far more prestige in Russia than in Western Europe, where it was often second

to opera on the bill. Under the Frenchman Marius Petipa, the St Petersburg Imperial Ballet rose to world prominence. He choreographed over 60 works, including *Swan Lake*, *The Nutcracker* and *The Sleeping Beauty*, and developed ballet as a large-scale spectacle. Anna Pavlova, Mikhail Fokine and Vaslav Nijinsky, all graduates of the Imperial Ballet school, came to the fore in the early 20th century.

Fokine, who has *Les Sylphides*, *The Firebird* and *Petrushka* to his credit, succeeded Petipa as the leading choreographer. Influenced by the World of Art group (see the Art section in this chapter), he saw ballet as a synthesis of the arts. The Ballets Russes, with designs by Leon Bakst, took Paris by storm in 1909 and brought about a revival of ballet in Europe as a whole.

After the revolution, though many leading lights went West, Soviet ballet maintained its technical standards. Socialist Realism demanded a good story line: new works included *The Red Poppy* (1927) and Prokofiev's *Romeo and Juliet* (1946). The first outstanding dancers of the Soviet period were Galina Ulanova and Maya Plisetskaya.

In the 1950s, Moscow's Bolshoy Ballet, which emphasised drama where Leningrad's Kirov Ballet focused on elegance, made its first triumphant tours of the West. Yury Grigorovich emerged as its bright, new choreographer, with *Spartacus*, *Ivan the Terrible* and other successes.

But by the late 1980s, Grigorovich was at loggerheads with leading dancers such as Plisetskaya, Yekaterina Maximova, Vladimir Vasiliev and Gediminas Taranda; he was accused of stifling choreographers and dancers he did not favour – including Vasiliev and Plisetskaya – and his style was earning such epithets as 'brutal' and 'Stalinist'. Leading Soviet dancers including Rudolf Nureyev, Natalia Makarova and Mikhail Baryshnikov – all from the Kirov – had been moving to the West since the 1960s for greater challenges and more money, and the Bolshoy feuds, combined with glasnost, sped up this process. Plisetskaya and Irek

Mukhamedov, both in 1990, were only two of its leading lights to go West.

The row went on, with both President Yeltsin and the State Duma, Russia's parliament, getting involved before Grigorovich finally resigned in 1995, prompting dancers loyal to him to stage the Bolshoy's first-ever strike. He was replaced by Vasiliev.

Things were more harmonious at the Kirov, where director Oleg Vinogradov staged a more adventurous repertoire with, it's generally acknowledged, higher standards than the Bolshoy. Altynai Asylmuratova emerged as the latest superstar at the end of the 1980s.

Both St Petersburg and Moscow have several other ballet companies in addition to the Kirov and Bolshoy.

Music
Classical The roots of Russian music lie in folk song and dance and Orthodox Church chants. Mikhail Glinka (1804-57), in operas which include *Ivan Susanin* (or *A Life for the Tsar*) and *Ruslan and Lyudmila*, was the first to merge these with Western forms. He influenced the composers known as the Mighty Handful, who lacked formal musical training until adulthood and were concerned to explore and develop Slav roots. Their orchestral works include *Pictures from an Exhibition* by Modest Mussorgsky (1839-81) and *Scheherazade* by Nikolai Rimsky-Korsakov (1844-1908). Mussorgsky's *Boris Godunov*, and *Prince Igor* by Alexandr Borodin (1833-87), are two of the best loved Russian operas.

Pyotr Tchaikovsky (1840-93) also used folk motifs but was closer to the Western tradition. His *1812 Overture*, his concertos and symphonies, the ballets *Swan Lake*, *The Sleeping Beauty* and *The Nutcracker*, and his opera *Yevgeny Onegin* are still among the world's most popular music.

The next generation included the great bass singer and pianist Fyodor Chaliapin (1873-1938), the pianist-composer Alexandr Scriabin (1872-1915), the Romantic composer Sergey Rachmaninov (1873-1943) and the innovator Igor Stravinsky (1882-

1971). The last two fled the revolution. Stravinsky's *The Rite of Spring* – which created a furore at its first performance in Paris – and *The Firebird* were influenced by Russian folk music. Sergey Prokofiev (1891-1953), who also left but returned in 1934, wrote the scores for Eisenstein's films *Alexander Nevsky* and *Ivan the Terrible*, the ballet *Romeo and Juliet*, and *Peter and the Wolf*, beloved of teachers of music to young children. His work was condemned for 'formalism' towards the end of his life.

Dmitry Shostakovich (1906-75) won international acclaim, chiefly for his symphonies, while working, not without conflict, in the Soviet Union. Other innovative composers were silenced. Major performers to emerge in the Soviet era – though some left for the West – included violinist David Oystrakh (1908-74), pianist Svyatoslav Richter (born 1914), cellist/conductor Mstislav Rostropovich (born 1927) and pianist/conductor Vladimir Ashkenazy.

Modest Mussorgsky

Progressive new music surfaced only slowly in the post-Stalin era, with outside contacts limited. Alfred Schnittke's First Symphony, probably the most important work of this major experimental modern Russian composer, had to be premiered by its champion, conductor Gennady Rozhdestvensky, in the provincial city of Gorky (now Nizhny Novgorod) in 1974 and wasn't played in Moscow till 1986.

Leading contemporary Russian composers – most of whom, like Schnittke, now live in Western Europe – include Andrey Volkonsky, Sofia Gubaydulina, Edison Denisov, Valentin Silvestrov and, in the newest generation, Alexandr Knayfel, Dmitry Smirnov and Yelena Firsova. Among virtuosi are Boris Berezovsky (piano), Natalia Gutman (cello), Gidon Kremer (violin) and Alexey Lyubimov (piano).

Rock Russian rock was born in the 1960s, when the 'bourgeois' Beatles filtered through despite official disapproval. Rock developed underground, starved of decent equipment and the chance to record or perform to big audiences, but gathered a huge following among the disaffected, distrustful youth of the 1970s (the Soviet hippie era) and 1980s.

Bands in the 1970s started by imitating Western counterparts, but eventually a home-grown music emerged, whose lyrics often reflected real social issues. Some artists, like Boris Grebenshikov – a kind of Russian Bob Dylan cum John Lennon – and his band Akvarium (Aquarium), became household names but still needed other jobs to get by. Music was circulated by illegal tapes known as *magizdat*, the musical equivalent of samizdat; concerts were held, if at all, in remote halls in city suburbs, and even to attend them could be risky.

Punk and heavy metal came into fashion in the early 1980s. Under glasnost, the authorities eventually allowed the true voices of youth to sound out: rock festivals were held in outlying Soviet republics such as Georgia and Estonia, big concerts took place in major cities, and the state record company, Melodia, started to produce albums by previously unacceptable groups.

Come glasnost, rock initially flowered, with New Wave music, fashionable from about the mid-1980s, appealing to a Russian taste for theatricality. The tone of many of the more 'serious' groups of the 1980s was one of protest about, or a gloomy resignation to, the frustration and alienation of Soviet life – messages that still find a big response in 1990s Russia, where many of the same groups remain popular. The tortured dronings of Viktor Tsoy and the chunky riffs of his band Kino were archetypal. Tsoy died in 1990 but other 1980s bands are still leaders in the field today, among them Akvarium; Va Bank from Moscow and DDT from St Petersburg, both punk-influenced; Orkestr Populyarnaya Mekhanika (Popular Mechanics Orchestra), a St Petersburg 'performance rock' outfit; and Nautilus Pompilius, an electronic New Wave band from Yekaterinburg.

Rock groups now play openly in music clubs and nightclubs and there's little that's 'underground' about them any more, though the Russian rock scene remains homely and amateurish by Western standards. The loss of the underground/protest niche perhaps explains the shortage of major new bands to come to the fore since the early 1990s. The two top newcomers are Dva Samolyota (Two Aeroplanes), good-time ska messengers from St Petersburg, and Nogu Svelo (Cramp in the Leg) from Moscow, which plays a mixture of styles from pop to reggae, postpunk and German beer-hall music.

Russian pop is as popular as ever. Two top acts to look out for are Bravo, a Moscow band playing polished bebop/rockabilly, and the everlasting Alla Pugachyova, a female solo singer who puts tons of energy into her shows.

Architecture

Until Soviet times most building was in wood. The *izba*, or single-storey wooden cottage, still fairly common in the countryside, was the typical Russian dwelling. Stone and brick were usually the preserves of the Church, royalty and nobility.

Early Russia Kievan Rus adopted the 'cross in square' church plan developed in Byzantium in the 9th century. At its simplest this consisted of three aisles, each with an eastern apse (semicircular end), a dome or 'cupola' over the central aisle next to its apse, and high vaulted roofs forming a crucifix shape centred on the dome. As Russian culture moved north, Novgorod, Pskov and Vladimir-Suzdal developed the pattern with varying emphases in the 11th and 12th centuries. Roofs grew steeper to prevent heavy northern snows collecting and crushing them, and windows grew narrower to keep the cold out. Pskov invented the little *kokoshnik* gable, which was semicircular or spade-shaped and was usually found in rows supporting a dome or drum. Stone often replaced brick, and in Vladimir-Suzdal was carved into a glorious cacophony of decorative images. Another Vladimir-Suzdal hallmark was the 'blind arcade' – a wall decoration resembling a row of arches.

Moscow Moscow in the 15th century looked to these earlier centres for inspiration in its grand building programme. Though the architects of two of the Kremlin's three great cathedrals built between 1475 and 1510 were Italian, they took Vladimir's churches as their models; the third cathedral was by builders from Pskov.

Later in the 16th century the translation into brick of north Russian wooden church features, such as the tent roof *(shatyor)* and the onion dome on a tall drum, added up to a new, uniquely Russian architecture, more vertical and spiring in effect than the Byzantine shape. St Basil's Cathedral, the Ivan the Great Belltower in the Moscow Kremlin and the Ascension Church at Kolomenskoe are three high points of this era. In the 17th century builders in Moscow added tiers of kokoshniki, colourful tiles and brick patterning to create jolly, merchant-financed churches such as St Nicholas of the Weavers, and the Trinity in Nikitniki. In mid-century

Patriarch Nikon outlawed such frippery, but elaboration returned later in the century with the Western-influenced Moscow Baroque, which featured ornate white detailing against red-brick walls. The Church of the Intercession at Fili is a high point of this.

Baroque Mainstream Baroque reached Russia with Peter the Great's big opening up to Western influences. The focus was on his new capital, St Petersburg, as he banned new stone buildings elsewhere. The great Baroque architect was an Italian, Bartolomeo Rastrelli, who created an inspired series of buildings, the style of which merged into Rococo, for Empress Elizabeth. Three of the most brilliant were the Winter Palace and Smolny Cathedral, both in St Petersburg, and Catherine Place at nearby Pushkin.

Classicism In the later 18th century, Catherine the Great turned away from Rococo 'excess' toward Europe's new wave of classicism – an attempt to recreate the ambience of an idealised ancient Rome and Greece with their mathematical proportions, rows of columns, pediments and domes. Catherine and her successors built waves of grand classical edifices in a bid to make St Petersburg the continent's most imposing capital.

From the simpler classicism of her own reign, exemplified by the Pavlovsk Palace near St Petersburg, the more grandiose Russian Empire style developed under Alexander, with such buildings as the Admiralty and Kazan Cathedral in St Petersburg. The heavy St Isaac's Cathedral, built for Nicholas I, was the last big project of this wave of classicism in St Petersburg. Moscow abounds with Empire-style buildings since much of it had to be rebuilt after the fire of 1812.

Revivals A series of architectural revivals, notably of early Russian styles, began in the later 19th century. The first, pseudo-Russian phase produced the GUM (Gosudarstvenny Univermag), or state department store, the History Museum and the Leningrad Station in Moscow, and the Moscow Station and the

Resurrection Church in St Petersburg. The early 20th-century Neo-Russian movement brought forth the extraordinary Kazan Station in Moscow, which imitates no fewer than seven earlier styles, while Style Moderne (Russian Art Nouveau) yielded the bizarre Yaroslavl Station on the other side of the same square.

Soviet Era The revolution gave rein to young Constructivist architects, who rejected superficial decoration in favour of buildings whose appearance was a direct function of their uses and materials – a new architecture for a new society. They used lots of glass and concrete in uncompromising geometric forms.

Konstantin Melnikov was probably the most famous Constructivist and his own house off ulitsa Arbat in Moscow is one of the most interesting examples of the style. Moscow's *Pravda* and *Izvestia* offices are others. In the 1930s the Constructivists were denounced, and a 400-metre-high design by perpetrators of yet another revival – monumental classicism – was chosen for Stalin's pet project, a Palace of Soviets in Moscow, which mercifully never got off the ground.

Like the US and German governments of the 1930s, Stalin favoured neoclassical architecture, which echoed ancient Athens – 'the only culture of the past to approach the ideal', according to Anatoly Lunacharsky, the first Soviet Commissar of Education. Stalin liked it to be on a gigantic scale to underline the might of the Soviet state. Convict labour was used, with a high death toll, to create enormous structures around the country. They reached their apogee in the 'Seven Sisters', seven skyscrapers, Gothic in effect, which popped up around Moscow soon after WW II.

Then in 1955 came a decree ordering architects to avoid 'excesses', after which a bland International Modern style – Constructivism without the spark, you might say – was used for prestige buildings, while drab blocks of cramped flats sprouted country-wide to house the people. The past few years have seen big architectural energies going into restoration of decayed churches and monasteries.

Painting

Icons Icons – images intended to aid the veneration of the holy subjects they depict, and sometimes believed able to grant luck, wishes or even miracles – were the key art form up to the time of Peter the Great, though only in the 20th century did they really come to be seen as 'works of art'. They're most commonly found on the iconostasis of a church, a large screen in front of the east-end sanctuary.

Icons were originally painted by monks as a spiritual exercise, and Byzantine rules decreed that only Christ, the Virgin, the angels, saints and scriptural events could be painted – all of which were supposed to be copies of a limited number of approved prototype images. Christ images include the Pantokrator (All-Ruler) and the Mandilion, the latter called 'not made by hand' because it was supposedly developed from the imprint of Christ's face on St Veronica's handkerchief. Icons were traditionally

A Russian icon,
spiritual exercise become art form

painted in tempera – inorganic pigment mixed with a binder such as egg yolk – on wood. When they faded they were often touched up, obscuring the original work.

The first 'Russian' icons were painted by Byzantine monks in Kiev. The beginning of a distinct Russian icon tradition came when artists in Novgorod started to draw on local folk art in their representation of people, producing sharply outlined figures with softer faces and introducing lighter colours including pale yellows and greens.

The earliest outstanding painter was Theophanes the Greek (Feofan Grek, about 1340-1405), who worked in Byzantium, then Novgorod, then Moscow, and brought a new delicacy and grace to the form. His finest works are in the Annunciation Cathedral of the Moscow Kremlin.

Andrey Rublyov, a monk at the Trinity Monastery of St Sergius, Sergiev Posad, and the Andronikov Monastery, Moscow, and by 20 years Theophanes' junior, was the greatest Russian icon painter. His most famous work is the dreamy *Old Testament Trinity*, in Moscow's Tretyakov Gallery.

The layman Dionysius, the leading late 15th-century painter, elongated his figures and refined the use of colour. Sixteenth-century icons grew smaller and more crowded, their figures more realistic and Russian-looking. In 17th-century Moscow, Simon Ushakov moved towards Western religious painting with the use of perspective and architectural backgrounds.

Peredvizhniki In the 18th century, when Peter the Great encouraged Western trends in Russian art, Dmitry Levitsky's portraits were the outstanding achievement. The major artistic force of the 19th century was the Peredvizhniki (Wanderers) movement, which saw art as a force for national awareness and social change. The movement gained its name from the touring exhibitions with which it widened its audience. Patronised by the industrialists Savva Mamontov – whose Abramtsevo estate near Moscow became an artists' colony – and Pavel Tretyakov, they included Vasily Surikov, who painted vivid Russian historical scenes, Nikolai Ge (biblical and historical scenes), and Ilya Repin, perhaps the best loved of all Russian artists, who ranged from social criticism (*Volga Bargemen*) through history (*Zaporozhie Cossacks Writing a Letter to the Turkish Sultan*) to portraits of the famous.

Isaak Levitan, who revealed the beauty of the Russian landscape, was one of many others associated with the Peredvizhniki. The end-of-century genius Mikhail Vrubel, inspired by sparkling Byzantine and Venetian mosaics, showed early traces of Western influence.

Futurism Around the turn of the century the World of Art (Mir Iskusstva) movement in St Petersburg, led by Alexandr Benois and Sergey Diaghilev under the motto 'Art pure and unfettered', opened Russia up to Western innovations such as Impressionism, Art Nouveau and Symbolism. From about 1905 Russian art became a maelstrom of groups, styles and 'isms' as it absorbed decades of European change in a few years before giving birth to its own avant-garde Futurist movements, which in turn helped Western art go head over heels.

Mikhail Larionov and Natalia Goncharova were the centre of the Cézanne-influenced Knave of Diamonds group (with which Vasily Kandinsky was associated) before developing Neo-Primitivism, based on popular arts and primitive icons.

In 1915 Kazimir Malevich announced the arrival of Suprematism, declaring that his utterly abstract geometrical shapes – with the black square representing the ultimate 'zero form' – finally freed art from having to depict the material world and made it a doorway to higher realities. Another famed Futurist, who managed to escape subordinate isms, was Vladimir Mayakovsky, who was also a major poet.

Soviet Era Futurists turned to the needs of the revolution – education, posters, banners – with enthusiasm. They had a chance to act on their theories of how art shapes society.

Marx, Engels and Lenin gazed out over Soviet society from countless Futurist posters

But at the end of the 1920s, Formalist (abstract) art fell out of favour. The Communist Party wanted Socialist Realism (see the Literature section). Images of striving workers, heroic soldiers and inspiring leaders took over; two million sculptures of Lenin and Stalin dotted the country; Malevich ended up painting portraits (penetrating ones) and doing designs for Red Square parades; Mayakovsky committed suicide.

After Stalin, an avant-garde 'Conceptualist' underground was allowed to form. Ilya Kabakov painted or sometimes just arranged the debris of everyday life to show the gap between the promises and realities of Soviet existence. Erik Bulatov's 'Sotsart' pointed to the devaluation of language by ironically reproducing Soviet slogans or depicting words disappearing over the horizon. In 1962 the authorities set up a show of such 'unofficial' art at the Moscow Manezh; Khrushchev called it 'dogshit' and sent it back underground. In the mid-1970s it resurfaced in the Moscow suburbs – only to be literally bulldozed back down.

Eventually a thaw set in and the avant-garde became international big business. In 1988, *A Fundamental Lexicon* by Grisha Bruskin, a multipanelled iconostasis-like work satirising both Soviet propaganda and

the Church, sold for UK£242,000 at a Sotheby's sale in Moscow.

The avant-garde of the 1990s is a disparate cluster of artists of varying ability, with Malevich, Kabakov and Bulatov among its gurus and Andrey Roiter, Vadim Zakharov, Kostia Shchvedeshchotov, Andrey Monastyrsky and Ivan Chuikov among its leading lights. Like all avant-gardes, this one is largely ignored by the general public. To see its work you must usually find your way to one of the few specialist galleries.

The most popular painter in Russia is the religious artist Ilya Glazunov, a staunch defender of the Russian Orthodox cultural tradition. Hundreds of thousands of people visit exhibitions of his work.

Moscow's Tretyakov Gallery and St Petersburg's Russian Museum have the country's chief collections of Russian art, while the Hermitage (St Petersburg) and the Pushkin Fine Arts Museum (Moscow) have world-famous West European collections. Both cities also stage dozens of temporary exhibitions.

Film

Cinema still has an importance in Russia which it lost in the West with the coming of TV. On average, a Russian goes to the movies more than once a month. But in recent years the Russian film industry has suffered from an end to state funding and a flood of lousy foreign films into its cinemas.

Russian – or rather Soviet – cinema first flourished shortly after the revolution. Sergey Eisenstein's *Battleship Potemkin* (1925) remains one of the landmarks of world cinema, its famous Odessa Steps sequence possibly the most cribbed three minutes on celluloid; Charlie Chaplin described it as 'the best film in the world'. (For more details, see Odessa in the Southern Ukraine chapter.) Eisenstein's *Alexandr Nevsky* (1938) contains one of cinema's great battle scenes; his *Ivan the Terrible* (1945) shows the coming to power of the great tsar amid intrigues and his eventual triumph over his enemies – a discreet commentary on Stalinism.

Mikhail Kalatozov's *The Cranes are Flying* (1957) – a love story set during WW II – was judged Best Film at Cannes in 1958. Of later Soviet directors, probably the dominant figure was Andrey Tarkovsky, whose films include *Andrey Rublyov* (1966), *Solaris* (1972) – the Russian answer to *2001* – and *Stalker* (1980), which summed up the Brezhnev era pretty well with its characters wandering puzzled through a landscape of clanking trains, rusting metal and overgrown concrete. Tarkovsky died in exile in 1987. In Russia, Alexey German's *My Friend Ivan Lapshin* (1982) is widely reckoned one of the best Soviet films: set in 1935, it shows with a light touch the amorous and professional ups and downs of a provincial police investigator, yet catches the real horror of life under Stalin with its underlying sense of impending terror.

Glasnost brought new excitement as film makers were allowed to reassess Soviet life with unprecedented freedom, and audiences flocked to see the latest exposure of youth culture or Stalinism. (There was also a steady stream of releases of previously banned films.) Vasily Pichul's *Little Vera* caused a sensation in 1989 with its frank portrayal of a family in chaos (exhausted wife, drunken husband, rebellious daughter) and its sexual frankness – mild by Western standards but

startling to the Soviet audience. Since then pornography has become commonplace.

Folk Culture

Loosely defined, 'folk culture' is what ordinary people have traditionally done to enrich their lives in a way that distinguishes them from other groups or regions. Despite Soviet standardisation and sterilisation of some forms, Russian folk culture is still very visible, especially in music, dance, and applied and decorative art.

Big music and dance ensembles such as the Igor Moiseev Folk Dance Ensemble, the Osipov Russian Folk Orchestra and the Pyatnitsky Russian Folk Chorus have repertoires with roots as old as Kievan Rus, including heroic ballads and the familiar Slavic *trepak* or stamping dances. Smaller bands in restaurants may do similar things – or put on gipsy song-and-dance shows, once the traditional accompaniment of tsarist officers on drinking and womanising binges.

Isolated by vast distances and long winters, Russians evolved an amazing spectrum of richly decorated folk art. Perhaps most familiar are the intricately painted, enamelled wood boxes called Palekh, after the village east of Moscow that's famous for them; and *finift*, luminous enamelled metal miniatures from Rostov-Veliky. From Gzhel, also east of Moscow, came glazed earthenware in the 18th century and its trademark blue-and-white porcelain in the 19th. Gus-Khrustalny, south of Vladimir, maintains a glass-making tradition as old as Rus. Every region also has its own style of embroidery and some specialise in knitted and other fine fabrics.

Most common is woodcarving, represented by toys, distaffs and gingerbread moulds in the museums, and in its most clichéd form by the nested *matryoshka* dolls – surely the most familiar symbol of Russia – and the red, black and gold lacquered-pine bowls called *khokhloma* which overflow from souvenir shops. Most uniquely Slavic are the 'gingerbread' houses of western and northern Russia and Siberia with their carved window frames, lintels and trim. The art of carpentry flourished in 17th and 18th-century houses and churches.

Late in the Soviet period, these things could increasingly be found only in homes or in museum collections. But the coming of the free market and a revived interest in national traditions has brought much more good craftwork into the open. The process is also being catalysed by the restoration of churches and mosques and their artwork.

Circus

Russian popular culture is not confined to TV soap operas, discos and video halls. At the circus, despite economic difficulties since the demise of support from the Soviet state, you're still sure to see adults as well as children at ease and in unreserved good humour. The Russian circus tradition has roots in the medieval travelling minstrels called *skomorokhi*. The country's first permanent circus was established in St Petersburg in 1877.

While Western circuses grow smaller and more scarce, the Russian versions are like those we went to as kids – prancing horses with acrobats on their backs, snarling lions and tigers, heart-stopping high-wire artists

Preventing Animal Cruelty

While the animal-rights situation in Russia has shown some improvement over the past few years, it's still light years behind that in Western countries. Zoo and circus animals are mistreated to an extent that would be criminal in other countries, and there is not yet a national network of animal shelters; strays are routinely rounded up and drowned.

Some animal trainers and zoo workers defend the standard practices – chaining elephants by a back leg to the ground on a one-metre lead; placing horses, lions, bears, tigers and other large animals in tiny cages – by saying that the country has enough trouble providing its pensioners with food and shelter, and that it can't be worried about animals.

Others see absolutely nothing wrong with any of it. Janice Cox of the World Society for the Protection of Animals (WSPA, pronounced 'wispa') says that she's spoken with circus trainers in Moscow who defend the use of ice-skating polar bears with the explanation, 'It's their natural habitat...They're on the ice'.

Though the treatment of zoo and circus animals has improved tremendously in Moscow and St Petersburg, where the money and attention brought by tourism have led to better conditions, more food and cleaner cages, the problem is still enormous. And the situation in the rest of the country is still heartbreaking, as any visitor to a regional zoo or circus can attest.

If you should see inhumane treatment of animals in zoos or circuses during your trip, you can help to do something about it. Take photographs if you can, or take notes of the animals' condition and exact location, and report it to Janice Cox, Central & Eastern European Department, WSPA (☎ (0171) 793 0540; fax (0171) 793 0208), 2 Langley Lane, London SW8 ITJ, or to Zoo Check (☎ (0306) 71 2091), an international organisation that monitors and investigates the conditions in which animals are housed in zoos and seeks widespread reforms. It's part of the Born Free Foundation, at Coldharbour, Dorking, Surrey RH5 6HA, UK.

Ironically, animal abuse in St Petersburg was a contributing factor in the establishment of the USA's main animal-protection organisation. Henry Bergh, a wealthy American socialite, was sent to St Petersburg as Abraham Lincoln's legate, to serve under ambassador Cassius Clay in the early 1860s. One snowy day, as Bergh was making his way through St Petersburg's streets, he came upon a Russian peasant who was mercilessly flogging his fallen horse. Bergh leapt off his coach and disarmed the man, but the incident affected Bergh profoundly.

Soon after, Bergh resigned his position (he and Clay had never got on). He stopped in London on his way back to the USA and met there with members of the RSPCA, which had been founded in 1824 by Richard 'Humanity Dick' Martin. Bergh was so impressed that on his return to New York he set about using his social and political connections and in 1866 established the American Society for the Prevention of Cruelty to Animals. ■

and clowns that are hilarious in spite of the language barrier. Many cities have their own troupes and most at least have an arena for visiting companies. Best known is the Moscow Circus, which is really several troupes, with 7000 artists in all. In summer, circuses go on tour to each other's cities. Tickets everywhere are US$1 or US$2.

Sport

The harvests of Olympic medals won by athletes of the USSR were the product of a 1949 Communist Party Central Committee demand for 'world supremacy in major sports in the immediate future'. The collapse of the Soviet Union also meant the collapse of the system that channelled a sporting elite towards international success: Gossport, the all-powerful state sports committee which paid the salaries of 25,000 athletes and 1200 coaches, was abolished in 1991. But in the 1992 Olympics the 'Combined Team', representing all the ex-Soviet nations except the Baltic states, still did well. Since then Russia has started to compete separately in international events.

Russia's three major spectator sports – soccer (*futbol*), ice hockey (*khokkey*) and basketball (*basketbol*) – have suffered in recent years from the departure of top players to rich foreign clubs, revelations of corruption, and the replacement of Soviet leagues with purely Russian ones. Still, in the past decade Russian soccer at least has begun to produce teams of greater flair – if, ultimately, little more successful – than the dour Brezhnev-era outfits. Spartak of Moscow has been the dominant club in recent years. Other top teams include Dinamo, TsSKA, Lokomotiv and Torpedo (all from Moscow), Rotor Volgograd and Lokomotiv Nizhny Novgorod. The Supreme League (Vysshaya Liga) has 18 teams, with promotion and relegation between divisions. The season runs from March to October. There's also an FA Cup-type competition, the Kubka Rossii, whose final rounds are played between April and June.

Ice hockey has a 14-team Vysshaya Liga which includes teams from Ukraine, Belarus and Latvia. The season runs from September to March. Top clubs include TsSKA, Dinamo and Krylya Sovietov (all Moscow), Torpedo Yaroslavl, Torpedo Nizhny Novgorod, Itil Kazan and Khimik Voskresensk.

Horse racing (*skachki*) is popular and many cities have a course (*ippodrom*) with regular meetings. Sometimes the horses race in harness – and in winter there's *troyka* racing.

RELIGION
Russian Orthodox Church

After decades of closures and confiscations of property, and victimisation, deportations and executions of believers under the Soviet regime, the Russian Orthodox Church (Russkaya Pravoslavnaya Tserkov) is enjoying a big revival. By 1991 it already had an estimated 50 million members. Numbers have grown thanks not only to the new religious freedom initiated by Mikhail Gorbachev and enshrined in Russia's 1993 constitution, but also because of the growth of Russian nationalism, for the Church is an intimate part of many Russians' notions of Russia and 'Russianness'. This is still the case despite recriminations over the Church's infiltration by the KGB during the Soviet era (three metropolitans – senior bishops – were accused in 1992 of having been KGB agents).

Closed and neglected churches are being restored all over the country, and churches and monasteries that had been turned into museums, archive stores, even prisons, have been returned to church hands. Services have been held in the ancient cathedrals of the Moscow Kremlin, and in Moscow the total number of active churches rose from 47 in 1989 to 300 by 1993. There are probably close to 20,000 in the whole country, as against under 7000 in 1988. The biggest symbol of the Church's revival will be the Cathedral of Christ the Saviour, a massive Moscow landmark accommodating 10,000 worshippers, which was blown up by Stalin's orders but which is now being rebuilt for US$250 million.

In 1917 Russia had over 50,000 churches.

Lenin adapted Marx's view of religion as 'the opium of the people' to a Russian context, and likened it to home brew. Stalin seemed to be trying to wipe it out altogether until 1941, when he decided the war effort needed the patriotism religion could stir up. Khrushchev returned to the attack in the 1950s, closing about 15,000 churches – some became museums of atheism! – and only under Gorbachev did a new liberalisation happen.

History & Hierarchy Constantinople (modern Istanbul, ancient Byzantium, the capital of the Eastern Roman Empire after 395 AD) was the eastern centre of Christianity in the Middle Ages, and Rome was its western centre. For doctrinal, cultural and political reasons, the two gradually drew apart. The final date of the split between the 'Eastern Orthodox' and 'Roman Catholic' churches is usually put at 1054.

Prince Vladimir of Kiev effectively founded the Russian Orthodox Church in 988 by adopting Christianity from Constantinople. The Church's headquarters stayed at Kiev until 1300, when it moved north to Vladimir. In the 1320s it moved again, from Vladimir to Moscow.

Patriarch Alexy of Moscow & All Russia is head of the Church. The Patriarch's residence is the Danilov Monastery, Moscow, though some Church business is still conducted at the Trinity Monastery of St Sergius at Sergiev Posad, his residence until the late 1980s. The Yelokhovsky Cathedral is currently the senior church in Moscow. The Church's senior bishops bear the title Metropolitan. The Russian Orthodox Church is one of the main fellowship of 15 autocephalous ('self-headed') Orthodox churches, in which Constantinople is a kind of first among equals.

Beliefs & Practice Russian Orthodoxy is highly traditional, and the atmosphere inside a church is formal and solemn. Priests dress imposingly, the smell of candles and incense permeates the air, old women bustle about sweeping and polishing. Churches have no

seats, no music (only chanting) and no statues – but many icons (see Art in Arts & Culture), before which people will often be seen praying, and even kissing the ground. Men bare their heads and women usually cover theirs.

As a rule, working churches are open to one and all, but as a visitor take care not to disturb any devotions or offend sensibilities. Hands in pockets attract frowns. Women visitors can often get away without covering their heads but miniskirts are unwelcome and even trousers sometimes attract disapproval. Photography at services is generally not welcome, though you might get a yes if you ask. At other times you should still feel out the situation first and ask if in doubt.

The Virgin Mary (Bogomater, Mother of God) is greatly honoured. The language of the liturgy is 'Church Slavonic', the old Bulgarian dialect into which the Bible was first translated for Slavs. Easter (Paskha) is the focus of the Church year, with festive midnight services to launch Easter Day. Christmas (Rozhdestvo) falls on 7 January because the Church still uses the Julian calendar that the Soviet state abandoned in 1918.

In most churches, Divine Liturgy (Bozhestvennaya Liturgia), lasting about two hours, is at 8, 9 or 10 am Monday to Saturday, and usually at 7 and 10 am on Sunday and festival days. Most churches also hold services at 5 or 6 pm daily. Some of these include an akathistos (akafist), a series of chants to the Virgin or saints.

Church Design Churches are decorated with frescoes, mosaics and icons with the aim of conveying Christian teachings and assisting veneration. Different subjects are assigned traditional places in the church (the Last Judgement, for instance, appears on the west wall). An often elaborately decorated iconostasis (icon stand) divides the main body of the church from the sanctuary, or altar area, at the east end, which is off limits to all but the priest. During a service the priest comes and goes through the Holy or

Royal Door, an opening in the middle of the iconostasis.

The iconostasis is composed of up to six tiers of icons. The biggest is the deesis row *(deisusnyy ryad)*, whose central group of icons, known as the deesis, consists of Christ enthroned as the judge of the world, with the Virgin and John the Baptist interceding for humanity on either side. Archangels, apostles and Eastern Church fathers may also appear on this row. Below the deesis row are one or two rows of smaller icons: the bottom one is the local row *(mestnyy ryad)* showing saints with local links. Above the deesis row are the festival row *(prazdnichnyy ryad)* showing the annual festivals of the Church, then the prophet row *(prorocheskiy ryad)* showing Old Testament prophets, and sometimes a further patriarch row *(praotechesky ryad)* showing the Old Testament patriarchs.

Church Names In Russian, *sobor* means cathedral; *tserkov* and *khram* mean church. Common church names include:

Blagoveshchenskay	(Annunciation)
Borisoglebskaya	(SS Boris & Gleb)
Nikolskaya	(St Nicholas)
Petropavlovskaya	(SS Peter & Paul)
Pokrovskaya	(Intercession of the Virgin)
Preobrazhenskaya	(Transfiguration)
Rizopolozhenskaya	(Deposition of the Holy Robe)
Rozhdestvenskaya	(Nativity)
Troitskaya	(Trinity)
Uspenskaya	(Assumption or Dormition)
Vladimirskaya	(St Vladimir)
Voskresenskaya	(Resurrection)
Voznesenskaya	(Ascension)
Znamenskaya	(Holy Sign)

Old Believers The Russian Church was split in 1653 by the reforms of Patriarch Nikon, who thought it had departed from its roots. He insisted, among other things, that the translation of the Bible be altered to conform with the Greek original, and that the sign of the cross be made with three fingers, not two. Those who couldn't accept these changes became known as Old Believers (Starovery) and came in for persecution. Some fled to the Siberian forests or remote parts of Central Asia, where one group who had never heard

of Lenin, electricity or the revolution was found in the 1980s. Only in 1771-1827, 1905-18 and again recently have Old Believers had real freedom of worship. They probably number over a million but in 1917 there were as many as 20 million.

Other Christian Churches

Russia has small numbers of Roman Catholics, and Lutheran and Baptist Protestants, mostly among the German and other non-Russian ethnic groups. Other groups such as the Mormons, Seventh-Day Adventists and the Salvation Army are sending missionaries into the potentially fertile ground of a country where God officially didn't exist for 70 years.

St Basil's Cathedral, Red Square, Moscow

Islam

European Russia has about 12 million active and nominal Muslims, mainly among the Tatar and Bashkir peoples east of Moscow and several of the Caucasus ethnic groups (see Population & People). Nearly all are Sunni Muslims, except for some Shia Muslims in Dagestan. Soviet 'militant atheism' led to the closure of nearly all the mosques and *madrassas* (Muslim religious schools) in Russia. Under Stalin there were mass deportations and liquidation of the Muslim elite. Policies eased marginally after WW II.

Islam has, like Christianity, enjoyed growth since the mid-1980s. Though it has been some Muslim peoples – notably the Chechens and Tatars – who have been the most resistant of Russia's minorities to being brought within the Russian national fold since the fall of the Soviet Union in 1991, nationalism has played at least as big a part as religion in this, and militant Islam has as yet barely raised its head in Russia.

Islam in Russia is fairly secularised – eg women are not veiled, the Friday Sabbath is not a commercial holiday.

Working mosques are closed to women and often to non-Muslim men, though men may occasionally be invited in. There seems to be no way around this. If you are asked in, you'll have to take your shoes off (and hope your socks are clean! – dirty socks, like dirty feet, may be an insult to the mosque).

Judaism

Many of Russia's 700,000 or so Jews are assimilated to Russian culture and do not seriously practise Judaism. However, there were approximately 30 synagogues by 1991. Unlike the country's other religious groups, Jews have no central coordinating body, though a *yeshiva*, or rabbinical academy, opened in Moscow in 1956.

Buddhism

The 145,000 Kalmyks who are the largest ethnic group in the Kalmyk Republic, north-west of the Caspian Sea, are traditionally members of the Gelugpa or 'Yellow-Hat'

sect of Tibetan Buddhism, whose spiritual leader is the Dalai Lama. The Kalmyks fled to their present region in the 17th century from wars in western Mongolia, where Buddhism had reached them not long before. Buddhism was tolerated by the Soviet state until Stalin nearly wiped it out in the 1930s. Today there are just a few temples in the Kalmyk Republic.

Shamanism

The religion of most of the 700,000 Mari and some of the 800,000 Udmurts, both Finno-Ugric peoples in the middle Volga region, remains largely animist and shamanist. Animism is a belief in the presence of spirits or spiritual qualities in objects of the natural world. People contact these spirits for guidance through a medium or shaman ('witch doctor').

LANGUAGE

Just about everyone in Russia speaks Russian, though there are also dozens of other languages spoken by ethnic minorities. Russian and most of the other languages are written in variants of the Cyrillic alphabet. It's easy to find English-speakers in the big cities but not so easy in small towns (sometimes not even in tourist hotels).

Russian grammar may be daunting, but your travels will be far more interesting if you at least take the time to learn the Cyrillic alphabet, so that you can read maps and street signs.

Since most of what's in this section is aimed at spoken situations, we have accompanied the Cyrillic forms mostly with phonetic translations rather than direct transliterations.

Books

A good teach-yourself set (a book and two tapes) is the BBC's *Get By in Russian*. Another good book-and-cassette set for beginners is *Colloquial Russian* by Svetlana le Fleming & Susan E Kay. The paperback *Penguin Russian Course* is good for more devoted learners. When you go, take along Lonely Planet's detailed and useful *Russian*

Phrasebook and a small dictionary such as the *Pocket Oxford Russian Dictionary*.

Two recent books are worthy of mention. The four-kg *Random House Russian-English Dictionary of Idioms* by Sophia Lubensky is a must for any serious student of Russian. Developed over 12 years, originally to help spooks speak (it was undertaken by the US National Cryptologic School, Department of Defense), it contains over 7500 idioms and set expressions not found in traditional Russian-English dictionaries. It's not much fun for beginners – all the Russian listings are in Cyrillic, and no direct (only idiomatic) translations are given. Also note that the meanings and spellings are in American English. *Russian Proverbs* by Chris Skillen & Vladimir Lubarov is a lovely little hardcover with a selection of the most charming Russian proverbs – from 'it's madness to bring a samovar to Tula' to 'a bad peace is better than a good fight'. It lists both Russian and English and has very nice illustrations (though a couple are in the wrong place!) throughout.

Cyrillic Alphabet

The Cyrillic alphabet resembles Greek with some extra characters. Each language that uses Cyrillic has a slightly different variant. The alphabet chart in Appendix I at the back of the book shows the letters used in Russian, Ukrainian and Belarusian with their Roman-letter equivalents and common pronunciations.

Pronunciation The sounds of a, o, e and я are 'weaker' when the stress in the word does not fall on them – eg in вода (*voda*, water) the stress falls on the second syllable, so it's pronounced '*va-DA*', with the unstressed pronunciation for o and the stressed pronunciation for a. The vowel й only follows other vowels in so-called diphthongs, eg ой '*oy*', ей '*ey, yey*'. Russians usually print ё without the dots, a source of confusion in pronunciation.

The 'voiced' consonants б, в, г, д, ж and з are not voiced at the end of words (eg хлеб, bread, is pronounced '*khlyep*') or before voiceless consonants. The г in the common

adjective endings -его and -ого is pronounced '*v*'.

Two letters have no sound but only modify others. A consonant followed by the 'soft sign' ь is spoken with the tongue flat against the palate, as if followed by the faint beginnings of a '*y*'. The rare 'hard sign' ъ after a consonant inserts a slight pause before the next vowel.

Transliteration There's no ideal system for going from Cyrillic to Roman letters; the more faithfully a system indicates pronunciation, the more complicated it is. We use the simple US Library of Congress System I, good for deciphering printed words and rendering proper names in familiar form.

In this system Cyrillic е (spoken '*ye*') is written as Roman *e* except at the start of words where it's *ye* (eg Yeltsin). The combination кс becomes *x*. At the end of words certain pairs get special forms: -ия is written -*ia*, -ье -*ie*, -ьи -*yi*. Russian names are simplified by making final -ый and -ий into plain -*y*.

In a few cases we make exceptions for common usage. The names of 18th to 19th-century Russian rulers are anglicised – eg Peter the Great not Pyotr, Tsar Nicholas not Nikolay. For names ending in -чёв we write -*chev* not -*chyov* (eg Gorbachev); similarly for -шёв and -щёв. Other familiar exceptions – which would all be spelled differently if we stuck adamantly to the system – are *rouble*, *nyet*, *soviet*, *perestroika*, Baikal, Tchaikovsky, even Intourist.

Grammar

This drives even serious students crackers. Nouns have gender and six possible endings; verbs also decline, as in Latin. One result is that things named after people have odd endings – Lenin Ave is prospekt Lenina, Tchaikovsky Square is ploshchad Chaykovskogo and so on. For a beginner the best way around this is to ignore it; you can pick up the meanings of printed words without worrying much about endings.

There are simplifications, too. Russian has no 'a' or 'the'. The verb 'to be' commonly drops out of simple sentences – eg 'I am an American' (male) is я-американец ('*ya uh-mi-ri-KAHN-yits*'). Russians also don't normally use the verb 'to have'. Instead they use the preposition у, which means 'at' or 'by', and the third person singular of the verb 'to be': eg 'I have' is у меня есть ('*u min-YA yest*'), literally 'by me (is)'.

Questions The easiest way to turn a statement into a question is just to say it with a rising tone and a questioning look, or follow it with a quizzical *da?* – eg 'is this Moscow?', это Москва, да? ('*EH-ta mahsk-VA, da?*').

Negation A sentence is made negative by putting не before its main word, eg 'this is not Moscow', это не Москва ('*EH-ta nye mahsk-VA*').

Pronouns Normally, plural 'you', вы, is used in conversation. The singular ты is for talking to children, relatives and close friends.

I, we
  ya, mih
  я, мы
you (singular), you (plural)
  tih, vih
  ты, Вы
he, she, it, they
  ohn, a-NA, a-NO, a-NI
  он, она, оно, они

Useful Words & Phrases

Two words you're sure to use are Здравствуйте ('*ZDRAST-vooy-tyeh*'), the universal 'hello' (but if you say it a second time in one day to the same person, they'll think you forgot you already saw them!), and Пожалуйста ('*pa-ZHAHL-ooh-stuh*'), the multipurpose word for 'please' (commonly in- cluded in all polite requests), 'you're welcome', 'pardon me', 'after you' and more.

Good morning.
  DOH-bra-yuh OO-tra
  Доброе утро.

Good afternoon.
  DOH-bri dyen
  Добрый день.

Good evening.
  DOH-bri VYEH-chir
  Добрый вечер.

Goodbye.
  das-fi-DA-nya
  До свидания.

Goodbye (casual).
  pah-KAH
  Пока.

How are you?
  kak dyi-LAH?
  Как дела?

yes, no
  da, nyet
  да, нет

Thank you (very much).
  spuh-SEE-ba (bal-SHOY-uh)
  Спасибо (большое).

Pardon me.
  pra-STEE-tyeh, pa-ZHAHL-ooh-stuh
  Простите, пожалуйста.

No problem/Never mind.
  ni-che-VOH (literally, 'nothing')
  Ничего.

good/OK
  kha-ra-SHOH
  хорошо

bad
  PLOH-kha
  плохо

this, that
  EH-ta, toh
  это, то

I don't speak Russian.
  ya nye ga-var-YU pa-RU-ski
  Я не говорю по-русски.

I don't understand.
  ya nye pah-ni-MAH-yu
  Я не понимаю.

Do you speak English?
  vih ga-var-EE-tyeh pa-an-GLEE-ski?
  Вы говорите по-английски?

Will you write it down, please?
  zuh-pi-SHEE-tyeh, pa-ZHAHL-ooh-stuh?
  Запишите, пожалуйста.

I like (it).
mnyeh NRAH-veet-suh
Мне нравится.

Can you help me?
pa-ma-GEET-yeh mnyeh pa-ZHAHL-ooh-stuh?
Помогите мне пожалуйста?

May I take a photo?
fa-ta-gruh-FEE-ra-vut MOZH-na?
Фотографировать можно?

I need...
mnyeh NOOZH-na...
Мне нужно...

Where is...?
gdyeh...?
Где...?

toilet
tu-al-YET
туалет

translator
pi-ri-VOHT-chik
переводчик

Names & Introductions

In introducing yourself you can use your first name, or first and last. Russians often address each other by first name plus patronymic, a middle name based on their father's first name – eg Natalya Borisovna (Natalya, daughter of Boris), Pavel Nikolaevich (Pavel, son of Nikolay). This requires careful attention when someone is being introduced to you!

What's your name?
kahk vahs za-VOOT?
Как Вас зовут?

My name is...
min-YA za-VOOT...
Меня зовут...

Pleased to meet you.
OH-chin pree-YAHT-na
Очень приятно.

my husband
moy moozh
мой муж

my wife
ma-YA zhi-NA
моя жена

my boyfriend
moy drook
мой друг

my girlfriend
ma-YA pa-DROOG-uh
моя подруга

Countries

Where are you from?
aht-KUH-dah vi?
Откуда вы?

Australia
uf-STRAH-li-uh
Австралия

Canada
ka-NA-duh
Канада

France
FRAHN-tsi-yuh
Франция

Germany
gehr-MAH-ni-yuh
Германия

Great Britain
vi-LEE-ka-bri-TA-ni-uh
Великобритания

Ireland
eer-LAHN-di-yuh
Ирландия

New Zealand
NOH-vuh-yuh zyeh-LAHN-di-yuh
Новая Зеландия

USA, America
seh sheh ah, uh-MYEH-ri-kuh
США, Америка

Signs

under reconstruction
ri-MONT
РЕМОНТ

men's (toilet)
MOOZH-skoy tu-al-YET
МУЖСКОЙ ТУАЛЕТ (М)

women's (toilet)
ZHEN-ski tu-al-YET
ЖЕНСКИЙ ТУАЛЕТ (Ж)

EUROPEAN RUSSIA

entrance, exit
fkhot, VIH-khut
ВХОД, ВЫХОД

pedestrian crossing/passage
pi-ri-KHOT
ПЕРЕХОД

cashier, ticket office
KAHS-suh
КАССА

information desk
SPRAHV-ki, SPRAH-vuch-na-yuh
byu-ROH
СПРАВКИ, СПРАВОЧНОЕ БЮРО

no smoking
nyi ku-REET
НЕ КУРИТЬ

no vacancy
myest nyet
МЕСТ НЕТ

Transport – general

map, transport map
KAR-tuh, SKHEM-uh trahns-POR-tuh
карта, схема транспорта

ticket, tickets
bee-LYET, bee-LYET-i
билет, билеты

baggage
buh-GAHZH
багаж

arrival
pri-BIH-ti-yeh
прибытие

departure
aht-pruv-LYEN-i-yeh
отправление

one-way
vah-DYIN ka-NYETS , ye-DYIN-i
в один конец, единый

return, round-trip
tu-DA ee a-BRAHT-na, a-BRAHT-ni
туда и обратно, обратный

free, occupied
sfa-BOD-nuh, ZAH-nyuh-tuh
свободно, занято

What town is this?
kuh-KOY EH-tuh GOR-ut?
Какой это город?

Transport – air

airport
ah-EH-ra-port
аэропорт

check-in
ri-gi-STRAHT-si-uh
регистрация

customs
tuh-MOHZH-nyah
таможня

When does it leave?
kug-DA aht-li-TA-yit?
Когда отлетает?

Transport – bus, trolleybus, tram, metro

The usual way to get to the exit in a crowded bus is to say to anyone in the way, *vykhodite?* (*'vih-KHO-di-tyeh'*), 'Are you getting off?'.

bus
uf-TOH-boos
автобус

trolleybus
trahl-YEY-boos
троллейбус

tram
trum-VAI
трамвай

fixed-route minibus
marsh-ROOT-na-yuh tahk-SEE
маршрутное такси

bus stop
ah-sta-NOV-kuh
остановка

city bus, trolleybus or tram ticket, tickets
tuh-LOHN, tuh-LOHN-i
талон, талоны

metro token, tokens
zhi-TOHN, zhi-TOHN-i
жетон, жетоны

Transport – train

railway station
zhi-LYEZ-nuh-da-ROHZH-ni vahg-ZAHL
железнодорожный (ж. д.) вокзал

When does it leave?
kug-DA aht-KHO-dyit?
Когда отходит?

train
  PO-yest
  поезд
carriage
  va-GON
  вагон
compartment
  ku-PEH
  купе
seat, place
  MYES-ta
  место
soft or 1st-class (compartment)
  MYAKH-ki
  мягкий
hard or 2nd-class (compartment)
  ku-PYEY-ni
  купейный
reserved-place or 3rd-class (carriage)
  plahts-KART-ni
  плацкартный
local train
  eh-lik-TREECH-kuh or *PREE-gahr-ahd-nih PO-yest*
  электричка or пригородный поезд
'fast' long-distance train
  SKOH-ri PO-yest
  скорый поезд
slower (literally, 'passenger') intercity train
  puh-suh-ZHEER-ski PO-yest
  пассажирский поезд
carriage attendant
  pra-VOHD-nyik (m), *pra-VOHD-nyit-suh* (f)
  проводник, проводница

Transport – taxi & car
taxi
  tahk-SEE
  такси
petrol station, service station
  za-PRAHV-ahch-nuh-yuh STAHNT-si-uh
  заправочная станция

Transport – boat
river station
  reech-NOY vahg-ZAHL
  речной вокзал

pier/quay
  pri-CHAHL or *pri-STAHN*
  причал or пристань
steamship
  pa-ra-KHOT
  пароход
hydrofoil (literally, 'high-speed')
  ska-rast-NAH-yuh
  скоростная

Around Town
House numbers are not always in step on opposite sides of the street. Russian addresses are written back-to-front; see Post & Telecommunications in the European Russia Facts for the Visitor chapter.

square/plaza
  PLOH-shchut
  площадь (пл.)
street
  OO-leet-suh
  улица (ул.)
avenue
  pra-SPYEKT
  проспект (просп.)
lane
  pi-ri-OO-lahk
  переулок (пер.)
descent/slope
  spoosk
  спуск
boulevard
  bool-VAHR
  бульвар
highway
  sha-SEH
  шоссе
embankment
  nuh-bir-YEZH-nuh-yuh
  набережная (наб.)
building
  KOR-poos
  корпус
museum
  mu-ZYEY
  музей

theatre
ti-ATR
театр

church
TSER-kuf
церковь

circus
tsirk
цирк

north, south
SYEH-vir, yook
север, юг

east
va-STOK
восток

west
ZAH-puht
запад

to (on) the left
nuh-LYEH-va
налево

to (on) the right
nuh-PRAH-va
направо

straight on
PRYAH-ma
прямо

(go) back
nuh-ZAHT
назад

here, there
toot, tahm
тут, там

I'm lost.
ya zuh-blu-DEEL-suh (m), *ya zuh-blu-DEE-lus* (f)
Я заблудился, я заблудилась.

Accommodation

hotel
gus-TEE-nit-suh
гостиница

floor/storey
eh-TAZH
этаж

room
NOHM-yer
номер

How much is a room?
SKOL-ka STO-eet NOHM-yer?
Сколько стоит номер?

Do you have a cheaper room?
u vahs yest dye-SHYEV-lye NOHM-yer?
У вас есть дешевле номер?

floor supervisor (literally, 'on duty')
di-ZHOOR-nuh-yuh
дежурная

key
klyooch
ключ

boiled water
kee-pyuh-TOK
кипяток

soap
MIH-la
мыло

toilet paper
tu-a-LYET-nuh-yuh bu-MA-guh
туалетная бумага

towel
pa-la-TYEN-tsuh
полотенце

blanket
ah-di-YAH-la
одеяло

too hot/stuffy
ZHAR-ka/DOOSH-na
жарко/душно

The...isn't working.
...ni ruh-BOH-tuh-yit
...не работает.

toilet
tu-ah-LYET
туалет

tap/faucet
krahn
кран

heating
a-ta-PLEN-i-yeh
отопление

light
sfyet
свет

electricity
eh-lik-TREE-chist-va
электричество

Food

For a longer list of words and phrases related to ordering meals, and specific foods, dishes and drinks, see Food & Drink in the European Russia Facts for the Visitor chapter.

breakfast
  ZAHF-truk
  завтрак
lunch (afternoon meal)
  a-BYET
  обед
dinner, supper
  OO-zhin
  ужин
restaurant
  ri-sta-RAHN
  ресторан
café
  ka-FYEH
  кафе
canteen
  sta-LO-vuh-yuh
  столовая
snack bar
  bu-FYET
  буфет
buffet/smorgasbord/Swedish Table
  SHFET-ski stol
  шведский стол
to take away
  S sa-BOY
  с собой

Money, Post & Telecommunications

money
  DYEN-gi
  деньги
currency exchange
  ahb-MYEHN vahl-YU-tuh
  обмен валюты
bank
  bahnk
  банк
travellers' cheques
  da-ROHZH-nih-yeh CHEH-ki
  дорожные чеки
small change (eg for telephone)
  ruz-MYEN
  размен

post office
  pohch-TAH
  почта
stamp
  MAR-kuh
  марка
postcard
  aht-KRIT-kuh
  открытка
telephone
  ti-li-FOHN
  телефон
intercity/international telephone office
  mizh-du-gahr-OHD-ni/mizh-du nah-ROHD-ni ti-li-FOHN-i punkt
  междугородный/международный телефонныйпункт
fax
  fahx
  факс ог телефакс

Shopping

shop
  muh-guh-ZYIN
  магазин
bookshop
  KNEEZH-ni muh-guh-ZYIN
  книжный магазин
department store
  u-ni-vir-SAHL-ni muh-guh-ZYIN
  универсальный магазин
newsstand
  ga-ZET-nyi ki-OSK
  газетный киоск
market
  RIH-nuk
  рынок
(colour) film
  (TSFYET-nuh-yuh) PLYON-kuh
  (цветная) плёнка
pharmacy
  up-TYEK-a
  аптека
souvenirs
  su-vin-EER-i
  сувениры
open, closed
  aht-KRIT, zuh-KRIT
  открыт, закрыт

working, not working (opening hours)
ruh-BOH-tuh-yit, ni ruh-BOH-tuh-yit
работает, не работает
Please show me.
pa-kuh-ZHEE-tyeh, pa-ZHAHL-ooh-stuh
Покажите пожалуйста.
How much is it?
SKOL-ka STO-eet?
Сколько стоит?
Do you have...?
u VAHS...?
У Вас...?

Numbers

In Russian a comma is used in place of the English decimal point. In numbers over 10,000, the groups of three digits are separated by a space (usually) or a full point.

How many?	
SKOL-ka	Сколько?
zero	
nohl	ноль
one	
ah-DYIN	один
two	
dva	два
three	
tree	три
four	
chi-TIR-yeh	четыре
five	
pyaht	пять
six	
shest	шесть
seven	
syem	семь
eight	
VO-syim	восемь
nine	
DYEV-yut	девять
10	
DYES-yut	десять
11	
ah-DYIN-ut-sut	одиннадцать
12	
dvi-NAHT-sut	двенадцать
13	
tri-NAHT-sut	тринадцать
20	
DVAHT-sut	двадцать

21	
DVAHT-sut	двадцать один
ah-DYIN	
30	
TREET-sut	тридцать
40	
SO-ruk	сорок
50	
pi-dis-YAHT	пятьдесят
60	
shiz-dis-YAHT	шестьдесят
70	
SYEM-dis-yit	семьдесят
80	
VO-sim-dis-yit	восемьдесят
90	
di-vyi-NOH-sta	девяносто
100	
stoh	сто
200	
DVYE-sti	двести
300	
TRI-stuh	триста
400	
chyi-TIR-i-stuh	четыреста
500	
pyuht-SOHT	пятьсот
600	
shyist-SOHT	шестьсот
700	
syim-SOHT	семьсот
800	
vah-syim-SOHT	восемьсот
900	
dyiv-yut-SOHT	девятьсот
1000	
TIH-suh-chuh	тысяча
2000	
dvyeh TIH-suh-chi	две тысячи
3000	
tree TIH-suh-chi	три тысячи
4000	
chi-TIR-yeh TIH-suh-chi	четыре тысячи
5000	
pyaht TIH-suhch	пять тысяч
6000	
shest TIH-suhch	шесть тысяч

10,000
DYES-yut TIH-suhch
десять тысяч

20,000
DVAHT-sut TIH-suhch
двадцать тысяч

30,000
TREET-sut TIH-suhch
тридцать тысячи

73,568
SYEM-dis-yit tree TIH-suh-chi pyuht-SOHT shiz-dis-YAHT VO-syim
семьдесят три тысячи пятьсот шестьдесят восемь

100,000
stoh TIH-suhch
сто тысяч

one million
ah-DYIN mi-li-OHN
один миллион

Time

Round hours are fairly easy, except that there are three different ways of saying the Russian equivalent of 'o'clock', depending on the hour. Thus one o'clock is *'ah-DYIN chahs'* (or simply *'chahs'*), two o'clock is *'dva chuh-SAH'* (and similarly for three and four o'clock) and five o'clock is *'pyaht chuh-SOF'* (and similarly up to 20). For in-between times the standard formula gives brain-twisters like 'without-25-five' for 4.35. You'll be understood if you say the hour followed by the minutes: eg 9.20 is девять-двадцать (*'DYEV-yut DVAHD-sut'*). For minutes under 10 insert zero, ноль (*'nohl'*): eg 2.08 is два-ноль-восемь (*'dva nohl VOH-sem'*). Timetables use a 24-hour clock: eg 3 pm is пятнадцать часов (*'pyit-NAHT-sut chuh-SOF'*).

hour
chahs
час

minute
mi-NOOT-uh
минута

What time is it?
ka-TOR-i chahs
Который час?

At what time?
fka-TOR-um chuh-SOO?
В котором часу?

am/in the morning
oo-TRA
утра

pm/in the afternoon
dnya
дня

in the evening
VYEH-chi-ruh
вечера

local time
MYEST-na-yuh VREM-yuh
местное время

Moscow time
muh-SKOF-skuh-yeh VREM-yuh
московское время

Days & Dates

Dates are given as day-month-year, with the month usually in Roman numerals. Days of the week are often represented by numbers in timetables; Monday is 1.

when?
kahg-DA?   когда?

today
si-VOHD-nyuh   сегодня

yesterday
fchi-RA   вчера

tomorrow
ZAHF-truh   завтра

day after tomorrow
pa-sli-ZAHF-truh   послезавтра

Monday
pa-ni-DEL-nik   понедельник

Tuesday
FTOR-nik   вторник

Wednesday
sri-DA   среда

Thursday
chit-VERK   четверг

Friday
PYAT-nit-suh   пятница

Saturday
su-BOHT-uh   суббота

Sunday
vas-kri-SEN-yuh   воскресенье

Museum Dates

Centuries are represented with Roman numerals.

century, centuries	в., вв.
year, years	г., гг.
beginning, middle, end	начало, середина, конец
AD (literally, 'our era')	н.э.
BC (literally, 'before our era')	до н.э.
10th century AD	X в. н.э.
7th century BC	VII в. до н.э.

Emergencies

I'm sick.
   ya BOH-lyin (m), ya bahl-NA (f)
   Я болен, я больна.

I need a doctor.
   mnyeh NU-zhin vrahch
   Мне нужен врач.

hospital
   BOHL-nit-suh
   больница

police
   mi-LEET-si-yuh
   милиция

Fire!
   pa-ZHAR!
   Пожар!

Help!
   na POH-mushch! or *pa-ma-GEET-yeh!*
   На помощь! or Помогите!

Thief!
   vor!
   Вор!

Facts for the Visitor

PLANNING YOUR TRIP

The days of Intourist's monopoly over everything tourism-related, of mandatory prepaid travel, of hard-currency vouchers and of KGB spooks who followed you around the countryside are history. But the Soviet legacy of an inefficient tourism infrastructure, Byzantine visa procedures and a lack of standard information outlets means that making arrangements is still a challenging business.

The change in government has resulted in a country that's wide open and ready for exploration. Nowadays almost all cities, towns and villages are open to the public – 'closed' cities are rare birds indeed, and the places that are closed here would be closed anywhere, even in the West: military installations, rocket-launch sites etc.

The level of difficulty involved in arranging a trip to Russia increases in direct proportion to the level of independence you're after. These days an impulsive weekend trip to St Petersburg or Moscow from, say, Finland, can be arranged in one day. But a trek across the wilds of western Karelia or the eastern Kola Peninsula would call for a bit more legwork to sort out visa requirements and other red tape. This is not by any means to say that it's as difficult as before the fall of communism – it's far, far easier and far more open. But there are still rules to follow, fees to pay, papers to be stamped and customs checks to be passed through.

This section discusses the things you should think about before you travel to Russia. Further details on agencies, programmes, costs and routes into the country are presented in the European Russia Getting There & Away chapter.

Who's in Charge?

When you figure this out, please contact the Kremlin and let the Russian president in on it. As with nearly every other formerly state-run entity in Russia, Intourist, the CCTE and Sputnik have privatised. That is to say, they have exploded, cracked open like eggs fallen from the nest and shattered into hundreds, even thousands, of privately held companies with no real central state control. Intourist Moscow Ltd, Intourist New York, the St Petersburg Travel Company, VAO Intourist, Intourist Murmansk and the many other organisations that use the name 'Intourist' have no more connection with each other than does one travel agency with another back home, except perhaps through the network of contacts built up between their staff in the old days when all were part of one company. Sputnik (which handled 'youth' tourism during the Soviet era) and the CCTE (which handled trade union exchanges) have become general tourism agencies competing in the market like all the others.

The result is that other, smaller and, perhaps, better travel agencies have managed to get a look in where before they could not. Travel agents and individuals can book hotels directly, plan itineraries, buy train and plane tickets (let's not even mention what's happened to Aeroflot just yet; see the European Russia Getting Around and Getting There & Away chapters for more information), and perform in a matter of hours all the functions that used to take weeks.

This lack of a centralised 'tourism control centre' has made travel throughout the country easy: you make your own arrangements and go – even on the spur of the moment.

Tourism information offices are covered under Tourist Offices in this chapter. Foreign and Russian travel agencies that specialise in flights and packages to European Russia are examined in the European Russia Getting There & Away chapter.

Saving Money

Prices are at their most outrageous and hotel space at its tightest in 'high season' (mid-

May to mid-September, or mid-March to the end of October, depending on the programme); in popular centres (the Moscow region, St Petersburg, the Black Sea resorts); and at short notice. But outside these 'hot spots', hotel prices remain essentially constant throughout the year.

You'll save a lot by going with a friend. Two in a double room pay just a few dollars more than one. The cost of transfers (transport to/from your hotel) and excursions for individuals is calculated by the carload. Another way to cut costs is to drive in from Europe and stay in campsites or camp alongside roads, an activity which is legal and (with the exception of major highways) relatively safe.

The biggest savings are in group rates – for hotels (at least 15% below individual rates), excursions (a fraction of individual prices) and packages (to take a tour through a Polish, Czech or Hungarian operator can cost less than half as much as going on your own). Some agencies let individuals join their groups on a flight-only, tour-only or flight-and-hotel basis.

In a Group or on Your Own?

Lonely Planet readers as a rule need no introduction to the virtues of independent travel, but, in the case of Russia, group travel has some advantages worth noting. Bottom-end group travel is a very cheap way to see European Russia, rivalled only by private or business visits. Bed-and-breakfast accommodation can be another alternative to group travel, a bit more expensive than bottom-end group travel but less so than accommodation in hotels; and you get benefits such as city tours, home-cooked meals and the chance to get to know your Russian host.

Service is better everywhere for groups, and, once in a city, there's nothing to stop you from skipping the excursions and rambling on your own. Most special-interest travel is done in groups.

Group Travel Tours can start at home or in Russia, last for a long weekend or for months, in conditions that range from Spartan to shamefully luxurious, with full board or do-it-yourself meals. Many feature a smorgasbord of guided excursions and entertainment (which you can take or leave), while some B&B packages leave you mostly on your own.

For some specific programmes see the Getting There & Away chapter. Tours of interest are also noted in the regional chapters.

Individual Travel To head out on your own equipped with a few Russian phrases and a map is no harder here than anywhere else. In the past individual travel could only be arranged through Intourist, which regarded it as an unpalatable but profitable sideline. With the collapse of all that nonsense, individual travel is certainly the most exciting, if not absolutely the cheapest, way to see any part of Russia.

The central obstacle is that theoretically, no Russian embassy or consulate will issue a tourist visa without confirmation of every night's accommodation, so you must (again, theoretically) develop a day-by-day itinerary – which details at least all accommodation – that meets with the embassy's approval. This is a nerve-wracking exercise best done through a travel agency.

It's worth choosing an agency carefully. Those with experience and contacts can get fast answers from Russian hotels, set the visa process in motion before hotel bookings are in hand and nail down cheap transport in spite of last-minute changes.

You can rejig your itinerary and extend your visa once you're in Russia, though under new visa regulations this takes a good deal of time and will cost you extra.

But there are other ways around this and, happily, they're easier and in many cases cheaper. The HI St Petersburg Hostel and other members of the Russian Youth Hostel Association (see Accommodation later in this chapter) will issue invitations good for a tourist visa based on a booked night – and they'll tack on additional weeks for good measure. The hostel invitations (including those from Travellers Guest House, Moscow, both the HI St Petersburg Hostel and Holiday Hostel in St Petersburg, and others) can also be tailored to fit your needs, even if it means a business invitation, which gives you much more flexibility in terms of extensions, changes etc. A full discussion of visas, including types, regulations, fees, red tape, changes etc, is in the Visas & Embassies section following.

Excursions Excursions and trips can be booked wherever you are. If you're planning something ambitious, unusual or off the beaten track, it's probably wise to try to book it in advance. See the European Russia Getting There & Away chapter, and Getting There & Away sections of city chapters, for information on useful travel agencies.

Where Not to Go

Though there are obviously some places off limits to visitors in any country, a detailed list of open and closed cities isn't really part of the game any more (see Visas & Embassies for more details). If you have doubts about whether a place is safe – eg because of a natural disaster or civil unrest – contact your government's foreign affairs department (see Dangers & Annoyances).

VISAS & EMBASSIES
Visas

All foreigners visiting Russia need visas. To get one you must technically have confirmed accommodation for every night you'll be in the country, though in practice there are countless ways around this.

At the time of writing, a Russian visa is a passport-sized paper document; nothing goes into your passport. There are, however, discussions taking place about changing over to stamps in your passport. A visa lists entry/exit dates, your passport number, any children travelling with you, and visa type (see below). It also lists cities, but this doesn't matter much in terms of where you can go. It's an exit permit, too, so if you lose it (or overstay), leaving the country can be harder than getting in.

The following sections give general information about visa procedures both before

you go to Russia and once you're there. For further information on procedures in Moscow, which have some special local features, see the Moscow chapter.

For information on visas for neighbouring countries and other former Soviet states, see the European Russia Getting There & Away chapter and the Trans-Siberian Railway chapter.

Registration When you check in to a hotel, campsite or hostel, you surrender passport and visa so the hotel can register you with OVIR (Otdel Viz i Registratsii), the Department of Visas and Registration. You'll get your documents back the next morning if you ask (though nobody seems to remember them for you at check-out time).

If you're travelling on your own, you must remember that all Russian visas must be registered with OVIR within three working days of your arrival in Russia. No ifs or buts about it. Many companies, including some Finnish travel agencies in Helsinki, will claim that their 'visas needn't be registered'. This is not so: *all* Russian visas – whether issued by the Moscow Travellers Guest House or by the office of the Russian president – need to be registered with the nearest office of OVIR within three working days of arrival in the country. Be highly suspicious of any company that tells you otherwise. Sometimes you have to pay a registration fee of US$5 to US$10.

Extending a visa that's not registered can be impossible, and getting out of the country with an unregistered visa could be a very expensive proposition. You might waltz out with just a lecture or even unhindered. On the other hand, travellers report that fines of up to US$500 have been levied at the Finnish and Norwegian borders, and St Petersburg and Moscow airport officials aren't about to let a juicy penalty walk past them. It's not worth the risk.

Registration Problems The company or organisation that invited you to Russia is responsible for your registration, and no other company can support your visa. You can't take a visa that was issued on the invitation of, say, the HI St Petersburg Hostel and have it registered in Moscow by the Travellers Guest House.

If you're not sure which organisation invited you (if the sponsorship line – on tourist visas this begins with the words *V uchrezhdenie* – has a name you've never heard of), one option is to spend a night at one of the major (expensive) hotels, which will register your visa for you for varying fees.

The other way is a bit time-consuming, but a lot cheaper if you have a place to stay. Your embassy may be able to help you find the organisation's address, or you can get assistance in finding it at the Association of Joint Ventures, International Unions and Organisations (AJVIUO), Gorbachev Foundation Building, Leningradsky prospekt 55, Moscow. They will charge US$10 for a search that finds your sponsor, or US$30 for a fruitless search (you work it out). The search takes one day.

If you've found your sponsor's address, you must go there and ask someone to help you register. If they welcome you with open arms, you're set! They'll take in your visa and register it for you. If they refuse to do anything for you, have them write a letter to OVIR/UVIR (see below) stating that they refuse to take responsibility for you (you can use this at OVIR/UVIR to support your case for a new visa).

If the search for your sponsor turned up the fact that your sponsor is not a registered company (in other words, your visa was obtained using a fraudulent sponsorship letter), you'll need that in writing from the AJVIUO. Armed with that letter, head to OVIR/UVIR.

UVIR Different offices of OVIR handle things differently; one office may be able to perform a service that another can't. If you're having visa problems or trying to extend a visa, the national headquarters, known as UVIR (Upravlenia Viz i Registratsii; ☎ (095) 207 01 13), is the place to come. It's in Moscow at ulitsa Pokrovka 42 (formerly ulitsa Chernyshevskogo, and some signs still say that). The nearest metro

▲▲

Stop Press: New Visa Requirements in the Pipeline
Midway through 1995, at least two Moscow newspapers published stories regarding plans by the Russian Ministry of Foreign Affairs (MID) to change significantly the procedure for obtaining a visa invitation. The proposal would require the Russian entity issuing the invitation – whether an individual or a business, for a tourist or a business visa – to obtain from the Office of Visas and Registration (UVIR) a pre-printed invitation and mail this to the foreign visa applicant. Facsimiles of this form would not be acceptable.

The stated reason for this was that the visa situation had grown uncontrollable, and that many organisations were issuing visa invitations in exchange for money (true), which was leading to security problems (not true).

The potential ramifications of such an act are manifold. At the very least it would result either in significant delays in transmission of these invitations by post or in a substantial addition to the cost of delivery as senders resorted to the use of Western express-mail companies. But should the ministry prove to be cracking down on the quality, rather than the quantity, of visa invitations issued, many requests for business or other long-term, non-specific visas might be rejected out of hand. Such a move could severely impede independent travellers.

According to an article in the *Moscow Times*, the foreign ministry said that the new measures would come into effect in September or October 1995. The forms, the article continued, would be 'introduced gradually, first in Moscow and then in St Petersburg and other cities'.

Lonely Planet will continue to monitor the situation, and will publish in its newsletter, *Planet Talk*, as well as on its Internet information service, the latest information available on Russian visa requirements. ■

stations are Krasnye Vorota and Kurskaya. There are English-speaking officers, but you should be prepared for a long wait. The office is open Monday, Tuesday and Thursday from 10 am to 1 pm and 3 to 6 pm, Friday from 10 am to 1 pm and 3 to 5 pm, and Saturday, for emergencies only, from 10 am to 1 pm. It is closed on Sunday and Wednesday.

HIV/AIDS Testing The Russian government has gone back and forth on this issue. At the time of writing, we understand that from August 1995 foreigners who wish to stay in the Russian Federation for longer than three months will be required to take an HIV/AIDS test. Details on enforcement are sketchy. The Russian Embassy in Washington, DC, said that a certificate from your doctor at home would be required before a long-term visa would be issued. Questions remain about testing once inside Russia, and about the situation of those people who had already been issued a visa without such a certificate. Note that this would, by definition, *not* affect tourist visas, which are not valid for periods long enough to fall under the regulations.

Types of Visa Six types of visa are available to foreign visitors and are listed below.

For all visas you'll need:

- a passport valid for at least a month beyond your return date plus photocopies of the passport validity and personal data pages. A UK Visitor's passport or other temporary papers won't do. You may be able to get away with giving the embassy or consulate just the photocopies of the passport validity and personal data pages instead of the whole passport;
- three passport-sized (4 by 4.5 cm), full-face photos not more than a year old. Vending-machine photos with white background are fine if they're essentially identical. It's probably wise not to make radical changes in your appearance between photo time and your arrival in Russia;
- a completed application form, including entry/exit dates;
- a handling fee of an amount that varies from country to country and according to your citizenship.

Tourist Visa A tourist visa is issued to – well, to tourists: those who have booked hotel or hostel space and are in Russia for purposes other than business. As the visa game goes, these are the most straightforward and inflexible available. In theory you're supposed to have booked accommodation for every night you'll be in the country, but in practice you can often get away with booking only a few, even just one – ask the travel agent, hotel or hostel through which you book.

It is not easy to extend a tourist visa and, even if you can, it's usually only for a short time, up to a maximum of three months. Tourist visas are best for those trips when you know exactly what you're doing, and when, where and for how long you'll be doing it. To obtain a tourist visa, you'll need, in addition to the above:

- confirmation of hotel reservations, which can be a faxed copy on hotel letterhead signed and stamped by the hotel; confirmation of bookings from Intourist or a travel agent; or a visa-support letter from an organisation authorised to issue one, such as the Russian Youth Hostel Association (RYHA) or any of its member hostels or Peter Tourist Information and Postal Services (Peter TIPS). (See the next section regarding tourist visa-support fees charged by some hostels, guesthouses and companies in Russia.)

Business Visa Far more flexible and desirable to the independent traveller is a business, or commercial, visa supported by a Russian company. The company's invitation eliminates the need for prearranged hotel confirmations, as the company inviting you ostensibly puts you up for the duration of your stay. While a visa to Russia supposedly allows you to travel anywhere, holders of tourist visas may have a harder time getting lodging in smaller cities that are not listed on their visas than will holders of business visas doing the same thing.

To obtain a business visa you must have:

- a letter of invitation from a registered Russian company. This *must* be signed by a Russian director of that company (a Western friend's signature – even that of the Western director or partner in a Russian joint-stock company – will probably be turned down), guaranteeing to provide accommodation during the entire length of your stay.

There are many organisations that will send you a business invitation for a fee, usually not an outrageous one. The fastest and most reliable way to get a business invitation is through hostels: the Travellers Guest House in Moscow and the HI St Petersburg Hostel both issue business invitations. You'll need to send them a fax or e-mail containing your name as it appears in your passport, date and place of birth, nationality, passport number and expiry date, dates of entry to and exit from Russia (these can be approximate) and the consulate at which you intend to apply for your visa. Below are some sample fees for visa-support services which include an invitation and registration services upon arrival:

Travellers Guest House/IRO Travel, Moscow (☎ (095) 971 40 59, fax (095) 280 76 86; e-mail tgh@glas.apc.org) – All with reservation. Tourist visa: one month's single-entry US$30. Business visa: three months single-entry US$45; three months multiple-entry US$150; six months multiple-entry US$175; one year's multiple-entry $250.

HI St Petersburg Hostel (☎ (812) 329 80 18; fax (812) 329 80 19; e-mail ryh@ryh.spb.su for hostel information, bookings@ryh.spb.su to book) – Tourist visa: (with reservation; for accommodation booked plus two weeks of added time in country) US$10; (without reservation) US$25. Business visa: three months single-entry US$40; three months dual-entry US$60; six months multiple-entry (eight weeks advance notice required for MID (Ministry of Foreign Affairs) approval) US$150. Need credit card (Visa/MasterCard) or other payment in advance.

Peter TIPS, St Petersburg (☎ (812) 279 00 37) – Tourist visa-support letter: three months single-entry US$10; three months extendable US$20. Conversion from single to multiple-entry US$200. Registration US$15.

Russian Youth Hostels & Tourism (RYHT), Redondo Beach, USA (☎ (310) 618 2014; fax (310) 618 1140; e-mail 71573.2010@compuserve.com) – Tourist visa (with reservation at HI St Petersburg or Moscow hostels or Travellers Guest House in Moscow) US$40; (without reservation) US$55; Business visa: three months single-entry US$60; three months dual-entry US$90; six months mul-

tiple-entry (eight weeks advance notice required for MID approval) US$175. Need credit card or other payment in advance. Includes guaranteed processing by Russian embassy/consulate.

There are scores of other companies willing to issue business visa invitations, some cheaper, some more expensive. We are listing the above because we know them to be reliable and experienced, and because they follow through with registration.

Student Visa Student visas can be wonderful things: flexible, extendable, and they even entitle you to pay Russian prices for airfares, train tickets, and other items affected under the country's dual-pricing system (see Costs, below). The problem here is that you pretty well have to be legit: you'll need proof of enrolment at an accredited Russian school or university, which usually requires a lot of prepayment. For information on language courses and other study in Russia, see the Activities section in this chapter.

'Private' Visa This is what you get for a visit by personal invitation. The visa itself is as easy to get as a tourist visa once you have an invitation, but getting the invitation is complex.

The person who is to invite you must go to their local office of OVIR (or, in smaller towns, to the police) and fill out an invitation form for approval of the invitation. Approval, which takes several weeks, comes in the form of a notice of permission (izveshchenie), good for one year, which the person inviting must send to you. With this and the standard application form you apply for the visa, valid for as long as 60 days in your host's town.

For information on inviting a Russian citizen to your country, see the end of this Visas section.

'On-the-Spot' Visa These are basically fast-track business visas, freed from the requirement for advance invitations. Individuals who arrive from abroad at Moscow's

Sheremetevo-2 or St Petersburg's Pulkovo-2 airport can get short-term visas at a special Intourist office before passport control. To get one of these, you'll have to arrange to be met at the airport by a representative of a Russian company, who will 'invite' you to Russia.

Typically, they're good for up to a month, and cost a fee of about US$150 to US$250. Though expensive and problematic, this may be one way around the paper chase.

Transit Visa This is for 'passing through', which is interpreted loosely. For transit by air it's usually good for 48 hours. For a nonstop Trans-Siberian Railway journey it's valid for 10 days, giving westbound passengers a few days in Moscow without the obligatory hotel prebooking (eastbounders can't linger in Moscow). Under certain circumstances, travellers passing through Russia who hold valid entry/exit visas to Armenia, Belarus, Kazakhstan, Kyrgyzstan, Tajikistan or Uzbekistan need not apply for a Russian transit visa. The requirements on this are sketchy, and while a Russian consulate may say it's unnecessary, the odds of being allowed into or out of Russia on the premise that you're holding a Tajik visa are slim. Many border guards are not familiar with the latest regulations handed down in Moscow, so it's always best to play it safe, especially when travelling to border crossings in remote areas.

Visa-Free Travel Prebooked cruise passengers can visit Russian ports for up to four days without a visa if they sleep aboard the ship. In 1994, the Russian government added a 2 am curfew to that restriction, but this may change in the future. This won't work for return passengers on ordinary scheduled sailings. Visa-free cruises are available to several cities; see the European Russia Getting There & Away chapter for more information.

When to Apply Apply as soon as you have all the documents you need (but not more than two months ahead). Business, tourist,

private and student visas all take the same amount of time to process once you have the paper – be it invitation, confirmation or izveshchenie. This ought to be 10 working days, but at busy embassies such as London's it may be longer. You can pay a higher fee for quicker service at most embassies. Transit visas take seven working days – or as little as a few hours at the Russian Embassy in Beijing.

How to Apply Russian visa procedures are straight out of Kafka. Individuals can arrange their own visas, though long queues at embassies and consulates are common in high season and Russian consular officials are sometimes somewhat less than bright and perky – and they rarely answer the telephone. If you're booking your flight or accommodation through a travel agency, they'll get your visa too for an extra fee, usually between US$5 and US$30 (agencies in Hong Kong, which must go to Bangkok for visas, nail you for more). For group tours, the agency does the work. (See the European Russia Getting There & Away chapter and the Trans-Siberian Railway chapter for information on some useful travel agencies.)

Visa Agencies Certain agencies specialise in getting visas: eg, in the USA, Visa Services (☎ (202) 387 0300), 1519 Connecticut Ave NW, Washington, DC 20036; in the UK, Worldwide Visas (☎ (0171) 379 0419), 9 Adelaide Street, Charing Cross, London WC2 N4HZ. Unless you're really pressed for time or especially badly affected by impersonal bureaucracies, it seems a bit lavish, really. An agency will put your paperwork together and forward it to the embassy for you – for a fee of up to US$65.

In Person To do it yourself, go to the nearest Russian embassy or consulate (if you're not near one, see the following By Mail section). Bring your passport or photocopies of the pages covering your personal information and passport validity, your photographs and your hotel confirmation, hostel or business invitation, proof of enrolment, izveshchenie or through tickets. Ask for, and complete, the visa application, and then wait.

How long you wait depends on how much you're willing to pay. Rush fees vary not just by country but by individual consulate, but, as an example, the Russian consulate in San Francisco charges US$40 for service in seven to eight days, US$50 for five to six-day service, US$60 for three to four-day service and US$80 for next-day service. A two-hour rush visa (or one that is mailed back to you the same day) costs US$120. For information on obtaining a Russian transit visa in Beijing, see the Trans-Siberian Railway chapter.

While Russian consular officials in some locations are friendly and even smile once in a while, those at others are often not. Unfortunately, there's not much you can do except be very polite and get out of there as quickly as you can. You *do* have the right to shop around: nothing is stopping you from taking care of your visa by mail at a known friendly consular office (in our experience) such as Helsinki, Warsaw or San Francisco.

By Mail It's possible to do it all by mail, with stamped, self-addressed envelopes or Federal Express, Airborne, DHL or TNT airbills complete with your account number, if you have one, for all requested forms and completed documents. When you get the visa check it carefully, including expiry, entry and exit dates and any restrictions on entry or exit points.

Fax-Back Service In the USA (or if you use a US telephone carrier to get '1-800' service from overseas) you can obtain current visa requirements and application forms by fax by calling the Russian Fax-Back Service (1-800 634 4296). A voice and touch-tone-driven menu will offer you choices of available documents. You may select up to four. The fax-back service will send within 10 minutes all the documents you select to any fax machine in the world (for international calls enter the code 011 plus your country and city codes). The service is free.

London Interactive Telephone Service For callers in the UK, the Russian embassy's consular section in London offers an interactive recorded message about visas (☎ (0891) 171 271). This is a premium-rate number which costs £0.49/minute peak, £0.38/minute cheap, but it tells you most of what you'll need to know in five to 10 minutes. Choose from six messages dealing with different types of visa. You then have to visit or write to the consulate to get the relevant forms. Even if (by some administrative oversight) you were so lucky as to get through on the main consulate number, you'd be referred to this recording anyway.

Extensions & Changes Extensions have become time-consuming, if not downright difficult. A tourist visa can now only be extended in Moscow, only through official hotels (not hostels) and with a great deal of advance notice and perhaps of money.

Transit visas at the time of writing are getting more and more difficult to extend for longer than five days. Trans-Siberian passengers from Beijing have had little trouble getting one three-day extension by claiming they couldn't get a westward train booking. This takes less than a day at the Moscow office of UVIR (☎ (095) 207 01 13), ulitsa Pokrovka 42 (see the earlier section on UVIR for details). If you're asked where you're staying, probably the safest thing to say is that you're sleeping at the Travellers Guest House. You may be asked for your outbound ticket, so it's best to bring it along. See the Moscow chapter for more information on extending your transit visa.

Visitors on private visas have succeeded in extending them by going to the local OVIR or police office and presenting telegrams from friends elsewhere in Russia inviting them to visit.

Where Can You Go? Some cities in Russia are still off limits to foreigners but these are few and far between. Any visa is technically valid for all of Russia except these closed cities.

Practically speaking, no one cares where

you go. During the research of this book, Nick Selby (who went to 29 cities and dozens of small towns) had a visa with no list of towns – just the words 'For Abroad' – and the only people to raise a stink about it were two hotel administrators. John Noble had difficulty in only two cities, Richard Nebesky in only one. It really seems a question of whether the person you're dealing with is familiar with the rules.

You may have trouble with a tourist visa in a hotel in a strange city, though this can usually be talked around. If you will be venturing off the beaten path, it's best to play it safe and get a business visa, which essentially allows you the run of the country.

Lost or Stolen Passport or Visa In order to facilitate replacement of your documents, it is imperative that you make and carry photocopies of them, especially your Russian visa. Without this photocopy, replacing a lost or stolen visa can be a nightmare: you may even have to contact the issuing embassy and ask them to find your visa number.

Your embassy or consulate in Russia can replace a lost or stolen passport, but if you lose your visa you must go to the local visa office, OVIR (in Moscow, UVIR). A Russian travel agent, Intourist, your hotel service bureau or the youth hostels can help with this, including reporting the loss to the police. Again, both procedures are much easier if you've stashed a few passport-sized photos, your visa number and photocopies of your visa and your passport's personal information and validity pages.

Inviting Russians to Your Country
Inviting a Russian to visit you in your country involves less hassle for you than getting into Russia on their invitation, but just as much hassle for them. Most of the details that follow apply to the situation in the USA; in other countries, begin by consulting the Department of Foreign Affairs or its equivalent.

In early 1995, in response to many complaints and news reports of poor treatment of Russians by US consular officials, the US Embassy in Moscow announced that it was 'streamlining' visa procedures for Russians applying to enter the USA. In general, a letter of invitation is no longer required for tourist invitations (though US State Department officials stress that one helps). Those applying for business, research, scientific or other types of visas still need a bona fide letter of invitation.

Generally speaking, Russian citizens are now issued a three-year multiple-entry visa to the USA for a fee of US$120 plus a non-refundable US$20 application fee. Four new categories have been created to reduce crowds. *Express* is for people over 60; adults with immediate relatives who are US citizens; students; exchange visitors returning to the USA; or those who have travelled twice to the USA on short visits; *Group* is for groups of five or more going to the USA for non-tourist purposes such as business seminars and educational exchanges. *Foreign Commercial Service* caters for US businesspeople living in Russia who wish to invite Russian colleagues to the USA for business purposes. And *Travel Agency* lets Russian businesspeople submit applications through selected travel agencies.

For more information once in Moscow, contact the US embassy consular section's receptionist under the American flag at Novinsky bulvar 19/23.

In any event, a letter of invitation helps. You'll need to write a letter to your intended guest that includes their name and address and yours, your relationship, the proposed visit period, and a statement to the effect that you will accommodate your guest and give financial support if necessary.

In the USA, take it to a notary public, who will witness your signature. In the UK, a solicitor or Commissioner for Oaths will do this, after which the Russian Embassy in London says you should take it to the Foreign Office for endorsement.

Send the letter to your friend, who uses it to apply for a passport and/or exit permit and an entry visa to your country. (If you've ever fumed about the wait to get service at a

Russian consulate, you should have sympathy for anyone coming up against US visa staff in Russia: they will have at least as hard a time as you did.) If their application is turned down, US citizens can appeal to the consular section, but note that visas to the US can be refused by the consular officer based solely on their opinion of the applicant and their application. If you do appeal, send copies to your congressman or woman, and try and sound as flag-waving as possible when dealing with consular staff.

Russian Embassies & Consulates

Like many things about Russia, the information contained in this section is vulnerable to change. Consulates are moving and changing their contact telephone numbers, and some may even be closed in years to come. You should verify in formation given here before you mail off your travel documents and payments. Unless otherwise specified, the details listed below are for embassies.

Armenia
    Hotel Hrazdan, 72 Pionerakan St, 375019 Yerevan (☎ (8852) 52 45 22, 52 44 24)
Australia
    78 Canberra Ave, Griffith, Canberra, ACT 2603 (☎ (06) 295 9033, 295 9474; fax (06) 295 1847)
    Consulate: 7-9 Fullerton St, Woollahra, NSW 2025 (☎ (02) 327 5065)
Austria
    Reisnerstr 45-47, A-1030 Vienna (☎ (0222) 712 1229, 712 3233, 713 1215; fax (0222) 712 3388)
    Consulate: Bürgelsteinstr 2, A-5020 Salzburg (☎ (0662) 62 41 84; fax (0662) 621 7434)
Azerbaijan
    Hotel Azerbaijan, 370133 Baku (☎ (8922) 98 60 16; fax (9822) 98 60 83)
Belarus
    vulitsa Staravilenskaja 48, 220002 Minsk (☎ (0172) 345 497; fax (0172) 503 664)
Belgium
    66 Avenue de Fre, B-1180 Brussels (☎ (02) 374 3406, 374 6886, 374 3106; fax (02) 374 2613, 346 2453)
Canada
    285 Charlotte St, Ottawa, Ontario K1N 8L5 (☎ (613) 235 4341, 235 5376, 236 1413; fax (613) 236 6342)
    Consular Section: 52 Range Rd, Ottawa, Ontario K1N 8J5 (☎ (613) 236 6215, 236 7220; fax (613) 238 6158)

    Consulate: 3655 Avenue du Musée, Montreal, Quebec H3G 2E1 (☎ (514) 843 5901, 842 5343; fax (514) 842 2012)
China
    4 Baizhongjie, Beijing 100600 (☎ (10) 532 2051, visa section 532 1267)
    Consulate: 20 Huangpu Lu, Shanghai 200080 (☎ (21) 324 2682)
Croatia
    Bosanska 44, HR-41000 Zagreb (☎ (041) 57 54 44, 57 54 35; fax (041) 57 22 60)
Czech Republic
    Podkaštany 1, Prague 6 (☎ (02) 38 19 43, 38 19 40; fax (02) 37 38 00)
    Consulate: Hlinky 1462, CZ-60300 Brno (☎ (05) 33 44 27; fax (05) 33 44 29); Petra Velikého 18, CZ-36001 Karlovy Vary (☎ (017) 2 26 09; fax (017) 2 62 61)
Denmark
    Kristianiagade 5, DK-2100 Copenhagen (☎ 31 38 23 70, 31 42 55 85; fax 31 42 37 41)
Estonia
    Pikk 19, EE-0001 Tallinn (☎ (22) 44 30 14; fax (22) 44 37 73)
    Consulate: Vilde 8, EE-2020 Narva (☎ & fax (235) 3 13 67)
Finland
    Tehtaankatu 1B, FIN-00140 Helsinki (☎ (90) 66 14 49, 66 18 76/7, 60 70 50; fax (90) 66 10 06)
    Consulate: Vartiovuorenkatu 2, 20700 Turku (☎ (21) 233 64 41; fax (21) 231 97 79)
France
    40-50 Boulevard Lannes, F-75116 Paris (☎ (1) 45 04 05 50, 45 04 71 71; fax (1) 45 04 17 65)
    Consulate: 8 Ambroise Pare, F-13008 Marseille (☎ 91 77 15 25; fax 91 77 34 54)
Germany
    PO Box 200908, Waldstr 42, D-53177 Bonn (☎ (0228) 31 20 85/6/7, 31 25 29/32, 31 20 74; fax (0228) 31 15 63)
    Consulate: (☎ (0228) 31 20 75; fax (0228) 38 45 61)
    Consulate Berlin: Unter den Linden 63-65, D-10117 Berlin (☎ (030) 2 29 14 20; fax (030) 2 29 93 97)
    Consulate Hamburg: Am Feenteich 20, D-22085 Hamburg (☎ (040) 2 29 52 01; fax (040) 2 29 77 27)
    Consulate Leipzig: Kickerlingsberg 18, D-04105 Leipzig (☎ (0341) 5 18 76; fax (0341) 5 85 24 04)
    Consulate Munich: Seidelstr 8, D-80355 Munich (☎ (089) 59 25 03; fax (089) 5 50 38 28)
    Consulate Rostock: Tuhnenstr 3, D-18057 Rostock (☎ (0381) 2 26 42; fax (0381) 2 27 43)
Greece
    Paleo Psikhico, 28 Nikiforou Litra St, GR-15452 Athens (☎ (01) 672 5235, 672 6130, 671 4504; fax (01) 647 9708)

Hungary
Bajza utea 35, H-1062 Budapest V1 (☎ (1) 132 0911, 112 1013; fax (1) 252 5077)

Ireland
186 Orwell Rd, Rathgar, Dublin (☎ (01) 492 3525, 492 2048; fax (01) 492 3525)

Israel
120 Rehov Hayarkon, Tel Aviv 63573 (☎ (3) 522 6744, 522 6733/6; fax (3) 522 6713)

Italy
Via Gaeta 5, I-00186 Rome (☎ (06) 494 1680/1, 494 1649; fax (06) 49 10 31)
Consulate: Via St Aquilino 3, I-20148 Milan (☎ (02) 48 70 59 12, 48 70 60 41)

Japan
2-1-1 Azabudai, Minato-ku, Tokyo 106 (☎ (3) 3583 5982, 3858 4297; fax (3) 3505 0593)
Consulate: (☎ (3) 3586 0707; fax (3) 3505 0593)
Consulate Osaka-Fu: Toyonaka-Shi, Nishimi-dorigaoka 1-2-2, Osaka-Fu (☎ (6) 848 3452; fax (6) 848 3453)
Consulate Sapporo: 826 Nishi, 12-chome, Minami 14 Jo, Chuo-ku, Sapporo 064 (☎ (11) 561 3171/2; fax (11) 561 8897)

Kazakhstan
ulitsa Dzhandosova 4, Almaty (☎ (3272) 44 83 32, visa enquiries 44 66 44)

Kyrgyzstan
ulitsa Pervomayskaya 17, Bishkek (☎ (3312) 22 16 91; fax (3312) 22 18 23, 22 17 10)

Latvia
Paeglesiela 2, LV-1397 Riga (☎ (2) 33 21 51, 22 06 93; fax (2) 21 25 79)

Lithuania
Juozapavičiaus gatvė 11, LT-2000 Vilnius (☎ (22) 35 17 63; fax (22) 35 38 77)

Moldova
bulvar Stefan del Mare 151, 277019 Chisinau (☎ & fax (2) 23 26 00)

Mongolia
Friendship St A 6, Ulan Bator (☎ (1) 7 28 51, 2 68 36, 2 75 06)

Netherlands
Andries Bickerweg 2, NL-2517 JP The Hague (☎ (070) 345 13 00/1, 346 88 88, 34 10 75 06; fax (070) 361 7960)
Consulate: (☎ (070) 346 7940)

New Zealand
57 Messines Rd, Wellington (☎ (04) 476 6113; fax (04) 476 3843)

North Korea
Choson Minjujuii inmin, Chuji Soryong Tesagwan, Conghwaguck, Pyongyang (☎ (2) 81 31 01/2)

Norway
Drammensveen 74, 0271 Oslo (☎ 22 55 32 78/9; fax 22 55 00 70)

Poland
ulitsa Belwederska 49, PL-00-761 Warsaw

(☎ (022) 21 34 53, 21 59 54; fax (02) 625 3016)
Consulate: ulitsa Batorego 15, PL-80-251 Gdansk-Wrzeszcz (☎ (058) 41 42 00, 41 96 39)
Consulate Kracow: ulitsa Westerplatte 11, PL-31-033 Kracow (☎ (012) 22 26 47, 22 92 33, 22 83 88)
Consulate Poznan: ulitsa Dukowska 53A, PL-60-567 Poznan (☎ (061) 41 75 23, 41 77 40)
Consulate Szezecin: ulitsa P Skargi 14, PL-71-422 Szezecin (☎ (091) 22 22 45, 22 48 77, 22 21 19, 22 03 33)

Portugal
Rua Visconde de Santarem 59, P-1000 Lisbon (☎ (01) 8462424, 8462524, 8462623; fax (01) 8463008)

Romania
Sioseaua Kiseleff 6, Bucharest (☎ (1) 617 0120/8/9, 617 23 22, 617 0129; fax (1) 617 7659, 312 8405)
Consulate: Str Mihai Viteazul 5, Constantina (☎ (41) 61 51 68, 61 11 06)

Slovakia
Godrova 4, SK-81106 Bratislava (☎ (7) 31 34 68; fax (7) 33 49 10)

Slovenia
Cesta II.st 7, SLO-61000 Ljubljana (☎ (061) 26 11 89; fax (061) 125 4141)

South Africa
PO Box 6743 Pretoria 0001, Butano Building, 316 Brooks St, Menlo Park 0081 (☎ (12) 43 27 31/2; fax (12) 43 28 42)
Consular Section: 135 Bourke St, Sunnyside 0002 (☎ (12) 344 4820, 344 4812; fax (12) 343 8636)
Consulate: 8 Riebeeck St, Cape Town 8001 (☎ (21) 418 3656/7, 419 2651; fax (21) 419 2651)

South Korea
10001-13/14/15 Dacchi-Dng, Kangnam-Ku, Seoul (☎ (2) 554 9674, 555 8051; fax (2) 558 5608, 563 3589)

Spain
Velázquez 155, E-28002 Madrid (☎ (91) 411 0807, 562 2264; fax (91) 562 9712)
Consulate: Avenida Pearson 40-42, E-08034 Barcelona (☎ (93) 204 0246; fax (93) 280 5541)

Sweden
Gjoerwellsgatan 31, S-11260 Stockholm (☎ (08) 13 04 41/2/0, 53 37 32; fax (08) 618 2703)

Switzerland
Brunnadernrain 37, CH-3006 Bern (☎ (031) 352 05 66, 352 64 65; fax (031) 352 55 95)
Consulate: Brunnadernrain 53, CH-30006 Bern (☎ (031) 352 05 67, 352 64 25; fax (031) 352 64 60)
Consulate Geneva: 24 Rue Jean Schaub CH-1202 Geneva (☎ (022) 734 79 55, 734 90 83)

Turkey
Karyagdi Sok 5, Cankaya TR-06692 Ankara (☎ (312) 440 8217, 439 2122/3; fax (312) 438 3952)

Turkmenistan
11 Turkmenbashy Shaely, 744004 Ashkhabad (☎ (3632) 25 39 57, 29 84 66; fax (3632) 29 84 66)

Ukraine
vulitsya Kutuzova 8, UKR-252000 Kiev (☎ (044) 294 79 36; fax (044) 292 66 31)

UK
13 Kensington Palace Gardens, London W8 4QX (☎ (0171) 229 3628/9; fax (0171) 727 8624/5, 299 5804)
Consular Section: 5 Kensington Palace Gardens, London W8 4QS (☎ (0171) 229 8027, visa message (0891) 171271; fax (0171) 229 3215)
Consulate: 9 Coates Cres, Edinburgh E 113 7RL (☎ (0131) 225 7098; fax (0131) 225 9587)

USA
2650 Wisconsin Ave NW, Washington, DC 20007 (☎ (202) 298 5700, 298 5772; fax (202) 298 5749)
Visa Department: 1825 Phelps Pl NW, Washington, DC 20008 (☎ (202) 939 8907; fax (202) 939 8909)
Consulate Seattle: 2323 Westin Bldg, 2001 Sixth Ave, Seattle, WA 98121-2617 (☎ (206) 728 1910; fax (206) 728 1871; e-mail consul@consul. seanet.com; Internet http://www.seanet.com/ RussianPage/RussianPage.html)
Consulate San Francisco: 2790 Green St, San Francisco, CA 94123-4609 (☎ (415) 928 6878; fax (415) 929 0306)
Consulate New York: 9 East 91st St, New York, NY 10128 (☎ (212) 348 0926, 348 0955; fax (212) 831 9162)

Uzbekistan
ulitsa Nukusskaya (formerly ulitsa Poltoratskaya) 83, 750015 Tashkent (☎ (3712) 54 36 41, 55 92 18, 55 91 57; fax (3712) 55 87 74)

Vietnam
58 Tran Phu, Hanoi (☎ (4) 25 46 31/2; fax (4) 25 61 77)

Yugoslavia
Deligradska 32, YU-11000 Belgrade (☎ (11) 65 67 24, 64 53 45)

Foreign Embassies & Consulates in Russia

Embassies in Russia are listed under Information in the Moscow chapter; consulates are listed under various cities. St Petersburg has US, Canadian, British, German, French, Finnish, Dutch and scores of other consulates; see the St Petersburg chapter for more information. UK, US, Canadian, Australian and NZ consular offices have 24-hour duty lines for general emergencies. The US Embassy likes Americans to register their itineraries, but others may not care if they hear from you unless you're in jail or hospital. They'll help you replace a lost passport and advise on a lost visa and other emergencies. They're willing to help someone at home make emergency contact with you if other efforts have failed. They won't hold mail for travellers.

DOCUMENTS

Besides your passport and visa, documents you may need – some, you definitely will – include:

• photocopies of your visa and passport, to make life a bowl of cherries in case something happens to the originals, which you should store separately (see Lost or Stolen Passport or Visa in the preceding Visas section).

• travel insurance: advisable for theft/loss and medical purposes – see the Health section.

• customs declaration (deklaratsia): see the Customs section. The deklaratsia is as valuable as your visa. It lists valuables and money you brought with you into the country. If you don't have it when you leave, customs could theoretically confiscate your foreign cash – on the theory that any cash you have must have been made during your stay. It does happen, though in practice you might just run into red tape that results in your missing your flight or being sent back from a border. If you haven't got a deklaratsia, or had one but have lost it, one way to avoid the risk of having your cash confiscated is to buy travellers' cheques with your foreign cash before you leave Russia.

• receipts: save receipts for objects of art, souvenirs and books, anything old or valuable. Export tax on these items is calculated by the purchase price and the lack of a receipt allows the customs official to assess the value of an item on the spot – and they're not exactly in your corner.

• hotel pass: more common in small towns than in major cities, this little card (handed to you when you check in) proves your status as a hotel guest, and is also temporary identification while the hotel has your passport and visa.

• student card: the ISIC student card brings discounts at some museums and sometimes on rail fares.

• drivers' documents: the most important are your driving licence, an international driving permit or authorised Russian translation of your document, registration and insurance papers for those with their own cars, and, for those in rented cars, a rental agreement. See Car & Motorbike in the European Russia Getting There & Away and Getting Around chapters.

health certificates: at the time of writing, despite heavy publicity, no HIV/AIDS test is required, nor are there plans to require a test of short-term visa holders. For more details see HIV/AIDS Testing in the Visas & Embassies section. Anyone required to take medication containing a narcotic drug should have a doctor's certificate.

CUSTOMS

Customs agents seem as little interested in extra hassle as travellers are, and rarely seem to make wilful trouble. Except on trains, bags aren't rifled through any more, but they are X-rayed.

On arrival, fill out a customs declaration (deklaratsia). This lists all your money and valuables, including jewellery, cameras, portable electronics etc, and is designed to prevent you from taking *out* more than you brought *in*. There is no 'green line' through customs – everyone's checked except diplomats.

You may be waved right through, but don't count on it. The deklaratsia is duly written on, stamped with a smart bang and returned to you. When you leave Russia you give it to customs, as well as another declaration of what you're taking out.

What You Can Bring In

You may bring in modest amounts of anything for personal use except illegal drugs (even today several foreigners are serving stiff jail terms in Russia), weapons and roubles. Cameras, notebook computers, video cameras, radios and Walkmans, and video and audio tapes are OK.

A few pairs of jeans and up to 250 cigarettes are fine but large amounts of anything sellable are suspect. Food is allowed (except for some fresh fruit and vegetables) and a litre of hard liquor or wine.

You can get a receipt (kvitantsia) for any confiscated item and you *might* succeed in reclaiming it when you leave.

What You Can Take Out

Anything bought from a Western-style shop or department store can go out, but save your receipts. You can't take Russian currency with you, though they won't usually check your pockets or wallet.

Anything vaguely 'arty', such as manuscripts, instruments, coins, jewellery (except obviously inexpensive jewellery; but, even so, keep your receipts), antiques or antiquarian books (meaning those published before 1975) must be assessed by the Ministry of Culture in Moscow (☎ (095) 921 32 58) at room 29, 3rd floor, Neglinnaya ulitsa 8/10, or in St Petersburg (☎ (812) 314 82 34) at naberezhnaya kanala Griboedova 107. There, bean-counting bureaucrats will issue a receipt for tax paid (usually 100% of the purchase price – bring your sales receipt) which you show to customs on your way out of the country. In case you're counting on a benevolent customs agent on the way out, bear in mind that uncleared art commands tax in excess of 600% at customs.

A painting bought at a tourist art market, or in a department store or a commercial gallery, is probably not a cultural treasure, though it should be declared and receipts should be kept.

Since 1990, the removal from the country of certain consumer goods – including furs, caviar, tea, fabrics, clothing, carpets, leather, photo equipment, electrical appliances and precious metal and stones (but not fine art) – has been prohibited. As this book went to print, however, the US State Department was informing travellers that caviar, at least, could be taken out of Russia with a receipt showing that it had been bought from a shop licensed to sell to foreigners. Other items may be similarly affected. But beware: customs agents in Russian airports seem to have magic noses capable of sniffing caviar at 100 metres and will happily rip through bags to find it.

Generally speaking, customs procedures in airports are much stricter and more thorough than at other border crossings. Drug dealers routinely carry their cargo on trains, and thorough car searches are a rare thing indeed – but they do happen occasionally, so beware.

Lost Deklaratsia

It's a good idea to photocopy your deklaratsia after you have entered Russia in case you lose it. If you do lose it, your embassy can give you a letter to Central Customs (☎ (095) 975 44 60, 975 32 89), Komsomolskaya ploshchad 1A, Moscow, requesting a replacement, but you might not get it if you've been in Russia more than a few weeks or didn't enter at Moscow. If you can't get one, arrange to have an absolute minimum of foreign currency in cash when you leave, and hope the customs inspector will let you just fill out another. Play dumb.

MONEY
Currency

The Russian currency is the rouble (rubl). Nominally the rouble is divided into 100 kopecks or kopeki (pronounced ka-PYEK-i), but, since one rouble buys nothing, you won't find much priced in kopecks any more.

Like any country with a currency that has been dropping steadily, Russia is liable to introduce new higher denomination banknotes at any time. Denominations already range from R100 to R100,000. There are also coins from R1 to R100.

Pre-1993 banknotes are no longer legal tender – so don't accept any blue R5000 or red R10,000 notes, or any notes bearing a picture of Lenin, unless you're looking for souvenirs. The denominations and colours of the new, legal notes are R100 (blue), R200 (pink), R500 (green), R1000 (green), R5000 (red), R10,000 (lighter green), R50,000 (beige-orange) and R100,000 (yellowish; just being introduced as we went to press).

By law, virtually all transactions are supposed to be in roubles, not in any foreign currency – even when they're special (high) prices charged only to foreigners (see the Costs section for more on these). Some restaurants, foreign shops and hotels may mark prices in US dollars or Deutschmarks, but these are converted to roubles at the day's exchange rate when you pay. However,

'cash-in-hand' payments such as to taxi drivers or vendors at art markets can often be made in dollars – indeed, you may well be asked for dollars. This is, strictly speaking, illegal.

Prices in this book are given in US dollar equivalents because they're more likely to stay reasonably accurate that way. You still have to pay in roubles.

Exchange Rates

In 1995, after several years of rapid decline in the rouble's value, the government said it would hold the currency at between 4300 and 4900 to the US dollar. Whether this would last remained to be seen. Future movements are impossible to guess. Approximate exchange rates at the time of writing included:

USA	US$1	=	R4565
United Kingdom	UK£1	=	R7190
Australia	A$1	=	R3400
New Zealand	NZ$1	=	R3020
Canada	C$1	=	R3390
Germany	DM1	=	R3205
Finland	Fmk1	=	R1060
France	FFr1	=	R930
Switzerland	SwFr1	=	R3985
Japan	¥100	=	R4560
Sweden	SKr1	=	R650
Norway	NKr1	=	R730
Denmark	DKr1	=	R825

Cash, Travellers' Cheques or Credit/Charge Cards?

Take all three if you can, with the cash and preferably the travellers' cheques in US dollars. Cash is nearly always the preferred method of payment, though cards are making big inroads, especially in the larger cities.

The fact that travellers' cheques are refundable makes them the safest way to carry your money, and you can also use them to pay direct for some goods and services. But outside Moscow and St Petersburg, travellers' cheques can be difficult, often impossible, to cash, and as difficult as cash to replace.

Cash advances on credit cards are easy enough to obtain in Moscow and St Petersburg, but elsewhere can be more difficult.

Unfortunately, the potential difficulties of obtaining cash from travellers' cheques and credit cards outside the two major cities mean that when you travel away from them you should carry most of the money you need in cash. To safeguard it, divide it up and carry it in several different places on your person and in your baggage.

Cash US dollars are by far the best currency to take. Any establishment that exchanges foreign currency will take US dollars. Deutschmarks are second best, with other main Western European currencies such as Swiss or French francs or pounds sterling further behind. Try to get rid of any Eastern European or ex-Soviet states' currencies before you come to Russia – they attract poor exchange rates, if you can change them at all.

Whatever currency you're carrying, make certain that it's all in pristine condition. Worn, damaged, faded or written-on notes will be refused. Take a mixture of denominations: larger notes are often more readily accepted than smaller ones, but you should always also have the equivalent of at least US$100 in small denominations for times when you're stuck changing money at an awful rate.

If you're taking US dollars, try to make sure all your banknotes – and definitely the US$50 and US$100 notes – were minted after 1991 (the date is shown on the bills). As an anti-counterfeit device, these newer US$50 and US$100 notes have an embedded thread (microprinted with the currency face value) running from top to bottom approximately beneath the words 'This Note Is Legal Tender...'. This is visible when held against the light and Russian moneychangers always check for it.

Travellers' Cheques US dollar travellers' cheques are your best bet. Take both small denominations (for buying roubles when the rate is awful) and big ones (to minimise commission, which may be charged per cheque, when you need to cash a lot of money). American Express is the most widely recognised brand in Russia, and has full-service offices in Moscow (☎ (095) 956 90 00) and St Petersburg (☎ (812) 119 60 09). These charge commission on cashing travellers' cheques, just as banks and other places do. Commission is typically 3% to 5%. For emergency refund of American Express travellers' cheques outside office hours, call the British number (44 273) 571600.

Thomas Cook is another widely recognised international brand. If your cheques are lost or stolen, you are required to call the company's world headquarters in the UK (☎ (44 1733) 502 995), which will assess your claim and, if happy, will authorise a refund through their Moscow or St Petersburg offices.

Visa travellers' cheques can be cashed in Moscow and St Petersburg relatively easily. Westpac travellers' cheques are very difficult to cash in Russia.

Credit/Charge Cards These are accepted at many of the more up-market restaurants, hotels and shops, especially in Moscow and St Petersburg. Cash advances against Visa and MasterCard are also a simple matter in the two main cities. Carry your passport when using a credit card as you will often be asked to show it as a precaution against fraud.

Before you go to Russia, make sure you note your card's details and the numbers to contact if it should be lost or stolen.

Generally, there's a 3% to 5% commission tacked on to the amount of a cash advance. The US consulate in St Petersburg recommends that you use a bank, as opposed to an exchange office, for cash advances of large sums; if you're really rich and want sums of US$10,000 or more, one day's notice is usually required. There have been tales of thieves targeting people coming out of buildings with cash advances, so always take care.

It's harder to get cash advances in smaller towns and cities, but credit and charge cards are being accepted for payments in more and more places. Visa, MasterCard/Eurocard, and American Express/Optima are the most widely accepted cards. Some places also accept Diners Club and JCB. The Discover card is not accepted in Russia.

Be careful when paying by card that you see how many slips are being made of your card, that you destroy all carbons, and that as few people as possible get hold of your card number and expiry date. You're usually safe in Western-owned establishments, but one major hotel had problems with its staff making multiple copies of cards. The stolen credit card market in Russia is booming, so protect your card as much as possible.

Sometimes a Visa sign is just decoration. Russians love colourful Western stickers, and Visa signs are 'pretty'. Even if you see the sign, ask whether the card is accepted before you go and order.

If your card is lost or stolen, here are the Moscow numbers you can report it to: American Express (☎ (095) 956 90 00; outside office hours call American Express in Britain on ☎ (44 273) 696 933)); Visa (☎ (095) 284 48 02); Eurocard/MasterCard (☎ (095) 284 47 94); Diners Club (☎ (095) 284 48 73). You can also report the loss of a Visa, Diners Club or Eurocard/MasterCard to United Card Services (☎ (095) 216 68 71, 216 56 39), at Stroenie (Building) 2, Grafsky pereulok 10/12 – or call the lost-card number in your home country.

Cashing Cheques If you're an American Express or Optima card-holder, you can use your personal cheque to get cash or buy travellers' cheques from the American Express offices in Moscow and St Petersburg. Limits depend on your card type and/or credit limit. Every 21 days you can get up to US$1000 on a green card, US$5000 on a gold card, and US$10,000 on a platinum card (on Optima cards you're also limited by the amount of available credit).

Changing Cash into Roubles

There are 100% legal exchange offices practically everywhere in Moscow and St Petersburg – in hotels, restaurants, boutiques, back alleys, vegetable shops etc. Many are open for long hours, often well into the evening. Look for signs that say 'Currency Exchange' (in English) or Обмен валюты (which means the same). Those in hotels and shops, or otherwise away from street crowds, are more secure places to change your money.

Other Russian cities and towns have exchange offices as well, though the smaller the place, the lighter the concentration. Exchange offices are generally easier places to deal with than full-blown bank branches, though you may have to use banks in some places. If you're travelling to remote areas it's best to change money in a large city along the way.

Banks and exchange offices are competitive; representative rates are printed in the *Moscow Times* and the *St Petersburg Press*, so comparing rates before you go shopping is quite easy. Rates are usually posted up on the premises. Generally speaking, rates in private exchange offices are a few points higher than the central bank rate, and rates are slightly better in Moscow than in St Petersburg. The best rates, of course, attract the longest queues.

Whether you change in a bank or an exchange office, you should be given an official receipt showing your name, the date and the currency and exchange rate. This is for your records only; you no longer need this receipt to reconvert roubles or to show to customs when you leave the country.

In small towns, it may pay to bring along your passport, visa and customs declaration to the exchange office. Word of reform in Russia filters down slowly, and a faceless bureaucrat is best stared down with valid paperwork.

Whenever you change money, the changer will subject your cash to some of the most ridiculous counterfeit detection methods you'll ever see. Try not to feel insulted, and, if there is a question about your note, point out watermarks and other counterfeit prevention features. If you're turned away, hit the next exchange office.

The Black Market Russia's famous black marketeers are as quaint as the dictatorship of the proletariat, but those *fartsovshchiky* are a resilient lot. Despite the fact that legal, privately owned exchange booths are as plentiful in Moscow and St Petersburg as they are in Amsterdam, the question 'Change money?' will still ring in the ears of foreigners as they walk Russia's streets or visit its tourist hotels or markets, and even as they wait at exchange offices! (The black marketeers who hang around the exchange booths at Moscow's Sheremetevo-2 airport, by the way, are almost guaranteed to do you down.)

Some black marketeers are ordinary folks trying to supplement their income; others are illegal full-time. They're the visible tip of Russia's enormous black economy, the sprawling mesh of small and big-time embezzlement, bribery, smuggling, under-the-counter trade, prostitution, protection rackets and gangsterism that the Western press loves to call the 'Mafia'.

The only situation in which changing money with these guys (they're always men) might be to your advantage is when you're in a town that has a shortage of legal outlets. When you have a legal alternative, avoid the black marketeers completely. Their rates are not much (or at all) better than the official rate. They have been at this game for a long time and given a great deal of thought to the best way to separate you from your money – and practice does make perfect.

If you decide to change money with them, take every precaution and use common sense.

- Isolate yourself and the changer from his friends – move to the side, never let yourself be at the centre of a crowd (even a crowd of three).
- Beware of out-of-date notes (see the earlier Currency section). These are the favourite trick of black-market money changers at Moscow's Sheremetevo-2 airport.
- Don't hand over your currency until your roubles are in your pocket – a changer who won't let you do that is trying to switch piles of counted roubles with old or phoney notes.
- Only take along the amount you want to change;

if you have to carry more, keep it in a separate pocket and don't show it.
- Trust your judgment: if it feels wrong, walk away.
- Beware of diversionary tactics: a shout of *'Militsia!'* or 'Police!' means someone's just about to try to take your money.
- Leave the area as soon as the transaction is completed (and your roubles are safely in your pocket) – don't let the changer try to make you stick around until he 'counts your money'.
- A changer who examines your money, scowls, folds it up and hands it back to you, saying it's 'no good' or 'counterfeit' has most likely just switched it for a lower denomination note. Don't let anyone examine your currency until you have your roubles safely in your pocket; don't accept folded notes.

Dealing on the black market is, of course, illegal, though generally tourists have to be careless or unlucky to end up in police hands for small-scale deals. Jail is technically a possible punishment for those who get caught, but they're more likely to be hauled down to the station and reprimanded.

Taking Care of Your Money
Don't leave money – in any form – lying around your room. Preferably, keep it in several different places about your person and baggage. When you go out, carry what you'll need in your pockets (but avoid eye-catching wallet bulges), with any more tucked away under your clothing – best in a money belt or shoulder wallet.

Keep the Change!
Hang on to coins and small-denomination notes. Otherwise you'll often be paying over the odds to people who 'haven't any change'.

Wire Transfers
Wire-transferring money to Russia is far easier than it used to be, though the price is high. The fastest way to transfer money from the US, Canada, UK, New Zealand, Australia, Germany, France and Finland, as well as the most expensive, is through Western Union, which has offices in the following Russian cities:

Artem, Astrakhan, Cheboxary, Izhevsk, Kaliningrad,

Kaluga, Krasnodar, Magadan, Moscow, Nizhny Novgorod, Novosibirsk, Penza, Omsk, Petropavlovsk-Kamchatsky, Petrodvorets, Rostov-on-Don, Ryazan, St Petersburg, Sochi, Tula, Vladivostok, Volgograd, Yoshkar-Ola.

Western Union charges US$40 for a US$500 transfer, US$15 for a US$100 transfer. It has several offices in Moscow (central office ☎ (095) 119 82 50) and money is forwarded from there to its member banks in the cities above, generally for an additional 5% handling fee.

Direct bank-to-bank wire transfer is also possible. You may need to open an account at a bank. Usually a commission of 1% to 4% of the amount transferred is charged. Depending on the bank, service takes from one to five days. See the Moscow and St Petersburg chapters for more information on banks to contact.

In emergencies, friends and relatives can wire funds to a US citizen in Russia through the State Department (☎ (202) 647 5225). The money is usually ready to be collected from the US embassy in Moscow after two days.

Rules & Regulations

You can bring any amount of foreign currency or travellers' cheques, plus (at the time of writing) R500,000, into Russia, but you must put it all down on your customs declaration (deklaratsia) when you enter the country – otherwise you may not be allowed to take it all out again. The declaration is designed to thwart those who would take out more money than they brought in. If you write that you're bringing in US$1000, then later try to take out US$2000, you may have the difference confiscated. On the other hand if you write that you're bringing in US$5000, customs agents may ask you to show them the money, to prove that you're not padding to cover an amount that you're coming to Russia to pick up, or that you plan on earning while in the country.

There's no restriction on changing unspent roubles back into foreign currency before you leave the country.

Costs

Our European Russia authors each spent about US$350 to US$400 a week in Russia during the course of research for this book, not counting travel to/from Russia, travel insurance, visa fees or other pre-arrival costs. It's possible to spend less – half that, if you're really frugal – by always seeking out the very cheapest accommodation options and avoiding aeroplanes, taxis, international phone calls and decent restaurants. If you always stay in comfortable hotels and eat in reasonable restaurants two or three times a day you're looking at US$600 or more a week. It's possible to spend US$350 or US$400 in 12 hours, and go nowhere, by having dinner in a top Moscow or St Petersburg restaurant, then sleeping it off in one of their best hotels.

The traveller's major costs in Russia, in roughly descending order, are accommodation, meals, transport and drinks. If you fly a lot, you can put transport near the top of the list. Lesser expenditure items are entry fees to museums and the like; city transport; excursions; books, maps, gifts and souvenirs; telephone calls etc; and entertainment.

Costs of accommodation, restaurants and some museums in Moscow and St Petersburg are on a different scale to the rest of the country. In these two main cities, you need to stay in hostels, guesthouses, student dorms or cheap homestays, and control your restaurant outings, to keep your budget in line with the US$30 to US$50 you'd typically spend elsewhere on moderate hotels and two or three restaurant meals a day. A few typical prices to help you estimate spending include:

- single/double room in a bottom-end hotel US$15/20; in Moscow or St Petersburg US$25/35
- single/double room in a mid-range hotel US$35/50; in Moscow or St Petersburg US$70/90
- train from Moscow to St Petersburg US$25; plane from Moscow to St Petersburg US$75
- train from Moscow to Astrakhan US$45; plane from Moscow to Astrakhan US$130
- lunch or dinner with drinks in a hotel or reasonable restaurant US$5 (US$10 to US$25 in Moscow or St Petersburg); in a top restaurant

US$15 (US$50 in Moscow and US$30 in St Petersburg)

• bus, tram, trolleybus or metro ride US$0.10
• taxi to/from the airport in most cities US$3 to US$5; in Moscow US$25 to US$40; in St Petersburg US$10 to US$15 *to* the airport, US$20 to US$35 *from* the airport
• entry to most museums under US$1; entry to the Hermitage, St Petersburg US$9
• excursion from St Petersburg to Petrodvorets US$15 per person in a group; US$100 for up to six people in St Petersburg Travel Company car with guide; US$5 unguided using public hydrofoil

Ways to save money include:

• share sleeping accommodation with one or more other people – double, triple and quadruple rooms generally cost a lot less per person than singles
• take overnight trains, saving hotel costs
• buy food in shops and markets
• get Russian prices where you can on trains, at museums and so on
• carry an ISIC student card, which can bring discounts at some museums and on some train fares
• don't go out at night, don't drink, don't visit the Kremlin or the Hermitage...
• go to Russia on a group tour: that way you can get decent accommodation, three meals a day, internal transport and excursions for as little as US$30 to US$50 a day

Dual-Pricing System You can call it an outrage, you can call it unfair, but at the end of the day you'll call it 1000% more for foreigners than for Russians at many museums, 300% more at many hotels, around 30% to 50% more for train fares and about 200% for airfares. Ask a Russian why this is so and you'll get a variety of justifications, some of the most frequent being: 'It is not so much for you, I think'; 'You have more money than us'; and 'This museum is here for Russians, not for foreigners' (that last came from the head curator of St Petersburg's Hermitage, who was 'explaining' an entry fee of US$9 for foreigners and US$0.20 for Russians).

There's nothing you can do but try as often as you can to get the Russian rate. Speak Russian as best you can, don't show your passport until the last possible second, proffer the amount Russians pay, and have Russian friends buy train, bus and theatre tickets for you wherever possible.

Tipping
A few, mainly top-end, hotels and restaurants add 5% to 15% service charge to your bill. Porters in hotels and railway stations expect tips – US$1 or US$2 in a hotel, US$1 plus US$0.40 per bag, if you have more than two, at a station is enough. In restaurants with waiter service most people tip 5% to 10% if the service is OK.

Bargaining
Shops have fixed prices but in markets – food, art or souvenir – some bargaining is usually expected. For food, initial asking prices tend to be in a sane proportion to the expected outcome. Sellers will be genuinely surprised if you reply to their '5000' with '1000'. They're more likely expecting 3500, 4000 or 4500 in the end. But press your luck further in places like art and craft markets which are heavily patronised by tourists.

Consumer Taxes
Russia has a 23% value-added tax. This is almost always included in quoted prices, but just occasionally it's in small print at the bottom of a menu, or a top-end hotel price might be quoted as US$200 plus 23%. Occasionally there are odd little local taxes such as the US$1 per night tourist tax that Moscow introduced in 1994 – again, included in quoted prices.

WHEN TO GO
July and August are the warmest months and the main holiday season for both foreigners and Russians. They're also the dampest months in most parts of European Russia, with as many as one rainy day in three. For these reasons, early summer (May, June) and late summer/early autumn (September and the first half of October) are many people's favourite seasons. Early autumn brings stunning colours as the leaves turn; locals disappear into the forests to gather buckets of mushrooms and berries.

Winter, if you're prepared for it, can be a

great season. The theatres open, the furs and vodka come out, the snow makes everything picturesque, and the insides of buildings are kept warm. Least liked everywhere are the first snows and the spring thaw, which turn everything to slush and mud.

WHAT TO BRING

Before you leave for Russia, make photocopies of your visa, and the personal information and validity pages of your passport, and take them with you. Also take some spare passport photos. After you have entered Russia, try to get a photocopy of your customs declaration (deklaratsia). All these will be very useful if your documents go astray.

Of course, bring as little as you can. If you're flying you'll avoid waits, headaches and even theft if you can compress your belongings to carry-on size. Aeroflot and other Russian and Eastern European carriers may levy big fees for overweight baggage.

For information on a useful medical kit and photography ideas, see the Health and Film & Photography sections in this chapter; for phrasebooks and dictionaries, see Language in Facts about European Russia.

Luggage

Unless you're here to trek it doesn't much matter what you carry it all in. A 'sausage' bag with a shoulder strap handles well in a crowded bus. A convertible, internal-framed backpack (with a handle and a flap to hide the straps) looks respectable when necessary. A light day-pack is very useful for excursions. But brightly coloured day packs, flags, English-language patches and other 'Hi, I'm a foreigner' accoutrements should not be used.

Clothing

Brightly coloured clothes mark you out as a foreigner and may attract unwanted attention. Russians mostly wear really dull colours – grey, dark blue, brown and black.

For winter you'll need a thick, windproof coat, preferably long; a hat with ear-flaps to guard against frostbite; gloves and scarf; and

thermal underwear. Because buildings are well heated inside, many light, removable layers work better than a few heavy ones. Footwear should be warm, thick-soled and waterproof (even insulated, for the north or Siberia).

In spring, summer and autumn, come equipped for sudden chills and rain. In autumn you'll need a hat and a raincoat or light overcoat. Late autumn and early winter tend to be wet and slushy. Shoes should be stout and water-resistant. Even in the hottest weather Soviet people rarely wear shorts or halter-tops except at resorts.

Except for some posh restaurants in Moscow and St Petersburg you can dress casually for an evening out – though the effort many Russian women put into dressing up may make women travellers glad of something a little smart for evening meals and theatres.

You'll need something modest for visiting churches and mosques, possibly including a head-scarf for women.

Other Items

Toiletries are readily available, even in small towns, so it's not a catastrophe if you forget soap, shampoo, toothpaste, razors, shaving cream etc. Tampons are readily available in big cities, but you'll probably want to bring along your own if you have a brand loyalty. Bring your own contraceptives, especially condoms, as Russian and Eastern European ones might as well be made from mosquito netting. If you're desperate, condoms (prezervativy) are sold in kiosks and pharmacies in most major cities (if you didn't bring any and didn't buy any and now you wish you had, see Health). Don't trust Russian-made birth-control pills.

You may want to bring your own light towel because Russian hotel towels are tiny and don't get changed as often as one might like. Tourist hotels have toilet paper and soap but public toilets rarely do, so these are essential day-pack items; pre-moistened cleansing tissues are convenient. Soviet loo paper is as delicate as newsprint and always seems to tear lengthwise.

An electric water-heating element enables you to purify water and make inexpensive hot drinks at will. A thermos flask, mug and spoon are a boon for long train or road journeys. And you'll need a bottle opener for all the mineral water you'll probably drink.

If you'll be spending a fair amount of time in St Petersburg or camping you may want to bring along a portable anti-microbial water filter. The Sweetwater filter, available for about US$50 from companies such as Recreational Equipment Inc (REI) of Sumner, Washington (☎ (206) 891 2500 or (800) 426 4840), is compact and effective. Pur brand makes a variety of portable units from about US$40. These or similar filters are available from camping equipment suppliers in many Western countries. Filters will not remove all pathogens, however: you should be sure that your filter removes at least *Giardia lamblia* (see Health later in this chapter).

In summer you'll need strong insect repellent in wooded countryside at almost any latitude. If you're camping or if you're in St Petersburg or any point north, you want industrial-strength product, such as REI Jungle Juice, available by mail through REI, or other repellent that's at least 95% DEET. This or mosquito coils or a net is essential. In northern Karelia and on the Kola Peninsula, huge, screaming, evil, dive-bombing mossies survive well into September.

Other items to consider are a water bottle, Swiss army knife, universal bathroom plug, laundry soap, washing line and a few clothes pegs, torch (flashlight) with spare batteries, sunglasses, compass, sunscreen and lip salve. News freaks may want a short-wave radio. If you're camping or trekking, you'll need a sleeping bag.

Gift Ideas
Small gifts go a long way, as acts of kindness or shameless bribes. Convenient and popular are music tapes, good coffee, disposable lighters, American chewing gum, stamps and postcards from home, spare medical items such as aspirin and antiseptic, souvenir key-rings or bottle openers, photo calendars and pocket calculators. All these items are available in Russia, but they can be expensive.

For your favourite floor lady (see Hotels in the later Accommodation section) try chocolate or scented soaps. For young children try crayons or alphabet books; for older ones, action figures (whatever the flavour of the day should be; at the time of writing it was X-Men, Mighty Morphin' Power Rangers, Polly Pockets and Barbie).

Marlboro cigarettes possess but a ghost of their former powers of persuasion, but they're always handy as a tip or a gift. Just don't expect people to grovel. You can buy them – and other Western cigarette brands including Winston and Camel – for about US$10 a carton (*blok*) at street kiosks in Russia.

Don't bring goods to sell unless you're incredibly desperate. It's a buyer's market in Russia, and standing outside a metro station flogging Levis takes business away from the rest of the people standing out there who probably need the money more than you do.

Food
Tea bags, instant coffee and sugar are widely available in Russia but you might take a few to keep you going till you can buy some. Bring your own powdered milk or coffee creamer – if you're coming from Poland or the Czech Republic, you can get tubes of concentrated, sweetened *mleko* that stores well and tastes better than powders.

Vitamins are probably worthwhile for long trips. Vegetarians may want them in any case, plus a cache of dry foods – eg nuts, grains, dried fruit, health-food bars, hot-drink and soup mixes – as alternatives to eating boiled cabbage and being serenaded by the chanting Hare Krishnas who run some of Russia's few vegetarian restaurants. Dry foods and other nonperishable snacks such as pot noodles, tinned fish, sausage and chocolate also make good supplies for Trans-Siberian travellers and for drivers.

TOURIST OFFICES
Local Tourist Information
Perhaps the best tourist information centre in

the country today is in St Petersburg, and is called Peter TIPS. It's a privately owned company whose friendly and knowledgeable staff offer a number of very helpful free services in addition to some for-profit products such as tours and excursions. See the Tourist Offices section in the St Petersburg chapter for more information. Elsewhere, you're dependent for information mainly on the moods of hotel receptionists/administrators, service bureaus and travel firms. Service bureaus and travel firms exist primarily to sell services such as accommodation, excursions and transport. If you don't look as though you're thinking of booking something, they may or may not be willing to answer questions.

Info on helpful agencies and bureaus is given in city sections. Some of the 100 or so branches of Sputnik around Russia are among the more sympathetic to travellers on modest budgets, thanks to Sputnik's traditional association with youth tourism.

Tourist Offices Abroad

Russia now has an overseas Russian National Tourist Office in New York City (☎ (212) 758 1162) that is purportedly independent of Intourist and all the rest; it's at 800 Third Avenue Suite 3101, New York NY 10022. Its director, Valentin Manturov, says you can write but you may not get information!

In London there's a telephone-only Russian Tourist Information Service on ☎ (0891) 516 951. Calls are charged at £0.48 a minute. Topics covered include visas, accommodation, tourist attractions, climate, transport, health and money.

Intourist has offices overseas, but they are of widely varying usefulness and only a couple – London comes to mind – can offer much more than any other travel agent. None can give good information on truly off-the-beaten-track travel. For more on travel agencies outside Russia, see the European Russia Getting There & Away chapter.

USEFUL ORGANISATIONS

Among 'friendship' societies specialising in person-to-person contacts are the Australia-Russia & Affiliated States Friendship Society, Inc., (☎ (02) 564 2866), 15 Crystal Street, Petersham, NSW 2049, Australia (in suburban Sydney). It assists with humanitarian and welfare projects, and brings together organisations and individuals with professional, scientific and cultural interests.

The Harvard University Russian Studies Center (☎ (617) 495 1000) has a small library of Russian periodicals, Western and Russian-language books and textbooks, and a very helpful staff.

The Britain Russia Centre (☎ (0171) 235 2116), 14 Grosvenor Place, London SW1X 7HW, UK, encourages nonpolitical UK-Russia contacts, with talks, films and other events. The Society for Cultural Relations with Russia (☎ (0171) 274 2282), 320 Brixton Rd, London SW9 6AB, UK, leans to artistic and cultural exchanges and study tours. Both have good libraries and offer student membership.

BUSINESS HOURS & HOLIDAYS

Business Hours

Government offices, should you need them, open Monday to Friday from 9 or 10 am to 5 or 6 pm. Banks usually open from 9 am to noon, Monday to Friday; those in major cities often also open from 1 to 6 pm. Currency-exchange booths open long hours, often until mid-evening, and on Saturday and sometimes Sunday too.

Most shops are open Monday to Saturday. Food shops tend to open from 8 am to 8 pm except for a break (pereryv) from 1 to 2 pm or 2 to 3 pm; some close later, some open Sunday until 5 pm. Other shops mostly operate from 10 or 11 am to 7 or 8 pm with a 2 to 3 pm break. Department stores may run from 8 am to 8 or 9 pm without a break. A few shops stay open through the weekend and close on Monday.

Restaurants typically open from noon to midnight except for a break between afternoon and evening meals (yes, for lunch). Cafes may open and close earlier.

Museum hours change like quicksilver, as do their weekly days off. Most shut entrance doors 30 minutes or an hour before closing time and may have shorter hours on the day *before* their day off. Some just seem to close without reason and a few stay that way for years.

Beware the *sanitarnyy den* (sanitary day). Once a month, usually near the end of the month (the last Tuesday, for example), nearly all establishments – shops, museums, restaurants, hotel dining rooms – shut down for cleaning, each on its own day and not always with much publicity.

Public Holidays

After more than seven decades of official atheism, religious holidays are once again kosher in Russia.

The main public holidays are:

1 January
New Year's Day
7 January
Russian Orthodox Christmas Day
23 February
Defenders of the Motherland Day – a new holiday from 1996 to celebrate the anniversary of the founding of the Red Army
8 March
International Women's Day
1 & 2 May
International Labour Day/Spring Festival
9 May
Victory (1945) Day
12 June
Russian Independence Day
7 November
Great October Socialist Revolution Anniversary

FESTIVALS

Russian festivals have shaken off the joyous-workers'-march-past image. A miscellany:

7 January
Russian Orthodox Christmas (Rozhdestvo) – begins with midnight church services
Late February, early March
Goodbye Russian Winter – takes place around St Petersburg, Petrozavodsk and some other Karelian cities. Festivities centre outside the city, with troyka rides, folk shows.
Last Week of March
Festival of the North – Murmansk and other towns of Murmansk region; reindeer races, ski marathon etc

March/April
Easter (Paskha) – main festival of Orthodox Church year. Easter Day begins with celebratory midnight services, after which people eat special dome-shaped cakes called *kulichy* and curd-cakes called *paskha*, and may exchange painted wooden Easter eggs. The devout deny themselves meat, milk, alcohol and sex in the 40-day pre-Easter fasting period of Lent.
April/May
St Petersburg Music Spring – international classical music festival
1st Sunday in June (and the two preceding days)
Pushkin Festival – at old Pushkin family estate of Mikhailovskoe and surrounding hamlets, near Pushkinsky Gory, 130 km south of Pskov
Last 10 days of June
St Petersburg White Nights – general merrymaking and staying out late, plus dance festival
Second Sunday in July
Fishermen's Day (Den Rybaka) – games, stalls, evening music and dance in fishing ports
Autumn (odd-numbered years)
Moscow Film Festival
7 November
Great October Socialist Revolution Anniversary – see the generals on TV staying heroically upright as they salute the tribal roars of their troops from open limos bouncing over the Red Square cobbles. Just kidding; it's actually not celebrated as such, though it is still a holiday.
Mid-November
Osenie Ritmy (Autumn Rhythms) – jazz festival, St Petersburg
20 December to 8 January
Christmas Musical Meetings in Northern Palmyra – a classical music festival held since 1991 in St Petersburg. Runs for three weeks, from the week before Western Christmas to Orthodox Christmas; hence exact dates may vary slightly.
25 December to 5 January
Russian Winter Festival – tourist-oriented troyka rides, folklore shows, games, vodka. Still celebrated in St Petersburg (Olgino) and possibly Suzdal, Novgorod and Moscow.
31 December & 1 January
Sylvestr and New Year – the main winter and gift-giving festival. Gifts are put under the traditional fir tree *(yolka)*. See out the old year with vodka and welcome the new one with champagne while listening to the Kremlin chimes on TV.

POST & TELECOMMUNICATIONS
Post

Outward post is slow but fairly reliable. Airmail letters take two to three weeks from Moscow and St Petersburg to the UK, longer

The Russian Calendar

Why do Russians celebrate Christmas in January? Why is the October Revolution holiday in November?

The Julian calendar was developed by the Roman Empire to approximate the true astronomical year. Over the centuries discrepancies accumulated, so that by the 16th century the calendar was 10 days out of step with the seasons. In 1582, Pope Gregory XIII decreed a new calendar with refinements (such as leap years) that gave a better fit.

Meanwhile, Russia was plodding along with a calendar left over from the Byzantine Empire. With extraordinarily bad timing, Peter the Great replaced this in 1700 with the Julian one – just as the Protestant countries of Europe were finally jettisoning it and grudgingly adopting the 'Catholic' Gregorian version.

By 1917, Russia's Julian dates were almost two weeks behind and the Soviet government decided to join the rest of the world on the Gregorian calendar. The day after 31 January 1918 was decreed to be 14 February. Working backwards, the establishment of Soviet power on Julian 25 October 1917 occurred on Gregorian 7 November. Russian Orthodox holy days are still based on the Julian calendar, which is why Christmas is celebrated on 7 January.

In this book we date events by the calendar officially in use in Russia at the time – ie Julian before 1918, Gregorian thereafter. Events for which this might be confusing are those which occurred in Russia in 1917, and those of international importance in the 17th to 19th centuries. To convert 20th century Julian dates to Gregorian ones, add 13 days. The correction is 12 days for the 19th century, 11 days for the 18th and 10 days for the 17th. ■

from other cities and three to four weeks to the USA or Australasia. Inward post is decidedly unreliable, with delivery times ranging from three weeks to never.

Pochtamt is any post office. A main post office is a *glavpochtamt*, an international one is a *mezhdunarodnyy glavpochtamt*. The main ones are open from 8 am to 8 or 9 pm, with shorter hours on Saturday and Sunday; in big cities one office may stay open 24 hours a day. The small ones in tourist hotels keep short hours – eg 10 am to 3 pm at Moscow's Hotel Intourist.

To send an airmail letter (up to 20 grams) or postcard to any foreign address costs US$0.30. Registration (*zakaznoe*) – a good idea for anything of value – is another US$0.60.

Books and printed matter are cheaper to send by surface mail at small-packet (*melkiy paket*) rates – eg about US$5.70 for 1 kg as opposed to US$14.60 by air. Registration, again, is another US$0.60. An international parcel of anything else is more expensive (eg US$11 for 1 kg, surface) and must go from a city's designated international post office; go to any window marked *posylki* (parcels).

In addition to selling stamps, envelopes and postcards, a few hotel post offices also do registration and express services, and will wrap and post books and printed matter (only). They usually register these and do the required customs forms, too (they must be filled out in Russian).

Some 'postcards' on sale in souvenir kiosks are not meant to be posted as such. They have a message on the back like ОТПРАВЛЯТЬ ПО ПОЧТЕ ТОЛЬКО В КОНВЕРТЕ (to be sent through the post only in an envelope). If you send these as postcards they may not make it.

Express Services The term Express Mail Service (EMS), a service provided by EMS Garantpost and available in some post offices or Garantpost offices, is a relative one: packages take about a week to get where they're going, though they generally do get there. The price, which used to be a bargain, is now just slightly less than those charged by Western-owned express mail services. Prices are by country zone, a list of which is available from EMS. A 100-gram document package to the USA costs US$31; the same package to Western Europe or Canada is US$34; to Australia or New Zealand, US$39 (none of these prices include the 23% VAT).

The three main Western express mail services in Russia offer two-day delivery to Europe and the USA/Canada, three-day to Australia/New Zealand.

TNT Express Worldwide is the cheapest of the Western-run firms: a 500-gram package to the UK/Europe costs US$38.50; to the USA/Canada, US$43; and to Australia/NZ, US$47.50.

DHL has been in Russia the longest. It offers overnight service between St Petersburg and Moscow. A 500-gram package to the USA/Canada costs US$54.12; to the UK/Europe, US$55.35; and to Australia/NZ, US$77.49.

Federal Express services are more limited since the reshuffling of FedEx offices worldwide spelt the end for intra-European service. It's also the most expensive of the Western services; a 500-gram letter from Russia to the USA/Canada (three days) costs US$65; to Australia/NZ (five days) it's US$73.

Addresses, Russian Style You can address outgoing international mail as you would from any country, in your own language, though it might help to *precede* it with the country name in Cyrillic. Some Cyrillic country names:

America (USA) – Америка (США)
Australia – Австралия
Canada – Канада
France – Франция
Germany – Германия
Great Britain – Великобритания
New Zealand – Новая Зиландия

Russian addresses are written opposite to Western ones, starting with the country and ending with the addressee's name – eg Россия 103123, г. Москва, улица Островского, д. 32 кв. 14, ИВАНОВ А. В. (Rossia 103123, g. Moskva, ulitsa Ostrovskogo, d. 32 kv. 14, Ivanov A V). The return address is written below the main address.

The six-digit number is the postal index. Before the place-name may be written *gorod* or *g.* (town), *posyolok* (settlement), *derevnya* (village) or, in some remote addresses, *kolkhoz* (collective farm), *sovkhoz* (state farm) or *selsoviet* (rural council).

Common street-address words are *ploshchad* or *pl.* (square), *ulitsa* or *ul.* (street), *prospekt* or *prosp.* (avenue), *pereulok* or *per.* (lane), *bulvar* or *bul.* (boulevard), *naberezhnaya* or *nab.* (embankment), *proezd* (passage) and *shosse* (highway).

The number of the house, building or complex may be preceded by *dom* or *d.* (house); two numbers separated by a slash (*/*) usually indicate a corner, the second number being the address on the cross-street. *Korpus* or *korp.* or *k.* indicates a building number within a complex, *vkhod* or *podezd* or *pod.* an entrance number, *etazh* the floor, *kvartira* or *kv.* the apartment. Floors are numbered American-style, the ground floor being the first.

Some people use a post-office address like *glavpochtamt, do vostrebovania* (main post office, for collection).

Receiving Mail on the Road Incoming mail service is so flaky that it's rare for anyone on the move to find anything, but you can try.

The most reliable option for those not staying in luxury hotels (which all provide mail service via Finland or other Scandinavian countries) is limited to American Express and Optima card-holders in Moscow and St Petersburg. American Express will hold mail (letters only, no packages) for up to 30 days before returning it. Mail to the St Petersburg office, which goes to a Finnish post box and is therefore much faster than to Moscow, takes about eight days from the USA and about five days from the UK, France and Germany. For St Petersburg (☎ 119 60 09) the address is (Card-holder Name), c/o American Express, PO Box 87, SF-53501 Lappeenranta, Finland, from where it's trucked down to the St Petersburg American Express office at the Grand Hotel Europe every day. If you'll be picking up in

Moscow (☎ 956 90 00), the address is Rossia 103001, g. Moskva, ulitsa Sadovaya-Kudrinskaya d. 21A, LAST NAME, First Name, c/o American Express Travel Services; in either office you'll need to bring your card or cheques with you to get your mail.

Private mail firms such as Westpost in St Petersburg (see the St Petersburg chapter) offer incoming mail services to nonclients for a small fee. Westpost will hold mail at its office in St Petersburg for a fee of US$1 per item; address letters to PL 8, SF-53501 Lappeenranta, Finland.

Poste restante is completely unreliable, but if you want to try, have a good time. It's called *do vostrebovania*, and here's how to address mail:

Rossia (postal code, if known)
City or Town Name
Glavpochtamt
Do Vostrebovania
JOHNSON, Hercules

Россия (eg) 101000
г. (eg) Москва
Главпочтамт
до востребования
ДЖОНСОН Геркулиз

Bring along your passport to get your mail. Forget parcels through poste restante.

When sending mail from abroad to Russia, it's best, as in the above example, to put Roman characters on top to get it to Russia, and Cyrillic on the bottom to get it to its ultimate destination.

Embassies and consulates won't hold mail for transient visitors.

Telephone

The world of international, and even domestic, telecommunications has changed immensely since 1991; it's now possible to do all sorts of magical things like dial a number in another country and have it connect. But with the improvement in services, there's been an explosion of providers that can get confusing and, if you're not careful, expensive.

Note that hotel room telephones nearly all have their own individual numbers; if someone is calling you, they don't have to go through a hotel operator first.

Local Calls Local calls can be made free from your room, or with tokens *(talony)* – or even, in some cities, free – at payphones *(taxofony)* on the street, in metro stations etc. In some cities the tokens you need are metro tokens; in Moscow they are different from metro tokens but sold at metro stations. In other large cities, tokens are for sale at kiosks where you can also buy bus and tram talony. Deposit your token in the cradle atop the phone, dial your number and when your party answers the coin will drop. You should get three minutes. Many payphones don't work; others work without tokens. In many cities that haven't got around to making tokens, the public phones are free for local calls – just pick up the receiver and dial the number!

Intercity Intercity calls within Russia, and between Russia and other ex-Soviet states can often be dialled direct from your room by dialling the hotel's external-call code (if any), then 8, then waiting for a new tone, then dialling the city code and number. If you can't dial direct you can book the call through hotel reception. Some tourist hotels have their own intercity *(mezhdugorodnyy)* direct-dial booths, for which you can buy tokens on the spot.

Another option is a public telephone centre *(telefonnyy punkt)*, where you order your call, then wait to be called to a booth, or at any phone box marked 'Mezhdugorodnyy' (Междугородный). These have their own special tokens, available at telephone centres. All these intercity phones work almost the same way as local payphones, with the added step of pushing the red button, marked *'Otvet'* (Ответ), on the face of the phone when your party answers.

Calls within European Russia or to the Baltic states, Belarus, Ukraine or Transcaucasia cost about US$0.45 a minute from 8 am to 6 pm, US$0.15 at other times.

City telephone codes in European Russia include: Moscow 095, St Petersburg 812, Arkhangelsk 818, Astrakhan 85100, Kaliningrad 0112, Kazan 8432, Mineralnye Vody 86531, Murmansk 815, Perm 3422, Pskov 81122, Suzdal 09231, Tver 08222, Vladimir 09222, Volgograd 8442, Vologda 81722, Yaroslavl 0852. Others are given under Information in city sections.

International The conventional way to make an international call from places outside St Petersburg and Moscow is to book it with hotel reception (which books it with the operator), wait in your room for an hour or so, and pay afterwards.

Alternatively, nearly all towns and cities have public telephone centres *(telefonnye punkty)* where you can make international calls. These may be in or next to the main post or telegraph office. You prepay for a fixed call duration. In a very few places you can dial direct but normally you have to order the call, then wait. Queues and waits can be long, but are not always. Some cities also have privately run communications centres and business centres where you can usually call more speedily but at greater expense.

From Moscow or St Petersburg, direct international dialling is the norm, and is usually available at hotels, hostels or private flats. Dial 8, wait for the second tone, dial 10, then the country code, area (city) code and the number you're dialling.

International call rates change constantly, though, surprisingly, there is no difference in price between a private telephone and a telephone centre. In summer 1995 peak rates were: to the USA, Canada, Australia and New Zealand, US$2.95 per minute; to Continental Europe and the UK, US$1.25 per minute. Peak rates apply on weekdays between 8 am and 8 pm (midnight to 7 am and 2 to 7 pm for Australia and New Zealand); at other times there are reductions of between 33% and 50% on calls to these countries.

Some useful country codes are: USA and Canada 1, UK 44, Australia 61, New Zealand 64, France 33, Denmark 45, Sweden 46, Norway 47, Poland 48, Germany 49, Finland 358, Lithuania 370, Latvia 371, Estonia 372, Moldova 373. For some countries you omit the first digit of the area code when dialling internationally – eg for the UK and Australia, omit the initial 0.

For incoming international calls, Russia's country code is 7. Do *not* drop any digits from city codes: for Moscow, for instance, you dial the international access code, then 7 095, then the number.

Satellite Phones Many hotels now have direct-dial phone booths, run by any of a number of satellite providers. You buy and insert a fixed-value card, dial country code and number, and you're there. Rates are high: one minute within Russia could cost US$1.50; to Europe US$3.30; to North America US$6.45; to the rest of the world US$7.95.

Private Telephones From a private phone in major cities, dialling outside Russia is very simple, but the prices keep rising and are now even higher than equivalent calls from the West to Russia. Dial 8, wait for the second tone, dial 10, followed by the country code, area code and number you're dialling.

At certain times it may be more difficult than at others; if you're ready to hurl the phone through a window, you can *try* ordering the call through the international operator (in St Petersburg on ☎ 315 00 12, in Moscow on ☎ 8 190 or 8 194); if you need to, say loudly and clearly 'English' and you'll usually get an English-speaking operator (you can also say *'ya nye ga-va-RYU pa-ROOSS-ki'*). The operator-assisted rate is the same as a direct-dial rate.

If you have a home telephone, you can discern incoming long-distance (international or domestic) from local calls by the length of the ring; local calls have a short ring, long-distance and international have a very long, incessant ring. Try not to answer international calls until after the beginning

Surfing to Russia...on the Internet

Getting information, other than the bare basics, out of Russian government sources can be a frustrating and fruitless task. So it's good to know that it's easy to get heaps of practical local information from Russia via the Internet and the World Wide Web. You don't even need a pocket protector or a degree in computer engineering: just a computer, a modem capable of transmitting and receiving at at least 9600 bits per second, a telephone connection and an Internet service provider.

The advent of graphical browsing software, like Netscape and Mosaic, has made jumping from site to site on the World Wide Web as easy as operating a Macintosh computer or a PC running Windows. Point-and-click 'surfing', or moving from point to point within the Web, has brought millions of new users in touch with electronic resources stored on computers all over the world.

In Russia, use of the Internet has spread like wildfire. As you would imagine, in a country where long-distance telephones hardly work at all, any technology that allows people to communicate reliably and inexpensively draws significant interest. There are Internet service providers and World Wide Web sites in almost every large Russian city, offering information on hundreds of subjects.

The upshot of all this is that getting information out of Russia is easier than ever. Russian sites offer loads of information, with Internet links back and forth around the globe to universities and Russian studies centres. But this is not all educational and dry, academic stuff being tossed about in the ether. It's club dates and KGB documents, media information and guided photo tours of the Hermitage, gay and lesbian resources and the nitty-gritty on registering a Russian company.

You can find out more about the Internet and the World Wide Web in books such as *The Whole Internet User's Guide* (O'Reilly & Associates), or even the embarrassing to buy but helpful *The Internet for Dummies* (IDG Books) available at good bookshops or computer shops everywhere. Once you choose a provider and get wired, drop in to Lonely Planet's home page (http://www.lonelyplanet.com), where you'll find travel news, information, the best travel health resource centre in the business, readers' letters, 'On the Road' features (articles from LP authors) and much more.

The addresses below will get you connected enough to surf freely on the Russian Web. For the non-English sections you run into, you'll need to get KOI8 or other Cyrillic fonts and install them, though if you don't speak Russian it won't matter if you go without.

- http://www.spb.su/ – St Petersburg Relcom home page, one of the cooler places to hang out; includes the *St Petersburg Press* (see next listing), *Severo Zapad*, *St Petersburg Business Journal*, St Petersburg Picture Gallery, The Other St Petersburg, Eco-Chronicle

---

of the second ring to avoid cutting off your party.

Country Direct Country Direct service is making infant steps in Russia. This service allows you to dial a Moscow number and be connected with an operator from the USA, who can put through collect or calling-card calls to the USA and, in some cases, calling-card calls to other countries. Providers of this service are: AT&T (☎ (095) 155 50 42 for an English-speaking operator, (095) 155 55 55 for a Russian-speaking operator); and SPRINT (☎ (095) 155 61 33 for English, (095) 938 61 33 for Russian).

MCI was the first foreign provider to allow access directly from both St Petersburg and Moscow (dial 8, wait for the tone, dial 10, then 800 497 7222).

Cellular Service Cellular telephone service is available in the entire north-western corridor from Moscow straight up to the tip of the Kola Peninsula and as far east as Arkhangelsk. See the city chapters for information about cellular service providers. Cell phone service is unbeatable outside the cities, where the state telephone system is effectively nonexistent. It allows immediate access to international, as well as domestic, phone lines.

Russia's cellular service operates on the

- http://www.spb.su/sppress/index.html – *St Petersburg Press* home page; weekly newspaper packed with practical information, listings, cultural information, exchange rates etc.
- http://www.glas.apc.org – Glasnet, including a mirror site of Econet, with connections to ecological resources and information from all over the world, Al-Anon, Judaism and Jewish life in Russia and other helpful and educational resources.
- http://www.sovam.com/ – Sovam Teleport home page, with connections to everywhere: software, Russian Web mailing-list archive, FSUMedia mailing-list archive, search engines, FAQ lists etc.
- http://sunsite.unc.edu/pjones/russian/outline.html – Exhibition of formerly secret documents from the Soviet Union, including a 1979 KGB report detailing serious design flaws at the Chornobyl (Chernobyl) nuclear reactor. Reports are available in facsimile of original documents or in translated form.
- http://www.mplik.ru/ – Ural Relcom home page, Yekaterinburg. Mostly Russian-language information (KOI8 fonts required), but a very comprehensive list of Russian Web servers, and a clickable map to help find them.
- http://www.kiae.su/www.wtr/kremlin/begin.html – A virtual walking tour of the Moscow Kremlin, complete with scary but unenforceable copyright infringement threats.
- http://www.sunsite.oit.unc.edu/sergei/Grandsons.html – Dazhdbog's Grandchildren, a quirky but interesting site run by a guy at the University of North Carolina Chapel Hill. Also links to other Russian servers.
- http://www.ic.gov/94fact/country/200.html – Pop quiz: Russia is a member of all of the following organisations *except*...:UNESCO, UNIDO, UNIKOM, UNOMOZ, UNICORN. Find out which on (we swear, it's true) the CIA's home page, which has lists and lists of mind-numbing facts about Russia and the former Soviet Union.
- http://www.elvis.msk.su/ – Elvis server. No, it's not info on a dead, bloated old pop star, but a site that has a couple of useful features, like an interactive Russian-English dictionary (KOI8 fonts required)

Off the Internet, on-line services such as The CompuServe Travel Forum and America On Line offer travel forums (Go:travsig or Keyword:Traveler, respectively) and US State Department Travel Advisories for foreign countries (Go:state or Keyword:Travel Advisories, respectively). These services both also offer bulletin-board-type listings and discussion groups on Eastern Europe, Russia and Russian cities.

Nick Selby, 74442.3034@compuserve.com

450 MHz Scandinavian standard; if you have a Scandinavian cell phone you can 'roam' – automatically transfer service to local cellular providers as you move – in Russian cities for varying fees. In Helsinki and other Finnish cities you can rent cellular phones that work in Russia. The cost is not low: expect to put down a deposit of at least US$1000 and pay prices of US$1 to US$3 per minute on calls to Finland, and much higher to the rest of the world. Rentals are also available in Moscow, St Petersburg and Murmansk, where the price is also sky-high.

Telegram
Telegrams are an easy, cheap, reliable way to reach the outside world. International telegrams can be sent from all but the smallest hotels and post offices and usually arrive within 24 hours, almost always within 72. Ask for a *blank mezhdunarodnaya telegramma* (international telegram form). A message in English is no problem if it's clearly printed. The cost is about US$0.10 per word.

Incoming telegrams work, too, addressed to you at your hotel with your date of arrival.

Fax & Telex
International fax and telex services are available at many city central telephone, telegraph and post offices, and at privately run

communication and business centres. Fax costs are similar to telephone charges. See city sections for details.

Electronic Mail

Electronic mail (e-mail) is probably the most reliable and inexpensive method of communication between Russia and the rest of the world. The vast majority of foreign residents in Russia use e-mail as one of their primary communications methods, so service is readily available.

To use e-mail, you'll need a computer with a modem and the software to run it, a telephone line, and an account with an e-mail provider. Generally speaking, e-mail service providers give a local access number, through which you access the service and your e-mail account. Depending on the service to which you subscribe, e-mail messages reach their destination from 15 minutes to three days after you post them through the service (the bigger companies such as Glasnet, Relcom, Sovam and SprintNet usually take no longer than an hour to send your message).

Many e-mail providers also allow access to the Internet, an international computer network. Applied at its most basic level, this allows you to send e-mail between providers, for example between CompuServe and MCIMail or, more practically, between a Russian e-mail provider and your e-mail provider back home. An Internet e-mail address looks like this: 74442.3034@compuserve .com or selby@gate.net or talk2us@ lonelyplanet.com.au.

A drawback is that you can only send e-mail to other people with e-mail service. But even if the person you're trying to contact doesn't have e-mail, you can send an e-mail message by fax, and the cost is still usually less than it would be to use a traditional fax machine, as the message is transmitted faster.

If you're currently a subscriber to CompuServe, SprintNet, MCIMail or SFMT, you can access your account in Russia (see below for access numbers and how to subscribe before you arrive) but surcharges will apply (with CompuServe this can get expensive at US$49 per hour!).

Signing on in Russia to a service such as Glasnet, Sovam, Relcom or Demos/+ generally entails a one-time fee plus a flat monthly charge in addition to 'air-time' charges. Note that because of Russia's notoriously poor local telephone lines, you'll need a modem with 'built-in error correction', or 'MNP' – software error correction is not enough.

If you're just trying to get word home, you can use the e-mail at places such as the HI St Petersburg Hostel or the Travellers Guest House in Moscow for a small fee. Sovam Teleport has offices in Moscow (☎ (095) 229 72 95) and St Petersburg (☎ (812) 311 84 12, Nevsky prospekt 30) and will sometimes allow visitors to use the in-house e-mail to send a message or two for a small fee, but no longer officially sets up temporary accounts.

Below are contact numbers and information for some of the e-mail providers operating in Russia, and their voice telephone numbers for contact before you arrive in Russia. The home page addresses are for people with World Wide Web browsers.

Sovam Teleport
  ☎ (095) 229 72 95; fax (095) 229 41 21; e-mail spbsales@sovam.com; St Petersburg access number ☎ (812) 311 03 65 (2400 baud); Moscow access number ☎ (095) 932 67 65, 932 69 65 (2400 baud); home page http://www.sovam.com/

Glasnet
  ☎ (812) 168 55 89; fax (095) 207 08 89; e-mail support@glas.apc.org; St Petersburg access number ☎ (812) 168 54 74; home page http://www.glas.apc.org/ or http://www.glasnet .ru/, whichever works best for you

A/O Relcom
  ☎ (095) 194 25 40; fax (095) 194 33 28; home page http://www.spb.su/

Demos/+
  ☎ (812) 233 00 34; fax (812) 233 50 16; e-mail info@demos.su

CompuServe
  Usenet news group alt.onlineservice.compu serve; Moscow access number ☎ (095) 110 77 92 NTW = SPR (2400 baud); international subscription numbers (Australia) ☎ 1 800 025 240, (UK) ☎ 0800 289 458, (USA) ☎ 1 800 848 8990

Sprint Network

☎ (095) 201 68 90; fax (095) 923 23 44; St Petersburg access number ☎ (812) 110 77 92 (2400 baud); international subscription numbers (Australia) ☎ (02) 218 4825, (UK) ☎ 0800 289 751, (USA) ☎ 1 800 877 1997

MCIMail

e-mail mcihelp@mcimail.com; Moscow access number ☎ (095) 971 51 01 (2400 baud); international subscription numbers (USA) ☎ 800 444 6245, (US number for rest of world) ☎ (1 202) 833 8484

Emergency Contact

In an emergency the most straightforward way for someone to reach you from outside Russia is by telephone to your hotel or hostel – language problems, bad connections, slack service and changeable numbers notwithstanding.

International calls to major cities in Russia can be dialled directly, and operators can assist in reaching many of even the smallest towns. Next best is a fax or telegram, care of your hotel, though the staff won't always chase you up if one arrives. A telegram takes one to two days.

As a last resort, most foreign affairs ministries maintain 24-hour emergency operators – eg the British Foreign Office (☎ (0171) 270 3000), the US State Department (☎ (202) 647 5225; 647 4000 outside business hours), and the Australian Department of Foreign Affairs & Trade (☎ (06) 261 3331) – who can call your embassy in Russia. Embassies prefer that other means have been exhausted before they're contacted. Your itinerary will be of help in the hunt for you, so leave a copy with someone at home.

TIME

From the early hours of the last Sunday in September to the early hours of the last Sunday in March, Moscow and St Petersburg time is GMT/UTC plus three hours. From the last Sunday in March to the last Sunday in September, 'summer time' is in force and it's GMT/UTC plus four hours.

Most of European Russia is in the same time zone as Moscow and St Petersburg. The exceptions are the Kaliningrad region in the west, which is on Moscow time minus one hour, and some regions in the east, where Samara and Izhevsk are on Moscow time plus one hour, and Ufa, Perm and Orenburg are on Moscow time plus two hours. East of the Ural Mountains, Yekaterinburg is on Moscow time plus two hours, Irkutsk on Moscow time plus five hours, Vladivostok on Moscow time plus seven hours, and Petropavlovsk-Kamchatsky on Moscow time plus nine hours.

Russian railway timetables (except for suburban trains) are in Moscow time everywhere – and so are station clocks in most places.

The following international relationships will be wrong by an hour for short periods when other cities change to 'summer time' on different dates.

When it's noon in Moscow and St Petersburg, it's...

1 am in San Francisco;
4 am in New York and Toronto;
9 am in London;
10 am in Paris, Berlin, Warsaw, Prague and Budapest;
11 am in Helsinki, Tallinn, Riga, Vilnius, Minsk, Kiev, Chisinau, Bucharest and Ankara;
noon in Tbilisi, Yerevan and Baku (1 pm in Yerevan and Baku in winter);
1 pm in Tashkent (2 pm in winter);
2 pm in Bishkek;
3 pm in Almaty;
4 pm in Beijing (5 pm in winter);
5 pm in Ulan Bator;
6 pm in winter Sydney, 8 pm in summer Sydney;
8 pm in winter Auckland, 10 pm in summer Auckland.

ELECTRICITY

Standard voltage is 220 volts, 50 cycles AC, though a few places still have an old 127-volt system. Sockets require a continental or European plug with two round pins. Travel adapters will enable many appliances from countries with different electrical set-ups to work in Russia. Look for voltage (V) and frequency (Hz) labels on your appliances. Some trains and hotel bathrooms have 110 and 220-volt shaver plugs.

LAUNDRY

You can get laundry done in most hotels. Ask

the floor attendant. It usually takes two days. If you're doing it yourself, bring along a universal sink plug.

TOILETS

Hotel room toilets are generally fine. Make sure you use them before you go out because public toilets are rare and, where they do exist, often disgusting, even in otherwise good restaurants (McDonald's is an honourable exception here). One of Mikhail Gorbachev's best innovations was the private-enterprise toilet, where you pay US$0.20 or so for the privilege of relieving yourself in clean surroundings. Initially controversial because they acknowledged social inequality, they're still uncommon – though less so in bigger cities, especially Moscow and St Petersburg. They're identified by the words платный туалет (*platny tualet*, pay toilet). In any toilet Ж stands for *zhenskiy*, women's; M for *muzhskoy*, men's.

WEIGHTS & MEASURES

Russia operates on the metric system (see the back of the book for conversions from other units). Restaurant menus often list the weight of food and drink servings in grams, and in particular you order drinks by weight; a teaglass is about 200 grams, a shot-glass about 50 grams. The unit of items sold by the piece, such as eggs, is *shtuka* or *sht.*, which literally means 'thing' or 'piece'.

A verst *(versta)*, an old Russian unit of measurement you come across in 19th-century novels etc, is 1.067 km. It's divided into 500 *sazheni*; a *sazhen* is divided into three *arshiny*; and an *arshin* is divided into 16 *vershoky*.

MUSEUMS

Russia probably has more museums per head than any other country. The Russian *muzey* has a wider meaning than the English 'museum' and includes some palaces, art galleries and nonworking churches. One interesting type is the museum of folk or wooden architecture *(muzey narodnoy/ derevyannoy arkhitektury)*, where fine old buildings are grouped in park-like surround-

ings. Most big towns have a history museum, plus often art, natural history, and decorative and applied art museums, and museums dedicated to local celebrities (usually in their old homes). A 'regional' or 'local lore' museum *(kraevedcheskiy muzey)* combines human and natural history. A 'panorama' (the Russian word is the same) is a pavilion with a giant painting in the round that you stand inside. It'll usually depict a famous battle – Borodino, Stalingrad, Sevastopol – and its soundless 360° gestalt of bloodshed should be enough to make anyone a pacifist.

Almost all gone now are the multitudes of museums once dedicated to Lenin. In Soviet times, almost every house where Lenin had slept or held a clandestine meeting was a museum. The only two now remaining, as far as we know, are at Gorki Leninskie, where Lenin died (see Around Moscow), and Ulyanovsk, where he was born (see The Volga Region).

Russian museums rarely have any explanatory info in languages other than Russian – so going with a guide is sometimes worth the expense. Take a dictionary if you decide it's not. See Language in the Facts about European Russia chapter for the way dates are shown.

Opening days and hours change crazily. In this book we give the most recent as a pointer. Last entry is usually 30 minutes or an hour before closing time. Costs depend basically on the importance of the museum and many museums post separate prices for foreigners and Russians. In most cases, getting the Russian price is as simple as asking for your ticket in Russian – *'ah-DYIN bil-YET, pa-ZHAHL-stuh'* – while in others (the Hermitage in St Petersburg pops to mind) the staff is so zealous in its quest to root out foreigners and their money that even Russians from remote villages sometimes get hassled. However an ISIC student card gets you in for half the foreigners' price in some places. Some price samples:

Kremlin, Moscow: US$0.10 to enter the grounds; US$2.50 for foreigners, US$0.20 for Russians, for each cathedral or museum inside

Hermitage Museum, St Petersburg: US$9 for foreigners, less than US$0.20 for Russians

Menshikov Palace, St Petersburg: US$4.50 for foreigners; US$1 for Russians

Turgenev Estate, Spasskoe Lutovinovo: US$0.50 for foreigners, US$0.10 for Russians

Regional History Museum, Arkhangelsk: US$0.30 for foreigners, US$0.05 for Russians

All museums charge a fee for taking photographs, a higher fee for video cameras, and almost all ban lights and tripods.

At a few museums individual visitors are supposed to join Russian-language guided tours. Once inside it may be possible to 'lose' these groups if you wish.

BOOKS

Most books are published in different editions by different publishers in different countries. As a result, a book might be a hardcover rarity in one country while it's readily available in paperback in another. Fortunately, bookshops and libraries search by title or author, so your local bookshop or library is best placed to advise you on the availability of the following recommendations and those in later chapters.

General

Much of *USSR: From an Original Idea by Karl Marx* by Marc Polonsky & Russell Taylor is still all too relevant. It's a 1980s street-wise look at the headaches of travel by authors who ran a company specialising in 'real life' Soviet tours – funny enough to keep you up when the trip gets you down.

Imperium by Ryszard Kapuscinski is a 1994 collection of essays, journalism and recollections of the Soviet empire by the Polish correspondent and travel writer. Kapuscinski's boyhood town, Pinsk, was in the part of Poland taken over by the USSR in 1939 (it's in Belarus today). His teacher and some classmates were then deported, and the experience left him with a loathing of the Soviet system which comes across strongly.

The New Russians by Hedrick Smith is a former *New York Times* correspondent's overview of Russian life – a 1990 update of the original version but still useful. The USSR, incidentally, produced its own equivalent of Hedrick Smith back in the 1960s in the shape of *Those Americans* by N Mikhailov & Z Kossenko, published in English by Henry Regnery (1962). (Normal Americans these authors encountered made remarks such as 'Capitalism has degraded America to the point that...the individual is on the verge of decay...')

Women's Glasnost vs Naglost by Tatyana Mamonova (1994) combines essays by this Russian women's movement leader with interviews of a cross-section of women in a country where wife-beating and abortion reach incredible levels.

Guidebooks

Trekking in Russia & Central Asia by Frith Maier (1994) is an unrivalled guide to getting out into the former Soviet Union's wild places by an American who first started exploring them as a student in St Petersburg in 1984, and later pioneered the US firm REI's adventure travel programme in the ex-USSR. It's full of route descriptions, maps, and useful background and planning info. The main focus is Siberia, the Russian Far East and Central Asia, but there are 35 pages on the Caucasus. The book is published in the USA by The Mountaineers, Seattle (☎ 800 553 4453); in Canada by Douglas & McIntyre, Vancouver; and in Britain by Cordee, Leicester.

Ian Watson's *The Baltics and Russia Through The Back Door* is an excellent, short, bare-bones practical guide that covers St Petersburg and Moscow. It's aimed at budget travellers and is published annually with up-to-date prices, though it makes no attempt to cover history or background, or any part of Russia except the two big cities.

Robert Greenall's *An Explorer's Guide to Russia* (1994) has a lot of good info for independent travellers but, despite its title, only covers central and northern European Russia. It's particularly good for those with the time and inclination to explore small, off-the-beaten-track places around Moscow.

Insight Guides Russia (1994) is a nice

read, with nice pictures, but practicalities are not a high priority; it gives historical and cultural background and has features on modern Russian life by Russian authors.

Louis Motorist's Guide to the Soviet Union (1987) by Victor & Jennifer Louis, covers most places that were open to Westerners in the mid-1980s, by the Soviet method of piling fact upon fact, but is studded with gaps and distortions, and its maps are almost useless. However it has an enormous phrase list covering everything that could go wrong with your car – eg 'Oil is leaking from the reduction gear of the rear axle' – and some things that you'd pray didn't, such as 'The engine fails at all rpm'.

Many cities and regions are covered in English-language guides from Russian publishers, available locally. They're useless on practicalities and unreliable on history but mostly have nice pictures.

Lonely Planet has guides to many neighbouring countries including Finland, the Baltic States & Kaliningrad, Poland, the Czech & Slovak Republics, Hungary and Central Asia.

Books on Moscow & St Petersburg

Blue Guide Moscow & Leningrad by Evan Mawdsley (1991) does a fine-tooth comb job on the architecture and history of both cities, dense with detail about every doorway you pass – an excellent reference book.

Discovering Moscow by Helen Boldyreff Semler is a lovingly compiled guide to just about every pre-1917 building of interest in the capital, full of detail about their inhabitants that brings the past alive.

There are plenty of guidebooks to St Petersburg, including Lonely Planet's new *St Petersburg City Guide*. Another practical information guide is *The Fresh Guide to St Petersburg*, researched and printed annually and available locally.

Moscow: A Traveller's Companion and *St Petersburg: A Traveller's Companion*, both edited by Laurence Kelly, are collections of extracts from centuries of locals' and visitors' writings about the two cities, covering many places you're likely to visit.

St Petersburg – History, Art and Architecture by Kathleen Berton Murrell is a lovely book of just what it says it is – complete with colour photographs. It's produced by the Russian publisher Troika, and is available in many shops in St Petersburg and Moscow.

Travellers' Tales

Several years before glasnost, Colin Thubron taught himself Russian and drove just about every open motor route alone, visiting many of today's most frequented destinations. The result, *Among the Russians* (published in some countries as *Where Nights Are Longest*) is a rather humourless but precise and eloquent account of the personal experience of travel in Soviet times – and a lot hasn't changed since.

Letters From Russia by the Marquis de Custine is a French aristocrat's rather jollier account of visiting St Petersburg and Moscow and hobnobbing with the tsar and high society in 1839. His description of St Basil's Cathedral hasn't been bettered yet: 'a sort of irregular fruit bristling with excrescences, a cantaloup melon with embroidered edges...a crystallisation of a thousand colours...this confectionery box'.

Caucasian Journey, by wandering fisherman Negley Farson, describes journeyings among the northern Caucasian tribal peoples in the 1920s, before the full force of Bolshevism hit them. In the 1990s Negley's son Daniel Farson took off down the Volga to the same destination and the result is *A Dry Ship to the Mountains* (1994).

There are some fine pieces on Russia, including one about a Volga trip, in Bruce Chatwin's last collection, *What Am I Doing Here*.

History

General & Pre-Soviet Era Sir Fitzroy Maclean, a Scot whose lifetime affair with Russia and other ex-Soviet republics goes back to days as a diplomat in Moscow in the 1930s, has written several entertaining, intelligent books on the country. His *Holy Russia* (1978) is a good short Russian history by a great storyteller, plus a walk through

Moscow, St Petersburg and other history-rich cities. His *All the Russias: The End of an Empire* (1992) covers the whole ex-USSR. The USSR section of his *Eastern Approaches* (which also covers WW II adventures elsewhere) focuses mainly on travels in outlying republics but does include a chilling account of the 1938 show trial of the veteran revolutionary Bukharin.

A History of Russia by Nicholas Riasanovsky is one of the best single-volume versions of the whole Russian story. It goes up to 1992.

A Traveller's History of Russia & the USSR by Peter Neville is quite a good, quick read, and good on pre-Gorbachev Russia, but, despite its supposed post-Soviet timing, it repeatedly refers to the USSR in the present tense.

One of the best books on any single strand of pre-Soviet history is *Peter the Great – His Life & World* by Robert K Massie – a good read about one of Russia's most famous and influential rulers.

Soviet Era *The Rise & Fall of the Soviet Empire* by Stephen Dalziel describes what its title says it does in lively style, covering the years 1917-92, with some good photos. *A History of the Soviet Union* by Geoffrey Hosking is a dense, analytical look at the Soviet era up to 1985. If you need to know why Kamenev fell out with Kalinin or why Left SRs loathed Kadets, Hosking's your man.

Ten Days That Shook the World is a melodramatic, enthusiastic, contemporary account of the Bolsheviks' 1917 power grab by American journalist John Reed.

The 900 Days: The Siege of Leningrad by Harrison Salisbury tells of that city's sufferings in WW II.

Recent History *Lenin's Tomb* by David Remnick, the *Washington Post*'s Moscow correspondent from 1988 to 1992, won a Pulitzer Prize for its flowing account of the Gorbachev era and its end, combining analytic history with interviews of hundreds of people of all kinds. *The Second Russian Rev-*

olution by Angus Roxburgh focuses on the political power struggles of the Gorbachev years – a fascinating blow-by-blow account, which ends, alas, before the 1991 coup. If Roxburgh brings out a sequel, don't miss it. *Eternal Russia* by Jonathan Steele, the *Guardian*'s Moscow correspondent from 1988, covers the Gorbachev years and continues up to the 1993 White House shoot-out and subsequent elections, looking back into the past to question whether Russia can ever really become the true capitalist democracy that Western politicians long for.

Martin Walker's Russia, a collection of articles by Steele's *Guardian* predecessor in Moscow, is worth reading for the excitement it conveys of early glasnost. Walker was encouraged to write about daily life as much as politics. *The Waking Giant* is Walker's more considered account of the Gorbachev revolution. Though written before Gorbachev's limitations became clear, it's still a fascinating assemblage of information.

Geoffrey Hosking published a sequel to his earlier work with *The Awakening of the Soviet Union* (1991).

Flora, Fauna & Environment
Two gloriously illustrated hardbacks, each based on a British TV series, have a wealth of information on the natural history of Russia and the ex-USSR. *The Nature of Russia* by John Massey Stewart (Boxtree, London, 1992) is the more comprehensive and wide-ranging, and more useful as a reference tool, with attention to many serious environmental problems. *Realms of the Russian Bear* by John Sparks (BBC Books, 1992) homes in on a few specific areas of exceptional interest. Both cost around £19.

The Soviet Environment: Problems, Policies & Politics, edited by John Massey Stewart (Cambridge University Press, 1992), collects experts' analyses of many of the main problems.

Arts
Back in the USSR by the urbane Russian rock writer Artemy Troitsky is the definitive history of Russian and Soviet rock music up

to the late 1980s. *Tusovka* by the same author is a 1990 sequel which profiles Troitsky's favourite figures on the rock/fashion/dance/art scene, many of whom are still around. Both take you inside the real Soviet youth culture.

Tamara Talbot Rice's *A Concise History of Russian Art* covers painting, architecture and applied arts. *The Art and Architecture of Russia*, a Pelican publication by George Heard Hamilton, is in a fairly academic style, but traces the history of those art forms thoroughly. Both books stop at the revolution. Camilla Gray's *The Russian Experiment in Art 1863-1922*, in the widely available softback Thames & Hudson World of Art series, is a good account of one of the most exciting periods in world art.

Lots of Russian-produced coffee-table art books, with good reproductions or photos of works in Russian museums, are sold in Russia.

Reference Books

The Traveller's Yellow Pages Moscow and *The Traveller's Yellow Pages St Petersburg* are comprehensive, mostly accurate, pocket-sized listings of thousands of useful addresses and numbers. They also contain maps, explanatory essays on many topics, seating plans to major theatres, and indexes in English, Russian, German and French. A North-West Russia volume is in the pipeline. Contact InfoService International Inc (☎ (516) 549 0064; fax (516) 549 2032), 1 St Marks Place, Cold Spring Harbor, NY 11724, USA, to order. Prices without shipping are between US$8 and US$14.

The similarly priced *Where In Moscow* and *Where in St Petersburg* from Russian Information Services (☎ (802) 223 4955; fax (802) 223 6105) of 89 Main St, Suite 2, Montpelier VT 05602, USA, have more selective listings but are still compact and useful. They're updated annually and have good maps. The same publisher's *Russia Survival Guide* is aimed primarily at business travellers; its *Russian Life* monthly magazine is worth following for travel news, visa regulation changes etc. Send for the *Access Russia* catalogue of Russia books available by mail order from the Montpelier address.

Bookshops

Russia Russians are avid readers and Russian bookshops are plentiful and busy – though in some cases they may be busy because they're selling washing machines, cigarettes, gym equipment and almost anything except books, which don't score much on the profit side.

The days of censorship are long gone; if a title is hard to find nowadays it's probably because of, yes, paper shortages, in the country famed for its infinite pine forests. But Russians have reaped the benefits of copyright laws that until recently allowed pirating of almost anything on paper. Cheap and hastily translated editions of Western favourites (ie 'anything by Harlequin') fill bookshelves and pedestrian subway tables (another source of books).

Foreign-language books can be found in quite a few Russian bookshops and often at bookstalls in main tourist hotels. Info on them is given in city sections. The Russian for bookshop is *knizhnyy magazin*. Individual bookshops have such imaginative names as Dom Knigi (Book House), Knizhny Mir (Book World) and, most exciting of all, Knigi (Books). Russia's best source of English-language books is Zwemmer bookshop in Moscow.

Overseas Zwemmer (☎ (0171) 379 6253) at 28 Denmark St, London WC2H 8NJ, is a bookshop devoted entirely to Russia, the former USSR and Eastern Europe. You can send for a comprehensive catalogue.

Many specialist map and travel bookshops have a good range on Russia. In London these include the Travellers' Bookshop at 25 Cecil Court, WC2N 4EZ, the Travel Bookshop at 13 Blenheim Crescent, W11 2EE, and Edward Stanford at 12-14 Long Acre, WC2E 9LP. In New York, The Complete Traveller (☎ (212) 685 9007) at 199 Madison Avenue, 10016, is quite good.

MAPS

The Soviet Union may have been the only country in the world with a black market in maps. Stalin put the state cartographic office under the control of the NKVD, forerunner of the KGB, which began systematically to distort maps for the sake of secrecy. (That is, it distorted maps of the USSR; Soviet maps of the Middle East were quite accurate, thank you very much.) Streets, neighbourhoods, whole towns were erased, rivers and highways were rerouted, mountain ranges disappeared.

In 1989 the cartographic office began to produce the first proper maps in almost 60 years, and today accurate maps of many cities and regions can be found.

Russian Sources

Good, topographically accurate Russian maps of many cities and regions are now published, and are cheap, but availability is very patchy. Also still around are a lot of inaccurate Soviet-era 'tourist maps' of cities, and modern maps based on these, mostly called *Turisticheskaya Skhema* or *Plan Goroda*. Pick up a map that's useful to you whenever you see it, even if you're thousands of km from the place it shows: you may never see it again.

A few cities have specialist map shops; otherwise, look in bookshops, hotels and street kiosks.

The Russian-language *Atlas avtomobilnykh dorog (Road Atlas)* (Trivium, Minsk, 1993), with 120 pages of fairly accurate regional road maps covering the whole ex-USSR, and some city maps, is reasonably compact, inexpensive and well worth having, and not just for drivers. It costs about US$5. In Moscow look for it at the Slavyanka map shop and from vendors in the pedestrian subway outside the Central Telegraph.

Overseas Sources

The *CIS* map from the German publisher Hallwag is one of the clearest all-Russia maps, covering the whole country and the rest of the CIS (main roads and railways included) on one sheet at a scale of 1:7,000,000 (1 cm to 70 km). A minor disadvantage to English-language users is that it uses an unfamiliar transliteration system. *Hildebrand's Travel Map CIS* is also good.

Bartholomew publishes a European Russia map at 1:2,000,000. Freytag & Berndt's CIS map has European Russia at 1:2,000,000 on one side, and the whole country at 1:8,000,000 on the other.

The most accurate, if not necessarily the most useful, commercially available maps of smaller regions of Russia are produced by the United States Defense Mapping Agency. These bring home just how ludicrous it was of the Soviets to confiscate tourists' snapshots of railway stations: the maps are based on CIA satellite imagery, and yes, you *can* see the dew on a mosquito's bum from 45,000 km above the earth! They're available for US$13.95 each (the country's broken into many sections) through A Galaxy of Maps (AGOM; ☎ (305) 477 4854), 3644 North Andrews Avenue, Oakland Park, FL 33309, USA and through universities and better map stores throughout the world. AGOM ships internationally.

Navigation charts make fine wall hangings but are expensive at about US$10 a sheet. The American ONC series at 1:1,000,000 covers the whole country. The American TPC series at 1:500,000 and British DMS charts at both scales are available for European Russia and other European parts of the ex-USSR.

The best commercially available English-language maps of Moscow and St Petersburg are published by Northern Cartographic of 4050 Williston Rd, South Burlington, VT 05403, USA, and are available from the publisher or through Russian Information Services (see the earlier Books – Reference section). They're for sale individually *(The New Moscow City Map & Guide* and *The New St Petersburg City Map & Guide)* and are also incorporated in *Where in Moscow* and *Where in St Petersburg*. They're easy to read and pretty accurate, though a Russian-language index and transport lines would make them handier.

Just such an index is included on the city maps in *The Traveller's Yellow Pages* for Moscow and St Petersburg (see Reference Books under Books); these maps, also available separately, are a bit less accurate and cover less ground than Northern Cartographic's, and they have large illustrations of major sights which can be distracting, but they have transport details and they're accurate enough for anything you'll need to do.

Edward Stanford (see Bookshops – Overseas) is the UK's best general map shop. Another good European source is ILH GeoCenter (☎ (0711) 788 93 40), Schockenriedstrasse 40a, Postfach 80 08 30, 7000 Stuttgart 80, Germany.

MEDIA

The Russian media are now as free as one would expect; the mass privatisation of Ostankino and other television and radio outlets, and almost all print media, has seen to that. There are still over 8,000 newspapers and periodicals in print in Russia despite paper shortages and harsh economic realities. And while Western involvement in radio and television is growing, Russian-owned outlets are developing a distinctive style that's a hybrid of slick 'But wait...there's more' shucksterism and Russian sensationalism.

Russian-Language Print Media

Russian print media has come an awfully long way; scandals are sought out and exposed, sometimes to the detriment of the reporter (several have been killed over the past years while investigating corruption and mismanagement of the military and intelligence organs). Hard-hitting investigative stories in papers such as *Izvestia* and *Moskovsky Komsomolets* have brought to light scandals including those that led to the killing of *MK* reporter Dmitry Kholodov, as well as the MMM financial debacle. All Moscow's dailies – including *Kommersant*, *Nezavisymaya Gazeta*, *Segodnya*, *Komsomolskaya Pravda* and *Obshchaya Gazeta* – reported in vivid detail the setbacks and tragedies of the war in Chechnya.

Despite a drop-off of over 25,000 subscribers, the in-depth reporting of the weekly *Argumenty i Fakty (Arguments & Facts)* has kept it the most widely read periodical in Russia. Foreign writers are translated into Russian in *Izvestia's* monthly *Inostrannaya Literatura*, while the weekly humour tabloid *Krokodil* keeps people chuckling happily.

In a nation of voracious readers, real cultural dialogue goes on in the so-called 'fat journals', or monthly literary journals. Most popular is *Izvestia's Novy Mir (New World)*, a ground-breaker even in 1973 for its excerpts from Solzhenitsyn's *One Day in the Life of Ivan Denisovich*.

Most of the dozens of Russian-language newspapers in St Petersburg are mouthpieces for one political party or another, or are involved in some form of sensationalism. The monthly *Sovershenno Sekretno (Top Secret)* claims that all its articles are based on info culled from secret Soviet archives: who knows?

Express Gazeta claims the dubious distinction of being 'Russia's first tabloid', and *Chas Pik (Rush Hour)* is a daily rag that's as serious as you'd want. There are several information and listings papers, including *Vsyo Dlya Vas (Everything for You)* which is a free, classified-advertisement paper, *To Da Syo (This and That)*, which is full of 'what's-on' listings, and *Chto Pochyom (What Costs What)*, which lists prices around town for everything from construction materials to tanning salons. *SPID Info (AIDS Info)* is a highly deceptive title: it claims to be a 'popular scientific' paper, but perhaps its popularity is due to the fact that it contains nothing but smut of the 'I never thought I'd be writing to you, but last week...' variety.

English-Language Print Media

The undisputed king of the hill in locally published English-language news is the *Moscow Times*, a first-rate daily staffed by top-notch journalists and editors covering Russian and international issues. It's available free (for the time being) at hotels, business centres and restaurants, and also by subscription. It also publishes a weekly international edition, which sums up Russian news only (see Subscriptions). Another Moscow daily, the *Moscow Tribune*, is available as well.

The *St Petersburg Press*, once an upstart with lofty ideas, is now an integral part of life in that city. Though a decidedly lower budget affair than either of the Moscow papers, it's a reliably good weekly. Newsstands in the bigger hotels in major cities usually have a few good Western newspapers of the *International Herald-Tribune*, *Times*, *Guardian* variety. These often reach Moscow and St Petersburg on the day of publication. They cost about one and a half times more than back home.

Like Grace Jones, Dame Edna and other large, uninvited guests who just won't give up and go home, the *Moscow News*, the English-language mouthpiece of the glasnost age, is still around. The Russian-language version of the same paper, *Moskovskie Novosti*, has a circulation of 200,000 copies a week; the English version, which is a joint venture between the Moscow News Corp and the American East View Publications, has a much smaller circulation of about 12,000 a week. The US edition is planning a 'help wanted' page for Russian companies recruiting Western talent.

Subscriptions Russian Information Services (see Books) handles US and Canadian subscriptions to the weekly edition of the *Moscow Times;* Europe and the rest of the world is handled by the *MT*'s Dutch partner, Van Eeghenstraat (☎ (31 20) 676 0701; US$130/6 months in Europe, US$155 in the USA). The *St Petersburg Press* is available by international subscription (US$135/year) by writing to Akadeemia 21G, EE-0026 Tallinn, Estonia (☎ (372 2) 531 171). *Moscow News* subscriptions are US$99/year in the USA (US$50/year for students) and are available through East View Publications (☎ (1 612) 550 0961; e-mail admin@ eastview.com), 3020 Harbor Lane North, Plymouth, MN 55447, USA.

Russian-Language TV

TV schedules and highlights are published daily in the *Moscow Times*. On view in Moscow are:

- Channel 1, Ostankino, Russian public television, which covers all of Russia; heavy on concerts and culture, news and analysis, current affairs, films;
- Channel 2, Russian TV, showing classic Russian entertainment like the American soap opera 'Santa Barbara' (twice daily) and Disney on Fridays. Also does some business and public-interest broadcasting;
- NTV, a very popular commercial television network covering most of urban European Russia;
- Channel 5, St Petersburg Channel (see St Petersburg Television below);
- Channel 6, which has a frenetic, CNN and MTV-filled schedule with some foreign serial dramas, films and music news;
- Moscow Channel, the local channel. BBC news

The Moscow Times

The Moscow Tribune

Moscow's two English-language daily newspapers

in English at 7 am, plus films and serial shows from the West;
• Educational Channel, a local teaching channel with documentaries, instructional shows, English courses and films.

In St Petersburg you can see the two national channels plus two local ones:

• St Petersburg Television, with some pithy, unconventional current-affairs programmes that have gained a wide audience;
• Channel 4, evening educational TV.

Elsewhere you'll usually see a national channel and a mixed national/local one. The button numbers on your hotel-room TV don't always correspond to channel numbers.

The most popular programmes are 'Vremya' ('Time' – a news' show, we believe), NTV's political analysis programme 'Itogi', and anything that's remotely sensational.

English-Language TV
In most large hotels in St Petersburg and Moscow, and all luxury hotels everywhere, there's satellite television, showing a wide variety of Western programmes from CNN, CNBC, the Discovery Channel, MTV (of course), BBC, and TV 5 from France, Pro7.

Russian-Language Radio
From the little *radio tochka* box in many hotel rooms you can usually tune in to a local station plus Radio Rossii, whose hourly renditions of *Moscow Nights* will give you nightmares if you fall asleep with the radio tochka on. The switch on the box will be set either to 'off' or 'loud'.

Radio in Russia is broken into three bands: AM, UKV (the lower band of FM from 66 to 77 MHz) and FM (100 to 107 MHz). A Western-made FM radio usually won't go lower than 85 MHz.

The Yanks are here, and in droves, making (generally album-oriented rock) noise. Private Russian-language radio has come a long way, and it's worth listening to, though it's rare to hear any Russian bands other than

oldies-but-goodies such as Akvarium, Kino and Time Machine. Check the *Moscow Times* or the *St Petersburg Press* for radio listings. Some stations are:

• Yevropa Plus, with one of the most annoying jingles on earth, which plays a lot of Western disco and rock. You'll hear a fair bit of ABBA and Donna Summer. It's constantly expanding to more cities; check locally for listings as it broadcasts on all bands;
• Open Radio in Moscow, a joint-stock company, which does news, talk and ranting, apparently modelling itself after North American 'all-news, everywhere-you-turn, in-your-face, all-the-time' stations. It's on 918 kHz AM and 102.5 FM;
• Radio 7, an American/Russian joint venture in Moscow, which does AC format music at 104.7 FM and 73.4 UKV;
• Radio Maximum, the slickest of the lot, serving Moscow and St Petersburg with all US money and equipment and a compressed, tight, h-h-hot sound at 103.7 FM.

English-Language Radio
Aside from the Russian stations that also have some English-language content, there's always the BBC. The clearest BBC World Service short-wave (SW) frequencies in the morning, late evening and at night are near 9410, 12,095 (the best) and 15,070 MHz – though the exact setting varies with location in Russia. If you're in St Petersburg or Moscow, you can get the BBC:

from midnight to 2 am GMT/UTC, at 6180 and 7325 MHz
from 2 to 5 am, at 6195
from 2 to 7 am, at 9410
from 4 am to 8.30 pm, at 12,095
from 1 to 8 pm, at 13,070
and from 8 pm to midnight, at 5930, 6180 and 7325.

Voice of America is clearest near 6040 MHz (SW) from 2 to 10 pm; in St Petersburg it's at 6866 MHz 24 hours a day. Among Russian stations (see the previous section), Radio Maximum does an hour-long jazz show in English on Monday at midnight, and Kasey Kasem's Top 40 Countdown is on Sunday from 9 am to 1 pm if you're really that desperate. In Moscow, Radio 7 does a comedic morning zoo show in English and news in English at half past the hour round the clock, and Open Radio broadcasts some English-language news and current affairs. St Petersburg English-language radio also includes Radio Modern, 104 FM, on Saturday at 11.15 am and Tuesday at 6.15 pm; and the BBC World Service every day at 1260 on the AM band.

FILM & PHOTOGRAPHY

There are no customs limits on camera equipment and film for personal use. Avoid running films through airport X-ray machines. No matter what the attendant says, these machines are not film-safe; effects are cumulative and too much will fog your pictures. Lead 'film-safe' pouches help, but the best solution is to have your film and camera inspected by hand. You can minimise officials' annoyance by having all film in a few clear plastic bags.

Subject Restrictions

A number of rules and regulations still exist on paper. It's forbidden to photograph military facilities or equipment. Other places of military value – railway bridges and tunnels, seaports, factories, dams, radio and electrical facilities – are also technically no-nos; though railway and river stations and airports are fine. You can't take pictures within the country's 25-km-wide border zones, nor from the air over Russian territory. Never mind that the CIA has it all mapped; if you're caught, your film can be confiscated.

But relax, these are pre-glasnost rules. Obvious military subjects and border zones are still theoretically taboo, but many rules are unevenly enforced. (In late 1994, Nick was *invited* by a Russian naval officer to photograph nuclear submarines docked in the closed city of Severodvinsk; while researching the first edition of this book John K was *invited* to photograph several of the Soviet Union's biggest hydroelectric dams.)

Some museums and galleries forbid flash pictures, some ban all photos. Caretakers in a few churches and other historical buildings charge mercilessly for the privilege.

If you've just taken some irreplaceable pictures and/or are thinking of shooting anything sensitive, consider inserting a fresh roll right away, so you won't lose the good ones if the film is confiscated.

Etiquette

When taking photographs of people, it's always better to ask first; if people don't want to be photographed, respect their privacy.

A lifetime with the KGB may make older people uneasy about having their picture taken. A (genuine) offer to send a copy can loosen a subject up. Many people are touchy about your photographing *embarrassing* things like drunks, run-down housing or consumer queues.

The Russian for 'may I take a photograph?' is *fotografirovat mozhno?* ('fa-ta-gruh-FEE-ra-vut MOZH-na?'). You can also use the more informal *mozhno vas snimat* ('MOZH-na vas sni-MAHT'), but this can also be construed as flirting with someone, so hold your camera high when you say it.

Hazards

Cold Camera batteries get sluggish in the cold. Carry your camera inside your coat and keep some spare batteries warm in your pocket. In the prolonged Siberian winter you may be better off with a manual camera than a do-everything battery-operated one; film gets brittle at very low temperatures and a motor-drive's fast advance or rewind can break it. It may also leave static marks on the film.

Condensation If it's very cold outside you can avoid ruinous moisture on camera innards and film by putting it in a plastic bag *before* going indoors and leaving it there until it's warm.

Heat To avoid magenta-tinted pictures of hot territories, protect film from fierce summer heat. If you don't like leaving it at the hotel, line a stuff-sack with a piece cut from an aluminised mylar 'survival blanket'; film will stay cool inside all day.

Shooting Tips

Frame-filling expanses of snow come out a bit grey unless you deliberately *overexpose* about one-half to one stop. Deep cold can play tricks with exposure, so 'bracket' your best pictures with additional shots about one stop under and overexposed.

Film

Kodak outlets can be found all over the country, even in smaller cities, selling 110-size and 35 mm print film, Ektachrome (but not Kodachrome) slide film and video cassettes. Prices are about as they are in Western Europe, but freshness is dodgy in remote areas, so bring film with you from the West. Moscow and St Petersburg each have several outlets, along with suppliers of Fuji and Agfa.

Some Russian films need to be rolled into a cartridge before use. If you've somehow forgotten your darkroom, this can be inconvenient.

Processing

Many of Kodak's locations around the country offer one-hour (or fast, anyway) developing, Western-made film, photo equipment and knick-knacks. Only a few places will develop slide film. They include the Kodak shop in Moscow's Hotel Mezhdunarodnaya, and Fuji on naberezhnaya reki Fontanki in St Petersburg: these can process Ektachrome, Fujichrome and some other brands (E6 process), but not Kodachrome. Russian-made colour film is reportedly compatible with Agfa processes but not Kodak, and is best developed in Russia.

Passport Photos

Passport photos – either from a machine or a passport photo specialist – are dirt cheap in Russia and it's worth stocking up if you do a lot of travelling. Look for signs saying Паспорт Фото.

HEALTH

Staying healthy while on the road depends on predeparture planning, day-to-day care and how you handle problems and emergencies. Despite the spread of several serious diseases in Russia because of deteriorating health care and sanitation, rising poverty and easing of travel restrictions, with a little forethought you may not even suffer a grumpy stomach while you're there.

The Russian health system is pretty dismal but routine care can be arranged through a hotel, and foreigners usually get the best available in any area.

Travel Health Guides

Travel with Children (Lonely Planet, 1995) includes basic advice on travel health for young children.

Predeparture Planning

Insurance A travel insurance policy to cover theft, loss and medical problems is a very wise idea. You may need to use one of the expensive Western-run medical services or ambulances in Moscow or St Petersburg. A 'medevac' policy, which covers the costs of being flown out of the country for treatment is a distinct plus, given the limited facilities in Russia. If you need to charter a flight to get you out really fast, the bill can approach US$30,000!

Medex Assistance (☎ (800) 537 2029 in the USA; ☎ (0800) 891 536 in the UK) offers the comprehensive Medex Plus programme, with worldwide evacuation coordination coverage that includes all of Russia. You carry a Russian-language membership card with instructions to your doctor to contact the American Medical Center in Moscow or St Petersburg, which will coordinate your treatment and, if necessary, arrange air-ambulance evacuation (usually to a Finnish hospital) or repatriation. The cost is US$125 a year for up to 90 consecutive days of travel or US$148 for unlimited consecutive travel days within one year.

There is a wide variety of other policies and your travel agent will be able to make recommendations. If you're a frequent traveller it's possible to get year-round insurance at reasonable rates (one such policy is offered by American Express). Check the small print: some policies exclude 'dangerous activities', which can include white-water rafting or even trekking, though you may be able to pay more for an amendment which covers these activities.

Very few fee-charging medical services in Russia will accept your foreign insurance documents as payment. You have to pay on the spot, get receipts for everything (and save all other paperwork) and claim later.

Medical Kits A basic kit should include tweezers, scissors, a thermometer (though mercury thermometers are prohibited by most airlines), aspirin or paracetemol (acetaminophen in the USA), antiseptic, bandages and Band-aids, a few gauze pads and some adhesive tape, and alcohol wipes or a small bottle of alcohol and some sterile pads which can be used for cleaning small wounds. Also bring something for putting an abrupt stop to diarrhoea (a kaolin preparation – eg Pepto-Bismol – or Imodium or Lomotil). For treatment of severe diarrhoea, especially in children, it's a good idea to bring a rehydration mixture. Water-purification tablets, iodine tincture or an electric water-heating element are useful if you can't find water that you trust (see Basic Rules).

In summer you'll need insect repellent for protection against mosquitoes almost everywhere, and against ticks and lesser annoyances if you'll be in the countryside (see What to Bring). You may also need sunscreen.

If you fear your diet may be inadequate, consider taking vitamin and iron pills with you.

A broad-spectrum antibiotic like tetracycline or penicillin is useful if you'll be off the beaten track, but be sure you have no allergies to it. Take only the recommended dose and take it for the prescribed period. Antibiotics should never taken indiscriminately: they are quite specific to the infections they can treat. Stop immediately if there is any serious reaction and don't use the drug at all if you're unsure whether you have the right one.

For this and any other prescription drug,

bring the prescription too, as proof that you use the drug legally. Don't count on refills in Russia (though a prescription for the generic rather than brand-name medication is easier to fill). If you're required to take a narcotic drug, carry a doctor's letter confirming this. Keep medicines in their original, labelled containers and in your hand luggage.

If you wear corrective lenses remember to take a spare pair of glasses and the prescription.

Considering the potential for contamination through dirty needles, some travellers now routinely carry a sterile pack of disposable syringes for any emergency shots that might be needed. Ask your doctor for a prescription for them and carry it with you to Russia, lest customs agents seize them (and possibly you) for possession of 'narcotic paraphernalia'. Try to get needles of three different sizes – 3cc, 22Gx1.5"; 3cc, 25Gx5/8", and a couple of 10-cc syringes with attachable 21Gx1.5" needles.

Kit Suppliers SAFA (☎ (0151) 709 6075), 59 Hill Street, Liverpool LP 5SE, England, specialises in travel medical kits for developing countries or other remote areas. All its kits contain plasters, bandages, swabs and medi-wipes. Its model 690 'Wallet Kit' (£11.90 plus VAT), available without prescription, contains two 25Gx5/8" and two 19Gx1.5" single-use hypodermic needles plus syringes and sutures. There are also more expensive 'AIDS Prevention Kits' (including artificial blood) and 'Upcountry Kits' (model 700) used by geologists, Peace Corps volunteers and others in remote areas for long periods. SAFA will ship anywhere in the world; its international fax order number is (44 151) 708 7211.

Immunisations & Documents Plan well ahead for immunisations since some should not be given simultaneously. Some also require courses of more than one shot. You can get advice from your doctor or from travel health advice centres. In Britain, you can obtain a printed health brief for any country, including a list of recommended

EUROPEAN RUSSIA

immunisations and info on seasonal diseases, by calling MASTA (Medical Advisory Services for Travellers Abroad) on ☎ (0891) 224 100. The brief, prepared from a database validated by the London School of Hygiene & Tropical Medicine, is free but the phone call costs £0.49 a minute (£0.39 at cheap rate). In the USA, you can call the Centers for Disease Control travellers' hotline (☎ (404) 332 4559), or the International Medicine Program at Cornell University Medical Center, New York (☎ (212) 746 5454). In Australia, call the Australian Government Health Service (part of the Commonwealth Department of Human Services & Health) or consult a clinic such as the Traveller's Medical & Vaccination Centre (☎ (03) 670 3969) at Level 2, 393 Little Bourke St, Melbourne.

Vaccinations can be carried out by your doctor or, in some countries, government health centres – travel agents can advise you where to go. In Britain there's also a network of British Airways Travel Clinics (☎ (0171) 831 5333).

Vaccinations should be recorded on an International Health Certificate, available where you receive them. Anyone required to take medication containing a narcotic drug should have a doctor's certificate. For prescription drugs or any disposable syringes that you carry, bring the prescription. From August 1995 foreigners who wish to stay in the Russian Federation for longer than three months may be required to take an HIV/AIDS test. See HIV/AIDS Testing in the section on Visas earlier in this chapter for more details.

Tetanus & Diphtheria Protection is highly recommended. Immunisation against diphtheria (usually combined with tetanus) is now recommended for Russia as there have been recent outbreaks of this potentially fatal disease, once declared eradicated in the USSR. Reported cases were running at a rate of over 20,000 a year in early 1994, many of them in Moscow and St Petersburg. Many people will have been immunised against diphtheria in childhood but boosters are necessary every 10 years. If you have never been immunised, a full course involves three doses at monthly intervals. In some countries diphtheria vaccine may be in short supply: in Britain call the Department of Health (☎ (0171) 972 4480) for information.

Polio A booster of either the oral or injected vaccine is required every 10 years to maintain our immunity from vaccination during childhood. Polio is a very serious, easily transmitted disease which is still prevalent in Russia.

Typhoid Immunisation is available either as an injection or oral capsules. Protection lasts for three years. You may get some side effects such as pain at the injection site, fever, headache and a general unwell feeling. A new single-dose injectable vaccine, which appears to have few side effects, is now available but is more expensive. Side effects are unusual with the oral form but occasionally an individual will have stomach cramps.

Hepatitis A The risk of contracting hepatitis A in Russia is moderate, though it increases with the length of your stay. Common-sense eating and drinking habits greatly reduce your chances of getting hepatitis A. Immunisation can be provided in two ways – either with gammaglobulin or with the recently developed vaccine Havrix, which provides long-term immunity (possibly more than 10 years) after two injections a month apart. It takes about three weeks to provide satisfactory protection. A gammaglobulin injection is not a vaccination but a dose of a ready-made antibody. It should be given as close as possible to departure because it is at its most effective in the first few weeks after administration and the effectiveness tapers off gradually between three and six months later.

Hepatitis B The immunisation schedule for hepatitis B, which has been increasing in Russia, requires three injections over a six-month period. You should have this if you anticipate contact with blood or other bodily secretions in Russia, either as a health-care worker or through sexual contact with the local population, particularly if you intend to stay in the country for a long time.

Cholera Russia's worst cholera outbreak since the 1970s occurred in Dagestan in 1994, killing at least 18 people and reportedly brought by Muslim pilgrims returning from Saudi Arabia. The risk of cholera is only significant in some areas, however. The cholera vaccine is not very effective, only lasts six months and is not recommended if you're pregnant. Cholera is contracted from contaminated water, so care with what you eat and drink is the best protection.

Encephalitis From May to September there's a risk of tick-borne encephalitis in forested areas. Hikers, campers and others going to forested areas during those months should consider immunisation with either a vaccine or a specific tick-borne encephalitis immunoglobulin. These are readily available in the UK and elsewhere in Europe, but are not available in Australia at the time of writing and may not become so since the need is not considered great.

Tuberculosis (TB) Vaccination for children under 12 travelling in endemic areas is sensible. An epidemic of TB broke out in Tomsk, Siberia, in 1994.

Medical Assistance

Hotels and guides can call a doctor; some hotels keep one on call. Polyclinics *(polikliniki)*, which are like district surgeries or health centres, provide free medical attention, though you may have to pay a little for medications. But the Russian medical system is in a dismal state due to lack of funds, poor equipment and poor training, and some common medications are unavailable. The average Russian pharmacy *(apteka)* doesn't have many supplies. In Moscow and St Petersburg there are some expensive Western-run medical services and pharmacies as well as some higher-quality Russian clinics and hospitals which are used to

dealing with foreigners (see those city sections for details). Many foreign residents fly out to the West when significant medical treatment is required.

For problems beyond the level of first aid – including any involving hospitalisation – contact your embassy or consulate for advice. If it's something really serious requiring evacuation to the West, they can usually give some help in organising it. In such cases, if you don't have medevac insurance (see Predeparture Planning), you'll need access to mountains of cash, or at least a credit card with a very generous credit limit. The following are among those companies that can provide emergency medical evacuations from Russia (usually to Finland):

- Delta Consulting (☎ (095) 229 65 36, 229 78 92), apartment 38, building 3, Bolshaya Dmitrovka ulitsa (formerly Pushkinskaya ulitsa) 7/5, Moscow 103009
- Jet Flite, Vantaa, Finland (☎ (358 0) 822 766)
- Euro-Flite, Vantaa, Finland (☎ (358 0) 870 2544)
- SOS International, Geneva, Switzerland (☎ (41 22) 47 61 61)
- Air Ambulance America, Austin, Texas, USA (☎ (1 512) 479 8000) – call collect

Several airlines, including SAS and Lufthansa, can provide medical evacuations on the next flight out. You have to buy a bunch of seats to put your stretcher and doctor on.

Basic Rules

Many problems can be avoided with common sense – eg get out of the sun when it's blazing hot, and carry enough clothes for potential plunges in temperature. Wash your hands frequently – it's easy to contaminate your own food.

Food & Drink Being cautious about what you eat and drink is the best protection against diseases of insanitation such as diarrhoea, giardiasis, cholera and hepatitis A. Tap water is best avoided in some places, and there have been many reported cases of unfit food being sold, but there's no need to get too paranoid about these.

In some Russian cities tap water is safe to drink; in others – notably St Petersburg – it definitely isn't. To play safe, don't drink it; that includes avoiding ice in your drinks and brushing your teeth with it. Five-star hotels will have their own water-purifying systems, however. Other decent hotels and restaurants should have safe bottled mineral water. Mineral water from shops and kiosks may not be pure. Imported bottled water is available in some shops in larger towns. An electric water heating element is a useful thing to carry for boiling your own water.

Cheap vodka bought from shops or kiosks can make you ill.

In tourist hotels and good restaurants, food can be considered safe. But choose food from street vendors and cafeterias (stolovaya) with care. Go for hot, fresh-looking dishes. Don't eat anything you don't like the look, taste or smell of. Avoid salads. Be suspicious of fish and shellfish and avoid undercooked meat. Peel fruit yourself or wash it in water you trust. Ice cream is OK, except possibly the 'softee' extruded kind. In remote areas milk may be unpasteurised (with a risk of tuberculosis), although yoghurt or *kefir* (sour milk) are usually hygienic.

If the place is clean and the vendor looks clean and healthy then the food is probably safe. Busy places are usually OK.

Water Purification The best way to purify water is to boil it for 10 minutes. If you can't boil it, treat it chemically. Iodine treatment kills bacteria, amoebas and the giardia parasite and is safe for short-term use unless you're pregnant or have thyroid problems. It's available in tablet form (eg Potable Aqua or Globaline), or a 2% tincture of iodine can be used. Add four drops per litre or quart of clear water and let it stand half an hour. Iodine degrades if it's exposed to air or dampness, so keep it sealed.

Chlorine tablets (eg Puritabs, Steritabs) won't kill amoebic cysts or giardia. A water filter (see What to Bring) may be useful but simple filtration will not remove all pathogens.

Nutrition Most hotel and restaurant food is tolerably nutritious. In places that are poorly provided with eateries try not to let the hassles of finding meals and dealing with rude staff make you skip meals and put your health at risk.

Keep your diet balanced. Eggs, beans, lentils and nuts are safe protein sources. Fruit you can peel is always safe and a good vitamin source. Don't forget grains (eg rice) and bread. Though well-cooked food is safer, when overcooked it loses much of its nutritional value. If your diet isn't well balanced or if your food intake is insufficient, it's a good idea to take vitamin and iron pills.

Diagnostics Normal body temperature is 37°C (98.6°F). More than 2°C higher indicates a 'high' fever. The normal adult pulse rate is 60 to 80 per minute (children 80 to 100, babies 100 to 140). As a rule, pulse increases about 20 beats per minute for each 1°C rise in fever. Breathing rate is another indicator of illness. Adults and older children breathe about 12 to 20 times a minute (up to 30 for young children, 40 for babies). People with high fever or serious respiratory illness breathe faster than normal. Over 40 shallow breaths a minute may indicate pneumonia.

Environmental Hazards

Sunburn Extreme heat is rare in Russia, but in heatwaves or at high altitude you can get sunburnt very fast, so a sunscreen is essential. Calamine lotion eases the pain of mild sunburn.

Hypothermia Trekkers run a risk of getting hypothermia, in which the body loses heat faster than it can generate it and the body's core temperature drops. It's surprisingly easy to go from chilly to dangerously cold when exposed to a combination of wind, wet clothing (from rain or sweat), fatigue and hunger, even when the air temperature is above freezing.

Symptoms are exhaustion, numbness

(especially in toes and fingers), shivering, slurred speech, clumsiness, lethargy, dizzy spells, muscle cramps, irrational behaviour and violent bursts of energy.

To prevent hypothermia, dress in easily donned layers. Silk, wool and a few artificial fibres insulate well even when wet; cotton doesn't. A hat makes a big difference, as a lot of heat is lost through the head. A waterproof outer layer is obviously important. Water will prevent dehydration and sugary snacks help to generate heat quickly.

To treat it, take shelter and replace wet clothing with dry. Drink hot liquids (not alcohol) and eat high-calorie, easily digestible snacks. It may be necessary to put the affected person in a sleeping bag and get in with them. Don't rub a hypothermia sufferer down or put them near a fire. The early recognition and treatment of mild hypothermia is the only way to prevent severe hypothermia, which is a critical condition.

Altitude Sickness Reduced oxygen at high altitudes affects most people to some extent. Take it very easy at first, drink lots of fluids and eat well. Even with acclimatisation you may still have headaches, dizziness, breathlessness, insomnia or low appetite. The symptoms usually go away after a day or two, but if they persist or worsen the only treatment is to descend – even a few hundred metres can help. Continuing breathlessness, severe headache, nausea, lack of appetite or dry cough are cause for concern. Profound tiredness, confusion, lack of coordination and balance are real danger signs. Acute Mountain Sickness (AMS) can be fatal.

There's no hard-and-fast rule about how high is too high – AMS has been fatal at 3000 metres, although 3500 to 4500 metres is when AMS usually becomes life-theatening. It's wise to sleep at a lower altitude than the greatest height reached during the day.

Pollution Though terrible pollution in many parts of Russia causes health problems for residents in those areas, short-term visitors should have little cause for concern unless they are victims of a freak accident. Radia-tion or chemical-affected food supplies, metal-polluted water, and foul air have cumulative effects which are not likely to harm people passing through. But if you're presented with a two-headed tomato or other obviously mutant vegetable, it's wise to pass! For more information on Chornobyl (Chernobyl) see the Health section in the Ukraine Facts for the Visitor chapter.

Sanitation-Related Diseases

Diarrhoea A change of water, food or climate, even jet lag, can bring on the runs, but a few desperate dashes to the loo, with no other symptoms, is nothing to worry about. More serious is diarrhoea due to contaminated food or water.

Dehydration is the main danger, particularly for children, so fluid replenishment is essential. Weak black tea with a little sugar, or soft drinks allowed to go flat and diluted with purified water, are good. In severe cases a rehydrating solution is necessary to replace minerals and salts. If you didn't bring a commercial mix, you can fake it by adding eight teaspoons of sugar to a litre of purified water; sip it slowly all day and eat salted cracker biscuits. Stick to a bland diet as you recover.

Lomotil or Imodium plugs you up but doesn't cure you. Use such drugs only if absolutely necessary – eg if you *must* travel. Don't use these preparations if you have a fever or are severely dehydrated. Antibiotics can be used to treat watery diarrhoea that's accompanied by fever, lethargy, blood or mucus; diarrhoea not improving after 48 hours; or severe diarrhoea, if you have to travel.

Giardiasis The water of St Petersburg and possibly surrounding towns is known to be contaminated with *Giardia lamblia*, a parasite found in contaminated water. Symptoms of infection – stomach cramps, nausea, bloated stomach, watery, foul-smelling diarrhoea and frequent gas – may not appear until weeks after exposure, and can come and go for weeks or months. The infection sometimes disappears of its own accord. There is no preventative drug. Tinidazole, known as Fasigyn, or metronidazole (Flagyl) are the recommended drugs for treatment. Either can be used in a single treatment dose.

The parasite can be killed by boiling your drinking water or treating it with iodine. Stay away from tap water, salads (which may have been washed in it) and ice.

Dysentery The main symptom of this serious illness, caused by contaminated food or water, is severe diarrhoea, often with traces of blood or mucus. There are two forms. Bacillary (or bacterial) dysentery shows rapid onset, high fever, headache, vomiting and stomach pains. It generally doesn't last more than a week, but it's highly contagious.

Amoebic dysentery is often more gradual in onset, with cramping abdominal pain and vomiting less likely; fever may not be present. It will persist until treated and can recur and cause long-term health problems. Only a stool test can reliably distinguish the two, and they must be treated differently. In an emergency the drugs norfloxacin or ciprofloxacin can be used for bacillary dysentery, and metronidazole (Flagyl) for amoebic dysentery. A useful alternative for bacillary dysentery is co-trimoxazole 160/800mg (Bactrim, Septrin, Resprim) twice daily for seven days, but this must not be used in people with a known sulpha allergy. An alternative to Flagyl is Fasigyn, taken as a two-gram daily dose for three days.

Cholera The bacteria responsible for cholera are waterborne, so care with what you eat and drink are the best protection. Outbreaks of cholera are usually widely reported, so you can often avoid problem areas.

The disease is characterised by a sudden onset of acute diarrhoea with 'rice water' stools, vomiting, muscular cramps, and extreme weakness. You need medical help – but, as a first step, treat for dehydration, which can be extreme, and if there is an appreciable delay in getting to hospital, then begin taking tetracycline. The adult dose is 250 mg four times daily, but it is not recommended for children aged eight or under, or for pregnant women. An alternative drug is Ampicillin. Remember that while antibiotics might kill the bacteria, it is a toxin produced by the bacteria which causes the massive fluid loss. Fluid replacement is by far the most important aspect of treatment.

Viral Gastroenteritis This intestinal infection caused by a virus is characterised by stomach cramps and diarrhoea and sometimes by vomiting and/or a slight fever. All you can do is rest and drink lots of fluids.

Hepatitis A Hepatitis A is spread by contaminated food, water or utensils. The symptoms include fever, chills, fatigue, aches and pains, followed by loss of appetite, nausea, vomiting, abdominal pain, dark urine, light-coloured faeces and jaundiced skin. The whites of the eyes may turn yellow. You should seek medical advice, but in general there is not much you can do apart from resting, drinking lots of fluids, eating lightly and avoiding fatty foods. You have to forego alcohol for six months after the illness.

Typhoid Typhoid fever is a very serious gut infection from contaminated water or food. Vaccination is not totally effective. At first you may feel like you have a bad cold or flu, with headache, sore throat, and a fever that rises a little each day to 40°C or more. The pulse may be abnormally slow and gets slower as the fever rises (in a typical fever it speeds up). There may also be vomiting, diarrhoea or constipation.

By the second week pink spots may appear on the body, along with trembling, delirium, weakness, weight loss and dehydration. If there are no complications, the fever and symptoms can disappear in the third week but medical help is essential before this, as common complications are pneumonia or perforated bowel, and the disease is very infectious.

The victim should be kept cool and made to drink a lot of fluids. The drug of choice is ciprofloxacin but this may not be available.

One alternative, chloramphenicol, is still the recommended antibiotic in many countries but there are fewer side affects with ampicillin. People who are allergic to penicillin should not be given ampicillin.

Diseases Spread by People, Animals & Insects

Hepatitis B Hepatitis B is spread through contact with infected blood, blood products or bodily fluids, eg through sexual contact, unsterilised needles and blood transfusions. Avoid injections, or carry your own disposable syringes. Symptoms are much the same as for hepatitis A, but more severe, and may lead to irreparable liver damage or even liver cancer. There is no treatment, but an effective vaccine is available (see Predeparture Planning).

Tuberculosis (TB) TB is a bacterial infection which is widespread in many developing countries. It is usually transmitted from person to person by coughing but may be transmitted through consumption of unpasteurised milk. Milk that has been boiled is safe to drink; the souring of milk to make yoghurt or cheese also kills the bacilli. Typically many months of contact with the infected person are required before the disease is passed on so it is not considered a serious risk to travellers. Most infected people never develop symptoms. In those who do, especially infants, symptoms may arise within weeks of the infection occurring and may be severe. In most, however, the disease lies dormant for many years until, for some reason, the infected person becomes physically run down.

Symptoms include fever, weight loss, night sweats and cough. Treatment is complex and requires medical supervision. Vaccination against tuberculosis may prevent serious disease so is recommended especially for children under 12 who are likely to be heavily exposed to infected people. Russian doctors reportedly have some odd ideas on how to treat it so steer clear of them.

Diphtheria Diphtheria can be a potentially fatal throat infection, caused by the inhalation of infected cough or sneeze droplets, or a less dangerous skin infection, spread by contaminated dust contacting the skin.

There's a higher risk of getting the throat infection in cities and crowded places: Moscow had over 13% of Russia's cases in 1994. Symptoms of the throat infection include coughing, short breath and a swollen pharynx. Vaccination is available to prevent it; you can also reduce risk by avoiding close contact with other people – eg kissing, sharing bottles or glasses.

The mainstay of treatment of the diphtheria throat infection is an intravenous infusion of diphtheria antitoxin. This antitoxin is produced in horses, so it may cause allergic reactions in some people. Because of this, it must be administered under close medical supervision. Antibiotics such as erythromycin or penicillin are then given to eradicate the diphtheria bacteria from the patient so that it is not transmitted to others.

Frequent washing and keeping the skin dry will help prevent the skin infection.

Encephalitis, Lyme Disease & Typhus

These diseases are a risk for hikers, campers and others going to some forested and rural areas in certain seasons.

Encephalitis is inflammation of the brain tissue. It has multiple causes including the Japanese B encephalitis virus (transmitted through mosquito bites) and the various microorganisms with which a person might become infected through a tick bite. Symptoms include fever, headache, vomiting, neck stiffness, pain in the eyes when looking at light, alteration in consciousness, seizures and paralysis or muscle weakness. Correct diagnosis and treatment require hospitalisation. Tick encephalitis is a risk from May to September in rural areas almost anywhere in Russia. Ticks may be found on the edge of forests and in clearings, long grass and hedgerows. A vaccine is available (see Immunisations & Documents earlier in this section).

You can avoid insect bites by covering

bare skin, by screening windows or beds or by using insect repellents.

Lyme disease, another tick-borne infection, is prevalent mainly in rural areas around Moscow, St Petersburg, Tver and in the Golden Ring area east of Moscow, from April to September. No vaccine is available. The illness usually begins with a spreading rash at the site of the bite accompanied by fever, headache, extreme fatigue, aching joints and muscles, and mild neck stiffness. If untreated, these symptoms usually resolve over several weeks, but over subsequent weeks or months disorders of the nervous system, heart and joints may develop. The response to treatment is best early in the illness. The longer the delay, the longer the recovery period. Treatment involves the use of antibiotics, often tetracycline, 250 mg, four times a day for at least 10 days. Alternative or additional treatment would depend upon the patient and the severity of symptoms.

Ticks can also spread typhus, which begins with fever, chills, headache and muscle pains, followed a few days later by a body rash. There is often a large painful sore at the site of the bite and nearby lymph nodes are swollen and painful. Treatment is with tetracycline, or chloramphenicol under medical supervision.

Measures to avoid tick bites include covering bare skin or using a strong insect repellent. Serious walkers in areas where ticks are endemic should consider having their boots and trousers impregnated with benzyl benzoate and dibutylphthalate. Check your body if you have been walking through a tick-infested area. Vaseline, alcohol or oil will persuade a tick to let go.

Sexually Transmitted Diseases Abstinence is the only sure preventative for diseases spread by sexual contact, but use of a condom is very effective (but exercise great caution with Russian condoms – see the earlier What to Bring section). Gonorrhoea and syphilis (which is on the increase in Russia) are the most common diseases; symptoms include sores, blisters or a rash around the genitals, and discharge or pain when urinating. Symptoms may be less marked or absent in women. Syphilis symptoms eventually disappear, but the disease continues and can cause severe problems in later years. Treatment of gonorrhoea or syphilis is by antibiotics, available at some Western-run clinics, including the American Medical Centers, in St Petersburg and Moscow, and at Skin and Venereal Dispensaries (Kozhno-Venerichskie Dispansery), found throughout the country, which offer diagnosis and treatment of sexually transmitted diseases.

There are numerous other sexually transmitted diseases, for most of which effective treatment is available.

HIV/AIDS HIV, the Human Immunodeficiency Virus, may develop into AIDS, Acquired Immune Deficiency Syndrome, for which there is no cure. Any exposure to blood, blood products or bodily fluids may put the individual at risk. In industrialised countries transmission is mostly through contact between homosexual or bisexual males, or via contaminated needles shared by intravenous drug users. Abstinence and condoms (not Russian condoms – see What to Bring) are the most effective preventives.

HIV/AIDS can also be spread through infected blood transfusions and by dirty needles – vaccinations, acupuncture, tattooing and ear or nose piercing are potentially as dangerous as intravenous drug use if the equipment is not clean. If you have to have an injection in Russia, ask to see the syringe unwrapped in front of you, or better still, bring a needle and syringe pack to Russia with you (see Medical Kits).

From August 1995 foreigners who wish to stay in the Russian Federation for longer than three months may be required to take an HIV/AIDS test. See HIV/AIDS Testing in the section on Visas earlier in this chapter for more details.

Women's Health
Gynaecological Problems Poor diet, lowered resistance from the use of antibiot-

ics, even contraceptive pills can pave the way for vaginal infections in hot weather. Maintaining good personal hygiene, wearing skirts or loose-fitting trousers and cotton underwear will minimise the risk.

Yeast infections, characterised by a rash, itch and discharge, can be treated with a vinegar or lemon-juice douche or with yoghurt. Nystatin suppositories are the usual medical prescription.

Trichomonas is a more serious infection, with a discharge and a burning sensation when urinating. Male sexual partners must also be treated and if a vinegar-water douche is not effective medical attention should be sought. Metronidazole (brand name Flagyl) is the prescribed drug.

Pregnancy Most miscarriages occur during the first three months of pregnancy so this is the riskiest time to travel. The last three months should also be spent within reach of

good medical care. Pregnant women should avoid unnecessary medication. Good diet and rest are doubly important during pregnancy.

WOMEN TRAVELLERS

Bring sanitary towels or tampons. You may find tampons but you can't count on it (see What to Bring). Western and Russian-made soap and other toiletries are widely available but you might want to bring your own soap as hotels supply meagre quantities.

You're unlikely to experience sexual harassment on the streets in most parts of the country, though sexual stereotyping remains strong. However, in places such as Astrakhan and Makhachkala in southern European Russia we have seen Russian women being harassed by non-Russian men. In remoter areas, the idea that women are somehow less capable than men may persist, and in some Muslim areas women are treated as second-

---

Russians' Health

The legacy left by Soviet environmental degradation and scientific isolation, combined with more recent economic dislocation, has led to a crisis in Russians' health. A few statistics:

- One Russian newspaper reported in 1992 that the average 40-year-old would have consumed 28 kg of toxic chemicals in food grown in the former Soviet Union.
- In 1992 Russian government scientists calculated that 15% of the country was 'ecologically unsafe' for people due to dumping of toxic wastes, the effects of nuclear explosions and accidents, and other causes. About 2.6 million people were living in parts of Russia – mostly in the western Bryansk region – affected by the 1986 Chornobyl (Chernobyl) disaster in Ukraine. Some 400,000 of these were in areas from which they should be moved. Big increases in cancer, heart disease and other health problems have been reported in these areas.
- In 1993 the average Russian consumed 15% less fruit and vegetables than in 1989, 23% less meat, fish and their products, and 25% less dairy produce, but 5% more bread and 13% more potatoes, according to the Russian Academy of Medical Sciences. In 1994 a government health chief claimed 8.5% of meat was unfit for consumption.
- Russian men's average life expectancy has fallen dramatically to 57 years (in the West it's over 70); Russian women's is about 70. Deaths are exceeding births at such a rate that the population is expected to fall from 150 million to about 140 million by 2005. Some 61% of men smoke. Alcoholism is endemic. Infant mortality is increasing. There are complications in over 40% of births. In 1995 the Education Ministry classed only 20% of children as healthy.
- Some 30% of polikliniki don't have hot water, and 7% have no water at all. The figures are higher for hospitals. School kitchens are so dirty that in 1992 a quarter of all intestinal infections in the whole population were occurring in kindergarten children.
- Diphtheria, tuberculosis, syphilis, hepatitis B and whooping cough all showed serious growth between 1993 and 1994. ■

Gay & Lesbian Issues

Article 121.1 of the Russian Criminal Code, which punished homosexual acts with up to three years imprisonment, was repealed in May 1993. But Russia's organised gay and lesbian movement goes back to 1990, when a press conference was held to announce the establishment of the gay and lesbian newspaper *Tema* and the formation of the Moscow Union of Sexual Minorities. On 9 October 1991, Krilya (Wings), the first gay and lesbian association in the country's history, was officially registered.

There is an active gay and lesbian scene in Moscow and St Petersburg, but it's still in its infancy. Organisations are cagy about contact details (understandably so, given the volatile political climate in the country), and there's nothing that approaches the kind of community support infrastructure common in the West.

Key reading is *The Rights of Lesbians & Gay Men in the Russian Federation*, a 130-page, US$15 book in Russian and English published by the International Gay & Lesbian Human Rights Commission (☎ (415) 255 8680; fax (415) 255 8662), 1360 Mission Street, Suite 200, San Francisco, CA 94103, USA.

As far as on-the-ground resources go, *Probuzhdenie (Awakening)* is a monthly magazine with news, essays, poetry, stories and, most important, personal ads from all over the country. There are separate editions for gay men and lesbians. Newspapers such as the *Moscow Times* and the *St Petersburg Press* have shown an interest in (and, in the case of the latter, a commitment to) publicising gay and lesbian issues and events.

The Spartacus guide lists several organisations, clubs, cruising areas and health services, though their listings tend to be dated: some gay travellers have reported problems when relying on an out-of-date listing, so be sure to confirm details.

In Moscow, contact the AESOP Center (☎ & fax (095) 141 83 15, satellite (502) 224 31 18; e-mail aesop@glas.apc.org), PO Box 27, Moscow 121552, which is a gay and lesbian resource centre that also does awareness and AIDS support group work, or the Moscow Union of Lesbians (☎ (095) 152 16 57). In St Petersburg, Krilya (☎ (812) 312 31 80) is a political and social action group which organises AIDS awareness drives and lobbies for gay and lesbian rights. The Tchaikovsky Fund (☎ (812) 311 09 37) is a gay resource centre. The Independent Women's Club is a lesbian information centre (☎ (812) 511 91 16).

Nick Selby

class people. Anywhere in the country, revealing clothing will probably attract unwanted attention. With lawlessness and crime on the rise, you need to be wary; a woman alone should certainly avoid private taxis at night.

Any young or youngish woman alone in or near flashy bars frequented by foreigners risks being mistaken for a prostitute. Susan Forsyth, who travelled with John Noble in Russia, recalls:

I was sitting on a bench outside a bar in a St Petersburg hotel, quietly gazing at the birds in the hotel aviary, when a man sidled up and sat uncomfortably close to me. He opened one of his palms to reveal his hotel pass, on which his room number was prominently displayed. 'Hundred dollars, US', he said in faltering English (this was the going rate for a hard-currency prostitute). I vehemently defended my status as a hotel guest, whereat he moved on.

In towns and cities, Russian women dress up and wear lots of make-up. If you wear casual gear, you might feel uncomfortable at dinner in a restaurant, or at a theatre or ballet. So consider packing something 'smart' to change into at the end of a day's travel or sightseeing. See the Religion section for how women are expected to dress in Orthodox churches.

You might be treated rudely or ignored by female service bureau staff while a man standing next to you is getting smiles and answers to his questions. Persevere to get the help you need. Interacting with Russian women outside the unreal world of tourist hotels can be enjoyable. Among other places, markets provide a chance to communicate with the local people. Even if your Russian isn't up to much you can get by, and get behind those unsmiling masks.

DANGERS & ANNOYANCES
Danger Regions
It's obviously foolish to go where there's fighting going on or bandits on the loose. The Caucasus is the most volatile area. No one needs reminding about Chechnya. Northern Ossetia, scene of violent ethnic clashes between the Ossetians and the Ingush, was quiet by 1994 – with armed police guards on intercity buses. Mineralnye Vody and its airport was plagued by a spate of hijackings and kidnappings in 1994. There were reports of buses being held up in the countryside in Dagestan, but the cities there seemed safe.

If you're going anywhere you think might be dangerous, check with your government's foreign affairs ministry at home or your embassy in Russia: the British Foreign Office has a travel advice unit (☎ (0171) 270 4129); the US State Department has a 24-hour number for the same purpose, ☎ (202) 647 5225; State Department information is also available on-line through CompuServe (GO: STATE); in Australia the Department of Foreign Affairs & Trade (☎ (06) 261 3305) can give advice on risks in specific countries.

Transport Safety
See the Getting Around chapter for information on the hazards of flying and precautions to take on some trains.

Annoyances
The single most annoying thing the majority of travellers encounter in Russia is that combination of bureaucracy and apathy which turns some people in 'service' industries into surly, ill-mannered, obstructive goblins. Things have improved somewhat with the introduction of private enterprise, but at times you still have to contend with hotel desk staff struck deaf, or at best monosyllabic, by your arrival, restaurants packed with 'waiters' too 'busy' to go anywhere near your table, shop 'assistants' with strange paralyses that make them unable to turn to face customers, and so on.

Happily, these petty Oblomovs are balanced by numbers of polite, kindly characters still aware that we're all members of the same species. For every grumpy, insolent reception clerk there'll be a floor lady who'll happily boil up her samovar time and again for your cups of tea.

As a foreigner you're protected from many of the worst aspects of Russian reality. Russians as a rule are profoundly proud of their country, and will often intervene on a foreigner's behalf lest he or she take home a less than rosy view of Russians. When butting heads with a recalcitrant 'service' professional, the line 'Is this is the way you treat foreigners here?' will often work wonders.

One thing you can't do anything about, though, is the tangle of opening hours whereby every shop, museum and café seems to be having its lunch or afternoon break, or day off, or is *remont* (closed for repairs), or is simply closed full stop, just when you want to visit.

Other things you might find annoying are alcoholic late-night comings, goings and door-banging in hotel corridors; engine-revving, car-alarm testing, tyre-screeching and more door-banging outside hotels after the restaurant closes; the brain-numbing volume of restaurant bands; the clouds of cigarette smoke that billow from most gatherings of more than one Russian citizen; and fartsovshchiky (black marketeers) and prostitutes who *still* walk into your hotel room offering caviar, sex, currency deals or Soviet military watches.

Crime
The 'Mafia' The Western media have had a field day talking about the dangers of the Russian Mafia, painting a portrait of a country inundated with Al Capone types who race through the streets indiscriminately firing Kalashnikovs. In fact, the organised crime problem in Russia is far more

complex, and far less of a threat to visitors, than one might guess from reading an issue of *Newsweek*.

In general, when people discuss the Mafia they're speaking of the black marketeers and criminal gangs that blossomed with glasnost's removal of the state's channels of fear. Some of the more vicious gangsters do indeed occasionally settle scores with Kalashnikovs. But 'Mafia' is a loosely applied term that can also range from financiers, bureaucrats or business people involved in fraud, corruption or embezzlement (often in association with the gangster-types) to corrupt police or small-time kiosk owners forced to pay for 'protection'. Mafia fingers are in all sorts of pies, including transport, staple goods distribution, drug trafficking, bootlegging, gunrunning and prostitution. In the Caucasus, friends warned John N that three men he'd been talking with were 'Cossack champagne Mafia'!

Crime against foreigners has increased as well, but the Western press has gone completely over the top. Unless you're involved in high-flying currency speculation, organised criminals really aren't going to waste their time with you. What you do have to watch for is the very real threat of street crime carried out by drunken or angry punks and hoods.

Street Crime Moscow and St Petersburg's streets are about as safe, or as dangerous, as those of New York, Mexico City, London or Amsterdam. There's petty theft, pocket-picking, purse-snatching and all the other crimes that are endemic in big-city life anywhere in the world. Travellers have reported muggings in broad daylight along Moscow's Novy Arbat and St Petersburg's Nevsky prospekt. Many have reported problems with groups of children who surround foreigners, ostensibly to beg, and end up closing in, with dozens of hands probing Westerners' pockets or worse (see Dangers & Annoyances in the Moscow chapter for more on this phenomenon).

The key here is to be neither paranoid nor insouciant. Common sense must be applied, and you should be aware that it's pretty obvious you're a Westerner. Some anti-crime tips:

- Dress down, avoiding bright colours and obviously foreign clothes.
- Bum bags (fanny packs) are out; they're easily cut with a razor and hey, wasn't that your wallet? If you're going to use a pouch, use a strong leather one or, better yet, an under-the-clothes model so your money is next to your skin. But carry around enough cash so you won't have to pull your pants down to buy a Pepsi.
- An exciting way to meet Russian photo enthusiasts is to walk down the Arbat or Nevsky prospekt with your Nikon slung carelessly over your shoulder. Bag it – preferably in a cheap, locally bought bag, which will help disguise your foreignness.
- Don't do anything you wouldn't normally do at home. If you flash jewellery or cash, wander alone down dark alleys at night or speak on your cellular phone while walking down the street, you invite trouble.
- If you must carry a wallet, keep it in your front pants pocket – not your back pocket or inside jacket pocket. Watch out when in crowds and on public transport. Assume any displays of anger or altercations in crowds to be diversionary tactics and act accordingly.
- Don't change money on the street unless absolutely necessary, and then take as much control as you can of the situation and stay alert (see the Money section for more tips).
- Keep photocopies of your passport, visa (especially) and other important documents in a safe place – you'll be glad of them if you *do* lose the originals (see Lost or Stolen Passport or Visa in the Visas & Embassies section earlier in this chapter).
- Don't get into a taxi whose occupants outnumber you.

Burglary Break-ins to flats and cars are epidemic so don't leave anything of worth – this includes sunglasses, cassette tapes, windscreen wipers and cigarettes – in a car. Valuables lying around hotel rooms are also tempting providence. At campsites watch for things being stolen from clotheslines or even cabins. If you'll be living in a flat, invest in a steel door (see *The Traveller's Yellow Pages* or *Where in Moscow/St Petersburg* for suppliers).

Airport Crime There have been countless

reports of crime at Sheremetevo airport, Moscow, usually involving checked baggage which has been slit open and ransacked. The culprits concentrate on foreign flights (they seem to have a fondness for flights to Germany and the USA, but they'll get anyone) and go for easy targets – unlocked hard suitcases, rucksacks and soft cloth bags.

There's not much you can do about it except try to prevent it. Never pack valuables in checked luggage, and try as best you can to fit everything into carry-on.

Reporting Theft & Loss

If you're here in a group, your tour guide or service bureau should be your first resort if you want to report a theft or loss. You may end up talking to the police (militsia): their phone number is 02 in large cities, and if you don't speak Russian you'll need a translator. *Vorovstvo* and *krazha* both mean theft in Russian. For lost passports or visas, see Visas & Embassies in this chapter. Lost travellers' cheques may be replaceable – see Money in this chapter – but if you're kopek-less in the wilderness, find the nearest city administration building (ask: *Gde administratsia goroda?*). It's your best bet for contact with your embassy and its people may arrange for you to travel there.

Lost luggage is a nightmare, especially if you don't speak Russian. In Moscow the consular section of your embassy may help. Airport lost-luggage offices rarely answer the phone. At Sheremetevo they just usher you into a vast room full of bags and let you rummage around.

KGB

The Committee for State Security (Komitet Gosudarstvennoy Bezopastnosti, or KGB) is on the scrap-heap of Soviet history. Its successor, the Federal Security Service (Federalnaya Sluzhba Bezopastnosti; ☎ (095) 924 31 58) has far better things to do with its time than run around after a bunch of tourists.

Arrest

If you are arrested, the Russian authorities are obliged to inform your embassy or consulate immediately and allow you to communicate with it without delay. You can insist on seeing an embassy or consular official straight away. Be polite and respectful towards officials and things will go far more smoothly for you. *'pa-ZHAHL-stuh, ya kha-TYEL bi pahz-vah-NEET v pah-SOLST-vih ma-YEY STRAHN-ih'* means 'I'd like to call my embassy'.

ACTIVITIES
Adventure Travel

One of the ways you can tell that adventure travel in Russia is going to be adventurous is that it's such an adventure finding a reputable adventure travel agent. John Noble asked the travel editor of the *Moscow Times* which Russian adventure travel firms she would recommend, and she said 'Just one'. Fly-by-night and underfinanced firms are rife, and you really should take time to check out what you're getting before you commit any funds. Check out Frith Maier's *Trekking in Russia & Central Asia* (see Books), which is considered *the* source on adventure travel in Russia and the former Soviet Union. A good place to hook up with adventure travel groups, especially Russian mountaineers and outdoor enthusiasts, is through the geological expeditions which are based in many Russian cities and towns; another good bet is to look for Russian adventure travel clubs, which also pop up in towns and cities.

Much more information on possibilities and contacts in European Russia, Siberia and the Russian Far East can be found in the regional chapters and in Facts about Siberia & the Far East.

The firm the travel editor of the *Moscow Times* was thinking of is Pilgrim Tours (in Russian it's Moskovskoe Turisticheskoe Agentstvo Piligrim) (☎ (7 095) 365 45 63, 207 32 43; fax (7 095) 369 03 89; e-mail pilgrimtours@glas.apc.org), 1-y Kirpichny pereulok 17, Moscow; it's also mentioned in Frith Maier's book. It offers excursions, hiking, trekking or mountaineering trips in

EUROPEAN RUSSIA

Working in Russia

There are few people who came to Russia to get rich (the ones who did tend to be less like you and me and more like, say, Duane Andreas, chairman of the high-rolling, US government-sub-sidised, commodity brokering agro-giant Archer Daniels Midland Corporation). But working your way through Russia, especially if you've got some Russian language and a sophisticated sense of humour, is a great way to really get to know the country and its people.

While regulations on foreigners working in Russia are arcane and visa procedures Byzantine, getting permission to work here is, practically speaking, more a question of lining up your gig than fumbling with paperwork. Once you have an employer, all the red tape seems to disappear as though by magic, and a multiple-entry business visa will be yours once your new company's facilitators are on the job. There are taxes and duties and residence problems to be coped with, but these change so quickly and so regularly that committing them to ink is folly (though we're a follyful lot; see Visas & Embassies earlier in this chapter for some key regulations).

The question any applicant will face is whether to work for a Western or a Russian company. There are advantages and disadvantages to both, and it's really a question of what you're in it for that will decide. Generally speaking, though, a Western company will provide you with a level of financial security that will be unmatched by many Russian companies. This means that you will probably be paid.

Be especially careful if you're considering working for a large Russian company that has been doing business for years: that type of firm generally takes the longest to switch over to the idea that employees are people the company hires to do a job of work in exchange for money. Late payments, perhaps accompanied by colourful tales of corporate penury, are frequent, and non-payment is not uncommon. And should you complain too much, you'll no doubt be reminded of those poor bastards slaving away in Kamchatkan tractor combines who haven't been paid for seven months, or were last paid in tampons or spark plugs, and how much did those lovely Nike running shoes cost you back home in the decadent West where you live with your rich family?

If you can hold out financially, though, working for a Russian company can be rewarding in other ways, such as the chance to work on your command of the language and learn the ropes from a truly Russian perspective, and the possibility of pleasure and business trips with co-workers that will gain you entrée to activities and places that would probably be closed to foreigners under normal circumstances. If you're looking to live like a Russian, you should probably start by being paid like one.

---

the Caucasus, Kamchatka and other parts of the ex-USSR, plus kayaking, bicycling, cross-country and downhill skiing, helicopter skiing and what it refers to as a 'leisurely expedition to the North Pole'. Prices are reasonable, and the company comes highly recommended. It's also used by REI Adventures (see below).

Other Moscow firms offering adventure travel include Travel Russia (☎ (7 095) 290 34 39, 290 30 88; fax (7 095) 291 87 83) at korpus 2, Trubnikovsky pereulok 21, Moscow 121069; CCTE-Intour (☎ (7 095) 235 44 26; fax (7 095) 230 27 84), Ozerkovskaya naberezhnaya 50, Moscow 113532; and Sputnik (☎ (7 095) 939 80 65; fax (7 095) 938 11 92, 956 10 68), Hotel

Orlyonok, ulitsa Kosygina 15, Moscow 117946.

One excellent information source for north-western Russian adventure travel is the Scandinavian Study Centre, formerly the Econord Ecological Information Centre (☎ in Norway (47 78) 91 4010, then wait for a second tone and dial 118; ☎ in Apatity, Russia (7 81533) 3 72 62). This is a non-profit educational and cultural exchange centre, a joint venture between the Scandinavian and Russian 'Open University Systems'. See the Kola Peninsula section in Northern European Russia for more information.

Though some Western adventure travel firms have scaled down their activities in

Getting a job at a Western firm isn't as easy as it was in the early days, when all the CV you needed was your Western passport and your willingness to stay in the country. Today there's stiff competition for positions in Russia, which are seen as side-door entry ports to multinational corporations, or if you're already in the front door, a hardship post – to be followed by a cushy assignment at the end of your Russian tenure.

Along with the competition, there's also the fact that foreign companies consider your on-the-ground presence to be a profound plus; setting up the gig beforehand is much more difficult when you're competing with someone already established in Russia. Unless you've already got Russian contacts to assist you, the best strategy is simply to show up and establish yourself, and count on the job coming through some time after you've got a flat and you know the city. A huge percentage of long-term resident expatriates did things just that way.

Use resources overseas to get your search started. Operate on the theory that you won't get anything till you get there, but you can make things much easier by making as many connections as you can beforehand – a good rule of thumb is that if you can't get someone to meet you at the airport, you don't yet have enough connections. Check the *Moscow Times* and *St Petersburg Press* classified sections for jobs postings as well as employment services (headhunters). Check the *Russian Life's* adverts also. Use Internet connections to get into Russian business circles and establish a presence before you arrive. Check *The Traveller's Yellow Pages* and *Where In Moscow/St Petersburg* for companies in your field that are in Moscow, and contact their overseas offices.

The Expat Community

The expatriate community in Russia is a close-knit one; the feeling of being ground-breakers in a hostile territory is, though diminished over the last couple of years, still a major factor. Foreign business associations are well established in Moscow (which has an estimated 100,000 resident foreigners) and St Petersburg, and anywhere there are foreigners – from Texan oil workers in Nefteyugansk or Arkhangelsk to Canadian construction specialists at the Black Sea resorts to the Australian and North American geophysicists lurking about Karelia and the Kola Peninsula – there's at the very least a watering hole cum war-story forum. The network of expatriates looks after its own, and once you're accepted as a serious resident, it's as chummy as any old-boy network the West has to offer.

Nick Selby

Russia because of rising costs, several still offer a range of programmes including trekking, rafting, mountaineering and more. A good bet for a first contact in North America is REI Adventures (☎ (206) 891 2631, toll-free 800 622 2236; fax (206) 395 4744), PO Box 1938, Sumner, WA 98380-0880, USA, the most established American firm dealing in Russian adventure travel. Its trips cater to all levels, and REI offers discounts on packages purchased well in advance.

Inside Russia Sojourns (☎ (704) 265 4060) at RR 2 Box 324, Boone, NC 28607, USA, does bicycle trips together with its partner, the St Petersburg Bicycle Club. The trips run between St Petersburg and Moscow, and require moderate cycling skills. They use hotels and hostels when in cities and camp along the way. Inclusive packages for the two-week trips are around US$825 (airfare not included). The company also arranges homestays in St Petersburg, including city tours, and theatre/opera excursions. For groups of 10 or more, the price for inclusive ground packages (staying in flats) is US$350/person.

In Britain, experienced companies offering adventure trips – including treks, climbs, riding and skiing – in parts of Russia and the ex-Soviet Union include Exodus (☎ (0181) 675 5550, 673 0859; fax (0181) 673 0779) of 9 Weir Road, London SW12 0LT, and Steppes East (☎ (01285) 810 267; fax (01285) 810 693) of Castle Eaton, Swindon,

Wiltshire, SN6 6JU. Explore Worldwide (☎ (01252) 344 161) does trekking in the Caucasus and overland trips to the Golden Ring; it's at 1 Frederick Street, Aldershot, Hampshire, GU11 1LQ. Wild Explorer Holidays (☎ & fax (01471) 822 487) at Skye Environmental Centre, Broadford, Isle of Skye, IV49 9AQ, offers wolf and bear-watching trips.

Study

Many of the agencies that specialise in Russian travel (see European Russia – Getting There & Away) will offer Russian-language courses as a tour, which usually includes B&B and general-interest tours. For more serious students of Russian, a university course in Russia, complete with credit at your home university, can easily be arranged. Thanks to many factors, the Russian educational network is a wide-open scene these days, and educational exchange (in all areas, not just language studies) has never been easier. Check with universities in your city about exchange programmes.

The AAASS at Stanford University (fax (415) 725 7737) publishes an annual list of exchanges available; contact them directly for more information and a list of over 50 such programmes. Classic Tours (☎ (0171) 613 4441; fax (0171) 613 4024), 148 Curtain Road, London EC2A 3AR, offers 'Living Russian Language Programmes' in St Petersburg, which include side-trips to Moscow.

HIGHLIGHTS

Moscow and St Petersburg are by far Russia's two most fascinating cities – and a big contrast, so try to fit both into your plans. As well as the best palaces, museums and theatres, they have the best restaurants, the best nightlife and the best hotels – plus decent hostel-type accommodation geared to international budget travellers. There are many excellent short trips to be made out from both cities, too – especially to the 'Golden Ring' area of historic towns east of Moscow and the magnificent tsarist palaces and parks outside St Petersburg.

North of St Petersburg, the forests, rivers and lakes of Karelia offer some fine hiking and kayaking, as well as an extraordinary collection of old Russian wooden buildings on Kizhi Island in Lake Onega. Still further north, there's the curiosity of a port city inside the Arctic Circle (Murmansk) and some good climbing and skiing on the Kola Peninsula. From Arkhangelsk you can visit the Solovetsky Islands in the White Sea, with their monastery that was once one of Stalin's most infamous Gulag camps, and (with luck) get a glimpse of nuclear submarines at Severodvinsk.

Domes of the Cathedral of the Transfiguration, Kizhi Island

The mighty Volga is not so mighty now that it has been harnessed for hydroelectricity but you can see it in a relatively unfettered state at Golden Ring towns such as Yaroslavl or, further east, Nizhny Novgorod. Astrakhan, near the delta where the Volga enters the Caspian Sea, is an old Russian city but has reminders that Central Asia is close.

In the deep south are the spectacularly beautiful Caucasus mountains, with superb wild flowers in summer, relics of little-known ancient cultures and a fascinating ethnic mix among their modern inhabitants – though the conflicts that some of these have been embroiled in mean you shouldn't travel to parts of the Caucasus.

ACCOMMODATION

You're free to stay in any type of accommodation you can find in Russia. Gone are the days when tourists were restricted to specified hotels and a few grotty campsites, all of which had to be booked before you could even get a visa. You may need, or at least find it useful, to book a few nights before you get to Russia (see Visas & Embassies), but you're now rarely required to book the whole lot.

Details on specific places to stay, including (where relevant) how to book, can of course be found in Places to Stay sections in the various city chapters.

Hostels & Guesthouses

Moscow, St Petersburg and Novgorod now each have one or more youth or backpackers' hostels, all more or less in the international mould, most of them partly run by foreigners. Some are called 'Guest House' rather than 'Hostel'. These are easy places to stay as they're mostly geared to foreign budget travellers. Most of them are easy to book from outside Russia and can also provide the support you need for a visa (see Visas & Embassies). For the moment, most of them also have beds available if you just turn up at the door.

Accommodation is normally in five or six-bed dormitories or double rooms, each with their own toilet and bathroom, at around US$15 per person, and there are usually cooking facilities and/or cooked meals available.

One of the St Petersburg hostels is a member of Hostelling International (HI), the organisation that used to be called the International Youth Hostel Federation. The same hostel is also the hub of the non-profit national Russian Youth Hostel Association (RYHA; in Russia ☎ (812) 329 80 18, in the USA ☎ (310) 618 2014; fax (310) 618 1140; e-mail ryh@ryh.spb.su), which represents seven hostels and guesthouses in Russia. RYHA acts as a coordinating body for reservations and advance payments for, and information about, its member hostels, and can arrange visa invitations and paperwork for travellers staying at any of its hostels as well. By the time this book goes to press, RYHA may well have become a fully fledged member of Hostelling International; should that happen (and it looks likely), travellers will be able to make reservations through any HI member hostel via HI's International Booking Network (IBN). RYHA member hostels at the time of writing include: Travellers Guest House and G&R Hostel in Moscow, HI St Petersburg Hostel, Holiday Hostel and the Summer Hostel in St Petersburg, the Novgorod Youth Hostel in Novgorod and Baikalkomplex in Irkutsk (which accommodates travellers in private homes). You can, of course, reserve and contact all the above hostels directly, without going through RYHA: see city chapters for contact information.

Private Homes

It's not hard in many places to find a room in a private flat, shared with the owners. One good point about this type of accommodation – often referred as 'bed & breakfast' (B&B) or 'homestay' – is that it enables you to glimpse how Russians really live. Typically you get a two-bed room, use of a bathroom, and possibly cooking facilities. Most flats that take in guests are clean and respectable – though they're rarely large! If you stay in a few you'll be surprised, despite outward similarities, how different their owners can make them.

Moscow and St Petersburg have organisations specifically geared to accommodate foreign visitors in private flats at around US$20 or US$30 per person, normally with English-speaking hosts, breakfast included and other services such as excursions and extra meals available. Many travel agencies and tourism firms in these and other cities can also find you a place for something like US$15 per person, but the price may depend on things like how far the flat is from the city centre, whether the hosts speak English, and whether any meals are provided. It's also possible to pay the price Russians pay for staying in a private flat – about US$7 a night – by going with one of the people who approach travellers arriving off major trains in Moscow and St Petersburg, or finding a *kvartirnoe byuro*, which is an agency that places short-term guests in private flats. You'll want to be sure that you trust anyone who approaches you at a station (many of them really are genuine folks just in need of some extra cash) and establish how far from the city centre their place is before accompanying them. It's better to avoid committing yourself before you actually see the place. Kvartirnye byura are usually located in airports or Aeroflot offices and sometimes train or bus stations. In some places home-owners also wait around the entrances or lobbies of certain hotels offering rooms in their flats. Always establish the location first. If you're alone, it's possible you'll find yourself sharing the room with another guest.

Booking Homestays from Overseas

You can contact many Russian homestay agents from overseas (if you do, check that they can provide visa support too), but you can also book through many travel agencies in your own country.

One Russian organisation we have had good reports about is the St Petersburg-based Host Families Association (HOFA; ☎ & fax (7 812) 275 1992; e-mail alexei@hofak.stu .spb.su), which also has agents in the USA

(☎ (202) 333 9343), the UK (☎ (01295) 710 648) and Australia (☎ (03) 9725 8555). HOFA can provide places in St Petersburg, Moscow, Pskov, Saratov, Volgograd, some Siberian cities and nine cities in other ex-Soviet countries. It offers visa support.

The following are among agents in other countries that specialise to varying degrees in Russian homestays. Some can offer places in a wide range of Russian and other former Soviet Union cities (see Travel Agencies in the European Russia Getting There & Away chapter for contact details of the UK and Australian outfits):

Australia
    Eastern Europe Travel Bureau
    Gateway Travel
    Iris Hotels
    Red Bear Tours
UK
    Goodwill Holidays
    Zwemmer Travel
USA
    American-International Homestays (☎ toll-free 1 800 876 2048), PO Box 7178, Boulder, CO 80306-7178
    Helen Kates (☎ & fax (603) 585 6534), PO Box 221, Fitzwilliam, NH 03447 – the US agent for Moscow Bed & Breakfast
    Home & Host International (☎ (612) 871 0596; fax (612) 871 8853), 2445 Park Avenue, Minneapolis, Minnesota 55404
    International Bed & Breakfast (☎ toll-free 800 422 5283; fax (215) 663 8580), PO Box 823, Huntingdon Valley, PA 19006

Normal prices are between US$25 and US$50 per person a night, usually with breakfast and English-speaking hosts included. HOFA offers discounts for students, for stays of a week or more, and other things. Some of these companies also offer more expensive packages including excursions, all meals, and so on. It's worth knowing that your host family usually only gets a small fraction of the price you pay the agent.

Student Dormitories

In Moscow, St Petersburg and one or two other places it's possible to stay in Russian student accommodation. Prices range from about US$2.50 to US$15 a night. The accommodation is not unlike what you get in a hostel or guest house. Getting in can sometimes be a bit iffy – it depends on availability or even the administrator's mood. A student card, and looking like a student, certainly help.

Hotels

Russian hotels run the gamut from flyblown licetraps where for a couple of dollars you can, if you wish, share a room (and a single unflushable toilet down the corridor) with a gang of male market traders from the 'southern republics', to international five-star palaces full of Western business people whose slumbers cost their companies US$400 a night.

Most hotels have one price for Russians and another, about four times as high, for foreigners. There's little you can do about this (even if you go with Russian friends you'll often still have to pay the foreigner price). The only exceptions are a few hotels, mostly in out-of-the-way places, that get very few foreigners and haven't heard there are such things as foreigner prices. (Don't tell them!)

At most hotels, you can just walk in and get a room on the spot. If you can't, it will probably be for one of four reasons:

- the hotel is genuinely full (extremely rare);
- the receptionist/administrator thinks that because you haven't got their town named on your visa you can't stay there (almost as rare) – they're wrong, but there may not be much you can do about it;
- they say their hotel doesn't take foreigners – either because they think it's so bad you couldn't possibly want to stay there (they can usually be persuaded otherwise, though when you've seen round some places you might agree with them) or because they didn't take foreigners in Soviet times and they don't know times have changed (this happens more often in out-of-the-way places);
- or the hotel belongs to some institute or organisation and only takes people booked in through special channels.

Procedures & Populace At virtually all hotels you have to show your passport and

visa when you check in – and they may keep it till next day to register your presence with the local OVIR. Don't worry about this – it's normal – but do remember to get your passport and visa back before you leave. It's possible that no one will remind you. At decent hotels you get a little card or slip of paper with your room number and the hotel's details on it. Carry this with you: you may be asked to show it to get back into the hotel when you've been out.

In most hotels except the cheapest and the expensive new foreign ones, each floor has a floor lady (dezhurnaya) to keep an eye on it. They're well worth making friends with. Often the dezhurnaya and the room cleaners are the nicest people in the place, almost always able to supply you with snacks, bottled drinks or boiled water.

Once you've got your room, it's worth having a good look round the hotel to find out where and when you can eat and drink. Take the lift up to the highest floor for a view over the city – often spectacular and useful in getting your bearings.

Hotels with significant numbers of foreigners attract prostitutes – which is what any well-dressed young Russian woman hanging around a lobby or bar without other apparent purpose is likely to be.

Checkout time is usually noon, but no one usually minds if you stay an extra hour or two. If you want to store your luggage somewhere safe for a late departure, arrange it with the dezhurnaya.

Rooms Many hotels have a range of rooms at widely differing prices but may automatically offer foreigners the most expensive, often claiming that cheaper ones are 'not suitable' or that there are 'many gipsies' on the cheaper floors. A little persistence may be needed if you want a cheaper room.

Not all hotels have genuine single rooms and 'single' prices often refer to single occupancy of a double room. If a hotel has real singles, but they're all full, it may let a single traveller occupy a double for the single-room rate. Another option occasionally offered is to share a double with someone else. Some hotels, mainly in the bottom end and lower middle range, have rooms for three or four people where the price per person comes to much less than in a single or double.

Some hotels offer lower rates for second and subsequent nights of your stay.

An average hotel room measures about four by five metres and has its own bathroom containing a toilet, washbasin, shower and/or bath, loo paper, soap and a couple of small towels. Hot water supplies are fairly reliable: but since hot water is supplied on a district basis, whole neighbourhoods can be without it for a month or more in summer when the system is shut down for maintenance (the best hotels, however, somehow manage to avoid this).

Virtually all beds are single. Russian pillows are large and square: folding them in half is one way to make them comfortable. Some sheets are double-layered and have big holes in the middle so that blankets can be stuffed into them to make a kind of quilt in winter.

A *lyux* room is a kind of suite, with a sitting room in addition to the bedroom and bathroom.

Bottom End These are the places they didn't let foreigners see (or save money in) in Soviet times. A bottom-end hotel typically costs around US$15/20 (US$20/30 in St Petersburg, US$25/35 in Moscow) for singles/doubles, though if it hasn't discovered foreigner prices you may pay US$6/8 or so. You can even bargain a bit in a few places. Some have cheap, dormitory-type rooms where you share with whoever else happens to be there.

Rooms may have their own toilet, washbasin or shower, or you may have to use facilities shared by the whole corridor. Some places are clean, if fusty, and even run to TV or a fridge in the rooms; others are decaying, dirty, smelly and lack decent toilets and washing facilities. In some cheap hotels you do have to take care with security. Don't leave money or other valuables anywhere obvious in the room when you go out.

Middle Range These are mainly Soviet-era tourist hotels, typically concrete and glass rectangles, though some of the older ones have a bit more style. They have clean, reasonably comfortable rooms with proper bathrooms and often small balconies. They'll have a restaurant or two – often with a dance floor and an ear-numbing pop group – plus a couple of bars or the snack bars called *bufety*, буфеты ('*bu-FYET-i*'), sometimes secreted away at the end of the corridor on the 11th floor, and, increasingly often, a casino haunted by sleazy mafiosi (they'll steer clear of you if you steer clear of them). Singles/doubles can cost from US$25/35 to US$50/80 (in St Petersburg US$30/35 to US$120/140, in Moscow US$50/70 to US$130/150 – it should be said that standards are often higher in the two big cities).

To date, Russia has disappointingly few of the small, cosy, moderately priced new hotels that have sprung up in the Baltic states, for instance. The only serious attempt at setting up new middle-range hotels has been made by Mikof-Iris Hotels, which runs a chain of decent hotels attached to eye microsurgery clinics across Russia. Unfortunately many of them are a long way from city centres and we found several that were at least temporarily closed. The Mikof-Iris office in Moscow (☎ (095) 483 04 60; fax (095) 485 59 54) is at Suite 266, Beskudnikovsky bulvar 59A. Its foreign partner is Iris Hotels (☎ (02) 580 6466; fax (02) 580 7256), PO Box 60, Hurstville, NSW 2220, Australia.

Top End The real top end is the new wave of mostly Western-run luxury hotels, nearly all in Moscow and St Petersburg. These are up to the best international standards, with very comfortable rooms boasting satellite TV, minibars, hair dryers etc, good service, fine restaurants, health clubs, and prices to match, from around US$200/250 to US$350/400 a single/double (and that's before you even think about a suite).

Outside the two big cities the 'top end', where it exists, is composed mainly of the very best Soviet-era tourist hotels, along with the occasional former Communist Party hotel or small new private venture. You may pay from US$60/100 to US$130/150.

You may get better prices for top-end hotels if you prebook through a travel agent in Russia or abroad.

Tourbases

A tourbase (turbaza) is a holiday camp for Russians, usually owned by a factory or large company for the use of its employees. They range from absolutely Spartan to somewhat luxurious, and many are now open to foreign tourists. Lodging options usually consist of a large common room with six or more beds, smaller doubles and private cottages. All are cheap: usually US$10/15 or less. There are reasons: many have no indoor plumbing, and usually the only place to eat is a stolovaya (canteen). But, if you bring a good supply of food and a sense of adventure, these are a great way to get a feel for the average Russian's holiday. At some, you can arrange boating, skiing, hiking or mountaineering trips.

Camping

Camping in the wild is legal in many places, except where posted (Не разбивать палатку, 'No putting up of tents', and/or Не разжигать костов, 'No campfires') and if you're off the beaten track it is usually legal and fine just to put up a tent and hit the hay. Check with locals if you're in doubt.

Organised camp sites (kempingi) are increasingly rare (some now house troops returned from Germany, the Baltics etc) and are usually open only from some time in June to some time in September. They're not quite like camp sites in the West: small wooden cabins often take up much of the space, leaving little room for tents. Some kempingi are on the fringes of cities but may be in quite attractive woodland settings; however, communal toilets and washrooms are often filthy and other facilities few.

FOOD

Things have improved beyond recognition since late Soviet times, but eating in Russia (outside Moscow and St Petersburg) is not yet quite a matter of just popping into the local café for a quick bite.

Restaurants, shops and markets do have food, and usually a fair choice of it. It's just that, in some towns, there aren't very many of them. You won't starve – you needn't usually go hungry – but sometimes you may have to walk a long way to find a meal. Things are different in Moscow and, especially, St Petersburg, where there are dozens of good places to eat.

Most eateries are now easy to get into – bribe-demanding door attendants, and waiters who say 'full' when the number of empty tables could give you agoraphobia, are now, thankfully, more or less creatures of the past. Reservations are advisable only at a few genuinely busy places, mainly in Moscow and St Petersburg. Service is still grumpy in some places but at least the waiters no longer pretend you're not there.

One thing you need to watch out for, though, is opening and closing times. All too often outside the two big cities an eatery is not yet open, or just closing, right when you feel hungry. The best times to be sure of getting a meal are between 1 and 2 pm for lunch and between 6.30 and 8 pm for dinner.

Food in run-of-the-mill Russian restaurants tends to be bland, rich, heavy on meat, potatoes and overboiled or pickled vegetables, and light on fresh vegetables, dairy products and fresh fruit. Try to get into the Russian way of starting with a few zakuski (hors d'oeuvres), which are often the most interesting items on the menu. 'Main' courses are smaller than Westerners are used to and can be very uninspired.

There's been a big growth in non-Russian restaurants and in Moscow or St Petersburg you can eat excellent Italian, Mexican, Indian, French, American and many other meals. Most of these have foreign management and foreign standards of service – though, often, foreign price levels too. They're a lot thinner on the ground outside the two big cities but still pop up here and there.

Don't miss the cuisine of the former

Soviet republic of Georgia, with unique, spicy dishes that do justice to both meat and vegetables. There are quite a few Georgian restaurants in European Russia.

Fast food, too, has arrived in Russia – a blessing when you don't want to waste one or two hours just staving off hunger.

Dress in all but the top-end restaurants is modest but informal. Russian women often put some effort into their appearance when eating out.

Where to Eat

Self-Catering Now that the long queues and empty window displays of leaner times are history, self-catering can be a good and interesting option.

Food Shops Moscow and St Petersburg have lots of foreign-run supermarkets where you can get most of what you're used to back home. Cheaper everywhere are Russian food shops, a few of which are like supermarkets themselves, with a big range of goods, while others specialise in certain types of food. Most are pretty well stocked, often with imported as well as Russian food, though many still have the infuriating system whereby you have to queue three times for each purchase – once to find out its price, once to pay, and once to collect it. It's advisable to take your own bag to put your purchases in.

One inexpensive staple Russian food you might want to buy for long journeys is *kolbasa*, salami-like sausage, which is eaten cold, in slices, and can go down pretty well with bread, tomato and raw onion. It comes in various types and guises – thin or fat, herby or garlicky, but always long.

Types of food shop include:

Булочная (*'BOO-luch-nuh-yuh'*) – bakery; Russian bread is generally good

Гастроном (*'guh-stra-NOHM'*) – grocery or speciality-food shop

Кондитерская (*'kun-DEE-tir-skuh-yuh'*) – confectionery

Кулинария (*'ku-li-NAR-ee-ya'*) – with prepared foods like cabbage salad and ready-to-heat cutlets; some have cheap on-site cafés too

Markets Every sizeable town has a market, рынок (*'RIH-nuk'*), where locals sell spare potatoes and carrots from their dacha plots and bigger traders offload truckfuls of melons, oranges, bananas – you name it – often from the Transcaucasus or even Central Asia. You'll often find dried fruit, cheese, nuts, honey, meat and other foods in markets too. Take your own shopping bag. Markets are colourful places to visit even if you don't need to buy; go early in the morning for the liveliest scene and best selection.

You can usually bargain a bit over prices. Watch carefully that the vendor doesn't select the most rotten or shrivelled items to pop into your bag.

Hotel Restaurants All hotels, except a few bottom-end places, always have *somewhere* you can eat, and most of them are open to non-residents too. A standard provincial hotel will typically have a restaurant (ресторан, *'ri-sta-RAHN'*) serving Russian food, a bar (бар) which serves a few snacks, and one or two bufety tucked away on the upper floors. A bufet sells cold meats, boiled eggs, salads, bread, pastries etc, plus tea/coffee and soft and alcoholic drinks. If you want to take something back to your room, say *soboy* (*'sa-BOY'*).

Better hotels have a choice of restaurants – one or two of which may be reserved for tour groups – and maybe a couple of cafés/bars serving light meals. Worse ones may only have a sloppy stolovaya, столовая (*'sta-LO-vuh-yuh'*), or canteen.

It's worth checking out the hours of your hotel's eateries when you arrive: the main restaurant will serve breakfast from around 8 to 10 am; lunch from around noon to 3 or 4 pm; and dinner from around 6 to 10 pm – but may run out of enthusiasm about halfway through each session, notably for breakfast, which can often be hard to get after 9 am. A lunch or dinner of a couple of zakuski, soup, a main course, a beer and a coffee might cost US$8, but prices are variable.

Hotel restaurants often have a dance floor and in the evening may be plagued by gale-force music from live pop bands, and groups of revellers who get more and more drunk as the night proceeds. You can usually avoid these by going early – say by 7 pm – for dinner. You may get better service then too, as the restaurant will be less busy. Bars and bufety open at bizarre hours whose logic may be understood by their staff but certainly isn't by anyone else – but at least the times are usually posted on the door.

Some tourist hotels have a Swedish Table, шведский стол ('SHFET-ski stol') – a cafe-teria where you can eat as much as you like for a moderate price. They're convenient but the food's usually pretty stodgy.

Other Restaurants These run the gamut from excellent to awful. Best are generally the privately run ones. You can tell these by their individualistic appearance: from signs and décor to what the waiters wear and the way the menu is laid out – they're all different. Privately-run restaurants range from expensive foreign ones (mostly in Moscow and St Petersburg) to more modest Russian, Georgian and other places which usually still put some effort into their food. They open longish hours – typically from about noon to 10 pm, maybe with a break from about 5 to 6 pm. You can pay US$40 or more for a full dinner with drinks in a top Moscow or St Petersburg restaurant, or under US$10 for a meal elsewhere.

State-run restaurants mostly look like hangovers from Soviet times – and they are – with 1970s-style signs and décor, and unenthusiastic waiters. They serve almost exclusively Russian food, which can be good or can be bland, overcooked and greasy. They open similar hours to hotel restaurants and have similar prices.

Cafés A kafe, кафе ('kah-FYEH'), can be anything from an ice-cream parlour to an elegant small restaurant. Most are mini-restaurants which concentrate on a limited menu: pizza, hot sausages, pelmeni, the odd salad, sweet dishes. They tend to open and close earlier than restaurants and be a bit cheaper. A gril-bar is usually a café that specialises in grilled chicken.

Stolovaya A stolovaya is the common person's eatery. It's dreary but cheap (you can often fill up for under US$1) with a small, less-than-mouthwatering choice of cutlet or fish or meatballs, soup, boiled vegetables, bread, tea and coffee. Slide your tray along the counter and the staff will ladle out what you point at. You'll often find them in market or station areas. They have poetic names such as Stolovaya No 32. Some are decent, some very grotty.

Fast Food A few Western fast-food chains have hit Moscow and St Petersburg, where they're incredibly popular. The original Moscow McDonald's is reckoned to be the world's busiest restaurant. Elsewhere Russian imitators are getting in on the act with outlets which may be a street kiosk or even a van, or may be a café with tables. Pizza (in some unique local forms – the worst has a thick, soggy base and couple of curling sausage slices on top) is common, burgers (similarly variable) and kebabs (often the Russian shashlyk form) reasonably so.

Snack Shops Around parks and markets, on streets, near railway and bus stations are cheap, often stand-up places selling one or two items plus a drink. They're usually a poor introduction to their respective products but they're handy and cheap. 'Takeaway' is на вынос ('na VIH-nus'). Types of snack shop include:

Блинная ('BLEE-nuh-yuh') serves bliny, pancakes with savoury or sweet fillings

Бутербродная ('bu-tir-BROD-nuh-yuh') serves little open sandwiches

Закусочная ('zuh-KU-such-nuh-yuh') serves miscellaneous snacks

Пельменная ('pil-MYEN-uh-yuh') serves pelmeni, meat ravioli

Пирожковая ('pi-ra-SHKO-vuh-yuh') serves pirozhki, deep-fried meat or vegetable turnovers

Сосиская ('sa-SEES-kuh-yuh') serves sausages with bread and mustard

Чебуречная ('chi-bu-RECH-nuh-yuh') serves Georgian or Armenian chebureki, spicy deep-fried mutton pies

Шашлычная ('shush-LICH-nuh-yuh') serves shashlyk, charcoal-grilled meat kebabs

Ice-Cream Parlours Russians love ice cream, bought anywhere you see the label morozhenoe, мороженое ('ma-ROH-zhi-nah-yuh'). It's not unusual to see people gobbling dishfuls of it at outdoor tables in freezing weather. An ice-cream parlour is a kafe-morozhenoe. There's a lot of imported ice cream now, but the Russian variety is good too.

Booking Restaurants

If you do reserve a table at a restaurant, it's worth specifying chistyy stol ('clean table') to avoid finding an expensive array of zakuski already laid out on your table when you arrive. It's not too difficult, with a little Russian, to book a table by phone. Otherwise, go along and ask for the manager. Phrases you may find useful include:

Who is the manager?
kto ud-mi-ni-STRAH-tor?
Кто администратор?
I want to book a table.
ya kha-CHU zuh-kuh-ZAHT STO-lik
Я хочу заказать столик.
How many people?
SKOL-ka chi-la-VYEK-av?
Сколько человеков?
Two (three, four) people.
dva (tri, chi-TIR-yeh) chi-la-VYEK-uh
Два (три, четыре) человека.
At what time?
fka-TOR-um chuh-SOO?
В котором часу?
1 o'clock
ah-DYIN chas
(один) час

2 (3, 4) o'clock
dva (tri, chi-TIR-yeh) chuh-SAH
два (три, четыре) часа
5 (6, 7, 8, 9) o'clock
pyat (shest, sem, VO-syim, DYEV-yut)
chu-SOF
пять (шесть, семь, восемь, девять) часов
today
si-VOHD-nyuh
сегодня
tomorrow
ZAHF-truh
завтра
in the evening
VYEH-chi-rum
вечером
Surname?
fuh-MEE-li-uh?
фамилия?
When do you open (close)?
kug-DA ot-KRIT-uh (zuh-KRIT-uh)?
Когда открыто (закрыто)?
break (between afternoon and evening meal)
pee-ree-RIF
Перерыв

Ordering & Paying

Foreign-run restaurants and others with foreign customers (such as those in tourist hotels) have English (or French or German) language menus. If a menu is in Russian only, you may in some places get some translation help from the waiter. On menus, only items with prices beside them are 'on', and if you're unlucky some of these will have run out too. Some menus are such faint carbon copies, with a mess of corrections and additions typed or written over them, that even Russians can't understand them. If the menu defeats you – as it often does – you can just say 'What do you recommend?', Что вы посоветуете? ('shto vih pa-sa-VYEH-tu-yeh-tyeh?'). Or you could point at what others have. Visits to the kitchen are frowned upon.

If a waiter – or your food – is taking an eternity to appear, ponder a word Russian has given to the universal vocabulary of eating. After the victory over Napoleon, impatient

Russian soldiers in Paris cafés would bang their tables and shout *bystro, bystro!* (quickly, quickly!), from which came the bistro. Only since the Soviet Union collapsed in 1991, it seems, has the idea started to catch on back at home.

waiter, waitress
 ah-fit-si-AHNT , ah-fit-si-AHNT-kuh
 официант,официантка
menu
 min-YU
 меню
hot
 gar-YA-chi
 горячий
cold
 kha-LOHD-ni
 холодный
more
 yee-SHCHO
 ещё
May we order?
 MOZH-na zuh-kuh-ZAHT?
 Можно заказать?
Please bring...
 pri-nyeh-SEE-tyeh, pa-ZHAHL-stuh...
 Принесите, пожалуйста...
That's all.
 vsyo
 Всё.
Bon appetit!
 pri-AHT-na-va ah-pih-TEET-a!
 Приятного аппетита!

When you're done you'll have to chase up the bill, счёт *('schyot')*. If there's a service charge, noted on the menu by the words за обслуживание (for service), there's no need to tip further unless the service has been exceptional (see also Money – Tipping).

Breakfast
Breakfast or *zavtrak*, завтрак *('ZAHF-truk')*, in hotels can range from a large help-yourself buffet spread to bread, butter, jam, tea and a boiled egg (or, worse, a pair of cold meatballs). Items you might find include:

Блины *('blee-NIH')* – *bliny* or leavened buckwheat pancakes; as блинчики, *blinchiki*, they're rolled around meat or cheese and browned
Каша – *kasha* or Russian-style buckwheat porridge
Сырники *('SEER-ni-ki')* – fritters of cottage cheese, flour and milk
Творог *('tva-ROK')* – cottage cheese
Яйцо *('yai-TSOH')* – egg
 всмятку *('FSMYAT-ku')* – soft-boiled
 крутое *('kru-TOY-eh')* – hard-boiled
 омлет *('ahm-LYET')* – omelette
 яичница *('yuh-EECH-nit-suh')* – fried
кефир *('kyi-FEER')* – yoghurt-like sour milk, served as a drink

Bliny, kasha and syrniki can be delicious if topped with some combination of jam, sugar and the universal Russian condiment, sour cream, сметана *('smi-TAH-nuh')*.

Lunch & Dinner
Russians often like a fairly heavy early-afternoon meal, *obed*, обед *('ah-BYET')*, and a lighter evening meal, *uzhin*, ужин *('OO-zhin')*, but a night-out supper can go on and on.

Meals (and menus) are divided into courses:

Закуски – *zakuski* or appetisers, often grouped into холодные закуски (cold zakuski) and горячие закуски (hot zakuski)
Первые блюда – first courses, usually soups
Вторые блюда – second courses or 'main' dishes, also called горячие блюда (hot courses)
Сладкие блюда – sweet courses or desserts

Main dishes may be further divided into:

Фирменные – house specials
Национальные – national or ethnic dishes
Порционные – special orders
Мясные – meat
Рыбные – fish
Из птицы – poultry
Овощные – vegetable

Appetisers The fancier zakuski rival main courses for price. Of course try the caviar, икра (*'ee-KRA'*). The best is black (sturgeon) caviar, *ikra chyornaya*, also called *zernistaya*. Much cheaper and saltier is red (salmon) caviar, *ikra krasnaya*, also called *ketovaya*. Russians spread it on buttered toast or bliny and wash it down with a slug of vodka. There's also ersatz caviar made entirely from aubergine or other vegetables.

A few other zakuski worth trying include:

Блины со сметаной (*'blee-NIH sa-smi-TA-noy'*) – pancakes with sour cream
Грибы в сметане (*'gree-BIH fsmi-TA-nyeh'*) or жульен из грибов (*'zhool-YEN eez gree-BOF'*) – mushrooms baked in sour cream, obscenely good
Рыба солёная (*'RIH-buh sahl-YO-nuh-yuh'*) – salted fish
Сёмга копчёная (*'SYOM-guh kahp-CHO-nuh-yuh'*) – smoked salmon

Salad, салат (*'suh-LAHT'*), is an appetiser too. Most likely you'll be offered one with tomatoes, из помидоров (*'eez pa-mi-DOR-uf'*), or cucumbers, из огурцов (*'eez a-goort-SOF'*), or the ubiquitous салат столичный (*'suh-LAHT sta-LEECH-ni'*), comprised of vegetable and beef bits, potato and egg in sour cream and mayonnaise.

Soup Rich soups may be the pinnacle of Slavic cooking. There are dozens of varieties, often served with a dollop of sour cream. Most are made from meat stock. The Russian word sounds the same, суп.

Among the most common soups are:

Борщ (*'borshch'*) – beetroot soup with vegetables and meat
Лапша (*'LAHP-shuh'*) – chicken noodle soup
Окрошка (*'a-KROHSH-kuh'*) – cold or hot soup made from cucumbers, sour cream, potatoes, egg, meat and *kvas* (a beer-like drink)
Рассольник (*'rah-SOL-nik'*) – soup of marinated cucumber and kidney
Солянка (*'sahl-YAHNK-uh'*) – thick meat or fish soup with salted cucumbers and other vegetables
Уха (*'OO-khuh'*) – fish soup with potatoes and vegetables
Харчо (*'khar-CHOH'*) – garlicky mutton soup, Caucasian-style
Щи (*'shchi'*) – cabbage or sauerkraut soup (many varieties)

Poultry & Meat Poultry is птица (*'PTEET-suh'*) – and is usually chicken, курица (*'KOO-rit-suh'*) or цыплёнок (*'tsi-PLYOH-nuk'*). Meat is мясо (*'MYA-suh'*); in particular:

Баранина (*'buh-RA-ni-nuh'*) – mutton
Говядина (*'gav-YA-di-nuh'*) – beef
Свинина (*'sfi-NEE-nuh'*) – pork

Cooking Styles Words you might spot on the menu:

Варёный (*'var-YOH-ni'*) – boiled
Жареный (*'ZHAR-ih-ni'*) – roast, baked or fried
Отварной (*'aht-var-NOY'*) – poached or boiled
Печёный (*'pi-CHOH-ni'*) – baked
Фри (*'free'*) – fried

Dishes The list of possible dishes (and possible names) is huge, but following are some common meat and poultry dishes:

Антрекот (*'ahn-tri-KOHT'*) – entrecôte, boned sirloin steak
Бефстроганов (*'byef-STRO-guh-nof'*) – beef Stroganoff, beef slices in a rich sauce
Бифштекс (*'bif-SHTEKS'*) – 'steak', usually a glorified hamburger filling
Голубцы (*'ga-loop-TSIH'*) – *golubtsy*, cabbage rolls stuffed with meat
Жаркое (*'zhar-KOY-eh'*) – meat or poultry stewed in a clay pot; most common seems to be жаркое по-домашнему (*'...pa-da-MAHSH-ni-mu'*), 'home-style', with mushrooms, potatoes and vegetables
Котлета (*'kaht-LYET-uh'*) – this is usually a croquette of ground meat; котлета по-

пожарская ('...pa-pa-ZHAR-ska-ya') is minced chicken

Котлета по-киевски ('kaht-LYET-uh pa-KEE-iv-ski') – chicken Kiev, fried boneless chicken breast stuffed with butter (watch out, it squirts!)

Пельмени ('pil-MYEN-i') – pelmeni or Siberian-style meat dumplings

Плов – plov or pilaf, rice with mutton bits, from Central Asia

Цыплёнок табака ('tsi-PLYOH-nuk tuh-buh-KAH') – chicken Tabaka, grilled chicken Caucasian-style

Шашлык – shashlyk, skewered and grilled mutton or other meat, adapted from Central Asia and Transcaucasia

Fish Fish is рыба ('RIH-buh'). Some common varieties are:

Омуль ('OH-mool') – omul, like salmon, from Lake Baikal

Осётр ('a-SYOTR'), осетрина ('a-si-TREE-nuh') or севрюга ('siv-RYU-guh') – sturgeon

Сёмга ('SYOM-guh') – salmon

Судак ('su-DAHK') – pike perch

Форель ('far-YEL') – trout

Two good sturgeon dishes are:

Осетрина отварная ('a-si-TREE-nuh aht-VAR-nuh-yuh') – poached sturgeon

Осетрина с грибами ('a-si-TREE-nuh zgree-BUH-mi') – with mushrooms

Vegetables Vegetables are овощи ('OH-va-shchi'); greens are зелень ('ZYEH-lin'). Any vegetable garnish is гарниры ('gar-NEE-ri'). Common vegetables include:

Горо ('ga-ROKH') – peas

Капуста ('kuh-POOS-tuh') – cabbage

Картошка ('kar-TOSH-kuh'), картофель ('kar-TOF-il') – potato

Морковь ('mar-KOF') – carrots

Огурец ('a-gur-YETS') – cucumber

Помидор ('pa-mi-DOR') – tomato

Fruit Fruits are фрукты ('FROOK-ti'). In the market (or if you're lucky, in a restaurant) you might find:

Абрикос ('uh-bri-KOS') – apricot

Арбуз ('ar-BOOS') – watermelon

Виноград ('vi-na-GRAHT') – grapes

Груша ('GROO-shuh') – pear

Дыня ('DIN-yuh') – melon

Яблоко ('YA-bla-ka') – apple

Other Foods On every table are stacks of bread, хлеб ('khlep'). Best is Russian 'black' bread, a vitamin-rich sour rye.

Russians are mad about wild mushrooms, грибы ('gree-BIH'); in late summer and early autumn they troop into the woods with their buckets. Other items:

Рис ('rees') – rice

Сыр ('seer') – cheese

Масло ('MAHS-la') – butter

Перец ('PYER-its') – pepper

Сахар ('SA-khar') – sugar

Соль ('sol') – salt

Desserts Perhaps most Russians are exhausted or drunk by dessert time, since this is the least imaginative course. Most likely you'll get ice cream, мороженое ('ma-ROH-zhi-nah-yuh'). Other possibilities are:

Блинчики ('BLEEN-chi-ki') – pancakes with jam or other sweet filling

Кисель ('ki-SEL') – fruit jelly (jell-o to Yanks)

Компот ('kahm-POHT') – fruit in syrup (probably from a tin)

Оладьи ('a-LAH-dyi') – fritters topped with syrup

Пирожное ('pi-ROZH-na-yuh') – pastries

For Vegetarians

Russia is rough on a vegetarian – though some private restaurants have caught on. Main dishes are heavy on meat and poultry, vegetables are boiled to death and even the good vegetable and fish soups are usually made from meat stock.

If you're vegetarian, say so, early and often. You'll see a lot of cucumber and tomato salads, and will develop an eagle eye for the rare good fish and dairy dishes. Zakuski include quite a lot of meatless things like eggs, salted fish and mushrooms. If you spot обощи свежие, fresh (raw) vegetables on the menu, you're in luck!

Menus often have a category like овощные, молочные, яичные, мучные блюда (vegetable, milk, egg and flour dishes) – but don't get your hopes up. You may have to just run down the names of things you can eat, rather than relying on the waiter to think of something.

By the way, potatoes *(kartoshka, kartofel)* aren't filed under 'vegetable' in the Russian mind, so you must name them separately: 'potatoes and vegetables'.

I'm a vegetarian (f).
　ya vi-gi-ta-ri-AHN-ka
　Я вегетарианка.
I'm a vegetarian (m).
　ya vi-gi-ta-ri-AHN-yets
　Я вегетарианец.
I cannot eat meat.
　ya ni yem myis-NOH-va
　Я не ем мясного.
without meat
　bis MYA-suh
　без мяса
only vegetables
　TOL-ka OH-va-shchi
　только овощи

Lobio, a dish made with haricot beans and walnuts

DRINKS

'Drinking is the joy of the Rus. We cannot live without it.' With these words Vladimir of Kiev, the father of the Russian state, is said to have rejected abstinent Islam on his people's behalf in the 10th century. And who wouldn't want to bend their minds now and then during those long, cold, dark winters? Russians sometimes drink vodka in moderation, but more often it's tipped down in swift shots, with a beer, with the aim of getting legless.

The *average* Russian drinks more than 12 litres of pure alcohol a year – equivalent to over a bottle of vodka a week – and men drink much more than women.

The nearest thing to a pub is a *traktir* (tavern), but these are not common. Nor, except in hotels, are bars that serve nothing but drink. A lot of public drinking (other than on park benches) goes on in restaurants and cafés – and, since many of these are in hotels, the average tourist is likely to encounter quite a lot of it. In restaurants, in combination with music and dancing, drinking produces some pretty unrestrained behaviour by the end of many evenings. This makes restaurants fun places *if* you're in the mood. If you find yourself sharing a table with locals, it's odds-on they'll press you to drink with them. Even people from distant tables, spotting foreigners, may be seized with hospitable urges. If it's vodka that's being drunk, they'll want a man to down the shot – neat of course – in one; women are usually excused. This can be fun to start with as you toast international friendship etc, but vodka has a knack of creeping up on you from behind and if that happens just after you've started tucking into steak, chips and fried egg, the consequences can be appalling. A slice of heavily buttered bread before each shot, or a beer the morning after, are reckoned to be vodka antidotes.

Refusing a drink can be very difficult. Russians may continue to insist until they win you over, especially on some train rides. If you can't manage to stand quite firm, take it in small gulps with copious thanks, while saying how you'd love to indulge but have to be up early in the morning etc. And if you're really not in the mood, the only tested and true method of warding off all offers (as well as making them feel quite awful) is to say *'Ya alkogolik'* (*'alkogolichka'* for women) – 'I'm an alcoholic'.

Alcohol

You can buy it everywhere. Kiosks, shops, bars, restaurants – you name it. Foreign brands as well as Russian are common. But be very suspicious of kiosk spirits. There's a lot of bad cheap stuff around that can make you ill. Only buy screw-top – never tin-top – bottles. Always check to see that the seal is not broken. Taste carefully any liquor you've bought at a kiosk to make sure it's really what it's supposed to be, and that it hasn't been diluted or tampered with. Err on the side of caution.

In a restaurant you can order drinks by the bottle (which could be half-litre, three-quarter-litre or litre) or, for smaller quantities, by weight: 50 grams, equal to 50 ml, for one shot, maybe 200 grams in a small flask for a few shots.

Vodka Vodka is distilled from wheat, rye or occasionally potatoes. The word comes from *voda* (water), and means something like 'a wee drop'. Its flavour (if any) comes from what's added after distillation. Two common 'plain' vodkas are Stolichnaya, which is in fact slightly sweetened with sugar, and Moskovskaya, which has a touch of sodium bicarbonate. Tastier, more colourful and rarer are Zolotoe Koltso (Golden Ring), Pertsovka (pepper vodka), Starka (with apple and pear leaves), Limonnaya (lemon vodka), and Okhotnichya (Hunter's), which has about a dozen ingredients, including peppers, juniper berries, ginger and cloves. Zubrovka, one of God's gifts to humanity, is flavoured with bison grass but is unfortunately very hard to find outside Poland.

Sure enough, the fashion for Western products has extended even unto vodka. The more popular imports are Smirnoff (made in Connecticut, USA), Absolut (and all its varieties), Gorbachow, Rasputin and New Yorkskaya.

Supermarket and liquor store prices range from around US$2.50 for a half-litre of Stolichnaya or Moskovskaya to US$18 for the most exotic ones. Average kiosk prices in 1994 were: Russkaya US$1, Stolichnaya US$1.50 to US$3, Absolut plain US$10, Absolut Citron US$13.50, Absolut Kurant US$15.

Beer Ordinary Russian beer is hoppy. It's also not pasteurised, so after a couple of days those hops try to start a little hop farm of their own right in the bottle – the date on the bottle is the date of production, not the 'sell-by' date. Beer's safe for about three days after its production.

Regular brands are generally named after the cities they come from – Moskovskoe, St Petersburgskoe, Zhigulevskoe (from Zhigulevsk on the Volga) – and a bottle of one of these costs around US$0.25 to US$0.40 in shops or kiosks. But new joint-venture brewers are starting up all over the country, and bringing quality and taste up to

Western norms. Probably the best of the brews is St Petersburg's Baltika, a fresh, slightly bitter Pilsner-type beer that's obscenely good, believe it or not, with a crushed clove of garlic added to it. Baltika is sold at kiosks and from wire baskets in front of metro stations, as well as in shops. There are several grades; you only want grade 3, 4 or 6. Another St Petersburg brewery, a joint venture, is Piterbir.

The beer carts and kiosks that say Пиво and are surrounded by jar-holding Russians are selling fresh draft. Go on, get hold of a glass or a jar and give it a try...

Champagne, Wine & Brandy Soviet champagne (it's still called this – isn't it interesting that two of the things that Russians hold most dear – passports and champagne – still say 'Soviet'?) comes very dry *(bryut)*, dry *(sukhoe)*, semidry *(polusukhoe)*, semisweet *(polusladkoe)* and sweet *(sladkoe)*. Anything above dry is sweet enough to turn your mouth inside out. A three-quarter-litre (750 gram) bottle is about US$6 in a restaurant, US$5 in a supermarket, kiosk or liquor store. Most other wine comes from outside the former USSR (Eastern European brands are the cheapest), though you can still find Georgian, Moldovan or Crimean wine.

Brandy is popular and it's all called *konyak*, though local varieties certainly aren't Cognac. The best non-Western konyak in Russia is Armenian, and five star is fine.

Kvas & Mead *Kvas* is fermented rye bread water, dispensed on the street for a few kopecks a glass from big, wheeled tanks with Квас printed on the side. It's mildly alcoholic, tastes not unlike ginger beer, and is cool and refreshing in summer.

Mead *(myod)*, brewed from honey, is a great winter warmer. It crops up here and there.

Alcohol Words
alcohol
   al-ka-GOHL
   алкоголь

glass
   stuh-KAHN
   стакан
bottle
   bu-TIL-kuh
   бутылка
50 grams
   pit-dis-YAHT grahm
   пятьдесят грамм
200 grams
   DVYES-t i grahm
   двести грамм
750 grams (three-quarter litre)
   sim-SOT pit-dis-YAHT grahm
   семьсот пятьдесят грамм
litre
   LEE-tr
   литр
vodka
   VOHT-kuh
   водка
Soviet champagne
   sav-YET-ska-yuh sham-PAN-ska-yuh
   Советское шампанское
very dry
   bryut
   брют
dry
   soo-KHOY-eh
   сухое
semidry
   pah-loo-soo-KHOY-eh
   полусухое
semisweet
   pah-loo-SLAT-kah-yeh
   полусладкое
sweet
   SLAT-kah-yeh
   сладкое
wine
   vi-NOH
   вино
white wine
   BYEL-ah-yuh vi-NOH
   белое вино
red wine
   KRAHS-na-yuh vi-NOH
   красное вино

dry (wine)
  soo-KHOY
  сухой
sweet (wine)
  SLAT-ky
  сладкий
brandy
  ka-NYAK
  коньяк
beer
  PEE-vah
  пиво
beer bar
  piv-NOY bar
  пивной бар
kvas
  kvahs
  квас
mead
  myoht
  мёд
takeaway
  sa-BOY
  с собой
To your health!
  za VA-sheh zda-ROH-vyeh!
  За ваше здоровье

Nonalcoholic Drinks

Water & Mineral Water Tap water is suspect in some cities and should definitely be avoided in St Petersburg. Many people stick to mineral water, which is ubiquitous and cheap (see the Health section for more on water).

Tea & Coffee These normally come black, though warming, milky coffee turns up in some places in winter.

The traditional Russian tea-making method is to brew an extremely strong pot, pour small shots of it into glasses and fill the glasses with hot water from the *samovar*, an urn with an inner tube filled with hot charcoal. The pot is kept warm on top of the samovar. Modern samovars have electric elements, like a kettle, instead of the charcoal tube. Putting jam, instead of sugar, in tea is quite common.

Coffee comes in small cups and is supposed to be thick, but quality – and sometimes supplies – are erratic. Almost any cafe, restaurant or bufet, and some bakery shops, will offer tea or coffee or both.

If you're a serious coffee or tea drinker, carry a thermos, mug, your own tea bags and/or coffee, and powdered milk and sugar if you use them. It's easy to get the thermos filled with boiling water by your dezhurnaya or at a hotel bufet.

Sok, Napitok & Limonad *Sok* is juice – of a kind – usually sweetened, flavoured and heavily diluted. It never resembles the original fruit, but a jugful with a meal often goes down a treat. *Napitok* means beverage but in practice it's often a fancy sok, maybe with some real fruit thrown in. *Limonad* ('lemonade') is a fizzy drink apparently made from industrial waste and tasting like mouthwash.

Other Drinks Jugs of *kefir*, liquid yoghurt, are served as a breakfast drink. Milk is common and is sold cheaply in dairy shops (*molochnaya*) – but is often not pasteurised. Pepsi, Coke and their relatives are widely available.

Alcohol-Free Words
water
  va-DAH
  вода
boiled water
  ki-pya-TOHK
  кипяток
mineral water
  mi-ni-RAL-nuh-yuh va-DAH
  минеральная вода
soda water
  ga-zi-ROH-va-nuh-yuh va-DAH
  газированная вода
coffee
  KOF-yeh
  кофе
tea
  chai
  чай

EUROPEAN RUSSIA

with sugar
  s SAKH-ar-am
  с сахаром
with jam
  s far-YEN-yim
  с вареньем
juice
  sohk
  сок

apple juice
  YAHB-luch-ny sohk
  яблочный сок
orange juice
  ah-pil-SIN-ah-vy sohk
  апельсиновый сок
grape juice
  vi-na-GRAD-ny sohk
  виноградный сок

'My name is Gennady, and I'm an alcoholic...'

The extent of Russian reform can be measured by many criteria, but the sight of 15 men and women in a small St Petersburg flat working their way through a 12-step alcoholic-recovery programme is as good a measure as any. As recently as 10 years ago, the penalty for alcoholism was incarceration and immediate revocation of a driving licence; the rule was kept on the books as a punitive option, used to detain and harass.

Russia is a country in which drinking to excess is not only tolerated but culturally encouraged. Despite ham-fisted efforts by the Gorbachev administration to clamp down on drinking, Russian alcohol consumption remains among the highest in the world. Public drunkenness is so common that it rarely draws even a 'tsk-tsk' from passers-by. 'I was walking down Kamennoostrovsky prospekt', said one Western visitor, 'and for a second I thought I was getting dizzy. Then I realised that everyone on the street in front of me was staggering down the pavement!'

Such public displays are nothing when compared with what goes on in private homes and restaurants. A Russian dinner party for six may drain four litres of vodka before the last guest staggers home – and if the vodka runs out, people will happily hit the *konyak* and champagne, without a thought of hangover or liver damage. And it's considered rude for a host to leave an empty bottle on a table.

For the relatively few teetotallers in Russia, a social life is a difficult, embarrassing and uncomfortable thing to maintain. So when Alcoholics Anonymous meetings began in Moscow, many found solace in numbers and the sort of organised support network familiar to many in the West.

'It's saved my life', says Mikhail, a young Muscovite who regularly attends meetings. 'People would press me to keep drinking even though I knew it was killing me – I've been in hospital several times – but here I have real friends. And it's nice to know that I'm not crazy and I'm not alone.' The feeling of isolation is a common one, especially in a country where admission of alcoholism is considered a sign of weakness, unmanliness or insanity.

Alcoholics Anonymous (AA) is a member-supported worldwide network of recovering alcoholics that holds meetings in which members can discuss how they're coping with their recovery. Membership is open to anyone with a desire to stop drinking, and dues (which go towards rent of the meeting space, advertising, and miscellaneous items such as coffee, tea and cakes for the meetings) are voluntary and based on what members can afford.

For many AA members, meetings are a ritual, a part of daily life. And because of the worldwide nature of AA, travellers are able to attend meetings practically wherever they go. 'They're an important part of my daily schedule', says one American planning a trip to Russia, 'and also a great way to meet people in a new city, country etc, who share a similar and important goal. This is a very reassuring fact for travellers in my position.'

There are English-language meetings in Moscow and St Petersburg, and Russian-language meetings in those and several other cities. Information on meetings is sensitive, so we can't list them here, but you can check with AA Worldwide Services at home, which can give you meeting lists and contact numbers in Moscow and St Petersburg. For more information in the USA, call ☎ (212) 870 3400; in the UK ☎ (0171) 352 3001; and in Australia ☎ (02) 799 1199 or 799 1705. ■

beverage
na-PEET-ak
напиток
'lemonade'
li-ma-NAHD
лимонад
soft drink
biz-al-ka-GOHL-ni nuh-PEE-tuk
безалкогольный напиток
milk
ma-la-KOH
молоко

ENTERTAINMENT

This section is about the practicalities of finding out what's on and getting to see it. Local specifics appear in the relevant city chapters. Classical, jazz and rock music, ballet, opera, drama, circus and cinema all thrive in Russia, the cultural flagships being St Petersburg's Kirov Ballet & Opera, Moscow's Bolshoy Ballet & Opera, and orchestras including the State Symphony Orchestra, the Russian National Symphony Orchestra and the St Petersburg Philharmonic. Many major cities have their own ballet and opera companies, orchestras or circuses.

Rock, pop and jazz are as popular as they are in the West – and Russia has its own megastars. Also worth tracking down are shows by the country's top folk dance and music troupes, which include the Igor Moiseev Folk Dance Ensemble or the Pyatnitsky Russian Folk Chorus.

Russia's big rock bands may play in big sports, culture or youth palaces (*dvortsy sporta, dvortsy kultury, dvortsy molodyozhi*) or in big-city clubs. Big – and faded – Western names often pop up too.

If the year before last's Russian Top 10 is what you're after, any tourist hotel restaurant band will oblige.

Much culture and entertainment lies dormant between about June and September as companies go away on tour or holiday.

More information on the arts will be found under Arts & Culture in Facts about European Russia.

Information & Tickets

Some entertainment listings are given in the English-language *Moscow Times, St Petersburg Press* and *Moscow Tribune*, but the ability to decipher Cyrillic is a huge advantage. A lot of information, including that about rock and sports events, is published on posters. You can also learn a lot from the what's-on charts in hotel service bureaus, at concierge desks and in the ticket kiosks that dot sizeable cities (these last are identified by the words *teatralnaya kassa*, Театральная касса, or just *teatr*, ТЕАТР. For sports fixtures, you can also check such newspapers as *Sport Express* or *Futbol*.

You can buy face-value tickets from the kassa (ticket office) at the venue itself (typically open for advance or same-day sales from early afternoon till the start of the evening show), or a teatralnaya kassa, or any other outlets listed on posters – look for words like продажа (sale) and билеты (tickets). It can be surprisingly easy to get tickets this way with a few words of Russian. For sports events you can often pay at the gate.

If these avenues fail, you can resort to a hotel service bureau or a ticket agency. Here you'll often pay a huge premium over the face value of the ticket (which is usually tiny). For things like the Bolshoy Ballet, US$50 to US$65 for a US$7 ticket is not unusual. Still, service bureaus and concierges generally get better tickets than you otherwise could, and for some events they might be the only places able to sell you a ticket at all.

Then there are the touts. It's standard practice when tickets are scarce for people with spares, as well as the professional touts, to sell a few off outside the main entrance in the half-hour or so before starting time. Prices are a free-for-all and of course you run the risk of obstructed view, wrong date and other hazards, but sellers will normally let you have a look at the ticket before you pay for it. Make sure that the ticket's for the date, performance and section you want (see the boxed table of theatre terms that follows).

See the Moscow and St Petersburg Entertainment sections for more information and strategies.

Maybe We Could Sell Them...

The bus doesn't go there anymore. The exhibition is under renovation. Your money was refused by the rocket scientist at the exchange office because it has a *pen mark* on it, you haven't eaten since that God-awful kotlet last night, and you've just begun to wonder whether bringing along the little darlings was such a hot idea after all.

Well, don't panic. Russia may not be Disney World (for that matter, it's not even Euro Disney), but there's plenty for you and your kids to do. Say what you will about the way Russians treat their tourists, but when it comes to children, even the sternest museum coat-check babushka is a downright pushover.

Most small cities have amusement parks with bumper cars, merry-go-rounds and swings, and the Russian idea of a video arcade is fun in a cheezy, hokey sort of way. Russian sporting goods shops usually have a good selection of winter sports equipment – like cross-country skis, sledges and ice skates – and they're usually a fraction of their price back home. In winter, frozen lakes are skating rinks, and Russia's countryside is filled with cross-country skiers. Many larger cities have 'children's cafés', where children feast on ice cream and sweets in a decidedly kookla-ish atmosphere, and it's hard to go wrong heading for the nearest kafe morozhenoe.

Moscow and St Petersburg are both as child-friendly as it gets in Russian cities. In St Petersburg, there's the rowing boats on Yelagin Island, tour boats up and down the Neva, water taxis through the canals or, perhaps most fun, in summer you can take the hydrofoil out to Petrodvorets, where kids go wild playing with the 'secret' trick fountain triggers.

As far as museums in St Petersburg go, the Arctic & Antarctic Museum, with exhibitions on polar exploration and ratty taxidermy exhibitions, is a good bet, as is the Kunstkammer, where ghoulish horrors await. If the little ones are at a violent stage, they can climb all over the cannon displayed in and around the Artillery Museum behind the Peter & Paul Fortress. For kids under 10, the City Children's Park in the former Tauride Gardens is a great place in summer, with rides to get dizzy on and little bridges to run rampant over.

The circus is another option, and your money might even go towards improving conditions there. The best source for toys in St Petersburg is usually the ground floor of DLT, at ulitsa Bolshaya Konyushennaya 21/23, which is packed to the rafters with Russian and foreign-made toys and games. But there's also a Barbie shop on Nevsky prospekt, and many shops now sell toys and games. Finally, if all else fails, park 'em in front of the tube: the HI St Petersburg Hostel's video room shows English-language movies.

Moscow's river-borne options are no less shabby, with cruises up the Moskva leaving constantly during the day. Detsky Mir, next to the Lubyanka and near GUM and Red Square, is now chock full of toys, games, fun displays and more grown-up offerings like cars and cameras. If you haven't overloaded your kids on things military, head for the Armed Forces Museum, featuring tanks, guns, cannon and an enormous selection of toy soldiers. There are *three* circuses in Moscow, and a zoo to boot. Gorky Park and the other 'Parks of Culture and Recreation' are packed with rides, paddle boats and other attractions. And at the Obraztsov Puppet Theatre language is no barrier to the hilarity, even for adults.

Nick Selby

Nightlife

It's amazing. In a few short years Russian nightlife has come from restaurant lounge singers hacking 'Feelings' to shreds to all-night raves, folk-music cafés, and dozens of 'holes in the wall' featuring exciting and talented modern performers in a friendly, even chic, atmosphere. The 1990s are Russia's Summer of Love, and many Russians are out there riding the wave for as long as they can.

You can dig the groovy vibes at one of Moscow's love-in-style basement rock clubs, where stylish young Muscovites pack into smoke-filled rooms and network, or hit a head-bashing punk or acid rock venue. Jazz clubs are on the upswing, and there are so many discos in the two big cities that it's hard to keep up with them.

If you like to leave your night-time entertainment to chance, the new breed of Russian

Some Useful Words & Phrases

theatre	*teatr*	театр
opera & ballet theatre	*teatr opery i baleta*	театр оперы и балета
drama theatre	*dramaticheskiy teatr*	драматический театр
concert hall	*kontsertnyy zal*	концертный зал
circus	*tsirk*	цирк
cinema	*kinoteatr, kino*	кинотеатр, кино
Have you got tickets for...?	*u vas bilety ('bil-YET-i') na...?*	У вас билеты на...?
Extra tickets?	*Lishnie bilety?*	Лишние билеты?
cheap tickets	*deshyovye bilety*	дешёвые билеты
best tickets	*luchshchie bilety*	лучшие билеты
stalls, lowest tier of seating	*amfiteatr, parter, kresla*	амфитеатр, партер, кресла
dress circle (one tier up from stalls)	*bel-etazh*	бель-этаж
box	*lozha*	ложа
balcony	*balkon*	балкон
first tier (eg of balcony)	*pervyy yarus*	первый (1-й) ярус
second tier	*vtoroy ('fta-ROY') yarus*	второй (2-ой) ярус
third tier	*tretiy yarus*	третий (3-й) ярус
row	*ryad ('ryat')*	ряд
inconvenient place (eg obstructed view)	*neudobnoe mesto ('nye-oo-DOHB-nah-yeh MYEST-ah')*	неудобное место
matinee	*utrenniy kontsert*	утренний концерт
cloakroom	*garderob ('gar-di-ROP')*	гардероб
guest stars	*gastroli*	гастроли
Swan Lake	*Lebedinoe ozero*	Лебединое озеро
Sleeping Beauty	*Spyachkaya krasavitsa*	Спячкая красавица
The Nutcracker	*Shchelkunchik*	Щелкунчик

casino can be found throughout the country. These run the gamut from megasleazy to top-flight and they're always open. The more popular games in Russia at the time of writing are roulette, slot machines and blackjack.

Outside the major cities, it's more difficult, and you're back in the restaurant with that lounge singer again.

See the city chapters for listings and more information.

THINGS TO BUY

There are plenty of attractive things to buy if you know where to look. Most regions still have some local craft specialities, even if the Soviet years have killed off others. Visits to a couple of the places mentioned in the Things to Buy section of the Moscow chapter would be a good introduction to the possibilities and their prices.

Regulations

The export of antiques, art and other objects of cultural value (fairly widely defined) is restricted – which is unfortunate because there are some real bargains to be had. Anything from a Western-style shop or department store should be OK to go, but you can never really be sure: apparently even samovars have 'cultural value' and musical instruments of any sort from a department store need to be cleared before export. See Customs in this chapter for the rules.

Sources
Joint-Venture & Flashy Russian Shops
These mainly sell imported Western goods and most focus on clothes, groceries or toiletries. Moscow and St Petersburg have several joint-venture supermarkets each, and countless joint-venture shops, selling everything from perfume to furs, ice cream to sex toys, and Hyundai to Mercedes Benz cars. Many tourist hotels have small joint-venture shops which sell Western toiletries, film, magazines and so on.

Beryozkas Once the Soviet Union's main outlet for things Western, *beryozkas* have lost all their allure for Russians with the advent of Western shops. Some still remain in big cities and tourist centres, selling Russian souvenirs, luxury goods, a few toiletries, booze and smokes. A few specialise in things like electronic goods, furs or books, but none of these offer any advantage over, say, Stockmann or any other Western chain in GUM (see Department Stores).

Department Stores All sizeable towns have at least one department store (*universalnyy magazin*, *univermag* for short). Many are called TsUM, Tsentralny (Central) Univermag, or GUM, Gosudarstvenny (State) Univermag. They're often worth a look. Detsky Mir (Children's World) shops are department stores with toys, clothes and school equipment.

Other Shops The old saying is that it takes a team of three to shop in Russia – one to inspect the goods, one to pay for them, one to collect them. The traditional method of purchase is to decide what you want, then pay the cashier for it and get a receipt, then exchange the receipt at the counter for your chosen item. Some shops have moved to saner systems but long queues can build up at each stage in those that haven't.

A *komissionnyy magazin* – the sign

usually just says *Komissionnyy*, Комиссионный – is a shop that sells private citizens' goods for a commission, at reduced prices. They're quite common and sometimes have bargains – jewellery, antiques etc. Specialist shops are usually named according to what they sell. A *yuvelirnaya* is a jeweller's, a *parfyumeria* is a perfumery. *Obuvi* and *tkani* denote shoe and cloth shops, *odezhda* denotes clothes, *podarki* indicates gifts.

Markets A *rynok* (market) is mainly for food, though clothes and flea markets spring up beside some. In a few cities there are art and craft markets – notably at Moscow's Izmaylovsky Park on weekends. Izmaylovsky Park has about the biggest and most interesting range of things to buy in the whole country. At such informal places you must negotiate a price – and sometimes a currency – with the seller. You won't get any receipts or paperwork.

Black Market Fartsovshchiky (black market traders) hang around wherever tourists do, offering not only to change money but to sell rabbit hats, caviar, Palekh boxes, 'CCCP' T-shirts, Soviet military watches and all manner of other bric-a-brac. Many small-scale black market dealers seem to operate without fear of the law but, while there might be nothing illegal about some purchases, the dealer is probably on the wrong side of the law at least some of the time, so take care. You also wouldn't want to get mixed up with any serious black market big wheels.

What to Look For
The trademark Russian souvenir is the matryoshka, the set of wooden dolls within dolls. Glasnost enabled them to become something of a true folk art, with all manner of intricate painted designs. But post-glasnost matryoshkas can be seedy little things, poorly painted dolls depicting Soviet and Russian leaders, the Keystone Cops – you name it.

These days you can buy small, mass-produced sets for a couple of dollars but the best examples may set you back US$100. For this price you can also take along a family photo to Izmaylovsky Park and come back the following week to collect your very own personalised matryoshka set.

Quality is similarly varied with the enamelled wooden boxes known as *palekh* (after the town east of Moscow where they originated), each with an intricate scene painted in its lid – but they're usually even more expensive. Several hundred dollars are asked for the best. Cheaper but cheerful are the gold, red and black wooden bowls, mugs and spoons from Khokhloma, a bit further east, which are widely available.

Another attractive Russian craft is the blue-and-white ornamental china called Gzhel (after its home town, also east of Moscow).

Matryoshkas

The trademark Russian textile is the 'Babushka scarf' – officially the Pavlovsky Posad kerchief *(platok Pavlovo Posad)*, again named after its home town east of Moscow. These fine woollen scarves with floral designs go for anything from US$2 to US$10 or more in shops. Other Russian textiles include wool shawls so fine they look almost like lace.

Amber *(yantar)* from the Baltic coast is a jewellery speciality, though beware of fake stuff in St Petersburg and Moscow markets and shops. A good necklace or ring might be US$50 to US$100. Russian records and cassettes – rock, jazz, classical – are a bargain at about US$1 to US$2 from Melodia shops around the country – though many Melodia shops have now diversified so far that they have hardly any music any more. Fortunately you can also get cassettes at street kiosks. A great gift idea is Russian-made albums of Western pop superstars such as the Битлз or Джими Хендрикс. They're also quite cheap but going fast.

Artificial fur hats – you may welcome one in winter – come as cheap as US$10 from shops, and maybe US$15 or US$20 from markets. Rabbit, the cheapest real fur, is not much dearer. Other furs are priced up to the sky. See the St Petersburg Markets section for information about that city's fur market.

More ideas: paintings from street artists and art markets (some talent amid the kitsch); art and children's books from bookshops; posters, both old Socialist exhortation and modern social commentary, from bookshops or specialist *plakaty* shops; little Lenin busts for US$5 to US$10 at street stands and in tourist markets.

If you like something, buy it. Don't wait for it to crop up again better, cheaper, or nearer the end of your trip. It probably won't.

Getting There & Away

European Russia has land borders with 11 other countries. You do not have to use the same agent to book your transport into the country as the one you're using to arrange any ground services in Russia – you can get there by the cheapest or most desirable means you can find. One happy situation is that, with the exception of transit visas, visa applications do not hinge on transport into *or out of* the country. Unless you have a transit visa, you can always enter Russia on a one-way ticket (even if your visa is only good for one day, no one will ever ask you to see your outgoing ticket), so you have a great deal of flexibility once inside Russia to determine the cheapest way of getting out again.

This chapter looks at ways to get into and out of European Russia, the agencies through which you can book trips, and the visa situation for neighbouring and nearby countries.

Information on travel between European Russia and Ukraine and Belarus is given in the Ukraine and Belarus Getting There & Away chapters; information on travel between European Russia and Siberia, the Russian Far East, Mongolia and China is given in the Trans-Siberian Railway chapter and/or the Siberia & the Russian Far East Getting There & Away chapter. For further details, and for some information on travel between European Russia and the former Soviet states in Transcaucasia and Central Asia, see the relevant city sections.

AIR

There's daily service to Moscow from all major European capitals and New York, as well as from Hong Kong and other Asian travel centres. There's also daily service from several European cities to St Petersburg. There isn't any direct service to European Russia from Australasia; you'll need to get to an Asian, European or American gateway and connect from there.

Airlines with daily service to Moscow, and at least several weekly flights to St Petersburg, include British Airways, Lufthansa, Finnair, Delta and SAS. Other airlines with regular flights to one or both main Russian cities include Aeroflot, Air China (CAAC), Air France, Air India, MIAT Mongolian, Alaska Airlines, Alitalia, ANA (All Nippon Airways), Balkan, ČSA, JAL, KLM, Korean Air, LOT Polish, Malév, PIA, Sabena, SAS, Swissair, THY (Turkish Airlines) and Transaero. Major airlines all have offices in Moscow, and there are also many in St Petersburg (see those chapters for addresses).

Only a few other European Russian airports have regular direct flights from outside the former USSR: they include Petrozavodsk (from Helsinki and Joensuu, Finland), Murmansk (from Oslo and Tromsø, Norway), and Sochi (from Turkey).

From nearly all the other ex-Soviet states there are regular (in some cases daily) flights to Moscow and some other European Russian cities by various Russian airlines (including Aeroflot) or by airlines of the new states. However there is a big question mark over safety on some of these, as well as on internal Russian flights (see the European Russia Getting Around chapter).

If you haven't prebooked your departure from Russia, you can arrange an outward flight through one of the many airlines that have Moscow or St Petersburg offices, a travel agent, VAO Intourist or your hotel's receptionist or service bureau can arrange a flight. See Travel Agencies in the Information section of the Moscow and St Petersburg chapters for details of several agents offering discounted tickets from these cities.

Bargain Tickets & Flights

Airlines don't offer the cheapest tickets but their best deals – usually advance-purchase tickets – will give you a reference point.

Some airlines drop prices as the departure date nears. With Apex fares, you get sizeable discounts by booking well ahead (for example, a 28-day advance booking knocks 25% off the London/Moscow return fare). Phone travel agents for bargains.

Cheap tickets are available in two distinct categories: official and unofficial. Official ones have a variety of names including advance-purchase fares, budget fares, Apex and super-Apex. Unofficial tickets are simply discounted tickets that the airlines release through selected travel agents. The cheapest tickets are often nonrefundable and require an extra fee for changing your flight. Many travel insurance policies will cover this loss if you have to change your flight for emergency reasons. Return (round-trip) tickets usually work out cheaper than two one-way fares – often *much* cheaper.

Use the fares quoted in this book as a guide only. They are approximate and based on the rates advertised by travel agents and airlines at press time. Quoted airfares do not necessarily constitute a recommendation for the carrier.

Bucket Shops In London and other large cities, 'bucket shops' (see Air Travel Glossary) offer some of the best bargains in the Western hemisphere, but of course none hand over a ticket until the last minute and some are just crooks in disguise. Check that they're licensed by the International Air Transport Association (IATA) or an equivalent national body, and get the tickets before you pay. In London, bucket shops advertise in Sunday newspaper travel sections, the 'What's On' section of *Time Out* (the weekly entertainment guide) and the free weekly *The News & Travel (TNT) Magazine*. In Germany, try *In München*, a free biweekly available in cafés and bars.

In the USA, travel sections in major city newspapers (especially on Sunday) often have classified flight ads. Bucket shops advertise in papers such as the *Village Voice*, the *San Jose Mercury News* and the *New Times* (Miami).

In Australia, the *Sydney Morning Herald*

and the Melbourne *Age* weekend travel sections have advertisements for bucket shops and bargains. Good Asian bucket-shop cities are Bangkok, Hong Kong, Singapore and Delhi.

Once you have your ticket, write down its number, together with the flight number and other details, and keep the information somewhere separate. If the ticket is lost or stolen, this will help you get a replacement.

Other Discounters You may decide to pay more than the rock-bottom fare by opting for the safety of a better known travel agent. These agencies include STA Travel, whose offices include:

74 Old Brompton Rd SW7, London, UK (☎ (0171) 937 9962)
10 Downing St, New York, NY 10014, USA (☎ (212) 627 3111), and many other offices in the USA including San Francisco (☎ (415) 391 8407), Los Angeles (☎ (213) 934 8722) and Boston (☎ (617) 266 6014); elsewhere in the US and Canada call (☎ (800) 777 0112)
224 Faraday St, Carlton, Melbourne 3053 (☎ (03) 9347 6911), and 732 Harris St, Ultimo, Sydney 2007 (☎ (02) 281 9866), Australia
10 High St, Auckland, New Zealand (☎ (09) 309 9995).

STA Travel also has offices in Hong Kong, Tokyo, Singapore, Bangkok and Kuala Lumpur. They don't do tours but they do get cheap-as-possible bookings on all major airlines.

Council Travel (☎ (212) 661 1450) or from the USA and Canada (☎ (800) 226 8624), 16th Floor, 205 East 42nd St, New York, is the head office of a US chain of student travel offices, doing essentially the same thing as STA but on a larger scale in that country.

Flight Centre International is a major dealer in cheap airfares, with offices throughout Australia and New Zealand. Flight Centre's main offices are: 19 Bourke St, Melbourne 3000 (☎ (03) 9650 2899); 317 Swanston St, Melbourne 3000 (☎ (03) 9663 1304); and 82 Elizabeth St, Sydney 2000 (☎ (02) 235 3522).

Other agencies that specialise in low fares

Air Travel Glossary

Apex Apex, or 'Advance Purchase Excursion', is a discounted ticket which must be paid for in advance. There are penalties if you wish to change it.

Baggage Allowance This will be written on your ticket: usually one 20-kg item to go in the hold, plus one item of hand luggage.

Bucket Shop An unbonded travel agency specialising in discounted airline tickets.

Bumped Just because you have a confirmed seat doesn't mean you're going to get on the plane (see Overbooking).

Cancellation Penalties If you have to cancel or change an Apex ticket there are often heavy penalties involved. Insurance can sometimes be taken out against these penalties. Some airlines impose penalties on regular tickets as well, particularly against 'no-show' passengers (see No-Shows).

Check In Airlines ask you to check in a certain time ahead of the flight departure (usually 1½ hours on international flights). If you fail to check in on time, and it the flight is overbooked, the airline can cancel your booking and give your seat to somebody else.

Confirmation Having a ticket written out with the flight and date you want doesn't mean you have a seat until the agent has checked with the airline that your status is confirmed. Meanwhile you could just be 'on request'.

Discounted Tickets There are two types of discounted fares – officially discounted (see Promotional Fares) and unofficially discounted. The lowest prices often impose drawbacks like flying with unpopular airlines, inconvenient schedules or unpleasant routes and connections. A discounted ticket can save you other things than money – you may be able to pay Apex prices without the associated Apex advance booking and other requirements. Discounted tickets only exist where there is fierce competition.

Full Fares Airlines traditionally offer first-class (coded F), business-class (coded J) and economy-class (coded Y) tickets. These days there are so many promotional and discounted fares available from the regular economy class that few passengers pay full economy fare.

Lost Tickets If you lose your airline ticket an airline will usually treat it like a travellers' cheque and, after inquiries, issue you with another one. Legally, however, an airline is entitled to treat it like cash – that is, if you lose it then it's gone forever. So take good care of your tickets.

No-Shows No-shows are passengers who fail to show up for their flight, sometimes due to unexpected delays or disasters, sometimes due to simply forgetting and sometimes because they made more than one booking and didn't bother to cancel the one they didn't want. Full-fare passengers who fail to turn up are sometimes entitled to travel on a later flight. The rest are penalised (see Cancellation Penalties).

On Request An unconfirmed booking for a flight (see Confirmation).

Open Jaws A return ticket where you fly out to one place but return from another. If available, this can save you backtracking to your arrival point.

are Trailfinders and Campus Travel in London and other UK cities; Kilroy Travel in many Scandinavian cities; Travel Overland in Munich and Bremen and Die Neue Reisewelle in Berlin, Germany; and Travel Cuts in Canada and the UK.

Round-the-World Tickets

If you're on an extended trip it's possible to string together flights with cooperating airlines into surprisingly cheap round-the-

world (RTW) tickets with six or 12 months validity. It's become a complicated business, with partnerships that may include 10 or 12 carriers. It's perhaps wise to go to an airfare specialist for these.

Sample Airfares

While airfares are volatile and prices change constantly, published fares can give you a reference point from which to make a realistic assessment of the cost of the average

Overbooking Airlines hate to fly with empty seats and since every flight has some passengers who fail to show up (see No-shows) airlines often book more passengers than they have seats. Usually the excess passengers balance those who fail to show up but occasionally somebody gets bumped. If this happens guess who it is most likely to happen to? The passengers who check in late.

Promotional Fares Officially discounted fares like Apex fares which are available from travel agents or direct from the airline.

Reconfirmation At least 72 hours prior to departure time of an onward or return flight you must contact the airline and 'reconfirm' that you intend to be on the flight. If you don't do this the airline can delete your name from the passenger list and you could lose your seat. You don't have to reconfirm the first flight on your itinerary or if your stopover is less than 72 hours. It doesn't hurt to reconfirm more than once.

Restrictions Discounted tickets often have various restrictions on them – advance purchase is the most usual one (see Apex). Others are restrictions on the minimum and maximum period you must be away, such as a minimum of 14 days or a maximum of one year (see Cancellation Penalties).

Standby A discounted ticket where you only fly if there is a seat free at the last moment. Standby fares are usually only available on domestic routes.

Tickets Out An entry requirement for many countries is that you have an onward or return ticket, in other words, a ticket out of the country. If you're not sure what you intend to do next, the easiest solution is to buy the cheapest onward ticket to a neighbouring country, or a ticket from a reliable airline which can later be refunded if you do not use it.

Transferred Tickets Airline tickets cannot be transferred from one person to another. Travellers sometimes try to sell the return half of their ticket, but officials can ask you to prove that you are the person named on the ticket. This is unlikely to happen on domestic flights, but on an international flight tickets may be compared with passports.

Travel Agencies Travel agencies vary widely and you should ensure that you use one that suits your needs. Some simply handle tours while full-service agencies handle everything from tours and tickets to car rental and hotel bookings. A good one will do all these things and can save you a lot of money. But if all you want is a ticket at the lowest possible price, then you really need an agency specialising in discounted tickets. A discounted ticket agency, however, may not be useful for other things, like hotel bookings.

Travel Periods Some officially discounted fares, Apex fares in particular, vary with the time of year. There is often a low (off-peak) season and a high (peak) season. Sometimes there's an intermediate or shoulder season as well. At peak times, when everyone wants to fly, not only will the officially discounted fares be higher but so will unofficially discounted fares, or there may simply be no discounted tickets available. Usually the fare depends on your outward flight – if you depart in the high season and return in the low season, you pay the high-season fare. ∎

---

ticket. At the time of writing, a sample of the lowest published (not bucket shop) return airfares to Moscow, and some of the restrictions that apply, included:

Los Angeles
US$1308 with LOT Polish (includes free stopover in Chicago, New York or Warsaw). Penalty for changing reservations/routing prior to departure is US$150 but the fare may be discounted for a child or infant. The ticket requires a minimum stay of seven days and a maximum stay of one month and the ticket is for travel Monday to Thursday from 1 June to 15 September.

New York
US$910 with ČSA. No refund after ticketing; reservation must be made at the time of ticketing; the minimum stay is until the first Sunday after departure from originating city; and it's a ten-day maximum stay.

London
US$510 with British Airways. Tickets may not be changed, rerouting is not permitted at any time, and the ticket is nonrefundable and must be issued on the same day as the reservation is made. There is a minimum stay of until the first Sunday after departure, a maximum stay of one month. The ticket is for travel between 15 June and 31

August, may be issued on or after 15 June and must be issued by 12 July.

Sydney

US$1850 with Qantas, British Airways or Thai Air and Aeroflot, changing aircraft in Bangkok, Singapore or Kuala Lumpur. The ticket is valid for one year. For about an extra US$40 you can fly on Vietnam Airlines with a stopover in Vietnam in both directions.

Paris

US$807 with all airlines on the route. The penalty for cancellation or no show is 25% of purchase price. This ticket requires 14-day advance reservation and a minimum stay of until the first Sunday after departure, and maximum stay of two months.

Frankfurt

US$667 with Transaero. This is a student fare, valid only for those who are full-time students or people between 12 and 27, and requires a minimum stay of six days and a maximum stay of one month.

US$923 with Aeroflot. Cancellation prior to departure incurs a penalty fee of DM100; ticket must be purchased within one day once reservation is made; minimum stay until the first Sunday after departure, maximum stay six months.

Tokyo

US$2,736. Several airlines offer this fare, which is the lowest published. Cancellation prior to departure incurs a penalty fee of ¥10,000 for adults and ¥5000 for a child. Tickets must be purchased within three days after a reservation is made, and allow a minimum stay of four days and a maximum stay of three months.

Hong Kong

US$2007. Several airlines offer this fare, which is the lowest published. It has no penalties for cancellation, alterations etc, and allows a maximum stay of nine months.

LAND

You may need visas for countries you pass through (see Visas for Other Countries in this chapter).

Bus

To/From Estonia There is a bus to St Petersburg leaving from Tallinn's Autobussijaam every night at 9.45 pm. Expect to arrive in St Petersburg rumpled and cranky, with limbs aching, eight hours and 50 minutes later.

To/From Finland Finnord and Sovtransavto Express Bus have daily services between Helsinki, Vyborg and St Petersburg, stopping in the city centre and at several hotels. See Getting There & Away in the St Petersburg chapter for more details. Further north, from Ivalo, a postbus heads to Kostamuksha in western Karelia, from where you can get connecting ground transport to Petrozavodsk.

To/From Norway The Kola Peninsula has a short Arctic border with Norway. There are no Norwegian rail links to the furthermost big town of Kirkenes, but there is daily coach service. See the Murmansk – Getting There & Away section for more information on bus and coach service between Kirkenes and Murmansk.

Train

The main western rail gateways to European Russia are Helsinki, Warsaw, Prague and Budapest. Through trains or through carriages also run from Athens, Berlin, Brussels, Bucharest, Frankfurt and Venice to Moscow, and from Berlin and Brussels to St Petersburg. Daily service is also available from Paris and Amsterdam to Moscow, with a change of train at Warsaw.

To/From the Czech Republic The night train from Prague to Warsaw arrives at Warsaw's Central Station at about 6.50 am, and connects with the 9 am Warsaw-Moscow train (20 to 24 hours; 38 hours Prague-Moscow). If you want to go to St Petersburg, you can catch the night train at about 12.44 am from Warsaw's Gdansk Station (29 to 39 hours). There's also a daily Prague-Moscow service via Chop, Lviv and Kiev, but it takes 48 hours.

The foreigners' fare from Moscow (2nd class; three or four-person couchette) is around US$140.

To/From Estonia There are two daily sleepers to St Petersburg which leave Tallinn at 8.10 and 11 pm, and arrive in St Petersburg at 7.15 and 9.45 am. To Moscow, trains leave Tallinn at 4.10 and 6.25 pm, arriving at 1.17 pm and 11.31 am, respectively.

To/From Finland On the heavily travelled

Helsinki-Vyborg-St Petersburg corridor the rail crossing is at Vainikkala (Luzhayka on the Russian side). There are two trains a day from Helsinki making the six to seven-hour journey to St Petersburg, and one a day to Moscow (see the Getting There & Away sections in the St Petersburg and Moscow chapters for more information). The foreigners' fare from Moscow (2nd class; three or four-person couchette) is around US$110.

To/From Hungary There's a daily train from Budapest to Moscow, taking 41 hours via Chop, Lviv and Kiev in Ukraine. The foreigners' fare from Moscow (2nd class; three or four-person couchette) is around US$170.

To/From Latvia Two trains run daily from Riga to Moscow (16 hours), crossing into Russia east of Ludza. From Riga to St Petersburg, train No 38 departs daily at 6.38 pm (12 hours).

To/From Lithuania Two trains run daily from Vilnius to Moscow (18 hours) via Minsk in Belarus. Train No 192 departs from Vilnius daily for St Petersburg (17 hours).

To/From Poland There's a twice-daily service between Warsaw's Central Station and Moscow (20 or 24 hours), and daily service between Warsaw and St Petersburg (29 to 39 hours). The St Petersburg trains leave Poland at Kuźnica, which is near Hrodna (Grodno) in Belarus. You'll change wheels just outside the Białystok Station, which takes about three hours. For information on services to Kaliningrad from Poland and Germany, see Kaliningrad in the Western European Russia chapter. The foreigners' fare from Moscow (2nd class; three or four-person couchette) is around US$60.

To/From Romania & Moldova There's a train from Bucharest North Station to Moscow three times a week, taking 43 hours via Chisinau (Moldova) and Kiev (Ukraine). Two trains daily link Chisinau and Moscow.

Car & Motorbike

Foreigners can now legally drive on almost all of Russia's highways, even with motorbikes. On the debit side, driving in Russia, while truly an unfiltered Russian experience, is *truly* an unfiltered Russian experience. Poor roads, maddeningly inadequate signposting, poor-quality petrol (usually 76 octane, though higher octane grades are becoming more readily available) and keen highway patrolmen can often lead to frustration and dismay.

That said, it's a fantastic way to see the country. With a car you're infinitely more mobile and it's better than relying on Russian trains and buses (you needn't get up early to catch that 4.48 am bus to Miserygorsk). And in the open countryside, where camping is now legal, you can save a lot of money by pitching a tent or sleeping in your van. See Accommodation in the European Russia Facts for the Visitor chapter for information on camping.

Motorbikes, while legal, undergo vigorous scrutiny by border officials and highway police, especially if you're driving anything vaguely Ninja-ish. But one traveller reported that while riding his hand-built motorcycle across the entire former Soviet Union, the only attention he attracted from the police consisted of admiring questions and comments.

Motorbikes are definitely not wise in St Petersburg and Moscow, where crime is high and traffic police widespread. Finally, while foreign automobile companies now have an established presence in Moscow, St Petersburg and other cities, motorcycles in the former Soviet Union are almost exclusively Russian or East German-made – it is to be doubted that a Ural cylinder-head gasket will fit your Hog.

Most of the Russian border is lined on the inside with a strip 25 km deep, within which access is controlled even for Russian citizens who live there. In these zones photos are frowned on and individuals are unlikely to get away with genuinely independent movement – you may be sent out of the area by police or border patrols unless you have a business visa and a letter from a Russian company stating why you need to be in the area.

The Basics To be allowed to drive your own car/motorbike in Russia you'll need a driving licence and either an international driving permit with a Russian translation of your licence's information or a certified Russian translation of your full licence (you can certify translations at a Russian embassy or consulate).

You will also need vehicle registration and proof of insurance. Be sure your insurance covers you in Russia. Russian insurance should be available at the border through Ingosstrakh (head office ($\mathbf{\varpi}$ (095) 233 17 59, 233 05 50, 233 20 70; fax (095) 230 25 18), Pyatnitskaya ulitsa 12, Moscow); through your insurance agent at home; or through one in Finland, which may also be able to get you a policy covering Russian driving.

Finally, a customs declaration promising to take your vehicle with you when you leave is also required.

For more information on driving/riding, see the European Russia Getting Around chapter.

Border Crossing You'll first pass the neighbouring country's border point, where you'll need to show your auto registration and insurance papers (including Finnish or Scandinavian proof of coverage if you're coming from Finland or Norway), your driving licence, passport and visa. Scandinavian formalities are usually minimal for Western citizens.

On the Russian side, chances are your vehicle will be subjected to a cursory inspection by border guards (your life will be made much easier if you open all doors and the boot yourself, and shine a torch for the guards at night). You pass through customs separately from your car, walking through a metal detector and possibly having hand luggage X-rayed.

You no longer need to file an itinerary, or state in which direction you're headed.

To/From Belarus, Ukraine & the West With the exception of roads into the Kaliningrad region from Lithuania and Poland, approaches to Russia from Lithuania, Poland, the Czech Republic, Slovakia, Hungary, Romania, Moldova and places further west all cross Belarus or Ukraine. See the Ukraine and Belarus Getting There & Away chapters for more information.

To/From Estonia The nearest border crossing from Tallinn is at Narva.

To/From Finland Highways cross at the Finnish border posts of Nuijamaa (Brusnichnoe on the Russian side) and Vaalimaa (Russian side, Torfyanovka). From there to St Petersburg the road is said by everyone to be infested with modern-day highwaymen (though we've never had any difficulties). Don't stop for anybody, fill up with petrol on the Finnish side (preferably before you get to the border petrol station, which is more expensive than others and closes early). There's a speed-trap just outside the St Petersburg city line, where the limit is 60 km/h. On this route especially, be sure to watch for all road signs; a few involve tricky curves and singposting is not all it should be. It's best to make this drive for the first time during daylight hours.

Further north, from Ivalo, a road which may or may not be open during your visit goes to Murmansk via the Finnish town of Raja Jooseppi; see the Murmansk – Getting There & Away section for more information on that and other crossings to the Kola Peninsula/northern Karelia.

To/From Latvia The M9 Riga-Moscow road crosses the border east of Rezekne (Latvia). The A212 road from Riga leads to Pskov, crossing a corner of Estonia en route.

SEA
To/From Finland
The Baltic Shipping Company runs visa-free cruises from Helsinki to St Petersburg aboard the *Konstantin Simonov* on which you can also book a straight one-way or

return passage (though you'll need a visa in that case). See Getting There & Away in the St Petersburg chapter for more information.

To/From Norway

Sovjetreiser offers sailings between Norway and Murmansk several times a week in summer, as does the Baltic Shipping Company (see Murmansk – Getting There & Away in the Northern European Russia chapter for more details).

To/From Sweden & Germany

The Baltic Shipping Company has sailings aboard the *Anna Karenina* between Stockholm, St Petersburg and Kiel, Germany (see the St Petersburg chapter for more information).

To/From Ukraine

Passenger and vehicle shipping services still, in theory, run to Sochi on Russia's Black Sea coast from Odessa and Yalta in Ukraine, with possible connections to/from other Black Sea and Mediterranean ports, but schedules are unreliable. See the Ukraine Getting There & Away chapter for more information. There are passenger and vehicle ferries between Kerch (at the eastern tip of the Crimean Peninsula in Ukraine) and Temryuk (near Russia's Sea of Azov coast), and between Kerch and Anapa and Novorossiysk (both on Russia's Black Sea coast).

To/From the UK

In the UK, CTC Lines (☎ (0171) 896 8844; fax (0171) 839 2483), 1 Lower Regent St, London SW1Y 4NN, offers a 14-day 'Baltic Capitals & St Petersburg' cruise. The cruise departs from Tilbury and stops in Amsterdam, Copenhagen, Stockholm, Helsinki, St Petersburg, Tallinn, Visby (Sweden) and several other places; the least expensive cabin is £873, the most expensive £2553.

To/From Turkey, Georgia & Abkhazia

There are some passenger services between these countries and Sochi on the Russian Black Sea coast (see the Caucasus chapter).

To/From Kazakhstan & Turkmenistan

It might be possible to get passage on a freighter crossing the Caspian Sea between Makhachkala, Dagestan, and Aqtau (formerly Shevchenko; Kazakhstan) or Turkmenbashi (formerly Krasnovodsk; Turkmenistan) – see the Caucasus chapter. Otherwise there is a service between Turkmenbashi and Baku (Azerbaijan) aboard cargo ships that can carry up to 300 passengers. There is no timetable and the ships simply sail when there is a load to be taken – on average, about three times a week. The crossing takes about 12 hours and costs around US$25.

TRAVEL AGENCIES & TOURS

Nowadays, virtually any travel agent in the world can assist you getting bookings, confirmations and many domestic travel tickets for many areas of Russia. You needn't go through a Russia specialist or Intourist to book trips into Russia, though the more experience your agent has, the better off you'll probably be. If you're just looking for a cheap ticket to the country, you should go with whatever agency has the best deal at the time you're flying (see also Air in this chapter).

The prices of some tour programmes vary with the time of year: 'high season' usually means mid-May to mid-September but can sometimes mean mid-March to the end of October.

Outside Russia

The following are a few travel firms outside Russia specialising in European Russia (and often other former USSR) travel. There are many more. For Intourist offices worldwide, see under Intourist later. For some agencies offering trips to specific areas, see the regional chapters. For firms specialising in adventure/activity travel and accommodation in private homes, see Activities and Accommodation in the European Russia Facts for the Visitor chapter.

UK Intourist Travel (☎ (0171) 538 8600; fax (0171) 538 5967) may be one of the best

Intourist offices around; too bad it's way out in the docklands at 219 Marsh Wall, Isle of Dogs, London E14 9FJ. It does a range of tours including cut-rate Moscow/St Petersburg trips in the £400 to £600 range, plus river cruises, individual travel and visa services.

Two long-established agencies specialising in Russia and ex-USSR travel are Regent Holidays (☎ (0117) 921 1711; fax (0117) 925 4866), 15 John St, Bristol, BS1 2HR, and Progressive Tours (☎ (0171) 262 1676; fax (0171) 724 6941), 12 Porchester Place, London W2 2BS. Both offer flight and accommodation deals.

Zwemmer Travel (☎ (0171) 374 6249; fax (0171) 379 6383), 28 Denmark St, London WC2 H8NJ, does discount bookings for Aeroflot flights from Heathrow and Manchester to Moscow and from Heathrow to St Petersburg. Zwemmer also arranges a number of other services.

Goodwill Holidays (☎ (01438) 716421), Manor Chambers, The Green, School Lane, Welwyn, Herts AL6 9EB, does Russian city tours including Arkhangelsk. Travel For The Arts (☎ (0171) 483 4466; fax (0171) 586 0639) does luxury 'culture' based tours to St Petersburg and other European cities; it's at 117 Regent's Park Rd, London NW1 8UR.

East-West Travel (☎ (0171) 938 3211; fax (0171) 938 1077), 15 Kensington High St, London W8 5NP, is a specialist in ex-USSR business travel and tourism.

USA Russian Youth Hostels & Tourism (RYHT; ☎ (310) 379 4316; fax (310) 379 8420), 409 North Pacific Hwy, Building 106, Suite 390, Redondo Beach, CA 90277, is the US partner and handling agent for all three St Petersburg youth hostels, as well as the one in Novgorod and the Travellers Guest House, Moscow. RYHT arranges trans-Siberian journeys and other independent Russian trips, as well as visa support and, if you're in the USA, visa processing (they take your visa into the Russian consulate and deal with it). This is one of the most honest companies in the USA to deal with in visa matters.

General Tours (☎ (617) 621 0977 or ☎ (800) 221 2216), 139 Main St, Cambridge, MA 02142, is a well-established company offering 'to your right is the Kremlin' packages to Moscow, St Petersburg and the Golden Ring for a wide range of prices. Prices in high season are about US$1500 per person for eight days in Moscow/St Petersburg including airfares, transfers, transport, tours, excursions and two meals a day (usually the guide arranges for lunch, which is paid separately).

Pioneer Tours (☎ (617) 547 1127), 203 Allston St, Cambridge, MA, specialises in independent travel packages which can consist of à la carte hotel bookings or homestays and airfare.

EuroCruises (☎ (212) 691 2099 or toll-free in the USA and Canada (800) 688 3876), 303 West 13th St, New York, NY 10014, is the US agent for the Baltic Shipping Company, the Russian company that organises visa-free cruises from Scandinavian cities to St Petersburg and on Russian inland waterways.

The Russian Nature Travel Company (☎ (603) 835 6369 or toll-free within the USA and Canada (800) 304 6369; e-mail: s.levin2@genie.geis.com), in South Acworth, NH, does trips to nature reserves all over Russia, from Lapplandsky to the Far East, and works closely with conservation organisations. In late 1995 it offered an expedition to the Russian Far East and to the Siberian tiger project's primary research site in the Sikhote-Alin Biosphere Nature Reserve. It plans to run several similar excursions each year. The price for that one was US$4250 per person from Boston, MA, or US$3850 per person from Seattle, WA, including airfare and US and Russian accommodation for the two-week excursion.

Australia A good place to arrange a visa with an invitation and no prepaid accommodation is Red Bear Tours (☎ (03) 9824 7183 or toll-free 008 337 031; fax (03) 9822 3956), c/- Passport Travel, 320B Glenferrie Rd, Malvern, Melbourne 3144. Red Bear can also arrange skiing tours, language courses, and trans-Siberian and Far East trips.

Gateway Travel (☎ (02) 745 3333; fax (02) 745 3237), 48 The Boulevarde, Strathfield, Sydney 2135, arranges homestays, youth hostels, apartments and hotels from A$40 to A$215, and can also arrange tours and river cruises.

Eastern Europe Travel Bureau (☎ (02) 262 1144; fax (02) 262 4479), Level 5, 75 King St, Sydney, does budget tours (they don't include airfares) including: Moscow, four days A$270; Moscow/St Petersburg, six days A$525. Cruises include: Moscow to St Petersburg by river and canal, 15 days from A$1075.

Safeway Travel (☎ (03) 9534 4866; fax (03) 9534 4206), 288 Carlisle St, Balaclava, Melbourne 3182, offers flights, tours and relatively inexpensive cruises.

Iris Hotels (☎ (02) 580 6466; fax (02) 580 7256), PO Box 60, Hurstville, Sydney 2220, is the Australian partner of the Russian Mikof-Iris mid-range hotel chain, and also offers packages.

Hong Kong & China Monkey Business (☎ 2723 1376; e-mail 100267.2570@ compuserve.com), Chungking Mansions, Nathan Rd 36-44 E-Block, 4th Floor, Flat 6, Kowloon, Hong Kong and (☎ (861) 301 2244, ext 716; e-mail 100267.2570@compuserve.com), Beijing Commercial Business Complex, No 1 Building Yu Lin Yi Office, Room 406 4th floor, You An Men Wai district, 100054 Beijing, China, is a well-established trans-Siberian specialist, which does trans-Siberian bookings, flights, and bookings for the Moscow Travellers Guest House and the HI St Petersburg Hostel. There were several complaints about Monkey Business in 1994 from travellers who felt they had been overcharged for some services and given inaccurate accounts of on-the-ground costs. But the company has been around a while and handles lots of people, and should not be ruled out on the strength of a few complaints.

Global Union Express (☎ 868 3231; fax (852) 845 5078), Room 22-23, New Henry House, 10 Ice House St, Central, Hong Kong can make reservations for the Travellers

Guest House as well. They also have cheap flights and other services.

Estonia Karol (☎ (22) 454 900, 446 240; fax (26) 313 918), Lembitu 4, EE0001, Tallinn, was a major player in the establishment of a St Petersburg-Helsinki-Estonia youth hostel cooperation network, and specialises in cheap independent travel to Russia, including full visa support.

Virone (☎ (22) 448 960), Pronksi 11, Tallinn, 200010, does simple packages from Tallinn to St Petersburg including hotel and city tours with driver.

Finland The very helpful and friendly Eurohostel (☎ (90) 664 452; fax (90) 655 044) works closely with the Russian Youth Hostel Association, and can help with paperwork, visa support, bus reservations and car rentals. It also offers discounted train tickets from Helsinki to St Petersburg at US$15 below the retail price in the railway station. It's part of the 'Hostel the Baltic Triangle' group, which arranges hostelling stays at member hostels in the Finnish, Estonian and Russian YHAs. They're just off the Silja Lines port in Helsinki at Linnankatu 9.

Finnsov Tours (☎ (90) 694 2011), formerly privately owned but now owned by Intourist Moscow Ltd, offers short but expensive package tours from Helsinki to St Petersburg and dozens of other Russian cities by train, bus and ship. It has a five-day St Petersburg-Tallinn tour by train at US$805. If you're game, so are they: you'll find them at Eerikinkatu 3, Helsinki.

Russian Agencies
Russia has hundreds of travel firms which would be only too pleased to arrange aspects of your visit. But a good many of them are small, inexperienced and after quick bucks. You'll find details of some of the more useful ones in the Travel Agencies sections of city and regional chapters.

State Tourism Agencies – Where Are They Now? The once mighty state organs of tourism have been reshuffled and rejigged to the point that they're practically unrecognisable if you do more than glance at them. While Intourist (which was the main tourism company for travel to the USSR), Sputnik (which handled student exchanges and youth travel) and the CCTE (which proudly marched happy delegates of trade union groups around metal-reinforced concrete-slab fabricating plants and so on) all still exist, their functions have changed. These days they're all doing general tourism, and are merely the largest of a rapidly growing network of tour and travel agencies that are popping up around the country; almost half their business comes from outbound Russian tourists.

Intourist The largest of the three, Intourist is alive and well and living in Moscow. They don't talk much of the divorce, from which several Intourist offshoots were created; they feel that's really none of our business. VAO Intourist (☎ (095) 292 22 60, 292 23 65, 292 12 78; fax (095) 292 20 34, 292 25 47), Mokhovaya ulitsa 13, Moscow, has a network of offices in Moscow, St Petersburg and dozens of other Russian cities that deal with inbound and, increasingly, outbound tourism. This is the organisation that is most akin to the old Intourist (generally speaking, when you wander into an office marked 'Intourist', it's now a privately owned, affiliated office of VAO Intourist), and it performs standard tourist agency functions such as booking tours, excursions, train, air, boat and car trips etc. Intourist offices also offer full package services, including guides, domestic travel arrangements, accommodation, transfers and visa assistance for travel to all republics of the former Soviet Union.

Intourist air booking centres offer outbound package tours for Russians to beach resorts and vaguely Western European places such as Turkey, the Black Sea resorts and the UK.

From abroad, Intourist still provides a large range of packages to Russia, for both groups and individuals. Sample rates for a seven-night package from London to Moscow/St Petersburg including airfares, accommodation, transfers and train to St Petersburg (in 1994) was £459 low season, £559 high-season (airfare only on British Airways £295; on SAS £270).

Intourist Holding Company (☎ (095) 250 24 46, 251 55 59; fax (095) 251 69 94, 250 46 30), 1-ya Brestskaya ulitsa 35, 125047 Moscow, founded in 1992 by a group of Russian travel sector companies including Intourtrans and Intourservice, calls itself a 'travel sector investment company' and mainly concerns itself with construction and management of hotels and motels.

An offshoot of Intourist Holding is Novintour (☎ (095) 250 41 84, 250 41 80, 250 84 29; fax (095) 251 69 94), which has offices in the same building as Intourist Holding Company. Novintour does essentially the same thing as VAO Intourist's offices – though it concentrates on 'areas formerly closed to foreign tourists' - in addition to the standard offerings of tours and excursions to Moscow, St Petersburg, the Golden Ring etc.

Below are foreign offices of agencies calling themselves 'Intourist':

Australia
    37-49 Pitt St, Sydney 2000 (☎ (02) 247 7652; fax (02) 251 6196)
Austria
    Schwedenplatz A-1010 Vienna (☎ (0222) 533 7150, 533 4119; fax (0222) 535 0755)
Canada
    1013 Bloor St, West Toronto, ON M6H 1M1 (☎ (416) 537 2165; fax (416) 537 1627)
    1801 McGill College Ave 630, Montreal, PQ H3A 2N4 (☎ (514) 849 6394; fax (514) 849 6743)
Czech Republic
    Pramo, ulice V Wolkerova 13, CZ-16000 Prague 6 (☎ (02) 24 13 41; fax (02) 32 33 64)
France
    7 Boulevard des Capucines, F-75002 Paris (☎ (1) 47 42 47 40; fax (1) 47 42 87 28)
India
    c/- Russian Trade Representation, Plot 6-7 Block 50E, Nyaya Marg Chanakyapuri, New Delhi 110021 (☎ (11) 687 6336; fax (11) 687 3503)
Italy
    Piazza Buenos Aires 6-7, I-00198 Rome (☎ (06) 855 3892; fax (06) 855 3633, 855 7749)

Japan
    Roppongi Heights 1-16, 4-chome Roppongi,
    Minato-ku, Tokyo 106 (☎ (3) 35 84 66 18; fax (3)
    35 84 66 17)
Norway
    Bygdo Alle 62, N-0265 Oslo 2 (☎ 22 44 17 85;
    fax 22 83 65 85)
Poland
    ulica Krucza 47, PL-00-509 Warsaw (☎ (022) 29
    02 02, 29 67 67; fax (022) 29 02 02)
    Intour Orbis
    15 ulica Podwale, PL-00-252 Warsaw (☎ (022)
    31 63 56, 31 00 81; fax (02) 635 7849)
Sweden
    Framresor AB, Drottninggatan 25, S-10322
    Stockholm (☎ (08) 21 59 34; fax (08) 21 63 10)
Switzerland
    Bleicherweg 15A CH-8002 Zurich (☎ (01) 281
    1124; fax (01) 281 1124)
UK
    219 Marsh Wall, Isle of Dogs, London E14 9FJ
    (☎ (0171) 538 8600, 538 5966, 538 3202; fax
    (0171) 538 5967)
USA
    630 Fifth Ave, Suite 868, New York, NY 10111
    (☎ (212) 757 3884/85; fax (212) 459 0031)

Sputnik Sputnik's tentacles are almost as
far-reaching as VAO Intourist's, and in some
cities (such as Arkhangelsk) Sputnik may be
the best shot you'll have of a tourist information centre. Sputnik's head office (☎ (095)
939 80 65; fax (095) 938 11 92) is at the Hotel
Orlyonok, ulitsa Kosygina 15, 117946
Moscow. There are 107 branch offices across
the CIS, some owned outright, some part-
owned, by Sputnik. All these offices provide
tourist information, book air, boat and rail
travel and arrange tours and excursions.

CCTE CCTE-Intour (☎ (095) 235 62 77, 235
82 22, 235 44 26; fax (095) 230 27 84),
Ozerkovskaya naberezhnaya 50, 113532
Moscow, is a 'stock' company offering
essentially similar services to VAO Intourist
with the addition of specialised sport, adventure and walking tours. Its listed hotel prices
for St Petersburg during 1994 were 5% to
10% higher than standard rates from the
hotels directly.

VISAS FOR OTHER COUNTRIES
If you're combining other countries with
your trip to European Russia, you may need
visas for several of the countries you pass
through. For some countries it's not difficult
to get visas in Russia; for others, it's a frustrating, time-consuming business just to find
out whether you need one, let alone get it.
Overall it's better to get these visas before
you come to Russia – and to allow lots of
time for visas for any of the ex-Soviet states.
Note that transit visas, which are cheaper
than tourist visas, are available for some
countries. These will probably be suitable if
you'll only be there a few days.

Foreign embassies in Russia – including
those of all the former Soviet republics – are
in Moscow; some countries also have consulates in St Petersburg and/or other cities
(see city sections for details) which can
usually issue visas as well.

The visa requirements of most of the
former Soviet states would seem to have
been drafted by the same genius who brought
us Russian visa regulations. All are also volatile, and the regulations below will likely
change before you've finished reading this
book. Some of these countries may go the
way of Estonia and ex-members of the
Warsaw Pact, dropping visa regulations for
some Western nationalities. In countries
where former Soviet states don't have their
own embassies, their visas are often available from Russian embassies.

Here are current visa requirements for
former Soviet states and other countries near
European Russia, with some information on
procedures in Moscow in case you have to
apply there. See the Trans-Siberian Railway
chapter for information on Chinese and
Mongolian visas.

Armenia
    The Moscow Embassy says that a Russian visa is
    good for now, though you will need to register
    the visa at the local branch of OVIR on arrival.
Azerbaijan
    From Russia you don't need a visa to get in, but
    you'll lose your Russian visa if it's only a single-
    entry one. It's best to apply at an Azerbaijani
    consulate for a visa to play it safe; you can get an
    on-the-spot visa at the Baku airport but it's
    reportedly not fun.

Belarus

An invitation or booked accommodation is required to get any visa except a transit visa. Sindbad Travel, the HI St Petersburg Hostel and the Travellers Guest House in Moscow can assist with accommodation vouchers. Belarus tourist visas are *not* issued at the Russia-Belarus border, but transit visas are issued to passengers returning to Europe from Russia through Belarus at no charge.

Your Russian visa, if still valid, will act as a transit visa while crossing Belarus from Europe to Russia, provided you don't leave the train; if you're in transit from Russia to Europe, a transit visa should be issued at no charge at the Belarus-Russia border. If you're picking up a continuing ticket at Hrodna (Grodno) – for example, to Warsaw – you should be allowed to go to the Intourist ticket counter in the Hrodna station without creating problems for yourself. See the Belarus Facts for the Visitor chapter for more information.

Czech Republic

UK, US and Western European passport holders need no visa; those with Canadian, Australian and NZ passports need one. Same-day visas at the Moscow embassy are about US$20; take two photos.

Estonia

Citizens of the following countries *do not* need a visa: UK, USA, Canada, Australia, New Zealand, Japan, Denmark, the Czech Republic, Slovakia, Hungary, Poland, Bulgaria, Liechtenstein, Vatican City, Andorra, Monaco and San Marino. Estonian visas are good for travel in the other Baltic states as well.

Be prepared to be awoken at 2 am for customs procedures on the night train from St Petersburg to Tallinn. In Moscow a tourist visa costs US$10 for three-working-day service, US$20 for same-day service.

Finland

No visa is needed by US, Canadian, UK, Australian or NZ passport holders for up to three months stay.

Georgia

Visa required; consult the embassy in Moscow. Fighting may be continuing. On-the-spot visas are said to be given at the airport in Tblisi but don't count on it.

Hungary

US, Canadian, UK, and Western European citizens do not need a visa. Australian and NZ passport holders can get 48-hour transit visas or 30-day tourist visas on arrival by air or road but not by rail. Visas for those who need them are available at the Moscow embassy the same day for US$12; take two photos.

Kazakhstan

Travellers have had negligible problems spending five or even seven days transiting Kazakhstan on a valid Russian visa; officially the limit is three days. Kazakhstan visas require sponsorship by a Kazakhstan organisation or individual; processing takes one week from submission of all documents (including a photocopy of your Russian visa), and costs US$60 for a two-week visa, US$70 for three weeks, US$100 for one month or more.

Kyrgyzstan

A Russian visa will get you in, but travellers who plan on staying for more than a few days will need a visa. These are easier to obtain than for most Central Asian states, from Kyrgyz embassies in places such as Brussels, Washington DC, even Moscow, where they're available immediately for US$40.

Latvia

It's a rubber-stamp process; fill in an application, give them two photos and US$10 for two-working-day service, US$45 for next-working-day service (for tourist visas) and you're in. Citizens of the UK and other Baltic and Eastern European countries don't need a visa.

Lithuania

Almost the same as in Latvia except that tourist visas are US$20 for one-week service, US$30 for the next working day; and you only need one photo. Citizens from the UK, Denmark, Iceland, Switzerland and Norway do not need a visa.

Moldova

Requires visas from visitors of all nationalities. They can be obtained at any Moldovan Embassy for US$50 to US$80, depending on your nationality, with no formal invitation needed. You can also pick up your visa on the spot at some European airports such as Frankfurt – check with the nearest Moldovan Consulate – but *not* at Chisinau airport or at borders. Two passport photos are required.

Norway

No visa is needed by US, Canadian, UK, Australian or NZ passport holders.

Poland

No visa is needed for citizens of the USA, Germany or the Netherlands, but UK, Canadian, Australian, French and NZ citizens need a visa. At the Moscow embassy, transit visas are US$10, tourist visas US$18; student discount is possible on tourist visas; take two photos.

Slovakia

Most (but not all) Europeans and North Americans don't need visas; same-day visas cost about US$20 (two photos).

Tajikistan

Shooting should keep you away from here, but if you really want to go, contact the Russian Consulate nearest you or the Tajik Consulate in Moscow.

Turkmenistan

Turkmen embassies (in Vienna, Paris, Washington, DC, and elsewhere) can issue tourist visas more or less immediately for around US$30; you can also get visas on arrival at Ashghabat airport for US$20. The Moscow embassy told us it did not issue visas.

Ukraine

Visas at the Moscow embassy can take 10 days to process and cost as much as US$100. You'll need a completed Ukrainian application form, a valid passport, three passport-sized photos and an invitation or booked accommodation. But there are easier ways – see the Ukraine Facts for the Visitor chapter for more information.

Uzbekistan

To get a visa you must either book services through an accredited Uzbek travel agency, or obtain an officially approved invitation from Uzbekistan. Uzbek and Russian embassies may be able to let you know of travel agencies in your country that can help. Tourist visas are available through Uzbekturizm (☎ (095) 238 89 59, 238 56 32), rooms 53 and 54, ulitsa Bolshaya Polyanka 41, Moscow, in conjunction with accommodation bookings in Uzbekistan; seven-day visa US$40, eight to 15 days US$50, takes 10 days.

WARNING

The information in this chapter is particularly vulnerable to change: prices for international travel are volatile, routes are introduced and cancelled, schedules change, special deals come and go, and rules and visa requirements are amended. Airlines and governments seem to take a perverse pleasure in making price structures and regulations as complicated as possible. You should check directly with the airline or a travel agent to make sure you understand how a fare (and ticket you may buy) works. In addition, the travel industry is highly competitive and there are many lurks and perks.

The upshot of this is that you should get opinions, quotes and advice from as many airlines and travel agents as possible before you part with your hard-earned cash. The details given in this chapter should be regarded as pointers and are not a substitute for your own careful, up-to-date research.

Getting Around

You're free to go virtually anywhere you want in European Russia, and new ways of getting around are being discovered all the time.

AIR

The former Soviet state airline, Aeroflot (Air Fleet) has been decentralised into hundreds of smaller airlines ('baby-flots') at such an alarming rate that not even the Russian Department of Air Transport (RDAT) can say how many exist. The International Airline Passenger Association (IAPA), a Washington DC-based consumer watchdog group, estimates that the number exceeds 300. These airlines came about when Aeroflot left aircraft parked at airfields around the country – in many cases, employees or managers of an airfield with a couple of Aeroflot planes on its tarmac simply commandeered them and started an airline.

The upshot of this orgy of aerobatic entrepreneurship is virtually unregulated skies and the worst regional safety record in the world (according to the IAPA), ahead of China, Central Africa, Colombia and all developing Asian nations.

One problem is that badly financed airlines can't pay for proper maintenance, spare parts or even proper fuel payloads: by 1995 half of Russia's aircraft were past their recommended lifespan. In addition, a lack of reliable radar and communications equipment has led to several near misses involving Russian and foreign jumbo jets. Unpredictable infrastructure aggravates the situation; on 7 December 1993 a state-owned electric company turned off the power to a major air-traffic control centre which had not paid its electricity bill. Among the thousands of people aboard planes flying in the affected area at the time was Russian president Boris Yeltsin, who was none too thrilled about the incident when he learned of it later.

As a result of these incidents (and many fatal crashes), the IAPA stated in January 1994 (and restated to Lonely Planet in January 1995) such blunt and hard-to-ignore warnings as 'Do not fly to, in or over Russia, even on our honor roll airlines' and 'only a fool with no regard for personal safety would fly Aeroflot at any price'. The US government subsequently banned its employees from flying on Russian-owned airlines unless there was absolutely no alternative (the ban has since been amended to include only airlines not certified by the RDAT to be of international standards, something the IAPA says is a victory of 'politics over common sense').

While this all sounds grim, there are some mitigating factors. The routes that link Moscow and St Petersburg to Western Europe are considered safe. The corridor between the two cities is probably the safest air route in the country. And the airlines that are certified to operate internationally by the RDAT are safer than those not so certified. The list of airlines thus certified includes Aeroflot Russian International Airways (which is the company that took over the bulk of Aeroflot's long-haul aircraft), and Transaero Airlines, a high-quality Russian airline offering good service aboard mostly Western-made aircraft (mainly Boeing 737s and 757s) doing long-haul flights to many cities in Russia and the former Soviet Union.

Cheap flights are available, but with all the safety questions in Russian airspace, we recommend that you fly only when necessary, and then choose internationally certified carriers (a list of internationally certified Russian-owned carriers is available from the US Embassy Moscow's Consular Information). See the next section for how to find out what airlines fly particular routes.

Timetables

These are often fantasy-based. Many flights (except those between major cities) are delayed, often for hours and with no explanation offered. Rerouting of aircraft *in mid-flight* is not uncommon, as many airports are now demanding hard-currency payment for landing fees (which is illegal but practised).

If you're lucky enough to see a domestic flights timetable, and able to decipher it, you'll find that all the airlines are listed together (if you look very closely you'll see that each has a different flight code). You may never actually know which airline you're flying on because they generally share the same ticket outlets and check-in facilities – and many of them still haven't got round to writing their own names on their planes in place of 'Aeroflot'.

Some routes are served by two or even three different airlines, others by just one. Aeroflot no longer flies any internal Russian routes, though it flies a few routes between Russia and other ex-Soviet republics.

Service
Except on Transaero, service is absolutely no-frills – a small cup of mineral water may be all you're given (one traveller reported that on an 11-hour flight he was *also* given a hard-boiled egg), so follow the example of fellow passengers and prepare your own lunch for a long flight! Transaero's service is pretty good, offering a separate business class, polite flight attendants, edible food, and a generally pleasant environment.

Check-In & Luggage
Some airports have special check-in and waiting-room facilities for foreigners, which make procedures easier. This may enable you to board early and miss out on any mad scrambles when flights are overbooked. Check-in is 90 to 40 minutes before departure and airlines are entitled to bump you if you come later than that. To minimise the danger of loss or theft, try not to check in any baggage: many planes have special stowage areas for large carry-on pieces. Flights are generally one class only and seating is usually a free-for-all.

Getting Tickets
Air tickets for virtually all domestic Russian airlines, and airlines of former Soviet republics, can be purchased from Aeroflot offices in cities all over Russia (see city chapters for locations) and through travel agents in Russia or abroad. Transaero also has its own network of ticket offices, including Okhotny ryad 2, Moscow (☎ (095) 292 7513, 578 05 37/8/9; fax (095) 292 7682) and Schiphol Airport, Holland (☎ (02503) 52151; fax (02503) 51023).

Generally speaking, you'll do better booking internal flights once you arrive in Russia, where more flights and flight information are available, and where prices may be lower.

Whenever you book airline tickets in Russia you'll need your passport and visa. Most Aeroflot offices in the country have a special window for foreigners and international flights, so you won't have to wait in huge queues, though you will pay foreigners' rates unless you have a student or diplomatic visa. At crowded ticket offices it's a good idea to get to any window you can and show your passport, making it clear that you're a foreigner. Since foreigners have to pay about three times as much as Russians for their tickets, staff are often keen to sell to foreigners and may even find seats on supposedly full planes. Flight tickets can also be purchased at the airport right up to the departure of the plane and sometimes even if the city/town centre office says that the plane is full.

Costs
On some routes there are fare differences depending on which airline you fly, where the plane stops, and sometimes the time of departure or arrival. The only ways to find out about these are to scrutinise timetables – if you can find them – or ask at ticket outlets. On all flights foreigners have to pay about three times as much as Russians, and as you have to show your passport when you buy the ticket there's no getting around this.

Return fares are usually just double the one-way fares. The following approximate one-way foreigners' fares and flying times from Moscow to other Russian and ex-

EUROPEAN RUSSIA

Soviet cities are representative of those throughout the country:

Almaty – US$250, five hours
Arkhangelsk – US$115, three hours
Astrakhan – US$130, 2¼ hours
Baku – US$160, three hours
Irkutsk – US$250, 7½ hours
Kiev – US$130, 1½ hours
Minsk – US$100, 1½ hours
Murmansk – US$145, three hours
Novgorod – US$85, 1½ hours
Novosibirsk – US$210, four hours
Petrozavodsk – US$75, 2½ hours
Pskov – US$90, 1½ hours
Sochi – US$130, 2½ hours
St Petersburg – US$75, 1½ hours (Pulkovo Air)
    US$85, 1½ hours (Transaero)
Tallinn – US$110, 1½ hours
Tashkent – US$220, four hours
Riga – US$115, 1½ hours
Vilnius – US$90, 1½ hours
Vladivostok – US$400, nine hours
Yekaterinburg – US$115, 2½ hours

BUS

All Russian buses can now be taken by foreigners and are a great way to travel when journeying between small towns. In some regions, like border areas, central Karelia, south-western Russia and the Kola Peninsula, bus travel may be the only option you have. There are no foreigners' prices on buses – you pay the same as Russians. But Russia's long-distance bus stations – like long-distance bus stations everywhere – are scoundrel magnets, and are rarely pleasant places to visit after dark.

Getting Tickets

Forget Intourist and many travel agents, who feel that bus travel is not for foreigners. Most cities have a main intercity bus station (*avtovokzal*, '*af-tah-vahk-ZAHL*'), usually called the *tsentralnyy avtovokzal* (central bus station) even if it's on the edge of town. There are several services a day to main regional destinations. Prices are comparable to Russian-price 2nd-class train fares; journey times depend on road conditions but probably average somewhere between those of a *skoryy* and a *passazhirskiy* train.

Tickets are sold at the station, where

smouldering queues wait quasi-patiently for the window to begin selling seats. This usually happens an hour or two before a bus is scheduled to depart. Ticket prices are usually listed on the timetable and posted on a wall. As often as not you'll get a ticket with a seat assignment.

If tickets seem to be sold out, you can, of course, negotiate with the driver. There will be competition for the remaining floor space, and you'll need to act sharp and stay alert. Find out what platform your bus is leaving from and get there NOW. Proffer the correct ticket price – many drivers will let you buy the ticket without a mark-up if you keep your mouth shut and act as though you do this every day. If that's refused, work your way upwards. Note that it's illegal for buses to carry more passengers than they have seats; drivers may ask those standing to duck when the bus passes road checkpoints.

Costs

Some sample one-way bus fares include the following:

Moscow-Kazan – US$20
Moscow-Nizhny Novgorod – US$6
Moscow-Novgorod – US$13
Moscow-Suzdal – US$3
Moscow-Voronezh – US$13
Moscow-Yaroslavl – US$6
Bryansk-Smolensk – US$4.30
Krasnodar-Sochi – US$2.40
Makhachkala-Derbent – US$1.50
Mineralnye Vody-Terskol (Mt Elbrus) – US$2.50
Murmansk-Apatity – US$7
Murmansk-Petrozavodsk – US$9.50
Oryol-Kursk – US$3.50
Petrozavodsk-Kem – US$7.50
St Petersburg-Novgorod – US$10
Vologda-Arkhangelsk – US$14
Voronezh-Tambov – US$5.60

TRAIN

European Russia is crisscrossed with an extensive rail network that makes rail a viable means of getting to practically anywhere. Train journeys are cheap and relatively comfortable but they usually take a long, long time. If you like trains, and if you or your travelling partner speaks good

Russian, they're an excellent way to get around, see the countryside and meet Russians from all walks of life. A good 1st or 2nd-class berth on a Russian sleeper train could prove more civilised than one in Western Europe as they're often larger and more comfortable.

The whole Russian rail network runs on Moscow time. You'll find timetables and station clocks on Moscow time. The only general exception is suburban rail services, which stick to local time.

Types of Train

There is nothing quite like the smell of a Russian train: it's a mixture of coal smoke and coffee, cigarettes and sweat, sausage and vodka, garlic and beef pie and dozens of other elements that combine to form an aroma that's neither bad nor good but so distinctive it will be permanently etched in your mind's nose.

Long Haul The regular long-distance service is a *skoryy poezd* (fast train). It stops more often than the typical intercity train in the West and rarely gets up enough speed really to merit the 'fast' label. Foreigners booking rail tickets through agencies are usually put on a skoryy train. The best skoryy trains often have names. These name trains (*firmennye poezdy*) generally have cleaner cars, polite(er) attendants and more convenient arrival/departure hours; and sometimes fewer stops, more 1st-class accommodation or functioning restaurants. There are over 50 name trains from Moscow and they're usually identifiable on timetables as their names are often given there. They have names like Baykal (to Irkutsk), Vologodskie Zori (to Vologda), Intourist, Express, Beryozka and others (to St Petersburg), Moskva Express (to Berlin) and so on.

A *passazhirskiy poezd* (passenger train) is an intercity stopping train, found mostly on routes of 1000 km or less. These can take an awfully long time as they clank and lurch from one small town to the next.

Short Haul A *prigorodnyy poezd* (suburban train), also called an *elektrichka*, is a local service linking a city and its suburbs or nearby towns, or groups of adjacent towns – often useful for day trips, though they can be fearfully crowded. There's no need to book ahead for these – just buy your ticket and go. In bigger stations there may be separate timetables, ticket halls (usually called the *prigorodnyy zal*) and platforms for these trains.

Classes

With a reservation, your ticket will normally give the numbers of your carriage (*vagon*) and seat (*mesto*).

1st Class Compartments in a 1st-class carriage, also called soft class (*myagkiy*) or sleeping car (*spalnyy vagon, SV* or *lyux*), have upholstered seats and convert to comfortable sleeping compartments for two people. You will be given two sheets, a washcloth, a pillowcase and a blanket. Your mattress will be rolled up on the seats at the beginning of the journey. Mattresses are usually rather...shall we say, *lived in*, but the sheets are almost always clean and manage to cover things adequately.

2nd Class Compartments in a 2nd-class carriage, also called *kupeynyy* or *kupe* (compartmentalised) or hard class (*zhyostkiy*), are four-person (occasionally three-person) couchettes. The four and three-person varieties are sometimes given as 2/4 and 2/3 on fare lists (1/2 is 1st-class, two-person). Seats are leather or plastic and also form the lower pair of bunks. You have to pay a fee to the conductor (*provodnik*) for your bedding, usually about US$1 to US$1.50.

Other Classes *Platskartnyy* (reserved-place), sometimes also called hard class or 3rd class, has open bunk accommodation. Groups of hard bunks are partitioned, but not closed off, from each other, and many more are squeezed in than in 1st or 2nd class.

Obshchiy (general), also called 4th class, is unreserved bench-type seating. At times there might be room to lie down, while at other times there might not be enough room to sit. Prigorodnyy trains normally have only this type of accommodation. On a few shorter haul intercity trains there are higher grade obshchiy carriages with more comfortable, reserved chairs. Obshchiy is rare on skoryy trains.

Travelling with Children On many trains there will be a special wagon for people travelling with children. There are also special ticket windows (see Getting Tickets later in this chapter) for passengers with children. These wagons are watched over by an especially matronly wagon attendant who keeps, you can be sure, the riffraff out.

On the Journey
The compartments are comfortable but can get a little close after several hours. You can stow your luggage in the steel bins beneath the lower bunks or above the door – the bins are safer. Smoking is forbidden in the compartments (young toughs usually have arguments with the attendants about this rule), but permitted in the spaces at the ends of the cars, past the toilets or the attendant's room. Here there'll almost always be a tin can wired to the door which will serve as an ashtray; otherwise, it's usual to throw your butts on the floor.

The provodnik or provodnitsa may not smile too often, but they are generally among the best hearted service workers in the country, providing cups of tea from their samovars – though you shouldn't rely on these for all your liquid intake – and often a wake-up call (or bellow) on arrival. On long trips it's well worth your while to be friendly to the attendant.

Many passengers bring comfortable 'lounging' clothes for the trip such as track suits and slippers. Sleeping compartments are mixed sex; when women show that they want to change or get out of bed, men go out and loiter in the corridor.

Food & Drink Take as much food and drink with you as you think you'll need for the whole trip. The food in restaurant cars, if there is any, is repugnant, and you're unlikely to find much edible at halts along the way. On long trips Russian travellers bring great bundles of food which they spread out and – as dictated by railway etiquette – offer to each other; you should do the same. Good rail foods are sausage, Marmite, Vegemite and peanut butter, ham, pot noodles, bread, cheese and chocolate: basically, any dense food that doesn't require refrigeration. Always remember to bring along bottled water for the trip as there'll be none available on the train. Almost every train in Russia has a samovar at the end of the carriage filled with boiling water that's safe to drink.

At many stations, hawkers will come aboard selling beer, soft drinks, sandwiches and other food and, near borders, cigarettes and vodka. Be suspicious of all food sold like this, though hard-boiled eggs are generally all right to eat. Most city stations have a bufet but it won't be anything special.

Information
Some major stations used by tourists have Intourist offices, which you can call at if you need help. Ask for Intourist or *mezhdunarodnyy sektor* (international section).

Left Luggage
Many railway stations have either a left-luggage room (*kamera khranenia*, камера хранения) or left-luggage lockers (*avtomaticheskie kamery khranenia*, автоматические камеры хранения). These are generally secure, but make sure you note down their opening and closing hours and, if in doubt, establish how long you can leave your stuff for.

Here is how to work the left-luggage lockers (they're generally the same everywhere). Be suspicious of people who offer to help you work them, above all when it comes to selecting your combination.

1. Buy two tokens *(zhetony)* from the attendant – these may even be old 15 kopeck coins.
2. Find an empty locker.

3. Put your stuff in.
4. Decide on a combination of one Russian letter and three numbers and for God's sake *write it down*. Write down your locker number, too.
5. Set the combination on the inside of the locker door.
6. Put one token in the slot.
7. Close the locker.

To open the locker, set your combination on the outside of your locker door. Note that even though it seems as if the knobs on the outside of the door should correspond directly with those on the inside, the letter is always the left-most knob, followed by three numbers, on both the inside and the outside. After you've set your combination, put a token in the slot. You'll probably start to freak when nothing happens; wait a second or two for the electrical humming sound and then pull open the locker.

Getting Tickets

Outside St Petersburg and Moscow (see those city sections), getting tickets for the Russian price is generally no big deal, though getting tickets for Russian trains is an art in and of itself. Most railway station ticket windows are maddeningly inefficient, and long waits are the rule. But as far as paying the Russian price, it's quite a simple matter as long as you're willing to do what Russians do to get *their* tickets.

Russian railway stations can be very confusing places for a foreigner. Bigger cities do have special ticket offices for foreigners, which may be in the station but are usually several km away, that are easier to deal with. (You'll have to pay foreigner prices at these.)

Ticket windows are a uniquely Russian experience; they're invariably thick glass with a postage-stamp-sized opening through which you have to shout your request, sometimes with a microphone/speaker system that renders any spoken word unintelligible. There are several ticket windows in larger stations, usually one or more general ticket windows (for the purchase of all ticket types), and one or more 'special' windows exclusively for veterans, the elderly or infirm, heroes of the Great Patriotic War and passengers travelling with children. Queuing at one of the special windows means risking a long wait only to be told you're in the wrong queue.

The correct window will invariably be the one behind which an attendant is reading a newspaper, blissfully unaware of the pleas of the crowds that are pressing against the glass, mumbling obscenities and jockeying for position. Crowds are lighter at certain times of the day, depending on rail schedules; sometimes you'll wait only a few minutes, while at other times you can wait hours. There's just no way around standing in a massive queue unless you're willing to risk not getting a seat and paying highly inflated prices by bribing your way on to the train, which is iffy.

The final obstacle is the astounding *tekhnologicheskiy pereryv* (the 'technical break'). This may happen four times a day, and is strictly observed in as much as each window is closed for *at least* the posted times. People often queue at a window that's scheduled to reopen in 15 minutes or so.

Once (if) you get to the front of the queue, you can usually get the ticket you want fairly easily provided you have all the information as you need – your destination, the train number, the date and time of departure, the type of accommodation and the number of tickets – and even more easily if you have all this written down in Cyrillic. Use ordinary (Arabic) numerals for the day of the month and Roman numerals for the month (see the boxed aside Reading a Train Timetable later in this chapter for more information).

If you just can't cope with all this, you can attempt to enlist the help of a station official, who may even try to help a foreigner. Some key words are: *nachalnik* (boss), *administrator* (manager) and *dispetcher* (dispatcher). Asking for help from anyone usually brings some reward, but, obviously, ordinary mortals have less clout than station officials.

You can usually get a seat on a 'sold-out' train by speaking with a carriage attendant – *provodnik* (male) or *provodnitsa* (female). If you don't have a ticket, try to find a friendly provodnik, state your destination, and offer a price. To estimate prices for Russian citizens, subtract a third to a half from the prices in the table. Offer the face ticket price first and move slowly upwards from there – you can usually reach an agreement.

Suburban Trains Tickets for these – which are very cheap – are often sold at separate windows. There are also machines (*avtomaticheskie kassy*) which would work if a system of tokens could be agreed upon. A table beside the machine tells you which price zone *(zona)* your destination is in. You deposit coins or tokens (when they're available) and press buttons for one-way *(tuda)* or return *(obratno)*, full fare *(polny)* or child *(detsky)*.

Costs

If there's a method used by Russian Rail in calculating their fares, it's probably a corollary of Fermat's last theorem. The most important facts are:

'If/Then' logical statements should not be relied on, no matter how great the temptation. For example, the statement 'If the train from Vologda to Moscow, which takes eight hours, costs US$12.50, then the train to St Petersburg (10½ hours) should cost about US$14' would be incorrect. The train to St Petersburg may take longer yet cost less.

Foreigners are supposed to pay special fares, higher than those Russians pay. In practice this is often not enforced if you buy your tickets at stations – you don't need a passport or visa to book a train ticket: speak Russian or write your destination and desired train number, time, date and class down in Russian and you'll probably pay the Russian rate. This is more difficult on a few major tourist routes, including the Moscow-St Petersburg line and the main trans-Siberian trains, where even if you manage to get a Russian-price ticket, you run the risk of costly 'fines' along the way. Westerners booking through Intourist and related agencies will always pay foreigner rates. The difference between foreigner and Russian fares goes up and down – and also varies between routes: at the time of writing foreigner fares were mostly 50% to 100% higher than Russian fares.

Different trains on the same route may have different fares – in particular a firmennyy poezd is likely to be anywhere in between 10% and 50% more expensive than other trains.

You'll always pay more for a train ticket from abroad than if you were to buy it in Russia – even at the full foreigner rate; availability is such that there's not much advantage in buying tickets abroad.

First-class fares are generally 60% to 100% higher than 2nd-class; 3rd-class is about 40% less than 2nd-class; 4th-class is about 60% less than 2nd-class. If you have children, one child under five travels free; other children under 10 pay half-fare.

Fares are frequently hiked upward by large amounts to compensate for inflation. In this book we don't generally give rail fares in regional chapters, as they are so variable. The following table is a rough guide only. At the time of writing, these are typical 2nd-class foreigners' fares between Moscow and a number of Russian and ex-Soviet cities on skoryy trains (including bedding charges) purchased from railway stations or other official sources:

Almaty – US$93.50
Arkhangelsk – US$38
Astrakhan – US$45
Brest – US$35.50
Irkutsk – US$120
Kaliningrad – US$40.50
Kazan – US$29
Kiev – US$45
Khabarovsk – US$229
Kursk – US$26
Minsk – US$29
Murmansk – US$53
Nizhny Novgorod – US$26
Novgorod – US$27.50
Novosibirsk – US$110
Odessa – US$45
Oryol – US$22.50
Perm – US$42
Pskov – US$27.50
Pyatigorsk – US$52
Riga – US$34
Rostov-on-Don – US$42
Simferopol – US$42
Smolensk – US$26
Sochi – US$53.50
St Petersburg $28
Tallinn – US$34
Tashkent – US$85
Ulan-Ude – US$119.50
Vilnius – US$37
Vladikavkaz US$56.50
Vladivostok – US$235
Vologda – US$24
Vyborg – US$29
Yekaterinburg – US$50

Dangers & Annoyances

Some intercity trains – especially train No 35/36 between Moscow and St Petersburg – have been plagued by midnight rip-offs. Make certain on all sleepers that your baggage is stowed, preferably in the steel bins beneath the lower bunks. When you lock your door, remember that it can be unlocked with a rather simple key; on the left side of the door about three-quarters of the way up there's a small steel switch that flips up, blocking the door from opening more

Reading a Train Timetable

Russian rail timetables vary from place to place, but generally list: a destination; train number; category of train; frequency of service; and time of departure and arrival, in *Moscow time* unless otherwise noted (see the following).

Trains in smaller city stations generally begin somewhere else, so you'll see a starting point and a destination on the timetable. For example, when catching a train from Petrozavodsk to Murmansk, the timetable may list Moscow as an origination point and Murmansk as the destination. The following are a few key points to look out for.

Number *Nomer*, Номер. The higher the number of a train, the slower it is; anything over 900 is likely to be a mail train (mail posted from Minsk during the early Pleistocene epoch is just now arriving in Belgorod).

Category Скорый, Пассажирский, Почтовый-багажный, Пригородный (*Skoryy, Passazhirskiy, Pochtovyy-bagazhnyy, Prigorodnyy*) and various abbreviations thereof, are train categories and refer, respectively, to fast, passenger, post-cargo and suburban trains. There may also be the name of the train, usually in Russian quotation marks, eg "Нижегородец" ('*Nizhegorodets*').

Frequency ежедневно (*yezhednevno*, daily); чётные (*chyotnye*, even dates); нечётные (*nechyotnye*, odd dates); отменён (*otmenyon*, cancelled). All of these, as well, can appear in various abbreviations. Days of the week are listed usually as numbers (where 1 is Monday and 7 Sunday) or as abbreviations of the name of the day (Пон, Вт, Ср, Чт, Пт, Сб and Вск are, respectively, Monday to Sunday).

On some trains, frequency depends on the time of year, in which case details are usually given in hard-to-decipher, abbreviated, small print: eg '27/VI – 31/VIII Ч; 1/IX – 25/VI 2,5' means that from 27 June to 31 August the train runs on even dates, while from 1 September to 25 June it runs on Tuesday and Friday. See, it's really quite straightforward (once you've wrapped your mind around the fact that Russians use Roman numerals to denote months!).

Arrival & Departure Times Most train times are given in a 24-hour time format, and almost always in Moscow time (Московское время, *Moskovskoe vremya*). But suburban trains are usually marked in local time (местное время, *mestnoe vremya*). From here in it gets tricky (as though the rest isn't), so don't confuse the following:

время отправления (*vremya otpravlenia*), which means time of departure;
Время отправления с начального пункта (*vremya otpravlenia s nachalnogo punkta*), the time of departure from the train's starting point;
время прибытия (*vremya pribytia*), the time of arrival at the station you're in;
время прибытия на конечный пункт (*vremya pribytia na konechnyy punkt*), the time of arrival at the destination;
время в пути (*vremya v puti*), the duration of the journey.

Corresponding trains running in opposite directions on the same route may appear on the same line of the timetable. In this case you may find route entries like время отправления с конечного пункта (*vremya otpravlenia s konechnogo punkta*), or the time the return train leaves its station of origin.

Distance You may sometimes see the растояние (*rastoyanie*), distance in km, on the timetable as well, but they're probably lying.

John Noble & Nick Selby

than a few cm. Flip this switch up and make sure to stuff some balled-up toilet paper or a piece of cork in the cavity so it can't be flipped back down by a bent coat-hanger.

Generally, Russians love speaking with foreigners; on long train rides, they love drinking with them as well. Turning this down is not always as easy as it would seem. Choose your drinking partners very carefully on trains, and only drink from new bottles and only when you can watch the seal being broken. If you have a bad feeling about someone, saying '*Ya alkogolik/alkogolichka*' ('I'm an alcoholic', in masculine and feminine forms) will usually stop them from pressing.

CAR & MOTORBIKE

Driving in Russia isn't everybody's cup of tea but if you've got a sense of humour and don't mind some fairly rugged road conditions, a few hassles finding petrol, and getting lost now and then, it's a great way to see European Russia. You experience at least one aspect of Russian reality as the locals do, see more of the countryside, and have total independence from the Russian transportation system until you run out of petrol.

See the previous Getting There & Away chapter for information on planning and preparing a trip to Russia with your own vehicle.

Road Rules

Russians drive on the right. Speed limits are generally 60 km/h in towns and 110 km/h on the open highway, though sometimes signs indicate other limits. There may be a 90 km/h zone, enforced by speed traps, as you leave a city.

Technically the maximum legal blood-alcohol content is 0.04%, but in practice it is illegal to drive after consuming *any* alcohol at all. This is a rule that is strictly enforced. The normal way of establishing alcohol in the blood is by a blood test (it's best to carry syringes; see the Health section in the European Russia Facts for the Visitor chapter) but apparently you can be deemed under its influence even without any test.

The GAI The State Automobile Inspectorate, GAI ('*gah-yee*', short for Gosudarstvennaya Avtomobilnaya Inspektsia) skulks about on the roadsides, waiting for speeding, headlightless or other miscreant vehicles. Officers of the GAI are authorised to stop you (they do this by pointing their striped, sometimes lighted, stick at you and waving you towards the side), issue on-the-spot fines (in roubles only – you should get a receipt) and, worst of all, shoot at your car if you refuse to pull over. (While shooting is not common, neither is it uncommon. One trouble-making expatriate US resident had 18 bullet holes in his car after he refused to stop!) The GAI also hosts the occasional speed trap – the Moscow-Brest, Moscow-Oryol and Vyborg-St Petersburg roads have reputations for this. In cities, the GAI is everywhere, especially before big events. There are permanent GAI checkpoints at the boundary of every Russian city and many Russian towns. For serious infractions, the GAI can confiscate your licence and you'll have to retrieve it from the main station. GAI guys have been known to shake down foreigners. Don't give them any hard currency. Get receipts for any fine you pay and if you think you've been ripped off, head for the nearest GAI office and complain. Get the shield number of the 'arresting' officer.

Imposters There are GAI imposters in and around St Petersburg and Moscow, and on the roads between those cities and St Petersburg and Vyborg. If you're being flagged down by someone who looks like an officer, slow down and take a very good look before you stop.

The most important elements of a GAI uniform are the shield (badge) and the radio. The outfit itself is easy to come by, but shields and radios are zealously guarded.

The shield is silver with red lettering saying ГАИ (GAI) and a tricoloured Russian flag as well as a shield number. Any shield without the flag is bogus or left over from the Soviet era. Even if an officer is not wearing a uniform (they run short during major events like the Goodwill Games in St Petersburg), if he's got a shield he's probably legit.

The radio is another hard-to-come-by item. They're about as large as inexpensive CB radios from Radio Shack (Tandy), and usually have a leather holder on a leather sling. In some larger cities, GAI officers are now being issued more stylish (and smaller) Western-made Kenwood or Motorola radios.

Look to see that the officer is neatly groomed; if he's a slob, he's probably a fake.

Finally, real GAI officers will give you a preposterous little salute, and say something along the lines of 'Good day, I am officer (blah blah blah) of GAI,' and then tell you what you allegedly did wrong. Any other opening lines are against regulations.

If you're very sure you've been pulled over by a fake, make sure – very sure – that your fake is not armed, pull away as soon as you can and head for the nearest town border, where you'll find a real GAI station at which to report the incident. They actually do care; in 1994 the Moscow Times reported that a police commander had warned Russian citizens of these imposters, and recommended they take the action outlined above.

Fuel
Supplies of petrol (benzin) are erratic; this is obvious from the long lines of cars at petrol stations. Drivers pushing cars by hand (in order to save fuel) as the queue inches forward may become a familiar sight.

Petrol comes in four main grades – 76, 93, 95 and 98 octane. Unleaded is virtually non-existent. Most Western engines prefer 95 but often 93, or even only 76, is all that's available.

Some cities, including Vyborg, St Petersburg and Moscow, have Western joint-venture petrol stations; Neste is the most common. Petrol here costs slightly less than in Western Europe; in 1995, the cost for 76 octane was about US$0.25/litre.

The procedure at petrol stations is still Soviet-style. A petrol hose wound round the pump or on the ground means the pump is empty. If it's working the nozzle will be in the holder. When your turn comes, you stick the nozzle in your tank, run over and pay at the cashier's window – which is usually minuscule and gated, probably to protect the cashier from irate motorists – and the pump will be switched on to deliver the amount you have paid for. You might also have to press something on the pump to get the fuel flowing at last. Be absolutely certain that the attendant isn't trying to help you by offering you diesel for a vehicle they think would run well on it – like a pick-up truck or (in Nick's case) a Jeep Cherokee. Ask if the pump you're using is benzin or diesel (it sounds the same in Russian: dizel). You're not looking for premixed oil and petrol, either, unless your vehicle has a two-stroke engine.

Petrol stations aren't often more than 100 km apart, but don't rely on it.

Oil is maslo ('MAHS-lah'); the Russian version of Multigrade is called M10GI. Transmission oil is TAD-171 and antifreeze is TOSOL A-40. Air is vozdukh ('VOZ-dukh') and water is voda.

On the Road
The Atlas avtomobilnykh dorog road atlas of the former USSR (see Maps in the European Russia Facts for the Visitor chapter) is a useful thing to carry. Russian main roads are a mixed bag – sometimes smooth, straight dual carriageways, sometimes rough, narrow, winding and choked with the diesel fumes of the slow, heavy vehicles that make up a high proportion of Russian traffic. Driving much more than 300 km in a day usually gets pretty tiring.

Russian drivers use indicators far less than they should, and like to overtake everything on the road – on the inside. Priority rules at roundabouts seem to vary from area to area: all you can do is follow local practice. Russian drivers rarely switch on anything more than sidelights – and often not even those – until it's pitch black at night. Some say this is to avoid dazzling others, as for some reason dipping headlights is not a common practice. But maybe it's because they all have clapped-out batteries.

Don't expect to find many places for a decent meal between cities. You may even

A Day with One of Russia's Most Hated Public Servants

In the United States, it's the IRS. In the Soviet Union, it was the KGB. In England it's Manchester United fans, but in the new Russia, motorists and passengers alike loathe, fear and despise the ubiquitous members of the Gosavtoinspektsia: GAI.

GAI ('gah-yee') are traffic officers that stand at intersections throughout the country looking for signs of vehicular misbehaviour. Actually, they can pull you over for anything they want. And they do. But what makes them really annoying is that they're entitled to impose on-the-spot fines. Oh, yeah, one more thing: if you don't stop when they wave you over, they can shoot at your vehicle.

On my last trip to Russia I got pulled over twice in one day, while riding in two separate vehicles. I thought, 'What makes these guys tick?'. How do they decide whom to pull over? And is it exciting to be an armed traffic cop? I mean, their New York City counterparts would give a limb for the opportunity. In the interests of fair play, I spent a Monday morning with some of the guys at St Petersburg GAI Central.

[7 am. Roll Call] No big surprise, kinda like Hill Street Blues with shabbier uniforms. Hot sheet covered, accidents discussed, criminal element lamented. I learn that GAI guys work two days on, two days off, and they have regular beats.

[9 am. Upstairs Office] Meeting with Sergei (not his real name), a captain. Yes, we can shoot at your car. No, I can't tell you how many officers we have, but there are enough to keep control of the situation. I asked him what foreigners can do if they disagree with an officer's charges against him. 'Well, their documents will be confiscated and then they can go to the address on the ticket the officer gives them and get them back...' Oh.

[10 am. Car Pool] Sergei leads the way to his spanking new Ford Escort GAImobile. We're off to check out the boys on patrol. Obeying the seat-belt law, I fasten mine. Sergei ignores his, peels out of the parking space, turns on the revolving blue light and, in blatant violation of every St Petersburg traffic law, does 120 km/h (80 mph) through narrow city streets; he runs all red traffic lights, honks and shoots truly terrifying looks at motorists he passes – which is all of them.

[10.30 am. Checkpoint on the St Petersburg-Murmansk Highway] There are GAI checkpoints at all major roads leading out of the city. We arrive in time to see one incoming and one outgoing car being tossed by Kalashnikov automatic rifle-wielding officers. They salute Sergei, who leads me into the checkpoint station house where he proudly shows off the station sauna (it's a four-seater). Has another officer demonstrate the state-of-the-art computer system (it's a 386 running MTEZ). They dial in to the GAI Server and the officer stumbles through the log-in. After five minutes he gives up and instead proffers the hand-written hot sheet.

[11.15 am. Through the City] Screeching through residential neighbourhoods, Sergei is explaining how the officers we're whizzing by are trained professionals – they spend six months in the GAI academy after their army service. We pass about half a dozen stopped cars, and Sergei

---

drive a whole day without passing anywhere that sells hot drinks.

Traffic lights that flicker green are about to change to yellow, then red. Flickering yellow traffic lights mean that the junction isn't regulated by the lights.

Radar detectors are legal in Russia, and are probably a handy bit of equipment to have along.

Breakdowns In case of breakdown or accident the best thing to do is get help as soon as possible from the nearest Intourist office or from the GAI, the latter of which is obliged to help you arrange repairs. Automobile Towing Service (Avtotransportnoe Predpriyatie; ☎ (095) 188 65 01) in Moscow says it does towing within the hour. In St Petersburg, a joint-venture towing firm called Spas 001 (☎ 001) will do quick tows and/or repairs. See *The Traveller's Yellow Pages Moscow* and *The Traveller's Yellow Pages St Petersburg* for listings of automobile repair shops. *Louis Motorist's Guide to the Soviet Union* (see Books in the European Russia Facts for the Visitor chapter) has several pages of phrases to describe anything that could go wrong with a car.

is saying, 'He's checking documents...This one's checking insurance...that one's investigating a stolen car...' He can tell all that by passing them at speed. Amazing. Sergei says he's been in 'many' high-speed car chases and I believe him totally. Not out of idle curiosity, I ask him how long it takes to fill in an accident report. He says a minimum of one hour.

[11.40 am. Checkpoint on the St Petersburg-Vyborg Highway] This is exactly the same as the first checkpoint, except this one is on the road leading to Finland and there's no sauna. There's an enormous pile of cash on the desk. Checkpoint officer tells me that their radar gun is 'out for repair', but helpfully points out one of the other pieces of crime-fighting equipment present: the telephone. Sergei says that radar detectors are 'unfortunately not prohibited here'. That's Russian cop lingo for 'They're legal'.

[12.10 pm. Petrograd Side] As we career home, Sergei spots a stalled pick-up truck. His face a mask of pure anger, he screeches to a halt, tickets the hapless driver, calls in his number plates (to ensure follow-up action) and we drive away. As we tear back to the station house, Sergei suddenly stops to let a dump truck, for which the signal is green, pass through an intersection, and (I swear) says solemnly, 'You know, even though I have this siren on, I still have a responsibility to maintain safety on the roads.'

And people say these guys aren't dedicated public servants.

Nick Selby

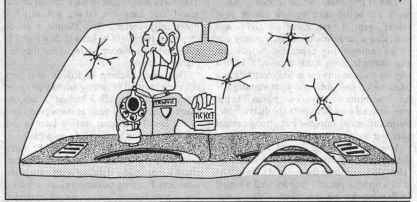

Driving in Cities Driving yourself isn't a bad way of getting around cities if you avoid morning and evening peak hours and don't mind adding to the pollution or getting caught up in some nasty one-way systems. But signposting in cities is poor – and in particular, the signposts to your hotel virtually always peter out just before that vital last turning, leaving you lost and rewarding you with several km of additional travelling at the end of a day's drive. Watch out for tram lines, which can make a horrible, buckled mess of the road surface; trolleybuses which swing a long way out as they leave a stop; traffic

lights obscured by jumbles of wires; and signs obscured by overhanging foliage.

Trams always have right of way over other vehicles and sometimes assert this right rather violently. Vehicles have right of way over pedestrians.

Parking On-street parking poses few problems in general, but break-ins are all too frequent. Some hotels have locked-up compounds where you can leave your car overnight, but often you just have to leave it out the front. Leave nothing of value on or inside it. 'Value' here means any value at all:

remove sunglasses, cigarettes, cassette tapes, and especially windscreen wipers.

Car Rental

In a few cities you can rent self-drive cars from Russian or joint-venture outfits. See Getting Around in the Moscow and St Petersburg chapters and other city sections for more information. You can book self-drive rental cars in St Petersburg and Moscow through travel agents in the West, though it will be expensive. If you're intending to use a rental car for intercity travel, or if your plans otherwise rely on having one, you need to make absolutely sure it will be available before you confirm.

This is important. Some serious groundwork has to be done by you and/or your travel agent if your dates are tight, and reserving a car from outside the country can be an outrageously expensive proposition (for example, Avis wants almost US$170 a day for an economy car in St Petersburg and Moscow). Look into non-joint-venture car hire and work out a plan B to put into action if a car turns out to be unavailable. Some offices of Intourist can arrange rental cars, but not from abroad.

You could do worse than a Lada. They're the butt of many a poor joke in the West – Q: 'How do you double the value of a Lada?' A: 'Fill it up with petrol' – but are well adapted to Russian driving conditions. Other rental cars in Russia tend to be either Fords (usually with driver; see the following section), Nissans or Mitsubishis.

With all rental agencies, check whether there are any limits on where you can take the vehicle, and look carefully into the insurance situation and other small print.

Ask to borrow a petrol canister. Your life will be made a whole lot easier if you can get one.

Chauffeur-Driven Cars If your budget is big enough, a chauffeur-driven car can be a reasonable way to get from one city to another where other transport services are weak. The cost is about US$12 an hour plus a per-km charge. This works out about the same as, or a little less than, a self-drive rental car for trips up to 125 km, but much more for longer distances – about US$175 for a 250-km trip, for instance. If you want to make any stops or side trips in a chauffeured car, specify them when you make the booking. If you don't, the driver may refuse to do anything other than go from A to B as fast as possible. Depending on the company, cars may be Volgas (the same make as official Russian taxis), but more frequently are Nissans, Mitsubishis or Fords.

HITCHING

Hitching is never entirely safe in any country in the world, and we don't recommend it. Travellers who decide to hitch should understand that they are taking a small but potentially serious risk. People who do choose to hitch will be safer if they travel in pairs and let someone know where they are planning to go.

That said, hitching in Russia is a very common method of getting around. In cities, hitching rides is called hailing a cab, no matter what type of vehicle stops (see Taxis in the Local Transport section later in this chapter). In the countryside, especially in remote areas not well served by public transport, hitching is a major mode of transport. Rides are hailed by standing at the side of the road and flagging passing vehicles with a low, up-and-down wave (not an extended thumb). You're expected to pitch in for petrol; paying what would be the normal bus fare for a long-haul ride is considered appropriate.

While hitching is widely accepted here – and therefore safer than in some other countries – there are always yahoos and lunatics puttering down the nation's highways and byways. Use common sense and keep safe. Avoid hitching at night. Women should exercise extreme caution and everyone should avoid hitching alone.

BOAT

The great rivers that wind across the flat expanses of Russia are the country's oldest highways. A millennium ago the early Russians based their power on control of the waterborne trade between the Baltic and Black seas. River transport remains important and in summer it's possible to travel long distances across Russia on passenger boats. You can do this either by taking a cruise, bookable through agencies in the West (often expensive) or in Russia, or by using scheduled river passenger services. The season runs from late May to mid-October but is shorter on some routes.

On timetables and fare tables, Raketa, Kometa and Meteor are all types of hydrofoil; *skoraya* (fast) usually refers to steamships; *gidrofoyl*, *skorostnaya* (high-speed) or *na podvodnykh krylyakh* (underwaterwinged) to hydrofoils. *Vverkh* means upstream, *vnizu* downstream; *tuda* means one way, *krugovoy* return.

Major Routes

European Russia's main waterway network extends from St Petersburg to Astrakhan, near the Volga's delta on the Caspian Sea, via the Neva, Svir and Volga rivers and a series of linking canals. Moscow is part of this system.

The main passenger services ply between Moscow and St Petersburg, and between Moscow and various points on the Volga and Don including Yaroslavl, Nizhny Novgorod, Volgograd and Astrakhan.

At the time of writing there don't appear to be any scheduled services on the Moscow-St Petersburg route, only cruises. The common Moscow-St Petersburg cruise route heads north via Uglich to Lake Onega, with stops in Petrozavodsk and Kizhi Island, then south-west to Lake Ladoga, north to Valaam, and south to the Neva and St Petersburg. Some trips detour down the Volga from Uglich to places such as Yaroslavl, Kostroma, Plyos and Nizhny Novgorod. A 13-day locally booked cruise from Moscow to St Petersburg might cost anywhere between US$260 and US$413 depending on the class of cabin, the ship and so on.

The Volga routes are served by both scheduled services and cruises. You can use

the scheduled services for short hops from one city to the next: they have a huge range of fares depending on the class of cabin: Moscow to Yaroslavl costs from US$7 to US$117; and Moscow to Astrakhan, US$25 to US$450 (food not included). Cruises are mostly return: Moscow-Yaroslavl-Moscow, four or five days, costs from US$70 to US$180; and Moscow-Astrakhan-Moscow, 18 to 20 days, from US$425 to US$4275.

See the Moscow, Around Moscow, St Petersburg and Volga Region chapters for more detail on services and bookings in Russia. In St Petersburg, cruises can be booked through the offices of Sindbad Travel, Peter TIPS, or the St Petersburg Travel Company.

Other Routes

Other river or sea passenger services in Russia, some served by hydrofoil, include: along the Neva River and the Gulf of Finland from St Petersburg to Petrodvorets, Kronstadt and Lomonosov; from St Petersburg to Valaam in Lake Ladoga; on Lake Onega, from Petrozavodsk to Kizhi; from Kem (Karelia) and Arkhangelsk to the Solovetsky Islands; from Pskov to Tartu (Estonia); between Novgorod and Staraya Russa; along the Kuban River from Krasnodar; and along the Black Sea coast between Sochi, Novorossiysk and other places.

Overseas Booking Agencies

You can book Moscow-St Petersburg and Volga cruises through travel agents including some of those listed under Travel Agencies in the European Russia Getting There & Away chapter. Agencies in the USA that specialise in Russian river cruises include:

Marketing International (☎ (800) 578 7742 or (415) 592 1397), Belmont, CA – operates luxury cruises on the *Lev Tolstoy*; 20-day cruises start at US$1399 per person in double cabins, US$1499 for single cabins;

EuroCruises (☎ (800) 688 3876 or (212) 691 2099), 303 West 13th St, New York, NY 10014 – runs 12-day packages between St Petersburg and Moscow aboard the *Sergey Kirov* from US$2959 per person double occupancy including airfares (ex-New York; cruise only can be arranged). They also run trips between St Petersburg and Rostov-on-Don including 17-night cruises aboard the *Alexey Surkov* at US$3639 per person including airfares, transfers and Moscow hotel and tours;

Odessa America Cruise Company (☎ (516) 747 8880; fax (516) 747 8367), 170 Old Country Rd, Mineola, NY 11501 – does Moscow-St Petersburg cruises aboard the *Lenin* and the *Andropov*. These 14-day cruises cost between US$895 and US$1595;

Cruise Tours (☎ (800) 248 6542), Slate Hill, NY – runs 12-day tours aboard the *Alexander Griboedov*; prices start at about US$899 per person in double cabins;

GT Cruises (☎ (718) 934 4100), 2610 East 16th St, Brooklyn, NY 11235 – runs 15-day cruises between Moscow and St Petersburg (with four days in both cities including excursions) on the *Russ*; cheapest cabins start at US$699 per person in a quad.

LOCAL TRANSPORT

Most cities have good public transport systems combining bus, trolleybus and tram; the biggest cities also have metro systems. Public transport is very cheap, and is easy to use, especially if you can decipher Cyrillic. Taxis are fairly plentiful, and are usually cheap by Western standards.

Orientation & Maps

Tourist hotels are often among the highest buildings in town, and a ride up to the top floor by lift is often a fine way of getting your bearings in a new city.

A few tourist maps show some bus routes and so on; in some cities there are also transport maps called *Skhema passazhirskogo transporta*, which again are extremely useful if you can decipher Cyrillic.

Potentially confusing is the wave of street name changes over recent years, with Soviet-era names being replaced by new ones honouring modern heroes or by revived, pre-communist names. We mention old street names in the Moscow and St Petersburg chapters and in other city sections where the changes could cause problems.

Metro

Moscow and St Petersburg have metro systems. If the rest of the Soviet Union had worked as efficiently as the metro, it would have kicked Western butt: these metros leave their Western counterparts in the dust. Once you've learnt a couple of basics, they're even easy to use.

Stations are mostly identified from outside by big M signs. Metro tokens (zhetony) are sold at the ticket window; in 1995, a ride on the Moscow or St Petersburg metro cost US$0.10. The lobby has a row of low gates through which you pass to enter the system, and usually the last map of the system you'll see before you board the train. Put your token in the slot beside the gate, wait until the little light changes from red to green (or approximations of those colours), then go. If you try to go before the lights change, metal arms come across to stop you.

Down at platform level, signs in Cyrillic list the stations to which trains go from the different platforms. If you can't decipher them, just tell someone the name of your destination station. The supervisors at the bottom of escalators or in lobbies are also adept at helping lost passengers, even without a word of common language.

Digital clocks at the end of platforms tell you the time and how long it is since the last train left. Five minutes is a long time. Just before a departing train's doors close, a recorded voice, still full of the optimism of socialist progress, announces 'Ostorozhno! Dveri zakryvayutsya. Sleduyushchaya stantsia (name of next station)'. This means 'Careful! The doors are closing. Next station (name of next station)'. Just before it stops at the next station, the words are 'Stantsia (name of station)'. In case you don't catch these, or they come confusingly close together, as they often do in St Petersburg, the surest way of getting off at the right station is to count the stops. You can't rely on spotting signs on the platforms as you pull in.

To exit to the street, follow signs saying Выход в город (*Vykhod v gorod*, Exit to the city). If there's more than one exit, each sign names the street you come out on. If you need to change to another line, the process is much the same whether it passes through the same station or through a nearby one linked by underground walkways. The word to look for is Переход (*Perekhod*, Change), often with a blue-background man-on-stairs sign, followed by на станцию... (*na stantsiyu...*, to...station) or на...линию (*na...liniyu*, to...line), then usually к поездам до станций... (*k poezdam do stantsiy...*, to trains to...stations).

Bus, Trolleybus & Tram

These three forms of transport are often the only means of getting around towns, and even in cities with metros you often need above-ground transport, too. Services are frequent in city centres, but more erratic as you move out towards the edges. They can get jam-packed in the late afternoon or on poorly served routes.

A stop is usually marked by a roadside A (*avtobus*, *'uf-TOH-boos'*) sign for buses, T or П for trolleybuses (*'tra-LEY-boos'*), and ТРАМВАЙ (*'trum-VAI'*) or a T hanging over the road for trams. The normal fare in 1995 was under US$0.10.

Payment methods vary from city to city, but the most common method is to punch a ticket in little machines fixed inside the vehicle. You buy the tickets (*talony, 'tuh-LOHN-i'*) in strips of five or 10 from drivers – a sign in the window between the driver's compartment and the passenger area saying Талоны нет (*talony nyet*) means that the driver's out of tickets – from street kiosks displaying them in the window, or sometimes from sellers outside metro or railway stations. Ticket checkers are rare in some cities but widespread in others, including St Petersburg, where in 1995 the fine (*shtraf*) for riding without a ticket was US$4.75. Most passengers are honest and patiently pass each other's tickets up and down to the nearest punch, which is what you should do if someone pokes you and hands you a ticket.

Other payment methods include depositing a coin in a box and rolling out a ticket, or paying your fare to an absurdly dressed conductor (usually a woman with several rolls of tickets hanging from a rope round her neck).

On crowded transport people usually give up seats to women with children or a lot of baggage, and to old people. People manoeuvre their way out by asking anyone in the way: '*Vy vykhodite seychas?*' ('*vih vih-KHO-dee-tyeh sih-SHASS?*', 'Are you getting off now?'); or just '*Vykhodite?*' ('Getting off?'). If you're asked this, and you aren't getting off, step aside.

Marshrutnoe Taxi

A *marshrutnoe taxi* ('*marsh-ROOT-na-yuh tahk-SEE*') is a minibus running along a fixed route. You can get on at fixed stops but can get off anywhere; try saying '*Zdes pozhaluysta*' ('Here, please'). Their routes are hard to ascertain and their schedules erratic – it's easier to stick to other transport. Fares depend on the distance travelled.

Taxi

What's a Taxi? There are two main types of taxis in Russia: the official ones (four-door Volga sedans with a chequerboard strip down the side and a green light in the front window); and 'private' taxis (any other vehicle you may see; see also Hitching earlier in this chapter).

Official taxis have a meter that they sometimes use, though you can always negotiate an off-the-meter price. There's a flag-fall charge, and the number on the meter must be multiplied by the multiplier listed on a sign that *should* be on the dashboard or somewhere visible. Extra charges are incurred for radio calls and some night-time calls.

Unofficial or private taxis are anything you can stop. Stand at the side of the road, extend your arm and wait until something stops – it could be an ambulance, off-duty city bus, army jeep or just a passenger car. When someone stops for you, it's common to negotiate destination and fare either speaking through the passenger-side window or through a partially open door. State your destination, and if the driver's game, one of a couple of things will happen. If the driver asks you to *saditse* (sit down), just get in and when you reach the destination you pay what you feel the ride was worth. If the driver states a price, you can negotiate. Your offer has been rejected if the driver takes off in a huff.

Lastly, the driver may just ask you how much it's worth to you. For this you'll need to have spoken with locals to determine the average taxi fare in that city at the time of your visit; taxi prices around the country vary widely. Practice saying your destination and the amount you want to pay so it comes out properly. The more smoothly you speak, the lower the fare.

In 1995, a short trip through the centre of Moscow or St Petersburg was about US$3, from Sheremetevo-2 Airport to the Moscow Travellers Guest House was about US$30, and from Pulkovo-2 to the HI St Petersburg Hostel was about US$15 to US$20. A trip across the centre of Arkhangelsk was US$3, and from Murmansk's port to the 69th Parallel Hotel was about US$4. If possible, let a Russian friend negotiate for you: they'll do better than you will.

Risks & Precautions Now and then tales crop up of rip-offs or robberies in taxis. More of the tales involve the Sheremetevo Airport run in Moscow than anywhere else, and Russian citizens, rather than foreigners, seem to be the chief victims. The sort of things reported stolen are VCRs, personal computers and so on, brought back by citizens who have been abroad – but there are also sudden demands for a fare rise along the way. That's why it's important to make absolutely clear at the outset how much you'll pay.

Avoid taxis lurking outside foreign-run establishments, luxury hotels etc. They charge far too much and get uppity when you try to talk them down. Know your route, be familiar with how to get there and how long

it should take. Never get into a taxi with more than one person in it, especially after dark. Keep your fare money in a separate pocket to avoid flashing large wads of cash. Have the taxi stop at the corner nearest your destination, not the exact address, if you're staying at a private residence. Trust your instincts. If a driver looks creepy, take the next car. Check the back seat of the car for hidden friends before you get in.

Boat

In St Petersburg, Moscow and several other cities on rivers, coasts, lakes or reservoirs, public ferries and water excursions give a different perspective on the place. For details, see the relevant city chapters or sections.

TOURS

A guided tour in English can be a helpful introduction to a new city, or an easy way into a busy or restricted-access sight, or just a way of finding out more about a place. Package travellers will have several tours included in their itineraries. For individuals in Moscow and St Petersburg, local companies organise open group excursions to the main places of interest. In other cities, or for lesser sights in Moscow and St Petersburg, individuals who want an English-speaking guide must pay local travel agency, Intourist or Sputnik prices – or persuade a service bureau or tour group to let them join the group on one of its excursions, which is often quite easy. A good place to find English-speaking guides is an English-language institute (pedagogical institute), of which practically every town has at least one. Here you can meet English-language students who are as keen to speak with you as you are to speak with them. Your hotel administrator is in many cases another good source of English-speaking contacts.

On some excursions, it's worth trying to pin down exactly where you'll go and how you'll spend the time. Otherwise, if you have your heart set on a particular goal, you may be disappointed.

Even if you don't speak Russian, you

could consider joining the trips organised for Russian people by city excursion bureaus, shown on tourist maps as *gorodskoe byuro* *exkursiy*. These are very cheap – about US$1 or US$2 an hour – and some go to places that foreigners' tours don't.

Moscow
Москва

Population: nine million
(unofficial estimate: 13 to 14 million)
Some people love Moscow. Some hate it. Most do both. It's glittering, it's grey. It's friendly, it's surly. It's beautiful, it's bleak. It's flashy, it's suburban.

It's the epicentre of the new Russia, with shops, restaurants and nightlife that most provincial Russians can still only dream about (though they may pale by comparison with those in most Western cities). As never before in the lifetimes of its people, Moscow is a city of excitement and opportunity where anything can happen. It also epitomises all that's wrong with the new Russia, scared of increasing street crime and rising prices, riddled with Mafia, and spattered with large numbers of drunks and beggars.

Much more than most major cities, Moscow rewards those who take the time and trouble to get to know it. For the capital of the world's biggest country and the fulcrum of half the 20th-century world order, to many newcomers it seems oddly quiet and village-like. Within a day or two you may find yourself wondering where the *real* action is – the buzzing big-city hub of bright lights and street glamour, where you can feel the pulse of the city. You won't find it in Moscow.

The slur that St Petersburgers cast on Moscow – that it's 'just a big village', not a 'real city' – is partly true. Moscow indeed began life as a provincial outpost and grew slowly, with different neighbourhoods taking distinct identities. Now, with one foot in Europe and the other turned towards Asia, it's more like several thousand villages. Each street, courtyard and staircase has its own character. Moscow has its great buildings, historic sites, seats of the high and mighty, broad avenues, famous theatres, busy restaurants, parks and squares, but the real flavour of this city is in its small nooks and crannies,

each of them unique. Perhaps the unrevealing nature of its public face is a legacy of a past where safety lay in secrecy and privacy.

Pass beneath the Kremlin walls and stroll around the historic precinct within. Walk on Red Square, feast your eyes on St Basil's Cathedral. Then start to explore, wherever your fancy takes you. Markets, parks, small quiet streets off the main avenues. The beautiful old convent of Novodevichy and the cemetery next door, where multitudes of the famous are buried. The Tretyakov or Pushkin fine arts museums, which house world-famous collections of Russian and Impressionist art. The old royal country palace of Kolomenskoe on its bluff above a bend of the sinuous Moscow River. Take a boat ride along the river itself. Go to a concert or a club. Start to notice how subtly many buildings are floodlit after dark.

Above all, if you have any contacts among residents here, follow them up. The inside of one Muscovite flat will tell you more about the city than 10 museums. Any hospitality you receive is likely to be warm, and through Muscovite eyes you'll begin to discover the real Moscow.

HISTORY
The Kremlin and its surrounds were probably settled by the 11th century, but the

founding of Moscow is traditionally ascribed to Yury Dolgoruky, Prince of Suzdal, who is recorded as giving a feast here, on what was the western fringe of his realm, in 1147. In 1237-38 Moscow was sacked along with the rest of the Vladimir-Suzdal realm by Tatars led by Batu, Jenghiz Khan's grandson. These Tatars set up a capital at Saray on the southern Volga and became known as the Golden Horde. Moscow, near river trade routes, survived to become a princedom in its own right from the time of Daniil (1276-1303), and emerged as the Golden Horde's chief northern tribute collector. Prince Ivan I (1325-40), nicknamed Kalita (Moneybags) for his tax-gathering abilities, gained the title Grand Prince of Rus in 1328. In the 1320s Metropolitan Pyotr, head of the Russian Church, moved from Vladimir to Moscow, and by the middle of the century Moscow had absorbed Vladimir and Suzdal. A rampart and a series of fortified monasteries were built around the line of the modern Boulevard Ring.

Moscow came to lead the struggle to push back the Golden Horde, with Ivan Kalita's grandson Grand Prince Dmitry inflicting their first heavy defeat at Kulikovo on the Don in 1380. This earned him the name Dmitry Donskoy. But two years later, the horde was still able to burn Moscow down. Not until the late 15th century, under Ivan III, called the Great, could Moscow cease paying tribute to the horde. By the end of Ivan's reign, Moscow's control stretched from Novgorod in the west to Tula in the south, towards the Urals in the east and to the Barents Sea in the north. Ivan brought Italian architects to build cathedrals in the Kremlin and styled himself ruler 'of all Russia' as he set about reuniting the lands of old Kievan Rus.

Ivan IV (1533-84), named Grozny ('Awesome', but for this man translated as 'Terrible'), became grand prince at the age of three and spent his childhood amid vicious palace power struggles in which his mother was murdered. He had himself crowned tsar (caesar) at 16 and went on to marry six times (though Elizabeth I of England turned him down), terrorise the nobles and kill his eldest son in a fit of rage. He expanded Muscovite territory by launching the conquest of Siberia and winning control of the Volga from the Golden Horde khanates of Kazan and Astrakhan – St Basil's Cathedral was built in celebration – but he failed to win the Baltic region.

By 1571, when the Crimean Tatars burnt all Moscow except the Kremlin, the city probably had over 100,000 people and was one of the biggest in the world. The Kitay-Gorod, east of the Kremlin, was the main part of the town. By 1600 a nine-km white stone wall with 27 towers stood round the line of the Boulevard Ring, and a 16-km rampart around the Garden Ring. The area inside the white wall came to be known as the Bely Gorod (White City).

Tsar Boris Godunov (1598-1605) – formerly an adviser to Ivan the Terrible's son and successor, Fyodor – faced both famine and the Polish-backed invasion of the first False Dmitry. The seven years after Boris' death were the Time of Troubles – characterised by the first False Dmitry proclaiming himself tsar, then being murdered, a second False Dmitry popping up, civil wars, invasions and Moscow being occupied by Poland. Finally the Poles were driven out, and 16-year-old Mikhail Romanov was elected tsar by a council of nobles, launching the 300-year Romanov dynasty and a period of consolidation during which Muscovy's territory spread southwards.

Peter I (the Great), impressed in his youth by visits to Moscow's foreigners' quarter on the Yauza River, toured Europe in 1697-98. He built a new capital, St Petersburg, on the Baltic to open Russia up to Western trade and ideas and consolidate military victories over Sweden. He disliked Moscow, where as a boy he had seen his uncle and his mother's advisers killed in a palace coup, and forced the nobility to move to St Petersburg and wear Western-style clothes, slapping a tax on beards, symbol of the old, inward-looking Russia.

But Moscow remained important enough to be Napoleon's main goal when his troops marched on Russia in 1812. After the bloody

Battle of Borodino 130 km west of the city, the Russians abandoned Moscow and allowed Napoleon to march in and install himself in the Kremlin. The night he arrived a great fire broke out which burnt most of the city, including the stores. With winter coming, the French had to pull out little more than a month after they had arrived.

Moscow was feverishly rebuilt in just a few years, and it was around this time that its two outer defence rings were replaced by the tree-lined Boulevard Ring and Garden Ring roads. As new industrial suburbs grew up beyond the 'class barrier' of the Garden Ring, the city's population grew from 350,000 in the 1840s to 1.4 million in 1914.

October 1917 saw more savage street fighting in Moscow than in St Petersburg. The Bolsheviks occupied, lost and retook the Kremlin over an eight-day period. In 1918 the government moved back to Moscow after two centuries' absence, fearing that Petrograd (as St Petersburg was then called) might come under German attack. Moscow became the epicentre of the total reorganisation – in some cases devastation – of a huge country, and scene of its main 1930s show trials.

Under Stalin, one of the world's first comprehensive urban plans was devised for Moscow. The first line of the metro was completed in 1935. The broad thoroughfares he deemed necessary for his capital were created in the 1930s – ulitsa Gorkogo (now Tverskaya ulitsa), prospekt Marxa (now Mokhovaya ulitsa, Okhotny ryad and Teatralny proezd), prospekt Mira, Leninsky and Leningradsky prospekts. The Garden Ring was cleared of trees and made wide enough for warplanes to land. In the late 1940s and early 1950s the 'Seven Sisters' or 'Stalin Wedding Cakes', seven great, grey neo-Gothic skyscrapers (see Landmarks under Orientation), poked up into Moscow's sky. Meanwhile, by some estimates, Stalin had had half of Moscow's artistic and historical landmarks demolished – most notoriously the enormous Cathedral of Christ the Saviour, a major city landmark which is now being rebuilt.

German troops came within about 40 km of the Kremlin in December 1941.

After WW II huge housing estates grew up round the outskirts: many of the less high-rise ones hurriedly erected under Khrushchev in the mid-1950s are nicknamed *khrushchoby*, after *trushchoby* (slums); later blocks were built higher as planners tried to keep the city within its outer ring road.

Moscow has been in the forefront of political change, and a thorn in the flesh of the national leaders, since the first whispers of glasnost in the mid-1980s. Boris Yeltsin, made the city's new Communist Party chief in 1985, became hugely popular as he sacked hundreds of corrupt commercial managers, set up new food markets with supplies direct from the countryside, allowed ulitsa Arbat to become a centre of unofficial entertainment, and permitted demonstrations to be held in the city. This last was too much for the communist old guard and led to Yeltsin's resignation in 1987.

When Moscow elected a new, reforming city council in 1990, with the economist Gavriil Popov as mayor, Popov immediately embarked on the 'decommunisation' of the city, selling off housing and state businesses, restoring pre-Revolutionary street names, and permitting an unofficial May Day demonstration in Red Square in 1990, which forced Mikhail Gorbachev, humiliated, to retreat from the reviewing stand beside Lenin's tomb.

It was the rallying of Muscovites behind Yeltsin at Moscow's 'White House', seat of the parliament of the Russian Republic, that foiled the old-guard coup in 1991 and precipitated the ultimate collapse of the Soviet Union. Two years later, when disenchantment with Yeltsin and politics in general had set in, Muscovites attended another confrontation at the White House – between tanks sent by Yeltsin, now Russian President, and his obstructive foes in parliament. This time the people were spectators, not participants.

By the mid-1990s Moscow was very much the vanguard of the 'new Russia', filling up with all the things Russians had expected capitalism to bring but which had barely begun to percolate down to the provinces: banks, stock exchanges, casinos, advertising, BMWs, bright new shops, hotels, restaurants and nightlife – *money*. And, of course, one thing no-one had wanted – crime. The Mafia had its fingers in just about everything, and no-one seemed able to do a thing about it. Not just gangsters, but bankers, businesspeople, politicians and TV stars were gunned down or blown up. The crime wave overshadowed the benefits of economic change in most Muscovites' minds.

ORIENTATION

The Kremlin, a north-pointing triangle with sides 750 metres long, is at the heart of Moscow in every way. Red Square lies along its east side, the Moscow River flows past its south side. Picture Moscow as four road rings that spread out from this centre. Radial roads spear out across the rings, and the Moscow River meanders across everything from north-west to south-east with the Kremlin sitting at the northern tip of its biggest loop.

This chapter divides Moscow into 11 areas, as shown on the Moscow map: the City Centre, bound by the first ring; six 'Inner' areas, stretching from the first ring to just outside the third ring; and four 'Outer' areas, within the fourth ring.

The Four Rings

The first of the four rings, a semicircle round the north of the Kremlin, between 250 and 750 metres out, is formed by the streets Mokhovaya ulitsa, Okhotny ryad and Teatralny proezd, and the squares Novaya ploshchad and Staraya ploshchad. Three other important squares, Manezhnaya ploshchad, Teatralnaya ploshchad and Lubyanskaya ploshchad, punctuate this ring. The area bound by these streets and squares forms this chapter's City Centre area.

Next is the Boulevard Ring (Bulvarnoe Koltso), three-quarters of a circle 750 to 1500 metres from the Kremlin. It's mostly dual carriageway, with a park strip down the middle. Each section has a different name,

always ending in 'bulvar'. The Boulevard Ring ends as it approaches the Moscow River in the south-west and south-east.

Third is the Garden Ring (Sadovoe Koltso), a full circle between two and 2.5 km out, which crosses the river twice. Most of its northern sections are called Sadovaya-something (Garden-something) ulitsa; several of its southern sections are called ulitsa something val, recalling its origins as a rampart *(val)*. This chapter's 'Inner' areas, which contain most of Moscow's historic sights, museums, theatres, restaurants, shops and better hotels, extend to one km or so beyond the Garden Ring. Beyond this, the suburbs begin. It's easy to remember the difference between the Garden and Boulevard rings: the Garden Ring is the one *without* any gardens. It was once a tree-lined boulevard, but was widened into a busy ring road and lined with large buildings in the 1930s.

The fourth ring, much further out, is Moscow's outer ring road, the Moskovskaya Koltsevaya Avtomobilnaya Doroga, some 15 km from the Kremlin in the east and west, and 19 km in the north and south. A few protuberances apart, it forms the city limits.

Radial Roads

Moscow's main radial roads spear across these rings like spokes of a wheel, many beginning from the innermost ring.

The north-west exit from Manezhnaya ploshchad is Tverskaya ulitsa (formerly ulitsa Gorkogo), the start of the road to St Petersburg. It crosses the Boulevard Ring at Pushkinskaya ploshchad and becomes Leningradsky prospekt soon after the Garden Ring.

Ulitsa Vozdvizhenka heads west from Mokhovaya ulitsa, changing its name to ulitsa Novy Arbat at the Boulevard Ring, then to Kutuzovsky prospekt after it crosses the Moscow River, and becomes the main road for Smolensk, Minsk, Poland and Paris.

Bolshoy Kamenny Bridge at the south-west corner of the Kremlin leads over the river to Bolshaya Yakimanka ulitsa, which changes its name and becomes Leninsky

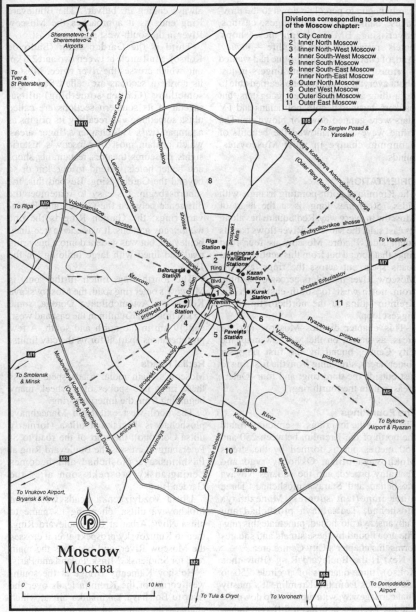

prospekt, the main south-westward artery, after it crosses the Garden Ring.

Bolshoy Moskvoretsky Bridge at the south-east corner of the Kremlin leads to ulitsa Bolshaya Ordynka which eventually becomes Varshavskoe shosse, the main road south towards Tula, Oryol and Ukraine.

Bolshaya Lubyanka ulitsa, north-east from Lubyanskaya ploshchad, becomes prospekt Mira, the Yaroslavl road.

Landmarks

The only elevation worth the name in the whole flat expanse is the Sparrow Hills, six km south-west of the Kremlin, topped by the Moscow University skyscraper. The Sparrow Hills afford the most panoramic view the city has to offer except for the Ostankino TV tower in the north. Moscow has few useful landmarks for getting your bearings from a distance: probably the most prominent buildings are the 'Seven Sisters' – the Ukraina and Leningradsky hotels, the university tower on the Sparrow Hills, the Foreign Affairs and Transport Construction ministries, the Kudrinskaya ploshchad and the Kotelnicheskaya apartment buildings – but they're all so similar that they're a positive handicap to finding your way around.

Transport Termini

Moscow's five airports are all beyond the outer ring road, 30 to 40 km from the city centre. Sheremetevo-2 (where you'll arrive if you fly in from outside the former Soviet Union) and Sheremetevo-1 airports are to the north-west, linked to the centre by Leningradskoe shosse, then Leningradsky prospekt. Domodedovo and Bykovo airports are to the south-east, Vnukovo to the south-west.

Moscow's nine main railway terminals are all on or just outside the Garden Ring, four or five km from the centre. All have metro stations on the spot. If you come from the west, you'll probably arrive at the Belorussia Station, north-west of the centre; from Latvia, at the Riga Station (north); from the north-west, at the Leningrad Station (north-east); from the east, at the Yaroslavl or Kazan stations (north-east); from the south, at the Kiev (south-west), Pavelets (south) or Kursk (east) stations.

Street Names

Moscow has indulged in an orgy of renaming streets and squares in an official effort to bury the Soviet past. In most cases the old pre-Soviet names have simply been restored. Unfortunately for newcomers, not only do Muscovites continue to call many streets by their Soviet names, but the city authorities haven't yet got round to changing all the street signs. Some streets even have both names up in different places. In this chapter we use the new names in text and maps, but mention old names in text too. The table on the next page gives a list of new and old names.

INFORMATION
Tourist Offices

Moscow has as yet no tourist information offices in the normal sense – places where you can go and get a map, ask about places to stay, opening times of sights, and so on. If you're after a particular service, there are a number of 'service bureaus' which offer general city tours, visits to sights, hotel bookings, transport tickets, and so on. Most of these you can do or obtain yourself for less money, but sometimes it may be worth paying for the convenience of having someone else do it for you. If it's just information you want, you might be able to get it out of a service bureau, but don't count on it. Hotel reception desks are also worth trying.

Intourist has a central service bureau (☎ 292 23 65, 292 12 78; fax 292 25 47) at Mokhovaya ulitsa 13, open from 9 am to 8 pm daily. Walking from the Hotel National, pass the doors of the Intourist main offices and go in the single door a little further along, slightly set back from the street. The office has desks which deal with sightseeing trips in and around Moscow, entertainment tickets, air tickets (☎ 292 22 93), train tickets (☎ 292 23 94), hotel bookings and tours elsewhere in the ex-USSR, and visa matters.

Intourist also has service bureaus in about

Street Names

If the sign on a Moscow street doesn't show the name you are expecting, you may not be lost. It may just be that the new name hasn't been put up yet.

New Name	Old Name
prospekt Akademika Sakharova	Novokirovsky prospekt
Andronevskaya ploshchad	Pryamikova ploshchad
Arkhangelsky pereulok	Telegrafny pereulok
Bogoyavlensky pereulok	Kuybyshevsky proezd
Bolshaya Dmitrovka ulitsa	Pushkinskaya ulitsa
Bolshaya Lubyanka ulitsa	ulitsa Dzerzhinskogo
Bolshaya Nikitskaya ulitsa	ulitsa Gertsena
Bolshaya Tatarskaya ulitsa	ulitsa Zemlyachki
Bolshaya Yakimanka ulitsa	ulitsa Dimitrova
Bolshoy Afanasevsky pereulok	ulitsa Myaskovskogo
Bolshoy Kislovsky pereulok	ulitsa Semashko
Bolshoy Kozikhinsky pereulok	Ostuzheva ulitsa
Bolshoy Nikolopeskovsky pereulok	ulitsa Vakhtangova
Bolshoy Palashevsky pereulok	Yuzhinsky pereulok
Bolshoy Patriarshy pereulok	ulitsa Adama Mitskevicha
Bolshoy Spasoplinishchevsky pereulok	ulitsa Arkhipova
Borisoglebsky pereulok	ulitsa Pisemskogo
Bryusov pereulok	ulitsa Nezhdanovoy
ulitsa Chayanova	ulitsa Gotvalda
Denezhny pereulok	ulitsa Vesnina
Dolgorukovskaya ulitsa	Kalyaevskaya ulitsa
Filippovsky pereulok	pereulok Axakova
Gagarinsky pereulok	ulitsa Ryleeva
Gazetny pereulok	ulitsa Ogaryova
Glazovsky pereulok	ulitsa Lunacharskogo
Glinishchevsky pereulok	Ulitsa Nemirovicha-Danchenko
Goncharnaya ulitsa	ulitsa Volodarskogo
Granatny pereulok	ulitsa Shchuseva
Gustyanikov pereulok	Bolshevistsky pereulok
ulitsa Ilinka	ulitsa Kuybysheva
ulitsa Ivanteevskaya	ulitsa Podbelskogo
Kaluzhskaya ploshchad	Oktyabrskaya ploshchad
Kamergersky pereulok	proezd Khudozhestvennogo Teatra
Kitaygorodsky proezd	Kitaysky proezd
Kolymazhnaya ulitsa	ulitsa Marshala Shaposhnikova
ulitsa Korovy Val	ulitsa Dobryninskaya
Kosmodamianskaya ulitsa	naberezhnaya Maxima Gorkogo
Kudrinskaya ploshchad	ploshchad Vosstania
Leontevsky pereulok	ulitsa stanislavskogo
Lubyanskaya ploshchad	ploshchad Dzerzhinskogo
Lubyansky proezd	proezd Serova
Malaya Dmitrovka ulitsa	ulitsa Chekhova
Malaya Nikitskaya ulitsa	ulitsa Kachalova
Malaya Ordynka ulitsa	ulitsa Ostrovskogo
Maly Kharitonevsky pereulok	ulitsa Griboedova
Maly Kislovsky pereulok	Sobinovsky pereulok
Maly Patriarshy pereulok	Maly Pionersky pereulok
Maly Rzhevsky pereulok	ulitsa Paliashvili

Maly Znamensky pereulok	ulitsa Marxa i Engelsa
Mamonovsky pereulok	pereulok Sadovskikh
Manezhnaya ploshchad	ploshchad 50-letia Oktyabrya
ulitsa Maroseyka	ulitsa Bogdana Khmelnitskogo
Milyutinsky pereulok	ulitsa Markhlevskogo
Mokhovaya ulitsa	prospekt Marxa
Myasnitskaya ulitsa	ulitsa Kirova
ploshchad Myasnitskie Vorota	ploshchad Kirovskie Vorota
Nikitsky bulvar	Suvorovsky bulvar
Nikitsky pereulok	ulitsa Belinskogo
Nikoloyamskaya ulitsa	Ulyanovskaya ulitsa
Nikolskaya ulitsa	ulitsa 25-go Oktryabrya
Nikolsky pereulok	proezd Vladimirova
Novinsky bulvar	ulitsa Chaykovskogo
ulitsa Novy Arbat	prospekt Kalinina
Nozhovy pereulok	ulitsa Paliashvili
Ogorodnoy slobody pereulok	pereulok Stopani
Okhotny ryad	prospekt Marxa
Paveletskaya ploshchad	Leninskaya ploshchad
Petrovsky pereulok	ulitsa Moskvina
ulitsa Pokrovka	ulitsa Chernyshevskogo
Povarskaya ulitsa	ulitsa Vorovskogo
Prechistenka ulitsa	Kropotkinskaya ulitsa
Prechistensky pereulok	pereulok Ostrovskogo
Predtechinsky pereulok	ulitsa Bolshevistskaya
Protopopovsky pereulok	Bezbozhny pereulok
ploshchad Rogozhskaya Zastava	ploshchad Ilicha
Romanov pereulok	ulitsa Granovskogo
Sadovnicheskaya ulitsa	ulitsa Osipenko
Serpukhovskaya ploshchad	Dobryninskaya ploshchad
Slavyanskaya ploshchad	ploshchad Nogina
Sofiyskaya naberezhnaya	naberezhnaya Morisa Toreza
ulitsa Spiridonovka	ulitsa Alexeya Tolstogo
Staraya Basmannaya ulitsa	ulitsa Karla Marxa
Staropimenovsky pereulok	ulitsa Medvedeva
Sukharevskaya ploshchad	Kolkhoznaya ploshchad
Suvorovskaya ploshchad	ploshchad Kommuny
Teatralnaya ploshchad	ploshchad Sverdlova
Triumfalnaya ploshchad	ploshchad Mayakovskogo
Tverskaya ploshchad	Sovietskaya ploshchad
Tverskaya ulitsa	ulitsa Gorkogo
Tverskaya Zastava ploshchad	ploshchad Belorusskogo Vokzala
1-ya Tverskaya-Yamskaya ulitsa	ulitsa Gorkogo
ulitsa Varvarka	ulitsa Razina
Vetoshny pereulok	proezd Sapunova
ulitsa Vorontsovo Pole	ulitsa Obukha
ulitsa Vozdvizhenka	prospekt Kalinina
Voznesensky pereulok	ulitsa Stankevich
Yauzskaya ulitsa	Internatsionalnaya ulitsa
Yelokhovskaya ploshchad	Baumanskaya ploshchad
Yermolaevsky pereulok	ulitsa Zholtovskogo
ulitsa Zemlyanoy Val	ulitsa Chkalova
ulitsa Znamenka	ulitsa Frunze
Zvonarsky pereulok	2-y Neglinny pereulok

10 middle and top-range hotels around the city. Each offers some of the same services as the central bureau.

Intourservice, a separate outfit from Intourist, has bureaus at Nikitsky pereulok (formerly ulitsa Belinskogo) 4A (☎ 203 80 16), off Tverskaya ulitsa near the Hotel Intourist, and in a few hotels, which offer more sightseeing trips and chauffeur-car hire.

In addition to these you'll find other desks or offices in hotels, and a range of travel and other agencies around the city, which offer specific services.

More information on what individual bureaus and agencies offer appears under Visas, Travel Agencies, Organised Tours, Entertainment, Getting There & Away, and other headings in this chapter.

Money

Don't change money with people who approach you at the money-changing booths at Sheremetevo-2 airport: they have been known to give worthless, out-of-date banknotes.

As everywhere else in Russia, take care with your money in Moscow: don't leave it lying around your room, and if you go out with money, carry just a small amount in your pocket and tuck the rest away under your clothing, preferably in a money belt or shoulder wallet.

There are hundreds of currency-exchange booths in hotels, shops, transport terminals and booking offices, even some post and telephone offices, and on the street all over the city. Look for 'Currency Exchange' or 'Money Changer' signs in English, or 'Obmen Valyuty' in Russian. Many are open long hours. Booths in hotels and shops, or otherwise away from street crowds, are more secure places to change your money. Nearly all booths take cash only. They like US dollars or Deutschmarks best, but many will also change other Western and some Eastern European currencies. Rates vary a bit so it's worth checking a few before you part with your money: the US$ and other rates are usually posted up.

Travellers' Cheques Moscow has more places to change major-brand travellers' cheques than elsewhere in Russia, but still relatively few. Among the more convenient places are the branches of various banks in the Intourist, Moskva, Metropol, Radisson Slavyanskaya, Baltschug-Kempinski, Olympic Penta and Mezhdunarodnaya-1 hotels, and the Pochta hall of the Central Telegraph. You can also change American Express travellers' cheques into Western currency or roubles at the American Express office. Nearly all charge 3% to 5% commission.

Places that sell travellers' cheques include American Express and some of the above hotel-based bank branches.

For some information on replacing lost travellers' cheques, see the European Russia Facts for the Visitor chapter.

Credit Cards Major credit cards are accepted at many hotels, restaurants, shops and businesses, but check whether there's a surcharge. You can get cash advances on Visa, Eurocard/MasterCard and Diners Club cards at numerous places; you'll usually be charged 1% to 5% commission. The bank in the Olympic Penta Hotel levies 2% on Visa cards. Other places where you can obtain cash advances include the Moskva, Metropol, Intourist, Baltschug-Kempinski and Salyut hotels (for Visa, Eurocard/MasterCard and Diners Club); the Pochta hall of the Central Telegraph, the Ukraina, Izmaylovo and Pullman Iris hotels and the Aeroflot office at ulitsa Petrovka 20 (Visa); and the Radisson Slavyanskaya Hotel (Eurocard/MasterCard). Automatic teller machines (ATMs) in the Pochta hall of the Central Telegraph, and in the Novoarbatsky Gastronom supermarket at ulitsa Novy Arbat (formerly prospekt Kalinina) 13, will give cash US dollars to holders of Eurocard/MasterCard and Cirrus Maestro cards. Some Plus Network cards may soon be accepted, too. Check with your bank before you leave.

See the European Russia Facts for the Visitor chapter for more information on credit cards, including how to report theft or loss.

American Express American Express (☎ 956 90 00; fax 956 90 05) is on the western Garden Ring at Sadovaya-Kudrinskaya ulitsa 21A (metro: Mayakovskaya); open Monday to Friday from 9 am to 5 pm, Saturday from 9 am to 1 pm. Among other things, it cashes American Express travellers' cheques at 3% commission, helps with lost American Express cards and travellers' cheques, sells travellers' cheques, and runs client mail-holding and travel services. An American Express card will also get you a cash advance from the office (against a personal cheque) or, outside working hours, from cash dispensers at the office and in the Hotel Mezhdunarodnaya-1 lobby.

Wire Transfers Cash wires from several Western countries can be arranged through Western Union. The Western Union office in Moscow (☎ 119 82 50; Monday to Friday from 11 am to 3.30 pm) can list the banks in the city through which you can do this: the more central ones include Rossiysky Kredit Bank at Tverskaya ulitsa 19A (just north of Pushkinskaya ploshchad), and Inkombank at Sadovaya-Triumfalnaya ulitsa 14/12. Western Union or the banks themselves will tell you the procedure to follow.

Dialogbank, in the Radisson Slavyanskaya Hotel and elsewhere, and Mosbusinessbank at ulitsa Kuznetsky Most 15 are among banks that can cash transfers without requiring you to open an account with them. For more on wire transfers, see the Money section in European Russia Facts for the Visitor.

Post
The usual warnings on delays and disappearances of incoming and outgoing mail (see European Russia Facts for the Visitor) apply to Moscow.

Sending Mail Most of the bigger hotels have small post offices of their own, where you can buy postcards, envelopes and stamps, and send postcards and letters. A convenient, centrally located post office is in the Central Telegraph (Tsentralny Telegraf) at Tverskaya ulitsa 7, just up the hill from the Hotel Intourist (Inner North-West; metro: Okhotny Ryad). For postal services go to the 'Pochta' hall, half-right inside the building entrance. Postal counters are open from 8 am to 2 pm and 3 to 9 pm Monday to Friday, 8 am to 2 pm and 3 to 7 pm Saturday, and 9 am to 2 pm and 3 to 7 pm Sunday. You can buy stamps, envelopes and postcards and send domestic and international mail. EMS express mail is at window No 6. In the same building are moneychangers and a range of telecommunications services.

Another convenient post office is at ulitsa Novy Arbat (formerly prospekt Kalinina) 2, in the Artel Business Centre (Inner South-West; metro: Arbatskaya). There's also Moscow's head post office (Moskovsky Glavpochtamt) at Myasnitskaya ulitsa (formerly ulitsa Kirova) 26, on the corner of Chistoprudny bulvar (Inner North-East; metro: Turgenevskaya or Chistye Prudy). It's open from 8 am to 8 pm Monday to Friday, 8 am to 7 pm Saturday and 9 am to 7 pm Sunday, and has a philatelic counter. If you have international mail that for some reason any of these offices can't handle, make your way out to the International Post Office (Mezhdunarodny Pochtamt, Международный почтамт) at Varshavskoe shosse 37, about 500 metres north of Nagatinskaya metro.

EMS is available at all these offices. Several international courier services can also be found in Moscow. TNT Express Worldwide (☎ 201 25 85) is at Denczhny pereulok (formerly ulitsa Vesnina) 1 (Inner South-West: metro: Smolenskaya). DHL (☎ 956 10 00) is at pereulok Chernyshevskogo 3 (Inner North; nearest metro: Novoslobodskaya), the Radisson-Slavyanskaya Hotel (☎ 941 86 21), the Olympic Penta Hotel (☎ 971 61 01) and the Hotel Mezhdunarodnaya, entrance 3, room

902 (☎ 253 11 94). Federal Express (☎ 253 16 41) is in the Hotel Mezhdunarodnaya, entrance 3, 1st floor.

Receiving Mail If you have an American Express card or American Express travellers' cheques, you can have mail (letters only, no packages) addressed to the American Express office in Moscow, where it will be held for you to collect. The postal address of American Express is Sadovaya-Kudrinskaya ulitsa 21A, Moscow 103001. A reliable private address, where you know mail will be kept for you, would be about as good. Otherwise, the do vostrebovania service, equivalent to poste restante, at the Moscow head post office (see the previous section), is probably as reliable as anywhere. Have do vostrebovania mail addressed to:

Russia 101000
Moscow
Moskovsky glavpochtamt
Do vostrebovania
your name (surname first, in CAPITALS)

Россия 101000
г. Москва
Московский главпочтамт
До востребования
your name (surname first, in CAPITALS)

To collect do vostrebovania mail, take your passport to the post office between 8 am and 8 pm Monday to Saturday, or 8 am and 7 pm Sunday. For the do vostrebovania section, walk down Myasnitskaya ulitsa from the post office's main entrance, go through the first arch on the left and in the door marked выдача корреспонденции до востребования. The do vostrebovania section is one floor up.

Having your mail sent to a hotel is not generally a good idea, as it might easily be mislaid. The Travellers Guest House, however, holds mail pretty reliably, and for ages.

Telecommunications
Telephone You can make any kind of call – local (within the Moscow area code), long-distance or international – from most hotels, usually from your room. You should be able to dial direct to most parts of the world; if not, you have to get an operator, who'll ring you back with the call sooner or later. The reception or your dezhurnaya (floor lady) will be able to clarify this and tell you about dialling prefixes and costs, and will often book calls for you themselves if necessary. Local calls are generally free, but for other calls hotels may add their own surcharge. Check prices before you call: for some calls it will probably be worth going out to one of the public telephone offices, or making the briefest possible call from your hotel to ask your party to call you back in your room. Most hotel room telephones have their own direct-dial number for incoming calls (on a card in the room, or ask reception), so there's no need to be connected through the hotel switchboard.

Some hotels have direct-dial cardphone booths in their lobbies, or business centres with telephone facilities, but these are often extremely expensive.

Local calls (within the Moscow area code) can be made from payphones on the street and in metro stations. The tokens *(zhetony)* you need for these are sold in metro stations at the same windows as metro tokens. Ask for *zhetony dlya taxofonov*. They cost a few cents each.

See the European Russia Facts for the Visitor chapter for information on Home Country Direct services. Moscow's telephone code for incoming long-distance and international calls is 095. Don't ever drop the 0.

Telephone Offices If you're not calling from your accommodation, for long-distance calls within Russia and to other former Soviet republics you need an intercity telephone office *(mezhdugorodnyy telefonnyy punkt)*, and for calls to other countries you need an international telephone office *(mezhdunarodnyy telefonnyy punkt)*. The convenient Central Telegraph (Tsentralny Telegraf) at Tverskaya ulitsa 7, just up the hill from the Hotel Intourist (Inner North-

West; metro: Okhotny Ryad), has both of these. The first room on the left inside the building, Zal 3, is for calls within Russia or the ex-USSR only. It's open from 7 am to 10 pm daily, and you dial direct. The next, bigger, room (Zal 1) and the smaller Zal 2 beyond it are for both international calls and calls within the ex-USSR. In Zal 1, open 24 hours daily, you order your call at the counter and are called to a booth when it's connected. In Zal 2, open from 7 am to 10 pm daily, you yourself dial direct (dialling instructions are posted up in English). Charges are posted up in both rooms: at the time of research both rooms charged about the same as peak-rate charges from private phones. Because you dial direct, Zal 2 is quicker than Zal 1 unless the queues are unusually long: you're unlikely to have to wait more than a few minutes for a booth. A deposit of around US$3 for ex-USSR calls and US$13 for international calls is required in all rooms.

Another direct-dial long-distance and international telephone office, with similar rates, is just along the street from the Central Telegraph in a decommissioned church at Gazetny pereulok (formerly ulitsa Ogaryova) 15. Queues may be shorter here than at the Central Telegraph. It's open from 7.30 am to 10 pm daily. You pay either by placing a deposit (the same amounts as at the Central Telegraph) or by buying a card and inserting it when you get a dial tone.

Two other fairly central places to make long-distance and international phone calls are on ulitsa Novy Arbat, near metro Arbatskaya (Inner South-West). The Artel Business Centre at ulitsa Novy Arbat 2, opposite the Praga restaurant, is open from 8.30 am to 9.45 pm daily. The telephone lines are good, there's usually no waiting time, and some staff speak English. At the time of research rates to Europe were around 50% higher than at the other places mentioned in this section, but to other countries they were about the same. The alternative is a small ground-floor office just west of the Irish House supermarket, between the first and second high-rise blocks, with 'Mezhdunarodnyy Telefon' and 'Mezhdugorodnyy

telefon-avtomat' signs. It's open from 8 am to 8 pm daily, works on a card system like the Gazetny pereulok office, and charges similar rates to the Central Telegraph.

If you're staying at the Travellers Guest House, there's a telephone office nearby with international direct-dial facilities and similar prices to the Central Telegraph. It's on prospekt Mira just north of Kapelsky pereulok, the street leading to the Olympic Penta Hotel.

Fax Many business and tourist hotels have 'business centres' with fax service but these can be very expensive. There are cheaper alternatives.

The Central Telegraph, the telephone office at Gazetny pereulok 15, the Artel Business Centre and the Moscow head post office (see the Telephone and Post sections for locations) all offer worldwide fax service.

At the Central Telegraph there are services both in Zal 1 (to the left as you enter the building) and in the Pochta hall (half-right). In Zal 1, the service is at counter No 1, open from 9 am to 8.30 pm daily, with prices at the time of research of about US$2.10 a minute to Europe, US$3.50 to Asia, US$3.50 to the Americas or Australasia, and US$4.25 to Africa. Transmission may not be immediate. In the Pochta hall, open from 8 am to 10 pm daily, there's an immediate transmission service at window No 8, with prices 50% higher. At window No 13, Global Sprint Fax charged per page about US$2 to US$2.50 to Europe, or US$5.25 to the Americas or Australasia, for transmission within four hours. Whether this is cheaper than the others depends on how long your pages take to go through and is something of a gamble.

The Gazetny pereulok office has fax service from 9 am to 9 pm daily, with the same prices as Zal 1 of the Central Telegraph.

Artel, open from 8.30 am to 9.45 pm daily, charged per page US$2.50 to US$3 to Europe, US$3 to North America, US$4 to Asia, US$4.50 to Africa and US$6.50 to Australasia.

Moscow's head post office has a fax service with international rates, at the time of research, of around US$1.80 a minute to Europe and US$4.50 to North America or Australasia.

All these places also have incoming fax services.

Telegrams Telegrams are a fairly quick way of communicating if you don't have a phone or fax number to contact. International rates were between US$0.15 and US$0.25 per word at the time of writing. Places from which you can send domestic or international telegrams include most hotel post offices, window No 12 in the Central Telegraph Pochta hall, the post office in the Artel Business Centre, and the Moscow head post office.

Photocopying You can get photocopies at the following places:

- the business centre on floor 2 of GUM, in the middle of GUM's Red Square side (City Centre; metro: Ploshchad Revolyutsii)
- the Dom Pedagogicheskoy Knigi bookshop on the corner of Bolshaya Dmitrovka ulitsa (formerly Pushkinskaya ulitsa) and Kamergersky pereulok (formerly proezd Khudozhestvennogo Teatra; Inner North metro: Teatralnaya)
- the Artel Business Centre at ulitsa Novy Arbat 2 (Inner South-West; metro: Arbatskaya)
- the business centre in the Radisson Slavyanskaya Hotel (Inner South-West; metro: Kievskaya)
- the Xerox Centres at Novinsky bulvar (formerly ulitsa Chaykovskogo) 15, a few steps south of the US embassy (Inner North-West; metro: Barrikadnaya), and in the Hotel Mezhdunarodnaya-1 (Inner North-West; nearest metro: Ulitsa 1905 Goda). An A4 page costs around US$0.20.

Foreign Embassies
Western embassy attitudes towards their citizens as tourists in Russia vary. The US Embassy encourages Americans to register their itinerary (take your passport to the American Citizen Services Unit and they'll keep your details on file till your stated date of departure), but other countries feel no need to hear about you unless you're in jail or hospital. But most are on the end of the

phone 24 hours a day if you need them. At some embassies you may have to push through crowds of Russians seeking visas to your country.

About 130 countries have embassies in Moscow. Most are open from 9 or 10 am to noon or 1 pm, Monday to Friday. Some are open afternoons as well. For notes on getting visas for other countries, see the European Russia Getting There & Away chapter and (for Chinese and Mongolian visas) the Trans-Siberian Railway chapter.

When applying for a visa in Moscow, it helps to be at the embassy by opening time. It's worth telephoning to check the hours before you go (but it may be hard to get further info by telephone, since many Moscow embassies are very busy and some speak little English).

Some embassies will speed up their normal processes on payment of an 'urgent' fee. You may be able to ease your path through some of the more labyrinthine visa procedures, for a fee, by using the help of a travel agency or visa agency (see the sections on these later in this chapter).

Embassies in Moscow include:

Armenia
    Armyansky pereulok 2 (☎ 924 12 69)
Australia
    Kropotkinsky pereulok 13 (☎ 956 60 70)
Austria
    Starokonyushenny pereulok 1 (☎ 201 73 17)
Azerbaijan
    Leontevsky pereulok (formerly ulitsa Stanislav-skogo) 16 (☎ 229 16 49)
Belarus
    Maroseyka ulitsa 17/6 (☎ 924 70 31; for visa enquiries 924 70 95)
Belgium
    ulitsa Malaya Molchanovka 7 (☎ 291 60 27)
Bulgaria
    ulitsa Mosfilmovskaya 66 (☎ 147 90 00)
Canada
    Starokonyushenny pereulok 23 (☎ 956 66 66)
China
    ulitsa Druzhby 6 (☎ 143 15 40; for visa enquiries 143 15 43)
Czech Republic
    ulitsa Yuliusa Fuchika 12/14 (☎ 251 05 40)
Denmark
    Prechistensky pereulok (formerly pereulok Ostrovskogo) 9 (☎ 201 78 60)

Estonia
Kalashny pereulok 8 (☎ 290 46 55, 290 50 13)

Finland
Kropotkinsky pereulok 15/17 (☎ 246 40 27)

France
Bolshaya Yakimanka ulitsa (formerly ulitsa Dimitrova) 45 (☎ 236 00 03)

Georgia
Nozhovy pereulok (formerly ulitsa Paliashvili) 6 (☎ 291 66 02, 291 69 02)
Consular section: ulitsa Arbat 42 (☎ 241 97 67)

Germany
ulitsa Mosfilmovskaya 56 (☎ 956 10 80)
Consular section: Leninsky prospekt 95A (☎ 936 24 01)

Greece
Leontevsky pereulok (formerly ulitsa Stanislavskogo) 4 (☎ 290 22 74)

Hungary
ulitsa Mosfilmovskaya 62 (☎ 143 86 11)

Iceland
Khlebny pereulok 28 (☎ 290 47 42)

India
ulitsa Vorontsovo Pole (formerly ulitsa Obukha) 6-8 (☎ 297 08 20)

Ireland
Grokholsky pereulok 5 (☎ 288 41 01, 230 27 63)

Israel
ulitsa Bolshaya Ordynka 56 (☎ 238 27 32, 230 67 00)

Italy
Denezhny pereulok (formerly ulitsa Vesnina) 5 (☎ 241 15 33)

Japan
Kalashny pereulok 12 (☎ 291 85 00)

Kazakhstan
Chistoprudny bulvar 3A (☎ 208 98 52, 927 18 36)

Kyrgyzstan
ulitsa Bolshaya Ordynka 64 (☎ 237 44 81, 237 48 82)

Latvia
ulitsa Chaplygina 3 (☎ 925 27 07)

Lithuania
Borisoglebsky pereulok (formerly ulitsa Pisemskogo) 10 (☎ 291 26 43)

Moldova
ulitsa Kuznetsky Most 18 (☎ 928 54 05)

Mongolia
Borisoglebsky pereulok (formerly ulitsa Pisemskogo) 11 (☎ 290 67 92)
Consular section (for visas): Spasopeskovsky pereulok 7 (☎ 244 78 67)

Netherlands
Kalashny pereulok 6 (☎ 291 29 99)

New Zealand
Povarskaya ulitsa (formerly ulitsa Vorovskogo) 44 (☎ 956 35 79)

North Korea
ulitsa Mosfilmovskaya 72 (☎ 143 62 49)

Norway
Povarskaya ulitsa (formerly ulitsa Vorovskogo) 7 (☎ 290 38 72)

Poland
ulitsa Klimashkina 4 (☎ 255 00 17; visa section 254 36 21)

Portugal
Botanichesky pereulok 1 (☎ 230 24 35)

Romania
ulitsa Mosfilmovskaya 64 (☎ 143 04 24, 143 04 27)

Slovakia
ulitsa Yuliusa Fuchika 12/14 (☎ 251 05 40, 251 10 70)

South Africa
Bolshoy Strochenovsky pereulok 22/25 (☎ 230 68 69)

Spain
Bolshaya Nikitskaya ulitsa (formerly ulitsa Gertsena) 50/8 (☎ 202 21 61)

Sweden
ulitsa Mosfilmovskaya 60 (☎ 956 12 00)

Switzerland
Ogorodnoy Slobody pereulok (formerly pereulok Stopani) 2/5 (☎ 925 53 22)

Tajikistan
Skatertny pereulok 19 (☎ 290 61 02)

Turkey
7-y Rostovsky pereulok 12 (☎ 245 67 35)

Turkmenistan
Filippovsky pereulok (formerly pereulok Axakova) 22 (☎ 291 66 36)

Ukraine
Leontevsky pereulok (formerly ulitsa Stanislavskogo) 18 (☎ 229 10 79; for visa enquiries 229 07 84, 229 91 60)

UK
Sofiyskaya naberezhnaya (formerly naberezhnaya Morisa Toreza) 14 (☎ 956 74 00)

USA
Novinsky bulvar (formerly ulitsa Chaykovskogo) 19/23 (☎ 252 24 51; after-hours duty officer 252 18 98; American Citizen Services, open Monday to Friday from 9 am to 5 pm, 956 42 95)

Uzbekistan
Pogorelsky pereulok 12 (☎ 230 00 76, 238 98 11; for visa enquiries 230 00 54)

Yugoslavia
ulitsa Mosfilmovskaya 46 (☎ 147 41 06)

Russian Visas
See European Russia Facts for the Visitor for general information on Russian visas.

Registration Normally your visa's sponsor (which is often your hotel or host) will register your visa for you. You can ask whether this is being done. The sponsor's name appears on your visa (on tourist visas it appears beside the words *V uchrezhdenie*).

One case in which your visa might not get registered is if you obtained it with an invitation or sponsorship that you bought from an organisation unconnected with your travel or accommodation in Russia. In such cases you may have to seek out the sponsor in Russia to get your visa registered. In Moscow, hotels with Intourist service bureaus can usually register tourist visas for guests whose visas are not sponsored by Intourist, but other hotels can generally only register visas sponsored by themselves and may not accept you as a guest if your visa is not already registered. The main Intourist service bureau at Mokhovaya ulitsa 13 can register tourist visas. It can also tell you how to register other visas – normally through UVIR (Upravlenia Viz i Registratsii; ☎ 207 01 13), the city's main visa and registration office, at ulitsa Pokrovka (formerly ulitsa Chernyshevskogo) 42 (Inner North-East; metro: Kurskaya or Krasnye Vorota).

If you know your sponsor's name but not where it is, your embassy may be able to help you find its address, or you can try going to the Association of Joint Ventures, International Unions and Organisations in the Gorbachev Foundation building at Leningradsky prospekt 55, to obtain either the sponsor's address or a report stating that the sponsor is not a registered tourist agency (which means that the visa was obtained with a fraudulent sponsorship letter). The fee for this service is US$10 if the sponsor is in the files, US$30 if not. A report saying that your sponsor is not a registered tourist agency may be accepted by UVIR or Intourist for registration purposes.

Extending a Transit Visa Extending a Russian transit visa is a fairly straightforward process at UVIR (see the preceding section). The staff are used to dealing with foreigners and speak English. UVIR's hours

are 10 am to 1 pm and 3 to 6 pm Monday, Tuesday and Thursday; 10 am to 1 pm and 3 to 5 pm Friday; and 10 am to 1 pm on Saturday for emergencies only. It's closed Wednesday and Sunday. If you go early in the day you should be able to complete the process the same day.

Your extension begins the day you apply for it, so don't apply for it too soon. How long it will be for seems to depend partly on the official who deals with you. Some travellers have had no trouble extending a 10-day transit visa by 10 days. More frequently, though, the maximum given is only a five-day extension. Certainly there's no harm asking for as much as you want. Beware of any officials who invite you to leave the queue and pay extra sums for extensions. This is illegal and probably won't bring you any benefits. Take your passport and visa to Room 1, to the left on the 1st floor of the UVIR building. If you have a ticket out of Russia with an appropriate date on it, that may also be useful though it's not generally needed. Fill in a form with your name, date of birth, address in Russia, passport number, and the words 'I want to extend my visa until (date)' under 'Zayavlenie', sign it and hand it in. You'll be given a chit to take to the Sberegatelny Bank (Savings Bank) along the street and told to come back to UVIR the same day or the next working day.

The Sberegatelny Bank is at ulitsa Pokrovka 31, about 300 metres west of UVIR on the other side of the street. It's open Monday to Friday from 8.30 am to 2 pm and 3 to 7.30 pm. At the bank you must show your chit from UVIR, fill in another form, pay a fee of US$4, and get a receipt (and the chit back) to take back to UVIR.

Extending or Changing a Tourist Visa A tourist visa has the word *Turizm* inserted beside the words *Tsel poezdki*. Its sponsor (named beside the words *V uchrezhdenie*) is responsible for requesting extensions or changes to it.

In Moscow, Intourist can deal directly with extensions of up to one month or changes to tourist visas sponsored by itself, or tourist visas with no sponsor written on them (which means the Russian consulate issuing the visa made a mistake). It may, however, need a lot of advance notice. If your hotel has an Intourist service bureau, that should be able to handle the change or extension for you; if not, go to the main Intourist service bureau at Mokhovaya ulitsa 13. If another Russian tourist agency was the sponsor, it should be able to organise the extension or change through Intourist; if not, obtain a letter from the agency explaining why the extension or change is needed and take it to Intourist. The normal Intourist fee for visa extensions and changes is at least US$50 plus VAT.

If you know your sponsor's name but not where it is, you can try following the procedures already outlined under Registration.

Extending or Changing Other Visas
Changes and extensions to other visas are handled not by Intourist but by UVIR (see preceding sections) or its district branches, known as OVIR (Otdel Viz i Registratsii). Again, your sponsor is legally responsible for requesting them, and should be able to handle the matter for you. If your sponsor is unwilling to do this, ask the sponsor for a letter requesting what needs to be done, which can be taken to UVIR/OVIR or, failing that, a letter saying that the sponsor is unwilling to act.

Lost or Stolen Visas Be sure to carry photocopies of your passport and visa to reduce the headache of replacing them. Visas, in particular, are easier to replace if you have a photocopy. Your embassy should be able to help, at least with advice on what you need to do. If your visa was a tourist visa, the matter will be handled by Intourist: contact its main service bureau at Mokhovaya ulitsa 13 or its other service bureaus in several major hotels. If you had a transit, business or private visa, the matter will be handled by UVIR (see Registration). You'll need to report the loss to the local police (*militsia*) and obtain a certificate from them. Your sponsor's help will also be needed: if your

sponsor won't deal direct with Intourist or UVIR for you, you'll at least need a letter from your sponsor requesting replacement of your visa. If you don't know who your sponsor was, you may need to contact the travel agent through which you obtained the visa, or even the Russian consulate that issued it, to find out. If you know your sponsor's name but not how to contact it, ask your embassy's help. You may have to follow the procedure already outlined under Registration to find out.

If your passport is lost too, tickets or other evidence showing when you entered Russia will be useful.

Leaving Russia Without a Valid Visa If your visa is out of date, or lost, or you never had one (which might happen if you entered from another ex-Soviet state and weren't checked by immigration on entry), trying to leave Russia from Sheremetevo-2 airport is problematic. You may have fewer difficulties by land. With a visa that's less than one month out of date, you may still be allowed to leave but may be fined up to US$100. If your visa is more than a month out of date, or you have no visa, you will probably not be allowed to leave without going back to UVIR to sort your papers out. Officially, fines on people who entered Russia without a visa can total more than US$250, but you may be able to obtain advance advice and help in this and other situations from the Russian Ministry of Foreign Affairs consular point (Konsulsky Punkt; ☎ 578 76 20, 578 31 71), open from 7 am to 8.30 pm daily, at Sheremetevo-2. The consular point is between departure gates 12 and 13, but you won't be able to reach it without an escort since it's behind the border guard.

Visa Agencies If extending, changing or replacing your visa, or getting one if you never had one, is proving difficult, you could consider contacting one of the visa agencies listed in *The Traveller's Yellow Pages Moscow* (see Books in this chapter) or *Moscow Express Directory* (see Media in this chapter), or advertised in the small ads sections of the *Moscow Times* or *Moscow Tribune*. You might want to check the legality of their services.

Cultural Centres & Libraries

The American Cultural Center Library (☎ 915 36 69, 297 69 85), open Monday to Friday from 10 am to 8 pm, the French Cultural Centre (☎ 915 36 69), open Monday to Friday from 1 to 6 pm, and the British Council Resource Centre (☎ 915 35 11), open Monday to Friday from 10 am to 8 pm, are all on floor 3 of the Foreign Literature Library at Nikoloyamskaya ulitsa (formerly Ulyanovskaya ulitsa) 1. Take your passport. Nearest metro stations are Taganskaya and Kitay-Gorod.

The Russian State Library (Russkaya Gosudarstvennaya Biblioteka) at ulitsa Vozdvizhenka (formerly part of prospekt Kalinina) 3 on the corner of Mokhovaya ulitsa (metro: Biblioteka im Lenina), is the world's largest, with over 20 million volumes. If you seriously want to peruse some of these, take along your passport and one passport photo. You have to fill in a form or two at the library's information office, to the right just inside the main entrance, in order to get a pass *(propusk)*. Foreigners are then directed to Reading Room No 1, which they share with members of the Academy of Science and professors! To obtain books you have to fill in request forms (for which you may have to consult the catalogues) and hand them to the librarians. You may then have to wait 24 hours to receive the book. The library's opening hours are 9 am to 10 pm daily, except Sunday in summer and the last Monday of each month.

Travel Agencies

The break-up of the old state tourism monopolies has spawned dozens of travel agencies, small and large, in Moscow. You can use one to book transport or accommodation, excursions, tours or adventure trips in other parts of Russia, and more, if you don't want to do it all yourself and can afford the profits they

take. Many can provide visa support if you make arrangements through them before coming to Russia. Useful agencies include:

Alpha-Omega Travel (☎ 928 94 59; fax 928 60 39, ☎ & fax 928 99 58), Lubyansky proezd (formerly proezd Serova) 3, floor 3 No 12, 101958 Moscow – services include discounted international airfares

Asia Express (☎ 166 11 96, 166 12 95; fax 166 16 67), Rooms 1526/1527, Korpus Beta, Hotel Izmaylovo, Izmaylovskoe shosse 71, 105613 Moscow – services include discounted international airfares

Barry Martin Group (☎ 271 26 09; fax 271 92 42), ulitsa Vorontsovskaya 29, 109044 Moscow – Moscow office of a British business-travel agency

CCTE-Intour (☎ 235 44 26; fax 230 27 84), Ozerkovskaya naberezhnaya 50, 113532 Moscow – deals primarily in prebooked tours

East-West Travel (☎ 924 06 29; fax 925 04 60), Bolshaya Lubyanka ulitsa (formerly ulitsa Dzerzhinskogo) 24/15, 101000 Moscow – British business and tourist travel agency offering international and domestic travel tickets, ex-USSR visa service and hotel bookings

Globus Agency (☎ 203 72 42; fax 229 26 65), Bolshaya Nikitskaya ulitsa (formerly ulitsa Gertsena) 13, 103009 Moscow – middle and top-end hotel bookings, air tickets

Griphon Travel (☎ 243 23 95; fax 243 30 02), Rooms 743/744, Hotel Ukraina, Kutuzovsky prospekt 2/1, 121248 Moscow – services include discounted international airfares

Intourist (☎ 292 23 65, 292 12 78; fax 292 25 47), Mokhovaya ulitsa 13, 103009 Moscow (also desks in many Moscow hotels) – hotel and travel bookings and tours in Russia and ex-USSR, excursions, registration, extension and replacement of visas

Intourtrans (☎ 929 88 55, 927 11 81, 927 11 05; fax 921 19 96), ulitsa Petrovka 15/13, 103031 Moscow – domestic and international train tickets, domestic and some international air tickets

IRO Travel (☎ 971 40 59, 280 85 62; fax 280 76 86), ulitsa Bolshaya Pereyaslavskaya 50, 10th floor, 129041 Moscow – based at the Travellers Guest House and part of the same operation, offering domestic and international rail and air tickets (including cheap international airfares), visa support service, trans-Siberian and Central Asia packages

Moscow City Excursion Bureau (Moskovskoe Gorodskoe Byuro Exkursy; ☎ 924 94 46; fax 921 74 59), ulitsa Rozhdestvenka 5, 103031 Moscow – hotel, homestay and student dorm accommodation (a couple of days' notice needed), Moscow walking tours, tours in other parts of Russia and ex-USSR, visa support for customers

Pilgrim Tours (Moskovskoe Turisticheskoe Agentstvo Piligrim; ☎ 365 45 63; fax 369 03 89), 1-y Kirpichny pereulok 17, 105118 Moscow, – leading, experienced adventure travel firm, offering trekking, mountaineering, skiing, kayaking, biking etc trips throughout the ex-USSR

Shipra Travels (☎ 438 57 56), Room 514, Tsentralny Dom Turista, Leninsky prospekt 146, 117604 Moscow – services include discounted international airfares

Sputnik (☎ 939 80 65; fax 938 11 92, 956 10 68), Hotel Orlyonok, ulitsa Kosygina 15, 117946 Moscow – deals primarily in prebooked accommodation and tours

Ticket Express (☎ 244 72 60), Building 2, Novokonyushenny pereulok 9/2 – air ticket agency

Travel Russia (☎ 290 34 39, 291 03 47; fax 291 87 83), korpus 2, Trubnikovsky pereulok 21, 121069 Moscow – adventure trips in many parts of ex-USSR

Books & Bookshops

Guides and other books on Moscow are covered in the European Russia Facts for the Visitor chapter.

Reference Publications If you're staying in Moscow for long you should get hold of either (or both) of two very useful, American-published reference sources, *Where in Moscow*, published annually since 1991, and *The Traveller's Yellow Pages Moscow*, first published in 1995. Both have very useful listings of Moscow services and businesses, plus good city maps. Outside Russia, they are sold in some Russia-specialist or travel bookshops, or you can order them from the publishers (see Books – Reference in the European Russia Facts for the Visitor chapter). Places they're sold in Moscow include most of the major hotels, some foreign shops, some of the bookshops listed here, and the Artel Business Centre at ulitsa Novy Arbat 2.

Information Moscow is a long-established, Moscow-published compendium of Moscow names, addresses and facts, also available abroad. The monthly *Moscow Business Telephone Guide* is a useful, newspaper-style listing of addresses, phone and fax numbers of thousands of Moscow enterprises, distributed free to hotels, supermarkets, restaurants and so on.

Bookshops Zwemmer (Zvemmer Knigi; ☎ 928 20 21) at ulitsa Kuznetsky Most 18 (Inner North; metro; Kuznetsky Most) is a full-scale English-language bookshop with shelves of mainly imported books, including many on Moscow and the rest of Russia and lots of novels and general English-language reading.

The Travellers Guest House (☎ 971 40 59, 280 85 62) at ulitsa Bolshaya Pereyaslavskaya 50, 10th floor (Inner North; metro: Prospekt Mira) sells a wide range of Lonely Planet and other guides.

There are bookstalls in most of the major hotels, some of which sell quite a range of English-language publications.

Torgovy Dom Biblio-Globus at Myasnitskaya ulitsa 6, near the Lubyanka (City Centre; metro: Lubyanka), has lots of art and photography books, some in English, and dictionaries.

Knigi at Malaya Nikitskaya ulitsa (formerly ulitsa Kachalova) 16 (Inner North-West; nearest metros Barrikadnaya and Arbatskaya) sells second-hand foreign books, from cheap paperbacks to antiquarian collectors' items.

Dom Knigi at ulitsa Novy Arbat 26 (Inner South-West; metro: Arbatskaya), once Moscow's premier bookshop, is now a disappointing place much given over to selling souvenirs, cassette tapes and household goods. But you might pick up a bargain dictionary from the stalls outside.

Ulitsa Arbat (Inner South-West), and the Inner North streets Kamergersky pereulok (formerly proezd Khudozhestvennogo Teatra), Stoleshnikov pereulok and ulitsa Kuznetsky Most, are dotted with Russian antiquarian and second-hand bookshops.

Maps

Bookstalls in most major hotels sell city maps. The best generally available one we know is the *New Moscow City Map & Guide* (see Maps in European Russia Facts for the Visitor), which is actually the map pages of *Where in Moscow* in single-sheet form. It has a good street index. You can get it from most of the same outlets as *Where in Moscow* (see Books & Bookshops) for about US$7.

Slavyanka at ulitsa Kuznetsky Most 9 has a great selection of maps of Russian regions and parts of other ex-Soviet states, especially Ukraine and Belarus. It also sells the *Moskva Transport* map, a good Russian city map showing public transport routes.

Torgovy Dom Biblio-Globus at Myasnitskaya ulitsa 6 has inexpensive city and Moscow region maps.

You'll also find a variety of maps sold at stalls on ploshchad Revolyutsii and in the pedestrian underpass beneath Tverskaya ulitsa near the Central Telegraph.

Media

Print Moscow has two English-language newspapers produced mainly by native English-speakers, the *Moscow Times* and the *Moscow Tribune*. Both are published daily except Sunday and Monday, and distributed free. You can pick up copies at most places where numbers of English-speakers are found – hotels, restaurants, foreign-run supermarkets and so on. Both are well worth reading for their coverage of Moscow, Russian and international news, the *Moscow Times* especially so.

Other English-language publications worth picking up, and distributed in the same way, are *Moscow News*, the weekly English-language version of the Russian *Moskovskie Novosti*, full of political, social, economic and cultural comment – a Russian counterpoint to the foreign-dominated dailies; the pamphlet-form *Moscow Express Directory*, 'updated once in two weeks', with listings of things such as places where you can change travellers' cheques or get cash on credit cards; and the monthly *Moscow Business Telephone Guide*, with thousands of business addresses, phone and fax numbers.

See the Entertainment section for publications giving details of what's on in Moscow.

Many major foreign newspapers and magazines reach Moscow on the day of publication and are sold at newsstands in the main hotels. The diverse Russian press is sold at newsstands all over the city.

Broadcast Ordinary TVs in Moscow can receive six or seven channels; for details, see the Media section of the European Russia Facts for the Visitor chapter. About 40 international satellite channels are also available here, and many top-end hotel rooms have them.

Moscow has dozens of official and commercial radio stations. Open Radio on 918 kHz AM and 102.5 MHz FM broadcasts some English-language news and current affairs. Radio 7 (73.4 and 104.7 MHz FM) has rock music and news in English at half past the hour, round the clock. Radio Maximum (103.7 MHz FM) is a good music station playing 'adult and contemporary' rock, and pop. Radio Prestige (101.7 MHz FM) plays jazz and blues and has some English-language news.

Film & Photography

There are numerous Kodak shops in Moscow, many of them offering quick print developing as well as selling film, batteries and cameras. Some of the more convenient locations are on Tverskaya ulitsa opposite the Hotel Intourist; in the GUM, Detsky Mir and Petrovsky Passazh department stores; in the Radisson Slavyanskaya Hotel; Yupiter shop at ulitsa Novy Arbat 25; and Knigi shop at ulitsa Petrovka 15.

There are Fuji photo stores at Stoleshnikov pereulok 5/20 and ulitsa Novy Arbat 25.

Passport Photos You can get instant passport photos in many places around the city, including about 18 Polaroid Express studios. Four photos at Polaroid Express cost about US$4. Convenient locations include: Bolshaya Dmitrovka ulitsa (formerly Pushkinskaya ulitsa) 14, Detsky Mir and GUM department stores, and ulitsa Novy Arbat 30/9.

Medical Services

See the Health section of European Russia Facts for the Visitor for general comments on health and medical services. Moscow tap water has always been OK to drink in our experience, but some people (including Muscovites) won't drink it, so you might want to play safe and do the same.

Remember that very few medical services in Russia accept non-Russian medical insurance plans, so if you use one you have to pay on the spot, get receipts, and hope to claim the cost back on your travel insurance policy (if you have one).

Your embassy will be able to recommend doctors or medical services, and should be able to offer logistical support in serious cases. In an emergency get your hotel or host to call a doctor or ambulance. You're unlikely to have to pay for a Russian doctor called by your hotel or for the public ambulance service.

There is now quite a wide range of foreign-run health services available in Moscow, though their facilities are limited; if you need hospitalisation they'll refer you to one of the better Russian hospitals or advise medical evacuation. They're also mostly pretty expensive, even for basic consultations, and on top of everything else, most toss in a 'first-visit' fee for new patients which may be one-third of the consultation charge.

One of the less expensive outfits, which will also accept some foreign medical insurances, is the European Medical Centre (☎ 253 07 03) in the tourists' polyclinic at korpus 2, Gruzinsky pereulok 3 (Inner North-West; metro: Belorusskaya). It has a French doctor and offers consultations, minor surgery and immunisations. Cost for a consultation is about US$70 (US$60 for students and young people). Opening hours are 9.30 am to 6.30 pm Monday to Friday.

Other foreign medical services include:

American Medical Center (☎ 956 33 66), 2-y Tverskoy-Yamskoy pereulok 10 (Inner North-West; metro: Mayakovskaya) – wide-ranging facilities including 24-hour emergency service for members (short-term membership available), North American and European doctors, but particularly expensive

International Medical Clinic (☎ 280 71 38, 280 83 74), 10th floor, Polyclinic No 1, Grokholsky pereulok 31 (Inner North; metro: Prospekt Mira) – international doctors and nurses, minor surgery, immunisations, ambulance service, phones answered any time, consultation about US$60, membership not required

US Global Health (☎ 974 23 32), 4th floor, 4-y Dobryninsky pereulok 4 (Inner South; metro: Oktyabrskaya) – US-certified doctors, 24-hour emergency physician access

Russian medical services include:

Botkin Hospital (☎ 237 83 38 for information, 945 79 82 for reception), 2-y Botkinsky proezd 5 (Outer North; metro: Dinamo) – the main Moscow hospital for foreigners, well equipped by Russian standards, with emergency and after-hours service

Tourists' Polyclinic (☎ 254 43 96), korpus 2, Gruzinsky pereulok 3 (metro: Belorusskaya) – out-patient clinic for minor injuries and illnesses

Ambulance The Euro-Medical Club (☎ 250 99 00, 143 25 03) has a 24-hour ambulance service with English-speaking dispatchers and Western-standard equipment on board. A fee of US$150 is charged at pick-up and you'll be taken to the Michurinsky Hospital, Michurinsky prospekt 6, which is equipped for emergencies and has an intensive-care unit. The hospital charges on admission.

The International Medical Clinic also has an ambulance service.

The Moscow city ambulance service is on ☎ 03.

Dentists As with other medical services, watch out for costs at foreign-run dentists in Moscow. One that has received good recommendations is the dental clinic at the Adventist Health Center (☎ 126 75 54), prospekt 60-letia Oktyabrya 21A (metro: Leninsky Prospekt). Others include:

Intermed (☎ 284 74 03), korpus 5, ulitsa Durova 26 (metro: Prospekt Mira) – a German/Russian joint venture

Mosta Dental Clinic (☎ 927 07 65), Bolshoy Cherkassky pereulok 15 (metro: Lubyanka) – English-speaking Japanese dentists

US Dental Care (☎ 236 81 06), ulitsa Shabolovka 8, building 3, ground floor (metro: Oktyabrskaya) – an English-speaking, US-run dental clinic charging US$40 for examinations and US$60 for cleaning

Pharmacies The International Medical Clinic and the American Medical Center both have pharmacies stocked with Western medicines. The one at the American Medical Center is open daily. Medicine Man (☎ 155 70 80) at ulitsa Chernyakhovskogo 4 (metro: Aeroport) is a Swiss-Russian joint-venture pharmacy with Western medicines, open Monday to Friday from 10 am to 8 pm, Saturday from 10 am to 4 pm. There are also pharmacies in several of the major hotels.

Emergency

Emergency telephone numbers (with Russian-speaking operators) are 01 for fire, 02 for police, 03 for ambulance. See the preceding Medical Services section for more on health emergencies. Most hotels have a police (militsia) department assigned to them. Your embassy will be able to provide some advice or help in most emergencies.

Dangers & Annoyances

See this chapter's Getting There & Away section for warnings relating to Sheremetevo-2 airport and Moscow-St Petersburg trains.

Crime Despite the glut of Mafia killings in Moscow and Muscovites' paranoia about rising crime, visitors generally have little to fear from big-time organised crime, which concentrates on other targets. But you certainly need to be on your guard against pickpockets and muggers.

The commonest hazard anywhere in central Moscow is the gangs of urchins, generally referred to as 'gipsy kids', who are after your bag, camera, or anything loose on your body. These come in groups of eight, 10 or more and may be as young as seven or eight years old. Often the youngest will begin by asking you for money or some little gift, and if you stop the others will then appear, swarm around you, and try to grab anything they can from your person. They also sometimes spray a stinging concoction in your face to temporarily blind you. They are a danger anywhere in central areas of the city including main tourist haunts such as the Alexandrovsky Garden outside the Kremlin, Teatralnaya ploshchad in front of the Bolshoy Theatre, and the Triumfalnaya ploshchad area. They're easily recognisable because they're exceptionally dirty and unkempt. If you see them coming give them as wide a berth as possible. Moscow residents say the best thing to do if they approach you is to thump the first one hard – admittedly difficult to do to a seven-year-old girl.

The following precautions will reduce the risk of such attacks and other street crime:

- Dress down, avoiding bright colours and clothes that mark you out as a foreigner.
- Carry only a minimum of money, or anything else, in your pockets (if you need extra, secrete it under your clothes).
- Carry anything you need to carry in a locally bought bag (cheap plastic carrier bags are widely available) – this helps to disguise your foreignness.
- Take special care in underground walkways and anywhere crowded such as railway stations, the metro or markets.
- Take great care where you go after dark.
- Keep photocopies of your passport, visa and other important documents in a safe place.
- Take care when leaving a club or bar, or returning to your accommodation, after drinking – thieves have targeted foreigners who have been drinking.
- If you're staying in private accommodation where foreigners are known to live, take care near the building and in the lift, lobby or staircase, especially in the evening. Foreigners have been targeted by thieves in such places.
- Don't get into a taxi of any kind that already has anyone other than the driver inside.

If your visa or passport is stolen, you'll need to report it to the police in order to get a replacement. Your embassy can advise on procedures (see also the Russian Visas section earlier in this chapter). You will probably also need a police report if you want to make any insurance claims.

THE KREMLIN

The Moscow Kremlin (Kreml) is the kernel of its city and country, the place to which all Russian roads lead and from which most Russian power emanates. Here Ivan the Terrible and Stalin orchestrated their terrors; Napoleon watched Moscow burn; Lenin fashioned the dictatorship of the proletariat; Khrushchev led communism in the Cold War; Gorbachev unleashed perestroika; and Yeltsin struggled to keep reform afloat. Today the white, blue and red Russian flag flies over the Kremlin, the Soviet red flag having been hauled down on 25 December 1991.

In what was for decades a den of militant atheism, it may come as a surprise that the Kremlin's chief glories, the bases from which most of its famous gold domes rise, are cathedrals. The Kremlin was once the centre of Russia's Church as well as its state.

The Kremlin occupies a roughly triangular plot of land covering little Borovitsky Hill on the north bank of the Moscow River, probably first settled in the 11th century. Today it's enclosed by high walls 2.25 km long. Red Square lies outside the east wall. The best views of the Kremlin are from Sofiyskaya naberezhnaya, across the river, and the upper floors of the Rossia and Intourist hotels.

A kremlin is a town's fortified stronghold, and the first short, wooden wall around Moscow's was built in the 1150s. The Kremlin grew with the importance of Moscow's princes and in the 1320s became the headquarters of the Russian Church, which shifted from Vladimir. The 'White Stone Kremlin' – which had limestone walls – was built in the 1360s with almost the present boundaries. This lasted till the 1475-1516 rebuilding launched by Ivan the Great, when master builders from Pskov and Italy came to supervise new walls and towers (most of which still stand), the three great cathedrals and more. The other buildings have been added piecemeal since then.

Even after Peter the Great shifted his capital and Church headquarters to St Petersburg, tsars were crowned here. But none of today's Kremlin would be standing if Catherine the Great hadn't run out of money and interest after drawing up plans for a new, classical-style Kremlin in the 1770s, or if Napoleon's troops hadn't been prevented by rain and the timely arrival of Russian soldiers from blowing the whole place up as they left in 1812.

Getting In

The Kremlin is open to visitors not wearing shorts from 10 am to 5 pm daily except Thursday. The main visitors' entrance is the Kutafya Tower on Manezhnaya ulitsa (metro: Alexandrovsky Sad, Borovitskaya or Biblioteka im Lenina). Ticket offices, which close at 4.30 pm, are on either side of the Kutafya tower and in the Alexandrovsky Garden a short distance to the south. Beneath the Kutafya Tower is a left-luggage office (kamera khranenia), open from 9 am to 6.30 pm, where you must leave large bags or backpacks for US$0.20 apiece.

A ticket for the grounds is US$0.10, then there are extra charges for tickets to the cathedrals and museums inside: you can get the extra tickets you want either at the ticket offices (where prices are posted in English) or at the door of each cathedral or museum that you decide to visit. Charges for foreigners were US$2.50 each for six buildings clustered around the Kremlin's central Sobornaya ploshchad (Cathedral Square) – the Assumption, Archangel and Annunciation cathedrals, the Church of the Deposition of the Robe, the Patriarch's Palace, and the Ivan the Great Bell Tower – and US$10 for the Armoury. The ISIC card gets you half-price tickets. Prices for Russians are about one-tenth of the foreigners' prices but the ticket cashiers are very adept at distinguishing non-Russian accents.

Inside the grounds, police blow whistles to stop you straying into out-of-bounds areas, which include the government buildings.

Tours Intourist and Intourservice offer guided tours in English of the Kremlin

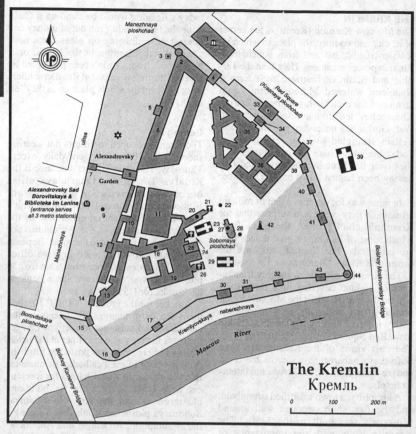

The Kremlin
Кремль

grounds (without entering any of the cathedrals or museums except the Armoury) for about US$20 per person, and of the Diamond Fund Exhibition for about US$24, daily except Thursday. You can book at their main bureaus (see the Tourist Offices section earlier in this chapter) or at their desks in many main hotels. Cheaper Kremlin tours are available through Patriarchi Dom and the Moscow City Excursion Bureau (see the Organised Tours section later in this chapter). Patriarchi Dom's tours include the Armoury, but only go about once or twice a week.

Northern & Western Buildings

The **Kutafya Tower** (Kutafya bashnya), which forms the main visitors' entrance today, stands away from the Kremlin's west wall, at the end of a ramp over the Alexandrovsky Garden. The ramp was once a bridge over the Neglinnaya River, which used to be part of the Kremlin's defences but has flowed underground, beneath the Alexandrovsky Garden, since the early 19th century. The Kutafya Tower is the last survivor of a number of outer bridge towers that once stood on this side of the Kremlin.

From the Kutafya Tower you walk up the

1	State History Museum Государственный исторический музей	15	Borovitskaya Gate Tower Боровицкая башня	31	First Nameless Tower Первая Безымянная башня
2	Corner Arsenal Tower Угловая Арсенальная башня	16	Water-Drawing Tower Водовзводная башня	32	Second Nameless Tower Вторая Безымянная башня
3	Tomb of the Unknown Soldier Могила неизвестного солдата	17	Annunciation Tower Благовещенская башня		
		18	Terem Palace Теремной дворец	33	Lenin's Tomb Мавзолей В.И. Ленина
4	Nikolskaya Tower Никольская башня	19	Great Kremlin Palace Большой кремлёвский дворец	34	Senate Tower Сенатская башня
5	Middle Arsenal Tower Средняя арсенальная башня	20	Patriarch's Palace Патриарший дворец	35	Senate Сенат
		21	Church of the Twelve Apostles Собор двенадцати апостолов	36	Supreme Soviet Верховный Совет
6	Arsenal Арсенал			37	Saviour Gatetower Спасская башня
7	Kutafya Tower & Ticket Offices Кутафья башня и кассы музеев Кремля	22	Tsar Cannon Царь-пушка	38	Tsar Tower Царская башня
		23	Assumption Cathedral Успенский собор	39	St Basil's Cathedral Собор Василия Блаженного
8	Trinity Gate Tower Троицкая башня	24	Church of the Deposi- tion of the Robe Церковь ризположения		
9	Ticket Office Кассы музеев Кремля	25	Hall of Facets Грановитая палата	40	Alarm Tower Набатная башня
10	Poteshny Palace Потешный дворец	26	Annunciation Cathedral Благовещенский собор	41	Konstantin-Yelena Tower Константино-Елен инская башня
11	State Kremlin Palace Государственный Кремлёвский дворец	27	Ivan the Great Bell Tower Колокольня Ивана Великого		
12	Commandant Tower Комендантская башня			42	Lenin Statue Памятник Ленину
13	Armoury & Diamond Fund Exhibition Оружейная и выставка алмазного фонда	28	Tsar Bell Царь-колокол	43	Peter Tower Петровская башня
		29	Archangel Cathedral Архангельский собор	44	Beklemishevskaya Tower Беклемишевская башня
14	Armoury Tower Оружейная башня	30	Secrets Tower Тайницкая башня		

ramp and pass through the Kremlin walls beneath the **Trinity Gate Tower** (Troitskaya bashnya). On your way to Sobornaya ploshchad you now pass, or can see, the following buildings that are closed to visitors.

The lane to the right (south), immediately inside the Trinity Gate Tower, runs between the 17th-century **Poteshny Palace** (Poteshny dvorets), where Stalin lived, and the marble, glass and concrete **State Kremlin Palace** (Gosudarstvenny Kremlyovsky dvorets), built in 1960-61 for Communist Party congresses and as a concert and ballet auditorium. It holds 6000 people and its acoustics are said to be superb. North of the State Kremlin Palace, the 18th-century **Arsenal** (Arsenal) is ringed with 800 captured Napoleonic gun barrels. The ultimate seat of power in the modern Kremlin, the offices of the president of Russia, are in the yellow, triangular former **Senate** (Senat) building, a fine 18th-century classical edifice, east of the Arsenal. Next to it is a 1930s **Supreme Soviet** (Verkhovny Soviet) building.

Assumption Cathedral

The first building open to visitors that you reach, just past the State Kremlin Palace, is the Patriarch's Palace (Patriarshy dvorets), but you'll probably prefer to pass by it for the time being and continue into Sobornaya ploshchad, the heart of the Kremlin, surrounded by magnificent buildings.

On the north side of Sobornaya ploshchad, with five golden helmet domes, and four semicircular gables facing the square, is the Assumption Cathedral (Uspensky sobor), the focal church of pre-Revolutionary Russia and burial place of most of the heads of the Russian Orthodox Church from the 1320s to 1700. The Assumption Cathedral was built between 1475 and 1479 after the Bolognese architect Aristotle Fioravanti had toured Novgorod, Suzdal and Vladimir to acquaint himself with Russian architecture. His design is based on the Assumption Cathedral at Vladimir, with some Western features added. It replaced a smaller 1326 cathedral on the same site. In 1812 French troops used the cathedral as a stable and ran off with 295 kg of gold and over five tonnes of silver, but much of it was recovered. Occasional special services are now held in the Assumption Cathedral after a gap from 1918 to 1989.

A striking 1660s fresco of the Virgin Mary faces Sobornaya ploshchad above the door that was used for royal processions. The visitors' entrance is at the west end. The interior is unusually bright and spacious, full of warm golds, reds and blues. The tombs of many of the leaders of the Russian Church (metropolitans up to 1590, patriarchs from 1590 to 1700) are against the north, west and south walls. Near the south wall is a tent-roofed wooden throne made in 1551 for Ivan the Terrible, known as the Throne of Monomakh because of its carved scenes from the career of 12th-century Grand Prince Vladimir Monomakh of Kiev.

The iconostasis dates from 1652 but its lowest level contains some older icons. Among them are, second from the right, the 1340s *Saviour with the Angry Eye (Spas yaroe oko)* and, on the left of the central door, the *Virgin of Vladimir*, an early 15th-century Rublyov-school copy of Russia's most revered image, the *Vladimir Icon of the Mother of God*. (The 12th-century original, now in the Tretyakov Gallery, stood in the Assumption Cathedral from the 1480s to 1930.) One of the oldest Russian icons, the 12th-century red-clothed *St George* from Novgorod, formerly positioned to the right of the iconostasis' south door, was away for restoration when we last visited.

Most of the existing murals on the cathedral walls were painted on a gilt base in the 1640s, but three grouped together on the south wall – *The Apocalypse (Apokalipsis), The Life of Metropolitan Pyotr,* and *All Creatures Rejoice in Thee (O tebe raduetsya)* – are attributed to Dionysius and his followers, the cathedral's original 15th-century mural painters.

Church of the Deposition of the Robe

This delicate little single-domed church (Tserkov Rizpolozhenia) beside the west door of the Assumption Cathedral was built between 1484 and 1486 in exclusively Russian style as the private chapel of the heads of the Church, who tended to be highly suspicious of such people as Italian architects. Later the tsars used it. The interior walls, ceilings and pillars are covered with 17th-century frescoes. It houses an exhibition of 15th to 17th-century woodcarving.

Ivan the Great Bell Tower

With its two golden domes rising above the east side of Sobornaya ploshchad, the Ivan the Great Bell Tower (Kolokolnya Ivana Velikogo) is the Kremlin's tallest structure – a Moscow landmark visible from 30 km away. Before the 20th century it was forbidden to build higher in Moscow. The southern tower had just two octagonal tiers beneath a drum and dome when designed by the Italian Marco Bono in 1505-08. Boris Godunov raised it to 81 metres (which the inscription just below the dome tells us at some length). The building's central section, with a 65-tonne bell, dates from between 1532 and 1543 and is another Russian/Italian stylistic combination; the northern end is 19th-century. Just whom the building's name refers to is obscure: the only seemingly sure thing is that it's not Ivan the Great. Exhibitions from the Kremlin collections are shown on the ground floor.

Tsar Bell

Beside the bell tower stands the world's biggest bell, the Tsar-kolokol, a 202-tonne monster that never rang. It was cast in the 1730s for Empress Anna Ivanovna using remains of Tsar Alexey's 130-tonne 1655 version, which had shattered in a fall from its own special belfry in a 1701 fire. In another fire in 1737 an 11.5-tonne piece cracked off the new bell. Alexey's and Anna's likenesses adorn it.

Tsar Cannon

North of the bell tower is the Tsar Cannon (Tsar-pushka). It was cast in 1586 for Fyodor I, whose portrait is on the barrel. Shot has probably never sullied its 89-cm bore – certainly not the cannonballs beside it, which are too big even for this elephantine firearm.

Archangel Cathedral

Back on Sobornaya ploshchad, the Archangel Cathedral (Arkhangelsky sobor) at the square's south-east corner was for centuries the coronation, wedding and burial church of tsars. The tombs of all Muscovy's rulers but one from the 1320s to the 1690s are here (the

The Tsar Bell, broken before it was ever rung

The Tsar Cannon, probably never fired

absentee is Boris Godunov, who is buried at Sergiev Posad.) The cathedral was built between 1505 and 1508 by the Italian Alevisio Novi and dedicated to Archangel Michael, guardian of the Moscow princes. Like the Assumption Cathedral, it is five-domed and essentially Byzantine-Russian in style. But the exterior has many Venetian Renaissance features – notably the distinctive scallop-shell gables.

The rows of sarcophagi which take up much of the floor space were carved in the 17th century. Tsarevich Dmitry, a son of Ivan the Terrible who died mysteriously in 1591, then was impersonated by the False Dmitrys during the Time of Troubles, lies beneath a painted stone canopy. Frustratingly, Ivan's own tomb is out of sight behind the iconostasis, along with his other sons Ivan (whom he killed) and Fyodor (who succeeded him). From Peter the Great onwards, emperors and empresses were buried in St Petersburg; the exception is Peter II, who died in Moscow in 1730 and is here in the Archangel Cathedral.

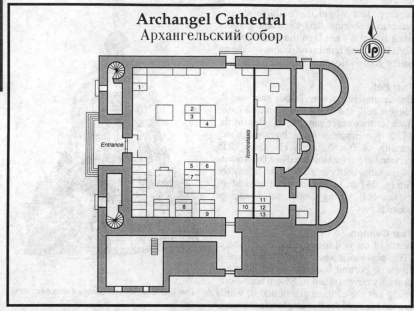

Archangel Cathedral
Архангельский собор

Entrance

Iconostasis

1	Vasily Shuysky 1606-10	6	Tsarevich Dmitry	11	Fyodor I 1584-98
	Василий Шуйский		Царевич Дмитрий		Фёдор I
2	Ivan V 1682-96	7	Mikhail Romanov 1613-45	12	Tsarevich Ivan
	Иван V		Михаил Романов		Царевич Иван
3	Fyodor III 1676-82	8	Dmitry Donskoy 1359-89	13	Ivan IV the Terrible 1547-84
	Фёдор III		Дмитрий Донской		Иван IV Грозный
4	Peter II 1727-30	9	Ivan I Kalita 1325-40		
	Пётр II		Иван I Калита		
5	Alexey Romanov 1645-76	10	Ivan III the Great 1462-1505		*Dates are rulers' years on the throne*
	Алексей Романов		Иван III Великий		

The murals – revealed from under later layers during 1950s restorations – are from the 17th century. The south wall depicts many of the people buried here; on the pillars are some of their predecessors, including Andrey Bogolyubsky, Prince Daniil and his father, Alexandr Nevsky.

Annunciation Cathedral

The Annunciation Cathedral (Blago-veshchensky sobor) at the south-west corner of Sobornaya ploshchad contains probably the greatest icons of possibly the greatest icon painter, Theophanes the Greek. They have a timeless beauty which appeals even to those usually left cold by icons.

This cathedral, built between 1484 and 1489 by Pskov masters, was the royal family's private chapel. Originally it had just three domes and an open gallery round three sides. Ivan the Terrible, whose taste was more elaborate, added six more domes and chapels at each corner, enclosed the gallery and covered the roof with gold. His fourth marriage disqualified him under Orthodox law from entering the church proper, so he had the southern arm of the gallery converted into the Archangel Gabriel Chapel, from which he could watch services through a grille.

Many of the murals in the gallery date from the 1560s. Among them are the *Capture of Jericho* in the porch, *Jonah and the Whale* on the south side of the northern arm of the gallery, *Virgil* on the west arm's west wall, the *Trinity* on its east wall, and the *Tree of Jesse* (showing Christ's ancestors) on its ceiling.

The small central part of the cathedral has a lovely jasper floor and several 16th-century frescoes – including Russian princes on the north pillar and Byzantine emperors on the south, both with apocalypse scenes above them. But its real treasure is the iconostasis, where 1920s restorers uncovered early 15th-century icons probably painted for a previous church on the site by three of the greatest medieval Russian artists.

Theophanes is usually thought to have painted the six icons at the right-hand end of the deesis row, the biggest of the iconostasis' six tiers. From left to right, these are the *Virgin Mary*, *Christ Enthroned*, *St John the Baptist*, the *Archangel Gabriel*, the *Apostle Paul* and *St John Chrysostom*. What sets them apart from most other icons is the genuine emotion visible in their faces and movements. These are real people, not cardboard cutouts.

The third icon from the left, *Archangel Michael*, is ascribed to Andrey Rublyov, who may also have done the adjacent *St Peter.* Rublyov is also reckoned the artist of the first, second, sixth, seventh and probably the third and fifth icons from the left of the festival row, above the deesis row. Prokhor of Gorodets is thought to have painted the seven at the right-hand end.

The Archangel Gabriel Chapel (Pridel Arkhangela Gavriila) can be entered either from the south end of the west arm of the gallery or from the central part of the cathedral. It has a colourful iconostasis dating from 1564 (when the chapel was consecrated) and an exhibition of other icons.

Hall of Facets & Terem Palace

On the west side of Sobornaya ploshchad, and named after its Italian Renaissance stone facing, is the square Hall of Facets (Granovitaya palata). Its upper floor housed the tsar's throne room, scene of banquets and ceremonies, and was reached by outside staircases from the square below. Designed by Marco Ruffo and Pietro Solario and built between 1487 and 1491, it's closed to tourists. The 16th and 17th-century Terem Palace (Teremnoy dvorets), most splendid of all the Kremlin palaces, is also closed. You can glimpse its sumptuous cluster of golden domes and chequered roof behind and above the Church of the Deposition of the Robe.

Patriarch's Palace

Immediately north of the Assumption Cathedral, this palace was mostly built in the mid-17th century for Patriarch Nikon, who ordered a return to the early Moscow style. It contains a Museum of 17th-Century Russian Applied Art & Life. This houses mostly church vestments, icons, illuminated books and so on, but also incorporates the five-domed Church of the Twelve Apostles, which Nikon had built as a new patriarch's chapel, and the large Hall of the Cross (Krestovaya Palata), once the patriarch's official reception hall.

Armoury

A numbingly opulent collection of treasures accumulated over centuries by the Russian state and Church is housed in the Armoury (Oruzheynaya palata) in the south west corner of the Kremlin. Normally you can enter (with a ticket) at any time the Kremlin is open, but during some busy periods entry may only be permitted at certain specific times, which will be posted at the Armoury door or the Kutafya Tower ticket offices. In such cases your ticket will be for one particular entry time (*seans*).

The collection is in nine rooms: Nos 1 to 5 upstairs, Nos 6 to 9 downstairs. Room 3 (18th to 20th-century Russian gold and silver) has the renowned Easter eggs of precious metals and jewels by the St Petersburg jewellers Fabergé. Each opens to reveal amazingly detailed miniature objects – most famously a clockwork trans-Siberian train made of gold, with a platinum locomotive and ruby headlamp.

Room 6 is one of the most fascinating: it's full of thrones and royal regalia. There's the joint coronation throne of boy tsars Peter (the Great) and his half-brother Ivan V, with a secret compartment from which Regent Sofia was able to prompt them; the 800-diamond throne of Peter's father Tsar Alexey; the jewel-studded, sable-trimmed, gold Cap of Monomakh, worn for coronations for two centuries until 1682; and the coronation dresses of 18th-century empresses. (Empress Elizabeth, we're told, had 15,000 other dresses, and lots of unpaid bills.)

Among the coaches in room 9 is the sleigh in which Elizabeth rode from St Petersburg to Moscow for her coronation, which was pulled by 23 horses at a time – about 800 in all for the trip.

Between the Armoury and the Annunciation Cathedral stretches the 700-room Great Kremlin Palace (Bolshoy Kremlyovsky dvorets), built in the period from 1838 to 1849 as an imperial residence. It's not open to the public.

Diamond Fund Exhibition

If the Armoury hasn't sated your diamond lust, there are more in the separate Diamond Fund Exhibition (Vystavka almaznogo fonda) in the same building, but you have to pre-book a group tour to see them (see the Getting In section). The collection, mainly of precious stones and jewellery garnered by tsars and empresses, includes such weighty beasts as the 190-carat diamond given to Catherine the Great by her lover Grigory Orlov.

Towers

The Kremlin walls have 19 distinctive towers, mostly built between 1485 and 1500, with tent roofs added in the 17th century. Some had to be rebuilt after Napoleonic vandalism. The **Saviour Gate Tower** (Spasskaya bashnya) over the Kremlin's 'official' exit on to Red Square is Moscow's Big Ben – its chimes are relayed over state radio. This gate was used for processions in tsarist days. Ivan the Terrible watched executions from the nearby spot where the **Tsar Tower** (Tsarskaya bashnya) was later built. The **Konstantin-Yelena Tower** (Konstantino-Yeleninskaya bashnya) is also known as the Torture Tower. The **Secrets Tower** (Taynitskaya bashnya) facing the river was both a gate and the start of a secret passage to the river. Ivan the Terrible used the **Annunciation Tower** (Blagoveshchenskaya bashnya), next along, as a prison.

Alexandrovsky Garden

This park (Alexandrovsky Sad) along the Kremlin's west wall, open to everybody for nothing, is a pleasant spot in which to cool down on a hot day. The Tomb of the Unknown Soldier (Mogila neizvestnogo soldata) at its north end is a kind of national pilgrimage spot, where newlyweds have their pictures taken. The tomb contains the remains of one soldier who died in December 1941 at Km 41 of Leningradskoe shosse – the nearest the Nazis came to Moscow. Its inscription reads 'Your name is unknown, your deeds immortal'. There's an eternal flame, and other inscriptions listing the Soviet hero cities of WW II and honouring 'those who fell for the motherland' between 1941 and 1945.

CITY CENTRE

The heart of the city lies in the arc round the Kremlin bound by the streets Mokhovaya ulitsa, Okhotny ryad, Teatralny proezd and Lubyansky proezd.

Red Square

Red Square (Krasnaya ploshchad) lies immediately outside the Kremlin's northeast wall. As you step on to the square, indulge your eyes on the building that, more than any other, says 'Russia': St Basil's Cathedral, which rises from the slope at the south end of the square.

Red Square is closed to traffic except for the limousines that whizz in and out of the Kremlin's Saviour Gate from time to time. Most people on the square are sightseers but that doesn't reduce the frisson of walking on these 400 by 150 metres of cobbles so central to Russian history. It's particularly atmospheric when floodlit at night.

Red Square used to be a market square and has always been a place the Kremlin's occupants chose to make points to their people. Ivan the Terrible publicly confessed his misdeeds here in 1547, built St Basil's to commemorate his victories in the 1550s, and later had numerous perceived enemies executed here. Cossack rebel Stepan Razin (dismembered in 1671) and Peter the Great's 2000-strong mutinous palace guard, the Streltsy, executed en masse in 1698, died here too. Soviet rulers chose Red Square for their main twice-yearly military parades – perhaps most poignantly on 7 November 1941, when tanks rolled straight off to the front line outside Moscow, and during the Cold War, when lines of ICBMs rumbled across the square to remind the West of Soviet military might.

The name Krasnaya ploshchad has nothing to do with either communism or the blood that's flowed here. *Krasnyy* originally meant beautiful: only in the 20th century did it come to mean 'red' too.

Lenin's Tomb Lenin's granite tomb (Mavzoley V I Lenina) stands at the foot of the Kremlin wall, which somewhat dwarfs it. Despite calls by Moscow's mayor and others for Lenin to be removed to a more secluded resting place, by 1995 the embalmed leader still remained on show in the place he had occupied for most of the time since his death in 1924 (apart from a retreat to Siberia during WW II). From 1953 to 1961 Lenin shared the tomb with Stalin, who when alive had initiated the tradition that Soviet leaders stand

atop the tomb to inspect the annual May Day and 7 November parades. The ceremonial, goose-stepping changing of the guard at the tomb every hour was discontinued in October 1993 in the wake of the battle at Moscow's White House.

The tomb is open to the public, free of charge, from 10 am to 1 pm daily except Monday and Friday. Just join the queue at the north-west corner of Red Square and within a few minutes you'll be descending the stairs into the tomb. Guards tell visitors to remove hats as they enter. Without stopping, you walk round three sides of the glass case in which Lenin lies, like a saint's body in a Catholic church. A surprisingly small figure wearing a spotted tie, with features that seem a mite touched up, he looks for all the world like a plaster cast.

From the tomb you emerge into a plot beneath the Kremlin wall where lie the remains of many more Soviet-era luminaries. Special notables are represented by busts above their graves in a special plot between Lenin's tomb and the Kremlin wall – including Stalin; Leonid Brezhnev and his two successors as Soviet Communist Party general secretary, Yury Andropov and Konstantin Chernenko; Felix Dzerzhinsky, founder of the Cheka (forerunner of the KGB); Yakov Sverdlov, a key organiser of the October Revolution and the first official head of the Soviet state; Andrey Zhdanov, Stalin's cultural chief and the second-most powerful man in the USSR immediately after WW II; and Mikhail Frunze, the Red Army leader who secured Central Asia for the Soviet Union in the 1920s. Other graves include those of Lenin's lover Inessa Armand and the American John Reed (Dzhon Rid), author of *Ten Days that Shook the World*. Plaques in the wall mark the spots where the ashes of many more heroes lie, including Yury Gagarin, the first astronaut; Marshal Georgy Zhukov, who commanded the defeat of Hitler; Alexey Kosygin, Brezhnev's initial partner in power in the 1960s; and Igor Kurchatov, leader of the team that developed the Soviet hydrogen bomb.

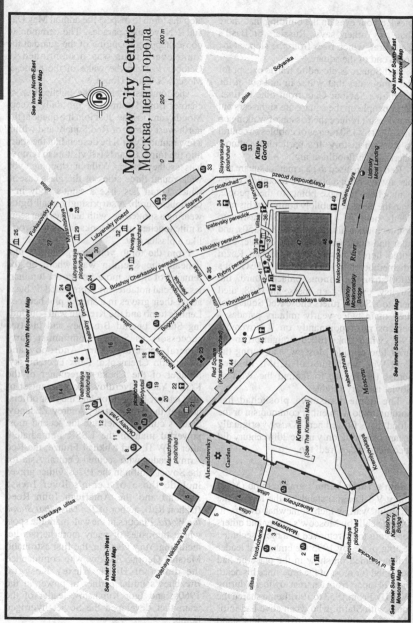

Moscow City Centre
Москва, центр города

PLACES TO STAY

7 Hotel National
Гостиница Националь
10 Hotel Moskva
Гостиница Москва
16 Hotel Metropol
Гостиница Метрополь
47 Hotel Rossia
Гостиница Россия

OTHER

1 Pashkov House
Дом Пашкова
3 Russian State Library
Российская государственная
библиотека
4 Central Exhibition Hall
Центральный выставочный зал
5 Moscow State University
Московский государственный
университет
6 Intourist
Интурист
9 - Transaero
Трансаэро
11 State Duma
Государственная дума
12 House of Unions
Дом союзов
14 Bolshoy Theatre
Большой театр
15 Maly Theatre
Малый театр
17 Old Printing House
Старый печатный двор
18 Zaikonospassky Monastery Church
Церковь Заиконоспасского монастыря
20 Former Central Lenin Museum
Бывший Центральный
музей В. И. Ленина
21 State History Museum
Государственный исторический музей
22 Kazan Cathedral
Казанский собор
23 GUM Department Store
ГУМ
25 Detsky Mir
Детский мир
26 KGB Museum
Музей К.Г.Б.
27 Lubyanka
Лубянка
28 Torgovy Dom Biblio-Globus
Торговый дом Библио-Глобус

29 Mayakovsky Museum
Музей В.В. Маяковского
30 Memorial to Victims of Totalitarianism
Памятник жертвах тоталитарного
режима
31 Moscow City History Museum
Музей истории города Москвы
32 Polytechnical Museum
Политехнический музей
34 Church of the Trinity in Nikitniki
Церковь Троицы в Никитниках
35 Old Stock Exchange
36 St George's Church
Церковь Георгия
37 Chambers in Zaryadie Museum
Музей палаты в Зарядье
38 Monks' Building
Братский корпус
39 Monastery of the Sign Cathedral
Собор знаменского монастыря
40 Monastery of the Sign Belltower
Колокольня знаменского монастыря
41 St Maxim the Blessed's Church
Церковь Максима Блаженного
42 English House
Палаты старого английского двора
43 Place of Skulls
Лобное место
44 Lenin's Tomb
Мавзолей В.И. Ленина
45 St Basil's Cathedral
Собор Василия Блаженного
46 St Barbara's Church
Церковь Варвары
48 Central Concert Hall
Центральный концертный зал
49 Church of St Anne's Conception
Церковь зачатия Анны

METRO STATIONS

2 Borovitskaya, Alexandrovsky Sad &
Biblioteka im Lenina
Боровицкая, Александровский
Сад и Библиотека имени Ленина
8 Okhotny Ryad (two locations)
Охотный Ряд
13 Teatralnaya
Театральная
19 Ploshchad Revolyutsii (two locations)
Площадь Революции
24 Lubyanka (two locations)
Лубянка
33 Kitay-Gorod (four locations)
Китай-Город

St Basil's Cathedral No picture can prepare you for St Basil's (Sobor Vasilia Blazhennogo), which rises like a fairy tale at the south end of Red Square. This building's unique cluster of colours and shapes, in some lights ominous and foreboding, in others joyous and playful, is the ultimate symbol of Russia; and, despite its Oriental-looking turban domes, the cathedral is in fact the culmination in brick of a wholly Russian style that had been developed in building wooden churches.

St Basil's was created between 1555 and 1561, replacing an existing church on the site, to celebrate Ivan the Terrible's taking of the Tatar stronghold of Kazan on 1 October 1552, the feast of the Intercession – hence its official name, the Pokrovsky (Intercession) Cathedral. The architect is thought to have been called Posnik Yakovlev. Legend has it that Ivan had this genius blinded so that he could never build anything to compare with St Basil's. The cathedral owes its usual name to the barefoot holy fool Vasily (Basil) the Blessed, who predicted Ivan's damnation and added (correctly), as the army left for Kazan, that Ivan would murder a son. Vasily died while Kazan was under siege and was buried beside the church which St Basil's soon replaced. He was later canonised.

St Basil's seeming anarchy of shapes in fact hides a comprehensible plan of nine main chapels: the tall, tent-roofed one in the centre; four big, octagonal-towered ones, topped with the four biggest domes, on the north, south, east and west; and four smaller ones in between. A couple of extra tent roofs on the stairways, an extra north-east chapel over Vasily the Blessed's grave, and a tent-roofed south-east bell tower were added later. Only in the 1670s were the domes patterned and St Basil's given its present, highly colourful appearance.

The interior is open to visitors from 11 am to 3.30 pm daily except Tuesday (US$1.30 for foreigners). The ground floor holds a small exhibition on St Basil's itself, and there are some lovely frescoes of flower patterns and saints. The inside of the central tower is supported by a forest of scaffolding.

In front of St Basil's stands a statue of the butcher Kuzma Minin and Prince Dmitry Pozharsky, who raised and led the army that ejected the occupying Poles from the Kremlin in 1612. Just up the slope is the round, walled Lobnoe Mesto (Place of Skulls), traditional site of Red Square executions.

GUM The Gosudarstvenny Universalny Magazin (State Department Store), which lines the north-east side of Red Square, was built in the 19th century to house over 1000 shops. A remarkable transformation has taken place here since the perestroika years, when GUM symbolised all that was worst about Soviet shopping – long queues and shelves empty of all but a few drab goods. Privatised in 1993, GUM is now a symbol of the positive side of economic reform, a bright, bustling place full of attractive shops stocked with imported and Russian goods of all kinds, and the best single place to look for anything you want to buy in Moscow, from shoes to souvenirs and computers to cosmetics. Benetton, Yves Rocher, Galerie Lafayette and many other big foreign names are here. There are a few snack places, and

The fairy-tale domes of St Basil's Cathedral

pay toilets at the south end of the ground floor.

Kazan Cathedral The pretty Kazan Cathedral (Kazansky sobor) on the corner of Red Square and Nikolskaya ulitsa (formerly ulitsa 25 Oktyabrya), opposite the north end of GUM, looks, and is, both old and brand-new at the same time. Founded in 1636 in thanks for the 1612 expulsion of Polish invaders, it housed for two centuries the *Virgin of Kazan* icon which had supposedly helped to rout the Poles, and became a highly venerated symbol of Moscow's and Russia's survival. Then in 1936 it was demolished, allegedly because it impeded the flow of celebrating workers in May Day and Revolution Day parades. In 1993, with the revival of the Church, it was rebuilt as before. It's open to visitors from 8 am to 7 pm daily. Evening service is held at 8 pm on Mondays.

History & Lenin Museums The State History Museum (Gosudarstvenny istorichesky muzey) at the north end of Red Square has a ginormous collection covering the whole Russian empire from the Stone Age on, but at the time of writing it was still closed for restoration, as it had been since 1986. Disputes over the ownership of items requisitioned from churches and private estates after the October Revolution, as well as the time taken over the reconstruction, have delayed the reopening. If and when the museum reopens, the building itself, which dates from the late 19th century, will be an attraction as well as its exhibits: each room is in the style of a different period or region, some with highly decorated walls which echo old Russian churches.

The former Central Lenin Museum (Tsentralny muzey V I Lenina) across the street at ploshchad Revolyutsii 2, once the big daddy of all the Lenin museums peppered around the USSR (the others were branches of this one), was closed in 1993 after the White House shoot-out. It may be used to house the Moscow city duma (council) or become a commercial centre.

Kitay-Gorod
The narrow old streets east of Red Square are known as the Kitay-Gorod, which means Chinatown, but it probably has nothing to do with China. This is one of the oldest parts of Moscow, settled since the 13th century and long a trade and financial centre.

Nikolskaya ulitsa, which leaves Red Square between GUM and the Kazan Cathedral and leads to Lubyanskaya ploshchad, is the Kitay-Gorod's busiest street, lined with numerous shops and thronged with pedestrians. It used to be the centre of a busy trade in icons, and had three monasteries. The dilapidated, but now again occasionally active, church of the **Zaikonospassky Monastery** (Zaikonospassky monastyr), built between 1661 and 1720, stands in the courtyard of No 9. The ornate green-and-white building a block east, with a lion and unicorn above its entrance, is the old **printing house** (pechatny dvor) on whose site in 1563-64 Ivan Fyodorov reputedly produced Russia's first printed book, the *Acts of the Apostles*.

Moscow's financial heart used to be along ulitsa Ilinka (formerly ulitsa Kuybysheva), a block south of Nikolskaya ulitsa: the **old stock exchange** (byvshaya birzha) is at No 2.

Ulitsa Varvarka (formerly ulitsa Razina) has the Kitay-Gorod's greatest concentration of interesting buildings, though they're grotesquely dwarfed by the Hotel Rossia. The pink-and-white **St Barbara's Church** (Tserkov Varvary), now government offices, dates from the years 1795 to 1804. The reconstructed 16th-century **English House** (Palaty starogo angliyskogo dvora), white with peaked wooden roofs, was the residence of England's first emissaries to Russia (sent by Elizabeth I to Ivan the Terrible) and the base for the English merchants who, in exchange for military supplies to Ivan, were allowed to trade duty-free in Russia.

The yellow **St Maxim the Blessed's Church** (Tserkov Maxima Blazhennogo) at ulitsa Varvarka 4, built in 1698, is now a folk-art exhibition/sales hall. Next along is the pointed bell tower of the 17th-century **Monastery of the Sign** (Znamensky monastyr); between the street and the western half of the Rossia's access ramp are the monastery's monks' building (now a crafts shop) and its golden-domed cathedral. Between the street and the east half of the ramp is the small but interesting **Chambers in Zaryadie Museum** (Muzey palaty v Zaryadie), devoted to the lives of the Romanov family in the days before they became tsars and were mere boyars. The house was built by Nikita Romanov, who was Ivan the Terrible's first brother-in-law, and whose grandson Mikhail later became the first of the 300-year Romanov dynasty. Restored in the 19th century, the house has two storeys on its street side but four facing the Hotel Rossia. It's open on Wednesday from 11 am to 6 pm, and Thursday to Monday from 10 am to 5 pm; it's closed on Tuesday and the first Monday of the month. The entrance is on the Hotel Rossia side. The colourful **St George's Church** (Tserkov Georgia) at ulitsa Varvarka 12, yet another crafts gallery, dates from 1658. Off the south-east corner of the Hotel Rossia is the pretty little 15th and 16th-century Pskov-style **Church of St Anne's Conception** (Tserkov zachatya Anny).

Opposite St George's Church, Ipatevsky pereulok leads to the 1630s **Church of the Trinity in Nikitniki** (Tserkov Troitsy v Nikitnikakh), one of Moscow's finest, with onion domes and lovely tiers of red-and-white spade gables rising from a square tower. The inside is covered with 1650s gospel frescoes by Simon Ushakov and others which reveal much about 17th-century Russia. The 1640s iconostasis also has Ushakov work, including *Our Lady of Vladimir*, surrounded by the tsars' family tree. A carved doorway leads into St Nikita the Martyr's chapel, above the vault of the Nikitnikov merchant family, one of whom had the church built. The church is open as a museum Friday to Monday from 10 am to 6 pm, Wednesday and Thursday from noon to 8 pm, and closed Tuesday and the first Monday of the month.

Around Manezhnaya Ploshchad

Wide Manezhnaya ploshchad (formerly ploshchad 50-letia Oktyabrya), north of the State History Museum at the north end of Red Square, is where several key Moscow streets converge. Busy Tverskaya ulitsa runs up to the north-west (see the Inner North-West section); Okhotny ryad leads north-east to Teatralnaya ploshchad; Mokhovaya ulitsa heads south-west to Borovitskaya ploshchad at the south-west corner of the Kremlin. From 1961 to 1990 Mokhovaya ulitsa, Okhotny ryad and its eastward continuation Teatralny proezd all went under one name, prospekt Marxa; then the old names were restored. Mokhovaya ulitsa is named after an old market in moss *(mokh)*, which was used for insulation; Okhotny ryad (Hunting Row) is where fish and game were once sold.

In Moscow's most ambitious modern development project, Manezhnaya ploshchad is being turned into a pedestrian zone with an underground shopping mall. This began in 1994 and is due to be finished for the city's 850th anniversary celebrations in 1997. Until 1938 the square was full of buildings: archaeologists have unearthed some centuries-old structures during the recent works.

The long, low building on the south-west side of the square is the **Central Exhibition Hall** (Tsentralny vystavochny zal), home to some of Moscow's most popular art exhibitions, open daily except Tuesday from 11 am to 8 pm. It's known as the Manezh, having originally been built, in 1825, as a military riding school (French: *manège*). On the north-west side of the square are the fine old edifices of **Moscow State University** (Moskovsky gosudarstvennaya universitet), built in 1793; the grandiose **Intourist headquarters** (1934), formerly the US embassy; and the **Hotel National**, built in 1903 and recently remodelled. The 1930s **Hotel Moskva**, fronting the north-east side of the square, is half-Constructivist, half-Stalinesque in style. The story goes that Uncle Joe was shown two possible designs for the hotel. Not realising they were alternatives, he approved both. Not daring to point out his error, the builders built half in each style.

Along Mokhovaya ulitsa, at its corner

with ulitsa Vozdvizhenka (formerly part of prospekt Kalinina), is the **Russian State Library** (Rossiyskaya gosudarstvenny biblioteka), the world's biggest with over 20 million volumes. Built between the two world wars, the library is in dire need of modernisation, and reading places are way short of demand. It incorporates one of Moscow's finest classical buildings, the 1784-87 **Pashkov House** (Dom Pashkova), named after its original owner, at the south end of Mokhovaya ulitsa. Use of the library requires some persistence (see the earlier Cultural Centres & Libraries section).

North-east of Manezhnaya ploshchad, Okhotny ryad passes between the Hotel Moskva and the glowering **State Duma** (Gosudarstvennaya duma), where Russia's parliament now sits. This building was erected in the 1930s for Gosplan (the Soviet State Planning Department) and was the source of the USSR's Five Year Plans. Next door is the green-columned **House of Unions** (Dom soyuzov), which dates from the 1780s and used to be the Nobles' Club. Its Hall of Columns (originally a ballroom, now a concert hall) was the scene of one of Stalin's grotesquest show trials, that of Nikolai Bukharin, a leading Communist Party theorist who had been a close associate of Lenin, in 1938. (This trial is chillingly described in Fitzroy Maclean's *Eastern Approaches*.) Other show trials during the 1930s purges took place in the October Hall in the same building.

Teatralnaya Ploshchad

Teatralnaya ploshchad (formerly ploshchad Sverdlova) opens out on both sides of Okhotny ryad, 200 metres from Manezhnaya ploshchad. The northern half of the square is dominated by the **Bolshoy Theatre**. There has been a theatre here since the late 18th century and Tchaikovsky's *Swan Lake* was premiered (unsuccessfully) here in 1877. Initially overshadowed by St Petersburg's Mariinsky Theatre, the Bolshoy didn't really hit the high notes until the 1950s, 1960s and 1970s, when foreign tours won big acclaim for its ballet and opera companies. More

recently the theatre has been a hotbed of controversy (see Entertainment). The busy streets behind the Bolshoy constitute Moscow's main shopping centre (see the Inner North section). Across ulitsa Petrovka from the Bolshoy (Big), is the **Maly** (Small) **Theatre**, a drama theatre. On the southern half of Teatralnaya ploshchad the tiled, sculptured front of the luxury **Hotel Metropol** has been restored to its original turn-of-the-century elegance. A **Karl Marx Statue** remains on the square before it.

From Teatralnaya ploshchad, Teatralny proezd runs uphill to Lubyanskaya ploshchad, passing the big **Detsky Mir** (Children's World) department store.

Around Lubyanskaya Ploshchad

For several decades the broad square at the top of Teatralny proezd meant just three chilling letters to most Russians: KGB, the initials of the Komitet Gosudarstvennoy Bezopasnosti (Committee for State Security). Today the red-and-grey building looming on its north-east side, known to one and all as the **Lubyanka**, is the headquarters of the KGB's successor the FSB (Federalnaya Sluzhba Bezopastnosti, Federal Security Service). The FSB doesn't run Russia's spies abroad, as the KGB did (that job is now done by a separate External Intelligence Service, the SVR) but still manages to find work for 75,000 people. A plaque to Yury Andropov, once the KGB's chief, is embedded in the Lubyanka wall fronting the square. The main entrance is round the back, on Furkasovsky pereulok. Behind the Lubyanka at Bolshaya Lubyanka ulitsa 12/1 is a four-room **KGB Museum** devoted to the history and paraphernalia of the Soviet intelligence services. Klaus Fuchs and Kim Philby make appearances. The museum is not open to casual callers but Patriarchi Dom (see Organised Tours) occasionally takes groups there.

From 1926 to 1990 Lubyanskaya ploshchad was called ploshchad Dzerzhinskogo, after Felix Dzerzhinsky, who founded the Cheka, the KGB's ancestor, soon after the revolution. A tall statue of

Dzerzhinsky which dominated the square was memorably removed by angry crowds, with the assistance of a couple of cranes, when the 1991 coup collapsed. The much humbler **Memorial to the Victims of Totalitarianism** (Pamyatnik zhertvakh totalitarnogo rezhima) stands in the little garden on the south-east side of the square. This single stone slab comes from the territory of an infamous 1930s labour camp on the Solovetsky Islands in the White Sea. The inscription says it was placed here in 1990 'in memory of the millions of victims of the totalitarian regime' by Memorial, an organisation devoted to digging out the truth about Stalinism.

Through an archway facing the Lubyanka on Myasnitskaya ulitsa (formerly ulitsa Kirova) is the excellent **Mayakovsky Museum** (Muzey V V Mayakovskogo), opened in 1989 in the building where the great avant-garde poet and artist Vladimir Mayakovsky lived from 1919. At first a fervent supporter of the revolution, Mayakovsky later grew disenchanted – and out of favour – with it, and shot himself in this building in 1930. The museum, whose address is actually Lubyansky proezd (formerly proezd Serova) 3/6, is open Monday, Tuesday, Friday, Saturday and Sunday from 10 am to 6 pm, Thursday from 1 to 9 pm. It's closed on Wednesday and the last Friday of the month.

The little **Moscow City History Museum** (Muzey istorii goroda Moskvy) at Novaya ploshchad 12 faces the huge **Polytechnical Museum** (Politekhnichesky muzey), which occupies a whole block at No 3/4. The former, open daily except Monday and the last day of the month, shows well how the city has spread from its starting point at the Kremlin. The Polytechnical Museum, open the same days, covers the history of Russian science, technology and industry.

INNER NORTH

The area that stretches about two km north of the Bolshoy Theatre is full of narrow, winding streets and intriguing nooks and crannies. In this part of the city are a range of eateries, several theatres, the Old Circus and, just behind the Bolshoy, Moscow's glossiest central shopping area (see the earlier Books & Bookshops section, and the later Things to Buy, for more information on specific shops).

Ulitsa Petrovka

Now restored to its pre-Revolutionary fashionable status, ulitsa Petrovka begins beside the Bolshoy Theatre. The big department store **TsUM** at No 2 is, like its slightly superior counterpart GUM, a bright, busy place now given over to multitudes of separate shops. It was built in 1909 as the Scottish-owned Muir & Merrilees. **Petrovsky Passazh** at No 10 has become Moscow's sleekest shopping arcade, like a smaller, glitzier version of GUM, dominated by foreign names. It, too, dates from the 1900s. There are a couple of worthwhile little Russian crafts shops just north of Petrovsky Passazh opposite Stoleshnikov pereulok.

The **Upper St Peter Monastery** (Vysoko-Petrovsky monastyr) at the corner of ulitsa Petrovka and Petrovsky bulvar (part of the Boulevard Ring) was founded in the 1380s as part of an early defensive ring round Moscow. Its present buildings date mostly from the late 17th century. You can enter from Petrovsky bulvar or Krapivensky pereulok. The main Virgin of Bogolyubovo Church has five onion domes on towers above spade gables. The loveliest structure is the brick Church of Metropolitan Pyotr in the middle of the grounds, restored with a shingle roof. It was built in 1690 by Peter the Great's mother in thanks for his ousting of the Regent Sofia.

Ulitsa Kuznetsky Most

Another street that has now been restored to its pre-Revolutionary smartness, ulitsa Kuznetsky Most has some interesting shops – particularly good for books and maps – and several airline offices. The Moscow Artists' Union's **Moscow Galleries** at Nos 11 and 20 are worth looking into.

The grand 19th-century **Sandunovskie Baths** (Sandunovskie bany, Sanduny for short), north of ulitsa Kuznetsky Most on Zvonarsky pereulok (formerly 2-y Neglinny pereulok), is Moscow's most famous public bathhouse. See the boxed item on Russian bathhouse behaviour under Petrozavodsk in the Northern European Russia chapter for background and etiquette. If you fancy having a go, the cost of a session at Sanduny ranges from US$5 to US$10 depending which section of the baths you choose.

Bolshaya Dmitrovka Ulitsa (Pushkinskaya Ulitsa)

Bolshaya Dmitrovka ulitsa, which runs north from Okhotny ryad, is one of those streets that will probably continue to be known by its Soviet-era name – Pushkinskaya ulitsa – for years, even if the city authorities do eventually get round to changing the signs. It's a good street for eateries with rock-bottom prices and has a few theatres too. Moscow's most famous drama theatre, plus a few better eateries and interesting shops, are in adjoining streets such as Kamergersky pereulok and Stoleshnikov pereulok.

The **Chekhov Moscow Art Theatre** at Kamergersky pereulok (formerly proezd Khudozhestvennogo Teatra) 3 gave the world Chekhov, revolutionised Russian drama, and heavily influenced Western theatre. Founded by actor-director Konstantin Stanislavsky and playwright-director Vladimir Nemirovich-Danchenko over an 18-hour restaurant lunch in 1898, the Art Theatre adopted a 'realist' approach which stressed truthful portrayal of characters and society, teamwork by the cast (not relying on stars), and respect for the writer. 'We declared war on all the conventionalities of the theatre...in the acting, the properties, the scenery, or the interpretation of the play', Stanislavsky wrote.

This treatment of *The Seagull* rescued Chekhov from despair after the play had flopped in St Petersburg. *Uncle Vanya*, *Three Sisters* and *The Cherry Orchard* were all premiered here. Gorky's *The Lower Depths* was another success. Chekhov is still staged here regularly. There's a stylised seagull emblem on the street frontage. The elegant interior was left simple to avoid distracting the audience. The theatre is known by its Russian initials MKhAT, short for Moskovsky Khudozhestvenny Akademichesky Teatr (Moscow Academic Art Theatre). The words 'imeni Chekhova' ('named after Chekhov') are now tacked on to the end to distinguish it from the newer Moscow Art Theatre named after Gorky (MKhAT imeni Gorkogo).

North of the Boulevard Ring

Moscow's **Old Circus** (Stary tsirk) is at Tsvetnoy bulvar 13, down the street from Tsvetnoy Bulvar metro. An oasis of light and chattering children on dark winter nights, it has been here since 1880, though the existing building is modern, having been rebuilt between 1987 and 1989. The **Central Market** (Tsentralny rynok) next door is closed for reconstruction.

Further north, beyond the Garden Ring, are several **museums** you might seek out if you have a special interest:

Glinka Museum of Musical Culture (Muzey muzikalnoy kultury imeni Glinki), ulitsa Fadeeva 4. Instruments and exhibits on Russian 19th-century composers. Open from 2 to 5 pm daily except Monday, plus other hours some days. About 750 metres from Novoslobodskaya or Mayakovskaya metro.

Museums of Decorative & Folk Art (Muzei dekorativnogo i narodnogo iskusstva), Delegatskaya ulitsa 3 and 5, almost on the Garden Ring. Good two-room Palekh collection. Also examples of finift, multilayered glazed or painted miniatures on metal from 18th and 19th-century Rostov-Veliky. Bigger than the Folk Art Museum on Leontevsky pereulok. Open Monday, Wednesday, Saturday and Sunday from 10 am to 6 pm, Tuesday and Thursday from 12.30 to 8 pm, closed Friday and last Thursday of month. Metro: Tsvetnoy Bulvar.

Armed Forces Museum (Muzey vooruzhennykh sil), ulitsa Sovietskoy Armii 2. History of Soviet and Russian forces since 1917, with the captured German standards paraded in Red Square in 1945 and parts of the US U-2 spy plane brought down in Siberia in 1960. Plus tanks, planes, guns etc. Open from 10 am to 5 pm daily except Monday and the second-last Tuesday of the month. Novoslobodskaya metro is 1.25 km west.

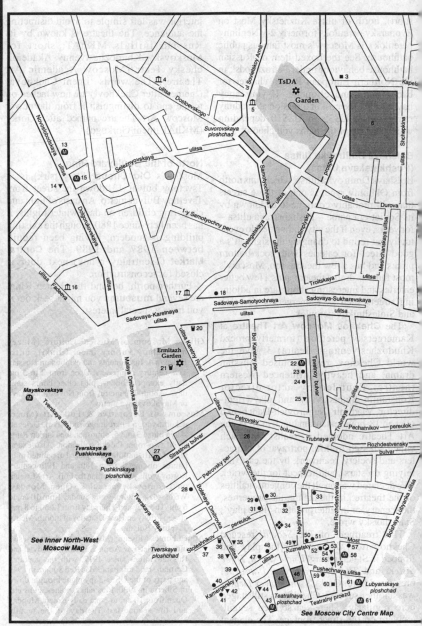

TsDA
Garden

ul Sovietskoy Armii

Kapels

ulitsa Shchepkina

ulitsa Dostoevskogo

Novoslobodskaya ulitsa

Seleznyovskaya ulitsa

Dolgorukovskaya ulitsa

ulitsa Fadeeva

Suvorovskaya ploshchad

Samotyochnaya ulitsa

Delegatskaya ulitsa

Olimpysky prospekt

ulitsa

Durova

Meshchanskaya ulitsa

Troitskaya ulitsa

1-y Samotyochny per

Sadovaya-Karetnaya ulitsa

Sadovaya-Samotyochnaya ulitsa

Sadovaya-Sukharevskaya ulitsa

ulitsa Karetny Ryad

Ermitazh Garden

Malaya Dmitrovka ulitsa

Mayakovskaya

Tverskaya ulitsa

Tverskaya & Pushkinskaya

Pushkinskaya ploshchad

Strastnoy bulvar

Petrovsky per

Bolshaya Dmitrovka

Petrovka

Petrovsky bulvar

Bol Karetny per

Tsvetnoy bulvar

Trubnaya ulitsa

Trubnaya pl

Pechatnikov — pereulok

Rozhdestvensky bulvar

Tverskaya ulitsa

pereulok

Neglinnaya ulitsa

ulitsa Rozhdestvenka

Bolshaya Lubyanka ulitsa

See Inner North-West
Moscow Map

Tverskaya ploshchad

Stoleshnikov per

ulitsa

ulitsa

Kuznetsky

Most

Pushechnaya ulitsa

Bolshaya Lubyanka ulitsa

Lubyanskaya ploshchad

Kamergersky per

Teatralnaya ploshchad

Teatralny proezd

See Moscow City Centre Map

PLACES TO STAY

1 Travellers Guest House
   Гостиница цмипкс
3 Olympic Penta Hotel
   Гостиница Олимпик Пента
32 Hotel Budapest
   Гостиница Будапешт
60 Hotel Savoy
   Гостиница Савой

PLACES TO EAT

8 Flamingo
   Фламинго
9 Kombi's
   Комбис
10 Restoran Pescatore 90
   Ресторан Пескаторе 90
14 Azteca
   Азтека
25 Gril-Bar Annushka
   Гриль-бар Аннушка
35 Zelyonyu Ogonyok & Shokoladnaya
   Зулёный огонёк и шоколадная
37 Kafe Stoleshniki / Uncle Guilly's
   Кафе Столешники/У Гиляровского
38 Oladyi
   Оладьи
42 Artistico's
44 Kafe Sadko
   Кафе Садко
49 Rokki
   Рокки
54 Restoran Iberia
   Ресторан Иберия
56 Pizzeria Ca Pizza

OTHER

2 Telephone Office
   Телефонный Пункт
4 Dostoevsky Flat-Museum
   Музей-квартира Ф.М. Достоевского
5 Armed Forces Museum
   Музей вооружённых сил
6 Olympic Sports Complex
   Спорткомплекс "Олимпийский..
11 International Medical Clinic
   Международное Медицинское
   Клиника
12 Irish Embassy
   Ирландское посольство
16 Glinka Museum of Musical Culture
   Музей музыкальной культуры
   имени Глинки

continued next page

Inner North Moscow
Москва, внчтренняя северная часть

0   250   500 m

continued from previous page

17 Museums of Decorative & Folk Art
     Музеи декоративного и
     народного искусства
18 Obraztsov Puppet Theatre
     Театр кукол под руководством
     С.В. Образцова
20 BB King
     Б. Б. Кинг
21 Hermitage Club
     Клуб Эрмитаж
23 Central Market
     Центральный рынок
24 Old Circus
     Старый цирк
26 Upper St Peter Monastery
     Высоко-петровский монастырь
28 Stanislavsky & Nemirovich-Danchenko
     Musical Theatre
     Музыкальный театр имени К.С.
     Станиславского и В.И.
     Немировича-Данченко
29 Intourtrans
     Интуртранс
30 Aeroflot
     Аэрофлот
31 Mekha Fur Shop
     Магазин Меха
33 Sandunovskie Baths
     Сандуновские бани
34 Petrovsky Passazh
     Петровский Пассаж
36 Pivnoy Bar
     Пивной бар
39 Golovnye Ubory Hat Shop
     Магазин Головные уборы
40 Chekhov Moscow Art Theatre
     МХАТ имени Чехова
41 Finnair & Malév
45 Bolshoy Theatre
     Большой театр

46 TsUM
     ЦУМ
47 Air China
48 JAL & SAS
50 Slavyanka Shop
     Магазин славянка
51 Moscow Gallery
     Московская галерея
52 Zwemmer Knigi
     Звеммер книги
53 Moldovan Embassy
     Посольство Молдовы
55 Moscow City Excursion Bureau
     Московское городское бюро
     экскурсий
57 Moscow Gallery
     Московская галерея
59 Alitalia

METRO STATIONS

7   Prospekt Mira (2 locations)
     Проспект Мира
13 Mendeleevskaya
     Менделеевская
15 Novoslobodskaya
     Новослободская
19 Sukharevskaya
     Сухаревская
22 Tsvetnoy Bulvar
     Цветной бульвар
27 Chekhovskaya
     Чеховская
43 Teatralnaya
     Театральная
58 Kuznetsky Most
     Кузнецкий Мост
61 Lubyanka (2 locations)
     Лубянка

Dostoevsky Flat-Museum (Muzey-kvartira F M Dostoevskogo), ulitsa Dostoevskogo 2, in the grounds of the hospital, now named after the writer, where Dostoevsky's father was a doctor. Dostoevsky spent his childhood here. Some explanatory material in English. Open Thursday, Saturday and Sunday from 11 am to 5 pm; Wednesday and Friday 2 to 8 pm. Nearest metro: Mendeleevskaya.

INNER NORTH-WEST

The area that stretches north-west from the city centre lies between two of Moscow's busiest arteries – Tverskaya ulitsa (formerly ulitsa Gorkogo), which runs north-west from Manezhnaya ploshchad, and ulitsa Novy Arbat (formerly prospekt Kalinina), which heads west to the Kalininsky Bridge over the Moscow River. Between the two is a network of quiet, old streets dotted with artistic venues and museums. On the bank of the Moscow River, towards the area's western extremity, stands the Moscow White House. (Ulitsa Novy Arbat itself is covered in the following Inner South-West section.)

Inner Tverskaya Ulitsa

In spite of soulless reconstruction in the 1930s, it's hard to imagine Moscow without Tverskaya ulitsa, the start of the road to St Petersburg. The bottom end of the street, by the National and Intourist hotels, is regarded as the city's hub by many tourists. Numerous places to eat, the Central Telegraph, and some of Moscow's classier shops are dotted up the slope to the intersection with the Boulevard Ring at Pushkinskaya ploshchad. Trolleybus Nos 12 and 20 run up and down Tverskaya ulitsa as far as the Belorussia Station.

Through the arch across the start of Bryusov pereulok (formerly ulitsa Nezhdanovoy) is the unexpected little gold-domed **Church of the Resurrection** (Tserkov Voskresenia). The main building, built in 1629, is full of fine icons saved from churches that were torn down during the Soviet era. The refectory and bell tower date from 1820.

A bit further up Tverskaya ulitsa is **Tverskaya ploshchad** (formerly Soviet-skaya ploshchad), just a space around a statue of Yury Dolgoruky, traditionally considered Moscow's founder. The five-storey building that faces it is the seat of civic power in Moscow, **City Hall**, with the office of the mayor.

On the east side of Tverskaya ulitsa at No 14, shortly before Pushkinskaya ploshchad, is the ornate **Yeliseevsky Magazin**. Originally a mansion, it was remodelled in 1901 as a kind of Harrod's of Russian grocery shops, with chandeliers, stained glass and marble columns. After being as empty as every other food shop in the perestroika years, it's now full of goods again, but the stupid system of queueing three times (first to find out the price, then to pay it, then to collect your purchase) survives. In the Brezhnev years, Yeliseev's (poetically known at the time as Gastronom No 1) was at the centre of a major scandal over shady dealings in food; after a trial in 1984 its manager, Yury Sokolov, was executed.

Around Pushkinskaya Ploshchad

The parks that open out on either side of Tverskaya ulitsa at the intersection with the Boulevard Ring constitute Pushkinskaya ploshchad, famous as the site of Russia's original **McDonald's**, still hugely popular and with wonderfully clean toilets. Pushkinskaya ploshchad is also the nearest thing to a Russian Fleet Street. On the north side, east of Tverskaya ulitsa, squat the offices of *Izvestia (News)*, the former newspaper of the USSR Supreme Soviet. Unlike its erstwhile partner in misinformation *Pravda (Truth)*, *Izvestia* changed its tone in the late 1980s, started to take advertising and began supporting political reformers against conservatives. Now privatised and controlled by its own staff, it's carving a niche as a serious paper of record that also manages to make money – something no other Russian paper has managed to do – despite a circulation down to below one million from 11 million in 1989.

Opposite *Izvestia* on the south side of Pushkinskaya ploshchad is **Moskovskie Novosti** *(Moscow News)*, published in several languages and a standard-bearer of reform since the 1980s. Then, the street in front of it was a kind of open-air debating club, with constant crowds gathered to use the new freedom to air their views. Occasional demonstrations still take place at Pushkinskaya ploshchad but more often it's just full of people relaxing, especially around the fountains on warm afternoons.

On Nastasinsky pereulok, a block north of Pushkinskaya ploshchad, is the trade union gazette **Trud** *(Labour)*; the Art Nouveau building was home to *Pravda* in the 1920s.

Just off Pushkinskaya ploshchad, at Malaya Dmitrovka ulitsa (formerly ulitsa Chekhova) 4, stand the multiple tent roofs of the **Church of the Nativity of the Virgin in Putinki** (Tserkov rozhdestva Bogoroditsy v Putinkakh). Curiously, these contributed to a ban on tent roofs on churches by Patriarch Nikon in 1652, the year this church was

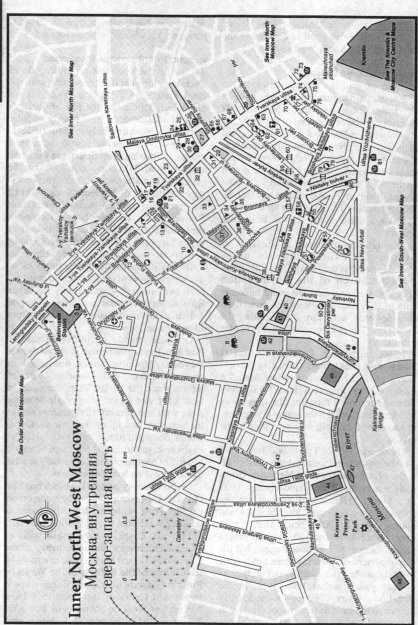

Inner North-West Moscow

Москва, внутренняя
северо-западная часть

PLACES TO STAY

4   Palace Hotel
    Гостиница Палас
13   Hotel Pekin
    Гостиница Пекин
23   Hotel Tverskaya
    Гостиница Тверская
36   Marco Polo Presnya
    Hotel
    Гостиница Марко
    Поло Пресня
44   Hotels
    Mezhdunarodnaya-1,
    Mezhdunarodnaya-2 &
    International
    Trade Centre
    Гостиницы
    Международная-1 и
    Международная-2 и
    центр
    международной
    ѓторговли
47   Inflotel
    Инфлотел
68   Hotel Tsentralnaya
    Гостиница Центральная
75   Hotel Intourist
    Гостиница Интурист

PLACES TO EAT

14   Patio Pasta
    Патио Паста
17   American Bar & Grill &
    Kombi's
    Американский бар и
    гриль и Комбис
18   Baku
    Баку
19   Restoran Tandur
    Ресторан Тандур
24   Bistro
    Бистро
31   McDonald's
    Макдоналдс
33   Moskovskie Zori
    Московские Зори
34   Kafe Margarita
    Кафе Маргарита
35   Kafe Begemot
    Кафе Бегемот
45   Restaurant Santa Fe
    Ресторан Санта Фе
46   Sadko Centre
    Садко центр
67   Pizza Hut
    Пицца Хат

70   McDonald's
    Макдоналдс
72   Kombi's
    Комбис
74   La Kantina
    Ла Кантина

OTHER

1   Central Railway
    Agency & River Boat
    Ticket Office
    Центральное
    железнодорожное
    агенство и Речная
    касса
2   Tverskaya Zastava
    ploshchad
    Тверская застава
    площадь
5   Tourists' Polyclinic
    Поликлиника
7   Polish Embassy
    Польское посольство
8   Zoo
    Зоопарк
9   American Express
    Американский Экспресс
10   Garden Ring Supermarket
    Универсам "Золотое
    Кольцо..
11   Czech & Slovak
    Embassies
    Посольства Чешской
    Республики и
    Словакии
12   CSA
    ЧСА
15   Triumfalnaya ploshchad
    Триумфальная площадь
16   Sadovaya-Triumfalnaya
    Садовая-триумфальная
21   Tchaikovsky Concert Hall
    Консертный зал имени
    Чайковского
22   Russian Artists' Union
    Exhibition Hall
    Выставочный зал
    Российского союза
    хдожников
25   Church of the Nativity
    of the Virgin in Putinki
    Церковь рождества
    Богородицы в
    Путинках
27   Pushkinskaya
    ploshchad
    Пушкинская площадь

28   Izvestia
    Известия
29   Trud
    Труд
32   Revolution Museum
    Музей революции
37   Patriarch's Pond
    Патриарший пруд
38   Chekhov House-
    Museum
    Дом-музей Чехова
40   Kudrinskaya ploshchad
    Кудринская площадь
41   Apartment Block
    Многоквартирный дом
43   Pilot Club
    Клуб пилот
48   White House
    Белый дом (Дом
    правительства
    Российской
    федерации)
49   Former Comecon
    Building
    Бывшее здание СЕВа
50   US Embassy
    Посольство США
51   New Zealand Embassy
    Посольство Новой
    Зеландии
52   Lithuanian Embassy
    Посольство Литвы
53   LAL
    ЛАЛ
54   Bookshop
    Книги
55   Georgian Embassy
    Посольство Грузии
56   Church of the Grand
    Ascension
    Церковь Большого
    Вознесения
57   Gorky House-Museum
    Дом-музей Горького
58   ITAR-TASS
    ИТАР-ТАСС
59   Museum of Folk Art
    Музей народного
    искусства
60   Stanislavsky
    House-Museum
    Дом-музей
    Станиславского
61   Church of the
    Resurrection
    Церковь Воскресения

continued next page

completed. Nikon thought them too Russian, too secular, too far from Byzantine roots.

Boulevard Ring

Pushkinskaya ploshchad forms part of Moscow's oddest-shaped park, eight km long and 20 metres wide, between the two carriageways of the Boulevard Ring (Bulvarnoe Koltso). Though hemmed in by traffic, the shady path down the middle of the road makes a great stroll, with intriguing 'bench people', families, and musicians toting violas. The Boulevard Ring was created in the late 18th and early 19th centuries, replacing Moscow's old defensive walls with boulevards and terraces of handsome buildings, and some of that era's elegance lingers in the neighbourhoods south-west of Pushkinskaya ploshchad, off Tverskoy bulvar – the oldest section – and Nikitsky bulvar (formerly Suvorovsky bulvar). Trolleybus Nos 15 and 31 run both ways along the ring between Trubnaya ploshchad, 1.25 km east of Pushkinskaya ploshchad, and Kropotkinskaya metro 2.75 km south.

Patriarch's Pond

Beside outer Malaya Bronnaya ulitsa, a pleasant one-km walk west from Pushkinskaya ploshchad, is the Patriarshy prud, a peaceful fishpond (and winter skating rink). It was immortalised by writer Mikhail Bulgakov, who made the devil appear here in *The Master and Margarita*, one of the most loved Russian novels of the 20th century. There are some pleasant small cafés and restaurants nearby.

Outer Tverskaya Ulitsa

Just north of Pushkinskaya ploshchad at Tverskaya ulitsa 21 is the **Revolution Museum** (Muzey revolyutsii), with a wrecked trolleybus in its forecourt. The bus got the worse of an encounter with a military vehicle when acting as a barricade near the White House during the 1991 coup. Inside the museum, a mish-mash of material tries to provide an honest account of Soviet history from the 1905 and 1917 revolutions up to the 1980s. Guided tours in English, which add a lot to the interest of the museum, have been available on Saturday and Sunday, so it may be best to go on those days. There are letters written by labour-camp inmates, photos of the 1930s destruction of churches, and one of the few 1940s issues of *Pravda* that didn't picture Stalin on the front page. Look for the picture of the giant Palace of Soviets

(Dvorets Sovietov) that Stalin was going to build on the site of the blown-up Cathedral of Christ the Saviour (Khram Khrista Spasitelya), and check the outfit of Yakov Sverdlov, the first official head of the Soviet state, who made leather trendy long before Marlon Brando donned it in *The Wild One*. Fellow revolutionary Anatoly Lunacharsky wrote of Sverdlov: 'He adopted a costume which visibly expressed his whole inner personality. He took to wearing leather from head to foot...The man was like ice.' The museum's hours are: Tuesday, Thursday and Saturday from 10 am to 6 pm; Wednesday, 11 am to 7 pm; Friday, 10 am to 6 pm; Sunday, 10 am to 5 pm; Monday, closed. Entrance is US$0.70 for foreigners. There's a good café, open from 11 am to 5 pm, and a souvenir shop.

Further up Tverskaya ulitsa at No 25, the Russian Artists' Union has an **art & handicrafts exhibition hall**.

Tverskaya ulitsa crosses the Garden Ring at **Triumfalnaya ploshchad** (formerly ploshchad Mayakovskogo), with several good restaurants, the Tchaikovsky Concert Hall (Kontsertny zal imeni Chaykovskogo) and a few theatres clustered nearby. Though Revolutionary bard Vladimir Mayakovsky no longer lends his name to the square, his statue still surveys it and the metro station beneath is still called Mayakovskaya.

Bolshaya Nikitskaya Ulitsa (Ulitsa Gertsena)

Bolshaya Nikitskaya ulitsa, still widely known by its Soviet name, ulitsa Gertsena, dissects the Inner North-West area, running from the Moscow State University buildings on Mokhovaya ulitsa out to the Garden Ring. In the backstreets along here many old mansions have survived, some renovated, some falling to pieces. Most of those inside the Boulevard Ring were built by the 18th-century aristocracy; most of those outside, by rising 19th-century industrialists. With little traffic, this is an excellent area for a quiet ramble.

The **Tchaikovsky Conservatory** (Konservatoria imeni Chaykovskogo) at No 13 is one of Russia's leading schools for musicians, with two concert halls of its own.

At Leontevsky pereulok (formerly ulitsa Stanislavskogo) 7, north off Bolshaya Nikitskaya ulitsa, is the **Museum of Folk Art** (Muzey narodnogo iskusstva), a one-room sampler of traditional and contemporary Russian handicrafts. It's open daily except Monday from 11 am to 6 pm. Don't confuse it with the more splendid Museums of Decorative & Folk Art at ulitsa Delegatskaya 3 and 5 (see the Inner North section). Across the street at Leontevsky pereulok 6 is the **Stanislavsky House-Museum** (Dom-muzey Stanislavskogo), the mansion of Chekhov's patron and founder of the Moscow Art Theatre, Konstantin Stanislavsky; it's open Thursday, Saturday and Sunday from 11 am to 6 pm, Wednesday and Friday from 2 to 9 pm, and closed Monday and Tuesday.

Ploshchad Nikitskie Vorota, where Bolshaya Nikitskaya ulitsa crosses the Boulevard Ring, is named after the Nikitsky Gates in the city walls that the ring has replaced. On its east side is the headquarters of **ITAR-TASS**, the official Russian news agency, with its windows full of news photos. South down the Boulevard Ring here, the **Museum of Oriental Art** (Muzey iskusstva narodov vostoka) at Nikitsky bulvar (formerly Suvorovsky bulvar) 12A mounts professional exhibitions from a big collection of art and religious artefacts from Asia and Africa. It's open from 11 am to 8 pm daily except Monday and the last Friday of the month. Further down towards Arbatskaya ploshchad at Nikitsky bulvar 7 are the **Gogol Memorial Rooms** (Memorialnye komnaty N V Gogolya), where 19th-century writer Nikolai Gogol spent his last, tortured months – open daily except Tuesday and Friday from at least 1 to 5.45 pm. In the courtyard a gloomy Gogol statue has some of his best known characters in bas-relief around the base: they include the Inspector General, the clerk of *The Overcoat* and others.

In 1831 the poet Alexandr Pushkin married Natalia Goncharova at the **Church**

of the Grand Ascension (Tserkov Bol-shogo Voznesenia) on the west side of ploshchad Nikitskie Vorota. Six years later he died, defending her honour in a duel in St Petersburg. The plain, heavy church building is now *remont* (closed for repairs). Immediately north, at Malaya Nikitskaya ulitsa (formerly ulitsa Kachalova) 6/2, is the fascinating 1906 Art Nouveau **Gorky House-Museum** (Dom-muzey Gorkogo). It's fascinating more for Art Nouveau than for Gorky. Designed by Fyodor Shekhtel for a banker named Ryabushinsky and bought by Gorky in 1931, it's a visual fantasy, from the sculpted doorways, ceiling murals, stained glass and carved-stone staircase to the exterior tilework. There's a tale that Stalin hastened Gorky's death (in 1936) by having the walls of the small ground-floor bedroom covered with toxic paint. The museum is free: enter at the back. Opening hours are Thursday, Saturday and Sunday from 10 am to 5 pm, Wednesday and Friday from noon to 7 pm. It's closed Monday, Tuesday and the last Thursday of the month.

Garden Ring
The **skyscraper** at Kudrinskaya ploshchad (formerly ploshchad Vosstania), where Bolshaya Nikitskaya ulitsa meets the Garden Ring, is an apartment block, one of Stalin's neo-Gothic juggernauts. This wide, noisy stretch of the Garden Ring makes it easy to believe the story that the ring's widening and the felling of its trees in the 1930s was done to enable warplanes to land there. These alterations robbed the ring, created in the early 19th century as a tree-lined boulevard in place of Moscow's old outer rampart, of its charm. If you fancy a trip round the entire 16 km of the Garden Ring, hop on trolleybus No Б in either direction. It'll eventually bring you back to where you started (though you may have to change to another No Б at the Kursk Station).

The neighbourhood around Kudrinskaya ploshchad, Barrikadnaya, saw heavy street fighting during the 1905 and 1917 uprisings. Just north, on the inner side of the Garden Ring at Sadovaya-Kudrinskaya ulitsa 6, is

the **Chekhov House-Museum** (Dom-muzey Chekhova), where Chekhov forsook medicine for writing. It's open four days a week from 11 am to 6 pm, Wednesday and Friday from 2 to 8 pm, and closed Monday.

Behind Kudrinskaya ploshchad at the corner of Barrikadnaya ulitsa and Bolshaya Gruzinskaya ulitsa (opposite metro Krasnopresnenskaya) is the main entrance to the big **Moscow Zoo** (Moskovsky zoopark), vaguely depressing but set among trees. It's open daily from 9 am to 8 pm in summer, 6 pm in spring and autumn, 5 pm in winter. Part of the eastern half of the zoo (east of Bolshaya Gruzinskaya ulitsa) was under repair, so if you wanted to visit the monkeys, apes, terrarium or children's zoo, you had to use a separate entrance on the Garden Ring opposite the Chekhov Museum.

A block south of Kudrinskaya ploshchad, on the Garden Ring at Novinsky bulvar (formerly ulitsa Chaykovskogo) 19/23 is the **US Embassy** – easy to spot thanks to the crowds of anxious visa applicants. Around the corner on Bolshoy Devyatinsky pereulok a replacement embassy, built in the 1980s, stands largely empty. The Americans found it had been riddled with high-tech Soviet eavesdropping devices during construction and haven't decided whether to build it again.

White House
Moscow's White House (Bely dom), scene of two crucial episodes in Russian history in the 1990s, stands at Krasnopresnenskaya naberezhnaya 2, just north of the Kalininsky Bridge, a short walk west of the US embassy (Krasnopresnenskaya and Barrikadnaya are the nearest metro stations). It was at the White House that Boris Yeltsin rallied the opposition that scrambled the 1991 hardline coup, then two years later sent in tanks and troops to blast out conservative rivals – some of them the same people who had backed him in 1991. The images of Yeltsin climbing on a tank in front of the White House in 1991, and of the same building ablaze after the 1993 assault, are among the most unforgettable from those tumultuous years.

The White House – now back to its origi-

The *Other* White House

The White House was built in the 1970s as the House of Soviets (administrative headquarters) for the Russian Republic of the USSR. When Russians elected a new Congress of People's Deputies, or parliament, to replace their republic's old rubber-stamp Supreme Soviet in 1990, the White House became its seat. Boris Yeltsin was picked by the new parliament as its chairman, and then in June 1991 was elected president of Russia (which was still part of the USSR) in a direct popular vote. He used the parliament as his power base in his ongoing combat with Mikhail Gorbachev, president of the USSR, an entity whose hold over Russia he sought to weaken.

When the old-guard coup against Gorbachev unfolded in Moscow on 19 August 1991, it was to the White House that Yeltsin went, narrowly avoiding arrest by the KGB, to rally opposition to the coup. Summoned by his appeals, people arrived to surround the White House and barricade its approaches with buses, building materials and scrap metal. Yeltsin persuaded troops surrounding the building to switch to his side, famously clambering on to a tank to urge Russia to resist the coup. Troops ordered to storm the building refused to do so. By the following day more than 100,000 people had gathered to protect the White House. In the face of this and other massive popular opposition, plans for an armed assault on the building were abandoned, and the coup collapsed. Only three people had died, in confrontations with armoured cars on the Garden Ring near the White House. Within days the Communist Party was banned and Gorbachev's other power base, the Soviet Union, was dying. By the end of 1991 Yeltsin was installed in the Kremlin, where now the Russian, not the Soviet, flag flew.

But over the next two years a new conflict brewed, turning the White House from Yeltsin's power base into that of his greatest rivals. The parliament there had been elected only a short time after non-communist parties were legalised in 1990, and was dominated by communists and Russian nationalists. Though these people had for the most part opposed the 1991 coup, they also opposed Yeltsin's economic market reforms and his increasing personal power. With a Russian constitution left over from Soviet times that failed to define whether president or parliament was supreme, the parliament counteracted many of Yeltsin's presidential decrees, leading to a political impasse.

The Kremlin-White House rift came to a head in September 1993 when parliament convened with plans to remove many of the president's powers. On 21 September Yeltsin declared the parliament dissolved, pending new elections under an amended constitution later in the year. Parliament refused to accept this and in turn declared Yeltsin stripped of all his powers, voting vice-president Alexandr Rutskoi 'president' in Yeltsin's place. Rutskoi, a mustachioed ex-air force pilot, and the parliament's chairman, Ruslan Khasbulatov, had been key anti-coup leaders alongside Yeltsin in 1991, but had since split from him. Again barricades went up around the White House, but this time it was Yeltsin who sent the troops to encircle it, ordering the members to leave by 4 October. Many did, but on 2 October street violence began on the Garden Ring. On 3 October pro-parliament demonstrators overwhelmed the troops around the White House, stormed the nearby Moscow city government offices, and then attacked the Ostankino TV centre in northern Moscow. The Ostankino attack failed but 62 died in the overnight battle.

Next morning tanks and machine guns bombarded the White House and troops stormed it, turning it into a blazing 'Black-and-White House' while Muscovites watched the spectacle from the Kalininsky Bridge. Resistance was short-lived: at least 70 died and Rutskoi and Khasbulatov were arrested.

Today, the White House contains the office of Russia's prime minister and national government offices. The new, less powerful parliament, the State Duma, sits near the Kremlin, in the former Gosplan building on Okhotny ryad. The skyscraper near the White House that looks like a telephone book standing on end (built for Comecon, the communist world's economic coordinating body, in the 1960s) is again in use as city government offices. ∎

---

nal whiteness and officially called the House of Government of the Russian Federation (Dom pravitelstva Rossiyskoy federatsii) – fronts one of the Moscow River's stateliest bends, with the Stalinesque Hotel Ukraina rising on the far bank. This corner of Moscow is particularly appealing when these buildings and the Kalininsky Bridge are lit up at night. The White House is not open to visitors but the epoch-making events that took place here make it one of Moscow's not-to-be-missed sights. In the park behind it one or two memorials mark places where people died in the 1993 battle.

INNER SOUTH-WEST

The south-western segment of inner Moscow, bound by ulitsa Novy Arbat in the north and stretching down a long tongue of land within a great loop of the Moscow River, is packed with interest, from the shops, buskers and restaurants of pedestrianised ulitsa Arbat to Moscow's top foreign-art collection, in the Pushkin Fine Arts Museum, and the historic, beautiful Novodevichy Convent and Cemetery. Within the Garden Ring is a web of old streets with some fine churches and other good museums, which is a delight to wander through (not alone!) after dark when many of its buildings are subtly lit.

Ulitsa Vozdvizhenka & Ulitsa Novy Arbat

Ulitsa Vozdvizhenka, running west from the Kremlin, and ulitsa Novy Arbat, its continuation to the Moscow River, form the start of the road west to Smolensk and the west. Their combined name in Soviet times was prospekt Kalinina.

The 'Moorish Castle' studded with sea-shells at ulitsa Vozdvizhenka 16 was built in 1899 for an eccentric merchant named Arseny Morozov, who was inspired by a real one in Spain. The inside is sumptuous and equally over-the-top. It's now the **House of Friendship with Peoples of Foreign Countries** (Dom druzhby s narodom zarubezhnykh stran). They might let you in for a look. See for yourself why, according to one story, Morozov's mother said when she saw it, 'Until now, only I knew you were mad; now everyone will'.

Ulitsa Novy Arbat, which begins beyond the Boulevard Ring, was created in the 1960s, with four matching ministry high-rises. In Soviet times it was Moscow's 'modern' shopping centre, but now it seems rather run-down apart from oases such as the **Arbat Irish House** supermarket (Irlandsky dom na Arbate) and **Bar Shamrock** at No 13. **Dom Knigi** at no 26, once Moscow's best general bookshop, is a shadow of its old self. The **Mikhail Lermontov House-Museum** (Dom-muzey Lermontova) at Malaya Molchanovka ulitsa 2, north off ulitsa Novy Arbat, displays the background of the 19th-century author of *A Hero of Our Time*. It's open Wednesday to Sunday from at least 2 to 5 pm.

The Moscow White House is beside the river just past the west end of ulitsa Novy Arbat – see Inner North-West.

Ulitsa Arbat

Ulitsa Arbat is a 1.25-km-long pedestrian mall which stretches from Arbatskaya ploshchad (metro: Arbatskaya) on the Boulevard Ring to Smolenskaya ploshchad on the Garden Ring (metro: Smolenskaya). The street art market, complete with instant portrait painters, soapbox poets and jugglers who made it an early oasis of free expression during perestroika, has gone now. But some of the buskers (and some of the pickpockets) remain; the Arbat is still an interesting walk, dotted with old, pastel-coloured merchant houses and tourist-oriented shops and places to eat.

The names of nearby lanes – Khlebny (Bread), Skatertny (Tablecloth), Serebryany (Silver), Plotnikov (Carpenters') – and that of the peaceful quarter south of the Arbat, called Staraya Konyushennaya (Old Stables) from earlier times, identify the area as an old settlement of court attendants. These were eventually displaced by artists and aristocrats. Until the 1960s ulitsa Arbat was Moscow's main westward artery. Then a swathe was bulldozed through streets to its north to create the present ulitsa Novy Arbat thoroughfare, taking out the old Arbatskaya ploshchad, a monastery and half a dozen churches. Ulitsa Arbat itself lay like a severed limb until restored as a pedestrian precinct in the 1980s. A relic of ulitsa Arbat's perestroika-era atmosphere is the **Wall of**

Peace (Stena Mira) near its east end, composed of hundreds of individually painted tiles on an international-friendship theme. In a side street at Krivoarbatsky pereulok 10 stands the refreshingly bizarre – though recently obscured by scaffolding – **Melnikov House** (Dom Melnikova). This concoction of brick, plaster and lozenge-shaped windows was built in 1927 by Konstantin Melnikov, the great Constructivist architect who was denounced in the 1930s and banned from ever working again. Melnikov lived on in the house, one of the few privately owned houses in the USSR, until he died in 1974. Today it's in a sad state of disrepair, with attempts to restore it as a Melnikov museum confounded by a legal battle over ownership between Melnikov's children. Towards the west end of the Arbat is the **Gruzia Tsentr**, a Georgian cultural centre with a small wax museum (figures of Stalin, Gorbachev and co), and towering over this whole end of the street is one of Stalin's 'Seven Sisters', the **Foreign Affairs Ministry** (Ministerstvo innostrannykh del), whose upper reaches look like a fairy-tale castle when floodlit after dark.

Pushkin Fine Arts Museum

Moscow's premier foreign-art museum is just a hop, skip and jump from the south-west corner of the Kremlin at ulitsa Volkhonka 12 (metro: Kropotkinskaya). The Pushkin (Muzey izobrazitelnykh iskusstv imeni A S Pushkina) is famous for its Impressionist and postimpressionist paintings, but also has a broad selection of European works from the Renaissance onward – mostly appropriated from private collections after the revolution – and a good display of ancient Egyptian art. Keep an eye open for any special exhibitions at the Pushkin, too: in recent years the museum, like the Hermitage in St Petersburg, has revealed some fabulous art hoards kept secret since they were seized by the Red Army from Germany at the end of WW II. In 1993 the Pushkin admitted that it held the gold of ancient Troy, found by the archaeologist Heinrich Schliemann in the 19th century; then in 1995 it unveiled a stash of

63 works by the likes of Degas, Renoir, Goya, El Greco and Tintoretto that had been thought lost for 50 years.

The highlight of the museum's permanent display is certainly the four rooms **(17, 18, 21 & 22)** of Impressionist and postimpressionist paintings and sculpture. Room 22 has 11 Monets and several Renoirs; 18 has many Gauguins and Cézannes; 17 has Picasso, Matisse and Rousseau; 21 has several Van Goghs and Degas. But don't neglect the Italian Renaissance paintings **(4 & 5)**, the 17th-century Dutch and Flemish paintings, including six Rembrandt portraits **(8, 9 & 10)**, and the ancient Egyptian collection in **room 1** (enter via rooms 3, 4 & 2). Some rooms have labels in English. Art freaks should allow several hours.

The museum is open daily except Monday from 10 am to 7 pm. Admission for foreigners is US$5 (US$2 with an ISIC card). There's a bufet downstairs next to the cloakroom.

Around the Pushkin Fine Arts Museum

Next door to the Pushkin at ulitsa Volkhonka 14 is the **Museum of Private Collections** (Sobranie lichnykh kollektsiy). This shows art collections donated by private individuals, many of whom amassed the works during the Soviet era. The museum's collection is based on 2300 works donated by Ilya Silberstein (1905-88), whose idea the museum was. The collectors, as well as the art, are featured. The museum is open Wednesday to Sunday from 10 am to 4 pm.

Along Maly Znamensky pereulok (formerly ulitsa Marxa i Engelsa), the lane between the Pushkin and Private Collections museums, a **Rerikh Museum** (Muzey imeni N K Rerikha) and **International Rerikh Centre** (Mezhdunarodny tsentr Rerikha) are being built. Nikolay Rerikh (known internationally as Nicholas Roerich) was a mystical Russian artist of the late 19th and early 20th centuries who now has an international following. He spent a lot of time in Central Asia, India and the Altay mountains of Siberia, painting some very distinctive landscapes and mythological scenes. Next door is a

EUROPEAN RUSSIA

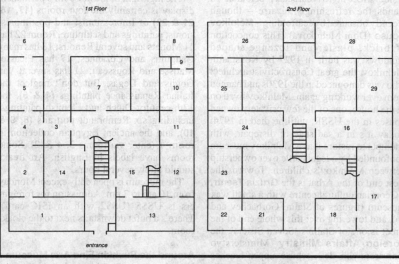

Pushkin Fine Arts Museum
Музей изобразительных искусств имени А.С. Пушкина

1st Floor

6		8
		9
5	7	10
4	3	11
2	14	15	12
1	13	

entrance

2nd Floor

26		28
25		29
	24	16
23		17
22	21	18

1	Art of Ancient Egypt	
2	Art of Ancient Assyria, Babylon, Cyprus, Armenia, Parthia, India	
3	Roman, Egyptian & Byzantine Art, 2nd to 15th Century	
4	Italian Painting, 13th to 15th Century	
5	Italian Painting, 15th & 16th Century	
6	Italian Painting, 16th Century	
7	Greek, Roman & Black Sea Coast Art, 6th Century BC to 4th Century AD	
8-10	Flemish & Dutch Painting, 17th Century	
11	Flemish & Spanish Painting, 17th Century	
12	Italian Painting, 17th & 18th Century	
13	French painting, 17th & 18th Century	
14	Copies of Greek Sculpture, 5th & 4th Century BC	
15	Copies of Medieval & Renaissance European Monuments, Church Art etc	

16	Copies of Greek Sculpture, 5th Century BC
17	French & Spanish Painting & Sculpture, Early 20th Century
18	French Painting & Sculpture, Late 19th Century
21	French & Dutch Art, Late 19th & Early 20th Century
22	French Painting, Late 19th Century
23	French Painting & Sculpture, 19th Century
24	Copies of Greek Sculpture, 4th to 1st Century BC
25	Copies of Roman Sculpture, 6th Century BC to 4th Century AD
26	Copies of Medieval Sculpture
28	Copies of Italian Renaissance Sculpture
29	Casts of Works by Michelangelo

Cathedral of Christ the Saviour Rises Again

The plot of land where the Cathedral of Christ the Saviour is being resurrected has one of the most chequered pasts in Moscow. To commemorate the victory over Napoleon, Tsar Alexander I commissioned a church for the Sparrow Hills, where Moscow University now stands. After Alexander's death, Tsar Nicholas I had it redesigned and relocated on ulitsa Volkhonka, closer to the Kremlin. The lavish cathedral rose slowly. When finished in 1883 it was 103 metres high, big enough for 10,000 worshippers, and its golden dome, 30 metres wide, was a major landmark.

Then in 1934 it was simply blown up, to make way for the ultimate Stalinist edifice, a 'Palace of Soviets' which, at 315 metres high and topped by a 100-metre Lenin statue (the world's biggest statue, of course), would naturally have been the tallest building in the world. But the excavation kept filling with water (divine wrath?) and Khrushchev finally abandoned the project, sensibly turning the site into the outdoor Moskva Swimming Pool. This wasn't without a few giant statistics of its own: 13,000 sq metres of water surface, and up to 20,000 swimmers a day.

But steam from the pool, which was heated in winter, caused damage at the Pushkin Fine Arts Museum, so the pool was closed in the early 1990s. The site lay desolate until 1994, when the Orthodox Church, no doubt keen to stamp its image anew on the Moscow skyline, decided to rebuild the cathedral. It was something of a mystery where the estimated US$250 million cost would come from – state funds and private donations were both requested, but there were objections to the use of government money for the project. At any rate, the cornerstone was ceremonially laid in 1995 and the basic reconstruction is intended to be complete by 1997. Decoration of the interior probably won't finish till 2000. The Vatican apparently has the cathedral's original iconostasis but has promised to give it back. ∎

dilapidated, turquoise-coloured mansion, under reconstruction, which used to be the Marx & Engels Museum but now houses the **Nobility League** (Dvoryanskoe Sobranie)! The two-storey building to its side is a 1930s replica of the house in Manchester, England, where Friedrich Engels, the pioneer of communist thought, lived in the 19th century. The lopsided church beside the Pushkin Fine Arts Museum at Kolymazhnaya ulitsa (formerly ulitsa Marshala Shaposhnikova) 8 is **St Antipy-by-the-Carriagehouse** (Tserkov Antipia na kolymazhnom dvore). It was supposedly commissioned by Malyuta Skuratov, the psychopath who ran Ivan the Terrible's secret police. More convivial is **Rosie O'Grady's** pub, a block north where Maly Znamensky pereulok crosses ulitsa Znamenka (formerly ulitsa Frunze). This major expat hang-out is a fun place to pause during your Moscow explorations.

The gigantic block a couple of streets further back, on ulitsa Znamenka at the Boulevard Ring, is the **Ministry of Defence** (Ministerstvo oborony) – Russia's Pentagon.

Between ulitsa Volkhonka and the Moscow River, on the old site of the Moskva Swimming Pool, the **Cathedral of Christ the Saviour** (Khram Khrista Spasitelya), a giant Moscow

The original Cathedral of Christ the Saviour

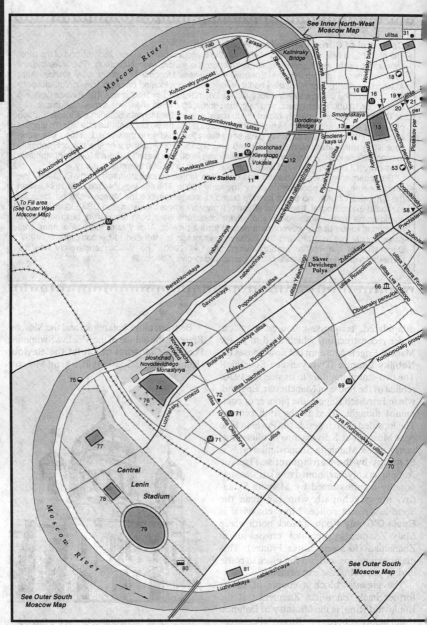

See Inner North-West
Moscow Map

Moscow River

nab Tarasa
Shevchenko

1

Kalininsky
Bridge

Smolenskaya naberezhnaya

Novinsky bulvar

ulitsa 31

Kutuzovsky prospekt

2

3

18

16 M 16

4

17

19

21

Bol Dorogomilovskaya ulitsa

5

Smolenskaya
pl

20 per

Borodinsky
Bridge

13

Smolenskaya ul

14

15

Denezhny pereulok

Piotakov per

Kutuzovsky prospekt

6

7

10 ploshchad
Kievskogo
Vokzala

9 M

Kievskaya ulitsa

12

Smolensky bulvar

53

ulitsa Mozhaysky Val

Studenchskaya ulitsa

Kiev Station

11

Rostovskaya naberezhnaya

Krogodinsky

58

Prechisten

To Fili area
(See Outer West
Moscow Map)

M
8

Berezhkovskaya naberezhnaya

Plyushchikha ulitsa

Smolenskaya ulitsa

Zubovsk

Savvinskaya naberezhnaya

Pogodinskaya ulitsa

ulitsa Yelanskogo

Skver
Devichego
Polya

Zubovskaya ulitsa

ulitsa Rossolimo

ulitsa Lva Tolstogo

ulitsa Timura Frun

66

Obdlensky pereulok

Novodevichy
proezd

73

Bolshaya Pirogovskaya ulitsa

Komsomolsky prospek

ploshchad
Novodevichego
Monastyrya

Malaya Pirogovskaya ul

74

ulitsa Usacheva

75

69 M

Luzhnetsky proezd

76

72

ulitsa proezd

1Oelte Okzyabrya

ulitsa Yefremova

2-ya Frunzenskaya ulitsa

77

71

M 71

M

Central
Lenin
Stadium

70

78

79

Moscow River

80

81

Luzhnetskaya naberezhnaya

See Outer South
Moscow Map

See Outer South
Moscow Map

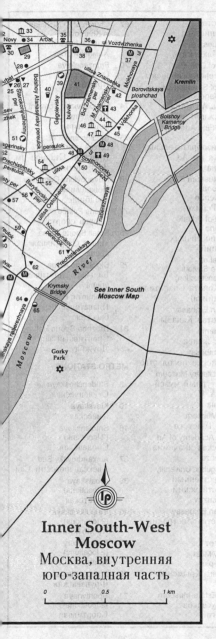

**Inner South-West
Moscow
Москва, внутренняя
юго-западная часть**

0   0.5   1 km

PLACES TO STAY

1	Hotel Ukraina
	Гостиница Украина
9	Hotel Kievskaya
	Гостиница Киевская
11	Radisson Slavyanskaya Hotel
	Гостиница Радиссон Славянская
13	Hotel Belgrad
	Гостиница Белград
14	Hotel Zolotoe Koltso
	Гостиница Золотое Кольцо

PLACES TO EAT

4	Pizza Hut
	Пицца Хат
17	McDonald's
	Макдоналдс
19	Restoran Mziuri
	Ресторан Мзюри
20	Bar Italian Restaurant
	Бар итальянский ресторан
21	Bar Italian Pizzeria
23	Kafe Rioni
	Кафе Риони
25	Kafe Rosa
	Кафе Роса
27	Restoran San Marco Pizzeria
	Ресторан Сан Марко Пиццерия
29	Bar Shamrock & Palms Coffee Shop
	Бар Шамрок и Кафе Палмс
32	Sports Bar
42	Rosie O'Grady's
	Рози О'Грэди'с
45	Patio Pizza
	Патио Пицца
50	Tren Mos Bistro
	Трен Мос Бистро
56	U Mamy Zoi
	У мамы Зои
58	Kropotkinskaya 36
	Кропоткинская 36
61	Le Chalet
62	Chayka Swimming Pool Restaurant
	Бассейн Чайка
68	Guria Kafe
	Кафе Гурия
72	Kafe Arena
	Кафе Арена
73	U Pirosmany
	У Пиросмани

continued next page

EUROPEAN RUSSIA

continued from previous page

OTHER

2 Russky Suvenir
   Русский сувенир
3 Tsentralny Salon
   Центральный салон
5 Sadko Supermarket
   Магазин Садко
6 Central Railway Agency
   Центральное
   железнодорожное
   агентство
7 Dorogomilovsky Market
   Дорогомиловский рынок
12 Kievsky Vokzal Landing
    Пристань Киевский
    вокзал
15 Foreign Affairs Ministry
    Министерство
    иностранных дел
18 Mongolian Consulate
    Монгольское
    консульство
19 Gruzia Tsentr
    Грузия центр
22 Melnikov House
    Дом Мельникова
24 Mekha Fur Shop
26 Arbatskaya Lavitsa
    Shop
    Арбатская лавица
28 Wall of Peace
    Стена мира
29 Arbat Irish House
    Supermarket &
    Novoarbatsky
    Gastronom
    Ирландский дом на
    Арбате и
    Новоарбатский
    гастроном
30 Telephone Office
    Телефонный пункт
31 Melodia Music Shop
    Мелодия
33 Mikhail Lermontov
    House-Museum
    Дом-музей Лермонтова
34 Dom Knigi
    Дом книги
35 Artel Business Centre
    Артель бизнес-центр
36 House of Friendship
    with Peoples of
    Foreign Countries
    Дом дружбы
39 Turkmen Embassy

Посольство
Туркменистана
40 Arbat Blues Club
    Арбат блюз клуб
41 Ministry of Defence
    Министерство обороны
43 Church of St Antipy-by-
    the-Carriagehouse
    Церковь Антипиа на
    колымажном дворе
44 Pushkin Fine Arts
    Museum
    Музей изобразительных
    искусств им А.С.
    Пушкина
46 Rerikh Museum &
    International
    Rerikh Centre
    Музей Рериха
47 Museum of Private
    Collections
    Собрание личных
    коллекций
49 Cathedral of
    Christ the Saviour
    (under construction)
    Храм Христа Спасителя
    (строящийся)
51 Canadian Embassy
    Посольство Канады
52 Krisis Zhanra
    Крисис жанра
53 Italian Embassy
    Итальянское посольство
54 Pushkin Literary Museum
    Литературный музей
    имени А. С.
    Пушкина
55 Tolstoy Museum
    Музей Толстого
57 Russian Academy of Art
    Российская академия
    художеств
59 State Linguistic University
    Государственный
    лингвистический
    университет
60 Australian Embassy
    Посольство Австралии
64 Aeroflot
    Аэрофлот
65 Krymsky Most
    Landing-pier
    Пристань Крымский
    мост
66 Tolstoy Estate-Museum
    Музей-усадьба
    Толстого

67 Church of St Nicholas
    in Khamovniki
    Никольская церковь в
    Хамовниках
70 Frunzenskaya
    Landing-pier
    Пристань
    Фрунзенская
74 Novodevichy Convent
    Новодевичий
    монастырь
75 Stadion imeni VI
    Lenina Landing-pier
    Пристань Стадион им.
    В. И. Ленина
76 Novodevichy Cemetery
    Новодевичье
    кладбище
77 Sports Palace
    Дворец спорта
78 Small Sports Arena
    Малая спортивная
    арена
79 Big Sports Arena
    Большая спортивная
    арена
80 Swimming Pool
    Плавательный
    бассейн
81 Druzhba Sports Hall
    Спортивный зал
    Дружба

METRO STATIONS

8 Studencheskaya
   Студенческая
10 Kievskaya
    Киевская
16 Smolenskaya
    (2 locations)
    Смоленская
37 Alexandrovsky Sad
    Александровский Сад
38 Arbatskaya
    (2 locations)
    Арбатская
48 Kropotkinskaya
    (2 locations)
    Кропоткинская
63 Park Kultury
    (2 locations)
    Парк Культуры
69 Frunzenskaya
    Фрунзенская
71 Sportivnaya
    (2 locations)
    Спортивная

landmark that was blown up by Stalin, is rising again. Since the original took 44 years to build, the modern Russian builders will for once look speedy!

Prechistenka Ulitsa & Beyond

Prechistenka ulitsa (formerly Kropotkinskaya ulitsa), which heads south-west from Kropotkinskaya metro, is a virtual museum of classical mansions, most of which date from the Empire-style rebuilding after the great fire of 1812. Have a look at No 12, which houses the **Pushkin Literary Museum** (Literaturny muzey imeni Pushkina), devoted to the poet's life and work, open Wednesday to Sunday from 11 am to 6 pm; No 11, now a **Tolstoy Museum** (Muzey Tolstogo), with the writer's manuscripts, letters and sketches, open from 11 am to 6 pm daily except Monday and the last Friday of the month; **No 20**, now home of GlavUpDK, the Main Diplomatic Corps Service Bureau, which provides foreign diplomats with drivers, secretaries and other assistance; **No 17**; and No 19-21, now the **Russian Academy of Art** (Rossiyskaya akademia khudozhestv), with an exhibition hall.

There's more Tolstoyana across the busy Garden Ring from the end of Prechistenka ulitsa. Down the second street on the left – opposite the shady **Skver Devichego Polya** (Maiden's Field) park, with its own brooding Tolstoy statue – is the interesting **Tolstoy Estate-Museum** (Muzey-usadba Tolstogo) at ulitsa Lva Tolstogo 21. Park Kultury is the nearest metro. The house was the writer's winter home in the 1880s and 1890s. It's neither particularly big nor especially opulent, but fitting for junior nobility, which Tolstoy was. Rimsky-Korsakov and Rachmaninov played the piano in the upstairs reception room; Tolstoy's training weights and bicycle repose outside his study. You can wander around without a guide or group and there are explanatory notices in English. The house is open from 10 am to 6 pm in summer, to 4 pm in winter, closed Monday and the last Friday of the month.

At the south end of ulitsa Lva Tolstogo, the beautiful **Church of St Nicholas of the Weavers** (Tserkov Nikoli v Khamovnikakh) vies with St Basil's Cathedral as the most colourful in Moscow. Commissioned by the Moscow weavers' guild in 1676, it indeed looks like a great, jolly, green-and-orange tapestry. Inside are equally rich frescoes and icons.

Novodevichy

A cluster of sparkling domes behind handsome turreted walls near a bank of the Moscow River, Novodevichy Convent (Novodevichy monastyr) is one of the city's most beautiful groups of buildings, full of history and treasures. The adjacent Novodevichy Cemetery is Moscow's most prestigious resting place after the Kremlin wall, with many famous tombs. The name Novodevichy (New Maidens) probably comes from a market, once held in the locality, where Tatars bought Russian girls to sell to Muslim harems.

Trolleybus Nos 5 and 15 come here down Prechistenka ulitsa and Bolshaya Pirogovskaya ulitsa from Kropotkinskaya metro station. Sportivnaya metro is 500 metres to the south.

Convent The convent entrance is on ploshchad Novodevichego Monastyrya beside Bolshaya Pirogovskaya ulitsa. The best views of it are from across the pond to its north.

The convent is being returned to religious use and is open to visitors from 8 am to 6 pm daily, free. One or two rooms house temporary exhibitions of various kinds, for which tickets are sold at the ticket office inside the grounds. It was founded in 1524 to celebrate the taking of Smolensk from Lithuania, an important step in Moscow's conquest of the old Kievan Rus lands. From early on, noblewomen would retire here, some willingly, some not. Novodevichy was rebuilt by Peter the Great's half-sister Sofia, who used it as a second residence when she ruled Russia during his boyhood in the 1680s. By

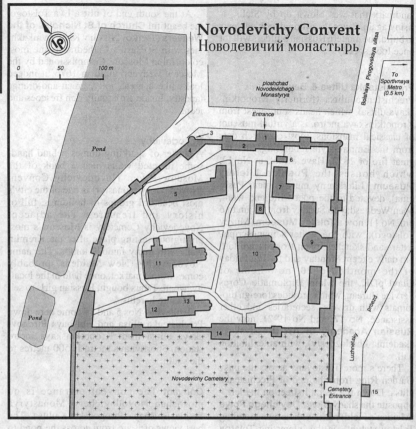

Novodevichy Convent
Новодевичий монастырь

ploshchad
Novodevichego
Monastyrya

Bolshaya Pirogovskaya ulitsa

To
Sportivnaya
Metro
(0.5 km)

Entrance

Pond

Pond

Novodevichy Cemetery

Luzhnetsky proezd

Cemetery
Entrance

1	Transfiguration Gate-Church Преображенская надвратная церковь	7	Exhibition Room Выставочный зал	13	St Ambrose's Church Амбросиевская церковь
2	Lopukhin Building Лопухинский корпус	8	Prokhorov Chapel (1911) Часовня Прохоровых	14	Intercession Gate-Church Покровская надвратная церковь
3	Pond Tower Напрудная башня	9	Bell Tower Колокольня	15	Novodevichy Cemetery Ticket Office Касса - Новодевичье кладбище
4	Sofia's Chambers Палаты Софии	10	Smolensk Cathedral Смоленский собор		
5	Monks' Quarters Братский корпус	11	Assumption Church Успенская церковь		
6	Ticket Office Касса	12	Irina Godunov Building Ирининские палаты		

this time the convent was a major landowner: it had 36 villages and 15,000 serfs around Russia. When Peter, aged 17, deposed Sofia in 1689 he confined her to Novodevichy, and in 1698 she was imprisoned here for life after being implicated in a rebellion by the Streltsy, the palace guard. It's said Peter had some of her supporters hanged outside her window to remind her not to meddle. Sofia was joined in her retirement by Yevdokia Lopukhina, Peter's first wife, whom he considered a nag and divorced.

You enter the convent under the red-and-white Moscow Baroque **Transfiguration Gate-Church** (Preobrazhenskaya nadvratnaya tserkov), built between 1687 and 1689, on the north wall. The first building in front of you on the left contains a room for temporary exhibitions. Yevdokia Lopukhina lived in the **Lopukhin Building** (Lopukhinsky korpus) against the north wall and Sofia, probably, in chambers adjoining the Pond Tower (Naprudnaya bashnya). The oldest and dominant building in the grounds is the white **Smolensk Cathedral** (Smolensky sobor), built in 1524-25 and based on the Assumption Cathedral in the Kremlin. Its beautifully proportioned domes were added in the 17th century. For the moment it's only open in summer, as a museum. The walls of the sumptuous interior are covered in 16th-century frescoes and there's a huge iconostasis given by Sofia, with icons from both her time and Boris Godunov's. The tombs of Sofia, a couple of her sisters, and Yevdokia Lopukhina are in the south nave. There's also a noble and royal burial vault in the basement.

The **bell tower** (kolokolnya) against the convent's east wall, completed in 1690 with a gold dome topping six red-brick tiers with white details, is generally regarded as Moscow's finest. The red-and-white **Assumption Church** (Uspenskaya tserkov) and its refectory date from 1685 to 1687. The 16th-century **St Ambrose's Church** (Ambrosievskaya tserkov) is adjoined by another refectory and the **Irina Godunov Building** (Irininskie palaty), where Boris Godunov's sister lived.

Cemetery Novodevichy Cemetery (Novodevichie kladbishche) contains the tombs of Khrushchev, Chekhov, Gogol, Mayakovsky, Stanislavsky, Prokofiev, Eisenstein, Gromyko and a mixed bag of many other Russian and Soviet notables. It's open daily from 10 am to 5 pm. Tickets (US$1) are sold at a kiosk across the street from the entrance on Luzhnetsky proezd, the continuation of Bolshaya Pirogovskaya ulitsa. If you want to investigate this place in depth, buy the Russian map on sale at the kiosk, which pinpoints nearly 200 graves.

In Soviet times Novodevichy Cemetery was used for some very eminent people – notably Khrushchev – whom the authorities judged unsuitable for the Kremlin wall. Other famous bodies were moved here when their original cemeteries were destroyed under Stalin. For many years until the late 1980s the cemetery was closed to the general public to prevent too many people from paying their respects to Khrushchev. It's a fascinating place, with tombstones ranging from the modest to the three-metre-long tank above one general's grave and the big stone aeroplane on an aircraft designer's.

The intertwined white and black blocks round Khrushchev's bust were intended by their sculptor Ernst Neizvestny to represent Khrushchev's good and bad sides: Neizvestny and Khrushchev's family had to fight long and hard to be allowed anything more than a simple slab. The tombstone of Nadezhda Allilueva, Stalin's second wife, is surrounded by unbreakable glass to prevent vandalism: her nose was once broken off. Allilueva committed suicide in 1932, apparently after a phone call from one of Stalin's bodyguards telling her that the great leader was in bed with another woman.

And yes, Vyacheslav Molotov is he of the cocktail (it was named after him) and also the man who signed the infamous Molotov-Ribbentrop Pact, which established non-aggression between the USSR and Nazi Germany in 1939.

Luzhniki

The area within the river bend south-west of Novodevichy contains a group of 1950s

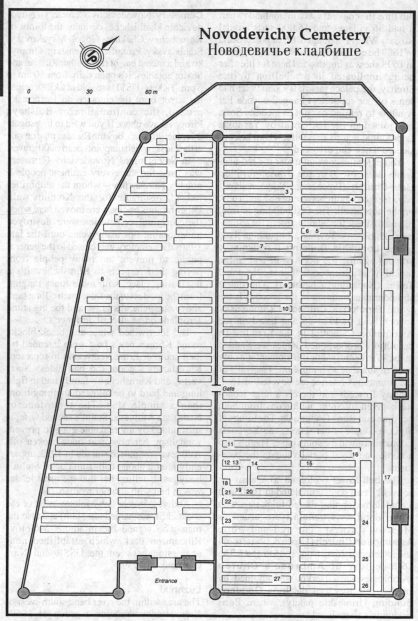

Novodevichy Cemetery
Новодевичье кладбище

1   Nikita Khrushchev (1894-1971), Soviet
    First Secretary & Premier 1957-64
    Никита Хрущёв
2   David Oystrakh (1908-74), Violinist
    Давид Ойстрах
3   Fyodor Chaliapin (1873-1938), Singer
    Фёдор Шаляпин
4   Sergey Prokofiev (1891-1953), Composer
    Сергей Прокофьев
5   Nikolay Rubinstein (1835-85),
    Pianist & Conductor
    Николай Рубинштейн
6   Alexandr Scriabin (1872-1915),
    Composer
    Александр Скрябин
7   Sergey Elsenstein (1898-1948),
    Film Director
    Сергей Эйсенштейн
8   Andrey Tupolev (1888-1972),
    Aircraft Designer
    Андрей Туполев
9   Pyotr Kropotkin (1842-1921), Anarchist
    Пётр Кропоткин
10 Andrey Gromyko (1909-89),
    Soviet Foreign Minister 1957-85
    Андрей Громыко
11 Nikolay Gogol (1809-52), Writer
    Николай Гоголь
12 Anton Chekhov (1860-1904), Writer
    Антон Чехов
13 Olga Knipper-Chekhova (1868-1959),
    Actor & Wife of Anton Chekhov
    Ольга Книппер-Чехова
14 Vladimir Nemirovich Danchenko
    (1858-1943), Co-Founder of
    Moscow Art Theatre
    Владимир Немирович Данченко

15 Pavel & Sergey Tretyakov (1832-98,
    1834-92), Founders of Tretyakov
    Gallery
    Павел и Сергей Третьяков
16 Vladimir Mayakovsky (1893-1930), Poet
    Владимир Маяковский
17 Alexandra Kollontay (1872-1952),
    Writer & Diplomat
    Александра Коллонтай
18 Konstantin Stanislavsky (1863-1938),
    Theatre Director & Co-Founder of
    Moscow Art Theatre
    Константин Станиславский
19 Mikhail Bulgakov (1891-1940), Writer
    Михаил Булгаков
20 Valentin Serov (1865-1911), Artist
    Валентин Серов
21 Maria Yermolova (1853-1928), Actor
    Мария Ермолова
22 Isaak Levitan (1860-1900), Artist
    Исаак Левитан
23 Mikhail Nesterov (1862-1942), Artist
    Михаил Нестеров
24 Alexey Shchusev (1873-1949), Architect
    Алексей Щусев
25 Vyacheslav Molotov (1890-1986), Soviet
    Foreign Minister 1939-49, 1953-56
    Вячеслав Молотов
26 Nadezhda Allilueva (1901-32), Stalin's
    Second Wife
    Надежда Аллилуева
27 Dmitry Shostakovich (1906-75),
    Composer
    Дмитрий Шостакович

sporting stadia together known as the Central Lenin Stadium (Tsentralny stadion imeni V I Lenina) or Luzhniki ('Marshes', which is what the area used to be). The main 103,000-capacity Big Sports Arena was the chief venue for the 1980 Olympics.

INNER SOUTH

The Zamoskvorechie (Beyond-Moscow-River Area) stretches south from opposite the Kremlin, inside a big river loop. In this part of the city you'll find Moscow's most famous park, its premier gallery of Russian art, and the modern-day headquarters of the Russian Orthodox Church.

The Vodootvodny (Drainage) Canal slices across the top of the Zamoskvorechie, preventing spring floods in the city centre and creating a sliver of island opposite the Kremlin. South was the direction from which Tatars used to attack, so Moscow's defensive forces were stationed in the Zamoskvorechie, along with merchants and quarters devoted to servicing the royal court. After the Tatar threat died out and the court moved to St Petersburg, the merchants were joined by nobles, then by 19th-century factories and their workers. Little damaged by Stalin, it's still a varied, intriguing area of Moscow.

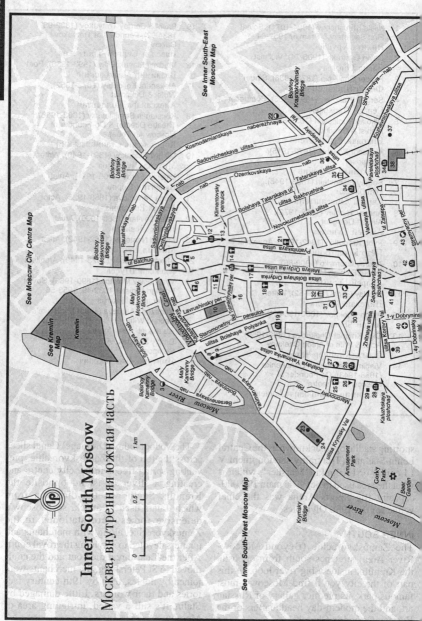

Inner South Moscow
Москва, внутренняя южная часть

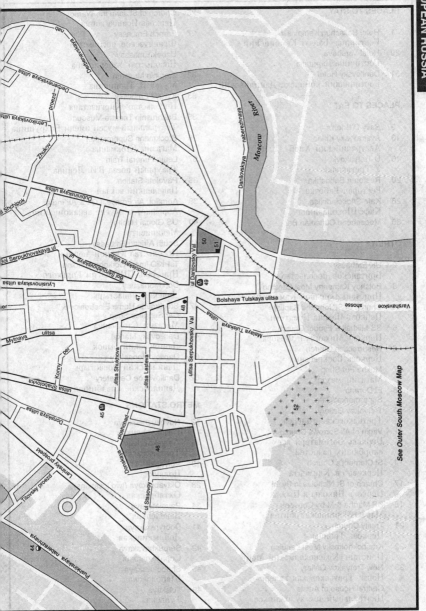

Moscow River

See Outer South Moscow Map

PLACES TO STAY

1 Hotel Baltschug Kempinski
   Гостиница Балчуг-Кемпинский
29 Hotel Varshava
   Гостиница Варшава
51 Danilovsky Hotel
   Гостиничний комплекс Даниловский

PLACES TO EAT

9 Sally O'Brien's
13 Avstraliysky Khleb
   Австралийский Хлеб
16 U Tretyakovki
   У Третяковки
20 Restoran Babochka
   Ресторан Бабочка
26 Kafe Shokoladnitsa
   Кафе Шоколадница
30 Moosehead Canadian Bar

OTHER

2 UK Embassy
   Британское посольство
3 Bolshoy Kamenny Most Landing
   Пристань Большой Каменный Мост
4 Church of St John the Baptist
   Церковь Иоанна Предтечи
5 SS Mikhail & Fyodor Church
   Церковь Михаила и Фёдора
6 Resurrection Church
   Церковь Воскресения
7 Mekha Fur Shop
   Магазин меха
8 El Dorado
   Supermarket/Café
10 Tretyakov Gallery
   Третьяковская галерея
11 Virgin of All Sorrows Church
   Церковь Богоматери всех
   скорбящих радостей
14 St Clement's Church
   Церковь св. Климента
17 Church of St Nicholas in Pyzhi
   Церковь Николы в Пыжах
18 SS Martha & Mary Convent
   Марфо-Мариинская обитель
21 Trinity Church
   Церковь Троицы
22 Krasnokholmsky Most Landing
   Пристань Краснохолмский Мост
23 New Tretyakov Gallery
   Новая Третьяковская галерея
24 Central House of Artists
   Центральный дом художников

25 Church of St John the Warrior
   Церковь Иоанна воина
27 French Embassy
   Французское посольство
31 Uzbek Embassy
   Посольство Узбекистана
32 Tropinin Museum
   Музей В. Тропинина
33 Kyrgyz Embassy
   Посольство Киргизстана
35 Bakhrushin Theatre-Museum
   Театральный музей имени Бахрушина
36 Stockmann Supermarket
   Магазин Стокманна
37 Lenin Funeral Train
   Траурный поезд В.И. Ленина
38 Pavelets Station
   Павелецкий вокзал
39 Aeroflot, Air France, LOT & Air India
   Аэрофлот и другие авиакомпании
40 US Global Health
   Мединцентр
43 South African Embassy
   Посольство Южной Африки
44 TsPKiO imeni Gorkogo Landing
   Пристань ЦПКиО им Горького
46 Don Monastery
   Донской монастырь
47 Stockmann Home Electronics &
   Car Supplies Shop
   Магазин Стокманна
48 Danilovsky Market
   Даниловский рынок
50 Danilov Monastery
   Даниловский монастырь
52 Danilovskoe Cemetery
   Даниловское кладбиище

METRO STATIONS

12 Novokuznetskaya
   Новокузнецкая
15 Tretyakovskaya
   Третьяковская
19 Polyanka
   Полянка
28 Oktyabrskaya (two locations)
   Октябрьская
34 Paveletskaya
   Павелецкая
41 Dobryninskaya
   Добрынинская
42 Serpukhovskaya
   Серпуховская
45 Shabolovskaya
   Шаболовская
49 Tulskaya
   Тульская

Gorky Park

Stretching almost three km along the river upstream of the Krymsky Bridge, Gorky Park is full of that sometimes rare species, the happy Russian. Officially the Central Park of Culture & Rest named after Maxim Gorky (Tsentralny Park Kultury i Otdykha imeni A M Gorkogo), it's the original Soviet culture park. In part it's straight ornamental park, with black swans cruising between the pedal boats to make even Australians feel a little bit at home. But that's not all. Gorky Park's new 'Disneyland on the Moskva' image is a result of a small new Western amusement park on the north-west side of the park; the two Western roller coasters (including one with a full 360° loop) and almost a dozen other terror-inducing attractions can get expensive, though, with rides from US$2 to US$4. There are also stages and auditoria where you might run across anything from science lectures to rock concerts. The less kempt area beyond the Green (Zelyony) Theatre about halfway along is called the Neskuchny Sad (Nonboring Garden).

Dotted between the attractions are a number of snack bars and, behind the new amusement park, a 2000-seat German beer hall (though it serves Dutch beer), complete with litre glasses and excellent grilled chicken. In winter the ponds freeze and the paths are flooded to make a giant skating rink – you can rent skates if you take along some ID such as your passport. The park's main entrance is on ulitsa Krymsky Val, half a km from either Park Kultury or Oktyabrskaya metro. Admission to the park is US$1.20.

Around Gorky Park

The big block at ulitsa Krymsky Val 10, opposite Gorky Park's main entrance, houses both the **Central House of Artists** (Tsentralny dom khudozhnikov and the **New Tretyakov Gallery** (Novaya Tretyakovskaya galereya). The latter is *not* the famous Tretyakov Gallery. The Central House of Artists, facing the road, puts on good contemporary art shows. The New Tretyakov Gallery, behind, has a permanent collection of mainly Soviet-era art but also puts on some good exhibitions. Both are open from 11 am to 8 pm daily except Monday. In front of the Central House of Artists there's a busy street art market most days. Near the rear of the building is a collection of statues of Soviet leaders – Stalin, Dzerzhinsky, Kalinin, Sverdlov – dumped here when they were removed from their pedestals around Moscow in the wave of anti-Soviet feeling after the 1991 coup.

Nearby on Bolshaya Yakimanka ulitsa (formerly ulitsa Dimitrova) stands the finest of all Zamoskvorcchie churches, **St John the Warrior** (Tserkov Ivana voina), with its colourful, tiled domes. Said to have been partly designed by Peter the Great in thanks for his 1709 victory over Sweden at Poltava, it mixes Moscow and European Baroque styles. It's a working church but often locked: the big, 17th-century iconostasis is reputedly a masterpiece. You can see the Kremlin in the distance from here.

Tretyakov Gallery

The Tretyakov Gallery (Tretyakovskaya galereya) reopened in 1995 after a nine-year renovation. It was worth the wait: the restoration work was world-class, and the collection is nothing short of spectacular. The Tretyakov houses the world's best collection of Russian icons and an outstanding collection of other pre-Revolutionary Russian art, particularly the 19th-century Peredvizhniki (for who and what they were, see Arts & Culture in the Facts about European Russia chapter). There may be more masterpieces per sq metre in the Tretyakov than anywhere else.

The collection is based on that of the 19th-century industrialist brothers Pavel and Sergey Tretyakov. Pavel was a patron of the Peredvizhniki. The original part of the building was created in the likeness of an old boyar castle by Viktor Vasnetsov between 1900 and 1905.

Much of the Tretyakov's collection of religious art came to it when confiscated from churches during the Soviet era. Now that the Orthodox Church wants its icons back, the

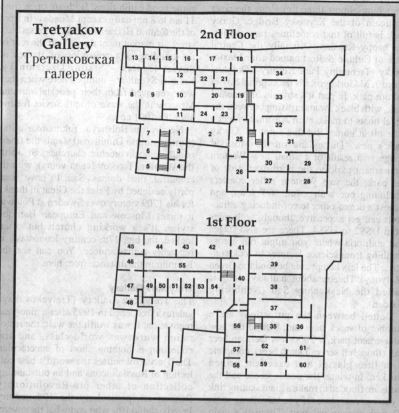

Tretyakov Gallery
Третьяковская галерея

2nd Floor

1st Floor

Painting and Sculpture in the Tretyakov Gallery

The listings progress chronologically beginning on the 2nd floor, in room 1; there are only a couple of twists and turns in the layout (see map). Rooms are listed in bold print.

Second Floor, Rooms 1-7 18th-century painting and sculpture including **1** *Anichkov Palace and Nevsky Prospekt*, by an unknown artist, Nikitin's *Portrait of Anna Petrovna* and a larger one of her by Caravaggio; **2** sculptures, mainly by Shubin but others including Martos' *Portrait of N V Panina*, and his *Tombstone for S S Volkonskaya*, Rastrelli's *Portrait of an Unknown Man* and Kozlovsky's very sweet *Cupid with an Arrow*; **3** Rokotov on the left wall, right wall dominated by Antropov's enormous *Portrait of Peter III*; **4** paintings from graduates of the Russian Academy of Arts, which accepted children of nobility as well as serfs for the 15-year course which began at age 5, including Shibanov's *Celebration of a Wedding Agreement* and Argunov's *Portrait of a Woman in a Russian Dress*; **5** mainly Levitsky, including *Portrait of the Artist's Daughter* and *Portrait of P A Demidov*; **6** arranged around the enormous *Actaeon* by Martos and including Shchedrin's *Stone Bridge in Gatchina*, Alekseev's *View of the Palace Embankment from the Peter*

& *Paul Fortress* and *View of the Roman Colosseum* by Matveev; **7** Borovikovsky's wonderful *Portrait of M I Lopukhina* and *Portrait of the Princesses Gagarin*.

Rooms 8-19 19th-century painting and sculpture including **8** Kiprensky, his mega-famous *Portrait of A S Pushkin*, what may be the artist's *self-portrait*, and *Newspaper Readers in Naples*, Shchedrin's *Arbour Covered in Vines*, *New Rome*, *Castle Sant Angelo*, and *Genre-Scene: Pilgrims*; **9** mostly Bryullov, including *Equestrian*, *Self-portrait*, Gentseric's *Invasion of Rome* and his sketch of *The Last Day of Pompeii*; **10** Ivanov, dominated by his enormous *Christ's Appearance to the People*, and, on the wall to the right of this, preliminary character sketches for this piece; **11** Ivanov, also Shternberg's *Gambling in a Neapolitan Hostel* and *October Feast Day in Rome* and Solnitsev's *Peasant Family before Dinner*; **12** Ivanov, including *Man Looking Upwards* and *Two Heads in Turbans...*; **13** Tropinin's lovely *The Lace Maker* and *The Guitarist* as well as *Peasant Whittling a Crutch*, a *Self-portrait* and another lovely *Portrait of the Artist's Son*; **14** Venetsianov's *Ploughing in Spring* and *Harvesting in Summer*, *Wet Nurse with Baby* and *Zakharka*, as well as Tyranov's *Weavers*; **15** Sorokin's moving *Spanish Beggar Girl*, and on the right centre wall, Fedotov's *Aristocrat's Breakfast*, *The Major's Proposal* and one of our favourites, *The Fresh Cavalier – An Official on the Morning after Receiving an Award*; **16**, containing the first paintings bought by Tretyakov in 1856 from the artists: Khudyakov's *Skirmish with Finnish Smugglers* and Shilder's *Temptation*, as well as Pukirev's discomfiting *The Unequal Marriage* and Flavitsky's *Princess Tarakanova*, in which she is depicted during a flood, imprisoned in the Peter & Paul Fortress' dungeons for pretending to be the daughter of Tsaritsa Elizabeth Petrovna; **17** Perov, dominated by his *Dispute over Faith* and featuring his *Portrait of Dostoevsky*; **18**, which is half Savrasov, including *Country Road*, and half Vasilev, including *The Thaw* and *After the Rain*; **19** Lavaretsky's sinister *Bacchus*, Bogolyubov's fantastic *Horse Rides on the Neva* and Ayvazovsky's grim *The Black Sea* and *Sea Shore*.

Rooms 20, 23-24 and part of 25 Peredvizhniki, including **20** Kramskoy's *Unknown Lady*, *Christ in the Wilderness* and portraits of *Tolstoy* and *Nekrasov*; **23** Myasoedov's *The Zemstvo Having Lunch* and Zhuravlyov's *Merchant's Funeral Banquet*; **24** including Yaroshenko's *There Is Life Everywhere* and *General Staff meeting in Fili*, Boddanov-Belsky's charming *Counting Out Loud* and Makovsky's *The Party*; and half of **25** including Shishkin's *Morning in a Pine Forest* and *Rye*.

Rooms 21, 22 and 26-27 More 19th-century paintings and sculptures including **21** Kuindzhi's *Moonlight Night on the Dnepr* and *On the Island of Valaam*; **22** including Makovsky's *Children Running from the Approaching Storm* and Bakalovich's *The Maecenas' Waiting Room*, while the centrepiece is Brodzhki's *Cupid in a Shell*; **26** Vasnetsov's *Knights*, *Alenushka*, *Telegram from the War*, *Tsarevich Ivan on a Grey Wolf* and *The Flying Carpet*; **27** Vereshchagin's panoramic *Shipka-Sheynovo: Skobolev near Shipka*, in which the artist places himself on the darker horse behind the general and next to the flag-bearer, and his *Apotheosis of War*, which is pretty self-explanatory: an enormous pile of skulls being picked through by vultures.

Room 28 Surikov, including *Morning of the Execution of the Streltsy* and *Boyarina Morozova*, an Old Believer being dragged off to prison.

Rooms 29-30 Repin, including *Dragonfly*, *Portrait of Turgenev*, the fantabulous *A Religious Procession Through Kursk*, a sketch of *The Volga Bargemen* which will have to suffice until the masterpiece returns (if it ever does) from tours abroad, *Ivan the Terrible and His Son*, and *E V Pavlov in an Operating Theatre*.

Room 31 Ge, including *The Last Supper*, *Peter the Great Interrogating the Tsarevich* and *Golgotha*.

Rooms 32-33 Vrubel, including *The Swan Princess, Pan, Portrait of M I Artsybusheva* and *Seated Demon.*

Room 34 Nesterov, including *Silence, The Hermit* and *House Arrest.*

Ground Floor, Room 35 Polenov, including *Harem Ash-Sharif*, the lovely *Courtyard in Moscow*, which depicts the 19th-century Arbat, and, two paintings down, the closer view of his *Grandmother's Garden*; **36** Stepanov's *Cranes Are Flying* and Kuznetsov's *Portrait of Tchaikovsky* and *Portrait of A P Chekhov.*

Rooms 37-39 Late 19th and early 20th-century works, including **37** mainly Levitan landscapes, including *March* and *The Evening Bells Ringing*, plus two small wall sections of tiny Pokhitonov paintings, including *Laundresses* and *La Panne – The Beach*; **38** including Grabar's technicolour *February Azure*, Rerikh's *Visitors from Overseas* and Malyavin's loud *Whirlwind*; **39** in the first half Korovin, including *Portrait of N D Chichagov, The Northern Idyll* and *Winter in Lapplandia*, in the second half Serov, including *Girl with Peaches, Mika Morozov* and *By the Window.*

Rooms 40-41 Works from the beginning of the 20th century, including **41** Zinaida Serebryakova's *At the Dressing Table – Self-portrait*; Borisov-Musatov, including *Lady in a Rocking Chair* and *The Pool*, and a portrait of the artist by Matveev directly under the large video camera on the right as you enter.

Rooms 42-45 Early 20th-century art, including **42** Kuznetsov, Saryan including *Street – Midday – Constantinople* and *Date Palm*, along with Krynov; **43** Larionov's *Cock* and *Soldier Resting*, and Goncharova's *Boys Skating*; **44** including Larionov, Mashkov, Kuprin, Rozhdestvensky's *Still Life with Liqueur* and *Bull Fight* and Lentulov's truly weird *Woman with a Child – Requiem*; **45** Mainly Petrov-Vodkin, including *Girls on the Volga* and *An Old Milk Seller*, as well as Altman's *Self-portrait.*

Room 46 Chagall, including *The Window* and much more when it's not on tour, but when it is you can still see works by Georgian artist Pirosmanashvili (Pirosmani), whose legendary romantic tendencies led him to sell everything he owned so he could buy his love, Margarita, a million roses to dissuade her from leaving for Paris (she left anyway), including *Fisherman among the Cliffs* and *Barn in a Georgian Village*. This room also begins the cubist exhibition, with Annenkov's *Day Dreams of a Provincial.*

Room 47 More cubism, including Rozanova, Udaltsova, Tatlin's *Staro Basmannaya – Board No 1.*

Room 48 'Masterpieces of Modern Art' including Klyun's *Suprematism* and *Black Square*, and Kandinsky, including various *Improvisation*s and Filonov's *Composition.*

Rooms 49-54 With no labelling in English, these rooms feature lithographs, sketches, water colours by dozens of artists including **52** Levitan landscapes, **53** drawings and water colours by Vrubel and **54** Mir Iskusstva neoclassicism *and* avant garde including Kandinsky, Popova, Filonov and Chagall.

Rooms 55-62 Icons and religious art. Novgorod school icons include: **56** the 12th-century *Ustyug Annunciation* and 13th-century *St Nicholas*, both brought to Moscow by Ivan the Terrible, and the ubiquitous 15th-century *The Miracle of St George and the Dragon* (a favourite subject in Russian art; this victory is seen as a symbol of Good triumphing over Evil and appears on the emblem of old Muscovy); and **61** *Last Judgement, The Miracle of SS Florus & Laurus* and *Entombment*, all 15th-century.

Room 57 The *Vladimir Icon of the Mother of God (Vladimirskaya ikona Bozhiey Materi)* is Russia's most revered icon. An image of the Virgin and infant Christ, it is credited with having saved Moscow from Timur (Tamerlane) and with all manner of other wonders, and is believed crucial to the welfare of Russia as a whole. It resided in Kiev, Vladimir and Moscow while each city was the Russian capital. Almost certainly painted by a 12th-century Byzantine, it probably reached Kiev from Constantinople in about 1130, was moved secretly by Andrey Bogolyubov to Vladimir's Assumption Cathedral in 1155, then stood in the Moscow Kremlin's Assumption Cathedral from the 1480s to 1930. Patriarch Alexey was allowed to borrow it from the Tretyakov for one day in 1993 so that he could pray to it for an avoidance of bloodshed at the White House. His prayers failed.

Room 59 The late 14th-century *Virgin of the Don* by Theophanes the Greek is said to have brought Dmitry Donskoy victory over the Tatars at the Battle of Kulikovo in 1380.

Room 60 Andrey Rublyov's early 15th-century *Holy Trinity (Svyataya Troitsa)*, from the Trinity Monastery of St Sergius, Sergiev Posad, is widely regarded as the greatest Russian icon of all. It depicts the Old Testament Trinity – three angels who appeared to Abraham in an episode from Genesis and are seen as a prefiguration of the New Testament Trinity. On the rear wall of this room, the Deesis Row of an iconostasis features (centre) *The Saviour*, (left of centre) *The Virgin Mother*, (right of centre) *John the Baptist*, (left) *Archangel Michael* and (right) *Archangel Gabriel*. These works were painted by Rublyov and Daniil Chyorny in Moscow in 1408. To the left of this are other Moscow school icons, *Archangel Michael*, *Christ* and *St Paul*.

Room 61 Works by Dionysius (late 15th, early 16th centuries) and Simon Ushakov (17th century). ■

Tretyakov has had to battle to keep its most precious treasures. For the moment at least, it has fended off the pressure by also restoring the **Church of St Nicholas** within its grounds. About 200 icons are displayed there, and the building functions as both church and museum.

The gallery is open daily except Monday from 10 am to 7 pm; the ticket counter closes at 6.30 pm. The telephone number is ☎ 231 13 62. It is one km south of the Kremlin, at Lavrushinsky pereulok 10 (metro: Tretyakovskaya). Admission is US$6 for foreigners, US$3 for ISIC holders, US$1.20 for Russians, and US$0.60 for Russian students. Photography is not permitted. You may take notes, but only in pencil.

Orientation The rooms are numbered, and generally progress in chronological order. Paintings and sculptures begin on the 2nd floor, in room 1, and progress through the majority of the ground floor. Most Peredvizhniki are in rooms 20, 23 and 24, except in those cases where a Peredvizhniki artist has a hall dedicated to exhibiting his work (they were all men).

Icons reside on the ground floor in rooms 55 to 62. The entrance to the gallery is through a courtyard so neat it could be an architect's rendering; the ticket counters face the main entry staircase. Show up early on weekends: by 10.45 am the queue reaches the street and winds north.

The entire gallery is accessible to wheelchairs by means of staircase-ascender/descender lifts.

Russian-language tours leave every half-hour or so from the lobby. Russian language cassette tours are available – with players – for US$1 from the desk just to the left of the main entry staircase. There are no English cassettes available yet, though most of the paintings are labelled in both Russian and English. Sadly, the icons and the graphic art are described only in Russian – see the Language section in the Facts about European Russia chapter for more information on how to interpret museum dates and listings.

To the right as you enter, two kiosks and a small shop sell excellent (though poorly bound) and reasonably priced books and maps about the Tretyakov and other museums. Downstairs are two cafés, also very clean and reasonably priced, which sell snacks, drinks and (happily) Ben & Jerry's ice cream.

Toilets are past the ticket counters to the right. The cloakroom is at the far wall opposite the main entry staircase; bags should be left in the room opposite it, next to the stairs.

Ulitsa Bolshaya Ordynka & Pyatnitskaya Ulitsa

The atmosphere of 19th-century Moscow lives on in the low buildings, old courtyards and clusters of onion domes along narrow ulitsa Bolshaya Ordynka, which runs two km down the middle of the Zamoskvorechie to Serpukhovskaya ploshchad (formerly Dobryninskaya ploshchad), and on Pyatnitskaya ulitsa, which is roughly parallel to it and 200 metres to the east. The many churches, several of them recently reopened or being restored in readiness for reopening, make up a scrapbook of Moscow architectural styles. The name Ordynka comes from *orda* (horde): until the 16th century this was the start of the road to the Golden Horde's capital on the Volga, and Tatar ambassadors lived here. Tretyakovskaya, Novokuznetskaya, Serpukhovskaya and Dobryninskaya metro stations are all in the area.

Heading south from Maly Moskvoretsky Bridge, the first lane on the right, 2-y Kadashevsky pereulok, contains the tall **Resurrection Church** (Tserkov Voskresenia), recently turned into a restoration centre for other churches. Its rich, late 17th-century decoration, including five domes on thin towers which earned it the nickname

'Candle', is a fine example of so-called Moscow Baroque.

In Chernigovsky pereulok the small, white **SS Mikhail & Fyodor Church** (Tserkos Mikhaila i Fyodora), with two rows of spade gables and five domes on a thin tower, is being restored as a working church, while the bigger **St John the Baptist Church** (Tserkov Ioanna Predtechi) houses an exhibition of unusual Russian glassware. Both date from the late 17th century, though St John's bell tower, a Zamoskvorechie landmark which fronts Pyatnitskaya ulitsa, was added in 1753.

The yellow-and-white, Empire-style **Virgin of All Sorrows Church** (Tserkov Bogomateri vsekh skorbyashchikh radostey) at ulitsa Bolshaya Ordynka 20, a working church, dates mostly from between 1828 and 1833. The mansion over the road was built for the same patron, the merchant Dolgov. Klimentovsky pereulok leads to **St Clement's Church** (Tserkov Klimenta Papy Rimskogo), built between 1742 and 1774, at Pyatnitskaya ulitsa 26 (lately closed for rebuilding), a rare Moscow example of the true Baroque favoured by Empress Elizabeth.

The blue-and-white **Church of St Nicholas in Pyzhi** (Tserkov Nikoly v Pyzhakh) at ulitsa Bolshaya Ordynka 27A, a working church, is a typical five-domed, mid-17th century church, with spade gables and thin onion domes. **SS Martha & Mary Convent** (Marfo-Mariiskaya obitel) at No 34A, with its pretty, single-domed, white Intercession Church (now housing church restoration offices), was founded in the early 20th century by Grand Princess Yelisaveta, the last tsarina's sister, after her husband, Grand Duke Sergey, was assassinated.

The little **Tropinin Museum** (Muzey V Tropinina) at Shchetininsky pereulok 10, a block west of ulitsa Bolshaya Ordynka, contains 19th-century Russian art, much of it by the serf-born Romantic Vasily Tropinin; it's open Monday, Thursday and Friday from noon to 6.30 pm, Saturday and Sunday from 10 am to 4.30 pm. Over on Pyatnitskaya ulitsa and slightly further north, the 1824-26

Empire-style **Trinity Church** (Tserkov Troitsy) is being restored.

Around Paveletskaya Ploshchad

This wide square (formerly Leninskaya ploshchad) on the Garden Ring is dominated by the Pavelets Station, terminus for trains to the Volga region. The finest loco in the neighbourhood, however, stands idle in an air-conditioned pavilion just east of the station. This is the **Lenin Funeral Train** (Traurny poezd V 1 Lenina) which brought Lenin's body to Moscow from Gorki Leninskie, where he died, in January 1924. Once a shrine of Lenin pilgrimages, it now shares its quarters with an imported-car showroom. The old steam engine is in beautiful condition.

The **Bakhrushin Theatre Museum** (Teatralny muzey imeni Bakhrushina), Russia's foremost stage museum, is on the north side of Paveletskaya ploshchad at ulitsa Bakhrushina 31/12. Founded in 1894, it makes a fascinating walk through Russian drama, ballet and opera. There are model stage sets, photos and original costumes, including Nijinsky's ballet shoes. It's open from noon to 6 pm daily except Tuesday and the last Monday of the month.

Don Monastery

The youngest of Moscow's fortified monasteries, founded in 1591 on the spot where the Muscovite army had just camped before repulsing the last Tatar raid on Moscow, is a five-minute walk from Shabolovskaya metro. Turn right out of the metro down ulitsa Shabolovka, then take the first street on the right, Donskaya ploshchad. The Don Monastery (Donskoy monastyr) was built to house the *Virgin of the Don* icon, revered for its help at the battle of Kulikovo (1380) and again in 1591 when, it's said, the Tatar khan Giri retreated without a fight after the icon (now in the Tretyakov Gallery) showered him with burning arrows in a dream.

Most of the monastery, surrounded by a brick wall with 12 towers, was built between 1684 and 1733 under Regent Sofia and Peter the Great. By 1764 it had 7000 serfs. From 1918 to 1927 it was the headquarters of the Russian Orthodox Church, then it was closed as a monastery, falling into neglect despite being partly used as an architecture museum. Restored in 1990 and 1991, it's now back in Church hands. The **Virgin of Tikhvin Church** (Tserkov Tikhvinskoy Bogomateri) over the north gate, built in 1713 and 1714, is one of the last examples of Moscow Baroque. In the centre of the grounds is the large, brick **New Cathedral** (Novy Sobor), built between 1684 and 1693; just to its south is the smaller **Old Cathedral** (Stary Sobor), dating from 1591 to 1593, where Patriarch Tikhon, who led the Orthodox Church from 1917 until his death in 1924, lies in a marble tomb. Both cathedrals are now working.

After a plague in 1771, when burials in central Moscow were banned, the Don Monastery became a graveyard for the nobility, and it is littered with elaborate tombs and chapels.

Danilov Monastery

The headquarters of the Russian Orthodox Church stands behind white fortress walls on ulitsa Danilovsky Val, five minutes' walk east of Tulskaya metro. The Danilov Monastery (Svyato-Danilovsky monastyr) was built in the late 13th century by Daniil, the first Prince of Moscow, as an outer city defence. Ivan the Terrible rebuilt it, and it was later repeatedly altered. After the revolution it spent time as a factory and as a detention centre before being returned to the Church in 1983. It was restored in time to replace Sergiev Posad (formerly Zagorsk) as the Church's spiritual and administrative centre and the official residence of its head, the Patriarch of Moscow & All Russia, during Russian Orthodoxy's 1988 millennium celebrations.

It's OK to wander in and look round, but be on your best behaviour: no photos or smoking, and men must remove hats inside the churches. On holy days in particular the place seethes with worshippers crossing themselves, lighting candles and ladling

EUROPEAN RUSSIA

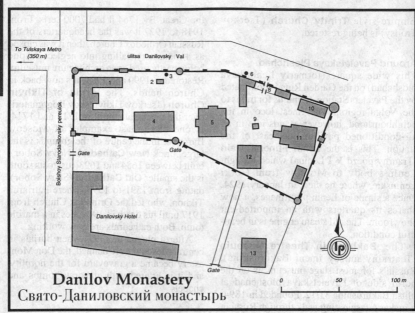

Danilov Monastery
Свято-Даниловский монастырь

1	Patriarch's Official Residence Служебная резиденция патриарха	6	Shop Иконная лавка	11	Church of the Holy Fathers of the Seven Ecumenical Councils Храм св. отцов семи вселенских соборов
2	Chapel Часовня	7	Entrance Вход		
3	Khachkhar Хачхар	8	St Simeon Stylites Gate-Church Надвратная церковь Симеона Столпника	12	Refectory Дом настоятеля
4	External Affairs Department Корпус ОВЦС	9	Chapel Часовня	13	Church of the Resurrection of the Holy Word Церковь Воскресения Словущего
5	Trinity Cathedral Троицкий собор	10	Monks' Building Братский корпус		

holy water into jugs at the tiny chapel inside the gates. The older women do this as though it were their last chance on earth!

You enter beneath the pink **St Simeon Stylites Gate-Church** (Nadvratnaya tserkov Simeona Stolpnika) on the north wall on ulitsa Danilovsky Val. Its bells are the first in Moscow to ring on holy days. The bell tower was built anew in 1984, in its original 1730s form. The monastery's oldest and busiest church, where worship goes on continuously from 10 am to 5 pm daily, is the **Church of the Holy Fathers of the Seven Ecumenical Councils** (Tserkov sv ottsov semi vselenskikh soborov). Founded in the 17th century and rebuilt repeatedly since, the church contains several chapels on two floors: the main one upstairs is flanked by side chapels to St Daniil (the prince, on the north side) and SS Boris & Gleb (south). On the ground floor the small main chapel is dedicated to the Protecting Veil, the northern one to the prophet Daniel. Many of the church's icons are new; others have been brought from other churches.

The yellow, classical **Trinity Cathedral** (Troitsky sobor), built in the 1830s, restored in the 1980s, holds 5 pm services on Friday and Sunday, others on holy days, and also special services such as funerals and baptisms. West of the cathedral are the patriarchate's **External Affairs Department** (Korpus OVTsS) and, at the far end of the grounds, the **Patriarch's official residence** (Sluzhebnaya rezidentsia patriarkha) and synodal premises. Against the north wall in this part of the monastery is a 13th-century Armenian **carved-stone cross** or *khachkar*, a gift from the Armenian Church.

The church guesthouse in the southern part of the monastery grounds has been turned into an elegant hotel (see Places to Stay).

INNER SOUTH-EAST
Around Taganskaya Ploshchad

Taganskaya ploshchad (metro: Taganskaya), on the Garden Ring, is a monster intersection, loud, dusty and crowded. But it's the hub of the Zayauzie, the area south of the little Yauza River, the territory of the 17th-century blacksmiths' and other guilds and later an Old Believers' quarter. The square's personality disappeared with a reconstruction in the 1970s and 1980s but traces remain in the streets that radiate from it. The great block on Taganskaya ploshchad at Verkhnyaya Radishchevskaya ulitsa is the **Taganka Theatre**, famous in the Soviet era for director Yury Lyubimov's vaguely subversive repertoire, from contemporised Chekhov to modern Russian and Western works, which annoyed the Soviet authorities and delighted everyone else. The theatre owed a share of its popularity to the actor-singer-poet Vladimir Vysotsky, beloved of Muscovites, who sang of the coarse and

funny Russian soul and drank himself to death in 1980.

Behind metro Taganskaya is the sombre 1712 **Taganka Gates Church of St Nicholas** (Tserkov Nikoly u Taganskikh vorot). More fetching is the **Potters' Church of the Assumption** (Tserkov Uspenia Bogoroditsy v goncharovoy slobode), built in 1654, with its star-spangled domes, a block away at Goncharnaya ulitsa (formerly ulitsa Volodarskogo) 29. Note the tilework under the 'extra' refectory dome.

Goncharnaya ulitsa leads north to two impressive classical mansions, at No 12 and No 16, and the **Church of St Nikita Beyond the Yauza** (Tserkov Nikoly za Yauzoy), under restoration but partly in use, with 15th-century foundations, 16th-century walls, 17th-century chapels and an 18th-century bell tower. The church is dwarfed by the **Kotelnicheskaya Apartments** block (Mnogokvartirny dom Kotelnicheskaya), one of the Stalin Gothic 'Seven Sisters' skyscrapers built around 1950. To the east, above the Yauza at Yauzskaya ulitsa (formerly Internatsionalnaya ulitsa) 9-11 is the huge **Batashyov Palace** (Dvorets Batashyova), an industrialist's manor house built in 1802 with lion gates and its own church. It's now a hospital.

North-east of Taganskaya, at Bolshaya Kommunisticheskaya ulitsa 15, you can't miss the grand **Cathedral of St Martin the Confessor** (Khram sv Martina Ispovednika), built in 1792 in shameless imitation of St Paul's Cathedral in London. Badly neglected during the Soviet period, it's now open and being renovated. This whole neighbourhood has a look of abandoned grace.

Andronikov Monastery & Andrey Rublyov Museum

The fortified Andronikov Monastery (Spaso-Andronikov monastyr) on the banks of the Yauza at Andronevskaya ploshchad (formerly ploshchad Pryamikova; metro: Ploshchad Ilicha), just over one km north-east of Taganskaya ploshchad, dates from

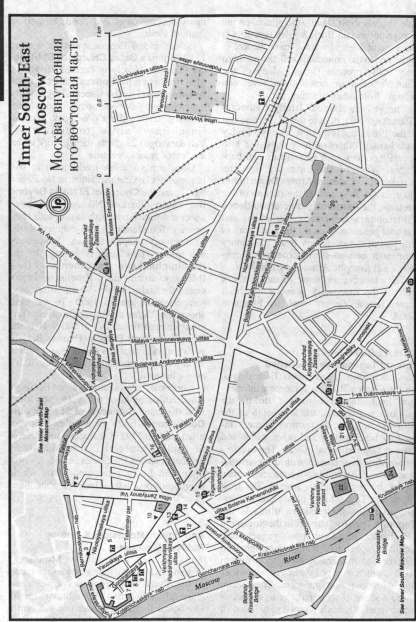

Inner South-East Moscow

Москва, внутренняя юго-восточная часть

ploschad Rogozhskaya Zastava

shosse Entuziastov

ulitsa Zolotorozhsky Val

Dushinskaya ulitsa

Petrovsky proezd

Rodimtseva ulitsa

ulitsa Voytovicha

Radochaya ulitsa

Nizhegorodskaya ulitsa

Novorogozhskaya ulitsa

Bolshaya Kalitnikovskaya ulitsa

Srednyaya Kalitnikovskaya ulitsa

Malaya Kalitnikovskaya ulitsa

ulitsa Sergeya Radonezhskogo

Malaya Andronevskaya ulitsa

Bolshaya Andronevskaya ulitsa

Andronevskaya ploschad

ulitsa Sergeya

See Inner North-East Moscow Map

Yauza River

Nikoloyamskaya nab

Nikoloyamskaya ulitsa

ulitsa Zemlyanoy Val

Taganskaya ulitsa

Taganskaya ploschad

Bol. Fakelny pereulok

Bolshie Kamenshchiki

Marksistskaya ulitsa

ploschad Krestyanskaya Zastava

Volgogradsky prospekt

1-ya Dubrovskaya ul

ulitsa M Melnikova

Volgogradsky prospekt

3-y Krutitsky

Dinamovskaya ulitsa

Vorontsovskaya ulitsa

Verkhny Novospassky proezd

Krutitskaya nab

Novospassky Bridge

Bernikovskaya — nab

Nikoloyamskaya ulitsa

Tetennsky per

Yauzskaya ulitsa

Goncharnaya ul

Verkhnaya Radishchevskaya ulitsa

Goncharnaya nab

Krasnokholmskaya nab

Podgorskaya nab

Kotelnicheskaya — nab

Moscow River

Bolshoy Krasnokholmsky Bridge

See Inner South Moscow Map

Nabolraya ul

Novospasskaya ploschad

PLACES TO EAT

2 American Bar & Grill 2
   Американский бар и грилл 2
10 Taganka Blues
   Таганка блюз

OTHER

1 Andronikov Monastery & Andrey Rublyov
   Museum
   Спасо-Андроников монастырь и
   музей имени Андрея Рублёва
3 Foreign Literature Library
   Библиотека иностранной литературы
4 Kotelnicheskaya Apartments
   Многоквартирный дом
   Котельническая
5 Batashyov Palace
   Дворец Баташёва
7 Church of St Nikita Beyond the Yauza
   Церковь Никиты за Яузой
8 18th-Century Mansion
   Городская усадьба XVII В.
9 19th-Century Mansion
   Городская усадьба XIX В.
11 Taganka Theatre
   Театр на Таганке
12 Potters' Church of the Assumption
   Церковь Успения Богородицы
   в Гончаровой слободе
13 Taganka Gates Church of St Nicholas
   Церковь Николы у таганских ворот

16 Cathedral of St Martin the Confessor
   Храм Св. Мартина Исповедника
17 Rogozhskoe Cemetery
   Рогожское кладбище
18 Intercession Church
   Церковь Покрова
19 Pet Market
   Птичий рынок
20 Kalitnikovskoe Cemetery
   Калитниковское кладбище
22 Novospassky Monastery
   Новоспасский монастырь
23 Novospassky Most Landing
   Пристань Новоспасский Мост
24 Krutitskoe Podvorie
   Крутицкое подворье

METRO STATIONS

6 Ploshchad Ilicha
   Площадь Ильича
14 Taganskaya (2 locations)
   Таганская
15 Marxistskaya
   Марксистская
21 Proletarskaya (3 locations)
   Пролетарская
25 Volgogradsky Prospekt
   Волгоградский Проспект

1360. It's famous because Andrey Rublyov, the master of icon-painting, was a monk here in the 15th century. Rublyov is buried in the grounds; no-one quite knows where.

In the centre of the grounds, topped by a posy of kokoshnik gables, is the compact **Saviour's Cathedral** (Spassky Sobor), built in 1427, the oldest stone building in Moscow, and now being restored. To the left is the combined rectory and 17th-century Moscow Baroque **Church of the Archangel Michael** (Tserkov Arkhangela Mikhaila). To the right of that, in the old monks' quarters, is the **Andrey Rublyov Museum of Early Russian Culture & Art** (Muzey Drevnerusskoy Kultury i Iskusstva imeni Andreya Rublyova), a museum of icons but with nothing by Rublyov himself. What there is, however, is lovely, including a few strong,

luminous 14th to 16th-century works from the Novgorod, Rostov and Moscow schools, interestingly juxtaposed. The museum is open from 11 am to 6 pm daily except Wednesday and the last Friday of the month.

Novospassky Monastery

One km south of Taganskaya ploshchad, on Verkhny Novospassky proezd (metro: Proletarskaya), is another of Moscow's fort-monasteries. Novospassky (Novospassky monastyr; the New Monastery of the Saviour) dates from the 15th century, when it was relocated from inside the Kremlin. Under restoration for at least 30 years, it became a working monastery again in the early 1990s. During the day you can walk in beneath the 18th-century wedding-cake bell tower. English-speaking guides are available if you want one.

The centrepiece is the **Transfiguration Cathedral** (Spaso-Preobrazhensky Sobor), built by the imperial Romanov family in the 1640s in imitation of the Kremlin's Assumption Cathedral. Frescoes inside depict the history of Christianity in Russia, with the Romanov family tree, which goes back to the Viking Prince Rurik, climbing one wall.

To the left is the **Intercession Church** (Pokrovskaya Tserkov, 1675), which is joined to the refectory (trapezny) and bakery buildings. Behind the cathedral is the **Church of the Sign** (Tserkov Znamenia), which was finished in 1808 as a memorial chapel for the noble Sheremetev family.

Outside near the river is a pond. Under the bank, beneath one of the monastery towers, is the site of a mass grave for thousands of victims of Stalin's 1930s reign of terror.

Krutitskoe Podvorie

Across the road south of Novospassky is a sumptuous *podvorie* (ecclesiastical residence) used by the Moscow metropolitans from the 16th century, when they lost their place in the Kremlin with the founding of the Russian patriarchate. At the north end is the **Assumption Cathedral** (Uspensky Sobor), a symphony of brickwork now under restoration, and towards the river is what may be a reconstructed metropolitan's house. But the best part is in between – an extraordinary Moscow Baroque **gate tower** (teremok), with friezes in unexpected yellows and blues, frescoes of the Saviour, Virgin and (possibly) John the Baptist, and of the Assumption of the Virgin. You can visit daily except Tuesday, from 10 am to 6 pm.

Pet Market

Muscovites have a big interest in the non-human world despite – or more likely because of – their utterly urban environment. The Ptichy Rynok (literally, Bird Market) on Bolshaya Kalitnikovskaya ulitsa, two km east of Taganskaya ploshchad, heaves with humanity hawking dogs, cats, budgerigars, parrots, the odd goat and any creature you could dream up for your home aquarium. Rumour has it even crocodiles have been sold here. It's open daily except Monday and is busiest in the mornings, especially on Saturday and Sunday. Get there by trolleybus No 16 or 26 from Nizhnyaya Radishchevskaya ulitsa, the short street behind Taganskaya metro – it's about five stops. If stuck, follow anyone with a kitten peeping out of their pocket!

A corner of Kalitnikovskoe Cemetery near the market was a dumping ground for the bodies of people the KGB killed in the Lubyanka in the 1930s.

Rogozhskoe Old Believers' Community

One of Russia's most atmospheric religious centres is the Old Believers' cemetery and churches at Rogozhskoe, three km east of Taganskaya ploshchad. The Old Believers split from the main Russian Orthodox Church in 1653 when they refused to accept certain reforms by Patriarch Nikon (see Religion in Facts about European Russia), and have maintained old forms of worship and customs such as the wearing of beards ever since. In the late 18th century, during a brief period free of persecution , rich Old Believer merchants set up perhaps the most important Old Believer community around their Rogozhskoe Cemetery (Rogozhskoe kladbishche), and the place remains an island of old Russia to this day, with dark, mysterious churches.

To get there take trolleybus No 16 or 26, or bus No 51, east from Taganskaya ploshchad along Taganskaya ulitsa and Nizhegorodskaya ulitsa, and get off after crossing a railway. Rogozhskoe's tall, green-domed 20th-century **bell tower** is visible to the north (left). The yellow classical-style **Intercession Church** (Tserkov Pokrova) contains one of Moscow's finest collections of icons, all dating from before 1653. The oldest is the 14th-century *Saviour with the Angry Eye (Spas yaroe oko)*, protected by glass near the south door. Six icons on the deesis row (the biggest row) of the iconostasis are believed to be by the Rublyov school, and the seventh, *The Saviour (Spas)*, is attributed to Andrey Rublyov himself.

The other churches here are the **Church of the Nativity** (Tserkov Rozhdestva) and the tiny **Church of St Nicholas** (Tserkov Nikoly). Another **Church of St Nicholas** provides a picturesque entry to the **cemetery**, which contains the family tombs of Old Believer merchants from the Morozov, Ryabushinsksy and Soldatenkov families, among others, as well as a bishop's residence, almshouses and other buildings.

INNER NORTH-EAST
Around Komsomolskaya Ploshchad

This square with three main rail termini, 0.75 km outside the Garden Ring, is proof that Moscow really is the place where Europe and Asia meet. Leave your valuables at home (unless you have to take them on a train) as the crowds that constantly pass through it contain some very impoverished characters and drunks. Komsomolskaya ploshchad is also an amazing architectural variety show of bizarre styles.

The **Leningrad Station** (Leningradsky vokzal) on the north side of the square, with

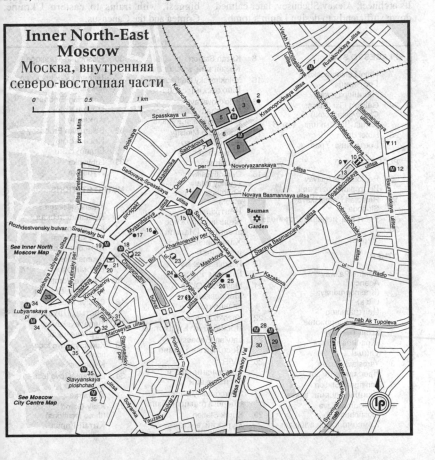

Inner North-East Moscow
Москва, внутренняя северо-восточная части

its tall clock tower, is Moscow's oldest, built in 1851 and very similar to its opposite number at the far end of the line, the Moscow Station in St Petersburg. The **Yaroslavl Station** (Yaroslavsky vokzal) next door, start of the Trans-Siberian Railway, is a 1902-04 Art Nouveau fantasy by Fyodor Shekhtel with turrets that would look at home in Disneyland. The **Kazan Station** (Kazansky vokzal), built between 1912 and 1926 on the south side of the square, which serves Central Asia and western Siberia, is a retrospective of seven building styles going back to a 16th-century Tatar tower in Kazan. Its architect, Alexey Shchusev, later calmed down sufficiently to design Lenin's tomb.

The Yaroslavl and Kazan stations bring an exotic flavour to Moscow as travellers from Asian regions settle among bags, parcels, families and animals to await trains.

The 26-storey wedding cake west of Komsomolskaya ploshchad is the **Hotel Leningradskaya** (Gostinitsa Leningradskaya). Another of Stalin's Seven Sisters, which was originally the Transport Construction Ministry and is now the **Agriculture Ministry** (Ministerstvo selskogo khozyaystva), is 600 metres south on the Garden Ring. The **Kursk Station** (Kursky vokzal), a further 1.5 km south, is Moscow's biggest, with trains to eastern Ukraine, Crimea and the Caucasus.

PLACES TO STAY

7   Hotel Leningradskaya
Гостиница
Ленинградская

24   Galina's Flat (Ulitsa Chaplygina Dom8)
улица Чаплыгина, дом 8

25   Hotel Ural
Гостиница Урал

PLACES TO EAT

9   Restoran Razgulyay
Ресторан Разгуляй

11   Restoran Nemetskaya Sloboda
Ресторан немецкая слобода

20   Turist
Турист

OTHER

2   Central Railway Agency (Krasnoprudnaya ulitsa)
Центральное железнодорожное агенство (Краснопрудная улица)

3   Yaroslavl Station
Ярославский вокзал

5   Leningrad Station
Ленинградский вокзал

6   Komsomolskaya Ploshchad
Комсомольская площадь

8   Kazan Station
Казанский вокзал

10   Yelokhovsky Cathedral
Елоховский собор

13   Yelokhovskaya Ploshchad
Елоховская площадь

14   Agriculture Ministry
Министерство сельского хозяйства

16   Central Railway Agency (Maly Kharitonevsky pereulok)
Центральное железнодорожное агенство (Малый Харитоневский переулок)

17   Ridzhina Gallery
Галерея Риджина

21   Main Post Office
Московский главпочтамт

22   Kazakh Embassy
Посольство Казахстана

23   Latvian Embassy
Посольство Латвии

26   UVIR
Управления виз и регистрации

27   Sberegatelny Bank
Сберегательный банк

29   Kursk Station
Курский вокзал

30   Ploshchad Kurskogo Vokzala
Площадь Курского вокзала

31   Armenian Embassy
Посольство Армении

32   Belarusian Embassy
Посольство Белоруссии

33   Lubyanka
Лубянка

METRO STATIONS

1   Krasnoselskaya
Красносельская

4   Komsomolskaya (two locations)
Комсомольская

12   Baumanskaya
Бауманская

15   Krasnye Vorota
Красные Ворота

18   Chistye Prudy
Чистые Пруды

19   Turgenevskaya
Тургеневская

28   Kurskaya (two locations)
Курская

34   Lubyanka (two locations)
Лубянка

35   Kitay-Gorod (three locations)
Китай-Город

Yelokhovsky Cathedral

Spartakovskaya ulitsa 15, near Bauman-skaya metro, is the unlikely address of Moscow's senior Orthodox cathedral. This role was given to the Church of the Epiphany in Yelokhovo (Yelokhovsky Cathedral, Yelokhovsky Sobor) in 1943. (The Patriarch had been evicted from the Kremlin's Assumption Cathedral in 1918.) The Patriarch leads important services here today. Built between 1837 and 1845 with five domes in a Russian eclectic style, the cathedral is full of gilt, icons, and bescarved old women polishing, lighting candles, kneeling, crossing themselves, or kissing the floor. In the northern part of the cathedral is the tomb of St Nicholas the Miracle Worker (Svyatoy Nikolay Ugodnik), who is believed to make wishes come true if you light a candle and pray to him. A shrine in front of the right side of the iconostasis contains the remains of St Alexey, a 14th-century metropolitan.

OUTER NORTH
Sokolniki Park

This park (Park Sokolniki) is twice as big as Gorky Park, with a lot of sports facilities. In winter you can ice-skate or cross-country ski here and rent the gear on the spot. The 400-metre walk to the main entrance from Sokolniki metro passes the good-looking 1909-13 **Resurrection Church** (Tserkov Voskresenia, Церковь Воскресения).

All-Russia Exhibition Centre

No other place sums up the rise and fall of the Soviet dream quite so well as the All-Russia Exhibition Centre (Vserossiysky Vystavochny Tsentr, VVTs). The old initials by which it's still commonly known, VDNKh (*'Vey-dey-en-kha'*), tell half the story. They stand for Vystavka Dostizheny Narodnogo Khozyaystva SSSR, or USSR Economic Achievements Exhibition.

VDNKh was created in the 1950s and 1960s to impress upon one and all the success of the Soviet economic system. Stretching two km from end to end and one km from side to side, it's composed of wide pedestrian avenues and grandiose pavilions that glorified every aspect of Socialist construction from education and health to agriculture, technology and science. Here and there stand the kitschest of Socialist Realist statues, pointedly painted a golder gold than any church dome.

VDNKh was an early casualty when those in power finally admitted that the Soviet economy had become a disaster. Funds were cut off from it by 1990. Today VDNKh is the VVTs, a commercial centre, its pavilions given over to sales of the very imported goods Soviet propaganda insisted were inferior. Much of the merchandise on sale is low-priced clothing and the like from China. The domed Kosmos (Space) pavilion towards the far end houses more expensive imported cars. Lenin's slogan 'Socialism is Soviet power plus electrification' still adorns the electrification pavilion to its right.

The VVTs's main entrance, 500 metres from prospekt Mira, is approached by its own imposing avenues from the Hotel Kosmos or VDNKh metro station. It's open daily.

The soaring 100-metre titanium obelisk beside VDNKh metro is a monument to Soviet space flight. In its base is the **Cosmonautics Museum** (Музей космонавтики), open from 10 am to 7 pm daily except Monday and the last Friday of the month.

Ostankino

The **Ostankino TV Tower** (Ostankinskaya televizionnaya bashnya, Останкинская телевизионная башня), which rises 540 metres beside ulitsa Akademika Korolyova, 1.75 km west of VDNKh metro, has viewing platforms and restaurants at around 330 metres, with 35 to 40-km views on clear days. It's open to visitors daily except Monday from 9 am to 8.30 pm. To get a ticket (US$1) take your passport and visa to the building marked 'Exkursii na Telebashnya' beside the tower. Then walk over to the tower, pass through security control, and the lift will whisk you up at 25 km/h to the viewing level. There are a couple of restaurants up here too but the food is poor.

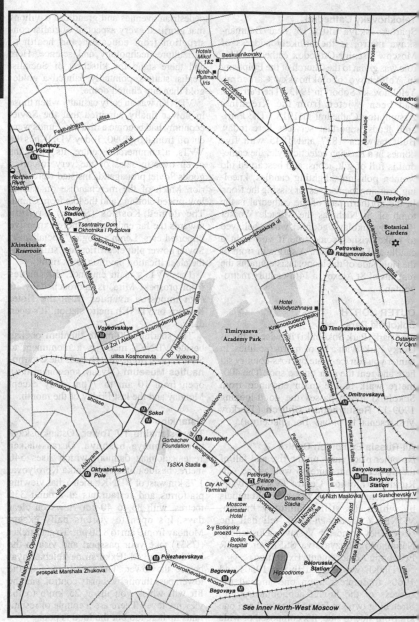

See Inner North-West Moscow

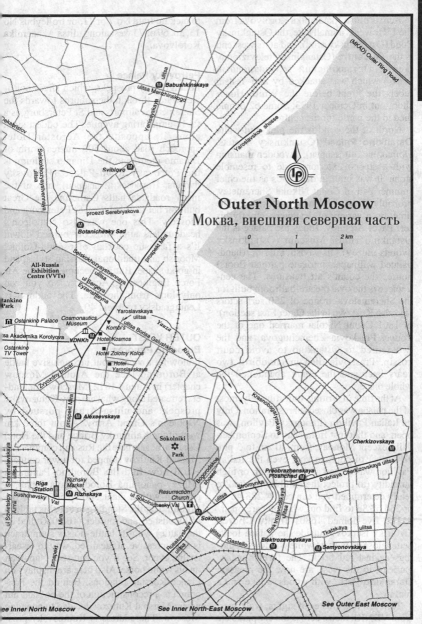

Outer North Moscow
Моква, внешняя северная часть

0   1   2 km

(MKAD) Outer Ring Road

Yaroslavskoe shosse

ulitsa Menzhinskogo

ulitsa ■ Babushkinskaya

Yenisejskaya

Dekabristov

Selskokhozyaystvennaya ulitsa

Sviblovo Ⓜ

proezd Serebryakova

Ⓜ Botanichesky Sad

Selskokhozyaystvennaya ulitsa

ul Sergeya Eyzenshteyna

prospekt Mira

All-Russia Exhibition Centre (VVTs)

stankino Park

🏛 Ostankino Palace

ssa Akademika Korolyova

Ostankino TV Tower

Zvyozdny bulvar

Yaroslavskaya ulitsa

Cosmonautics Museum

▼ Kombi's

ulitsa Borisa Galushkina

🏛 VDNKh   Hotel Kosmos

■ Hotel Zolotoy Kolos

■ Hotel Yaroslavskaya

Yauza River

prospekt Mira

Ⓜ Alexeevskaya

Krasnobogatyrskaya

ul Sovetsky

Sheremetevsky ulitsa

Riga Station

Sushchevsky Val

Ⓜ Rizhskaya

Rizhsky Market

prospekt Mira

Sokolniki ✿ Park

Bogorodskoe shosse

Cherkizovskaya Ⓜ

ulitsa

Preobrazhenskaya Ploshchad Ⓜ

Bolshaya Cherkizovskaya ulitsa

Stromynka

Resurrection Church

ul Sokolnichesky Val

🚩 Sokolniki

Russkolniksaya ulitsa

Gastello

Elektrozavodskaya ulitsa

Elektrozavodskaya Ⓜ

Tkatskaya ulitsa

Ⓜ Semyonovskaya

See Inner North Moscow   See Inner North-East Moscow   See Outer East Moscow

Across ulitsa Akademika Korolyova from the TV tower is a small lake, the Ostankinsky Pond (Ostankinsky prud), and at its west end is the **TV Centre** (Ostankinsky televizionny tsentr, Останкинский телевизионный центр) which was attacked by anti-Yeltsin rebels the night before the White House shoot-out in October 1993. Some 62 people died in the battle for the centre.

North of the pond is the pink-and-white **Ostankino Palace** (Ostankinsky dvorets, Останкинский дворец), a wooden mansion with a stucco exterior made to resemble stone. It was built in the 1790s as the chief summer pad of Count Nikolai Sheremetev, probably Russia's richest aristocrat of the time, by a variety of designers, chiefly his serf Pavel Argunov. Today the palace is the Ostankino House-Museum (Ostankinsky dvorets-muzey). Its lavish interior (hand-painted wallpaper, intricate parquet floors) houses the count's art treasures. The centrepiece is the oval theatre-ballroom built for the Sheremetevs' troupe of 250 serf actors (see also Kuskovo in the Outer East section). In 1801 Count Nikolai married one of the troupe, Praskovia Zhemchugova, and the two retired to Ostankino to avoid court gossip. Praskovia died in childbirth two years later and the count abandoned the whole place.

At the time of writing, unfortunately, most of the palace was closed for restoration. Only its Italian Pavilion (Italiansky Pavilon) was open, and that just from May to September, daily except Monday, from 10 am to 3 pm. To further discourage you, even the Italian Pavilion was closed at times of rain or high humidity (to protect the exhibits). If you're really determined you can call ☎ 283 46 45 or 286 62 88 to find out what bits are open.

The five-domed 1680s **Trinity Church** (Troitsky tserkov) outside the palace looks better close up with its white window mouldings against red brick. The former palace gardens, to the west, are now the pleasant **Ostankino Park**, with woods, a lake and a funfair.

To reach this cluster of sights, walk west from VDNKh metro across the car parks etc to pick up tram No 7 or 11, or trolleybus No 13, 36, 69 or 73 west along ulitsa Akademika Korolyova.

Petrovsky Palace
Leningradsky prospekt, which slices north-westwards through the suburbs towards the Sheremetevo airports and St Petersburg, is a fairly uninspiring avenue. The oddest sight along it, opposite the Aerostar Hotel approach road about 500 metres north of Dinamo metro and the Dinamo stadium, is the Petrovsky Road-Palace (Petrovsky dvorets, Петровский дворец), one of the many roadside halts Catherine the Great built for her trips between St Petersburg and Moscow. This one was also Napoleon's headquarters after Moscow burned down. It's a fantastic cocktail of pseudo-Gothic, Moorish and traditional Russian styles, and in good shape. But it's occupied by the Air Force Engineering Academy, so you can only look from the gate. The address is Leningradsky prospekt 40.

OUTER WEST
Borodino Panorama
Following a vicious but inconclusive battle at Borodino (see the Around Moscow chapter) in August 1812, Moscow's defenders retreated along what are now Kutuzovsky prospekt and ulitsa Arbat, pursued by Napoleon's Grand Army. About three km west of the Kalininsky Bridge and the Hotel Ukraina, near where the Russian commander Mikhail Kutuzov stopped for a war council, you'll now find the Borodino Panorama (Muzey-panorama Borodinskaya bitva), a pavilion with a giant 360° painting of the Borodino battle. Standing inside this tableau of bloodshed and murder (100,000 died in the battle) with its battle-noises soundtrack is an impressive, if idealised, way to visualise the event. See if you can spot Napoleon on his white horse. Also here are displays on Franco-Russian relations. Behind the Panorama is a reconstruction of the peasant hut where Marshal Kutuzov decided to abandon Moscow. The address is Kutuzovsky pros-

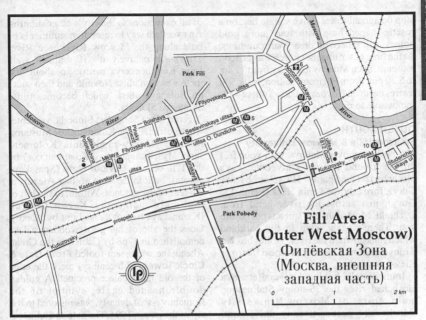

Park Fili

Novozavodskaya ulitsa

Filyovskaya ulitsa

Bolshaya

Pinsky proyezd

ulitsa Poloskuha

Seslavinskaya ulitsa

ulitsa O. Dundicha

ulitsa Barklaya

Malaya Filyovskaya ulitsa

Minskaya

Kastanaevskaya ulitsa

ulitsa 1812 Goda

Kutuzovsky prospekt

Studencheskaya ul.

Park Pobedy

prospekt

Kutuzovsky

ulitsa

River

River

Moscow

**Fili Area
(Outer West Moscow)**
Филёвская Зона
(Москва, внешняя
западная часть)

0   1   2 km

METRO STATIONS		OTHER	
1	Kuntsevskaya Кунцевская	2	M'ARS Gallery Галерея М'АРС
3	Pionerskaya Пионерская	6	Fili Church of the Intercession Церковь Покрова в Филях
4	Filyovsky Park Филёвский парк	8	Triumphal Arch Триумфальная арка
5	Bagrationovskaya Багратионовская	9	Borodino Panorama Музей-панорама Бородинская битва
7	Fili Фили		
10	Kutuzovskaya Кутузовская		

---

pekt 38 (nearest metro: Kutuzovskaya). The panorama and hut are open from 10 am to 6 pm daily, except Friday and the last Thursday of the month.

The **Triumphal Arch** (Triumfalnaya arka) a bit further out on Kutuzovsky prospekt celebrates Napoleon's eventual defeat. It was demolished at its original site in front of the Belorussia Station in the 1930s and recon-

structed here in a fit of post-WW II public spirit.

Fili Church of the Intercession
About 1.5 km north of the Borodino Panorama in the neighbourhood called Fili is the 1690s Church of the Intercession (Tserkov Pokrova v Filyakh), a beautiful red-brick, Moscow Baroque confection – gold dome

atop octagonal tower above square tier, on a rosette-shaped base with four more gold domes – in otherwise dreary surroundings. At the time of writing the church was an icon museum, open Monday to Friday from 11 am to 5.30 pm. From Fili metro station, walk 500 metres north on Novozavodskaya ulitsa – it's impossible to miss.

OUTER SOUTH
Sparrow Hills & Moscow University

The best view over Moscow with your feet on the ground is from Universitetskaya ploshchad on the Sparrow Hills (Vorobyovie Gory), formerly the Lenin Hills (Leninskie Gory), just across the river bend from Luzhniki. Most of the city spreads out before you. There's a ski jump in the parkland which runs down to the river. Trolleybus No 7 runs here from Leninsky Prospekt metro or Kievskaya metro.

Immediately behind Universitetskaya ploshchad rises the 36-storey Stalinesque main spire of Moscow University (Moskovsky gosudarstvenny universitet, Московский государственный университет), visible from most places in the city thanks to its elevated site; it was built by convict labour between 1949 and 1953. Other university buildings are planted around it. Bus Nos 1, 113 and 119 travel between the back of the main building and Universitet metro.

Ploshchad Gagarina

The huge monument to Yury Gagarin on Leninsky prospekt (metro: Leninsky Prospekt), looking as though he's about to high-dive into the plaza, stands where Moscow turned out to welcome the world's first astronaut and a badly needed Soviet hero-figure. The semicircular buildings that look like a giant's gateway are apartment blocks, started in 1940 when they were indeed at the outer edge of the city.

Kolomenskoe

Kolomenskoe, an ancient royal country seat amid four sq km of parkland on a bluff above a bend of the Moscow River, is the choicest of all excursions to the city's outer suburbs. An excellent way to reach it in summer is by boat along the Moscow River (see River Trips). Alternatively, it's 10 minutes' walk from Kolomenskaya metro: go about 400 metres east on ulitsa Novinki and then south on Bolshaya ulitsa, which becomes ulitsa Shtatnaya Sloboda.

From ulitsa Shtatnaya Sloboda, you enter what's officially the Kolomenskoe Museum-Reserve (Muzey-zapovednik Kolomenskoe, Музей-заповедник Коломенское) by the 17th-century **Saviour Gate** (Spasskaya vorota), built in the time of Tsar Alexey, at the rear of the grounds. Within, to the left of the main path, the **Kazan Church** (Kazanskaya tserkov), also built by Alexey, faces the site of his great wooden palace demolished in 1768 by Catherine the Great. Ahead, the white, tent-roofed **Front Gate & Clock Tower** (17th century) mark the edge of the old inner palace precinct. A golden double-headed eagle, symbol of the Romanov tsarist dynasty, was restored to the top of the gate in 1994. The gate and adjacent buildings house an interesting museum with a bit of everything: a model of Alexey's wooden palace, material on rebellions associated with Kolomenskoe, and Russian crafts from clocks and tiles to woodcarving and metalwork.

Just outside the front gate, overlooking the river, rises Kolomenskoe's loveliest structure: the tall, almost rocket-like **Ascension Church** (Voznesensky tserkov) is nearly as quintessentially Russian as St Basil's Cathedral. The Ascension Church was built between 1530 and 1532 for Grand Prince Vasily III, probably to celebrate the birth of his heir – Ivan the Terrible. It was an important departure for Russian architecture, and paved the way for St Basil's a quarter of a century later by reproducing the shapes of Russian wooden churches in brick for the first time. Immediately south of it are the round 16th-century **St George's Bell Tower** (Kolokolnya Georgia) and a 17th-century falcon tower or water tower – no-one seems sure which.

Some 300 metres further south across a

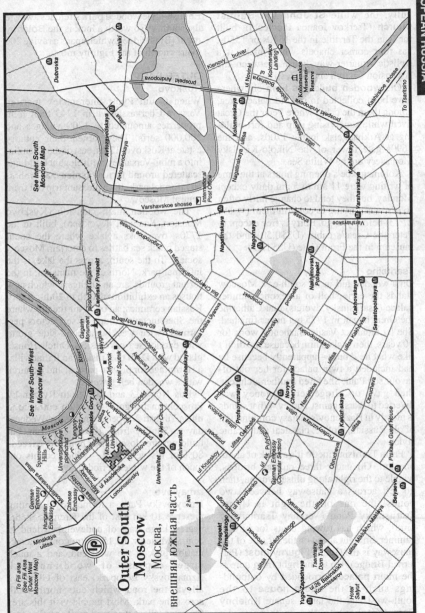

Outer South Moscow
Москва,
внешняя южная часть

LP

Minskaya ulitsa

To Fili area
(See Fili Area /
Outer West
Moscow Map)

German
Embassy

Hungarian
Embassy

Chinese
Embassy

Sparrow
Hills

Universitetskaya ploshchad

Universitetskiye
Hills

Vorobyovy Gory

Leninsky Landing

River Moscow

See Inner South-West
Moscow Map

Gagarin
Monument

ploshchad Gagarina

Leninsky Prospekt

Bol Cheryomushkinskaya

Zagorodnoe shosse

See Inner South
Moscow Map

Avtozavodskaya

Avtozavodskaya

ulitsa

prospekt Andropova

Pechatniki

Dubrovka

Klenovy bulvar

ul Novinki

Bolshaya

Kolomenskoe Landing

Kolomenskoe
Museum-
Reserve

Kolomenskaya

Nagatinskaya ulitsa

Kashirskoe shosse

To Tsaritsino

Kashirskaya

Varshavskoe shosse

International
Post Office

Varshavskoe shosse

Varshavskoe shosse

Nagatinskaya

Nagornaya

Nakhimovsky
Prospekt

Kakhovskaya

Sevastopolskaya

ulitsa Kakhovka

Kashirskoe shosse

Hotel Orlyonok
Hotel Sputnik

New Circus

Keldysh

Leninsky prospekt

ulitsa Vavilova

Lensovet

Gubkina

ulitsa Akademika Khriunova

ulitsa Dmitria Ulyanova

60-letia Oktyabrya
prospekt

Akademicheskaya

Profsoyuznaya

Nakhimovsky prospekt

Novye
Cheryomushki

Menelona

Profsoyuznaya

Obrucheva

ulitsa Garibaldi

ulitsa Profsoyuznaya

Sevastopolsky

Profsoyuznaya

Universitet

ulitsa Kravchenko

Leninsky prospekt

ul Kravchenko

German Embassy
(Consular Section)

ul 26 Bakinskikh
Kominssarov

Prakash Guest House

Kaluzskaya

Obrucheva

Belyaevo

Vernadskogo prospekt

ul Krupskoy

Prospekt
Vernadskogo

ulitsa Lobachevskogo

Yugo-Zapadnaya

ulitsa Miklukho-Maklaya

Tsentralny
Dom Turista

Hotel
Salyut

0   1   2 km

gully, the white **St John the Baptist Church** (Tserkov Ioanna Predtechi), built for Ivan the Terrible in the 1540s or 1550s, has four corner chapels which make it a stylistic 'quarter-way house' between the Ascension Church and St Basil's.

Old **wooden buildings** from elsewhere have been collected in the old palace area, among them the cabin where Peter the Great lived while supervising ship and fort building at Arkhangelsk in the 1700s, and the 1690s gate tower of the Nikolo-Karelsky Monastery on the White Sea.

Kolomenskoe's opening hours at the time of writing were 11 am to 5 pm daily except Monday, but they tend to change fairly often so it's worth trying to confirm them (☎ 115 27 13) before you go. Entry is free except to Peter the Great's cabin (US$0.50) and the museum in the Front Gate (US$1.25).

Tsaritsino

On a wooded hill in far south-east Moscow stands the eerie shell of an exotic summer palace (Tsaritsinsky dvorets) that Catherine the Great began in 1775 but never finished. She let architect Vasily Bazhenov work for 10 years, then sacked him because she didn't like what he'd built – apparently because he had included a twin palace for her out-of-favour son Paul. She hired another architect, then gave up altogether as money was diverted to wars against Turkey. What stands is mostly in Bazhenov's fantasy combination of old Russian, Gothic, classical and Arabic styles.

From Tsaritsino metro it's a walk of about one km. Go under three railway bridges, wiggle to the right along ulitsa Tyurina, then go left across a causeway between two ponds: the one on the right is Upper Tsaritsinsky Pond (Verkhny Tsaritsinsky prud), which has rowing boats for hire in summer. Straight ahead on the far side of the causeway is the Gothic **Figurny most** (Patterned Bridge). Up to the right from here is the **main palace**, surrounded by outbuildings such as the **opera house** to the south-west and the large, square **Khlebny Dom** (Kitchen) to the north-east. An

English-style wooded **park** stretches away to the south. Also worth a look is the **Bolshoy most** (Big Bridge), which spans a ravine 200 metres north of the Figurny most.

OUTER EAST
Kuskovo

When Count Pyotr Sheremetev married Varvara Cherkassakava in 1743 their joint properties amounted to 1200 villages and 200,000 serfs. They turned their country estate at Kuskovo, 12 km east of the Kremlin, into a mini-Versailles, with elegant buildings scattered around formal gardens, as well as an informal park. It's a pleasant trip out from central Moscow.

The wooden main mansion (Kyskovo Mansion, Усадьба Кусково), built in the 1770s, overlooks a lake where the count staged mock sea battles to entertain Moscow society. To the south, across the lake, is the informal park. North of the mansion, in the formal grounds, are an Orangery which now houses an exhibition of 18th to 20th-century Russian ceramics; an open-air theatre where the Sheremetevs' troupe of serf actors performed twice weekly; a pond-side grotto with exotic 'sea caverns'; a Dutch House, glazed with Delft tiles inside; an Italian villa; a Hermitage for private parties; and a church with a wooden bell tower.

Bus Nos 133 and 208 from Ryazansky Prospekt metro go to the main entrance at ulitsa Yunosti 2. Opening hours are Wednesday to Sunday from 10 am to 6 pm, but buildings are closed when humidity exceeds 80% or it's very cold – which counts out much of the winter period.

Izmaylovo

Izmaylovsky Park, a former royal hunting preserve 10 km east of the Kremlin, is the nearest large tract of undeveloped land to central Moscow. Its 15 sq km contain a recreation park at the west end, and a much larger expanse of woodland park (Izmaylovsky Lesopark) east of Glavnaya alleya, the road which cuts north-south across the park. Most people visit this area for its excellent weekend crafts market (see

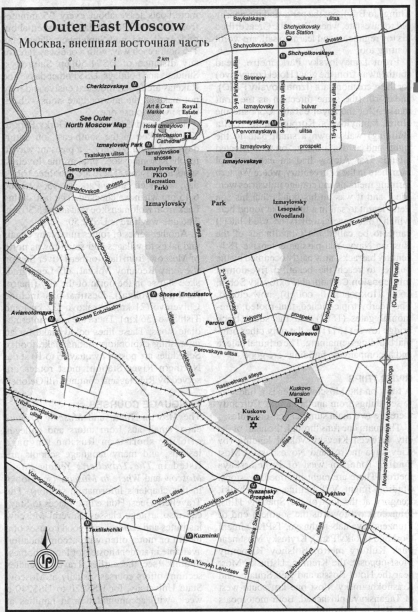

Outer East Moscow
Москва, внешняя восточная часть

0   1   2 km

Baykalskaya   ulitsa

Shchyolkovsky
Bus Station

Shchyolkovskoe   shosse

Ⓜ Shchyolkovskaya

Sirenevy   bulvar

Cherkizovskaya Ⓜ

Izmaylovsky   bulvar

Art & Craft
Market   Royal
              Estate

Pervomayskaya

Hotel Izmaylovo

Intercession
Cathedral

Pervomayskaya   ulitsa

Izmaylovsky Park Ⓜ

Izmaylovsky   prospekt

Tkatskaya ulitsa

Ismaylovskoe
shosse

Ⓜ Izmaylovskaya

Semyonovskaya Ⓜ

Izmaylovsky
PKiO
(Recreation
Park)

Izmaylovskoe   shosse

Izmaylovsky   Park   Izmaylovsky
                                   Lesopark
                                   (Woodland)

See Outer
North Moscow Map

prospekt Budyonnogo

Glavnaya

alleya

shosse Entuziastov

ulitsa Gospitalny Val

Aviamotornaya

Ⓜ Aviamotornaya

Ⓜ Shosse Entuziastov

shosse Entuziastov

2-ya Vladimirskaya

Perovo   Zelyony

ulitsa

Svoboda prospekt

Novogireevo

Perovskaya ulitsa

Nizhegorodskaya
ulitsa

Plekhanova

Rassvetnaya alleya

Kuskovo
Mansion

Kuskovo
Park

ulitsa Yunosti

ulitsa Moldagulovy

Svobodny prospekt

shosse Entuziastov

(Outer Ring Road)

Kievnotornaya ulitsa

Ryazansky

Volgogradsky prospekt

Oxkaya ulitsa

Zelenodolskaya ulitsa

Ryazansky
Prospekt

prospekt

Ⓜ Vykhino

Ⓜ Textilshchiki

Ⓜ Kuzminki

Akademika Skryabina

ulitsa Yunykh Lenintsev

Tashkentskaya ulitsa

Moskovskaya Koltsevaya Avtomobilnaya Doroga

Things to Buy), but the parks and the nearby old royal estate, where Peter the Great drilled his toy regiments and learnt to sail, are worth visiting too.

From Izmaylovsky Park metro, head south (away from the giant Hotel Izmaylovo) for the recreation park (**Izmaylovsky PKiO**), and north (the same direction as the craft market) for the **royal estate**. Opposite the Hotel Izmaylovo's Korpus Delta (Delta Building) walk down a small path to the right, and across a bridge on to a moated island. Tsar Alexey had an experimental farm here in the 17th century, where Western farming methods and cottage industries were tried, and it was on his ponds that his son Peter learnt to sail in a little boat found here which (like several others he used later!) came to be called the Grandfather of the Russian Navy. You pass an extensive 18th-century barracks, now partly occupied by the police, to reach the beautiful five-domed **Intercession Cathedral** (Pokrovsky Sobor, 1679, Покровский собор), now closed. The nearby triple-arched, tent-roofed, ceremonial gates (1682) and the squat brick bridge tower (1671) are the only other original buildings remaining. The original palace and accompanying buildings are gone.

RIVER TRIPS

A ferry on the Moscow River is a fine way to see things from another angle. Currently there are two main summer-season routes.

The main one runs through the heart of the city between Kievsky Vokzal landing (by Kievskaya metro) and Novospassky Most landing (one km west of Proletarskaya metro). There are eight intermediate stops: Stadion imeni V I Lenina at Luzhniki, Lengory at the foot of the Sparrow Hills, Frunzenskaya towards the southern end of Frunzenskaya naberezhnaya, TsPKiO imeni Gorkogo (Gorky Park), Krymsky Most near Park Kultury metro, Bolshoy Kamenny Most opposite the Kremlin, Ustinsky Most near the Hotel Rossia and Red Square, and Krasnokholmsky Most one km south-west of Taganskaya ploshchad. Both motorboats and Raketa hydrofoils ply this route. The

motorboats leave about every 25 minutes from noon to 8.30 pm daily between about mid-April and mid-September. They take 1½ hours each way, with a one-way fare for any distance of US$1.50 on Saturdays, Sundays and holidays, US$1 other days. The Raketas are faster, more expensive and may not make all the intermediate stops – check if you want to use one.

The second line runs from Gorky Park to Kolomenskoe in the south-east, on Saturdays and Sundays only – a pleasant way to reach Kolomenskoe, one of the loveliest spots in Moscow. There are just three trips a day, which left Gorky Park at 1.45, 4.15 and 6.45 pm when we checked. The last sailing back from Kolomenskoe is at about 5.30 pm. The one-way fare is US$1.50.

Another series of routes runs along canals and lakes to villages and small towns north of Moscow, from the Northern River Station (Severny Rechnoy Vokzal) off Leningradskoe shosse in the north of the city (metro: Rechnoy Vokzal). Destinations include Chiverevo (21 km), Axakovo (32 km) and Tishkovo (36 km). There are many intermediate stops. These lines could make for an interesting exploratory outing (take food!). Schedules are posted by quays 6 to 10 at the Northern River Station; most routes are served by Raketas and continue till October.

LANGUAGE COURSES

The *Moscow Times* and *Moscow Tribune* carry small ads from tutors and colleges offering short-term Russian-language lessons, and many language schools are listed in *The Traveller's Yellow Pages Moscow* and *Where in Moscow* (see Books in this chapter's Information section). The Travellers Guest House (see Places to Stay) can also arrange classes. Several Moscow institutes and colleges run good courses of a month or more, often with accommodation available in student hostels or family homes. Sputnik (see the earlier Travel Agencies section) offers courses, usually at Moscow State University, for US$220 to US$240 a week, with accommodation in families at US$20 a night. Another place to ask is the

State Linguistic University (Gosudarstvenny Lingvistichesky Universitet; ☎ 246 28 07; fax 230 26 21) at ulitsa Ostozhenka 38, Moscow 119837 (metro: Park Kultury). Berlitz (☎ 253 82 23; fax 253 27 81) is at the International Trade Centre at Krasnopresnenskaya naberezhnaya 12 (the same complex as the Hotel Mezhdunarodnaya).

It's possible to organise courses from overseas. Enquire at universities and colleges in your home country which have Russian departments. Red Bear Tours (see the Travel Agencies section in the European Russia Getting There & Away chapter) has offered four-week small-class courses at the good Institute of Youth for around US$1000 including accommodation. Red Bear has also offered Russian politics courses in Moscow. Others who have advertised small-group or individual language courses in Moscow include The Eastern Company (☎ (0181) 566 1668), BCM Box 2022, London WC1N 3XX, England, and Kreml 2000 (☎ (0181) 544 1718), 7 Courtney Rd, Colliers Wood, London SW 19.

ORGANISED TOURS

For Kremlin tours, see the earlier Kremlin section.

Patriarchi Dom (☎ 255 41 93, ☎ & fax 255 45 15), a joint American/Russian organisation, runs a very varied and interesting programme of English-language tours in and around Moscow. Its printed programmes are fairly widely distributed in expatriate and tourist haunts. Call between 9 am and 7 pm for information, to book places and find out the starting points of tours. Two or three different tours are offered each day. Those within Moscow normally last two or three hours and cost around US$8 to US$13 per person; outside the city they are usually eight hours or more in duration and can cost anywhere from US$15 to US$48 depending on the time, distance and whether lunch is included.

Tours within Moscow cover main tourist sites including the Kremlin, Novodevichy, Kolomenskoe or the Tretyakov Gallery; neighbourhood walks in the Arbat,

Lubyanka, Prechistenka and other areas; 'theme' tours on topics such as icons, specific writers or architectural styles, Stalin's Moscow, crafts or contemporary art; and speciality tours such as the KGB Museum, *Izvestia* newspaper, Moscow State University, a Moscow school or the Red October chocolate factory. Outside Moscow, there are trips to less visited places like the Khimki Channel dacha area, Alexandrov, Peredelkino and Zvenigorod. There are also trips to more famous destinations such as Sergiev Posad, Vladimir and Suzdal, Pereslavl-Zalessky and Rostov-Veliky, Tula and Yasnaya Polyana. Patriarchi Dom can also arrange 'bespoke tours' for individuals or groups. For up to 10 people the cost is US$10 to US$12 an hour per group with guide only, or around US$20 to US$30 an hour if transport is needed (meals and admission fees extra).

The Moscow City Excursion Bureau (Moskovskoe Gorodskoe Byuro Exkursy; ☎ 924 94 46; fax 921 74 59) offers a range of over 400 tours, most available in English, to just about anywhere you could want to go in and around Moscow. Visit its office at ulitsa Rozhdestvenka 5 (metro: Lubyanka) to arrange one. There are theme trips – to places associated with literary and artistic figures such as Mikhail Bulgakov and Boris Pasternak, for example – as well as visits to particular sites. Two-hour walking tours cost US$10 per person; three to five-hour car tours in the city are US$25 to US$45 per carload; out-of-town trips are about US$7 per hour per carload, plus lunch at US$8 per person.

Intourist and Intourservice run open tours to a few main tourist sites, including daily three-hour general city tours for around US$10 per person. Prices for tours within Moscow are similar to those charged by Patriarchi Dom and the Moscow City Excursion Bureau; out-of-town trips are dearer. You can check their programmes and book at their main bureaus (see the earlier Tourist Offices section) or their desks in major hotels.

Many travel agencies and hotels offer

tours and guides for their clients. Some are cheaper than the above: Sputnik's rates for Kremlin Diamond Fund and Armoury tours, for instance, are US$15 and US$12, respectively.

PLACES TO STAY

Moscow hotels are mostly expensive for what you get, but there are exceptions – and there are economical non-hotel options too. Many hotels, plus all the hostels/guesthouses listed in this section and some homestays, can be booked before you come to Russia, either direct by fax or through a travel agency. If you're considering booking direct, and Moscow is your first stop in Russia, make enquiries several weeks in advance and ask whether the accommodation can provide visa support. For a selection of useful travel agencies, see the European Russia Getting There & Away chapter. Each agency will normally have a selection of places it can book you into, sometimes at cheaper rates than the 'off-the-street' prices given here, sometimes more expensive. Prices given in this section are those for individual foreigners. Rates in many hotels are considerably lower for groups and much lower for Russians.

If Moscow is your first stop in Russia, you should make sure your visa is registered here: this is done automatically at most accommodation places, but if you want to stay somewhere that hasn't sponsored your visa, you may have difficulties. For more details, see the Russian Visas section under Information in this chapter, and the Visas & Embassies section in European Russia Facts for the Visitor.

PLACES TO STAY – BOTTOM END

This price bracket covers places where two people can stay for up to US$55 a night. There are options all the way up from around US$14 (US$7 for one person). Where places to stay are not grouped by area (Inner North-West etc), the maps on which they appear in this chapter are given in brackets.

Private Homes

The Russian price for a bed in a private flat (usually in a twin room) is around US$7 and it's quite possible for travellers to pay this. Travellers arriving off major long-distance (particularly trans-Siberian) trains, may be approached at the station by people offering rooms. Obviously you have to be careful about security with these people – and if you're thinking of going with them, establish just how far from the city centre their flat is. Probably safer is to go with one of the people who wait in certain known places offering rooms. These people are expecting mainly Russian customers and are unlikely to be on the lookout for tourists to rip off. One place they wait is the doorway of the Hotel Kievskaya (see Hotels – Inner South-West); another is the doorway of korpus (building) 3 of the Hotel Zolotoy Kolos (see Hotels – Outer North).

One home which travellers have recommended to us is the flat of a 'kind, hospitable' English-speaking woman called *Galina* (☎ 921 60 38) at ulitsa Chaplygina 8, flat 35, 1.5 km south-west of the Yaroslavl, Leningrad and Kazan stations (Inner North-East). The address in Russian is Moscow 103062, ulitsa Chaplygina, dom 8, kv 35. Turgenevskaya and Chistye Prudy metro stations are about 750 metres west. Six beds are available at US$8 each in two rooms in this clean, comfortable flat, with bath and kitchen. Galina also provides a good, big breakfast for US$1.50 if you want it. She sometimes approaches trans-Siberian travellers arriving at the Yaroslavl Station.

The *Moscow City Excursion Bureau* (Moskovskoe Gorodskoe Byuro Exkursy; ☎ 921 41 10; fax 921 74 59), centrally located at ulitsa Rozhdestvenka 5 (Inner North), can arrange homestays for US$10 to US$15, but may need a couple of days to organise it. You can contact the bureau from other countries to make a booking and get visa support.

Another possibility is to go to a *kvartirnoe byuro*, an agency offering beds in private homes. There's one just off the lobby of the Hotel Kievskaya, which offers places in two-bed rooms in flats in the outlying Kuntsevo district, for US$7 a person. There are at least three on the ground floor of the City Air Terminal (Gorodskoy aerovokzal, Городской аэровокзал) at Leningradsky prospekt 37 (Outer North), including one at kassa (ticket window) No 1A. Prices for places in flats around the city are all about US$6 or US$7.

Moscow Bed & Breakfast (☎ & fax 457 35 08) is an agency which specialises in homestays for foreigners, with English-speaking hosts. Prices (including breakfast) are US$40 a night per person in central Moscow, or US$25/30 for singles/doubles outside the centre. Flats without a host family are also available, for US$50 or US$60 a night per flat in the centre, or US$40 away from the centre. These can accommodate up to four people. For US$20 the agency can provide visa support if you book before coming to Russia – fax your details to it. Moscow Bed & Breakfast also offers transport booking, station and airport transfers, guide/interpreter services and tours.

The Traveller's Yellow Pages Moscow lists several other homestay organisations under 'Bed & Breakfast'.

Booking from Overseas Several overseas agencies can also arrange Moscow homestays (and visas) for you. In the USA you can book for Moscow Bed & Breakfast and arrange visas through their agent Helen Kates (☎ & fax (603) 585 6534) at PO Box 221, Fitzwilliam, NH 03447. Other agencies that offer Moscow homestays include Gateway Travel, Eastern Europe Travel Bureau, Iris Hotels and Red Bear Tours (Australia); Goodwill Holidays and Zwemmer Travel (Britain); and American-International Homestays and Home & Host International (USA). Normal prices are between US$25 and US$50 a night, usually with English-speaking hosts and breakfast included; some of these companies also offer more expensive packages which include excursions, all meals, and so on.

HOFA (Host Families Association), a St Petersburg-based organisation with agents in the USA, Britain and Australia, offers B&B in Moscow for US$30/50 per single/double, with discounts for students or stays of a week, and central apartment rentals from June to August from US$30 a night or US$180 a week.

See Accommodation in the European Russia Facts for the Visitor chapter for contact details of the US agencies, and Travel Agencies in European Russia Getting There & Away for the others.

Student Dormitories

The *Moscow City Excursion Bureau* (see the preceding Private Homes section) can also arrange places in student dorms, some centrally located, for US$10. The bureau says it only uses secure dorms. It may need a couple of days to organise things.

Other student dorm possibilities may crop up but take care with security.

Hostels & Guesthouses

The *Travellers Guest House* (☎ 971 40 59, 280 85 62; fax 280 76 86; e-mail tgh@glas.apc.org) is to date the only guesthouse in Moscow that's really geared to international budget travellers. It's on floor 10 at Bolshaya Pereyaslavskaya ulitsa 50 (Inner North), four km north of the Kremlin, 1.75 km from the Yaroslavl, Leningrad and Kazan stations, and a 10-minute walk north of Prospekt Mira metro. The only sign on the building says ЦМИПКС.

Run by a joint American/Russian team, the Travellers Guest House can take up to 140 people, at US$15 for a place in a five-bed dorm, or US$30/40 for single/double rooms. Rooms are basic but clean; each shares a toilet and bathroom with one other room. There's a common room where travellers get together, a kitchen, useful notice boards, and a place to leave luggage. Part of the same operation is the travel agency IRO Travel, offering a good Russian visa support service (see Visas & Embassies in European Russia Facts for the Visitor), good international airfares, rail tickets at foreigners' prices, and trans-Siberian and Central Asia packages. Down on the 3rd floor of the building there's a bufet serving coffee, drinks and some snacks. The Travellers Guest House also sells a wide range of Lonely Planet books!

Prakash Guest House (Гостиница Пракаш; ☎ & fax 334 25 98) at Profsoyuznaya ulitsa 83 (Outer South) offers similar accommodation to the Travellers Guest House though without the communal facilities. Run by a friendly Indian team, with many guests from the subcontinent, it's 13 km from the Kremlin but just a minute's walk north of Belyaevo metro. A place in a four-bed dormitory costs US$10; singles/doubles with breakfast, TV and phone are US$30/40. Some pairs of rooms share a bathroom and toilet. Indian (vegetarian and non-vegetarian) and continental meals are available at US$5 for breakfast, US$10 for lunch or dinner. There's room for about 70 guests but it's worth ringing first to check availability. Prakash also offers visa support, domestic travel bookings and airport transfers. It's in korpus (building) 1 at Profsoyuznaya ulitsa 83: enter by the far door on the south side of this building (the side facing towards the metro). There are no signs.

If the *G&R International Centre For Education and Culture* (☎ 374 74 30; fax 374 73 66) were more conveniently located it would make a fine option, but it's ever so far from the city centre (more than 40 minutes by public transport) and at first difficult to find. A bed in a double room is US$17 per person, or US$20 including breakfast. The centre offers full visa support and registration and will arrange transport and transfers for guests; the room price includes a tour of Red Square. It's set in lovely grounds in the Institut Molodyozhi (Institute of Youth) compound; this used to be a high Komsomol school. Nearby is Park Kuskovo, with a peaceful lake and the fine estate of Count Sheremetev.

Reservations can be made directly, or through the organisation's reservation partners (which include Red Bear Tours (see Travel Agencies in European Russia Getting There & Away) in Australia) and the Russian Youth Hostel Association (see Accommodation in European Russia Facts for the Visitor). The address is ulitsa Yunosti 5/1 korpus 6, office 35. By public transport, go to metro Vykhino (southern end of the Tagansko-Krasnopresnenskaya line), then take bus No 197 or 697 (just in front of the metro) for five to seven stops – ask the driver for 'Institut Molodyozhi'.

Hotels

Hotels in the bottom price range are mostly grey places that were poor relations even in Soviet times. But if you don't mind too much about atmosphere, those listed here will provide adequate rooms, often with in-house eating options and other services. Most are in outer areas of the city but many are close to metro stations.

Inner North-West The *Hotel Tsentralnaya* (☎ 229 89 57), centrally located at Tverskaya ulitsa 10, is due to be reconstructed into a middle-range hotel, but until that happens it has good big singles/doubles for US$30/50. Rooms have washbasin only; toilets and showers are shared with other rooms in the corridor, but they're OK. Staff are not very accustomed to foreigners. Pushkinskaya and Tverskaya metros are five minutes' walk north.

Inner South-West Reception staff at the *Hotel Kievskaya* (☎ 240 12 34), by the Kiev Station at ulitsa Kievskaya 2, may try to deter you by warning that there are 'many gipsies' in the hotel – their way of saying 'beware of theft'. The hotel has singles/doubles with private bathroom for US$35/40 or US$48/50. Singles with toilet only at US$25 are OK, too. There are also singles/doubles sharing toilets on the corridor for US$13/15 or US$18/20. All rooms have phone, TV and fridge. Kievskaya metro is just down the street.

Inner South The *Hotel Varshava (Warsaw)* (☎ 238 19 70) at Kaluzhskaya ploshchad (formerly Oktyabrskaya ploshchad; metro: Oktyabrskaya) 1/2 has comfortable singles/doubles at US$45/55 (plus 25% for the first night) but won't take individuals unless they're on a business visa and have been booked in by their Russian counterpart.

Inner North-East The *Hotel Ural* (☎ 917 42 58, 227 32 89), 2.5 km east of the Kremlin at ulitsa Pokrovka (formerly ulitsa Chernyshevskogo) 40, close to the UVIR office, was about the best bottom-end hotel in inner Moscow. Sad to say, it was closed for renovations for at least a year as of mid-1995. Before closing, it had clean, decent-sized 'third-category' singles/doubles for US$18/23 with washbasin, fridge, TV and phone (showers and toilets in the corridor). Rooms with private bathroom were US$27/47 to US$33/63. The hotel has a restaurant, bar and stolovaya and they're used to foreigners here. The nearest metros are Krasnye Vorota and Kurskaya, both 750 metres away.

Outer North The *Hotel Molodyozhnaya* (Гостиница Молодёжная ☎ 210 45 65, 210 45 77; fax 210 43 11), a towering blue block at Dmitrovskoe shosse 27, eight km north of the Kremlin, was built for student and youth tourists in the Soviet era (its name means 'Youth'). Rooms are on the small side but clean. Through the main reception they cost US$32/34, but *Firma Jasmin* (☎ 210 98 29), an independent firm which runs a group of rooms on floor 20, charges lower prices for similar standards: doubles sharing bathroom and toilet with one other room for around US$17, or with private bath, phone and TV for around US$30. Take the lift to floor 20 and find their office: they may be unwilling to discuss prices over the phone. The Molodyozhnaya has a variety of average cafés, bars and restaurants. It's 400 metres north of Timiryazevskaya metro; numerous buses and trolleybuses pass by, too.

Close to Vodny Stadion metro, on the way out to Sheremetevo airport, the *Tsentralny Dom Okhotnika i Rybolova* (TsDOR, Central House of Hunters and Fishers, Централь-ный дом охотника и рыболова; ☎ 452 13 63) has clean, comfortable doubles with shower for US$30. Unexpected foreigners are viewed with some puzzlement, but they should take you. It's the red-brick building across the bus yard from the metro station – the address is Golovinskoe shosse 1A.

Behind the middle-range Hotel Kosmos, eight km north-east of the Kremlin, are a couple of cheaper but quite adequate hotels. The *Hotel Zolotoy Kolos* (Гостиница Золотой Колос; ☎ 286 27 03, 217 43 55) at ulitsa Yaroslavskaya 15 on the corner of ulitsa Kosmonavtov, offers foreigners 'first-category' singles/doubles with bathroom, phone and TV for US$26/30 the first night, US$22/27 for subsequent nights. Reception is in korpus (building) 3. *Hotel Yaroslav-skaya* (Гостиница Ярославская; ☎ 217 62 43) down the street at ulitsa Yaroslavskaya 8, is another multi-korpus place with similar first-category rooms at US$30 or US$35 (prices are the same for single or double occupancy) and other rooms ranging from US$20 to US$60. It has a restaurant in korpus 6. VDNKh metro is close.

Outer South The *Hotel Orlyonok* (Гостиница Орлёнок; ☎ 939 88 84, 939 88 53; fax 938 19 56) at ulitsa Kosygina 15 in a pleasant part of the city six km south-west of the Kremlin, used to be the main Moscow hotel for Sputnik, the Soviet youth travel outfit. But it's no longer particularly youthful or busy – or cheap unless you have a business visa and your Russian counterpart has booked you in here. In that case the rate for singles/doubles is US$18/24. Otherwise they'll only put you in the best rooms – with fine views – on floors 17 and 18, at US$32 a single or double. There are restaurants on floors 2 and 20, with main dishes around US$3 to US$7, plus a few bufety and bars. Transport is inconvenient: you need to get to Leninsky Prospekt metro then walk 20 minutes or take trolleybus No 7.

The nearby *Hotel Sputnik* (Гостиница Спутник; ☎ 938 71 06, 938 70 96) at Leninsky prospekt 38 has basic rooms with no bath, only shower, at US$22/34 for singles/doubles. Reception views foreigners with some suspicion but will probably let you in if you're willing to pay a US$17 telephone deposit! There's a restaurant. From Leninsky Prospekt metro, it's a 15-minute walk or take bus No 111 or trolleybus No 4, 33, 62 or 84.

Outer East The *Hotel Izmaylovo*, built for the 1980 Olympics at Izmaylovskoe shosse 71, nine km from the Kremlin, has about 8000 beds, which apparently makes it Europe's biggest hotel. Fortunately it's divided into six korpuses (blocks) – five for accommodation, one for entertainment – which makes the scale seem relatively human. The atmosphere is brighter than in other bottom-end hotels. The hotel is right outside Izmaylovsky Park metro.

Each block is separately run and though all the rooms – virtually identical in plan – are comfortable, modernish and a reasonable size with bathroom, TV and phone, there's some difference in prices mainly because of variations in fixtures and fittings. Cheapest is Korpus Alfa (A; ☎ 166 01 45; fax 166 00 60) with singles/doubles at US$30/40. Korpus Beta (Б; ☎ 166 27 63) has singles/doubles at US$42/54. A reasonably priced help-yourself breakfast is served in Alfa's 2nd-floor restaurant. Korpus Gamma (Г; ☎ 166 37 36) and Korpus Delta (Д; ☎ 166 41 27; fax 166 74 86) adjoin each other. Gamma's rates are US$33/46; Delta's begin at US$43 for a single and go up to US$105. Delta has an Intourist service bureau, an air ticket booking office, and several restaurants and cafés, some of which it shares with Gamma (see Places to Eat – Inexpensive & Moderate). CCTE-Intour (see Travel Agencies in European Russia Getting There & Away) has its own group of superior rooms in Delta, renovated in 1994, at US$40/50 including breakfast. Korpus Vega (B) is the most expensive block – staff say this is because it has Finnish furniture – at US$40/60 (go to the service bureau to get this price – reception quotes more). There's an international fax and telephone office in Vega.

PLACES TO STAY – MIDDLE

Double rooms in this bracket cost from US$70 to US$160, with most places towards the lower end of that range. Rooms have private bathrooms, TV and almost always phone. Many of these hotels are Soviet-era constructions, and 10 years ago they were about the best Moscow could offer. Their prices have been kept in check, and service standards pepped up a bit, by competition from the new wave of superior top-end hotels, but even so the prices foreigners have to pay often seem expensive for what you get. These hotels' foreign customers are largely middle-budget tourists and businesspeople.

City Centre

The *Hotel Moskva* (☎ 292 10 00, 292 20 08; fax 925 01 55) occupies the block between Manezhnaya ploshchad and Teatralnaya ploshchad at Okhotny ryad 2 (metro: Okhotny Ryad). Once a reserve of Communist Party apparatchiks, its atmosphere is appropriately sombre – apart from a smattering of prostitutes and pimps in the lobby – but the rooms are comfortable and the dezhurnayas are still in the old motherly-friendly mould. Singles/doubles vary from US$60/70 to US$70/80. The hotel has an Intourist service bureau and a grand but moderately priced restaurant overlooking Manezhnaya ploshchad (see Places to Eat). A reconstruction is planned.

The *Hotel Rossia* (☎ 298 54 00, 298 53 44; fax 298 55 41) at ulitsa Varvarka (formerly ulitsa Razina) 6, has over 5000 beds (but it's not Moscow's biggest hotel – that 'honour' goes to the Hotel Izmaylovo). This grotesquely enormous 1960s block, with sides 250 metres long, dwarfs the neighbouring old churches and mansions of the Kitay-Gorod, but fortunately it's set just far enough back from St Basil's Cathedral not to spoil that. Partly closed in 1994 to get rid of its cockroaches and rats, it's reputedly to be renovated and divided into four smaller hotels. In the meantime, the average-sized rooms go for US$50/70 a single/double. There are numerous bufety (one on floor 12 has great views of the Kremlin), a few restaurants, and Intourist and Intourservice service bureaus. Kitay-Gorod is the nearest metro.

Inner North

Hotel Budapest (☎ 921 10 60, 924 88 20; fax 921 12 66) at Petrovskie linii 2/18, one km north of the Kremlin (metro: Kuznetsky Most) is a comfortable medium-sized hotel, one of the best in its price range. The 125 rooms, all with cable TV, cost US$100 for singles, US$120 to US$170 for doubles, and there's a stylish restaurant.

Inner North-West

The *Hotel Intourist* (☎ 956 84 00, 956 84 44; fax 956 84 50), a landmark 22-storey slab at Tverskaya ulitsa 3/5, used to be one of the brighter places in town but has been superseded by the new wave of top-end hotels since the late 1980s. It's to be taken over by the Marriott group and there's a possibility that it will be demolished altogether to make way for a new hotel. Singles or doubles were US$155 though several travel agencies, including Intourist overseas offices, could book you in for around two-thirds of that. There are numerous restaurants, bars and cafés and an Intourservice bureau. Okhoty Ryad metro is just down the street.

Hotel Pekin (☎ 209 43 22; fax 200 14 20) at Bolshaya Sadovaya ulitsa 5 on Triumfalnaya ploshchad (formerly ploshchad Mayakovskogo; metro: Mayakovskaya) has largeish but faded singles/doubles for US$94/130. There's a Chinese restaurant.

The *Inflotel* (☎ 255 92 78; fax 253 95 78, 255 92 83) at Krasnopresnenskaya naberezhnaya 12 is actually the cruise ship *Alexandr Blok* moored on the Moscow River by the Hotel Mezhdunarodnaya. It has been here several years. Rooms (cabins) are clean, with bathroom and TV, but tiny: singles/doubles range from US$75/95 to US$143/172. There's a Greek restaurant and a bar/café. Public transport is bad: it's a one-km walk from Ulitsa 1905 Goda metro,

or the occasional bus No 4 comes along the embankment from the Kalininsky Bridge.

Inner South-West

The *Hotel Belgrad* (☎ 248 16 76; fax 230 21 29) at Smolenskaya ulitsa 8 has poky singles/doubles at US$82/92 but is functional and conveniently placed near the west end of ulitsa Arbat. The identical *Hotel Zolotoe Koltso* (Golden Ring Hotel; ☎ 248 68 43; fax 248 74 63), across the road at Smolenskaya ulitsa 5, charges US$70/80. If you book through Sputnik the rate at the Zolotoe Koltso is US$60/75. Both hotels have service bureaus and a couple of restaurants. Smolenskaya metro is just north on the Boulevard Ring but note that the entrances on either side of the road go to different lines.

The *Hotel Ukraina* (☎ 243 30 30; fax 243 30 92), a 1000-room Stalin wedding cake at Kutuzovsky prospekt 2/1 by the Kalininsky Bridge, faces the White House across the Moscow River. It's the most atmospheric and offers among the best value of the hotels in the middle range, with echoes of Stalinesque pomp in its spacious hallways and comfortable, modernised, almost stately rooms. Mostly with terrific views, these go for US$80/110 including a buffet breakfast. There are two restaurants, at least three bufety or bars, an Intourist service bureau and a business centre. Kievskaya is the nearest metro but trolleybus No 2 goes along ulitsa Novy Arbat to the Kremlin.

Inner North-East

The *Hotel Leningradskaya* (☎ 975 30 32; fax 975 18 02), another Stalin skyscraper, is at Kalanchyovskaya ulitsa 21/40 near the Leningrad, Yaroslavl and Kazan stations (metro: Komsomolskaya). It's unmodernised with singles at US$61 and doubles from US$92.

Outer North

The *Hotel Kosmos* (Гостиница Космос; ☎ 217 07 85, 217 07 86; fax 215 88 80) at prospekt Mira 150 is another Soviet monster – it has 3500 beds – eight km from the Kremlin but over the road from VDNKh metro. Rooms are US$100, single or double.

It has a big name for prostitution and there are few advantages to staying out here, except perhaps for the many in-house restaurants, the business centre and the pool. The ground-floor Vecherny Kosmos restaurant does a US$5 all-you-can-eat breakfast. Intourist has a service bureau and there's an Intourtrans transport booking desk.

Mikof-Iris Hotels, the chain of hotels at eye microsurgery clinics across Russia, has the *Hotel Mikof 1* (Гостиница Микоф 1) at Beskudnikovsky bulvar 59A, 15 km northwest of the Kremlin. Public transport is a pain – a 15-minute ride on bus No 114 or 167 from Petrovsko-Razumovskoe metro – but the city-centre shuttle bus of the neighbouring Hotel Pullman Iris (see Places to Stay – Top End) is available for US$12 return. The rooms are tasteful, modern and very clean, with singles/doubles for US$62/80 including breakfast. The hotel is on floor 4 of the 'Pansionat' building at the clinic; there's a restaurant on floor 8. You'll see patients with patches over their eyes walking around other floors! The cheaper *Hotel Mikof 2* (Гостиница Микоф 2), with doubles at US$100 in another block at the same address, was temporarily shut for renovation when we visited. You may get lower rates for both places if you book through overseas agents such as Iris Hotels (see Travel Agencies in the European Russia Getting There & Away chapter). In Russia you should make an advance reservation through the Mikof-Iris office (☎ 483 04 60; fax 485 59 54) in suite 266 at Beskudnikovsky bulvar 59A (in a different block from the hotel). It's hardly worth the trouble of organising a stay out here if you're already in Moscow, but if you've been booked in from overseas, the accommodation is good.

Outer South

Out at Leninsky prospekt 146, 13 km from the Kremlin, is the *Tsentralny Dom Turista* (Central Tourist House, Центральный дом туриста; ☎ 438 55 10; fax 434 31 97), once the flagship hotel of Soviet trade union tourism. Rooms are clean and functional, with TV, phone, fridge and private bathrooms, and cost US$42/63 for singles/doubles. The hotel has a service bureau and a handful of restaurants and cafés. From Yugo-Zapadnaya metro, take any bus, or trolleybus No 62 or 84, two stops up ulitsa 26 Bakinskikh Komissarov.

The 2000-bed *Hotel Salyut* (Гостиница Салют; ☎ 438 63 65) at Leninsky prospekt 158 is even further – 16 km – from the centre but it's not a bad place, relatively well priced at US$80/100 for clean, comfortable singles/doubles. Sputnik offers about 25% off these prices. The hotel has a service bureau, several eateries, and a pool and massage room. From Yugo-Zapadnaya metro, take bus No 227, 250, 281 or 502 two stops south along prospekt Vernadskogo.

PLACES TO STAY – TOP END

Moscow's top-end hotels offer international standards of comfort and service that barely existed before the late 1980s. Nearly all are new since then, or are older hotels that have undergone dramatic upgradings. Most are run by Western hotel chains such as Renaissance, Inter-Continental, Marco Polo, Radisson, Kempinski and Pullman, and you can book these through their offices abroad. Businesspeople make up the overwhelming majority of the clientele. Prices range from the high to the stratospheric. Expect satellite and/or cable TV, international direct-dial phones, air-con, minibars and room service in very comfortable modern or modernised rooms, and a range of expensive restaurants, shops, bars and services. Many hotels have health clubs or exercise rooms with pool, sauna, massage and the like.

Those without bottomless expense accounts can usually sample the atmosphere of privilege by visiting the shops in these hotels' lobbies or – for a few dollars – taking a coffee and cake at one of their cafés.

City Centre

The *Hotel National* (☎ 258 70 00; fax 258 71 00) at Okhotny ryad 14/1 occupies the choicest location of all Moscow hotels, facing the Kremlin across Manezhnaya ploshchad, at the foot of Tverskaya ulitsa (metro: Okhotny Ryad). Built in 1903, its chandeliers and frescoed ceilings survived the revolution and the hotel remained one of Moscow's best until the 1980s. It's now decidedly back in that category after a four-year renovation. It makes much of its historical associations: H G Wells, Henri Barbusse, Anatole France, John Reed and, of course, Lenin slept here (though there are arguments about where V I spent the night: it's down to room 101, 107 or 115). The National is on a relatively modest scale with 231 rooms and suites. It's owned by the city of Moscow and its management team is supervised by consultants from Forte Hotels, led by Swen Vermilen, who headed up the team responsible for St Petersburg's Grand Hotel Europe – Russia's first (many say best) five-star hotel. The National also has the smilingest staff we've ever seen in a Russian hotel – even the security guards are polite and friendly.

The luxury doubles in the old wing (US$420 to US$460) are actually slightly smaller than the standard doubles (US$350 to US$390) in the new, but warrant the higher tariff because their views into Red Square are spectacular; many bedroom windows stare right at St Basil's. The four National Suites (US$1200) are the prime property here.

Single rooms are leased out on long-term contracts, and are not generally available. The hotel has four restaurants (including the Moscow branch of Maxim's of Paris), several bars, an atrium café and all the perks, including a small pool, whirlpool and health club.

The *Hotel Metropol* (☎ 927 60 00; fax 927 60 10) at Teatralny proezd 1, opposite the Bolshoy Theatre (metro: Ploshchad Revolyutsii), is another pre-Revolutionary hotel, restored to past glories a few years before the National. Bedecked with art nouveau décor, it has 400 rooms and suites, large lobbies and lounges, a beautiful main dining hall and two other restaurants. Singles/doubles are US$340/390 and up. The Metropol is one of the Inter-Continental Hotels Group.

Inner North

The *Hotel Savoy* (☎ 929 85 00, 929 85 58; fax 230 21 86), very centrally located at ulitsa Rozhdestvenka 3 (metro: Lubyanka), was the first of Moscow's new-wave luxury hotels when it reopened in 1989. Founded as a top-line hotel in 1912, it sank to second-class status under the name Berlin in Soviet times, before being restored in the late 1980s. The gilt, murals and chandeliers maintain the atmosphere of pre-Revolution-ary privilege. There are just 86 rooms and suites, with the cheapest singles/doubles going for US$350/380 (including buffet breakfast). There's a business centre too. The bars and restaurant are reserved for residents. The hotel is owned by an Intourist-Finnair joint venture and you can book through Finnair.

The *Moscow Olympic Penta Renaissance Hotel* (Olympic Penta for short; ☎ 931 90 00; fax 931 90 20) at Olimpiysky prospekt 18, four km north of the Kremlin, was built for the 1980 Olympics, as was the enormous indoor Olympic Sports Complex across the road. It was upgraded with Lufthansa's help around 1990 and is now German-run. The 500 rooms and suites cost from US$314/363 for singles/doubles. Thanks to its athletic origins, the hotel boasts probably the best hotel fitness club in Moscow, with a 22-metre pool. There's a range of quality eateries. Prospekt Mira metro is 10 minutes' walk east.

Inner North-West

The *Hotel Tverskaya* at Tverkskaya ulitsa 24 between the Boulevard and Garden Rings (metro: Mayakovskaya), two km from the Kremlin, is one of the international Best Western chain, scheduled over-optimisti-cally to open in 1995. You can get info and book through Best Western reservation centres worldwide.

A further 1.25 km out at 1-ya Tverskaya-Yamskaya ulitsa 19 (metro: Belorusskaya), the *Palace Hotel* (☎ 956 31 52; fax 956 31 51) has singles/doubles at US$338/412 including buffet breakfast. But overseas agencies, including Intourist branches, can often book you in for significantly less. One of the Austrian Marco Polo Hotels group, it's in smart modern style, with 221 rooms and suites, and some top-class restaurants (see Places to Eat – Expensive).

A smaller Marco Polo hotel, with just 64 rooms and slightly less luxurious, is the *Marco Polo Presnya Hotel* (☎ 202 03 81; fax 230 27 04) at Spiridonevsky pereulok 9 in the quiet Patriarch's Pond area two km north-west of the Kremlin. Singles are US$227 to US$246, doubles US$270. Nearest metros are Tverskaya and Pushkinskaya.

The city's longest-serving top-end hotel is the business-oriented *Hotel Mezhdunarodnaya-1* (☎ 253 13 91; fax 253 24 00) at Krasnoprenenskaya naberezhnaya 12, beside the Moscow River 3.5 km west of the Kremlin. Known as 'the Mezh' to its friends, it was built around 1980 with the International Trade Centre which adjoins it. The style is modern Western, the 300-odd rooms comfortable but not huge, the restaurants, bars and shops numerous. The lobby sports a fountain, panoramic glass lifts and some very obvious prostitutes. Singles/doubles are US$205/238 in July and August, US$228/264 at other times. The *Mezhdunarodnaya-2* at the north end of the complex is an apartment hotel, more expensive. Transport is poor: it's a one-km walk from Ulitsa 1905 Goda metro.

Inner South-West

The bright, American-managed *Radisson Slavyanskaya Hotel* (☎ 941 80 20; fax 941 80 00) is 3.5 km west of the Kremlin at Berezhkovskaya naberezhnaya 2 by the Kiev station (metro: Kievskaya). It's almost a village in itself with spacious lounge areas, a big business centre, its own shopping mall, a host of cafés and restaurants (see Places to Eat), and a big pool. Several foreign news organisations have offices here and there's an international press club, too. There are 430 rooms and suites, with standard singles/doubles at US$277/301.

Inner South

The *Hotel Baltschug Kempinski* (☎ 230 65 00;

fax 230 65 02) is on the Moscow River bank, opposite the Kremlin at ulitsa Balchug 1. Opened in 1992 after a total reconstruction of a turn-of-the-century hotel, it has 234 rooms from around US$380 to US$425, suites from US$705 to US$1600, two restaurants and a business centre. Breakfast is reputedly the best in Moscow. Tretyakovskaya metro is 750 metres south.

One of the most interesting top-end choices is the 111-room *Danilovsky Hotel* (☎ 954 05 03; fax 954 07 50) at Bolshoy Starodanilovsky pereulok 5, 4.5 km south of the Kremlin (metro: Tulskaya). This belongs to the Moscow Patriarchate of the Russian Orthodox Church, and is located in the grounds of the Danilov Monastery, the Church's headquarters. It operates as a normal hotel and has quite a flow of tourists. Opened in 1991, it's modern and elegant, with singles/doubles at US$200/230. There's a good, not too expensive Russian and international restaurant, a bar, a communications centre and an Intourservice bureau. Reception advises faxing two weeks in advance for a reservation.

Outer North

The *Moscow Aerostar Hotel* (Гостиница Аэростар Москва; ☎ 213 90 00; fax 213 90 01), Canada's entry in the Moscow hotel game, is fairly conveniently placed six km from the Kremlin at Leningradsky prospekt 37, on the road in from Sheremetevo airport. There are 415 rooms, three restaurants (lunch buffet in the Café Taiga is relatively economical at US$16) and friendly service. Singles/doubles are US$264/314 and up, including buffet breakfast.

The French-run *Hotel Pullman Iris* (Гостиница Пульман Ирис; ☎ 488 80 00; fax 906 01 05) is a long way from the centre, 15 km out at Korovinskoe shosse 10 – convenient for Sheremetevo airport if nothing else. Built in grounds next to an eye surgery clinic, it's constructed in a sort of upright half-oval shape to maintain the eye theme, with an atrium inside. The hotel's ambience is stylishly French. There are 195 rooms and suites, with standard singles/doubles at

US$230/ 275, plus a restaurant and coffee shop. There's a free hourly shuttle bus to/from the city centre.

At Sheremetevo-2 airport itself is the 500-room *Novotel* (☎ 578 91 10; fax 578 27 94), also with French eateries and a city-centre shuttle bus. Singles/doubles are around US$180/200.

PLACES TO STAY – APARTMENT RENTALS

If you're staying in Moscow a while, you can cut costs sharply by renting your own apartment. There are many available all over the city at all sorts of prices, and lots of agencies – some Western-run – ready to rent them to you. Ask around, check the ads in the *Moscow Times* and *Moscow Tribune*, or consult the 'Apartments' section of *Where in Moscow*. Security should be a factor in your choice of apartment.

PLACES TO EAT

Thanks mainly to foreign incomers, Moscow now has a fairly wide range of good eateries that have decent service and aren't a pain to get into. Some – McDonald's and other fast-food outlets among them – are a positive delight if you've been wandering the culinary wastes of provincial Russia. Pricewise, though Moscow is far from a budget eater's paradise, there are enough places where you can feed well for a few dollars. There are also lots of costly places, some of which are worth the money if you want to dine in style. Disappointingly, though you can enjoy dozens of foreign cuisines here, there's rather a scarcity of good, reasonably priced Russian restaurants.

At some popular restaurants, reservations are advisable for dinner but you can usually get into the same places for lunch or an early evening meal (6 or 6.30 pm) without booking. We've indicated in the following pages where bookings are advisable. These can usually be made fairly easily by phone. Someone will normally speak at least some English; otherwise, a little Russian can go a long way – see the Food section in the European Russia Facts for the Visitor chapter for some useful phrases. Some of the more expensive restaurants add 23% VAT to your bill – prices given here include such add-ons but not any tips you may feel inclined to give.

Almost all the hotels mentioned in the Places to Stay section have restaurants where you can get a fair (or better) meal at most times of day. These are mentioned in this section only if they're worth going out of your way for.

Self-Catering

You can cut costs considerably by buying some of your own food and drinks in shops and markets, which nowadays are well stocked. You can shop in Russian food shops, Western supermarkets, or several food markets dotted around the city.

Russian Food Shops These are everywhere, and range from street stalls to big supermarkets. They are often well stocked and with fair prices, but in some you still have to contend with the archaic Soviet-style system of queueing three times – once to find out the price of what you want, once to pay for it, and once to collect it. Fortunately the queues aren't too long any more. Many Russian shops sell packaged imports as well as Russian food. One of the best Russian food stores is the Novoarbatsky Gastronom at ulitsa Novy Arbat 13, underneath the Arbat Irish House (see below).

Supermarkets You can get all the familiar packaged goods from back home at Western-run supermarkets, and they're easy places to cope with, but you're paying import prices. There are lots of them, and more and more are staying open 24 hours a day. Some of the best and most convenient are:

Arbat Irish House, ulitsa Novy Arbat 13 (Inner South-West; metro: Arbatskaya)
Foodland, Sadko Arcade (Inner North-West; nearest metro: Ulitsa 1905 Goda)
Garden Ring Supermarket, Bolshaya Sadovaya ulitsa 1 (Inner North-West; metro: Mayakovskaya)
Sadko, Bolshaya Dorogomilovskaya 16 (Inner South-West; metro: Kievskaya)

Stockmann, ulitsa Zatsepsky Val 4/8 (Inner South; metro: Paveletskaya)

Markets Moscow's food markets (*rynky*) are full of interest as well as fruit, vegetables, cheese, honey and meat. Many of the traders and their goods are from former southern republics of the Soviet Union. Take your own bag. Prices are good if you bargain a bit – and keep an eye on the quality of the items that are being popped into your bag. The most central markets are:

Danilovsky Market, Mytnaya ulitsa 74 (Inner South; metro: Tulskaya)
Rizhsky Market, prospekt Mira 94-96 (Outer North; metro: Rizhskaya)
Dorogomilovsky Market, ulitsa Mozhaysky Val 10, with an overflow section along Kievskaya ulitsa to the Kiev Station (Inner South-West; metro: Kievskaya)

The real Central Market (Tsentralny rynok) on Tsvetnoy bulvar (Inner North; metro: Tsvetnoy Bulvar) is under reconstruction for what looks as though it may be years.

PLACES TO EAT – INEXPENSIVE & MODERATE

This section covers places where you can get a meal for US$15 or less (often much less).

City Centre

GUM *Rostik's*, upstairs at the north end of GUM on Red Square, is good for quick

grilled chicken. Order from the cashier at the entrance, pick up your order from the counter, and sit at a table to eat. Three pieces of chicken plus chips, salad and a bread roll will set you back just US$3. Hours are 10 am to 10 pm daily. Also in GUM, at the far (south) end is *Kafe Kopakabana*, serving burgers or salads for US$2 and hot chocolate for US$1. There are a few other snack and drink places in GUM: you can get a good coffee in the upstairs *Business Centre*, halfway along the Red Square side.

Hotels The *Hotel Moskva* has a grandiose green-pillared, high-ceilinged restaurant overlooking Manezhnaya ploshchad, with reasonable fare, service and prices. At lunchtimes part of it is given over to the *Stol Russkoy Kukhni*, a US$5 help-yourself Russian buffet – nothing spectacular but you can fill up. In the main part of the restaurant, zakuski range from US$0.50 to US$3.50, and most fish, chicken or meat main courses are US$1.50 to US$4. You need to start with a couple of zakuski to assuage any real hunger. Hours are 8 to 10 am, noon to 5 pm, and 6 to 10 pm. To find the restaurant, take the lift on the right side of the hotel lobby as you enter.

Also in the Hotel Moskva building, but most easily entered from Manezhnaya ploshchad, is the popular *Rincon Español* (☎ 292 28 93), which serves good Spanish

---

Home Delivery

There are currently at least three pizza delivery services in Moscow, all doing pies in the US$15 to US$20 range.

Pizza Express (☎ 198 60 73, 943 6317), a new American entry, promises to serve New York City-style pizza (which, as we all know, has been scientifically proven to be the world's best). Delivery is free, and prices range from US$15 to US$18 for thin-crust pies. It's open Sunday to Thursday from 11 am to 10 pm, Friday and Saturday from 11 am to midnight.

Jack's (☎ 956 61 96) does thicker crust pies and a limited selection of other Italian dishes in about the same price range. It's open Monday to Friday from 4 to 10 pm, Saturday and Sunday from 11 am to 10 pm.

Pizza Hut (☎ 229 90 13) delivers its stuff as well. Hours and prices are as in the restaurant, with a minimum order of US$30. ■

food – and potent sangria – from noon to midnight. Most main meat dishes are US$8 to US$14. Musicians liven things up in the evening.

For a snack with a view, head up to the bufet at the west end of floor 12 of the *Hotel Rossia*, which has a great panorama of the Kremlin. A few reasonable, inexpensive hot and cold snacks are available. There's a *Baskin-Robbins* ice-cream place on the outside of the hotel's west side.

Inner North

Around TsUM *Restoran Iberia* (☎ 928 26 72) at ulitsa Rozhdestvenka 5, half a block behind the Hotel Savoy, is a pleasant, clean Georgian restaurant, where a meal with a drink costs around US$15. It's open from noon to 5 pm and 6 to 11 pm. See the entry on U Mamy Zoi in Inner South-West for more on Georgian food. On the corner of ulitsa Rozhdestvenka and Pushechnaya ulitsa is the new *Pizzeria Ca Pizza*, doing good salads, vegetarian dishes and omelettes in the US$3 range, and pizza slices for US$2.50.

Inside TsUM, you can get a quick but ordinary bite of pizza, bliny or grilled chicken for US$2 to US$3.50 at *Pitstsa Bystro* on floors 3 and 4.

Behind TsUM on the corner of ulitsa Kuznetsky Most and Neglinnaya ulitsa, *Rokki* serves up good portions of burgers, fish & chips, chilli con carne and the like in Americanised surroundings for US$8 to US$11. It has a bar, too.

Bolshaya Dmitrovka Ulitsa If you're looking for a very cheap meal, wander up Bolshaya Dmitrovka ulitsa (formerly Pushkinskaya ulitsa). This street has several very plain Russian eateries where you can feed adequately. One of the first places you come to heading up the street from Okhotny ryad, *Kafe Sadko*, is actually a cut above the others, with waiters, individually prepared food, and drinks: a bifshteks, chicken or fish main course is around US$5. *Oladyi*, further up the street, is a small stand-up place

serving excellent small bliny with sour cream and berries – a great snack at US$0.40 for four. Almost opposite, with separate doors in the same building, are *Zelyonyu Ogonyok*, a stand-up stolovaya where salad, soup and main course costs about US$1.50, and *Shokoladnaya*, a sit-down place with more appetising food (order from the friendly women in the kitchen): a selection such as chicken and mashed potato, a small tomato salad, bread roll, slivki (cream dessert), two éclairs and a drink is around US$3. Both these places are open from 8 am to 8 pm daily. The basement *Pivnoy Bar* (Beer Bar) at the corner of Stoleshnikov pereulok is a shabby dive but with a respectable (all-male) clientele. Open from 9 am to 8 pm, it serves half-litre mugs of Russian beer for US$0.25.

Artistico's (☎ 292 40 42) is the proverbial 'lovely little Italian place I know quite near here'; it's a great place for an intimate evening. The place has been a restaurant since pre-Revolutionary times, and there's a fantastic ceiling mural (that's been restored, changing some of the frowns to smiles). The specialities are definitely Italian, as is the atmosphere. Main pasta dishes average US$10 to US$12, specialities (such as Bistecca alla Pizzaiola are pricey at about US$22, but chicken dishes average US$12. Make reservations for the evening. It's off Bolshaya Dmitrovka ulitsa on Kamergersky pereulok (formerly proezd Khudozhest-vennogo Teatra), though the address is Bolshaya Dmitrovka ulitsa 5/6.

Another good place to eat in this part of town is *Kafe Stoleshniki* (☎ 229 20 50), which also calls itself *Uncle Guilly's* after a Russian writer called Gilyarovsky. It's off Bolshaya Dmitrovka ulitsa at Stoleshnikov pereulok 6. Though the steakhouse here falls within our Expensive category, there's also a small bar where good food is served at half-a-dozen tables: a chef's salad costs US$10, steaks US$12 to US$18, burgers and sandwiches around US$8 to US$9. Hours of opening are noon to midnight. A reservation may be useful if you want to be sure of a table after about 7 pm.

Prospekt Mira If you're staying at the Travellers Guest House, two places on prospekt Mira opposite the orange line entrance of Prospekt Mira metro station are handy. From 10 am to 10 pm daily, *Kombi's* (Комби'с) at prospekt Mira 46 serves up subs (long sandwich rolls) and croissants with a big choice of fillings for US$3 to US$5, small tubs of salad for US$0.50 to US$1.50, plus cakes, milk shakes, coffee and beer. It's a bright place, one of four Kombi's around the city, good for breakfast or a bite later. *Flamingo* next door at No 48, a waiter-service place open from 1 pm to midnight, serves chicken in a variety of ways – grilled, fried, tabaka (spicy Georgian-style), Rus (Russian), Kentaki (Kentucky) or shashlyk – for US$6 to US$8, plus an eclectic range of starters including khumos (hummus), tabouli, soups and salads for US$2 to US$4.

Moscow's fourth *McDonald's* is to open in the brick building next to the Prospekt Mira metro station.

Tsvetnoy Bulvar Near the Old Circus and Tsvetnoy Bulvar metro, *Gril-Bar Annushka* at Tsvetnoy bulvar 7 does fair portions of grilled chicken for US$0.60 from 11 am to 10 pm daily. There are soup, salads and lavash (Georgian flat bread), too.

Inner North-West
Tverskaya Ulitsa and Nearby This busy thoroughfare and its immediate environs have several good fast-food and other easy eating options. The *Hotel Intourist* at Tverskaya ulitsa 3 has numerous eateries. The most straightforward – but very ordinary – option was the serve-yourself buffet in the Tourist's Hall on floor 2. For US$5 at breakfast (7.30 to 10.30 am) and US$10 at lunch (noon to 3 pm) you could eat all you wanted, though there wasn't very much that you'd go back for more of.

Directly in front of the Hotel Intourist, the wonderful *Patio Pizza* chain has built yet another pleasant Italian place, this one open 24 hours. They do the same as the rest of the Patio chain (see Inner South-West), for the same prices, and they lost money on Nick at

the all-you-can-eat salad bar for US$7. They also serve a breakfast buffet (all you can eat) from 5 to 10.30 am for US$9.

Kombi's at No 4, opposite the Hotel Intourist, is good for subs and filled croissants from 10 am to 10 pm daily. Menu and prices are the same as at Kombi's on prospekt Mira (see Inner North).

La Kantina (☎ 292 53 88) at No 5, a few steps up the street from the Hotel Intourist, is a Tex-Mex place of jolly atmosphere and middling cuisine. It's always busy. Starters such as nachos, guacamole and corn chips, or chilli con carne are about US$6; main dishes, which include fajitas, spare ribs, chicken and enchiladas, are mostly US$12 to US$15.

McDonald's has two places just steps off Tverskaya ulitsa. One is at Gazetny pereulok (formerly ulitsa Ogaryova) 17/9, facing the Central Telegraph; the other, one km further up at Bolshaya Bronnaya ulitsa 29 on Pushkinskaya ploshchad, was Russia's original McDonald's (opened in 1990). It has a large outside terrace, good for watching the crowds in summer; though the days are gone of half-km queues and opportunists reselling hour-old Big Macs at Moscow's markets, this is still reckoned the world's busiest restaurant, getting through 30,000 or more customers a day. Russian McDonald's outlets serve the same fare as everywhere else: the price lists are in Russian but the staff can take your order in English. A plain hamburger is US$0.85; a Big Mac with a big portion of chips is US$3. Both branches are open from 9 am (10 am on Saturday and Sunday) to 10 pm.

Between the two McDonald's, *Pizza Hut*, at Tverskaya ulitsa 12, does one-person pizzas for US$4.50 to US$8, two-person pizzas for US$6.50 to US$14, and a three/four-person size for US$10 to US$19. It's open from 11 am to 10 pm daily. It also has a takeaway slice bar from 11 am to 8 pm, (US$1.50 a slice), and you can call ☎ 229 90 13 for free delivery.

Just north of the eastern part of Pushkinskaya ploshchad, *Bistro*, a café at Malaya Dmitrovka ulitsa (formerly ulitsa

Chekhova) 6, does fair soups (US$2.25), shashlyk and chicken tabaka (around US$5) from noon to 10 pm.

The café in the *Muzey Revolyutsii* at Tverskaya ulitsa 21, just north of Pushkinskaya ploshchad, has good snacks and light hot dishes up to US$3.25. It's open from 11 am to 5 pm daily.

Gam or Chiz? – How to Read a Moscow McDonald's Menu

гамбургер
hamburger

двойной (тройной) гамбургер
double (triple) hamburger

чизбургер
cheeseburger

биг мак
Big Mac

филе-о-фиш
fillet-o'-fish

(большая) порция картофеля фри
(big) portion of chips

яблочный пирожок
apple pie

БИГ МАК

Patriarch's Pond Area In the quiet Patriarch's Pond area about 750 metres west of Pushkinskaya ploshchad, *Moskovskie Zory* (☎ 299 57 25) at Maly Kozikhinsky pereulok 11 is a good small Russian restaurant, with a little outdoor area where a couple of tables are set in summer. Service is good and the atmosphere pleasant – reservations are advised for dinner (opening hours are noon to 11 pm daily, bookings are taken from 10 am to 1 pm). The good, fresh zakuski are the highlight – choices such as ovoshchie naturalnye (fresh vegetables), mushrooms dishes or caviar are mostly US$6 to US$12, though soup is just US$1.50. Main courses – such as beef Stroganoff, pelmeni, or bifshteks – are uninspired but sizeable at US$5 to US$7.50.

Right across the street from Patriarch's Pond, on the corner of Malaya Bronnaya ulitsa and Maly Kozikhinsky pereulok, is *Kafe Margarita*, popular with a studenty, artsy crowd in the evenings, when there's a US$1 entry fee and sometimes live music. Food is mostly light but presentable; stuffed tomatoes (pomidory farshirovannye), and bliny with mushrooms (s gribami) or caviar (s ikroy) are among the choices, all around US$4 to US$5. There's champagne, brandy and so on, too.

Kafe Begemot a block south at Spiridonevsky pereulok 10 is a pleasant, small café with meat and vegetable zakuski from US$1 to US$1.75 and main meat dishes for US$3 or US$4.

Triumfalnaya Ploshchad This square (formerly ploshchad Mayakovskogo), where Tverskaya ulitsa crosses the Garden Ring, is home to several good Western-style eateries, all within steps of Mayakovskaya metro. Turn left at the top of the metro escalator and cross the street from the exit to the *American Bar & Grill* (☎ 251 79 99), one of Moscow's very best restaurants for all-round value. Open 24 hours, it efficiently and smilingly serves up just what you'd expect in any self-respecting restaurant of its kind in the West – which makes it outstanding in Moscow. You can't get a better start to a

Moscow day (or end to a Moscow night) than an ABG breakfast, served from 4 to 11 am (to 12.30 pm Saturday and Sunday): a generous plate of eggs, fried potatoes and toast, with a bottomless cup of coffee, is US$5 or US$6. At other times there are burgers or burritos at US$6 to US$9, salads at US$5 to US$10, barbecued chicken or pork ribs around US$14, steaks around US$22. Bookings are useful for dinner. The address is 1-ya Tverskaya-Yamskaya ulitsa 2/1, though it's actually just off that street.

Next door to the American Bar & Grill is a branch of the good subs-and-croissants chain *Kombi's*, open from 10 am to 10 pm, with the same menu and prices as at the prospekt Mira branch (see Inner North).

A few steps down Tverskaya ulitsa towards the city centre is the Moscow branch of *Restoran Tandoor* (☎ 209 55 65), a terrific Indian restaurant run by the folks who run the one of the same name in St Petersburg. Everything's good, but order chicken well done. Starters, including their great veg samosa, cost about US$3, fish about US$7, Tandoori chicken US$10, and other chicken and lamb dishes from US$7 to US$15. There's an extensive vegetarian selection priced from US$4 to US$8. The Tandoor takes all major credit cards, and it's best to reserve for the evenings. It's open from 11 am to 11 pm every day. A few doors down on the same side of the street, *Baku* is a stand-up and takeaway Lebanese place (there's also a sit-down restaurant) that gives you a filling meal of falafel and salad for less than US$2. Go left as you enter to sit down, or to the right for the stand-up café.

A short distance north of Triumfalnaya ploshchad, *Patio Pasta* (☎ 251 58 61) at 1-ya Tverskaya-Yamskaya ulitsa 1/3 is from the same stable as the excellent Patio Pizza (see Inner South-West), with the same unlimited salad bar for US$7. Pasta dishes are US$5 to US$15, with spaghetti Bolognese at US$5 for a generous plateful. It's open from noon to midnight.

Krasnaya Presnya Moscow's top Tex-Mex specialist is the hugely popular *Restaurant Santa Fe* (☎ 256 21 26), at Mantulinskaya ulitsa 5/1, stroenie (building) 6, at the entrance to Krasnaya Presnya Park, four km from the Kremlin. Good service and big portions of tasty food are its merry recipe. It's a big place but if you want an evening table you should still make a reservation, go early, or be prepared to wait for as long as an hour. Fortunately there's a bar and lounge where you can wait if you have to. Appetisers such as quesadillas, black bean soup or gazpacho run from US$3 to US$8, salads are US$4 to US$14, burgers US$6 to US$10, and most main courses US$10 to US$14 (steaks are US$22). The Santa Fe is open from noon to 4 am. From Ulitsa 1905 Goda metro it's quite a pleasant one-km walk in daylight, or you can take bus No 12, tram No 23 or trolleybus No 18, 54 or 66, which go down ulitsa Tryokhgorny Val, then along Shmitovsky proezd, one block north of Mantulinskaya ulitsa. The restaurant will provide a free ride back to the metro after you have eaten.

In the same area is the *Sadko Arcade*, a complex of Western shops and restaurants at Krasnopresnenskaya naberezhnaya 14, one km west along the river embankment from the Hotel Mezhdunarodnaya. There are several popular restaurants here, with something to suit most tastes, if not quite every pocket (see also Places to Eat – Expensive). Most are open from around noon to 11 pm daily. The easiest way to reach Sadko Arcade is by taxi, though the walk along the river from the Mezhdunarodnaya is nice enough in daylight. Alternatively, you can follow the directions for the Santa Fe, then continue south through the park and turn right along the embankment. The majority of eateries are through the back of the arcade: on the way through are a couple of great patisserie/cafés with slices of cake/gateau for US$2.50-plus. The best priced place in the arcade, through the back, is the *Chicken Grill*, where reasonable portions of grilled chicken cost US$3 and chips US$0.90; nearby are *Pizza Pazza* with pizzas for US$8 to US$17 and an all-you-can-eat salad bar for US$8, and a German *Beer House* with varieties of sausage from US$8 to US$12, grilled pork knuckle (a speciality) around US$18, plus apple strudel and big mugs of beer.

Inner South-West

Ulitsa Novy Arbat *Bar Shamrock*, upstairs in the Irish House supermarket building at ulitsa Novy Arbat 13 (the first high-rise block as you come from Arbatskaya metro), is a friendly Irish bar serving toasted sandwiches and beef & bean or chilli & cheese burritos for US$3, and other bar food, alongside its US$4 mugs of Guinness. It's open from 11 am to midnight. Football hooligans from all nations and stations of life congregate along the street on the far side, at the *Sports Bar*, at ulitsa Novy Arbat 10, a real American place where large-screen TVs blare out five or so channels of sport. The food's very good: Maryland crab cakes (US$8), vegetables with blue-cheese dip (US$9) and spicy chicken wings (US$8.50, two-for-one on Tuesdays) are good bar snacks, while more substantial burgers (US$8 to US$10) and steaks (US$17) satisfy the most demanding carnivore. There are US$2 (real) pints of Heineken draft on Wednesday from noon to 5 am and every day from 6 to 8 pm. The *Palms Coffee Shop* in the Tsentr Valday in the east end of the Irish House building is a good, clean place with a variety of eats from snacks such as vegetable cutlets (kotlety ovoshchnye) or masala samosa at US$3 or US$4 to main platters for up to US$10.

Ulitsa Arbat *Restoran San Marco Pizzeria*, about 300 metres along the Arbat from Arbatskaya metro, is a busy place serving up respectable pizza and pasta in the US$6 to US$12 range. Further along, *Kafe Rosa* and *Kafe Rioni* both do hot dishes for US$3 to US$4, plus snacks and small salads.

Bar Italian Pizzeria, towards the west end of the street, is a nice place with a large pavement café in summer and pizzas which average US$8 to US$12. It's run by the same folks who bring you *Bar Italian Restaurant* just a bit further down the street, which is

more expensive, but popular. Lunch is US$17, and there are outdoor tables in summer. Opposite, the Gruzia Tsentr (Georgian Centre) contains the reasonably priced Georgian *Restoran Mziuri*.

At No 50-52, almost at the end of the street, is a big *McDonald's*. Prices and hours – 9 am (10 am on Saturday and Sunday) to 10 pm – are the same as at Moscow's other McDonald's (see Inner North-West). Smolenskaya is the nearest metro.

West of the River There's a *Pizza Hut*, one of the world's biggest, at Kutuzovsky prospekt 17, about 700 metres west of the Hotel Ukraina. It has the same hours and prices as the Tverskaya ulitsa Pizza Hut (see Inner North-West), and a takeaway section too.

Most of the many eateries in the Radisson Slavyanskaya Hotel come into the Expensive category, but the *Skandia Restaurant* in the hotel's mall does buffet breakfasts from 7.30 to 11 am for US$10 (continental) or US$15 (hot).

Kievskaya is the nearest metro to both these places.

Near the Pushkin Fine Arts Museum *Patio Pizza* (☎ 201 50 00) at ulitsa Volkhonka 13 almost opposite the museum (metro: Kropotkinskaya) is Moscow's best Italian eatery for all-round value. Go for lunch or an early dinner to avoid queues. Vegetarians thrive on the US$6 all-you-can-eat salad bar (go back for more as many times as you like), while the pizzas, mostly at US$5 to US$10, are plenty for one person and enough for two who aren't especially hungry. There's also lasagne, spaghetti and trout from US$6 to US$8. Service is good and there's a bit of a buzz in the atmosphere of the greenery-surrounded, glassed-in patio. Hours are noon to midnight daily.

More a place to drink than eat, but one of the most convivial spots in Moscow, is *Rosie O'Grady's* on the corner of ulitsa Znamenka (formerly ulitsa Frunze) and Maly Znamensky pereulok (formerly ulitsa Marxa i Engelsa). This real Irish pub is always busy with a mainly foreign crowd that spills out into the street whenever the weather's not unbearable. A 'pint' of Guinness (actually 0.4 litres, three-quarters of a pint) is US$5.25. There are sandwiches (US$3.25) and snacks which include Irish stew (US$5.60), and a hot roast-beef lunch on Sunday. It's open from noon to 1 am (to midnight on Sunday). Borovitskaya is the nearest metro.

A Georgian treat lies in store if you can find *U Mamy Zoi* on Barykovsky pereulok. Georgia has a unique, spicy, semi-Middle Eastern cuisine that does justice to both meat and vegetables ('real food', as one relieved trans-Siberian traveller uttered on reaching U Mamy Zoi. If you're not going to Georgia you should sample it in Moscow. Try to get to U Mamy Zoi, one of the city's most enjoyable Georgian restaurants, by about 7 pm if you don't want to wait for a table. At kiosks outside the nearby Kropotkinskaya metro station you can buy bottles of wine to take to the restaurant (cheaper than its own Georgian wine, which is about US$4 a bottle). From the metro walk along Prechistenka ulitsa (formerly Kropotkinskaya ulitsa), take the third street on the left (Barykovsky pereulok) and go through the first arch on the right. The entrance to the small, subterranean restaurant is at the back of the courtyard. Best is to order a spread to share between you. A filling meal should come to less than US$10 per person. Choices include lobio (beans), kharcho (spicy mutton and rice soup), satsivi (turkey with walnut sauce at room temperature), shashlyk, khinkali (dumplings), chakhokhbili (chicken in tomato and onion sauce), pkhali and baklazhany s orekhom (both aubergine-and-walnut combinations). Order at least one khachapuri (hot flat bread with a cheese filling) each. Georgian musicians serenade diners, but don't make a request unless you're prepared to pay for it. U Mamy Zoi is open from noon to 10 pm daily.

Near Park Kultury Metro The restaurant at the *Chayka Swimming Pool* on Novokrymsky proezd is open to everyone and does sizeable portions of good Russian food from noon to 9.30 pm daily. Cold zakuski are mostly around US$2.50, bliny US$4, main courses including svinina (pork) and osetrina (sturgeon) from US$5 to US$9.

The *Guria Kafe* at the back of Komsomolsky prospekt 7, opposite the spectacular Church of St Nicholas of the Weavers, is another Georgian restaurant with good food at similar prices to U Mamy Zoi, though service can be grumpy. You can bring your own drinks. It's open from lunch to 9 pm.

The well-known *Kropotkinskaya 36* restaurant at Prechistenka ulitsa (formerly Kropotkinskaya ulitsa) 36 is listed in our Expensive section, but the shop next door, under the same management, has a few café tables and good light meals such as soups, filled baguettes, and ramshteks (rump steak) in the US$1.50 to US$3 range. It's open from 10 am to 9 pm.

Near Novodevichy Convent *U Pirosmany* (☎ 247 19 26) at Novodevichy proezd 4, opposite the pond outside the convent, is one of Moscow's best Georgian restaurants. It's named after a famous Georgian 'primitive' artist and has pleasing wood-and-whitewash décor. It's a bit smarter and more expensive than U Mamy Zoi but the fare, particularly the starters, is good: the menu is on a board in the lobby. Hours are noon to 4.30 pm and 8 to 10.30 pm: reservations are advisable in the evening, when there's usually low-key music.

For fairly quick food try the *Kafe Arena* beside the Hotel Arena entrance on the corner of ulitsa 10-letia Oktyabrya and ulitsa Usacheva. There's a long menu with many zakuski, and main dishes around US$3 or US$4. It's open from 1 to 4 pm and 6 to 10 pm daily except Monday. Don't confuse it with the dreary *Arena Restoran*. The hotel next door accommodates many circus artistes.

Inner South
Near the Tretyakov Gallery If you renovate it...they will come. Just across the street from the main entrance of the gallery, at Bolshoy Tolmachyovsky pereulok 3, *U Tretyakova*

has a fully fledged restaurant that doesn't look too great, but next door there is a lovely courtyard café serving drinks, salads, sandwiches and pelmeni, all for around US$2.50. It's open from 10 am to 6 pm daily.

Sally O'Brien's is yet another congenial Irish pub, which does pints of the black stuff for US$5, and has a happy hour Friday to Sunday from 8.30 to 9.30 pm during which bottled Mexican beers are US$2.40. Bar food is in the US$10 to US$12 range. It's at 1/3 ulitsa Bolshaya Polyanka 1/3, just across the Maly Kamenny bridge from the Kremlin. Just next door, at the corner, inside the *El Dorado* 24-hour supermarket (which has everything), there's a stylish café, which serves pastries, drinks and reasonably priced hot dishes, such as grilled trout for US$8.

Just next to metro Novokuznetskaya, the *Avstraliysky Khleb* (Australian Bread) bakery does very good breads and rolls. Australians craving a genuine MCG or SCG-style meat pie can satisfy their yearning here as well for around US$0.60 to US$1 a shot. Non-Australians be warned: these square parcels of pale pastry and minced meat are an acquired taste! For the rest of us, happily, the Aussie bakers also make four different fruit versions.

Elsewhere in the Inner South The café in the *New Tretyakov Gallery* at ulitsa Krymsky Val 10, opposite the main entrance to Gorky Park, has good, cheap coffee and pastries. There are also a few snack places in *Gorky Park* itself, including a 2000-seat beer garden with genuine oom-pah-pah atmosphere. Half-litres of Grolsch (it's Dutch, but live a little) cost US$3, excellent grilled chicken with potatoes and salad US$4, and apple dumplings in cinnamon sauce US$2. It's open from 10 am to 10 pm behind the new Western-style amusement park on the west side of the park.

Kafe Shokoladnitsa at the north-west corner of Kaluzhskaya ploshchad (formerly Oktyabrskaya ploshchad; metro: Oktyabrskaya) is well known for its speciality of pancakes with chocolate sauce (blinchiki shokoladnitsa) for US$1.20. You can wash

them down with mead (myod naturalnyy) at US$0.20. The solyanka soup is good but the main courses (US$2 to US$5) are less exciting. The trick is not to order too much: this way your pancakes won't go cold if, as is likely, everything reaches your table at once. The café is open from 11 am to 10 pm, and Sunday from noon to 9 pm.

Moosehead Canadian Bar at ulitsa Bolshaya Polyanka 54 is a Canadian-run foreigners' haunt which serves all the usual imported beer and spirits, along with soups (US$4 to US$5) and bar food including burgers and beef curry (US$7 to US$10). It's open Tuesday to Saturday from noon to 5 am, Sunday and Monday from noon to midnight. The nearest metro is Oktyabrskaya.

The restaurant in the top-end *Danilovsky Hotel* in the grounds of the Danilov Monastery at Bolshoy Starodanilovsky pereulok 5 (metro: Tulskaya) is good and surprisingly economical, with a long international and Russian menu. Several main dishes are US$5 or less, others up to US$10.

Inner South-East

The *American Bar & Grill 2* (☎ 912 36 15), a 10-minute walk or two bus stops south of Kurskaya metro, is the more pleasant of the two, with an outdoor garden in summer, an indoor atrium and, in winter, the tantalising aroma of pizza and wood smoke wafting from the wood-fired brick pizza oven. The menu and prices are the same as those at the ABG in the Inner North-West section, making this the other 'best all-round value' restaurant in Moscow. It's open 24 hours and does the ABG breakfast as well. The address is ulitsa Zemlyanoy Val 59, on the south bank of the Yauza River. It's physically closer to metro Taganskaya but is easier to reach from Kurskaya.

Taganka Blues (☎ 915 10 04) at Verkhnyaya Radishchevskaya ulitsa 15, along the street from the Taganka Theatre, is a good place for an evening meal with entertainment. The dinner price of US$13 includes a 1½-hour Russian folklore show and two hours of jazz. You need to book. The restaurant is open from 2 pm to midnight daily.

Inner North-East

The Kazan Station has a branch of the good *Rostik's* quick grilled-chicken diner (see City Centre), open from 10 am to 10 pm daily.

You can also warm up with good grilled chicken, for US$0.50 a portion, and tea at *Turist*, a stand-up café 200 metres towards the city centre along Myasnitskaya ulitsa (formerly ulitsa Kirova) from the head post office.

Near the Yelokhovsky Cathedral at Baumanskaya ulitsa 23 (metro: Baumanskaya), *Restoran Nemetskaya Sloboda* (☎ 267 44 76) is an inexpensive, friendly and good little Russian restaurant with clean-cut modern décor. Zakuski cost from US$2 to US$5, and there's a big choice of hot main dishes around US$5. The restaurant is open from noon to 11 pm daily. Its name is on the front of Baumanskaya ulitsa 23; the entrance is at the back, round the left side of the building.

Outer North

There's a *Kombi's* (see Inner North) at prospekt Mira 180, just up the road from the Hotel Kosmos. It's open from 10 am to 10 pm daily.

Outer East

For food or drink in the Izmaylovo area, the best place to pop into is Korpus (building) Delta of the *Hotel Izmaylovo* (Гостиница Измайлово). You pass this as you walk from Izmaylovsky Park metro to the crafts market. On the ground floor there's a café with good tea and delicious Greek pastries, plus a Jeverstube beer bar with food. Upstairs on floor 3 are Mexican, Chinese and Indian restaurants, all with main dishes around US$7 to US$9.

PLACES TO EAT – EXPENSIVE
City Centre

There are several offerings at the Hotel National. The *Slavyansky Restaurant* serves buffet breakfast, lunch and dinner for US$20/42/53, with pasta dishes from US$11 to US$17 and other main courses US$19 to US$32. The next two face right on to the

Kremlin: the *Moskovsky*, the National's Russian restaurant, with a small stage and dance floor, is open for dinner at similar prices to the Slavyansky. The *St Petersburg*, with its strumming guitar ambience, does continental cuisine, with pastas from US$15 to US$21 and meat and fish dishes from US$36 to US$48. It also serves a continental breakfast for US$15.

When we visited, *Maxim's of Paris* was in the process of re-renovating the lobby-level restaurant – pulling out even the marble floors – to make it exactly like the one in Paris. Prices, sad to say, were not yet available. Guesses, anyone?

The *Alexandrovsky*, inside the National's ground-floor atrium, does very nice French pastries and cakes, an afternoon tea from 3 to 6 pm (US$19) and cappuccino (US$5). Or, if you're feeling more than peckish, you could part with US$18 or so for a club sandwich. Yes, US$18 for a sandwich.

The *Hotel Metropol* serves very expensive buffet meals beneath the stained-glass ceiling of its splendid, fountained main dining hall. Here, a sandwich in the lobby lounge will set you back only US$8 or so.

Inner North

Kafe Stoleshniki/Uncle Guilly's (☎ 229 20 50) at Stoleshnikov pereulok 6 has a good steakhouse open from noon to midnight. Steak with soup or salad is in the US$25 to US$40 region. You should book for an evening meal. There's also a cheaper bar/restaurant here (see Places to Eat – Inexpensive & Moderate). Stoleshnikov pereulok runs from Bolshaya Dmitrovka ulitsa (formerly Pushkinskaya ulitsa) to Tverskaya ulitsa.

Just south of the Prospekt Mira circle line metro entrance, *Restoran Pescatore 90* at prospekt Mira 36 is a good Italian restaurant with plenty of continental atmosphere. It has a lengthy menu of pastas around US$15 and other main dishes around US$25. It's open from noon to 11.30 pm daily.

The *Vienna Café* in the Olympic Penta Hotel at Olimpiysky prospekt 18, 10 minutes' walk west of the Prospekt Mira orange line metro entrance, does buffet meals: US$21 for breakfast (until 11 am), US$46 for lunch.

The *Azteca* at Novoslobodskaya ulitsa 11, opposite Novoslobodskaya metro, is a 24-hour oasis of beautiful, bright Mexican colours and good Mexican food. Starters are around US$5 to US$10, main courses about US$13 to US$20. You can enjoy a margarita or Mexican beer, too. The waiters, in Mexican costume, are Russian and Cuban.

Inner North-West

Until the Hotel Intourist's reconstruction, about the best food in this monolith at Tverskaya ulitsa 3 was served in the little, independently run *Azteca* Mexican restaurant on floor 20, but whether this will survive the reconstruction is unknown.

The Austrian-run Palace Hotel, 3.25 km from the Kremlin on 1-ya Tverskaya-Yamskaya ulitsa (the continuation of Tverskaya ulitsa), has three top-class restaurants. One, the *Yakor* (Anchor), is probably Moscow's best place for fish and seafood. The *Vena* (Vienna) restaurant serves up haute cuisine with an Austrian touch. The third, the *Lomonosov*, has a Russian and international menu and music at night. Two courses at any of these, without drinks, would set you back US$40 or more. You can sample the Palace quality more economically with a US$3.50 slice of cake at the hotel's ground-floor *Café Mozart*! Nearest metro is Belorusskaya.

The restaurant at the *Marco Polo Presnya Hotel*, Spiridonevsky pereulok 9, part of the same chain as the Palace, also gets good reports.

The Sadko Arcade at Krasnopresnenskaya naberezhnaya 14, four km west of the Kremlin (for how to get there see Places to Eat – Inexpensive & Moderate), has an array of expat-pleasing restaurants. These include a *Swiss House* with fish and meat main courses around US$25 to US$30, a *Steak House* with main dishes from US$26 to US$33, and a *Trattoria* with pasta at US$12 to US$18 and Italian main dishes for US$22 to US$32. There's a similarly international array of eateries inside the nearby *Hotel Mezhdunarodnaya-1*.

Inner South-West

Le Chalet (☎ 202 01 06) is a Swiss place, and vegetarians need not bother. The menu's getting pricey, but it has very nice views of Gorky Park, and customers get a ride home after dinner. Fish dishes cost between US$14 and US$29, fondues (meat and cheese) about US$48 for two, and the desserts are all made in-house and look great. It's about a five-minute walk from metro Park Kultury, at Korobeynikov pereulok 1/2.

The Radisson Slavyanskaya Hotel near Kievskaya metro has one of Moscow's top steak houses, *The Exchange*, and the *Amadeus Café*, with an international menu, among its many eateries.

Kropotkinskaya 36 (☎ 201 75 00) at Prechistenka ulitsa (formerly Kropotkinskaya ulitsa) 36 is the oldest privately owned restaurant in Moscow, and dates from the early years of perestroika. It remains a quality place, serving good Russian food on two floors (the downstairs room is less formal). A full meal including drinks comes to around US$30.

Inner South

Restoran Babochka or *U Babushki* ('At Grandma's'; ☎ 230 27 97), downstairs at Bolshaya Ordynka 42, 300 metres south of Tretyakovskaya metro, serves up good home-style Russian cooking in homely surroundings from 1 to 11 pm daily except Monday. Zakuski are US$4 to US$15, main dishes US$13 to US$18 – except pelmeni, which are US$6.

Inner North-East

Restoran Razgulyay (☎ 267 76 13) at Spartakovskaya ulitsa 11, on the little square in front of the Yelokhovsky Cathedral (metro: Baumanskaya) is a long-time favourite Russian restaurant among the foreign community in Moscow. With one room decorated in Gzhel-pottery-style blue and white, and the other in Khokhloma-ware-like reds and oranges, it offers good zakuski from US$3 to US$7 and main dishes from around US$8. Sometimes a gipsy group sings. Bookings are taken from 11 am to 3 pm.

ENTERTAINMENT

Moscow can keep anyone entertained for months. A ballet at the Bolshoy, a concert in the Kremlin or a night at the Moscow circus is a unique experience – and there's a lively club scene, too.

Unfortunately for summer visitors, much of the entertainment industry goes on holiday or tour between late June and early September, when choice is limited and quality lower. However, the circuses are an exception, and there are usually a few good one-off events.

Information

The keys to finding out what's on are the weekly 'Happenings' guide in the Friday *Moscow Times*, the fortnightly magazine *Moscow Revue*, and the Friday 'Time Out' section in the *Moscow Tribune*. All have useful listings in English of music, dance, theatre, nightlife, art exhibitions and more, with the one in the *Moscow Times* seemingly the best informed. They are distributed free to hotels, restaurants and other places where foreigners congregate. The Russian weekly *Dosug v Moskve (Leisure in Moscow)*, published on Saturdays, has good listings, too (those for theatres and concert halls are for the next week but one). It's sold at newsstands.

Theatre and concert-hall programmes for a month or so ahead are also displayed in Russian at the venues themselves, on street posters, and on charts at ticket kiosks (see the following section) around the city.

Tickets

Tickets for most stage events, concerts and sports are easy enough to get, though, as happens anywhere in the world, a few very popular events sell out early. Service bureaus in hotels, and the main Intourist service bureau at Mokhovaya ulitsa 13, sell tickets for a few main events – and sometimes have tickets when other outlets have run out – but

charge often very hefty commissions on what are usually very cheap face values. It's cheaper just to go along to the ticket office at the venue (most are open for advance or same-day sales for several hours most days, right up to the start of the performance if there are tickets left), or a street ticket kiosk. The street kiosks are marked 'Teatralnaya Kassa' (or just театр) and sell tickets for concerts, circuses, theatres, shows and sports events at close to their face value. Often the tickets they have available are displayed in the window. Locations of some useful kiosks are: Manezhnaya ploshchad in front of Intourist headquarters; ploshchad Revolyutsii near the metro exit; the west side of Teatralnaya ploshchad; ulitsa Petrovka opposite the Bolshoy Theatre; Tverskaya ulitsa opposite the Hotel National; Pushkinskaya ploshchad near the corner of Malaya Dmitrovka ulitsa (formerly ulitsa Chekhova); and outside Prospekt Mira circle line metro station.

Typical face-value prices for theatres and classical concerts are US$2 or less, and for the circuses US$1 to US$5. If your Russian is inadequate, copy the name of the event and the date on a piece of paper and show it to the cashier. Often there will be a range of ticket prices available. For some useful words related to ticket-buying, see Entertainment in European Russia Facts for the Visitor.

Tickets for the Bolshoy Theatre, the circuses and a few other things are a bit harder – but still quite possible – to come by. You'll be extremely lucky to pay the face value for a Bolshoy ticket. A common practice when tickets are hard to get is to go to the venue half an hour before the show starts and look for someone with spare tickets to sell. Ticket touts with Bolshoy tickets hang around Teatralnaya ploshchad most of the day – but the nearer you get to curtain up, the cheaper the tickets are likely to be. Of course you'll pay above the face value, and you have to watch out for rip-offs: check the date, time and other details of the ticket as carefully as you can and watch out for the words *neudobnoe mesto* (inconvenient place), which usually means it's a seat with a restricted view.

Virtually all evening theatre, concert and circus performances start at 7 pm.

Clubs and music venues usually have a pay-at-the-door system, with cover prices anywhere from US$5 to US$40. For specially popular nights, it may pay to go along and try to make a reservation in advance – but check whether this will cost extra.

Ballet & Opera

The Bolshoy Ballet & Opera, whose theatre dominates Teatralnaya ploshchad, has been an unhappy, divided place in recent years. Its longtime ballet director Boris Grigorovich, who had been lionised in the 1960s and 1970s, finally resigned in 1995 after years at loggerheads with other officials and leading stars, who accused him of dictatorial policies and artistic sterility. Numerous stars left for the West or to set up independent ballet companies in Russia. Some others showed him great loyalty, and the day he resigned some of the cast of *Romeo & Juliet* came on stage to tell the audience that sorry, they were too upset to dance that night. Thus began the first strike in the Bolshoy's 220-year history. Grigorovich's replacement is Vladimir Vasiliev, a former leading Bolshoy dancer and opponent of Grigorovich. His appointment opens the way for a much more adventurous range of ballets and choreography than Bolshoy audiences have seen for decades, but Vasiliev faces a battle to raise both standards and cash for the struggling Bolshoy.

Whatever the Bolshoy's behind-the-scenes troubles, an evening there remains one of Moscow's best nights out. The atmosphere in the glittering, six-tier auditorium is electric – though the 18th-century theatre, whose foundations are sinking, is due to close for restoration in 1997, with performances shifting to a new auditorium adjoining Teatralnaya ploshchad. Both the ballet and opera companies, with several hundred artists between them, perform a range of Russian and foreign works. Sometimes other Russian companies perform here, too – it's always wise to check that it's

the actual Bolshoy Ballet or Opera that you're paying to see.

Normally you can't get Bolshoy tickets from the theatre's box office or from a teatralnaya kassa. You might conceivably be lucky a week or more in advance – or at 3.30 pm on the day of the performance, when any unsold tickets may go on sale at the theatre's box office. But generally you either have to buy a ticket from one of a few specific outlets (as far ahead as you can, though you might still be lucky on the day), or hang around outside the theatre before the performance and get one from a tout (see the preceding Tickets section). Either way you'll pay many times its face value – perhaps five to 10 times from touts, whose cheapest tickets are between US$5 and US$15, and 15 times from outlets such as the Travellers Guest House (see Places to Stay – Bottom End), EPS (☎ 927 69 82) in the Hotel Metropol lobby (see Places to Stay – Top End), and Intourist service bureaus (see the Tourist Offices section under Information). The Travellers Guest House has a full range of tickets from US$10 to US$60, while IPS and Intourist sell only the more expensive tickets at up to US$60 for the ballet or US$50 for the opera. These are still a snip compared with the prices charged by similarly prestigious ballet and opera houses in the West.

Each ticket displays the section of the theatre in which the seat is located: the *parter* is the stalls, the *lozhi benuara* are boxes at the sides of the parter, the *amfiteatr* is behind the parter, and the *bel-etazh* is the dress circle above the lozhi benuara and amfiteatr. Above the bel-etazh is the *balkon* (circle), with four *yarusy* (tiers) numbered one to four from the bottom up.

The Bolshoy does not have a monopoly on ballet and opera in Moscow. Leading dancers also appear with the Kremlin Ballet and the Moscow Classical Ballet Theatre, both of which perform in the State Kremlin Palace. There is, too, the Stanislavsky & Nemirovich-Danchenko Musical Theatre at Bolshaya Dmitrovka ulitsa (formerly Pushkinskaya ulitsa) 17 – another opera and ballet theatre, with a similar classics-based repertoire to the Bolshoy's, and standards often as high.

Classical Music

The two top concert venues are the Tchaikovsky Concert Hall, which seats over 1600, on Triumfalnaya ploshchad (formerly ploshchad Mayakovskogo), and the Tchaikovsky Conservatory (also the country's biggest music school) at Bolshaya Nikitskaya ulitsa (formerly ulitsa Gertsena) 13. The Conservatory has both a Big Hall (Bolshoy Zal) and a Small Hall (Maly Zal). Among other settings for concerts are the atmospheric old Ostankino Palace, and the Sheremetev Palace at Kuskovo (see the Outer North and Outer East sections).

The Tchaikovsky Concert Hall is the base for the famous State Symphony Orchestra (Gosudarstvenny Akademichesky Simfonichesky Orkestr), directed and often conducted by Yevgeny Svetlanov. Another orchestra to look out for is the young but acclaimed Russian National Symphony Orchestra, run without state funding by Mikhail Pletnev. There's quite a succession of music festivals throughout the season in Moscow. Probably the most famous of them is the International Tchaikovsky Competition, in which hundreds of musicians compete for the titles of best pianist, singer, cellist and violinist, but it is held only every four years (the next is due in 1998). The *Moscow Times* listings have pointers to outstanding concerts.

Rock, Pop & Nightlife

Occasional big concerts by top Russian and foreign bands (and a few somewhat faded Western visitors) are staged at various venues around the city such as the Central Lenin Stadium, the Central Concert Hall (Tsentralny Kontsertny Zal) at the Hotel Rossia and even the State Kremlin Palace. Watch the press and posters.

Several clubs have regular live bands, and many of them stay open in the summer. Friday and Saturday are the best nights everywhere. Of course, it's a changing scene,

but three established places with relaxed but lively atmospheres are the Hermitage Club, Krisis Zhanra and Pilot.

The Hermitage Club, in the Ermitazh Garden at Karetny ryad 3 (Inner North; metro: Chekhovskaya or Tsvetnoy Bulvar), attracts an artsy, studenty crowd to its two large, adjoining rooms. One is given over to music; the other is a bar with tables. Basically it's a Friday-to-Sunday disco (10 pm to 6 am) but it gets liveliest when there's a band on, which could be anything from world music to Russian rave. Events are advertised in the Travellers Guest House for the benefit of those staying there. Entry is normally US$10, with half price before 11 pm (it's worth arriving in good time if there's an event on), and drinks are around US$3.

Krisis Zhanra is a cosy basement bar, popular among resident foreigners, with live blues, folk or jazz from about 9 pm most nights. Its address is Prechistensky pereulok (formerly pereulok Ostrovskogo) 22 (Inner South-West; metro: Kropotkinskaya) – the entrance is round the back, actually off Bolshoy Vlasevsky pereulok. It's open from noon to 1 am daily except Monday, with a cover charge of US$3 after 6 pm; drinks are around US$3 and hot food is available.

Pilot, at ulitsa Tryokhgorny Val 6 (Inner North-West; metro: Ulitsa 1905 Goda), attracts a mainly Russian student crowd for its good dance tracks and varied rock bands, Wednesday or Thursday to Saturday or Sunday, from 11 pm to 6 am. Cover is US$10 for men, US$5 for women.

Blues fans have a couple of good places to head for. The Arbat Blues Club, at Filippovsky pereulok (formerly pereulok Axakova) 11 (Inner South-West; metro: Arbatskaya), has some really excellent Russian blues bands from around 8.30 pm to the small hours on Friday and Saturday nights. Entry is US$10. B B King, a shiny basement bar at Sadovaya-Samotyochnaya ulitsa 4/2 (Inner North; metro: Tsvetnoy Bulvar), has live blues from around 9 pm on Thursday and Saturday. Drinks are about US$4 and there's food from US$4 to US$15 (no cover).

A good, not-too-costly night out of a different kind can be had at Taganka Blues, a restaurant with a nightly jazz band and Russian folklore show (see Places to Eat – Inexpensive & Moderate, Inner South-East).

Among the best of the more up-market nightclubs is Manhattan Express at the north-west corner of the Hotel Rossia (City Centre; metro: Kitay-Gorod) which is modelled on New York's Studio 54. Open from 7 pm to 5 am nightly, it's a restaurant as well as a club, with a cover charge of US$20 to US$30 after 9 pm. There's a different theme each night – techno on Monday, students on Tuesday, 1960s to 1980s disco on Thursday (when foreigners with passports can get in free until midnight), radio DJs on Friday, and special events such as live bands or floor shows on other nights. Many of the other more expensive clubs, which often have casinos attached, are in the topless-show-and-Mafia mould.

Check the Friday *Moscow Times* for latest details of all these places and also for new clubs.

Circus

Moscow has two separate circuses and despite economic problems since the fall of the Soviet Union they still put on glittering shows, with Muscovites of all ages relaxing and enjoying themselves in the audience. The first half of the show is likely to be a modern mix of dance, cabaret and rock music before animals and acrobats reassert themselves. The 3400-seat New Circus (Novy Tsirk, Новый цирк) at prospekt Vernadskogo 7 (Outer South; metro: Universitet) has the highest reputation, but the more centrally located Old Circus (Stary Tsirk), in its modernised 19th-century building at Tsvetnoy bulvar 13 (Inner North; metro: Tsvetnoy Bulvar), runs close. There are performances at one or both circuses almost daily all year round. Shows are normally at 7 pm, with extra shows at 3 pm and often 11 or 11.30 am on Saturday and Sunday. Tickets are around US$1 to US$2 and you can buy them in advance at the circuses or from teatralnye kassy (see the

earlier Tickets section). If you turn up just before the performance you may find the show is sold out, but touts will usually have tickets for around US$10. In summer there is often a tent circus in Gorky Park.

Folk Ensembles

Several Russian folk dance and music ensembles put on colourful, entertaining shows. These are often staged at the big Tchaikovsky Concert Hall, which is a testament to their popularity. Three particularly worth catching are the Igor Moiseev Folk Dance Ensemble, the Osipov Russian Folk Orchestra and the Pyatnitsky Russian Folk Chorus.

Theatre

Moscow has around 20 professional and numerous amateur theatres. A wide range of plays – contemporary and classic, Russian and foreign – is staged at most of them, but except for occasional visiting companies from other countries, everything is in Russian so its appeal to the average visitor is limited. One theatre where language is little barrier, however, is the Obraztsov Puppet Theatre (Teatr kukol pod rukovodstvom S V Obraztsova) at Sadovaya-Samotyochnaya ulitsa 3 (Inner North; metro: Tsvetnoy Bulvar), which has often hilarious shows for adults which are well worth taking in, as well as for children. The Obraztsov's *Don Juan* has been running since the Soviet era, when it introduced Russia's first full-frontal nude puppet.

The listings press has good information on what's on at the Obraztsov and other theatres, the best of which include the Chekhov Moscow Art Theatre at Kamergersky pereulok 3, famous for its associations with Chekhov (Inner North); the Yermolova Theatre next to the Hotel Intourist at Tverskaya ulitsa 5, the Mossoviet Theatre at Bolshaya Sadovaya ulitsa 16, the Teatr Yunogo Zritelya (Young Spectators' Theatre) at Mamonovsky pereulok (formerly pereulok Sadovskikh) 10, the Malaya Bronnaya Theatre at Malaya Bronnaya ulitsa 4, and the Pushkin Theatre at Tverskoy bulvar 23 (all Inner North-West); the Taganka Theatre on Taganskaya ploshchad (Inner South-East), famous for its daring productions in the Soviet years; and the Sovremennik (Contemporary) Theatre at Chistoprudny bulvar 19A (Inner North-East).

Cinema

The Americom House of Cinema in the Radisson Slavyanskaya Hotel (Inner South-West) sometimes shows recent-release movies in English. Otherwise, everything is in Russian or with Russian voice-over. Serious Russian films and many foreign classics are shown at the Moskva Cinema at Triumfalnaya ploshchad 1, and the Cinema Centre and Cinema Museum, both at Druzhinnikovskaya ulitsa 15 (all Inner North-West).

Exhibitions

There's always a fascinating range of short-term art, historical, cultural and other exhibitions around Moscow. Many museums have special sections for temporary exhibitions; other good shows can be found in the city's numerous art galleries.

Press listings will help you to pick out highlights and give dates and times. Galleries that often have something interesting on include:

Central Exhibition Hall, Manezhnaya ploshchad (City Centre; metro: Okhotny Ryad) – mainstream exhibitions

Central House of Artists, ulitsa Krymsky Val 10 (Inner South; metro: Park Kultury) – a major contemporary art centre, usually several concurrent shows

M'ARS Gallery, Malaya Filyovskaya ulitsa 32 (Outer West; metro: Pionerskaya) – contemporary art gallery of several years' standing, founded by artists banned in the Soviet era

Moscow Gallery, ulitsa Kuznetsky Most 11 & 20 (Inner North; metro: Kuznetsky Most) – modern

Ridzhina Gallery, Myasnitskaya ulitsa 36 (Inner North-East; metro: Turgenevskaya) – modern and contemporary

Russian Academy of Arts, Prechistenka ulitsa 21 (Inner South-West; metro: Kropotkinskaya) – modern and contemporary but not avant-garde

Spectator Sport

Moscow has five or more soccer teams – Spartak, Dinamo, Torpedo, Lokomotiv and TsSKA (Tsentralny Sportivny Klub Armii) usually among them – in the Russian Premier League most seasons. It also usually has two or three representatives in European club competitions. Many of these clubs' home games, plus international matches, are played at the Big Sports Arena in the Central Lenin Stadium (Inner South-West; metro: Sportivnaya), which is rarely anything like full. Other games may be at the Dinamo (Стадионы Динамо) or TsSKA (Стадионы ЦСКА) stadia on Leningradsky prospekt (Outer North; metros: Dinamo, Aeroport). You can pay at the gate, or buy advance tickets for big games from teatralnye kassy.

Moscow's leading ice hockey teams are TsSKA, Dinamo, Spartak and Krylya Sovietov. TsSKA, with sponsorship from McDonald's, is the big name. Games may be at the clubs' own stadia or at the Central Lenin Stadium's Sports Palace or Small Sports Arena. Again, few games are very well attended and you can pay at the gate.

Buy Russian sports newspapers such as *Sport Express* and *Futbol* to find out what's on.

There's harness racing and (in winter) troyka racing at the 160-year-old Hippodrome (Ippodrom, Ипподром; ☎ 945 43 67) on Begovaya alleya (Outer North; metro: Begovaya), whose faded elegance is a nice backdrop for an off-beat (read: weird) afternoon. Racing is on Sunday, from noon or 1 pm, and Wednesday and Thursday evening from about 7 pm. The crowds are overwhelmingly male and hard-drinking (vodka's sold by the litre at the concession stands).

Entry tickets are US$0.05, and a programme (which includes admission) US$0.60. Betting windows are on ground level, beneath the stands. There are windows for bets of 10 roubles, 100 roubles and, for the big spenders, 1000 roubles. At the time of writing this translated to windows for bets of US$0.002, US$0.02 and US$0.20. The system of betting in use here is fantastically convoluted. To win one option, the 'Express 7', the punter must pick correctly the order of the first seven horses across the line in several races; the odds are five million to one – but they try! Try your luck with a *Troynoy Odinar* or the winning horse in three races. Make sure to pick only one horse from each race at first (later you can add place and show bets, but that's complex). The odds board shows a three-digit number; the lower the number, the greater the amount of money bet on a horse.

To break free of the riffraff, walk through the metal detector at the Klub Royal, at the southern end of the track, and have some Ben & Jerry's ice cream for US$2 a bowl. And if you see a guy named Kazbek, tell him he owes Nick money.

THINGS TO BUY

By far the best place to go for a wide selection of Russian arts and crafts, which make great souvenirs and presents, is the weekend market out east at Izmaylovsky Park. But there are also lots of shops around the city centre which deal in the same sorts of thing. The big central department stores GUM and TsUM are good for all manner of everyday requisites from a pen or film to shoes or luggage.

Moscow's main city-centre shopping areas are ulitsa Petrovka, ulitsa Kuznetsky Most and other streets behind the Bolshoy Theatre, and Tverskaya ulitsa, which is dotted with classy shops almost all the way out to the Belorussia Station. Though these may still lack the eye-catching window displays familiar to shoppers in the West, many have a wide range of attractive goods inside.

Moscow shops are generally open Monday to Friday from 9 or 10 am to 2 pm, and 3 to 7 pm, and Saturday from 9 or 10 am to 2 pm and 3 to 5 or 6 pm. They're closed on Sunday. The big department stores and most Western-run shops do without the early afternoon break. Food shops may stay open an hour longer at night.

If you're thinking of buying anything that might be classed an art treasure or an antique,

beware of export restrictions – see Customs in European Russia Facts for the Visitor.

Art & Crafts

Markets The Saturday and Sunday 'Vernisazh' (Вернисаж) market at Izmaylovsky Park (Outer East; metro: Izmaylovsky Park) is a sprawling area packed with attractive art and handmade crafts. You'll find not just Moscow's biggest and most original range of matryoshkas, Palekh and Khokhloma ware, and dozens of artists selling their own work (with many appealing town and landscapes), but also lots of rugs from the Caucasus and Central Asia, some very attractive pottery, antique samovars, handmade clothes, jewellery, fur hats, chess sets, toys and much more. Quality is mostly high and many of the items are truly original. Prices can be reasonable but you have to bargain for them. Be wary of buying icons, as many of these have been stolen from churches. The market is two minutes' walk from Izmaylovksy Park metro; follow the crowds past the big hotel complex outside the station.

Many other artists set up their stalls on ulitsa Krymsky Val opposite the entrance to Gorky Park (Inner South; metro: Park Kultury), particularly on Saturday and Sunday. The art here is a mite less commercial than at Izmaylovksy Park, and there are only a few crafts.

Shops Shops in top hotels and several smart foreign-run shops sell good Russian crafts, but you'll find lower prices elsewhere. Some of the shops in GUM (City Centre; metro: Ploshchad Revolyutsii) have a good range of crafts. There are also two shops with some original work on ulitsa Petrovka, opposite Stoleshnikov pereulok (Inner North; metro: Kuznetsky Most). The Arbatskaya Lavitsa shop at ulitsa Arbat 27 (Inner South-West; metro: Arbatskaya) stocks lots of colourful souvenirs including Khokhloma, Palekh and Gzhel. Torgovy Dom Biblio-Globus on Myasnitskaya ulitsa by the Lubyanka (City Centre; metro: Lubyanka) has more.

Tsentralny Salon at Ukrainsky bulvar 6

(Inner South-West; metro: Kievskaya), is one of Moscow's biggest craft shops, with many unusual items including some fine ceramics from US$8, hundreds of paintings, painted wooden eggs, and Caucasian and Central Asian carpets (though there's a better and probably less expensive range of these at Izmaylovksy Park). Russky Suvenir, round the corner at Kutuzovsky prospekt 9, has a fairly big range of typical souvenirs. Both these shops can stamp your receipt to provide export clearance.

The shop at the Danilov Monastery (Inner South; metro: Tulskaya) has some quality miniature icon reproductions and attractive painted wooden eggs.

Hats & Furs
A Russian fur hat is a very practical item in the Russian winter as well as a good souvenir, and perfectly adequate rabbit or lamb's-wool hats are sold for US$10 to US$20 in shops such as Mekha on the corner of ulitsa Petrovka and Stoleshnikov pereulok, which also sells fur coats, and Golovnye ubory on Bolshaya Dmitrovka ulitsa (formerly Pushkinskaya ulitsa) just north of ulitsa Kuznetsky Most (both Inner North; metro: Kuznetsky Most). Two more Mekha shops are on ulitsa Arbat at the corner of Bolshoy Nikolopeskovsky pereulok (Inner South-West; metro: Arbatskaya), and at Pyatnitskaya ulitsa 13 (Inner South; metro: Novokuznetskaya). The latter sells coats, too.

Department Stores
Central Moscow has four big department stores, which are all interesting for a browse even if you don't need to buy anything. All are now mostly given over to many separate private-enterprise shops and have a huge range of both Russian and imported goods. The biggest is GUM on Red Square (City Centre; metro: Ploshchad Revolyutsii), where you can find almost anything you need. TsUM, across ulitsa Petrovka from the Bolshoy Theatre, is a slightly down-market version of GUM, almost as big, while Petrovsky Passazh at ulitsa Petrovka 10 is

the glitziest, dominated by expensive foreign names (both Inner North; metro: Kuznetsky Most). Detsky Mir (Children's World) at Teatralny proezd 5 (City Centre; metro: Lubyanka) now sports a few imported cars as well as toys, school goods and children's clothes.

Music
Melodia at ulitsa Novy Arbat 22 has a decent range of popular and classical Russian cassettes (US$1 to US$1.50), CDs (US$5 to US$20) and records (US$0.50 to US$4). Kiosks outside on the street sell more.

Imported Goods
There are clusters of shops selling imported Western products in places such as GUM, Petrovsky Passazh, the Radisson Slavyanskaya Hotel shopping mall (Inner South-West; metro: Kievskaya), the Sadko Arcade and the Hotel Mezhdunarodnaya (both Inner North-West; nearest metro: Ulitsa 1905 Goda).

GETTING THERE & AWAY
For an overview of international routes to Moscow, see the European Russia Getting There & Away chapter.

If you're travelling to, or even just through, another country – even a former Soviet state such as Ukraine or Belarus – check out the visa requirements before you buy your ticket. Some information is given in the Ukraine and Belarus Facts for the Visitor chapters.

Air
See the European Russia Getting Around chapter for safety information on flying in the former Soviet Union.

To/From Countries Outside the ex-USSR
Sheremetevo-2 airport, 30 km north-west of the city centre, handles flights to/from places outside the former Soviet Union. Neighbouring Sheremetevo-1 is supposed to be under expansion so that it, too, can take these flights – so it's wise to double-check your departure airport. There are daily flights by

numerous airlines to/from nearly all European and many other world capitals, and many provincial cities, too. A flight from London or Paris takes about three hours, from New York about 10 hours. In recent years Sheremetevo-2 has had to handle far more passengers than it was designed for and arrival queues at immigration can be up to an hour long. It also has a reputation for thefts from checked-in luggage.

For Sheremetevo-2 flight departure information ring ☎ 578 78 16, 578 75 18 or 578 82 86; for flight arrivals call 578 82 24.

Tickets If you need a flight to a country outside the ex-USSR, there are a number of agencies that sell heavily discounted fares, including some on major Western airlines. Details of some of these are given under Travel Agencies in the Moscow Information section. Others advertise in the English-language press. Scheduled fares on Aeroflot are no better than those on other airlines.

To/From Russia and the ex-USSR Four Moscow airports are devoted to flights to/from places within Russia and the 14 other ex-Soviet states (Armenia, Azerbaijan, Belarus, Estonia, Georgia, Kazakhstan, Kyrgyzstan, Latvia, Lithuania, Moldova, Tajikistan, Turkmenistan, Ukraine and Uzbekistan). Most flights to/from St Petersburg, the Baltic states, Belarus and northern European Russia, and all flights by Transaero Airlines, use Sheremetevo-1 airport. Most flights to/from the east (including the Volga cities and Siberia) and the Central Asian states use Domodedovo airport, about 40 km south of the city centre. Most flights to/from the Russian Caucasus, Moldova and Kaliningrad use Vnukovo airport, 30 km south-west. Flights to/from Ukraine, Georgia and Armenia use either Sheremetevo-1 or Vnukovo; Azerbaijan flights use either Sheremetevo-1 or Domodedovo. Bykovo airport, 30 km south-east, handles a miscellany of medium-range destinations including Petrozavodsk, Nalchik and Penza. Naturally there are

exceptions to these guidelines so always check.

Sheremetevo-1 flight information is available on ☎ 578 23 72 (departures), 578 36 10 (arrivals).

Tickets Though the old Aeroflot monopoly on internal air travel has been broken up into dozens of separate Russian regional airlines and national airlines of the former Soviet republics, tickets for nearly all of them are sold by the same outlets and they're all listed together on timetables.

There's little to choose between different domestic airlines in terms of safety and comfort (or lack of them), though Transaero, which flies Boeings almost exclusively, is a cut above the others (see Schedules for its destinations). Aeroflot, Transaero, and LAL (Lithuanian Airlines) are among the few significant ex-USSR-based airlines with their own ticket offices in Moscow – though you can also buy their tickets at general outlets.

Most of the agencies that sell air tickets to places outside the ex-USSR (see Travel Agencies in the Moscow Information section) sell them to places within it as well, but there are also some fairly convenient ticket offices you can deal with yourself. The handiest is Intourtrans (☎ 927 11 81, 921 83 94; fax 921 19 96), through the archway at ulitsa Petrovka 15/13 (Inner North; metro: Kuznetsky Most). Go to floor 2 for tickets on Baltic states airlines, floor 3 for all other flights within the ex-USSR and for information in English from the Avia Spravka desk (you're supposed to pay US$0.50 for information). Intourtrans' opening times are Monday to Friday from 9 am to 8 pm, Saturday and Sunday from 9 am to 7 pm, but each counter closes for various periods within those hours, so if there are queues try to pick a counter that isn't going to shut just as you reach it (their rest periods – *pereryvy* – are posted up).

Intourist's central service bureau at Mokhovaya ulitsa 13 (City Centre; metro: Okhotny Ryad) sells tickets for virtually all flights within the ex-USSR from Moscow, including on Transaero and the Baltic states airlines LAL, Estonian Air and Latavio, but charges slightly higher prices than Intourtrans. The air ticket desk (☎ 292 22 93) is open from 9 am to 1 pm and 2 to 8 pm daily.

Less convenient is the City Air Terminal (Gorodskoy aerovokzal; ☎ 155 09 22) at Leningradsky prospekt 37 (Outer North). To reach it you have to take the metro to Dinamo, then any trolleybus or tram north on Leningradsky prospekt for one km. Ticket window Nos 27 to 32, at the north end of the hall, sell 'domestic' tickets for foreigners from 8 am to 7.30 pm Monday to Friday, 8 am to 6.30 pm Saturday, Sunday, holidays and the day before holidays. Window Nos 7 to 9 sell 'international' tickets – which may or may not include some of the non-Russian ex-USSR states – from 10 am to 1 pm and 2 to 5 pm Monday to Thursday, and 10 am to 1 pm and 2 to 4 pm on Friday (Saturday and Sunday closed). Transaero tickets are sold at window No 4.

Transaero (☎ 578 05 37, 578 05 80; fax 292 76 82) also has ticket offices at Okhotny ryad 2 on the western corner of the Hotel Moskva building (City Centre; metro: Okhotny Ryad), and at Sheremetevo-1 airport.

The Aeroflot offices (all ☎ 156 80 19) at ulitsa Petrovka 20 (opposite Intourtrans), Frunzenskaya naberezhnaya 4 (Inner South-West; metro: Park Kultury), and ulitsa Korovy Val (formerly Dobryninskaya ulitsa) 7 (Inner South; metro: Oktyabrskaya) are supposed to sell Aeroflot tickets to Aeroflot's non-Russian ex-USSR destinations – Tallinn, Riga, Vilnius, Kiev, Baku and Yerevan at the time of writing. They don't always realise they're supposed to sell these tickets, but may be worth calling into if you happen to be nearby.

Schedules These change all the time. Timetables barely exist (except for Transaero) because they are so quickly outdated, and the only reliable sources of schedule information are ticket sales outlets. There are about six daily flights to St Petersburg, and two or three a day nonstop to major Russian desti-

nations including Arkhangelsk, Astrakhan, Irkutsk, Khabarovsk, Krasnoyarsk, Mineralnye Vody, Murmansk, Nizhny Novgorod, Novosibirsk, Rostov-on-Don, Vladivostok and Yekaterinburg. You can fly to dozens of smaller places daily or a few days a week. There are even daily nonstop flights to places in the far east such as Magadan, Petropavlovsk-Kamchatsky, Yakutsk and Yuzhno-Sakhalinsk. Flights to Ukraine, Belarus and other ex-Soviet states are generally less frequent, though there are daily flights to most of these countries' capitals and service of some kind to various other cities. More services may develop.

Transaero's destinations are Almaty, Baku, Kiev, Minsk, Novosibirsk, Odessa, Riga, St Petersburg, Sochi, Tashkent, Vladivostok and Yekaterinburg. Many of these are served daily. Flights to Ashghabat, Bishkek, Irkutsk and Lviv are planned.

Fares See European Russia Getting Around for fare information. There's usually little variation in fares between ticket outlets.

Airport Procedures Check-in for flights within the ex-USSR is supposed to close 40 minutes before take-off, but be sure to reach the airport well before that. It may take some time to find the right check-in desk and you may even have to locate a special foreigners' check-in. In Domodedovo's large terminal building, foreigners must find the 'Intourist' door (towards the left-hand end of the building as you enter), where you will be put on a bus to take you to a special check-in desk. It can take half an hour from arriving at the airport to reaching check-in.

Airline Offices Airline offices in Moscow include:

Aeroflot
    ulitsa Petrovka 20 (☎ 156 80 19)
    Frunzenskaya naberezhnaya 4 (☎ 156 80 19)
    ulitsa Korovy Val (formerly Dobryninskaya ulitsa) 7 (☎ 156 80 19)
    Sheremetevo-2 Airport (☎ 578 01 60)

Air China
    stroenie (building) 5, ulitsa Kuznetsky Most 1/8
    (☎ 292 33 87, airport 578 27 25)
Air France
    ulitsa Korovy Val (formerly Dobryninskaya
    ulitsa) 7 (☎ 237 23 25, airport 578 27 57)
Air India
    ulitsa Korovy Val (formerly Dobryninskaya
    ulitsa) 7 (☎ 237 74 94, airport 578 27 47)
Alitalia
    ulitsa Pushechnaya 7 (☎ 923 98 40, airport 578 27 67)
Austrian Airlines
    Office 1805, Hotel Mezhdunarodnaya,
    Krasnopresnenskaya naberezhnaya 12 (☎ 253 16
    70, airport 578 27 34)
British Airways
    Office 1905, Hotel Mezhdunarodnaya,
    Krasnopresnenskaya naberezhnaya 12 (☎ 253 24
    92, airport 578 29 23)
Continental Airlines
    Neglinnaya ulitsa 15 (☎ 925 12 91)
ČSA (Czechoslovak Airlines)
    2-ya Brestskaya ulitsa 21/27 (☎ 250 45 71,
    airport 578 27 04)
Delta Airlines
    Office 1102A, Hotel Mezhdunarodnaya,
    Krasnopresnenskaya naberezhnaya 12 (☎ 253 26
    58, airport 578 27 38)
Finnair
    Kamergersky pereulok (formerly proezd
    Khudozhestvennogo Teatra) 6 (☎ 292 87 88,
    airport 578 27 18)
Iberia
    Sheremetevo-2 airport (☎ 578 27 91)
JAL (Japan Air Lines)
    ulitsa Kuznetsky Most 3 (☎ 921 64 48, airport
    578 29 42)
KLM
    ulitsa Usacheva 35, 1st floor (☎ 258 36 00,
    airport 578 27 62)
LAL (Lithuanian Airlines)
    Povarskaya ulitsa (formerly ulitsa Vorovskogo)
    24 (☎ 203 75 02)
LOT (Polish Airlines)
    Office 5, ulitsa Korovy Val (formerly
    Dobryninskaya ulitsa) 7 (☎ 238 00 03, airport
    578 27 06)
Lufthansa
    Olympic Penta Hotel, Olimpiysky prospekt 18
    (☎ 975 25 01, airport 578 31 51)
Malév Hungarian Airlines
    Kamergersky pereulok (formerly proezd
    Khudozhestvennogo Teatra) 6 (☎ 292 04 34,
    airport 578 27 10)
Sabena
    Sheremetevo-2 Airport (☎ 578 27 13)
SAS
    ulitsa Kuznetsky Most 3 (☎ 925 47 47, airport
    578 27 27)

Swissair
    Office 2005, Hotel Mezhdunarodnaya,
    Krasnopresnenskaya naberezhnaya 12 (☎ 253 89
    88, airport 578 27 40)
Transaero
    Okhotny ryad 2 (☎ 578 05 37)

Bus
Buses run to a number of towns and cities
within about 700 km of Moscow. There are
no foreigners' prices on buses and to most
places the fares are similar to the Russian
fares for kupeynyy class on trains. Buses are
reasonably comfortable but to most places
they're a bit slower than trains, and less
frequent.

To/From St Petersburg Ticket window No
21 in Moscow's Leningrad train station sells
tickets for the Galaktika company's 'comfortable Mercedes Benz' bus to St
Petersburg, leaving the station at 8 pm
nightly for an 8½-hour trip costing US$14.

To/From Other Places To book a seat you
have to go out to the long-distance bus terminal, the Shchyolkovsky Avtovokzal
(Щёлковский автовокзал), beside
Shchyolkovskaya metro station in the east of
the city, where queues can be bad – and it is
generally advisable to book ahead, especially for travel on Friday, Saturday or
Sunday.

Places to which it's most worth considering a bus are those with poor train services
such as Pereslavl-Zalessky (which is not on
a railway) and Vladimir (which has few
afternoon trains from Moscow). Services (all
daily) from Shchyolkovsky include:

Cheboxary – US$9.50, 12 to 14 hours, three buses
Kazan – US$20, 16½ hours, 6.30 pm
Kharkiv (Kharkov) – US$19, 20 hours, 8.30 pm
Kostroma – US$8, eight hours, four buses
Kursk – US$13, 14 hours, 4.50 pm
Nizhny Novgorod – US$6, nine hours, four buses
Novgorod – US$13, 11½ hours, 8.30 pm
Pereslavl-Zalessky – US$3.25, 2½ to 3½ hours, four
    buses
Plyos – US$7, 8½ hours, 11 am and 8.45 pm
Suzdal – US$3, 4¼ hours, 5 pm
Vladimir – US$2.75, 3½ hours, five buses from 1.30
    to 7.30 pm

Voronezh – US$13, 12½ hours, 8 am
Yaroslavl – US$6, six hours, 9 am and 1.50 pm

Train

Moscow has rail links to most parts of Russia, most former Soviet states, numerous countries in Eastern and Western Europe, and China and Mongolia.

See the European Russia Getting Around chapter for general information on train travel, fares, tickets, and deciphering timetables. Take care of your belongings at Moscow's stations and their nearby metro stations, all of which are nearly always very crowded, and on trains. Night trains between Moscow and St Petersburg in particular have been notorious for thefts, though the situation seems to have improved somewhat. Some thieves even used a (reportedly harmless) gas to make sure travellers didn't wake up while they rifled their luggage. You might like to invest in a chain and padlock or a length of strong wire to secure your compartment door. One place you can buy these in Moscow is the Stockmann Home Electronics & Car Supplies shop at Lyusinovskaya ulitsa 70, one block north of Tulskaya metro (Inner South).

One important distinction to grasp when taking trains from Moscow is the difference between long-distance and 'suburban' trains. Long-distance trains run to places at least three or four hours out of Moscow, with limited stops and a range of accommodation classes. Suburban trains, known as *prigorodnye poezdy* or *elektrichky*, run to within just 100 or 200 km of Moscow, stop almost everywhere, and have a single class of hard bench seats. You simply buy your ticket before the train leaves, and there's no limit on capacity – so you may have to stand for some of the trip. Most Moscow stations have a separate ticket hall for suburban trains, usually called the Prigorodny Zal and often tucked away at the side or back of the station building (information on locations of these is given under the relevant destinations in the Around Moscow chapter). Suburban trains are also usually listed on separate timetables, and may go from a separate group of platforms.

Stations Moscow's nine main stations, all with metro stations on the spot, are:

Belorussia Station (Belorussky vokzal), Tverskaya Zastava ploshchad (formerly ploshchad Belorusskogo Vokzala; Inner North-West; metro: Belorusskaya) – trains to/from Smolensk, Kaliningrad, Belarus, Lithuania, Poland, Germany, Belgium; some trains to/from the Czech Republic; suburban trains to/from the west including Mozhaysk, Borodino, Zvenigorod

Kazan Station (Kazansky vokzal), Komsomolskaya ploshchad (Inner North-East; metro: Komsomolskaya) – trains to/from Cheboxary, Yoshkar-Ola, Kazan, Izhevsk, Ufa, Ryazan, Penza, Ulyanovsk, Samara, Novorossiysk, Central Asia; some trains to/from Vladimir, Nizhny Novgorod, Urals, Siberia, Saratov, Rostov-on-Don; suburban trains to/from the south-east including Bykovo Airport, Kolomna, Gzhel, Ryazan

Kiev Station (Kievsky vokzal), ploshchad Kievskogo Vokzala (Inner South-West; metro: Kievskaya) – trains to/from Bryansk, Kiev, western Ukraine, Moldova, Slovakia, Hungary, Austria, Romania, Bulgaria, Croatia, Serbia, Greece, Venice; some trains to/from the Czech Republic; suburban trains to/from the south-west including Peredelkino, Kaluga

Kursk Station (Kursky vokzal), ploshchad Kurskogo Vokzala (Inner North-East; metro: Kurskaya) – trains to/from Oryol, Kursk, Krasnodar, Adler, the Caucasus, eastern Ukraine, Crimea, Georgia, Azerbaijan; some trains to/from Rostov-on-Don, Vladimir, Nizhny Novgorod, Perm; suburban trains to/from the east and south including Petushki, Vladimir, Podolsk, Chekhov, Serpukhov, Tula

Leningrad Station (Leningradsky vokzal), Komsomolskaya ploshchad (Inner North-East; metro: Komsomolskaya) – trains to/from Tver, Novgorod, Pskov, St Petersburg, Vyborg, Murmansk, Estonia, Helsinki; suburban trains to/from the north-west including Klin, Tver

Pavelets Station (Paveletsky vokzal), Paveletskaya ploshchad (formerly Leninskaya ploshchad; Inner South; metro: Paveletskaya) – trains to/from Yelets, Lipetsk, Voronezh, Tambov, Volgograd, Astrakhan; some trains to/from Saratov; suburban trains to/from the south-east including Leninskaya

Riga Station (Rizhsky vokzal), Rizhskaya ploshchad (Outer North; metro: Rizhskaya) – trains to/from Latvia; suburban trains to/from the north-west including Istra, Novoierusalimskaya

Savyolov Station (Savyolovsky vokzal), ploshchad Savyolovskogo Vokzala (Outer North; metro: Savyolovskaya) – trains to/from Cherepovets; some trains to/from Kostroma, Vologda; suburban trains to/from the north

Yaroslavl Station (Yaroslavsky vokzal), Komsomolskaya ploshchad (Inner North-East; metro: Komsomolskaya) – trains to/from Yaroslavl, Arkhangelsk, Vorkuta, Russian Far East, Mongolia, China, North Korea; some trains to/from Vladimir, Nizhny Novgorod, Kostroma, Vologda, Perm, Urals, Siberia; suburban trains to/from the north-east including Abramtsevo, Khotkovo, Sergiev Posad, Alexandrov

Trains Hundreds of trains leave Moscow's stations daily, with several a day to most main cities. The quickest and most comfortable long-distance trains are generally the 'name trains' *(firmennye poezdy)*. These also tend to start and end their journeys at relatively convenient hours. They can also be more expensive than other trains.

The table on the following pages shows name trains and other best services to/from some main terminus cities. There are many other services too, to the same cities and others. All trains of course stop at many places along their routes; thus, for example, you could use the Abakan-bound 'Khakasia' to reach Kazan, Yekaterinburg or Novosibirsk.

Timetables showing these and the other services are displayed at stations and ticket offices, but are not very easy to decipher. Note also that railway timetables (and ticket clerks) often use old names for some cities – you may find Sverdlovsk instead of Yekaterinburg, Gorky instead of Nizhny Novgorod, Kalinin instead of Tver, even Leningrad instead of St Petersburg.

There's hardly any fare variation between the different trains to St Petersburg. For further info on fares, see the following Tickets section and the Train section of the European Russia Getting Around chapter. You may be able to get up-to-date fare information from the Central Railway Agency on ☎ 927 21 05 or 262 42 02.

Schedules do change from time to time, but usually only by a few minutes. Frequencies may change occasionally.

Further information on services to/from specific places can be found in the relevant city sections. For full coverage of trans-Siberian services, see the Trans-Siberian Railway chapter.

Tickets For long-distance trains it's best to get your ticket as far in advance as you can. Tickets on some trains may be available on the day of departure, but this is less likely in summer. Take your passport along when you go to buy a ticket, even if you're trying to get a Russian-price ticket, as you may need to show some identification.

Russian-Price Tickets Getting Russian-price tickets (except for suburban trains, which do not have foreigners' fares) is harder in Moscow than in most Russian cities. Station ticket clerks may send you away to one of the special foreigners' ticket offices where you can't avoid paying a foreigners' price – or you may be lucky and get a ticket with no questions asked. Another consideration is that on some of the trains from Moscow most used by foreigners – particularly trains to St Petersburg and the main trans-Siberian trains – there's a risk of conductors or provodniks demanding 'fines' if they find foreigners travelling on Russian-price tickets.

If you *are* trying for a Russian-price ticket, you have to be prepared to queue, and you also have to try to make sure you're queueing at the right ticket window. Some stations have one set of ticket windows for departures within 24 hours, and another set for advance tickets (usually available up to 30, or even 45, days before travel). Advance ticket windows are usually labelled 'Predvaritelnaya Kassa' or something similar.

In the Leningrad Station, the Russian ticket windows in the first hall are for trains departing within 24 hours; the advance ticket windows are up the stairs at the right-hand end of the second hall. The Yaroslavl Station Russian ticket windows (upstairs) only sell tickets for trains leaving within 24 hours.

Destination	Name	Number*	Moscow Station	Departure Time**	Trip Time (Hours)	Notes
Abakan	Khakasia	68/67	Kazan	11.42 pm	75	
Adler	Sochi	1/2	Kursk	7.09 pm	39	
Adler		23/24	Kursk	1.35 pm	40	
Almaty	Kazakhstan	8/7	Kazan	10.15 pm	76	
Arkhangelsk		16/15	Yaroslavl	12.05 pm	21	
Astrakhan	Lotos	5/6	Pavelets	9.10 am	31	departs Moscow even dates only
Astrakhan		183/184	Pavelets	11.05 pm	33	
Athens	Pushkin	9/10	Kiev	9.56 am	69	departs Moscow Tuesday, Thursday, Saturday, Sunday
Baku		5/6	Kursk	1.45 am	54	
Barnaul	Altay	36/35	Kazan	4.10 pm	63	departs Moscow odd dates only
Barnaul		96/95	Kazan	9.30 pm	68	departs Moscow even dates only
Beijing		4/3	Yaroslavl	7.45 pm	135	'Trans-Mongolian', departs Moscow Tuesday only
Beijing		20/19	Yaroslavl	8.25 pm	149	'Trans-Manchurian', departs Moscow Friday & Saturday only
Belgrade	Pushkin	9/10	Kiev	9.56 am	46	
Berlin	Moskva Express	13/14	Belorussia	1.09 pm	33	
Bishkek	Kirgizia	18/17	Kazan	11.02 pm	76	
Bratislava	Slovakia Express	51/52	Kiev	11.47 am	43	
Brest		73/74	Belorussia	5.45 pm	17	
Brussels	Vostok-Zapad Express	15/16	Belorussia	8.15 pm	4	connection for London
Bryansk	Desna	99/100	Kiev	10.43 pm	7	
Bucharest	Rumynia Express	5/6	Kiev	4.45 pm	43	departs Moscow Sunday, Wednesday, Thursday only
Budapest	Tissa Express	15/16	Kiev	8.32 pm	41	
Chisinau (Kishinyov)	Moldova	47/48	Kiev	10.50 pm	31	
Donetsk	Donbass	9/10	Kursk	1.20 pm	21	
Dushanbe		24/23	Kazan	1.00 am	89	departs Moscow odd dates only
Frankfurt	Moskva Express	13/14	Belorussia	1.09 pm	44	
Grozny	Terek	88/87	Kazan	3.44 pm	40	departs Moscow even dates only
Helsinki	Tolstoy	32/31	Leningrad	6.17 pm	15	
Homel (Gomel)	Sozh	55/56	Belorussia	7.49 pm	16	
Hrodna (Grodno)	Nyoman	77/78	Belorussia	2.38 pm	20	

Destination	Name	Number*	Moscow Station	Departure Time**	Trip Time (Hours)	Notes
Irkutsk	Baikal	10/9	Yaroslavl	9.05 pm	84	departs Moscow daily in summer, odd dates only in winter
Irkutsk		118/117	Yaroslavl	7.45 pm	80	twice weekly
Kaliningrad	Yantar	29/30	Belorussia	1.23 pm	24	
Kaliningrad		149/150	Belorussia	10.07 pm	26	
Kazan	Tatarstan	28/27	Kazan	6.15 pm	14	
Kazan		92/91	Kazan	10.45 pm	15	departs Moscow odd dates only
Kharkiv (Kharkov)	Kharkov	19/20	Kursk	8.40 pm	14	
Kiev	Ukraina	1/2	Kiev	7.03 pm	15	
Kiev	Kiev	3/4	Kiev	2.20 pm	16	
Kislovodsk	Kavkaz	3/4	Kursk	4.22 pm	36	via Mineralnye Vody
Krasnoyarsk	Yenisey	56/55	Kazan	12.51 pm	64	departs Moscow three days a week
Krasnoyarsk		90/89	Kazan	00.34 am	72	departs Moscow daily in summer, four days weekly in winter
Kursk	Solovey	105/106	Kursk	8.45 pm	10	
London						see Brussels
Lviv (Lvov)	Verkhovina	73/74	Kiev	9.17 am	29	
Makhachkala	Dagestan	78/79	Kursk	6.51 pm	42	
Minsk	Belorussia	1/2	Belorussia	7.15 pm	13	
Minsk	Minsk	3/4	Belorussia	9.32 pm	13	
Minsk	Svisloch	25/26	Belorussia	10.47 am	13	
Murmansk	Arktika	16/15	Leningrad	00.30 am	36	
Murmansk		182/181	Leningrad	7.29 pm	41	
Nalchik	Elbrus	61/62	Kursk	2.48 pm	39	via Mineralnye Vody
Nizhny Novgorod	Yarmarka	2/1	Kazan	9.40 pm	9	
Nizhny Novgorod	Nizhe-gorodets	38/37	Yaroslavl	11.10 pm	8	
Novgorod	Ilmen	42/41	Leningrad	10.10 pm	9	
Novosibirsk	Sibiryak	26/25	Yaroslavl	2.25 pm	52	
Odessa	Odessa	23/24	Kiev	7.44 pm	28	
Omsk	Irtysh	48/47	Kazan	7.10 pm	44	
Perm	Kama	22/21	Kursk	3.45 pm	24	
Petrozavodsk	Karelia	18/17	Leningrad	6.22 pm	16	
Polatsk (Polotsk)	Dvina	277/278	Belorussia	4.15 pm	13	
Poltava	Poltava	91/92	Kursk	7.37 pm	18	
Prague	Dukla Express	7/8	Kiev	1.00 pm	48	via Kiev, Lvov
Prague		21/22	Belorussia	7.01 pm	38	via Brest, Warsaw
Pskov		70/69	Leningrad	7.45 pm	13	
Riga	Latvia Express	1/2	Riga	7.53 pm	16	via Rezekne
Riga	Yurmala	3/4	Riga	9.08 pm	16	via Rezekne
Rostov-on-Don	Tikhy Don	20/19	Kazan	6.50 pm	22	
St Petersburg	Krasnaya Strela	2/1	Leningrad	11.55 pm	8½	

Destination	Name	Number*	Moscow Station	Departure Time**	Trip Time (Hours)	Notes
St Petersburg	Express	4/3	Leningrad	11.59 pm	8½	
St Petersburg	Inturist	6/5	Leningrad	11.10 pm	8	
St Petersburg	Beryozka	10/9	Leningrad	00.52 am	8	
St Petersburg	Yunost	24/23	Leningrad	12.26 pm	8	
St Petersburg	Smena	26/25	Leningrad	11.00 pm	8	
St Petersburg	Sankt-Peterburg	36/35	Leningrad	00.05 am	9	has been notorious for thefts
St Petersburg	ER 200	158/157	Leningrad	12.21 pm	5	departs Moscow Friday only
St Petersburg	Avrora	160/159	Leningrad	5.18 pm	6	
Samara	Zhiguli	10/9	Kazan	12.20 pm	19	
Saratov	Saratov	9/10	Pavelets	3.00 pm	17	
Simferopol	Krym	31/32	Kursk	10.25 am	27	
Simferopol	Simferopol	67/68	Kursk	2.55 pm	26	
Smolensk	Smolensk	103/104	Belorussia	4.00 pm	8	
Sofia	Sofia Express	59/60	Kiev	2.44 pm	53	
Tallinn	Estonia	34/33	Leningrad	5.25 pm	17	via Narva
Tallinn		176/175	Leningrad	4.00 pm	20	via Pskov, Tartu
Tashkent	Uzbekistan	6/5	Kazan	11.52 pm	59	
Ulan Bator		6/5	Yaroslavl	5.20 pm	110	departs Moscow Wednesday, Thursday only
Venice	Tissa Express	15/16	Kiev	8.32 pm	57	departs Moscow Wednesday & Sunday only
Vienna	Vostok-Zapad Express	15/16	Belorussia	8.15 pm	36	via Minsk, Warsaw
Vienna	Slovakia Express	51/52	Kiev	11.47 am	45	via Kiev, Bratislava
Vilnius	Lietuva	5/6	Belorussia	5.17 pm	18	
Vladikavkaz	Osetia	29/30	Kursk	1.15 pm	43	
Vladivostok	Rossia	2/1	Yaroslavl	2.00 pm	153	departs Moscow odd dates only
Volgograd	Volgograd	1/2	Pavelets	2.05 pm	22	
Vologda	Vologodskie Zori	148/147	Yaroslavl	10.20 pm	9	
Vyborg	A Nikitin	38/37	Leningrad	9.55 pm	11	
Warsaw	Interexpress/Polonez	9/10	Belorussia	3.17 pm	19	
Warsaw		21/22	Belorussia	7.01 pm	24	
Yaroslavl	Yaroslavl	122/121	Yaroslavl	4.15 pm	5	
Yaroslavl		124/123	Yaroslavl	7.40 am	5	
Yekaterinburg	Ural	16/15	Kazan	3.54 pm	29	
Yekaterinburg	Ural	8/7	Yaroslavl	2.00 pm	30	departs Moscow even dates only

* Number of train outbound from Moscow/inbound to Moscow
** Departure time from Moscow (daily unless stated otherwise)

The brown building between the Leningrad and Yaroslavl stations (behind the metro exit) sells advance tickets to Russians for destinations in the ex-USSR: it's a labyrinthine place with different rooms for different groups of destinations, open from 7 am to 8 pm Monday to Saturday, 7 am to 5 pm Sunday. Some rooms have interactive screens giving ticket availability for specific trains and dates.

Foreigners' Ticket Offices If you have been turned away from station ticket windows, or have simply decided on the more straightforward option of paying a foreigners' fare in any case, you can get the straight foreigners' fare at four offices of the Central Railway Agency (Tsentralnoe Zheleznodorozhnoe Agentstvo), all open daily from 8 am to 1 pm and 2 to 7 pm. The offices are:

Maly Kharitonevsky pereulok (formerly ulitsa Griboedova) 6 (☎ 262 06 04; Inner North-East; metro: Chistye Prudy or Krasnye Vorota) – window Nos 1 to 3 in zal (room) No 1 of korpus (building) No 1 sell tickets for ex-USSR destinations from 10 days ahead to the day of departure; window Nos 7 and 8 in the ground floor hall of korpus No 2 sell tickets to other countries from 30 days ahead to the day of departure

Krasnoprudnaya ulitsa 1 (☎ 266 00 04; Inner North-East; metro: Komsomolskaya), immediately east of the Yaroslavl Station (look for the 'Zheleznodorozhye Kassy' sign) – tickets from 30 days ahead to the day of departure, from window No 2 for ex-USSR destinations, window Nos 5 to 8 for other countries

Leningradsky prospekt 1 (☎ 262 33 42; Inner North-West; metro: Belorusskaya), on the corner of Nizhnyaya ulitsa, entered from the side lane of the west side of Leningradsksy prospekt, across the railway bridge from the Belorussia Station – tickets from 30 days ahead to day of departure from window Nos 9 and 10

ulitsa Mozhaysky Val 4/6 (☎ 240 05 05; Inner South-West; metro: Kievskaya), one km west of the Kiev Station – tickets to all destinations from 30 days ahead to day of departure

Foreigners' price tickets to St Petersburg and Tallinn within 24 hours of departure are also sold at window Nos 19 to 21 in the Leningrad Station (up the stairs on the right at the end of the station's second hall, then turn right,

then left). Hours are 8 am to noon and 1 to 7 pm, daily.

For tickets to Helsinki from 45 days ahead to the day of departure, you can also go to window Nos 35 and 36 in the second hall of the Leningrad Station. Opening hours are 8 am to 1 pm and 2 to 6.30 pm, but after 4 pm only same-day tickets are sold.

Other Ticket Outlets If you don't fancy the melee of a station or the effort of finding your way to a Central Railway Agency office, you can buy tickets from the following three places at mark-ups that vary between 5% and 25% on the basic foreigners' price. The amount of mark-up varies from train to train. On the whole Intourtrans seems to have the smallest mark-ups of the three, and Intourist the biggest.

Intourtrans (☎ 927 11 81), through the arch at ulitsa Petrovka 15/13 (Inner North; metro: Kuznetsky Most) – open Monday to Friday from 9 am to 8 pm, Saturday and Sunday from 9 am to 7 pm; rail ticket office is on floor 2

IRO Travel (☎ 971 40 59, 280 85 62; fax 280 76 86) at the Travellers Guest House, 10th floor, ulitsa Bolshaya Pereyaslavskaya 50 (Inner North; metro: Prospekt Mira)

Intourist central service bureau (☎ 292 23 94), Mokhovaya ulitsa 13 (City Centre; metro: Okhotny Ryad) – train ticket desk open from 9 am to 1 pm and 2 to 8 pm daily

Many other travel agencies can also provide train tickets (see Travel Agencies in this chapter's Information section).

Car & Motorbike

See the European Russia Getting Around chapter for general advice on driving.

Ten major highways, numbered M1 to M10 (but not in any logical order), fan out from Moscow to all points of the compass. Most are in fairly good condition at first but some get scraggy further out. The main road from Western Europe, the M1 from Poland via Brest, Minsk and Smolensk, is straight and dull but fairly quick. The M10 to St Petersburg is dual carriageway much of the way to Tver, 145 km out, but there are narrow stretches beyond. The first 110 km of the M2 to Oryol and Ukraine are excellent dual carriageway – something you'll remember like a dream as you hit some of the bumpy, narrow roads further south. The M7 east to Vladimir and the M8 north-east to Yaroslavl are in reasonable condition but are busy and slow.

Moscow has around 40 petrol stations which sell 93-grade petrol. There's a 24-hour Western-run petrol station, Nefto Agip, at Leningradskoe shosse 63 north of Rechnoy Vokzal metro. There are parts, service and repair specialists for many Western makes of car in Moscow. *The Traveller's Yellow Pages Moscow* and *Where in Moscow* list most of them. The Stockmann Home Electronics & Car Supplies shop at Lyusinovskaya ulitsa 70, one block north of Tulskaya metro (Inner South) sells some parts for many foreign makes.

Car Rental There's little reason for the average traveller to rent a car for getting about Moscow, as public transport is quite adequate. But you might want to consider it for trips out of the city. You'll need your passport, driving licence and major credit card.

There are lots of car-rental firms in Moscow, and most tourist hotels have a rental desk of some kind, but the scene has two special features: many firms won't let you take their cars out of the city, and others will only rent you a car with a driver. Companies' policies change frequently, so the only answer is to ring round some of those listed below to try to find what you want. Cars with drivers don't always work out more expensive than cars without, and save you the trouble of coping with Russian roads.

As you'd expect, the big international outfits charge quite a lot more than small Russian ones. From Hertz, for example, you're looking at US$145 per 24 hours for a self-drive Lada with unlimited km. At least you should be paying for a reliable car. You may get Ladas from smaller outfits for less than US$50 a day. If you have a Lada from anyone, and it goes wrong, there's always a

good chance another passing Lada driver will be able to fix it for you with the bits of wire and tube they all carry in the boot. Of the following companies, Avis, Hertz and Europcar have had cars available without driver for use anywhere in Russia. InNis, MGKP and Olga have had cars without driver available for the Moscow region. Hertz, MGKP and Rasko can offer Ladas.

Avis
    Berezhovskaya naberezhnaya 12 (☎ 240 98 63)
    Sheremetevo-2 Airport (☎ 578 56 46)
Europcar
    International Trade Centre, Krasnopresnenskaya naberezhnaya 12 (☎ 253 13 69)
    Novaya ploshchad 14 (☎ 923 97 49)
    Olympic Penta Hotel, Olimpiysky prospekt 18 (☎ 971 61 01)
    Sheremetevo-2 Airport (☎ 578 82 36)
Hertz
    Room 11, prospekt Mira 49 (☎ 284 43 91)
    Sheremetevo-2 Airport (☎ 578 75 32)
InNis
    ulitsa Bolshaya Ordynka 32 (☎ 238 30 77)
MGKP
    Hotel Rossia, ulitsa Varvarka (formerly ulitsa Razina) 6 (☎ 298 58 53)
    Kozhevnicheskaya ulitsa 6 (☎ 235 27 79)
Olga
    Hotel Metropol, Teatralny proezd 1 (☎ 927 69 72)
Rasko
    2-y Paveletsky proezd 6 (☎ 235 60 51)
    Hotel Kosmos, prospekt Mira 150 (☎ 235 82 08)
    Sheremetevo-2 Airport (☎ 578 71 79)

Boat

In summer, passenger boats from Moscow ply the rivers and canals of Russia all the way north to St Petersburg, and south to Astrakhan on the Volga delta near the Caspian Sea. The St Petersburg route follows the Moscow Canal and then the Volga River to the Rybinsk Reservoir, then the Volga-Baltic canal to Lake Onega, the Svir river to Lake Ladoga and the Neva River to St Petersburg. The main southbound route takes the Moscow Canal north to the Volga then follows the Volga east and then south all the way downstream to Astrakhan (10 days from Moscow), via Uglich, Yaroslavl, Kostroma, Nizhny Novgorod, Kazan, Ulyanovsk, Samara, Saratov and Volgograd.

The Moscow terminus for these sailings is the Northern River Station (Severny Rechnoy Vokzal; ☎ 459 74 76; fax 459 70 16) at Leningradskoe shosse 51 (Outer North; metro: Rechnoy Vokzal). The navigation season depends on the route. If you thought the break-up of Aeroflot was something, wait till you see what's happened to state-run ship services. As we write this, the state services are being pared down further and further, handing over their boats to private enterprises, but at the time of writing sailings between Moscow and Astrakhan via Yaroslavl, Nizhny Novgorod, and Kazan left about every other day from early June to mid-October.

You can take the boats to intermediate stops, and a short trip to Yaroslavl (1½ days) or Nizhny Novgorod (three days) could be an interesting way to see some of Russia. Fares depend on the class of cabin: there are at least eight classes. One-way fares – not including food – range from US$7 to US$117 to Yaroslavl; US$20 to US$200 to Nizhny Novgorod; US$41.50 to US$250 to Kazan; US$25 to US$450 to Astrakhan. At the time of writing, service to Rostov-on-Don and Ufa had been indefinitely suspended.

Tickets are sold at the Northern River Station and at an advance booking office at Leningradsky prospekt 1 (☎ 257 71 09) near the Belorussia Station (Inner North-West; metro: Belorusskaya). The advance booking office is actually just off Leningradsky prospekt, in Nizhnyaya ulitsa, across the railway bridge north of the station.

Also advertised at the Northern River Station, the Leningradsky prospekt ticket office, and elsewhere are 'cruises' run by private companies, likely to be on better vessels and to include food. Most of these are return trips although there are some one-way cruises to St Petersburg (indeed, these may now be the only sailings to St Petersburg). Thirteen-day cruises between Moscow and St Petersburg (via Uglich, Petrozavodsk, Kizhi Island in Lake Onega and Valaam Island in Lake Ladoga) run at least every two weeks. Typical prices range

from US$260 to US$413 including meals and excursions along the way. Four or five-day return cruises to Yaroslavl were from US$70 to US$180; short trips to Tver and back were from US$43 to US$990; and 18 to 20-day round-trip cruises to Astrakhan were from US$425 to US$4275. Foreigners, they say, are charged the same as Russians, so long as they're individuals, not members of a large group.

One organisation whose cruises have been recommended is the Centre for Creative Initiatives & Projects (☎ 245 02 82, or an English/Russian answering machine on ☎ 330 49 50) at room 516, Zubovsky bulvar 17, just north of Park Kultury metro station (Inner South-West). The centre offers a range of durations from three to 16 days on routes along the Volga as far as Nizhny Novgorod, and north to St Petersburg, with prices of US$30 to US$60 a day.

It's possible to book cruises from other countries: see the European Russia Getting Around chapter for information.

GETTING AROUND

The central area around the Kremlin, the Kitay-Gorod and the Bolshoy Theatre are best seen on foot. To almost anywhere else, the fastest, cheapest and easiest way to get around is on the metro and on foot, though buses, trolleybuses and trams come in useful sometimes.

To/From the Airports

You can get between all five airports and the city centre cheaply by a combination of bus and metro or suburban train, but if you're in a hurry, or are going early in the morning or late at night, or have a lot of baggage, you'll probably need a taxi. There have been occasional tales of theft or robbery in taxis going into the city from Sheremetevo-2, so be on your guard with these and don't get into any vehicle that already has anyone other than the driver in it.

The easiest and surest way to get from any airport into the city is to get your travel agent (if you have one) to book you a transfer. This means you'll be driven straight from the airport to your destination in the city. You may not have to pay any more than a normal taxi fare: Intourist, for instance, charges US$25 for transfers to/from Sheremetevo-2. Some travel firms have airport desks where you can book transfers on the spot.

The City Air Terminal (Gorodskoy aerovokzal) at Leningradsky prospekt 37 (Outer North) has bus services to/from all the airports, but as the terminal itself is not very convenient to reach, other routes to/from the airports are usually easier. Buses from the City Air Terminal also tend to be less frequent than the alternative services. To reach the City Air Terminal, take the metro to the Dinamo stop, then any trolleybus or tram north on Leningradsky prospekt for one km.

Leaving Moscow, your hotel or accommodation will always be able to arrange a taxi for you, but you can get one cheaper yourself. See the later Taxi section for how to order one. Don't rely on flagging one down on the street as it may take a long time to find a driver who is prepared to go out to an airport.

Sheremetevo Buses run between the airport and Rechnoy Vokzal metro station at the northern end of the green metro line. 'Express' buses link Sheremetevo-1 and Sheremetevo-2 with Rechnoy Vokzal metro every half an hour from 7 am to 9 pm for a fare of US$0.60. The slower city bus No 551 runs between the same places from about 5.30 am to 11 pm. It goes about every 20 minutes during the day but may be less frequent in the early morning and late evening. To find the bus stop at Sheremetevo-2, follow the road to the left immediately outside the arrivals hall: the stop is about 200 metres along, marked with 'Express' and '551' signs. You may have to work your way past a few taxi touts as leave the terminal.

Going out to the airport from Rechnoy Vokzal, leave the metro platform by the exit at the front end of your train. For the Express bus, turn right outside the station and you'll find the 'Express' stop about 75 metres along the road. The Express goes to Sheremetevo-2 first, then Sheremetevo-1. It takes about 25

minutes to Sheremetevo-2. For bus No 551, cross the road to the stop near the metro station's other exit. No 551 goes to Sheremetevo-1 first, then Sheremetevo-2. Allow 45 minutes to reach Sheremetevo-2.

Buses from the City Air Terminal go to Sheremetevo-2 (US$1, 35 minutes) only a few times a day – the schedule when we last checked was 8.30 and 11 am, and 1.30, 2.30, 4, 5.30, 7.30 and 10 pm. Buses from the City Air Terminal to Sheremetevo-1 (US$1, 45 minutes) go about hourly from 6.25 am to 11.30 pm.

A taxi between either Sheremetevo airport and the city centre takes about 45 minutes. It should cost US$30 to US$45, though absurd prices may be asked of tourists. At Sheremetevo-2 you'll be pestered by taxi drivers or their touts before you leave the terminal building – don't agree to anything till you see the car itself outside. You may be able to get a cab for a rock-bottom US$25 or so by going up to the departures level and finding one that has just dropped someone off.

Domodedovo The airport is linked by buses to Domodedovskaya metro station from 6 am to midnight. For buses from the airport to the metro, walk to the right when you exit the terminal: you'll find the buses in front of the building with the 'Avtobusy-Expressy' sign. They leave for Domodedovskaya metro when full (about every 15 to 20 minutes during the day). The trip takes 30 to 40 minutes and the fare is US$1.20. Other buses from the same parking area go to Oktyabrskaya metro and the City Air Terminal – take one if it suits you but if you want to go to Domodedovskaya, take no notice of touts who try to tell you that you really should go to Oktyabrskaya.

Going out to the airport, you should set off at least three hours before take-off. Pitfalls of the trip are variable metro journeying times, a metro branch line that goes the wrong way (to Kakhovskaya station on an adjacent line), possible waits for a bus at Domodedovskaya, and obscure check-in procedures at the airport (see Getting There

& Away – Air). At Domodedovskaya, the buses wait by the 'A/P Domodedovo' sign outside the metro station and leave when full (about every 15 to 20 minutes during the day): you may not get on the first one.

Buses leave the City Air Terminal for Domodedovskaya (US$1.50, 1½ hours) once or twice an hour from 5.30 am to 11 pm.

A third alternative is the suburban train (prigorodny poezd) between the airport and the Pavelets Station (Inner South; metro: Paveletskaya). The airport station is to the left as you exit the terminal building. The trains run almost hourly from 5 am to 10.30 pm and take 1¼ hours for a fare of US$0.20. Going out to the airport, make sure your train is going to Aeroport Domodedovo, which is on its own branch line, and not just to Domodedovo town.

A taxi to/from the city centre should cost US$25 to US$35. The trip takes one to 1½ hours depending on traffic.

Vnukovo Buses link the airport with Yugo-Zapadnaya metro station from 6.45 am to 10.15 pm. By 'Express' bus the trip takes 30 minutes and costs US$0.60. The buses leave when full (about every 15 to 20 minutes during the day). There's also the slower city bus No 511.

Buses leave the City Air Terminal for Vnukovo (one hour, US$1) hourly from 6 am to 11 pm.

A taxi to/from the city centre is about US$25.

Bykovo When we checked, buses left the City Airline Terminal for Bykovo (US$1.80, 1½ hours) at 6.35, 7.35, 9.05, 10.05 and 11.35 am, and 12.35, 2.35, 4.35 and 6.35 pm.

Suburban (prigorodnye) trains run between Bykovo train station, 400 metres from the airport, and the Kazan Station (Inner North-East; metro: Komsomolskaya). One of their stops en route is Vykhino, by Vykhino metro station. Going out to the airport, most trains heading for Platforma 47 Km, Vinogradovo, Shifernaya or Golutvin stop at Bykovo (as well as those marked 'Bykovo') but just a few go straight through,

so always check. The trains, which take about one hour, go about every 20 minutes from 5 am to 10 pm, and about every 40 minutes from 10 pm to midnight. At the Kazan Station, buy your ticket (about US$0.15) in the Prigorodny Zal (Room No 7), entered from the right-hand (west) end of the building.

A taxi to/from the city centre is about US$25 to US$30.

Between Airports To get between Sheremetevo-2 and Sheremetevo-1 take city bus No 551 or 517 (No 517 goes from the same stops as No 551 – see Sheremetevo, above).

Around five buses a day run between Domodedovo and Vnukovo airports, a 1½-hour trip for US$2. Departures from Domodedovo (from the same stop as buses to Domodedovskaya metro) when we checked were at 6.30, 9.30 and 11.30 am, and 1.30 and 3.30 pm.

To/From Train Stations

All the main stations are within four km of the Kremlin and all have metro stations on the spot. Taxis wait outside.

Metro

The metro is the easiest, quickest and cheapest way of getting around Moscow. With elegant, graffiti-free stations – many of them marble-faced, frescoed, gilded works of art – this is one Stalin-initiated project Muscovites are proud of, and nine million of them use it every day. The stations were meant to double as air-raid shelters, which is why the escalators seem to plunge halfway to the centre of the earth.

The 150-plus stations are marked outside with big 'M' signs. Buy a few tokens (zhetony) for about US$0.10 each from the windows inside the entrance, place one in the slot of the automatic entry gates, wait for its little lights to change, and you're on your way. (If you don't wait for the lights to change, metal arms will come across and bar your way.)

Stations have maps of the system, and

signs on each platform show the stations each train goes to. Interchange stations are linked by underground passages, indicated by 'perekhod' (crossover) signs which are usually blue with a stick figure running up the stairs. Once you've figured out which train you need you'll rarely wait more than two minutes for it. With an elementary idea of Cyrillic, and by counting stops, you can manage very well. If you get lost, the kindly women who supervise the escalators can point you in the right direction. Exits to street level are marked 'vykhod v gorod'. Eventually you'll start to recognise the recorded announcements in the cars: *'sleduyushchaya stantsia...'* ('next station...') followed by the station name, as the doors are closing, or *'stantsia...'* just before they open.

The basic layout of the system is straightforward. There's one circle line (the *koltsevaya linia*) with stops at seven of the city's main main-line railway stations, and eight radial lines that splay out from the city centre and all intersect with the circle line. A ninth radial line was due to open in 1995 and already appears on some metro maps. There are a few quirks, however. Sometimes three or four lines intersect in one place with as many stations linked by perekhod. Adjacent interchange stations often don't have the same names. Two stations, Arbatskaya and

Smolenskaya, appear with the same name on more than one line, with entrances and platforms near each other but not connected by perekhod; either will do for getting off but be sure which one you're getting on at. And the Leninskie Gory station has been 'temporarily' shut for years because of adjacent bridge repairs.

Stations open at about 5.30 am and close at 12.30 am. If you're on a train by 12.30 am you can ride it to the end of the line, but perekhody (interchange walkways) close at 1 am.

Some of our favourite stations are: Komsomolskaya, with mosaics of past Russian military heroes; the Kievskaya circle line stop, with mosaics of Ukrainian history; beautiful Mayakovskaya, grand prize winner at the 1938 International Exhibition; Novokuznetskaya, with military bas-reliefs and industrial ceiling mosaics; and Ploshchad Revolyutsii, where statues beside the escalators illustrate the means and ends of Socialism (from the bottom: force to carry out and protect the revolution, industry, agriculture, hunting, education, sport, childrearing).

Bus, Trolleybus & Tram

Buses, trolleybuses and trams run almost everywhere the metro doesn't go. They can be useful along a few radial or cross-town routes that the metro misses, and are necessary for reaching a few hotels or sights away from the city centre.

All routes are shown on the good Russian *Moskva Transport* map, but unfortunately it's not very widely available. One place we have found it is the Slavyanka map shop (see Maps in this chapter's Information section).

Buses, trolleybuses and trams run from 5 am to 1 am, though services are infrequent at the ends of the day. They can get very crowded at busy times. Bus stops are marked by 'A' signs (for *Avtobus)*, trolleybus stops by 'T' signs by the roadside, tram stops by a 'T' sign over the roadway – all of which usually indicate the line numbers, too. Stops may also have roadside signs with little pictures of a bus, trolleybus or tram.

Metro Station Names

Several Moscow metro stations have had their names changed since the end of the Soviet era. All metro signs and maps bear the new titles. Here they are:

New Name	Old Name
Alexandrovsky Sad	Kalininskaya
Alexeevskaya	Shcherbakovskaya
Chistye Prudy	Kirovskaya
Kitay-Gorod	Ploshchad Nogina
Krasnye Vorota	Lermontovskaya
Lubyanka	Dzerzhinskaya
Okhotny Ryad	Prospekt Marxa
Sukharevskaya	Kolkhoznaya
Teatralnaya	Ploshchad Sverdlova
Tsaritsino	Lenino
Tverskaya	Gorkovskaya

RICHARD NEBESKY

RICHARD NEBESKY

RICHARD NEBESKY

RICHARD NEBESKY

RICHARD NEBESKY

A: Assumption Cathedral, Moscow Kremlin
B: St Basil's Cathedral, Red Square, Moscow
C: Annunciation Cathedral, Kazan

D: St Basil's Cathedral, Red Square,
    Moscow
E: Moscow Kremlin

Moscow Metro
Московское метро

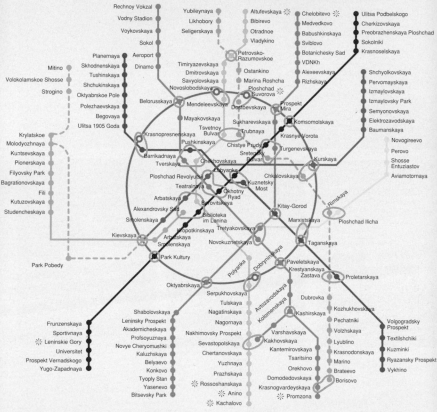

Rechnoy Vokzal · Vodny Stadion · Voykovskaya · Sokol · Aeroport · Planernaya · Skhodnenskaya · Tushinskaya · Shchukinskaya · Oktyabrskoe Pole · Polezhaevskaya · Begovaya · Ulitsa 1905 Goda · Dinamo · Mitino · Volokolamskoe Shosse · Strogino

Yubileynaya · Likhobory · Seligerskaya · Timiryazevskaya · Dmitrovskaya · Savyolovskaya · Novoslobodskaya · Belorusskaya · Mendeleevskaya · Mayakovskaya · Tsvetnoy Bulvar · Pushkinskaya · Krasnopresnenskaya · Barrikadnaya · Tverskaya · Chekhovskaya · Ploshchad Revolyutsii · Teatralnaya · Okhotny Ryad · Borovitskaya · Biblioteka im Lenina · Arbatskaya · Aleksandrovsky Sad · Smolenskaya · Kropotkinskaya · Arbatskaya · Smolenskaya

Altufevskaya · Bibirevo · Otradnoe · Vladykino · Petrovsko-Razumovskoe · Ostankino · Marina Roshcha · Ploshchad Suvorova · Dostoevskaya · Sukharevskaya · Trubnaya · Chistye Prudy · Sretensky Bulvar · Lubyanka · Kuznetsky Most

Chelobitevo · Medvedkovo · Babushkinskaya · Sviblovo · Botanichesky Sad · VDNKh · Alexeevskaya · Rizhskaya · Prospekt Mira · Komsomolskaya · Krasnye Vorota · Turgenevskaya · Chkalovskaya

Ulitsa Podbelskogo · Cherkizovskaya · Preobrazhenskaya Ploshchad · Sokolniki · Krasnoselskaya · Shchyolkovskaya · Pervomayskaya · Izmaylovskaya · Izmaylovsky Park · Semyonovskaya · Elektrozavodskaya · Baumanskaya · Kurskaya

Krylatskoe · Molodyozhnaya · Kuntsevskaya · Pionerskaya · Filyovsky Park · Bagrationovskaya · Fili · Kutuzovskaya · Studencheskaya · Kievskaya · Park Pobedy

Kitay-Gorod · Marxistskaya · Novokuznetskaya · Tretyakovskaya · Taganskaya · Ploshchad Ilicha · Rimskaya · Aviamotornaya · Shosse Entuziastov · Perovo · Novogireevo

Park Kultury · Oktyabrskaya · Serpukhovskaya · Tulskaya · Nagatinskaya · Shabolovskaya · Leninsky Prospekt · Akademicheskaya · Profsoyuznaya · Novye Cheryomushki · Kaluzhskaya · Belyaevo · Konkovo · Tyoply Stan · Yasenevo · Bitsevsky Park

Polyanka · Dobryninskaya · Paveletskaya · Krestyanskaya Zastava · Proletarskaya · Avtozavodskaya · Kolomenskaya · Kashirskaya · Dubrovka · Kozhukhovskaya · Pechatniki · Volzhskaya · Lyublino · Krasnodonskaya · Marino · Bratievo · Borisovo · Volgogradsky Prospekt · Textilshchiki · Kuzminki · Ryazansky Prospekt · Vykhino

Nagornaya · Nakhimovsky Prospekt · Varshavskaya · Sevastopolskaya · Kakhovskaya · Chertanovskaya · Kantemirovskaya · Yuzhnaya · Tsaritsino · Prazhskaya · Orekhovo · Domodedovskaya · Rossoshanskaya · Krasnogvardeyskaya · Anino · Promzona · Kachalovo

---

LEGEND

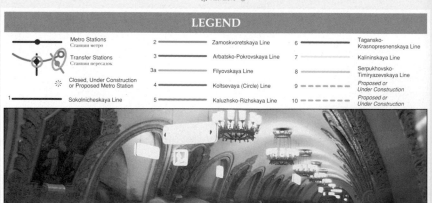

Metro Stations / Станции метро	
Transfer Stations / Станции пересадок	
Closed, Under Construction or Proposed Metro Station	

1 — Sokolnicheskaya Line	
2 — Zamoskvoretskaya Line	6 — Tagansko-Krasnopresnenskaya Line
3 — Arbatsko-Pokrovskaya Line	7 — Kalininskaya Line
3a — Filyovskaya Line	8 — Serpukhovsko-Timiryazevskaya Line
4 — Koltsevaya (Circle) Line	9 — Proposed or Under Construction
5 — Kaluzhsko-Rizhskaya Line	10 — Proposed or Under Construction

1-Sokolnicheskaya Line
СОКОЛЬНИЧЕСКАЯ ЛИНИЯ

УЛ. ПОДБЕЛЬСКОГО
Ul. Podbelskogo
ЧЕРКИЗОВСКАЯ
Cherkizovskaya
ПРЕОБРАЖЕНСКАЯ
ПЛОЩАДЬ
Preobrazhenskaya Ploshchad
СОКОЛЬНИКИ
Sokolniki
КРАСНОСЕЛЬСКАЯ
Krasnoselskaya
КОМСОМОЛЬСКАЯ
Komsomolskaya
КРАСНЫЕ ВОРОТА
Krasnye Vorota
ЧИСТЫЕ ПРУДЫ
Chistye Prudy
ЛУБЯНКА
Lubyanka
ОХОТНЫЙ РЯД
Okhotny Ryad
БИБЛИОТЕКА ИМ. ЛЕНИНА
Biblioteka im Lenina
КРОПОТКИНСКАЯ
Kropotkinskaya
ПАРК КУЛЬТУРЫ
Park Kultury
ФРУНЗЕНСКАЯ
Frunzenskaya
СПОРТИВНАЯ
Sportivnaya
ЛЕНИНСКИЕ ГОРЫ
Leninskie Gory
УНИВЕРСИТЕТ
Universitet
ПРОСПЕКТ ВЕРНАДСКОГО
Prospekt Vernadskogo
ЮГО-ЗАПАДНАЯ
Yugo-Zapadnaya

2-Zamoskvoretskaya Line
ЗАМОСКВОРЕЦКАЯ ЛИНИЯ

РЕЧНОЙ ВОКЗАЛ
Rechnoy Vokzal
ВОДНЫЙ СТАДИОН
Vodny Stadion
ВОЙКОВСКАЯ
Voykovskaya
СОКОЛ
Sokol
АЭРОПОРТ
Aeroport

ДИНАМО
Dinamo
БЕЛОРУССКАЯ
Belorusskaya
МАЯКОВСКАЯ
Mayakovskaya
ТВЕРСКАЯ
Tverskaya
ТЕАТРАЛЬНАЯ
Teatralnaya
НОВОКУЗНЕЦКАЯ
Novokuznetskaya
ПАВЕЛЕЦКАЯ
Paveletskaya
АВТОЗАВОДСКАЯ
Avtozavodskaya
КОЛОМЕНСКАЯ
Kolomenskaya
КАШИРСКАЯ
Kashirskaya
ВАРШАВСКАЯ
Varshavskaya
КАХОВСКАЯ
Kakhovskaya
КАНТЕМИРОВСКАЯ
Kantemirovskaya
ЦАРИЦЫНО
Tsaritsino
ОРЕХОВО
Orekhovo
ДОМОДЕДОВСКАЯ
Domodedovskaya
КРАСНОГВАРДЕЙСКАЯ
Krasnogvardeyskaya
ПРОМЗОНА
Promzona

3-Arbatsko-Pokrovskaya line
АРБАТСКО-ПОКРОВСКАЯ
ЛИНИЯ

КИЕВСКАЯ
Kievskaya
СМОЛЕНСКАЯ
Smolenskaya
АРБАТСКАЯ
Arbatskaya
ПЛОЩАДЬ РЕВОЛЮЦИИ
Ploshchad Revolutsii
КУРСКАЯ
Kurskaya
БАУМАНСКАЯ
Baumanskaya
ЭЛЕКТРОЗАВОДСКАЯ
Elektrozavodskaya
СЕМЁНОВСКАЯ
Semyonovskaya

ИЗМАЙЛОВСКИЙ
ПАРК
Izmaylovsky park
ИЗМАЙЛОВСКАЯ
Izmaylovskaya
ПЕРВОМАЙСКАЯ
Pervomayskaya
ЩЁЛКОВСКАЯ
Shchyolkovskaya

3A-Filyovskaya line
ФИЛЁВСКАЯ ЛИНИЯ

КРЫЛАТСКОЕ
Krylatskoe
МОЛОДЁЖНАЯ
Molodyozhnaya
КУНЦЕВСКАЯ
Kuntsevskaya
ПИОНЕРСКАЯ
Pionerskaya
ФИЛЁВСКИЙ ПАРК
Filyovsky Park
БАГРАТИОНОВСКАЯ
Bagrationovskaya
ФИЛИ
Fili
КУТУЗОВСКАЯ
Kutuzovskaya
СТУДЕНЧЕСКАЯ
Studencheskaya
КИЕВСКАЯ
Kievskaya
СМОЛЕНСКАЯ
Smolenskaya
АРБАТСКАЯ
Arbatskaya
АЛЕКСАНДРОВСКИЙ
САД
Alexandrovsky Sad

4-Koltsevaya Line
КОЛЬЦЕВАЯ ЛИНИЯ

КРАСНОПРЕСНЕНСКАЯ
Krasnopresnenskaya
БЕЛОРУССКАЯ
Belorusskaya
НОВОСЛОБОДСКАЯ
Novoslobodskaya
ПЛОЩАДЬ СУВОРОВА
Ploshchad Suvorova
ПРОСПЕКТ МИРА
Prospekt Mira
КОМСОМОЛЬСКАЯ
Komsomolskaya
continued next page

continued from previous page

КУРСКАЯ
Kurskaya

ТАГАНСКАЯ
Taganskaya

ПАВЕЛЕЦКАЯ
Paveletskaya

ДОБРЫНИНСКАЯ
Dobryninskaya

ОКТЯБРСКАЯ
Oktyabrskaya

ПАРК КУЛЬТУРЫ
Park Kultury

КИЕВСКАЯ
Kievskaya

5-Kaluzhsko-Rizhskaya Line
КАЛУЖСКО-РИЖСКАЯ
ЛИНИЯ

ЧЕЛОБИТЬЕВО
Chelobitevo

МЕДВЕДКОВО
Medvedkovo

БАБУШКИНСКАЯ
Babushkinskaya

СВИБЛОВО
Sviblovo

БОТАНИЧЕСКИЙ САД
Botanichesky Sad

ВДНХ
VDNKh

АЛЕКСЕЕВСКАЯ
Alexeevskaya

РИЖСКАЯ
Rizhskaya

ПРОСПЕКТ МИРА
Prospekt Mira

СУХАРЕВСКАЯ
Sukharevskaya

ТУРГЕНЕВСКАЯ
Turgenevskaya

КИТАЙ-ГОРОД
Kitay-Gorod

ТРЕТЬЯКОВСКАЯ
Tretyakovskaya

ОКТЯБРЬСКАЯ
Oktyabrskaya

ШАБОЛОВСКАЯ
Shabolovskaya

ЛЕНИНСКИЙ ПРОСПЕКТ
Leninsky Prospekt

АКАДЕМИЧЕСКАЯ
Akademicheskaya

ПРОФСОЮЗНАЯ
Profsoyuznaya

НОВЫЕ ЧЕРЁМУШКИ
Novye Cheryomushki

КАЛУЖСКАЯ
Kaluzhskaya

БЕЛЯЕВО
Belyaevo

КОНЬКОВО
Konkovo

ТЁПЛЫЙ СТАН
Tyoply Stan

ЯСЕНЕВО
Yasenevo

БИТЦЕВСКИЙ ПАРК
Bitsevsky Park

6-Tagansko-Krasnopresnenskaya Line
ТАГАНСКО-КРАСНОПРЕСНЕНСКАЯ
ЛИНИЯ

ПЛАНЕРНАЯ
Planernaya

СХОДНЕНСКАЯ
Skhodnenskaya

ТУШИНСКАЯ
Tushinskaya

ЩУКИНСКАЯ
Shchukinskaya

ОКТЯБРЬСКОЕ ПОЛЕ
Oktyabrskoe Pole

ПОЛЕЖАЕВСКАЯ
Polezhaevskaya

БЕГОВАЯ
Begovaya

УЛИЦА 1905 ГОДА
Ulitsa 1905 Goda

БАРРИКАДНАЯ
Barrikadnaya

ПУШКИНСКАЯ
Pushkinskaya

КУЗНЕЦКИЙ МОСТ
Kuznetsky Most

КИТАЙ-ГОРОД
Kitay-Gorod

ТАГАНСКАЯ
Taganskaya

ПРОЛЕТАРСКАЯ
Proletarskaya

ВОЛГОГРАДСКИЙ
ПРОСПЕКТ
Volgogradsky Prospekt

ТЕКСТИЛЬЩИКИ
Textilshchiki

КУЗЬМИНКИ
Kuzminki

РЯЗАНСКИЙ ПРОСПЕКТ
Ryazansky Prospekt

ВЫХИНО
Vykhino

7-Kalininskaya Line
КАЛИНИНСКАЯ ЛИНИЯ

НОВОГИРЕЕВО
Novogireevo

ПЕРОВО
Perovo

ШОССЕ ЭНТУЗИАСТОВ
Shosse Entuziastov

АВИАМОТОРНАЯ
Aviamotornaya

ПЛ. ИЛЬИЧА
Pl. Ilicha

МАРКСИСТСКАЯ
Marxistskaya

ТРЕТЬЯКОВСКАЯ
Tretyakovskaya

8-Serpukhovsko-Timiryazevskaya Line
СЕРПУХОВСКО-ТИМИРЯЗЕВСКАЯ
ЛИНИЯ

АЛТУФЬЕВСКАЯ
Altufevskaya

БИБИРЕВО
Bibirevo

ОТРАДНОЕ
Otradnoe

ВЛАДЫКИНО
Vladykino

ПЕТРОВСКО-РАЗУМОВСКОЕ
Petrovsko-Razumovskoe

ТИМИРЯЗЕВСКАЯ
Timiryazevskaya

ДМИТРОВСКАЯ
Dmitrovskaya

САВЁЛОВСКАЯ
Savyolovskaya

МЕНДЕЛЕЕВСКАЯ
Mendeleevskaya

ЦВЕТНОЙ БУЛЬВАР
Tsvetnoy Bulvar

ЧЕХОВСКАЯ
Chekhovskaya

БОРОВИЦКАЯ
Borovitskaya

ПОЛЯНКА Polyanka	**9-Proposed or Under Construction**	КОЖУХОВСКАЯ Kozhukhovskaya
СЕРПУХОВСКАЯ Serpukhovskaya	ЮБИЛЕЙНАЯ Yubileynaya	ПЕЧАТНИКИ Pechatniki
ТУЛЬСКАЯ Tulskaya	ЛИХОБОРЫ Likhobory	ВОЛЖСКАЯ Volzhskaya
НАГАТИНСКАЯ Nagatinskaya	СЕЛИГЕРСКАЯ Seligerskaya	ЛЮБЛИНО Lyublino
НАГОРНАЯ Nagornaya	ПЕТРОВСКО-РАЗУМОВСКОЕ Petrovsko-Razumovskoe	КРАСНОДОНСКАЯ Krasnodonskaya
НАХИМОВСКИЙ ПРОСПЕКТ Nakhimovsky Prospekt	ОСТАНКИНО Ostankino	МАРЬИНО Marino
СЕВАСТОПОЛЬСКАЯ Sevastopolskaya	МАРЬИНА РОЩА Marina Roshcha	БРАТЕЕВО Brateevo
ЧЕРТАНОВСКАЯ Chertanovskaya	ДОСТОЕВСКАЯ Dostoevskaya	БОРИСОВО Borisovo
ЮЖНАЯ Yuzhnaya	ТРУБНАЯ Trubnaya	**10-Proposed or Under Construction**
ПРАЖСКАЯ Prazhskaya	СРЕТЕНСКИЙ БУЛЬВАР Sretensky Bulvar	МИТИНО Mitino
РОССОШАНСКАЯ Rossoshanskaya	ЧКАЛОВСКАЯ Chkalovskaya	ВОЛОКАЛОМСКОЕ ШОССЕ Volokalomskoe Shosse
АНИНО Anino	РИМСКАЯ Rimskaya	СТРОГИНО Strogino
КАЧАЛОВО Kachalovo	КРЕСТЬЯНСКАЯ ЗАСТАВА Krestyanskaya Zastava	ПАРК ПОБЕДЫ Park Pobedy
	ДУБРОВКА Dubrovka	КИЕВСКАЯ Kievskaya

To ride a bus, trolleybus or tram you need a ticket *(talon)* which you punch in one of the ticket-punchers inside the vehicle. (In crowded vehicles people may pass tickets along to the person nearest the puncher to do this for them.) Talony, which cost around US$0.10 each, can be bought in strips of five or 10 from drivers, from street kiosks that display them, and sometimes in metro stations. The same talony are used for all three types of vehicle. Ticket inspections are rare indeed, and people often ride buses without a ticket, for which in theory they can be fined US$3.50.

Useful services for reaching specific places are given elsewhere in this chapter. Routes of general usefulness – and for cheap excursions – include trolleybus Nos 15 and 31, which run round the western half of the Boulevard Ring (between Tsvetnoy bulvar and Kropotkinskaya metro), and trolleybus No Б, which runs all the way round the Garden Ring. Useful radial routes to/from the city centre include:

North: Bolshaya Lubyanka ulitsa, Sretenka ulitsa and prospekt Mira (ulitsa Kuznetsky Most to VDNKh metro) – trolleybus Nos 9 and 48 (No 9 continues to Ostankino)

North-West: Tverskaya ulitsa (Manezhnaya ploshchad to the Belorussia Station) – trolleybus Nos 12 and 20)

West: Teatralnaya ploshchad, Manezhnaya ploshchad, Mokhovaya ulitsa, ulitsa Vozdvizhenka, ulitsa Novy Arbat, Kutuzovsky prospekt – trolleybus No 2

South-West: Arbatskaya ploshchad, Kropotkinskaya metro, Prechistenka ulitsa, Bolshaya Pirogovskaya ulitsa, Central Lenin Stadium – trolleybus Nos 5 and 15

South-East: Novaya ploshchad, ulitsa Solyanka, Taganskaya ulitsa – trolleybus No 63

Taxi

The simple way to get a taxi is to stand on the street and stick your arm out. Before too long a car will stop and, if the driver fancies going where you want to go, you're on your way. Many private car drivers cruise around as unofficial taxis ('gipsy cabs'), and other drivers will often take you if they're going in roughly the same direction. For a five-minute ride, a payment of US$1 is plenty; for 10 or 15 minutes, pay around US$1.50 to US$2.50. You can get across town for US$5 or so. You can also hire a cab by the hour – if you have a few visits to make, for instance – for around US$6 to US$10. Generally it's better to fix the fare before you get in – but for short rides it's usually OK just to proffer an appropriate amount when you get out. Official taxis, which carry a little chequerboard logo on the side and/or a small green light in the windscreen, charge about the same. No driver uses a meter, even if the cab has one, and few drivers ever admit to having any change. You'll probably have to pay more if you catch a taxi right in front of a hotel.

Don't hesitate to wave on a car whose occupant(s) you don't like the look of, or are obviously drunk – and it's better not to get into one whose occupants outnumber you. Problems may be more likely to crop up if you take a street cab waiting outside a nightclub or perhaps a tourist hotel or restaurant at night.

For longer rides, or if you need to be somewhere at a fixed time, you may need to book a taxi. Hotels can arrange this for you but it's cheaper if you do it yourself. You can call the Central Taxi Reservation Office (Tsentralnoe Byuro Zakazov Taxi; ☎ 927 00 00) at any time of day or night to order one, but you should give them at least one and preferably two or more hours notice,. You can book one the day before for an early start to an airport. Usually the dispatcher on the phone will speak a bit of English, though it may help if you can speak some Russian too. They'll want to ring you back a few minutes before pick-up, to confirm that you still want the booking and give you the car's registration number. You should be charged about US$4 for the booking then around US$0.50 a km.

There are also several reliable privately run taxi services. These include Martex (☎ 495 43 36), which will reportedly take you to Sheremetevo-2 airport for US$20, Globus Servis (☎ 298 61 46) Krasnaya, Gorka (☎ 381 27 46) and Pride (☎ 451 08 58). Again, a couple of hours' notice is usually needed. Some car-rental firms, including Hertz, also provide reasonably priced taxi service (see Getting There & Away – Car & Motorbike).

Moscow vs St Petersburg

The friendly competition between residents of Moscow and St Petersburg can get quite heated. Muscovites will claim that St Petersburgians are a bunch of foppish bumpkins who sit in the provinces drinking tea, looking at portraits and discussing the state of the world crisis. Similarly, St Petersburgians consider Muscovites to be opportunistic greedheads, who would sell their own mothers in order to raise the cash to import cigarettes that they would then sell to school children.

But most visitors who come to St Petersburg from Moscow agree that life in the former capital is certainly more laid back than in the present one, and that St Petersburg residents carry themselves with a brand of dignity not seen elsewhere in the country. A popular joke offers a unique insight into the differences between residents of the two big cities.

A young man from St Petersburg was lucky enough to have found a seat on the Moscow metro during rush hour. After he had gone a stop or two, an elderly woman carrying shopping bags got on the train and stood in front of him. The young man immediately got up and offered his seat to the old woman, who sat down contentedly.

'You must be from St Petersburg', the old woman said.

'Yes, I am', said the young man, 'but how did you know?'

'No Muscovite would ever be so polite as to give an old woman his seat', the woman said.

The young man considered this for a moment and then said, 'And you are from Moscow.'

'Yes, I am', replied the woman, 'but how did you know?'

'Well', replied the young man, 'in St Petersburg, when someone gives us a seat on the metro, we always say "thank you".'

Nick Selby

Around Moscow
Около Москвы

This chapter covers places within about 300 km of Moscow. A few are not far beyond the city's suburbs and most can be visited as day trips from the capital, but some of the more distant places are easier with an overnight (or longer) stop. The 'Golden Ring' of historic towns and villages north-east of Moscow – some of them set on the Volga River, others amid timeless countryside – is well worth a few days of your time.

This region is in many ways the heartland of Russia, with a subtly changing landscape crossed by many winding rivers, that typifies the provincial scene that's so dear to Russian hearts and has been immortalised by so many artists and writers. The towns and villages are an equally typical mixture of the old and picturesque and the modern and drab.

As soon as you leave Moscow the contrasts between the capital and the slower, more old-fashioned, less colourful and often poorer provincial world make themselves felt. Even one trip out of the big city will not only take you to some fascinating and beautiful corners of Russia but also open your eyes to the kind of life that the great majority of Russians lead.

GETTING THERE & AWAY
Train & Bus

Many places in this chapter can be reached by suburban trains from Moscow. These are some of the easiest, if not the quickest, forms of Russian transport to use: find the suburban ticket hall (пригородный зал, prigorodnyy zal) at the appropriate Moscow station, check the timetable for a train going where you want, buy your ticket, board the train and you're off. All carriages are one class and no advance bookings or compartment reservations are needed. Information on which trains you need is given under the relevant destinations. On timetables, abbreviations indicate frequency of service such as ежед (yezhednevno, daily), раб (rabochim, Monday to Friday), вых (vykhodnym, Saturday, Sunday and holidays), Сб (subbotam, Saturday) and Вск (voskresenyam, Sunday); and give information on where the train stops, such as везде (vezde, everywhere) or везде кроме... (vezde krome..., everywhere except...). For some places, you need buses or long-distance trains. For these, booking ahead is advisable if not always necessary.

Car & Taxi

A good way to go if you don't mind coping with Russian roads is to drive yourself. Some of the car-rental companies mentioned in Moscow – Getting There & Away will allow their vehicles to be taken out of the city. Another possibility is to hire a taxi as a chauffeur for a day or even longer: you'll have to negotiate a price, but for two or three people it may work out economically.

Boat

Long-distance passenger services along the Volga connect Moscow with Uglich, Yaroslavl, Kostroma, Plyos and cities all the way down to Astrakhan near the Caspian Sea. Cruises booked in Moscow or abroad will also take you to these places: see Moscow Getting There & Away and under relevant cities in this chapter for more information.

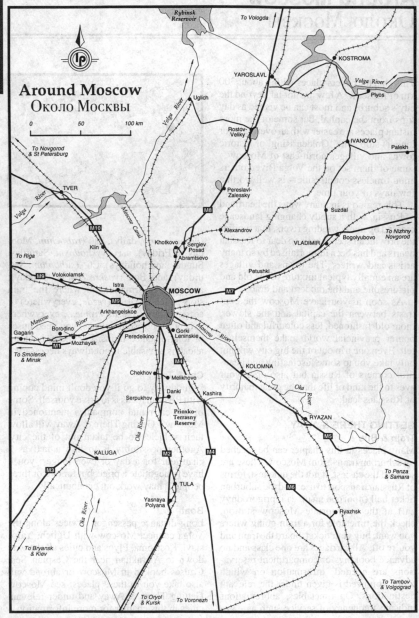

Around Moscow
Около Москвы

0   50   100 km

To Novgorod
& St Petersburg

Rybinsk
Reservoir

To Vologda

KOSTROMA

Volga River

Plyos

YAROSLAVL

Uglich

Rostov-
Veliky

IVANOVO

Palekh

Volga River

Pereslavl-
Zalessky

Suzdal

TVER

Alexandrov

To Riga

Klin

Khotkovo

Sergiev
Posad

Abramtsevo

M8

VLADIMIR

Bogolyubovo

To Nizhny
Novgorod

Moscow Canal

Volga

Petushki

M10

Volokolamsk

M9

Istra

MOSCOW

M7

Moscow
River

Arkhangelskoe

Moscow   River

Gagarin

Borodino

Mozhaysk

Peredelkino

Gorki
Leninskie

M1

KOLOMNA

To Smolensk
& Minsk

Oka River

To Riga

Chekhov

Melikhovo

M4

Kashira

Serpukhov

Danki

Prioksko-
Terrasny
Reserve

RYAZAN

Oka River

M5

KALUGA

M2

M4

To Penza
& Samara

M3

TULA

M6

Yasnaya
Polyana

Ryazhsk

Oka River

To Bryansk
& Kiev

To Tambov
& Volgograd

To Oryol
& Kursk

To Voronezh

Tours
Guided tours are available from Moscow to many of the places in this chapter, and can be an interesting, informative way to go, especially if your time is limited. See the Organised Tours and Travel Agencies sections of the Moscow chapter for some outfits offering these; Patriarchi Dom has a particularly interesting range of trips.

GETTING AROUND
Trains and/or buses link places around Moscow. You can travel along the Volga between Yaroslavl, Kostroma and Plyos by hydrofoil.

North-West
Северо-запад

KLIN
КЛИН
Tchaikovsky lived in Klin, 90 km north-west of central Moscow, from 1885 to 1893, the year of his death in St Petersburg. Here he wrote his *Pathetique* symphony and *Nutcracker* and *Sleeping Beauty* ballets. His last residence, at ulitsa Chaykovskogo 48, has been a museum (now the Dom-Muzey Chaykovskogo) since his brother Modest bought it after his death. It's still much as it was when Tchaikovsky lived there, full of personal effects including his Becker grand piano, now played only by top pianists on special occasions. The museum is open from 10 am to 6 pm daily except Wednesday, Thursday and the last Monday of the month.

Getting There & Away
Klin is on the road and railway from Moscow to Tver, Novgorod and St Petersburg, and it's possible to combine it with Tver in one lengthy day trip from Moscow if you're feeling energetic. Suburban trains from Moscow's Leningrad Station run to Klin two or three times an hour from 5 am, a trip of about 1½ hours. The suburban ticket hall at the Leningrad Station is along the alley between the right-hand side of the station building and Komsomolskaya metro. In addition to direct trains to Klin, trains heading for Zavidovo, Redkino, Tver (Kalinin), Konakovsky Mokh or Konakovo GRES will stop at Klin. The last train back to Moscow leaves Klin at about 9.30 pm. Services between Klin and Tver – a trip of just over one hour – are almost as frequent.

TVER
ТВЕРЬ
Population: 450,000
Tver, on the Volga 150 km north-west of Moscow, was the capital of an unruly ministate that was Moscow's chief rival in the 14th and 15th centuries. But its subsequent history reads like the Book of Job – punished for rising against the Mongol Tatars, conquered by Ivan III, savaged by Ivan the Terrible, seized by the Poles and completely destroyed by fire in 1763. Reborn in the 18th century after Catherine the Great made it one of her rest stops between St Petersburg and

Wooden nutcracker, early 20th century; Tchaikovsky wrote his *Nutcracker* ballet in Klin

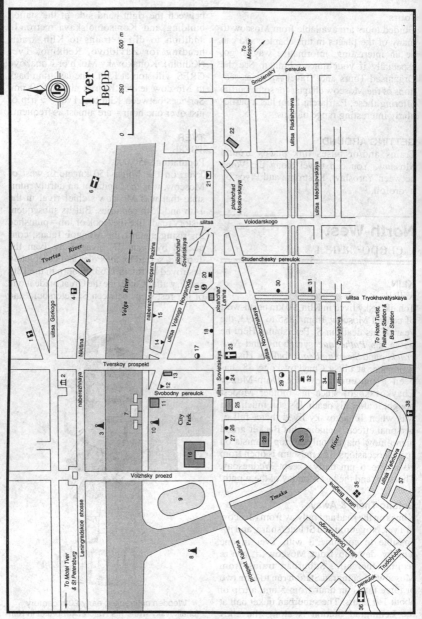

PLACES TO STAY	5	River Station Речной вокзал	22	Politicheskaya Kniga Bookshop Книжный магазин Политическая книга
28 Hotel Tsentralnaya Гостиница Центральная	6	Church Церковь		
34 Hotel Volga Гостиница Волга	7	Excursion-Boat Landings	23	Church of the Ascension Церковь Вознесения
PLACES TO EAT		Пристаны для речных экскурсий	24	Podarki Shop Подарки
12 Stolovaya No 32 Столовая N 32	8	WW II Victory Obelisk Обелиск победы	25	Drama Theatre Театр драмы
14 Stolovaya No 31 Столовая N 31	9	Old Stadium Старый стадион	26	Dom Ofitserov Дом офицеров
15 Restoran Ресторан	10	Pushkin Statue Памятник Пушкину	29	Tram Stop Остановка трамваев
20 Kafe Molodyozhnoe Кафе Молодёжное	11	Cinema Кинотеатр	30	Bookshop Книжный магазин
27 Retro Kafe Ретро Кафе	13	Bookshop Книжный магазин	33	Circus Цирк
31 Kafe Minutka Кафе Минутка	16	Catherine the Great's Palace	35	Univermag Tver Универмаг Тверь
32 Kafe Bagira Кафе Багира		Путевой дворец, Краеведческий музей и Картинная галерея	36	Church of the White Trinity Церковь Белой Троицы
OTHER	17	Tram Stop Остановка трамваев	37	Central Market Центральный рынок
1 Church Церковь	18	Bookshop Книжный магазин	38	Intercession Church Храм Покровка Богородицы
2 Museum of Tver Life Музей тверского быта	19	Bank Банк		
3 Nikitin Statue Памятник Никитину	21	Post Office Почтамт		
4 Assumption Church Успенская церковь				

Moscow, in places it now looks like a little rustic St Petersburg.

Though Tver's Baroque-classical architecture doesn't put it in the same league as some of the old Russian towns of the Golden Ring, it has just about enough attractions to make it an interesting day trip from Moscow. You might also want to stop here for the same reason Catherine did: it's on the Moscow-St Petersburg road (and railway, today). In winter the surrounding forests are apparently good for cross-country skiing.

Tver dumped its Soviet-era name, Kalinin (after Mikhail Kalinin, Stalin's puppet president during WW II, who was born here), back in 1990, but a lot of people – especially railway ticket clerks and timetable compilers – apparently haven't heard the news yet.

Orientation

The Volga runs roughly west-east through Tver, with the town centre on the south side. Ulitsa Sovietskaya is the main east-west street. It's crossed in the central area by Tverskoy prospekt, which changes its name to prospekt Chaykovskogo farther south. The railway station is four km south of the centre at the point where prospekt Chaykovskogo turns 90° east and becomes ulitsa Kominterna. The bus station is 300 metres east of the railway station along ulitsa Kominterna.

Information

There are several money-changing kiosks around the town centre. You can also change money at the bank on ploshchad Lenina.

The main post office is on ploshchad Moskovskaya and international phone calls can be made here. The Tver telephone code is 08222.

A good source of maps of Russian cities and regions, plus posters and arty postcards, is the Politicheskaya Kniga bookshop on ploshchad Moskovskaya.

Things to See

South of the River Classical former town houses and public buildings from the late 1700s and early 1800s line **ulitsa Sovietskaya** and the riverfront **naberezhnaya Stepana Razina**.

On the corner of ulitsa Sovietskaya and Tverskoy prospekt, the classical **Church of the Ascension** (Tserkov Voznesenia) has had a Soviet-era digital clock removed from its tower and is being restored.

At the west end of ulitsa Sovietskaya, fronted by a statue of Mikhail Kalinin, stands the town's most imposing building – Catherine the Great's 1775 'Road Palace' (Putevoy Dvorets). It houses Tver's **Regional Museum** (Tverskoy kraevedchesky muzey) and **Art Gallery** (Tverskaya kartinnaya galereya), both open from 11 am to 6 pm Wednesday to Sunday, plus Tuesday for tour groups only. The gallery has both Russian and Western European work. The **City Park** on the river bank behind the palace has a foppish statue of Pushkin and, if you're lucky, live music on summer weekends. In summer, Volga excursion boats sail from the piers in front of the park.

Somewhere on ulitsa Sovietskaya in April 1940, in Tver's NKVD headquarters, over 6000 Polish prisoners were shot one by one in a soundproof room at night. They were buried in trenches near Mednoe, 20 km west of Tver. Over 8000 other Polish prisoners were massacred near Smolensk and Kharkiv (Ukraine). Until the truth was revealed in 1990 and 1991, the Soviet authorities had always claimed that the Poles – who included the cream of the Polish officer corps, captured or arrested during the Soviet invasion of Poland – were killed by the Nazis.

Ulitsa Radishcheva, two blocks south of ulitsa Sovietskaya, is a pedestrian street which might be a little lively in summer but was devoid of street life on our visit one November weekend – apart from a few opportunists asking out-of-towners if they were Polish and had anything to sell.

More lively is the sprawling **Central Market** (Tsentralny rynok), south of the small Tmaka River. Just before the market, on ulitsa Yefimova, the old **Intercession Church** (Khram Pokrovka Bogoroditsy) is being restored and is open from 7.30 am to 7 pm.

The quaintest part of town is the streets of old wooden houses with carved eaves and window frames, west of the market across ulitsa Bragina. Here, on pereulok Trudolyubia, is Tver's oldest building, the stately **Church of the White Trinity** (Tserkov Beloy Troitsy), built in 1564; it has daily services.

North of the River You can cross the Volga at the north end of Tverskoy prospekt or on Volzhsky proezd which runs up beside the Road Palace. A promenade stretches along the north bank, giving a good view of the old houses on the south bank. The **statue** in the park here is of Afanasy Nikitin, a local merchant who went overland to India 30 years before Vasco da Gama sailed there, and wrote a best seller about it.

The **Museum of Tver Life** (Muzey Tverskogo Byta) in a short street off ulitsa Gorkogo is housed in an 18th-century merchant's manor house. It's worth a visit for its arts, crafts, furniture and other domestic artefacts ranging over several centuries. Hours are 11 am to 5 pm, Wednesday to Sunday.

Places to Stay

All hotels are out of the same Soviet concrete mould. The *Hotel Tsentralnaya* (☎ 3 81 57) at ulitsa Novotorzhskaya 33/8, opposite the circus, has plain but adequate rooms for US$22 a double with private bathroom, or US$12 with washbasin only and facilities along the corridor. It has a restaurant too. The

Hotel Volga (☎ 3 81 00) at ulitsa Zhelyabova 1 facing the Tmaka River has similar prices and standards, and a restaurant, but you may wait hours before someone appears at reception to check you in.

The *Hotel Turist* (☎ 3 61 78) on ulitsa Kominterna facing the railway station is still open despite messy renovations – not worth it at US$17/26 a single/double, and without a restaurant.

Some tour groups may find themselves in the shabby *Motel Tver* (☎ 5 96 96, 5 56 92), eight km west of town at Leningradskoe shosse 130. The rare bus No 7 runs between the motel and the town centre, while tram Nos 4, 5, 7 and 10 to/from the centre terminate two km from the motel (bus No 109 runs now and then between the motel and the tram stop).

Places to Eat

A fine place to head for quick eating is *Stolovaya No 32* near the Volga end of Svobodny pereulok. Inside, to the left, is an Arabskaya Kukhnya section serving decent pizza at US$1 a slice (no vegetarian varieties, unfortunately), shawarma kebab for US$0.75, portions of hot chips for US$0.50 and coffee. It's open from 10.30 am to 8 pm daily. There's also a standard stolovaya here, with main meat dishes or pelmeny at around US$0.30 and soup for US$0.10, open from 8 am to 8 pm daily. *Stolovaya No 31*, a block east along ulitsa Volnogo Novgoroda, is marginally cheaper and open from 9 am to 8 pm daily.

The *Retro Kafe* at ulitsa Sovietskaya 12, almost opposite the Road Palace, has slightly greater pretensions with a neat, clean décor and a quiet ambience. A variety of main dishes cost US$1 to US$3, and there are numerous salads up to US$1.20. Enter at the side of the building, and go upstairs.

There are a few other cafés on ulitsa Sovietskaya and ulitsa Radishcheva, including *Kafe Molodyozhnoe*, a younger-generation hang-out downstairs at ulitsa Sovietskaya 15, serving snacks from 10 am to 3 pm and 4 to 9 pm daily.

The *Restoran* at naberezhnaya Stepana Razina 10, facing the Volga, has a Desertny Zal with sweet snacks and drinks downstairs, and a bigger restaurant upstairs.

The Tsentralnaya and Volga hotels and the Motel Tver all have typical but adequate hotel restaurants where three courses will normally cost US$4 or US$5.

Entertainment

The Retro Kafe has jazz a few evenings a week; the Dom Ofitserov (House of Officers) next door on ulitsa Sovietskaya also advertises jazz. There's a circus opposite the Tsentralnaya Hotel, by the Tmaka River, and a drama theatre on ulitsa Sovietskaya.

Things to Buy

The little crafts/souvenir shop facing the Museum of Tver Life is worth a quick look. You might find something worthwhile in the Podarki (Gifts) shop on ulitsa Sovietskaya just west of Tverskoy prospekt. The town's department store is Univermag Tver on ulitsa Bragina just south of the Tmaka River.

Getting There & Away

There's a daily bus to Novgorod at 11.45 am, taking 8½ hours.

Suburban trains take 2½ to three hours to reach Tver (often still called Kalinin on timetables) from Moscow's Leningrad Station. See the Klin section for the location of the suburban ticket hall at the Leningrad Station. Departures are roughly hourly and the last train back to Moscow from Tver is at 8.35 pm.

Most trains between Moscow and St Petersburg also stop at Tver.

In summer, ferries and hydrofoils sail to regional destinations from the river station at the confluence of the Volga and Tvertsa rivers. The only boats to Moscow seem to be occasional cruise vessels.

Getting Around

Tram Nos 2, 5, 6 and 11 run from the bus and railway stations up prospekt Chaykovskogo and Tverskoy prospekt to the town centre, a 10-minute ride. Nos 5, 6 and 11 continue over the Volga from the north end of

Tverskoy prospekt; No 2 turns west along ulitsa Sovietskaya.

LAKE SELIGER
ОЗЕРО СЕЛИГЕР

Among pine forests 190 km west of Tver, near the headwaters of the Volga, is large, island-dotted Lake Seliger. The area has some of Russia's best canoeing, hiking, camping and hunting territory. From the pretty, old-fashioned town of Ostashkov on the south shore you can take boat trips to Khachin Island, the largest in the lake, or Stolbnoy Island, with a monastery which was turned into a Stalinist labour camp. The Polish prisoners killed at Tver in 1940 were held on Stolbnoy before their murders.

Ostashkov has a grotty hotel but there are several turbazy around the lake, especially in Zarechie.

Five to seven buses daily run from Tver to Ostashkov (4½ hours). From Moscow, there's an overnight train to Ostashkov (11½ hours) from the Leningrad Station, and an overnight bus (US$10; 8½ hours) from the Shchyolkovsky Bus Station.

West
Запад

ISTRA & NEW JERUSALEM MONASTERY
ИСТРА И НОВО-ИЕРУСАЛИМСКИЙ МОНАСТЫРЬ

In the 17th century, Nikon, the patriarch whose reforms drove the Old Believers from the Orthodox Church, decided to show one and all that Russia deserved to be the centre of the Christian world by building a little Holy City right at home, complete with its own Church of the Holy Sepulchre. This was the grandiose New Jerusalem Monastery (Novo-Ierusalimsky Monastyr), founded in 1656 near the picturesque though now polluted Istra River, 50 km west of central Moscow. The project was nearly stillborn when the abrasive Nikon lost his job.

Unlike other Moscow monasteries, this one had no military use, though with its perimeter walls and towers it looks like a fortress. In WW II the retreating Germans blew it to pieces but it's gradually being reconstructed. The monastery is now in Orthodox Church hands again, after years as a museum, and attracts a steady stream of worshippers. The nearby woods are a popular picnic spot. Another attraction is the Moscow region's Museum of Wooden Architecture, a collection of renovated 17th to 19th-century buildings that show off the traditional 'gingerbread' woodwork outside and give a glimpse of old rural life inside.

Monastery

In the centre of the monastery grounds, and intended by Nikon to look like Jerusalem's Church of the Holy Sepulchre, is the **Cathedral of the Resurrection** (Voskresensky sobor). Like its prototype, it's really several churches under one roof. The huge rotunda – very ambitious in 1685 – collapsed under its own weight a few decades after it went up and had to be constructed all over again. With much of the latest reconstruction still incomplete, the interior lacks its original sparkle, and in any case can only be seen on guided tours. Recently these were only available on summer Sundays, but the schedule may change now that the monastery is in Church hands. One part of the cathedral where reconstruction is complete is the unusual underground **Church of SS Konstantin & Yelena**, entered via an interior staircase, with a belfry peeping up above the ground outside the cathedral. Nikon was buried in the cathedral, beneath the Church of John the Baptist (Tserkov Ioanna Predtechi).

At the rear of the grounds is the Moscow Baroque **Nativity Church** (Rozhdestvenskaya tserkov), with chambers for the tsar on the left and the abbot on the right. It houses a two-floor museum of books, music scores, porcelain, paintings and old armour, with a section on the history of the monastery; however, the museum is said to be in danger of closure since the Church takeover.

Behind the monastery near the river is Nikon's former 'hermitage', a rather unmonastic three-storey affair.

Museum of Wooden Architecture

This collection of buildings (Muzey derevyannogo zodchestva) just outside the monastery's north wall includes a church built in 1647, an 18th-century house and inn, a 19th-century peasant's home, granaries and a windmill, all from the Moscow region.

Getting There & Away

Suburban trains run about twice an hour from Moscow's Riga Station to Istra (about one hour), from where buses run to the Muzey stop by the monastery. You can also pick up the trains at Tushino Station, by Tushinskaya metro.

By car, leave Moscow from Leningradsky prospekt and its continuation, Volokolamskoe shosse, and continue through Dedovsk to Istra. The monastery is two km west of Istra's town centre.

ARKHANGELSKOE
АРХАНГЕЛЬСКОЕ

On the Moscow River a short distance west of Moscow's outer ring road is one of the grandest estates in the region, Arkhangelskoe. Unhappily, the palace has been under restoration and closed for years, and a big question mark still hangs over the reopening date. However, the beautiful grounds are worth a visit in any case. Even if they're officially locked, people wander in through a gap in the fence.

A grandson of Dmitry Golitsyn, a statesman under Peter the Great, started work on a palace in the 1780s but lost interest and sold it all to Prince Nikolay Yusupov, one of the richest Russians of that time or since. During several ambassadorships and as Director of the Imperial Museums, Yusupov managed to accumulate an art collection of his own that outclassed many European museums. After a rough start – the house was pillaged by Napoleon's troops, trashed in a serfs' revolt and nearly burned down – Yusupov fixed up the house and filled it with his treasures.

Main House

The palace is mainly a series of elegant halls for showing off Yusupov's paintings, furniture, sculptures, tapestries, porcelain and glass. His paintings include an entire room devoted to the Italian master Tiepolo and – at least once upon a time, according to one source – portraits of each of his 300 mistresses.

Gardens

The multilevel, Italian-style park is full of 18th-century copies of classical statues, plus one of Pushkin. A colonnade on the east side was meant to be a Yusupov family mausoleum but was never finished.

Serf Theatre

Yusupov also organised a troupe of serf actors that eventually became one of the best known of its kind, and built them a theatre just west of the gardens.

Church

Predating everything else is the little white Church of the Archangel Michael (Arkhangelskaya Tserkov, 1667). Yusupov smothered it with the self-important Holy Gates (Svyatie Vorota) to link it with the estate.

Places to Eat

There's a bufet in the car park and the reasonable *Arkhangelskoe Restaurant* (☎ (095) 562 03 28) across the road. Or you can eat a bit more expensively at the *Russkaya Izba (Russian Cabin*; ☎ (095) 561 42 44) at ulitsa Naberezhnaya 1 in nearby Ilinskoe village, by the river bridge. Its traditional Russian food is said to be very good – especially the zakuski and soups. Both places are open from noon to 10 or 11 pm.

Getting There & Away

The estate is 22 km west of central Moscow. Bus No 549 to Bolnitsa No 62 (Hospital No 62) from Moscow's Tushinskaya Bus Station (Avtobusnaya Stantsia Tushinskaya), by Tushinskaya metro, stops at Arkhangelskoe, near the estate entrance, and

Ilinskoe. It runs about three times an hour from 6 am to 7.30 pm, with a few more services up to midnight.

If driving, go out along Leningradsky prospekt, stay to the left as it becomes Volokolamskoe shosse, then beyond the outer ring road, fork left into Ilinskoe shosse. It's a half-hour drive.

BORODINO
БОРОДИНО

In 1812 Napoleon invaded Russia, lured by the prospect of taking Moscow. For three months the Russians retreated, until on 26 August the two armies met in a bloody one-day battle of attrition at the village of Borodino, 130 km west of Moscow. In 15 hours more than one-third of each army was killed – over 100,000 soldiers in all. Europe would know nothing as terrible until WW I.

The French seemed to be the winners, as the Russians withdrew and abandoned Moscow to them. But in fact Borodino was the beginning of the end for Napoleon, who was soon in full, disastrous retreat. The entire battlefield – more than 100 sq km – is now the **State Borodino Military-Historical Museum-Preserve** (Gosudarstvenny Boro-

dinsky Voenno-Istorichesky Muzey-Zapovednik). It includes a museum and some three dozen monuments to generals and divisions (most erected at the battle's 1912 centennial), and further memorials to Soviet soldiers who died in a second Borodino battle in WW II.

If your interest is limited, a vivid 'snapshot' of the 1812 battle can be found at the Borodino Panorama in Moscow. But Borodino makes an easy detour if you happen to be driving between Moscow and Smolensk.

The front line of the 1812 battle was roughly along the line of the four-km road from Borodino village to Borodino railway station. The French were to its west, the Russians east. Most of the monuments are close to the road. The museum, about a km south of the village, has lots of maps and an illuminated model of the battle. It's open from 10 am to 6 pm daily except Monday and the last Friday of the month. There's a grubby café by its car park.

The hilltop monument about 400 metres in front of the museum is the grave of Prince Bagration, a heroic Georgian infantry general who was mortally wounded in the

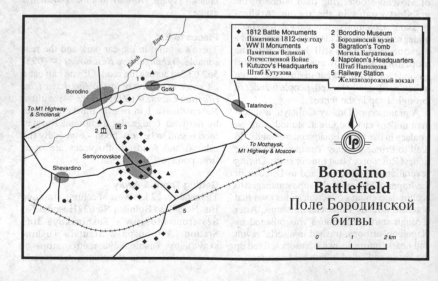

◆	1812 Battle Monuments	2	Borodino Museum
	Памятники 1812-ому году		Бородинский музей
▲	WW II Monuments	3	Bagration's Tomb
	Памятники Великой		Могила Багратиона
	Отечественной Войне	4	Napoleon's Headquarters
1	Kutuzov's Headquarters		Штаб Наполеона
	Штаб Кутузова	5	Railway Station
			Железнодорожный вокзал

Borodino Battlefield
Поле Бородинской битвы

0   1   2 km

battle. It's surrounded by WW II trenches. Farther south there's a concentration of monuments around Semyonovskoe village, scene of the battle's most frenzied fighting where Bagration's heroic Second Army, opposing far larger French forces, was virtually obliterated. The redoubts around Semyonovskoe changed hands eight times in the battle. It's thought the Russian commander, Mikhail Kutuzov, deliberately sacrificed Bagration's army to save his larger First Army, opposing lighter French forces in the northern part of the battlefield. Kutuzov's headquarters is marked by an obelisk in the village of Gorki. Another obelisk near the Shevardinsky redoubt to the south-west – paid for in 1912 with French donations – marks Napoleon's camp. Near the railway station are two WW II mass graves.

Getting There & Away

Suburban trains run every hour or so from Moscow's Belorussia Station to Borodino (2¼ hours). Most trains heading to Gagarin also stop at Borodino. For a day trip from Moscow the latest outward trains you should take are the 9.41 or 10.24 am. The suburban ticket hall at the Belorussia Station is at entrance No 4.

If driving from Moscow, stay on the M1 Minsk highway till the Mozhaysk turn-off, 95 km beyond the Moscow outer ring road. It's five km north to Mozhaysk, a sleepy old town, then 13 km west to Borodino village. Drivers from Smolensk should take the 'Borodino 17' turn-off, about nine km east of the turn-off for Gagarin (where Yury grew up), then after a few km go right at the 'Muzey Borodino 12' sign.

PEREDELKINO
ПЕРЕДЕЛКИНО

Boris Pasternak – poet, author of *Doctor Zhivago* and winner of the 1957 Nobel prize for literature – lived for a long time in a dacha in this now-trendy writers' colony on Moscow's south-west outskirts, just five km beyond the city's outer ring road. Though he was officially in disgrace when he died in

1960, thousands of people came to his funeral, and even before perestroika his grave had a steady stream of visitors. The grave is in a small cemetery *(kladbishche)* near Peredelkino railway station, in a little pine grove towards the rear on the right-hand side, and has a stone slab bearing Pasternak's profile. Above the graveyard is the tiny 15th-century Transfiguration Church (Preobrazhenskaya Tserkov).

Pasternak's dacha is now a museum, the **Dom-Muzey Pasternaka**. Visits are by guided tour in Russian. You'll see the room where he died and the room where he finished *Dr Zhivago*.

Villa Peredelkino (☎ (095) 435 14 78) at 1-ya Chobotovskaya alleya 2A, on the same street as Peredelkino's railway station, is an expensive Italian restaurant in the former dacha of Leonid Brezhnev's daughter, open from noon to midnight daily.

Getting There & Away

Frequent suburban trains take 20 minutes to reach Peredelkino, on the line to Kaluga-II station, from Moscow's Kiev Station. If you're driving, go out along Kutuzovsky prospekt, which becomes Mozhayskoe shosse. Beyond the outer ring road, continue on the Minskoe shosse (highway M1) and at the 21-km post turn left to Peredelkino.

South
Юг

MELIKHOVO
МЕЛИХОВО

The estate south of Moscow which Chekhov bought in 1892 and lived on until 1899 is open as a museum (Muzey A P Chekhova). Here Chekhov wrote *The Seagull* and *Uncle Vanya*, was responsible for building three local schools and a fire station, and continued to practise medicine. Melikhovo is about seven km east of the dual carriageway which parallels the old M2 Moscow-Oryol road, signposted 50 km south of the Moscow outer ring road. Suburban trains run from Moscow's Kursk Station to the town of Chekhov, 12 km west of Melikhovo, from where there are occasional buses to Melikhovo.

PRIOXKO-TERRASNY RESERVE
ПРИОКСКО-ТЕРРАСНЫЙ ЗАПОВЕДНИК

The Prioxko-Terrasny Biosphere Reserve (Prioxko-Terrasny Biosferny Zapovednik) covers a 50-sq-km area bordering the northern flood plain of the Oka River, a tributary of the Volga. It's a meeting point of northern fir groves and marshes with typical southern meadow steppe, and its varied fauna includes a herd of European bison, brought back from near extinction since WW II.

You can't wander freely in the reserve but tours in Russian are given a couple of times a day from its excursion bureau, and foreigners who turn up alone might be given an individual tour if any English-speaking staff are on hand. The reserve is open year-round except on public holidays.

There's a small museum near the office with stuffed specimens of the reserve's fauna, typical of European Russia, including beavers, elk, deer and boar. You're unlikely to see the real thing outside, except maybe elk or deer in winter. The reserve's pride, and the focus of most visits, is its European bison nursery (pitomnik zubrov). Two pairs of bison, one of Europe's largest mammals (some weigh over a tonne), were brought from Poland in 1948. Now there are about 60 and more than 200 have been sent out to other parts of the country. The bison come into the nursery in greatest numbers at feeding time – 7 am and 7 pm.

Getting There & Away

Public transport is difficult. You need to take a suburban train from Moscow's Kursk Station to Serpukhov (2¼ hours), then a rare bus to the village of Danki, with some pretty wooden houses, one km from the reserve's excursion bureau.

For drivers, the turn-off from the Moscow-Oryol highway is 76 km south of the Moscow outer ring road. Driving from Moscow, you have to turn west and then double back under the highway. Go through Danki then turn right to the reserve. It's five km from the highway to the excursion bureau.

TULA
ТУЛА

Population: 550,000

Tula, 170 km south of Moscow on the M2 highway to Oryol and Ukraine, is polluted and not very pretty, but has two interesting museums devoted to its famous products – guns and samovars – that may be worth a stop if you're coming this way. If you're driving and don't want to stop here, take the western bypass, since traffic in the city is heavy and the roads poor.

Tula lay in the path of Tatar armies advancing on Moscow and was fortified from the 15th century. It has long been famous in Russia for making guns – a craft begun in the 16th century and confirmed when Peter the Great founded a small arms factory here in 1712 – and samovars, both industries based on local iron ore and coal deposits. Tula was named a Soviet hero-city for repulsing 45 days of German attacks in 1941.

The city's economy has suffered from the fall-off in orders from the impoverished Russian army, but Tula has stayed in the forefront of military affairs through the 106th Guards Airborne Division, stationed locally. The elite paratroops' offer of support to Boris Yeltsin was crucial to the failure of the 1991 putsch in Moscow, and they were also among the troops which blasted Yeltsin's parliamentary enemies out of the Moscow White House in 1993.

Things to See

The **kremlin** is at the heart of the city on ploshchad Vosstania, through which the main north-south road through Tula passes. It was built in 1514-21 with thick limestone walls about a km round. Inside are the **Weapons Museum** (Muzey oruzhiey), incongruously sited in the former Epiphany

Cathedral (Bogoyavlensky sobor), and the five-domed **Assumption Cathedral** (Uspensky sobor). Among the conventional weapons (from muskets to kalashnikovs) in the museum are many curiosities such as the 'Velodog', a pistol designed for sale to British cyclists whom the makers imagined would need to gun down dangerous dogs in their path; and a pistol designed for astronauts who came to earth in dangerously wild or remote places. The Assumption Cathedral, recently returned to Church use, was founded in the 16th century and rebuilt in the mid-18th century. It has 18th-century frescoes.

The **Samovar Museum** (Muzey samovarov), outside the kremlin entrance, has as many of these quintessentially Russian tea urns as you could wish to see – including one in the shape of Lenin's tomb!

Places to Stay & Eat

The *Hotel Moskva* outside Tula's Moskovsky railway station seems to be the only place that considers itself good enough for foreigners. Not that that's much recommendation – the receptionist was nasty, and seedy thugs

A samovar, the Russian tea urn

lurked in the lobby. Small if clean doubles are US$25. There's a bufet on the hotel's 5th floor serving eggs, bread and coffee. You can change money here. The *Hotel Tula* by the bus station said it wasn't good enough for foreigners.

Babushkas around town sell a tasty local speciality called Tulsky pryanik – glazed gingerbread with an apricot-jam filling.

Getting There & Away

Suburban trains to Tula go from Moscow's Kursk Station. The trip takes four or five hours, so it's better if you can get on a long-distance train heading for Kursk or Ukraine, many of which stop at Tula.

There's a daily bus at 9 am from Moscow's Shchyolkovsky Bus Station, taking 4½ hours for US$2.70. After the ride you can cheer yourself up by looking at the sign on top of Tula's bus station – 'Glory to Soviet science'.

YASNAYA POLYANA
ЯСНАЯ ПОЛЯНА

Yasnaya Polyana (Bright Glade), the estate where the great Russian writer Count Lev Tolstoy was born, spent much of his life and is buried, is 14 km south of central Tula. Before you trek out here from Moscow, try to establish how much is open: when we visited, one of the two museums on the estate was shut, and for several years the place has been the subject of heated wrangling between local bureaucrats, who have administered it since Soviet times, and members of the Tolstoy family, who accuse the bureaucrats of planning to build a tourist complex on the estate and claim that it's badly staffed and threatened by pollution. The Tolstoys want one of the writer's great-great-grandsons, Vladimir Tolstoy, to take over as director.

Normally, the estate is open from 9 am to 5 pm, Wednesday to Sunday, except the last Wednesday of the month and during high humidity. The ticket office, plus a café and bookstall, are opposite the main gate. Russian, and occasionally foreign-language, guided tours of the grounds and/or museums

Lev Tolstoy, Squire of Yasnaya Polyana

Lev Tolstoy was born at Yasnaya Polyana in 1828. He inherited the estate in 1847, and spent in all more than 50 years here, including nearly all his writing life. He was a liberal member of the lesser nobility who tried to free his serfs before this became compulsory, taught their children himself and joined in manual labour on the estate. In 1910, terminally disenchanted with the squire's life, he left Yasnaya Polyana for the south to start a peasant's life in an *izba* (wooden village house), but caught pneumonia and died at a remote railway halt, Astapovo.

An avenue of birches leads from the estate gates to the house where Tolstoy and his family lived, now the Tolstoy House-Museum (Dom-Muzey Tolstogo), packed with the authentic memorabilia not just of its residents but of famous visitors like Chekhov, Repin and Turgenev. Tolstoy's library here had 22,000 volumes in 35 languages. The study in which he wrote *War and Peace* (1863-69) and *Anna Karenina* (1873-77) is upstairs. The short-sighted Tolstoy sat at his desk here on a low, child-sized chair so that he wouldn't have to bend to read. His wife, Sofia, would make a clean copy of his day's scribblings in the adjacent room in the evenings. She lost count of the number of times she wrote out *War and Peace*.

The house was originally just a wing of the main estate house, where Tolstoy was born. He sold the central part of the house in 1854: it was moved in 36 pieces to a nearby village and later demolished. The far wing, known as the Kuzminsky House, houses the Tolstoy Literary Museum (Literaturny Muzey imeni Tolstoya), devoted to his writing career. A path leads to Tolstoy's unmarked grave among trees in a quiet corner of the estate, a favourite pilgrimage spot for bridal parties. The other main structure in the grounds is the Volkonsky House, which in Tolstoy's time was the servants' quarters. ■

are normally given from 10 am to 2 pm. You need to take one of these if you want to enter the museums, but you can wander around the grounds without a guide.

Getting There & Away

Bus No 114 to Shchekino from Tula's bus station stops at the Yasnaya Polyana turn-off – with a blue 'Yasnaya Polyana' sign – on the main road south from central Tula. From here it's one km to the right (west) to the estate entrance.

If you're driving from Moscow, it's easier to follow Tula's western bypass all the way to its south end and then turn back north towards Tula, than to go through central Tula, which is clogged with bad roads and heavy traffic. The Yasnaya Polyana turn-off is about 24 km from the south end of the bypass on the road back towards central Tula.

GORKI LENINSKIE
ГОРКИ ЛЕНИНСКИЕ
Lenin and his family took occasional rests at the lovely little 1830s manor house on this wooded estate, 32 km south-east of the Kremlin, after he narrowly survived an assassination attempt in 1918. After strokes in 1922 and 1923, Lenin spent more and more time at Gorki Leninskie, leaving only once in the eight months before he died here on 21 January 1924. Now it's a museum, still open daily from 10 am to 6 pm except Tuesday and the last day of the month – though numbers of visitors have somewhat declined from the 500,000 who flocked (or were herded) here annually in Soviet times. Some of the rooms are kept as they were, and the clocks still stand at 6.50 (am), the time of Lenin's death. The grounds are pretty.

Getting There & Away
Suburban trains from Moscow's Pavelets Station take half an hour to reach Leninskaya station, and then it's a short ride on bus No 27 or 28 to the museum. By road, there are three turn-offs to the left from the M4 Kashirskoe shosse, about eight to 11 km beyond the Moscow outer ring road.

North-East – the Golden Ring
Северо-восток –
Золотое Кольцо

The 'Golden Ring' (Zolotoe Koltso) is a modern name for a loop of very old towns north-east of Moscow which preceded the present capital as the political and cultural heart of Russia. The towns' churches, monasteries, city-forts (kremlins) and museums make an incredibly picturesque portfolio of early Russian craftwork. Another attraction of the region is that some of the towns are

really little more than villages, providing a peaceful glimpse of country life as it is lived all over European Russia.

Best known is little Suzdal, officially protected against industrial development and littered with so many protected buildings that it's almost one big museum. The other towns are more lived-in but are equally rich in old buildings such as churches, monasteries or kremlins. Made from stone, these buildings have outlived most wooden structures.

You do run the risk of old-Russian-church overload here, so it pays to be selective in where you go. The most visited places are Sergiev Posad and Suzdal, but Vladimir and Bogolyubovo, Plyos, Kostroma, Yaroslavl, Rostov-Veliky and Pereslavl-Zalessky, in their different ways, all have big attractions too.

Most places in the Golden Ring can be visited individually in day or overnight trips from Moscow, but a better way to absorb the region's beauties and place in history, if you have time, is to devote a few days to taking in a combination of places. Transport and accommodation are easy enough to find as you go along. One or two-day excursions are also available from Moscow, and Golden Ring visits are a standard item on many package tours to Russia.

This section covers the Golden Ring in anticlockwise order, though if you're doing a full circuit you might prefer to travel in a clockwise direction, as the distances between the first few destinations are shorter that way.

History
The Golden Ring's main towns began as outposts of the Kievan Rus state and grew as people moved north with Kiev's decline. At the start of the 12th century, Prince Vladimir Monomakh of Kiev founded a fort at Vladimir and gave the Rostov-Suzdal principality, in which it lay, to his son Yury Dolgoruky. Yury made Suzdal his capital but concentrated his energies down south, eventually winning the title Grand Prince of Kiev and installing himself there. He still took the

precaution of fortifying the settlements of Pereslavl-Zalessky and Kostroma in his original territory, along with a small western outpost called Moscow.

After Yury died in 1157, his son and successor, Andrey Bogolyubov, spurned the chance of establishing himself in Kiev and moved back to the more secure northern territories. Andrey based himself at Vladimir, which became the effective capital of Russia in 1169 when Andrey went back and sacked Kiev, taking the Grand Prince title to the north. Under these princes and their successors, Suzdal grew rich as a commercial centre and Vladimir sprouted cathedrals, monasteries and massive city walls. Rostov, Yaroslavl and other centres later split off as separate principalities.

In 1237, darkness fell as the Mongol Tatars invaded Russia, sacking and burning everything. But having made their point, they were mostly content to rule and collect taxes through local princes, which they did for the next 2½ centuries. The region again prospered under Andrey's nephew Yaroslav and Yaroslav's son Alexandr Nevsky of Novgorod. But Moscow, given independence by Alexandr Nevsky in 1252, grew in influence as an intermediary between the Tatars and the other Russian princes. Moscow absorbed Pereslavl-Zalessky, Vladimir and Suzdal in the 14th century; the headquarters of the Russian Orthodox Church was transferred there from Vladimir in the 1320s; and by the end of the 15th century the entire region was part of Muscovy, the Moscow state.

Architecture & Art

The majority of the Golden Ring's surviving architectural monuments date from spurts of building and rebuilding after the collapse of Tatar power. Most were bankrolled in the 16th century by the Moscow princes (particularly the fort-monasteries of Suzdal), and from the 17th century by the Church (as happened in Rostov) and a new class of rich merchants (as in Yaroslavl).

But the buildings that gave the region a key place in the story of Russian architecture were constructed before the Tatars came. Most important are three 12th-century buildings in and near Vladimir: the cathedrals of the Assumption and St Dmitry and the Church of the Intercession on the Nerl. These are the vital link between the architecture of 11th-century Kiev and that of 15th-century Moscow – early northern interpretations, in majestic, finely carved white stone, of Kiev's Byzantine-style brick churches.

The Vladimir-Suzdal region was also a chief inheritor of Kiev's Byzantine artistic traditions, though only a few fragments of 12th and 13th-century frescoes now remain in the Vladimir and Suzdal cathedrals and in the old church at Kideshka. (Some icons also survive in Moscow and St Petersburg museums.) While still primarily Byzantine in style, these works show a bold use of colour and a range of human emotions that heralds later Russian developments. This 'Vladimir-Suzdal school' came to an end with the Tatar invasions and Novgorod was left to continue the development of Russian art. Art revived, prolifically, in the Golden Ring from the 15th century onwards but never regained its earlier pioneering role – though the colourful, realistic late 17th-century murals by Gury Nikitin of Kostroma and his followers, which adorn several Golden Ring churches, shouldn't be missed.

Wooden Architecture Along the roads and in the villages are many northern-style 'gingerbread' log houses, decorated with bright paintwork, carved doorways and window frames – and often a pensioner at the front with a bucket of vegetables for sale. At Suzdal, Kostroma and Palekh, old wooden houses and churches are assembled in museums of wooden architecture – a convenient way to see some beautiful feats of 16th to 19th-century carpentry.

Crafts The region is also famous for art on another scale. The villages of Palekh, Mstyora and Kholuy, all north-east of Vladimir, became icon-painting centres as early as the 13th century and later developed special skills at working in miniature. When the

1917 revolution destroyed the market for icons, many painters here turned to lacquer miniatures of legendary or historical scenes on papier-mâché boxes, a technique first developed in the 19th century around the village of Fedoskino, north of Moscow. Nowadays, most people know these tiny works of art as 'Palekh boxes'.

Other regional traditions include the crystal and glasswork of Gus-Khrustalny near Vladimir, the textiles of Ivanovo, and finift, the finely painted enamelware of Rostov-Veliky.

VLADIMIR
ВЛАДИМИР

Population: 350,000

The city that gave way to Moscow as Russia's capital is now little different from a hundred other medium-sized Russian industrial towns – except that it has two of the most beautiful buildings in Russia, and a third stands a few km away at Bogolyubovo. It's easy enough to take in the main sights in a few hours en route between Moscow and Suzdal.

History

Vladimir was founded by Vladimir Monomakh of Kiev in 1108 as a fort in the Rostov-Suzdal principality that he gave to one of his younger sons, Yury Dolgoruky. Under Yury's son Andrey Bogolyubov it became capital of the principality in 1157 or 1158, and capital of all Kievan Rus after Andrey sacked Kiev in 1169. Andrey and his brother Vsevolod III (1176-1212) consolidated themselves as the strongest Russian princes and brought builders and artists from as far away as Western Europe to give Vladimir a Kiev-like splendour.

Devastated by the Tatars in 1238 and 1293, the city recovered each time but its realm disintegrated into small princedoms with Moscow increasingly dominant. The head of the Russian Church resided here from 1300 to 1326 but then moved to Moscow. Worldly power finally shifted to Moscow around this time too. Even so, the

grand princes remained nominally Grand Princes of Vladimir until the 15th century. In the 20th century, Vladimir prospered anew on the back of textile, machine-building and chemical industries.

Orientation & Information

The main road through the city from west to east is called successively prospekt Lenina, ulitsa Pushkina, Moskovskaya ulitsa, ulitsa III Internatsionala, ulitsa Frunze and Dobroselskaya ulitsa. The Assumption and St Dmitry cathedrals are just off ulitsa III Internatsionala, standing impressively at the top of the tree-covered slope down to the Klyazma River. The rail and bus stations are both on Vokzalnaya ulitsa at the bottom of the same slope a short distance east. The M7 Moscow-Nizhny Novgorod road makes a loop round the north side of the city.

You can change money in the Vladimir and Zarya hotels and at an obmen valyuty office on ulitsa III Internatsionala opposite the two main cathedrals. The bookshop on the north side of prospekt Lenina, about 200 metres west of the Hotel Zarya, is good for maps. The Vladimir telephone code is 09222.

Assumption Cathedral

Andrey Bogolyubov announced Vladimir's succession to Kiev as the Russian capital with a northern white-stone version of Kiev's brick Byzantine-style churches. Begun in 1158, the Assumption Cathedral (Uspensky sobor) is simple but majestic in form and adorned (innovatively for the time) with fine carving. It was extended on all sides after a fire in the 1180s, becoming five aisles wide instead of three. The four outer domes were added then too. Since then it has changed little. In the 1470s the Italian architect Aristotle Fioravanti was instructed to use it as a model when he planned the Moscow Kremlin's own Assumption Cathedral.

Initially, the cathedral housed a Byzantine icon of the Virgin brought from Kiev by Andrey Bogolyubov, which already in his time was on its way to becoming Russia's

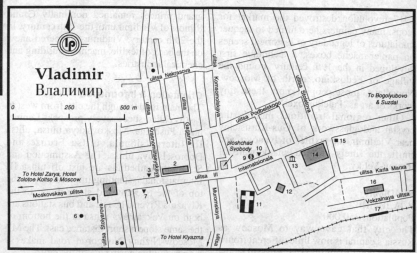

Vladimir
Владимир

0   250   500 m

To Bogolyubovo
& Suzdal

To Hotel Zarya, Hotel
Zolotoe Koltso & Moscow

To Hotel Klyazma

1	**Princess' Convent** Княгинин монастырь	
2	**Trading Arcades** Торговые ряды	
3	**Restoran U Zolotykh Vorot** Ресторан у Золотых ворот	
4	**Golden Gate** Золотые ворота	
5	**Crystal, Lacquer Miniatures & Embroidery Exhibition** Выставка хрусталя, лаковой миниатюры и вышивки	
6	**Lunacharsky Drama Theatre** Драматический театр имени Луначарского	
7	**Kafe Pitstsa** Кафе пицца	
8	**Old Vladimir Exhibition** Выставка Старый Владимир	
9	**Money Exchange** Обмен валюты	
10	**Bar/Restoran Stary Gorod** Бар/Ресторан Старый Город	
11	**Assumption Cathedral** Успенский собор	
12	**St Dmitry's Cathedral** Дмитриевский собор	
13	**Prerevolutionary History Museum** Музей истории дореволюционного прошлого Владимирского края	
14	**Former Nativity Monastery** Бывший Рождественский монастырь	
15	**Hotel Vladimir** Гостиница Владимир	
16	**Bus Station** Автовокзал	
17	**Railway Station** Вокзал	

most revered image, a national protector and granter of supreme status to the city that kept it. Moved to Moscow in 1390, it's now known as the *Vladimir Icon of the Mother of God* and since 1930 has been kept in the Tretyakov Gallery in Moscow.

Adjoining the cathedral on the north side

(beside the path up from ulitsa III Internatsionala) are an 1810 belltower and the 1862 St George's Chapel. The cathedral is a working church, open to visitors only from 1.30 to 4.30 pm daily (US$2.50 for foreigners).

A few restored 1158-60 murals of peacocks and prophets holding scrolls can be made out about halfway up the inner wall of the outer north aisle. When they were painted, this was an outside wall. The real treasures are the (also restored, though already slightly faded) *Last Judgment* frescoes by Andrey Rublyov and Daniil Chyorny, painted in 1408 in the central nave and inner south aisle, under the choir gallery towards the west end. Among them, in the central nave, are rows of haloed evangelists and angels, with realistic, sympathetic faces, and (on the ceiling) Christ with his right arm raised.

Cathedral of St Dmitry

Vladimir-Suzdal stone carving reached its most amazing heights on the Cathedral of St Dmitry (Dmitrievsky sobor, 1193-97), the only surviving part of Vsevolod III's palace complex. The western doorway and the upper parts of all four walls are covered in an amazing profusion of stone images – a few of them Christian but mostly animal, vegetable and mythological.

The top centre of the north, south and west walls all show King David bewitching the birds and beasts with music, which may be an oblique way of complimenting Vsevolod, who appears in person at the top left of the north wall, with a baby son on his knee and other sons kneeling on each side. Above the right-hand window of the south wall, Alexander the Great ascends into heaven, a symbol of princely might; on the west wall appear the labours of Hercules.

The cathedral is often locked, but if you ask at the nearby History Museum someone may let you in. Inside, on the larger, central vault beneath the princely gallery on the west side, are some beautiful 12th-century frescoes of apostles and angels, almost certainly by Byzantine artists.

Golden Gate

Vladimir's Golden Gate (Zolotye Vorota), part defensive tower, part triumphal arch, and modelled on the very similar structure in Kiev, was built by Andrey Bogolyubov to guard the main, western entrance to his city about half a km west of the Assumption Cathedral. The Golden Gate, restored under Catherine the Great, now houses a museum of Vladimir's military history, open from 10 am to 4 or 5 pm daily except Tuesday and the last Friday of the month. To the east, on ulitsa III Internatsionala, are the late 18th-century Trading Arcades (Torgovye ryady).

Other Attractions

The **Vladimir Region Pre-Revolutionary History Museum** (Muzey istorii dorevolyutsionnogo proshlogo Vladimirskogo kraya), at ulitsa III Internatsionala 64 close to the Cathedral of St Dmitry, includes the original coffin of Alexandr Nevsky of Novgorod, the 13th-century military leader who was also Prince of Vladimir. He was buried in the former Nativity Monastery farther along the street, once one of Russia's most important monasteries, but his remains were moved to St Petersburg in 1724 when Peter the Great allotted him Russian hero status. The museum is open from 10 am to 3.30 or 4.30 pm daily except Monday and the last Thursday of the month.

Interesting for its site as well as its contents is the **Old Vladimir Exhibition** (Vystavka Stary Vladimir) in an old water tower on Kozlov val (part of the old ramparts), open daily from 11 am to 6 pm except Monday. Near the Golden Gate, in the red-brick former Old Believers' Trinity Church (1913-16) at Moskovskaya ulitsa 2, is a **Crystal, Lacquer Miniatures & Embroidery Exhibition** (Vystavka khrustalya, lakovoy miniatyury i vyshivki) featuring the crafts of Gus-Khrustalny and other nearby towns.

The **Princess' Convent** (Knyagina monastyr) off ulitsa Nekrasova, founded by Vsevolod III's wife, Maria, is now a convent again after spending recent decades as a Museum of Orthodoxy & Atheism. The only substantial surviving building is its 16th-century Assumption Cathedral (Uspensky sobor), with many well-preserved 1640s frescoes.

Places to Stay

The *Hotel Vladimir* (☎ 6 06 00), conveniently located at ulitsa III Internatsionala 74 about half a km east of the Assumption Cathedral, has bare but clean doubles with private bathroom for US$15.

The best hotel is the *Hotel Zolotoe Koltso*, which opened in 1992 in the west of town on the corner of ulitsa Chaykovskogo and ulitsa Balakireva: go two km west along the main street from the Golden Gate, then one km north on ulitsa Chaykovskogo. It's a 350-bed place with a good restaurant. Comfortable enough singles/doubles with private bathroom go for US$25/40.

Nearer the centre with the same prices, but a bit run-down, is the *Hotel Zarya* (☎ 2 34 22) at ulitsa Pushkina 36, about one km west of the cathedrals. It seems to attract dubious business folk. It has two buildings, Korpus I (bigger and newer) and Korpus II (with the main reception).

About two km south of the town centre, beyond the Klyazma River, is the *Hotel Klyazma* (☎ 2 42 37) at Sudogodskoe shosse 15. Clean doubles with balconies and private bathrooms are US$31. To get there, take trolleybus No 6 from Muromskaya ulitsa, just south of the ulitsa III Internatsionala bridge, to the second stop.

Places to Eat

All the hotels mentioned have restaurants and Korpus II of the *Hotel Zarya* has a ground-floor café with a good choice of quick, acceptable food.

The inexpensive *Bar/Restoran Stary Gorod* on ulitsa III Internatsionala opposite the Cathedral of St Dmitry serves a couple of hot dishes, good coffee, ice cream and a few other snacks from noon to midnight daily. On ulitsa III Internatsionala just east of the Golden Gate there's pizza at the *Kafe Pitstsa* and standard restaurant fare at the *Restoran U Zolotykh Vorot*.

Getting There & Away

It's easy to get to Vladimir from Moscow or vice versa in the morning, but services in the afternoon and evening are inconvenient.

Bus There are five daily buses each way between Moscow's Shchyolkovsky Bus Station and Vladimir, taking 3½ hours for US$2.70. A further 20-odd daily buses to and from Moscow stop at Vladimir in transit, but buses from Vladimir to Moscow, like the trains, are mostly in the morning: in the afternoon the crowds wanting tickets to Moscow can be a nightmare.

Other buses from Vladimir run to Suzdal (US$0.25; one hour; 23 times daily from 6.40 am to 9.40 pm, tickets from kassa No 7), Nizhny Novgorod (five hours; seven times daily), Ivanovo (three hours; 12 times daily), Kostroma (5½ hours; 7.15 am and noon, daily) and Yaroslavl (six hours; 6.30 am daily and 3.40 pm Friday to Sunday).

Train In Moscow, the Kursk Station is the terminus for all suburban and most long-distance trains to/from Vladimir. Up to 14 long-distance trains daily run in each direction between Moscow and Nizhny Novgorod (still shown by its old name, Gorky, on many timetables), stopping at Vladimir. From Moscow, all these leave between about 9.30 pm and 9.30 am, except train No 46 (1.45 pm). The trip is about three hours. In the opposite direction, departures from Vladimir to Moscow are all between 12.30 am and 12.30 pm. After that, you usually need two suburban trains to get from Moscow to Vladimir or vice versa, changing about halfway at Petushki – a trip of anywhere from 3½ to six hours. Suburban trains run from the Kursk Station to Petushki about 15 times daily, at erratic intervals between 5.40 am and 10.45 pm, and from Petushki to Vladimir at 5 and 10.15 am and 1.05, 6.25, 7.50 and 10.18 pm, at the time of writing. On Saturday and Sunday only, there's one suburban train, at 6.40 am, all the way from the Kursk Station to Vladimir. Westbound from Vladimir, suburban trains run to Petushki at 6.20 and 8.50 am and 3.10, 5.30 and 8.15 pm, with waits of 30 minutes to 2½ hours for connections at Petushki. The only direct suburban services from Vladimir to Moscow are at 7.04 am on Saturdays and 1.58 pm on Saturday and Sunday.

Car Vladimir is a straightforward 180-km drive from Moscow. This is the beginning of the road to Siberia, walked by thousands of exiles in the old days. To reach Suzdal from central Vladimir, drive about six km east along the main street and then turn left along Suzdalsky prospekt, crossing the Vladimir bypass after a km or so.

Getting Around

Trolleybus No 5 from the rail and bus stations runs up to and along the main east-west street, passing the Hotel Vladimir, the two main cathedrals and the town centre, the Hotel Zarya, and on out to the western edge of Vladimir. Trolleybus No 1 runs from end to end of town along the main street. Trolleybus No 4 covers at least the Hotel Vladimir to Golden Gate section of the same route.

BOGOLYUBOVO
БОГОЛЮБОВО
Population: 4000

When Andrey Bogolyubov was returning north from Kiev in the late 1150s, his horses – so the story goes – stopped where Bogolyubovo ('ba-gal-YOO-ba-va') now stands, 11 km east of Vladimir, and wouldn't go a step farther. This is supposedly why Andrey made nearby Vladimir, and not his father's old base of Suzdal, his capital, and why the icon of the Mother of God that he was bearing became so closely tied to Vladimir's, and ultimately Russia's, fortunes. Whatever the legends, Andrey built a stone palace-cum-fort that dates from 1158-65 at this strategic spot near the meeting of the Nerl and Klyazma rivers. Nearby, in 1165, he built possibly the most perfect of all old Russian buildings, the Church of the Intercession on the Nerl.

Palace & Monastery

A tower and arch from Andrey Bogolyubov's palace survive amid a dilapidated but recently reopened 18th-century monastery by the Vladimir-Nizhny Novgorod road in the middle of Bogolyubovo. The dominant buildings today are the monastery's 1841 belltower beside the road, and its 1866

Assumption Cathedral (Uspensky sobor). Just east of the cathedral, Andrey's arch and tower – on whose stairs, according to a chronicle, Andrey was assassinated by hostile boyars – adjoin each other, and the arch adjoins the 18th-century Church of the Virgin's Nativity (Rozhdestvenskaya tserkov).

Church of the Intercession on the Nerl

To reach this famous little church (Tserkov Pokrova na Nerli), go back about 200 metres towards Vladimir from the monastery-palace group and then turn into ulitsa Frunze which winds downhill and under a railway bridge. Under the bridge, take the path to the left along the side of a small wood. The church appears across the meadows, about 1.25 km from the bridge. Its beauty lies in its simple but perfect proportions, a brilliantly chosen waterside site and sparing use of delicate carving. If it looks a mite top-heavy, it's because the original helmet dome was replaced by a cushion dome in 1803.

Legend has it that Andrey had the church built in memory of his favourite son, Izyaslav, who was killed in battle against the Bulgars. As on the Cathedral of St Dmitry in Vladimir, King David sits at the top of three façades, the birds and beasts entranced by his music. The inside has more carving, including 20 pairs of lions. If the church is closed, try asking at the house behind.

Getting There & Away

Buses to Penkino or Kameshnovo from Vladimir bus station stop at Bogolyubovo. There are at least seven daily, including departures at 7.15 and 10.40 am and 12.50, 1.55 and 5.30 pm – tickets from kassa No 6. There are also reportedly buses to Bogolyubovo from ulitsa Gagarina in Vladimir.

Drivers from central Vladimir should head straight out east along the main road. Drivers from Suzdal should turn left when they hit Vladimir's northern bypass and go five km.

SUZDAL

СУЗДАЛЬ

Population: 12,000

Suzdal (*'SOOZ-dal'*), 35 km north of Vladimir, is special not just for its lovely old monasteries, convents and churches but also because they haven't been strangled by 20th-century ugliness, noise and pollution. Bypassed by industry because the Moscow-Nizhny Novgorod railway was routed 30 km to its south, the town is now officially protected from unsightly development. As a result it remains the little rural settlement it always was, on low eminences above the winding Kamenka River, with green fields reaching right into the centre and its housing mostly comprised of one-storey izbas.

Suzdal is uniquely peaceful among Russian tourist towns, and the slightly unreal 'living museum' atmosphere resulting from its protected status is a small price to pay. It's even more peaceful today than in Soviet times, since the number of visitors – Russian and foreign – has fallen off dramatically. It's especially picturesque in snow, but there's nothing to shield Suzdal from winter winds whipping in from Siberia.

History

First mentioned in 1024, Suzdal was made the capital of the Rostov-Suzdal principality by Yury Dolgoruky in the first half of the 12th century. When Andrey Bogolyubov returned from Kiev in 1157 or 1158 he made Vladimir the capital, and from then on the principality was known as Vladimir-Suzdal. But, set in a fertile wheat-growing area, Suzdal remained a trade centre even after the Tatar invasions. It was an independent princedom from the early 13th to the mid-14th century, when it united with Nizhny Novgorod until both were annexed by Moscow in 1392.

Under Muscovite rule, Suzdal became a wealthy monastic centre, with particularly big building projects funded by tsars Vasily III and Ivan the Terrible in the 16th century. In the late 17th and 18th centuries, wealthy merchants paid for 30 gorgeous little churches, which still adorn the town.

Orientation

Many places you're likely to visit are on or near the central 1.5 km of the north-south main street, ulitsa Lenina. The chief exceptions are the Intercession Monastery and the GTK accommodation complex, one to 1.5 km north-west of the centre.

Information

In addition to their normal weekly closing days, most Suzdal museums and monuments are closed on the last Friday of the month. A few of the minor ones close altogether from October to April.

You can change money at the GTK (which also offers Visa-card cash advances), the bank on Krasnaya ploshchad (go upstairs) and a couple of obmen valyuty places in the Trading Arcades beside Torgovaya ploshchad. There's a post, telephone and telegraph office on Krasnaya ploshchad; the GTK provides these services too. Suzdal's telephone code is 09231.

There's a bookshop, which might have some Russian guidebooks in English, in the Trading Arcades.

Kremlin

The 1.4-km-long earth rampart of Suzdal's kremlin (fort), founded in the 11th century, today encloses a few streets of houses and a handful of churches as well as the main cathedral group on Kremlyovskaya ulitsa.

The **Nativity of the Virgin Cathedral** (Rozhdestvensky sobor), its blue domes spangled with gold, was founded in the 1220s but only its richly carved lower section is original white stone, the rest being 16th-century brick. The inside is sumptuous with frescoes from the 13th and 17th centuries (the best of the earlier ones are the figures of two elders in the upper part of the south apse) and 13th-century damascene (gold on copper) west and south doors – gospel scenes on the west, angels' deeds on the south.

The 15th to 18th-century **Archbishop's Chambers** line the south side of the cathedral yard, with an entrance to their 18th-century Cross Hall (Krestovaya palata) which was used for receptions. The **Suzdal**

History Exhibition (Istoricheskaya Expozitsia) is reached from the tent-roofed 1635 bell tower on the east side of the yard. The old Russian painting (Drevnerusskoy zhivopisi) display, also entered from the bell tower, is well worth a visit though it concentrates on 15th to 17th-century icons of the Vladimir-Suzdal school – well after the 12th to 13th-century high point of this school, the few surviving works of which are mostly in Moscow and St Petersburg museums.

The cathedral, Cross Hall and exhibitions are all open from 10 am to 4 or 5 pm daily except Tuesday and the last Friday of the month. Tickets for all of them are sold at the Cross Hall – but the cathedral is closed at times of low temperature or high humidity to protect its art.

Just south of this group stands the 1766 wooden St Nicholas' Church, brought from Glatovo village near Yuriev-Polsky. Another St Nicholas', one of Suzdal's own fine small churches, built in 1720-39, is on ulitsa Lebedeva just east of the cathedral group, with its pointed tower fronting the road.

Torgovaya Ploshchad

Suzdal's Torgovaya ploshchad (Trade Square) is dominated by the pillared Trading Arcades (1806-11) along its west side, with one pair of small churches in front of them and another pair behind, above the river. Though all these four are closed, the pretty, five-domed 1707 Emperor Constantine Church over in the square's north-eastern corner is a working church; the inside is ornate. The 1787 Virgin of All Sorrows Church next to it is smaller but has a big bell tower.

Monastery of the Deposition

The Monastery of the Deposition of the Holy Robe (Rizopolozhensky monastyr) is said to date from 1207 but the existing buildings are 16th to 19th century. It's now a dilapidated mess but has two pretty pyramidal entrance turrets (1688) on the south gate. Suzdal's tallest structure, a 72-metre 1813-19 bell tower, rises from the east wall. The central Deposition Cathedral (Rizopolozhensky

Sobor), with three helmet domes, dates from the first half of the 16th century; it is reminiscent of the Moscow Kremlin's Archangel Cathedral.

Alexandrovsky Convent

This little, white-painted convent (Alexandrovsky monastyr) at the top of the river embankment stands out for its simple, quiet beauty. Reputedly founded in 1240 by Alexandr Nevsky for noble women whose menfolk had been killed by the Tatars, its present Ascension Church (Voznesenskaya tserkov) and bell tower date from 1695.

Saviour Monastery of St Euthymius

Suzdal's biggest monastery (Spaso-Yevfimievsky monastyr), founded to protect the town's northern entry in the 14th century, grew mighty in the 16th and 17th centuries after Vasily III, Ivan the Terrible and the noble Pozharsky family funded impressive new stone buildings and big land and property acquisitions. It was girded with its great brick walls and towers in the 17th century. The entrance and ticket office are in the high gatetower in the south wall. Entry is US$1.50 for foreigners, plus US$1.50 or US$2.50 for each of four museums or exhibitions inside that you choose to visit. The monastery is open from 10 am to 4 or 5 pm. Unlike most other Suzdal sights, its closing days are Monday and the last Thursday of the month.

Inside, a tall 16th to 17th-century bell tower stands before the seven-domed **Cathedral of the Transfiguration of the Saviour** (Spaso-Preobrazhensky sobor). Every hour on the hour during opening times, a 10-minute concert of chimes is given on the bell tower's bells – well worth hearing. The bell ringer hawks cassette tapes of the bells afterwards. The cathedral was built in the 1590s in 12th to 13th-century Vladimir-Suzdal style. Inside, some bright 1689 frescoes recounting the monastery's history, by the school of the famous Gury Nikitin from Kostroma, have been uncovered. Entry is by ticket from the main kassa. The tomb of Prince Dmitry Pozharsky (1578-1642),

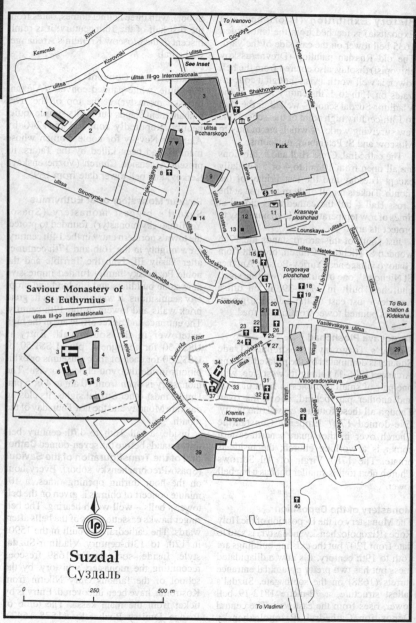

Saviour Monastery of St Euthymius

Suzdal
Суздаль

PLACES TO STAY

1   GTK Motel
    Мотель ГТК
2   GTK
    Главный туристический комплекс
13 Hotel Rizopolozhenskaya
    Гостиница Ризоположенская
14 Likhoninsky Dom
    Лихонинский Дом

PLACES TO EAT

7   Restoran Trapeznaya
    Ресторан Трапезная
25 Restoran Gostiny Dvor
    Ресторан Гостиный двор
27 Restoran Pogrebok
    Ресторан Погребок
36 Restoran Trapeznaya
    Ресторан Трапезная

OTHER

3   Saviour Monastery of St Euthymius
    Спасо-Евфимиевский
    монастырь
4   Our Lady of Smolensk Church
    Смоленская церковь
5   18th-Century Town House
    Жилой дом, XVIII в.
6   Intercession Convent
    Покровский монастырь
8   SS Peter & Paul Church (1694)
    Петропавловская церковь
9   Alexandrovsky Convent
    Александровский монастырь
10 Bank
    Банк
11 Post, Telephone & Telegraph Office
    Почтамт и телеграф
12 Monastery of the Deposition
    Ризоположенский монастырь
15 St Antipy's Church
    Антипьевская церковь
16 St Lazarus' Church (1667)
    Лазаревская церковь

17 Holy Cross Church (1770)
    Крестовская церковь
18 Virgin of All Sorrows Church (1787)
    Скорбященская церковь
19 Emperor Constantine Church (1707)
    Царевоконстантиновская церковь
20 Kazanskaya Church (1739)
    Казанская церковь
21 Trading Arcades
    Торговые ряды
22 Entry into Jerusalem Church (1707)
    Входоиерусалимская церковь
23 St Parasceva Pyatnitsa Church (1772)
    Параскева пятницкая церковь
24 Assumption Church (17th Century)
    Успенская церковь
26 Resurrection Church (1719)
    Воскресенская церковь
28 Food Market
    Рынок
29 St Basil's Monastery
    Васильевский монастырь
30 Pretechenskaya Church (1720)
    Предтеченская церковь
31 St Nicholas' Church
    Никольская церковь
32 Nativity of the Virgin Church
    Рождественская церковь
33 Cathedral Bell Tower (1635)
    Колокольня
34 Nativity of the Virgin Cathedral
    Рождественский собор
35 Archbishop's Chambers
    Архиерейские палаты
37 St Nicholas' Church (Wooden) (1766)
    Никольская церковь
    (деревянная)
38 SS Kosmas & Damian Church (1725)
    Козьмодемьянская церковь
39 Museum of Wooden Architecture &
    Peasant Life
    Музей деревянного зодчества и
    крестьянского быта
40 Church of the Sign (1749)
    Знаменская церковь

continued next page

---

leader of the Russian army that drove the Polish invaders from Moscow in 1612, is by the cathedral's east wall.

The 1525 **Assumption Church** (Uspenskaya tserkov) facing the bell tower adjoins

the old Father Superior's chambers, which houses a display of Russian books from the 15th century on. The **monks' quarters** across the compound contain a museum of modern Russian folk art. At the north end of

	Saviour Monastery of St Euthymius	5	Belltower
			Звонница
1	Prison	6	Assumption Church
	Тюрьма		Успенская церковь
2	Hospital & St Nicholas' Church	7	Father Superior's Chambers
	Больничные кельи и Никольская церковь		Камеры отца-игумена
3	Cathedral of the Transfiguration	8	Annunciation Gate-Church
	of the Saviour		Благовещенская надвратная церковь
	Спасо-Преображенский собор	9	Southern Gate-Tower
4	Monks' Quarters		Южные ворота
	Братский корпус		

the complex is the old monastery prison, set up in 1764 for religious dissidents, now closed to visitors, and the combined **hospital** and **St Nicholas' Church** (Bolnichnye kelyi i Nikolskaya tserkov, 1669), which contain a rich museum of 12th to 20th-century Russian applied art, much of it from Suzdal itself.

Across ulitsa Lenina from the south-east corner of the monastery are the 1696-1707 Our Lady of Smolensk Church and Suzdal's only surviving early **18th-century town house**; the latter is furnished in original style and open daily except Monday from 10 am to 4 or 5 pm.

Intercession Convent

The Intercession Convent (Pokrovsky monastyr), founded in 1364, has been handed back to the Church since Soviet times and a small community of black-robed nuns is in residence. The three-domed Intercession Cathedral (Pokrovsky sobor) in the centre, built in 1510-18, is again in use, and under renovation after becoming sadly dilapidated in Soviet times.

The convent was originally a place of exile for the unwanted wives of tsars – among them Solomonia Saburova, first wife of Vasily III, who was sent here in the 1520s because of her supposed infertility. The story goes that she finally became pregnant too late to avoid being divorced. She had a baby boy in Suzdal but, fearing he would be seen as a dangerous rival to any sons produced by Vasily's new wife, Yelena Glinska, secretly had him adopted, pretended he had died and

staged a mock burial. This was probably just as well for the boy since Yelena did indeed produce a son – Ivan the Terrible. The legend received dramatic corroboration in 1934 when researchers opened a small 16th-century tomb beside Solomonia's, in the crypt beneath the Intercession Cathedral. They found a silk and pearl shirt stuffed with rags – and no bones. The crypt is closed to visitors.

In Soviet times the convent was turned into a hotel, with accommodation in wooden izbas around the grounds. This was still functioning at the time of writing but was due to close by 1996. The same may happen to the museum of the convent's history, in a 17th-century building against the west wall, and the wooden building near the entrance with a display of Suzdal embroidery plus two rooms restored as nuns' cells. For the moment, these are open from 9.30 am to 3.30 or 4.30 pm, daily except Tuesday and the last Friday of the month. It's to be hoped that the restaurant in the 1551 Refectory Church of the Conception of St Anna (Trapeznaya tserkov Zachatia Sviatoi Anny), north of the Intercession Cathedral, stays open, as it serves the best food in Suzdal.

Museum of Wooden Architecture & Peasant Life

The highlights of this wooden 'model village' (Muzey derevyannogo zodchestva i krestyanskogo byta), illustrating old peasant life in this region of Russia, are more churches – notably the 1756 Transfiguration Church (Preobrazhenskaya tserkov) brought from Kozlyatievo village and the simpler 1776 Resurrection Church (Voskresenskaya tserkov) from Patakino. They're interesting to compare with Suzdal's brick churches from the same era. There are also log houses, windmills, a barn and lots of tools and handicrafts.

The museum is across the river south of the kremlin, open from 9.30 am to 3.30 or 4.30 pm daily except Tuesday and the last Friday of the month. Building interiors are open only from 1 May to 1 October.

Other Suzdal Buildings

Every little Suzdal church has its own charm. Our favourites include the simple **Resurrection Church** (Voskresenskaya tserkov) on Torgovaya ploshchad, built in 1719; the shabby but graceful **Pretechenskaya Church** (Pretechenskaya tserkov, 1720) on ulitsa Lenina; and the slender tower of **St Lazarus' Church** (Lazarevskaya tserkov, 1667) with its multicoloured stonework, on Staraya ulitsa. The **SS Kosmas & Damian Church** (Kosmodamianovskaya tserkov, 1725) is picturesquely placed on a bend in the river. Keep looking. You'll find more.

Suzdal's fifth monastery is **St Basil's** (Vasilevsky monastyr) on the Kideksha road. Its cathedral (Vasilevsky sobor) and Purification Church (Sretenskaya tserkov) are both 17th century.

Kideksha

The 1152 **Church of SS Boris & Gleb** (Borisoglebskaya tserkov) on the Nerl River in this quiet village four km east of Suzdal is the oldest in the district, built for Yury Dolgoruky who had a small wooden palace here.

The palace has disappeared and the church, rebuilt many times, has lost its original vault, roof and dome and gained a 19th-century porch. But the church's old floor, a metre below the modern one, gives a sense of the place's age, and drawings in the porch give an idea of what it may once have looked like. A few fragments of 12th-century frescoes remain, including two figures on horseback, probably Boris and Gleb, sons of

Vladimir of Kiev, who were killed by another son, Svyatopolk, and became the first Russian saints. The church is open from 10 am to 4 or 5 pm daily except Tuesday and the last Friday of the month. The other buildings in the compound are 18th century.

Rides

Horse-drawn carts (sleighs in winter) in Suzdal wait for customers around the kremlin and the south end of the Trading Arcades. Bargain with the drivers.

Places to Stay

In the decrepit Monastery of the Deposition is the equally decrepit *Hotel Rizopolozhenskaya* (☎ 2 14 08). Singles/doubles with private bath and toilet are just US$5.50/7.50 but there's no hot water and the whole place is pretty shabby. They don't get many foreigners but the price makes it tolerable for a night or two if your budget is tight.

The best place to stay in Suzdal, if you can afford US$30 per person and can get a room, is *Likhoninsky Dom* (☎ 2 19 01, 2 04 44 or (09222) 2 42 63, 2 52 78) at ulitsa Slobodskaya 34, a quiet street near the town centre. This is a 17th-century house, renovated and partly furnished in period style, which was used as a museum until recently turned into a small hotel by the Vladimir-Suzdal museum authorities. It has just three or four comfortable, pleasantly decorated rooms, including a single, all sharing clean bathrooms, and a pretty garden out the back. It's one of the most unusual and atmospheric hotels in Russia. The only drawback is that no meals are served. The building, with a white ground floor and wooden upper floor, is unmarked except for the number 34: ring the bell on the gate to enter. It's worth calling in advance to try to make a booking.

Another atmospheric but much more expensive place to stay is the old *Intercession Convent* (☎ 2 09 08). Though the convent has now been returned to the Church and has nuns in residence, the 30 comfortable rooms in wooden izba-style cabins installed here for visitors in Soviet times are due to stay open until 1996. Perhaps they'll last longer than that. They have a private bathroom and cost US$82.50, single or double.

The main tourist hotel is the aptly titled *Glavny Turistsky Komplex* (Main Tourist Complex, ☎ 2 15 30; fax 2 06 66), usually known by its initials GTK. It's a long, low-rise block on the north-west edge of town, off ulitsa Korovniki – fairly modern but shoddily built, with damp already affecting some rooms. It was built for groups, with rooms of average size and comfort (but some grubby bathrooms), a vast lobby, souvenir shop, cinema, swimming pool, a disco on weekends and gloomy staff. You should be able to get in here if nowhere else. Rooms are US$82, single or double, but one traveller told us he had pleaded poverty and obtained a 'room for Russians' – a single without TV or phone – for US$41. The adjacent motel rooms are even more extortionate at US$54.50/109.

Places to Eat

The *Restoran Trapeznaya* in the Intercession Convent's Conception of St Anna Refectory Church serves good Russian food, and it's to be hoped it doesn't close now that the convent has been returned to the Church. A couple of zakuski, a main course and a dessert come to around US$5. Save room for a dessert of bliny with honey, which is truly succulent. Ask for warming, mildly alcoholic mead *(medovukha)* to wash it all down. Hours are 9 am to 8 pm daily, though they're observed somewhat erratically.

Another *Restoran Trapeznaya*, in the Archbishop's Chambers in the kremlin, also does decent Russian fare – like thick pokhlyobka soup, zharkoe (individual meat and potato hotpots), the ubiquitous mushrooms baked in sour cream and more bliny and mead. It's open for lunch only, daily except Tuesday. Enter from the south side of the Archbishop's Chambers.

Around the centre of town are a few other cafés and restaurants, less inviting but passable. One is the inexpensive, busy and harassed *Restoran Pogrebok* on Kremlyovskaya ulitsa, open from 10 am to 6 pm daily except Monday. Another is the *Restoran Gostiny Dvor* at the south end of the Trading Arcades, open daily from 11 am to 3 pm and 4 to 8 pm.

Meals in the main upstairs restaurant at the *GTK* are reasonable, but individuals should book an exact time since the needs of groups get priority. On the ground floor is a dreadful stolovaya which fills you up quickly and cheaply if you're desperate; open until about 7 pm.

There's a small food market in the town centre.

Things to Buy

A few souvenir shops are dotted along Kremlyovskaya ulitsa and in the Trading Arcades and the GTK.

Getting There & Away

There's no railway here. Suzdal's bus station (avtovokzal) is 1.5 km east of the centre along Vasilevskaya ulitsa, at the junction of the town's eastern bypass.

If you're heading straight to Suzdal from Moscow, there's one daily bus from the Shchyolkovsky Bus Station at 5 pm, taking 4½ hours for US$3.25. This bus returns from Suzdal to Moscow at 5.30 am. A few Moscow-Ivanovo and Ivanovo-Moscow buses also stop at Suzdal.

The common alternative is to go via Vladimir. Buses run both ways between Suzdal and Vladimir bus stations 23 times daily. The one-hour trip costs US$0.25. Departures from Vladimir are from 6.40 am to 9.40 pm; from Suzdal they're from 5.20 am to 8 pm.

Heading north from Suzdal, you have to hope for a place on a bus coming through from Vladimir and you usually have to wait until it arrives before tickets are sold: there are two buses a day to Kostroma (4¼ hours from Suzdal), one or two to Yaroslavl (five hours) and about 12 to Ivanovo (two hours) where you should be able to change to a Kostroma or Yaroslavl bus.

Getting Around

The best way is on foot. There are short-cut

JOHN NOBLE

RICHARD NEBESKY

RICHARD NEBESKY

Top: St Dmitry's Cathedral, Vladimir
tom: Gate of Archangel Cathedral, Kremlin, Moscow
ight: Assumption Cathedral, Kremlin, Moscow

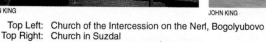

Top Left: Church of the Intercession on the Nerl, Bogolyubovo
Top Right: Church in Suzdal
Bottom Left: Iconostasis, Elijah Church, Yaroslavl
Bottom Right: Trinity Monastery of St Sergius, Zagorsk

paths in the town – like the footbridge over the river behind the GTK which cuts at least one km off the three km to the centre. Bus No 3 runs erratically through the day between the GTK and the bus station, via the town centre.

IVANOVO & PALEKH
ИВАНОВО И ПАЛЕХ

Ivanovo (population 550,000), 78 km north of Suzdal on the Suzdal-Kostroma road, is known for two (connected) features: its cotton textiles – it's one of Russia's biggest centres – and its women. The town's female population, swelled by the textile mills' labour needs, apparently once heavily outnumbered its male population and Ivanovo women are still renowned as very assertive, even aggressive, men-chasers. In appearance it's a very drab and dreary industrial town. You might have to change buses here if you're travelling between the northern and southern parts of the Golden Ring.

Ivanovo is occasionally used as a base for tour groups visiting Palekh, the village famous for icon painters and small lacquer boxes, 65 km south-east on the Nizhny Novgorod road. Palekh has a good museum of local icons and boxes (closed Monday and the last Friday of the month), fine restored 14th to 19th-century icons in the Raising of the Cross Church (Krestovo-Sdvizhenskaya tserkov) and a few shops and exhibitions selling Palekh boxes. Though most visitors to Palekh come in groups, there are buses from Ivanovo and one a day from Vladimir via Suzdal.

Places to Stay
If you have to stay in Ivanovo there are three reasonable hotels in the rather spread-out city centre, all charging around US$25/40 for singles/doubles: the *Tsentralnaya Hotel* (☎ (09322) 2 81 22) at ulitsa Engelsa 1, the *Hotel Turist* at the corner of ulitsa Baturina and ulitsa Kalinina and the *Hotel Sovietskaya* (☎ (09322) 7 85 57) on prospekt Lenina. The *Hotel Ivanovo* on ulitsa Karla Marxa off ulitsa Engelsa might be cheaper.

There's also a very basic *hotel* in the middle of Palekh.

Getting There & Away
You can fly to Ivanovo from Moscow's Bykovo Airport. In Ivanovo, the rail station is at the north end of ulitsa Engelsa; the bus station is several km away in the south of town. Buses run to/from Moscow's Shchyolkovsky Bus Station (US$4.50; 6½ hours) about eight times daily; to/from Suzdal (two hours) and Vladimir (three hours) about 12 times daily; to/from Kostroma (two hours) about 12 times daily; and to/from Yaroslavl (two hours) two or three times daily. Trains to Ivanovo run from Moscow's Yaroslavl Station, taking six to eight hours.

PLYOS
ПЛЁС

Plyos is a tranquil little town of trees, wooden houses and hilly streets winding down to the Volga waterfront, 62 km north-east of Ivanovo and 63 km south-east of Kostroma. It's a regular stop on Volga cruises but you can also get there by bus from Ivanovo or (on Sunday only) Kostroma, and – best – in summer by hydrofoil from Kostroma or Yaroslavl (see those cities' Getting There & Away sections).

Though fortified from the 15th century and later a Volga trade centre, its renown today stems from its late 19th-century role as an artists' retreat. Isaak Levitan, possibly the greatest Russian landscape artist, found inspiration here in the summers of 1888-90. The playwright Chekhov commented that Plyos put a smile in Levitan's paintings.

Walk along the riverfront and take in the lovely views from the hill topped by the simple Assumption Cathedral (Uspensky sobor), which stands within the ramparts of the old fort. The Levitan House Museum (Dom-Muzey Levitana) in the eastern part of the town, across the small Shokhonka River, displays work of other artists who visited Plyos, as well as works by Levitan.

KOSTROMA
КОСТРОМА
Population: 300,000

Though founded in the 1150s and once one of the Golden Ring's most important cultural and commercial centres, Kostroma ('*kastra-MA*'), on the Volga 95 km north of Ivanovo, now looks like it came from somewhere else. In 1773 a fire destroyed everything wooden and the centre was rebuilt all at once, in uninspiring Russian classical style.

But the town's pride is the Monastery of St Ipaty (Ipatevsky monastyr), founded in 1332 by a Tatar ancestor of Tsar Boris Godunov and later patronised – like Kostroma in general – by the Romanov dynasty. The frescoes in its beautiful cathedral are by a school of 17th-century Kostroma painters, headed by Gury Nikitin, whose work can be seen all over the Golden Ring.

Orientation
The main part of the town lies along the north bank of the Volga, with the bus and rail stations out in the east end of town and the St Ipaty Monastery to the west, across the tributary Kostroma River.

Kostroma is in the process of changing street names: some streets have both old and new signs up; buses may show either name. The central square, ploshchad Susaninskaya, was formerly ploshchad Revolyutsii. Old street names are given here in brackets.

Information
You can change money at the Hotel Volga, the Ametist shop on Sovietskaya ulitsa or the Motel Kostroma. The post, telephone and telegraph office is on Sovietskaya ulitsa, half a km east of the centre, and has a fax service. The Kostroma telephone code is 0942 for six-digit numbers, 09422 for five-digit numbers.

Monastery of St Ipaty
The monastery's past was closely tied to both the Godunov and Romanov families, fierce rivals in high-level Russian power games before the Romanovs established their 300-year dynasty in the 17th century. The Godunovs, descended from a 14th-century Tatar chief who converted to Christianity, built the monastery's Trinity Cathedral (Troitsky sobor) – first a wooden one, then the present white-stone building with gold domes in 1590. Inside are over 80 old frescoes by Kostroma painters (plus some 20th-century additions) and a gorgeous iconostasis of gold and carved wood.

In 1600 Boris Godunov, the only member of his family to become tsar, exiled the head of the Romanov family, Fyodor, to the monastery, along with other Romanovs including Fyodor's son Mikhail. Mikhail Romanov was in Kostroma at the time he was elected tsar in 1613, at the end of the Time of Troubles, and in honour of the event all his Romanov successors made a point of visiting the monastery's red Romanov Chambers (Palaty Romanov), opposite the cathedral.

The monastery is open from 9 am to 4.30 pm daily from May to October, otherwise from 10 am, and closed Friday. It's 2.5 km west of the town centre. Bus No 8 goes there from ulitsa Yeleninskaya (ulitsa Lenina), off the central ploshchad Susaninskaya (ploshchad Revolyutsii).

Museum of Wooden Architecture
A group of garishly painted wooden houses behind the monastery have nothing at all to do with traditional architecture but were a set for the Russian-Italian film *Black Eyes*. But beyond them is an attractive outdoor museum of northern-style wooden buildings (Muzey derevyannogo zodchestva), including peasant houses, churches (one built without nails) and a windmill. The museum has the same opening hours as the monastery.

Town Centre
Ploshchad Susaninskaya (still ploshchad Revolyutsii on some street and bus signs) was built as an ensemble under Catherine the Great's patronage after the 1773 fire and looks like a movie set. Clockwise around the north side are: a 19th-century fire tower (still used as one, and under UNESCO protection) with a little museum on fire-fighting; a

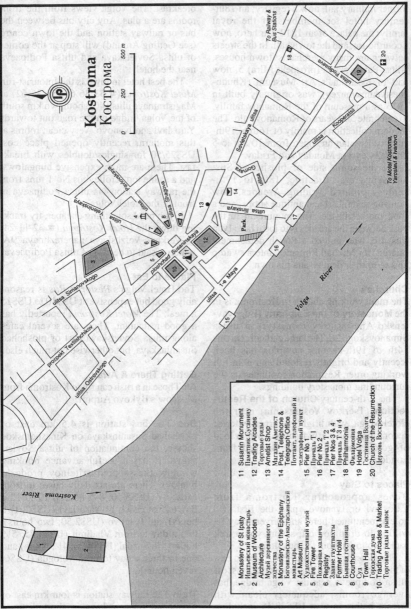

Kostroma
Кострома

To Railway &
Bus Stations

To Motel Kostroma,
Yaroslavl & Ivanovo

Volga River

Kostroma River

0   250   500 m

1	Monastery of St Ipaty / Ипатьевский монастырь
2	Museum of Wooden Architecture / Музей деревянного зодчества
3	Monastery of the Epiphany / Богоявленско-Анастасьинский монастырь
4	Art Museum / Художественный музей
5	Fire Tower / Пожарная каланча
6	Former Hotel / Здание гауптвахты
7	Former Hotel / Бывшая гостиница
8	Courthouse / Суд
9	Town Hall / Городская дума
10	Trading Arcades & Market / Торговые ряды и рынок

11	Susanin Monument / Памятник Сусанину
12	Trading Arcades / Торговые ряды
13	Ametist Shop / Магазин Аметист
14	Post, Telephone & Telegraph Office / Почтамт, телефонный и телеграфный пункт
15	Pier No 1 / Причал Т 1
16	Pier No 2 / Причал Т 2
17	Pier Nos 3 & 4 / Причалы Т 3 и 4
18	Philharmonia / Филармония
19	Hotel Volga / Гостиница Волга
20	Church of the Resurrection / Церковь Воскресения

former military jail, now a registry; an 18th-century hotel for members of the royal family; the palace of an 1812 war hero, now a courthouse; and the town hall. In the streets between are many merchants' town houses. Ulitsa Pavlovskaya (prospekt Mira) 5, now part of Kostroma's Art Museum (Khudozhestvenny muzey), was originally built in 1913 as a museum of the Romanov family, to celebrate 300 years of Romanov rule. The modern collection is mainly of 16th to 19th-century Russian art; open from 10 am to 5 pm daily except Monday and Friday.

On the south side of ploshchad Susaninskaya are attractive, 18th to 19th-century pillared Trading Arcades, now housing several art and antique shops, and a food market inside. The monument in the park between the arcades is to local hero Ivan Susanin, who guided a Polish detachment hunting for Mikhail Romanov into a swamp and so to their deaths, and his own.

Churches

The main working church in Kostroma is in the **Monastery of the Epiphany** (Bogoyavlensko-Anastasinsky monastyr) at ulitsa Simanovskogo 26. The large cathedral in this 14th to 19th-century complex has been recently and brightly restored and is in full working order. Restoration continues on the surrounding monastery buildings.

The 17th-century **Church of the Resurrection** (Tserkov Voskresenia) near the Hotel Volga, with bright patterned exterior decoration, was partly financed with a load of gold coins mistakenly shipped from London.

Places to Stay

Buses approaching Kostroma from Yaroslavl or Ivanovo pass the first two hotels mentioned here, and drivers may be willing to drop you off, saving you a trek back into town from the bus station.

The *Hotel Volga* (☎ 4 61 83), two km east of the centre at ulitsa Yunosheskaya 1 just off ulitsa Podipaeva near the Volga bridge, has average rooms, adequately clean with private bathrooms, at US$28/45 including breakfast. The Volga views from the front rooms are a plus. Any city bus between the bus or railway station and the town centre (see Getting Around) will stop at the corner of ulitsa Sovietskaya and ulitsa Podipaeva near the hotel.

The best hotel in town is the Intourist-run *Motel Kostroma* (☎ 53 36 61, 53 36 62) at Magistralnaya ulitsa 40, about two km south of the Volga bridge on the road out towards Yaroslavl and Ivanovo. Very clean rooms at this modern, recently opened place cost US$25/50 for singles/doubles with breakfast. There are more expensive bungalows, and a sauna too. Trolleybus No 1 runs from the railway station via ulitsa Podipaeva in front of the Hotel Volga.

If you need something cheaper, try tracking down the *Hotel Kostroma* (☎ 32 11 24) at Verkhne-Volzhskaya naberezhnaya 9A, which is said to be east of ulitsa Podipaeva.

Places to Eat

The Hotel Volga's *Restoran Rus* is reasonably good but expensive at US$10 to US$15 a meal. The *Motel Kostroma* reportedly has a good restaurant. There are several cafés along ulitsa Sovietskaya east of ploshchad Susaninskaya, but otherwise not much else.

Getting There & Away

Air Those in a rush can fly to Kostroma from Moscow's Bykovo Airport.

Bus The bus station is 4.5 km east of ploshchad Susaninskaya on Kineshemskoe shosse, the continuation of ulitsa Sovietskaya. It has a useful advance booking window (kassa predvaritelnoy prodazhi biletov). There are six daily buses to/from Moscow (US$8.50; 8½ hours), 10 to 12 a day to/from each of Yaroslavl (US$2; two hours) and Ivanovo (US$2.50; two hours), two a day to/from Vladimir (US$4.75; 5½ hours) via Suzdal (US$4.20; 4¼ hours) and one to three a day to/from Vologda (US$6; seven hours).

Train The railway station is four km east of ploshchad Susaninskaya, a short distance north of ulitsa Sovietskaya. There are three or four daily suburban trains to/from Yaroslavl (three hours), one daily overnight skoryy train to/from Moscow's Savyolov Station (8½ hours) and a daily train to/from Khabarovsk in the Russian Far East, but nothing to/from Ivanovo or Vladimir.

River In summer, hydrofoils from Pier (Prichal) No 2 sail up the Volga at least as far as Yaroslavl (1½ hours) five times a day, and downstream to Plyos (1¼ hours) or beyond six times daily. One daily sailing (at 6.30 am when we checked) goes as far as Nizhny Novgorod and Cheboxary. Timetables are posted at the pier and tickets are sold there 15 minutes before departure. One-way fares are US$1.60 to Yaroslavl, US$1.20 to Plyos and US$4.70 to Nizhny Novgorod. Long-distance river boats between Moscow and points down the Volga as far as Astrakhan also call at Kostroma (Pier No 3 or 4). Pier No 1 is for local services.

Getting Around

Bus No 13 links the airport and the bus and railway stations. Bus Nos 1, 2, 9, 9 Expres, 14K, 19 and others run between the bus station and the central ploshchad Susaninskaya, along the full length of ulitsa Sovietskaya. Trolleybus No 2 runs between the railway station and ploshchad Susaninskaya.

YAROSLAVL
ЯРОСЛАВЛЬ
Population: 680,000

Yaroslavl ('yee-ra-SLAV-l'), on the Volga 250 km north-east of Moscow and 70 km west of Kostroma, has wide, orderly, tree-lined streets and a fascinating old heart. Being the biggest place between Moscow and Arkhangelsk, it has a much more metropolitan feel than anywhere else in the Golden Ring – yet is still a pleasantly quiet and relaxed city.

In 1010, the Kievan prince Yaroslav the Wise took an interest in a trading post where the Kotorosl River enters the Volga. According to legend the locals responded by setting a sacred bear on him. Yaroslav killed the bear with his axe and founded a town on the spot, putting the bear and the axe in its coat of arms.

Yaroslavl was the centre of an independent principality by the time the Tatars came. It was developed in the 16th and 17th centuries as the Volga's first port, and grew into Russia's second-biggest city of the time, fat on trade with the Middle East and Europe.

Rich merchants of that time competed to build churches bigger than Moscow's, with bright decoration and frescoes on modern themes. Though the city's pride is the Monastery of the Transfiguration of the Saviour, the merchant churches are what's special here.

Orientation

The old part of town, and the modern centre, are roughly between the Volga and the Pervomayskaya ulitsa inner ring road. Inside, streets radiate from Sovietskaya ploshchad to three other squares on the ring: Bogoyavlenskaya ploshchad (formerly ploshchad Podbelskogo, and some of the old signs remain) with the landmark Transfiguration Monastery; ploshchad Volkova with the large classical-fronted 19th-century Volkov Theatre; and Krasnaya ploshchad near the River Station.

Information

You can change money at the Yaroslavsky Bank on ulitsa Kirova, open from 8 am to 2 pm and 3 to 6.30 pm daily, except Sunday and the second-last Tuesday of the month. Dom Knigi almost next door may have some useful maps. The main post, telephone and telegraph office, with fax service, is on Bogoyavlenskaya ploshchad (formerly ploshchad Podbelskogo) opposite the Transfiguration Monastery. The Yaroslavl telephone code is 0852.

Monastery & Around

The white walls and towers of the **Monastery of the Transfiguration of the Saviour** (Spaso-Preobrazhensky monastyr) front Bogoyavlenskaya ploshchad. Founded in

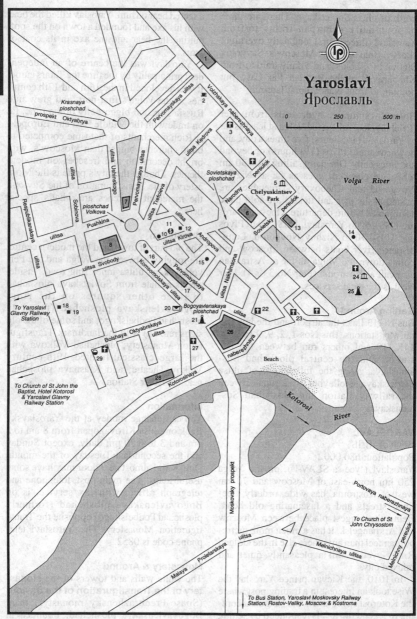

Yaroslavl
Ярославль

0   250   500 m

Krasnaya ploshchad

prospekt Oktyabrya

ulitsa Ushinskogo

Pervomayskaya ulitsa

Voznskaya naberezhnaya

ulitsa Kedrova

Pervomayskaya ulitsa

ulitsa Trefeleva

ploshchad Volkova

Pushkina

Sovietskaya ploshchad

Narodny pereulok

Chelyuskintsev Park

Sovietsky pereulok

Volga River

Respublikanskaya

Sobinova

ulitsa

ulitsa

ulitsa

ulitsa Svobody

ulitsa Kirova

Andropova

Pervomayskaya ulitsa

Komsomolskaya ulitsa

ulitsa Nakhimsona

Bogoyavlenskaya ploshchad

To Yaroslavl Glavny Railway Station

Bolshaya Oktyabrskaya

ulitsa

naberezhnaya

Beach

Kotorosl River

To Church of St John the Baptist, Hotel Kotorosl & Yaroslavl Glavny Railway Station

Kotoroslnaya

Moskovsky prospekt

Portovaya naberezhnaya

To Church of St John Chrysostom

Melnichny pereulok

ulitsa

Melnichnaya ulitsa

Malaya Proletarskaya

To Bus Station, Yaroslavl Moskovsky Railway Station, Rostov-Veliky, Moscow & Kostroma

the 12th century, this was one of Russia's richest and best fortified monasteries by the 1500s. The oldest surviving structures, dating from 1516 but heavily altered since then, are the Holy Gate (Svyatye vorota) on the river side – where the modern entrance is – and the central Cathedral of the Transfiguration (Preobrazhensky sobor), which is under restoration. Entry to the grounds is free but there are charges for a number of museums and exhibitions within. The best of these is devoted to old icons and crafts (Drevnerusskoe i narodnogo prikladnoe iskusstvo) and costs US$1.25. Another (Medveditsa Masha) consists of a solitary live bear in a tiny enclosure in the south-west corner. But the most exciting thing to do here, for US$0.75, is climb the belltower (zvonnitsa) for a panorama of the city and a close-up view of the amazing spiked gold baubles that top some of the monastery buildings. The grounds are open from 10 am to 5 pm daily.

Also off Bogoyavlenskaya ploshchad is the vaulted, red-brick 17th-century **Church of the Epiphany** (Tserkov Bogoyavlenia). It has bright exterior ceramic tiles (a Yaroslavl speciality) and a carved iconostasis; open from 10 am to 1 pm and 2 to 5 pm daily except Tuesday (US$0.75). The square's

The 17th-century Church of the Epiphany

central **statue of Yaroslav the Wise** (Pamyatnik Yaroslavu Mudromu) was unveiled by presidents Yeltsin of Russia and Kravchuk of Ukraine in 1993.

Along Pervomayskaya ulitsa, past the 19th-century Trading Arcades (Gostiny Dvor), is the **Znamenskaya Watchtower** (Znamenskaya bashnya), built in 1658 on what was then the edge of the city.

Church of Elijah the Prophet

This church (Tserkov Ilyi Proroka) on Sovietskaya ploshchad in the centre of the old town has some of the Golden Ring's brightest frescoes, by the ubiquitous Gury Nikitin of Kostroma and his school. Dating, like the church, from the 17th century, they depict religious and secular scenes in realistic style. Closed from October to April and during wet spells, the church is otherwise open from 10 am to 1 pm and 2 to 6 pm, except Wednesday. Entry is US$1.25, plus US$2.50 if you want to take photos.

Broad Sovietskaya ploshchad, surrounded by government buildings and with streets radiating in all directions, was planned as the hub of town in an 18th-century rebuilding programme.

River Embankments

The Volga and Kotorosl embankments from the Church of Elijah the Prophet back to the Transfiguration Monastery make an enjoyable 1.5-km walk. A pedestrian promenade runs along the bank of the Volga below the level of the street, Volzhskaya naberezhnaya.

From the Church of Elijah the Prophet, head towards the river on Narodny pereulok. Here, the **Church of St Nicholas the Miracle-Worker** (Tserkov Nikoly Nadeina) was the first of Yaroslavl's merchant churches, built in 1622. It has a sparkling Baroque iconostasis and frescoes showing the life and works of the said St Nicholas, who's highly popular among Russians, and is open as a museum from 10 am to 5 pm daily except Sunday and Monday.

Just south at Volzhskaya naberezhnaya 23, facing the Volga, is the main building of the **Yaroslavl Art Museum** (Yaroslavsky Khudozhestvenny Muzey), with 18th to 20th-century Russian art; open from 10 am to 6 or 7 pm daily except Friday. The **House of Matveev** (Dom Matveeva) on Sovietsky pereulok, built in the late 18th century, is one of several merchants' town houses still standing in the blocks near the embankment. A little farther along the embankment are the **Volga Bastion** (Volzhskaya bashnya), built as a watchtower in the 1660s, a fine early 19th-century church, and the 17th-century former Metropolitan's Palace housing the old Yaroslavl art section of the **Art Museum**, with icons and other work from the 13th to 19th centuries; open from 10 am to 5.30 pm daily except Friday.

In the leafy park behind the museum is a stone-slab **monument** marking the spot where Yaroslav founded the city in 1010. The park stretches right out onto the tip of land between the Volga and the Kotorosl. Above the Kotorosl you can discern raised embankments indicating the site of Yaroslavl's old kremlin. Also along here are three more **17th-century churches**.

Churches South of the Kotorosl

Two 17th-century churches south of the Kotorosl River are well worth searching out. In the settlement of Korovniki, picturesquely placed on the south side of the mouth of the Kotorosl, is the summer **Church of St John Chrysostom** (Tserkov Ioanna Zlatusta), an elegant conglomeration of domes, brick towers and dazzling tilework. Next to it are a winter church, and a belltower called 'the Candle of Yaroslavl'. Take bus No 4 from Bogoyavlenskaya ploshchad for two stops, or walk across the Kotorosl on Moskovsky prospekt and then head left for about 1.5 km.

Also south of the Kotorosl is the unique 15-domed **Church of St John the Baptist** (Tserkov Ioanna Predtechi), with intricate brick and tilework. Take tram No 3 west along Bolshaya Oktyabrskaya ulitsa to the third stop, then walk one km south down prospekt Tolbukhina and across the bridge; the church is near the river on the right.

River Trips

Summer services from the River Station on the Volga at the north end of Pervomayskaya ulitsa include a range of slow suburban (prigorodny) boats to local destinations like Nekrasovskoe (halfway to Kostroma, 2½ hours) and Konstantinovo (2¼ hours upstream), with lots of stops. The best trip is probably to Tolga, 35 minutes from Yaroslavl on the Konstantinovo route, which has a convent with lovely 17th-century buildings near the river, now handed back to a community of nuns and being restored after being used as a Soviet prison. Konstantinovo boats only go two or three times daily, however; the hourly service to Dolmatovo (25 minutes) might make a more convenient shoestring cruise. For longer-distance sailings from the River Station, see Getting There & Away.

Places to Stay

The all-round best value is at the *Hotel Yubileynaya* (☎ 22 41 59), handily located at Kotoroslnaya naberezhnaya 11A, close to the Transfiguration Monastery and overlooking the Kotorosl River. Staff are used to foreigners (most tour groups come here). The rooms are comfortable but totally unexceptional, costing US$26/41 for singles/doubles with private bathroom. There's a decent restaurant and a busy bar serving snacks.

If you're on a tighter budget, you have two options. Both might offer mild discouragement of the 'We're not good enough for you' kind, but will relent. One is the *Hotel Volga* (☎ 22 91 31) at ulitsa Kirova 10 right in the middle of the old city. It's a dowdy old place but not unfriendly, with a range of rooms costing from US$13/26 with washbasin only (toilet and shower in the corridor) to US$17.50/35 with private bathroom and sitting room. The *Hotel Vest* in a tall red brick tower at Respublikanskaya ulitsa 79, off Bolshaya Oktyabrskaya ulitsa two blocks west of Bogoyavlenskaya ploshchad, has great views. Rooms are US$10/14 with toilet and washbasin (shower in the corridor) or US$12/18 with private toilet and shower ('polulyux'). Rooms with TV and/or phone are considerably pricier.

Round the back of the Hotel Vest, with the same address, is the small *Hotel Yuta* (☎ 21 87 93), run by something called the Business Cooperation Association. Comfy rooms with private bathroom, TV and phone are from US$35 to US$48, single or double.

A bit farther west at Bolshaya Oktyabrskaya ulitsa 87, past the prospekt Tolbukhina corner and on the route of tram No 3 (see Getting Around), the *Hotel Kotorosl* (☎ 21 24 15) is another respectable place, charging US$28.50/57 for rooms sharing toilet and shower with one other room. It has a café.

The *Hotel Yaroslavl* (☎ 22 12 75) on noisy ploshchad Volkova is not worth it at US$37 for doubles with bathroom and toilet in the corridor, or US$85 for 'lyux' rooms with private bathroom.

Places to Eat

The restaurant at the *Hotel Yubileynaya* is about the best. It will do a good breakfast for US$1; lunch or dinner costs about US$5 –

Friend or Foe

My patience was already running a bit thin as I stepped off a jam-packed city bus and into a rain shower outside Yaroslavl bus station, towards the end of a six-week trip from Moscow to the Mongolian border and back. Inside the bus station, having located the tiny hole in a wall that sold tickets to Kostroma, I joined the would-be passengers milling in front of it. After a while, I had edged near enough to the window to think that my turn would be next. Two young men in suits suddenly appeared from nowhere and with a confident 'Devochka!' grabbed the ticket clerk's attention and pushed in front of me. Several minutes later, just as they seemed to be nearing the end of their chat with her, I sensed a war-bemedalled old man trying to edge in front of me on another side. 'You wait your bloody turn!' I said to him in English, powers of translation vanishing under stress. Sheepishly, he answered 'Ya ne ponimayu', and held back, seemingly wondering if I was someone important. I felt a little ashamed at having been so rude to someone so powerless.

'Do you have one ticket to Kostroma at 2.15?' I asked the ticket clerk (in Russian now). She continued to silently scrutinise the desk a few inches below her eyes.

'Do you have one ticket to Kostroma at 2.15?' I repeated.

After a pause, she looked up. 'Give me the money!' she shrieked at me, as if any sane person would have done this already – before finding out what the ticket cost, or even if it was available.

'Skolko (How much)?' I bellowed back at her, trying to instil maximum fury into that frustratingly short word.

She told me, I banged the money down, she banged the ticket down, and I turned away wishing I knew a lot of Russian insults – and that I hadn't, in the heat of the moment, forgotten the few I did know.

That ticket clerk was a fairly extreme case, but she seemed to sum up all that's worst about dealing with ticket clerks, hotel receptionists, shop assistants and other low-ranking 'service' industry workers who confront the public in Russia.

Why *are* these people so often so stunningly rude? It's not just foreigners who get this treatment, nor just foreigners who are taken aback by it. I remember one Russian man in Tyumen railway station, Siberia, getting into such an abusive quarrel with an obstructive 'information window' clerk that she was even moved to leave her cubicle to harangue him face to face.

It has to be way of life, a conditioned form of behaviour for people low down on the institutional ladder who actually have to deal with the public. The job's lousy, the pay and the working environment are lousy, no-one wants to bribe you, the bosses have it easy and everyone with any money is a crook; the only worthwhile thing about it all is the chance of a natter with your mates at break times. And the customers – well, they're just a nuisance. They're certainly not members of the same species just trying to get through life like you are. Yet, I reflected as I waited for the Kostroma bus to arrive, my ticket clerk was probably sweet as pie to her friends and family. And there, I realised, lay a clue to my riddle. Friends and family *are* a different species from the public. Even more than most countries, Russia runs on friendships, contacts, favours. A Russian who knows someone working at a bus station simply asks the friend to arrange a ticket, and it's all done with smiles and small talk, behind the counter. But the panes of glass separating the ticket

---

start early if you want to avoid the band in the evening.

Restoran Staroe Mesto on Komsomolskaya ulitsa just off ploshchad Volkova is an agreeable cellar restaurant serving Russian standards for around US$3; open from noon to 10 pm daily.

Kafe Lira at Volzhskaya naberezhnaya 43 just south of the River Station does tolerable light meals – such as pizza or file (meat and veg) for US$2 to US$3. It's open daily from noon to 11 pm and has a young crowd in the evenings. The *Restoran Volga* at the River Station is a reasonable stolovaya by day, and a reasonable restaurant, with main courses around US$2.50, from 7 pm to midnight.

There's a small food market off ulitsa Andropova in the centre.

Getting There & Away

Bus The bus station is two km south of the Kotorosl River on Moskovsky prospekt,

clerk from the contactless unfortunates outside are the frontier between her own world, cosy and trustworthy, and the outside world which, it seems, she finds threatening and hostile.

I have also met so many exceptionally warm, generous, helpful and hospitable Russians that at times I need reminding that the Yaroslavl bus station clerk and her ilk aren't just a bad dream. But both types are equally real – and the same person could be both at different times. I've realised that most Russians who have treated me kindly are those I've met informally – by asking the way on the street, getting into conversation on a train or by meeting them through other friends. That way I've had a (however brief) personal relationship with them, and have become to them a real person, different from the crowds of passers-by. (Where the crowds are thinner, you're more likely to strike lucky, as co-author Andrew Humphreys relates: 'In small Siberian villages I would ask someone for directions to the nearest hotel and instead be taken home, fed, introduced to the neighbourhood and given a bed for the night'.)

But when you deal with a Russian official as a member of the public you're, well, just a number. Even tour guides, having been entertaining, amusing and charming for three, six, 12 hours, may slink away with at best a quick formal goodbye at the end. And as for individual foreign travellers, who don't fit into known categories of what foreigners are supposed to do in Russia, well, they're not even numbers!

Russians' homes demonstrate as well as anything the great divide between the outside world and the inner world of friends and family. No-one seems to care a jot how drab and dilapidated the outsides of their blocks are, how much rubbish is strewn around them, nor how stinking are the shared stairwells. But once you pass the thick doors into an individual flat, you're entering an inner world, likely to be as carefully tended, neat and cosy as its surrounds are neglected and ugly.

Why have Russians such a wealth of hospitality to 'known' people and such thin traditions of politeness to humanity at large? It's easy to answer 'communism', under which *was* surely true that anyone you didn't know you could trust might be an enemy – a habit of mind that could take generations to change. But it may all go back longer than that. The Russian state and its servants, of whatever political complexion, have never been exactly friendly to Russian people. And Russia is such a *big* place, with such a tough climate and environment and, even now, such difficult communications, that life has always been lived by most people on an intensely local level. In such circumstances suspicion, even fear, of the outsider – even from the next village – is almost inevitable. Russian 19th-century novels bear this out, even if you don't take into account the long history of threats and invasions to Russia as a whole by a string of outsiders from Jenghiz Khan to Adolf Hitler.

Nor have things improved since communism fell. In fact, they have got worse. Such certainties as there were about the outside world have evaporated. In these troubled, shifting times friends and contacts are, if anything, even more important, and the unknown, anonymous outsider even more of a threat.

John Noble

---

beside Yaroslavl Moskovsky railway station. There are one or two buses daily to/from Moscow's Shchyolkovsky Bus Station (US$6.50; six hours), plus about five buses stopping here in transit. Most of these will stop at Pereslavl-Zalessky and Sergiev Posad. Other daily departures include:

Ivanovo (two hours) – two or three buses
Kostroma (two hours) – 10 to 12 buses
Pereslavl-Zalessky (three hours) – three to five buses

Rostov-Veliky (1½ hours) – eight buses
Uglich (4½ hours) – one or two buses
Vladimir (six hours) – one or two buses
Vologda (five hours) – one to three buses in transit

Train The main station is Yaroslavl Glavny, three km west of the centre along ulitsa Svobody. If your train coming into Yaroslavl happens to stop at the lesser Yaroslavl Moskovsky station, two km south of the Kotorosl River on Moskovsky prospekt, there's no harm getting off there as transport to the centre is no harder.

Around 20 trains a day run to/from Moscow's Yaroslavl Station, a trip of about five hours, but most are travelling to/from places far to the north (like Arkhangelsk) or east (Yekaterinburg, Novosibirsk, Vladivostok, Beijing). It may be easiest to get tickets on train No 124, leaving Moscow at 7.40 am, or No 122, leaving at 4.15 pm (both skoryy), which terminate at Yaroslavl. Going back to Moscow, No 121 leaves Yaroslavl at 7 am and No 123 at 12.15 am.

If you want to head on past the Ural Mountains from the Golden Ring, Yaroslavl is the place to start from. There's also daily service to/from St Petersburg and Nizhny Novgorod. For closer destinations, it's easiest to get suburban trains. For Rostov-Veliky (two hours), take any suburban train to Rostov itself, Beklemishevo or Alexandrov (about eight to 12 daily). Three or four suburban trains run daily to Kostroma (three hours).

River In summer from the River Station at the north end of Pervomayskaya ulitsa, there's a range of passenger services on the Volga to places as far away as Astrakhan. Timetables are posted at the River Station, which also has an information window.

The six or seven daily hydrofoils to downstream *(vniz)* destinations will all take you to Kostroma in 1½ hours for US$1.60. Most also go to Plyos (three hours). Tickets go on sale about 30 minutes before departure.

From about early June to early October, long-distance Volga passenger steamers stop every couple of days in Yaroslavl on their way between Moscow (1½ days away) and cities like Nizhny Novgorod, Kazan and Astrakhan (about eight days). The ships are rarely full and tickets are normally available at short notice. Fares depend on your class of cabin: to Moscow they range from US$7 to US$45, except for the Lyux A class which is US$123. Some cruises from Moscow also come here (see Moscow – Getting There & Away).

Getting Around

From Yaroslavl Glavny station, tram No 3 from the stop on ulitsa Ukhtomskogo, 200 metres to the right when you exit the station, goes along Bolshaya Oktyabrskaya ulitsa to the tram terminus a short walk west of Bogoyavlenskaya ploshchad. This is good enough for all hotels. Trolleybus No 1 runs between the station and ploshchad Volkova and Krasnaya ploshchad: you can get off at the Ploshchad Yunosti stop for the Vest and Yuta hotels.

From the bus station and Yaroslavl Moskovsky railway station, trolleybus No 5 or 9 from the far side of the main road outside will get you to Bogoyavlenskaya ploshchad; No 5 goes on to Krasnaya ploshchad.

ROSTOV-VELIKY
РОСТОВ-ВЕЛИКИЙ

Population: 40,000

Also called Rostov-Yaroslavsky, this town *('rah-STOV-vi-LEEK-i')* is one of Russia's oldest, first chronicled in 862. Today it's a sleepy, rustic little place, 57 km towards Moscow from Yaroslavl, with some magnificent old buildings magically sited by a shimmering lake. Much less tourist-oriented than Suzdal, the most comparable place in the Golden Ring, Rostov lets you feel you're discovering it for yourself. And you can stay right in among those wonderful old buildings.

Perhaps to flatter its home-grown aristocracy, Yury Dolgoruky gave Rostov the name Veliky (Great) in the 12th century, while making Suzdal the capital of his Rostov-Suzdal principality. By the early 13th century the Rostov region had split off from Suzdal and then into smaller pieces. The Tatars didn't leave much of it standing, and in the late 1600s an ambitious Orthodox Church metropolitan, Iona Sysoevich, cleared almost everything else away for a wonderful private kremlin on the shore of Lake Nero.

On the highway in from the south, look out for fairy-tale views across the lake to the kremlin and the Monastery of St Jacob.

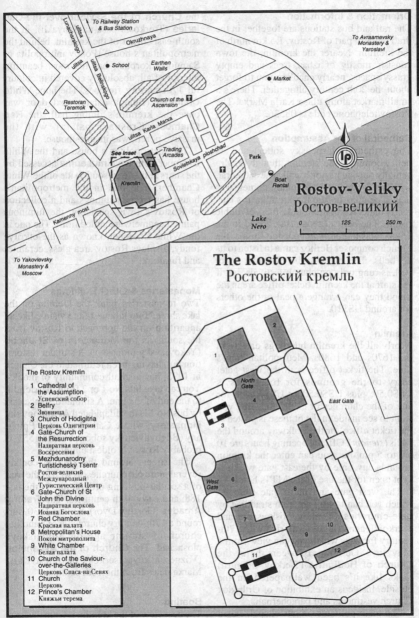

Rostov-Veliky
Ростов-великий

Lake Nero

0   125   250 m

The Rostov Kremlin
Ростовский кремль

The Rostov Kremlin

1 Cathedral of
   the Assumption
   Успенский собор
2 Belfry
   Звонница
3 Church of Hodigitria
   Церковь Одигитрии
4 Gate-Church of
   the Resurrection
   Надвратная церковь
   Воскресения
5 Mezhdunarodny
   Turistichesky Tsentr
   Ростов-великий
   Международный
   Туристический Центр
6 Gate-Church of St
   John the Divine
   Надвратная церковь
   Иоанна Богослова
7 Red Chamber
   Красная палата
8 Metropolitan's House
   Покои митрополита
9 White Chamber
   Белая палата
10 Church of the Saviour-
   over-the-Galleries
   Церковь Спаса-на-Сенях
11 Church
   Церковь
12 Prince's Chamber
   Княжьи терема

Orientation & Information

The rail and bus stations are together in the drab modern part of Rostov, 1.5 km north of the kremlin. Nearer the kremlin, the town consists mostly of izbas, trees and empty grassy spaces, nearly enabling you to forget about the 20th century altogether. There's a small market along ulitsa Karla Marxa. The Rostov telephone code is 08536.

Cathedral of the Assumption

The cathedral (Uspensky sobor) and its belfry dominate the kremlin, though they're actually outside its north wall. The cathedral, with its five magnificent onion domes, was here a century before the kremlin. It's currently under restoration, and a mess of rubble inside. The belfry (zvonnitsa), added in the 1680s, was famous even outside Russia; the French composer Berlioz came to listen to its 13 bells. The biggest, the 32-tonne Sysoi bell, is rung only on church festivals, but if the staff at the kremlin ticket office are in the mood they can arrange a peal of the others for around US$10.

Kremlin

Nearly all the kremlin buildings date from the 1670s and 1680s, Metropolitan Iona's time. The ticket office is in the west gate: entry to the grounds for foreigners is US$0.50, plus US$0.50 or US$1 each for any of the churches or exhibitions that you want to see inside (a list of these is posted at the ticket office) or the walkway around the walls *(stenam)*. Official opening hours are 10 am to 5 pm, but you can enter the kremlin grounds any time by the east gate which is kept open for the use of the MTTs hotel.

The west gate and north gate (through which you can't pass) are both straddled by gate-churches (Tserkov Voskresenia and Tserkov Ioanna Bogoslova), rich with 17th-century frescoes which you can view from 1 May to 1 October. Between them, the Church of Hodigitria (Tserkov Odigitrii) looks like it's been wallpapered on the outside. Inside is an exhibition of Orthodox Church vestments and paraphernalia.

The metropolitan's private chapel, called the Church of the Saviour-over-the-Galleries (Tserkov Spasa-na-Senyakh), in the south-east corner of the kremlin, behind the metropolitan's house (Pokoy mitropolita or Samuilov korpus), has the most beautiful interior of all, absolutely covered in colourful 17th-century frescoes. The huge White Chamber (Belaya palata) next door was once the kremlin's dining hall; the Red Chamber (Krasnaya palata), with the massive porch, was its guesthouse.

The metropolitan's house and the White Chamber both have museums accessed by the stairs at the rear (south) side of the White Chamber. The one in the metropolitan's house has icons, paintings and a collection of Rostov's own speciality, the luminous painted enamelware called finift. The one in the White Chamber, known as the otkritye fondy, displays Rostov-area glass, ceramics and furniture.

Monasteries & Other Buildings

Two monasteries flank the kremlin on the lake shore. Two km west (and visible like an apparition on the approach to Rostov from the south) is the Monastery of St Jacob (Yakovlevsky monastyr). It's under restoration but, having been returned to the Church in 1993, has a small community of monks. You can take bus No 1 or 2 from the kremlin to the end of the line. A similar distance east by bus No 1 is the dilapidated Avraamevsky Monastery, whose Cathedral of the Epiphany (Bogoyavlensky sobor), built in 1553, is probably Rostov's oldest building.

The streets around the kremlin contain several more old churches, as well as the fruit of a secular-building programme in the late 18th and early 19th centuries. The Trading Arcades (Gostiny Dvor), built in 1830, surround a 17th-century church; there's another church of similar age on Sovietskaya ploshchad. The Church of the Ascension (Voznesenskaya tserkov) on ulitsa Karla Marxa dates from the 16th century.

Boating

The best view of the kremlin is from the lake.

You can hire a rowing boat by the park east of the centre.

Places to Stay & Eat

The *Rostov-Veliky Mezhdunarodny Turisti-chesky Tsentr* (MTTs, or International Tourist Centre; ☎ 3 12 44), also called the *Dom na Pogrebakh*, right inside the kremlin, is among the most atmospheric places to stay in Russia. The clean, wood-panelled rooms are all US$22/44 for singles/doubles though they vary somewhat in size. All share clean toilets and showers. In the basement of the same building are the *Bufet Pogrebok*, with drinks and cakes (watch your head as you enter!), and a *Kafe* with more substantial fare.

The best meals – and friendly service too – are at the *Restoran Teremok*, a short distance north of the kremlin. The fare is standard Russian but above-average, and you can get three courses with a drink for around US$4. Hours are noon to midnight, daily.

Getting There & Away

To/From Yaroslavl There are up to 12 suburban trains each way daily, taking two hours, the last from Rostov leaving at 10.57 pm. Eight buses a day run from Rostov to Yaroslavl and vice versa, a 1½-hour trip, the last from Rostov leaving at 5.35 pm. In addition, there are numerous buses stopping at Rostov in transit to Yaroslavl; any tickets available for these are sold when the bus arrives.

To/From Pereslavl-Zalessky, Sergiev Posad, Uglich & Moscow There are seven daily in-transit buses to and from Moscow's Shchyolkovsky Bus Station, taking four to five hours, which also stop at Pereslavl-Zalessky and Sergiev Posad. There are also three or four in-transit buses just to Pereslavl-Zalessky and two to Uglich (three hours).

By train to/from Moscow's Yaroslavl Station, you can either try for a ticket on one of the six daily long-distance trains stopping at Rostov (four hours), or go by suburban

train, changing trains halfway at Alexandrov, which takes about five hours. Between Alexandrov and Rostov there are only four daily trains each way. The 5.48 and 9.35 am and 3.01 and 5.51 pm trains from Moscow to Alexandrov (all stopping at Sergiev Posad en route) should connect with the 8.20 am and 12.35, 5.30 and 8.20 pm trains from Alexandrov to Rostov. The suburban ticket hall at Moscow's Yaroslavl Station is at the rear left of the building. Trains leave Rostov for Alexandrov at 4.55 and 7.22 am and 1.15 and 4.25 pm.

Getting Around

Rostov is a pleasant place to walk around, but bus No 6 runs between the railway station and the centre if you need to save time.

UGLICH
УГЛИЧ

An old-fashioned but shabby town on the Volga 90 km north-west of Rostov-Veliky, Uglich can be reached by bus from Rostov or Yaroslavl, though most tourists come to it as a stop on Volga cruises. Locals hawk Uglich-made watches to cruise passengers.

It was here in 1591 that Ivan the Terrible's son Dmitry – later to be impersonated by the string of False Dmitrys in the Time of Troubles – was murdered, probably on Boris Godunov's orders. Within the waterside kremlin area, the red **Church of St Dmitry on the Blood** (Tserkov Dmitria-na-krovi), with its cluster of spangled blue domes, was built in the 1690s on the spot where the body was found. Also in the kremlin, but open erratically, are the five-domed **Transfiguration Cathedral** (Preobrazhensky sobor) and the 15th-century **Prince's Chambers**, with turrets added in the 19th century and a craft exhibition inside. Opposite each other, along ulitsa Karla Marxa from the kremlin, are two other fine buildings from the 1690s: the **Church of the Nativity of John the Baptist** (Tserkov Rozhdenia Ioanna Predtechi), similar in design to the Church of St Dmitry on the Blood, and the large but badly dilapidated **Monastery of the Resurrection** (Voskresensky monastyr).

PERESLAVL-ZALESSKY
ПЕРЕСЛАВЛЬ-ЗАЛЕССКИЙ
Population: 45,000

On the shore of Lake Pleshcheevo almost exactly halfway between Moscow and Yaroslavl, Pereslavl-Zalessky's history and monuments aren't in the Golden Ring's first division, but it's a good place to come if, like the many Muscovites who have dachas here, you want to soak up the atmosphere of a peaceful old Russian village. The southern half of the town is full of one-storey izbas, with pretty gardens in summer, and narrow dirt lanes.

Pereslavl-Zalessky – the name means Pereslavl Beyond the Woods – was made a town in 1152 by Yury Dolgoruky, and Alexandr Nevsky was born here. But the present town is a shadow of earlier days, having been sacked five times by the Mongol Tatars and stormed frequently by neighbouring princes and foreign armies. Its earth walls and the little Cathedral of the Transfiguration are as old as the town. Lake Pleshcheevo takes credit as one of the birthplaces of the Russian navy, having been one of the places where Peter the Great developed his obsession with the sea, studying navigation and building a flotilla of over 100 little ships by the time he was 20.

Orientation
Pereslavl is pretty much a one-street town, with the bus station at the south-west end, two km from the centre. Apart from the kremlin area, most of the historic sights are out past the bus station.

Central Area
The walls of Yury Dolgoruky's **kremlin** are now a grassy ring around the central town. You can walk along the top most of the way round. Inside, the simple **Cathedral of the Transfiguration of the Saviour** (Spaso-Preobrazhensky sobor), started in 1152, is one of the oldest standing buildings in

Pereslavl-Zalessky
Переславль-Залесский

0   0.5   1 km

Footbridges

Lake Pleshcheevo

Trubezh River

Narodnaya ploshchad

Rostovskaya ulitsa

To Market,
Rostov-Veliky &
Yaroslavl

Kremlin Walls

Trubezh River

Podgornaya ulitsa

To Botik Museum

Sovetskaya ulitsa

ulitsa Kardovskogo

To Fyodorovsky Monastery,
Sergiev Posad & Moscow

1 Hotel Pereslavl &
   Traktir na Ozernoe
   Гостиница Переславль
   и Трактир на Озерном
2 Church of St Simeon
   Симеоновская церковь
3 Forty Saints' Church
   Сорокосвятская церковь
4 Cathedral of the
   Transfiguration of the Saviour
   Спасо-Преображенский собор

5 Church of Peter
   the Metropolitan
   Церковь Петра
   митрополита
6 Bus Station
   Автовокзал
7 Goritsky Monastery
   Горицкий монастырь
8 Purification Church of
   Alexandr Nevsky
   Церковь Александра
   Невского Сретенского
9 Danilovsky Monastery
   Даниловский монастырь

Russia, though its frescoes are 19th-century touch-ups. A bust of Alexandr Nevsky stands in front. Across the grassy square, the tent-roofed **Church of Peter the Metropolitan** (Tserkov Petra mitropolita), built in 1585 and renovated in 1957, now looks abandoned. Nearby are twin churches built in 1745.

The **Trubezh River** winds two km from the kremlin to the lake, fringed by trees and narrow lanes. It's a focus of local relaxation with people rowing their narrow boats up and down it until well after dark on summer evenings. You can follow the northern riverbank most of the way to the lake by a combination of paths and streets. Foot-bridges cross to the south bank. The **Forty Saints' Church** (Sorokosvyatskaya tserkov) sits picturesquely on the south side of the river mouth.

South End of Town

The **Goritsky Monastery** (Goritsky monastyr) was founded in the 14th century, though today the oldest buildings are the 17th-century gates, gate-church and belfry. From the bus station, walk 200 metres towards Moscow then turn right: it's up on the hill after 300 metres. The centrepiece is the Baroque Assumption Cathedral (Uspensky sobor) with its beautiful carved iconostasis. In the refectory is a museum (open 10 am to 5 pm, closed Tuesday and the last Monday of the month) with icons and incredible carved-wood furnishings. Mounted outside the gates is a stunningly incongruous WW II tank.

Across the highway from Goritsky, the 1785 **Purification Church of Alexandr Nevsky** (Tserkov Alexandra Nevskogo Sretenskaya) is a working church. To the east, on a hillock overlooking fields and dachas, is the half-abandoned **Danilovsky Monastery** (Danilovsky monastyr), whose tent-roofed Trinity Cathedral (Troitsky sobor) was built in the 1530s. Another 16th-century walled monastery is the **Fyodorovsky Monastery** (Fyodorovsky monastyr), about two km south on the Moscow road.

Four km along the road past the Goritsky Monastery, at the south end of the lake, is the small **Botik Museum** (Muzey Botika) with assorted nautical gear and the sailboat *Fortuna*, the only one of Peter the Great's boats (except one in the St Petersburg Naval Museum) to survive fires and neglect. It's open from 10 am to 5 pm; closed Monday. To make up for Pereslavl's lack of a mainline railway, you can reach the Botik on a tiny two-carriage train which rattles along its single track from the back of the bus station at 9 am and 1 and 4.30 pm, returning at about 12.30, 4 and 8.30 pm. Past the Botik, the train continues round to Kupan, north of the lake.

Places to Stay & Eat

The *Hotel Pereslavl* at Rostovskaya ulitsa 7, 400 metres north of the Trubezh River, was only built in 1985 but is already undergoing repairs. The rooms are all right, costing US$13.50/22 for singles/doubles with private bathroom. The hotel has an upstairs restaurant, and a ground-floor bar serving food too. There's also the cosier *Traktir na Ozernoe* restaurant, with a separate entrance at the north end of the building. A market is a few hundred metres up the Rostov road from the hotel.

Getting There & Away

Pereslavl has no mainline railway station so if you don't have your own transport you must use buses. Ticket sellers at Pereslavl bus station won't usually sell tickets until shortly before departure, which causes unnecessary queuing.

To/from Moscow's Shchyolkovsky Bus Station there are four daily buses starting or finishing at Pereslavl (US$3.50; 2½ to 3½ hours). To/from Sergiev Posad (US$1.60; 1¼ hours) there are three to five buses daily (the last departure from Sergiev Posad is at 6.30 pm, the last from Pereslavl at 4 pm Monday to Friday and 7.45 pm on weekends) plus others in transit. To/from Yaroslavl (three hours), also stopping at Rostov-Veliky (1½ hours), there are three to five buses daily. Other buses pass through in transit to Moscow, Yaroslavl and Kostroma.

Getting Around

Bus No 1, often very crowded, runs up and down the main street. Heading into town from the bus station, the stop is about 100 metres south of the bus station (away from the town centre, towards Moscow); heading out to the bus station from the centre, you can catch it just north of the river.

SERGIEV POSAD
СЕРГИЕВ ПОСАД

Population: 100,000

Sergiev Posad is the town around the Trinity Monastery of St Sergius (Troitse-Sergieva Lavra), one of Russia's most important religious and historical landmarks and a place of both spiritual and nationalist pilgrimage. Still often referred to by its Soviet-era name, Zagorsk, Sergiev Posad is 60 km from the edge of Moscow on the Yaroslavl road. If you have time for just one trip out of Moscow, this is the obvious choice.

The monastery was founded in about 1340 by Sergius of Radonezh, a monk (now patron saint of Russia) who wielded enough moral authority to unite the country against Mongol Tatar rule, blessing Dmitry Donskoy's army before it gave the Tatars their first beating in 1380. The monastery's status as defender of the motherland grew during the Time of Troubles; with Moscow occupied by the Poles, it withstood a 16-month siege and then encouraged the uprising that drove them out.

As a *lavra*, or exalted monastery, and the main link in a chain of fort-monasteries defending Moscow, it grew enormously wealthy on the gifts of tsars, nobles and merchants looking for divine support. Closed by the Bolsheviks, it was reopened after WW II as the Zagorsk Historical & Art Museum and the residence of the Patriarch of the Russian Orthodox Church, again becoming a working monastery. The patriarch, and the administrative centre of the Church, moved to the Danilovsky Monastery in Moscow in 1988, but the Trinity Monastery of St Sergius remains one of Russia's most important monasteries and spiritual sites. For concentrated wealth and artistry, beautiful churches and a sense of the interlocking history of Church and state, it shouldn't be missed. Medieval Russia still seems alive here in the incense and chanting and the armies of pilgrims and supplicants.

Orientation & Information

Prospekt Krasnoy Armii is the main street, running north-south through the town centre. The railway station (vokzal) and bus station (avtostantsia) are on opposite corners of a wide yard to the east of prospekt Krasnoy Armii. The left-luggage room (kamera khranenia) in the railway station is open daily from 8 am to noon and 1 to 7 pm. To reach the monastery, leave the yard along 1-ya Rybnaya ulitsa beside the bus station, with the rail tracks behind you, and turn right on prospekt Krasnoy Armii after about 250 metres. The monastery is about 400 metres along, on the left.

There are money-exchange points inside the monastery. Another in the Hotel Zagorsk offers Visa-card cash advances. There's a post, telephone and telegraph office outside the south-east wall of the monastery. Stalls outside the monastery entrance sell lots of matryoshka dolls, Palekh boxes, babushka scarves, etc.

Trinity Monastery of St Sergius

The monastery grounds are open daily from 10 am to 6 pm. Entry to the grounds is free but there's a US$3 charge to use a camera. There are additional charges to visit the museums inside or walk along the walls (all open from 10 am to 5 pm daily except Monday and their monthly closing days). If you want to visit the monastery's opulent treasury (see Museums), it's advisable to buy your ticket when you arrive. Tours of the grounds and churches (not the museums), given by English-speaking monks, cost US$12.50 for one person, or US$10 each for more than one person – ask at the office next to the Gate-Church of John the Baptist.

Devout women visitors wear headscarves, and all men should remove hats in the churches.

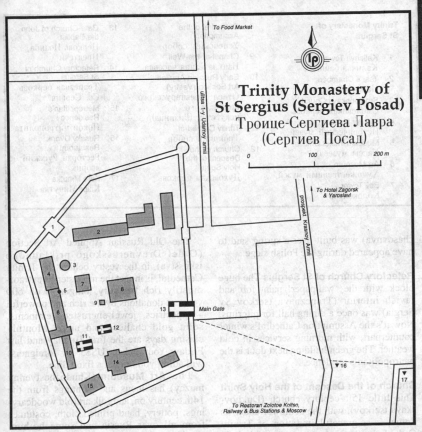

Trinity Monastery of St Sergius (Sergiev Posad)
Троице-Сергиева Лавра (Сергиев Посад)

To Food Market

To Hotel Zagorsk & Yaroslavl

0   100   200 m

ulitsa 1-y Udarnoy armii

prospekt Krasnoy Armii

1

2

3

4

5

6

7

8

9

10

11

12

13 Main Gate

14

15

16

17

To Restoran Zolotoe Koltso,
Railway & Bus Stations & Moscow

Trinity Cathedral Built in the 1420s, this squat, dark yet beautiful church (Troitsky sobor) is the heart of the monastery – and in its way the heart of Russian Orthodoxy. A memorial service for St Sergius (whose tomb stands in the south-east corner, with people lining up to light candles in front of it) goes on all day, every day, lit only by oil lamps. Most of the icons are by the great medieval painter Andrey Rublyov and his disciples, though Rublyov's masterpiece icon of the Old Testament Trinity, to the right of the centre of the iconostasis, is a copy, the original being in Moscow's Tretyakov Gallery.

Cathedral of the Assumption This cathedral (Uspensky Sobor), with its star-spangled domes, was modelled on the cathedral of the same name in the Moscow Kremlin. It was finished in 1585 with money left by Ivan the Terrible in a fit of remorse for killing his son. Services are held here in summer but outside service times you may find it closed.

Outside the west door is the grave of Boris Godunov, the only tsar not buried in the Moscow Kremlin or St Petersburg's SS Peter & Paul Cathedral. Nearby, the resplendent Chapel-at-the-Well (Nadkladeznaya

Trinity Monastery of St Sergius		8	Cathedral of the Assumption Успенский собор	13	Gate-Church of John the Baptist Церковь Иоанна Предтечи
1	Kalichya Tower Каличья башня	9	Chapel-at-the-Well Надкладезная часовня	14	Refectory Church of St Sergius Трапезная церковь Св. Сергия
2	Tsar's Chambers Царские палаты	10	Early Russian Applied Art Section (Vestry) Отдел Древнерусского прикладного искусства (Ризница)	15	Metropolitan's Residence Покои митрополита
3	Smolenskaya Church Смоленская церковь			16	Russky Dvorik Restaurant Ресторан Русский дворик
4	History Museum Исторический музей	11	Trinity Cathedral Троицкий собор		
5	Museum Ticket Offices Кассы музеев	12	Church of the Descent of the Holy Spirit Духовская церковь	17	Kafe Minutka Кафе Минутка
6	Art Museum Художественный музей				
7	Bell Tower Колокольня				

chasovnya) was built over a spring said to have appeared during the Polish siege.

Refectory Church of St Sergius The huge block with the 'wallpaper' paint job and lavish interior (Trapeznaya tserkov Sv Sergia) was once a dining hall for pilgrims. Now it's the Assumption Cathedral's winter counterpart, with morning services in cold weather. The green building next door is the metropolitan's residence.

Church of the Descent of the Holy Spirit This little 15th-century church (Dukhovskaya tserkov), with the belltower under its dome, is a graceful imitation of Trinity Cathedral. It's used only on special occasions. It contains, among other things, the grave of the first Bishop of Alaska.

Belltower This five-tier Baroque wedding cake took 30 years to build in the 18th century, and once had 40 bells.

Tsar's Chambers The 17th-century royal palaces (Tsarskie palaty) at the north end of the monastery are now part of an Ecclesiastical Academy.

Museums Tickets for the three museums are sold at the kassa at the north end of the Art Museum.

The Old Russian Applied Art Section (Otdel Drevnerusskogo prikladnogo iskusstva), in the vestry behind the Trinity Cathedral, is in fact the monastery's extraordinarily rich **treasury**, bulging with 600 years of donations by the rich and powerful – tapestries, jewel-encrusted vestments, solid gold chalices and more. Monthly closing days are the first Tuesday and last Friday. Your ticket (US$5 for foreigners) will admit you only at a fixed time.

The **Art Museum** (Khudozhestvenny muzey) has icons and paintings from the 14th century on, and folk art (old woodcarvings, pottery, hand-printed cloth, costumes from all over Russia and some ho-hum Soviet-era stuff). Tickets are US$3. In the old hospital is the monastery's **History & Architecture Museum** (Istorichesky muzey). Tickets are US$1. Both these museums' monthly closing day is the last Wednesday.

Walls & Tower For a walk along part of the walls (Krepostnye steny), and a climb up the 18th-century Kalichya Tower (Kalichya bashny) for a good view over the monastery and town, take the passage between the art and history museums. Tickets are US$1.

Places to Stay
The *Hotel Zagorsk* on Sovietskaya ploshchad, about 500 metres north along

prospekt Krasnoy Armii from the monastery gate, has singles/doubles with private bathroom for an expensive US$34/68. Oddly, reception may demand to see 'Sergiev Posad' or 'Zagorsk' on your visa if you want to stay, but will probably back down if you're persistent.

Places to Eat

The *Russky Dvorik* restaurant across the road from the monastery entrance was under repair but looks as if it might be OK when it reopens. On the street corner behind it, the *Kafe Minutka* does soups, salads and reasonable, if modest, hot main dishes for US$1 to US$1.50. There are a few more small eateries along prospekt Krasnoy Armii north of the monastery. For a bigger meal, go for the set lunch (US$4) or dinner (US$2.25) in the restaurant at the *Hotel Zagorsk*, or head to the *Restoran Zolotoe Koltso*, probably the best in town, on prospekt Krasnoy Armii almost opposite 1-ya Rybnaya ulitsa, the street leading from the stations. A salad, soup, main course, drink and coffee at the Zolotoe Koltso will be up to US$10; service is fairly good, though it may get busy with tour groups around 1 or 2 pm.

There's a *food market* about 500 metres north of the monastery up ulitsa 1-y Udarnoy Armii.

Getting There & Away

Sergiev Posad is still called Zagorsk on some timetables.

Suburban trains run every half-hour or so to/from Moscow's Yaroslavl Station, where the suburban ticket hall is at the rear left of the building. The trip takes a little over 1½ hours; take any train bound for Sergiev Posad or Alexandrov. You can continue on to Rostov-Veliky (3½ hours) or Yaroslavl (five to 5½ hours) by taking the 7.22 or 11.13 am or 4.34 or 7.13 pm train to Alexandrov, and changing there to a Yaroslavl-bound suburban train.

Buses starting at Sergiev Posad run to Pereslavl-Zalessky (US$1.60; 1¼ hours) three to five times daily. About nine northbound buses a day stop here in transit to Yaroslavl, Kostroma or Rybinsk; all these will take you to Pereslavl-Zalessky, Rostov-Veliky or Yaroslavl if you can get a ticket. There are also about nine in-transit buses to Moscow.

ABRAMTSEVO & KHOTKOVO
АБРАМЦЕВО И ХОТКОВО

The small Abramtsevo estate 15 km southwest of Sergiev Posad was a seedbed for several 19th-century movements aiming to preserve patriarchal Russian religious, social and aesthetic values. In the 1840s and 1850s it was the home of Sergey Axakov, pioneer novelist of Russian realism, and a refuge for upper-class intellectuals.

In 1870 a railway tycoon and art patron named Savva Mamontov bought Abramtsevo and turned it into an artists' colony dedicated to a renaissance of traditional Russian art and architecture, which was to have a strong influence on painting, sculpture, applied art and even theatre. The list of resident painters alone is a who's who of 'Neo-Russianism' – it includes Ilya Repin, landscape artist Isaak Levitan, portraitist Valentin Serov and the quite un-Slavophilic painter and ceramicist Mikhail Vrubel.

Other projects included woodworking and ceramics workshops, Mamontov's private opera (where Fyodor Chaliapin made his debut) and several buildings designed, built and decorated in traditional style as group efforts.

All this is now the **Abramtsevo Estate Museum-Preserve** (Abramtsevo Usadba Muzey-Zapovednik), a good museum, in peaceful surroundings, about an important stream of 19th-century artistic thought, and a good addition to a day trip to Sergiev Posad. It's normally open from 10 am to 5 pm daily except Monday, Tuesday and the 30th of each month – but may also be closed for the entire months of April and October.

Main House

Several rooms have been preserved intact. Axakov's dining room and study contain paintings and sculptures of family and friends, but most of the house is devoted to the Mamontov years. The main attraction is Mamontov's dining room, featuring Repin's portraits of the patron and his wife, and the luminous *Girl with Peaches* by Serov. A striking majolica bench by Vrubel is in the garden.

Saviour Church 'Not Made by Hand'
The prettiest building in the grounds, this small church (Tserkov Spasa Nerukotvorny) seems to symbolise Mamontov's intentions – it's a carefully researched homage by half a dozen artists to 14th-century Novgorod architecture. The iconostasis is by Repin and Vasily Polenov.

Hut on Chicken Legs
This just goes to show that serious art doesn't have to be serious. The Slavophile painter Viktor Vasnetsov conjured up the fairy tale of Baba Yaga the witch with this playhouse with feet, near the church.

Convent of the Intercession
Between Abramtsevo and Sergiev Posad, in the village of Khotkovo, is the Convent of the Intercession (Pokrovsky monastyr); it was founded in 1308 though the present buildings are 18th century or newer. The parents of Sergius of Radonezh, Russia's patron saint and founder of the Trinity Mon-

astery of St Sergius at Sergiev Posad, are buried in the convent's recently restored Intercession Cathedral (Pokrovsky sobor). The biggest building is the early 20th-century St Nicholas' Cathedral.

Places to Eat
There is a restaurant near the museum at Abramtsevo, or if you're driving stop at the *Skazka (Fairy Tale)* restaurant (☎ (095) 584 34 36), with its over-the-top wooden décor and excellent soups, on the highway at the 43-km post from Moscow.

Getting There & Away
There are occasional buses (No 155) to Abramtsevo from Sergiev Posad bus station. Abramtsevo is three stops and Khotkovo two before Sergiev Posad on suburban trains from Moscow's Yaroslavl Station. Most trains heading to Sergiev Posad or Alexandrov stop at both places (but a few miss out Abramtsevo, so check).

By car, turn west off the M8 Moscow-Yaroslavl highway just north of the 61-km post. The turn-off is marked by signs to Khotkovo and Abramtsevo. For the Khotkovo convent, turn left just before the rail tracks in the village; for Abramtsevo continue over the railway and on for a few more km.

St Petersburg
Санкт Петербург

Population: five million

If Moscow is Europe's most Asiatic capital, St Petersburg is Russia's most European city. Created by Peter the Great as his 'window on the West' at the only point where traditional Russian territory meets a seaway to Northern Europe, it was built with 18th and 19th-century European pomp and orderliness by mainly European architects. The result is a city that remains one of Europe's most beautiful: where Moscow intimidates, St Petersburg enchants.

The vistas of elegant buildings across the wide Neva River and along the canals and avenues recall Paris, Amsterdam, Venice and Berlin. But St Petersburg's beauty, happily little harmed by Stalinist reconstruction, is of a brand all its own.

The jolly onion domes of Moscow seem almost passé here, where a more Western outlook was taken at every stage of planning and construction. Even the city's colours – the green and gold of the Winter Palace, the red beside the Anichkov Bridge, the blue of Smolny Cathedral – reflect a closer stylistic allegiance to the courts of Europe than to the Kremlin. The buildings' playful Baroque façades exude the riotous opulence of tsarist Russia. Today, despite their well-publicised problems, residents feel enough affection for their city to call it simply 'Piter' – and visitors' taste buds are now receiving a much improved welcome from new private and foreign restaurant ventures. Reform and transformation are bringing the city a face-lift that's about 73 years overdue.

The spirit of reform is so alive here it's palpable. Small, Russian-owned businesses are popping up everywhere, Western businesses are following suit (enter Subway, McDonald's and the rest), and even the city itself is getting in on the money train by accepting corporate sponsorship of street signs – it's not your imagination, that street sign does say 'USA Today'. And the deification process has turned 180 degrees: the Order of Lenin plaque at the Ploshchad Vosstania metro station has been replaced with a Marlboro cigarette ad.

St Petersburg is chock-full of history: from here autocratic tsars ruled Russia for two centuries with the splendour and stubbornness that led to their downfall at the hands of its workers and soldiers in March 1917. That same year, Lenin came back here from exile to drive his Bolshevik Party to power. The city's two centuries as Russia's capital bequeathed it an artistic and entertainment scene which still at least equals Moscow's. Russian ballet was born in St Petersburg and the 19th-century flowering of Russian music was centred here. Nijinsky, Tchaikovsky and Rimsky-Korsakov, to name but a few, spent important periods here. Pushkin was educated in, exiled from, readmitted to and killed in St Petersburg; Dostoevsky set *Crime and Punishment* here.

At one end of the cultural spectrum today are the Hermitage, one of the world's great art galleries, housed in the tsars' superb Winter Palace, and the Kirov Ballet, which has recently overshadowed Moscow's Bolshoy. At the other end, St Petersburg has produced many of Russia's top rock bands; wealthy young Russians spend sultry summer evenings partying in dozens of Western-style nightclubs or at rave parties that run all night long – with laser shows, top dance hits and DJs imported from the UK, Sweden and, in many cases, Africa. For a change of pace, venture out to one of the sublime suburban palaces and parks such as Petrodvorets or Pavlovsk.

St Petersburg's latitude – level with Seward, Alaska and Cape Farewell, Greenland – gives it nearly 24-hour daylight in midsummer but long, grey winters. From June to August, when temperatures usually reach 20°C, the city is absolutely packed with foreign and Russian tourists. From December to March, when the Neva is ice and temperatures rarely exceed freezing, the long nights have a twinkling magic; the sun lazily lobs itself skyward at around 10 am and decides to call it a day around 3 pm.

HISTORY

Alexandr of Novgorod defeated the Swedes near the mouth of the Neva in 1240 – earning the title Nevsky (of the Neva). Sweden took control of the region in the 17th century and it was Peter the Great's desire to crush this rival and make Russia a European power that led to the founding of the city. At the start of the Great Northern War (1700-21) he captured the Swedish outposts on the Neva, and in 1703 he founded the Peter & Paul Fortress on the Neva a few km in from the sea. After Peter trounced the Swedes at Poltava in 1709, the city he named, in Dutch style, Sankt Pieter Burkh, really began to grow. Canals were dug to drain the marshy south bank and in 1712 he made the place his capital, forcing administrators, nobles and merchants to move here and build new homes. Peasants were drafted in for forced labour, many dying for their pains. Architects and artisans were brought from all over Europe. By Peter's death in 1725 his city had a population of 40,000 and 90% of Russia's foreign trade passed through it. The south bank around the Admiralty had become the city centre.

Peter's immediate successors moved the capital back to Moscow but Empress Anna

Statue of Peter I by Falconet

Ivanovna (1730-40) returned to St Petersburg. Between 1741 and 1825 under Empress Elizabeth, Catherine the Great and Alexander I it became a cosmopolitan city with a royal court of famed splendour. These monarchs commissioned great series of palaces, government buildings and churches, which turned it into one of Europe's grandest capitals.

The emancipation of the serfs in 1861 and industrialisation, which peaked in the 1890s, brought a flood of poor workers into the city, leading to overcrowding, poor sanitation, epidemics and festering discontent. St Petersburg became a hotbed of strikes and political violence and was the hub of the 1905 revolution, sparked by 'Bloody Sunday' – 9 January 1905 – when a strikers' march to petition the tsar in the Winter Palace was fired on by troops. By 1914, when in a wave of patriotism at the start of WW I the city's name was changed to the Russian-style Petrograd, it had 2.1 million people.

Petrograd was again the cradle of revolution in 1917. It was here that workers' protests turned into a general strike and troops mutinied, forcing the end of the monarchy in March. The Petrograd Soviet, a socialist focus for workers' and soldiers' demands, started meeting in the city's Tauride Palace alongside the country's reformist Provisional Government. It was to Petrograd's Finland Station that Lenin travelled in April to organise the Bolshevik Party, and against Petrograd that the loyalist General Kornilov marched his troops in August, only to be headed off by rebel soldiers and armed workers from the city. A former girls' college in the city, the Smolny Institute, became the focus of activity as the Bolsheviks took control of the Petrograd Soviet, which had installed itself there.

The actual revolution came after Bolsheviks occupied key positions in Petrograd on 24 October. Next day the All-Russian Congress of Soviets, meeting in the Smolny, appointed a Bolshevik government. That night, after some exchanges of gunfire and a blank shot from the cruiser *Aurora* on the Neva, the Provisional Government in the Winter Palace surrendered to the Bolsheviks.

The new government operated from the Smolny until March 1918, when it moved to Moscow, fearing a German attack on Petrograd. The privations of the Civil War caused Petrograd's population to drop to about 700,000, and in 1921 strikes in the city and a revolt by the sailors of nearby Kronstadt helped to bring about Lenin's more liberal New Economic Policy.

Petrograd was renamed Leningrad after Lenin's death in 1924. It was a hub of Stalin's 1930s industrialisation programme and by 1939 had 3.1 million people and 11% of Soviet industrial output. But Stalin feared it as a rival power base and the 1934 assassination of the local communist chief Sergey Kirov at Smolny was the start of his 1930s Communist Party purge.

When the Germans attacked the USSR in June 1941 it took them only two-and-a-half months to reach Leningrad. As the birthplace of Bolshevism, Hitler hated the place and he swore to wipe it from the face of the earth. His troops besieged it from 8 September 1941 until 27 January 1944. Many people

(and three-quarters of the industrial plant) had been evacuated. Nevertheless, between 500,000 and a million died from shelling, starvation and disease in what's called the '900 Days' (actually 872). By comparison the USA and UK suffered about 700,000 dead between them in all of WW II. Leningraders dropped dead of hunger or cold in the streets and when no cats or rats were left they ate glue off the back of wallpaper. The city was saved from an even worse fate by the winter 'Road of Life' across frozen Lake Ladoga to the east, a thin supply line which remained in Soviet hands.

After the war, Leningrad was reconstructed and reborn, though it took until 1960 for its population to exceed pre-WW II levels. The city centre and most of the inner areas have been reconstructed, though the outlying areas (as is the case practically everywhere in Russia) are lined with horrific, depressing, uniformly grey and chunky blocks of flats that go on forever.

In 1989, Anatoly Sobchak, a reform (and honorarium-) minded candidate was elected mayor. His plans called for rapid growth in joint-venture projects and the opening of trade with the West.

During the 1991 putsch, in true Leningrad style, the army refused to come to the aid of Moscow's coup leaders. Sobchak talked the Army out of arresting him (a warrant for his arrest had been issued in Moscow). And when Leningrad residents turned on their TVs and saw *Swan Lake* they took to the streets in protest (for some reason *Swan Lake* is the programme of choice during governmental upheaval in Russia; a curator at the Russian Museum said that the next time he hears it he's hopping on a plane to Finland). As hundreds of thousands of Leningraders filled Palace Square, Sobchak appeared on local TV denouncing the coup and asking local residents to do the same. Fearful but determined, residents spent a jittery evening awaiting the tanks that Moscow had threatened to send in, but which never appeared.

Almost as soon as Dzerzhinsky's statue hit the asphalt in Moscow, the Leningrad city council was proposing to change the city's name back to St Petersburg, a measure that easily won approval (though it's interesting that the region around the city refused to join in the fun and to this day calls itself the Leningradsky oblast).

Plans for making St Petersburg a tax-free port went the way of the dodo, but foreign business in the city is booming. Corny as it may sound, St Petersburg did re-establish itself as Russia's window on the West.

The Goodwill Games of 1994 were (as perhaps all Goodwill Games are) a disappointment in terms of turnout, but the preparations for them were a huge shot in the arm for the city, which invested millions of dollars in repairs and generally sprucing up the place. Roads were patched, stadiums fixed up, buildings painted and English-language signs began to sprout up everywhere. The police and traffic police even received new uniforms, and, since the traffic cops are absolutely everywhere, even that helped the city's image.

Today St Petersburg is a cosmopolitan city with a lively cultural and artistic core. Foreign and Russian business is quickly sending down roots. St Petersburg is Russia's biggest port, and a huge industrial centre. And with all Moscow's infighting, dirty politics and entrenched lobbyist sub-culture, more than a few people are thinking that maybe Peter the Great had the right idea in moving a tumultuous country's capital northward, to the city on the Neva.

ORIENTATION

St Petersburg sprawls across and around the delta of the Neva River, at the end of the easternmost arm of the Baltic Sea, known as the Gulf of Finland. Entering St Petersburg at its south-eastern corner, the Neva first flows north and then turns west across the middle of the city, dividing there into several branches and forming the islands which make up the delta. The two biggest branches, which diverge where the Winter Palace

---

St Petersburg's Architecture

Unrestricted by winding old streets or buildings from the past, the early European and Europe-trained designers of St Petersburg created a unique waterside city of straight avenues, wide plazas and grand edifices in the Baroque, Rococo and classical styles of the 18th and early 19th centuries.

Few major buildings had reached their final form by Peter the Great's death in 1725, though his version of Petergof Palace was complete and SS Peter & Paul Cathedral and the Twelve Colleges were well under way. Empress Elizabeth (1741-61) commissioned the first grand wave of buildings, from Bartolomeo Rastrelli, an Italian, who engraved Elizabeth's love of fun on the city's profile. His inspired creations, such as the Winter Palace, Smolny Cathedral and the Great Palace at Pushkin, playful in their Rococo detail yet majestic in form, mirrored her glittering court, which drew European diplomats, artists and travellers.

Catherine the Great and Alexander I launched fleets of projects to make St Petersburg Europe's most imposing capital, employing an international array of designers to beat the West at its own architectural games. Both monarchs rode the new wave of classical taste, whose increasing severity can be traced through some of their chief buildings. The Academy of Arts by J B M Vallin de la Mothe (France), Pavlovsk Palace by Charles Cameron (England) and the Hermitage Theatre by Giacomo Quarenghi (Italy) display the simpler, earlier classicism of Catherine's reign. Quarenghi's Smolny Institute for Alexander was halfway towards the later, heavier works of another Italian, Carlo Rossi, who created the Mikhail Palace (now the Russian Museum), the General Staff building and ploshchad Ostrovskogo.

The more grandiose branch of later classicism known as Russian Empire style is typified by the Kazan Cathedral and the Admiralty, both built by Russians for Alexander. The huge-domed St Isaac's Cathedral by Ricard de Montferrand (France), mostly built under Nicholas I (1825-55), was the city's last major classical building. ∎

stands on the south bank, are the Bolshaya (Big) and Malaya (Small) Neva; they flow into the sea either side of Vasilevsky Island.

The heart of St Petersburg is the area spreading back from the Winter Palace and the Admiralty on the south bank, its skyline dominated by the golden dome of St Isaac's Cathedral. Nevsky prospekt, stretching east-south-east from the Admiralty, is the main street, with many of the city's sights, shops and restaurants. Nevsky prospekt crosses three waterways cutting across from the Neva to the sea, the biggest being the Fontanka River.

The north side of the city has three main areas. The westernmost is Vasilevsky Island, at whose east end – the Strelka – many of the city's fine early buildings still stand. The middle area is Petrograd Side, a cluster of delta islands whose south end is marked by the tall gold spire of the SS Peter & Paul Cathedral. This is where the city began.

The third, eastern, area is Vyborg Side, divided from Petrograd Side by the Bolshaya Nevka channel (not to be confused with the Bolshaya Neva) and stretching east along the north bank of the Neva.

Street Names

While St Petersburg is still in the process of renaming many of its streets – in many cases simply restoring the pre-communist names – there have already been such fundamental changes to the names of the city's streets that any map more than three years old is hopelessly and irretrievably useless. More infuriating, residents will continue to refer to renamed streets, even major ones, by their old names. The list headed Street Name Changes in St Petersburg shows those that were in place in May 1995; newer changes may be found in publications such as the *St Petersburg Press* or *The Traveller's Yellow Pages* (see under Books & Bookshops later in this chapter's Information section). In this chapter, we use the new names, and if it's a street that's stubbornly referred to by its old one as well, we've put that in parentheses after the new name.

St Petersburg has two streets called Bolshoy prospekt: one on Petrograd Side, one on Vasilevsky Island. The two sides of some Vasilevsky Island streets are known as lines *(linii)* and opposite sides of these streets have different names – thus 4-ya linia (4th line) and 5-ya linia (5th line) are the east and west sides of the same street – which collectively is called 4-ya i 5-ya linii (4th and 5th lines).

INFORMATION
Visa Registration Offices

OVIR (see Visas in European Russia Facts for the Visitor) offices in the city are:

Main Office
  Saltykova-Shchedrina ulitsa 4 (☎ 278 24 81, 273 90 38), open Monday to Friday from 9.30 am to 5.30 pm
Dzerzhinsky District
  Chekhova ulitsa 15 (☎ 272 55 56)
Frunzensky District
  Obvodnogo kanal naberezhnaya 48 (☎ 166 14 68)
Kalininsky District
  Mineralnaya ulitsa 3 (☎ 540 39 87)
Kirovsky District
  Stachek prospekt 18 (☎ 252 77 14)
Krasnoselsky District
  Avangardnaya ulitsa 35 (☎ 136 89 06)
Kuybyshevsky District
  Krylova pereulok 3 (☎ 310 41 17)
Leninsky District
  Sovietsky pereulok 9 (☎ 292 43 56)
Moskovsky District
  Moskovsky prospekt 95 (☎ 294 81 55; 298 18 27)
Novocherkassky District
  Krasnodonskaya ulitsa 14 (☎ 224 01 96)
Oktyabrsky District
  Bolshaya Podyacheskaya ulitsa 26 (☎ 314 49 01)
Petrogradsky District
  Bolshaya Monetnaya ulitsa 20 (☎ 232 11 19)
Primorsky District
  Generalnaya Khruleva ulitsa 15 (☎ 394 72 13)
Smolninsky District
  Mytninskaya ulitsa 3 (☎ 274 57 10)
Vasileostrovsky District
  19-ya liniya 10 (☎ 355 75 24)
Vyborgsky District
  Lesnoy prospekt 20 (☎ 542 21 72)

Tourist Offices
The pioneering, nonprofit Tourist Information

EUROPEAN RUSSIA

Name Changes in St Petersburg

Street Names

New Name	Old Name
Admiralteysky kanal	kanal Krushteyna
Atamanskaya ulitsa	ulitsa Krasnogo Elektrika
Bolnichny pereulok	ulitsa Santyago de Kuba
Bolshaya Konyushennaya ulitsa	ulitsa Zhelyabova
Bolshaya Monetnaya ulitsa	ulitsa Skorokhodova
ulitsa Bolshaya Morskaya	ulitsa Gertsena
Bolshoy Sampsonevsky prospekt	prospekt Karla Marxa
Dachny prospekt	Suslova prospekt
Furshtadtskaya ulitsa	ulitsa Petra Lavrova
Galernaya ulitsa	Krasnaya ulitsa
Gorokhovaya ulitsa	ulitsa Dzerzhinskogo
Grafsky pereulok	ulitsa Marii Ulyanovoy
Italyanskaya ulitsa	ulitsa Rakova
Kamennoostrovsky prospekt	Kirovsky prospekt
Karavannaya ulitsa	ulitsa Tolmacheva
Kavalergardskaya ulitsa	ulitsa Krasnoy Konnitsy
Kazanskaya ulitsa	ulitsa Plekhanova *
Konnogvardeysky bulvar	bulvar Profsoyuzov
Kronverksky prospekt	prospekt Maxim Gorkogo
Lanskoye shosse	prospekt N I Smirnova
Malaya Konyushennaya ulitsa	ulitsa Sofie Perovskoy
Malaya Morskaya ulitsa	ulitsa Gogolya
Malaya Posadskaya ulitsa	Bratev Vasilevykh ulitsa
Maly prospekt (Petrogradskoy storony)	prospekt Shchorsa
Maly Sampsonievsky prospekt	ulitsa Bratstva
ulitsa Mikhailovskaya	ulitsa Brodskogo
Millionnaya ulitsa	ulitsa Khalturina
Moshkov pereulok	Zaporozhsky pereulok
Nikolskaya ploshchad	ploshchad Kommunarov
Novocherkassky prospekt	Krasnogvardeysky prospekt
Panteleymonovskaya ulitsa	ulitsa Pestelya
Pochtamtskaya ulitsa	ulitsa Soyuza Svyazy
Pochtamtsky pereulok	pereulok Podbelskogo
Polozova ulitsa	ulitsa Anny Ulyanovoy
Preobrazhenskaya ploshchad	Radishcheva ploshchad
Pribrezhnaya ulitsa	Kodatskogo ulitsa and Pogranichikov prospekt

Centre (TIC) in the lobby of the Astoria Hotel closed in the spring of 1995, but several organisations now fill the gap left by the TIC's demise.

Peter TIPS The first fully fledged tourist information centre to operate entirely independently of the organs of state tourism opened in 1995 at Nevsky prospekt 86, in Dom Aktyor, the House of Actors. It's a subsidiary of Ost-West Contact Service, a German-owned travel services company. Peter TIPS (☎ 279 00 37) is a very friendly place that hands out free city maps, city information, pamphlets and brochures, practical information about transportation in and

Rizhsky prospekt	prospekt Ogorodnikova
Sennaya ploshchad	ploshchad Mira
Shpalernaya ulitsa	ulitsa Voynova
Sirenevy bulvar	Pelshe ulitsa
Staro-Petergofsky prospekt	prospekt Gaza
Troitskaya ploshchad	ploshchad Revolutsii
Vitebskaya ulitsa	ulitsa Voytika
Voznesensky prospekt	prospekt Mayorova
Vvedenskaya ulitsa	ulitsa Olega Koshevogo
Yekatarinski Kanal	Kanal Griboedova **
Yeletskaya ulitsa	ulitsa Fotevoy
Yenotaevskaya ulitsa	ulitsa Fofanovoy
Zakharevskaya ulitsa	ulitsa Kalyaeva

* This street-name change had been suspended – there was already another Kazanskaya ulitsa – and authorities were arguing about it as we wrote this. Meanwhile everyone calls it ulitsa Plekhanova.
** This street is still generally referred to only by its Soviet-era name; in this book we bow to general usage and use the old name.

Bridge Names

New Name	Old Name
Kharlamov most	Komsomolsky most
Panteleymonovsky most	most Pestelya
Sampsonevsky most	most Svobody
Silin most	Pionersky most
Troitsky most	Kirovsky most

Park Names

New Name	Old Name
Alexandrovsky Sad	Sad imeni A M Gorkogo
Lopukhinsky Sad	Sad imeni F E Dzerzhinskogo
Udelny Park	Chelyuskintsev Park

Metro Names

New Name	Old Name
Devyatkino	Komsomolskaya
Novocherkasskaya	Krasnogvardeyskaya
Sennaya Ploshchad	Ploshchad Mira

around St Petersburg, offers free hotel booking services and are generally good eggs.

For a fee, it arranges city and regional tours and excursions – for example, a one-hour bus tour of St Petersburg is US$15; a German-language tour to Novgorod, including transport and lunch, is US$140 for one person, then US$25 for each additional person. It sells tickets to all the city's cultural outlets at the Russian price plus a 10% mark-up; Kirov Ballet tickets would therefore cost US$3.75 at the time of writing.

It also issues and supports tourist, business and cultural exchange visas – a three-month invitation costs US$10, and conversion of a single to multiple-entry visa is US$200.

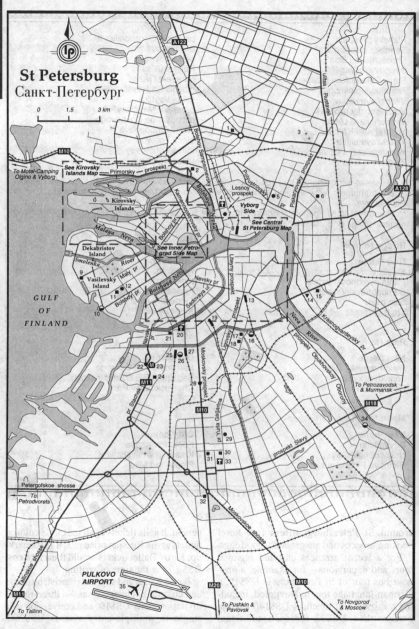

St Petersburg
Санкт-Петербург

0   1.5   3 km

See Kirovsky Islands Map

To Motel-Camping Olgino & Vyborg

Primorsky — prospekt

Kirovsky Islands

Malaya Neva

Dekabristov Island

Smolenka

River

Vasilevsky Island

GULF
OF
FINLAND

Bolshoy pr

Maly pr

Bolshoy pr

See Inner Petro-grad Side Map

Lesnoy prospekt

Vyborg Side

See Central St Petersburg Map

Nevsky pr

Sadovaya ul

Nevsky pr

Liteyny prospekt

Nevsky

pr

Nevsky River

Krasnogvardeysky pr

To Petrozavodsk & Murmansk

Moskovsky prospekt

pr Stachek

pr Yuria Gagarina

prospekt Slavy

Petergofskoe shosse

To Petrodvorets

Moskovskoe shosse

Tallinskoe shosse

PULKOVO
AIRPORT

To Tallinn

To Pushkin & Pavlovsk

To Novgorod & Moscow

PLACES TO STAY

1 Hotel Sputnik
   Гостиница Спутник
2 Vyborgskaya Hotel
   Гостиница Выборгская
6 Hotel Karelia
   Гостиница Карелия
9 Pribaltiyskaya Hotel
   Гостиница Приморская
11 Hotel Gavan
   Гостиница Гавань
15 Hotel Deson-Ladoga
   Гостиница Десон-Ладога
17 Kievskaya Hotel
   Гостиница Киевская
18 Hotel Zarya
   Гостиница Заря
21 Hotel Sovietskaya
   Гостиница Советская
24 Summer Hostel
   Летний Хостел
30 Hotel Mir
   Гостиница Мир
32 Hotel Pulkovskaya
   Гостиница Пулковская

PLACES TO EAT

14 Shvabsky Domik Restaurant
   Ресторан Швабский домик

OTHER

3 Piskaryovka Cemetery
   Пискарёвское кладбище
4 St Sampson's Cathedral
   Самсоновский собор
5 Krondatevsky Market
   Крондатевский Рынок

7 Vyborgsky Culture Palace
   Выборгский дворец культуры
8 Finland Station
   Финляндский вокзал
10 Passenger Sea Terminal
   Морской вокзал
12 Kirov Culture Palace
   Дворец культуры имени С.М. Кирова
13 Moscow Station
   Московский вокзал
16 Bus Station (Avtovokzal) No 2
   Автовокзал 2
19 Vitebsk Station
   Витебский вокзал
20 Trinity Cathedral
   Троицкий собор
22 Narva Arch
   Нарвские ворота
23 Metro Narvskaya
   Метро Нарвская
25 Baltic Station
   Балтийский вокзал
26 Bus Station (Avtovoksal) No 1
   Автовокзал 1
27 Warsaw Station
   Варшавский вокзал
28 Moscow Triumphal Arch
   Московские ворота
29 Lenin Sports-Concert Complex
   Спортивно-концертный комплекс
   имени В.И. Ленина
31 Chesma Palace
   Чесменский дворец
33 Chesma Church
   Чесменская церковь
34 River Terminal
   Речной вокзал
35 Pulkovo Airport
   Пулково Аэропорт

Contact Ost-West (☎ 279 36 35) for more information.

HI St Petersburg Hostel The registration desk at the HI St Petersburg Hostel (☎ 277 05 69) is staffed by helpful English-speaking staff who are very experienced in getting around the city cheaply. There's also a budget travel agency downstairs, Sindbad Travel (see Travel Agencies later in this section), and they sell domestically and

internationally published guidebooks (including Lonely Planet guides).

St Petersburg Travel Company The St Petersburg Travel Company (formerly Intourist; ☎ 315 51 29) has a desk in the Astoria, where it arranges city tours and provides a wide range of other (albeit for profit) services, including car rental, theatre and Kirov tickets etc. It is open daily.

Hotels The concierge desks in the Grand Hotel Europe and the Nevskij Palace Hotel have extremely knowledgeable and helpful staff, and they'll usually help you even if you don't look like a millionaire, but it's best to dress neatly. They can also arrange everything that you'd expect a city travel desk to do: tours, excursions, car rentals, theatre tickets etc.

Money

As in the rest of the country, moneychanging offices are now legal and blooming everywhere. In fact, they seem to be in every nook and cranny in the entire city. Private exchange offices are rampant, and it's a question of finding the best rate. A weekly random comparison of banks is printed in the *St Petersburg Press*, and you can check for posted rates wherever you happen to be. Below are just a few offices.

Promstroy (Industry & Construction) Bank
 Head office Nevsky prospekt 38, entrance in Mikhailovskaya ulitsa across from the Grand Hotel Europe (though it has small offices all over town) – offers cash advances on Visa/Master Card/Eurocard
Saint Petersburg Savings
 Head office Nevsky prospekt 38, entrance in Mikhailovskaya ulitsa across from the Grand Hotel Europe – offers cash advances on Visa/MasterCard/Eurocard, buys and sells travellers' cheques
Astrobank
 Nevsky prospekt 58 is a moneychanging office
Hotels
 Astoria, Grand Hotel Europe, Nevskij Palace, Oktyabrskaya, Moskva, Saint Petersburg, Pribaltiyskaya, Hotelship Peterhof, Helen, Pulkovskaya and others – many offer advances on Visa/MasterCard/Eurocard; the Grand Hotel Europe and Nevskij Palace Hotel can organise travellers' cheques as well

Post

For information concerning postal services in European Russia as a whole, see the earlier Facts about European Russia chapter.

St Petersburg's main international and domestic post and telegraph office (glavpochtamt) is at ulitsa Pochtamtskaya 9,

two blocks south-west of St Isaac's Cathedral; there are also over 400 branch offices in the city. The services provided by branches is usually in proportion to their size – most can cope with international letters and postcards, some can even send international telegrams.

Visitors can usually find what they need – postcards, envelopes and stamps – at the small postal desks in tourist hotels. You can also post books and printed matter abroad from these desks. They tend to open from about 10 am to 3 pm.

Non-book parcels, such as clothing, must go from the main post office. For the moment, window No 26 is for international mail, though it keeps being shuffled so just walk to the far left side of the counter at the opposite end of where you enter the hall and look for a sign; window No 38 is for fax, photocopying and domestic and international telegrams.

Packages for Express Mail Service (EMS) must be taken to Garantpost (☎ 311 96 71, 311 78 21), bulvar Konnogvardeysky 6, Dom 4.

Westpost (☎ 275 07 84) is a privately run, US-managed international mail service at Dom Aktyor, Nevsky prospekt 86, for monthly and one-time clients. Mail is trucked daily from St Petersburg to Lappeenranta, Finland (which seems to be the Switzerland of matters postal around here), and is mailed from there. One-time users pay a fee – US$1 for a letter or postcard or US$4 a kilo – plus Finnish postage. Westpost is located through the main entrance and through the first door on the right-hand side.

A similar, though less flashy, Russian-run post service, Post International (☎ 219 44 72), sends letters 'several times a week', dropping them into the US or British postal system. For letters to the USA and Europe, the cost is US$2 for the first ounce (28.5 grams), US$1 for each additional ounce; express mail to the USA for nonmembers is US$23. It's at Nevsky prospekt 20, through the door with the 'Fuji' sign, straight back through a second door, turn left and left again, past the staircase, then right and into the office. Whoo.

The three main Western express mail services have offices in St Petersburg. TNT Express Worldwide (☎ 122 96 70, 104 36 84) is at Liteyny prospekt 50. DHL has two locations here: the main office is at naberezhnaya kanala Griboedova 5 kv. 325 (☎ 311 26 49); the other is at the Nevskij Palace Hotel (☎ 119 61 00, 119 61 17). Federal Express (☎ 279 12 87) is at ulitsa Mayokovskogo 2.

Receiving Mail in St Petersburg

The wonderful folk at American Express (☎ 119 60 09) will hold mail (letters only; no parcels) and messages for card-holders and users of American Express travellers' cheques for up to 30 days at the company's office in the Grand Hotel Europe; the mailing address for St Petersburg is American Express, PO Box 87, SF-53501 Lappeenranta, Finland – mail is brought from Lappeenranta to the American Express office daily, at no charge. You'll need to bring your card or travellers' cheques with you, along with your passport or other ID, to get your mail. From the USA, Canada and Western Europe, mail takes about a week to arrive.

Westpost (☎ 275 07 84; e-mail wp@sas.spb.su) at Dom Aktyor, Nevsky prospekt 86, offers post boxes in Lappeenranta, with daily pick-up and delivery to its offices, or, for corporate clients, to its address in St Petersburg. You can become a basic Westpost client for US$20 per month, and it also offers a US-magazine subscription service. Nonclient visitors can have mail delivered for a US$1 fee to PL 8, SF-53501 Lappeenranta, Finland; you can pick it up at the Westpost office.

For US$50 a month, Post International (see earlier in this section for details) offers a post box in the USA from which mail is forwarded to you in St Petersburg. It's just not as convenient as Westpost, but it is an alternative.

Poste restante is notoriously useless, but if you want to try it, the St Petersburg branch is at Nevsky prospekt 6 (rather than the glavpochtamt). The postal code is 190400. Bring along your passport to get your mail.

Telecommunications

Telephone See European Russia Facts for the Visitor for a general discussion of telephone options. St Petersburg's telephone code is 812.

Pay Telephones Payphones, Таксофон ('taksa-FON'), are located throughout the city and are generally in working order. They accept metro tokens (zhetony) as payment. Place the token in the slot on top of the phone and dial the number; when the party answers, the token should drop. A series of beeps means place another token in the slot or risk disconnection.

Domestic (which means within Russia or to any former Soviet republic) long-distance calls may be made from pay telephones marked междугородный (mezhdugorodny); using different, wrinkled-metal tokens, they work on a similar principle, but you need to push the Ответ (otvet) button on the phone's face when your party answers. Dial 8, wait for the second tone, and dial the city code (including noughts) and the number. New card-operated pay telephones are all over the city; you can buy cards at the central telephone office, Peter TIPS, and the major hotels. These phones can be used for local, long-distance and international calls (see the section on Private Telephone Companies for further information).

State/Central Telephone Office The State-run long-distance telephone office is at ulitsa Bolshaya Morskaya (ulitsa Gertsena) 3/5. Generally speaking, you can make telephone calls from here with no waiting; international calls are placed from window No 13 or 14. Through the wooden doors are international phone booths that take yet a different sort of token; get an international token from any cash desk, dial as you would from a home phone (see below), and push the button marked Ответ (otvet) when your party answers. Prices are identical to those of home ('private') phones.

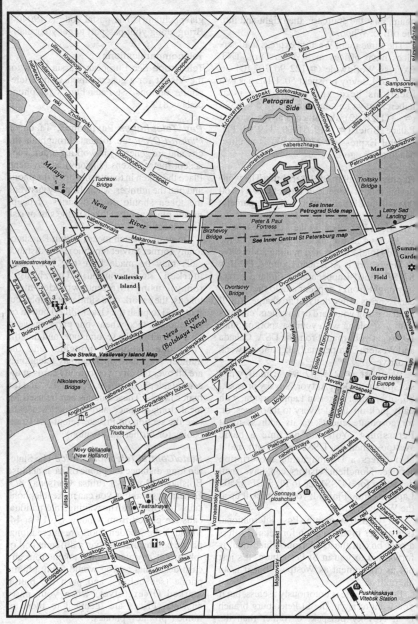

Central St Petersburg
Центральный Санкт-Петербурга

Vyborg Side

Finlyandsky pr

cruiser
Aurora

Finland
Station

ploshchad Lenina

Arsenalnaya naberezhnaya

Komsomola ulitsa

Mikhaylova ulitsa

ulitsa Akademika Lebedeva

Vyborgskaya naberezhnaya

Liteyny Bridge

Neva

River

Sphinx Monuments

naberezhnaya

Robespera

Shpalernaya ulitsa

Tauride Gardens

ulitsa Chaykovskogo

ulitsa Furshtadtskaya

ulitsa Saltykova-Shchedrina

Mokhovaya

Liteyny prospekt

ulitsa

Hotel Rus

ulitsa Mayakovskogo

ulitsa Nekrasova

Fontanka River

ulitsa Zhukovskogo

ulitsa Voinstania

Peter TIPS

Nevsky prospekt

Vladimirsky prospekt

Nevskij Palace Hotel

Oktyabrskaya Hotel

3-ya Sovietskaya u.

HI St Petersburg Hostel & Sindbad Travel

prospekt Bakunina

Suvorovsky prospekt

ulitsa Proletarskoy Diktatury

Bolshoy Okhtinsky Bridge (closed for repairs until 1997)

Nevsky prospekt

Moscow Station

Kuznechny pereulok

Razezzhaya ulitsa

Marata

Ligovsky prospekt

See Inner Central St Petersburg map

Sinopskaya

naberezhnaya

See Smolny Region Map

Alexandra Nevskogo Bridge

Pl. Alexandra Nevskogo

13

14

0   0.5   1 km

PLACES TO STAY

1	Hotelship Peterhof Гостиница Петергоф
13	Hotel Moskva Гостиница Москва
16	Holiday Hostel
17	Hotel St Petersburg Гостиница С-Петербург

PLACES TO EAT

5	Kafe Fregat Кафе Фрегат

OTHER

2	Morskaya Pristan Landing Морская пристань
3	Church Церковь
4	Church Церковь

6	St Petersburg History Museum Музей истории санкт Петербурга
7	Shamrock Pub Шамрок Пуб
8	Conservatory Консерватория
9	Mariinsky Theatre Мариинский театр оперы и балета
10	St Nicholas' Cathedral Николский собор
11	The Jazz Club Центр джазовой музыки
12	Rimsky-Korsakov Flat-Museum Музей-квартира Римского-Корсакова
14	Alexandr Nevsky Lavra (Monastery) Лавра Александра Невского
15	Kresty Prison Кресты Тюрма
18	Stockmann's

Private Telephones From a private phone in St Petersburg, dialling outside Russia is very simple, but the prices keep rising and are even higher now than equivalent calls from the West to Russia. To dial internationally, dial 8, wait for the second dial tone, dial 10 then the country code (without preceding noughts) and the number. In 1995, daytime international telephone prices were:

US$2.95 to the USA, Canada, Australasia
US$1.25 per minute to Continental Europe and the UK

Private Telephone Companies MCI offers country direct service from St Petersburg (dial 8, wait for the tone, dial (10 800) 497 72 22). Other companies at the time of writing must be accessed through Moscow: they are AT&T (☎ (095) 155 50 42 for an English-speaking operator, 155 55 55 for a Russian-speaking operator) and SPRINT (☎ (095) 155 61 33 English, 938 61 33 Russian).

BCL (☎ 311 14 88) has card-operated pay telephones all over town at a surprising number of locations. You can buy cards from anywhere that has a BCL payphone.

Peterstar (☎ 119 60 60) also operates credit-card-operated pay telephones around town at similar rates.

The St Petersburg Taksofon Company (☎ 059) sells phone debit cards as well, which work in its booths at telephone and telegraph offices, where you can also buy the cards.

Calling from a Hotel If you're staying at a hotel that doesn't offer satellite service, international calls may be booked with hotel reception. You might have to wait for up to an hour from the agreed time, and you pay afterwards. You could dial the international operator yourself (☎ 312 00 12) but your hotel will probably do just as well, maybe better.

The Grand Hotel Europe, Nevskij Palace, Okhtinskaya, Astoria, Pribaltiyskaya and other hotels, as well as the HI St Petersburg Hostel, have satellite-linked, international direct-dial telephones, with no waiting, for varying outrageous fees. Of these, the HI St Petersburg Hostel has the lowest rates (US$4 per minute to the USA/Canada/Australia/New Zealand, US$2 to the UK/Europe).

Most hotel-room telephones have their own direct-dial number for incoming calls (on a card in the room, or ask reception), which saves you having to be connected through the switchboard.

Domestic long-distance calls can also be booked through reception. Local calls can be made free from your room (sometimes directly, sometimes with a prefix number).

Cellular Service Cellular telephone service has been available in and around St Petersburg since 1991. Rental phones are available here, but the price is sky-high. There are currently three cellular service providers in town, and roaming is available on all, but it isn't cheap by any means:

North West (☎ 528 47 47), at the Hotel Moskva, ploshchad Alexandra Nevskogo 2, operates on the GSM system and has rates comparable to private telephone charges (see Private Telephone Companies earlier);

SPT Motorola (☎ 311 55 93), at ploshchad Ostrovskogo 5, rents phones that work on the NAMPS system for US$23 to US$27 a day plus airtime;

Delta Telecom (☎ 314 61 26), at ulitsa Bolshaya Morskaya (ulitsa Gertsena) 22, was the first company to offer cellular service in St Petersburg. Delta's other claim to fame is as the world's most expensive cell service provider. Air charges are US$0.15 to US$0.69 per minute within St Petersburg, US$5 per minute to the USA, UK, Canada, Australia, New Zealand, and unless you have an NMT-450 (Scandinavian standard) phone, you'll have to buy one. However, Delta is reliable and has a good concentration of cells in the city and on the road up to Vyborg. If you're upwardly mobile or if you just *need* a cell phone for a few days during your stay, you can rent one from Delta starting at US$25 per day, including 25 minutes of local airtime.

Fax Faxes can be sent and received at the Central Telephone Office: (incoming fax number 314 33 60). Generally speaking, faxes are sent out within 48 hours of your dropping them off, but you can request *srochny* (express) and have it sent out immediately for twice the price. Faxes can also be received at all major hotels and at the two youth hostels (see the Places to Stay listings for incoming fax number) at varying prices.

You can also send and receive faxes at the American Business Center, ulitsa Bolshaya Morskaya (ulitsa Gertsena) 57, near St Isaac's and the Central Post Office (☎ 110 60 42; fax 311 07 94; international ☎ (7 812) 850 1900; incoming international fax (7 812) 850 19 01). This place provides a range of other useful services, including photocopying, rental of PCs, guides and translators.

Faxes can also be sent via electronic mail (see following section).

Fax Prices At the time of writing, the cost per page of sending or receiving a fax at the American Business Center was:

US$3.60 to the USA and Canada
US$2.70 to Europe
US$1.50 to Finland and the Baltics
US$4.50 to the rest of the world
US$0.25 for incoming faxes

At the time of writing, prices per page for faxes sent or received at the central telephone office were:

US$3.95 to the USA, Canada and Australasia
US$1.70 to Continental Europe and the UK
US$0.60 for incoming faxes

Electronic Mail See the European Russia Facts for the Visitor chapter for a full discussion of electronic mail (e-mail), as well as local access numbers in St Petersburg for CompuServe, SprintNet, MCIMail, SFMT, Glasnet, Relcom and Demos/+, as well as subscription information.

If you're just trying to get word home, you can do so at the HI St Petersburg Hostel, or at Sovam Teleport (☎ 311 84 12), Nevsky prospekt 30, which will sometimes allow visitors to use its in-house e-mail to send a message or two for a small fee, but no longer sets up temporary accounts.

Telegrams International telegrams can be sent from many of the larger post offices, as well as from window No 38 at the main post office. If you speak Russian, or can get an English-speaking operator, you can also arrange telegrams from a private telephone (☎ 066). Telegrams can take from three to five days to arrive at their destination. Incoming telegrams work, too; they should be addressed to you at your hotel and marked with your date of arrival.

Foreign Consulates

Consulates in St Petersburg include:

Bulgaria
  Ryleeva ulitsa 27 (☎ 273 73 47; fax 272 57 18)
Canada
  Malodetskoselsky prospekt 32 (☎ 119 84 48; fax 119 83 93)
China
  naberezhnaya kanala Griboedova 134 (☎ 114 62 30)
Cuba
  Ryleeva ulitsa 37 (☎ 272 53 03)
Czech and Slovak Republics
  ulitsa Tverskaya 5 (☎ 271 04 59, 271 61 01; fax 271 46 15)
Denmark
  Bolshaya alleya 13, Kamenny Ostrov (☎ 234 37 55)
Estonia
  Bolshaya Monetnaya ulitsa 14 (☎ 233 55 48)
Finland
  ulitsa Chaykovskogo 71 (☎ 273 73 21; emergency ☎ 116 06 52)
  Commercial Department: 4-ya Krasnoarmeyskaya ulitsa 4a (☎ 316 16 41)
France
  naberezhnaya reki Moyki 15 (☎ 314 14 43)
Germany
  ulitsa Furshtadtskaya 39 (☎ 273 55 98, 279 32 07)
Hungary
  ulitsa Marata 15 (☎ 312 67 53; 312 64 58)
India
  Ryleeva ulitsa 35 (☎ 272 19 88)
Italy
  Teatralnaya ploshchad 10 (☎ 312 32 17, 312 31 06)
Japan
  naberezhnaya reki Moyki 29 (☎ 314 14 18, 314 14 34)
Latvia
  Galernaya ulitsa 69 (☎ 315 17 74)
Netherlands
  prospekt Morisa Toreza (☎ 554 48 90, 554 49 00)
Poland
  5-ya Sovetskaya ulitsa 12 (☎ 274 43 18; 274 41 70)
South Africa
  naberezhnaya reki Moyki 11 (☎ 119 63 63)
Sweden
  10-ya linia No 11, Vasilevsky Island (☎ 213 4 91)
UK
  ploshchad Proletarskoy Diktatury 5 (☎ 119 6 36)
  Visa Department (☎ 119 61 66)
USA
  ulitsa Furshtadtskaya 15 (metro: Chernyshev skaya; ☎ 274 86 89, 274 85 68, 275 17 01). It' open for routine business for US citizens from am to 5.30 pm Monday to Friday, Notarial ser vices until 12 pm Monday to Friday. There's 24-hour duty officer for emergencies.

Cultural Centres

There's a whole lot o' culture going on a naberezhnaya reki Fontanki 46. There sit the British Council St Petersburg (☎ 119 6 74), part of the organisation that 'represent Britain in the areas of culture...in over 10 countries'. Now, just hold on a second; it' more than just upper-middle-aged rock bands and Monty Python stars being shame lessly junketed by the old boy network; this is serious stuff. The Council sponsors classi cal concerts, theatre and other performances and arranges for exchanges of students, pro fessionals and (frighteningly) economists between the two countries. It's on the 3rd floor of the building.

Down one flight of stairs, the Prince George Vladimirovich Golitsyna Memorial Library (☎ 311 13 33) is a lovely reading room containing books in English and Russian pertaining to Russian culture and British-Russian links. It also has encyclopae dias and other reference books, and it allows you to photocopy sections at no charge.

The Goethe Institute St Petersburg (☎ 219 49 75) is in the same building but is hard to find: walk into the lobby, go straight to the back, turn right, follow the narrow hallway and take the flight of stairs up to find the German Cultural Centre. It works on similar lines to the British Council.

Travel Agencies

This is a fledgling field, and dozens of agen cies are popping out of the woodwork. Be careful, and check with the airlines to see if the agent is actually getting you a better deal

)efore you use one. Concierges at the better
1otels can perform some standard booking
;ervices, though at a price.

Sindbad Travel (☎ 327 83 84; fax 329 80
19; e-mail sindbad@ryh.spb.su), owned by
he HI St Petersburg Hostel, is a genuine
Western-style student and discount air-ticket
)ffice, specialising in one-way and short or
10-advance purchase tickets. They're also
full service ticketing centres for Kilroy
Travel and STA, and can book onward youth
hostel bookings through the IBN system.
Basically they offer all the same services as
:he big guys they represent, and they have
friendly service from people who understand
what they're booking. They're at the HI St
Petersburg Hostel, 3-ya Sovietskaya ulitsa
28, on the ground floor.

American Express (at the Grand Hotel
Europe), believe it or not, does discounted
return tickets to European and American des-
:inations on Deutsche BA and other airlines.
Check their specials, sometimes advertised
in the *St Petersburg Press*. Other travel agencies are popping up all the time, so check the
St Petersburg Press for adverts.

Books & Bookshops
Reference Publications The 'big two'
books that are popular with local expatriates
are *The Traveller's Yellow Pages St Petersburg* and *Where in St Petersburg*, both
essentially pocket-sized yellow pages, the
latter more selective and narrower in scope
than the former. Both feature maps of the
city. See Books in the European Russia Facts
for the Visitor chapter for information on
how to get these (they're published and distributed in the USA), and on travel guides
and other books about St Petersburg. *Ves
Peterburg* (All Petersburg) is a full-sized,
Russian-published yellow pages available at
bookshops and kiosks throughout the city.

Bookshops So far there are no Western-
style bookshops here, but the Russian-run
bookshops are getting better all the time.
Start at Dom Knigi, the biggest bookshop in
town, which has some books in Western
languages plus books on Russian-language

courses, science and engineering, school
texts and, upstairs, maps and postcards. It's
on the corner of naberezhnaya kanala
Griboedova and Nevsky prospekt in the pre-
Revolutionary St Petersburg headquarters of
the Singer Sewing Machine company; walk
in, go to the back past the stairs, then turn left
and left again.

Grouped near the corner of Nevsky prospekt and ulitsa Bolshaya Morskaya (ulitsa
Gertsena) you'll find four bookshops facing
each other. Iskusstv, on the south-west
corner, is tiny but has a good collection of
real art books. Of the four, the one next door
to Iskusstv is the cheapest, and features some
Western-language books, Euro-Cart maps
and some stationery. It's also got a tacky
souvenir shop and a Baltiysky Bank cash
exchange desk that says it gives cash
advances for Visa and MasterCard. Across
Nevsky and west of the corner, the art bookshop is pretty much a rip-off, while on the
east side, Staraya Knigi has a good collection
of old books (including, perhaps, some
second-hand novels in English) and
other...er...old stuff.

Nevsky prospekt is lined from top to
bottom with smaller book and map shops
(there's another good one at Nevsky prospekt 141), and there are various others
around the city. Pedestrian subways are rife
with book stalls.

The HI St Petersburg Hostel sells internationally and locally produced travel guides,
including Lonely Planet guides.

Maps
It's no longer a big deal finding maps for
walking around; hotels and restaurants hand
them out as a matter of routine, and city,
regional and even country maps are readily
available at bookshops and kiosks. The
Russian-made regional topographical maps
that are available at larger bookshops are
generally quite good, though they're cumbersome as they can take up to 25 large
pages.

The most readily available commercially
produced map of St Petersburg is the US-
published *New St Petersburg City Map &*

Guide, available in English and Russian. *The Traveller's Yellow Pages City Map*, published in the USA by InfoServices Russia and printed by an Estonian firm, is good but the scale is somewhat erratic and the maps have little pictures of major sights which can be distracting. It does, however, have a unique and extremely useful English/Russian street index that pushes it ahead of the crowd. See Maps in the earlier European Russia Facts for the Visitor chapter for where to obtain these maps abroad. In St Petersburg you can find them in some hotels, shops and bookshops, and at the Airport Duty Free. *The New St Petersburg City Map & Guide* is also available from Russian Information Services (☎ 254 92 75).

The *Marshruty Gorodskogo Transporta* (*Municipal Transit Routes*) map published by St Petersburg's Culture and Tourism office is very useful and is available at kiosks along Nevsky prospekt. The *Turistskaya Skhema* (*Tourist Map*) is also now readily available at bookshops along Nevsky prospekt (try Art Books at Nevsky prospekt 20; Dom Knigi at No 28; or Knigi at No 141) and at kiosks on the busier streets. It's available in Russian, English and German.

Interesting for the central areas – and useful now that many streets are reverting to pre-communist names – is *Peterburg Leningrad Starye i Novye Grodskie Nazvania* (*Peterburg Leningrad Old and New City Names*), which gives the 1989 and 1878 names of most streets. We found it on sale at the Russian Museum and you could also try in antiquarian bookshops on Nevsky and Liteyny prospekts.

Media

Newspapers & Magazines The *St Petersburg Press* is making a real go of being a reliable and readable weekly English-language information paper. Its 'Prospekts' section is packed with practical information and listings of clubs, pubs, restaurants, museums, theatres etc. It's available at bookshops, hotels, restaurants and the youth hostels. It's also available online through the Internet, and runs a home page on the World Wide Web (point your browser at http://www.spb.su/) that features the paper as well as other services like photos of the city, room-by-room tours of the Hermitage etc. It's worth checking out.

Pulse is a slick colour monthly with tons of club, pub, nightlife and other information about the city, written with a very young and fresh outlook. It's available free in outlets all over the city.

The city's other English-language offering, the *Neva News*, is pathetic and sometimes laughably incoherent. The *Moscow Times* is available at the HI St Petersburg Hostel and Holiday Hostel and in some hotels, and so far it's free.

TV & Radio In addition to the national stations (see the European Russia Facts for the Visitor chapter for information on these as well as English-language radio), there's St Petersburg Television – a mix of news, soap operas and educational programming – and all the luxury hotels offer cable or satellite TV. Radio 1, 71.66 MHz, is a US-run venture that plays modern rock with some dabs of pop and alternative music thrown in. Radio Rox (102 FM) does rock and roll and cool traffic reports.

Film & Photography

Kodak Express has nine drop-off locations and two full-service shops in town, doing fast developing and selling a range of film at European prices. Main branches are at ulitsa Bolshaya Morskaya (ulitsa Gertsena) 32 (☎ 110 64 03) and Malaya Konyushennaya 7 (☎ 110 64 97). Agfa (☎ 311 99 74) does fast (if not one-hour) developing, and sells film and camera supplies on the 3rd floor of Nevsky prospekt 20. Fuji's shop near the Anichkov Bridge (☎ 314 49 36) does about the same; it's at naberezhnaya reki Fontanki 23. A great deal on Russian photo equipment can be had at the Photo Shop No 76 (☎ 232 19 02), Bolshoy prospekt (Petrograd Side) 63; it's open from 10 am to 7 pm. Specials at the time of writing included a Zenit body with 50 mm lens for US$50 and a top-of-the-line FC 122 with a huge lens for US$155.

For cheap passport photographs (US$0.50 for four) head for the machine inside the shop at Nevsky prospekt 128, which also has an exchange booth.

Warning

Whatever you do, don't drink St Petersburg tap water – it harbours *Giardia lamblia*, an intestinal parasite which can cause diarrhoea and at a time like that, fibrous Russian toilet paper feels like a steel file across your nether quarters), stomach cramps and nausea. Stick to bottled water, which is readily available at supermarkcts, 24-hour shops and hotels; avoid ice and, ideally, raw fruit and vegetables that may have come into contact with tap water. See the Health section in the earlier European Russia Facts for the Visitor chapter for more information.

Medical Services

Unless you're an uninsured US or South African resident and citizen, medical treatment in St Petersburg will be beneath the standards you're used to receiving at home. Nonetheless, St Petersburg is second only to Moscow and offers adequate treatment for most routine, and some emergency, treatment. More serious medical emergencies are best treated outside Russia; Finland is the best option. See European Russia Facts for the Visitor for information on health and health insurance issues.

The best bet for Western-quality treatment in St Petersburg is the American Medical Center (AMC; ☎ 119 61 01; fax 119 61 20), a US-run facility offering a huge range of medical services including prenatal, gynaecological and paediatric care, dentistry, 24-hour emergency care, on-site urgent care facilities, private ambulance services, house calls and 24-hour coordination of medical evacuations from the CIS. They also have a complete western pharmacy. 'Course, it's gonna cost ya: prices are stellar, with a basic check-up clocking in at a robust US$135 for members and US$185 for nonmembers and it's all uphill from there. HIV screening costs US$35, but you'll also need

a counselling session; the total package price for a visa AIDS test is US$75.

But for routine matters, a Russian poliklinika is often able to provide perfectly adequate care. We asked AMC doctors where they'd send their family members if the AMC weren't an option: they all said Poliklinika No 2 (☎ 292 62 72), the former clinic of choice for diplomatic staff, at Moskovsky prospekt 22; or Gastello Hospital (☎ 291 79 60; 293 70 10) at ulitsa Gastello 20. For more listings, check *The Traveller's Yellow Pages*.

Ambulance The state-run ambulance service is still free; Russian-speakers can get help by dialling (☎ 03). Saying it's for a foreigner may help get faster and better service. Private ambulance service is available through the AMC, and house calls are available 24 hours a day.

Pharmacies Pharmacies (singular *apteka*, which is what you should ask for) are located all over the city. Generally, pharmacies in St Petersburg are almost, but not really, well stocked, and many have Western medications. The higher quality ones have everything you might need.

Apteka Petrofarm is an all-night pharmacy that's packed with Western everything. The entrance is at the corner of Nevsky and Bolshaya Konyushennaya. The night entrance (for use from 9 pm to 8 am) is around the corner at Bolshaya Konyushennaya 14; go through the archway, turn to the right and it's at the top of the small staircase. Apteka No 4 at Nevsky prospekt 5 is a good pharmacy with a large range of Western stuff and tampons. There's also a full Western pharmacy at the AMC.

Religious Services

There are a number of English and other Western-language services in town; check the *St Petersburg Press* for current information during your stay. Some services in English (E), German (G), Hebrew (H), Russian (R) and Latin (L), and places of worship, follow:

Anglican/Episcopalian Open Christianity Centre (☎ 277 87 50), Chernoretsky Pereulok 4/6, metro Ploshchad Alexandra Nevskogo – services first Sunday of month at 10 am (E)

Armenian Church of St Catherine (☎ 311 57 95), Nevsky prospekt 40/42

Church of Jesus Christ of Latter Day Saints (☎ 119 61 48), Dom Aktyor, Nevsky prospekt 86 – services daily at 9.30 am and 1 pm, Sunday school etc (E, R)

Christ Church (☎ 110 18 70), Professora Popova ulitsa 47 – services Wednesday and Sunday (E, R)

Chabad-Lubavitch (☎ 113 62 09), Lermontovsky prospekt 2 – Shabbas services Friday at sundown, daily services at 9.30 am etc (H)

Evangelical Lutheran Church (☎ 311 24 23), St Anne's Church (Spartak Cinema), Saltikova-Shchedrina ulitsa 8, metro Cherneshevskaya – service at 10.30 am Sunday (G)

Mosque of the Congregation of Muslims (☎ 233 98 19), Kronverksky prospekt 7 – open daily from 10 am to 7 pm

Buddhist Temple (☎ 239 13 41), Primorsky prospekt 91, metro Chyornaya Rechka

Nondenominational Services (☎ 292 06 05), Oranienbaumskaya ulitsa 5, room 50, 3rd floor, – bible classes, services etc (E, R)

Our Lady of Lourdes (Roman Catholic; ☎ 272 50 02), Kovensky pereulok 7 (near ulitsa Mayakovskaya) – Sunday Mass 11.30 am (L, R), 1.30 pm (E), 5 pm (G)

Russian Orthodox services are available at several locations throughout the city. Check the *St Petersburg Press*, *The Traveller's Yellow Pages* or *Where in St Petersburg* for listings.

THE HISTORIC HEART

For two centuries the Russian government was centred along the half-km strip of territory that stretched from the Winter Palace to ploshchad Dekabristov. Today its great buildings are empty of political muscle but stand as monuments to the extravagant splendours of tsardom.

Dvortsovaya Ploshchad

From Nevsky Prospekt or Gostiny Dvor metro, a 15-minute walk along Nevsky prospekt – or a quick bus or trolleybus ride – brings you to Dvortsovaya ploshchad (Palace Square), where the stunning green, white and gold **Winter Palace** (Zimny dvorets) appears like a mirage, its Rococo profusion of columns, windows and recesses topped by rows of larger-than-life statues. A residence of tsars from 1762 to 1917, it' now the biggest part of the Hermitage ar museum.

During Bloody Sunday (9 January 1905) tsarist troops fired on workers who had peaceably gathered in the square – the shoot ings sparked the 1905 revolution. And it wa across Dvortsovaya ploshchad that the much exaggerated storming of the Winter Palace took place during the 1917 October Revolu tion. There *was* gunfire before the Provisional government in the palace surren dered to the revolutionaries, but the famou charge across the square was largely invented by the film maker Eisenstein.

The 47.5 metre Alexander Column in the square commemorates the 1812 victory ove Napoleon and is named after Alexander I The former General Staff buildings of the Russian army (1819-29) curve round the south of the square in two great blocks joined by arches over ulitsa Bolshaya Morskaya which are topped by a chariot of victory which is another monument to the Napole onic wars.

Admiralty

The gilded spire of the old Admiralty across the road from Dvortsovaya ploshchad is an easy St Petersburg landmark. It's visible along most of the three streets – Gorokhovaya ulitsa, Vosnesensky and Nevsky prospekts, which originate practi cally at its front door. This spot was the headquarters of the Russian navy from 1711 to 1917, and today the building houses a naval college. Constructed in 1806-23 to the designs of Andreyan Zakharov, it's a fore most example of the Russian Empire style of classical architecture, with its rows of white columns and plentiful reliefs and statuary. One feature you can get a close look at is the nymphs holding giant globes flanking the main gate. Its gardens and fountains are par ticularly lovely in summer – it's worth walking three or four blocks out of your way to or from the Hermitage to pass through these.

Ploshchad Dekabristov

West of the Admiralty, ploshchad Dekabristov (Decembrists' Square) is named after the first feeble attempt at a Russian revolution – the Decembrists' Uprising of 14 December 1825. Inspired by radical ideas from France during the Napoleonic campaigns, young officers tried to depose the new Tsar Nicholas I by drawing up troops in the square. But they allowed their opponents to argue with them and were finally dispersed with grapeshot. Most of the leaders ended up on the gallows or in Siberia.

The most famous statue of Peter the Great, the **Bronze Horseman**, with his mount rearing above the snake of treason, stands at the river end of the square. This statue, along with the view of the SS Peter & Paul Fortress against raised drawbridges during summer white nights (when the sun doesn't set), has become the trademark image of the new spirit of St Petersburg. The inscription reads *To Peter I from Catherine II – 1782*. It was cast for Catherine the Great by the Frenchman Etienne Falconet.

Most of the west side of the square is occupied by the Central State Historical Archives in the former Senate and Synod buildings, built in 1829-34. These institutions had been set up by Peter the Great to run the civil administration and the Orthodox Church.

The **Manege Central Exhibition Hall** (☎ 314 82 53) across the street used to be the Horse Guards' Riding School (constructed 1804-07 from a design by Quarenghi). It's now got rotating exhibitions and is open daily, except Thursday, from 11 am to 7 pm. Admission for foreigners is US$0.40.

St Isaac's Cathedral

The golden dome of bulky St Isaac's Cathedral

St Isaac's Cathedral

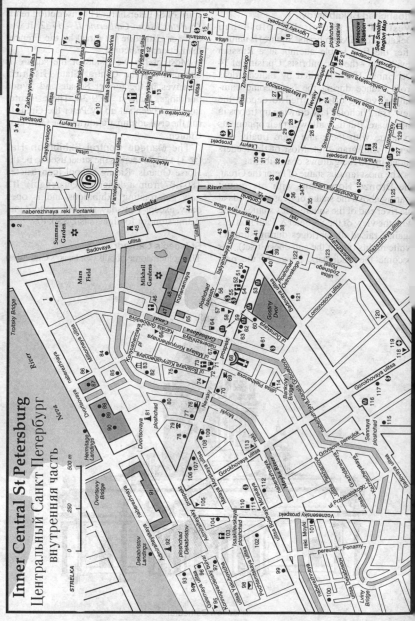

Inner Central St Petersburg
Центральный Санкт Петербург
внутренняя часть

PLACES TO STAY

13 Hotel Rus
   Гостиница Русь
19 Hotel Oktyabrskaya
   Гостиница Октябрьская
26 Nevskij Palace Hotel
   Гостиница Невский
   Дворец
57 Grand Hotel Europe
110 Hotel Astoria
   Гостиница Астория
114 Student Dormitory
   Общежитие

PLACES TO EAT

5 Kiosks
   Киоски
7 Café (Summer only)
   Кафе
16 Springtime Shwarma
   Шварма
18 Carrols Restaurant
   Ресторан Карролс
22 Baskin Robbins Café
   Кафе Мороженое Баскин
23 John Bull Pub
   Джон Бул Пуб
24 Restoran Nevsky
   Ресторан Невский
28 Afrodite
   Restaurant/Beer
   Garden
   Ресторан Афродита
42 Kafe 01
   Кафе 01
52 Grillmaster
   Грилмастер
55 Nevsky 40
   Невский 40
58 Sadko's
   Ресторан Садко
63 Nevsky 27 Bakery
   Булочная кондитерская
64 Chayka Café
   Кафе Чайка
66 Restaurant\Café St
   Petersburg
   Ресторан и Кафе Санкт
   Петербург
69 Café Bon Jour
   Кафе Бон Жур
74 Subway
   Метро
76 Kafe Literaturnoe
   Кафе Литературное

86 1001 Nights
   Ресторан 1001 Ночь
94 Senat Bar
   Сенат Бар
95 Le Bistro Café
   Кафе - Бистро
105 Tandoor Indian
   Restaurant
   Ресторан Тандур
113 Pizza Hut
   Пицца Хат
118 Restoran Na Fontanke
   Ресторан на Фонтанке
120 Montreal Steak
125 Mollies Irish Bar
   Молис ирландский бар

OTHER

1 Marble Palace
   Мраморный дворец
2 Summer Palace
   Летний дворец
3 GAI Checkpoint
   ГАИ
4 MVD (aka KGB's 'Big
   House')
   МВД
6 Mir Musika
7 US Consulate
   Консульство США
10 Central OVIR
   ОВИР
11 Spaso-
   Preobrazhensky
   Cathederal
   Спасо-Преображенский
   собор
12 Bulgarian Consulate
   Консульство Болгарии
14 Bolshoy Teatr Kukol
   (Big Puppet Theatre)
   Большой театр кукол
15 Holiday 24-Hour
   Market
   Супермаркет (24-часа)
17 TNT Express World-
   wide
21 Pharmacy
   Аптека
27 Federal Express
29 Westpost and Peter
   TIPS
30 Sporting Goods
   Спортивний магазин
31 Babylon
   Вавилон

32 Cosmos Supermarket
   (24 hours)
   Супермаркет Космос
33 Domenico's
   Клуб Доменикоз
34 Police Station
   Полицейское
   управление
35 Cultural Centres
   Культурный центр
36 Beloselsky-
   Belozersky Palace
   Белосельский-
   Белозерский дворец
37 Anichkov Bridge
   Landing
   Аничков мост пристань
38 Anichkov Palace
   Аничков дворец
39 Catherine II Statue
   from Art Market
   Памятник Екатерини
   II из картинный
   рынок
40 Public Library
   Библиотека
41 Yeliseevsky Market
   Гастроном
   Елисеевский
43 Zimny Stadion
   Зимний стадион
44 Circus
   Цирк
45 Engineers' Castle
   Инженерный замок
46 Church of the Resur-
   rection of Christ
   Храм Воскресения
   Христова
47 Benois Building
   Корпус Бенуа
48 Russian Museum
   Русский музей
49 Museum of
   Ethnography
   Музей этнографии
50 Passazh Department
   Store
   Универмаг Пассаж
51 Supermarket
   Супермаркет
54 Armenian Church
   Армянская церковь
56 Philharmonia Large
   Hall
   Большой зал
   Филармонии
   continued next page

continued from previous page

60 Theatre Booking
    Office
    Театральная касса
61 Train Ticket Centre
    Железнодорожные
    билетные кассы
62 Central Art Salon
    Центральный
    художественный
    салон
65 Maly Theatre
    Малый театр
67 Dom Knigi
    Дом книги
68 Kazan Cathedral
    Казанский собор
70 Stroganov Palace
    Строгановский дворец
71 Koff Beer Garden
72 24-hour Pharmacy
    Аптека (24-Час)
73 Dutch Church
    Голландская Церков
75 DLT Department
    Store
77 Staraya Kniga
    Старая книга
78 Nevsky Prospekt 14
    Невский проспект 14
79 Central Telephone
    Office
    Телефон
80 General Staff Building
    Здание Главного штаба
81 Alexander Column
    Александровская колонна
82 Glinka Capella
    Хоровая капелла имени
    М.И. Глинки
83 Pushkin Flat-Museum
    Музей-квартира А.С.
    Пушкина
84 French Consulate
    Консульство Франции
85 Japanese Consulate
    Консульство Японии
87 Hermitage Theatre
    Эрмитажный театр
88 Large Hermitage
    Великой Эрмитаж

89 Little Hermitage
    Малый Эрмитаж
90 Winter Palace
    Зимний дворец
91 Admiralty
    Адмиралтейство
92 Bronze Horseman
    Медный всадник
93 Senate
    Сенат
96 Synod
    Синод
97 Central Exhibition
    Hall
    Центральный
    выставочный зал
98 Main Post Office
    Главпочтамт
99 American Business
    Center
    Американский деловой
    центр
100 Yusupov Palace
    Юсуповский дворец
101 Lufthansa Office
    Луфтханса
102 St Petersburg Travel
    Company
    С. Петербурская компания
    путешествий
103 St Isaac's Cathedral
    Исаакиевский собор
104 Finnair Office
    Финнаир
106 Beryozka
    Берёзка
107 Aeroflot
    Аэрофлот
108 Bookshop
    Книги
109 Bookshop
    Книги
111 Air France
    Аир Франце
112 Airline Offices
    Конторы авиакомпаний
115 Le Shop
117 Aeroflot Ticket Office
    Аэрофлот

119 American Medical
    Center
    Американский
    Медицинский Центр
121 Vorontsov Palace
    Дворец Воронцова
122 Pushkin Theatre
    Театр драмы имени
    А.С. Пушкина
123 Vaganova School of
    Choreography
    Хореографическое
    училище имени
    Профессора А.Я.
    Ваганова
124 Maly Dramatic
    Theatre
    Малый драмати-
    ческий театр
127 Kuznechny Market
    Кузнечный рынок
128 Vladimir Church
    Владимирская
    церковь
129 Dostoevsky Museum
    Музей Ф.М.
    Достоевского
130 Arctic & Antarctic
    Museum
    Арктический и
    Антарктический
    музей

METRO STATIONS

8   Chernyshevskaya
    Чернышевская
20 Ploshchad Vosstania
    Площадь Восстания
25 Mayakovskaya
    Маяковская
53 Gostiny Dvor
    Гостиный двор
59 Nevsky Prospekt
    Невский проспект
116 Sennaya Ploshchad
    Сенная площадь
126 Vladimirskaya
    Владимирская

(Isaakievsky sobor; ☎ 315 97 32, 210 92 06), looming just south of ploshchad Dekabristov, is a dominant piece of the St Petersburg skyline. The Frenchman Ricard de Montferrand won a competition organised by Alexander I to design the cathedral in 1818. It took so long to build – until 1858 – that Alexander's successor Nicholas I was able to insist on a more grandiose structure than Montferrand had planned. Special ships and a railway had to be built to carry the granite for the huge pillars from Finland. There's a statue of Montferrand holding a model of the cathedral on the west façade.

Inside, St Isaac's is open as a museum from 11 am to 6 pm Thursday to Monday, to 5 pm Tuesday and is closed Wednesday and the last Monday of the month. It's obscenely lavish. Since 1990, after a 62-year gap, services have been held here on major religious holidays and St Isaac's may return to full Church control before long. Admission is about US$8.50 (US$4.25 for ISIC holders), photos (no tripods or flashes) cost another US$8.50 and video cameras command a whopping US$21.

Don't miss the sublime city views from the colonnade (kolonnada) around the drum of the dome, which is open from 11 am to 5 pm Thursday to Monday, to 4 pm Tuesday, closed Wednesday. You need separate tickets for the colonnade, and there are often long queues to pay the US$2.80 (US$1 for ISIC holders), another US$3.10 for photos and US$10.50 for video. You could avoid the crowds by joining any tour from the usual suspects – try St Petersburg Travel Company across the street (St Isaac's is often combined with the Peter & Paul Fortress). Note that it's several hundred steps up the spiral staircase to the colonnade, and there are no escalators. Every printed resource on this matter seems to come up with a different number; we got bored after counting 180, though 262 seems to be reasonable, but a couple of guides put the number at 562; send your totals to Lonely Planet Steps Contest, c/o the Federal Counter-Intelligence Service, Lubyanka ulitsa 1/3, Moscow.

St Petersburg History Museum

About 600 metres west of ploshchad Dekabristov, at naberezhnaya Krasnogo Flota 44, this museum focuses on St Petersburg since the 1917 revolution. Though there's no material in English, it's good on the 1941-44 siege; it's open from 11 am to 5 or 6 pm, closed Wednesday.

THE HERMITAGE

One of the world's great art galleries, set in a magnificent palace from which tsars ruled Russia for one-and-a-half centuries, the State Hermitage (Gosudarstvenny ermitazh) fully lives up to its reputation as one of the country's chief glories. You can be absorbed for days by its treasures and still come out wishing for more.

The enormous collection amounts almost to a history of Western European art, displaying the full range of artists such as Rembrandt, Rubens and Picasso, and schools including the Florentine and Venetian Renaissance, Impressionism and postimpressionism. And there are also Prehistoric, Egyptian, Russian and Oriental sections plus excellent temporary exhibitions.

The vastness of the place – five main buildings, of which the Winter Palace alone has 1057 rooms and 117 staircases – and its huge numbers of visitors demand a little planning. It may be useful to make a reconnaissance tour first, then return another day to enjoy your favourite bits.

The State Hermitage consists of five linked buildings along riverside Dvortsovaya naberezhnaya. From west to east they are the Winter Palace, the Little Hermitage, the Old and New Hermitages (sometimes grouped together and called the Large Hermitage) and the Hermitage Theatre.

The art collection is on all three floors of the Winter Palace and the main two floors of the Little and Large Hermitages. The Hermitage Theatre isn't generally open.

See the following pages for floor plans and a guide to the Hermitage's stupendous collection.

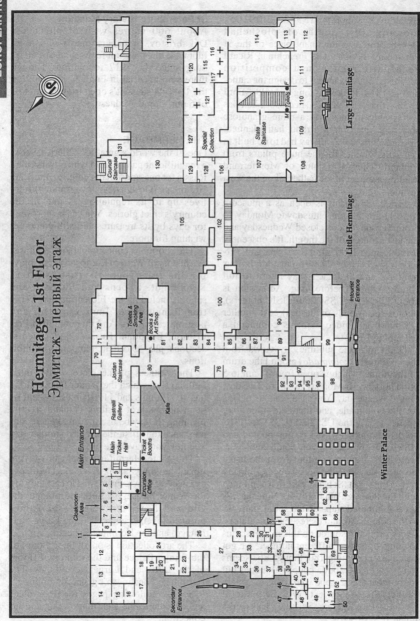

Hermitage – 1st Floor
Эрмитаж – первый этаж

Large Hermitage

Little Hermitage

Winter Palace

Council Staircase

Special Collection

State Staircase

M Toilets F

Jordan Staircase

Rastrelli Gallery

Kafe

Toilets & Smoking Area

Books & Art Shop

Main Entrance

Main Ticket Hall

Ticket Booths

Excursion Office

Chakroom Area

Intourist Entrance

Secondary Entrance

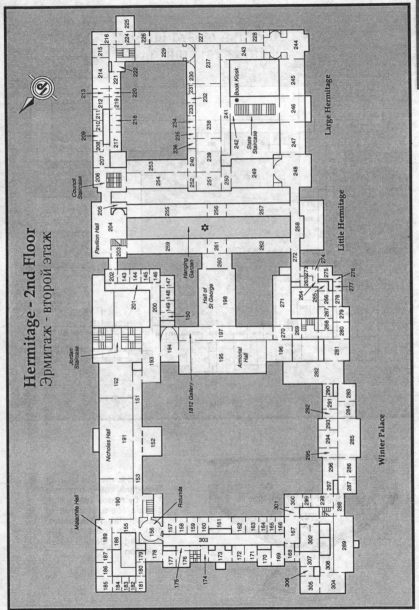

Hermitage - 2nd Floor
Эрмитаж - второй этаж

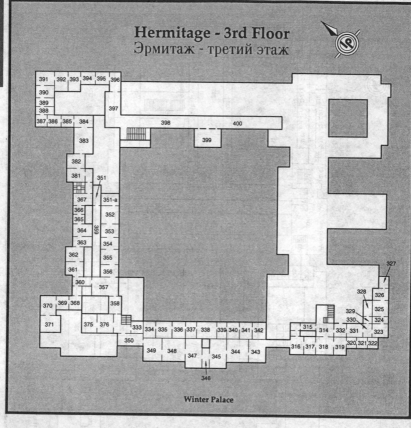

Hermitage - 3rd Floor
Эрмитаж - третий этаж

Winter Palace

The two-tonne Cauldron of Tamerlane, cast in bronze in 1399 by master smith Abd-al-Aziz for a mosque in present-day Kazakhstan, and now part of the Hermitage's Central Asian collection

The Hermitage Collection

This is a list of many of the items within the Hermitage, verified in May 1995. While changes do occur, the head curator has said that things should remain static for the next few years at least. That said, consider these words of wisdom: 'Everything will remain exactly where it is except for those things which do not.'

Winter Palace, 1st floor 1-33 Russian Prehistoric artefacts: **11** Palaeolithic and Mesolithic, 300th to 6th millennia BC; **12** Neolithic and Bronze Ages 5th to 1st millennia BC, including petroglyphs from the second half of the third millenia BC taken from the northeast shores of Lake Ozero; **13** Bronze Age, western steppes 4th to 2nd millennia BC; **14** Bronze Age, southern Siberia and Kazakhstan 2nd millennium to 9th century BC, fine bronze animals; **15-18** Scythian culture 7th to 3rd centuries BC – but the best Scythian material is in the Special Collection; **19-20** forest steppes 7th to 4th centuries BC; **21-23 & 26** material from Altai Mountain burial mounds, including **26** human and horse corpses preserved for over 2000 years complete with hair and teeth; **24** Iron Age, Eastern Europe, including Finno-Ugrians and Balts, 8th century BC to 12th century AD; **33** southern steppes tribes 3rd century BC to 10th century AD – some fine Sarmatian gold.

34-69 The Russian 'East': **34-39** Central Asia, 4th century BC to 13th century AD; **55-66** Caucasus and Transcaucasia 10th century BC to 16th century AD, including **56** Urartu 9th to 7th century BC, **59** Dagestan 6th to 11th centuries AD, **66** 14th-century Italian colonies in Crimea; **67-69** Golden Horde 13th to 14th centuries.

100 Ancient Egypt: a fine collection, much of it found by Russian archaeologists; sadly no labelling in English, except the signs saying 'Please Do Not Touch'.

Little Hermitage, 1st floor 101-102 Roman marble.

New Hermitage, 1st floor Ancient classical culture: **106-109 & 127** Roman sculpture 1st century BC to 4th century AD; **111-114** Ancient Greece 8th to 2nd centuries BC, mostly ceramics and sculpture; **115-117 & 121** Greek colonies around northern Black Sea, 7th century BC to 3rd century AD; **128** the huge 19th-century jasper Kolyvanskaya Vase from Siberia; **130-131** Ancient Italy 7th to 2nd centuries BC, including Etruscan vases and bronze mirrors.

Winter Palace – 2nd floor 143-146 Spanish art from the 16th to 19th centuries, **147-189** Russian culture and art: **147-150** 10th to 15th centuries; **151** 15th to 17th centuries; **152** icons, ceramics, jewellery etc from 'Moscow Baroque' period, first half 17th century; **153** items relating to Peter the Great; **155-166** late 17th, early 18th century, including **155** Moorish Dining Room, and **156** Rotunda with a bust of Peter the Great and a brass Triumphal Pillar, topped by a Rastrelli-created statue of Peter; **157-first half of 161** Petrovskaya Gallereya, including lathing machinery used by Peter, and **160** mosaic of Peter by Lomonosov, **161** a chandelier partly built by the Great Guy; **167-173** mid to end 18th century – spot the bizarre 1772 tapestry image of Australia (167); **175-187** (start at **187** and work your way back) Rooms occupied by the last imperial family, now displaying 19th-century interior design, including **178** Nicholas II's Gothic library; **188** Small Dining Room (Malaya stolovaya), where the Provisional Government was arrested by the Bolsheviks on 26 October 1917; **189** Malachite Hall (Malakhitovy zal) with two tonnes of gorgeous green malachite columns, boxes, bowls and urns.

190-192 Neva Enfilade, one of two sets of state rooms for ceremonies and balls: **190** Concert Hall (Kontsertny zal) for small balls, with an 18th-century silver coffin for the remains of Alexandr

Nevsky; **191** Great or Nicholas Hall (Bolshoy zal), scene of great winter balls now used, like **192**, the Fore Hall, for temporary exhibitions.

193-198 Great Enfilade, the second series of state rooms: **193** Field Marshals' Hall; **194** Peter the Great's Hall (Petrovsky zal), with his throne; **195** Armorial Hall, bright and gilt encrusted, displaying 16th to 19th-century west European silver.

197 The 1812 Gallery: hung with portraits of Russian and allied Napoleonic war leaders.

198 Hall of St George or Great Throne Room: once a state room, now used for temporary exhibitions.

200-202 West European tapestry 16th to 19th centuries.

263-268 German art 15th to 18th centuries, including Dürer and Lucas Cranach the Elder.

269-271 West European 18th-century porcelain (**271** was the tsars' cathedral).

272-289 French art 15th to 18th centuries, including: **272-273** tapestries, ceramics, metalwork; **279** Poussin; **280** Lorrain; **284** Watteau.

298-302 British art 16th to 19th centuries, including: **299** Reynolds; **300** Gainsborough's *Lady in Blue.*

303 'Dark Corridor': West European tapestry 16th to 18th centuries, mainly Flanders. Follow the confusing trail through **167** and **308** to get to **304**, a wonderful collection of Western European stone engravings from the 13th to the 19th centuries; **305** the Burgundy Hall, containing English and French Porcelain; **306** Maria Alexandrovna's bedroom; and **307** the Blue Bedroom, French, Austrian and German porcelain.

Little Hermitage – 2nd floor 204 Pavilion Hall (Pavilonny zal): a sparkling white-and-gold room with lovely chandeliers, tables, galleries, and columns. The south windows look on to Catherine the Great's hanging garden; the floor mosaic in front of them is copied from a Roman bath. Roman and Florentine mosaics from the 18th and 19th centuries, and the amazing *Peacock Clock,* a revolving dial in one of the toadstools which tells the time and on the hour (when it's working) has the peacock, toadstools, owl and cock come to life.

258 Flemish art 17th century.

259 West European applied art 11th to 15th centuries.

261-262 Dutch art 15th and 16th centuries.

Large Hermitage – 2nd floor 206 next to the Council (Soviet) Staircase with its marble, malachite and glass triumphal arch; **207-215** Florentine art 13th to 16th centuries: **209** 15th century, including Fra Angelico; **213** 15th and early 16th centuries, including two small Botticellis, Filippino Lippi, Perugino; **214** Russia's only two Leonardo da Vincis – the *Benois Madonna* and the strikingly different *Madonna Litta,* both named after their last owners; **215** Leonardo's pupils, including Correggio and Andrea del Sarto.
216 Italian Mannerist art 16th century – and a view over the little Winter Canal to the Hermitage Theatre.

217-222 Venetian art, mainly 16th century: **217** Giorgione's *Judith (Yudif)*; **219** Titian's *Portrait of a Young Woman (Portret molodoy zhenshchinu)* and *Flight into Egypt (Begstvo v Egipet)*, and more by Giorgione; **221** more Titian, including *Danaë* and *St Sebastian*; **222** Paolo Veronese's *Mourning of Christ (Oplakivanie Khrista)*.

226-227 Loggia of Raphael: Quarenghi's 1780s copy of a gallery in the Vatican with murals by Raphael.

228-238 Italian art 16th to 18th centuries: **228** 16th-century ceramics; **229** Raphael and disciples, including his *Madonna Conestabile* and *Holy Family (Svyatoe Semeystvo)*, plus wonderful ceramics and decorations AND Russia's only Michelangelo, a marble statue of a Crouching Boy; **230-236** always seem closed, but they should contain, **232** Caravaggio and Bernini; **237** 16th-century paintings, including Paolo Veronese and Tintoretto; **238** 17th and 18th-century painters, including Canaletto and Tiepolo, also two huge 19th-century Russian malachite vases. **237 & 238** have lovely ceilings.

239-240 (temporarily in 143-146) Spanish art 16th to 18th centuries: **239** Goya's *Portrait of the Actress Antonia Zarate (Antonii Sarate)*, Murillo's *Boy with a Dog*, Diego Velazquez' *Breakfast*; **240** El Greco's marvellous *St Peter and St Paul*.

241 Marble sculptures, Antonio Canova and Albert Thorwaldsen; **243** The Giddyap Room; Western European armour and weaponry from the 15th to 17th centuries, featuring four 16th-century German suits of armour atop armoured (and, thankfully, stuffed) horses.

244-247 (closed at the time of writing for renovation, allegedly until 1997) Flemish art 17th century: **245** savage hunting and market scenes by Snyders; **246** Van Dyck portraits; **247** a large room displaying the amazing range of Rubens, including *Descent from the Cross (Snyatie c kresta)*, *Bacchus (Bakkh)*, *The Union of Earth and Water (Soyuz zemli i vody)*, *Portrait of a Curly-Haired Old Man (Golova starika)*, and *Roman Charity (Ottselyubie rimlyanki)*.

248-252 & 254 Dutch art 17th century: **249** landscapes and portraits by Ruisdael, Hals, Bol and others; **250** 18th-century Delft ceramics; **254** more than 20 Rembrandts ranging from lighter, more detailed early canvases like *Abraham's Sacrifice of Isaac (Zhertvoprinoshenie Avraama)* and *Danaë* through *The Holy Family (Svyatoe semeystvo)* of 1645 to darker, penetrating late works like *The Return of the Prodigal Son* and two canvases entitled *Portrait of an Old Man (Portret starika)*, plus work by Rembrandt's pupils, including Bol.

Winter Palace, 3rd floor An approximately chronological order in which to view the French art collection is **314, 332-328** in descending order, **325-315** in descending order and **343-350** in ascending order. The staircase beside room **269** on floor 2 brings you out by room**314**.

314-320, 321-325, 328-332 French art 19th century: **321-325, 328, 329** mostly Barbizon School, including Corot, Courbet, Millet; **331** Delacroix.

315 Impressionists and postimpressionists: **315** Rodin sculptures; **316** Gauguin, Tahitian works; **317** Van Gogh, Rousseau, Forain, Latour; **318** Cézanne, Pissarro; **319** Pissarro, Monet, Sisley; **320** Renoir, Degas.

334 20th-century European and American art.

334-342 European art 19th century, including landscapes by Caspar David Friedrich.

343, 349-350 French art 19th to 20th centuries: Bonnard, Vlaminck, Marquet, Leger and others.

344-345 Picasso: **344** mainly blue and Cubist periods; **345** Cubist and later periods.

346-348 Matisse.

351-371, 381-396 Oriental culture and art: **351-357, 359-364** China and Tibet, an excellent collection; **358** Indonesia; **365-367** Mongolia; **368-371** India; **381-387** Byzantium, Near and Middle East.

398 & 400 Coins.

Special Collection To get into this mind-bending display of crafted gold, silver and jewels off **121** you must either book in with a group at hotel concierge desks or at the St Petersburg Travel Company, or hire a guide from the deep thinkers in the Hermitage's excursion office. Even at these prices places are scarce, so try to book it as soon as you reach St Petersburg. The excursion office at the museum is to the right as you enter, up the small staircase and towards the back, and it's the last door on the left-hand side.

The focus is a hoard of fabulously worked Scythian and Greek gold and silver from the Caucasus, Crimea and Ukraine, dating from the 7th to 2nd centuries BC when the Scythians, who dominated the region, and the Greeks, in colonies around the northern Black Sea, crafted the pieces to accompany the dead into the afterlife. The treasure was unearthed from graves in the late 19th century. The rest of the collection is European jewellery, precious metals and stones of the 16th to 19th centuries, amassed by tsars from Peter the Great onwards. ■

History

The present Baroque/Rococo Winter Palace was commissioned from Rastrelli in 1754 by Empress Elizabeth. Catherine the Great and her successors had most of the interior remodelled in classical style by 1837. That year a fire destroyed most of the interior, but it was restored virtually identically. It remained an imperial home until 1917, though the last two tsars spent more time in other St Petersburg palaces.

The classical Little Hermitage was built for Catherine the Great as a retreat that would also house the art collection started by Peter the Great, which she expanded. At the river end of the Large Hermitage is the Old Hermitage, which also dates from her time. At its south end, facing ulitsa Millionnaya, is

the New Hermitage, which was built for Nicholas II to hold the still-growing art collection and was opened to the public for the first time in 1852. The Hermitage Theatre was built in the 1780s by the Classicist Quarenghi, who thought it one of his finest works.

The art collection benefited when the state took over aristocrats' collections after the revolution, but Stalin sold some treasures – including about 15 Rembrandts – for foreign currency. The famous Impressionist and postimpressionist collections of the pre-Revolutionary Moscow industrialists Sergey Shchukin and Ivan Morozov were moved to the Hermitage in 1948.

In 1995 the Hermitage ran a highly controversial temporary display, called 'Hidden

Treasures Revealed', composed entirely of art captured by the Red Army in 1945. The exhibit contained 74 paintings, among them notably works by Monet, Degas, Renoir, Cezanne, Picasso, Matisse and zillions more, almost all never before publicly displayed. After the exhibition ended in October 1995, the collection was to be returned to storage, though a huge political debate raged as to whether the paintings belonged back in Germany, where they might see the light of exhibition once again. Stay tuned.

Admission

The Hermitage (☎ 311 34 65) is open from 10.30 am to 5.30 or 6 pm daily, except Sunday and Monday; until 5 pm Sunday and closed Monday. The main ticket hall is inside the main entrance on the river side of the Winter Palace. In summer only there are also ticket kiosks outside a secondary entrance at the west end of the Winter Palace, but neither kiosks nor entrance are always open.

The dual pricing system in place here (whereby Westerners pay the rouble equivalent of about US$8 to US$9 while Russians pay less than US$0.20) infuriates many visitors, but it is not about to change. Still photographs, but not tripods or flashes, are permitted, though you'll have to pay a US$3 charge; to bring in a video camera costs US$7. Unless your Russian's good, forget about getting in for the Russian price – these babushkas have an eagle eye for Western running shoes, bum bags, University of Whatever sweatshirts etc.

Tickets entitle you to wander freely (crowds permitting!), and the last are sold an hour before closing time. At busy times the queues can be horrendous and you might wait well over an hour to get in. On a wet November Tuesday, there'll hardly be a queue at all.

To avoid queues altogether, you can join a standard tour, which whizzes round the main parts in about an hour and a half but at least provides an introduction to the place in English. It's easy enough to 'lose' the group and stay on till closing time. The tours take place most afternoons. Tours can be arranged at hotels, the St Petersburg Travel Company, other travel agents, or with the Hermitage itself; the tours' office is down the corridor to the right as you enter, up the stairs and the last door on the left.

The bufet is hardly worth queuing for; take your own snacks if you plan a long visit.

Orientation

The rooms are numbered. The river is on the north side and Dvortsovaya ploshchad is south. There's only space to show 15% to 20% of the collection, so the works on view are changed from time to time and sometimes rooms are closed. Only a few sections have any English labelling.

From the main ticket hall, the Rastrelli Gallery (which has a few book and card stalls usually selling small Hermitage plans in Russian) leads to the white marble Jordan Staircase, with windows and mirrors on all sides, which takes you up to floor 2 of the Winter Palace. The staircase is one of the few parts of the interior to maintain its original Rastrelli appearance.

See the list under The Hermitage Collection for a thorough run-down on what's in all the rooms at the time of writing. If your time is limited, the following route takes in the major highlights (room numbers are in bold type):

Winter Palace, 2nd floor 189 Malachite Hall; 190-198 great state rooms.

Large Hermitage, 2nd floor 207-215 Florentine art 13th to 16th centuries; 217-222 & 237 Venetian art 16th century; 229-236 more Italian art 16th century; 238 Italian art of the 17th and 18th centuries; 239-240 (temporarily located in 143-146) Spanish art 16th to 18th centuries; 245-247 Flemish art 17th century; 249-252 & 254 Dutch art 17th century.

Winter Palace, 3rd floor 315-320 Impressionists and postimpressionists; 344-348 Picasso and Matisse.

NEVSKY PROSPEKT

Russia's most famous street runs four km from the Admiralty to the Alexandr Nevsky Monastery, from which it takes its name. The inner two-and-a-half km to Moscow Station is St Petersburg's seething main avenue, the city's shopping centre and focus of its entertainment and street life. Pushing through its shopping-bag-clutching crowds is an essential St Petersburg experience.

Today a walk down Nevsky is a walk into the heart of the new Russia: a buzzing, swirling mishmash of new and colourful shop fronts, restaurants, bars, toy shops, art galleries, banks and perfumeries that's packed to overflowing with tourists and natives, workers and beggars, scamrunners, pickpockets, purse snatchers, yahoos and religious fanatics, Russians and expats – and all of them are shoving past on their way to the action.

Nevsky prospekt was laid out in the early years of St Petersburg as the start of the main road to Novgorod and soon became dotted with fine buildings, squares and bridges. Today five metro stations – Nevsky Prospekt, Gostiny Dvor, Mayakovskaya, Ploshchad Vosstania and Ploshchad Alexandra Nevskogo – are scattered along its length, and buses and trolleybuses hunt in packs: see the Getting Around section later in this chapter for useful numbers.

The 1994 Goodwill Games brought fresh coats of paint for all Nevsky's treasures, and a new layer of asphalt for St Petersburg's surface-of-the-moon-like streets; Nevsky's brightly coloured buildings – including the newly renovated Nevskij Palace Hotel, the Belozersky Palace, the House of Journalists, Yeliseevsky's food shop (back to private ownership after 74 years), the Grand Hotel Europe, Dom Knigi and the Kazansky Sobor – have not looked this good since St Petersburg's heyday at the turn of the 20th century.

Admiralty End

Inner Nevsky, ulitsa Gogolya and ulitsa Bolshaya Morskaya (ulitsa Gertsena) were the heart of the pre-Revolutionary financial district, and if Credit Lyonnais Russie (back in Russia after the 'late unpleasantness'), The Russian Bank of Trade and Industry and Baltiysky Bank get their way, it will be again; all of these institutions have headquarters or offices in this area today.

Tchaikovsky died at ulitsa Gogolya 13. The wall of Nevsky prospekt 14, a school, bears a blue-and-white **stencilled sign** maintained since WW II: starting Граждане! (*'Grazhdane!'*), it translates: 'Citizens! At times of artillery bombardment this side of the street is most dangerous!'

Just before the Moyka River, the **Literaturnoe Kafe** is, despite its repugnant 'food', one of St Petersburg's most interesting, for its Pushkin associations and ambience. Across the Moyka, Rastrelli's green **Stroganov Palace** (1752-54) has kept most of its original appearance.

Kazan Cathedral Area

A block beyond the Moyka, the great colonnaded arms of the Kazan Cathedral (Kazansky sobor) reach out towards the north side of the avenue. Its design, by Andrey Voronikhin, a former serf, was influenced by St Peter's in Rome. Built in 1801-11, it's named after the supposedly miraculous Kazan icon which it once housed. The square in front of it has been a site for political demonstrations since before the revolution.

The cathedral houses the Museum of the History of Religion (☎ 311 04 95); the museum genuinely covers the history as well as the infamies of many religions. In the north transept is the grave of Field Marshal Kutuzov, the Russian commander against Napoleon in 1812. There's no explanatory material in English, so if you're particularly interested, go with a group. The museum is open Monday, Tuesday, Thursday and Friday from 11 am to 5 pm, Saturday and Sunday from 12.30 to 5 pm; entrance fees for foreigners are US$3 (US$1.50 for ISIC holders, children and pensioners), and the Russian rate is about US$0.25. It's easy to get the Russian rate.

Opposite, St Petersburg's biggest bookshop, **Dom Knigi**, is topped by the globe emblem of the Singer sewing machine company, which constructed the building in 1902-04. Just behind the Kazan Cathedral, a bit south of the Central Train Ticket Centre, sits the **Bankovy Bridge**, one of St Petersburg's loveliest bridges. Suspended by cables emerging from the mouths of golden-winged griffins, the wooden bridge affords a splendid view north up the Griboedova Canal past Nevsky prospekt to the Church of the Resurrection of Christ. In the next block of Nevsky prospekt, pavement artists cluster in front of the **Central Art Salon** (Tsentralny khudozhestvenny salon).

Griboedova Canal to the Fontanka

This section of Nevsky is perhaps the busiest; a whirlwind of activity and colour of which the **Grand Hotel Europe** (the Yevropeyskaya under the Sovs) is the epicentre. The unbelievably lavish hotel was completely renovated from 1989-91, and is once again one of the city's architectural gems, boasting shameless splendour: marble and gilt, sweeping staircases, antique furnishings, casino, four restaurants with imported food, a caviar bar and billiards room, and modern touches like a shopping arcade, health club and satellite TV. If you're feeling wicked enough to visit, you can lounge about in the atrium – you don't even have to buy one of its US$3 cups of coffee.

Diagonally across Nevsky, the arcades of **Gostiny Dvor** department store stand across ulitsa Dumskaya from the clocktower of the former **Town Duma**, seat of the pre-Revolutionary city government. One of the world's first indoor shopping malls, the 'Merchant Yard' dates from 1757-85, and is another Rastrelli creation. The St Petersburg equivalent of Moscow's GUM, Gostiny Dvor housed hundreds of small shops, counters and stalls. Under the Sovs, of course, it became one giant place in which to find the same nothing stretched out over a large area, which was freezing in winter, broiling in summer and inconvenient year-round. In recent years, though, it's been progressively improving, and if they ever finish the renovation of the façade, it will probably look good as well. The wooden fence lining Nevsky prospekt has become a kind of Day-Glo Hyde Park Speaker's Corner, attracting

representatives of the most reprehensible lunatic-fringe political groups, religious proselytisers, and purveyors of posters featuring a range of subjects from smut to 1970s vintage Erik Estrada and Fonzy.

On the other side of Nevsky, in the arcade at No 48, the **Passazh** department store was the first St Petersburg shop to move to self-financing, independent of the state supply network. Today, Passazh is everything that Gostiny Dvor wants to be: stylish, packed with desirable goods and, more important, shoppers with cash to spend. Downstairs in the basement, there's a fully fledged and well-stocked Western supermarket. (See Self-catering later in this chapter.)

Tucked in a recess between the banks and the café near ulitsa Mikhailovskaya, the **Armenian Church** (1771-80), one of two in St Petersburg, is open, though under extensive renovation. The Soviet regime deemed it reasonable to bash the place to bits and install a 2nd floor, which blocked the view of the cupola. The renovation, performed by members of the congregation, has included removal of that 2nd floor and restoration of the cupola and several icons, but there is still a long way to go. It's in the process of creating a new iconostasis as well.

The **Vorontsov Palace** on Sadovaya ulitsa, opposite the south-east side of Gostiny Dvor, is another noble town house by Rastrelli. It's now a military school.

Ploshchad Ostrovskogo

Formerly the home of a 'Tourist Art Market' which has gone the way of the dodo, this airy square was created by Carlo Rossi in the 1820s and 1830s, and its west side is taken up by the **Saltykov-Shchedrin Public Library**, St Petersburg's biggest – it's even got an English-language section. Rossi's **Pushkin Theatre** (formerly the Alexandrinsky) at the south end of the square is one of Russia's most important. In 1896 the opening night of Chekhov's *The Seagull* was so badly received here that the playwright fled to wander anonymously among the crowds on Nevsky prospekt.

Behind the theatre, ulitsa Zodchego Rossi,

a continuation of Rossi's ensemble, is proportion deified: it's 22 metres wide and high and 220 metres long. The **Vaganova School of Choreography** situated here is the Kirov Ballet's training school, where Pavlova, Nijinsky, Nureyev and others learned their art.

The **Anichkov Palace**, between ploshchad Ostrovskogo and the Fontanka River (its main façade faces the river), was home to several imperial favourites, including Catherine the Great's lover Grigory Potyomkin.

Anichkov Bridge & Beyond

Nevsky prospekt crosses the Fontanka on the **Anichkov Bridge**, with famous 1840s statues of rearing horses at its four corners. A photogenic Baroque backdrop is provided by the red 1840s **Beloselsky-Belozersky Palace**. Between the Fontanka and Moscow Station, Nevsky prospekt has fewer historic buildings but heaps more shops and cinemas. This is one of the most concentrated areas of chi-chi shops and restaurants, and in the centre of the strip the **Nevskij Palace Hotel** is in the former Baltiyskaya Hotel building. Another spectacular renovation (actually a gut rehab), the Nevskij Palace boasts fine restaurants, bars and nightclubs. Across the street, behind the Afrodite restaurant, is one of St Petersburg's most popular summer beer gardens.

Ploshchad Vosstania (Uprising Square), whose landmark is the giant granite pillar with the Commie star, marks the division of Nevsky prospekt and Stary Nevsky prospekt, which juts off the square at a 45° angle headed south-east, to the Alexandra Nevskogo bridge.

Stary Nevsky's charm is in its relative desolation; despite the appearance of Benetton, some tourist-oriented art galleries and a Len West shoe shop, the mood on Stary Nevsky is far more laid back.

Alexandr Nevsky Monastery

The working Alexandr Nevsky Monastery, with the graves of some of Russia's most famous artistic figures, is entered from ploshchad Alexandra Nevskogo opposite the Hotel Moskva. It was founded in 1713 by Peter the Great, who wrongly thought this was where Alexandr of Novgorod had beaten the Swedes in 1240. In 1797 it became a lavra (superior monastery). Today it is open to the public and, sadly, the courtyard is filled with homeless beggars.

You can wander freely around most of the grounds but for the two most important graveyards, if you're not already on a tour, you're supposed to join a group tour in Russian. Tickets for foreigners cost US$0.75 or US$0.35 for ISIC holders and US$0.25 for Russians; photographs are an additional US$0.25. They are sold outside the main gate (to your right as you enter) and in summer you may have to book an hour or two ahead. Opening hours are from 11 am to 6 pm, except Thursday and the first Tuesday of the month. Alternatively, travellers have been known to act dumb and just wander past the elderly babushka who guards the gate and on to the graveyards from the path inside the main gate.

The **Tikhvin Cemetery** (Tikhvinskoe kladbishche), on the right, contains the most famous graves. In the far right-hand corner from its gate, a bust of Tchaikovsky surmounts his grave. Nearby are Rubinshteyn, Borodin, Mussorgsky, Rimsky-Korsakov and Glinka. Following the wall back towards the gate you reach the tomb of Dostoevsky. The **Lazarus Cemetery** (Lazarevskoe kladbishche), facing the Tikhvin across the entrance path, contains several late great St Petersburg architects – among them Starov, Voronikhin, Quarenghi, Zakharov and Rossi.

Across the canal in the main lavra complex, the first main building on the left is the 1717-22 Baroque **Annunciation Church** (Blagoveshchenskaya tserkov), now the City Sculpture Museum (Muzey gorodskoy skulptury) and closed for renovation. About 100 metres further on is the monastery's 1776-90 classical **Trinity Cathedral** (Troitsky sobor). It is open for worship Saturday, Sunday and holidays from 6 am to the end of evening services (closed for cleaning between 2 and 5 pm); early liturgy from 7 am, late liturgy from 10 am and all-night vigils begin at 6 pm. Hundreds crowd in on 12 September to celebrate the feast of Alexandr Nevsky, now a saint.

Opposite the cathedral is the St Petersburg **Metropolitan's House**. On the far right of the grounds facing the canal is St Petersburg's **Orthodox Academy**, one of only a handful in Russia (another is at Sergiev Posad).

BETWEEN NEVSKY & NEVA

It's a pleasure to stroll in the gardens, waterways and squares of the old area north of Nevsky prospekt and west of the Fontanka River. Here are some of St Petersburg's best museums. Further east, don't miss Smolny Cathedral.

Ploshchad Iskusstv

Just a block north of Nevsky Prospekt metro, quiet ploshchad Iskusstv (Arts Square) is named after its cluster of museums and concert halls – notably the **Russian Museum**, one of St Petersburg's best, and the **Ethnography Museum**, which should probably be skipped, the **Large Hall** (Bolshoy zal) of the St Petersburg Philharmonia, venue for top classical concerts, and the **Maly Theatre**, the city's second fiddle to the Mariinsky for opera and ballet.

The **Brodsky House-Museum** at No 3 is a former home of Isaak Brodsky, one of the favoured artists of the revolution. It has works by top 19th-century painters like Repin, Levitan and Kramskoy, but the Russian Museum has better collections by the same artists. A statue of Pushkin stands in the middle of ploshchad Iskusstv. The square, and ulitsa Mikhailovskaya which joins it to Nevsky prospekt, were designed as a unit by Rossi in the 1820s and 1830s.

Russian Museum The former Mikhail Palace, now the Russian Museum (Gosudarstvenny Russky muzey), houses one of the country's two finest collections of Russian art (the other is in Moscow's Tretyakov Gallery). It's open daily, except Tuesday, from 10 am to 6 pm. There's a decent little café inside on the same basement level as the kassa. Admission is US$1.90 for foreigners, US$1 for students.

The palace was built in 1819-29 for Grand Duke Mikhail, brother of Alexander I and Nicholas I. The Museum was founded in 1898, under Alexander II. The Benois building, which is now connected to the original palace and accessible through an entrance on naberezhnaya kanala Griboedova, was constructed in 1916.

The museum has been under constant renovation for years, and it is not possible to get a firm date on when it will finally be finished; there have been major changes in exhibition layouts, though the curator tells us that the layout has been finalised pending only the return of a small portion of the museum's collection (albeit an important one, including the museum's entire Chagall collection, currently on world tour).

Peter Ilyich Tchaikovsky

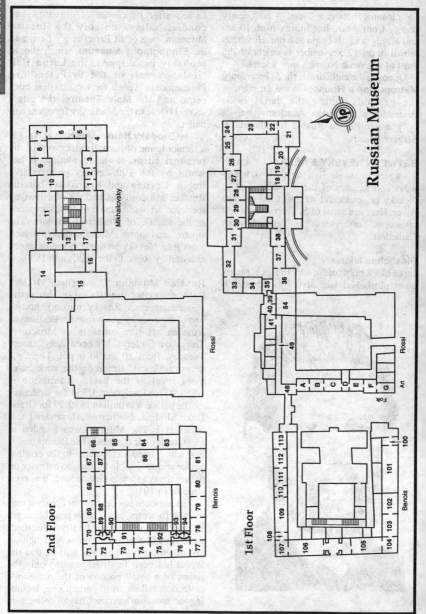

Numbering in the museum is not always chronological, and the layout below follows an essentially straightforward walk through the rooms that are open to the public. Rooms 1-15 are on the 2nd floor (upstairs from the State Vestibule, originally the main entrance), and rooms 18-38 are on the ground floor, of the Mikhail Palace. Rooms 39-54 are on the ground floor and rooms 66-113 are on the 2nd floor of the Benois Building.

Rooms 1-4: 12th to 15th-century icons – we liked the *Siege of Novgorod by the Suzdalians* (2) and *Apostle Peter* and *Apostle Paul* by Andrey Rublyov and others (3).

5-9: 17th to 18th-century sculpture, portraits and tapestries.

10, 12, 14: late 18th-century, early 19th-century paintings and sculpture – interesting old St Petersburg townscapes in **14**.

11: the White Hall, the finest in the palace, with period furniture by Rossi.

15: big 19th-century canvasses mainly by graduates of the official Academy – Aivazovsky's Crimea seascapes stand out.

18-22: first half of the 19th century focusing (**19**) on the beginnings of the socially aware 'Critical Realist' tradition.

23-38: Peredvizhniki and associated artists including (**24, 27, 28**) landscapes; (**25**) Kramskoy; and (**26**) Nikolai Ge, including his fearsome *Peter I interrogating Tsarevich Alexey at Peterhof*.

32: Polencov, including his *Christ and the Singer*, Antakolsky sculptures.

33, 34, 35 and **54:** a permanent exhibition of the work of Repin, probably Russia's best-loved artist; **33** has portraits and *The Volga Bargeman*, an indictment of Russian 'social justice'; **34** has *Zaporozhie Cossacks writing a letter to the Turkish Sultan* (officially entitled *Zaprozhtse*); and **54** contains the massive *Meeting of the State Council*, Repin's rendering of the meeting at the Mariinsky Palace on 7 May 1901 (it's full of tsarist hot shots: there's a scheme in the room to help you tell who's who).

36: Russian history, portraits by Surikov, a national revivalist.

37 and **38:** landscapes by Kuingi.

39: popular 19th-century painter Malyavin's paintings of stereotypical Russian mothers and maidens.

40: Ryabushkin on pre-Peter-the-Great 17th-century Russian history, includes the very telling and humorous *Yedut*, or *They Are Coming*, depicting the perturbed-looking reception committee for the first foreigners allowed in Russia.

41: Vasnetsov, including *Russian Knight at the Crossroads* and other 'sketches' for his mosaics.

42-47: currently under renovation and will be used to permanently exhibit Levitan and other late 19th-century painters.

48: Antakolski sculptures (exits to the right lead to the ten halls of Russian Folk art exhibition, including handicrafts, wood work, carvings, pottery, toys etc).

49: actually a long corridor; it houses panels prepared by Korovin for the 1900 Paris Exhibition depicting northern Russian scenes; white nights, northern Russian nature etc.

66: the Vrubel room featuring his epic *Russian Hero* (it's a fat man on a fat horse and, when compared with *Russian Knight at the Crossroads*, points out the fascinating contrast between the two sides of the Russian nature), *The Demon* and *The Six-Winged Seraph*. It's through the windowed corridor leading to the Benois building and up the stairs.

67: Nesterov's religious paintings of the history of the Orthodox Church; Konenkov sculptures.

68: work from the Fellowship of The World of Fine Arts: Benois, Somov, Dobuzhinsky, Bakst and others (we liked the portrait of SP Diaghilev).

69: Borisov-Musatov, considered by many to be the father of Russian modern art; Meteev's sculpture.

70, 71: Serov, portraits of Russian aristocracy and other high-rollers; Trubitskoy sculptures of same.

72: Impressionists Korovin, Grabar and Serebryakova; and Trubitskoy's sculptures of Lev Tolstoy and *Unknown Woman*.

73: Kustodiev's paintings of 'stereotypical' Russians.

74: Rerikh fans unite, it's The Rerikh Room, cocktails free to those who can name the street on which he used to live.

75-79: Russian Avante Garde, symbolism, neoclassical works of artists, including Saryan Kuznetsov, Petrov-Vodkin, Grigoriev, Shukhaev, Altman, Lenturov etc; note that **79** will be the home of the museum's Chagall and Malevich collection as soon as it returns from revenue-producing exhibitions abroad (in other words, don't hold your breath).

83-113: rotating exhibition halls.

Ethnography Museum The State Museum of Ethnography (☎ 219 11 74) displays the traditional crafts, customs and beliefs of many of the peoples who make up the former Soviet Union's impossibly fragile ethnic mosaic – the mosaic whose members are currently throwing bombs at one another. There's a lot of pretty blatant propaganda going on here, but there are some notable exceptions: the sections on Transcaucasia and Central Asia, upstairs, are fascinating, with wonderful rugs and two full-size yurts (nomads' portable tent-houses). Throughout the museum, a guide makes a lot of difference to how much you understand.

It's open daily from 10 am to 6 pm, except Monday and the last Friday of the month. Admission for foreigners is US$1.60 (a whole US$0.05 for ISIC holders, children and pensioners); for Russians it's US$0.05, half that for kids.

Resurrection Church

The multi-domed **Church of the Resurrection of Christ** (Khram Voskresenia Khristova) on the Griboedova Canal just off ploshchad Iskusstv was built in 1887-1907 on the spot where Alexander II, despite his reforms, was blown up by the People's Will terrorist group in 1881. Because of its site it's also known as the Church of the Saviour of the Spilled Blood (Khram Spasa na Krovi), and because various translations of *that* term float around you may hear it called several other names by tour guides and hotel concierges, such as 'Church of the Spilled Blood', 'Church of the Bleeding Saviour' etc. It can get confusing.

It's partly modelled on St Basil's in Moscow, as part of an effort to revive earlier Russian architecture. The scaffolding that had marred the exterior for as long as anyone can remember was finally removed in 1992, and it is a gift that today the exterior can be enjoyed: while there are some fine mosaics inside, until the job of turning it into a museum of mosaics is completed you won't be able to see the interior.

Pushkin Flat-Museum

Pushkin's last home (he only lived here for a year), at naberezhnaya reki Moyki 12, is beside one of the prettiest curves of the Moyka River – between two small bridges and almost opposite the little Winter Canal, which branches off to the Neva beneath the Hermitage arches. This is where the poet died after his duel in 1837. His killer was a French soldier of fortune, d'Anthes, who had been paying public and insulting court to Pushkin's beautiful wife, Natalia. The affair was widely seen as a put-up job on behalf of the tsar, who found the famed poet's radical politics inconvenient – and who, gossip said, may himself have been the one who was really stalking Natalia. The little house is now the Pushkin Flat-Museum (☎ 312 19 62), open daily from 11 am to 6 pm, except Tuesday and the last Friday of the month; admission for foreigners is about US$1.40 (US$0.45 for ISIC holders, children and pensioners) and includes a Russian-language tour (English tours can be arranged on advance notice).

Mars Field

The Mars Field (Marsovo pole) is the open space south of the Kirovsky Bridge. Don't take a short cut across the grass – you may be walking on graves from the 1917 revolution, the civil war, or of later communist luminaries also buried here. There's a monument to the luminaries in the middle. The field is so named because it was the scene of 19th-century military parades.

Across ulitsa Millionnaya, in the courtyard of the Marble Palace, there's a pedestal where the armoured car once stood from which Vlad Lenin uttered his rallying call '*Da zdrastvuet sotsialisticheskaya revolyutsia*' ('Long live socialist revolution') at the Finland Station on 3 April 1917. Now it's sort of a rotating exhibition pedestal: in summer 1994, it sported a full-sized, marbelised Ford Mondeo.

The **Marble Palace**, built for Catherine the Great's lover Grigory Orlov in 1768-85, formerly housed a Lenin Museum; currently it is a branch of the Russian Museum (☎ 312 91 96), featuring rotating exhibitions. A three-year exhibition of 18th-20th-century handicrafts and portraits was scheduled to begin in late 1995. It's open daily except Tuesday from 10 am to 6 pm; admission for foreigners is US$5.40 (US$2.25 for ISIC holders, children and pensioners), photo and video cameras are US$2.25.

Summer Garden

Perhaps St Petersburg's loveliest park, the Summer Garden (Letny sad) is between the Mars Field and the Fontanka River. You can enter at the north or south ends. It opens at

8 am daily, except in April when it's shut, and closes at 10 pm from May to August, 8 pm in September and 7 pm from October to March.

Laid out for Peter the Great with fountains, pavilions and a geometrical plan to resemble the park at Versailles, the garden became a strolling place for St Petersburg's 19th-century leisured classes. Though changed, it maintains a formal elegance, with thousands of lime trees shading its straight paths and lines of statues. In winter individual wooden huts are placed over the statues to protect them from the cold.

The modest, two-storey **Summer Palace** in the north-east corner was St Petersburg's first palace, built for Peter in 1704-14, and is pretty well intact. Little reliefs around the walls depict Russian naval victories. Today it's open as a museum (Muzey letny dvorets Petra I; ☎ 314 03 74) from early May to early November daily from 11 am to 6 pm, except Tuesday and the last Monday of the month. Many rooms are stocked with early 18th-century furnishings. Tickets are sold in the nearby **Tea House** (Chayny domik) for Russian-language group tours, usually from 11 am to late afternoon. Admission for foreigners is US$1.60, US$0.80 for children and students.

Neither the Tea House nor the Coffee House (Kofeyny domik) behind it offers tea, coffee or anything else to eat or drink. Nor does anywhere else in the garden. Surprise, surprise. But they do hold various small exhibitions – art openings and the like. Get tickets from the Tea House.

South of the Summer Garden

A much greater Summer Palace used to stand across the canal from the south end of the Summer Garden. But Rastrelli's almost fairy-tale wooden creation for Empress Elizabeth was knocked down in the 1790s to make way for the bulky, brick **Engineers' Castle** of Paul I, an insanely cruel tsar who lived in fear of assassination and was indeed suffocated in his bed a month after moving into the castle. Later it became a military engineering school (hence the name). The

pleasant **Mikhail Gardens** are over the road, while the yellow **Sheremetev Palace** across the Fontanka, built in 1750-55, houses a recently opened museum to the great, long-persecuted poet Anna Akhmatova (1889-1960).

SMOLNY REGION
City Children's Park & Tauride Palace

The former Tauride Gardens, now the City Children's Park (Gorodskoy detsky park), are worth a stop on the way to Smolny. It's a great place for children under ten; the kiddie rides are among the best in Russia. Even though the beauty of this lovely park's canals and little bridges has been somewhat marred, you can watch Russians enjoying themselves and have a look across the lake at the fine Tauride Palace (Tavrichesky dvorets), built in 1783-89 for Catherine the Great's lover Potyomkin.

The palace takes its name from the Ukrainian region of Crimea (once called Tavria), which Potyomkin was responsible for conquering. Between 1905 and 1917 the State Duma, the Provisional Government and the Petrograd Soviet all met here. Today it's home to the Parliamentary Assembly of the Member States of the CIS and you can't go in. The gardens are a block-and-a-half east of Chernyshevskaya metro. Bus Nos 5, 46, 58 and 134 to Smolny pass along side.

Flowers Exhibition Hall

One of the finest ways to escape momentarily from a St Petersburg winter is to head for the Flowers Exhibition Hall, an indoor tropical paradise just north-west of the City Children's Gardens at the corner of ulitsa Potyomkinskaya and ulitsa Shpalernaya. Dig the 'monster' tree to the right of the entrance. It also has a wishing well, and there's a flower-selling stall at the front. It's open year-round, daily from 11 am to 7 pm, except Monday and Thursday.

Smolny

The **cathedral** at Smolny, three km east of the Summer Garden, is one of the most fabulous of all Rastrelli's buildings, and the

Smolny Region
Смольнынский район

0   250   500 m

PLACES TO STAY

7	Student Dormitory
	Общежитие
47	HI St Petersburg Hostel & Sindbad Travel
50	Oktyabrskaya Hotel
	Гостинца Октябрьская

PLACES TO EAT

17	Café/Saloon
	Кафе
18	Vechernee Kafe
	ВечернееКафе
21	Kiosks
	Киоски
22	Café (Summer only)
	Кафе
25	Café Bagdad
	Кафе Багдад
34	Verona Pizzeria
	Пицериа Верона
41	Springtime Shwarma
	Шварма
43	Ariran Restaurant
	Ресторан Ариан
48	Carrols Restaurant
	Ресторан Царролс
54	Baskin Robbins Café
	Кафе Мороженое Роббинс
55	John Bull Pub
	Джон Бул Пуб

OTHER

1	Garmonia Lyux
	Гармониа Люкс
2	Flower Shop
	Интерфлора

Smolny Institute next door was the hub of the October Revolution. Buses here include No 6 from the Admiralty via much of Nevsky prospekt, and trolleybus No 5 or 7 from ploshchad Vosstania.

The cathedral is the centrepiece of a convent mostly built, to Rastrelli's designs, in 1748-57. His inspiration was to combine Baroque details with the forests of towers and onion domes typical of an old Russian monastery. There's special genius in the proportions of the cathedral, to which the convent buildings are a perfect foil. Rastrelli also planned a gigantic belltower needling up at the west end of the convent, facing down ulitsa Voynova, but funds ran out. Today the convent houses the city administration's offices while the cathedral

is a concert hall, usually open only for performances.

The **Smolny Institute**, built by Quarenghi in 1806-08 as a school for aristocratic girls, had fame thrust upon it in 1917 when Trotsky and Lenin directed the October Revolution from the headquarters of the Bolshevik Central Committee and the Petrograd Soviet which had been set up here. In its Hall of Acts (Aktovy zal) on 25 October, the All-Russian Congress of Soviets conferred power on a Bolshevik government led by Lenin, which ran the country from here until March 1918.

SOUTH & WEST OF NEVSKY PROSPEKT
Sennaya Ploshchad Area

This teeming and rather dirty square, now

dominated by a gaping site that seems to be a permanent exhibition of construction equipment, is the gateway to Dostoevsky-ville. The peripatetic writer, who occupied around 20 residences in his 28-year stay in the city, once spent a couple of days in debtors' prison in what is now called the Senior Officer's Barracks, just across the square from the Sennaya Ploshchad metro station. At the site of the metro station, in turn, was once a large cathedral that dominated the square. By the way, Dostoevsky had been thrown in there by his publisher, for missing a deadline ('Had we but thought of it...' – T Wheeler).

Just west of the square and across the river, at ulitsa Kaznacheyskaya 7, is the flat where he wrote *Crime and Punishment*; Raskolnikov's route to the murder passed directly under the author's window. The old woman lived at flat 74, naberezhnaya kanala Griboedova 104; you can visit the hallway outside the flat (residents are quite used to it). Entering from the canal side, walk straight back to entrance No 5 (apartments 22-81); the flat's on the 3rd floor.

Vladimirskaya Ploshchad Area

Around Vladimirskaya ploshchad are the indoor **Kuznechny market**, St Petersburg's biggest and best stocked (open daily), plus a clutch of entertainment venues, a bitchin' Irish pub, small museums and a smattering of eateries and shops. The onion-domed working **Vladimir Church** (1761-83) dominates the square.

Dostoevsky wrote most of *The Brothers Karamazov* in a flat at Kuznechny pereulok 5, just past the market, and died there in 1881. It's now a small **Dostoevsky Museum** (☎ 311 18 04), open from 11 am to 5 pm daily except Monday and the last Wednesday of the month. Admission for foreigners is US$2, US$1 for students.

The **Arctic & Antarctic Museum** (☎ 113 19 98) on ulitsa Marata focuses on Soviet polar exploration and ratty taxidermy exhibitions. Admission is US$0.15. It's open Wednesday to Sunday from 10 am to 6 pm. There's a small **Rimsky-Korsakov Flat-Museum** at Zagorodny prospekt 28, open from 9 am to 8 pm Wednesday to Saturday, 11 am to 6 pm Sunday. Zagorodny prospekt continues past Pionerskaya ploshchad, where in 1849 Dostoevsky and 20 others, sentenced to death for socialist leanings, were lined up to be shot – only to be told at the last moment that their sentences had been commuted.

Teatralnaya Ploshchad Area

Known throughout the world during the Soviet reign as the Kirov, the **Mariinsky Theatre** resumed its original name in 1992 – though the ballet company still uses the name Kirov. Its home at Teatralnaya ploshchad is the focus of an area of quiet old canal side streets (and another nice Irish pub, the Shamrock). Teatralnaya ploshchad has been a St Petersburg entertainment centre since fairs were held here in the mid-18th century.

One good foot route there is along the south side of the Moyka River from Isaakievskaya ploshchad. On the way, you'll pass the old **Yusupov Palace** (☎ 311 53 53) at naberezhnaya reki Moyki 94, where in 1916 Rasputin, invited to dinner by Prince Felix Yusupov and friends, was filled with poisoned food, cakes, cookies and drink. After he ate and drank all this and was happily (and healthily) licking his fingers, the Yusupov gang did what they probably should have done in the first place: shot ol' Raspy repeatedly. But like a tsarist-era Terminator, he refused to die, and when Yusupov knelt over him, Rasputin grabbed him by the throat! At that point, Yusupov did what any sane man would do: he ran away. When he returned with reinforcements, they found Rasputin had dragged himself outside. They shot him a few more times, beat him with sticks for good measure, and finally stuffed him through the ice of the frozen river. As a footnote, legend has it that Rasputin did not die until he was submerged – water was found in his lungs.

The palace's ground and 2nd floors are open to visitors (US$1.60) but to see the basement chamber in which Raspy ate the poisoned puffy stuff, you'll need to prearrange a 'Rasputin Tour' with the museum administrator, who generally wants US$8 per person for a group of at least three. Consolation: you'll see wax figures of Rasputin and Felix.

A route no less fraught with bloody historical associations is along the Griboedova Canal from the Kazan Cathedral, passing close to Sennaya ploshchad.

North-east of Teatralnaya ploshchad, before it twists south-east, the canal runs under another of St Petersburg's beautiful beast-supported bridges – the **Lviny most**, with cables emerging from the mouths of golden lions. Bus Nos 3, 22 and 27 from Nevsky prospekt, Nos 2 and 100 from ploshchad Lenina via the Mars Field and Nevsky prospekt, and tram No 31 from Kronverksky prospekt on Petrograd Side via the Admiralty all serve Teatralnaya ploshchad.

Outside performance times you can usually wander into the Mariinsky Theatre's (☎ 114 12 11) foyer, and maybe peep into its lovely auditorium. The Mariinsky, built in 1860, has played a pivotal role in Russian ballet and opera ever since. The St Petersburg Conservatory faces it. See the Entertainment section later in this chapter for information on getting tickets for the Kirov/Mariinsky.

The Baroque spires and domes of **St Nicholas' Cathedral** (1753-62), rising among the trees at the bottom of ulitsa Glinki, shelter many 18th-century icons and a fine carved wooden iconostasis. A graceful belltower overlooks the Kryukov Canal, crossed by the Staro-Nikolsky bridge. South along this canal and across a footbridge over the Fontanka is blue-domed **Trinity Cathedral** on Izmaylovsky prospekt, an impressive 1828-35 classical edifice; sadly, it was boarded up when we visited.

Moskovsky Prospekt

This long avenue south from Sennaya ploshchad is the start of the main road to Moscow. The iron **Moscow Triumphal Arch** three-and-a-half km along, looking very like Berlin's Brandenburg Gate, was built in 1838 to mark victories over Turks, Persians and Poles, demolished in 1936 then rebuilt in 1959-60. Local legend has it that the gate is built on the spot where travellers entering the city in the early days had to show that they had brought with them bricks or stones to be used in the construction of buildings.

Ulitsa Gastello, east off Moskovsky prospekt a couple of km further down, contains the **Chesma Palace**, which has a ground plan like a radiation warning sign, built for Catherine the Great to rest en route to the city of Tsarskoe Selo (now Pushkin). More interesting is the red-and-white 18th-century Gothic **Chesma Church**, behind the Hotel Mir at No 17. The church, built in honour of the Battle of Çeşme (1770) when the Russian fleet sailed from the Baltic to the Aegean to beat the Turks, houses the curious Chesma Victory Museum, currently under renovation and scheduled to reopen in 1997; it has a lurid diorama of the battle.

Wide Moskovskaya ploshchad, a little way south of ulitsa Gastello, was intended under a 1930s plan to become the centre of St Petersburg, replacing the old tsarist centre. It is a testament to the stubbornness of St Petersburgians that during the time of Stalin's terror, this plan was universally ignored. Moskovsky prospekt ends a few hundred metres further on at ploshchad Pobedy, where the **Monument to the Heroic Defenders of Leningrad**, commemorating WW II and the siege, makes a striking first impression on entering St Petersburg.

VASILEVSKY ISLAND

The interesting parts of Vasilevsky Island are its eastern 'nose', the Strelka (Tongue of Land), where Peter the Great first wanted his new city's administrative and intellectual centre, and the embankment facing the Admiralty.

In fact, the Strelka became the focus of St Petersburg's maritime trade, symbolised by the white colonnaded **Stock Exchange**. The two **Rostral Columns** on the point, studded with ships' prows, were oil-fired navigation

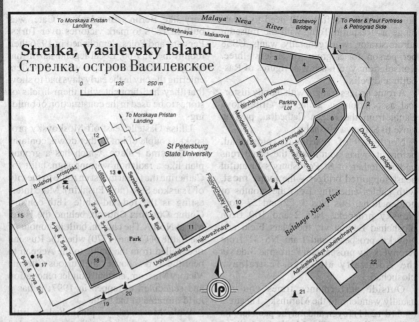

Strelka, Vasilevsky Island
Стрелка, остров Василевское

1	Rostral Column Ростральная колонна
2	Rostral Column Ростральная колонна
3	Institute of Russian Literature (Pushkin House) Институт русской литературы (Пушкинский дом)
4	Museum of Agriculture Музей сельского хозяйства
5	Central Naval Museum Центральный военно-морской музей
6	Museum of Zoology Зоологический музей
7	Museum of Anthropology & Ethnography (Kuntskammer) Музей антропологии и этнографии (Кунтскаммера)
8	Lomonosov Statue Памятник Ломоносову
9	Twelve Colleges Двенадцать коллегий
10	Philological Faculty Филологический факультет Государственного Университета
11	Menshikov Palace Дворец Меншикова
12	Church of St Catherine Церковь св. Екатерины
13	Sirin Restaurant Ресторан Сирин
14	Kafe Nika (De Konick) Кафе Ника
15	Market Рынок
16	Pivo Stand Пиво
17	Salon Best Салон Бест
18	Academy of Arts Museum Музей академии художеств
19	Sphinx Monument Свинкс
20	Sphinx Monument Свинкс
21	Bronze Horseman Медный всадник
22	Admiralty Адмиралтейство

beacons in the 1800s (on some holidays gas torches are still lit on them). The area remains an intellectual centre, with the St Petersburg State University, the Academy of Arts and a veritable 'museum ghetto'.

The Strelka also has one of the best views in the city: you look left to the Peter & Paul Fortress and right to the Hermitage, the Admiralty and St Isaac's Cathedral.

At the inner end of the island many north-south streets have separate names and independent numbering for each side or 'line' (linia). Thus the street beside Menshikov Palace is Sezdovskaya linia on the east side and 1-ya (*pervaya*, first) linia on the west, the next street is 2-ya linia on the east and 3-ya on the west, and so on.

Museums near the Strelka

The Stock Exchange is now the **Central Naval Museum** (Tsentralny Voenno-Morskoy muzey; ☎ 218 25 02), full of maps, excellent model-ships, flags and photos of and about the Russian navy right up to the present. Also on display is the *Botik*, Peter's first boat, the granddaddy of them all; a pre-turn-of-the-century submarine (it's a two-seater) and some big oars. It's open from 10.30 am to 5.30 pm (last entry at 4.45 pm), closed Monday, Tuesday and the last Thursday of the month. Admission for foreigners is US$1, US$2 for a Russian-language excursion and US$1 for photos or video cameras.

To the right (north) of the Exchange is a former maritime warehouse and former Museum of Agriculture. Beyond this the old Customs House, topped with statues and a dome, is now called Pushkin House (Pushkinsky dom), and is home to the **Institute of Russian Literature**, and a Literary Museum with exhibits on Tolstoy, Gogol, Lermontov, Turgenev, Gorky and others. It's open from 11 am to 5.30 pm, closed Monday and Tuesday.

To the left of the Exchange in another ex-warehouse is the **Museum of Zoology** (Zoologichesky Muzey; ☎ 218 01 12), said to be one of the biggest and best in the world, with more stuffed animals than you can

shake a stick at, plus insects and fish from all over the world. Among the dioramas and the tens of thousands of mounted beasties is a complete woolly mammoth (!) thawed out of the Siberian ice in 1902. The museum's open from 11 am to 6 pm (last entry 5 pm), closed Friday. And it's a bargain: admission for foreigners is US$0.20 (US$0.02 for ISIC holders, children and pensioners). Guided tours for groups of up to 30 people can be had for US$14.25 (US$11.50 for ISIC holders, children and pensioners). On Thursday, the administrator said, admission is free except for excursions.

Museum of Anthropology & Ethnography

The blue-and-white building with the steeple was the city's first museum, founded in 1714 by Peter himself. In contrast to the State Museum of Ethnography, this museum (Muzey Antropologii i Etnografii; ☎ 218 01 18) is about peoples outside the former USSR, with wonderfully campy dioramas and displays on the cultures of Asia, Oceania, Africa and the Americas. The old anatomy theatre at the city centre is the big draw, with selections from Peter's original *kunstkammer*. While this translates from German to 'art chamber', the bloodthirsty crowds are really here to see Peter's collection of 'curiosities': bugs and snakes, gold ornaments from Siberian tombs and a truly ghoulish collection of preserved freaks, foetuses and body parts. It's fun for the whole family.

The museum is open from 11 am to 6 pm (last entry 4.45 pm), closed Thursday and Friday. Admission for all is US$1.70. The entrance is around the corner in Tamozhyonny pereulok.

Menshikov Palace

Alexandr Menshikov was a close friend (many now say lover) of Peter the Great. For helping the tsar defeat the Swedes he was made Governor General of St Petersburg and given Vasilevsky Island. Peter later took the island back, but in 1707 Menshikov put up one of the city's first buildings, a riverside palace (Dvorets Menshikova) just west of the Twelve Colleges. He effectively ran Russia from here for three years between Peter's death and his own exile.

Later the palace was a military academy and then it went to seed until Lenin suggested it be saved. Now its lavish interiors are again filled with period art and furniture as a museum of 'Russian Culture of the First Third of the 18th century' (☎ 213 11 22). It's open from 10.30 am to 4.30 pm, closed Monday; admission for foreigners is US$4.50 (US$3.40 for ISIC holders and children), photos are US$2.85, video cameras US$7.60. Russian-language excursions, which start every ten minutes, are included in the price.

Academy of Arts Museum

Two blocks west of the Menshikov Palace, at Universitetskaya naberezhnaya 17, is the Russian Academy of Arts' Research Museum (Muzey Akademii Khudozhestv; ☎ 213 64 96; excursion desk 213 35 78), guarded by two imported Egyptian sphinxes said to be about 3500 years old. Inside are works done by Academy students and faculty since its founding, plus changing exhibitions, sometimes by foreign artists. The classical entrance hall with its dusty statues is itself a sight. It's open from 11 am to 7 pm (last entry 5 pm), closed Monday and Tuesday. Admission for foreigners is US$3 (US$1.40 for ISIC holders, children and pensioners), US$0.50 for photos and video cameras. A Russian-language excursion is about US$12.

Churches

Four untended, mostly unused classical churches are in the blocks just west of the university. The handsomest is the former **Lutheran Church of St Catherine** (Tserkov Yekateriny, 1771) at Bolshoy prospekt 1, now a Melodia sound studio.

More intriguing is what looks like a homage to Istanbul's Sancta Sofia Cathedral, behind high walls at the west end of Bolshoy prospekt. This Byzantine mystery is now a naval training school so there's no way in.

Take bus No 7 or trolleybus No 10 from the Hermitage.

Twelve Colleges

West of the Anthropology Museum and marked by a statue of the scientist-poet Mikhail Lomonosov is Mendeleevskaya linia and the skinny, 400-metre-long Twelve Colleges building. Meant originally for Peter's government ministries, it's now part of the university, which stretches out behind it.

PETROGRAD SIDE
Inner Petrograd Side

Petrograd Side (Petrogradskaya storona) is a cluster of delta islands between the Malaya Neva and Bolshaya Nevka channels. On little Zayachy Island, Peter the Great first broke ground for St Petersburg and built the Peter & Paul Fortress. Most of Petrograd Side's other sights are near the fortress, though the Kirovsky Islands feature some vast parklands and old dacha-palaces which are currently the stomping ground of government big-wigs, large gentlemen of indeterminate occupation who drive Mercedes Benzes, rich foreign businessmen and the occasional Danish diplomat.

Peter & Paul Fortress Founded in 1703, the Peter & Paul Fortress (Petropavlovskaya krepost) is the oldest building in St Petersburg. Peter planned it as a defence against the Swedes but defeated them before it was finished. Its main use up to 1917 was as a political prison; one of its first inmates was Peter's own son Alexey, whose torture Peter is said to have overseen personally. Other famous residents were Dostoevsky, Gorky, Trotsky and Lenin's older brother, Alexandr. Most worth seeing are the **Cathedral of SS Peter & Paul**, with its landmark needle-thin spire, and the Trubetskoy Bastion.

The cathedral, though plain on the outside, was radically different from traditional Orthodox churches. If you haven't overdosed on churches, don't miss its magnificent Baroque interior. All of Russia's pre-Revolutionary rulers from Peter the

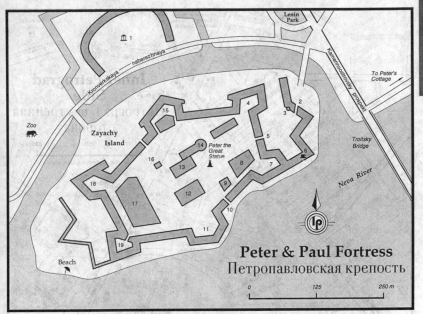

Peter & Paul Fortress
Петропавловская крепость

0   125   250 m

1	Artillery Museum Артиллерийский музей	8	Engineers' Building Инженерный корпус	14	Grand-Ducal Mausoleum Усыпальница

1 Artillery Museum
   Артиллерийский музей
2 St John Gate
   Иоанновские ворота
3 Ticket Office
   Касса
4 Menshikov Bastion
   Меншиковский бастион
5 St Peter Gate
   Петровские ворота
6 Summer Rooftop Café
   Летний Кафе
7 Peter I Bastion
   Петровский бастион

8 Engineers' Building
   Инженерный корпус
9 Senior Officers'
   Barracks
   Гауптвахта
10 Nevsky Gate
   Невские ворота
11 Naryshkin Bastion
   Нарышкинский бастион
12 Commandant's House
   Обер-комендантский дом
13 SS Peter & Paul
   Cathedral
   Петропавловский собор

14 Grand-Ducal
   Mausoleum
   Усыпальница
15 Golovkin Bastion
   Головкинский
   бастион
16 Boat House
   Домик ботика
17 Mint
   Монетный двор
18 Zotov Bastion
   Зотовский бастион
19 Trubetskoy Bastion
   Трубецкой бастион

Great onwards, except Peter II, Ivan VI and
Nicholas II, are buried here. Peter I's grave
is at front right, and people still leave fresh
flowers on it. Individuals might avoid
queues by discreetly moving upstream
through the crowds exiting into the adjoining
Grand-Ducal Mausoleum. The mauso-

leum, built at the turn of this century, has a
free exhibit on the reconstruction of the fortress.

In the fort's south-west corner are reconstructions of the grim cells of the
Trubetskoy Bastion, where Peter supervised the torture to death of his son and

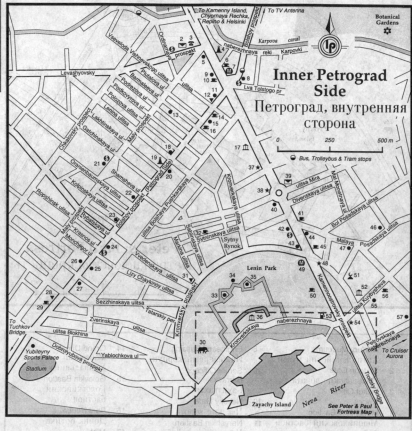

continued from previous page

OTHER

2 Post Office
   Почта
3 Telegraph/Telephone
   Office
   Телеграф и Телефон
4 Popov Statue
   Памятник Попова
5 Cinema
   Кино
8 Teatr Experiment
   Театр Эксперимент
9 Bookshop
   Книжный Магазин
11 Babylon
   Вавилон
13 Kodak One Hour
   Кодак 1-Час
15 Photo Shop
   Фото
17 Kirov Museum
   Музей Кирова
18 Kodak One Hour Photo
   Кодак 1-Час
19 Lenin Statue
   Памятник В. И. Ленину
20 Melodiya
   Мелодия
21 Babylon Super
   Вавилон супер

22 Bally
   Баллы
23 Babylon Toys
24 Babylon Photo Express
25 Staraya Knigf
   Старая Книга
26 'Everything For
   Fishermen'
   Всё для рыболовов
27 Newton (Electronic
   Dept Store)
   Нютоп
30 Zoo
   Зоопарк
33 Music Hall
   Мюзик Хол
35 Planetarium
   Планетариум
36 Artillery Museum
   Артиллерийский музей
37 GAI Checkpoint
   ГАИ
38 GAI Checkpoint
   ГАИ
39 Post Office
   Почта
40 Gril Diez
   Грил Диез
42 Toy Shop
   Игрушки
43 Perfume/Cosmetics
   Shop
   Духи

44 Florist/Mercedes
   Dealership
   Цветы и
   Корона-Логоваз
46 Banya 50
   Баня 50
47 Sport Complex
   Комплекс спортивный
48 GAI Checkpoint
   ГАИ
51 Mosque
   Мечеть
52 Museum of Political
   History
   Музей Русской
   Политической
   Истории
53 Petrol Station
   Бензоколонка
54 GAI Checkpoint
   ГАИ
55 Diana Sporting Goods
   Магазин Диана
57 Peter's Cabin
   Домик Петра

METRO STATIONS

7 Petrogradskaya
   Петроградская
49 Gorkovskaya
   Горьковская

which were used by later tsars to keep a lid on original thinking in the empire.

In the south wall is **Nevsky Gate**, a later addition, where prisoners were loaded on boats for execution elsewhere. Notice the plaques showing water levels of famous floods. Outside are fine views of the whole central waterfront. Around to the left in summer is a fascinating collection of fishers, joggers and standing sunbathers (standing's said to give you a *proper* tan), and in winter you might see people swimming in holes cut through the ice (an activity that's said to be 'good for the health'). Above this is a summer café, on the artillery platform, serving chicken, sandwiches, beer and soft drinks.

At noon every day a cannon is fired from the **Naryshkin Bastion**, scaring the daylights out of the tourists.

The **Commandant's House** is a Museum of the History of St Petersburg up to the 1917 revolution, and includes a room restored to its 1820s appearance. It's been under renovation for quite some time. The **Engineers' Building** has a museum on the city's architecture.

Entry to the fort is free but for most buildings inside you'll need a ticket from the kiosk at the east end, or to make a payment at the door.

The fort is open from 11 am to 6 pm (to 4 pm Tuesday), closed Wednesday and the last Tuesday of the month. The closest you can get by bus from near the Hermitage is on a No 10 or 45 to the zoo, but it's a very pleasant walk along Dvortsovaya naberezhnaya, and across the Troitsky Bridge to Kamenno-ostrovskiy prospekt and the entrance. Gorkovskaya metro is in Lenin Park, a three-minute walk from the fortress.

Behind the Fortress Across the moat, in the fort's original arsenal, is the **Artillery Museum** (Artilleriysky Muzey; ☎ 232 02 96), open from 11 am to 6 pm, closed Monday and Tuesday. It's a great place if you like weapons: it seems to have one of everything right back to the Stone Age. It's also got Lenin's armoured car parked in its drive-way. Admission for foreigners is US$2.40.

West of that is the **St Petersburg Zoo** (☎ 232 28 39), which, though it's not as bad as it was, is still pretty gruesome and full of miserable animals and happy kids. The zoo suffers from a lack of funds and it's a sad sight indeed; it's open from 10 am to 6 pm daily, admission is about US$0.60.

Just north of the zoo is a new permanent **Amusement Park**, complete with bumper cars, a couple of small roller coasters, and the like: rides cost about US$0.25.

East and behind the museum is **Lenin Park**, cool in summer but too close to traffic to be peaceful. At the back, the **Planetarium/Baltiysky Dom** theatre complex keeps post-communist youth off the streets by throwing wild raves, all-night dance parties and drink-a-thons in summer.

East of the park across Kamennoostrovsky prospekt is a working **mosque**, built in 1912 and modelled on Samarkand's Gur Emir Mausoleum where Timur (Tamerlaine) is buried. Its fluted azure dome and minarets have been under renovation for years – the crane seems to be a permanent fixture behind the fortress's spire.

Museum of Political History East of Kamennoostrovsky prospekt at ulitsa Kuybysheva 4 is the Ksheshinskaya Palace which contains the Museum of Political History in Russia (Muzey Politicheskoy Istorii Rossii; ☎ 233 71 13), which is more interesting than it sounds. The Bolsheviks made their headquarters, and Lenin often gave speeches, from the balcony of this elegant Art Nouveau palace that once belonged to Matilda Kshesinskaya, famous ballet dancer and one-time lover of Tsar Nicholas II. Even if you can't read Russian go in to see the house itself, the paintings and photos from the lead up to the revolution, and the glossy dioramas and mini-films. It's open from 10 am to 5.30 pm, closed Thursday. Admission is US$0.80

Perhaps best of all, the **Wax Museum**, accessible through the east-side entrance (under the arch and to the left), is a hoot; if you ever thought that maybe the Russians were telling a little stinky one about Lenin's body being 'preserved' in that glass box, you'll know for sure after you see this. You'll also see a quite senile-looking Krushchev, Brezhnev holding a bent cigarette, a preter-naturally sober-looking Yeltsin pointing at a Gorbachev who appears to be saying, 'Calm down, everything will be all right...' and Vlad himself looking quite chipper. The wax museum's open daily from 10 am to 6 pm; the US$0.50 admission is supposed to include a sombre Russian-language excur-sion by an unusually dolorous guide, but you can slip that and just look at the display, which only takes a couple of minutes.

In mid-1995 the wax figures moved out and reportedly have been temporarily relo-cated to the Municipal Cultural Centre at 41 Nevsky prospekt, with an admission fee of US$3. The 20th century figures were not included in the new exhibit, and it's up in the air whether the whole thing will stay there, move back or what. Check when you're in town, because this exhibition is worth seeing.

Peter's Cabin In a patch of trees east of the fortress at Petrovskaya naberezhnaya 6 is a little stone building. In here is preserved St Petersburg's first residence, a log cabin where Peter lived in 1703 while supervising the construction of the fortress and city. Peter's Cabin (Domik Petra; ☎ 232 45 76) is open from 10 am to 8 pm, except Tuesday and the last Monday of the month. Admis-sion is about US$1.50 (US$0.75 for ISIC holders, children and pensioners). It feels more like a shrine than a museum.

Cruiser *Aurora* In the Nevka opposite the Hotel St Petersburg is the *Aurora* (or *Avrora*), a cruiser mothballed from the Russo-Japanese War. From a downstream mooring on the night of 25 October 1917, its crew fired a blank round from the forward gun, demoralising the Winter Palace's defenders and marking the start of the October Revolution. During WW II, the Russians sank it to protect it from German bombs. Now, refloated, restored and painted up in awfully pretty colours, it's a museum, free of charge and open from 10.30 am to 4 pm, closed Monday, Tuesday and the last Wednesday of the month. It's swarming with kids on weekends.

Botanical Gardens This quiet jungle in eastern Aptekarsky (Apothecary) Island, just north-east of the Petrogradskaya metro station and across the Karpova Canal, was once a garden of medicinal plants which gave the island its name. The botanical gardens on the site today offers one of St Petersburg's most peaceful strolling grounds. The Dutch-built greenhouse is difficult to get into but the lovely gardens are, for now, free. The entrance is at ulitsa Professora Popova 2, but if they decide to start charging, there are holes in the fence near the intersection of the Karpova Canal and Aptekarskaya naberezhnaya.

TV Antenna Here's a weird one (but exclusive: you read it here first): the Leningrad Radio-Tele Broadcasting Centre's antenna (☎ 234 78 87), at the northern end of Petrograd Side, is open for excursions by arrangement with Peter TIPS (see Tourist Offices in the Information section earlier in this chapter). The 50,000-watt transmitter tower stands 310 metres over the city, and it has just recently been allowed to let the public inside. It's a great place to bring kids; it offers excellent views of the entire city and environs, and you can take photos.

The tower was the first of its kind in the Soviet Union when constructed in 1963, so they weren't thinking about revolving restaurants or other amenities yet (the Ostankino tower in Moscow is modelled on this one), but these days there's a bar/café on the 2nd observation level (200 metres). It was originally 316 metres (taller than the Eiffel Tower), but they had to lop off the last six due to stress from high winds.

The itty-bitty lift (once the fastest in the country) makes the trip from ground level to the first viewing platform (197 metres) in a minute and three-quarters; from there you can walk up to the café level, where you can access the outside catwalk. The tower sways up to 50 cm on windy days, and you can feel it! A fun fact: the tower's construction was supervised by an all-female crew; the forewoman still lives in St Petersburg.

All the city's TV and radio signals originate here, but residents within almost a km around the antenna still get bad reception, as the signal goes right over their heads.

Peter TIPS (☎ 279 00 37) will take foreigners for US$10 a head, Russians for US$1.20, and needs at least a day's notice. To reach the TV Antenna start at Petrogradskaya metro, take trolleybus No 31 north up Bolshoy prospekt from the stop in front of Teatr Experiment for two stops; get off when you see the tower (if you cross the big bridge you've missed it). Walk down to naberezhnaya Kantemirovsky, turn right and walk to the city centre gates facing the river.

Kirovsky Islands

This is the collective name for the outer delta islands of Petrograd Side – Kamenny, Yelagin and Krestovsky. The first of these is known as Kamenny ostrov; its Soviet-era name, Trudyashchikhsya – meaning 'Of the Workers' – is on some older maps but nobody *ever* uses it. Once marshy jungles, the islands were granted to 18th and 19th-century court favourites and developed into elegant playgrounds. But they're still mostly parkland, huge leafy venues for picnics, river sports and white-nights cavorting.

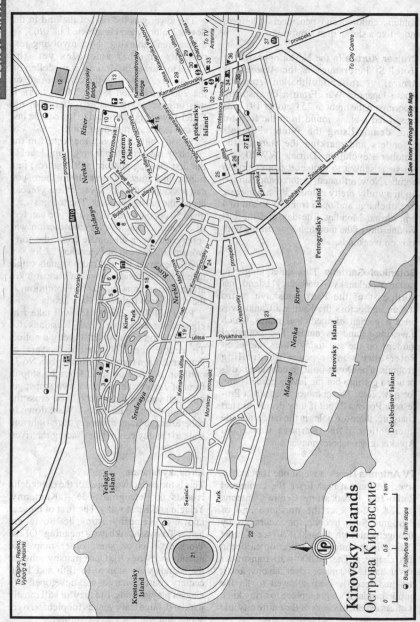

Kirovsky Islands
Острова Кировские

PLACES TO STAY

25 Dvorets Molodyozhy Hotel
    Гостиница Дворец молодёжи
30 Hotel Druzhba
    Гостиница Дружба

PLACES TO EAT

4   Kafe
    Кафе
19 Kafe
    Кафе
24 Restaurant Tryum
    Ресторан Трюм
32 Chick-King
    Чик-Кинг
33 Kafe
    Кафе
34 Kafe
    Кафе
36 Imperial Restaurant
    Ресторан Империал

OTHER

1   Buddhist Temple
    Буддисткий дацан
2   Boat Rental
    Прокат лодок

3   Amusement Park
    Аттракционы
5   Stables
    Конюшенный корпус
6   Kitchen Building
    Кухонный корпус
7   Yelagin Palace
    Елагинский дворец
8   Polovtsev House
    Дом Половцева
9   Danish Consulate General
    Здание генерального консула Дании
10 Sports Hall
    Спортывний зал
12 Military Naval Academy
    Военно-Морская Академия
13 Kamenno-Ostrovsky Palace
    Каменно-Островский дворец
14 Church of St John the Baptist
    Церковь Иоанна Предтечи
15 Sphinx Monuments
    Свинкс
16 Peters Tree
    Дуб Петра 1
17 Kamenny Ostrov Theatre
    Каменно-Островский театр

18 Water Bikes
    Водный велосипед
20 Ferry Landing
    Пристань
21 Kirov Stadium
    Стадион имени Кирова
22 Ferry Landing
    Пристань
23 Dinamo Stadium
    Стадион Динамо
26 Petrograd Central GAI Station
    ГАИ
27 Church
    Церковь
28 Market
    Рынок
29 TV Antenna
    Центр телевизионного вещания
31 Rifle Shop
    Магазин Рифл
35 Future Hotel Site

METRO STATIONS

11 Chyornaya Rechka
    Чёрная Речка
37 Petrogradskaya
    Петроградская

Kamenny ostrov (Stone Island) This island's charm, seclusion and turn-of-the-century dachas, combined with winding lanes and a series of canals, lakes and ponds, make a stroll here pleasant at any time of year (though the walk across the bridge from the Aptekarsky side gets a mite chilly in winter). At the east end of the island the **Church of St John the Baptist** (Tserkov Ioanna Predtechi, 1778) seems to have found better use as a basketball court. Behind it the big, classical **Kamennoostrovsky Palace**, built by Catherine the Great for her son, is now a weedy military sanatorium.

2-ya Beryozovaya alleya, which dissects the island in an upside-down 'v' from the roundabout off Kamennoostrovsky prospekt in the centre of the island's eastern side,

sports some lovely dachas, including some former party and KGB retreats, which now rent out space to wealthy Russians and foreigners, as well as some of the upper strata of St Petersburg Mafiagentsia.

The island also boasts a government retreat, used by the president when he's in town and by other big wigs when he's not. Look for the **tree**, said to have been planted by Peter the Great, almost blocking naberezhnaya reki Krestovki just west of its intersection with 2-ya Beryozovaya alleya.

The centre of the island has lots of turn-of-the-century summer houses. A pretty example is a wooden gingerbread mansion, with high gables like hats, at the end of Polevaya alleya, next to the kindergarten. A grander example on the north-west shore is the lavish mansion of one Senator Polovtsev, who had barely moved in when the Bolsheviks took it away. Nearby is an ungainly, though sweet, wooden summer theatre first put up in the 1820s, and a footbridge to Yelagin Island. The **Danish Consulate-General** has, *hands-down*, the coolest diplomat property in town; they're in a massive dacha on Bolshaya alleya, towards the centre of the island.

Kamenny Ostrov is a short walk from Yelagin island; 15 minutes' walk north of metro Petrogradskaya and ten minutes south of metro Chyornaya Rechka.

Yelagin Island This island's centrepiece is the **Yelagin Palace** (Yelaginsky dvorets), built for his mother by Tsar Alexander I, who had architect Carlo Rossi landscape the entire island while he was at it. The palace is to your right as you cross the footbridge from Kamenny Ostrov.

The very beautiful restored interiors of the main house include old furnishings on loan from the Europe and Astoria hotels; don't miss the stupendous 1890s carved-walnut study ensemble from Europe and the incredible inlaid-wood floors. The house is open from 10 am to 6 pm, closed Monday and Tuesday. Other nearby estate buildings sometimes have exhibitions too. Admission is US$1 for foreigners, US$0.10 for Russians, US$0.05 for students and children. Other nearby estate buildings sometimes have exhibitions, too.

The rest of the island is a lovely network of paths, greenery, lakes and channels – you can rent rowing boats – and a plaza at the west end looking out to the Gulf of Finland. It's all now the Central Park of Culture & Rest (named after, still, Kirov), two km long and pedestrian only. Several small cafés are open in summer.

The rowing boat rental stand is at the northern end of the island, at the 3-ya Yelagin bridge, which runs between the island and Primorsky prospekt to the north. The water bicycle rental stand is almost due south of the Yelagin Palace. Rates are about US$1 per hour, and you can explore the network of canals and lakes on the island. If you stop for a picnic, keep the boat in sight!

Krestovsky Island The biggest of the three islands, Krestovsky consists mostly of the vast **Seaside Park of Victory** (Primorsky Park Pobedy), dotted with sports fields and the 100,000 seat **Kirov Stadium**, where you can see St Petersburg's reprehensible football team, Zenit, lose to whatever team it's taking on.

Bus No 71a from metro Petrogradskaya goes the length of Krestovsky Island to Kirov Stadium. Bus No 71 from near metro Petrogradskaya, bus No 45 from inner Nevsky prospekt and the Hermitage, and tram No 12 from metro Gostiny Dvor or metro Gorkovskaya all terminate on Krestovsky near the footbridge to Yelagin.

Buddhist Temple From Yelagin Island a footbridge crosses north to the mainland. There, at Primorsky prospekt 91 by Lipovaya alleya, is a Buddhist *datsan* (temple), of all things. (Russia's Buddhist community is centred in the Buryatia Republic in Siberia.) A neglected but handsome and richly coloured three-storey building with walls sloping in Tibetan style, it was built from 1900-15 at the instigation of Pyotr Badmaev, a Buddhist physician to Tsar Nicholas II.

From anywhere but Yelagin Island, take any tram or trolleybus west from metro Chyornaya Rechka to the Lipovaya alleya stop.

VYBORG SIDE

Peter the Great had no apparent interest in the far side of the Neva, and today, beyond the embankment and Finland Station, among the factories and railway lines, there are few attractions, though if you're looking for a fur hat, the **Kondratevsky rynok** at Polyustrovsky prospekt is just the ticket (see Things to Buy later in this chapter).

Finland Station

Finland Station (Finlyandsky vokzal) is where, in 1917, Lenin arrived from exile in

Switzerland (having ridden in a sealed railway carriage through Germany, Sweden and Finland) and gave his legendary speech from the top of an armoured car, in the square where his statue now stands. After fleeing a second time he again arrived here from Finland, this time disguised as a rail fireman, and the locomotive he rode in is displayed on the platform. It's not really the same station, having been rebuilt following WW II. The Ploshchad Lenina metro station is next door.

Kresty Prison

Kresty is St Petersburg's main holding prison; if you're busted here, Kresty's where they take you to await whatever it is that awaits you (it's also conveniently located just next door to the Holiday Hostel). But what distinguishes Kresty from, say, New York's Riker's Island, is that Kresty is located on a main boulevard, and prisoners can get to the windows. Russian families are quite close, and with true Russian exuberance, the families of the accused line the street outside, bonding with their inmates.

On any given day you can see dozens of these well wishers lining Arsenalnaya naberezhnaya. Mothers, fathers and sometimes even drunken friends stand crying. Wives and girlfriends stand close to the concrete fence, moving their arms in what may look like complicated dance moves, but what is in fact a crude code, known to inmates and prison guards alike.

The prisoner, let's call him the receiver, makes himself known by holding an article of clothing out the window (they stick their arms through the bars or through holes in the steel mesh). When the sender, down on the street, identifies their man, they start waving their arms about, tracing Cyrillic characters in the air.

The receiver waves up and down to signal 'I understand', and side to side to signal 'repeat'. Under this method, after three or four minutes of waving, one can clearly discern the message, 'I-c-a-l-l-e-d-y-o-u-r-f-r-i-e-n-d-M-i-s-h-a'!

The process, understandably, is time consuming (a message like 'I called your lawyer but he was out to lunch' could take half an hour or so), but the family and friends on the street below (again in true Russian style) bring along sausage, bread, cheese and thermoses filled with hot tea. Of course, some bring along a bottle of vodka just to pass the time.

The best time to go is in the early evening; bring along a snack, and try not to be obtrusive or rude.

Piskaryovka Cemetery

For two and a half years during WW II the Germans besieged Leningrad and between half a million and one million people died, mostly of cold and starvation. Almost half a million were buried in mass graves in this cemetery (Piskaryovskoe memorialnoe kladbishche). With acres of slightly raised mounds marked by year, it's a sobering place. At the entrance is an exhibit of photographs that need no captions. Here you'll understand the Russian obsession with that war.

The cemetery is a long way out; about a 40-minute trip from the city centre on public transport. From Ploshchad Muzhestva metro station turn left, cross prospekt Nepokoryonnykh and take bus No 123 about seven minutes east to the square granite pavilion.

St Sampson's Cathedral

Peter the Great defeated the Swedes at Poltava in 1709, on the feast day of St Sampson. In commemoration a wooden church (Sampsonevsky sobor) was built at what is now Bolshoy Sampsonevsky prospekt 41, and the five-domed stone church that replaced it in the 1730s is now among the city's oldest buildings. The comely church, with galleries on either side and a kerb-side bell tower, has been closed and is in the hands of a team of Polish restorers.

ACTIVITIES
Banya

Tired? Overworked? A good beating may be all you need, and St Petersburg's public banyas are as good a place as any to get one! See 'A Russian Banya' in the Petrozavodsk section of the Northern European Russia chapter for background and banya etiquette. Here are a few of the better public banyas:

Banya 13 (☎ 550 09 85), Karbysheva ulitsa 29A (metro: Ploshchad Muzhestva), has a large outdoor heated pool

Banya 50 (☎ 233 50 92), ulitsa Malaya Passadskaya 28, is a nice, clean and friendly place

Nevskie Bani, ulitsa Marata 5/7 (metro: Mayakovskaya), the largest in town, is smack in the city centre

Hash House Harriers
A 'drinking club with a running problem', the HHH started in Kuala Lumpur, Malaysia, and has since spread to British consulates all over the world. The runs are usually of five km or less, followed by a 'down-down' chug-a-lug session during which you wear practically as much beer as you drink. It's great fun in a football-hooligan sort of a way. They meet every Sunday at 2 pm near the statue of Pushkin in ploshchad Iskusstv – bring running gear, and, if you like, new running shoes. For more information contact Lesley Saunderson at the British Consulate (☎ 119 60 36).

Rowing Boat Rental
In summer, a lovely way to while away a day (or to keep the kids somewhat amused) is paddling through the canals and lakes on Yelagin Island. The rowing boat rental stand is at the northern end of the island at the 3-ya Yelagin bridge, which runs between the island and Primorsky prospekt to the north. The water bicycle rental stand is almost due south of the Yelagin Palace. Rates are about US$1 per hour, and you can explore the network of canals and lakes on the island. If you stop for a picnic, keep the boat in sight!

Tanning
Looking sallow? St Petersburg's full of tanning salons, usually costing about US$6 for half an hour. Try Luda (☎ 275 53 82), Nevsky prospekt 18, Casa Antonio (☎ 114 37 55), on Soyuza Pechatnikov ulitsa, or the salon at Leninsky prospekt 115 (☎ 153 94 63). There's also a solarium at the Summer Hostel.

Working Out
The Summer Hostel has a health club, with free weights and aerobics classes for about US$1 an hour. The Grand Hotel Europe, Nevskij Palace and Astoria hotels also have health clubs that admit visitors. Prices range from about US$10 to US$20 per day.

RIVER & CANAL TRIPS
In summer – roughly May to September – St Petersburg makes good use of its rivers and canals. In addition to the hydrofoil sailings to Petrodvorets and Lomonosov, excursion boats leave the Anichkov Bridge landing on the Fontanka River just off Nevsky prospekt every 15 minutes from 10.45 am to 8 pm for a 75-minute, US$2.50 tootle around the canals and smaller rivers, sometimes with commentary in Russian.

There are also 80-minute 'City on the Neva' cruises, up the river and back from Hermitage No 2 landing, every 40 minutes or so for US$0.75. Forty-minute trips also sometimes go from Letny Sad (Summer Garden). You'll generally putter into the Neva, headed east, go around the horn and south to the Smolny, where you turn back and head for home. The boats' cafés sell snacks, beer and champagne – bring an ice bucket.

Queues for these public boats can be long but, should you be of the wealthy persuasion or in a group of four, you can hire a water taxi (motorboat) at various landings throughout the city, particularly just north of Nevsky prospekt at the Griboedova Canal, and further south, at the landing just north of the Bankovy Bridge. You can also catch water taxis on the Moyka at Nevsky prospekt, and one landing south of there, near ulitsa Gorokhavaya. The benefit of this (other than the obvious lack of screaming children and vomiting and sometimes belligerent co-passengers) is that you can choose the canals you want to see and take them at a pace you set.

The price for water-taxi trips is as much as you're willing to pay, with a rock bottom starting price of about US$30; expect to pay at least US$35 unless you're a good negotiator.

ORGANISED TOURS

There are so many agencies offering tours of the city that there's no point in trying to list them all; check the *St Petersburg Press*, or *The Traveller's Yellow Pages* for tour agencies. Peter TIPS (see Information earlier in this chapter) offers a wide range of city tours, including a one-hour orientation tour for US$15. The HI St Petersburg Hostel has a minivan and offers city orientation tours and special events.

A couple of agencies, including the St Petersburg Travel Company, have desks in the Astoria Hotel, which is convenient. They offer city orientation tours for about US$10; specialised tours (museums, churches, rivers etc) can be arranged there as well. All of the city's luxury hotels' concierge desks or service bureaus offer tours ranging from standard coach affairs to absolutely lavish treats, such as chartered river-boat soirees etc.

Helicopter Tours

Now that aviation restrictions have loosened, helicopter tours are a much more common option. You still can't fly directly over the city centre, but you can fly over the Neva, between the Admiralty and the Peter & Paul Fortress, and over to the Smolny.

Air Len (☎ 350 89 79, 350 07 60) is probably the most reliable company in town (it won the contract for aerial shots of the Goodwill Games), and its flights leave from the SKK Sports Complex, near metro Park Pobedy, many times a day during summer months. You can show up and wait to join a tour (about US$15 for 20 minutes) or you can charter the chopper by the hour for US$500 to US$700 depending on the destination. You can fit up to 20 people in the Mi8 helicopters, so this is not a bad deal for groups – especially for the ten-minute jaunt down to Pushkin! It'll also do charters to

Kizhi, Staraya Russa, Novgorod, Pskov and Petrozavodsk.

FESTIVALS

During the white nights of the last 10 days of June, when night never falls, many St Petersburgers stay out celebrating – quietly or otherwise – all night, particularly at weekends. There's a tourist-oriented *White Nights Dance Festival* with events ranging from folk to ballet, but the main Kirov company doesn't always take part – more often its students do. The *Russian Winter* (25 December to 5 January) and *Goodbye Russian Winter* (late February to early March) festivities centre outside the city, with troika rides, folk shows and performing bears.

Less tourist oriented are the *Christmas Musical Meetings in Northern Palmyra*, a classical music festival held, since 1991, during the week before Christmas. The locations change; check the *St Petersburg Press* for specifics. The *St Petersburg Music Spring*, an international classical music festival held in April or May, and the mid-November international jazz festival, Osenie Ritmy (Autumn Rhythms), are built around St Petersburg's jazz clubs.

PLACES TO STAY

St Petersburg's accommodation scene has improved to the point that it's unrecognisable to returning visitors. And the changes have affected every price range; it's not just that big money moved in and built luxury places (which it did), but there are now no fewer than two youth hostels and several B&B-arranging companies. Even the former Intourist hotels have begun performing heretofore unheard of acts, such as smiling, cleaning the rooms, charging on the basis of value and so on.

Some St Petersburg hotels are plagued by crowds of noisy, cheap-drink-sodden Finns, who make even Russians seem like teetotallers.

But the increase in available bedspace does not by any means mean that St Petersburg accommodation is a big bargain – it's not, at least when compared to the rest of the country outside Moscow.

For a traditional hotel room, playing it straight (admitting you're a foreigner and using a Western passport), rock bottom is about US$12 to US$17, but you'll have to get out of the city centre for it. The youth hostels range from US$12 to US$15 for a bed, and B&Bs can, if you're very choosy and not picky about being far from the city centre, run as little as US$20, but average US$25 to US$35 for a couple. All the above prices include breakfast. There are, of course, ways to get into hotels for cheaper prices, but you'll need help from a Russian friend, or, better, a Russian company.

PLACES TO STAY – BOTTOM END
City Centre

Russia's first and to date only Hostelling International (HI) member hostel, the HI St Petersburg Hostel (☎ 329 80 18; fax 329 80 19; see next paragraph for e-mail) has the cheapest rooms in the city centre at US$15 per bed in rooms with two to six beds. The hostel's been open since early 1992, and is run by an American and his two Russian partners. It's about a five-minute walk north-east of Moscow Station and ploshchad Vosstannia (see the Smolny Region map), and the rooms are very clean and comfortable. Breakfast is included, the staff's preternaturally friendly, and the hostel's visa support service is one of the best around. There's a video-café downstairs showing movies a couple of times a week. It also has a fully fledged budget travel agency, Sindbad Travel (see Travel Agencies in the Information section earlier in this chapter).

Reservations can be made by faxing directly on (7 812) 329 80 19, through any HI hostel on the International Booking Network (IBN), or, in the USA, through RYHT (☎ (1 310) 618 2014; fax (1 310) 618 1140). You can e-mail them at ryh@ryh.spb.su for general questions about the hostel; and bookings@ryh.spb.su to book. It will also accept reservations for Holiday Hostel and others in the Russian Youth Hostel Association. If you've got an Internet browser, http://www.spb.su/ryh/ gets you to get to the hostel's home page.

Unless you feel like spending upwards of US$300 per night, you can't get a much better location than the *Student Dormitory* (☎ 314 74 72) at ulitsa Plekhanova 6, 120 metres behind the Kazan Cathedral, but this is an iffy proposition. Technically, you should be allowed to get into its clean, comfortable (have we mentioned perfectly located?) singles/doubles for US$12/14.50, but management runs from a bit unpredictable to downright dodgy, and availability is very tight, especially in summer. Calling first may help, or you can just try showing up. Be friendly.

The *Bolshoy Teatr Kukol Hotel* (yes, that does mean the 'Big Puppet Theatre Hotel'; ☎ 273 39 96) at ulitsa Nekrasova 12, has singles/doubles at US$15/22. Hmmm.

The *Oktyabrskaya* (☎ 277 63 30) at Ligovsky prospekt 10, a crumbling old hotel smack in ploshchad Vosstania, is a fair place with a terrific location. It has comfortable, but well-worn, singles/doubles at US$24/28, and it's a fair deal. Rumour has it that it's being taken over by a foreign firm (many people say Holiday Inn), and slated to be gutted and converted to a luxury hotel, but for the moment it's still an option to be considered. It's opposite Moscow Station.

The *Hotel Rus* (☎ 273 46 83, 272 66 54) is a large, modern and popular place not far at all from the city centre, and it's a good bet at US$28 for a single, US$40 for a double with bath included and US$50 for a two-room 'suite' (which has a couch that sleeps a third person comfortably, if on a wonky angle). It's at ulitsa Artilleryskaya 1, a one-block street just south of ploshchad Radishcheva, near metro Chernyshevskaya.

Petrograd & Vyborg Sides

The *Holiday Hostel* (☎ & fax 542 73 64) at ulitsa Mikhailova 1, 3rd floor, became St Petersburg's second western-style youth hostel in 1994. Its location just south of Finland Station, has its pros and cons. Pro is definitely the view – in summer, its rooftop café offers the classic panorama of Peter &

Paul Fortress against the backdrop of raised drawbridges. Among the cons is that, aside from Finland Station, there's not much out there. On top of that, the incessant shouting you hear is the families of inmates calling to loved ones being held at Kresty Prison, which is right next door. The hostel itself is clean and fun, though slightly run-down. It doesn't offer as much in the way of services as the HI St Petersburg Hostel, though the staff is very friendly and they try hard. It has two to five beds to a room (no surcharge if you're lucky enough to get a double); a bed is US$12 (US$14 in summer), and there's a US$10 fee for the visa invitation. From Finland Station (metro: Ploshchad Lenina) turn left, walk to ulitsa Mikhailova, turn right, cross the street; the entrance to the yard is on the left (you'll see the big, red-brick prison wall) and the hostel entrance is in the south-west corner of the courtyard. The code for the front door is 1648 and the hostel's on the 3rd floor.

The small, old *Hotel Druzhba* (☎ 234 18 44) at ulitsa Chapygina 4, at the foot of the city's TV mast in northern Petrograd would be a great place with a great location, but apparently it doesn't take foreigners. And thank God. The lobby's patrolled by Kalashnikov-toting guards and management is cold but polite. If it did accept foreigners the price would be US$17/20 for singles/doubles. It's a pleasant 10-minute walk or a quick bus ride down Kamenno-ostrovsky prospekt to Petrogradskaya metro. (See the Kirovsky Islands map.)

If there is a room left over at the *Dvorets Molodyozhy* (Palace of Youth; ☎ 234 32 78) at ulitsa Professora Popova 47, index 197022, it's only because it hasn't yet been rented out by some fly-by-night company as office space. It's a very quiet location, but bus No 25 to Nevsky prospekt doesn't come by often, and it's a 25-minute walk to Petrogradskaya metro. It's big and Soviet-modern outside, plain inside. Rooms are doubles and triples with attached showers (some baths). There is one pleasant guests-only restaurant without music, and a forlorn grill-bar. If you can get in, it's got singles for

US$13.50 and doubles from US$30 to US$50 not including breakfast (which might be a good thing; its breakfast consists of a bowl of glop).

On the mainland, north of Kamenny Ostrov near metro Chyornaya Rechka, is the *Vyborgskaya* (☎ 246 91 41, 246 23 19) at Torzhkovskaya ulitsa 3, index 197342. Its three buildings have singles, doubles and suites from US$14/24/50, some with attached bath, some communal. There are two decent restaurants, both with bands, a bufet and a cheap sauna that fits three. Nearby Chyornaya Rechka metro makes it convenient to the city centre. (See the St Petersburg map.)

Just a 10-minute walk away (or a short bus ride north-west from Ploshchad Muzhestva metro) the *Hotel Sputnik* (☎ 552 56 32) at prospekt Morisa Toreza 34, index 194021, is far away from the centre but in a quiet neighbourhood of apartment blocks. Foreigners get singles or doubles with attached bath, a restaurant with live music and three bufety. It's not a bad place, though it's getting pricey at US$30 to US$40 a single and US$40 to US$50 a double. (See the St Petersburg map.)

The crumbling *Hotel Karelia* (☎ 226 35 15/19) at ulitsa Tukhachevskogo 27/2, index 195253, is a dump for the money and worth avoiding. Plain, quiet singles/doubles with attached showers are US$26/38.50 the first night, US$20.50/31 for each additional night. The staff is pretty slack and the location lousy, 10 km from the city centre. It's a dreary 25-minute ride by trolleybus No 3 or 19 to metro Ploshchad Lenina.

Vasilevsky Island

The *Hotel Gavan* (☎ 356 85 04), Sredny prospekt 88, index 199106, is reasonably modern inside, with two restaurants (one with live music), two bufety and a bar. Rooms – mostly doubles with attached bath – are old and plain but clean. Aside from a small park the neighbourhood is featureless. From the hotel, bus No 30 goes to the Hermitage and outer Nevsky prospekt; tram No

63 goes to the Hermitage and the Strelka. (See the St Petersburg map.)

South & East of the City Centre

See the St Petersburg map for all the hotels in this section.

The newly opened *Summer Hostel* (☎ 252 75 63; fax 252 40 19) is not exactly centrally located (it's about a 10-minute metro ride from ploshchad Vosstania), but it's the cheapest hostel bed in town at US$6 per person (US$8 in the renovated wing), including tax and breakfast.

Part of the state-run Industrial Teachers' College, the hostel employs English-language students as staff to keep costs down. There are two wings, both on the 3rd floor; the renovated wing has a much nicer common area (with a TV and a pool table) and kitchen (three refrigerators and four hotplates; there are two very good Western supermarkets nearby – see Places to Eat, Self-Catering). But both wings are clean and the rooms perfectly adequate – as adequate as in hotels that cost 10 times as much!

The building also has a sauna, health club and hairdresser, all available (at extra fees of about US$1 to US$3) to guests.

It's at ulitsa Baltiyskaya 26; from metro Narvskaya walk left, down prospekt Stachek away from the Narva Gate to ulitsa Baltiyskaya; the hostel is then 300 metres ahead on the left-hand side. As you enter, fight past the babushka/door guards, turn left down the hallway, right into the stairwell and up to the 3rd floor.

The hostel is a member of the Russian Youth Hostel Association, so bookings may be made through the HI International Booking Network, or through the RYHA (see Accommodation section in Facts About European Russia), the RYHT office in Redondo Beach, California, USA (see HI St Petersburg Hostel earlier in this section), or directly with the hostel.

The dumpy but cheerful *Kievskaya Hotel* (☎ 166 04 56), Dnepropetrovskaya ulitsa 49, index 192202, and the *Hotel Zarya* (☎ 166 83 98), a block away at Kurskaya ulitsa 40, are both city-run under a single management, and both charge a reasonable US$18/28 for singles/doubles. The Kievskaya has attached showers, the Zarya has baths. Each has a bufet and a plain guests-only restaurant without music. They're out in a boring neighbourhood on the Obvodny Canal, though transport is easy. Bus No 25 from the local bus terminal next door is a mini-tour to Gostiny Dvor metro, Nevsky prospekt and Petrograd Side. Between nearby Ligovsky prospekt and metro Ploshchad Vosstania, take anything except bus No 14; the nearest stop is Obvodny Canal.

Far south at ulitsa Gastello 17, index 196135, staff at the last-resort, down-at-heel *Hotel Mir* (☎ 118 51 66) seem to spend most of their time on the phone. Half the rooms have attached toilets and showers, half don't. Avoid it, but if you fail, the closest metro is Moskovskaya, or take bus No 16 from Park Pobedy metro. Rooms are US$24/33 for singles/doubles.

North-West Outskirts

Unless you're driving from Finland and are so tired you can't possible go a km further, skip the *Motel-Camping Olgino* (☎ 238 35 50), about 18 km north-west of the city centre at Primorskoe shosse 59 (index 197229). It's far away and inconvenient to public transport, and not in a particularly safe part of town, but at least from here you can walk through the pine woods to the Baltic shore to clear your head. Double rooms are US$35 to US$45 (cheaper from Sunday to Thursday).

A taxi to the city (they know you need to get there) will be at least US$10. By public transport count on at least an hour and a half: the nearest metro is Chyornaya Rechka, about 11 km away by country bus No 411 or 416 (US$0.50) or city bus No 110. From the metro station, walk north across the park and over the road to the bus stop. The last bus at night leaves here about 10.45 pm. At Olgino, the stop is about 400 metres towards St Petersburg from the motel entrance. (See the Around St Petersburg map.)

Private Homes

There are several agencies advertising in Russian and Western press.

The Travellers Guest House in Moscow (☎ (095) 971 40 59; e-mail tgh@glas.apc.org) organises placements in flats in St Petersburg for as little as US$10 per person per night.

We've received numerous favourable letters about the St Petersburg Host Family Association (HOFA; fax 275 19 92; e-mail alexei@hofak.spb.stu.su); there have also been several more positive reports on CompuServe's travel forums, and we've communicated with travellers who've used the service and they say it's a good deal. It's been around, they say, for four years, and originated at St Petersburg (then Leningrad) University.

HOFA places travellers with Russian families, generally academics and professionals, in their apartments around town. You'll usually get a private room and a shared bath, and breakfast is included. HOFA says that at least one member of the family will speak English. Their basic price for one or two people is US$25/40 per night; US$150/240 week for an apartment near the city centre. This includes a business visa invitation that HOFA will register with OVIR on your arrival. Payment is in cash, to the family you're staying with. HOFA also has agents in the USA, UK and Australia (see Accommodation in the European Russia Facts for the Visitor chapter), and offers accommodation in several other Russian cities.

Shakti (☎ 279 51 98; e-mail cas@spec tron.spb.su) is a younger company that can arrange similar homestays with similar types of families; the basic price is US$30/45 per night for apartments near the city centre. This also includes a business visa and OVIR registration, though be sure to insist on registration as they tend to think little of the authorities. The flats we saw were quite nice and very clean.

Both of these companies also offer guides, excursions, Russian lessons and other add-ons; contact them directly for more information.

There are also babushkas and other touts hanging around in Moscow and Finland Sta-

tions with 'Room for Rent' signs. Most of these are people trying to pick up some cash, but be absolutely sure of what you're getting before you pay for anything. Demand to see the room or flat before committing, and use caution and common sense.

Lloyd Donaldson, editor of the *St Petersburg Press*, wrote of a very nice experience with one of these women when he was finding a place to stay for a friend. The woman approached them in Moscow Station with a hand-written sign around her neck, and

...was offering hotel rooms for US$5.50 in the northern suburbs. When I said we were looking for something in the centre with a family, she said 'Come with me, I'll take you to the despatcher.'

When we got there we discovered that the system that operates in Budapest is now also operating in a very small way here in St Petersburg - the idea of a little bureau in the railway stations that acts as an agent for people with rooms to rent in their apartments.

The despatcher had 14 places on her list. One of the landladies spoke English. The price was US$11 a night, without meals, to be paid each day. When I said we were looking for something for a month, she said, 'Well, we normally only do stays for up to 10 days... but if you and the landlady like each other then you could extend it.'

The bureau is in Dom Kultury (the House of Culture) which is on Ligovsky prospekt, next to Moscow Station. To find the bureau (which is literally just one woman at a shabby desk stationed in one corner of a corridor) go in the main entrance, turn right, and walk about four metres. It's on your right near the window.

My feeling about the whole deal, as an experienced traveller and someone who has lived in Russia for three years, was that it was totally OK. There was no question at all of 'foreigners' discrimination' in terms of pricing, and I had no hesitation in dealing with either women. They both seemed very decent, very normal women. (The one on the platform was a pensioner who gets 120,000 roubles (US$27) a month.)

PLACES TO STAY – MIDDLE
City Centre

The *Hotel Moskva* (☎ 274 30 01, 274 20 51) is, like the Hotel St Petersburg, a big three-star place not far from the city centre, just opposite the Alexander Nevsky Monastery. But it comes second to the St Petersburg in everything except access (Ploshchad Alexandra Nevskogo metro is right under the hotel). Service is slacker, the lobby dimmer, rooms smaller – though comfortable and clean – and the feeling more institutional. For what you get, the rack rate of US$67/82 (it accepts Visa, Eurocard, MasterCard, American Express), is a bit steep, but a lot of packages use the Moskva, and then the price drops considerably. Try for a room at the back where it's quiet.

Downstairs in the lobby, the Neva Star, formerly a hard-currency shop, now a posh boutique selling discounted imported clothes and food at western European prices, is a welcome feature. The restaurants and cafés are so-so, and there's an expensive all-you-can-eat buffet (see Places to Eat later in this chapter). The hotel is at ploshchad Alexandra Nevskogo 2 (index 143317) at the end of Nevsky prospekt. (See the Central St Petersburg map.)

The big Hotel Helen-Sovietskaya (☎ 259 25 52) at Lermontovsky prospekt 43, index 198106, is only three km south-west of the Hermitage, along the Fontanka River, but is poorly served by public transport. The hotel is a Finnish/Russian joint venture. Rooms are of about three-star standard, and come with TV, telephone and bath; service is decent, and there is a big beryozka, an almost-real and not-very expensive Bierstube, three restaurants and three cafés. Singles/doubles cost US$65/105, and it accepts Visa, Eurocard and MasterCard. Occasionally there are some thugs milling about in the lobby, but they're usually not a problem.

The nearest metro is Baltiyskaya, 750 metres south, but if you're already paying the price to stay at the hotel, you won't mind a bit getting a US$3 taxi ride from the city centre. Trolleybus Nos 3 and 8 follow Zagorodny prospekt to Nevsky prospekt; bus No 49 and tram No 1 go to the Mariinsky Theatre en route to ploshchad Truda. (See the St Petersburg map.) Reservations can also be made through the joint-venture partner, Arctia Hotels in Helsinki (☎ (358 0) 694 80 22).

Vyborg Side

The big, three star Hotel St Petersburg (☎ 542 90 31, 542 95 60) has standard post-Intourist accommodations and facilities, with clean but dull rooms. It's opposite the Cruiser Aurora at Vyborgskaya naberezhnaya 5/2, index 194300, which gives the front rooms great views over the Neva towards the Hermitage – but also traffic noise if you open the windows. Eating facilities are good, the service bureau big but erratic in attitude. At US$75/95 for singles/doubles, it's not a bad deal, though the staff is still struggling to crawl out from under the rock of Intourist training. There's a good restaurant, beer hall and even a concert hall downstairs. It accepts Visa, Eurocard, MasterCard and American Express.

The place halfway burned down in 1991 after a Russian-made TV set popped its cork and torched a couple of floors, but it's been renovated back to standards. The extension may some day be finished.

On the down side, public transport is mediocre for a place so close to the city centre. It's a 15-minute walk to the nearest metro, Ploshchad Lenina; and you may wait 20 minutes on prospekt Finlyandsky, behind the hotel, for the westbound tram No 6 or 63 to take you across the Sampsonevsky Bridge over to metro Gorkovskaya. Tram No 63 continues to the Strelka. There are also buses and trams from ploshchad Lenina. (See the Central St Petersburg map.)

The Hotel Okhtinskaya (☎ 227 44 38) is an under-publicised French/Russian joint-venture hotel that has been made absolutely inconvenient due to the closing of the Bolshoy Okhtinsky Bridge that connected it to the eastern half of the city centre at the Smolny. The bridge is scheduled to reopen in 1997. The Okhtinskaya, at ulitsa Okhtinskaya 4 (it's really on Sverdlovskaya naberezhnaya, about 200 metres south of the Nevsky Melody restaurant) is a fine business-class hotel, with very clean and modern rooms with river views (though the views aren't exactly of St Petersburg's finest sections).

What's good about it is its staff, the dining

rooms and the saunas. What's bad is its location, and because of that only, the US$80/88 for single/double rooms seems a bit out of line.

Vasilevsky Island

The *Hotelship Peterhof* (☎ 213 63 21), moored off naberezhnaya Makarova, just north of the Tuchkov Bridge, is a Swiss-managed, Russian-staffed hotel-ship that's certainly got staying power. Billing itself as 'A Little Slice of Switzerland in St Petersburg,' it's kind of a fun place, not too inconveniently located from the city centre – it's about five blocks from metro Vasileostrovskaya which is one stop from the Gostiny Dvor/Nevsky Prospekt metro stations.

The rooms aren't huge – in fact, they're cabins – but they're certainly clean and the ship has a good restaurant downstairs (they do 'theme nights', and its Italian food is darn good) and a full bar and sort of disco-ette upstairs. The staff is very courteous and helpful. Whether the good service justifies a US$115/190 price tag is a toss up, but they certainly try. They accept Visa, Eurocard and MasterCard. (See the Central St Petersburg map.)

The *Pribaltiyskaya Hotel* (☎ 356 41 35, 356 45 63) is an Intourist-built behemoth on the Gulf of Finland that's very popular with package tour groups (perhaps you caught its movie debut in *The Russia House*). It's at ulitsa Korablestroyteley (Shipbuilders' St) 14, index 199226. There's fair service, big, clean rooms (no singles) with stunning views of the Gulf of Finland if you're lucky: ask. The rack rate of US$155 for a double is laughable; no one ever pays that, and it can be a very economical place to stay if you're here on a package. It accepts Visa, Eurocard, MasterCard and American Express.

The good news is that, perhaps because it's a bit inconvenient, it's got a lot of extras – such as a bowling alley, a Baltic Star shop (formerly a hard-currency shop), a good business and conference centre, money-changers and an in-house (though pricey)

taxi service. The huge service bureau, though, offers more bureau than service, and charges you extra for CNN. It has four restaurants and three bars, none of which will set the world alight. But it's blessed with a good three-meal-a-day Swedish Table, a bufet on almost every floor, and close proximity to the Venezia Italian restaurant and pizzeria. Flanking the hotel on both sides is St Petersburg's biggest beryozka.

It's far away on the Gulf of Finland, at the windy (whoo!) end of Vasilevsky Island, half an hour from the city centre. From Nevsky prospekt, the fastest way is to metro Primorskaya, and then a bus No 41 to the hotel. Bus Nos 7 and 44 go all the way down Nevsky prospekt, No 30 goes to the Hermitage, or take No 128 or 152 to metro Primorskaya (but No 44, 128 or 151 back, for four stops).

South & East of the City Centre

The main advantage of Intourist's modern *Pulkovskaya Hotel* (☎ 264 51 22), eight km south of the city centre at ploshchad Pobedy 1, index 196143, is its proximity to the airport – 15 minutes by bus No 13 that stops right in front, or by taxi for US$3 (don't take the in-house taxi service: walk a little north, away from the hotel, and flag one down on Moskovsky prospekt to avoid paying a 'tourist price').

No doubt the Pulkovskaya's rates (US$120/140 singles/doubles) are to pay for all those Finnish lighting fixtures, but the rooms (all with baths) are comfortable and clean, and service is good.

Two cavernous restaurants with floor shows are no good for a quiet meal, though the food isn't bad. Happily a Swedish Table serves decent breakfast and lunch, and there's a good lobby bar. The hotel is about 750 metres south of Moskovskaya metro by the Defenders of Leningrad Monument; or bus Nos 3 and 39-Э (not 39) go to ulitsa Bolshaya Morskaya (ulitsa Gertsena) via Nevsky prospekt. (See the St Petersburg map.)

The *Hotel Deson-Ladoga* (☎ 528 53 93),

prospekt Shaumyana 26, a dreary block in a sea of dreary blocks, is across the Neva from Nevsky Monastery. Single and double rooms have attached showers (US$78/104), and there's a restaurant with live music. It's east of Krasnogvardeyskaya metro station (take exit stairs No 8). The only bright spot in the neighbourhood is the Shvabsky Domik restaurant by the metro.

PLACES TO STAY – TOP END

St Petersburg's luxury hotels are now truly luxurious. The appearance of the Grand Hotel Europe and the Nevskij Palace, along with other contenders (notably the late luxury hotel-ships Olympia and the US-run Commodore, which steamed out in 1994 but hinted at returning), has resulted in a fundamental improvement in service levels. The luxury hotels all offer heaps of amenities, which include, at the very least, a health club, satellite TV, telephone, business centres, shops, newsstands, drinkable coffee and a concierge desk to take the hassle out of buying tickets (the latter, to be sure, at a premium price).

All the top-end hotels are in the city centre, all accept major credit cards and offer several categories of rooms. In the following listings, we list bottom and top prices per category.

Top of the Russian-owned line and most inexpensive in the luxury category is the *Hotel Astoria* (☎ 210 57 57; fax 315 96 68; telex 121213 ASTOR SU), ulitsa Bolshaya Morskaya (ulitsa Gertsena) 39, index 190000, right in front of St Isaac's cathedral. It has been renovated; the original Astoria appears in its Art Nouveau glory, and period furniture that wasn't stolen, looted or damaged can be seen in some of the more expensive rooms.

The hotel's in two sections, new and old (the old wing flanks the corner of ulitsa Bolshaya Morskaya (ulitsa Gertsena)), and you'll have to walk outside to get to either from the other. The old wing's grand rooms and suites are large and luxurious, while the new wing's rooms are large and comfortable.

Give the hotel's restaurants a big swerve; the lobby bar is actually quite nice for business drinks, and there's a nice little café on the 3rd floor and in the lobby of the old wing. Service is desperately fighting Intourist upbringing (with a good amount of success) – it's clearly the best of the non-joint-venture hotels. Singles cost US$170 to US$220; doubles US$210 to US$300; two-room suites US$370 to US$400; and three-room apartments (these are *nice*) for US$600. (See the Inner Central St Petersburg map.)

The *Nevskij Palace Hotel* (☎ 275 20 01; telex 121279 herms su), run by the Austrian Marco Polo Hotels and Resorts chain, is a fantabulously renovated place, with about as much luxury as one can stand. All rooms are what you'd expect from any Austrian luxury hotel, and its lobby is a great place to hang out on rainy days; it's a gold and marble multilevel atrium, with chi-chi shops, a *Bierstube*, and a general feeling of opulence. The hotel offers full conference facilities.

The hotel's restaurants are perhaps the best in town (see Places to Eat), and the service is excellent all round – if it's not, grab a manager and they'll set it right, right away (as they did when a slightly uppity clerk at the reception desk wouldn't give us an envelope!). The concierge service is good. Singles cost US$280, doubles US$334; a small suite of two rooms US$365; a regular suite US$456; and the presidential suite US$851 (1 bedroom), US$1155 (2 bedrooms); prices include breakfast and VAT. Reservations can be made directly with the hotel, through Steigenberger Reservation Service agents, or by contacting Marco Polo International in Vienna (☎ (43 1) 715 55 30-424). The hotel's address is Nevsky prospekt 57 (postal code 191025); the nearest metro is Mayakovskaya, 200 metres east.

The *Grand Hotel Europe* (☎ 119 60 00; fax 119 60 01; telex 64 121073) – the Yevropeyskaya in Soviet times – is perhaps the finest property in town if you go by location and architecture. It's certainly the most expensive.

A joint venture between Reso Hotels, SIAB construction and the City of St Petersburg (who always squabble and whose partners always threaten to back out), has enabled the original and breathtaking Art Nouveau interiors, along with a baroque façade designed by Rossi, to be completely restored to their turn-of-the-century glory.

The Europe restaurant's ceiling has got to be seen, even if that's the only reason you set foot in the hotel. The vaulted affair is covered with phenomenally beautiful and intricate stained glass, perhaps as a foil to keep your eyes off the prices, which are stellar. The atrium coffee bar is pleasant; the lobby bar would be nice if it would get some higher bar stools. The hotel has a total of four restaurants, a caviar bar and a 'nightclub'.

Rooms are comfortable, but a bit smaller than you'd think, and service is about as good as you get in Russia. The address is Mikhailovskaya ulitsa 1/7, (postal code 191073). Singles cost US$295 to US$335; doubles US$335 to US$375; belle chambre or terrace room (single/double) US$375/415; penthouse US$415 to US$530; two-room suites US$530 to US$710; executive suite US$850; and 'Lidvall' or 'Rossi' suites for US$975. These prices, by the way, do not include breakfast (which is only another US$20!) but do include VAT. In case you don't have your own limousine, Nevsky Prospekt metro is around the corner. (See the Inner Central St Petersburg map.)

PLACES TO EAT

When you're sitting in a St Petersburg, say, Indian restaurant, having a lamb vindaloo spicy enough to blow a hole in your head, a gorgeous Tandoori chicken and a decent bottle of wine, it's hard to conjure up those TV news images of bread queues, meat shortages and empty shelves. Fact is, those cold-war visions are as dated as junk bonds, Duran Duran, power ties and Charles and Diana.

Restaurants here tend to be civilised affairs, and there're plenty of them. The Soviet way of doing things (where the thug standing in the restaurant's doorway asked the couple, dressed for dinner and approaching the entrance at dinner time, 'What do *you* want?!') has mostly gone the way of the

five-year plan. You won't have to make reservations except in very popular places, and if you're told there are no seats there probably aren't any.

Undeniably, an increase in price has come along with the increase in quality; you can still eat cheaply at stolovayas, unpretentious cafés and Russian snack bars, but if you patronise the chic new eateries, bistros or cafés you'll pay near Western prices – and the shock value of a bill from some of the city's finer restaurants is as worthy of a '*Mon Dieu!*' as any that Paris has to offer. But with all this, the wide range of choices can only be good news. Whatever you fancy – from Uzbek to Arabian, Chinese to Italian, Georgian to fast food, Western European to good ol' Russian home cooking – it's here and in abundance.

Self-Catering

Self-catering is now not only possible, but plausible. The city has seen an explosion in food shops, and Western-style supermarkets are popping up like weeds all over the place. Teeming with fresh meats, cheese, vegetables, tinned goods, frozen prepared foods (such as pizza, some dinners and even fresh-frozen prawns), and usually booze, in many of these places you'd swear you'd been transported back home to a Safeway or Coles supermarket. Chains such as *Babylon* and *Holiday* have many extended-trading or 24-hour grocery shops in several areas of the city; there are a few along Nevsky prospekt alone, and a good one for quick snacks at ploshchad Vosstania, just east of Moscow Station.

The biggest supermarket in the city centre is called – surprise, surprise! – *Supermarket*, and is found in the basement of Passazh shopping centre; it's open from 9 am to 9 pm. Another good bet in the city centre is the *Babylon* at the corner of Nevsky prospekt and ulitsa Mayakovskaya, which has a collection of tinned and packaged foods, western soft drinks and a varying stock of other stuff, and accepts credit cards. The *Frukti Conservi* vegetable shop at the corner of Marata and Nevsky has a great deal of veges, Finnish drinking water, Western booze and a Russian juice bar (about US$0.05 a glass).

Yeliseevsky market, on Nevsky prospekt opposite ploshchad Ostrovskogo, is Russia's most beautiful, if not most famous, food shop. A turn-of-the-century rich people's food court, the place has now been mostly restored to its pre-Soviet splendour. Meat, chicken and fish are through the right-hand entrance, and Western and top-end Russian packaged and bulk dry goods are to the left.

Lower on Nevsky prospekt, the *Antanta Market*, in a basement on ulitsa Malaya Konyushennaya 9, is a sprawling labyrinth of imported foods and enough varieties of booze to look like a US liquor store; prices are going northward, however. It's open Monday to Friday from noon to 10 pm, and Saturday to 8 pm.

Out on Petrograd Side, the *Babylon Super* has a terrific selection of exotic (for Russia) fresh veges, like ginger root and avocado, and frozen veges, as well as a French-inspired bakery section that makes wonderful breads and awesome pastries several times daily. There are also lots of wines and beers. It accepts Visa, Eurocard, MasterCard and American Express and, if you'll be in town long, you can set up a Babylon Super credit card. It's at Maly prospekt 54, and is open Monday to Saturday from 10 am to 9 pm, and Sunday from noon to 8 pm. While you're out there on Petrograd Side, check out the florist (☎ 238 19 15) at Kamennoostrovsky prospekt 5. It sells flowers, plants and, oh yes, a full line of Mercedes Benz sedans. It's open daily from 9 am to 7 pm.

The *Kalinka Stockmann's*, behind the Hotel St Petersburg at Finlandsky prospekt 1, is a smaller affair, with good Finnish milk supplies – good for stopping off for decadent Western luxuries to cook up at the Holiday Hostel. It also sells some international newspapers and magazines.

And if you're in that Finnish-food mode, head for one of *Spar Market*'s two locations: Slavy prospekt 30 (way out in southern

nowhere; metro Moskovskaya, then trolleybus No 27 or 29 east; it's just past the Kupichinsky department store) and at the much more conveniently located, but smaller, prospekt Stachek 1 (metro: Narvskaya), which also has a small café doing very nice pastries and coffee for about US$1.50.

If you're staying at the Summer Hostel, the prospekt Stachek location is ideal; if it hasn't got what you're after, try diagonally across the street towards the hostel on ulitsa Baltiyskaya, 30 metres past the corner of prospekt Stachek, where a VIT *St Petersburg* supermarket has fruit, veges, frozen foods and booze from beer and wine to the hard stuff.

Bakeries Even in the old days the standard Russian bulochnaya turned out some terrific, rich, sour brown bread. There are still bakeries in every neighbourhood, as well as speciality and joint-venture bakers. *Karavay Bakery*, just across from the City Children's Park, has scrumptious bread, cakes and buns. It's at Tavricheskaya ulitsa 33, and is open from 8 am to 8 pm.

Nevsky 27, across from the Grand Hotel Europe, is another joint-venture place doing exceptionally good bread; there are long queues before it closes at lunch time for a break. It's open from 8 am to 1 pm and 2 to 7 pm. The *Bahlsen Bakery*, next to Le Kafe at Nevsky prospekt 142, does good bread and cakes. It's open Monday to Saturday from 8 am to 8 pm.

Markets With the advent of widespread supermarket and 24-hour shop penetration, St Petersburg's markets (rynky; singular rynok) no longer cause St Petersburgers to drop their jaws to pavement level and drool in envy, but they're still fascinating places to visit and fabulous sources of fresh produce, meats and other food.

In buildings large enough to house a small football field, the markets are held daily, and food and produce from all over the former Soviet Union can be found, including exotic fruits and vegetables that you may never have seen before (and sometimes wish you never had!). Most of the markets also feature fresh meats – as in so fresh they're still in the process of being hacked off the carcass. Markets are also a good place to pick up honey and honey products (try before you buy – it's free), cottage cheese, heavy cream and sometimes even flowers.

Two of the liveliest and most central (and most expensive) markets are the *Kuznechny* on Kuznechny pereulok, two minutes' walk from Vladimirskaya metro, and the *Maltsevsky* at ulitsa Nekrasova 52 close to Ploshchad Vosstania metro. Some others are: the *Sytny* at Sytninskaya ploshchad 3/5 (Gorkovskaya metro, behind Alexandrovsky park and up towards the Tbilisi restaurant); the *Torzhkovsky* at Torzhkovskaya ulitsa 20 (Chyornaya Rechka metro), noted as much for its selection of fine poultry as its gangland slayings; the *Kalininsky* at Polyustrovsky prospekt 45 (Ploshchad Lenina metro, then tram No 6 or 19, bus No 100, 107, 136 or 137 or any trolleybus except No 8), with its terrific fur (as well as pet) market out the back, where it has great hats; the *Moskovsky* at ulitsa Reshetnikova 12 (almost opposite Elektrosila metro); the *Sennoy* at Moskovsky prospekt 4 (Ploshchad Mira metro); and the more inexpensive *Vasileostrovsky* at Bolshoy prospekt 18 on Vasilevsky Island (Vasileostrovskaya metro).

Restaurants

City Centre The *Korean House* serves up some of the best Korean food in Eastern Europe, and after some problems with the last location, resettled (so recently that it's not on our maps) at Izmailovsky prospekt 2, in the Tekhnologichesky Institut area. They have signs in both English and Russian on the street, but the entrance itself is not very conspicuous – go in the building's entrance and on the right you'll see the Korean House sign. At its last location the food was awesome, with a decidedly heavy hand on the garlic and spices, and the staff were incredibly friendly. Specialities were Korean-style beef (marinated and cooked at

the table), and marinated carrots and kim chi (marinated cabbage). They also did darn good cold and hot noodle soups and dishes in both vegetarian and carnivorous varieties. Main courses ranged from US$3 to US$5.

Another excellent food spot on the move is *Restaurant Shen Yan*, a (you guessed it) Chinese place at Rubinshteyna 12. It planned to move at the time of writing, but hadn't quite figured out to where; find out when you get here. The food is exquisite, plentiful and cheap, with sweet and sour pork (US$6.50), interesting 'squirrel made out of fish' (US$7) and scrumptious roast vegetables (US$4.50). It is closed for one month in winter when the staff heads home to China to see the family.

Metekhi (☎ 272 33 61) at Belinskogo ulitsa 3, near the Belinskogo bridge, serves Georgian specialities at reasonable prices; main courses cost US$3 to US$6 and entrées US$1 to US$4. It also serves good veggie dishes, and has fine service. It's closest to metro Gostiny Dvor.

1001 Nights (☎ 312 22 65) is an Uzbek place near the Hermitage that has good Central Asian food, a very nice atmosphere and, considering its primo location, very reasonable prices, with main courses averaging US$3.35 to US$4.75. Definitely try the manty, which are enormous spicy dumplings, for US$1.90 and the very tasty kebab garshochke at a steeper US$4.30. Service is slow, but it's because staff expect you to relax and take a while – tell them if you're in a hurry! There's belly dancing in the evenings. The restaurant's at Millionnaya ulitsa 21/6, downstairs; it's open from 11 to 1 am.

Nearby at ulitsa Furmanova (which runs parallel to and on the west of the Fontanka), *Russky Bliny* does just those in a cosy setting for incredibly cheap prices – US$1.10 for a minced chicken pancake is as high as things go. It's only open for lunch and an early dinner, Monday to Friday from 11 am to 6 pm.

Shanghai (☎ 314 31 38), a big old Soviet-style eating palace, has some surprisingly good food, though it's erratic which dish will be good on which day, so it's generally a dodgy bet. The restaurant's at Sadovaya ulitsa 12/23, just around the corner from the Nevsky Prospekt metro; main courses range from US$4 to US$10. It's open from noon to midnight. There's a casino upstairs.

Tandoor (☎ 312 38 86) is *the* Indian place in town, with a full traditional Indian menu for about US$2.50 for an entrée, US$5 to US$9 per main, and a limited wine list. The only drawback we found was a tendency to undercook chicken dishes – specify well done. It has a number of vegetarian items on the menu, as well as a good selection of traditional Indian breads and desserts. If you like things spicy, insist on *spicy*. It's worth going to at least once, maybe more often. The restaurant is at Vosnesensky prospekt 2, just off Isaakievskaya ploshchad; it's open from noon to 11 pm.

Saigon's (☎ 315 87 72) Asian interior (complete with a bamboo bridge) belies its Russian menu; steaks for US$7, chicken tabaka at US$4.75 and salmon for $6 are all fine. It's at ulitsa Plekhanova 33, and is open from noon to 10.30 pm.

St Petersburg's very nice *Pizza Hut*, at 71/76 naberezhnaya reki Moyki, does nine varieties of pizza (medium plain US$5.50, medium vegetarian US$7.50 and medium super supreme US$11), and sells beer, wine and cappuccino, and has a salad bar. It also does deliveries in a very limited area. It's a good place to eat, though the 'thin and crispy' pizza dough tastes like a little like a Saltine cracker – get the pan-style and pig out.

There's a decent Armenian restaurant, the *Nairy* (☎ 314 80 93), on ulitsa Dekabristov near metro Sadovaya/Sennaya Ploshchad. It's open from 11 am to midnight.

Bahlsen – Le Café (☎ 271 28 11) at Nevsky prospekt 142, just east of ploshchad Vosstania, is both an inexpensive stand-up café, serving hot dogs, pizzas and snacks for less than US$3, and a sit-down bistro with Swiss-ish prices. It's a good place for a chat, and it serves a good spaghetti bolognese for US$7.80, a Spanish omelette for US$5.80 and a cheeseburger with fries and a salad for US$7.85. It's open from noon to midnight,

and it accepts Visa, Eurocard, MasterCard, American Express, JCB and Diners Club.

Chopsticks (☎ 119 60 00) at the Grand Hotel Europe, has meagre servings of dependable Chinese food in a stylish setting; main courses range from US$8 to US$22, and it accepts Visa, Eurocard, MasterCard, American Express, JCB and Diners Club. It's open from 1 to 11 pm. It's at the entrance closest to Nevsky prospekt, and is the restaurant on the right as you enter the hotel.

Nikolai (Dom Arkhitektora) (☎ 311 14 02), in the House of Architects at Bolshaya Morskaya (ulitsa Gertsena) 52, does its best to serve up European and even Brazilian food. It has a nice layout, and main courses average from US$16 to US$25.

Bistro le Francais (☎ 210 96 22, 315 24 65) is just that – the genuine French chef greets guests with a jaunty '*Bonjour*' – but *sans* surly maître d' who pretends not to speak English. It has very nice, very rich specialities from US$8 to US$20, and there's a video screening club that also rents films in the restaurant (see Entertainment later in this chapter). It's at ulitsa Galernaya 20.

The *Restoran Nevsky* (☎ 311 30 93) at Nevsky prospekt 71 (above metro Mayakovskaya) seems to be doing its best to keep alive the traditions of the communist dining experience. It's popular with tourists because of listings in aged guidebooks, and if you haven't yet experienced overpriced, mediocre food and poor service, you might stop in for a bite. It's open from noon to 11 pm.

Bella Leone (☎ 113 16 70) at Vladimirsky prospekt 9 is a cheerful and very western place which serves Italian and European food. Make reservations as it's very popular; it accepts American Express.

The *Queen* (☎ 314 07 18) at ulitsa Gorokhovaya 27 (near Sennaya Ploshchad metro) is a quiet and small but excellent spot for Russian and European food. The service is terrific, and the food quite good. The sturgeon and salmon for US$10, veal toscano at US$19 and fillet of chicken at US$16 are all fine, but a portion of butter is US$1 – that's getting greedy. It's open until midnight, and call ahead for reservations as it's small.

The *Club Ambassador* (☎ 272 91 81) at naberezhnaya reki Fontanki 14 is a slick place, with lovely, cosy rooms and good food. It's unfortunate that a high number of large, cell-phone-carrying types have discovered this. However, it's a very nice place for a meal, and it prepares Russian and French food quite well. It's open from 1 pm to midnight, with a fixed-price lunch from 1 to 4 pm.

Syurpriz is, in fact, *syurpriz*ingly good – with a café to the left (see Cafés, Bistros, Fast Food & Snack Bars later in this section) and full restaurant to the right, it's a modern place with friendly service. It has good shrimp and beef dishes, though they range upward from, respectively, US$12 and US$15. It's open from 10 am to 10 pm, and is located at Nevsky prospekt 113 (which is technically Stary Nevsky).

Ariran (☎ 274 04 66) at 8-ya Sovietskaya 20, is a Korean restaurant that has gotten good reviews, but when we went there the place smelt pretty stale and the prices were astronomical: main dishes (starting with stir-fried vegetables) range from an unforgivable US$15 up to US$40. If its prices come down it's worth trying but, if not, forget it. It's open from 11 am to 11 pm.

The *Senat Bar* (☎ 314 92 53) at Galernaya ulitsa 1-3 is a first-class Russian place, with an odd, but interesting, interior designed by local artists and a beautiful vaulted ceiling. The food is good, on the expensive side (at about US$15 a main course), and beer lovers will love the extensive beer list. It's open from 11 am to 5 am.

Restaurant Adamant (☎ 311 55 75) is a high-end Russian place at naberezhnaya reki Moyki 72, which serves Russian food in a hushed and dark, but tasteful, atmosphere. Hot entrées cost US$4 to US$7, meat and fish dishes US$5 to US$15 and US$7 to US$20 respectively. American Express is accepted.

The Brasserie (☎ 119 60 00) is the Grand Hotel Europe's casually elegant dining option; a more relaxed atmosphere than its Restaurant Europe without letting its hair down so low that it becomes Sadko's (see Cafés, Bistros, Fast Food & Snack Bars later in this section). It has excellent food and service, and would be good for a business lunch, with main courses in the US$12 to US$18 range and entrée dishes US$4 to US$10. Visa, Eurocard, MasterCard, American Express, JCB and Diners Club are accepted, and it's open Monday to Saturday from 11 am to 11 pm, Sunday to 11 pm.

Afrodite (☎ 275 76 20) at Nevsky prospekt 86, just across the street from the Nevskij Palace Hotel, specialises in seafood, but it has a good all-round menu, and an extensive wine list. It's a nice setting, with good food and good service, and it can afford it – at US$12 to US$18 for main courses, it's pricey but good for a treat. It accepts Visa, Eurocard and MasterCard. Behind it, in summer, the Beer Garden is a very cool place to hang out (see Pubs, Bars & Beer Gardens later in this section).

The *Restaurant St Petersburg* (☎ 314 49 47), opposite the Resurrection Cathedral on the Griboedova Canal, is a nice setting, though the whole places feels a bit like a tourist trap; during dinner (beef and lamb US$17 to US$20; chicken US$15 and fish US$14 to US$20), a floorshow occurs in which Peter the Great flounces about the place...it's too much! The food's good, and the service is fine. It's open from noon to 2 am, and the floorshow begins at 9 pm. If you do go, the glass and tile work, done by local artists, is worth looking at.

The Grand Hotel Europe's flagship *Restaurant Europe* (☎ 119 60 00) has the most beautiful setting in town, if not the country. This extravagantly luxurious place, with its stained-glass ceilings and luminous history (you want celebrities, we got celebrities, from the King of Siam to Khrushchev to Buzz Aldrin to Michael Caine...) serves spectacular food at celestial prices – so celestial, in fact, that they're spelled out: 'thirty two dollars' etc. It also serves a luxuriously sumptuous Sunday Jazz Brunch ('thirty dollars') from noon to 3 pm. If someone well off is taking you out to dinner, this is the place to have them take you. It's open for breakfast ('twenty dollars') from 7 to 10 am, and dinner from 6 to 11 pm.

Dinner at the Nevskij Palace's *Imperial Restaurant*, where guests also have their buffet breakfast, is a superb buffet affair, with continental and international specialities and live music on most evenings. Here is where it also holds its blow-out Sunday Jazz brunches (US$32). On the 2nd floor, the *Admiralty Restaurant* has fine Russian and seafood specialities, in a sort of 'Ahhhr, matey' setting, with ship models from the St Petersburg naval museum. Main courses cost from US$23 to US$28, entrées US$10 to US$21 and salads US$9 to US$15. It's not quite as sexy as the rooftop *Landskrona*, thought by many to be St Petersburg's finest restaurant. The European and Russian specialities are served in a gorgeous setting, and there's dancing and live music; in summer, an open-air terrace offers panoramic views of the city. Main courses range from US$29 to US$34; entrées US$15 to US$21 and salads US$7 to US$9. In each of these restaurants the service is impeccable, and they all accept Visa, Eurocard, MasterCard, American Express, JCB and Diners Club.

Petrograd Side The *Grand Café Antwerpen* (☎ 233 97 46) at Kronverksky prospekt 13/2, just opposite the Gorkovskaya metro station, is a stylish place with fantastic stuffed mushrooms (US$5), decent Russian/European food (entrées US$3 to US$10, main courses US$8 to US$15) and darn good Belgian beer on draught and in bottles. It has an atrium café attached to the main dining room, and it's open from noon to midnight.

Kafe Tbilisi (☎ 232 93 31), St Petersburg's first cooperative, serves great Georgian food, except on the days it doesn't, in which case it can be pretty dire – most of the time it's good. Definitely try the homemade cheese, and its lavash and khachipuri breads. Its Satsivi chicken is usually great, as is its shashlyk. Main courses range from about US$2 to US$4 and entrée dishes cost from US$1 to US$3. The restaurant's at Sytninskaya ulitsa 10, and is open from noon to 10 or 11 pm depending on the crowd. Dig the crazy doorman in traditional Georgian garb. It also has a tiny bar, and service is very good.

Kafe Tet-a-Tet (☎ 232 75 48), Bolshoy prospekt 65 (Petrograd Side), is a perfect name for this place; all the tables are quiet, cosy and for two. The food's fine, and there's a pianist tinkling away while you dine – worth it on a date. It's open from 1 to 5 pm and 7 pm to midnight.

Khaibei (☎ 233 20 46) at Bolshoy prospekt 61 (Petrograd Side) has average Chinese food, give or take the occasional pebble in your food. Prices are heading up; at the time of writing main courses averaged from US$4.75 to US$6. The restaurant's upstairs from the express café (see Cafés, Bistros, Fast Food & Snack Bars later in this section).

Demyanova Ukha (☎ 232 80 90) has quietly remained one of St Petersburg's more reliable seafood places for years. It has a very relaxed atmosphere (lots of wood) and pleasant staff. Seafood dishes range from about US$5 to US$9; shashlyk US$6. It may pay to reserve in advance. It's behind the Peter and Paul Fortress at prospekt Kronverksky 53.

The *Petrogradskoe* at Bolshoy prospekt 88/1 (Petrograd Side), has perfectly ordinary food in a pleasant place. Beef and chicken dishes cost up to US$6.50. The nearest metro is Petrogradskaya.

Petrostar (☎ 232 40 47) at Bolshaya Pusharskaya ulitsa 30 (Petrograd Side) is said to have a good selection of Russian cuisine at reasonable prices (under US$10 for main courses). It's open from 1 pm to midnight.

Pirosmani (☎ 235 46 66) at Bolshoy prospekt 14 (Petrograd Side) has excellent Georgian food in a...well, in a unique setting. It's not advisable to go if you're subject to hallucinogenic episodes – the rear wall of the restaurant is psychedelically sculpted in what's billed as a tribute to the Georgian artist's work, and there are rivers flowing through the restaurant. When all's said and done, though, the food is what brings you back, even though the average meal will cost you US$14 (its basturma is US$7.95;

shashlyk US$7.15 and khachapuri bread is US$1.90). It's just not convenient to public transport; from metro Petrogradskaya take any trolleybus south along Bolshoy prospekt. It's open from noon to 11 pm.

The *Imperial Restaurant* (☎ 234 17 42; not to be confused with the Imperial Restaurant at the Nevskij Palace Hotel) has excellent Russian food and good service, though you'll need to get past its Soviet-style doorman to discover this (just be polite and keep saying 'Dinner'). It's popular, so reserve in advance. It has a good bar and a very nice dining room; try the baked mushrooms (US$15) and the Surovsky beef (also US$15); the prices go up from there. It's at Kamennoostrovsky prospekt 53, just across the Karpova Canal on Aptekarsky island, about a ten-minute walk from metro Petrogradskaya.

Vyborg Side People say great things about *Staraya Derevnaya* (☎ 239 00 00), a family-run traditional Russian restaurant at ulitsa Savushkina ulitsa 72 (nearest metro is Chyornaya Rechka, then take tram No 2, 31 or 37). It's said to have great service, and because it's small, it's very intimate and cosy – make reservations. On weekend evenings, there's musical entertainment in the form of traditional Russian ballads. Main courses range from US$4 to US$7, entrées US$2 to US$5.

Schwabskiy Domik (☎ 528 22 11) at Novocherkassky prospekt 28 (at metro Novocherkasskaya) was one of the earliest joint-venture restaurants in town. The Bavarian décor is pushing the hokey barrier but it's still fun, and the food – schnitzel, sauerkraut, sausage and roast pork – is good. There are two entrances; the one on the left is the former hard-currency place that is intended for Westerners to use, the one on the right is for Russians and is cheaper.

Vasilevsky Island *Svir* (☎ 213 63 21) is the Hotelship Peterhof's restaurant, and it's quite a nice place to spend an evening. The dining room is on the lower level of the ship, moored off naberezhnaya Makarova just west of the Tuchkov Bridge at the north-east end of Vasilevsky Island, so there's a nice Neva view, and the food and service are both very good. It has food festivals, rotating monthly, during which it highlights specific cuisines. Main courses range from US$12 to US$25, entrée dishes US$4 to US$10.

Restoran Kalinka (☎ 213 37 18) has Russian romance, guitar-strumming and Russian food: good baked mushrooms 'po-Tolstovsky' (US$11), interesting pancake nests with heavy cream and caviar at US$13, shchi and borshch at US$6 and more expensive seafood. It's at Sezdovskaya 9, north of Bolshoy prospekt, and it's open from noon to midnight. Don't panic: the wolf at the front entrance is stuffed.

The *Venezia* (☎ 352 14 32) at ulitsa Korablestroyteley 21, near the Pribaltiyskaya Hotel, has two distinct sections; downstairs it's got take-away pizzas for about US$2, and upstairs it's a more formal Italian restaurant with fair service and good enough food, though it gets pricey; main courses are US$8 to US$25. It accepts Visa, Eurocard and MasterCard, and it's open from 12.30 to 11.30 pm. It's close to metro Primorskaya. You can phone in orders to take away; it's flirting with the idea of delivery but...

South of the City Centre *Pizza House* (☎ 316 26 66), formerly Pizza Express, has been serving up Finnish-style pizzas and decent Italian food for several years now. It also has a good selection of Italian food, a huge wine list and tons of liquor – and it delivers. It's near metro Tekhnologichesky Institut at ulitsa Podolskaya 23, and its pizzas range from an average of US$8 to US$10. Prices are in Finnish Markka, and it accepts Visa, Eurocard and MasterCard. Delivery's free if you order five dishes or more. It's a comfortable place to sit.

Daddy's Steak Room (☎ 298 95 52) is a bit out of the way, south of the city centre at Moskovsky prospekt 73 (just next to metro Frunzenskaya), but the trip is worth it. St Petersburg's first Western-style steak house, this Finnish-run godsend serves great slabs of beef at very reasonable prices; you can get a good, large steak, garlic potatoes and a couple of trips to the salad bar for about US$10, and it has an extensive wine list, though that can get pricey. It's also starting to do a limited Mexican menu. The place gives you good value for the money. It accepts Visa, Eurocard and MasterCard, and prices are in Finnish markka.

Troyka (☎ 310 25 47), a Swiss-Russian joint venture, is like a night at an execrable variety show – in fact, it's so awful it might even be worth the US$45 set price. There's Russian food, and a lot of red and gold and sort of pseudo exotic dancers and big hats. It's in the basement at Zagorodny prospekt 27, which is about equal distance from the Pushkinskaya and Vladimirskaya metros.

Cafés, Bistros, Fast Food & Snack Bars

The availability of quick snack food in St Petersburg has multiplied exponentially; practically every street in the city centre has several places where you can grab a bite of something. This list is not by any means complete, though it does cover the major bases and will help you to keep your stomach ship-shape until time for dinner.

In addition to these places, the standard Russian blinnayas, bistros, kafe morozhenoes, kafeterii, stolovayas and bufety are all over the place, and these days most of them have what they say they have! Nevsky prospekt, for example, has a something every 100 metres or so, it's really a question of what you're *craving* as opposed to what you *can* have.

City Centre – Inner Nevsky Prospekt

At the Admiralty end of Nevsky, the *Kafe Druzhba* at Nevsky prospekt 15, has good chicken and bliny from US$1.50 to US$3. There's also a small disco in the evening from 7 to 11 pm. It's open from 11 am to 11 pm. This lower Nevsky area, west of Griboedova Canal, is also home to several good *Kafe Morozhenoe*; we like the one at Nevsky prospekt 3 (open from 10 am to 9 pm), though these ice-cream cafés can be spotted throughout the entire stretch of Nevsky prospekt.

Balkany is a pitta/felafel café that also changes money and sells T-shirts (you work it out) at Nevsky prospekt 27. You can buy the mid-Eastern goodies through its street window or go inside, where the little café sells only snacks and drinks. The felafel is good at about US$1, and there is a good deal on moussaka for three people at US$4.50.

The *Pyshki-Pyshechnaya* Doughnut Shop near the DLT department store on ulitsa Konyushennaya serves great plain doughnuts (covered with confectioners' sugar when its around) and drinkable coffee from 9 am to 8 pm. A bit higher on the culinary chain, the *Kafe St Petersburg* two blocks east (adjacent to the Restaurant St Petersburg across the Griboedova Canal from the Resurrection Cathedral) is an incredibly popular place with great food for very reasonable prices. You may have to queue amongst all the foreign students trying to grab a portion of the baked mushrooms in cream sauce, which is splendid, for about US$1.50. It's open from 9 am to 11 pm (break between 1 and 2 pm).

We list the *Literaturnoe Kafe* because it's in so many other guidebooks you might wander in thinking it's a good place. It may have had its day back in Pushkin's time (his last meal was eaten here...) but today, despite the lovely setting and the very civilised string quartet playing away in the back, the Lit Kaf is nothing more than a highly priced tourist trap, with terrible food, sloppy service and variable prices.

Nevsky 27 is a stand-up café/bakery/pastry shop right near the Grand Hotel Europe, with decent coffee and pastries for dirt cheap prices.

With the opening of *Grillmaster* (☎ 110 40 55) at Nevsky prospekt 46 in the summer of 1994, this German concern officially beat the US-based McDonald's chain in the race to open St Petersburg's first Western-style *schnell*-food hamburger joint. If Ray Kroc were alive he'd be going McGreen with envy watching the crowds fight to get at the US$2.10 jumbo burgers, US$1.35 hot dogs and the US$2.05 chicken fillet sandwiches. It's open from 8.30 am to 10 pm, and it also has fish, pizza and ice cream, but no toilet.

More (and some say better) fast-food burgers and the like are available at *Carrols* (☎ 279 17 36), a Finnish-run place doing fast-food set meals for under US$5: a plain burger with salad is US$1.25, a fishburger's US$2.20. It's at ulitsa Vosstania 5, just north of Ploshchad Vosstania metro, and is open from 9 am to 11 pm daily. Another location may be opening at the corner of Nevsky prospekt and ulitsa Rubinshteyna.

The *Transcarpathian Kafe* (☎ 110 69 97) is a classy kind of place in a sleazeball sort of way just off Nevsky prospekt on ulitsa Bolshaya Morskaya (ulitsa Gertsena); meat main courses range from US$4.30 to US$4.50, soups for US$2.50 to US$3. Next door, the *Bistro* is still a good option, a standard Russian stand-up with cheap chicken, salads and sandwiches.

Kafe 01 (☎ 312 11 36) at ulitsa Karavannaya 15, was an unpretentious bistro, serving up great food at great prices, but it's been out of the bag for a couple of years now and it's very hard to get a seat, what with all those henchmen in there flexing their muscles and making cell-phone calls. The food's still very good, as are the prices; fried pike or perch at US$4 and pork 'po-karsky' at US$5. Make reservations or forget about it.

The tiny *Kafe* at Dvortsovaya naberezhnaya 28 does cheap hamburgers, hot dogs and hot chocolate and is open from 11 am to 5 pm.

We passed by the *Priboy Kafe* (☎ 311 82 85) at naberezhnaya reki Moyki 19; it looked worth trying out. It's got bliny (jam and sour cream for US$1.40; caviar for US$3.35), a pork grill at US$3.50 and chicken dishes at around US$2.85. It's open from 11 am to 10 pm.

Kafe Vienna (☎ 275 20 01) at the Nevskij Palace Hotel is, well, a Viennese café, and serves good pastries, coffee and hot chocolate. Visa, Eurocard, MasterCard, American Express, JCB and Diners Club are accepted. It's open from 10 am to 11 pm.

Gino Ginelli's (☎ 312 46 31) at naberezhnaya kanala Griboedova 14 is an Italian ice and ice-cream place next to Chaika bar. It's open from 10 am to 1 am.

If you're in the mood for some micro-waved pizza for about US$6, head for *Nevsky 40*, a place whose location is far better than it deserves, just opposite Gostiny Dvor. It's also got a lovely café/bar in the easternmost entrance – lots of wood and mirrors. Nice for a rest.

Polar Fast Food, a Finnish/Russian joint-venture snack shack, has burgers, microwaved pizzas etc at Finnish prices. It has a branch in ploshchad Iskusstv, behind the Grand Hotel Europe, and another just outside the Frunzenskaya metro station.

For its first year, *Sadko's* (☎ 119 60 00) at the Grand Hotel Europe was so popular (it charged in roubles but felt like a Western bar) that it became unmanageable. It seemed that every business deal – dirty or otherwise – involving foreigners that went down in town was discussed here, and speculators used to hop from table to table to schmooze. In 1992, when it turned to hard currency in an attempt to flush out the riffraff, it was such a big deal that it was reported in *Newsweek*. Today, Sadko's is a huge, Texan-inspired barn of a bar, still very popular but by no means what it was. It serves decent, though pricey, food (burger and fries US$10, entrées US$8 to US$10) and it has a great beer selection (US$3 to US$9), but its 'speciality cocktails' – like a piddle of whiskey at the bottom of a cup of coffee – are getting out of line at US$10. It has karaoke and good live bands on weekends, when the place starts jumping. It's open till midnight, and it accepts Visa, Eurocard, MasterCard, American Express, JCB and Diners Club.

Sandwich fans will be pleased to know that the largest *Subway* sandwich shop in the world opened at Nevsky prospekt 20 in December 1994, and it's killer. All the sub-marine-style sandwiches it makes come with cheese, onions, lettuce, tomato, pickles, green peppers, olives, salt and pepper at no extra charge, and most of the food is imported. But the prices aren't: the cheapest is vege & cheese at US$2.25; the most expensive is roast beef at US$3.85, and in between there's tuna and ham. It's open from 10 am to 10 pm daily.

Just across ulitsa Plekhanova from the

Kazansky sobor at No 3 is *Bon Jour Fast Food* (☎ 219 47 89), which serves burgers, sandwiches and fries at decent prices. Le burger with cheese is US$2.60 and le vege and cheese roll is US$1.45. It's open from 9 am to 10 pm daily.

The *Pizzeria* at ulitsa Rubinshteyna 30 has been around forever, it seems. It serves Russian-style pizzas – eat in, takeaway, no waiting, and cheap.

City Centre – Outer Nevsky Prospekt

Baskin Robbins (☎ 164 64 56) at Nevsky prospekt 79 is just one of the US ice-cream parlour chain's locations in St Petersburg (it also has a branch out near the Planetarium behind the Peter & Paul Fortress) and it's spreading throughout the country. Ice creams cost about US$0.50 per scoop.

Bahlsen – Le Kafe (☎ 271 28 11) at Nevsky prospekt 142, just east of ploshchad Vosstania, is an inexpensive stand-up café, serving hot dogs, pizzas and snacks for less than US$3. It's open from noon to midnight, and it accepts Visa, Eurocard, MasterCard, American Express, JCB and Diners Club.

Guess what's cooking at café *Hot Dog*, downstairs at Nevsky prospekt 103? You're right! They're sizzling, along with burgers, from 11 am to 9 pm with a break from 2 to 3 pm.

There's a nice and very cheap *Roast Chicken Kafe* at Nevsky prospekt 147, up towards the Hotel Moskva. It has very cheap roast chicken and fountain Coke, Fanta and Sprite. It's open from 8 am to 8 pm, with a break from 1 to 2 pm.

And speaking of the Hotel Moskva, its *Russian Kafe* at the north-east end of the hotel serves decent pastries, ice cream and coffee.

Syurpriz café, next to Syurpriz restaurant at Nevsky prospekt 113, is a nice little sit-down pizza joint that does very good pizzas (US$2.40 to US$5), and other snacky things, including a good chicken Kiev for US$3.60. It's also got Tuborg on draught, and it's open from 10 am to 10 pm.

City Centre – North & East of Nevsky Prospekt

Bagdad Kafe (☎ 272 23 55) at ulitsa Furshtadtskaya 27 is still cookin' and cooler than ever. Excellent huge and tasty manty dumplings (US$2.40), shashlyk (US$3.60), soups and plov (US$1.90) are served – this basement café is an old standby. It's open from noon to 11 pm.

Hostellers go for the *Bar Don Kikhot*, at naberezhnaya reki Fontanki 21, a Spanish/Russian joint venture doing grilled chicken (US$3.35), burgers (US$1.40) and Polish sausage (US$1). It has an English sign in the window. It's open from 10 am to 6 pm.

North-east of the hostel, at Suvorovsky prospekt 43, the *Pizzeria Verona* (☎ 275 77 62) does decent pizzas for US$2.25 to US$3.20. It's open from 10 am to 10 pm, and also has soft drinks and beer.

Kafe Maxim (☎ 312 26 12) at Millionnaya ulitsa 10 does kotlet (US$3.10), pelmeni (US$3.10) and other café food in a pleasant, two-room setting. It's open from 11 am to 10 pm.

Springtime Shwarma Bistro is our favourite Middle-Eastern place in town because it's so darn cheap and good. You can get a gyro or felafel for under US$1 (though they are a bit on the small side) and it has a large selection of other Middle-Eastern specialities, especially vegetarian ones. It's at the corner of ulitsa Radishcheva and ulitsa Nekrasova at ulitsa Radishcheva 20, four long blocks east of Liteyny prospekt. Of course, when it comes to Middle-Eastern food, there's always dissenting opinion: the *St Petersburg Press*' editors argue that *Shakherezada* at Razyeszhaya 3 has the best felafel and hummus in town. You decide. It's pretty good for vegetarians, and it's open from 11 am to 11 pm. It's near metro Dostoevskogo.

Vechernee Kafe is an OK basement affair which serves hot dogs (US$2.40), kotlet (US$1.90) or steak (US$3.35) mainly to wash down various blue and pink liqueurs and Western beer. It's at ulitsa Chaykovskogo 75, just a bit east of the Finnish consulate. Around the corner, *Kafe Medved* calls itself a business-club/saloon; it's in the basement of ulitsa Potyomkinskaya 7, and it serves cheap snacks, beers etc.

It's good if you're trying to renew your German passport at the consulate around the corner and staff make you wait for hours and hours. Next door, the *Kafe Saloon* has draught DeKoninck beer and a seedier atmosphere.

Petrograd Side If you're peckish at Petrogradskaya metro, there's the *Sandwich Kafe* (☎ 232 70 28) just across the street, through the spooky tunnel. This little bastion of civility does very good sandwiches, salads and ice cream, and the highest price is about US$1.90. It's open from 11 am to 8 pm. Of course, a bit closer to the metro (adjacent to it, in fact) is *2+2*, which has sandwiches, salads, pizzas and other snacks, nuked up to your liking. It's open from 10 am to 9 pm.

If only there was a *Gril Diez* (☎ 232 42 55) everywhere; this wonderful place does whole spit-roast chicken (though on some days they can be a tad scrawny) for about US$2. It's at Kamennoostrovsky prospekt 16, on the roundabout. One frustrating aspect; they seem to wait until all chickens are sold until putting up another broiler-full, which creates huge and stagnant queues – and the guy in front of you (the one with the huge rucksack) is going to buy the last seven. It's open from 10 am to 8 pm.

Heading south from metro Petrogradskaya, all vegetarians will kindly form a line and hit *Troitsky Most*, aka the *Hare Krishna Kafe* (☎ 232 66 93), which does excellent vegetarian dishes, herb tea, mindwashing potion – er, pizzas etc. You can sample small dishes of everything on the menu (mainly lentil and white beans in curry sauce; curried, cloved and sultana'd rice and kasha) for under US$2, and what's more there's minimal chanting required. It's at ulitsa Malaya Passadskaya 2, across the road from the Mercedes-Benz dealership/florist, and is open from 11 am to 8 pm, with a break from 3 to 4 pm.

Way down at the south-west end of Bolshoy prospekt (Petrograd Side) next to Pirosmani restaurant is the *Pirosmani* pavement café, doing lavish bread, pastries, hot dogs and hamburgers. Everything's less than US$1, except the copious quantities of booze available.

Someone should speak with the owner of the *Grot* café (☎ 238 46 90), in Admiraltiysky Park behind the Peter & Paul Fortress, about the way that name sounds in English. The Grotto, which is what it means, actually looks like one, and is a very nice place for a mid-afternoon coffee. It's open from 11 am to 9 pm, and there is no smoking allowed inside.

Kafe at Kamennoostrovsky prospekt 50, just north of the Karpova Canal, has hot chocolate, cakes, coffee and a really nice cat; it's open from 9 am to 9 pm (break between 1 and 2 pm). And on the opposite side of the street, the *Kafe* at Kamennoostrovsky prospekt 54, near the Hotel Druzhba (actually under a sign that says Druzhba), is very cheap and has good coffee and hot chocolate. It's even a pleasant place to sit. It's open from 7 am to 8 pm (break between 1 and 2 pm).

Chick-King (☎ 232 49 22) at Kamennoostrovsky prospekt 54, diagonally opposite the Imperial restaurant, is a fast-food chicken place doing decent schnitzel (US$2.50), fried chicken (US$2) and great deep-fried potato chunks and fried onions (US$0.60). In front is a Koff bar serving pints for US$2. It's open from 11 am to 11 pm.

Express Kafe (☎ 233 20 46), just downstairs from Khaibei restaurant at Bolshoy prospekt (Petrograd Side) 61, is cheap and serves fast Chinese and Russian food. Pick from the samples on the counter; everything's less than US$2.40, and mostly everything is tasty – especially the dumplings. It's open from 10 am to 7 pm.

Vasilevsky Island The tiny *Sirin Bar* (☎ 213 22 48, 213 72 82) at 1-ya linia 16, has surprisingly good and cheap Russian food: chicken dishes and 'Hungarian Meat' at US$2.60; it's open from 11 am to midnight.

Kafe Grilette at 1-ya linia 40 has ice cream and hot sandwiches for less than US$1.

Kafe Nika (DeKoninck) (☎ 213 22 79), at Bolshoy prospekt 8, is yet another café to sport this Belgian beer logo; it's got some substantial café food, like a pork grill

(US$3.10), hunter's sausage (US$2.15) and a beef grill for US$2.85 – a nice place.

The food at the *Gril-Bar Vo Dvore* (☎ 213 24 21), just next to Nika (under the arch), looks pretty good; it's got pita-kebabs for US$1.20, chicken dishes at US$1.90 and a big pork cutlet for US$2.15. It's open from 11 am to 11 pm.

Salon Best at 6-ya linia 9 is a little shop that also sells good grilled chickens for US$2.85 apiece; it's also got bottled beer and draught Coke, Sprite and Fanta. It's worth a shot if you're starving on the Strelka. Panic not if you think the beer's too expensive – there's a *pivo kiosk* just outside serving up the suds, and it's even got beer mugs.

Sun Deck Kafe (☎ 213 63 21) at the Hotelship Peterhof is – in summer, anyway – a pleasant, deck-top café serving hot and cold snacks, sandwiches, drinks etc at Swiss prices. It's on board the Hotelship, moored along naberezhnaya Makarova just northwest of the Tuchkov bridge.

Pubs, Bars & Beer Gardens

In summer there are a couple of *Koff beer gardens* in the city centre, one opposite the Grand Hotel Europe, between the former Duma and Gostiny Dvor, and one in front of Tserkov Svyatogo Petra. Both have draught and bottled beers, for about US$2.85 and US$2.15, respectively.

In 1994 most foreign residents here danced a wee jig when *Mollies Irish Bar* (☎ 319 97 68) brought a bit o' the black to the City on the Neva: draught Guinness pints for US$4 and lagers for US$3. This place became hugely popular very fast for its great beer, classic pub décor, friendly service, and Christian Walsh, who trained at the school Tom Cruise went to for the movie *Cocktail*: he stands back there twirling bottles, breaking hearts and making management nervous. It serves pub food; sandwiches for about US$4 to US$5, soups US$2. It's at ulitsa Rubinshteyna 36, and it's open from 11 am to 3 am every day. Never know who might turn up – one night Nick met Ireland's Minister of Education!

The cool and cavernous *Shamrock* (☎ 219 46 25) at ulitsa Dekabristov 27, just across the street from the Mariinsky theatre, is claiming that *its* Guinness is shipped straight from Dublin, while 'other' pubs use English stuff. Its location couldn't be better; we'll see how the battle of the Irish pubs goes. Pints cost US$5.

The *Dog and Fox* (☎ 242 22 68), on the 3rd floor at naberezhnaya Chyornaya Rechka 41 (corner of ulitsa Grafova), has imported beer and cider, as well as pub and vegetarian food. The large place looks and feels like a large English pub (lots o' Union Jack, though switch the flags and it could be a Texas two-step joint). It has live music on some nights, and it's open from noon to 3 am daily. From metro Chyornaya Rechka, walk north about 150 metres, across the canal (that's Chyorna Rechka, or 'Black River'), then turn right and the pub is 400 metres ahead on the left-hand side of the street. The location could be a lot more central, but a good reason to go out of your way to have a pint here is that 50% of the profits go directly to the Red Kidz charity. It's involved in a host of worthy projects in town, helping abandoned and disfigured children as well as constructing shelters for the homeless.

The Beer Garden, behind Afrodite restaurant (Nevsky prospekt 86) and opposite the Nevskij Palace Hotel, is a great summer spot. It's in a secluded courtyard, and it plays music and serves Finnish beer, blue liqueurs and Finnish snacks, and it's a very enjoyable place to spend an evening. It's popular with, it seems, everyone – expats, Russians and travellers alike.

If you're wondering how *The John Bull Pub* (☎ 164 98 77), at Nevsky prospekt 79 near metro Mayakovskaya, managed to get an English pub to St Petersburg, the answer is: on a truck – the whole kit and caboodle. After all that trouble, it goes and serves John Bull bitter and Skol lager at US$4 for a bit less than a pint. Still, it's a fun place to sit and have a beer after a long day of walking up and down Nevsky prospekt. Order a 'both toastie' and relax (don't try to steal any of the knick-knacks – they're nailed down!). It's open from noon to midnight, and it has an adjacent restaurant serving Russian food.

At the weekend, *Sadko*'s (☎ 119 60 00) huge, Texan-inspired barn of a bar gets packed, people have a great time and one can glean why it used to be the most popular place in town (well, it was fun, cheap and the *only* place in town for a while, but that's nit-picking, isn't it?). It has karaoke and good live bands on Friday and Saturday, and a huge selection of booze and beer, snacks and full meals in the adjacent restaurant section. It's open till midnight, and it accepts Visa, Eurocard, MasterCard, American Express, JCB and Diners Club.

The Warsteiner Forum (☎ 277 29 14) at ploshchad Vosstania isn't very popular, but it's a nice place with good German beer and good schnitzel. Beers range from about US$5, and the schnitzel is US$12; its 'peasant breakfast' (sausage, eggs, toast) is US$7, and a plate of sausages is a mean US$6. It's open from noon to 2 am.

The *Bierstube* in the Nevskij Palace Hotel is pretty much what you'd expect; waitresses in dirndl, an Austrian setting, snacks and good – but dear – beer. Draughts (0.5 litres) are US$6. It accepts Visa, Eurocard, MasterCard, American Express, JCB and Diners Club, and it's open from 10 am (for those in need of a *Frühschoppen*) to 11 pm.

The Grand Hotel Europe's *Lobby Bar* is a very civilised place, best visited if you're on an expense account. Beers are US$7 a bottle, and mixed drinks get expensive! It also serves coffee, espresso and cappuccino. It accepts Visa, Eurocard, MasterCard, American Express, JCB and Diners Club. There's piano entertainment in the evenings, and you can walk through the archway into the library to read the paper.

The *Marine Bar* at the US Consulate (☎ 274 86 89) isn't really open to the public, but it does have Friday night get-togethers, barbecues, movie nights etc that are open to citizens of most Western – and even some Eastern European – countries by invitation only. The bar itself is kind of cool, and there's a pool table. You'll have to check at the consulate to see if anything's happening, and

you *will* need to be invited by one of the Marines – don't just show up.

On any given night, the *Chaika* (☎ 312 46 31) bar is filled with foreign businessmen, German tour groups singing *Schunkellieder* and swarms of prostitutes who'll sidle up to males at the bar and say something coolly seductive like 'I want peanuts' or 'Buy me beer'. In the past there have been suggestions that customers who stayed late may have been overcharged by tacking on imaginary beers to the punch-cards that are used to calculate the bill. This place is worth avoiding if you're picking up the tab. It's at naberezhnaya kanala Griboedova 14, near the corner of Nevsky prospekt.

The *Nightclub* on the top floor of the Grand Hotel Europe has a small dance floor.

A Final Word on Beer The queues you see early in the morning at places around town – at the corner of naberezhnaya reki Fontanki and ploshchad Lomonosova, for example – are folks waiting to fill up their jars at *The Odd Stray Beer Cart*, a fine tradition that should be experienced at least once during a stay in St Petersburg. The beer is fresh and usually – well, it won't kill you. Bring your own jar. It's dirt cheap, which is fitting.

ENTERTAINMENT

St Petersburg is the entertainment equal of many Western cities, and you are no longer required to like opera or ballet. Sure, the classical entertainment in the city is amongst the best in the world – ballet, opera, classical music and theatre – but there's a new world here of rock clubs, jazz joints and discos that has St Petersburg nightlife soaring to heights never before witnessed in Russia.

Check the *St Petersburg Press* for listings. You can also find out some what's-on information from street posters or timetables in theatres, concert halls or from the combined theatre-booking offices (teatralne kassy) around the city.

Tickets
Face-value tickets for concerts, theatres and so on are sold at the venues themselves

(usually from 11 am to 3 pm and 4 to 6 pm, and best bought in advance), or through the combined booking offices. Excluding the Kirov, the dearest tickets are rarely more than US$2.

For the Kirov, tickets can be a problem, as Westerners are charged as much as they possibly can be and official tickets are rationed out to the larger hotels and tour companies well in advance. You can try at the box office, where the face price of tickets is about US$4, but since ticket sales usually start 20 days in advance, your chances are slim. Go as early as you can (the booking office is open from 11 am to 7 pm; performances start at 7 pm). Once you get turned away from there you have several choices, including Peter TIPS, which sells tickets at the Russian price plus a 10% mark-up; the teatralne kassy around town; other tourist agencies such as the St Petersburg Travel Company; concierge desks at the larger hotels; and, if it comes down to it, from touts in front of the theatre itself.

The best bet for tickets through a booking office is the Teatralnaya Kassa (☎ 314 93 85) at Nevsky prospekt 42, opposite Gostiny Dvor, and in the middle of Dumskaya ulitsa on the west side of Gostiny Dvor. Here you can get tickets for everything, including the Kirov, but they sell out quickly. Offering to buy tickets s nagruzkoy, or along with a bunch of other tickets to shows no one wants to see, can help otherwise unavailable tickets to appear, and this usually works out to be cheaper than any other option. In May 1995, Nick was offered good tickets to a performance of Swan Lake at the Mariinsky for US$2.60 at this office (s nagruzkoy was unnecessary), but during the high season prices are higher and availability is diminished.

Concierge desks at the better hotels will be only too pleased to sell you Kirov tickets for upwards of US$60, though if you've got a limited amount of time and you're happy with that, they do get some of the best seats in the house. The HI St Petersburg Hostel and Holiday Hostel will try to get you tickets at a less breathtaking mark-up.

When all else fails, just as in any city, there are touts, usually young speculators, who hang out in front of the venue before a performance. Make sure that the ticket's for the date and section you want: the stalls (on the ground floor) are the parter; the dress circle (one level up) is the bel-etazh; and the balcony is the balkon or yarus (see Entertainment in the European Russia Facts for the Visitor chapter for more useful words and phrases). Go along to the venue an hour or so before the performance – a standard tout price you shouldn't feel fleeced paying (even though you're being fleeced) is US$30.

Tickets to special advertised rock concerts are often sold through nonstandard outlets – look for words like prodazha (sale) and bileti (tickets) on posters to find out where. Sometimes people sell tickets from tables in pedestrian subways; check the underpasses at Nevsky Prospekt and Gostiny Dvor metros.

Whatever the method, good tickets go fast! Most theatres and concert halls are closed on Monday. There are usually matinees on Sunday and sometimes on Saturday.

Ballet, Opera & Classical Music

September to early summer is the main performing season – the cultural scene goes into neutral for the rest of the summer, with companies away on tour. An exception is the last 10 days of June, when St Petersburg stages the White Nights Dance Festival. Extra events of variable quality are mounted throughout the summer tourist season at halls such as the Vyborgsky Culture Palace at ulitsa Komissara Smirnova 15 off Lesnoy prospekt (metro: Ploshchad Lenina), the Lensovieta Culture Palace at Kamennoostrovsky prospekt 42 (metro: Petrogradskaya) and the Oktyabrsky Concert Hall at Ligovsky prospekt 6 (metro: Ploshchad Vosstania).

Ballet & Opera St Petersburg was the birthplace of Russian ballet back in 1738; the Kirov premiered Tchaikovsky's Sleeping Beauty and Nutcracker, and nurtured Nijinsky, Pavlova, Nureyev, Makarova and

Baryshnikov. Today, under director Oleg Vinogradov, the Kirov has a reputation for more varied and sensitive productions than Moscow's Bolshoy. Don't miss it if you get the chance. The Kirov Opera is also a treat. Both are at the Mariinsky Theatre at Teatralnaya ploshchad 1. Russian and international classics are in the repertoire, with about five ballets and five operas performed each month.

The companies tend to go away on tour for about two months in the summer and unpredictably the rest of the year. Be sure it's the Kirov company itself, and not the Russian Ballet, that you're paying to see – sometimes visiting ensembles perform here too.

Cheaper and easier-to-get-into ballet and opera performances are staged at the Maly (Small) Theatre (Peterburgsky Gosudarstvenny Akademichesky Maly Teatr opery i baleta imeni M P Mussorgskogo) at ploshchad Iskusstv 1. It mounts more contemporary works than the Kirov and standards are respectable. The Conservatory, on Teatralnaya ploshchad, also stages some operas.

Classical Music The St Petersburg Philharmonia's symphony orchestra is particularly renowned. It has two concert halls – the Bolshoy Zal (Big Hall; ☎ 311 74 89) on ploshchad Iskusstv, and the Maly Zal imeni M I Glinki (Small Hall named after M I Glinka – not to be confused with the Maly Theatre, or the Maly Dramatic Theatre, or the Glinka Capella) nearby at Nevsky prospekt 30. The Glinka Capella (Akademicheskaya Khorovaya Kapella imeni M I Glinki; ☎ 314 10 58) at naberezhnaya reki Moyki 20 also has high standards, focusing on choral, chamber and organ concerts. Other venues include Smolny Cathedral (☎ 271 91 82), which usually features choral works, and the Peterburgsky Concert Hall at ploshchad Lenina 1.

Jazz
A really fun time can be had at the New Jazz Club (☎ 275 60 90) at the east side of the Tavrichesky Gardens. It has good bands (not only jazz), a good bar and it's a comfortable place to hang out for a while. From metro Chernyshevskaya, turn right on to ulitsa Furshtadtskaya, then right to the park; the club's in the yellow opera house at the far right-hand corner. It's open from 7.30 to 11 pm, and admission is US$1.90.

Down at Okoshki Art Kafe, the setting is by far the most, er, laid back in town – it seems pretty thrown together, and the jazz and blues entertainment is inconsistent. It's at ulitsa Bolshaya Morskaya (ulitsa Gertsena) 58; use the small door on the left.

The Jazz Philharmonic Hall, formerly the Jazz Club, is a weird place for Russia as there's no smoking. Two bands – straight jazz and an attempt at Dixieland (it's not bad, and can be fun) – plus guests doing mainstream and modern jazz, are all hosted by the co-founder, David Goloshchyokin, who runs about being seen. Tickets for foreigners are US$3.80 (US$4.75 on Sunday); for Russians it's US$1.40/2.85. The club is at Zagorodny prospekt, a ten-minute walk to the southwest from metro Dostoevskaya.

Also in that neighbourhood, the clubbier Kvadrat Jazz Club at Pravdy ulitsa does traditional and mainstream jazz; from metro Dostoevskaya, head for Bolshaya Moskovskaya, and follow it south-west until it turns into Pravdy.

Rock
St Petersburg can lay a strong claim to being the Russian rock capital, having produced top 1980s bands like Akvarium, Alisa, Kino, DDT, AVIA, Televizor and Populyarnaya Mekhanika. And now that the government's out of the creative process, the rock scene in St Petersburg is far less bleak than before. It's not Amsterdam or London yet, but it's got the attitude of early CBGBs and ever more venues to let steam off. Check the *St Petersburg Press*' weekly Music Scene and Club Guide for listings of who's in town.

The TaMtAm Club (maybe it's the TaMtaM club – who knows?) is the ticket for head-banging rock 'n' roll; it goes in and out of fashion, but low prices keep the place full of interesting people and relatively thug-free; admission's a paltry US$1. It's open Thursday to Saturday from 8 to 11 pm and is on the corner of Maly prospekt (Vasilevsky Island) and 16-ya linia.

Other good obstreperous venues include the Ten Club out in the middle of nowhere at naberezhnaya Obvodnogo kanala 62 (from metro Pushkinskaya walk south to the canal and east for about seven minutes – it's in the yellow building just past the factory. Admission is US$2.40. More convenient (but *just*) to the city centre is the Wild Side (☎ 186 34 66), a couple of blocks from metro Narvskaya. It has live rock and pop shows and a disco for a US$4.75 admission fee. It's at 12 naberezhnaya Bumazhnogo kanala.

The Archwall Club at 10 Pravdy ulitsa (metro: Dostoevskaya) has live rock concerts, but it's a bit tame – it also has a disco night on Saturday. Admission is US$1.90 to US$2.85 for concerts.

Rock around the Clock (☎ 310 12 16) at Sadovaya ulitsa 20, between Nevsky prospekt and metro Sennaya Ploshchad, is a bar/restaurant that also has classic rock from 9 pm to 6 am. Admission from Sunday to Wednesday is US$4.75; Thursday to Saturday prices are anyone's guess, up to and including US$19.

Nightclubs & Discos

The Western influence has taken its toll here; almost all new clubs are decidedly Western, and many import DJs from cities renowned for their nightlife – Paris and New York come to mind – and sometimes from more unlikely places – like Ouagadougou, Lagos and London. St Petersburg's raves are all-night affairs, usually in a converted theatre or sport complex somewhere, where thousands of young Russians and a smattering of foreigners party to acid-house and trance, replete with laser shows, naked people – the works. The raves that were held at the sport complex on Petrograd Side (near the corner of ulitsa Malaya Passadskaya and Konny pereulok) had all this, and the added bonus of an Olympic-sized swimming pool and an upstairs solarium! There's usually a high

enough door fee to keep the riffraff out. Check the radio for ads or ask Russian friends.

St Petersburg's nightclubs seem to run through a definite life cycle: inception; buzz and hype; 'what-a-place'; discovery by gangsters, thugs and hoodlums; discovery by tourists; and decline. That said, there are more than enough places to boogie here, and the list grows all the time. Most large hotels offer some sort of night bar, possibly with a disco.

Domenico's (☎ 272 57 17) opened in 1994 and became very popular with expatriates and Russians alike. It's teamed up in the past with the management of Mollies Irish Pub to stage joint promotional nights (like midwinter beach blowouts awarding free drinks to those who show up in swimming trunks). It's also a class-act disco and nightclub. The address is Nevsky prospekt 70, near the corner of Fontanka and Nevsky. Admission before 9 pm is free, after 9 pm is US$30, beers are US$4 to US$5. Its food is rich but good; steak is a speciality at US$11; pasta dishes from US$7 to US$9, fish US$11 to US$13.

We like the Tunnel (☎ 233 25 62) because it's popular and because it's in a bomb shelter, where it plays house and trance music. It's open Thursday to Saturday from midnight to 6 am, and is located on Lubyansky pereulok at the corner with Zverinskaya ulitsa (the closest metro's Gorkovskaya).

Joy (☎ 311 35 40) is a popular place with Mercedes-Benz owners. It's perfectly located and we *love* that polyester look. Admission is about US$14, and it's open from 10 pm to 5 am at 1/27 Lomonosova ulitsa (it's the sort of roundy thing on the corner).

Nevsky Melody (☎ 227 26 76) would be more popular if it were closer to the city centre; it's out on Sverdlovskaya naberezhnaya, but if you don't mind shelling out a lot it's a great place to spend an evening. It's got a disco downstairs, along with a casino, and it has erotic shows at about 1 am (it also has an amateur strip night that's sometimes good for a laugh). It's open from 10 pm to 4 or 5 am.

The Stardust Nightclub at the planetarium just behind the Peter & Paul Fortress is, depending on the night, fantastic fun or perfectly fine. It's huge and jammin', and it has live rock concerts, disco nights and some erotic evening shows. It's in Alexandrovsky Park, five minutes' walk from Gorkovskaya metro.

Stiers Club (☎ 186 95 22) at ploshchad Stachek, opposite the Narvskaya metro station, is a pretty standard disco/nightclub that charges US$14 to get in. It's got two bars, and it's open Wednesday to Sunday from 10 pm to 6 am.

Courier Disco (☎ 311 46 78), next to the Okoshki Art Kafe, at ulitsa Bolshaya Morskaya (ulitsa Gertsena) 58, is a traditional meat market, with ladies' nights on Saturday, when women pay US$3.80 and men pay US$7. It plays dance and house music.

Gay & Lesbian Venues

Don't expect these listings to stretch on for pages; St Petersburg has, at the time of writing, only three bars/clubs that cater to gays and lesbians, and they're not exactly advertising heavily. To get in, either say you're gay (*ya goluboy*) or lesbian (*ya lesbianka*) to the hulking goon at the door; foreigners will probably be allowed in regardless of sexual orientation. Back rooms, called *chyornaya komnata* (black rooms), are not common, and are frowned upon by gay-rights activists because their legality is iffy at best.

The Klub/Disco at ulitsa Galernaya 33 is a weekend disco with a US$4 entry fee.

There's another weekend nightclub/disco downstairs at Teatr Experiment just near metro Petrogradskaya, and a small daily nightclub at ulitsa Mokhovaya 15.

Circus & Puppets

The St Petersburg State Circus (☎ 210 46 49) has a permanent building at naberezhnaya reki Fontanki 3, half a km south of the Summer Garden. There are nightly shows at

7.30 pm, plus afternoon and lunch-time performances at weekends. Tickets bought here cost up to US$2.

For puppets, the main venue is the Bolshoy Teatr Kukol (☎ 272 88 08) at ulitsa Nekrasova 10, with shows on Saturday and Sunday at 11.30 am and 2 pm; tickets for everyone (Russian or not, kid or not) cost between US$0.30 and US$0.60. The Teatr Kukol-Marionetok (☎ 311 19 00) at Nevsky prospekt 52 does, as the name suggests, puppet and marionette shows on a varying schedule. Tickets cost between US$0.20 and US$1.

Theatre

The premier drama theatre is the Pushkin at ploshchad Ostrovskogo 2, which stages (in Russian) the likes of Shakespeare, Aristophanes and even Arthur 'Aeroport' Hailey as well as home-grown plays. The Lensoviet Theatre, at Vladimirsky prospekt 12, and the Gorky Bolshoy Dramatic Theatre, at naberezhnaya reki Fontanki 65, are the other top mainstream drama theatres. For experimental fare, try the Maly Dramatic Theatre at ulitsa Rubinshteyna 18. Music-hall variety shows are staged at the Komsomol Theatre at Park Lenina 4 and the Teatr Estrady at ulitsa Zhelyabova 27. Teatr Experiment at the corner of Kamennoostrovsky and Bolshoy prospekts (Petrograd Side), has performances as well, but it's also a gay and lesbian nightclub at the weekend.

Cinema & Video

Most of the cinemas in St Petersburg play US or other foreign movies that have been heinously translated and dubbed using a single male voice (the man is called a *lektor*) for all characters, which is only amusing during love scenes. The French recently lost their title as the world's worst translators (the line: 'Shot of rotgut – in a dirty glass'; the subtitle: *'Un apéritif, s'il vous plaît'*) when the Russian team, translating the movie *Wayne's World*, learned the Americanism 'hurl'. Cinemas charge less than US$1 for entry and films run continuously from about 1 to 10 pm.

When you tire of trying to pick out the English from beneath the lektor's voice, you can either attend a video screening or rent an English-language video.

The VideoStar Club (☎ 210 96 22 or 315 24 65) at Bistro le Francais, ulitsa Galernaya 20, screens a movie on Wednesday and Thursday evenings and two on Sunday (Sunday afternoons are going to be family movies). The screenings are free and you can buy café snacks (great chocolate truffles), beer and soft drinks; it also rents English-language videos to club members. Membership is US$30 per year, a US$50 security deposit and US$3 for one film, US$5 for two and US$7.50 for three; rentals are for 48 hours. It'll rent you a video player as well at a cost of US$20 for two days. If you're in town for a while, it has a home delivery service available, a US$2 charge is added to the rental price. It's open from noon to midnight daily.

The HI St Petersburg Hostel has weekly video screenings in its lounge, which is open to the public; it charges US$2 for Coke and popcorn.

THINGS TO BUY

Ahh, what to buy? No one comes here for the shopping, but a lot of people leave with their wallets a lot lighter now that St Petersburg has almost everything you'd want – and oftentimes it's cheaper than at home.

Most St Petersburg shops are open from 11 am to 7 or 8 pm, but beryozkas and department stores give you an extra hour or two at both ends. Virtually everything is closed from 2 to 3 pm for lunch and, except for beryozkas, all day Sunday.

Arts & Antiques

See the European Russia Facts for the Visitor chapter on the nightmare of getting art out of the country, customs fees etc. There are dozens of art and antique shops throughout the city; only some of them – generally the more expensive – will walk you through the customs clearing procedures.

Palitra (☎ 277 12 16) is a gallery owned and operated by St Petersburg artists, and it's the real thing. It's at the end of Stary Nevsky

at No 166, and is open Tuesday to Saturday from 11 am to 7 pm. It serves coffee.

Dimion (☎ 275 34 94) at Nevsky prospekt 3 has a good selection of groovy rock-crystal items; it's open Monday to Friday from 10 am to 5 pm and Saturday and Sunday from 11 am to 7 p m.

The Exhibition Hall at the Union of Artists (☎ 314 30 60) displays some of the finest art works in St Petersburg, though prices here are higher and the artists give up a cut to the union. It's at ulitsa Bolshaya Morskaya (ulitsa Gertsena) 38, near Isaakievskaya ploshchad, and is open Tuesday to Sunday from 1 to 7 pm.

Ananov at the Grand Hotel Europe (☎ 119 60 00) has that Fabergé egg you've been planning to buy to add elegance to the study; its prices are high enough to ensure that you'll have no problems clearing customs on the way out. It's open from 11 am to 8 pm.

There's an artists' market for tourists on both sides of Nevsky prospekt near the Nevsky Prospekt metro station entrance on ulitsa Mikhailovskaya. On the south side of the street portrait artists sit beneath the arches, while purveyors of matryoshkas and other crapola wind around the corner opposite Gostiny Dvor. Opposite, the space just west of the Grand Hotel Europe's Sadko restaurant is reserved for 'painting' and other 'locally' produced 'art'.

Petersburg (☎ 273 03 41) is an antique salon with an exquisite selection of antique furniture, almost none of which you'll be able to get out of the country under normal circumstances. If you'll be living in town for a while, or if you've got connections, it's a great place to shop. It's at ulitsa Furshtadtskaya 42, and is open Monday to Saturday from 11 am to 2 pm and 3 to 5 pm.

Na Liteynom antiquarian bookshop (☎ 275 38 73), in the courtyard at Liteyny prospekt 61, has a good selection of old books, as well as a small antique collection. It's open daily except Sunday from 11 am to 7 pm.

Other Shops Along Nevsky Prospekt

Optika Exclusive at No 13 is good for

Western glasses and frames. There is also a couple of good pharmacies along Nevsky – see under Medical Services near the start of this chapter.

Nike has its shop at No 34 selling running shoes and accessories at high European prices; it's open from 11 am to 8 pm, and accepts cash only. Barbie at No 63 is the place to go to get that special something for that special someone: a fountain mermaid Barbie is US$17, a magic change hair set US$5.20, and it's also got Ken dolls and turbo colour Hot Wheels for US$5.40. It's open from 10 am to 7 pm.

Fabergé Egg

Original Levis at No 102 has just that at Western European prices.

See also the Bookshops and Self-catering sections earlier in this chapter.

Department Stores

The city's dotted with department stores; service and supplies are better than ever and it's great fun to join the thronging crowds in the big ones. Gostiny Dvor is St Pete's answer to Moscow's GUM, though the selection and service just aren't up to those in its big brother across the street, Passazh. Both are covered in the Nevsky Prospekt section earlier in this chapter.

DLT at Bolshaya Konyushennaya ulitsa 21/23 began as a children's department store but now has a great supply of everything. It's still, however, the best place to start looking for imported and Russian-made toys and games, children's clothing etc. It also has a great selection of sporting goods at the back of the store.

All the department stores in the city have moneychanging offices, and many let out space to Western firms such as Littlewoods, which sell a variety of Western goods (usually, though, not the best).

Western Speciality Shops

Throughout the city, Western-owned (or appearing to be Western) shops pop up now and then, the most obvious examples being Barbie, Nike and Reebok on Nevsky prospekt. There are many more opening every day: Bally's mind-blowingly expensive accessories and trinkets shop (sports jacket – US$709) at Bolshoy prospekt (Petrograd Side) comes to mind. A miscellany: Lancôme, Yves Rocher and Nina Ricci all have shops along Nevsky prospekt selling designer perfume, trinkets, cologne etc; Diesel and Marco Pizzo at the Petrogradskaya metro sell, respectively, casual wear (including jeans and sweaters) and (decent) shoes; just across the Karpovka, Rifle Jeans sells a great selection of out-of-season stock.

The Dutch-run Babylon chain has shops all over town; each specialises in something;

look on Liteyny prospekt (housewares) and ulitsa Sadovaya (men's clothing). There are also three shops along Bolshoy prospekt (Petrograd Side): at Kamennoostrovsky prospekt (women's clothing), north of ulitsa Rybatskaya (children's toys) and south of ulitsa Rybatskaya (photo supplies, film and cameras). There's also a 24-hour Super Babylon food shop at Maly prospekt 16.

Music & Video Cassettes

Copyright? Huh? You can find bootlegged music cassettes at kiosks around the city. Usually labelled in Russian or bad English, the tapes are of varying quality. For higher quality, try Garmonia Lyux, downstairs next to the florist at Shpalerna ulitsa 44 (☎ 272 16 88). The walls are covered with computer print-outs of the selections available. Pick what you want, either give staff a tape or buy one and come back in about a week to pick up your cassette. Mir Muzika at ulitsa Furshtadtskaya 42 has a small collection of CDs at US prices (about US$11 to US$14). For works rejected by the rest of the world, head for the Kodak shop on outer Nevsky prospekt, which has the very best of ABBA, Tom Jones and Mr Julio Iglesias from US$15 to US$20. Melodia is still around at Nevsky prospekt 47, though these days it stocks more blenders than record albums. A real Melodia (☎ 232 11 39), which stocks a great selection of CDs and LPs of mainly Russian musicians (Russian CD US$11, Western artist CD US$17 to US$21; LP US$1.50 to US$3), still exists at Bolshoy prospekt (Petrograd Side) 47, and is open from 11 am to 7 pm daily.

Kiosk Cities

Throughout the city, usually (though not always) adjacent to metro stations, dozens of kiosks group en masse selling generally the same stuff – counterfeit clothing from China, Finnish juice drinks, Western beer, cheap vodka, blue liquors, bootleg video cassettes, and Western cigarettes (average price for a pack of 20 Marlboro and Winston in 1995 was US$1.25). Some, like the ones near Petrogradskaya, Chernyshevskaya, Ploshchad Muzhestva and Ploshchad Vosstania metros, are reliable suppliers of staple items, music cassettes and other goods, while others, like the one at metro Primorskaya, are just a blight on the landscape. The city of St Petersburg has passed regulations forcing kiosks to conform to aesthetic standards, so the kiosk cities are getting, albeit marginally, prettier.

Markets

Markets are mainly for food, but the Kondratevsky rynok's fur market (see Self-catering in the earlier Places to Eat section) has some fantastic buys, though it's getting pricey. Always check the inside for mismatched fur, poor stitching etc.

GETTING THERE & AWAY
Air

St Petersburg has direct air links with most major European capitals and airlines, many offering several connections each week (Lufthansa offers six flights a week to/from Frankfurt). Most major airlines have a representative office either in town or at the airport. Airline offices in St Petersburg include:

Aeroflot
   Nevsky prospekt 7 on the corner of ulitsa Gogolya (☎ 104 38 22)
Air France
   at Pulkovo-2 (☎ 104 34 33)
Austrian Airlines
   Nevskij Palace Hotel (☎ 104 38 22)
Balkan Bulgarian Airlines
   ulitsa Bolshaya Morskaya (ulitsa Gertsena) 36 (☎ 315 50 30)
British Airways
   ulitsa Bolshaya Morskaya (ulitsa Gertsena) 36 (☎ 311 58 20)
ČSA Czech Airlines
   ulitsa Bolshaya Morskaya (ulitsa Gertsena) 36 (☎ 315 52 59)
Delta Airlines (USA)
   ulitsa Bolshaya Morskaya (ulitsa Gertsena) 36 (☎ 311 58 20)
Finnair
   Gogolya ulitsa 19 (☎ 315 97 36)
KLM
   at Pulkovo-2 (☎ 104 34 40)
LOT Polish Airlines
   Karavannaya ulitsa 1 at ploshchad Manezhnaya (☎ 273 57 21)

Lufthansa
Vosnesensky prospekt 7 (☎ 314 49 79, 314 59 17)
Malév Hungarian Airlines
Vosnesensky prospekt 7 (☎ 314 63 80, 315 54 55)
Scandinavian Airlines System (SAS)
Nevskij Palace Hotel (☎ 314 50 86)
Swissair
Nevskij Palace Hotel (☎ 314 50 86)
Transaero (Agent) Sindbad Travel
(☎ 327 83 84, fax 329 80 19; e-mail sindbad@ryh.spb.su) 3-ya Sovietskaya 28, and Liteyny prospekt 50, above the TNT office with the entrance to the left of the TNT office.

Note that international airline tickets are one of the few items in Russia that are still charged in Western currency, usually US dollars but sometimes Deutschmarks.

Domestically, you can fly just about anywhere you want, but only a few times a week in some cases. There are several Moscow flights a day (US$75 to US$150, 1½ hours), and other daily services include Kiev, Minsk, Murmansk, Odessa, Petrozavodsk, Pskov and Tbilisi. St Petersburg's airport code is LED.

To/From Moscow In May 1995 the Russian Department of Air Transport granted Transaero, a high-quality Russian airline offering Western-standard service aboard mostly Western-made aircraft (mainly Boeing 737s and 757s), the right to compete with Pulkovo Airlines, the 'baby-flot' that previously had the route monopoly. Pulkovo had held exclusive rights to the route since Soviet times, when it was the Leningrad division of Aeroflot. The result of the new arrangement is better service and – dare we say it – choice. Prices between the two carriers are competitive, with Transaero coming in a bit cheaper in economy class; return airfare between the cities is US$170 (economy class) and US$350 (business class) on Transaero and US$178 (economy) and US$230 (business) on Pulkovo. Tickets for both Pulkovo and Transaero can be purchased at Aeroflot offices, travel agencies such as Sindbad Travel and IRO Travel in Moscow, and through Transaero agents in both cities.

Bus
St Petersburg's two long-distance bus stations are Avtovokzal 1 at naberezhnaya Obvodnogo kanala 118 (near metro Baltiyskaya) which serves northern destinations such as Vyborg, Karelia etc, and Avtovokzal 2 at naberezhnaya Obvodnogo kanala 36 (10 minutes from metro Ligovsky Prospekt) which serves Baltic countries (Estonia included), and destinations to the south and east such as Novgorod, Pskov, Vologda, Moscow and beyond.

Finnord (☎ 314 89 51) runs buses to/from Helsinki, Vyborg and Lakhti from its office at ulitsa Italyanskaya 37 and at the Hotel Pribaltiyskaya.

To/From Helsinki There are three bus companies offering shuttle services between Helsinki's autobus station and St Petersburg. St Petersburg Express is the cheapest of the bus services; at the time of writing they charged US$43.50 for the trip from St Petersburg to Helsinki. Buses leave from the Hotel Astoria at 12.30 pm and arrive in Helsinki 7.35 pm.

Finnord (☎ 314 89 51) runs buses to/from Helsinki, Vyborg and Lakhti from its office at ulitsa Italyanskaya 37, and via the Hotel Astoria; the cost of a one-way ticket is US$46. Buses leave the Astoria at 3.10 pm, arriving at Helsinki at 10.15 pm.

Sovtransavto Express Bus (☎ 264 51 25) has coaches leaving every day from the Pulkovskaya Hotel, Astoria Hotel, Grand Hotel Europe and St Petersburg Hotel to/from Helsinki, Lapeenranta, and from Vyborg to/from Lapeenranta. The bus for Helsinki costs US$46, and leaves from the Grand Hotel Europe at 8.45 am, arriving at 3.45 pm. See the service desk or concierge at these hotels for more information, or call Sovtransavto.

From Helsinki, buses leave the bus station for St Petersburg at 7.15 am (St Petersburg Express), 9.00 am (Finnord and Sovtransavto).

Train
St Petersburg has four chief main-railway-line stations, all south of the river, except the

Finland Station (Finlyandsky vokzal) which is on ploshchad Lenina, Vyborg Side, and serves trains on the Helsinki railway line. Moscow Station (Moskovsky vokzal), at ploshchad Vosstania on Nevsky prospekt, handles trains to/from Moscow, the far north, Crimea, the Caucasus, Georgia and Central Asia; Vitebsk Station (Vitebsky vokzal), at Zagorodny prospekt 52, deals with Smolensk, Belarus, Kiev, Odessa and Moldova; and Warsaw Station (Varshavsky vokzal), at naberezhnaya Obvodnogo kanala 118, covers the Baltic republics, Pskov, Lviv (Lvov) and Eastern Europe. Baltic Station (Baltiysky vokzal), just along the road from the Warsaw Station, is mainly for suburban trains.

Information & Tickets Domestic and international train information and tickets are available from the Intourist counter (No 13) at the Central Train Ticket Centre at naberezhnaya kanala Griboedova 24 (open Monday to Saturday from 8 am to 4 pm; Sunday to 4 pm). The problem here, as regards information, is one of definition: Intourist has apparently confused 'capitalism' with 'extortion'; it charges US$0.15 *per question* about train times and prices. You can also get tickets, and information about domestic trains, from the Intourist counter at Moscow Station. If you enter the main hall from ploshchad Vosstania, it's the first small door on the right after passing the schedules.

Sindbad Travel at the HI St Petersburg Hostel has a ticket-buying service for those who just can't cope with the folks at the station or the train centre; for this they tack a flat US$5 on to the ticket price. They also sell discounted tickets to Helsinki (see the To/From Helsinki section).

Moscow tickets can be purchased at any of these three places, or from any luxury hotel at a huge mark-up (the Grand Hotel Europe charges US$65 for tickets). Note that foreigners are required to pay the foreigner rate for tickets between Moscow and St Petersburg; many (non-Russian-speaking) foreigners trying to use the cheaper tickets for Russians are told that they must pay the conductor the difference between the Russian and foreigner tickets or they can't board the train (this is essentially a bribe to the conductor). If your Russian is good, give it a shot, but if you're caught the bribe to the conductor can be higher than even the face value of the foreigner tickets.

To/From Moscow Most of the 12 or more daily Moscow trains take seven to 8½ hours. Several are overnight sleepers, which save time and a night's hotel costs. To Moscow the best overnight trains are Nos 1 (11.55 pm), 3 (11.59 pm) and 5 (11.38 pm). From Moscow, Nos 2 (11.55 pm), 4 (11.59 pm) and 6 (11.10 pm) are the best. There's also the once-weekly, high-speed ER200, which covers the 650 km in less than five hours – it leaves St Petersburg on Thursday at 12.15 pm, and Moscow on Friday at 12.20 pm - it's the same price as the others.

To/From Helsinki There are two daily trains between St Petersburg and Helsinki. The *Repin*, a Russian-run train that's cleaner than most Russian trains, departs from St Petersburg's Finlyandsky vokzal at 8.05 am and arrives at Helsinki at 2.03 pm. The return trip leaves Helsinki at 3.32 pm and arrives at St Petersburg at 11.20 pm. The *Sibelius*, a quite civilised Finnish Railways-run train that's more convenient, more pleasant, faster and (if you're travelling in 1st class) *cheaper*, leaves St Petersburg at 3.55 pm, arrives Helsinki 9.34 pm; leaves Helsinki at 6.30 am and arrives at St Petersburg at 1.55 pm. Tickets can be purchased at Window 46 (Repino) or 53 (Sibelius); the booth is open Monday to Saturday from 8 am to 1 pm and 2 to 7 pm, until 1 pm and 2 to 4 pm Sunday.

You can save yourself around a quarter of the 2nd-class fare to Helsinki by allowing yourself a lot of time: from Finlyandsky vokzal, take an *elektrichka* (suburban train) to Vyborg railway station, where you meet the Helsinki-bound *Repin* at 10.16 am and the *Sibelius* at 6.15 pm. You can save even more by catching a bus from Vyborg instead; see the Vyborg Getting There & Away section in the Northern European Russia chapter for more information. The trip to Vyborg by elektrichka takes about 2½ hours. Sindbad Travel (see the Travel Agents section earlier in this chapter for details) sells tickets from St Petersburg to Helsinki at US$15 off retail price. In Helsinki, the same discount can be obtained through Eurohostel (see the European Russia Getting There & Away chapter).

To/From Other Destinations There are trains at least daily to/from Novgorod, which is served by both the Moscow and Vitebsk railway stations, Pskov (four to five hours), Petrozavodsk (ten hours), Murmansk (18 to 35 hours), Vologda (ten to 12 hours), Tallinn (seven to 8½ hours), Riga (ten to 11 hours), Vilnius (12 to 14 hours), Minsk (16 hours), Kiev (24 to 30 hours), Lviv (Lvov; 24 to 28 hours), Warsaw (23 to 26 hours) and Berlin (34 hours). For Budapest, Prague, Sofia and Bucharest, there are through-carriages from St Petersburg, though they're hitched on to new trains at Lviv (Lvov) in Ukraine.

Car & Motorbike
The roads from Tallinn, Pskov and Moscow feed into Moskovsky prospekt, which runs straight as a die about eight km north to Sennaya ploshchad on the southern edge of the city centre. The main road from Finland, which has a reputation for occasional highway robbery, is via the Vaalimaa-Torfyanovka border point (230 km from St Petersburg), Vyborg (160 km) and Zelenogorsk. Helsinki is 460 km away. The road passes the Olgino motel-campsite on the way into St Petersburg, then becomes Primorsky prospekt – there's a speed trap just before the city limits, where the speed limit is a preposterous 60 km/h. Also be careful leaving Vyborg; see the European Russia Getting There & Away chapter, and Vyborg in the Northern European Russia chapter, for more on this route; and Getting Around later in this chapter for tips on St Petersburg itself.

Rental Renting a car in St Petersburg is now

a pretty simple thing; listed below are some self and chauffeur-drive rental agencies:

Astoria Rent A Car (☎ 210 58 58), Astoria Hotel, rents Nissans with or without drivers for about US$75 per day.

Avis, Pulkovo-2 International airport (☎ 235 64 44) with a second office at Remeslennaya ulitsa 13 (same ☎), has *got* to be kidding; Renault Lagunas are US$165 per day, with 100 km free and US$1.10 per km for each additional km. It also has less expensive cars, but they rent out very very quickly in summer.

Hertz's office in St Petersburg was temporarily closed in 1995. Even when it's open it only rents chauffeur-driven cars (you must pay for the rental plus your chauffeur).

Svit (☎ 356 93 29), Prebaltiyskaya Hotel, rents Fords with drivers; they cost US$15 per hour, US$12 an hour for long-term rentals.

Transvell (☎ 113 72 53, 113 72 28) rents self and chauffeur-drive cars. It also has an office in Helsinki, and you can drive its cars between Finland and Russia. Phone the Helsinki office (☎ (358 0) 351 33 00) or Harri's mobile phone (☎ (949) 728 793). In St Petersburg, its cars start at US$48 a day plus VAT and insurance, but from Finland when VAT and insurance are added on the cost can total US$200 a day or more.

Boat
The Baltic Shipping Company's *Konstantin Simonov, Anna Karenina* and *Ilich* sail from Finland, Kiel/Stockholm and Stockholm to St Petersburg. You can use the ships for straight transport (one way or return) or book a cruise. A huge advantage of the cruise option is that it's visa free – as long as you sleep on the ship, you don't need a visa.

The high season runs from mid-May to mid-September, and mid-December to the second week in January. Sailing schedules change from year to year, but expect the *Konstantin Simonov* to sail to/from Helsinki twice a week (currently Monday and Thursday) from May to November. A bed in a quad room for a one-way trip is US$70/65 for the high and the low season. The cheapest four-day cruises, including return passage, start at US$150/135 for the high/low season in a four-person inside cabin.

The *Anna Karenina* sails from Kiel on Saturday and Nynashamn (45 minutes from Stockholm) on Sunday, and arrives at St

Petersburg on Tuesday at 9 am. The cheapest one-way fare from Kiel is US$285/245 and the cheapest visa-free cruise is US$370/320; from Nynashamn it's US$110/100, US$205/175.

The *Ilich* sails between Stockholm and Riga and Stockholm and St Petersburg; schedules and prices are very complicated. Contact the Baltic Shipping Company for more information (see its telephone numbers in this section).

Passenger ships dock at the Sea Terminal (Morskoy vokzal) at the west end of Bolshoy prospekt on Vasilevsky Island (take bus No 128 from Vasileostrovskaya metro or trolleybus No 10 from Nevsky prospekt or Primorskaya metro). Telephone numbers for the Baltic Shipping Company are:

St Petersburg (☎ 355 16 16, 355 61 40)
Helsinki (☎ (358 9) 665 755)
Stockholm (☎ (46 0) 20 00 29)
Kiel (☎ (49 431) 982 0000)
US Agent (EuroCruises; ☎ (800) 688 3876, (212) 691 2099)

There's information on the Russian inland waterways network in the European Russia Getting Around chapter. In St Petersburg, cruises can be booked through the offices of Sindbad Travel, Peter TIPS, or the St Petersburg Travel Company.

GETTING AROUND

The central area on both sides of the Neva is best seen on foot. Some hotels and tourist sites are far from the city centre, though most are convenient to public transport.

The metro is not as extensive as Moscow's so you're more likely to use buses, trolleybuses and trams. For these options there is a good transport map published by PolyPlan called *Skhema Marshrutov Gorodskogo Transporta (Plan of City Transit Routes)* sold – along with metro maps – from news kiosks and from Dom Knigi on Nevsky prospekt. Both the Transit Routes and metro maps are in Russian.

Most transport shuts down between 1 and 6 am, and when the river isn't frozen the following Neva bridges *(mosty)* are raised at night to let seagoing ships through. Most St Petersburgers (and many visitors) have stories of being marooned, and the fun of paying triple price to have a taxi race at break-neck speed to try to beat a bridge opening wears thin quickly – don't get caught on the wrong side! Below are times when the bridges are up:

Most Alexandra Nevskogo, 2.35 to 4.50 am
Bolshoy Okhtinsky Most, closed for repairs until 1997; normally up from 2.45 to 4.45 am
Liteyny Most, 2.10 to 4.40 am
Troitsky Most, 2 to 4.40 am
Dvortsovy Most, 1.35 to 3.05 and 3.15 to 4.45 am
Most Leytenanta Shmidta, 1.55 to 4.50 am
Most Birzhevoy, 2.25 to 3.20 and 3.40 to 4.40 am
Tuchkov Most, 2.20 to 3.10 and 3.40 to 4.40 am

Exceptions to the schedule are only made during all-night festivals such as White Nights.

To/From the Airport

St Petersburg's airport is at Pulkovo, about 17 km south of the city centre. The cheapest do-it-yourself transport is bus-plus-metro. From Moskovskaya metro (not Moskovskie Vorota), bus No 39 runs to Pulkovo-1, the domestic terminal, and No 13 to Pulkovo-2, the international terminal, stopping at the Hotel Pulkovskaya en route. They go whenever they feel like it, take 15 minutes and cost less than US$0.50. This is a difficult airport to reach by bus.

There is a US$1 Express bus that takes 45 minutes to the domestic terminal only, from a small Aeroflot office at ulitsa Bolshaya Morskaya (ulitsa Gertsena) 13, a block off Nevsky prospekt. It goes about every half hour throughout the day, and every hour and a half at night; there's a timetable in the office window. The bus is labelled Городской Аэровокзал Аэропорт Пулково ('Gorodskoy Aerovokzal – Aeroport Pulkovo'). Shuttles run between the domestic and international terminals, but you'll probably have to pay about US$2 to US$5 for the journey.

Buses accept cash or the tickets called

St Petersburg Metro
Санкт Петербургское метро

Parnasskaya
ПАРНАССКАЯ

Prospekt Prosveshenia
ПРОСПЕКТ ПРОСВЕЩЕНИЯ

Ozerki
ОЗЕРКИ

Udelnaya
УДЕЛЬНАЯ

Pionerskaya
ПИОНЕРСКАЯ

Chyornaya Rechka
ЧЁРНАЯ РЕЧКА

Primorskaya
ПРИМОРСКАЯ

Petrogradskaya
ПЕТРОГРАДСКАЯ

Vasileostrovskaya
ВАСИЛЕОСТРОВСКАЯ

Gorkovskaya
ГОРЬКОВСКАЯ

Devyatkino
ДЕВЯТКИНО

Grazhdansky Prospekt
ГРАЖДАНСКИЙ ПРОСПЕКТ

Akademicheskaya
АКАДЕМИЧЕСКАЯ

Politekhnicheskaya
ПОЛИТЕХНИЧЕСКАЯ

Ploshchad Muzhestva
ПЛОЩАДЬ МУЖЕСТВА

Lesnaya
ЛЕСНАЯ

Vyborgskaya
ВЫБОРГСКАЯ

Ploshchad Lenina
ПЛОЩАДЬ ЛЕНИНА

Finland Station
ФИНЛЯНДСКИЙ ВОКЗАЛ

Neva River

Chernyshevskaya
ЧЕРНЫШЕВСКАЯ

Nevsky Prospekt
НЕВСКИЙ ПРОСПЕКТ

Ploshchad Vosstania
ПЛОЩАДЬ ВОССТАНИЯ

Gostiny Dvor
ГОСТИНЫЙ ДВОР

Mayakovskaya
МАЯКОВСКАЯ

Sadovaya
САДОВАЯ

Dostoevskaya
ДОСТОЕВСКАЯ

Moscow Station
МОСКОВСКИЙ ВОКЗАЛ

Sennaya ploshchad
СЕННАЯ ПЛОЩАДЬ

Vladimirskaya
ВЛАДИМИРСКАЯ

Ligovsky Prospekt
ЛИГОВСКИЙ ПРОСПЕКТ

Pushkinskaya
ПУШКИНСКАЯ

Tekhnologichesky Institut
ТЕХНОЛОГИЧЕСКИЙ ИНСТИТУТ

Vitebsk Station
ВИТЕБСКИЙ ВОКЗАЛ

Ploshchad Alexandra Nevskogo
ПЛОЩАДЬ АЛЕКСАНДРА НЕВСКОГО

Novocherkasskaya
НОВОЧЕРКАССКАЯ

Obvodnyy Canal

Warsaw Station
ВАРШАВСКИЙ ВОКЗАЛ

Baltic Station БАЛТИЙСКИЙ ВОКЗАЛ

Baltiyskaya
БАЛТИЙСКАЯ

Narvskaya
НАРВСКАЯ

Kirovsky Zavod
КИРОВСКИЙ ЗАВОД

Avtovo
АВТОВО

Leninsky Prospekt
ЛЕНИНСКИЙ ПРОСПЕКТ

Prospekt Veteranov
ПРОПЕКТ ВЕТЕРАНОВ

Frunzenskaya
ФРУНЗЕНСКАЯ

Moskovskie Vorota
МОСКОВСКИЕ ВОРОТА

Elektrosila
ЭЛЕКТРОСИЛА

Park Pobedy
ПАРК ПОБЕДЫ

Moskovskaya
МОСКОВСКАЯ

Zvyozdnaya
ЗВЁЗДНАЯ

Kupchino
КУПЧИНО

Yelizarovskaya
ЕЛИЗАРОВСКАЯ

Lomonosovskaya
ЛОМОНОСОВСКАЯ

Proletarskaya
ПРОЛЕТАРСКАЯ

Obukhovo
ОБУХОВО

Rybatskoe
РЫБАЦКОЕ

Ladozhskaya
ЛАДОЖСКАЯ

Prospekt Bolchevikov
ПРОСПЕКТ БОЛЬШЕВИКОВ

Ulitsa Dybenko
УЛИЦА ДЫБЕНКО

LEGEND

⬤ Transfer Stations / Станции пересадок	1 Kirovsko-Vyborgskaya Line / Кировско-Выборгская линия	4 Pravoberezhnaya Line / Правобережная линия
● Metro Stations / Станции метро	2 Moskovsko-Petrogradskaya Line / Московско-Петроградская линия	
▬ Railway Stations / Железнодорожные вокзал	3 Nevsko-Vasileostrovskaya Line / Невско-Василеостровская линия	*Please note: Map not to scale* Ⓛ

NICK SELBY

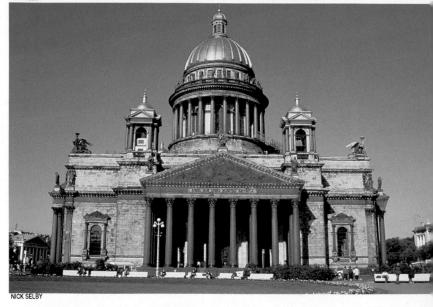

NICK SELBY

Top: The Bronze Horseman, St Petersburg
Bottom: St Isaac's Cathedral, St Petersburg

talony, which you can buy in strips of 10 from drivers for US$1.50, and which are useful on all city buses, trolleybuses and trams.

It's cheaper to get a taxi to the airport (about US$6 to US$10) than from it (at least US$20 unless your Russian's great, then at least US$10). One good way to reduce the bill is metro-plus-taxi from Moskovskaya metro; a taxi will only cost about US$3 to US$5.

The drivers that hang out at the airport are your introduction to what everyone calls the 'Mafia' and what is actually a bunch of thugs who control who can park their car there and wait for fares.

A smart way to do it is to arrange to be met at the airport by faxing one of the more reliable (read expensive) taxi services before you get on the plane. It'll be waiting for you when you arrive with your name on a sign. Expect to pay about US$25 to US$35 for a ride to the city centre using these services (see under Taxis later in this section for contact numbers), but for this price you won't have to hassle and haggle after your customs ordeal. It could be worth it.

If you're staying at any of the luxury hotels in town, or if your hotel package includes transfers, you'll be met by bus or minivan.

To/From the Seaport & Railway Stations

The Vasilevsky Island seaport is on the bus No 7 and trolleybus No 10 lines from near the Hermitage. The St Petersburg Travel Company, as well as the more expensive taxi services like SVIT, offer transfers to/from railway stations/hotels and the seaport for about US$35 per car load. Every railway terminus has a metro station next door, and taxis are easy to get if you walk a block or two away from the station before trying.

Metro

Though less majestic than Moscow's, the St Petersburg metro leaves other 'undergrounds' in the dust. You'll rarely wait more than three minutes for a train (even at 6 am on Sunday), and the clock at the end of the platform shows elapsed time since the last train departed.

It's the quickest way around the wider city and tokens (zhetony) cost US$0.10! Buy your tokens at the booths in the stations, place them in the entry gates, wait for the coins to drop and walk through (memo to potential fare-beaters: spring-mounted, pneumatically-fired gates slam shut once you pass the beam of an electric eye – even if it doesn't hurt so much, this makes a lot of noise and gate activation will certainly earn you the wrath of several screaming babushkas and possibly a policeman). If you're staying in town more than a week, you may want to get a monthly or half-monthly pass, sold at stations and in kiosks – show the pass to the person watching the open gate at the end of the entry gate row.

Since 1993, the lines have been numbered, which has simplified typing this paragraph only. Colours vary depending on the map you're looking at, but looking at the southern-most part of any map, Line 1 is always at the left; Line 4 at the right.

The grandest looking stations seem to be on Line 1. Stations open at 5.30 am and close at 1 am, and the metro begins closing down at about 12.30 am.

St Petersburg's metro is not as extensive as Moscow's, nor as user-friendly. Many station platforms (eg, on Line 3 to Vasilevsky Island and many stations on Line 2 north of Nevsky prospekt) have outer safety doors, so you can't see the station from an arriving train. The announcements in the cars are also confusing: on arrival, both the current station (*stantsia*) and the next (*sleduyushchaya stantsia*) are identified, often just as the doors slam open. So you need to count stations, ask other passengers and/or learn Cyrillic to read the maps.

Bus, Trolleybus & Tram

At the time of writing a ticket or talon, used on all buses, trolleybuses and trams, was US$0.08. They're sold in kiosks at major interchanges, by hawkers at the railway stations, and often in strips of 10 by drivers.

Bus stops are marked by 'A' signs (for

avtobus), trolleybus stops by T or т signs by the roadside and tram stops by a т sign over the roadway – all usually indicating the line numbers too. Stops may also have roadside signs with little pictures of a bus, trolleybus or tram. Most transport runs from 6 am to 1 am.

Following are some important long routes across the city.

Along Nevsky prospekt between the Admiralty and Moscow Station: bus Nos 7, 44; trolleybus Nos 1, 7, 10, 22. Trolleybus Nos 1 and 22 continue out to Hotel Moskva and Alexandr Nevsky Monastery.

Around the Sadovaya ulitsa ring road south of Nevsky prospekt: tram Nos 3, 13, 14. Tram No 3 continues north of Nevsky prospekt and crosses the Kirovsky Bridge into Petrograd Side.

From the Hermitage to the Pribaltiyskaya Hotel on Vasilevsky Island: bus Nos 7, 30, 44; trolleybus No 12.

From the Hermitage to Krestovsky Island (Petrograd Side): bus No 45 terminates at the bridge to Yelagin Island. From metro Gostiny Dvor via Liteyny Bridge to the same terminus: tram No 12.

From the Hermitage via prospekt Kronverksky to Kamennoostrovsky prospekt (Petrograd Side): tram No 63.

Along Kamennoostrovsky prospekt (Petrograd Side): bus Nos 46, 65. These cross the Neva on the Troitsky Bridge.

Along Lesnoy prospekt (Vyborg Side): trolleybus No 23; tram Nos 20, 32. These all cross the Neva on the Liteyny Bridge.

Taxi

See the European Russia Facts for the Visitor chapter for a full discussion of taxis and taxi safety tips. Prices at the time of writing for an official, metered taxi were US$0.30 flag fall, US$0.30 per km, US$1 for reservation charge and US$3 an hour waiting time. Average prices for a ride across the centre of town in a private car were about US$2; from metro Petrogradskaya to Pulkovo-2 was US$10 to US$15, and from Finlyandsky vokzal to the HI St Petersburg Hostel was US$5.

Calling to order a taxi is the most reliable way. If you're a Russian-speaker or you know one, the City Taxi Service is the easiest. Call when you need the taxi – calling far in advance just makes the dispatcher cranky.

City Taxi Service (☎ 265 13 33)
SVIT (☎ 356 93 29; fax 356 00 94, 356 38 45) will arrange to meet you at the airport if you fax them a day in advance.
Interavto (☎ 277 40 32) will pick you up from the airport if you call them a day in advance, but it's harder to reach.

Car

It's true, the best way of getting around the city by car is by bus. St Petersburg's roads are gnarled, its laws are strange, and the eyes of the eternally vigilant GAI guys (traffic cops), who are empowered to stop and fine motorists on the spot – and more – are always on you. If they wave you to the side of the road, it's best to pull over. For more information, see European Russia Getting Around.

Left turns are illegal except where posted; you'll have to make three rights or a short U-turn (and this is safer?). Street signs are inadequate, street lights are almost nonexistent except in the city centre, and Russian drivers make Italian drivers seem downright cuddly! Are you still game? For national driving regulations, see European Russia Getting Around.

Boat

In this 'Venice of the North' it's surprising that there should be no waterborne public transport other than hydrofoil and ferry services to Petrodvorets, Kronstadt and Lomonosov. See the section on River & Canal Trips for information about water taxis and organised boat tours.

Around St Petersburg
Окрестность Санкт-Петербурга

Between 25 and 45 km from central St Petersburg lie five splendid old tsarist palaces surrounded by lovely parks – all fine outings from the city. The time to see Petrodvorets on the coast is summer, when its famous fountains are flowing and it can be reached by hydrofoil from St Petersburg. Pushkin has another glorious palace, and Pavlovsk has probably the loveliest park. These last two, lying close together south of the city, can be combined in one trip. Then there's Lomonosov, beyond Petrodvorets, and Gatchina, further south than Pushkin and Pavlovsk. All except Lomonosov suffered varying degrees of ruin in WW II and some are still being restored.

Best of all, you don't need to book a tour or hire a guide; all of these obscenely lavish estates are open to the public and easily accessible by inexpensive public transport. If you do want a tour of the palaces, those that leave from in front of the Kazan Cathedral on Nevsky prospekt are a great option; look for the person with the megaphone. Tickets can also be booked at the excursion booth just outside Gostiny Dvor on ulitsa Dumskaya. Both of these places charge less than US$2 or US$3 for a tour

including transport. The St Petersburg Travel Company and hotel concierge desks offer coach tours to all the palaces from upwards of US$20 per person.

The most frequently visited sites are Petrodvorets, Pushkin and Pavlovsk. It's a good idea to take your own snacks to the palaces as most of them only have minimal (none, in the case of Lomonosov) offerings.

The old town of Vyborg, near the Finnish border, is mainly a stop en route between St Petersburg and Helsinki. On the shores of Lake Ladoga, north-east of St Petersburg, is the Nizhnezvirsky Nature Reserve, which can be visited by those interested in its populations of freshwater animals and migratory birds.

Petrodvorets

467

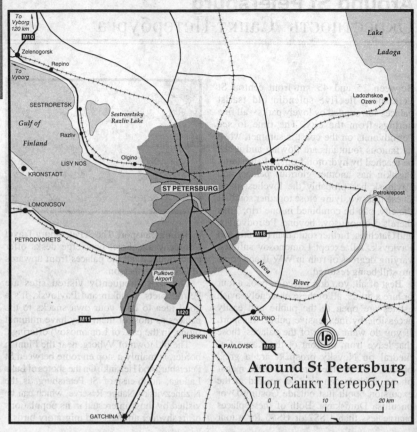

Around St Petersburg
Под Санкт Петербург

0   10   20 km

VYBORG
ВЫБОРГ
Population: 100,000

Vyborg *('VIH-bork')* is not so much a place to go to as a place to come from – it is a Gulf of Finland port, a rail junction and the main border town on the Helsinki-St Petersburg road. This is a shame, as Vyborg is a lovely 13th-century city filled with old buildings, winding cobblestone streets and a romantic, if dishevelled, harbour. Most visitors, though, seem to be Finns on coach tours to St Petersburg or on weekend drinking binges – it works out cheaper for them to book

transport, accommodation and drink here than to remain in Helsinki.

One of the oldest cities in Europe, Vyborg's central feature is the imposing medieval Vyborg Castle, built by the Swedes in 1293 when they first captured Karelia from Novgorod. Since then borders have jumped back and forth around Vyborg.

Peter the Great added it to Russia in 1710. A century later it fell within autonomous Finland, and after the October Revolution it remained part of independent Finland (since when the Finns have called it Viipuri). Stalin took it in 1939, lost it to the Finns and Germans during WW II, and on getting it back deported all the Finnish people.

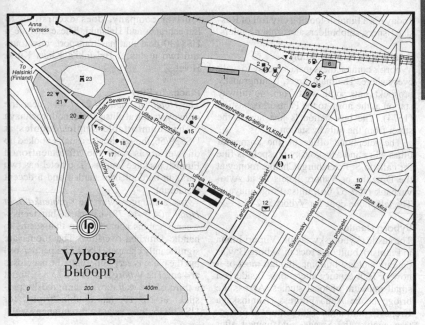

Vyborg
Выборг

0   200   400m

PLACES TO STAY

1 Korolenko Boat Hotel
   Гостиница Короленко
2 Hotel Druzhba
   Гостиница Дружба
11 Vyborg Hotel
   Гостиница Выборг

PLACES TO EAT

3 Bar Kahvila Favorit
   Бар Кавила Фаворит
4 Pogrebok
   Ресторан Погребок
7 Willehemina Kafe
   Кафе Вильхемина
9 Neste Kafe
   Кафе Несте
17 Restoran Samira
   Ресторан Самира

19 Kafe Luzhny Val
   Кафе Лужный Вал
20 Café-Boat
   Кафе
21 Snack Boat
   Лодка Снек
22 Pizza Boat
   Лодка Пищерия

OTHER

5 Petrol Station
   ABC (Бензоколонка)
6 Railway Station
   Железнодорожный
   Вокзал
8 Bus Station
   Автовокзал
9 Neste Petrol Station
   ABC Несте
   (Бензоколонка)

10 Telephone Office
   Телефон - Телеграф
12 Post Office
   Почта
13 Spaso-
   Preobrazhensky
   Cathedral
   Спасо-
   Преображенский
   Собор
14 City Hall Tower
   Башня ратуши
15 Round Tower
   Круглая Башня
16 Market
   Рынок
18 Clock Tower
   Башня часов
23 Vyborg Castle
   Выборгский замок

Today it's a Finnish-looking city full of Russian fishers, shipbuilders and timber-haulers.

Orientation & Information

Vyborg's compactness makes it easy to walk everywhere. The main street, Leningradsky prospekt, cuts south-west from the railway station at the north to the Pantserlax bastion (1574). The bus station is just across the street from the railway station.

The telephone office on the corner of ulitsa Mira and Moskovsky prospekt is fine for calls to St Petersburg. Change money at the Druzhba or Vyborg hotels or at Avtovazbank (☎ 2 57 06), ulitsa Progonnaya 1. The telephone code for Vyborg is 278.

Vyborg Castle

The castle (Vyborgsky zamok, Viipuri Linna in Finnish), built on a rock in Vyborg Bay, is the city's oldest building, though most of it now is 16th-century alterations. Inside is a small museum of local studies. Across the bridge is the Anna Fortress (Anninskaya Krepost), built in the 18th century as protection against the Swedes and named after Empress Anna Ivanovna.

Other Things to See

While the castle's the only genuine 'attraction' in the city, there are also some lovely streets with centuries-old churches, bell towers and cathedrals. A short walk from the castle takes you to the **Kruglaya bashnya** (Round Tower, 16th century), **Sobor Petra i Pavla** (Peter & Paul Cathedral, 1799) and the **Spaso-Preobrazhensky sobor** (Cathedral of the Transfiguration, 1787) which are all worth visiting. Some of the town's earlier buildings have been converted into office space for new Russian companies. There's a lovely little neighbourhood on the spit, just south of the bridge that passes the castle, with charming streets, old buildings and the occasional beer-bar and grocery shop. The main street in this area is Krepostnaya ulitsa.

Organised Tours

In the lobby of the Hotel Druzhba, Saimaa Lines OY (☎ 2 47 60), a Finnish joint-venture tourism company, does excursions to Lapeenranta and Helsinki. These include a US$130 deal that has transport, city tours and two nights at Helsinki's Klaus Kurki Hotel.

Places to Stay

The *Hotel Druzhba* (☎ 2 57 44), near the railway station at ulitsa Zheleznodorozhnaya 5, has comfortable singles/doubles at US$39/56, though they're usually booked up on weekends with the aforementioned Finnish package tourists. The hotel has two bars, an outdoor beer garden and a decent restaurant.

Just a swagger away, the *Korolenko Boat Hotel* (☎ 3 44 78) has clean but teensy-weensy cabins aboard a ship that seems to handle Druzhba overflow. The rooms are significantly cheaper (US$17.85 per person) but the place is very noisy until the bar closes at 4 am. The *Vyborg Hotel* (☎ 2 23 83), about a third of the way down Leningradsky prospekt at No 19, has doubles/triples for US$28/36; they've got a restaurant as well.

Places to Eat

The market just north of the Round Tower has fresh produce for the self caterer.

The *Restaurant Pogrebok* (cellar) near the Druzhba and Korolenko hotels has very good meat and chicken dishes for less than US$2.85. It's down a creepy staircase at ulitsa Zheleznodorozhnaya 2. Across the street, the *Bar Kahvila Favorit* is a hastily-constructed affair that mainly serves hard liquor; it's open from noon until the last person lurches out.

The *Neste Kafe*, at the Neste filling station opposite the railway station, has good sandwiches and pizzas in a decidedly Western setting. It's open 24 hours a day. Nearby, the *Willehemina Kafe* (a shack really) has edible hamburgers and hot dogs. Avoid the snack shack just next to the station doors.

The big surprise in this town is the pleasant Chinese restaurant *Samira* (☎ 2 19 10) at Storozhevoy Bashni ulitsa 10, near the 15th-century watchtower of the old cathedral. Their very tasty pork is the highest priced dish at US$2.85. They also do great beef dumplings and Chinese tea, though there are no vegetarian dishes. The restaurant's open from 11 am to midnight.

The two *boat-restaurants* moored at the bridge next to the castle are quite civilised with expensive pizza (US$7.50) and beer.

Just near the port, the *Lyuzhny Val* (☎ 9 32 99) is a very pleasant and cavernous cellar bar/snack bar, with good service. It's at ulitsa Yuzhny Val 4, and open from noon to midnight.

Getting There & Away

Bus From St Petersburg, all buses to Helsinki stop at Vyborg, but you'd do much better taking the elektrichka. To Helsinki, there's a daily Russian bus at 3.30 pm (four hours, US$27.50). There are also buses from St Petersburg that pass through (see the St Petersburg – Getting There & Away section for more information). There are daily buses to Lappeenranta (Finland) at 9.15 am (Russian-run) and 7 pm (Finnish-run); both cost about US$12. Buses leave from the bus station, which is near the railway station and the Hotel Druzhba.

Train Vyborg is 2½ hours by suburban train from St Petersburg's Finland Station, rather stretching the idea of 'suburban'. Trains go every hour all day, and every hour or two in the evenings; on the big board at the Finland Station they're called Vyborgskoe.

The two daily fast trains from St Petersburg to Helsinki stop at Vyborg and at the border crossing of Luzhayka (Vainikkala on the Finnish side). If you're trying to save money on the way out of St Petersburg by coming to Vyborg by elektrichka and then catching the Helsinki train, you'll be wanting window No 5 at Vyborg; trains to Helsinki leave Vyborg at 10.16 am and 6.15 pm.

Car & Motorbike St Petersburg is 160 km away and Helsinki is 300 km away. There are two crossings to Finland: at Torfyanovka (to Vaalimaa); and at Brusnichnoe (to Nuijamaa). The former is the direct route to Helsinki, while the latter is more scenic, passing along the Saimaa Canal towards the lake of the same name. At the border, the Frontier Duty Free Shop has some great deals on Levis, liquor, VCRs and other home electronics. The road between the border and St Petersburg has a reputation for the occasional highway robbery, so don't stop for a picnic.

If you need to fill up there's the Neste, which is almost twice as expensive as the Russian-owned filling station that's closer to the railway station, but Neste takes credit cards and is open 24 hours.

Boat There are only rare sailings to/from Finnish ports; sometimes cruise ships dock here too.

PETRODVORETS
ПЕТРОДВОРЕЦ

Peter the Great had a cabin 29 km west of St Petersburg on the Gulf of Finland, to oversee construction of his Kronstadt (or Kronshtadt) naval base. He liked it so much there that he built a villa, Monplaisir, and then a whole series of palaces across an estate originally called Petergof, which has been called Petrodvorets (Peter's Palace) since 1944 (there was a brief attempt to rename the place Petergof in 1992, but it fizzled). All are set within a spectacular ensemble of gravity-powered fountains that are now the site's main attraction. This 'Russian Versailles' is probably the most impressive of St Petersburg's suburban palaces.

Petrodvorets (*'pet-ra-dvar-YETS'*) was completely trashed by the Germans in WW II and is largely a reconstruction from photos, drawings and anecdotes.

There will almost always be something closed while you are there because, inexplicably, each site has its own closing days: Grand Palace, Monday and last Tuesday of the month; Marly, Tuesday and last Wednesday; Monplaisir, Hermitage and Catherine Building, Wednesday and last Thursday; Cottage, Friday and last Thursday. Normal hours are 9 am to 10 pm daily, while the museums are open from 11 am to 8 pm daily from the end of May to the end of September.

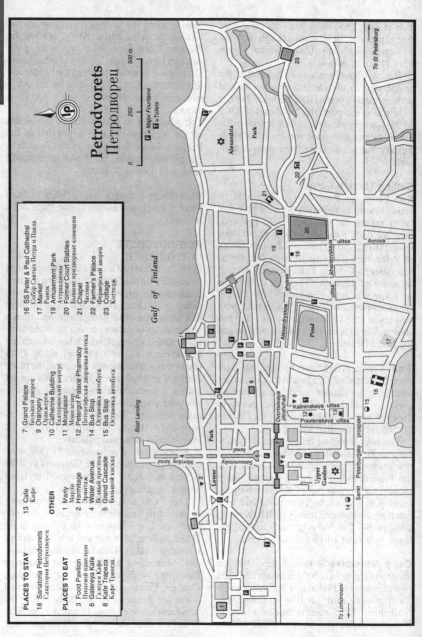

Petrodvorets
Петродворец

= Major Fountains
= Toilets

Gulf of Finland

PLACES TO STAY
18 Sanatoria Petrodvorets
    Санатория Петродворец

PLACES TO EAT
3   Food Pavilion
    Пищевой павильон
6   Galereya Kafe
    Галерея Кафе
8   Kafe Trapeza
    Кафе Трапеза
13 Cafe
    Кафе

OTHER
1   Marly
    Марли
2   Hermitage
    Эрмитаж
4   Water Avenue
    Водяной проспект
5   Grand Cascade
    Большой каскад
7   Grand Palace
    Большой дворец
9   Orangery
    Оранжерея
10 Catherine Building
    Екатеринский корпус
11 Monplaisir
    Монплезир
12 Petergof Palace Pharmacy
    Петергофская дворцовая аптека
14 Bus Stop
    Остановка автобуса
15 Bus Stop
    Остановка автобуса
16 SS Peter & Paul Cathedral
    Собор Святых Петра и Павла
17 Market
    Рынок
19 Amusement Park
    Аттракционы
20 Former Court Stables
    Бывшие придворные конюшни
21 Chapel
    Часовня
22 Farmer's Palace
    Фермерский дворец
23 Cottage
    Коттедж

The Lower Park and Alexandria Park are open every day.

Because of the confounded opening hours, it's only possible to take in all the museums and palaces in a single day during weekends, when, naturally, the place is swarming with visitors. All the attractions charge separate admissions. Admission to the grounds is payable at the cash booth on the jetty.

Grand Cascade

The uncontested centrepiece is the Grand Cascade & Water Avenue, a symphony of fountains (over 140) and canals partly engineered by Peter himself. The central statue of Samson tearing open a lion's jaws celebrates – as so many things in St Petersburg do – Peter's victory over the Swedes.

To the disappointment of visitors since 1990, the cascade has been shut down for restoration. With luck it will be squirting again in the near future, though it's difficult to say for certain. Other fountains are functional, and the trick fountains – triggered by hidden switches (hidden, that is, by hordes of kids jumping on them) – are designed to squirt any unsuspecting passers-by. Normally the fountains play from 11 am to 8 pm daily from May to September.

Grand Palace

Between the cascade and the formal Upper Garden is the *Bolshoy dvorets* ('Grand Palace'). Peter's modest project, finished just before his death, was grossly enlarged by Rastrelli for Empress Elizabeth and later redecorated for Catherine the Great. It's now a vast museum of lavish rooms and galleries – a monument above all to the craft of reconstruction (which is still going on). Anything not nailed down was removed before the Germans arrived, so the paintings, furniture and chandeliers are original.

Highlights include the Chesma Hall, full of huge paintings of Russia's destruction of the Turkish fleet at Çeşme in 1770, all by the same German artist. After the battle Catherine arranged for a ship to be blown up so he could paint it properly. In its pathological single-mindedness, the room is not unlike a Lenin museum. Two 'Chinese' rooms have walls of rich lacquered wood. Between them is another bizarre gallery: 360 portraits of eight young girls by the Italian Pietro Rotari, sold *en bloc* to Catherine by his widow, who managed to slip in a few elderly subjects too.

Of some 20 rooms, the last, without a trace of Catherine, is the finest – Peter's simple, beautiful study, apparently the only room to survive the Germans. It has 14 fantastic carved-wood panels, of which six reconstructions (in lighter wood) are no less impressive; each took 1½ years to do.

The palace is a must-see, preferably with a guide. Peter the Great still looks like the tsar with the best taste.

You'll need to join a tour group to enter (US$5.50 for foreigners, US$1 for Russians; photos US$2.15, video US$5.50). Tickets are sold inside, near the lobby where you pick up your tapochki.

Monplaisir

Peter's outwardly more humble villa, with study and galleries facing the sea, remained his favourite and it's not hard to see why: wood-panelled, snug and elegant, peaceful even when there's a crowd – which there used to be all the time, what with Peter's mandatory partying ('misbehaving' guests were required to gulp down huge quantities of wine). The main hall has marble floors and a richly painted ceiling; the kitchen is Dutch style, a little study is Chinese. Admission for foreigners/Russians is US$4.50/0.19 while photos/videos are US$1/2.

To the left is an annexe called the Catherine Building because Catherine the Great was living here – establishing an alibi? – when her husband Peter III was overthrown. Catherine Building admission is US$2.75/0.19, and US$1/2 for photos/video. Tickets are sold around the east side of the building.

Lower Park & Other Pavilions

Along the Gulf shore is the Lower Park, with more fountains – big and small, elegant and silly (watch out for the trick fountains) – and more pavilions.

Near the shoreline, and finished soon after the Grand Palace, is a two-storey pink-and-white box called the Hermitage, which features the ultimate in private dining on the second floor. Special elevators hoist a fully laid table into the imperial presence, thereby eliminating any hindrance by servants. The elevators are circular and directly in front of each diner, whose plate would be lowered, replenished and replaced. Admission for foreigners/Russians is US$2.85/0.09, while photos/videos are US$1/2.

Further west is Marly, another of Peter's mini-palaces and guesthouses. To the east an old Orangery – which would appear to be a rest house for Russian tourists – houses the Historical Museum of Wax Figures, containing 49 figures of big-wigged Russians (from Peter I to Nicholas II) from the 18th and 19th centuries. Admission to the museum is US$2.85/0.09 while photos/videos are US$1/2.40. Get tickets in the small shack outside. It's open every day from 11 am to 6 pm.

Alexandria Park

Even on summer weekends, the rambling, overgrown Alexandria Park is peaceful and empty, and ideal for a leisurely walk. It was built for Tsar Nicholas I (and named for his tsarina) and it looks as though his heart wasn't in his royal work. Besides a mock-Gothic chapel, its diversions include the Farmer's Palace (1831), which vaguely resembles a stone farmstead and is currently in ruins, and the Cottage (1829), which is modelled on an English country cottage and is intact.

Now a museum, the Cottage's rooms – neo-Gothic, Rococo or Art Nouveau depending on later renovations – are full of imperial bric-a-brac and hundreds of works by minor Russian artists. In the boudoir is a clock with 66 faces, one for each pre-Revolutionary province.

On the way back, what looks like a Gothic college campus was once the imperial stables and is now a retirement home (for humans, we suspect).

Petergof Palace Pharmacy

This peculiar tourist attraction is a brand-new, old-style apothecary shop with drawers full of medicinal plants – it looks (and smells) like the real thing. They'll whip up a herb drink for you, and if your Russian's good enough you can talk to them about your ingrown whatsit. They've also got a fair selection of Western remedies, like Panadol. They're open 8 am to 8 pm and closed Saturday. It's just east of the Upper Garden.

Petrodvorets Town

Outside the grounds is Petrodvorets town. Don't overlook the five-domed SS Peter & Paul Cathedral across the road, in traditional style but built only at the turn of the century. If you're around at 9.45 am and 4.45 pm you'll hear the church bells play a lovely tune. The cathedral holds evening services at 5 pm, and closes at 6 or 7 pm except on holidays, when night services are held.

Six km east of Petrodvorets is Strelna, another estate with parklands and two palaces built for Peter (later enlarged for Empress Elizabeth by Rastrelli).

Places to Stay

There's a dorm or two in all this. The *Baza Otdykha Petergof* (☎ 427 54 03) at Alexandryskaya (formerly Sovietskaya) ploshchad 7, in front of the entrance to the lower gardens, has clean rooms for US$20 per person. The same sort of room at the slightly less ostentatious *Sanitariya Petrodvorets* (no phone) at the end of ulitsa Avrova (No 2) costs US$7.50 per person, and a bit more in summer.

Places to Eat

Just across from the pharmacy, the *Kafe Trapeza* (☎ 427 93 93), at Kalininskaya ulitsa 9, is a nice and cosy place doing veal with fried potatoes and chicken Kiev for about US$3.80. The round pavilion near the boat landing has an adequate *café, grill-bar* and *canteen*. It's open from 1 to 9 pm, and closed Saturday. Behind the Grand Palace is the newish *Galereya Kafe* (☎ 427 98 84), doing decent snacks and light lunches for

US$2 to US$4. It's open from 10 am to 8 pm daily except Monday.

Getting There & Away

Suburban trains take 40 minutes from St Petersburg's Baltic Station to Novy Petrodvorets (not Stary Petrodvorets), departing every 30 to 60 minutes until early evening. Buy tickets from the cash desk. From Novy Petrodvorets Station, take any bus but No 357 to the fifth stop (the fourth is a church), which takes about 10 minutes, to the park; ask for 'fontana'. As you enter, arrowed signs direct you to the lower park, Monplaisir, Marly and the booking office.

By road it's about an hour; there's plenty of street parking outside the grounds.

For beating queues, a coach tour is a good idea, but be sure of what you'll see besides the grounds. An individual excursion with guide and hire car could be a complete waste of money. You could get a taxi from the state taxi service in St Petersburg to take you there, wait for you and bring you back for about US$30.

From May to September, a fine alternative is the *Meteor* hydrofoil from the jetty in front of St Petersburg's Hermitage, which goes every 20 to 30 minutes from 9.30 am to at least 7 pm, or a much slower ferry every 20 to 40 minutes from Sea Wharf (Morskaya pristan) near Tuchkov Bridge on naberezhnaya Morskaya, Vasilevsky Island. The hydrofoil trip takes half an hour and costs US$4, plus the US$1 park entry fee (US$0.05 for Russians) payable on the way out from St Petersburg.

To see the sights with the locals, queue at the ticket booths and join a tour narrated in Russian.

LOMONOSOV
ЛОМОНОСОВ

While Peter was building Monplaisir, his right-hand man, Alexandr Menshikov, began his own palace, **Oranienbaum**, 12 km further down the coast. Menshikov never saw the finished product; following Peter's death and Menshikov's exile, the estate served briefly as a hospital and then passed to Tsar Peter III, who didn't much like ruling Russia and spent a lot of time at Oranienbaum. After doing away with him, his wife Catherine (the Great) made it her private pleasure ground.

Oranienbaum was not occupied by the Nazis. After WW II it was for some reason renamed for the scientist-poet Mikhail Lomonosov and now doubles as a museum and public park, with boat rentals and carnival rides alongside the remaining buildings. The park is open from 9 am to 10 pm, but the palace-museums are open only from 11 am to 6 pm (to 5 pm Monday), and closed Tuesday, the last Monday of the month, and in winter.

Biggest of all, with semicircular galleries and lower garden, is Menshikov's **Grand Palace** (Большой дворец), which is (still) under restoration, though a finishing date of 1995/6 has been given. Once a canal linked it to the Gulf. Beyond the pond is **Peterstadt Palace** (Дворец Петерштадт), Peter III's boxy toy palace, with rich, uncomfortable-looking interiors and some Chinese-style lacquer-on-wood paintings. It's approached through the Gate of Honour (Въездные ворота), which is all that remains of a toy fortress where he amused himself drilling his soldiers.

But most worth seeing is Catherine's over-the-top **Chinese Palace** (Китайский дворец). It's Baroque outside and extravagantly Rococo inside, with a private retreat designed by Antonio Rinaldi that includes painted ceilings, fine inlaid-wood floors and walls, and decoration probably unequalled in any of the other St Petersburg palaces. The most blindingly sumptuous is the **Large Chinese Room**, designed in the 'Oriental' style of the day. The house, though restored, is not a reconstruction but the real thing. The nearby kitchen house has a small exhibition of furnishings. It's open Monday and Wednesday to Friday from 11 am to 6 pm, Saturday and Sunday from 10 am to 6 pm, and closed Tuesday and the last Monday of the month.

The building that looks like a blue-and-white wedding cake is the **Coasting-Hill Pavilion** (Павильон катальной горки). It

Lomonosov
Ломоносов

0   250   500 m

prospekt Yunogo Lenintsa

Coasting-Hill Pavilion

Lower Garden

Grand Palace

Boat Rental

Pond

Amusement Park

Chinese Palace

Kitchen House

Gate of Honour

Poterstadt Palace

Manezh

Lenin Statue/ Gate

Railway Station

Shkipersky kanal

To Lomonosov Pier

Bus Station

Railway Station

To St Petersburg

---

was the launching-pad for Catherine's private roller coaster: a multistorey wooden slide which courtiers would fly down on little carts or toboggans. The slide is gone but the pavilion's extravagant inner rooms are worth a look. Tickets for foreigners/Russians are US$2/0.10 and sold inside the main entrance to the Porcelain and White rooms.

Perhaps Lomonosov's best feature is the several kilometres of quiet paths through pine woods and sombre gardens, with relatively small crowds – a rarity on the Russian tourist trail. The town of Lomonosov has nothing to offer, not even food.

Getting There & Away

The suburban train from St Petersburg's Baltic Station to Petrodvorets continues to Lomonosov. Get off at Oranienbaum-I (not II) Station, an hour from St Petersburg. From the station, walk past a church and then cross prospekt Yunogo Lenintsa to the park entrance, a small stone gatehouse by a Lenin statue.

From May to September, hydrofoils come here from naberezhnaya Makarova, near the Hotelship Peterhof and the Tuchkov bridge on Vasilevsky Island, every 30 minutes from about 7.30 am to at least 6 pm. The cost is

US$5. The route is Morskaya-Kronstadt-Lomonosov-Morskaya. Note that in 1995 boat service to Lomonosov was not running due to renovation; it's unclear when it will start again.

KRONSTADT
КРОНШТАДТ

Within a year of founding St Petersburg, Peter – desirous of protecting the city and his new Baltic toehold – started work on the fortress of Kronstadt on Kotlin Island, 30 km out in the Gulf of Finland. It's been a pivotal Soviet and Russian naval base ever since.

In March 1921 the base was the scene of a short-lived mutiny against the Bolsheviks, one of the last overt signs of opposition to the revolution until perestroika. The city of Kronstadt, which is still off-limits to foreigners, reportedly has a beautiful Byzantine-style cathedral.

Hydrofoils to Lomonosov stop here.

PUSHKIN & PAVLOVSK
ПУШКИН И ПАВЛОВСК

The sumptuous palaces and big, beautiful parks at Pushkin and Pavlovsk, neighbours 25 km and 29 km south of St Petersburg, can be combined in a day's visit – but since they're both good places to relax, you might want to take them more slowly.

Pushkin's palaces and parks were created under Empresses Elizabeth and Catherine the Great between 1744 and 1796. The centrepiece is the vast 1752-56 Baroque Catherine Palace (Yekaterininsky dvorets), designed by Rastrelli and named after Elizabeth's mother, Peter the Great's second wife. Pushkin used to be called Tsarskoe selo (Tsar's Village) but was renamed after Russia's favourite poet, who studied here in 1937. The country's first railway opened in 1837 to carry the royal family between here and St Petersburg.

Pavlovsk's park of woodland, rivers, lakes, little valleys, avenues, Classical statues and temples, is one of the most exquisite in Russia, while its Great Palace is a Classical contrast to the Catherine Palace. Palace and park were originally designed by

Charles Cameron between 1781 and 1786, on Catherine the Great's orders, for her son, the future Paul I.

Information

At both places, getting into the parks and lesser exhibitions is little or no problem, but tickets for the two main palaces are zealously guarded by stern babushki who, like their comrades in the Hermitage, can smell Reeboks at 1000 metres: expect to pay the foreigner price (US$7.25, as opposed to US$0.50 for Russians) unless your Russian is good. Russian-language tours run at set times between noon and 5 pm, and tickets are sold from 10 am until they run out – which they may do in an hour or two on busy days. So if you're keen to see the inside of a palace, you may save disappointment by taking an excursion – the St Petersburg Travel Company in St Petersburg usually run separate trips for the two places lasting about four hours each. You could make your own way back to the city if you want to stay on afterwards. The interior of the Catherine Palace is the more sumptuous, if you have to choose between the two.

The parks are open every day, but the Catherine Palace is closed on Tuesdays and the last Monday of the month, while the Great Palace is closed Friday and the first Monday of the month.

Catherine Palace

As at the Winter Palace, Catherine the Great had many of Rastrelli's original interiors remodelled in Classical style. Charles Cameron, reputedly an aristocratic Scot but probably a London builder's son with a flair for self-invention, was her chief redesigner. The palace was used in varying degrees by different tsars until 1917, but was ruined by the Germans in WW II. So far, most of Rastrelli's wonderful exterior and 20-odd rooms of the interior have been restored with no mean skill – compare it to the photographs of the devastation left by the Germans and you'll be suitably impressed. The palace is 300 metres long, with the golden domes of its chapel rising at its north end, and

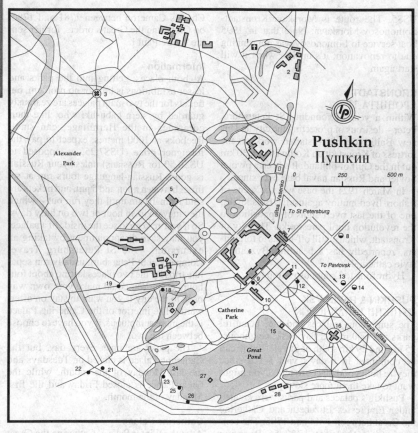

Pushkin
Пушкин

0   250   500 m

ulitsa Vasenko

To St Petersburg

To Pavlovsk

Komsomolskaya ulitsa

Alexander
Park

Catherine
Park

Great
Pond

outbuildings enclosing a courtyard on the
west side. The visitors' entrance and ticket
office are in the middle of the courtyard side.

All the rooms on show are upstairs. Visits
normally start with the white State Staircase,
an 1860 addition. South of here, only two
rooms – both by Rastrelli – have been
restored: the Gentlemen-in-Waiting's
Dining Room (Kavalerskaya stolovaya) and,
beyond, the Great Hall (Bolshoy zal), which
is the largest room in the palace, and is all
light and glitter from its windows, mirrors
and gilded woodcarvings.

North of the State Staircase, on the court-

yard side, are the State Dining Room, the
Crimson and Green Pilaster Rooms, the Portrait Room and finally the Amber Room
(Yantarnaya komnata). This Amber Room
was decorated by Rastrelli with gilded
woodcarvings, mirrors, agate and jasper
mosaics, and exquisitely engraved amber
panels given to Peter the Great by the King
of Prussia in 1716. But its treasures were
plundered by the Nazis and went missing in
Kaliningrad (then Königsberg) in 1945.
Next is the large, sumptuous Picture Hall
(Kartinny zal).

Most of the north end is Cameron's early

Classical work. The elegant proportions of the Green Dining Room (Zelyonaya stolovaya) on the courtyard side are typical. Also on the courtyard side are three rooms with fabulous, patterned silk wall-coverings: the Blue Drawing Room (Golubaya gostinaya), the Chinese Blue Drawing Room (Kitayskaya golubaya gostinaya) – a severely Classical design enlivened by the 18th-century fashion for Oriental motifs, all recreated since WW II from photos – and the Choir Anteroom (Predkhornaya), whose gold silk, woven with swans and pheasants, is the original from the 18th century. The anteroom leads into the Choir (Khory) and the chapel (designed by Rastrelli) and is painted blue and gold. On the park side, next to the Chinese Blue Drawing Room, is an elegant monarchical bedroom.

On the ground floor beneath the chapel are rooms used for temporary exhibitions, entered from the road outside, across which is the entrance to a branch of the Pushkin Museum. This museum has more than 20 rooms and the only way in is by queuing for a guided tour – it's mainly for enthusiasts of poetic paraphernalia and 19th-century Russia.

The Catherine Palace is open from 11 am to 6 pm in summer (until 5 pm in winter) and closed Tuesday and the last Monday of the month.

Pushkin Parks

Around the south and east of the Catherine Palace extends the lovely Catherine Park (Yekaterininsky Park). The main entrance is on Komsomolskaya ulitsa in front of the palace.

The park's inner, formal section runs down terraces in front of the palace to Rastrelli's blue-and-white Hermitage building. Just off the south-east corner of the palace, Cameron's Cold Baths building, containing his extravagant Agate Rooms (Agatovye komnaty), is sometimes open. His Cameron Gallery next door, with a display of 18th and 19th-century costumes and carriages, is open daily except Tuesday. Its upper arcade was made so Catherine the Great could enjoy the views. Between the gallery and the palace, notice the south-pointing ramp which Cameron added for the ageing empress to walk down into the park.

The park's outer section focuses on the Great Pond, where you can rent a boat in summer. This section is dotted with an intriguing array of structures ranging from the 'Pyramid', where Catherine the Great buried her favourite dogs, to the Creaking Summerhouse (or Chinese Pavilion), the Marble Bridge (copied from one at Wilton, England) and the Ruined Tower, which was built 'ready-ruined' in keeping with a 1770s romantic fashion – maybe an 18th-century empress's equivalent of the current taste for distressed denim!

A short distance north of the Catherine Palace along ulitsa Vasenko, the Classical Alexander Palace was built by Quarenghi in 1792-96 for the future Alexander I. It isn't open to the public. Nor officially, it seems, is the wild and empty Alexander Park, which extends on three sides of it, adjoining the Catherine Park in the south. But usually you'll find the odd gate open or a section of fencing missing, enabling people to wander into the park without any problems. One such gate is behind the Catherine Palace.

Pavlovsk Great Palace
Cameron's original palace was a three-storey,

domed square with single-storey wings curving only halfway round the existing courtyard. Paul loathed his mother, and with his wife, Maria Fyodorovna, wanted a more restrained, more French approach to building than Cameron's. The Englishman was replaced by his assistant Vincenzo Brenna, who disproportionately enlarged the wings and, along with other noted architect/designers like Quarenghi and Rossi, completed the interior. The palace, a royal residence until 1917, burnt down in WW II but was fully restored by 1970.

The finest rooms are on the middle floor of the square central block. Cameron designed the round Italian Hall beneath the dome, and the Grecian Hall to its west, though the lovely green fluted columns were added by Brenna. Flanking these are two private suites mainly designed by Brenna – Paul's along the north side of the block and Maria Fyodorovna's on the south. The insane, military-obsessed Paul's Hall of War – he's also responsible for the Engineers' Castle in St Petersburg – contrasts with Maria's Hall of Peace, which is decorated with musical instruments and flowers.

1	Railway Station Железнодорожный вокзал	11	Old Woods Старая сильвия	22	Pavilion of the Three Graces Павильон трех граций
2	Bus Stop Автобусная остановка	12	Visconti Bridge Висконтьев мост	23	Great Palace Большой дворец
3	Novoshaleynye Ponds Новошалейные пруды	13	Great Cascade Большой каскад	24	Great Circles (Two Sites) Большие круги
4	Beautiful Valley Pond Краснодолинный пруд	14	Summer Theatre Летний театр	25	Treble Lime Alley Тройная липовая аллея
5	Beautiful Valley Pavilion Краснодолинный павильон	15	Apollo Colonnade Колоннада Аполонна	26	Bus Stop Автобусная остановка
6	Ruin Руины	16	Cold Baths Холодная баня	27	Aviary Птичник
7	New Woods Новая сильвия	17	Humpback Bridge Горбатый мостик	28	Labyrinths Лабиринты
8	Mausoleum Мавзолей	18	Birch Circle Хоровод берёз	29	Rossi Pavilion Павильон Росси
9	Birch Circle Хоровод берёз	19	Temple of Friendship Храм дружбы	30	Grave of Revolutionaries Могила жертв революции
10	Rose Pavilion Роз Павильон	20	Black Bridge Чёрный мост		
		21	Private (Royal) Garden Собственный садик		

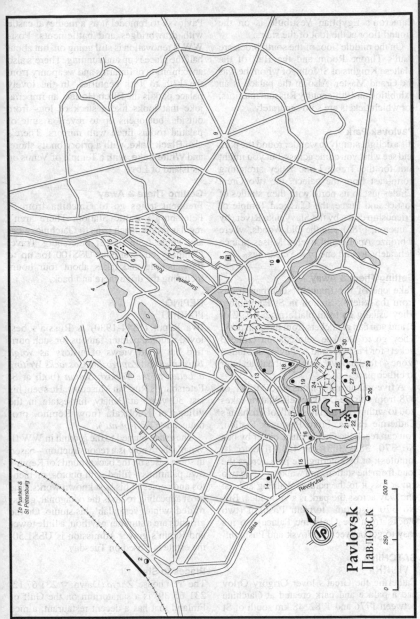

Pavlovsk
Павловск

To Pushkin &
St Petersburg

ulitsa Revolyutsii

Slavyanka River

500 m
250
0

Cameron's Egyptian Vestibule is on the ground floor at the foot of the stairs.

On the middle floor of the south block are Paul's Throne Room and the Hall of the Maltese Knights of St John, of whom he was the Grand Master. Also in the palace is an exhibition on 19th-century Russian interiors, for which tickets are sold separately.

Pavlovsk Park

It's a delight simply to wander round the park and see what you come across, but you might aim for the Treble Lime Alley stretching north-east from the palace, the two Great Circles just to its north with their statues of Justice and Peace, the Classical Temple of Friendship down by the Slavyanka River (by Cameron, 1782), and the Old Woods, where a bronze Apollo and twelve Muses prance delicately around one of the clearings.

Getting There & Away

Take one of the frequent suburban trains from the Vitebsk Station in St Petersburg. They usually go from platforms No 1, 2 or 3, and you can get tickets from the cash desk. They go to Detskoe selo Station (zone 3 ticket) for Pushkin, and to Pavlovsk Station (zone 4) for Pavlovsk. It's about half an hour to either place.

A five-minute ride on bus No 370, 371, or 378 from outside Detskoe selo Station takes you to within two minutes walk of Pushkin's Catherine Palace. From Pavlovsk Station, you can reach the Great Palace either by bus No 370, 383, 383A or 493 (five to 10 minutes); or by entering the park across the road from the station, and walking 1.5 to two km across it to the palace. Walking at least one way across the park is a good idea. Bus No 370 also runs to/from Pushkin (two blocks from the Catherine Palace), so it's easy to get between Pavlovsk and Pushkin.

GATCHINA
ГАТЧИНА

Catherine the Great's lover Grigory Orlov had a palace and park created at Gatchina between 1776 and 1782, 48 km south of St Petersburg. Later, Paul I moved here from

Pavlovsk to remodel it as a medieval castle with drawbridges and battlements. Post-WW II renovation is still going on, but about half the place is up and running. There's also an exhibition of firearms and weaponry from the 17th to 19th centuries. In the lovely palace park is the **Birch House**, an imperial joke that looks like a stack of logs from outside, but opens up to reveal a suite of palatial rooms lined with mirrors. There's also **Black Lake**, with a priory on its shore, and **White Lake**, with a Temple of Venus on its Island of Love.

Getting There & Away

Frequent trains go to Gatchina from St Petersburg's Baltic Station. There aren't regular group coach trips to Gatchina: a car and guide from the St Petersburg Travel Company costs around US$100 for up to three people and takes about four hours including the drive there and back.

REPINO
РЕПИНО

Ilya Repin (1844-1930) is Russia's best loved national painter, famous for such purified but vivid views of history as *Volga Bargemen* and *Zaporozhie Cossacks Writing a Letter to the Turkish Sultan* (both at St Petersburg's Russian Museum). He spent his last 30 years at Penaty, his estate in the village of Kuokkala (now Repino, pronounced '*RYEH-pi-na*').

The estate burned to the ground in WW II. What's there now is a reconstruction – based in some cases on the backgrounds of Repin's own paintings – filled with photos, mementos and copies of his best known works. The most appealing room is the octagonal, glass-roofed 'winter verandah', his studio. On the grounds are a summer pavilion, a little tower and Repin's grave. Admission is US$1.50; the estate is closed on Tuesday.

Places to Stay

The 'rest house' *Zarya* (Dawn; ☎ 231 67 12, 231 65 39) is a sanatorium on the Gulf of Finland that has a decent restaurant, a nice sauna and very comfortable rooms. It's at

Primorskoe shosse 423, not far from the Repin museum. Prices are US$15/25.

Getting There & Away

At 50 km from the centre of St Petersburg, Repino is rather far to go unless you're driving on to Vyborg or Helsinki. There are suburban trains to Repino Station, about a km from Penaty, from St Petersburg's Finland Station. From the station, walk to the gulf and left on ulitsa Repina for 300 or 400 metres. A taxi might want US$30 to US$50 for a return trip from St Petersburg. Regional bus No 411 goes there, via Olgino and Sestroretsk, from metro Chyornaya Rechka, but it's a very long haul on public transport.

NIZHNEZVIRSKY NATURE RESERVE
НИЖНЕЗВИРСКИЙ
ГОСУДАРСТВЕННЫ ЗАПОВЕДНИК

On the south-eastern shore of Lake Ladoga, the 414-sq-km Nizhnezvirsky Nature Reserve is an important stopover for migra-

tory birds and home to a variety of animals, among them the Lake Ladoga ringed seal *(Phoca hispida ladogensis)*, a freshwater subspecies peculiar to the area. It also covers the coastal zone and the mouth of the Svir River, where salmon and trout spawn. Arrangements to visit the reserve can be made through the American Association for the Support of Ecological Initiatives, (☎ (1 203) 347 2967; fax (1 203) 347 8459; e-mail wwasch@eagle.wesleyan.edu), 150 Coleman Road, Middletown CT 06457, USA. Bill Wasch Sr and Jr, who run the organisation, are both intimately involved with the reserve and others like it, and are great sources of information.

From St Petersburg, contact Alexandr Karpenko, head of Adonis (☎ 307 09 18; e-mail alexk@aasei.spb.su), at Komandantsky prospekt 40, korpus 2, flat 236. The above agencies are nonprofit, and can arrange stays at other European Russian reserves as well.

Western European Russia
Европейская Россия, западная часть

Western European Russia, between Moscow and St Petersburg and the borders of Ukraine, Belarus, Latvia and Estonia, is an area of rolling hills, endless steppe, and long-contested borders. This area saw the heaviest fighting in the country during WW II; towns in the southernmost region like Kursk, Oryol, Bryansk and Smolensk, have all been destroyed by war on several occasions.

By a quirk of geo-political fate, this region also includes Kaliningrad, the strategically important wedge of Russia between Lithuania, Poland and the Baltic Sea. Not included in this chapter are European Russia's two largest cities – Moscow and St Petersburg – or the areas nearby, which are covered in those city chapters and 'Around Moscow' and 'Around St Petersburg' chapters.

HISTORY

The region was settled by the Slavs, migrating from the west, in about the sixth to eighth centuries AD. At the same time Varangians (Vikings) from Scandinavia began trading and raiding across the region en route to the Black Sea. In 862, supposedly at the invitation of local Slavic tribes, Varangians under Prince Rurik came to rule and establish order in the land of 'Rus'. Their first permanent settlement, Novgorod, is seen by many as Russia's birthplace. Rurik's successor Oleg founded the Kievan Rus state, and the upstart principalities of Vladimir and Muscovy are descended from the same line.

By the 12th century, Novgorod was a European political and commercial centre that began expanding aggressively, increasingly attracting the attention of the Swedes, who had held sway in most of present-day north-west Russia. The friction, at first economic, became ostensibly religious as Swedish crusaders tried to push back the Orthodox 'heathens'. Novgorod's Prince Alexandr Nevsky is considered a Russian hero for thrashing both the Swedish and Teutonic crusaders in the 1240s, putting an end to western Christian intentions in Russia.

Though the Mongol Tatars only got as far as the swamps outside Novgorod, the city's princes sensibly accepted the Tatars as rulers. By 1480 Ivan III had driven out the Tatars and annexed Novgorod and all its northern lands for Moscow. South of Moscow, towns such as Oryol and Voronezh were founded as fortifications against the Tatars.

From 1558-83, Ivan IV (the Terrible) fought Poles, Lithuanians and Swedes in an unsuccessful grab for Baltic real estate. Soon afterwards, with Russia in a shambles during the Time of Troubles, Sweden and Russia took bits of western Russian territory including Smolensk and the east end of the Gulf of Finland.

Under the reign of the early Romanovs (1613-82), Russia gradually expanded its territories west and south of Moscow, but experienced revolts from Cossack communities, including those from Voronezh, near the Don River.

Determined to defeat the Swedes and reach the Baltic, Peter the Great made an alliance with Poland and Denmark, and forced his way to the Gulf of Finland, pausing only to lay the foundations of St Petersburg. With his new navy, he won the

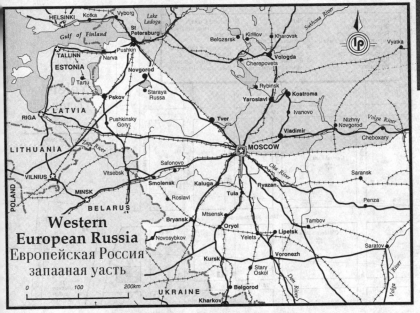

Western
European Russia
Европейская Россия
запааная уасть

Great Northern War (1700-21), winning everything back from Sweden, plus the Baltic coastline down to Riga in Latvia. Russia's western territories expanded further – to include Lithuania, Belarus and much of Poland – with the Partitions of Poland between 1772 and 1795.

In 1920 Soviet Russia recognised the independence of Estonia, Latvia and Lithuania. During the early stages of WW II secret deals that had been struck with Nazi Germany allowed the USSR's western European border to expand again. Hitler subsequently invaded the western USSR, including the Baltic states but lost it all (plus Kaliningrad, a previously German City) to the Red Army towards the end of the war. The new independence of the Baltic states, Belarus and Ukraine since the tumultuous events of 1990-91 has once again made Russia's western boundaries into borders between countries, rather than just between republics of the Soviet Union.

South of Moscow
На юг от Москвы

Three main routes head south from the Moscow region. The easternmost route, along the M4 highway, leads to Yelets and Voronezh. The central route, taken by the M2 highway and the railway heading for Kharkiv (Kharkov) in Ukraine, leads through Oryol, Kursk and Belgorod. The south-western route, heading ultimately for Kiev, leads to Bryansk, just off the M3 highway. All these routes take you over rolling, always changing steppe.

YELETS
ЕЛЕТС
Population: 120,000
Yelets was founded along the Sosna River in 1146 as a fortification against the Polovtsy. It was sacked by Tatars three times and

EUROPEAN RUSSIA

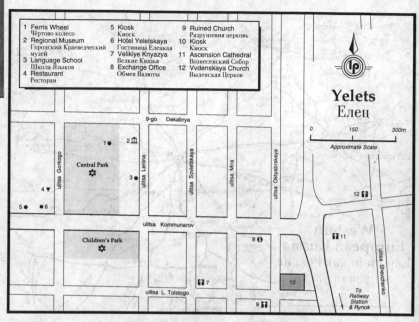

1 Ferris Wheel
Чёртово колесо
2 Regional Museum
Городский Краеведческий
музей
3 Language School
Школа Языков
4 Restaurant
Ресторан
5 Kiosk
Киоск
6 Hotel Yeletskaya
Гостиница Елецкая
7 Velikiye Knyazya
Велкие Князья
8 Exchange Office
Обмен Валюты
9 Ruined Church
Разрушения церковь
10 Kiosk
Киоск
11 Ascension Cathedral
Вознесенский Собор
12 Vvdenskaya Church
Выденская Церков

Yelets
Елец

0   150   300m
Approximate Scale

rebuilt in the 16th century, though what remains of the town today is like a perfect movie set of mid-19th-century Russian life. The city is laid out in a logical grid, and the streets are lined with colonnaded buildings, wooden and brick 19th-century houses and only the occasional post-war Soviet monstrosity.

The town's showpiece, visible from miles around, is the beautiful Ascension Cathedral (Vosnesensky sobor), which was designed by Konstantin Ton (1794-1881), the architect who brought us St Petersburg's Moskovsky and Moscow's Leningradsky railway stations (there's a great view of it from the bridge crossing the Sosna, just east of the town). And tucked into the town's tidy streets are about half a dozen working churches and cathedrals, plus the ruins of several more.

Recently reopened (it was a 'closed' city), Yelets doesn't have much to offer in the way of amenities or information (the Intourist office in Oryol simply says that Yelets is 'not on the tourist route'). Although it is a charming and relaxing town in the midst of some beautiful countryside, it's at best a day trip, or perhaps an overnighter, from Oryol or Voronezh. Yelets is 78 km west of Lipetsk, 180 km south of Tula, 170 km east of Oryol, and 140 km north-west of Voronezh.

Orientation & Information
From the railway station, walk to the east end of the platform and take bus No 1 into the city centre. It stops just past the Hotel Yelets on ulitsa Kommunarov, the city's main street. There are no tourist offices or maps to be found, and information is difficult to get from Intourist outside Yelets. While hotel staff are pleasant and helpful (especially when answering questions about the town and its churches), they are certainly not used to visits from foreigners, and they get a bit confused about visa regulations and for-

eigner prices. There's an office for changing money at ulitsa Kommunarov 7, though the place wasn't open when we visited.

Dangers & Annoyances While nothing untoward happened during our visit, and most of the townspeople seemed very friendly, helpful and open, Yelets suffers from a disproportionately high number of Adidas-tracksuited thugs milling about the streets and around kiosks. This author walked the town streets until 11 pm without even a hint of trouble, but travellers should exercise caution when walking around late at night.

Things to See & Do

The town is very compact and easy to get around. There's not much to see, but what there is is like a museum of a town from a century ago, albeit one with silly street names. The town's **Central Park** (Tsentralny Park) is quite relaxing, with the rusting hulk of a Ferris wheel marking the site of a former amusement park. There's a small **children's park** across the street, with basic playground equipment that is used by lots of smiling kids.

Churches are scattered throughout the town: the working **Ascension Cathedral**, which sits at the east end of ulitsa Kommunarov, is open (and packed) for services from 8 to 11 am and 5 to 7 pm. The nonworking and somewhat crumbling **Vydenskaya Church**, on ulitsa Shevchenko, is a nice church diagonally opposite a perfect example of an ornate, late 18th-century wooden house.

A devastated and scaffolded **cathedral**, for some reason referred to even by elderly residents merely as '33', is on the corner of Oktyabrskaya ulitsa and ulitsa L Tolstogo, while two blocks away the collapsing **Church of the Veliky Knaz** is open for worship from 8 to 11 am and 5 to 7 pm but no services are performed (their donation cup isn't exactly brimming with funds and they'd appreciate it if visitors would leave something).

What's that? You've been to Oryol and you want to see *another* Bunin Museum? Look no further than ulitsa Gorkogo 15; it's open daily except Monday and Tuesday from 10 am to 6 pm. The town's **Regional Museum**, on ulitsa Lenina just off 9-go Dekabrya ulitsa and open the same hours as the Bunin Museum, houses artefacts from Yelets' colourful past.

The town's main **shopping street**, ulitsa Mira, is perhaps the most picturesque street in town (the kind of street where horse-drawn coal carts look perfectly appropriate). At the south end of ulitsa Mira sits the town's **main square**, ploshchad Lenina, a cobble-stoned affair.

Places to Stay & Eat

The town's only hotel, *Hotel Yelets*, is located on the corner of ulitsa Kommunarov and ulitsa Gorkogo, in the ugliest building in town. The staff are not used to visiting foreigners, and there's some confusion about the prices foreigners are to be charged; on one night, singles/doubles were US$7.50/15, while on another the price was US$15/20. Rooms are absolutely standard, though clean, and the staff are friendly. The hotel's restaurant, located around the corner on ulitsa Gorkogo, serves up ghastly food but the service is pleasant.

There's an unexciting *market* about a kilometre east of the Sosna, with fresh fruit and produce. There are also several state shops, including a good *bulochnaya*, on ulitsa Mira, and a cluster of *kiosks* on the corner of ulitsa Oktyabrskaya and ulitsa L Tolstogo selling foreign soft drinks, liquor and cigarettes etc.

Getting There & Away

Buses to Yelets from Tula, Oryol and Voronezh take six hours and cost around US$3.50. Yelets is on the M4 highway between Moscow and Voronezh, and is on the Moscow-Donetsk railway, with daily service to Moscow (10 hours), Tula (five hours) and Oryol (seven hours).

VORONEZH
ВОРОНЕЖ

Population: 1 million

Voronezh is an average-sized Russian industrial city set in pleasant surroundings on the bank of the Voronezh River, about 18 kilometres from the Don River. The city and region are fondly remembered by most Russians as it has an extremely interesting folkloric history.

The black soil of the Voronezh region is similar as the world famous Ukrainian soil which is known for its high agricultural yield. The potato is the major crop of the region and among the finest in all of Russia (apparently the reason is due to both the rich black soil and an ideal growing climate). Potatoes, however, were not always grown here. A tale exists about Peter the Great's propitious decision to grow potatoes in the region.

> The tsar issued a decree about growing and preparing potatoes or 'apples of the earth' as he preferred to call them. However, the enthusiastic Russians discovered a problem. One of Peter the Great's tips was to harvest the potatoes when the buds bloomed. Apparently the peasants were not told which part to harvest so, after trying to eat every part of the potato, except the root, they became ill. The peasants, understandably angry and disappointed, burned the crop leaving only the roots remaining. Thankfully, someone tasted the inside of the charred potato and the plant was here to stay.

History

Voronezh was first mentioned in 12th-century chronicles, but was officially founded in 1585 as a fortress against the invading Tatars. Cossack *stanitsas* (villages) were established in this frontier region, and uprisings against Russian domination were common. Some of the more legendary uprisings were led by Gerasim Krivusha (1648) and Stenka Razin in (1670-71).

During the reign of Peter the Great, the first Russian warship – the *Predestinatia* – was built here in 1696; more than 200 warships from the Voronezh dockyards followed to form the new Russian fleet.

During WW II the city suffered frontline fighting for 200 days, when over 90% of the city's buildings were destroyed (especially during the most intense skirmishes between July and August 1942).

Orientation & Information

The main street is prospekt Revolyutsii; its northern tip is connected to the railway station by ulitsa Bunina, while the southern tip, past ploshchad imeni Lenina, becomes ulitsa Kirova. The other main street, ulitsa Plekhanovskaya, intersects at ploshchad imeni Lenina. The eastern bank of Voronezh is newer and was founded in 1928.

Intourist (☎ 52 37 46) is at ulitsa Platonova 12, but is not very helpful. Much more informative is Sputnik (☎ 33 05 56), Dorozhnaya 15A, where the friendly and knowledgable staff can fill you in on Voronezh and the surrounding region which boasts a mineral spring and nature reserve.

There are several places to change US dollars and Deutschmarks. Voronezhsky Bank, at ulitsa Plekhanovskaya 12, is one of the more convenient and is open Monday to Saturday from 9 am to 5 pm. A foreign exchange office in Russky Dom Selenga, on the corner of ulitsa Plekhanovskaya and ulitsa Koltsovskaya, is open daily from 9 am to 7 pm. The post office is at prospekt Revolyutsii 23 while the telephone office is at prospekt Revolyutsii 33. Out of date and inaccurate maps are available from Knigi at prospekt Revolyutsii 37, while GUM on the opposite side of the prospect, sells Kodak film.

The Voronezh telephone code is 0732.

Museums

The **I N Kramsky Regional Fine Arts Museum** (Oblastnoy khudozhestvenny muzey I N Kramskogo), at prospekt Revolyutsii 18, is reached through a passage, and is the second building on the left in the courtyard. There is a collection of Russian painting and sculpture, as well as Greek and Roman sculpture, and an Egyptian sarcophagus. It is open Tuesday to Sunday from 10 am to 5.15 pm, and the entry fee is US$0.10.

The interesting **Museum of Local**

Studies (Kraevedchesky muzey) at Plekhanovskaya 29 has exhibits on Peter the Great and early 20th-century tools. It is open Tuesday, Thursday and Friday from 11 am to 7 pm, and Wednesday, Saturday and Sunday from 10 am to 6 pm. The entry fee is US$0.40.

There is a large two-storey **Army Museum of the Great Patriotic War 1941-1945** (Velikaya otechestvennaya voyna 1941-1945) in the Arsenal (Expozitsia) at ulitsa Stepana Razina 43. It has the usual photos and weapons so often found in WW II museums. Its map of Europe is wildly inaccurate showing Czechoslovakia in place of Austria, Austria in place of Switzerland, with poor Switzerland left completely off the map. Outside are a few tanks and a *katyusha* (rocket-launching truck). Opening times and entry fee are the same as the above-mentioned Museum of Local Studies.

There is also the **Regional Museum of Zoology & Geology** (Zoologichesky i geologichesky muzey) in the university at Universitetskaya ploshchad 1.

There are three artist's museums in Voronezh: the **I S Nikitin House-Museum** (Dom-muzey I S Nikitina) at ulitsa Nikitinskaya 19, which is open Thursday to Tuesday from 10 am 6 pm (US$0.04); the **A V Koltsov Museum** (Muzey A V Koltsova) at Plekhanovskaya 3, which was temporarily closed at the time of writing; and the **A L Durov House-Museum** (Dom-muzey A L Durova) at ulitsa Durova 2.

Churches & Monastery

There are six churches, a cathedral and a working monastery in town. The 19th-century, blue-tinged **Akatov Monastery Complex** (Komplex Akatova monastyrya) at ulitsa Osvobozhdenia Truda 1, founded in 1674, has been fully restored with monks and nuns in service.

Another well-preserved place is the **Nicholas Church** (Nikolskaya tserkov, 1720), ulitsa Taranchenko 19-a, which has an interior of fresco-covered walls and a plain 18th-century iconostasis. All that survives of the 19th-century **Intercession Cathedral** (Pokrovsky Kafedralny sobor), ulitsa Bekhterena, are the walls which have been restored but the interior is obviously rather bare. The 18th-century **Vvedenskaya Church** (Vvedenskaya tserkov), ulitsa Osvobozhdenia Truda 20, was under restoration at the time of writing.

Places to Stay

There are often people hanging around the railway station or Hotel Brno attempting to rent their rooms for the asking price of US$5, but the rooms could be cheaper after bargaining. Out of the six hotels in Voronezh only two readily accepted foreigners. The gloomy *Hotel Rossia* (☎ 55 58 98), ulitsa Tsentralnaya 23, has dingy singles/doubles starting at US$14.80/20.50. The main Intourist hotel is *Hotel Brno* (☎ 50 92 02), Plekhanovskaya 9, which has pleasant staff. Its smallish and fairly clean rooms cost US$22/28. Further along Plekhanovskaya, at No 8, across the large ploshchad imeni Lenina, is *Hotel Don* (☎ 55 58 98), with rooms for US$19/25. They only accept foreigners if they are sent by Intourist or Hotel Brno, but this could also depend on the willingness of the receptionist to let you stay.

Places to Eat

Good food and pleasant service can be had at *Hotel Brno's* restaurant. The dishes cost around US$2 to US$3, and Kotleta po-kievsky is worth a try. *Kafe Milan*, at prospekt Revolyutsii 44, has imported coffee and good gelati. It is open daily from 10 am to 10 pm. At Plekhanovskaya 15 is *Anna Kafe*, which is not bad for cakes, while *Kafe Minutka*, at ploshchad imeni Lenina 8, is also recommended.

Entertainment

The *Regional Philharmonia* (Oblastnaya filarmonia) is at ploshchad imeni Lenina 11a; tickets are on sale from noon to 8 pm. The *State Theatre of Opera & Ballet* (Gosudarstvenny teatr opery i baleta) is at ploshchad imeni Lenina 7 and the *Regional Puppet Theatre* (Oblastnoy teatr kukol) can be found at prospekt Revolyutsii 50.

Getting There & Away

The RDS, on the corner of Plekhanovskaya and Koltsovskaya, is the centre for Aeroflot, rail and bus advance-booking offices, and also includes a foreign exchange office that is open daily from 9 am to 7 pm.

Air There are several daily flights to/from Moscow (Domodedovo) for US$63. Daily flights to St Petersburg/Sochi are US$96/95. Mineralnye Vody has three flights a week for US$87.

Bus Some sample bus fares are Tambov (US$5.60, plus US$0.40 per baggage, five hours), Saratov (US$8.50, plus US$0.70 per baggage) and Moscow (US$10.80, plus US$0.70 per baggage).

Train Trains to Moscow take about 12 hours. Trains to other destinations include: Saratov (18 hours); Pyatigorsk (25 hours); and St Petersburg (24 hours).

Getting Around

To/From the Airport Buses to the airport depart from the railway station or RDS, and take about 40 minutes.

Bus, trolleybus and tram fares cost US$0.03; tickets are available from ticket booths or the driver.

Bus The main bus station is at Moskovsky prospekt 17. To get there from the railway station take tram No 12 to ulitsa Plekhanovskaya and from there take trolleybus No 6, 7 or 12.

Train The railway station is at ploshchad Chernyakhovskogo. To get to the centre of town around ploshchad imeni Lenina, take bus No 12 or trolleybus No 2, 3 or 11.

RAMON
РАМОНЬ

The **19th-century chateau** of Princess Oldenbruskoy near Ramon, 36 km north of Voronezh, off the M4 highway, has a collection of antique furniture. To get there take one of the hourly (from 6.15 am to 7.10 pm)

buses that depart from the bus station at Moskovskaya prospekt in Voronezh. The fare for normal/soft class is US$0.40/0.50 for the 36-km trip.

STARY OSKOL
СТАРЫЙ ОСКОЛ
Population: 230,000

A testament to the abuse of the earth's natural resources, Stary Oskol is four hours south of Yelets on the Moscow-Donetsk railway (14 hours south of Moscow). The only thing old here is the ring of houses near the railway station. The centre is small and dull, and the town is filled with factories, smog, pollution, and a disconcerting number of residents with birth defects.

While it may appear on the map to be a tempting stopping point between Yelets or Voronezh and Kursk or Belgorod, the only reasons one should be here are a) one's car broke down; b) one took the wrong turn somewhere; and c) one's gone mad.

Outside the centre, a horrific, soul-depressing *mikrorayon* ('micro-region') houses the bulk of the city's population which work in the environment-fouling culprits: black-metal and metal smelting, tractor and motorcycle-part manufacturing. The 'micro-region' is about six times larger than the town.

It is a depressing place, and needless to say, the tourism industry here isn't exactly jumpin'.

Orientation & Information

The railway station is two km east of the centre; take the rare and slow bus No 5 from there to ulitsa Lenina in the town's centre. The bus station is about four km east of the centre; almost every city bus goes between the station and the centre.

The post office is at ulitsa Lenina 50, the telegraph office is at ulitsa Lenina 56, and there's an intercity telephone office ('Send me a ticket out of here!') at the railway station. The telephone code is 07252.

Things to See

To become converted to a greenie, stand on

ulitsa Komsomolskaya, halfway between ulitsa Lenina and ulitsa Druzhba, and look at the 'micro-region'.

Places to Stay & Eat

The mosquito-ridden *Hotel Oskol* (☎ 22 57 92) at ulitsa Lenina 59 is a run-down, dank and dreary place that offers smoking and non-smoking rooms and no showers. It has dormitory-style rooms with two beds for US$3.75 per person and singles for US$6.00. Management are unconcerned where you come from (they don't even check passports), so the rates are the same for foreigners and Russians. The hotel's administrator suggests that foreigners would be more comfortable at the *Hotel Rossia* (☎ 24 44 32), at bulvar Druzhba in the 'micro-region', which has clean singles/ doubles for US$14/22. Take bus No 3 from ulitsa Lenina to the Dom Knigi stop, the hotel is on the opposite side of the street about 200 metres away. The Hotel Rossia also has a fair restaurant.

Kafe Snezhinki, near the fountain on ulitsa Lenina, and opposite No 27, has cakes, meat-filled pies and ice cream.

Getting There & Away

Stary Oskol is accessible by bus (US$2, four hours) and train (four hours) from Yelets and Belgorod. There's a twice-daily train service to Moscow (16 hours).

ORYOL

ОРЮЛ

Population: 346,000

Founded in 1566 as a fortress against the Tatars, Oryol ('arr-YOL'; the name means 'eagle') is a fine provincial town with some industry and a pleasant, while unexciting, town centre. The town straddles the junction of the Oka and Orlik rivers, 370 km south of central Moscow.

The feeling of old provincial Russia lingers in parts of Oryol thanks to several old low-rise buildings, including colonnaded shops along ulitsa Moskovskaya south of the Oka, and a few 18th and early 19th-century churches.

Oryol is also the birthplace of the writer Ivan Turgenev who was born in 1818, and who often returned here from his family estate at Spasskoe Lutovinovo, 70 km north. There's a big statue of him overlooking the Oka on the slope known as the Turgenev Bank (Turgenevsky spusk) off ploshchad Lenina. There's also a bust of him in the public garden named after his novel, *A Nest of the Gentry* (which mirrors life in tsarist Oryol), overlooking the Orlik at the end of Oktyabrskaya ulitsa.

Turgenev was one of a surprising number of gentry that called Oryol home (19,000 out of a population of 32,000 in 1853), and writers thrived here; 12 of them are remembered in the city's museums.

The town has held up quite well despite being devastated several times by armies, most recently in 1943 when the Red Army took it back from the Nazis (5 August, the anniversary of the liberation, is an important local holiday).

For a provincial town, it seems quite cosmopolitan; locals attribute this to Yegor Stroiev, an agricultural specialist who happened to be a great chum of Gorbachev's. In 1985, Stroiev was appointed regional administrator and, confident of his position due to his ties to the Kremlin, he announced that the distribution of Oryol's significant agricultural output would favour Oryol, rather than Moscow. While this helped the immediate situation only somewhat, it gave a sense of independence which could have been partly responsible for the high level of post-Soviet privatisation which is readily apparent today.

Orientation

The railway station is two km north-east, and the bus station is three km south, of ploshchad Lenina.

Running between ploshchad Karla Marxa and ploshchad Lenina, ulitsa Lenina serves as the centre's main street, connecting the old city centre to Moskovskaya prospekt. The cobblestone street is divided by wide flower planters, and if you stand at the top (off ploshchad Lenina) and look down the hill there's a great view of what was once a cathedral but is now a bread factory No 3.

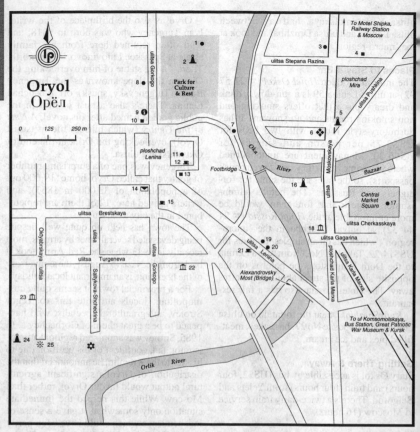

Oryol
Орёл

0   125   250 m

To Motel Shipka,
Railway Station
& Moscow

ulitsa Stepana Razina

ploshchad
Mira

Park for
Culture
& Rest

ulitsa Gorkogo

ploshchad
Lenina

Footbridge

Oka   River

Moskovskaya

Bazaar

Central
Market
Square

ulitsa Cherkasskaya

ulitsa Brestskaya

ulitsa Gagarina

Oktyabrskaya

ulitsa Saltykova-Shchedrina

ulitsa Turgeneva

ulitsa Gorkogo

ulitsa Lenina

Alexandrovsky
Most (Bridge)

ploshchad Karla Marxa

ulitsa Karla Marxa

To ul Komsomolskaya,
Bus Station, Great Patriotic
War Museum & Kursk

Orlik   River

Information

Tourist Office Intourist, at ulitsa Gorkogo 37 (☎ 7 46 95/6, 9 59 09), has a couple of English-speaking staff and some ancient tourist maps of the city, though they're working on a new one that looks promising. The reception desk at the Hotel Russia (see Places to Stay later) is an invaluable information source, with very friendly and exceptionally helpful English-speaking administrators.

Money Change money at offices on the 2nd floor of the main post office. Okabank, ulitsa

Moskovskaya 29, seems to take their opening hours of 9 am to 1 pm, Monday to Friday as more of a suggestion than a rule.

Post & Telecommunications The post office is on the corner of ulitsa Gorkogo and ploshchad Lenina.

International and intercity telephone calls can be booked at the Rossia, Salyut and Shipka hotels or at the international telephone office at ulitsa Lenina 34; in any event you'll have to pay in advance and there are no refunds. The telephone code for Oryol is 08622.

Museums

Spasskoe Lutovinovo (see under that heading later) is the best literary museum in the district, but Oryol has its own **Turgenev Museum** at ulitsa Turgeneva 11; it's open daily except Friday from 9 am to 6 pm. With the same opening hours, the **Oryol Writer's Museum**, next door at No 13, and the home of 19th-century historian **T N Granovsky**, at ulitsa 7 Noyabrya 24, are each devoted to five more Oryol-related writers. Ivan Bunin, featured in the Writer's Museum, is the only one other than Turgenev to approach fame. Bunin buffs should visit the **Ivan Bunin Museum**, at Georgevsky pereulok 1, open daily except Friday from 10 am to 6 pm. This two-room affair features belongings from the writer's Paris apartment. Still not sated? There's a statue of Bunin (though everyone in town avers it bears no resemblance to him) in front of the, yes, **Bunin Library** at ulitsa Gorkogo 41, opposite the Park of Rest and Culture.

The birthplace of Oryol writer **Leonid Andreev** is a typical late 19th-century Oryol house at 2-ya Pushkarna ulitsa 41, open daily except Friday from 10 am to 6 pm. It opened in 1991 and is at the south end of town, west of the Orlik.

The **Great Patriotic War Museum**, on the corner of Komsomolskaya ulitsa and Normandia Neman, is open daily except Monday from 10 am to 6 pm, and has a basic collection of weaponry, recruitment and propaganda posters and a panorama depicting the liberation of Oryol as Red Army troops advanced on Kursk. Admission is US$0.05, though foreign groups are charged US$7.

Other Things to See & Do

The **Park for Culture and Rest** (Park Kultury i Otdykha) is a lovely step back to a gentler time. It's just a somewhat average small city park, but there's an amusement park at the north-east end, with a rusting but functional Ferris wheel as well as a 'tilt-a-whirl' (a circular platform with a surrounding fence that the rider is strapped to; when the ride starts, the platform begins spinning and tilting upwards), motorised swings and even pretty respectable bumper-cars. There is also a kiddie ride section. The rides stay open until about 11 pm.

A walk down the steep embankment to the Oka, between the park and junction of the Oka and Orlik rivers brings you to the town's **rowing-boat rental stand**, open in summer from 9 am to 9 pm, which rents sturdy wooden rowing boats for US$0.50 an hour. The banks of the Oka draw huge crowds of bathers and carpet washers on sunny days.

Ploshchad Mira, or **Peace Square**, is located on the corner of ulitsa Moskovskaya and ulitsa Pushkina and is easily identified by its WW II tank. The fighting machine, which perches precariously atop a granite base, is a time-honoured spot for newlyweds to pose for family photos on the big day. It's also the site for the city's residents to pay respects to those who fought and died in battle. There is a marble memorial, with maps, behind the tank.

Places to Stay

The *Motel Shipka* (☎ 3 07 04), at Moskov-skoe shosse 175, is the town's cheapest option, but it's eight km north of the centre, on the road out to the north end of the Oryol bypass (which is three km past the motel). Reception and staff are helpful, and the rooms are fine, with some having balconies, and others having intermittently functioning refrigerators. Singles/doubles are US$17/20, and the director (who also runs the local Intourist office) says that you can cut a US$30 to US$40 room deal which includes all meals as well as tours and excursions. Bus Nos 8 and the slower 8K leave for the city centre about three times an hour; taxis run (cost US$2.50 to US$3.50) in either direction.

Central location comes at a price; the soul-less *Hotel Salyut*, with only the occasional whimper of staff helpfulness, on the south-east corner of ploshchad Lenina, has singles/doubles for US$34/68, and a casino downstairs. Just across the ploshchad at ulitsa Gorkogo 37, the *Hotel Rossia* (☎ 6 75 50) has much nicer rooms for the same price, and extremely helpful and friendly staff,

many of whom speak English. The *Hotel Oryol* at ploshchad Mira says it doesn't accept foreigners.

Places to Eat

Locals say that the best place for a blow-out meal is the *Motel Shipka's* dining hall, where meat and fish dishes with appetisers cost between US$5 to US$8; there's some live music (though it's no longer a dance hall) and two bars and a casino, as well as a realist mural.

The *Rossia*, *Salyut* and *Oryol* hotels (from better to worse, respectively) have standard Soviet-style restaurants, featuring ear-numbingly loud music and meals in the US$6 to US$8 price range.

Kafe Aktyor, at the south-east side of the Turgenev Theatre on ploshchad Lenina, has excellent beef and chicken dishes for US$6 to US$10. It also has very good service, but it is so dark inside one gets the feeling that management has responded to the desires of its clientele to dine incognito. *Kafe Russkie Bliny* doesn't have any pancakes, but it does sell pastries, milky coffee and hard-boiled eggs of a certain age; it's on ulitsa Gorkogo just off ploshchad Lenina. The *café* on the 3rd floor of the Orlovsky Univermag has good, cheap eats, with basic meat/chicken dishes and salads for about US$1.50. *Yagonka*, at ulitsa Lenina 25, is a very nice café, featuring coffee, pastries, pizzas and occasional supplies of imported soft-serve ice cream. There's a *bakery* at No 26, with bread, good pastries and cakes.

Things to Buy

There's a teeming daily market on the south bank of the Oka just east of ulitsa Moskovskaya. Along the riverbank, a very colourful bazaar sells just about everything from VCRs and TVs to a large selection of fresh produce from the Caucasus. This bazaar is adjacent to the market, from which tables spill out into the surrounding square.

Just on the other side of the Oka, the Orlovsky Univermag has a wide range of Russian, Soviet and foreign appliances, clocks and watches. There is a café, on the ground floor, and women's clothing and Russian souvenirs can be found on the 2nd floor. Along ulitsa Lenina, at No 32, the Igrushki toy store has dolls, models, toy cars etc, as well as basic art supplies. Magazin 18 has a good selection of meat and dairy goods, produce and drinks. Photographic film and one-hour film (but not slide) developing is available from Kodak at the Hotel Salyut's ulitsa Lenina entrance.

Getting There & Away

Air There are flights from Moscow (Vnukovo) several times a week (US$64, 1¼ hours), and St Petersburg (Pulkovo I) three times weekly (US$107, 1½ hours). Oryol's airport code is OEL.

Bus & Train Oryol is on the Moscow-Kharkiv (Kharkov) railway, with numerous daily services. Buses head to Moscow several times a day (six hours), and there is rail and bus service to Kursk, Belgorod, Lipetsk, Yelets, and Bryansk. There is a bus, but no direct rail service to Smolensk.

Car & Motorbike From Moscow the road is of varied quality – excellent dual carriageway out of Moscow, but badly surfaced and narrow for 40 km either side of Tula. South to Kursk is 152 km, with the road to Kiev (518 km) branching west 55 km south of Oryol.

Getting Around

From the railway station, tram No 2 stops at ulitsa Karla Marxa, on the south-east foot of the Alexandrovsky most (bridge) leading to ulitsa Lenina. From ploshchad Karla Marxa, take trolleybus No 4 or 6 to the bus station.

SPASSKOE LUTOVINOVO
СПАССКОЕ-ЛУТОВИНОВО

The manor of 19th-century novelist Ivan Turgenev is open as a museum daily except Tuesday (and the last day of each month) from 10 am to 5 pm. Turgenev, born in Oryol (70 km south) in 1818, grew up at his family's estate here. The land was given to

the family by Ivan the Terrible, and the local landscape and people inspired much of Turgenev's writing.

Though he spent much of his life in Moscow, St Petersburg, Germany and France, he thought of Spasskoe Lutovinovo as his homeland and returned here many times. The beauty of the estate makes this easy to understand.

Turgenev was exiled here from St Petersburg in 1852-53 as a result of his work *The Hunter's Sketches*. He completed his most famous novel, *Fathers and Sons*, at Spasskoe Lutovinovo.

The house, restored in the 1970s (which was when the coal stoves were installed), contains a fair-sized collection of period furniture, though the interior is almost completely devoid of personality despite the fact that some of the writer's personal items and a substantial percentage of his books still remain. There's an icon hanging in Turgenev's study that was given to the family by Ivan the Terrible. The entrance to the house was formerly the kitchen.

Several buildings remain in the grounds, including the family banya and church, both of which were closed to the public when we visited. The big oak tree planted as a sapling by Turgenev, and the writer's 'exile house', where he lived in 1852-53, are just away from the house.

Outside the estate, the farming families of the peasants that were dependent on the family still live and work on tiny farms.

Admission to the estate is US$0.50 which includes a Russian-language guided tour and US$0.75 for the museum, plus a 'grounds fee' of US$0.50. The foreigner rate is a steeper US$3.50, though it's quite simple to pay the Russian price with minimal language skills. Photographers are charged US$2.50 and 'videographers' are supposed to pay US$45! Once inside the house, if you're not in a group and they're not too crowded, the caretakers will happily give you a free Russian-language tour.

There's a disappointing café opposite the estate entrance serving tea, coffee and small cakes.

Spasskoe Lutovinovo
Спасское-Лутовиново

1 Oak tree planted by Turgenev
2 Turgenev House
3 Family Church
4 Ticket Office
5 Cafe
6 Kiosks
7 Banya
8 Toilets (outhouse)
9 Monument
10 Bus Stop to Peasant Farms & Mtsensk

0   0.5   1 km
Approximate Scale

To Mtsensk →

Bastyevo Train Station

To Peasant Farms

To Oryol ↓

Getting There & Away

Intourist offers excursions, which leave from either the Oryol Intourist office or the Motel Shipka, for about US$20 per person. A much more fulfilling experience is to see it on your own as it offers a look at the surrounding areas.

Bus Take the Mtsensk bus from Oryol (they leave twice an hour from 5.30 am to 9.30 pm every day, 45 minutes, US$0.60), and switch at Mtsensk's bus station for a Spasskoe Lutovinovo bus (40 minutes, US$0.25).

Train Elektrichkas leave from Oryol at 6.40 and 8.55 am for Bastyevo (1½ hours). From the north end of the railway station, walk east 3.5 km (it's the road to the left), or catch the bus which runs hourly from Mtsensk via Bastyevo (in theory they're supposed to meet the train, but...) to the estate. Trains return to Oryol at 1.50 and 5.59 pm.

Car & Motorbike By road, it's seven km west of the Moscow-Oryol road from a turning 65 km north of Oryol and nine km north of Mtsensk.

KURSK
КУРСК
Population: 420,000

Founded (most likely) in the 9th century, Kursk was destroyed by the Tatars in 1240. It then lay in Lithuanian territory for a couple of centuries before being annexed by Moscow and emerging as a southern frontier fort in the late 16th century. In the 18th and 19th centuries it became a grain-trade and industrial centre and an important railway junction. Much of its appearance is a result of rebuilding after severe damage during WW II.

The main road from the north approaches central Kursk down ulitsa Lenina.

Orientation & Information

Kursk's centre is divided by the north/south-running ulitsa Lenina, with Krasnaya ploshchad at the south end. Ulitsa Dzerzhinskogo heads quite steeply downhill from the west side of Krasnaya ploshchad to the valley of a small, now invisible, river where you'll find the busy Central Market. Make phone calls from your hotel; there's also a telegraph office at Krasnaya ploshchad.

Intourist is at the Solovinaya Roshcha

JOHN KING

JOHN KING

NICK SELBY

JOHN NOBLE

NICK SELBY

NICK SELBY

<table>
<tr><td>B</td></tr>
<tr><td>D</td></tr>
<tr><td>F</td></tr>
</table>

A: Cathedral of SS Peter & Paul, Petrodvorets
B: Cruiser *Aurora*, St Petersburg
C: St Petersburg courtyard
D: Beloselsky-Belozersky Palace

E: Detail, Beloselsky-Belozersky Palace, St Petersburg
F: Posters, St Petersburg

Left: City administration building, Kursk
Right: Millennium Monument, Novgorod
Bottom: Petrodvorets

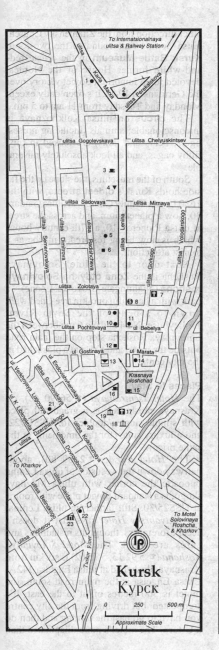

PLACES TO STAY

6 Hotel Kurskaya
   Гостиница Курская
12 Hotel Tsentralnaya
   Госиница Центральная

PLACES TO EAT

3 Lakonka Café
   Лаконка Кафе
4 Restoran Oktyabrsky
   Ресторан Октябрьский
15 Voskhod Café
   Восхад Кафе
16 Bakery/Café
   Булочная-Кафе

OTHER

1 Northern Market
   Северний Рынок
2 Kursk Medical Institute
   Курский медицинский институт
5 Pushkin Theatre
   Пушкинский театр
7 Sergievo-Kazansky Cathedral
   Сергиево-Казанский кафедральный
   Собор
8 Bank
   Банк
9 Detsky Mir
   Детский Мир
10 Univermag
   Универмаг
11 Dom Knigi
   Дом Книги
13 Post Office
   Почтамт
14 House of Soviets
   Дом советов
17 Znamensky Church
   Знаменская Церковь
18 Kursk Battle Museum
   Музей Курской битвы
19 Regional Museum
   Областной краеведческий
   музей
20 Circus
   Цирк
21 Central Market
   Центральный рынок
22 Planetarium
   Планетарий
23 17th-Century House
   Дом ЧМШШ в.

motel. They have little to do, except sulk that there are no foreign tourists. They can, however, arrange a city tour for US$30.

A good bet for changing money is the Sberbank counter at the railway station; there's a small counter marked 'Kantor' in the Detsky Mir department store's entrance off ulitsa Ufimtseva that may be open. The Sberbank, at ulitsa Lenina diagonally across the street, has surly service and hoods lurking around the exchange counter.

The bookshop at ulitsa Lenina 11 has a good selection of Russian books, some maps, and an electronic musical instrument shop, in case you forgot your digital sampler. The telephone code for Kursk is 07100.

Sergievo-Kazansky Cathedral

About halfway down ulitsa Lenina and a block to the east, on pleasant, tree-lined ulitsa Gorkogo, is the fine Baroque Sergievo-Kazansky Cathedral, a working church, built in 1752-78 to a design by Rastrelli. Turn down ulitsa Mozhayskogo opposite the Hotel Kursk to reach it. It's green and white with blue domes. Inside are, in fact, two churches, one on top of the other, for summer and winter use.

Krasnaya Ploshchad

The foot of ulitsa Lenina opens into Krasnaya ploshchad, surrounded by imposing classical-style buildings – the House of Soviets on the east side, the post office on the west, the Hotel Tsentralnaya on the north-west and the matching city council building on the north-east. At the south end of the square is Kursk's most distinctive building, the domed Znamensky Church (1816-28), functioning again after having been so zealously converted by the Soviets into a cinema that the atmosphere inside is still like praying in the lobby of the Bijou.

Other Attractions

Just down the hill from the Znamensky Church, in the 1826-53 former bishop's palace, is the regional museum; it's open daily except Friday and the last Thursday of the month from 10.30 am to 6 pm. In the

other direction from the Znamensky Church, ulitsa Sonina runs round to the two-room Kursk Battle Museum in the ornate red-and-white former House of the Nobles, devoted to an important Soviet victory over the Germans in 1943. It's open daily except Monday and Tuesday from 11 am to 5 pm.

The circus on ulitsa Kolkhoznaya is unconscionable: animals (including horses, tigers, bears and lions) are locked in tiny, filthy cages, and all look absolutely miserable.

South of the museums, the slope up the far side holds Kursk's oldest streets, with the 1680 Lower Trinity Church, at ulitsa Gaidara 30, now a planetarium, and across the street at ulitsa Pionerov 10, a 17th-century house which is now being restored – maybe as a tourist attraction.

Next door to the Motel Solovinaya Roshcha is the Zona otdykha Solovinaya roshcha (Nightingale Grove Rest Zone) – a park with a beautiful one-km tree-lined walk down to a bend of the Seym River. Trolleybuses No 4 and No 6 run between the Solovinaya Roshcha stop on the main road outside the motel and Krasnaya ploshchad in the city centre.

Places to Stay

The *Hotel Tsentralnaya* (☎ 56 90 48), on Krasnaya ploshchad, is a grand old place with simple singles/doubles for US$11/22, and a luxury suite (for the time being at the same price).

The *Hotel Kursk* (☎ 2 69 80), about halfway down the west side of ulitsa Lenina opposite the corner with ulitsa Mozhayskogo, is a standard Soviet place with rooms at US$25/30. Still farther up ulitsa Lenina, the *Oktyabrsky Hotel* says that it doesn't accept foreigners, though its restaurants and cafés are open. The *Motel Solovinaya Roshcha* (☎ 5 92 13, 5 75 62) is six km from Krasnaya ploshchad at ulitsa Engelsa 142A. Ulitsa Engelsa is the main road south, the motel is 300 metres off it to the east. It's signposted, but driving from the city centre you have to go past the turning and then do a U-turn. The motel's more dilapidated than ever but what's intolerable is that it's the most expensive place in town despite its preposterous location, with rooms for US$32.50/57. Its restaurant has a tendency to fob you off with schnitzel and rice for breakfast but will produce eggs if you insist.

Places to Eat
The hotel restaurants are all average. Meals generally run from US$2 to US$3 without liquor. The bufet at the *Motel Solovinaya Roshcha* is pretty dire, while those at the *Hotel Tsentralnaya and Oktyabrsky Hotel* are fine, serving cakes, sandwiches, 'pizza' and drinks. The *Hotel Kursk* has a restaurant with live music and also the *Bar Turist*, which is a large hall (upstairs, facing ulitsa Lenina) with coffee and rock videos.

Outside the Oktyabrsky, the *Grill* serves up good roast chicken, sold by weight. In summer you can dine 'al fresco' in their garden, where they place tables next to the rubbish skips.

Across the street from the Znamensky Church is *Kafe Voskhod*, a stolovaya really, serving decent roast chicken, execrable kotlet, and boiled potatoes and cabbage (which, inexplicably, has a nice spicy kick to it!). A full meal costs less than US$1.

In Krasnaya ploshchad, on the corner of ulitsa Dzerzhinskogo, there's a well-stocked bakery/pastry shop selling a good selection of local speciality breads including *khleb Kursky* as well as imported sausages and cheeses. They also have a small *café* serving snacks and drinks.

Kafe Lakonka, three-quarters of the way up ulitsa Lenina, has very nice cakes, buns and milky cocoa, all for about US$0.50.

There's massive penetration of Western ice cream – Snickers, Mars, Dove Bar – and you'll find it in virtually every shop. It's priced as in the west but it's heaven-sent if your stomach's grumbling.

Things to Buy
Across the street from the bookshop, the town's big department store has a lot of Western cosmetics, some sporting goods and soft drinks. Next door is Detsky Mir, with

some toys and children's clothes. The town's two markets, the Central (Tsentralny, down ulitsa Dzerzhinskogo) and the Northern (Severny, on ulitsa Karla Marxa) sell food, produce and clothes (the sort that will make you say, 'So *that*'s where they get it!').

Getting There & Away
Air There are four weekly flights from Moscow to Kursk (US$74, Monday 9.50 am and Monday, Wednesday and Friday 8.30 pm), and a weekly flight from St Petersburg (US$114). Kursk's airport code is URS.

Bus Kursk is accessible by frequent bus service from Belgorod, Oryol, Moscow and Kharkiv (Kharkov). If you're arriving at Kursk by bus from the south, have the driver let you off at the Solovinaya Roshcha, from where you can get trolleybus No 4 or 6 to the centre, saving an hour of doubling back.

Train Like Oryol, Kursk is on the Moscow-Kharkiv (Kharkov) railway with trains to Moscow every half hour, sometimes more. Moscow is eight hours away, Kharkiv (Kharkov) three hours, and there are also daily trains to/from the Caucasus and Crimea. The station is about three km north-east of Krasnaya ploshchad on Internatsionalnaya ulitsa.

Car & Motorbike After a vile start through Kursk's southern industrial areas and another rough 25 km or so, the 200-km road to Belgorod and Kharkiv (Kharkov) is mostly smooth and wide. Kursk has a western bypass, looping round from 12 km north of the town centre to 19 km south of it.

Getting Around
Bus No 19 goes up ulitsa Lenina to the railway station but it's a rarity; Marshrutnoe taxis ply the route more often for about US$0.20. Bus No 11 goes between the airport and the central market.

Bus No 1 goes between the railroad station, past the corner of ulitsa Karla Marxa and ulitsa Perekalskova (in front of the

Medical Institute), and the bus station, north-west of the centre.

KURSK BATTLE MEMORIAL
ПАМЯТНИК КУРСКОЙ БИТВЫ
The battle from 5 July to 5 August 1943, known as the Battle of the Kursk Bulge, was one of the Red Army's most important victories in WW II. German tanks attempting a pincer movement on Kursk – at the time the most forward Soviet-held town on this front – were halted by minefields and then driven back, turning Germany's 1943 counteroffensive into a retreat that saw the Red Army pass the Dnepr River by the end of September. The Kursk battle sprawled over a wide area, liberating places as far apart as Oryol and Belgorod, but the main memorial to it is beside the Kursk-Belgorod highway, 115 km from Kursk and 40 km south of Oboyan. A T-43 tank and a YaK fighter plane commemorate the part played by Soviet tankmen and airmen in the battle. Antitank guns stand on either side of a long wall sculpted with tank crew faces, beneath which is the War Glory Hall (Zal boyevoy slavy), open daily except Monday from 10 am to 5 pm. At the north end of the memorial area, past the plane, is a monument naming the Soviet units that took part in the battle. Gun emplacements and trenches are preserved in the tree area to the right of the tank.

Eight km further south, at the south end of the village of Yakovlevo – scene of particularly fierce fighting in the battle – there's a cannon monument.

BELGOROD
БЕЛГОРОД
Population: 230,000
First mentioned in 1237, Belgorod (the name means 'White City') became a major fortress against the Crimean Tatars in the late 17th century. During WW II, the town was smashed to bits as the Kursk battle raged in and around it.

Today, Belgorod is an administrative centre and a border town, and it feels it – a sprawling, congested metropolis packed with industry, state enterprise offices (especially Energomash), and dozens of ministries of this and that. What's left of the town centre is filled with militia, and the only hotel in town that will take foreigners charges exorbitant rates. Only stop here if you're desperate.

Information
The central post office is at ulitsa Frunze 70, on the corner of ulitsa Revolyutsii, with phone, fax, intercity telephone and EMS mail services. The Detsky Mir department store near ploshchad Lenina has a small book stall. The telephone code for Belgorod is 0722.

Places to Stay & Eat
If you're desperate, you'll be wanting the *Tsentralnaya Hotel* (☎ 2 17 55, 2 39 41), at ulitsa Kommunisticheskaya 86, opposite the Detsky Mir department store near ploshchad Lenina. They gouge US$51/85 for singles/doubles that are absolutely standard. They also have a restaurant downstairs. The much nicer *Belgorod Hotel* (☎ 2 25 12), at ulitsa Revolyutsii 1, is worth a try; they say that they don't take foreigners but they might if you prove persuasive.

Getting There & Away
Belgorod is on the Moscow-Kharkiv (Kharkov) railway, and buses between those cities stop here as well. By road, Belgorod is about 35 km north of the Ukrainian border, and about 70 km from the centre of Kharkiv (Kharkov).

BRYANSK
БРЯНСК
Population: 450,000
Founded in 985 by Prince Vladimir, Bryansk has been transformed from an idyllic riverside town to a military and industrial behemoth. The city has been associated with things military since the days of Peter the Great, who established a shipbuilding factory here which constructed, between 1737-39, the Bryansk Flotilla.

From 1941-43, occupying German troops were kept maddeningly busy fighting off as

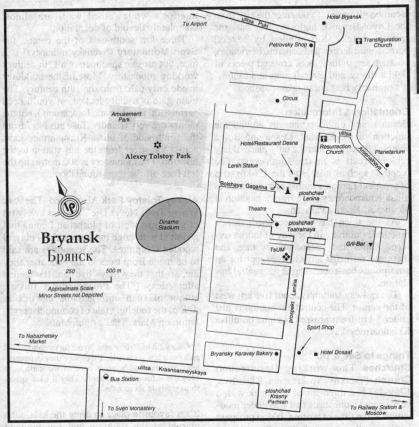

Bryansk
Брянск

0   250   500 m
Approximate Scale
Minor Streets not Depicted

To Airport

ulitsa Puki

Hotel Bryansk

Petrovsky Shop

Transfiguration Church

Circus

Amusement Park

Alexey Tolstoy Park

Hotel/Restaurant Desna

ulitsa

Resurrection Church

Planetarium

Arsenalskaya

Lenin Statue

Bolshaya Gagarina ul

ploshchad Lenina

Theatre

ploshchad Teatralnaya

Dinamo Stadium

TsUM

Gril-Bar

prospekt Lenina

To Nabazhetsky Market

Sport Shop

Hotel Dosaaf

ulitsa Krasnoarmeyskaya

Bryansky Karavay Bakery

Bus Station

ploshchad Krasny Partisan

To Sven Monastery

To Railway Station & Moscow

many as 60,000 local partisans, who took to the forests and sabotaged everything they could, which turned out to be a great deal. Partisans are credited (albeit by Soviet-era history books) with killing over 150,000 Germans. In an unsuccessful effort to flush out these pesky folks, German troops set to defoliating the forests surrounding the city.

During the Battle of Kursk, Bryansk was decimated; today less than 10% of Bryansk's pre-war buildings remain.

The accident at the Chernobyl atomic power plant was particularly devastating to the Bryansk region. Locals claim that the military bases at Bryansk and Oryol were ordered to fire cloud-seeding missiles to cause rain to fall over Bryansk, ostensibly to spare Moscow from the approaching radiation. Whether true or not – it is worth noting that during the 1994 Goodwill Games at St Petersburg, Russian scientists claimed to perform similar cloud seeding to prevent rain from washing out the event – no one argues that the Bryansk region received a huge dose of radiation from the accident. Western scientists say that short visits to Bryansk are safe.

The military base is still pretty active, and

it can be glimpsed if you enter the city from the Oryol-Bryansk highway, just past the railway tracks. Surrounded by several barbed-wire fences and concrete barricades, you can see thousands of covered pieces of field artillery, anti-aircraft guns and canon – it's probably best not to take snapshots.

Orientation & Information
Bryansk sits on four plateaus around the junction of the Snezhet, Desna and Bolva rivers. The action (and the only place of any real interest) is in the south-west. The 'centre', such as it is, hugs the 1.5-km strip of prospekt Lenina, running perpendicular to ulitsa Krasnoarmeyskaya from a junction at ploshchad Krasny Partisan.

As the town has just reopened, there's practically nothing in the way of tourist services. Cafés and restaurants are rare, and there are no maps anywhere except for an amorphous bus-route map at the central bus station.

The railway station is about five km west of the centre. The central bus station is just under a km from prospekt Lenina on ulitsa Krasnoarmeyskaya.

Things to See & Do
Churches The working **Resurrection Church** (Tserkov Voskresenia Khristova, 1739-41) is a three-spired landmark with a very ornate iconostasis that was under renovation at the time of writing. It's on prospekt Lenina on the corner of ulitsa Arsenalnaya. An 18th-century church around the corner on ulitsa Arsenalnaya (opposite No 15), is now the regional planetarium, open daily except Saturday from 9 am to 7 pm (though they were closed when the author visited on a Sunday). Nearby, the **Federova Residence**, at ulitsa Arsenalnaya 25, is a charming 19th-century log cabin.

The **Transfiguration Church** (Preobrazhensky khram), also called the 'New Girl's Monastery' (Novo-Devychy monastyr), next to the Hotel Bryansk, has recently been reconverted. From the outside, it's a fine pseudo-Russian cathedral, loosely based on Moscow's St Basil's, but the interior's whitewashed walls are almost completely devoid of decoration.

Three km south-east of the centre, the **Sven Monastery** (Svensky monastyr) is a nice, but prosaic specimen of a 13th-century working monastery. Most of the buildings inside only date from the 18th century. The main gate is usually locked, so you'll need permission to get in and look around, but the monks are very friendly. Take bus No 7 from the south side of ulitsa Krasnoarmeyskaya across the street from the bus station to the last stop. The monastery is 300 metres up the left fork off the semi-roundabout.

Alexey Tolstoy Park Also called 'The Park Where Trees Never Die', this is a lovely bit of green just west of ploshchad Lenina that is dotted with huge but intricate and playful wooden sculptures. The sculptures are said to be made from trees in the park after they die, so that they may 'live' on. It's named after Alexy ('The Propagandist') Tolstoy, author of such unforgettable classics as *Aelita*, the touching tale of communist revolution on Mars. That's right, Mars.

'...Gusev cut in. "Here's the layout for tomorrow...I'll pick out a few good lads...I'll capture the electromagnetic stations and wire at once to the earth – to Moscow – for reinforcements. They'll have spaceships ready in six months"...'

It's a favourite place to bring the kids, who marvel at the fountain and run rampant through the amusement park in summer. Follow Bolshaya Gagarina ulitsa west off ploshchad Lenina, and veer right past the Dinamo stadium. There are also nice parks to the east of ploshchad Lenina and ploshchad Teatralnaya.

Circus This is an old-fashioned one-ring circus (Bryansky tsirk) that had to be the model for the one used in the film *Moscow on the Hudson*. There's also a bouncy room for kids upstairs.

Places to Stay & Eat
The *Bryansky Karavay* bakery, on prospekt

Lenina just north of ploshchad Krasny Partisan, has the best bread in the region. The city has two central *markets*, the Tsentralny and the Nabezhetsky. Bus No 10 goes down prospekt Lenina and ulitsa Krasnoarmeyskaya to the Nabezhetsky, while bus No 10K runs the 10 km between the two.

There's a small *café* in Tolstoy Park serving cakes and juice, and in the small park to the east of ploshchad Teatralnaya a *Gril-Bar* has good shashlyk, roast chicken, cakes, and a lot of imported, albeit predominantly blue, liquors. Skip the *Kafe U Vokzala* at the railway station, but the bus station's *café* has some Finnish ice cream, and the *café* in the central department store has good hot dogs and some sandwiches.

The *Hotel Bryansk* (☎ 6 68 44), at the northern end of prospekt Lenina, has basic singles/doubles for US$15/16. It also has a big eating hall and grotty bufety on the 7th and 13th floors. Across the street, a small shop, *Petrovsky*, sells imported cheese, sausages and soft drinks.

Down at ploshchad Lenina, the *Hotel Desna* has marginally nicer rooms for US$15/22.50, and a nicer restaurant. It has a kiosk in the lobby selling imported cheese, sausages, cold beer and soda. Its bufet was closed when we visited, but it's on the 2nd floor.

Further south on prospekt Lenina, the *Hotel Dosaaf* doesn't take foreigners, but that may be good news from the looks of it. Some administrators at the Desna and Bryansk hotels seem to be blissfully ignorant of the recent shift in governmental policy in Russia and say that one needs Bryansk in one's visa to register at the hotels. Should this happen, wait until their shift is over and try again.

Things to Buy
The central department store (TsUM), just past the bridge on prospekt Lenina, is well stocked. There's a great sporting goods shop just opposite the Bryansky Karavay bakery.

Getting There & Away
Bryansk is on the Moscow-Kiev railway; almost every train out of Moscow's Kievsky Station stops here. It's accessible by bus and rail (two hours) from Oryol, and by bus only to/from Smolensk (five hours, no direct rail connection). Bryansk is off the M3 (Moscow-Kiev) highway from a turning 325 km south-west of Moscow. Schedules for flights to Bryansk are unpredictable; the cost is US$66 from Moscow. Bryansk's airport code is BZK.

Getting Around
From the railway station, take trolleybus No 1 or 2 from in front of the Kafe U Vokzala to ploshchad Krasni Partisan. Trolleybuses No 3, No 4 and No 10 run past the bus station, up prospekt Lenina to the Hotel Bryansk. Bus No 4 runs between prospekt Lenina and the airport.

Smolensk Region
Смоленская область

SMOLENSK
СМОЛЕНСК
Population: 340,000
First mentioned in 863 as the capital of the Slavic Krivichi tribes and a major trade centre, Smolensk's position on the upper Dnepr River gave it early control over trade routes between Moscow and the West and between the Baltic and Black seas – 'from the Varangians to the Greeks'. It became part of Kievan Rus, but after being sacked by the Tatars in about 1237, Smolensk passed to Lithuania. Moscow captured it in 1340, Lithuania in 1408, Moscow again in 1514, Poland in 1611 after a 20-month siege, and Russia in 1654.

There was a big battle between the Russians and Napoleon's army outside Smolensk in 1812 and more heavy fighting in 1941 and 1943, despite which quite a number of original or restored old buildings remain, notably churches and long sections of the city walls with fine towers reminiscent of the Moscow Kremlin. These and the

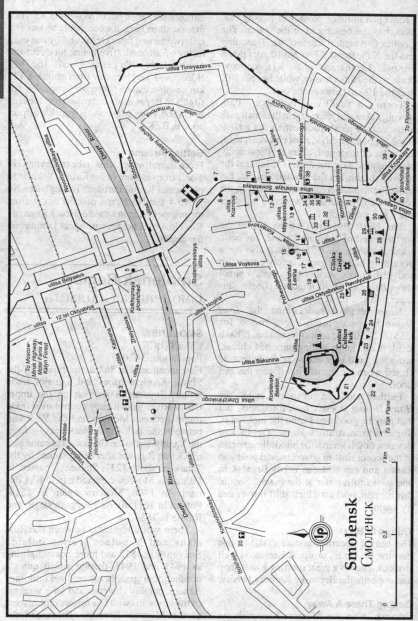

Smolensk
СМОЛЕНСК

PLACES TO STAY		
16	Hotel Tsentralnaya	
	Гостиница Центральная	
22	Hotel Rossia	
	Гостиница Россия	
31	Hotel Smolenskaya	
	Гостиница Смоленская	

PLACES TO EAT		
11	U Kristina Café	
	Кафе У Кристина	
12	Buterbrodnaya	
	Бутербродная Кафе	
14	Kafe Zarya	
	Кафе Заря	
23	Bistro	
	Бистро	
30	Bar U Samovara	
	Бар у самовара	
34	Bar Holsten 777	
	Бар Голстен 777	
35	Bar Russky Chay	
	Бар Русский Чай	
36	Bar Bulion	
	Бар Бульон	
37	Bar Blinnaya	
	Бар Блинная	

OTHER		
1	Railway Station	
	Железнодорожный	
	вокзал	

2	St Barbara's Convent
	Монастырь Св. Варвары
3	SS Peter and Paul Church
	Петропавловская церковь
4	Bus Station
	Автовокзал
5	Zadneprovsky Market
	Заднепровский рынок
6	Assumption Cathedral
	Успенский собор
7	Smolensk Flax Exhibition
	Выставка Смоленский лён
8	Trinity Monastery Bell Tower
	Колокольня Троицкого монастыря
9	Bookshop
	Книжный магазин
10	Bookshop
	Книжный магазин
13	Melodia (Record Shop)
	Магазин Мелодия
15	Intourist
	Интурист
17	Drama Theatre
	Драматический театр
18	House of Soviets
	Дом Советов
19	Defenders of 1812 Memorial
	Памятник обороняющимся 1812 г.

20	Svirskaya Church
	Свирская церковь
21	Spartak Stadium
	Стадион Спартак
24	Wading Pool/Waterfall
	Бассейн/Водопад
25	Post Office
	Почтамт
26	Gromovaya Tower
	Громовая Башня
27	WW II Memorial
	Памятник Великой Отечественной войны
28	1812 Monument
	Памятник 1812-ому году
29	WW II Museum
	Музей Великой Отечественной войны
32	Konenkov Sculpture Museum
	Музей С. Т. Коненкова
33	History Museum
	Исторический музей
38	Dnepr Bank
	Днепр Банк
39	Art Gallery
	Картинная галерея
40	Department Store
	ЦУМ

scenic slopes above the river make Smolensk well worth exploring, though few visitors have spent more than a night here as they speed between Poland and Moscow. Smolensk is also the home of the successful YaK 42 airliner.

Orientation

Central Smolensk, surrounded by lengths of ancient wall, stands on a hill on the south bank of the Dnepr. The formal city centre is ploshchad Lenina with the Glinka Garden (Gorodsky sad imeni M I Glinki) on its south side and the House of Soviets, Drama Theatre and Hotel Tsentralnaya on the north side. The railway station and Kolkhoznaya

ploshchad, site of the main market, are north of the river. Ulitsa Bolshaya Sovietskaya leads across the river and up the hill from Kolkhoznaya ploshchad to the centre. The Moscow-Minsk highway passes about 13 km north of Smolensk.

Information

Tourist Office The city Intourist office (☎ 3 35 08) is at ulitsa Konenkova 3, a couple of doors down from the Hotel Tsentralnaya. It's now a joint stock company, run by the suave Mikhail Soldatenkof. They do city tours for groups of six or more for US$3 to US$5 per person, and run excursions to Novospasskaya (Glinka's birthplace) and the

Przhevalsky National Park (see Around Smolensk).

Money Changing money is a hassle here; though you'll see a lot of 'change money' signs around, there aren't too many places that do exactly that. Try the Dnepr Commercial Bank on the corner of Bolshaya Sovietskaya and Tukhashevskogo, which will deign to change your foreign money if you bring your passport to enter the building (an ISIC card eventually worked). It's at Room 26, on the 2nd floor, at the top of the stairs and left, and first door on the left. They're supposed to be moving to ulitsa Gagarina in 1996. Their user-friendly hours are 9.30 am to 12.45 pm.

Post & Telecommunications The central post, telegraph and telephone office is at ulitsa Oktyabrskoy Revolyutsii 6. You may find an English-language map of Smolensk in either of the two bookshops facing each other across ulitsa Bolshaya Sovietskaya a block down from ulitsa Lenina. There's a fax and computer business centre, Everything For You (Vsyo Dla Vas) (☎ 9 67 01/9 63 63, fax 9 69 00, e-mail bemy!gela@mastak.msk .su), at ulitsa Lenina 16 on the 2nd floor.

The telephone code for Smolensk is 08100.

Fortress Walls
The 6-km-long, 5.5-metre-thick, 15-metre-high walls of the Smolensk fortress were built in 1596-1602. Originally they had 38 towers, 17 of which stand today. The Central Culture Park (Tsentralny park kultury i otdykha) backs a longish south-west stretch of the walls. Overlooking the Spartak Stadium just outside the line of the walls on the west side of the park, the Korolevsky Bastion is a high earth rampart built by the Poles who captured Smolensk in 1611. It saw heavy fighting in 1654 and 1812. The park has a 26-metre-high cast-iron monument to the 1812 defenders.

You can enter the Gromovaya Tower on the west side of ulitsa Oktyabrskoy Revolyutsii from 10 am to 6 pm daily except Monday. At the foot of the walls east of here you'll find

an eternal flame memorial to the dead of WW II and the graves of some of the Soviet soldiers who died in Smolensk's WW II defence, plus a WW II museum (open daily from 10 am to 6 pm, except Monday) and another monument to the heroes of 1812.

Assumption Cathedral
Smolensk's big green-and-white working cathedral rises at the top of a flight of steps halfway up ulitsa Bolshaya Sovietskaya. A cathedral has stood here since 1101 but this one was built in the late 17th and early 18th centuries. Topped by five domes, it has a spectacular gilded interior. Napoleon is said to have been so impressed that he set a guard to stop his own men from vandalising it.

To your right as you enter, you can recognise – by all the candles around it – a supposedly wonder-working icon of the Virgin. This is a 16th-century copy of the original, said to be by St Luke, which had been on this site since 1103 and was stolen in 1923. The cathedral bell tower, at the top of the steps, dates from a St Petersburg Baroque-style revamp in 1763-72. There's a good view from the terrace at the east end of the cathedral.

Flax Exhibition
A little further up the hill, ulitsa Bolshaya Sovietskaya cuts through the former Trinity Monastery. The bell tower is on the west side; on the east side the pink monastery church now houses the Smolensk Flax Exhibition, open daily except Monday from 10 am to 6 pm. The latter unwittingly tells a sad tale of how the revolution and mechanisation replaced colourful, varied, traditional textile designs with mass-produced uniformity.

SS Peter & Paul Church
This lovely old Kiev-style brick church – built in the 1140s and heavily restored in the 1960s – stands at ulitsa Kashena 20A north of the river, near the ulitsa Dzerzhinskogo bridge. The 17th and 18th-century buildings of St Barbara's Convent are next door. A footbridge leads to SS Peter & Paul from the railway station – or walk from Kolkhoznaya ploshchad.

Archangel Michael Church

The pinky-grey Archangel Michael Church or Svirskaya tserkov, just off Bolshaya Krasnoflotskaya ulitsa, south of the river, is another fine 12th-century building (1180-97), restored after damage in WW II.

History Museum & Art Gallery

Smolensk's History Museum, at ulitsa Lenina 8, is open daily except Monday from 10 am to 6 pm. The art gallery is at ulitsa Krupskaya 7.

Konenkov Sculpture Museum

Smolensk's sculpture museum is at ulitsa Mayakovskaya 7. You'll find some very playful and interesting woodworks by Sergey Konenkov here. Upstairs, past the frightening Prorok statue, is a small but very good collection of steel, bronze and aluminium statuettes, and another room housing pure kitsch – if you've been itching to see a matryoshka doll, they have some good ones here. It's open daily from 10 am to 6 pm.

YaK

Want to see a YaK 42? There's one on ulitsa Bagrationa. A tram (No 3 or 6) stops east of the Hotel Rossia. It's worth a look.

Places to Stay

Outside the city, the standard Motel Fenix (☎ 2 14 88), lies 1.5 km north (away from Smolensk) from the main Smolensk junction on the Moscow-Minsk highway, four km out of town. It's dilapidated – some rooms leak when it rains – and you must fight hard for service, but it's the cheapest place around and for US$16 the rooms aren't that bad (though they are a bit damp). The camp site next door is, according to Smolensk Intourist, being used to house soldiers who have returned from East Germany and is therefore closed to the public. Bus Nos 102 and 137 (rare though) go from the motel to Smolensk's Kolkhoznaya ploshchad, a 30 to 40-minute ride, from where there are trams to the city centre (see Getting Around later).

The Hotel Rossia (☎ 9 66 51, 3 39 70), at ulitsa Dzerzhinskogo 23/2, may be big and uninspiring, but it has the cleanest singles/doubles in town for US$22/40. The staff, however, aren't exactly enthusiastic. The Hotel Tsentralnaya (☎ 3 36 04), on the corner of ploshchad Lenina and ulitsa Konenkova, has cleaned up its act and is now a reasonable deal with timeworn rooms for US$30/60.

The pre-WW II Hotel Smolensk (☎ 3 03 97), at ulitsa Glinki 11/30, has cantankerous staff, expensive and grotty rooms (US$33/90 with bath, US$23/45 without) that lack toilet paper and, in some cases, toilet seats. There is hot and cold water – though not, of course, simultaneously.

Places to Eat

Smolensk's main market is the Zadneprovsky on Kolkhoznaya ploshchad north of the river.

The Hotel Rossia has two large but ochin plokhoy (very bad) restaurants, a good bufet on the 7th floor and two shops in the lobby that sell Western goods. The lobby bar at the Hotel Tsentralnaya serves good cakes and real coffee, and there's a Beryozka imported goods shop there as well.

Bar Holsten 777, on the corner of ulitsa Lenina and ulitsa Bolshaya Sovietskaya is a slick cellar bar/café with good food, expensive imported beer and thugs in the lobby. It's open from noon to 5 am. Next door, on ulitsa Bolshaya Sovietskaya, is Bar Russky Chay, a very popular café despite the lack of a sign. It has good coffee, sandwiches, roast chicken, fruit, ice cream, a few small salads and is open from noon to 4 pm and 5 to 10 pm. It's also very smoky. Next door is the Bar Bulion, which doesn't allow smoking or serve good food. And two doors down from there is the Bar Blinnaya, a stolovaya with good borshch.

U Kristina, opposite Bolshaya Sovietskaya 14, is an interesting maze of dining rooms in a cellar café that serves hot meals and drinks. Walk through the entrance tunnel, turn left, turn left again and down the stairs. It's no smoking, and it's open from 10 am to 3 pm and 4 to 10 pm. Just off ulitsa Bolshoya Sovietskaya near the bookshops, the *Buterbrodnaya* is a very charming but small, cellar sandwich shop, also serving rolls, cakes, coffee and drinks. It's open from 10.30 am to 6.30 pm.

Bar U Samovara, at ulitsa Dzerzhinskogo 4, is a quiet cellar café serving tea, juice and good cakes daily except Monday from 1 to 3 pm and 4 to 9 pm. Dig the log slices on the walls. The *Kafe Zarya*, opposite the Hotel Tsentralnaya, is OK for pastries but its restaurant section is poor.

A different *Bar Blinnaya*, near the Hotel Rossia, between ulitsa Dzerzhinskogo's wall and the central culture park, has very good bliny, very bad kotlet and good salads and is open from 10 am to 3 pm, and 4 to 6 pm. In summer, a nice outdoor *café* next to the Fenix Chess Club (Shakhmatny Fenix Klub) at ulitsa Lenina 12, serves pizza, pies and cakes. There's a rather smelly restaurant next door at No 14. The *Bistro* on ulitsa Mayakovskaya, just up the street from the Konenkov Sculpture Museum, serves pizza and sandwiches.

Things to Buy
The central department store on ploshchad Smirnova, now run by a joint stock company, has a big children's section, with model kits (hopefully they'll keep up supplies of Warsaw Pact planes, tanks and troops), toys, clothes, and a Kodak 1-Hour photoshop that develops and sells film. There's a kiosk city outside the central market.

Getting There & Away
Air Daily flights to/from Moscow cost US$72; from St Petersburg US$91; and there are several flights a week from Minsk for US$55. Smolensk's airport code is LNX.

Bus Smolensk bus station, just south of the railway station, serves most of the region's smaller towns with frequent daily service, and several times daily service to St Petersburg and Moscow.

Train Smolensk is on the Moscow-Minsk-Warsaw railway with several daily trains to/from Moscow (7 hours), Minsk (4 hours),

Brest (7½ hours), Warsaw (12 to 14 hours). The ticket queues at the Smolensk Station are intolerable.

There are also daily rail links with Western Europe (see European Russia – Getting There & Away and Moscow – Getting There & Away).

Car & Motorbike By road it's 390 km to Moscow, and 330 km to Minsk. Both are among Russia's better, though duller, stretches of highway, being mostly flat, straight and empty.

Getting Around
From the railway station, trams Nos 1 and 4 go to Kolkhoznaya ploshchad and up ulitsa Bolshaya Sovietskaya to the Assumption Cathedral and the edge of the town centre. No 3 goes to the Hotel Rossia. Bus Nos 2, 5 and 7 also go up ulitsa Bolshaya Sovietskaya from Kolkhoznaya ploshchad.

AROUND SMOLENSK
ОКРЕСТОСТЬ СМОЛЕНСКА
Flyonovo
Флёново
In the late 19th and early 20th centuries, top Russian art and music names like Stravinsky, Chaliapin, Vrubel and Serov visited the Flyonovo estate of the artist Princess Maria Tenisheva, near Talashkino, about 15 km south of Smolensk on the Roslavl road. The visitors joined in applied-art workshops, which the princess organised for her peasants, and helped in building projects.

The most striking result is a series of dramatic murals and mosaics on the brick Holy Spirit Church – particularly the one of Christ over the entrance. One house called Teremok, decorated with ornate peasant-style carving, is now a folk-art museum, open daily except Mondays. Intourist runs four-hour excursions here from Smolensk: the cost for up to three individual travellers would be around US$70. On your own, take bus No 104 from the bus station to Talashkino.

Katyn Forest
КАТЫН ЛЕС

In 1990 the Soviet authorities finally admitted that the NKVD (predecessor of the KGB) had shot over 6000 Polish officers in the back of the head in the Katyn Forest near Smolensk in 1940. The bodies of the officers, who had been imprisoned by the Soviet occupation troops in Poland in 1939, were left in four mass graves.

Vladimir Tokarev, 89 years old, admits he took part in the executions. He described, according to the *Times* of London, how executioners, sent on direct orders of the Politburo, shot the Poles 'one by one, in a soundproof prison cell, at the rate of 250 a night'.

The atrocity became a cause célèbre because until 1990 the Soviet authorities insisted on blaming it on the Nazis. The victims were trucked from Gnezdovo, a country station, to Kozy Gory, site of the graves. The graves have not been disturbed and are now marked by memorials. About 11,000 other Polish officers almost certainly died similar deaths elsewhere in the USSR.

Less well known is that the Katyn Forest was also, according to a 1989 *Moscow News* report, the site of massacres of 135,000 Soviet prisoners of war by the Nazis (out of an estimated one million Soviet POWs shot by the Germans in WW II) and of thousands of Soviet 'enemies of the state' exterminated by the NKVD in the 1930s. *Moscow News* recounted the tale of a man named Petrov, who:

... burst into NKVD headquarters one morning before the war and insisted he hadn't done anything wrong and had been shot by mistake. It was discovered that he had been on the list of those sentenced to be shot, but hadn't died, only stayed unconscious for a long time. When he came to in Katyn Forest, he burrowed out of the pit and made tracks to the town. Embarrassed by the absurd situation, the NKVD issued him new identity papers in the name of Ivanov and packed him off out of the region.

Getting There & Away Getting there on your own is simple; take bus No 101 (direction: Smolenk Smetanino) from the Smolensk bus station to Kozy Gory. It's easy to miss so look for the sign saying '*Memorial Polsky ofitseram pogibshim v Katyni*' about a km past the highway flyover. If you get to Katyn, you've gone too far. The memorial is in two spots: one with a simple wood cross, and a marble headstone dedicated to Russian dead; and the more impressive Polish memorial further up the path. The forest is spooky, but the memorials are moving.

Przhevalsky National Park
Национальний Парк имёИржевалского

Lying 60 km from the city, the birthplace of adventurer Przhevalsky is said to be a stunningly beautiful national park, though you'll need reservations to get in. Activities in the park include camping, horse riding, hiking and fishing. Intourist Smolensk can arrange a trip on a month's notice for approximately US$20 to US$30 a day including meals and activities; other Russian travel agents may be able to book it as well.

Novgorod Region
Новгородская область

NOVGOROD
НОВГОРОД
Population: 190,000

The name means 'new town', but Novgorod was here by the 9th century and for 600 years was Russia's most pioneering artistic and political centre. Today it's mostly known for its history, and for some of the most diverse and beautiful architecture in the country.

Methodically trashed by the Nazis, it's a sign of the city's historical importance that its old kremlin was one of the Soviet government's first reconstruction projects. Today the town crawls with Russians, foreign tourists and school groups, but it's an easy and rewarding overnight stop. Novgorod's only three hours by road from St Petersburg and is found just off the M10 highway connecting Moscow and St Petersburg.

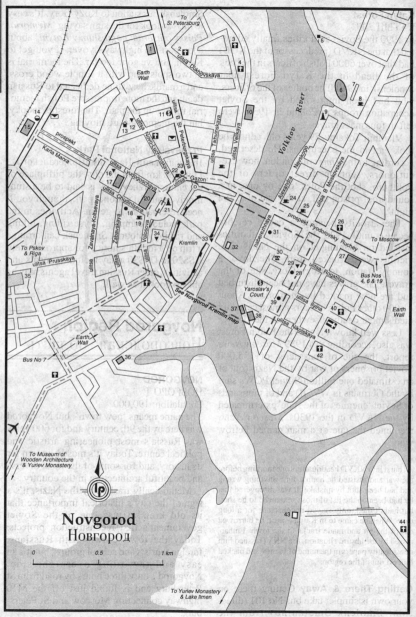

Novgorod
Новгород

0   0.5   1 km

To St Petersburg

Earth Wall

ulitsa Dukhovskaya

ulitsa B St Petersburgskaya

Novo-Luchanskaya

ulitsa Tikhvinskaya

ulitsa Velikaya

Volkhov River

prospekt Karla Marxa

ulitsa Lyudogoscha

ulitsa Chudintseva

Zavalnaya-Koltsevaya

Zabavskaya

Volosova

ulitsa

ulitsa Prusskaya

Gazon

Kremlin

See Novgorod Kremlin map

Earth Wall

Bus No 7

To Pskov & Riga

To Museum of Wooden Architecture & Yuriev Monastery

To Yuriev Monastery & Lake Ilmen

Alexandra Nevskogo

naberezhnaya

prospekt Fyodorovsky Ruchey

ulitsa B Moskovskaya

ulitsa Rogatitsa

ulitsa Ilyina

ulitsa Nikolskaya

Yaroslav's Court

Earth Wall

To Moscow

Bus Nos 4, 6 & 19

Bus Nos 4, 6 & 19

PLACES TO STAY	OTHER		26	Church of St Theodore Stratelates Церковь Федора Стратилата

PLACES TO STAY

5	Beresta Palace Hotel Отель Береста Паласе
10	Hotel Intourist Гостиница Интурист
13	Novgorod Youth Hostel Гостиница ПУУ
17	Hotel Volkhov Гостиница Волхов
27	Hotel Sadko Гостиница Садко
38	Hotel Rossia Гостиница Россия

PLACES TO EAT

8	Kafe Karusel Кафе Карусель
12	Pivnoy Restaurant Пивной Ресторан
16	Restaurant Pri Dvore Ресторан При Дворе
19	Kafe Charodeyka Кафе Чародейка
22	Baskin Robbins Kiosk Баскин Роббинс киоск
24	Kafe Merl Кафе Мерл
25	Baskin Robbins Stand Баскин Роббинс кафе
29	Kafe Posad Кафе Посад
33	Summer Shashlyk Stand Летний шашлычный киоск
34	Gril Bar Грил Бар

OTHER

1	Central Department Store ЦУМ
2	Trinity Church Церковь Троицы
3	Church of the Intercession Покровская церковь
4	Church of SS Peter & Paul Петропавловская церковь
6	Stadium Стадион
7	Ferris Wheel Чёртово колесо
9	Alexander Nevsky Statue Памятник Александра Невского
11	Sberbank Сбербанк
14	Bus Station Автовокзал
15	Railway Station Железнодорожный вокзал
18	Beryozka Магазин Берёзка
20	Regional Administration Building Областная администрация
21	Sofiyskaya ploshchad & Lenin Statue Памятник Ленину
23	Bookshop Книжный магазин

26	Church of St Theodore Stratelates Церковь Федора Стратилата
28	Oktyabr Cinema Кино Октябрь
30	Telephone Office Телефон
31	Banya Баня
32	Kremlin Landing Причал Кремля
35	Market Рынок
36	Tower Башня
37	River Station Речной вокзал
39	Bookshop Книжный магазин
40	Church of Our Saviour-at-Ilino Церковь Спаса-на-Ильине
41	Cathedral of Our Lady of the Sign Знаменский собор
42	Church of the Apostle Philip Церковь Апостола Филлипа
43	Seltso Landing Причал Сельцо
44	Church of Our Saviour-at-Neredilsa Церковь Спаса-на-Нередице

History

In a sense, Russian history began here. This was the first permanent settlement of the Varangian Norsemen who established the embryonic Russian state. By the 12th century the city, called 'Lord Novgorod the Great', was Russia's biggest: an independent quasi-democracy whose princes were hired and fired by a citizens' assembly, and whose strong, spare style of church architecture, icon-painting and down-to-earth *byliny* (epic songs) were to become distinct idioms.

Spared from the Mongol Tatars, who got bogged down in the surrounding swamps, Novgorod suffered most at the hands of other Russians. Ivan III of Moscow attacked and annexed it in 1477, and Ivan the Terrible, whose storm-troopers razed the city and slaughtered 60,000 people in a savage pogrom, broke its back. The founding of St Petersburg finished it off as a trading centre.

Orientation & Information

The town has two main centres: the kremlin on the west bank of the Volkhov River, and the old market district, Yaroslav's Court, on

New Street Names in Novgorod

New Name	Old Name
ulitsa Andreevskaya	ulitsa Mstinskaya
ulitsa Bolshaya St Peterburgskaya	ulitsa Leningradskaya
ulitsa Bolshoy Dvortsovaya	ulitsa Gertsena
ulitsa Bolshoy Moskovskaya	prospekt Lenina
ulitsa BolshoyVlasevskaya	ulitsa Chernyshevskogo
ulitsa Boyana	ulitsa Bolshevikov
ulitsa Chudintseva	ulitsa L Tolstogo
ulitsa Danslavnya	ulitsa Yakovlevskaya
ulitsa Dobrynya	ulitsa Sverdlova
ulitsa Dukhovskaya	ulitsa Musy Dzhalilya
prospekt Fyodorovsky Ruchey	prospekt Yuria Gagarina
ulitsa Gazon	ulitsa Gorkogo
ulitsa Ilyina	ulitsa Pervogo Maya
ulitsa Ivanskaya	ulitsa Bez Nazvania
ulitsa Konyukhova	ulitsa Cheremnova
ulitsa Kozmodemyanskaya	ulitsa Dekabristov
ulitsa Lubyanitsa	ulitsa Pushkinskaya
ulitsa Lyudogoschaya	ulitsa Sovietskaya
ulitsa Lyukina	ulitsa Litvinova
ulitsa M Vlasevskaya	ulitsa Sovietskaya
ulitsa Manitsina	ulitsa Gerasimenko
ulitsa Mikhailova	ulitsa Kirovskaya
ulitsa Nikitin by	ulitsa Mstinskyi by
ulitsa Nikolskaya	ulitsa Suvorovskaya
ulitsa Novo-Lyuchanskaya	ulitsa Komsomolskaya
ulitsa Nutnaya	ulitsa Borovichskaya
ulitsa Olovyanka	ulitsa T Frunze
ulitsa Predtechenskaya	ulitsa Nekrasova
ulitsa Prusskaya	ulitsa Zhelyabova
ulitsa Rogatitsa	ulitsa Bolshevikov
ulitsa Rozvazha	ulitsa Gorkogo
ulitsa Ryadyatina	ulitsa Telegina
Sennaya ploshchad	Truda ploshchad
ulitsa Slavkov by	ulitsa Slavny by
Sofiyskaya ploshchad	ploshchad Pobedy
ulitsa Staro-Moskovskaya	ulitsa Mstinskaya
ulitsa Stratilatovskaya	ulitsa Lermontova
ulitsa Tikhvinskaya	ulitsa Komarova
ulitsa Troitskaya-Proboynaya Frolovskaya	ulitsa Proletarskaya
ulitsa Tshitnaya	ulitsa Krasnaya ulitsa
ulitsa Velikaya	ulitsa Dmitreyskaya
ulitsa Volosova	ulitsa Meretskova
ulitsa Vozdvizhenskaya	ulitsa Lukinskaya
ulitsa Yakovleva	ulitsa Shtykova
ulitsa Zabavskaya	ulitsa Nekrasova
ulitsa Zapolskaya	ulitsa Pankratova
ulitsa Zavalnaya	ulitsa Pankratova
ulitsa Zavalnaya-Koltsevaya	ulitsa Chernyakhovskogo
ulitsa Znamenskaya	ulitsa Krasilova
ulitsa Zverinskaya	ulitsa Bredova

the east bank. The kremlin side sprawls outward like a pheasant's tail, while the east side is grid-like.

Intourist's office at the Hotel Intourist is staffed by folk who can't speak English at all (though they'll snap right to it if you utter the phrase 'joint venture'). The main post office is on ulitsa Bolshaya St Peterburgskaya (ulitsa Leningradskaya), with a small branch at the Hotel Intourist. Change money at hotels, or at branches of Novobank – its main branch is at ulitsa Slavnaya 50 (east of the Volkhov), and it has branches all over town, including at the Beresta Palace and Intourist hotels. City maps are rare but can be found on sale at the Beresta Palace Hotel, at the Hotel Intourist's post office and at kiosks near the kremlin. There's a market on Saturdays and Wednesdays at the west end of ulitsa Prusskaya (ulitsa Zhelyabova). Novgorod's telephone code is 816.

Street Name Changes Like St Petersburg and Moscow, Novgorod has turned its back on anything remotely connected to things communist and, since 1991, has changed the vast majority of its street names. The box shows new and old street names as of summer 1994. Note that while the town has renamed practically every street, its implementation strategy is right out of the movie *Brazil*; old names continue to be used by locals, and many streets now boast *two* street signs – with no indication of which is the old and which is the new name! If you ask for a street and are greeted with bewilderment, try the old name. It'll probably work.

In this chapter, because of all this, we use the new street name followed by the old street name in parenthesis.

The Kremlin

Part park, part tourist attraction, part archive, this is worth seeing with a group tour (cost around US$5, that is, if you can find a willing group), or through the Beresta Palace Hotel's tour service. On your own, tickets for the cathedral (free), palace (US$1.40, children US$0.70) and museum (US$1.20, photos US$1.40) are available at the main museum. The buildings are open from 10 am to 6 pm; the cathedral is closed on Wednesdays and the last Monday of the month, the palace on Tuesdays and the last Friday, and the museum on Tuesdays and the last Thursday.

Cathedral of St Sophia Finished in 1050, the handsome, Byzantine Cathedral of St Sophia (Sofiysky sobor) is the town's centrepiece and possibly the oldest building in Russia. The west doors, captured from the Swedes, have tiny cast-bronze biblical scenes and even portraits of the artists. The icons inside go back to the 14th century, and older ones are in the museum. In comparison, the frescoes are barely dry, being less than a century old. Nearby are the 15th-century belfry and a leaning 17th-century clock tower.

Millennium of Russia Monument Watch the crowds go round and round this bronze birthday cake, unveiled in 1862 on the 1000th anniversary of the Varangian Prince Rurik's arrival. The Nazis cut it up, intending to ship it to Germany, but the Red Army saved the day.

The women at the top are Mother Russia and the Orthodox Church. Around the middle, clockwise from the south, are Rurik, Prince Vladimir of Kiev (who introduced Christianity), tsars Mikhail Romanov, Peter the Great and Ivan III, and Dmitry Donskoy trampling a Mongol Tatar. In the bottom band on the east side are nobles and rulers, including Catherine the Great with an armload of laurels for all her lovers. Alexandr Nevsky and other military heroes are on the north side, and literary and artistic figures are on the west.

Chamber of Facets The Gothic Chamber of Facets (Granovitaya palata), part of a reception hall built in 1433, now has a collection of icons and lavish church booty from the region. Individuals must join a group at the ticket office.

Museum of History & Art This is said to be one of the best research museums of its kind in Russia, with a huge collection of early icons, birch-bark manuscripts, paintings, early wood sculpture and applied art.

Yaroslav's Court

Across a footbridge from the kremlin is old Novgorod's market, with the remnants of a 17th-century arcade facing the river. Beyond that is the market gatehouse, an array of churches sponsored by 13th to 16th-century merchant guilds, and a 'road palace' built in the 18th century as a rest stop for Catherine the Great.

The Court Cathedral of St Nicholas (Nikolo-Dvorishchensky sobor, 1136) is all that remains of the early palace complex of the Novgorod princes, from which the area gets its name of Yaroslav's Court (Yaroslavskoe dvorishche). Inside, fragments of old frescoes include one of Job, covered in boils, with his wife passing him food on the end of a pole. The other frescoes are 19th-century restorations. The cathedral is open from 10 am to 6 pm, and closed Monday.

Novgorod, for six centuries a thriving centre of Russian art, is a treasure trove of icons such as this Byzantine-influenced one of Christ from the 12th century

Church of Our Saviour-at-Ilino

The 14th-century Church of Our Saviour-at-Ilino (Tserkov Spasa-na-Iline) has to be one of the most charming buildings in all of Russia. Outside, its graffiti-like ornaments and lopsided gables are almost playful. Inside are the only surviving frescoes by the legendary Byzantine painter Theophanes the Greek (and they came close to extinction when the church served as a Nazi machine-gun nest). Note the figure of Christ Pantokrator up in the dome.

This is pure Novgorod style (in contrast to the lumbering 17th-century Moscow-style Cathedral of Our Lady of the Sign across the street). It's at ulitsa Pervogo Maya 26a, and is only open from noon to 4 pm; it's closed Monday to Wednesday and also in cold or wet weather.

Other Churches

Some other churches with personality in the Novgorod style are **Church of SS Peter & Paul** (1406) on ulitsa Zverinskaya (ulitsa Bredova), behind No 14, near the Hotel Intourist, and the **Church of St Theodore Stratelates** (Tserkov Fedora Stratilata, 1361) at prospekt Fyodorovsky Ruchey (prospect Yuria Gagarina) 19. An appealing church in the angular Moscow style is **Trinity Church** (Tserkov Troitsy, 1557) at ulitsa Dukhovskaya (ulitsa Musy Dzhalilya).

The **Church of Our Saviour-at-Nereditsa** (Tserkov Spasa-na-Nereditse, 1198), which has a few bits of 12th-century frescoes, is in the village of Seltso, five minutes by boat from the kremlin landing, plus a 1.5-km walk.

Services are held at the **Church of the Intercession**, near the Hotel Intourist, and at the **Church of the Apostle Philip**, east of the river.

Yuriev Monastery & Museum of Wooden Architecture

In the southern marshes is this dilapidated 12th-century monastery with its heavily reconstructed Cathedral of St George and a clutch of 19th-century add-ons. It's not as striking as many places closer to town,

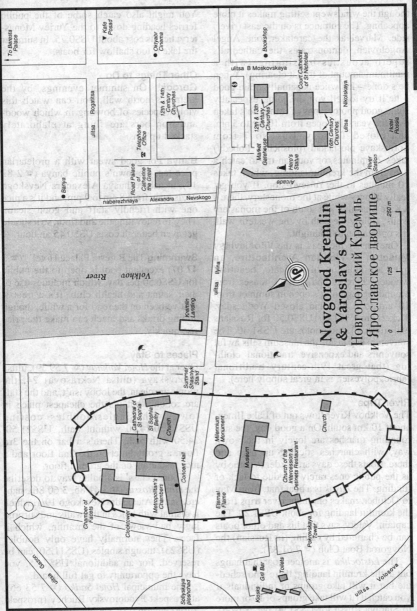

Novgorod Kremlin
& Yaroslav's Court
Новгородский Кремль
и Ярославское дворище

though the windswept setting makes it more appealing. The entrance is on the east (river) side. Marvel as the caretaker, one Angel Angelovich, demonstrates the cathedral's superb acoustics by singing (with a minimum amount of throat clearing). When he's done – his voice is actually quite good – he'll try to sell you the joint, especially some good photographs of it that he's taken over the years. It's open from 10 am to 5 pm, and closed Tuesday. Bus No 7 from Sofiyskaya ploshchad (ploshchad Pobedy) takes 20 minutes, or you can try to catch a boat from the kremlin landing, which takes 10 minutes to the Yurievo stop. If you get really hungry while at the monastery, there's a Kafe Shashlyk just south of the monastery walls; follow the path by the western wall. It's open noon to midnight.

One km up the road is the **Vitoslavlitsy Museum of Wooden Architecture**, an open-air museum of intricate, beautiful wooden churches and peasant houses from around the region. It's open in summer from 10 am to 6 pm, and closed Wednesday. Tickets are US$1.20 (US$0.50 for Russians and students), and photos are US$1.40. The souvenir shop inside the museum sells awful souvenirs and expensive 'traditional' clothing (that great 19th-century traditional fabric, polyester, is in great supply here).

River Trips

The Volkhov River flows out of Lake Ilmen, about 10 km south. On a good day, the surrounding marshes are lovely in their own way, with churches sticking up here and there. Boats these days are harder to come by as the public ones rarely run due to lack of funding. The *Zuyok* is a boat that, from May to October, makes one-hour river trips from the kremlin landing for about US$1.20. The captain, Valery, says that his and other boats can be chartered by calling (in Russian) the Novgorod Boat Club (☎ 7 61 85).

The *Lastochka* is another boat that hangs out at the kremlin landing; there's no schedule but it will take groups or individuals if you catch it (it will take groups of 10 or more to Staraya Russa for US$1.90 per person).

You might also catch some of the public ferries heading down to the Yuriev Monastery; tickets cost about US$0.75. In summer the lake is too shallow for boats.

Other Things to Do

Gorodki On summer evenings, by the kremlin's north wall, you can watch this violent species of bowling in which wood-and-iron bars are flung at elaborately stacked-up pins.

Banya For good sweat with a proletarian price tag, the town's public banya (☎ 2 82 13), at naberezhnaya Alexandra Nevskogo 24, is open from 8 am to 9 pm, and it's a nice one with friendly staff and good steam. They're renovating the 2nd floor, so it should get even better. It costs US$0.45 an hour.

Swimming The Beresta Palace Hotel's (☎ 3 47 07) excellent pool is open to the public for US$6.50 per day, which includes use of their sauna and health club. It's a treat if you've been on the road for a while, though adding drinks and lunch can make the price rise quickly.

Places to Stay

Over at the *Hotel Volkhov* (☎ 7 59 39), ulitsa Zabavskaya (ulitsa Nekrasova) 24, the rooms are clean, the lobby isn't, and the staff are robotic, but it's the cheapest place in town with singles/doubles costing US$11.50/14.50 without bath, US$21.50/34.50 with bath. There's a bar on the 3rd floor, a grotty bufet on the 2nd floor and a nice restaurant on the ground floor.

'Tourist class' is a polite way to describe the *Hotel Rossia* (☎ 3 41 85, 3 60 86), naberezhnaya Alexandra Nevskogo 19/1, which is dismal with holes in the walls and surprisingly bad views of the kremlin, which it faces. They normally have only doubles (US$23), though singles (US$11.50) can be reserved. For an additional US$7.15, you have the opportunity to get full board.

The municipal *Hotel Sadko* (☎ 7 53 66), at prospekt Fyodorovsky Ruchey (prospekt Yuria Gagarina) 16, has nice rooms and staff, though they're a bit out of the centre at the eastern end of town. It's not a bad deal at US$14.50/22.85.

Novgorod's *Youth Hostel* (☎ 7 20 33, 7 14 58), a member of the Russian Youth Hostel Association, is a former teachers' dormitory (Gostinitsa PUU) just outside the centre on the west side of town, near the earth fortifications at ulitsa Zavalnaya-Koltsevaya (ulitsa Chernyakhovskogo) 27A. Rooms are clean and there's a nice common area, but a definite drawback are the gangsters who patronise the café downstairs. They're all friendly enough, and they don't menace the guests, but they seem to have car burglar-alarm testing contests at 2 am. Ask for a room at the back and it will be quieter. The hostel has singles/doubles/triples for US$17.25/ 14.85/18.50. Rooms can be booked through the HI St Petersburg Hostel, or through any Russian Youth Hostels Association member. The sign on the door of this building says 'Roza Betrov', and the interior's pretty pink.

The *Hotel Intourist* (☎ 7 50 89; fax 7 41 57, e-mail root@intour.nov.su), by the river at ulitsa Velikaya (ulitsa Dmitreyskaya) 16, has clean rooms, polite staff and a decent restaurant. They also have a good lobby café serving real coffee. The expansion work that's been going on since 1989 continues (a guy comes by every now and then and bangs on a piece of it); hotel officials say it will be completed in March 1996, but a former director of the hotel says: 'March is believable...March of what year – now there is the mystery'. They've got singles, doubles and luxury suites for US$33.50/39/66.50. There's also a guarded car park under the building.

The *Beresta Palace Hotel* (☎ 3 47 07) is a luxury hotel located on the east bank of the Volkhov. It was established by the Marco Polo chain, which pulled out of management in November 1994, and we haven't visited since before the change. But the reason this place deserved this much ink is that the prices – while decidedly high – are very reasonable considering what you get, and they offer services to non-guests at the same rate as guests.

The best deal is their weekend getaway: US$293 per couple including two nights stay, breakfast and dinner, city tours and use of the hotel's pool, health club, sauna and tennis courts.

The standard rates are US$130/160 high season, and US$100/130 low season, though management says that far better deals can be had through travel agents in Russia or abroad. The hotel has a restaurant, two banquet halls, a nightclub, pub and Bier-stube, a decent money exchange, a dental clinic (?!) and a hairstylist. It was a great place under Marco Polo (the current management team has been trained by Marco Polo and has come from the Intourist Hotel across the river), so good luck to them.

The *Savino* (or *Novgorodsky*) camp site (☎ 7 24 48), with tent sites and cabins, is 12 km east of town, but everyone – even Intourist – says to steer clear of it.

Places to Eat

West Side For great Russian dishes and a first-rate location, try the *Detinets Restaurant* in a former church beside the kremlin's Pokrovskaya Tower; bar and casual booths downstairs, restaurant upstairs. The *Restaurant Pri Dvore* at ulitsa Lyudogoshchaya (ulitsa Sovietskaya) 3 is nicely renovated and has good service, very good food and clean toilets. They also have an outdoor café with great shashlyk, pizza and barbecue sausages, soft drinks, beer and wine.

The food at the *Hotel Intourist* restaurant is limited but good and it's open all day. In summer there's a *shashlyk stand* just outside the kremlin's eastern gate before the footbridge. *Café Charodeyka*, at ulitsa Volosova (ulitsa Meretskova) 1/1, is newly renovated and has good pizza, sandwiches, beer and juices. It's open from 10 to 1 am.

Just outside the kremlin park's west side is a *Gril-Bar* serving great roast chicken by the gram. Nearby, the *Kafe Fenix* at ulitsa Gazon (ulitsa Gorkogo) 15 is somewhat creepy but does decent sandwiches, hot dogs and salads. And if your sweet tooth is playing up, there's a *Baskin Robbins* ice-cream café with great ice cream but erratic supplies (a local said that sometimes they have 20 flavours, and sometimes none). It's at ulitsa Gazon (ulitsa Gorkogo) 5/2, and is open from 10 am to 10 pm.

East Side The cooperative *Kafe Posad* (☎ 9 48 49), ulitsa Rogatitsa (ulitsa Bolshevikov) 14, is more inventive (even serving Beef Francaise which is a steak covered with American-style cheese and breadcrumbs) but still cheap; main courses cost up to US$1.50. It's open from noon to midnight (supper from 6 to 8 pm), and closed Sunday.

Near the amusement park opposite ulitsa Bolshaya Moskovskaya 84/1, the *Kafe Karusel* has good mushrooms in cream sauce, shashlyk and soups in the US$2 to US$3 range. The restaurant at the *Hotel Sadko* is quite good, with meat and fish dishes from US$1.40 to US$1.90; they're open from 11 am to 11 pm, with music from 8 pm onwards.

The restaurant at the *Beresta Palace Hotel* has an expensive breakfast at US$7, but their set lunch for US$7 is well worth it. Dinners are also good value: chicken Kiev (US$4.50), fried fish (US$3.50), cheeseburger with fries and salad (US$5.50), and pizza Quattro Staggioni (US$5.50) feature on the menu. Avoid the local mineral water sold at the bar, and opt instead for the imported stuff.

Kafe Merl, at naberezhnaya Alexandra Nevskogo 26, does decent shashlyk and sells German draft beer for US$1.40 a half litre. It's a nice place to sit in summer.

There's another *Baskin Robbins* kiosk at the west end of ulitsa Fedorovsky Ruchey (prospect Yuria Gagarina).

Getting There & Away

Air The tiny airport is on the road to Yuriev Monastery. There are daily flights from Moscow's Bykovo Airport for US$83, and every day or so in summer from St Petersburg (US$54) and Kiev (US$114). Novgorod's airport code is NVR.

Bus There are several daily buses from Moscow and about a dozen from St Peters-

burg, from which, bus is far more convenient than any other means of getting here. Buses leave from St Petersburg's Avtovokzal 2 about once an hour, cost about US$10 and take three hours. The last bus back to St Petersburg is at 7.05 pm; for tickets to St Petersburg from Novgorod, use cash window No 1 at Novgorod bus station, on the left as you enter the ticket hall. There's also a direct bus service to/from Smolensk and Pskov.

Train The railway and bus stations are 1.5 km west of the kremlin, at the end of prospect Karla Marxa. A daily fast train from St Petersburg's Moscow Station takes four hours (190 km) and there's a slower passazhirskiy train from St Petersburg's Vitsebsk Station. A train also comes from Moscow's Leningrad Station, taking 9½ hours.

Car & Motorbike Novgorod is on the Moscow-St Petersburg highway, and the road to Pskov and Riga is open.

Getting Around

Bus Nos 4, 6 and 19 pass near the Sadko and Volkhov hotels on their way to the railway station, and within half a km of the Intourist Hotel (Univermag stop). Bus Nos 4 and 20 go from ulitsa Chudintseva (ulitsa L Tolstogo) to the Beresta Palace Hotel. Bus No 7 goes to the airport from Sofiyskaya ploshchad (ploshchad Pobedy) near the kremlin. A taxi from the Hotel Intourist is under US$2 to the railway station and about US$4 to the airport.

STARAYA RUSSA
СТАРАЯ РУССА

This small town, south beyond Lake Ilmen, was a riverside trading post even in Varangian days. It's now best known as one of Dostoevsky's retreats, where he wrote *The Brothers Karamazov*, *The Possessed* and *The Adolescent*.

These days the author's house is open as a **museum** (☎ 2 14 77). It's a fine log cabin on the riverside and, unlike many other 'writer's house-museums' in Russia, it really feels as if someone lived and worked there. Russian-language guides lead you through in a zombie-like tone, pointing out every detail – family photos, books read at the time, identifying the people in photos on the walls of his study etc. They'll even tell you what the master liked to eat for breakfast, but we won't spoil the surprise by revealing it here. Admission for foreigners is US$1.20, while Russians pay a mere US$0.19. The museum is open Tuesday to Friday from 10 am to 6 pm, and Saturday and Sunday from 10 am to 5 pm. It's closed on Monday.

In town, you can also see the **Transfiguration Cathedral** (Spaso-Preobrazhensky sobor, 1198) and the 17th-century **Purification Church** (Tserkov Sretenia). There are plans afoot to restore the whole town centre, which was a model for many of the settings in *The Brothers Karamazov*, though no one can say where the money would come from for such a change. If you're hungry, the Kafe at ploshchad Revolyutsii is said to have tea and cookies, though it was closed when we visited in the middle of the day.

Getting There & Away

Daily ferries take two hours to cross the lake, except in summer, when you must go by car or bus. Buses leave Novgorod's bus station about every two hours (starting at 5.40 am), and take about two hours. The cost is US$1.90. From the Staraya Russa bus station, buses No 1, No 7 and No 114 (slow and erratic service) head to the centre.

Pskov Region
Псковская область

PSKOV
ПСКОВ
Population: 205,000

Pskov is as old as Russia but has always been Novgorod's 'little brother', even as the centre of an independent principality in the 14th and 15th centuries. It is, in fact, like a small, less glamorised Novgorod – built around a riverside kremlin with a beautiful cathedral inside, and bursting with churches designed by its own schools of architects and icon-painters.

Pskov has many of the same kind of sights as Novgorod, and so those pushed for time might feel that it's unnecessary to visit both. However, it's a worthy alternative on the way from St Petersburg to Tallinn or Riga, and has surprisingly few tourists.

As a border town (30 km from Estonia), Pskov's history is saturated with 700 years of war for control of the Baltic coast. The German Teutonic knights captured it in 1240, but Alexandr Nevsky routed them two years later in a famous battle on the ice of Lake Peipus (Chudskoe ozero to Russians). The Poles laid siege to it in the 16th century and the Swedes wrecked it the following century. Peter the Great used it as a base for his drive to the sea, and the Red Army fought its first serious battle with Nazi troops nearby.

This is also Pushkin country. The poet's grave and Mikhailovskoe, his family's estate, are a two-hour drive away.

Orientation & Information

The Rizhskaya Hotel is three long blocks west of the Velikaya River, while almost everything else is on the east side. The town's axis is Oktyabrsky prospekt, ending at Oktyabrskaya ploshchad.

VAO Intourist is in Room 211 of the Rizhskaya. The main post office and central department store are on Oktyabrskaya ploshchad and the telephone and telegraph office is two blocks up Oktyabrsky prospekt. The biggest bookshop is about half a km west of the Hotel Rizhskaya. Change money at the Sberbank at Rizhsky prospekt 29, or across the street at the flashier Partner Bank, Rizhsky prospekt 40b, window 10. Staff at the exchange office in the Hotel Rizhskaya on the 2nd floor are rude and surly, but they do say that they offer Visa cash advances.

The telephone code is 81122.

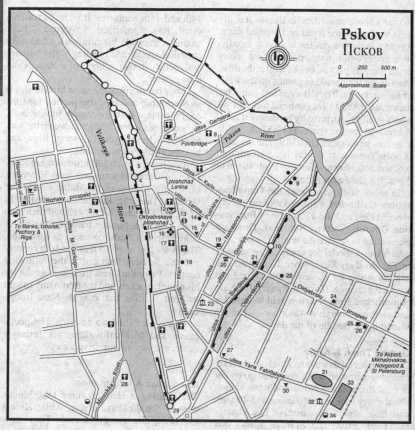

Pskov
Псков

0   250   500 m

Approximate Scale

Old City

Pskov's walls formerly had four layers. The kremlin or *krom* was the religious and ceremonial centre. Its stone walls and the southern annexe, Dovmont Town (Dovmontov gorod), date from the 13th century. The Central Town (Sredny gorod), around ulitsa Pushkina, was the commercial centre, though little remains of it or its 14th-century walls. The walls and towers of the Outer Town (Okolny gorod, 15th to 16th centuries) can still be seen along ulitsa Sverdlova, the Velikaya River embankment and across the tributary Pskova River.

The Kremlin & Dovmont Town In Dovmont Town (named after an early prince) the foundations of a dozen 12th to 15th-century churches are scattered around like discarded shoes. Through a passage is the kremlin, where the *veche* (citizens' assembly) elected its princes and sent them off to war, and Trinity Cathedral where many of the princes are buried. Some of the kremlin's towers and galleries are open. You can climb to the top of Vasilevskaya Tower, by the embankment outside Dovmont Town.

Trinity Cathedral The Trinity Cathedral

PLACES TO STAY

1 Hotel Rizhskaya
Гостиница Рижская
3 Krom Hotel
Гостиница Кром
22 Hotel Oktyabrskaya
Гостиница Октябрьская

PLACES TO EAT

2 Kuorio Restaurant
Ресторан Куорио
7 Cafés
Кафе
15 Kafe Cheburechnaya
Кафе Чебуречная
25 Globus Café
Кафе Глобус
27 Restaurant Gera
Ресторан Гера
30 Market and Restaurant
Рынок и Ресторан

OTHER

4 Vasilevskaya Tower
Васильевская башня

5 Dovmont Town
Довмонтов город
6 Kremlin & Trinity
Cathedral
Кремль и Троицкий собор
8 Epiphany Church
Церковь Богоявленская
9 Merchant Houses
Дома торговцев
10 Petrovskaya Tower
Петровская башня
11 River Station
Речной вокзал
12 Post Office
Почтамт
13 Bank
Банк
14 Moto Shoe Repair
Мото
16 Department Store
ЦУМ
17 Church of St Nicholas-
on-Usokha
Церковь Николы-на-
Усохе
18 Merchant Houses
Дома торговцев
19 Bakery/Pizzeria
Булочная/Пицерия

20 Telephone &
Telegraph Office
Телефон и телеграф
21 Coca Cola Kiosk
Кока Кола Киоск
23 Pogankin Palaces &
Museum
Поганкина палаты и
музей
24 Sewing Supplies
26 Technical Book shop
Политехнические
книги
28 Mirozhsky Monastery
Мирожский
монастырь
29 Pokrovskaya Tower
Покровская башня
31 Stadion Lokomotiv
Стадион локомотив
32 Railway Museum
Железнодорожный
музей
33 Railway Station
Железнодорожный
вокзал
34 Bus Station
Автовокзал

(Troitsky sobor, 1699) is the best reason to visit Pskov. The gilded centre dome, as high as a 28-storey building, can be seen from 30 km away on a clear day. It's a working church and the daily morning and evening services are like a medieval scene – supplicants outside, black-robed, leather-booted acolytes at the door, chanting priests in heavy robes, and hymns from the gallery. All of this occurs beneath 17th-century frescoes and a seven-tiered iconostasis. Visitors are welcome (modestly dressed); there's no charge but donations are appreciated.

Mirozhsky Monastery
The attraction here is the UNESCO-protected Cathedral of the Transfiguration of the Saviour (Spaso-Preobrazhensky sobor) with its striking 12th-century Greek frescoes, which mark the earliest appearance of the grand, sombre 'Pskov style'. The cathedral

has been under restoration since the 1960s. It's open daily, except Mondays and in damp weather, from noon to 6 pm (in 1½ hour slots to keep the humidity down). It's across the Velikaya River; bus No 2 from near the Hotel Rizhskaya runs nearby.

Pogankin Palaces & Museum
The Pogankin Palaces (Pogankiny palaty) aren't palaces (though the walls are two metres thick) but the house and treasury of a very rich 17th-century merchant. They now house the Pskov History & Art Museum.

Skip Soviet history in the new wing. In the courtyard, past an art gallery and silverwork exhibit, the main house features the history of ancient Pskov, with icons, icon-maps and the Sword of Dovmont that passed from prince to prince. Upstairs are photos and furnishings of 19th to 20th-century peasant life. Note the house's massive, tiled stove-heaters. It's open daily, except Monday and the last Tuesday of the month, from noon to 7 pm. Entry is through the new wing on Komsomolsky pereulok.

More modest merchant houses include several at, and behind, ulitsa Sovietskaya 52, and at ulitsa Gogolya 42 and 43.

Churches

There are dozens of churches, of which two appealing ones are the Church of St Nicholas-on-Usokha (Tserkov Nikoly-na-Usokhe), on the west side of ulitsa Sovietskaya, near the main square (open from 11 am to 2 pm and from 4 to 7 pm, and closed Monday), and the visibly crumbling Epiphany Church (Tserkov Bogoyavlenskaya, 1495), with its big Pskov-style belfry, across the Pskova footbridge.

Places to Stay

The Stalinesque *Hotel Oktyabrskaya* (☎ 2 55 93) is conveniently located between the centre and the railway station, at Oktyabrsky prospekt 36. It's also the cheapest place in town, with singles/doubles for US$18/30. The bland but quiet *Hotel Rizhskaya* (☎ 6 22 23), west of the Velikaya River at Rizhsky prospekt 25, has decent rooms, more friendly staff and more light. Their cute little rooms (all with TV and phone) are US$20.50/34. The *Krom* hotel, under (seemingly) perpetual construction on the river bank, should (according to VAO Intourist) be open in summer 1995.

But there's a catch for all these hotels; be aware that the whole city has hot water problems.

Places to Eat

The main farmers' *market* is at ulitsa Karla Marxa and ulitsa Pushkina, with small *markets* across the road west of the Hotel Rizhskaya

The most cheerful place in town is the cooperative Georgian *Kafe Cheburechnaya*, which serves greasy *chebureki* (deep-fried meat dumplings), shashlyk, salad and Turkish coffee. It's at Oktyabrsky prospekt 10; entrance is around the back. The *bakery*

opposite the telephone/telegraph office has good bread and Doka pizza for US$1.70.

The *Riga restaurant* in the Hotel Rizhskaya has good food but small helpings. Locals prefer the *Kuorio*, a Finnish café, one block east of the hotel, and the *Novgorod*, 1.5 km further west, just off Rizhsky prospekt. The *Avrora* at the Hotel Oktyabrskaya serves up a darn good shashlyk for US$2.25, which includes the toughs at the surrounding tables at no extra charge!

Things To Buy

Shoe Repair If your shoes have had it, head to Moto Shoe Repair, at ulitsa Pushkina 4. They've got Western machines and service standards for resoles, repairs etc.

Getting There & Away

Air Pskov's small airport has daily flights from St Petersburg (US$51) and Moscow (Bykovo) (US$89) and several per week from Kiev's Borispil and Zhulyany airports (US$103). The Pskov airport code is PKV.

Bus & Train There are no easy connections to Novgorod by train, but by bus it's much easier from the central bus station; there are at least two a day. The bus station, near the railway station, is handy for Izborsk (US$1.50) and Pechory (US$2). St Petersburg (Warsaw Station) is 4½ hours away by fast train; there are several trains a day. One train goes to Tallinn at 4.58 am (eight hours) and two a day go to Moscow (12 hours). There's a daily train to Riga. While waiting for your train, you can pop in to the tiny railway museum across the street.

Car & Motorbike The roads to Vitsebsk (37 km), St Petersburg (265 km), Novgorod (200 km), Riga (280 km) and Tallinn (370 km) are open to foreign drivers.

Getting Around

From the airport, bus No 1 goes to the Hotel Oktyabrskaya. For the Hotel Rizhskaya a taxi (about US$3) is simplest; otherwise take bus No 10 or 12 from the airport to the railway station, then bus No 17 from there to the hotel (Tipografia stop).

AROUND PSKOV
ОКОЛО ПСКОВА

Izborsk
Изборск

On a ridge with huge views over the countryside, Izborsk was once the equal of Pskov. Now it's a sleepy village by the ruins of a fortress as old as Pskov's. Inside the ruins is the 14th-century **Church of St Nicholas** – the parish church – and a stone tower older than the walls. Outside is the 17th-century **Church of St Sergius**, which has a little exhibit on local archaeology; some pieces date from the 8th century.

Getting There & Away It's 32 km from Pskov to Izborsk on the Riga road. VAO Intourist's overpriced all-day excursion to here and to Pechory Monastery is US$80 for up to three people. Remember that the Novy Izborsk Railway Station is nowhere near Izborsk!

Mikhailovskoe
Михайловское

The family house of Russia's most loved writer is open as part of the **Pushkin Museum Reserve**, a three-hour bus ride from Pskov.

Alexander Pushkin

Pushkin spent many productive years at Mikhailovskoe, his family's estate near the settlement of Pushkinsky Gory (Pushkin Hills), 130 km south of Pskov. The family first came to the area in the late 1700s, when Pushkin's great-grandfather Abram Hannibal was given the land by Empress Elizabeth. The family house was destroyed during WW II and has since been rebuilt.

The 20-hectare park is open daily, except Monday and the last day of the month, from 9 am to 4.30 pm. Entry is about US$1, and excursions (Russian-language) are available for about US$2.50.

At Pushkinsky Gory, about 800 metres north of the bus stop, is the **Svyatogorsky Monastery**, where Pushkin was buried.

It's lovely countryside, and it can be seen as part of a day trip.

Getting There & Away VAO Intourist Pskov will take individuals on an excursion for US$132 per person, or you can do it yourself by catching a bus to Pushkinsky Gory from the Pskov bus station. There are several buses a day (US$1.50, three hours) – buses to Novosokolniki, Novorzhev and Loknya all stop at Pushkinsky Gory, four km from the Pushkin house.

From Pushkinsky Gory bus station, catch a bus heading to Mikhailovskoe, and get off at the Bugrovo stop. Walk north to the fork in the road, bear left (past the rock with Pushkin's face carved in it) and walk to the end of Yelovaya alleya, to the family house. There are only three buses a day between Pushkinsky Gory and Mikhailovskoe. The last one leaves Mikhailovskoe at 6 pm. The last bus back to Pskov from Pushkinsky Gory leaves at around 7 pm.

Pechory Monastery
Печоры Монастырь

Founded in 1473 in a ravine full of hermits' caves, this has been a working cloister ever since. With all the high ground outside it's an improbable stronghold, but several tsars fortified it and depended on it.

A path descends under the St Nicholas Church (1564) into a sea of colours and architectural styles, where about 70 monks still live. Taking photos of the buildings is OK but not of the monks. The central yellow church is really two buildings – at ground level is the original Assumption Cathedral, built into the caves, and upstairs is the 18th-century Baroque Intercession Church. Below the belfry on the left is the entrance to the caves, where some 10,000 bodies – monks, benefactors and others – are bricked up in vaults, with more dying to get in.

Before WW II, this area was in independent Estonia and one-third of the townspeople are Estonian-speakers. The caves and churches can be visited, but only in the mornings and you'll have to negotiate with the monks who usually charge about US$5 for a tour. Intourist Pskov will be more than pleased to take you there for US$89 per person. There are buses and trains to the area (Pechory is an hour west of Pskov on the Riga and Tallinn lines).

Kaliningrad Region
Калининградская область

A disconnected wedge of Russia too strategic to have been left in anyone else's hands, the 15,100 sq km of the Kaliningrad Region (population 900,000 plus an estimated 200,000 to 400,000 military personnel) lies severed from the rest of Russia, between Lithuania, Poland and the Baltic Sea. From the 13th century until 1945, Kaliningrad was German, part of the core territory of the Teutonic knights and their successors the dukes and kings of Prussia. Its capital, now named Kaliningrad, was the famous German city Königsberg.

After WW I, East Prussia (the northern half of which the Kaliningrad Region approximates) was separated from the rest of Germany. Hitler's desire to reunite it was one of the sparks that lit WW II. The three-month campaign by which the Red Army took it in 1945 was one of the fiercest of the war, with hundreds of thousands of casualties on both sides.

Virtually the entire German population of the Kaliningrad Region was evacuated or fled to Germany during WW II, and most of those who remained were shot or deported to Siberia after the war. They were replaced with people from various regions of the USSR. Recent years have seen a steady flow of Russian-Germans from the Volga region migrating to their former homeland.

Until 1990 the Kaliningrad Region was closed to outsiders. Now, despite the preponderance of military vehicles on the roads and numerous uniforms on the streets, it's open and hoping to establish itself as a free-trade zone. In 1993 the region declared itself a free port, with local companies exempt from import and export duty. Foreign investment is slowly filtering in and major Western companies, such as Fuji and Rank Xerox, are already represented. Commercial links with neighbouring Poland are also flourishing.

Tourism in the region is mainly confined to large parties of Germans, many of whom are here to visit ancestral lands. However, individual travel is possible and if the concrete horror of the Soviet city of Kaliningrad isn't to your taste then the surrounding countryside and the coast, with the two seaside resorts of Svetlogorsk and Zelenogradsk, are very attractive and full of haunting reminders of the region's opulent Prussian past. The countryside is low-lying and rolling with a lot of farmland and about 20% woodland. Many of the roads are lined with avenues of trees mostly planted during the German period.

Visas
Unless you're flying, to reach the Kaliningrad Region from anywhere else in Russia – or vice versa – will entail leaving Russia and crossing through the Baltic States and maybe Belarus too – all of which have their own visa requirements (see the European Russia Getting There & Away chapter). Visas for the Baltic States must be acquired beforehand (since November 1994 the three countries have stopped issuing them on the border)

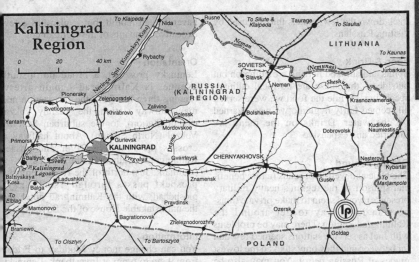

Kaliningrad
Region

0   20   40 km

To Klaipeda, Nida, Rusne, To Silute & Klaipeda, Taurage, To Siauliai, LITHUANIA, To Kaunas, Rybachy, Neman, SOVIETSK, Jurbarkas, Slavsk, (Nemunas), Pionersky, Zelenogradsk, Zalivino, RUSSIA (KALININGRAD REGION), Neman, Sheshupe, Krasnoznamensk, Svetlogorsk, Khrabrovo, Polessk, Bolshakovo, Dobrovolsk, Kudirkos-Naumiestis, Yantarny, Mordovskoe, Gurievsk, KALININGRAD, Primorsk, Nesterov, Baltiysk, Svetly, Pregolya, Gvardeysk, CHERNYAKHOVSK, Kybartai, Kaliningrad Lagoon, Gusev, To Marijampole, Baltiyskaya Kosa, Ladushkin, Znamensk, Balga, To Elblag, Pravdinsk, Ozersk, Mamonovo, Bagrationovsk, Zheleznodorozhny, Goldap, Braniewo, To Olsztyn, To Bartoszyce, POLAND

although citizens of some Western nations need only a valid passport to enter Estonia, Latvia or Lithuania.

Also, an overland trip between the Kaliningrad Region and anywhere else in Russia means you must be in possession of a double or multi-entry Russian visa because it involves crossing on to foreign territory before then re-entering the country. Kaliningrad should also be named on your Russian visa, otherwise you risk being turned back at the Kaliningrad border. Most hotels thoroughly scrutinise your visa.

Telephone

There are three basic types of phone call, each with a different procedure: local (within the town or city that you're in); long-distance (within the Kaliningrad Region, Lithuania, Latvia, Estonia or Russia); and international (to the rest of the world).

Local calls can be made from any telephone booth but the phones only accept special tokens, sold from post offices for US$0.15. Long-distance calls must be made from the special long-distance telephones found at telephone offices. Again, these phones are token-operated – one token being

good for about three minutes. The telephone office will have a list of the different telephone codes. International calls are also made from the telephone office: give the number you want at the desk, then sit and wait until your connection is made. After the call you will be billed for the time.

Books

If you can read German, try to get hold of the excellent guide *Königsberg Kaliningrad* by Henning Sietz (Edition Temmen, Bremen, 1992). Otherwise, the only thing available in English is a coffee-table album, *Leben Danach/Life After* (published in Finland, 1994), containing some highly evocative photos of the region taken between 1988 and 1992. However, you're likely to have more success finding the book in neighbouring Lithuania, or in Estonia or Finland, than you are in the Kaliningrad Region itself.

Accommodation

The accommodation scene in the Kaliningrad Region has developed specifically to the needs of the visiting Germans – or rather to their wallets: it's expensive. Those looking for something cheaper will have to track down the few hostels that are used by visiting Russians.

Food & Drink

Sprats and smoked herring are common but outside of that these are no local culinary specialities. While the food we were served all seemed fairly hygienic we were warned off the water. Drinks on the menu are imported and expensive.

Getting Around

The wide and well-kept roads (a rare beneficial spin-off of the region's heavy military presence) would seem to make private transport an ideal way to get around the Kaliningrad Region. There may be problems with fuel as service stations seemed few and far between and they only stocked the lowest grades of Russian petrol. You may also be inconvenienced on major roads by frequent military spot-checks, with under-sized soldiers in out-sized uniforms squinting at you along the barrel of their assault rifles. Make sure you have all your documents (vehicle registration, driving licence, passport, visa) in order and to hand, and try not to act too nervously.

KALININGRAD
КАЛИНИНГРАД
Population: 400,000

Founded as a Teutonic order fort in 1255, Königsberg joined the Hanseatic League in 1340 and from 1457 to 1618 was the residence of the Grand Masters of the Teutonic order and their successors the dukes of Prussia. The first Prussian king was crowned here in 1701. The city was nearly flattened by British air raids in 1944 and the Red Army assault from April 6 to 9 1945. Many of the surviving Germans were sent to Siberia – the last 25,000 were deported to Germany in 1947-48. The city was renamed (after Mikhail Kalinin, one of Lenin's henchmen who also found favour with Stalin), rebuilt and re-peopled mostly by Russians. Today it has a lot of drab Soviet architecture and desolate empty spaces where cleared areas

haven't been rebuilt, but it also has a few evocative remnants of the German era.

Orientation

Leninsky prospekt, a broad north-south avenue, is Kaliningrad's main artery running three km from the bus station and main railway station, the Yuzhny Vokzal (South Station), to the suburban Severny Vokzal (North Station). About halfway it crosses the Pregolya River and passes Kaliningrad's cathedral, the town's major landmark. Just north of the river, Leninsky prospekt passes through Tsentralnaya ploshchad, with the Kaliningrad hotel and the unmistakable House of the Soviets.

Information

You can change money Monday to Friday from 9 am to 6 pm at Investbank, Leninsky prospekt 28, at another Investbank on ulitsa Ivannikova off ulitsa Chernyakhovskogo and at most hotels. The exchange bureau at the Hotel Kaliningrad is particularly useful and is open until 11 pm. The main post, telephone and telegraph office is in an out-of-the-way location at ulitsa Kosmonavta Leonova 22, about 700 metres north of prospekt Mira. There is another, more central telephone office at ulitsa Teatralnaya 13/19 and also a telephone and telegraph office beside the Yuzhny Vokzal. The Hotel Kaliningrad has an international telephone, fax and telex office.

The Kaliningrad city telephone code is 22 if you're dialling from within the Kaliningrad Region or 0112 from elsewhere.

Things to See

The outstanding German remnant is the red brick Gothic shell of the **Dom**, or cathedral, founded in 1333. The **Tomb of Immanuel Kant**, the 18th-century philosopher who was born in, studied and taught in Königsberg, is on the outer north side. The fine but run-down blue Renaissance-style building just across the river to the south of the cathedral is the old **Stock Exchange** built in the 1870s, now a 'Sailors' Culture Palace', housing, amongst other things, a café and popular disco.

At the east end of wide Tsentralnaya ploshchad, on the site of the 1255 castle (whose ruins were dynamited in 1965), stands the unfinished upright H-shaped **House of the Soviets** (Dom Sovietov), one of the ugliest creations of Soviet architecture (no mean achievement). Just north of Tsentralnaya ploshchad, on ulitsa Universitetskaya near the university, is the much visited **Bunker Museum** (Muzey Blindazh) which was the German command post in 1945 (it's open daily from 10 am to 5.30 pm).

North of the House of Soviets stretches the **Lower Pond** (Prud Nizhny), in German times the Schlossteich, a favourite recreation and relaxation spot. Kaliningrad's **History & Art Museum** is housed in a reconstructed 1912 concert hall on the east bank. It's open daily, except Monday, from 11 am to 7 pm. Ulitsa Chernyakhovskogo separates the pond's north end from the larger **Upper Pond** (Prud Verkhny). On the south-east corner of Prud Verkhny is the fat, red-brick **Dohna Tower** (Bashnya Dona), a bastion of the city's old defensive ring which is now the **Amber Museum**. It's open daily except Mondays from 10 am to 6 pm. There is also the **Rossgarten Gate** which is one of the original German city gates. Another bastion, now in Soviet military use, is the rotund **Wrangel Tower**, which stands near the south-west corner of the pond. From here ulitsa Profesora Baranova heads west to ploshchad Pobedy, passing the **central market** on ulitsa Chernyakhovskogo just to the south.

On **Ploshchad Pobedy** (formerly Hansaplatz) is the 1930 **Kaliningrad North Station** (Severny Vokzal) and the 1923 **city hall**. About 300 metres west along prospekt Mira is the 1927 **Kaliningrad Drama Theatre**, restored in 1980, and then about a half-km further, just before the entrance to **Kalinin Park** (or PKiO Kalinina, and formerly known as the Luisenwahl, a favourite Königsberg park), is the splendid **Cosmonaut Monument**, a real gem of Soviet iconography.

Places to Stay

The accommodation choices in Kaliningrad are poor. Most tour groups stay in the town's principal hotel, the *Hotel Kaliningrad* (☎ 46 94 40), handily placed on Tsentralnaya ploshchad at Leninsky prospekt 81. It's a standard 1970s Soviet hotel which, despite having had a half-hearted stab at some renovation, is still overpricing its singles/doubles at US$30/45. The large *Hotel Moskva* (☎ 27 20 89) at prospekt Mira 19, about 800 metres west of ploshchad Pobedy, has shabby but adequately clean rooms at a variety of prices: singles from US$7 to US$14; doubles from US$9 to US$18. With so few cheap options in town this place is often full, so try to book in advance if possible.

There is another cheapish option a little out of the centre in the *Hotel Patriot* (☎ 27 50 23), three km north of the city at ulitsa Ozernaya 25A: take Tram Nos 6 or 10 north up ulitsa Gorkogo from the central market. Ozernaya is the first street on the right after ulitsa Gorkogo crosses a bridge over the railway. Walk 200-300 metres along ulitsa Ozernaya then turn into the side road beside No 25 on the north side. Keep going through a number of unpromising yards until you see the newish nine-storey slab of the Patriot ahead.

Among the more expensive options are the three resting cruise ships moored to the north bank of the Pregolya, just west of the Leninsky prospekt bridge. Of the three the *Hotelschiff Hansa* (☎ and fax 43 38 06) is the cleanest and most comfortable and all the cabins have their own private shower and toilet. It's also the most expensive with rooms at US$58/105. The Hansa takes credit cards. The second in line is the *Hotelschiff Baltcompany* (☎ and fax 46 16 04), which is much less swank but its rooms are cheaper at US$50/67. Four hundred metres further is the *Hotelschiff Baltpergo* (☎ 47 15 22), which borders on the seedy. Toilets and showers are shared between a whole corridor. Rooms are US$25/42.

Places to Eat

The best food and the most satisfying menu

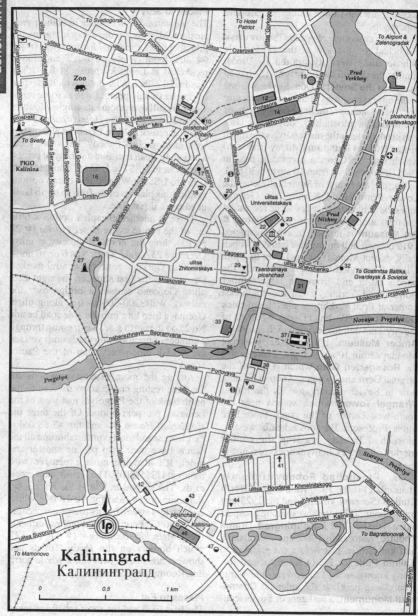

To Svetlogorsk
To Hotel Patriot
To Airport & Zelenogradsk

ulitsa Kosmonavta
Leonova
ulitsa Chaykovskogo
ulitsa Zooopicheskaya
Kirova
ulitsa Sovetsky prospekt
ulitsa Gorkogo
Proletarskaya
ulitsa Ozerova

Prud Verkhny

13 15

Zoo

prospekt Mira
12 Professora
Baranova
14
ploshchad Vasilevskogo

prospekt 2
ulitsa Grekova
ulitsa Serzhanta Koloskova
8 9
ploshchad Pobedy
ulitsa Chernyakhovskogo
10
ulitsa 21

PKiO Kalinina

ulitsa Svobodnaya
ulitsa Gostinaya
3 4 5
6
7
11
ulitsa ulitsa Ivanikova

16

ulitsa Dmitry
Odesskaya
17
Leninsky
19
ulitsa Universitetskaya

Prud Nizhny
25

Gvardeysky prospekt
ulitsa Generala Galitskogo
Teatralnaya
18
prospekt
20
22
23
24

ulitsa Shevchenko
Klinicheskaya
Amalia
ulitsa 9-go

26
27
ulitsa Vagnera
28
30
29
32

ulitsa Zhitomirskaya
Tsentralnaya ploshchad
31

Moskovsky prospekt
Moskovsky prospekt

33
Novaya Pregolya

naberezhnaya Bagramyana
37

34 35 36

Pregolya
ulitsa Portovaya
38
39 40

Oktyabrskaya

ulitsa Polotskaya
Zheleznodorozhnaya
Staraya Pregolya

Leninsky prospekt
ulitsa Bagrationa
41

42
43
ulitsa Bogdana Khmelnitskogo
44
ulitsa Olshtynskaya
45
Dzerzhinskogo

To Mamonovo
ploshchad Kalinina
46
prospekt Kalinina
To Bagrationovsk

47

alleya Smelykh

Kaliningrad
Калининград

0   0.5   1 km

To Gostinitsa Baltika, Gvardeysk & Sovietsk
To Svetly
ulitsa Suvorova

PLACES TO STAY

3 Hotel Moskva
Гостиница Москва
30 Hotel Kaliningrad
Гостиница Калининград
34 Hotel Baltinpergo
Гостиница Балтинперго
35 Hotelschiff Baltcompany
Гостиница Балтийской компании
36 Hotel Hansa
Гостиница Ханса

PLACES TO EAT

4 Kafe Express
Кафе Экспресс
7 Kafe Teatralnaya
Кафе Театральная
11 Restoran Chayka
Ресторан Чайка
20 Italian Café
Итальянское Кафе
29 Restoran Belarus
Ресторан Беларусь
33 Dvorets Sporta Yunost
Дворец спорта Юность
38 Restoran Brigantina
Ресторан Бригантина
40 Pinguin Bistro
Бистро Пингвин
44 Restoran Olshtyn
Ресторан Олштин

OTHER

1 Post, Telephone & Telegraph Office
Почта, телефон, телеграф
2 Cosmonaut Monument
Памятник Космонавтам
5 Kaliningrad Drama Theatre
Калининградский драматический театр
6 Schiller Statue
Памятник Шиллеру
8 Severny Vokzal (North Station)
Северный вокзал
9 Old North Station Building
Здание старого Северного вокзала
10 Lenin Statue
Памятник Ленину
12 Former Technology House
Бывший Дом Технологии
13 Wrangel Tower
Башня Врангеля

14 Central Market
Центральный рынок
15 Amber Museum, Dohna Tower &
Rossgarten Gate
Янтарный музей, башня Дохна
и ворота розария
16 Baltika Stadium
Стадион Балтика
17 Mother Russia Statue
Памятник России-матери
18 Telephone Office
Телефонная станция
19 Investbank
Инвестбанк
21 Hospital
Госпиталь
22 University
Университет
23 Kant Statue
Памятник Канту
24 Bunker Museum
Музей бункер
25 History & Art Museum
Исторический и художественный
музей
26 Astronomers' Bastion
Бастион Астрономов
27 11th Guards Army Monument
Памятник 11-ой армейской
гвардии
28 Investbank
Инвестбанк
31 House of Soviets
Дом Советов
32 Palace of Weddings
Дворец Бракосочетания
37 Cathedral
Собор
38 Former Stock Exchange
Бывшее Здание Биржы
39 Amberkönigbank
Амберкенингбанк
41 Church
Церковь
42 Brandenburg Gate
Бранденбургские Ворота
43 Aeroflot
Аэрофлот
45 Friedland Gate
Фриндландские Ворота
46 Yuzhny Vokzal (South Station)
Южный вокзал
47 Bus Station
Автовокзал

is to be found at the *restaurant* at the Hotels-chiff Hansa (☎ 43 37 37). However, this doesn't come cheap: soups are around the US$3 mark and main dishes are from US$10 to US$12. Right in front of the Hansa is the large *Dvorets Sporta Yunost* (Youth Sports Palace) which has a café popular with locals. The food is nothing spectacular but it's quite cheap and reasonably substantial.

Two restaurants reckoned among the best in town (but not recommended for those who don't appreciate loud dance music with their food) are the *Restoran Olshtyn* at ulitsa Olshtynskaya 1, near the Yuzhny Vokzal, and the *Restoran Brigantina* in the old stock exchange, now the Sailors' Culture Palace at Leninsky prospekt 83. Quieter, and conveniently central, is the *Restoran Belarus* at ulitsa Zhitomirskaya 14, facing the west side of Tsentralnaya ploshchad.

A little further north, and the most Western in appearance of all Kaliningrad's restaurants, is the *Italian Café* (☎ 43 07 53) at Leninsky prospekt 27-31. As the name might suggest, the menu is heavy on pizza (US$3) and pasta (from US$1.80 to US$4), but there are also meals like omelettes for US$2 and grilled chicken for US$3.50. Close by is the *Kafe Teatralnaya* at ulitsa Teatralnaya 38, which branches west off Leninsky prospekt. It's a large, typically Russian dining room – right down to the MTV – serving the standard stroganoff, cutlets and shashlyk for around US$2. A little further along, on prospekt Mira on the corner of ulitsa Grekova, the *Kafe Express* lives up to its name with quick counter service for snacks such as *buterbrody* (open sandwiches), cakes, juice and coffee. Exactly the same sort of fare, plus hot dogs and ice cream, is offered at the *Pinguin*, at Leninsky prospekt 95, just south of the bridge, which is open from 10 am to 10 pm.

Getting There & Away

Air The only scheduled flights at the time of writing were to/from the CIS with Aeroflot. Aeroflot's main office (☎ 44 66 66 or ☎ 44 66 57) is on the north side of ploshchad Kalinina. Scheduled flights to/from Poland, Denmark and Germany (with Lufthansa) may also be up and running by now.

Bus The bus station is on ploshchad Kalinina at the southern end of Leninsky prospekt.

There are cheap daily buses from Kaliningrad to Vilnius, the capital of Lithuania, from where it's possible to connect with services to Warsaw, Minsk or north to Latvia and Estonia. There is also a direct overnight service to/from Tallinn, the Estonian capital, a city which has excellent rail links with St Petersburg and Moscow; this bus goes via Riga.

There are a number of bus services between north-eastern Poland and Kaliningrad, operated jointly by König Auto (☎ 43 04 80) of Kaliningrad and various Polish companies. The starting points in Poland include Olsztyn, Białystok, Elblag and Gdańsk.

Buses also serve all towns in the Kaliningrad Region and are a comfortable way of getting around. Tickets, however, should be bought as far in advance as possible, especially during the summer months when the buses become full very quickly.

Train Kaliningrad has two railway stations: Severny vokzal (North Station) just off ploshchad Pobedy; and Yuzhny vokzal (South Station). All long-distance and many of the local trains go from Yuzhny vokzal, passing through, but not always stopping at, Severny vokzal.

From the west, Kaliningrad can be reached by direct train from Berlin via Gdańsk and also from Gdynia via Gdańsk and Braniewo (Branevo) in north-east Poland. Between Braniewo and Warsaw, a trip of five or six hours, you need to change trains at Olsztyn. From the east, there are numerous daily trains from St Petersburg or Moscow going via either Kaunas or Vilnius in Lithuania.

There are frequent services to almost all towns in the Kaliningrad Region. Trains have the advantage over the buses, with their limited seating, because you're always sure to find a seat on one. Even so the trains running out to the coast, particularly to Zelenogradsk and Svetlogorsk, do become crowded and if you're slow boarding you can end up standing, nose wedged in somebody's armpit for the whole journey.

Car & Motorbike At present, the vehicle ferry from Germany (see following), if it's still running, offers motorists the only way in from the south as the road borders are open only to buses. It has been announced that some time in 1995 a new road link between Kaliningrad and Goldap in Poland will open, but don't hold your breath: for several years now work has been under way on the old 'Reichsbahn' connecting Berlin and Kaliningrad but there are still no signs of it opening. The Lithuanian border is more promising. The road through Sovietsk is the most well-used route but a much more scenic alternative is to drive via the Lithuanian town of Klaipėda and down the long Kurshskaya kosa sandspit (known as Kuršiu nerija or Neringa to Lithuanians).

See Car & Motorbike in the Kaliningrad Region section for more on driving.

Sea The uncertainty over Kaliningrad's future means that shipping services have a habit of being short-lived. There should at least be a service from Gdańsk, possibly still with the Alexandr Line (contact Biuro Turystyki Cliff Tour (☎ (058) 56 35 13; fax (058) 53 49 32) in Gdańsk for further information), whose ferry did sail three times a week each way during summer and docked at Svetly, 25 km west of the city of Kaliningrad. The trip takes around five hours and used to cost US$25 one way. Buses run four or five times an hour between Svetly and Kaliningrad bus station. There may also be a summer hydrofoil service operating on the same route (contact Baltic Foils (☎ (058) 47 97 35) in Gdańsk for further information). A weekly ferry, the *Mercuri-I*, from Kiel in northern Germany, entered service in 1992 and may still be running; contact Schneider Reisen (☎ (040) 380 20 60) in Hamburg or Baltisches Reisebüro (☎ (089) 59 36 53; fax (089) 52 59 13) in Munich for current details.

Getting Around
Local Transport Trams, trolleybuses and buses cover the city thoroughly, though they can get uncomfortably crowded. The usual ticket-punching system is used. Tickets are sold at kiosks around town and also by some drivers. Tram Nos 2 and 3 are particularly useful going from ploshchad Kalinina (the square before the Yuzhny Vokzal and bus station) along Leninsky prospekt to ploshchad Pobedy, stopping at the Hotel Kaliningrad on the way.

Taxis Taxis are common and cheap. Private drivers are also often prepared to act as makeshift taxis if they're going in your general direction. Cars prepared to do this have a white sticker in their window giving the price per km – US$0.05 at the time of writing.

SVETLOGORSK
СВЕТЛОГОРСК
Svetlogorsk (formerly the German Rauschen) is a pleasant and green coastal town, 35 km north-west of the city of Kaliningrad. The narrow beach is backed by high, steep sandy slopes and the small town is dotted with wooden houses, some of which were used in the Soviet era as sanatoriums for workers and officials. Svetlogorsk is an easy day visit from Kaliningrad but conversely could also be a pleasant base from which to make forays to the city.

Orientation & Information
Svetlogorsk is slightly confusing in that it has two railway stations: Svetlogorsk I and Svetlogorsk II. Svetlogorsk II, which is where the trains terminate (with the exception of the last couple, late in the evening), is the station you should get off at.

Immediately south of the station, ulitsa Lenina runs roughly from east to west, parallel to the tracks. The town's market, post office and telephone and telegraph office are east of the station, 450 metres along ulitsa

Lenina then south down ulitsa Oktyabr-skaya. There is also a small *univermag* (department store) at the end of ulitsa Oktyabrskaya.

Svetlogorsk's telephone code is 2533.

Things to See & Do

The **beach** lies 200 metres north of the Svetlogorsk II Station and can be reached by the neighbouring chair lift (a ride costs US$0.25). On ulitsa Oktyabrskaya is the 25-metre **water tower** and the curious red-tile-domed Jugendstil (the German version of Art Nouveau) **bathhouse**. About 200 metres east along ulitsa Lenina from the ulitsa Oktyabrskaya corner, is another small crossroad where a left (north) turn takes you to the main steps down to the beach. Near the bottom of these steps is a very large, colourful **sundial**.

Places to Stay

The best bet is the *Hotel Volna* (☎ 3005) at Kaliningradsky prospekt 68a. It's a large, fairly drab Soviet block but it's lent some appeal by its grassy and wooded surrounds. The adequate singles/doubles come with private bathroom and cost US$20/28. To get there from Svetlogorsk II Station, go east along ulitsa Lenina (that's left if your back is to the tracks) and take ulitsa Karla Marxa, the first street on your right. At the end of ulitsa Karla Marxa, turn right along Kaliningradsky prospekt and the hotel should be about 700 metres on your left, set back off the road a little beside a huge zig-gurat-style brick building.

There's also a small, very basic-looking *Gostinitsa* (Hotel) at the other end of Kaliningradsky prospekt, just past the east end of the lake, and we heard of another hotel, the *Hotel Baltika*, said to be not far from the beach, which has rooms with private shower and toilet.

Getting There & Away

There are about 20 to 25 trains a day from Kaliningrad to Svetlogorsk. Direct trains take about one hour; those going via Zelenogradsk take about 1½ hours.

ZELENOGRADSK
ЗЕЛЕНОГРАДСК

Zelenogradsk (formerly the German Kranz), 30 km north of Kaliningrad, is the most popular resort of the region and has been since the 19th century. On hot summer days thousands of people arrive from Kaliningrad to sunbathe on the long, sandy, wide beach. However, unlike neighbouring Svetlogorsk, Zelenogradsk has lost much of the charm it would have had in the German era.

Orientation & Information

The railway and bus stations are side by side on the south side of ulitsa Lenina, the main east-west street running through town. To reach the beach cross ulitsa Lenina and take any street heading north. The beach is about 200 metres ahead. The telephone and tele-graph office is 200 metres east of the station along ulitsa Lenina, where it widens into a square of sorts, with the post office about 100 metres down the street off to the south. A further 400 metres east along ulitsa Lenina is Blick, by far the best handicraft shop we found in the Kaliningrad Region, where you can change money.

Things to See & Do

Other than the beach there really isn't too much in Zelenogradsk, though there's a nice, kitsch silver-painted **statue** of Lenin in front of the sanatorium on ulitsa Lenina.

Getting There & Away

About 20 trains a day run from Kaliningrad to Zelenogradsk (a trip of 30 to 40 minutes), many of them continuing on to Svetlogorsk. There are also about 12 buses a day to/from Kaliningrad, plus six daily to/from the Lith-uanian village of Smiltynė at the northern tip of the Kurshskaya kosa sandspit, opposite Klaipėda. If your onward plans include a trip to Lithuania then this coastal route is an extremely attractive option rather than going back inland and via Sovietsk.

Northern European Russia
Европейская Россия, северная часть

Northern European Russia – from the Gulf of Finland to the Arctic Barents Sea and from Finland to the Ural Mountains – is a fabric of pine and birch forest, marshes, tens of thousands of lakes and, in the far north, tundra and dwarf forests. It's a potential paradise for hikers, boaters, campers and skiers, boasting gigantic areas of pristine wilderness. This, coupled with its recent accessibility, makes it one of the world's most attractive outdoor sporting destinations. And it's cheap.

The White Sea, cutting in deeply from the Barents, defines the geography of the far north. Sandwiched between it and Finland is Russia's Karelian Republic. Its capital, Petrozavodsk, is the base for seeing the extraordinary wooden buildings of Kizhi Island. Beyond the White Sea on the Arctic-facing Kola Peninsula – 'Russian Lappland' – is the port of Murmansk, the world's largest city inside the Arctic Circle. Farther east, the newly discovered oil and gold reserves of the Arkhangelsk Region has lent it a gold-rush atmosphere, as thousands of prospectors and dozens of multinational conglomerates swarm to cash in.

In the central north, from the Vologda Region towards Arkhangelsk and Kola, lie dozens of monasteries and churches, dating from before the reign of Ivan the Terrible. Some of these, such as those on the Solovetsky Islands in the White Sea, were converted under the Soviets to Gulags, and almost all are possible to visit today.

HISTORY

Early Russian incursions into the region came from Novgorod (see Western European Russia). By the 12th century, Novgorod was a European political and commercial centre that began expanding aggressively up Karelia's rivers and lakes to the White Sea. Today most of the north's permanent Russians are descendants of Novgorodian merchants, adventurers, hunters and fishers, and are known as Pomory (the phrase *'po more'* means 'up to the sea').

The Swedes, who held sway in most of present-day north-western Russia, up to and including the Kola Peninsula, began to feel the effects of the Pomory expansion. The friction, at first economic, became ostensibly religious as Swedish crusaders tried to push back the Orthodox 'heathens'. Novgorod's Prince Alexandr Nevsky is considered a Russian hero for thrashing both the Swedish and Teutonic crusaders in the 1240s, putting an end to Western Christian intentions in Russia.

The Norwegians were more easily persuaded to give up claims to the Kola Peninsula. For several centuries Russians, Norwegians, Finns and Swedes exploited fish, fur and the indigenous Lapp reindeer-herders in the peninsula.

The first Western European visitors to the region were Dutch and English explorers who crashed into the Arctic island of Novaya Zemlya in the 16th century.

During the Time of Troubles (1606-13), a period of domestic anarchy and foreign invasions, Sweden again took over a swathe of territory from the Baltic to the White Sea.

Determined to defeat the Swedes and

Northern European
Russia
Европейская Россия
северная часть

reach the Baltic, Peter the Great made an alliance with Poland and Denmark, and forced his way to the Gulf of Finland, pausing only to lay the foundations of St Petersburg. With his new navy, he won the Great Northern War (1700-21), winning everything back from Sweden, plus Vyborg and the Baltic coastline down to Riga. The Swedes were pushed back even further, and in 1809 they forfeited Finland.

The north rose to prominence again as a WW I supply route. An Arctic port was built at Murmansk and a rail line laid down to Petrozavodsk and St Petersburg. After the October Revolution, the Allies occupied Murmansk and Arkhangelsk for two years, advancing south almost to Petrozavodsk.

Stalin invaded Finland and the Baltic states in 1939-40, confident from his secret pact with Hitler that they were 'his'. Finland, having achieved independence after the revolution, fought the Red Army to a standstill but had to give up its entire Arctic coastline and Vyborg. Hoping to retrieve this territory, Finland allied itself with Germany during WW II, and Hitler launched attacks along the entire Soviet-Finnish border. Murmansk again became a supply port, a lifeline from the allies to Russia's defenders, and was later bombed to rubble for its importance.

CLIMATE

The entire region has a continental climate. In the far north summers are cool and short, and winters snowy but dry. Petrozavodsk is about 5°C cooler than St Petersburg in any season, while Murmansk and Arkhangelsk can be decidedly winter-like as early as the first week in September. Though Kola Peninsula winters are bitter, the Gulf Stream makes the weather in Murmansk changeable, but, on average, less extreme than St Petersburg. See Appendix III for climate charts.

PEOPLE

About half the country's 140,000 Karelians, cousins of the Finns, are concentrated in the Karelia Republic along the Finnish border. The other large indigenous group in the region are the 500,000 or so Komi, who mainly live in their eponymous autonomous republic east of the White Sea. Its capital is Syktyvkar (see the aside on Syktyvkar later in this chapter). Only about 1500 of the once numerous Saami (Lapp) reindeer-herders remain in the far north; most other Lapps are in northern Scandinavia.

ACCOMMODATION

In addition to the standard hotels, motels and camp sites in the north, there are also *turbazy* (tour bases), which are places to stay in remote areas that act as Russian holiday centres. Here you can arrange outdoor sport tours, such as boating, skiing, hiking or mountaineering, and set out on group treks for periods of five to 30 days. Equipment rental is usually available, and trained guides lead the groups. See individual sections for more information.

GETTING THERE & AWAY

Most international connections are through St Petersburg. There's air service daily to Petrozavodsk, Arkhangelsk and Murmansk from St Petersburg and Moscow. SAS and Finnair fly to the region, serving Petrozavodsk and Murmansk from Finland and Norway, respectively. There are overland routes to Murmansk from Norway, and to Petrozavodsk and Murmansk from Finland (see the Getting There & Away sections for those cities).

GETTING AROUND

If you're not driving, overnight trains are the way to go. In summer it's a beautiful journey across Karelia and the Kola Peninsula, with the track never far from a river bank or lake shore, endless forest and tundra stretching beyond and, Petrozavodsk aside, crystal-clear air.

Within regions, such as Karelia or the Kola Peninsula, long-distance buses provide convenient and inexpensive transport. Rubber rafting is a favourite sport in these areas; you'll see thousands of 'weekend sailors' crowding Petrozavodsk's railway station on Fridays and Sundays to partake in the activity. Foreigners can drive freely in the entire area, except in designated military zones, and for most stretches the St Petersburg-Murmansk highway is a fine road. Within regions, especially in the Kola Peninsula, a car can be quite convenient, though car break-ins are frequent in the big cities.

Karelia
Карелия

Karelia is a vast wilderness stretching from St Petersburg to the Arctic Circle – half is forest and much of the rest is water. Its 60,000 lakes include Ladoga and Onega lakes, the two largest in Europe.

The original Karelians are related to Finns, and western Karelia has at various times been part of Sweden, Finland and Russia. Tourism officials boast of 55 nationalities in the capital, Petrozavodsk, though 70% of the people who live here are Russian. Many are the offspring of prisoners and deportees sent by Stalin in 1931-33 to dig the White Sea Canal that links rivers and lakes into a domestic water route to the Arctic.

Karelia is a republic within Russia. Its main outputs are timber and minerals. Finnish, the closest thing outside Russian that the Karelians have to a national language, is commonly used along with Russian (though Karelian, a Finno-Ugric language, is spoken by some).

PETROZAVODSK
ПЕТРОЗАВОДСК
Population: 280,000
Tourists come here for one thing: to see the collection of old wooden buildings on Kizhi Island, 55 km north-east of the city across Lake Onega, and especially the 22-domed Church of the Transfiguration, the flower of Russian wooden architecture.

Petrozavodsk itself has a short, grim history. It was created in 1703 as an iron foundry and armaments plant for Peter the Great (its name means 'Peter's Factory'), and the town was subsequently used by both

the tsars and the Bolsheviks as a place of exile for St Petersburg's troublemakers. The city's main attractions are a respectable Fine Arts Museum, a lively and traditional Karelian music ensemble and its good-natured people.

Orientation & Information
The city straddles the Lososinka River where it enters Lake Onega (Onezhskoe ozero). Its axis, prospekt Marxa, runs all the way to the ferry terminal (vodnyy vokzal).

Intourist is at the Hotel Severnaya. The post, telephone and telegraph offices are on the corner of ulitsa Dzerzhinskogo and ulitsa Sverdlova. Change money at Intourist, or one of the dozens of banks all over town competing for your bucks: there is a Sberbank on the corner of prospekt Lenina and ulitsa Engelsa and another at ulitsa Kirova 5; and a Tekobank at ulitsa Kirova 22 (downstairs, next to the stolovaya) with another at prospekt Lenina 11. City maps in Russian are for sale at most bookshops (try Ex-Libris at prospekt Lenina 23 or Knigi at prospekt Marxa 14, which also has a good selection of pens, paper and postcards).

Kodak 1-Hour, at ulitsa Sverdlova 23, does print developing for US$0.70 per print, and they also sell film. There's a well-stocked pharmacy at prospekt Lenina 36, near the railway station, which is open Monday to Friday from 9 am to 8 pm, and Saturday and Sunday from 10 am to 5 pm.

Until the city can replace all the old ones, public telephones operate free of charge for local calls. The telephone code for Petrozavodsk is 814

Things to See & Do
Fine Arts Museum The Fine Arts Museum, prospekt Marxa 8, has a good collection of 15th to 17th-century Karelian icons and some 18th to 20th-century Russian paintings; it's open from 11 am to 6 pm and closed Monday. Admission for foreigners is US$1.60 (no student price); tours in Russian are US$9.50, and in English (☎ 7 40 03) by special arrangement only. This museum and the uninspiring Classical 'crescent' of ploshchad Lenina are the oldest buildings in town.

Museum of Local Studies In a converted church at prospekt Uritskogo 32, the small Museum of Local Studies (Kraevedchesky muzey) features research and folk art on the Karelian epic poem *Kalevala*, though non-Russian-speakers may not be able to make much of it. It is currently closed for renovation, and it is unclear whether it will reopen.

Geological Museum Foreign geologists rave about the museum at the Petrozavodsk Geological Institute at the Russian Academy of Sciences, ulitsa Pushkinskaya 11 (look for the rocks out front). It is said to house a collection that is interesting enough to attract even non-geologists. It's open Monday to Friday from 9 am to 7 pm.

Duluth Statue Duluth, Minnesota, Petrozavodsk's US sister city, commissioned Rafael Consuegra to sculpt a huge metal statue that would capture the real Petrozavodskian spirit. The result is *The Fishermen*, which seems to be *The Old Man and the Sea* meets Edvard Munch's *The Scream*. It's on the lakefront just near the Geological Museum.

Cathedral of the Ralsing of the Cross The blue-domed Cathedral of the Raising of the Cross (Krestovo-Sdvizhensky sobor) on ulitsa Pravdy is an active church with a melancholic graveyard.

Banya The best place in town for a Russian banya is at ulitsa Kirova 4 (open daily from 8 am to 10 pm). It's standard but clean and friendly; it costs US$0.40 per hour in the public section, or you can rent the whole sauna with a group of up to 10 for US$19 for 1½ hours.

Amusement Park There's a sweet amusement park behind the ferry terminal, open in summer, that is geared to smaller children. It's got a mini-Ferris wheel, plus various swing rides and pony rides. Closer to the lake shore is a small roller coaster, a very popular tilt-a-whirl and a 25-metre-high Ferris wheel for grown-ups that is slow and affords no view whatsoever of the city.

Afghan War Memorial In the park behind Pervomaysky prospekt sits one of Russia's few memorials to veterans of the Afghanistan war. The stone monument lists local residents who died in the conflict.

Places to Stay

The cheapest place in town is the hard-to-get-to *Karel Skan* (☎ 4 67 65), at ulitsa Murmanskaya 28, which has dormitory beds (two or three to a room) for US$6.75. Rooms have separate bath and toilets, and cooking facilities are available. The *Hotel Severnaya* (☎ 7 19 58, 7 07 03), at prospekt Lenina 21, is plain and slightly run-down, but its central location – and the fact that it's the second-cheapest place in town – makes up for most of that. It also has the roughest loo paper in Russia (which would seem to be A4-sized writing paper cut into four), but everything works and the staff are pleasant enough. The cheapest singles/doubles are US$11.50/32, with separate bathrooms accessed from the hallway. The staff may try to charge you to use these.

At the city's northern line, on the road out to the airport, the *Hotel Pietari* (☎ 4 53 97), Shuyskaya shosse 16, was Karelia's first privately owned hotel, and is the current favourite of Finnish truckies passing through. It's family run, has a nice restaurant with fixed-price menus, clean singles/doubles/triples for US$18/28/36, a sauna (US$4 per hour), and huge, scary dogs guarding the car park (US$7 per night).

The *Karelia Hotel* (☎ 5 88 97), at naberezhnaya Gyullinga 2, a five-minute walk from the ferry terminal, is a standard but more modern hotel. Ask for a view of the lake. Rooms are small but clean, at US$28.50/38, and the hotel's restaurant is good. If you're going to spend that much money for a room though, you'd probably be much better off at the *Karelian Government Hotel* (☎ 7 56 61) at ulitsa Sverdlova 10, formerly the Communist Party's recreational pad. It's been renovated by Finns and is by far the nicest place in town. Very comfortable singles/doubles/suites cost US$30/51/71, and there's also a great sauna and

A Russian Banya

There's a level of clean that can only be attained, Russians say, through the rigorous action of a ritual Russian *banya*. A combination of dry sauna, steam bath, massage and plunges into ice-cold water, the banya is a weekly event that is as much a part of Russian life as, say, bowling in Bedrock. The word 'banya' has come to mean far more than its dictionary definition, which is 'bathhouse'.

Preparation begins at home, where thermos flasks are filled to their cork-plugged brims with specially-brewed tea. These teas are peculiar to the banya; a mixture of jams, fruits, spices, tea and heaps of sugar. Armed with this brew, the bather heads out. (A couple of beers picked up along the way is not unheard-of either.)

Based on any number of scheduling concerns, people usually go to the banya on the same day each week and, with others there on the same day, a close circle is formed; the closest equivalent in the West would probably be your workout buddies.

After a 'warm up' in the dry sauna (the word's the same in Russian, pronounced 'SA-oo-na'), where the temperature is in the low 100's Celsius (lower 200's Fahrenheit), you're ready for the *parilka* – the dreaded steam room.

The parilka will have a furnace that's heating rocks. Onto these, bathers throw water, usually mixed with eucalyptus oil, with a long-handled ladle-like implement made specially for the purpose. When the room's got a good head of steam going, the bathers grab hold of bundles of dried birch leaves *(vennki)*, dip them in hot water and, well, beat each other with them. The beating (which isn't violent, and feels a lot better than it sounds) is said to rid your body of toxins.

As you might suspect, all that steam makes the air even hotter; bathers continue to throw water on until visibility is nil and the room is unbearably hot, at which point everyone runs out coughing. And as if the relatively cold air outside the parilka isn't enough of a shock to one's system, the next step is a plunge into the icy cold waters of the *basseyn* (pool), whose health benefits I've yet to work out (they're probably incredibly important).

After the plunge, it's out to the locker rooms wrapped up in sheets (available from the attendant or somewhere in the locker room), where the events of the world are discussed over the tea (or whatever). Then the process begins again; sessions can go on for two or three hours.

Every Russian town has a public banya, larger towns and cities have several. Baths are segregated by sex, and depending on the size of the place, there are either separate sections for men and women or the baths admit different sexes on different days. One more thing. Alcohol affects you faster in a banya, so if you do partake, be careful and do it slowly. It's considered bad form to lose your lunch in a steam room!

Nick Selby

English-speaking staff. One step down is the *Hotel Fregat* (☎ 6 17 70) at the lake side of the ferry terminal. This much smaller Finnish-renovated hotel has well-appointed rooms on the pricier side at US$38/57 including breakfast, as well as a nice sauna with a cooking area. The entrance is unmarked, next to the Fregat Restoran entrance; ring the hard-to-see bell on the left side of the door.

Places to Eat

There is a market on ulitsa Antikaynena, which is small but very clean and has a good selection of fresh produce and meat (behind is a clothing market, mostly selling Chinese knock-offs). The Produkti-Ruokatavaraa shop, at ulitsa Kirova 6, is well stocked with foreign foodstuffs, plus fresh fruit, meat, chicken and sausage.

Cafés *Ben & Jerry's Ice Cream*, the American super-premium ice cream manufacturer, runs what is arguably Russia's finest scoop shop at Krasnaya ulitsa 8. They serve up locally produced versions of the company's sinfully fat-and-chunk-packed flavours, including Cherry Garcia, cappuccino, blueberry and, of course, chocolate and vanilla, all done up in freshly made, hand-rolled cones. The staff's polite, and two scoops is a paltry US$0.50! It's worth noting that in place here is the company's laudable 'five to one' policy, under which the highest paid worker (up to and including the Chairman of the Board) makes no more than five times that of the lowest paid worker. Along with their huge donations to environmental and human rights causes, this works to make Ben & Jerry's a very socially responsible company.

Pizza-Kebab at the railway station has just that; real pizza and good gyro (though they call it 'kebab') for under US$2 and the setting is agreeable. The Finnish-Russian joint venture also sells beer and fountain Coke (with a 'cup charge' of about US$0.20 – you can avoid this by bringing your own cup, but they refuse to pour the Coke into your hands!). It's open from 11.30 am to 11.30 pm. In the grassy area on prospekt Lenina, between ulitsa Andropova and ulitsa Dzerzhinskogo, are three small shack-cafés that have outside tables in summer. One of these, *Kavkaz*, has shashlyk, another has Russian beer, and the third, *Gamburg*, has pre-packaged Finnish-made pizzas (that they heat by microwave) for US$1.75. Nearby, on ulitsa Andropova, *Kafe Express* has coffee, juices, ice cream and sandwiches (they'll also fry you up some eggs if you ask nicely). The bufet on the 2nd floor at the *Hotel Severnaya* is good and cheap, while the downstairs restaurant is fair. In summer, the restaurant spills out into a sidewalk café, serving pizza, sandwiches and drinks.

While *Kafe Morozhenoe*, on the corner of prospekt Marxa and ulitsa Kuybysheva (near the statue of Marx and Engels deciding where to eat), may not be Ben & Jerry's, they do try hard. There's also a reasonable *snack bar* in the ferry terminal; they serve sandwiches, shashlyk and real coffee, and in summer there are seats outside.

Restaurants The *Petrovsky Restoran* (☎ 7 09 92), ulitsa Andropova 1, has northern dishes at reasonable prices, and there's no music. Try the local speciality, Myaso po Petrovsky (a meat casserole with mushrooms) at US$2; other main courses range from US$1.50 to US$4.75. It's open until 2 am, and there is also a creepy bar at the front. *Restoran Maxim* (☎ 7 50 18), prospekt Lenina 10, is a very slick, stylish place with good steaks and fish dishes from US$3; it can get expensive if you include drinks, and there's an American-style bar. There's music from 7 pm; leave before 9.30 pm if you don't want to see the strip show. The restaurant is open from noon to 1 am.

The *Restoran Neubrandenburg* (☎ 7 50 38), prospekt Lenina 23, has good food in a hokey, Christmas-like atmosphere. There is no live music, but there are stereos in the bar and dining room, which has main courses from US$2 to US$3.50. The *Business Klub*, behind the Hotel Severnaya, is an expensive and exclusive spot with an English-style pub and a casino. It's open from 8 pm to 5 am.

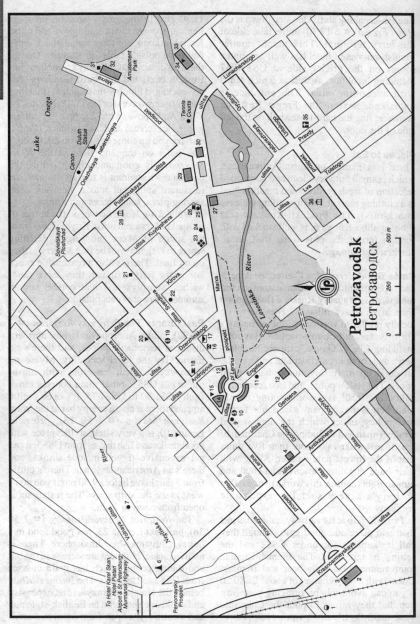

Petrozavodsk
Петрозаводск

PLACES TO STAY

14 Hotel Severnaya
Гостиница Северная
21 Karelian Government Hotel
Гостиница Государства Карелии
31 Hotel Fregat
Гостиница Фрегат
33 Karelia Hotel
Гостиница Карелия

PLACES TO EAT

3 Pizza-Kebab
Пицца-Кебаб
8 Ben & Jerry's Ice Cream
Бен и Джеррис Мороженое
13 Petrovsky Restaurant
Ресторан Петровский
15 Business Klub
.ЛВИЩюБиснес Клуб .ЬВТЬю
18 Kafe Express
Кафе Экспресс
20 Maxim Restaurant
Ресторан Максим
26 Kafe Morozhenoe
Кафе Мороженое
34 Restoran Tok
Ресторан Ток

OTHER

1 Bus Station
Автовокзал
2 Railway Station
Железнодорожный вокзал
4 Aeroflot City Terminal
Аэрофлот
5 Central Market
Центральный рынок
6 Afghan War Memorial
Памятник Афганской войны
7 Drinking Well
Колодец
9 Bookshop
Книжный магазин
10 Sberbank
Сбербанк
11 Finnair
Финаир
12 Philharmonic Hall
Филармония
14 Moto Shoe Repair
Мото
16 Telephone & Telegraph Office
Телефон и телеграф
17 Post Office
Почтамт
19 Tekobank
Текобанк

22 Kodak
Кодак
23 Department Store
ЦУМ
24 Exhibition Hall
Выставочный зал
25 Bookshop
Книжный магазин
27 National Theatre
Национальный Театр
28 Geological Museum
Геологический музей
29 Fine Arts Museum
Музей изобразительных искусств
30 Russian Theatre
Русский театр
32 Ferry Terminal
Водный вокзал
35 Cathedral of the Raising of the Cross
Крестово-Воздвиженский собор
36 Museum of Local Studies
Краеведческий музей

The restaurant at the *Hotel Karelia* serves up, eventually, some very good food; the music, unfortunately, is very loud. Specialties are chicken and fish dishes, with main courses from US$2 to US$3. Also at the Hotel Karelia, with a separate entrance, is the *Restoran Tok* (☎ 5 57 00) with a more polished atmosphere, OK service and average food; main courses range from US$1.75 to US$3. A bit cheaper, but with decidedly mixed reviews, is the *Hotel Fregat's* restaurant (☎ 6 14 98), which does a decent steak at US$2. Upstairs is an American-style bar with everything reasonably priced except wines.

Entertainment

Kantele, a jolly Karelian folk ensemble, per-forms at the National Theatre (formerly the Finnish Theatre), prospekt Marxa 19, or at the Philharmonic Hall, ulitsa Gogolya 6. You can buy tickets at the theatres or through Intourist.

Things to Buy

Karelian embroidery and traditional-style clothing are sometimes available at non-tourist prices in the department stores. If you're feeling under the weather, the local firewater Karelsky Balzam – made from 20 herbs – is said to have tremendous powers of healing. And at 45% alcohol it bloody well should! There's a non-English speaking folk-art gallery at prospekt Marxa 13 that sells locally produced art. The local Detsky Mir, ulitsa Dzerzhinskogo 7, is a good source of toys, prams, bicycles and hammocks, and upstairs they have clothes and coats.

There's also a great office supplier called Office Klub (☎ 9 99 82) at the ferry terminal, prospekt Marxa 1A. They sell pens, paper, copiers, computers, faxes, phones and parts as well as other miscellaneous office goods.

Getting There & Away

Air Petrozavodsk's adorable little airport – it's a little wooden house and the field's in the back yard – is 400 km north-east of St Petersburg. There are flights daily from St Petersburg's Pulkovo-1 (US$66) and Moscow's Bykovo (US$92) and three flights a week from Arkhangelsk (US$74) and Murmansk (US$99). Finnair flies on Mondays, Wednesdays and Fridays from Helsinki via Joensuu, Finland, with a return APEX fare of US$220 (maximum stay one month), and a regular fare of US$267.49. Note that you clear Finnish customs at Joensuu, so the flight leaves and arrives at Helsinki's domestic air terminal (a Finnair employee, when asked why a flight to Russia left from the domestic terminal said, 'We're practising!'). The airport code for Petrozavodsk is PES.

Bus For destinations in northern Karelia, catch buses at the main bus station, behind the railway station. A Finnish postbus from Petrozavodsk to Helsinki that stops at Sortavala leaves the Severnaya Hotel every Sunday, Wednesday and Friday at 8.30 am and arrives in Sortavala at 3.45 pm, but the cost is an outrageous US$43. Turistiliikenne, in Kuhmo, Finland, operates a daily bus from Kuhmo to Kostomuksha on the western border of Karelia with connecting bus service to Belomorsk for about US$17.

Train The overnight passazhirskiy train from St Petersburg (Moscow Station) is convenient and saves the cost of a hotel. Trains leave for St Petersburg (six per day, seven to 17 hours); Moscow (six per day, 15 to 20 hours); and Murmansk (eight per day, 21 to 35 hours). The railway station is at the west end of prospekt Lenina.

Car & Motorbike The motorway from St Petersburg (420 km) is open. Intourist in Petrozavodsk suggests that it's possible to cross at Vyartsilya (500 km from Petrozavodsk via Olonets) to Tohmajrvi and on to Joensuu in Finland.

Boat In summer the St Petersburg Travel Company runs a seven-day cruise from St Petersburg via the Neva River and the White Sea Canal to Petrozavodsk and Kizhi.

Getting Around

To/From the Airport From the Hotel Severnaya, a taxi to the airport is about US$5. Less convenient is the bus between the airport and Aeroflot's city office on ulitsa Antikaynena; it runs hourly from mid-morning to early evening and takes half an hour. Bus No 16 links the railway station, Severnaya and ferry terminal.

Bus For the Hotel Karel Skan take trolleybus No 3 from the railway station to the corner of ulitsa Murmanskaya and Pervomayskaya prospekt; the hotel's to the north on ulitsa Murmanskaya and on the left, in the building that's tucked back in from the street.

AROUND PETROZAVODSK
ОКРЕСТНОСТЬ ПЕТРОЗАВОДСКА

To the north and west of the city lies one of the most beautiful and accessible regions for hunting, fishing, hiking and camping in Russia. Finns have been quietly revelling in the area for some time (it used to be theirs, after all) and Finnish tourists can be found all over Karelia.

Other than in the 120-km 'border zone', in which you'll need a business visa and perhaps a note from a company explaining your presence, you're free to roam at will. Camping and campfires are permitted almost anywhere, except where posted (Не разбивать палатку 'no putting up of tents' and/or Не разжигать костров 'no camp-fires'), and if you're off the beaten track it is usually legal and fine just to put up a tent and hit the hay. Check with locals if you're in doubt.

The region's lakes and rivers make for great kayaking and rubber-rafting, though there aren't many rapids. Karelians are keen boaters. Be careful about border zones, though: two Germans reported being sent packing back to Petrozavodsk by a 'border' patrol when, they say, they were well over 200 km from the border.

Intourist runs ho-hum excursions to Russia's first mineral spa, founded by Peter the Great at Martsialnye Vody, and to the waterfall and nature reserve at Kivach. A lack of a bus service makes Kivach difficult if you're without a car, as it's about 50 km north of the city.

Kizhi Island
Остров Кижи

An old pagan ritual site, Kizhi Island made a natural 'parish' for 12th-century Russian colonists, though none of the earliest churches remain.

Its centrepiece is the fairy-tale **Cathedral of the Transfiguration** (Preobrazhensky sobor, 1714), with a chorus of 22 domes, gables and ingenious decorations to keep water off the walls. Even so, it's now so rickety that it's been closed, and in spite of UNESCO protection nobody can agree on how to restore it. Next door is the nine-domed **Church of the Intercession** (Pokrovskaya tserkov, 1764). The icons from the cathedral are on display here and in the Petrozavodsk Fine Arts Museum.

The other buildings in the collection were brought from the region around Lake Onega. Nineteenth-century peasant houses, some more ornate than others, are nicely restored inside. The little 14th-century **Church of the Resurrection of Lazarus** may be the oldest wooden building in Russia. The **Chapel of the Archangel Michael** has an exhibit on Christianity in Karelia, and music students from Petrozavodsk play its bells in the summer.

There are more wooden churches outside the 'museum', and a hamlet with houses like the ones inside, but occupied. From the landing it's three km north to another village and five km to the end of the island. The

Kizhi Island
остров Кижи

0   250   500 m

silence, fresh air and views on a sunny day are reason enough to come here (but beware of poisonous snakes in the remoter parts).

Museum entry fees are steep for foreigners at US$9.50 (though we paid the Russian price simply by saying '*odin bilet, pozhaluysta*' – 'one ticket, please'); Russians pay about US$0.50, and Russian students pay less than US$0.05. Karelian residents enter free.

Places to Eat A *restoran* is near the landing, but it seems to want to sell drinks more than food. Just opposite the pier is a small kiosk cluster, including an 'art shop' selling heinously overpriced souvenirs, and a *kafe* that has some snacks. There's a map of the museum and island 50 metres south-east of the kiosk cluster.

Getting There & Away Going on your own is easy – hydrofoils make the 80-minute direct trip several times a day from the Petrozavodsk ferry terminal; others stop first at Sennaya Guba on the next island. A return ticket is US$9.50 (but again, it's easy to get the Russian price of US$3.50; buy your return ticket early). You can only go during 'navigation season', which is mid-May to mid-November.

Kosalma
Косалма

One hour's bus ride north of Petrozavodsk, and a bit past the dacha villages of Shua and Tsarevich, brings you to Kosalma (*'KAH-sul-ma'*), a resort town for local factory workers. Boris Yeltsin comes here now and then to stay at the former Communist Party dacha, which is now a privately owned hotel. Locals come to get away from the city and to take advantage of the Ukshizero and Kunchizero lakes, while Russian tourists use it as a starting point for river or ski tours of south-eastern Karelia.

Other than the simple pleasure of relaxation, Kosalma has little to offer. It has two shops with basic goods, open from 8 am to midnight, at the Kosalma bus stop, along with an expensive, mediocre café. The

Turbaza Kosalma can arrange for some fine Karelian adventures, like cross-country skiing and camping trips, hiking and other outdoor nature excursions.

Places to Stay & Eat *Baza Otdykha PLMK*, 100 metres south of the Kosalma city line (not the Turbaza Kosalma) offers a true look at Karelian workers' holiday-making. The spartan (outside toilets and no hot water), but dirt-cheap, camp has a bunkhouse with a bed in a six-bed room for US$1.75, and four-bed cottages for US$4.75. It's roughing it, but gently, and foreigners are welcome. It's on Lake Ukshizero, and rowing boats are available at no cost. There's a small canteen, and cooking facilities are available. The entrance is 100 metres south of the city line, down the hill. Administration is on the right, near the docks.

The *Turbaza Kosalma*, two km north of the Kosalma bus stop on the left (Petrozavodsk ☎ 7 35 45), postal index 186108, offers 12-day tours (boating and kayaking in summer, skiing in winter) which take you around some of Karelia's loveliest areas for about US$125 including meals, lodging and equipment (you can also bring your own equipment). Just sticking around the base picking berries and mushrooms can be pleasant enough – there's a banya and sauna, and a bar/stolovaya. They also have a bus, available for excursions, though this is expensive. A Finnish-Russian joint venture is forming, which would include building cottages on the site. You can reserve (in Russian) places at the Turbaza office in Petrozavodsk, ulitsa Sverdlova 30, or try your luck and just show up at the base.

At the other end of the spectrum is the *Russky Sever Hotel* (Petrozavodsk ☎ 9 99 66), 1.5 km north of the Kosalma bus stop, a modern place with good service, nice singles/doubles overlooking the lake and a private sauna for US$16/24. It also has a good, but somewhat pricey, restaurant.

Getting There & Away Kosalma is on the St Petersburg-Murmansk highway, 43 km north of Petrozavodsk. Buses leave Petrozavodsk's bus station at least six times a day.

VALAAM
ВАЛААМ

The Valaam Archipelago, which consists of Valaam Island and about 50 smaller ones, sits in north-western Lake Ladoga (*'LAH-da-ga'*) south of south-western Karelia and north of St Petersburg. The main attractions here are the 14th-century **Valaam Transfiguration Monastery** (Spaso-Preobrazhenskii Valaamsky monastyr), its cathedral and buildings, and the pleasant town that surrounds it.

There is some dispute about the identity of the first settlers – some sources say that they were 10th-century monks – but most agree that the monastery was first settled in the late 14th century as a fortress against Swedish invaders, who managed to destroy it completely in 1611. Rebuilt with money from Peter the Great, the monastery doubled as a prison.

Many of the monks and much of the monastery's treasure were moved to Finland, which controlled the territory between 1918 and 1940, when it fell back into Soviet hands. The Soviet authorities closed the monastery, took whatever was left and built what they referred to as an 'urban-type settlement' there.

Today the buildings are protected architectural landmarks, but neglect has taken its toll. Many of the buildings are decrepit and in need of immediate repair. Concerned people are trying hard, but in many cases arguments about how to proceed with the restoration have impeded progress, and lack of funding compounds the difficulties.

There are about 600 residents on the main island, including army service personnel, restoration workers, guides and clergy, most of whom get around in horse-drawn carriages or motorboats.

Getting There & Away
The most common way to get to Valaam and, once there, to get around is on tour boats which leave from St Petersburg at night,

arrive in the morning, do about a six-hour tour of the islands, and then head back, arriving in St Petersburg the following morning. Getting here from Karelia, while less common, can be a more satisfying adventure.

To/From St Petersburg Cruise ships leave the St Petersburg River Terminal frequently, but on uncertain schedules; check with Sindbad Travel (☎ 327 83 84) or Peter TIPS (☎ 279 00 37) to see when they'll go during your stay. The river terminal (☎ 262 02 39, 262 13 18) is at prospekt Obukhovskoy oborony 195, near metro Proletarskaya. It's open daily from 9 am to 9 pm. The cruise, which lasts for two nights and one day, costs from US$54 to US$78 including full board. If you add Kizhi, the trip becomes one of four nights and three days and costs from US$145 to US$208 including full board.

These prices are the same for Russians and foreigners, though foreigners are required to buy a 'voucher' – essentially a surcharge – which costs US$30 for Valaam, US$60 for Valaam and Kizhi. Tickets can be booked at the river terminal or through Sindbad Travel, which charges a service fee of US$10 per ticket.

To/From Southern Karelia From southern Karelia, the gateway to Valaam is the sleepy town of Sortavala, about 300 km west of Petrozavodsk. Sortavala is in an iffy border zone, but police say that foreigners don't need special permission or visas to make the trip – something even Intourist Petrozavodsk wasn't aware of. This route has just been opened to foreigners, so there's a fair amount of this kind of confusion. Be prepared for rules to change and officials to be unfamiliar with them.

A Finnish postbus from Petrozavodsk to Helsinki that stops in Sortavala departs from the Severnaya Hotel every Sunday, Wednesday and Friday at 8.30 am and arrives in Sortavala at 3.45 pm, but the cost is an outrageous US$43. The better bet is train No 656, a clean and uncrowded train which leaves Petrozavodsk every night at 12.30 am and arrives at Sortavala at 9.45 the next morning: a platskart ticket is about US$5! It's a local train though, so much of the ride is stop-and-go. Once you get to Sortavala it's an easy 15-minute walk from the railway station to the boat pier. Head north along the train tracks – the direction from which the train comes into the station – until you get to the bridge, then turn right, then right again past (probably) the nude Finnish sunbathers to get to the pier. Many of the visiting Finns were born in this area or even on Valaam and are returning for the first time to the land from which they fled many years ago.

Three boats are usually docked there: a hydrofoil, which takes 40 minutes to get to Valaam; a large boat, which takes a bit more than an hour; and a smaller boat, which takes three hours. The hydrofoil costs about US$5 per person. Boats go to Valaam from about mid-May (just after the ice has thawed) to August.

Two intrepid travellers who made their way to Valaam from Sortavala in spring 1995 had this to say:

The walk from the pier near the main monastery where we arrived to the larger harbour from the bay, where boats to/from St Petersburg dock, is five to six km through beautiful forests and meadows on an unpaved road. So if you're coming from Sortavala and want to take the boat to St. Pete, be prepared for this walk or try to hitch a ride on a boat or cart. We were lucky enough to hitch a ride from a friendly guy who kind of looked like your Uncle Jeb or Cousin Bob but who turned out to be the *mayor*, and the owner of the only (?) car on the island. Coming here through Karelia was totally worth it and a good way of taking a detour off of the well-worn tourist trail.

Margaret Phillips & Eriko Kojima

BELOMORSK
БЕЛОМОРСК
Population: 17,000

For three years only, during WW II, Belomorsk was the capital of the Karelian Republic of the USSR, and the fact that there's nothing here may account for that. Boats no longer run between here and the Solovetsky Islands, despite what Intourist Petrozavodsk may tell you.

The town, with an industry that revolves mainly around sea fishing and wood working, has a legitimate attraction in the ancient petroglyphs (stone carvings) found here, but virtually nothing to support a tourist industry.

Things to See & Do
The small but very good **regional museum**, currently at ulitsa Oktyabrsky 36 but alleged to be moving to the Hotel Gandvik sometime, has some petroglyphs and a very good historical exhibition on the creation of the town. It's open Monday to Friday from 10 am to 6 pm and closed on Saturday and Sunday. Admission is US$1.90.

The **petroglyphs**, made in the 6th to 5th-centuries BC by the forebears of the region's Saami reindeer-herders, can be seen on a tour arranged by the museum. They're fascinating, though a horrible building has been erected around one grouping of petroglyphs to protect them from vandals. Another larger group, however, remains outdoors. Doing it by yourself is difficult, as routes are unmarked and often difficult through the woods. The tours cost about US$2 and take about three hours.

The **White Sea Canal** (Belomorkanal) smells as bad as the cigarettes which are its namesake. It connects the White Sea with Lake Ladoga, and was constructed entirely by Gulag labour during 1931-33. As the Great Soviet Encyclopedia gushes: 'Despite complex geological conditions, the work was completed within 20 months'. You can arrange through the museum to see one of the canal's 19 locks, a slight detour along the way to viewing the petroglyphs.

Places to Stay & Eat
The town's only option is the *Hotel Gandvik* (☎ 2 25 69), ulitsa Pervomayskaya 18, and it's a dire one. Rooms are dilapidated and there's a faulty hot water system. Singles/doubles are US$18/22. There's a *stolovaya* around the corner that has good fish dishes.

Getting There & Around
Belomorsk is on the Moscow-St Petersburg-

Murmansk railway, with several trains daily to each. Buses to Kostomuksha, near the Finnish border (where connecting buses can be caught to Ivalo and, from there, Helsinki) run on Fridays and Sundays (four hours). Check for the times (which change) at the railway station, just across the river to the north of the centre (bus No 5 runs between them). Turistiliikenne, in Kuhmo, Finland, operates a daily bus from Kuhmo to Kostomuksha on the western border of Karelia with a connecting bus service to Belomorsk for FIM80 (about US$17).

KEM
КЕМЬ

Population: 18,000

Kem ('Kyem'), a pleasant town founded in the 16th century, also doesn't tax visitors with too many things to do. As a jump-off point for the Solovetsky Islands, it's a perfectly rational place to stop, as it's a much faster sea journey from here than from Arkhangelsk. The Turbaza Kem (see Places to Stay & Eat) is run by friendly people who can help arrange the two-hour boat journey.

The town has a collection of wooden houses on the south-east side of town, near the lovely wooden **Uspensky Cathedral**. Just north of the eastern end of the town's main drag, prospekt Proletarskaya, is the crumbling **Blagoveshchensky Cathedral**, which is open for services, but only just – it's interior and exterior are scaffolded, and you need to walk down a plank to get to the entrance.

The telephone code for Kem is 34581 from St Petersburg, or 581 from Petrozavodsk.

Places to Stay & Eat

The *Turbaza Kem* (☎ 2 03 85) is at ulitsa Energetikov 22, postal index 186600. The pleasant stone and wood building is fine for a night or two (they can offer some skiing or hiking tours around the region), but the main reason to stay here is if you're planning on catching the boat to the Solovetsky Islands. The turbaza can also arrange day tours of the

islands. Singles/doubles are about US$10/15, and there's a restaurant downstairs. The *Kafe Nadezhda* across the street served the worst meal Nick ever experienced in almost four years of Eastern European living.

Getting There & Away

Kem is a stop on the St Petersburg-Moscow-Murmansk railway. For information on boats from Kem to the Solovetsky Islands, see The Solovetsky Islands section. Bus No 1 runs from Kem's railway station to the port, which is actually in the village of Podvore, a 35-minute ride away.

Kola Peninsula
Кольский Полуостров

The Kola Peninsula (Kolsky Poluostrov) is a 100,000-sq-km knob of tundra, forest and low mountains between the White Sea and the Arctic Barents Sea. Originally populated only by Saami (Lapp) reindeer-herders and a few Russian trappers and fishers, the discovery of a northern sea route in the 16th century turned the tiny settlement of Kola into an Arctic trading post. In 1916, under pressure from the British to establish a supply port, Murmansk was founded (the first buildings being British-built wood houses).

The discovery of huge ore and mineral deposits sped up growth and generated an environmental mess in some areas. Thousands of sq km of forests are dying of sulphur poisoning from nickel smelters in the towns of Nikel and Monchegorsk.

The Kola Inlet from the Barents, ice-free year-round thanks to an eddy from the Gulf Stream, was the ideal site for the port of Murmansk, and now, at nearby Severomorsk, for the Russian Northern Fleet's home base. Thanks to the latter, the Kola Peninsula today has the somewhat dubious distinction of being home to the world's greatest concentration of military and naval forces.

The Soviet regime became quite excited by the region's suitability for Gulag camps. The camps, now abandoned, are generally not reachable without off-road vehicles or boat, but some visits can be arranged through the Scandinavian Study Centre (see Organised Tours) in Apatity. And if you've always wanted to tour a Soviet nuclear power plant, the Kola Peninsula won't disappoint – just head for Polyarnye Zory, which boasts atomic fun for the whole family.

Speaking of things nuclear, there were at least two above-ground nuclear detonations (for 'civil' purposes, not above-ground testing) in the region, involving one and four-kilotonne devices. Both were in the Khibiny mountain range, and one was as recent as autumn 1984. However, radiation monitoring by the Russian government, Norwegian observers and independent verification by the Apatity Science Centre has stated that background radiation in the entire region is at or below international norms.

Aside from the unique geological interest that the region holds, it also offers some exceptional hiking and other outdoor sport. The Khibiny mountain range has some good mountaineering opportunities (new granite up to 700 metres), and skiers will have more than enough to keep them inexpensively busy downhill at Kirovsk (the Russian north's best ski destination, where European and Russian competitions are held annually), and cross-country practically anywhere. North and west of the ecologically ruined city of Monchegorsk lies the relatively pristine **Lappland Nature Reserve**, a 3000-sq-km natural wonderland, which can be accessed by permission only, though permission isn't too difficult to obtain (see below).

Information

Outside of Murmansk there are no Intourist offices, but tourist information and assistance can be obtained from the Apatity City Administration (☎ (81533) 3 15 04, 3 48 30; fax 3 27 59), ploshchad Lenina 1, and from the Scandinavian Study Centre in Apatity. The Apatity City Administration can be contacted to arrange full visa support, hotel reservations, homestays and excursions, including one to the otherwise closed town of Severomorsk. The administration can also arrange hunting and fishing licences for independent travellers. Send a fax, in English, with your name, passport number, routes, purpose (hunting, fishing etc), dates and type of equipment you'll be using, a week or more in advance.

Organised Tours

The Scandinavian Study Centre (Norwegian ☎ (47 78) 91 4010, wait for second tone and then dial 118; local ☎ (81533) 3 72 62), formerly the Econord Ecological Information Centre, a non-profit educational and cultural exchange centre, is a joint venture between the Scandinavian and Russian 'Open University Systems'. They're involved in a number of projects that are a boon to independent travellers to the region. Working closely with the Kola (Apatity) Geological Expedition, the Scandinavian Study Centre acts as a liaison between foreigners and local public and private firms that arrange trekking, mountain climbing, camping, skiing and, according to Swedish employee Peder Axenstein, 'any other low-key nature experiences: no helicopters!'

They'll also arrange for accommodation in hotels, homestays, health resorts or for camping (with or without equipment rental), and offer full visa support. They don't charge for their liaison services, and don't mark up prices for services they arrange, which they say they try to keep as low as possible.

They also take individuals or groups (they prefer groups) into the Lappland Nature Reserve, a UNESCO-protected nature reserve in the central west of the peninsula for camping, trekking and nature excursions. You can obtain a copy of their glossy journal, *Econord*, by contacting them.

A reputable, privately held Russian firm in Apatity, Tekom (Norwegian ☎ (47 78) 91 4010, wait for tone and then dial 126), offers mountaineering, snow, ice and rock climbing, ski tours through the southern Kola Peninsula, and hiking tours that include building igloos – in which you sleep. Their 1994 seven-day ski marathon around the Kola Peninsula was a great success, and they hope to make it an annual event. During the marathon, held in September, 'points' are issued for rubbish collected along the way. Their climbing courses run from beginner to advanced. You can also book their services through the Apatity City administration and the Scandinavian Study Centre.

Festival of the North

The Festival of the North is not yet a tourism gimmick but an annual regional celebration held since 1934, with each town hosting its own events. It's officially the last week in March but usually lasts longer. Murmansk has reindeer and deer-plus-ski races (in which a reindeer pulls a contestant on skis), an international ski marathon and biathlon, ice hockey, 'polar-bear' swimming and a general carnival atmosphere. Hotels get booked up well in advance. Most events in Murmansk are held at the south end of town in Dolina Uyuta (Cosy Valley), a 25-minute ride from the railway station on bus No 12. There's through-the-ice swimming at Lake Semyonovskaya, and snowmobile rides can be arranged through Intourist Murmansk.

MURMANSK
МУРМАНСК
Population: 450,000

The most novel thing about Murmansk is its location – halfway between Moscow and the North Pole, 200 km north of the Arctic Circle. Temperatures can be fierce, ranging from -8°C to -13°C in January, and 8°C to 14°C in July. The best time to visit Murmansk is from February to March; it's freezing but clear, and the nights are often lit by the aurora borealis.

Murmansk's permanent residents are mostly Russians; many more temporary residents are lured by high pay and other perks to work in fish processing or ship repair. Saami are rarely seen except during the Festival of the North, when they come to compete in traditional games.

Life here looks pretty hard. 'Polar night' means nonstop darkness for all of December and most of January, though locals say they 'feel' it by the end of October. Outside the town there is just tundra. Little wonder that the population turnover is 20% a year.

Except during the festival there is little to do other than visit a couple of museums and take a cruise on the inlet. Security is ingrained, and not just because the Northern Fleet (including nuclear submarines and a large part of the country's nuclear arsenal) is in the nearby city of Severomorsk. Murmansk is also the home port of Russia's nuclear-powered ice-breakers.

Orientation

The city is on three levels: port, centre and surrounding heights full of housing blocks. Dominating the centre is the municipal Hotel Arktika on ploshchad Sovietskoy Konstitutsii, also known as Five-Corners (Pyat-Ugla). Above and north of this is Lake Semyonovskaya and an immense, concrete war-memorial soldier the locals call 'Alyosha'. The main artery, prospekt Lenina, follows a broken line through town.

Information

Intourist is at the Hotel Polyarny Zory (☎ 5 43 85, 5 43 72). They offer the usual fare, plus car rental with driver for US$6 per hour.

Money Changing money in Murmansk can be difficult, as banks have infuriatingly unpredictable hours, surly staff and they frequently run out of roubles. (This undoubtedly explains the well-organised and professional groups of black marketeers huddling outside banks and near exchange counters.) The main branch of Sberbank is at Five-Corners between the Arktika and Meridian hotels, open Monday to Friday from 8.30 am to 7 pm (break from 2 to 3 pm), Saturday from 8.30 am to 6 pm (break from 2 to 3 pm), and closed Sunday. There are branches at the Meridien and at prospekt Lenina 80. The Arktika Hotel's bank has, typically, erratic

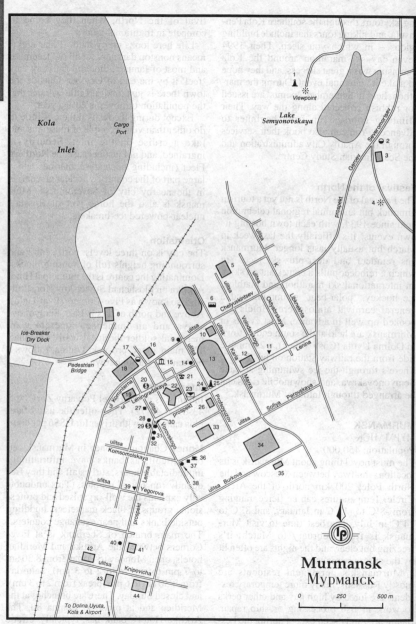

Murmansk
Мурманск

0   250   500 m

hours (they were closed on eight visits over the course of one week!). The Hotel Polyarny Zory has a booth in the lobby, as does the 69th Parallel Hotel. The art salon, at prospekt Lenina 80 next to the bank branch, also has an exchange desk.

Post & Telecommunications The main post, telephone and telegraph offices are just behind the Hotel Arktika. Satellite phones, about the same price as the state phones, can be used by the public on the 4th floor of the Arktika. NMT-450 standard cellular phones

work here, as well as in the rest of the Kola Peninsula. Tele-Nord (☎ 5 70 67), ulitsa Karla Marxa 25A, is a Finnish company that will rent cellular phones for US$10 per day with a US$1000 cash deposit.

Note that when making local calls within Murmansk you must add the digit 5 at the beginning (for example, Tele-Nord's number, when dialled from within Murmansk, would therefore be ☎ 55 70 67). The telephone code for Murmansk is 815.

Foreign Consulates The Norwegian Consulate General (☎ 1 00 37, 24-hour emergency number ☎ 75 12 95), currently at ulitsa Pushkinskaya 10 but planning to move in late 1995 to ulitsa Sofia Perovskaya 5, is also the honorary Swedish Consulate General. They say that they'll also help out other Scandinavian citizens. Finland has a consular branch office (☎ 4 32 75, Finnish phone (358 697) 669 006), at ulitsa Karla Marxa 25A, that does minimal services for Finns and visa services for others. There's an Australian trade mission next door at ulitsa Karla Marxa 25, but they're really just there to establish trade links and they offer no consular services.

Bookshops The biggest bookshop is a long trudge up to ulitsa Burkova but there's a smaller one at prospekt Lenina 67.

Things to See & Do
St Nicholas Church The Kola Peninsula's central cathedral would be impressive enough, even if it didn't have such a colourful history.

The site of the present cathedral was that of a wooden church, built in 1946. In 1984, the congregation decided to build a new church, and began doing so in secret. It's hard to hide a cathedral, and when the government found out about it in 1985, they sent in miners with orders to blow it up. This raised a holy stink, and demonstrators sat around the site, blocking the miners; simultaneous protests were held in front of the Moscow city executive committee.

The government capitulated to some extent, letting what was left of the building stand but forbidding any further work on it. After perestroika greased the country's religious wheels, construction resumed in 1987 and continued over the next five summers.

Today the St Nicholas Church (Svyato-Nikolskaya tserkov), named for the patron saint of sailors, is the Kola Peninsula's religious administrative centre.

To get there from the railway station, take trolleybus No 4 for four stops, walk past the pond and up the stairs, then along a dirt trail to the main road, and the church is to the right. Services are held Monday, Saturday and Sunday at 8 am and 6 pm.

Murmansk Fine Arts Museum The Fine Arts Museum (Khudozhestvenny muzey), ulitsa Kominterna 13, was established in Murmansk's oldest stone building in 1989, but only got a permanent collection in 1994, which is now housed on the 2nd floor. The small but interesting collection includes graphic arts, paintings, decorative applied arts and bone carvings, all on an 'image-of-the-north' theme. It features seven prints by Boris Nepomnyashchy, including *Purgatory*, and biblical figures including *Cain and Abel*. The 3rd floor houses temporary exhibitions, which change monthly. Admission is about US$0.50 for foreigners, US$0.25 for Russians and ISIC holders, and it's open daily except Monday from 11 am to 6 pm.

Museum of Regional Studies This museum, at prospekt Lenina 90, is good even without a guide. The 2nd floor features geology (minerals are a major resource on the peninsula), natural history and oceanography. Anthropology, Saami and Pomory history, the Anglo-American occupation and exhibits of WW II are on the 3rd floor. It's open Saturday to Wednesday from 11 am to 6 pm. Admission is less than US$0.10.

Art Gallery On the 2nd floor of the city administration building, ulitsa Sofia Perovskaya 3, the Regional Centre of Crafts holds a permanent exhibition of art from Kola Peninsula artists, including 'paintings' from coloured crushed stone powder – a technique developed in Apatity. Some of the works are for sale. The gallery is open daily except Monday from 10 am to 6 pm.

Polar Research Institute The small museum of the Polar Research Institute, ulitsa Knipovicha 6, is groups-only and mainly for specialists.

Naval Museum The hard-to-find Military Museum of the North Sea Fleet (Muzey Militarny Severnogo Morskogo Flota), ulitsa Tortseva 15, is a must if you're a WW II or naval buff. It's got six rooms on the Great Patriotic War and one on the modern fleet – torpedos, mines, model ships, diving and chemical warfare suits. A guided tour is about US$2.50, otherwise admission is free. It's open Thursday to Monday from 9 am to 5 pm (break from 1 to 2 pm). Take trolleybus No 4 north to the last stop, cross the street, then take bus No 10 for four stops (look for the smokestack). Walk towards the smokestack, and turn left at the *tovari* shop.

Port It's hit or miss, but in summer there's a chance to see one of the Murmansk Shipping Company's four **atomic-powered ice-breakers** at the port's dock. Photography, except in the port itself, is perfectly legal now, and you can photograph anything you see from the railway and passenger sea terminals and on board the ferries. With permission (and a good reason) you can arrange to see the ice-breaker port 10 km north of the city, through the Murmansk Shipping Company (see the Northern European Russia Getting There & Away chapter).

Lake Semyonovskaya Semyonovskaya is named for the unfortunate would-be hermit Semyon Korzhnev, an old tsarist soldier who retired at the turn of the century to a cabin on the shore, and was the only resident for miles around. Imagine his disappointment when they decided to put Murmansk here.

The lake and 'Alyosha' are on a plateau above town. The view isn't very romantic, but it's open land where old women still collect bilberries to sell in the market. To get there, take trolleybus No 3 up prospekt Lenina.

Views are better from up the road behind the lake. There is said to be a cemetery on the same road for British and American soldiers of the 1918-20 occupation.

Anatoly Bredov Statue Anatoly Bredov was a hero of the Great Patriotic War who, finding himself surrounded by Nazi troops, detonated a grenade he was holding, taking several fascist bad guys with him. He's famous all over the Kola Peninsula. There is a great statue of Anatoly on prospekt Lenina,

just in front of the stadium, which depicts him seconds before the big boom.

Swimming Murmansk's excellent municipal swimming pool is at ulitsa Chelyuskintsev just behind the central stadium. It's amazing: 50 metres long, with three, five, seven and 10-metre diving boards. There are two kiddie pools downstairs plus two saunas. A check room is available for valuables. It's open October to June from 7 am to 10 pm, and admission is about US$1.

Organised Tours
Intourist has an interesting deer-sledding exhibition in winter, 40 km out of town. A folk ensemble meets your group and takes you around a lake on ice-sleds, then provides outdoor dinner and folk dancing by a fire. The cost is US$55 per person in groups of 10 or more. They can also arrange five-day snowmobiling and 'tundra tours'.

In summer, weather and sea permitting, you can also join a one-hour Intourist excursion on Kola Inlet (Kolsky Zaliv) for US$5. You'll go south towards Kola but not very far north (you won't see the Northern Fleet but you will see the city Severomorsk). Mostly you see shipyards and tundra. To do it solo, go to the Passenger Ferry Terminal and hop on a ferry going to Mishukovo. Ferries leave six times a day, and the 30-minute journey is about US$0.75 each way. For shorter trips, you can catch ferries to Abram-Mys, Tri-Ruchya or Minkino.

Places to Stay
The cheapest option in the city centre, just across from the Hotel Arktika, is the *Meridian Hotel* (☎ 5 78 76), at ulitsa Vorovskogo 5/23. Run-down but clean and comfortable singles/doubles are US$22.75/42. It has very friendly service, and the bufet on the 4th floor serves up a great ham and egg breakfast.

Somewhat out of the centre is the *69th Parallel Hotel* (Gostinitsa Shestdesyat-Devyataya Parallel, ☎ 6 56 45) at Lyzhny proezd 14 in Dolina Uyuta (Cosy Valley), index 183042. Take trolleybus No 1 or 6 from the centre for about 10 minutes. During the Festival of the North, which is held nearby, this normally inconvenient and perfectly ordinary place becomes very convenient and in demand. For some reason, triples cost less than doubles (and two people can stay in a triple). Rooms go for US$21/30.50/25; all have phones and TVs, many have balconies and some have fridges. There is an expensive café in the lobby.

The *Hotel Polyarny Zory* (☎ 5 02 82), ulitsa Knipovicha 17, near the Detsky Mir bus stop on prospekt Lenina, has large, clean and cheerful rooms at US$28/42 (students with a Russian student ID pay the Russian rate). There's a lot of construction nearby, but the noise isn't bad at all. They've got a lobby bar, a bufet and a good restaurant downstairs.

An excellent but pricier option is the *Administratsii Hotel* (☎ 5 92 37), ulitsa Sofia Perovskaya 3, in the city administration building. It's said to have very nice rooms for US$60/80, but they wouldn't let me look at the rooms (the lobby, however, did look nice).

The *Hotel Arktika* (☎ 5 79 88) on Five-Corners, prospekt Lenina 82, postal index 183038, is scandalously overpriced for what you get – even the front-desk receptionist said so! The rooms with attached bath are plain and drafty, and for US$79/104 you'd think they could slap some paint on the walls. The exception to this is the 4th floor, which has been renovated and furnished by a Swedish firm to Western business standards. If you're on an expense account, the 4th floor's very nice rooms go for US$124/132; all have satellite TV, and there's a satellite phone and fax near the dezhurnaya's desk. All major credit cards are accepted.

If you are determined to spend that much money, do what Mr and Mrs Jane Fonda did and stay at the sinfully luxurious (but awkwardly located) *Ogni Murmanskaya* (☎ 59 87 78; Finnish fax (358 9) 4929 2459), at the top of the hill (great city views) at ulitsa Furmanova 11. This secluded hotel is a shining example of how all Russian-managed hotels should be: simplex and

duplex doubles are US$100/120 including breakfast, and all are Western-standard luxury – even the bathroom floors are heated. The hotel will pick you up at the airport with two days' notice. They have high security and the restaurant is thankfully short on thugs.

Places to Eat

A seasonal item is reindeer meat, and of course there are lots of fish, especially cod. Try the 'severyanka', which is the local chowder.

For self-caterers there's a small market at the bottom of ulitsa Volodarskogo.

Restaurants & Cafés The *Panorama Restoran* near Lake Semyonovskaya has good food and, in winter, a good view of the city lights. Meat and fish main courses are US$1 to US$4; take trolleybus No 3 on prospekt Lenina three stops north, and from the stop at the top of the hill, walk south-east 300 metres. The restaurant is on the left. The *Petrovsky Restoran*, at ulitsa Lobova 43 near the Naval Museum, is said to be good; cheap for lunch, though expensive for dinner.

Burger Bar, at prospekt Lenina 72, has good hamburgers at an expensive US$7. The café in front is non smoking, and the bar and restaurant are to the rear. If your idea of pizza is sausage and eggs on a greasy cracker, then the *Pizzeria*, on prospekt Lenina north-east of ulitsa Volodarskogo, sells pizza, while the *Kafe Yunost*, behind the Arktika, is OK for ice cream and coffee.

Kafe Svetlana, at the Administratsii Hotel, Sofia Perovskaya 3, is very clean and good, with stingy portions of fresh fish with vegetables for US$0.50, and plov for about US$1 – it's non smoking and entry is at the side of the building. There's a surprisingly clean and cheerful *bufet* at the Passenger Ferry Terminal, with sandwiches, hard-boiled eggs and so forth, while the *Pingvin* ice cream café at the Rodina cinema is popular and crowded.

Hotels The *Hotel Arktika* has a stodgy *shvedsky stol* (Swedish Table) at which you can eat all you want for about US$5. It's open from 7.30 to 10 am, noon to 3 pm and 6 to

8 pm. The hotel also has a restaurant, and four rapaciously expensive bufety, with surly staff to boot, upstairs. The restaurant at the *Hotel Polyarny Zory* has good food, with main courses from US$1.50 to US$3, while the Meridian Hotel's *restoran* is standard in every respect.

Entertainment

The Seamen's Club, ulitsa Karla Marxa 1, has a bar, library, occasional social events for foreign sailors, and weekend disco nights attended mainly by drunken North Fleet sailors. Tourists, and their money, are welcome. It's open from 3.30 to 11 pm, and closed Sunday. The Kirov Palace of Culture, near the Hotel Arktika, has films and exhibits and, if you're lonely, they have weekend singles dances.

The Regional Puppet Theatre on the 1st floor of the Regional Science Library, ulitsa Sofia Perovskaya 21A, holds children's puppet shows from September to June every Saturday and Sunday at 11 am, 1 and 3 pm.

Classical concerts are held at the Philharmonic Concert Hall (Kontsertny zal filarmonii), a newly renovated 700-seat auditorium at the city administration building, ulitsa Sofia Perovskaya 3. Tickets and information are available there.

Things to Buy

There seems to be little in the way of Saami handicrafts. If you didn't bring your woollies, the Volna department store on ulitsa Leningradskaya has everything you'll need. The city's Detsky Mir is not particularly inspiring.

The once mighty beryozka at prospekt Lenina 67 has fallen on hard times and now rents out counter space to other firms, all selling cheap (as in tacky) imported stuff, while on the corner of prospekt Lenina and ulitsa Vorovskogo, the Pyat-Ugla Art Book/Souvenir shop has a good selection of art books, and even has some maps available. It's closed Sunday and Monday. If your children are feeling fashion-impaired, and you want to throw some money into the wind, there's a Benetton 013 at Prospekt Lenina 67.

Getting There & Away

Air The Aeroflot office is at prospekt Lenina 19, one trolleybus stop past Detsky Mir; the international department is upstairs. There are flights daily to/from Moscow (Sheremetevo) for US$144; to/from St Petersburg two or three times a day for US$134; to/from Arkhangelsk for US$139. In summer, Aeroflot and Finnair each has a weekly flight to/from Helsinki via Rovaniemi in Finland for US$390 return, and, at least in June and July, SAS makes a weekly hop to Kirkenes (KKN) in Norway for US$199. Murmansk's airport code is MMK.

Bus From Murmansk, bus is the fastest way to get around the Kola Peninsula. The bus station is just next to the railway station. Buses leave at least twice a day to Apatity (US$7; five hours) and Kandalaksha (US$10; eight hours), stopping at other cities and towns in the Kola Peninsula's western corridor along the way. Buses also leave frequently to other cities near Murmansk and on the peninsula, whether 'closed' or not (you'll be able to buy the ticket without a problem, but if you're trying to get into a closed city without permission you'll be nabbed when you try to enter – soldiers board the bus at the city line of wherever it is you're trying to go so do be careful). There is a Finnish postbus making the trip between Ivalvo (where connections to Rovaniemi and Helsinki await) and the Hotel Arktika; tickets range from US$32 to US$35. The buses leave daily from Ivalvo's post office at 3 pm and arrive in Murmansk at 10.30 pm; the return trip leaves the Arktika at 7.30 am and arrives in Ivalvo at 1 pm.

Train Depending on the season, there are one or two daily fast trains from St Petersburg's Moscow Station (27 hours), and from Moscow's Leningrad Station (34 hours). There are other, slower trains as well. A line also goes 200 km to the Norwegian border at Borisoglebsk, near Nikel, though there's no line on the other side, only a road. There is one train a day to Arkhangelsk, but there's only one wagon for the journey (25 hours).

If there are no places, get a ticket on the same train to Obozersky, where you can get another ticket for Arkhangelsk. To Petrozavodsk, there are several trains a day (21 to 35 hours).

Car & Motorbike Good news: the Murmansk-St Petersburg highway is now open all the way, and for the most part it's smooth sailing. Weather permitting, you can drive to Murmansk from Norway. From Kirkenes the official road crossing is at Storskog near Nikel, 220 km from Murmansk, and the border is open Wednesday, Friday and Sunday. Sovjetreiser (☎ (47) 78 99 19 81), a Norwegian company, runs a passenger bus service to Murmansk from Kirkenes for NOK350 (about US$40); buses leave Kirkenes at 3 pm, and arrive in Murmansk at the Hotel Arktika at 10 pm. The return journey departs on Wednesday, Friday and Sunday at 9 am, arriving in Kirkenes at 1 pm.

The only official border crossing from Finland to the Kola Peninsula is near the Finnish town of Ivalo, 240 km west via the Lotta River valley. The Finnish border town is Raja Jooseppi, which has links with Helsinki (the Russian border town is Lotta). Murmansk Intourist says it's open to foreigners but that's if you're hauling freight or if you spend quite a bit of baksheesh to get through as an individual traveller – right now, it is essentially not an open border, but Kola officials say that it should be fully open to passenger traffic in late 1995.

Boat The sea terminal (*morskoy vokzal*) is mainly for transport on the inlet and weekly or twice-weekly summer connections along the Barents coast. Take the footbridge across the railyard from the right side of the railway station if you're facing the harbour, then 150 metres to the right.

From Vadso, Norway, Murmansk Shipping Company runs a ferry service aboard the *Kanin* for NOK500 each way. In summer (June to August) the service runs three times a week, with a visa-free return trip that gives you a day in Murmansk. The trip is made at night, takes 12 hours and includes breakfast.

In winter (September to June), boats run to Vadso on the second and fourth Wednesday, and return to Murmansk on the second and fourth Thursday of each month. Contact Vadso Reisburo (☎ (47) 78 95 10 79, fax 78 95 10 31) for more information.

From Kirkenes there's a catamaran that sails daily except Wednesday and Sunday for NOK550; check with Sovjetreiser for details (see Car & Motorbike above).

There is talk of reopening the ferry service to Arkhangelsk, but as the line has been unprofitable, it's best to contact Murmansk Shipping Company (MSC) to check. MSC also runs a coastal service to areas of the Kola Peninsula that are not accessible by road; these are mainly 'closed' areas, but MSC may be able to get you on if you've got a good reason. Every possible restriction will apply but if you're game, contact MSC's extremely helpful foreign relations manager, Alexandr Timofeev (☎ (47) 78 91 04 42). He's very busy so don't call on a lark or a whim.

If you're really rich and want the experience of a lifetime, MSC's atomic-powered ice-breakers offer passenger service between Murmansk and Providenia, just across the Bering Strait from Anchorage, Alaska, once a year. The 21-day journey cuts through the ice and stops at Wrangel Island, the Novosibirskie Islands, Severnaya Zemlya, the North Pole (where you party on the ice), Zemlya Frantsa-Iosifa (Franz Josef Land), Novaya Zemlya and Murmansk. Prices *start* at US$18,950 per person, double occupancy. The price includes two hours of helicopter flight time as well as hotels in Helsinki and Providenia, but not airfare. Contact Quark Expeditions (☎ 800 356 5699, toll free within USA and Canada only), 980 Post Rd, Darien, CT, 06820 USA.

Getting Around

A taxi from the airport to the centre is about US$7. Bus Nos 106 and 106-Э (express) run between the airport and the railway station every 20 to 30 minutes for 50 kopecks; the express takes half an hour. The Hotel Polyarny Zory is near the Detsky Mir bus stop;

the Hotel Arktika is just across from the railway station. For the 69th Parallel Hotel, get off at Detsky Mir and go back on trolley-bus No 1 or 6.

AROUND MURMANSK
ОКРЕСТНОСТЬ МУРМАНСКА
Kola
Кола
There isn't much of the past left in Kola. An exception, however, is the homely **Annunciation Cathedral** (Blagoveshchensky sobor, 1809) which has a little museum on Pomory life (but you can see a display of this, the town's wooden fortress and more, at the Murmansk Museum of Regional Studies). It's open from 10 am to 5.30 pm (4 pm on weekends), and closed Monday.

To get there, take bus No 106 (not No 106-Э) from the railway station for 15 km to the Kola stop, then walk for 10 minutes to the west from the Lotta turn-off.

Severomorsk
Североморск
Population: 70,000
The headquarters of the Russian North Fleet is mostly closed, but it's possible to get here. What you need is a good reason, and there seem to be three of those (on all the following, no-one will mention prices or guarantee anything until each case is reviewed).

Submarine K-21 This WW II-era submarine saw quite a bit of action and is now a museum. Intourist Murmansk can arrange a tour with 'a lot of notice' and heavy bureaucratic intervention.

Safonovo The Military Aircraft Museum in Safonovo, near Severomorsk, is said by expats and by Murmansk's Regional Cultural Administrator to house a spectacular exhibition of military aviation. It is also visitable through Intourist Murmansk under similar conditions.

Cruiser *Admiral Khimov* The Apatity City Administration can arrange a look at the atomic cruiser *Admiral Khimov* when it's in

port at Severomorsk. The city administration needs at least one month's notice (see Apatity later). The trip would also include a city tour of Severomorsk.

Polyarny
Полярный
Population: 29,000
The headquarters of the Russian Nuclear Submarine Fleet is completely closed to foreigners. Forget it.

MONCHEGORSK
МОНЧЕГОРСК
Population: 70,000
The immediately obvious ecological devastation in and around Monchegorsk (the name in Saami means 'beautiful tundra') is appalling: the ground is literally scorched black, and there is a total absence of plant life due to both the pollution and plant-burning campaigns by the city administration, which felt that black ground was more 'attractive' than dying vegetation. Recent events have transformed the town's story from merely tragic to tragically ironic.

The culprits are the Soviet government's flagrant disregard for the environment in favour of industrial output (which was idiotic both economically and environmentally), and its brainchild, the Severonikel Kombinat plant which produces nickel and copper. Between 1980 and 1993, this plant and its sister, Pechemnikel, in the border town of Nikel, spewed 600,000 tonnes of sulfur dioxide into the atmosphere, along with 10,000 tonnes of nickel powder and other heavy metals, according to Valery Berlin of the Peoples Ecological Centre in Apatity. In 1994 and 1995 emissions had been cut roughly in half, due mainly to lower production.

The irony is, since the fall of the Soviet Union and the related decline in military orders, the plant's main clients are now subcontractors for US and Japanese auto manufacturers, who use the plant's products to manufacture catalytic converters that reduce emissions on Western automobiles.

If there's any good news, it's that reduced

demand by the military has led to a 30% reduction in pollution, which has had noticeable effects already. But without drastic foreign assistance in the form of 'conversion' (from military production to the manufacture of civilian goods), the situation will only get worse. Already over 1000 sq km of trees have been destroyed in Monchegorsk and the Kola Peninsula's northern corridor.

The only attraction here, unless you're an ecologist or just want to see environmental hell, is the nearby Lappland Nature Reserve.

All calls from outside the town must go through the operator in Murmansk

Places to Stay & Eat

The town's two hotels are the *Lapplandia* (☎ 2 45 26), at prospekt Metallurgov 32, which has singles/doubles from US$14.25/20, and the somewhat nicer *Sever* (☎ 2 26 55), at prospekt Metallurgov 4 (nearer the bus station). The Sever has slightly better rooms and it's cheaper, with rooms for US$5.75/7.75. The restaurant at the Lapplandia is open from noon to 11 pm, and the Sever has a bufet on the 1st floor.

Getting There & Away

Buses leave to/from Murmansk's bus station several times a day (US$4.50; three hours).

LAPPLAND NATURE RESERVE
ЛАППЛАНДСКИЙ ГОСУДАРСТВЕННЫ ЗАПОВЕДНИК

Near the ecologically devastated city of Monchegorsk, and spanning north and west towards Norway and Finland, the UNESCO-protected Lappland Nature Reserve (☎ 2 22 67 – through Murmansk operator only; e-mail root@zap.mgus.murmansk.su – limited English) consists of 2684 sq km of almost pristine wilderness: about half of it is virgin tundra, and the rest consists of alpine grasslands, marshes, rivers and lakes. The reserve was founded in 1932 to protect the area's reindeer herds; these herds are still among Europe's largest. Along with over 220 species of vertebrates and 180 bird species, there are more than 800 species of higher plants, mosses and lichens. Today, the park

can be visited by individuals or small groups (fewer than 12 people) under limited conditions by advance arrangement.

The threat to the ecological balance of the park's flora and fauna is multi-faceted: on one hand, while the Khibiny mountain range manages to stave off most of the damage that Monchegorsk's nickel plant threatens to inflict, the easternmost section of the park has been decimated. Inside the park itself poachers, illegal loggers and other trespassers inflict damage, too. These miscreants, along with the usual culprits – local and regional government corruption, lack of funding – make keeping the park alive more difficult. The Russian government, along with non-governmental organisations including the Scandinavian Study Centre, the World Wide Fund for Nature and the American Association for the Support of Ecological Initiatives, is scrambling to provide funding and expertise.

Inside, visitors can trek through the wilderness – the best times to visit are March-April and July-August – or traverse it on cross-country skis or snowshoes. There are cottages dotted throughout the park, about every 15 km along trails, and the area is patrolled by very helpful and friendly rangers. The rangers, and the 20 or so people who live on the reserve, make their base camp (and the tourist base camp as well) at Chunozerskaya, Lapplandsky's administrative centre. You'll probably run into reindeer and wolves, at the very least, along your way.

Wolves are common in the reserve

Costs vary but are generally very low – this is a non-profit centre.

What to Bring

Very warm clothes, in layers – the outer layer waterproof. Good, comfortable trekking boots. Equipment is available but Western equipment, especially sleeping bags, will probably be of higher quality. Russian tents are fine but heavy. If you'll be trekking, you may want to bring along trail mix and other high-protein food, and you'll need navigational equipment – at the very least a sighting compass, and a Global Positioning System unit (see GPS in Siberia & the Far East Facts for the Visitor) isn't a bad idea at all. Snowshoes and skis are available locally for loan or inexpensive rental.

Getting There & Away

The reserve is best reached through Monchegorsk. Arrangements must be made in advance, and there are several agencies that can handle this for you, notably the Scandinavian Study Centre (formerly the Econord Ecological Information Centre; Norwegian ☎ (47) 78 91 40 10, wait for second tone and then dial 118; or, from Apatity, ☎ 3 72 62). You can also make arrangements through the very friendly folks at the American Association for the Support of Ecological Initiatives (☎ (1 203) 347 2967; fax (1 203) 347 8459; e-mail wwasch@eagle.wesleyan.edu), 150 Coleman Rd, Middletown CT 06457, USA. Bill Wasch Sr and Jr are both intimately involved with the reserve and others like it, and are great sources of information.

From St Petersburg, contact Alexandr Karpenko, head of Adonis (☎ 307 09 18; e-mail alexk@aasei.spb.su), at Komandantsky prospekt 40, korpus 2, flat 236. All the above agencies are not-for-profit, and all can arrange stays at other European Russian reserves as well.

APATITY

АПАТИТЫ
Population: 80,000
The Kola Peninsula's second-largest city was founded as a geological studies centre in 1966, on the site of a former Gulag camp. Today it is a mining centre, named after the apatite ore, used in the production of phosphorous fertilisers. The Kola Peninsula has the world's largest deposit of apatite ore.

While the city itself isn't very attractive to those outside scientific circles, Apatity is an excellent jump-off point for hiking, climbing and skiing expeditions in the nearby Khibiny mountains, and hunting trips – who knows, you may even get a chance to see Yeti, the Big Foot-like forest loiterer (42-cm-long footprints have been found) who is said to pop into the region now and again, apparently just to walk around leaving his mark. Apatity is also a cultural centre for arts and crafts.

Orientation

Apatity has two main sections, the 'Academic Town' and the city proper. The main shopping streets are ulitsa Fersmana and ulitsa Lenina. The city's main railway station is at the south-western end of town, while the bus station is north of the centre, just east of the Academic Town.

Information

The Scandinavian Study Centre (☎ 3 72 62) is a terrific source of information; they're in the Academic Town, in Laboratory 8A. The Apatity City Administration (☎ 3 15 04, 3 48 30) is at ploshchad Lenina 1; they can help with hotel bookings or tourist information in Russian. See the Kola Peninsula Tourist Information section for more on the useful services these places can offer travellers.

You can change money at one of the two banks next to each other on ploshchad Geologicheskaya: Sberbank, open Monday to Friday from 8 am to 8 pm, Saturday 11 am to 5 pm; and Apititkom Bank, open Monday to Friday from 9.30 am to 12.30 pm.

The central post, telephone and fax offices are on ploshchad Lenina.

The best bookshop in town is next to the post and telephone offices on ploshchad Lenina. Maps of the region (1:1,000,000) are available from the sporting goods shop

EUROPEAN RUSSIA

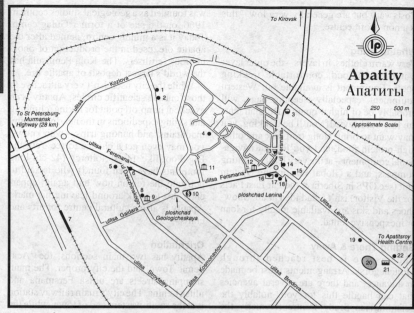

1	Library Библиотека	9	Regional Museum Краеведческий музей севера	16	Post, Telephone & Telegraph Почтамт, Телефон и Телеграф
2	Bookshop Книжный Магазин	10	Bank Банк	17	Cinema Кино
3	Bus Station Автовокзал	11	Museum of the Geo- logical Exhibition Музей Геологической Выставкой	18	Bookshop Книжний магазин
4	Scandinavian Study Centre (Econord) Скандинавский центр			19	Dom Kultury Дом Культури
5	Central Market Центральный рынок	12	Geological Exploration Museum Музей Геологических Экспедиций	20	Skating Rink Каток
6	Salma Art Gallery Салма Арт			21	Swimming Pool Бассейн
7	Railway Station Железнодорожный вокзал	13	Pelmennaya Пельменная	22	Sporting Goods Shop Магазин Спортивных принадлежностей
		14	City Administration Городская Администрация		
8	Sporting Goods Shop Магазин Спортивных принадлежностей	15	Hotel Ametist Гостиница Аметист		

around the corner from the Regional Museum, on the corner of ulitsa Dzerzhinskogo and ulitsa Gaidara.

The city's telephone code is 81533.

Museums

Rock fans won't be disappointed in Apatity, home to the massive **Museum of the Geological Exhibition**, at ulitsa Fersmana 26A (entrance is on the west side of the building). It's geared to specialists, and it's open Monday to Friday from 9 am to 5 pm, with a break from 12.40 to 2 pm. Just down the street at No 6 is the more user-friendly **Regional Geological Museum**, a much smaller affair but with very good exhibitions of rocks and minerals unique to the area, as well as some local crafts. It's open Monday to Friday from 9 am to 6 pm. The **Regional Museum**, on the corner of ulitsa Dzerzhinskogo and ulitsa Gaidara, has a ho-hum collection if you've seen the one in Murmansk, but worth it if you haven't. There are Saami costumes, tools and sledges, and an interesting 14th-century Swedish map of the region. It's open (ostensibly) daily except Sunday and Monday from 10 am to 6 pm, but sometimes you have to beg to get in.

Places to Stay

The *Hotel Amatist* (☎ 3 32 01), ulitsa Lenina 3, has clean singles/doubles for US$25/32; ask for a room with a view of the mountains. There's a smoky bufet/bar on the 2nd floor, open until midnight. The *Tsentr Zdorovya Apatitstroya* (Apititsroy Health Centre, ☎ 4 08 27), at the eastern edge of town, was formerly the rest and health clinic of the huge Apititsroy construction company, which has now opened the clinic to the public because they've fallen on hard times. This spa is a spotlessly clean resort complete with a very nice pool and sauna/banya, winter garden and two restaurants. New prices haven't been set yet, but in 1994, a 21-day stay including accommodation, meals and health treatments (sitz baths, mud treatments, homeopathic milkshakes and massage) was an amazing US$166! Nightly, weekly and monthly stays are available, and the city administration uses the place as a base for its hunting and fishing excursions. Contact either the city administration or the Scandinavian Study Centre to book.

The *Dacha*, next door to the health-centre, is a great deal for groups: it's a four-room hotel with queen-sized beds, and downstairs is a living room, winter garden, sauna and cold-pool. All this for US$71 per night.

Service is excellent, and while food isn't provided the staff will cook up any food you bring them. Contact either the city administration or the Scandinavian Study Centre to book.

Places to Eat

There aren't really any local specialities to speak of, but the locally made, round-loaf bread, Pomorsky Khleb, is great stuff; local bakeries also make a mean Rom Baba (though you'll be hard-pressed to find any rum in them!).

There's a restaurant at the *Hotel Amatist* that is big, loud and typical. Across the street, a *stolovaya* serves up stolovaya fare. The best fast food in town is at the *Pelmennaya*, ulitsa Fersmana 9, which has excellent pelmeni dumplings, 'chebureki', which is like a deep-fried Jamaican beef pie, and edible sausage. A gut-busting pelmeni session will cost about US$1.25. The *Gril-Bar*, at ulitsa Lenina 20, has sandwiches and chicken for about US$0.90 to US$1.75. Ulitsa Fersmana is a central shopping street, and it and ulitsa Lenina are both lined with well-stocked food shops.

Entertainment

Bi-weekly classical concerts are held at the Salma Art Salon (☎ 4 11 83), ulitsa Dzerzhinskogo 1. Musicians and music lovers from all over the region gather here for free or inexpensive concerts and recitals. Information is available at Salma, or at the Scandinavian Study Centre.

Things to Buy

Apatity is an artistic centre, and a locally invented method of 'painting', using coloured dust from crushed local minerals, is now catching on all over the Russian north. The wonderful Salma Art Salon, at ulitsa Dzerzhinskogo 1, is a true cooperative venture: it's privately owned and shows and sells the work of over 200 Kola Peninsula artists. Prices are low, and the management can arrange for customs papers to get the stuff out (they'll even significantly under-value pieces on your receipts to thwart exorbitant customs levies, and they said we could print that!). The exhibition hall to the front holds new exhibitions of arts and craft plus applied decorative art every month, and a shop is at the back.

Getting There & Away

Air Apatity's new Khibiny Airport is served from Moscow (daily except Saturday and Sunday); tickets are US$124 or R150,000 for Russians. Flights to/from St Petersburg leave Monday, Tuesday, Friday and Sunday and are US$106. There are no flights from Murmansk. Apatity's airport code, KVK, stands for Krovsk, but it means Apatity.

Bus & Train Buses are the easiest way to get in from Murmansk, and they run at least twice a day from Murmansk's bus station (US$7; four hours). Trains are cheaper and take longer (five to eight hours); take any train heading south from Murmansk. From Moscow and St Petersburg, most trains to Murmansk stop in Apatity.

Car & Motorbike Apatity is 30 km east of the St Petersburg-Murmansk highway, from a turning 35 km south of Monchegorsk, and it's well sign-posted.

Getting Around

Bus Nos 5 and 13 (not 13K) run between the railway station and the centre. There's an hourly bus to Khibiny Airport. Bus Nos 101, 102 and 105 go between Apatity and Kirovsk.

KIROVSK
КИРОВСК
Population: 45,000

There's not much to do in Kirovsk except ski, but the skiing here is definitely the finest in north-west Russia – the city hosts the annual All-Europe Downhill Freestyle Competition. In addition, the city's five ski schools hold lessons in ballet skiing, ski-jumping, mogul skiing and has annual giant slalom and speed ski competitions. If you break your leg while you're at it, the city's newest church boasts a 'healing' icon that'll get you fixed up in a jiffy!

Orientation & Information

Kirovsk, and its 'microregion', known not by its Russian name (Kukisvumchorr) but simply by the moniker 'Kirovsk-25' (signifying its distance from Apatity, a convention adopted by early geological crews who would use distance markers to identify dig sites), are nestled in the Khibiny mountains, separated by a winding mountain road. The centre is tiny and easy to navigate, while all the skiing takes place near Kirovsk-25. The central post and telephone offices are at ulitsa Lenina 1; there is no sign for the post office, but the door on the right is for a bank (that doesn't change money), that also accepts packages and letters, while the door on the left is for the telephone office. To get there, walk up the stairs, then go through an unmarked door on the left side of the 2nd floor. International calls can be made on – get this – three days' notice, but you can get a *srochny*, or express, call placed within two hours at no additional charge if you ask specifically for it. It's open from 8 am to 5.30 pm every day. To call Kirovsk from outside the region try the operator at Murmansk.

Maps are available at the city administration building. The city's best bookshop (which is not saying much) is at ulitsa Lenina 22. Change money next door at the Sberbank, open Monday to Saturday from 9 am to 4.30 pm, with a break from 2 to 3 pm.

Things to See & Do

Orthodox Church The Kazanskaya Church (Kazanskaya tserkov), just outside Kirovsk-25, was built on the site of another church that had been moved from Kirovsk. The newly built church is, well, unorthodox in that it was converted from a typical north Russian wooden house. The inside is lovely, however, with an impressive iconostasis and the allegedly miraculous **Icon of St Nicholas**. On the night of 21 May 1994, the icon incredibly restored itself, and now works its miracles Monday to Friday from 9 am to 6 pm with a break between 2 and 3 pm. Take bus No 1, 12 or 105 from Kirovsk centre towards Kirovsk-25, and ask for the church. From the bus stop, walk west (back towards Kirovsk), turn south (left), then turn east (left again) and the church is 200 metres on the right-hand side of the road.

Kirovsk-25 This 'microregion' has a **Regional Museum** that seems to be perpetually closed, but the best sight is the surrounding mountains, or rather the lack of half of them. A veteran geophysicist for a major Western minerals concern said that he knew of no way to accomplish such a neat removal of literally half a mountain (they look like those models you used to see in school of a cutaway section of a volcano), other than a nuclear detonation, but local scientists insist that this was accomplished by the use of earth movers and heavy equipment. Nevertheless, it's an awesome and disturbing sight to behold. Take bus No 1, 12 or 105 from Kirovsk to the northern end of Kirovsk-25.

Skiing The city's ski slopes may look easy, but those mountains sure are steep! The slopes' 17 lifts are mainly towropes, and lift tickets are US$0.50 per ride, or US$4.50 for a day pass. There are eight trails, as well as a children's trail and lift. Bring your own equipment – while rentals are available, the place only has about 20 pairs of skis and boots to go round, and this place is popular! Ski packages can be arranged through the Scandinavian Study Centre in Apatity, or through Vice-Mayor Mikhail Viktorovich Shevakh, at the city administration office (☎ 2 14 35; Norwegian fax (47) 78 91 49 10, wait for tone then dial 120), ulitsa Lenina 16, which can also help with hotel bookings.

Places to Stay
All hotels are rather crowded in winter. The *Hotel Polyarnaya* (no telephone), ulitsa Lenina 18, next to the city hall, is very cold and drafty, but it's clean and the cheapest

place in town (and they'll give you extra blankets). Doubles/quads go for US$8.20/5 per person, and they'll let two people take a quad room. The Hungarian-built *Hotel Severnaya* (☎ 2 04 42), ulitsa Lenina 11, opened in February 1994 and is a truly Western-standard hotel (except for the tiny Russian hotel beds) smack in the centre of the city. At US$50, however, the singles are not worth it in the slightest, but for the same price you can get a double with a very nice bathroom, and the deluxe is US$47 (?!) per person, though they'll stick someone else in there if you're alone and only pay for yourself. There are also a lobby bar and a restaurant.

The *Khibinsky Sportkomplex* (Khibiny mountains Sports Complex) is a large turbaza that was closed when we visited but was scheduled to reopen in 1995. It's said to have singles/doubles/triples, and a restaurant. It's the hotel closest to the ski slopes, and you can get there by taking a rare bus No 12.

Places to Eat
There's a good market on ploshchad Lenina opposite the Lenin statue that has imported food, drinks etc. It's open from 11 am to 7 pm.

The restaurant at the *Hotel Severnaya* has OK food and loud music. *Kafe Zodiak*, at ulitsa Lenina 13 (the sign says *Morozhenoe Kafe*), is somewhat pricey and doesn't have much, though they say that that will change soon. *Restoran Vechernee*, ulitsa Khibinogorskaya 29, is the best place in town; there's a café upstairs and it's open every day but Monday from noon to 8 pm.

Getting There & Around
Bus Nos 101, 102 and 105 go between Apatity and Kirovsk. Bus Nos 1, 12 and 105 run between Kirovsk and Kirovsk-25. Kirovsk's railway station, like many of the 'Potyomkin villages' that would pop up around Russia (constructed only to impress visiting officials) is hardly ever used, and locals joke that its first and last passenger was Iosif Stalin.

POLYARNYE ZORY
ПОЛЯРНЫЕ ЗОРИ
Population: 20,000
This 'energy city' is right chuffed to be home to the Kola Nuclear Power Plant, a VVER-440-213 and VVER-440-230-type plant. All through the town, cheerful references to the wonders of Mr Atom abound, with slogans like 'An Atom Should be a Worker, not a Soldier' decorating local apartment blocks.

The town's railway and bus station is 1.5 km due west of the Nevsky Berega Hotel and there's a market just across the street from the station, though it only sells clothes. Next to the railway station is the **Museum of the Polar Partisan**, open daily except Wednesday and Thursday from 10 am to 7 pm, which is worth a visit if you're waiting for a train.

Telephone calls to Polyarnye Zory from outside the region must be routed through Murmansk. The telephone code is 81555.

Organised Tours
For something with a difference, the plant's Public Relations Director, Peter Danilov (☎ 6 81 40, 6 39 10), will happily arrange a tour on five days' notice. Marvel at the fish (trout, salmon and others) that swim in the tank filled with the plant's output coolant water (this purportedly demonstrates the plant's cleanliness).

Place to Stay & Eat
The town's hotel, the *Nevsky Berega* (☎ 6 41 51), ulitsa Lomonosova 1, is spotlessly clean, with comfortable doubles for US$22.75. Most rooms have terraces overlooking the forest. The hotel's restaurant is very nice, though it can afford to be; main courses start at US$4. The steak and onions for US$5 is good but the portions are small. It's non smoking in the restaurant, and room service is available.

The *Pivnoy Bar* next to the market is good for a snack.

Getting There & Away
The city is between Kandalaksha and Apatity, and can be reached by both train and bus, several times a day, from either place. In town, there aren't any buses between the railway or bus stations and the hotel.

KANDALAKSHA
КАНДАЛАКША
Population: 50,000
The Kola Peninsula's most important port after Murmansk, Kandalaksha is now a rather grim industrial city, home to one of the military's most important aluminium plants. The Pomory fishing village, around which the town was founded and which dates from the 17th century, is still inhabited. The telephone code is 81533.

Things to See & Do
Kandalaksha's large **nature reserve and sea-bird sanctuary** (Kandalakshisky Gosudarstvenny Zapovednik) is on the White Sea islands south-west of its coast. Over 250 species of sea birds call it home including eiders, gulls, murres, kittiwakes, razorbills and black guillemots, which nest in the rookeries of the Kuvshin and Kharlov islands. Trips to the islands can be arranged, in summer only, through the city administration office (☎ 2 49 57), the city excursions bureau (☎ 5 03 96), or at the reserve's administration centre, at the southern end of town. For more information on getting in, you can also contact the American Association for the Support of Ecological Initiatives (☎ (1 203) 347 2967; fax (1 203) 347 8459; e-mail wwasch@eagle.wesleyan.edu), 150 Coleman Rd, Middletown CT 06457, USA.

From St Petersburg, contact Alexandr Karpenko, head of Adonis (☎ 307 09 18; e-mail alexk@aasei.spb.su), at Komandant-sky prospekt 40, korpus 2, flat 236. Both of the above agencies are not-for-profit, and both can arrange stays at other European Russian reserves as well.

To get to the reserve, take bus No 1 from the railway station to the last stop and walk towards the port; the administration centre will be on the left-hand side, across the river from the Pomor village.

In the area west of the town, there is said to be the wreckage of US and British planes downed during WW II.

Places to Stay & Eat

The *Belomore Hotel* (☎ 2 31 00, 2 20 13), at ulitsa 50-letia Oktyabrya dom 1 (opposite the tank), has surly staff and grotty singles/doubles for US$21.50/33.50, with a restaurant that opens 'in the evening'. The *Hotel Spolokhi* (☎ 5 57 68), ulitsa Naberezhnaya 130 (due east of the centre, towards the riverbank), manages to be both new and a dump – the desk clerk thought the author was using his compass to measure background radiation and she didn't seem surprised in the least that someone would measure radiation in the hotel lobby – with rooms at US$23/34.50. There's a restaurant in the hotel that is open Friday to Sunday from 8 pm, and a bufet open Monday to Friday from 10 am to 4 pm. There is also a *Gril-Bar* next door to the Belomore Hotel.

Getting There & Around

Kandalaksha is served by several buses a day to Apatity and one a day to Murmansk. Any train heading to or from Murmansk stops here as well. Any local bus goes from the railway and bus station at the north-east end of town to the centre, which is to the south-west, across the railway tracks.

Arkhangelsk Region
Архаигельская област

ARKHANGELSK
АРХАИГЕЛЬСК
Population: 800,000

Arkhangelsk's rough and grim history, a product of its strategic location, has ensured that since its inception many of its residents have worn some sort of uniform (see History below).

However, Arkhangelsk is now a tidy, staid and utilitarian city, pleasant enough but with few attractions (unless you happen to be in the oil or diamond business). It's more likely that you'll be using the city as a jump-off point for one of the region's several other offerings, such as Malye Karely or the Solovetsky Islands.

The centre is an interesting mixture of turn-of-the-century wooden buildings, many with wood-burning stoves (for which stacks of logs wait outside) and water wells, which sit adjacent to Soviet-styled concrete apartment blocks and department stores.

History

The construction of present-day Arkhangelsk was decreed by Ivan the Terrible in 1574, 21 years after the arrival of the first British traders there. The *Edward Bonaventure*, captained by Richard Chancellor, along with the *Bona Confidentia* and the *Bona Spiranza*, left England in 1553 in search of a northern access route to China, but ended up in what was then a remote fishing settlement along the Severnaya Dvina River.

Armed with a note from England's King Edward VI, Chancellor bounded overland to Moscow, where he met with Ivan (then still in his pre-Terrible period), who immediately and enthusiastically established trade ties with England. The Brits, keen to discover an enormous new market for their wool (and relishing the idea of thumbing their noses at the Flemish, who had already been trading quite profitably at Novgorod), established the Muscovy Company in late 1553.

In 1693 Peter the Great, fully charged with his vision of a great Russian navy, built an admiralty and seaport at Arkhangelsk, from where he launched the Russian navy's tiny first ship, the *Svyatoy Pavel*, in 1694.

The importance of Arkhangelsk's port as a centre for trade, especially with Western Europe, led to an enormous bazaar or trade fair, which reached the height of its power in the late 1700s.

The 19th century and the early 20th century established Arkhangelsk as a major lumber centre (by 1914 there were 29 sawmills employing around 11,000 workers), which it remains today.

Allied troops have twice played an important role in the city's history. During Russia's civil war, the allied 'interventionists'

The Texan Invasion

If you should overhear someone in Arkhangelsk saying that they 'wunder if we kin git sum Meskin food roun here', you've probably run into one of the gaggle of Texas oil men who stampeded into town over the past few years. Conoco led the charge, establishing a joint venture with Arkhangelsk Geologia, a Russian oil company which needed a bit of help to develop a field that it had been working on. At present, Conoco has about 60 people in and around the region, most of whom call Arkhangelsk home. Not long after they moved in, Conoco's Texans were joined by other Texans from Texaco, Mobil etc. They in turn were joined by representatives of mineral giants such as 'the big Australian', BHP, who have been having a fine old time extracting the area's diamonds, thank you very much. It is to be expected that the upshot of such high-rolling folks putting their feet up on desks around here will be an increase in the cost of living; prices in Arkhangelsk are already approaching Moscovian levels. ■

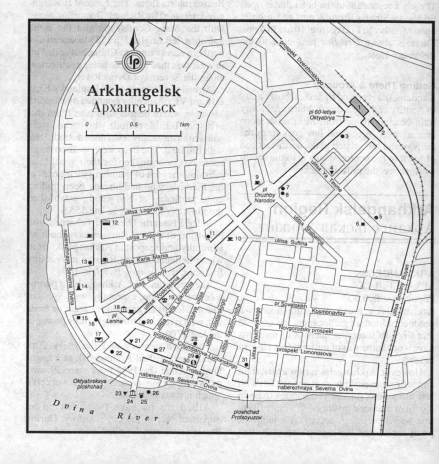

managed to land at Arkhangelsk on 2 August 1918, but aside from the heroic landing operation, they accomplished nothing because of confusion within their own ranks (the multinational force comprised of Brits, Americans, French, Poles, Italians and others was constantly, some say hilariously, hindered by breakdowns in internal communications).

During WW II Arkhangelsk, along with Murmansk, became a key supply port bringing desperately needed foreign equipment to the Russian army, and food to supply the besieged city of Leningrad.

Orientation

Arkhangelsk sits on a peninsula jutting into the Severnaya Dvina River. The city's streets sprawl in a rough 'V' shape with an axis formed by ulitsa Voskresenia (formerly ulitsa Engelsa), which cuts from the river at the south-west to the railway and bus stations at the north-east. The most obvious landmark is the towering skyscraper on ploshchad Lenina.

Arkhangelsk is just beginning the process of changing its street names. The following are name changes as of September 1994:

New Name	Old Name
naberezhnaya Severnaya	naberezhnaya VI Lenina-Dvina
prospekt Troitsky	prospekt Vinogradova
ulitsa Voskresenia	ulitsa Engelsa

Information

Tourist Office Because the city was 'closed' for so long there's a distinct lack of tourist information to be had; Sputnik's office (☎ 43 20 30), at Room 101 in the city administration building off ploshchad Lenina, is mainly

PLACES TO STAY		2	Bus Station Автовокзал	19	Telephone Office Телефон
6	Hotel Belamorskaya Гостиница Беламорская	3	Aeroflot Office Аэрофлот	20	Dom Knigi Дом Книги
15	Pur Navilok Hotel Гостиница Пур Навилок	5	Market Рынок	22	Lomonosov Drama Theatre Драматический театр им. Ломоносова
27	Hotel Dvina Гостиница Двина	7	Art/Souvenir Shop Сувениров Магазин		
		8	Ford Sport Centre Форд Спортивный Центр	24	Krasnaya Pristan Pier, Zapovednik Museum Красная Пристань, Музей-заповедник Малые Карелы
PLACES TO EAT					
4	Pelmennaya Пельменная	11	Book Shop Книжный магазин		
9	Kafe Belye Nochi Кафе Белье Ночи	12	Swimming Pool Бассейн	26	Pier Причал
10	Kafe Bylina Кафе Былина	13	Concert Hall Консертный зал	28	House Of Propaganda... Дом пропаганды
21	Gril Bar Грил Бар	14	Great Patriotic War Monument Памятник Великой Отечественной Войны	29	Department Store ЦУМ
23	U Alyosha Restaurant Ресторан у Алёша			30	Sberbank Сбербанк
25	Seabridge Bar Сийбридж Бар	16	Administration Building Административное здание	31	Central Market Централь ний рынок
OTHER		17	Post Office Почтамт		
1	Railway Station Железнодорожный вокзал	18	Fine Arts Museum Художествений музей		

geared to sending Russians to Asia and Europe but their staff are friendly and helpful. The Intourist office (☎ 49 00 00, 49 14 30) was devoid of staff when we visited, but they're also said to be helpful.

Money Change money at one of the two Sberbanks: one is on the corner of prospekt Lomonosova and ulitsa Voskresenia and another is at ulitsa Volodarskogo just north of naberezhnaya Severnaya Dvina. There is also a private moneychanging office at naberezhnaya Severnaya Dvina 88 while the Pur Navilok hotel has an exchange booth.

Post & Telecommunications The main post office is on the west side of ploshchad Lenina at ulitsa Voskresenia 5. Send telegrams from window Nos 2 and 3, and international post from window No 8, though there's no international EMS yet. The central telephone office, with its Alice in Wonderland motif, is on the corner of prospekt Lomonosova and ulitsa Voskresenia; it gets incredibly crowded in the evenings so get there early.

The telephone code for Arkhangelsk is 818.

Bookshops City maps are available at the main Dom Knigi bookshop on ploshchad Lenina, which also has a fair book selection and an adjacent newsstand that sells Russian newspapers from all over the country. You can also find maps at the souvenir shop just east of ploshchad Druzhby Narodov on ulitsa Voskresenia.

The city's only English-language newspaper is the *Arkhangelsk Business News*, an atrociously edited bi-monthly (some articles begin with the word 'Nevertheless') that occasionally and inadvertently proffers a tidbit or two of practical information.

Things to See & Do
Fine Arts Museum The city's surprisingly good Fine Arts Museum on the north-east side of ploshchad Lenina boasts an impressive selection of 16th to 18th-century religious artworks on the 2nd floor. Towards the rear of the 2nd floor you'll also find 19th-century textiles, samovars, some applied decorative art and a tiny collection of period costumes from the late 19th century.

The 1st floor, if you can get past the stern babushkas who try to ward off those not in a group (be persistent; it may help to carry a notebook and look student-like), houses a good selection of paintings and portraits with 'northern' themes, and an extensive Imperial Portrait Gallery. Look for Stanislav Khlebovsky's portraits (1861) of Catherine II and the dead Prince Oranskogo.

The mezzanine level, looking very much like a tiny New York Soho loftspace, is host to classical and jazz concerts; schedules are posted in the lobby, where you'll also find a small stand of art books and the museum's excellent local crafts shop, which sells very good handicrafts at excellent prices. Admission is US$2 for foreigners and US$0.15 for Russians and ISIC card-holders. It's open every day except Wednesday from 10 am to 5 pm.

Regional Studies Museum The main reason to come here (also on the north-east side of ploshchad Lenina a few doors down from the Fine Arts Museum) is the exhibition on the 2nd floor dedicated to local soldiers who died in the Afghanistan war. The albums containing snapshots taken by Russian soldiers during the conflict gives a first-hand view of conditions in that country, and there is a moving display of personal effects and letters sent home from soldiers who died. Adjacent to this exhibition is a large but unspectacular collection of Soviet propaganda posters, and a room dedicated to Saami sledges, crafts and textiles. The 1st floor houses a taxidermy collection that's interesting in a ghoulish sort of way, with guidebooks in Russian describing local sea life. Admission is US$0.30, US$0.15 for ISIC card-holders, and it's US$1 for still photographs. It's open every day except Friday and the last Thursday of the month from 10 am to 6 pm.

House of Propaganda of Monuments of History & Culture The name (said with a straight face by museum officials) is misleading; this is an exhibition hall in a landmark wooden house on a lovely street that local officials are trying to rebuild as Arkhangelsk's answer to Moscow's Arbat. The exhibitions, which are rotated monthly, are usually by local painters or photographers (be sure to check if they're running anything by local photo-journalist Vitaly Krekhalev, whose images of everyday life under the Soviets are a gritty treat). The museum, just south-east of Pomorskaya ulitsa on prospekt Chumbarova Luchinskogo, is open daily from 10 am to 6 pm.

Zapad Sailboat Museum The *Zapad*, a Finnish-built sailing ship, can be seen at its dry-dock perch on the Krasnaya Pristan pier. It's pretty, but skip the US$0.50 unguided tour, from which you'll emerge saying, 'Yup, it's a boat, alright'.

Severnaya Dvina Embankment Walking along the Severnaya Dvina embankment can make for a lovely stroll at any time of year. The former admiralty building near the Zapad museum isn't hard to look at, and Star Trek fans will appreciate the shape of the city's Great Patriotic War monument just south of ulitsa Karla Marxa. Turning up ulitsa Karla Marxa brings you to the city's concert hall (Kamerny kontsertny zal), which is one of the more aesthetically successful Soviet church conversions – the acoustics are superb. Concerts are held several times a month; check with the cash desk at the hall.

Sports The city's 50-metre-long municipal **swimming pool** (with five-metre diving boards), at ulitsa Loginova 6, is open every day from October to June from 10 am to 9 pm. Admission is US$1.20 per hour. However, the pool is closed on several occasions during the day for swimming instruction. The city's **skating rink**, at naberezhnaya Severnaya Dvina 30, is also open to the public for sessions on Sunday at

4 and 6 pm. Admission is US$1 for adults, and US$0.50 for children. Skate rental is available but in limited supply. There's said to be a sauna as well (US$5 per hour) but it is difficult to get into.

Places to Stay

This is definitely the city's weak spot, as accommodation is either cheap and nasty or acceptable and expensive. In addition, the whole city has heating and hot water problems. The monstrous, 500-room *Dvina* (☎ 49 55 02) at prospekt Troitsky 52 is OK, with clean singles/doubles for US$33/48 and decent (though expensive) bufety. The *Hotel Belomorskaya* (☎ 46 26 67), at ulitsa Ya Timme 3, has dilapidated rooms for US$52/71 and a seedy lobby filled with shady characters (and a sign that says 'Need money? You can sell your belongings to our shop on the second floor!'). The most 'luxurious' option, and the place of choice for foreign residents, is the *Pur Navilok* (☎ 43 01 26, 43 23 89) at naberezhnaya Severnaya Dvina 88. It has bay-windowed rooms with very nice river views for US$100/120; a single without a bay window is US$80. There's a bufet on the 1st floor, and the place takes American Express cards.

Places to Eat

The town's well-stocked central market is on the corner of prospekt Chumbarova Luchinskogo, at ulitsa Vyucheyskogo, near the River Station (look for the cubic Rynok sign), and there's a second (less attractive) market opposite the Hotel Belomorskaya.

The newly refurbished *Yubileyny* restaurant at the Dvina hotel should be as good as the old one, while the *Hotel Belomorskaya's* restaurant should be avoided. A Western-style supermarket in the Belomorskaya's lobby, scheduled to open at the time of writing in early 1995, promises to sell a good selection of imported packaged foods. The *Pur Navilok* hotel has a restaurant and a bufet but the food is expensive.

Restoran Sever is a big, Soviet-style eating hall at the river terminal; its downstairs bufet has meat pies, pastries and coffee. Speaking of Soviet-style eating halls, the other one is the *Dvina* on the corner of prospekt Troitsky and ulitsa Pomorskaya (entrance is on prospekt Troitsky; the restaurant's upstairs and to the rear). Main courses range from US$1.75 to US$3.50. Downstairs, the *Bar Primorsky* is a flashy place with small, expensive though tasty pizza (US$2), slightly cheaper sandwiches and a lot of blue alcohol. All, except the Sever's bufet which closes at 8 pm, are open till midnight.

Fine dining can be had at the *U Alyosha*, a restaurant/ship moored at the Krasnaya Pristan pier that has a very cosy atmosphere and good food with meat and fish main courses from US$4 to US$6. Just across the pier is the *Seabridge* bar and restaurant, an American-owned, Finnish-managed affair on a sailing ship. This is the city's expat watering hole, and it's easy to forget you're not on Sydney's Circular Quay or in New York's South Street Seaport. Prices are expensive: upstairs you can get pizzas, hot dogs and hamburgers from US$3 to US$8, and in the downstairs bar Finnish beers go for about US$4 a pint. Both floors are open until 3 am, and all major credit cards are accepted.

The *Gril-Bar*, on prospekt Troitsky just opposite the Lomonosov Drama Theatre, has good roast chicken; a thigh and drumstick portion is about US$0.75. It's open from 9 am to 7 pm, and closed from 2 to 3 pm. There's another *chicken grill* at the central market. *Kafe Bylina* ('epic'), on ulitsa Voskresenia near ulitsa Suftina, has cheap and better than average stolovaya fare and pouty teenaged waitresses who spend a good deal of time hugging their boyfriends near the cash desk. *Belye Nochi*, ulitsa Priorova 6 at ploshchad Druzhby Narodov, has sandwiches and ice cream, along with a huge selection of alcohol, which makes it a popular night spot.

There's a good *pelmennaya* at ulitsa Ya Timme 10, serving beef-filled dumplings that you can wash down with Russian draft beer. You can fill yourself up for less than US$5, but it's only open until 8 pm.

Entertainment

The best nightclub in town is Relax (☎ 49 49 34), at the Sailor's Cultural Centre, ulitsa Shubina 9, with an entrance on prospekt Lomonosova. It's hugely popular and security is very tight; everyone is frisked, all handbags are searched at the entrance, and guests are asked to check their weapons at the door (I'm not kidding – if you are packing a weapon, you can pick up your piece as you exit from the friendly weapon check-room attendant). There's live music on Wednesday, Friday, Saturday and Sunday nights (closed Monday and Tuesday), and the place serves drinks but no food. Admission is US$5. To get there, take tram No 1 or 5 to the ulitsa Shuvorova stop, and ask for 'Relax'.

Getting There & Away

Air There is daily service to/from Moscow's Sheremetevo-1 (US$112; three hours), St Petersburg's Pulkovo-1 (US$97; three hours), and Murmansk (US$139; one hour) airports. There are three flights a week (Monday, Wednesday and Friday) to the Solovetsky Islands for US$24 each way.

The Aeroflot office is at ulitsa Voskresenia 116, just west of the railway and bus stations. It's open Monday to Friday from 10 am to 4.30 pm (break from 2 to 3 pm), and Saturday and Sunday from 10 am to 2 pm. Foreigners must use window No 9.

The airport code for Arkhangelsk is ARH.

Train There is at least one direct train a day (25 hours) to/from Moscow's Yaroslavl Station. Indirect trains can be taken through Vologda and then further north. There's a daily train to/from St Petersburg through Vologda (35 to 40 hours). There is one train to/from Murmansk a day, but there's only one wagon for the journey (25 hours). If there are no places, get a ticket on the same train to Obozersky where you can get another ticket for Arkhangelsk.

Car & Motorbike The Russian 'tourist automobile route' from Vologda is now open to foreigners, passing through Velsk and

Shenkursk, and along the Dvina to Arkhangelsk. Contact the Vologda Tours & Excursions Bureau (see Vologda later) for more information. From Moscow, take the M8 north – bring some extra shock absorbers – it's about 1100 km. The M8 goes through Vologda.

Boat For a port, there is precious little access for passenger ships, probably because of Arkhangelsk's large naval presence. There is a service to/from the Solovetsky Islands (14 hours; see the Solovetsky Islands section for details) and in future it may be possible to get a cruise from Murmansk through the Baltic Shipping Company (see the Murmansk Getting There & Away section earlier in this chapter). Regular passenger service had been cancelled in 1994 due to unprofitability.

Getting Around

There is an extensive network of buses and trams. Bus No 54 goes from the railway station to the centre. Bus No 531 runs between the railway station and Arkhangelsk Airport once an hour from 7.25 am to 7.30 pm; the first bus is at 5.55 am. Bus No 12 also runs between the railway station and the airport.

MALYE KARELY
МАЛЫЕ КАРЕЛЫ

The open-air **Wooden Architecture Museum** (☎ 99 57 44) at Malye Karely, 25 km east of Arkhangelsk, features 19th-century wooden buildings, wind and watermills, bell towers and the impressive five-domed **Vosnesenskaya cathedral**, all brought here from the Kargopol region. The architecture and construction are similar to that found in Kizhi, and the natural scenery around the reserve is quite pleasant.

The museum is open every day from 10 am to 5 pm; closed Tuesday. Admission is US$2.50 for foreigners and US$0.25 for Russians and students (they may or may not accept your ISIC as student identification).

Follow the large map of the grounds to your left as you enter. The church, **chyornye izby** (or 'black cottages', so called because the lack of a full chimney resulted in smoke

staining the outside walls), and most other buildings can only be viewed from outside, though there's a 'living room' which you can enter for a US$0.25 fee; once inside you have the privilege of ordering a US$2 cup of tea.

Another attraction, up the wooden 'ecological trail', is a second, smaller village, plus the **Georgevskaya tserkov** (1672), and some other wooden peasant houses.

At the main museum area, **horse rides** are offered, though they're expensive (US$1.50 for adults, US$0.50 for children) for the amount of time you'll actually have on the beastie.

Getting There & Away

Bus No 104 goes from Arkhangelsk's avtovokzal (bus station) and Morskoe Vokzal (sea/river terminal) to Malye Karely and back, with buses running every half-hour until 10.30 pm. Take it to the last stop, cross the street and the wooden footbridge and follow the wooden road to the cash desk.

SEVERODVINSK
СЕВЕРОДВИНСК

The main reason to visit Severodvinsk, 40 km south-west of Arkhangelsk, is to catch a glimpse of the atomic and diesel submarines parked in its harbour. Unfortunately, Severodvinsk is also a closed military city because of the atomic and diesel submarines parked in the harbour. Legal visits can be arranged, however, if enough notice is given, through the Severodvinsk city administration (☎ 2 34 97), but you'll have to give them a darned good reason. Otherwise deportation and possible arrest await anyone entering the area without permission. Bear in mind that Lonely Planet does not advise illegal travel in restricted areas.

We visited, without a visa, on a sunny September weekday and not only weren't we bothered but we were actually invited to photograph the subs and tour the bridge and weapons deck of a Russian Navy destroyer by naval officers (who later remarked that they 'really ought to set up a cash desk on the pier!'). Keep in mind that we speak passable Russian and most of the talking to the officers was done by a Russian friend, so they may not have understood that we were foreigners.

The city was the main base for the construction and staging of atomic materials (including subs) for use in the above-ground nuclear testing range on the islands of Novaya Zemlya, 500 km north-east of Arkhangelsk. Those activities have thankfully been brought to a halt, and with a drop-off in military orders, the factory isn't working much these days.

Despite its military nature, the town is quite lovely, with wide tree-lined streets and wooden Stalin-era houses.

Orientation & Information

Severodvinsk is laid out in a sensible grid, with the railway station at the north-east end of town on ulitsa Zheleznodorozhnikov, which is due north of the harbour. There are no information offices or maps available anywhere, but there is an English school in Room 403 of the Belamore Hotel, near the harbour, that apparently offers English-speaking guides. The Aeroflot office is at ulitsa Trudy 12, and it's open Monday to Friday from 8 am to 7 pm, and Saturday and Sunday from 8 am to 5 pm. The central post, telephone and telegraph office is at ulitsa Plyusina 1, off ploshchad Lenina.

Things to See & Do

The **submarines** are across the harbour from the naval base, which is at the northern end of ulitsa Portovaya. Take bus No 3, which circles the city anti-clockwise from the railway station, to ulitsa Trudy (in front of the statue labelled 'Geroi Truda'). Walk north on ulitsa Trudy, left on Pervomayskaya ulitsa and take the first right onto Portovaya

---

'We could charge people for this...'

Severodvinsk is a 'closed' city in the Arkhangelsk Region. It's closed because it's a storage area for nuclear submarines and formerly a staging area for the nuclear gear that used to be transported to the islands of Novaya Zemlya back when the Soviet Union was doing above-ground nuclear testing.

I had gone because an expatriate living in Arkhangelsk had told me that Severodvinsk was 'closed, but not *that* closed', and that I could get a great view of the subs across the harbour. After about an hour of looking, I finally asked a kid where the subs were ('Excuse me, where are the nuclear submarines?') and was directed to a fence at the end of a long, deserted street.

The 'fence' turned out to be the entrance to some sort of naval facility, and as I passed the boundary (there was no one guarding it) I realised that from that point on, no amount of pleaded ignorance would help me if I – an American with a camera in a Russian military facility – were caught. The water was now in sight, and moored at the docks were two rather large gunships, sporting several large and vicious-looking guns fore and aft. A man with a face of stone and wearing an officer's uniform stood between me and the subs.

'Hi!', I said with a smile, 'may I take a photograph?' The officer looked me and grinned, and said, 'Why not?'. There were about eight black submarines parked just across the water, but far enough away to make my photographs look as if they were taken from a spy satellite in the 1960s. Still, I got the shots. I looked over to one of the gunships and saw on board a young woman in a pink coat looking around near the bridge. As I walked back past the gang-plank, I asked the officer if I could take a look around on board. He smiled again and said, 'Of course, go right up.'

I saw the bridge and the guns but I started to get a little nervous; my Russian is good enough to say what I had said so far, but anything else would be a hopeless stretch, and I wanted to get out of there fast. On my way out, a much more senior-looking officer approached me with a look of investigatory intent.

'What is *he* doing here?', he asked, looking at me but speaking to the officer who had let me on board. 'He's taking an excursion', said the first.

The senior officer looked at me, rubbed his chin thoughtfully and said to the officer, 'You know, we really ought to set up a ticket booth out here.'

Nick Selby

ulitsa. (If you get lost, you could do what we did, which was to imitate Ensign Chekhov in *Star Trek V* and say, 'We are looking for nuclear wessles' – '*Gde atomnye podvodnye lodki*'.)

At the end of Portovaya you'll come to a (probably unstaffed) gate; this is the entrance to the base. As soon as you cross this point you are irretrievably in violation of Russian law and no amount of 'But officer, I didn't see the sign' will help you.

At the water, turn left and walk along the piers. The subs are just across the harbour to the north-west. If you should happen upon someone in uniform, it's best to ask permission – in Russian – to stick around.

Regional Studies Museum The large Regional Studies Museum, at ulitsa Pionerskaya just off ulitsa Sovietskaya, is open Monday to Wednesday and Friday from 10 am to 5 pm, and Thursday from 9 am to 5 pm. It was closed when we visited.

Amusement Park The city's amusement park is great, with the best bumper-cars in Russia. Clean and fun, there're plenty of rides for the whole family, including a Russian video arcade that has no fewer than six submarine video games. It's in the Park of Rest & Culture, off ulitsa Sovietskaya. Bus No 3 stops right in front.

Chess Club There's a frightfully busy Chess Club at ulitsa Sovietskaya 39. It's open Tuesday to Friday from 6 to 10 pm, and Saturday and Sunday from 10 am to 7 pm.

Places to Stay
To stay here, you'll need Severodvinsk to be specifically written on your visa, something that can only be obtained through an official invitation from the city administration or through the military. The cheapest option is the *Belamore Hotel* (☎ 3 63 42) at ulitsa Trudy 2, with basic singles/doubles for US$5.50/9. There's a good kiosk in the lobby, as well as a café. The newer and cleaner *Nikolsky Posad Hotel* (☎ 4 09 80), at ulitsa Karla Marxa 21, has rooms for

US$7/10.50, plus a US$1 per day 'registration fee' for foreigners. There's a coffee shop next door.

Places to Eat
The town's central market, just next to the railway station, is a massive and very busy place, with a great deal of clothing outside and a somewhat disappointing, but adequate, selection of food inside.

The *Stolovaya*, on ulitsa Zheleznodorozhnikov, 600 metres south of the railway station, had small stones in the plov, but just 20 metres further south is the *Doka Pizzeria*, serving up Western-style pizzas (in Western-style pizza boxes) for US$1.50.

There's a restaurant at the *Nikolsky Posad Hotel* that looks all right. Just down the road from the Belamore Hotel is *Lagonka*, a good bakery and sweets café serving ice cream and very imaginative cupcakes, coffee and juice. At ploshchad Lenina, opposite the House of Culture, a *Kafe* serves up a good steak for a paltry US$1, and they have some good salads.

Getting There & Away
Bus No 133 from the Arkhangelsk bus station makes the 70-minute trip frequently, and every 15 minutes between 11.30 am and 8.30 pm. It costs US$0.75, and tickets are available inside the station. Getting back is as easy; buy tickets at the bus section of the Severodvinsk Railway Station. By train it is incredibly inconvenient, being infrequent and taking three times as long – it's just not worth it.

THE SOLOVETSKY ISLANDS
СОЛОВЕЦКИЕ ОСТРОВА
The fiercely isolated Solovetsky Islands, a tiny archipelago in the White Sea between Karelia and Arkhangelsk, are home to the monastery in which Stalin's government housed one of the Soviet Union's most infamous Gulag camps until the late 1930s. Many Russians refer to the islands by their diminutive nickname, Solevki.

The monastery's grounds, on the largest of the archipelago's islands, are surrounded by formidable stone walls (between eight and 11 metres high, and four to six metres thick), with seven gates and eight towers. The island has been an architectural, historical and nature reserve since 1974.

History

The islands were settled in the 1420s and 1430s by two monks from the Kirill-Belozersk Monastery (see the Vologda Region section), Zosima and Savvaty, who found the lack of scary monsters there reassuring enough to build a monastery.

Over the next hundred years, the monks' dedication and ingenuity resulted in the construction of a huge stone kremlin, factories and smelters; the island's fortress proved good fortification against attacks from Livonians and Swedes (in 1571, 1582 and 1611).

By the 1660s, the monastery owned over 50 saltworks, and by the mid-17th century the island's industry employed 600 workers, and it was home to over 300 monks. The monks had also, inadvertently, become prosperous enough to ensure that they would be the subject of attacks from tsars and Soviet forces for years to come.

In 1668, the monks took advantage of the ousting of Patriarch Nikon to announce their independence from the central church control. Over the next eight years, the monks and their allies (mainly disgruntled workers and Old Believers, with a few fugitive Cossacks thrown in for good measure) held out against constant attacks by the tsar's armies.

They probably could have held out for a good deal longer if it weren't for the turncoat monk, Feoktist, who led tsarist troops to an undefended section of the monastery's White Tower, from where they launched a decisive offensive. The monks were defeated in January 1676; tsarist forces killed almost every participant.

On 6-7 July 1854, at the outset of the Crimean War, the English ships *Eurydice*, *Brisk* and *Miranda* were sent to the White Sea area to look for an auxiliary port for the English navy. When they got to Solevki they engaged in a battle in which both the Rus-

sians and the English claimed decisive victory – the Russians said that a hail of cannon fire from the monastery sank one ship, while the English aver that they lost interest after firing red-hot shots at the monastery, landing forces, blowing up buildings and sailing away, fleet intact.

Under the Soviet regime (1923-39), the seemingly made-to-order prison (what better use for a good, strong stone fortress in Soviet Russia?) was converted into a Gulag camp, one of the most feared and infamous in the 'Gulag Archipelago'. In Solzhenitsyn's book of that title, he described the treatment of prisoners in the 'punishment cells' at the island's Sekirnaya Hill:

Poles the thickness of an arm were set from wall to wall and prisoners were ordered to sit on these poles all day...The height of the poles was set so that one's feet could not reach the ground...the prisoner spent the entire day trying to maintain his balance. If he fell, the jailers jumped in and beat him...or else they took him outside to a flight of stairs...(and) tied a person lengthwise to a beam, for added weight, and rolled him down (and there wasn't even one landing, and the steps were so steep that the log with the human being on it would go all the way down without stopping).

The Gulag camp closed in 1939.

The Kremlin

Inside the kremlin, most of which dates from the 16th century, you can tour the buildings and churches, including the **St Nicholas Church** (Glavny Nikolsky tserkov, 1831-33), the **refectory** (a massive single-pillared chamber) which connects to the **Assumption Cathedral** (Uspensky sobor, 1552-57) and the **Transfiguration Cathedral** (Preobrazhensky sobor, 1556-64).

There are day tours of the island outside the kremlin, plus visits to Sekirnaya Hill and the Khutor Gorka botanical gardens.

Getting There & Away

To/From Kem There are two boats: the *Bezuprechny* (favoured by the Turbaza Kem), which is US$7 each way; and the cooperatively owned *Savatii*, which charges US$9.50. Each boat makes the trip daily, weather permitting, during the 'season'. This is allegedly from 20 May until 15 October, but realistically, the season ends around 1 September when storms around Solevki kick up in earnest. Turbaza Kem can also arrange day tours of the island.

To/From Arkhangelsk There is weekly passenger service aboard the *Yushar* to/from the Solovetsky Islands (14 hours). The boat makes the trip from June to September every seventh day from the third of the month; it leaves Arkhangelsk at 5.30 pm and arrives in Solovetsky at 8.30 am. The return trip leaves Solovetsky at 5 pm and arrives in Arkhangelsk at 7.30 am; the cost is US$15 each way. Arkhangelsk Sputnik can book you on or, alternatively, charter boats may be booked, for varying outrageous prices, at the Arkhangelsk pier near the *Zapad* sailboat museum. By air, flights leave Arkhangelsk on Monday, Wednesday and Friday and cost US$24 one way.

Vologda Region
Вологодская область

VOLOGDA
ВОЛОГДА
Population: 205,000

'Liberated' by Novgorod from the Finns in the 12th century, Vologda thenceforth led a reasonably happy existence thumbing its nose at the Novgorodians. Taking Moscow's side against all comers seemingly from the moment of its inception, Vologda was rewarded by Ivan the Terrible, who deemed the quaint city was perhaps worthy of his living there (Vologdians are steadfast in their belief that the city was a contender for Russian capital), and a perfect site for a grand cathedral.

Vologda was an important centre of industry, commerce and arts – Vologda lace is still a coveted luxury item – up to the 17th century, but with the increasing importance of Arkhangelsk as a port and the founding of

St Petersburg, Vologda's economic powerhouse status was revoked. With the construction in the late 19th century of a railway linking it to Moscow, St Petersburg and Arkhangelsk, Vologda became known more as a gateway between power centres than a force of its own.

Today Vologda is a pleasant provincial city with a high concentration of churches and monasteries, and many lovely parks and wooden buildings. Its surrounding areas also hold great monastic treasure, and its proximity to both Moscow, the Golden Ring and St Petersburg make a diversionary trip here well worth the effort.

Orientation
Vologda straddles the Vologda River, with the town's centre mainly concentrated on the southern side. The town's main axis, ulitsa Mira, runs from the railway and bus station north to the junction of Oktyabrskaya ulitsa, where it juts north-east, and crosses the Vologda. The Archbishop's Courtyard, which is often referred to as the Vologda Kremlin, is on the south bank of the Vologda, west of the main bridge, on Kremlyovskaya ploshchad.

Information
Tourist Office For some reason, Vologda boasts an unusually helpful tourist office, the Vologda Tours & Excursions Bureau (☎ 2 25 93, 2 43 89) at Kremlyovskaya ploshchad 8. The staff seem ever eager to arrange tours of the outlying areas (which you may want to take them up on) and city tours (which, as the city's so small, you're better off doing on your own). The 90% privatised company has English and (they say) German guides and the director's name is Natalia Pavlovna Tlekhugova.

Money Change money at the central department store, in the pedestrian zone one block north of ulitsa Mira's north-east jig; there's a booth in the lobby, or try the booth at the Birzha Building, across ulitsa Batyushkova at No 12. It's open Tuesday to Friday from 10 am to 2 pm and from 3 to 6 pm. If they get too surly, try Vologda Bank at ulitsa Mira 36, on

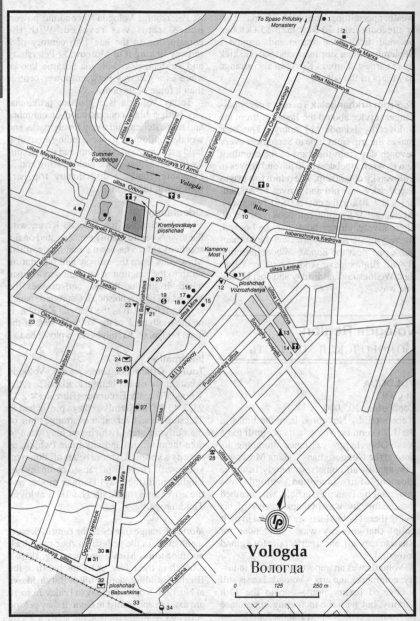

Vologda
Вологда

0   125   250 m

PLACES TO STAY

2	Oktyabr Hotel Гостиница Октябрь
3	Sretenskaya Church Dorm Сретенская Церковь Общежитие
23	Hotel Oktyabrskaya Гостиница Октябрьская
30	Vologda Hotel Гостиница Вологда
31	Sputnik Hotel Гостиница Спутник

PLACES TO EAT

12	Pirozhkovaya Пирожковая
21	Tsentralnaya Restaurant Центральный Ресторан
22	Birzha Биржа

OTHER

| 1 | Bakery
Булочная |
| 4 | Exhibition Hall
Выставочный зал |

5	Kiddie Boat Rental Прокат лодок для детей
6	Kremlin (Archbishop's Courtyard) Кремль (Архиерейское подворье)
7	Saint Sofia's Cathedral Софийский Собор
8	Alexander Nevsky Church Церковь Александра Невского
9	Church of St Dmitrius of Preluki Церковь Дмитрия Прилуцкого
10	Boat Rental (summer) Прокат лодок (летом)
11	Sport Shop Спортивный магазин
13	Teeny Lenin Statue Памятник маленького Ленина
14	Church of St John the Baptist Церковь Иоанна Предтечи
15	Detsky Mir (Toy shop) Детский Мир
16	Book Shop Книжный магазин

17	Istochnik Antique Books Источник Антиквариат
18	Book Shop Книжный магазин
19	Central Department Store & Money Exchange ЦУМ и обмен валюты
20	Central Market Центральний рынок
24	Post Office Почта
25	Vologda Bank Вологда Банк
26	Dom Knigi (Bookshop) Дом Книги
27	T-34 Tank Танк Т-34
28	Telephone Office Телефон
29	Banya Баня
32	Central Post Office Центральный почтамт
33	Railway Station Железнодорожный вокзал
34	Bus Station Автовокзал

the corner of ulitsa Oktyabrskaya. It's open Monday to Friday from 9.30 am to 12.30 pm.

Post & Telecommunications The main post office is on ploshchad Babushkina, but there's a perfectly functional office on the corner of ulitsa Mira and ulitsa Oktyabrskaya. The main telephone office (despite the huge neon sign saying it's on ploshchad Babushkina) is at ulitsa Gertsena 29, on the corner of ulitsa Menzhinskogo. Here you'll find dial-it-yourself intercity phones: pay in advance at the cash desk, dial the city code (without prefix, eg St Petersburg is 812), and press the button on the phone when your party answers. If you talk for less than you paid for you get change! It's open from 9 am to 10 pm. The telephone code for Vologda is 81722.

Things to See & Do
Archbishop's Courtyard Vologda's Archbishop's Courtyard is the city's historical centrepiece, a multi-towered stone fortress (1671-75) containing several noteworthy buildings. Among the main buildings are the Treasurer's Palace (Kazenny Prikaz, 1659); the house of Iosif Zolotoy (Iosifovsky Korpus, 1764-69); and the Baroque (but not crazily so) Voskresensky Cathedral (1772-76) which was built in place of the north-east tower and which (since 1952) is an art and picture gallery. The courtyard also houses the town's Museum of History & Architecture.

The courtyard was, according to the sign above the entrance, 'generously donated' by the church to the victorious Soviet atheists just after the Great October Revolution.

The courtyard is open to visitors, and the art gallery has rotating exhibitions on varying schedules; check with the courtyard's administrative offices in the centre of the yard for details during your stay.

St Sofia's Cathedral & Bell Tower Directly outside the courtyard's walls sits Vologda's most famous cathedral, St Sofia's, said to be built on the direct orders of Ivan the Terrible. Ivan's ruthlessness at Novgorod – where he ruthlessly sacked his own city and tortured its inhabitants, even going so far as to roast them on spits and fry them alive in enormous frying pans especially made for the occasion – was well known throughout Russia. So the workers jumped: the massive stone cathedral Ivan wanted so badly was erected in just two years (1568-70) – and they only worked in summer.

But haste, of course, makes waste. Local legend and some guidebook histories say that Ivan, upon walking into St Sofia's for the first time, was struck on the head by a 'red tile' that had been carelessly grouted to the ceiling. Ivan angrily stormed out of the cathedral and, for whatever reason (who knows with this guy – some say he might have left because he had a bad meal) he never returned. The cathedral was finally consecrated after the feisty tsar's death. The cathedral was decorated between 1680 and 1686, but the iconostasis you'll see today was made in 1724-38 by designer Maxim Iskritsky. The frescoes were restored in 1962-78. You can gain access to the cathedral daily from 10 am to 5 pm by arrangement with the Archbishop's Courtyard administration or the Vologda Tourist Office.

Next to the cathedral, the St Sofia's Bell Tower (Kolokolnya Sofiyskogo Sobora; 1869-70) is a reconstruction of the original, which was built in 1659 and which was allegedly 78.5 metres tall. You can climb the much shorter reconstruction, which boasts an original clock installed in 1871 by – the sign says – the Brothers Butenop Company, Monday to Friday from 10 am to 5 pm by arrangement with the administration of the Archbishop's Courtyard (the cost is about US$1.50).

Museum of History & Architecture This is a fun museum. Vologda's commercial and military past is re-lived through whimsical exhibits including a two-metre rifle used to defend the kremlin, huge padlocks, handcuffs and torture devices, all sorts of taxidermy, old Russian newspapers, lots of communist propaganda (and lots of pictures of Stalin), local carvings, and woven birch boxes. The famous and delicate Vologda lace is represented by a handmade lace 'Gerb Sovietskogo Soyuza' – hammer and sickle! OK, OK, the Gerb is just one among many other excellent examples like dresses, wedding dresses and tablecloths. The museum's open Wednesday to Sunday from 10.30 am to 4.30 pm. Admission is US$0.01 for Russians, US$0.70 for foreigners, and still photos are US$2.25 (the staff are tight on enforcement).

Leningradskaya Ulitsa This peaceful, tree-lined street, which cuts southward from the Vologda River just west of the kremlin, features stately 19th-century merchant homes. At No 6, the **Regional Exhibition Hall** has art and photo exhibitions rotating monthly. It's open Wednesday to Sunday from 10 am to 4.30 pm. Admission is US$0.01 for Russians and US$0.70 for foreigners.

Intercession Church Around the corner from St Sofia's, this 17th-century church (Khram Pokrova Presvyatoy Bogoroditsy) has been renovated after spending the last 70 years in mothballs. Services are held daily at 8 am and feature an excellent choir.

Church of St John the Baptist On ploshchad Revolyutsii, where you'll also find a Great Patriotic War Memorial and eternal flame, the disused Church of St John the Baptist (1710; the bell tower was built in 1717) makes a truly classy backdrop for the smallest Lenin statue around (it's a huge pedestal supporting an itty-bitty statue; anyone who's seen the Stonehenge scene in the film *Spinal Tap* will appreciate this). It's at the eastern end of the park near ulitsa Menzhinskogo.

Church of St Dmitrius of Preluki This lovely little church (1711; the bell tower was built in 1750), diagonally across the river from the kremlin, is currently closed for what looks like a lengthy renovation.

Spaso-Prilutsky Monastery This working monastery, which dates from the 14th century, looms on the outskirts of the city. It's a bit muddy, but the monastery welcomes guests, and a visit makes for an interesting afternoon, especially if you can get inside its centrepiece, the 16th-century **Cathedral of the Saviour**. The entrance is on the north-west side of the monastery walls. The monks really want to get groups of five or more (the cost is US$3), but if you show up alone, act interested and are polite, they'll let you walk the grounds unescorted at no cost. Bus No 103 passes right by the entrance, or you can take bus No 102 to the Zheleznodorozhna stop (where the road forks), take the left fork, cross the railway tracks and the entrance is about 200 metres on the left. You can get a great photo of the place from the middle of the railway bridge that crosses the Vologda.

Boat Rental In summer you may be able to rent rowing boats for short cruises up the Vologda from the rental station, just east of the ulitsa Chernyshevskogo bridge across from the Dmitry Priluchkogo Church. Kiddie boat rentals can be had in the children's play-ground just behind the kremlin.

Banya The city's largest banya is at ulitsa Mira 40. It's clean, staff are friendly and it's open daily from 9 am to 9 pm. Prices are US$1.10 for men and US$0.90 for women.

Places to Stay

The coolest and cheapest place in town is the converted *Sretenskaya Church Dorm* (Sretenskaya tserkov, 1731) (☎ 2 94 42), naberezhnaya VI Armii 85, directly across the Vologda from the kremlin. Now a dormitory for students in the Ministry of Culture's study programme, the friendly (if perplexed) management says it will let foreigners stay there if they call first (speak Russian), but

they'll probably let you in even if you just show up (they think you won't like it but it's fun and a crash pad as good as any). Rooms have 12 beds. The price is US$2.40 per bed per night; there are cooking facilities but no hot water. In summer there's a floating bridge leading almost to the kremlin gate.

One step down in quality and up in price is the *Oktyabr* (☎ 2 05 69), at ulitsa Karla Marxa 7, two bus stops north of the Vologda. The friendly staff don't make the Stalinist-era wooden building any less grotty or make up for the lack of showers or hot water, but it's cheap – rooms with three beds are US$3.15 per bed; with four beds it's US$2.75 per bed. You can get good cakes and bread at the bakery around the corner on ulitsa Chernyshevskogo.

Truckies go for the *Sputnik* (☎ 2 27 52), Puteyskaya ulitsa 14A, near the railway and bus stations. Shabby but standard singles/doubles are US$14.25/28.50 without bath; US$23.80/47.60 with bath. It can get loud at night, and there's a bar downstairs.

A more reasonable option is the *Hotel Vologda* (☎ 2 30 79), also near the railway station at ulitsa Mira 92. It has clean rooms and friendlier staff. It's a bit more than the Sputnik with rooms at US$16.65/33.50 without bath (showers are on the 3rd floor), but a world apart.

The town's top-end offering is the *Oktyabrskaya* (☎ 2 01 45), on ulitsa Oktyabrskaya 25 (on the corner of ulitsa Avksentevskogo). It's a genuinely modern place with bright lights, a pleasant lobby that boasts an exchange booth, chi-chi shops and standard (but *green*) rooms for a surprisingly reasonable US$24.75/49.50 with bath.

Places to Eat

The town's good central market is near the corner of prospekt Pobedy and ulitsa Batyushkova.

Cheap fast food can be had (along with the occasional roast chicken) at the *Pirozhkovaya*, on ulitsa Mira near Kamenny Most (bridge), which also has dumplings, pizza, milky coffee and rolls.

The restaurant at the *Vologda* is quite good

and reasonably priced; there's also a very good bufet on the 2nd floor at the end of the hall that does a good kotlet for about US$0.50. The café/bar and restaurant at the *Oktyabrskaya* are also worth checking out: the café has good service and German beer is about US$1.10 per can. The *Tsentralnaya* restaurant, upstairs on the corner of ulitsa Batyushkova and the pedestrian zone, has a bar section serving small pizzas and main courses from US$1 to US$3 but the rest of it is to be avoided.

The *restoran* in the railway station is surprisingly decent, and it has good stew and salads for about US$0.50 to US$3. It's open from 8 am to 3 pm and from 4 to 11 pm.

There's a *cafeteria* in the south entrance of the Birzha Building, ulitsa Batyushkova 11, that has decent borshch and another, the *Dorozhnaya*, at ulitsa Kalinina 70 near the railway station.

Things to Buy

Vologda lace is the big hit; you can try the department stores, small shops in the centre or at the market. Detsky Mir, at ulitsa Mira 11, has a fair selection of board games, cars, helicopters, the last metal cap guns in Russia, dolls, prams and kids' bikes. The sport shop, at Kamenny Most 6, has rubber rafts, skis and poles, leather hunting belts and pouches, Russian weights, bicycles and motorcycles.

Getting There & Away

Air There are daily flights to St Petersburg Pulkovo-1 (US$89); Moscow Bykovo (US$89); and a Tuesday flight from Arkhangelsk (US$97). Vologda's airport code is VGD.

Bus Bus service from Kostroma to Vologda runs one to three times daily; the seven-hour trip costs US$5.50 *myagkiy*, and US$4 *zhyostkiy*. From Ivanovo via Yaroslavl there's one bus on odd dates (five hours; US$4 from Yaroslavl). Buses also leave from St Petersburg several times a day.

Train Daily connections to Moscow (Yaroslavl Station; eight hours) and St Petersburg (Moscow Station; 10 hours) are easy travelling. The train from Arkhangelsk to Vologda departs daily at 10.25 am and arrives at 12.25 am (14 hours); the return journey departs at 3.35 pm, arriving in Arkhangelsk at 5.45 am.

Car & Motorbike The Moscow-Arkhangelsk highway (M8) cuts almost straight up to Vologda via Yaroslavl; it's about 500 km from Moscow, 600 km from Arkhangelsk.

Getting Around

Vologda is very compact, which makes getting around on foot ideal.

KIRILLOV
КИРИЛЛОВ

The **Kirilla-Belozersky Museum of History, Architecture & Fine Arts**, housed in a spectacular, but non-working, 14th-century monastery of the same name, is the reason to come here, two hours north-west of the city by bus. Legend has it that the monastery's founder, Kirill, was living at the Similovsky monastery when he had a vision of the Virgin Mary showing him the towers of a new monastery. There's an icon depicting the vision inside the monastery.

The monastery's massive walls surround four main areas: the **Large Assumption Monastery**, the **Small Ivanov Monastery**, the **Stockaded Town**, and the **New Town**, all of which are open daily except Monday from 9 am to 5 pm. The main exhibition, which includes a tour of the churches, cathedrals and buildings, a regional history and history of the monastery, costs US$2.85. An additional US$2.85 buys a tour of the catwalks and towers along the monastery's massive stone walls, built to stave off attacks from Lithuanians and Swedes. Also open for visitation (separate admissions usually apply) are the wooden chapel (the original settlement site), the Wooden Church of the Laying of the Robes, and prison cells which date from the 17th century – even Patriarch Nikon did time here, and in his boredom he is said to have turned to carpentry.

The museum also holds rotating exhibitions and sometimes demonstrates icon restoration techniques.

At **Feranpontov**, five km west of Kirillov, is another monastery which has been converted to a branch of the Kirillov museum. Dionysius came here to paint frescoes which can be viewed.

Getting There & Away

From Vologda's bus station, buses leave at 6.10 and 7.40 am and 12.20, 1.20 and 2.30 pm for the two-hour (US$2.15) journey. Several buses a day run back to Vologda, with the last leaving at 6.30 pm. When you arrive in Kirillov, ask the driver to let you off in the centre; you'll see the monastery from there.

To Ferapontov from Vologda, catch a bus to Lipinvor which stops right there; they leave at 9.20 and 11.35 am and 4.50 pm.

Volga Region
Поволже

Though the region called Povolzhe (which means Along the Volga River) meanders over a great deal of European Russia, historically and sentimentally it belongs in a chapter of its own, as it has been the main artery of the Russian heartland for over a millennium.

While ancient Tver, Yaroslavl and Kostroma (covered in the Around Moscow chapter) decorate the upper river, many of the cities of the middle and lower Volga are industrial ports, with lots of history but in some cases limited cultural appeal. Many of their visitors come on river cruises, which perhaps is the only style of sightseeing that flatters these places. Among the most attractive destinations are cities which were completely or partly closed in Soviet times, such as Nizhny Novgorod, Kazan and Astrakhan.

This chapter covers the Volga and its cities from Nizhny Novgorod to Astrakhan, plus the Perm and Ufa areas located up the eastern tributaries of the Volga, and the Rostov-on-Don area on the Sea of Azov in the south, which since 1952 has been linked to the Volga by the 100-km-long Lenin (or Volga-Don) Ship Canal.

HISTORY

The Volga, Don and neighbouring rivers were trade routes before Russia even existed, with Slav and Norse adventurers trading along them from the Baltic Sea to Byzantium. For the Russian state the southern reaches were a perpetual headache. In the 13th century the entire region was conquered by the Tatar Golden Horde, who eventually made their capital near present-day Volgograd and hammered at Russia for two more centuries.

The Golden Horde began falling apart after being defeated by Moscow's Prince Dmitry Donskoy at Kulikovo on the Don in

1380, and a thrashing by Timur (Tamerlane) soon after. By the mid-15th century the Tatars had collapsed into separate khanates at Kazan, Astrakhan and in the Crimea. Tsar Ivan III played them off against one another, and Ivan the Terrible took Kazan and Astrakhan in the 1550s, leaving only a subservient Crimean enclave.

Cossacks

Serfs, paupers and dropouts began fleeing south from Russia, Poland and Lithuania in the 15th century, organising themselves into military-agricultural communities in the Dnipro (Dnepr) River area in Ukraine, the Don River basin, the Caucasus and western Kazakhstan. Those in a given region, for example the Don Cossacks, also constituted an army (voysko), within which the men of each village (stanitsa) elected their own leader (ataman).

The Russian government, mindful of the trouble these people could make, later offered them autonomy in return for military services, but they made trouble anyway. Three peasant uprisings in the Volga-Don region were led by Cossacks – Stepan (Stenka) Razin in 1670, Kondraty Bulavin in 1707 and Yemelyan Pugachov in 1773. Razin's army seized the entire lower Volga basin before being routed at Simbirsk (Ulya-

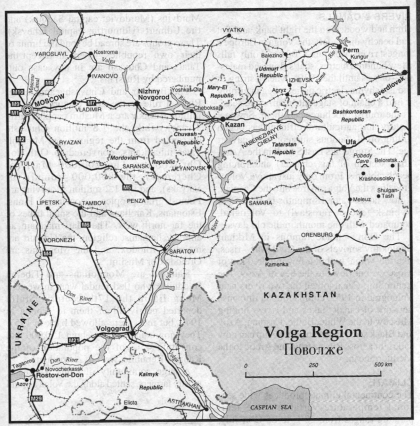

VYATKA

YAROSLAVL
Kostroma
Volga
IVANOVO

Perm
Kungur
Balezino
Udmurt
Republic
IZHEVSK
Kama
Sverdlovsk

MOSCOW
M10
M9
M8
Moscow
Canal
M7
VLADIMIR
Nizhny
Novgorod
Yoshkar-Ola
Mary-El
Republic
Cheboksary
Agryz
Kazan
Bashkortostan
Republic

M1

M2
RYAZAN
Chuvash
Republic
NABEREZHNYYE
CHELNY
Tatarstan
Republic
Ufa
Pobedy
Cave
Beloretsk

TULA
Mordovian
Republic
SARANSK
ULYANOVSK
Krasnousolsky

M5
Meleuz
Shulgan-
Tash

LIPETSK
TAMBOV
PENZA
SAMARA

M6
VORONEZH
ORENBURG

M4
SARATOV

Kamenka

KAZAKHSTAN

Don River

UKRAINE

Volgograd

Volga Region
Поволжье

M21

Don River
Taganrog
Novocherkassk
Rostov-on-Don
Azov
M29

0   250   500 km

Kalmyk
Republic

Elista
ASTRAKHAN

CASPIAN SEA

novsk), and Razin became a national folk hero.

After quashing Pugachov's rebellion, Catherine the Great put an end to Cossack autonomy, disbanded the Dnieper (Zaporozhie) Cossacks and made the whole lower Don an administrative territory, with the capital at Novocherkassk.

Civil War

The lower Volga and Don basins put up furious resistance to the Great October Revolution. The Don Cossacks elected an anti-Bolshevik ataman in 1917. Of the three main White Army offensives in 1919, the one that most nearly undid the Bolsheviks – with southern Cossacks as its backbone – originated here.

WW II

The Germans' furthest penetration into the Soviet Union was to Stalingrad (now Volgograd) and the North Caucasus. Rostov-on-Don was occupied, and the battle for Stalingrad in the winter of 1942 was a turning point in Russian resistance to Hitler, and probably in the war as a whole.

RIVERS & CANALS

High and wooded on the right bank, and flat and beachy on the left, the Volga is Europe's longest river. Along its 3700 km it only falls a few hundred metres, so it's slow and majestic – or was until the 1930s, when a string of monster hydroelectric projects began turning it into a chain of stagnant 'man-made seas', as the tourist brochures call them. Sewage, factory and agricultural effluent has begun killing off its famous sturgeon (and caviar; see 'The Sturgeon's Last Stand' in the Astrakhan section of this chapter) and forcing beach closures. From only just above Volgograd does the Volga run free into the Caspian. It now takes water 18 months to flow from Rybinsk (above Yaroslavl) to Volgograd, compared with one month in the old days.

The Don – made famous in Mikhail Sholokhov's novels of the Civil War – rises, like the Volga, within a few hundred km of Moscow, but flows to the Sea of Azov. The Lenin Ship Canal joined the two rivers near Volgograd in 1952, completing an immense network of canals, lakes and rivers linking Moscow to the White, Baltic, Caspian, Azov and Black seas; an ocean-going ship can now sail right across Russia from the Arctic to the Mediterranean.

CLIMATE

The continental climate produces wide seasonal temperature variations; the temperature ranges from 20°C to 25°C in July, but from -10°C to -15°C in January. Humidity is fairly low. Locals say the period from May to September is the best.

PEOPLE

Besides Russians, the largest ethnic group in the region is the Tatars, who have their own republic of Tatarstan centred at Kazan. The system of republics in this region stems from Soviet attempts to limit the influence of the Tatars, historic rivals of the Russians. Other groups with republics in the same region are the Bashkir (Bashkortostan; capital Ufa), the Chuvash (Chuvashia; capital Cheboxary), the Kalmyks (Kalmykia; capital Elista), the Mari (Mary-El; capital Yoshkar-Ola), the

Mordvins (Mordovia; capital Saransk) and the Udmurt (Udmurtia; capital Izhevsk). These groups are spread beyond the limits of their 'own' republics, where all except the Tatars and Chuvash are in any case outnumbered by Russians.

The Bashkir and Chuvash came under Russian rule in the 16th century. The 1.5 million Bashkir are a Muslim people (partly Turkic), while the 1.8 million Chuvash, descended from the region's pre-Mongol-Tatar inhabitants, converted to Orthodox Christianity. The 700,000 Mari (or Cheremys), the 800,000 Udmurt (or Votyaks), and the 1.2 million Mordvins are Finno-Ugrian peoples – cousins of Finns, Estonians, Karelians and the small tribes of the far north-west. The Mari maintain an animist/shamanist religion, the Udmurt are mainly Orthodox, and the Mordvins are Orthodox or Muslim.

Kalmyks are Mongolians and Tibetan Buddhists who fled feudal wars in western Mongolia in the 17th century. Stalin deported nearly all of them to Siberia in 1943, but most were allowed back in 1957. They now number only about 150,000 and constitute 45% of the population of the Kalmyk Republic, west of Astrakhan.

A large community of ethnic Germans, mostly farmers, settled along the Volga around

Russian child dressed for winter

Saratov in the 18th and 19th centuries and even got their own autonomous republic within Russia in 1924. However, this was abolished during WW II, and emigration and deportation have since thinned their numbers out.

GETTING THERE & AROUND

The obvious way to travel between Volga region cities is on the Volga. Considering the river's historical importance, this is how the heart of Russia ought to be seen. In recent years services have been cut due to lack of passengers, but in summer it is still possible to catch a boat daily in either direction between major cities.

Intercity steamships ply the Volga and Don daily from around late May to late September, but it is difficult to book these outside Russia. Sample fares for the wide range of cabin classes available include Moscow-Ulyanovsk (US$14 to US$263; four days), Ulyanovsk-Volgograd (US$12 to US$209; three days), Volgograd-Rostov via the canal (US$7.60 to US$136; 43 hours). Steamers go from Moscow to Rostov-on-Don or Astrakhan in a brisk 10½ days.

Daily intercity flights and slow trains offer few views of the river.

Volga-Don Cruises A cruise is not everyone's idea of travel. The middle and lower Volga-Don route starts (or ends) at Moscow and may take in Kazan, Ulyanovsk, Volgograd, the Volga-Don Canal and Rostov-on-Don, or you could stay on the Volga and end up in Astrakhan. Furious bouts of city sightseeing alternate with slack days chugging down the reservoirs, relieved by shashlyk picnics and visits to hydroelectric stations. Accommodation is on board.

During the Ulyanovsk-Volgograd section you have mostly river banks to look at. The most interesting segment is Volgograd to Rostov-on-Don via the canal's 15 locks, and the Zhiguli hills near Samara. The section from Volgograd to Astrakhan is also fairly interesting with some picturesque villages and fishermen to see.

Intourist used to run three cruises each summer between Kazan and Rostov-on-Don, and Rechflot (the former Soviet state boat company) still does, but the accommodation and service is very basic on these. Most foreign travel agents can make bookings only on the expensive luxury liners of the Russian Waterways Cruises managed by Cruise Marketing International (☎ (415) 592 1347; fax (415) 591 4970), who are located at Suite A, 1601 Industrial Way, Belmont, CA 94002, USA. They offer a 21-day Moscow-Volgograd cruise for US$1399 to US$1899 per person, or a 15-day Moscow-St Petersburg cruise for US$1099 to US$1599 (excluding international flights). There are some exceptions in Australia where Safeway Travel (☎ (03) 9534 4866; fax (03) 9534 4206) at 288 Carlisle St, Balaclava, Victoria 3182, can book passengers on the cheaper but more basic cruise boats. See also the European Russia Getting Around chapter for more info on Volga and Don rivers services.

NIZHNY NOVGOROD
НУЖНИЙ НОВГОРОД
Population: 1.5 million
Nizhny Novgorod is a pleasant enough city with a rather bare Kremlin, museums and churches which are being restored. It is also economically bustling and has a lively street scene. Nizhny Novgorod (not to be confused with Novgorod) belongs historically with the Golden Ring towns near Moscow. It was founded in 1221 as a prelude to a challenge by the Rostov-Suzdal principality on the Bulgar people's hold on the region between the Volga and the Ural Mountains – a challenge that was pre-empted by the Mongol-Tatar invasion of the 1230s. Nizhny Novgorod was named Gorky in Soviet times after the writer Maxim Gorky (born here in 1868), who disapproved of the idea. Nowadays, Russia's third-largest city is best known as the place where the late physicist, dissident and Nobel laureate Andrey Sakharov was exiled until 1986.

Other than Sakharov, the town's most important citizen was probably one Kuzma Minin, a 17th-century mayor who helped raise the army that drove the Poles from Moscow and snapped Russia out of its Time of Troubles. In late 1990 the city was opened to foreigners, and went back to its original name.

Today, the town holds the International Trade Fair, which also assists in the drive to reform through privatisation and in improving the local economy. The success of privatisation in industry and agriculture here has become a model for other Russian cities to follow. The key to success was gradual privatisation and financial support through funds and bank loans for young enterprises. Some of the major local industries involve the production of MiG fighters, GAZ cars, ships and submarines.

The district is also known for traditional crafts, including the world-famous *matryoshka* doll. Another major craft is the spoons, cups and dishes with their gold and black base partially covered by designs of flowers – known as Khokhloma ware after a town about 100 km north of Nizhny Novgorod. The lesser known crafts include

chopping boards and cast copper alloys. Many of these can be bought in a shop at Bolshaya Pokrovskaya 43.

Orientation & Information

The town lies on the southern bank of the Volga River and is also split by the Oka River. The western bank includes the railway station and one of the main hotels, the Tsentralnaya on ploshchad Lenina. The eastern bank has the museums, and the Kremlin on ploshchad Minina, from which span out the main streets, including Bolshaya Pokrovskaya with many shops and restaurants.

The Intourist office is in Hotel Tsentralnaya on ploshchad Lenina, and is open Monday to Friday from 9 am to 5 pm. There are many places that change US dollars and German marks. Visa cash advances are available at NBD Bank (☎ 34 39 90), Gorky ploshchad 9. Travellers' cheques are exchanged with a 4% commission and cash advances on MasterCard are given at Hotel Oktyabrskaya on Verkhne-Volzhskaya nabe-

---

A Sign of the Times

The GAZ (ГАЗ) emblem with the deer on a red background is well known in Russia and other former Eastern Bloc countries. The acronym stands for Gorky Avtozavod (Gorky Automobile Works), and it adorns the Volga sedan car and trucks that the company has been producing since 1932, when the GAZ factory was built from Henry Ford blueprints and Stalin declared it one of the triumphs of socialism. By 1994 the giant company had grown to be much more than just another car maker. It had 350,000 employees and its assets included 120 kindergartens, 10,000 cows, a sanatorium in Sochi on the Black Sea coast, an 1100-bed hospital and many other extras. In Soviet times the well-known and sturdy six-cylinder Volga sedan was commonly used by rank-and-file Communist Party members or as a taxi, while the Chaika limousine served the socialist elite as their high-status vehicle. Trucks and armoured vehicles were produced by GAZ for the army. Today the privatised factory is in trouble, not only from declining sales of its product. A more serious threat is the claims of corruption within the company, where millions of roubles are reportedly missing. As in other companies that have been privatised, the leadership is still the same and work practices have not changed a great deal. ■

rezhnaya. The Western Union money-wire service is at Vokyneshtorbank (☎ 2 35 07 03), Maxim Gorky ulitsa 115, and is open Monday to Friday from 9.30 am to 12.30 pm. The pochtamt is on the corner of ulitsa Bolshaya Pokrovskaya and ulitsa Malaya Pokrovskaya, and there is also a post office at the railway station. The city's telephone code is 8312.

At the time of writing there were no local maps available. Kodak film was widely available from several Kodak shops along ulitsa Bolshaya Pokrovskaya. There is a monthly publication in English, The *Nizhny Novgorod Times*, which lists some restaurants and events.

Kremlin

The Kremlin is perched on the hill above the Volga River but the entrance is from the other side of ploshchad Minina. The present walls with 11 towers are from the 16th century, but none of the original buildings is left, apart from the 17th-century Cathedral of the Archangel Michael (Arkhangelskoe sobor, 1631). Most of the other buildings within the Kremlin's walls house the local administrative government. At the north-eastern end of the Kremlin is the former governor's house, which was built in the 1840s, and which has the Art Museum (Khudozhestvenny muzey; ☎ 39 13 73). Exhibits range from 18th-century icons to 20th-century paintings by such artists as Rerikh and Borovikovsky. The Art Museum is open Thursday to Monday from 10 am to 5 pm and Wednesday from noon to 7 pm; the entry fee is US$1. Behind the main entrance gate (with the picture of Jesus Christ on it) from the square is a small exhibit of WW II tanks and armoured cars. A monument to the heroes of WW II overlooks the Volga on the northern side of the Kremlin.

Churches & Monasteries

Nizhny Novgorod has many churches, most of which have been or are being renovated after the neglect and destruction of the past 70 years.

The **Assumption Church** (Uspenskaya tserkov) is on top of a hill across from pereulok Krutoy, the continuation of ulitsa Dobrolyubova which crosses Bolshaya Pokrovskaya. This 17th-century stone church is unique in Russia as the design was normally used for building wooden churches. The baroque **Stroganov or Nativity Church** (Stroganovskaya tserkov), built at the turn of the 18th century, has retained its magnificent stone carvings, but the interior is still rather bare after its reconstruction. It is just above ulitsa Mayakovskaya, which is the main street leading from the railway station to the Kremlin. The large, impressive looking dome of the **Saviour Old Market Cathedral** (Spassky Staroyarmarochny sobor, 1822) can be found in a maze of streets behind the exhibition building (Yarmarka) on ploshchad Lenina.

The town's two monasteries are not easy to reach and can be viewed from the outside only. The **Annunciation Monastery** (Blagoveshchenskaya monastyr) is above ulitsa Chernigovskaya. It was founded in the 13th century but most of the structures are from the 18th century. **Pechorskaya Monastery** (Pechorskaya monastyr) is off ulitsa Rodinova, behind the Pechory cinema. The present buildings are from the 17th century and are used by local government.

Museums

The **Museum of History & Architecture** (Istoriko-arkhitekturny muzey; ☎ 36 76 61) at Verkhne-Volzhskaya naberezhnaya 7 incorporates within its rooms the usual exhibits of local history, flora and fauna. Closer to the Kremlin at No 5 Verkhne-Volzhskaya Naberezhnaya is the **Radio Museum** (Muzey Radiolaboratorii; ☎ 36 67 55), which is open Monday to Friday from 10 am to 4 pm, but only to groups of 20 or more visitors.

The **Sakharov Museum** (Muzey A D Sakharova; ☎ 66 86 23) at prospekt Gagarina 214 is actually the flat Sakharov shared with his wife Yelena Bonner while they were exiled here. Not much original furniture remains. One room has an exhibit on prisoners of conscience. It is open Saturday to

Thursday from 9 am to 6 pm. To get there catch a bus travelling from ploshchad Minina towards Shcherbinka housing complex and get off at the Muzey Akademika Sakharova bus stop. There is also a rather ordinary **Gorky Museum** (Muzey A M Gorkogo; ☎ 36 15 29) at ulitsa Semashko 19, where Maxim Gorky lived.

Places to Stay

For those with a valid train ticket it is possible to stay in the railway accommodation *Komnaty Otdykha*. Basic single rooms cost US$15.60, or a bed in a twin share is US$7.80. The main older-style hotel is *Tsentralnaya* (☎ 4 42 70) on the fourth floor of Sovietsky dom 12 at ploshchad Lenina, on the western side of the Oka River. Take tram No 1 one stop from the railway station. Reasonable rooms with bath and breakfast cost US$30.50/45. There is a foreign exchange in the hotel, as well as a café and restaurant.

The ageing *Hotel Rossia* (☎ 39 19 71) at Verkhne-Volzhskaya naberezhnaya has basic rooms without bath for US$27 and with bath for US$61. The newest hotel in town is *Oktyabrskaya* (☎ 32 01 71; fax 32 05 50), located further east up the Verkhne-Volzhskaya naberezhnaya at 9A. The nice rooms cost US$50/80.

Places to Eat

Ulitsa Bolshaya Pokrovskaya is the main commercial street, with many restaurants and cafés that tend to change owners and names frequently. Restaurants around town include *Novomatic* in the middle of the square, opposite the main entrance to the Kremlin. This fairly pleasant place serves drinks and simple Russian meals for around US$2.50.

The majestic *Gardinia Restaurant* (☎ 36 41 01) overlooks the Volga from Verkhne-Volzhskaya naberezhnaya, opposite the

---

Andrey Sakharov, Conscience of the Reform Movement

Dr Andrey Dmitrievich Sakharov (1921-89) was a leading nuclear physicist who became a human rights advocate and one of the main figures opposing the Soviet regime from within. He was born in Moscow and followed in his father's footsteps as a physicist. By the age of 32 he was a full member of the Soviet Academy of Sciences, and was one of the two leading scientists involved in developing the first hydrogen bomb in the Soviet Union.

From the 1960s on, Sakharov became vocal in opposing nuclear arms production. He also started speaking out against human rights abuses and in 1970 was a co-founder of the Committee for Human Rights. In 1975 Sakharov was awarded the Nobel peace prize, but he never dared to go and pick it up. He was afraid to leave the USSR because the authorities might not let him return. Once outside the country he would lose the ability to pressure the communist regime through his dissident activities. His actions brought him into conflict with the government, and in 1980 he was exiled to Nizhny Novgorod (then named Gorky) after he criticised the Soviet invasion of Afghanistan. His wife, Yelena Bonner, joined him in 1984, by which time he had undertaken several hunger strikes.

Even though the Soviet government revoked all his titles and confiscated his medals, Sakharov remained a member of the Soviet Academy of Sciences. He was released in 1986 by Mikhail Gorbachev, and became a member of the Congress of People's Deputies (or Parliament) in 1989, the year it was first established. He continued to criticise the Soviet leadership as a member of the congress, and by the time of his death was widely regarded as the conscience of the reform movement.

The Soviet Union's former secret police, the KGB, had an estimated 520 files on this famous dissident, who disclosed human rights abuses and criticised the nuclear arms programme and Soviet foreign policy. Some of these files were released in 1994 and revealed that the Politburo's fear of Sakharov verged on hysteria. They thought that Sakharov's high profile must mean he was a Western spy – and even his wife was strongly suspected of espionage. ■

Oktyabrskaya Hotel. It is an American-style fast-food place serving chicken, macaroni and other such delights that cost around US$2 to US$3.50, while techno music vibrates through the ears. The *Buryatskaya (Sloboda)* restaurant near the Kremlin, overlooking the River Volga, has a full meal with drinks for about US$12, including a good fish shashlyk. One of the better restaurants is the *U Shakhovky* at ulitsa Piskunovo, near the corner of Bolshaya Pokrovskaya, with good, well-presented Russian food. Bookings are essential for dinner when only the well-dressed clientele are admitted.

Most hotels, like Tsentralnaya or Rossia, also have the usual Russian restaurants. The one at the Rossia has a tasty goulash (US$2.50).

The *Vera Pavlovas Dmitrievsky* shop on ulitsa Piskunovo, near the corner of Bolshaya Pokrovskaya, has a good selection of cheeses and imported foods.

Getting There & Away
Air The Aeroflot office is at prospekt Lenina 7 (☎ 44 20 46). A one-way flight to/from Moscow costs US$70.

Bus There are four daily buses to/from Moscow (Schyolkovsky bus station) between 9.40 am and 9.25 pm. The nine-hour trip costs US$13.

Train The railway station is on the western bank of the Oka River at ploshchad Revolyutsii. The most convenient train to take from Moscow's Yaroslavl station is the night train No 38 which leaves at 11.10 pm and arrives at 7.25 am. In the opposite direction, train No 37 leaves Nizhny Novgorod for Moscow at 10.20 pm. There are also three daily trains to Nizhny Novgorod from Moscow's Kursk station and one from its Kazan station. Note that Nizhny Novgorod is still called Gorky on some railway timetables. There are also daily trains to Kazan.

Boat In summer months it is possible to get to or from Moscow, Yaroslavl (US$6 in 3B to US$102 in lyux A), Kazan and other major Volga ports daily by the boats going up and down the Volga.

Getting Around
Public Transport Trams, trolleybuses and buses tend to be more crowded than in other Russian cities, maybe because they don't run that often. The tickets cost US$0.08 and US$0.05, respectively, and can be bought from *talony* booths. Tram No 1 is convenient, starting from the railway station and passing Tsentralnaya Hotel, the exhibition buildings, the river port and the Kremlin. There is a metro but it only runs south from the railway station and does not go anywhere near the old part of town.

Taxi Prices seem fluid as in many other parts of Russia and bargaining is necessary. We paid US$3 to get from the railway station to the Kremlin. The asking price to the airport is US$10.

Car Rental It is possible to hire a Scorpion car with a driver for US$7.60 per hour at Hotel Oktyabrskaya.

KAZAN
КАЗАНЬ
Population: 1.10 million
Kazan, founded in the 13th century, is one of the oldest Tatar cities in Russia, and was the capital of part of the Golden Horde in the 15th and 16th centuries. Tatars are a Turkic people and speak a dialect of the Turkic language. They are descended from the Mongol-Tatar armies of Jenghiz Khan and his successors, and also from earlier Hunnic, Turkic and Finno-Ugric settlers on the middle Volga. In a neat historical inversion, the Kazan Khanate at one point even allied itself with Moscow as a vassal state. In 1552 Ivan the Terrible ravaged the city, forced the Muslim khan to become Christian and moved the Tatars to the suburbs. St Basil's Cathedral in Moscow was built to celebrate Kazan's downfall. The town was seized in a revolt during 1773-74 and destroyed, but was soon rebuilt.

The city later flourished as a gateway to Siberia. Leo Tolstoy was educated in the city.

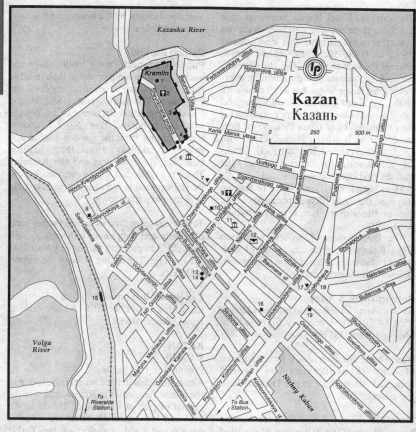

Some of Russia's first Marxists surfaced here and Lenin was in fact thrown out of Kazan University for being too bolshy. Under the Soviet Union, Kazan became the capital of a new Tatar Autonomous Republic. In autumn 1990, this oil-rich and strongly nationalist region (now renamed Tatarstan) declared its autonomy from the rest of Russia, launching several years of political warfare with the central government in Moscow. Of the 3.7 million people within the republic, only 48% are Tatars; with 43% being Russian, the dreams of an independent state might be hard to achieve and sustain.

Tatar nationalism is strong in this city. There are no Russian flags flying over the city, only the green, white and red-striped Tatar flag. All the streets are also bilingually signposted.

Orientation & Information

Once located well up the tributary Kazanka River, Kazan is now lapped by the flat waters behind Kuybyshev Dam, 400 km downstream. The riverside station is at the foot of ulitsa Tatarstan. At Kuybyshevskaya ploshchad, ulitsa Tatarstan meets ulitsa Baumana, the main street for shopping, food

PLACES TO STAY		OTHER		11	Tatarstan Regional History Museum
8	Hotel Volga Гостиница Волга	1	Syuyumbike Tower Башня Сююмбике		Музей истории связи Татарстана
10	Hotel Kazan Гостиница Казань	2	Annunciation Cathedral Благовещенский собор	12	Post Office Почтамт
16	Hotel Duslik Гостиница Дуслик	3	Konsistorskaya Tower Консисторская башня	13	Aeroflot Office Аэрофлот
19	Hotel Tatarstan Гостиница Татарстан	4	South-eastern Tower Юго-Восточная башня	14	Railway Booking Office Железнодорожные билетные кассы
PLACES TO EAT		5	Spasskyh Tower Спасская башня	15	Main Train Station Железнодорожный вокзал
7	Bar Grot Бар „Грот"	6	Folk Art Museum Краеведческий музей	18	Kuybysheva Square Площадь Куйбышева
17	Vostok Restoran Ресторан Восток	9	Peter & Paul Cathedral Петро-павловский собор		

and hotels. This street also has a heavy police presence in the evening due to the city's high juvenile crime rate.

Intourist (☎ 32 41 95) has an office in the Hotel Kazan, ulitsa Baumana 9/15, but is not very useful. We couldn't even get a train ticket booked here and were told to go and do it ourselves at the railway booking office. Many places, including the hotels, change US dollars and German marks only. The main post office is on ulitsa Baumana. The Kazan telephone code is 8432.

Good, new city maps with public transport information are sold at the bookshop in the Hotel Tatarstan.

The Kremlin

The city fortress, at the river end of ulitsa Lenina and ulitsa Baumana, has been rebuilt a number of times over the last five centuries. Ivan the Terrible blew it up and had Pskov masons redo it in white limestone during the 16th and 17th centuries. The Annunciation Cathedral (Blagoveshchensky sobor, 1562) was designed by the same architect who did St Basil's Cathedral. The leaning 17th-century, 59-metre-high Syuyumbike Tower (Bashnya Syuyumbike) is named after a long-suffering princess married to three successive khans.

There are many legends associated with

the tower and the Tatar Queen. One of them states that the cause of the Russian siege of Kazan by Ivan IV was Syuyumbike's refusal to marry the tsar. To save her city, Syuyumbike agreed to marry the tsar only if a tower higher than any other mosque in Kazan could be built in a week. After the tower's completion, Syuyumbike found it impossible to leave her native city and killed herself by jumping from the upper terrace of the tower.

From Syuyumbike Tower or from the Spassky Tower (with the clock in it), you can see over the city and to the levees holding back the Volga. Once through the Spassky Tower, the first lane on the right in the administrative buildings leads to two other towers, Konsistorskaya and Yugo-Vostochnaya, which have a small exhibit of old Kazan photographs. The towers are open from 10 am to 5 pm and the entry fee is US$0.10.

Museums

Across Pervomayskaya ploshchad, at ulitsa Lenina 2, is a **museum** of Tatar Folk Art (Kraevedchesky muzey). It's open Sunday to Friday from 10 am to 5 pm. The **Tatarstan Regional History Museum** (Muzey istorii svyazi respubliki Tatarstan) is at ulitsa Baumana and is open Monday to Friday from 10 am to noon.

SS Peter & Paul Cathedral

The colourful twin-towered Petropavlovsky sobor is on Musy Dzhalilya ulitsa, between ulitsa Lenina and ulitsa Profsoyuznaya. This 18th-century baroque cathedral has a heavily decorated façade and the unusual Russian feature of being divided into two storeys. It was built in honour of Tsar Peter I after he visited Kazan in 1722.

Mosques

Just off ulitsa Tatarstan, on ulitsa Nasiri near Lake Kaban (Kabanskoe Ozero), are several 18th-century mosques.

Places to Stay & Eat

Cruiseniks usually stay on board. There is a dormitory-style hotel called *Molodezhny Tsentr* (☎ 32 79 54) at ulitsa Dekabristov 1, where basic rooms with no TV and a share bath and toilet cost US$7.60 per person. There is also a basic restaurant here. To get here take either tram No 9 or trolleybus No 1, 4 or 10.

One of the few hotels to accept foreigners is *Duslik* (☎ 32 53 20) at ulitsa Pravo-Bulachnaya 49. The run-down and not-so-clean rooms cost about US$26.50/55.60. To get here take trolleybus No 4 from the railway station, get off at the first stop past the bridge and walk back to it. The hotel is on your right.

The conveniently located *Hotel Volga* (☎ 32 18 94), ulitsa Said-Galeeva 1A, just a few minutes walk north-west from the railway station, has a sleazy clientele hanging around the front door and the reception area. The rooms cost US$27/69.70.

The old *Hotel Kazan* (☎ 32 77 57), ulitsa Baumana 9/15, with its fading grandiose interior, has rooms for US$28.50/56.70 and deluxe rooms for US$82.60. Its restaurant is in the same style as the hotel and the food is the usual Russian fare for under US$1.

The more modern, prefabricated *Hotel Tatarstan* (☎ 32 69 79) at ulitsa Kuybysheva 2 is the main Intourist hotel with a money-changer, post and telephone office, restaurant and a nightclub. The rather sterile rooms cost US$26.30/52.60. The restaurant serves ordinary Russian and Tatar dishes for around US$2 – but be careful: fish and chicken prices are per 100 grams, so ask how much the whole portion will be. To get here from the railway station take tram No 2 or trolleybus No 7.

Opposite the Tatarstan at No 13 is the *Restoran Vostok* (☎ 32 61 71), which is a popular place with the locals. A place with some old-world character is simply called *Bar Grot* (☎ 32 41 21), and can be found at ulitsa Chernishevskogo 5 – they also serve inexpensive local and Russian dishes.

Getting There & Away

Air There are daily 1½-hour flights to/from Moscow (Domodedovo) for US$93. The Aeroflot office is on the corner of Levo-Bulachnaya ulitsa and Martyna Mezhlauka ulitsa.

Bus There is one daily bus to/from Moscow (Schyolkovsky bus station, departing at 6.30 pm) and the 16½-hour trip costs US$20. There are also daily buses to Ulyanovsk and Nizhny Novgorod. The bus station is near the river port on the corner of Kamilya Yakuba ulitsa and Portovaya ulitsa.

Train The railway station is on Ukhtom-skogo ulitsa. It is best to buy advance train tickets from the railway booking office on the corner of Martyna Mezhlauka and Levo-Bulachnaya. A fast train from Moscow's Kazan station takes 13 to 15 hours. There is also an easier night train to Kazan and a similar train to Ulyanovsk. There is no direct service to Perm and it is necessary to first get a train to Balezino, which takes 10 hours.

Boat The river port is at the end of ulitsa Portovaya, which is the continuation of Tatarstan ulitsa. From June to September there are regular boats between Moscow and Astrakhan, most of which continue to Rostov. Some sample fares in lyux A and 3B are: Moscow US$236 and US$13; Nizhny Novgorod US$108 and US$6, and Astrakhan US$290 and US$16.20.

Getting Around

Bus, tram or trolleybus tickets cost US$0.05 and are available from the usual ticket booths or the driver. Bus No 56 goes to the airport from a bus stand near the corner of Baumana ulitsa and Kuybysheva ulitsa.

AROUND KAZAN
ОКРЕСТНОСТЬ КАЗАНЯ
Raifa Monastery
Раифский монастырь
The Raifa Monastery (Raifsky Bogrodisky monastyr) was consecrated in 1665 but suffered much damage during the Soviet years, as it was used as a site to produce pump-making equipment and as a reformatory for young offenders. It has been under restoration since 1990 but so far only the church has been fully restored.

The monastery lies about 20 km west of Kazan in the village of Raifa. To get there take bus No 104 from just outside the railway station. The trip takes about 50 minutes and the fare is US$0.30. Once the bus turns right off the main road, get off at the second bus stop on the left. Raifa Monastery is a five-minute walk from here along the smaller road.

PERM
ПЕРМЬ
Population 1.09 million
Perm is a large industrial city, located on the trans-Siberian Railway line, which for many years was closed to foreigners due to the large military and industrial complex concentrated there. It was founded around the same time as the establishment of some copper-smelting works in 1723 on the Kama River, at the southern foothills of the Ural Mountains. Perm is a gateway to Siberia and Asia from Europe and its industrial development was ensured with the passing of the Siberian Post Road, and later the Trans-Siberian Railway, through it. Empress Catherine the Great decreed that Perm be made a provincial capital in 1780. Between 1940 and 1957 the town was temporarily renamed Molotov, after Vyacheslav Mikhailovich Molotov, a foreign minister during the Stalin rule who lost his post and status after a disagreement during the Khrushchev days – Molotov cocktails are also named after him.

Perm is the cultural centre of the Ural Mountains region, especially with regard to folklore. It is also a good starting point for hiking, rafting and skiing in the wilderness of the Ural Mountains.

Orientation
Perm is a large, sprawling city, with the Kama River flowing past its northern edge. The city is centred around the intersection of ulitsa Lenina and Komsomolsky prospekt. Going east along ulitsa Lenina takes you to the Perm II railway station. Along this part of the street are most of the shops, offices and theatres.

Information
Intourist (☎ 33 55 85) is at ulitsa Popova 9.

Many places change US dollars and Deutschmarks, but only the Permkombank (☎ 48 16 22) at bulvar Gagarina 65 changes American Express and Thomas Cook travellers' cheques, as well as providing cash advances for Visa, Diners and MasterCard. Tram No 7 goes there from near the corner of ulitsa Lenina and Komsomolsky prospekt. Take this tram to the end of the line and walk back a couple of hundred metres – Permkombank is on the right.

The main post office and telephone office are on the corner of ulitsa Lenina and ulitsa Popova. The city's telephone code is 3422. Perm is two hours ahead of Moscow time.

Old style maps are available from a bookshop next to the Univermag on the corner of ulitsa Lenina and Komsomosky prospekt. Univermag has a one-hour Kodak processing lab which sells most of the usual Kodak products, and is also a good place to buy souvenirs.

Things to See
The spire and cupola-like dome of the **art gallery** (Permskaya Gosudarstvennaya Galeria) at the top end of Komsomolsky prospekt are part of a former cathedral. The iconostasis is part of the gallery and the

EUROPEAN RUSSIA

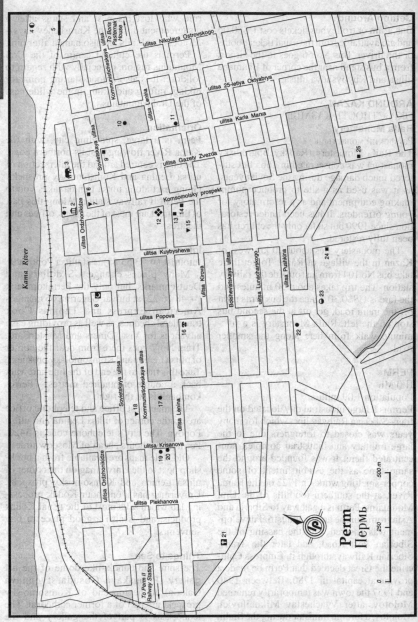

ulitsa Nikolaya Ostrovskogo

To Boris
Pasternak
House

Kommunisticheskaya ulitsa

ulitsa 25-letiya Oktyabrya

ulitsa Lenina

ulitsa Karla Marxa

Soyetskaya ulitsa

ulitsa Gazety Zvezda

Kama River

ulitsa Ordzhonikidze

Komsomolsky prospekt

ulitsa Kuybysheva

ulitsa Kirova

Bolshevistskaya ulitsa

ulitsa Lunacharskogo

ulitsa Pushkina

ulitsa Popova

Soyetskaya ulitsa

Kommunistcheskaya ulitsa

ulitsa Lenina

ulitsa Krisanova

ulitsa Ordzhonikidze

ulitsa Plekhanova

To Perm II
Railway Station

Perm
Пермь

500 m

250

0

PLACES TO STAY

6 Hotel Turist
Гостиница Турист

9 Hotel Tsentralnaya
Гостиница Центральная

13 Hotel Ural
Гостиница Урал

14 Hotel Prikame
Гостиница Прикамье

24 Hotel Sportivnaya
Гостиница Спортивная

25 Hotel Vostochnaya
Гостиница Восточная

PLACES TO EAT

7 Priglashaem Kafe
Кафе Приглашаем

15 Neva Restoran &
Open-Air Market
Ресторан Нева и рынок

18 Yevropeysky Restoran
Европейский Ресторан

OTHER

1 Art Gallery
Галерия

2 Regional Ethno-
graphic Museum
Областной краеведческий
музей

3 Zoo
Зоопарк

4 River Port
Речной порт

5 Perm Railway Station
Вокзал Пермь

8 Mosque
Мечеть

10 Academic Theatre
Академический театр

11 Evrasia Travel
Евразия трэвэл

12 Department Store
Универмаг

16 Telephone Exchange
Центральный
переговорный пункт

17 Panfilov Municipal
Ballet Company
Городской балет
Панфилова

19 Railway Booking Office
Железнодорожные
билетные кассы

20 Aeroflot Office
Аэрофлот

21 Kazan Church
Казанская церковь

22 Market
Центральный Рынок

23 Bus Station
Автобусный вокзал

middle and top parts of it can be closely viewed from either of the two floors on which other paintings and sculptures are exhibited. The art gallery was opened in 1922 and today it houses one of the largest collections in the country. There is an impressive wooden sculpture exhibit of items from the 17th to 19th centuries, as well as many paintings by such artists as Boris Kustodiev and Natalia Goncharova. The gallery is open Tuesday to Sunday from 11 am to 6 pm, and the entry fee is US$1.

On the corner of Komsomolsky prospekt 6 and ulitsa Ordzhonikidze is the **Ethnography Museum** (Permsky oblastnoy kraevedchesky muzey), which only has exhibits of prehistory and Soviet propaganda in the form of exhibits concerning the era from the Russian Revolution to the 1930s. It is open Saturday to Thursday from 10 am to 6 pm, and the entry fee is US$0.25.

There is an **aquarium** (akvaterrarium) on the Kama River side of the art gallery which is open Monday to Saturday from 10 am to 5 pm.

There are several churches around town but they need to be restored and entry is generally not possible. The **Kazan Church**

(Kazanskaya tserkov) on ulitsa Plekhanova has frescoes by Nikolay Rerikh, but only the outside one can be seen. There is a **mosque** (mechet) on ulitsa Ordzhonikidze, two blocks east of the art gallery.

Boris Pasternak lived and wrote *Dr Zhivago* in a blue house with white rims on ulitsa Lenina, near the corner of Golgova. In the novel the town Yuryatin is actually Perm.

Places to Stay

Only a handful of Perm's run-down hotels accept foreigners. *Hotel Prikame* (☎ 34 86 62) at Komsomolsky prospekt 27 has shabby rooms for US$25/35 with bath, toilet and TV; without these amenities rooms are US$12.50/20. The breakfast is not worth it, even though it only costs US$0.85.

The *Hotel Tsentralnaya* (☎ 32 60 10) at ulitsa Karla Marxa is fairly run-down and the rooms cost US$22.50 for one, two or three people. The rather more reasonable *Hotel Sportivnaya* (☎ 34 95 18) at ulitsa Kuybysheva 49 has standard rooms for US$17.50/25.

The still-to-be-completed *Hotel Ural* (☎ 34 44 17) on the corner of ulitsa Lenina and Komsomolsky prospekt is the newest

Intourist place to stay. Their standard rooms cost US$25/40. The only problem here was a regular supply of hot water – in fact, the hotel would not let us stay here without a prior reservation because the Russian prime minister was occupying one of the rooms, and it was only during his stay of two days that the hotel had hot water. However, many Russian cities or areas have their hot water cut off for weeks in summer for maintenance of the systems, so this may not be a permanent problem.

Places to Eat

Perm has some reasonable restaurants. The *Kafe Priglashaem*, on the corner of Komsomolsky prospekt and Ordzhonikidze ulitsa, is popular with young people. It's open from 11 am to 9 pm. One of the best places is part of the Hotel Prikame: the *Prikame Restoran* is clean and has a fading, turn-of-the-century look and reasonably pleasant service. The dishes start at US$2. There is also a bar and evening entertainment. Another good restaurant is *Neva*, at ulitsa Kuybysheva 31, behind the Hotel Ural and next to the open-air market. Most dishes cost around US$2 and a two-course meal including a soft drink and a bottle of wine is about US$10.

One of the best and most expensive restaurants, according to a good friend, is *Yevropeysky* at ulitsa Lenina 73A, opposite the modern opera building. Of course, they specialise in good European food.

A good but pricey place for breakfast is *Maxim Cafe* on the 7th floor of Hotel Ural. A set breakfast of ham, egg, bread, jam and coffee is US$4 and is served between 8 and 10 am. During the rest of the day, light snacks and drinks are available.

Fresh vegetables and fruit are available at two markets: the main one is next to the main bus station on Tsentralny rynok and the smaller one is behind the Hotel Ural.

Entertainment

The Academic Theatre of Opera & Ballet (Akademichesky teatr opery i baleta) in Sad Reshetnikova is the third-best ballet school in Russia, and is a very good place to see ballet and opera. The other place for ballet is the Municipal Ballet Company at the Gorodskoy Ballet Theatre on ulitsa Lenina, west of Hotel Ural.

Russian bands play most evenings at Prikame Restoran.

Getting There & Away

Air The Aeroflot office (☎ 33 46 68) is at ulitsa Krisanova near the corner of ulitsa Lenina. There are daily flights to/from Moscow (US$118), Ufa (US$78) and Saratov (US$113). To Nizhny Novgorod there is only a Monday flight (US$102) and to Volgograd there are four flights a week (US$127).

Train Perm is on the main trans-Siberian rail route from Moscow (22 to 24 hours). Yekaterinburg (6½ hours) is the next major city as you head east.

Perm has two railway stations on opposing sides of the city: Vokzal Perm in the east and Perm II Vokzal in the west. Most trains use Perm II. There are daily trains between Moscow and Perm. There are no direct trains to Kazan or Ufa. To get to Kazan a change at Balezino is required and the whole journey can take up to 16 hours, while to Ufa a change at Yekaterinburg is necessary and the journey can take nearly 24 hours.

Remember that Perm is two hours ahead of Moscow time and that all rail transport operates on Moscow time.

Boat The river port is at the eastern end of ulitsa Ordzhonikidze, close to the Perm railway station. At the time of writing boats departed twice a week from May to September to travel up and down the Kama River. This service has been drastically cut in the last few years and not many people use it. Its future might be doubtful. In July and August there are two weekly boats to Volgograd on the Volga River, taking six days and costing up to US$100 in lyux A – these boats also stop at Ulyanovsk and Samara.

Getting Around

To get to the airport, there are either buses from outside the Aeroflot office or from the bus station at Tsentralny rynok. Buses No 110, No 119 and No 120 cost US$0.25 and take about 35 minutes. A taxi costs about US$7.50.

Take any bus or trolleybus, or tram No 7, to get from the Perm II railway station to the hotels Ural and Prikame and the centre of the town. The ticket booths charge a flat fee of US$0.25.

AROUND PERM
ОКРЕСТНОСТЬ ПЕРМЬЯ

There are many sights that are difficult to reach in the Perm region. However, it is possible to participate in many outdoor activities like skiing, hiking, canoeing or rafting. Several companies operate such trips not only in the Perm region but also to other parts of Russia. Two agencies have been recommended: Evresia Travel (☎ 32 64 31; fax 32 69 14; e-mail BSZ3458(REC)) at ulitsa K Marxa 8; and Cruise (☎ 25 69 72; fax 34 49 26), ulitsa Stakchanovskaya 2-69. One available tour is a 15-day journey along the Chusovaya River, east of Perm – at the time of research this trip cost US$510 per person for one or two people, cheaper if the group is bigger. Another trip is a 14-day horse riding tour along the same river, costing US$850 per person for a group of three to five, less for a larger group.

Khokhlovka
Хохловка

At Khokhlovka, about 45 km north of Perm, is an open-air museum of Perm's ethnographic architecture (Arkhitekturno-etnograficheskiy muzey Khokhlovka). There are at present eight wooden buildings. Two churches date back to the turn of the 18th century, while the other structures are from the 19th or early 20th century. Some buildings still have furniture and tools inside.

The best time to visit this sight is during the first weekend of May, when a folk and culture festival celebrates the coming of spring.

Khokhlovka is a difficult spot to get to as there are only a couple of buses daily from Perm. It's about a 45-minute drive by car.

Kungur & Around
Кунгур и Окрестность

Situated 90 km south-east of Perm, Kungur is one of the oldest towns in the Ural Mountains. It lies in 'a gigantic natural bowl where three rivers meet'. Kungur's population is 80,000 and it has many picturesque natural attractions around it. It was founded in 1648 and was the centre of Perm province until 1781. In the 19th century the merchants of Kungur established trade relations with Asia and became the largest tea dealers in the country.

The post and telephone office is at ulitsa Lenina 17. The city's telephone code is 271.

Things to See Kungur's attractions include the **All Saints Church** (Vsekh Svyatikh tserkov), and also a **Regional Museum** at ulitsa Gogolya 36 which is open from 11 am to 5 pm and costs US$0.25 to get in. Other places of interest are the old **governor's house**, dating from the 17th century, and a unique row of shops called **Gostiny dvor**.

About five km from Kungur is the **Kungur Ice Cave** (Lednaya peshchera), which is famous for the unique karst and ice formations with frozen waterfalls and transparent lakes. The cave is open from 10 am to 4 pm and the entry fee, which allows you to see one km out of the cave's entire length of 4.6 km, is US$5.

Another place to visit is the **White Mountain Monastery** (Belogorsky monastyr) which is partially ruined. During the Soviet era it was used as a mental hospital and today it is waiting to be restored.

Places to Stay & Eat The *Hotel Iren* (☎ 3 21 57) is at ulitsa Lenina 30, Kungur. The restaurant *Ermak* (☎ 3 50 28) at ulitsa K Marxa 11 has been recommended.

It is possible to stay a five-minute walk from the Ice Cave at *Stalagmit Hotel* (☎ 3 42 81 or 3 36 25) for US$25 in a deluxe room. There is a restaurant in the hotel, which is also a travel agency.

Getting There & Away The train and bus stations in Kungur are at ulitsa Bachurina. The bus fare to/from Perm is US$2.30.

There are daily buses between Kungur's railway station and the Ice Cave (half an hour), but there is no public transport to the White Mountain Monastery. The dirt road is practically impassable for vehicles when wet. It is also possible to see the Kungur sights on a tour with Evrasia Travel (see the Around Perm introduction).

Perm 36
Пермь 36

Perm 36 is about 10 km from the town of Chusovoy, which is 100 km east of Perm. This was one of the infamous labour camps of the Gulag Archipelago where many dissidents were persecuted. It opened in 1918 for the detention of political prisoners and closed in 1988. Such well-known dissidents as Gleb Yakunin and Anatoly Shcharansky did their time here, but other non-Russians such as the Lithuanian Balis Gajauskas, the Estonian Mart Niklus, the Belarusian Vasil Stus and the Ukrainian Lev Lukyanenko were also imprisoned here. Perm 36 has a memorial to the victims of the Gulag system and there is a plan to make it into a museum and research centre, but that will depend on whether the necessary funds will be available.

Perm 36 is difficult to reach as there is no public transport connections with Chusovoy. There are, however, buses and trains between Chusovoy and Perm.

UFA
УФА

Population: 1.08 million

Ufa is the capital of Bashkortostan and was founded in 1574, little more than 22 years after the Bashkirs were incorporated into the growing Russian Empire by Ivan the Terrible. The Bashkir are Turkic people who make up less than a quarter of Bashkortostan's population of three million. They settled in the region during the Mongol khanate invasions, between the 13th and 15th centuries.

Orientation & Information

Ufa is a medium-sized, quiet and pleasant city, whose wide, tree-lined streets and few high-rise buildings make it look like a town, not a city. It sits on the bank of the Belaya River. There are three major streets: in the older part of town is ulitsa Lenina with some hotels and the post office; a couple of streets west is ulitsa K Marxa with many shops and an Aeroflot office; and further north-east on prospekt Oktyabrya is the centre of the newer part of town which contains univermag Ufa.

The major shopping hub is around ploshchad Oktyabrya, also known as Tsentralny rynok, through which all public transport passes on the way between ulitsa Lenina, the railway station and prospekt Oktyabrya.

The Bashkir Regional Tourist Office (☎ 24 36 74) is in the Hotel Turist at ulitsa R Zorge, but at the time of writing was not very helpful. Only US dollars or Deutschmarks can be changed in the various exchange counters around town or in hotels like Bashkiria or Turist. The pochtamt is on the corner of ulitsa Lenina and ulitsa Kommunisticheskaya, while the telephone office is on the opposite corner. The Ufa telephone code is 3472. The kiosk selling newspapers next to Hotel Bashkiria also sells poor-quality city maps.

Things to See

The **Lenin Museum** (Muzey V I Lenina) on the corner of ulitsa Kirova and ulitsa Krupskoy has not only the house where Lenin stayed (No 45, which is at the ulitsa Dostoevskogo end of the museum) but also a whole street of wooden Bashkir houses. Most of these are used as government offices, except for No 34 and No 39, which comprise a museum of Bashkir history and folklore. Opening hours are Tuesday to Sunday from 10 am to 6 pm.

Also on Kirova at No 17 is another **museum** which has regularly changing exhibitions. It is open Monday to Friday from 10 am to 6 pm.

Places to Stay

The cheapest but least appealing hotel is *Ufa* at ulitsa K Marxa 23. Rooms without any facilities cost US$17.50/33 and those with bath and toilet are US$52.50/83. Slightly better but not the cleanest place is the former deluxe *Hotel Bashkiria* on the corner of ulitsa Lenina and ulitsa Kirova. Grubby singles with a sink and TV are US$25, while other singles/doubles including bath and toilet cost US$60/65.

The *Hotel Atidel* (☎ 22 56 80) at ulitsa Lenina 18 has rooms for US$36.50/61.50. There is a similar looking *Hotel Turist* (☎ 24 36 56) at ulitsa R Zorge 15. The most modern hotel in town is *Rossia* (☎ 34 31 81) at prospekt Oktyabrya 81. The fine rooms in this prefabricated building are US$40/100. The hotel has a currency exchange which accepts Visa cards, an Aeroflot office and a restaurant.

Places to Eat

A good place for fresh fruit and vegetables is the market *(bazar)* at ulitsa Tsyurupi off ploshchad Oktyabrya, which is known as Tsentralny rynok.

Opposite the bazar on the corner of ulitsa Tsyurupi and ploshchad Oktyabrya is *Kafe Unish*, with the usual Russian bufet food. *Restoran Ufa* on the corner of ulitsa Lenina and ulitsa Kommunisticheskaya has an unfortunate, kitschy Bashkir décor. The dishes are rather ordinary (US$1.50 to US$2.50) and the toilet is a squat. Russian bands play most evenings. A place with similar food, prices and entertainment is *Bashkortostan Restorani* at ploshchad Oktyabrya.

An up-market place to eat is *Restaurant Jespr* at ulitsa Lenina, next to the post office. Entrées cost around US$10 and main dishes cost up to US$21.50. The hotel *Rossia*'s restaurant is cheaper (US$2 to US$4 per dish) and has classier looking surroundings to enjoy the meal in. In front of the hotel is the *Bar/kafe Kaiserdom* which has imported beer.

Getting There & Away

Air The Aeroflot office is at ulitsa K Marxa 28, and there are branches in some hotels like the Bashkiria and the Rossia. There are six daily flights to/from Moscow, costing US$115. There are also daily flights to Saratov, Kazan and Mineralnye Vody. There are flights twice a day to/from Beloretsk, costing US$15.

Bus The bus station is at the intersection of ulitsa R Zorge and ulitsa Mingazheva. Buses depart from here to other towns around Bashkortostan. To Beloretsk there are two buses daily taking 6½ hours and the fare is US$4.30. There are four buses daily to Meleuz, taking almost five hours and costing US$3.30.

Train The railway station is at the northern end of ulitsa Lenina. There are daily trains to/from Moscow, taking 30 hours, and nightly trains to Ulyanovsk, taking anywhere between 10 to 19 hours depending on the train.

Boat There are only 11 services to/from Moscow between mid-June and early September. The river port is behind the railway station.

Getting Around

Bus No 101 costs US$0.15 from the airport all the way through the heart of the city, along ulitsa Lenina and Tsentralny rynok (ploshchad Oktyabrya), past the bus station to the railway station. It takes about 35 minutes from the airport to Tsentralny rynok.

All buses, trolleybuses and trams cost US$0.04 per ride, and tickets are sold by provodniks on them. There are also small buses that cost US$0.08 and tend to be faster and less crowded. One of these, No 2, plies the route from Hotel Atidel, along ulitsa Lenina, through Tsentralny rynok to Hotel Rossia. The ordinary bus No 106 takes a similar route.

As with most places in Russia, taxi drivers are open to bargaining and start by asking US$5 from the railway station to the centre of Ufa.

AROUND UFA
ОКРЕСТНОСТЬ УФЫ

There are two caves south of Ufa. The **Shulgan-Tash (Kapova) Cave** is near the village of Starobukhangulov, which is accessible from the town of Beloretsk. You can explore three levels of the cave, which also has a lake. It is known for its Palaeolithic cave drawings, including mammoths, horses and a rhinoceros.

The other cave is **Pobedy (Victory)** and is near the village of Krasnousolsky, which can be reached from Sterlitamak or Beloretsk. This cave has the usual stalactites and stalagmites but some are formed from ice, and there is some stunning natural scenery involving gorges and forests.

ULYANOVSK
УЛЬЯНОВСК

Population: 640,000

Founded as Simbirsk in the 17th century, Ulyanovsk (*'ool-YAN-ovsk'*) is a tourist stop for only one reason: it's the birthplace and boyhood home of Lenin (born Vladimir Ilich Ulyanov) and thus a former Soviet shrine. Its few Western visitors are day-tripping from Volga cruise ships. It's of interest only to see the big place Lenin still occupies in the national psyche.

Ulyanovsk was initially a fortified town and Moscow's border guard post. Due to its geographic position it became a centre for trade with Asia. During the 18th century the nobles nicknamed this town 'Noble's Nest' as Russia's rich used to retire there for their holidays. The famous Russian author Ivan Goncharov was born and lived here.

Despite a new name on Lenin's death, the city stayed a backwater until the centenary of his birth in 1970. Then, in a Brezhnevian orgy of redevelopment, the city centre became a 'memorial zone' with museum complex, yawning plazas and the restoration of seven Ulyanov family houses and one entire neighbourhood.

The city itself is bland, conservative and devoid of churches (Stalin knocked most of them down) or other signs of age. It's on the banks of what used to be the Volga River, now Kuybyshev Reservoir.

Orientation & Information

The main memorial zone occupies the high Volga banks from ploshchad Lenina to the giant Lenin Memorial Centre. Two blocks east is ulitsa Goncharova, the shopping district.

Intourist is at the Hotel Venets (floor 3, north door). The Venets has post and telegraph offices, a bank (which accepts Visa for payment only) and a kiosk with Russian maps. Inkom Bank near the corner of ulitsa Goncharova and ulitsa Bebelya changes US dollars and German marks, charging a high commission. The main post office is on ulitsa Goncharova on the corner of ulitsa Tolstogo. The Ulyanovsk telephone code is 84222.

Memorial Zone

Memorial Centre The **Big Hall** (Bolshoy Zal) is built around three Ulyanov family houses. Upstairs are a zillion Lenin portraits, dioramas of old Simbirsk and a vast, glossy museum of the revolution, full of photos and artefacts but obscure without a guide. Off to one side a **statue** of The Man stands in a hall whose sacramental overtones would have made him squirm. The centre is open from 10 am to 6 pm.

Near the Memorial Centre Down the banks behind the centre is a string of mini-parks built by the Soviet republics in 1970, now weedy and crumbling, rich in unintended symbolism. Above them a cable car descends to the river.

In a former cloth-merchant's house in ulitsa Gimova is the Soviet answer to church weddings, the **Palace of Marriages** (Dvorets Brakosochetania). Wedding parties go straight from there to lay flowers at Lenin's statue.

At the southern end of Kommunisticheskaya ulitsa is **Lenin's grammar school**. The headmaster's son was Alexandr Kerensky, later to head the provisional government Lenin overthrew. At the other end of the

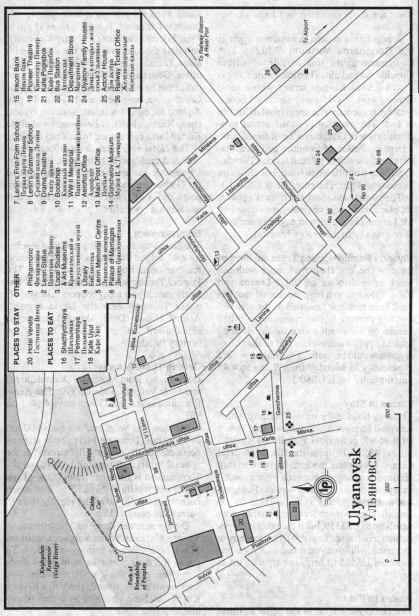

street are the regional art and local studies museums.

A non-Lenin or non-communist sight is the **Goncharov Museum** (Muzey I A Goncharova) on the corner of ulitsa Goncharova and ulitsa Lenina. Goncharov is a well-known Russian writer whose most famous work is *Oblomov*, which is about a wealthy nobleman who spent most of his life in bed. The museum is in the actual two-storey house of Goncharov's childhood, with a large collection of furniture and memorabilia from the author's life. It is open Tuesday to Sunday from 10 am to 6 pm, but closes on Tuesday at 4 pm. The entry fee is US$0.10.

The promenade above the river is a peaceful place when you've finally overdosed on Mr Lenin. The old men in pyjamas are WW II veterans from the nearby hospital.

Ulyanov Family Houses There are three of these at the Big Hall, four more within a block of each other on ulitsa Lenina and ulitsa Tolstogo, in a neighbourhood that has itself been restored. Lenin aside, the area and the too-perfect house-museum at ulitsa Lenina 68 are worth a visit for the detailed look at upper-middle-class life of that time. A guide would be useful. Opening times are Wednesday to Monday from 9 am to 4.45 pm; the entry fee is US$0.15.

Places to Stay
The only hotel at the time of writing which accepted foreigners was the two-star *Venets* (☎ 9 45 95) at Sovietskaya ulitsa 15, postal index 432600, opposite the Memorial Centre. It's central, modern, fairly clean (not all linen is changed after each visitor) and – except for the supper band – quiet. The hotel has a unique pricing system. Their rooms cost 10 times as much for foreigners, in other words up to US$150, but if the hotel is empty (which most of the time it is) the nice lady at reception will give you a bed in a four-bed room for US$25 (it helps to bargain a bit as well).

Places to Eat
The co-op *Kafe Uyut* in the cellar at ulitsa

Karla Marxa 5 has good little pizzas and salads at fair prices. It is open from 11 am to 7 pm. For cakes and ice cream, try *Kafeterny*, on ulitsa Goncharova near the corner with ulitsa Lenina. There are other cafés along ulitsa Goncharova. Shashlyk, cakes and coffee can be tried in *Shachlychnaya* at ulitsa Goncharova, open between 10 am and 6 pm. A place for early breakfast, with the typical cheap Russian bufet, is *Pelmennaya* at ulitsa Karla Marxa 6; it's open from 7 am to 6 pm.

The *Hotel Venets* has a mediocre restaurant and café and a bufet near the lobby. Ulyanovsk was apparently a testing ground for Gorbachev's abortive anti-alcohol campaign and is still nearly dry – no restaurants or cafés are open after 7 pm.

Entertainment
The Kafe Pogrebok (Cellar), ulitsa Goncharova 44 behind the Venets, is a Komsomol-run bar open from 11 am to 8 pm. The Pioneer Theatre at ulitsa Karla Marxa 11 has a café and club for teenyboppers. Located off ulitsa Tolstogo near the Lenin houses, Actors' House (Dom Aktyora) has occasional films and an arresting turn-of-the century façade.

Getting There & Away
Daily flights from Moscow (Domodedovo) and from Volgograd are US$90. The Aeroflot office is at ulitsa Goncharova 4 (☎ 1 65 93).

Moscow and Volgograd are both 900 km away by rail. There are two railway stations north-east of the centre: Ulyanovsk-I is for special tourist trains and Ulyanovsk-Tsentralnaya is for other trains. One of the best trains to Ufa is No 255 as it is much faster than the No 609. The nightly train to Saratov takes up to 15 hours.

During summer there are daily boats to Samara, Kazan and other Volga destinations. The 1st-class fare to Saratov is US$54. To get to the river port take tram No 4 from Hotel Venets for five stops, from where you walk down a lane towards the Volga River's Kuybyshev Reservoir. You cross the railway line on a pedestrian bridge.

Getting Around

From the airport, bus No 6 takes half an hour to the end of the line (Tsentr stop) on ulitsa Goncharova behind the Hotel Venets. A taxi is about US$6. Ulyanovsk-I railway station is 2.5 km from Tsentr on bus No 1 or 2; Ulyanovsk-Tsentralnaya is 4.5 km by bus No 4, 2 or 117, or tram No 4.

Ulyanovsk has the cheapest public transport we found anywhere in Russia. The trams and buses cost US$0.01 per ride, and tickets are available from ticket booths.

SARATOV
САРАТОВ
Population: 900,000

This pleasant city has a thriving commercial centre with not many sights but enjoyable tree-filled streets to promenade along. The tree-lined pedestrian mall of prospekt Kirova has many shops, cafés and restaurants and is a very relaxing spot to walk through or enjoy a drink or a meal. The bridge which spans the Volga from Saratov was built in 1965 and is one of the largest in Europe.

Saratov was established in 1590. It was initially a fortress forming a line of defence for the trade route along the Volga. The city was moved in 1616 and 1674, the second time after a fortress was destroyed during a rebellion. The city was occupied during WW II by the Germans and has monuments to its heroes.

Orientation & Information

The centre of town is the pedestrian mall on prospekt Kirova (Nemetskaya), stretching over one km from the covered market at ulitsa Chapaeva to ulitsa Radishcheva. One block north along Radishcheva is Muzeysky ploshchad from which the busy commercial prospekt Lenina (Moskovsky) is linked by trolleybus No 1 or 9 to the river port and the Hotel Volga.

Intourist (☎ 24 18 23) is at prospekt Kirova 34. As usual there are many places changing US dollars and Deutschmarks but nothing else. Tsentralny Bank is at prospekt Kirova 7. The Western Union money wire service is at Komplexbank (☎ 2 26 45 61), ulitsa Michurina 103, and is open Monday to Friday from 10 am to 1 pm. The pochtamt is on the corner of ulitsa Lenina and ulitsa Chapaeva. The city's telephone code is 8452. Maps of the city with public transport information are available from a bookshop called Saratov kniga on the corner of prospekt Kirova and ulitsa Volskaya for US$2.25.

Things to See

The 17th-century **Trinity Cathedral** (Troitsky sobor) at ploshchad Muzeynaya has a heavily decorated interior, including an elaborate iconostasis. Another interesting religious structure is the **Utoli Moya Pechali Church** (1903) on the corner of ulitsa Radishcheva and ulitsa Volzhskaya, the roof of which is dotted with many mini-onion domes.

The **Art Museum** (Khudozhestveny muzey, also known as Radishchev muzey) is at ploshchad Revolyutsii and is open Tuesday to Sunday from 10 am to 5 pm, but closes on Tuesday at 4 pm. The **Regional Folklore Museum** (Oblastnoy muzey kraevedenia) at Muzeynaya ploshchad is open Tuesday to Sunday from 10 am to 5 pm. In the same square is the **Old Cathedral** (Stary sobor). The **Chernishevsky House Museum** is on the corner of ulitsa Chernishevsky and ulitsa Nekrasov and has the usual artist home exhibits.

Places to Stay

Both the railway station and river port have hotels for ticket holders but as yet these do not accept foreigners, just as many other hotels in town don't.

A reasonable place to stay is *Hotel Volga* (☎ 24 36 45) at prospekt Kirova 34, where rooms for one or two guests cost from US$16 to US$80. There is also a restaurant. The most up-market but least friendly place is *Hotel Slovakia* (☎ 26 76 18) at naberezhnaya Kosmonavtov, near the river port. They do not like independent travellers and will only allow foreigners to stay here if Saratov is written in their visa. The fairly modern rooms with good views of the Volga River cost US$45/52.50.

You could also try the *Hotel Olympia* (☎ 25 14 41) at ulitsa Chernishevskaya 54.

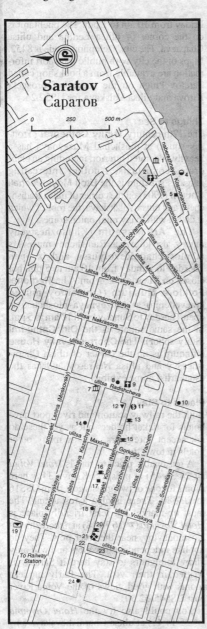

Saratov
Саратов

0   250   500 m

PLACES TO STAY

5   Hotel Slovakia
    Гостиница Словакия
17 Hotel Volga
    Гостиница Волга

PLACES TO EAT

12 Restoran Pira
    Ресторан Пира
13 Konditerskaya Kafe
    Кондитерская Кафе
15 Aroman Kafe
    Ароман Кафе
16 Stolovaya Kafe
    Столовая Кафе
20 Semeynoe Kafe
    Семейное Кафе

OTHER

1   Regional Folklore Museum
    Областной музей краеведения
2   ploshchad Muzeynaya
    площадь Музейная
3   Trinity Cathedral
    Троицкий собор
4   River Port
    Речной вокзал
6   ploshchad Fedika
    площадь Федика
7   Art Museum
    Художественый музей
8   ploshchad Revolutsii
    площадь Революции
9   Utoli Moya Pechali Church
    Храм Утоли Моя Печали
10 Philharmonic Theatre
    Филармония
11 Tsentralny Bank
    Центральный Банк
14 Opera and Ballet Theatre
    Театр оперы и балета
18 Bookshop
    Саратов книга
19 Main Post Office
    Почтамт
21 Department Store
    Универмаг
22 ploshchad Kirova
    площадь Кирова
23 Central Market
    Торговый-Дом-Центральный
24 Aeroflot Office
    Аэрофлот

Places to Eat

The best place for fresh fruit and vegetables is the lively and thriving *market* (Torgovy-Dom-Tsentralny or TDTs) on the corner of ulitsa Sakko i Vancetti and ulitsa Chapaeva.

The *Bilina Kafe* at prospekt Kirova 50 has soups and cheap shashlyk. Next door, *Torti* is good for cakes. At No 48 is the bufet *Delikatessen-Sarkompexim*, a joint Russian-Swiss venture selling European food products including yoghurt and many snacks and cakes. In the same building as Hotel Volga is another joint venture bufet *Pinguin bistro delikatessen*, with a larger and better choice of snacks and desserts.

Kafe Stolovaya at No 30 tempts customers with its BBQ chicken outside the store. There are also other items on the menu like fish or bifshteks, all under US$0.50 per dish. A nice view of the square at the end of Kirova No 4 can be enjoyed from the 1st-floor terrace of the *Restoran Pira*. The ordinary Russian dishes cost around US$3.50.

Entertainment

Opera and ballet performances can be seen at Teatr opery i baleta at ploshchad Revolyutsii. The classical concerts are on at the Philharmonic Theatre (Filarmonia) on ulitsa Radishcheva.

Getting There & Away

Aeroflot (☎ 4 44 52) is at ulitsa Stepana Razina 42. There are daily flights to/from Moscow for US$93.

The railway station is on Privokzalnaya ploshchad, at the end of prospekt Lenina. Saratov is on the Moscow-Astrakhan line and the trains also stop in Kazan, Ulyanovsk and Volgograd. An overnight train to/from Volgograd takes 9½ hours. The nightly train to Ulyanovsk takes up to 15 hours.

The river port is at naberezhnaya Kosmonavtov, the eastern end of Lenina prospekt. The Volga boats travelling between Moscow and Astrakhan or Rostov-on-Don pass through Saratov twice a day between May and September. The trip to Volgograd takes about 20 hours and costs US$26 in 1st class.

Getting Around

Unlike in many other Russian cities all

The Volga Germans

The Volga Germans have been around since the second half of the 18th century, when they were invited by Catherine the Great to modernise farming techniques in Russia. Most of the Germans who came were Catholics or Mennonites, and they arrived in three waves between 1764 and 1862. Their adopted name comes from the Volga River, near which most of them settled; the second major settlement was along the Black Sea coast. The Germans had their own autonomous republic along the Volga, east, south, and south-east of Saratov, but after the German invasion of 1941 Stalin had them moved to Siberia and Central Asia. The Soviet authorities doubted the loyalty of the Volga Germans. Many members of other nationalities who were living at the time in the USSR, as well as large numbers of Russians, sided with the German invaders (that is why the communists referred to the struggle of WW II as the Great Patriotic War), and the same was feared of the Volga Germans. They were never allowed to return.

Recently there has been some talk of setting up a new Volga German Republic in the vicinity of the old one, around Saratov. This seems unlikely as there are only about 20,000 people of German descent left in the region. The remainder, whose numbers are estimated at two to five million, would have to be brought in from Siberia and Central Asia and resettled in the area. This would be an expensive and logistically enormous task. As well, there is the question of the local Russians, and whether they would be willing to live in such a state. No one is certain how many ethnic Germans want to settle along the Volga, but most are keen to leave their homes in Central Asia. Many have recently chosen to move to Germany – in 1991, 147,320 Germans left the CIS and 700,000 applied to leave. ■

public transport tickets are not exchangeable and a bus requires a different ticket to a trolleybus or tram, which can be bought from booths marked *Prodazha abonementnikh biletov* for US$0.05. The trolleybus Nos 2 and 2A stop at the market (TDTs) that is a short walk from ulitsa Kirova pedestrian zone, which can be reached by walking north along ulitsa Chapaeva to ploshchad Kirova. The main thoroughfare of prospekt Lenina is plied by trolleybus No 9, which starts its route at the railway station and stops at Muzeynaya ploshchad, a short walk from the river port and Hotel Slovakia.

VOLGOGRAD
ВОЛГОГРАД
Population: 1 million

The city was founded in 1589 as Tsaritsyn and was only a fortress. Volgograd is better known by its pre-1961 name, Stalingrad, the focus of one of the most decisive battles of WW II.

In July 1942 German soldiers besieged Stalingrad, and for four months house-to-house fighting raged and German dive-bombers pounded the city. Hitler insisted that there be no retreat from the symbolically and strategically important Volga port

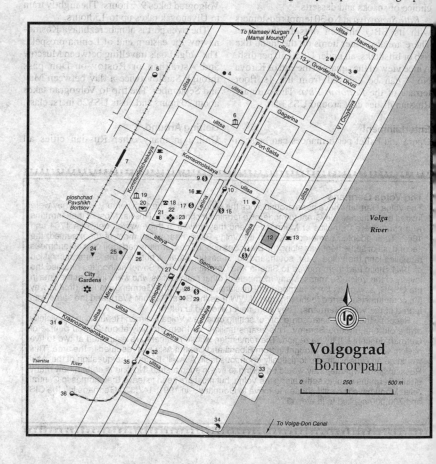

Volgograd
Волгоград

Soviet forces split the German armies in November, thwarted a German attempt to bring up reinforcements in December, and surrounded and defeated the Germans, who surrendered in February 1943.

In the battle an estimated one million Soviet soldiers and 200,000 Germans died and the city was completely destroyed. Only about 6000 out of 91,000 Germans taken as prisoners of war returned back to their homeland. You have to remind yourself that this heavily industrialised port, rail junction and regional capital has been rebuilt from scratch since 1945.

And its history has a repetitious quality. Just as the Nazis hoped to strangle Stalin's Caspian Sea oil here, the Red Army had earlier fought a bloody Civil War battle over

the city (then called Tsaritsyn) to keep Moscow's food supplies out of White soldiers hands. Stalin organised the city defences and in honour of him it was later renamed Stalingrad.

The 'hero-city' has been well rewarded. Despite the heavy scent of patriotism and a narrow range of attractions, the centre is clean, prosperous and friendly, filled on summer evenings with strolling families. A big portion of visitors are veterans, both Russian and German.

If you've made the effort to get here, don't miss the battlefield memorial at Mamaev Kurgan (Mamai Mound) with its famous statue of a sword-wielding Mother Russia, and the museum and panorama of the battle.

PLACES TO STAY

21	Hotel Intourist
	Гостиница Интурист
26	Hotel Volgograd
	Гостиница Волгоград

PLACES TO EAT

8	Kafe Pelmennaya
	Кафе Пельменная
13	Kafe Garni
	Кафе Гарни
16	Kafe Prietenie
	Кафе Приетение
24	Oktyabrskaya Hotel
	Гостиница Октябрьская
30	Restoran Dragon
	Ресторан Дракон

OTHER

1	ploshchad Lenina Tram Stop
	Остановка площадь Ленина
2	Pavlov House
	Павловский Домик
3	Battle of Stalingrad Panorama
	Панорама Сталинградская битва
4	Planetarium
	Планетарий

5	Central Bus Station
	Центральный автовокзал
6	Fine Arts Museum
	Музей изобразительных искусств
7	Train Station
	Железнодорожный вокзал
9	Exchange Office
	Обмен валюты
10	Komsomolskaya Tram Stop
	Комсомольская остановка
11	Central Market
	Колхозный рынок
12	Musical Comedy Theatre
	Театр музыкальной комедии
14	Beryozka
	Магазин Берёзка
15	Main Bank
	Банк
17	Bank
	Банк
18	International Telephone Office
	Международный телефон
19	Memorial History Museum
	Мемориально-исторический музей
20	Main Post & Telegraph Office
	Главпочтамт

22	Central Department Store
	ЦУМ
23	Puppet Theatre
	Театр кукол
25	Gorky Drama Theatre
	Драматический театр имени М. Горького
27	Airport Bus Stop
	Автобус на аэропорт
28	Aeroflot Office
	Аэрофлот
29	Exchange Office
	Обмен валюты
31	Circus
	Цирк
32	Artists' Union Exhibition Hall
	Выставочный зал Союза художников
33	River Station
	Речной вокзал
34	Small Beach
	Маленький пляж
35	Pionerskaya Tram Stop
	Пионерская остановка
36	Tram Terminal
	Конечная остановка трамвая

Orientation & Information

Volgograd stretches 75 km along the river but averages only four km in width. Its main lengthwise artery is prospekt Lenina. From the central ploshchad Pavshikh Bortsov (Fallen Warriors' Square) a promenade, alleya Geroev (Ave of Heroes), crosses prospekt Lenina to the river terminal.

The Hotel Intourist on the square has an Intourist office, bank and post office. Also on the square is the central post and telegraph office (topped by an immense sign proclaiming 'the ideas of V I Lenin will live and triumph'). Overseas calls can be made from your hotel or the office behind the Hotel Intourist on ulitsa Mira. The Volgograd telephone code is 8442.

The main bank is at prospekt Lenina 18, but there are many other exchange offices around. Maps are sold in the hotel lobby or at news kiosks.

Mamaev Kurgan (Mamai Mound)

This hill (known as Hill 102 during the battle) located three km north of the centre, the site of the battle's fiercest fighting for four months, is now a memorial to all who died at Stalingrad. Though your first reaction may be that it's pretty schmaltzy, the total effect is somehow very moving – and it's hard not to be impressed with that statue of Mother Russia.

From the road you climb past a series of sculptures: a bare-chested soldier, the city's ruined walls (complete with battle sounds) and a row of figures by a pond. On the wall by the pond is a quote from a Russian war correspondent:

A steel wind hit them in the face, but they all went forward, and again the enemy was gripped with superstitious terror: were these living people that were attacking, or the dead?

Above is the Pantheon, inscribed with 7200 names, picked at random, of soldiers who died here. The syrupy music is Schumann's *Traümerei*, the choice meant as a reminder that there's no grudge against ordinary Germans. Spare a thought for the guards,

tottering in the heat, who have to listen to it over and over. At the top of the hill is the 72-metre-high sword-wielding statue of Mother Russia.

To get there, go north on prospekt Lenina by taxi or on the high-speed tram or trolleybus Nos 1, 8 and 11, or on bus No 17 from Komsomolskaya ulitsa.

Panorama, Museum & Pavlov House

The Panorama is a 360° illustration of the view from atop Mamaev Kurgan. It's a gruesomely fascinating composite painting of various heroic deeds including the taking of the hill by the Russians. Individuals can join a Russian group at the door but a translator is helpful. If you can't find an amenable group of cruiseniks, Intourist will rent you a guide for US$7.50. To see it on your own is US$0.50. Photos are not allowed.

Afterwards, stop by the Museum of the Defence on the lower level around the back, which has dioramas, models of the ruined centre, weapons, uniforms etc. Everything is open 10 am to 5 pm, closed Monday and the last Friday of the month.

Next door are the ruins of a flour mill, and across the street is Pavlov House, named for an officer who, with a handful of men, defended it for 2 months. The complex is two blocks east of the Ploshchad Lenina high-speed tram stop.

Other Museums

The little **Fine Arts Museum** is a pleasant surprise, with its collection of Russian paintings, Palekh boxes, porcelain and carved ivory. It's through a small door on ulitsa Port-Saida off prospekt Lenina, and is open 10 am to 6 pm, closed Wednesday. The entry fee is US$0.20. The **Memorial History Museum** (Memorialno-istorichesky muzey) on the corner of ulitsa Kommunisticheskaya and ploshchad Pavshikh Bortsov has a collection of Russian aviation, cosmonautics, photos and pilots uniforms. It is open Wednesday to Monday from 10 am to 5.30 pm and the entry fee is US$0.10.

Cathedral of the Transfiguration, Kizhi Island, Petrozavodsk

A	B
C	D
E	

A: Window of Lenin Museum, Ufa
B: Russian town house, Perm
C: Flour mill ruins & tanks, Volgograd

D: Nikolskaya Church, Voronezh
E: Glacier & peaks from trail to
Mt Elbrus, Caucasus

Planetarium

The Planetarium, ulitsa Gagarina 14, has hourly shows from 10 am to 4 pm for US$0.50, and occasional US$0.25 tours to the telescope; you should also ask Intourist about the Battle of Stalingrad documentary which is shown here.

Parks

In alleya Geroev is a **monument** to 3500 Red Civil War partisans who are buried beneath ploshchad Pavshikh Bortsov. At the east end of the park, an ostentatious colonnaded stairway descends to the Volga.

The **City Gardens** (Gorodskie Sada) is a big leafy place west of ploshchad Pavshikh Bortsov, with a hotel where many government officials stay.

River Trips

You can go downstream on excursion boats past 30 km of Volgograd to the first lock of the Volga-Don Canal. Tickets are at window 1 at the river terminal's north end; boats leave from the south end. The one-hour hydrofoil trip is claustrophobic. The slower open-decked boat takes about three hours; ask for *medlennaya lodka* (slow boat) or *tri chasa* (three hours). It may also be possible to go 20 km upstream to the poetically named 'XXII Party Congress Hydroelectric Project'. Skip Intourist's all-day bus trip to the dam.

Places to Stay

The only hotel that accepts foreigners all the time is Hotel Intourist; some of the other hotels might accept a foreigner but it depends both on who is at the reception and your nationality.

Intourist runs the *Hotel Intourist* (☎ 36 45 53) on the corner of ulitsa Mira 14 and ploshchad and also uses the *Hotel Volgograd* (☎ 36 17 72) which is across ploshchad Pavshikh Bortsov. They are light-years apart in quality. The Intourist is a treat: it has rooms of faded elegance ranging from suites to bathless singles, laid-back staff, and no parking lot full of post-adolescent evening revellers. The rooms cost US$65/80, includ-

ing breakfast, and payment is possible by Visa, MasterCard or Amex. The Volgograd is just big and old. Their rooms cost US$40/57.50.

The spartan *Hotel Yuzhnaya* (☎ 44 09 38) is at ulitsa Raboche-Krestyanskaya 18 (the southern extension of prospekt Lenina). Close by on the bank of the Volga River is *Hotel Turist* (☎ 34 12 43) at ulitsa Naberezhnaya 62-y.

The top-end hotel is *Oktyabrskaya* (☎ 33 81 20) at Kommunisticheskaya 5a, on the northern tip of the City Gardens where it meets with ploshchad Pavshikh Bortsov, behind a burned-out building. Their rooms cost US$50/60.

Places to Eat

For the best meal in town, dress up and eat with the elite at the *Oktyabrskaya Hotel*, a luxurious, unmarked place for state guests and government officials in the north-west corner of the City Gardens. Enter from the park, through the lobby. There's also a well-supplied bufet, and prices are reasonable.

The restaurant at the *Hotel Intourist* has a small menu of diminutive lukewarm portions (US$2 to US$4.50) and one music-free room. Beer is plentiful. The cavernous *Volgograd Restaurant* (beside the hotel of the same name) has adequate food and crabby service.

The Chinese *Restoran Dragon* at prospekt Lenina 10 has reasonable dishes (a bit salty with Russian flavouring) – most are pork done in various styles for around US$4.50. They are open from noon to 4 pm and 6 pm to midnight. Beware of being a suspected westerner because you will be taken to the 'dollar room' and, as the Intourist lady told us, 'You will pay through the nose' for the same meal.

There are several mediocre cafés in the City Gardens. Other central cafés include *Prietenie* at prospekt Lenina 6 and *Garni* behind the Musical Comedy Theatre. You'll find coffee and ice cream along both sides of alleya Geroev.

The Central Market is on the corner of Komsomolskaya ulitsa and Sovietskaya ulitsa.

Entertainment

The circus is at Krasnoznamenskaya ulitsa 15, opposite the City Gardens, and the Puppet Theatre is at prospekt Lenina 15, at alleya Geroev.

Getting There & Away

Air Aeroflot (☎ 33 59 66) is at alleya Geroev 5. Daily 1½-hour flights from Moscow (Domodedovo) are US$103, and from Ulyanovsk it's US$93. At the airport, the old yellow building is for foreigners.

Train Three trains a day run to/from Moscow (Pavelets station), with more operating in summer. The trip takes over 20 hours. To Ulyanovsk it takes 23 hours and there are also trains to Rostov-on-Don. The railway station is two blocks west of ploshchad Pavshikh Bortsov on Kommunisticheskaya ulitsa; a second station one km north is for special tourist trains.

Boat Steamers go upstream to Ulyanovsk (three days, US$11.60 to US$209 in 3B to lyux A) and Moscow (seven days, US$20.80 to US$374.20); downstream via the canal and Don River to Rostov-on-Don (two days, US$7.60 to US$136.10); and almost to the Caspian Sea at Astrakhan (19 hours, US$6.90 to US$122.90). Between Yaroslavl and Volgograd the cost is US$17 to US$305. In July and August there are also two weekly boats to Perm on the Kama River, taking six days and costing up to US$100 in 1st class.

Getting Around

To/From the Airport From prospekt Lenina opposite Aeroflot, an Express bus does the 30-minute trip to the airport every 15 to 30 minutes for US$0.50; a city bus from there is US$0.15 but takes almost an hour. Inbound, ask for alleya Geroev. A taxi is about US$5 but they're scarce. There are two rail crossings on the way, each with possible delays of half an hour or more, so head out at least 2½ hours before departure time.

Public Transport The city centre is accessible on foot, and everywhere else by the high-speed tram *skorostnoy tramvay* (CT on Russian maps). The tram is a kind of mini-metro along or under prospekt Lenina and a bargain at US$0.05 a ride. Stations and many stops have automatic ticket machines. There are also buses and trolleybuses that cost the same as the tram but their tickets are available from booths marked in Cyrillic Абонементние талоны.

ASTRAKHAN
АСТРАХАНЬ
Population 500,000

This city of canals, bridges and a mix of nationalities is at the upper end of the Volga River delta, about 100 km from the Caspian Sea, making it both a river and a sea port. Astrakhan is pleasant with an impressive Kremlin and traditional wooden Russian houses, but in summer it gets very hot and dusty. It is full of history, which the white walls of the Kremlin have witnessed.

The Golden Horde took over the area in the 13th century and it was at the end of the same century that a city called Astrakhan was founded on the right bank of the Volga River by the Tatar khanate. However, this city was destroyed by Timur (Tamerlane) in 1395. After Kazan fell to Ivan the Terrible, the rest of the Volga River region was easily taken by Ivan's troops. The same fate befell Astrakhan, whose ruler Derbish-Ali deserted the city without defending it. Today's Kremlin was built on the left bank of the river in 1558 by Ivan's troops, and a city was founded on the new site. It was a major trading centre for Central Asia and Caucasus and has always prospered economically.

Orientation & Information

The centre of Astrakhan is on an island surrounded by the Volga River and the canals imeni 1 Maya and the Kutum. The Kremlin holds a central position, with the pedestrian zone running along Sovietskaya ulitsa. The major thoroughfare of ulitsa Pobedy cuts through the eastern part of the island and goes north to the railway station. Most of the traffic and public transport diverts from ulitsa Pobedy on the central island to ulitsa

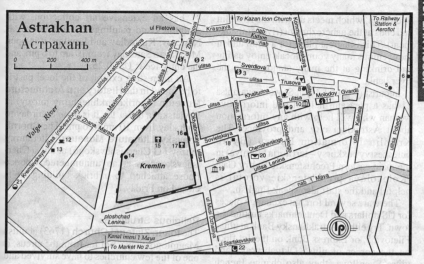

Astrakhan
Астрахань

PLACES TO STAY	
13	Hotel Lotos Гостиница Лотос
18	Novomoskovskaya Hotel Гостиница Ново-Московская
PLACES TO EAT	
4	Restoran Modern Ресторан Модернь
12	Kafe Volzhanka Кафе Волжанка
OTHER	
1	Astrakhansky Bank Астраханский Банк
2	Currency Exchange Counter Обмен валюты
3	Express Bank Експресс Банк
5	Kustodiev Art Gallery Картинная галерия им. Б. М. Кустодиева
6	Market No 1 Рынок 1
7	Regional Philharmonic Orchestra Областная филармония

8	Shatrovaya Tower Шатровая башня
9	October Cinema Кино Октябрь
10	History and Architecture Museum Историко-архитектурный музей
11	Intourist Интурист
14	Red Tower Красные ворота
15	Trinity Cathedral Троицкий собор
16	Prechistenskie Belfry Gate Колокольня Пречистенские ворота
17	Assumption Cathedral Успенский собор
19	Chernishevsky Literature Museum Литературный музей И. Г. Чернышевского
20	Main Post Office Почтамт
21	River Port Речной вокзал
22	Mosque Мусулман мечет Но 1

Sverdlova, which meets up with the Kremlin and ends at the naberezhnaya (river embankment). This is a great place for a stroll and in the evenings many young locals enjoy eating and drinking at the many stands along the river bank.

Intourist (☎ 24 63 44) at Sovietskaya ulitsa 21 has a pleasant, helpful and informative woman who will help with any information about Astrakhan city and province. The Kremlin Information Bureau (Byuro puteshestvy i exkursy – territoria kremlya) in the main eastern Prechistenskie Belfry Gate (Kolokolnya prechistenskie vorota) is helpful and the staff also speak English.

There are several foreign exchange places for US dollars and Deutschmarks around the town. Try either Astrakhansky Bank at ulitsa Filetova 5, or Express Bank on the 1st floor on the corner of ulitsa Oktyabrskaya and ulitsa Sverdlova (they also change French francs). The main post and telegraph office is on the corner of ulitsa Kirova (No 27/10) and ulitsa Chernishevskogo. The Astrakhan telephone code is 85100.

City maps are available either from the magazine stand on the 1st floor of the main railway station or Hotel Lotos.

The Kremlin

The large 16th-century fortress on top of Zayachy Hill was the realisation of the architect Dorofey Myakishiev's dream. It can be entered through the main eastern Prechistenskie Belfry Gate (1908-12) which looks like a church tower. The **Assumption Cathedral** (Uspensky sobor, 1698-1710) is behind the gate and is being restored. In the central part of the Kremlin is the yet to be restored **Trinity Cathedral** (Troitsky sobor, 18th century). At the western end, in the **Red Tower** (Krasnye vorota, 16th century), is the Kremlin's only exhibition of Astrakhan historical photos. The Red Tower is open Tuesday to Sunday from 11 am to 4 pm, and the entry fee is US$0.15.

Museums

The **Kustodiev Art Gallery** (Kartinnaya galeria B M Kustodieva) at ulitsa Sverdlova 81 has an extensive art collection, with sculptures and paintings by such artists as Nesterov, Kustodiev and Levitan. It is open Monday to Saturday from 10 am to 6 pm, and the entry fee is US$0.25.

An interesting exhibit of the local past is to be found in the **History and Architecture Museum** (Istoriko-arkhitekturny muzey) at Sovietskaya ulitsa 15. It is open Saturday to Thursday from 10 am to 6 pm. The **Chernishevsky Literature Museum** (Literaturny muzey I G Chernishevskogo) at ulitsa Cherishevskogo is at an unnumbered wooden house attached to a brick building. It is closed on Friday.

Religious Structures

The **Ioann Zlatoust Church** (1763) at ulitsa Magnitogorskaya, not far from the circus, is one of the few churches to have survived and has been fully restored, including the frescoes. One that was almost ruined is the **Kazan Icon Church** (Khram Kazansky ikonu) at ulitsa Chekhova 10a, which is being restored – its frescoes are barely visible on the walls. The 16th-century Spaso-preobrazhenskogo Monastery was not so lucky as only the **Shatrovaya Tower** on the corner of ulitsa Trusova and Kommunisti-cheskaya ulitsa remains.

There is also a **mosque** (Musulman mechet No 1) at ulitsa Spartakovskaya, with a plain interior but a classical exterior.

October Cinema

The October cinema (Oktyabr kino) at ulitsa Volodarskogo 13 has many tropical plants inside the foyer and is a sort of botanical indoor centre. One of its features is the 100-year-old date palm.

Organised Tours

Intourist can organise tours of the Volga delta to see the flora and fauna of the biosphere reserve. They also have city of Astrakhan tours. In August, there are also special 'Lotus' tours on boats from the harbour to see the red lotuses blooming.

Places to Stay
At the time of writing only Hotel Korvet and Hotel Lotos would accept foreigners, but we later heard that *Novomoskovskaya* (☎ 24 63 89) at ulitsa Sovietskaya 4 let them stay for US$20 per person.

The fairly modern and otherwise clean rooms at the *Hotel Lotos* (☎ 22 95 00), at Kremlevskaya ulitsa (labelled on some maps as 'naberezhnaya') 4, just north-east of the river port, also have dirty floors. They cost from US$26/32, including TV, shower, toilet and a good view of the Volga River. There is a rather uninspiring restaurant and a café at ground level.

The best place to stay is the new and privately established *Hotel Korvet* (☎ 34 03 78) at ulitsa Boevaya 50A. It is a short distance off the street – walk through the small park between No 50 and No 52. Reception is on the 1st floor of the turn-of-the-century building. To get there from the railway station, take tram or trolleybus No 1, 2 or 4, or bus No 5 or 18, to the stop 'Klub TRZ'. The spacious, clean, new rooms with TV, refrigerator, bath and toilet cost only US$50/60.

Places to Eat
There are two main markets. The first is on the corner of ulitsa Pobedy and Krasnaya naberezhnaya 108 and the second is at ploshchad Svobody. There is another fruit and vegetable street market on ulitsa Voevaya, opposite the Hotel Korvet. For a few extra roubles all drink vendors will sell you a 'cold' soft drink or a beer.

Next to the Hotel Lotos is *Kafe Volzhanka*, which is a fine spot for a drink and cheap local food. The ground-floor café at the *Hotel Lotos* has good lentil and vegetable soup plus grilled chicken for around US$3. Late at night the hotel's casino bar (entry US$0.50) serves a grilled chicken for US$5 and also other snacks. The hotel's *Restoran Lotos* has the standard hotel food and entertainment.

A reasonable place to eat is *Restoran Modern* on the corner of ulitsa Trusova (No 35) and Kommunisticheskaya ulitsa. It has a simple, small menu including sturgeon – dishes cost between US$1.30 and US$2.30.

The best place to eat is *Restoran Korvet* in the hotel of the same name. They have a good but small selection of dishes costing only US$1.50 to US$2. Recommended by a friend is *Restoran Sekret*, in a boat on the Volga River at Komsomolskaya naberezhnaya, opposite the northern tip of Gorodskoy Island. It is an expensive place referred to as a 'dollar restaurant', as prices are in US dollars.

Entertainment
The Regional Philharmonic (Oblastnoya filarmonia) is at ulitsa Molodoy Gvardii 4. The circus (Tsirk) is at ulitsa Pobedy, near the corner with Ryleeva.

Getting There & Away
There are two daily flights to/from Moscow costing US$137 which take two hours and twenty minutes. There are three flights a week to Mineralnye Vody, as well as flights to other destinations like St Petersburg, Rostov-on-Don and Aktau (formerly Shevchenko) in Kazakhstan. The Aeroflot office (☎ 54 74 9) is at ulitsa Pobedy 54.

The railway station is at Privokzalnaya ulitsa, and advance tickets are also available from the Railway Ticket Office at ulitsa Kommunisticheskaya 52. There are daily trains to/from Moscow (31 hours or more), Volgograd (10 hours) and Makhachkala (15 hours). The line to Makhachkala passes through eastern Chechnya.

There are no regular passenger boats to the other Caspian Sea ports. It is possible to find a freighter that takes passengers, but *only* if the passengers have the correct visa for the country of destination. Astrakhan is the end point of cruises on the Volga and the river port is at (naberezhnaya) ulitsa Zhelyabova 1. It takes about 10½ days to get here from Moscow at a cost of US$20 in 3B and US$356 in lyux A.

EUROPEAN RUSSIA

The Sturgeon's Last Stand?

The delta of the lower Volga River, where the river divides into about 800 branches, comprises the Astrakhan State Biosphere Reserve. It is home to an immense treasure of flora and fauna. Among the reeds are found beavers, raccoons, wild boars, musk rats, foxes, otters and desmans, not to mention many different species of fish including the famous sturgeon. Unfortunately, the sturgeon now only inhabit the waters south of Volgograd, as few seem to be capable of getting past the many dams along the Volga or surviving in the reservoirs. The dams along the Volga have created an environmental disaster as well as an industrial one. Due to the flatness of the land the water does not flow fast enough to power the turbines, which consequently do not produce as much electricity as was originally envisaged. In addition, the bottoms of the reservoirs store much of the pollution dumped into the Volga. As the water carrying the contaminants flows towards the dam and is stored in the reservoir, the pollution settles to the bottom. There it stays because there is never a sufficiently strong current to flush it out. In this environment it is impossible for the sturgeon and other fish to survive. Restricted to a smaller area, and threatened by pollution and overfishing, the sturgeon is in danger of being destroyed. This in turn puts the caviar industry at risk.

Caviar, the salty roe, or raw eggs, of the sturgeon, is a major commodity for local consumption and export. There are five basic types of caviar, named according to the variety of sturgeon each comes from: the smallest, greenish-black type is from the 'sevruga'; the larger, greyish, grey-green or brown type is 'osetrova'; the largest, black or grey type, 'beluga'; the rarest caviar is the golden roe of the 'sterlet'; and the cheapest is the 'payusnaya', which is made from imperfect or lower grades of eggs. Russia produces about 150 to 200 tonnes of caviar a year, of which about 20% is exported; the other major exporter is Iran, which produces 240 tonnes, of which 200 tonnes are exported. In 1993 the countries bordering the Caspian Sea (Russia, Kazakhstan, Turkmenistan, Iran and Azerbaijan) formed the Organisation of Caviar Exporting Countries (OCEC) to coordinate the world marketing of caviar.

All this may be too late for the Russian caviar industry and the sturgeon, to judge by the ever-diminishing annual catch. In 1978, what was then the USSR exported 2000 tonnes of caviar; in 1993 Russia produced a total of only 180 tonnes. The rapid decline in the last few years has been blamed on poaching, which has greatly increased with the break-up of the USSR. There is now no authority to enforce the quota laws and very little possibility of any kind of punishment for offenders. The problem is made worse by the fact that sturgeon take between 12 and 20 years to reach maturity before they return up the Volga to spawn. At present they are being poached before this cycle is completed, and ever fewer fish are making the journey back up the river to breed. Another consequence of the poaching of young sturgeon is an increase in inferior caviar from immature fish. At the time of writing, it was feared that poaching had the potential to eliminate the caviar industry within five years. ■

Getting Around

Bus No 5 and trolleybus No 3 go to/from the airport, railway station and ploshchad Lenina, and can be found at any bus stop along ulitsa Pobedy, ulitsa Sverdlova or ulitsa Zhelyabova. There is also an airport bus departing from the Aeroflot office to connect with all the flights.

Bus, trolleybus and tram tickets cost US$0.05 and are available from conductors on the public transport. Bus Nos 2, 2B and 5, as well as trolleybus Nos 1, 2, 3 and 4 run to/from the railway station and ploshchad Lenina.

ROSTOV-ON-DON
РОСТОВ-НА-ДОНУ
Population: 1 million

The downstream terminus for Volga-Don cruises, Rostov-on-Don (Rostov-na-Donu) is the industrial centre of a farming region known for its wine, among other things. Though pleasant and relatively prosperous, it's not very exciting, but it's a base for some excursions of historical interest, including two old Don Cossack capitals, the remains of a Genoese trading centre and a 3rd-century BC Greek colony.

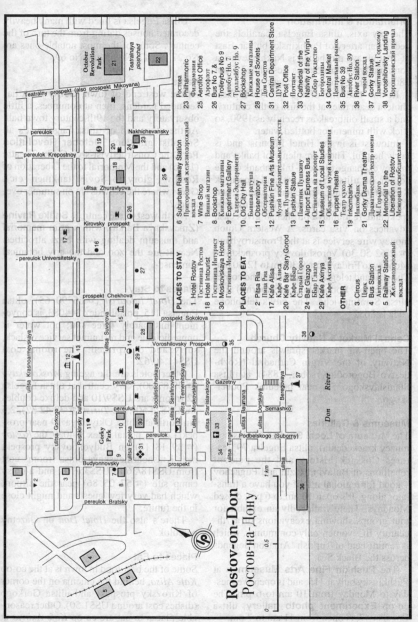

Rostov-on-Don
Ростов-на-Дону

PLACES TO STAY

1 Hotel Rostov
Гостиница Ростов
18 Hotel Intourist
Гостиница Интурист
30 Moskovskaya Hotel
Гостиница Московская

PLACES TO EAT

2 Pitsa Ria
Пицца Риа
17 Kafe Alisa
Кафе Алиса
20 Kafe Bar Stary Gorod
Кафе Бар Старый Город
24 Bar Glazgo
Бар Глазго
29 Kafe Axinya
Кафе Аксинья

OTHER

3 Circus
Цирк
4 Bus Station
Автовокзал
5 Railway Station
Железнодорожный вокзал
6 Suburban Railway Station
Пригородный железнодорожный вокзал
7 Wine Shop
Винный магазин
8 Bookshop
Книжные магазины
9 Experiment Gallery
Галерея Эксперимент
10 Old City Hall
Бывшая ратуша
11 Observatory
Обсерватория
12 Pushkin Fine Arts Museum
Музей изобразительных искусств им. Пушкина
13 Pushkin Statue
Памятник Пушкину
14 Airport Express Bus
Остановка на аэропорт
15 Museum of Local Studies
Областной музей краеведения
16 Puppet Theatre
Театр кукол
19 Inkombank
Инкомбанк
21 Gorky Drama Theatre
Драматический театр имени М. Горького
22 Memorial to the Liberation of Rostov
Мемориал освободителям
23 Philharmonic
Филармония
25 Aeroflot Office
Аэрофлот
26 Bus No 7 &
Trolleybus No 9
Автобус No. 7,
Троллейбус No. 9
27 Bookshop
Книжные магазины
28 House of Soviets
Дом Советов
31 Central Department Store
ЦУМ
32 Post Office
Почтамт
33 Nativity of the Virgin
Собор Рождество Богородицы
34 Central Market
Центральный рынок
35 Bus No 39
Автобус No. 39
36 River Station
Речной вокзал
37 Gorky Statue
Памятник М. Горькому
38 Voroshilovsky Landing
Ворошиловский причал

Orientation & Information

The city axis, ulitsa Engelsa, parallels the pedestrian artery of Pushkinsky bulvar. East of Teatralnaya ploshchad is Nakhichevan, a community of Armenians descended from 18th-century Crimean deportees.

Rostov had one of the world's highest cholera death rates at the turn of the century, and a small outbreak as recently as 1990, so stick with mineral or bottled water.

Intourist is in the Hotel Intourist and is fairly helpful. There are plenty of banks and money exchange offices – Inkombank on the corner of ulitsa Suvorova and pereulok Krepostnoy changes travellers' cheques, and Kredobank on the corner of Teatralny prospekt and Teatralnaya ploshchad gives cash advances on Visa cards. A Western Union money wire service is at the Promstroybank (☎ 2 62 50 36) Voroshilovsky prospekt 43, Monday to Friday from 9.30 am to 12.30 pm. The post and telegraph office is on the corner of pereulok Podbelskogo (Suborny) and ulitsa Serafinovicha. The city's telephone code is 8632.

Central Market & Nativity Church

The open-air market sprawls around the Nativity of the Virgin Cathedral (Rozhdestvo Bogoroditsy sobor, 1884), at ulitsa Stanislavskogo 58, near pereulok Podbelskogo.

Museums & Galleries

The **Museum of Local Studies** (Oblastnoy muzey kraevedenia), ulitsa Engelsa 79, features Cossack history and the peasant rebellions of Bulavin, Razin and Pugachov – good for regional info if you have a translator along. It's open 10 am to 6 pm, closed Mondays. There's allegedly an exhibit for tour groups showing excavations of a 7th-century BC women-only community, which is reminiscent of Turkish 'Amazon' legends across the Black Sea.

The **Pushkin Fine Arts Museum** is at Pushkinsky bulvar 115, and is open Wednesday to Monday from 10 am to 6 pm. The co-op **Experiment photo gallery**, ulitsa Engelsa 47, is open from 11 am to 7 pm.

Ulitsa Engelsa is lined with many heavily decorated houses dating from the turn of the century. Some of the most notable ones are No 27, No 47, No 55 and No 69.

Parks

At the west end of town, **Gorky Park** has secluded gardens, men at dominoes, a little observatory and the 19th-century town hall. At the other end of ulitsa Engelsa it's all Socialist grandeur: **October Revolution Park**, the Constructivist-style Gorky Theatre (1936) and the Memorial to the Liberation of Rostov ('glory to Soviet tankmen' etc). Guess where the crowds are on summer evenings?

North-west of the centre is **Snake Ravine** (Zmevskaya Balka), with a grim memorial and museum dealing with Nazi atrocities. Near it are the zoo and the city botanical gardens.

Places to Stay

The *Hotel Intourist* (☎ 65 90 65), ulitsa Engelsa 115, postal index 344083, is convenient but barely three star; hot water is unpredictable and restaurant service is slack, surly and overpriced. The rooms cost US$41.40/62.

Other hotels are the ageing *Moskovskaya* (☎ 38 87 00), very central at ulitsa Engelsa 62 (rooms are US$9/10 and deluxe doubles are US$24.50); the *Turist* (☎ 38 42 32), 2.5 km north at ulitsa Oktyabrya 19 near prospekt Lenina, postal index 344039; the *Rostov* (☎ 39 18 18) on Budyonnovsky prospekt near Krasnoarmeyskaya ulitsa (rooms cost from US$18/36 to US$35/70); and a noisy camp site (☎ 57 05 86) near the airport, which had very few guests and might close in the future.

There's also the *Hotel Don* on Gazetny pereulok.

Places to Eat

Some of the best food in town is at the co-op *Kafe Alisa*, behind the cinema on the corner of Kirovsky prospekt and ulitsa Gorkogo (dishes cost around US$1.50). Other reasonable places to eat are co-op *Kafe Axinya* at ulitsa Engelsa 86 and co-op *Pitsa Ria* on Krasnoarmeyskaya ulitsa west of Budyonnovsky.

In the park beside the Hotel Intourist is the cheap *Kafe Raduga*. The jolly *Bar Glazgo* east of the hotel and across the street has good ice cream (with fresh berries in summer) and Turkish coffee. The interesting old-world *Kafe bar Stary Gorod* is under street level on pereulok Krepostnoy, just east of the Hotel Intourist. The tasty dishes cost between US$1.50 and US$3.50, but there's a sign at the entrance explaining that a fee of US$2.50 is charged for sitting at the bar and US$7.50 for sitting at a table; strangely, we were not charged this fee.

Across the Don at Petrovsky Prichal (prichal means landing), in a replica of one of Peter the Great's frigates, is a *restaurant* favoured by Intourist but which has an uncertain future. Join a group or take the boat from the Voroshilovsky landing and walk two km up the beach.

You can buy regional wine and champagne at the state wine shop on Budyonnovsky prospekt next to Dom Knigi.

Getting There & Away

Air Daily flights to Moscow (Vnukovo) are US$107. The Aeroflot office (☎ 65 71 60) is at ulitsa Socialisticheskaya 144-146. Cheap flights to/from Germany may be available through Luftbrücke (☎ 58 50 33). In Germany, Luftbrücke (☎ (02132) 93160; fax 4485) is at Moerserstrasse 100A, 40667 Meerbusch or at Düsseldorf airport (☎ (0211) 421 6831/33/34; fax (0211) 421 6832).

Train At the west end of ulitsa Engelsa are suburban and long-distance stations. A fast train from Moscow's Kazan station takes over 20 hours. Some trains from Moscow go via Kharkiv (Kharkov) in Ukraine: check the Ukraine visa situation if you're thinking of taking one of these. Trains also run to Sochi, Krasnodar, Volgograd and elsewhere.

Boat The river station is at the south-eastern end of Budyonnovsky prospekt. Berths 5 and 6 are for long-distance steamships. Berths 7 to 12 are for hydrofoil ferries, including those heading upstream to Starocherkassk and downstream to Azov and Taganrog. Ticket windows are upstairs, one for upstream (vverkh), one for downstream (vnizu).

The boats to/from Moscow go up the canal and the Volga, stopping at many towns and costing between US$24 in 3B and US$428 in lyux A – a one-way trip takes 11 days. To/from Yaroslavl the cost is US$20 and US$366.

Getting Around

The best airport transport is a taxi, which will cost about US$5 from the Hotel Intourist. At the railway station the taxi mafia ask US$2.50 but the locals pay about US$1. Cheap, aggravating alternatives are the yellow No 62 bus (misnamed Express), costing US$0.05 from ulitsa Engelsa near Voroshilovsky prospekt, and bus No 7 and trolleybus No 9 eastbound from in front of the Hotel Intourist. Allow 45 minutes on any bus during peak hours.

Up and down ulitsa Engelsa, use bus No 7, 12 or 13, trolleybus No 1, 9 or 15, or take a taxi for US$0.05.

Boats cross the river for US$0.05 from Voroshilovsky landing by the bridge. Do-it-yourself river excursions are easy. River station berth 1 has 1½-hour round-trips hourly. There are also boats up the river to Tangarog (US$1.60) or downriver to Azov (US$2).

AROUND ROSTOV-ON-DON
ОКОЛО РОСТОВА-НА-ДОНУ

The following are available as Intourist excursions, though Starocherkassk is easy on your own.

Starocherkassk
Старочеркасск

Founded in 1593, the stanitsa of Old Cherkassk was the Don Cossack capital for two centuries. Once a fortified town of 20,000, it's now a village of vegetable farmers with a little main street restored to its turn-of-the-century appearance, including sites connected with the uprisings of Razin and Bulavin. There are remains of a fortress three km down the River Don, called Cherkassk Krepost.

Peter the Great, visiting here, allegedly came across a drunken Cossack sitting on a barrel, wearing only a rifle. This image of a soldier who'd sooner lose his clothes than his gun so impressed the tsar that he had it drawn up as the Don Cossack army seal. They hated it, but still used it on their letters to St Petersburg.

Near the west end of the main street is Bulavin's fortified house (1709) where he was eventually killed. East from the plain SS Peter & Paul Church (1751) and the old market square are more sturdy Cossack forthouses.

In a brick building beyond these is a good **museum** illustrating 16th to 20th-century Cossack life and the rebellions. It is open from 9 am to 5 pm daily except Tuesday and Friday, and costs US$0.15. The only problem is that there are three museum buildings and each one has different closing days – it is only on Monday and Sunday that all the buildings are open. Next door is the **Church of Our Lady of the Don** (1761), which was the private church of a Cossack ataman, and behind it is his Classical 'palace'.

At the east end is the square where in 1670 Razin rallied his followers and where he was later clapped in chains. In the **Resurrection Cathedral** (Voskresensky sobor, 1719) the beautiful iconostasis and baroque chandelier are a reminder that some Cossacks did pretty well for themselves. The entry fee costs US$0.20 and tickets are available from the Museum.

On the last Sunday of each month in summer a 'Cossack fair' features music, dancing, crafts and horseback riding.

Getting There & Away Starocherkassk is 30 km up the Don from Rostov. The most pleasant way is by river; hydrofoils go seven times a day for US$0.60, taking about 40 minutes. From the pier, head right to the cannon at the fort's south-west corner, then left and right and you're in the main street. Intourist runs a day excursion from Rostov-on-Don by car or coach in summer. It costs US$70 for up to seven individuals.

Novocherkassk
Новочеркасск

The Don Cossacks moved their capital to New Cherkassk in 1805. It's now a town of 200,000, 40 km north-east of Rostov. This is supposedly the setting for Nobel laureate Mikhail Sholokhov's *And Quiet Flows the Don*. Still a hero here is Ataman Matvey Platov, a Cossack general who was part of the force that chased Napoleon back to Paris; two arches commemorate his return.

In 1962, during the Khrushchev years, Soviet troops killed at least 22 striking workers here in a Stalin-like security operation that was covered up until 1989.

The **History of the Don Cossacks Museum**, at Sovietskaya ulitsa 38, has a big collection of memorabilia including a sword presented to Platov in England. It's open Tuesday to Sunday from 10 am to 5 pm.

Also worth a look is the beautiful **Ascension Cathedral** (Voznesensky sobor, 1905), a working church. The cathedral is at ploshchad Yermaka. To get here, take bus No 1 from the train or bus station.

Intourist's half-day Novocherkassk excursion from Rostov-on-Don costs US$50 for up to three individuals. From Rostov-on-Don, buses take 40 minutes and trains take 75 minutes.

Tanaïs & Azov
Танаис и Азов

From at least the 3rd century BC until the 4th century AD, the Greek colony of Tanaïs flourished on the Sea of Azov at the mouth of the Don. Genoese merchants in the 13th century established a trading settlement and Silk Road entrepôt nearby, calling it Tana. Later the Turks built a fortress to keep the Russians out of the Black Sea. The Cossacks took it for several years (its gate-latch and hinges are still in Starocherkassk), and Peter the Great captured it in 1696.

The industrial city of Azov has two attractions. **Azov Fort** (Azovskaya Krepost) is open to the public, while there is also an interesting **museum** containing exhibits on Cossack life and history. The museum is at ulitsa Moskovskaya 38/40, on the corner of Petrovsky prospekt, and is open Tuesday to Sunday from 10 am to 5 pm. Intourist runs half-day coach tours from Rostov-on-Don for US$55. Hydrofoils travel the 45 km down to Azov city from Rostov every 30 to 60 minutes for US$0.70.

Near Nedvigovka village on the road from Rostov-on-Don to Taganrog are excavations of the original Tanaïs and a little **museum**. Displays in the museum include statues of Greek gods, bronze oil lamps and amphorae. The museum is open mid-April to mid-November from 9 am to 1 pm and 2 to 5 pm, but closes on Monday at 1 pm. Intourist normally goes there.

Taganrog
Таганрог

Peter the Great originally meant this Azov sea port, 75 km west of Rostov, to be his big naval base. It's the birthplace of writer Anton Chekhov and Intourist offers an all-day tour to Trinity Fort and various Chekhov spots – it's not really worth it even at the group price of US$65.

The sights, however, include a **Literary Museum** at ulitsa Dktyabrskaya 9, in the school where Chekhov studied. This school has been reconstructed and contains various manuscripts. The museum is open Tuesday to Sunday from 10 am to 6 pm.

Both **Domik Chekhova** at ulitsa Chekhova 69 and **Lavka Chekhovykh** at ulitsa Sverlova (the shop where the Chekhovs lived from 1869 to 1874) have been reconstructed and are interesting period museums. Both museums are open Tuesday to Sunday, the former from 9 am to 5 pm and the latter from 10 am to 6 pm.

Buses go to Taganrog hourly throughout the day from the bus station in Rostov-on-Don for US$0.20. Hydrofoils make the trip from Rostov-on-Don six times a day for US$1.60.

Caucasus
Кавказ

The dramatic Caucasus mountain range striding from the Black Sea to the Caspian Sea forms Russia's southern border. This chapter covers the northern (Russian) side of the range, the foothills and steppe to the north, and the Russian coastal strip along the Black Sea at the west end of the Caucasus. The steeper southern side of the Caucasus lies in the now independent states of Georgia and Azerbaijan. Though parts of the Caucasus region have been tragically beset by war and ethnic conflict, its untroubled areas can make for some of the most exciting travel in Russia. It's not only different from everything to the north, but is also immensely varied within itself. Below the mountains' jagged 3000, 4000 and 5000-metre peaks lie valleys which are home to dozens of peoples speaking dozens of languages, practising Christianity or Islam, with a varied range of cultures.

The Caucasus is the most spectacular part of European Russia. Even if you're no walker or mountaineer, try to get up among the real hills by visiting Dombay, or the Baxan Valley beneath 5642-metre Mt Elbrus, which is Europe's highest peak if you accept the traditional view that the main Caucasus watershed – just south of Elbrus – is the border between Europe and Asia. The main northern approach to the Caucasus is from Rostov-on-Don across the slowly rising Kuban Steppe and through the mineral water spa area (Kavkazskie Mineralnye Vody) in the foothills of the central Caucasus. Where the Caucasus meets the Black Sea is Russia's holiday coast, the main resort being Sochi. At the east end of the Caucasus lies Dagestan, a complicated ethnic jigsaw with an Asiatic atmosphere, extending from the mountains to the Caspian Sea.

The violent upheavals that parts of the region have been going through can make

travel unsafe or impossible in places. Keep tabs on any danger areas as you make your plans. See Dangers & Annoyances in the European Russia Facts for the Visitor chapter. Recent travellers, if you can track any down, are amongst the best source of advice on how safe it is to visit a place.

At the time of writing travel was not possible to Chechnya, with parts of Ingushetia and Dagestan also in doubt. There was also reportedly the danger of hold-ups while travelling in the countryside in Dagestan, North Ossetia and Ingushetia.

HISTORY
The northern Caucasus has been at the crossroads of Mediterranean, Central Asian, Middle Eastern and Eastern European cultures since the Bronze Age. The result is an extraordinary mix of races with three main linguistic groups: Caucasian, Indo-European and Turkic. There are also several religions represented in the region, Islam and Orthodox Christianity having the greatest numbers of adherents. The Caucasus has, of course, suffered from many invasions and occupations through the course of history. Since long before Christ, it has been squeezed between rival empires – among them the Roman, Persian, Byzantine, Arab, Ottoman and Russian. During the most recent occupa-

tion, in the 19th century, it took the Russians several decades to subjugate the tribes of the region. This led to the 20th-century Soviet policy, which was to divide and conquer in order to rule. The effects of this policy on the region's nationalities were profound, and culminated in the separatist wars of the early 1990s.

Early Days

Little is known of the prehistory of the area but there have been several prehistoric and Stone-Age finds. Some of the earliest traces of human habitation are from the time of the Neolithic revolution, when hunting and gathering was being replaced with farming and the first communities were being established. These finds come from Dagestan's dry valleys and are dated to the same era as other early developments of agriculture in the Middle East and Japan, making the northern part of the Caucasus one of the cradles of civilisation.

Apart from archaeological finds, not much else is known of the early northern Caucasian people. It is known that they used copper and iron tools around 1000 BC, during the time of the so-called Koban

culture. The region was connected by well-established routes to the Greek civilisation, with which it had significant trading ties; this activity peaked around the 7th century BC.

Early Invasions

The era of the great migrations brought many different peoples to the Caucasus. The Scythians arrived from the east along the northern Black Sea coast in the 8th century BC, followed by the Sarmatians, also from the east, in about the 3rd century BC. In the first millennium AD, groups such as the Kipchaks (ancestors of the present-day Balkar), the Huns, the Pechenegs and the Khazars all left their mark, some settling and mixing with the existing inhabitants.

Alans

The Alans, ancestors of the modern Ossetians, are thought to have been originally a fusion of Sarmatians, pushed into the mountains by the Huns, with local tribes. The Alan state came to prominence during the 10th century AD, and at its peak ruled most of the northern Caucasus, with established trade routes to all the major empires surrounding it. The Alans were also Christians, probably

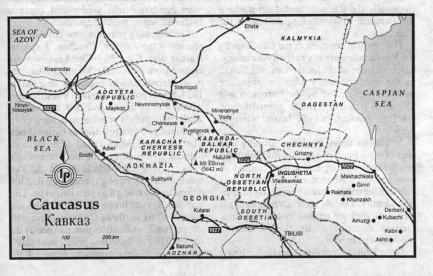

having been introduced to the religion by the Georgians.

During the 11th century, such Turkic tribes as the Kipchak, Polovtsy and Nogai constantly raided the region, and some members of these tribes ended up settling in parts of the northern Caucasus. The next major invasion was that of the Mongol Tatars in the early 13th century, which destroyed the Alan state. But a much more brutal invasion and occupation, which destroyed the last remains of the Alan state, came with Timur (Tamerlane), who also brought a new Asian terror to much of the Middle East. Many of the surviving Alans left the region or went higher up into the mountains.

Arrival of the Russians

In the foothills of the northern Caucasus the Adygey and Abaza replaced the Tatars.

Russian peasants and adventurers who escaped from the oppressive serf system began to settle in the lower Terek River region. It was not until the late 1550s that Russian military power reached the area as a result of a marriage between Tsar Ivan the Terrible and Maria Temrukovna, daughter of the Kabarda prince. Russian economic and military influence grew in the region, and eventually the Russians ended up pushing the Ottoman (Turkish) Empire out of the Caucasus.

The physical conquest of the Caucasus by the Russians began early in the 19th century. The resistance of the local tribes was fierce, as the predominantly Muslim populace resented being ruled by the European and Christian Russians. Bitter guerrilla-type warfare ensued, which lasted several decades.

At various times in history, usually at a time of crisis (such as a foreign invasion), the northern Caucasian tribes have united to form a military alliance, and it is sometimes said that the tribes share a *gorsky* (mountaineer) identity. Despite their diverse national identities, they are unified by cultural similarities engendered by their common mountainous habitat.

In the 19th century it was the leader Imam Shamil who united the Dagestanis and Chechens of the north-eastern Caucasus and fought the Russians for 30 years. Shamil and his followers were defeated in 1859 when Russian army units surrounded them in Gunib, Dagestan. Surrender came after a 15-day siege. As a result of this defeat, many of the tribes with strong Muslim beliefs ended up fleeing to Ottoman territory. The Ossetians, however, did not; they were Christians and never joined the struggle against the Russians. It is suspected that they did not want to be part of a state governed by Koranic law, which was the aim of Shamil's proposed northern Caucasian state.

Russian Rule

At the time of the Russian Revolution in 1917, many of the northern Caucasian tribes united to form the Mountain Republic. They did not, however, manage to keep their independence for long. Once the Soviet forces had consolidated power over Russia, they also conquered most other parts of the former Tsarist Imperial Empire. The Mountain Republic was taken back in 1921 and in the same year it was given the status of an Autonomous Republic within the Soviet Union. The various nationalities of Dagestan were combined into a new and separate Dagestan Autonomous Republic.

The following year four new autonomous regions – the Adygey, Chechen, Kabarda-Balkar and Karachay-Cherkess – were created from parts of the Mountain Autonomous Republic, which ceased to exist in 1924. Soviet policy was quite clear in its aim, which was to divide and rule by creating small autonomous regions that sometimes combined two totally different nationalities. The Soviet regime also used other methods to break up the unity of the mountain people – like giving each ethnic group its own national identity through promoting folk traditions and devising a written language. This way the Soviets broke up the troublesome groups of the northern Caucasus, and with stepped-up Russification aimed to pacify the region. The results of this policy are today's sometimes violent conflicts between the

Ossetians and the Ingush, the Chechens and the Russians, among others.

Deportations

In 1944, on Stalin's orders, most of the Balkar, Chechen, Ingush and Karachay people were deported to Central Asia and Siberia. The real reason was never given but the official reason – suspected collaboration with the German forces – was unfounded: some of those groups never even came into contact with the occupying forces during WW II. The people lost their property, and land was absorbed into surrounding republics. This move created even greater bitterness and hatred towards the Russians, but it also fuelled resentment and hatred between those nationalities that stayed and those who were deported. This was because the groups that stayed ended up taking the property and land of the deported groups, to whom it was never returned and who were never compensated for their loss.

It was only after Stalin's death that Khrushchev, in 1956, allowed the return of the above-mentioned groups to their former lands. During the rest of the Soviet period there seemed to be no problems between the various nationalities, mainly due to the oppressive and dictatorial nature of the Soviet regime. This changed very quickly after the failed 1991 coup in Moscow.

Post-Soviet Era

The result of the demise of the Soviet Union was the political restructuring of Russia. Many of the autonomous republics or regions were transformed into federal republics. Six of these were formed in northern Caucasus: Karachay-Cherkess, Kabarda-Balkar, North Ossetia, Dagestan, Adygeya and Checheno-Ingushetia. This last later broke up into the two separate republics of Chechnya and Ingushetia. The biggest problems for the Russians came from the Ingush and the Chechens.

Ingush

In June 1992, the Ingushetia Republic was created after constant calls by the indepen-

dently minded Ingush. At the same time the Ingush minority living in neighbouring North Ossetia, resentful that Ingush territory and property had not been given back to them after their return from exile in 1956, demanded unification with their kinfolk in the newly created Ingushetia Republic. In North Ossetia, the tension between the Ingush and Ossetians culminated in bloody clashes from 22 October 1992, in which hundreds of people died. Russian forces were sent in to control the situation, but according to local accounts they sided with the Ossetians and participated in the atrocities against the Ingush. The Ingush were no match for the combined force of Ossetians and the Russian Army. North Ossetia's whole Ingush population of over 50,000 was forced to flee into Ingushetia and live in extremely poor conditions, while most of their property in North Ossetia was destroyed or confiscated.

Chechens

Neighbouring Chechnya unilaterally declared independence from the Russian Federation in 1991. Leading the republic then and still leading it as this book went to press was President Dzhokar Dudaev, a former Soviet bomber pilot and air-force general. Within a few days of the declaration, the Russian President Boris Yeltsin declared a state of emergency in Chechnya and 650 Russian troops were sent there to occupy strategic places like the airport and government buildings. The Russians were soon forced to withdraw not only because the state of emergency was rejected by the Russian parliament, but also because they realised that their positions were not defensible owing to the armed resistance of the Chechens.

The newly declared independent country was not recognised internationally. As Chechnya was a landlocked country surrounded by Russia and CIS states, it was easy for the Russians to isolate it from the rest of the world and thus it never succeeded in developing into an independent state. Constant Chechen cries for self-determination resulted in an armed conflict with Russia, which failed to subdue Chechnya by clandestine operations involving anti-Dudaev armed groups (propped up by a handful of Russians). On 11 December 1994, in the face of much opposition in Russia and around the world against the action, Russian troops openly invaded Chechnya. They surrounded the capital Grozny and almost bombed it into submission, while Yeltsin tried to negotiate the total surrender of Dudaev's army. The attack on Grozny commenced on 31 December 1994, but the Chechens repulsed the attack and remained victorious for a few days. The demoralised Russian forces suffered heavy losses as a result of the poor planning of the whole operation. The Russian army's main problem was the use of untrained, raw recruits, who were poorly fed and poorly dressed for the winter conflict, instead of experienced units. But in spring 1995, after a new offensive with experienced troops, the Chechen capital fell. The hardy defenders left for the mountains of their homeland, from where they continued to fight. It seemed that Russia was in for a prolonged guerrilla war. (For more information, see the boxed aside later in this chapter.)

CLIMATE

The Black Sea coast is the mildest place in Russia in winter, rarely freezing. In summer it's warm and humid, reaching around 25°C from June to September. North of the Caucasus there's a continental climate – three or four freezing winter months but temperatures typically reaching around 30°C from June to August.

The higher you go the cooler it gets – many Caucasus peaks are permanently snow-covered – but on a sunny summer day you'll still be sweating at 3000 metres. November to April/May is the wettest season, but only on the Black Sea coastal plain (where around 1200 to 1800 mm of rain falls each year) does it get significantly wet.

POPULATION, PEOPLE & LANGUAGE

Around 13 million people inhabit the southern regions of Russia included in this chapter. Most Caucasian societies are strongly patriarchal, but the tribal nature of the mountain peoples has been diluted by Soviet education, collectivisation and urbanisation.

The region's ethnic complexity is revealed by its administrative divisions: strung across the north side of the Caucasus are seven republics within the Russian Federation, their names indicating some of the peoples that inhabit them: from west to east, they are Adygeya, the Karachay-Cherkess and Kabarda-Balkar republics, North Ossetia, Ingushetia, Chechnya and Dagestan.

Classified by language, of which 40 or so are spoken, the region's peoples divide into three main families. (Russian is spoken just about everywhere.)

Caucasians

About 2.5 million people in the region use some 30 indigenous Caucasian languages. They fall into north-western and north-eastern groups. All the written languages use the Cyrillic alphabet.

The north-western group, with about 600,000 people, includes the Kabarda, the Adygeya, the Abaza in the Karachay-Cherkess Republic (all also known as Circassians), as well as the Abkhazians of Abkhazia (who are beyond the scope of this book). Many more Circassians now live in Turkey, Syria, Jordan and Iraq.

North-east Caucasians divide into speakers of Nakh languages (chiefly the 800,000 Chechen and 200,000 Ingush) and speakers of the 30 or so Dagestan languages. The latter, all from Dagestan or Azerbaijan, are mostly nonwritten and have less than 10,000 speakers. All their speakers are loosely known as Lezgians – a term that still flutters Russian hearts by association with tribes whom it took Russia more than half the 19th century to tame. But Lezgi (or Kuri) is also the name of one of the more important individual languages, with 200,000 speakers in Dagestan and 170,000 in Azerbaijan. Others are Avar, with about 500,000 speakers, Lakh with 100,000, and Dargwa with 300,000.

A southern group of Caucasian languages, Kartvelian, is spoken by Georgians.

Indo-Europeans

The Indo-European language family is thought to have originated in western Turkey and to have spread over most of Europe and south and south-west Asia by 1000 BC. The Slavs, mainly Russians and Ukrainians who make up 80% of the population north of the Caucasus, are Indo-European. Prominent among speakers of other Indo-European languages in the Caucasus are the Ossetians, who number around 550,000 and are thought to be descended from Sarmatians pushed south into the Caucasus by the Huns in the 4th century. Most Ossetians live on the north (Russian) side of the Caucasus but at some stage others spilled through to the south side into what's now South Ossetia, in Georgia.

Turks

Turkic peoples in the region include 240,000 Kumyk and 60,000 Nogay in Dagestan, and the 100,000 Karachay and 70,000 Balkar in the west and central Caucasus.

RELIGION

Some Caucasus mountain peoples like the Kabarda, Karachay, Chechens and Balkar are Muslim, but Russian Orthodoxy predominates.

GETTING THERE & AWAY
Air

You can fly to several places in the region including Krasnodar on the steppe, Mineralnye Vody on the northern edge of the Caucasus (though this airport was subject to a spate of hijackings and kidnappings in 1994), Sochi on the Black Sea, Vladikavkaz and Nalchik in the Caucasus, and Makhachkala on the Caspian Sea.

Train

The main railways into the region funnel through Rostov-on-Don and then diverge – one to Mineralnye Vody and Makhachkala and on to Baku, the other to Krasnodar then down the Russian Black Sea coast and on

into Abkhazia and Georgia. There are trains all the way from Moscow taking 1½ to two days: some go via Kharkiv (Kharkov) in Ukraine so if you're thinking of taking one of these check the Ukraine visa situation first.

The railways are really more useful for shorter hops. Owing to the Chechnya conflict the line between Mineralnye Vody and Makhachkala was closed at the time of writing and trains were being diverted a very long way round via Astrakhan.

Car & Motorbike

Check with Intourist or their successors, or the police, for the latest information on where it is possible to drive. The main route through the region runs from Rostov-on-Don to the Georgian capital Tbilisi via Mineralnye Vody, Nalchik, Vladikavkaz and the spectacular Georgian Military Highway over the Caucasus. This road was open at the time of writing but there is a constant question of safety due to the Ossetian and Chechen conflicts. The branch through Chechnya, leading to Dagestan and Baku, was closed. The other main north-south road loops round from Rostov through Krasnodar to Sochi on the Black Sea; its continuation to Sukhumi (Abkhazia) and Batumi (western Georgia), then on to Georgia's road border with Turkey at Sarpi, is at times questionable due to the Abkhazian-Georgian conflict.

Boat

Novorossiysk and Sochi are served by irregular passenger ferries and hydrofoils. It might be possible to get passage on a freighter between Makhachkala in Dagestan and Turkmenbashi (formerly Krasnovodsk) in Turkmenistan or Aqtau (formerly Shevchenko) in Kazakhstan.

For Abkhazian, Georgian and Turkish destinations, see the Sochi section later in this chapter.

Tours

Foreign companies which offer trips to the Mt Elbrus area and Dagestan are mentioned in those sections.

GETTING AROUND

Groups usually travel by coach, with maybe the occasional train or plane thrown in. For individuals, car travel is the most flexible but bus and train are cheap. Roads in parts of the region are not the safest due to crime against foreigners, who at best end up paying bribes to police, military and the Mafia. The problem areas are in parts of the Caucasus. Chechnya at the time of writing was in a state of war with Russia. Dagestan and Ingushetia had Mafia roadblocks and the roads were not safe for travelling.

Bus

Buses fill the gap where the trains do not go or if the train is full they are an alternative. Apart from cars and taxis, buses are the only available transport into the mountainous areas. There are many overnight buses to all major destinations, and these long-distance buses can actually be faster than most of the trains, but can be very crowded. They are a cheap and efficient way to travel, but in Dagestan and Ingushetia they are reportedly an occasional target for armed hold-ups. Many buses are getting old and run down but the best ones are the Hungarian-made ones.

Train

It is fairly easy to hop onto most trains. Buying a ticket three or more days in advance is easy, but buying a ticket one or two days in advance is often impossible – in the latter case you will have to buy it two hours before the train leaves. In most cases they should have some 3rd-class (plats-kartnyy) sleepers left. The conditions on trains in this part of Russia are worse than in the northern parts of the country. The trains are noisier and dirtier, the toilets are filthy, the sleeping mattresses occasionally smell and the sheets can be soiled.

Car & Motorbike

Main roads are generally in a decent condition but the many animals wandering over them behave more sensibly than some of the drivers, who sometimes like to overtake in truly lunatic situations. Accidents are common.

Cable Car

One unusual (in Soviet terms) form of transport you may well find yourself riding in this region is the cable car. Highly exotic to northern Russians, who never see a hill from one year to the next, these are strung across any landscape with the merest hint of a slope – not just up mountains but over parks, lakes, even along flat valleys. Maybe the centralised Soviet cable car factory was oversupplied with parts and materials one year, and just kept churning the things out...

Kuban Steppe
Кубанская степь

From Rostov-on-Don, the overland routes to the Caucasus and the Black Sea coast cross the intensively cultivated Kuban Steppe, named after its major river, which flows from Elbrus into the Sea of Azov. This region had a high Cossack population and its peasants were among the chief victims of the grain requisitioning and forced collectivisation of the late 1920s and early 1930s, with apparently millions of them being starved, shot or deported.

The trip from Rostov to Pyatigorsk or Kislovodsk on the northern fringe of the Caucasus can be made in a day – by road it's just under 500 km. Mikhail Gorbachev's unexciting home town, Stavropol, is off the main road.

STAVROPOL
СТАВРОПОЛЬ
Population: 300,000

Stavropol was the Russian military supply centre throughout the Caucasus campaigns which lasted until the 1850s. The town's on a plateau, with an economy based on the agriculture of the surrounding steppe. Gorbachev grew up in the village of Privolnoe, 145 km to the north. His academic record took him to Moscow to study, then he returned to Stavropol with his wife Raisa to begin his rise up the Party ladder while she taught at the local university.

Orientation & Information

The main streets are prospekt Karla Marxa, a dual carriageway leading west from the railway station to the Hotel Stavropol, and ulitsa Dzerzhinskogo, running parallel a block south. For information try Stavropolintour (☎ 2 45 25 or 3 52 18) at ulitsa Ryleeva 5. The Stavropol telephone code is 86522.

Things to See

The 19th-century **St Andrew's Cathedral** (Andreevsky sobor) at ulitsa Dzerzhinskogo 155 is a working church. The **Regional Museum** (Kraevedchesky muzey) is at ulitsa Dzerzhinskogo 135 near the Hotel Kavkaz and includes an exhibit of army uniforms from Napoleon's army, as well as many Russian and local (Khoper) Cossack ones.

The Cossacks, who were granted control of the Kuban in 1792, are famed horse-riders

The Kuban Cossacks

The Kuban Cossacks (for background on Cossacks see the History and Population & People sections in the Facts about European Russia chapter) are a relatively young group, formed as a result of an imperial decree. In 1792, in the aftermath of the three Tatar Wars, the Empress Catherine II granted all the Kuban lands to the Black Sea Cossacks. This group was mostly made up of the Zaporizhzhya (Zaporozhie) and Don Cossack stanitsy (the traditional self-governing units of the Cossacks) and was led by ataman Chepega. Other people from Ukraine and the Don River basin were later brought in to help populate the uninhabited Kuban. The region developed its own blend of Ukrainian and Russian culture, which was also influenced by Caucasian mountain culture, mainly in dance and clothing design. As is well known, the Kuban Cossacks helped the Russian army to defeat the tribes of the Caucasus. This was not the only regional conflict in which the Cossacks participated; they had a hand in the Crimean War and the liberation of Bulgaria. The Cossacks were as good at farming as they were at fighting, and practised a system of communal farming. Each man was given a plot by the community, to be his for life; this plot could be inherited by his descendants but never sold.

Today, after they were all but wiped out under Soviet rule, Cossacks all over Russia are experiencing a revival. The Russian Parliament has passed laws to revive a Cossack nation and the traditional Cossack way of life. Some Cossack units have been created in the Russian armed forces. In the Kuban as well as in other parts of Russia, the Cossacks are re-forming into their stanitsy and electing the ataman as their leader. They are searching out their identity, which often has strong military overtones. The Cossack capital of Novocherkassk is the seat of the military college of Kadetsky Korpus, which is attended by Cossack boys. Some individuals have taken to fighting in conflicts beyond Russia, including those in Abkhazia, Bosnia-Hercegovina and Moldova. ■

There's an **Art Museum** at ulitsa Dzerzhinskogo 115.

Places to Stay

The new *Hotel Intourist* (☎ 3 77 55) at prospekt Marxa 42 costs from US$36/42 (US$7 per person more including breakfast) in one of the 106 standard rooms. Facilities include a restaurant, several bars and a pool with a sauna. The two-star *Hotel Kavkaz* (☎ 3 23 76/66) at ulitsa Kominterna 1, just north of ulitsa Dzerzhinskogo, costs US$21/34. At the time of writing the following hotels did not allow independent travellers to stay in them, but the situation may change in the future: *Hotel Stavropol* (☎ 5 97 36 or 3 76 14) at prospekt Karla Marxa 42 (corner of Kazachya ulitsa); the *Hotel Elbrus* (☎ 5 96 00) at ulitsa Gorkogo 43, a short walk north of the Stavropol; and the *Hotel Turist* (☎ 5 19 92/43), west of the centre at ulitsa Lenina 273.

Getting There & Away

Stavropol is 52 km north of the Rostov-Pyatigorsk road, 413 km from Rostov and 190 km from Pyatigorsk. There are daily flights from Moscow (US$118), less often from other cities. Aeroflot (☎ 4 58 37) is at Pereulok Zootekhnichesky 13A. Stavropol is on a branch line off the Rostov-Mineralnye Vody-Baku railway but has daily services to/from places on that line.

KRASNODAR

КРАСНОДАР

Population: 600,000

Krasnodar (called Yekaterinodar in tsarist times) was founded as a Cossack fort on the Kuban River in 1793. Recently the area won notoriety thanks to the Kuban Sea (Kubanskoe More), a huge reservoir created a few km upstream in the 1970s. The water table rose so high, according to the Soviet press, that 3500 sq km of farmland were flooded and the foundations of 27,000 blocks of flats waterlogged.

Orientation & Information

Krasnaya ulitsa is the 2-km long main street. The road from Rostov-on-Don feeds into its north end, a tree-lined dual carriageway. Numbering starts from the south. Parallel, two blocks east, is ulitsa Kommunarov; one block west is ulitsa Shaumyana. Main cross streets include, in south-north order, ulitsa Mira, ulitsa Sverdlova and Severnaya ulitsa.

The Intourist office (☎ 57 66 17) is at the Hotel Intourist. The main bookshop, Dom Knigi, is at Krasnaya ulitsa 43. There's a bank at ulitsa Ordzhonikidze 29, a telegraph office at ulitsa Sverdlova 64, and the main post office is at ulitsa Shaumyana 6. The Krasnodar telephone code is 8612.

Things to See & Do

The **Regional Museum** (Kraevedchesky muzey) at ulitsa Voroshilova 67 includes Scythian and ancient Greek figures. It's two blocks north and one east from the Hotel Tsentralnaya. The **Art Museum** (Khudozhestvenny muzey) is at Krasnaya ulitsa 13. Both are closed Tuesday. Intourist offers motor boat or hydrofoil trips on the Kuban, but it might be simpler and cheaper to do them independently.

Places to Stay & Eat

Intourist offers the big three-star *Hotel Intourist* (☎ 55 88 97) about halfway along Krasnaya ulitsa at No 109. The reasonable rooms cost US$32/42, including cockroaches. Forget the breakfast here. There are also several bars and a disco on the 13th floor. The cheaper *Motel Yuzhny* (☎ 5 93 36) is on the north-east side of town at Moskovskaya ulitsa 40, half a km east of Krasnodar-II railway station. The rooms cost US$20/34. For the motel, if coming from Rostov, turn left off the south end of Rostovskoe shosse, before the railway.

The following places to stay did not at the time of writing accept foreigners: *Hotel Tsentralnaya* (☎ 2 26 24, 2 90 57) at Krasnaya ulitsa 25 (corner of ulitsa Mira), and the *Hotel Turist* (☎ 9 25 04, 2 35 91) near the river at ulitsa Kubano-naberezhnaya 5, along Sovietskaya ulitsa three blocks west of the south end of Krasnaya ulitsa.

The *Central Market* (Tsentralny rynok) is

opposite the circus at ulitsa Budennogo 129, a block west of the Hotel Intourist.

Getting There & Away

Air There are several flights from Moscow (US$120) daily, and a few a week from other places like Vladikavkaz, Nalchik and Tbilisi. Aeroflot (☎ 57 60 07) is at Krasnaya ulitsa 129, just north of the Hotel Intourist.

Bus The intercity bus station (Avtovokzal Mezhdugorodnykh Soobshcheniy) is opposite the railway station; buses go to all destinations in the region. Sample fares and times to some destinations are Novorossiysk (US$1.80, three hours), Rostov-on-Don (US$2.40, five hours and 40 minutes) and Sochi (US$3, eight hours and 20 minutes). Luggage costs extra.

Train Several trains a day pass through on the Rostov-Sochi route. Rostov is four to six hours away, Sochi six or seven hours. Krasnodar-I station is on Privokzalnaya ploshchad at the east end of ulitsa Mira, next to the intercity bus station and convenient for the south end of Krasnaya ulitsa; Krasnodar-II is at ulitsa Kommunarov 282, two blocks east of the north end of Krasnaya ulitsa.

Car & Motorbike Krasnodar is 275 km from Rostov-on-Don and 420 km from Dagomys. The former official foreigners' route south goes west through Abynsk and Krymsk to the coast at Novorossiysk – but there is the more direct road through Teuchezhsk and Goryachy Klyuch.

Mineral Water Spas
Кавказские Минеральные Воды

The central Caucasus begins to rise from the steppe in an eerie landscape studded with mineral springs and dead volcanoes. The springs' curative powers have attracted unhealthy, hypochondriac, or plain holiday-minded Russians ever since someone noticed in the late 18th century that wounded soldiers got better quicker when they bathed in them. The area had passed from Turkish to Russian hands in 1774 but still came under attack from local tribes. Early patients sometimes had to take refuge in the forts.

Today the area, known in Russian as Kavkazskie Mineralnye Vody (Caucasian Mineral Waters), is a very popular holiday resort, with hordes of sanatoria where the healthy seem to outnumber the ailing. There are hotels too. The atmosphere is relaxed, the air mostly fresh, and the walks lovely. The parks and elegant spa buildings recall the 19th century, when fashionable society trekked down from Moscow and St Petersburg to see, be seen, attend balls and look for a spouse. The key to appearing an old hand is to carry a mug or flask with which to take the waters from the most favoured springs in the handsome old purpose-built galleries.

There are five main towns – the resorts of Pyatigorsk, Kislovodsk, Yessentuki and Zheleznovodsk and the industrial and transport centre, Mineralnye Vody (Minvody for short). The whole area is haunted by the Romantic writer Mikhail Lermontov, whose story 'Princess Mary', in his novel *A Hero of Our Time*, is set here and who, in an uncanny echo of its plot, was killed in a duel at Pyatigorsk in 1841. Many local sites crop up in the book, which also contains an episode set on the Georgian Military Highway. This short – by Russian standards very short – novel makes a great travelling companion.

Over 130 springs in the region, variously believed to benefit disorders of the muscles, bones, heart, circulation, nervous system or skin, gush out 60 million litres of mineral water a day. The towns have numerous buildings labelled 'istochnik' ('spring') where you can simply enter and drink for free. But you can't usually just wander into one of the bath houses *(vanny)* and take a reviving dip. Even Russian citizens need a *kurortnaya knizhka* (spa pass) to use these and they appear to be issued only to those undergoing treatment or staying at sanatoria. Your best

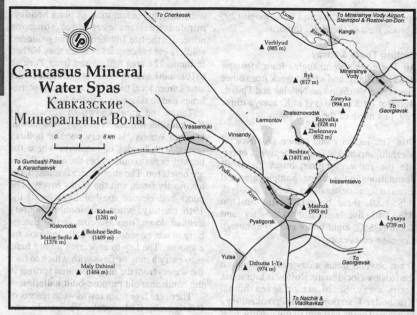

Caucasus Mineral Water Spas
Кавказские Минеральные Волы

chance of getting into the famous Narzan Baths at Kislovodsk or Lermontov Baths at Pyatigorsk is through Stavropolintour.

The climate is relatively mild and autumn is considered the best season, with the leaves turning. Spring is wet.

Getting There & Away

The airport and mainline railway station at Mineralnye Vody are linked to the spa towns by buses and a good local train service. In addition, a few mainline trains run along the branch line into Pyatigorsk and Kislovodsk.

Air Daily services to/from Mineralnye Vody in summer include: Moscow (US$121; 2¼ hours; three daily), Baku (four per week), Batumi (once a week), St Petersburg (US$153; one a week), Rostov-on-Don (US$66.60; six a week), Tashkent (four a week), Tbilisi (US$61; daily) and Yerevan (US$77.50; daily). The rest of the year there are still several flights a week to/from these places.

There are also two flights a week with Aeroflot to/from Sochi, and with a new regional airline Mineralovodskaya aviakompania (☎ (86531) 3 03 01) once a week. There are air ticket offices at Oktyabrskaya ulitsa 42 in Pyatigorsk, and next to the railway station on Privokzalnaya ploshchad in Kislovodsk.

Bus The Rostov-Tbilisi road goes through Mineralnye Vody and round Pyatigorsk on a bypass. Intercity buses serve the spa towns.

Train It's much of a muchness whether you use Mineralnye Vody's station, on the main Moscow-Rostov-Baku line, and then transfer by local transport, or take one of the fewer long-distance trains which go down the branch line. Mineralnye Vody has several trains a day to/from Moscow (about 29 hours) and Rostov-on-Don (nine hours), plus daily trains to/from Stavropol (10 hours), Nalchik and Vladikavkaz. Pyatigorsk and Kislovodsk are served by just a couple of daily trains direct to/from (in summer) Sochi, Rostov and Moscow.

Getting Around

Bus Nos 9 and 10 from the Mineralnye Vody airport go to the town's railway station, where you can hop on a local electric train to the spas. There are also buses from the airport about hourly to Pyatigorsk (US$0.60, taking 35 minutes), more often to Zhelezno-vodsk and Kislovodsk. There's a taxi stand at the front of the airport. Stavropolintour can transfer you by car between Mineralnye Vody and another town. For Kislovodsk, the price is about US$52 for the vehicle.

The busy but quick electric trains (*elek-tropoezdy*) run roughly half-hourly from about 4 am to 11 pm between Mineralnye Vody and Kislovodsk. Pyatigorsk is nearly halfway along the line, 35 minutes from Mineralnye Vody, and one hour from Kislovodsk. Stops between Pyatigorsk and Kislovodsk include Skachki and Yessentuki. The Zheleznovodsk line, branching off between Mineralnye Vody and Pyatigorsk, has fewer trains. Tickets are cheap and are available from ticket offices in the railway stations. For some outlying spots, taxis are best – hotels will usually book them for you.

The towns are generally small enough to walk around; where necessary, bus numbers etc are listed for outlying sites. Within the towns there are usually buses and trams available.

PYATIGORSK

ПЯТИГОРСК

Population: 110,000

The 'capital' of the spa region sprawls around the foot of 993-metre Mt Mashuk but its name is a Russification of Beshtau (Five Peaks), the Turkish title of the highest moun-tain in the neighbourhood. Pyatigorsk is 550 metres high and began life as a fort, called Konstantinovskaya, in 1780.

Orientation

The town spreads west and south from Mt Mashuk. The main street is the tree-lined prospekt Kirova, running west from below

the Academic Gallery near the foot of Mashuk, through the town centre to the railway station. The jagged crags of Beshtau (1401 metres) rise to the north-west, with the town's suburbs stretching to their feet. Elbrus' twin snow-covered peaks to the south can be seen from several points around town on a clear day.

Information

The Stavropolintour (☎ 5 95 60/7; fax 5 95 57), in the Hotel Intourist at ploshchad Lenina 13 (floor C), is an independent tourist company. They provide excellent informa-tion about the area and can organise a stay in the baths as well as hiking, skiing, hang gliding, mountaineering, hunting and fishing. Most equipment is not available for hire and if it is it's of poor quality, so bring your own. They can also book plane and train tickets if you give them at least a week's notice. The State Bank is on the corner of prospekt Kirova and ulitsa Sakko i Vantsetti. The bank is open for exchange Monday to Saturday from 8.30 am to noon. The main post office is on prospekt Kirova at the corner of ulitsa Kraynego, and the telegraph office is on the opposite side, just a bit further north on ulitsa Kraynego. The regional tele-phone code is 86533.

Mt Mashuk & Around

A cable car whisks you from the upper part of the town to the top of the near-perfect cone of Mt Mashuk for fresh breezes and a great panorama. It operates from 10 am to 6 pm (last ride is at 5.15 pm); a return ticket is US$0.50. In the park below the lower station are a few *istochnik* pavilions – some of the town's sources of free mineral water. Many Pyatigorsk springs are warm – up to 60°C – and sometimes sulphurous too.

From the lower cable car station the road circles round Mashuk. Off the road among trees is the little domed pavilion called the **Aeolian Harp**, which has long been a favour-ite lookout point. It was built in 1831 to replace a real harp plucked by a weather vane. Today ethereal electronic chords emanate from the dome while sightseers

Pyatigorsk
Пятигорск

0   250   500 m

To Mineralnye Vody
To Proval
To Lermontov Duel Site

ulitsa Panagyurishte

ulitsa Mira

Moskovskaya ulitsa

prospekt 40 let Oktyabrya

Kalinina

ulitsa Kraznogo

Mt Mashuk

ulitsa Pastukhova

ulitsa Akademika Pavlova

Krasnoarmeyskaya ulitsa

ulitsa Buachidze

ulitsa Khetagurova

Kozlova

Universitetskaya ulitsa

ulitsa Marynina

Oktyabrskaya

Kirova prospekt

ulitsa Dzerzhinskogo

ulitsa Sakko i Vancetti

ulitsa Anadzhievskogo

Dunaevskogo

To Motel-Camping Volna & Racecourse

To Nalchik & Vladikavkaz

To Bus Station

Lermontova

ulitsa Marza

Kirova prospekt

Park Tsvetnik

Teploсемaya ulitsa

Podkumok River

Stroeevaya ulitsa

PYATIGORSK

---

pose beside donkeys. From here you can walk down via **Lermontov's Grotto**, a small cave which the writer used to visit, to the **Academic Gallery** (formerly the Elizabeth Gallery), built in 1851 by an English architect, Upton, to house one of Pyatigorsk's best known springs. Today there is a small art gallery, and a coffee shop in the gallery too. It's here that Lermontov's antihero, Pechorin, first sets eyes on Princess Mary.

About a half-hour walk from the Aeolian Harp, past the **Spa Exhibition** (on Pyatigorsk's history; closed Monday) at bulvar Gagarina 2, is **Proval**, a cave open to the sky

where 19th-century couples would dance on a bridge over the pond of light blue sulphurous water.

The site of Lermontov's fatal duel is marked by a **monument** a further hour or so's walk round the road behind Mt Mashuk. Lermontov had been banished twice from St Petersburg to serve in the Caucasus army – first after blaming the tsarist authorities for the death of another 'troublesome' writer, Pushkin, in a duel, and second for duelling himself. In Pyatigorsk, Lermontov was challenged to a further duel for a jest about the clothes of one Major Martynov. Lermontov,

	PLACES TO STAY	6	Cable Car, Upper Station Канатная дорога, верхняя станция	21	Regional Museum Музей краеведения
1	Motel Мотель			22	State Bank Государственный банк
3	Hotel Beshtau Гостиница Бештау	7	Cable Car, Lower Station Канатная дорога, нижняя станция	23	Spa Research Institute Институт курортологии
26	Hotel Intourist Гостиница Интурист	8	Spa Exhibition Курортная выставка	24	Tarkhany Sanatorium Санаторий Тарханы
37	Hotel Pyatigorsk Гостиница Пятигорск	9	Aeolian Harp Эолова арфа	25	Lermontov Museum-Reserve Музей-заповедник М.Ю. Лермонтова
	PLACES TO EAT	10	Academic Gallery Академическая галерея		
27	Kafe Teremok Кафе Теремок	11	Lermontov's Grotto Грот М.Ю. Лермонтова	29	Dom Knigi (Bookshop) Магазин Дом книги
28	Kafe Кафе	12	Pushkin Baths Пушкинские ванны	30	Lermontov Statue Памятник М.Ю. Лермонтову
32	Gril Bar Гриль Бар	13	Musical Comedy Theatre Театр музыкальной комедии	31	Tolstoy Monument Памятник Л.Н. Толстому
33	Kafe Diana Кафе Диана				
36	Kafe Pingvin Кафе Пингвин	14	Chinese Pavilion Китайская беседка	34	Main Post Office Главный почтамт
38	Kafe Sofia & Kafe u Lukomorya Кафе София и Кафе у Лукоморья	15	Eagle Sculpture Скульптура орла	35	Telephone & Telegraph Office Центральный переговорный пункт
		16	Lermontov & Yermolov Baths Лермонтовские и Ермоловские ванны		
	OTHER	17	Lermontov Gallery Лермонтовская галерея	39	Post Office Почтамт
2	Lermontov Duel Site Место дуэли М.Ю. Лермонтова	18	Spring No 2 Источник No 2	40	Upper Market Верхний рынок
4	Mt Mashuk Summit Гора Машук, вершина	19	Diana's Grotto Грот Дианы	41	Aeroflot Ticket Office Кассы Аэрофлота
5	Proval Провал	20	Post Office Почтамт	42	Train Station Железнодорожный вокзал

firing first, aimed into the air, but was in return shot through the heart. Many saw his death, like Pushkin's, as orchestrated by the authorities.

You can reach the cable car, the Aeolian Harp and Proval by bus No 1 from the railway station via prospekt Kirova and ulitsa Andzhievskogo, or bus No 15 from the Upper Market; the nearest you can approach the duel site by public transport is by bus No 16 from the railway station via prospekt Kalinina, which re-emerges, after a back street wiggle, on prospekt Kalinina near a sign to 'Mesto dueli M Yu Lermontova'

('Lermontov Duel Site'), a 15-minute walk away.

Park Tsvetnik

The central Flower Park – as much buildings as vegetation – contains the blue **Lermontov Gallery** (1901), a sort of glass-and-iron Brighton Pavilion, plus the Lermontov (1831) and Yermolov (1880) Baths, and spring No 2. A path past **Diana's Grotto**, a small artificial cave, leads up to **Goryachaya (Hot) Hill**, with a much-photographed eagle sculpture and a Chinese lookout pavilion.

The **Spa Research Institute**, which develops mineral water treatments, is housed in the Classical Institut Kurortologii building at prospekt Kirova 34 near the park entrance. It was once the Restoratsia, Pyatigorsk's first hotel and the scene of balls described in *A Hero of Our Time*. **The Regional Museum** at ulitsa Sakko i Vantsetti 2 is open 10 am to 5.30 pm daily except Wednesday.

Lermontov Statue & Museum

The man himself stares towards Elbrus from his pedestal in the, yes, Lermontov Garden, near the foot of ulitsa Andzhievskogo. The thatched cottage where he spent his last two months is up the hill in the Lermontov Museum-Reserve, an extended family of Lermontov-related buildings and exhibitions in a walled, off-street area. It's open 10 am to 5 pm, except Tuesdays and the last Thursday of the month. The entrance is on ulitsa Karla Marxa.

Places to Stay

The three-star *Hotel Intourist* (☎ 5 91 72) at ploshchad Lenina 14, postal index 357521, is central, modern, clean and comfortable with great views from some rooms, all of which have balconies. The rooms cost from US$30/45 and are payable by Visa card. Breakfast is US$2 extra – OK for the standard-type eggs and sausage.

The motel rooms at the *Motel-Camping Volna* (☎ 5 05 28), though two-star and cheaper, are lousy value at US$13/20 – they're damp, fly-ridden, noisy and about 5 km west of the centre on Ogorodnaya ulitsa. The camp site cabins are self-contained and cleaner. There's little space for tents. Signposts to the place are hard to spot (it's about half a km south of ulitsa Tolyatti, which branches south off Fevralskaya ulitsa leading west from the railway station). The nearest stop for tram No 2 to the railway station and prospekt Kirova is on ulitsa Tolyatti.

At the time of writing neither of the following places accepted foreigners: the *Hotel Beshtau* (☎ 9 96 62/95) at ulitsa Patrisa Lumumby 17, off prospekt Kalinina, and an older motel (☎ 9 20 42/22) a further km or so north on prospekt Kalinina, in the suburb of Belaya Romashka. Bus Nos 16 and 113 up prospekt Kalinina from prospekt Kirova will get you to both places; Nos 4, 6, 9 and 15 go to the Beshtau only.

Places to Eat

Food at the *Hotel Intourist* is good – normal Intourist fare but well prepared and with decent variety. The catering block has at least three bars or cafés besides its two restaurants – both of which have evening shows, the smaller being the quieter. The restaurant at the *Motel-Camping Volna* is pot luck – you might get an excellent meal with friendly service, or it might be sloppy fare, sulkily presented. The band is dire.

There's a handful of cafés along prospekt Kirova. Mostly they close around 6 to 7 pm. At the corner with ulitsa Dzerzhinskogo (take the stairs below the street level) is *Gril Bar* with cheap grilled chicken (US$0.50) and drinks. The *Upper Market* (Verkhny Rynok) on ulitsa Mira functions daily till about 4 pm and in summer until later in the evening.

Another plus being this far south in summer is that due to the constant heat, it is possible to buy cold drinks and beer from just about any kiosk, café or restaurant for an extra few roubles.

Entertainment & Activities

In summer there are race meetings about twice a week on the course beside Skachki station in the west of the town. Stavropolintour may be able to fix a visit to the Tchersky stud farm, apparently the source of many champions, out towards Mineralnye Vody.

For your 'health', Stavropolintour can arrange applications of curative mud packs or inhalations of a variety of vile fumes at US$10 to US$15 a session. A one-off mineral bath or mud wallow is harder to arrange but may be possible. Stavropolintour has also advertised hang gliding from Mt Yutsa, 15 km out of town, but you have to bring your own hang glider.

The Friday and Saturday evening classical

concerts in town have been recommended by British visitors – tickets are US$1.50 at the door but about US$5 through Stavropolintour. The Musical Comedy Theatre (Teatr Muzikalnoy Komedii) at prospekt Kirova 17 is popular, with several shows in repertory. In summer there's often a night-time disco in Park Tsvetnik.

A good place for taped rock music and drinks is Kafe u Lukomorya, on the roof of a shopping complex at the corner of ulitsa Khetagurova and Kraynego. There is a view of the city and the place is open until 11 pm.

KISLOVODSK
КИСЛОВОДСК
Population: 100,000
Kislovodsk (Sour Waters) is hillier, greener, higher (822 metres) and quieter than Pyatigorsk. 'Love affairs that begin at the foot of Mashuk reach happy endings here,' Lermontov wrote. If you're not staying here, the beautiful park alone is worth a day trip.

Kislovodsk springs are mainly carbonic. Another famous Russian writer and dissident, Alexander Solzhenitsyn, was born here.

Orientation & Information
The railway station and Narzan Gallery (Narzannaya galereya), at the east and west ends of ulitsa Karla Marxa, are pretty much the centre of things, with the park spreading to their south. The main post, telephone and telegraph office is on Oktyabrskaya ploshchad, at the north end of traffic-free bulvar Kurortny, which runs north from the Narzan Gallery. The bus station is on the Yessentuki road on the northern edge of town. The advance Railway Ticket Office (Zheleznodorozhnye biletnye kassy) is at ulitsa Karla Marxa 6.

The regional telephone code is 86537.

Narzan Gallery & Baths
The rich, carbonic Narzan Spring around

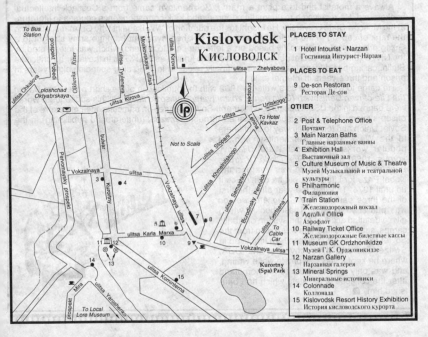

Kislovodsk
КИСЛОВОДСК

PLACES TO STAY
1 Hotel Intourist - Narzan
   Гостиница Интурист-Нарзан

PLACES TO EAT
9 De-son Restoran
   Ресторан Де-сон

OTHER
2 Post & Telephone Office
   Почтамт
3 Main Narzan Baths
   Главные нарзанные ванны
4 Exhibition Hall
   Выставочный зал
5 Culture Museum of Music & Theatre
   Музей Музыкальной и театральной
   культуры
6 Philharmonic
   Филармония
7 Train Station
   Железнодорожный вокзал
8 Aeroflot Office
   Аэрофлот
10 Railway Ticket Office
   Железнодорожные билетные кассы
11 Museum GK Ordzhonikidze
   Музей Г. К. Орджоникидзе
12 Narzan Gallery
   Нарзанная галерея
13 Mineral Springs
   Минеральные источники
14 Colonnade
   Коллонада
15 Kislovodsk Resort History Exhibition
   История кисловодского курорта

which Kislovodsk grew now whooshes up inside its own glass dome in a long Gothic gallery designed for it by the Englishman Upton in the 1850s. In the gallery you can rent a glass to taste a variety of local waters from labelled taps – it's open 7 to 9.30 am, 10.30 am to 3 pm, and 4 to 7 pm. The main Narzan Baths are in a 1903 Indian temple-style building on bulvar Kurortny. Bathing in Narzan – which means Drink of Giants in a local language – is said to prolong life and ease pain.

Kurortny Park

Kislovodsk's large, varied Kurortny (Spa) Park, opening out immediately south of the Narzan Gallery, dates from the early 19th century and has several great viewpoints.

Alexander Solzhenitsyn

Alexander Isayevich Solzhenitsyn is one of Russia's greatest dissidents. He exposed Soviet crimes against humanity and the atrocities of the Gulag forced-labour camps through his writings. He was born on 11 December 1918 in Kislovodsk, near Mineralnye Vody in the northern foothills of the Caucasus Mountains, six months after his father's death in an accident.

In June 1994, Solzhenitsyn returned to his mother country after 20 years in exile. It was a grand entrance. The BBC had paid Russian Railways approximately US$28,000 to enable Solzhenitsyn to undertake a two-month journey on a special train across the country from Vladivostok to Moscow. Solzhenitsyn visited many places along the way making speeches, but mostly he wanted to find out what people thought of the new Russia. Apparently he was impressed by the people's resolve to work their problems out and move ahead. One of the most moving experiences for him was to stop in the old villages of Bamlag and Amurlag in Siberia, which had been part of the 'Gulag Archipelago' he made infamous in the West. Here he asked to be left alone for a while.

Always a moralist and to a point a martyr, Solzhenitsyn came from a Cossack intellectual background. He received a mathematics degree, and took correspondence courses in literature at the Moscow State University. He fought for the duration of WW II against the Germans, attaining the rank of captain in the artillery. After the war Solzhenitsyn went from the army straight to a Gulag prison after a trial mostly based on a letter he sent to a friend, which was intercepted by the NKVD (the Soviet secret police, later to become known as the KGB). In the letter he criticised Stalin, calling him a 'gang leader'. He was finally released in 1956 after spending eight years in prison and three years in internal exile.

He came to wide notice as a writer in 1962 with the publication of the short novel *One Day in the Life of Ivan Denisovich (Odin den iz zhizni Ivana Denisovicha)*, but all his subsequent works were banned in the USSR because of their anti-Soviet nature – in particular, their exposure of the prison system. They were usually published through *samizdat* (underground publishing) in the Soviet Union and found their way to publishers in the West. Two of Solzhenitsyn's most popular works are *Cancer Ward (Rakovy korpus*; 1968) and *The First Circle (V kruge pervom*; 1968). In 1970 he was awarded the Nobel Prize for Literature, but he didn't pick it up until 1974. This was the year after the first of the three parts of *The Gulag Archipelago* was published in Paris. These books, which give a detailed account of the system of labour camps, sealed his fate – he was exiled from the Soviet Union for life. Solzhenitsyn first lived in Switzerland and then moved to the USA, where he kept a very low profile while writing, and was only able to return to his homeland after the collapse of the state which had banished him. ∎

The main path from the gallery, initially beside the little Olkhovka River, passes the **Kislovodsk Resort History Exhibition** (Istoria Kislovodskogo kurorta) and a **Lermontov statue**, both on the ulitsa Kominterna side of the park. It then heads uphill via a rose garden to the **Red Rocks** (Krasnye Kamni, coloured by their iron content), beyond which are the **Grey Rocks** (Serye Kamni), two km from the gallery, featuring an eagle sculpture and good views. Walking routes (marshruty) of varying lengths are marked around the park: No 3 brings you at least this far.

A few hundred metres past the Grey Rocks you can either continue up to Krasnoe Solnyshko hill (with views of Elbrus on a good day) or turn right to the cable car which will sweep you over Krasnoe Solnyshko to the top of 1376-metre **Mt Maloe Sedlo** (Little Saddle). Here is a great panorama of the valleys and upland plateaux into which this end of the spa region is carved. It looks easy enough to walk 5 km south-east along the tops to Mt Maly Dzhinal, at 1484 metres. Mt Bolshoe Sedlo, 1409 metres, is one km north-east. The cable car (Kanatnaya doroga Kislovodskaya sportbaza) runs from 10 am to 1.30 pm and 2.30 to 7 pm, except on Mondays or in fog, wind or rain. Tickets are US$0.50 one way – you can't buy returns.

Other Attractions

The prospekt Lenina and prospekt Dzerzhinskogo area has some grand and curious old houses, many now sanatoria. The **Local Lore Museum** (Kraevedchesky muzey), which has displays on local archaeology and history, is at ulitsa Zhukovskogo 12; it's open 10 am to 5 pm daily except Monday (US$0.10). Take bus No 2, 4, 8 or 9 from the railway station or Hotel Kavkaz to the Sanatorii Moskva stop.

Other museums include the **Culture Museum of Music & Theatre** (Muzey muzykalnoy i teatralnoy kultury) at prospekt Karla Marxa, **Art Museum** (Khudozhestvenny muzey) at ulitsa Yaroshenko 1 and the **G K Ordzhonikidze Museum** at Kurortny prospekt.

The **Lermontov Cliff** (Lermontovskaya Skala) where the climactic duel took place in *A Hero of Our Time* is about four km south-east of the town centre in the valley of the Olkhovka River.

Places to Stay

The new *Hotel Intourist – Narzan* (☎ 3 60 53; fax 5 97 57) at ulitsa Zhelyabova 5 near the corner of ulitsa Kirova is a luxury hotel with health spa facilities costing US$10 a day per person. Rooms start from US$30/40, including breakfast.

The *Hotel Kavkaz* (☎ 3 62 35) is at prospekt Dzerzhinskogo 24. It's a decent two-star place with balconies, views, a restaurant and a 'bar' which is more like a nightclub. The rooms cost US$18/27. Bus No 2, 4, 8 or 9 comes here from the railway station.

Places to Eat

The *Restoran Zamok*, in the Alikanovki River gorge about three km west of the centre, is one of the region's best known restaurants, as much for its food as for its setting beside the rock called the Castle of Treachery & Love (Zamok Kovarstva i Lyubvi).

The story goes that a shepherd boy and a rich girl fell in love but were forbidden to marry. They made a death pact. He jumped off the rock. She, seeing the mess, didn't.

It's advisable to book for dinner but this is not usually necessary for lunch. Taxi is the easiest transport, costing about US$1 one way.

There is also an ordinary Chinese restaurant, *De-son*, at Vokzalnaya ulitsa at the north-western edge of Kurortny park.

The *café* on top of Mt Maloe Sedlo does very welcome shashlyk, coffee and biscuits. The most central *market* is on prospekt Mira at the corner of ulitsa Yermolova.

The restaurant in the *Hotel Intourist-Narzan* is a good but expensive place to eat. In the evening they have unfortunate variety shows.

Entertainment

The Philharmonic is at ulitsa Karla Marxa 1.

YESSENTUKI
ЕССЕНТУКИ
Population: 75,000

The least attractive of the four spas, Yessentuki is the place to come if you need a serious course of mud baths. Internatsionalnaya ulitsa leads down from the station to the main square and the park entrance. Among the buildings in the park is another Gothic pavilion by Upton where you can drink from several springs, including No 17, which is supposed to be one of the best in the region. The **Semashko mud baths** are in a Greek-style building on Semashko ulitsa.

The *Restoran Zastava*, serving Cossack food, is one of the best.

ZHELEZNOVODSK
ЖЕЛЕЗНОВОДСК
Population: 15,000

The smallest of the spa towns, Zheleznovodsk (Iron Waters) lies at the foot of 852-metre Mt Zheleznaya, on the north side of Mt Beshtau. It's six km west of the Mineralnye Vody-Pyatigorsk road and served by its own spur of the local railway. The nice park here spreads up the mountain towards the natural forest. Zhelezhnovodsk waters are used for digestive, kidney and metabolic problems. Several springs are in the upper reaches of the park; on the way up are the red-and-white African-style **Ostrovsky Baths** (1893), the blue-and-white iron-and-glass **Pushkin Gallery** (1901), and the Emir of Bukhara's turn-of-the-century palace, now the **Tehlmann Sanatorium**, a mixture of Art Nouveau and Muslim styles. From the park a 3.5-km ring road leads round the mountain. There's also a spiral path to the top – a climb taking about 1¼ hours.

Central Caucasus
Центральный Кавказ

The spectacular Caucasus, about 1000 km long with peaks of 3000-plus metres found along three-quarters of its length, is not only a geographical but a political and ethnic barrier, its watershed forming the boundary between Russia and Georgia and Azerbaijan. The two Russian Caucasus mountain destinations most visited by foreigners are Dombay and the Baksan Valley. Towns in the foothills, like Pyatigorsk and Kislovodsk in the Mineral Water Spas area (see the previous section), Nalchik and Vladikavkaz, are the stepping-off points for these places and other mountain trips.

The main road crossing the central Caucasus is the Georgian Military Highway from Vladikavkaz to Tbilisi in Georgia.

Sometimes called the Great Caucasus to distinguish it from the separate Little Caucasus further south around the borders of Georgia, Armenia and Azerbaijan, the Caucasus is about 25 million years old, with over 2000 glaciers, 70% of them on the north (Russian) side, some as long as 13 or 14 km. The highest peaks are mostly in the middle third of the range where it's relatively narrow (further east and west it's up to 150 km wide). They include from west to east: Dombay-Yolgen (on the Russia-Abkhazia boundary), 4000 metres; Elbrus (Russia), 5642 metres; Ushba (Georgia), 4700 metres; Shkhara (Georgia), 5068 metres; Dykhtau (Russia), 5204 metres; and Kazbek (Georgia), 5033 metres. Further east are Tebulosmta, 4493 metres, and Bazardyuzyu, 4466 metres.

The name Caucasus comes from the Greek Kaukasos, and maybe before that from Kazkaz, a Hittite name for people living on the south shore of the Black Sea.

DOMBAY
ДОМБАЙ

The village of Dombay is 1500 metres high in a forested west Caucasus valley, surrounded by massive mountains needling up to snowcapped peaks. Three deep valleys watered by glacier-fed torrents – the Alibek from the west, the Amanauz from the south, the Dombay-Yolgen from the east – meet here to flow north, becoming the Teberda River a few km downstream. The scenery is magnificent, and even if you're no hiker or

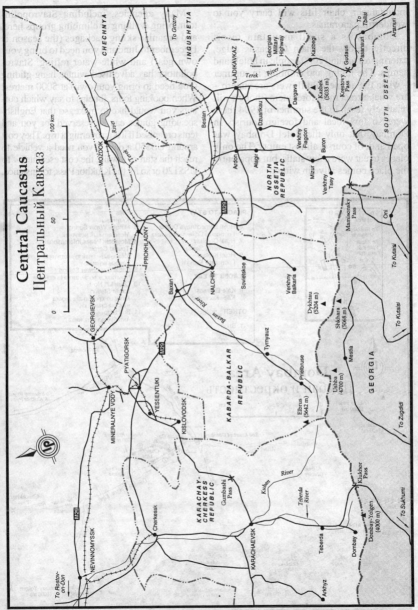

Central Caucasus
Центральный Кавказ

mountaineer, chair lifts will carry you to wonderful panoramas.

Dombay is a small mountain resort directly below the main Caucasus ridge, catering for around 2000 people in hotels and camps. The hiking and climbing in summer – when the alpine wild flowers are superb – are what attract most foreigners (though still relatively few). In the summer of 1994 there were so few local and foreign tourists in Dombay that only the Hotel Dombay was open and, of course, almost empty. The only places to eat were a few stalls, but apparently the place comes alive in winter.

Many agencies, including Stavropolintour, bring walking or climbing groups here, and organise skiing packages (the season is December to June and you need to bring your own gear) and white-water rafting. Stavropolintour has advertised winter hang-gliding (you need to bring your own) at 5000 metres! When booking tours, it helps to say which outings you would like to make, so that English-speaking guides can be reserved for you and tents organised if it is an overnight trip. They cost around US$50 a day; if you need a vehicle to reach the start of a walk, the cost escalates – to US$120 or so for the Klukhor Pass, for instance.

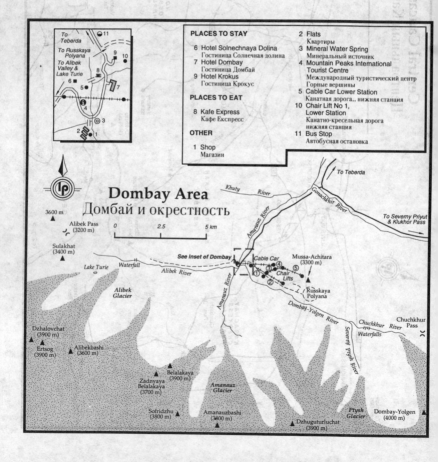

PLACES TO STAY	2 Flats
	Квартиры
6 Hotel Solnechnaya Dolina	3 Mineral Water Spring
Гостиница Солнечная долина	Минеральный источник
7 Hotel Dombay	4 Mountain Peaks International
Гостиница Домбай	Tourist Centre
9 Hotel Krokus	Международный туристический центр
Гостиница Крокус	Горные вершины
	5 Cable Car Lower Station
PLACES TO EAT	Канатная дорога,, нижняя станция
	10 Chair Lift No 1,
8 Kafe Express	Lower Station
Кафе Експресс	Канатно-кресельная дорога
	нижняя станция
OTHER	11 Bus Stop
	Автобусная остановка
1 Shop
Магазин

Dombay Area
Домбай и окрестность

RICHARD NEBESKÝ

RICHARD NEBESKÝ

RICHARD NEBESKY

RICHARD NEBESKY

RICHARD NEBESKY

A: Mt Ine & Dzhuguturluchat
   Glacier, Caucasus
B: Dombay-Yolgen River, Dombay, Caucasus

C: Wild flowers, Dombay, Caucasus
D: Wild flowers, Dombay, Caucasus
E: Wild flowers, Dombay, Caucasus

Scene on walk from Severny Priyut to Klukhor Pass, Caucasus

Dombay is at the heart of the Teberdinsky Nature Reserve, which stretches up to 20 km either side of a line from Teberda to the crest of the Caucasus main ridge. The reserve has a herd of European bison, reintroduced after being wiped out here in the 1920s, plus lynx, bear, deer, a unique flora and bird life that includes the black griffon. Guides are genuinely essential on many routes as trails are not marked.

After the Russians, the second-biggest ethnic group in the 400,000-plus population of the Karachay-Cherkess Republic (Karachaevo-Cherkesskaya Respublika), in which Dombay lies, are the 100,000-plus Karachay. They are a Muslim Turko-Tatar mountain people who, until the revolution, lived mainly on meat and milk. Their old, wooden-hut capital, Uchkulan in the upper Kuban Valley east of Teberda, was replaced in 1926 by the new town of Karachaevsk. The Karachay were exiled en masse to Siberia for allegedly siding with the Germans in WW II, but allowed back in 1957.

Information

There's nowhere official to change money, so do that before you come to Dombay. There's a post and telegraph office in the Hotel Dombay.

Kiosks outside some of Dombay's hotels sometimes have district maps. But you are more likely to find maps in Teberda.

Mussa-Achitara

The 3000-metre Mussa-Achitara (Horse Thief) ridge on the north side of the Dombay-Yolgen Valley has views all round the Dombay peaks, valleys and glaciers. First, take two chair lifts – No 1 behind the Hotel Krokus, then No 3 straight up the mountain to the upper cable car station (2260 metres). Two further chair lifts then rise to the ridge, where on a clear day you can make out Elbrus to the east. Total cost either way is around US$5. It's about a 45-minute walk to the nearby 3300-metre summit; some fairly strenuous ridge walking is also possible. The cable car was closed in summer at the time of writing, but is supposedly open in winter.

Walks

Chuchkhur Waterfalls & Ptysh Valley It's an easy, scenic six km from the end of chair lift No 2 to two fine waterfalls on the Chuchkhur River. First you follow a vehicle track, then you branch across Russkaya Polyana clearing. Past the waterfalls, a steep path leads towards the Chuchkhur Glacier. Twenty minutes downstream from the falls, a path forks south for a steady two-km walk up the Severny (North) Ptysh Valley. Chair lift No 2 stops about 4 pm.

Amanauz Valley A marked trail, steep in parts, leads south from the end of the Dombay housing estate and goes for about four km, up through two sets of woods to a waterfall and the Devil's Throat viewpoint.

Alibek Glacier The track behind the Hotel Solnechnaya Dolina leads about six km up the Alibek Valley to a mountaineers' hostel, passing a climbers' cemetery after two km. From the hostel there's a path up to little Lake Turie near the Alibek Glacier, nine km from Dombay. A strenuous variation is to fork left from the path after the hostel, and head through woods to the dramatic Alibek Falls. If you cross the dodgy bridge at the foot of the falls and then scramble up the left side you can walk on the glacier and up the scree on its right side to Lake Turie. A longer trip is to the Alibek Pass at the head of the valley.

Klukhor Pass You need transport for this most spectacular of the regular day-hikes, which starts from Severny Priyut (Northern Shelter, 2040 metres), 17 km up the Gonachkhir Valley road. The goal is a 2782-metre pass over the Caucasus watershed, which still carries remnants of the Sukhumi Military Highway, built to help the Russians subdue the west Caucasus in the 19th century. The path leads up beside a stream through glorious alpine meadows to Lake Klukhor – with ice floes even in August –

then to the pass itself, on the Georgian border. The last part of the climb is littered with bizarre monuments to the WW II defenders of the pass.

The walk is six km each way, takes about six hours there and back including stops, and is usually only open from mid-June to mid-October. Over the pass, the path descends 20-odd km to Yuzhny Priyut (Southern Shelter) on the Abkhazian side, a 110-km drive from Sukhumi.

Other Walks Crystal Pass is a 20-km, 10 to 12-hour trip up over the north side of the Alibek Valley – with more great views. The treks to the Murudzhinskie and Azgekskie lake groups, in the ranges east and west of the Dombay-Teberda road respectively, involve overnight camping.

Climbs
Peaks tackled from Dombay include Sofridzhu (3800 metres), Dombay-Yolgen (4000 metres) and Klukhor Bashi (3600 metres) on the main Caucasus ridge, and Sulakhat (3400 metres) and Semenov-Bashi (3600 metres) above the Alibek Valley.

Other Activities
You can swim in the evenings in the Gornye Vershiny's pool, after passing a cursory medical on floor 4. The Gornye Vershiny and Solnechnaya Dolina both have decent saunas. Both of these hotels are only open in winter.

Even though we did not get to ski here in winter the skiing terrain looks excellent in the form of European Alps. There are a few good long and steep runs for experienced skiers from below the Mussa-Achitara peak where the chairlift No 5 ends at 3008 metres and down to 1620 meters. There is also some possibility of tree skiing. Around chairlift No 4 there are a couple of t-bars for inexperienced skiers. There is plenty of terrain for ski touring if you have a local guide, but beware of avalanches. It is advisable to bring your own ski equipment as rental equipment is over-used and too old.

Places to Stay & Eat
In the summer of 1994 there was such a lack of local and foreign visitors that only the *Hotel Dombay* (☎ 7 82 69) was open (the village apparently is livelier in the winter). It is a decent if purely functional establishment, with two-star standard rooms costing US$15/30, but we only payed US$7.50 for a single room. The rooms are clean, with balconies, private baths and great views. Meals in the restaurant (in winter only), at fixed times, are bland but filling.

The other places to stay are apparently open in winter. *Mountain Peaks International Tourist Centre* (Mezhdunarodny Turistsky Tsentr Gornye Vershiny) (☎ 2 60 2 36) is a little more Spartan than the Dombay. The best hotel is the comfortable, wooden, trade union-run *Hotel Solnechnaya Dolina (Sunny Valley)*. The reasonably priced co-op restaurant at its south end has the best food in Dombay and is open to anyone. It also has an upstairs coffee and tea bar. Dombay's postal index is 357191.

In summer the only place to eat in the evening was *Kafe Express*, in a caravan opposite Hotel Dombay. Their cheap borsch was good, but the chicken tasted like a hen – very tough. Otherwise, during the day there were several stalls selling shashlyk, sweets and drinks at the bus station, and at the top of chairlifts 1 and 3.

Entertainment
In winter the convivial disco-bar on floor 9 of the Gornye Vershiny is the nocturnal hot spot. Sometimes there's alcohol available. There's champagne and ice cream in the 2nd-floor bar of the Hotel Dombay, and an atmosphereless disco in its basement.

Getting There & Away
The only way is by road. Coaches from Pyatigorsk usually take the 225-km route through Cherkessk and Karachaevsk – which takes about five hours – but there's a shorter, more scenic route along the A157 road over the 2044-metre Gumbashi Pass (with good views of Elbrus) between Kislovodsk and Karachaevsk. The fastest

way for individual travellers is a Stavropol-intour chauffeured car, for about US$89 one way from Pyatigorsk, or US$105 with a guide. A normal taxi can do the trip to/from Mineralnye Vody to Teberda for under US$49, depending on your bargaining skills.

Buses might not get you to Dombay on your appointed day: there are two a day between Teberda and Dombay (US$0.30, 20 minutes), around three daily to Teberda from Mineralnye Vody (five hours), one from Stavropol and none from Pyatigorsk. The nearest mainline railway station is Nevin-nomyssk, 180 km north. There are about three buses daily between there and Teberda. It's possible to visit Dombay as a day trip from Pyatigorsk.

TEBERDA
ТЕБЕРДА
Twenty km down the valley from Dombay, Teberda is larger and older. Both the *Hotel Teberda* (☎ 7 14 25) and *Hotel Klukhori* were closed at the time of writing, so there was nowhere to stay if you missed the bus. Many outings are common to both resorts, but the walks to the Dzhamagatskie Narzany mineral springs (west up the Dzhamagat Valley, six to seven hours round trip) and the Mukhinsky Pass (east) start here. The town has a nature museum and small zoo with animals from the Teberdinsky Reserve.

NALCHIK
НАЛЬЧИК
Population: 250,000
The town of Nalchik, 550 metres high in the foothills of the Caucasus, which rises to its west and south, began life in 1822 as a Russian fort. This is the nearest starting point for a day trip to the Elbrus foothills, if you don't want to sleep up there.

Nalchik is the capital of the Kabarda-Balkar Republic (Kabardino-Balkarskaya Respublika) within the Russian Federation. Around 360,000 of the republic's 800,000 people are Kabarda, and some 70,000 people, most of whom live in the mountains, are Balkar. The Kabarda are the most numerous of the peoples known as Circassian or

Adyge. They're famous for horse-breeding. In 1557 they united with Russia in the face of a Turkish invasion, the first Caucasus people to do so. Both the Kabarda and the Balkar are Muslim and heavily patriarchal.

Orientation & Information
The main streets are prospekt Lenina, running south from the railway station through the town centre, and prospekt A Shogentsukova (formerly ulitsa Respub-likanskaya) two blocks east. The Nart and Nalchik hotels are on ulitsa Lermontova, just east off prospekt Shogentsukova, and the main post, telephone and telegraph office is at prospekt Shogentsukova 5 on the corner of ulitsa Lermontova. The bank for foreign exchange – open from 10 am to 1 pm, Monday to Friday – is a block away on the corner of ulitsa Golovko.

The local Intourist office (☎ 7 77 86 or 9 93 71) is at ulitsa Pushkina 56. Knizhny Magazin Elbrus on the corner of prospekt Lenina and ulitsa Golovko has a good stock of maps of places near and far. The regional telephone code is 86622.

Things to See
A large, fine park stretches over two km south from the Nart and Nalchik hotels. From its southern end a chair lift and a cable car cross lakes to wooded hills. The interesting **Kabardino-Balkar Regional Museum** (Obedinenny muzey), open daily from 10 am to 6 pm at ulitsa Gorkogo 52, just off ulitsa Tolstogo, has good carpets *(kiiz)*. The **Fine Arts Museum** at prospekt Lenina 35 is open 11 am to 7 pm except Friday.

Chegem Canyon The canyon road turns west at the south end of Chegem-2 village, about 17 km north of Nalchik. The spectacular part of the canyon, about 44 km up, not far past the 30 metre Chegem Waterfall, is 250 metres high but only 20 metres wide (through which river and road both squeeze). Around Verkhny Chegem, a further 20 or so km up, are several archaeological sites, including Lygyt village with the remains of

Muslim and Christian temples and tombs going back to the 10th century.

Golubye Ozera The Golubye Ozera (Blue Lakes) are three or four pretty lakes 39 km up the Cherek Valley from Urvan, about 13 km east of Nalchik. Take the left fork after Sovietskoe village in the valley. The right fork leads to Bezengi, below the Bezengi section of the Caucasus, which has several 5000-metre peaks, like Dykhtau and Shkhara.

Places to Stay & Eat

The good-looking four-star *Hotel Druzhba* (☎ 222 23 10) at ulitsa Pirogova 8, about four km south of town on a landscaped hillside, has seven storeys with 134 standard rooms. There is also a restaurant, several bars and a swimming pool. It is also possible to stay in the two-star *Hotel Nart* (☎ 2 70 26/8, 2 74 80) at ulitsa Lermontova 2, a medium-sized 1970s tower block where rooms cost US$16.20/24.50. But the *Hotel Nalchik*, next door at prospekt Shogentsukova 3, has more atmosphere. It's smaller, older (built 1935, renovated 1980), and also two star and similarly priced. Rooms in both hotels have attached bathrooms – and while both restaurants have loud music, the Nalchik's is more convivial than the Nart's echoing dungeon. Both hotels' postal index is 360000.

The *Restoran Elbrus* in the park is open till 10 pm daily. The *Restoran Sosruko* at the head of the chair lift is constructed in the giant likeness of Sosruko, the Kabardian Prometheus. The *market* is just off ulitsa Gorkogo, half a block north of ulitsa Tolstogo.

Getting There & Away

Direct services to Nalchik are poor apart from daily buses to Mineralnye Vody, so it's often best to use a train or plane to Mineralnye Vody, 115 km north. Nalchik flights include Moscow daily (US$123, 2½ hours), and Yerevan, Krasnodar, Baku, Rostov-on-Don and Simferopol on some days. The only direct long-distance trains seem to be the daily 39-hour services to/from Moscow, through Mineralnye Vody and Rostov-on-Don. For short hops from Pyatigorsk, 100 km north, or Vladikavkaz, 115 km south-east, buses are also good.

Getting Around

Bus No 17, which runs between the airport and Dolinsk suburb, stops on prospekt Shogentsukova at the corner of ulitsa Lermontova (close to the centre and the Nart and Nalchik hotels) and near the park chair lift. Bus No 1 covers the same stretch of prospekt Shogentsukova.

ELBRUS AREA
ПРИЭЛЬБРУСЬЕ

Elbrus rises on a northern spur of the main Caucasus ridge at the west end of the Baxan Valley. Tourist facilities littered along the valley floor make it less attractive than Dombay, but the mountains are just as majestic and there are fine walks, climbs and skiing above the human detritus. The area – known in Russian as Prielbruse (Around-Elbrus Area) – pulls in a more seriously 'Outward Bound' crowd than Dombay, but day-trippers from Nalchik or the Caucasus mineral water spas can use chair lifts or cable cars to reach the slopes of Elbrus, or view its peaks from across the valley. The highest peak on the south side is Ushba (4700 metres) but several others exceed 4000 metres.

The upper Baxan Valley is a chief home of the Balkar, a Muslim Turko-Tatar people who, like the Karachay to their west, were exiled for supposed collaboration in WW II but returned in 1957. Many farmsteads stand empty but occasional horsemen tend herds of goats or cattle. The ramshackle Balkar villages are a far cry from standard Soviet-era settlements.

Information

The village of Terskol is at the upper part of the Azau Valley along which are sprinkled several hotels. At the western end of the valley, the road ends where the Azau cable car and the Elbrus mountain trail begin.

The vast majority of tourists come here with a tour group and as there are no restaurants (except one café in Terskol) everyone takes meals in their hotel, which need to be ordered one day in advance if you have not payed for it with your room. In the village of Terskol there is a mountain (ski) rescue, post office and two sparsely stocked general stores. There are no banks or money exchange counters. All the foreigners we met were in groups just to climb Elbrus and other mountains. It seems that mountain guides are still necessary, so make certain that if you want to camp you let them know when making your booking, so the guides can be prepared for high-altitude camping.

Elbrus

Elbrus is nearly 1000 metres above anything else in the vicinity. It's a volcanic cone with two peaks, the western being the higher at 5642 metres; the eastern peak is 5621 metres. Some people claim it to be the highest mountain in Europe as it lies on the Caucasus ridge that is the geographical border of Europe and Asia. The upper slopes are said to be coated in ice up to 200 metres thick, numerous glaciers slide down its flanks and several rivers, including the Kuban, start here. Its name, meaning Two Heads, comes from Persian. In the Balkar language it's Mingi-Tau (Thousands – ie Very Big – Mountain).

The first unconfirmed climb of Elbrus was in 1829 by a Russian expedition, but it was a lone Circassian hunter named Killar who was hired as a guide and he apparently reached the peak on his own. The lower east peak was not officially conquered until 31 July 1868 by a British expedition with D W Freshfield, A W Moore, C C Tucker, a guide François Devouassoud and two local hunters. It was not until 28 July 1874 that the higher west peak was climbed by another British expedition, consisting of F Gardiner, F C Grove, H Walker and P Knubel. The Soviet regime of course had to do things en

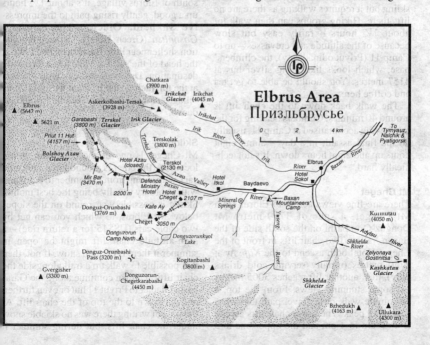

masse, the proletarian way for propaganda purposes, and in the 1980s had groups of up to 400 climbers at one time reaching the peak. Nowadays, the ascent and descent have apparently been done in many ways just to be different: on skis, by the landing of light aircraft, hang gliding and para-gliding; but the most unusual one was apparently on a motorcycle fitted with skis.

The Azau cable car rises in two stages (US$15 return) from 2350 metres to the Mir Bar at 3500 metres, which is open in the main ski season, and from where you can see both the twin peaks and the main Caucasus ridge. The last cable car down is at about 3.30 pm, but the day we wished to take it the departure time was 3.20 pm (maybe the operators were running according to their Caucasus time) and we ended up walking down. A chair lift continues to 3800 metres, which in some summers might be above the snowline, with year-round skiing – and cold! The area above the chair lift is definitely good for summer skiing but it requires walking as there are no lifts there. Hiking groups can then walk for about 1½ hours – fairly easy but slow because of the altitude and crevasses – up to Camp 11 (Priyut odinadtsaty), the climbers' base, which looks like a big silver bus at 4157 metres. You should be able to get tea and coffee here.

The walk back down to the chair lift is around 40 minutes. Climbers heading for the top, having acclimatised at Camp 11, usually do the final assault in a day – about eight hours up and eight hours down. It's not technically hard.

Mt Cheget

There are fine views across to Elbrus from Mt Cheget, a spur of 3769-metre Mt Donguz-Orunbashi on the south side of the Baxan Valley. Two chair lifts in front of the Cheget Hotel both ascend to the *Kafe Ay* at 2750 metres (usually serving cold drinks only), then another lift reaches 3005 metres for some stunning views. From the top, a 45-minute walk on a gravel path takes you to a small peak. The lower chair lifts ascend from 9 am to 4 pm and the upper one to 3

pm. You can descend until about half an hour after ascents stop. A one-way trip on one chair costs US$1.

From Kafe Ay there's an easy path of about seven km round the side of Mt Cheget, passing Donguzorunkyol Lake, to Donguzorun Camp North (Severny priyut Donguzorun) at 2500 metres, south of Mt Donguz-Orunbashi. Mt Donguzorun-Chegetkarabashi, which is about 4450 metres, soars behind the lake. From Camp North it's three steep km up to the snow-covered Donguz-Orunbashi or Nakra Pass on the Georgian border.

Other Walks

An easy walk, two to three hours one way, leads up the Terskol Valley from behind Terskol village to a dramatic view of Elbrus behind the 'hanging' Terskol Glacier, which drips over a hill's edge.

From the paved road up the Adylsu Valley south of Elbrus village, it's about 1½ hours up a good, gently rising path to the impressive Shkhelda Glacier. The *Zelyonaya Gostinitsa* (Green Hotel), an accommodation shelter near little Bashkarinskoe Lake at the head of the Adylsu Valley, is a day-walk destination. Day-walk valleys with glaciers at the top include the Irikchat west of Elbrus village, and the Yusengi, south from Baydaevo.

Skiing

Mt Cheget is one of the two main skiing locations (the other is around the Azau cable car), with skiing from December to April and with February usually being the best month. Skiing is possible year-round on the slopes below Mt Elbrus, to which you can get by two cable cars (US$15 for a return ride) – a high-altitude chair lift might be open in summer if there is enough snow. If not, then it is possible to walk up a trail alongside the chair lifts and then continue along the Garabashi Glacier to Priyut 11 hut or even further, and ski down to the top of the chair lift. At the time of writing there was no skiable snow under the chair lifts, but during summer it

Summer Skiing under Mt Elbrus

I arrived at Hotel Cheget in the Azau Valley from Pyatigorsk, in the central Caucasus range of southern Russia, under low cloud and drizzle. My disappointment did not last long, as within a couple of hours the heavy clouds lifted and high and mighty peaks dominated the view from the valley on every side – even the twin peaks of Mt Elbrus were visible. While gathering information for this book, I was also trying to find out whether it was possible to do some summer skiing, and where I could hire some ski equipment. Everyone assured me that it was possible to ski but that I would have to walk from where the chair lift ended, as this was where the snow began. There was nowhere to hire ski equipment as there was no snow under the chair lift. But then the Russian guide of a trekking group suggested I try the Mountain Rescue Service. There I managed to bargain down the price of skis, boots, poles and gloves to US$5. The price must have included the three glasses of cheap Russian vodka I had to drink to cement the deal. The equipment was in decent condition and included Atomic giant slalom skis and Salomon racing boots. Such good gear I would not get at a rental place.

The next day I rose early and after breakfast caught a bus from Hotel Cheget to the village of Terskol, from where I had to walk for 40 minutes to the cable car farther up at the end of the Azau Valley. The tourist price of US$9 return included both the cable cars, which took me to Mir Bar point (3470 metres). The chair lift from Mir up to Garabashi (3800 metres) was not running as expected. I had no choice but to walk up, which was pleasant in the cool mountain breeze and the warmth of the summer sun. The views of the glaciated mountains were breathtaking, while the twin peaks of Mt Elbrus dominated the view above the chair lift. On reaching the snow line at Garabashi, I put my ski boots on and continued walking up through the snow. It was 1 pm and I was running out of time: the last cable car returned at 3.30 pm and if I was to have a decent ski, I had at least to reach Camp 11 (Priyut odinadtsaty) at a height of 4157 metres. I noticed a snow-clearing machine transporter with a driver at the chair lift's hut. His asking price to Priyut odinadtsaty was US$15 and no bargaining. As I was running out of time and I wanted to ski, there was not much choice.

The view of the snow-covered peaks and deep valleys from Priut was even more magnificent – just like in the Alps but a little higher (not that a mortal can really tell). It was quite warm as the sun beat down mercilessly on the snow, which reflected the sun's rays. I had lunch below Priut hut, which is where most climbers stay before they set out to conquer Mt Elbrus. Unfortunately, the beauty of the glacier around the hut is spoiled by an unbelievable pile of rubbish, mostly rusting building material, kitchen utensils and discarded containers. While having lunch I had to overlook this mess to enjoy the view of the faraway mountains and glaciers.

It was time to make my first ever turns in the Caucasus. Unfortunately, it was already too late in the day for optimum summer snow conditions. The snow was very wet and sticky but once I got my rhythm it became enjoyable. Just like most other glaciers, the terrain was not very steep and before I knew it I was back at Garabashi.

Along the way I skied past three groups of climbers. Elbrus is a very popular mountain to climb and there were hordes of Germans, Scandinavians, Canadians and Americans there to place their flags on the peak of what is (technically speaking) Europe's highest mountain, since it sits in the middle of the dividing range between the European and Asian continents.

As I made my way back to the Mir station, the cable car departed according to some local Caucasus timetable – 10 minutes early – stranding me and two Russians. While one of the Russians started walking down, Oleg (from St Petersburg) and I waited. Gradually we realised that the cable car was not returning and we would have to walk down. As we commenced our descent, the weather closed in. There was no trail and we could only follow the remains of a dirt road that was barely visible through the fog. The walk was made more pleasant by having someone to chat to and, like most conversations in Russia, after the initial talk about work and family it centred around Russian and Central European politics and economics.

We arrived at the middle station in just over an hour, and were pleasantly surprised to find people here as it was one hour after the official closing time. They promised to take us down, but in 10 minutes time. We would have gladly waited half an hour or more to avoid walking in the rain again for at least another 1½ hours. As it was, there was still another hour's walk waiting for us along the Azau Valley to the village of Terskol and then back to Hotel Cheget.

Richard Nebesky

might, according to some locals, be possible to ski here.

It should be possible during the winter season to hire gear in the basement of the Cheget Hotel, but in summer they might be closed, especially if there is not enough snow below the chairlift. Also, as there are very few tourists here, facilities might not be open in the summer. It is better to bring your own equipment as the local rental equipment is old and well used (not safe). The lifts are pretty primitive and the accident rate for climbers and skiers is reportedly alarming. The skiing on the gently sloping Garabashi Glacier is slow, but in winter skiing around and under the Azau cable car looks great, with long, steep and challenging runs.

Organised Tours

Several companies run tours to the area and one you might like to try is Exodus (☎ (0181) 675 5550, 673 0859; fax (0181) 673 0779) at 9 Weir Rd, London SW12 0LT, UK. Their 16-day climbing tour of Elbrus is UK£1030, and they have other tours into the region. Another is Steppes East (☎ (01285) 810 267/567; fax (01285) 810 693) at Castle Eaton, Swindon, Wiltshire, SN6 6JU, UK. They have 14-day tours of climbing Mt Elbrus and trekking around the base of it, as well as helicopter skiing holidays.

US firms offering Mt Elbrus climbs include REI Adventures (☎ (206) 891 2631, toll-free 800 622 2236; fax (206) 395 4744), PO Box 1938, Sumner, WA 98390; Mountain Travel Sobek (☎ (510) 527 8100, toll-free 1 800 227 2384; fax (510) 525 7710) of 6420 Fairmount Avenue, El Cerrito, CA 94530; and Mountain Madness (☎ (206) 937 8389; fax (206) 937 1772) of 4218 SW Alaska St, Suite 206, Seattle, WA 98116.

One of the few reliable Russian tour companies that we found is Pilgrim Tours (Moskovskoe Turisticheskoe Agentstvo Piligrim) (☎ (095) 365 45 63 or (095) 207 32 43; fax (095) 369 03 89; e-mail pilgrimtours@ glas.apc.org.) at 1-y Kirpichny pereulok 17, 105118 Moscow, which has been used by REI Adventures. They have many tours of the Elbrus area. The climb of Mt Elbrus is an 11-day excursion that costs US$750 per person (in a group of six to nine people), not including air fares. Other tours include a ski tour, circle trek, rest in the mountains and heli-skiing (five days worth for US$2000 per person in a group of 10 to 12 people), all in the Elbrus area.

Places to Stay & Eat

Western groups are nearly always based at the miserable, two-star Hotel Itkol (☎ 5 12 47, 5 18 80) between Baydaevo and Terskol (postal index 361605). Its rooms have balconies, but in the bathrooms everything leaks and cockroaches thrive. Meals are barely palatable and rarely identifiable, though the packed lunches are fine. All this for US$16 per person. There's a post office and a downstairs bar offering brandy and ice cream in the evenings. Another place you might possibly be lodged in is the Hotel Sokol, a small collection of wooden buildings just southwest of Elbrus village. The dorms for climbers at Camp 11 on Elbrus are quite comfortable though the toilets are grim – but what a view!

The Hotel Cheget has a bar, a market (only souvenirs most days) nearby and kiosks at the foot of the chair lifts, selling things like shashlyk, pichin (a meat-filled flat bread), shchorpa (a Balkar soup) and soft drinks. The small rooms are OK from US$20/30, but the three meals per day (US$3) are cheap and dull. In Terskol there's a Defence Ministry hotel with a swimming pool and a popular bar. At the mineral springs, 15 minutes walk down the valley from the Hotel Itkol, is a bar selling fish pâté, wine and cheap lunches. It closes at about 4 pm.

Getting There & Away

The way to the Elbrus area is up the Baxan River valley from the Baxan town bypass on the Pyatigorsk-Nalchik road – it's 110 km to Azau Valley at the head of the valley road. The Baxan valley is of majestic proportions but scarred by power lines and pipelines, quarries and other 20th-century debris. Bits of the road are often washed away and it's under constant repair. Zhankhoteko village, near the start of the valley, has a roadside market selling colourful local woollens. Further up, the Balkar town of Tyrnyauz, built to mine molybdenum and tungsten – used in the Soviet space effort – has a real Satanic mills feel.

A Stavropolintour full-day excursion from Pyatigorsk costs around US$92 for individuals, US$30 for group members, including a guide. Buses go all the way to Azau and Terskol from Mineralnye Vody (US$2.50, four hours) twice a day and some can drop you off on the outskirts of Pyatigorsk (US$2). There are about three a day to Nalchik (US$1.10). It's an extra US$0.30 for luggage.

Getting Around

Between 9 am and 5 pm there is an hourly bus along Azau Valley from Terskol down to the Hotel Sokol and back up the valley. The fare is US$0.10.

VLADIKAVKAZ
ВЛАДИКАВКАЗ
Population: 300,000

An untidy town, hinting that the edge of Europe isn't far away, Vladikavkaz (Queen of the Caucasus) was called Ordzhonikidze from 1931-44 and 1954-90 after the Georgian Grigory 'Sergo' Ordzhonikidze, who led the imposition of Bolshevism on the Caucasus region in the 1920s. Some locals say he pursued his mission with near-genocidal enthusiasm.

Vladikavkaz is 740 metres high on the swift Terek River, at the north end of the Georgian Military Highway to Tbilisi. There have been settlements here intermittently since the 3rd millennium BC. The Russians built a fort in 1784. The Germans were stopped just a few km north in WW II.

The real attractions of the area are the bizarre relics of old Ossetian settlements out in the valleys to the west. You need at least half a day, preferably more, for these.

Vladikavkaz is the capital of North Ossetia (Severo-Osetinskaya Respublika), a republic within the Russian Federation. About 630,000 of the republic's populace are Ossetians, who are thought to be descended from a group of Sarmatians, an Indo-European people from east Iran, who arrived on the steppe to the north in the last centuries BC and were pushed into the Caucasus by the Huns in the 4th century AD. They assimilated with local tribes to form a people called the Alans or Alani, whose state lasted from about the 8th century to the 13th, when it was destroyed by the Tatars. Some escaped deep into the mountains and by the 18th century their descendants – the Ossetians – were mainly to be found in the valleys west of Vladikavkaz. Ossetia was incorporated into Russia, apparently peacefully, in 1774.

Most Ossetians are now Christian but maintain some animistic practices like ram sacrifice. Their main traditional festival is Jurgala, which lasts for 9 days from the second last Sunday of November. South Ossetia is across the Caucasus in Georgia.

The other main group that lived in eastern South Ossetia was the Ingush, who would have preferred to be part of neighbouring Ingushetia. (Today it is the Russians who make up the largest minority in South Ossetia.) This problem, aside from the usual ethnic hatred going back hundreds of years, dates back to 1944, when under Stalin's orders most Ingush were deported to Siberia for allegedly collaborating with the German invaders. They were rehabilitated during Khrushchev's rule in 1957 and allowed to return home. Another legacy of the Stalin era was the allocation of the western part of Ingushetia (known as Checheno-Ingushetia at the time) to North Ossetia. The returning Ingush found most of their property occupied by Ossetians.

Under communist rule both groups, Ossetians and Ingush, coexisted peaceably but this was an illusion. In June 1992, the Russian Duma passed a motion setting up an autonomous Ingushetia, which triggered some unfortunate events. The two groups engaged in bloody clashes from 22 October 1992, resulting in the deaths of hundreds of people. Russian forces were sent in to try to defuse the conflict. According to local accounts they sided with the Ossetians,

Vladikavkaz
Владикавказ

0   250   500 m

committing atrocities in the process. The combined force of the Russians and the Ossetians eventually forced the entire Ingush population of over 50,000 into Ingushetia, to live in extremely poor conditions – most of their houses in North Ossetia were destroyed and their property confiscated.

Orientation & Information

The Hotel Vladikavkaz is on the west bank of the Terek River, a half-km walk from the main street, prospekt Mira. For information there is Osetia-Intur (☎ 3 35 04) at prospekt Mira 19. There are post, telephone and tele-

graph offices on ulitsa Vatutina at the corner of ulitsa Kuybysheva, and opposite the railway station at the corner of ulitsa Markova and ulitsa Kirova.

The Vladikavkaz telephone code is 86722. For books and maps, try Knigi at prospekt Mira 31 or Voennaya Kniga on ulitsa Kuybysheva.

Mosque

Most postcards of Vladikavkaz show the Sunni mosque, located 100 metres from the Hotel Vladikavkaz beside the Terek. It's the most eye-catching building in town with its

PLACES TO STAY

13 Hotel Vladikavkaz
    Гостиница Владикавказ
17 Hotel Kavkaz
    Гостиница Кавказ

PLACES TO EAT

3   Kafe Metelitsa &
    Bread Shop
    Кафе Метелица и
    хлебный магазин

OTHER

1   Train Station
    Железнодорожный
    вокзал
2   Post, Telegraph &
    Telephone Office
    Почта, телеграф и
    телефон
4   Knigi (Bookshop)
    Книги
5   Detsky Mir
    Магазин Детский мир
6   Voennaya Kniga
    (Bookshop)
    Магазин Военная книга

7   Market
    Рынок
8   Post, Telegraph &
    Telephone Office
    Почта, телеграф и
    телефон
9   Telegraph &
    Telephone Office
    Телеграф и телефон
10 Russian Drama
    Theatre
    Русский драматический
    театр
11 North Ossetian Art
    Museum
    Северо-осетинский
    художественный
    музей
12 Former Intourist Hotel
    Бывшая гостиница
    Интуриста
14 Mosque
    Мечеть
15 North Ossetian History,
    Architecture &
    Literature Museum
    Музей истории,
    архитектуры и

литературы
Северной Осетии
16 Khetagurov
    House-Museum
    Дом-музей К.Л.
    Хетагурова
18 North Ossetian State
    University
    Северо-осетинский
    государственный
    университет
19 Bank
    Банк
20 Khetagurov Ossetian
    Literature Museum
    Музей осетинской
    литературы имени
    К.Л. Хетагурова
21 Pushkin Statue
    Памятник А.С.
    Пушкину
22 North Ossetia Council
    of Ministers
    Государственное
    министерство
    Северо-Осетинской
    Республики

blue dome, twin towers, and 300 Koranic inscriptions on the walls, but is utterly untypical. Built in 1906-08 by a Baku oil magnate with an Ossetian wife, it's now open as a museum from 10 am to 5.30 pm daily except Tuesday and Saturday.

Town Centre

The centre is low-rise, with a number of oldish buildings on ulitsa Gorkogo, ulitsa Butyrina, and prospekt Mira, a 1.25-km tree-lined boulevard given over to pedestrians and trams. The **North Ossetian History, Architecture & Literature Museum** at No 11, open 10 am to 7 pm daily except Monday, has some amazingly deformed old Alani skulls. The **North Ossetian Art Museum**, closed Wednesdays, is at No 12.

The **Khetagurov Ossetian Literature Museum** at ulitsa Botoeva 3, in an unusual old church, is named after Kosta Khetagurov

(1859-1906), who more or less invented that field of culture. It's closed Tuesday. Khetagurov's house, at ulitsa Butyrina 19, is also a museum; closed Monday.

Places to Stay & Eat

The *Hotel Vladikavkaz* (☎ 5 65 54, 5 20 28) at ulitsa Kotsoeva 75, postal index 362015, overlooks the Terek. The comfortable rooms have balconies (US$40/50), the staff are agreeable and the restaurants are reasonable. It is also possible to stay in the inexpensive and basic rooms of the *bus station*, between 7 pm to 6 am only, for US$4 per person.

The **Osnovnoy Zal** (Main Hall) on floor 2 of the hotel has a standard restaurant band and more varied food. There's also a bar on floor 2 with coffee, brandy, cakes and balcony tables.

Outside the hotel, apart from the large, well-stocked fruit and vegetable market on

The Situation in Chechnya

The Chechens of the northern Caucasus belong linguistically to the Nakh group and are Sunni Muslims. They are by reputation very proud, independently minded and unruly. They live by strict codes of honour and revenge, and clan blood feuds are well entrenched in their patriarchal culture. As a nation they have suffered greatly at the hands of the Russians, who conquered them, along with other neighbouring nationalities, in 1859 after a 30-year war. In 1944, with great loss of life, many Chechens were deported to Siberia for allegedly collaborating with the Germans – though it is hard to see how they could have done so since the Germans did not reach Chechnya. In effect, this was Stalin's pretext for disposing of potentially troublesome nationalities. The survivors were allowed to return after Khrushchev's amnesty in 1957.

Many Russians regard the Chechens with fear as a nation of brutal mafiosi who run a large underworld in Moscow and most other parts of Russia, involved in extortion, drug dealing, prostitution and other organised crime. It is believed that there are three major Chechen gangs in Moscow, while others have extended their operations into Central and Western Europe as well as the USA. The conflict between such Mafia groups is one of the factors that make Chechnya hard to rule. Contrary to popular belief, however, most Chechens are not mafiosi who drive Mercedes Benz cars and wear expensive suits. Such people make up only a very small part of the population, while many more are poor and frustrated with the political and economic situation, and were so even before the Russian onslaught which began in 1994.

In the summer of 1994 it was possible, but not advisable, to visit Chechnya. The capital, Grozny, whose name in Russian means 'awesome' or 'terrible' (Ivan the Terrible was Ivan Grozny in his native tongue) was a depressing, grey and dusty place with oil fields on its outskirts. There was only one very dilapidated hotel, the Hotel Kavkaz, where the largest group of guests was the presidential guard. The streets of the city seemed to be run by mafiosi, while other young men (presumably members of the Chechen army) drove around in Volvos and Mercedes Benzes and brandished Kalashnikov AK-47s. As of September 1994 Chechnya was in a state of civil war, and the situation continued to deteriorate during the time of writing of this book.

According to the Russian Federation, Chechnya is one of its republics in the northern Caucasus, bordered by the Russian province of Stavropol, the republics of Ingushetia, North Ossetia and Dagestan, and Georgia, a separate CIS nation. The independently minded Chechens think otherwise: they declared independence from the Russian Federation in 1991. Leading the republic at the time of writing is President Dzhokar Dudaev, a former Soviet bomber pilot and air-force general.

---

ulitsa Kuybysheva, the food scene is sad. On prospekt Mira we found only a few state-run cafés, the promising but never open basement *Kafe Metelitsa*, and a *restaurant* in the back garden (cum building site) of the former Hotel Intourist at No 19. There, the menu and food are reasonable but the surliness of the staff takes all possible pleasure out of eating – if you can get any food out of them in the first place! There's a good bread shop called *Khleb* above Kafe Metelitsa.

Getting There & Away

Air The airport is at Beslan, 22 km north. There are daily flights to/from Moscow (US$130), and less frequent ones elsewhere including Krasnodar, Rostov-on-Don, Sochi, Tbilisi and Yerevan.

Train Vladikavkaz is on a branch railway line that brings just a single skoryy train a day from Moscow (43 hours) via Rostov-on-Don and Mineralnye Vody (3¾ hours). There's a slow train to/from Adler (via Sochi) every two days.

Road Public buses run at least as far as Mineralnye Vody. By car it's an easy 115 km from Nalchik. To the south the spectacular Georgian Military Highway winds over the Caucasus – it's 70 km to Kazbegi, 220 km to Tbilisi.

Be warned, though, that the roads around the region are apparently unsafe and hold-ups of cars, trucks and even buses do occasionally occur. We did see some armed men on a few of these buses.

The road to invasion was paved in October 1991, when Dudaev was elected president, apparently by a small minority, and declared Chechnya independent. Within a few days Russian President Boris Yeltsin declared a state of emergency, but this was rejected by the Russian parliament as unconstitutional and undemocratic. Meanwhile, 650 Russian troops were sent to Chechnya and occupied strategic places such as the airport and government buildings. However, they quickly withdrew, not only because the state of emergency was rejected by the parliament, but also because they realised that they could not defend their positions against the armed resistance of the Chechens. A war of words ensued and Chechnya was left isolated, surrounded by Russian and CIS territory.

Chechen tactics included hijacking. Five hijacks were conducted between 1991 and 1993, then in 1994 came three hijackings of buses at Mineralnye Vody airport. During the third of these, five Russians died and 16 were injured when the local Russian OMON (or security police) force botched a rescue attempt. In September 1994, the situation deteriorated further. Chechen rebels opposed to Dudaev's regime were formed into military units with Russian backing. The rebel leader Umar Avturkhanov seemed to have the support of Ruslan Khasbulatov, the former speaker of the Russian parliament who was one of the leaders of the failed putsch against President Yeltsin in 1993. The rebels tried several times to take Grozny and during their last attempt they reached the presidential palace, but although assisted by the Russian air force and some of its troops the attack was repulsed.

After efforts to defeat the Chechen regime by lending support to rebel groups failed, Yeltsin made several requests for all armed groups to surrender their weapons to the Russians so that order could be restored. Russian patience ran out on 11 December 1994 and Chechnya was invaded, in spite of opposition to the action within Russia. Grozny was surrounded and almost bombed into submission, while Yeltsin tried to negotiate the total surrender of Dudaev's army. The attack on Grozny commenced on 31 December but was at first repulsed by the Chechens, who remained victorious for a few days. The now demoralised Russian forces had been badly led and had suffered heavy losses due to the bad planning of the whole operation – conscripts had been used instead of experienced troops.

Once the Russian forces were reinforced by combat-hardened troops, the fall of Grozny was only a matter of time. It is not yet clear when Russian troops actually took Grozny, since they claimed several times to have done so while fighting in the city continued.

continued on next page

AROUND VLADIKAVKAZ
ОКОЛО ВЛАДИКАВКАЗА

West of Vladikavkaz, a series of valleys pierces south from the plains into the Caucasus, narrowing in places to gorges. For thousands of years these have provided a refuge or permanent home for those who could defend them. The bleak mountainsides are dotted with the tall stone towers used for defence and living purposes by the 14th to 18th-century Ossetians/Alans, as well as with tombs of various shapes and sizes and other relics, making this one of the most bizarre landscapes in all of Russia. Hold-ups have occurred on the roads in this region.

You need four or five hours by car for Dargavs and the Kurtati Valley, about eight for the Tsey area.

Dargavs
Даргавс

This so-called 'village of the dead', some 40 km from Vladikavkaz in the Giseldon Valley, is the cemetery of an old Ossetian village, with 44 big, stone, beehive-shaped family tombs scattered up a hillside. Skeletons are visible through holes in the bases of these tombs. Dargavs is the most spectacular of many similar cemeteries in the district, which are likely to have been established by members of an ancestor cult. Some of the tombs are partly restored. To reach Dargavs, turn left at Gizel on the Vladikavkaz-Alagir road; fork left to Karmadon when the valley divides; then cross into the next valley to the west by a dirt road over the top from Karmadon.

But by the end of February 1995 Grozny was firmly in Russian control – a ruined city, where even the most basic amenities did not function. In the countryside the war continued well into the summer, but it was clear that, apart from the high mountains of the Caucasus and some thickly forested areas, the Russian army would eventually gain almost full control of Chechnya.

The fighting between the army and small groups of Chechens might go on for years, but what is more frightening for Russia is the prospect of more episodes like the one in the town of Budyonnovsk. In June 1995 a group of Chechens bribed their way through Russian checkpoints along the Russia-Chechnya border to a hospital in Budyonnovsk, more than 100 km into southern Russia. There they took about 1000 Russians hostage. While negotiations went on, armed confrontations between the Chechens and Russian security forces resulted in the deaths of around 120 of the hostages and 15 Chechen fighters. The Russian forces bungled again, and eventually the surviving Chechens negotiated their way back home. Russia provided buses to take them, and some hostages, back to the rebel-held parts of Chechnya, from where both groups walked away free.

By July 1995 both sides appeared keen to sign a peace treaty, since it seemed that without one the war could last for many years. Talks between the Russians and the Chechens were supervised by the Organisation for Security and Co-operation in Europe, and an agreement was signed on 30 July. Its terms were a ceasefire, the release of prisoners and the demilitarisation of Chechnya. The greatest problem, and one which both sides foresaw, was the difficulty of implementing the agreement. In parts of the country fighting continued and the signing of a comprehensive peace treaty may not occur in the foreseeable future. The major sticking-point – the fact that the Chechens demand total independence, while the Russians are only willing to grant them autonomy – was barely touched on in the 30 July agreement.

President Yeltsin and many other Russians fear that if Chechnya should become independent, they might then lose more of Russia's 88 regions (including 20 republics), and the Russian Federation might disintegrate, as the Soviet Union did only a few years ago. No Russian seems to want this, but a protracted guerrilla war with many casualties might be an even worse nightmare for the nation. Nor does Russia want to lose control of the oil pipelines that pass through Chechnya from Azerbaijan and Kazakhstan to Tuapse and Novorossiysk on Russia's Black Sea coast. ■

Kurtati Valley

Куртатинское ущелье

You can approach the glacier-watered Kurtati Valley (Kurtatinskoe ushchelie) either from Dzuarikau at its foot, on the Vladikavkaz-Alagir road, or by a dirt road over the top from a couple of km above Dargavs in the next valley east. The latter comes down near the small mining town of Verkhny Fiagdon. On the slopes west of Verkhny Fiagdon are the towers and cemetery of Tsimity, the valley's old main settlement. There are more towers and defence works around Kharisdzhin, a few km further up the valley. Between Verkhny Fiagdon and Dzuarikau the valley narrows to a gorge. At Dzivgis, just above the gorge, a high stone wall across a cave above the village betrays an old refuge against invaders.

Ardon Valley & Ossetian Military Highway

Ардонское ущелье и Военно-Осетинская дорога

The Ardon Valley runs south from Alagir, 40 km west of Vladikavkaz. Nuzal, above the mining village of Mizur, about 30 km from Alagir, has an old cemetery and towers, and a frescoed 12th or 13th-century chapel where David Soslan, the husband of Queen Tamara of Georgia, was buried.

The wooden **Rekom Church** at Verkhny Tsey, in the Tseyadon Valley about 15 km west of Buron (which is eight km up the Ardon from Mizur), is Ossetia's most revered shrine. Probably built in the 15th or 16th century, it's dedicated to St George but was probably originally a ram cult shrine. The upper Tseyadon Valley is surrounded by glaciers.

At the top of the Ardon Valley, the road winds over the 2819-metre Mamisonsky Pass to Kutaisi in Georgia, following the old Ossetian Military Highway (Voenno-Osetinskaya doroga), which was built to help the Russians control the region in the 19th century. A few tour buses take it – check with Stavropolintour.

Dagestan
Дагестан

Dagestan means the Mountain Kingdom. This republic, stretching deep into the north-east Caucasus from its 400-km Caspian coast, is the most complex and traditional part of the Caucasian ethnic jigsaw. It has about 30 languages divided into 81 national-ities, a result of its position on a great migration corridor between the Caspian and the Caucasus. Some of the largest groups are Avar, Dargin, Kumyk, Lezghin, Lakh and Tabasarans. One non-ethnic but distinctive group is the *abreks*, or the marauders, who made their living from robbery; their coup was to attack a wedding and take off with the bride. Over two-thirds of the largely Muslim population of nearly two million live in inland villages. Most of the ethnic groups in Dagestan are fervently Muslim and appar-ently around 2000 mosques were destroyed on Stalin's orders. Some have been rebuilt and many more are on the drawing board.

The weather is quite hot and dry in the lowlands, where the average daily maximum July temperature is 26°C but often exceeds 30°C. It tends to be cooler in the mountains where the sun can still get very hot. The mountain areas also have a shorter summer and the passes are only open from late June to late September. Winters are much colder with the average daily maximum tempera-ture in the lowlands being -4°C, lower in the mountains.

The history of Dagestan reaches back into ancient times. A settlement more than 10,000 years old was found near the village of Tschoch, which can be reached on foot from another village, Gunib. Russian biologists and archaeologists have asserted that Dagestan was one of the places where culti-vation and domestication first began on earth, and is thus one of the cradles of civilisation.

Dagestan has a bloodied recent history of many struggles for independence against Turks and Russians. Russia annexed Dagestan in 1813 after an arrangement with Persia. The local tribes did not take to Russian occupation easily and the fight against the Russian Imperial forces during the 19th century was led by Imam Shamil, a Lezghian, who is a local folk hero who led a war against the Orthodox invaders from 1845 until his surrender in 1859. He still holds a very romantic and legendary place in the nationalistic heart of the people. The Russians still did not establish full control until 1877. It is this sort of strong nationalism and independence that made Stalin fear them and he had whole groups of villages trans-ferred to Siberia at the end of WW II for alleged collaboration with the German invaders. The charges were false, since the local tribes could not be involved in such activities because the Germans never reached this area.

Despite its highly complicated ethnic mix, Dagestan has to date been free of serious post-Soviet ethnic conflict; it could be that its people, aware that their republic is a potential racial tinder box, are treading extra carefully to avoid the problems of other parts of Caucasus.

Folklore and handicraft traditions, espe-cially in the mountainous southern half where villages cling to steep hillsides, are as rich as anywhere in Russia. Dagestan's intri-cately patterned carpets and textiles are the most renowned of the region's crafts. Their rug designs are quite varied depending on what nationality makes them.

The best place to see Dagestan's carpets is the Derbent Sunday market, but there are other places for crafts. A factory in Rakhata village near Botlikh in west Dagestan is one place making the *bourka*, a multi-purpose, water and spear-proof shaggy felt cloak with wide, square shoulders, which stands up alone when not being worn. There are regional museums in Derbent and the capital, Makhachkala, on the Caspian coast. Other places you might visit include Kubachi, a jewellery-making village in the south-east, and villages on the Khunzakh Plateau in the west.

There are also some special local dishes like dumplings in ram's broth, served with garlic sauce known as *khinkal*.

Warning

In general, health is a problem in Dagestan. In 1994 the whole republic suffered a cholera outbreak, resulting in several deaths. The disease also spread to other areas, such as Azerbaijan. There were even cases reported in faraway Crimea.

MAKHACHKALA
МАХАЧКАЛА

The capital city of Dagestan is a port on the banks of the Caspian Sea. The whole place has the feeling of Asia and no wonder, as that continent is not far away. It is a typically large industrialised Soviet city that is dusty and characterless, with no restaurants. The only thing that makes up for this glumness is the friendliness and generosity of local people, but on the other hand not all can be trusted as the streets are apparently unsafe at night. The port's modern Soviet-style look is a result of a devastating earthquake in 1970, after which it had to be rebuilt. It is good to just stay overnight, while heading to other destinations, giving you time to see the interesting museum of Dagestani culture and history.

Orientation & Information

The main avenue is Leninsky prospekt, which has ploshchad Lenina at the north-western end, with the museum. The railway station is a five-minute walk east of here and on the other side of the railway tracks is the port. Leninsky prospekt stretches for several km in a south-easterly direction to Hotel Leningrad, department stores, the theatre, the Aeroflot office and the market.

Intourist (☎ 5 23 21 or 7 70 27) is in the Hotel Kaspy at ulitsa Buynaxnogo 8, south-east of the railway station. Dagpromstribank at Leninsky prospekt 39 (the north-western end) changes US dollars and German marks. The post and telegraph office has a branch at the Hotel Leningrad.

The Makhachkala telephone code is 8720 for 6-digit numbers, 08200 for 5-digit numbers.

Things to See

The **Dagestan History & Architecture Museum** (Dagestansky istorichesky i arkhitekturny muzey) on ploshchad Lenina is a very interesting museum with a good collection of Dagestan's costumes and tools on the 3rd floor. There is also a historical exhibit on the same floor, mainly of the Russian conquest of Dagestan. All the labels are in Russian. It is open Tuesday to Sunday from 10 am to 5 pm, and the entry fee is US$0.20.

The **Art Museum** (Muzey iskusstvo) at the corner of ulitsa Gorkogo and Markova has 19th-century and modern paintings. The most interesting exhibits are on the 1st floor including Dagestani carpets, ceramics, pottery, jewellery and decorated weapons. The Art Museum has the same hours as the History Museum.

A beach with good sand is not far from the railway station. Here the locals enjoy sunbathing, beach volleyball and Frisbee throwing. There are also snacks, shashlyk and kvas sellers in the area. To get there from the railway station, follow ulitsa V Emirova in a south-easterly direction until you reach ulitsa Gasanova on your left, before Hotel Kaspy, which takes you to the pedestrian bridge over the railway line and to the beach.

Organised Tours

Exodus Expeditions (☎ (0181) 675 5550; fax (0181) 673 0779), 9 Weir Rd, London SW12 OLT, UK, offer two-week walking tours around the major sights of Dagestan, with several nights in village homes, at an all-in cost of around UK£1110. The tours depart from London.

Places to Stay & Eat

At the time of writing only two hotels would accept foreigners, and surprisingly even Hotel Kaspy, which has the Intourist office, refused us a room.

The not-so-central *Hotel Turist* (☎ 2 73 41) is at the corner of prospekt Kalinina 100 and prospekt Kommsomolskaya. The doubles cost US$20.40 and are comparatively reasonable, but the staff are unfriendly and avaricious. To get here take trolleybus No 2 from the railway station.

The top place to stay is the ordinary-looking high-rise *Hotel Leningrad* (☎ 7 71 54) at Leninsky prospekt, which is anything but modern. It is, however, well guarded as several times when we could not be bothered to wait for the only working lift, we were met on the stairs by security guards running up and down with their Kalashnikov machine guns. The very basic rooms include TV, fridge, bathroom and toilet for US$20/25. To get here from the railway station take bus No 1 or 3 (US$0.10), or a taxi for US$1. At the rear of the hotel is a *kafe* which is only open during the day and which does not have an extensive menu.

Another place for lunch is the *restaurant* at the railway station. The day we had lunch there it was chicken paprika with mashed potatoes and the usual tomato/cucumber salad. It was actually tasty and only cost US$1, but this might have been an exception rather than a rule. There was not one restaurant open for dinner in all of Makhachkala. By the time we found this out, the grocery shops and the market were closed, but luckily the ladies at the reception of Hotel Leningrad put us on to some of the hotel's cleaning ladies who sold us some food. We were not alone this day as we heard of two Argentinians in a similar predicament. *Kafe Morozhenoe* in the Hotel Dagestan at ulitsa Buinaxnogo, opposite Hotel Kaspy, serves drinks and ice cream during the day.

Another plus being this far south in summer is that due to the constant heat, it is possible to buy cold drinks and beer from just about any kiosk, café or restaurant for a few extra roubles.

Getting There & Away

Air Makhachkala has daily flights to/from Moscow (US$136) and Volgograd (US$84). There are six flights a week to Mineralnye Vody (US$42) to other Caucasian regional centres. The Aeroflot office is at Leninsky prospekt 119, and airport buses meet the flights from here one hour before the flight's departure – the trip costs US$0.50 and takes 30 minutes. Taxis are at least US$5.

Bus The main bus station (Yuzhny vokzal) for all transport south of Makhachkala is in the southern part of town, on the main road that intersects with the edge of the town. Considering the run-down condition of the buses it is faster and surer to take the train. Our bus broke down several times on the return trip from Derbent.

Buses to Derbent (US$1.50, 2½ hours), Baku and other destinations depart from the main station. To get there take bus No 18 or 19 from the railway station, or take bus No 20 or trolleybus No 1 from ploshchad Lenina.

Train The railway station is at ulitsa V Emirova. The Rostov-on-Don to Baku railway goes through Derbent and there are several trains a day. There's a daily service to/from Moscow. The train to/from Astrakhan takes 15½ hours. The problem with all the Mineralnye Vody, Rostov-on-Don and Sochi trains is that due to the Chechnya conflict, since the end of 1994 all the trains have been diverted via Astrakhan, taking so much longer that it is worth flying.

Boat It is possible to cross the Caspian Sea on a freighter to Aqtau (formerly Shevchenko) in Kazakhstan, or Turkmenbashi (formerly Krasnovodsk) in Turkmenistan, if you have a visa for the country of your destination and have the skill and some Russian language skills to find a boat.

Getting Around

Buses and trolleybuses can get you anywhere in town and cost US$0.05. There are also minibuses which cost US$0.25. Taxis around town cost US$1 to US$2 depending on your destination.

DERBENT
ДЕРБЕНТ

Derbent was founded in the 6th century, and its great fortress of Naryn is mentioned in the story of Ali Baba. The old town's maze of streets lie below the fortress. To the Greeks and Romans, Derbent was the Caspian Gate – a mythical passage to the region of myths. The town has a real Asian feel to it with much of the action on the dusty streets of the town. Most of the people trading and sitting around are local Dagestanis – very few Russians are seen in the streets.

The streets around the bus station make up the town's huge street market where anything is sold daily, and this stretches to the walls of the old town and the Armenian Church. On Sundays a carpet market, which is a tradition dating back to the 12th century, is held on the outer north side of the town's long defensive wall, which was built by the Persians in the 6th century to stop nomads getting through the narrow pass between the Caspian and Caucasus here. Derbent was once famous for its madder dye used in carpets, but artificial colours have been used since the 19th century and traditional designs have mostly given way to more standard commercial patterns. Exceptions include the classically designed Soumakh rugs from villages like Ikra and Kabir in south Dagestan, which are sold in village shops or the Derbent market.

Orientation & Information

The small dusty port is dominated by the Naryn fortress and bordered on the eastern side by the Caspian Sea. It is easy to orient oneself by the Naryn fortress, which is visible from any point in Derbent.

Things to See

The 6th-century **Naryn Fort** (Krepost Naryn) looks impressive from the streets of Derbent but loses a lot up close, with nothing to see within its walls. There is, however, a great view of Derbent and the Caspian Sea

from the fort; the entry fee is US$0.10 and the fort is a 30-minute walk uphill from the town.

Below Naryn is the old walled town of Derbent, with interesting stone gates to walk through and a labyrinth of medieval dusty streets, amongst which is a **mosque**. Just east of the walls is the **Folk Craft Museum** (Muzey kobra i narodno-prikladnogo iskusstva) in the former Armenian Church (Armyansky khram) at ulitsa Razyaeva, about a five-minute walk north of the bus station. There is a good collection of Dagestani jewellery, belts, vases and carpets. The church itself is also interesting, especially its interior with attractive windows. It is open Wednesday to Monday, from 9 am to 5 pm, and the entry fee is US$0.05.

Getting There & Away

There are many daily buses to/from Makhachkala (US$1.50, 2½ hours) and Baku. The less frequent trains are more reliable as the unmaintained buses tend to have breakdowns.

OTHER DESTINATIONS IN DAGESTAN
ДРУГИЕ МЕСТА ДАГЕСТАНА

West of Makhachkala is the village of **Gimri**, which was the birthplace of Imam Shamil. One of the most spectacular gorges is **Arakanskoe** (Arakanskoe ushchelie), about 100 km west of Makhachkala. Further south is the 100-metre-long **Khunzakhsky waterfall** (vodopad), on the Tobot River, near Khunzakh. In **Goneb** is an old Russian fort and this is where Shamil surrendered to the Russians in 1859. There is also a very basic hotel in which to stay here. North-west of Derbent, along the Ulluchay River, is the town of Kubachi, from which it is possible to reach the village of **Amuzgi** on foot. Amuzgi has been known since the 12th century for its manufacture of armour and for local horse-riding skills. In **Akhti**, which is located near the Azerbaijani border with southern Dagestan, there are hot springs built for the Tsar's troops and a local museum in a former mosque. About 30 km further west is the village of **Rutul**, with a ruined mosque.

Black Sea Coast
Побережье Чёрного Моря

The foothills of the western 400 km of the Caucasus provide a scenic backdrop to a string of Black Sea resorts and ports with a fine subtropical climate – in summer, it's usually hot without being too humid, and the sea is warm. The leading resorts are Sochi and Dagomys. Dagomys, with its shiny resort complex in attractive coastal grounds, is *the* trendy vacation spot in the country. It would certainly win any Russia's Beach Bodies Beautiful contest and is a fine spot in which to relax after hectic Caucasian travels.

The most direct route for motorists from the north is via Rostov-on-Don and Krasnodar. It's 420 km from Krasnodar to Dagomys. South of Novorossiysk the road is scenic, touching the coast at several points but often climbing inland between towns. Trains from Rostov-on-Don reach the coast at Tuapse.

NOVOROSSIYSK
НОВОРОССИЙСК
Population: 200,000
This port on a deep, sheltered bay is being rebuilt for the Russian Black Sea fleet which has lost its bases in Ukraine. Novorossiysk can expect quite a growth in the near future. The road from Krasnodar comes in along Anapskoe shosse, with the *Hotel Brigantina* (with a restaurant) at No 18, then continues straight into the main street, ulitsa Sovietov, with the port just to its east, on the west side of the bay. The **Town History Museum** (Muzey istorii goroda) is on ulitsa Sovietov, a block south of the central ploshchad Geroev. Sukhumskoe shosse, which you take if you're heading for the south, leaves town along the far side of the bay.

WW II Memorials
In 1943 a small Soviet landing party held out for 225 days at the south end of the Malaya Zemlya peninsula on the west side of the bay, to form a bridgehead for the Soviet counter-offensive against the occupying Germans. Novorossiysk is peppered with WW II memorials. On Malaya Zemlya there are clusters at the south end of prospekt Lenina, where the party landed, and further round at Dolina Smerti (Death Valley), where it came under the fiercest bombardment.

Getting There & Away
Driving is the easiest way. There are trains from Krasnodar but not from the south, and buses from many destinations around, including Krasnodar (US$1.80; three hours) and Sochi (US$3; eight hours). Irregular boats and hydrofoils ply the route here from several other Russian Black Sea ports, including Sochi (US$8.30; four hours).

NOVOROSSIYSK TO DAGOMYS
МЕЖДУ НОВОРОССИЙСКОМ И ДАГОМЫСОМ
South of Novorossiysk, **Gelendzhik** is a resort of 32,000 people on an oval bay. The small beach is pebbly and the water is shallow. There is a *camping ground*, and the possibility of private accommodation as well as *Hotel Privenlivni Vereg* (☎ 2 35 44). The road then climbs through forest to the Mikhailov Pass (Mikhailovsky pereval, 250 metres) and Pshad Pass (Pshadsky pereval, 550 metres). **Dzhubga** is a small resort with a five-km sandy beach. **Tuapse** (population 65,000) is a port and industrial town surrounded by tea plantations, which are found all the way down this coast into Georgia.

SOCHI & DAGOMYS
СОЧИ И ДАГОМЫС
Population (Sochi): 300,000
The Dagomys resort, a showpiece created out of nothing by Intourist in the 1980s, is a holiday-makers' ghetto, isolated even from the small town of Dagomys, but a successful one, spaciously designed and with better facilities than probably any other Intourist establishment in the country – in many ways it's a Soviet dream come true, though standards are unfortunately beginning to decline. Sochi, older and much bigger – it has been under development as a resort since 1933 –

suffers by comparison but is still one of Russia's favourite resorts and a much more typical Soviet experience.

Orientation

Sochi stretches about seven km down the coast from the Sochi River to the southern suburb of Matsesta. The train and bus stations (side by side), the harbour and the shopping centre cluster at the north end. Kurortny prospekt, the main north-south street, runs the length of town a few blocks in from the sea.

Dagomys is 12 km north of Sochi on the main coast road. The resort stands in its own hilly grounds between the untidy town centre and the sea, and is reached by a two-km approach road.

Information

In Sochi, the Hotel Zhemchuzhina has the most clued-up bureau (the tourist office of Joint Stock Company of Zhemchuzhina; ☎ 92 60 84; fax 92 87 97) and a large beryozka. They run tours around Sochi and the surrounding region as well as the Caucasus and Abkhazia. A city tour costs US$5 per person. The Hotel Intourist-Kamelia also has a beryozka. Most major hotels change money, but only Radisson Hotel Lazurnaya and the Banka Menatel branch at the bus station change travellers' cheques of American Express, Thomas Cook, Visa and Citicorp, as well as giving cash advances for Visa cards. Sochi's main post office is on Kurortny prospekt at the corner of ulitsa Vorovskogo, but the main hotels have their own. The Hotel Lazurnaya's exchange rates are lower than most other places.

In Dagomys, there are tourist bureaus at the Olimpiysky and Dagomys hotels. The latter has a moneychanging office and a sizeable beryozka.

The local area code is 8622.

Dagomys Resort & Beach

If you're not already staying there, Dagomys resort is worth considering as a trip out from Sochi, if only to use the beach – it's just as

Sochi
Сочи

0   400   800 m

Arboretum
(Botanical Garden)

BLACK

SEA

Bytkha
▲ Hill

To Radisson Hotel Lazurnaya,
Maron Restaurant,
Mezhdunarodny Molodyozhny
Tsentr Sputnik, Matsesta, Adler,
Airport & Sukhumi

PLACES TO STAY		OTHER		14	Sochi Art Museum
9	Hotel Moskva	1	Zelyony Teatr		Сочинский
	Гостиница Москва		Зелёный театр		художественный
13	Hotel Leningrad	2	Kavkazskaya Rivera		музей
	Гостиница Ленинград		Sanatorium	16	Town History Museum
15	Hotel Sochi-Magnolia		Санаторий Кавказская		Музей истории
	Гостиница		Ривьера		города
	Сочи-Магнолия	3	Market	17	Zimny Teatr
18	Hotel Zhemchuzhina		Рынок		Зимний театр
	Гостиница Жемчужина	4	Post Office	20	Letny Teatr
22	Hotel Kavkaz		Почтамт		Летний театр
	Гостиница Кавказ	5	Bookshops	21	Circus
25	Hotel Intourist-Kamelia		Книжные магазины		Цирк
	Гостиница Интурист-	6	Aeroflot Office	23	Cable Car
	Камелия		Аэрофлот		Канатно-кресельная
		7	Bus Station		дорога
PLACES TO EAT			Автовокзал	24	Stadium
12	Restoran Kaskad	8	Train Station		Стадион
	Ресторан Каскал		Железнодорожный	26	Metallurg Sanatorium
19	Kafe Iveria		вокзал		Санаторий
	Кафе Иверия	10	Sea Terminal		Металлург
27	Staraya Melnitsa		Морской вокзал	28	Ordzhonikidze
	Restaurant	11	Festivalny Concert Hall		Sanatorium
	Ресторан Старая		Концертный зал		Санаторий имени С.
	мельница		Фестивальный		Орджоникидзе

pebbly as Sochi's but less crowded and with waters which at least feel a lot cleaner. Boards are provided for lying on and there's a decent range of food and drink bars on the spot. There's rarely any check on who crosses the bridge at the seaward edge of the resort grounds to the panoramic lift that descends to the beach.

Sochi Town Centre

The flea markets on Moskovskaya ulitsa, opposite the bus station, and on ulitsa Voikova, near the harbour, are interesting for seeing what the locals like as much as for buying anything. The main shops are along ulitsa Navaginskaya. From the harbour, a pedestrian promenade stretches south along the jam-packed beaches, which are backed for much of their length by steep slopes with a wooded park on top.

Museums

The **Sochi Art Museum**, at Kurortny prospekt 51, has some good visiting exhibitions as well as its permanent collection – it's open daily except Monday from 10 am to noon and 1 to 5 pm. Half a km further south and a block towards the sea is the **Town History Museum**, at ulitsa Ordzhonikidze 29.

Arboretum

Sochi's version of a botanic garden contains more than 1500 species of trees and shrubs from the world over, attractively laid out and well worth seeing. It extends on both sides of Kurortny prospekt, about two km south of the town centre. There are Mediterranean, Caucasus, Far East, Himalayan, Australian and American sections in the upper part. It is the third-largest in the CIS. The arboretum (dendrariy) is open from 8 am daily, to 8 pm in summer and 6 pm in winter.

Bytkha Hill

This 300-metre hill (Gora Bytkha) behind Sochi has good views over the town and coast. Ulitsa Bytkha, which turns off Kurortny prospekt about a km south of the

Arboretum, leads to the top. Bus No 22 'Avtovokzal-Bytkha' goes at least part way up, and Nos 19 and 23 may go all the way up. The Staraya Melnitsa restaurant is at the top.

Places to Stay

Sochi At the railway station, the Apartment Bureau (Kvartirnoe byuro) finds places to stay in private accommodation. Passengers of arriving trains are also approached for private accommodation which is about US$10 for one or two people, or less depending on how good you are at bargaining.

The very new and western-style luxury *Radisson Hotel Lazurnaya* (☎ 97 59 74; fax 97 45 77) at 103 Kurortny Prospect is just like other Radissons around the world with similar facilities and service, including a private beach, casino and health centre. Rooms start from US$168. Airport buses go past the hotel and from the railway station take bus No 3, 4 or 17 to Primore stop.

The 1700-bed *Hotel Zhemchuzhina* (☎ 92 44 94) has its own beach and a decent range of facilities. It's at Chyornomorskaya ulitsa 3, by the sea about two km from the centre, a half-km walk down from Kurortny prospekt past the Zimny Teatr. The comfortable standard rooms cost US$60/80 and the nicely renovated rooms on upper floors are more expensive. Breakfast is included and is good, and the waiting staff are friendly.

The *Hotel Intourist-Kamelia* (☎ 99 05 90), about four km south of the centre at Kurortny prospekt 91, comprises a rambling, quasi-palace edifice, and a modernish block beside it, which is slightly ageing but still comfortable. The rooms cost US$42/68. There are pleasant gardens, a private beach and tennis courts. The Intourist-Kamelia is halfway between the Sanatory Metallurg and Stadion bus stops, necessitating a half-km walk up or down a carbon monoxide-choked hill.

The large *Hotel Moskva* (☎ 92 36 17) at Kurortny prospekt 18, with three restaurants, looks one of the best bets in town, with rooms from US$26/30. The *Hotel Leningrad* (☎ 92 52 67) at Morskoy pereulok 2 is a step

down in quality at US$40/60; the *Hotel Sochi-Magnolia* (☎ 99 56 27) at Kurortny prospekt 50 at US$21/31.50 and the *Hotel Kavkaz* (☎ 92 35 66) at Kurortny prospekt 72 at US$28/45 are two steps down. Another possibility is the *Hotel Gorizont-Priboy* (☎ 44 16 77) at Prosveshchenia ulitsa 24 in the smaller resort of Adler, about 30 km south of Sochi. Red Bus No 4 goes to Adler from Sochi bus station and Kurortny prospekt.

The *Mezhdunarodny Molodyozhny Tsentr Sputnik* (Sputnik International Youth Centre; ☎ 96 02 88) is at Novorossiyskoe shosse 17/1, index 354062, near the main road in Matsesta. Their rooms cost US$30/32.50 with full board.

There is also the *Pansionat Svetlana* (☎ 92 07 79, 92 14 06) at Kurortny prospekt 75, index 354002, and the *Turbaza Sokol* (☎ 92 27 74/9) at ulitsa Voikova 48, index 354012. The Svetlana has at least three modernish blocks; the Sokol is a number of small buildings set sanatorium-like in pleasant wooded grounds, but its 'restaurant' is a pretty dire stolovaya. Both of these places require prior bookings; it is not possible to get accommodation by walking in off the street.

Dagomys The Dagomys complex consists of two hotels, one motel and one camp site. One approach road, ulitsa Leningradskaya, leads to all of them. The whole place is clean, its many facilities really work, and the staff are mostly helpful.

The centre of things, towering pyramid-like at the end of the approach road, is the comfortable, four-star, 1650-bed *Hotel Dagomys* (☎ 32 25 95, 99 38 40). The rooms cost US$34/56, including breakfast, and there is also a casino. On the way up you pass the three-star *Hotel Olimpiysky* and *Motel Meridian*, which are not much cheaper at US$36/50 with breakfast. There is also the *Camping Dagomys* whose 'cabins' are in fact caravans with the cooking fixtures removed costing US$20 for three people – they're as clean and comfortable as any accommodation in a Russian camp site. The caravans have their own toilets and there are separate shower blocks. All rooms in the hotels and motel have balconies. Resort facilities include the beach, indoor and outdoor pools, the sports centre with tennis courts, a concert hall-cum-cinema, a library with several shelves of books in English, and even acupuncture facilities. All are open to anyone staying in any of the four accommodation sections. The postal index is 354224.

Places to Eat

Sochi In Sochi, the food and service is some of the best that we experienced in Russia, especially in some of the hotels. In the Zhemchuzhina Hotel is the *Restoran Zhemchug*, where you can get breakfast and then Russian food in the evening, which includes a dance show. There are several other restaurants which serve Caucasian and Cossack food and also stage folk dancing and singing. The Zhemchuzhina also has several bars and cafés, including the co-op *Kafe Iveria* on the hotel's beach, which serves reasonable fish, chicken and salad.

The *Kafe Ldinka* outside the Letny Teatr serves drinks and cheap food (US$1) between 10 am and midnight. The *Maron*, on the sea side of Kurortny prospekt in Matsesta, does Chinese food. It's recognisably Chinese from the outside.

The *Restoran Kavkasky Aul (Caucasian Village)* (☎ 97 08 17) is in Agura Valley off the road to Adler, just inland from Matseta. It's in an isolated and appealing spot and serves Caucasian meals. There is no menu; food is prepared on the basis of how much one is willing to pay and what is available. The restaurant is open daily from 11 am to midnight. If taking bus No 4, ask to be dropped off at a spot called Sputnik, from where the restaurant is a 20-minute walk along the road. Another option is a taxi, which is better late at night for a return trip as the road is unlit.

The *Staraya Melnitsa (Old Mill)* on Bytkha Hill has also been recommended.

The *Kuban Restaurant* is one of three at Radisson Hotel Lazurnaya, Kurortny prospekt 103 in Matsesta. It is a luxury restaurant with main dishes costing around US$7 to US$10.

The *Sochi market*, on Moskovskaya ulitsa, a short walk north of the bus station, has fresh fruit and vegetables.

Dagomys There are many restaurants in the Dagomys complex, such as *Restoran Agat* in the Hotel Dagomys and the main *Restoran Olimpiysky* in the Hotel Olimpiysky. At both, the food is reportedly not as good as at the following places: the open-air *Restoran Dubrava* (Russian food) and *Kavkazskaya Kukhnya* (Caucasian) in the grounds; and the *Restoran Satan*, with Russian food, and the *Restoran Rubin*, both in the Hotel Dagomys.

There are so many bars and cafés – with and without alcohol – in the complex that you'd need a month to find them all. The one up on floor 22 of the Hotel Dagomys has the freshest of fresh air, while the bar on its main lobby floor offers air-conditioned seclusion. There's a beer bar selling the stuff by the jug between the two hotels. Don't be lured by the vile 'pizza' in the Turist Bar of the Hotel Olimpiysky.

The *Restoran Sakura* (☎ 31 57 43) (English is spoken) is a 'Japanese' co-op on the main road in Dagomys, 400 metres north of the resort approach road. For the trout, the blackboard gives the price per 100 grams. An average fish is about 300 grams.

Entertainment

The Dagomys complex has a cinema-cum-concert hall, a disco (in the sports centre) and a few restaurants with shows or live groups to dance to – see Places to Eat above.

In Sochi, the Hotel Moskva has a disco, and there are more restaurants with shows or music. Visiting rock acts quite often play Sochi's Letny Teatr (Summer Theatre) in Park Frunze or the Zelyony (Green) Teatr in Park Rivera, just north of the river. For opera, ballet and drama, check the huge Zimny (Winter) Teatr on Teatralnaya ploshchad which functions during some of the summer too. The Hotel Sochi-Magnolia has a casino. The Joint Stock Company of Zhemchuzhina office in Hotel Zhemchuzhina sells tickets to most theatre performances.

Getting There & Away

Air Flights to/from Sochi are much more frequent in summer, up to September/October, than in winter. In summer there are several daily flights to/from Moscow (US$128, 2½ hours), but in winter only a few a week. Other services include St Petersburg (US$160, three hours, daily), Rostov-on-Don (US$78, 1½ hours), Simferopol (US$84, 1½ hours), Tbilisi (US$78, one hour) and Yerevan (US$86, 1½ hours) – mostly several days a week in summer, a couple a week in winter. There are also some small airlines like Sochi Airlines-Aviaprima (at Adler airport ☎ (8620) 44 31 69; fax (8620) 44 22 55), which flies to Turkey, three times a week.

One of the best new airlines in the country is Transaero which only flies to/from Moscow in Boeings for US$215. Its ticket office is Agentstvo Vozdushnykh Soobshcheny (☎ 92 36 03) at ulitsa Navaginskaya 16.

In Sochi, Aeroflot (☎ 92 29 36) is on ulitsa Navaginskaya, with a couple of bookshops adjacent to it.

Bus Bus services, which could be affected by the political situation in Abkhazia and Georgia, include about a dozen daily to Sukhumi (five hours), a couple to Tskhaltubo (13 hours), and one overnight to Batumi. Daily buses to Krasnodar take eight hours (US$3) and are slightly cheaper to Novorossiysk (seven hours).

Train There are several trains a day between Sochi and Moscow (36 to 38 hours) via Rostov-on-Don. Trains to Mineralnye Vody take 13 hours. Southbound there are three or four daily to/from Sukhumi (four hours) and Tbilisi (14 to 16 hours) and one each for Yerevan (24 hours) and Batumi.

Car & Motorbike It's 155 km from Sochi to Sukhumi, 629 km to Tbilisi – a fairly straight, well-surfaced road on which you can make good time. However, travel depends on the political situation; visas might also be required in the future.

Boat Sochi is a major port of call for the irregular passenger ferries and hydrofoils travelling in summer up and down the Black Sea coast of Russia, between Sochi and Novorossiysk (US$19.70), via other ports like Gelendzhik and Tuapse. The day we wanted to take the boat it was not running due a breakdown, so the boats do not always run as regularly as they should.

There are also boats to Sukhumi (Abkhazia), Batumi (Georgia), Rize and Trabzon (both in Turkey, US$48, five hours, three times a week) but the ticket seller made it very clear that they would only sell a boat ticket to people with appropriate visas and/or permits for their destination.

Getting Around

To/From the Airport The airport is about 30 km south of Sochi, 40 km from Dagomys, on the ring road at the east side of Adler. The Joint Stock Company of Zhemchuzhina charges about US$28 for transfers to/from Dagomys – a drive of just 30 to 40 minutes if traffic is light.

Alternatively take a taxi or red bus No 84, an express, which runs between the airport and Sochi bus station every 10 to 40 minutes from 4.30 am to 11 pm, taking about 50 minutes and costing US$0.30 (plus a small charge for baggage) for the trip. Yellow bus Nos 4 and 4C also link the airport and bus station but are slower. Allow 2½ hours to reach the airport from Dagomys by bus.

Between Sochi & Dagomys It's a half-hour bus ride between Dagomys and Sochi. Bus No 47 'Sochi-Dagomys Komplex' terminates nearly a km up the Dagomys resort approach road, saving that much walking. Nos 45Э, 46, 48 and 49 stop on the main road at the foot of the resort approach road.

In Sochi, all buses go to the bus station. There's one every 15 to 20 minutes from 7 am to 7 pm, and just a few after that. A taxi between Sochi and Dagomys shouldn't be more than US$10, even late at night – it's much less if you bargain and don't take taxis from in front of the main hotels.

Sochi Bus Nos 3, 4 and 17 all travel from the bus station to Kurortny prospekt, then along Kurortny prospekt at least as far south as Matsesta. Tickets were available from provodniki (conductors) on the buses but occasionally buses did not have conductors.

AROUND SOCHI & DAGOMYS
ОКОЛО СОЧИ И ДАГОМЫСА
The Joint Stock Company of Zhemchuzhina offers dozens of trips to waterfalls, viewpoints, farms etc in the district. Most are hard to do independently without your own transport. You can also make trips to places in Abkhazia like Lake Ritsa, Gagra, Pitsunda, Novy Afon and Sukhumi.

Agura Valley
Агурское ущелье
An inland turning at Matsesta leads to a car park where you can walk to a small lake and a couple of waterfalls, one 25 metres high. The Orlinye Skaly (Eagle Cliffs) tower above. The Kavkazsky Aul restaurant is in the valley too.

Mt Bolshoy Akhun
Гора Большой Архун
An 11-km road signposted 'Akhun', shortly south of the Agura turning, leads up this hill with a lookout tower on top. There are views to the Caucasus and the coast. A path runs down to the Agura Valley.

Tea Farm
The four-hour trip to a tea farm near Dagomys costs over US$20, even for group members, but the apple cake they give you is said to be delicious!

Krasnaya Polyana
Красная Поляна
Krasnaya Polyana (Beautiful Glade), 600 metres high, is a small settlement surrounded by mountains and alpine meadows, about 70 km from Sochi. The spectacular road up from Adler follows the Mzymta River, passing through a deep, steep gorge after the village of Monastyrka. There are nature and minerals museums at Krasnaya Polyana.

The place is being developed as a ski resort – while it only has a few lifts for intermediate skiing, there is helicopter skiing for the experienced. The Joint Stock Company of Zhemchuzhina can take you there by road. Groups of seven or more cost US$60 per person, including a picnic (less without food), or a taxi costs about US$100.

From Adler's central market you can take bus No 135.

TRANS-SIBERIAN RAILWAY

The Trans-Siberian Railway

The Trans-Siberian Railway and connecting routes comprise one of the most famous, romantic and potentially enjoyable of all the world's great train journeys. Rolling out of Europe and into Asia, through eight time zones and over 9289 km of taiga, steppe and desert, the Trans-Siberian makes all other train rides seem like once around the block with Thomas the Tank Engine. Extending from Moscow to the Pacific coast, the Trans-Siberian is the world's longest single-service railway, and with its European and Asian extensions it's also the world's foremost overland 'highway'.

Any attempt to find the 'Trans-Siberian Railway' on a timetable, however, will meet with about as much success as a search through an atlas for the fabled Shangrila. The term 'Trans-Siberian' is used generically for three main lines and some of the numerous trains that run on them.

The main line, and the one with the strongest claim to the title Trans-Siberian Railway, runs from Moscow's Yaroslavl Station on a continuous unbroken track through and beyond Siberia to Vladivostok, in the Russian Far East. The *Rossia* departs every other day (on odd-numbered dates) from each of the two termini to begin its 6½-day marathon haul across the length of Russia. However, the routes that travel hacks and brochure compilers have traditionally referred to as the Trans-Siberian Railway are the two branches that veer off the main line in Eastern Siberia and depart from Russian territory to make a beeline for Beijing. The 7865-km Trans-Mongolian Railway makes its way along the Moscow-Vladivostok line as far as Lake Baikal, where it diverts to reach the Chinese capital via Ulan Bator, while the 9001-km Trans-Manchurian Railway leaves the line at Tarskaya to reach Beijing by way of Harbin and north-eastern China. The sense of passage engendered by getting on a train in European Russia and stepping off at the other end into a pungent,

dusty cloud of orientalism (or vice versa) has long made these routes a favourite with foreign travellers.

In the past, the romance of the all-Russian Moscow-Vladivostok line was impaired by the fact that foreigners were never allowed to ride the train all the way to its intended eastern terminus. Instead they had to disembark from the *Rossia* in Khabarovsk and switch to a train bound for the dreary commercial port of Nakhodka, at which point they were all but blindfolded and led on to a ferry for Japan or simply turned around and put back on the next train bound west. Today, Trans-Siberian travellers are free to complete their journey to Vladivostok, stepping off the train at the harbour-side heart of the vibrant Pacific city. From Vladivostok it's possible to pick up a train to Harbin and there change for Beijing, making a mammoth Trans-Siberian, Moscow-Beijing journey of roughly 12,000 km, taking 10½ days.

HISTORY
Beginnings
Russia's initial conquest of Siberia had been by means of its rivers, with the boats dragged from one watercourse to the next. Later transport took the form of horse-drawn carriages, sledges or *tarantass* (a coach body resting on three thick poles, dragged by horses) following the Great Siberia Post Road (Veliky trakt) – little more than a trail through the snow, mud or dust. At best, to travel across Siberia was a three or four-month undertaking, but for the exiles and poorer emigrants who were forced to go on foot, the journey could take a year or more. It was quicker to travel from St Petersburg to Vladivostok by crossing the Atlantic, North America and the Pacific, than it was to go overland across Siberia.

With the region's burgeoning population, and both Japan and China coveting Russian Far Eastern territories, the Empire clearly needed better communication links with its

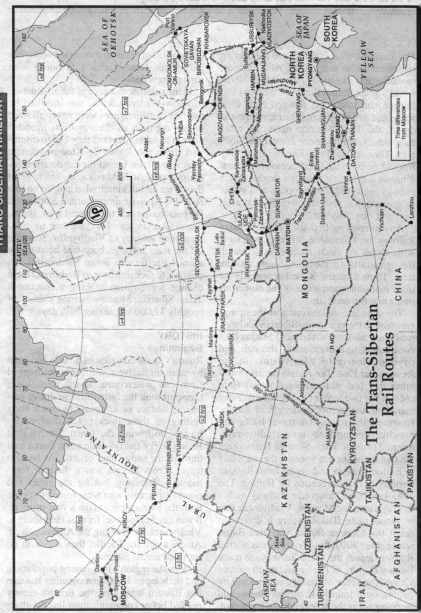

The Trans-Siberian
Rail Routes

extremities. Throughout the 19th century, ideas for a railway across Siberia were floated and ignored, including the 1857 proposal by an American banker, Perry McDonough Collins, for a rail and riverboat link from Irkutsk to the Pacific.

In 1869, the Americans completed their own coast-to-coast railway, and 1885 saw the opening of the Canadian Pacific. The following year, Tsar Alexander III finally authorised the building of a 7500-km line from Chelyabinsk (then Russia's eastern railhead) to Vladivostok, running along the route of the old post road and connecting all the major towns that had developed along it. In May 1891, Tsarevich Nicholas, visiting Vladivostok, ceremoniously emptied a wheelbarrow of dirt, so signifying that work on the new railway had begun.

Construction

The right of way was cut across the steppe and through the taiga with hand tools. The labour force was made up of a mixture of exiles and convicts (offered reduced sentences as an incentive to work), soldiers and imported, paid Chinese labourers. Thanks to the terrain, climate, floods and landslides, disease, war and bandit attacks, not to mention shoddy materials and bad planning, the railway took 26 years to build (and often rebuild). Nevertheless, it remains the most brilliant engineering feat of its time.

The railway was divided up into six sections so that construction could take place simultaneously all along the route. First under way was the Ussuri line (Vladivostok-Khabarovsk), built between 1891 and 1897, followed by the Western Siberian line (Chelyabinsk-Novosibirsk) in 1892-96 and the Mid-Siberian line (Novosibirsk via Irkutsk to Port Baikal) in 1893-98. In just seven years since the inaugural tipping of soil, Russia had a Trans-Siberian line that stretched from Moscow 5200 km to the western shore of Lake Baikal.

Baikal was initially crossed by two icebreakers built at Newcastle-upon-Tyne in England and sent in pieces to be assembled in Irkutsk. The huge, four-funnelled *Baikal*

was the larger of the two ('rather like a barn that had slipped afloat', recorded one contemporary traveller), and her decks were laid with three lines of track that could accommodate an entire express train and its load. The smaller sister ship, the *Angara*, was used for passengers. But when the Russo-Japanese war broke out in the winter of 1904, to speed the supply of troops and munitions to the front, temporary rails were actually laid across the frozen lake. The first test locomotive plunged through the ice, making a hole 22 km long. Undaunted, the Russians relaid the tracks, disassembled the locomotives and used teams of horses and men to pull the carriages and flat cars instead.

Completion

In the same year that Russia went to war with Japan, the final stretch of the 200-km Round-Baikal (or Circumbaikal) line around the lake's southern end was hurriedly completed, unplugging the Lake Baikal bottleneck. The Trans-Baikal line, from Mysovaya, where the ferries had docked on the lake's eastern shore, to Sretensk, just beyond Chita, had been built between 1895 and 1900. From there, early travellers boated down the Shilka and Amur rivers to Khabarovsk or rode to Vladivostok on the East China line, which had been laid across Manchuria in 1897-1903 on a narrow strip of land over which the Russians had wangled an 80-year lease. By 1904, it was finally possible to take a train all the way from St Petersburg through to Vladivostok. However, propelled by fears that they might lose control of the East China line to the Japanese, the Russians soon embarked upon an alternative Amur line, from Sretensk to Khabarovsk. Finished in 1916, with the bridge over the Amur River at Khabarovsk, it was the final link in the world's longest railway.

Early Services

Following Russia's orgy of self-publicity at the Paris Universal Exposition of 1900, the earliest Trans-Siberian travellers were lured on to the rails even before the line was fully completed. To attract overseas clientele, the *State Express* (as it was then known) was presented at the Exposition as a palace on wheels, but with the kind of scenery that not even Versailles could muster. A mock-up of a Trans-Siberian train was displayed amidst a landscape of stuffed seals, papier-mâché icebergs and mannequins of native hunters. Interspersed with the sleeping carriages were a gymnasium car, a restaurant car with a large, tiled bathroom, reading lounge and piano, and even a fully functioning church car crowned with a belfry. The same year saw the first precursor of the book you have in your hands: the official *Guide to the Great Siberian Railway*, published in St Petersburg.

However, the primary reason for the construction of the railway had been to further the economic and social development of Siberia, and the bulk of the passengers were emigrants escaping overpopulation in European Russia. Their travelling conditions were a far cry from the sumptuousness on offer to the international set – 'stables on wheels' was one eyewitness description. However, a few weeks of hardship on the rails was far preferable to the year-long trek that migration had previously entailed, and

in 1908 alone three-quarters of a million peasants rode east.

Post-Revolution

Civil war interrupted the development of the railway, but when the Reds finally prevailed, upgrading the Trans-Siberian was a major priority. The line was vital for the Bolsheviks' plans for economic rebirth, linking the iron-ore reserves of the Ural region with the Kuznetsk coalfields and the great industrial plants in development throughout Western Siberia.

In the 1920s, as part of the industrialisation of Western Siberia, the railway was extended south-west from Novosibirsk via Semipalatinsk to Almaty in Kazakhstan (the present-day Turkestan-Siberian Railway, known as the Turk-Sib). In 1940, a branch line was built between Ulan Ude and Naushki, on the border with Mongolia. By 1949 it had connected with Ulan Bator, the Mongolian capital. The line from Ulan Bator to Beijing was begun four years later and completed by 1956.

Travelling on the Trans-Siberian in the late 1970s, writer Eric Newby recorded being rattled by freight trains passing in the opposite direction at the rate of about one

An E-72 3 2-8-0 locomotive – successor to the old Shoh class, Trans-Siberian Railway

every two minutes. Heading west were flat cars loaded with tree trunks and steel girders, tractors under tarpaulins and brightly coloured containers sent overland from Nakhodka; heading east would be food and consumer goods. In the words of one commentator, the Trans-Siberian Railway had become the iron ribbon that held the Soviet Union together.

Despite the ascendancy of the aeroplane and the demise of the Soviet system, the importance of the Trans-Siberian Railway has not diminished. There is still no continuous motorable road across Siberia, and rail is still the only viable option for heavy freight. The Trans-Siberian also retains its role as a vital psycho-political prop. Russia's Far Eastern territories, though firmly established as Slavic domains for well over 100 years, still feel the threat of their Oriental neighbours (even if that perceived threat is now economic rather than military). The railway is a cast-iron safety cord, securing the far-flung territories to Moscow's motherly presence.

The BAM

In the 1930s, work was begun on a second trans-Siberian line, the 3100-km Baikal-Amur Mainline (Baikalo-Amurskaya Magistral, or BAM). This line was to extend from Tayshet on the existing Trans-Siberian line to the north, around the tip of Lake Baikal, and on to the previously inaccessible timber-rich Lena Basin and its coal, iron-ore and gold mines. Abandoned in WW II and stripped (its tracks were used to lay a relief line to the besieged city of Stalingrad), it was essentially started all over again in 1974. In the meantime, the line had gained in strategic importance as an alternative to the existing Trans-Siberian, which, in places lying within 100 km of the border, was felt to be too vulnerable to attack by potentially hostile China.

The BAM was called the 'Hero Project of the Century', and the youth of all the Soviet Union was called to rally to the challenge. That they did respond is evident in the names of some of the towns along the line – Estbam, Latbam and Litbam, named for the workers from the Baltic states who built them – and in the striking absence of elderly people in these communities today. The BAM towns and the necessary infrastructure sprang up at a pace with the railway because, unlike the Trans-Siberian, which connected existing settlements, the new line was being forced through completely virgin wilderness. Overcoming Siberia's swamps and mountains, its seemingly infinite number of rivers and, in particular, its vast swathe of permafrost forced the cost of the project to a staggering US$25 billion (the original Trans-Siberian is estimated to have cost the equivalent of US$500 million). Officially opened in 1991, the line still isn't finished. Although it is possible to travel the whole length of the BAM, from Tayshet, west of Lake Baikal, to Sovietskaya Gavan on the Pacific coast, the incomplete Severomuisk tunnel is currently bypassed by a temporary line, which is extremely susceptible to landslides.

The cost of the BAM was such that no money was left to invest in developing the industries that the railway was laid to service. As a consequence there's very little traffic on the line. More tragic has been the cost in human terms. The large workforce that was called in to gouge through the taiga, laying tracks and the foundations of new towns, has found itself with its work on the railway done but no new jobs awaiting. A number of settlements beside the tracks have already become ghost towns and many of the others are seeing their populations dwindle as residents leave in search of work elsewhere. Rather than the model of modern engineering which the BAM was proclaimed to be, it lies as a testament to the grand folly of Soviet planning.

ROUTES & TRAINS

For the first four days out of Moscow, the Trans-Siberian, Trans-Manchurian and Trans-Mongolian all follow the same double-track main line, through the Urals and into Western Siberia, over the River Yenisey (which marks the beginning of Eastern Siberia) and on to Irkutsk. On the fifth day, after rounding the southern tip of Lake Baikal, the Trans-Mongolian route branches off, heading south for the border 250 km away. The Trans-Manchurian stays with the main line for another 12 hours past Lake Baikal, before it too peels off, heading south for Zabaikalsk on the Chinese border, some 368 km distant. The Trans-Manchurian takes half a day longer to reach Beijing but it avoids the need for a Mongolian visa. However, it also means missing out on ever-popular Ulan Bator.

Every carriage has a timetable (in Cyrillic, of course) posted in the corridor, which also notes how long the train will stop at each station. Usually, halts last from two to five minutes, but about twice a day the train stops for 15 or 20 minutes, allowing passengers time to get off and stretch their legs or stock up from the platform kiosks. There are small white km-posts on the southern side of the line marking the distance from Moscow, although these are sometimes difficult to spot because they're so close to the track.

For the Turk-Sib Railway, which runs from Novosibirsk in Western Siberia to Almaty in Kazakhstan, with a branch line to Ürümqi in China, see Siberia & the Russian Far East's Getting There & Away section. Details of the Ussuriysk-Pyongyang service are also given in that section.

The Trans-Siberian

This is the Moscow-Vladivostok route, via the principal cities of Vyatka, Perm, Yekaterinburg, Omsk, Novosibirsk, Krasnoyarsk, Irkutsk, Ulan Ude, Chita and Khabarovsk.

The land is mostly flat in the west (except for the Ural Mountains – although these would hardly count as mountains if the surrounding landscape wasn't so flat) and hilly in the east. From Moscow through Western Siberia, the land on either side of the tracks is pastoral with small, isolated farmsteads in Cinemascope landscapes, but east of Krasnoyarsk the endless birch and pine forests of the taiga start to appear, and a real sense of wilderness sets in. Entering the Chita region, the taiga gives way to rolling meadows, hills and deciduous woodlands.

Between the cities are log-cabin settlements, some as immaculate and brightly painted as story-book illustrations.

The only train to traverse the whole length of the main line is the Moscow-Vladivostok express, the *Rossia*, given on the timetable as train No 1/2 (eastbound trains have even numbers, westbound odd). Train No 2 departs from Moscow's Yaroslavl Station every other day – odd-numbered dates – at 2 pm, arriving some 6½ days later in Vladivostok at 9.45 am local time. From Vladivostok, train No 1 departs each second day – odd-numbered dates – at just after 1 am local time, arriving in Moscow at about 6.45 am.

Another train often favoured by tour agencies (and therefore kept polished, vacuumed and well stocked with food and beer, and often with English-speaking provodniks/ provodnitsas) is the No 9/10 Moscow-Irkutsk service, the *Baikal Express*. Train No 10 leaves Moscow's Yaroslavl Station at 9.05 pm each day, arriving in Irkutsk 3½ days later at around 9 am Moscow time, or 2 pm local time.

Less well-maintained services that run out of Moscow and into Siberia include the daily No 25/26 *Sibiryak* Moscow-Novosibirsk and the No 183/194 Moscow-Khabarovsk; the summer-only, four-times-weekly No 70/80 Moscow-Chita; and the twice-weekly No 101/102 Moscow-Ulan Ude services.

Trans-Siberian Landmarks The km figures given in this section correspond to the white markers beside the railway line.

0 km: Moscow Departure from Yaroslavl Station. One minute late onto the platform and you'll see a rapidly receding dot way down the line. That's your train. It leaves bang on time.

73 km: Sergiev Posad Trinity St Sergius Monastery. Look to the north for the blue and gold domes.

282 km: Yaroslavl A stop of a few minutes. As the train crosses the bridge over the Volga River, the views of Yaroslavl are excellent.

357 km: Danilov A 15-minute halt.

957 km: Vyatka A 15-minute halt.

1365 km: Local time becomes Moscow time plus one hour, and shortly afterwards Moscow time plus two hours.

1433 km: Perm A 15-minute halt. A big city, it was until recently closed to foreigners because of its military-industrial installations.

1600-1900 km: The Ural Mountains. Look hard or you might not notice them.

1777 km: On the southern side of the tracks is a large white obelisk marking the boundary between Europe and Asia.

1818 km: Yekaterinburg A 20-minute halt. Tsar Nicholas II and his family were murdered here. It's also Boris Yeltsin's home town. There are several places to get food in and just outside the station.

2144 km: Tyumen A brief halt. This is the oldest city in Siberia, though you wouldn't know it from the railway.

2510 km: Local time becomes Moscow time plus three hours.

2716 km: Omsk A 15-minute halt in the city of Dostoevsky's exile. The train crosses the Irtysh River here.

3332 km: Cross a bridge over the Ob, one of the world's longest rivers.

3343 km: Novosibirsk Siberia's biggest, but not loveliest, city, and the junction for the Turk-Sib Railway. A 20-minute halt – if you're quick, there's just enough time to grab something from the kiosk city on the station forecourt.

3488 km: Local time becomes Moscow time plus four hours.

3571 km: Taiga This marks the branch line to Tomsk and the closed defence-industry city of Tomsk-7.

3719 km: Mariinsk A 15-minute halt.

3932 km: A small white obelisk to the south of the tracks marks the halfway point between Moscow and Beijing (via Ulan Bator).

4104 km: Krasnoyarsk A 20-minute halt. There are two bufety in the station building. If you run through the ticket hall and out onto the station forecourt you'll see a large mural of Lenin & Co adorning the wall of the post office. Krasnoyarsk is the best place to

change trains for the BAM. Heading east out of the station you cross a km-long bridge over the Yenisey River.

4484 km: Local time becomes Moscow time plus five hours.

4522 km: Tayshet The train makes a one or two-minute halt at this junction with the BAM heading north to Bratsk and Severobaikalsk.

4600-4700 km: Foothills of the Western Sayan Mountains.

4940 km: Zima The name means winter. A 15-minute halt.

5191 km: Irkutsk Approaching the city, the skyline is dominated by the Raising of the Cross Church, across on the eastern bank of the Angara River. The train stops for 20 minutes at what is Siberia's liveliest station. If you're quick, you can run through the station to the ranks of well-stocked kiosks and shashlyk sellers on the street outside.

5228 km: North of the line an improbably cheery Lenin waves from the hillside.

5300-5500 km: This is the most attractive stretch of the Trans-Siberian, as the line runs along the shore of Lake Baikal and through a series of tunnels blasted through the cliffs along the water's edge.

5312 km: Slyudyanka This is an unattractive mining town on the southern shore of Lake Baikal. There's a 15-minute halt here, which is just enough time to run down to the lake and dip in a hand.

The station at Taiga

5630 km: Cross the Selenga River.

5647 km: Ulan Ude Capital of Buryatia, and a 15-minute halt. There are plenty of kiosks on the platform, including one filled with different kinds of breads. The topiary mother and baby bear have been there since at least 1980, when they were noted by a passing journalist.

5655 km: Zaudinsky Trans-Mongolian junction.

5771 km: Local time becomes Moscow time plus six hours.

5790 km: Petrovsk-Zabaikalsky Known as Petrovsky Zavod when some of the Decembrists were jailed here in 1830-39 – an event commemorated in a large, photogenic mural at the station. A 12-minute halt.

5800-6300 km: Yablonovy Mountains.

5884 km: Bada A small town based around an aerodrome. Look for the MiG fighter monument and the cluster of old aircraft on the runway to the north. There is no halt here.

6204 km: Chita Little of sustenance is to be found on the platform, but in the station's cavernous waiting rooms there are two good bufety. A 15-minute halt.

6293 km: Karymskoe A 12-minute halt.

6312 km: Tarskaya Trans-Manchurian junction.

6446 km: Shilka A 15-minute halt.

7000 km: For the next 700 km the line runs, on average, only 50 km north of the Amur River, the border with China. At one time, strategic sensitivity meant that carriages containing foreigners had their window blinds fastened down during this stretch.

7012 km: Amazar There's a graveyard of steam locomotives here, but the brief halt of eight minutes or so doesn't give much time to explore.

7119 km: Yerofey Pavlovich Named in honour of the Siberian explorer Yerofey Pavlovich Khaberov (the remainder of his name went to the big city further down the line). A 10-minute halt.

7273 km: Bam A line branches off to connect with the BAM a few hundred km north.

7306 km: Skovorodino A 10-minute halt. The next station east after Skovorodino is

Bolshoy Never (Great Never), from where a desolate highway runs 1200 km north to Yakutsk.

7873 km: Belogorsk The junction with the branch line to Blagoveshchensk on the Amur River, a possible border crossing into China. A 15-minute halt.

8088 km: Arkhara A 15-minute halt.

8185 km: The boundary between Siberia and the Russian Far East. Local time becomes Moscow time plus seven hours.

8358 km: Birobidzhan The train makes a halt of a couple of minutes at the capital of the Jewish Autonomous Region – note the station name in Hebrew letters.

8487 km: Volochaevka This was the site of the final battle of the Civil War.

8531 km: Khabarovsk Approaching Khabarovsk from the west, the train crosses a 2.5-km bridge over the Amur River, the longest span on the whole line and the last stretch of the Trans-Siberian Railway to be completed (1916). From Khabarovsk you can connect with the BAM at Komsomolsk, or take a train direct to Port Vanino for a boat to Sakhalin Island. A statue of Yerofey Pavlovich Khaberov stands in the square outside the station, and in the ticket hall there are a couple of unsavoury snack places. A 25-minute halt.

9177 km: Ussuriysk Formerly named Nikolskoe in honour of the Tsarevich's 1891 visit, this town was once of a greater size and importance than nearby Vladivostok. There is a twice-weekly train from here to Pyongyang, the North Korean capital. A 10-minute halt.

9289 km: Vladivostok From here you can make train connections to Harbin in northeast China or catch a boat across to Japan.

The Trans-Mongolian

This branch line has been open since the mid-1950s and has become the rail route most synonymous with the 'Trans-Siberian' tag. The itinerary is identical to that of the Trans-Siberian until shortly after Lake Baikal at a place called Zaudinsky, when the line forks south across Buryatia to the Russian border town of Naushki. Entering

Mongolia brings a rapid change of scenery; the forests thin out into the lush green fields and pastures of the fertile Selenge Gol (Selenge River) basin. Ulan Bator is just 311 km south of the border, after which the line winds through billiard-baize plains and gently swelling hills, which soon give way to the harsh steppes of the Gobi Desert. After crossing into China's Inner Mongolia region, the train passes twice through the Great Wall to arrive in Beijing 5½ days after leaving Moscow.

Most tourists ride the weekly Chinese train (No 4), which departs from Moscow's Yaroslavl Station at 7.55 pm every Tuesday and arrives in Beijing at 3.33 pm the following Monday. In the reverse direction, Chinese train No 3 departs from Beijing at 7.40 am every Wednesday, reaching Moscow the following Monday at 5.10 pm. There is also a Moscow-Ulan Bator express (train No 5/6), which runs twice a week year-round, and a daily Irkutsk-Ulan Bator express (train No 263/264). From Ulan Bator there are two connections to Beijing: the twice-weekly train No 89/90 and the weekly train No 23/24.

Trans-Mongolian Landmarks Follow the Trans-Siberian landmarks until Zaudinsky. Both Mongolia and China have their own km markers. In Mongolia, 0 km is the border with Russia at Naushki; in China 0 km is Beijing.

5701 & 5885 km: Cross the Selenga River.
5902/0 km: Naushki A small, modern town that serves as the Russian border post. Stops here are usually at least two hours.
21 km: Sukhe Bator Also known as Suhbaatar, this is Mongolia's chief border town. You will be subject to customs procedures here. There is little in the town to look at, and the railway station is probably the building of greatest interest.
123 km: Darhan With a population of just over 80,000, this is Mongolia's second-largest city. It was designed by the Russians in the days when grey concrete slabs and

statues of Lenin were the in thing. A 10-minute halt.
404 km: Ulan Bator The sprawling Mongolian capital has a population of 600,000. The train stops here for half an hour, but as the city centre is a km away your wanderings will be confined to the station. There's a cafeteria and the usual assortment of kiosks, plus a large number of steam engines at the northern end of the platform.
649 km: Choyr A small, obscure village which, prior to 1992, was home to the biggest Soviet military airbase in Mongolia. The only MiGs to be seen now are mounted on plinths. A 15-minute halt.
876 km: Saynshand A 15-minute stop is made at a small (population 14,000), dusty, dry town out in the middle of the Gobi Desert.
1113 km: Dzamin-Uud Mongolian border post.
842 km: Erlian (Erenhot) The Chinese border post, and your first or last chance to shop at the Friendship Store. Bogies (support wheels) are changed.
415 km: Fengzhan There's nothing of note here, but about 30 km after this station you will get your first glimpse of the Great Wall as the line passes through it.
317 km: Datong Once Northern China's imperial centre, this is now one of the country's most depressing cities. A 10-minute halt.
193 km: Zhangjiakou A 10-minute halt.
82 km: Kanzuang Spectacular crossing of the Great Wall.
0 km: Beijing

The Trans-Manchurian

The segment of this route from the junction at Tarskaya (100 km east of Chita) to Shenyang in China was laid by the Russians in 1897-1903 as part of the East China line to Vladivostok and Dalian (Port Arthur). It goes via Manzhouli and Harbin in north-east China, crossing steppes, the Great Khingan Mountains (Da Hinggan Ling, to the Chinese) and, after Shenyang, coastal flat lands.

Tourists ride the weekly Russian trains

(No 20), which leave Moscow every Friday and Saturday at 8.35 pm and arrive in Beijing, some 6½ days later, the following Friday and Saturday mornings at 6.32 am. In the reverse direction, Russian train No 19 leaves Beijing at 8.32 pm every Friday and Saturday and gets to Moscow at 8.20 pm the following Friday or Saturday.

Trans-Manchurian Landmarks Follow the Trans-Siberian landmarks as far as Tarskaya. Once in China, the km markers show the distance from Harbin; after Harbin they show the distance to Beijing.

6666 km: Zabaikalsk Russian border post. You can eat in the restaurant here while the train's bogies are changed.
935 km: Manzhouli The Chinese border post. The train spends a further two hours or so here, so you can eat again or go shopping at the Friendship Store. One attraction is the large number of steam locomotives still at work in the shunting yards. After leaving Manzhouli, look to the south for the Dalai Lake, which unexpectedly pops up out of the grasslands like a great inland sea. It is Inner Mongolia's largest lake.
950-650 km: Great Khingan Mountains.
539 km: Boketu A 15-minute halt.
270 km: Angangxi A 15-minute halt.
0 km: Harbin A large industrial city with a very visible Russian imprint – lots of onion-domed Orthodox churches to be spotted. Many White Russians took refuge here, fleeing the Bolsheviks. It's now famous for its ice festival, held every year from 5 January until late February. A 20-minute halt.
841 km: Shenyang A major industrial city with a population of six million. A 15-minute halt.
415 km: Shanhaiguan The eastern end of the Great Wall, where it meets the sea. This happens four km from the centre of town and isn't visible from the train, but there are plenty of other great views.
133 km: Tianjin Now a sprawling munici-pality of eight million people, but in the 19th century it was a port city which attracted the

interest of almost every European nation that had a ship to put to sea. The evidence is in the fact that Tianjin is now a living museum of turn-of-the-century European architec-ture. It also possesses one of the cleanest and most modern railway stations in China. A 15-minute halt.
0 km: Beijing

The BAM

The Baikal-Amur Mainline has effectively only been in operation since 1991 and, as of writing, there's still no service that runs along its entire length. When compared with the famed Trans-Siberian and the chain of historic settlements it connects, the BAM doesn't seem to offer too much. Other than a beautiful switchback route through the lake-filled mountains between Bratsk and Severobaikalsk, in general the scenery on the 3000-km route is bleak and foreboding. It hasn't been improved by the intervention of man, either. Almost without exception, all the towns along the BAM have grown up in the last 40 or 50 years – not a period that is ever likely to be regarded as a golden age of Russian architecture.

The possible attraction of the BAM is that it is virgin territory: you're travelling across a part of Siberia that few other foreigners have ever seen (and few will ever want to). While not particularly absorbing in them-selves, the towns along the line can serve as bases for exploration of the surrounding wil-derness, and there are good opportunities for adventure tourism, though at present there is little supporting infrastructure.

From its junction with the Trans-Siberian at Tayshet, the principal towns of the BAM are Bratsk, Severobaikalsk, Tynda and Komsomolsk-on-Amur. From Tynda, a short stretch of the Yakutia Railway (which was to connect Yakutsk to the BAM) runs north, but at present the line is only in use as far as Aldan. From Komsomolsk, a line also extends further east to Sovietskaya Gavan on the Pacific coast.

There is a direct Moscow-Tynda express (train No 75/76), which goes every other day, alternating with the Moscow-Neryungri service (train No 77/78). A daily service connects Tynda with Komsomolsk (train No 203/204), and between Komsomolsk and Sovietskaya Gavan there are three daily trains. There's also a daily Krasnoyarsk-Severobaikalsk train (No 197/198) and one or two other services to Severobaikalsk from Irkutsk via Tayshet.

For anyone travelling on this little-known line, an invaluable aid is *The Siberian BAM Railway Guidebook* written by Athol Yates and published by Red Bear Tours/Trailblazer Publications (1995).

BREAKING YOUR JOURNEY

Mainly as a result of Soviet-era restrictions, stopovers have traditionally only been made at Irkutsk and the Mongolian capital of Ulan Bator. However, now that visitors are more or less free to travel around at will, there's no reason why other towns and cities shouldn't be visited. Of the big Western Siberian cities, Yekaterinburg has historic associations with the end of the Romanov dynasty, and Krasnoyarsk is well worth visiting. Severobaikalsk is a good place to enjoy the unsullied shores of Lake Baikal, and Ulan Ude's fascinating Buryat Buddhist heritage makes it an essential stopover. Further along the Trans-Siberian route, a couple of days each ought to be allowed for Khabarovsk and Vladivostok.

No such thing as a stopover ticket exists. If you are travelling from Moscow to Beijing, spending a night or two in Irkutsk and Ulan Bator, then you'll need three separate tickets: one Moscow-Irkutsk, another Irkutsk-Ulan Bator and a third valid for Ulan Bator-Beijing. All your tickets will be for a specific berth on a specific train on a specified day. Generally, ticket offices can only sell places on trains leaving from that particular station – for instance, the Irkutsk-Ulan Bator ticket would have to be bought in Irkutsk and the Ulan Bator-Beijing ticket in the Mongolian capital – but if you prefer, you can go through an agency which will be able to make all bookings in advance. For anyone flexible, independent rail travel within Russia is easy enough, and tickets for the

Moscow-Vladivostok route in particular are rarely hard to get. In addition to the long-distance services, there are numerous daily short-haul trains on which it's always possible, without advance booking, to get a berth. In 10 weeks of Siberian touring, Andrew Humphreys never bought a rail ticket more than 48 hours beforehand. It's even easy enough to make a short-notice booking on the daily Irkutsk-Ulan Bator train.

Problems may arise when getting tickets in Ulan Bator, as there are only four trains a week travelling onwards to Beijing. It may be worth booking this portion of your trip in advance, taking into account any stopovers to be made between the Mongolian capital and Beijing. On the Trans-Manchurian route, Shanhaiguan and Tianjin are worth a day or two, and getting off at either of these cities shouldn't be a problem as they are both relatively close to Beijing and connected by frequent daily services.

All Russian railway stations have prominent and reasonably decipherable timetables (see the European Russia Getting Around chapter for more information on timetables, and remember that the train times will be given in Moscow time). Some of the larger cities have foreigners' ticketing desks.

BOOKING
When to Go

See Siberia & the Russian Far East's Facts for the Visitor section for general climatic considerations. Ticket prices are the same year-round, but off-season travel-agency packages may be discounted. Summer tickets for the Trans-Manchurian and Trans-Mongolian must be booked further ahead – allow a couple of months.

Classes of Travel

The standard accommodation on all long-distance, Trans-Siberian-related trains is in 2nd-class (also called hard or kupeynyy) carriages. These carriages are divided into nine enclosed compartments, each with four reasonably comfortable berths, a fold-down table and just enough room between the

The Trans-Siberian
Moscow-Vladivostok (Train No 1/2 *Rossia*)

Station name		Stop (mins)	Departure time Eastbound	Westbound	Local Time Zone
Moscow	Москва		14.00	06.45*	Moscow time
Yaroslavl	Ярославль	5	18.30	02.10	
Danilov	Данилов	15	20.05	00.50	
Vyatka	Вятка	15	04.58	16.08	Moscow +1
Perm	Пермь	15	12.18	08.44	Moscow +2
Yekaterinburg	Екатеринбург	20	19.06	02.14	
Tyumen	Тюмень	10	23.39	21.29	
Ishim	Ишим	8	03.13	17.37	
Omsk	Омск	15	07.03	13.25	Moscow +3
Novosibirsk	Новосибирск	20	16.50	04.32	
Taiga	Тайга	10	20.57	00.33	Moscow +4
Mariinsk	Мариинск	15	23.38	22.07	
Krasnoyarsk	Красноярск	20	06.23	14.34	
Tayshet	Тайшет	2	13.44	06.34	
Zima	Зима	15	20.49	23.39	Moscow +5
Irkutsk	Иркутск	20	01.38	19.01	
Slyudyanka	Слюдянка	15	04.33	16.24	
Ulan Ude	Улан Удэ	15	10.10	11.02	
Petrovsk-Zabaikalsky	Петровск-Забайкальский	12	12.42	08.41	Moscow +6
Chita	Чита	15	19.47	01.51	
Karymskoe	Карымское	12	21.56	23.44	
Shilka	Шилка	15	24.34	21.06	
Amazar	Амазар	8	11.37	09.33	
Skovorodino	Сковородино	10	17.03	04.07	
Belogorsk	Белогорск	15	01.53	18.41	
Khabarovsk	Хабаровск	25	13.35	07.35	Moscow +7
Ussuriysk	Уссурийск	10	00.43	20.21	
Vladivostok	Владивосток		02.45*	18.05	

All times given in Moscow time
Times shown are departure times except * (arrival times) – subtract stop for arrival time

bunks to turn around, providing you're not excessively broad-shouldered.

On the Chinese train, 1st class (soft or myagkiy) has softer beds but hardly any more space than 2nd class and is not worth the considerably higher fare charged. The real luxury comes with Chinese deluxe class: roomy, wood-panelled two-berth compartments with a sofa, and a shower cubicle shared with the adjacent compartment.

First-class compartments on the Russian train are the same as 2nd-class, except that because there are only two berths you'll have

more room and more privacy. First class also has a slight advantage in that there are only half as many people queuing to use the toilet every morning. Other than in the deluxe class on the Chinese train, there are no showers.

There is another (lower) category of accommodation, not available on the Trans-Manchurian and Trans-Mongolian but common to all other trains in Russia, and that is *platskartnyy*. This is essentially an uncompartmentalised dormitory carriage with hard bunks that are slightly shorter than standard to accommodate more berths

The Trans-Mongolian
Moscow-Beijing (Train No 3/4 *The Chinese Train*)

Station name		Stop (mins)	Departure time Eastbound	Departure time Westbound	Local Time Zone
Moscow	Москва		19.55	17.10*	Moscow time
Yaroslavl	Ярославль	5	00.15	12.55	
Perm	Пермь	15	17.52	19.19	Moscow +2
Yekaterinburg	Екатеринбург	15	00.09	12.37	
Novosibirsk	Новосибирск	15	20.24	16.35	Moscow +3
Krasnoyarsk	Красноярск	15	09.34	03.43	Moscow +4
Irkutsk	Иркутск	15	03.49	09.20	Moscow +5
Ulan Ude	Улан Удэ	20	11.49	01.23	
Gusinoe Ozero	Гусиное Озеро	2	14.42	22.15	
Naushki	Наушки	120	18.20	20.25	
Sukhe Bator	Сухэ Батор	60	01.20	22.05	Ulan Bator time
Darhan	Дархан	10	03.11	19.00	(Moscow +5)
Ulan Bator	Улан Батор	30	09.30	13.50	
Choyr	Чойр	15	14.06	09.02	
Saynshand	Сайншанд	15	17.52	05.00	
Dzamin-Uud	Дзамин-Ууд	60	22.33	00.40	
Erlian		120	01.51	23.15	Beijing time
Jining		10	06.28	16.29	(Moscow +5)
Datong		10	08.34	14.25	
Zhangjiakou		10	11.00	11.47	
Kanzhuang		8	12.34	10.01	
Beijing			15.33*	07.40	

Times shown are departure times except * (arrival times) – subtract stop for arrival time

lengthways along the corridor. Privacy is out of the question. Instead of the usual maximum of three fellow travellers, in platskartnyy you have in effect close to 60 inquisitive companions. The scene often resembles a refugee camp, with clothing strung between bunks, a great swapping of bread and fish and shared jars of tea, and babies sitting on potties while their snot-nosed siblings tear up and down the corridor.

Platskartnyy tickets cost half to two-thirds the price of a 2nd-class berth. Avoid the top bunk, as it doesn't have enough head clearance to allow you to sit upright. This becomes a problem if the people on the two lower bunks elect to spend all day in bed, condemning you to endless hours lying on your back with your nose little more than a hand's breadth from the compartment ceiling.

Costs
In the past, one of the reasons Trans-Siberian routes appealed to travellers was that they represented one of the cheapest ways of travelling one-third of the way around the world. These days, however, with airline companies in desperate competition, slashing prices, throwing in free car rental, penthouse suites and a two-week sitter for the cat, that's no longer the case. The standard foreigners' price of a Moscow-Beijing ticket is US$265/470 for 2nd/1st-class passage on the Trans-Mongolian, and US$225/340 on the Trans-Manchurian route. From Moscow to Vladivostok it's US$235/449. As with hotels and domestic air tickets, a two-tier price system is in operation and Russians get to pay around half these fares. While it is possible for you to get a Russian colleague to

The Trans-Manchurian
Moscow-Beijing (Train No 19/20 *The Russian Train*)

Station name		Stop (mins)	Departure time Eastbound	Westbound	Local Time Zone
Moscow	Москва		20.35	20.20*	Moscow time
Yaroslavl	Ярославль	5	0.55	16.05	
Perm	Пермь	20	18.23	23.03	Moscow +2
Yekaterinburg	Екатеринбург	15	0.39	16.31	
Novosibirsk	Новосибирск	25	21.31	19.57	Moscow +3
Krasnoyarsk	Красноярск	20	10.17	07.01	Moscow +4
Irkutsk	Иркутск	20	04.30	12.30	Moscow +5
Ulan Ude	Улан Удэ	15	12.23	04.33	
Chita	Чита	15	21.43	18.50	Moscow +6
Zabaikalsk	Забайкалск	120	14.06	07.01	
Manzhouli		120	22.07	07.01	Beijing time
Hailar		10	00.42	02.31	(Moscow +5)
Xinganling		10	03.35	00.12	
Boketu		15	04.22	23.08	
Angangxi		15	08.25	18.56	
Daqing		10	10.01	17.10	
Harbin		20	12.08	14.53	
Changchun		12	15.52	11.30	
Shenyang		15	19.42	07.20	
Jinzhou		12	22.59	04.12	
Shanghaiguan		12	01.24	01.53	
Tianjin		15	05.00	22.19	
Beijing			06.32*	20.32	

Times shown are departure times except * (arrival times) – subtract stop for arrival time

purchase your ticket at the lower price, on long journeys the ticket will be checked; it's illegal for a foreigner to travel on a Russian-priced ticket, and if you are rumbled you're likely to be fined and thrown off the train.

The price of the train ticket is only one expense. The other major dent in your credit card is likely to be made by the cost of getting to the train's departure point and then home again at the end of the ride. In all likelihood, this will involve a flight or train to Moscow, and then a return journey from Beijing or Vladivostok (or vice versa). The number of stopovers should also figure in your accounting, as hotel rates in Russia are comparatively high. Depending on the level of comfort that you require, you can expect to be spending on average US$30 to US$35 on accommodation per night. Considering this expense, some of the packages offered by the travel agencies may turn out to be good deals.

Visas

Trans-Siberian travellers will need a Russian visa of some sort, and also perhaps Chinese and Mongolian visas, depending on the route. It's safer to obtain all visas in your home country before setting out. Some tour companies arrange your visas as part of their Trans-Siberian package. Bear in mind, if you are also travelling through Belarus, Ukraine, the Baltic States, etc, you will also need visas for some of those countries. See European Russia Getting There & Away for information on visas for Eastern European countries and ex-Soviet states.

Russian If you are not making any stops in Russia other than an initial/final night or two in Moscow, a transit visa (usually valid for a maximum of 10 days) is sufficient for a Trans-Siberian journey. It makes life easier if you can make do with a transit visa because the paperwork is much simpler and quicker (see European Russia Facts for the Visitor) – you just require proof that you are leaving the country (such as a visa for the next destination or your rail ticket).

If you pick up your Russian transit visa in China, it will usually give you three or four days in Moscow at the end of your journey. In Beijing, the Russian Embassy (☎ 532 20 51, visa section ☎ 532 12 67) is at 4 Baizhongjie, just off Dongzhimen and west of the Sanlitun Embassy Compound. A transit visa (or a tourist visa if you are armed with the required paperwork) takes three days to process and costs US$40, or you can pay US$60 for same-day express service. There is also a seemingly arbitrary consular fee: citizens of Australia, New Zealand, the UK and the USA are exempt, but other nationalities have to pay between US$1 and US$100 (someone has it in for the Burkina-Fasoians) on top of the standard processing charge. You also need three photos, your passport (or photocopies of the relevant pages), train ticket or ticket voucher and the exact money in dollars. Consular hours are Monday, Wednesday and Friday from 9.30 am to noon.

In Mongolia, the Russian Embassy (☎ 2 52 07) is on the south side of Peace Ave, one block west of the central post office in Ulan Bator.

Mongolian If you are travelling on the Trans-Mongolian train, which goes via Ulan Bator, then you will need some kind of Mongolian visa. Like the Russian visa, the Mongolian visa comes in two forms, transit or tourist, with the same sort of regulations applying. The transit visa is easy enough to get (just present a through-ticket and a visa for your onward destination), but it's only valid for three days in Mongolia. Unlike Russian transit visas, Mongolian transit visas cannot be extended, and if you are caught in the country after your visa has expired you'll be fined heavily and presented with a filing cabinet of forms to fill in, before being cuffed about the head and kicked out of the country. Obtaining a tourist visa (usually issued for two weeks) involves the same bureaucratic somersaults as the Russian tourist visa requires. The easiest way to bypass the red tape is to book a tour with a private operator which will obtain the tourist visa for you. Tourist visas can be extended (at the Ministry of Foreign Affairs at the junction of Marx and Peace Aves in Ulan Bator), making it possible to prolong your stay and do some independent wandering. However, check all travel arrangements carefully in advance because tickets for trains out of Mongolia are hard to get at short notice.

In Moscow, the Mongolian Embassy (☎ 244 78 67) is at Spasopeskovsky pereulok 7, close to the Smolenskaya metro. It's open from 9 am to 1 pm, and transit visas can be collected the same day between 4.30 and 5 pm. There is also a visa-issuing consulate in Irkutsk (see the Eastern Siberia chapter).

In Beijing, the Mongolian Embassy (☎ 532 12 03) is at 2 Xiushui Beilu, Jianguomenwai. The visa section of the embassy is open Monday, Tuesday, Thursday and Friday from 8.30 to 11.30 am.

A transit visa generally costs US$15 and takes three days to issue; US$30 for same-day or next-day service. Tourist visas are US$25; US$50 for express-processed service. Visas are free for Finnish and Indian nationals. All Mongolian embassies shut down for the week of National Day (*Naadam*), which officially falls around 11 to 13 July.

Chinese Visas for individual travel in China are easy to get – though the queues and confusion at the Chinese Embassy (☎ (095) 143 15 43) in Moscow, at ulitsa Druzhby 6, near the Universitet metro, make this far from the best place to apply. They reportedly also ask to see an onward ticket from China, something most other Chinese embassies don't require. The embassy is open Monday,

Wednesday and Friday from 9 am to noon. If you're passing through, there's also a Chinese consulate in Khabarovsk which can process visas in two days (see the Russian Far East chapter). A standard single-entry tourist visa is usually valid for a period of one or two months and costs US$50. If you want more time, ask and you may be given it; if not, it is quite easy to get visa extensions in most major cities once you are within China.

Getting To/From the Train

Unless you're using the Trans-Siberian or one of its offshoots as a transit route, getting to/from the train is liable to be your greatest expense. If you are picking up the train in Moscow, see the European Russia Getting There & Away chapter and the Moscow chapter for travel alternatives and costs. From Moscow, there are domestic flights to Vladivostok (US$398 one-way). From the USA, Alaska Airlines also flies a Seattle-Anchorage-Vladivostok route. Aeroflot connects the Russian Pacific port with Niigata (US$310 one-way) on Japan's western coast, and there's also a weekly ferry (2nd-class cabin US$300) which sails the same route, but only between May and October. See also Siberia & the Russian Far East's Getting There & Away section for further options.

To connect with the Trans-Manchurian or Trans-Mongolian at their eastern terminal, you should look into flights to Hong Kong. These are often cheaper than flying to Beijing, and connections between the two cities are straightforward.

Travel Agencies

Most travel agencies have their hands tied by Russian visa regulations, and if you're buying a Trans-Siberian ticket from them, to get the Russian visa you also have to preplan and book all accommodation and other transport. The simplest way around this is to employ the services of one of the small, independent travel companies that are registered in Russia and can issue their own invitations (a system known as visa support

– see European Russia Facts for the Visitor for further details). The HI St Petersburg Hostel and the Moscow Travellers Guest House are good examples. These companies usually require that you also make use of their services, either buying rail tickets or booking a couple of nights' accommodation with them, but it's a fairly small price to pay for complete freedom from fixed itineraries.

If you decide to take a package, it is important to note that most tour packages do not include your flights to/from the train – only your ticket, stopover accommodation, transfers and city tours and guides.

From Australasia Gateway Travel (☎ (02) 745 3333; fax (02) 745 3237), 48 The Boulevarde, Strathfield, NSW 2135, Australia, offers 2nd-class through-tickets on the Trans-Manchurian, Trans-Mongolian and Trans-Siberian routes for US$435, US$510 and US$450, respectively. It also offers fully escorted Trans-Manchurian/Mongolian tours and some expensive stopovers in Irkutsk.

Red Bear Tours (☎ (03) 9824 7183; toll free (008) 9337 031; fax (03) 9822 3956) at 320B Glenferrie Rd, Malvern, Victoria 3144, Australia, specialises in Russia, Mongolia and North Korea. It offers rail-only tickets and packages for the Trans-Manchurian, Trans-Mongolian, Trans-Siberian and Turk-Sib. The firm pioneered BAM tours, and offers 10-day trips along its length from Komsomolsk to Severobaikalsk. Red Bear can also provide homestays in various cities and secure three-month, multicity Russian visas.

Iris Hotels (☎ (02) 580 6466; fax (02) 580 7256), PO Box 60, Hurstville, NSW 2220, Australia, runs two or three Trans-Sib packages using the Mikof-Iris eye-surgery hotels (see Accommodation in the European Russia Facts for the Visitor chapter) as stopover bases. The 14-day tour starts in Khabarovsk (make your own way there) and takes in Irkutsk and Lake Baikal, Novosibirsk, Yekaterinburg and Moscow. The starting price of US$1295 includes eight nights' hotel accommodation, sightseeing, guides and a night at the opera or ballet. An alternative programme drops Novosibirsk in favour of two nights in St Petersburg. For budget travellers, Iris has a 22-day itinerary with homestays in Khabarovsk, Irkutsk, Novosibirsk and Yekaterinburg and hostel accommodation in Moscow. The price of US$1130 (US$955 twin) doesn't include flights.

The New Zealand-based operator Suntravel (☎ (09) 525 3074; fax (09) 525 3065) at 407 Great South Rd (PO Box 12-424), Penrose, Auckland, has what it calls 'basic express packages' on the Trans-Manchurian and Trans-Mongolian. They start in Beijing and include three nights' accommodation there, plus a night each in Irkutsk, Moscow and St Petersburg, a 2nd-class ticket to Moscow and then either a flight on to London or a train ticket to Helsinki, Berlin or Warsaw, from where you make your own way home. Prices are from NZ$2390 to NZ$2690. You can pick up the tour in Hong Kong for a further NZ$600. Suntravel offers something similar on the Trans-Siberian for NZ$2550 to NZ$2800, starting from Niigata.

From Canada Exotik Tours (☎ (514) 284 3324; fax (514) 843 5493) of 1117 Ste-Catherine O, Suite 806, Montreal H3B 1H9, is able to make reservations on the Trans-Siberian trains; however, they need a minimum of two months' notice. The staff can also help with visas, but only if you prebook all accommodation and other travel arrangements.

From Germany Lernidee Reisen (☎ (030) 786 5056; fax (030) 786 5596) of Duden strasse 78, 10965 Berlin, sells the following 2nd-class tickets: Beijing-Moscow (DM 775), Moscow-Beijing (DM 735), Beijing-Ulan Bator (DM 335), Ulan Bator-Beijing (DM 295), Ulan Bator-Moscow (DM 540) and Moscow-Ulan Bator (DM 585). Lernidee can also make bookings for the weekly Vladivostok-Niigata ferry, and will take care of visas.

Deutsches Reiseburo (☎ (069) 95 8800) of Emil-von-Behring strasse 6, 6000 Frankfurt am Main 50, offers a number of Trans-Siberian packages, including a 15-day Moscow-Irkutsk-Khabarovsk package, returning to Moscow by air, starting from DM 2645; a 16-day Moscow-Irkutsk-Ulan Bator-Gobi Desert package, returning to Moscow by air, for DM 4395; and several tours which mix Trans-Siberian destinations with Central Asia in the DM 3000 to DM4000 range. All prices include a return Germany-Moscow flight. TSA Reisen (07371) 8522; fax (07371) 12593) of Schulgasse 1, 88499 Riedlingen, is a Trans-Siberian specialist, offering all manner of permutations on the various routes and a variety of stopover options. It has some interesting side trips, like jeep excursions into the Gobi, and even a 13-day all-inclusive BAM package for DM 4760.

From Hong Kong & China Try Moonsky Star (also known as Monkey Business) (☎ (852) 2723 1376; fax (852) 723 6653, e-mail CompuServe 100267,2570) at Chungking Mansions, 36-44 Nathan Rd, E-block, 4th floor, Flat 6, Kowloon, Hong Kong, or (☎ (861) 301 2244, ext 716; fax (861) 301 2244, ext 444) at Qiao Yuan Hotel, Room 716, Dongbinhe Rd, Youanmenwai, 100054 Beijing, China. The company has a lot of experience in booking Trans-Siberian trains for independent travellers, and gives their customers a useful information package. However, we've heard a lot of complaints along the lines of poor organisation, indifferent service and, in particular, inflated prices. The basic, 2nd-class nonstop Moscow-Beijing ticket is US$375 to US$395; from Beijing to Moscow it's US$349 on the Trans-Manchurian or US$599 on the Trans-Mongolian (in deluxe class – because of safety fears, Moonsky won't book 2nd-class berths on this train). With one-day stopovers in Irkutsk and Ulan Bator, the price is US$695 from Moscow and US$749 from Beijing. Other packages offer various extensions to stopovers, including excursions, performances, sightseeing, transfers, meals and accommodation. For example, an all-in package with four days in Irkutsk and six in Mongolia costs US$1255. Packages include one night's accommodation in Moscow plus Russian and Mongolian visa support.

There are other ticket agencies in Hong Kong worth calling to compare against Monkey Business. They include Time Travel (☎ (852) 2366 6222; fax (852) 2739 5413) at Block A, 16th floor, Chungking Mansions, 40 Nathan Rd, Tsim Sha Tsui, Kowloon; Travel Advisers (☎ (852) 2312 7138; fax (852) 2312 7231), Room 906, South Seas Centre, Tower 2, 75 Mody Rd, Tsim Sha Tsui East, Kowloon; and Wallem Travel (☎ (852) 2821 3863; fax (852) 2865 2652) on the 46th floor, Hopewell Centre, 183 Queen's Rd East, Wanchai. In Beijing, the alternative to Monkey Business is to buy your ticket from CITS (China International Travel Service).

From Russia The 1995 programme for the Travellers Guesthouse/IRO Travel (☎ (095) 974 17 81, (095) 280 43 00; fax (095) 280 76 86) at ulitsa Bolshaya Pereyaslavskaya 50, 10th floor, Moscow, Russia 129401, offered eight different trips from Moscow to Beijing, with or without stopovers in Irkutsk and Mongolia. As an example, a package including visas, four nights' accommodation in Irkutsk and four in Mongolia was US$1050. Prices for trains only, without meals, hotels, transfers or visa support, were: Trans-Siberian to Vladivostok US$260/499 (2nd/1st class); Trans-Mongolian to Beijing US$295/495 (the Chinese train, No 4); and Trans-Manchurian to Beijing US$245/365 (the Russian train, No 20). The Guesthouse could also do Moscow-Ulan Bator (train No 6) for US$140/260.

Anyone already in Moscow can buy their own Trans-Siberian tickets from the building at ulitsa Krasnoprudnaya 1, next door to Yaroslavl Station. The office is on the 1st floor, marked *zheleznodorozhnoye kassy* (railway ticket office). Windows five to eight are for ticket sales, and you tell the staff (who only speak Russian) your destination, what train you want, the date and class of travel. They also need to know your name and passport number. If you don't speak Russian, just write it all out. You'll be handed a slip of paper to take to window nine or 10, where you pay and are handed a receipt to exchange for your ticket at the first window. It can be a laborious process, particularly in summer when the queues are long. Also, in summer you should try to come a few weeks in advance to be sure of getting a ticket on the train you want.

Intour-Khabarovsk (☎ (4212) 399 99 19, international ☎ (509) 31 42 22 51; fax (4212) 33 87 74) of Amursky bulvar 2, Khabarovsk 680065, Russia, does a 12-day excursion along the BAM. The package starts in Khabarovsk and includes Komsomolsk, Tynda, Chara and Severobaikalsk, wrapping up in Irkutsk.

From the UK The China Travel Service & Information Centre (☎ (0171) 388 8838; fax (0171) 388 8828) at 124 Euston Rd, London NW1 2AL, sells tickets for trains out of Beijing: a hard sleeper to Moscow is £245 (deluxe £310), to Irkutsk £150 (deluxe £205) and to Ulan Bator £135 (deluxe £180). The China Travel Service (☎ (0171) 836 9911; fax (0171) 836 3121) at 24 Cambridge Circus, London WC2H 8HD, sells tickets for trips both way and is considerably cheaper, eg Beijing-Moscow from £190 (though, curiously, Moscow-Beijing is £290) and Beijing-Ulan Bator from £95. For west-bound travellers, some form of accommodation in Moscow must be booked in order to get the Russian visa.

Goodwill Holidays (☎ (01438) 71 6421; fax (01438) 84 0228) of Manor Chambers, The Green, School Lane, Welwyn, Herts AL6 9EB, can make Trans-Siberian arrangements for individual travellers. It offers Moscow-Irkutsk tickets for £110 and Moscow-Vladivostok for £200 (the flight back, Vladivostok-Moscow, is £250). It also offers a full Russian visa service for £35 or visa support for private visits at £25.

Intourist Travel (☎ (0171) 538 8600; fax (0171) 538 5967) of Intourist House, 219 Marsh Wall, London E14 9FJ, offers 2nd-class Moscow-Vladivostok tickets for £215, and can also arrange for you to fly certain sections if time is at a premium. A 2nd-class, basic Moscow-Beijing ticket starts at £275, and there are several set itineraries with different permutations of stopovers. Intourist will organise all visas on the proviso that two nights' accommodation is booked with them (four nights if the stay in Russia exceeds two weeks), and recommends booking at least six weeks in advance.

One Europe Travel (☎ (0181) 566 9424; fax (0181) 566 8845) at Research House, Fraser Rd, Perivale, Middlesex UB6 7AQ, has about five basic Trans-Siberian packages, which it can also offer with extensions to St Petersburg or Hong Kong. Two nights in Moscow and a Trans-Manchurian ticket to Beijing goes for £355, while a Trans-Mongolian trip including two nights in Moscow, two nights in Ulan Bator and two nights in Beijing costs £549 for an individual, or £450 twin. Adding an extra night in Moscow and two in a homestay on the shores of Lake Baikal pushes the price up to £760, or £690 twin. One Europe can also work Severobaikalsk and Ulan Ude into itineraries and organise BAM trips to Komsomolsk.

Progressive Tours (☎ (0171) 262 1676) of 12 Porchester Place, Marble Arch, London W2 2BS, can book a 2nd-class sleeper for Moscow-Ulan Bator for £200 and Ulan Bator-Beijing for £67. The 2nd-class fare for Moscow-Vladivostok is £230. They can also book berths on the Vladivostok-Niigata ferry from £218. An out-of-season package (October to May) for Moscow-Beijing costs £285, which includes one night in Moscow and two sightseeing trips, a 2nd-class berth on the train and three meals a day within Russia. For a supplementary fee, your stay in Moscow can be extended and a stopover can be included in Irkutsk.

Regent Holidays (☎ (0117) 921 1711; fax (0117) 925 4866) of 15 John St, Bristol BS1 2HR, offers 10 or so different packages covering all routes, with prices starting at £310 for a basic one night in Moscow and a 2nd-class no-stopovers ticket to Beijing. Prices go up to around £500 if you add overnight stops in St Petersburg and Irkutsk.

Steppes East (☎ (01285) 81 0267; fax (01285) 81 0693) of Castle Eaton, Swindon, Wiltshire SN6 6JU, adventure-holiday specialists, does an 11-day, 1st-class accommodation, Trans-Mongolian trip with stopovers in Irkutsk and Ulan Bator for £1195/1150, depending on the direction of travel. Flights are not included. It also sells 2nd-class Trans-Mongolian tickets without stopovers from £195. Sundowners (☎ (0181) 742 8612; fax (0181) 742 3045) of 14 Barley Mow Passage, Chiswick W4 4PH, offers a 19-day Trans-Siberian package starting in Vladivostok (make your own way there) which gives you three nights in Irkutsk, Moscow and St Petersburg and a flight back to London for £2275. It also does a 29-day tour beginning in Hong Kong (make your own way there), taking in Guilin, Xian, Beijing, Ulan Bator, Irkutsk, Moscow and St Petersburg and ending with a flight back to London, for £3455. You can do the same thing but begin the tour from Nepal for £4530.

Voyages Jules Verne (☎ (0171) 723 5066; fax (0171) 723 8629) of 21 Dorset Square, London NW1 6QG, offers places on something called the 'Red Arrow Express', which involves a 21-day train journey from London via Moscow, Irkutsk, Ulan Bator and Beijing to Guangzhou in Canton. The price is just short of £2000 (and you make your own way home).

WHAT TO BRING

The list of travelling essentials for a Trans-Siberian jaunt doesn't differ too much from that given in this book's Facts for the Visitor sections, except perhaps that even greater stress should be given to toilet paper. Also bring your own plug (or a squash ball, which works just as well) for the toilet sink. Another recommended addition is some soft, slip-on footwear – thongs (flip-flops), Chinese cloth sandals, or something similar. Tracksuit or shell-suit trousers (something loose and comfortable) aren't a bad idea either – you're going to be doing a lot of slobbing around. You won't need a sleeping bag, but you might want to take your own lightweight sheet because the bedding handed out on the trains is often still damp from laundering.

Boiling water is always available from a samovar at the end of each carriage, so take a plastic mug and a teaspoon (although if you forget, the provodnitsa has beakers), along with sachets of instant coffee, hot chocolate or soup, or tea bags (sugar and creamer too, if needed). There's a dining car attached to most long-distance trains, and at every station halt you'll find clusters of kiosks and grannies selling home produce, so it isn't necessary to bring too much in the way of foodstuffs. Bring fruit, things like cheese slices or tinned meat to put on bread (easily available at stations) and snacks such as biscuits or chocolate bars. Juice or water in a plastic bottle is also a good idea.

How many books, games and other distractions you take along depends on whether you're travelling alone or with companions (and whether you want to talk to those companions). Unless you're a particularly voracious reader, a couple of light paperbacks should see you through as there's plenty en route to keep you occupied. Cards or chess might be a good idea, or something similar to break the ice with any non-English speakers you may encounter.

Baggage Space

If you're sensible you'll travel light, in which case you'll have no problems storing your luggage in your compartment. There is a luggage bin underneath each of the lower berths (50 cm wide, 40 cm in height, 110 cm long) and also enough space beside, under the bunk, to squeeze in another medium-sized canvas bag. Above the doorway there's a coffin-like space 160 cm long, 67 cm wide and 30 cm in height, which at a push, kick and shove will accommodate a couple of rucksacks.

There are no baggage restrictions travelling from the Moscow end, but in Beijing there is an enforced 35-kg allowance. Passengers with excess baggage are supposed to present it (along with passport, ticket and customs entry declaration) the day before departure at the Luggage Shipment Office, which is on the right-hand side of the main railway station in Beijing. The excess is charged at about US$11 per 10 kg, with a maximum excess of 40 kg allowed.

BOOKS

For general Russian reading see also the European Russia and Siberia & the Russian Far East Facts for the Visitor chapters.

There are a couple of good journey-enhancing volumes, the most essential of which is *The Trans-Siberian Handbook* (Trailblazer Publications, 1994) by Bryn Thomas – 320 pages of maps, diagrams, timetables and km-by-km route descriptions (anyone playing the Lenin-spotting game has an unassailable advantage armed with this). *The Trans-Siberian Rail Guide* (Compass Publications, 1995) by Robert Strauss is similar, but rather than Thomas' hyper-density of information, Strauss has favoured lengthy extracts culled from a century of Trans-Sib journalists.

The Big Red Train Ride (Penguin, 1978) by Eric Newby is the travelogue to take along. His account of a couple of weeks hopping on and off the *Rossia* between Moscow and Nakhodka is a little outdated but there's still plenty of colour and detail. Sometimes he's even as funny as he thinks he is. The Trans-Siberian forms a chapter of Christopher Portway's *The Great Railway Adventure* (Oxford Illustrated Press; now out of print), while another great train traveller, Paul Theroux, includes an amusingly caustic account of a Trans-Siberian journey in *The Great Rail Bazaar* (Penguin, 1977). He seems in little better mood 10 years later when he boards the Trans-Mongolian as the prelude to an exhaustive rail exploration of China, recounted in *Riding the Iron Rooster* (Penguin, 1988).

During the late 1980s, Brad Newsham was 'toting a bale of misery' (his words) around Japan and China and, via the Trans-Mongolian, to Moscow. He describes his woes, and little else, in *All the Right Places* (Sceptre, 1991). At around the same time, Mary Morris, also labouring under a cloud of self-created gloom, was following a similar self-absorbed route, related in *Wall to Wall: From Beijing to Berlin* (Flamingo, 1993). Both of these books will be of greater interest to psychoanalysts than to Trans-Siberian travellers. A good antidote to modern-day whingeing is Peter Fleming's *One's Company* (Penguin, 1956), in which a tumble down an embankment on board the Trans-Siberian is described with admirable sang-froid. Written in 1933, the style of the time was such that Fleming could get away with sentences such as, 'One of the most curious things about modern Russia is the startling and universal ugliness of the women'.

Fleming is just one of the dozens of writers extracted in *The Trans-Siberian Railway: A Travellers' Anthology*, edited by Deborah Manley (Century Hutchinson hardback, 1988). This is an excellent background read, now unfortunately out of print but worth tracking down. Also recommended is *Red Express* (Simon & Schuster hardback, 1990) by Michael Cordell & Peter Solness, a lavish photo album produced to accompany the Australian TV series of the same name that examined modern-day life in the ex-communist realms from East Berlin to China, following the route of the railway.

THE JOURNEY

Travellers respond in different ways to being sealed in a vaguely claustrophobic carriage with a crowd of strangers for six or more days, looking out at a landscape that hardly changes, with ambiguously shifting time zones and nothing insistent but hunger and bodily functions. Paul Theroux in *The Great Railway Bazaar* likened the trip to being in bed with a high fever, with each drowsy day broken into many smaller ones by naps and dreams. But not everybody is quite as saturnine, and for some the whole point of the trip is to have one nonstop rolling party with a menagerie of new friends and experiences.

Even before the suburbs of Moscow have disappeared, passengers have begun to make themselves at home. As Laurens van der Post

noted, unlike most Europeans or Americans, who travel in a train fully aware that it belongs to either a state or company, the Russians just take them over, moving into a carriage as though they were there for good. The compartments these days aren't quite as homely as they were when Van der Post travelled in the 1970s. Then, each was equipped with four tumblers, packaged biscuits, unwrapped sugar lumps and a folder holding a timetable and some reading matter – typically speeches by Lenin or Marx, or a report from the 17th Annual All-Union Tractor Kombinat Workers' Fair. Still, they're fairly snug, kept warm even in deepest winter by a coal-fired boiler in each carriage.

The biggest discomfort is the sanitary arrangements. There are two toilet/wash cubicles in each carriage; however, the one next to the provodnitsas' room is often kept locked for their own private use. That means 36 people have to make use of one toilet, and one stainless-steel basin for the purposes of washing. The tap water is cold, but if you have a plug you can get a cupful of hot water from the samovar to mix with it. The toilets are cleaned every morning, but prolonged exposure to them can still damage your sense of smell. There is a shaving point (220 V) in the toilet cubicle, but to get the electricity switched on you have to ask the provodnitsa. And if the garbage in your compartment starts to spill off the table, there's a bin under the triangular seat opposite the toilet door.

Smokers are relegated to the areas around the doors that link the carriages. The windows here are the only ones that aren't screwed shut. The rest stay sealed throughout the whole journey, although during the summer the provodnitsa might be persuaded to open one or two in the corridor.

Time Zones

With potentially eight time zones to choose from when riding a Trans-Siberian train, it can get a little confusing. As Mary Morris wrote in her account of a Beijing-Moscow trip, *Wall to Wall*:

No-one on the train knew what time it was. Some people said the train travelled on Moscow time but operated on local time, if you can figure that out. But half the people were on Beijing time and one diplomat said he was on Tokyo time, which was the same for some reason as Ulan Bator time. Our Chinese porter changed his watch 15 minutes every few hours or so but this was a system of his own devising.

The train timetables are in Moscow time but meals and lights out – and of course everything outside – are on local time. Clocks are set progressively later the further east you are, so when it's noon in Moscow it's 3 pm in Omsk, 5 pm in Irkutsk and 7 pm in Khabarovsk, giving rise to a gently disorienting 'train lag'. After a few days, your body clock quits in disgust.

Officially, China and Mongolia only have one time zone, five hours later than Moscow time. Local time is thus unchanged from Irkutsk to Beijing, except in late April or early May and again in September, when you may find a one-hour shift at the border. This is because of differences in when Russia, Mongolia and China switch to daylight-saving or summer time.

At most stations in Russia, there are two timetables displayed: one in Moscow time (*Moskovskoe vremya*) and one in local time (*mestnoe vremya*).

Attendants

Your provodnitsa (most of them are women), provodnik (the male variant) or *fuwuren* (on the Chinese train) may be the main thing you remember about your trip. Each carriage has two provodnitsas who work alternate shifts from their own compartment, keeping things clean, stoking the boiler, making tea, handing out new linen every few days and keeping track of passengers at stops. Some are like mothers – babushkas with hearts of Siberian gold beneath Wagnerian exteriors – while the other common type are the peroxided post-adolescents who spend most of their time flirting with the waiter in the dining car. In summer, on shorter express runs (eg Moscow-Irkutsk), many are students on holiday. It can improve your journey greatly if you get on well with the provodnitsa: you might get a window opened, be allowed to use their private and usually better cared for toilet, or even be moved to an empty compartment if one comes up.

They're unlikely to accept tips but you might leave them a small gift at the end of your trip.

Travelling Companions

If your tickets came through a company that does a lot of Trans-Sib business, it's likely you are going to be sharing a compartment with other travellers. However, these are working trains, not tourist specials, and you have a good chance of sharing a compartment with locals. Just as there is no segregation between foreigners and natives, neither is there any division of the sexes. Who you end up with is very much a lottery. With potentially six days together, sharing a space the size of a port-a-loo, exposed to the unmitigated smells, noises and eating habits of each other, much depends on your compartment mates. Your memories of the trip will be entirely different if you're sharing with an alcoholic Belarusian *biznesman* and his 11 suitcases than if three Japanese schoolgirls are your companions. You may want to consider this when it comes to booking your ticket. If it comes to the worst and you don't feel comfortable or safe with the characters sharing your compartment, then your provodnitsa may be able to engineer an exchange.

Station Halts

These are welcome respites for fresh air and exercise and to see what kind of food and drink the platform traders have to sell. Toilets are locked during stops, and that can be a long time at the border. The 'pok pok' you hear is a maintenance worker testing the bogies with a little hammer.

Stops last from one to 25 minutes; durations are given on the timetable posted in each carriage. Check this out or ask the provodnitsa, because departure comes without a whistle and the trains slip out almost soundlessly. Also be careful about crossing tracks.

t's quite common for another train to pull in between the platform and your train, in which case you have to climb through. Much worse is if the line between you and your train happens to be carrying a slow, three-km-long freight train just at departure time. It has happened. Nobody was sent to the salt mines. Instead, you'll most likely be put in a taxi to catch up, or perhaps your luggage will be off-loaded down the line for you to pick up as you continue your journey on another train.

Food & Drink

On a long-haul train, the dining car can easily become the centre of attraction, favoured more for its makeshift role as a social centre than for any gastronomic qualities. It becomes the place to meet, hang out, drink beer, play cards and enjoy a line of sight that doesn't abruptly end after a metre and a half with a Formica-boarded compartment wall.

The dining cars are changed at each border, so en route to Beijing you get Russian, Chinese and possibly Mongolian versions (ie travelling on the Chinese train doesn't mean you'll get a Chinese dining car all the way). Occasionally, between the Russian border and Ulan Bator there is no dining car, so be prepared. Everyone agrees that food and service are best in the Chinese dining car – no doubt prejudiced by the fact that until recently it was the only one that sold alcohol. There's no menu and no choice, but what you normally get is a number of stir-fried dishes with rice, and this set meal costs about US$6. In the Russian and Mongolian cars, the food is basic and boring but adequate – typically, grilled chicken or cutlet and rice, *gulyash* and boiled potatoes and green or tomato salads – and costs around the equivalent of US$4. On Russian services other than the main line *Rossia* and *Baikal Express*, prices can get even higher; for instance, on the Krasnoyarsk-Severobaikalsk train, a scrawny piece of grilled chicken with salad was an unbelievable US$7. You pay in roubles in the Russian car, RMB in the Chinese and dollars in the Mongolian.

Dining cars are open from approximately 9 am to 9 pm local time, making it a constant guessing game.

In the dining car there's often a table of pot noodles, chocolate, beer, juice and the like being peddled by the staff. The prices are overinflated and there's nothing that isn't available from the kiosks at the station halts.

Platform Supplies Kiosks and freelance entrepreneurs (typically babushkas squatting on upturned buckets) can unpredictably be found on station platforms. Platform kiosks are stocked with the standard Russian goods – that is, Marlboro cigarettes, Absolut vodka and Snickers bars well past their sell-by date. From Irkutsk onwards, the main staple is Chinese pot noodles (add hot water from the carriage samovar).

More interesting are the babushkas, who have farm produce such as milk, ice cream, grilled chicken or boiled potatoes, home cooking such as *pelmeni* or *pirozhki* and, depending on the season, buckets of forest berries and smoked fish. Between Moscow and Ulan Ude it's possible to eat perfectly well on supplies bought solely from the babushkas; however, further east and down into Mongolia there seems to be less on offer. There's little to be had along the BAM either, except in autumn when there are huge jars of fresh caviar for sale at amazingly low prices at the stations between Tynda and Komsomolsk.

Border Formalities

Border stops can take anything between one hour and six as customs officials go through the travelling warehouses that are the Chinese traders' compartments. For foreign travellers the procedure is uncomplicated – dull, even: passports, visas and currency forms are examined, with baggage searches rare (for this reason you may be approached by a trader and asked to carry their bag across the border – this is *not* a good idea). It's easier than entering the UK or Australia. While the customs formalities are being carried out, passengers are free to get off the train and wander up and down the platform. This is necessary because while the train is halted, the toilets on board are locked. There are banks at the border stations, and these represent the last chance to get rid of your roubles before leaving Russia, or RMB if you're on the way out of China. Even if you have no local currency to get rid of, you'll need to change some money to use in the dining car (dining cars are changed at the border and they only accept the currency of the country they belong to).

At the Chinese-Mongolian and Chinese-Russian borders, about two hours is spent hoisting the train aloft so that its bogies can be changed (the old Soviet Union used a wider gauge of track than all of its neighbours). If you're riding the Trans-Mongolian and want to witness this odd operation, stay on the train when it disgorges its passengers at Erlian Station, on the Chinese side of the China-Mongolia border. The train then pulls into a large shed half a km away. Get off before the staff lock the doors. It's OK to walk around and take photos, then stroll back down the line to the station.

In which case you have to climb through. Much worse is if the line between you and the ...

Safety

Despite the circulation of stories about people being drugged and gassed on the Trans-Siberian, safety on the rails isn't something to give any cause for worry. Common sense applies. Don't leave valuables lying about, and don't leave hand baggage unattended in a compartment while you get off at a station halt. The least safe places are those with the greatest exposure to foreign visitors, namely Moscow, Irkutsk, Ulan Bator and Beijing. A few years ago the train that connects all four, the Trans-Mongolian, had quite a bad reputation, but militia now ride the trains and matters have improved. For added safety, lock your cabins from the inside and also make use of the security clip on the upper left-hand part of the door (the clip can be flipped open from the outside with a knife, but not if you stuff the hole with paper).

SIBERIA &
THE RUSSIAN FAR EAST

Facts about Siberia & the Russian Far East

Salt mines, snowbound exile, frozen corpses – for most foreigners the images conjured by the name Siberia are somewhat less than welcoming. For most Russians, and other peoples of the ex-Soviet republics, these and similar images are graven in a great scar on the psyche. For four centuries this immense back yard has been used, first by the tsars and then by the Party, to dispose of undesirable elements in the populace. First to go were the criminals, then the political dissenters, followed by those who had through their labours inched materially ahead of their neighbours. Next went the religious, the leaders and their communities dispatched east over the Ural Mountains. They were followed by an en masse exile of the stubborn citizens of troublesome nationalities. Finally, no reason at all was needed to be sent to Siberia and it became the fear of everybody.

The writer Maxim Gorky gave voice to the national dread of Siberia when he described it as 'a land of chains and ice'. But it was also – and still is – a land able to encompass the serenity of Lake Baikal, the pristine geometry of the Altay Mountains, the fiery volcanic landscapes of Kamchatka, the sparkling, blue brilliance of the Arctic and the lush semitropical forests of the Pacific coast. Of the early exiles, many chose to stay on after their sentences had ended, seduced by the wide-open spaces and, strangely enough, the sense of freedom.

Siberia ('Sibir' in Russian, from the Mongolian Altay language, meaning 'Sleeping Land') takes in essentially the entire North Asian continent, east to the Pacific and south to China and Mongolia. This means BIG – 7000 km by 3500 km, wrapped around a third of the northern hemisphere. Viewed from the air, the flat land goes on and on, punctuated by meandering rivers, slashes of development and long banners of industrial

smoke. The journalist George Kennan, in his 1891 *Siberia and the Exile System*, wrote:

You can take the whole of the United States...and set it down in the middle of Siberia without touching anywhere the boundaries of the latter's territory; you can then take Alaska and all the countries of Europe, with the exception of Russia, and fit them into the remaining margin like the pieces of a dissected map. After having thus accommodated all [this] you will still have more than 300,000 square miles of Siberian territory to spare...an area half as large again as the Empire of Germany.

A hundred years on, with the world shrunk by air transport and satellite communications, Siberia has resisted all efforts to make it containable – or habitable: the population of this great land is only three times that of metropolitan Moscow, with most of it huddled along the railway in the south. Travellers today still write, not of journeys in Siberia, but of voyages or odysseys.

For visitors, the main experience of all this size has been unending views of *taiga* (Siberian forest) from the cocoon of a Trans-Siberian Railway carriage, perhaps with a stop in a big city along the route. Tourist development has stuck close to the railway and is still sparse, but new destinations are opening up all the time. Lake Baikal and the remote Kamchatka Peninsula, both areas of outstanding natural beauty and wonder, are trying to raise their profiles by establishing themselves as UNESCO world heritage sites, while the cities of the Far East, such as Khabarovsk and Vladivostok, are working all out to attract foreign business, revive the local economy and reinvent themselves as thriving, modern rivals to the traditional centres of attention in European Russia.

HISTORY

The first known Siberians were Palaeolithic (early Stone Age) tribes who lived around Lake Baikal and the headwaters of the Ob and Yenisey rivers. Remains of Neolithic (late Stone Age) settlements have been found all over Siberia. Indeed, many northern tribes were still basically at the Neolithic stage when the Russians arrived. As late as the Iron Age, the steppes and forests from the Ural Mountains to Baikal were populated by tribes of herders whose origins lay in the Caucasus (Abakan's regional museum contains relics from burial mounds of this period). Soon afterwards the earliest Mongolians appeared.

By the 3rd century BC, the southern region of what is now Siberia was under the control of the Huns. Descendants of these nomads were later driven west, to the terror of Russia and Europe. In the first few centuries AD, Turkic tribes moved in from Central Asia. Their most prominent descendants were the Khyagas, or 'Yenisey Kyrgyz', whose 6th to 13th-century empire, which took in much of Central Asia and central Siberia, was the Mongol Tatars' first big conquest. Another Turkic dynasty, the Bohai, dominated the south-east.

The first Russians in Siberia were fur traders from Novgorod who reached the northern Ob River in the late 11th century.

Mongol Tatars

Jenghiz Khan got his start in the early 13th century as a warlord south-east of Lake Baikal. His confederation of armies (called Tatars, after a prominent neighbouring tribe who were among Jenghiz' first conquests) pushed the Khyagas into Kyrgyzstan, went on to subdue most of Asia except far northern Siberia and, in the end, crossed Russia into Europe to create history's largest land empire. Of its later fragments, the Golden Horde dominated Russia until the mid-1400s and the splinters of the Golden Horde loosely controlled the Volga region and much of Siberia for another century.

The Opening of Siberia

If the Russians appreciate Ivan the Terrible for anything, it is for his seizure of the Tatar strongholds of Kazan (in 1552) and Astrakhan (in 1556), which put the entire Volga in Russian hands and swung open the door to Siberia. Seeing the writing on the wall, Yediger, the Khan of the Sibir Tatars, offered Ivan a tribute of sable pelts and became his vassal.

In 1558, the tsar authorised the powerful Stroganov family of merchants to open trading posts east of the Ural Mountains under the protection of Cossack mercenaries. When Yediger's successor, Kuchum, began plundering these settlements, a band of Cossacks and soldiers led by a convict named Yermak Timofeevich set out to teach him a lesson. In 1582, they took the Tatar capital of Kashlyk (present-day Tobolsk). In recognition of this achievement, Ivan pardoned Yermak for his past crimes and this bandit is now honoured as the 'conqueror of Siberia'.

Three years later Yermak plunged into a river to escape a Tatar ambush and was drowned. Nevertheless, the settlement of Siberia had begun and the next half-century saw one of history's most explosive expansions. Fuelled by a lust for furs, waves of Cossacks, trappers, traders and misfits had reached the Ob River by the 1580s. Until then this had represented the eastern limit of the known world. They had pushed on to the Yenisey by the end of the 16th century, the Lena by the 1620s and, in 1639, they made the Pacific coast at Okhotsk.

Behind the pioneers came the tsar's officials and soldiers to exact tributes (known as *yassak*) in the form of pelts. The export of furs became Russia's biggest moneymaker.

Indigenous tribes may have found the new-comers a welcome change from the Tatars but, despite their greater numbers, with only bows and arrows against Russian muskets they had no choice in the matter anyway. Only the Tatars, the Buryats, who lived around Lake Baikal, and the Chukchi in the north-east put up much resistance. Benson Bobrick, in his history of Siberia, likens the scenario to the push across the plains of the American West, with the Cossacks as cowboys, the Buryats etc as Indians and the tsarist army as the cavalry. Instead of a gold rush, Siberia experienced a fur frenzy.

Military stockades grew into towns – Tyumen in 1586, Tomsk in 1604, Krasnoyarsk in 1627, Yakutsk in 1632, Okhotsk in 1647, Irkutsk in 1651 and Chita in 1655. Settlement was encouraged with promises of easy land and freedom from serfdom. By the late 1600s there were as many settlers, traders, soldiers and missionaries as there were indigenous Siberians. As expeditions began to size up Siberia's huge mineral wealth, Peter the Great also sent engineers and geologists.

Edging into Manchuria

Rumours that the Amur and Ussuri river basins in the east contained desperately scarce arable land were confirmed by an exploratory expedition. In 1650, the tsar commissioned the Cossack trader Yerofey Khabarov (after whom Khabarovsk is named) to open up the region, but his rapacious barbarity was so great that the local tribes appealed to their Manchu overlords for help. Following a Chinese show of might, Khabarov withdrew well north of the Amur.

Like the schoolyard game in which children creep stealthily toward one colleague facing a wall, then freeze when this 'guard' suddenly spins round, the Russians surreptitiously filtered back into Manchu territory. Even allowing for a couple of retreats, the Russians were in occupation of the north bank of the Amur by 1689. The Manchus, threatened already by the Mongols, couldn't afford to enter into war on another front, but nor could Russia afford to lose the Chinese market, where most of its furs were sold. The two powers came to terms in the Treaty of Nerchinsk, which sealed a peace between them that lasted for more than 150 years.

Russians in America

Under the Treaty of Nerchinsk, Russia had to give up all claims to the Amur valley, and instead the government began to concentrate its efforts on the largely unknown far north-eastern territories. In 1648, the Cossack Semyon Dezhnev had been the first to sail round the north-east corner of Asia, from the Pacific Ocean into the Arctic. However, the glory went to Vitus Bering, a Danish officer in the Russian navy, who discovered the strait (which now bears his name) all over again in 1728. Four years later, Tsar Peter the Great called Bering to head the Great Northern Expedition. This was ostensibly a scientific survey of Kamchatka (claimed for the tsar in 1697 by the explorer Atlasov) and the eastern seaboard, but in reality its aim was to expand Russia's Pacific sphere of influence as far south as Japan and across to North America.

Bering succeeded in discovering Alaska, landing in 1741. Unfortunately, on the return voyage his ship was wrecked off an island just 250 km east of the Kamchatkan coast. Bering died on the island, and it, too, now carries his name. (Archaeologists digging on the island in 1991 discovered his grave and the bones were flown to Moscow for scientific examination. They've since been returned to the island and reburied with full naval ceremony.)

Survivors of Bering's crew brought back reports of an abundance of foxes, fur seals and otters inhabiting the islands off the mainland, triggering a fresh wave of fur-inspired expansion. An Irkutsk trader, Grigory Shelekhov, landed on Kodiak Island (in present-day Alaska) in 1784 and, 15 years later, his successor founded Sitka (originally called New Archangel), until 1900 the capital of Alaska. In 1804 the Russians reached Honolulu, and in 1806 Russian ships sailed into San Francisco Bay. Soon afterwards, an outpost was established at what is now called

Fort Ross (originally Fort Russ), California, where the imperial flag flew and a marker was buried on which was inscribed, 'Land of the Russian Empire'.

Russia's American territories hardly expanded beyond the initial boatload of settlers and looked very vulnerable in the face of British advancement through Canada, the Spanish moving from the south and the Americans themselves pushing overland through the mid-West. It seemed expedient in 1867 for Tsar Alexander II to sell the imperial lands to the USA for US$7.2 million (less than $5 a sq km) – a deal that at the time looked like a steal for the Russians.

Early Exiles

From about 1650, the authorities began dumping criminals in Siberia. In the 1700s, as Siberia's natural wealth became obvious, those dumped were put to work digging it up. As the demand for labour increased, so did the list of punishable offences: prize-fighting, prostitution, vagrancy, even fortune-telling all became grounds for banishment.

The death penalty was abolished and replaced with exile and forced labour, and people were soon being sent to Siberia without trial. POWs, religious dissenters and, more or less, anyone with an irritating opinion was soon joining the criminals on the long trail east. Exile had become big business. The Great Siberian Trakt, or Post Road, long the only route through the Ural Mountains and the taiga beyond, was developed to include a complex system of exile stations and holding prisons. By 1890, some 3400 exiles a week were marched in shackles to Irkutsk, although up to 15% would fail to survive the journey.

Once in Siberia, lesser offenders were simply released into villages (exiles were permitted to comprise up to a third of the population of any settlement) though they were forbidden to return west. More serious offenders were set to work in prisons or labour camps, the most notorious of which were the mines at Nerchinsk, east of Chita, and Kara, in the Ural Mountains. Popular mythology links Siberia with salt mines but

in fact there were few: at Nerchinsk it was silver the convicts dug for, while Kara was a source of gold.

Decembrists & Other Political Exiles

The most celebrated exiles were the Dekabristy, or Decembrists, army officers and aristocrats who bungled a revolt against Tsar Nicholas I in December 1825. Five were executed, but 116 were sent to Siberia for terms of hard labour, mostly in rural parts of the Chita region. After serving their sentences, these exiles could move to towns, personae non gratae but allowed to carry on as best they could. Their presence had a marked effect on the educational and cultural life in their adopted towns. Pardoned by Tsar Alexander II in 1856, many chose to stay on in Irkutsk and elsewhere.

After Napoleon's defeat, Russia had taken control of Poland, and in 1863-64 an uprising nearly overthrew the puppet government. Huge numbers of Polish rebels, many well educated, were shipped to Siberia. Other famous exiles were novelist Fyodor Dostoevsky, Leon Trotsky, Iosif Stalin and, of course, Lenin, who spent nearly three years near Abakan.

More Expansion & the Railway

In the mid-1800s, China was racked with civil strife and the Opium Wars, and the Russians, made bold by the concessions Great Britain had wrung from the weakened Manchus, stepped up the pace of expansion in the Far East. In the 1850s, ignoring old treaties, the Governor General of Eastern Siberia, Count Nikolay Muravev, repossessed and colonised the Amur basin (for which the grateful tsar added 'Amursky' to Muravev's name). Far from precipitating a Sino-Russian war, expansionist Russia also gained the Primorsky region (the dogleg of land between the Ussuri River and the Pacific) as a reward for its help in negotiating the lifting of an Anglo-French siege against Beijing.

Under Muravev's direction, in 1853 Sakhalin had also been added to the Russians' grab bag of territories, though they were forced to share the island with the Japanese, who had already staked a claim to the southern half. In 1875 Japan withdrew its claim in exchange for recognition of its sovereignty over the Kuril Islands. By 1900, the Russians held all of Manchuria and had naval bases at Port Arthur and Dalny (now Lüshen and Dalian).

Siberian development was hamstrung by vast distances and poor communications. It wasn't until 1886, when Tsar Alexander III authorised the building of 7500 km of railroad between Chelyabinsk (then Russia's eastern railhead) and Vladivostok, that things shifted up a few gears. Cities grew like mushrooms along the line. In less than 25 years to 1911, the immigrant population leapt above eight million. Most were peasants, who put Siberian agriculture at the head of the class in grain, stock and dairy farming (before the October Revolution, Europeans had Siberian butter on their tables). This growth was to collapse with Stalin's forcible collectivisation of agriculture in the 1930s.

The Russo-Japanese War

Feeling threatened by Russian expansion across Manchuria, wary of Slavic ambitions on Korea and keenly aware that the imminent completion of the Trans-Siberian Railway would facilitate rapid troop movement into the Far East, in February 1904 the Japanese launched a sudden naval attack on the Russian fleet at Port Arthur. Tsar Nicholas II ordered the Baltic fleet to sail clear around the world to join the battle, where it was immediately annihilated in the Tsushima Straits. In September 1905, a badly beaten Russia signed the Treaty of Portsmouth (Portsmouth, New Hampshire), under the terms of which it gave up Port Arthur, Dalny and southern Sakhalin and forsook any claims to Korea – but at least retained its pre-eminent position in Manchuria.

Civil War

Soviet rule was proclaimed in Siberia's major towns soon after the October Revolution, but in spite of all those exiled dissidents, this was not fertile ground for the Bolsheviks. Cossacks, merchants and a fairly contented peasantry were uneasy about Lenin's promises. Local heroes tended to be upper-class explorers, scientists or Decembrists.

In May 1918, a general counter-revolution swept across Siberia, sparked by a force of 45,000 Czechoslovakian POWs. The Czechoslovaks, who had been fighting alongside the Russians against the Germans, were heading home via Vladivostok when caught out by the Revolution and Russia's decision to pull out of WW I. Convinced that the new Soviet government was going to hand them over to the Germans, the fully armed Czechoslovaks seized virtually the entire Trans-Siberian Railway. The regional Bolshevik government in the Far East was thrown into retreat and by mid-September all Siberia was 'White'.

Meanwhile, the tsarist Admiral Alexandr Kolchak, stranded in the USA by the revolution, landed at Vladivostok and headed west at the head of a White army. His cause was boosted when the entire area from the Pacific to Lake Baikal was occupied by foreign troops – 72,000 Japanese, 7000 Americans, 6400 British, 4400 Canadians and others – all there, ostensibly, to help the Czechoslovaks.

In November 1918, Kolchak pushed into European Russia. Joining with armies from the Don basin and north-west Russia, he very nearly overthrew the Bolsheviks before being pushed back to Omsk, where his forces were decisively routed. Kolchak hastily retreated to Irkutsk. There he was captured and shot in 1920, which effectively ended the Civil War – except in the Far East, where it raged on until the Red victory at Volochaevka, west of Khabarovsk, in February 1922.

Soviet Consolidation

At that point almost all the foreigners withdrew. The Japanese, however, who rather fancied the land they had been occupying, from Baikal to the Sea of Japan, stayed put. To keep things cool, the Soviet government made this area into a buffer zone, declaring

SIBERIA & RUSSIAN FAR EAST

it the independent Far East Republic, with its capital at Chita. When the Japanese left in 1922, it was promptly absorbed into the USSR. A Canadian expedition that in 1922 had claimed for the British Empire little Wrangel Island (ostrov Vrangelya), north of the Bering Strait, was evicted at gun point five years later. No more was said about it.

Siberia was never a battlefield in WW II but in virtually the closing days of the war, with Japan on its knees, the Soviet Union occupied southern Sakhalin and the Kuril Islands. Japan accepted the loss but has continued to this day to maintain a claim to the southern islands in the Kuril chain, which at their closest point are approximately 14 km from Hokkaido.

The Gulag

The exile system was abolished at the turn of the century, but Stalin brought it back with a vengeance, expanding it into a full-blown, home-grown slave trade. He established a vast bureaucracy of resettlement programmes, transit prisons and labour colonies, concentration camps and special psychiatric hospitals all over Russia, commonly known as the Gulag (**G**lavny **U**pravlenie **Lag**erey, or Main Administration for Camps). Its inmates – some of whose only 'offence' was to be Jewish or a modern artist or a high-profile Buryat, or simply to have shaken the hand of such a person – cut trees, dug canals, laid railway tracks and worked in factories in remote areas, especially Siberia and the Far East. A huge slice of the north-east was set aside exclusively for labour camps, and whole cities such as Komsomolsk-on-Amur and Magadan were developed as Gulag centres. It was during Stalin's rule that Siberia became synonymous with death; while Iosif Vissarionovich sat in the Kremlin, an estimated 20 million people died in the Gulag. Nadezhda Mandelstam, whose poet husband, Osip, was taken by the Cheka and sent to Siberia, where he perished, wrote that a wife considered herself a widow from the moment of her husband's arrest.

Post-Stalinist Siberia

Following Stalin's death in 1953, amnesties freed up to two-thirds of all Siberia's prisoners. Exile and labour camps remained as corrective tools of the state right up until the dissolution of the USSR, but in a vastly reduced form. For Russians, the word that replaced 'Gulag' in the Siberian word association game was 'gigantomania'. The 1950s saw a proliferation of Olympian schemes that were variously bigger, wider, taller or more powerful than anything that had gone before (and in many cases costlier, less efficient and more environmentally disastrous, too). A series of hydroelectric power plants was constructed along the Angara and Yenisey rivers to supply power for the huge *kombinaty* (plants), such as aluminium smelters and pulp mills, that sprang up in their wake. At one point, Soviet planners even proposed building a barrage of mammoth dams along the Arctic coast to reverse the flow of the rivers and flood parts of central Siberia. Fortunately, that scheme never got off the drawing board, but work was begun on the Baikal-Amur Mainline (BAM), a second, no less ambitious trans-Siberian railway.

To attract the workforce needed for the colossal schemes, salaries three times higher than in European Russia were offered, as well as bonus schemes, longer holidays and tax exemptions. Youthful pioneers from all over the Soviet Union arrived in the taiga, eager to wield pick, spade and mosquito repellent. Cities sprang up deep in the virgin forest, rivers were dammed and plants set up for production, but the once-enthusiastic workforce was ultimately defeated, not by the terrain or other natural hardships, but by broken promises. Wages failed to keep up with inflation, bonuses were cut back and, worst of all, the work dried up. The much-heralded glory days never came. Figures quoted in a 1990 *National Geographic* article claimed that for the 26,000 immigrants that were arriving annually in the western Siberian city of Kemerovo, 24,000 former citizens were packing up and leaving. In 1989, and again in 1991, the miners of

Siberia's Kuzbas region went on strike for more money and better conditions. In the history of the Soviet Union they were the first ever to employ such openly defiant tactics. The government was almost brought to its knees.

The miners were voicing complaints common right across from the Ural Mountains to the Pacific, namely that the central government wasn't interested in developing the region but simply in milking it. In the words of Valentin Rasputin, a famed Siberian writer and activist, Moscow views Siberia as 'a barge moored to Russia that brings in its wealth and goods and then is pushed away from the shore'.

For more than 60 years, until the coming of glasnost emboldened the miners to take action, Siberia was shielded from foreign attention. It became a major centre of Cold War activity, with Novaya Zemlya and Kamchatka used for thermonuclear testing, nuclear weapons facilities at Lake Irtysh and Tomsk 7 and a radar station, which in the words of Eduard Shevardnadze was 'the size of the Egyptian pyramids', at Krasnoyarsk. The border with China and the Pacific seaboard bristled with antennae, tank barrels and missiles. Siberia briefly gained world attention in 1960, when a US U2 spy-plane dared these defences and was brought down over Sverdlovsk (present-day Yekaterinburg); and again in 1983, when Korean airliner KAL 007 was intercepted and destroyed just off the island of Sakhalin.

The collapse of the Soviet empire has given Siberia and Russia's Far East a greater degree of self-determination but has also left them underdeveloped, sparsely populated and short on cash. The region is rich in resources – oil, gas, coal, diamonds, bauxite, gold and other precious metals, fish and timber – and is, in fact, the potential saviour of Russia. However, most of this eldorado lies in remote regions, deep below the surface and securely locked in ice. How to get at it, and to whom the spoils (Moscow? the local inhabitants? foreign investors?) are the questions that currently dominate Siberia. They're the same questions that

have always dominated. Even now, more than 350 years after the first explorations, Siberia and the Russian Far East remain untamed frontier territory.

GEOGRAPHY

Siberia and the Russian Far East – defined for the purposes of this book as the Ural Mountains and all the land to their east, though strictly speaking Russians do not class the Ural region as part of Siberia – cover nearly 14 million sq km, an area greater than any other country in the world. The easternmost point, Big Diomede Island (ostrov Ratmanova) in the Bering Strait, is just 45 km from the Alaskan mainland.

The dividing line between Siberia and the Far East lies along the borders of the Khabarovsk Territory and Magadan Region, 150 to 1200 km inland from Russia's eastern seaboard on the Sea of Japan, Sea of Okhotsk, Bering Sea and Bering Strait. This eastern seaboard is 15,500 km long – which gives Russia more 'Pacific Rim' than any other country.

The region is washed in the north by the Arctic Kara, Laptev and East Siberian seas, with the Severnaya Zemlya islands between the first two constituting its northernmost extension. In the south it has land borders with Kazakhstan, Mongolia, China and North Korea.

On a map, Siberia's dominant geographical features are its 53,000 rivers and more than a million lakes. From west to east the major rivers are the Ob, Yenisey and Lena – all of which flow north to the Arctic – and the Amur, which flows east towards the Pacific. These four drain about two-thirds of the entire area of Siberia and the Russian Far East. The Ob rises in the Altay Republic, flows through Novosibirsk and empties into the Kara Sea via the 900-km-long Ob Gulf (Obskaya Guba) between the Yamal and Gydansky peninsulas. Combined with its tributary the Irtysh, which rises in Kazakhstan and flows through Omsk and Tobolsk, the Ob is the world's fifth-longest river at 5570 km. Only 20 km shorter is the combined Yenisey-Angara. The Yenisey rises in

Tuva and flows through Krasnoyarsk to enter the Kara Sea between the Gydansky and Taymyr peninsulas. Its tributary the Angara flows out of Lake Baikal and through Irkutsk and Bratsk to join the Yenisey north of Krasnoyarsk. The 4400-km Lena rises in the mountains west of Lake Baikal and flows through Yakutsk to the Laptev Sea. The 4416-km Amur forms a long stretch of the Russia-China border before flowing through Khabarovsk and into the Tatar Strait between the mainland and the large island of Sakhalin (which divides the seas of Japan and Okhotsk). The Amur's southern tributary the Ussuri, which meets it at Khabarovsk, forms another long stretch of the Chinese border.

Beautiful Lake Baikal, the world's deepest lake, holds nearly one-fifth of all the world's lake water.

As you travel across Siberia, one overwhelming impression is of the taiga – the dense, swampy forests of birch, pine, spruce and larch that trans-Siberian passengers watch for days on end. In parts of the south are areas of flat, dry steppe reaching southward into Central Asia and Mongolia. To the north is tundra, or 'cold desert', with shallow, delicate vegetation. Much of it is on the permanently frozen bog called permafrost, hard as rock to a depth of hundreds of metres, with at most the top few metres thawing in summer. Under pressure of a wheel, a railroad track or a foundation, permafrost turns to mud. To keep them from sinking, roadbeds in the tundra must be insulated and buildings erected on legs.

Another overwhelming impression – especially if you travel along the railway which runs near its southern border most of the way – is of Siberia's flatness. Between the Ural Mountains – which rarely top 1000 metres and are barely noticeable in their middle reaches west of Yekaterinburg – and the Yenisey River stretches the marshy West Siberian Plain, all of it below 200 metres. The Ob River, crossing this plain, falls only 100 metres in its last 2000 km. Between the Yenisey and the Lena is the Central Siberian Plateau, nearly all between 200 and 1000 metres.

In southern regions, and from Lake Baikal and the Lena eastwards, there's more relief. South-east of Novosibirsk are the beautiful Altay Mountains, which stretch over into Kazakhstan and Mongolia and peak at 4506 metre Mt Belukha on the Kazakhstan border. A little further east, the Western and Eastern Sayan ranges, which reach around 3000 metres, separate the Tuva from the rest of Russia. Mountains surround most of Lake Baikal and continue, occasionally topping 3000 metres, most of the way to the Sikhote Alin range in Ussuriland, east of Khabarovsk.

In the north-east there's a tangle of ranges all the way up to the Chukotka Peninsula facing Alaska, the most dramatic – indeed probably the most dramatic of all Russia's mountains – being the 200-odd volcanoes of the 1200-km-long Kamchatka Peninsula. About 30 of these – including Siberia and the Russian Far East's highest peak, 4750-metre Klyuchevskaya – are active, some highly so. The volcanic chain continues south in the form of the Kuril Islands, strung all the way from Kamchatka to Japan, which contain a further 40 active volcanoes.

CLIMATE

Siberia's climate is sharply continental but not as fearsome as you might imagine. Winter is bitingly cold in Trans-Siberian Railway towns – average January night temperatures are -20°C to -25°C, with cold snaps to -35°C – but, from January onwards, is mitigated by low humidity and lots of sun (and a sense that this is, after all, the time to see the 'genuine' Siberia). Siberians claim they feel cold if they go to St Petersburg in winter – where temperatures are a good 10°C higher – because of the humidity there. Spring comes in late April or May, later in the mountains.

July and August can be quite warm, with temperatures averaging 15°C or 20°C and reaching as high as 30°C. There are mosquitoes but, in most areas, not enough to ruin a visit. Of course, if you're trekking or doing anything else at high altitudes in summer, it can still get cold. September is the time for mushrooms, wild berries and brilliant foliage; residents claim that this is the most beautiful time of year in the Far East. The months of September and October bring unstable weather. The first frost usually occurs in October, and most snow falls in November and December.

You'll find it nippier if you stray northwards. Verkhoyansk, 650 km north of Yakutsk, is the coldest inhabited spot on earth. Winter temperatures here have dropped to -71°C (but summers can be surprisingly warm). And south doesn't necessarily mean warm: the zone of year-round permafrost, a good indicator of nasty cold, reaches right down across the Trans-Siberian Railway east of Lake Baikal.

Ussuriland, south-east of Khabarovsk, has a northern monsoonal climate. This means more rain (30% to 40% rainy days from May to September) and slightly milder winters – a balmy -13°C on a typical January day.

See Appendix III at the back of the book for climate charts.

FLORA, FAUNA & ENVIRONMENT

Siberia is divided into three distinct, broad east-west bands of vegetation type. In the northernmost extremes, fringed by the Arctic Ocean, is the icy tundra. These bleak, seemingly barren flatlands extend from 60 to 420 km south from the coast. They gradually become more amicable to life and build up to taiga, the vast, dense forest that characterises and covers the greater part of Siberia. At its southern fringes, close to the borders with Kazakhstan, Mongolia and, in parts, China, the taiga peters out to become a treeless, gently undulating grassland, or steppe.

Both tundra and taiga extend across to the Pacific coast, but the Russian Far East also has two other unusual vegetative zones. Kamchatka, a peninsula in the far north-east of Russia, is an active volcanic region with, in some places, a moon-like landscape and, elsewhere, weird and wonderful gigantic plant life. Ussuriland, as a result of its lower latitude in the extreme Russian south-east, experiences tropical air and rains. The forests covering this region – and their indigenous animals and vegetation – more closely resemble those of South-East Asia than anything typically associated with Siberia.

Tundra

Falling almost completely within the Arctic Circle, the tundra is the most inhospitable of Siberian terrain. The ground is permanently frozen (in places, recorded to a depth of 1450 metres) like one great block of ice, with just a thin, fragile carpet of vegetation lying on top. The few trees and bushes that manage to cling tenaciously to existence are stunted dwarfs, the permafrost refusing to yield to their roots. For nine months of the year the beleaguered greenery is also buried beneath a mattress of snow. When the brief, warming summer comes, the permafrost prevents drainage and the tundra becomes a spongy wetland, pocked with lakes, pools and puddles – breeding grounds for clouds of predatory mosquitoes and gnats and a haven for wildfowl. But, in general, wildlife has a hard time of it on the tundra and there are few species that can survive its climate and desolation. The reindeer, however, has few problems and there are thought to be around four million of them in Russia's tundra regions. They can endure temperatures as low as -50°C and, like the camel, they can store reserves of food. The reindeer sustains itself on lichen and grasses, in winter sniffing them out and pawing away the snow cover.

A similar diet sustains the lemming, a small, round, fat rodent, fixed in the popular consciousness for its proclivity for launching itself en masse from cliff tops. More amazing is its rate of reproduction. Lemmings can produce five or six litters annually, each of five or six young. The young in turn begin reproducing after only two months. With a gestation period of just three weeks, one pair could theoretically spawn close to 10,000 more lemmings in a 12-month period. That's a lot of birthdays to remember. In reality, predators and insufficient food supplies keep the numbers down.

Other tundra mammals include the Arctic fox, a smaller, more furry cousin of the European fox and a big lemming fan, and the wolf, which, although it prefers the taiga, will range far and wide drawn by the lure of reindeer meat.

Taiga

Siberia's taiga is the world's largest forest. It covers about five million sq km (an area big enough to blanket the whole of India) and accounts for about 25% of the world's wood reserves. Travelling on the BAM through the depths of Siberia, two or three days can go by with nothing but the impenetrable and foreboding dark wall of the forest visible outside the train: 'Where it ends', wrote Chekhov, 'only the migrating birds know'. Few people choose to live in the gloomy depths of the forest, and the towns and villages cling tightly to the railways and large rivers. It's as though any settlement that strayed away would be swallowed up and lost forever.

Though the conditions are less severe than in the Arctic region, it's still harsh and bitterly cold in the winter. The trees best suited for survival, and the main components of the taiga, are the pine, larch, spruce and firs. In the coldest (eastern) regions the deciduous larch predominates; shedding leaves cuts down on water loss, and its shallow roots give it the best chance of survival in permafrost conditions. Forest-floor vegetation isn't particularly dense (though it is wiry and spring-loaded, making it difficult for humans to move through) because of the permanent shade, but there is a great variety of grasses, moss, lichens, berries and mushrooms. These provide ample nourishment for the animals at the lower end of the food chain, which, in turn, become food for others. Wildlife flourishes. The indigenous cast includes squirrels and chipmunks (which dine well on pine-cone seeds), voles and lemmings, as well as small carnivores such as pole cats, foxes, wolverines and, less commonly, the sable, a weasel-like creature whose luxuriant pelt played such a great role in the early exploration of Siberia.

The most common species of large mammal in the taiga is the elk, a large deer that can measure over two metres at the shoulder and weighs almost as much as bear. The brown bear itself is also extremely numerous: a farmer on the northern shores o Lake Baikal said that on any given nigh during the summer (the bear hibernate through the colder months) he could guaran tee tracking one down.

Kamchatka

The fantastic array of vegetation and wildlife on Kamchatka is a result of the geotherma bubbling, brewing and rumbling that goes or below the peninsula's surface and manifests itself periodically in the eruption of one o around 30 active volcanoes. The minerals deposited by these eruptions have produced some incredibly fertile earth, which is capable of nurturing giant plants with accelerated growth rates. John Massey Stewart, in his book *The Nature of Russia*, gives the example of the dropwort, normally a small unremarkable plant, which in Kamchatka can grow as much as 10 cm in 24 hours and reaches a height of up to four metres. This effect is at its most fantastic in the calderas (craters) of collapsed volcanoes. Here, hot springs and thermal vents maintain a high temperature year round, creating almost greenhouse-like conditions for plants. Waterfowl and all manner of animals make their way here to shelter from the worst of winter, and Massey Stewart likens it to a 'Russian Garden of Eden'.

The volcanic ash also enriches the peninsula's rivers, leading to far greater spawnings of salmon than are experienced anywhere else. And in thermally warmed pools the salmon also gain weight at a much increased rate. All of which is good news for the region's predatory mammals and large sea birds (and for local fishers). The bears, in particular, benefit and the numerous Kamchatkan brown bears are the biggest of their species in Russia: a fully grown male stands at over three metres tall and weighs close to a tonne. Other well-fed fish eaters are the peninsula's sea otters (a protected species), seals and the great sea eagle, one of the world's largest birds of prey, with a 2.5-metre wingspan. The coastline is particularly favoured by birds, with over 200 recognised species including auks, tufted puffins and swans.

Ussuriland

Completely different to the taiga, tundra or steppe, Ussuriland is largely covered by a monsoon forest filled with an exotic array of plant life and animals – from tree frogs to tigers – found nowhere else in Russia. The mix of plants and wildlife draws from the taiga to the north, and also from neighbouring China and Korea and from the Himalaya. The topography is dominated by the Sikhote Alin Mountains, which run for more than 1000 km in a spine parallel to the coast. Unlike the sparsely vegetated woodland floor of the taiga, the forests of Ussuriland have a lush undergrowth, with lianas and vines twined around trunks and draped from branches. However, it's the animal life that arouses most interest – not the wolves, the sable or the Asian black bear, a tree-climbing, herbivorous cousin to the more common brown bear (also found here), so much as Russia's own tiger, the Siberian or Amur tiger.

The Siberian tiger is the largest subspecies of tiger and the largest member of the cat family. Animals have been measured at up to 3.5 metres in length. Little wonder that the native Nanai used to worship this incredible beast. There are estimated to be around 200 to 300 of the tigers in Ussuriland (out of a total world population of 350 to 450), which is something of a success considering that they had been hunted down to between 20 and 30 by the 1940s. The tiger was designated a protected species in 1948, and since then six reserves have been set up in the region, partly to help monitor and safeguard the cats. The tigers' favoured prey is boar, though they've been observed to hunt and kill bears, livestock and even humans (a partially devoured tractor driver was found in 1976).

Ussuriland is also home to the Amur leopard, a big cat significantly rarer than the tiger, though less impressive and consequently less often mentioned. Around 20 to 25 leopards roam the lands bordering China and North Korea.

Parks & Reserves

The following are some of the major reserves (zapovedniki) within the area of Siberia and the Russian Far East. Many are closed to unauthorised personnel, sealed off for scientific study. In most cases they are also extremely difficult to reach, being well away from civilisation and accessible only by helicopter. Exceptions are Sikhote Alin and Lazovsky, which can be visited from Vladivostok. It is also possible to get permission to visit Kronotsky, which requires a short flight from Petropavlovsk-Kamchatsky (see Kamchatka in the Russian Far East chapter).

There is a book, *Nature Reserves of the USSR* by M Davydova & V Koshevoi, published in English (1989) by the Moscow-based Progress Publishers, which may be available from specialist Russian bookshops.

Barguzin
: Covers an area of 2632 sq km on the north-east shore of Lake Baikal. It's a special reserve for the sable and also 38 other species of mammal including the Baikal seal and the flying squirrel.

The Siberian tiger, largest member of the cat family, is found mainly in Ussuriland

Central Siberian
A reserve of virgin taiga on the Yenisey River.

Kronotsky
A protected area of 10,990 sq km on the Kamchatka Peninsula with bears, sea lions and sea eagles. Within the reserve's boundaries is also the spectacular Valley of Geysers.

Lazovsky
A monsoon forest reserve on the Pacific coast

100 km north of Vladivostok, hunting ground of the Siberian tiger.

Sikhote Alin
The biggest Ussuriland reserve at 3476 sq km, stretching from the coast up into the mountains. It's home to over 340 species of bird and to the Siberian tiger.

Taymyr Peninsula
North of Norilsk, jutting out into the Arctic

Ecotourism on Hold

Although at times it has been conducted with a rapaciousness that has threatened entire species with extinction, hunting is a traditional Siberian livelihood in a region which offers few other means of existence. For a Siberian peasant living deep in the taiga, surrounded by forests of snuffling, grubbing and clawing creatures, a dead deer, boar or bear is food on the table, cash in the pocket and maybe even a new coat in the wardrobe – with temperatures stuck at -20°C for a quarter of the year and not an outdoor-clothing shop in sight, the wearing of fur garments is not a matter for debate but one of survival. To misquote a famous advertisement: 'It takes 40 dumb animals to make a fur coat, but in Siberia it takes an even dumber one not to wear it'.

In a land which also offers few obvious big-money tourist draws, Siberian and Far Eastern tour companies are dead keen to get up hunting parties, their pulses racing at the thought of the kill – US$6000 maybe from some poor sap of a foreign businessman. For locals, bagging a big brownie is just a case of turning off the TV, digging the rifle out of the cupboard and tramping off into the forest; but once a foreigner gets involved, hunting suddenly requires helicopter charters, boat rides, cross-country drives and half a year's salary as down payment. Which is all good news for Siberia's shootable wildlife – saved by greed.

On occasion in Siberia, the human species has slipped a couple of links down the food chain and found itself on the menu. In Ussuriland, the region around Vladivostok, the Siberian tiger is feared as a predator that has devoured men, women and pets. Tigers have been known to stalk villages. So it is that in recent years, local Ussuri residents have looked on with bemusement as an international posse of ecological groups moves in to save the tiger.

That the tiger needs saving is not in doubt. There are only about 250 to 350 of these fine animals left in Russia; in the past, up to 90 a year have fallen prey to poachers. Tiger skins can sell for up to US$5000, while their bones and organs fetch a good price from the Chinese, who value them for their supposed medicinal and aphrodisiac qualities.

It's the poachers who have the sympathy of many locals, the majority of whom are in dire economic straits. They feel that they would be far more worthy beneficiaries of all the money that's going the way of the big cats. It's a local contention that when times are good for the people, they will also be good for the tiger.

One route that might satisfy all comers would be the development of ecotourism. Foreigners bearing hard currency could boost the local economy while also bolstering the budgets of the nature reserves created to protect the tigers. However, ecotourism is not an easy concept for the average Siberian to grasp. Particularly perplexed was a fisherman I met on the northern shores of Lake Baikal, famous for its freshwater seals. When asked whether he'd be prepared to take visitors out on the lake to see the seals, he thought for a minute, then asked whether it wouldn't be a better idea if he just caught one and penned in it his back yard. Sensing that we weren't quite on the same wavelength, I explained that any visitors would probably want to see the seals in the lake, in the wild, flumping around on the rocks.

'Ah. They want to hunt', he said, his eyes lighting up.

'No', I replied, 'they probably would not want to hunt.'

'So. They can watch me hunt. They'll see the seals very good in the nets.'

'Couldn't they just go out onto the lake, see the seals and come back?', I persisted. He thought I was just about the funniest guy in the world.

Andrew Humphreys

Ocean, this is 13,483 sq km of protected tundra. It contains a host of wildlife including the rare red-breasted goose and musk ox.

Ust-Lensky
Russia's largest reserve covers 14,330 sq km of tundra at the mouth of the Lena River.

Wrangel Island
140 km off the coast of the far north-east of Russia, since 1976 this island has been a haven for polar bears, walruses and snow geese.

Conservation

While it has undoubtedly been a great source of wealth for Russia, the oil and gas industry, through greed, inattention and a failing infrastructure, has been perhaps the country's greatest environmental desecrator, causing some of the longest term damage. The fragile Arctic tundra has very obviously suffered massive degradation from oil spills. Environmental degradation from oil exploration and production in the West Siberian Plain has reached such levels that the huge Ob River flowing across it is almost dead. Less acknowledged, though equally harmful, is the destabilisation of the delicate tundra ecosystem by the construction of buildings, roads and railways and the extraction of the underground resources. Parts of the low-lying Yamal Peninsula at the mouth of the Ob, which contains some of the world's biggest gas reserves, have been literally melting into the sea as the permafrost melts near gas installations. The traditional hunting and reindeer-herding way of life of west Siberian native peoples such as the Nentsy, Khanty and Mansi is in danger of being killed off by the oil and gas industries. The tundra is also suffering the effects of acid rain, most of it the result of one smelting plant at Norilsk.

The catalogue of environmental wreckage in Siberia and the Far East is as varied as it is awful. In Chukotka in the far north-east, a past nuclear testing site, the local natives have been subjected to as much radiation as they would have if they'd been hanging around Chornobyl (Chernobyl) in 1986. But in Chukotka there were no warnings or evacuations. Now there is close to a 100% incidence of tuberculosis and a child mortal-

ity rate of 10%. Recent disclosures have revealed that the Russian Navy has been secretly dumping nuclear waste, including used reactors from submarines, in both the Sea of Japan, off Vladivostok, and the Arctic Ocean. Meanwhile, multinational logging concerns from the USA, South Korea and Japan, in partnership with Russia, are queueing up to clear-fell the Siberian forests, which are currently being devoured at an estimated four million hectares a year. And that's not to mention some of the northern hemisphere's worst polluted rivers, swathes of dead taiga, and air around some Siberian industrial towns that is so defiled that there'll never be any need for tinted windscreens.

The most documented instance of environmental degradation has centred around Lake Baikal. When two large pulp and cellulose plants began using the lake as a dump for waste products, it proved a rallying cause not just for locals but for concerned parties in all parts of the country. Baikal became the focus of the Soviet Union's first and most voluble environmental campaign, and the catalyst for the creation of a Russian green movement. Such was the groundswell of nationwide popular support that the government was forced to act and the offending plants were allegedly cleaned up, though scientists say there has been little actual improvement.

The limited success at Baikal was followed up with a victory for the native inhabitants of the Yamal peninsula on the Arctic coastline of Western Siberia, who managed to halt construction of a railway and gas pipeline that would have interfered with reindeer migration routes. Since 1991, international agencies have been able to add their weight to the Russian environmental cause; Friends of the Earth, for instance, is cooperating in saving the tiger and forests of Ussuriland, UNESCO is funding research around Lake Baikal and Greenpeace is active in opposing indiscriminate logging in the taiga.

GOVERNMENT

All of Siberia and the Russian Far East falls within the territory of the Russian Federation and is subject to rule from Moscow. To make this vast region more manageable, Siberia is split up into oblasti (regions), krai (territories) and republics, each with their own local government and administration. The republics – Altay, Khakassia, Tuva, Buryatia and Sakha (formerly Yakutia) – have significant non-Russian populations and nominally have greater powers of self-determination, but in practice are just as bound by the edicts of central government as everyone else. The system is a continuation of that established during the Soviet era but there's no Party any more. Those holding positions of power under the communists simply bought themselves new hats and carried on business as usual. Central government is responsible for defence, long-distance communications and the like, while regions are responsible for local services and privatisation. Both, in theory, are jointly responsible for foreign investment and the development of natural resources, but in practice Moscow still calls the shots – and, to the chagrin of Siberians, bags the cash.

In March 1992, more than 500 delegates from all over Siberia confronted Yeltsin's government, threatening to take Siberia out of the Federation unless their region was granted greater economic powers. Siberian and Russian Far Eastern products – especially timber, minerals, petroleum, gold, diamonds and furs – still generate half Russia's total hard-currency income but the regions from which this wealth emanates are seeing few of the benefits. Siberians are worse fed, have a lower life expectancy and produce fewer and less healthy children than their counterparts in western Russia. In 1993, Primorsky kray on the Pacific coast threatened to secede and become a fully fledged republic if it didn't get greater control over its economic assets. This was little more than bluff. For its part, Moscow is unwilling to give any measure of autonomy to the regions of Siberia and the Far East for fear any concessions would set a dangerous precedent. To see just how unwilling Moscow can be, the Siberians need only look to the ruins of Grozny.

ECONOMY

It may well be that in terms of raw materials, Russia is the richest country on earth, and much of this natural wealth lies in Siberia and the Far Eastern territories. The gold and diamond seams there are thought to exceed those in South Africa, the oil and gas fields are as bountiful as those in the Arabian Gulf and there is more timber than in all Brazil. The region also holds a third of the world's proven coal reserves.

Traditionally, Siberian society was agrarian, although as early as 1740 its precious metal mines were making a significant contribution to the wealth of the Russian Empire. Large-scale industrialisation began under the socialist government, facilitated by the development of the Kuznetsk coal basin, which fuelled growth along the route of the Trans-Siberian line. Iron foundries were established at Magnitogorsk, an enormous tractor factory at Chelyabinsk, locomotive and aircraft works at Ulan Ude, and so on. The town of Norilsk, now the largest anywhere within the Arctic Circle, was founded in 1922 to exploit the copper, nickel and other deposits of the far northern Taymyr Peninsula. WW II hastened the industrial evolution when many of European Russia's large manufacturing plants were dismantled and moved east of the Urals, well out of reach of the advancing Germans.

Oil was first discovered in Siberia in 1965. Brezhnev poured billions of roubles into extensive oilfields, principally located north of Tyumen and Omsk. In 1990 it was estimated that every second, 12 tonnes of oil were pumped out of the Tyumen region alone. The world's largest gas deposits lie even further north, around Urengoy and Yamburg east of the Ob Gulf and on the Yamal Peninsula to its west. The oil and gas industries, so vital to Russia's economy, have caused untold environmental damage and threatened the existence of some northern minority peoples.

The Far East accounts for only 5% of Russia's industrial output but the region contributes in other significant ways. It has a near monopoly on diamonds and gold, as well as antimony and tungsten, and the Pacific seaboard accounts for 60% of Russia's annual fish haul. The government is tight-lipped about the quantity of precious substances the open-cast mines of Sakha might yield, but in recent years hundreds of millions of dollars' worth of precious stones originating in Russia have appeared on the international market, seriously challenging South Africa's long-standing primacy.

However, a combination of counterproductive Soviet-era central planning, daunting physical conditions and inappropriate technology has meant that most of Siberia's resources are as yet untouched. The policy turnarounds that came as a result of the events of 1991 have provided a way out by opening the region to foreign investment – albeit reluctantly. The Far East in particular has taken the initiative, seeing its future welfare best secured by closer cooperation with other Pacific Rim nations. Cities such as Khabarovsk and Vladivostok are much closer, geographically, to Seoul and Tokyo – even to San Francisco – than they are to Moscow. It is far cheaper to import from these near neighbours than from an erratic central Russia. The former closed cities are now also even going so far as to offer foreign companies tax breaks to attract investment in the local economies. Reaction so far is cautious but there have been a few bites. Japan has already invested heavily in the fishing industry and gold mining, and Mitsubishi and Mitsui are part of a consortium, along with the Dutch/UK Shell and US and Russian companies, that is developing oil and gas fields off Sakhalin.

POPULATION & PEOPLE

About 33 million people live in Siberia and the Far East – just 22% of Russia's population, in 75% of its territory. Most settlements, including all the big cities (the biggest are Novosibirsk, Yekaterinburg, Omsk and Chelyabinsk, each with between 1.1 and 1.5 million people), are strung across the south, on or near the Trans-Siberian Railway.

The population includes over 30 indigenous peoples but these only make up 4% of the total. The rest are mainly Russian but there are also Ukrainians, Tatars, Germans, Jews, Latvians, Lithuanians, Estonians, Kazakhs and most other nationalities of the ex-Soviet Union, who came as pioneers, settlers, exiles or prisoners. Of all the region's oblasti, territories and republics, only Tuva has a majority native population.

The indigenous population is a welter of peoples of uncertain origin, mostly small in number. They speak many languages. Most were originally shamanist and nearly all were nomadic herders (of sheep, horses and cattle in the south and of reindeer in the north); some were fishers, trappers and hunters (of game inland and of walrus, seal and whale on the north coast). Very few had written languages until after the Revolution. There are few nomads nowadays, owing to Soviet policies of forced settlement, collectivisation and industrialisation.

Few of these people have lived in great harmony with the immigrants from the west who have been arriving since the 16th century, as their territories have been exploited by Moscow for a series of economic purposes – furs, agriculture, mining, industry and, most recently, oil and gas – and their cultures, languages and identities have been threatened by Russification and, in the Soviet period, collectivisation, industrialisation and environmental damage. The very existence of some of the smaller groups is now threatened. Few indigenous peoples wield real power in 'their' republics or districts and nearly all are swamped by Russians and other non-native populations. The most numerous peoples – the Buryats, Yakuts, Tuvans, Khakass and Altay – have their 'own' republics within the Russian Federation. Eight districts (okrugi) within other regions or territories are named after their native inhabitants, who are, however, in nearly all cases small minorities within them. Some of the small northern minorities are among the most disadvantaged peoples in Russia, with low life expectancy (35 to 40 for men), poor housing, high disease and suicide rates, and a way of life that is endangered by environmental damage.

SIBERIA & RUSSIAN FAR EAST

Unless you venture into rural areas, you're unlikely to see (or, at any rate, recognise) any but the more numerous Buryats, Tuvans and Yakuts. Most native peoples have adopted Russian dress.

In the Soviet era there was little racial tension, probably because the indigenous population was so small and so politically powerless. Stalin sent insubordinate indigenous leaders to the Gulag in the 1930s. Since the late 1980s, however, there have been stirrings of nationalism and anti-Russian sentiment, most notably in Tuva, Buryatia and Sakha (Yakutia). Tuva, the only republic with an indigenous majority, saw a wave of anti-Russian violence in the early 1990s, since which large numbers of Russians have left.

More on many of the Siberian peoples can be found in the Arts & Culture and Religion sections of this chapter, and in the regional chapters.

Buryats

This Mongol people is the largest indigenous group, 420,000 strong in Russia. Just over half of them live in the Republic of Buryatia (capital: Ulan Ude) south and east of Lake Baikal, which was Jenghiz Khan's home territory. Others are in rural autonomous districts (*okrugi*) west of Irkutsk and near Chita, as well as in Mongolia and northern Xinjiang. Many Buryats converted to Tibetan Buddhism in the 18th century, though many western Buryats later turned to Orthodox Christianity. The Buryats put up the strongest resistance to the early Russian presence.

Yakuts

At about 380,000, the Yakuts of the Lena River basin form the second-biggest native group. They are probably the most culturally advanced, with vigorous arts and literature. Yakuts form only about 33% of the population of the Republic of Sakha (formerly Yakutia; capital: Yakutsk) but hold many high governmental posts. Sakha has all Russia's diamond reserves and most of its gold as well as rich timber and coal

resources. The Yakuts are a Turkic people, skilled with horses, thought to have migrated centuries ago from the south-west and to be related to the Kazakhs and Kyrgyz. Unlike their cousins, however, they are shamanists.

Tuvans

The 210,000 Tuvans in Russia are, like the Buryats, a Tibetan Buddhist Mongol people, but are Turkic-speaking. Nearly all of them live in the Republic of Tuva (capital: Kyzyl), in the upper Yenisey basin on the Mongolian border, where they form 64% of the population. Traditionally, they have been hunters or herders of cattle, horses, sheep and yak. Tuva was part of the Chinese Empire in the 18th and 19th centuries, and later the nominally independent communist republic of Tannu Tuva from 1921 to 1944. Mongolia also has a sizeable Tuvan population.

Khakass

North of the Tuvans is another Turkic

A Buryat archer in traditional dress

people. Partly shamanist and partly Christian, the Khakass number about 80,000 but make up only about 11% of the population of the Republic of Khakassia (capital: Abakan). Formerly nomad herders, they are the local remnants of the 'Yenisey Kyrgyz' Empire, which stretched from Kazakhstan to Lake Baikal from the 6th to the 13th century.

Altay
This 71,000-strong Turkic-speaking people forms about 28% of the population of the mountainous Altay Republic (capital: Gorno-Altaysk) on the Kazakhstan and Mongolian borders south-east of Novosibirsk. From the 15th to the 18th century they were ruled by the fearsome Oyrats of western Mongolia, who scared the Kazakhs into joining Russia in the 18th century. They came under Russian control in the 19th century.

Evenki
Probably the most ancient of the Siberian tribes are the 30,000-strong Evenki or Tungus, spread widely from the middle Yenisey River to the eastern seaboard and south to Lake Baikal, the Amur River and Manchuria. Their language is related to Chinese, though they're culturally closer to Mongolians. They form 14% of the population of the huge Evenk Autonomous District (Okrug) north of Krasnoyarsk.

Related tribes are the Evens, hunter-fishers who number 17,000 scattered around the north-east, and the 12,000-strong Nanai, in the lower Amur River basin.

Nentsy
The 35,000 Nentsy are the biggest of the 25 small groups known as the 'Peoples of the North'. Together with three smaller peoples they are called the Samoyed (though some don't like this name because, in Russian, it sounds like 'cannibal'). Many Nentsy are still hunters and herders along the Arctic coast east and west of the northern Ural Mountains, but they face increasing destruction of their and their reindeer herds' habitat by the oil and gas industries.

Khanty
Also called Ostyaks, these former hunters and fishers are a Finno-Ugric people, related to the Finns, Estonians, Karelians and some Volga peoples. They were the first indigenous people seen by 11th-century Novgorodian explorers. The 22,000 Khanty and another small Finno-Ugric people, the 8000 Mansi (or Voguls), have a swampy joint autonomous district on the middle Ob River, where their share in the population has declined to just over 1% and their way of life has been shattered by the massive exploitation of the Samotlor oilfield, discovered in the 1960s.

Other Native Peoples
The six Palaeoasiatic, or Palaeosiberian, peoples are a miscellany, with languages that don't belong in any other category. Totalling about 34,000, most live in the far north-east. The most numerous are the 15,000 Chukchi and 9000 Koryaks. Their Stone Age forebears, who crossed the Bering Strait ice to America and Greenland, may also be remote ancestors of the American Indians.

Also in the far north-east are 1700 Eskimos and 700 Aleuts. Even less numerous are the Oroks of Sakhalin Island, who were counted at just 190 in the 1989 census.

Jews
In 1934 a Jewish Autonomous Region (Yevreyskaya Avtonomnaya Oblast) was created in the Far East in the same spirit as other autonomous divisions, with Hebrew as its 'national' language. The exercise was a resounding failure, partly because of the incredibly harsh and remote location. Only about 0.5% of the Soviet Union's Jews went there and stayed, and today the region's 15,000 Jewish inhabitants are outnumbered by 13 to one. Most live in the capital, Birobidzhan, west of Khabarovsk.

ARTS & CULTURE
Literature
Siberia has produced generals, adventurers and even politicians of note, but there have been very few writers, artists or composers.

In fact, when it comes to literature, Siberia is far more usually associated with the deaths of writers than with their genesis. The poet Osip Mandelstam, exiled for criticism of Stalin, died in 1938 in a transit camp on the outskirts of Vladivostok. The same year, Ukrainian poet Mikhaylo Dray-Kharma failed to survive winter in a camp at Kolyma. Dostoevsky was amongst the writers who did survive Siberia, and his four years of hard labour in a camp near Omsk are recounted in *The House of the Dead* (1862). In latter times, Anatoly Rybakov, author of *Children of the Arbat*, was sentenced to hard labour in Siberia, an experience which, no doubt, provided much source material for his Gulag novel *Fear*, published in 1993.

One writer whose origins are in Siberia, as distinct from those who were sent there in exile, is Yuz Aleshkovsky, born in Krasnoyarsk on the banks of the Yenisey – though that still didn't save him from being sent further east for a period in the camps. Aleshkovsky, who since 1978 has lived in the USA, has two books published in English, *Kangaroo* (1978) and *The Hand* (1980). The most famed native Siberian writer is Valentin Rasputin, known for his stories decrying the destruction of the land and spirit of the Russian people. His best known work is *Farewell to Matyora* (1979), about a Siberian village flooded when a hydroelectric dam is built. Rasputin also lent a prominent voice to the protests over the pollution of Lake Baikal.

Architecture

Architecture in Siberia has scarcely evolved beyond the basic need for shelter. The original nomads' dwellings were made of poles and skins (eg the cylindrical tent-house called a *yurta*, or yurt) or, in the south, a framework of poles covered with brush and earth. Yurts are still in use in rural Tuva and Altay. Examples of these dwellings can also be found in open-air museums including those near Bratsk, Irkutsk and Ulan Ude. The buildings of the Russian settlers are, not surprisingly, similar to those west of the Ural Mountains but fewer and more functional. Siberian variations on the traditional Russian and Ukrainian log house (izba) with 'wooden-lace' window frames and eaves can still be seen. The best preserved are in Irkutsk.

Siberia's churches were rarely anything grand, although the functional wooden structures did possess a stark beauty born of simplicity. Ironically, most of these early churches were later destroyed and the best examples now remain preserved in once-Russian Alaska.

Native Culture

Native art and culture has been relegated to the exhibit cases in regional museums, squeezed between the stuffed seals and the railway builders' theodolites. Outside the museums, the only other place to see native crafts is in the big city art salons, which are supplied by a small cottage industry of artisans. The Evenki keep the souvenir shops of Irkutsk stocked with small carved wooden items, while in Khabarovsk you can pick up cylindrical containers made of birch bark by local Nanai.

One art form that has survived is dance. The Buryat peoples retain their unique steps and patterns, which they put on show every summer at the Buryatia festival, but more interesting are the Koryaks of northern Kamchatka. The Koryaks use dance to tell stories, not just traditional myths and legends but also contemporary tales and anecdotes – 'the day I got my fingers trapped in the snowmobile tracks', that sort of thing – done

Wooden-shuttered Siberian windows

as a fluid, ensemble mime. Dance troupes sometimes travel down to perform in the regional capital, Petropavlovsk-Kamchatsky.

Another unique example of living native Siberian culture is Tuvan throat singing. You may be lucky enough to hear this at festivals or celebrations such as weddings in Tuva. It's a kind of very deep, tuneful chanting, produced from somewhere deep down in the throat – quite startling when you first hear it. Tuvan throat singers have made international tours, and recordings of their music are available in the West; one CD, *Voices from the Distant Steppe*, is released on the UK Realworld label.

RELIGION
Shamanism
Long before the coming of Christianity, the common religion of the indigenous tribes of Siberia was shamanism, a form of pagan earth-worship which dates back to the Stone Age, based on the observance of lunar rituals and sacred natural sites. All natural objects were believed to have a spirit and people contacted these spirits for guidance by means of a shaman: a high priest, prophet and doctor rolled into one. A few shamans still exist, particularly in the Buryatia region, although they are often regarded as curious anachronisms or outright quacks. Some spectacular old shamans' outfits can be seen in several Siberian museums, for example the regional museums at Irkutsk and Kyzyl.

Christianity
The Church made its first appearance at some time in the 1570s in the form of a collapsible tent carried over the Ural Mountains by a mercantile-sponsored band of marauding explorers. The first permanent church structure in Siberia was built in Tyumen in 1586. Soon afterwards, as part of their methods of subjugation, the Russians began forcibly baptising the natives – in some cases, tying a couple to poles and ducking them into water through a hole cut in the ice. Unsurprisingly, Christianity was never a big hit.

The state initially backed the Church in Siberia, perceiving it as an excellent tool of colonisation. Eventually, however, as the wealth and influence of the Church grew, it came to be viewed as a threat to secular power and a determined attempt was made to make it subordinate to the state. After the Russian Church reforms of 1653, there were those who couldn't accept the changes and continued to worship in the old ways. These 'Old Believers' became subject to persecution and many fled to Siberia. Their beliefs still survive in villages in the Buryatia region, particularly in the vicinity of Ulan Ude. As well as the Old Believers, many other religious communities either were exiled to Siberia or simply settled there hoping to find freedom of worship. The Skoptsy were a fanatical Christian sect exiled to Olekminsk in Yakutia during the 18th century. They believed in sexual abstinence, and to remove the threat of temptation young males were castrated.

Many of Siberia's Russian Orthodox churches were destroyed in the civil war, or at least suffered some damage, which gave the Bolsheviks an excellent excuse to complete the demolition and erect patriotic statues and monuments to the Party instead. Those churches that survived were usually converted to some secular use: the Church of the Trinity in Irkutsk became a planetarium; a Lutheran church in Vladivostok was commandeered for a naval museum and the Orthodox Hodigitira Cathedral in Ulan Ude was designated, bizarrely, a museum of atheism. The Church in Siberia has yet to exhibit any signs of recovery.

For further details on Christianity in Russia, see Facts about European Russia.

Buddhism
Buddhists in the Russian Federation number over half a million, a figure that has been growing steadily in the years since glasnost began to allow for free expression of religion. All Russia's Buddhists are members of the Gelugpa or 'Yellow-Hat' sect of Tibetan Buddhism, whose spiritual leader is the Dalai Lama. All of them are descendants of

SIBERIA & RUSSIAN FAR EAST

peoples who originally lived on the border with Mongolia, where Buddhism reached them in the 17th and early 18th centuries – Buryats near Lake Baikal and Tuvans to their west.

Contemplative and essentially atheistic, Buddhism was never a direct threat to the state and was tolerated until Stalin attempted to wipe it out in the 1930s, closing its 250 temples and 50 monasteries (datsans) and exiling or executing thousands of lamas, or priests. At the end of WW II, two datsans were opened, a new one at Ivolginsk near Ulan Ude and an old one at Aginsk, near Chita.

Since 1950 Buddhism has been organised under a Buddhist Religious Board at Ivolginsk, headed by the chief lama, the Bandido Hambo Lama. Until glasnost the only approved work for Buddhist organisations was to maintain a profile in various world-peace movements. Now they are free to reopen monasteries, and are doing so. The Dalai Lama has visited both Buryatia and Tuva.

Judaism
Even before the Soviet creation of the Jewish Autonomous Region centred around Birobidzhan, Siberia was home to large numbers of Jews. At one time they accounted for one-third of the population of Sretensk (a port town on the banks of the Shilka River, 300 km east of Chita) and in the 1880s Kansk, near Krasnoyarsk, was so predominantly Jewish that it was known as the Jerusalem of Siberia. There was also a synagogue in Verkhneudinsk (later Ulan Ude), and the one in Irkutsk is still standing and now operates as a Jewish cultural centre.

LANGUAGE
Though the minority peoples of Siberia and the Far East have their own languages, Russian is the predominant tongue virtually everywhere. See Facts about European Russia for the basics.

Facts for the Visitor

Though it's something for which the old Soviet system is frequently derided, the degree of homogeneity that it installed throughout such a vast territory – one which encompasses such a variety of peoples, traditions and geography – is nothing short of remarkable. People in Vladivostok, a city east of Calcutta, Bangkok and Beijing, drink from the same type of easy-stain mugs as those in Kaliningrad, just north of Poland. They drive curry-coloured cars of exactly the same model and park them outside identical, prematurely aged, grey 1970s tower blocks full of apartments painted either seasick green or cat's-tongue pink. Europe, which covers a far smaller area with less ethnic variation and has, in Brussels, a whole city of bureaucrats working towards the goal of common aggregation, comes nowhere close to mirroring the Soviet achievement. What this means in a practical sense is that most of the information given in the European Russia Facts for the Visitor chapter also holds true for Siberia and the Russian Far East; check there for more on some of the topics mentioned in this chapter and for information on Visas & Embassies, Documents, Customs, Tourist Offices, Business Hours & Holidays, Post & Telecommunications, Electricity, Laundry, Toilets, Weights & Measures, Entertainment, Museums and Things to Buy. The Trans-Siberian Railway chapter has further information on visas relevant to Siberian travellers.

MONEY

Unfortunately, the advice has to be to carry cash – preferably US dollars, and lots of them. The yen is commonly accepted in Khabarovsk, Vladivostok and on Sakhalin, and Chinese RMB can be exchanged at places in Irkutsk, Ulan Ude and Khabarovsk, but elsewhere you'll have trouble offloading anything other than US dollars. Bank tellers in Siberia are also extremely finicky about the dollars they will accept. If a bill is defaced in any way – written on, torn, dirty or badly worn – it'll be handed straight back. Some tellers won't accept any bills printed before 1990. In Irkutsk Andrew gave US$100 to a cashier, in what looked to him like pristine US$10 bills, only to have seven of them sniffily rejected. The same tellers will have no qualms about handing you a pile of Russian notes that look as though they did service in a kindergarten art class. Don't accept them: nobody else will.

Travellers' cheques are near useless. In the whole of Siberia and the Russian Far East we came across no more than two places that would touch them. Credit cards are a better bet, in particular Visa, which seemed to be the most widely recognised. Quite a few of the up-market hotels and restaurants accepted payment by credit card and in Irkutsk, Khabarovsk, Vladivostok and Yuzhno-Sakhalinsk it was possible to get a cash advance on Visa.

For those who have to carry large wads of cash, the only consolation to be offered is that security isn't the problem you might imagine. Take sensible precautions such as dividing your money into three or four stashes hidden out of view about your person (neck purse, money belt etc, all worn under your clothing), and there shouldn't be any problems. Money tends to go missing only when potential thieves are presented with easy opportunities. We haven't heard of any tourists in Siberia being mugged or attacked for their cash. Don't be unduly worried; just be careful.

Costs

A 1994 survey conducted by a Swiss-based consultancy firm rated Moscow as the third most expensive city in the world in which to live, after Tokyo and Osaka. But, according to a Labour Ministry report quoted in the *Moscow Times*, the Russian Far East is up to three times as expensive as the capital. As a general rule of thumb, the farther east you go, the more expensive it gets. One of the main reasons for this is that everything is shipped out from Moscow. Another is that, as you approach the Pacific, you're coming up against Japanese spending power.

Depending on the level of comfort required, accommodation in Siberia is going to cost an average US$25 to US$35 per night for a double room. In the Russian Far East that goes up to US$30 to US$50 per night, with the added disadvantage that cheaper options become thinner on the ground. Dining out in Siberia, it's possible to get away at under US$5 per head, but in cities such as Khabarovsk or Vladivostok that's ice-cream money – the outlay for a decent meal is at least US$10. Of course, it is possible to eat much more cheaply, maybe for just US$3 or US$4, but it's not guaranteed to be a pleasant experience. If you're not looking to cut corners and economise constantly, a reasonable budget would be around US$40 per day in Siberia and US$50 farther east, including train fares but not flights.

WHEN TO GO

When to go depends a great deal on which Siberia you want to see and what you want to do there. In summer getting around is easier and the bustle of street life and pavement traders adds an upbeat air to what can otherwise be some fairly charmless cities. But winter brings to life the Siberia of the imagination: starkly beautiful, sugar-frosted landscapes, and townscapes that resemble a succession of Christmas-card scenes. Much of the urban grime disappears, hidden beneath a great, white cloak. Temperatures as low as -25°C, though, might not be to everybody's liking. Winter can also make overland travel other than by rail difficult as roads become blocked.

April and May tend to be wet and slushy, and early summer is the worst time for biting insects. If you are considering any trekking or hiking, or even just spending time away from the cities, avoid May, June and July because the mosquitoes and horseflies are murderous. It's far better to go between late

August and early October, when the midges are more or less gone, the temperature is still quite mild (jumper or jacket required, but no coat) and the deciduous vegetation, particularly in the east, takes on a glorious russet palette.

Very few hotels offer out-of-season rates, just a couple of the large ex-Intourist places like the Intourist hotels in Irkutsk and Khabarovsk, which offer a discount of around 20%. See also Climate in Facts About Siberia & the Far East.

WHAT TO BRING

A summer or autumn trip to Siberia doesn't require you to pack anything much that's not on the list given in European Russia Facts for the Visitor. You might, however, want to make sure you have more than enough camera film because once you leave Moscow it could be many days and missed photo opportunities before you next have the chance to stock up. Similarly, batteries are hard to find, and there's no reading matter in English to be had anywhere between the Ural Mountains and the Pacific Ocean. A small torch is also useful for all the unlit hotel corridors and bathrooms with missing bulbs.

For day trips out of town, mosquito repellent is essential, especially in early summer. If you think you might be spending any amount of time in the taiga or around rivers, to avoid acquiring a complexion like blowtorched paint we would recommend a scarf to wrap around your face or even a head net, and some thick gloves.

Until mid-October a jumper (sweater) and a jacket are enough to keep you warm, but from then until late May you're going to need considerably more. Thermal underwear is a must, as are thick woollen socks, gloves, a scarf, a heavy coat and a woollen hat. It's also advisable to wear thick-soled shoes, if not boots. Lip salve and skin-moisturising creams are also a good idea. You might also want to take a heating coil (not all hotels have a dezhurnaya to supply hot water) and some sachets of instant coffee, hot chocolate or soup.

GPS – For the Traveller Who Has Everything

One of the biggest challenges in the Russian wilderness is knowing where you're going, and bad or hard-to-find maps make the situation worse. I was considering this very problem on the boat back to Petrozavodsk from Kizhi Island when I ran into a lovely American doctor doing advance work in the area for a minerals concern. She invited me to dinner, where I sat down for the first time ever with a bunch of guys who really know where they're going: geologists.

That evening, they invited me to join them on a field trip out to an area near the Karelian town of Sortavala, from where one could pick up a hydrofoil or ferry to the island of Valaam. Fair enough, I thought, we're always looking for fresh ways to get from point A to point B. I agreed and met them the next morning at their hotel.

On the trip out I noticed two things about all their gear: it was cooler than mine, and they carried less than I did. I was speaking with a couple of them about compass declination – a subject on which one could fill rooms with what I don't know – and other orienteering tips when the team leader reached into his pocket and produced something I'd only seen in magazines: a GPS unit.

The Global Positioning System (GPS) was developed by the US military. It involves 24 satellites that operate in six orbital planes at an altitude of 20,200 km. These put out coded signals that can be received by small units on earth. With the help of computer chips that can solve the several sets of simultaneous equations the readings produce, these instruments can determine their absolute location with surprising precision. This little piece of gizmotronics tells you:

- where you are on earth (within about 50 to 100 metres)
- where you've been
- where you're going (bearing, distance from any specific destination)
- how fast you're going
- when you'll get there
- what your altitude is above sea level
- and, of course, the time

Without a second's hesitation, I tried to invent various justifications for spending *whatever* it would cost. I knew I had to have one. The geologists let me play with this toy of theirs during the dig (which was, by the way, a fascinating experience) and I was hooked. In Melbourne for Lonely Planet's 21st-anniversary celebration, fellow gear-freak David Else (author of *Trekking in East Africa*) and I decided to inspect the new Silva GPS (US$1000) at a local sporting-goods shop. We were blown away. But not wishing to spend that much money, I went with the less expensive, smaller – and, many say, much better – Garmin GPS-40, which cost US$329 at a shop in Florida.

I've now used the thing extensively, and I must report that for rough guidance it's unbeatable. If you know where you want to get to, you can enter the coordinates of your destination (latitude and longitude culled from, say, a good atlas or map) and the Garmin will show you an electronic 'highway' (a graphical representation of a road leading off to the horizon). If the 'road' bends left, you turn left at the same angle. As long as you keep the electronic 'road' on the screen pointing straight, you're going towards your destination. I wish I'd had it in the wilds of Karelia and the Kola Peninsula, but I was only able to use it in some Russian cities. I've also used it for practice in Munich, Germany and in the Florida Everglades, where it's an invaluable piece of gear.

Handy features are the maps – you can enter coordinates as you go along and it draws a digital map of your entire journey – and 'real ground speed'. Less handy are that coverage varies depending on where you are – city readings are usually not very accurate – and vertical readings are fantasy. Once it told me I was 119 metres below sea level – in the Alps. Finally, they're not that easy to use – they have a terminology all their own and it takes a good while to get the hang of it.

As a guide, a GPS unit will come in handy when travelling in remote areas without roads – ie if you're boating, flying, parasailing, trekking, canoeing, hiking, biking or writing a guidebook. And if you'll be travelling anywhere off the beaten track in Russia – especially in remote areas such as Siberia, Karelia, the Kola Peninsula or the Ural Mountains – these jammies are choice equipment.

Just don't expect a GPS unit to serve as your *only* orienteering tool. Unless you've spent a lot of money and/or had a lot of experience with them, bring along a good compass as well for critical measurements.

Oh, yeah – that declination thing. The team agreed that you should leave the compass set at zero and calculate the declination later. Whatever.

Nick Selby

USEFUL ORGANISATIONS

These include:

Australia
   Australia, Russia & Affiliates Society, 15 Crystal St, Petersham, NSW 2049
Canada
   Friends of the Russian National Parks Society, 2816 Seaview Rd, Victoria, BC V8N 1K8
USA
   Baikal Watch, Earth Island Institute, 300 Broadway, Suite 28, San Francisco, CA 94133: a Russian-American environmental research group active in the protection and preservation of Lake Baikal
   Hornocker Wildlife Research Institute, PO Box 3246, University Station, Moscow, ID 83843 (e-mail dalm@glas.apc.org): conducts joint research with the Russians on the Siberian tiger

CULTURAL EVENTS & FESTIVALS

See also European Russia Facts for the Visitor for general Russian festivals and celebrations.

Late January (16 days)
   Tibetan Buddhist New Year (Tsagaalgan). A moveable feast, which celebrates the lunar new year and hence advances by about 10 days a year. In 1996 the first sighting of the new moon will be in late January. Mainly celebrated at family level in Buryatia and Tuva. Known as Shagaa in Tuva.
Early June
   Tun-Payram. Khakass opening-of-summer-pastures festival. Traditional food, costumes, sports. It is celebrated in Abakan, usually on first or second Sunday of month, and then in villages.
Early July
   Maitreya Buddha Festival. At Ivogolinsk datsan near Ulan Ude.
July
   Buryatia Folk Festival. Celebrated at the ethnographic museum in Ulan Ude.
Late July
   Ysyakh. Yakut opening-of-pastures festival. Traditional food and costumes.
Mid-August
   Naadym. Tuvan summer festival, with Tuvan wrestling *(khuresh)*, throat-singing and long-distance horse races.
25 December-5 January
   Russian Winter Festival. Tourist-oriented troyka rides and folklore performances at Irkutsk.

TIME

Siberia and the Far East spread across no fewer than eight time zones, which can have a strangely disorienting effect if you're travelling steadily across them (see the Trans-Siberian Railway chapter). To add to the confusion, some regions have been playing around with time as an expression of local independence: for a brief period not long ago, half the large city of Novosibirsk was in one time zone while the other half was in another. Hopefully, things have settled down as follows.

When it's noon in Moscow, it's...
   2 pm in Yekaterinburg and Tyumen
   3 pm in Omsk and Novosibirsk
   4 pm in Barnaul, Gorno-Altaysk, Krasnoyarsk, Abakan and Kyzyl
   5 pm in Bratsk, Irkutsk and Ulan Ude
   6 pm in Chita, Blagoveshchensk and Yakutsk
   7 pm in Khabarovsk and Vladivostok
   8 pm in Sakhalin and Magadan
   9 pm in Kamchatka and Providenia.

Long-distance train timetables, most railway station clocks and some air timetables are on Moscow time.

BOOKS

See also the Books section in the Trans-Siberian Railway chapter and, for more general background reading, European Russia Facts for the Visitor.

General

For basic background reading, Benson Bobrick's *East of the Sun* (Heinemann, 1992) is an excellent and very readable history of the conquest and settlement of Siberia and the Russian Far East, good on things like who mutilated whom and in what way. A more academic treatment is given in *The Russian Far East: A History* (Stanford University Press, 1994) by John J Stephan. *A History of the Peoples of Siberia* (Cambridge, 1994) by James Forsyth covers the same ground but from the perspective of the indigenous tribes. Forsyth's book is rather heavy going and those with a more casual interest might prefer *The Forgotten Peoples of Siberia* (Scalo, 1993) by Fred Mayer, a beautiful photographic essay on the living conditions and traditions of groups such as the reindeer-herding Koryaks and the walrus-hunting Chukchi.

The animal and plant life of Siberia and parts east comes under scrutiny in chapters of *The Realms of the Russian Bear* (BBC Books, 1992) by John Sparks and *The Nature of Russia* (Boxtree, 1992) by John Massey Stewart, both written with the novice naturalist in mind and lavishly illustrated. Also heavy on photographs is another natural-wonders book, *Baikal, Sacred Sea of Siberia* (Thames & Hudson), a pictorial tribute to the great lake with a text by travel writer and novelist Peter Matthiessen.

Travelogues

During the summer of 1991, Frederick Kempe followed the Tom River north from Novokuznetsk to the Ob and on to the Arctic Sea, a journey recalled in *Siberian Odyssey: A Voyage Into the Russian Soul* (G P Putnam's Sons, 1992). The style is journalistic (Kempe is the Berlin bureau chief with the *Wall Street Journal*) and concentrates on exposing the evils of the Soviet system through interviews with some of the dozens of people he met en route. At around the same time Italian journalist Tiziano Terzani was sailing down the Amur River when he heard news of a coup in the Kremlin. *Goodnight Mr Lenin* (Picador, 1992) records the lack of immediate impact that the death of communism had in the Russian Far East and follows the writer's efforts to scramble for Moscow and get in on the story.

Cycling may not seem like the obvious way to get across Siberia, and a book describing the attempt sounds a less than thrilling prospect, but it's to the credit of two authors who undertook two different, recent transcontinental Russian bike rides that their books are so engrossing. The first expedition was undertaken by a joint US-USSR team in summer 1989, setting off from Vladivostok and following roughly the route of the Trans-Siberian Railway. The resulting account, *Off the Map* (Robert Hale, 1993) by Mark Jenkins, is extremely well written but its focus on group dynamics pushes everything

else into the background. In *Between the Hammer and the Sickle* (Sinclair Stevenson, 1992), author Simon Vickers doesn't mention whether his team, which crossed Russia from west to east the following year, knew that they'd been beaten to the achievement, but he can take some consolation in the fact that his is the better book. Vickers' description of the often nightmarish journey (a recurring phrase is 'hideously ugly') provides a surprisingly absorbing, empathetic and evocative picture of both Soviet suburban living and life in rural Siberia.

If the cyclists made good reading out of potentially train-spotterish material, Christina Dodwell has managed the reverse. In *Beyond Siberia* (Sceptre, 1994) she describes several weeks in Kamchatka, amongst dramatic landscapes of smouldering volcanoes and precarious snow bridges, skiing around lumbering bears and scooting up clouds of snow while riding with an aerobatically inclined helicopter pilot. But what could have been a fascinating account is rendered unflaggingly dull by some excruciatingly bad prose. Better to travel with Laurens van der Post, who, in his *Journey into Russia* (Penguin, 1964), never got anywhere quite as exciting as Kamchatka (he visited Bratsk, Irkutsk and Khabarovsk) but recorded what he saw with an intelligence and insight still valid more than 30 years on.

Tuva or Bust! by the Californian Ralph Leighton (Penguin) is not so much a travelogue as a pre-travelogue, describing his own and Nobel physics laureate Richard Feynman's growing obsession with Tuva, which began at a dinner-table geography guessing-game in 1977, and the pair's years of trying to unravel Soviet bureaucracy in order to visit Tuva. You learn a lot about the place though Leighton doesn't actually get there till the book's Epilogue. Feynman had died just before the final go-ahead for their trip was received, in 1988.

Guides

There are no general guides to Siberia but there are a couple of excellent specialised publications which are well worth getting

SIBERIA & RUSSIAN FAR EAST

hold of if you are planning to visit the areas they touch upon. *Trekking in Russia & Central Asia* (1994) by Frith Maier is let down by maps that don't always relate very well to the text but it has good coverage of the wilderness regions of the Altay and Sayan mountains, the Lake Baikal region, Ussuriland, Sakhalin, Chukotka and Kamchatka. It's published in the USA by The Mountaineers, Seattle; in Canada by Douglas & McIntyre, Vancouver; and in Britain by Cordee, Leicester. *The Siberian BAM Railway Guidebook* (Red Bear Tours/Trailblazers, 1995) by Athol Yates covers in detail all the major settlements along this little-known line including Severobaikalsk (and the north end of Lake Baikal) and Komsomolsk. It also includes river routes with BAM rail connections, such as Khabarovsk to Nikolaevsk-on-Amur (along the Amur), and Ust-Kut to Yakutsk along the Lena.

Literature

Siberia's premier writer, Valentin Rasputin, is published in English translation by the Northwestern University Press, Illinois. Amongst his works so far available are *Farewell to Matyora*, a novel about a Siberian village flooded when a hydroelectric dam is built, and the collection *Siberia on Fire: Stories and Essays*, both in paperback. Anatoly Rybakov, best known for his *Children of the Arbat*, has since written *Fear*, an account of Stalin's purges as seen through the eyes of a young man sent into Siberian exile. However, the book that has probably done more than any other to shape Siberia in the Western popular consciousness is Alexander Solzhenitsyn's *The Gulag Archipelago*, a heavy read but a good one for those three-day train journeys (and Trans-Siberian passengers no longer need to rip the covers off to prevent its being identified and confiscated by the border guards).

MAPS

There isn't a map exclusively of Siberia; instead you should aim to pick up a good one of the Russian Federation as a whole (see European Russia Facts for the Visitor). A company called Russia/Central Asia Travel Resources, of 117 North 40th, Seattle, WA 98103 USA, has 1:200,000 Russian military topographical maps (recently declassified) which it sells in regional sets for US$125.

Once in Siberia, bookshops often sell maps of neighbouring cities or regions but not necessarily of their own. If you see a map or plan of a place you may be going to, pick it up because it's quite possible you won't find one when you get there.

MEDIA

For a general overview of the Russian media see European Russia Facts for the Visitor. Every major town and city throughout Siberia and the Far East has its own newspapers and periodicals, while each oblast or kray also has its own TV channel – usually a mix of local news and yet more imported soaps. Anyone who turns on the TV in some remote, unspoilt wilderness den and is confronted with *Santa Barbara*, followed by 30 minutes of whooping, high-kicking Australian aerobics, will soon start to see a grain of sense in the nationalistic rantings of Vladimir Zhirinovsky.

There are English-language newspapers out in Vladivostok and Yuzhno-Sakhalinsk, both very tightly focused on regional minutiae. Other than these, there's nothing to be found in English, not even in the top-class hotels, although one or two of them in Khabarovsk and Vladivostok do have CNN and other satellite channels. If you can speak Japanese you'll benefit from the Hokkaido-based TV transmissions that can be picked up on southern Sakhalin and the Japanese-language newspapers available at a few hotels in the Russian Far East.

FILM & PHOTOGRAPHY

See European Russia Facts for the Visitor for general comments. Taking photographs in Siberia only presents problems in deep winter when temperatures are way down in the minuses. At extremely low temperatures camera batteries won't function and film becomes very brittle. If cameras are exposed to cold and humidity for too long they acquire a frosty coating which can later work its way inside and cause havoc within the camera body.

There no longer appear to be any restrictions on what can or cannot be photographed, though, obviously, discretion is still required in border zones. And if you go around pointing your camera at soldiers and tanks, they're quite likely to point back; this could mean trouble.

Film stocks can be replenished in Novosibirsk (where there is a Kodak Express outlet which sells and processes print film), Khabarovsk and Vladivostok, where there are Fuji labs which offer high-quality, 24-hour processing.

HEALTH

See the Health section of European Russia Facts for the Visitor for overall coverage of health in Russia. A specific local hazard in some Siberian and Far East areas, from May to September, is encephalitis. Tick-borne encephalitis, a risk anywhere in rural Russia during these months, is apparently a particular danger in Ussuriland, while Japanese encephalitis (caused by mosquito bites) is a danger in rural areas bordering Mongolia, China and North Korea. Trekkers, campers and others going to rural areas should consider immunisation, which is available for both types of encephalitis. For more information on encephalitis, see under Immunisations & Documents and Diseases Spread by People, Animals & Insects in the Health section of European Russia Facts for the Visitor.

An epidemic of tuberculosis (TB) broke out in Tomsk in 1994. Beware Russian 'treatment' for this – bizarre methods used by desperate doctors have reportedly included tapping some of the patient's blood, subjecting it to ultraviolet radiation, then reinjecting it; and pumping large amounts of drugs into the chest via a tube through the nose, while instructing the patient not to cough.

WOMEN TRAVELLERS

Read the section in European Russia Facts for the Visitor – anything it says is hard to get in the better-supplied, western part of the country is going to be nearly impossible to get in Siberia. East of the Urals, the idea that women are less knowledgeable and, on the whole, less capable than men still persists. Andrew and his fiancée, travelling together, found that men in Siberia would always direct their speech to him even though he usually hadn't asked the question and his grasp of the Russian language was obviously inferior to his partner's. It can get very irritating, but at least you don't have to live there: Siberian women relish the chance to talk alone with a foreign woman, and the first thing they'll tell you is just how hopeless their menfolk are.

DANGERS & ANNOYANCES

A photographer for the magazine *National Geographic* characterised Siberia as the 'kind of place where you can't count on the light coming on when you flip the switch'. We'd go further: it's the kind of place where you can't count on water coming out when you turn on the tap; on getting into the hotel restaurant just because you're a guest there; or on the fact that, just because a bus took you out to some isolated little village, there will also be one to get you back to town.

Siberia and the Russian Far East have few dangers but they're loaded with annoyances. Some specific hazards include bears if you're trekking in Kamchatka, tick-borne encephalitis in Ussuriland (see Health above), and the food in the Hotel Intourist, Khabarovsk; but, generally speaking, you're far safer out here than in Moscow or St Petersburg. The paucity of tourists in Siberia means that there are few pickings for the kind of sharks sometimes encountered in European Russia. If any foreigners are likely to be targets for pickpockets, thieves or muggers, then it's going to be the visibly affluent Oriental businessmen much in evidence in Russia's Far Eastern cities.

The possible exception is Irkutsk, long a popular stopover for Trans-Mongolian and

SIBERIA & RUSSIAN FAR EAST

Trans-Manchurian passengers. Travellers have reported problems here such as the theft of bags, especially around the railway station, and even the occasional mugging. This is one place to take care, especially at night.

WORK

Opportunities for work are almost non-existent. There are no private English-language schools – the principal source of employment for English-speaking travellers worldwide – in Siberia or the Russian Far East. Being taken on as a teacher by a local state school is possible but it's an administrative nightmare and can take months to set up. The best chances of finding employment are in Khabarovsk and Vladivostok, cities that have a large number of foreign enterprises such as Australian-run restaurants, Canadian-owned motels and, maybe coming soon, a chain of US-backed supermarkets. There's a semi-annual publication called the *Register* which is an information directory for the Russian Far East and lists, amongst other things, all the foreign businesses in the region, along with their contact details. It may be a good place to start. The *Register* is available from all the major hotels in the Far East, from the international terminal at Khabarovsk airport and from the Radisson Slavyanskaya Hotel in Moscow. Alternatively, it can be ordered from Register USA Inc, PO Box 100, Fortville, IN 46040, USA for US$25, plus US$4 (US$10 overseas) for postage and handling.

ACTIVITIES

Siberia and the Far East is little more than a wilderness on which humanity has scarcely made a scratch. As such it's ideal adventure-holiday terrain, hampered only by the present lack of any tourism infrastructure. However, activities such as mountaineering, rafting and canoeing have always been popular with Russians (mainly because they were never allowed out of their own back yard) and many small towns have well-established outdoor clubs. One vital thing to be aware of is that you can't just turn up and expect to do things. Even if you arrive armed

with addresses and phone numbers it can take two or three days to make contact with anyone – and then maybe a further couple of days for them to figure out exactly what it is that you want of them. Give people as much advance warning as possible and, even if you can't hammer out all the details, give them an idea of what you are interested in. Above all, be flexible, be patient, and don't expect things to always go smoothly.

Foreign travel firms offer some activity-centred and adventure trips to Siberia which, at a price, take the effort out of setting it all up (see Siberia & the Far East Getting There & Away), and there are a few Russian-based agencies which might be helpful. Pilgrim Tours (in Russian, Moskovskoe Turisticheskoe Agentstvo Piligrim; ☎ (095) 365 45 63; fax (095) 369 03 89; e-mail pilgrimtours@glas.apc.org) at 1-y Kirpichny pereulok 17, Moscow 105118, comes highly recommended. This firm does a large number of adventure-based tours and its thick catalogue is well worth getting hold of. Travel Russia (☎ (095) 290 34 39, 290 30 88; fax (095) 291 87 83) at Trubnikovsky pereulok 21, korpus 2, Moscow 121069, which specialises in outdoor holidays, is also experienced in dealing with foreigners and reportedly provides good service.

Knowledgeable and experienced local specialists we can recommend who can fix up a wide range of activities in their regions – from rafting or skiing to trekking, riding or climbing, as appropriate – include:

Ural Mountains & Yekaterinburg Region
  Konstantin Brylyakov (☎(3432) 51 91 57; fax (3432) 51 34 83), Chief Specialist, Sputnik International Travel Bureau, ulitsa Pushkina 5, Yekaterinburg 620151 – Konstantin and his brother Yakov have extensive knowledge of the region
Altay
  Sibalp (☎(3832) 49 59 22; fax (3832) 46 90 59; e-mail sibalp@niee.nsk.su), apartment (kv.) 47, ulitsa Nemirovicha-Danchenko 155/1, Novosibirsk 630087 – a travel firm led by highly experienced Altay-bred mountaineer Sergey Kurgin
Khabarovsky Kray & BAM
  Alexandr Shelopugin (☎ (42172) 4 21 96; fax (42172) 4 21 96), Exotour Tourist Centre, prospekt Mira, Komsomolsk-on-Amur – activities

include archaeological and ornithological tours, caving, rafting and skiing; the centre has a lot of equipment including kayaks, tents and rock-climbing gear, and staff are highly experienced in using it

Other useful organisations are mentioned in the following sections and in regional chapters.

Trekking

Much of Siberia is covered in thick taiga forest which is extremely difficult to move through and fairly boring as far as scenery goes. The best trekking is found where the forest is broken by other physical features such as mountains or rivers. Kamchatka, with its awesome volcanic landscapes, and the very beautiful Altay Mountains are great places to explore, and a series of walks up the western coast of Lake Baikal, perhaps using a boat for backup, could be very rewarding. Less ambitiously, many of the towns along the BAM are good bases for heading out into the wilds. The western part of the line passes through some quite mountainous terrain, complete with high-altitude lakes and hot springs, and abandoned Gulag camps hidden in high canyons. Athol Yates' *The Siberian BAM Railway Guidebook* has good coverage of the region, including lots of remote places of interest and details of how to hike there.

Frith Maier in *Trekking in Russia & Central Asia* also recommends Sakhalin as a good trekking destination. Some companies that organise trekking expeditions are listed in Siberia & the Far East Getting There & Away, and under Tours and Contacts in the Kamchatka section.

Climbing

Possibilities for climbing exist in the Ural Mountains, the Altay (south of Novosibirsk on the Kazakhstan and Mongolian borders), the Kuznetsky Alatau (a range north of the Altay with less elevation but easier to reach from the Kuznetsk basin cities), the Sayan Mountains (on the Mongolian border), in the Baikalsky range (on the western shore of Lake Baikal) and amongst the volcanoes of the Kamchatka Peninsula. Again, Frith Maier's book is a good general guide, offering information on worthwhile climbs and the difficulties they present.

Sibalp (see the introduction to this Activities section) is a good firm to contact for organising an Altay climbing trip. Stalker (☎ (3952) 43 34 66; fax (3952) 43 23 22; telex 133153 INST SU) at PO Box 3673, Irkutsk 664 074, is a group of local climbers who act as guides in the mountains around Lake Baikal. Members of the Kedr Tourist Club also have valuable experience in the northern Baikalsky Mountains and are willing to act as guides; contact Anatoly Semilat (☎ (39566) 2 84 73; fax (39566) 2 26 05) at room 403, 4th hostel, 8th Kvartel, Zheleznogorsk Ilimsky 665680.

Pilgrim Tours (see the introductory paragraphs) arranged the first US ascent of Klyuchevskaya sopka, Kamchatka's highest volcano (4813 metres), and between 1 June and 31 August is prepared to lead other teams up to the summit in a 23-day expedition.

Rafting & Canoeing

With its 53,000-plus rivers, Siberia has plenty of potential for waterborne adventuring. As a consequence most tour companies offer some kind of rafting, canoeing or boating programme. The Altay and Baikal areas have some of the best possibilities. For contact addresses of the following firms, and others, see the regional sections. Ulan Ude-based Buryat-Intour does a 15-day trip which combines hiking and 150 km of rafting down the Temnik River, any time from June through to August. In the same region, Siberian Guides Inc will organise four days of kayaking around the picturesque Chivyrkuy Bay, which contains the warmest water in the whole of Lake Baikal, but the experience is expensive at upwards of US$85 per day. Baikalcomplex in Irkutsk, over on the other side of the water, will hire out kayaks for western-shore exploration at US$30 per day. BAMtour, in Severobaikalsk, can organise rafting of different degrees of difficulty along the rivers that flow into the northern end of Lake Baikal. The advantage here is that the organisation is completely flexible and you can tailor your own trip and negotiate your own price.

In the Russian Far East, Exotour in Komsomolsk (see the introductory paragraphs) organises rafting on tributaries of the Amur, while Ussurisky Wilderness Tours in Vladivostok takes out rafting parties in the Primorsky region. BOL Tours in the remote Magadan region also offers a range of rafting excursions of varying duration, for both novice and experienced groups.

Horse Riding

A tour company called Vostoksviaz, which operates out of Irkutsk, has access to a stable of horses near the village of Shida on the western shore of Lake Baikal and organises seven or eight-day horseback tours of the region. See the Around Irkutsk section in the Eastern Siberia chapter. Five days of riding in the same lake-side mountains and valleys also forms the base of a 12-day tour led by Steppes East (see Siberia & the Far East Getting There & Away), a UK-based adventure-tourism company.

Skiing

Almost all the skiing done in Siberia is of the cross-country variety. Any local tour agency can help out with finding a pair of skis and point you in the right direction. Alpha Tour in Kamchatka can organise skiing on the slopes of volcanoes. There are no ski resorts as such, and the closest thing is the Gorny Vozdukh (Mountain Air) tourist centre, three km outside Yuzhno-Sakhalinsk on the island of Sakhalin. It has a couple of straight downhill runs, a slalom route and 70 and 90-metre ski jumps. A hotel, the Santa Resort, is conveniently located nearby. There is also a 340-metre ski slope with chair lifts at Solnechny Springs near Severobaikalsk.

Fishing

Siberia and particularly the Russian Far East are an anglers' paradise with rivers swollen with grayling and various species of salmon. However, this sitting around for hours dangling a piece of string off the end of a pole and into the water can be a heart-stoppingly expensive business. Intour-Khabarovsk, for example, asks from US$800 to US$2000 for a week's organised fishing. Slightly cheaper, Cruise Ltd (☎ (3422) 25 69 72; fax (3422) 34 49 26) of ulitsa Stakchanovskaya 2-69, Perm 614004, will take parties for two weeks' salmon fishing in the Magadan region for US$690, a figure that doesn't include the cost of getting to Magadan. Iris Hotels (see Siberia & the Far East Getting There & Away) offers a seven-day sport-fishing programme in Kamchatka, angling for king salmon (June and July only), silver salmon (August and September only), and trout, grayling and char year round. Prices start at US$915, flight to Kamchatka not included.

While it is possible to go it alone and just head off with rod and tackle, most regions have strict restrictions on fishing.

ACCOMMODATION

Hotels in Siberia, unused to the expectations and requirements of foreign visitors, tend to be worse than those encountered in European Russia. Paying US$50 per night still does not guarantee having hot water. Andrew had a run of five consecutive hotels in two towns, not one of which had hot water, a functioning light in the bathroom or a seat on the toilet. Occasionally, you may experience the flip side and encounter a hidden gem of a hotel, which ought to command sky-high prices but instead is dirt cheap; however, such things are rare.

The Russian Far East, already visited by large numbers of Japanese and Koreans, has a number of good, up-market hotels, usually joint foreign-Russian ventures. These places have a high standard of amenities (in one case not just any toilet seats but thermostatically controlled, heated toilet seats) and charge correspondingly high prices.

A lot of the small, independent tourist companies are pushing homestays as a cheap alternative to hotels. The standard price seems to be about US$15, for which you should get a bed for the night, with clean sheets, and maybe breakfast. Russia-based agencies which can arrange homestays include the Travellers Guest House in Moscow (for Irkutsk and surrounds), HOFA in St Petersburg (for Irkutsk, Khabarovsk and Vladivostok; other cities on request with one month's notice), BAMtour in Severobaikalsk (all along the BAM) and Baikalcomplex in Irkutsk – see the relevant city sections for more details. Overseas, American-International Homestays (☎ toll-free (1800) 876 2048), PO Box 7178, Boulder, CO 80306-7178, USA specialises in this field and can place clients with families throughout Siberia. Australia's Iris Hotels (see Siberia & the Far East Getting There & Away) can arrange homestays in the Trans-Siberian cities of Yekaterinburg, Novosibirsk, Irkutsk and Khabarovsk for around US$34 single, US$25 per person for twin. See also the Accommodation section in European Russia Facts for the Visitor for further possibilities.

FOOD
Unfortunately, dining in Siberia is still stuck firmly in the Soviet era. In Russia's Far East, even the close proximity of China, Korea and Japan hasn't managed to enliven or improve the local cuisine. The only noticeable influence the Orient has had is to replace stodgy, grey potatoes with clots of stodgy, grey rice. In most provincial towns and cities the only restaurants generally belong to hotels, with other options being limited to a desultory handful of cafés and stolovayi. In such places it's wise to arrive with provisions to relieve the tedium of potato salad and salami. There are exceptions: Irkutsk, Khabarovsk and Vladivostok are all good on the stomach. All three have a number of fine private restaurants in which, variously, it's possible to eat sushi, mu-shu pork, cheesecake or kangaroo.

Most hotel food, however, is Russian or Ukrainian with just a 'Siberian' tacked on to the name – like *myaso po Sibirsky* (meat Siberian style), beef topped with cheese, or *vyrezka po tayozhnomu* (taiga tender loin), cubed steak cooked with herbs. The Siberian staple is *pelmeni*, steamed or boiled small, doughy packets stuffed with meat – a bit like a heavier version of ravioli. Pelmeni are usually served heaped on a plate with sour cream or butter. Further east, pelmeni are often served in a stock soup, flavoured with fennel and sometimes with a pastry covering. In Buryatia there's a bigger, palm-sized version of pelmeni called *poza*, sometimes spiced and commonly sold by roadside vendors at about US$0.50 each – two or three make a good, greasy meal. There's something similar served in the Far East called *kvaldum*, which is stuffed with cabbage in addition to meat.

Fish is plentiful, especially in the late summer and autumn when salmon (*syomga*) or sturgeon (*osyotr*) is far more likely to grace the table than meat. Around Baikal, these fish are supplemented by *omul*, a cousin of the salmon and trout, endemic to the lake and considered a local delicacy. Russians serve it smoked, broiled or raw on a slice of bread as an appetiser, in the same manner as that most ubiquitous of Siberian zakuski, caviar. Caviar (*ikra*) usually comes in two types: black (from the sturgeon), the best and most expensive; and red (from the salmon), which is saltier, cheaper and far more common. Far from being the food of princes, every Siberian household has a great jar of the stuff stored somewhere cool, and on station platforms and in pavement stalls babushki sell it by the litre for about US$8.

Seafood replaces freshwater fish in the Pacific coast region, especially around Vladivostok. Standard items on the menu include *kalmari*, *kraby* and *grebeshki* (scallops).

Few Siberians ever eat out because the meals served in restaurants could never match those dished up at home, which are prepared using ingredients fresh from the allotment, forest or river. If you are lucky enough to be invited back to a Siberian family household to eat, chances are it will be the finest meal of the trip.

DRINKS
As in European Russia, vodka and *shampanskoe* predominate, but with a heavy presence in shops and kiosks east of the Yenisey River of silty Chinese beers and sugary fruit drinks.

Getting There & Away

As recently as the 1980s, Moscow was just about the only gateway into Siberia and the Russian Far East other than the Trans-Siberian rail routes from China. This ridiculous situation meant that to get to, say, Khabarovsk from Tokyo, an air distance of around 1500 km, you would first have to fly 7740 km to Moscow, then 6200 km back to Khabarovsk, adding a third of the distance round the world to your journey. Today, even though Moscow still accounts for by far the bulk of traffic into Siberia, there are more

and more air routes being opened up by regional administrations eager to develop their own international business relations and attract foreign tourism.

Some of the new connections under consideration go way beyond the opening of just a new air service. The Hokkaido regional government and local officials on Sakhalin have for years been discussing the possibility of a 40-km bridge between the two islands, with perhaps a second span which would link northern Sakhalin to the Russian mainland.

So You Think You're a Traveller?

Kosh-Agach, in the middle of a barren plain 50 km from the Mongolian border in Siberia's remote Altay Republic, is so isolated and desolate that you wonder why it exists. It's certainly not the kind of place you expect to bump into anyone from anywhere near home. So I was not a little surprised to notice a van daubed with French stickers and a map of the route from Paris to Ulan Bator parked outside the town hall. Could be some adventurous characters with interesting tales to tell, I thought.

The surprises were only beginning. A fair-haired girl of perhaps 13 was getting out of the cab. Very adventurous, I thought, calling out 'Êtes-vous Française?' as I ran over.

'Scottish, actually,' she answered pleasantly.

'Oh...er...what are you doing here?'

'Going round the world in a horse and cart with my mum, dad and brothers,' she said, as matter-of-factly as if I'd asked her the time of day.

'Ah...a horse and cart...er...and this?' I pointed to the van.

'Oh, we just got a lift with them from the border. My dad's in there (the town hall) trying to sort out our paperwork. They won't let us cross into Mongolia.'

'So...whose is this van? And where's your horse and cart?

'It belongs to some French guys. They can't get across the border either. We're all stuck there and one of them has come here with Dad to try to sort out the paperwork.'

'And your mum and brothers are down at the border with the horse and cart?'

'My brothers are. Mum's had to go back to Britain for a few weeks; she's meeting up with us in Ulan Bator.'

Dad turned out to be called David Grant and yes, they were circumnavigating the world by horse-drawn caravan. They had been going two years so far – from Scotland to Tashanta, the border post 50 km south-east of Kosh-Agach, via Central Europe, Ukraine, Russia, a great loop round southern Kazakhstan, and a road (that doesn't appear on most maps) across the Altay from Leninogorsk in north-east Kazakhstan. The Frenchman of the van, Alexis de Suremain, lived and worked in Nizhny Novgorod but his two companions (also waiting at Tashanta) had come from Paris.

'Come down to the caravan and have a cup of tea,' David suggested. An unrefusable offer.

Fifty km across the desolate plain later, we reached Tashanta. If Kosh-Agach had been the end of the world, Tashanta was about the third circle of hell. A steppe wind blew gusts of cold rain in our faces as we picked our way through the mud past the line of rusty trucks waiting at the border post. A few shabby buildings made up the rest of Tashanta. The caravan was parked on

Meanwhile, the governor of Russia's north-easternmost republic, Chukotka, has been holding discussions with his Alaskan counterpart about the possibility of constructing a US$40 billion rail tunnel under the Bering Strait, thus creating a 'land link' between the two former Cold War adversaries. The Clinton administration has reportedly already invested US$5 million in a feasibility study.

At present, besides the Moscow gateways of Domodedovo domestic airport and Yaroslavl and Kazan railway stations, there are two other basic border passages into Siberia and the Russian Far East. From the south, there are the well-travelled Trans-Mongolian and Trans-Manchurian rail routes, both of which originate in Beijing.

There's also the less well-known Turk-Sib Railway, which runs from Almaty in Kazakhstan, Central Asia, plus trains from Kharkiv (Kharkov) in Ukraine and, in summer only, services from the Crimea, the Caucasus and the Russian Black Sea coast going at least as far as Irkutsk.

The other main way of approaching Siberia and the Russian Far East is direct from the Pacific Rim region. There are international flights from China, Japan, Korea, Singapore and the USA, boats from Japan and a rail route from either Pyongyang or Beijing via Harbin in north-east China.

---

a patch of grass off the road, the horse grazing nearby. The boys, who were *younger* than their sister, were waiting inside with the other two Frenchmen.

'She's getting tired, those hills in the Altay took a lot out of her,' said David, pointing to the horse. 'Has she brought you all the way from Scotland?'

'She's the second. We bought her in Holland.' David was worried, with reason. They all had Mongolian visas (from the Mongolian embassy in Almaty, Kazakhstan) and they'd had word that the Mongolian border guards would let them into Mongolia. But the Russian guards wouldn't let them out of Russia. This crossing was for commercial traffic only, they said. The official crossing was 1250 km east across several mountain ranges – and more like 3000 km by road. The beginning of winter was only two to three months off and they couldn't travel in the Siberian winter. They had plans to winter in Ulan Bator, the Mongolian capital. At their average 15 to 20 km a day, they could get there in time if they crossed here at Tashanta. The other route was out of question – 'And I'm not spending the winter in Kosh-Agach!' added David ferociously.

Bribery, it seemed, wasn't going to work. Right now David's hopes lay with one of President Yeltsin's personal envoys whom, amazingly enough, he had happened to bump into a week or so back in Kosh-Agach, where the envoy had been visiting on a regional fact-finding mission. The envoy had told him she would try to swing things with the border guards' bosses back in Moscow, but David was still waiting on the outcome.

Over delectable mugs of tea, we snuggled round the caravan's table and David summed up the thinking behind their mode of transport: 'Wanted to do it under our own steam. Can't sail, didn't want to drive.' The boys, growing a little quarrelsome having been kept indoors by the rain, were told to sit down and get on with some schoolwork; their parents were seeing to their formal education as well as majoring them in the school of life.

Looking through their albums – which included close-up photos of a rocket launch at Russia's Baykonur space centre in Kazakhstan ('We met a guy who invited the children in; the people inside weren't too pleased but it didn't matter') – I tried and failed to think of some way I could help. And then I had to leave. I had other places to get to and rather less than two years at my disposal.

A few weeks later I had got back to Britain by a combination of all the lazy person's forms of transport that the Grants had rejected. Were they still in Tashanta, I wondered? The Frenchmen had their van to take them back to civilisation if the border really wouldn't open for them. But did the Grants face winter in Kosh-Agach?

David, Kate, Torcuil, Eilidh and Fionn – wherever you are now, we're all with you in spirit.

John Noble

SIBERIA & RUSSIAN FAR EAST

AIR

For most people, flying to Siberia necessitates arriving at Moscow's Sheremetevo International Airport and then facing the hassle of transferring across town to either Domodedovo or Vnukovo, the two domestic airports from which all Siberia-bound services fly out. See Moscow – Getting Around for how to travel to, from and between the Moscow airports. Every Siberian city or large town has an airport with direct Moscow flights. Usually these flights go daily; in some cases they're twice daily, as with Khabarovsk and Vladivostok, three times daily, as in the case of Irkutsk, or even four times daily, as with Novosibirsk. Transaero (see European Russia Getting Around) links Moscow with Yekaterinburg, Norilsk, Novosibirsk and Vladivostok. There are also flights from St Petersburg to Yekaterinburg, Novosibirsk, Krasnoyarsk and Irkutsk.

Other flights direct to Siberia or the Russian Far East are as follows.

To/From Europe

Lufthansa flies from Frankfurt to Yekaterinburg and Novosibirsk twice a week each, but much cheaper flights are available through Luftbrücke (☎ (02132) 9 31 60; fax (02132) 44 85), Moerser Str 100A, 40667 Meerbusch, which runs charter flights from Düsseldorf to Yekaterinburg, Chelyabinsk, Omsk and Novosibirsk for around DM1100 return. Luftbrücke also has a Düsseldorf airport office (☎ (0211) 4 21 68 33/34; fax (0211) 4 21 68 32).

To/From the USA

Aeroflot flies twice a week between San Francisco and Khabarovsk, via Anchorage, for US$2870 return; and once a week between Khabarovsk and Seattle, via Anchorage, for US$2538 return. Alaska Airlines flies Khabarovsk-Anchorage and Vladivostok-Anchorage (both via Magadan) once a week for a return fare of just over US$1000, and has connecting flights to Seattle. Soon the same airline should also be flying an Anchorage-Petropavlovsk-Kamchatsky route, possibly in summer only.

ATIS America (☎ (510) 845 2801; fax (510) 845 7137), a California-based company, represents Kolyma-Indigirka Aviation, a charter air service operating out of the Republic of Sakha, which flies between Anchorage, Providenia and Magadan. The US commuter airline Bering Air (☎ (907) 443 5620) runs charter flights between Nome, in Alaska, and Providenia and Anadyr, on the Chukotka Peninsula, and can also help out with visas through its Russian agent.

Russia is on the other side of the International Date Line from the USA. Thus, when it's noon on Tuesday in Chukotka, it's 3 pm on Monday in Alaska (ie there's a 21-hour difference).

To/From China, Japan & South-East Asia

From Irkutsk, Aeroflot flies three times a week to Niigata (Japan) and daily to Shenyang (China). From Khabarovsk, Aeroflot flies three times a week to Niigata (US$696 return), twice a week to Harbin in northern China (US$270 return) and once a week to both Seoul and Singapore (US$2660 return). According to the timetable issued by Aeroflot's head office in Moscow there are also direct flights from Khabarovsk to Shenyang and Shanghai once a week, Manila once a week, Osaka twice a week and Pyongyang (North Korea) once a week, but these were not listed on the departure board at Khabarovsk's international terminal and may no longer be operating. Flights into Khabarovsk operated by other airlines include China Northern's twice-weekly Harbin connection, a weekly Niigata service with Japan Airlines and a weekly Seoul service with Asiana Airlines.

From Vladivostok, Aeroflot flies to Niigata four times a week (a two-hour flight) for US$622 return. Korean Air has flights to/from Seoul every Saturday for US$720 return. There are also flights between Hokodate, on Hokkaido, Japan's northernmost island, and Yuzhno-Sakhalinsk, on Sakhalin.

To/From Central Asia & Mongolia

There are flights three times a week between

Ulan Bator and Irkutsk and twice a week between Almaty, in Kazakhstan, and Irkutsk. Almaty also has a daily connection to Khabarovsk and once or twice-weekly flights to Novosibirsk, Yekaterinburg, Barnaul and Krasnoyarsk. There may also be flights to a few Siberian cities from Tashkent (Uzbekistan), Bishkek (Kyrgyzstan) and lesser cities in Kazakhstan, though schedules were in flux at the time of writing.

LAND
Train
Of course, the way to do this is on the Trans-Siberian Railway from Moscow, from Japan (via ship or plane to Vladivostok), or from Beijing on branch lines through Mongolia or north-eastern China. All the details are in the separate Trans-Siberian Railway chapter.

Other services linking Siberia with the west include trains between St Petersburg, Yekaterinburg and Omsk; a train which goes all the way from Kharkiv (Kharkov) in Ukraine to Vladivostok every two days; and, in summer, trains from the Crimea, the Caucasus and the Russian Black Sea coast, which go at least as far east as Irkutsk.

From Almaty in Kazakhstan, the Turkestan-Siberia or Turk-Sib Railway runs north to Novosibirsk in western Siberia, with daily service between the two cities. A thrice-weekly service from Tashkent (Uzbekistan) and Almaty to Barnaul, Novosibirsk, Krasnoyarsk and Irkutsk also uses this line, as do trains to Krasnoyarsk from Almaty, and to Krasnoyarsk from Bishkek (Kyrgyzstan) via Almaty, on alternate days. Twice-weekly trains and daily buses link Almaty with Ürümqi in China.

Another railway runs up the centre of Kazakhstan and carries trains between Tashkent, Almaty, Bishkek and Yekaterinburg.

A twice-weekly, two-night (41-hour) train (No 41/42) runs between Ussuriysk (on the line between Khabarovsk and Vladivostok) and the North Korean capital of Pyongyang, with further connections from there to Beijing. The trip is reportedly very enjoyable: the train is frequently half-empty and is composed of old carriages which date from a time when travel by rail was a much more stately affair. Steam locomotives, though not used for this service, are still in common use in North Korea.

SEA
Once a week during the summer, the *Antonia Nezhdanova* sails from Vladivostok to Niigata and Fushiki on the west coast of Japan. The voyage takes 42 hours, and 3rd-class passage (lower deck, four berths per cabin) costs US$280; 2nd-class (as for 3rd-class but on the main deck) is US$300; while 1st-class (twin-bed cabins) is US$730. All meals are included in the price. You may be able to get cheaper fares that don't include meals: ask. Passage can be booked in Vladivostok at the Marine Terminal (*Morskoy Vokzal*) behind the railway station; in Japan, try the Japan-Russia Travel Bureau (☎ (03) 3432 6161; fax (03) 3436 5530) in Tokyo – see Travel Agencies for the full address. For more information on the *Antonia Nezhdanova* see the Vladivostok section.

A cheaper option from Japan may be to take the ferry to Shanghai and ride the rails via Beijing. There's also a twice-weekly ferry from Wakkanai, a small town on the very northern tip of Hokkaido, about 300 km north of Sapporo, over to Korsakov, the southernmost port on the Russian island of Sakhalin, from where it's a US$133 flight to Vladivostok or less than US$10 for a ferry to the mainland.

From Fuyuan, a small port on the Amur River in north-eastern China, a hydrofoil sails every other day to Khabarovsk.

TOURS
The following agencies either offer complete package tours or can help to make Siberian travel arrangements. Most of them will organise your visa, but check to be sure this is part of the deal. However, the majority of companies that deal with this region tend to concentrate on the Trans-Siberian rail routes, and there's a comprehensive list of their addresses in the Trans-Siberian Railway chapter. See also European Russia Getting

There & Away for more general Russia-oriented agents.

From Australasia

Gateway Travel (☎ (02) 745 3333; fax (02) 745 3237) at 48 The Boulevarde, Strathfield, NSW 2135, Australia, is a Russia specialist and can offer a variety of tours for groups and individuals. These include specialist packages based around hunting, fishing, mountaineering and ecotourism. Visits to Kamchatka and Sakhalin can also be arranged via Gateway's contacts with Intourist. Iris Hotels (☎ (02) 580 6466; fax (02) 580 7256), PO Box 60, Hurstville, NSW 2220, Australia, can put together tailor-made tours which include the Trans-Siberian cities of Yekaterinburg, Novosibirsk, Irkutsk and Khabarovsk. Accommodation is in Mikof-Iris hotels (see European Russia – Facts for the Visitor, Accommodation) or in home-stays. Iris also runs a number of different programmes in Kamchatka including hiking tours, cross-country skiing and sport fishing.

From Canada

Exotik Tours (☎ (514) 284 3324; fax (514) 843 5493) of 1117 ste-Catherine O, suite 806, Montreal H3B 1H9, Quebec, doesn't offer any pre-set tours but can reserve services in Siberia upon request, for groups and individuals, ranging from hotels and transportation to transfers, sightseeing and interpreters. Exotik will book flights with Aeroflot on its twice-weekly Montreal-Moscow direct service.

From Japan

The Japan-Russia Travel Bureau (☎ (03) 3432 6161; fax (03) 3436 5530) at Kamiyacho Building, 3rd Floor, 5-12-12, Toranomon, Minato-ku, Tokyo 105, can arrange flights to Khabarovsk and Vladivostok. Staff there can also secure tickets for the ferry across from Niigata to Vladivostok (summer only) or for the boat to Shanghai, from where it's possible to take a train to Beijing and then on into Russia.

From South-East Asia

Global Union Express Ltd (☎ 868 3231 or 845 4232; fax 845 5078 or 537 2605) at Room 22-23, New Henry House, 10 Ice House St, Central, Hong Kong, is a general sales agent for Aeroflot and can arrange group or individual tours in Siberia including some homestays.

From the USA

American-International Homestays (☎ toll-free (1800) 876 2048), PO Box 7178, Boulder, CO 80306-7178, arranges all-inclusive homestay trips, which take in Moscow, Bishkek, Irkutsk and Lake Baikal and last 17 days, for US$2990 including return flight from New York, all meals and sightseeing. REI Adventures (☎ (206) 891 2631, (206) 395 8111 or toll-free (800) 622 2236; fax (206) 395 4744) at PO Box 1938, Sumner, WA 98390-0880, is a Russia specialist and runs several unusual Siberian expeditions. Its 1995 programme included a 17-day exploration of Lake Baikal with hiking in Zabaikalsky national park and a cruise to the Ushkany Islands, home to nerpa seals (prices from US$1700); or striking out from Baikal on a 21-day trek through the Sayan Mountains down into Mongolia and across the steppe to Ulan Bator (prices from US$2750). REI also has two Kamchatka tours, one a strenuous 14-day trek among the Klyuchevskaya volcano group (prices from US$1950), the other a more leisurely seven-day helicopter-assisted look at some of the peninsula's natural wonders including the Valley of the Geysers and the southern volcanoes (prices from US$1750). All the quoted prices are land costs only and don't include air fares.

Russia Far East/Asia Connection (☎ (907) 243 0313; fax (907) 243 0333; e-mail rfec@aol.com) of 6624 McGill Way, Anchorage, Alaska 99502, organises one-week escorted trips to near-neighbour Magadan which visit reindeer farms, Gulags and abandoned mines. Prices start at US$1350 flying from Anchorage and US$1650 from Los Angeles. REI also takes parties for 14 days of fishing, hiking and rafting in Kamchatka, starting at US$3350 per person, flying from Anchorage.

Mountain Travel Sobek (☎ (510) 527 8100, toll-free (1800) 227 2384; fax (510) 525 7710) of 6420 Fairmount Ave, El Cerrito, CA 94530-3606, offers a 15-day trip with seven days' rafting on the Katun River in the Altay Mountains from US$3150, and a 21-day summer Arctic cruise (19 days on board) from Murmansk to Providenia by way of Novaya Zemlya, Severnaya Zemlya, the Novosibirskie Islands, Wrangel Island and Big Diomede Island, for which prices start at US$10,995!

From the UK

Exodus Discovery Holidays (☎ (0181) 673 0859, 675 5550; fax (0181) 673 0779) of 9 Weir Rd, London SW12 0LT, does a fascinating 22-day 'footsteps of Jenghiz Khan' tour, which starts in Irkutsk and crosses Lake Baikal to Ulan Ude before heading deep into Mongolia, then looping round via Lake Hovsgol into the Sayan Mountains and back to Irkutsk. The fully inclusive price is £2190. Goodwill Holidays (☎ (01438) 71 6421; fax (01438) 84 0228) of Manor Chambers, The Green, School Lane, Welwyn, Herts AL6 9EB, will compose tours for groups and individuals in Siberia using trains or domestic flights, or a combination of both, and staying in homestays or hotels. Prices are from £26 per person per night for half-board accommodation with a family.

The 'tailor-made travel' section of Intourist Travel Ltd can book hotels almost anywhere throughout Siberia and the Russian Far East and organise transportation, transfers and sightseeing: see Travel Agencies in European Russia – Getting There & Away for further details. Steppes East (☎ (01285) 81 0267; fax (01285) 81 0693; telex 444102 STEPPE G) of Castle Eaton, Swindon, Wiltshire SN6 6JU, has only one set Siberian tour – a 12-day horseback exploration of the mountains around Lake Baikal at a fully inclusive price of £2200 – but specialises in catering to offbeat requirements (for instance, this company made all the Kamchatka arrangements for Christina Dodwell, author of *Beyond Siberia*) and has plenty of experience in the region.

Another specialist company is Field Studies Council Overseas (☎ (01743) 85 0164) of Montford Bridge, Shrewsbury SY4 1HW, an educational charity dedicated to environmental understanding. It runs about 50 trips abroad every year to places of special wildlife or botanical interest and its 1995 programme included a two-week excursion to Ussuriland, while for 1996 it's planning trips to Kamchatka.

From the Netherlands

Wilderness Expeditions (☎ (0545) 27 10 74; fax (0545) 27 37 56) at Kluverskamp 29, 7271 XM Borculo, specialises in expeditions to remote areas of Siberia, Kamchatka, Ussuriland, the Lake Baikal area, the Altay Mountains and even places like Wrangel Island and the Putgrana Plateau near Norilsk are all on their list. They also organise ornithological, trekking, rafting and cross-country skiing trips. They employ experienced and professional guides, mountaineers and porters.

SIBERIA & RUSSIAN FAR EAST

Getting Around

Getting around in Siberia and the Russian Far East isn't so much travel as a series of expeditions. In fact, foreign visitors to the region have traditionally regarded getting around – in the form of a trip on the Trans-Siberian Railway – as constituting the whole experience. Spare a thought for those poor unfortunates who had to do it on the hoof before the first railway tracks were laid. For them the journey from A, somewhere west of the Ural Mountains, to B, somewhere in Siberia, could easily consume a year or more of their footsore lives. The distances involved are vast. From Yekaterinburg at the western limits of Siberia to Vladivostok on the Pacific coast is about the same distance as from Berlin to New York, while even a relatively short overland hop, such as the one from Irkutsk in eastern Siberia to its near neighbour Khabarovsk, is still roughly equivalent to the distance from London to Cairo. And you were wondering about taking a bus?

Much of the information on flying, classes of train travel, Russian petrol types etc given in the European Russia Getting Around chapter is also relevant here, and the two chapters should be read in conjunction.

AIR

Because of the vast distances involved in travelling in Siberia and the Russian Far East and the limited extent of the road and rail network, flying is sometimes the only practical way of getting around. Aircraft take on the role of buses, especially on short-haul flights. Passengers frequently have to carry their own baggage aboard and dump it at the rear before scrumming for seats, and those who lose out end up standing for the duration of the flight.

Almost every small town has its airport (although 'airport', which tends to connote a great, high-tech temple to air transport, is perhaps a misleading term: most of these places have fewer facilities than the average

bus shelter). If nothing else, it will at leas[t] have frequent flights to the nearest big tow[n] or city, and from there you'll be able to mak[e] nationwide connections. Recent years hav[e] seen the emergence of small, regional air lines, but as most use old Aeroflot machines often still painted in the Aeroflot livery, an[d] sell tickets out of Aeroflot sales offices, ai[r] travellers are hardly aware of their existence

All the standard idiosyncrasies of Russia[n] travel apply to flying in Siberia (see Euro-pean Russia Getting Around for genera[l] comments). One that can prove particularl[y] troublesome is the difficulty of bookin[g] onward tickets. At the time of writing, fo[r] example, when flying from Vladivostok t[o] Yuzhno-Sakhalinsk, then later on t[o] Petropavlovsk-Kamchatsky, the tickets fo[r] the second leg of the journey could only b[e] purchased on Sakhalin. However, it's quite possible that the traveller might arrive there to find all Kamchatka flights booked up for weeks ahead. In this way, Andrew found himself stuck in Magadan with the prospect of 10 days to kill in the ex-Gulag centre, and the only way out was to return from where he'd come. One way to avoid this is to get the first ticket office to phone ahead and check onward availability, maybe making a reservation. If you're a foreigner paying double the local rate, it's quite likely they will oblige.

Unfortunately, there's usually no way around paying the higher foreigners' fare when flying since passports and tickets have to be presented repeatedly right up until boarding. For paying extra, you do get to wait in the separate Intourist lounge (if there is one) and will often be escorted onto the plane before everyone else. However, as the temperature on board is always a good 10°C below that in the departure hall, this is a privilege you could well do without. On landing, baggage belonging to foreign passengers is usually (though not always) diverted from the proletarian baggage-claim rea and delivered to the Intourist hall, but it rrives long after everybody else has collected theirs and left. This constitutes st-class treatment. Short-hop flights in emote areas – for instance, those within the Kamchatka Peninsula or around the island of Sakhalin – can be ridiculously cheap because to one has ever imagined that a foreigner might show up, and there's no two-tier pricing in place.

Tickets are bought from Aeroflot sales offices, located in the centre of every town of any size that possesses an airport. The offices are usually open six days a week, sometimes seven, from early morning to late evening.

Flight times are always given in Moscow ime (Moskovskoe vremya) – except when they're not. Then they're in local time (mestnoe vremya). Check carefully. Twice.

Costs

A return fare normally costs the equivalent of twice the one-way fare. Some sample one-way foreigners' airfares and flying times are:

Moscow–Novosibirsk – US$210, four hours
Moscow–Irkutsk – US$250, seven hours
Moscow–Vladivostok – US$400, nine hours
Moscow–Petropavlovsk-Kamchatsky – US$582, nine hours
Irkutsk–Khabarovsk – US$170, 2½ hours
Khabarovsk–Magadan – US$195, 2½ hours
Vladivostok–Yuzhno-Sakhalinsk – US$133, 1¾ hours

BUS

The distances are too great and the roads too bad for buses to be viable as intercity transport in Siberia and the Russian Far East. Buses provide only city-airport, suburban and local links. Each region seems to have been left to scavenge for its own fleet, and proud is the city that can boast more than a handful of the Hungarian-made Ikarus buses which are ubiquitous elsewhere in Russia. Instead, most of the vehicles employed for passenger transportation look like converted tractors or chicken shacks on wheels. They are, however, well used, and tickets for bus

journeys ought to be bought as far in advance as possible, usually from the town's central bus station. Baggage is usually charged for at a rate of about US$0.50 per item.

TRAIN

The railway is the main artery of life in Siberia and the Russian Far East, sustaining and nurturing the towns and cities along its length. For the traveller, this makes the railway the ideal mode of transport because it connects almost every place of any significance. (Towns that were once wealthy and important shrivelled and all but died after the railway bypassed them.) There are no longer any restrictions on which routes travellers can go by or which trains they can take, and since airlines began pitching foreigners' prices at international levels, the railway is the cheapest means of getting around. It is also, without doubt, the most comfortable.

The same types of train run in Siberia as in European Russia (see European Russia Getting Around) – skoryy poezd (fast train) and passazhirskiy poezd (passenger train) – but these distinctions are not vital unless you're intending to get off at some minor halt down the line. In this case you need to catch a stopping service. As most train journeys in Siberia, other than on suburban services, are measured in days rather than hours, accommodation is always in coupes (kupeynyy), or the open-plan, travelling-village version, platskartnyy (see the Trans-Siberian Railway chapter). First-class compartments, with two berths as opposed to four, are available only on long-distance trains such as the Moscow-Vladivostok (*Rossia*) and the Moscow-Irkutsk (*Baikal Express*) services. Making use of overnight trains saves on hotel bills.

In Siberia, in theory, all main-line services run on Moscow time (Moskovskoe vremya). Local time (mestnoe vremya) creeps back into usage in Russia's Far East, where stations generally have two timetables, one following each system. Provided you can understand Cyrillic script, the information they give is fairly easy to decipher and purchasing a ticket is straightforward. If you don't speak Russian, simply copy down your destination (in Cyrillic), the number of the train and the day of departure: today, сегодня (*'si-VOHD-nya'*); tonight, сегодня вечером (*'si-VOHD-nya VYEH-chi-rum'*); tomorrow, завтра (*'ZAHF-tra'*); the day after tomorrow, после завтра (*'pa-sli-ZAHF-tra'*). Foreigners are supposed to be charged more for their rail tickets but the difference is usually only 20% or 30%. Off the main line, there's sometimes no difference in price at all.

Most of the larger stations, such as Yekaterinburg, Irkutsk or Vladivostok, have one ticketing hall for local (prigorodnyy) services and one for long-distance trains. Some cities also have a special office – sometimes called 'Intourist' (Интурист) – for ticket sales to foreigners, which may be staffed by someone who speaks English. At these offices you'll always be charged the full foreigners' price for the ticket (whereas if you buy from the normal station windows you might well get away with paying local price), but sometimes tickets may be available at these places when the other cashiers claim the train is full.

Every station has a left luggage room (kamera khranenia) and, more often than not, two – one with lockers that take items up to the size of a medium sausage-bag, and a second for bulky packs and boxes, including rucksacks. It generally costs about US$0.50 to deposit hand luggage and US$1 or US$1.50 for the bigger items. Apart from a couple of hour-long breaks, the kamery are usually open round the clock.

Costs

Fares vary from train to train, and also go up and down with price hikes and (when you look at them in US dollar terms) exchange rates. Those given here are 2nd-class (kupeynyy) fares and are current at the time of writing; 1st-class, where available, is usually just less than double. Some fares and travelling times are:

Moscow-Vladivostok – US$235, 157 hours
Moscow-Irkutsk – US$110, 84 hours

Novosibirsk-Irkutsk – US$32, 36 hours
Krasnoyarsk-Severobaikalsk – US$22, 32 hours
Irkutsk-Khabarovsk – US$40, 36 hours
Khabarovsk-Komsomolsk – US$15, 9½ hours

CAR & MOTORBIKE

Siberia is traversed today, as it was a century ago, by only one highway. This doesn't even merit the title transcontinental because i peters out in the swamps east of Chita and doesn't re-emerge as a drivable surface fo another couple of hundred km. Road construction has always been far too expensive and, compared with a railway's capacity to carry thousands of tonnes of freight, the payoffs have always been too small.

The usual advantages of independen motoring aren't there in Siberia. There are almost no out-of-the-way places to be discovered, as the majority of settlements cling tenaciously to the lifeline of the railway. The roads play second fiddle to the railway follow its course closely and generally only deviate in the company of a branch line. For a motorist, the scenery is also numbingly monotonous, though the driver's eyes are better trained on the road in any case, watching for potholes. There is also the difficulty of obtaining petrol, or spares in the event of a breakdown.

People have driven from Alaska to London and, famously, from Beijing via Mongolia and Siberia to Paris. Groups have even cycled from St Petersburg to Vladivostok, and the reverse. These, though, were all

A less common mode of transport in Siberia

ll-blown expeditions, accompanied by the
level of careful planning and equipping that
oes into an attempt on Mt Everest or a trek
cross the Sahara. Motoring in Siberia can
e done, but it's a challenge, and a potential
ource of stories for your grandchildren
ather than a viable means of getting around.

There are one or two exceptions. The
Altay Mountains, Khakassia and Tuva,
Ussuriland and Sakhalin are reasonably
ompact, self-contained areas with better
oad systems than rail, making them well
uited to exploration by car. All have dramatic or at least interesting scenery, with a
air number of scattered towns and villages
o provide accommodation. Car hire is pos-
ible in Khabarovsk, Vladivostok and
Yuzhno-Sakhalinsk from the service bureaus
at the major hotels or from Intourist (see the
European Russia Getting Around chapter for
general comments on car hire in Russia).

BOAT

Considering that Siberia and Russia's Far
East were first opened up by boat, the
region's rivers are now a very much under-
used means of transportation. The main
reason for this, of course, is that for six to
eight months of the year all the great waterways are locked solid with ice.

During summer, though, the Yenisey,
Lena and Amur rivers are put to use as
aquatic highways, and Lake Baikal is also
plied by numerous ferry services. On the
Yenisey, regular passenger services run
between Krasnoyarsk and various points
north as far as Dudinka, and upstream from
Kyzyl in Tuva. The Lena provides the main
supply route for Yakutsk, a city isolated in

the taiga a thousand km north of any railway
line. During the navigation season (from late
May or early June until October) there is a
constant flow of river traffic between
Yakutsk and Ust-Kut, a port on the BAM.
Passengers are also taken. On the Amur
River there are daily hydrofoil passenger
services, which link Khabarovsk to
Komsomolsk and Komsomolsk to
Nikolaevsk near the river's mouth.

On Lake Baikal poor maintenance and a
lack of spare parts seem to cause shipping
schedules to change from season to season.
The only guaranteed services are those
between Irkutsk and Severobaikalsk on the
lake's northern shore, the twice-weekly
sailing between Irkutsk and Ust-Barguzin on
the eastern shore, and the shuttles which go
three or four times daily between Irkutsk and
Listvyanka. Other boats do provide a ferry
link up the western shore but on a very erratic
basis. The hydrofoil service that used to
connect Irkutsk with Bratsk, downriver on
the Angara, has been discontinued.

On the Pacific seaboard, passage on a ship
taken from Port Vanino provides a cheap
alternative to flying across to the island of
Sakhalin (though not for Russians, who can
still fly for loose change), and there are also
irregular sailings from Korsakov, on
Sakhalin, across to Yuzhno-Kurilsk in the
Kuril island chain. For the truly adventurous
– with a month or so to spare – it is possible
to hitch a lift on one of the supply ships that
sail out of Nakhodka and Vladivostok up to
the Arctic Circle towns of Anadyr and Providenia.

More details are given in the regional
chapters of the book.

Western Siberia
Западный Сибирь

This chapter covers Russia from the Ural Mountains, officially just west of Siberia, to the Yenisey River, which is the natural boundary between the low-lying West Siberian Plain and the higher Central Siberian Plateau. Believe it or not, the climate west of the Yenisey is warm compared to the region east of it, allowing pine, spruce and fir to dominate the forests (the even hardier larch takes over beyond the Yenisey).

Siberia's biggest cities are all here, chief among them Yekaterinburg, with much historical interest, and the younger Novosibirsk. The developed bits of western Siberia lie along or near the Trans-Siberian Railway, in the Ural foothills, and to a lesser extent in the oil, gas and mineral fields of the north. But the most exciting travel here is away from the railway, the cities and the industry – above all in two remote, beautiful, fascinating southern regions bordering Mongolia from which foreign visitors used to be restricted or banned. These are the Altay Republic south of Novosibirsk and the Republic of Tuva south of Krasnoyarsk.

The Urals
Урал

The Ural Mountains stretch 2000 km from the fringes of Kazakhstan in the south to the fringes of the Arctic Kara Sea in the north. They're low as famous mountain ranges go, failing to top 2000 metres anywhere, and if you just pass through on the train you may hardly notice them at all. They have been vital to Russia for almost 300 years as a major source of key metals and minerals, which gave rise to a number of industrial cities on their fringes, of which Yekaterinburg, the biggest, is western Siberia's most interesting city.

YEKATERINBURG
ЕКАТЕРИНБУРГ
Population: 1.4 million

Yekaterinburg is 41 km inside Asia but still 260 km short of the official beginning of Siberia. The continental boundary is marked by obelisks beside both the railway and the road from Perm, about 40 km west of Yekaterinburg.

The city was founded as a factory-fort in 1723 as part of Peter the Great's push to exploit the Ural region's mineral riches, and named after two Yekaterinas – Peter's wife (later Empress Catherine I), and the Russian patron saint of mining. A year later it would have been named after only one Yekaterina, or maybe someone else altogether, for by then Peter had discovered that his wife had a lover, and had had his head cut off and placed in a jar of surgical spirit in her bedroom.

By the 19th century Yekaterinburg was an engineering centre supplying the Ural region's mines with machinery. It was also the centre of that century's Urals gold rush, producing some immensely rich gold barons.

In July 1918, Tsar Nicholas II and his wife and children were killed by the Bolsheviks in the basement of a house where they had been held here. Six years later, the town was renamed Sverdlovsk, after Yakov Sverdlov, a leading Bolshevik thought to have arranged the murders. WW II turned it into a major

ANDREW HUMPHREYS

RICHARD NEBESKY

ROBERT STRAUSS

op: Old steam train, Trans-Siberian Railway
eft: Soviet-era train emblem
ht: Warning sign: 'Do not cross in front of train'

WALTER COLEBATCH

WALTER COLEBATCH

WALTER COLEBATCH

Top: Alternative transport, Siberia
Middle: Dawn in Taiga forest
Bottom: Siberian village houses

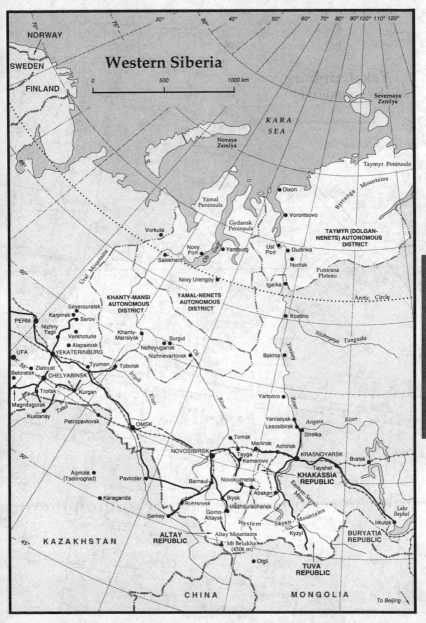

Western Siberia

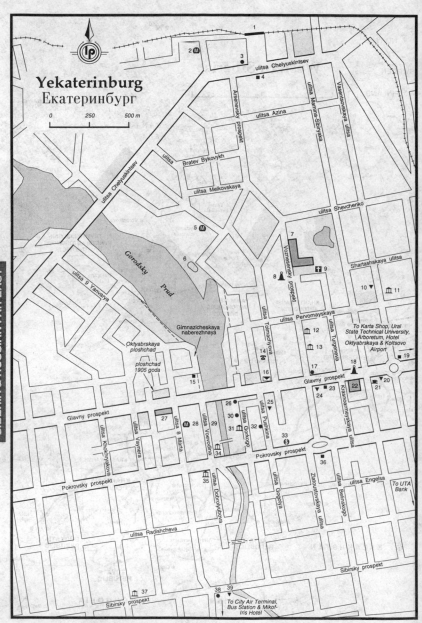

Yekaterinburg
Екатеринбург

0   250   500 m

ulitsa Chelyuskintsev

ulitsa Azina

ulitsa Bratev Bykovykh

ulitsa Melkovskaya

Gorodsky Prud

ulitsa 9 Yanvarya

ulitsa Chelyuskintsev

Arsenevsky prospekt

ulitsa Mamina-Sibiryaka

Vaissonsovskaya ulitsa

ulitsa Shevchenko

Shartashskaya ulitsa

Voznesensky prospekt

ulitsa Pervomayskaya

ulitsa Turgeneva

Tolmacheyova

Gimnazicheskaya naberezhnaya

Oktyabrskaya ploshchad

ploshchad 1905 goda

Glavny prospekt

ulitsa Khokhryakova

ulitsa Vaynera

ulitsa 8 Marta

ulitsa Voyevodina

ulitsa Gorkogo

ulitsa Pushkina

Glavny prospekt

Krasnoarmeyskaya ulitsa

Pokrovsky prospekt

ulitsa Dobrolyubova

ulitsa Gogolya

Zlatoustovskaya ulitsa

ulitsa Belinskogo

ulitsa Engelsa

To UTA Bank

Pokrovsky prospekt

ulitsa Radishcheva

Sibirsky prospekt

Sibirsky prospekt

To Karta Shop, Ural State Technical University, Arboretum, Hotel Oktyabrskaya & Koltsovo Airport

To City Air Terminal, Bus Station & Mikof-Iris Hotel

PLACES TO STAY

4 Hotel Sverdlovsk
   Гостиница Свердловск
15 Dom mira i Druzhby
   Дом мира и дружбы
19 Hotel Iset
   Гостиница Исет
23 Hotel Yubileynaya
   Гостиница Юбилейная
36 Hotel Tsentralnaya
   Гостиница Центральная

PLACES TO EAT

10 Uralskie Tsyplyata
   Restaurant
   Ресторан Уральские
   Цыплята
20 Gastronom Tsentralny
   Гастроном Центральный
21 Kafe Teatralnoe
   Кафе Театральное
24 Restoran Okean
   Ресторан Океан
25 Dom Rabotnikov
   Kultury
   Дом работников культуры
39 Kharbin Restaurant
   Ресторан Харбин

OTHER

1 Railway Station
   Железнодорожный вокзал
3 Knigi Shop
   Магазин Книги
6 Dinamo Stadium
   Стадион Динамо

7 Rastorguev-
   Kharitonov Mansion
   Усадьба Харитонова-
   Расторгуева
8 Romanov Death Site
   Место убийства Романовых
9 Ascension Church
   Вознесенская церковь
11 Dom Ofitserov &
   Military
   History Museum
   Дом Офицеров и Военно-
   исторический музей
12 Youth Museum
   Музей молодёжи
13 Political History
   Museum
   Музей политической
   истории
14 Inter-City Telephone
   Office
   Междугородный
   переговорный пункт
16 Post Office
   Почтамт
17 Sovkino Cinema
   Кинотеатр Совкино
18 Sverdlov Statue
   Памятник Я. М. Свердлову
22 Opera & Ballet Theatre
   Театр оперы и балета
26 Water Tower
   Водонапорная башня
27 City Hall
   Городской Совет
29 Geological Alley
   Геологическая аллея
30 Nature Department
   Отдел природы

31 Museum of City
   Architecture &
   Urals Industrial
   Technology
   Музей истории
   архитектуры
   города и
   промышленной
   техники Урала
32 Sputnik
   Спутник
33 Svak-Bank
   Свак-банк
34 Fine Arts Museum
   Музей
   изобразительных
   искусств
35 History & Local
   Studies Museum
   Историко-
   краеведческий
   музей
37 Geology Museum
   Уральский
   геологический
   музей
38 Circus
   Цирк

METRO STATIONS

2 Sverdlovskaya
   Свердловская
5 Dinamo (under
   construction)
   Динамо (строящееся)
28 Ploshchad 1905 Goda
   (under construction)
   Площадь 1905 Года
   (строящаяся)

SIBERIA & RUSSIAN FAR EAST

industrial centre as hundreds of factories were transferred here from vulnerable areas west of the Ural Mountains, and it was closed to foreigners until 1990 because of its many defence plants. In 1960, the US pilot Gary Powers was shot down in his U2 spy plane in this area, wrecking that year's Paris summit. (Powers, who baled out, was exchanged for a Soviet spy in 1962.) In 1979 64 people died of anthrax after a leak from a biological weapons plant, Sverdlovsk-17, in the city.

In 1991, Yekaterinburg took back its original name – though many people (and rail time-tables) continue to call it Sverdlovsk.

It turns out to be a rather interesting place – especially, perhaps, to geologists and industrial archaeologists – with pride in its place as the capital of the Ural region and its historical role in the area's development. While not exactly beautiful, it has a lot more pre-Soviet buildings than most cities further east – though all but six of its 50 churches, cathedrals and monasteries were demolished in the 1930s because they 'interfered with traffic movement' or their bells 'disturbed the people's sleep'. Like most Russian indus-trial cities, Yekaterinburg has endured an economic depression since the collapse of the Soviet Union. Among others, its industrial flagship, the giant Uralmash machine tool factory in the north of the city, had to lay off many of its 50,000 workers.

Orientation

Yekaterinburg has changed some street names but not many signs. We use the new names in the expectation/hope that they'll gradually win currency.

New Name	Old Name
Arsenevsky prospekt	ulitsa Sverdlova
Gimnazicheskaya - naberezhnaya	naberezhnaya Rabochey - Molodyozhi
Glavny prospekt	prospekt Lenina
Pokrovsky prospekt	ulitsa Malysheva
Sibirsky prospekt	ulitsa Kuybysheva
Vasentsovskaya ulitsa	ulitsa Lunacharskogo
Voznesensky prospekt	ulitsa Karla Libknekhta
Zlatoustovskaya ulitsa	ulitsa Rozy Lyuxemburg

The main boulevard is the east-west Glavny prospekt and the city centre is basically the few blocks around its intersection with Voznesensky prospekt, which leads 2.5 km north to the railway station. Glavny prospekt crosses the Iset River three blocks west of this intersection.

Information

Money There's a currency exchange office in the Hotel Tsentralnaya. You can also change money at Svak-Bank, half a block west of the hotel on Pokrovsky prospekt. UTA Bank at ulitsa Dekabristov 14, 1.3 km south off Vasentsovskaya ulitsa, can give Visa card cash advances.

Post & Telecommunications The Biznes-Servis-Byuro (☎ 53 62 48) in room 248 at the Hotel Sverdlovsk has international and domestic telephone and fax services and photocopying – open from 9 am to 6 pm, Monday to Friday. The main post office, on Glavny prospekt two blocks west of Voznesensky prospekt, has a fax service too. It's open from 8 am to 1 pm and 2 to 6 pm

Yeltsin & Yekaterinburg

Yekaterinburg's best known son is Boris Yeltsin, who was born of peasant parents in the village of Butka, 190 km east. Yeltsin studied civil engineering at what is now Yekaterinburg's technical university (and met his wife Naya there), worked his way up from foreman to head of the city's house-building organisation, then moved into Communist Party work, becoming head of the Sverdlovsk regional Party by 1976. He was popular as Party bosses went, as he was in the habit of riding the trams like everyone else and paying regular visits to local factories. He left after being promoted to head the Moscow Party in 1985. In 1991, during the old guard coup in Moscow, plans were drawn up for Yeltsin to run Russia's government from bunkers near Yekaterinburg if the coup succeeded. In 1992, as Russian president, he ordered the city's Sverdlovsk-17 biological weapons plant closed.

Russians under 30, by the way, are equally likely to know of Yekaterinburg as the birthplace of the top rock band Nautilus Pompilius. ■

Monday to Friday, and 10 am to 1 pm on Saturdays. The intercity telephone office is nearby at ulitsa Tolmachyova 24. The Yekaterinburg telephone code is 3432.

Foreign Consulate There's a US consulate (☎ 60 11 43; fax 60 11 81) in Yekaterinburg: at the time of research it provided only emergency services for US citizens and was based in one of the hotels. Call the US embassy in Moscow if you have trouble contacting it.

Travel Agencies If you're looking for any kind of help or guidance in or around Yekaterinburg you can't do better than contact Konstantin Brylyakov at the Sputnik office (☎ 51 91 57; fax 51 34 83) at ulitsa Pushkina 5. This enthusiastic young 'Chief Specialist' speaks excellent English, knows a lot about the city and the Ural region, and is full of ideas for inexpensive trips out of the city (see Around Yekaterinburg). He can also arrange guided city walks (he'll probably be your guide himself) and accommodation.

There's an Intourist office on floor 4 of the Hotel Yubileynaya, open from 8.30 am to 1 pm and 2 to 5.30 pm Monday to Friday, but they don't seem to like to do much. If pressed, they can book you into the Hotel Oktyabrskaya, sell you foreigner-price train tickets and probably arrange other services.

The Hotel Oktyabrskaya has a service bureau.

Maps Knigi shop, near the railway station opposite the end of Arsenevsky prospekt, is good for maps of the city and surrounding areas, including hiking and river maps of parts of the Ural region. Karta shop at ulitsa Pervomayskaya 74 is an excellent source of large-scale topographical maps of many areas of the ex-USSR. To find it, take a tram east along Glavny prospekt to Vostochnaya ulitsa (where Glavny prospekt goes under a railway bridge), then walk 350 metres north on Vostochnaya ulitsa, and a block to the right along ulitsa Pervomayskaya.

Romanov Death Site

The spot where the Romanov dynasty met its final gruesome end on the night of 16-17 July 1918 is beside Voznesensky prospekt, 600 metres north of Glavny prospekt. This bleak place is simply but movingly marked by a cross bearing photos of the murdered royal family, and a stone slab with the names Nikolay (Tsar Nicholas II), Alexandra (the tsarina), and Alexey, Olga, Tatyana, Maria and Anastasia (their five children). A wooden church is being built behind (eventually to be replaced by a larger, more permanent structure), and to one side, already completed, is the little wooden Chapel of the Revered Martyr Grand Princess Yelisaveta Fyodorovna (Chasovnya vo imya Prepodobnomuchenitsy Velikoi Knyagini Yelisavety Fyodorovny). Grand Princess Yelisaveta was a great-aunt of the royal family who, soon after her relatives' murders, reportedly met an even worse end – when she survived being thrown down a mine, poisonous gas was pumped in and the shaft filled with earth. Inside the chapel are modern paintings of her and the royal family.

The Romanovs were actually killed in the cellar of a house which stood here until Boris Yeltsin had it demolished (on Politburo orders, he says) in 1977. Imprisoned by the Bolsheviks after the revolution, the royal family was moved from place to place, eventually being brought here in April 1918. The Soviet government must have decided, with civil war spreading across Siberia, that the royal family was too good a potential White figurehead to leave alive. Late one night they were taken down to the cellar, told they were going to die, and shot repeatedly. The girls, protected by 'bullet-proof vests' of jewels sewn into their underclothes, had to be finished off with bayonets.

The house was known as Dom Ipateva, after its owner, one Nikolay Ipatev. It was later used as a museum of the revolution then as offices before being demolished.

At the back of the little park across the street from the Romanov site, the Ascension Church (Voznesenskaya Tserkov) is being restored. The ostentatious classical-fronted building lining the slope down to the north was the mansion of a rich 19th-century gold

SIBERIA & RUSSIAN FAR EAST

family called Rastorguev-Kharitonov. A park spreads out behind the mansion. In the cellars, it's said, the Rastorguev-Kharitonovs minted their own gold coins and tortured their enemies – perhaps an inspiration for the Romanovs' guards.

Istorichesky Skver & Around

Three blocks west of Voznesensky propekt, Glavny prospekt crosses a small dam forming the Gorodskoy prud (City Pond) on its north side, with the Iset River funnelled through a narrow channel on the south side.

The Riddle of the Romanov Remains

What happened to the bodies of the Romanovs after their deaths is a mixture of the macabre, the mysterious and the plain messy. After decades of rumour and speculation, expert investigations since 1991 have finally pieced the story together – almost.

When in 1991 archaeologists opened a shallow pit near Yekaterinburg, believed to be the Romanovs' grave, they found the bones of nine people. These were tentatively identified as Tsar Nicholas II, his wife Tsarina Alexandra, three of their four daughters, the royal doctor and three servants. Absent were any remains of the royal couple's one son, Tsarevich Alexey, aged 13 at the time of the killings. Also notably absent was the fourth daughter, which gave a new lease of life to theories that the youngest daughter, Anastasia (aged 17 in 1918), had somehow escaped the killings. Best known of several people who had claimed to be Anastasia was Anna Anderson, who appeared in Berlin in 1920 with convincing stories of life among the Romanovs which led many people to believe her. She died in the USA in 1984.

In 1992 bone samples from the excavated skeletons were sent to the British government's Forensic Science Service, to be tested by DNA identification techniques pioneered by British scientists. Using blood and hair samples from the Duke of Edinburgh (a grandson of the tsarina's sister) and two descendants of the tsar, by 1993 the scientists had established with 'more than 98.5%' certainty that the bones were those of the tsar, the tsarina and three of their daughters.

An official Russian inquiry team in Yekaterinburg then managed to piece together the skulls found in the pit – some badly damaged by rifle butts, hand grenades and acid – and built plaster models of the faces they had once borne. This, together with the DNA tests and dental records, satisfied them by 1994 that the three daughters found were Olga and Tatyana (the two oldest) – and Anastasia.

The missing daughter was Maria. Her and Alexey's remains were still undiscovered, but the Russians said they at least knew how they had been disposed of. And what a tale of ghoulish bungling it was. According to the Russian team, all five children had died with their parents in the cellar of the Dom Ipateva. The bodies were then trucked to an abandoned mine 30 km away and thrown in, followed by several grenades intended to collapse the mine shaft. The mine, however, did not collapse. The bodies were pulled out and an acids expert summoned. He brought 160 litres of acid but fell off his horse, broke a leg and couldn't help. It was then decided to distribute the bodies among various smaller mines and pour acid on them. But the lorry carrying them became bogged in a swamp, so the disposal team – by now understandably desperate – opted to bury them on the spot. They tried burning Alexey and Maria in preparation, but realised it would take days to burn all the bodies properly, so the others were just put in a pit and doused with acid. Even then, most of the acid soaked away into the ground – leaving the bones to be uncovered 73 years later.

For masterminding all this, Yakov Sverdlov got a city named after him.

The royal remains are likely to be buried in St Petersburg's SS Peter & Paul Cathedral, the resting place of most of Nicholas II's predecessors back to Peter the Great. ∎

Tsarina Alexandra and her four daughters, murdered in 1918

This was where Yekaterinburg began back in 1723. Water from the dam (reconstructed twice since that date) powered an iron forge below it. A mint and a stone-cutting works soon followed. On either side of the river today is a plaza-cum-park called Istorichesky skver (Historical Square), which is surrounded by a clutch of old buildings and museums. All the museums are open from 11 am to 6 pm daily except Tuesday. The architecture and technology museum also closes on Sunday.

On the east side are an old **water tower**, the **Nature Department** (Otdel prirody) of the local museum, and the combined **Museum of City Architecture & Ural Industrial Technology** (Muzey istorii arkhitektury goroda i promyshlennoy tekhniki Urala). These last two are housed in an old (though not the original) mining-equipment factory and mint buildings. The Nature Department displays minerals and precious stones from the Ural region, where emeralds, aquamarines, tourmalines, malachite, jasper and many more stones are mined. The architecture and industrial museum has antique machinery and an exhibition on the growth of the city.

On the west side of the river is **Geological Alley** (Geologicheskaya alleya), a small park dotted with large, labelled rock specimens from the Ural region. At the alley's south end stands the **Fine Arts Museum** (Muzey izobrazitelnykh iskusstv), which has unusual sections devoted to cast-iron art (including the elaborate Kasli Iron Pavilion which won prizes in Paris in 1900), precious-stone cutting (a local speciality), and the local craft of engraving or painting trays, known as Uralskie podnosy (Ural trays), as well as rooms of pre-Revolutionary Russian painting – all in all, well worth the US$1 entry fee for foreigners.

Just across the street corner from the Fine Arts Museum, at Pokrovsky prospekt 46, is the **History & Local Studies Museum** Istoriko-kraevedchesky muzey), which has some interesting exhibits on the Romanov murders, Old Believers in the Ural region, and old Yekaterinburg.

If your appetite for rocks isn't yet sated, visit the **Ural Geology Museum** (Uralsky Geologichesky Muzey), a further two blocks west and two south, at the corner of ulitsa Khokhryakova and Sibirsky prospekt. It has over 500 Ural region minerals and a collection of meteorites.

Political History & Youth Museums

On Voznesensky prospekt just north of Glavny prospekt are the Political History Museum (Muzey politicheskoy istorii), at No 26, open from 11 am to 6 pm daily except Friday, and the Museum of Youth (Muzey molodyozhi), at No 32, open from 11 am to 7 pm Tuesday to Saturday. Both have modernised their exhibits and are reportedly worth seeing.

Sverdlov Statue

Yakov Sverdlov remains (for the time being) atop his rock facing the Opera & Ballet Theatre on Glavny prospekt. With his downward-pointing finger he seems to be saying 'Take 'em to the cellar and shoot 'em'.

Military History Museum

This museum (Voenno-istorichesky muzey) is in the Dom Ofitserov (House of Officers) building at the corner of ulitsa Pervomayskaya and Vasentsovskaya ulitsa. The entrance is on ulitsa Pervomayskaya – but it's open to you and me only on Saturdays from 9.30 am to 4 pm. On other days it's shut or reserved for 'collective' visits. Even on Saturdays, the babushkas in charge follow you around, switching on the lights one room at a time – and not until they consider you've spent enough time in the room before. Exhibits cover the revolution, WW II, and the Soviet forces after WW II. In the yard behind there's a collection of tanks, planes and even a space capsule. The whereabouts of the wreckage of Gary Powers' US plane, which apparently were once in the museum, are a puzzle, if not a secret. Museum staff directed John to room No 109 in the Dom Ofitserov, where an important-looking officer said the plane was in another museum in a military area *(voinskaya chast)* out in the north of the city. It's probably easiest located from a spy plane.

University & Arboretum

The Ural State Technical University (Uralsky gosudarstvenny tekhnichesky universitet), an imposing 1930s Soviet classical edifice at the east end of Glavny prospekt, three km from the centre, is the biggest Russian university east of the Ural Mountains. It's generally known as UPI – the initials of its old name, Uralsky Politekhnichesky Institut (Ural Polytechnical Institute). In the Soviet era, despite (or maybe because of) its technological emphasis, it was renowned as a stepping stone to high political office – for Boris Yeltsin, among many others.

There's a nice, quiet open-air arboretum (Dendrologichesky Park-Vystavka) a block north of the university, at the corner of ulitsa Pervomayskaya and ulitsa Mira. You can reach the university by tram No 4, 13, 15 or 18 or bus No 28 east along Glavny prospekt. Get off the trams when they turn right down ulitsa Gagarina, a block before the university.

Other Attractions

Many old **wooden houses**, with picturesque, carved window frames, remain along streets like Zlatoustovskaya ulitsa and ulitsa Belinskogo, south of Pokrovsky prospekt. There are several large woodland parks (*lesoparki*), some with lakes, around the perimeter of the city.

Numerous quarries of different minerals lie within 20 km or so of Yekaterinburg. Sputnik (see Information) can organise visits.

Places to Stay

The *Hotel Iset* (☎ 55 69 43) at Glavny prospekt 69 is a decaying Constructivist building with a ground plan in the shape of a hammer and sickle. It has some of the cheaper accommodation in town and standard singles/doubles at US$15/30 with private bathroom and TV are quite clean and comfortable. On the 4th floor there are shabbier doubles with toilet only for US$17.50 (the staff hint there may be a security risk from 'gipsies' on that floor, though that could

just be a way of getting you to take a costlier room). There are also suites up to US$35/70.

Dom Mira i Druzhby (Peace & Friendship House; ☎ 51 77 52, 51 07 73; fax 57 08 02), a block north of Glavny prospekt at Gimnazicheskaya naberezhnaya 2, on the west side of the Gorodskóy prud, has very comfortable three-bedroom flats accommodating up to six people for US$50 a night – not bad value even for two or three, compared with what the same price would get you in a hotel. It's run by the Regional Association for Friendship & International Cooperation. They advise booking ahead but you may be lucky even if you don't.

The big *Hotel Sverdlovsk* (☎ 53 62 61) at ulitsa Chelyuskintsev 106, facing the railway station, is as good as other hotels in its price range. It also has convenient eating options. Standard singles/doubles with private bathroom are US$37/45 with a drab breakfast included. Doubles with an extra room range from US$75 to the 'improved' (*uluchshennyy*) variety at US$140.

The *Hotel Yubileynaya* (☎ 51 57 58) at Glavny prospekt 44 has a dark, gloomy lobby but brighter rooms at US$45 a single or double with private bathroom.

The *Hotel Tsentralnaya* (☎ 55 69 71) at Pokrovsky prospekt 74 (the south end of Voznesensky prospekt) is a better kept place with singles/doubles with attached bathroom for US$43/78.

There's a *Mikof-Iris* hotel (☎ 28 91 45, 28 44 78; fax 28 62 92) five km south-west of the centre at ulitsa Bardina 4A. It was closed for renovation when we visited but is said to be very comfortable with two-room suites at US$70 a single or double, including breakfast. For information on Mikof-Iris hotels, see Accommodation in European Russia Facts for the Visitor.

The best hotel, formerly belonging to the Communist Party, is the *Hotel Oktyabrskaya* (☎ 44 51 46; fax 44 50 16), in a quiet treed neighbourhood 3.5 km east of the centre, at ulitsa Sofyi Kovalevskoy 17, off ulitsa Pervomayskaya. Comfortable standard singles/doubles are US$83/110 the first night, US$55/88 for the following nights. There are also suites for two people at US$147 (two rooms) and US$166 (three rooms) the first night, US$98 and US$110 thereafter. The hotel has a restaurant and a service bureau. Bus No 28 along Glavny prospekt from the city centre stops on ulitsa Pervomayskaya near the Kovalevskoy corner. From the Ural State Technical University, walk a block north to ulitsa Pervomayskaya, then a block to the right, then turn left into ulitsa Sofyi Kovalevskoy. The hotel is a red-brick building with only a small sign on the door to give away its name.

Sputnik (see Information) is renovating an interesting tower-like building across the street from its ulitsa Pushkina office into what should be good middle-range accommodation. It can also arrange stays in the luxury *Uralsky Dvor* dachas, formerly used by high Communist Party officials, near Lake Baltym, 25 km north of the city. The Uralsky Dvor office in Yekaterinburg (fax 23 04 79) is at Moskovskaya ulitsa 29.

Places to Eat

The *Hotel Sverdlovsk*'s ground-floor restaurant does fairly good food for lunch and dinner – meat main courses such as langet (steak) are around US$2. If the main part of the restaurant is closed, a small room at the back should still be open. The hotel also has bars on floors 5 and 7 with a good range of light eats.

The *Hotel Tsentralnaya* restaurant is one of the best. It's smaller and more attractive than most hotel restaurants, with fair service and a long list of zakuski from US$0.50 to US$5.50 plus some good main dishes like kotlet po-kievsky (chicken Kiev) or chakhokhbili (Georgian-style chicken) for around US$3. There's a small dance floor and a band in the evenings – go early if you want a quiet dinner.

The *Hotel Yubileynaya* has a bufet on the 2nd floor.

The *Kafe* in the Dom Rabotnikov Kultury on ulitsa Pushkina near Istorichesky skver is OK for a basic feed of langet or befstroganoff for around US$1 – it also has a few zakuski.

It's open from 10.30 am to 4 pm and 5 to 7.30 pm.

Restoran Okean on Glavny prospekt a few steps east of Voznesensky prospekt is a popular fish restaurant, with main dishes around US$5 to US$7.

The *Kafe Teatralnoe* two blocks east, facing the side of the Opera & Ballet Theatre on ulitsa Mamina-Sibiryaka, has a restaurant section with quite a good range of zakuski at US$1.50 to US$4, pizza at US$1.50 to US$3, and main dishes at US$3 to US$5.50. There's also a snack bar with ice cream and other snacks, and it's open from 10 am to 4 pm and 5 to 9 pm. The big Gastronom Tsentralny food shop round the corner on Glavny prospekt has an *Express Bar* inside at its west end, with a few basic snacks.

The little *Uralskie Tsyplyata* (Ural Chicken) restaurant at Vasentsovskaya ulitsa 111, almost opposite the Dom Ofitserov, does good portions of grilled bird with a bit of tomato and cucumber for US$2.50. It's open from 10 am to 4 pm and 5 to 10 pm.

Probably the best – and most expensive – restaurant is the Chinese *Kharbin* (Harbin), south of the centre at Sibirsky prospekt 38. You can't miss the building – it's done up like a Chinese temple outside. The four-course set meal is US$25 a head and said to be excellent. There's a bar too (individual diners must eat in here, as there's a minimum of two requirement for the restaurant tables). Hours are noon to 4 pm and 6 to 11 pm and it gets busy in the evenings so you should go early to ensure a table. To get there, you can take tram No 32 from the Hotel Iset.

There are several places to get a bite in and just outside the railway station.

Things to Buy

Locally engraved or painted trays known as Uralskie podnosy are on sale in the Fine Art Museum for up to US$5.

Getting There & Away

Air The main airport is at Koltsovo, 15 km south-east of the city centre, with daily flights by Transaero and other airlines to/from Moscow (US$115; 2½ hours).

Lufthansa flies direct to/from Frankfurt and there are cheaper charters from Düsseldorf with Luftbrücke (see Siberia & the Far East Getting There & Away). Other flights go daily to/from Irkutsk, several times a week to/from St Petersburg, Omsk, Novosibirsk and Vladivostok, and a few times a week to/from Krasnoyarsk, Perm, Almaty (Kazakhstan) and Tashkent (Uzbekistan). Another airport at Uktus in the south of the city has only a few local flights.

Lufthansa (☎ 26 61 64, 26 89 15) is at the airport; Luftbrücke is on ☎ 26 62 21. Other air tickets for foreigners are sold at windows 25 and 26 in the city air terminal (Aerovokzal) at ulitsa Bolshakova 99A, south of the centre off ulitsa 8 Marta. Hours are 8 am to 1 pm and 2 to 5 pm, Monday to Friday. The Intourist office at the airport will sell same-day tickets to foreigners, if they're available. The office is in the stone-faced block, to the right of the colonnaded entrance – go through the 'Intourist' door and up the stairs.

Bus From the bus station south of the centre at ulitsa 8 Marta 145, on the corner of ulitsa Shchorsa, there are two daily buses to Tyumen, 23 to Chelyabinsk, and four to Nizhny Tagil. Bus No 589 to Chelyabinsk (US$5) leaves Yekaterinburg railway station at 6 and 7.30 am. Tickets are sold at a kiosk at the north-eastern corner of the station square.

Train Yekaterinburg is the major stop on the Trans-Siberian Railway between Perm (6½ hours west) and Novosibirsk (22 hours east). Apart from the Trans-Siberian, Trans-Mongolian and Trans-Manchurian trains to/from Vladivostok or Beijing, there are numerous other daily trains to different cities on and off the main trans-Siberian route. Eastbound, some go via Tyumen, others via Kurgan and Petropavlovsk (Kazakhstan): the two branches meet up again at Omsk. Westbound, some Moscow trains go via Kazan rather than Perm. The station's always full of people waiting for one train or another. To/from Moscow (Kazan Station), the daily 'Ural' (No 15/16), which starts and

finishes at Yekaterinburg and travels via Kazan, is a good choice, taking 29 hours.

Other services run to/from St Petersburg (twice daily), and Tashkent, Almaty and Bishkek (every two days).

In the station, which is north of the centre on ulitsa Chelyuskintsev, the main ticket windows are upstairs. You can get foreigner-price tickets from Intourist (see Information). Tickets for suburban services such as to Nizhny Tagil are sold at the 'prigorodnye kassy' on the ground floor, towards the east end of the station building.

Getting Around
To/From the Airport Express bus No 168 – often very crowded – runs between Koltsovo airport and the railway station. For the city centre, get off at the Kinoteatr Sovkino (Sovkino Cinema) stop at the corner of Glavny prospekt and Voznesensky prospekt. Service is about every 30 minutes from 6 am to 7 pm, then occasionally through the night. At the airport, buy tickets at the bus stand in the forecourt; at the station, there's a ticket office at the north-eastern corner of the station square. The fare is US$0.75. There's also express bus No 167 between the city air terminal and the airport.

Public Transport Many trolleybuses run up and down Voznesensky prospekt between the railway station and Glavny prospekt. Tram Nos 4, 13, 15 and 18 and bus No 28 cover long stretches of Glavny prospekt, with tram Nos 4 and 15 also serving the bus station.

Bus No 23 and tram No 5 run between the railway and bus stations. You can get off at the corner of Sibirsky prospekt for the Kharbin restaurant or at ulitsa Bolshakova for the city air terminal. Many other trams run up and down ulitsa 8 Marta between ulitsa Radishcheva and the bus station.

A metro is being built. The first section only connects the railway station with the giant Uralmash machine tool factory in the north of the city, but an extension from the station to ploshchad 1905 goda in the centre, just west of Istorichesky skver, was due to be completed soon.

The Urals

Geography Geographers divide the Urals into five sections. Yekaterinburg is on the east side of the longest, broadest and generally lowest stretch, the Middle Urals (Sredny Ural). The Middle Urals are at their highest, reaching over 1500 metres, towards their north end. The Southern Urals (Yuzhny Ural) stretch south from around Zlatoust, climbing to 1638 metres at Mt Yaman Tau, near Beloretsk. The Northern Urals (Severny Ural) begin north of Severouralsk and reach 1617 metres at Mt Telposiz. North of the Northern Urals (if this makes sense) come the Subarctic Urals (Pripolyarny Ural), a short stretch but with the highest peak in the whole range, 1894-metre Mt Narodnaya. The Arctic Urals (Polyarny Ural), whose highest peak is 1499-metre Mt Pay-Yer, take the range almost to the Kara Sea. The Arctic Novaya Zemlya islands, one of the Soviet Union's nuclear bomb testing grounds, are effectively a northern outcrop of the Urals.

Most of the Urals are covered in taiga, with rocky outcrops forming the peaks, but there are apparently some more dramatic rock walls on the northern peaks.

While the foothills of the Middle and Southern Urals are well populated, with several heavy industrial towns and cities (all considered to be in the Ural region, not Siberia), the more northerly Urals are very remote, with unexploited mineral riches, clear rivers and a tiny population mainly of Khanty and Nentsy hunters and reindeer herders.

History Nentsy, Khanty and Mansi natives had traded furs, walrus ivory and other products across the Urals from the 12th century, and early Russian invaders and merchants crossed the Urals from the 1580s, but it was the region's reserves of iron ore, metals, coal and gemstones that first aroused serious Russian interest. Peter the Great sent pioneer industrialists to set up ironworks and metalworks, with mainly military purposes in mind, in the early 18th century. Industrial centres like Yekaterinburg, Chelyabinsk, Nizhny Tagil, and Perm to the west of the Urals, date from that time. At the same time indiscriminate felling of forests and pollution of lakes and rivers began. WW II brought a new industrial boom as Stalin moved over 1000 factories east of the Urals, and this growth continued after the war.

Gold and platinum were found in the Urals in the 19th century, and the element ruthenium was discovered here. Amethyst, topaz and aquamarine are among the gems mined in the region, notably in the Murzinka fields near Nizhny Tagil. Malachite is quarried at Nizhny Tagil and near Yekaterinburg.

The Urals arms industry tradition, meanwhile, has continued: more or less the whole region was off limits to foreigners until 1990 and today some towns are still closed to outsiders for military reasons. Five of the 10 secret cities of the Soviet Union's 'nuclear archipelago' for weapons research and production were placed in the Urals – Sverdlovsk-44, Sverdlovsk-45, Chelyabinsk-65, Chelyabinsk-70 and Zlatoust-36 (the numbers are their postcodes). Chelyabinsk-70 and Arzamas-16, about 100 km south of Nizhny Novgorod, were the key research centres: the others were mainly uranium and plutonium production centres. Some have reportedly now gone over at least partly to civilian work. Chelyabinsk-65 (formerly Chelyabinsk-40) was the scene of the world's worst nuclear accident before Chernobyl, back in 1957 (though it wasn't admitted for decades). A nuclear waste tank exploded, severely contaminating an area eight km wide and 100 km long, with about 10,000 people eventually moved out and 23 villages bulldozed. The 1957 explosion, along with deliberate 1950s dumping of radioactive wastes into the nearby Techa River and Lake Karachay (which later dried up, allowing the wind to scatter radioactive dust), have led to grave health and environmental problems in the area. Don't go poking around – radiation levels monitored on the shores of Lake Karachay in 1990 would have given a fatal dose in one hour.

Activities *Trekking in Russia & Central Asia*, by Frith Maier (see Books in Siberia & the Far East Facts for the Visitor), describes a two to three-day hike up 1569-metre Konzhakovsky Kamen, the highest peak in the Middle Urals, and a nine to 10-day trek in the Mt Narodnaya area. July and August are the best months. The approach to the Mt Narodnaya area is from Pechora on the Moscow-Vorkuta railway on the west side of the Urals, then by hydrofoil up the Pechora River.

Cross-country skiing and rafting or kayaking are other locally popular Urals activities. Trips on relatively easy rivers like the Chusovaya, Serga, Usva and Vilva in the Middle Urals and the Vishera in the Northern Urals can be arranged through agencies like Sputnik in Yekaterinburg, or Cruise or Evresia in Perm (see the Around Perm section of the Volga Region chapter). ∎

SIBERIA & RUSSIAN FAR EAST

AROUND YEKATERINBURG
ОКОЛО ЕКАТЕРИНБУРГА

The Yekaterinburg and Ural region is far from geared up to foreign travellers and some trips and activities are hard to manage on your own. If you want help, Sputnik (see the Yekaterinburg Information section) is a good choice. It can arrange inexpensive accommodation in several places around the region, often in sanatoria, and has access to the Zelyony Mys (Green Cape) holiday centre near the closed atomic-energy town of Verkhny Neyvinsky, about 90 km north-west of Yekaterinburg, which it says is the best accommodation in the region, having been created for atomic scientists. Sputnik offers a big range of tours, rafting and kayaking trips in the region, some with an ecological or geological focus, and can probably help set up any itinerary you request.

Nizhnyaya Sinyachikha
Нижняя Синячиха

This village, about 150 km north-east of Yekaterinburg and 12 km north of the town of Alapaevsk, is home to an open-air architecture museum of old Ural region log buildings, with displays of period furniture, tools and domestic articles. There's one stone building – a cathedral, housing a museum of Ural region art. But it's very hard to reach by public transport from Yekaterinburg – about six hours by occasional trains, four or five hours by equally rare buses. Maps show a hotel in Alapaevsk, which also has Tchaikovsky Museum in a house where the composer once lived. A day trip by taxi from Yekaterinburg might be the answer. Sputnik offers trips with an overnight stay in sanatorium.

Nizhny Tagil
Нижний Тагил
Population: 400,000

The name of this industrial town 140 km north of Yekaterinburg was once synonymous with the Demidov clan of industrialists and landowners descended from Nikita Demidovich Antufev, sent by Peter the Great to set up weapons factories in the Ural region. His dynasty ended up with mansions in St Petersburg, Moscow and abroad, only visiting their Ural empire every decade or two.

Today the town is home to the Nizhny Tagil Museum-Reserve of Middle Urals Mining (Nizhny-Tagilsky muzey-zapovednik gornozavodskogo dela srednego Urala), a recently developed complex devoted to the region's industrial and other history, housed in various historic buildings in the town, focused on the Regional Studies Museum (Kraevedchesky muzey). The large collection includes blocks of malachite weighing 300 and 500 kg, found in Nizhny Tagil's Mednorudyansky mine in 1835. One section of the museum, at ulitsa Verkhne-Cherepanova 1, is devoted to the inventors (in 1834) of Russia's first steam engine, Yefim and Miron Cherepanov, with a model of the engine. On Tagilskaya ulitsa are the Museum of the Life & Trades of the Mining Population (Muzey byta i remesel gornozavodskogo naseleniya), with examples of local metal crafts and folk costume, and the Museum of Tray Manufacture (Muzey podnosnogo promysla) devoted to a well-known local craft.

The *Hotel Tagil* at Sadovaya ulitsa 6, opposite the railway station, is inexpensive. There's also the *Hotel Severny Ural*, two km west at prospekt Lenina 6. Several northbound long-distance trains from Yekaterinburg to places like Priobie, Nizhnyaya Tura, Kachkanar and Karpinsk stop in Nizhny Tagil, and there are suburban trains roughly hourly. The trip is three to four hours.

Verkhoturie
Верхотурье

This small country town on the Tura River about 170 km north of Nizhny Tagil was once the most important centre of Christianity in eastern Russia; today its dozen cathedrals, churches and monasteries are all in varying degrees of evocative decay. The main cathedral is second in size only to St Isaac's in St Petersburg. Overnight trains from Yekaterinburg to Severouralsk and Karpinsk go through Privokzalny, 10 km west.

Tyumen & Omsk Regions
Тюменская и Омская области

The old Siberian capital of Tobolsk, north of the Trans-Siberian Railway, is the most interesting destination in these regions between Yekaterinburg and Novosibirsk.

TYUMEN
ТЮМЕНЬ
Population: 400,000
Tyumen, 325 km east of Yekaterinburg on the main trans-Siberian rail line, is the capital of Russia's largest *oblast* (region), which stretches all the way to the Yamal and Gydansk peninsulas on the Arctic Kara Sea. Since the region has vast reserves of oil (produced mainly around Surgut and Nizhnevartovsk) and gas (further north), and is Russia's largest oil-exporting area, Tyumen is something of a business capital and seems economically less depressed than many other Siberian cities, but there's little to detain the casual visitor.

The first Russian fort in Siberia was founded here in 1586, near the site of Chimgi-Tura, an old capital of the Mongol-Tatar Taibuga clan which succeeded the Golden Horde in the west Siberian forests. During WW II, Lenin's corpse was kept in Tyumen, safe from the invading Germans.

Orientation & Information
The main street, running roughly east-west right across town, is ulitsa Respubliki. The city centre is the area east of its intersection with ulitsa Pervomayskaya, with the post office and long-distance telephone office two and three blocks, respectively, along to the east. The railway station is about 1.5 km south along ulitsa Pervomayskaya.

You can change money at the Hotel Prometey or, from 10 am to 4 pm Monday to Friday, at the Aeroflot office. There's a Sputnik office at ulitsa Respubliki 19, 1½

blocks west of ulitsa Pervomayskaya. The Tyumen telephone code is 3452.

Things to See
Three blocks west along ulitsa Respubliki from ulitsa Pervomayskaya, then half a block north on ulitsa Semakova, is the fine, green-and-white, multidomed **Church of the Holy Sign** (Znamenskaya tserkov), built in 1786 in Russian Baroque style. It's a working church. This area of town is full of old wooden houses, with the Tura River flowing by at the foot of a steep bank. You can walk further west to a **monastery**, undergoing restoration, in a fine position at the top of the river bank.

The Fine Arts Museum (Muzey izobrazitelnykh iskusstv) just along the street from the Hotel Prometey was closed for renovation.

Places to Stay & Eat
There's a *Gostinitsa* (hotel) upstairs in the railway station, with rooms at US$5/8.25 a single/double.

The *Hotel Vostok* (☎ 22 53 05), a long way east at ulitsa Respubliki 159, has basic singles/doubles with private bath for US$25.50/30.50 or US$30/36, and suites at US$51 a double. Trolleybus No 14 along ulitsa Respubliki gets you there from the centre in about 15 minutes – the hotel is a long, grey seven-storey building between the ulitsa Gorkogo and ulitsa Odesskaya corners.

The top place is the *Hotel Prometey* (☎ 25 14 23) on ulitsa 8 Marta, a modern place with rooms at US$70 a single or double, a restaurant and a bar. To reach it, go two blocks east on ulitsa Respubliki from ulitsa Pervomayskaya, then two blocks north on ulitsa 8 Marta.

Pitstsa Univek on ulitsa Respubliki just east of ulitsa Pervomayskaya does whole pizzas for US$3.50, slices for US$0.40, from 8 am to 8 pm.

Getting There & Away
You can fly to/from Moscow two or three times daily, or to/from Novosibirsk, Irkutsk,

St Petersburg or Tashkent a few times a week. The Aeroflot office, for tickets, is on a corner of the small park on the south side of ulitsa Respubliki, one block east of ulitsa Pervomayskaya. It's open daily. Several eastbound and westbound trains a day on the main trans-Siberian line stop at Tyumen: Yekaterinburg is about five hours away, Omsk eight hours, Novosibirsk 18 hours, Moscow 35 hours. There are also three trains a day to/from Tobolsk.

Getting Around
Any bus from the railway station will take you along ulitsa Pervomayskaya to ulitsa Respubliki or ulitsa Lenina, a block before. Returning to the railway station, you can pick buses up in front of the city hall (Gorodskoy Duma) on ulitsa Pervomayskaya, just south of ulitsa Lenina. Beware of ticket inspectors, who pounce when you reach the station – they levy US$1.25 fines if you don't have a ticket.

TOBOLSK
ТОБОЛЈСК
Tobolsk, 240 km north-east of Tyumen at the confluence of the Irtysh and Tobol rivers, is a historic town which could make an interesting trip from Tyumen. It was founded as a fort in 1587, near the site of Kashlyk (also called Sibir), the capital of the west Siberian khanate conquered for Russia by Yermak Timofeevich in 1582. Strategically located on the Irtysh, Tobolsk was the capital of Russian Siberia until 1824, and from 1621 the seat of Siberia's first bishopric – set up, incidentally, with the express purpose of stamping out incest, wife-renting and wife-stealing by sexually frustrated soldiers. But Tobolsk lost importance from the 1760s, when the new Great Siberian Trakt road to the east took a more southerly route.

The centrepiece is the elegant old **kremlin** on a clifftop overlooking the Irtysh. Within, visit the **Intercession Cathedral** (Pokrovsky Sobor), dating from the 1740s, the 1780

SIBERIA & RUSSIAN FAR EAST

Rasputin's Roots
Grigory Rasputin, the priest of sex who had such an infamous influence on the Russian royal family in the years before the Revolution, was born (in 1869) and grew up in the village of Pokrovskoe, 50 km along the road from Tyumen to Tobolsk, on the Tura River. His father was a farmer and cart driver. Rasputin married locally at the age of 18 and had three children. Though his house in Pokrovskoe has been demolished, in 1993 a BBC television crew managed to find villagers who could tell them about his time there. Like many other Russian men, Rasputin drank a lot. Though not a monk as is sometimes supposed, he did pray a lot. Then, in his mid-20s, he experienced a vision of the Virgin while working in the fields, and left Pokrovskoe to seek enlightenment. On his wanderings he seems to have come to believe, as did the contemporary Khlyst (Whip) sect, that sinning (especially through sex), then repenting, could bring people close to God.

Early in the 20th century Rasputin reached St Petersburg, where some sectors of high society, with little better to do, took a big interest in holy peasants. Rasputin's soothing talk, compassion and generosity, and his teaching that promiscuity could bring redemption, made him very popular with some aristocratic women. His magnetic personality was apparently heightened by what the French ambassador called 'a strong animal smell, like that of a goat'.

Eventually Rasputin was summoned by Tsarina Alexandra and seemed able, thanks to some kind of hypnotic power, to cure the uncontrollable bleeding of her haemophiliac son, Tsarevich Alexey, the heir to the throne. As he continued his drunken, lecherous life, replete with famous orgies, Rasputin's influence on the royal family grew to the point where he could make or break the careers of ministers and generals. Naturally, this made him increasingly unpopular and many blamed him for the disasters of WW I. Rasputin's end finally came late in 1916 when Prince Felix Yusupov and others decided he had to be got rid of. (For the difficulties they encountered in achieving this, see the Teatralnaya Ploshchad Area section of the St Petersburg chapter.) ■

Bishop's Chambers (Zimny Riznitsa), the old Trading Arcades (Gostiny Dvor), and the **Bell tower** (Zvonnitsa) where a huge bronze imperial eagle, taken from the roof during the revolution, still lies on the floor. Between the foot of the cliff and the river is the old town, with many wooden houses and three decaying churches. The upper town, apart from the kremlin, is an ugly Soviet city with a petrochemical complex in the background.

If you need to stay over, the best, but most expensive, place is said to be the *Hotel Tobolsk*.

A few trains and buses run daily from Tyumen, but it should be possible to rent a taxi in Tyumen (try at the railway station there) for around US$25 or US$30 for a day trip. The drive is 2½ hours.

OMSK
ОМСК

Population: 1.3 million

This sprawling industrial city lies on the Trans-Siberian Railway at the point where the Om River enters the Irtysh, 900 km east of Yekaterinburg and 800 km west of Novosibirsk. Omsk started out in 1716 as a Cossack outpost, then in 1824 replaced Tobolsk as the seat of the governor general of Siberia. It became a major dumping ground for exiles, the best known of whom was Fyodor Dostoevsky. In *Buried Alive in Siberia*, he wrote about his wretched years in prison here (1849-53), during which he nearly died from a flogging. In the Civil War, Admiral Kolchak made Omsk the seat of his anti-Bolshevik government – until it was overrun in 1919.

Today it's a resoundingly ordinary place with lots and lots of apartment blocks ('Why do they live in such small flats in the middle of endless, empty Siberia?' asked one traveller), the Stary (Old) Krepost and Novy (New) Krepost 18th-century forts, a large 19th-century cathedral, a few neighbourhoods of dilapidated wooden houses, a park with an enormous WW II memorial, and a beach on the Irtysh. You can take boat excursions from the River Station. The *Irtysh* and *Turist* are probably the two best hotels.

There are flights three or four times a day to/from Moscow (3½ hours), most days to/from Yekaterinburg and Novosibirsk, and a few times a week to places like Krasnoyarsk, Irkutsk and Abakan. There's also the ambitious Omsk Airlines, which flies to/from Stuttgart, Düsseldorf and Hanover! By train, Yekaterinburg is about 12 hours away, Tyumen eight hours, Novosibirsk 9½ hours, and Moscow 42 hours.

Novosibirsk & Tomsk Regions
Новосибирская и Томская области

Novosibirsk, Siberia's biggest city, is a fairly common stopover on trans-Siberian packages, being conveniently about halfway between the Ural Mountains and Lake Baikal. If you want to see an archetypal Soviet city – it has grown from almost nothing since the 1920s – check it out. It's a fairly friendly, if very functional, place. Otherwise, the best thing about it is that you can head south to the Altay Mountains.

NOVOSIBIRSK
НОВОСИБИРСК

Population: 1.5 million

Novosibirsk, a city spawned by the Trans-Siberian Railway, was founded at the rail crossing of the Ob River in 1893, which makes it the youngest of Siberia's big cities. Until 1925, it was known as Novonikolaevsk. Its mushroom-like growth began in the 1920s when it was purpose-built as an industrial and transport centre, between the coal fields of the developing Kuzbass area to the east (centred on Kemerovo and Novokuznetsk) and the mineral deposits of the Ural region to the west. In the 1930s the building of the Turk-Sib railway south from Novosibirsk to Almaty in Kazakhstan made

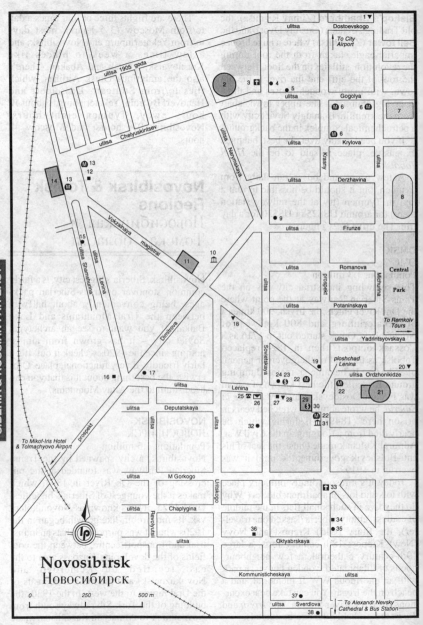

SIBERIA & RUSSIAN FAR EAST

To City Airport

ulitsa Dostoevskogo

ulitsa 1905 goda

ulitsa Chelyuskintsev

ulitsa Narymskaya

Gogolya

Krylova

Derzhavina

Frunze

Romanova

Potaninskaya

Yadrintsyovskaya

ploshchad Lenina

ulitsa Ordzhonikidze

Central Park

To Remkolv Tours

ulitsa 1905 goda

Vokzalnaya magistral

ulitsa Shamshurina

ulitsa Lenina

Dimitrova

Sovetskaya

Lenina

Deputatskaya

Uritskogo

M Gorkogo

Chaplygina

Oktyabrskaya

Kommunisticheskaya

Sverdlova

prospekt

Krasny

prospekt

Michurina

Revolyutsii

To Mikof-Iris Hotel & Tolmachyovo Airport

To Alexandr Nevsky Cathedral & Bus Station

Novosibirsk
Новосибирск

0   250   500 m

SIBERIA & RUSSIAN FAR EAST

the city a crucial transport link between Russia and Central Asia.

This is a very Soviet place – grey, functional, industrial and fond of statistics: biggest city (biggest railway station, biggest library) in Siberia, most sprawling after Moscow and St Petersburg, big airport, big dam. Pride of place goes to the Opera & Ballet Theatre, 'Siberia's Bolshoy', the biggest theatre in the country and the home of a respected ballet company and school.

Somehow the city manages to inspire a lot of loyalty among its natives.

You can make a trip out to Akademgorodok, the purpose-built 'Academy Township' created by the Soviet Academy of Sciences south of the city, near the Ob Sea reservoir.

Orientation
The city straddles the Ob, with the centre on its east side. The hub is ploshchad Lenina,

with the Opera & Ballet Theatre, and the two main axes are Krasny prospekt, running north-south through ploshchad Lenina, and Vokzalnaya magistral, running north-west from ploshchad Lenina to the railway station.

Information

Money Places you can change money include currency exchange desks in the main post office (Monday to Friday, 11 am to noon and 1 to 5 pm), the TsUM department store, and the lobby of the Hotel Sibir, Sibirsky Bank at ulitsa Lenina 4 (Monday to Friday, 9.30 am to 1 pm and 2 to 4 pm) and Sibirsky Torgovy Bank in the Tsentralny Komplex building facing ploshchad Lenina (Monday to Friday, 10.30 am to 1 pm and 2 to 6 pm). Sibirsky Bank offers Visa card cash advances.

Post & Telecommunications The main post office and the long-distance telephone office are a few doors apart on ulitsa Lenina. The post office has fax, telegram and EMS express post services. The Novosibirsk telephone code is 3832.

Travel Agencies For virtually any kind of trip in the Altay, you probably can't find better help than Sibalp (☎ 49 59 22; fax/answering machine 46 90 59; e-mail sibalp@niee.nsk.su). Its office is west of the Ob at ulitsa Nemirovicha-Danchenko 155/1, kvartira 47, but the director, Sergey Kurgin, can usually meet clients at their hotel. See the Altay Republic section for more on what Sibalp can offer. The Tourist Guides Union (Soyuz Provodnikov; ☎ 29 75 61, 29 57 78; fax 23 95 29) at ulitsa Lenina 30/2 may also be worth contacting – they specialise in rafting and sport-fishing in the Altay, Tuva and the far north.

There's a helpful Intourist service bureau in the Hotel Sibir lobby.

Maps Tsentralny Dom Kniga (Central House of Books), on ploshchad Lenina, has good 1:200,000 (one cm: two km) maps of some areas of Siberia, including parts of the Altay Mountains – worth looking at if you're heading for the hills or the outback. A plaque outside says Alexey Kosygin (Brezhnev's early partner in power) worked there from 1926 to 1930, when presumably it wasn't a bookshop. The kiosk in the Hotel Sibir foyer sells a decent city map for US$1.50.

Time Novosibirsk time is Moscow time plus three hours.

Film & Photography There's a Kodak Express print-processing outlet, with print film for sale too, in the TsUM department store on Vokzalnaya magistral.

Opera & Ballet Theatre

With the silver dome, giant portico and rich interior, this is indeed grand; many residents consider it the city's main attraction. They also agree that the sculptural ensemble out front is pretty ugly – Lenin, the *de rigueur* peasant, soldier and worker piece, and a couple representing the Socialist future but looking like they're directing traffic.

The classical ballet and opera inside are still good, too, despite recent financial problems, and it's easier to get in and see them here than it is in Moscow or St Petersburg. It's fun to watch Russian culture-vultures on a night out here – they look much happier than the people on the street. Novosibirsk takes ballet seriously. Its ballet school is among Russia's best.

The box office (kassa) is down on the left side of the theatre. Try to get tickets a day ahead.

Museums & Galleries

The **Local Studies Museum** (Kraevedchesky muzey) has two branches. The one at Vokzalnaya magistral 11 – actually a few yards up prospekt Dimitrova behind TsUM – ranges from a mammoth skeleton and stuffed animals through Siberian rocks and minerals to the development of Novosibirsk and the 'Uralo-Kuznetsky Kombinat' (basically the supplying of iron ore from the Ural region to the Kuzbass, and coal vice-versa – which accounts for a great deal of the freight traffic on the Trans-Siberian Railway). This branch is open Monday to Friday from 10 am to 6 pm but the displays are uninspired. More worthwhile is the museum's Krasny prospekt 19 branch, just off ploshchad Lenina, which focuses on applied art – mostly ceramics, with a very interesting collection of folk pottery from around Russia, some of it strangely reminiscent of Mexican folk pottery. Hours are 10 am to 4 pm, Monday to Friday. Next door is a hall for temporary exhibitions.

A few blocks down, at Krasny prospekt 5 on the corner of ulitsa Sverdlova, the **Art Gallery** (Kartinnaya galereya) includes 16 works by the turn-of-the-century Russian mystical painter Nikolay Rerikh (donated by him), plus changing exhibitions. Rerikh, who now enjoys international cult status, was obsessed for a while by the beauty and mystical qualities of the Altay Mountains south of Novosibirsk. The gallery is open from 11 am to 7 pm, closed Tuesday. Behind it, at ulitsa Sverdlova 13, the **Union of Artists' Gallery** (Vystavochny zal Soyuza khudozhnikov) shows ongoing exhibitions of local talent on the ground floor – open from 10 am to 6 pm except Monday – while upstairs is the commercial **Siberian Trade Bank Gallery** (Galereya Sibirskogo Torgovogo Banka).

Novosibirsk's **Russian Institute of Archaeology & Ethnography**, well known for its archaeological discoveries in the Altay Mountains, apparently has two very good museums: one with archaeological and ethnographic collections from throughout Siberia, the other an open-air museum of Siberian wooden architecture – try one of the travel agencies if you want to arrange visits.

Churches

The pretty little **Chapel of St Nicholas** (Chasovnya Svyatitelya Nikolaya), in the middle of Krasny prospekt two blocks south of ploshchad Lenina, is reckoned to be at the geographical centre of Russia. Originally built in 1915 to celebrate (two years late) 300 years of the Romanov dynasty, it was knocked down in the 1930s but rebuilt in 1993 for Novosibirsk's centenary. About 700 metres further down Krasny prospekt, the **Alexandr Nevsky Cathedral** (Sobor Alexandra Nevskogo), one of the city's first stone buildings, is under reconstruction.

The **Cathedral of the Ascension** (Vosnesenky Sobor) at ulitsa Sovietskaya 91, near the circus, has nice blue and gold domes, is beautiful inside, and dates from the early 1900s.

Other Attractions

Central Park (Tsentralny Park), north of the Opera & Ballet Theatre, has horse-drawn carts, a kids' railway, cafés, and outdoor music on summer weekends.

Cold? A traditional Russian **bathhouse** at ulitsa Sovietskaya 36 is open from 10 am to 10 pm daily except Wednesday. Only women are admitted on Tuesday, Friday and Sunday, only men on the other days. See 'A Russian Banya' under Petrozavodsk in the Northern European Russia chapter for background and etiquette.

Places to Stay

Travellers have told us that Inna Shmuriev of Remkolv Tours (☎ 22 88 84; fax 91 04 30), ulitsa Yadrintsyovskaya 48, kvartira 12, can arrange inexpensive accommodation in private flats or cheap hotels. Another possibility is the small 16-room *Hotel Sapfir* (Sapphire) at ulitsa Oktyabrskaya 49, with basic rooms at around US$6 to US$9 per person.

The huge *Hotel Novosibirsk* (☎ 20 11 20), opposite the railway station at Vokzalnaya magistral 1, has 888 typical rooms and, it says, the same prices for foreigners as for Russians. A 'II kategoria' double room with fridge, TV and phone but using shared bathrooms is US$22. Singles/doubles in 'I kategoria', with private bathrooms, are US$20/35. There are also 'lyux' suites at US$41 a double. The hotel has a restaurant, four bufety, and numerous shops and kiosks off the lobby.

The *Hotel Tsentralnaya* (☎ 22 72 94), in the city centre at ulitsa Lenina 3, is an older place with a range of dowdy but fairly clean

SIBERIA & RUSSIAN FAR EAST

and comfy rooms. The cheapest, at US$15/20 for singles/doubles, are 'kategoria III', with TV and washbasin but sharing clean toilets with other rooms (no showers). With private bathroom, fridge and TV (which may not work) you pay US$26/35. Other rooms go up to US$56 a double. There's a bufet on the 3rd floor.

The *Hotel Ob* (☎ 66 74 01), on the river bank three km south of the centre, a 750-metre walk south from Rechnoy Vokzal metro station, is an uninviting glass-and-concrete slab with singles at US$18, doubles at US$20 to US$28, and suites at US$35. All rooms have private bathroom, phone and TV.

Intourist's glossy, modern *Hotel Sibir* (☎ 23 12 15; fax 23 87 66) at ulitsa Lenina 21, on the corner of prospekt Dimitrova, has pleasant, comfortable rooms – and so it should have at US$85/100 for singles/doubles, US$125 for a suite. There's a good restaurant, a bufet on floor 7, and an Intourist service bureau.

The nicest place to stay is the small, independent *Otel Tsentr Rossii* (☎ 23 02 22; fax 23 49 52) at Krasny prospekt 28, 2½ blocks south of ploshchad Lenina. Aimed mainly at foreign business people, it has about 20 very comfortable suites for one, two or three people at US$110 to US$250 per suite. The hotel has its own good café and restaurant – and a great collection of landscape paintings adorning the walls.

There's a *Mikof-Iris Hotel* (☎ 41 01 55, 41 94 08; fax 40 37 37) several km west of the centre at ulitsa Kolkhidskaya 10, charging US$65/80 for singles/doubles including breakfast, or US$94/110 in suites. Ask a taxi driver for 'MNTK Mikrokhirurgii Glaza' (МНТК Микрохирургии ГлазаЪ).

Places to Eat

The Tsentralny Komplex building facing the west side of ploshchad Lenina has three eating places. Downstairs, the *Restoran Tsentralny*, on the ulitsa Lenina side, and the *Desertny Bar*, on the park side, are both gathering places for the city's young in the evenings. The restoran has good, quick light meals, snacks and drinks (the US$2 zharkoe

meat-and-vegetable hotpot is excellent), while the Desertny Bar has cakes, sweet dishes and fruit salad for US$0.50 or less – it's open from 10 am to 9.30 pm. Upstairs is a larger restaurant with a band and dancing in the evenings, when there's a US$2.50 entry charge. It stays open till the early hours.

Kafe Yunost on ulitsa Ordzhonikidze, behind the Opera & Ballet Theatre, is a relaxed café/restaurant with friendly service. The menu is limited to half a dozen zakuski (US$1 to US$3.50), one or two main meat dishes (US$1.50), and cakes and desserts – but the food goes down well. Hours are 11 am to 4 pm and 5 to 11 pm. Every evening there's live jazz from 7 pm.

A reasonable place for a main meal in the city centre is the *Restoran Druzhba* next door to the Hotel Tsentralnaya on ulitsa Lenina, open from noon to 5 pm and 7 pm to 1 am. Fare is standard Russian but good. A full meal with a drink or two comes to about US$10 or US$15. There's a band in the evening but it doesn't get wild.

Novosibirsk has two rather different Korean restaurants. *Stolovaya-Restoran Khekymgan* on Vokzalnaya magistral is a large cafeteria doing meatballs and noodles. You can eat quickly for US$2 or so. *Kafe Sobek* is a small, good Korean café, though with a few too many thickset men around, at ulitsa Dostoevskogo 19 (closest metro, Krasny Prospekt). A meal without drinks costs US$4 or US$5. Look for openers like che-namul (spicy, cold carrot salad) or kuksa (broth with egg, meat, carrots and hand-made noodles). Bulgogi is a beef dish, dakgogi is chicken. It's open from noon to 11 pm, closed Monday. Go at noon on the dot or between 2.30 and 4.30 pm – that way you miss the peak-hour lunch crowds and the evening mafia presence.

A full meal with a drink or two in the *Hotel Sibir's* excellent main 2nd-floor restaurant will come to around US$12 to US$15. You can also get a good breakfast in the hotel for about US$5.

The *Zolotoy Kolos* bakery, opposite the Hotel Tsentralnaya, has snacks, good coffee, ice cream, popcorn and a big choice of bread and cakes – a good place to stock up on Trans-Siberian supplies. Good bread is sold at stalls outside, too. The well-stocked central market is by Krasny Prospekt metro.

Entertainment

Aside from opera and ballet, the big theatre on ploshchad Lenina also houses the concert hall of the excellent Novosibirsk Philharmonic Society. Pop and rock concerts are sometimes held here. There's nightly jazz in the Kafe Yunost (see Places to Eat), and occasional recitals and chamber concerts in the Conservatory on ulitsa Sovietskaya. There's a circus on ulitsa Chelyuskintsev.

Things to Buy

The Hotel Sibir has a souvenir stall and the Krasny prospekt branch of the Local Studies Museum sells some appealing folk pottery. The railway station forecourt is filled, and Vokzalnaya magistral lined, with kiosks selling everything from popcorn to plimsolls – nothing exotic but probably the best places to look for everyday needs. The main department store in the city centre is TsUM on Vokzalnaya magistral. A huge flea market called the Barakholka (barakhlo means junk) goes on at weekends in the east of the city. Buses run from Rechnoy Vokzal metro. Hang on to your wallet.

Getting There & Away

Air Novosibirsk has two airports. Tolmachyovo, 20 km west of the centre off the Omsk road, is for most longer flights; the City Airport (Gorodskoy aeroport, also called Aeroport Novosibirsk), at the north end of Krasny prospekt, six km from ploshchad Lenina, is for shorter ones.

Lufthansa flies to/from Frankfurt twice a week and there are cheaper charter flights with Luftbrücke from Düsseldorf (see Siberia & the Far East Getting There & Away). Other scheduled flights to/from Tolmachyovo include Moscow (four hours) a few times daily (including by Transaero); Yekaterinburg and Irkutsk daily; St Petersburg, Omsk and Yakutsk most days; and Abakan, Almaty (Kazakhstan), Barnaul,

Bishkek (Kyrgyzstan), Magadan and Tomsk one to three times a week. At the City Airport, flights are scheduled to/from Krasnoyarsk and Kyzyl daily, and Gorno-Altaysk and a few cities in northern Kazakhstan a few days a week. You may find some flights are cancelled.

Lufthansa (☎ 22 71 51, 69 69 58) is at Tolmachyovo, and Transaero (☎ 23 19 17) is at Krasny prospekt 28. Luftbrücke is on ☎ 23 35 89. Other tickets for foreigners are sold at the Aeroflot international sector (mezhdunarodnyy sektor) office at ulitsa Gogolya 3, open Monday to Saturday from 9 am to 12.30 pm and 2 to 6 pm (on Thursdays it doesn't open till 11 am and on Saturdays it closes at 5 pm). Officially this office does not sell tickets on the day of travel (you're supposed to get those at the airports) but the scent of a foreigners' dollars may bring special help – and can also help you jump the queues.

Bus The bus station is an unmarked grey building at Krasny prospekt 4, 1.5 km south of ploshchad Lenina. There are buses about hourly to Barnaul (five hours) from 8 am to 7 pm, two a day to Biysk (7½ hours) and six a day to Tomsk (six hours). A private-enterprise 'Kommerchesky Express' bus runs to the bus station from the railway station forecourt, half-hourly from 7.15 to 11.45 am and 2.15 to 8.15 pm.

Train Numerous long-distance trains run through Novosibirsk daily. They go not only east and west across Siberia, but also south along the Turk-Sib line to Almaty, Bishkek and Tashkent. The station is Novosibirsk Glavny, at the west end of Vokzalnaya magistral.

The Trans-Siberian, Trans-Mongolian and Trans-Manchurian trains all come through but you're usually better off getting one of the other trains, which are less likely to be booked up. To/from Yekaterinburg and Moscow (Yaroslavl Station), one of the best is the daily 'Sibiryak', No 25/26. It takes 51 hours to Moscow. Eastbound, there are usually two or three trains a day going as far as Vladivostok (4½ days), six or seven to Irkutsk (31 to 35 hours), and nine or 10 to Krasnoyarsk (13 to 14 hours). The twice-weekly Moscow-Ulan Bator service (No 5/6) also comes through. Services to places off the main trans-Siberian line include trains at least daily to Barnaul, Biysk and Abakan, and most days to Severobaikalsk and Tynda on the BAM line.

On the Turk-Sib, there's service at least daily to/from Almaty (32 to 37 hours) via Semey (Semipalatinsk), and trains three or four times a week to/from Bishkek and Tashkent.

Tickets Novosibirsk has two special train ticket offices for foreigners, both away from the station and of course charging foreigners' prices – though queues are shorter than at the Russians' offices. For journeys within the ex-USSR (which includes Kazakhstan and Central Asia), same-day and advance tickets are sold at ulitsa Shamshurina 10, about 250 metres south of the station. This office is open Monday to Friday from 9 am to 1 pm and 2 to 5 pm. Destinations outside the ex-USSR (eg Mongolia or China) are handled by the Intourist office (☎ 98 23 33) at prospekt Dimitrova 2 in the Bank Vostok building near the Hotel Sibir, which is open Monday to Friday from 9 am to noon and 1 to 6 pm (closing at 5 pm on Fridays). Owing to the existence of these offices, you might have difficulty getting Russian-price tickets, but there's nothing to stop you trying. At the station, window Nos 11 to 14 are supposedly for same-day departures. There's an advance-booking office (predvaritelnye zheleznodorozhnye kassy) at ulitsa Soviet-skaya 50, open Monday to Saturday from 9 am to 1 pm and 2 to 7 pm.

Getting Around
To/From the Airports Express bus No 111Э runs back and forth between the two airports via the railway station and various other stops in the centre, including the Hotel Sibir and Krasny Prospekt metro. Service is roughly half-hourly from 5.30 am to 7 pm, except for two gaps in the schedule from

about 9 to 10.30 am and 3 to 4.30 pm. Outbound, be careful that your bus is going to the right airport. The trip from the station to Tolmachyovo is about 50 minutes, to the City Airport about 20 minutes. Bus No 122 runs between the station (from the street in front of the Hotel Novosibirsk) and Tolmachyovo every half-hour or so from 5.15 am to 11 pm. Trolleybus No 5 runs between the City Airport and Oktyabrskaya metro.

A taxi to the City Airport should be about US$2.50, to Tolmachyovo about US$4.

Metro Buses and trolleybuses around the city centre don't seem to follow any handy routes but Novosibirsk has a useful metro system. Currently there's just one line, running beneath Krasny prospekt much of its length, with a one-stop branch to the tongue-twisting Ploshchad Garina-Mikhaylovskogo station, which is at the railway station. The interchange station is Sibirskaya/Krasny Prospekt. Ploshchad Lenina is one stop south of Krasny Prospekt.

Boat From the River Station (Rechnoy Vokzal) by the Hotel Ob (metro Rechnoy Vokzal) there are local boats in summer (April/May to September/October) to various points within a few hours up and down the Ob, including occasionally to places on the Ob Sea like Zavyalovo, Ordynsk and Chingisy. These could make interesting excursions, but double-check schedules as services have been curtailed in recent years.

AKADEMGORODOK & THE OB SEA
АКАДЕМГОРОДОК И ОБСКОЕ МОРЕ
This 'academic township' nestled in the taiga 30 km south of Novosibirsk was founded in the 1950s by the Siberian branch of the Soviet Academy of Sciences as a think-tank for its scholars and researchers. With 23 institutes on everything from economics to genetics, 65,000 workers and their families, well-stocked shops and two-storey dachas for top academics, it was a highly prestigious

place to be educated and used to give a revealing glimpse of how the Soviet elite lived. But, like every other state enterprise, it has suffered from the economic slump and now seems a slightly forlorn place.

There isn't really much to *see* in Akademgorodok. The best part is the setting – quiet, wooded, full of birdsong, and a 15-minute walk from the 'Ob Sea' (Obskoe More), the 200-km-long reservoir behind a nearby dam on the Ob. It's said to be good for swimming, and local people come in droves on summer weekends.

If you want to learn much about Akademgorodok, and enter the institutes' museums, you should come on a guided trip – try Intourist or other travel agencies in Novosibirsk. The museums aren't generally open to casual callers, and there aren't enough tour groups any more to rely on tagging along with one. A highlight is the Geological Museum (Geologichesky Muzey) in the Institute of Geology (Institut Geologii) at Universitetsky prospekt 3, with a dazzling Siberian mineral collection. The Museum of the History & Culture of Siberian Peoples (Muzey Istorii i Kultury Narodov Sibiri) is an academic version of the Novosibirsk Museum of Local Studies.

Orientation & Information

The Novosibirsk map sold in the city's Hotel Sibir includes Akademgorodok. From Akademgorodok's Obskoe More station, the Ob Sea beach is down to the right (west) of the tracks, while Akademgorodok itself begins one km to the left, through the woods. A good way to orient yourself is to turn right along the main road that you hit 200 metres inland from the station, then take the first road on the left, which is Morskoy prospekt. The first street left off Morskoy prospekt is ulitsa Zhemchuzhnaya and the second is ulitsa Ilicha, with Akademgorodok's main shops, a fee-charging information kiosk and the Hotel Zolotaya Dolina. Head 200 metres to the right through the trees opposite the Hotel Zolotaya Dolina to come out on Universitetsky prospekt.

Places to Stay & Eat

The *Hotel Zolotaya Dolina* (☎ (3832) 35 66 09) at ulitsa Ilicha 10 has singles/doubles with private bathroom, fridge and TV for about US$25/60, plus a restaurant and a bufet. There's cheap food in the cafeteria (kafeterii) upstairs in the *Torgovy Tsentr* (Trade Centre), a shopping centre on the same street.

Getting There & Away

Suburban trains run from Novosibirsk Glavny station to Obskoe More station 16 to 20 times daily. The trip is 50 minutes. You can also pick them up at Rechnoy Vokzal railway station, across the road behind Rechnoy Vokzal metro station. You need any train that's heading for Berdsk, Iskitim, Lozhok, Linevo or Cherepanovo. Alternatively, from Rechnoy Vokzal metro take bus No 8Э (45 minutes to Akademgorodok) or the slower bus No 22. Returning to Novosibirsk, you can pick up the buses at the stop on ulitsa Zhemchuzhnaya just off Morskoy prospekt. On summer weekends (and some other times too) both buses and trains are packed solid.

TOMSK
ТОМСК
Population: 520,000

Tomsk, 270 km north-east of Novosibirsk, is perhaps Siberia's greatest might-have-been city. One of Siberia's oldest cities (founded 1604), until the Trans-Siberian Railway was built, it was also one of the most important – an administrative and commercial town on the Great Siberian Trakt at its Tom River crossing.

When it was bypassed by the railway (one story says it was a ghastly miscalculation by the city fathers, who felt that trains would just bring noise, dirt and disruption), Tomsk faded. In the Soviet era Tomsk was closed to foreigners because of Tomsk-7 (population 110,000), 16 km north, part of the 'nuclear archipelago' of 10 secret weapons research and production centres. Since Tomsk was opened, events haven't exactly encouraged people to visit. In 1993 an explosion at

Tomsk-7 scattered radioactivity over an estimated 120-sq-km area. Its spread was limited because snow was falling at the time, and no-one was evacuated. Then in 1994 Tomsk was the centre of a tuberculosis epidemic.

Nevertheless, it's apparently still a stately town, with some of the finest examples of Siberian wooden houses, with filigree-like decoration and carved façades. The library and medical school here were among Russia's earliest. There are fine arts and local studies museums, a botanical garden, the SS Peter & Paul Cathedral, and a Polish Catholic cathedral.

The *Oktyabrskaya* and *Rubin* are said to be the best hotels.

Getting There & Away

Tomsk is 80 km up a branch line from the Trans-Siberian Railway at Tayga. Through trains run from Novosibirsk and Moscow, and there are buses from Novosibirsk. From the east, you have to change trains at Tayga. There are flights from Novosibirsk, Krasnoyarsk and Moscow and elsewhere. The hydrofoil service along the Ob and Tom rivers from Novosibirsk was cancelled at the time of research.

Altay Republic
Республика Алтай

The Altay Mountains are one of the most beautiful and pristine parts of Siberia. They rise in the Altay Republic (Respublika Altay), which begins 450 km south-east of Novosibirsk, and stretch south into Kazakhstan, China and Mongolia. Siberia's highest peak, 4506-metre Mt Belukha, stands on the Kazakhstan border. To reach the Altay Republic from Novosibirsk, you must cross the separate Altay Territory (Altaysky kray) and usually make transport connections in one of its two main towns, Barnaul or Biysk.

Few foreigners get to this remote corner

of Siberia but those who do – to trek, climb, raft its wild rivers or track down its archaeological sites – won't forget its haunting beauty. The turn-of-the-century Russian mystical artist Nikolay Rerikh considered this one of the world's charmed places and captured its drama in many canvases. Foreigners who do come are mostly on organised adventure packages from other countries, but it's quite possible to travel in the Altay on your own – and to find good adventure guides in Novosibirsk or even locally. June to August are the best months here, though it can rain at any time.

The Altay Republic's highest country is in the south and east, and the mountains are divided by several river valleys, mostly running south-east to north-west. There's a great variety of landscape, from steppe to taiga to glaciers to semidesert, plus 7000 lakes, wild rivers and beautiful waterfalls. The Katun River, flowing down the centre of the republic from the Gebler glacier on Mt Belukha, and the Chulyshman River in the east, flowing into Lake Teletskoe, provide some of Russia's most challenging whitewater rafting. The Katun is dotted with rapids all the way from Ust-Koxa in the south-west of the republic to Gorno-Altaysk in the north – though there are calmer stretches along the way. Altay fauna includes bears, wolves, lynx, mountain goats, elk, deer, even snow leopards, and the flora is equally varied, with glorious alpine flowers in summer.

Foreign tourists are supposed to pay US$100 for a special voucher to enter the Altay Republic. Travel companies are supposed to collect this but local ones may be able to find ways of reducing or avoiding it, and if you go on your own you may well escape it.

Altay Republic time is Moscow time plus four hours.

History

The Denisova Cave in the Anuy River valley, about 100 km south-west of Gorno-Altaysk, was inhabited from the early Palaeolithic (Old Stone Age) period, possibly as early as

Altay Republic
Республика Алтай

0   50   100 km

300,000 BC, to the Middle Ages. Many important finds from different epochs have been made here.

The Altay is best known among archaeologists for its seminomadic, horse-riding, sheep-herding Pazyryk culture of the 6th to 2nd centuries BC. Pazyryk is considered part of the Scytho-Siberian cluster of cultures which stretched all the way to the steppes north of the Black Sea, which were dominated about the same time by the famous Scythians. The Pazyryks and Scythians had similar art styles.

Thanks to the Altay climate and the struc-

ture of their tombs, built underground beneath mounds *(kurgany)*, many Pazyryk burials have been wonderfully preserved. Rain or melting snow would seep into the tombs, which would then freeze and remain encased in ice for thousands of years. The Hermitage in St Petersburg displays mummified corpses, a funeral chariot, wood carvings and a wool carpet from a group of Pazyryk chieftains' tombs in the Ust-Ulagan Valley, opened in the 1940s by archaeologists from Novosibirsk's Russian Institute of Archaeology & Ethnography. The next major Pazyryk find didn't come until 1993, when the institute's diggers uncovered a noblewoman's tomb on the bleak Ukok Plateau, 2200 metres high in the far south-west of the Altay Republic. Along with a mummified corpse – decorated with tattoos of deer – were found sacrificed horses in regalia, silk and wool clothes, and gilded ornaments. This find is described in detail in the October 1994 *National Geographic*. Other Pazyryk tomb-mounds, some in groups, are at Sooru (west of Onguday), near Tuekta and Chemal, and north-east of Tashanta.

Also dotted around the republic are several groups of interesting petroglyphs (rock drawings). Their origins are debatable, but they're possibly from the Altay people's old shamanistic nature religion.

The Altay was within the northern range of the Turkic peoples who controlled much of southern Siberia and Central Asia from about the 6th century AD, and the modern Altay language is Turkic. From about the 15th century the Altay was under the rule of the Oyrats or Dzungarians from western Mongolia, until the Oyrats were wiped out by the Chinese in the 1750s. This was followed by a century of quarrels between

Russia and China over the region, until Russia prevailed in 1864.

Some Altay people were converted to Orthodox Christianity, but in 1904 a unique local religion, known to Russians as Burkhanism and combining elements of Buddhism with non-Buddhist Oyrat folk traditions, was born when an Altay shepherd called Chet Chelpan learned in a vision that a messianic figure called Oirot would come to lead his people to freedom. This stimulated anti-Russian feeling and was banned by the communists in 1933, by which time the formerly seminomadic Altay people had been largely collectivised. Whether or not Burkhanism will revive, elements of the old nature religion, such as horse hides hung on branches or sticks, still survive.

Formerly the Gorno-Altayskaya Autonomous Region, the Altay Republic became a full republic within Russia in 1991.

People

The Altay Republic is sparsely populated, with just 200,000 people. About 60% are Russians, 28% are native Altay people, and 5% are Kazakhs (mainly in the far southeast). The Altay, a Turkic-speaking people, are mostly village-dwellers, but a few are still seminomadic, moving with their herds to different pastures according to the season and living in yurts in summer. Settled families still sometimes keep yurts in their gardens as an extra room or kitchen for summer use. In the remoter areas the horse is still the main means of transport. Watch out for drunks.

The mainstays of the rural economy are sheep, goats, cattle, yaks and horses. Maral deer – whose antlers are considered to have aphrodisiac properties – and camels are bred on a few farms.

Information

Travel Agencies The popularity of the Altay among Western adventure travel firms goes up and down. Costs in Russia have been a deterrent to some, but companies who have offered trips in recent years include Exodus, Steppes East, Mountain Travel Sobek and

Modern Altay calendar

Wilderness Expeditions – see Travel Agencies in Siberia & the Far East Getting There & Away for more on these firms. Otto Frei Kulturreisen (☎ (031) 859 73 24; fax (031) 859 73 25) of Moosstrasse 8A, CH-3322 Schönbühl, Switzerland, has offered archaeological trips based at the Russian Institute of Archaeology & Ethnography's hotel near Denisova Cave. Australia's Red Bear Tours (see Independent Travel in the Trans-Siberian Railway chapter) may also do Altay archaeological trips.

The Moscow firms Pilgrim Tours, Travel Russia, Sputnik and CCTE-Intour also offer Altay trips – for details of these firms, see the Activities sections in European Russia Facts for the Visitor and Siberia & the Far East Facts for the Visitor.

More locally, for virtually any kind of trip in the Altay, one excellent firm to contact is Sibalp in Novosibirsk (see Information in the Novosibirsk section). This small agency, run by an experienced and knowledgeable Altay-born climber, Sergey Kurgin, has worked with several Western travel firms. Sibalp says it can arrange trips with about two days' notice, possibly longer for rafting. Typical costs for groups of four or more are US$50 or US$60 per person per day. Smaller groups will have to pay more per person. The Tourist Guides Union and Intourist in Novosibirsk are also worth contacting.

Maps Good 1:200,000 (one cm: two km) maps of parts of the Altay are sold at Tsentralny Dom Kniga in Novosibirsk.

BARNAUL
БАРНАУЛ

Barnaul, a rather old-fashioned medium-sized city 230 km south of Novosibirsk, is a possible staging post on the way to or from the Altay Mountains. Founded in 1739 as a fort, it's now the capital of a region called the Altay Territory (Altaysky Kray), which is distinct from the Altay Republic, where the mountains are. Between Novosibirsk and Barnaul you enter a new time zone: Barnaul is on Moscow time plus four hours.

Handily, the railway and bus stations are right next door to each other, on ploshchad Pobedy. If you have time to waste and want to see the city centre, go one km to the left from ploshchad Pobedy to Oktyabrskaya ploshchad, then one km to the right along prospekt Lenina to ploshchad Sovietov. Or head to the Local Studies Museum (Altaysky kraevoy kraevedchesky muzey), the oldest museum in Siberia, founded in 1823 and open Wednesday to Sunday from 10 am to 6 pm. This is 2.5 km straight ahead along ulitsa Krasnoarmeyskaya past the Hotel Barnaul as you leave ploshchad Pobedy, then a short distance left on ulitsa Polzunova.

If you need to stay, the *Hotel Barnaul* (☎ (3852) 25 25 81) at ulitsa Pobedy 9, across the street from ploshchad Pobedy, is decaying but has friendly staff. Standard rooms (without shower) are US$28 a single or double; 'lyux' rooms with bathroom are US$56. The hotel has an adequate restaurant with a band in the evenings, and a *Kafe*, open from 8 am to 8 pm, where you can eat more quietly.

Getting There & Away

If you can't get convenient direct transport between Novosibirsk and Biysk or Gorno-Altaysk, you could come to Barnaul and change. This is the place where the road to the Altay Mountains (and the railway as far as Biysk) split from the road and railway south to Kazakhstan. Leaving Barnaul, buses are generally an easier option than trains, as most trains are in transit and it can be hard to get tickets.

You can fly to/from Novosibirsk, Krasnoyarsk, Gorno-Altaysk, even Moscow, if the flights aren't cancelled. There are about 12 buses and several trains daily to/from Novosibirsk (five to six hours); 17 buses and four trains to/from Biysk (3½ hours); and seven buses to/from Gorno-Altaysk (5½ hours). There are also daily trains to/from Moscow (Kazan Station) and Almaty in Kazakhstan, and every couple of days to/from Krasnoyarsk, Irkutsk, Bishkek and Tashkent. To/from Semey (Semipalatinsk), the nearest city in Kazakhstan, there's one daily bus and four or five trains, all taking about 10 hours.

BIYSK
БИЙСК

Biysk, 160 km south-east of Barnaul, is the nearest railhead to the Altay Mountains and, like Barnaul, is a place you may need to change transport on the way to/from the mountains. Again, the bus and railway stations are next door to each other. One or two overnight trains (11 hours) and two daytime buses (7½ hours) come daily from Novosibirsk. There are nine buses to/from Gorno-Altaysk (2½ hours), departing from 7.20 am to 8.30 pm, and also daily buses to Shebalino, Onguday and Chemal, beyond Gorno-Altaysk, all leaving between 10.30 am and 3 pm. See Barnaul for transport to/from there. The *Hotel Tsentralnaya*, a km or two east of the stations, apparently has rooms for about US$25 a double.

GORNO-ALTAYSK
ГОРНО-АЛТАЙСК

Population: 47,000

The capital of the Altay Republic is an unlovely Soviet-style place just across the border from the Altaysky Kray, 467 km from Novosibirsk, 264 km from Barnaul and 103 km from Biysk. It's useful only for transport connections and to stock up on supplies. The town is seven km south-east off the main M52 road, from a turn-off at Mayma. About the only thing of interest is the **Local Studies Museum** (Kraevedchesky muzey) which has a reconstructed Pazyryk burial and material on Palaeolithic sites, petroglyphs, fauna and the history of the Chuysky Trakt road to the Mongolian border. The museum is on ulitsa Gorno-Altayskaya, which is parallel to the main street, Kommunisticheskaya ulitsa. Walk out the back of the bus station and head left for a couple of hundred metres. Opening days are Wednesday to Sunday, from 10 am to 5 pm.

Places to Stay

The *Hotel Turist* next to the bus station has reasonable rooms with private toilets (but no showers) for US$12 a double, US$15 a triple. About one km up Kommunisticheskaya ulitsa then to the right on the short ulitsa Babushkina, facing a park with a Lenin statue, the *Hotel Gorny Altay* has grumpy management and doubles with toilet for US$15, or 'lyux' rooms with a sitting room, shower and toilet (but no hot water) for US$50.

Getting There & Away

Flights from Novosibirsk are scheduled three times a week but they had been cancelled at the time of research. There may be flights from Barnaul and to Kosh-Agach and Ust-Koxa, which have airstrips. It may also be possible to hire helicopters. Try calling the airport (☎ (3854) 21 96, 52 25) to ask. The Aeroflot ticket office is next to the bus station. The airport is 12 km from town, off the M52, five km south of Mayma. Buses run between the airport and the bus station (40 minutes) a few times a day.

By land you have to get to Barnaul or Biysk (see those sections) then take a bus. A good way from Novosibirsk is the overnight train to Biysk. Buses run to Gorno-Altaysk from Barnaul (5½ hours) seven times daily and from Biysk (2½ hours) 13 times.

Bus services around the Altay Republic may be curtailed by petrol shortages. An alternative is to hitchhike by trying to flag vehicles down. Locals usually pay the equivalent of the bus fare for a ride (the 465-km bus trip from Gorno-Altaysk to Kosh-Agach costs US$7.50). From Gorno-Altaysk, once-daily buses were scheduled at the time of research to Manzherok (one hour; 2.50 pm), Shebalino (three hours; 10.35 am), Onguday (six hours; 3.30 pm), Aktash (11 hours; 8.40 am), Kosh-Agach (12½ hours; 7.05 am), Kokorya (13 hours; 6.40 am), and Tyungur (28 hours including an overnight stop in Ust-Kan; 1.05 pm).

CHUYSKY TRAKT
ЧУЙСКИЙ ТРАКТ

The Chuysky Trakt is the 510-km stretch of the M52 from Mayma near Gorno-Altaysk to Tashanta on the Mongolian border. The border was open only to local commercial traffic at the time of research, and individual travellers are unlikely to get across unless the rules have been eased. The best chance might be to try for a ride in a commercial vehicle (ie a truck).

The Chuysky Trakt was built before WW II, at least partly by Gulag labour. It's said that workers who died were buried beneath the road. The road runs near the Katun River as far as Ust-Sema, about 70 km from Gorno-Altaysk, briefly rejoins the Katun before Inya (375 km), then follows the tributary Chuya River from Inya to Kosh-Agach. It passes through a variety of valley landscapes and reaches some pretty out-of-the-way places, with long distances between the few villages. Despite its 'M' label, the road is often narrow and unpaved. Seven daily buses run from Gorno-Altaysk to various places on and off the trakt (see the Gorno-Altaysk section).

Lake Aya
Озеро Ая
The warm water of little Lake Aya, 25 km from Gorno-Altaysk, makes it a popular local outing. Follow the 'Aya 8' sign pointing to the right (west), 14 km south of Mayma, crossing a wooden suspension bridge over the Katun, and after three km turn left at the crossroads with 'Beryozka' and 'Ozero Aya' signs. It's then less than one km to the lake. The modern Yugoslav-built Aya Otel (☎ (38542) 4 14 91 or (38541) 2 27 64) by the lake has comfortable double and triple rooms at US$35 or US$40 per person, some with balconies overlooking the lake, and a decent restaurant. Three-hour easy rafting trips on a fairly sedate stretch of the Katun can be arranged at the hotel for US$7.50 per person. A taxi to Lake Aya from Gorno-Altaysk is about US$7.50.

Manzherok
Манжерок
About 30 km south of Mayma is the little private-enterprise Turkomplex Manzherok (☎ (3852) 44 32 18; ☎ & fax (3852) 41 77 13), beautifully sited in a pine grove on the

bank of the Katun. Here you can rent a two-person tent for US$2 or a two or three-bed room, with bathroom, for US$10. The friendly owners can provide three meals a day for US$6 and set up horse or raft trips. The site, with a bus stop outside on the main road, is one km north of Manzherok village, and 700 metres south of a black statue on a grey pedestal by the river bank. The statue is of Vyacheslav Shushkov, a Siberian engineer and writer who planned the Chuysky Trakt.

Cherga & Shebalino
Черга и Шебалино
The villages of Cherga, about 75 km from Mayma, and Shebalino (110 km) have maral deer farms. The one at Shebalino is five or six km along the road leading west up a valley from the south end of the village.

Seminsky Pass
Семинский перевал
On this pass (Seminsky pereval) over the Seminsky Range, a northern outlier of the Altay, 145 km from Mayma, is the Uchebno Trenirovochny Tsentr (UTTS), a state-run sports training centre, with the Czech-owned Hotel Lena (☎ (38547) 2 21 31). The hotel has cottages with two double rooms, a bathroom and a sitting room, as well as comfortable hotel rooms with bathroom for up to four people. The quoted price for foreigners is US$40 per person including meals in the stolovaya (cafeteria), but you can probably do a deal without food and pay US$25 or so. There are good walks in the surrounding hills.

Onguday
Онгудай
There's an extremely basic little hotel behind the bus stop in the middle of this village, just down to the west of the road, 190 km from Mayma. Bare rooms are US$2 per person. The toilet is out the back. At Sooru, west of Onguday, is the 'Tsar' group of Pazyryk aristocrats' burial mounds, in a picturesque valley.

Ilgumen Rapids, Yaloman & Inya
Пороги Ильгумень, Яломан и Иня

The Chuysky Trakt rejoins the Katun for a brief stretch between the river's wild Ilgumen rapids, about 60 km after Onguday, and Inya. The rapids are a starting place for white-water rafting trips down to Chemal. The bluff overlooking the start of the rapids, between the Katun and the tributary Ilgumen River, is a good place to camp.

Yaloman, the next village, has an unusual microclimate which enables its Altay people to grow cherries and apples.

Directly across the road from the 721 Km marker, between Inya and Iodro, is a crag with many petroglyphs. If you have no guide you'll have to look hard to find them but you should succeed. Maral deer and hunters are easily identifiable, and there's something that looks like a tiger, but one design which crops up a few times is harder to make out – it might be a shaman, it might be abstract, some Russians reckon it's a rocket.

Lake Shavlo
Озеро Шавлинское

From Chibit, about 350 km from Mayma, a track leads south to beautiful Lake Shavlo (Ozero Shavlinskoe), a two-day walk away at the foot of the Chuysky Range (see Southern Altay Republic).

Aktash
Акташ

A turn-off to the north here, 100 km before Kosh-Agach, leads to Ust-Ulagan (60 km), near the famous Pazyryk burial mounds opened in the 1940s. There's a daily bus service to Ust-Ulagan. Aktash has a depressing dump of a *hotel* on ulitsa Staraya Mokhova, facing the Produkty shop, that charges US$2.75 per person. The rooms have nothing except beds; there's a communal washbasin in another room. You probably won't find anyone around till late afternoon.

Ortolyk
Ортолык

A few km before Kosh-Agach, this is the first Kazakh village along the Chuysky Trakt.

Kosh-Agach
Кош-Агач

The 'capital' of the south-east of the Altay Republic, Kosh-Agach is like the end of the world – a small town spread for no apparent reason in the middle of a wide, bleak, high, bare plain stretching in either direction to forbidding distant mountains. If you want to go somewhere that's a bit different, try it. Most of the people here are Kazakh, with a few Altay and Russians. Here, in the middle of nowhere, they have an airstrip, a few streets of one-storey houses, a town hall, a small market, a petrol station and, naturally, a Dom Kultury (House of Culture). There's even the *Hotel Tsentralnaya* on the square facing the Dom Kultury, with basic rooms for US$2.75 per person. It has a washroom inside but the toilet is a shed out the back.

Kokorya, across the plain to the east, is an Altay village. Tashanta, the border post on the Russian side of the Mongolian border, is 50 km down the road (see the 'So You Think You're a Traveller?' aside in the Siberia & the Russian Far East Getting There & Away chapter).

SOUTHERN ALTAY REPUBLIC
РЕСПУБЛИКА АЛТАЙ, ЮГО-ЗАПАДНАЯ ЧАСТЬ

The Altay Republic's highest mountains are in the south-west – the Katunsky Range, culminating in Mt Belukha, and the Northern Chuysky Range, running east-west between the Chuya and Argut rivers, with several challenging peaks topped by 4173-metre Mt Aktru. These areas offer some of the best trekking and climbing in the Altay.

According to some Asian legends, the Belukha area is the future location of Shambhala, a paradisiac realm that will come into existence after humanity destroys itself. Others believe Shambhala is a state of heightened energy and awareness induced by supernatural phenomena or inner means – or perhaps simply by experiencing the wild beauty of Belukha!

The road to Belukha goes through some remote areas, with scattered villages. At Ust-Kan there's a basic *hotel* and in the nearby

Altay village of Mendur-Sokkon is an **Altay ethnographic museum**. Ust-Koxa, at the confluence of the Koxa and Katun rivers, has an airstrip, and Verkhny Uymon has a **Nikolay Rerikh House-Museum**. A daily bus (486 km with an overnight stop at Ust-Kan) is scheduled from Gorno-Altaysk to Tyungur, on the Katun River, the usual starting point of treks in the Belukha area.

At Tolono, on the high bank of the Katun downstream of Tyungur, are some **Turkic stone sculptures** of warriors killed in battle, dating from about 500 AD. There's a small **Rafters' Museum** where the Argut flows into the Katun.

Trekking

The basic trek, a minimum of five days, covers the northern approaches to Belukha. From Tyungur the route is south up the Kucherla River valley to beautiful Lake Kucherla. The *Turistichesky Komplex Kucherla* (☎ (3852) 25 66 72) has cabins for two or three people at Tyungur and Lake Kucherla and also offers hiking, rafting, boating, horse-riding and climbing trips.

Yaks inhabit the high pastures of the Altay Republic

There's a petroglyph site in the Kucherla valley. From Lake Kucherla you cross the 2800-metre Kara-Tyurek Pass to Lake Akkem, in the next valley east, parallel to the Kucherla. From Lake Akkem there are great views of Belukha and its ice wall if you're lucky with the weather. There are mountaineers' huts here where you may be able to stay. You descend the Akkem valley, crossing north-west over the Kiziyak Pass back to Tyungur. This trek is described in *Trekking in Russia & Central Asia* (see Books in Siberia & the Far East Facts for the Visitor).

Variations on the basic route include side-hikes to Darashkol Lake from Lake Kucherla, or up to the Akkem Glacier above Lake Akkem (this is the normal mountaineers' approach to Belukha itself). There is also a six or seven-day eastward extension across the Argut River to Lake Shavlo and Chibit on the Chuysky Trakt. Lake Shavlo is a base for climbs in the Northern Chuysky Range.

EASTERN ALTAY REPUBLIC
РЕСПУБЛИКА АЛТАЙ, ВОСТОЧНАЯ ЧАСТЬ

Lake Teletskoe is the Altay's biggest lake, surrounded by forests and very deep at 325 metres. A few local tourism bases are dotted along its shores, including cabins at the north end (Zolotoe Ozero) and the south end, and ferries run along its length. Trekking is possible around here in late spring and early autumn as well as in summer. Treks to the south end of the lake from Edigan, about 50 km south of Chemal (highest pass, 2600 metres), and from Balyktuyul, about 15 km north of Ust-Ulagan, with passes up to 2000 metres, are described in *Trekking in Russia & Central Asia*. The Chulyshman River flowing into the south end of the lake is a white-water favourite. East of the lake and the Chulyshman, the **Altay Nature Reserve** (Altaysky zapovednik) stretches to the borders of Khakassia and Tuva. At the time of research buses from Gorno-Altaysk to Artybash at the north end of the lake, the only village on the lake reached by road, had been cancelled.

SIBERIA & RUSSIAN FAR EAST

Krasnoyarsk Territory
Красноярский край

The Krasnoyarsk Territory (Krasnoyarsky Kray) is a region of great mineral and forest wealth stretching from south of its capital, Krasnoyarsk, all the way to the Arctic coast. The dominant geographical feature is the Yenisey River, running the length of the territory. In summer passenger boats travel the Yenisey from Krasnoyarsk almost to the Arctic Kara Sea. Krasnoyarsk is the nearest big city to the republics of Khakassia and Tuva, to its south.

KRASNOYARSK
КРАСНОЯРСК

Population: 1 million

Krasnoyarsk grew from a 17th-century Cossack fort to its present size thanks to the discovery of gold in the 19th century, the arrival of the Trans-Siberian Railway and the shifting of factories here during WW II. Just upstream is a hydroelectric dam with a reservoir stretching 350 km up the Yenisey.

It's a less metropolitan but more eye-pleasing place than the comparable Novosibirsk, with a sense of space imparted by outlying hills and the two-km-wide Yenisey flowing through the centre. There are quite a few 19th-century buildings (though it seems nothing remains from the early days) and the centre is relatively quiet and unpolluted.

Krasnoyarsk was closed to foreigners until late in the Soviet period because of a concentration of defence-related industries, including the Krasnoyarsk-26 and Krasnoyarsk-45 secret nuclear-weapons cities nearby. Krasnoyarsk-26 has underground housing, factories and a nuclear reactor, linked by tunnels rumoured to be 10 times longer than the Moscow metro. These cities have now diversified – Krasnoyarsk-45 makes BASF cassettes, Krasnoyarsk-26 makes Samsung TVs.

If you have come from the west, it's a sobering thought that at Krasnoyarsk you're still nearer to Russia's western borders than to its eastern tip.

Orientation
The Yenisey flows roughly west-east through Krasnoyarsk, with the city centre a strip about four blocks wide on the north bank. The main street is east-west prospekt Mira, two blocks north of the river, and the best orientation point is the Hotel Krasnoyarsk, 1½ blocks south of prospekt Mira and overlooking the bridge over the two-km-wide Yenisey.

Information
There are currency exchange points at the airport (not always open); at Sinto Bank, prospekt Mira 87, open Monday to Friday from 10 am to noon and 2 to 4 pm; and at the Central Aeroflot Agency. Avtovazbank at prospekt Mira 30 offers Visa and Eurocard/MasterCard cash advances.

The main post office and the long-distance telephone office are at ulitsa Lenina 49. The Krasnoyarsk telephone code is 3912.

Knizhny Mir bookshop at prospekt Mira 86 has some 1:200,000 and 1:500,000 maps of Russian regions. Akademkniga next door is worth a look too.

Krasnoyarsk time is Moscow time plus four hours.

Museums
The leading 19th-century Russian historical painter Vasily Surikov was born in Krasnoyarsk and lived here. His house at ulitsa Lenina 98 is now the **Surikov Museum-Estate** (Muzey-usadba V I Surikova), worth a visit. Don't confuse this with the **Surikov Art Museum** (Khudozhestvenny muzey imeni V I Surikova) at ulitsa Parizhskoy Kommuny 20, on the corner of ulitsa Karla Marxa, which is a wider ranging museum showing Russian art from the 18th to 20th centuries – it's open from 10 am to 6 pm daily except Monday. The **Local Studies Museum** (Kraevedchesky muzey) at ulitsa Dubrovinskogo 84, beside the Yenisey bridge, has exotic Egyptian-style decoration

SIBERIA & RUSSIAN FAR EAST

Top: Lake Baikal region
Middle: Lake Baikal fisherman
Bottom: Village on Lake Baikal

ANDREW HUMPHREYS

Decorated wooden doorway, Ulan Ude

outside but at the time of research was 'remont'.

The **Sv Nikolai Paddle Steamer**, which carried Lenin up the Yenisey to exile in Shushenskoe (see Around Abakan) in 1897, rests at the eastern end of ulitsa Dubrovinskogo, near the Philharmonia. It was under some kind of renovation when we visited.

Churches

Krasnoyarsk's main working church is the **Intercession Cathedral** (Pokrovsky Kafedralny Sobor), a salmon-pink and white building with gold domes on ulitsa Surikova, built in the late 18th century. The **Annunciation Cathedral** (Blagoveshchensky Sobor) at the corner of ulitsa Lenina and ulitsa 9 Yanvarya is being renovated. The red-brick neo-Gothic **Catholic church** on ulitsa Gorkogo is now working again after being used as an organ concert hall in Soviet times. On Sundays, mass is celebrated in German

and Polish simultaneously at 9.30 am (for the local German and Polish communities), and in Russian at 11 am.

Central Park

Tsentralny Park, entered opposite a big Lenin statue on ulitsa Karla Marxa, one km west of the Hotel Krasnoyarsk, has views over the river from its southern end.

St Parasceva Pyatnitsa Chapel

This tower-like hilltop chapel (Chasovnya Svyatoy Velikomuchenitsy Paraskevy Pyatnitsy), visible to the north from some places in the city centre, makes a nice walk from the centre. It's been recently restored inside. Walk to the northern end of ulitsa Veynbauma or ulitsa Perensona, go left along the road (ulitsa Bryanskaya) then up the wooden staircase on the hillside – about 40 minutes from the city centre.

SIBERIA & RUSSIAN FAR EAST

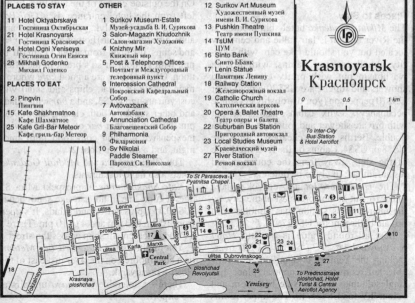

PLACES TO STAY		
11	Hotel Oktyabrskaya	Гостиница Октябрьская
21	Hotel Krasnoyarsk	Гостиница Красноярск
24	Hotel Ogni Yeniseya	Гостиница Огни Енисея
26	Mikhail Godenko	Михаил Годенко

PLACES TO EAT		
2	Pingvin	Пингвин
15	Kafe Shakhmatnoe	Кафе Шахматное
25	Kafe Gril-Bar Meteor	Кафе гриль-бар Метеор

OTHER		
1	Surikov Museum-Estate	Музей-усадьба В. И. Сурикова
3	Salon-Magazin Khudozhnik	Салон-магазин Художник
4	Knizhny Mir	Книжный мир
5	Post & Telephone Offices	Почтамт и Международный телефонный пункт
6	Intercession Cathedral	Покровский Кафедральный Собор
7	Avtovazbank	Автовазбанк
8	Annunciation Cathedral	Благовещенский Собор
9	Philharmonia	Филармония
10	Sv Nikolai Paddle Steamer	Пароход Св. Николаи

12	Surikov Art Museum	Художественный музей имени В. И. Сурихова
13	Pushkin Theatre	Театр имени Пушкина
14	TsUM	ЦУМ
16	Sinto Bank	Синто ББанк
17	Lenin Statue	Памятник Ленину
18	Railway Station	Железнорожный вокзал
19	Catholic Church	Католическая церковь
20	Opera & Ballet Theatre	Театр оперы и балета
22	Suburban Bus Station	Пригородный автовокзал
23	Local Studies Museum	Краеведческий музей
27	River Station	Речной вокзал

Krasnoyarsk
Красноярск

0   0.5   1 km

To Inter-City Bus Station & Hotel Aeroflot

To St Parasceva-Pyatnitsa Chapel

To Predmostnaya ploshchad, Hotel Turist & Central Aeroflot Agency

Yenisey

Stolby Nature Reserve

The best thing to do in Krasnoyarsk is to walk in the Stolby Nature Reserve (Zapovednik Stolby), a hilly area of woods and strange rock pillars *(stolby)* on the southwest edge of the city. Take any tram heading towards the Yenisey bridge from in front of the Hotel Krasnoyarsk, to the second stop, Predmostnaya ploshchad at the south end of the bridge, then bus No 7 from Predmostnaya ploshchad to the end of the line.

Divnogorsk

In summer (1 May to 1 September), hourly boats sail 30 km up the Yenisey to Divnogorsk, site of the hydroelectric dam holding back the long Krasnoyarsk Reservoir (Krasnoyarskoe vodokhranilishche) on the Yenisey. Sailings from Krasnoyarsk are from 8 am to 7 pm and the last back from Divnogorsk is at 8 pm. Buses to Divnogorsk go from the Suburban Bus Station (Prigorodny Avtovokzal) at the back of the Hotel Krasnoyarsk.

Places to Stay

The *Mikhail Godenko* hotel-ship moored at the River Station is fair value and centrally located but you should take care with security. Small 1st-class cabins, with private washbasin but with pretty clean shared showers and toilets, are US$20 a double or US$10 per person (you'd probably get single occupancy). 'Lyux' cabins, also small but with private shower and toilet, are US$30 a double. Berths in the cheapest cabins are US$8 or US$4. Cabins on the riverward side of the ship, away from the entrance and restaurant, are likely to be quieter.

The *Hotel Aeroflot* at Aerovokzalnaya ulitsa 16, out in the north-east of the city, by the intercity bus station, has doubles with private bathroom for US$27.

Best all-round value is the big *Hotel Krasnoyarsk* (☎ 27 37 54, 27 37 69) overlooking the Yenisey bridge. This comfortable and conveniently central place has singles/doubles with private bathroom and colour TV for US$35/40. The upper rooms at the front have great views over the river. The hotel has an excellent range of eating options (see Places to Eat) and staff are friendly.

Two inferior hotels – the dingy *Hotel Ogni Yeniseya* (☎ 27 82 62) at ulitsa Dubrovinskogo 80, a block east of the Yenisey bridge, and the *Hotel Turist* (☎ 36 14 70, 36 18 30) on Predmostnaya ploshchad at the south end of the bridge, both charge US$50 for doubles. They're not worth it.

The most expensive place is the *Hotel Oktyabrskaya* (☎ 27 19 16, 27 69 68) at prospekt Mira 15, on the corner of ulitsa 9 Yanvarya. Singles/doubles with private bathroom are US$40/60, and suites are US$80 or US$100. It's a good hotel but doesn't really offer anything more than the Krasnoyarsk, except a casino. Bus No 42 comes east along prospekt Mira to ulitsa 9 Yanvarya.

Places to Eat

The Hotel Krasnoyarsk has several good options aside from its loud main restaurant. On the outside corner of the building, to the left from the hotel entrance, is a *Gril-Bar* serving good shashlyk, grilled chicken and aubergine (baklazhan) hotpot for US$2 or so, and soups. It's open from about 11 am till 10 pm, with an hour or so's break in the afternoon. Off the lobby are a good *kafe* where a main course of meat, chips and salad will cost you around US$3, and a *bar* with salads and other snacks – both closing about 9.30 pm. There's another *bar* on floor 3, serving inexpensive hot and cold food until midnight, and a *bufet* on floor 2.

The *Oktyabrskaya* and *Mikhail Godenko* hotels also have restaurants.

Kafe Shakhmatnoe at prospekt Mira 85 does a good line in hot sausage sandwiches (US$0.75), plus coffee and salads. It's open from 10 am to 3 pm and 4 to 10 pm. There's a *Pingvin* ice-cream shop across the street.

You might try the *Kafe Gril-Bar Meteor*, on a boat moored on the river just east of the Hotel Krasnoyarsk.

There's a tolerable *stolovaya* upstairs at the airport.

Entertainment

There's a big Opera & Ballet Theatre beside the Hotel Krasnoyarsk and an even bigger Philharmonia at the east end of prospekt Mira.

Things to Buy

Salon-Magazin Khudozhnik on prospekt Mira between ulitsa Kirova and ulitsa Diktatury Proletariata sells paintings and wood carvings and is worth a look. TsUM at ulitsa Karla Marxa 102 is the main city centre department store.

Getting There & Away

Air Krasnoyarsk has two airports only three km apart but both about 45 km north-west of the city. Yemelyanovo, the main one, has flights once or more daily to/from Moscow (4½ hours), Abakan, Barnaul, Bratsk, Irkutsk (2½ hours), Kyzyl, Norilsk (2½ hours), Novosibirsk and Omsk; on most days to/from St Petersburg (six hours) and Khabarovsk (four hours); and a few times weekly to/from Yekaterinburg, Tomsk and Yakutsk. Cheremshanka Airport serves a few extra flights to/from some of the same places, and also Igarka and Dudinka a few days a week.

Tickets are sold at the Central Aeroflot Agency (Tsentralnoe Agentstvo Aeroflota) on Predmostnaya ploshchad at the south end of the Yenisey bridge. Foreigners can go to the Dispetcher Mezhdunarodnykh Perevozok window for quick service. Take any tram heading towards the bridge from in front of the Hotel Krasnoyarsk, to the second stop.

Bus The intercity bus station (Mezhdugorodny Avtovkzal) is out in the north-east of the city at Aerovokzalnaya ulitsa 22. Buses leave in the morning for Abakan (9½ hours), Shushenskoe (10½ hours) and Sayanogorsk (11 hours).

Train The station is 2.5 km west of the centre on Vokzalnaya ulitsa. Several eastbound and westbound trains across Siberia stop here daily and Krasnoyarsk is on the routes of the trans-Siberian, trans-Mongolian and trans-Manchurian trains and the twice-weekly Moscow-Ulan Bator service (No 5/6). The three-times-weekly 'Yenisey', train No 55/56, is a good service to/from Moscow (Kazan Station), taking 64 hours, but there are six or seven other trains a day. Nine or 10 trains run daily to/from Novosibirsk (13 to 14 hours). Eastbound, there are about six trains a day to/from Irkutsk (about 19 hours) and two as far as Vladivostok. There are two daily trains along the BAM – one to Severobaikalsk, the other to Tynda and Neryungri on alternate days. The BAM splits from the main trans-Siberian line at Tayshet, 390 km east of Krasnoyarsk.

To/from Abakan, train No 23/24 (12 hours) is four or five hours quicker than Nos 657/658 and 659/660. Trains also go daily to/from Almaty (Kazakhstan), every two days to/from Bishkek (Kyrgyzstan) and three times a week to/from Tashkent (Uzbekistan).

Boat Long-distance passenger boats ply the Yenisey in summer from Krasnoyarsk's River Station (Rechnoy Vokzal) to places as far north as Vorontsovo, more than 2000 km away on the Yenisey Gulf (Yeniseysky zaliv), which opens on to the Arctic Kara Sea. The main service is to the seagoing port of Dudinka, 1989 km north and well within the Arctic Circle. The voyage to Dudinka takes nearly four days (and nearly six days coming back, against the current). You can fly out of Dudinka. Sailings to Dudinka are every two to four days from early June to the beginning of October. Stops include Yeniseysk (413 km; 18 hours), Bakhta (1023 km; 44 hours) and Igarka (1744 km; 79 hours). There's a ticket office in the River Station, open from 8 am to 7 pm: the boats are not usually full, but you may not get the class you want very close to departure. One-way fares to Dudinka range from US$45 to US$115. The top price gets you a place in a 1st-class two-person cabin with washbasin; a four-berth 2nd-class cabin is US$80 per person. It's also possible to take far more expensive cruises on the same route on the

Swiss-managed *Anton Chekhov*: contact Reisebüro Mittelthurgau (☎ (072) 218 585; fax (072) 223 407), Marktplatz 5, 8570 Weinfelden, Switzerland, or Euro Cruises (☎ (212) 691 2099, or toll-free in the USA and Canada (800) 688 3876), 303 West 13th St, New York, NY 10014, USA.

Other routes from Krasnoyarsk go to Podtesovo and Yartsevo, both north of Yeniseysk, and Vorontsovo (a nearly five-day trip). There are also services from Podtesovo to Boguchany on the Angara, from Boguchany to Kezhma further up the Angara, and from Potapovo (94 km south of Dudinka) to Nosok, where the Yenisey enters the Yenisey Gulf. Timetables are displayed in the Krasnoyarsk River Station.

Getting Around

To/From the Airports Bus No 135 runs between both airports and the city's suburban bus station (Prigorodny Avtovokzal) behind the Hotel Krasnoyarsk, about half-hourly from 5.40 am to 10.50 pm, then occasionally through the night. It can be packed and to ensure a place going out to the airport, you should buy a ticket in advance from kassa No 4 (open from 6.30 am to 5.30 pm) at the suburban bus station. The ride to Cheremshanka is about 40 minutes, to Yemelyanovo 50 minutes. The fare is US$0.25.

A taxi from either airport to the centre is about US$20.

Local Transport Trolleybus No 2 runs between the railway station forecourt and the intercity bus station, via the city centre. Going to the intercity bus station you can pick it up on ulitsa Karla Marxa by the suburban bus station. Trolleybus No 7 runs between the railway station and the Medinstitut stop at the foot of Aerovokzalnaya ulitsa, about half a km from the intercity bus station, also via the city centre.

Other services from the railway station to the centre include bus No 17 and trolleybus No 14 from the station forecourt, and bus No 11 from the road out the front. Some of these come into the centre on ulitsa Karla Marxa,

others on prospekt Mira. From the centre to the railway station, you can pick up bus No 11 and trolleybus Nos 7 and 14 on ulitsa Lenina between ulitsa Surikova and ulitsa Perensona.

NORTHERN KRASNOYARSK TERRITORY
СЕВЕРНЫЙ КРАСНОЯРСКИЙ КРАЙ

The northern part of the Krasnoyarsk Territory, beyond the Arctic Circle, offers a few possibilities if you *really* want to get off the beaten track. In summer, bring lots of mosquito repellent. Official restrictions on tourism have been imposed in some areas, notably parts of the Taymyr Peninsula, so you should try to check out the situation before coming.

Getting There & Away

You can reach the region by boat, and fly out, or vice-versa. In summer, passenger boats travel from Krasnoyarsk all the way down the Yenisey to Igarka, Dudinka and Vorontsovo, on the Yenisey Gulf beyond the river's mouth (See Krasnoyarsk Getting There & Away). There are flights from Krasnoyarsk and elsewhere to Igarka, Dudinka and Norilsk. There are also flights between Norilsk and Moscow, including by Transaero. What's claimed to be the world's northernmost railway runs between Dudinka and Norilsk, a slow four-hour trip.

Travel Agencies The Tourist Guides Union in Novosibirsk (see the Novosibirsk Information section) is one outfit offering trips to the Putorana Plateau. Taymyrintur (☎ (3919) 35 48 90; ☎ & fax (3919) 35 10 42) is a Norilsk travel agency which says it specialises in active tourism. Wilderness Expeditions in the Netherlands (see Travel Agencies in the Siberia & the Far East Getting There & Away chapter) can arrange expeditions to the Putorana Plateau and the Taymyr Peninsula.

If you want to go even further north, Pilgrim Tours in Moscow (see Activities in Siberia & the Far East Facts for the Visitor) and a firm called BARC in St Petersburg

☎ (812) 352 20 77; fax (812) 352 24 70) have both 10-day to 12-day tours to the North Pole and the Severnaya Zemlya and Zemlya Frantsa-Iosifa island groups, with stops in Norilsk or Dixon, at the mouth of the Yenisey Gulf. Prices from Moscow or St Petersburg are US$3700 and up.

Igarka & Dudinka
Игарка и Дудинка
These are seagoing ports on the lower Yenisey. Dudinka is the capital of the Taymyr (Dolgan-Nenets) Autonomous District, in which the Dolgan and Nenets peoples are far outnumbered by Russians. The condition of these formerly nomadic hunters and reindeer herders is apparently among the worst of all Siberian native peoples. In Dudinka the only place to stay is apparently the *Hotel Ogni Yeniseya*, with cheap but reasonable rooms.

Norilsk
Норильск
This nickel-processing city 80 km east of Dudinka, now with 280,000 people, was founded in the 1920s to exploit big reserves of copper, nickel, cobalt and coal, and much of it was built by Gulag forced labour. Norilsk is responsible for acid rain over a wide area of the Siberian tundra. The city has a museum about its own construction and the horrors of the Gulag.

Putorana Plateau
Плато Путорана
The Putorana Plateau is a range of glacier-worn mountains of volcanic origin beginning about 75 km east of Norilsk and stretching about 350 km farther east. It harbours some truly magnificent waterfalls and canyons, top-grade white-water rafting on the Kureyka River, and superb fishing. The top of the plateau is flat, barren, windswept and moonlike, with temperatures often below freezing even in summer, and wind-chill of as much as 40°C. The area is uninhabited except for a few hunters and nomads in summer. Expeditions have reached the plateau by boat along rivers and lakes from Norilsk.

Taymyr Peninsula
Полуостров Таймыр
This most northerly part of the Russian mainland has a winter 'night' two months long, with temperatures staying below freezing for eight months, and a summer 'day' lasting nearly three months. The Taymyr has over 400,000 wild reindeer, and over 13,000 sq km of the peninsula's tundra form the Taymyr Nature Reserve (Zapovednik Taymyr), Russia's second-biggest. There are also huge coal reserves up here.

Khakassia
Хакасия

The Republic of Khakassia, a patch of steppe and mountains about the size of Ireland, lies on the upper Yenisey River south-west of Krasnoyarsk. Like the neighbouring Altay and Tuva republics, it's one of the cradles of Siberian civilisation. Some of the stone idols and the thousands of burial mounds here date back at least 3000 to 5000 years. The most impressive are from the Khyagas, or 'Yenisey Kyrgyz', Empire, which spanned much of Central Asia and central Siberia in the 6th to 12th centuries.

The destruction of the Khyagas by the Mongol Tatars ended the region's golden age. Worn out by futile resistance to Jenghiz Khan's son Jochi, most Khyagas finally migrated to what is now Kyrgyzstan. Those who remained – the forebears of the present-day Khakass people – were picked on by neighbours until, in 1701, they *asked* to join the Russian Empire. The Russians, who founded Abakan, modern Khakassia's capital, as a fort soon after this, offered tax incentives to encourage the Khakass to become Christians and now outnumber the indigenous population here 10 to one.

Abakan is mainly of interest as a base for exploring the broad, fertile Minusinsk Basin in which it sits and the Western Sayan Mountains along the border of Tuva to the south, a beautiful, well-endowed region with dry, sunny Central Asian weather and a wide variety of scenery – steppe and taiga, fresh and salt lakes, rivers, and mountains as high as 3000 metres.

Khakassia time is Moscow time plus four hours.

ABAKAN
АБАКАН

Population: 170,000

The clean, leafy, 20th-century town of Abakan has an interesting museum and zoo – and an amazing amount of marble, of which there's a surplus from Khakassia's quarries, lining its hotel staircases, bathrooms etc.

The Yenisey north from Abakan has been converted into the Krasnoyarsk Reservoir, a flat pond stretching 350 km to the Divnogorsk dam near Krasnoyarsk.

Orientation

Abakan, surrounded by suburbs of dachas and vegetable gardens, is on the west shore of the Krasnoyarsk Reservoir, where the tributary Abakan River enters the Yenisey. Most of what's important is on or near ulitsa Shchetinkina, the north-south axis.

Information

You can change money at the airport, at the Aeroflot office on ulitsa Chertygasheva, or at Abakan Tours in the Hotel Intourist. The main post and telephone office is on ulitsa Shchetinkina near prospekt Lenina. The Abakan telephone code is 39172.

Abakan Tours (☎ & fax 6 37 60), which is actually the local Intourist branch gone independent, has some of the most helpful and energetic staff you'll find in any travel agency in Russia. They can change money, book discount rooms in the Hotel Sibir and sell air tickets at no extra cost, as well as organise trips around Khakassia and to Tuva. The office is in the little Hotel Intourist, off Khakasskaya ulitsa, and is open from 8 am to 5 pm.

Khakassia Local Studies Museum

The good Khakassky Respublikansky Muzey Kraevedenia concentrates on the history and prehistory of Khakassia. In the lobby is a forest of burial totems. The earliest of these – showing a sun with a face – is at least 3000 years old. Others date from periods of matriarchal rule. On the walls are copies of striking stone paintings; the originals predate the totems by at least a millennium.

Inside, archaeology and anthropology are the best sections. The former has Stone Age implements, Bronze Age paintings, Iron Age tools, complex Khyagas jewellery, totems and burial items. The latter is mostly about the impact of Cossacks and settlers on the Khakass. A guide would be useful.

The museum is at ulitsa Pushkina 96, near the railway station, and is open from 10 am to 6 pm; it's closed on Monday and on the last day of each month.

Zoo

Abakan has a zoo with a collection of 70 Siberian and Russian Far East species including a rare Amur (Ussuri) tiger and camels from Tuva. It's on ulitsa Pushkina three km west of the railway station, open from 10 am to 3 pm daily (the ticket office closes at 2 pm). Take trolleybus No 2 or 4 from anywhere on ulitsa Pushkina to the Myaso Kombinat stop; you can also get No 4 southbound at the post office.

Other Things to See & Do

The clean **Central Baths** (Tsentralnye bani), with hot and cold pools, massage and tea, are on ulitsa Kirova, off ulitsa Shchetinkina. You'll find a wooded **park** with a small beach two km east on prospekt Lenina.

Festivals

The Khakass festival of Tun-Payram celebrates the opening of summer pastures. A gathering in Abakan (usually on the first or second Sunday in June – dates vary) enjoys horse racing, wrestling, archery and other competitions, traditional food and brilliant

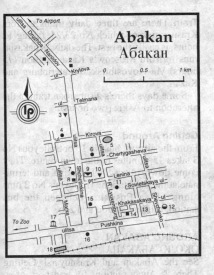

Abakan
Абакан

To Airport
ulitsa Druzhba Narodov
Krylova
0   0.5   1 km
ul
Telmana
ul
Kirova
ulitsa
Chertygasheva
ul
Shchetinkina
Lenina
pr
Sovietskaya ul
K Lyxembrg
Marxa
Khakasskaya
Shchenko
To Zoo
ulitsa
Pushkina

1	Hotel Druzhba Гостиница Дружба
2	Hotel Sibir Гостиница Сибирь
3	Pitstseria Пиццерия
4	Central Baths Центральные бани
5	Stadium Стадион
6	Aeroflot Аэрофлот
7	Bookshop Книжный магазин
8	Hotel Khakasia Гостиница Хакасия
9	Post & Telephone Offices Главпочтамт и Международный телефонный пункт
10	Kafe Lakomka Кафе Лакомка
11	TV Tower Телебашня
12	Bus Station Автовокзал
13	Central Market Центральный рынок
14	Hotel Intourist Гостиница Интурист
15	Regional Drama Theatre Областной драматический театр
16	Department Store Универмаг
17	Khakassia Local Studies Museum Хакасский Республиканский музей краеведения
18	Railway Station Железнодорожный вокзал

costumes. Then everybody carries on in their own villages for several more days.

Places to Stay

The *Hotel Khakasia* (☎ 6 37 02) has reasonable, no-frills singles/doubles with private bathroom for US$27.50/35. It's very central, at prospekt Lenina 88, on the corner of ulitsa Shchetinkina.

The *Hotel Druzhba* (☎ 5 09 55) at the north end of ulitsa Shchetinkina, 1.5 km from the centre, is a bit cheaper at US$25/30 for rooms with attached showers, but it's shabby and can be noisy, and despite its name ('Friendship') its receptionists can be iffy about unexpected foreigners without 'Abakan' on their visas.

The choice place to stay is the little *Hotel Intourist* (☎ 6 60 33; ☎ & fax 6 37 60), an unmarked light brown brick building in a grove of trees at Khakasskaya ulitsa 54A. The handful of rooms, accommodating a total of 12 people, are really comfortable, even luxurious, and cost US$40 per person. There's a restaurant too.

The *Hotel Sibir* (☎ 6 77 11) at ulitsa Druzhba Narodov 9, in the north of town, has good rooms with kitchen for US$30 to

US$50 per person if you book through Abakan Tours. At the hotel they're more expensive. There's a restaurant with a band in the evening.

Places to Eat

Khakass food is Central Asian, with lots of onion, garlic and peppers, but they use pork as well as mutton. Laghman – fried noodles, vegetables and mutton – is common. Keep an eye out for oat biscuits called talkan. Airan is the local equivalent of yoghurt and araka is vodka made from fermented milk!

There's a decent *Pitstseria* (Pizzeria) on ulitsa Shchetinkina north of the centre. Thick-base one-person pizzas are US$1.50 to US$2.50 and they also have salad and drinks. Hours are 11 am to 4 pm and 5 to 10.30 pm. The restaurant at the *Hotel Druzhba* is big and loud, but there's a bufet on floor 4. *Kafe Lakomka*, on prospekt Lenina, serves plain, cheap, fried chicken and light meals.

There are a few shashlyk stands at the market and in front of the railway station.

The central market is on ulitsa Chkalova near ulitsa Pushkina. Local tomatoes are 'famous' and in autumn apples, melons and berries are good.

Getting There & Away

Air Flight schedules are subject to change and cancellations. Scheduled flights include:

Krasnoyarsk (one hour), three or four daily
Novosibirsk (1½ hours), one or two daily
Irkutsk (3½ hours), one daily
Moscow (4½ hours), one or two daily

Flights to/from Kyzyl had been cancelled at the time of research but may restart – try to book early if they do. The Aeroflot office is on ulitsa Chertygasheva but you can buy tickets more easily from Abakan Tours at the same price.

Bus The bus station on ulitsa Shevchenko is a rather chaotic place with minimal timetable information. There's one morning bus to Krasnoyarsk (9½ hours). Several direct buses a day go to Minusinsk, Shushenskoe, Sayanogorsk and Askiz, but some get very crowded. For Minusinsk you pay on the bus, but for Shushenskoe you need to get a ticket in advance at the bus station – and on peak summer weekends these can be sold out a day or more ahead.

Buses to Kyzyl (US$9; 8½ hours) leave from the railway station at 7 and 11.30 am and 7 pm, and tickets are sold at a window inside the station from 6.30 am to noon and 4.30 to 7 pm. Book as far ahead as you can, especially if the flights are not going.

Train There are three daily trains to/from Krasnoyarsk of which No 23/24, taking 12 hours, is easily the best. The daily 'Khakasia' runs to/from Moscow's Kazan Station (75 hours) via Novosibirsk, Yekaterinburg and Kazan.

Some days there's a suburban train in the afternoon to Askiz (two hours).

Getting Around

From the airport, bus No 15 or trolleybus No 3 takes 15 minutes to the town centre. They come down ulitsa Shchetinkina and terminate at the bus station. Trolleybus No 2 runs along ulitsa Pushkina between the bus station, railway station and zoo.

AROUND ABAKAN
ОКОЛО АБАКАНА

See the Abakan and Krasnoyarsk Getting There & Away sections for transport information to the following places. Abakan Tours can arrange trips to all of them, and archaeological and horse-riding trips too: a full-day car trip to Shushenskoe or the Sayano-Shushenskaya dam is US$100.

Minusinsk
Минусинск
Population: 70,000

This 18th-century town, 20 km from Abakan on the Kyzyl road, has all the architecture Abakan lacks, well preserved and lived-in. In the old part of Minusinsk, on an island in a branch of the Yenisey, are the original church (still in use) and wood, stone and brick houses built by 19th-century Siberian gold merchants who travelled the world and built in European style.

In 1877, a pharmacist named Martyanov opened a museum in Minusinsk with his collection of rocks and bugs. It is now a big, well-presented collection featuring archaeology (Bronze Age barrows, Scythian weapons), immigrants and exiles (some Decembrists served labour terms here), and the museum's library is still as it was when Lenin used it. The museum is closed on Mondays.

Shushenskoe
Шушенское

Population: 17,000

Founded in the 18th century by immigrant peasants, Shushenskoe (*'SHU-shen-ska-ya'*), 85 km south of Abakan, is pleasant, shady and dead as a doornail. Its claim to fame is as the place where Lenin was exiled from St Petersburg from 1897 to 1900, and the place where he married fellow revolutionary Nadezhda Krupskaya, who had followed him here in 1898 with her mother.

On the 1970 centennial of Lenin's birth, the whole village centre was reconstructed to look as it had done in 1870 (with a few houses inserted from the poor side of town for the sake of illustration) and was named the 'Lenin's Siberian Exile' Memorial Museum-Preserve. Lenin or no Lenin, the place is a good way to visualise a fairly prosperous turn-of-the-century village of 1500 people. The houses where Lenin stayed are done up in detail, with original furniture. On adjacent streets are the village hall and jail, a pub and several dozen more houses, including those of a rich shopkeeper and lots of 'poor peasants'.

The complex, close to the Shush River where it enters the Yenisey, is open from 10 am to 6 pm daily and admission is US$1.50 (extra for photos). The cheap *Hotel Sayany* on ulitsa Michurina and *Hotel Turist* on prospekt XXVII sezda KPSS are both within two or three blocks east of the museum area. The *Ogni Sayan (Sayan Lights)* restaurant, near the centre of town, is reasonable.

Sayano-Shushenskaya Dam
Саяно-Шушенская дамба

Russia's biggest hydroelectric dam, with 10 640,000 KW turbines, is in the Karlovy Gorge of the upper Yenisey, 150 km upstream from Abakan. Begun in 1975, construction took nearly 20 years. Don't confuse it with the little Maynskaya Dam downstream. The access road is paved with marble, the only material available from local quarries. Unfortunately visitors aren't allowed behind the dam to see the reservoir,

which snakes 300 km back through the Sayan Mountains into Tuva.

If you come, you'll see en route the 'new town' of Sayanogorsk, with its modern aluminium smelter, and its alter ego, the 250-year-old mining town of Mayna, with old wooden houses full of transplanted urban pensioners. In the foothills near the dam is the tidy workers' colony of Cheryomushki ('Wild Cherries').

The trip gives you a sample of the Siberian vegetation regions – rolling steppe (ribbed with poplars against wind erosion) near Abakan, woodland steppe at Mayna, taiga around Sayanogorsk and mountains in the background everywhere.

The *Meridian* restaurant at Sayanogorsk is reportedly good. Cheryomushki has a decent café in the central plaza.

SOUTH-WEST KHAKASSIA
ЮЖНО-ЗАПАДНАЯ ХАКАСИЯ

The A161 road via the iron-ore-mining town of Abaza is a possible alternative route through the Western Sayan Mountains to Tuva, for those with their own transport. It's 420 km from Abakan to Ak-Dovurak in western Tuva. Askiz, 90 km south-west of Abakan, is a Khakass village and a centre of Tun-Payram festivities. Abakan Tours offers trips here with the chance to see Khakass costume, sample Khakass cooking and hear and buy Khakass musical instruments. There are two good *Kempingy* ('Campings') along the way which Abakan Tours can tell you about and book. One, about 20 minutes from Abaza, is really a small hotel with double and triple rooms and a sauna. The other is three km off the road, in the taiga at Stoktysh, on the Stok River near the Tuva border, and has wooden cottages.

Tuva
Тува

The Republic of Tuva (spelt Тыва in Tuvan), south of Khakassia across the Western Sayan Mountains, is one of the least known and most curious corners of Russia. The Tuvans, who form about two-thirds of its 300,000 population (most of the rest are Russians), are nomadic pastoralists by nature, Buddhist and shamanist by religion, Mongolian by cultural heritage, and Turkic by language. Their republic is a transition zone between the Siberian taiga and the Mongolian steppe, with areas of rolling green hills, plains, semi-desert and forest, hemmed in by 2000-metre-plus mountains on all sides (the Western and Eastern Sayan ranges in the north, the fringes of the Altay in the west, the Tannu Ola in the south, and a jumble of ranges in the east). The Bolshoy (Big) and Maly (Little) Yenisey rivers – Biy-Khem and Ka-Khem to Tuvans – flow down from the eastern mountains to meet and form the Yenisey (Ulug-Khem) at the capital, Kyzyl. White-water rafting is possible on the Maly Yenisey.

Despite Soviet efforts at collectivisation, much of the Tuvan population is still semi-nomadic, moving their herds out from their villages to summer pastures where they live in yurts – you'll see these if you travel around rural Tuva, especially towards the mountainous fringes. The range of animals they herd reflects Tuva's crossroads character – camels, yaks, cows, horses, goats, sheep, even reindeer in the eastern forests.

Culturally the Tuvans go in for cross-country horse racing, a special form of wrestling called *khuresh*, carving the soft stone agalmatolite, and most famously for throat-singing – a spine-tingling, deep-down, tuneful chanting which apparently comes in four styles, called *khöömey, sygyt, kargyraa* and *borbangnadyr.*

Though Kyzyl, the only place in Tuva easily accessible from the outside world, is a concrete city out of the Soviet mould, it's quite possible to get out and about from there. Though (or perhaps because) Tuvans are among the poorest people in Russia, they're by and large remarkably friendly to foreigners.

Some hotels in Kyzyl like to see Kyzyl named on your Russian visa, so it's worth listing it as one of your destinations when you apply for the visa.

Tuva time is Moscow time plus four hours.

History
First inhabited at least 40,000 years ago, Tuva fell under Turkic rule in the 6th century AD, was conquered by the Uyghurs from modern Xinjiang (China) in the 8th century, taken over by the Turkic 'Yenisey Kyrgyz' empire in the 9th century, then, like neighbouring regions to the east and west, ruled by Jenghiz Khan's Mongolian successors from about the 13th century. When the last independent Mongolian state, that of the western Mongolian Oyrats, was wiped out by the Manchu Chinese in the 1750s, Tuva became an outpost of China but was left fairly well alone under local chiefs. It was during the Chinese period that Buddhism, of the Yellow-Hat Tibetan variety led by the Dalai Lama, came to Tuva, where it coexisted with the older shamanist nature religion. By 1929 there were 22 monasteries in Tuva, the most important being at Chadan, and about one man in 15 was a lama.

Russian traders, gold prospectors and peasants first began to settle in Tuva in the 19th century. Come the Chinese revolution of 1911, Russia stirred up a separatist movement in Tuva and took it 'under protection' in 1914 (an 'exceptionally progressive event', according to one Soviet Tuvan history). After the Bolshevik Revolution and ensuing Civil War, Tuva became a nominally independent people's republic (Tannu-Tuva) in 1921. Though under Soviet supervision, prime minister Donduk's government declared Buddhism the state religion and Mongolian the official language, and favoured reunification with Mongolia.

Not surprisingly, in 1929 Moscow installed a dependable communist, Solchak

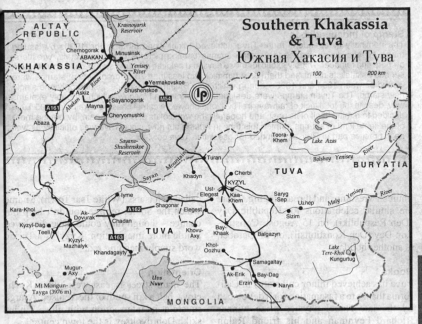

Toka, as prime minister. Tuvan, the vernacular Turkic tongue, became the official language, initially written in the Latin alphabet but later converted to Cyrillic. In 1944 Stalin took away Tuva's remnants of autonomy, renamed it, with impeccable logic, the Tuvinian Autonomous Region, and incorporated it into the USSR. Russian immigration increased, Buddhism and shamanism were stamped on, and the seminomadic Tuvans were collectivised, many slaughtering their animals rather than hand them over. Limited agriculture and industry were introduced in the 1950s. However, seminomadism survived to some extent in the mountainous fringes and the east, where there were no roads, and so, for a while at least, did shamanism.

Poverty has fuelled ethnic tensions. After anti-Russian riots in 1990, more than 3000 skilled Russian workers left Tuva, and the drain has continued as many Russians see little future here with Tuvans now dominant

in the government. Tuva proclaimed itself a full republic within Russia in 1991 and Sherig-Ool Oorzhak was elected its first president in 1992. Some Tuvans yearn for full independence or reunification with Mongolia but such dreams seem unrealistic given Tuva's economic reliance on Moscow, which still provides most of the Tuvan budget.

Buddhism is slowly reviving and new temples have been founded in Kyzyl and elsewhere. The Dalai Lama visited Tuva in 1992 and 1994.

Language
Tuvans speak Tuvan but most of them also speak Russian. 'Hello' in Tuvan is *Ekii*.

Festivals
The main Tuvan festivals are Shagaa, the Buddhist New Year, which is in mid to late January in 1997 and advances about 10 days a year, and Naadym, in July, which is an occasion for long-distance horse racing,

---

Stamp of Independence

The nominally independent Tannu-Tuva achieved minor world fame in the 1930s by issuing triangular and diamond-shaped postage stamps bearing pictures of yaks, camels, wrestlers, archers and reindeer – highly exotic for those days and beloved of young stamp-collectors, though serious philatelists dismissed them as a gimmick. No less than 70 different sets of stamps were issued between 1934 and 1936 – during which time Britain, for instance, issued only one single new stamp. The Tuvan stamps were designed and printed in Moscow, which probably explains why, despite the total lack of railways in Tuva, one showed a camel chasing a train. In 1995 Tuva decided to remind itself of its past, and hopefully the world of its existence again, by issuing more of the same kind of stamps, printed this time in Austria but now, since Tuva was officially as well as in practice part of Russia, intended for use within Tuva only. ■

---

khuresh wrestling, and throat-singing. There are similar celebrations for Republic Day (Den Respubliki), on 15 August. Constitution Day (Den Konstitutsii), on 21 October, is another holiday.

Books

Tuva has achieved minor cult status in California thanks to a fascination for it developed by the late Nobel physics prize winner Richard Feynman and his friend Ralph Leighton. They set up an organisation called Friends of Tuva which has been instrumental in, among other things, taking Tuvan throat-singers and exhibitions of Tuvan artefacts to the West. The story of their obsession is told in Leighton's *Tuva or Bust!* (see Books in Siberia & the Far East Facts for the Visitor). Those who are seriously interested could also seek out *Unknown Mongolia* by Douglas Carruthers, a British explorer who reached Tuva in 1911, and *Nomads of South Siberia* by Sevyan Vaynshteyn, probably the leading Russian Tuva expert (Cambridge University Press, 1980).

KYZYL
КЫЗЫЛ
Population: 80,000

The capital of Tuva sits on a broad plain, with the Bolshoy and Maly Yenisey rivers meeting on the northern edge of town. It's a Soviet-style place of straight streets and concrete buildings, quite unromantic. Founded as a Russian settlement in 1914, it used to be called Belotsarsk (White Tsar Town), a name which the Soviet regime couldn't help but change – though they could have displayed a little more imagination: Kyzyl is a Turkic word simply meaning red.

Orientation

The main street is east-west ulitsa Kochetova, half a km south of the Yenisey. A large square at its intersection with ulitsa Tuvinskikh Dobrovoltsev is the town centre.

Information

The post and telephone offices are together on ulitsa Kochetova on the south side of the central square. Next door is the Biznes-Tsentr, open Monday to Friday from 8 am to 5 pm, which has fax service. The Kyzyl telephone code is 39422 for five-digit numbers, 3942 for six-digit numbers.

The Kyzyl branch of Sputnik (☎ 3 25 29), in the Hotel Kottedzh at ulitsa Krasnykh Partizan 38, is about the best travel agency in town. For groups of five or more, it offers several six to 15-day programmes in Tuva, costing about US$60 a day per person. It can also organise short or long individual trips, and can arrange helicopters to fly to destinations around Tuva – for one such day trip involving 40-minute flights there and back, we were quoted US$750! The office is open Monday to Friday from 8 am to 5 pm.

Central Square

The square at the intersection of ulitsa Koch-

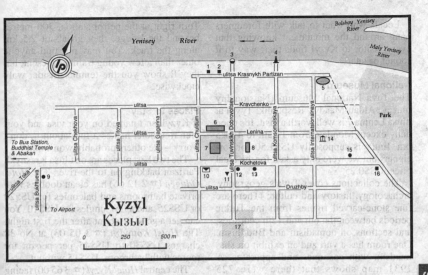

Kyzyl
Кызыл

0   250   500 m

1	Hotel Kottedzh Гостиница Коттэдж	7	Theatre Театр	12	Cinema Кино
2	Hotel Odugen Гостиница Одуген	8	Hotel Kyzyl Гостиница Кызыл	13	Knigi Bookshop Книги
3	Boat Quay Причал	9	Aeroflot Аэрофлот	14	Tuva National Museum Национальный музей „Алдан-Маадыр" Республики Тыва
4	Centre of Asia Monument Памятник Центр Азии	10	Post & Telephone Offices Почтамт и Междугородный телефонный пункт	15	TNIIYaLI ТНИИЯЛИ
5	Stadium Стадион	11	Restoran Ulug Khem Ресторан Улуг Хем	16	Hotel Mongulek Гостиница Монгулек
6	Supreme Khural Верховный Хурал			17	Market Рынок

etova and ulitsa Tuvinskikh Dobrovoltsev has a big theatre in the middle, with some exotic Tuvan woodcarvings around its upper levels, and government buildings on two sides – the one on the north is the Supreme Khural (Verkhovny Khural) or Parliament. The statue east of the theatre is of Solchak Toka, Tuva's communist prime minister in the 1930s.

Centre of Asia Monument
Kyzyl's focal attraction stands on the bank of the Yenisey at the end of ulitsa Komso-

molskaya. Everyone says this stone globe and obelisk – or at least their forerunners – were erected here by a mysterious 19th-century English adventurer to mark the geographical centre of Asia. The same eccentric gent had apparently already done the same for a couple of other continents. According to Ralph Leighton in *Tuva or Bust!*, the centre of Asia is just about here if you balance a map of Asia drawn by the obscure Gall's stereographic projection on a pin, but hundreds of km away by other methods of calculating it.

Locals who want to talk with foreigners hang around the monument knowing that every visitor to Kyzyl finds their way to it sooner or later.

National Museum

The Tuva National Museum (Natsionalny muzey 'Aldan-Maadyr' Respubliki Tyva) at ulitsa Lenina 7 is well worth a visit. It's open daily except Monday, from 11 am to 4 or 5 pm. Entry is supposedly US$1.50 for foreigners but we were only asked for the local price, US$0.25.

The collections cover Tuva's geography, archaeology, history and culture. There are fine stone-carved figures from the Turkic periods between the 6th and 12th centuries, and sections on nomadism and Buddhism. One room has a yurt and an exhibit on shamanism, with costumes and apparatus. A 1931 map shows that there were 725 shamans in Tuva then, nearly half of them women. Have a look out the back, where there are more ancient stone carvings.

TNIIYaLI

Kyzyl's Language, Literature & History Research Institute (Tuvinsky Nauchno-Issledovatelskii Institut Yazyka, Literatura i Istorii, TNIIYaLI for short), at ulitsa Kochetova 4, has an interesting ethnography museum but it doesn't admit casual callers. Sputnik can get you in.

Park

A large woodland park stretches east from the end of ulitsa Kochetova, with the Maly Yenisey flowing along its north side.

Buddhist Temple

The little Tuvdan Chaykhorlin temple across the Yenisey from the town was built in 1992 and is Tuva's leading Buddhist temple. You can just see its golden roof from some places in town. It's just the beginning of what's planned to be a larger complex. To reach it, walk or take a 'Vostok-Avtovokzal' bus west along ulitsa Kochetova to the roundabout, 1.5 km from the central square, then walk north across the bridge over the Yenisey.

Turn right at the petrol station, 700 metres beyond the bridge, then go about 2.5 km along the track. You may not find anyone other than a few young trainees present, but they'll show you the temple. Inside, walk clockwise.

Places to Stay

If Kyzyl isn't named on your visa and your preferred hotel makes a fuss about it, don't worry – the others probably won't mind.

The two best places are on ulitsa Krasnykh Partizan backing on to the river. The *Hotel Odugen* (☎ 2 12 66) has clean doubles with private bathrooms and balconies for US$20 or US$25, and a few singles for US$10. You can get a good discount after the first night. The *Hotel Kottedzh* (☎ 3 05 03) at No 38 charges US$30 to US$45 per person for rooms with bathroom, US$15 without.

The central *Hotel Kyzyl* (☎ 3 65 00) facing ulitsa Tuvinskikh Dobrovoltsev has a range of tired old rooms, with foreigners usually steered towards the 'lyux' ones – quite comfortable with sitting room and attached bathroom at US$25/50. Standard rooms with attached bathroom are US$25/26, and rooms using shared facilities are US$15/20.

The *Hotel Mongulek* (☎ 3 16 03) at the east end of ulitsa Kochetova has a range of shabby rooms, and wants foreigners to stay on the 5th floor, the most expensive, where suites with attached shower cost US$19 per person. There's also one single room up there, for US$13.

Places to Eat

Restoran Ulug Khem on ulitsa Tuvinskikh Dobrovoltsev just south of ulitsa Kochetova is an erratically open stolovaya – soup, a main course and dessert costs about US$2. There's another stolovaya in the *Hotel Odugen* – though it may only have pelmeni. The *Hotel Kyzyl* has a café and the *Hotel Mongulek* has a restaurant. The *market* at the south end of ulitsa Tuvinskikh Dobrovoltsev has shashlyk stands and some fresh produce. You may find the typical Central Asian drinks kumyss (fermented mare's milk) and khaipak (a milder version of the same) here.

Things to Buy

Sputnik has a few agalmatolite carvings for sale and you may be offered others.

Getting There & Away

At the time of research Tuva had no generally open borders with Mongolia: the road crossings south of Erzin and Khandagayty were restricted to local commercial traffic. It might conceivably be possible to get a ride across in a truck if you have a Mongolian visa.

Air The airport is seven km south-west of the centre. Flights are subject to cancellation for a host of reasons, including lack of fuel and bad weather, but they're scheduled to/from Krasnoyarsk and Novosibirsk daily, Irkutsk four times a week, Ulan Ude twice a week, Biysk once a week, and Tuvan regional centres like Mugur-Axy, Kyzyl-Mazhalyk and Kungurtuk on most days, with other destinations served two or three days a week. Flights to/from Abakan may recommence.

Tickets are sold at the Aeroflot office at ulitsa Bukhtueva, open from 8 am to 5 pm daily.

Bus The bus station is out in the west end of town, about three km from the centre. Buses go to/from Abakan (US$9; 8½ hours) three times daily – a fine trip over the Western Sayan, with a halt in Turan. Buses also run daily to numerous places around Tuva. It's seven hours to Erzin (US$3), 2½ hours to Shagonar, about six hours to Ak-Dovurak, and eight hours to Teeli. The Tsentr Turistsky agency (☎ 30 10 33) in room 2 at the Hotel Mongulek runs one or two weekly buses to Abakan (US$14) and Novosibirsk (US$32; 28 hours).

Car It shouldn't be too hard to find a driver who'll take you out of town for a day or two, provided petrol is in adequate supply. Try at the bus station.

Boat In summer, boats go every two or three days up the Bolshoy Yenisey to Toora-Khem near Lake Azas. The trip upstream is 12

Soft stone carving from Tuva

hours, but eight hours coming back downstream. Departures are usually at 8 am – ask at the Tuvinskaya Sudokhodnaya Kompania office by the quay at the end of ulitsa Tuvinskikh Dobrovoltsev. Tickets for foreigners officially cost US$26 but you may be able to get the local price of US$13. They're sold an hour or two before departure – take your passport.

Getting Around

Bus No 1, 'Vostok-Aeroport', from the airport enters the town along ulitsa Bukhtueva then runs along ulitsa Kochetova at least as far as the Hotel Mongulek. Bus fares are US$0.10 – pay the conductor.

The 'Vostok-Avtovokzal' bus runs from the bus station along ulitsa Kochetova through the centre. A taxi between the bus station and the town centre is US$1 or US$2.

EASTERN TUVA
ВОСТОЧНАЯ ТУВА

The east is mainly forested and roadless, with more rivers and lakes than the rest of Tuva.

Toora-Khem & Lake Azas
Тоора-Хем и Озеро Азас

Lake Azas (also called Lake Todzha) is big and beautiful, surrounded by forest and mountains. The way to come is by boat from Kyzyl up the Bolshoy Yenisey to Toora-Khem, about 30 km west of the lake (see Kyzyl Getting There & Away). The river trip is beautiful though the seating on the boat is enclosed and it's hard to see some of the views. There's a *hotel* at Toora-Khem charging US$4 per person with food available.

If no bus appears to take you from Toora-Khem to the lake, you should be able to find a taxi or hitch a lift. At the lake there's a cheap *Turbaza* with four-bed cabins and basic food available – soup, bread, tinned sardines and ham. You can hire boats on the lake or take walks. Locals say there are bears in the area.

Erzheey
Эржеей

This is a Russian Old Believers' village reached from Sizim on the Maly Yenisey. Two km from the village, there's a *kemping* with four huts, a café and showers, where you can organise horse trips up the river to Uzhep.

Kungurtug
Кунгуртуг

Kungurtug is a village in the south-east with flights from Kyzyl – though the weather is often poor and you may not be able to fly back when you want. You can visit nearby Lake Tere-Khol, with an island almost entirely covered by the ruins of an Uyghur fortress-palace of the 8th century. The man who excavated it in the 1950s, Sevyan Vaynshteyn, was baffled by how so much building material could have been carried there by water. However, he heard a local legend that the lake appeared after the fortress was built.

SOUTHERN TUVA
ЮЖНАЯ ТУВА

The village of **Samagaltay**, 165 km south of Kyzyl, has a Buddhist temple. Families here carve and sell small Buddha figures from agalmatolite.

Erzin, 220 km from Kyzyl, is a town of almost entirely Tuvan people, with a *hotel* charging US$3 per person and a decent *stolovaya* nearby. Desert begins to the south, across the Tes-Khem River. **Bay-Dag**, north of Erzin, has camel herds.

WESTERN TUVA
ЗАПАДНАЯ ТУВА

Thirty km west of Kyzyl, **Ust-Elegest**, is another place with camel herds. From **Ak-Dovurak**, 300 km from Kyzyl, an alternative road into Khakassia crosses the Western Sayan. **Kyzyl-Dag** near Teeli has a new Buddhist temple, bigger than the one at Kyzyl. Maps show hotels in Shagonar, Chadan, Kyzyl-Mazhalyk and Teeli.

The Mongun-Tayga district in the far south-west is a mountainous region with lakes, yak pastures and 3976-metre Mt Mongun-Tayga, the highest in Tuva. The main settlement is **Mugur-Axy** village, to which there are flights from Kyzyl.

Eastern Siberia
Восточный Сибир

Eastern Siberia lies bounded by the great Yenisey River and the maritime territories of the Russian Far East. In the north it stretches to the Arctic shoreline and in the south it's bordered by Mongolia and China. The major towns and cities are all grouped in the south along the roughly parallel routes of the Trans-Siberian and BAM railways. Further north the settlements become extremely isolated and are accessible only by air.

The Western BAM & Northern Lake Baikal
Западный БАМ и северный Байкал

TAYSHET
ТАЙШЕТ
Population: 70,000
About the only point of interest in Tayshet is that it's the Trans-Siberian's westernmost junction with the Baikal-Amur Mainline (BAM). There's no reason to stop off here unless you're changing trains, and even that isn't recommended as most of the eastbound services out of Moscow pass through in the early hours of the morning. Should you find

yourself in Tayshet at that time, the railway station has rest dormitories (one room for men, with about a dozen beds, plus several smaller rooms for women) for about US$2 a night. Across the street is the *Hotel Birusa* (☎ 3 03 18) with singles/doubles at US$6/10. The hotel has a restaurant, and there's a stolovaya 100 metres down the street (ulitsa Transportnaya), open from 7 am to 7 pm, and on weekends from 10 am to 11 pm.

BRATSK
БРАТСК
Population: 280,000
There was a fort here on the Angara River as early as the 17th century, but it and about 40 other villages are now at the bottom of the 'Bratsk Sea', an artificial lake created in 1955 by the building of the Bratsk Hydroelectric Station (Bratskaya Gidro-Elektricheskaya Stantsia). The present-day town of Bratsk only marginally pre-dates the dam. It rose out of virgin taiga through the labour of 1500 volunteer workers, who at the beginning had to live under canvas, enduring winter temperatures as low as -58°C and swarms of summer midges that nearly blotted out the sun – or so the legend goes.

Almost 40 years after being turned on, the gargantuan Bratsk dam – one of four along the Angara – is still producing power at only 50% capacity, for lack of customers. The Soviet solution was to bring customers out to the dam, and these included the world's largest aluminium smelting plant, 20 km west of the centre, and an equally big cellulose factory five km south.

Consequently the area has become a ghetto of belching factories and the thick, grey air is amongst the foulest in the country. Forests are dead or dying for 100 km around. An uncomfortable joke refers to the 'Bratsk method of birth control': a visiting public-health specialist claimed that two years at the

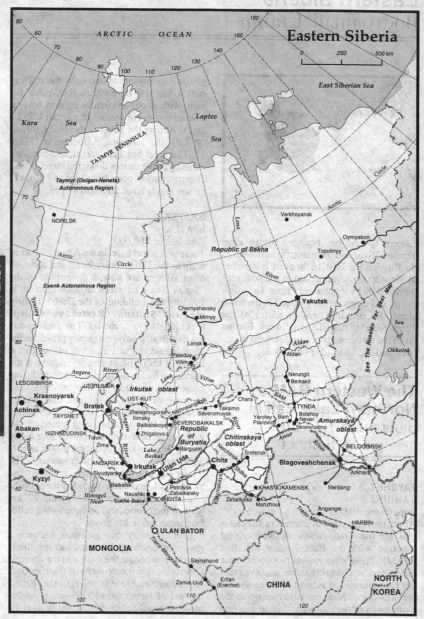

Eastern Siberia

ARCTIC OCEAN

East Siberian Sea

Kara Sea

Laptev Sea

TAYMYR PENINSULA

Taymyr (Dolgan-Nenets) Autonomous Region

NORILSK

Arctic Circle

Verkhoyansk

Oymyakon

Republic of Sakha

Topoliyy

Evenk Autonomous Region

Yakutsk

Chernyshevsky

Mimyy

Lena River

Aldan

Sea of Okhotsk

See the Russian Far East Map

Lensk

Peleduy

Vitim

Aldan

Nerungri

Berkakit

LESOSIBIRSK

Angara River

UST-ILIMSK

UST-KUT

Lena River

Vitim

Chara

BAM

TYNDA

Krasnoyarsk

Bratsk

Achinsk

TAYSHET

Zhelenogorsk

Ilimsky

Baikalskoye

Zhigalovo

Nizhneangarsk

Taksimo

Severomuysk

Yerofey Pavlovich

Bolshoy Never

Skovorodino

Bam

Amurskaya oblast

Manzhouli

Abakan

NIZHNEUDINSK

Zima

Tulun

SEVEROBAIKALSK

Republic of Buryatia

Barguzin

Chitinskaya oblast

Nerchinsk

Sretensk

BELOGORSK

Kyzyl

ANGARSK

Irkutsk

Slyudyanka

Lake Baikal

Ulan Ude

Chita

Blagoveshchensk

Arkhara

Baikalsk

Petrovsk

KRASNOKAMENSK

Hovsgol Nuur

Naushki

Zabaikalsky

KYAKHTA

Sukhe Bator

Kaymanskaya

Shilka

Zabaikalsk

Manzhouli

Nenjiang

Angangxi

HARBIN

ULAN BATOR

MONGOLIA

Trans-Mongolian

Trans-Manchurian

Saynshand

Zamia Uud

Erlian (Erenhot)

CHINA

NORTH KOREA

1	Museum of Regional Studies Краеведческий музей
2	Hotel Taiga Гостиница Тайга
3	Telephone & Telegraph Office Телефон и Телеграф
4	Hotel Bratsk Гостиница Братск
5	Aeroflot Аэрофлот
6	Bookshop Книжный магазин
7	Post Office Почтамт
8	Market Рынок
9	Bus Station Автовокзал
10	Suburban Railway Station Пригородный железнодорожный вокзал

Bratsk
Братск

0   250   500 m

aluminium plant was enough to make many of its workers sterile.

So why come? Well, according to local Intourist literature, 'An American public figure remarked that any educated man who hasn't seen the Bratsk hydropower station can hardly consider his education complete'. The town itself, isolated in the taiga, is at least a good place to see the scale of Soviet industrial fantasies and marvel at what Russians can do when they're inspired.

Orientation & Information

The city is actually a necklace of several small settlements around the shore of the Bratsk Sea, each originally a centre for a different aspect of the dam's construction. The two principal hotels, the Taiga and Bratsk, are in the central district (*Tsentralny Rayon*), a forest of apartment blocks 35 km south-west of the dam.

Intourist (☎ 44 39 51; fax 44 65 22) is on the 1st floor of the Hotel Taiga, and there's an exchange bureau downstairs in the foyer. The telephone and telegraph office is just down the street at ulitsa Mira 27, and there is a post office a block east on ulitsa Kirova, with a bookshop opposite.

Bratsk time is Moscow time plus five hours. The Bratsk telephone code is 3953.

Things to See & Do

Bratsk Intourist city tours are US$20, and after telling us this the young woman at the service desk added, 'But there's nothing interesting round here'. While the central district is completely without charm, neighbouring **Padun**, 40 minutes' walk from the dam, has a pleasant promenade, an old log watchtower and the city's only working church. From the central district take northbound bus No 118 along ulitsa Mira to the end.

As long as you're here, you should have a look at the **dam & power station**. The dam itself is one-km long with a road and the BAM railway running across the top. Inside the powerhouse, you can punch 'English' on an automated display and learn all you ever wanted to know about Siberian dams. Photography is allowed. Intourist's two-hour outing costs a stiff US$45, but without their guide you might have difficulty gaining entry to the powerhouse. From the Hotel Taiga or Hotel Bratsk, bus No 107, northbound on ulitsa Mira, takes 45 minutes to the dam. It only goes by every hour or so and is jammed full, but it stops right on the dam, from which a zillion steps descend to the powerhouse.

Bratsk's other attraction is the **Angara Village**, an open-air ethnographic museum containing a reconstructed Evenk camp, another watchtower from the old fort and the obligatory 'three farmsteads of varying economic level' from the 19th century. It's 15 km north of the central district, at least four km off the road, and there's no bus to it. Intourist can arrange an excursion there for US$40 or you might take a taxi. The museum is closed by mud in the spring but it's open in the summer from 10 am to 5 pm, closed Monday.

Places to Stay

Intourist runs the old but sturdy *Hotel Taiga* (☎ 44 39 79) at ulitsa Mira 35. It has clean, plain singles/doubles for US$40/50 with attached showers (with hot water). Nearby is the municipal *Hotel Bratsk* (☎ 4 46 44) at ulitsa Deputatskaya 32. Singles/doubles with attached showers (no hot water) are US$24/46 while those with shared facilities are slightly cheaper. There's no extra charge for the cockroaches.

Closer to the dam, in the Energetik settlement, is the *Hotel Turist* (☎ 37 09 95) at ulitsa Naymushina 28.

Places to Eat

The *Hotel Bratsk* has a restaurant but one look inside and we passed. The restaurant on the 1st floor of the *Hotel Taiga* is better. The service is professional and the food is good, particularly the pelmeni (small meat-filled dumplings) served in either sour cream (smetana) or butter (maslo) at US$1 for a heaped plate. Other dishes on the menu cost US$3 to US$4. There is also a small *café* on the ground floor where, if you ask, they can produce a menu in English. The adjacent bar seems to be the most popular night haunt in town.

If you don't fancy the options for dining out, there are two stores next to the bookshop on ulitsa Kirova. These have a lot of imported foodstuffs, with which you might be able to sustain yourself.

Getting There & Away

Air Daily flights go to/from Krasnoyarsk, Irkutsk (US$80 one way, one hour), Moscow, Novosibirsk, Omsk and Vladivostok. There are also flights to/from Yekaterinburg six times a week, Khabarovsk three times a week, Magadan twice a week and Yakutsk once a week. The Aeroflot office is at ulitsa Deputatskaya 17, open from 8 am to 7 pm. At the airport the foreigners' area (mezhdunarodnyy sektor) is at the far left end as you face the planes.

Train The strung-out town has four stations on the BAM. Anzyobi station (also called Chekanovsky) is closest to the Taiga and Bratsk hotels; Padunskie Porogi, the next station north, is closest to the Hotel Turist. The branch line into the central district is only for suburban trains. Two fast trains daily go west to Moscow and one to Krasnoyarsk, while another three go as far as the Trans-Siberian main line at Tayshet (315 km, 7½ hours). Eastbound there are daily trains to Severobaikalsk (740 km, 18 hours) and Tynda/Neryungri (change here for Komsomolsk).

Boat There used to be a hydrofoil link between Bratsk and Irkutsk, a 13-hour trip along the Angara River. However, in 1994 the service had been discontinued because of a lack of passengers; you could contact Intourist to see whether it's since been revived.

Getting Around

From the airport, express bus No 110 goes past the Hotel Taiga to the central district bus station on ulitsa Yuzhnaya every hour throughout the day. The trip takes about 50 minutes. Bus No 103 goes to the Hotel Turist. A taxi trip will put your heart in your throat but it's the surest way *to* the airport.

Bus No 27A shuttles between Anzyobi railway station and the central district bus station on ulitsa Yuzhnaya. From Padunskie

Porogi station take bus No 103 for a 10-minute ride to the Hotel Turist.

AROUND BRATSK
ОКЛО БРАТСКА

Intourist offers numerous programmes for tourism in the taiga along the Kova River (a tributary of the Angara) and at Lake Baikal's northern end. Among the offerings are three days of hiking from cabins on the Kova for US$580, two days of hiking and three days of white-water boating on the Kova for US$770, and two weeks of boating on the Kova and lower Angara for US$880. A week of skiing around Bratsk and the Kova costs US$560.

ZHELEZNOGORSK ILIMSKY
ЖЕЛЕЗНОГОРСК-ИЛИМСКИЙ
Population: 33,000
Though not actually on the railway, Zheleznogorsk Ilimsky is a BAM town, created in the 1960s around an iron-ore processing plant (Zheleznogorsk means 'mountain of iron'). It's situated 150 km east of Bratsk and several km north of the BAM station Korshunikha. It's notable for its exceptionally clean and well-maintained appearance and for its density of museums; there's a local museum, a Museum of Russian-Japanese Friendship, the Yangel Museum and the Museum of the House of Yangel – which is a lot of history for a town just 30 years old. The celebrated Yangel is one Mikhail Yangel, a leading space-race scientist who was closely involved with Yury Gagarin's epoch-making first-man-in-space flight. Yangel died in 1971.

One reason for visiting Zheleznogorsk Ilimsky might be to use it as a base for exploring the surrounding wilderness: with its craggy mountains and lake-filled valleys, this is one of the most picturesque regions of all Siberia. The Kedr Tourist Club can offer experienced guides for US$10 per day who are willing to accompany or lead trekkers, mountaineers or canoeing/rafting parties (the club has canoes for hire at US$4.50 per day). The club can also arrange *homestays* at US$5 per person. Contact Anatoly Semilet

(☎ (39566) 2 84 73, 2 28 28; fax (39566) 2 26 05) at room 430, 4th Hostel, 8th Kvartal, Zheleznogorsk Ilimsky 665680. Alternative accommodation can be found in the *Hotel Magnetit* (☎ (39566) 2 17 58), which has rooms with attached showers for US$6/10.

UST-KUT
УСТЬ КУТ
Population: 70,000
Although now reached by the BAM railway, Ust-Kut originally grew as a port on the great Lena River. It was founded in 1631 by the explorer Yerofey Khabarov, who used it as a supply base for Yakutsk some 1988 km downriver. Ust-Kut can also lay claim to one of Siberia's fabled, but in fact few, salt mines, which was operating up until the time of the Revolution.

The town's points of interest include the Osetrovo shipbuilding works, founded in the 17th century, the nearby museum, and also the mud spas. However, the main reason for visiting would be to recreate Khabarov's route and take a boat down the Lena. During the navigation season, from late May to late September, about two boats per week make the 4½-day trip to Yakutsk. Passage in a 1st-class, two-berth, upper-deck cabin is US$106, while a place in a four-berth, upper-deck cabin is US$78. A place in a four-berth, 1st deck cabin is US$60, in an eight-berth, 1st-deck cabin it's US$40; while if you don't mind being deep in the bowels of the ship on the lowest deck you can get a berth for as little as US$32. There are also hydrofoils which depart every other day at 7 am heading downriver as far as Vitim and Peleduy, a 14-hour journey costing US$50. In the opposite direction, hydrofoils depart every other day for Zhigalovo, 342 km upstream, an 11-hour journey for US$24. (There is a road linking Zhigalovo to Irkutsk and it may be possible to get a bus between the two.) Bookings should be made at the Osetrovo river port (☎ (39565) 2 63 97; fax (39565) 2 07 29) at ulitsa Kalinina 8, across from the railway station.

Accommodation in Ust-Kut is at the 220-bed *Lena Hotel* (☎ (39565) 2 15 07; fax

(39565) 2 07 29 marked 'attn Lena Hotel') at ulitsa Kirova 88, close to the railway station. A double room with attached toilet and shower is US$33, while a similar single is US$27. The *river port building* also has fairly basic rest rooms, where a place in a four-bed dormitory costs US$5 and a bed in a double room US$7.50.

Ust-Kut also has a small airfield with flights to Chita, Irkutsk and Yakutsk. To get to the airfield take bus No 101 from outside the railway station.

SEVEROBAIKALSK
СЕВЕРОБАЙКАЛЬСК
Population: 35,000

Before the coming of the BAM railway there was no town called Severobaikalsk, just virgin taiga crowding to the edge of Lake Baikal. The town appeared almost overnight in the early 1970s. The first dwellings were temporary – railroad carriages and shacks built from scavenged railway construction materials – but a small, permanent, concrete-block town followed, built by workers from Leningrad (they're commemorated in a monument in front of Severobaikalsk's ski-slope-roofed railway station). However, the money ran out long before everyone was properly housed, and a large percentage of Severobaikalsk's residents still live in the ramshackle home-made shanty town, ironically referred to by locals as the 'Old Town'. The industries that were part of the Severobaikalsk blueprint also never got further than a Leningrad city-planner's drawing board. Now that their work on the BAM is finished, it's unclear how most of the town's residents are to make a living. Most are apparently prepared to take their chances where they are, beside the lake, rather than uproot.

Despite the fact that the best views of Baikal are those from the railway yard and the coal-fired electricity plant, Severobaikalsk is not an unattractive place. Its small size means that in minutes a bus can have you out of the concrete and in the wilderness beside cool, clear rivers that run gurgling from rounded olive-green mountains. The town makes an excellent base from which to explore the northern end of the lake and it has some very good accommodation. The hydrofoil link with Irkutsk also makes Severobaikalsk easily accessible from the main Trans-Siberian rail route.

Orientation & Information
Severobaikalsk is compact. The main street, Leningradsky prospekt, runs north from the railway station 600 metres to ploshchad Tsentralny (Central Square) – and that's about the extent of the town. From the square, Leningradsky prospekt continues north-west to the Old Town. Running from east to west in front of the railway station is the snappily named prospekt 60 let Soyuz Sovietskikh Sotsialisticheskikh Respublik (60 Years of the USSR Ave). Taking a right-hand turn at the east end of this street will bring you to the port on Lake Baikal, 1.5 km south of the railway station.

Most of the town's amenities are on or around ploshchad Tsentralny. On the east side of the square is the trade centre (Torgovy Tsentr), a miniature department store, and just to the south is the post office, open on weekdays from 10 am to 6 pm, Saturday from 10 am to 2 pm, and closed on Sunday. The telephone and telegraph office is behind the trade centre, housed in a three-storey block, and open 24 hours daily. The local bank, the only place in town to change money, is next to the telephone office. It's closed at weekends.

One person who will be able to help with accommodation, tours and information in the Severobaikalsk area is Rashit Yahin of the one-man outfit BAMtour (☎ 2 15 60; fax 2 25 15; telex 154215 DWC SU: mark all faxes and telexes 'attn Rashit Yahin, BAMtour'). The company has few actual resources apart from Yahin himself, who came to North Baikal 20 years ago to work on the BAM and since 1990 has been operating as an occasional guide and interpreter. He can book accommodation in and around Severobaikalsk (and right along the length of the BAM) and can also arrange homestays. Yahin can also help to organise any day trips or expeditions and arrange for the hire of boats, kayaks, rafts, bicycles etc. Prices are always negotiable as these things are borrowed from neighbours and local organisations.

The time in Severobaikalsk is Moscow time plus five hours. The telephone code is 30139.

Things to See & Do

There is a **local museum** and an adjacent **art gallery**, both located at ulitsa Mira 2, and open from 10 am to 5 pm daily except Monday. The museum is dedicated to the building of the BAM and also has a small display of Buryat artefacts. The gallery has a limited collection of work by local artists.

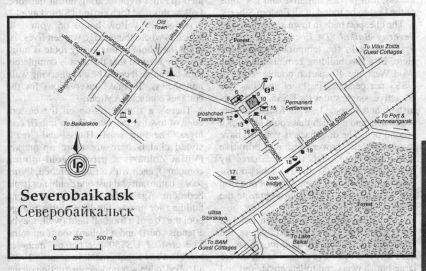

Severobaikalsk
Северобайкальск

SIBERIA & RUSSIAN FAR EAST

PLACES TO STAY		OTHER		12	Local Government Building Государственное здание
1	Hotel Severny Baikal Гостиница Северный Байкал	2	Monument to the Great Patriotic War Памятник Великой Отечественной Войны	13	Bookshop Книжный магазин
PLACES TO EAT		3	Local Museum Местный музей	15	Post Office Почтамт
6	Kafe Visit Кафе Визит	4	Art Gallery Художественная галерея	16	Supormarket Магазин
9	Restoran Leningrad Ресторан Ленинград	5	Palace of Culture Дворец культуры	18	Bus Station Автовокзал
10	Bakery Пекарня	7	Telephone & Telegraph Office Телефон и Телеграф	19	Market Рынок
14	Kafe Anya Кафе Аня	8	Bank Банк	20	Railway Station Железнодорожный вокзал
17	Kafe Russ Кафе Русь	11	Trade Centre Торговый центр		

Neither is particularly enlightening and neither justifies the foreigners' admission charge of US$1.50.

Places to Stay

Severobaikalsk was never built with tourism in mind and so, blessedly, there's no Intourist presence. All the accommodation in town is the result of private initiative and it's some of the best to be found in all Eastern Siberia.

The cheapest beds in town are at the *Hotel Severny Baikal* (☎ 77 12) on ulitsa Sportivnaya in the temporary settlement. Here, in a low building reminiscent of the Wild West, are 40 spartan double rooms at US$3 per person. The hotel also has two attractive, single suites for US$5, nicely furnished and carpeted, with fridge, phone, washbasin and a couch that could serve as a second bed. The drawback is you still have to use the one shower room and primitive hole-in-the-floor toilets that are shared by the whole hotel. Take the No 1 bus northwest from ploshchad Tsentralny for one stop and walk on, taking a left turn opposite the 'Baikal' store.

The closest thing to a state-run hotel in Severobaikalsk is at the port, where the *harbour administration building* has 20 double rooms at US$15 each. The rooms are large but showers and toilets are shared and there are no other facilities. Still, if you're arriving by hydrofoil from Irkutsk it's a good option for the first night. From the railway station, take bus No 103 and after two km, as the road runs down to the lake side, you'll see the red-brick harbour building off to your right.

Also close to the lake, in a woodland setting, are the four *BAM guest cottages* – owned by the railway company. Each of these two-storey wooden chalets has three beautifully furnished double bedrooms, a large living room with telephone and TV, two bathrooms and an immaculate, fully equipped kitchen for residents to prepare their own meals. There's also a separate sauna building with plunge pool and party room – unfortunately, this is also a big hit with local businessmen. The cottages are ideal if you're travelling in a group, and even for individuals or pairs they are a great alternative to faceless, grey hotel rooms and a bargain to boot at only US$12 per person per night. The cottages are 25 minutes' walk from the railway station, over the footbridge, then right along the road parallel to the tracks; take the first surfaced road on the left, then the first right, bearing left at the fork. Follow this road for a km until Sibirskaya 12, a two-storey yellow house on your left, which is where the cottage warden lives. At night the whole of this lonely route is unlit: we were assured that the area is completely safe, but alone it could be an unnerving walk nonetheless. To make reservations for the cottages contact BAMtour.

There's a similar set-up on the eastern edge of town at the *Vitim Zolda tourist cottages*. The four small Hansel-and-Gretel-styled chalets here are more up-market (Vitim Zolda is a private gold-mining company), each with a fitted kitchen, living room, bathroom and just one double or triple bedroom. Again there's a separate sauna building for guests, but here with a plunge pool the size of a football field (well, maybe a tennis court) and a billiard room upstairs. The cost of US$50 per person includes breakfast and a main meal. In autumn 1994, a 16-bed lodge was under construction on the site and by now may well be finished and offering cheaper beds. Vitim Zolda can also arrange boating or fishing on Baikal, shoreline trekking or even panning for gold (and, they claim, you get to keep anything you find). Contact Yevgenia Kuznitzovna (☎ 2 13 02 – Russian only) or book through BAMtour. To reach the cottages from the railway station it's a 20-minute walk; follow prospekt 60 let SSSR east to the T-junction, where it's left, then first right. The cottages are down an unsurfaced slip road 400 metres along on the left.

Places to Eat

The *Leningrad* is supposedly the town's top restaurant but the fact that its proprietors have ignored the events of recent years and stuck with the discredited Soviet city name is an early warning of what to expect: true pre-perestroika service, dishes you never ordered and a bill full of mysterious surcharges, including a mandatory 15% tip per diner. Much better is the *Russ*, a bar/restaurant on prospekt 60 let SSSR with a cosy atmosphere and efficient service. The menu is limited to three different kinds of pelmeni and some fishy selections (US$1.50 to US$4) but the food is good. There's also beer brewed on the premises, sold in great flagons for US$1. The Russ is open from early evening until midnight.

In the Palace of Culture on ploshchad Tsentralny is the *Kafe Visit* which has a 'meat and potatoes' menu but is far more popular with the locals as a drinking and dancing venue. It's open from noon to 3 pm and 7 to 11 pm. Across the square, on the corner of Leningradsky prospekt, *Kafe Ayana* is a canteen which serves a set daily meal of a salad, soup, main dish and drink for around US$1.50.

For shopping, the supermarket (and that's a very loose usage of the word) is on Leningradsky prospekt and there's a small market 100 metres east of the railway station. Fresh bread can be found at the bakery around the rear of the trade centre.

Getting There & Away
Air There's no airport at Severobaikalsk but from neighbouring Nizhneangarsk, 20 km away to the north-east, there are four or five flights a week to Ulan Ude (US$80, 80 minutes) and less frequently to Bratsk and Irkutsk.

Train There are daily westbound trains to Tayshet, Krasnoyarsk and Moscow; eastbound there are two daily services to Tynda/Neryungri, where you can connect for Komsomolsk.

Boat From June to September a hydrofoil service runs the length of Lake Baikal between Severobaikalsk and Irkutsk. The hydrofoil departs at 6.40 am every other day from the port at Severobaikalsk (or 6.20 am

from Nizhneangarsk) and reaches Irkutsk 10 hours later after a change of craft at Port Baikal. Seats can be booked in advance before noon at an office on the 1st floor of the local government building on ploshchad Tsentralny. A one-way ticket from Severobaikalsk to Port Baikal is US$25, with another US$3.50 for the fare from Port Baikal to Irkutsk.

Getting Around
Bus No 103 to Nizhneangarsk, which passes Severobaikalsk port, runs every hour from 5.50 am until 9 pm from the railway station forecourt. Bus Nos 1 and 2 go north-west from ploshchad Tsentralny along Leningradsky prospekt, No 2 turning left along ulitsa Mira to pass the local museum and art gallery.

AROUND SEVEROBAIKALSK (NORTH BAIKAL)
ОКРЕСТНОСТЬ СЕВЕРОБАЙКАЛЬСКА (СЕВЕРНЫЙ БАЙКАЛ)
While the southern end of Lake Baikal has been well visited since the opening of the Trans-Siberian Railway at the beginning of this century, the northern end of the lake is still almost completely unknown. Consequently it is the best area to visit to enjoy the serenity of the lakeside scenery and the perfect place for camping or indulging in other wilderness pursuits such as trekking, rafting, mountaineering or, in winter, skiing. However, as yet there is absolutely no tourism infrastructure. Rashit Yahin of BAMtour (for details see Severobaikalsk Information) is the local expert and the best person to contact for tours, activities and accommodation in the area.

Other than the lake, the biggest attractions of the area for locals are the hot springs. There are several popular sites where water emerges from the ground at 50°C and the locals, who firmly believe in its curative powers, have fashioned baths supplied by the springs. The closest spring to Severobaikalsk is at Solnechny, 45 minutes west along the BAM. The station is called Goudzhekit – about three trains a day stop there – and the chalet that serves as the bathhouse is 10 minutes' walk from the railway (to the right along the dirt track behind the station for 400 metres, then left at the sign that says 'goriachy kliuchy'). More attractive are Khakusy Springs, on the eastern shore of Lake Baikal directly across from Severobaikalsk. Nine km inland from Khakusy is a beautiful, high-altitude mountain lake, Frolikha. The two can be combined in an exhausting day trip but you would need to hire a boat to get across the lake.

Boats, in fact, represent the main means of getting around Baikal's northern end, as there are no roads or railway lines along the lake shore. Rashit Yahin suggests taking a few days to explore the lake's western shore in a series of boat hops. A chain of basic hunters' cabins dotted along the coast (including at Cape Kotelnikovsky – see below) could provide overnight accommodation. It's possible, Yahin says, to get down as far as Cheremshany Cape where there's a

lodge that sleeps six (US$15 per night). However, such an expedition would entail spending about US$50 per day for the boat and captain, and you'll probably need a guide – maybe another US$30. BAMtour has a good English-language map of the north-western Baikal region, which is available directly from the company.

Nizhneangarsk
Нижнеангарск
Nizhneangarsk, a small fishing village (population 10,000) about 20 km north-east of Severobaikalsk, is home to the regional airstrip and a fish-processing plant. Neither of these, admittedly, is a prime tourist attraction, but there is a local museum which traces the history of the settlement back to the 17th century. As well, there's a souvenir shop at ulitsa Kooperativnaya, near the airfield, which sells attractive local handicrafts – though animal lovers might prefer to give the sealskin hats a miss. The hydrofoil for Irkutsk begins its journey in Nizhneangarsk, departing every other day at 6.20 am.

Bus No 103 from Severobaikalsk railway station departs hourly for Nizhneangarsk, and takes 30 minutes to get there.

Kholodnaya (Evenk Village)
Холодная
The Evenki are one of the original indigenous peoples of the North Baikal region, although today there's little to distinguish them from the later Russian settlers. Their village of Kholodnaya, 20 km north-east of Nizhneangarsk, which was originally an encampment of birch-bark yurts, is still quite attractive and offers a good insight into traditional life in deepest Siberia. Of course, the reindeer herds which the Evenki have historically tended are long gone (confiscated with forced collectivisation in the 1930s), and instead many villagers are employed at a local polar-fox farm producing fur hats and souvenirs.

About 10 km from Kholodnaya are the remains of a Stalinist Gulag camp where, in the late 1930s, prisoners laboured mining mica. The camp was closed shortly before

North Baikal / Северный Байкал

BURYATIA

IRKUTSK OBLAST

Kholodnaya
Dushkachan
Verkhne Zaimka
Verkhne Angara River
BAM Railway
Nizhneangarsk
Goudzhekit
Severobaikalsk
Lake Frolikha
Khakusy
Baikalskoe

Mt Chersky
Cape Kotelnikovsky

0   12.5   25 km

Lake Baikal

BAIKALSKY RANGE

Cheremshany Cape

Barguzin Nature Reserve

Baikal-Lena Nature Reserve

Davsha

WW II but several decaying and weather-beaten buildings survive, along with towers, barbed-wire fences and three abandoned – and most likely dangerous – mine shafts. The camp is located in the Akikan valley and the strenuous trek to reach it takes between three and four hours. Head out from Kholodnaya railway station on the Kichera road, cross the river and continue up the hill until the 42-km marker. A little beyond, off to the left, is an overgrown dirt track which eventually, after about an hour, becomes a path beside a stream and winds up the valley to the Gulag camp.

Bus No 106 departs from Severobaikalsk railway station for Kholodnaya daily at 7.20 am and 1 and 5 pm. The journey takes about an hour and then 40 minutes later the bus makes the return trip. From Severobaikalsk, some eastbound local commuter trains also stop at Kholodnaya.

Baikalskoe
Байкальское

Sited on a lakeside bluff at the foot of a steep, emerald-green hill, the tiny fishing village of Baikalskoe is absurdly picturesque. There's no concrete or asphalt, just a hundred or so picture-pretty weatherboard cottages with bright-blue shutters and small, neat, green and flowery gardens. The first cottages were built here over a hundred years ago but the style of life in the village has changed so little since then that they are indistinguishable from the more recent houses. The water for all the houses is still drawn from a well and the settlement's electricity is generated by a trawler moored at the jetty.

It takes less than half an hour to explore the village but the surrounding area is good for walking. There's a decent path which leads up past a small hillside cemetery (filled with the graves of fishermen who died on the lake) and continues along the top of some steep cliffs.

If the fishers aren't too busy, Baikalskoe is the place to hire a skippered boat for excursions down to Cape Kotelnikovsky (see below) or possibly, depending on the time of year, to visit the seal colonies out on the lake – although an excursion such as this needs some advance planning. If you speak Russian, simply ask around the village whether there's anyone with a boat willing to take you out; if you don't, you may need to use the services of BAMtour. You should expect to pay something like US$10 per hour for boat hire. One fisherman in the village that we spoke with also guaranteed that he could lead visitors to bears in the forest, though he seemed a little perplexed by the idea that someone might just want to watch the animals and not shoot them.

Bus No 104 from the railway station at Severobaikalsk leaves for Baikalskoe daily at 7 am, noon and 5 pm. The journey takes an hour and the bus makes the return trip after a 30-minute halt.

Cape Kotelnikovsky
Мыс Котельниковский

Kotelnikovsky is a remote, uninhabited spot on the western shore of Lake Baikal about 65 km south of Severobaikalsk, and is known locally for its hot springs. Ten km inland from the springs are the peaks of the Baikalsky range, a spine of mountains which stretch from the northern end of the lake to a point roughly halfway to its southern tip. The scenery around the highest peak, Mt Chersky (2588 metres), 40 km directly inland from Kotelnikovsky, is said to be some of the most spectacular in Siberia, with waterfall cascades and glacial lakes. There is a small, basic lodge at Kotelnikovsky with 16 beds at US$10 per night. You could contact Alexandr Kluchakhin or Eugene Maryasov of the Davan Tourist Club in Severobaikalsk (ulitsa Rabochaya 19A, Severobaikalsk, Buryatia 671717), both of whom have extensive knowledge of the region.

It is possible to make a day trip to Kotelnikovsky by chartering a skippered boat from Baikalskoe (see above). The trip down the lake takes about 2½ hours each way, so if you're staying in Severobaikalsk and need to be back in Baikalskoe for the last bus (which departs at 6.30 pm), that gives you about four hours at Kotelnikovsky. For the day's hire of a boat with room aboard for four passengers you should expect to pay around US$50.

TYNDA
ТЫНДА

Population: 70,000

Tynda, 1320 km east of Severobaikalsk, is *the* BAM town; the BAM construction company's headquarters are here, as are the editorial offices of the railway's weekly, the *BAM*. It's from Tynda that the, as yet unfinished, Yakutia Railway (or AYAM) extends north towards Yakutsk, while a branch line goes south to connect with the Trans-Siberian at the town of Bam. The town is also home to the best of the BAM museums. Housed in the city library at ulitsa Profsoyuznaya 3, the museum has not only models and photographs pertaining to the railway, but also indigenous Evenk artefacts and a small section on the Gulag. It's open Saturday to Thursday from 10 am to 1 pm and 2 to 6 pm.

Equally worth visiting – to shed some of the accumulated grime of your journey – is the town's public *banya* (Russian sauna). The attendant has freshly cut birch branches for sale to enable bathers to whip themselves up into a sweat-soaked state of nirvana. See 'A Russian Banya' in the Petrozavodsk section of the Northern European Russia chapter for background and banya etiquette. The banya is on ulitsa Amurskaya, next door to the great sledgehammer-wielding statue.

If you are overnighting in Tynda give the centrally located and prominent *Hotel Yunost* (☎ (41656) 3 27 08) on Krasnaya Presnya a miss. It charges over US$100 for pokey doubles. Better value is the *Hotel Nadezhda* (☎ (41656) 2 96 55), which is behind the Yunost at ulitsa Festivalnaya 1. The hotel is on the 3rd floor of the building and has dormitory-style accommodation, with a few beds in each room at US$10 per person. There's also the *Hotel Orbita*, which is a large guesthouse in a wooded location, 15 minutes' walk from the town centre. The rooms are US$16 a night and the hotel also has a very good restaurant. To get there from the railway station, head for the centre of

town but don't turn on to Krasnaya Presnya, the main street; carry on another 500 metres and take a left into ulitsa Nadezhdy. At the end of ulitsa Nadezhdy, fork left and through the hedge into the grounds of the hotel.

Getting There & Away
Trains depart westward from Tynda daily for Severobaikalsk (train No 206) and, via Bratsk and Tayshet, for Moscow (train No 75/76 or 77/78). Towards the east there is a daily Tynda-Komsomolsk service (train No 204), which takes 40 hours between the two towns. Twice a week during the summer months (starting in early June), on Monday and Thursday at 9.25 pm, train No 261 departs from Tynda for Kislovodsk, near Stavropol, transporting Siberians to the holiday spas of the Caucasus region of southern Russia.

Buses run from in front of the railway station south to the town of Bolshoy Never, 20 km east of Skovorodino on the Trans-Siberian Railway.

Irkutsk & Southern Lake Baikal
Иркутск и южный Байкал

IRKUTSK
ИРКУТСК

Population: 630,000

With the cultural heritage of its aristocratic exiles, the Asiatic influences of nearby Mongolia and China, and the easy accessibility of Lake Baikal, Irkutsk is one of the most appealing cities on the Trans-Siberian trail.

Irkutsk was founded in 1651 as a Cossack garrison, to bring the indigenous Buryats into line. In the 1700s, it was the springboard for expeditions to the far north and east and, under trader Grigory Shelekhov, across the Bering Strait into Alaska and California (referred to locally at that time as the 'American district of Irkutsk'). Furs and ivory were

Lake Baikal
Озеро Байкал

There is probably no more beautiful place in all Russia than Lake Baikal, the 'Pearl of Siberia' – crystal clear (and, for the most part, drinkably pure), set round with mountains and lined with little settlements of wood cabins.

It's also one of the most interesting bodies of water on earth. Tour guides positively overflow with statistics. This 636-km-long slash in the taiga, although only the world's seventh-largest lake, is still bigger than Belgium. It's also the world's deepest lake: 1637 metres (or over a mile) to the bottom near the western shore. In it is nearly one-fifth of the world's fresh water – more water than North America's five Great Lakes combined. Swimmers brave enough to face Baikal's icy waters (never warmer than about 15°C except in a few bays) risk vertigo, as it's possible to see down as far as 40 metres.

Baikal's weather is unpredictable in all seasons, with especially foul and dangerous storms in November. The first snows fall around this time and by December, beginning from the marshes at the northern tip, the lake has begun to freeze. From February to April it's the world's biggest skating rink. Covered by ice a metre or more thick, the lake serves as a road, temporarily forming a navigable land route between the settlements at its northern and southern ends. During the Russo-Japanese war, when it was imperative that troops be got to the front line quickly, a railway track was even laid across the frozen lake. However, warm currents thin out the ice in places and the bottom of the lake is said to be a graveyard of cars and trucks. Nevertheless, despite its potentially deadly nature, Baikal is at its most spectacularly beautiful in winter.

Ecology From the seven-km thickness of sediment at the bottom, scientists calculate that Baikal has been in existence for over 25 million years, making it by far the world's most ancient lake (almost all earth's other lakes are less than 20,000 years old). Like the Galapagos Islands, where animal and plant life have evolved in complete isolation from the rest of the planet, Baikal is a living museum of flora and fauna. Of over 2000 recorded plant and animal species, 70% to 80% are found nowhere else. The lake is home to varieties of fish and sponges that, elsewhere, live only in salt water. The *nerpa*, Baikal's freshwater seal, is separated by over 3000 km from its nearest relative, the Arctic ringed seal, and nobody has the faintest idea how it got here.

Another curiosity is the big-eyed golomyanka fish, little more than a blob of pinkish fat with a backbone. It lives at extreme pressures at a depth of one to 1.5 km and, when brought to the surface, dissolves into an oily spot. More edible fish include immense sturgeon and Baikal's endemic delicacy, the omul (a relative of the salmon and trout).

But the lake's ecosystem has proved delicate. The omul population nose-dived in the 1950s as a result of overfishing and the building of the Irkutsk dam (which raised the lake level and destroyed many of the fish's shallow-water feeding grounds). The omul has also taken a battering from the pollution carried into Baikal by the Selenga River, a vast tributary which alone supplies half the water that flows into the lake. Rising south of Russia's border, the Selenga collects pollutants from three large Mongolian cities, human and industrial waste from Ulan Ude, the Buryat capital, and effluents from a pulp mill at Selenginsk. Omul fishing is now restricted.

In the 1960s a newly built cellulose plant at Baikalsk began to dump wastes into the lake, raising a level of protest previously unheard of in the then Soviet Union. Baikal became a banner for the country's new environmental movement and the precursor of all Soviet-era environmental activism. The cellulose plant is now probably the most cleaned-up factory in the whole of Russia although, despite claims to the contrary, it's believed that dumping continues.

There are three nature reserves around the lake, which total more than a million hectares, all off limits to everyone but scientists and naturalists. Additionally, over 250 km of shore line, including the entire western shore as far north as Olkhon Island, is now contained within two national parks. Still, many Siberians think the lake is not getting the protection it deserves. Lake Baikal's salvation may lie in its adoption as a UNESCO World Heritage Site, a matter under consideration at the time of writing. ■

SIBERIA & RUSSIAN FAR EAST

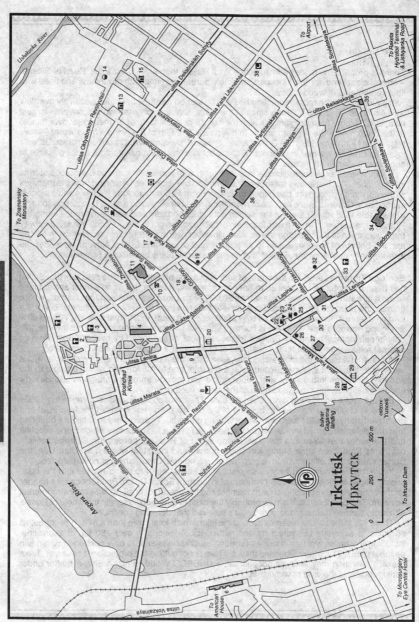

Irkutsk
Иркутск

PLACES TO STAY		
4	Hotel Angara	
	Гостиница Ангара	
7	Hotel Intourist	
	Гостиница Интурист	
9	Hotel Sibir	
	Гостиница Сибирь	

PLACES TO EAT		
11	Restoran Aura & Kafe Peshera	
	Ресторан Аура и Кафе Пещера	
12	Kafe Yunost	
	Кафе Юность	
17	Niva Bakery	
	Пекария Нива	
21	Restoran Dragon	
	Ресторан Дракон	
22	Theatre Kafe	
	Кафе Театр	
23	Bylina	
	Былина	
24	Karlson Kafe	
	Кафе Карлсон	
30	Restoran Fikhtelberg	
	Ресторан Фихтельберг	

OTHER		
1	Epiphany Church	
	Богоявленская церковь	
2	Church of the Saviour	
	Спасская церковь	
3	Catholic Church	
	Католическая церковь	
5	Trinity Church	
	Троицкая церковь	
6	Railway Station	
	Железнодорожный вокзал	
8	Post Office	
	Почтамт	
10	Telephone & Telegraph Office	
	Телефон и Телеграф	
11	Circus	
	Цирк	
13	Trubetskoy House	
	Дом Трубецкого	
14	Bus Station	
	Автовокзал	
15	Volkonsky House	
	Дом Волконского	
16	Synagogue	
	Синагога	
18	Aeroflot	
	Аэрофлот	
19	Rodnik Bookshop	
	Книжный магазин Родник	
20	Art Museum	
	Художественный музей	
22	Vampilov Theatre	
	Театр имени Вампилова	
25	Knigotorga Bookshop	
	Книготорга	
26	Antey Bookshop	
	Книжный магазин Антей	
27	Okhlopkov Drama Theatre	
	Драматический театр имени Охлопкова	
28	White House	
	Белый Дом	
29	Museum of Regional Studies	
	Краеведческий музей	
31	Philharmonic Hall	
	Филармония	
32	Mongolian Consulate	
	Консульство Монголии	
33	Raising of the Cross Church	
	Крестовосдвиженская церковь	
34	Musical Theatre	
	Музыкальный театр	
35	Puppet Theatre	
	Театр Кукол	
36	Department Store	
	Универмаг	
37	Central Market	
	Центральный рынок	
38	Mosque	
	Мечеть	

SIBERIA & RUSSIAN FAR EAST

sent to Irkutsk from all over eastern Siberia and carried to Mongolia, Tibet and China in exchange for silk and tea. Mingling with the merchants were scientists, missionaries and the first cast-off convicts.

As the administrative centre of East Siberia, Irkutsk became a major junction on the exile road. Its most illustrious 19th-century exiles were Decembrists and Polish rebels, many of whom chose to stay – a rough-hewn aristocracy, who kept education, the arts and political awareness at a high level. Several Decembrists' houses have been restored as museums of the time.

Disaster struck in 1879 when fire destroyed almost three-quarters of the city. However, after gold was discovered in the Lena basin in the 1880s, the city didn't simply recover, it boomed. On the charred remains of log cabins, the newly rich built brick mansions and grand public buildings. The city's Russian classical architecture dates from this period. The shops filled with luxuries and imported goods, and Irkutsk became known as 'the Paris of Siberia'.

A city of well-to-do merchants and high-brow society, Irkutsk did not welcome the news of the Great October Socialist Revolution. Passing power into the hands of the working people sounded like a terrible idea and the city became a centre of resistance to Bolshevism. It wasn't until 1920, with the capture in Irkutsk of Admiral Kolchak, the head of the White army, and his summary execution, that the city finally succumbed to the Red tide.

Soviet-era planning had Irkutsk develop as an industrial and scientific centre and the face of the city was brutalised with graceless institutional architecture. Following the same blueprint, the Angara River was dammed in the 1950s, another step in the taming and modernising of Siberia.

The city still retains vestiges of its cosmopolitan and eclectic heritage. The scores of old gingerbread log houses are gradually losing out to the ugly stucco blocks loved by the Russians (understandably, since the latter come with such things as indoor plumbing) but they are still prevalent in the centre.

The single biggest attraction here is, of course, Lake Baikal, near enough for a day trip.

Orientation

The city centre is on the east bank of the Angara, above the confluence with its tributaries, the Ushakovka and the Irkut. Five km upstream is the Irkutsk hydroelectric station; boats to Lake Baikal leave from south of the dam.

The city's axes are ulitsa Karla Marxa (the main shopping street and once the boundary between town and garrison) and ulitsa Lenina, which runs parallel to the Angara 500 metres inland. The administrative centre is ploshchad Kirova at the north end of Lenina, with its Stalin-era Party headquarters. Across the Angara are the bustling railway station, university research institutes and new apartment blocks.

Irkutsk Drama Theatre

Maps of Irkutsk can be picked up at the news kiosk in the foyer of the Hotel Intourist.

Information

Money There is a concentration of currency-exchange places on ulitsa Lenina, but a good one to remember is the bureau in the service department at the Hotel Intourist, which works 24 hours. The Russo-Asiatic Bank at ulitsa Lenina 3, opposite the site of the Hotel Siberia, will cash American Express and Citicorp travellers' cheques, and is open from 9 am to 3 pm daily. Cash advances on a Visa card are possible at the exchange bureau in the Hotel Intourist.

Post & Telecommunications The main post office, at ulitsa Stepana Rezina, is open from 8 am to 8 pm, and on weekends from 9 am to 6 pm. Faxes can be sent from a desk at the post office between 8 am and 5 pm on weekdays only. To Australia a fax costs US$6.50 per minute, to the UK US$5 and to the USA US$6. The central telephone and telegraph office is on ulitsa Sverdlova, opposite the circus. Phone calls to Australia and the USA cost US$5 per minute, while calls to Europe are US$2 a minute. The telephone office is open 24 hours daily, with fax service between 8 am and 8 pm and a telex room open from 8 am to 5 pm.

Irkutsk time is Moscow time plus five hours. The Irkutsk telephone code is 3952.

Foreign Consulates The Mongolian Consulate (☎ 34 24 47) at ulitsa Lapina 11 will give you a transit visa for the Trans-Mongolian trip to Beijing. It's open for visas Monday to Saturday from 9 am to 1 pm and 2 to 6 pm. Bring your passport, train ticket and a passport-sized photo; the fee is US$30 for an immediate visa or US$15 if you can wait for a couple of days. The staff don't speak English but they understand 'transit visa'.

Travel Agencies Staff at Irkutsk-Baikal Intourist (☎ 29 02 66; fax 27 78 72; telex 231716 TURNE SU) are not only efficient and helpful, they even display initiative –

capitalising on the absence of a McDonald's or Pizza Hut, the tour company has its own smart, logo-emblazoned catering trailer out on Irkutsk's busiest streets, where it does a roaring trade in Intour-burgers, pizza and Coke. More conventionally, Intourist offers a range of themed city tours (museums, ethnic cultures, 'Russian romance') and a dozen or so Baikal-based packages. It also rents bicycles (US$2 per hour) and rowing boats (US$3 per hour) and can arrange helicopter sightseeing trips. Its offices are at the Hotel Intourist.

The smaller, private company Baikal-complex (☎ 36 54 19, 43 20 60; fax 43 23 22; telex 231522 PTB SU; e-mail loa@ibc2.irkutsk.su – all communications should be marked 'attn Nemirovsky, Baikal-complex') specialises in exploring Lake Baikal by boat. A cruise programme is normally five to 10 days with excursions to the shore at the more interesting places. The ship has berths for six but can take 12 if passengers sleep ashore in tents, and costs US$250 per day to hire. Baikalcomplex also rents out bicycles (US$4 per day) and canoes (US$30 per day) and can help to secure rail tickets to Beijing and Ulan Bator at short notice. Its mailing address is PO Box 3598, Irkutsk 29, 664029 Russia.

Bookshops None of Irkutsk's bookshops has anything in English but Antey, at ulitsa Karla Marxa 20 near ulitsa Lenina (behind the statue of Lenin hailing a taxi), does have a selection of maps including a good one of the general Baikal region. Other bookshops are Knigotorga (across the square at ulitsa Lenina 15) and Rodnik, at the corner of ulitsa Karla Marxa and ulitsa Litvinova.

Decembrist Houses
After completing their term of labour near Chita, many Decembrists settled in Irkutsk. So, too, did the wives of nine of them and the girlfriends of another two, who had followed them into exile. The first of these women was Yekaterina Trubetskaya, the wife of Prince Sergey Trubetskoy, who was allowed to go to Siberia on condition that she forfeit all

titles and hereditary claims to them. She died here, and her husband subsequently returned to Moscow.

The restored houses of Trubetskoy and Count Sergey Volkonsky, with furnishings and pictures of family and friends, are now rather touching museums, although a little meaningless without the explanations of a guide. (Alternatively, get hold of *The Princess of Siberia* (London, 1984), Christine Sutherland's account of the life of Maria Volkonskaya.) Trubetskoy's house, with maps and paintings of exile life in the cellar, is at ulitsa Dzerzhinskogo 64, open from 10 am to 6 pm, closed Tuesday. Admission is US$2.50. The Volkonsky house is one block east, just off ulitsa Timiryazeva – follow the dusty road that runs down the side of the church and it's a big bluish-grey building, unmarked. Enter through the courtyard. It's open from 10 am to 6 pm every day except Monday, and admission costs US$3.50.

Irkutsk Museum & Around
The red-brick piece of Victoriana at ulitsa Karla Marxa 2, near the river, was in the 1870s the museum of the Siberian Geographical Society, a club of explorers and researchers, whose names adorn the exterior. It's now the Irkutsk Museum of Regional Studies and is open from 10 am to 6 pm, closed on Monday. Admission is US$2.50, or US$1.50 with student ID.

The best exhibits feature indigenous tribes from the time when, under the influence of Russian settlers, they were abandoning nomadic ways: house mock-ups; shamans' robes and amazing headgear; an Evenk coat made of feathers; and fearsome Buryat idols. Upstairs, lively displays trace the history of Irkutsk through the coming of the Trans-Siberian Railway and two world wars, and bring it bang up to date with Snickers wrappers and jeans made in China. The porcelain Nubian heads and cuddly toy monkeys are, an English-speaking attendant said, thrown in for decoration.

The **obelisk** across the road from the museum was erected on the 10th anniversary of the arrival of the Trans-Siberian Railway.

SIBERIA & RUSSIAN FAR EAST

The faces are those of Yermak (the 'conqueror of Siberia'), Count Muravev-Amursky (the governor general who took the Amur River back from the Chinese) and Speransky, another governor. Yury Gagarin, the first person in space, despite having no Irkutsk connections, is commemorated with a monument 300 metres further north along the corniche. Almost opposite the monument is a small side street, ulitsa Gasheka, named after the Czech novelist Jaroslav Hašek, creator of the classic *The Good Soldier Švejk*. In the immediate post-Revolutionary period Hašek lived in Irkutsk, where he worked for the Bolsheviks (a move born out of expediency rather than any political conviction) as an editor and political commissar.

The small, tree-covered island just upstream of the Trans-Siberian obelisk is **Youth Island** (ostrov Yunosti). It has a small, rocky beach and what looks like a miniature Sydney Opera House but is, in fact, a dance bandstand.

Other Museums

The **Church of the Saviour** (Spasskaya tserkov), north of ploshchad Kirova, houses

Traditional folk singers, Angara River

the Irkutsk Museum's natural-history collection of stuffed animals and early Evenk, Buryat and Yakut clothing. Upstairs there's an exhibition hall and, ascending a claustrophobic's nightmare of a staircase, a display of local church history. It's open from 10 am to 6 pm except on Tuesday, and admission is US$2. Across the road, the **Epiphany Church** (Bogoyavlenskaya tserkov) is a museum of Russian icons. It's open from 10 am to 6 pm, closed on Monday and Tuesday; admission US$2. The **Irkutsk Art Museum** at ulitsa Lenina 5 has a weak collection composed of indigenous Siberian art, icons, Russian painting and Chinese porcelain, which few are going to find worth the US$4 admission charge. Opening hours are 10 am to 6 pm daily except Tuesday.

Moored within sight of the Raketa river terminal (for hydrofoils to Lake Baikal) is the icebreaker-ferry *Angara*, one of two old boats, manufactured in England and shipped here in pieces, that originally ferried Trans-Siberian passengers, and the train, across the lake. It now houses the **Museum of Baikal Navigation**, and is open daily except Monday.

Wooden Houses & Other Old Buildings

Though they're steadily disappearing, the city still has whole neighbourhoods of wooden cabins. The heaviest concentration is in the streets between ulitsa Karla Marxa and ulitsa Timiryazeva. Some of these buildings look as though they've just endured a 24-hour vodka binge (dishevelled, unsanitary and on the point of keeling over) but others are exquisite, with beautiful, lace-like, carved wood decoration. Two side by side on bulvar Gagarina, south of ulitsa Karla Marxa, illustrate the stylistic differences between early Siberian (No 14, with women's quarters upstairs facing the courtyard and few front windows) and later Russian (No 16, with 'wooden lace' decoration and many high windows facing the street).

Opposite the Irkutsk Museum on ulitsa Karla Marxa is the **White House** (Bely Dom), built in 1804 as the residence of the governors general of Eastern Siberia. It's now a university science library. At ulitsa Zhelyabova 5, opposite the circus, is the huge, ornate **Pioneers' Palace** (the Pioneers were not explorers but a Soviet youth organisation), built in 1897 for a rich and eccentric gold merchant named Vtorov but commandeered by the Soviets following the Revolution.

Churches

The heart of old Irkutsk was the magnificent Annunciation Cathedral, at the north end of ploshchad Kirova; but, after suffering extensive damage in the Civil War, the cathedral was demolished to make way for the hulking Party headquarters. It is still visible in photos exhibited in the belfry of the Church of the Saviour (Spasskaya tserkov, 1706), which stands behind the Party building. The exterior of the whitewashed Saviour's church is decorated with fresco panels, one of which depicts the baptism of Buryats. Across the road is the Epiphany Church (Bogoyavlenskaya tserkov, 1723). Both are now museum branches (see Museums).

A block south on ulitsa Sukhe-Batora is Siberia's only Gothic building, a Catholic church built by Polish exiles in 1881. In the 1930s it became a concert hall (it's still used for organ recitals), while around the same time the Trinity Church (Troitskaya tserkov) on ulitsa Chkalova, near the river, was made into a planetarium. The Baroque Raising of the Cross Church (Krestovozdvizhenskaya tserkov, 1758), on ulitsa Sedova near the stadium, is one of the few churches that remained open to worshippers during the Soviet era. It dominates the skyline of Irkutsk seen from the Trans-Siberian.

There is a dilapidated synagogue at ulitsa Karla Libknekhta 23 and a mosque four blocks further south on the same street.

Znamensky Monastery

This former nunnery is the headquarters of the Orthodox diocese of Irkutsk, Chita, Buryatia and Sakha. Inside is the working Church of the Sign (Znamenskaya tserkov, 1763), restored by exiled nuns and reopened

after WW II. Services are held at 10 am and 5 pm on weekends and Church holidays, and possibly at other times.

In the cemetery is the grave of the merchant-explorer Grigory Shelekhov and those of Princess Trubetskaya, wife of the exiled Decembrist, and three of her children. Another grave, marked by a stone tree with no branches, is said to be that of a merchant who had 11 daughters and no sons. The monastery is across the Ushakovka River via trolleybus No 3, or a 1.5-km walk from the south end of ploshchad Kirova.

Places to Stay

Until the restoration and reopening of Irkutsk's historical Hotel Grand, a project under discussion at the time of writing, the top accommodation in town is at the *Hotel Intourist* (☎ 29 63 35; fax 27 78 72) at bulvar Gagarina 44. It's no beauty, but it does benefit from a fine setting on the Angara River, and is within easy walking distance of the centre. Rooms with showers and baths are plain and clean, and there's a multitude of services including four bars, three restaurants and two cafés. Single rooms range from US$60 to US$82, doubles from US$72 to US$92. At one time the *Hotel Angara* (☎ 24 16 31) was an acceptable substitute to the Intourist but these days it's extremely seedy, the only redeeming feature being its location on the city's central square, ploshchad Kirova. The rooms all have their own showers. Singles are US$30 to US$40, while doubles are US$44. Across the square at ulitsa Lenina 18 are the remains of the *Hotel Sibir* (☎ 29 37 51), well-known haunt of one of Irkutsk's rival Mafia gangs. When the hotel caught fire (cause unknown) in early 1995, the local fire brigade happened to be 15 km out of town attending to another mysterious blaze; by the time they raced back, the Sibir had been completely consumed.

Definitely not a hang-out of men who play with matches, and highly recommended, is the hotel attached to the *Microsurgery Eye Centre* (☎ 46 25 69; fax 46 17 62) at ulitsa Lermontova 337. It's a 10-minute bus ride across to the west bank of the Angara, but the place is clean (clinically so) and modern, with bathrooms that make you feel you've just entered a four-sq-metre annexe of Sweden. The staff are friendly and there's a caf, and a sauna for guests' use. A single room is US$38, or a bed in a double US$23. To get there take trolleybus No 1, No 7 or No 2 from ploshchad Kirova, or No 6 from the airport, and get off at the Mikro Gerurgsky stop in front of the seven-storey Microsurgery building.

There are a couple of other cheap options away from the centre of town. The *Hotel Profkurs* (☎ 23 55 66 ext 362, or 28 77 29 in the evening) at ulitsa Baikalskaya 263 is a hostel attached to a technological institute, quite close to the Raketa hydrofoil terminal. Clean double rooms with shower and toilet are US$10 per person. To get there from the city centre take tram No 5 from ulitsa Partizanskaya, behind the central market, and get off at the penultimate stop, Vostokznergoremont (Востокзнерг оремонт in metre-high letters on an office block to your left); the hotel is in the building directly in front as you step off the tram. To reach the hotel from the Raketa terminal, walk directly inland and pass through two housing estates. On crossing a second major road you should arrive at a car park with a chain-link fence; the hotel is beyond the car park and the small cluster of apartment blocks, beside the tram tracks. In all, it's a 15-minute walk.

The *Hotel Dossaf* (☎ 27 27 40, 27 00 20) at ulitsa Kultukskaya 9B feels very much like student accommodation. Guests are given an apartment with kitchen, bathroom and living room/bedroom, which sleeps two to four persons. Like most student accommodation, the place has taken a battering, but a bed is only US$7. Take tram No 5 from behind the market, or bus No 20 from the railway station, to a stop called Pervay Sovietsky, at the junction of ulitsa Sovietskaya and ulitsa Dekabrskikh Sobyty. Beside the junction is a tank on a plinth; you need to go the way its barrel points (north along ulitsa Sovietskaya), taking the first left. As you reach two tall chimneys off to

the right, you can see the red-brick Dosaf building adjacent to a long, five-storey apartment block.

One other highly recommended option is to stay at *American House* (☎ 43 26 89). This is a large private home 20 minutes' walk from the railway station, where Lida Scolocchini and her son Mark offer bed and fantastic breakfast for US$15. Only six people can be accommodated so reservations must be made well in advance. The address is ulitsa Ostrovsky 19, Irkutsk, Russia 664029. To get there take the short flight of steps across the road from the south end of the railway station. Take the unsurfaced road at the top of the steps and then head left, up the hill for a km. After crossing two roads, you'll pass a garage with red stars on the doors (a fire station) on your right, and from there you take the third turning on the right. Alternatively, take a taxi from in front of the railway station and ask for Dom Amerikansky – you should pay about US$2.

Baikalcomplex (see Information) can also arrange *homestays* (average US$30), not only in Irkutsk but in Listvyanka and other lakeside settlements.

Places to Eat

While not exactly a gastronomic gold mine, Irkutsk does have a number of decent places to eat. Of the three pricey restaurants at the Hotel Intourist, the *Sibirsky Traktir*, with decor to delight a furrier, serves traditional Russian dishes, while the *Peking* has a good Chinese menu. Better and cheaper oriental food can be found at the *Dragon*, a Russian-Chinese joint venture at ulitsa Pyatoy Armii (5-y Armii) 67. Recommended are the crispy chicken (krustyashaya kuritsa), the spicy beef (govyadina 'Iva') and the deep-fried squid (kalmari zhareny), all at around US$2 a dish. Place a side order for *depeshny farshirovany*, which are a bit like meat-filled nan breads (US$1.50 for two). The Dragon is open from 11 am to 4 pm and 6 to 11 pm. Booking is recommended.

Fikhtelberg is a cavernous (getting a table is never a problem) but elegant East German-built restaurant with heavy, slightly greasy but good Russian and Bavarian dishes: lots of pork (svinina) and nothing vegetarian. A meal for two without drinks will come to about US$8. The restaurant is at ulitsa Lenina 46, beside the stadium, and it's open from noon to 4 pm and 6 to 11 pm. At the *Aura*, a tiny restaurant on the top floor of the circus building (round to the left of the main entrance), the food is far better than the blandness of the menu would suggest – in fact it's probably the best to be had dining out in Irkutsk. At weekends there's a live cabaret and a boisterous, smoky, speakeasy atmosphere. The bill will come to around US$12 per person including a supplement for the entertainment. The Aura is open from noon to 3 pm and 5 pm to midnight, and booking is essential.

Also in the circus building (round to the right of the main entrance) is the *Kafe Peshera*, a good place for a daytime snack or coffee stop. The chunky playpen furniture and camouflage netting on the ceiling suggest the place was designed with kids in mind, and the racks of vodka behind the bar seem a little incongruous. However, it's the vodka that sets the tone, so much so that in the evening the Peshera is somewhere that any safety-minded, self-preservationist individual would do well to avoid. It's open from 11 am to 10 pm. The *Karlson Kafe* at ulitsa Lenina 15 is inspired by the character of the same name created by Swedish children's author Astrid Lindgren. In a tiny, pretty, glazed-brick interior, large pottery figures and scenes from the book adorn the walls. It's charming and kids would probably love it, but here, too, the clientele the caf, attracts is far more interested in alcohol than ice cream.

Other cheap, quick cafés include the *Yunost*, on ulitsa Karla Marxa near ulitsa Karla Libknekhta, a cheery place which specialises in pizza; and the *Bylina*, at ulitsa Lenina 13, which serves a couple of basic but good dishes (usually macaroni and meat) for about US$0.75. Both are open from 10 am to 10 pm.

The best coffee in town is served at the back of the *Niva* bakery, at ulitsa Karla Marxa 37; but there's no seating, just chest-high counters to lean against. Judging by the queues, the Niva also does the best bread in town. For somewhere to sit and linger, the *Theatre Kafe* on the corner of ulitsa Karla Marxa and ulitsa Lenina has a colourful cast of patrons and large picture windows onto the street.

For Trans-Siberian food stocks, try the lively central market on ulitsa Chekhova, with fish from the barrel, berries by the bucket and kiosks of Chinese noodles and beer.

Entertainment

The circus, on ulitsa Zhelyabova just east of ploshchad Kirova, is seasonal but during the summer break the auditorium is used by other travelling shows. Check the foyer posters for details. Despite its dilapidated appearance, the 1890 Philharmonic Hall, opposite the stadium on ulitsa Lenina, still has regular performances. Along the same street, towards the junction with ulitsa Karla Marxa, is the basement Vampilov Theatre which is home to a youthful fringe company.

Getting There & Away

Air There are two or three flights a day to Moscow (US$250, seven hours) and two a week to St Petersburg. Siberian connections include daily flights to Bratsk (US$80, one hour), Khabarovsk (US$165, 2¾ hours), Krasnoyarsk, Novosibirsk (US$130, 2½ hours) and Ulan Ude (US$58, 50 minutes). There are also flights once or twice a week to Petropavlovsk-Kamchatsky, Magadan and Yakutsk (US$222, 3½ hours). International connections include flights to/from Niigata in Japan, Shenyang in China, and Ulan Bator. At the airport, Intourist is in the left-hand building as you face the planes.

There is a typically dismal Aeroflot office (☎ 27 69 17) in town at ulitsa Gorkogo 29, which is open daily from 8 am to 7 pm.

Bus Five buses a day run to Listvyanka on Lake Baikal from the bus station on ulitsa Oktyabrskoy Revolyutsii.

Train Irkutsk is 88 hours from Moscow by daily express train. The best choice is the *Baikal Express* (westbound train No 9, eastbound No 10), which departs from Moscow's Yaroslavl station every day at 9.05 pm. There are generally no problems getting places on this train. Other alternatives are the daily Moscow-Vladivostok train (No 1/2), the *Rossia*, train No 79/80 Moscow-Chita, or train No 183/184 Moscow-Khabarovsk. The Moscow-Irkutsk fare in a four-berth sleeper was around US$110. For details of travelling on the weekly Trans-Mongolian train, No 3/4, or Trans-Manchurian train, No 19/20, and breaking your journey in Irkutsk, see the Trans-Siberian Railway chapter.

There are several daily services that will take you on to Ulan Ude (eight hours) – it's worth trying to catch an early morning train and travel what is one of the most scenic sections of the Siberian railways during daylight. You can get to Yekaterinburg (53 hours), Novosibirsk (32 hours), Krasnoyarsk (19 hours), Chita (18 hours), Khabarovsk (58 hours) and Vladivostok (72 hours) on the services mentioned above.

When facing Irkutsk railway station from the front, the long-distance ticket hall is on the far left and the left-luggage office is on the far right in a separate building beyond the toilet block.

Boat Every other day from June to late September, a hydrofoil makes the 10-hour trip up Lake Baikal to the northerly towns of Severobaikalsk and Nizhneangarsk. It leaves at 7 am from the Raketa terminal, south of the dam, and a one-way ticket costs US$30. During the same summer months, there's also a hydrofoil service to Ust-Barguzin on the lake's eastern shore, which departs at 9 am every Monday and Thursday and gets to Ust-Barguzin at 4 pm. It's wise to check the timetables (pinned up outside the ticket office at Raketa) as services are subject to change and possibly cancellation.

See the Around Irkutsk section for details of hydrofoil services to Listvyanka and up the western shore of the lake.

Getting Around

From the airport, bus No 20 runs to the railway station, stopping on ploshchad Kirova for the Angara and Sibir hotels and at the Planetariy stop, just before the river bridge, 10 minutes' walk along the corniche from the Hotel Intourist. Two trolleybuses also serve the airport: No 4 runs into town and terminates opposite the Hotel Sibir; No 6 runs across the dam and passes the Microsurgery Eye Hospital.

From the railway station, tram Nos 1 and 2 and bus Nos 7, 16 and 20 cross the river; all stop at Planetariy, the first stop after the bridge, but only the buses stop on ploshchad Kirova.

To reach the Raketa terminal for hydrofoils, take southbound bus No 16 from the railway station, ploshchad Kirova or the stadium. Raketa is the fourth stop after the *Angara* steamship (look for it on the right). From ploshchad Kirova to the hydrofoil terminal is a 25-minute ride. On buses you pay the conductor (US$0.08, plus US$0.04 for any large items of baggage), while on trams and trolleybuses tickets are bought from the driver (five for US$0.50) and punched. A taxi from the Raketa terminal, or the airport, to ploshchad Kirova should cost no more than US$5.

Local ferries make a good shoestring excursion, upstream to the dam and downstream to half a dozen *sadovodstva*, suburban districts with vegetable allotments and dachas. The most convenient pier is bulvar Gagarina, near the Hotel Intourist. Small boats do a one-hour return trip up to the dam, leaving every half-hour or so from 6.30 am to late evening. Bigger Moskva boats go about 10 km downstream, a 3½-hour round trip. Buy tickets on board. The navigation season is from late April to early October.

AROUND IRKUTSK (SOUTH-WEST BAIKAL)
ОКРЕСТНОСТЬ ИРКУТСКА
(ЮЖНО-ЗАПАДНЫЙ БАЙКАЛ)

There are 336 rivers feeding into Lake Baikal and just one, the Angara, flowing out. An over-quoted legend tells of Old Man

Baikal and his 337 daughters, one of whom fell in love with Yenisey and ran away to join him. In a rage the old man hurled a huge rock after her, the so-called Shaman Rock. The rock lies in the Angara where it flows out from the lake's south-western end, but since the building of the Irkutsk dam only a thumbnail shows above the risen waters. Just east of the outlet are the Hotel Baikal and, about four km up the shore, the village of Listvyanka. On the other side of the outlet is Port Baikal, from where early Trans-Siberian passengers were ferried across the lake. Port Baikal later became a station on

the Round-Baikal line, whose rusty tracks stretch down the shore.

The immense view from here south toward the Khamar-Daban Mountains in Buryatia takes in perhaps 5% of the lake. There's a good, large map of the lake available from the Limnological Institute in Listvyanka or the kiosk beside the ticket office at the Raketa hydrofoil terminal in Irkutsk.

Baikalcomplex in Irkutsk (see Travel Agencies) can arrange homestays at various sites along the lake's western shore, including at Listvyanka. The price depends on the

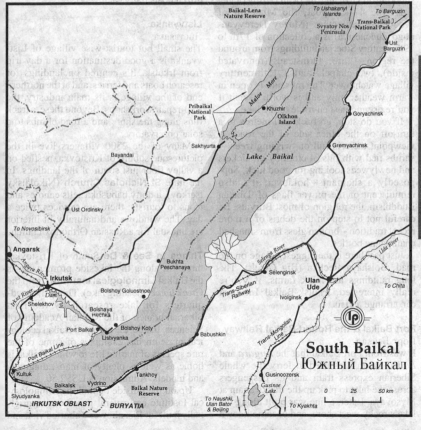

SIBERIA & RUSSIAN FAR EAST

type of accommodation, but full board in a wooden cabin is around US$27 per person for the first night and drops to US$19 for any further length of time.

Baikal Road & Museum of Wooden Architecture

Иркутск-Байкальская Дорога м Музей Деревянного Зодчества

The 65-km Irkutsk-Baikal road was built in an incredible two months in 1960 after US President Eisenhower was invited to visit the great lake (some of his ancestors were allegedly Siberian gold merchants). The trip was cancelled amid the fiasco that followed the shooting down of an American U2 spy plane.

At the 47-km post, the Museum of Wooden Architecture (Muzey Derevyannogo Zodchestva) is a collection of 17th to 19th-century Siberian buildings from around the region – three farmsteads (renovated inside), two chapels and a 15th-century village watchtower. The museum is open in warm weather only and is worth a visit if you're driving past en route to the lake.

If you do stop, go back 100 metres to a turn-off on the other side of the road. A viewpoint there is full of 'wishing trees' – shrubs tied with bits of cloth by picnickers and newlyweds looking for good luck. Supposedly a shamanist holdover, it's also reminiscent of the prayer flags of Tibetan Buddhism, the religion of most Buryats. Be careful not to step on the debris of a more recent tradition – broken glass from smashed champagne bottles.

Just past here is the biggest village on the road, Bolshaya Rechka (Big Creek). The long buildings are mink farms; if you're really interested, Irkutsk-Baikal Intourist can arrange a visit.

Port Baikal & the Round-Baikal Railway

Порт Байкал

It was from Port Baikal that the *Angara* and *Baikal* steamships used to ferry the whole Siberian express train and its passengers across the lake to pick up the tracks again at Mysovaya. Later, a line was built along the lake's rocky west shore, and became known

as the Round-Baikal (or Circumbaikal) Railway. With a tunnel almost every km, this proved the most challenging section of the Trans-Siberian to build. When the dam submerged the tracks between Irkutsk and Port Baikal and a short cut was laid from Irkutsk to Kultuk, the remaining 94 km of the Round-Baikal Railway became a neglected branch line. Now only the occasional train trudges to and fro with supplies for Port Baikal's 700 people and its fading ship-repair yards.

A visit to the dilapidated cabins of Port Baikal makes a melancholy day trip, starting with a boat ride from Listvyanka (half a dozen boats daily each way).

Listvyanka

Листвянка

The small but tourist-wise village of Listvyanka is a good destination for a day trip from Irkutsk. It's centred on landings for research boats and ferries, and at the northern end of the village is its main industry, the ship-repair workshops. Beyond these, a track runs along the shore and a road climbs to a solar observatory.

Many of the 2500 villagers live in the picturesque suburb of Kristovka, nestled on a valley floor just south of the landings. In the little **St Nicholas Church** (Nikolaisky tserkov), a dotty babushka sells candles and icons to tourists; there are services twice a day. The windows and naturally lit interior are unusual for a Russian Orthodox church.

Things to See & Do South of Kristovka, three km along the lakeside promenade, is the **Baikal Limnological Institute** (from the Greek *limne*, meaning lake). This is the headquarters for lake research by the East Siberian branch of the Russian Academy of Sciences. Inside, the cramped Baikal ecological museum has examples of some of the rare species of marine life to which Baikal is home as well as plenty of maps, diagrams and models. Admission is US$2.50.

Up on the hillside behind the Limnological Institute are several guesthouses, originally built for Eisenhower's aborted visit and now part of a heart sanatorium for the privileged. Beyond them is the Hotel Baikal. From the hotel a 2.5-km path climbs to an observation point with excellent views of the lake and mountains, Port Baikal and the Angara River.

Places to Stay The 118-bed *Hotel Baikal* (☎ (3952) 29 03 91) is a one-km climb from the highway via the access road or through the Limnological Institute grounds. Singles/doubles at US$64/102 are comfortable, and half of them have unmatched views of the lake (for an extra US$5). In the village, 150 metres south of the hydrofoil jetty, is a green, weather-beaten, two-storied *turbaza*. It has a large dormitory and a couple of cell-like rooms (complete with filthy, bare plaster walls engraved with graffiti), but they're not particularly appealing. Toilet facilities are basic and when we visited there was no running water – but what do you expect for less than US$2 per night?

Places to Eat The Russian/Siberian food at the *Hotel Baikal* is excellent, the service is polite and there's no band. Down in the village, opposite the hydrofoil landing, the *Restoran Baikal* is a little more earthy and is patronised by locals. They do basic soup, salad, meat and potatoes, which is quite edible and very cheap.

Getting There & Away Between 9 am and 7 pm daily there are six buses from Irkutsk bus station to Listvyanka. From Listvyanka landing, the first departure is at 7 am and the last at 7 pm. You can check the timetable at the Hotel Baikal or with whoever's serving in the little cafeteria beside the village bus stop. The bus also stops near the Limnological Institute. A seat one-way is US$2.

The hydrofoil service between Irkutsk (leaving from the Raketa terminal) and Listvyanka has three or four departures a day from mid-May to late September. The one-way trip takes just over an hour and costs US$3. The earliest sailing from Irkutsk is at

10 am and the last hydrofoil leaves Listvyanka at 6.30 pm but double-check the schedules.

It's quite possible to hitchhike to Baikal but hard to find a good place to do it; the roundabout at the turn-off to the dam (along the route of trolleybus No 1 or bus No 16) seemed to be a good place. Bear in mind that when you hitch in Russia the driver usually expects to be paid.

Up the West Shore
Западное Побережье Байкала
Ferries and hydrofoils go to several landings along the west shore – but, then again, maybe they don't. Maintenance problems, lack of spare parts, financial constraints and the weather all play deciding roles in what services are running. It's very difficult to get accurate and up-to-date information, and the only sure way is to go down to the Raketa terminal in Irkutsk and ask. And then ask again, just to be sure.

One fairly reliable destination is **Bolshoy Koty**, a biological research station and a worked-out 19th-century gold field, 15 km north of Listvyanka. The 10 am hydrofoil from Irkutsk, via Listvyanka, provides Bolshoy Koty's sole daily transport link. It arrives around midday and makes the return journey two hours later. Two hours is more than enough to explore the tiny village; there's a sad, small museum and aquarium (open from noon to 1 pm only), one kiosk and an empty store. If you intend to eat, bring a packed lunch. A hike over the wooded hills back to Listvyanka might make a good half-day expedition.

Supposedly, a daily (except Wednesdays), open-decked Moskva ferry chugs from Irkutsk (departs at 8.30 am) to Listvyanka (arrives at 12.30 pm) and on to **Bolshoy Goluostnoe**, 50 km north. This is a more attractive proposition than the claustrophobic hydrofoil but you only have about 30 minutes at Bolshoy Goluostnoe before the boat starts on its return journey. **Bukhta Peschanaya** (Sandy Bay), 80 km from Listvyanka, is potentially the furthest north

SIBERIA & RUSSIAN FAR EAST

you can go in a day trip. From Listvyanka, a hydrofoil leaves at 9 am and it's a 3½-hour trip. This leaves a further three hours to explore the beach, bounded by dramatic capes at either end, before the hydrofoil departs back to Listvyanka. At both Bolshoy Goluostnoe and Bukhta Peschanaya there's accommodation in the form of wooden cabins with saunas, double rooms and either shared or attached toilets, or in large, single-sex dormitories. Book beforehand through Irkutsk-Baikal Intourist.

Olkhon, the large island off Baikal's western shore (and at 70 km long, the largest of the lake's 27 islands), was at one time served by ferry from Irkutsk but is now only accessible by bus. It's a popular destination for holidaying Russians from the region's cities, mainly because the channel between the island and the lake shore (known as Maloe More, or 'Small Sea') is one of the few places in Baikal where the water is temperate enough for swimming. Unfortunately, as a consequence, much of the coastal area at the south of the island is blighted by concrete and litter. In the interior of the island are half a dozen lakes and the 1300-metre Izhmey Peak, with the only settlement of any size being the fishing village of Khuzhir. The northern end of Olkhon, once the domain of religious shamans, is reportedly a good place to see Baikal seals. Buses leave Irkutsk bus station for Olkhon every morning at 8 am, taking eight torturous hours over pot-holed roads to reach Sakhyurta, the nearest mainland village to the southern tip of the island (there's a ferry crossing point a few km up the road).

The tour company Vostoksvyaz, based in Irkutsk, offers eight and nine-day packages of horse riding around the mainland shore of Maloe More, with accommodation at the settlement of Shida; the price including transfers, meals etc is US$525 per person. It may be possible (and we weren't able to speak to the company to confirm this) for people to make their own way to Shida on the Olkhon bus and just use the Shida accommodation and stable of horses. Contact Dmitry Gavoroukhin (☎ (3952) 43 27 36) or Vitaly Bourlakov (fax (3952) 43 23 79; telex 613726 ANSWERBACK:EXPLORE SU). Irkutsk-Baikal Intourist can also help with exploring the lake's west coast, and Baikalcomplex seems very flexible and willing to tailor individual itineraries.

EASTERN SHORE OF LAKE BAIKAL
ВОСТОЧНОЕ ПОБЕРЕЖЬЕ БАЙКАЛА

The eastern shore of Lake Baikal is some of Buryatia's wildest and least explored territory, not only untrodden by hiking-booted backpackers but relatively uncolonised even by local Buryats and Russians. At a certain point, all roads and tracks stop dead. Farther to the north there's not the slightest trace of civilisation for some hundreds of km until the single-minded swathe of the BAM ploughs through the taiga beyond the northern end of the lake. The most ecologically interesting parts – those which throughout history have remained free of habitation or development – now fall within the bounds of the **Barguzin National Reserve** (Barguzinsky zapovednik). Created in 1917, this is Russia's oldest national reserve. With over 263,000 hectares of protected flora and fauna, the park has long provided valuable virgin research territory for small armies of scientists hermited away in the small coastal settlement of Davsha. Davsha, linked only by boat to Ust-Barguzin 120 km to the south, also acts as a reception centre for visitors, and it may be possible for travellers to get up there and see some of the park's unique mammal, bird and plant life.

Immediately south of the Barguzin Reserve is the **Trans-Baikal National Park** (Zabaikalsky Natsionalny Park), a more accessible, but still controlled, stretch of forested Baikal coastline. Within the bounds of the national park, 12 km off the Svyatoy Nos Peninsula, are the Ushkany Islands, four small mountain peaks out in the lake that are the favourite basking place of Baikal's nerpa seals.

Access to Zabaikalsky is by road from Ust-Barguzin, a timber town connected by bus to Ulan Ude and by ferry to Irkutsk.

Ust-Barguzin
Усть Баргузин

What was once a neat Siberian village on the estuary of the Barguzin River has been disfigured by prefab concrete apartment blocks, but Ust-Barguzin still has appeal as a convenient base for exploration of Baikal's wild eastern shoreline. You need to hire some kind of transport to visit the national park (admission US$1.50) and it's preferable to have an idea of where you're heading for; locals can suggest good scenic spots to visit, one of which will undoubtedly be the popular hot springs (admission US$5) not too far to the north. More interesting would be to take a boat over to the Svyatoy Nos Peninsula or even around its southern tip and out to the Ushkany Islands for a chance at seal-watching. A local tourism entrepreneur, Sasha Loginov (☎ 9 25 91), can help to find a boat and captain for hire. Anyone interested in heading deeper into the reserve, or possibly visiting Davsha, should visit the national park headquarters (☎ 9 25 78) in the centre of town; ask anybody where it is.

There are a couple of decent places to stay in Ust-Barguzin, including the basic but adequate *Hotel Baikal,* which charges the equivalent of US$3 or US$4 a night, and a friendly six-room *guesthouse* (☎ 9 22 77) at ulitsa Lenina 31 that charges US$15 per night for full board and has a sauna.

The ferry for Irkutsk departs twice a week at 9 am, taking a leisurely seven hours for the crossing. There's a daily bus south to Ulan Ude (US$2.50 one-way), which departs at 8.30 am and arrives around 4 pm, including a couple of welcome rest stops along the way.

Southern Buryatia
Южная Бурятия

The mountainous republic of Buryatia covers an area of over 350,000 sq km, spreading around the north and east of Lake Baikal and forming an 800-km 'panhandle' south-west along the Mongolian border. For most of its history the region has been under Asiatic influence, something clearly visible in the facial features of the 250,000 indigenous Buryats. In the 1st century BC, the Huns invaded and subjugated the native tribes. Later waves of nomadic peoples arrived, migrating north from what is present-day Mongolia. Jenghiz Khan's mother is said to have come from the settlement of Barguzin, close to the eastern shore of Baikal. When Mrs Khan's son grew to become the terror of the western world, Buryat tribes roamed as part of his horde.

The defeat of the Huns allowed for unchecked Russian expansion and in the 17th century the first Cossacks arrived amongst the Buryats. The Cossacks were followed by migrating peasants who introduced the natives to agriculture. While the western tribes took to this new static lifestyle, the Eastern Buryats remained nomadic cattle herders and hunters. Buryatia became a great source of wealth for Russia, supplying timber, furs and gold, although the Buryats themselves, soon outnumbered by the fair-skinned squatters (today, Buryats make up 25% of the regional population), benefited little. In the Soviet period, Buryatia became an autonomous republic, and then, with the USSR's demise, a republic within Russia.

The Buryats have managed to keep alive their language – although it's not widely spoken and its use is mainly confined to the home – and it is now being taught again in schools. There is also an attempt to reintroduce the Buryatian script (written from top to bottom of the page), which they were coerced into abandoning for Cyrillic in the 1930s.

Buryats are also found in two smaller 'autonomous districts' – Aginsk, south of Chita, and the very Russianised Ust-Ordynsky, west of Baikal – as well as in Mongolia and in China's Inner Mongolia autonomous region.

Religion
Buddhism In pre-Revolutionary Russia, Buddhism was an officially recognised religion and there were 46 high monasteries (datsans) and 150 temples in the Buryatia,

Chita and Irkutsk regions. Stalin sent thousands of lamas (priests) and others to the Gulag and destroyed all but two of the datsans – though, in recognition of wartime support from religious groups, he allowed a few to be rebuilt (the datsan at Ivolginsk, near Ulan Ude, was one of these). Since the events of 1991 there has been a re-emergence of interest in Buddhist traditions and there are about 20 new and restored datsans in Buryatia; the datsan at Atsagat (40 km due east of Ulan Ude) is one that has been recently re-established. The village of Atsagat is the home of Agvan Dorzhiev, Buddhist philosopher, reformer and teacher of the 13th Dalai Lama. The present incarnation of the Dalai Lama (the 14th) has visited the datsan at Ivolginsk several times, most recently in autumn 1994.

Buddhists celebrate – openly now – six *hurals* each year. Tsagaalgan, the Buddhist New Year, carries on for 16 days at the time of the lunar new year, mostly at the family level with ceremonial food and dress. During the hural to Maitreya, Buddha of the future, held in early July, a Maitreya statue is carried in a colourful procession around the datsan grounds at Ivolginsk.

Shamanism Despite adopting Buddhism in the 18th century, the Buryats were not inclined to give up their shamanistic beliefs and practised the two religions side by side. Many of the shamanistic sacred places *(obos)* and rock paintings are still known, and Siberian Guides Inc (see Ulan Ude, Information) includes a few in its 'Religious Tour of Buryatia' package. Buryat-Intour can also arrange day trips to some of the closer sites.

Old Believers As well as the shamanism, Buddhism and mainstream Russian Orthodoxy, Buryatia is a home to the Semeyski, or Old Believers. These are the descendants of conservative 17th-century Russian Orthodox breakaways who fled here from persecution in northern Russia. There are still a number of Semeyski villages, noted for their brightly painted houses, and visits can

be arranged through either Buryat-Intour or Siberian Guides Inc (see Ulan Ude – Information).

ULAN UDE
УЛАН УДЕ
Population: 360,000

Despite an archetypal Stalinist centre dominated by a surreally large head of Lenin, Ulan Ude is a very un-Russian place. In fact, it's downright weird. As well as Lenin's boulderous bonce (inspired, it's said, by the outsized head of Marx on his London tomb), the visitor to Ulan Ude can also inspect a hidden horde of Buddhist treasures and an authentically kitsch temple on the plains.

While nearby Irkutsk struts its tsarist history and traditions, Ulan Ude, capital of Buryatia, seems more conscious of the Asian-ness that comes with its proximity to Mongolia and China. Founded in the 17th century as a Cossack garrison on the Selenga River and chartered as Verkhne-Udinsk in 1775, Ulan Ude grew as a trading post on the tea road route between Irkutsk and China. At the turn of the century the town's population stood at 10,000, but by 1930 this had risen tenfold with the onset of Soviet industrialisation.

The indigenous people of the region, the Buryats, put up stiff resistance to Sovietisation, as they had to earlier Russian colonisation, and grimly clung to their language, their cultural identity and the Tibetan-Buddhist faith they had adopted in the early 18th century from their cousins in Mongolia. In 1934, as part of the Soviet recognition of national minorities, the city got its present name, Buryat for Red Uda (the Uda River is a local tributary).

Because of Soviet installations on the Mongolian border, until 1987 the city was tightly closed and could only be visited by special permission (Eric Newby managed to spend several days here in 1977 during his big red train ride). Heavy industry remains the backbone of the region with a large locomotive works (the local Intourist office can arrange visits for railway enthusiasts), an aircraft factory and a metal-processing plant.

Orientation

Tree-lined ulitsa Lenina is the city's axis, with the parade square, ploshchad Sovietov, at the north end and shopping areas around the old trading arcades towards the south. To reach ploshchad Sovietov from the railway station, cross the footbridge over the tracks and walk south along ulitsa Borsoeva for 300 metres, then take the small side road on the right immediately after the Okean shop. Bear slightly left, toward the red-brick Hotel Geser, and the central square is a few minutes walk beyond.

The newer parts of town lie south of the river and north of the railway line. There's a fairly crude Russian-language town map available from the Buryat-Intour office at the Hotel Geser; a good map of the whole republic, also in Russian and called *Respublika Buryatia*, can also be found in Ulan Ude.

Information

There are exchange bureaus at the Hotel Geser (open from 9 am to 4 pm) and at the Hotel Buryatia (open from 9 am to 7 pm). The Mosbiznesbank at ulitsa Lenina 27 and the Agroprombank at ulitsa Lenina 13 also change money but you won't find any place that accepts either travellers' cheques or credit cards. The main post office is on ulitsa Sukhe-Batora, at the north-west corner of ploshchad Sovietov. It's open Monday to Friday from 9 am to 1 pm and 2 to 5 pm. It has an international telephone desk which charges US$6 per minute for anywhere outside Russia. The main telephone and telegraph office is on ulitsa Borsoeva, by the railway footbridge. The rates here are cheaper than at the post office and it's open 24 hours daily.

Buryat-Intour (☎ 2 69 54; fax 2 92 67; telex 219112 KRUIZ SU) is the new incarnation of the old Ulan Ude Intourist and has two offices in town, the one in the Hotel Geser being the easiest to find. The friendly, English-speaking staff run a variety of tours around the area including rafting, hiking and a 'Robinson Crusoe' programme which has you abandoned for five days on the Svyatoy Nos peninsula on Lake Baikal, left to seek your own shelter and forage for food. Siberian Guides Inc (☎ 4 75 11; fax 6 32 44 marked 'attn BOX 157') at ulitsa Zchukovsky 23, Ulan Ude 670020, specialises in adventure holidays based on Lake Baikal and the mountain ranges along its eastern shore, and can also organise day trips to local religious and cultural sites. The general director of Siberian Guides Inc, Anatoly Khunkhenov, speaks excellent English.

Ulan Ude time is Moscow time plus five hours. The telephone code is 30122.

Merchants' Quarter

The town's historical main artery was ulitsa Bolshoy, now renamed ulitsa Lenina, and most of its elegant, faded architecture dates from the mid-19th century. The brown mansion with statues, near ulitsa Kalandarashvili, was built in 1907 by a rich merchant. The fine, classically styled frontage along ulitsa Kuybysheva, now a clinic, was once a Merchants' Inn (Gostiny Dvor, 1825). Opposite are crumbling trading arcades (*torgovy ryad*), with the central department store now built into the middle of them. On the corner of ulitsa Kirova and Kommunisticheskaya is a large, pink house, home earlier this century to an American soldier, Colonel Morrow. The mercenary Morrow was aiding the Whites in the Civil War but some blatant profiteering (stealing gold from the Barguzin valley) caused a local surge of support for the Reds and he was run out of town. South of ulitsa Kuybysheva is the oldest quarter with some beautifully decorated log houses and, to the east, Hodigitria Cathedral.

Hodigitria Cathedral & the Fond

The broken-down Hodigitria Cathedral (Odigitrichesky sobor, 1785), at the southern end of ulitsa Lenina, was probably the pride of Verkhne-Udinsk. Now it looks abandoned, the perfect camouflage for its truly stupendous contents – the collected remains of pre-Revolutionary Buddhism in Russia, salvaged from Buryatia's monasteries and temples on the eve of their destruction.

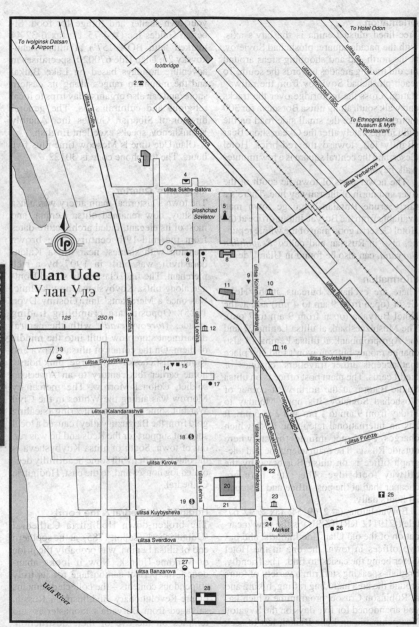

Ulan Ude
Улан Удэ

Behind a succession of solidly padlocked doors, dusty shelves are crammed with hundreds, if not thousands, of Buddha figures, Tantric sculptures, tangkas and banners, vestments and masks, musical instruments and sacred volumes, along with homeless huddles of Soviet kitsch.

The artefacts found their way here when, after the Revolution, a museum of Oriental art and ethnography was proposed and a serious collection was started, culled from datsans forced into more secular channels. In the 1930s, the datsans were demolished and the collection turned into an antireligious museum (its devoted curators presumably pretending to be atheists). This ironic twist is probably what saved it from destruction.

Although there are plans to build a museum to house the collection (referred to as the 'fond', meaning reserve or archives), in its present, stored state it's not open to the public. However, Buryat-Intour can arrange a guided tour for US$5 per person if you let them know a day or two in advance.

Ethnographical Museum

The open-air ethnographical museum (Etnografichesky muzey) of reconstructed buildings is one of the best in the country for a portrayal of indigenous and early Russian life. The exhibits begin just inside the entrance, with reconstructions of prehistoric burial mounds and stone totems, and trace the region's vernacular history through to the wooden buildings of earlier this century.

A complex at the right rear includes yurts (nomadic tent houses, more recently used as summer outbuildings) as well as cabins adopted by the eastern Buryats when they settled down in the 19th century. Nearby, a small Buddhist temple, in a Buryat synthesis of Tibetan, Chinese and other styles, has an exhibit on temple architecture. The buildings that look like a cross between a yurt and a house are typical of the western Buryats. Note the icons inside: western Buryats converted to Christianity. Also here are clothes and utensils for Tsagaalgan celebrations. A low yurt at the rear has a still for making that

SIBERIA & RUSSIAN FAR EAST

Central Asian standby, kumyss (fermented mare's milk).

There are also examples of an Old Believers' settlement, including an exquisite village gate (1906) and a tiny chapel. Through the woods to the right is a complex of Evenk bark-and-skin *tipis*. The shaman's yard has totems of the higher world – fish, moose and bear – in front of his house and those of the lower, or dark, world at the rear, along with birds as 'guards'.

The museum is open daily except Monday from 10 am to 6 pm all year round. It's six km from ploshchad Sovietov on bus No 8 (which leaves you about a km away but runs frequently) or bus No 35 (which goes to the entrance but runs less often), both caught from the local bus station on ulitsa Banzarova.

Other Museums

Ulan Ude's museums are small and of marginal interest. The **Fine Arts Museum** (the grey edifice on ulitsa Kuybysheva) features Buryat and other Eastern decorative and fine art. It's open from 11 am to 7 pm and closed on Monday. The **Museum of Oriental Art & Buryat History** is on ulitsa Profsoyuznaya, at the corner of ulitsa Kommunisticheskaya. Close by, letters, manuscripts and sepia photos make up the collection of the **Buryatia Literary Museum** at Sovietskaya 27, which is open Tuesday to Saturday from 10 am to 5.30 pm. The **Nature Museum**, at ulitsa Lenina 46, concentrates on the wildlife of Lake Baikal and the wetlands of the Selenga Delta; it's open from 11 am to 7 pm daily except Monday.

Places to Stay

Though only completed since the demise of the Soviet Union, Ulan Ude's flagship hotel, the *Buryatia* (☎ 2 18 35), seems keen to revive the spirit of the good old, bad old days with service that is unrepentantly Brezhnevesque, a restaurant given over to riotously partying locals, and a caf, on a par with the worst railway station stolovaya. It's possible that, approached in the right frame of mind, the Buryatia could be fun; and the rooms

themselves are reasonably comfortable at US$28/46 for a single/double. It's at ulitsa Kommunisticheskaya 41a. The *Hotel Baikal* (☎ 237 18), on ploshchad Sovietov, is no fun at all. The bedding was damp, bare wires protruded from the TV, only one light bulb worked out of three and the chair collapsed when Andrew sat on it (that there was no hot water or toilet seat goes without saying). This place is reasonably cheap at US$17/27, but for masochists only.

The most comfortable place in town to stay is the old Party hang-out, the *Hotel Geser* (☎ 2 81 51) at ulitsa Ranzhurova 11. This is a modern, well-maintained hotel trying hard, and coming close, to achieving an international standard of service. It has an international telephone in the foyer, a sauna and a billiard room. Singles/doubles are US$32/50. The best of the cheaper hotels is the *Hotel Barguzin* (☎ 2 57 46) on ulitsa Sovietskaya. Though it doesn't have hot water, it's not as seedy as the Baikal and the staff are quite friendly. Singles are US$14, doubles US$23.

The cheapest beds in town are at the *Hotel Odon* (☎ 434 80), a large, sombre establishment at ulitsa Gagarina 43, two km from ploshchad Sovietov. There are 200-plus rooms priced on average at about US$5. To get there from the railway station, come out of the front entrance and turn right, walk to the end of the street, then head east along ulitsa Yerbanova. Ulitsa Gagarina is the third turning on your left.

Places to Eat

The restaurant at the *Hotel Buryatia* is popular as the town's number-one party spot. If you prefer to eat, the food is reasonable enough and includes some local specialities such as poza, the Buryat version of meat dumplings. The food at the *Hotel Baikal* is cheap but near inedible. For the same price, much better is the *Restoran Turistsky*, next door to the Hotel Barguzin. Soup, a dish of meat and potatoes and tea will come to US$2; it's open from 11 am to 4 pm and 6 to 11 pm.

The *Hotel Geser* has two eating options:

the cafeteria (open from 8 am to 8 pm) serves one or two set meals throughout the day for around US$4, while the restaurant (open from 11 am to midnight) has a more extensive menu but higher prices. The best food in town (it has some discernible flavour and the meat, potatoes and vegetables aren't all the same colour) is served at the *Myth*, which is a couple of km out on the road to the ethnographic museum. The main dishes are all around US$2 each but as this is a somewhat exclusive restaurant, some sizeable surcharges are slapped on the bill. To get there take tram No 1 from ulitsa Kommunisticheskaya east along ulitsa Yerbanova until it forks at the Kino Oktyabra; the Myth is on the ground floor of the grey building 100 metres along the left-hand fork.

For snacks, there's the *Buterbrody*, by the tram stop on ulitsa Kommunisticheskaya, a small café that does sandwiches and pastries. There are also a few food stalls around the central market, east on ulitsa Kuybysheva.

Getting There & Away

Air There are direct flights almost daily to/from Bratsk, Irkutsk, Moscow and Vladivostok. Other Siberian connections include three a week to Novosibirsk and two a week to Petropavlovsk-Kamchatsky, Yakutsk and Yuzhno-Sakhalinsk. There are also twice-weekly flights to/from Ulan Bator. The Aeroflot office is on the corner of ploshchad Sovietov and ulitsa Lenina; it's open Monday to Friday from 9 am to 1 pm and 2 to 7 pm, and on Saturday from 9 am to 1 pm and 2 to 6 pm.

Bus There are daily buses north to Ust-Barguzin, from where it's possible to take a twice-weekly ferry across Lake Baikal to Irkutsk; and south to Kyakhta on the Russia-Mongolia border (see the Kyakhta section for comments on crossing the border).

Train The *Rossia* arrives daily, bound for Moscow (train No 1), at 4.34 pm local time, and bound for Vladivostok (train No 2) at 1.30 pm. There are two other daily services to Moscow, as well as one to Novosibirsk

and one to Irkutsk. There are additional daily trains heading east to Chita, Blagoveshchensk and Khabarovsk.

Ulan Ude is the first or last major Russian city (depending on which way you are travelling) for Trans-Mongolian (train No 3/4) travellers en route between Moscow and Beijing. Train No 5/6, the Moscow-Ulan Bator express, and train No 263/264, Irkutsk-Ulan Bator (change at Naushki), also halt at Ulan Ude. See the Trans-Siberian Railway section for further details.

Getting Around

Bus No 10 and express bus No 34 go between the airport and ploshchad Sovietov, near the Hotel Baikal. On bus No 34, which runs every half-hour, the journey takes 25 minutes and costs US$0.25. East from ploshchad Sovietov, the No 10 bus goes to the railway station.

IVOLGINSK DATSAN
ИВОЛГИНСК

This monastery at the foot of the Khamar-Daban Mountains – though Lhasa it's not – is reason enough to visit Ulan Ude. It held out as the centre of Buddhism in the USSR and today there are about 30 lamas here, mostly trained in Mongolia.

Near the front gate is the main temple, built in 1972. Its interior is a riot of colour, with hundreds of Buddha images and *tangkas* (icon-tapestries) saved from other temples or donated from around the world. The four 'guardians' at the rear are recent paintings by Buryat artists. In the right front corner of the compound is a smaller temple, and to the left there's a round shrine to Maitreya.

To the left of the main temple is a museum containing the pride of the monastery: a beautiful 108-volume, handmade, richly illuminated Ganjur, or Buddhist scripture, in Tibetan, plus the 225-volume Danjur (commentaries) in Sanskrit, and hundreds of quaint and kitschy gifts to the monastery.

Other buildings include a library, behind the main temple, and the datsan's first building, a green temple at right rear. Nearby are sacred reliquaries called stupas and a tree said to be grown from a cutting of the original bodhi tree. The lamas' houses are at the back and the one with the stone lions is for the head lama, who is also head of all Buddhists in Russia.

Around the perimeter are prayer wheels. These cylinders full of prayers on scraps of paper are turned clockwise to 'activate' them. In fact, everything is done clockwise so as to keep one's right side to venerated objects. Visitors are welcome in the temples and may observe the ceremonies, which tend to start by around 8 or 9 am and go on for two or three hours. The lama at the rear of the hall is the one to ask about taking photos. The temple is closed in the evening.

Getting There & Away Ivolginsk is 30 km west of Ulan Ude. From the bus station, bus No 104 to Kalyonova (*'kal-YO-na-va'*), departing at 7.10 am, noon and 4 pm, will take you direct to the monastery, or bus No 130, which departs every 30 minutes throughout the day, will take you as far as the village of Ivolga. From there follow the road out of the village and you'll see the datsan glinting in the distance, off to your right. It's a four or five-km walk – but considerably longer if you attempt a short cut across the marshy plain with its many hidden streams.

There are buses from outside the monastery back to Ulan Ude at 1.30 and 5.30 pm.

KYAKHTA
КЯХТА

The town has no conventional tourist sights, but the marooned remainders of its former opulence and its proximity to the Russian-Mongolian border make Kyakhta a fascinating excursion for the romantically minded.

Kyakhta lies 200 km south of Ulan Ude, hidden in a valley amongst the hills that demarcate the Russian-Mongolian border. Although artefacts have been found in the area that date back as far as 2000 BC, the town itself was only founded in the early 18th century when the first Cossacks arrived and drove back the Mongol tribes who bred

their cattle and hunted here. As Kyakhta grew, it became a staging post on the tea route from China through Mongolia to European Russia. The shrewd townsfolk began to operate as intermediaries between merchants in Canton and Shanghai and the fur traders in the Russian cities of Siberia. By the mid-19th century, as many as 5000 cases of tea a day were arriving in Kyakhta and the town's trading links extended to Great Britain and even North America. It became a town of millionaires. Architects from Europe designed mansions for the town's merchants (a stash of gaudy crockery and figurines which once belonged to Kyakhtan merchants lies in dust-encased cabinets in Ulan Ude's Hodigitria Cathedral) and Kyakhta's cathedral was said to hold more treasures than any other church in Siberia and reputedly had solid-silver doors embedded with diamonds, rubies and emeralds.

The glorious state of affairs was brought to an end with the completion of the Trans-Siberian Railway. Almost overnight, all the tea was redirected via Vladivostok. By the time Luigi Barzini and his team drove through Kyakhta in 1907 (described in his book *Peking to Paris*), all the riches had dried up.

Kyakhta today is like a stage-set town. Its one main street (ulitsa Lenina) is lined with stately stone buildings and behind them is almost nothing: wooden shacks clustered limpet-like on the steep valley sides, and bare hills beyond. The town's main role is as a heavily militarised border post, and the road in from the north is lined with tanks, armoured vehicles and, distant in the fields, helicopters like colonies of big, black insects.

Things to See & Do
A few indications of Kyakhta's past wealth survive in the grand colonial-style blocks on ulitsa Lenina, buildings that seem completely out of scale for such a small, end-of-the-world village. One of these buildings, 400 metres north of the bus station, houses the impressive **local museum**, which is strong on geology and archaeology.

We were told there is also a 19th-century library with over 18,000 volumes in Russian, German, French and Latin, but we couldn't find it.

Just south of the bus station, in a small, green park, is the crumbling shell of what appears to have been quite an impressive church. The overgrown churchyard is home to a small fair but, like the church, the rides are long neglected and now little more than rusting skeletons. Some 800 metres further south along ulitsa Lenina is the town's still-functioning, well-maintained **Orthodox church**.

If two churches of such size seems excessive in a town of such modest proportions, then the best is yet to come. Three or four km on, beyond the Orthodox church, is what was once **Kyakhta cathedral**. Designed in part by an Italian architect, with its elegant classical porticoes, central dome flanked by smaller cupolas and graceful, four-tiered bell tower, the cathedral wouldn't look out of place in Rome or Paris. However, while externally it's fairly complete, inside the building has been gutted: there's no furniture, no decoration – nothing except a rubble-strewn hollow. To add to the incongruity, the cathedral stands almost alone on wasteland with few other buildings in the vicinity, just some tumbledown shacks and a small factory with a life-sized silver Lenin out front (he has an identical golden twin in town; both look as though they fell out of a cereal packet). This is in fact a crossing point on the **Russia-Mongolia border**.

Barely 50 metres south of the cathedral runs a chain-link fence with a guarded gate. Beyond is a customs house, then another fence and then the plains of Mongolia. There's usually a small camp of people waiting on the Russian side to cross. It's obvious from the makeshift camps and fires that crossing here involves a long wait. With no nearby amenities, the cathedral's bell tower functions as a public toilet.

An alternative way to reach the cathedral, other than by the main road, is to climb the hill behind the bus station and follow the tank tracks. The series of huge red-brick buildings down to the right are old **tea warehouses** (gostiny dvor).

Places to Stay & Eat

There's a pleasant old lodge, the *Hotel Druzhba*, with 40 neat rooms with attached toilets and washing facilities, for US$4 to US$8. It's on ulitsa Kuperovsky, one block west of ulitsa Lenina beside the Orthodox church. Other than a stolovaya across the road from the museum, the only place to eat is the *Restoran Lotus*, in the centre of town opposite the little golden Lenin. Despite the Japanese trappings the food remains stodgily Russian, but it is at least cheap. There are also a couple of shops on this corner that sell bread, cheese, sausage and other basic provisions.

Getting There & Away

There are three buses a day to/from Ulan Ude. The journey takes five to six hours but the scenery is pleasant. A one-way ticket costs US$6, or US$10 on the more comfortable Ikarus coach. Four buses a day also run between Kyakhta and Naushki, 25 km west, from where there is a daily train to/from Irkutsk, via Ulan Ude. Naushki, a small, modern settlement, is also the last Russian station on the Trans-Mongolian rail route. There's a train once a day from here to the Mongolian town of Sukhe Bator (also known as Suhbaatar).

Westerners are theoretically not permitted to cross the border at Kyakhta although a US tour group managed it a few years ago. Anyone wanting to make an attempt needs to catch the bus for Altanbulag, the nearest settlement on the Mongolian side. From there take a bus on to Sukhe Bator, 24 km west, a larger town with better transport connections.

East from Ulan Ude
На восток от Улан Уды

CHITA
ЧИТА
Population: 315,000
Chita began life in 1653 as a Cossack stockade at the confluence of the Ingoda River and its tributary the Chita. Its status was consid-

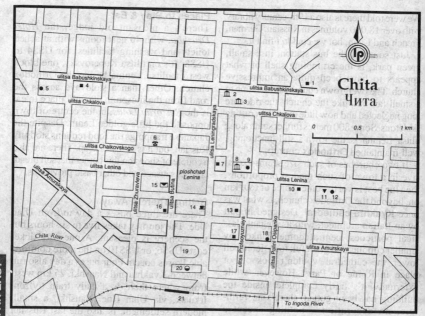

Chita
Чита

0   0.5   1 km

erably improved when in 1827 it became the residence of a group of the exiled Decembrists. After building their own prison, they went on to dig irrigation systems and cultivate the land, all initially as a means of improving their own lot but ultimately also benefiting the greater non-exile community. Under the influence of the exiles, Chita developed into a busy commercial and agricultural centre. The present-day city still has a commemorative ulitsa Dekabristov, though ulitsa Damskaya (or Ladies' Street), named in honour of the exiled Decembrists' wives and mentioned in the 1900 *Guide to the Great Siberian Railway*, seems to have disappeared.

The completion of the Trans-Baikal railway in 1900 consolidated Chita's importance, putting the town on line with both Vladivostok and Moscow. Since then, light engineering has grown to form the backbone of the regional economy. When the East Chinese Railway opened in 1901, Chita became the guardian of this route into Manchuria and home to a large military presence. For this reason the city was closed to foreign visitors until the late 1980s.

Now it's open and there isn't too much to get excited about. The city is, perhaps, worth only a day's visit. The ideal scenario would be to arrive in the morning and then take a train onwards in the late evening (in 1994, both the Khabarovsk and Vladivostok trains departed from Chita at around midnight, local time).

Orientation & Information

There's a currency-exchange bureau at the Hotel Dauria; the central post office is at ulitsa Butina 37 (on ploshchad Lenina) and the telephone and telegraph office is a block north, at ulitsa Chaikovskogo 24.

Central Chita is laid out on a grid pattern with the railway running along its southern edge. Immediately north of the railway station is the sports stadium and, two blocks

SIBERIA & RUSSIAN FAR EAST

PLACES TO STAY	PLACES TO EAT	
1 Hotel Turist Гостиница Турист	11 Restoran Argol Ресторан Аргол	8 Military Museum Военный музей
4 Hotel Baikal Гостиница Байкал	14 Kafe Sibir Кафе Сибирь	9 Army Officers' Club Дом офицеров армии
7 Hotel Zabaikal Гостиница Забайкалье	**OTHER**	12 Aeroflot Аэрофлот
10 Hotel Taiga Гостиница Тайга	2 Regional Museum Областной музей	15 Central Post Office Центральный почтамт
13 Hotel Ingoda Гостиница Ингода	3 Art Museum Художественный музей	18 Bookshop Dom Knigi Дом книги
16 Hotel Volna Гостиница Волна	5 Market Рынок	19 Stadium Стадион
17 Hotel Dauria Гостиница Даурия	6 Telephone & Telegraph Office Телефон и Телеграф	20 Bus Station Автовокзал
		21 Railway Station Железнодорожный вокзал

further, the awesome expanse of ploshchad Lenina. Bisecting the square, running east-west, is the wide, boulevard-like ulitsa Lenina, the city's main thoroughfare. Parallel to Lenina, three blocks south, is ulitsa Amurskaya (still sometimes called by its previous name, ulitsa Kalinina), the main shopping street. There's a Russian-language tourist map of Chita available from kiosks and at the Dom Knigi, Chita's best bookshop, at ulitsa Amurskaya 58.

Cossack horseman, Chita

Chita time is Moscow time plus six hours. The local telephone code is 30222.

Things To See & Do

There's a good **Military Museum**, housed in one of the most impressive buildings in town at ulitsa Lenina 86; it's open Wednesday to Friday from 10 am to 1 pm and 2 to 6 pm, and on Saturday and Sunday from 10 am to 1 pm and 2 to 5 pm. If you fancy being photographed next to a Red Army rocket launcher or Soviet armoured personnel carrier, there's a clutch of military hardware round the back. Next door to the military museum is the **Army Officers' Club** (Dom Ofitserov), which is worth a look-in for the chess room, a surprisingly noisy warren of activity and a great encapsulation of a Russia fast disappearing. It's upstairs on the 2nd floor through a door opposite the bar. There is also a fairly dull **Regional Museum** at ulitsa Babushkinskaya 113 and an **Art Museum** at ulitsa Chkalova 120.

If you have time to kill you could walk south across the bridge over the Chita River. One km further on is the larger Ingoda River.

Places to Stay

The invading hordes of traders from China make finding a bed for the night in Chita a difficult proposition. The *Hotel Turist* (☎ 6

SIBERIA & RUSSIAN FAR EAST

52 70), which belongs to the multistorey car-park school of architecture (the interior as well as the exterior), has supplemented all its signs and notices with scribbled Chinese translations in deference to the cross-border merchants who fill its rooms. It's at ulitsa Babushkinskaya 40 and rooms with showers are US$32/44. At the *Hotel Baikal*, three km west along ulitsa Babushkinskaya at No 149, next to the market, there is even less chance of finding a room: with boxes and bulging, black plastic-wrapped packages piled halfway to the ceiling, it's tough even to make it to the reception desk.

One hotel worth trying to book in advance is the elegant, 19th-century *Hotel Dauria* (☎ 6 23 65) at ulitsa Amurskaya 80 (entered round the corner on ulitsa Profsoyuznaya). The rooms are a little faded but still quite elegant with great, high ceilings; singles/ doubles with attached showers are US$16/24. There are a couple of other, undesirable fallbacks: the *Hotel Zabaikal* at Leningradskaya 36, central but extremely dingy, charges US$20 per night; while the *Hotel Taiga* at ulitsa Lenina 75 is a decrepit student hostel (though none of the students we saw had yet hit their teens) with places in four-bed dormitories at US$4 per person.

There are also a couple of hotels 'reserved' for official local administration guests (the *Hotel Ingoda* on ulitsa Profsoyuznaya, just up from the Dauria, and the *Hotel Volna* at ulitsa Butina 33). Good Russian and some persistence might get you a room if everywhere else is booked up.

Places to Eat

The only half-decent place in town seemed to be the *Kafe Dauria* attached to the hotel of the same name. The *Restoran Argol* at ulitsa Lenina 65, next to the Aeroflot offices, was *remont*, and the *Kafe Sibir* at ulitsa Leningradskaya 5, which was highly recommended, remained mysteriously closed for the whole of our stay.

Getting There & Away

Air Two flights daily link Chita with Moscow (7½ hours). There are also direct flights once a week to/from Beijing and Harbin. The Aeroflot office is at ulitsa Lenina 55.

Train Chita is 6200 km from Moscow and there's a direct train, No 79/80, which runs daily each way between the two cities. Other eastbound services to stop at Chita include trains to Blagoveshchensk, Khabarovsk and Vladivostok. Westbound from Chita, apart from Moscow, there are also services to Chelyabinsk, Kharkiv (Kharkov) and Novosibirsk. Chita is also the last major Russian city on the route of the Trans-Manchurian (No 19/20) before the line branches off for China 100 km east, at Tarskaya. It crosses the border at Zabaikalsk. Chita is the first station east of Tayshet from which it is possible to make a link with the northerly BAM railway; train No 192 runs daily to Tynda, branching from the Trans-Siberian route at the town of Bam.

BLAGOVESHCHENSK
БЛАГОВЕЩЕНСК
Population: 210,000

This industrial city and regional capital is interesting mainly for its location – across the Amur River from the Chinese town of Heihe – and its stormy history. It began as a military outpost in 1644, under the name Ust-Zaysk, and was seized by the Manchurians 45 years later. The Russians, under the command of Nikolay Muravev, took it back in 1856 and gave it its present name, which means 'Good News'.

By the end of the century Blagoveshchensk, thriving on Sino-Russian commerce, was larger and of greater importance than either Vladivostok or Khabarovsk. But in 1900, to avenge European deaths in the Chinese Boxer Rebellion, Cossacks slaughtered every Chinese in the city. The dead numbered in the thousands. During the years of the Cultural Revolution the Chinese subjected Blagoveshchensk to 24-hour propaganda blasted from loudspeakers across the river; the Soviets trained the guns of their tanks at China and fumed.

Nowadays, there is again a lively cross-border barter trade, encouraged by the free-trade zone that was declared between the Chinese and Russian cities in early 1994 (the first of its kind anywhere in Russia). There's an exchange of people also, with the shortage of labour in the Russian Amur region being remedied by importing Chinese workers. Russian and Chinese tourists cross to and fro, and since 1991 Westerners have been allowed through, too. To facilitate this cross-cultural commerce, a bridge has been proposed which would span the Amur and link the two countries.

The town still retains some traces of tsarist elegance and a bust of Chekhov on the wall of one of the oldest buildings records that he spent the night there in June 1890, on his way to Sakhalin. There are a number of hotels in town: the *Hotel Druzhba* (☎ 9 05 40) at ulitsa Kuznechnaya 1; the *Hotel Zeya* (☎ 2 11 00) at ulitsa Kalinina 8; and the *Hotel Yubileina* (☎ 2 11 19) at ulitsa Lenina 108.

Blagoveshchensk time is Moscow time plus six hours. The telephone code is 41622.

Getting There & Away

The city is 110 km off the Trans-Siberian on a branch line from Belogorsk, itself 660 km from Khabarovsk. There is a direct overnight Khabarovsk-Blagoveshchensk fast train (No 185), a 17-hour trip.

Sakha Republic
Республика Саха

YAKUTSK
ЯКУТСК
Population: 198,000

Yakutsk was founded in 1632 as a Cossack fort, and later served as a base for expeditions to the Pacific coast and the far north-east. The most unrepentant dissidents (including Decembrists and Bolsheviks) were exiled here. Yakutsk was, in fact, mainly a 'jail without doors'. There was no need for bars or locks: isolated amidst millions of sq km of bug-infested, swampy forest that became one great deepfreeze for eight months of the year, no-one was going anywhere. Some tried, but their bodies usually turned up in the spring, uncovered by the melting snow. Hence the runaways became known by the nickname 'snow-drops'.

When it became apparent in the late 19th century that the Yakutian earth had more to give up than just corpses, the fortunes of the town underwent a dramatic change. Prospectors, adventurers and mining companies needed a base from which to exploit the newly discovered mineral wealth of the Lena River basin, and Yakutsk became a kind of 'Wild East' version of Dodge City. Supplied by Lena shipping, the town was a boozy, bawdy rest-and-recreation centre for the region's gold-miners, who rolled in to blow their wages on drink and women. The biggest building in town was the vodka factory. It supplied countless bars and a ring of brothels staffed by girls from Moscow and Europe doing a little prospecting of their own. Drinking would progress to brawling and there'd be deaths, with some men murdered for their pay packets. When, one way or another, the money was gone it was back to the mines for another six months or a year of hard labour.

Today, Yakutsk – now capital of the Republic of Sakha (formerly Yakutia, or the Yakut Autonomous Republic) – is a drab, ugly town of collapsing wooden houses, mud and dust in the spring, grimy snow and black ice in the winter. January temperatures sometimes plummet to below -60°C but usually they teeter around -30°C – still cold enough to send the town into hibernation. As if that weren't sufficient to keep dogged travellers at bay, in 1994 local authorities imposed their own visa regime and all visitors arriving at Yakutsk airport now have to pay the equivalent of around US$75 admission. That's a lot of money for physical discomfort, bad food and a few small museums.

Of course, the people and landscapes of the far north, not Yakutsk, are the reason to visit this area, and there's no point coming

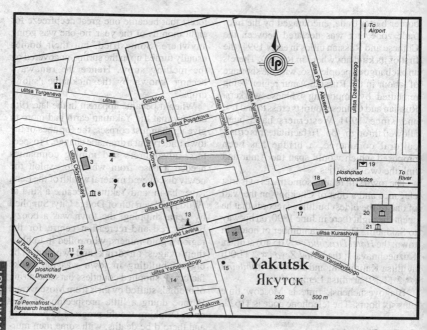

Yakutsk
Якутск

unless you're able to spend some money on excursions – along the Lena, into the tundra or to see Yakut or Evenk villages. Since the area was opened in 1989, most tourists have been those on Lena cruises.

Orientation & Information

The main street is prospekt Lenina, most of it between ploshchad Druzhby to the west and ploshchad Ordzhonikidze to the east. The Lena River is east of Ordzhonikidze and the port is reached by following ulitsa Khabarova north from prospekt Lenina and then bearing right. The bus station is more central, just 500 metres north of Lenina on ulitsa Oktyabrskaya. A transport map is sold in the bookshop opposite the Hotel Lena.

You can change money at the bank on ulitsa Kirova or at the Hotel Ontario; better yet, do it before you come. The main post and telegraph office is on ploshchad Ordzhonikidze. YakutIntour has its offices at

ulitsa Arzhakova 6, which is just south of ploshchad Lenina.

Yakutsk time is Moscow time plus six hours. The local telephone code is 41122.

Museum of History & Culture

This museum was founded at the turn of the century by Yemelyan Yaroslavsky, Yakutsk's favourite exile, who married a Yakut and later went west to join the Bolsheviks. It includes Ysyakh festival props, the interiors of Yakut summer and winter houses, a room devoted to Yakut shamans, a kayak from the first Russian polar expedition and the skeleton of a woolly mammoth. The museum, housed in what was once the residence of the Bishop of Yakutia (a long-defunct post), is at prospekt Lenina 5, near ploshchad Ordzhonikidze, and is open from 11 am to 6 pm every day except Monday. Also in the complex are a tower from the original Cossack fort, a whale skeleton and Yaroslavsky's house.

SIBERIA & RUSSIAN FAR EAST

PLACES TO STAY	5	Pioneer Palace	13	Lenin Statue
3 Hotel Yakutsk		Дворец пионеров		Памятник Ленину
Гостиница Якутск	6	Bank	14	Green Market
18 Hotel Lena		Банк		Зелёный рынок
Гостиница Лена	7	TV Tower	15	Department Store
		Телебашня		Eybdthvfu
PLACES TO EAT	8	Yakut Literary Museum	16	Russian Drama Theatre
4 Kafe Delfin		Якутский литературный		Русский
КафеДельфин		музей		драматический театр
11 Restoran Sever	9	Yakut Music & Drama	17	Bookshop
Ресторан Север		Theatre		Книжный магазин
		Якутский драматический	19	Post Office
OTHER		и музыкальный театр	20	Yaroslavsky House
1 St Nicholas Church	10	Academy of Science &		Museum
Никольская церковь		Geology		Дом-музей Ярославского
		Академия наук и	21	Museum of History &
2 Bus Station		геологии		Culture
Автовокзал	12	Bookshop		Музей истории и
		Книжный магазин		культуры

Other Museums

You can't miss the **Yakut Literary Museum**, shaped like a giant yurt, 1½ blocks north of prospekt Lenina on ulitsa Oktyabrskaya. Inside are exhibits on Yakut authors, musicians and playwrights and their Kazakh linguistic and literary roots. It's all quite well done, but obscure unless you have a guide. The Academy of Sciences building, on ulitsa Petrovskogo, has a starchy geological museum. There is also an **Academy of Sciences Institute of Permafrost**, which sounds about as exciting as a lump of frozen soil, but is actually worth a visit. Yakutsk is probably the only large city completely built on permafrost and, as such, it suffers some quite unique problems. Building on permafrost is like building on ice and, as the Yakutians have discovered, contact with a building's concrete or brick foundations thaws the frozen earth. The result is subsidence and there are many lopsided houses and blocks to be seen around town. Researchers have discovered that the only way to keep a building steady and upright is to sit it on stilts bored 10 metres into the ground. At the Permafrost Institute visitors can descend into a cavern at just such a depth, where the temperature remains constant at around -5°C.

Places to Stay

The best place to stay is the Canadian-Russian *Hotel Ontario* (☎ 6 50 58), about a 20-minute drive from the city centre. Outside, the Ontario looks like a traditional Yakut log cabin, but inside it's all modern Western conveniences including – the greatest luxury of all – hot water. Beds are around US$50 per night. In town, the *Hotel Yakutsk* (☎ 5 07 00) has thin walls, seatless toilets and chairs held together by string, but rooms do have showers. It's at ulitsa Oktyabrskaya 20/1, near the bus station. The *Hotel Lena* (☎ 4 48 90), prospekt Lenina 8, is about the same but close to airport buses and the Museum of History & Culture. Both hotels charge around US$40 per night.

Places to Eat

Guests at the *Hotel Ontario* also benefit from the best food in town, but at a price: a three-course dinner will come to around US$20. The restaurant at the *Hotel Yakutsk* has mediocre Russian standards; the one at the *Lena* is marginally better and there are also two bufety and a bar. Alternatives are a dreary stolovaya called *Kafe Delfin*, behind the Hotel Yakutsk, and the *Restoran Sever* on western prospekt Lenina. Food is expensive, probably due to the cost of getting it here.

SIBERIA & RUSSIAN FAR EAST

Entertainment

YakutIntour may be able to arrange a performance by the Yakut Dance Company, with polished versions of traditional music and dance. The Yakut Drama & Music Theatre is on ploshchad Druzhby and the Russian Drama Theatre is on prospekt Lenina.

Getting There & Away

The most convenient way to reach Yakutsk is by air. Daily direct flights from Moscow cost about US$300 and take six hours. There are also connections three times a week to/from Irkutsk, twice a week to/from Khabarovsk, Petropavlovsk-Kamchatsky and Vladivostok, and once a week to/from Magadan. The unmarked foreigners' check-in is around the right end of the terminal (facing the planes).

During summer there are twice-weekly sailings between Yakutsk and the port of Ust-Kut, nearly 2000 km upriver. See the earlier Ust-Kut section for further details – but note that, while it takes only 4½ days to sail to Yakutsk, the journey in the opposite direction, against the current, takes a whole week.

The other option, for the devotee of off-the-beaten-track travelling, is to take the bus – there is a 1200-km highway between Yakutsk and the town of Bolshoy Never on the Trans-Siberian line, passing through the BAM town of Tynda. We believe there is some kind of regular service but how frequent it is, the dates of travel or any other details we don't know. It's a fair bet, however, that the service doesn't operate in the winter.

Getting Around

From the airport, bus No 4 goes to ploshchad Ordzhonikidze (*'or-jo-ni-KEED-za'*), near the Hotel Lena. For the Hotel Yakutsk, transfer there to westbound bus No 6 or 8 and get off at the Avtovokzal stop. Southbound bus No 8, from in front of the bus station, goes to the river port (*rechnoy port*) at the end of the line.

AROUND YAKUTSK
ОКРЕСТНОСТЬ ЯКУТСКА

The territory of the Republic of Sakha covers approximately three million sq km, almost half of which is within the Arctic Circle and almost all within the permafrost zone. It's some of the most inhospitable terrain in the whole Russian Federation. The town of Verkhoyansk, 650 km north of Yakutsk, holds the record as the coldest inhabited spot on earth with temperatures recorded as low as -71°C (in the nearby valleys of the mountains of Oymyakon they go down to -82°C). At such times, according to Yakut lore, if you shout to a friend and he can't hear you it's because all the words have frozen in the air. But when the spring comes, all the words thaw and if you go back at the right time you can hear everything that was said months ago.

Summer is brief and quite uncomfortable: June, with its midsummer 'white nights', is blighted by rains and infested with mosquitoes (to such an extent that reindeer are said to have been suffocated by the midges swarming up their nostrils); July is hot and fetid; and August is perhaps the only agreeable month. Midsummer nights are 'white', with the sun barely setting. The average density of the republic's one million people (of whom 30% are Yakut) is about one for every three sq km. Most live along the Lena River and its tributaries.

In this austere, frozen wilderness the size of India, Evenk and Chukchi still hunt for a living on the Arctic coast, Yakuts tend horses and cattle as if this were Central Asia, and Russian engineers scratch away at stupendous underground riches – oil and gas, coal and tin, gold and diamonds. The heart of Sakha's diamond industry is the town of Mirny (population: 40,000), 800 km west of Yakutsk, while Aldan (accessible by rail from the BAM town of Tynda) is the servicing centre for the gold fields.

Yakut & Evenk Villages

YakutIntour will take you on a half-day coach trip to a Yakut village or fly you 500 km north-east to Topolinoe village for a look at Evenk life. Two nights and a city tour in Yakutsk plus two nights in Topolinoe cost about US$270, by advance arrangement only.

Lena Pillars
Ленские Столбы

Sakha's main highway is the 4400-km-long Lena River, which originates in the mountains to the west of Lake Baikal. It's navigable for five months of the year, but during the other months, frozen to a depth of five metres, it serves as an icy route for conventional wheeled traffic.

The Lena Pillars (Lenskie Stolby) are huge, tower-like sandstone formations that line the river for an 18-km stretch, about 140 km south of Yakutsk. There's a tourist hydrofoil which during summer makes regular four-hour sailings up to the rocks and allows time for picnicking or climbing before sailing back downstream to the city. The cost of the excursion is approximately US$100 and you should contact YakutIntour for further details.

YakutIntour also runs a 1200-km, 10-night luxury cruise up to Vitim and back, complete with on-board and onshore entertainment.

The Russian Far East
Дальний Восток

The Russian Far East is the geographical term for the territories that run along the Pacific seaboard, from Chukotka in the north, with its Arctic coastline, down to Primorsky kray (or Ussuriland), squeezed between China, Korea and the Sea of Japan. It includes the Kamchatka Peninsula and the string of Kuril Islands which arc down to Japan, enclosing the Sea of Okhotsk and the large, fish-shaped island of Sakhalin.

Khabarovsk Territory
Хабаровский Край

BIROBIDZHAN
БИРОБИДЖАН
Population: 90,000

At Birobidzhan, a small town 180 km west of Khabarovsk on the Trans-Siberian line, the sharp-eyed might spot some strange, non-Cyrillic lettering painted on the station building. It's only the station name but the language in which it's written is Hebrew. This is one of the scarce present-day indications of Birobidzhan's status as capital of the Jewish Autonomous Region (Yevreyskaya Avtonomnaya Oblast).

Faced with severe poverty among the Jews in European Russia, the young Soviet government proposed the creation of a rural 'homeland' to which Jews could migrate. After a search for a thinly populated area (to minimise local backlash), 36,000 sq km on the Bira and Bidzhan rivers, tributaries of the Amur, was opened to settlement in 1927. This had the extra advantage of plugging a borderland hole which was susceptible to Japanese ambitions.

But the region was unused for good reason – it was swampy and mosquito infested, with poor soil and bitterly cold winters (January average -26˚C, extremes to -40˚C). About 40,000 Jews, mainly from Belarus and Ukraine, made the trek, but only a third stayed. As a further sweetener, the area was declared the Jewish Autonomous Region in 1934. The anti-Semitism of the Stalin years killed off the project and all Jewish institutions in the region, including the schools and synagogue, were shut down. The Museum of Jewish Culture & History was razed to the ground and the use of Hebrew was banned.

Today, 15,000 Jews account for only 7% of the region's population. In recent years many have left for Israel. Ironically, the same benign political winds that blew open the gates to migration have also breathed life into Birobidzhan's long-dormant Jewish heritage. With the removal of Soviet-era fetters, schools are now returning to teaching Hebrew and Yiddish and efforts are under way to raise money for a new synagogue.

Orientation & Information
The city's main streets run east-west, parallel to and squeezed between the railway line and the River Bira to the south. From the station the streets are ulitsa Kalinina, ulitsa Lenina, ulitsa Sholom-Aleikhema (the main axis), ulitsa Pionerskaya and prospekt 60 let SSSR with its twin squares, ploshchad Lenina and ploshchad Sovetov.

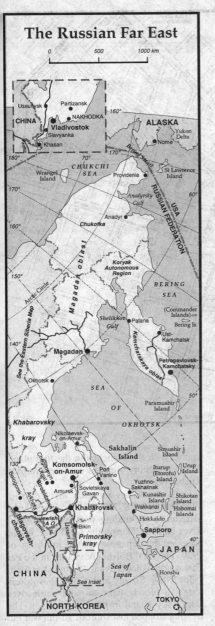

The Russian Far East

The main post, telephone and telegraph office is at prospekt 60 let SSSR 14. There is an office of Intour-Birobidzhan (☎ 6 15 73) at ulitsa Sholom-Aleikhema 55. The Hotel Vostok (☎ 6 53 30) is at ulitsa Sholom-Aleikhema 1.

Birobidzhan time is Moscow time plus seven hours. The local telephone code is 42162.

Things to See & Do

The **Museum of Local Studies** (Kraevedchesky muzey), at ulitsa Lenina 25, has a room devoted to the Jewish history of the region, and there's a working synagogue at Mayakovskogo 11 (follow ulitsa Sholom-Aleikhema east into ulitsa Komsomolskaya, on into ulitsa Sovietskaya, and Mayakovskogo is left at the end). Look out for the *Birobidzhaner Stern* (*Birobidzhan Star*), Russia's only Yiddish newspaper.

The town has a **Yiddish Music & Drama Theatre** (Yevreysky muzykalny i dramatichesky teatr) and several Jewish folk-music ensembles – enquire at the Intour-Birobidzhan office for details of performances and venues.

Getting There & Away

The *Rossia* and the Moscow-Khabarovsk train both make a brief halt at Birobidzhan, as do most other services. Alternatively, Birobidzhan is an easy day trip from Khabarovsk, just three hours down the line. Catch the No 103 Moscow train (departs from Khabarovsk at 6.45 am local time) or the No 601 Leninsk service (departs at 7 am local time) and return late afternoon on train No 2, the *Rossia*.

KHABAROVSK

ХАБАРОВСК

Population: 611,000

After the monotonous *taiga* of eastern Siberia and its severe wilderness towns, Khabarovsk comes as a welcome relief. It lies at the broad confluence of the Amur River and its tributary, the Ussuri, and the town has the air almost of a coastal resort. The main street, a leafy tree-lined boulevard

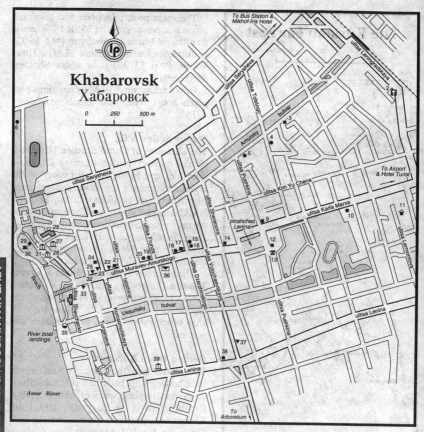

Khabarovsk
Хабаровск

0   250   500 m

To Bus Station &
Mikhof-Iris Hotel

To Airport
& Hotel Turist

To
Arboretum

ploshchad
Lenina

ulitsa Leningradskaya
ulitsa Serysheva
ulitsa Tolstogo
bulvar
Amursky
ulitsa Pushkina
ulitsa Kim Yu Chena
ulitsa Serysheva
ulitsa Frunze
ulitsa Sheronova
ulitsa Volochaevskaya
ulitsa Muravev-Amurskogo
ulitsa Dzerzhinskogo
ulitsa Istomina
ulitsa Karla Marxa
ulitsa Lenina
ulitsa Lenina
ulitsa Pushkina
ulitsa Lenina
ulitsa Lermontova
bulvar
Komsomolskaya
Ussurisky
Turgeneva
ulitsa Shevchenko
Beach
River boat
landings
Amur River

SIBERIA & RUSSIAN FAR EAST

with some very attractive 19th-century brick architecture, bustles with pizza-selling street vendors and animated window-shoppers who don't seem afraid to smile. Considering that it's almost the far side of Asia from Moscow and only 25 km from China, the centre of Khabarovsk has a surprisingly European feel.

The town was founded in 1858 as a military post in the campaign by the governor general of Eastern Siberia, Count Nikolay Muravev (later Muravev-Amursky), to take the Amur back from the Manchus. It was named for the man who got the Russians into

trouble with the Manchus in the first place, the 17th-century Russian explorer Yerofey Khabarov.

Until the Trans-Siberian arrived from Vladivostok in 1897, Khabarovsk was just a garrison, a fur-trading post and an Amur River landing. During the Civil War, it was occupied by Japanese troops for most of 1920. The final Bolshevik victory in the Far East was at Volochaevka, 45 km to the west.

In 1969, Soviet and Chinese soldiers fought a bloody hand-to-hand battle over Damansky Island in the Ussuri River. The fighting stopped just short of all-out war but

PLACES TO STAY

3 Hotel Mayak
Гостиница Маяк
11 Pedagogical Institute
Hostel
12 Hotel Tsentralnaya
Гостиница Центральная
14 Hotel Lyudmila and
Hotel of the
Regional
Administration
Гостиница Людмила
24 Hotel Sapporo
Гостиница Саппоро
28 Hotel Intourist
Гостиница Интурист
38 Hotel Amur
Гостиница Амур

PLACES TO EAT

17 Kafe Dauria
Кафе Даурия
21 Merkury Store & Kafe
Меркурий
магазин/Кафе
22 Restoran Russ
Ресторан Русь
23 Buterbrodna
Бутербродна
25 Restoran Sapporo
Ресторан Саппоро
30 Tower Kafe
Кафе Вышка

33 Restoran Kamali
Ресторан Камалий
37 Restoran Harbin
Ресторан Харбин

OTHER

1 Railway Station
Железнодорожный
вокзал
2 Church of Christ's Birth
Христорождественская
церковь
4 Circus
Цирк
5 Market
Рынок
6 Chinese Consulate
Консульство Китайское
7 Lenin Stadium
Стадион имени В. И.
Ленина
8 Aeroflot
Аэрофлот
9 Bookshop
Книжестный магазин
10 Theatre of Musical
Comedy
Театр музыкальной
комедии
13 Central Telephone,
Telegraph & Fax
Office
Главпочтамт

15 Kodak Photo Express
Кодак Фото Магазин
16 Drama Theatre
Драматический Театр
18 Department Store
Универмаг
19 Souvenir Shop
Магазин Сувениры
20 Childrens Bookshop
Детская книга
26 Art Museum
Художественный
музей
27 Military Museum
Военный музей
29 Casino Amur
Касино Амур
31 Museum of Local
Studies
Краеведческий музей
32 Ploshchad
Komsomolskaya
Площад
Комсомолская
34 Parus Business Centre
Парус Бизнес-центр
35 River Boat Ticket Office
Речной вокзал
36 Central Post Office
Центральный Почтамт
39 Museum of Geology
Геологический
музей

SIBERIA & RUSSIAN FAR EAST

it set in motion a huge military build-up. Since 1984, tensions have eased and there's now substantial cross-border trade: the Russians buy cheap clothing, junk food and trashy video games, the Chinese buy timber and fertilisers. In mid-1991 the Russians handed Damansky and several other islands back to the Chinese.

Now, the future of Khabarovsk seems again to be in foreign hands. The Japanese are back in occupation, not with soldiers this time but with businesses and tourists. They make up four-fifths of all foreign visitors here and their presence in town is demonstrated by the Japanese-run hotels and the couple of restaurants that specialise in sushi. South Koreans have also begun arriving in large numbers, opening many new busi-

nesses in Khabarovsk, including a large TV factory. As lumbering Soviet-era industries collapse, these new enterprises are providing much-needed work for locals. Unsurprisingly, Khabarovsk is actively courting further foreign interest and investment.

Khabarovskians are 80% Russian-speakers, with small Korean and Armenian communities. The only indigenous people here in any numbers are the Nanai, whose capital is Troitskoe, three hours down the Amur. Khabarovsk is the capital of a territory, Khabarovsky kray, that stretches 2000 km north along the Sea of Okhotsk.

Orientation

The city is on the high east bank of the Amur (which the Chinese call Heilongjiang, or

Count Nikolay Muravev-Amursky founded
Khabarovsk in 1858

Black Dragon River), just north of the confluence with the Ussuri. Topographically, the city is like a ploughed field with the three main streets running along parallel ridges. The busiest street and central attraction is ulitsa Muravev-Amurskogo, which becomes ulitsa Karla Marxa east of the parade square, ploshchad Lenina. South of Muravev-Amurskogo is ulitsa Lenina, while north is bleak Amursky bulvar with the railway station at its eastern end. Khabarovsk covers a large area (in fact, at 400 sq km, it's more than half the size of Moscow) and it's a 3.5-km walk from the railway station to the river front and Hotel Intourist. The Chinese border is 25 km across the hills to the southwest.

There are numerous maps of Khabarovsk available, in English, Russian or Chinese, gathered in an atlas (for US$4) or done in the form of a beautiful bird's-eye 3D drawing – look for them in the bookshops on Muravev-Amurskogo.

Information
Money There is a rash of currency-exchange offices across the city and even the museums have them. One late opener to remember is the kiosk in the foyer of the Sapporo restau-

rant, which is open for business until 9 pm. The exchange bureau at the Hotel Intourist will take travellers' cheques and also gives cash advances on Visa, Eurocard and MasterCard. It's open from 9.30 am to 8.15 pm.

Post & Telecommunications The main post and telegraph office is at ulitsa Muravev-Amurskogo 28, open from 8 am to 8 pm, and on weekends from 9 am to 7 pm. A letter from here to anywhere outside Russia will cost US$0.50. The main telephone and fax office is at ulitsa Pushkina 56, two doors along from the Hotel Tsentralnaya. Calls to the USA or Australia are charged at US$3 per minute and to Europe US$3.80 per minute; it's open daily from 8.30 am to 10 pm. There are credit-card-operated phones at the post office and the Hotel Intourist but calls are charged at a blanket rate of US$8 per minute.

Khabarovsk time is Moscow time plus seven hours. The local telephone code for Khabarovsk is 4212.

Foreign Consulates There is a Chinese consulate (☎ 34 85 37, or for visa hotline ☎ 33 83 90) in the north-west corner of the grounds of the Lenin Stadium. Visa applications are dealt with on Mondays, Wednesdays and Fridays at 9.30 am. The cost is US$70 for a single-entry visa and processing takes two days. The Japanese Consulate (☎ 33 26 23, visa hotline 33 87 75) is in room 208 at the Hotel Sapporo.

Travel Agencies Unfortunately, Intourist-Khabarovsk (☎ 39 90 44; ☎ & fax 33 87 74; telex 141114 KRUIZ SU) at Amursky bulvar 2, Khabarovsk 680065, is the only agency in town with any experience of dealing with foreigners, though as far as customer service goes, its staff appear to have learnt little: 'You want to go to Sakhalin? Ha! Don't think it is so easy.' They are, however, very innovative. In the summer of 1994 Intourist-Khabarovsk went into partnership with the Russian navy to lay on what they term 'military tourism'. US$600 can now buy a group excursion on a warship or diesel submarine, or a personal tour of a mechanised infantry division. US$700 puts you at the controls of a T-55 tank for an hour, while US$1440 turns the tables and gives you a shot at destruction with an anti-tank missile launcher. For the budget traveller, ripping off a round Rambo-style with a Kalashnikov assault rifle is just US$45.

Among the more conventional services Intourist-Khabarovsk offers are boat rides on the Amur, helicopter excursions (US$55 per person), and one-day trips to Fuyuan in China. By advance arrangement, Intourist will take Great White Hunters to shoot bears or just to camp out in the Khekhtsir taiga preserve.

Bookshops Khabarovsk is the best place east of Moscow for bookshops. The Knizhnoy Mir, at ulitsa Pushkina 56, allows customers to directly handle the books – an innovation that has yet to reach the capital. Knizhnoy Mir is also the best place for maps, which are all pinned up for examination and comparison. Ulitsa Muravev-Amurskogo 17 houses two bookshops, the Knigi and the Detskaya Knigi (Children's Books). The Knigi at ulitsa Karla Marxa 49 had the only English-language books that we saw in all Siberia and the Far East (Shakespeare's *The Tempest* and something on baby behaviour, if anyone's interested).

Film & Photography You can stock up on film at the Fuji shop in the basement of the Hotel Intourist, which also offers 24-hour print processing. A similar service is available at Kodak Express on the corner of ulitsa Dzerzhinskogo and Muravev-Amurskogo.

Ulitsa Muravev-Amurskogo & the Riverfront

Among those bits of architecture that survived the Civil War are the intricate red-brick façade of the territorial public library, built 1900 to 1902, and the headquarters of the Amur Steamship Company with its round, church-like tower. Both are on ploshchad Komsomolskaya. Dating from 1858, the attractive mint-green building at ulitsa Muravev-Amurskogo 9, now the Merkury food store, has an equally unusual interior with decorated ceilings and colourful, carved wooden figurines in the 1st-floor cafeteria.

Steps from ploshchad Komsomolskaya lead to the waterfront and a small beach. South is a string of summertime food stalls and the landing stages for the suburban river boats. A city park stretches 1.5 km downriver (north) and its leafy paths are a favourite place for locals to take an evening stroll. The giant satellite dish, not quite hidden by the trees, is to receive Moscow TV programmes. A few hundred metres north is a cliff-top tower, in which, so the story goes, a troupe of WW I Austro-Hungarian POW musicians was shot dead for refusing to play the Russian Imperial anthem. Now, it contains a café where you can drink coffee or beer and enjoy the view across the river.

Opposite the tower is a statue of Count Nikolay Muravev-Amursky, the man who secured Khabarovsk for the tsar. During Soviet times the count was displaced by the ubiquitous Lenin and has only recently reclaimed his plinth. Muravev's remains actually lie in Montparnasse Cemetery in Paris, the city in which he died in 1881. The monument at the foot of the cliff below the tower is to mark the spot where the city's founders first stepped ashore.

Church of Christ's Birth

The Bolsheviks succeeded in destroying almost all of Khabarovsk's churches including the grand cathedral which stood on what is now ploshchad Komsomolskaya. The result is that this city of more than half a million people has, incredibly, only three churches. Two of these, the Orthodox Alexander Nevsky Temple on ulitsa Yasnaya and the Innokentievsky Temple on ulitsa Turgeneva, are fairly unexceptional but the third, the Church of Christ's Birth (Khristo-rozhdestvenskaya tserkov) at ulitsa Leningradskaya 65, is worth a visit. Its simple wooden construction hides a kaleidoscopic interior of coloured glass and glitzy icons. If you can find out when services are held, then it's worth turning up to hear the mesmeric, polyphonic hymn singing.

Museum of Local Studies

This very good museum (Kraevedchesky muzey), founded in 1894, looks at the history, natural history and indigenous peoples of the Far East. Here you can see what an Ussuri tiger looks like (there are only a few hundred left in the wild). The archaeology section includes prehistoric rock paintings. Best are photos and exhibits featuring indigenous groups (many of them extinct or nearly so) with tools, religious art and clothing – including Nivkhi clothing made of fish skin. A 360° panorama depicts the battle at Volochaevka. There is also an arresting display about the Soviet Gulag. The museum is at ulitsa Shevchenko 11, 200 metres north of ploshchad Komsomolskaya, and is open from 10 am to 6 pm, closed on Monday.

Other Museums

Next door to the Museum of Local Studies is the **Art Museum** (Khudozhestvenny muzey) with a patchy assortment of religious icons, Japanese porcelain and 19th-century Russian painting on the upper floor, while the lower floors are given over to displays of ethnic handicrafts, a contemporary gallery and a gift shop. Admission is US$2 and it's open from 10 am to 6 pm, closed on Monday and Tuesday.

Across the road is the **Military Museum** (Voennogo muzey), which is heavy on the Russo-Japanese war and the battles fought in this area. There are some striking posters and kitschy bits of Soviet regalia and also a luxury officers-only Trans-Siberian rail carriage, but beware of being too selective with your attention because the babushka attendants are there to ensure that every exhibit receives attention – anyone skipping displays will be sent back. The babushkas also do a good sideline in hustling military cap badges and buttons (for US dollars only). Admission and opening hours are the same

as for the Art Museum. There is also a Museum of Geology at ulitsa Lenina 15.

Arboretum

South on ulitsa Volochaevskaya is the Arboretum (Dendrariy), a 12-hectare botanical garden. It has samples of all the trees and shrubs of the Russian Far East and is open daily from 9 am to 6 pm. Take bus No 9, 10, 25 or 29 along Volochaevskaya to the Ussuriyskaya stop, about three km from ulitsa Muravev-Amurskogo.

Places to Stay

With 270 rooms on 10 floors, the *Hotel Intourist* (☎ 39 93 13; fax 33 87 74; telex 141114 KRUIZ SU) at Amursky bulvar 2, accommodates almost all the packaged and prebooked tourists who hit town. The rooms all come with attached bathrooms, they're clean, and the hotel has a plethora of bars, cafés and other amenities. However, the hotel is overpriced, with singles at US$97, doubles US$120.

For a similar amount of money there is a much better alternative in the *Hotel Sapporo* (☎ 33 27 02; fax within Russia 33 28 30, fax from abroad 4088, fax from the USA 10 333 011 7 50931 41 4088) at ulitsa Komsomolskaya 79. Opened in 1993, this small hotel was precision engineered to suit the requirements of Japanese business personnel, from the two-metre-high Japanese flag in the lobby to the heated toilet seats. The singles at US$120 and doubles at US$160 must be booked well in advance. The *Hotel Lyudmila* (☎ 38 86 49) at ulitsa Muravev-Amurskogo 33, occupies the 3rd floor of an administrative block, converted into 'business class' accommodation. There are 18 three-room suites, nice but cluttered with furniture and superfluous domestic appliances, all chosen by someone with the tastes of Barbara Cartland. A suite costs US$100 a night.

There's a Mikof-Iris hotel (☎ 39 94 01) at ulitsa Tikhookeanskaya 211, which is a few km outside the city centre. See Accommodation in European Russia Facts for the Visitor chapter for information on this hotel chain.

Rooms are US$65 for a single or US$40 each in a double. There are also some two-room suites at US$94 for single occupancy, US$55 each for two people sharing, or US$43 each for a trio. To get to the Microsurgery centre, where the hotel is located, take tram No 5 from in front of the railway station and it's about a 40-minute ride.

The *Hotel Turist* (☎ 37 06 17) at ulitsa Karla Marxa 67 is a typical 1970s Soviet hotel, but its boxy rooms are well maintained with a TV, fridge and telephone and a clean, tiled bathroom. Singles are US$44, doubles US$56. At the *Hotel Tsentralnaya* (☎ 33 47 59), at ulitsa Pushkina 52, you can be neighbours with Lenin, who stands just a door down at the head of his parade square. Acceptable singles/doubles at US$30/37 come with attached shower and toilet. The hotel is popular with Chinese and out-of-town traders. The same clientele inhabit the *Hotel Amur* (☎ 22 12 23) at ulitsa Lenina 29, although this hotel is considerably more grotty than the Tsentralnaya. Singles are US$24, doubles US$20 per person, and a place in a three-bed room is US$15.

Several budget options exist, the cheapest of which is the *Hotel of the Regional Administration* (☎ 33 89 57) with a great location at ulitsa Muravev-Amurskogo 33. The rooms are fairly Spartan but they are only US$3 per person. The hotel and reception desk are on the 1st floor (the Russian 2nd) – the foyer reception is for the Hotel Lyudmila on the 3rd floor. The *Foreign Language Department of the Pedagogical Institute* has a student dormitory, at Lermontova 50, that accepts foreign visitors. The rooms are unfurnished, save for beds, and are fairly grim, as are the shared toilets and showers, but it's a good opportunity to meet local, English-speaking students. A single room is US$14, a bed in a double room is US$7, or in a triple-bed room, US$6. To get there, follow ulitsa Leningradskaya 80 metres south of the junction with ulitsa Karla Marxa, then cut to the right through a gap in the buildings after the Khabarovsky Kooperatok store; walk due west, past three apartment blocks, to reach the back of Lermontova 50. The entrance is round the front and the dormitory is on the 3rd floor.

The *Hotel Mayak* (☎ 33 09 35) is conveniently close to the railway station at ulitsa Kooperativnaya 11. It's housed in a fairly squalid-looking apartment block but the rooms aren't too bad; singles are US$15, doubles US$28. From the railway station walk 400 metres along Amursky bulvar, turning left immediately after No 48.

Places to Eat

The best food in town is at the *Restoran Harbin*, a pricey Chinese/Russian joint venture with cooks and ingredients from China. The restaurant has two dining rooms, with the one on the right being cheaper, but for an evening meal you can still figure on spending US$25, without booze. It's open from 11 am to 4 pm and 6 to 11 pm. The Harbin is at ulitsa Volochaevskaya 118, near ulitsa Lenina. 'Stunningly good but extortionate' is how a *Moscow Times* journalist described the *Unikhab*, a swish Japanese restaurant on the top floor of the Hotel Intourist. It caters to Japanese business personnel who pay for their Tokyo-quality sushi with fistfuls of yen. On the ground floor of the same hotel, the *Red Hall* (Krasny Zal) is appalling. The breakfast of water-logged omelette and rubberised pancakes (US$2.50) was completely inedible and in the evening the band was so loud that it had our undercooked vegetables doing a samba round the plate. Its saving graces are that it's cheap (dishes are US$1 to US$3) and open late: 8 am until 2 am.

By far our favourite place was the *Kamali* at ulitsa Muravev-Amurskogo 2, on ploshchad Komsomolskaya. With just five tables down in a basement, it has a very cosy, almost continental atmosphere, with chequered tablecloths, potted plants and a high, bar-like counter, behind which the waitresses stand and look sullen. The service is good and the food excellent, with dishes in the US$3 to US$4 range. It's open from 2 to 6 pm and 7 to 11 pm and a reservation is recommended in the evening.

Attracting a young, fashionable and well-heeled crowd, the most popular place in town seems to be the *Sapporo* at ulitsa Muravev-Amurskogo 3. Although the place looks flash the menu isn't too badly priced and the food is top-class. We had an excellent mushroom soup (US$0.80) and a very tasty myaso po-russky (US$3.50), which turned out to be beef and chopped vegetables in a creamy white sauce topped with melted cheese. The Sapporo is open from 8 am to 4 pm and 6 to 11 pm; reservations are essential after 8 pm.

The *Russ* at ulitsa Muravev-Amurskogo 5, is a down-market alternative to the Sapporo. The large, airy dining hall is on the 1st floor, with French windows that overlook the main street. In the afternoon it's a pleasant, lazy diner but we did notice an ominous-looking drum kit in the corner – best to eat early. Despite exotic-sounding titles (which meant nothing to our Russian companions, either), the fare is the same basic memories-of-school-days offerings, priced at US$1.50 to US$2.50. It's open from 11 am to 4 pm and 5 to 11 pm.

For snacks, ulitsa Muravev-Amurskogo has lots of cheap eateries. In warm weather, outdoor kiosks serve shashlyk and the local version of pizza – no tomato, no meat, just a little cheese and hunks of onion. *Kafe Dauria*, at ulitsa Muravev-Amurskogo 25, has cutlets and poza, while *Buterbrodna* at ulitsa Komsomolskaya 79, does sandwiches and juice and is a popular hang-out for students. The nicest place for a coffee, tea, beer or ice cream is the *Tower Kafe* in the park overlooking the river.

For Trans-Siberian supplies, the Merkury store at ulitsa Muravev-Amurskogo 9 has dried fruit, nuts, cheese, biscuits etc, or for fresh fruit, try the market on Amursky bulvar near ulitsa Tolstogo.

Entertainment
There are two casinos in town, one at the Hotel Turist, the other by the Tower Kafe. Both are frequented by a lot of rather dubious-looking characters. There's a pitch reserved for the circus on ulitsa Tolstogo, near the market, but the show only hits town for a few months of each year, usually in early summer. The Drama Theatre is at ulitsa Dzerzhinskogo 44 and there's a Theatre of Musical Comedy at ulitsa Karla Marxa 64 with a contemporary fine-arts gallery opposite. The Kino Gigant at ulitsa Muravev-Amurskogo 19, directly across from the central post office, screens recent Hollywood releases. Intour-Khabarovsk can also arrange concerts of Siberian music performed by local ensembles.

A pricey evening out with a difference exists in the 'champagne sunset flight' advertised by Russian Air Services (☎ 22 40 31), a dusk, sightseeing whirl in a helicopter along the Amur River.

Things to Buy
In Khabarovsk you'll find the same matryoshka dolls, painted boxes and dodgy watercolours common to all art salons and suveniry throughout Russia, the only difference being that here the price tags are in yen. The Khabarovskians, aware that the yen can out-slog the dollar any day, also charge more than anywhere else for the same standard goods. The art salons in the Military and Art museums are particularly outrageous in their pricing, and the best alternative is to go shopping along ulitsa Muravev-Amurskogo. Try the antique/ craft store at No 17 and the Univermag at No 23.

Getting There & Away
Air The airport at Khabarovsk is the largest in Siberia or the Russian Far East and it has direct connections with almost every other Russian airport of any size as well as international links with several Pacific Rim countries. Domestic flights include twice a day to/from Moscow (US$350, 8½ hours), Irkutsk (US$170, 2¾ hours) and Petropavlovsk-Kamchatsky (US$210, 2¾ hours), one flight a day to/from Magadan (US$195, 2½ hours), Vladivostok (US$95, 1¼ hours) and Yuzhno-Sakhalinsk (US$120, 1½ hours) and two flights a week to Yakutsk (US$185, 1½ hours).

International routes flown by Aeroflot include three times a week to/from Niigata (US$696 return), twice a week to/from

Harbin (US$270 return) and San Francisco (US$2870 return) via Anchorage and once a week to/from Seattle (US$2538 return) via Anchorage, Seoul and Singapore (US$2660 return). Several international operators also use Khabarovsk. Alaska Airlines (☎ 37 88 04) flies Khabarovsk-Magadan-Anchorage-Seattle once a week for a return fare of US$1008, bookable seven days in advance, maximum stay 90 days. Also, China Northern (☎ 37 34 40) flies to/from Harbin twice a week, and there are once a week services with Japan Airlines (☎ 37 06 86) to/from Niigata and with Asiana Airlines (☎ 37 88 04) to/from Seoul.

The foreign airlines all have offices on the upper floor of the airport's international terminal, a modern two-storey building to the far left of the main building. Aeroflot's sales office (☎ 34 84 57) is at Amursky bulvar 5. The front desk at the Hotel Intourist can also book seats on domestic flights and issue tickets.

All international flights are subject to a US$25 departure tax, to be paid at the terminal's information desk prior to checking in. Intourist passengers making domestic flights should check in at the old international terminal, which is the odd-looking porticoed building next to the new one.

Train On the daily *Rossia* (train No 1/2), Moscow is 130 hours away; a place in a four-berth sleeper costs around US$160. Irkutsk is 36 hours away, Vladivostok 13 hours. The line to Vladivostok runs in places only 10 km from the Chinese border and the *Rossia* (until recently, supposedly the only train to carry foreigners in this region) has always travelled this sensitive stretch cloaked by the darkness of night. However, there are now no less than eight other services which will take you from Khabarovsk to the Pacific port at almost any time you should choose.

Services westbound include the No 1 Vladivostok-Moscow train, the No 183 daily Khabarovsk-Moscow train, and trains to Novosibirsk, Kharkiv (Kharkov) and Blagoveshchensk.

There is a daily service to Tynda on the BAM and, on alternate days, one to Neryungri. Train No 67/68 runs to/from Komsomolsk-on-Amur, another BAM station, with connections to Sovietskaya Gavan and Port Vanino for the ferry across to Sakhalin Island.

Boat There is a river connection between Fuyuan in northern China and Khabarovsk; see the Around Khabarovsk section later in this chapter. Between May and October, there are also hydrofoils on the Amur River running between Khabarovsk and Komsomolsk (from where you can change for another boat to Nikolaevsk at the river's mouth). There's a ticket office by the riverboat landings south of the beach, from where you can enquire about schedules.

Getting Around
From the airport, seven km east of the centre, trolleybus No 1 passes the Hotel Turist (Leningradskaya stop) and continues to the end of the line at ploshchad Komsomolskaya, near the Hotel Intourist. It runs every few minutes and the trip takes half an hour. Tickets, costing US$0.05, are bought in strips of 10 from the driver. A taxi from the Hotel Intourist to the airport will cost the equivalent of US$6.

The railway station is at the east end of Amursky bulvar. From there, bus No 2 (caught front right as you leave the station) goes five or six stops to the Amursky bulvar stop, a block from the Hotel Intourist. The Hotel Turist is to the left from the railway station, one stop by any bus heading in that direction. The local bus station is on ulitsa Voronezhskaya: right out of the railway station, follow the tram tracks round, under the railway bridge, and it's a further 300 metres on the left – or take tram No 1, 2, 5 or 6 north from the railway station.

In summer, Intourist offers an open 1½-hour Amur River cruise but for considerably less, you can do your own 2½ to three-hour round trip by ferry to the marshy dacha suburbs from one of the landings (prichal) by the beach. Good choices might be the trip downstream to Green Island (Ostrov Zelyony) from landing No 5, upstream to Vladimirovka from landing No 2 or around the back channels to Priamurskaya from landing No 3. Timetables are posted beside the landings. Navigation season is May to October.

AROUND KHABAROVSK
ОКРЕСТНОСТЬ ХАБАРОВСКА

Fuyuan (China)
Фуюан

Every other day at 8.30 am, a hydrofoil departs from the river station at Khabarovsk for Fuyuan, a small town on the Chinese bank of the Amur River, three hours' sail away. If you return with the hydrofoil later the same day, no visa is required for the visit. Anyone wishing to travel on into China needs a valid visa (there's a Chinese consulate in Khabarovsk; see the earlier Information section). From Fuyuan they should take a bus to Jiamusi and then on to Harbin, the transportation hub of north-east China.

Intour-Khabarovsk can help book tickets for Fuyuan if necessary. The Amur Tourist Company (☎ 39 81 45) at ulitsa Muravev-Amurskogo 2, also uses this route for its tours to Jiamusi (US$200, four days) and Harbin (US$295, seven days), which are run mainly for the benefit of Russian traders.

Sikachi-Alyan
Сикачи-Алян

This is a small Nanai fishing settlement of perhaps 30 or so dwellings strung along the banks of the Amur, 40 km downriver of Khabarovsk. The main attractions are some 11th-century BC petroglyphs – aboriginal stone carvings adorning some of the boulders on the muddy flats at the water's edge. From the village, the boulders are quite difficult to find, involving a short boat ride and a trek along the wooded shore (from June through to October, infested with swarms of mosquitoes that can easily bite through cotton, so wear something more protective, and cover your hands and face too). You need a guide, or at least someone amongst you who can speak Russian well enough to ask

for directions and persuade some local to row you across the small stretch of water that separates the village and the carvings.

To get to Sikachi-Alyan take bus No 205 (Maleesheva) which runs from Khabarovsk every day at 7.15 am and 5 pm, making the return journey at 9 am and 6.45 pm. A single ticket is US$1.50. Take your own food as there is no shop in the village. Intour-Khabarovsk can arrange visits, with guide and including a traditional performance, for US$80 for individuals, or US$20 per person in a group (minimum of four people).

KOMSOMOLSK-ON-AMUR
КОМСОМОЛЬСК НА АМУРЕ

Population: 305,000

Komsomolsk-on-Amur (usually just shortened to Komsomolsk – 'City of Youth') is the largest city on the BAM but, at least in terms of population, getting smaller all the time. It's also probably the most depressing city on the BAM.

The city was founded in 1932 by enthusiastic members of the Young Communist League, Komsomol, who sailed up the Amur on a ship called the *Columbus*, alighting in the middle of a great swamp 290 km north of Khabarovsk.

Komsomolsk was established to strengthen the Soviet's Far Eastern defences, and it became the site for steelworks, a secretive aircraft factory and huge shipbuilding yards, turning out ice-breakers and submarines. It was also to form the eastern terminus of the planned BAM, the second trans-Siberian railway. The BAM project languished for 40 years until, with a fresh wave of glorious rhetoric and hyperbole, it was relaunched in the early 1970s. A new wave of idealistic young socialists arrived in Komsomolsk to have another crack at creating the proletarian paradise.

The demise of the Soviet Union has turned Komsomolsk from a socialist dream into a communal nightmare. The factories, producing goods that no-one wants any more, have been forced to lay off large numbers of employees, and in autumn 1994 many of those still in work hadn't received any wages for months. The BAM, though completed and open to traffic, has not proved the economic provider that everybody hoped it would be. As a result alcoholism is rampant, divorce rates have rocketed, and the only answer for many is to leave and return west.

All of which makes Komsomolsk a fairly dismal place to visit. Possible tourist attractions are limited to a museum of indigenous peoples and an art gallery, both on ulitsa Mira, and a museum of aviation, which is actually very good. The central, ex-Intourist hotel, which is about the only accommodation in town, is quite expensive at around US$45 to US$50 a night. It might be possible to organise a homestay or find some cheaper accommodation by contacting the travel agency Marika (☎ (42172) 3 47 63; fax (42172) 4 02 69) at ulitsa Shikhanova 10.

Getting There & Away

Komsomolsk has good rail connections with Khabarovsk (four trains daily: Nos 67/68, 187/188, 205/206 and 921/922) and daily trains to/from Vladivostok (No 205/206) and to/from Nakhodka (the No 187/188 Sovietskaya Gavan-Tikhookeanskaya service). Along the BAM, there are three trains a day to Sovietskaya Gavan, via Port Vanino, and one daily service to/from Tynda. The journey between Khabarovsk and Komsomolsk takes 9½ hours on the overnight train (No 67/68).

Between early June and the end of August it's possible to travel to/from Khabarovsk by way of the Amur River, using the regular daily hydrofoil service. Make enquiries at the river station. There is also a hydrofoil departing at 8 am every morning for Nikolaevsk, at the mouth of the Amur on the Pacific coast. The trip takes 12 hours and costs US$32.

SOVIETSKAYA GAVAN (& PORT VANINO)
СОВЕТСКАЯ ГАВАНЬ (ПОРТ ВАНИНО)
Population 32,000
Sovietskaya Gavan is a port on the Pacific coast linked to Komsomolsk, 500 km west,

by an extension of the BAM. It was founded in 1853 and originally named Imperatorskaya Gavan (Emperor's Harbour), changing to 'Harbour of the Soviets' in 1926. After Vladivostok and Petropavlovsk-Kamchatsky, it is Russia's third-largest naval base on the Pacific seaboard. Aside from a complex of concrete bunkers and gun emplacements constructed prior to WW II in anticipation of war with the Japanese, there's very little to see. Sovietskaya Gavan is often shortened to Sovgavan on rail timetables.

About 20 km north of Sovgavan, and a stop before it on the railway, is Port Vanino (population 30,000), a civilian harbour. Vanino was only founded in 1944 and it was known primarily as a waystation for prisoners being shipped up to the Kolyma Gulag camps. For visitors today, its main (and possibly only) distinction is that it's the place to board ship for Sakhalin Island.

There is no regular ferry service but about once or twice a week a freighter leaves Vanino for Kholmsk, on Sakhalin's west coast (for information on the week's sailing dates, phone Vanino harbour ☎ (42137) 5 73 00 or 5 78 57). Tickets are bought from a counter at Vanino railway station. The form seems to be that passengers roll in on the last train through (No 252, Khabarovsk-Sovgavan, arriving at Vanino at 10 pm), and camp down for a chilly few hours in the station waiting room. There's no schedule posted but there is a dot matrix board in the station hall and at some time in the early hours it flashes up the proposed departure time of the ship, which is usually 5 to 7 am. Soon after, tickets go on sale at US$5 plus US$1 per item of baggage. Buses appear at the station to pick everyone up and ferry them down to the quayside. Once on board, finding somewhere comfortable and warm to sit is a matter of improvisation. If you can find someone to open them up, there are some gloomy cabins down on the lower deck for an additional US$15. The best bet is just to follow the other Russian passengers and see what they do. There is a cafeteria on the ship serving hot meals, which opens around midday. The voyage lasts roughly 15 hours, arriving at Kholmsk, on Sakhalin, at about 10 pm.

Should you require a bed for the night in Port Vanino, there's the *Hotel Vanino* (☎ (42137) 59 91 40) at ulitsa Pervaya Linia 2.

Getting There & Away

Only three trains connect with Sovgavan, all also stopping at Port Vanino, and they are the No 187/188 to/from Tikhookeanskaya (Nakhodka), and the No 251/252 and No 921/922, both to/from Khabarovsk. All trains go via Komsomolsk. The journey time from Komsomolsk to Sovgavan is 15 hours.

NIKOLAEVSK-ON-AMUR
НИКОЛАЕВСК-НА-АМУРЕ
Population: 40,000

Fortress Nikolaevsk, named for the tsar, was founded in 1850 as guardian of the river mouth during Nikolay Muravev's push down the Amur into Manchu territory. When Sakhalin Island, just 20 km across the Tatar Strait, was transformed into a penal colony in 1875, Nikolaevsk became a staging post for the shiploads of convicts being sailed down the Amur. Following the trail of the prisoners, Chekhov spent a night in Nikolaevsk in 1890, recording in his journal that he couldn't find a bed for the night.

Despite its remote location, by 1910 the town had become quite cosmopolitan, boasting Chinese, Japanese and British consulates, an American club set up by Californian and Bostonian traders, and a brothel staffed by French girls. All of this was turned upside down when the Bolsheviks rode into town in 1920 and as their first action massacred every Japanese they could find. Things have been quiet since then.

Nikolaevsk today still retains an enchanting tsarist character, with narrow tree-lined streets squeezing between two-storey wooden houses. Things to see in town include a good museum and the remains of the 1850 fortress.

Getting There & Away

From June to October a hydrofoil connects Nikolaevsk with Komsomolsk, departing every morning at 6.30 am. The journey takes 12 hours and costs US$32 one-way. During February and March the ice on the river is thick enough for it to serve as a temporary road – though, unpredictably, not always. The rest of the year the town is served, weather permitting, by a small airfield.

Primorsky Kray
Приморский Край

VLADIVOSTOK
ВЛАДИВОСТОК
Population: 690,000

For more than 30 years Vladivostok – meaning 'Lord of the East' – was a closed city, known only as the secrecy-shrouded home of the Russian Pacific Fleet. But these days the Fleet is a rusting and disintegrating relic of a past that Vladivostok is keen to shake off. The new Vladivostok is looking to rapidly reinvent itself as Russia's money-making, fast-spending, high-living commercial and financial centre in Asia – a role with which it's not altogether unfamiliar.

Founded in 1860 during Russia's second push across the Amur River, Vladivostok abruptly became the main Russian Pacific naval base when Port Arthur fell in the Russo-Japanese War. In 1891, Tsarevich Nicholas made a visit to inaugurate the new Trans-Siberian rail line which was to link Vladivostok with Moscow and reinforce shaky Russian influence in the region. Korean and Chinese labourers had built the city and at the turn of the century they accounted for four out of every five of its citizens. In addition, cosmopolitan Vladivostok teemed with French hoteliers, German store owners, Swiss speculators and merchants and sailors of every nation in a manner more akin to Shanghai or Hong Kong than to Moscow.

When the Reds seized power in European Russia in 1917, Japanese, Americans, French and English poured ashore here to support the tsarist counterattack. After the head of the White army, Admiral Kolchak, was defeated and executed at Irkutsk in 1920, Vladivostok held out for another two years, until Soviet forces finally marched in and drew the curtain. In the 1920s, 40% of men of working age had been Chinese, but Stalin got rid of them by shooting several hundred in 1938 as alleged spies and deporting another 10,000. As the eastern terminus of the Trans-Siberian, Vladivostok also became the recipient of other deportees; the northern suburb of Vtoraya Rechka became a transit centre for hundreds of thousands of prisoners waiting to be shipped up to labour, and most likely perish, in the gold fields of Kolyma. The US consulate – the only Western diplomatic office in the Soviet Far East – was forced to close in 1948 and the city was closed entirely in 1958.

Some 45 years or so later, the US consulate has reopened, signifying the return of the outside world to Vladivostok. The difference is already visible. Four out of five motorists drive Japanese cars, while the local business personnel who brought the vehicles over throw around wads of US$100 bills in the Casino Versailles. And every week the local football team runs out onto the field wearing XXXX-emblazoned shirts, courtesy of their sponsoring Australian brewery. The city isn't quite yet on its feet; it is still looking a little pale and suffering from a nasty post-Soviet hangover, but it is recovering far faster than most other places. Vladivostok is one of the very few towns or cities in Siberia and the Russian Far East that doesn't just serve as a base for wilderness exploration but is worth visiting in its own right.

Orientation

Physically, Vladivostok is one of Russia's more attractive cities. The centre is ranged in tiers on the hills surrounding the crooked finger of the Golden Horn Bay (bukhta Zolotoy Rog). South of the bay are residential and business districts, while the main commercial centre is on the north side, with its main axis ulitsa Svetlanskaya (formerly Leninskaya) running parallel to the water-

front. Near Svetlanskaya's western end a couple of wide boulevards run off north, laboriously climbing the bayside hills; this area constitutes the city's 'downtown'. The city's main junction, site of traffic snarl-ups and congested pavements, is where ulitsa Aleutskaya (formerly ulitsa 25 Oktyabrya) intersects Svetlanskaya. About 800 km south of this crossroads, on ulitsa Aleutskaya, is the railway station. The majority of Vladivostok's hotels are west of Aleutskaya, all within 10 minutes walk of the station. Running north, ulitsa Aleutskaya feeds into other major roads to become the main highway out of the city, passing through the Sanatornaya region, where there's a grouping of good but pricey hotels, and on to the airport.

You might want to look out for the *Vladivostok turistskaya skhema*, a reasonably accurate map of the city centre, or a 1:125,000 map, *Vladivostok and its Suburbs*, which is useful if you're planning on making any trips out of town. Potential stockists of the two include the bus station, the airport, the Vlad Motor-Inn (north of the centre) and the Hotel Vladivostok.

Information

Money There are currency-exchange desks in all the major hotels, at the Marine Terminal (Morskoy Vokzal), at the Vostok Bank at ulitsa Aleutskaya 21 and at the CredoBank at ulitsa Aleutskaya 16. The CredoBank will also give cash advances on a Visa card (enter through the door at the back of the building).

Post & Telecommunications The main post office is on ulitsa Aleutskaya, opposite the railway station. Envelopes, stamps, post boxes etc are on the 1st floor (the stairs are on the left immediately as you enter the building), while on the ground floor is the international telephone and telegraph office, open 24 hours daily. A fax office is upstairs, open from 8 am to 7 pm. International calls can also be made without waiting at the business centre at Okeansky prospekt 24, but it's more expensive than at the post office. The business centre will also receive faxes

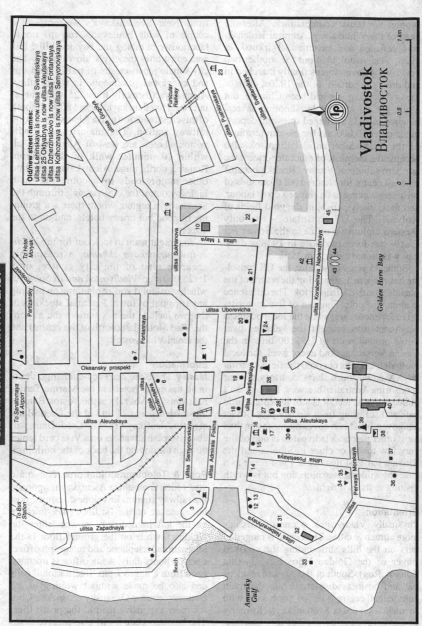

SIBERIA & RUSSIAN FAR EAST

Vladivostok
Владивосток

Old/new street names:
ulitsa Leninskaya is now ulitsa Svetlanskaya
ulitsa 25 Oktyabrya is now ulitsa Aleutskaya
ulitsa Dzerzinskovo is now ulitsa Fontannaya
ulitsa Kolhoznaya is now ulitsa Semyonovskaya

0   0.5   1 km

Golden Horn Bay

Amursky Gulf

Beach

Funicular Railway

To Hotel Moyak

To Sanatornaya & Airport

To Bus Station

ulitsa Gogolya

ulitsa Pushkinskaya

ulitsa Svetlanskaya

ulitsa Sukhanova

ulitsa 1 Maya

ulitsa Korabelnaya Naberezhnaya

Partizansky prospekt

Vtoskoi

ulitsa Fontannaya

ulitsa Uborevicha

Okeansky prospekt

ulitsa Mordovtseva

ulitsa Aleutskaya

ulitsa Semyonovskaya

ulitsa Admirala Fokina

ulitsa Svetlanskaya

ulitsa Aleutskaya

ulitsa Posetskaya

ulitsa Pervaya Morskaya

ulitsa Naberezhnaya

ulitsa Zapadnaya

SIBERIA & RUSSIAN FAR EAST

(fax 25 38 41, 26 47 05) for a small charge per page. The business centre at the Hotel Versailles is hooked up to e-mail but from our brief dealings with them, we imagine they're going to charge you big-time for access.

Vladivostok time is Moscow time plus seven hours. The local telephone code is 4232.

Foreign Consulates Apparently, city officials in neighbouring Khabarovsk were quite upset when the smattering of countries looking to establish their presence in the Russian Far East plumped for rival Vladivostok. Note: for anybody wishing to travel to Harbin or Beijing, Khabarovsk does have a Chinese consulate.

Foreign representations in Vladivostok include:

Australia
ulitsa Uborevicha 17, 4th floor (☎ 22 86 28; fax 22 87 78; telex 612520 SMAIL SU)

Japan
  ulitsa Mordovtseva 12 (☎ 26 75 02; fax 26 75 41) – visa applications accepted on weekdays except Wednesday from 10 am to noon
South Korea
  ulitsa Aleutskaya 45a, 5th floor (☎ 22 77 29; fax 22 94 71)
USA
  ulitsa Mordovtseva 12 (☎ 26 84 58 or visa hotline 26 85 54; fax 26 84 45)

Travel Agencies Ussuriysky Wilderness Tours, run by Andrey Kozhenovsky, organises trekking, camping and rafting in the Primorsky region and can also arrange visits to the villages of indigenous peoples and to the Chinese border. Contact Olga Bekhterava (☎ 46 32 82), who speaks good English. Primorsky Club (☎ 31 80 37; fax 32 07 10; Sprintmail c:ussr,a:sovmail,o:vlad, wood,un:primorsky) at ulitsa Russkaya 17, can help with ferry and airline bookings, and also make hotel reservations should you want to arrange your accommodation in advance.

Bookshops The city's two best bookshops are at ulitsa Svetlanskaya 41 and 43. They both have a small selection of maps and postcards and also a coffee-table book, *Old Vladivostok*, which is a beautifully produced pictorial history of the city (but just a little heavy in the rucksack and on the pocket). Useful, even if you're only here for a day or two, is the knowledgeable and detailed *Vladivostok: Your Essential Guide* written by Erik Azulay, one of the city's expat residents. It's available for a couple of dollars from the Nostalgia gift shop on ulitsa Pervaya Morskaya.

The city also has its own English-language newspaper, the *Vladivostok News*, a four-page weekly that might be of interest to anyone wanting to pick up a feel for what's happening in the region. The paper is available for a dollar or less at the major hotels.

Railway Station & Ulitsa Aleutskaya
Though not quite on the same scale as Moscow's Yaroslavl Station, the eastern terminus of the Trans-Siberian Railway, Vladivostok Central Station (1912), is an equally exotic architectural concoction. The ceiling in the main hall is decorated with some excellent bold and bright socialist paintings that have benefited, like the rest of the building, from recent renovation. The trains run in a cutting below street level and a bridge beside the station leads over the tracks to the large, characterless block of the Marine Terminal from where ships for Japan sail.

Across the road from the railway station is a small paved terrace where the drunks gather at the feet of an unusually animated Lenin who, curiously, as if he'd known all along how things were going to turn out, stands gesticulating toward Japan, the country whose money Vladivostok now so assiduously courts.

Ulitsa Aleutskaya, formerly ulitsa 25 Oktyabrya (the date on which the Bolsheviks 'liberated' Vladivostok during the Civil War), is lined with grand buildings, some of which were built by Japanese prisoners of war. The house at No 15 (the yellow building next door to the offices of the Far Eastern Shipping Company) once belonged to the family of Yul Brynner, born in Vladivostok in 1920. Brynner's grandfather, originally from Switzerland, had an import/export empire with offices throughout Manchuria and eastern Siberia. The one-day-to-be King of Siam never saw merchant service: he left Vladivostok aged four, carried to Paris by his mother, a newly abandoned wife. There's nothing to be seen at the house but there is a display devoted to Yul and the Brynner family in the Arsenev Regional Museum.

Waterfront & Ulitsa Svetlanskaya
The heart of Vladivostok is ploshchad Bortsov za Vlast Sovietov na Dalnem Vostokey (the Square of the Fighters for Soviet Power in the Far East) – it must be up for renaming soon – with a large monument to the Fighters as its centrepiece. The monument acts as a focal point for musicians, orators and sloganeers of all kinds. The square was Alexander Solzhenitsyn's first stop-off point on his internationally heralded return to Russia in 1994. A crowd of 4000 turned out on that occasion, but on any day

there's usually some small gathering listening to one of the resident bands. The monolithic slab at the western end of the paved plaza is the White House (Bely dom), home to the regional administration.

While the inhabitants of the White House are now responsible for shaping the city's future, until just a few years ago the real tower of power in Vladivostok was just a few hundred metres away on the harbour road (ulitsa Korabelnaya Naberezhnaya) in the form of the headquarters of the Pacific Fleet. Next door, an S-56 'Red Banner' submarine lies moored on a grassy plot as a reminder of the fleet's glory days. The submarine, which sank 10 enemy ships during WW II, serves as a museum, and while the mainly photographic collection isn't too enthralling, clambering around inside is fun. It's open daily from 9 am to 1 pm and 2 to 6 pm; admission US$1. Opposite floats the *Krasny Vimpel*, the Soviet Pacific Fleet's first ship, now also a museum.

Immediately north of the submarine, and before the ferry terminal (see Getting Around), a flight of steps leads up to connect with ulitsa Svetlanskaya. They emerge close to the GUM department store (No 33-35), originally built by Germans towards the end of last century and now filled with domestic appliances from Japan. Much of the architecture on this street dates from the late 19th century and bears a marked European influence.

City Museum

The Arsenev Regional Museum (Kraevedchesky muzey Arsenev) at ulitsa Svetlanskaya 20 (named for a turn-of-the-century ethnographer/writer) must be one of Russia's most eccentric museums. On the ground floor is the customary array of stuffed wildlife, snakes in jars etc, but the collection also includes a rare Amur leopard (unlikely to be seen anywhere else) and a Siberian tiger the size of a stretch limo. One wing is a real *Boy's Own* treat with a line-up of gleaming, chrome and enamel 1930s racing bikes, a motorcycle and sidecar with a great girder-length machine gun mounted between the

handlebars, and a collection of plastic model kits that as a young kid you might have disowned your parents for. On the 2nd floor, amongst other things, there are Japanese ceramics, a display dedicated to the Brynner family, some interesting bits of geology and a hall housing temporary exhibitions. The museum also offers a chance to purchase a little bit of history, in an antique and bric-a-brac store off the lobby, full of Soviet badges, coins and tablecloth-sized flags, assorted old bank notes, icons and other memorabilia. The prices are extremely reasonable. The museum is open from 10 am to 6.30 pm daily except Mondays: admission US$1.50.

Other Museums

The sight of a church surrounded by artillery pieces, tank hulls and missile spares might seem a little incongruous but this Lutheran house of worship was taken out of the service of the Lord a long time ago. It's now home to the **Museum of the Pacific Fleet** (Muzey Tikhookeanskogo flota), celebrating Russia's far-eastern naval activity from the 19th century to the present day. Just inside the door, on the left, is a fascinating pictorial map, painted in 1905, that illustrates very clearly the topography of the city. Visitors with a more morbid bent might find themselves held by a photograph of 'brutal interventionist' Japanese officers standing around a table, under which are planted several Bolshevik heads. The museum is at the junction of ulitsa Pushkinskaya 14 (ride any tram two stops east of the central square) and is open Wednesday to Sunday, from 10 am to 1 pm and 2 to 5.30 pm; admission US$1.

Directly behind the Pacific Fleet museum a **funicular railway** connects ulitsa Pushkinskaya with ulitsa Sukhanova, which is about 200 metres farther up the steeply sloping hillside. Even if the funicular isn't working (it wasn't when we visited), it's worth tackling the adjacent steps to gain the top and a superb panorama of the bay. A few minutes walk from the viewpoint (downhill, mercifully) is the **Sukhanov Museum** (Muzey Sukhanov), named for the turn-of-the-century city councillor whose home it was. The museum is simply his house preserved with its period furnishings. One room also serves as an antique store with a small selection of tsarist silverware, religious icons and other pricey odds and ends. It's at ulitsa Sukhanova 9, open from 10.30 am to 7 pm every day except Monday, with admission US$1.50.

Hemmed in by Japan, Korea and China, this southerly protuberance of Russia has an awful lot of border to police, so it shouldn't be too surprising that the **Border Guards' Museum** (Muzey boevoy slavy pogranvoisk) is quite as large and impressive as it is. Despite the fact that all the Primorsky region's potentially border-infringing neighbours are Orientals, most of the achievements celebrated in the museum are at the expense of the White, Anglo-Saxon USA. The museum is the big, blue building at ulitsa Semyonovskaya 17-19. It's open Tuesday to Saturday from 9 am to 5 pm.

The **Primorsky Art Museum** (Primorskaya kartinnaya galereya), at ulitsa Aleutskaya 12, is also something of a surprise, with a large number of 17th-century Dutch works and some excellent works by Russian painters, including a piece by Kandinsky (according to Erik Azulay they also have an early Chagall but we couldn't find it). Admission is US$2 and includes entry to the contemporary gallery on the ground floor. The museum is open Tuesday to Saturday from 10 am to 6.30 pm.

Aquarium

At the western end of ulitsa Svetlanskaya is a small park, busy with photographers and their props, food sellers and the odd busker. Beyond the park, there's a narrow strip of sandy beach before the chill waters of the Amursky Gulf (Amursky zaliv). A few hundred metres north of the beach, past the sports stadium, is the Okeanarium, a large aquarium with live fish and marine creatures and stuffed birds. A little further along the shoreline road is a pen containing some Beluga whales.

Places to Stay

Central Though they insist on pronouncing it *'ver-SAH-les'*, the *Hotel Versailles* (☎ 26 42 01; fax 26 51 24; e-mail /c=su/a=sovmail/ o=vladivostok/pn=vers@sprint.com) is suitably palatial, especially the long, low, vaulted reception hall which, unless you're packing a wallet full of gold American Express cards, is intimidating enough to send you scurrying back out to the gutter. The rooms are sumptuous, with every conceivable facility, but then they are US$180/240 per night. The hotel is at ulitsa Svetlanskaya 10.

At the *Hotel Vladivostok* (☎ 22 22 08), at ulitsa Naberezhnaya 10, the former flagship of the Soviet era, old habits die hard – no-one gets a room without an advance reservation and a visa must be produced that specifically mentions Vladivostok. Once past reception, the rooms are clean enough, with attached bathrooms, and half of them have great views over Amursky Gulf. Singles are US$40 to US$46, doubles US$70. The whole of the 4th floor of the Vladivostok has been leased to a private company which runs it as the *Hotel Visit* (☎ 21 20 53). The rooms have been renovated and refurbished and come with satellite TV, direct international phone lines and fridges stocked with beer and juice. Singles are US$100, doubles US$130.

There are two other concrete-hive hotels in the immediate vicinity of the Vladivostok. A couple of blocks north is the *Hotel Equator* (☎ 21 28 64) at ulitsa Naberezhnaya 20. It's a little more scruffy than its near neighbour but it's also substantially cheaper at US$28/58. The *Hotel Amursky Zaliv* (☎ 22 55 20) dug into the cliff side (the top floor is at street level) at ulitsa Naberezhnaya 9, has received some bad reports but we had no problems with it. The rooms were clean and comfortable and our bathroom had been newly tiled. All the rooms seemed to have balconies overlooking the bay. Singles are from US$34, doubles US$80.

Close to the railway station, the *Hotel Primore* (☎ 22 51 22) at ulitsa Posetskaya 20, is an aged establishment with a bleak interior used mainly by Russians. Rooms with attached shower are US$30/36. An interesting alternative exists in the *Hotel Vladimir* (☎ 22 57 69; fax 26 80 33; e-mail x.400(c:ussr,a:sovmail,o:vladivostok,un: dmsv)), a cruise ship operating as a floating hotel, moored in the Golden Horn Bay opposite the submarine on ulitsa Korabelnaya Naberezhnaya. The cabins are well looked after but the main problem is the size: for fans of telephone kiosks only. Also, as home to the city's most popular nightspot, the Vladimir can be very noisy at night. For the best chance of quiet, ask for a cabin port-side, towards the stern. Singles are US$34, doubles US$50.

Those whose optimum concern is money and not comfort or hygiene might want to check out the *Hotel Moryak* (☎ 25 38 15) at Partizansky prospekt 14. This place is popular with visiting Russian students and the rooms are only US$7. They were a little wary of giving a room to a foreigner but if you can speak some Russian there shouldn't be any problem. A student identity card might also help. To get there take any bus going north up Okeansky prospekt and get off at the Kartinnaya Galereya stop, right in front of the hotel – a looming chateau-like building with a twin flight of steps up to the front door.

Sanatornaya Sanatornaya is a wooded, coastal suburb, seven stops out on the train or a 30-minute drive north of the centre. Despite being about midway between the airport and the city there's no particularly good reason to stay out here – the tranquillity of the location is countered by the nightmarish traffic that clogs the sole highway into the city. However, several of the city's most exclusive hotels are situated here. The *Vlad Motor-Inn* (☎ 21 58 54, satellite phone ☎ (509) 851 51 11; fax (509) 851 51 16) a Canadian/Russian venture, describes itself as 'a little piece of Northern America'. The description is spot on and the rooms are as comfortable as any from California to North Carolina, with big soft beds to sprawl on while you watch MTV or CNN and suck on

a Bud. There's even guaranteed hot water. The adjacent restaurant has a menu full of burgers and cheesecake, and every Wednesday it's 'pizza and movie night'. There's a business centre next door which handles car hire. The double rooms are US$185 and credit cards are accepted. The postal address is ulitsa Vosmaya 1, Sanatornaya, 19th km, Vladivostok, Russia 690038.

Close by are the *Hotel Enkai* (☎ 21 54 22) at ulitsa Devyataya 6, a lavish ex-nomenklatura hang-out with rooms at US$100 and the slightly cheaper *Hotel Pansionat* (☎ 21 58 40) at Devyataya 14, originally built for the summit between Brezhnev and US President Gerald Ford which took place in 1974.

Places to Eat

It's possible to eat well in Vladivostok and it's possible to eat cheaply, but not both at the same time. The *Vlad Motor-Inn* serves fantastic food, concentrating on US staples (burgers, ribs, club sandwiches) but also including some more general continental dishes. The sweets are exceptional – particularly the cheesecakes – but you're looking at US$15 per head for a meal without drinks. Antipodean cuisine gets a look-in at the joint Russian-Australian *Captain Cook's* on the ground floor of the Hotel Pansionat. The steaks are good (around US$10), and there's kangaroo and crocodile, both of which will take a fair-sized bite out of your credit card.

Of the restaurants at the city's central hotels, the best are at the *Versailles* and *Vladimir* (open until 3 am) but they are both unwarrantedly expensive. Better value is *Nostalgia*, a restaurant which eschews the starkness of Soviet-era eating for tsarist lavishness. The small, low-ceilinged dining room is carpeted with a plush red pile which also covers the lower half of the walls; the upper half is papered with a heavy damask, all of which combines to give the effect of sitting inside a jewellery box. The menu is Russian traditional and the food is excellent. Dishes are US$5 to US$8. The restaurant (plus café and gift shop) is at ulitsa Pervaya Morskaya 6/25 and it's open from 10 am to

11 pm. The food at the *Zhemchuzhina* (Pearl), a stylish Italian restaurant off ulitsa Svetlanskaya, is also very good. The restaurant specialises in seafood (the calamari salad at US$3 is recommended) and meat in wine sauces (US$4 to US$5). Opening times are from noon to 4 pm and 6 to 11 pm, with reservations a must in the evening. The restaurant is 50 metres back from the street, just east of the junction with ulitsa 1 Maya.

Seafood also features heavily on the menu at *Okean*, an attractive restaurant with good service and views over Amursky Gulf, at ulitsa Naberezhnaya 3, next door to the cinema. Main courses are about US$6. Far less intimate, the *Volna* (Wave) occupies almost the whole of the top floor of the Marine Terminal in one great, gymnasium-like room. Perplexingly, the management have chosen to obscure the view across the harbour with folds of net curtains. The food isn't up to much either, and unless you're part of a group, the service is appalling.

For snacks, probably the best place is the *Nostalgia Kafe*, with soup, pancakes and pastries (open from 9 am to midnight), but the most popular eatery in town is *Magic Burger*, at ulitsa Svetlanskaya 44, a fast-food joint that will either make you give up burgers for good or pledge your life to McDonald's. Once beyond the queue at the door, the service is speedy and the papier-mâché pizzas and burgers are cheap (US$0.80 each). The *Kafe Fontan* on the 1st floor of the Marine Terminal is a stolovaya serving a couple of dishes (it seemed to be always kebab or sausage, with salad, for US$2) plus beverages. It's open from 6 am to 3 pm and 6 pm to 3 am. The bufet in the railway station does good pelmeni.

The *Kafe Chudesnista* at ulitsa Fokina 1, facing the park, has a pleasant seafront atmosphere – don't be put off by the shellsuited individuals hanging around; they're not mafiosi, but footballers from the stadium next door. Vegetarians could check out the *Krishna Kafe* at Okeansky prospekt 10/12; it's open from 10 am to 3 pm and 5 to 7 pm, and on Sundays from 10 am to 5 pm. The *Kafe Ldinka*, centrally located at ulitsa Aleutskaya 23, comes close to a Western-style café and is a good place to sit over coffee and ice cream. Open from 11 am to 3 pm and 4 to 10 pm.

Entertainment

Compared to the rest of Siberia and the Russian Far East, Vladivostok is party city. At ulitsa Svetlanskaya 13 are two cabaret venues: The Green Lantern puts on music and magic shows, while The Blue Star gets more earthy with striptease and erotic dancing. Both charge US$5 entrance fee and are open nightly except Monday. The nightclub on board the Hotel Vladimir is the most popular place after dark but admission is a staggering US$12. It's open from 9 pm to 5 am. A cheaper alternative is the bar at the Hotel Amursky Zaliv, open until 6 am. Like the Vladimir, it also attracts some dubious characters but at least they seem to have a sense of humour – the house band gets at least one request a night to play the theme to *The Godfather*. Both the hotels Versailles and Vladimir have casinos, open from 8 pm until the early hours.

The Gorky Theatre (Teatr Gorkogo), at ulitsa Svetlanskaya 49, is the city's main venue for drama, while the concert hall (Filarmonia) is at ulitsa Svetlanskaya 15. Kino Okean at ulitsa Naberezhnaya 3 shows overdubbed recent US releases, while the Ussuri on ulitsa Svetlanskaya has a more eclectic programme – Japanese Godzilla movies when we were there. If you are at all interested in sport, Erik Azulay's book recommends attending a game at the football stadium, where if the match leaves you less than thrilled the view from the stands across Amursky Gulf provides fine compensation. The local team Lush Vladivostok has been in the Russian Premier League recently. Since the top teams in this league qualify for European competitions, this raises the odd prospect, should Lush Vladivostok be successful, of Real Madrid, AC Milan, Blackburn Rovers etc having to travel to the very far side of Asia to play 'European' games.

Things to Buy

Although pricey, the traditional handicrafts on sale at Nostalgia (ulitsa Pervaya Morskaya 6/25) were by far the most beautiful that Andrew saw anywhere in Russia. Other places to look for lacquered boxes, matryoshka dolls, painted trays and jewellery are the Art Salon down the stairs at ulitsa Aleutskaya 14 and the Art Gallery on the ground floor of the same building. For souvenirs of Soviet Russia there's the shop in the City Museum or the Flotsky Magazin at Svetlanskaya 11, which used to be the army and navy supplies store and still has a counter selling buttons, badges and other small bits of military insignia.

The state department store, GUM, at ulitsa Svetlanskaya 35-37, is amazingly well stocked with a lot of stuff imported from Japan. It is also worth exploring if only because it's such a beautiful building. At Svetlanskaya 45, there's another large state store with the ground floor given over exclusively to Australian food products and suitably decorated in green and gold. For fresh fruit and vegetables, the market is at Pervaya Rechka every day from 10 am. Take tram No 7 from in front of the railway station, north for six stops.

Getting There & Away

Air There are flights twice daily to/from Khabarovsk (US$108, 1¼ hours) and Moscow (US$398, nine hours), twice a day four times a week to Irkutsk (US$212, four hours), daily to Petropavlovsk-Kamchatsky (US$242, four hours) and Yuzhno-Sakhalinsk (US$133, 1¾ hours), four times a week to Magadan and twice a week to Yakutsk. Transaero has three weekly flights to/from Moscow.

At the time of writing the only international route Aeroflot flies out of Vladivostok is to/from Niigata four times a week (US$622 return, two hours). Korean Air (☎ 22 20 00; office at the airport, room 702) has flights to/from Seoul every Saturday (US$720 return, 2½ hours), while Alaska Airlines flies to/from Anchorage and Seattle twice a week in summer via Magadan (for

further details phone the Primorsky Club travel agency, which is Alaska Airlines' Vladivostok agent).

The airport at Vladivostok must be one of the worst in Russia. The terminal resembles a bombed-out warehouse, with little to indicate where or when to check in and no boards to announce arrivals or take-offs. The departure hall is a vast, unheated, half-lit tin shed. If you have the option, fly from Khabarovsk.

Train Vladivostok is the eastern terminus for train No 1/2, the *Rossia*. Making the return journey to Moscow it departs every other day (odd-numbered dates) at a little after 1 am local time. Other trains west include the daily No 5 *Okean* overnight to Khabarovsk and No 7 *Sibir* to Novosibirsk; the No 53, which departs every other day to Kharkiv (Kharkov); and the daily No 185 to Blagoveshchensk. There is also a daily service to Komsomolsk (train No 206) for connections eastbound to Port Vanino/Sovgavan on the Pacific coast and ships to Sakhalin Island and, westbound, to Tynda and onwards along the BAM.

Several times a week an express train connects Vladivostok with Harbin in the Heilongjiang province of northern China, from where there are daily connections to Beijing. A one-way sleeper ticket to Harbin cost US$66 at the time of writing. The train crosses the border at the Chinese town of Suifenhe and also stops at Mudanjiang.

All tickets for long-distance trains are sold in the Marine Terminal, off to the left on the ground floor. The ticket office in the railway building is only for suburban services.

Boat Once a week (in 1994 it departed from Vladivostok on a Tuesday) from May to October, the *Antonina Nezhdanova* sails from Vladivostok to Niigata and then Fushiki on the west coast of Japan. The ship is said to be extremely well run with friendly cabin staff and very good food. The voyage takes 42 hours and 3rd-class passage (lower deck, four berths per cabin) is US$280, 2nd-class (as for 3rd but on the main deck) is US$300, while 1st (twin-bed cabins) is

US$730. All meals are included in the price – you may be able to get cheaper fares that don't have meals included: ask. The ship will also take motorbikes for US$80 and cars for US$156. The ticket office is in the Marine Terminal behind the railway station. Although we weren't able to confirm, there is possibly also a service to Pusan in South Korea. Make enquiries with the Far Eastern Shipping Company (FESCO) (☎ 22 81 56), ulitsa Aleutskaya 17 (next door to Yul's old haunt).

Getting Around

To/From the Airport There is no direct connection between the airport and the city centre. Instead, take any suburban train from the central station three stops to Vtoraya Rechka (Second River). There's a bus station 150 metres east of the railway along the main street, ulitsa Russkaya. From there take bus No 101, the express airport service. It leaves about every 20 minutes, costs US$1 and takes approximately 45 minutes. Count on about two hours for the whole journey. Coming from the airport it's the reverse procedure. From the platform at Vtoraya Rechka you get a first sight of the city to the south, so you know which direction train you should catch.

Public Transport A system of buses, trolley-buses and trams makes up the city transport network but within the centre you'll probably only need to use the trams. From in front of the railway station, tram Nos 4 and 5 run north then swing east onto ulitsa Svetlanskaya, running past the Pacific Fleet Museum and to the head of the bay; tram No 7 stays on ulitsa Aleutskaya, running north past the market. All public transport within the city is free.

Ferry From the terminal on ulitsa Korabelnaya Naberezhnaya, just beyond the submarine, ferries leave every 20 minutes for the other side of the bay. There isn't much over there but the ride itself is enjoyable, chugging past the rusting hulls of nuclear submarines.

AROUND VLADIVOSTOK
ОКРЕСТНОСТЬ ВЛАДИВОСТОКА

Vladivostok is the capital of Primorsky kray (or Maritime Territory), the arm of land that lies bounded by China on the east and the Sea of Japan to the west. The central region of Primorsky kray, bounded by the Ussuri and Bikin rivers and shielded from the sea by the Sikhote Alin Mountains, is also known as Ussuriland. The Ussuriland taiga was the setting for Akira Kurosawa's 1970 film *Dersu Uzala* (based on the book of the same name by Ussuri-born ethnographer, Arseniev). The southern forests are the world's most northerly monsoon forests and home to black and brown bear, Siberian boar, the rare Siberian tiger and the virtually extinct Amur leopard, plus hundreds of species of local migratory birds. See Flora & Fauna in the Facts about Siberia & the Far East chapter for more information. For anybody interested in exploring the Ussuriland region and visiting some of the six nature reserves, Frith Maier's *Trekking in Russia & Central Asia* (see Books in the Siberia & the Far East – Facts for the Visitor chapter) is highly recommended for its information on trails and hikes, flora and fauna and ideas for places to visit.

The locals prefer pleasures of a less arduous nature, and a popular day trip from Vladivostok is to take the ferry from the terminal on ulitsa Korabelnaya Naberezhnaya out and across the Amursky Gulf to the port of Slavyanka, 50 km south toward the North Korean border. The small town itself is quite attractive but the surrounding beaches are the real draw, and during the summer months they're filled by half the populace of Vladivostok. However, if you go far enough south it is possible to find seclusion. En route to Slavyanka some ferries stop off at Popov Island, one of the archipelago of islands south of Vladivostok, where many of the city's residents have small plots of land or dachas. The larger island to the north of Popov is Russky Island, property of the Pacific Fleet and reputed arms arsenal – one little accident there, we were told, and the whole of Vladivostok is gone. Needless to say, the island is out of bounds.

NAKHODKA
НАХОДКА

Population: 178,000

Nakhodka, which means 'discovery', was little more than a landing until after WW II (and was, in its infancy, called Amerikanka). Now it's a major fishing port, spread around a sheltered bay stumbled upon by a storm-tossed Russian ship in the 1850s (hence the present name). The town prospered as a result of being the only Soviet-era Pacific port open to foreign ships. It was also the eastern terminus of the Trans-Siberian, though few foreigners ever saw more than just the road from the railway station to the quay as they were quickly ushered on board the ferry for Japan. Paul Theroux managed to take a quick look round passing through one winter, and noted in *The Great Railway Bazaar* that Nakhodka 'gives the impression of being on the very edge of the world, in an atmosphere that does not quite support life...the sort of place that gives rise to the notion that the earth is flat'. With the reopening of Vladivostok, there is no reason at all to visit this place.

Sakhalin Island
Остров Сахалин

Geographically, this island, about the size of Scotland, is an offshore extension of the Sikhote-Alin Mountains in the south-east corner of Russia, though it looks just as much a northern extension of Japan. In fact, Russia and Japan have been wrangling over it for more than a century.

The first Japanese settlers came across from Hokkaido in the early 1800s, attracted by seas that were so full of fish, whales and seals that, in the words of an early explorer, 'the water looked as though it was boiling'. The island already had occupants in the form of the Nivkh, Orok and Ainu peoples, but just as this didn't give pause to the Japanese, the Russians were equally heedless when they claimed Sakhalin in 1853, as part of their campaign to secure the Amur region. Japan agreed to recognise Russian sovereignty in exchange for the rights to the Kuril Islands (incidentally, also inhabited by Nivkh, Orok and Ainu). Inspired by its extreme remoteness from European Russia, the tsar made the island into one huge penal colony, echoing Britain's use of Botany Bay as a dumping ground for its unwanted human refuse. Anton Chekhov visited in 1890 and wrote up his observations in *A Journey to Sakhalin*. They can be summarised in one extract: 'I have seen Ceylon which is paradise and Sakhalin which is hell'.

Japan restaked its claim to hell, seizing the island during the Russo-Japanese War and getting to keep the southern half under the terms of the concluding peace settlement (The Treaty of Portsmouth, 1905). The treaty was rubbished when, during the final days of WW II, the Soviet Union staged a successful invasion of Sakhalin and dug in. From being the world's biggest penal colony, it became

SIBERIA & RUSSIAN FAR EAST

the world's biggest aircraft carrier – a highly militarised eastern outpost of the Soviet empire loaded with aircraft, missiles and guns. Just how sensitive Sakhalin had become was illustrated in 1983 when Korean Airlines flight 007 went off course over the southern part of the island and was brought down by a scrambled jet interceptor. All 267 on board were killed instantly. The Americans charged the Russians with the deliberate mass murder of innocents, while the Russians accused the USA of callously putting those lives at risk by sending 007 on a spying mission.

Nowadays, Russia, the USA and Japan work shoulder to shoulder extracting oil while investors from around the Pacific Rim eye Sakhalin's other natural riches – gas, coal, uranium and silver, as well as timber, furs and a fine fishery. There are even plans on the drawing board for a bridge that would link southern Sakhalin with the northern Japanese island of Hokkaido, just 40 km away across La Perouse Strait. Meanwhile, unfortunately, Sakhalin gained world attention in May 1995 when it suffered one of the worst earthquakes in Russian history. Tremors which measured 7.5 on the Richter scale flattened the oil settlement of Neftegorsk, near the northern tip of the island, and claimed around 2000 lives.

The majority of the island's 710,000 population live on the southern half of the island, centred mainly in the capital, Yuzhno-Sakhalinsk, and the two ports, Kholmsk and Korsakov. The Sakhalinskaya oblast also includes the island of Moneron and the disputed Kuril chain.

YUZHNO-SAKHALINSK
ЮЖНО САХАЛИНСК
Population 170,000

Yuzhno-Sakhalinsk is a small town nestled sleepily amongst olive-green hills. While the town isn't particularly attractive, neither does it detract too much from the beauty of the surrounding landscape. There isn't much to do in Yuzhno-Sakhalinsk, but there are sufficient numbers of hotels and restaurants to make it a good base for further exploration of the island.

Yuzhno-Sakhalinsk was founded in 1881 as Vladimirovka, named after a major who directed the compulsory labour. At that time it was little more than a hamlet, composed of a few farmsteads worked by convicts. The main Russian settlements were further north, on the coast of the Tatar Strait, places that were more accessible from the mainland. It was the Japanese who developed Vladimirovka, renaming it Toiohara and, during their 40 years of occupation, building it into a thriving township and centre of regional administration. After the Japanese were booted out in 1945, the USSR tried to whip up enthusiasm on the mainland and get people to migrate to southern Sakhalin, with the intention that the island should be decisively and irreversibly Russified; Toiohara became Yuzhno-Sakhalinsk (Southern Sakhalin).

For 45 years the town developed in an unexceptional manner as a centre for light industry and food processing – specifically fish – before attracting widespread international attention in 1990 as the site of the 'Sakhalin experiment'. A newly appointed governor from Moscow, Valentin Fyodorov, a former economics professor, vowed to create capitalism on the island. He privatised retail trade, distributed land and turned Yuzhno-Sakhalinsk's Communist Party headquarters into a business centre. The experiment was not an unqualified success, with the majority of people claiming to have been left poorer by the free-market reforms. Fyodorov called it a day and hightailed it back to Moscow in April 1993.

This small, backwater town remains, however, the object of marked international interest, with four pricey joint-venture hotels in town, Korean and Japanese restaurants with prices that make those in Moscow seem provincial by comparison, and Hong Kong and US-sponsored satellite phone systems that put the place in direct credit-card-operated contact with the rest of the world. The reason for the disproportionate foreign presence is not hard to discern: Sakhalin is scented with the fragrance of oil. Most of the major multinational oil and gas companies have representatives in town – hence the hotels, restaurants and phone systems. When the oil starts flowing (at present it's held up, waiting for the Russian parliament to pass the necessary legislation), the effects on Yuzhno-Sakhalinsk could be significant – the talk is of country-and-western bars and McDonald's. Maybe you ought to get there now, before it's too late.

Orientation

Yuzhno-Sakhalinsk lies stretched along the floor of a narrow valley 25 km inland of Lososy Bay at the southern end of the island. The town's main axis, running roughly north-south, is ulitsa Lenina with ploshchad Lenina at its midpoint. Most of the shops are along ulitsa Lenina, within a km either side of the central square. Kommunistichesky prospekt runs east from the square with the island's main administrative buildings strung along it. There's a very good Russian-language map of Yuzhno-Sakhalinsk and the southern part of the island available at the Regional Museum's ticket desk and at a couple of the kiosks in the railway station.

Information

The island's main post office is at the northeast corner of ploshchad Lenina, with the telephone and telegraph office next door at ulitsa Lenina 220. There is, however, no need to bother with the cantankerous, old Russian telephone system because Sakhalin is the beneficiary of the most advanced telecommunications in the whole of Russia. Kriljon, a US-backed company, has installed direct-dial international credit-card-operated phones at the Eurasia, Sakhalin-Sapporo and Turist hotels and in the foyer of the Sakhin Centr (an international business centre at Kommunistichesky prospekt 32). The phones accept American Express, JCB, MasterCard and Visa, and calls are charged at US$5 per minute. SakhalinTelecom also has Yuzhno-Sakhalinsk linked into a satellite system with phones at, amongst other places, the Hotel Turist, the airport and their office

at Kommunistichesky prospekt 43. The phones take SakhalinTelecom phonecards, which come in values of US$12, US$25 and US$50 (US$12 got us about three minutes calling the UK) and are sold from outlets conveniently close to the phones. The SakhalinTelecom office also has a fax service for US$7 per minute to anywhere in the world.

Currency can be exchanged at the bureau in the lobby of the Hotel Sakhalin-Sapporo or Hotel Lada, while the Inkombank at the Sakhin Centr, room 316, will give a cash advance on a Visa card. Nowhere in town accepts travellers' cheques.

The town's sole travel agency is Intourist-Sakhalin (☎ 2 24 02) in room 436 at the Sakhin Centr. Its staff are unused to dealing with foreigners, except for Japanese, and it's quite likely you'll find no-one in their office who speaks any English, which is unfortunate as their brochure needs an awful lot of elaborating on – sample: 'Tour for entomologists – day 1, arrive to Yuzhno-Sakhalinsk; day 2-4, watch the insects; day 5, depart Yuzhno-Sakhalinsk'.

Yuzhno-Sakhalinsk has only two bookshops (at ulitsa Lenina 287 and 293), both of which are poorly stocked. It does, however, have its own weekly English-language newspaper, the *Free Sakhalin News*, a local government and economic digest that can be picked up in the foyer of the Hotel Sakhalin-Sapporo.

Sakhalin time is Moscow time plus eight hours. The Yuzhno-Sakhalinsk telephone code is 4244.

Things to See & Do

The pagoda-like roofs of the **Regional Museum** (Oblastnoy kraevedchesky muzey), at Kommunistichesky prospekt 29, are a strong visual reminder of Sakhalin's Japanese heritage – the building was home to the Karafuto administration (Karafuto was the Japanese name for Sakhalin) before the Soviet Union regained possession of the south of the island in 1945. On the ground floor, the museum's collections deal with the island's natural and climatic features, its pre-

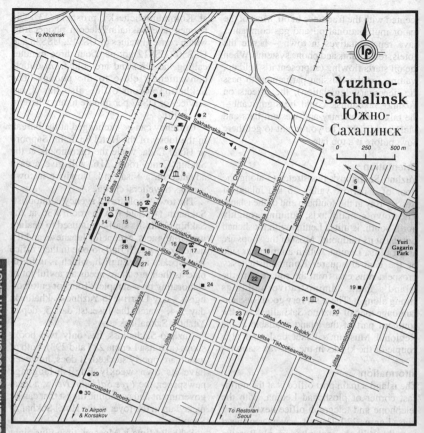

Yuzhno-Sakhalinsk
Южно-Сахалинск

0   250   500 m

history and some fascinating ethnography, including fish-skin robes and seal-hide tunics worn by the Ainu. The Siberian and Far Eastern penchant for taxidermy is also well in evidence, with the larger part of a whole colony of seals stuffed and on display. Upstairs is a presentation of Sakhalin's history from 1917 to 1960. There is a very good and professionally produced English-language museum guide available at the front desk. The museum is open daily from 11 am to 6 pm except Monday, closing at 5 pm on Tuesday. Admission is US$1.50.

In the gardens in front of the museum stand half a dozen squat pieces of ancient artillery (the sign at the front desk reading, 'To shoot please pay 3000 roubles' refers, probably, to camera-users), but for those with an interest in things that go bang, the **Officers' Club** (Dom Ofitserov), one block east, has a yard full of guns, armoured vehicles and tanks.

The bunker-like structure at ulitsa Lenina 137 was also built by the Japanese, in this case for use as a military command centre, but the architecture gives little clue to its Oriental origins and is as dull as the meagre collection of paintings it now houses in its

PLACES TO STAY					
5	Hotel Turist Гостиница Турист	4	Restoran Slavyanka Ресторан Славянка	15	Ploshchad Lenina Площадь Ленина
11	Hotel Moneron Гостиница Монерон	6	Midzumi Мидзуми	16	October Cinema Кинотеатр Октябрь
12	Hotel Eurasia Гостиница Евразия	25	Restoran Saigon Ресторан Сайгон	17	SakhalinTelecom Office Сахалин Телеком
19	Hotel Lada Гостиница Лада		**OTHER**	18	Sakhin Centr (Business Centre) Сахинцентр (Бизнесцентр)
24	Hotel Natalia Гостиница Наталия	1	Market Рынок		
26	Hotel Dalnevostochnik Гостиница Дальневосточник	2	Komsomolets Cinema Кинотеатр Комсомолец	20	Officer's Club Дом Офицеров
27	Hotel Sakhalin-Sapporo Гостиница Сахалин-Саппоро	7	Aeroflot Аэрофлот	21	Regional Museum Областной музей
		8	Art Museum Художественный музей	22	Chekhov Drama Theatre Драматический театр имени Чехова
28	Hotel Rybak Гостиница Рыбак	9	Telephone & Telegraph Office Телефон и Телеграф		
	PLACES TO EAT	10	Central Post Office Центральный почтамт	23	Central Department Store ЦУМ
3	Kafe Кафе	13	Bus Station Автовокзал	29	Bookshop Книжный магазин
		14	Railway Station Железнодорожный вокзал	30	Bookshop Книжный магазин

SIBERIA & RUSSIAN FAR EAST

present role as the regional **Art Museum** (Khudozhestvenny muzey).

Places to Stay

There are no less than four up-market, joint-venture hotels in Yuzhno-Sakhalinsk. Most prominent amongst them is the *Hotel Sakhalin-Sapporo* (☎ 3 26 34; fax (5044) 16 20 01) at ulitsa Lenina 181, an old breeze-block monstrosity that has been given a refit by the Japanese. The hotel is aimed at the business traveller and offers services such as interpreters and car hire. Singles range from US$60 to US$110 and doubles are US$130. The Japanese are also partners in the *Hotel Eurasia* (☎ 27 44 66) on ulitsa Vokzalnaya, next door to the railway station, with all rooms at US$90, and the Koreans are backing the *Hotel Natalia* (☎ 3 66 83), a very private and comfortable hotel at Anton Bujukly 38, with singles at US$68, doubles US$90.

The fourth joint-venture hotel is the pricey *Santa Resort Hotel* (☎ 5 92 65; fax (509) 856

55 55) at ulitsa Venskaya 3, a few km up on the hillside overlooking town. It's a good ski base with a downhill slope and chair lifts nearby.

Although it's 15 minutes walk from the town centre, the *Hotel Turist* (☎ 3 19 60) at Sakhalinskaya 2, is a good cheaper-end option. The rooms are large and clean (the sheets are changed every day) with attached shower and toilet and cost US$18/28. The oppressive *Hotel Lada* (☎ 3 31 45), about a km south at ulitsa Komsomolskaya 154, charges US$60/90 for similar.

There are a clutch of budget hotels around ploshchad Lenina: the *Hotel Moneron* (☎ 2 34 53), a big Wedgwood-blue building on the square's north side; the *Hotel Rybak* (☎ 2 37 68), opposite the Moneron; and the *Hotel Dalnevostochnik* at ulitsa Karla Marxa 43. All three hotels are run-down and decrepit and the guests hanging about the lobby looked like extras from a Dostoevsky novel. None of these hotels was willing to let a foreigner have a room, but if you can speak

Russian and put up a good fight then one of them might give way. Singles at the Moneron and Dalnevostochnik are roughly US$8 and doubles US$15, while the Rybak charges about twice that.

Places to Eat

The small and intimate *Katyusha* at the Sakhalin-Sapporo is a better than average hotel restaurant with good service. In season (late summer through autumn) the menu is heavy on salmon (baked, fried or shashlyk for US$5), but other options include omelettes at US$1.50, lamb shashlyk at US$4 and garlic chicken at US$5. It's open from 8 am to midnight. The restaurant at the Japanese-backed *Hotel Eurasia* is surprisingly seedy, with half of the room taken up by a dance floor and bandstand. The food is very mediocre (bifshteks po Sakhalinsky turned out to be nothing more exciting than a piece of fried meat with a halved geriatric tomato on top) and not particularly cheap at US$4 to US$6 per dish.

Excellent Siberian cuisine is served at the *Slavyanka* at ulitsa Sakhalinskaya 45, a small, self-consciously Russian restaurant decorated with painted wooden spoons, matryoshka dolls and embroidered shawls, and with a resident balalaika trio. The densely typed menu is in Russian only but just take pot luck – it all looked great. Main courses are US$2.50 to US$4.50 and reservations are recommended. As with the Slavyanka, at the *Saigon* a drab exterior disguises a very pleasant interior. In this case, the management has made a stab at evoking the Far East, with liberal use of rice-paper screens and bamboo, although the menu has about as much to do with Vietnam as Bill Clinton. The food is good, with prices similar to those at the Slavyanka. The Saigon is open from noon to 5 pm and 6 pm to midnight, and is located at ulitsa Karla Marxa 27.

The Japanese *Midzuumi* at ulitsa Lenina 182 and the Korean *Seoul* at prospekt Mira 245 are where Sakhalin's expat community head for when they're feeling overloaded on Russia and homesick, but at an average of US$50 and US$30 per head, respectively, the luxury of escape doesn't come cheap.

For snacks, there's a couple of cafés north along ulitsa Lenina, one of which, near the junction with ulitsa Sakhalinskaya, is also a good food store useful for picnic stocks. The small local market is just around the corner, on the western stretch of ulitsa Sakhalinskaya.

Getting There & Away

Air There are two flights a day to/from Khabarovsk (US$118, 1¼ hours), and one a day to/from Vladivostok (US$133, 1¾ hours) and to/from Moscow. The foreigners' departure hall is through a small door 15 metres to the left of the main entrance. There is a departure tax equivalent to US$8, payable on checking in.

The Aeroflot office (☎ 3 40 90) is at ulitsa Lenina 198 and the English-speaking Intourist desk is to your left as you enter. The office is open daily except Sunday, from 8 am to 7 pm.

Bus There are numerous buses each day to Kholmsk (US$4, 1½ hours). Daily buses also run north to Dolinsk and south to Korsakov.

Train The farthest point north on the island reached by the railway is Nogliki on the east coast, about a quarter of the way down from the tip. It's served by one train a day which departs from Yuzhno-Sakhalinsk at 10.20 pm, arriving at 1.48 pm the next day. There is also a 7.45 am daily train to Tymovskoe in the central region of the island. For other, closer towns such as Kholmsk or Korsakov, the bus provides a faster and much more frequent service.

Boat It's possible to board a ship for Port Vanino on the mainland from Kholmsk. From the port of Korsakov, there is a ferry link to Wakkanai, on Hokkaido, Japan's northernmost island.

Getting Around

All buses depart from in front of the railway

station on ploshchad Lenina. Bus Nos 108 and 120 run to the airport, a journey of about 25 minutes for US$0.50. Services begin at around 6.30 am, or one hour later on Sundays. There's an enquiry bureau (spravochny byuro) in the hall of the railway station. A taxi from the railway station to the airport will cost around US$10, but for early-morning flights cars should be ordered in advance (☎ 2 33 92) from the office at ulitsa Vokzalnaya 56A.

The Hotel Sakhalin-Sapporo has a car-rental service.

AROUND SAKHALIN
ДРУГИЕ МЕСТА САХАЛИНА

Almost three-quarters of the island is wild, mountain terrain, with the lower plains covered by three-metre-high grasses and bamboos. While the island is possessed of a rugged beauty, it's also very difficult to explore because of the lack of any decent transport system. Visitors will have to spend money on car hire or, alternatively, come prepared for some serious hiking and wilderness camping. The best base is Yuzhno-Sakhalinsk, which is the island's transport hub, such as it is, and has the only airport with mainland connections. There are small airfields elsewhere on the island at Okha and Nogliki to the north and Shakhtersk in the central region, all connected to Yuzhno-Sakhalinsk by scheduled short-hop air taxis.

One of the nicest places to go from Yuzhno-Sakhalinsk is the **Lake Tunaicha** region in the extreme south-east, where there's an archipelago of various-sized lakes, some only separated from the sea by narrow causeways a few metres wide. Amber gets washed up on the beaches of the region and this stretch of coastline is also favoured by seals. To get to Tunaicha, drive south out of Yuzhno-Sakhalinsk, past the right-hand turn for the airport, and at the next crossroads take a left turn in the direction of **Okhotskoe**. It's about 45 km. From Yuzhno-Sakhalinsk there should also be buses for Okhotskoe.

Thirty-five km due south of Yuzhno-Sakhalinsk is the grimy port of **Korsakov** (population 43,000), centre of the island's hugely profitable fishing industry. Korsakov is also the place to catch the twice-weekly Wakkanai ferry (☎ (42435) 2 23 52 for details of sailings). Southern Sakhalin's other major port, **Kholmsk** (population 40,000), is 40 km due west of the capital. It's another small fishing town, not worth anybody's time unless they're there for the boat to mainland Russia. The boat, which makes a 15-hour crossing to Port Vanino, leaves two or three times a week (☎ (42433) 2 53 00 for details of sailings – see also the Sovietskaya Gavan & Port Vanino section earlier). Both arriving and departing, the boat fails to make decent connections with buses to Yuzhno-Sakhalinsk and passengers will have to stay overnight in Kholmsk. Across the road and 100 metres south of the passenger shipping terminal is the *Hotel Kholmsk* (☎ (42433) 2 22 48) at ulitsa Sovietskaya 41. It's clean and well kept with singles for US$36, doubles US$48. The *Hotel Meridian* (☎ (42433) 3 28 55) at ulitsa Sovietskaya 136b might be a cheaper option. Kholmsk bus station is right at the north end of ulitsa Sovietskaya, about 2.5 km from the passenger shipping terminal.

To visit the north of Sakhalin, the best way is to take the railway that runs up the spine of the island as far as **Nogliki**, on the north-eastern coast. This is reputedly a good area to visit bird colonies and sea-lion rookeries. Another interesting trip might be to take the train just as far as Tymovskoe and from there take a bus to nearby **Alexandrovsk**, one of the first settlements the Russians established on Sakhalin and the place in which Chekhov spent most of his time during his 1890 visit to the island.

Kuril Islands
Курильские острова

Discovered and first charted in 1739 as part of Russia's Great Northern Expedition, the Kurils are a chain of 56 variously sized islands, arced like stepping stones between the southern tip of Kamchatka and the northern Japanese island of Hokkaido. However, if geographically the islands seem to form a link between Russia and Japan, then politically they are more of a wedge, driving the two powers apart.

A treaty of 1855 divided possession of the chain between Russia and Japan; the latter received the islands of Habomai, Shikotan, Kunashir and Etorofu. A second treaty, in 1875, gave Tokyo sovereignty over the whole lot in exchange for recognising the Russians' right to Sakhalin. But then, in the last days of WW II, with Japan collapsing under American assault, the Soviets reneged on the deal and invaded the Kurils. For three years the new Russian settlers and the existing Japanese residents lived side by side, but in 1948 Stalin ordered all the Japanese to leave. The Kurils have been a diplomatic minefield between the two nations ever since.

The islands, which form part of the Pacific 'Ring of Fire', are actually the tips of a volcanic, sea-bed mountain range. Amongst the peaks protruding from the sea are around 40 active volcanoes, many of which erupt frequently and violently. The islands are stunningly beautiful – the kind of places where they film James Bond movies, with perfectly circular azure-blue lagoons, bubbling, steaming rivers and some spectacular cliff formations (from which the bad guy gets thrown at the end). The main centres of habitation are Severo-Kurilsk on Paramushir Island, Kurilsk on Iturup Island and Yuzhno-Kurilsk on Kunashir, the southernmost and most accessible of the island chain.

Anyone planning on a visit to the Kurils should get hold of Frith Maier's *Trekking in Russia & Central Asia* which has a short chapter on the islands, with some good practical information on Kunashir.

Getting There & Away

This is tricky. About the only way to reach the Kurils is to fly from Yuzhno-Sakhalinsk, a flight of just over an hour. The problem is that the islands are often wreathed in a thick fog, caused by the meeting of hot and cold streams, making airborne approaches impossible. Although in theory flights are daily, you have to be prepared to hang around for up to four or five days waiting for the weather to improve. An alternative does exist in sailing. Once or twice a week, a ship departs from Korsakov, Sakhalin's southern port, taking a day to reach Yuzhno-Kurilsk, on the southernmost island of Kunashir. It's not a ferry service but fare-paying passengers are taken – for enquiries contact the sea terminal information desk in Korsakov (☎ (42435) 2 23 52) at pereulok Reidovy 2.

Magadan
Магадан

Population: 152,000

Magadan is barely a lifetime old but already it occupies a major place in one of the grimmest chapters of Russian history.

The origins of the town lie with the beginnings of the great terrors of the Stalin era. In 1932 gold was discovered in the Kolyma region. A new administration was brought into being, under the auspices of the NKVD, to excavate the gold and other precious metals – it was called Dalstroy. The same year, the first prisoner-laden ships arrived at a bare, swampy site on Nagaeva Bay, on the inhospitable northern shore of the Sea of Okhotsk. They were immediately set to labour, building docks and piers for the ships to follow, administrative blocks for their overseers and barracks for their guards. Eventually – though not before winter had come and thousands had died from working knee-deep in deathly cold waters and mud – they built their own flimsy accommodations.

Completed, the newly named town of Magadan served as a marshalling point for the human cargo destined for the hinterland gold fields of Kolyma. From the harbour, the already ragged and exhausted new arrivals were marched, shoved and prodded along the main street, ulitsa Berzin – named for the first director of Dalstroy. (Berzin was

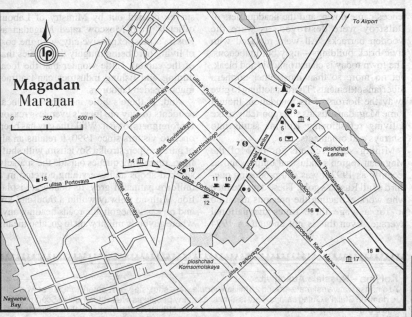

Magadan
Магадан

0   250   500 m

To Airport

ploshchad Lenina

ploshchad Komsomolskaya

Nagaeva Bay

PLACES TO STAY

5 Hotel Magadan
   Гостиница Магадан
15 Hotel Okean
   Гостиница Океан
16 Hotel
   Severovostokzoloto
18 Hotel Business Center
   Гостиница
   Бизнес-Центр

PLACES TO EAT

10 Kafe Russ
   Кафе Русь
11 Kafe Ariran
   Ариран

12 Kafe Globus
   Глобус

OTHER

1 Aircraft Monument
   Памятник Самолёт
2 Aeroflot
   Аэрофлот
3 Bus Station
   Автовокзал
4 Regional Museum
   Областной музей
6 Post, Telephone &
   Telegraph Office
   Почтамт, Телефон и
   Телеграф

7 Sberbank
   Сбирбанк
8 Bookshop
   Книжный магазин
9 Cinema
   Кино
13 Bookshop
   Книжный магазин
14 Geological & Mineral-
   ogical Museum
   Геологический и
   минеральный музей
17 Regional Museum
   Областной музей

---

recalled to Moscow and shot in 1938 for being too lenient on his Kolyma slave force; the street became ulitsa Stalina and then, in 1956, prospekt Lenina.) The prisoners were deposited in one of the town's many transit camps, there to await selection for the differ-

ent mines, 'corrective centres' and work troops out in the taiga. For many, Magadan was the last town they would ever see.

The town's trade in human lives began to end in the 1950s with the death of Stalin. The watchtowers and high, barbed-wire-topped fences came down, and the headquarters of Dalstroy were destroyed, as were the wooden barracks. All were replaced with civic brick buildings – ugly but innocuous. The town today is claustrophobic and bleak, but no more so than most other northern Siberian settlements. There is nothing to give away the horrors of its foundation, though some Magadan artisans still reportedly make a living refashioning Kolyma skulls into ashtrays and ornaments.

Mining still accounts for 60% of the Magadan region's industrial output, and as recently as 1992 it was still producing one-third of all Russia's gold. These days the men who work extracting the precious metal do so for a wage three times the national average. Even this is not enough. A 1994 survey carried out by Ministry of Labour officials from Moscow rated Magadan as Russia's most expensive city, with the cost of living here being roughly three times that of the capital. Little wonder that the local mining and fishing industries can't attract much-needed labourers.

And, if there's little incentive for local residents to stay on, there's even less reason for foreigners to visit. While the city has been open to visitors since 1990, it retains an air of pure pre-perestroika Sovietism, with shuffling, mumbling queues outside the sparsely stocked shops and everything covered in a uniform patina of grey. Its deliberate isolation, with no railway within a thousand km and no easily negotiable roads heading anywhere anybody might want to go, also means

Kolyma – Russia's Auschwitz

At a conservative estimate around 20 million people were shot, starved, beaten, tortured or worked to death in Stalin's Gulag camps. That is almost as many people as live in the whole of Scandinavia and a great many more than the entire population of Australia. Another conservative estimate has it that one-fifth of those Stalin-era victims died in the camps of the Kolyma region. There were so many corpses that their bones were used as beds for roads.

If Kolyma isn't a name as chillingly recognisable as Auschwitz, Belsen or Dachau, it is not because the horrors there were any less awful, but because they were perpetrated by a secretive government on its own citizens and because they took place in an isolated, fog-shrouded, ice-locked region, 9000 km from Moscow.

At any one moment, the camps in Kolyma held about half a million occupants. Kolyma consumed prisoners – those who survived the journey there. Prisoners were shipped up, thousands at a time, from Vladivostok, where they'd been waiting in transit camps after crossing the vastness of Russia crammed into cattle cars so tightly that some died of suffocation. The sea passage took a further eight or 10 days and was, if anything, an even more deadly journey. One ship left Vladivostok too late in the year and became stuck fast in the ice, finally reaching the Kolyma coast nine months later with not one of its thousands of prisoners still alive. Those aboard another prison ship revolted and the guards held them back with hoses, filling the hold with water. It was 40°C below zero. The 3000 prisoners were delivered to Magadan entombed in ice.

The port of Magadan, capital of the Kolyma region, was the 'gateway to hell'. From its harbour the already wasted prisoners, little more than living skeletons, were marched along the infamous 'road of bones' to one of the region's 100 or more camps. Many of these were simply named by their distance from the start of the march: the 23-km camp, the 72-km camp, the 220-km camp.

Once in the camps, most of the prisoners were put to work digging for gold. They worked 14 hours a day, barely sustained by a daily diet of 700 grams of bread and an evening bowl of cabbage soup. Quotas were set for the amount of gold they had to recover each day. The quotas were high and in the attempt to meet them prisoners often died of exhaustion. The alternative, for anyone who failed to meet the quota, was a cut in their food ration. As hunger took its toll, the shortfall in the quota would widen and the ration would become ever smaller. Eventually all that was left was the strength to crawl out of sight and succumb to the cold and the release of death. It's estimated that for every kg of gold mined one man died. ■

hat the only way in or out is by an expensive
light.

Orientation & Information

Magadan lies in a bowl, encircled by bare
hills with the west open to deep-water
Nagaeva Bay. The main thoroughfare is
prospekt Lenina with the central shopping
district lying between ploshchad Komsomolskaya and the junction with ulitsa
Proletarskaya. Immediately north of Pro-
etarskaya are the bus station and the
Aeroflot offices. Prospekt Lenina becomes
Komsomolskaya shosse as it climbs over the
ip of the hills and runs north-east 60 km to
he airport.

The main post, telephone and telegraph
office is on the north side of the desolate
ploshchad Lenina: open weekdays from 8
am to 8 pm, and on weekends until 6 pm. The
Sberbank at ulitsa Pushkina 4 has a currency-
exchange desk, as do the Hotel Business
Center and Hotel Okean.

BOL Tours (☎ 2 02 96; fax 2 30 28 attn
BS Levin) is an enthusiastic, one-man
agency run by Boris Levin, a geologist by
training. Levin has a lot of experience
leading youth groups around the region and
he can organise city sightseeing trips for
visitors, local flora and fauna excursions,
drives out to old Gulag camps, rafting expeditions, and boating trips to observe seals
and, occasionally, walrus. Although BOL
prefers to organise these things as seven and
eight-day packages costing US$600 to
US$700, you should be able to negotiate for
individual requirements. There's a slight
problem in that Levin speaks little English,
but with advance notice he can find interpreters. The postal address is Box 0/77, 685000
Magadan, Russia.

An English-language map called
Magadan and its Surroundings is available
for about US$0.50 from local bookshops
(the best is on prospekt Lenina and there's
another at the junction of ulitsa
Dzerzhinskogo and ulitsa Portovaya).

Magadan time is Moscow time plus eight
hours. The local telephone code is 41322.

Things to See & Do

At the approach to town, as prospekt Lenina
crosses a small river, in the shadow of some
squalid apartment blocks are what appear to
be the remains of a small-scale military skirmish. Two jet fighters on sticks swoop down
on the road, while behind them various other
discarded war machines, including a gutted
helicopter and some missile launchers, serve
as a children's playground. Like the flats
next to the aircraft, most of Magadan's architecture is unremittingly grim but there are
some good examples of **Stalinist Baroque**
in the buildings that line the southern end of
prospekt Lenina and the east end of ulitsa
Portovaya.

More conventional sights include a
Regional Museum (Kraevedchesky muzey)
split between two homes; the building at
prospekt Karla Marxa 55 has exhibits portraying life in the camps, while that at ulitsa
Proletarskaya 20/A has a model of a baby
mammoth recovered some years ago from a
glacier in the Magadan region. There is also
a **Geological & Mineralogical Museum** at
ulitsa Portovaya 16. Boris Levin of BOL
Tours knows the city well and can guide
visitors to the few remains of the Dalstroy
era, including the hospital where
Solzhenitsyn was treated when he was
marched through Magadan in the 1950s.

Places to Stay

Conveniently located across from the bus
station is the *Hotel Magadan* (☎ 2 10 14) at
Proletarskaya 8. It's large and gloomy with
impossibly long, unlit corridors – not recommended for anyone who has recently
watched *The Shining*. The rooms all have
attached bathrooms, but they're very seedy
and neglected. Prices are singles/doubles
US$17/32. The surroundings are slightly
more pleasant at the *Hotel Okean* (☎ 3 57 09)
at ulitsa Portovaya 36/10, 400 metres from
Nagaeva Bay (2.5 km from the bus station).
It's better looked after than the Magadan and
more used to foreign guests. There's a currency exchange and restaurant, and the bar
here is frequented by visiting foreign business reps. Singles start at US$35 and go up

to US$95, doubles are from US$56 to US$70.

The best accommodation in town is at the *Hotel Business Center* (☎ 5 81 57; fax 5 82 23) at Proletarskaya 84B (two km south of the bus station), a purpose-built business hotel with 14 clean, well-furnished rooms at US$60/76. The hotel, a modern, drab grey brick and glass construction, is 200 metres back from the road, beyond the multistorey apartment blocks. At the other end of the scale, the *Hotel Severovostokzoloto* (☎ 2 35 92) has the cheapest beds in town at US$8 for singles and US$12 for doubles, but the rooms are unpleasant and toilets and showers are shared – we doubt they've ever had a foreign visitor in the place. It's at ulitsa Gorkogo 14.

Places to Eat

Eating options are pretty much limited to the hotel restaurants. *At Max's* (☎ 5 81 57) in the Hotel Business Center is the best, but it's expensive and a drag to get out to for anyone staying somewhere more central. Of the other two, the dining room at the *Magadan* is a large, chill, unwelcoming place with staff who seem allergic to guests, while the restaurant at the *Okean* seemed OK, but both evenings I tried for a table I found the place booked by local wedding parties. There are several cafés around the junction of ulitsa Portovaya and prospekt Lenina: the *Globus* is at Portovaya 7 with the Korean *Ariran* opposite, and round the corner, across from the cinema, is the *Russ*, open Monday to Saturday, noon to 10 pm.

For imported dry foods, fresh vegetables and, more rarely, fruit, there is a small market at the junction of ulitsa Dzerzhinskogo and ulitsa Portovaya, and another on Komsomolskaya shosse, the road out to the airport, 800 metres north of the bus station.

Getting There & Away

With one exception, all roads out of Magadan go nowhere and terminate there. The one exception is the Kolyma Highway to Yakutsk, more than 1500 km to the east. The 'Road of Bones' (so named for the pris-

oners who built it) is roughshod and impassable in winter, and there are no regular bus services running its length even in summer. It exists as a sometime freight route and the only way of travelling along it is to hitch. As the nearest railway runs more than a thousand km south of Magadan, this means the only way in or out is by air. There are daily flights to/from Moscow and Khabarovsk, four flights a week to Vladivostok and Novosibirsk, and two flights a week to Irkutsk, Petropavlovsk-Kamchatsky and Yakutsk. The sole international service through Magadan airport is Alaska Airlines en route between Anchorage and Khabarovsk or Anchorage and Vladivostok, both flights dropping in once a week, each way.

The Aeroflot office (☎ 2 88 91) is behind and to the left of the bus station on prospekt Lenina, although foreigners may be sent to the airport to purchase their tickets from the international desk (as you face the main airport building, it's to your left, round the corner and through an unmarked door). Alternatively there's a foreigners' ticketing desk at the Hotel Business Center.

Getting Around

From early morning until late at night, two coaches run in relay between the bus station and airport forecourt. The journey takes 45 minutes and costs the equivalent of US$2.50 – pay the driver.

Kamchatka
Камчатка

Dubbed 'the land of fire and ice', Kamchatka is one of Russia's least explored but most scenically spectacular regions. A thousand-km-long peninsula separated from the mainland by the Okhotsk Sea, Kamchatka is hyperactively volcanic with terrain that bubbles, spurts and spews in a manner that suggests that here, Creation hasn't quite finished yet. The region can claim 200-plus volcanoes (sopky) in varying stages of activity, some long extinct, grassed over with aquamarine crater lakes, while 20 or more rank amongst the world's most volatile. Klyuchevskaya (the highest at 4750 metres) last erupted as recently as October 1994, sending so much ash into the air that international flights from North America to South-East Asia were disrupted.

The volcanoes are often surrounded by lava fields, and these lunar-like, pocked cinder landscapes served as the testing grounds for Russia's moon-walking vehicles. The thermal activity deep below the earth's surface also produces numerous hot springs, heated rivers and geysers. The most spectacular examples are to be found in the Valley of the Geysers (Dolina Geizerov) in the Kronotsky National Park, where around 200 geothermal pressure valves sporadically blast steam, mud and water heavenwards from the canyon floor. Away from the volcanoes, Kamchatka is covered by large areas of mixed forests and plains of giant grasses, home to a vast array of wildlife including between 10,000 and 20,000 brown bears and the sable, the animal that provided much of the impetus for early Russian explorations of the peninsula.

The man credited with the discovery of Kamchatka, in 1697, was the Cossack Vladimir Atlasov who, like most explorers of the time, was out to find new lands to plunder. He established two forts on the Kamchatka River which became bases for the Russian traders who followed, looking to exact tithes of furs from the locals. The native Koryak, Chukchi, Itelmen and Kamchadals warred with their new self-appointed overlords, but they fared badly and their numbers were greatly diminished. Today, the remnants of the Chukchi nation inhabit the isolated north-east of Kamchatka, while the Koryaks live on the west coast of the peninsula with their territorial capital at Palana. These peoples still maintain a traditional existence as reindeer herders and sea hunters, the animals being a source of food and raw materials for clothing. While much of their culture and language has been lost, the tradition of storytelling through mime, dance and song has survived – the writer Christina Dodwell, who spent time amongst the Koryaks, has described her travels with a dance troupe in *Beyond Siberia* (see Siberia & the Far East – Facts for the Visitor, Books section).

Kamchatka was long regarded as the least hospitable place in the Russian Empire – a land of primeval wilderness inhabited by a few primitives, half a year's journey distant and with nothing to offer beyond a dwindling supply of furs. When the Imperial lands in Alaska were sold off in 1867, Kamchatka might also have been up for grabs if the Americans had shown enough interest. Some 53 years later there was a taker, when an American named Washington Baker Vanderlip wanted to buy the province. He was offered a 60-year concession by Lenin but the two couldn't come to terms and the deal never went through.

After WW II, in the geography of the Cold

Kamchatka
Камчатка

Magdan Oblast

Talovka

Shelikhov Gulf

SEA OF OKHOTSK

Palana

BERING SEA

Karaginsky Island

Ust-Khayryuzovo

Klyuchi

Nizhne-Kamchatsk

Kozyrevsk
Esso
Atlasov

Ust-Kamchatsk

Mt Klyuchevskaya

Bering Island

Mt Kronotskaya

Kamchatka River

Milkovo

Kronotsky National Park

Commander Islands

Mednyy Island

Mt Koryakskaya

Valley of the Geysers

Petropavlovsk-Kamchatsky
Avacha Bay

Mt Khodukta

Southern volcanoes group

Kurilskoe Lake

Ozernovsky

PACIFIC OCEAN

0   150   300 km

War, Kamchatka took on new strategic importance and foreign interest was definitely no longer welcome. It became a base for military airfields and early warning radar systems, while the coastline sheltered parts of the Soviet Pacific Fleet. Isolated regions of Kamchatka also served as target areas for missile testings. No foreigners, nor even nonresident Russians were allowed anywhere near the peninsula. That all changed in 1990. These days the only hint of paranoias past is that visitors must have 'permission' to visit Kamchatka, which basically means having it listed on your visa (see Independent Travel later in this section). Touching down at Petropavlovsk-Kamchatsky airport today on a scheduled flight, there's no attempt to hide the silver pencil-snouts of fighter aircraft that protrude from the endless ranks of large grassy hummocks along the runway.

Ironically, visitors will have a far easier time spotting once-secret military hardware like fighter planes, nuclear submarines or radar stations than they will seeing anything else in Kamchatka. The main volcanoes, the geysers, the lakes and all of the region's most breathtaking scenery is well away from the regional capital, Petropavlovsk-Kamchatsky. Helicopters have to be hired or some serious hiking has to be embarked upon, requiring nights of wilderness camping. Either way, this is one place that has to be planned for in advance – without any forward planning, you're unlikely to make it out of the capital, and while Petropavlovsk is a reasonably attractive town, it just doesn't justify all the expense of getting there.

Where to Go

There are a couple of trips that can be made from Petropavlovsk without too much trouble or expense. There are hot springs at **Paratunka**, 25 km south of Yelizovo, the airport town. You may be able to get a bus there, or alternatively hitch a lift. The springs in Paratunka itself are not particularly attractive as they're heavily frequented by the locals, but if you can get there, there's a beautiful set of natural springs some 15 km

further south on the slopes of Goryachaya across the road from the volcanologists centre.

It's possible to ascend the slopes o **Avachinskaya** and **Koryakskaya**, the tw volcanoes that loom over Petropavlovsk The foot of the slopes and the start of th ascent begins about 30 km from the town but there's no road over there, so you nee to enlist the help of a local agency. Accordin to Frith Maier in *Trekking in Russia & Central Asia*, an ascent of Avachinskay should take about four to six hours hiking with crampons and ice axes recommende for the steep upper slopes. Koryakskaya i more difficult and Maier recommends tha it's attempted only by experienced climbers

According to local sources, the place mos worth visiting is the **Valley of the Geysers** This is an expensive excursion as it lies abou 150 km north of Petropavlovsk and the onl way there is by helicopter. Special permis sion is also required for visits to the valley At present the tourist agency Sogjoy (se Contacts) is the only organisation empow ered to grant access, but other tourist firm can arrange visits through Sogjoy. Anothe spectacular region is the grouping of th southern volcanoes, including **Mutnovsky** which erupted as recently as 1994. Th valleys between the peaks are filled with thermal rivers and boiling lakes. Furthe south, toward the tip of the peninsula, **Lake Kurilskoe** in the South Kamchatka reserve is the spawning ground for over one millior salmon each year and, consequently, home to the Stellar sea eagle, a bird with a wing span of around 2.5 metres.

For good hiking Frith Maier recommends the **Klyuchi volcanoes**, a wild, active grouping containing the region's giant Klyu chevskaya and its near twin Mt Kamen (jus a little shorter at 4617 metres). The towns o Kozyrevsk and Klyuchi are convenien bases.

Independent Travel

Officially, visitors still must have an invita tion specifically for Kamchatka, but Aeroflo didn't ask for any documentation before selling a ticket to Petropavlovsk. Problems may arise when you try checking into a hotel – a few receptionists did seem inordinately worried that we were there without any paperwork but, then again, nobody actually refused us a room or pointed us back in the direction of the airport. The best you can do is simply list Petropavlovsk-Kamchatsky as one of your proposed destinations when applying for your Russian visa and see whether it makes it onto the issued document. If it isn't included you could risk taking the flight anyway, and if there are any problems on arrival visit the OVIR office (☎ (41522) 7 14 63) in Petropavlovsk at ulitsa Leninskaya 14.

The other essential thing to do before departing is to get a copy of *Trekking in Russia & Central Asia* by Frith Maier (see Books in Siberia & the Far East – Facts for the Visitor), which contains a lot of solid, practical advice on solo travel and wilderness destinations in Kamchatka and elaborates on many of the points made here.

Once you've arrived at Petropavlovsk, the major problem is going to be getting around. With only one major road on the peninsula and no railways, the most common means of reaching A from B is flying. Lumbering, 12-seater Mil-8 helicopters operate like minibuses on Kamchatka, ferrying scientists, volcanologists and hunters between remote settlements and isolated cabins. However, for a foreigner, hitching a ride can be prohibitively expensive. As Frith Maier points out, so far the only foreign tourists on Kamchatka have been hunters willing to pay upwards of US$10,000 to bag a bear, and locals have set prices accordingly. For an hour's ride in a helicopter you're looking at a minimum of US$100. Even areas that are close enough not to necessitate helicopter transfers often, because of the lack of roads, require some kind of tracked all-terrain vehicle, or *vezidkhod*.

Scheduled, short-hop flights around Kamchatka are relatively cheap and some of these will get you fairly close to where you want to go. From Petropavlovsk you can reach the west-coast Koryak settlements of Palana and

Ust-Khayryuzovo; Ust-Kamchatsk, a small fishing town at the mouth of the Kamchatka River; Kozyrevsk 40 km from the volcano Klyuchevskaya; or Ozernovsky, toward the southern tip of the peninsula and just 15 km from Lake Kurilskoe.

Kozyrevsk can also be reached by a regular bus which runs from Petropavlovsk via Esso, before going on to Klyuchi and Ust-Kamchatsk. None of these places is set up to receive tourists and it's recommended that you take advice on accommodation before heading up there (see Contacts). Also, take advice on your route and its possible dangers. Many locals have died exploring Kamchatka, overcome by sulphurous fumes on the volcanoes or crashing through thin crusts into boiling pits below, caught by winter avalanches or mauled by one of the region's large bear population.

Travel Agents
It is far better to arrange as much as you can beforehand (see Tours & Programmes following) but if you're arriving on Kamchatka unprepared there are a few travel agencies around that might be able to help. Kamchatintour (☎ (41500) 3 42 08, 7 10 34; fax (50901) 64 00 86; telex 244124 INTUR SU) at ulitsa Leningradskaya 124b, Petropavlovsk-Kamchatsky, 683003 Russia, has had a lot of experience dealing with foreign visitors, but mostly Japanese, hunters and large parties, so is liable to be expensive. Staff also may be unwilling to help individuals or insufficiently large parties. Its offices are 150 metres behind the 16-storey octagonal tower (almost the only tower block in town), on the 4th floor. Alpha-Tour (☎ (41500) 5 58 50, 5 35 59; international ☎ & fax (50901) 64 00 81; telex 412062 OCTET SU (BOX 50652); e-mail tour@alpha.kamchatka.su), on the other hand, has been recommended as a company that can happily cope with independent travellers. It can arrange helicopters, vezidkhod and guides, fishing, skiing and rafting. Lost World (☎ (41500) 4 76 68; fax (41500) 7 45 01 attn Lost World; telex

244110PBTSU attn Lost World) at ulitsa Okeanskaya 58/10 is an unknown quantity but in its 1993 brochure advertised some well-priced three or four-day excursions down to the southern group of volcanoes.

Two other agencies possibly worth contacting are Kamchatka Adventures (☎ (41500) 2 46 15; fax (41500) 6 24 36; telex 244 131 OKEAN SU) at ulitsa Sovietskaya 2a, Petropavlovsk-Kamchatsky, and Snow Leopard (☎ (41500) 6 42 54; fax (41500) 2 43 64; e-mail service@ post.kamchatka.su) at 19-29 ulitsa Pogranichnaya, Yelizovo. Try Yegor and Natalia Vasiliev (☎ (41500) 7 67 28) or Mikhail Ivanovich (☎ (41500) 5 83 40) of the Hotel Geser for alternative quotes on helicopter rental.

Sogjoy (☎ (41500) 6 14 93, 6 29 84), the tourist company that holds the key to the Valley of the Geysers, is at ulitsa Sopochnaya 13 in Yelizovo, the settlement by the airport. Some of the companies above, however, should be able to get you access to the valley, either by dealing with Sogjoy themselves or by some other means.

Organised Tours For contact details of foreign firms mentioned in this section, see Travel Agencies in Siberia & the Far East Getting There & Away. For Russian firms, see Activities in Siberia & the Far East Facts for the Visitor.

REI Adventures in the USA is a Kamchatka specialist. Its 1995 programme included an eight-day 'Wonders of Kamchatka' tour taking in Lake Kurilskoe, the southern volcanoes and the Valley of the Geysers for a starting price of US$1750, and it also runs a 15-day trek around the Klyuchevskaya volcanoes for a basic US$1950. Neither package includes the cost of getting to Kamchatka.

UK-based Steppes East doesn't have any set packages but its speciality is in catering to off-beat requirements and it has plenty of experience in the region.

Australia's Iris Hotels group does a 12-day helicopter-supported tour of the Klyuchi and southern group of volcanoes, taking in

caldera lake visits and hot springs, and camping at the base of the volcanoes. Alternatively, it offers nine days of hiking and rafting in the Petropavlovsk region for US$1225 per person (no flights included) or specialist bird-watching or sports-fishing trips.

The Moscow-based Travel Russia has a number of different Kamchatka trekking programmes. For example, 15 days between mid-July and mid-September, with the route graded according to the clients' specifications and possibly including boat trips, cost around US$2568 (Moscow-Kamchatka return flight included) per person, for groups of four to seven people.

Pilgrim Tours, another reputable Moscow company, has in the past taken teams of foreign climbers to the summit of Klyuchevskaya (and will do it again for US$1920 – pay your own flight to Kamchatka). For the less intrepid, Pilgrim also organises moderately strenuous trekking around the southern volcanoes (12 days for US$1200, flights not included) and visits to the Valley of the Geysers (US$300 from Petropavlovsk).

PETROPAVLOVSK-KAMCHATSKY
ПЕТРОПАВЛОВСК КАМЧАТСКИЙ
Population: 273,000

Petropavlovsk-Kamchatsky is the administrative centre of the Kamchatka oblast and the only settlement of any size on the whole peninsula. However, the huddles of low-rise concrete blocks that make up the town are dwarfed by Avachinskaya and Koryakskaya, two brooding, active volcanoes. Both have erupted since 1990, though living in jerry-built Soviet structures, the town's residents fear earthquakes far more than they fear the smoky mountains.

Petropavlovsk was founded in 1741 by Vitus Bering, the Danish-born Russian captain who discovered the straits that bear his name. The town was named for Bering's two ships, the Svyatoy Pyotr (St Peter) and Svyatoy Pavel (St Paul) – the suffix Kamchatsky was added to distinguish it from all the other Petropavlovsks in Russia. It became the tsars' major Pacific sea port and

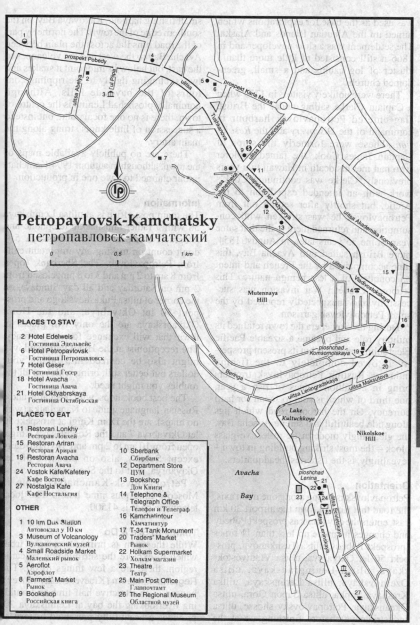

Petropavlovsk-Kamchatsky
петропавловск-камчатский

0   0.5   1 km

PLACES TO STAY

2 Hotel Edelweis
   Гостиница Эдельвейс
6 Hotel Petropavlovsk
   Гостиница Петропавловск
7 Hotel Geser
   Гостиница Гесер
18 Hotel Avacha
   Гостиница Авача
21 Hotel Oktyabrskaya
   Гостиница Октябрьская

PLACES TO EAT

11 Restoran Lonkhy
   Ресторан Лонкей
15 Restoran Ariran
   Ресторан Ариран
19 Restoran Avacha
   Ресторан Авача
24 Vostok Kafe/Kafetery
   Кафе Восток
27 Nostalgia Kafe
   Кафе Ностальгия

OTHER

1 10 km Bus Station
   Автовокзал у 10 км
3 Museum of Volcanology
   Вулканоческий музей
4 Small Roadside Market
   Маленький рынок
5 Aeroflot
   Аэрофлот
8 Farmers' Market
   Рынок
9 Bookshop
   Российская книга
10 Sberbank
   Сбербанк
12 Department Store
   ЦУМ
13 Bookshop
   Дом Книги
14 Telephone &
   Telegraph Office
   Телефон и Телеграф
16 Kamchatintour
   Камчатинтур
17 T-34 Tank Monument
20 Traders' Market
   Рынок
22 Holkam Supermarket
   Холкам магазин
23 Theatre
   Театр
25 Main Post Office
   Главпочтамт
26 The Regional Museum
   Областной музей

Mutennaya
Hill

ploshchad
Komsomolskaya

Lake
Kultuchkoye

Avacha

Bay

ploshchad
Lenina

Nikolskoe
Hill

was used as the base for explorations which turned up the Aleutian Islands and Alaska. The settlement was a slow developer and in 1866 it still consisted of little more than a cluster of log cabins and a small, green-domed church.

There were unlikely visitors in 1779 when a Captain Clerke sailing under the British flag entered Petropavlovsk harbour in command of the *Discovery* and the *Resolution*. These were formerly the ships of Captain James Cook, the famed explorer who had met his death in Hawaii two years previously. Clerke was continuing Cook's work with an intended expedition to the Arctic, but shortly after setting out from Petropavlovsk he was stricken with consumption and returned there to die that same year. Some 75 years later, in August 1854, more British sailed into Avacha Bay, this time accompanied by the French and intent on conquest of a less benign nature. This seaborne Crimean War invasion was successfully and unexpectedly repulsed by the small Petropavlovsk garrison.

During the Soviet era the town retained its military role and became a sizeable Pacific Fleet submarine base, but its present prosperity is owed completely to the fishing industry. Rusting Petropavlovsk trawlers bring in a million tonnes of fish a year, one-third of which is sold to Japan for hard currency. On the harbour road which jigs alongside beautiful and serene Avacha Bay, the gleamingly modernistic reflective-glass block – the most striking building in town – revealingly, is the fisheries' headquarters.

Orientation

Petropavlovsk is strung along one main axis, the road that runs in from the airport 30 km east, enters the city limits as prospekt Pobedy and changes its name no less than 11 times (prospekt Pobedy, ulitsa Tushkanova, prospekt 50 let Oktyabrya, ulitsa Vladivostokskaya, ulitsa Leningradskaya, ulitsa Ozernovskaya, ulitsa Leninskaya, ulitsa Krasnaya Sopka, ulitsa Sapon Gora, ulitsa Okeanskaya, Petropavlovsky shosse, ulitsa Industrialnaya) before finishing up at the

small fishing harbour, Rakovaya Bay, on the southern edge of the town. The northerly part of the road runs flat across the plain between Avacha Bay to the west and the volcanoes to the east, but below its midpoint it snakes and twists, clinging tightly to the rippling contours of the bay-side hills. Although nominally ploshchad Lenina is the centre of town, there is no one focal point, but instead a succession of little knots strung along the main artery.

There are no publicly available maps of the town, although in autumn 1994 Kamchat-intour claimed to have one in production.

Information

The main post office is at ulitsa Leninskaya 56 with a rather ramshackle telephone and telegraph office at Vladivostokskaya 5 – don't count on making any important calls from Petropavlovsk. The Sberbank (open from 8 am to 2 pm and 3 to 8 pm; closed from 2 pm on Saturday and all day Sunday), on the corner of ulitsa Pukashevskogo and prospekt 50 let Oktyabrya, and the Hotel Oktyabrskaya are the only two places in town that will exchange foreign currency. The receptionist at the Hotel Petropavlovsk might also be coerced into taking your dollars but better still, bring with you all the roubles you might need.

The best bookshops, with postcards and a Russian-language guide to Kamchatka (with no maps), are the Dom Knigi at prospekt 50 let Oktyabrya 7 and the Rossiyskaya Kniga, open from 10 am to 2 pm and 3 to 6 pm daily except Sunday, also on prospekt 50 let Oktyabrya, next to the Sberbank.

Petropavlovsk-Kamchatsky time is Moscow time plus nine hours. The local telephone code is 41500.

Things to See & Do

While the town is primarily a base from which to explore the surrounding volcanic region, there are a few things to do. The **Regional Museum** (Kraevedchesky muzey) housed in an attractive half-timbered building overlooking the bay at Leninskaya 20 provides a beautifully presented history of the region focusing mainly on prehistory and geology, native peoples and early settlers. There's an extremely interesting section on early Russian settlers in America with reconstructions of the first settlements. It's open Wednesday to Sunday from 10 am to 1 pm and 2 to 6 pm; admission US$1. There is also a **Museum of Volcanology** (☎ 5 93 61) at bulvar Piipa 9 and a **Museum of Geology** (☎ 3 98 67) at ulitsa Beringa 117.

In front of the classically styled regional administration building at Leninskaya 14 is the **monument to Captain Clerke**, a small obelisk erected by a delegation from the British Admiralty in 1913. There are more British graves, as well as some French graves, and up on Nikolskoe Hill there are monuments to those who fell in the failed Crimean War invasion in 1854.

Places to Stay

The hotel favoured by tour companies is the *Hotel Petropavlovsk* (☎ 5 03 74) at ulitsa Karla Marxa 31. It's a squat concrete block facing the volcanoes (and with its back to the main road, making it extremely difficult to identify). It's reasonably pleasant inside and all rooms have their own bathrooms; singles are US$42, doubles US$55. The Petropavlovsk is 100 metres back from ulitsa Tushkanova just north of the major road junction marked by a large obelisk. Also just north of the obelisk, a dusty side road leads off Tushkanova and down to the *Hotel Geser* (☎ 5 79 96), a great concrete edifice out in a windswept no-man's land. The place is very bleak and a little isolated (about a km from the main road) but it's also quite cheap: singles US$25, doubles US$36.

The *Hotel Oktyabrskaya* (☎ 2 46 84) at ulitsa Sovietskaya 51, is recommended for its location, close to ploshchad Lenina in the prettiest part of town. The hotel has been recently upgraded and it has a currency-exchange desk and the facility to make international calls. However, nobody has thought to put a sign on the building – it's a grey pebble-dashed building, three storeys high, with a pitched roof.

One to avoid is the *Hotel Avacha* (☎ 2 73 31), at ulitsa Leninskaya 61, opposite the T-34 tank monument. It's extremely seedy inside and despite some rooms having great views, they're not worth the US$50/80 that foreigners are charged.

On the northern edge of town, just five minutes walk, or one stop south, from the 10-km bus station, is the *Hotel Edelweis* (☎ 5 33 24) at prospekt Pobedy 27, occupying one floor of an apartment block. The hotel's dozen or so rooms are large and very clean but there's only one shower block and the toilets are shared between the whole floor – although they are well looked after. There's a kitchen for self-catering. Prices are US$22 to US$32 per person. The entrance to the hotel is off ulitsa Abelya: walk to the end of the first block on the left and go round to the other side.

Places to Eat

Despite being a little gloomy, the restaurant in the basement of the *Hotel Petropavlovsk* seems to be about the best the town has to offer. The menu leans heavily towards fish, which is well presented and reasonably priced. Upstairs, on the ground floor, there's a cheerful café-bar which serves decent food from an English-language menu. The large restaurant attached to the *Hotel Avacha* was undergoing extensive renovation in autumn 1994 but might be worth checking out. There is also the respectable-looking *Restoran Lonkhy* (open from noon to 5 pm and 7 to 11.30 pm) at prospekt 50 let Oktyabrya 24 and the *Restoran Ariran* (☎ 2 72 38) at ulitsa Leningradskaya 72.

For snacks, try the *Vostok Kafetirii/Vostok Kafe* at Leninskaya 60. The Kafetirii, open from 9 am to 7 pm, is a stolovaya serving salads, soup, sausage and cutlets, while the Kafe, open from 11 am to midnight, has a slightly expanded menu and seating. Just south of the Regional Museum is the *Nostalgia Kafe* which might be nice but was securely padlocked each time we visited. There's a snack bar on the 1st floor of the *Holkam supermarket*, at ulitsa Leninskaya 62, with sandwiches, pastries, cakes and

SIBERIA & RUSSIAN FAR EAST

coffee – open until 7 pm. The supermarket, a sparkling Dutch-Swiss-Russian venture, is also the best place to shop for food supplies. Other places include the traders' market just south of ploshchad Komsomolskaya and the farmers' market on ulitsa Voitsesheka.

Getting There & Away
The only way in or out of Petropavlovsk-Kamchatsky, and indeed the rest of Kamchatka, is to fly. There are flights twice daily to/from Moscow (US$582; nine hours) and Khabarovsk (US$204; three hours), daily to/from Vladivostok (US$222; three hours), and twice weekly to/from Magadan, Yakutsk and Yuzhno-Sakhalinsk.

An international terminal is due to open at Petropavlovsk airport in 1995, at which point Japan Airlines may start operating a Niigata-Kamchatka service. For the moment the only international operator flying into Petropavlovsk is Alaska Airlines with a weekly Anchorage service for around US$1000 return.

The Aeroflot office (☎ 5 61 19) is at ulitsa Karl Marxa 33/1, adjacent to the Hotel Petropavlovsk. The far counter in the 1st-

floor ticket hall is the Intourist desk, staffed by English-speakers.

Getting Around
The two services of most use are bus Nos 1 and No 22, big mustard-yellow buses (state-run and free of charge) which run almost the whole length of Petropavlovsk, from the 10-km station near the town's northern edge to the Regional Museum and, in the case of No 1, on down via Okeanskaya to Rakovaya Bay. Bus No 22 doubles back along ulitsa Sovietskaya at the Regional Museum. Most of the rest of the town's ramshackle bus fleet is privately owned, run by individuals taking advantage of the town's chronic shortage of public transport, and they charge from US$0.50 to US$1.

All buses for the airport go from the 10-km stop on prospekt Pobedy at the north end of town; take bus No 100, or anything marked 'Aeroport' or Yelizovo, which is the name of the settlement close by the airport. The journey takes about 45 minutes and a ticket costs US$1. Arriving at the airport, to get into town catch any bus on the forecourt that reads 'Petropavlovsk'.

UKRAINE

Facts about Ukraine

The word Ukraine means Borderland, a name coined centuries ago for what was the traditional crossroads between the Baltic and Black seas, the fringe between Europe and Central Asia. Settled since ancient times, Ukraine has a long tradition of cultural identity and statehood stemming back to Kievan Rus, which at its peak in the 10th century was one of the most powerful and established kingdoms in all of Europe. But like all borderlands, its fate was to be a battleground and coveted prize for a number of surrounding empires – namely the Poles and Lithuanians from the north and north-west and the Russians from the north-east, along with the Tatars and Turks from the south. Between the 14th and 19th centuries, its boundaries fluctuated during countless wars and broken alliances, with much suffering inflicted from outside. The majority of its population was eventually subjected to serfdom and Ukrainian culture was forcibly suppressed. Stalin starved over six million of its people to death in the early 1930s (to which there are almost no memorials), and WW II chose it as a chief battleground (to which seemingly countless memorials were erected).

Yet through the centuries of hardship, the Ukrainian people have endured, preserved their various identities and nurtured their cultures. The country's national anthem, 'Ukraine Has Not Yet Died', summarises the national psyche – one dominated by the age-long desire for sovereignty, combined with the ingrained will to survive. Ukrainians are tough, hard-working people, but they're also open and friendly, with a curious and hospitable attitude toward foreigners. A special sense of generosity and civil kindness prevails, stemming from long traditions of having to band together in order to survive. People have learned to rely on nothing but themselves, their tight self-sufficient communities and their own resourcefulness.

Ukraine today is a land of great economic importance, of smoggy industrial cities and countless old-fashioned villages of picket fences, duck ponds and overloaded horse carts. All grow out of the endlessly rolling, subtly changing steppe. The capital, Kiev, is the mother city of Ukraine, Russia and Belarus, the centre a millennium ago of the first recognisably Eastern Slav state. The many survivals from that and other eras – and a great riverside setting – make Kiev one of Europe's most fascinating cities. Down in Crimea, Yalta is deservedly the country's most famous sea resort, combining a spectacular setting with much of artistic and historic interest. Nearby, the town of Bakhchysaray is a haunt from the Tatar past. Odessa is a major port as well as an aristocratic resort, with a history of trade and commerce and an air of exotic intrigue. Lviv, in the west, is the heart and soul of Ukrainian patriotism and the most architecturally beautiful city, with a true Central European elegance. Further variety is gained by spending time in lesser known places like Kharkiv, an unassuming but likeable industrial city; Chernivtsi, a lively and scenic border town with a cross of cultures; Lutsk, which has a Polish past; Kamyanets-Podilsky, a fortified castle town; and Chernihiv, with its numerous relics of 11th-century Kievan Rus. For a real glimpse of charming, backwater rural Ukraine, head to one of the many pretty towns in the west like Pochayiv or Berezhany, where you'll surely be the only foreigner milling about.

Ukraine
Україна

HISTORY
Scythians, Greeks & Sarmatians

The Scythians, excellent horse riders who arrived from Central Asia, dominated the plains north of the Black Sea from the 7th to 4th centuries BC. In westerly areas they established a fairly settled state. The Greek Herodotus described sacrifices of 50 or more people to accompany a Scythian king's burial. He also reported that the royalty didn't wash but had vapour baths – and that for recreation they retired into tents and threw cannabis 'seeds' on to heated stones, which created 'a strong aroma that no Greek burnt offering can match' and made them dance and shout. Scythians are most famed for the superb gold work found in their tombs from the Caucasus to Hungary – often featuring highly detailed, lifelike animal or human representations. The finest collections are in Kiev's Caves Monastery and the Hermitage in St Petersburg.

Around the same time as the Scythians arrived on the Ukraine steppes, Greeks, mainly from western Asia Minor, established colonies around the Black Sea coast. The two groups traded, intermarried and sometimes fought. Much of the famed Scythian gold work was crafted by Greeks.

Between the 4th and 2nd centuries BC, a new wave from the east, the Sarmatians, displaced the Scythians everywhere except Crimea. The Amazon myth may go back to the Sarmatians, whose women apparently weren't allowed to marry until after they had killed in battle. The Sarmatians continued to trade with Greek Black Sea cities but harassed the fringes of the Roman Empire.

Ostrogoths, Huns, Slavs & Khazars

In the 2nd century AD, the Ostrogoths, a Germanic people from the vicinity of northern Poland, set up a state covering most of modern Ukraine. In about 370 they were subjugated by the Huns, the first of a new series of nomad invaders originating in Mongolia. The Huns set up a western steppe empire and threatened the Roman Empire. In the 6th and 7th centuries, the Slavs took advantage of the shake-up caused by the Huns to spread west, south and east – including throughout Ukraine – from the vicinity of the northern Carpathian Mountains and Vistula valley in present-day Poland.

In the 8th century, most of Ukraine came under the rule of the Khazars, originally a nomadic grouping of Turkic and Iranian tribes in the Caucasus, who built an empire combining the military advantages of nomadic horsemen with Iranian and Jewish trading skills. They adopted Judaism in the 9th century, and their capital was Itil, near the mouth of the Volga.

Kievan Rus

From the 6th century, Scandinavians had been exploring, trading and setting up small states east of the Baltic. Known as Varyagi (Varangians) or Rus to the Slavs, they had raided Constantinople and come into conflict with the Khazars before one of them, Oleh of Novgorod, declared himself ruler of Kiev in 882. Initially a southern Varangian outpost with control over only part of north-central Ukraine, Kiev grew to be capital of a large, unified Rus state which at its biggest – under Svyatoslav (962-72) – stretched from the Volga to the Danube to the Baltic; its prosperity was based on the control of trade from the Baltic to the Black Sea by the Dnipro and other waterways. Its Nordic lords were assimilated into their Slavic subjects' culture.

Svyatoslav crushed the Khazars, only to open the way for continual conflict with the fierce Turkic Pechenegs, who defeated and killed him in 972. Nor could he overcome Constantinople, from where his successor, Volodymyr (known to Russians as Vladimir), accepted Christianity in 988, marking the founding of what later became the Russian and Ukrainian Orthodox Church. With the new religion came Byzantine ideas of imperial authority, the beginnings of literature, systematic education and law. It also introduced Byzantine art (icons, mosaics, frescoes) and architecture, from which descended entire Eastern Slavic traditions.

Russia, Ukraine and Belarus all stemmed from this Eastern Slavic state. Present-day

Russia evolved from breakaway northern princedoms centred around the Novgorod and Vladimir-Suzdal regions, and present-day Ukraine from the original Kiev and breakaway western princedoms of Galicia and Volyn. Each subsequently evolved different linguistic and cultural identities. By the 11th and 12th centuries, the Kievan Rus state began to splinter, dividing into 10 to 15 rival princedoms. Vladimir Monomakh (1113-25) was the last ruler to hold it all together. When Prince Andriy Bogolyubov of Suzdal sacked Kiev in 1169, followed by the Mongols 70 years later, the end of an empire which had ruled for three and a half centuries was complete, and the power base moved to the north and west.

Galician-Volynian Principality

The western Galicia and Volyn regions (comprising most of present-day western, central and northern Ukraine, as well as parts of north-eastern Poland and southern Belarus) united into the Galician-Volynian Principality under Prince Roman Mstyslavych from Volyn, who in 1203 defeated his northern rivals in Suzdal and retained control of Kiev – briefly coming close to reuniting the once vast Eastern Slavic territories. The Romanovych dynasty is seen by many as the first 'Ukrainian' state, having arisen on modern Ukrainian territory with a political and cultural identity stemming from the heritage of Kiev. A period of relative prosperity was enjoyed under Prince Roman's dynamic son King Danylo and his son Lev, during which time the capital cities of Volodymyr (present-day Volodymyr-Volynsky), Halych and Lviv flourished along major east-west trade routes. The dynasty ended after only a few generations, with political control being absorbed by the expanding Polish and Lithuanian kingdoms in the mid-14th century. This marked the end of Ukraine's short period of self-determination, save for brief periods during the Cossack Hetmanate. During the ensuing centuries, the country chafed under the control of a variety of external powers.

Tatars & Turks

Jenghiz Khan never quite reached Ukraine, but his grandson Batu devastated Kiev in 1240. While the Galician-Volynian Principality was controlling western Ukraine, much of eastern and southern Ukraine, along with much of European Russia and a good chunk of Siberia, came under the power of the Volga-based Golden Horde.

The Golden Horde became Turkified and Islamicised, and traded with the Mediterranean through Italian colonies in Crimea. It was weakened in the 14th century by the Black Death, the growing military strength of Moscow in the north, the expansion of Poland and Lithuania in the west, and not least by Timur, the last great Central Asian conqueror, who invaded the region in 1395 and smashed the Golden Horde's capital, Sarai, on the Volga. The Golden Horde finally disintegrated in the 15th century, dividing into several still smaller khanates. One, the Crimean Khanate, became a vassal of the Constantinople-based Ottoman Turk Empire, which went on to control all coastal Ukraine by 1520. The Turks and the Crimean Tatars, as the people of the Crimean Khanate were known, were big thorns in Ukrainian, Russian and Polish sides until the 18th century.

Cossacks

The Ukraine steppe was sparsely populated due to military devastation and plague. A border region on the fringe of several expanding empires, it was the first land to be referred to as 'Ukrainian', and after the fall of the Galician-Volynian principality in the late 14th century, the focus of the region's history shifted here. During the late 15th century the area began to attract runaway serfs, criminals, Orthodox refugees and other misfits from more tightly controlled Polish and Lithuanian domains to the north-west. Along with a few semi-independent Tatar bands, the inhabitants formed self-governing militaristic communities and became known as *kazaks* (Cossacks), a Turkic word meaning outlaw, adventurer or free person. The people elected ruling *hetmans*, or chieftains. The most famous group of Ukrainian Cossacks, based below the rapids (*za porozhy*) on the lower Dnipro, were known as the Zaporizky, made famous by their fortified island community known as the Zaporizky Sich (see Khortytsya Island in the Zaporizhzhya section). Similar groups from Muscovy who went to the Don region were also called Cossacks. The Ukrainian Cossacks eventually developed a self-ruling Cossack Hetmanate, which to some degree reasserted the concept of Ukrainian self-determination, although it 'officially' was under Polish, and later Russian, rule. At the height of their power, the Cossacks waged a number of successful campaigns against the Turks, sacking the Black Sea cities of Varna and Kafa and even twice assaulting Constantinople, in 1615 and 1620.

In 1596 the Union of Brest set up the Uniate Church – commonly called the Ukrainian Catholic or Greek Catholic Church – which recognised the Roman pope as leader but followed Orthodox forms of worship that involved the Old Slavonic language. This brought millions of peasants in the eastern and southern border areas of the Polish-Lithuanian state (which had once been in Kievan Rus) into the Catholic fold of their rulers without really changing their religious practices. The Uniate Church became a binding cultural force for most Ruthenians, as these early Orthodox Ukrainians under Polish and Lithuanian control came to be known. The Cossacks, however, remained fully Orthodox.

Polish monarchs were often at odds with the Cossacks, suppressing their autonomy while continuing to use them as mercenaries. The local peasant population, the majority of whom were Ruthenian Ukrainians, also despised their Polish landlords. After a number of unsuccessful uprisings, a huge rebellion in 1648 led by the famous Cossack Hetman Bohdan Khmelnytsky (aided by Tatar cavalry) destroyed the Polish army at the battle of Pyliavtsi, near the present-day city of Khmelnytsky. Storming past Lviv, Khmelnytsky was poised for an invasion of Poland, but decided to accept an armistice and returned triumphantly to Kiev. The following year at another battle against Polish King Casimir, near Zboriv, Khmelnytsky was betrayed by his Tatar allies and forced to sign an armistice. A further forced armistice in 1651 made Khmelnytsky finally realise that foreign support was necessary for a decisive victory over the Poles. He engaged in a formal but controversial military alliance with Muscovy in 1654 (see the Pereyeslav-Khmelnytsky section in the Central Ukraine chapter). Subsequent conflicts and counteralliances with the Poles and the Swedes threw the situation into disarray. In 1660, a war broke out between Poland and Russia over control of Ukraine, ending in a treaty in 1667, and another in 1668, with Russia gaining control over Kiev and northern Ukraine east of the Dnipro and the Poles keeping the territory to the west – laying the foundation of the division between east and west Ukraine that remains evident today. Hetman Ivan Mazepa, aiming to unite Polish and Russian-dominated Ukraine, allied with Sweden against Russia's Peter the Great but was beaten at Poltava (1709). Following victories against the Ottomans, Catherine the Great disarmed and destroyed the Cossack Sich in 1775.

Russian Control

The absorption of Ukraine was pivotal in the emergence of the Russian Empire as a world power. During the 18th century, following a series of wars with the Turks, Russia expanded into southern Ukraine. The Partitions of Poland (1772-95) saw most of western Ukraine transferred from Polish to Russian hands, except for the far west, around Lviv, which went to the Habsburg Empire. Ukrainian nationalism was born in Kiev in the 1840s, its guru and moral leader being the prolific writer and poet Taras Shevchenko (see Arts & Culture – Literature later in this chapter). In 1863 and 1876 the tsarist authorities attempted to suppress the movement by banning the Ukrainian language in schools, journals and books. The focus of the nationalist movement shifted to Lviv, the centre of the Uniate Church, where

UKRAINE

the Ruthenian population resented the continuing dominance of Roman Catholic Poles in this eastern corner of the Habsburg Empire.

20th Century

Civil War Following WW I and the collapse of tsarist power, Ukraine finally had a chance to gain its independence, but none of the bewildering array of factions could win decisive support. A *rada* (council) in Kiev, elected by mainly urban dwellers, proclaimed the autonomous Ukrainian National Republic (UNR) in 1918, electing Mykhailo Hrushevsky, a Ukrainian leader returned from exile, as the first official president of Ukraine. Bolsheviks, under their leader Skrypnyk, set up a rival Congress of Soviets in Kharkiv. Civil war broke out and eventually developed into total anarchy, with six different armies vying for power and Kiev changing hands five times within a year. The Reds, with the help of Russian Bolsheviks, first took Kiev, but were driven out by the UNR with the help of Germans and Austrians, who in turn set up a quasi-Hetmanate state under General Skoropadsky in April 1918. Eight months later, the Directory, a rival government made up of former UNR members, took control of Kiev, but fell into conflict between its two leaders, socialist Vynnychenko and nationalist Petlyura. At the same time, a self-proclaimed anarchist, Makhno, gained support in the south. The Bolsheviks again invaded and retook Kiev in February 1919.

Meanwhile, in Lviv, the West Ukrainian National Republic (ZUNR) was proclaimed, beginning its own short war with Poland, which ended after seven months with an international decision to cede western Ukraine to Poland as a 'protectorate'. The remaining western Ukrainian troops joined with their eastern counterparts, and under the command of Petlyura engaged in battles against the Whites under General Denikin, and also against the Red Bolshevik Army, which eventually, heavily supported by Russia, got the upper hand. In alliance with Poland, Petlyura launched another counterassault in April 1920, retaking Kiev in May, only to be driven out and then cut out of another deal brokered between the two stronger powers. Ukraine was again divided under the Treaty of Riga, with Poland, along with Romania and Czechoslovakia, retaining portions of western Ukraine, while the Soviet forces were given control of the rest. Petlyura set up a government in exile, and was assassinated in Paris in 1926. During these battles, Jews were targeted by all sides – especially the Whites, who carried out numerous pogroms – with an estimated death of 35,000.

Soviet Power Ukraine was a nominally independent Soviet Socialist Republic until it became a founder member of the USSR in 1922. While the power structure of Moscow was taking shape, a sort of national revival took place in the 1920s, with an assertion of Ukrainian culture and identity. When Stalin took power in 1927, he looked upon Ukraine as a laboratory for executing Soviet restructuring while at the same time stamping out 'harmful' nationalism. In 1932-33 he engineered a famine. Farm land was collectivised and grain forcibly confiscated to fulfil unrealistic quotas, while the peasants who toiled the fields starved to death. The punishment for taking any amount of grain from the state-controlled collection agencies was execution, a practice commonly and randomly enforced. Estimates put the death toll at between five and seven million. Intellectual and political executions and deportations followed, along with the blatant and specific destruction and looting of numerous Ukrainian cathedrals, which were seen as national historical symbols. Over 250 buildings, churches, cemeteries and palaces were systematically razed to the ground. During the great purges of 1937-39, it is estimated that throughout the USSR another one million people were executed and between three and 12 million were sent to labour camps, with a high proportion coming from Ukraine. Kiev replaced Kharkiv as the capital of Soviet Ukraine in 1934.

Famine

What the Holocaust was to the Jews of Europe, the famine of 1932 to 1933 was to the Ukrainians. It was a tragedy on an unimaginable scale, which crippled the entire country. The deep psychological, social and political wounds affect the people even today.

The biggest tragedy of all was that this famine was artificially engineered and need never have happened. There was food, and plenty of it. In an experiment with collectivisation, Stalin ordered the production of unrealistic quotas of grain, while ordering that no grain from a collective farm could be distributed to the peasants until all quotas had been met. Party authorities had the authority to conduct house-to-house searches and confiscate all grain. Any man, woman or child caught stealing grain from a government storehouse could be executed. Internal passports were issued to prevent desperate people running off in search of food. Peasants literally starved to death under the gaze of gun-wielding Communist Party activists. Entire villages died of starvation. Cannibalism was commonly reported. Estimates put the death toll during 1932 and 1933 at between five and seven million.

Soviet authorities denied for years that a famine had occurred. Western governments, which at the time did not want to strain ties with the new Soviet state, played down the atrocities. No monuments were erected to the victims of the famine; meanwhile, thousands of Lenin statues and WW II monuments were raised across the country.

In the years leading up to, and after, independence, efforts were made to reveal the full extent of this great tragedy. International recognition of the famine may enable the Ukrainian people to heal an old wound. But this harrowing chapter in the country's history remains a symbol both of human brutality and of the will to survive. ■

'...but nothing to eat', reads the caption on this 1949 woodcut, which depicts 'the happy life' on a collective farm where even the cows are starving. Stalin's portrait hangs on the wall, and the messenger brings an armful of new decrees. The woodcut is from a series entitled 'Kolkhozes', one of several made and distributed by the Ukrainian Insurgent Army (UPA) during the years of Soviet rule in Ukraine.

UKRAINE

WW II The Red Army rolled into Polish Ukraine in September 1939. The Germans attacked in 1941 and by the end of the year controlled virtually all of Ukraine, occupying it for over two years. Two major factions of Ukrainian partisans emerged: Soviet partisans who were essentially controlled by Moscow, and the UPA (Ukrainian Insurgent Army), which was concentrated predominantly in the west and fought both German and Russian troops with the aim of establishing an independent Ukraine. By the end of 1943 Kharkiv and Kiev were retaken by the Soviet Red Army, which in early 1944 launched a massive offensive of 2.3 million men that pushed back the German forces and obliterated Ukraine in the process. An estimated six million Ukrainians died in the war, which left the majority of the country's cities in ruin.

After the war, the USSR kept the territory it had taken from Poland in 1939. Ukraine, like Belarus, got its own seat in the UN on the grounds of extra suffering during the war. A Ukrainian army under a government in exile led by Stepan Bandera (who was assassinated in Germany by a Soviet spy in 1959) continued a guerrilla existence up until the 1950s, while millions of Ukrainians were sent to Siberia for suspicion of 'disloyalty'. The Uniate Church, accused of collaboration with the Nazis and closely linked with Ukrainian nationalism, was forced to dissolve into a union with the Russian Orthodox Church in 1946.

It's estimated that the wars, famine and purges which occurred during the first half of the 20th century cost the lives of over half of the male and a quarter of the female population of Ukraine.

New Nationalism The 1986 Chornobyl disaster and, in the west, the Uniate Church were the first focuses of glasnost-era opposition to Soviet rule. With Chornobyl, discontent was provoked not just by the disaster itself but also by the appallingly slow official response to it and the ongoing cover-up of its consequences. The first

Kremlin announcement wasn't made until two days after the event, and May Day parades in Kiev went ahead three days after the announcement, despite the fact that fallout was blowing over the city by that time. The Uniate Church began to come out from underground in 1988, claiming four million adherents and rocking Lviv with marches and church takeovers. But with its large Russian and Orthodox populations the rest of Ukraine was slower off the nationalist mark. Rukh (Ukrainian People's Movement for Restructuring), the umbrella nationalist movement founded in Kiev by a number of prominent intellectuals and writers, won seats across the republic in 1990 local elections, particularly in the secession-minded west, where it took control of Lviv and other city councils. But the communists still kept a majority in the republican parliament.

In July 1990, this parliament issued a sovereignty – but not secession – declaration which proved too little for the growing independence movement. In October, a wave of protest marches in Kiev, inspired by hunger-striking students, forced the resignation of the old-guard prime minister. Another sign of growing nationalism was the revival of Ukraine's own autocephalous (self-governing) Orthodox Church, which had been forcibly amalgamated with the Russian Orthodox Church in 1686.

Independent Ukraine Shortly after the failed Soviet coup in August 1991, the Communist Party of Ukraine (CPU) was banned from power and on 24 August 1991, the Supreme Rada adopted a declaration of independence pending a nationwide referendum. In December of that year some 84% of the population voted overwhelmingly (90%) in favour of independence. Leonid Kravchuk, former chairman of the CPU, was elected as the first president of Ukraine, and a national armed forces was established.

Factions almost immediately arose within the newly formed government, disputing policy and the general direction of economic reform. The leadership, high in rhetoric but inexperienced, tended to revert to old centralist methods. Growing dissatisfaction eventually resulted in a second vote of no confidence, forcing the government to resign in September 1992. Difficulties also plagued the new government. Disagreements and tensions with Russia and the Western world concerning the future of Ukraine's cache of inherited nuclear weapons reached disturbing levels. Complications over ownership of the Black Sea fleet harboured in the Crimean port of Sevastopol further strained Ukrainian-Russian relationships. Finally, in January 1994, an agreement was reached between Ukraine, Russia and the USA. In exchange for security guarantees and just compensation, Ukraine began a process of denuclearisation. A temporary agreement was later also reached over the Black Sea fleet, with Ukraine granting partial ownership to Russia in lieu of an increasing oil debt.

Meanwhile, skyrocketing inflation, fuel shortages and plummeting consumer power caused widespread dissatisfaction with the government, rekindling age-old differences between the east and west. Western Ukrainians were concerned with achieving national independence and closer ties with the West, while the east lamented the economic situation and pushed for closer economic union with Russia. The presidential election campaign in July 1994 was largely fought on these differences, with pro-Russian reformer Leonid Kuchma winning over Leonid Kravchuk; the vote was drawn almost perfectly along the line of the Dnipro River.

The recent political and economic crisis has seen a rise in the popularity of the re-established Ukrainian Communist Party. In the 1994 elections, the Party won 86 seats. The next largest representation (20 seats) was won by Rukh, with the Peasants Party of Ukraine (a quasi-centrist-socialist pro-collectivised farming party) and the Socialist Party of Ukraine winning 18 and 14 seats, respectively. It seems it will be an uphill battle for reform-minded President Leonid Kuchma to get legislation passed. One good sign is Kuchma's seemingly dedicated campaign to purge his government of former communist hardliners who oppose dynamic economic restructuring.

Some economic reforms have been pushed through, winning the approval of the IMF and the World Bank, which both released much-needed loans. In February 1994, Ukraine became a member of NATO's Partnership for Peace programme. The future for Ukraine poses huge challenges, but hope lies in its large, well-educated and skilled population and the country's vast resources. For the first time in centuries Ukraine's destiny is in the hands of Ukrainians.

GEOGRAPHY

At 603,700 sq km, and stretching about 2000 km east to west and 1000 km north to south, Ukraine is the largest country wholly within Europe, scraping in just ahead of France. It's bordered by seven nations, with Russia to the east and north, Belarus to the north, Poland to the west and a large stretch Black Sea coast to the south. There are short borders with Slovakia, Hungary, Romania and Moldova to the south-west.

The topography consists almost entirely of steppe – gently rolling, partially wooded plains – at a mean height of 175 metres. The horizon is broken from the north-west near Lutsk to the south-east near the central Dnipro River valley by a belt of highland, with river-valley gorges and ravines, some over 300 metres deep. The only serious mountains are a short stretch of the Carpathians in the far west and the Crimean Mountains in the far south. In the north, there are forests and some scattered marshland; in the south, the steppe is open and sparsely wooded.

Approximately 3000 rivers flow through Ukraine, with 116 of them over 100 km long. The four major rivers cross the country from west to east: the Dnister, the Pivdenny (Southern) Buh, the Dnipro and the Siversky Donets River. The first three flow into the Black Sea (the Dnipro making a great 90° bend south of Dnipropetrovsk to do so), but the Siversky Donets flows into the Don, which enters the Sea of Azov.

A central 'black earth' belt of deep, thick,

humus-rich soil – one of the world's most fertile regions – covers nearly two-thirds of Ukraine. Regions of mineral wealth lie in the coal and iron belts of the far east and south-central regions.

CLIMATE

Inland Ukraine has a relatively moderate continental climate with little variation across the generally flat countryside. The hottest month is July, averaging 23°C, while January, the coldest month, averages around freezing. Kiev is completely frozen for at most only two to three months of the year, usually from December to February (compared to Moscow's five months). The eastern areas catch a few of the chilling Siberian breezes, while the west catches the tail end of the warm Mediterranean winds. The tiny corner of Zakarpatska, on the south-west side of the Carpathians, usually stays hotter and drier. On the coast, Yalta and Odessa are generally a few degrees warmer still, and are much milder in winter, rarely dipping below freezing during the day. Inland, June and July are the wettest months, while Yalta experiences most of its limited rainfall during December and January. Most of the country averages 114 cm of rain a year; Crimea has an annual average of only 40 cm. See Appendix III for climate charts.

FLORA, FAUNA & ENVIRONMENT

The majority of Ukraine lies in a belt of steppe, primarily flat, heavily cultivated grasslands, with a few patches of forest comprised of oak, maple, linden and ash. Willow and aspen grow along the rivers. A thin belt of forest runs across the north of the country, consisting mostly of silver fir, beech, oak and spruce, with a few swamps also scattered about. The Carpathians are heavily wooded, with oaks and beech at the lower elevations and pines, junipers and alpine meadows on higher ground. A narrow strip of Mediterranean vegetation runs along the southern coast of Crimea. Vineyards thrive in Crimea and Transcarpathia.

Agrarian Tradition

The majority of Ukraine's broad steppe consists of humus-rich *chornozem* (black earth), cultivated since the Scythians back in the 4th century BC. With age-old agrarian traditions, Ukrainian culture is deeply imbued with symbolic references to its crops, wild flowers and trees. The garden is sacred, and among the most treasured and best maintained possessions. Rural villages are patchworks of flowers and painted fences encircling neat rows of vegetables. Herbs, leaves and roots are still grown for medicinal purposes, mixed and concocted into healing recipes passed on for generations.

Fields & Flowers

Formerly known as the bread basket of the USSR, over half of the country is covered in silvery fields of wheat, barley, rye, oats and sugar beets. The calendar year was traditionally based on the harvest, a time for many celebrations. Large tracts are also set aside as grazing land, and in spring explode into brilliant, swaying seas of *maky* (red poppies), *sonyashnyky* (sunflowers) and golden mustard. Other wild flowers include *romani* (daisies), blue *blavati*, yellow *lotysh* harvest flowers and the small, white *kashka*, which grows between the grasses and on the hills in the west. *Bozy* (lilac) is a common favourite, as is the colourful and tall hollyhock. Dozens of flowers are specially cultivated for nectar and honey *(med)* production.

Trees

Most cities have venues for strolling lined with *kashtany* (chestnut trees), which are the official symbol of Kiev. The *kalina*, a deciduous bush with clusters of white flowers and red berries, was immortalised by Shevchenko and other poets as a national symbol, its fruit used for generations as a healthy juice and preserve. The *lipa* (linden tree) commonly lines country lanes, and its fragrant flowers are used to make a sweet tea. Orchards of *vyshnya* (cherry) and *yabluka* (apple) trees have long been vivid images in songs and poems – they were a favourite of Shevchenko, and Chekhov wrote the *Cherry*

Orchard while in Crimea. *Bereza* (birch) and *buk* (beech) trees grow in large groves, predominantly in the north and along rivers. With over 25 species in Ukraine, *verba* (willow trees) are traditionally used to make baskets, fences and household appliances. The largest concentration and variety of *sosna* (pines) is found in the small stretch of the Carpathian Mountains in the far southwest. *Dub* (oak trees) are concentrated around the Dnipro – the Zaporizky Sich was once built entirely from oak timbers.

Animals

The creatures you'll probably see most often are the millions of white geese and ducks which spot the green and black earth and fill countless ponds all over the countryside. The animal life of Ukraine is diverse, with over 100 species of mammals. Wolves, foxes, martens, deer, rabbits and other small furry animals stay out of sight and are limited mainly to wooded regions and the Carpathian and Crimean mountains, the latter also

Ukrainians are traditionally close to the earth and its creatures (from a 1949 woodcut series)

having wild pigs, gazelles and mountain sheep. The Crimean deer was once a hunting trophy prized by tsars and commissars. Ukraine is home to over 350 species of birds, the secret messengers of many folk songs and fairy tales, and over 200 species of fish swim in its streams and rivers.

Conservation

There are four types of state nature reserves. A *zapovidnyk* is the strictest, with tight controls on private use. There are about 10 such reserves in Ukraine, totalling 92,340 hectares. Those open to the public include the small Kaniv Nature Reserve south of Kiev, which includes 2000 hectares of pristine steppe forest and hills, with over 5000 plant species indigenous to the area. About 100 km east of Kherson is the Askaniya Nova Reserve, with 33,000 hectares of steppe, populated by wild animals first introduced to the site by a German settler in 1828, including herds of bison, zebras, wild horses, deer, Watusi cows and African ostrich. There's also a botanical park, and the entire park is open to visitors. The Chornomorsky (Black Sea) Nature Reserve is about 75 km southwest of Kherson and includes 57,000 hectares of estuary. The reserve was established in 1927 to protect various species of migratory birds. Limited excursions to the bird habitats are conducted in spring and autumn.

A *zakaznyk* is a less restricted nature reserve, usually entirely open to the public. There are 123 in the country, totalling more than 156,000 hectares.

National parks *(nasionalny zapovidni parky)* can be large swathes of wild nature, artificially landscaped parks, botanical gardens or wooded recreational areas on the outskirts of a city. They're all open to the public. The Carpathian State National Park south-west of Kolomyya is the largest in the country, with some of the highest peaks in the range covered in alpine vegetation. The Shasky National Park in the extreme northwestern corner of the country features a number of lakes densely wooded with birch and aspen. The Sofiyivka Park & Arboretum in the city of Uman is a famed 200-year-old landscaped park, with over 150 hectares of grottos, lakes and pavilions.

Zapovidno-myslyvski hospodarstva, or game reserves, are usually off limits and focus on the preservation of animals and their natural environments. There are four game reserves in Ukraine, totalling 133,000 hectares. The Crimean State Nature & Game Reserve in the mountains north of Yalta is the most important. Although it's off limits, the surrounding areas are equally picturesque and offer free hiking and camping.

The State Committee for Environmental Protection issues a list of numerous animals that are protected by law, including the Carpathian wildcat and the great bustard, a huge, crane-like bird. Plants under protection include the yew tree and the Carpathian rhododendron.

Pollution

The Chornobyl disaster was but the tip of an iceberg of neglect whose effects you breathe in virtually every time you walk down a city street or drive on a main road. During the entire tenure of the Soviet Union, the intense drive to industrialise was ruthless and exploitative, with little foresight or care given to possible environmental damage and repercussions. This legacy of irresponsibility is one that all the former Soviet republics now have to endure. In many areas, beautiful lands have been destroyed, and soils are contaminated with poisons that have also taken their toll on the population.

Besides the horrors of Chornobyl (increased rates of thyroid cancer, leukemia, birth defects etc), other alarming developments have occurred. In autumn 1988, 40,000 Chernivtsi children were temporarily evacuated after more than a hundred of them started going bald and seeing nightmare visions. The blame was laid on thallium poisoning, but researchers are still divided on the issue. Other occurrences of the condition, known as alopecia, have turned up in places like the Cherkasy region. Much of the Donbas and cities like Kryvy Rih and Zaporizhzhya have lingering clouds of pollution, causing increasing respiratory and other health problems. Acid rain has been reported in much of the Carpathians, around Kiev and along the southern stretches of the Dnipro River. Many of the rivers have been polluted by waste runoff from industry and agriculture, due to lax restrictions and minimal controls. Much of the silt carried downstream from Chornobyl is radioactively contaminated – how far down the river and to what extent is still not fully known.

The Green Party in Ukraine is the political wing of the environmental organisation Zeleny Svit (Green World), and, although small, it's a crucial voice in raising issues and encouraging politicians to clean, regulate and protect the environment. The State Committee for Environmental Protection is the official government agency assigned to deal with environmental and pollution problems.

GOVERNMENT
Constitution

A final decision on the precise wording of the constitution remains to be made. Major amendments were initially instigated in the early 1990s to provide for sovereignty as a nonsocialist state and for the inclusion of the executive presidency, but disagreement on the exact division of power stalled completion until 1993. After the 1994 elections, new discussions concerning further changes to the constitution began.

Government Structure

Executive power is in the hands of the president and prime minister, with legislative power vested in the 450-member Supreme Rada. The president, elected by popular vote for a five-year term, appoints the prime minister and the 35 cabinet ministers, but all appointments must be approved by the Supreme Rada, whose members are also elected by popular vote for terms of five years. Leonid Kuchma, who replaced Leonid Kravchuk, was the country's first president.

Political Parties

There are over 35 different political parties in Ukraine, ranging from the Ukrainian People's Movement for Restructuring (known as Rukh, the most powerful pro-reform party), the Communist Party of Ukraine (banned in 1991, re-established in May 1993 and attracting more members than any other party), the Socialist Party of Ukraine (a spin-off of former communists) and the Congress of National Democratic Forces (an alliance of 20 nationalist-conservative groups and parties). Parliamentary seats are campaigned primarily on the basis of party orientation.

Regional Structure
The country is broken up into 24 states or regional administrative divisions called *oblasts*, and one autonomous republic (Crimea), with each, save for the Volyn and Zakarpatska (Transcarpathia) regions in the west, named after its principal city. Each oblast is subsequently broken into *rayons* or smaller administrative counties, each also named after its principal town. Kiev is the official capital and the seat of the national government, with Lviv the cultural capital of the west and Kharkiv the centre of the east. Simferopol is the political capital of the Crimean Republic.

East-West Rift
Although Ukrainian was adopted as the state language in 1990, a controversy still brews over the language chosen to conduct government business. Many Supreme Rada meetings have ended in a row over this very issue, with representatives from the west demanding that sessions be held strictly in Ukrainian and members from the east retaliating in Russian. Such ingrained ideological differences between the two spheres have brought some degree of strife. However, the two sides openly acknowledge their differences and the serious issue of east-west separation rarely arises – both factions for the most part are committed to unity as a single state. The one topic which can get quite explosive is the issue of closer ties with Russia: the east favours the idea, the west does not. The idea of reunification with Russia, however, is not widespread.

Two regions which have been pushing for more autonomy are the Donbas region, mainly populated by Russian miners, and the Transcarpathian region, with its large Ruthenian population.

Crimean Question
The Republic of Crimea, with its 63% Russian population, is constantly prodding the idea of reunification with Russia – a continual source of tension between Simferopol and Kiev. The central government has the power to nullify any Crimean legislation which it deems violates internal security, and has already quashed the Crimean proposal for a peninsula-wide referendum concerning complete independence. This political battle is set to continue well into the future.

ECONOMY
Ukraine previously contributed 20% of Soviet production, but since independence many of its ageing factories have become virtually useless, relying on now-extinct raw materials and component parts previously supplied from other equally defunct industries elsewhere in the former Soviet Union. Wary of mass unemployment, the government has continued to subsidise these 'dinosaur' industries, slowing the country's economic reform. Crucial measures toward privatisation have been slow. By 1994, less than 10% of the country's enterprises and under 5% of the workforce were in the private sector, totalling only 20% of the nation's GDP, as opposed to 40% in Russia and well over 50% in countries like the Czech Republic and Poland. Unable to produce and to cope with market rates, Ukraine saw inflation skyrocket, reaching an annual rate of 3400% in 1993 and still rising rapidly. In 1994 the total value of the economy was estimated at between US$30 and US$35 billion.

To improve the production of *kolhosps* (collectivised farms), landmark legislation was introduced to allow full private ownership of agricultural land. However, few Ukrainians have the capital to buy sufficient equipment or the necessary fuel to run a

UKRAINE

productive private enterprise. Consumer prices have been liberalised at an average increased rate of 80% to 90% per month, but average monthly income remains dismally low, reducing the standard citizen's purchasing power to nil (this is a complaint you'll hear over and over). The average monthly salary is around US$10 to US$20, with pensioners often receiving less than US$2. No-one will starve, thanks to their gardens, but a new pair of shoes is often an unheard-of luxury. As outdated state industries flounder, higher unemployment seems inevitable.

Hope for the Future

Some foreign investment has occurred, with over 500 joint ventures established by mid-1992. Foreign aid from the IMF (US$371 million loaned in November 1994), the World Bank (US$500 million loaned in December 1994), the USA, Germany and others is finally coming in. Now that independence euphoria and high hopes have turned to despair, the government is finally coming to grips with its dire straits. Following the elections in summer 1994, tough reform packages were proposed that were aimed directly at stabilising inflation, revamping the banking system and pushing privatisation and pro-market reforms. How much actually gets accomplished is another matter.

Ukraine has the agricultural potential to achieve prosperity. It has the world's largest sugar-beet crops, huge grain and potato resources and some of the richest soil on earth. The soils around the estuaries in the Kherson region produce large melon crops.

However, about 40% of the grain harvest (around 40 to 50 tonnes per year) is lost due to theft and poor storage. Most of the population survives not on the beleaguered national agricultural industry but on the thousands of tiny, privately worked plots of land that surround each city. The virtual life-blood of the people, the plots are not only a major source of food but also provide extra income, with surplus goods sold in local markets.

Besides large coal and iron deposits (in the Donets Basin in the east, and in the south-central Kryvy Rih area), there are untapped reserves of petroleum and natural gas. Yet the country suffers desperate fuel shortages: those ubiquitous crowded trams, cancelled buses and reduced numbers of trains are constant reminders of its insufficient fuel reserves. Electricity supplies are met by belching thermal power stations and hydro-electric plants that harness the Dnipro, as well as the five questionably operational nuclear power plants.

POPULATION & PEOPLE

Ukraine has 52 million people, with over half the population living in urban areas. Five cities have over a million citizens – Kiev, Kharkiv, Dnipropetrovsk, Odessa and Donetsk. The other half of the population live in small towns and villages of between 1000 and 5000 inhabitants, relying primarily on an agricultural economy. The overall average population density is about 85 people per sq km.

Over 72% of the people are Ukrainian; another 22%, many of whom are concentrated in the east, are Russian. Apart from the Russians, the seven largest minority groups, all less than half a million in population, are: Jewish, Belarusian, Moldovan, Bulgarian, Polish, Hungarian and Romanian. The Jewish minority is almost entirely urban, while the other minorities live clustered around their respective borders. Almost all of the Tatar population, around 250,000, live in Crimea, their ancestral homeland (see History in the Crimea chapter). Around 2.5 million Ukrainians live outside the country: 1.5 million in North America, and a large population in the Kuban region of Sub-caucasian Russia.

East & West

There is definitely a difference between Ukrainians from the east and those from the west. Western Ukrainians consider themselves to be 100% Ukrainian and the vanguard of Ukrainian culture, speaking the language and proudly displaying their nationalism. In the east, where over 10 million ethnic Russians live, convictions of nationality are less intense, and most people speak Russian – the result of over 350 years of Russification. Only about half of these Ukrainians can speak their own language. There are also many 'half-Ukrainians', who consider themselves as much ethnically Russian as Ukrainian. Underlying tensions between Ukrainians and ethnic Russians stem partly from these conceptions.

Minority Tensions

Tensions between the ethnic Russians and Ukrainians also stem from historical grievances and a tradition of sour relations between the two peoples – the Ukrainians desiring to assert their identity, the Russians denying or belittling it. Similar tensions are also played out between the Polish minorities and Ukrainians in the west. Although these strains cause pressure, it's commonly felt that there is no chance of widespread violence or serious civil strife. The probability that a situation like that in the former Yugoslavia will erupt in Ukraine is very small.

EDUCATION

One of the primary aims of the newly independent government was the reversal of the Russified education system. In the 1980s, about half of the country's pupils were taught in the Russian language, although Ukrainians constituted over 70% of the population. After independence, Ukrainian tuition was made available for all students, but choice was still individual. Small funds were also allotted to provide education in the language of minorities such as Hungarian, Polish and Romanian. Ukrainian history and literature, rather than Russian and Soviet, were given a new emphasis in the curriculum. New schools were opened, including the reopening of the once renowned Kiev-Mohyla Academy (heavily backed by Kravchuk), the first higher education institution in Ukraine, dating from 1615.

After eight years of compulsory education, a student can opt to either go to work, enter a two-year trade-school course, or continue to the 11th grade in order to enter one of three types of institutions – a technical college, speciality institute or university.

ARTS & CULTURE
Cultural Identity

In the 18th century, Catherine the Great, who planned to further absorb Ukraine into her empire, coined the term Malorossy or 'Little Russians' for the inhabitants of Ukraine. This derogatory term aimed at belittling the individual identity of Ukrainian culture. For decades, the Western world perceived Ukraine simply as a part of Russia. Moscow's monopoly ensured that history books and cultural references placed Ukraine as an addendum to the dominant power, denying its unique and characteristic voice. Borscht, painted eggs and many of the famous Cossack song and dance traditions originated in Ukraine, not Russia.

Literature

Origins Ukraine's many literary personalities stand out as the most influential voices of national and cultural identity.

The origins of Ukrainian literature go back to ancient Slavic chronicles such as the 12th-century *Slovo o polku Ihorevim (The Tale of Ihor's Armament)*, considered to be a masterpiece of medieval Ukrainian literature, and the 16th-century *Peresopnytsia Gospel*, which incorporated Ukrainian colloquial expressions.

The beginnings of modern Ukrainian literature were propagated in the mid-18th century by Hryhorii Skovoroda, the 'Ukrainian Socrates'. A wandering philosopher and intellectual, Skovoroda wrote groups of poems and philosophical arguments in Ukrainian which were directed at the common person rather than the social elite. Ivan Kotlarevsky's 1798 version of Virgil's *Aeneid*, the first published work to be written in the vernacular Ukrainian language, was a reinterpretation of the Greek Classic, with the heroes being replaced by robust Cossacks and peasants. He later published his famous work *Natalka Poltavka*, a classic story which was subsequently reproduced as

UKRAINE

a ballet, a theatrical production and a motion picture.

Kharkiv Romantics At Kharkiv University in the 1820s, a number of young Ukrainian intellectuals led a movement to elevate the Ukrainian language so that it could achieve literary respectability. Ballads, prose and poetry were published, along with two influential anthologies of Ukrainian literature, the *Zaporizky Antiquities* and *Ukrainian Anthology*, which for the first time documented the numerous poems, songs and stories held in the country's significant oral traditions. In western Ukraine, an almanac of folk songs, poems and historical articles called *Rusalka Dnistrovaia (The Nymph of the Dnister)* was published in colloquial Ukrainian, giving the common person access for the first time to an elevated form of literature in the vernacular.

Shevchenko Taras Shevchenko stands unmatched as a Ukrainian writer, embodying and stirring the national consciousness. With his writings the Ukrainian language finally achieved literary respectability – at a time when suppression of the language was increasingly issuing from Moscow. Many claim that to understand Ukrainian heritage one must understand the significance of this national hero, the man after whom half the country is named. Born a serf in 1814, Shevchenko studied painting at the Academy of Arts in St Petersburg, where in 1840 he published, with great success, his first collection of poems, *Kobzar (The Bard)*.

His prolific work elevated the status of the Ukrainian language from that of a secondary peasant tongue to a vehicle of eloquent and poetic expression at the same levels of excellence and sophistication as other great writers of his time. By combining vernacular expressions and colloquial dialects with Church Slavonic, he formed a unique voice. At a time when many writers were directing their work to high society, Shevchenko wrote for the common people. A staunch antitsarist (once banished for 10 years to Siberia on the direct orders of Tsar Nicholas

I, which led to his premature death), Shevchenko preached social justice with compelling passion, in universal terms as well as specifically to the downtrodden peasant and to the Ukrainian nation as a whole. He referred to his country as 'This land of ours that is not our own'. In 1876, 15 years after Shevchenko's death, Tsar Alexander II officially banned all Ukrainian books and publishing, but Shevchenko's clear and ringing message was firmly gripped in the heart of a nation.

Shevchenko's Legacy After Shevchenko, many other great Ukrainian authors flourished, despite the oppressive conditions. Panteleimon Kulish, Shevchenko's contemporary, published several influential social and cultural works, including ethnographic collections and historic criticisms. National romanticism gave sway to a realism that sought to further expose social injustice. Ivan Nechui-Levytsky raised the issues of gross inequality between rich Polish landlords and poor Ukrainian peasants, a theme echoed in the work of Panas Myrnyi, whose book *Khiba revut voly? (Do Oxen Roar?)* attacked social injustice as the cause of evil within the oppressed. Stefan Rudansk was well known for his humorous wit when criticising political inequities. Leonid Hlibov wrote many allegorical fables which painted Ukraine's Polish and Russian oppressors as villains, and author Pavlo Hrabovsky was exiled to Siberia because his poems openly criticised the tsar's imperial policies. Volodymyr Vynnychenko, later an active politician and Ukrainian revolutionary, was a prolific and varied writer, whose early works like *Beauty and Power* portrayed class conflict in realistic terms. His later work *Beauty and Strength* expressed his concerns about the disintegration of village traditions. Novelist Mykhailo Kotsyubynsky used impressionistic writing to express social strife in rural Ukraine, often with an innovative sense of suspense. His *Shadows of Forgotten Ancestors* celebrated the strife and myth of village life in the Carpathians and was later made into a motion picture in 1965 by producer Serhii Paradzhanov.

Ivan Franko & Lesia Ukrainka Arguably the most talented and prolific writer of the early 20th century was Ivan Franko, whose work spanned all literary genres, including poetry, drama, fiction, social and philosophical debate, political prose and children's stories. His work was at once scholarly and moving, shedding light on the issues plaguing Ukrainian society, which eventually led to his arrest and temporary imprisonment. Some of his better known works include *The Turnip Farmer*, *The Converted Sinner* and *During Work*, where his skill at storytelling was used to convey social, moral and humanitarian ideals and their application to Ukrainian dilemmas.

Equally distinguished and prolific was Larysa Kosach, known by her pen name Lesia Ukrainka. Born into a prestigious Ukrainian family, and well educated, her frail health inspired her to compose deeply moving poetry expressing inner strength and inspiration – symbolic beatitudes for the Ukrainian people – typified in works such as *Hope Against Hope* and *On the Wings of Songs*. The universal expression of beauty in her work *The Forest Song* was later made into a ballet, an opera and a motion picture.

Postwar & Soviet Era Olena Teliha, executed by the Gestapo in 1944, was an inspirational voice for postwar writers. Her sensitive and patriotic writings are collected in her work *The Soul on Guard*. Dokia Humenna's description of the Ukrainian peasant's plight between the wars also won her fame, while Ivan Bahrianyi portrayed life as a political prisoner in his work *Why I Refuse to Return to the USSR*. *Starfall*, by Mykola Ponedilok, portrays with a wry humour the grief of Soviet life in Ukraine in the 1960s. A 1961 compilation of poems entitled *Journey of the Heart* propelled Lina Kostenko to international recognition. Poet and writer Vasyl Stus was eventually killed in a Soviet labour camp and most of his work was destroyed, but his *Winter Trees* (1968)

and *Candle in the Mirror* (1977) are poetic legacies depicting the turmoil experienced by Soviet dissidents. Other Ukrainian poets murdered during the Soviet regime include Alexi Tihy and Yuri Litvin.

Contemporary The Union of Ukrainian Writers in Kiev was a catalyst in the events leading up to independence, with works by writers such as Ivan Drach and Yuri Tarnavsky contributing to the public upheaval. Poet Ihor Kalyanets is a contemporary realist who relates the issues of the day using an experimental style of free verse. Other contemporary poets include Bohdan Boychuk and Maria Revakovych, and the essayist Solomea Pavlychko is also well known. Scholars Ivan Rudnytsky and Orest Subtelny are two excellent historians whose analysis of history focuses on its effect in shaping present-day Ukraine. The trio of poets out of Lviv who go by the title *Bu-Ba-Bu*, led by Yuriy Andrukhovych, are recognised by some as part of a wave of new postmodern writers. For a further listing of contemporary works, see the Books section in Ukraine Facts for the Visitor.

Theatre & Drama
Ukrainian theatre and drama originated from seasonal harvest festivals and staged events such as the traditional folk wedding and the Easter drama. Liturgical ceremonies played a strong role in developing a strong sense of theatrics. Modern dramatic theatre was first introduced in Kiev during the 17th century by students of the Caves Monastery, where the study of oratory rhetoric was obligatory. The Kiev-Mohyla Academy was the first to include drama and theatre as a part of the secular curriculum. In 1765 the staging of Ukrainian drama was banned because it was considered to be subversive and anti-Muscovite. Ukrainian drama moved underground and to the streets and marketplaces, where spontaneous productions became popular, usually based on the Cossack and Christian legends.

During the 19th century, Ukrainian theatre and drama resurfaced in the classical and romantic modes, typified by productions such as Kotlarevsky's *Natalka Poltavka*, and outstanding performances by actors such as Tetiana Danylova and Pavlo Chubynsky. Numerous amateur Ukrainian troupes formed and flourished until the 1876 decree by Tsar Alexander II which officially banned all Ukrainian books and publishing, including drama and theatre productions.

Ukrainian drama and theatre then shifted emphasis to the west. During the latter part of the century, the first professional Ukrainian theatre (the Besida) flourished in Lviv. In 1904 the Kiev Music & Drama School reopened, producing many fine actors such as Maria Zankovetska and Stepan Janovych. The subsequent political turmoil, war and revolution of the first half of the 20th century almost dissolved Ukrainian theatre, but under the leadership of directors Les Kurbas and Mykola Kulish, most cities had once again developed theatrical companies by 1930, the most prominent the Berezil group in Kharkiv.

The actress and director Lidia Krushelnytska has been prominent in the last few decades. She eventually emigrated to the USA and propelled the Ukrainian Theatre of America to international exposure. Most major cities have Ukrainian drama theatres which regularly host a wide range of productions, the most prominent being the Ivan Franko Theatre in Kiev. One group to look out for is the Kiev-based Ukrainian Theatre on Podol, raved about at a recent Edinburgh International Theatre Festival. The Kiev Karpenko Karyi Theatre Institute is also a hotbed of young new talent.

Dance

Ballet Classical ballet was introduced to Ukraine in the 18th century, performed by serfs as a form of entertainment for noblemen and women. In the 19th century, Ukrainian ballet switched to an operetta style, with performances such as *Zaporizhzhets za Dunayem* (*Zaporizky beyond the Danube*; 1863), before then turning to imitate the Russian, French and Italian counterparts of the time. The first ballets to be staged written solely by Ukrainian composers took place in the 1930s, and included Verykivsky's *The Nobleman Kanovsky*, which fused classical ballet with traditional folk dance.

During the Soviet era, Ukrainian ballet was dominated by Russian classics and performances of Soviet realism, a highlight being Homoliaka's 1957 *Black Gold*, depicting the drama of young Soviet life. Ukrainian composers and Ukrainian themes were slowly reintroduced, including Dankevych's *The Lily*, based on a Shevchenko poem, and *The Forest Song* by Skorulsky, based on a poem by Lesia Ukrainka. These productions helped to develop ballet into a genre of heroic drama and national symbolism.

In the 1970s, a fleeting trend of one-act avant-garde ballets focusing on philosophical literary works by authors such as Ivan Franko developed. The highlight of this movement is Maiorov's *The Dawn Poem*, based on traditional piano pieces by Korsenko.

During the 1980s and into the 1990s, more than 50 ballets were produced by Ukrainian composers, the predominant emphasis being the traditional synthesis of classic and folk themes, with the Kiev and Lviv opera and ballet theatres at the forefront.

Famous Ukrainian choreographers have included V Zavarykhyn, who ran his own school in Paris in the 1920s, and O Zaklynska, whose modern interpretations of folk dances won widespread admiration. V Periaslavets was a renowned ballerina before teaching at a range of international schools. Recently, Victor Litvinov, Kiev Ballet's artistic director, has teamed up with Kiev composer Yuri Shevchenko to produce some interesting work.

Ukraine's ballet and opera theatres are located in Kiev, Lviv, Kharkiv, Odessa, Donetsk and Dnipropetrovsk.

Folk Dance The inspiration for many Ukrainian ballets was the early folk dances which celebrated the traditions and ceremonies of peasant life. Often accompanied by folk music, many dances symbolised seasonal rituals based on the calendar feasts – *koliada* (winter), *vesnianky* (spring), *kupalo* (summer) and *obzhynky* (autumn or harvest). Combined with incantations *(zamovliannia)* and songs, special dances celebrated the rites of birth, marriage and death. Their themes depicted the complex sociological aspects of village life, from relationships between boys and girls to the coming of age, heroism and feminism. The *hahilky*, famous circle dances performed by girls during Easter, combined the rituals of prayer with the celebration of spring. *Khorovody* dance games stemmed from ancient folk traditions based on courtship and social interaction.

The most famous folk dances were those of the Cossacks. Born from the drunken celebrations which followed successful campaigns, they eventually developed styles and patterns which took on special meanings within the Cossack culture. These movements (like the 'duck-kick') eventually evolved into the famous dances which today so encapsulate the spirit and legend of the Cossacks.

Numerous Ukrainian folk-dance groups perform internationally as well as within the country. One of the best is the folk ensemble Karpatsky Vizerunok from Ivano-Frankivsk. Foreign Ukrainian dance groups, based mostly in Canada and the USA, also perform.

Music

Oral Literature Oral traditions were handed down from generation to generation. Nostalgic fascination for these traditions led to written anthologies of song and dance which became some of the first works published in the Ukrainian language.

Bylyny were lengthy epic narrative poems that told of the strength and courageous deeds of the *bahatyri*, or historic Ukrainian heroes mainly from the Kievan Rus era. They were usually accompanied by harp-like instruments and composed by *druzhyny*, official narrators of the court.

Dumas were long lyrical ballads that glorified the exploits of the Cossacks and were performed by *kobzars*, minstrel-like bards.

Other oral traditions characteristic of certain regional groups grew in fame. The *chumak* songs recounted the tales of the Cossack salt traders. The songs of the *burlaky* (landless peasants) came to be known as the sorrowful expressions of the peasant communities. Fables and proverbs intertwined with nostalgia for a better life.

Bandura & Kobza The heart and soul of Ukrainian folk music lies in the legendary *bandura* or *kobza* player, made famous by Shevchenko's first book of poems entitled *Kobzar* – the name given to a class of wandering minstrels from the 16th and 17th centuries whose songs and ballads were often accompanied by heroic tales and poems, narrated to the accompaniment of the kobza, a lute-like instrument. Welcomed everywhere, the kobza player was the sacred keeper of Ukrainian folklore and Cossack legends – to a Cossack, the kobza was a gift of God. The images of a lone Cossack strumming sentimental tunes over the vast steppe are resonant.

In the 18th century the kobza was replaced by the unrivalled bandura, a larger instrument with up to 45 strings. Popular bandura choirs were formed, accompanied by Ukrainian national songs and folk dances. Inheriting the mythical symbolism of the kobza, the bandura soon became a national symbol, with virtuosos like Ostap Verersai and F Kholodny composing many pieces

The bandura and its precursor, the kobza, have long been the archetypal instruments of Ukrainian folk music

UKRAINE

whose melodies later found their way into orchestras and symphonies. *A Bandura Handbook* by Zinovii Shtokalko, a virtuoso bandurist of the 20th century, is a theoretical study of the technical and cultural aspects of the bandura. The Ukrainian Bandura Chorus, from Kiev, still performs worldwide.

Folk Music From the traditions of the ballad and bandura, folk music became an integral part of the Ukrainian music spectrum, and inspired many of the country's classical composers. Respected today as a viable form of music, many groups with long-standing traditions have come to the fore, in particular the Ukrainian National Orchestra of Folk Instruments. Based in Kiev, they're considered one of the best such groups in the world and utilise a wide array of folk instruments, including the bandura, *sopilka*, *drymba* and *torban*. The Volyn and Transcarpatska folk choirs are also notable, and often perform on home turf. The Hayda Ensemble focuses on the rich folk music from the Carpathian region, while Krajany, a popular Ukrainian folk group out of Kiev, emulates the melodies of the early kobza ensembles. Around Christmas time you're sure to hear the traditional *koliady* or carol concerts.

Classical & Opera Ukrainian classical composer Mykola Diletsky's manual on music theory became the foremost music textbook in all of Ukraine and Russia in the late 17th century. The renowned 18th-century composers Dmytro Bortniansky and Maxym Berezovsky wrote a number of symphonies and operas which were performed in France and Italy to wide acclaim.

However, the best known Ukrainian composer was the legendary Mykola Lysenko, whose works in the late 19th century earned him the title 'father of Ukrainian national music'. His fame lies in his analytical study of Ukrainian folk songs and their application into serious pieces of classical music based on the piano. After his death in 1912, the music academy he founded in Kiev went on to produce many other talented composers.

Composer and conductor Mykola Kolessa gained fame for his mid-20th-century works that combined classical composition with motifs from Carpathian folk songs.

Contemporary composers such as the well-respected Ukrainian-American Virko Baley have done much to promote interest in Ukrainian music. Leading Ukrainian composers today include Bibik, Hrabovsky, Karabyts, Sylvestrov, Skoryk and Stankovych. Top on the list of contemporary Ukrainian classical musicians include cellist Natalie Khomo, virtuoso violinist Oleh Krysa and piano virtuosos Mykola Suk and Volodymyr Vynnytsky.

Opera legend Solomia Krushelnytska mesmerised her audiences during the early part of the 20th century with her leading roles in *Aida*, *Madam Butterfly* and the Ukrainian operetta *Zaporizhzhets za Dunayem*. Ukrainian operettas, which combine more acting and dancing than typical operas, are popular classics often performed at the Ukraine's six ballet and opera theatres. Michel Volkovytsky, artistic director of the Shevchenko National Opera in Kiev, has worked internationally and received recent acclaim for his production of Antin Rudnytsky's opera *Anna Yaroslavna*, which featured two of Ukraine's leading opera singers, V Pyvovarov and L Zabiliasta.

Rock & Jazz The former symbol of rebellious and dissident youth, rock culture in Ukraine is becoming more established and varied. Jazz seems less popular, but is still in circulation. The influx of Western music is no longer limited to the black market – nearly every street corner has a blaring kiosk selling a selection of bootleg copies. The music scene is varied, but still disorganised, with events being staged with little or no prior advertising. Two bands to look out for are Nebo Rock, a sort of avant-garde experimental jazz ensemble, and Plach Yeremiyi, a high-energy semipunk band. Singer-songwriter Nina Matvienko, a folk singer who draws heavily on ancient Ukrainian folk songs, is hugely popular; she won the prestigious Shevchenko Prize for the performing arts in 1988.

Architecture

Domestic When analysing architectural history or style, the predominant themes are usually the architecture of the Church, royalty and nobility, and not the typical wooden village house, which changed relatively little over the centuries. Yet much can be said about this tiny functional microcosm, and a visit to one of the many open-air architecture museums will show you their subtle variety and rich detail, providing a valuable insight into the daily life of days gone by. Typically, the wooden house, with a steeply thatched roof, had two rooms – one for sleeping and one for preparing food and eating – both on either side of an entry space and often entered off a fenced courtyard or wooden porch. This vernacular architecture can still be seen in some parts of the countryside, but prefabricated masonry construction has in recent years become the predominant technique of house construction.

Wooden Churches A unique genre of architecture worth special mention is the highly developed Ukrainian wooden church – a testament to ingenious vernacular artistry, proportion and environmental harmony. Typical features included gable construction with a pyramidal roof composed of octagonal tiers. Provincial church roofs varied from two to four-tiered, but the skill of some carpenters extended to five or even seven tiers capped with wooden-shingled onion domes and cupolas – such as St Nicholas' Church in the Lviv open-air museum and St George's Church in Drohobych. The roof eaves were overhung to cover low porches and often a number of smaller open galleries wrapped around the outside of the lower roof tiers. A steep-roofed, free-standing bell tower within the fenced-in grounds was also typical. The verticality of the tiered roofs and steepness of the gables varied with locations and climatic conditions. Some wooden churches even developed sophisticated side chapels and apses which contrasted with the traditionally more simple designs. Nails were rarely used in the construction, which consisted entirely of a complex system of wood joinery. For the best selection and variety of wooden churches, visit one of the delightful open-air museums of folk architecture, where you'll get to wander around re-created villages of wooden buildings and churches set in picturesque surroundings. The best of these museums are in Kiev, Lviv, Uzhhorod and Pereyeslav-Khmelnytsky.

Kievan Rus Kievan Rus adopted the cruciform church plan developed in Constantinople in the 9th century. At its simplest, this consisted of three parallel aisles (a small aisle on either side of the central aisle, or nave), each with an eastern apse ending in a semicircle, crossed by another aisle and a dome or cupola rising out of the intersection – basically a crucifix shape centred on the dome. Lesser domes might top the four arms of the cross or the corners of the building. The pinnacle of this achievement is displayed in St Sophia in Kiev, with two aisles on either side of the central nave (later doubled), five apses on its eastern side and 13 cupolas, with a pyramidal arrangement topping it all off. The Transfiguration Cathedral in Chernihiv is another example of early Byzantine architecture, with two side bell towers added later. Four other Byzantine cathedrals from the 11th and 12th centuries were destroyed in Kiev in the 1930s by Soviet authorities, the most prominent of which was St Michael's Golden Domed Monastery.

Variations to this basic design ensued, either for ornamental or functional reasons. Besides the central or twin bell towers flanking the entrance, rows of apses along the exterior north and south sides were added, which opened up into side chapels in the interior. Architectural influence from local wooden churches created a distinct Ukrainian-Byzantine mould. The Trinity and All Saints churches in the Caves Monastery in Kiev are high expressions of this style.

After the focus of Ukrainian culture moved to the west in the Galician-Volynian Principality, a more stoic castle-like architecture developed during the 14th century. Built of stone and with a primary function of defence, the imposing fortresses at Kamyanets-Podilsky, Khotyn and Lutsk are impressive examples. Even church architecture took on a fortress-like form, with the fortified monastery at Mezhyrich a direct descendant.

Renaissance The Renaissance influence of the 16th century was felt predominantly in the western region of Ukraine. Many of the castles were reworked with Renaissance detailing, including the addition of blind arcading – wall or tower ornamentation resembling a row of arches, as evident in Ostroh and Berezhany. The real hotbed of Renaissance architecture was Lviv, many of its buildings designed by Italian architects who used elements of Ukrainian Byzantine traditions – exemplified in the Dormition Cathedral with its Kornyakt Tower and Three Saints Chapel. The majority of buildings lining the ploshcha Rynok, as well as the ornate Boyim chapel in Lviv, are all purely proportioned Renaissance façades.

Baroque The late Renaissance blended with the early Baroque, adding curving lines and dynamic detailing as in the Jesuit College in Lviv. Pure Baroque design was used in palaces like the Mariyinsky Palace in Kiev, while church design developed into what is known as Ukrainian Baroque, a synthesis of Baroque detailing with Byzantine plan and massing. This style, with the green helmet-shaped dome as its trademark, developed as the predominant mode of design in the 17th and 18th centuries. St Sophia and St Cyril's in Kiev were remodelled and hundreds of new churches were designed – typified by St George's Cathedral in the Vydubytsky Monastery in Kiev, St Nicholas' Cathedral in Nizhyn and the most stylised version of all (bordering on Rococo), St Andrew's in Kiev, designed by the great Rastrelli. An equally stylised version of Ukrainian Baroque, with an emphasis on sculptural quality, is St George's Cathedral in Lviv. Perhaps the highest level of refinement of all examples of Ukrainian Baroque is found in the great

Uspensky Cathedral of the Pochayiv Monastery.

Some Ukrainian Baroque also combined features of traditional wooden architecture such as a colonnaded porch and free-standing belfries. Examples include the Church of the Nativity of the Virgin in the Caves Monastery, the Pokrovska Cathedral in Kharkiv and many of Kiev's churches in the Podil district, including the small, but lovely, Chapel-Church of Mykola Dobry.

Classicism The severity of the classical style, based on the simplistic geometry of Greek and Roman antiquity, imposed a restraining order on the exuberance of the Ukrainian Baroque of the 17th century. Brought on by the classically minded planning of St Petersburg, city planners in Ukraine followed suit, with the Khrula ploshcha (Round Square) in Poltava an excellent example. The Podil quarter of Kiev was redesigned according to a grid plan, and the city centres of newly developed cities like Odessa, where rational classical planning reached perfection with the grand Potemkin steps, were strongly influenced by classicism. Many buildings followed suit: the city halls in Lviv and Kolomyya, the University of Kiev, the bell tower of Kharkiv's Uspensky Cathedral, Odessa's Vorontsov Palace and the formal gardens of the Arboretum in Uman.

Revivals & Early 20th Century A series of architectural revivals developed at the end of the 19th century. St Volodymyr's Cathedral in Kiev revived ancient Ukrainian Byzantine traditions, while a number of opera houses, notably those in Kiev, Odessa and Lviv, were designed in a Renaissance revivalist mode with the addition of heavy Baroque and classical detailing – a Habsburg favourite.

A modern Ukrainian style based on Art Nouveau featured in the design of the Regional Museum Building in Poltava and the fantastically eclectic Metropolitan Palace and present-day university complex in Chernivtsi.

Soviet Era The beginnings of Soviet idealism were manifested in a stern Constructivist style, typified by Kharkiv's House of State Industry and university buildings surrounding the vast ploshcha Svobody. Soviet authority soon found a better expression in an inflated revivalist style known as Monumental Classicism, where enormous temple-like edifices were erected to house the notorious committees and ministries of the State. Kiev is full of these buildings – the Ministry of Foreign Affairs and Presidential Administration buildings are the most imposing. Eventually, all sense of aesthetics was lost when postwar development, in the name of the International Style (coined by German guru Mies van der Rohe), saw the mushrooming of unsightly housing blocks encroaching on and choking the outskirts of most cities.

By far the most architectural mayhem occurred in the early 1930s, when the Soviet regime, in an attempt to destroy Ukraine's national identity, demolished some of the country's most sacred buildings. Over 250 churches, cathedrals, cemeteries and palaces were obliterated, including historic cathedrals in cities like Poltava, Ternopil and Odessa. Kiev suffered the worst – no less than four 12th-century cathedrals that had withstood centuries of wars, fires and famine fell overnight to the Soviet wrecking ball. St Sophia in Kiev was also slated for destruction, and were it not for the convincing pleas from international organisations, it too would have been lost.

Visual Arts

Icons Religious art dominated all art well up to the 17th century, with its key expression being the icon – small holy images painted on limewood panels with tempera paint mixed with egg yolk and hot wax. Brought to Ukraine by Prince Volodymyr from the Greek Byzantine settlement of Chersonesus in Crimea, the icons were instantly attributed with healing and spiritual powers. Icon painters, mostly monks, developed strict codes of conformity, rarely ever signing their work, and depicting only Christ, the Virgin,

angels and saints. A Kiev school of iconography was set up during the 11th century at the Caves Monastery, its leading artists being Alimpy and Hryhorii, both of whom are entombed in the monastery's caves. Other schools were soon founded, in Zhovkva and Lviv, where the icon painters cultivated a less Byzantine and more European style, with the addition of landscapes and small narrative scenes. The development of the iconostasis – a tall screen lined with symbolic rows of icons, separating the altar from the congregation – increased the production of icons, with thousands created for hundreds of churches every year well up to the 18th century. For a look at some historic Ukrainian icons, see the National Museum in Lviv or the Museum of Ukrainian Fine Arts in Kiev.

Church murals, mosaics and frescoes, as well as manuscript illuminations, developed at the same time as the icon, and played an important role in the evolution of art in Ukraine. Some of the oldest frescoes are found in Kiev's St Sophia Cathedral, and almost all Orthodox church interiors are a parade of colourful wall paintings – some of the most striking are in Kiev's St Volodymyr's Cathedral.

Romanticism The first break from religious art occurred during the Cossack Hetmanate, with the beginnings of portrait painting (based on icon techniques). A secular, romantic trend of folk painting slowly developed, a common theme being the Kozak Mamay, or Cossack playing a bandura or kobza. Romanticism developed simultaneously with the national literary revival of the late 19th century. The massive output of over 1000 artistic works by the national poet Shevchenko (who was trained as an artist) began a trend towards a simplistic realism based on the romanticised themes of country life and folk traditions. Numerous artists emerged. Most remained unknown, but some, including Ukrainian-born artists Nikolai Ge and Ilya Repin (famous for his work *Zaporizky Cossacks Writing a Letter to the Turkish Sultan*) and others involved in the Peredvizhniki movement, drew international fame. Less well known but equally talented artists included romanticist F Krasyntsky, the symbolic O Novakivsky, and the expressive I Trush, whose beautiful images evoked a nostalgia that bordered on Impressionism. For a good look into the mass of Romantic work produced in Ukraine during the late 19th century, visit the art museums in Odessa and Kharkiv, as well as the National Museum in Lviv and the Museum of Ukrainian Fine Arts in Kiev.

Graphic Art The increased use of printing techniques including woodcuts and metal etching was propagated by an 1844 series of etchings by Shevchenko entitled *Zhyvopysna Ukraina (Picturesque Ukraine)*. Artists included the experimental Yuri Narbut and Olena Kulchystska, who concentrated on children's books and cultivated a highly sophisticated graphic-art movement based stylistically on Art-Nouveau aesthetics but applied to a Ukrainian national style.

Modern Styles The 1930s marked the emergence of a wide variety of styles in Ukrainian art, ranging from Impressionism to futurism, cubism and constructivism. Although the techniques and interpretations of aesthetics differed with each style, it's interesting to note that the majority of Ukrainian artists stuck to the similar themes of national folk culture developed by the Romantics a generation before. Fundamental to all new movements in Ukraine was the desire to develop a national consciousness and style rooted in traditions but experimental in technique. The work by M Boichuk, trained in Western Europe, stands out. His mural-style paintings, which blended modern trends with ancient Kievan and Italian Renaissance imagery, were considered too nationalistic for the authorities. He was subsequently sent to Siberia, where he was executed with his wife in 1937, and most of his works were destroyed.

Soviet Era The Soviet era had only one official art movement: Socialist Realism. This style was a method of propagating Soviet ideals – the industrialised peasant, the muscular worker and the glories of Soviet heroes. Although it imposed severe limitations on creativity, it produced some technically talented compositions, the best and worst examples often found in sculptural form. Both extremes are illustrated in Kiev's Museum of the Great Patriotic War, where the towering 'tin lady' is a blatant shock of bad taste, while nearby a series of sculptural relief work shows Social Realism with a highly developed sense of expression.

Those who didn't follow the State's accepted norms either emigrated or were disposed of. Ukrainian artists A Horska, O Zalyvakha and S Shabaitura were imprisoned and exiled during the 1970s, and Horska was executed.

Since independence, Ukrainian art has enjoyed a reawakening of style revivals, with the Academy of Fine Arts in both Kiev and Lviv producing new young artists, whose themes often combine the political and economic upheavals of the day. Some of the better known contemporary Ukrainian artists include Hlib Visheslavsky from Kiev and Vasyl Ryabchenko from Odessa, both of whose works are known in the West. Most art museums have temporary galleries which host a number of local artists – the best selection is in the large Ukrainsky Dim (Ukrainian House) in Kiev, a multimedia exhibition hall with four floors of temporary exhibits.

Folk Art In the midst of Soviet rule, the age-old traditions of folk art were seen as a type of nationalistic expression. The folk-art academies established in Kosiv, Rivne and Lviv, among other places, were seen as subversive hotbeds of dissident activism. The authorities even went so far as to impose temporary bans on folk embroidery.

Folk art in Ukraine is among the richest and most highly developed in the world, and is a highly regarded tradition among Ukrainians. Visit one of the many ethnographic museums for a good look at the wide variety of folk traditions. Some of the best are the

Folk art such as this woodcut from the 1949 series 'Ideals of the Ukrainian Liberation Movement' displayed a bold style and a strongly nationalistic message

Ethnographic Museum in Lviv, the Ukrainian Folk Decorative Art Museum in the Caves Monastery in Kiev, the Museum of Hutzul Folk Art in Kolomyya and the interiors of many folk houses in the numerous open-air architectural museums. For more details of folk and applied art, including *pysanky* (painted eggs), embroidery and woodwork, see the Things to Buy section in Ukraine Facts for the Visitor.

Film

A Fedetsky's early films *Train Arriving at Kharkiv Station* (1896) and *Dancing in Kinna Square* (1897) were landmark productions in early motion-picture experimentation. The first film studios in Ukraine were established in Kiev and Odessa in 1915, with the original screen production of the famous novel by Kotlarevsky, *Natalka Poltavka*, acted by the beloved actress Natalia Lissenko.

In 1924 one of the largest film studios in Eastern Europe, the Film Institute, was established in Kiev, and along with the Cinema School in Odessa included 25 independent film companies. The films produced during its short (six-year) heyday are considered some of the masterpieces of the silent-film era. Cinema giants included the Russian Sergey Eisenstein and the Ukrainian Alexander Dovzhenko, whose 1930 film *Zemlia (The Earth)* is a milestone of achievement and rated as one of the greatest films in the history of cinematography. Other acclaimed films by Dovzhenko were *Zvenyhora* (1927) and *Arsenal* (1929). These, along with *Zemlia*, were probing cinematic parables which dealt with the effects of the revolution in Ukraine.

During the Soviet era, Ukrainian cinema all but disappeared, until a revival in the 1950s saw the production of a number of documentary films based on historic Ukrainian themes and characters, such as Serhii Bondarchuk's documentary *Taras Shevchenko* in 1951. Slavko Novytsky, who emigrated to Canada in 1950, became the leading name during this time, producing documentaries ranging from *Pysanka: the Ukrainian Easter Egg*, a highly praised art documentary, to the moving *The Harvest of Despair* (1972), a shocking portrayal of the 1932-33 famine which won acclaim at the New York Film Festival.

The very gifted Serhii Paradzhanov, who died in 1990, produced his first film in 1965. Called *Shadows of Forgotten Ancestors*, it was based on a Kotsiubynsky novel about feudal Carpathian Ukraine, and featured dynamic film techniques and hypersensationalism. The work was spurned by the authorities but well received internationally. Jailed in the 1970s, Paradzhanov emerged to continue his work. In his last film, *Ashik Kerib* (1988), his hero flees through Transcaucasia after a rash love affair with a young Turkish woman.

The International Film Festival held in Kiev during the last week of October is a recent tradition that's bringing exposure to a swag of young, upcoming Ukrainian film

UKRAINE

directors. Yuri Illienko and I Hrabovsky are two of the better-established names.

RELIGION
Ukrainian Orthodox Church

Prior to independence, all Orthodox churches in Ukraine were banned except for the official Russian Orthodox Church. In 1990 the Ukrainian section of the Church was renamed the Ukrainian Orthodox Church (UOC), while still paying allegiance to the Moscow Patriarchate, and the metropolitan of Kiev was given semiautonomous authority. The Caves Monastery in Kiev belongs to this Church.

Ukrainian Autocephalous Orthodox Church

In 1686, the Orthodox Church in Ukraine was forced to recognise authority from Moscow, rather than Kiev, issuing in a long period of control by the Russian Orthodox Church. The Church was re-established in 1921 in a brief flowering of Ukrainian identity, and was known as the Ukrainian Autocephalous Orthodox Church (UAOC). In 1930 it was once again forced into the Russian Orthodox fold, although it secretly continued to practise. The Church shares identical practices with the other Orthodox churches, but its allegiance is to the Ukrainian Patriarchate in Kiev. Services are strictly in the Ukrainian language, and church hierarchy differs from that of the Russian Orthodox Church. In 1990 the Church was fully revived and has since drawn many followers.

For more on the history and practices of the Eastern Orthodox churches, see Religion in Facts about European Russia.

Uniate Church

Often referred to as Ukrainian Catholic or Greek Catholic, the Uniate Church is essentially the 'union' or combination of the Catholic and Orthodox churches which fatefully separated in 1054. The Uniate Church service follows Orthodox worship and ritual, but it recognises the Roman pope as its leader and doctrinal authority. The church was formed, largely for political reasons, at the Union of Brest in 1596 (see History), and abolished by Stalin in 1946, with all of its property confiscated or handed over to the Russian Orthodox Church. It survived underground, holding clandestine services in forests, and re-emerged in the late 1980s as a leader in the national drive for independence. The Church is heavily concentrated in the west of the country, and Uniate priests are the only Catholic priests in the world allowed to marry.

Other Religions

Most cities include a Polish Roman Catholic church as well as a Protestant church. Small Jewish minorities exist in all cities and Muslim communities, primarily Tatars, exist in Crimea.

LANGUAGE

Ukrainian, like Russian and Belarusian, is an Eastern Slavic language, and is arguably the closest of the three to the original 9th-century Slavonic used in Kiev before the more formal Church Slavonic from Bulgaria was introduced with Christianity in the 10th century. Because of Ukraine's history of domination by outside powers, the language was often considered inferior or subservient to the dominant language of the time – in the east, to Russian; in the west, Polish. In 1876 Tsar Alexander II forbade schooling in Ukrainian and banned all Ukrainian books and publishing, setting a precedent of Russification which has carried down to some degree to the present day. Yet, as in all communities struggling for independence and national identity, the concept of language is held sacred in Ukraine, and each successive national revival has taken it as a rallying-point.

Today, the Ukrainian language is slowly being revived, and in 1990 it was adopted as the official language. The western and eastern accents differ, with various dialects in the Carpathians. Russian is still spoken predominantly in the east and south, where over half the Ukrainians are relearning their own language. Crimea is almost entirely

Russian-speaking. Russian is understood everywhere by everyone, so although it may be diplomatic and polite to speak Ukrainian (especially in the west), you'll have no problem being understood if you speak Russian.

Books

If you have no knowledge of Ukrainian or Russian it would be wise to bring along a dictionary or phrasebook. Lonely Planet publishes detailed and useful phrasebooks to both languages.

Alphabet & Pronunciation

Around 70% of the Ukrainian language is identical or similar to Russian and Belarusian. It is written in the Cyrillic alphabet, using three additional letters not found in Russian, i, ї, and є, all of which are neutral vowel sounds (the Russian letter о is often replaced by a Ukrainian i). The Ukrainian г usually has a soft *h* sound. (See also the alphabet charts in Appendix I at the back of the book.) These differences between the two languages are sometimes quite simple in practice: for example, the town of Chernigov in Russian is Chernihiv in Ukrainian. Overall, Ukrainian is softer sounding and less guttural than Russian.

The -я *(-ya)* ending for nouns and names in Russian (especially street names) is dropped in Ukrainian, and we transliterate the letter и as *y* in Ukrainian, whereas in Russian we transliterate и as *i*. Hence, for example, a street named Deribasovskaya in Russian would be Derybasivska in Ukrainian.

The Ukrainian alphabet doesn't include the letters ё, ы and э, and has no hard sign, ъ, although it does include the soft sign, ь.

Useful Words & Phrases

yes
tak
так

no
nee
ні

Good day/hello.
DO-bree dehn
Добрий день.

Good morning.
DO-bree RAH-nok
Добрий ранок.

Good night.
DO-bree VEH-chir
Добрий вечір.

How are you?
yak zhih-VESH?
Як живеш?

Goodbye.
do po-BAH-chen-nya
До побачення.

Thank you (very much).
DYA-koo-yoo (DOO-zheh)
Дякую (дуже).

Please.
PRO-shoo (in the west),
bood LAHS-kah (in the east)
прошу, будь ласка

Pardon me.
peh-reh-PRO-sho-yoo
Перепрошую.

good/OK
DOB-reh
добре

bad
po-HAH-no
погано

when, where
ko-lih, deh
коли, де

here, there
toot, tahm
тут, там

I don't understand you.
ya neh ro-zoo-MEE-yu vahs.
Я не розумію вас.

I don't understand Ukrainian.
ya neh ro-zoo-MEE-yu
poh-oo-krah-YEEN-skih
Я не розумію по-Українськи.

Do you speak English?
chih vih ho-VO-rih-teh
poh-ahn-HLEEY-skih?
Чи ви говорите по-Англійськи?

I wish to extend my visa.
ya KHO-choo pro-DOV-zhi-ti VI-zoo
Я хочу продовжити візу.
I want (I'd like)...
ya KHO-choo...
Я хочу...
Where can I...?
deh MOZH-nah...?
Де можна...?

Getting Around
Where is the railway station?
deh vohk-ZAL?
Де вокзал?
Where is the bus station?
deh av-to-vohk-ZAL?
Де автовокзал?
Where is the...stop?
deh zoo-PIN-kah...?
Де зупинка...?
tram
trahm-VAH-yoo
трамваю
trolleybus
tro-LEY-boo-sah
тролейбуса
bus
ahv-TO-boo-sah
автобуса
metro
meh-TRO
метро

Accommodation & Food
Where is the hotel?
deh hos-tihn-NEETS-yah (HO-tehl)?
Де гостинниця (готель)?

Where is a restaurant?
deh rehs-to-RAHN?
Де ресторан?
Where is the toilet?
deh too-ah-LEHT?
Де туалет?

Shopping
Do you have...?
chih yeh oo vahs...?
Чи є у вас...?
I need...
meh-NEE TREH-bah...
Мені треба...
How much?
SKEEL-kih?
Скільки?
How much does this cost?
SKEEL-kih tseh kosh-TOO-yeh?
Скільки це коштує?

For information on the Russian language, plus words and phrases, see Facts about European Russia.

In the west, almost all street signs have been changed to Ukrainian, although not all maps have been updated. In the east, in cities such as Kharkiv, street signs are sometimes in Russian, sometimes Ukrainian, and sometimes both. In those cities where this may cause confusion, we give both. In Crimea we use a mixture, using the street name that is being predominantly used (mostly Russian), but putting the Ukrainian address term – for example, *vulitsya* for street, not *ulitsa*, and *ploshcha* for square, not *ploshchad*.

Facts for the Visitor

VISAS & EMBASSIES

Visas

All foreigners visiting Ukraine need visas, which are issued only by consular offices. 'Emergency' visas are obtainable at border points and a one-month visa can be obtained on the spot at the Boryspil Airport in Kiev (see the Emergency Visas section later in this chapter for details). The visa is stamped into your passport, and does not include other documentation. The requirements for visas applied for in advance are as follows:

- A valid passport, re-entry permit or refugee travel document. The expiration date of your passport should extend for at least one month beyond the date you intend to leave Ukraine. It's a good idea to get some photocopies of the pages containing personal and validity details.
- An official invitation from Ukraine or a hotel confirmation from a travel agency. This extra hassle was supposedly set up to combat the Mafia and other undesirable prospectors from crossing the border for quick deals, although it seems the people it mainly affects are potential tourists. See the Getting the Invitation section.
- One completed visa application form with affixed passport-size photograph. The form can be obtained at any Ukrainian consulate or embassy or can be faxed to you on the same day. The form is basically 12 simple identification questions, including purpose of travel (see Types of Visa), length of stay and proposed destinations. To be on the safe side, overestimate your intended length of stay. Travel is free and you're not limited to the destinations you state, but you should list only the places for which you have hotel vouchers, or the destination of your invitation. Take several extra photos with you, and make sure they look similar to the one on your passport. It's also best not to make radical changes in your appearance between photo time and your arrival in Ukraine. George got hassled for a while trying to leave the country because his aged passport showed him clean-shaven with long hair, but at the time he had a beard and short hair!

It's possible to get all this done by mail, including self-addressed stamped envelopes with requested forms, completed documents and required payment.

Types of Visa The type of visa you receive depends on what you state on your application form under 'purpose of travel' – either business, private, tourist or transit. All visas are invalid once you leave the country, unless you apply for a multiple-entry visa.

Any visa can be extended once you're in the country by applying at the passport office (OVIR) of the Ministry of Internal Affairs. See the Visa Extensions section. For further enquiries and the latest information, contact the nearest Ukraine embassy.

Business Visa A business visa requires an official invitation from a business contact in Ukraine, and is valid for a maximum of three months unless a multiple-entry visa is requested. The regular processing fee is US$30 (within nine business days), US$60 for rush processing (within three days) and US$100 for express (same-day) service. There are no travel restrictions.

Private Visa A private visa is valid for a maximum of three months, unless you apply for a multiple-entry visa, and requires an official invitation from a private party (person or organisation) in Ukraine. Prices are the same as for a business visa. There are no travel restrictions.

Tourist Visa A tourist visa is valid for a maximum of three months unless you apply for a multiple-entry visa. Basically, it's identical to a private visa but your invitation comes not from a private individual but in the form of a hotel or tour confirmation from a travel agency inside or outside Ukraine. Prices are the same as for a business visa. There are no travel restrictions, except for those imposed by your tour arrangements.

Transit Visa Basically, this is a visa allowing you to cross the country en route to another country – from Hungary to Russia for example. If you apply for one in advance you don't need an invitation or hotel confirmation, but you must send or show a copy of your train ticket and visa into the country of destination. The fee is US$15 for regular processing (within nine business days) and US$30 for express (same-day) service. A transit visa is valid for only 72 hours. It's possible to get an emergency visa at the border, also valid for 72 hours and basically the same as a transit visa.

Multiple-Entry Visa A multiple-entry visa can be applied to any visa and is valid for six months, costing US$120 for regular processing or US$240 for express processing. You can also apply for a dual-entry visa, costing US$60/120 for regular/express processing. The decision to award a multiple-entry visa supposedly rests with the Ukrainian Foreign Ministry, and you usually require a good reason for needing one, generally for business.

Emergency Visas Visas are issued at official border crossings for those who cross without one. These so-called 'emergency visas' cost US$50 and are good for only 72 hours, but you can get them extended at the passport office (OVIR) of the Ministry of Internal Affairs in Kiev or Lviv. Below is a description of the process according to method of entry.

If you fly into **Kiev's Boryspil Airport** without a visa, you can easily get one on the spot for a up to a month. This is absolutely the easiest method of entry. To receive your visa, you have to fill out a basic form and wait in two lines, one to pay the US$50 visa fee, then another for the additional voucher fee, which varies in price depending on how long you want your visa for – US$20 for one to seven days, US$30 for eight to 15 days, US$40 for 16 to 21 days and US$50 for 22 to 30 days (maximum). After receiving your visa (usually taking about one hour), you have to fill out a customs form before you're allowed to pass through.

If you cross into Ukraine **by rail** without a visa, the process involves a few antics. The visas issued at rail border stops are US$50

for a maximum of 72 hours – enough time for passing through but hardly enough for anything else. If you're late in leaving, you'll get hit with a fine.

Here's the procedure: your passport will be taken from you and you'll be escorted off the train to a stuffy passport-control waiting room with an endless stream of border guards and militiamen shaking hands with each other. You fill out a form, take another to a nearby bank to pay US$50, return the receipt and wait, before finally receiving your visa – at which time you hope the train hasn't already left. (At the Chop border crossing with Slovakia the train may have disappeared to change rail gauges – but it will return.) Apparently, the Polish and Slovakian borders are the smoothest. If the rare occasion arises when you and the border guard simply don't seem to get along, you can demand: 'I want to contact my consulate', *'ya KHO-choo zvee-ya-ZAH-tihs z mo-YEEM KON-sool-stvom'*.

If you're planning on entering Ukraine **from Russia** it's probably a good idea to get your Ukraine visa before you enter Russia, as procedures at the Ukraine embassy in Moscow can be lengthy and complicated. **Bus crossings**, most commonly from Slovakia, follow the same basic procedure.

Getting the Invitation The easiest way to get an invitation *(zaproshennya)* is if you have a friend, relative or contact in Ukraine who could send or fax the document, which they obtain through their local visa office (OVIR) of the Ministry of Internal Affairs.

But for the majority who don't have the option, this bureaucratic task can easily be taken care of by a travel agent who deals with travel in Ukraine (see Travel Agencies in the Ukraine Getting There & Away chapter). Agents can usually get an invitation for a private visa for up to one month, provided (here's the catch) you buy airline tickets from them. Otherwise, they can book you a prepaid hotel confirmation, necessary for a tourist visa, also up to one month. You don't need to have hotels reserved for the entire duration of your stay, just for the first few days. This can also be done personally, by contacting a hotel in Ukraine and having them send you the necessary confirmation. It's possible as well (with a relative degree of hassle) to get a visa without an invitation, at the border, and then extend it once you're in the country (see the following sections). Travel within the country is free and unrestricted, except for the city of Sevastopol and the usual military bases.

Visa Extensions

To have your emergency visa, or any visa, extended to a maximum of two months, you have to go to the passport and registration office of the Ministry of Internal Affairs, called OVIR (open weekdays only, usually from 9 or 10 am to 5 pm, closing at noon on Friday). Although there are local offices in every city, this procedure is best done in either Kiev or Lviv; Kiev can be very busy and hectic.

Kiev
   Vulitsya Bohomoltsa 10 (☎ (044) 291 18 30)
Lviv
   Vulitsya Rudanskoho 3, 3rd floor, right behind the Hotel Zhorzh

After you tell them you wish to extend your visa (see the Language section in Facts about Ukraine), and for how long (two months maximum), they'll give you a piece of paper with a few numbers on it. You'll then have to do a small bureaucratic tango – go to a specified bank and fill out a small form (place the numbers given to you on the form and scribble your name, address, etc), pay a minimal fee (about US$0.50), get a crucial stamp, then return the form to the OVIR office and pay a US$10 processing fee. You can usually have the entire process finished in a few hours if you're lucky and smile a lot. Seek help at the tourist office in the Hotel Zhorzh (Lviv), or Kievska Hotel (Kiev) if you have trouble.

Lost or Stolen Documents

Your embassy or consulate in Ukraine (see the Kiev chapter) can replace a lost passport, but to replace your visa you'll have to go to the OVIR office. Your hotel service bureau may be able to help. Both procedures are much easier if you've stashed a few passport-size photos, your visa number and photocopies of important pages from your passport.

Ukrainian Embassies & Consulates

Ukrainian representatives in other countries include:

Australia
   Consulate: 4 Bloom St, Moonee Ponds 3039 (☎ (03) 9320 0135; fax (03) 9326 0139)
Austria
   Elisabethstrasse 13, 1010 Vienna (☎ (0222) 586 9717; fax (0222) 586 3424)
Belarus
   vulitsa Kirava 17-306, Minsk (☎ (0172) 27 23 54; fax (0172) 27 28 61)
Canada
   331 Metcalfe St, Ottawa, Ont K2P 1S3 (☎ (613) 230 2961; fax (613) 230 2400)
Czech Republic
   Korunovační 34, Prague 6 (☎ (02) 37 43 66)
Finland
   Punavourenkatu, 21C, 00151 Helsinki (☎ (90) 608 563; fax (90) 607 968)
France
   21 Ave de Saxe, 75007 Paris (☎ (1) 43 06 07 37; fax (1) 43 06 02 94)
Germany
   Waldstrasse 42, 5300 Bonn 2 (☎ (0228) 31 21 39; fax (0228) 31 83 51)
   Consulate: Pienzenauerstrasse 15, 8000 Munich 80 (☎ (089) 982 87 71; fax (089) 982 71 71)
Greece
   33 Athens St, 15457 Neopsychikon, Athens (☎ (0) 671 8957; fax (0) 671 66 52)
Hungary
   H 1062, Budapest, Ut Nogradi 8 (☎ (1) 155 24 43; fax (1) 202 22 87)
Israel
   12 Stricker St, 62006 Tel Aviv (☎ (03) 604 01 41; fax (03) 604 25 12)
Italy
   Via Bastelfidardo 50, Roma 00185 (☎ (06) 447 00 172; fax (06) 447 00 181)
Poland
   Aleja Szucha 7, Warsaw (☎ (22) 625 0127; fax (22) 625 3230)
Romania
   Bucharest, Sector 1, Str Rabat 1 (☎ (4) 312 4514; fax (4) 312 4547)

UKRAINE

Russia
>   Leontevsky pereulok (formerly ulitsa Stanislavskogo) 18 (☎ (095) 229 10 79, 229 07 84, 229 91 60)

Turkey
>   Sheraton Hotel, Ankara (☎ (4) 68 54 54; fax (4) 67 11 36)

UK
>   78 Kensington Park Rd, London W11 2PL (☎ (0171) 727 6312; fax (0171) 792 1708)

USA
>   3350 M St, NW, Washington DC 20007 (☎ (202) 333 7507/08/09; fax (202) 333 7510)
>   Consulate: 240 East 49th St, New York, NY 10017 (☎ (212) 371 5690; fax (212) 371 5547)
>   Consulate: 10 East Huron St, Chicago, Ill 60611 (☎(312) 384 6032; fax (312) 642 4385)

Yugoslavia
>   Ulica Beligradska br 32, 11000 Belgrad (☎ (011) 65 75 33)

DOCUMENTS

Besides your passport with visa, documents you may need include:

* Vouchers: if you've prepaid accommodation through a travel agency prior to departure, hold on to all vouchers and receipts.
* Customs Declaration: this is as valuable as your visa. That small piece of paper you filled out and had stamped when you entered (see Customs) will be asked for when you leave – keep it safe.
* Receipts: save receipts for all currency exchanges, purchases of souvenirs, and hotel receipts. Officials rarely ask to see them, but it's always a good idea to have proof handy just in case.
* Hotel Pass: when you check in, most hotels hand you a little card with your room number on it. This gets you in and out of the hotel and procures your key.
* Driver's Documents: if you're driving your own vehicle you should keep your International Driving Permit, proof of insurance and registration handy. If renting, keep your rental agreement handy.
* Health Certificates: travellers coming from Asia and Africa, and possibly Latin America, may need smallpox and cholera vaccination certificates. Anyone requiring medication containing a narcotic drug should have a doctor's certificate. Foreigners planning to live in Ukraine for over three months may be required to have an AIDS test.
* Personal IDs: bring a few other photo IDs to prove you are actually the person in your passport.

CUSTOMS

When you arrive (or prior to arriving if travelling by train) you'll be given a small customs declaration form *(deklaratsia)* to fill out. On the train they often don't have one in English. If this is the case, the first six lines ask: your name, nationality, the country you are coming from, the country you are entering, purpose of visit and number of luggage items. The next six items labelled with Roman numerals ask you what you're bringing into the country. Put 'No' for the first four, which ask if you have any firearms, narcotics, antiques or Ukrainian currency or bonds. List all the money you have in all currencies in the following larger box. Finally, the last line asks if you're carrying anything for someone else. Put 'No'. Sign and date the form. On the back, list all the valuables you have, including major pieces of jewellery and cameras.

This form will be checked, stamped and handed back to you. When you leave the country, you'll have to fill out another identical form, which, along with your original, you hand over to the customs official.

What You Can Bring In

You can bring in any item for personal use as long as it isn't illegal drugs or weapons. For items not intended for personal use, you may have to pay a duty on anything over the following limits: 1.5 litres of hard alcohol, 2.1 litres of wine, up to 100 cigarettes, and any items or gifts (excluding alcohol, wine and tobacco) exceeding a total of US$5000 or 200 grams per person.

What You Can Take Out

Anything from a tourist shop (like Ukrainsky Suvenir) or gift shop is OK (but remember to save the receipts).

You're also not allowed to take out works of art or cultural/historical treasures without special permission from the Ministry of Culture (☎ (044) 224 49 11), located on vulitsya Ivana Franka 19 in Kiev. They've been especially cracking down on antique icons, which are apparently a hot item.

Certain consumer goods are officially not

supposed to be taken out of the country (except if bought in a tourist or gift shop for foreign currency), including jewellery made of precious metals or gems, household appliances, electronic equipment, tools, furs, meat or canned dairy products, and narcotics and military equipment (no nukes).

Duties are imposed on all items exported that are intended to be used to make a profit (whatever that means).

Officially, you can't take out more money than your customs form shows you came in with.

Lost Deklaratsia

If you lose your deklaratsia, your embassy can give you a letter to Central Customs (☎ (044) 446 51 86) provulok Politekhnichny 4A, Kiev, requesting a replacement. If you can't get one or just can't find it at the moment, arrange to have (or don't expose more than) the absolute minimum of hard-currency cash when you leave, and hope the customs inspector will let you just fill out another. The local Kiev customs office (☎ (044) 229 51 71, 229 78 92) is at vulitsya Reytarska 19. There's also a Boryspil Airport customs office (☎ (044) 296 70 46, 296 72 16).

MONEY
Currency

In November 1992 the rouble was replaced by the temporary *karbovanets* (kbv; plural: *karbovanatsi*), commonly known as the *kupon*. This was intended to be a transitional currency until inflation was stabilised and the 'real' currency, the *hryvnya* (named after the ancient coin of Kievan Rus), could be released. Well, it's been quite a few years and inflation is still out of control, the kupon is still around and all the hryvnya (printed in Canada) are still waiting in the wings. Official word has it, however, that the hryvnya may be released by late 1995 and hence be in use by the time you arrive.

The currency is comprised solely of notes, with larger and larger ones being printed up at the same rate as inflation. They range from a measly 10 kupon note (rare) up to a 200,000 kupon note. The most common are the 20,000, 50,000, and 100,000 kupon notes. Keep the small 500, 1000, 5000 and 10,000 kupon notes, otherwise you'll be repeatedly paying over the odds because people 'haven't any change'.

Exchange Rates

To give an idea of inflation, this is how the rate has changed over a two-year span.

January 1993: US$1	=	kbv700
June 1993: US$1	=	kbv3000
December 1993: US$	=	kbv13,000
August 1994: US$1	=	kbv40,000
October 1994: US$1	=	kbv80,000
December 1994: US$1	=	kbv130,000

From early 1995 the rate remained reasonably steady for a time at about kbv150,000 to the US dollar. Even so, it makes sense not to exchange large quantities at one time. But make sure you don't run out and be forced to have to drastically overpay in hard currency. Approximate exchange rates include:

Australia	A$1	=	kbv125,700
Canada	C$1	=	kbv125,325
Denmark	DKr1	=	kbv30,480
Germany	DM1	=	kbv118,475
France	FFr1	=	kbv34,280
Finland	Fmk1	=	kbv39,235
Norway	NKr1	=	kbv26,890
New Zealand	NZ$1	=	kbv111,735
Russia	R1	=	kbv37
Sweden	SKr1	=	kbv23,941
Switzerland	SwFr1	=	kbv147,250
USA	US$1	=	kbv168,725
United Kingdom	UK£1	=	kbv265,750
Japan	¥100	=	kbv168,499

Where to Change Money

The daily rates don't vary substantially from place to place but the hotels generally have the worst rates, while the numerous exchange kiosks (with the sign *obmin valyuty*) scattered along the main streets have the best rates. However, exchanging money at hotels, banks and shops is a bit more relaxed than at the street kiosks. Exchanging on the black market is illegal and, with the

UKRAINE

rates not much higher, doesn't have much going for it.

Hard currency can be changerd into kupons anywhere (banks, hotels and exchange kiosks), but travellers' cheques are only accepted at certain banks and exchange offices in a few of the larger cities. The best places to go are the Western Union/X-Change Points offices that are beginning to pop up in most cities. They exchange travellers' cheques, and they even make cash advances (in dollars or kupons) on major credit cards, and will receive money wired from anywhere in the world. At the time of writing there were branches in Kiev, Lviv, Odessa, Zhytomyr and Donetsk, with others to be opened in Ivano-Frankivsk, Ternopil and Chernivtsi. The nationwide bank chain UKR Exim Bank also exchanges travellers' cheques. In Kiev there are a few others, including the Ekonombank. Addresses and specific information regarding exchanging money are given in the Information section for each city.

What Money to Take

Travellers' cheques and credit cards are obviously the safest, and they can be exchanged into kupons or dollars at a few places, but only a very select group of top-end hotels and duty-free shops directly accept them. You'll have to take a lot of cash as well – the most common being the US dollar, with Deutschmarks also widely accepted. Other currencies, such as the British pound or French franc, are exchangeable in banks, but not necessarily around town (taxis, hard-currency shops, etc). A word of warning: don't take old, worn-out bills or ones that have tears or markings on them because they *won't* be accepted – even at banks. Bring new bills if you can. You should take smaller denominations, such as US$5, US$10 and US$20 notes, to change into kupons and pay for certain services, and a bunch of US$1 bills for bribes, quick tips, taxis etc.

In August 1995, the National Bank of Ukraine, in an attempt to strengthen the stability of the Ukrainian kupon, officially banned the use of hard currency as a means of payment in restaurants and retail shops. However, hotels, travel agencies, international transport companies, duty-free shops and other services directed at foreign tourists were to be exempt from the hard-currency ban. In other words, you'll have to pay hard currency for your international train or flight out of the country, any visa-related or legal fees, and a few hotels and tourist services. But everywhere else, including in restaurants, cafés and retail shops and on domestic transport, you'll officially have to pay in kupons (although many people may still find US dollars hard to resist).

You can expect to pay more than locals for certain services, just because you are a foreigner – for example, hotels and train tickets. However, the increment is often not too great, and the prices are still relatively cheap.

Taking Care of Your Money

It's obvious that all tourists carry large amounts of hard currency on them. With the present economy, this makes you a walking bank. Ordinary people are honest and safe, but there are those who hang out near the hotels and target tourists. Don't flash your money, stay low-key in appearance, and have more than one place on your body where you stash your cash. A 'fake' wallet isn't a bad idea, with the 'real' one concealed in a money belt or harness. Use your best judgement and be aware of your surroundings. However, even with rising crime rates, Kiev is still far safer than most comparable Western cities.

Rules & Regulations

There's no limit on the amount of foreign currency or travellers' cheques you can take into or out of the country, but make sure that the amount you take out is lower that what you came in with. You may want to check on this legality before you travel. You're not allowed to take out kupons, and it's near impossible to exchange them, so plan well. Save your receipts from hard-currency exchanges and purchases, just in case a customs official gets bored.

Barters & Bribes

It's no longer practical to barter with Western goods, like jeans, T-shirts or calculators, although these still make wildly appreciated gifts. As far as bartering or bribing, the almighty US dollar is what talks. A fresh pack of unopened Western cigarettes (such as Marlboro) may be tempting, but it has far less buying power. Sometimes a sold-out train ticket, a hotel room not usually open to Westerners, access to a closed site or a table in a restaurant can mysteriously be procured for well-placed kupons or dollars. This system of bribery should be handled discreetly and with caution. Often chocolates are given as a more innocent bribe, especially to the workers who take care of bureaucratic procedures such as visa extensions, tourist information, ticket booking etc.

Bargaining & Tips

No-one expects tips in local cafés and cafeteria-style eateries. At nicer restaurants, especially tourist-oriented establishments, a small tip of about 5% to 10% is usually expected, with many places including a 5% service charge in the bill. If you run across the rare occasion that a waiter or waitress is especially friendly, a tip will be appreciated and will reward their unusual kindness.

Hotels and established restaurants have set prices and don't take to bargaining. But at the country's many markets – food, art, souvenir, junk – a bit of bargaining is expected and prices are rarely marked. Bargaining is especially fierce at souvenir and craft markets. The vendors usually raise their prices by only about 15%.

Costs

Before You Go If you're on a package tour, or you've prearranged your accommodation, you will have to pay the bulk of your expenses before you set off. The prices and variety of services offered on packaged tours vary widely. Consult some of the travel agencies listed in Ukraine Getting There & Away. The average rate per day ranges from US$80 to US$150, including accommodation and meals but excluding airfare.

Accommodation The greatest travel expense in Ukraine is accommodation, although outside Kiev, prices are reasonably low. For example, it averaged between US$15 and US$20 per night for accommodation between August and November 1994, and it is often cheaper per person for double rooms. Many hotels in the larger cities – such as Kiev, Lviv, Odessa and Kharkiv – accept hard currency only.

Food Food is ridiculously cheap, especially if you eat in local cafeteria-style eateries, where a full plate is usually under US$1. At a decent restaurant, a full meal with drink costs anywhere from US$2 to US$5. At the nicest place in town, say a hotel or exclusive restaurant, a full meal will run to about US$6 to US$9 on average. A few restaurants may require hard currency only, but most accept kupons. Expect prices to be 15% to 30% higher in restaurants in Kiev. Street treats, such as ice cream, pastries and delicious cakes in small cafés, cost pennies.

Transport Transport costs in Ukraine are also low. A 2nd-class *(kupe)* sleeper on the train between Kiev and Lviv is about US$6, and between Odessa and Kiev it's about US$5. Most ticket offices for foreigners charge a very minimal fee for their services, and all domestic services can be paid for in kupons. The exception is the Kiev Intourist ticket office (☎ 224 25 59, 224 29 50), behind the Kievska Hotel, at vulitsya Hospitalna 12, where they charge about five times the price of the ticket for their services. Electric trains and buses between cities are ridiculously cheap, although the price of bus tickets has drastically increased. A few hours bus ride between Chernivtsi and Kamyanets-Podilsky or Lviv and Ivano-Frankivsk will cost about US$0.75. A local electric train from Simferopol to Bakhchysaray is about US$0.25. On public transport within cities, it costs a few cents for a bus, tram or metro ride. A monthly pass for all public transport in Kiev is about US$1.

Taxis are obviously the most expensive form of transport, with a varying range of

UKRAINE

prices depending on the location, destination, time and desperation of the situation. A 40-km taxi ride from Boryspil Airport to central Kiev, for example, costs about US$15 to US$20, while a simple ride across town will cost about US$3 to US$4; it costs about half this much in Lviv or Odessa. George took a cab about 50 km from Foros back to Yalta in Crimea for US$5, but the next day another cab wanted to charge him the same price for a journey of about 15 km. He also hired a cab as a personal chauffeur for a few hours in Poltava for about US$6.

Price Rises In November 1994, the IMF loaned US$371 million to Ukraine under the condition that it drop price subsidies and allow the free market to set the figures. This has been a slow and painful process for most Ukrainians, with a monthly price hike in consumer goods of up to 80% or 90%. Salaries meanwhile remain pathetically low (see Economy in Facts about Ukraine). How this affects the tourist is simple: prices for most consumer goods, including transport, are rising every month. Although still a fraction of Western costs, many of the prices quoted, although accurate at the time of research, may be slightly off. A loaf of bread, for example, cost only about US$0.08 in August 1994; by November it cost US$0.25. Although for a Western tourist that's still a pittance, for a pensioner who receives US$2 a month, it's a crisis. Hotels seem for the most part to be more stable in their prices, but nothing is certain.

WHEN TO GO

Ukraine isn't exactly the French Riviera as far as popular destinations go, so even during the high season things rarely get too crowded. The exception, as far as sights are concerned, are the Caves Monastery in Kiev, and the beaches in Odessa and Crimea in the summer, when large crowds do persist. Likewise, in Kiev, and especially Yalta, some of the cheaper hotels may be booked out in summer. Certain services are seasonal, such as the hydrofoil service down the Dnipro from Kiev, boat service around the beaches

of Odessa and sights around Yalta (see those sections for details). Nearly all museums and tourist sights are open year-round, with the exception of outdoor sights, which close earlier in winter.

The summer months are obviously the warmest, but also the wettest; see the Climate section in Facts about Ukraine and the Climate Charts in the Appendix at the back of the book for specific temperatures. In winter, it gets especially cold inland, in particular during December and January. However, there is a definite ambience to the muffled landscape lying quiet under its white blanket. It's a general Slavic tradition to have roasting interiors, so the insides of most buildings, especially homes, are always welcoming.

The most pleasant season to come to Ukraine is during the spring, from late April to early June, when the trees and flowers are in bloom and the temperatures are a few degrees cooler than in summer.

During the months of July and August the theatres close down for the season. Packaged tours through tourist companies are usually 15% to 25% cheaper in the low season, from October to April.

Food fluctuates with the seasons. The availability of fresh produce is substantially curtailed during the winter, when most people survive on jars of preserved fruits and vegetables. Dishes are usually heartier in winter, fresher in spring and summer. Each holiday season has its own special foods, such as Easter breads and Christmas cakes.

WHAT TO BRING

See the European Russia Facts for the Visitor chapter for ideas on this topic. The traveller who travels lightest is brightest. Air Ukraine charges stiff penalties (over US$100) for excess baggage over 22 kg for two pieces, plus a five-kg limit on hand luggage.

For information on a useful first-aid kit, see the Health section in European Russia Facts for the Visitor; for photography ideas, see the Ukraine and European Russia Facts for the Visitor chapters; and for phrasebooks, see Language in Facts about Ukraine.

Luggage

Unless you're here to trek, it doesn't much matter what you pack your belongings in. The best for mobility and ease of carrying (especially on trains, through busy stations, on unbelievably crowded public transport etc) are the soft packs that convert to a backpack with shoulder and waist straps. A smaller day pack is essential for excursions and carrying around necessary items.

Clothing

For winter, spring and autumn you'll need a waterproof jacket; the best ones are long, with a hood and lots of practical zipper pockets. Being lightweight and wind resistant, they allow you to wear substantial layers underneath. Wearing many light, removable layers not only better insulates you, it also allows you to adjust easily from indoors to out. Even in summer, a weatherproof jacket is recommended in case of sudden chills and rain. Around winter, early spring and late autumn, a hat, gloves and woollen socks are recommended.

Good footwear is crucial. A durable, weatherproof, thick-soled boot or similar shoe is best. A lightweight pair of plastic thongs is a good idea for the often questionable floors in hotel bathrooms and showers. In summer, you might appreciate an extra pair of sandals.

Even at the opera and better restaurants, you can get away with casual gear, but you'll get better service and feel less conspicuous if you have one outfit that dresses you up a bit, especially as most Ukrainians dress up on such occasions. In churches, dress should be modest and women should wear a loose headscarf.

Other Items

Bring all the toiletries you'll need for your entire trip (some hard-currency shops in Kiev sell items, but don't count on it), as well as contraceptives, tampons, contact-lens supplies, medicine, prescription drugs (bring your prescription with you), vitamins etc.

A few rolls of toilet paper are a good idea, because it's often sold only at the bazaars,

and only with a one-ply grit. No public toilets have toilet paper or soap, so carry a roll around with you, as well as a bar of soap in a plastic bag, or better yet, a couple of packets of antibacterial premoistened cleansing tissues. An all-purpose handkerchief and a small towel are also nice to have.

In summer, especially if you're camping, you'll need insect repellent in wooded countryside at almost any latitude. Campers may also want a mosquito net.

Other items to consider are a water bottle, Swiss army knife (with bottle opener, corkscrew, blades and scissors), spoon, all-purpose cup, universal bathroom plug, laundry soap, clothesline and a few clothes pegs, torch (flashlight), sunglasses, compass, sketchbook, pen or pencils, small calculator, safety pins, extra shoelaces, washcloth, good hat with brim, travel alarm clock, extra watch and camera batteries, sunscreen and lip salve, sewing kit and toenail clippers. It may also be a good idea to take water-purification tablets if you're not sure of water safety. Crimea had a serious cholera epidemic during the autumn of 1994, mainly due to unclean water supplies.

Gift Ideas

Small gifts go a long way, as acts of kindness or as shameless bribes. Convenient and popular are good coffee, chocolate, disposable lighters, American chewing gum, postcards from home, spare medical items like aspirin or antiseptic, souvenir key rings or bottle openers, photo calendars, pocket calculators, T-shirts with Western-looking logos (universities or tourist sights like Disneyland are a rave), cheap digital watches, sunglasses and pocket English dictionaries.

For your favourite floor lady, try chocolate or scented soaps. For small children try crayons, alphabet books, colourfully packaged confectionery, or balloons. The kids will crowd around you and make your heart swell. For older kids, small badges, baseball cards and lapel pins are popular.

Food

Since boiled water is available in most

places, a thermos flask and a stash of tea bags and powdered drinks are a good idea.

Vitamins are good for long trips, as well as a cache of lightweight foods like dry nuts, fruit, health-food bars, soup mixes etc. This is especially critical for vegetarians, whose only other option may be boiled cabbage and carrot salads. A stash of sweets is always nice to take the blues away.

TOURIST OFFICES
Local Tourist Information
Most countries have well-equipped tourist offices staffed with friendly and knowledgable personnel ready to help you with any questions you might have. Unfortunately, these organisations are just fairy tales in Ukraine – they simply don't exist. At best, in many hotels there's what's called a service bureau that performs specific functions and not much else – such as selling train tickets or arranging expensive excursions. Answering everyday questions is not in their job description, and it's a service that no-one seems to be willing to practise. Private tourist offices deal almost exclusively in arranging excursions, and nothing else. Practical, everyday advice and information, from how to make a phone call to finding local bus information, is nigh impossible to get.

A good place to try first, however, is that service bureau in your hotel, which might range from absolutely useless to partially helpful. Hotel receptionists are sometimes helpful. If you find a polite one, ask all you need to know then and there. Otherwise, the common person on the street is almost always the nicest and will often lead you by the hand to show you where to wait for the bus.

There is actually a State Committee of Ukraine for Tourism, but what its job is seems a mystery. In Lviv, look for it in the service bureau at the Hotel Zhorzh, ploshcha Mitskevycha 1 (☎ (032220) 72 67 51, 72 67 40, 79 84 65; fax 74 21 82); this service bureau is one of the country's best. In Kiev, it's at Yaroslaviv val 36 (☎ (044) 212 55 70; fax 212 46 24).

There are travel agencies inside Ukraine,

but rather than providing free general tourist information, they usually deal strictly with arranging private tours and excursions. For listings of these Ukrainian travel agencies see the Information sections for the major cities, and the Ukraine Getting Around chapter.

Tourist Offices Abroad
The best source of tourist information outside Ukraine is either your local Ukrainian consulate, or one of the many foreign travel agencies that deal with travel to Ukraine and can help you plan or book your trip. For a listing of these foreign travel agencies see Ukraine Getting There & Away.

USEFUL ORGANISATIONS
There are a number of special-interest organisations that are affiliated in one way or another with Ukraine. The following details only a small number of such organisations in North America. Most major cities in Europe, the Americas and Australia have Ukrainian cultural fraternal organisations – check your local listings.

Canada
    Canadian Institute of Ukrainian Studies, University of Toronto, 21 Sussex Ave, Toronto, Ont M5S 1A1

USA
    Children of Chornobyl, 272 Old Short Hills Rd, Short Hills NJ 07078 (☎ (201) 376 5140)
    The Harvard Ukrainian Research Institute, 1583 Massachusetts Ave, Cambridge MA 02138
    The Ukrainian Heritage Foundation, 2047 Wingate Rd, Poland OH 44514
    The Ukrainian Museum, 203 Second Ave, New York NY 10003
    The Ukrainian National Association, 30 Montgomery St, Jersey City, NJ 07302

BUSINESS HOURS & HOLIDAYS
Business Hours
Government offices are open on weekdays from 9 or 10 am to 5 or 6 pm, usually closing at noon on Friday. Banks are usually open on weekdays from 9 am to 1 pm.

Most shops are open Monday to Saturday from 8 or 9 am until 8 or 9 pm, but some smaller shops close earlier, at 5 or 6 pm.

UKRAINE

Nearly all shops close for an hour's break in the middle of the day, usually from 1 to 2 pm, sometimes an hour later, and sometimes for two hours.

Cafeteria-style eateries and cafés usually open at 8 or 9 am and close at 6 or 7 pm. Restaurants typically open from noon to midnight, except for a break between afternoon and evening meals, usually from 4 to 5 pm.

Museum hours are typically from about 9 am to 5 or 6 pm, but they vary, and there's always one or two days a week when they're closed. Most won't admit you in the 30 minutes before closing time.

Public transit usually operates from 6 am to midnight; the metro operates from 6 am to 1 am.

Beware the *sanitary den* (sanitary day). Once a month, usually during the fourth week, nearly everything – shops, restaurants, hotel dining rooms, museums – shuts down for cleaning, each having its own day and not always with much publicity. Equally notorious are sudden closures due to 'technical complications' – whatever that means.

Public Holidays

The main public holidays are:

1 January
New Year's Day
7 January
Orthodox Christmas Day
8 March
International Women's Day
1 & 2 May
International Labour Day
9 May
Victory (1945) Day & Mother's Day
24 August
Independence (1991) Day
28 October
Liberation (1944) Day
31 December
New Year's Eve

FESTIVALS

Thousands of small cultural events and festivals are held throughout the country in small communities, many in celebration of the seasons and local folk traditions. The larger festivals include:

7 January
Orthodox Christmas Day – a special time for families, it includes festivities in the afternoon as well as Christmas services.
March/April
Easter (Paskha) – the main festival of the Orthodox Church year. The day begins with celebratory midnight services, and in many small villages there's a parade around the village church.
May
National Virtuoso, Lviv – a month of musical and theatrical performances focusing on national and cultural themes.
Last Weekend of May
Kiev Days – a colourful spring celebration and festival in honour of the capital city.
6 June
Ivan Kupallo Day, Kiev – a celebration of Midsummer's Night, dating back to pagan origins.
August
Crimean Stars, Yalta – special events are scheduled throughout the month to celebrate Crimean history and culture.
24 August
Independence Day – each city hosts festivals and parades with performances and special events.
First week in October
Kiev International Music Festival – hundreds of international composers and musicians perform at numerous venues.
Last week in October
International Kiev Film Festival – usually held at the House of Cinema on the corner of vulitsya Saksahnskoho and vulitsya Kulbysheva near Palats Sportu metro stop. A great time to check out new cinematic talent.
28 October
Liberation Day (1944), Kiev – a large veterans-wearing-medals parade in the morning is followed by speeches and gala performances in the afternoon.
31 December & 1 January
New Year – gifts are placed under a traditional fir tree and special songs are sung. See out the old year with vodka and welcome in the new with champagne.

POST & TELECOMMUNICATIONS
Post
The post office is called a *poshta* or *pochta*. The main ones (sometimes called a *poshtamt*) are usually open from 8 am to 9 pm Monday to Friday, from 9 am to 7 pm on

UKRAINE

Saturday, and are closed on Sunday. The smaller post offices often close earlier, and don't open on Saturday. The small post offices in a few of the hotels close even earlier, between 1 and 3 pm.

Outward mail is slow but fairly reliable. Airmail letters take about two weeks from Ukraine to elsewhere in Europe, and two to three weeks to America or Australia. Incoming post is more unreliable, taking from three to six weeks to an eternity. Mail sent to Ukraine should not attract special attention or look especially Western.

You can buy stamped (often extra stamps will be added) airmail envelopes and postcards at the main post offices, then just drop them at your convenience into one of the blue postboxes on the street. Some of the larger post offices have more than one mail box. The box marked *za kordon* is for mail being sent outside the country.

It's faster and more reliable to send your mail express. International Express Mail (EMS) is available at most main post offices, and letters are supposed to reach anywhere within five days. You can send parcels up to 10 kg (22 lb) through EMS. Bring your packages unwrapped in case they wish to verify the contents. Books and printed matter go at a cheaper rate. If you want the utmost in reliability, there are DHL Worldwide Express offices in most major cities: Kiev (☎ (044) 221 50 95); Odessa (☎ (0482) 24 42 69); Kharkiv (☎ (0572) 20 13 42); Lviv (☎ (0322) 74 58 66); and Donetsk (☎ (0622) 35 90 08).

Addressing Mail When addressing outgoing mail, repeat the country destination before you print the addressee's name, in Cyrillic if you can. This is because all addresses in Ukraine are written in reverse order – for example Ukraina, m Kyiv, 252091, vul Franko 26/8, kv 12, Yuri Orestovich Vesolovsky. The return address is written smaller and below the main address.

Common words and abbreviations included in addresses are: *budynok* or *bud.* (building), *bulvar* or *bul.* (boulevard), *dim* or

d. (house), *etazh* (floor), *kolhosp* (collective farm), *korpus* or *k.* (building within a complex), *kvartyra* or *kv.* (apartment), *maydan* (square, usually park-like), *misto* or *m.* (city), *naberezhna* or *nab.* (embankment), *pasazh* (passage), *ploshcha* or *pl.* (square), *prospekt* or *pr.* (avenue), *provulok* or *prov.* (lane), *rayon* or *r-n* (country), *selishche* or *sel.* (settlement), *selo* or *s.* (village), *shose* (highway), *uzviz* (slope), *vkhid, podezd* or *pod.* (entrance number) and *vulitsya* or *vul.* (street).

Floors are numbered American-style, the ground floor being No 1. On an address, two numbers separated by a slash (/) usually indicate a corner, the second number being the address on the cross street.

See European Russia Facts for the Visitor for more information on address styles.

Receiving Mail The best way to receive or have mail held for you in Ukraine is through a personal contact, but many hotels (especially if you've prebooked) will hold clearly marked mail for you if you let them know when you're coming. Highly valuable post is risky, and forget about packages. Embassies and consulates won't hold mail for transient travellers, but you can try asking at the America House (vulitsya Melnikova 63) or British Council Office (Bessarabska ploshcha 9/1), both in Kiev (see Cultural Centres in the Kiev Information section). If an American Express Office ever pops up in Ukraine, they hold mail for card and cheque holders for up to two months.

Telephone

Local Calls Local calls are made from public phones on the street. They are usually free, but in Lviv they require a *telefon zheton* – a small coin purchased at kiosks. Not all public phones work, and in Kiev it seems that none of them do.

Intercity & International Making telephone calls in Ukraine is a true test of stamina and patience. To place a long-distance or international phone call you can *only* use a private phone in someone's home, or call from your hotel, the city telephone office or on a Utel direct-dial card phone (see Utel section). All public phones on the streets are for local calls only.

Sometimes, if you are using a private phone, you can get an international operator by dialling 079, or 073 for international assistance. In Kiev, you can reach an international operator in several languages by dialling 8 191 for French, 8 192 for English, 8 193 for German, 8 194 for Ukrainian or Russian or 8 195 for Spanish.

For international calls, dial 8 to get a dial tone, then 10 for international dialling, followed by the country code, city code and number. For intercity calls dial 8, followed by the city code and number. Calls to Russian, Belarusian and most former-USSR cities don't require the international code; this may change.

Some city telephone codes in Ukraine are as follows (numbers with a '2' in parentheses require an extra '2' when dialling five-digit numbers; it is not required if dialling a six-digit number): Chernihiv 04622, Chernivtsi 03859 or 03722, Dnipropetrovsk 0562, Donetsk 0622, Feodosiya 06562, Ivano-Frankivsk 0342(2), Kamyanets-Podilsky 03849, Kharkiv 0572, Khmelnytsky 03822, Kiev 044, Lutsk 03322, Lviv 0322, Odessa 0482, Poltava 0532(2), Rivne 0362(2), Simferopol 0652, Ternopil 0352(2), Vinnytsya 04322, Yalta 0654, Yevpatoria 06569, Zaporizhzhya 0612(2).

When calling Ukraine, the country code is 380. If dialling from abroad, the first '0' in the city code is not dialled: to call from the USA to Kiev, for example, you would dial 380 44, then the local number.

Utel The easiest way to call long distance is to purchase a Utel (Ukraine Telecom; ☎ 229 83 66), vulitsya Bohdana Khmelnystskoho 38, Kiev) fixed-value phone card, sold at the post office and major hotels, and used on Utel direct-dial card phones located at main post offices, hotels, airports and some restaurants. The connection is clear and quick, with no hassles. A US$10 card can give you three to five minutes to the USA or Australia, or about 10 minutes to Europe. You can also call within Ukraine with the card.

Calling from Hotels Most hotel receptions can call long distance for you (international or intercity), and sometimes you can call from your own room, but you'll have to pay hard currency for the call – US$0.60 a minute for Europe, US$2.50 a minute for the USA or Australia. If your hotel tells you to go to the local telephone office, go to another hotel.

Telephone Offices If you can't make a long-distance call at your hotel, the final option is the least preferred. Every city and town has a telephone office (some open 24 hours), frequently attached to the main post office and often a swarming frenzy of chaos. *Mizhhorodny*, or *mizhmisky*, means intercity, and *mizhnarodny* means international. At larger telephone offices there may be separate offices for either, and some small offices may not be able to place long-distance calls at all. Larger post offices may also have direct-dial intercity phones, from which you just dial the city code and number. If not, the basic procedure is as follows: hand the woman working the switchboard the number and city you wish to call, along with the desired length of your call and usually a 100,000 kupon bill to cover the cost. Then you wait – sometimes for over half an hour if it's crowded. Eventually, they'll call your city and assign you a booth *(kabina)* where your call will be put through – and sharply cut off when your time is up. Pick up your change before you leave. Sometimes you don't hand the number to the switchboard operator, just the money, and you dial the number yourself when a booth becomes available (which means you'll have to know the city code). Intercity calls are fairly cheap, less than US$1 for a five-minute call. International calls are US$0.60 a minute to Europe, US$2.50 a minute to the USA or Australia, and you pay in kupons when using the telephone offices.

UKRAINE

Telegram

Telegrams, although a bit archaic, are still used in Ukraine and are easy, cheap and fairly reliable. International telegrams can be sent (for kupons) from most post offices, as well as some hotels, usually arriving within 24 hours and almost always within 48 hours. Ask for a *blank mizhnarodnoho telegramma* (international telegram form). A message in English is no problem if it's clearly printed. You can also attempt to have incoming telegrams sent to you at your hotel, but this seems unreliable.

Telex & Fax

International telex and fax (both pronounced the same in Ukrainian as in English) are quickly replacing telegrams, and are available in most main post offices (in kupons) and the better hotels (in hard currency). Sending a fax, telex or telegram from your hotel is a lot easier than from the post office, but it is more expensive. Prices for faxes are about the same as for international phone calls. The main post office and most hotels will also receive faxes for you if you let them know ahead of time and tell them when you expect the fax to arrive.

TIME

Most of the country is on the same time zone – GMT/UTC plus two hours. Crimea, however, is on Moscow time – GMT/UTC plus three hours. The country shifts to summer time at midnight on the first Sunday in April by setting the clocks ahead by one hour. On the last Sunday in October the clocks are set back again.

When it's noon in Kiev, it's...

2 am in San Francisco;
5 am in New York and Toronto;
10 am in London;
11 am in Paris, Warsaw, Prague and Budapest;
noon in Minsk, Helsinki, Bucharest, Ankara and Cairo;
1 pm in Moscow and Simferopol;
5 pm in summer Beijing;
6 pm in Ulan Bator and winter Beijing;
7 pm in winter Sydney, 9 pm in summer Sydney;
9 pm in winter Auckland, 11 pm in summer Auckland.

ELECTRICITY

The system is the same as in Russia – see Electricity in European Russia Facts for the Visitor.

LAUNDRY

See Laundry in European Russia Facts for the Visitor.

TOILETS

Hotel-room toilets are usually passable, but public toilets are vile and nauseating. And so are many showers at camp sites, because people think they're toilets too. Often public toilets resemble no more than a stinky clogged hole with foot markers on either side. You'll be more likely to find moon rock than toilet paper (even in hotels), so keep a roll or two on you at all times and guard it with your life. Sometimes in bigger cities and railway stations there are pay toilets *(platny tualet)*, which thankfully tend to be slightly more bearable. Even in fine restaurants and opera houses don't expect a pleasant experience. Your best bet is the lobby services of the nicest hotel in town. In the countryside or small towns you may find yourself discreetly consulting nature, not an uncommon practice. Think of it all as one more insightful first-hand experience of the Ukrainian lifestyle.

Ж for *zhinochy* stands for women's rest room; Ч or М, for *cholovichy* or *muzhcheny*, stands for men's.

WEIGHTS & MEASURES

Ukraine uses the metric system – see European Russia Facts for the Visitor.

BOOKS

History, Politics & Current Events

Harvard Ukrainian Institute Publications (1583 Massachusetts Ave, Cambridge, MA 02138, USA) and CIUS Press (352 Athabasca Hall, University of Alberta, Edmonton, Alberta, Canada T6G 2E8) are two publishing houses that specialise in Ukrainian books, covering every imaginable topic. Their catalogues can be ordered. In Britain, the Zwemmer bookshop (☎ (0171) 379 6253) at 28 Denmark St, London WC2H 8NJ, specialises in the whole ex-USSR, including Ukraine. It, too, issues a catalogue.

Ukraine: A History by Orest Subtelny is probably the best concise history of Ukraine, easy to read and enjoyable, but way too big to bring along. *Famine in Ukraine, 1932-33* by Roman Serbyn & Bohdan Krawchenko and *The Harvest of Sorrow: Soviet Collectivization and the Terror-Famine* by Robert Conquest are two books that give the full historical account of the events leading up to the mass famine and its effects on the Ukrainian people and nation as a whole. *Life Sentence: Memoirs of a Ukrainian Political Prisoner* by Danylo Shumak is the amazing personal autobiography of Amnesty International's once most 'senior' political prisoner – describing over 30 years spent being shunted from one prison and labour camp to another, including being sentenced to death by communist authorities. *Chernobyl: A Documentary Story* by Iurii Shcherbak is probably the only book on the nuclear disaster based completely on interviews and eyewitness accounts. Written by an award-winning author and screen writer, it was published to much acclaim in both Ukraine and Russia.

Letters from Kiev by Solomea Pavlychko is an eyewitness account of the political and economic upheavals during 1990-91, written by one of the county's youngest upcoming literary figures. *Ukraine: From Chornobyl to Sovereignty*, edited by Roman Solchanyk, is a collection of 15 interviews with prominent figures that sheds light on the major current political issues facing Ukraine today. *The Poet as Mythmaker* by George Grabowicz is an in-depth study into the life and work of Ukraine's national hero, poet Taras Shevchenko, and his role in shaping the Ukrainian consciousness.

For a total resource, the weighty five-volume *Encyclopedia of Ukraine* is published by CIUS Press and covers the complete A to Z of all things Ukrainian. Also available through CIUS Press is *Ukraine & Ukrainians around the World*, edited by Lensyk Pawliczko, a reference book listing all the Ukrainian organisations worldwide.

Guidebooks

The selection of current guidebooks to Ukraine is limited, often including only Kiev. *Ukraine: A Tourist Guide* (1993), compiled by Osyp Zinkewych & Volodymr Hula, by Smoloskyp Publishers, is a thorough covering of the architectural and historical sights of each region in the country. It has lots of little pictures, facts and addresses, but is low on logistics and practical survival information.

Ukraine, Language and Travel Guide (1994) by Linda Hodges & George Chumak has excellent and extensive coverage of language and conversation divided into tourist-oriented sections. It also has some interesting related information but its travel information lacks practical details.

Eastern Europe by Steven Birbaum has a thorough section on Kiev, along with chapters on Lviv and Odessa.

Hiking Guide to Poland & Ukraine by Tim Bruford (published by Bradt, 41 Nortoft Rd, Chalfont St Peter, Bucks SL9 0LA, England) is an excellent resource which includes 148 pages on different hikes in Ukraine as well as general and background information.

Trekking in Russia & Central Asia by Frith Maicr (published by Cordee, Leicester, England; The Mountaineers, Seattle, USA; and Douglas & McIntyre, Vancouver, Canada) includes a 14-page chapter detailing walks, treks and climbs in Crimea.

For language books see the Language section in Facts about Ukraine.

MAPS
Country Maps

Country maps are easy to find, with loads of them proudly published immediately after independence and sold in all bookshops. Except for general references and distances, however, they're not too useful, with none of them sufficient if you're going to be driving. The best maps for clearly showing roads and accurate detail are the series of four maps

(1:750,000) covering Ukraine, Belarus, European Russia and the Caucasus published by the map company Marco Polo. Maps No 2/3 (Belarus-Russia-Ukraine) and No 4 (Ukraine, Crimea, Moldova) cover all of Ukraine. These maps are a good purchase prior to departure; they not available once you get there.

You may be lucky enough to find a few of the unbelievably detailed (1:200,000) Topographic Maps (Topografycheska Karta) series which cover each region of the country, showing every river, forest, road, contour and village. They're very hard to find – we bought all we could discover.

City Maps

You can usually buy a map of Kiev outside the country before you arrive, but for other cities, you'll have to wait until you get there. Cities like Kiev, Lviv (the best), Kharkiv and Yalta have fairly accurate and reliable maps (sold at bookshops and kiosks), but other cities might have at best grossly oversimplified old maps, showing former street names and sometimes with intentionally distorted features. City maps are called *plan mista* or *plan horoda*. Transport maps, called *skhema transporta*, can sometimes be found, but many are old and outdated. For smaller towns, commercially available maps just don't exist. Maps are cheap, so the general rule is to buy any that you find, as they might be the only ones available. Some regional maps, like the ones found in Crimea, have small overall city maps on the back.

MEDIA
Ukrainian-Language Print Media
Newspapers Since independence there's been relative freedom of press, although most of the 1787 officially registered newspapers are controlled organs of the Supreme Rada, a political organisation or a large professional body. About 70% of all newspapers are printed in the Ukrainian language.

Demokratychna Ukraina (Democratic Ukraine) is the misnamed formal voice of the Communist Party, and it basically hasn't changed much. *Holos Ukrainy (Voice of Ukraine)* and *Pravda Ukrainy (Ukrainian Truth)* are both controlled by the Supreme Rada, endorsing, raising or shrouding issues as the parliament sees it. *Literaturna Ukraina (Ukrainian Literature)* is the voice of the Union of Writers of Ukraine, a pro-reform, democratic, nationalist group of literary and intellectual thinkers who played an important part in the push for independence in 1991. *Nezavizimost (Independence)* is one of the only major newspapers that's just what its name implies – independent, covering events from a firm middle ground.

Svoboda (Freedom) is a Ukrainian daily published in the USA and Canada and widely read by North American Ukrainian diaspora.

Journals The 185 periodicals published in Ukraine are more liberal and less controlled by the government than the newspapers, and cover a wide range of general and speciality topics. About 60% are printed in Ukrainian. *Berezil*, formerly *Prapor*, is a long-standing, popular monthly journal featuring mostly fictional literature by popular writers. *Muzyka (Music), Obrazotvorche Mistetstvo (Fine Arts)* and *Ukrainsky Teatr (Ukrainian Theatre)* each cover their respective fields in the world of arts and culture. *Politika i Chas (Politics and Time)* is a monthly focusing on Ukrainian international relations and foreign affairs. For sport literates, *Start* is a monthly sport journal, while *Ranok (Morning)* is a journal with fiction and social writings aimed at the youth market.

English-Language Print Media
The *Ukrainian Weekly*, published by the Ukrainian National Assembly in the USA and Canada, is the best English-language newspaper covering all topics of Ukrainian life, people, politics, economics and general news. Published in Kiev, *News from Ukraine* and *Ukrainian Times* are two English-language newspapers that are worth finding for news, facts and information, and are especially pertinent to the capital. Outside Kiev they're hard to find. *Window on Ukraine* is an economics-oriented newspaper geared more towards the foreign

business community but with a handy e-mail and fax bulletin.

The America House and British Council libraries in Kiev (see Information in the Kiev chapter) are faithful bastions of English-language literature, newspapers and magazines, although the papers may be a day or two late, and the facilities' hours are limited.

International English-language papers are hard to find and expensive. Try the top hotels' lobby kiosks.

Ukrainian-Language TV

The funniest aspect of TV in Ukraine is its *reklamas*, or commercials, which naively try to imitate Western tactics. You quickly begin to memorise the same commercials which play over and over. On view in Kiev are:

- Channel 1, UT-1, the main Ukrainian TV channel, with news, concerts, sports and general programming;
- Channel 7, a commercial channel that sometimes broadcasts CNN news in English;
- Channel 8, a shared station used by Ukrainian and Russian TV channels;
- Channel 30, which sometimes airs educational programmes;
- Channel 32, ICTV, which has periodic Western news and music videos;
- Channel 37, which shows Ukrainian news;
- Ostankino, a Moscow-based channel with Russian news and programming.

Some older TVs seem to mix up these channel numbers, and you'll be lucky to get all seven on any one TV set – even luckier outside Kiev. In Lviv there's a popular Polish TV and news channel; in Kharkiv there are a few more Russian ones. Your hotel room usually has a TV, but more often than not it's just decoration.

English-Language TV

Top-end hotels, including the Kievska and Dnipro in Kiev, the Grand in Lviv and the Roxolana in Ivano-Frankivsk, have live CNN, SkyNet and some German stations by satellite – but then you might never leave your room! America House and the British Council in Kiev might one day have satellite TV in their facilities.

Ukrainian-Language Radio

The little plastic box hanging off your hotel-room wall usually transmits a local station or two plus the Ukrainian National Radio Broadcasting Company, the main national channel, with concerts, random music, news commentary etc. Russian radio is usually available. It's a good distraction from the noises from surrounding rooms which penetrate the paper-thin walls.

FILM & PHOTOGRAPHY

In general, Western film is available in most larger cities, but only for hard currency and it's more expensive than back home. Most places just stock print film; colour slide and B&W film is hard to find. It's best to bring all the film you need with you rather than depending on finding supplies on the road. The same applies to camera batteries, which are even harder to come by. There's some old Soviet film for sale here and there, but it's a mystery how you'll manage to get it developed outside the country.

In general, there are no restrictions on photography – the days of top-secret bridges and belching factories is over, but it's not recommended to photograph sensitive military installations and border stations (at least not obviously). A camera is still associated with spies, secret agents, the KGB and the press. A camera-toting tourist snapping shots just for pleasure is a strange phenomenon and often open to suspicion or intolerance.

For further photography information, tips, and etiquette see the Film & Photography section in European Russia Facts for the Visitor.

HEALTH

For general information on health-related problems and preventative measures, see the Health section in European Russia Facts for the Visitor, most of which is relevant to Ukraine – including the increase in cases of diphtheria and the incidence of tick encephalitis and Lyme disease in rural areas during summer. Before departing, travellers should check with their local public health service for information on current epidemic or health risks for travellers to Ukraine. Certain immunisations, such as tetanus, typhoid and diphtheria, should be current.

Chornobyl

The risk to short-term visitors is insignificant. The areas to stay away from, at least for long-term exposure, are the northern parts of the Zhytomyr and Kiev oblasts. Chernihiv, although only 80 km to the east of Chornobyl, was spared by favourable winds and is completely safe to visit. Although swimming in the Dnipro around Kiev is popular with locals, especially in summer, some authorities have advised against it – portions of silt have been contaminated by radioactive particles flowing downstream. The most absorptive foods are mushrooms and berries, two staples of Ukrainian diet that should be avoided if their origin is uncertain.

Cholera

Cholera, a disease of the intestine caused by waterborne bacteria, was in near epidemic proportions in and around Crimea during the autumn of 1994 – to the point that Turkey

---

Chornobyl

On 26 April 1986, reactor No 4 at the Chornobyl (Chernobyl in Russian) nuclear power station, 100 km north of Kiev, blew up during the testing of a generator. Nearly nine tonnes of radioactive material – 90 times as much as the Hiroshima bomb – were hurled into the sky. Winds over the following days, mostly blowing north and west, carried fallout into Belarus, as well as Russia, Poland and the Baltic region. Fallout affected 23% of Belarus, with 4.8% of Ukrainian territory and 0.5% of Russian land exposed. Thirty-one people died during the explosion, but how many thousands perished due to the ensuing acute radiation sickness is unknown. About 135,000 people were evacuated from a 30-km radius around the plant, with peripheral areas remaining at a high risk of exposure. The reactor was enclosed in a concrete-and-steel sarcophagus. Over the following years about 600,000 people – popularly known as 'the liquidators' – worked on clean-up operations inside the 30-km zone. Although scientists agree that there is no risk of the sarcophagus exploding, the status of the estimated 180 tonnes of radioactive material still remaining trapped or infused in the concrete is unclear.

The major effects of the explosion only became clear gradually and despite what plainly seemed to be official cover-up efforts, prompting an outbreak of political protest. Doctors in Kiev, Minsk and elsewhere noted significant increases in cancer-related diseases among people, particularly children, from contaminated areas. By 1991, clean-up organisations were saying that between 5000 and 10,000 of their number had died, against official figures of 300-odd. Radiation hot spots were scattered outside the 30-km zone, including enough radiation around Kiev to cause fears for the safety of its population. An estimated 4.9 million people in northern Ukraine, southern Belarus and the south-western corner of Russia were affected to some degree, many continuing to live on contaminated land and producing contaminated meat, milk and vegetables, which were finding their way into local markets.

Today, Ukraine has evacuated most of the highly contaminated areas, although a number of 'resettlers', anxious to return to their villages, have moved back within the forbidden zone, a practice the government mainly ignores. An international team of scientists has set up a 24-hour monitoring station at the plant but, with insufficient resources, the already economically desperate government is pleading for increased foreign aid to help with the immense clean-up costs. Over 15% of Ukraine's annual budget is consumed by Chornobyl-related clean-up and maintenance operations, an amount the government argues is nowhere close to sufficient, but all it can possibly afford. Agricultural and production losses, especially in Belarus, have also crippled the economy. With Ukraine importing over half its energy (90% from Russia, which demands market prices), in late 1993, to the distress of the international community, the government voted to reopen the remaining reactors at Chornobyl to help solve its energy crisis. Ukraine relies on its five Chornobyl-style reactors for one-third of its energy.

Western medical and governmental sources are unanimous that the risk to short-term visitors is insignificant. ■

suspended all shipping traffic arriving from Yalta and Odessa. Recently, the dangers have subsided, but to be on the safe side, drink only bottled water (easily obtainable in most food stores) in Crimea, and in the entire country if possible. It's a good idea to bring a water bottle and some water-purification tablets, especially if you plan on camping or doing a lot of walking.

WOMEN TRAVELLERS

See the Women Travellers section in European Russia Facts for the Visitor – the information provided there also applies to Ukraine.

DANGERS & ANNOYANCES

The biggest annoyance you'll experience is in dealing with the inherent bureaucracy and apathy which turns some people in 'service' industries into some of the most unpleasant people on earth. Don't expect people to be polite or helpful, or to provide any kind of service at all. Dumbstruck desk staff, blind waiters, paralysed shop assistants and the inevitable curtains being drawn shut to the sounds of laughter after you've waited an hour in the ticket line – these little annoyances won't surprise you at all. When the rare service bureau employee goes out of the way to take a particular interest in your problem or question, it will seem all the more heaven-sent.

Crime

Organised Mafia is big time in Ukraine, and some speculate that it has a hand in the government. But there are also thousands of small-scale mafiosi who run rings of kiosks, supply pensioners with cigarettes to sell and take part in the favourite pastime of the mobile elite – *kupuvati-prodati*, or buy, sell and pocket the profit. It's almost expected that all *biznesmeny* are a crooked lot and that capitalism is just controlled banditry, with you, as a Westerner, a representative of that golden capitalist dream.

Nevertheless, as a tourist you won't feel the effects of the Mafia. The biggest danger to tourists is the increasing number of mostly independent criminals who direct their attentions to ripping off naive tourists loaded with dollars. Because you're a Westerner, you're perceived to be rich and made of money. Undesirables often lurk around the hotels looking for targets. Don't flash your money or carry on conversations with shifty characters that approach you, and be careful at night going into and out of your hotel, especially in Kiev. You run a high risk trying to exchange currency on the black market. You should try to avoid being alone late at night on the metro in Kiev or in the parks around the centre.

In comparison to Western cities, however, even Kiev is relatively safe – nothing compared to such places as New York or Los Angeles. The usual safety and awareness precautions that all travellers normally take should be applied in Ukraine. See the Dangers & Annoyances section in European Russia Facts for the Visitor for further information and tips.

The emergency phone numbers accessible from any working phone in the country are:

Fire (pozhezhnoyi kluzhby) ☎ 01
Police (militsya) ☎ 02
Ambulance (shvidkoyi dopomohy) ☎ 03

WORK

Most foreigners in Ukraine are thought to be some sort of slick businesspeople, simply because the idea of someone coming to visit the country just as a tourist is unfathomable.

The majority of foreign workers in Ukraine are either part of large foreign joint-venture corporations such as Coca-Cola or Pac Tel, government workers such as embassy employees or political analysts, or part of some social-oriented organisation. The US Peace Corps has about 100 volunteers working in the country, either teaching English, consulting or doing social work. The Ukrainian National Association (UNA) of America regularly sends volunteers to teach at universities, as do the Soros Foundation and the associated Renaissance Foundation, which emphasise closer cultural interrelations through education. Journalists,

UKRAINE

scholars (such as Fulbright fellows) and other researchers, including archaeologists at Kamyanets-Podilsky and Khersones, are involved in only relatively small numbers. The floodgates have been opened as far as missionaries are concerned, and zealots are campaigning passionately.

But the freewheeling transient travellers so common in other parts of Europe, who pick up seasonal work from place to place, really don't exist in Ukraine. Wages, unless you work for a foreign company, are minuscule and without the aid of some organisation or personal contact, the vast complications of setting yourself up are insurmountable.

ACTIVITIES
Hiking, Trekking & Camping
The best prospects for hiking, trekking and camping are in Crimea (definitely the most popular) and the Carpathians in the south-west, along with a few scattered national parks (see Conservation under Flora & Fauna in Facts about Ukraine), where in the summer you'll probably be joined by other local enthusiasts.

A number of organisations (see the Ukraine Getting There & Away chapter) organise trekking adventures in Crimea, all focusing on the spectacular Crimean mountain range along the south coast. For independent travellers, the easy hikes to the two most accessible cave cities of Chufut-Kale and Manhup-Kale (see Crimea chapter) are popular, although many other more remote sites exist which have further excellent and scenic hikes. Other highlights of Crimean treks include the Bolshoy Kanyon, the deepest canyon in Crimea, at over 300 metres deep and only three km long; the Dzhur-Dzhur and Uchansu waterfalls; and the mramorna (marble) caves. You can also hike to the top of some of Crimea's highest peaks, such as Roman-Cosh, Demyr-Kapu and Kemal-Yeherek.

The picturesque Carpathians occupy a broad stretch of the south-west of the country, a region steeped in folklore. With a good map you can just about walk anywhere you like, with the vast majority of the moun-tains uninhabited, fairly remote and highly scenic – most of the towns and villages lie along the roads. A good place to start is the Carpathian State National Park, about 55 km south-west of Kolomyya.

Supplies are almost nonexistent, so if you're going to camp or trek, come well prepared and equipped with all you're going to need.

Other Activities
Boat trips down the Dnipro from Kiev to Odessa are becoming more and more popular, and are a fun and relaxing way to see the country. You can either travel independently from Kiev or Odessa during the summer or go on a prearranged trip organised through a tourist agency (see the Dnipro River Trips section in Ukraine Getting Around).

HIGHLIGHTS
Ukraine's highlights include:

- Kiev – the Caves Monastery, St Sophia Cathedral complex and the open-air architectural museum.
- Lviv – ploshcha Rynok, the Old Town and the open-air architecture museum;
- Crimea – Khans' Palace and Chufut-Kale at Bakhchisaray, as well as the combination of mountains, sea and sun of the south coast around Yalta;
- Odessa – the group of excellent museums around the centre, and a performance at the opera house.
- Kamyanets-Podilsky – the old town, castle and surrounding landscape;
- Pochayiv – the Pochayiv Monastery complex, including attending the services;
- Pereyaslav-Khmelnytsky – a boat ride and visit to the open-air museum;
- Chernivtsi – the old town centre;
- Chernihiv – the grouping of 11th and 12th-century ecclesiastic buildings in the Dytynets.

Simply travelling through the country on your own is perhaps the biggest attraction of all – always unpredictable, never straightforward, and regularly providing some form of unanticipated adventure and escapade that requires the wildest of imagination and utmost sense of humour to survive. These memories, along with the people you meet along the way, are the real highlights.

ACCOMMODATION

Accommodation will be one of the biggest expenses of your trip. The standards of accommodation are beneath those of the West, but most of the time they are acceptable. Prices and brief descriptions of most hotels and camping grounds are given in the Places to Stay sections of major cities. Unless stated otherwise, hotel prices listed in Ukraine chapters are for rooms with private toilet, shower and (sometimes) bath, and are payable in Ukrainian currency.

Camping

Camp sites, usually on the edge of major cities and difficult to reach by public transport, aren't too common but are the cheapest form of accommodation. Tent sites are usually hidden away in a small neglected corner, with most people staying in two to five-person bungalows which vary in comfort and price. Some have bathrooms and showers (Category A), some don't (Category B), and most are arranged in clusters close to one another. Privacy isn't high, but some sites have a slightly alpine ambience with pretty surroundings, while others are quite miserable. None are exceptionally clean, and the main site bathrooms are often disgusting. Most camp sites also have a restaurant and café and sometimes a small motel.

Hotels

As far as character goes, most of the hotels are tall, unsightly concrete rectangles built under the Soviet regime in the 1960s and 1970s. Fortunately, the rooms are reasonably comfortable, though well worn. A typical double is about four metres by five metres with two small single beds and a small entry area, off which lies a small bathroom in various degrees of cleanliness. Sheets and towels are usually provided but don't expect soap or toilet paper. Almost every hotel has at least one restaurant, and some of the larger hotels have several as well as a few cafés and upper-storey bufety. Off the lobby of better hotels there usually lies a variety of facilities, often including a gift shop, newsstand, travel bureau and exchange booth.

Some cities have turn-of-the-century hotels which are a delight but are either completely falling apart or completely renovated and very expensive.

All hotels, especially in Crimea and in the west, have water problems, often with no hot water and sometimes no water at all. Ask about the situation of the *voda* (water) when you check in, because there might be special times when there isn't a supply.

Checking In When you check in, it's best to start with a smile. The receptionist will ask where you're from and to see your passport, after which they'll reach for a special foreigners' list of prices. Many hotels require you to fill out a general identification information form prior to checking in – but trying to decipher it can be a problem. The receptionist will usually assist you. You're usually given a hotel card with your room number on it, which you then show to your floor lady (*dezhurna*), who then gives you your key. The dezhurna is usually the person you return the key to when you leave and the one to ask for toilet paper, extra blankets and hot water. Don't lose your hotel card. The receptionist will usually ask to keep your passport, but they should return it after you've paid and after they've registered you, which may take a few hours. If you get nervous tell them you need it back sooner to exchange money, although this always seems to cause irritation.

Top-End Hotels There are a few joint-venture luxury hotels in Ukraine which are well up to top Western standards but are overwhelmingly expensive. They're usually the only places staffed with reliable, courteous, English-speaking staff (what a delight) – who are often the best source of information. The toilets off the lobbies are the cleanest in town.

Unregistered Hotels In many cities there are so-called unregistered hotels that won't accept tourists, usually because they're beneath acceptable norms of cleanliness, mainly in the realm of bathrooms. They'll usually bluntly deny you service and redirect you to the most expensive hotel in town. However, in some of the small towns off the beaten path (Kremenets, for example), this might be the only hotel in town, so when they tell you 'no foreigners', you're stuck! Sometimes they'll let you stay just one night (if you 'don't tell anyone') but normally you have to have authorised permission – which entails your passport being stamped by the local passport and registration office (OVIR). This procedure could prove to be either simple or an impossible bureaucratic tightrope walk. It's best to get to small towns early in the day to give yourself options.

Other Accommodation

Homestays and exchanges are catching on, with an increasing number of travel agencies organising them (see Ukraine Getting There & Away). Usually the host family also acts as your personal guide and first-hand information resource.

As tourist traffic slowly increases, eager opportunists are offering rooms for hire in their houses and flats. This is still in the primitive stages, and great care should be made to find out what's involved; for example whether or not you have to share the double bed with snoring grandpa or need to take an hour's bus ride to get there. However, if you are lucky, this could be a refreshing and cheap accommodation alternative, with a great home-cooked meal thrown in. At railway stations, look out for people, usually older ladies, holding small signs which include the word 'kimnaty' (Ukrainian) or 'komnati' (Russian), meaning 'rooms'. Make sure you work out the price beforehand – in Kiev it was around US$10 per person per night, and about half that price in Odessa.

FOOD

Food and drinks in Ukraine have much in common with those you find in Russia. See the Food and Drinks sections in European Russia Facts for the Visitor for further information.

Ukrainian cuisine celebrates distinctive natural flavours and simple ingredients, being rarely heavily spiced or overly complicated but always hearty and rich. Many of the country's specialities stem from simple peasant dishes heavily based on grains and staple vegetables like potatoes, cabbage, beets and mushrooms, seasoned with garlic, dill and vinegar. Beef, pork, poultry and fish are widely used and most dishes are either boiled, fried or stewed. Desserts are usually heavily laden with honey and fruit, mainly cherries and plums, and often baked into sweet breads.

Unfortunately, and quite ironically, you often can't find good Ukrainian food in Ukraine. Most top-end restaurants serve trendy European cuisine, with Ukrainian fare relegated to skimpy appetisers. It's often doled out by the smaller cafeteria-style eateries, but their quality of ingredients often gives a bland impression of *varenyky* and borscht. You can still find good local cuisine but it may take a bit of effort. The best Ukrainian cooking is found in the home, and if you get invited to someone's house for a meal you'll be in for a treat.

Where to Eat

It's best to expect poor, inattentive service with sparse menu selections in most places. This way, when you're greeted with a waiter or waitress who acknowledges your existence above that of a nuisance, and when you're actually served something agreeable, it will seem all the more delightful.

Restaurants Hotel restaurants are the most reliable, but an increasing number of private places are popping up, offering a more inviting and intimate alternative to the gala ballroom overkill. Most restaurants are open from noon to midnight, closing for an hour or two in the afternoon to prepare for dinner. Reservations are only necessary in popular places; most of the time you walk right in.

Menus are basically useless. They're rarely in English, and even if you can read

Ukrainian it won't help because they're usually cheaply printed pieces of rice paper and barely decipherable. The chances that a waiter or waitress speaks English is about a million to one. If you're getting nowhere, just say a few words like borscht, *salat* (salad), *varenyky* (dumplings), *myaso* (meat), *kurka* (chicken), *kartoplya* (potatoes) or *ovochi* (vegetables). In general, service is slow and drawn out. For most Ukrainians, eating out is a major (and expensive) social event that goes on and on. Restaurants are usually not geared for customers in a hurry. Bring a book or good conversation. If you want a quiet meal, come before 7 pm, because around 8 pm the obligatory band (almost always tone deaf) comes out and everyone boogies.

Cafeterias If you want a quick meal with no hassles, head to one of the many cafeteria-style eateries, called *yidalnya*, *stolova* or sometimes just *kafe*. You usually pick up a tray and the woman in a white *shmok* behind the counter ladles out heaped portions of varenyky, scalding borscht, potatoes, meatballs, random salads and fruit-compote drinks. As it's ridiculously cheap, you don't feel so bad if it's not the best quality, but more often than not the food is hot, starchy and tasty – and quick. A *varenychna* is an eatery that just serves varenyky. A *shashlychna* is a sort of shashlyk stand. These cafeterias are usually open from 8 or 9 am to 6 or 7 pm.

Bufet A *bufet* is really just a small eatery or snack bar which sometimes can cook you a quick meal to order, but is more likely just to have a few precooked greasy snacks and small sandwiches. You find these in railway stations and on the upper floors of hotels. A *zakusochna* is an even smaller bufet.

Kafe A *kafe* is sometimes a cafeteria and sometimes more like a café in the West, where you can have a coffee or tea accompanied by a pastry or piece of cake. They're scattered throughout the centre of cities and vary quite a bit in ambience and menu.

Coffee is usually a frothy, grind-filled, Turkish-style beverage, and tea is usually black and strong – and both are overly sweetened, so if you don't want to gag on sugar say *bez tsukor* or *malo tsukor* (without or just a little sugar). Often jam is used to sweeten tea, as is honey and lemon. The cakes and pastries are delicious when fresh. A *pyrizhkova* is a sort of café/bakery that specialises in cakes and sweets.

Snack Kiosks Small snack kiosks cluster around railway and bus stations, usually selling drinks and just one species of snack, such as limp pieces of greasy pizza or even greasier *piroshky* – a sort of stuffed doughbomb. They're cheap, fast and often tempting. They sometimes call themselves a *zakusochna*.

Markets Always hectic, always colourful, the *rynok*, or marketplace/bazaar, is the supermarket of Ukraine, and the critical focal point of a local economy where the gardens' excess produce is sold. A daily trip, usually in the early morning, is a ritual sacred to each household, and for the tourist a reliable source of fresh vegetables, fruit, honey, nuts, cheese, eggs and various hanging chunks of meat – as well as a form of relentless entertainment. If you're camping or wanting to make sandwiches for the road, this is where to go. Some of the bigger markets have the dairy products in a separate *molocharna* section. In small towns they're open only in the mornings, and in all markets, this is when the selection is best.

Food Stores These are the least reliable source of food and inspiration – often barren shelves with two unlabelled jars and a couple of dusty cans. However, there are some *hastronoms*, or food stores, that do quite well, selling bottled water and bread, along with a random selection of fruit and vegetables and some meats and cheeses. Lines are usually long because prices are cheapest. A *bulochna* is a bakery, a *kondyterska* sells confectionery and a *kulynarna* is something like a delicatessen. Each store is basically a

UKRAINE

Salo

Salo, сало, otherwise known as pig fat or lard, is sacred to Ukrainians. The eating of salo is a centuries-old tradition that runs deep and thick in Ukrainian blood. Any local will describe the moment of the salo's dissolving on the tongue in terms of sheer ecstasy. Spread thick on bread, or wrapped separately in a newspaper bundle, it's a delicacy that accompanies many humble meals. During the Soviet years, meat was often unavailable or prohibitively expensive, but salo, the faithful alternative, was always there – and still is. Conveniently stored in vats, it needs no refrigeration and has the longevity of fine wine.

Not all salo is the same. Each region takes pride in the texture and flavour of its local salo, sometimes even mixing in tiny flecks of bacon or chunks of garlic for an extra crunch. A visit to any local marketplace will reveal buyers carefully scrutinising hunks of lard before selecting the one of the finest quality.

As for health considerations, most Ukrainians say that a little salo a day keeps the doctor away. It is even believed to absorb harmful radiation; there was a dramatic increase in salo consumption after the Chornobyl disaster. When asked whether salo clogs the arteries, most Ukrainians will argue that, on the contrary, it simply adds a protective lubricant. ∎

---

hit-or-miss thing, bread being the most common item sold. In larger cities, there are Western-style markets which sell Western products at high hard-currency prices.

Varenyky

Varenyky, вареники, sometimes known as *halusky*, are by far the most popular Ukrainian dish. Small dumplings made with rolled dough are filled with a variety of ingredients, thrown into a huge pot of scalding water and boiled for a few minutes until they float – very delicious and addictive, but tastiness varies according to the quality of the filling. Almost all restaurants serve them, usually with either cheese or meat, and almost always with sour cream or a grease-like sauce. *Pyrohy* usually refers to larger baked, pie-like varenyky filled with the same kinds of ingredients. Smaller, appetiser-sized versions of varenyky are called *pyrizhky*. Common combinations include:

з м'ясом (*'z MYA-som'*) – with meat
з сиром (*'z SIH-rom'*) – with cottage cheese
з голандським сиром (*'z ho-lahnd-SKIM SIH-rom'*) – with cheese
з картоплею (*'z kahr-TOP-leh-yu'*) – with potato
з капустою (*'z kah-POOS-to-yu'*) – with cabbage

з грибами (*'z hrih-BAH-mih'*) – with mushrooms
з вишнями (*'z VIHSH-nya-mih'*) – with cherries
з повидлом (*'z po-VIHD-lom'*) – with jam

Borscht

The national soup, and adopted by other Slavic cultures, borscht, борщ, is based on a beet and mixed-vegetable broth and comes in dozens of varieties. The most popular version is a clear broth, but cream is often added. A simple gauge of quality is the thickness of its ingredients – the best has loads of beets, beans, onions, carrots and potatoes, sometimes topped off with meat or sausage or tiny mushroom-filled varenyky and seasoned with garlic, dill, parsley and bay leaves. Often you'll simply get a watered-down version with a few sad slivers of beet pathetically floating around.

Holubtsi

Translated as 'little dove', *holubtsi*, голубці, are cabbage rolls stuffed with seasoned rice with meat or buckwheat, usually topped with a tomato-based sauce.

Kotleta po-Kyivsky

Known to the English-speaking world as chicken Kiev, *kotleta po-Kyivsky*, котлета по-київськи, does exist, but for some reason it's not easy to find. It's a chunk of boneless chicken stuffed with butter, seasoned, floured and deep fried – absolutely delicious if you can track down the 'elusive hen'.

Kasha

An ancient dish, *kasha*, каша, is basically a grain-based gruel. The most common kind is *hrechana kasha*, a buckwheat porridge, seasoned and eaten with a sauce as a side dish or used as a stuffing.

Khleeb

Khleeb, хліб, is the Ukrainian word for bread. Sweet breads and rolls *(bulochky)* are steeped with honey and tradition and are often associated with holidays or ceremonies. *Babka* is a sweet egg bread popular during Easter but available all year. *Kalach* is similar to babka but denser and braided into a circular shape. *Paska* is the official Easter bread, usually decorated and shaped into a cross. *Korovay* is a tall, cylindrical traditional wedding bread. *Pampushki* can be fresh rolls soaked in crushed garlic and oil, or a sort of sweet jam or fruit-filled baked roll. *Makivnik* is a sweet poppy-seed bread flavoured with honey and molasses, popular around Christmas. *Khrusty* are deep-fried strips of sweet dough coated with sugar, and *medivnyk* is a honey cake that can keep for days without going stale.

Appetisers

A meal will often begin with zakusky, закуски *('zah-KOOS-kih')*, generally one of the following:

сир *('sihr')* – cottage cheese
чорна, червона ікра *('CHOR-nah', 'cher-VO-nah eek-RAH')* – black, red caviar
суп, підлива *('soop', 'pid-LEE-vah')* – soup, sauce
салата *('sah-LAH-ta')* – salad
асорті *('ah-sor-TEE')* – mixed plate

Main Course

Main course is друге *('DROO-heh')*. Some commonly found options are:

без м'яса *('bez MYAH-sah')* – without meat
м'ясо, свинина *('MYA-so', 'svih-NIH-nah')* – meat, pork
шашлик *('shash-LIHK')* – shashlyk
теляча котлета *('teh-LYA-chah kot-LEH-tah')* – veal cutlet
курка *('KOOR-kah')* – chicken
птиця *('PTIH-tsyah')* – poultry
риба, форель, щука *('RIH-bah', 'fo-REHL', 'SHCHOO-kah')* – fish, trout, pike
ковбаса *('kohv-bah-SAH')* – sausage
фрикаделі *('frih-kah-DEH-li')* – meat balls
макарони *('mah-kah-RO-nee')* – pasta
рис *('rihs')* – rice

Vegetables

Vegetables are овочі *('O-vo-chee')*, and those on the menu may include:

картопля, бараболя *('kahr-TOP-lya, bah-rah-BOL-ya')* – potato
квасоля *('kvah-SOL-ya')* – beans
буряки *('boo-rya-KIH')* – beet
капуста *('kah-POOS-tah')* – cabbage
цибуля *('tsih-BOO-lya')* – onions
морква *('MORK-vah')* – carrots
горох *('ho-ROKH')* – peas
помідори *('po-mee-DO-rih')* – tomatoes
гриби *('hrih-BIH')* – mushrooms

Dessert

If you're still going when десерт *('deh-SEIIRT')*, is served, you may be offered:

тісто or тістечко, торт *('TEES-to' or 'TEES-tehch-ko', 'tort')* – pastry, cake
сирник *('SIHR-nihk')* – cheesecake, baked cheese
печиво *('PEH-chih-vo')* – biscuit, cookie
морозиво *('mo-RO-zih-vo')* – ice cream

Fruit & Nuts

Fruit, фрукти *('FROOK-tih')*, and nuts, горіхи *('ho-REE-khih')*, are an important part of many desserts as well as being sold fresh in markets:

яблука *('YAB-loo-kah')* – apples
вишні *('VIHSH-nee')* – cherries
апельсини *('ah-pehl-SIH-nih')* – oranges

банани *('bah-NAH-nih')* – bananas
лимони *('lih-MO-nih')* – lemons
абрикоси *('ahb-rih-KO-sih')* – apricots
виноград *('vih-no-HRAHD')* – grapes
персики *('PEHR-sih-kih')* – peaches
трускавки, суниці *('TROOS-khav-kih',
'soo-NIH-tsee')* – strawberries
сливи *('SLIH-vih')* – plums
порічки *('po-REECH-kih')* – red currants
мигдаль *('mih-HRAHL')* – almonds
волоські горіхи *('vo-LOHS-kee ho-RIH-
khee')* – walnuts
земляні горіхи *('zehm-lya-NEE ho-REE-
khih')* – peanuts
ізюм *('ee-ZYUM')* – raisins

Miscellaneous

Assorted useful words and phrases are:

сніданок *('snee-DAH-nok')* – breakfast
обід *('o-BEED')* – lunch
обід, вечеря *('o-BEED', 'veh-CHER-yah')*
– early dinner, late dinner
перекуска *('peh-reh-KOOS-kah')* – snack
гарчий *('har-YACH-ee')* – hot
холодний *('kho-LOHD-nee')* – cold
меню, рахунок *('mehn-YOO', 'rah-KHOO-
nok')* – menu, bill
офіціант (-ка) *('o-fee-tsee-AHNT(-kah)')* –
waiter (waitress)
Можна замовити? *('MOZH-nah za-MO-
vih-tih?')* – May I order?

DRINKS

Drinks, напої *('nah-PO-yee')*, are for the
most part similar to those found in European
Russia. Both Crimea and Transcarpathia
produce excellent wines.

сік, компот *('seek', 'KOHM-poht')* – juice,
fruit drink
молоко, йогурт *('mo-lo-KO', 'YO-hoort')*
– milk, yoghurt
гарячий шоколад *('har-YAH-chee
SHOK-o-lahd')* – hot chocolate
кава, чай *('KAH-vah', 'chai')* – coffee, tea
пиво, вино *('PIH-voh', 'vih-NOH')* – beer,
wine
горілка *('ho-REEL-kah')* – vodka

Козацький квас *('koh-ZATS-kee kvahs')* –
Cossack kvas
Українська горілка з перцем *('oo-krah-
YEENS-kah ho-REEL-kah z PEHR-
tsehm')* – Ukrainian pepper vodka

ENTERTAINMENT
Theatre

Treat yourself to the high-and-mighty opera
house: it may be the only time in your life a
ticket to the opera will cost you US$0.25,
and more often than not you'll see an excellent performance. The opera and ballet
houses in Lviv, Odessa and Kiev are spectacular, and other cities have them, too –
Kharkiv's has an exceptionally good troupe.
Each city also has its philharmonic and a
number of drama theatres, usually at least
one where performances are in Ukrainian
and one where they're in Russian. There's
also the obligatory puppet theatre and the
circus – a sort of theatre in its own right,
complete with bears on roller skates, live
music and screaming kids. Kiev's circus is
the largest.

To purchase tickets or find out what's
playing, head to the *teatralny kasa*, or ticket
office, usually with several locations in the
city centre. They predominantly sell only
advance tickets, with same-day tickets available at the theatre box office, sometimes that
morning but usually about one hour before
the performance. If the ticket office tells you
the show is sold out, go to the theatre anyway
– you'll probably be able to purchase a seat
beforehand. The service bureaus in some
hotels sell tickets, but for a higher price, of
course. Some cities publish cultural information gazettes with listings of events: *Vechirny
Kyiv (Evening Kiev)* is one.

Rock & Jazz Concerts

Large rock concerts are usually held in big
sports complexes or cultural palaces. Once
in a while you'll get an over-the-hill Western
performer sweeping up the tail end of a
mammoth world tour, but it's usually domestic bands with varying degrees of talent.
Each restaurant features their own rock band
in the evening – it's amazing how many of

these bands there are. They usually play deafening, synthesiser-laden 1970s pop tunes – sometimes in its own twisted way entertaining, but usually ear-splitting.

Some cities will have a bar or club with some decent jazz or folk, but it's a random thing. A number of jazz festivals do swing through. Look out for posters advertising these events.

Folk Shows

These are usually geared for tourists, but they're always colourful and entertaining. Ukrainian culture is rich in folk music and dance (see the Folk Dance section in Facts about Ukraine). The venues range from a reserved restaurant to a city theatre, and in summer they're staged at the open-air museums of folk architecture. Your hotel's service bureau may have information, as will the teatralny kasa. You can sometimes join a tour group's packaged folklore dinner-show if there's extra space.

THINGS TO BUY

Ukraine's rich folk culture is world renowned and there's much more to buy than just *pysanky*, the beautifully painted eggs. A trip to some of the places mentioned in Kiev's Things to Buy section would be a good introduction to what's out there.

Souvenirs & Gifts

The trademark Ukrainian souvenirs are the pysanky, or painted Easter eggs. Every region, even village, has hundreds of distinct patterns, and each pattern has a special meaning and ritual. Traditionally, the eggs were drained and decorated using a lengthy heated-wax procedure, but the wooden eggs mostly sold today are directly painted on, and produced not for ceremony but for tourists. They're cheap and easy to carry around.

Ukrainian embroidery (*vyshyvka*) is equally steeped in tradition, with each region having traditional patterns, colours and even unique stitches. The most common is the black and red cross-stitch or *khresty*. Shirts for men (*sorochky*), blouses for women (*blyuza*), as well as belts, skirts and table-

Some designs found on pysanky, or decorated eggs, are as old as the Egyptian pyramids

cloths are all attractively embroidered and sold. A hand-embroidered shirt, a labour-intensive endeavour, will cost anywhere from US$10 to US$40, depending on the embroidery's complexity and the quality of material. Also popular are the long, narrow embroidered towels called *rushnyky*. Woven kilims (rugs) are usually machine-made, so they don't have the attraction of the hand-made ones in the museums, but they're still a good deal.

The ceramics (*keramiky*) are usually folksy and attractive with lots of green and yellow flowery patterns, and ridiculously cheap. Keep an eye out for the black ceramic (often candlesticks) with a matt finish, common in Lviv as well as in Kiev.

Carved wooden boxes (*derevyani skrynki*), plates (*tarilka*) and candlesticks are plentiful and attractive. One technique is *enkrustasya* (encrustation), where the wood is decorated with colourful beads and metals inlaid into patterns.

There are a few antique stores around, mostly in Kiev, with the hot item being old hand-painted wooden icons – most of which are officially illegal to take out of the country (see the Customs section in this chapter).

Sources

During the days of state-controlled tourism, hard-currency shops in Ukraine, called *kashtan* ('chestnut'), were the only reliable places to buy Western goods (for hard cur-

UKRAINE

rency only). Today, they often sell nothing more than alcohol, chocolate and cheap Western perfumes, and are low on anything remotely resembling a souvenir. There are exceptions, though, so they're sometimes worth a peek.

Ukrainsky Suvenir One of the best sources for gifts and souvenirs is this nationwide chain of gift shops. The stocks and quality vary wildly between outlets, with Kiev's the best, Odessa's and Vinnytsya's good and Lviv's bad. But they're all worth a look for embroidery, ceramics, carved wooden boxes etc.

Department Stores Most sizeable towns have a TsUM (Tsentralny Univermag, or central department store) or GUM (Gosudarstvenny Univermag, or state department store). Both usually have a portion of a floor dedicated to gifts and souvenirs, and they're often the cheapest place. Selection is random, and finding the gift section difficult, with little order to the vast sprawl of former-Soviet consumer items. Smaller state-run stores called *khudozhestvenny salon* are like art stores and are a good place to look for crafts and gifts.

Craft Markets The recent influx of tourists has caused a number of craft markets to pop up catering to the tourist crowd. Sometimes it's just a few vendors near a park, but a few cities have established sites. The best are in Lviv near the Opera House, and along Andriyivsky uzviz in Kiev. Here women sell their handiwork, produced over many long winter hours. Not only folk crafts but paintings, jewellery, books, pins and ceramics all turn up at the markets. All prices are bargainable, but the handmade items usually don't get bargained down too low. The ultimate craft market, more like a craft fair, is held every Saturday in Kosiv, near Ivano-Frankivsk.

Bazaars, often attached to a produce market (rynok), are huge subcities of buying and selling mayhem. The items are targeted at locals, with everything from baby animals and cheap clothing to even cheaper electronic equipment, spare car parts and booze. They're fun to roam around in but you'll rarely find anything to tempt you.

Tourist Sights Often the best places to pick up folk crafts and gifts are the tourist sights themselves. Many museums have small gift tables off the lobby, and some places have full-blown gift shops – there are four well-stocked ones in Kiev's Caves Monastery, as well as one in the Golden Gate and two in the city's open-air museum of folk architecture.

Getting There & Away

Travel into Ukraine is unrestricted at all border points. Land entrance or exit can be made from Russia to the north and east; Belarus to the north; Poland, Slovakia and Hungary to the west; and Romania and Moldova to the south-west. By water you can enter or exit the country via the Black Sea ports of Odessa or Yalta, or terminate a long river trip on the Danube at the port city of Izmayil. By air, almost all international flights arrive and depart from Kiev's puny Boryspil International Airport – which is often the easiest way to get in or out of the country.

AIR

For a list of air travel terminology, see the Air Travel Glossary in the European Russia Getting There & Away chapter.

To/From Kiev

Most international flights enter and exit Ukraine at the Boryspil International Airport in Kiev, about 40 km south-east of the centre. Upon arrival, reserve about one hour to find your baggage among the pile outside on the tarmac, and pass through customs and passport control – and at least an extra hour if you need to apply for a visa. Facilities at the airport are meagre and slow, with construction going on, so when departing give yourself at least two hours prior to departure time for passport control and customs. For getting to/from the airport see the Kiev chapter.

Kiev is linked with most major European cities (Amsterdam, Berlin, Brussels, Budapest, Frankfurt, Helsinki, London, Manchester, Moscow, Munich, Paris, Prague, Vienna, Warsaw and Zurich), with the main European international airlines servicing Kiev to/from their home cities at least twice a week – including Air France, Austrian Airlines, Balkan Bulgarian Airlines, ČSA, Finnair, KLM, LOT Polish Airlines, Luft-

hansa, Malév Hungarian Airlines and Swissair.

There are two national airlines. Ukraine International Airlines deals with flights between Ukraine and most major Western European capitals, including weekly services between Kiev and Amsterdam, Berlin, Brussels, Frankfurt, London, Manchester, Munich, Paris, Vienna and Zurich. Air Ukraine provides services between Ukraine and North America, including weekly flights to Chicago, New York, Toronto and Washington, DC. Services to/from Kiev and Eastern Europe and along the south-eastern Mediterranean include weekly flights to Athens, Cairo, Istanbul, Prague, Tel Aviv and Warsaw. Air Ukraine is also the only domestic carrier (see Ukraine Getting Around).

For the addresses of all airline offices in Kiev see Kiev Getting There & Away. International contacts for Air Ukraine and Ukraine International include:

Air Ukraine
   New York – ☎ (212) 599 0555
   Washington, DC – ☎ (202) 833 4648
   Toronto – ☎ (416) 236 7547
Ukraine International
   Austria – ☎ (1) 712 96 83
   Belgium – ☎ (02) 722 31 32
   Canada – ☎ (1 800) 876 01 14
   France – ☎ (1) 40 74 00 04
   Germany – ☎ (069) 502 005
   Holland – ☎ (020) 604 12 04
   Switzerland – ☎ (411) 81 65 102
   UK – ☎ (01293) 502 005
   USA – ☎ (1 800) 876 0114

To/From Elsewhere in Ukraine

Outside Kiev, international flights are limited. The airport at Lviv is serviced by LOT Polish Airlines and ČSA, with weekly flights to/from Warsaw and Prague. Air Ukraine has weekly services between Chicago and Lviv. Ukraine International has weekly flights between Lviv and each of Amsterdam, Frankfurt, London and Manchester; and occasional, seasonal flights connecting Lviv with Berlin, Brussels, Vienna, Munich, Paris and Zürich. The airport at Odessa is serviced by Austrian Airlines, with two weekly flights to/from Vienna. Air Ukraine has a weekly service between Ivano-Frankivsk and New York. Ukraine International has seasonal flights between Ivano-Frankivsk and Manchester from June to the end of August. Aeroflot has weekly flights between Simferopol and Moscow and St Petersburg.

LAND

At the time of writing all official land border crossings into Ukraine were unrestricted, with emergency visas available for rail, bus and auto travellers. However, the issuing of emergency visas at the Russian border was rumoured to be unreliable, and it's probably best to get your visa beforehand.

Bus

Buses stop at the border for customs and passport controls. The most common bus crossing is between Uzhhorod and Michalovice in Slovakia.

Train

International trains cross into Ukraine at more than 10 different locations, coming from seven different countries.

Border crossings for those holding visas are a straightforward but drawn-out affair, with a steady stream of customs and ticket personnel scrutinising your passport one after another. About an hour or so before crossing the border, you'll be given a customs form to fill out (see Customs in Ukraine Facts for the Visitor). If you're leaving the country you'll have to provide the original customs document you received when entering. A soldier usually accompanies the customs officer, in order to check for stowaways and the like, and if you look suspicious you may have your bags checked, usually when leaving the country, to make sure you're not smuggling any icons or antiques. To apply for an emergency visa when entering the country you'll be escorted off the train at or near the border (see Visas in Ukraine Facts for the Visitor).

Car & Motorbike

There are about 11 main road routes into Ukraine through frontier border stations. To avoid possible complications, drivers should enter through one of these official routes, although there are some smaller, unregulated roads that cross over as well, especially along the Russian and Belarusian borders. Roads entering Ukraine often have two numbers: their international number, as well as their Ukrainian equivalent: for example, the E40 (A259) between Poland and Ukraine. You can also have your car or motorbike ferried into Odessa or Yalta from seaports throughout the Black Sea and the Mediterranean.

You'll need an International Driving Permit (from motorists' organisations like the UK's AA or RAC and the USA's AAA), the vehicle's registration papers and some form of auto insurance, preferably full coverage. Make sure your insurance carrier covers driving into the former USSR – apparently British insurance is not valid in any CIS country. Coverage can supposedly be purchased at the Uzhhorod border. The registration papers should preferably be in the form of an international motor vehicle certificate (also available from motorists' organisations). Crossings may involve some questionable extra 'road tax'.

According to RAC, a fire extinguisher, first-aid kit and warning triangle are compulsory – and it's a good idea to have them anyway, although in practice it may not be enforced. Fill up with petrol as late as you can before crossing the border (it's not always easy to get inside the country – see Car & Motorbike in Ukraine Getting Around) and have your vehicle thoroughly serviced beforehand. Take at least one spare petrol can and as many spare parts as you can possibly carry. Most important is a detailed road map, as these are hard to find inside the country (see Maps in Ukraine Facts for the Visitor). If your car is your most precious possession, don't drive it into Ukraine. For information about driving your car or motorbike inside Ukraine see the Ukraine Getting Around chapter.

To/From Russia

Bus A few buses a day go from Kharkiv's main bus station across the border into Russia on the E95 (M2) road, including a daily 20-hour trip to Moscow stopping in Kursk, Oryol and Tula on the way. The official frontier crossing is 40 km north of Kharkiv and 40 km south of Belgorno near the Russian border town of Zhuravlevka, just west of the rail crossing.

Train Most major Ukrainian cities have daily services to Moscow, with two border crossings: one used by trains heading to Kiev, the other by trains passing through Kharkiv.

Trains between Kiev and Moscow (15 hours, several daily) go via Bryansk (Russia) and Konotop (Ukraine), crossing at the Ukrainian border town of Seredyna-Buda. The best trains to take (numbers are southbound/northbound) between Moscow and Kiev are No 1/2, the *Ukrainia*, or No 3/4, the *Kiev*. The best trains between Moscow and Lviv (28 hours, daily via Kiev) are Nos 33/34 and 73/74. Between Moscow and Odessa (28 hours, daily via Kiev) there's the No 23/24, the *Odessa*. Between Moscow and Chernivtsi there are two daily trains, also travelling via Kiev and taking about 30 hours; one train goes on to Ivano-Frankivsk (39 hours).

Trains between Kharkiv and Moscow (12 to 13 hours, several times daily via Kursk) cross the border just 40 km north of Kharkiv, just east of the road crossing. The best train is No 19/20, the *Kharkiv*. Between Moscow and Simferopol (25 to 27 hours, daily via Kharkiv) the best trains are No 67/68, the *Simferopol*, and No 31/32, the *Krym*. Trains between Moscow and Donetsk (21 to 22 hours, twice daily), Dnipropetrovsk (19 to 20 hours, twice daily), Zaporizhzhya (19 hours, daily) and Sevastopol (29½ hours, daily) all go through Kharkiv.

There's also a long train every other day between Kharkiv and Vladivostok and back (No 54 eastbound, No 53 westbound) via Penza, Kurgan, Novosibirsk, Chita and Khabarovsk, among other places. In summer, trains travel between Crimea and places in Siberia at least as far east as Irkutsk. Many trains travelling between Moscow and the Caucasus go through Kharkiv, including the seasonal service to Rostov-on-Don (12 hours), Sochi (22 hours) and Tbilisi (31 hours).

Daily international trains passing through Ukraine to/from Moscow's Kievsky Vokzal include No 9/10, the *Pushkin*, Kiev-Lviv-Chop-Belgrade, with a carriage to Athens four times a week; No 51/52, the *Slovakia Express*, Kiev-Lviv-Chop-Bratislava-Vienna; No 15/16 Kiev-Lviv-Chop-Budapest, with a carriage to Venice twice a week; No 7/8, the *Dukla Express*, Kiev-Lviv-Chop-Uzhhorod-Prague; and No 59/60, the *Sofia Express*, Kiev-Chernivtsi-Sofia.

Car & Motorbike The main auto route taken between Kiev and Moscow starts off as the E93 (M20) north of Kiev, and then becomes the M3 when it branches off to the east halfway to Chernihiv. The M3 then goes all the way to Moscow, but the E93 branches off soon after the Russian border. Between this crossing and the one north of Kharkiv, many small roads cross the border, but they don't have official frontier posts.

Driving from Ukraine to the Caucasus, east of Donetsk the border frontier point is on the E40 (M19) road crossing just before the Russian town of Novoshakhtinsk at the Ukrainian border village of Dovzhansky, about 150 km east of Donetsk. Another major road crosses the border just south-east of Luhansk, as well as one to the south between Mariupol and Rostov along the northern edge of the Sea of Azov, but neither have official frontier posts.

Car Ferry Ferry services can carry you and your vehicle across the border from Kerch, at the extreme eastern tip of Crimea, usually to the Russian ports of Temryuk, 83 km around to the north, or Anapa (96 km) and Novorossiysk (150 km) around to the south.

Visas Everyone requires a visa to enter Russia (see Visas in European Russia Facts for the Visitor).

UKRAINE

To/From Belarus

Train There are five main rail crossings between Belarus and Ukraine. The busiest – used by both Kiev-Minsk trains (11 hours, daily) and Simferopol-Minsk trains (29 hours, daily) – crosses the border about 40 km south of Homel and about 70 km north of Chernihiv, near the town of Dobryanka on the Ukrainian side.

The Minsk-Kharkiv line (17 hours, daily via Sumy) crosses the border near the Ukrainian village of Derevyny, and its first major stop in Ukraine is in the town of Shchors.

The Minsk-Odessa train (27 hours, every other day) either goes through Kiev, crossing the border south of Homel, or takes a more direct route to the west through Zhytomyr, crossing the border about 45 km south of the Belarusian city of Mazyr at the Belarusian border village of Slavechna. The first major stop in Ukraine is in the town of Ovruch.

The Vilnius-Lviv (15 hours, twice daily) and Minsk-Lviv (17 hours, daily) trains pass through Baravanichy (Belarus) and Rivne (Ukraine), crossing at the border village of Buchlichy, about 50 km south of the Belarusian town of Lunynets and about 30 km north of the Ukrainian town of Dubrovytsya.

The Kiev-Brest (14 hours, three to four times daily), Odessa-Brest (16 hours, every other day) and Chernivtsi-Brest (21 hours, daily via Lviv) trains cross the border near Malaryta (Belarus), halfway between Brest and Kovel, the first major stop in Ukraine.

Car & Motorbike Six roads cross between Ukraine and Belarus but only two have official frontier stations. The main M20 motor route north from Chernihiv to Homel crosses near the rail crossing, just north of the Ukrainian village of Novy Yarylovichy and south of the Belarusian village of Novaja Huta.

The main M14 motor route between Brest and Kovel crosses the border north-east of the rail crossing, just south-east of the Belarus village of Makrany.

Visas Belarus does *not* issue visas at the borders, except under special circumstances (see Visas in Belarus Facts for the Visitor).

To/From Poland

Trains between Lviv and the Polish cities of Warsaw (13 hours, daily), Krakow (about seven hours; change in Przemysl) and Lublin (10½ hours, daily) cross at the well-used Ukrainian border stop of Mostiska, with Medyka on the Polish side, about 20 km east of Przemysl (2½ hours, three times daily to/from Lviv), where trains split to Warsaw to the north and Krakow to the west. The same crossing is used for road traffic on the E40 (A259) with Shehyni the frontier town on the Ukrainian side and Medyka in Poland. This crossing tends to be crowded at weekends.

The Warsaw-Kiev line (16 to 20 hours, two to three times daily), which passes through Lutsk, Rivne and Zhytomyr en route, crosses the border over the western Buh River just south of the Belarus border. Polish auto route 82 also crosses here, changing to the A255 in Ukraine. On the Ukraine side the border town is Jahodin and on the Polish side it's Dorohusk. For road travellers the Polish border town is Okopy Nowe.

Visas Americans and most Western Europeans do not require a visa to enter Poland, but Australian and New Zealand passport holders do require one. At the Munich consulate, a double-entry tourist visa costs DM100, a double-entry transit visa is DM85, and a multi-entry transit visa costs DM140.

To/From Slovakia

The Prague-Kiev (30 hours, daily) train (which stops at Košice in Slovakia and Lviv en route) crosses into Ukraine at the Slovak border post of Čierna nad Tisou and the Ukrainian border town of Chop. The E50 motor route from Košice and Michalovce crosses at Vysne Nemecke on the Slovak side to Uzhhorod in Ukraine, becoming the M17 in Ukraine. Daily buses also cross the border. Expect long queues on weekends due to local traffic.

Americans and most Western Europeans do not require a visa to enter either Slovakia or the Czech Republic, but Canadian, Australian and New Zealand passport holders should check their status.

To/From Hungary

Train The short border with Hungary has one major rail crossing, with trains running between Lviv and Budapest (12 hours, daily), crossing from Zahony on the Hungarian side to Chop on the Ukrainian side, 23 km from Uzhhorod.

Car & Motorbike There are four road frontier crossings. The main auto route from Debrecen and Nyiregyhaza, the E573 (M17), crosses at the same site as the rail crossing. There may be long waits during the weekends. The other three crossings, although official, may not be open all year. The crossing near the Ukrainian village of Dzvinkove is about 20 km south-east. About 35 km farther south-east, Hungarian road 41 crosses at the Hungarian border village of Beregsurany, just south-west of the Ukrainian town of Berehove. Still another 30 km south-east is the frontier crossing at Tiszabecs in Hungary and Vylok on the Ukrainian side (on Hungarian road 491).

Visas Americans and most Western Europeans do not require a visa to enter Hungary, but Canadian, Australian and New Zealand passport holders should check their status.

To/From Romania

The Bucharest-Chernivtsi (11 hours, daily) line crosses the border about 40 km south of Chernivtsi at the Romanian border town of Vadul Siret, with Hlyboka on the Ukrainian side. The E85 (A269) crosses at the same border frontier in Romania, with Porubne on the Ukrainian side. An unofficial road crossing is also found along the picturesque border area over the Tisa River at the Ukrainian town of Tyachiv, about 30 km west of Sighetu Marmatiei (Romania) and halfway between Khust and Rakhiv in Ukraine.

All nationalities require a visa to enter Romania. Visas can be issued at the border for around US$22 for two months, but it's always a good idea to take care of this beforehand.

To/From Moldova

Trains running between Chisinau and Odessa (six hours, twice daily) cross from the border town of Kuchurhan on the Ukrainian side to Pervomaise on the Moldovan side, 30 km from Tiraspol. The official motor route E581(M14) also crosses here, as does the Chisinau-Kiev (14 hours, daily) train line.

Trains (12 hours, daily) and vehicles between Chisinau and Chernivtsi cross the official frontier from the border town of Mamalyha in Ukraine to Criva in Moldova, about 50 km east of Chernivtsi.

The main M21 road heading north-east out of Chisinau, and leading eventually to Kirovohrad well into Ukraine, crosses the border frontier about 20 km north-east of the Moldovan town of Dubashari on the Dnister River. Another road, the A272, crosses the Dnister River along the northern border of Moldova, with the Ukrainian city of Mohyliv-Podilsky on the left bank and the Moldovan town of Otaci on the right bank.

Visas Moldova requires visas from all nationalities. They can be obtained at any Moldovan embassy, for between US$50 and US$80, with no formal invitation needed. You can also pick up your visa at some European airports, such as Frankfurt, but not at Chisinau. Two passport photos are required.

Some trains between Chernivtsi and other parts of Ukraine pass through Moldova en route. According to the Moldovan embassy in the USA, if you're not planning to leave the train in Moldova, and your ticket shows that your destination is in Ukraine and you'll be in Moldova less than 24 hours, no visa is needed.

SEA & RIVER
Black Sea

Entering or leaving Ukraine by ship can be done through the Black Sea ports of Odessa and Yalta, travelling to/from various ports in the Black Sea and the Mediterranean. When entering Ukraine, customs and passport control takes place at the Sea Port building *(morsky vokzal)*. The company that handles this service is the Black Sea Shipping Company (Chornomorsky Morsky Parokhodstvo), based in Odessa. They sail to Alexandria (Egypt), Beirut (Lebanon), Haifa (Israel), Istanbul (Turkey), Larnaka (Cyprus), Latakia (Syria), Limassol (Cyprus), Piraeus (Greece), Port Said (Egypt), Rhodes (Greece), Santorini (Greece), Sochi (Russia), Syracuse (Italy), Thessaloniki (Greece) and Varna (Bulgaria). Rare destinations include Algiers, Barcelona, Genoa, Marseilles, Naples and Valletta (Malta). Services to these destinations may not run year-round.

The main destinations that are dependable year-round are Haifa, Istanbul, Limassol, Piraeus and Port Said, with some of the Istanbul boats stopping in Varna on the way. Boats for these destinations generally sail weekly in summer and twice a month during winter. The most frequent and reliable is the Odessa to Istanbul journey, usually on a boat called the *Yunost*.

Prices have gone up drastically, making a voyage an expensive outing. One-way between Odessa and Istanbul is about US$100. A one-way ticket to Piraeus costs about US$200 for the cheapest possible accommodation, which is Category 4 – a four-berth cabin without washbasin. Category 1, a private cabin for two with bath and sitting room, runs to about US$145 per person between Odessa and Istanbul one-way. The prices are about one-third less during the off season, which is from October to March.

The Black Sea Shipping Company's headquarters (☎ (0482) 25 35 39; telex 23 27 16) is at Potyomkintsev ploshcha 1, Odessa 270026. Some of the travel agencies mentioned later in this chapter can also help with booking your trip. From the USA, you can contact the Odessa America Cruise Company (☎ (516) 747 8880 or toll-free 1 800 221 3254), 170 Old Century Rd, Mineola, NY 11501. It represents the Black Sea Shipping Company and can arrange 'Ukrainian waterways' tours between Kiev and Odessa aboard the *Gluchkov* from May to October.

The cruises cost between US$895 and US$1595.

Danube River

The Ukrainian Danube Shipping Company (Dunaye-More) runs scheduled summer boat services up and down the Danube between its home port of Izmayil, about 85 km from the mouth of the Black Sea, and a wealth of European cities including Passau (Germany), Vienna, Bratislava (Slovakia), Budapest, Belgrade, Nikopol (Bulgaria) and Guirgiu (Romania). However, due to the war in the former Yugoslavia, at the time of writing, all passenger-boat traffic south of Budapest had been suspended, making a journey down the Danube from Western Europe to the Black Sea temporarily impossible. The company also runs seasonal boat trips to other ports on the Black Sea including Odessa, Yalta, Varna (Bulgaria), Constanta (Romania), Sochi and Istanbul. These services have irregular schedules, and are prone to cancellations.

The Ukrainian Danube Shipping Company also arranges occasional special trips from Izmayil to Istanbul via boat to Varna (six hours), then overland by bus to Istanbul (12 hours), which seems to be the cheapest way to get there.

The company's headquarters is at prospekt Suvorova 2, Izmayil 272630, Ukraine (☎ (04841) 90 210); or contact Transkruyz, Morsky Vokzal, kom 35, vulitsya Komnata 34, Izmayil 272630, Ukraine (☎ (04841) 9 09 59; fax (04841) 2 30 64; telex 232 136).

Foreign cruise lines also ply the Danube. In the USA, the Danube Shipping Company (☎ (213) 641 8001 or toll-free (1 800) 999 0226), 5250 West Century Blvd, Los Angeles, CA 90045, offers a number of European river cruises, including Danube river trips, but unfortunately they have also temporarily suspended their services south of Budapest.

When entering Izmayil by boat from an international destination, customs and passport controls are conducted at the river/sea port terminal (morsky vokzal). For those who arrive at Izmayil by river to find that boats to Odessa are not running, there's a nightly train to Odessa (eight to nine hours). There's a year-round hydrofoil service heading east along the last tiny leg of the Danube to the Ukrainian towns of Kiliia (50 minutes) and Vylkove (two hours).

TRAVEL AGENCIES & TOURS

Back during the long years of State restrictions, in order to navigate their way through the bureaucratic mess, most people who wished to travel to Ukraine were forced to seek the help of one of the specialised private tourist offices based abroad. Although travel is now unrestricted, these agencies still provide a wide range of services and can now offer a greater variety and flexibility of tours – some even organise adventure-oriented trips and treks. For those with a specific reason for travelling or who like to have all the potential hassles eliminated (and who have a bit more money to spend), these agencies can provide a worry-free alternative to travel in Ukraine. Besides arranging all accommodation, transportation, excursions, meals, tour guides etc, the agencies also take care of your visa for you. They can often provide this visa service by itself, but usually only if you purchase airline tickets or book a hotel through them. The trips are usually pricey, ranging anywhere from US$75 to US$175 per day (excluding airfare), depending on the services provided.

Unless noted otherwise, the travel agencies mentioned here provide a standard range of seasonal package tours to Ukraine, as well as visa services and prepaid hotel confirmations.

Australia

Gateway Travel (☎ (02) 745 3333; fax (02) 745 3237), 48 The Boulevard, Strathfield 2135, is one of the best agencies, with a wide and specialised variety of tours, excursions and services, including arranging boat cruises down the Dnipro and homestays.

Another to consider is Baltic & East European Travel (☎ (08) 232 1228; fax (08) 244 5528), 1st Floor, 2 Hindmarsh Square, Adelaide 5000.

Canada

Agencies include Caravel Tours: Travel Ltd (☎ (403) 963 4575), Box 277, Stony Plain, Alberta T0E 2G0; East West Travel (☎ (403) 476 1577), 12952 82nd St, Edmonton, Alberta T5E 2T2; Kobza (☎ (416) 251 9110; fax (416) 253 9515), 3235 Lakeshore Blvd West, Toronto, Ontario M8V 1M3; and Travel Unlimited (☎ (204) 586 8059), 869 Main St, Winnipeg, Manitoba R2W 2L5.

UK

Exodus (☎ (0181) 675 5550; fax (0181) 673 0779), 9 Weir Rd, London SW12 0LT, provides similar services to those offered by REI Adventures in the USA.

Intourist Travel (☎ (0171) 538 8600; fax (0171) 538 5967), Intourist House, 219 Marsh Wall, London E14 9FJ, is one of the biggest agencies, with all the former Intourist contacts.

Rochdale Travel Centre (☎ (01706) 311 4446; fax (01706) 526 668), 66 Drake St, Rochdale, Lancashire 0L16 1PA, specialises in travel to Ukraine – besides providing a wide range of tours, services and information, it's also a direct sales agent for Air Ukraine in the UK.

Tour de Force Travel (☎ (0171) 323 0747; fax (0171) 631 3667), 200-208 Tottenham Court Rd, London W1P 9LA, specialises in botany, natural history and art appreciation tours. And then there's Ukrainian Travel (☎ (0161) 633 2232), 27 Henshaw St, Oldham, Lancashire.

USA

American-International Homestays (☎ (303) 642 3088 or toll-free (1800) 876 2048; fax (303) 642 3365), PO Box 7178, Boulder, CO 80306-7178, arranges home stays – individual or group trips with accommodation in the home(s) of host families supervised by the organisation. Most of their Ukrainian contacts are in Kiev.

Dunwoodie Travel (☎ (914) 969 4200), 771A Yonkers Ave, Yonkers, NY 10704, provides various tours, visa services and hotel confirmations.

Home & Host International (☎ (612) 871

0596; fax (612) 871 8853), 2445 Park Ave, Minneapolis, MN 55404, provides similar services to American-International Homestays.

Kobasniuk Travel (☎ (212) 254 8779; fax (212) 254 4005), 157 Second Ave, New York, NY 10003, offers a wide variety of tour packages, some of which include Eastern Europe, as well as boat cruises down the Dnipro, airline tickets and visa services.

REI Adventures (☎ (206) 891 2631 or toll-free (800) 622 2236; fax (206) 395 4744), PO Box 1938, Sumner, WA 98390-0800, specialises in treks and mountain-biking expeditions in the former USSR led by experienced and knowledgeable guides. Most treks are in Central Asia, but they do arrange expeditions to Crimea.

Scope Travel (☎ (201) 378 8998; fax (201) 378 7903), 1605 Springfield Ave, Rashway, NJ 07065, is one of the most experienced travel companies dealing with Ukraine and is a founding member of the Auscoprut joint venture, which runs the Hotel Roxolana in Ivano-Frankivsk.

Trans-Russia Travel (☎ (415) 925 0661; fax (415) 925 0358), 80 East Sir Francis Drake Blvd, Suite 3A, Larkspur, CA 94939, specialises in homestays and adventure programmes for groups and individuals.

Russia

The Host Families Association (HOFA; ☎ & fax (812) 275 19 92; e-mail alexei@hofak. stu.spb.su), St Petersburg, has agents in the USA (☎ (202) 333 9343), UK (☎ (01295) 710 648) and Australia (☎ (03) 725 8555).

For more details see Accommodation in European Russia Facts fror the Visitor.

Pilgrim Tours (☎ (095) 365 54 63; fax (095) 369 03 89; e-mail pilgrimtours@glas. apc.org), 1-y Kirpichny pereulok 17, Moscow 105118, organises travel adventures to Crimea.

Ukraine

There are several Ukrainian travel agencies based within the country that arrange city tours and various country excursions – for a list see Tours in Ukraine Getting Around.

WARNING

The information in this chapter is particularly vulnerable to change: prices for international travel are volatile, routes are introduced and cancelled, schedules change, special deals come and go, and rules and visa requirements are amended. Airlines and governments seem to take a perverse pleasure in making price structures and regulations as complicated as possible. You should check directly with the airline or a travel agent to make sure you understand how a fare (and ticket you may buy) works. In addition, the travel industry is highly competitive and there are many lurks and perks.

The upshot of this is that you should get opinions, quotes and advice from as many airlines and travel agents as possible before you part with your hard-earned cash. The details given in this chapter should be regarded as pointers and are not a substitute for your own careful, up-to-date research.

Getting Around

Travel within Ukraine, although not always easy, is completely unrestricted. All roads can be used by motor vehicles, and all cities, towns and villages are accessible – except the port city of Sevastopol, which remains one of the world's few 'closed cities'.

The country is linked by a system of trains, buses and roads, and the cities are navigable by trolleybuses, trams, city buses and – in Kiev and Kharkiv – a metro.

But things don't often go smoothly. A fuel crisis has severely curtailed all petrol-powered transportation (mainly city buses) and reliability of services has also declined. While major train routes between cities are still reliable, reasonably frequent and comfortable, local bus transportation, although still available, is often plagued by unannounced schedule changes, reduced services and cancellations. The urban public transportation system is so overwhelmingly overworked and underserviced that the crowds often become unbearable. Maintenance is low, with dirty trains and dirty buses, some of which should be in museums.

Information is also difficult to come by, and explanatory notices for the unaware tourist just don't exist. Schedules, ticket windows, platforms, directions etc are almost always a frantic mystery, often leaving you feeling helpless and frustrated.

But it *is* possible to reach your destination and survive the trip – and in the process rub shoulders with the average Ukrainian who has developed a pleasant sense of humour to combat the daily struggle.

AIR

Kiev, Odessa, Lviv and Ivano-Frankivsk all handle domestic as well as international flights (see Air in Ukraine Getting There & Away). The airports at Cherkasy, Chernivtsi, Dnipropetrovsk, Donetsk, Kharkiv, Kherson, Khmelnytsky, Kirovohrad, Kryvy Rih, Luhansk, Mariupol, Mykolayiv, Poltava, Rivne, Simferopol, Uzhhorod, Vinnytsya,

Zaporizhzhya and Zhytomyr can also handle domestic flights (along with an occasional flight to Moscow) – at least in theory. The majority of these runways are currently unused: domestic flights were one of the first services to be axed when Ukraine's economic perils began to include fuel shortages. Air Ukraine was the only carrier of domestic flights at the time of writing. The airports that were being serviced by domestic flights to/from Kiev included Donetsk, Ivano-Frankivsk, Kharkiv, Lviv, Odessa, Simferopol, Chernivtsi and Uzhhorod. In February 1995 prices (one way/return) from Kiev to Odessa were US$76/152, Kiev to Simferopol US$91/182 and Kiev to Lviv US$79/158.

All domestic aircraft were inherited from Aeroflot after the break-up of the Soviet Union; now they're painted blue and yellow. Don't expect the same standards that you're used to in the West. For information on all domestic flights in Ukraine, contact Air Ukraine in Kiev at vulitsya Karla Marxa 4 or vulitsya Dmytrivska 1 (☎ (044) 224 05 01, 225 32 17), vulitsya Hospitalna 12 (☎ (044) 224 10 45, 224 29 50) or call (from Kiev) ☎ 056. For information on offices outside Ukraine see the listing in Ukraine Getting There & Away.

BUS

Buses service almost every city and small town in the country and are best for those short trips outside main cities, such as to Zhovkva, Khotyn, Ostroh and Pochayiv, which are not serviced by trains. Between most major cities it's more convenient to take a night train, but for shorter distances such as from Lviv to Ivano-Frankivsk or Lviv to Lutsk, the bus is often quicker and more frequent.

There's a different, more hectic mentality to riding the buses, with less etiquette involved than on trains. They're always dirty and overcrowded, but there's no better way to mingle with the locals than on a bumpy, overheated and overcrowded bus ride through the countryside. In general, the buses are frequent but follow only a loose schedule, often changing agendas daily.

Bus stations are called either *avtovokzal* or *avtostantsya*. In small towns, there's just one, but in large cities there are several – one main one for the majority of buses, including those travelling longer distances, and a few smaller bus stations on the outskirts from which a few local destinations are serviced.

Getting Tickets

The most difficult task is buying tickets. Some cities, like Lviv, have excellent bus ticket offices where you can buy them in advance, but more often than not you have to buy them at the bus stations themselves. In smaller towns, where the bus is passing through en route, same-day tickets are often sold only when the bus arrives – which always causes confusion because the bus may already be full.

Times and destinations are usually written on small pieces of paper next to the ticket windows where they're sold. Каса повернення квитків, *kasa povernennya kvitkiv*, is the ticket window for return tickets, while каса попередього продажу квитків, *kasa poperednoho prodazhu kvitkiv*, is the ticket window for advance tickets. Bigger bus stations have large information wall posters, and almost all stations have a schematic map on the wall showing all the cities and towns serviced. In the bus station there's usually an information window marked довідкове бюро. Write down the name of your destination on a piece of paper and show it to the attendant.

Outside on the platforms are usually signs with the destinations and sometimes the schedules printed on them. You can also walk up to a platform with a crowd of people and ask them where and when the bus is going.

Most tickets (a tiny receipt) have reserved seats if you're buying the ticket at the originating station or in advance. Tickets sold somewhere en route are often without a number and are for standing room only. One

tactic that can be used if the ticket lines are long and you can't figure out which one to wait in, is simply to stand at the proper platform and when the bus arrives muscle your way on and move to the back. If someone kicks you out of your seat you'll have to stand. Eventually an attendant will move to the back and sell you a ticket on the spot, or else you can buy one from the driver as you board.

Every hour or so the bus will stop for a break, allowing passengers to stretch out and get some fresh air, smoke a cigarette or buy something to drink at a kiosk. The buses are never very clean, the seats cramped and the centre aisle always taken up by bodies and sacks of potatoes.

Although bus tickets have gone up drastically, a few hours bus ride, say between Chernivtsi and Kamyanets-Podilsky or Lviv and Ivano-Frankivsk, will still only cost about 75 cents.

TRAIN

Trains between major cities are frequent, relatively cheap and often a convenient night's journey. For listings of journey durations and destinations, see the Getting There & Away sections for each city concerned. The railway stations are called *zaliznychny vokzal* (railway station) or just *vokzal* (station). All trains run on Kiev time, except those in Crimea, which run on Moscow time – one hour later.

Types of Train

The regular long-distance service is a *skory poyizd* (fast train) that's really not that fast; the *expres poyizd* is a faster version of the skory which makes fewer stops. A *pasazhyrsky poyizd* (passenger train) is also like a skory, but it's slower with more stops and it usually doesn't leave the country.

Fanning out from most cities is a network of *prymiski poyizd* (suburban trains; *pryhorodny poyizd* in Russian); they're also called *elektrichka* because they're electric. They link a city to its suburbs and other nearby towns and cities – often useful for day rips. These trains only have upright, hard bench seats and don't run during the night.

Classes

Except for a few destinations in the west of the country, most major cities are conveniently located about one night's journey apart by train, so you'll want to get a sleeper. There are four types of accommodation:

Spalny vahon (SV; sleeping wagon) is a 1st-class couchette with an individual compartment for two people. It's perfect if you're travelling as a couple, but could be awkward if you're alone. Not all trains offer a spalny vahon.

Kupe or kupeyny is a 2nd-class sleeper with a compartment for four people. This is the most popular, and is quite comfortable even though the beds are a bit narrower than in the spalny vahon. It's comparable to most 2nd-class sleepers elsewhere in Europe, only a bit more run-down.

Platskart, which is what most locals take, is a 3rd-class sleeper and far less desirable. The entire train car is open (not separate compartments) with groups of six bunks in each alcove along with others along the aisle. It's usually overcrowded, dirty and extremely stuffy with the windows jammed shut.

Zahalny vahon (*obshchiy* in Russian) means an upright, hard bench seat for the entire journey – absolute torture. This is mainly used by people travelling short distances.

You should always purchase either a spalny vahon or a kupe. The tickets are relatively cheap so it's not worth suffering the low standards. All tickets have assigned places with your carriage (vahon) and bunk (mesto) numbers on your ticket. For a kupe, even bunk numbers are on the top, odd numbers on the bottom. Sheets, a pillow, blanket and towel are either already on the bed or available from the attendant, for a small fee. Sometimes platskart and zahalny vahon carriages have no assigned seats and are on a first-come, first-served basis.

On the Journey

Most people bring food and drink with them because relying on the dining car is foolish. Each sleeping carriage is looked after by an attendant called a *providnik* (male) or *provodnitsa* (female), who collects your ticket and gives you wake-up calls in the morning. They don't smile much but are generally among the best hearted service workers in the country, providing cups of tea from their samovars at the beginning and end of the journey (don't rely on these for all your liquid intake).

Getting Tickets

Generally, buying tickets at the railway station is absolute chaos. Thankfully, there are usually special offices that sell tickets to foreigners where there are no hassles and no long waits. A slight commission is usually added but it's well worth your sanity. Tickets for local electric trains are easy to buy at the station from the windows marked приміська каса, *prymiska kasa* (*pryhorodna kasa* in Russian). *Mizhnarodna kasa* is the window for international tickets.

Information

The best place to get train information is from the ticket offices for foreigners. In the railway stations there's usually someone behind the window marked довідкове бюро, *dovidkove byuro* (information office) who's supposed to answer your questions. Write down the name of your destination and show it to this attendant. There are train schedules posted on the wall but they take some figuring out. Some stations in the east and in Crimea might use Russian equivalents (see Language in Facts about European Russia). A few key words to know include:

відправлення (*'vid-PRAV-len-nyah'*) – departing trains
прибуття (*'pry-BOOT-ya'*) – arriving trains
непарні (*'neh-PAR-nee'*) – odd dates
парні (*'PAR-nee'*) – even dates
щоденно (*'shcho-DEN-no'*) – daily
постійно, щороку (*'POHS-tih-ee-no'*, *'shcho-ROK-oo'*) – year-round
час (*'chahs'*) – time
квиток, білет (*'kvi-TOK'*, *'bee-LEHT'*) – ticket
платформа (*'PLAT-for-ma'*) – platform
розклад (*'ROHZ-klahd'*) – timetable
колія (*'KOH-lee-yah'*) – track

вхід *('vkheed')* – entrance
вихід *('VIH-kheed')* – exit
приміськній, приг ородний   *('pri-mis-KEEY'*, *'PRI-ho-rod-neey')* – suburban
міжміський *('mizh-mis-KEEY')* – intercity
міжна родний *('mizh-nah-rod-NEEY')* – international

CAR & MOTORBIKE

With fuel hard to come by, spare parts rare, road conditions rugged and getting lost inevitable, driving or riding in Ukraine can be a liability and problematic – but always an adventure and the best way to really see the country. Learn a bit about general mechanics and don't take your brand-new car or bike into the country and expect it to stay that way.

Road Types

There are four main types of road in Ukraine. The first are the three main highways that cut across the country – the east-west E40 (M17) from Lviv to Kharkiv via Kiev, the E93 (M20) from Kiev to Odessa, and the E95 (M2) from Kharkiv to Simferopol. The only sections that are dual carriageways are the first 100 or so km outside of Kiev in either direction, with the rest being decently maintained but crowded and polluted with belching trucks. Other single-carriage highways include the E573/50/471 (M17) Chop-Uzhhorod-Lviv; M14 Brest-Lutsk-Ternopil-Chernivtsi; M21 Kirovohrad-Dnipropetrovsk-Donetsk-Luhansk; M23 Odessa-Kherson-Mariupol-Rostov-on-Don; and M25 Simferopol-Kerch.

The main cities and large towns are also linked by secondary single carriageways that begin with the letter 'A', like the A267 between Lviv and Ternopil. The next category of roads is the single-lane roads that link the small towns all over the country – narrower, often picturesque and more or less paved with frequent potholes – beginning with the letter 'P', like the P105 between Kremenets and Pochayiv. After this there are hundreds of smaller, mostly dirt or scantily paved tracks that link the villages. Roads are rarely marked by their numbers; mostly, a sign states the road's destination, which is usually the largest town down the line or its eventual termination point. This means two things: have a good map and the ability to read city names in Cyrillic, as only a few of the major routes, and usually just those in the west of the country, have multiple-language signs. Driving into the cities is always a trying experience: look out for the old Intourist signs that usually point the way to the hotel, or follow the signs that say 'Tsentr'.

Road Rules

People in Ukraine drive on the right. Speed limits are generally 60 km/h in towns and 110 km/h on the open highway, although signs sometimes indicate other limits such as the 80 or 90 km/h zone as you leave the city. Tickets and speed traps are not uncommon, although most drivers seem reckless and oblivious to the risk of being booked.

It's a criminal offence to drive after consuming any alcohol at all. The usual way to establish the presence of alcohol in the blood is with a blood test, but apparently you can be deemed to be under the influence even without any test.

The traffic police are called *Derzhavna Avto Inspektsia* (State Motor Inspectorate) or DAI (pronounced *'dah-ee'*), and are under the jurisdiction of the local regional government. These are the cocky guys who for no reason wave their little batons at cars on the main urban thoroughfares and highway junctions and demand to see your *dokumenty* – have your papers ready. On the outskirts of major cities there are sometimes control checkpoints where you'll also be asked to show your documents.

There's usually no problem parking in the cities. A yellow sign, yellow paint on the kerb or a sign with a red 'X' means 'no parking'. A diagonal red stripe indicates temporary parking only. There are paid parking lots around and most upper-end hotels have private lots. In small towns you can just about park your car anywhere. Don't leave any valuables exposed.

Fuel

Unleaded petrol is virtually unknown. Most of the petrol *(benzyn)* available is at low-octane levels (76 and 92) which may give high-compression engines trouble. Fuel is also not easy to get, and is of varying quality and price. Some road maps have petrol stations *(avtoservis)* marked on them but some of these will be shut down, empty or with long queues. Most people fill not only their cars but a few spare cans at each opportunity. Some stations have diesel. The usual method is to prepay the attendant in the small booth. Never let yourself get dangerously low and keep your spare can full. If you can help it, stay away from the people selling fuel on the side of the road – you don't know what you're getting. There are a few private stations that are more expensive but with higher-quality petrol and better service.

Repairs

Most people are secondary mechanics as a result of having to fix everything themselves. You may occasionally get a handy and friendly attendant at a station, but there are service garages *(dorozhniy servis,* or road service) offering varying degrees of expertise:

Kiev
    Winner Ford Kiev (☎ 271 79 50), vulitsya Narodnoho Opolchennya 16A
    Nissan-Ukraine (☎ 266 75 07), vulitsya Heroiv Oborony 4
    Mazda (☎ 553 15 95), vulitsya Bereznyakivska 23
    Kiev-Auto (☎ 269 09 45), vulitsya Perspektyvna 4
    Auto Summit (☎ 556 85 28), Kharkivske shose 179

Lviv
    Auto Route Servis Complex (☎ 9 24 52), between Lviv and Horodok on the E40, about 15 km outside the centre

Kharkiv
    Ukrinteravtoservis (☎ 23 31 32), vulitsya Biolohichna 4B

Odessa
    Road Service (☎ 24 90 32), at the 1612-km road mark on the E93
    Autoservice (☎ 33 95 54), Leningrad shose 27

Simferopol
    Autoservice (☎ 22 34 22), vulitsya Kyivska 148

The following Ukrainian words may come in handy:

машина *('mah-SHIH-nah')* – car
бензин *('behn-ZIHN')* – petrol
масло *('MAHS-lo')* – oil
вода *('VO-dah')* – water
акумулятор *('ah-koo-moo-LYA-tor')* – battery
шина *('SHIH-nah')* – tyre
свічки *('SVEECH-kih')* – spark plugs
ремінь *('reh-MEEN')* – fan belt
щітки *('SCHEET-kih')* – wiper
гальма *('hahl-MAH')* – brakes

Car Rental

Cars can be rented in Ukraine with or without a driver, but it may be cheaper to bargain with a taxi driver if you just want to go to one destination and back for a day trip. Car-rental prices range from US$8 to US$15 an hour or US$50 to US$300 a day, depending on the type of car and whether you have a private driver. Sometimes the charge is by the km, sometimes by the hour, sometimes by the day – and there's always a few hidden taxes and fees.

The reliability and availability of rental cars is sketchy, even if you have reservations, and make sure you read all the fine print on the rental agreement (usually in English). In Kiev a few of the major hotels, such as the Kievska and the Dnipro, have car rentals, as do the following agencies:

Kiev
    Intenergo-Kiev (☎ 291 76 76), vulitsya Bratska 10
    Nikita (☎ 550 32 26)
    Otema (☎ 212 01 29)
    Oto (☎ 220 84 70)

Lviv
    the service bureau in the Hotel Zhorzh (☎ 72 67 51, 79 84 65; fax 74 21 82), ploshcha Mitskevycha 1

Yalta
    the service bureau (☎ 35 01 50) in the Hotel Yalta, vulitsya Drazhynsko 50

UKRAINE

Motorbike

The same basic rules apply for motorbikes as for cars. There are a lot of old, beat-up motorbikes around complete with sidecars stuffed with potatoes or chickens. The more Western your motorbike looks the more attention it's going to get. You may get pulled over by the police more often, but usually only to ask you how much it costs and how fast it goes. In small villages you will be likened to an arriving UFO. In big cities it's best to park your bike in a paid, secure parking spot.

HITCHING

Hitching is never entirely safe in any country in the world, and we don't recommend it. Nevertheless, hitching is a very common method of getting around in Ukraine (see European Russia Getting Around). Travellers who decide to hitch should understand that they are taking a small but potentially serious risk. People who do choose to hitch will be safer if they travel in pairs and let someone know where they are planning to go. Avoid hitching at night. Women should exercise extreme caution and everyone should avoid hitching alone.

BOAT
Dnipro River Trips

The Dnipro flows for over 800 km through Russia and Belarus, gathering its main tributaries just as it begins its great 1000-km journey across Ukraine and splitting the country in two with a long diagonal bend before spilling out into the Black Sea. The river is a national symbol with all sorts of poetic, cultural and historical attachments, most of its course slicing through classic areas of steppe and along the haunts of the legendary Cossacks. It's also a major transportation artery flowing past some large and important cities – its water harnessed by huge hydroelectric power plants and dams, namely at the cities of Kremenchuk, Zaporizhzhya and Dnipropetrovsk.

Passenger hydrofoils travel up and down the 240 km between Kiev and Cherkasy (six hours) from the end of April to the middle of October. Passenger boats travel south of Cherkasy only from May to August, unless prearranged with a chartered boat or a tour package. During this time you can take a boat to a number of cities along the Dnipro, the main sites being Cherkasy, Kremenchuk, Dnipropetrovsk, Zaporizhzhya and Kherson, as well as the Black Sea ports of Yevpatoria and Odessa. The faster boats are called *rakety* or *meteory*. Hydrofoils between Kiev and Cherkasy are smaller with no deck space, but the passenger boats travelling farther distances are larger and have deck areas. There are some sleeping boats for trips beyond Dnipropetrovsk as well as overnight round-trip boats.

A trip between Kiev and Odessa normally takes about 2½ days with two boat changes en route, the first being in Kremenchuk (eight hours from Kiev), followed by Kherson (13 hours from Kremenchuk). From Kherson to Odessa is about three more hours, to Yevpatoria about six hours. Unless you're on a special direct boat or on a prepackaged tour, the normal passenger boats don't have direct connections, so you'll have to stay the night in Kremenchuk and Kherson between boat changes. There are some direct boats in summer from Kiev to Odessa which take all day and night (24 hours). Tickets and information are available at the river terminal (*richkovy vokzal*) in Kiev or the sea terminal (*morsky vokzal*) in Odessa.

Dnipro River cruises between Kiev and Odessa are a common package trip organised by travel agencies abroad (see the list in Ukraine Getting There & Away) as well as Ukrainian agencies in Kiev and Odessa (see listings in each city under Information). The boats used are often comfortable passenger ships with four-berth, double and single cabins. A typical prepackaged trip is a drawn-out 10-day cruise stopping at Kaniv, Kremenchuk, Dnipropetrovsk, Zaporizhzhya, Nova Kakhovka and Kherson along the way, with a day or two in Kiev and Odessa at either end. Small excursions and tours are usually arranged at each stop. Prices range from about US$700 to US$1400 per person. You can do this sort of trip yourself for less money, but with more hassles and possible unpredictable mishaps – and perhaps more fun.

Other River Trips

Besides Kiev, other small passenger boats *(katery)* shuttle travellers in and around the Yalta, Odessa and Feodosia areas. Infrequent boats also connect Black Sea and Crimean ports like Yalta, Feodosia, Yevpatoria, Odessa and Izmayil, but with fuel shortages much of this traffic has recently – and, we hope, only temporarily – ceased.

LOCAL TRANSPORT

Local transport will be the most daunting experience in Ukraine. It's hard to imagine just how intensely overcrowded and miserable some of the conditions are. There's no room for shyness and no time to be squeamish – push for push, you must learn to assert yourself to survive.

Few people can afford cars so everybody takes public transport. The metros in Kiev and Kharkiv are the best, most reliable and least crowded, simply because they run so often. City buses are the worst – the fuel shortage has rendered them so few and far between that they're almost useless. Trolleybuses and trams are better because they run on electricity, but they're still unbelievably crowded because there's just not enough of them. We've seen trolleybuses so full that the people are literally hanging out the windows with the entire vehicle on the verge of tipping over at every turn.

Tickets *(kvytok* or *bilet)* are ridiculously cheap (a few cents at most). You can buy them at most bus-stop kiosks and sometimes from the driver on trams only. Plastic metro tokens (zhetony) are bought at the metro

stations – go to the ticket window near the downstairs entrance. Some cities like Kiev sell monthly passes during the first week of the month for all modes of transportation, costing less than US$1. You can also buy these from the kiosks near the metro stations and bus stops, or from the ticket window near the downstairs metro entrance.

There's usually a small sign near each bus or trolley stop with the vehicle numbers and sometimes times, although these are highly unreliable. A stands for autobus or autobus stop, T stands for a tram or tram stop, Tp stands for a trolleybus or trolleybus stop and M stands for metro.

TOURS

Once you're in the country, there are many Ukrainian travel agencies which specialise in organising city tours and excursions throughout the country, such as a cruise down the Dnipro. Some agencies are well organised, while others are a pathetic waste of time. Many of these travel agencies are listed in city Information sections, but here are a few of the better ones:

Kievintour
    vulitsya Volodymyrska 47, Kiev (☎ (044) 229 31 15)
Londonskaya Travel Agency
    Hotel Londonskaya, Primorsky bulvar 11, Odessa (☎ (0482) 22 87 87, 25 03 38)
State Committee of Ukraine for Tourism
    Hotel Zhorzh, ploshcha Mitskevycha 1, Lviv (☎ (0322) 72 67 51; fax (0322) 74 21 82)
Travel & Service Bureau
    Hotel Yalta, vulitsya Drazhynsko 50, Yalta (☎ (0654) 35 01 50)
Ukrainian Services Corporation
    vulitsya Horkoho 125A, Kiev (☎ (044) 269 85 65)

UKRAINE

Kiev
Київ

Population: 2.6 million

Kiev (Kyiv in Ukrainian) is not only the capital of Ukraine but also the mother city for all Eastern Slavic peoples. Kievan Rus, the state from which Ukraine, Russia and Belarus are all descended, was established here between the 9th and 11th centuries. Kievan Rus was also the place of origin of the Russian Orthodox Church and all Eastern Slavic art and architecture. The state from which all later Eastern Slavic states were descended (Kievan Rus), the Russian Orthodox Church and Eastern Slavic art and architecture were all founded here between the 9th and 11th centuries. Russian is widely heard on the street, but most people also speak Ukrainian, which is slowly becoming more prevalent as Kiev tries to define and establish its independence in the aftermath of over 300 years of rule from Moscow.

St Sophia Cathedral and the Caves Monastery are two of the country's most fascinating sites, dating back to the days of Kievan Rus. The city's old areas stand on wooded hills above the west bank of the snaking Dnipro River. Modern Kiev's wide boulevards and broad squares can't match the allure of the city's heritage which has somehow managed to survive Mongol invasions, devastating fires, communist urban planning and the massive destruction of WW II. Today, Kiev has a big-city atmosphere, more cosmopolitan than any other in the country, but within its urban sprawl, gracious testaments to its tumultuous history can still be found.

HISTORY

Archaeology suggests Kiev has existed since the late 5th century (482 is the official date), although traces of earlier human settlements have been discovered in the area. An 11th-century chronicle written by the monks of the Caves Monastery says it was founded by the leaders of an Eastern Slav tribe – the three brothers Ky (after whom the city is said to be named), Shchek and Khoriv, and their sister Lybid, whose names today demark the topography of the city. In the 9th century, Scandinavians from Novgorod took control of Kiev from the Magyars, Asiatic vassals of the Khazars. The story goes that in 882, a Scandinavian called Oleh killed two other Scandinavians, Askold and Dir, who had had some kind of arrangement with the Magyars, and declared himself an independent ruler, inaugurating Kievan Rus. 'Rus' was the original name given by Eastern Slavs to the Scandinavian traders/settlers who eventually became their overlords; Kievan Rus became the name for the great state which was eventually ruled from Kiev by this Slavicised Scandinavian dynasty. Kiev thrived off the river trade, sending furs, honey and slaves to pay for the luxuries of Constantinople. Under the rule of Svyatoslav (962-72), the state governed an area spreading from the Volga to the Danube to Novgorod.

Constantinople was one rival that couldn't be defeated, and in 988 Svyatoslav's son Volodymyr, evidently deciding that if he couldn't beat them he might as well join them, married the emperor's sister and adopted Christianity as his state religion.

Kiev's pagan idols were destroyed, and its people baptised in the Dnipro.

Under Volodymyr's son Yaroslav the Wise (1017-54), Kiev became a cultural and political centre in the Byzantine mould. St Sophia Cathedral was built to proclaim the glory of both God and city. Like all great cities, it exploited its favourable geographic location, becoming the primary trading centre and economic hub between the Baltics, Western Europe and Constantinople. By the 12th century, Kiev reputedly had over 400 churches, but its economic prowess had already begun to wane. Power had shifted to a number of breakaway principalities, and in 1169 Andrey Bogolyubov, from the outlying, north-eastern Kievan principality of Suzdal, sacked Kiev and took the title of Grand Prince of Rus away from the city to the north.

In 1240 Kiev was sacked again by the Tatars. An Italian who visited the city six years later reported that barely 200 houses remained standing. Kiev shrank to the riverside area known as Podil – the area surrounding today's Kontraktova ploshcha – which remained its centre through centuries, first as a Lithuanian or Polish frontier town and then from 1667, following Cossack rule, as a Russian outpost. After the Second Partition of Poland, in 1793, much of Ukraine passed from Polish to Russian hands and Kiev's importance grew as the capital of Russian Ukraine. During the next century, tsarist policies encouraged Russian emigration and Russification, while suppressing Ukrainian national identity, a policy ruthlessly imitated by the early communists. After a fire in 1811, the city began to rapidly develop, spreading back up the hill, with industry and railways arriving in the second half of the 19th century. During the chaos following the Bolshevik Revolution, Kiev was the site of frequent battles between Red and White Ukrainian forces. Another industrial boom followed in the 1930s, fuelled by the arrival of large numbers of starving peasants from the surrounding rural areas. By 1912, Kiev had 626,000 people; by 1939, just before WW II, the population had risen to 846,000.

In August 1941, the advancing Germans killed or captured over half a million Soviet troops at Kiev (you won't find many memorials to this). The Germans also killed about 100,000 Jews and other minorities at Baby Yar, in the north of the city. Four in 10 buildings were destroyed and 80% of the city's inhabitants were homeless by the time the Red Army retook Kiev on 6 November 1943.

The postwar years saw even more rapid industrialisation with the construction of the unsightly suburbs which surround the city. During the late 1980s, nationalistic and democratic movements from Western Ukraine began to catch on in the capital city, and with the eventual collapse of the Soviet Union, the Supreme Rada of Ukraine declared Independence in Kiev on 24 August 1991.

ORIENTATION

The modern centre and the remains of the old city are both on the hilly west bank of the Dnipro River, and are broken up into three major districts. The Old Town, or Upper Town, is concentrated around the northern end of vulitsya Volodymyrska, near St Sophia Cathedral. Kiev's main commercial promenade is vulitsya Khreshchatyk, running parallel to vulitsya Volodymyrska along the bottom of a valley from Bessarabska ploshcha, and heading north towards maydan Nezalezhnosti, the city's main square.

North of the old town from around St Andrew's Church to Kontraktova ploshcha is the area known as Podil, or Lower Town, the historic merchants' quarter and river port.

From the northern end of Khreshchatyk, vulitsya Hrushevskoho runs south-east along a ridge to the district known as Pechersk, the historic ecclesiastical centre and site of the Caves Monastery. Woods and parks cover most of the west bank's slopes to form an attractive five-km 'nature strip'. Across the river on the east bank are a series of attractive islands with good beaches and parkland, beyond which lurk large depressing districts of concrete housing blocks.

UKRAINE

Kiev Київ

To Oryol & Moscow

To Boryspil Airport, Poltava & Kharkiv

To Zhytomyr, Brest, Luv & Vinnytsya

To Odessa

prospekt Henerala Vatutina

vulitsya Kurenivskoho

bulvar Perova

prospekt Brovarsky

prospekt Mira

Kharkivske shose

prospekt Mykoly Bazhana

Metro Bridge

Dolobetsky Island

Footbridge

Paton Bridge

prospekt Vozziednannia

Dnipro River

Trukhanov Island

Footbridge

Kariavka

prospekt Chervonykh

vulitsya Kostiantynivska

vulitsya Frunze

vulitsya Hrushevskoho

vulitsya Khreshchatyk

bulvar Lesi Ukrainky

Narodny

See Podil Map

vul Hlybochytsya

vulitsya Artema

vulitsya Tarasa Shevchenka

bulvar Taras Shevchenka

vulitsya Chervonoarmiyska

bulvar Druzhby Narodiv

prospekt Nauky

Nauka

Oleny Telihy

vulitsya Melnikova

vulitsya Dehtiarivska

prospekt Peremohy

vulitsya Borshchahivska

bulvar Industrialny

prospekt Povitroflotsky

See Central Kiev Map

prospekt Chervonozoryany

Moskovska ploshcha

vulitsya Vasylkivska

prospekt 40-richchya Zhovtnya

Okholona

prospekt Peremohy

prospekt 50-richchya Zhovtnya

vulitsya Kiltseva

doroha

prospekt Akademika Hlushkova

prospekt Akademika Zabolotnoho

0   2   4 km

PLACES TO STAY

1	Prolisok Camping & Motel Мотель-кемпінг Пролісок
15	Hotel Lybid Гостинниця Либідь
22	Hotel Bratislava Гостинниця Братислава
23	Autocamp Kiev Автокемпинг Київ
30	Hotel Druzhba Гостинниця Дружба
32	Hotel Myr Гостинниця Мир
35	Hotel Zoloty Kolos Гостинниця Золотий Колос
36	Hotel Holoseevskaya Гостинниця Голосеевская

PLACES TO EAT

21	Restoran Mlyn Ресторан Млин

OTHER

4	Baby Yar Monument Пам'ятник Бабій Яр
5	St Cyril's Church Кирилівська церква
7	Lokomotiv Pier Причал Локомотив
8	St Sophia's Cathedral Софійський собор

9	America House Американський дім
10	Zoo Зоопарк
12	Zhulyany Airport Аеропорт Жуляни
13	Railway Station Залізничний вокзал
16	Maydan Nezalezhnosti Майдан Незалежності
17	Bessarabska ploshcha Бессарабська площа
18	Rusanovsky Sady Pier Причал Русанівські сади
19	Dovbychka Pier Причал Довбичка
20	Hidropark Pier Причал Гідропарк
26	Caves Monastery Печерська Лавра
27	Defence of the Motherland Monument & Museum of the Great Patriotic War Пам'ятник Захисту Вітчизни та Музей Великої вітчизняної війни
33	Horse Racetrack Парк кінських перегонів
34	Ukrainian Exhibition of Economic Achievements ВДНГ (Виставка досягнень в народному господарстві України)

37	Long-Distance Bus Station Автобусний вокзал
39	Vydubytsky Monastery Видубицький монастир
40	Sady Nizhniy i Pier Сади Нижний причал
41	Folk Architecture Museum Музей народної архітектури

METRO STATIONS

2	Svyatoshyn Святошин
3	Shulyavska Шулявська
6	Petrivka Петрівка
11	Politekhnichny Instytut Політехнічний Інститут
14	Vokzalna Вокзальна
24	Darnytsya Дарниця
25	Hidropark Гідропарк
28	Palats Sportu Палац Спорту
29	Palats Ukraina Палац Україна
31	Lybidska Либідська
38	Druzhby Narodiv Дружби Народів

INFORMATION
Tourist Offices

Kiev still lacks an official central tourist office. The Hotel Kievska at vulitsya Hospitalna 12 has a service bureau, as does the Kiev Intourist Ticket & Information Office behind the hotel; the latter also provides air and train information. Along with the Kievska, the Rus and Dnipro hotels arrange city tours and also have small service bureaus.

Money

Nearly every hotel can exchange dollars to kupons, as will the numerous exchange kiosks around the city, marked 'obmin valyut'. The rate does not change substantially from place to place, but is usually worse at the hotels. To make cash advances on your credit card or to exchange travellers' cheques with a small commission, head to one of the following. Ekonombank (☎ 221 22 80), Khreshchatyk 32A, entered from the back of a courtyard off the street just south of vulitsya Porizna, is open Monday to

Friday from 9 am to 3 pm. Interbank, at vulitsya Yaroslaviv val 36, is open Monday to Friday from 9 am to 12.30 pm, and 2 to 3 pm. Interbank was planning to move outside the centre of town to vulitsya Industryalna 27. There's also a Western Union/X-Change Points office in the Hotel Lybid (☎ 221 77 31) off ploshcha Peremohy, as well as in the Arc/Diplomat Supermarket (☎ 286 75 57) at vulitsya Horkoho 165, open daily from 9 am to 7 pm. The Hotel Kievska will change travellers' cheques to dollars or kupons Monday to Friday from 8 am to 7 pm (closed from noon to 1 pm) and on Saturday and Sunday from 8 am to 5 pm.

Post & Telecommunications
The main post office is at vulitsya Khreshchatyk 22, on the corner of maydan Nezalezhnosti (open from 8 am to 9 pm Monday to Friday, 9 am to 7 pm on Saturday and closed on Sunday). Long-distance phones and fax are operational daily from 8 am to 10 pm. Zal No 1 is for letters and zal No 2 is for packages. There's a DHL Worldwide Express office (☎ 221 50 95) at Sportyvna ploshcha 1, room 101. Federal Express (☎ 229 97 12) is at bulvar Tarasa Shevchenka 5, and United Parcel Service (UPS; ☎ 212 22 89) is at Lvivska ploshcha 8.

To use a calling card or reach an international operator, you cannot use a public phone – ask to use your hotel's private phone. To place an international call, dial '8', wait for a second dial tone, then dial '10' followed by the country code and number. For long-distance calls within Ukraine, the '10' is not necessary. Foreign-language operators can be reached by dialling 8 192 (English), 8 191 (French), 8 193 (German) or 8 195 (Spanish). Typical charges are about US$0.60 for a two-minute call to Europe, or US$2.50 per minute to call the USA or Australia. You can reach an AT&T international operator by dialling 8 10011.

If your hotel receptionist can't help you to make the call, try the receptions of the Kievska or Dnipro hotels – much easier than dealing with the chaos of the telephones in

the main post office. Utel card phones can be found in the lobbies of most top-end hotels; see Facts for the Visitor – Post & Telecommunications.

Local calls are free from all public phones, if you can find one that works. Kiev's area code is 044.

Foreign Embassies & Consulates
For a complete listing consult the *Kiev in Your Pocket* booklet (see Bookshops, Maps & Media) or ask at any embassy.

Armenia
    Hotel Moskva (☎ 229 08 06/07)
Argentina
    vulitsya Staronavodnytska 8 (☎ 295 11 19)
Australia
    vulitsya Malopidvalna 8 (☎ 228 74 26)
Austria
    National Hotel, vulitsya Lypska 3 (☎ 291 88 48, 291 60 68)
    vulitsya Desyatynna 4B (☎ 229 23 60)
Belarus
    vulitsya Kutuzova 8 (☎ 294 82 12)
Belgium
    vulitsya B Khmelyntskoho 64 (☎ 224 31 49)
Bulgaria
    vulitsya Hospitalna 1 (☎ 225 51 19; fax 224 99 29)
Canada
    Yaroslaviv val 31 (☎ 212 22 35)
China
    vulitsya Hrushevskoho 32 (☎ 293 73 71)
Croatia
    vulitsya Volodymyrska 45 (fax 224 90 05)
Czech Republic
    Yaroslaviv val 34 (☎ 212 08 07)
Denmark
    vulitsya Volodymyrska 45 (☎ 229 45 37; fax 229 18 31)
Egypt
    vulitsya Observatorna 19 (☎ 212 13 27)
Finland
    vulitsya Striletska 14 (☎ 228 75 51; fax 228 20 32)
France
    vulitsya Reyterska 39 (☎ 228 87 28; fax 229 08 70)
Germany
    vulitsya Chkalova 84 (☎ 216 14 77; fax 216 92 33)
Greece
    National Hotel, vulitsya Lypska 3 (☎ 291 88 73)
Hungary
    vulitsya Reyterska 33 (☎ 212 40 04)

Israel
    bulvar L Ukrainky 34 (☎ 295 69 25)
Italy
    National Hotel, vulitsya Lypska 3 (☎ 291 89 92;
    fax 291 88 97)
Japan
    National Hotel, vulitsya Lypska 3 (☎ 291 89 18)
Korea
    vulitsya Volodymyrska 43 (☎ 224 23 19; fax 224
    03 64)
Kyrgyzstan
    vulitsya Kutuzova 8 (☎ 295 53 80)
Latvia
    vulitsya Desyatynna 4B (☎ 229 23 60)
Lithuania
    vulitsya Horoko 22 (☎ 227 43 72)
Moldova
    National Hotel, vulitsya Lypska 3 (☎ 291 87 44)
Mongolia
    vulitsya Kotsyubynskoho 3 (☎ 216 88 91)
Netherlands
    vulitsya Turhenivska (☎ 216 19 05; fax 216 81
    05)
Norway
    vulitsya Striletska 15 (☎ 224 00 66; fax 224 06
    55)
Poland
    Yaroslaviv val 12 (☎ 224 80 40)
Romania
    vulitsya Kotsyubynskoho 8 (☎ 224 52 61)
Russia
    vulitsya Kutuzova 8 (☎ 294 79 36)
Slovakia
    Yaroslaviv val 34 (☎ 212 03 10)
South Africa
    Hotel Dnipro (☎ 229 66 33, 229 40 61)
Spain
    vulitsya Dekhtiarivska 38 (☎ 213 04 81; fax 213
    00 31)
Sweden
    National Hotel, vulitsya Lypska 3 (☎ 291 89
    19/69)
Switzerland
    vulitsya Fedorova 12 (☎ 220 53 75; fax 227 86
    88)
Tunisia
    vulitsya Chervonoarmiyska 44, apt No 1 (☎ 220
    86 55)
Turkey
    vulitsya Arsenalna 18 (☎ 294 99 15; fax 295 64
    23)
UK
    vulitsya Desyatynna 9 (☎ 229 12 87; fax 228 39
    72)
UN office in Ukraine
    Sichnevoho Povstannya 6 (☎ 293 93 63)
USA
    vulitsya Kotsyubynskoho 10 (☎ 244 73 42/45;
    fax 244 73 50)

Cultural Centres

America House, part of the US Embassy information service, is at vulitsya Melnikova 63, and has a nice library and reading area where you can pick up a lot of information from the English-speaking staff. It's open only from 2 to 5 pm daily except Sunday. Take trolleybus No 16 from maydan Nezalezhnosti, getting off at the first stop after vulitsya Artema becomes Melnikova. The British Council library and reading room is at the Polytechnic Institute, Central House, room 258, and is open on weekdays from 11 am to 6 pm (one hour later on Tuesday and Thursday). Take the metro to the Politekhnichny Instytut stop. The British Embassy arranges architectural walks from time to time.

Travel Agencies

The many travel agencies that arrange city tours, as well as make arrangements for travel elsewhere in the country, include: Ukrainian Services Corp (☎ 269 85 65) at vulitsya Horkoho 125A; Kievintour (☎ 229 31 15) at vulitsya Volodymyrska 47; Extour (☎ 228 20 74) at bulvar Tarasa Shevchenko 16, room 216; Ukrintur (☎ 212 55 70) at vulitsya Yaroslaviv val 36; Relief (☎ 245 40 30) at vulitsya Solomyanska 20B; and Incomartour (☎ 517 06 91, 228 11 24). Most of these agencies only provide tour services, and aren't too helpful if you're an independent traveller who just wants some general information.

Bookshops & Useful Publications

Many kiosks sell city maps. The only one that shows public transportation seems to be that published by Incomartour, but it only shows the central area. Other maps may still have old street names or be published in Russian, so make sure you buy a recent publication.

An extremely useful booklet is the quarterly *Kiev in Your Pocket* guide, US$5 from most hotels and Air Ukraine offices. Before you visit the sights, you might want to get hold of a book or guide in English, like the outdated, but still useful, *Kiev Tourist Atlas*

UKRAINE

booklet. *Kiev: Architectural Landmarks and Art Museums* (Aurora, St Petersburg) or *Architectural Face of Kiev*, by S K Kilesso, have lots of interesting photos and plans. The booklets on St Sophia and the Caves Monastery by Mystetsvo Publishers of Kiev are very informative, with excellent illustrations, and are usually available at the sights. Druzhba at vulitsya Khreshchatyk 30 and Knihy Noty at Khreshchatyk 24 stock some of these. To the right of Kafe Khreshchatyk, at No 26, is another bookshop called Mystetsvo. Brooklyn Kyiv at pasazh 17, off Khreshchatyk, is perhaps the best bookshop in town.

News from Ukraine and *Ukrainian Times* are two English-language newspapers published in Kiev with up-to-date news, events and information. They're great if you can find them. Try hotel kiosks like the ones in the Dnipro and Kievska hotels. *Vechirny Kiev (Evening Kiev)* is an independent news guide in Ukrainian listing all events and entertainment possibilities.

Film & Photography
There's a Kodak film and processing outlet in a corner of the Druzhba bookshop at Khreshchatyk 30, open Monday to Saturday from 10 am to 8 pm, and on Sunday from 10 am to 6 pm. A Fuji photo centre is at Pushkinska vulitsya 20, open Monday to Friday from 10 am to 8 pm, and on Saturday 10 am to 3 pm; it's closed on Sunday. You can get Agfa film at Chervonoarmiyska vulitsya 52. Many hotel-lobby shops stock various film, as does the small store in the lobby of the main post office.

Fuel
Fuel is not always easily available in Kiev, with supplies and prices erratic and unreliable. You can expect to pay approximately the same prices as those in the West, with octane levels at 76, 92 and 93.

State-run filling stations include No 1 vulitsya Saratovska 63 (☎ 442 43 88); No 2 vulitsya Frunze 58 (☎ 417 33 15); No 9 vulitsya Oleny Telihi (☎ 440 75 11); No 17 Kharkivske shose (☎ 556 52 25); No 28

vulitsya Hlybochytska 12 (☎ 213 31 00); and No 29 prospekt Peremohy (☎ 444 14 18).

VULITSYA KHRESHCHATYK
Khreshchatyk, Kiev's mile-long commercial boulevard, is a bustling thoroughfare with wide pavements and lots of shops, crossable only via underground passages. Although it was completely rebuilt and more than doubled in width after the destruction of WW II, it still retains an air of cosmopolitan elegance, its long blocks lined with formal and imposing Soviet-style neoclassical façades. The **Bessarabsky Market** at Bessarabska ploshcha marks the southern end of Khreshchatyk. Built in 1910-12, the market was established for traders coming to Kiev from Bessarabia (essentially present-day Moldova), and today its aisles of fruit and vegetable vendors are a delight to wander through.

Ploshcha Lenkomsomola & Around
At the northern end of Khreshchatyk is ploshcha Lenkomsomola, a large circular intersection which will most likely have a new name by the time you arrive.

On the northern side of the intersection is the rectangular white-stone **Ukrainsky Dim** (Ukrainian House), the former Lenin Museum, now a multimedia exhibition hall with four floors of temporary exhibits as well as a theatre which periodically shows films. It's open daily from 11 am to 6.30 pm, closed on Monday, and has free public toilets downstairs. The tall draped box in the central foyer is actually covering a statue of Lenin, too large to remove from the building without having to tear out a wall. Across Volodymyrsky uzviz, which leads down to the river bank, is the 1882 **State Philharmonia building**, originally the Kiev Merchants' Assembly headquarters and currently under reconstruction. The controversial **rainbow arch**, a tasteless metallic parabola rising from the park behind the Philharmonia, is a monument to the 1654 'unification' of Russia and Ukraine, an event which many Ukrainians consider to be the beginning of the Russian yoke over their country. Directly behind the monument are sweeping views over the Dnipro and surrounding islands, with some paths that zigzag down the hillside to the pedestrian bridge below. Hidden in the midst of trees to the left stands a **statue of Prince Volodymyr** (reachable by walking halfway down Volodymyrsky uzviz), a monument to the ruler who in 988 brought Christianity to the Eastern Slavs and who baptised the citizens of Kiev en mass in the Dnipro, supposedly near this site.

Maydan Nezalezhnosti & Around

One long block south-west of ploshcha Lenkomsomola is the fountain-filled maydan Nezalezhnosti (Independence Square), the closest thing to a main square, and definitely the most popular outdoor meeting place for Kievians. It's crowded with sauntering locals and vendors all day and well into the night, when the fountains are impressively lit. Across the street, below the 1960s Hotel Moskva, is a broad marble platform where a massive red granite statue of Lenin once stood. To the right is the attractive column-lined façade of the **Tchaikovsky State Conservatory**, a frequent venue for concerts and music festivals. Khreshchatyk and Maydan Nezalezhnosti metro stations are both on vulitsya Khreshchatyk, with trolleybus No 20 running up and down.

Off the western side of maydan Nezalezhnosti are six streets fanning out uphill in a star-like configuration. Just up the second street from the left is the **Taras Shevchenko Memorial House Museum** at provulok Shevchenka No 6, a beautifully restored 19th-century wooden house and garden where the national poet lived for a short while in 1846. Inside, among the original furnishings, a number of Shevchenko's personal artefacts and a small collection of his works are on display. The museum is open from 10 am to 6 pm (noon to 8 pm on Tuesday) and is closed on Monday and the last Friday of the month.

UPPER TOWN

Along Volodymyrska vulitsya, which runs parallel and three blocks uphill west of Khreshchatyk, lie a number of Kiev's historic landmarks. On the corner of vulitsya Bohdana Khmelnytskoho and vulitsya Volodymyrska sits the ornate **Shevchenko Opera & Ballet Theatre**. Built in 1901, it's an impressive building, similar in scale and grandeur to the opera houses in Odessa and Lviv, and was the first theatre to perform classical operas translated into the Ukrainian language. Just down vulitsya Bohdana Khmelnytskoho, at No 15, is the **National Science Museum**, open daily from 10 am to 4.30 pm (closed on Wednesday and Thursday). Its extensive exhibits are broken up into four separate museums, which cover the disciplines of archaeology, geology, botany and zoology.

A block north, on the corner of vulitsya Volodymyrska and Yaroslaviv val, stands the **Golden Gate** (Zoloti Vorota), the historic main gateway into the ancient city during Yaroslav's rule, supposedly inspired by Constantinople's Golden Gate. Originally built in 1037, it was a strong link in Kiev's extensive fortification system, with ramparts once stretching out from both sides of the gate. What you see is a 1982 reconstruction of the original (in celebration of the city's 1500-year anniversary) which was first destroyed in a 1240 Mongol-Tatar raid, then covered with earth in 1750. Inside is a small museum of old Rus architecture. The site is open from March to November, 10 am to 5.30 pm (10 am to 4.30 pm on Wednesday and closed on Thursday). It has a series of stairways and balconies which look down onto two original walls. There's a gift shop on the 3rd floor. Nearby is the Zoloti Vorota metro station, connected to the Teatralna station.

Two long blocks farther north, Volodymyrska vulitsya opens up to **Sofiyska ploshcha**, the historic site where Kiev citizens triumphantly welcomed a victorious Bohdan Khmelnytsky after his battles with the Poles in the mid-17th century. A statue of the Cossack leader, with mace drawn and horse reared, rises from the middle of the square.

UKRAINE

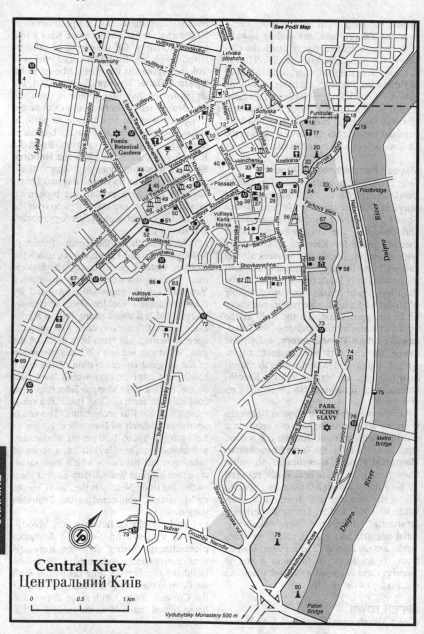

See Podil Map

Funicular

Footbridge

Fomin
Botanical
Gardens

Passazh

PARK
VICHNY
SLAVY

Metro
Bridge

Paton
Bridge

Vydubytsky Monastery 500 m

Central Kiev
Центральний Київ

0   0.5   1 km

UKRAINE

PLACES TO STAY

2 Hotel Lybid
Гостинниця Либідь

26 Hotel Dnipro
Гостинниця Дніпро

27 Hotel Khreshchatyk
Гостинниця Хрещатик

29 Hotel Moskva
Гостинниця Москва

50 Hotel Ukraina
Гостинниця Україна

61 National Hotel
Гостинниця Національна

63 Hotel Klevska
Гостинниця Київська

65 Hotel Rus
Гостинниця Русь

PLACES TO EAT

7 Bon-Bon Kafe
Кафе Бон-Бон

11 Kafe Yaroslava Val
Кафе Ярослава Вал

12 Restaurant Melodia
Ресторан Мелодія

13 Vesuvio Pizza
Везувіо Піщерія

33 Restaurant Lestnitsa
Ресторан Лестніца

34 Kafe Khreshchatyk
Кафе Хрещатик

36 Kafe Pasazh
Кафе Пасаж

37 Bon-Bon Kafe
Кафе Бон-Бон

46 Montanya Snack Bar
Монтаня бар

58 Kureni
Куреni

67 Eskimo Bar
Ескімо бар

OTHER

1 Circus
Цирк

4 Main Railway Station
Залізничний вокзал

6 St Volodymyr's Cathedral
Володимирський собор

8 Shevchenko Opera & Ballet Theatre
Театр опери та балету
ім. Т. Г. Шевченка

10 Golden Gate
Золоті ворота

14 St Sophia Cathedral
Софійський собор

15 Mykhaylivska ploshcha
Михайлівська площа

16 Kiev Contemporary Art Centre
Київський арт центр

17 Church of St John the Baptist
Іоанахрестителя церква

19 Main River Terminal
Річковий вокзал

20 Prince Volodymyr Statue
Пам'ятник князю Володимиру

21 Church of St Alexander
Костьол Св. Александра

22 Ukrainsky Dim
Український дім

23 Monument to Unification of Russia &
Ukraine
Монумент в ознаменування
возз'єднання України з Росією

24 Philharmonia
Філармонія

25 Ploshcha Lenkomsomola
Ленкомсомола площа

30 Maydan Nezalezhnosti
Майдан Незалежності

31 Taras Shevchenko Memorial House
Museum
Літературно-меморіальний дім
Т. Г. Шевченка

32 Main Post Office
Главпоштамт

39 Teatralna Kasa
Театральна каса

40 Teatralna Kasa
Театральна каса

42 Shevchenko State Museum
Музей Т. Г. Шевченка

43 Museum of Natural Sciences
Природознавчий музей України

44 Kiev University (Shevchenko
University)
Київський Університет ім.
Т. Г. Шевченка

45 Shevchenko Statue & Park
Пам'ятник Тарасу Шевченку та парк

48 Western & Oriental Art Museum
Музей західного та
східного мистецтва

49 Russian Art Museum
Музей Російського мистецтва

51 Teatralna Kasa
Театральна каса

52 Ukrainsky Suvenir
Український сувенір

UKRAINE

continued next page

continued from previous page

53 Bessarabsky Market
Бессарабський ринок

54 Ivan Franko Ukrainian Drama Theatre
Український драматичний театр
ім. Івана Франка

55 House of Monsters
(Horodetsky Building)
Дім страхіть (будинок Городецького)

56 Museum of Ukrainian Fine Arts
Музей Українського образотворчого
мистецтва

57 Dynamo Stadium
Стадіон Динамо

59 Mariyinsky Palace
Маріїнський палац

60 Parliament Building
Українська Верховна Рада

62 Kiev History Museum
Музей історії міста

68 St Nicholas' Church
Церква Св. Николая

69 Volodymyrsky Market
Володимирський ринок

71 Bus Ticket Office
Автобусна каса

74 Askold's Grave Rotunda
Аскольдова могиля ротонда

75 Metro Pier
Метро Причал

77 Caves Monastery Main Entrance
Печерська Лавра, головний вхід

78 Defence of Motherland Monument &
Museum of the Great Patriotic War
Монумент захисту Вітчизни та музей
Великої вітчизняної війни

80 Foundation of Kiev Monument
Пам'ятник засновникам Києва

METRO STATIONS

3 Vokzalna
Вокзальна

5 Universytet
Університет

9 Zoloti Vorota
Золоті Ворота

18 Poshtova Ploshcha
Поштова Площа

28 Maydan Nezalezhnosti
Майдан Незалежності

35 Maydan Nezalezhnosti
Майдан Незалежності

38 Khreshchatyk
Хрещатик

41 Teatralna
Театральна

47 Ploshcha Lva Tolstoho
Площа Льва Толстого

64 Palats Sportu
Палац Спорту

66 Respublikansky Stadion
Республіканський Стадіон

70 Palats Ukraina
Палац Україна

72 Klovska
Кловська

73 Arsenalna
Арсенальна

76 Dnipro
Дніпро

79 Druzhby Narodiv
Дружби народів

St Sophia Cathedral

The entire western side of the Sofiyska ploshcha is taken up by the St Sophia Cathedral & Monastery complex. Sofiysky Sobor, the city's oldest standing church, was built in 1017-31 in honour of Prince Yaroslav's victory over the Pechenegs, a rival tribe from the east. Named after Hagia Sofia (Holy Wisdom) Cathedral in Istanbul, Christendom's greatest church from 548 to 1453, its Byzantine plan and decoration announced the new religious and political authority of Kiev. St Sophia was also a centre of learning and culture, housing the first school and library in Kievan Rus. Being adjacent to the Royal Palace and the seat of the metropolitan (a leading religious figure), the cathedral also staged all royal ceremonies, including coronations, the signing of treaties and the receiving of foreign dignitaries.

St Sophia's basic structure and several of the interior mosaics and frescoes are original, but the building's outward appearance owes most to the helmet-domed Ukrainian Baroque style of the late 17th and early 18th centuries. St Sophia originally had a central nave with two aisles on each side, all with semicircular apses at the eastern end. By the

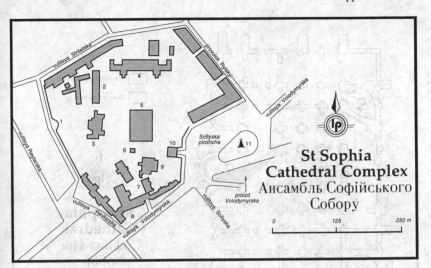

St Sophia Cathedral Complex
Ансамбль Софійського Собору

1	Zaborovsky Gate
	Брама Заборовського
2	Brethren's House
	Братський корпус
3	Metropolitan's House
	Дім митрополита
4	Seminary
	Бурса
5	St Sophia Cathedral
	Софійський собор
6	Ticket Booth
	Каса
7	Southern Gate Tower
	Башта південної брами
8	Consistory
	Консисторія
9	Refectory Church
	Трапезна
10	Bell Tower & Entrance
	Дзвінниця та вхід
11	Bohdan Khmelnytsky Monument
	Пам'ятник Богдану Хмельницькому

end of the 11th century two arcades had been added on the northern side, two on the south – almost doubling the width – and one on the west. The walls were of patterned pink brick, some of which can be seen on the exterior of the apses, and the roof was topped by 13 semicircular cupolas on drums (the number stands for Christ and the Disciples). The harmonious pyramidal outline and the sequences of semicircles in arches, roofs, windows and walls were characteristic features of later Ukrainian and Russian churches.

The two stair towers on the west side were probably added in the 12th century and the narthex (entrance hall) between them in the 19th century. Partly ruined by the Tatars in 1240 and further damaged during the period of Lithuanian-Polish rule, St Sophia lay abandoned until 1685-1707, when extensive repairs were made. The 18th-century 76-metre-high bell tower at the entrance to the grounds from Sofiyska ploshcha, built during the reconstruction, is embellished with wedding-cake Ukrainian Baroque plasterwork. You can compare the building's original 11th-century and present-day exteriors with the two excellent models on either end of the entrance narthex.

The main entrance into the complex is usually through the bell tower, but may be temporarily diverted around the corner to the Southern Gate Tower due to further restoration work. Trolleybus Nos 16 and 18 from the back of maydan Nezalezhnosti will drop you off a block north, on vulitsya Volodymyrska.

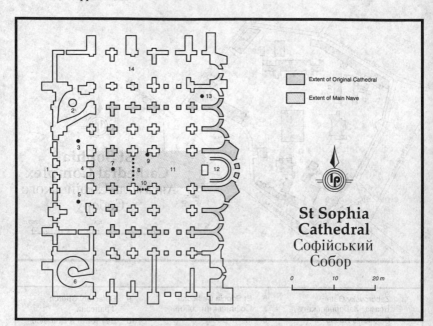

St Sophia Cathedral
Софійський Собор

1. Entrance
2. Stair Tower (closed)
3. Model (present day)
4. Gold-Plated Doors (13th century)
5. Model (11th century)
6. Stair Tower (closed)
7. Remains of Original Marble Threshold
8. Site of Now-Demolished Centre of Fresco of Yaroslav & Family Approaching Christ
9. Fragment of Child of Yaroslav (11th century)
10. Frescoes of Yaroslav's Children (18th & 19th-century restoration)
11. Central Crossing with Original Christ Pantokrator Mosaic on Dome
12. Central Apse with Virgin Orans Mosaic
13. Yaroslav's Marble Coffin
14. Exhibit Hall

Interior The original Byzantine decorative scheme was followed by Eastern Slavic Orthodox churches for 900 years. Each figure or scene had its allotted position and together they made the church into a giant three-dimensional symbol of the Orthodox world order. What we see today dates partly from the 11th century (some of it uncovered by 20th-century restorers), partly from the 17th to 19th centuries.

Start with the central dome, where the 11th-century mosaic of Christ Pantokrator (All-Ruler) stares disarmingly down. This is a Byzantine Christ, embodying God the Father as well as God the Son and holding the Book of Judgement. Of the four archangels around him, only one is original. Below them, between the windows of the drum, are the Apostles (only half of one, Paul, is original). Next in the hierarchy are the four Evangelists, in the corners between the arches below the drum. Mark is original.

Farther down, on the western sides of the pillars facing down the nave, the two highest-standing mosaic figures are the Archangel Gabriel and the Virgin of the Annunciation, together signifying the Incarnation.

The central apse is dominated by the six-metre-high 11th-century mosaic of the Virgin Orans – a peculiarly Orthodox concept of the Virgin as a symbol of the earthly Church interceding for the salvation of humanity. Due to her historic survival, this particular Virgin Orans is reputed to be indestructible. Below her, another mosaic shows the original Eucharist, with Christ presenting the chalice to his Apostles on one side, the wafer on the other. The main nave previously featured a highly individual touch: a fresco of Yaroslav and his family approaching Christ. Parts of the family procession are still to be seen – four pink and white figures on the south wall, restored in the 18th and 19th centuries, and part of one 11th-century original on the north.

In the north-east of the cathedral is Yaroslav's marble coffin, carved with early Christian symbols in the Near East in the 5th or 6th century and later brought to Kiev. The far northern arcade has a number of exhibits concerning the history of the cathedral. The far southern arcade is closed off, but peek through the iron gate into the south-western stair tower for a glimpse of some rare secular frescoes of Byzantine court life, including musicians, chariot races and hunting scenes.

Mykhaylivska Ploshcha & Around

Stretching east from Sofiyska ploshcha to Mykhaylivska ploshcha is a three-block-long green strip of park called proizd Volodymyrsky, with a few scattered statues of pagan gods amongst the trees. The entire north-western side of Mykhaylivska ploshcha is dominated by the massive and imposing 1937 neoclassical **Ministry of Foreign Affairs building**, the former headquarters of the Central Committee of the Ukraine Communist Party. Just east is the top of the 1905 funicular which runs down the steep hillside to Poshtova ploshcha. On vul-itsya Triokhsviatytelska 8, on the way to the funicular, is the **Kiev Contemporary Art Centre**, regularly hosting exhibits and evening concerts. On the western corner of the square is a small monument to the 1932-33 famine.

Off vulitsya Triokhsviatytelska is the pleasant 1713 **Church of St John the Baptist**, whitewashed, with an attractive wood-shingled roof. This small church is actually the refectory of the once magnificent St Mykhayl Monastery of the Golden Cupolas, a seven-cupola cathedral and bell tower, second in importance only to St Sophia. The monastery complex withstood the trials of time, surviving from 1108 until 1936, when the communist regime decided to tear it down to make space for a Central Committee building (a practice carried out all over the country). Ironically, nothing was built on the site and you can still see the overgrown foundations on the vacant lot directly north of the refectory. Inside the former refectory is an old photo of the monastery complex. Farther down, on the corner of Kostiolna vulitsya, is the 19th-century Polish Catholic **Church of St Alexander**, recognisable by its large central dome and twin bell towers.

St Andrew's Church & Around

Northern vulitsya Volodymyrska, beyond St Sophia, follows the line of the main street of Yaroslav's Kiev. **St Andrew's Church**, poised at the northern end of the street and at the top of the charming Andriyivsky uzviz, is an inspired 1746-61 Baroque interpretation of the traditional Ukrainian five-domed, cross-shaped church by Rastrelli, the Italian architect who designed many of St Petersburg's great buildings. The slender curves of its blue, white, gold and green exterior stand out against the skyline, perched high above the Podil district at the crest of the historic upper town, at the supposed site where the Apostle Andrew erected a cross. Its richly decorated interior features a three-tiered iconostasis and several paintings from the 18th century. The church is usually open as a museum, but has been closed for restoration.

Before reaching St Andrew's on vulitsya Volodymyrska, a small set of steps to your left leads to a flat-topped hillock and the reconstructed foundations of Kiev's first cathedral, known as the **Desyatynna** (Church of the One-Tenth) because its founder Volodymyr dedicated 10% of his income to it. Founded in 989, the church collapsed under the weight of the people who had taken refuge on its roof during the 1240 Tatar siege. It was a precursor in design and splendour to St Sophia and stood at the centre of Volodymyr's Kiev. Next to the foundations is a linden tree, planted in 1635 in memory of a Kiev metropolitan. Farther west is the **Ukraine History Museum**, open from 10 am to 6 pm, closed on Wednesday and every last Thursday of the month. Its extensive exhibits go back to the Scythians and the Greek Black Sea colonies right up to WW I, with strong exhibits on Kievan Rus and the Cossacks, as well as more recent folk art featuring a few 18th-century carved wooden horse carts.

ANDRIYIVSKY UZVIZ

Andriyivsky uzviz, Kiev's most charming street, attractively curves its way down from St Andrew's to the base of the Podil district. This steep lane is the official artists' headquarters of the city, and in recent times has become one of the most popular places to hang out. Lining its streets are galleries, gift shops, restaurants and cafés, creating the perfect magnet for tourists.

About halfway down on the right-hand side of the street, recognisable by its pointed turret, is the 19th-century **Castle of Richard the Lion-hearted**, which is to be reopened as a hotel. Just beyond, a flight of steps leads up to an outdoor terrace, with expansive views of the surrounding area. Farther down, at No 22, on the opposite side of the street, is a small **local history museum** dedicated to the history of Andriyivsky uzviz and the Podil district, with lots of fascinating old photos, open from 11 am to 6 pm, closed on Monday and Tuesday. Another staircase just

past the museum leads to the top of another hillock with excellent views towards St Andrew's and down over the Podil. Still farther down, at No 13, is the **Mikhail Bulgakov House Museum**, dedicated to the famous 20th-century Russian satirical writer, whose work was heavily censored by Soviet authorities. It's open from 10 am to 6 pm (closed on Wednesday). The lower floor contains old photos of Kiev, while the top floor is a re-creation of the author's studio and displays his personal belongings.

PODIL

Andriyivsky uzviz spills out into the Podil, the historic mercantile quarter and trading district of Kiev. Dating back to the earliest settlements, this flat area tucked beneath a row of hills quickly grew around the main port on the riverfront. Destroyed by Mongol-Tatar invasions in the 13th century, it was rebuilt, only to be devastated again in a three-day fire in 1811. However, it survived WW II better than most of the city, and because of this there's a more relaxed, small-scale atmosphere in its 19th-century grid of streets. The Kontraktova Ploshcha metro station will put you smack in the centre of Podil.

Kontraktova Ploshcha & Around

The heart of the Podil district is Kontraktova ploshcha, a park-like square named after the large, white arcaded **Kontraktova Dim** (House of Contracts) occupying the centre. Built in 1817, originally as a legal headquarters for the negotiating and signing of contracts between port merchants, it later became a hotel. It's been renovated and is beginning to fill with restaurants, galleries and businesses. Off its northern side is the **Samson Fountain**, a Baroque cupola rising above a sculpture of a rather wimpy Samson wrestling a lion; the original wooden sculpture is housed in the History of Kiev Museum. On the opposite side of the square is a statue of Hryhorii Skovoroda. Known as the 'Ukrainian Socrates', Skovoroda was a well-educated 18th-century scholar who abandoned his formal education for the life of a wandering philosopher.

Along vulitsya Spaska, off the north-eastern corner of Kontraktova ploshcha, is an ensemble of buildings comprising the **Kiev-Mohyla Akademy**, the first higher-education institution in Ukraine. Established in 1615, it was originally part of the now-defunct Bratsky Monastery (Brotherhood School). Under Peter the Great, the university became one of the most illustrious learning centres in all of Russia and Ukraine. A hotbed of Ukrainian nationalism, it was closed by the tsars and only reopened in 1992 after independence. The main building is the yellow curving façade with the large classical portico, although the oldest structure is the simple white building on the far northern corner with the dome of the 1703 Holy Spirit Church rising from its far eastern end.

Vulitsya Spaska runs north-east to the waterfront. There's an interesting **Chornobyl Museum** in a side street on the left of vulitsya Spaska, at provulok Zhoreviy 1, in the brick building with a tower (a former fire house). Inside are a number of photographs and exhibits documenting the worst nuclear tragedy in history (so far), including displays about the early clean-up crews, who were exposed to severe radiation. The museum is open daily except Sunday.

Just past the Restoran Spadshchyna, at Spaska No 12, is the excellent **Starodavni Kiev Gallery & Studio**, housed in a 150-year-old warehouse, displaying local talent and open daily from 10 am to 6 pm. Farther down, at Spaska 16B, set back from the street and housed in an attractive 17th-century house with a classical portico, is the **Museum Hetmanstva**. Recently restored, the small museum is dedicated to the hetmans, the Cossack chieftains of Ukraine. The house, budynok Mazepa, is named after the last great Ukrainian Cossack leader to rise up against Russian domination. Allied with the Swedes, Hetman Mazepa was wiped out by Russian troops in the battle of Poltava in 1709.

A block farther south-east is the corner **Naberezhno-Mykilska Church**, actually two small separate churches. The beige church in front serves as the bell tower and

dates from the 1860s, while the fanciful white Baroque church behind it is 100 years older. Farther down vulitsya Pochaynynska, at No 2, is yet another attractive little church, the 1692 **Illinska Church**, with a separate bell tower, Baroque gate and small rose garden inside the tiny compound.

Nestled to the west of Kontraktova ploshcha are a tight pack of ecclesiastical and historic buildings. Vulitsya Prytytsko Mykilska curves north-west to the **Florivsky Monastery**, a 15th-century women's convent, one of the few to defiantly remain open during communist times. It's entered through a unique 1740 bell tower with four classical pediments and a Renaissance cupola rising from the middle, designed by the same architect who designed the Kontraktova Dim. The first building in the complex is the three-cupola **Voznesenka Church** (1732), with a traditional Orthodox interior. Behind it is the 17th-century **Trapezna Church & Refectory**, with a large painting of St Serosky on an exterior wall. North of the church and refectory are pretty fenced gardens and 19th-century nuns' dormitories. The small 1824 **Voskresenska Krystovna Church**, built up against the hill at the eastern end of the complex, has a unique colonnaded rotunda façade. Across the street from the monastery is the Ukrainian National Guard Headquarters, which may explain the numbers of soldiers milling about.

Just next door, to the right of the Florivsky Monastery, at No 7, is the first pharmacy building in Kiev, dating from 1728. Although there were medicinal monks long before at the Pechersk Monastery, this was the first pharmacy in the city accessible to the general public, and it's still open today. It also houses the fascinating **Apteka Museum**, which traces the history of medicinal processing, from bat wings to natural herbs; it's open from 9 am to 4 pm, closed on Monday.

A short distance to the north, the street ends at the oldest standing structure in the Podil, the 1631 **Church of Mykola Prytysko**, its design based on an earlier wooden church which previously stood on the site. Its whitewashed, green-roofed exterior is a lovely example of early Ukrainian Baroque, and together with a spattering of older painted brick buildings nearby, the church gives the block a colourful character. Inside, past the long dark entrance narthex, are some angelic remains of an original 17th-century fresco above the apse.

A right turn east on vulitsya Khoryva leads to the white **House of Peter I**, with a unique two-storey porch supported by squat columns. Presumably Peter the Great stayed here in 1706 prior to engaging the invading Swedish armies marching towards Kiev.

South of Kontraktova ploshcha off vulitsya Pokrovska (sometimes called vulitsya Zelinskoho) are two fine 18th-century churches. At No 6 is the 1716 **Chapel Church of Mykola Dobry** (St Nicholas the Good). Its beautiful colonnaded upper gallery is reminiscent of ancient Kievan Rus wooden churches. Just farther south on the opposite side of the street, at No 7, stands the

1766 **Pokrovska Church & Bell Tower**. Built in the late Ukrainian Baroque style, it features eclectic detailing, with various pediments and small raised portals protruding from the exterior façades. Farther down vulitsya Pokrovska, at No 14, is a palace dating from 1808, which once housed the Podil history museum and is now the residence of the American ambassador. Farther south, vulitsya Petra Sahaydachnoho runs into Poshtova ploshcha, once the site of a river postal station. Off the square is the main river terminal (richkovy vokzal). On the opposite side is the 1905 funicular, which climbs the steep wooded slope up to Mykhaylivska ploshcha.

AROUND SHEVCHENKO PARK

Some interesting museums and other sights ring Shevchenko Park, at the junction of Volodymyrska vulitsya and bulvar Tarasa Shevchenka. Ploshcha Lva Tolstoho or Teatralna are the nearest metros. In the park

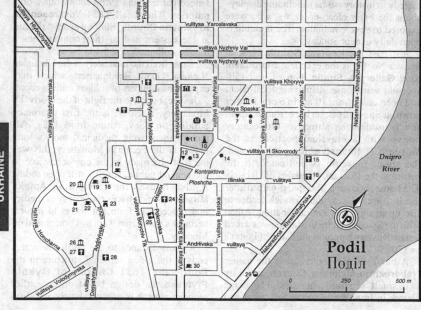

itself is a tall statue of the man half Ukraine is named after – Taras Shevchenko, the multitalented 19th-century nationalist poet-artist. The **Shevchenko State Museum** at bulvar Tarasa Shevchenka 12 has a collection of over 4000 of his own and his contemporaries' artistic and literary works, displayed in sumptuous settings to the sounds of classical music, including examples of his poetry books translated into a number of languages. It's open from 10 am to 6 pm, except Monday and the last Friday of the month.

On the eastern side of the park are the **Russian Art Museum** (vulitsya Tereshchenkivska 9) and the **Western & Oriental Art Museum** (vulitsya Tereshchenkivska 15). The Russian collection is one of the best outside the museums of Moscow and St Petersburg, and is open from 10 am to 6 pm,

Friday from noon to 8 pm and closed on Thursday. There are 35 rooms, with over 2000 paintings, including early Novgorod, Rostov-Suzdal and Moscow icons and a fine collection from the second half of the 19th century, including Repin, Levitan, Ayvazovsky, Vrubel – and Vasily Vereshchagin's powerful antiwar canvas, *The Conquerors*. The Western & Oriental collection was closed for restoration at the time of writing, but supposedly has lots of Byzantine icons and impressive artefacts from ancient Egypt, China and Japan.

The red classical building along the western side of the park is **Kiev University** (1837-43). Known also as the Shevchenko University this prestigious university was completely rebuilt after destruction in WW II. In 1901 Tsar Nicholas I supposedly ordered the building to be painted blood red in response to student protests against mandatory conscription into his army.

A block away and surrounded by a small leafy park, **St Volodymyr's Cathedral** (1862-96) has a seven-cupola neo-Bzyantine exterior with Baroque elements mixed into the three-dimensional façade. This working cathedral has a spectacular interior, dark yet highlighted with Art-Nouveau wall paintings emblazoned with gold accents. A series of striking paintings by Viktor Vasnetsov in the nave and main apse show scenes from eastern Orthodox history as well as standard Christian subjects. A number of sacred icons and masses of brightly flickering candles attract a steady stream of elderly faithful who make the cavernous interior their second home. On weekend afternoons it's interesting to watch mass wedding ceremonies, often three or four couples at a time.

Directly behind the Universytet metro station, a block west down bulvar Tarasa Shevchenka, are the spacious **Fomin Botanical Gardens**, laid out in 1841 and named after the prominent 1920s botanist and university faculty member Alexander Fomin.

FROM KHRESHCHATYK TO THE CAVES MONASTERY

The 2.5 km from the northern end of Khreshchatyk to the Caves Monastery is a pleasant route, with several possible stops along the way. Trolleybus No 20 running north on Khreshchatyk will take you all the way, running south-east along vulitsya Hrushevskoho, the main road stretching along the ridge high above the Dnipro. The series of parks and wooded slopes lining the street heading down to the river make for pleasant strolling, with numerous good viewpoints. Halfway between Khreshchatyk and the Caves Monastery is the Arsenalna metro station.

The few quiet backstreets branching south-east uphill from the northern end of vulitsya Khreshchatyk have numerous interesting buildings mingled in, making it worth a pleasant stroll. Across from the Hotel Moskva up a staircase high above vulitsya Instytutska is the 1840s **Palace of Culture**

& Arts, an occasional venue for concerts and exhibitions. Farther uphill, at No 9A, is the whimsical turn-of-the-century pseudo-Renaissance **National Bank of Ukraine Headquarters**, with several snarling lion heads staring down from the façade. Around the corner on vulitsya Bankivska 2 is the former palace residence of a sugar merchant, now the **Union of Ukrainian Writers**, home of a group of influential literary and intellectual dissidents who, forming the political party Rukh, played a crucial role in independence. Farther down, at No 10, is a building affectionately known as the **House of Monsters**. Designed by the local architect Horodetsky, the façade is covered with sculptural motifs of the animal kingdom – deer, rhinoceros and elephant heads, perched giant frogs and some mythical aquatic creatures adorning the top corners. Ironically, the real monsters reside within the massive and imposing **Presidential Administration Building** across the street. Nearby, off the pleasant park-like ploshcha Franka, is the popular **Ivan Franko Ukrainian Drama Theatre**.

At vulitsya Hrushevskoho 6 is the **Museum of Ukrainian Fine Arts**, its Doric temple front guarded by two large lions. Inside, 21 rooms give a comprehensive view of seven centuries of fine art in Ukraine, including a collection of old Ukrainian icons and wooden sculpture plus some impressive 19th-century paintings. About half a km farther on, behind the parliament building on the left-hand side on the road, is the blue-and-white Baroque **Mariyinsky Palace**, built in 1750-55 and based on a Rastrelli design. When not used by the president to formally receive foreign dignitaries, excursions can be arranged on Wednesday and Saturday through the nearby Kiev History Museum. There's a good lookout point beyond the palace.

To reach the **Kiev History Museum**, a former palace, turn right into the next street to the west, vulitsya Lypska, which ends at the museum three blocks down. Open from 10 am to 6 pm, closed on Friday, its 14 rooms and two floors take you on an excellent historical journey with numerous wall paintings, old maps, models of the city and hundreds of artefacts dating from the founding of Kiev up to the 20th century. The top floor has two special exhibits, one on the disaster of Chornobyl, and another honouring the Ukrainian political prisoners who died under the Soviet regime.

Beyond Arsenalna metro, vulitsya Hrushevskoho becomes vulitsya Sichnevoho Povstannya. In parkland to the left of Dniprovsky proizd, which forks down towards the river, is a small 1810 church-rotunda – on the supposed site of **Askold's grave**. In Eternal Glory Park (Park Vichny Slavy) alongside vulitsya Sichnevoho Povstannya is an eternal flame and the graves of WW II heroes.

CAVES MONASTERY

Founded three km south of where Kiev stood in 1051, the Caves Monastery (Pechersk Lavra) was Kievan Rus' first, and for a long time most famous, monastery. Spread across wooded slopes above the Dnipro, it's a unique array of gold-domed churches, underground labyrinths lined with mummified monks, and elegant monastic buildings turned museums, one of which has a hoard of Scythian gold to rival that of the Hermitage in St Petersburg. It's the single most fascinating and extensive tourist site in the city. You need a full day to get a half-decent introduction to the whole place, though you could visit the caves and a couple of other highlights in about three hours. *Kiev-Pechersk Lavra* (Mystetsvo Publishers) is an illustrated packet with lots of information and interesting details. The caves themselves are not for the seriously claustrophobic, since their underground passages are narrow, low and often crowded.

The monks dug out and lived in the caves, where their preserved bodies are now a tourist attraction. But the monastery so prospered that the Dormition Cathedral was built in 1073-89. This was Kiev's second great Byzantine-inspired church, which in turn inspired the early 12th-century churches of Russia's Golden Ring. The monastery

became Kievan Rus' intellectual centre, producing chronicles and icons and training builders and artists. Wrecked by the Tatars in 1240, it went through a series of revivals and disastrous fires before being mostly rebuilt in the 18th-century Ukrainian Baroque style which we see today. The monastery was made into a museum in 1926, but part of it – the Further Caves and their buildings, possibly as a prelude to the rest – was returned to the Orthodox Church in 1988.

Pechersk means 'of the caves'; a *lavra* is a senior monastery. The complex is divided into the Upper Lavra and, down to the south, the Lower Lavra. The latter contains the caves, themselves divided into Nearer and Further.

Getting There & Getting In

Trolleybus No 20 east along Khreshchatyk, or south along vulitsya Hrushevskoho and vulitsya Sichnevoho Povstannya, goes to the monastery. The monastery complex is open from 9.30 am to 6 pm, but they usually don't let anyone in after 5 pm. It's closed on Tuesday. Most of the museums and buildings close for about an hour in the afternoon. Two ticket booths are located just outside the Trinity Gate Church, the main entrance. Tickets cost US$2, and an extra US$3 for a camera, which no-one seems to enforce. This main ticket allows access into all the grounds and museums except for the bell tower, Historical Treasures Museum, the Museum of Microminiature and the caves. If you restrict your visit to the caves of the Lower Lavra, you only need to purchase a candle. You can arrange for a tour with a private English-speaking guide for about US$10 – go to the excursion office to your left as you enter. In the high season you may want to buy an advance ticket for one of the pre-set tours of the Historical Treasures Museum, as they may sell out.

Trinity Gate Church

The main entrance is through the striking Trinity Gate Church, a well-preserved piece of early 12th-century Rus architecture. Rebuilt in the 18th century, it once doubled as a watchtower and as part of the original

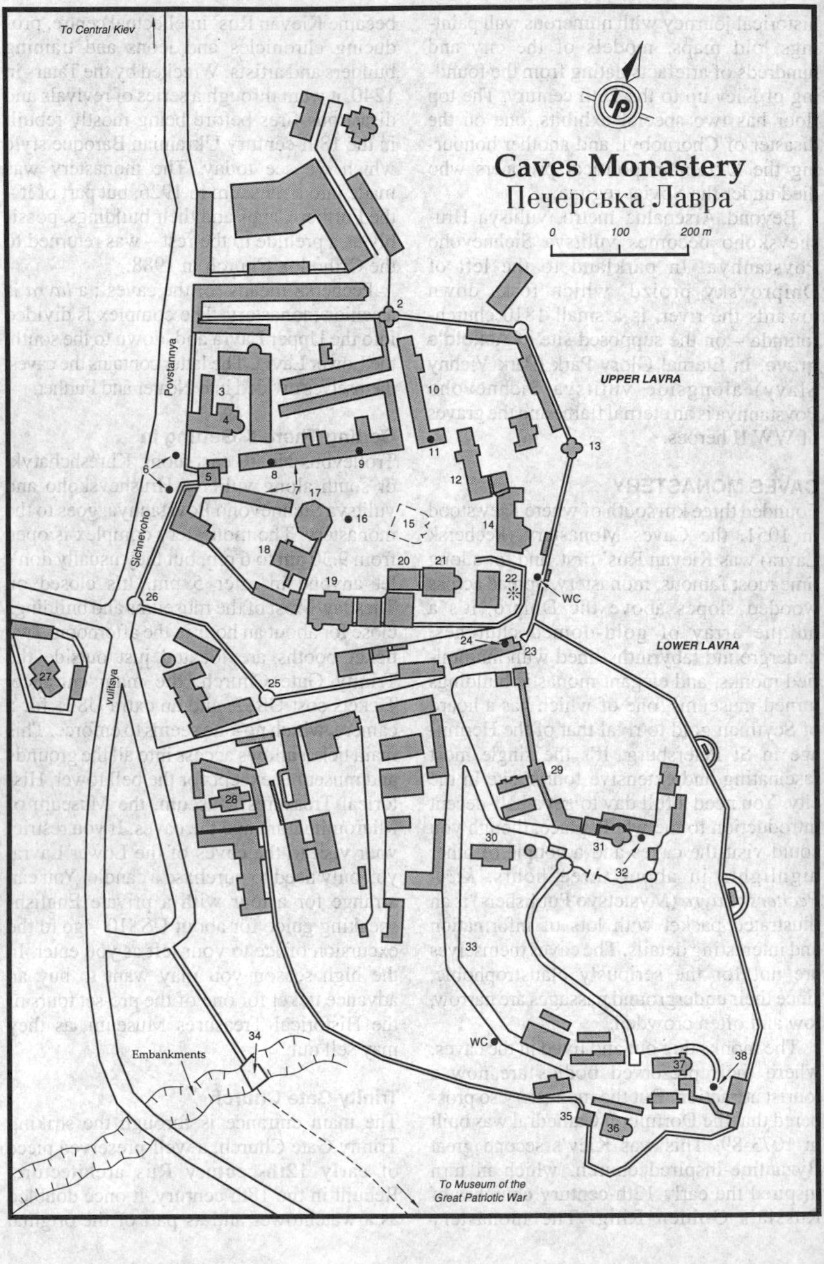

To Central Kiev

Caves Monastery
Печерська Лавра

0   100   200 m

UPPER LAVRA

LOWER LAVRA

Povstannya

Sichnevoho

Vulitsya

WC

Embankments

To Museum of the
Great Patriotic War

UKRAINE

UKRAINE

monastery fortifications. The entrance into the interior of the church is around the corner to the left after you enter the gate. Note the scorpions, fish and animals below the holy types in the entrance passage. The exterior and tiny interior were elaborately painted by leading Kiev artists in 1734-44. Note also the dramatic scene of Christ upsetting the temple marketplace, above the interior doorway. The carved and gilded wooden iconostasis is 17th century, and the wooden benches are 200 years old, reserved for the elderly monks who couldn't take the standing-only Orthodox rituals.

Monks' Dormitories

Two lines of 18th-century dormitories stretch out from the Gate Church. The one on the right houses two exhibitions: the first contains mostly 18th-century icons; the second has historical portraits of monks, metropolitans and other monastic figures. The dormitory to the left has two gift shops.

St Nicholas' Church & the Museum of Theatre, Music & Cinematic Art

Just north of Trinity Gate Church is the small 17th to 18th-century St Nicholas' Church, with its blue dome adorned with golden stars. Inside is a temporary exhibit hall with exhibits related to the history of the monastery. Farther around is the Museum of Theatre, Music & Cinematic Art, an excellent small museum filled with old photos, posters and paraphernalia tracing the history of Ukrainian theatre and cinema and some of its most famous personalities. Modern dramatic theatre was actually first introduced in Kiev during the 17th century by students of the Caves Monastery. Upstairs is a temporary exhibit space.

Dormition Cathedral & Bell Tower

In the centre of the Upper Lavra are the ruins of the once-magnificent Orthodox Dormition Cathedral. Its destruction was originally blamed on the Germans; it was later proven to have been intentionally mined by the Red Army, supposedly to 'slow' the advance of German forces (as if the cathedral was a major obstacle). Only one of the cathedral's gold domes still stands. The vaulted space beneath the dome still has fragments of frescoes.

Towering to the left of the ruins rises the cathedral's 96.5-metre-tall bell tower, built in 1731-44. To climb up the 239 steps you need to purchase a separate ticket at the kiosk in front (the former monastery well), costing about US$0.20; a charge of US$3 for camera or video is 'officially' required, but no-one asks. The view from the top offers 360-degree panoramas over the entire complex. Just before the top are the bells, once 12 in all, but only about six remain today.

Refectory & Church

Directly to the south of the ruined cathedral are the refectory and the Refectory Church of St Anthony & Theodosius, sporting the monastery's most famous gold-striped dome, built in 1885-1905. Now a working church, the main domed space is slightly reminiscent of Istanbul's Hagia Sophia, with its ring of small narrow windows along the base of the drum. The adjacent former refectory has two elegant rows of narrow columns. Both interiors are beautifully painted with Biblical scenes, saints and Art-Nouveau patterns – well worth close inspection.

Historical Treasures Museum

To the north of the ruined cathedral, this museum is devoted mainly to historic items and precious stones or metal found or made in Ukraine. Considering the wealth of the exhibits, the displays are in surprisingly shoddy cases. The highlight is the upstairs display of a fabulous hoard of gold jewellery worked for the Scythians by Greek Black Sea colonists, much of which comes from two 4th-century BC burial mounds – the Tolstaya grave in the Dnipropetrovsk region and the Gaimana grave in the Zaporizhzhya region. The jewellery is unbelievably well crafted, especially when one grasps how old it really is (around 2500 years old). From the Tolstaya grave comes possibly the most magnificent Scythian piece of all – a large mid-4th-century BC gold pectoral (a sort of large necklace) covered with superbly detailed animals and everyday scenes. Next to it is an equally striking detailed golden scabbard. Downstairs, past the 12th-century model of Kiev, are exhibits of richly ornamented goblets, crosses, chalices and icons, crafted by Ukrainian, Russian, Polish and Lithuanian masters. The gun-wielding, bored-looking security guard following close behind throughout the museum seems highly unnecessary.

The Historical Treasures Museum requires a special entrance ticket purchased at the kiosk in the building north of the museum. You're required to be part of a

45-minute excursion in Ukrainian or Russian, leaving about every 15 minutes and costing about US$0.20. English tours are usually given every hour during the high season and on weekends for about US$2, and are often pre-booked by large tour groups.

Ukrainian Museum of Books & Printing

Housed in the former 18th-century printshop, the entrance to this museum is just south of the Historical Treasures Museum. The exhibits include a large display of old books, printing presses, wood blocks, etchings and a number of exhibits on famous Ukrainian authors. Upstairs is a temporary exhibition hall.

Ukrainian Folk Decorative Art Museum

In the former Metropolitan's House (1727), this is one of the city's most fascinating museums, and the best of its kind in the country. Among the exhibits is an excellent display of the different folk dress from each oblast (region) within Ukraine, along with plenty of kilims, embroidery, pottery, ceramics, woodcarvings and glass. Upstairs around the main atrium space is a temporary exhibition area, usually filled with paintings.

Museum of Microminiature

Housed in the former 18th-century library, this unusual and popular exhibition displays various tiny complex creations, so small that microscopes are needed in order to view them. The work of Russian artist Nikolai Siadristy, the creations include the world's smallest electric motor, smallest book (with some verses of Shevchenko), smallest complete chess set (placed on the head of a nail) and a flea fitted with golden horseshoes. A separate ticket must be purchased at the kiosk in front of the bell tower.

All Saints' Church & the Church of the Saviour at Berestovo

The 1696-98 All Saints' Church over the monastery's northernmost service gate is a beautifully composed, little-altered example of early Ukrainian Baroque architecture. Its narrow and lofty interior has fine early 20th-

century murals with a youthful-looking Christ glaring down from the central dome. Under the gate is a gift shop that sells, among the typical folk souvenirs, some nice antique icons.

Farther north outside the service gate lies the Church of the Saviour at Berestovo, built by Volodymyr Monomakh as a burial church for his dynasty. Of the original church, only the western narthex stands, now forming the central crossing and transepts. Much of an original 12th-century fresco, *Christ Appearing to His Disciples at the Sea of Tiberias*, was uncovered during the 1970s above the arch on the western wall of the crossing. Most of the other murals are by 17th-century Greek artists from Mt Athos.

Nearer Caves

The Nearer Caves are reached by walking east under a short series of buttressed arches flying off the southern façade of the Museum of Books & Printing. Follow the path between the perimeter walls, past another gift shop (more antique icons) and then through the 1795 Southern Gate to enter the Lower Lavra. Before turning into the Nearer Caves, the path veers to the right and leads down past the **History of Religion & Culture Museum**, housed in a 19th-century monks' quarters. This museum requires a separate ticket, and includes a downstairs gallery with an interesting program of temporary exhibits. Across the path is the 1763 Bell Tower of the Nearer Caves. The **Church of the Raising of the Cross** (1700), with its colourful 1769 iconostasis, is beside the caves' entrance.

There's no fee to visit the caves, but it's courteous (and illuminating) to buy a candle from the stall before you enter, to carry with you throughout the passages. You follow a fixed route through about 200 metres of the Nearer Caves' reputed half-km of passages. Dozens of niches contain open coffins with mummified monks' bodies – many labelled in Cyrillic script, all tastefully covered apart from the occasional protruding toe or finger. There's also an underground dining hall and three subterranean churches, decorated during the 18th and 19th centuries. The tomb of Nestor, the presumed author of the 11th-century *Tales of Bygone Years*, the oldest Eastern Slavic chronicle, is on the right some way after St Varlaam's, the second church, just before the main concentration of burial niches. Also look for Antony, the monastery's first monk; the chroniclers Nikon the Great, Simon and Polikarp; the early Rus icon painters Alimpy and Hryhorii; and the 12th-century healers Damian and Agapit. Many of those entombed here are saints, making the caves a sacred site and a visit akin to a pilgrimage for Orthodox believers. Courteous and respectful behaviour should be followed, with men removing their hats. If you come when it's not crowded, it can be a very moving experience, but the occasion is often tainted if it's crowded.

Further Caves

The Further Caves were the originals; Antony only moved to the Nearer Caves when he felt crowded out by newcomers. The entrance is in the 1679 **Church of the Conception of St Ann**. Uphill is the beautiful seven-domed **Church of the Nativity of the Virgin** (1696), whose design was based on traditional wooden churches and includes a gate tower and covered portico. Rising to the right is the unusual high-Baroque 1761 **Bell Tower of the Further Caves**. Since the Further Caves and their associated buildings are now back in Church hands, you may see many black-robed monks wandering about. The Further Caves have about 280 metres of passages, but the visitors' route is a bit shorter than that through the Nearer Caves. The passages are also lined with ornamented mummified monks (spot the exposed hand) and contain three underground churches.

BEYOND THE CAVES MONASTERY

She Who Must Be Obeyed or Mother Russia are just two of the many names which have been coined for the giant 72-metre-high stainless-steel statue of a woman brandishing a sword and shield, surrounded by typical Soviet-style landscaping. Formally known as the **Defence of the Motherland Monu-**ment, she dominates any view of Kiev from the opposite bank of the Dnipro. Her original height had to be lowered so as not to rise above the Caves Monastery's bell tower.

Before reaching the statue, you will pass on the right the **Afghan War Museum**, offering a glimpse (rather one-sided) into the horrors of the nine-year conflict that most Westerners know very little about. Between the building and the monument is an outdoor museum of WW II-era Soviet military, including tanks, artillery, planes and armoured personnel carriers. The **Ukrainian Museum of the Great Patriotic War**, located directly beneath the statue, includes among its extensive displays a moving exhibit on the suffering of children during WW II. Both museums are open from 10 am to 5 pm; they're closed on Monday. Nearby there's an elevated walkway, beneath which are a number of sculptural bas-reliefs representing the genre of Socialist Realism at its best – false heroics of the common people running off to fight for the motherland against the fascists.

The lovely little **Vydubytsky Monastery** is about a km south of the motherland monument, on a small loop road off Na Dnepryanske shose, south of the busy Paton Bridge intersection. The walk is mostly downhill. Alternatively, tram Nos 27 and 35 from Arsenalna metro, or Nos 21, 31, 32 and 34 from Dnipro metro, go to Paton Bridge. Vydubytsky was founded in the 11th century, but was mostly rebuilt in the 17th and 18th centuries. Enter next to the 1727-33 blue-and-gold-roofed **bell tower**. Directly to your right is the centrepiece, the vertical five-domed **St George's Cathedral**, built in 1696-1701. Its detailing is exquisite, rising straight from a simple cruciform plan. Past the refectory buildings and at the foot of the grounds is the oldest building of the complex, **St Michael's Church**, the only building not covered with white plaster, exposing sections of original masonry. The church, dating back to 1070-88, is only partial, the bulk of the structure having fallen into the river in the 16th century, then rebuilt in the 1760s. To the right as you enter the church is the only original fresco, a dark and faded 11th-century Last Judgement scene. To the right of St Michael's are the mid-19th-century monks' dormitories. An attractive wooden well lies on the south side of the complex. Uphill and behind the monastery are the **Ukraine Academy of Sciences Botanical Gardens**, especially fragrant in spring and with attractive views of the Dnipro.

EAST BANK & RIVER TRIPS

The low-lying islands and promontories on the Dnipro's east bank are mainly woods and parkland. This is good strolling territory and the sandy beaches are busy in summer. To get to the islands, take the metro to Hidropark, cross the Dnipro footbridge directly below the rainbow arch or take the ferry from pier 5, half a km north of the main river terminal building, across to Lokomotiv pier (about 14 crossings daily in summer). On the east side, regular ferries link a number of spots such as Hidropark (near the metro), Spartak (south of the footbridge), Dovbychka and Rusanovsky Sady.

In summer, Kiev panorama boats leave the high-numbered piers just south of the main river terminal building every one or 1½ hours between 11 am and 7 pm; tickets are available on the spot. You'd see a good stretch of the city from regular ferries like those to the northern river beach, Uste Desny, from pier 5 (10 to 17 times daily), or Sady Nizhniy I and Sady Nizhniy II heading south from Metro Pier just north of Dnipro metro (every 40 or 80 minutes from 7.40 am to 8.20 pm, with the last boat back at 9.30 pm, and taking one hour each way).

Ferries normally stop when the Dnipro freezes – from some time in December to about early March. Due to the shortage of fuel they may stop running much earlier, decrease in frequency or possibly cease on certain routes.

ST CYRIL'S & BABY YAR

St Cyril's Church, on the corner of vulitsya Oleny Telihi and vulitsya Frunze, about five km north-west of the centre, has five cupolas of varying size which rise out of a wooded hillside. Dating to the 12th century, when it was part of a larger monastery, its present exterior is an 18th-century Ukrainian Baroque reconstruction. The striking interior has more medieval murals than anywhere else in Kiev, covering over 800 sq metres. Though mostly derivative of St Sophia and other churches, they're made accessible by some explanatory signs in English. St Cyril's is open as a museum daily except Friday.

About 1.5 km south-west of St Cyril's across the parkland, between vulitsya Oleny Telihi, vulitsya Melnikova and vulitsya Dorohozhitska, is a dramatic sculptural ensemble monument to the 100,000 *(sto tisyach)* Jews, Gipsies and partisans killed at the Baby Yar ravine by the Nazis in 1941. US president Bill Clinton visited Baby Yar in 1995.

Trolleybus No 27 goes to both places from Shulyavska and Petrivka metros. For St Cyril's, get off at the Muzey Kyrylivska Tserkva stop on vulitsya Oleny Telihi and walk up the stairs on the south side of the street. For the Baby Yar monument, get off at the Baby Yar stop on vulitsya Oleny Telihi, then walk south, crossing vulitsya Melnikova. The monument is over to the left. Trolley bus No 16 from maydan Nezalezhnosti will also take you down vulitsya Melnikova to Baby Yar.

FOLK ARCHITECTURE MUSEUM

The Ukraine Museum of Folk Architecture & Life is far south of the centre, but it's well worth the trip as it's the largest of its kind in the country. Spread out over scenic rolling hills dotted with groves of trees are a large number of quaint 17th to 20th-century wooden cottages, churches, farmsteads and windmills, many of them with manicured flower and vegetable gardens and interiors furnished with fascinating old textiles, traditional furniture and tools. The museum is divided into seven small villages representing the regional areas of Podolia, Carpathia, Polesia, Poltava, Southern Ukraine, Sloboda Ukraine and the Central Dnipro River Valley.

UKRAINE

Most of the structures were brought in from these regions.

There's a sunken restaurant in the Sloboda Ukraine village, but better still is the small restaurant in the old wooden ·19th-century *shynok*, or Cossack pub, in the Dnipro Valley region, the first village you come to. There's plenty of grassy open space and many people bring their own picnic. There's also a good gift shop in the Dnipro Valley region, near the shynok. You can usually find a young boy on a horse cart who, for a small price, can take you around and show you the highlights. Throughout the year there's often special events and festivals at the museum; for information call (☎ 266 24 16, 266 55 42) or ask at your hotel service bureau. It's open year-round from 10 am to 5 pm, closing on Monday and an hour earlier in winter.

To reach the museum, take trolleybus No 4 or 11 from Lybidska metro to VDNKh stop (the Ukrainian Exhibition of Economic Achievements), then bus No 24 to the end of the line. The museum is between Pyrohovo and Feofania villages, about 12 km from the city centre. The last bus back into the city leaves at 5.34 pm. A taxi would cost around US$10 each way.

PLACES TO STAY – BOTTOM END

Kiev definitely lacks good inexpensive accommodation, with many aged and decrepit establishments charging ridiculously exorbitant rates. Hopefully, this will change as the city begins to get a better idea of the facilities which should be available in a capital city. If US$50 is too much for you, your choice is unfortunately very limited. There is as yet no youth hostel, but growing numbers of people are beginning to learn the financial potential of renting out a spare bedroom to tourists. You may find someone at the railway station brandishing a small sign advertising a room to rent, but this is still highly unreliable. Make sure you work out the details carefully. We've also heard of people discreetly camping on the mostly deserted islands across the river from the centre of town, but this is not recommended.

Camping

From 1 May to 31 September you can camp or stay in a bungalow at the *Prolisok Camping & Motel* (☎ 444 03 95, 444 12 93), about 12 km west of the centre, 1.5 km beyond the ring road on prospekt Peremohy; it's a hassle to reach by public transport. Set amongst quiet pine trees, there are three-room bungalows with bath for up to seven people at US$4 per person, and smaller bungalows without bath for two people for US$3 per person. To pitch a tent costs US$5. There's also a standard hotel (open all year) at the entrance, costing US$65 for a double or single. There's a couple of cafés and a restaurant onsite. To get there, take the infrequent bus No 37 from the end metro station Svyatoshyn, west down prospekt Peremohy, or if you get tired of waiting, take the more frequent trolleybus No 7 halfway, getting off when it turns left off prospekt Peremohy. Continue walking for about 10 minutes. It's on the left-hand side of the road just before the pedestrian overpass.

There's also the *Autocamp Kiev*, near the Darnytsya metro station on the right bank of the city on prospekt Brovarsky 31. Stretched out among some trees on an island in the middle of the road, it's been closed for about two years and is now a parking lot. But who knows, it may reopen.

Hotels

There is one reasonably priced hotel conveniently accessible to a metro station. The *Hotel Druzhba* (☎ 268 34 06, 268 33 00) at bulvar Druzhby Narodiv 5 is a typical 1970s-style hotel with worn but satisfactory rooms costing US$10/20 for a single/double and $US30 for a triple, payable in kupons. There's a restaurant, bar and small gift shop located within the building. It's often booked out, so it's advisable to call ahead, especially during the summer. To get to the hotel, take the metro to the end station, Lybidska. Walk south down vulitsya Chervonoarmiyska (towards the freeway overpass) for 200 metres, then turn left on bulvar Druzhby Narodiv and it's on your left-hand side about 300 metres down.

The *Hotel Myr* (☎ 264 96 51, 264 96 46) at prospekt 40-richchya Zhovtnya 70 is also reasonable, but requires an additional, crowded two-stop ride on trolleybus No 4, 11 or 12 from Lybidska metro, a stop past the bus station. It's a modern and characterless structure, but the rooms are acceptable without undue luxury, at US$13/17/21 for a single/double/triple. There's a few 'deluxe' double rooms for around US$30. The entrance is up a side street next to the Flamingo Club. There's also the standard restaurant and bar in the hotel.

PLACES TO STAY – MIDDLE

If you're willing to fork out a bit more money, the best deals are the Hotel Moskva or the Hotel Ukraina. The *Hotel Moskva* (☎ 229 03 47), a 1960s Soviet-style replica of the original in the Russian capital, has a prime location, ceremoniously overlooking maydan Nezalezhnosti and with great views across to St Sophia Cathedral – that is if you get a room on the right side. The rooms are more spacious than average, but the entire place could use some fixing up. The staff is friendly and there's a restaurant, a few snack bars, souvenir kiosks and a sleazy slot-machine room. Rooms cost US$55/77 for a single/double. The hotel is located at vulitsya Instytutska 4, just up from the Maydan Nezalezhnosti metro station.

The *Hotel Ukraina* (☎ 229 27 07, 229 28 07) at bulvar Tarasa Shevchenka 5, on the corner of vulitsya Pushkinska, is the only hotel housed in an elegant prewar building. Built in 1908, and recently renovated, it has an excellent central location and the old-world charm and character that is desperately lacking in most other establishments, including a striking central staircase. Rooms have high ceilings and are cosy, costing US$72/88 for a single/double and US$110 for a triple, hard currency only. There's two restaurants, a few bars and a hard-currency shop in the lobby and on the 2nd floor. The Teatralna metro station is a block away.

The *Hotel Andriyivska* (☎ 416 22 56) has the best location of all, splendidly situated off the charming Andriyivsky uzviz at No 24, just down from St Andrew's Church (turn left down the side street). The hotel includes a relaxing courtyard with tables and a terrace, two restaurants and a café. Rooms cost US$70/126 for a single/double, and for larger, nicer rooms it's US$105/140, hard-currency only.

There's a couple of mid-range hotels on the bleak eastern side of the river. The best of these is the *Hotel Bratislava* (☎ 551 73 34) on vulitsya Malyshka 1, just off the Darnytsya metro station. It's a standard high-rise hotel with decent service and all amenities. Rooms are US$54/75/96 a single/double/triple, hard currency only.

Two other hotels, the *Hotel Holoseevskaya* (☎ 261 41 16) and the *Hotel Zoloty Kolos* (☎ 261 40 01), are farther west, past the Hotel Myr, at No 93 and No 95 prospekt 40-richchya Zhovtnya. Both are ridiculously overpriced (about US$90 per person), and not worth the hectic ride on trolleybus No 4, 11 or 12 from Lybidska metro to get there.

PLACES TO STAY – TOP END

The *Hotel Dnipro* (☎ 229 71 93), located on the far northern end of Khreshchatyk, at No 1/2, is an unbelievably overpriced, but somehow still busy, Intourist-style hotel. It's professionally staffed and reaches Western standards, with a good buffet breakfast included in the price. Rooms cost US$150/160 for a single/double (hard currency only) and there's a large restaurant, a couple of bars, a newsstand, exchange office and excursion bureau on the premises. Get off at Maydan Nezalezhnosti metro station.

The *Hotel Khreshchatyk* (☎ 229 71 93) is a bit more luxurious than the Moskva, slightly less so than the Dnipro, and is right in between, at Khreshchatyk 16. It's also overpriced at US$100/120 for a single/double, hard currency only. A number of airline offices are located off the lobby.

The highest standards of service, quality and exorbitant rates are awarded to the *Hotel Kievska* (☎ 220 41 44, 227 95 54) at vulitsya Hospitalna 12, formerly the Intourist Hotel. It's popular with large package groups and

UKRAINE

the friendly and professional staff are uncharacteristically eager to please. Within the complex are three restaurants, three hard-currency bars, a hard-currency casino, a hard-currency shop, a pharmacy and a tourist information and ticket office attached to the rear of the building. Prices, including breakfast buffet, are an astronomical US$183/193 for a single/double, hard currency only, of course. The hotel is in between the Palats Sportu and Klovska metro stations.

Nearby is the equally tall and bland façade of the *Hotel Rus* (☎ 220 56 46, 220 42 55) at vulitsya Hospitalna 4. It's not quite up to the standards of the Kievska, but it still offers good service for less money. Rooms cost US$75/100 for a single/double, with deluxe rooms for an additional US$50, hard currency only. The restaurant is on the 3rd floor, with a newsstand and gift shop off the lobby.

Off the hectic ploshcha Peremohy 1, at the far western end of bulvar Tarasa Shevchenka, is the *Hotel Lybid* (☎ 274 00 63), a tall, unkempt 1970s eyesore, formerly well used by Intourist groups. It has a number of facilities in the lobby, including a Western Union/X-Change Points office and gift shops. Standard rooms cost US$56/92 for a single/double (hard currency only); the restaurant is on the 2nd floor. It's about a 20-minute uphill walk to the Universytet metro station, but trolleybus Nos 8, 9 and 17 departing from in front of the Ukrainia department store by the hotel run down bulvar Tarasa Shevchenka to Bessarabska ploshcha; No 9 goes only about halfway.

The *Hotel Salyat* (☎ 290 61 30), at vulitsya Sichnevoho Povstannya 11A and built like a concrete space station, is not far from the Caves Monastery, but too overpriced to bother with at US$150 a single/double. The restaurant is reputed to be quite good. The *Hotel National* isn't an option, as it rents rooms to diplomats only.

PLACES TO EAT

Dining-out prospects in Kiev were once limited to the meat and potato dishes served at the tourist-oriented hotels. Since independence, however, many private restaurants have sprung up throughout the city, serving a wide variety of cuisines. The bulk of the patrons are still foreigners or business-people, as a meal out (although costing only a few dollars) is an enormous expense for most locals. You're more likely to see locals at the small cafés sipping a coffee, than eating at the restaurants.

Every hotel has at least one restaurant and usually a café or two. Most have reasonable food and are payable in kupons (check beforehand), with live music after 8 pm. Reputed to be the best and most expensive is the restaurant located in the *Hotel Dnipro*, with a diversified menu offering Ukrainian and European dishes, open from 7 am to 11 pm. The *Hotel Ukraina* restaurant has good atmosphere and Ukrainian cuisine. If you want a quiet meal, ask for the dining area away from the live music. It's open from noon to 12 am (closed between 5 and 6 pm).

Cafés

Andriyivsky uzviz has an increasing number of cafés and restaurants. The corner *Kafe Zamkove*, at No 24, is small and quaint, with steak and eggs for about US$2; it's open from 10 am to 9 pm. Around the corner are two restaurants and a terrace café in the *Hotel Andriyivska*. The *Restoran Podvirnya*, at No 19, has a nice wooden outdoor dining area at the rear, and serves European dishes for about US$8 to US10; it's open from 1 to 11 pm. At No 14 there's the small *Kafe Rami* – pricey but with pleasant outdoor seating. Across the street is the popular café *Svitlytsya*, at No 13A; it's open from 11 am to 9 pm, closed from 3 to 4 pm.

The bulk of the city's other cafés are along Khreshchatyk, and the best are along the Khreshchatyk pasazh, a small street through a large arched opening at vulitsya Khreshchatyk 15, north of the Khreshchatyk metro station. On either side of the archway are upper-balcony cafés blaring music and serving ice cream and drinks. The first café on your left past the apteka, *Kafe Pasazh*, serves tasty and cheap cakes and pastries. Farther down the small street are several Western hard-currency bars, including the

Bon-Bon Kafe, which has an excellent selection of exquisite, though slightly pricey, Hungarian cakes (payable in kupons).

Far nicer in atmosphere is the other *Bon-Bon Kafe*, on vulitsya Leontovycha 3, around the corner from St Volodymyr's Cathedral, with a pleasant outdoor patio. There's a café and restaurant downstairs in the *Exhibition Hall of the Arts* off Lvivska ploshcha. Ice cream is sold up and down Khreshchatyk. At the rear of maydan Nezalezhnosti, next to the bread shop, a small stall sells soft-serve ice cream in waffle cones. A *Pinguin* ice-cream shop is at vulitsya Chervonoarmiyska, down from ploshcha Lva Tolstoho, and there's another at vulitsya Khreshchatyk 46.

The *Niko Supermarket* at bulvar Tarasa Shevchenka 2, just up from vulitsya Khreshchatyk, sells Western food products for hard currency only.

Restaurants

Podil The *Hostynny Dvir* (☎ 416 68 76, 416 22 71), on the southern side of the Kontraktova Dim, in the centre of Kontraktova ploshcha, is a popular spot with an attractive painted and vaulted interior. Traditionally dressed waiters and waitresses serve a variety of fish, meat and Ukrainian dishes for about US$7 to US$10. You'll need reservations for dinner. It's open from noon to 11 pm (closed between 5 and 7 pm).

At vulitsya Spaska 8 is the low-key, relaxing *Restoran Spadshchyna*. Polite service and a variety of Ukrainian dishes for about US$2 to US$4 make it perfect for both lunch and dinner. The chicken cutlet (kotleta Spadshchyna) and various varenyky are the specialities.

Between Kontraktova ploshcha and Poshtova ploshcha, at vulitsya Petra Sahaydachnoho 10, is the bustling *Kafe Kozachenky*, serving heaped plates of hot food for less than US$2, with excellent borsch. The easiest way to order is to point to a plate that appears from the window to the right of the counter. It's open from 9 am to 5 pm.

If you've got lots of hard currency to spend, head to the *Bit Burger* restaurant on vulitsya Petra Sahaydachnoho 27, between Poshtova ploshcha and Kontraktova ploshcha.

Central Kiev *Maxim* (☎ 224-70-21), located near the opera house, at vulitsya Bohdana Khmelnytskoho 21, was one of the first private restaurants in town. It serves traditional dishes for moderately expensive prices, often with deafeningly loud music.

The *Restaurant Lestnitsa* (☎ 229 86 29) is next to the House of Architecture, at vulitsya Hrinchenko 7, just off maydan Nezalezhnosti. Downstairs, beyond the tacky lights around the entrance, lies a small dining room with traditional food for about US$5 to US8 for a full meal.

The *Kafe Khreshchatyk* at vulitsya Khreshchatyk 28, just north of vulitsya Porizna, is a long-established, inexpensive and quick upstairs eatery. The speciality is a small salad and a meat-and-potato stew baked in a small clay pot. It's open from 8 am to 8 pm.

For pizza try *Vesuvio Pizza* (☎ 228 34 48) on vulitsya Reytarska 25. It's small, friendly and smoke-free, and they serve a tasty variety of good-quality pizza, whole (US$5 to US$6) or by the slice (up to US$0.60); it's open from 10 am to 9 pm. *Restaurant Melodia* at vulitsya Volodymyrska 36 also serves good pizzas for US$3 to US$5, along with other meals, and is open from noon to midnight.

The *Montanya Snack Bar* at vulitsya Volodymyrska 70, south of vulitsya Lva Tolstoho, serves delicious Middle Eastern food, popular with foreign students; it's open from noon to 11 pm.

The *Eskimo Bar* at vulitsya Chervonoarmiyska 64, near the Respublikansky Stadion metro station, is an American-style restaurant/café serving hamburgers and french fries.

The small *Kafe Yaroslava Val* on the corner of Yaroslaviv val and vulitsya Ivana Franka has a quiet restaurant around the back where meat and potato dishes are served for about US$2; it's open from 1 to 11 pm.

For a real splurge, the *Apollo* at Khreshchatyk pasazh 15, just up from the Bon-Bon Kafe, has top service and food, a formal and elegant interior and hard-currency requirements.

Riverside For unique atmosphere try the *Kureni* (☎ 293 40 62) at Parkova aleia 19, an open-air restaurant set in a park-like setting scattered with a number of various-sized dining huts with thatched roofs – very pleasant in summer, when the place is hopping with people, especially if you can get a private hut to yourselves; reservations are recommended. The food is traditional Ukrainian, costing US$4 to US$6 for a full meal, and it's open from noon to midnight; closed between 5 and 6 pm. It's located just below the Mariyinsky Palace; a trail leads down the hillside to Parkova aleia.

The riverside *Restoran Mlyn* in Hidropark is housed in an old wooden mill, and serves good food in an inviting atmosphere. Head half-right when entering the park from Hidropark metro, and take care when walking on the island after dusk.

Market
The Bessarabsky Market is a bright and beautiful market hall with piles of fresh fruit, vegetables, nuts and assorted hanging hunks of meats, all wonderfully displayed by vendors who eagerly offer you samples of their best selection. The milk products, including various cheeses, are located off the southern side of the market hall in a smaller separate space, called the *mdocharna*. A block west of the Palats Ukraina metro station is the Volodymyrsky market – cheaper, more local but more hectic than the Bessarabsky Market.

ENTERTAINMENT
If you're feeling adventurous, you can attempt to translate *Vechirny Kiev* (Evening Kiev), an independent news guide in Ukrainian which lists events and entertainment possibilities.

Kiev has over 20 theatres presenting a wide range of performances, with ticket prices ridiculously low. Rather than picking up tickets through some hotels, which charge 10 times the price of the ticket in commission, buy them either at the theatre or at one of the many ticket offices found throughout the city. The ticket offices (teatralna kasa) also have schedules of all performances at all theatres. There's a small ticket office at Khreshchatyk 21, just north of vulitsya Liuteranska. Larger offices are located on vulitsya Chervonoarmiyska 16 (☎ 224 82 34), just north of ploshcha Lva Tolstoho, and at vulitsya Prorizna 9, next to the State Youth Theatre; both are open daily from 10 am to 7 pm. On the same day of the performance, tickets are usually only available at the theatre itself about an hour before the curtain goes up.

A performance at the lavish Shevchenko Opera & Ballet Theatre at vulitsya Volodymyrska 50 is a fine affair and highly recommended. Once the philharmonia on ploshcha Lenkomsomola is restored it will host a number of regular concerts. The Catholic Church of St Nicholas (between Respublikansky Stadion and Palats Ukraina metro stations) at Chervonoarmiyska vulitsya 75 is the only piece of truly Gothic architecture in the city and also regularly hosts organ and chamber-music concerts. The Ukrainian Drama Theatre is on ploshcha Franka, two blocks east of Khreshchatyk.

The Koleso Theatre at No 8 Andriyivsky uzviz is a small semi-avant-garde comedy/drama theatre, with performances on Thursday, Friday, Saturday and Monday during the theatre season. As with the other eateries in this area, its café is a popular hang-out in the evenings.

Kiev's circus, on ploshcha Peremohy, open year-round except July and August, pulls young and old alike, with live music, loads of acrobats and, unfortunately, bears on rollerskates – a real Kiev tradition.

The Kiev International Music Festival is held the first week in October, with hundreds of performances at numerous venues. The Annual International Kiev Film Festival is held the last week in October. Kiev Days Festival, centred around Andriyivsky uzviz, takes place during the last weekend in May.

Kiev's unofficial 'people's culture corner' is the subway beneath Khreshchatyk in front of the post office by maydan Nezalezhnosti. Musicians and poets with something to say perform here. Spontaneous street entertainment also sometimes occurs around the fountain in maydan Nezalezhnosti. Nearly every restaurant in town offers live music of varying degrees of ear-splitting quality. The Apollo bar (adjacent to the restaurant of the same name) and others around it on the Khreshchatyk pasazh offer a pub-like atmosphere.

The Dynamo Stadium, just off vulitsya Kirova, is home to Dynamo Kiev, one of Europe's leading soccer teams. The stadium is small, so if you want to see a game, check that they aren't using a bigger stadium.

THINGS TO BUY

Most hotels sell cheap souvenir items, but they're usually expensive and inferior. The stores at the tourist sites are better. There's a good gift shop selling embroidered shirts and folk souvenirs on the 3rd floor of the Golden Gate. In the Caves Monastery, there are four gift shops selling a wide variety of embroidery, carved and painted wooden trinkets and antique icons. There's also a good gift shop with folk art and embroidery in the Dnipro River valley area of the outdoor folk-architecture museum.

All along Andriyivsky uzviz there are street vendors selling more of the same, along with a number of art galleries. A few vendors, mostly selling books, line Khreshchatyk near maydan Nezalezhnosti. Ukrainsky Suvenir on vulitsya Chervonoarmiyska 23, just off ploshcha Lva Tolstoho, is the best in the country. They sell everything from embroidery and carpets to a wide variety of ceramics. The store at Khreshchatyk 32 sells a smaller range of similar items.

There are several antique stores, the best being downstairs at Horkoho 11, not far from the Ploshcha Lva Tolstoho metro station. Others are at Esplanada 2, not far from the Palats Sportu metro station; at Reytarska 29, two blocks south of Lvivska ploshcha; and at Khreshchatyk 46, off the street in a courtyard.

GETTING THERE & AWAY
Air

All international flights arrive at and depart from the small Boryspil International Airport (☎ 274 99 13), about 40 km east of Kiev. Facilities at the airport are limited. Some domestic flights use the smaller Zhulyany Airport, about 12 km from the centre.

You can fly direct from Kiev to over 15 countries in Europe on Ukraine International Airlines, including weekly flights to/from Amsterdam, Berlin, Brussels, Frankfurt, London, Manchester, Munich, Paris, Vienna and Zurich. Air Ukraine (an affiliated national airline) has weekly international flights to North America (including to Chicago, New York, Toronto and Washington), as well as weekly flights to Eastern European and Mediterranean destinations such as Prague, Warsaw, Athens, Cairo and Istanbul. Air Ukraine is also the only airline which services a number of domestic destinations, including Odessa, Lviv, Simferopol, Kharkiv, Donetsk, Uzhhorod, Ivano-Frankivsk, Donetsk and Chernivitsi. For all schedules, listings, prices and tickets, visit the Ukraine International Airlines office at prospekt Peremohy 14 (☎ 216 67 30), or the Air Ukraine office at vulitsya Karla Marxa 4 (☎ 224 05 01, 225 32 17), near maydan Nezalezhnosti. Information and tickets for both airlines can also be obtained at the Intourist ticket office behind the Hotel Kievska, at vulitsya Hospitalna 12 (☎ 224 29 50 (general information), 224 10 45 (airline information), 224 25 59 (train information). You can also call ☎ 056 for domestic flight information.

Most other airline offices, all of which offer transfer flights around the world, are located in the lobby of the Hotel Khreshchatyk at vulitsya Khreshchatyk 14.

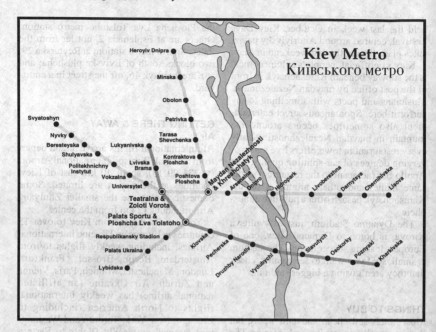

Kiev Metro
Київського метро

Heroyiv Dnipra

Minska

Obolon

Petrivka

Svyatoshyn

Nyvky

Beresteyska

Shulyavska

Politekhnichnyi Instytut

Vokzalna

Universytet

Lukyanivska

Lvivska Brama

Tarasa Shevchenka

Kontraktova Ploshcha

Poshtova Ploshcha

Maydan Nezalezhnosti & Khreshchatyk

Arsenalna

Dnipro

Hidropark

Livoberezhna

Darnytsya

Chernihivska

Lisova

Teatralna & Zoloti Vorota

Palats Sportu & Ploshcha Lva Tolstoho

Respublikansky Stadion

Palats Ukraina

Lybidska

Klovska

Pecherska

Druzhby Narodiv

Vydubychi

Slavutych

Osokorky

Poznyaki

Kharkivska

These include Air France (☎ 229-13-95), ČSA (☎ 228 02 96), LOT (228 71 50) and Lufthansa (☎ 229 36 61). Austrian Airlines, SAS and Swissair are at vulitsya Chervonoarmiyska 9/2 (☎ 229 13 95). KLM (☎ 268 90 23) is at vulitsya Horkoho 102. All airlines also have offices located at Boryspil Airport.

Bus

There are seven bus terminals in Kiev, although most buses run from the long-distance bus station (tsentralny avtobus vokzal) on Moskovska ploshcha, one stop from Lybidska metro station on trolleybus Nos 4, 11 or 12, or tram Nos 9 or 10. Make sure you get on the trolleybus going in the right direction; ask for 'avto vokzal'. You can buy tickets at the station, or sometimes even on the bus, but it's better to purchase them in advance at the ticket office (☎ 225-50-15) at bulvar Lesi Ukrainky 14.

Train

International The daily Berlin train takes 25½ hours via Warsaw (15½ hours) and Brest (10 hours). Other Warsaw and Brest services are slower. There are also daily trains to/from Prague (30 hours), Vienna (32 hours), Budapest (22 to 23 hours), Bucharest (22 to 23 hours), Sofia (34 hours) and Belgrade (30 hours). Several Moscow trains run daily, taking about 15 hours. Other trains go at least daily to Minsk (11 hours), Riga (21 hours), St Petersburg (23 to 30 hours), Rostov-on-Don (19 hours), Kishinev (14 hours) and Sochi (34 hours).

Domestic There are at least five daily trains to/from Lviv (12 hours) and Odessa (12 hours); three daily trains to/from Poltava (seven hours), Kharkiv (11 hours), Simferopol (18 to 19 hours) and Uzhhorod (20 to 21 hours); and two daily to Chernihiv (four hours) and Chernivtsi (14 hours).

UKRAINE

NORTH TO SOUTH LINE	Львівська Брама	Берестеиська
	Lvivska Brama	Beresteyska
Героїв Дніпра	Золоті Ворота	Шулявська
Heroyiv Dnipra	Zoloti Vorota	Shulyavska
Мінська	Площа Льва Толстого	Політехнічний Інститут
Minska	Ploshcha Lva Tolstoho	Politekhnichny Instytut
Оболонь	Кловська	Вокзальна
Obolon	Klovska	Vokzalna
Петрівка	Печерська	Університет
Petrivka	Pecherska	Universytet
Тараса Шевченка	Дружби Народів	Театральна
Tarasa Shevchenka	Druzhby Narodiv	Teatralna
Контрактова Площа	Видубичі	Хрещатик
Kontraktova Ploshcha	Vydubychi	Khreshchatyk
Поштова Площа	Славутич	Арсенальна
Poshtova Ploshcha	Slavutych	Arsenalna
Майдан Незалежності	Осокорки	Дніпро
Maydan Nezalezhnosti	Osokorky	Dnipro
Палац Спорту	Познякі	Гідропарк
Palats Sportu	Poznyaki	Hidropark
Республіканський Стадіон	Харківська	Лівобережна
Respublikansky Stadion	Kharkivska	Livoberezhna
Палац Україна		Дарниця
Palats Ukraina	WEST TO EAST LINE	Darnytsya
Либідська		Чернігівська
Lybidska	Святошин	Chernihivska
	Svyatoshyn	Лісова
NORTH-WEST TO EAST LINE	Нивки	Lisova
	Nyvky	
Лукянівська		
Lukyanivska		

The station is on the western fringe of the centre, at the end of ulitsa Kominternu, which branches off the middle of bulvar Tarasa Shevchenka. Vokzalna metro station is right outside the main station, with a curved colonnaded façade with a clock. The platform and ticket booths for electric trains which service local destinations are in between the main station and the metro.

Buying Tickets Don't bother with the chaos in the main ticket hall of the railway station. To buy same-day tickets at the station, go upstairs and turn to your left into the Zal Inturyst (Intourist Hall). Kasa No 42 is only for foreigners, mostly students (tickets payable in kupons), and there's rarely a long wait. You can try to buy advance tickets here, but they may tell you to go to the main ticket office at bulvar Tarasa Shevchenka 38, in the lobby of the Hotel Expres (at the intersection of ulitsa Kominternu and bulvar Tarasa Shevchenka). This is usually very crowded, with only a few of the many windows ever operating. If you want absolutely no hassles, go to the Intourist ticket office (☎ 224 25 59) behind the Hotel Kievska, at vulitsya Hospitalna 12; it's open daily from 9 am to 6 pm, closed between 1 and 2 pm. Unlike most ticket offices, this one really exploits the situation, with the tickets payable in hard currency only and costing about four to five times the usual price. A 2nd-class sleeper from Kiev to Lviv is US$23, as opposed to about US$6 at kasa No 42 upstairs in the Zal Inturyst at the railway station.

Car

For car-rental details see the Ukraine Getting Around section.

UKRAINE

Boat

Kiev is the most northerly hydrofoil and passenger boat port on the Dnipro and the usual starting or finishing point of Dnipro River cruises. The boat terminal and ticket office (rechnoy vokzal) is on Poshtova ploshcha, near the Poshtova Ploshcha metro station.

Hydrofoil services usually run from the end of April to the middle of October, and only travel south to Cherkasy (six hours), with 15 stops en route, including Kaniv (four hours) and Pereyeslav-Khmelnytsky (three hours). The hydrofoils are small and fast-moving vessels with no deck space and are often crowded; they have a tiny bufet on board. Get a window seat if you can.

During the summer there are four hydrofoils a day, with only two a day at the beginning and end of the season. On weekends they sometimes run overnight trips, where you leave on Friday night, spend a day at Kosiv and then take another night boat back. For trips farther than Cherkasy, service is limited from May to August except for specially chartered vessels, and they're usually larger passenger ships. It is possible to take a boat all the way down to Odessa but it will take about 2½ days. For more information, see the Ukraine Getting Around chapter.

Tickets can be purchased in advance at the ticket kasa downstairs in the boat terminal, next to an information kiosk. If you can't organise it yourself, one of the travel agencies mentioned in this chapter's Information section will be able to organise a cruise for you.

GETTING AROUND
To/From the Airport

An airport bus (☎ 295 67 01) runs the 40 km between ploshcha Peremohy and Boryspil Airport, taking about one hour each way. It's scheduled every 20 minutes, but with the fuel shortages it's far from reliable. For about US$15 to US$20 you can get a taxi. Zhulyany Airport is reached by taxi or a 40-minute ride on trolleybus No 9 from ploshcha Peremohy.

Local Transport

It's difficult to find a city map with public transport marked; the only one seems to be the map in English put out by Incomartour.

The three lines of Kiev's metro are very useful and the only frequent and regularly reliable form of transportation. There are buses, trolleybuses and trams, going just about everywhere, but they're almost always unbearably crowded and, due to fuel shortages, they never seem to keep to a schedule. If you're going to ride these secondary forms of public transport, you're going to have to learn to push and shove.

During the first week of each month you can buy a monthly pass, good for all forms of transportation, for about US$1. Otherwise, you can buy bus and tram tickets from the kiosks, although many people ride for free. The metro requires zhetony – coloured plastic tokens which are sold at all stations from a window near the entrance.

Taxis

Taxis congregate at the main railway station, in front of the Dnipro and Kievska hotels, and on ploshcha Peremohy.

Central Ukraine
Центральна Україна

Central Ukraine is the traditional bread-basket region and grows the bulk of the country's grain, wheat and other agricultural produce. The part that sweeps west from the Dnipro River is classic steppe, the traditional land of the Cossacks. It includes endless stretches of prairie-like land whose solitude is broken only by rural villages and simple farming towns.

This is also the region (especially in the south-east) that predominantly fell prey to Stalin's collectivisation experiment. It suffered famine in 1932-33 when an estimated five to seven million Ukrainians starved to death while the storehouses in Moscow remained full. Entire villages were wiped out, and many were re-populated with ethnic Russians. Today there are large Russian minorities in cities such as Dnipropetrovsk and the huge sprawling industrial city of Krivy Rih.

PEREYASLAV-KHMELNYTSKY
ПЕРЕЯСЛАВ-ХМЕЛЬНИЦЬКИЙ
Population: 24,000

A three-hour, roughly 90-km trip downriver from Kiev, Pereyaslav-Khmelnytsky makes an excellent and relaxing day trip from the capital. Dating from the 10th century, the city was a fortress town under Kievan Rus and later a strategic Cossack military base, with an important collegium founded in 1738. Designated as a Historical-Cultural Preserve, the sleepy provincial town boasts historic architecture and a number of interesting museums.

It was here that the great Cossack leader Bohdan Khmelnytsky, on 18 January 1654 and under controversial circumstances, signed the infamous Pereyaslav agreement, which accepted the tsar's overlordship of Ukraine, irrevocably tying the fate of the Ukraine and Russia. Originally the agreement was to be a military alliance among

equals, with the sovereignty of Ukraine respected. But a second agreement hastily signed in Pereyaslav five years later, after Khmelnytsky's death, by his son, Iruii, gave Russia the decisive upper hand and political control over much of Ukraine. This notorious agreement is the source of much dispute between historians, and for many Ukrainian nationalists, including Shevchenko, the day it was signed was the darkest day in the sad history of Ukraine, one that brought about the death of its sovereignty.

Pereyaslav-Khmelnytsky's telephone area code is 04467.

Folk Architecture Museum
The highlight of a visit here is the Folk Architecture Museum, which lies in a peaceful, wooded area between the town and the river boat station. From the small boat terminal, which is at the end of a long inlet off the main Dnipro, it's about one km to the museum and a km further to the town centre. Follow the road from the dock and turn right on to the main road, then take the first left down a long, tree-lined road that leads to the entrance. If you arrive in Pereyaslav-Khmelnytsky by bus, head south-east from the bus station for 1.5 km into the centre, continue down vulitsya Khmelnytsky and out of town for a km, then turn right down

979

the road to the museum entrance. The museum is open from 10 am to 5 pm Saturday to Tuesday and Thursday, from noon to 5 pm Friday, and is closed Wednesday. The entry fee is about US$0.50.

Along shaded paths set amongst picket fences and flower gardens are a number of beautiful wooden churches, windmills and farmhouses, several decked out on the inside with original furnishings and others set up as small museums. Most structures are originally from the central Dnipro region. Bring a picnic and settle in for a relaxing afternoon.

Town Centre

The town boasts a good number of impressive buildings and museums for its size, most around the central ploshcha Vozyednannya, which lies off the main street, vulitsya Khmelnytsky. To reach the town centre, from the opposite side of the museum cut across a wide field to the right of a pond. You'll see St Michael's Church a short distance away on your left, the tall bell tower of the Ascension Monastery in the distance to your right, and the Uspenska Church in the middle. Cross the small bridge and turn right on to vulitsya Lenina then left on to vulitsya Khmelnytsky.

A half block before reaching ploshcha Vozyednannya, on the right side of vulitsya Khmelnytsky 20, is the **Kobzar Museum** (Musey Kobzarstva), open Friday to Tuesday from 10 am to 5 pm, closed from 1 to 2 pm. Inside is a small exhibition of old, traditional string instruments and exhibits on the legendary kobzar and bandura player, Ukraine's version of the wandering, lute-toting bard who travelled from village to village playing songs and reciting stories (see Music in Facts about Ukraine).

Nearby (you can ask directions at the Kobzar Museum) is the **historical museum**, which includes a 500-year-old chess set and a sword supposed to have been Khmelnytsky's.

Straight ahead half a block from the Kobzar Museum is ploshcha Vozyednannya. Its south-western side is entirely taken by the **Ascension Monastery** (Voznesensky

monaster), including the 1700 Baroque **cathedral** and the highly ornate 1770 **bell tower**, which rises from the corner and dominates the skyline from far across the surrounding flat lands. The complex also includes a collegium built in 1753 and, oddly, a few pieces of WW II military equipment littering the grounds.

Two churches of interest lie south-east of ploshcha Vozyednannya. The **Uspenska Church** is at the end of vulitsya Moskovska, two blocks south-east of the Ascension Monastery. The small but lovely 1644 **St Michael Church** (Mykhaylivska tserkva) is hidden behind some cottage-lined streets near the small Trubezh River, around the south-western end of vulitsya Lenina. It has a charming 1745 bell tower at the entrance, and inside the church grounds is the **Regional Ethnographic Museum**.

Places to Stay

If you miss the last boat back or want to just hang out longer, there is a small *hotel* (☎ 5 14 52) at vulitsya Khmelnytsky 5, across the street from the Ascension Monastery on the southern corner of the main square, that charges US$3/5 for singles/doubles.

Getting There & Away

Most buses running between Kiev's main bus station and Cherkasy (at least six daily each way) stop at Pereyaslav-Khmelnytsky on the way. Some Cherkasy buses may take the route on the opposite side of the Dnipro through Kaniv, so make sure your bus is going through Pereyaslav-Khmelnytsky. The bus station is about 1.5 km north-west of the centre, on the opposite side of the town from the folk architecture museum. To get there from the centre, head straight north-west along vulitsya Khmelnytsky from ploshcha Vozyednannya.

But by far the most enjoyable way to get there is to take one of the daily seasonal hydrofoils which leave from Kiev's main river boat terminal (see Getting There & Away in Kiev). Pereyaslav-Khmelnytsky is the fifth stop, taking about 2½ to three hours.

KANIV
КАНІВ

When Taras Shevchenko died in 1861, he left his famous poem *Zapovit (Testament)* requesting his countrymen to bury him on a hill overlooking the great Dnipro River, where, after rising up and liberating the land they could 'freely, and with good intent, speak quietly of him'.

Kaniv, 10 stops, four hours and 162 km down the Dnipro from Kiev, is the spot. In 1925 the steep and scenic bluff overlooking the river called Taras' Hill (Tarasova Hora) was officially designated a State Cultural Preserve. The magnet and homage site for tourists is the **Shevchenko Monument & Literary Memorial Museum**. It can be reached by climbing the 400 steps which start near the Tarasova Hora pier and ascend past a fountain on the wooded hillside. The tomb is beneath the towering obelisk, which is crowned with a statue of the poet. There is an observation point in front and a grove of memorial oak and chestnut trees off to the side, making for a peaceful and reflective spot. The neoclassical Memorial Museum has an extensive account of Shevchenko's life and work. Behind it a path leads up to the tomb of Yadlovsky, the man who guarded Shevchenko's body from 1883 to 1933. The Tarasova Hora hotel is nearby.

About 15 km south of the city is the **Kaniv Nature Reserve** – about 2000 hectares of pristine forest and hills with over 5000 species of plants indigenous to the area.

Kaniv is an hour past Pereyaslav-Khmelnytsky and four hours from Kiev on the hydrofoil service from Kiev's main river boat terminal (see Getting There & Away in Kiev). A few of the Cherkasy buses from Kiev's main bus station stop in Kaniv along the way.

Kaniv's telephone area code is 04736.

CHERNIHIV
ЧЕРНІГІВ

Population: 313,000

Chernihiv, 140 km north of Kiev on the Desna River, was the capital of one of the most important princedoms within Kievan Rus. An impressive group of early religious buildings have survived, although some had to be rebuilt after WW II. Of the 25 architectural landmarks from the 11th to 12th century in Ukraine, five are in Chernihiv, making it well worth a trip if you have the time.

The city dates from the early 8th century, but didn't become significant until 100 years later as a Kievan Rus princedom and an important fortified crossroads. After being sacked by Tatars in 1239, the city was rebuilt with the addition of several new Byzantine churches and monasteries, a few of which survive today. The city subsequently fell to the Lithuanians, who built up the fortress in the 14th century, and then to Poland in the early 17th century, before eventually coming under Russian rule.

Orientation & Information

Vulitsya Lenina, the city's park-like main artery, runs north-west to south-east, with the main square, ploshcha Chervona, halfway along. At the south-east end of vulitsya Lenina is the Dytynets ('Ramparts'), the historic centre of the city. Two major monasteries lie to its south-west. The railway and bus stations are in ploshcha Vokzalna, about two km west of ploshcha Chervona.

There's a post and telephone office northwest of ploshcha Chervona, on the corner of vulitsya Lenina and prospekt Zhovtnevy Revolyutsiyi.

City Centre

Start at ploshcha Chervona, a wide open brick-paved square with parks running off each side. Boasting a sculpted frieze, the most prominent building is the neoclassical **Taras Shevchenko Music & Drama Theatre**, on the north-eastern side. Behind the theatre and in the middle of a park is the lovely and simple **Pyatnytska Church**, built in the 12th century. Most of what you see is a 1960s reconstruction that brings it close to its original Kievan Rus appearance. Inside on the left are a few photos showing its three very different reconstructions over the centuries (it was once much larger), each time after being destroyed in war – first by the

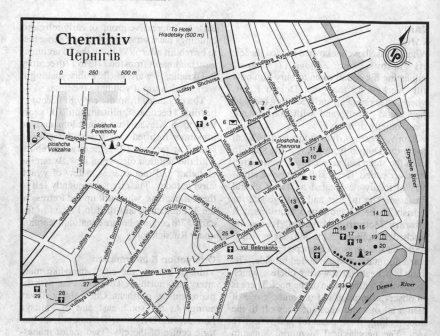

Chernihiv
Чернігів

0   250   500 m

To Hotel
Hradetsky (500 m)

vulitsya Shchorsa

vulitsya Kyivska

ploshcha
Peremohy

prospect Zhovtnevy

vulitsya Revolyutsyi

Frunze

Kokho

vulitsya

vulitsya

Vokzalna

prospect Zhovtnevy

Zhovtnevy

Revolyutsiy

Konstromska

Koisiubynskoho

ploshcha
Chervona

vulitsya Sverdlova

Seredniykova

Pushkina

Stryzhen River

ploshcha
Peremohy

ploshcha
Vokzalna

vulitsya

vulitsya Shchorsa

Malyasova

Ostrovskoho

vulitsya

Desnyaka

vulitsya Vorovskoho

Krugova

vulitsya Shevchenko

Lenina

vulitsya K Libknekta

vulitsya Karla Marxa

vulitsya Promeshenna

Suvorova

Vatutina

vulitsya Proletarska

vul Belinskoho

vulitsya Lva Tolstoho

vulitsya Uspenskoho

Luchna

Nakhimova

Antonova-Ovenka

vulitsya Leskovytska

vulitsya Lenina

vulitsya Nova

Desna River

Tatars, then by the Poles, and finally in WW
II. The exterior brickwork is superb. Behind
the church further in the park is a monument
of Khmelnytsky with his familiar feathered
hat.

Running south-east from ploshcha Chervona is the **Alley of Heroes**, a long park with
busts of a variety of noteworthy people,
many of whom were old communist heroes.
Farther along this axis are the five beautiful
golden domes of **St Catherine's Church**,
designed in the Ukrainian Baroque style in
the 17th and 18th centuries. The lofty white
interior reflects its pure cruciform plan and
houses the **Museum of Decorative Art**.
Dedicated mostly to an impressive display of
embroidery from the Chernihiv region, it's
open from 10 am to 5 pm, daily except
Wednesday.

Dytynets North-east of St Catherine Church
is the Dytynets, the area of first settlement

and, from the 10th century, the site of a
strategic fortress commanding trade routes
south to Kiev. Today it's a peaceful, leafy
park where, standing in a close cluster, are a
remarkable group of early religious buildings. The most striking is the **Spaso-
Preobrazhensky Cathedral**, which has two
distinctive, missile-like corner bell towers.
Dating from 1017, it's one of the oldest
churches of the Kievan Rus, partially reconstructed between the 17th and 19th centuries.
The interior is dark and mysterious, and
houses an 18th-century Baroque iconostasis
and the tombs of several Kievan Rus royalty,
including Prince Mstyslav Khorobry, the
younger brother of Yaroslav the Wise, who
had the cathedral built. The side aisles are
lined with a series of impressive wall paintings depicting scenes from the Old
Testament. Note the exposed original ionic
stone capital on the second column on the
northern transept, the far side from the
cathedral's entrance.

UKRAINE

Immediately north-west is the 12th-century **Boryso-Hlibsky Cathedral**, designed following ancient traditions with a central dome rising out of an essentially box-like base, its roof comprised of a series of interconnected vaults. The cathedral, named after the first Ukrainian saints, Borys and Hlib, was badly damaged in WW II and partially rebuilt 15 years later. Some foundations of the original are exposed on the north and south sides. Inside is a museum charting the history of the cathedral and the Dytynets area, open from 10 am to 5 pm daily. Among the artefacts are the 18th-century **Royal Doors**, commissioned by the famous Cossack leader Ivan Mazepa, depicting both

Borys and Hlib reclining at the base of the doors.

Farther north-west is the highly decorated former **collegium** (1710), standing out with its undulate tower. The exterior ornamentation is a strange combination of Byzantine and Baroque motifs. It was also rebuilt after being partially destroyed by a fire in WW II. Inside is a small museum which displays mostly icons from the 17th to 19th centuries, open daily from 11 am to 7 pm.

North-east of the Boryso-Hlibsky Cathedral is the former **Archbishop's residence** (1780), which has a classical portico, and now houses the city's archives. Further north-east, behind the bust of Pushkin, is the

UKRAINE

city's **art museum**, open from 10 am to 5 pm daily, with an impressive collection of historic European paintings upstairs and a temporary gallery downstairs. South-east of the art museum is the **Chernihiv History Museum**, housed in another neoclassical building, this time the former Governor's house (1804). Open from 10 am to 6 pm daily except Thursday, it has two floors of well-displayed historical exhibits, strong on Kievan Rus and with some good Cossack weaponry, including a Hetman sword, and a copy of the famous 1581 'Ostroh Bible', the first Bible to be printed in the old Slavonic language.

Lining the southern edge of the Dytynets are a row of mostly 18th-century **cannons** overlooking the embankments and once protecting the fortified southern entrance to the city. From here there are excellent views to the west, past St Catherine's to the Yeletsky Monastery and, farther, to the Troyitsko Monastery, their multi-domed ensembles dominating the skyline. Nearby is a seated statue of a young Taras Shevchenko. Directly south on the river bank is the **river boat terminal**, where (during summer) ferry boats take people up and down the Desna River.

Yeletsky Monastery

To reach this monastery, walk down vulitsya Belinskoho, south-west from St Catherine's past some old wooden houses, and head towards the 36-metre octagonal bell tower with its very bulbous onion dome. From the bell tower, turn right and then left, following the walls to the entrance gate. If this is closed there's a small gate on the opposite side of the walls.

The monastery is now a working convent, the centrepiece being the 12th-century **Uspensky Cathedral**, remodelled in the 17th century into a fine example of Ukrainian Baroque, with the distinctively shaped cupolas. To the right (south) is the **Peter & Paul Church** (Petropavlivska tserkva), site of the monks' original cells. The grounds are leafy and unkempt, but very peaceful.

Between the cathedral and bell tower is the small refectory.

Across the street from the Yeletsky Monastery on the corner of vulitsya Proletarska and vulitsya Vorovskoho is a small park with the **Black Grave**, a former archaeological site, where Prince Chorny (Black), the founder of Chernihiv, was supposedly buried in the 10th century.

Illinsky Church & Troyitsko Monastery

It's not far to walk (about two km) from the Black Grave to the monastery; or you could take trolley bus No 8, which runs down vulitsya Lva Tolstoho from the Dytynets right past the monastery. From the **Hill of Glory Monument** (dedicated to the unknown soldier) on the corner of vulitsya Uspenskoho and vulitsya Lva Tolstoho, you can walk up the flight of stairs and past the obelisk to the monastery. But a better approach is to turn left along the small vulitsya Uspenskoho. Lined with quaint wooden cottages, it runs along the base of the ridge until reaching **Illinsky Church** at No 33. A dirt path leads uphill past the Illinsky Church to Troyitsko Monastery.

The small Illinsky Church is part of the monastery complex although it's tucked away below the hillside. It's a charming church and dates from 1069, but the highlight is the connected **Antoniy Caves**, 315 metres of underground passageways and galleries, and five subterranean chapels. Constructed mostly from the 11th to 13th centuries, they differ from the Caves Monastery in Kiev in that these are well lit, with larger spaces, and many chapels are vaulted and decorated with plaster work. There are no monk's bodies, but there are a few neat piles of human bones lying around. There's a map of the caves on a wall next to the entrance, the kasa is in the wooden bell tower next door. The caves are open from 10 am to 6 pm daily except Thursday. You may have to ask the caretaker to let you in when there aren't too many tourists around.

Uphill, the magnificent five-tiered, 58-metre bell tower of the **Troyitsko Monastery** is High Baroque, similar to the one in the Caves Monastery in Kiev. Beyond the entrance next to the bell tower, which protrudes into the street, the grounds are well maintained. The large 1679 multi-cupola **Trinity Cathedral** (Troyitsky sobor) is yet another excellent example of Ukrainian Baroque, its main façade decorated with a series of niches. To the left (north-west) of the cathedral are two small, ornate chapels. On the opposite side of the cathedral (south-east) is the beige **Vedenska Church & Refectory** (1677), with its squat cupola. Opposite the cathedral are the monks' dormitories.

Market

There's a colourful and frantic market behind the **Voskresenska Church** at vulitsya Komsomolska 36, near the tall red and white radio tower. The small church was built in the mid-18th century in Ukrainian Classical style. Across the street is its more Baroque, squat bell tower.

Places to Stay

The best located hotel is the *Hotel Desna* (☎ 7 77 00), on the western corner of ploshcha Chervona. It's an older building with rooms that aren't kept up, but it is none the less comfortable. If no-one is in the lobby reception, check upstairs in the dezhurna's office on your right. Rooms are US$4/6 for singles/doubles. Make sure you ask for a room with a private bath.

The *Hotel Ukruina* (☎ 7 46 04) is like the Desna in quality but with perhaps a bit better service. It's two blocks north-west at vulitsya Lenina 33, on the corner of prospekt Zhovtnevy Revolyutsiyi, with rooms costing US$5/7 for singles/doubles with bath and a few cheap triples and quads without bath.

The *Hotel Hradetsky* (☎ 4 50 25) is the mandatory crumbling, tall, Intourist style hotel, a little farther from the centre, but with better rooms and service, and with staff more used to serving tourists than the other hotels. Rooms with bath go for US$6/8 a single/double. It's about two km north-west along vulitsya Lenina from ploshcha Chervona, at No 68.

Places to Eat

A small door on the south-east side of the Taras Shevchenko Theatre leads downstairs to the *Tsentral Kafe*, good for lunch or dinner, serving inexpensive and tasty food in relaxing surroundings; it's open from noon to 11 pm. Across the street and down at vulitsya Shevchenko 8, is a bakery (Magazin No 103) with nice cakes, cookies and coffee, open 10 am to 5 pm.

All the hotels have restaurants, the selection and quality of the food they serve varying with the availability of supplies. The best is in the *Hotel Hradetsky*, which also has small bufety on the 4th and 11th floors.

Getting There & Away

The railway and bus stations are next to each other, about two km west of the centre. Crowded trolleybus No 1 runs between the stations and the centre, stopping a block north of ploshcha Chervona.

Between Kiev and Chernihiv there are more buses than trains, making the bus probably the best means of getting there. Six to eight buses run daily (four hours from Kiev's main bus station), as opposed to about two daily trains (four to five hours). For a long alternate route via Nizhyn, electric trains run the two-hour trip from Chernihiv to this town about four times a day. From Nizhyn you can catch another electric train back to Kiev (2½ hours; 10 times daily).

Chernihiv is on the Kiev-St Petersburg railway line, which runs through Homel and Minsk, as well as the Minsk-Sevastopol line. Each has a train passing through once a day in each direction.

SEDNIV
СЕДНІВ

Sedniv, a small village 25 km north-east of Chernihiv on the Snov River, is an idyllic spot with a history reaching back to the Kievan Rus era. Set in a pristine, wooded valley, it has three fine churches and gives visitors a glimpse of the simple life. It's an easy day's excursion from Chernihiv, with at least five buses a day going to/from Horodnya, stopping in Sedniv along the way.

From the bus station continue on the road towards the 1860 **Uspensky Church** and bell tower in the centre of the village. **St George's** (1715), a beautiful wooden church constructed entirely without nails, and the **Resurrection Church** (Voskresenska tserkva; 1690), the oldest in the area, are both further along and set back off the road. The surrounding area, especially near the banks of the Snov River, is beautiful, particularly in spring.

NIZHYN
НІЖИН
Population: 83,000

The compact centre of Nizhyn is jam-packed with pristine white and green churches, testament to its colourful and rich history dating back to the 12th century, when it was an outlying fortress of the Chernihiv principality. Its citizens were cruelly punished by the Poles after rebellions in the 1630s. Soon after the Cossacks liberated the city, it fell under Russian control (in the late 17th century). It may not merit an entire trip in itself, but can be visited as a slight detour on the way between Chernihiv and Kiev.

Nizhyn's telephone area code is 04631.

City Centre
Most sights are off vulitsya Hoholya, the short and colourful main strip connecting large ploshcha Lenina in the west with vulitsya Moskovska one km to the east. Tree-filled Hohol Park is halfway along on the south side of the street.

Starting at the north-east corner of ploshcha Lenina and walking east on vulitsya Hoholya past the biblioteka (library), the first church rising on your left at No 4 is the 1752 **Church of St John the Baptist** (Ioanna Bohoslova). Farther along at No 10, across from **Hohol Park**, is the 1716 **Annunciation Cathedral**. Built in a formidable Byzantine style, it has five rusted domes rising above a well-chipped plaster base. A right at vulitsya Yavorskoho along the park will end in the old **town hall** and vulitsya Batyuka, where to your right at No 14 is the **Nizhyn Regional Museum**.

Continuing east on vulitsya Hoholya will take you to a cluster of impressive sparkling-white churches, the finest being the splendid 1668-70 **St Nicholas Cathedral**, off to your right. It is an outstanding example of Ukrainian Baroque, having five swooping, green helmet domes with golden cupolas, all rising from a pasty-white, heavily moulded cruciform base. Across the street is the classical 1780 **All Saint's Church**, sporting three porticoes and a single dome. Directly behind, almost touching, is another, smaller 18th-century **church**. Just across a small street to the east is the 1733 **Troyitska Church** with an interesting pseudo-classical bell tower.

A block further vulitsya Hoholya ends where it meets the bustling vulitsya Moskovska. To your left and across the street is the central **market** (rynok). On the opposite far corner is the *Stare Misto Kafe*. If you continue north on vulitsya Moskovska, across the Oster River to your right is the weathered brick Byzantine carcass of the 1757 **Spasa Church**.

The *Hotel Nizhyn* on the south-east corner of ploshcha Lenina at vulitsya Batyuka 1 may be able to provide accommodation. Off the lobby is the café *Rayduha*, which sells cakes, coffee and pizza.

Getting There & Away
Five electric trains daily travel to/from Chernihiv (two hours), and about 10 a day run to/from Kiev (2½ hours). The electric train platform for Kiev is south of the main platform and has the times posted. Buses also run to both locations as well as other destinations in the area. It's possible to leave Chernihiv early in the morning, stop in Nizhyn for a few hours, and then continue to Kiev in the same full day, or vice versa.

Getting Around
The town centre is about three km north of the bus and railway stations. From the railway station, cross the pedestrian bridge back over the tracks and walk past the bus station (on your right) to the main road, vulitsya Shevchenko, which leads to the right (north) to ploshcha Lenina after 2.5 km.

Any bus going in that direction (Nos 2, 3, 4, 6, 9) will pull up at the corner stop and take you there. This is much faster than waiting for the single bus No 3 that goes from the front of the railway station to the centre. A taxi to the centre from the station would cost about US$1.

VINNYTSYA
ВИННИЦЯ
Population: 387,000

Vinnytsya, 260 km south-west of Kiev, is a nicer overnight stop than Zhytomyr (125 km to the north) for road travellers heading east to Kiev. Founded in 1363, it was controlled by Lithuania or Poland with frequent Cossack uprisings until 1793, when it became Russian.

Most things are on or near vulitsya Lenina, which stretches about 2.5 km from ploshcha Gagarina in the west to ploshcha Zhovtneva (sometimes referred to as ploshcha Oktyabrya) in the east, crossing the Pivdenny (Southern) Buh River just west of ploshcha Zhovtneva.

During WW II a mass grave was discovered in Vinnytsya containing about 10,000 victims that had been shot by the NKVD during Stalin's terror purges of 1937-39.

Vinnytsya's telephone area code is 04322.

Vulitsya Lenina
On the east end of the street, No 14 is the former **Capuchin monastery**, now a Polish Catholic church. No 23 is a former 1758 **Dominican monastery**, now an Orthodox church with fragments of original frescoes on the far wall. No 17 is a former **Jesuit monastery** (17th century). Set back from the street at No 19 is the **regional museum**, open from 10 am to 6 pm daily except Monday. It houses, besides some ethnographic and archaeological displays, heavy exhibits on WW II, graphically portraying the horror, through hundreds of photos, that the Ukrainians had to endure. To the right is the city **picture gallery**, which displays 18th to 19th-century European paintings and ceramics, and is open from 10 am to 6 pm daily except Friday.

Other Things to See & Do
Vulitsya Kozytskoho intersects vulitsya Lenina about halfway along, just east from the neoclassical **Music & Drama Theatre**. A block north around the corner from the Hotel Ukraina stands a tall brick clock tower, built in 1902 on the site of the city's former walled defences. Inside is a **museum** (open from 9 am to 5 pm daily except Monday) dedicated to the soldiers from the Vinnytsya region who perished in the 1979-89 Afghan war, displaying photos, letters and personal artefacts.

In the opposite direction – south on vulitsya Kozytskoho – across the river and uphill to your right, is the fine wooden **Mykolayivska Church**, built in 1745, at vulitsya Mayakovsky 2. It's an excellent example of Podilian (from the historical region of Ukraine encompassing the centre and western parts of the country) folk architecture with three cupolas and a low arcaded gallery along the base.

Horkohe Culture Park through the strange-looking gateway off ploshcha Gagarina is a busy area with plenty of strolling venues lined with benches. One summer evening we found chess, soccer, a circus, an open-air disco, a funfair, table tennis and athletics all in action.

At No 17 on vulitsya Bevza, second left after you cross the bridge east of ploshcha Zhovtneva, is the **house-museum** of the Ukrainian literary figure Mykhaylo Kotsyubynsky, open from 10 am to 6 pm daily except Wednesday.

Outside the centre, south-west along vulitsya Pyrohova at No 157 is the **house-museum** of Mykola Pyrohov (Nikolai Pirogov in Russian), a noted Russian surgeon and medical scientist. On display are a number of early surgical implements and his rudimentary operating table.

Hitler's swimming pool, the only unexploded remnant of one of his wartime bunkers, is supposedly eight km north of Vinnytsya at Kolo-Mikhaylovka.

A WW II Partisans' camp in the forest near Kalinovka, 25 km north, is preserved as a museum.

Places to Stay & Eat

The *Hotel Zhovtnevy* (☎ 32 65 40) at vulitsya Pyrohova 2, just off ploshcha Gagarina, is ageing but still comfortable and costs US$6/8 for singles/doubles. There's a small service bureau and a moneychanging office off the lobby.

Halfway along vulitsya Lenina, on the corner of vulitsya Kozytskoho, the *Hotel Ukraina* (☎ 32 17 71) at vulitsya Kozytskoho 36, is an attractive turn-of-the-century building with bigger than average rooms for US$12 a single or double. A block west and set back from vulitsya Lenina at vulitsya Pushkina 4 is the more expensive *Hotel Podillya* (☎ 32 68 78), where singles/doubles cost US$18/26. The *Hotel Yuzhny Buh* (☎ 32 38 76) across the river on the busy ploshcha Zhovtneva is the least aesthetically appealing option with singles/ doubles/ triples for US$6/8/9.

The shop at vulitsya Lenina 29 sells good sausage and sweet plum wine by the glass or small bottle. The *Kafe Vinnytsya* at vulitsya Lenina 69 is a cafeteria-style eatery where you can have tasty borscht, schnitzel, holubtsi and a salad for less than US$1. The best hotel restaurant is supposedly in the *Hotel Podillya*, though the restaurant upstairs in the *Hotel Ukraina* has good chicken and beef dishes for about US$2. Below is a popular and pleasant café that does pizza and sandwiches as well as strong coffee and beer.

Things to Buy

Look into Ukrainsky Suvenir at vulitsya Lenina 41 for folk craft. The best bookshop in town is at vulitsya Lenina 101, just off the bottom of ploshcha Gagarina.

Getting There & Around

Bus There are two bus stations – if you arrive from Khmelnytsky or Chernivtsi you'll probably arrive at the smaller Zapada station. From here tram No 4 will take you, after about 10 stops, to the centre of town. The main bus station is at vulitsya Kyivska 8 just north of ploshcha Zhovtneva and just east across the river from the centre. Turn right after you cross the bridge half a block on vulitsya Kyivska. From this bus station there are over 10 daily buses to/from Kiev's main bus station (three hours), and about eight to 10 to/from Khmelnytsky (two hours) with half stopping at Medzhybizh along the way.

Train There are about 10 trains a day to/from Kiev (four hours), and about six to/from Lviv (eight hours via Khmelnytsky and Ternopil), as well as at least two a day to/from Chernivtsi (11 hours) and Odessa (seven to eight hours). The railway station is about 2.5 km across the river east of the centre. Tram Nos 1, 4 and 6 and trolleybus No 5 travel down vulitsya Lenina between the two.

UMAN
УМАНЬ
Population: 95,000

If you have your own transport and are driving between Kiev and Odessa, a good stop is Uman, 210 km from Kiev, 280 km from Odessa. Traffic from Vinnytsya to Odessa joins this route here also. In 1796 Polish Count Felix Pototsky, with the help of a Belgian engineer, laid out the 150-hectare **Sofiyivka Park** for his wife Sofia, a former Turkish slave whom he had bought for two million zloty. It's a fine piece of landscaping, with grottoes, lakes, waterfalls, fountains, pavilions and 500 species of trees. Most of the sights are strung out along the Kamenka River, especially around the upper and lower ponds, the former having the 'island of love' with a rose pavilion on it. Other sites include the 'Grotto of Fear and Doubts', the 'Fountain of Three Tears', and the 'Grotto of Venus'.

Off the town's main park-like square, west of Sofiyivka Park, is the Hotel Uman. The **Regional Ethnographic Museum** is farther west down vulitsya Zhovtneva 31.

Western Ukraine
Західна Україна

Western Ukraine has had the unfortunate luck of being a border country, battled over and tossed back and forth between rival states for as long as anyone can remember. Its history is littered with sieges, ruin, fires and plagues. Despite all this mayhem, the Western Ukrainians have always banded together, protecting their identity and culture as though they were sacred icons. Not under the repressive Russian sphere until WW II, Western Ukraine, although in an impoverished state, was allowed more liberty under Polish and Habsburg rule. As a result it has a less Russified identity, as well as an air of Central European flair to some of its cities. Whereas you'll hear mostly Russian spoken in the east and in the Crimea, only Ukrainian is spoken here. Western Ukrainians consider themselves a different people from their eastern kin. Cities like Lviv were in the vanguard of nationalism that helped speed independence in 1991.

Lviv Region
Львівська область

LVIV
ЛЬВІВ
Population: 810,000

Lviv, the capital of Western Ukraine, is a Central European city. Until 1939 it had never been ruled from Moscow and it was here that Ukrainian nationalism and the Ukrainian Catholic Church, or Uniate Church, re-emerged in the late 1980s. Escaping the urban destruction of WW II, Lviv's skyline of towers, spires and roofs against a hilly backdrop exudes history. There are buildings in most of the main Western styles from down the centuries: Gothic, Renaissance, Baroque, Rococo (from 4½ centuries

of Polish rule) and neoclassical (from the 19th-century Austro-Hungarian era). But Lviv is also a busy industrial and commercial centre with its share of decrepit communist-era industry and housing estates on the outskirts. Yet the narrow old streets and colourful historic core make it one of the best places in the country to visit.

History

Lviv was founded as a hilltop fort in the mid-13th century by Danylo Halytsky, prince of Galicia and Volyn, a former western principality of Kievan Rus. It was supposedly named after his son Lev, which means lion, hence the historic symbol of the city. The history of Lviv (Lemberg under the Austrians and Germans) goes hand in hand with the history of Galicia, the historic region centred around Western Ukraine. For centuries it's been the region's chief city, sited on the strategic east-west trade routes and controlling Carpathian passes.

In the early 14th century, Galician forces under nobleman Dmytro Detko warded off a Polish invasion lead by Prince Casimir the Great. But soon after, the Poles, aided by Hungarians, defeated the Ukrainians and began a long and bitter rule over Galicia. Over the centuries intense religious, social and ethnic conflicts between the resident

Ukrainians and the ruling Poles developed. Most of the Galician nobility (many sent over from Poland, Germany and Hungary) eventually adopted the Polish language and religion – Roman Catholicism – which introduced a Western European, particularly Italian, influence in the 16th century, evident in Lviv's architecture. But the peasants remained Orthodox. Some fled south-east, beyond Polish control, to set up early Cossack communities. Those who stayed were finally herded into the Ukrainian Catholic Church, set up in 1596, which acknowledged the Pope's spiritual supremacy but stuck to the area's Orthodox forms of worship. Lviv eventually became the 'capital' of this Church. In the first partition of Poland (1772), Galicia became part of the Habsburg Austro-Hungarian Empire but remained controlled by Poles.

Towards the end of the 19th century, Lviv became the centre of Ukrainian nationalism (suppressed by Russia in Kiev), which was centred on the Ukrainian Catholic Church and resentful of continuing Roman Catholic Polish domination. With the Habsburg Empire's collapse at the end of WW I, Lviv was, for a few days, the seat of an independent government of what was known variously as Ruthenia, Western Ukraine or East Galicia. But the troops of re-emergent Poland expelled the government and Lviv returned to Polish rule (apart from a brief Soviet takeover in 1920), until September 1939 when the Red Army walked in, asserting Moscow's control over the city for the first time in its long history.

Lviv was occupied by Germany from 1941 to 1944. Soviet sources say 136,000 people died in its Jewish ghetto and nearly 350,000 in its concentration camps. After the war, Soviet forces re-occupied Lviv and most of Galicia, repressing the nationally conscious Western Ukrainian people. The Ukrainian Catholic Church, forced underground by Stalin in 1946, re-emerged with glasnost in the late 1980s to play a big part in a new Ukrainian independence movement, centred in Lviv. Nationalists were voted into power unanimously in Western

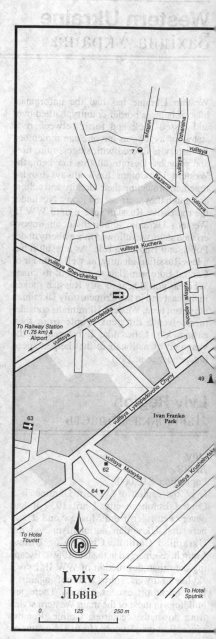

Lviv
Львів

0   125   250 m

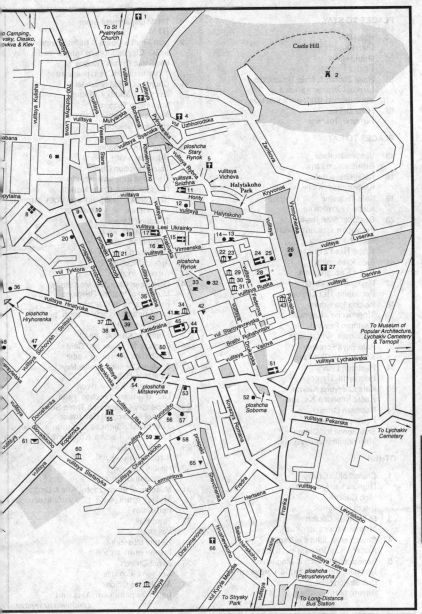

PLACES TO STAY

6   Hotel Lviv
    Гостинниця Львів
38 Grand Hotel
    Гранд Готель
53 Hotel Zhorzh & Train Ticket Office
    Готель Жорж та каса
    продажу залізничних квитків
62 Hotel Dnister
    Готель Дністер

PLACES TO EAT

13 Virmenska Kafe
    Вірменське кафе
16 Kofeyenaya Kafe
    Кофеиеная Кафе
19 Kafe Teatralne
    Кафе Театральне
23 Restoran Stari Royal
    Ресторан Старий Рояль
33 Kafe Pid Ratusha
    Кафе Під Ратушаою
41 Kafe Katedralna
    Кафе Катедральна
42 Restoran Pid Levom
    Ресторан Під Левом
46 Korona Ice Cream
    Морожене „Корона"
47 Restoran Festival
    Ресторан Фестиваль
50 Kafe Bilya Fontana
    Кафе Біля Фонтана
54 Restoran Lyux
    Ресторан Люкс
59 Kafe Chervona Kalyna
    Кафе Червона Калина
64 Restoran Grono
    Ресторан Гроно
65 Snihuronka Ice Cream
    Морожене Снігуронька

OTHER

1   Church of St Onefry
    Церква Св. Онуфря
2   High Castle
    Високий замок
3   St Nicholas Church
    Миколаївська церква
4   Church of St John the Baptist
    Костел Св. Іоанахрестителя
5   Benedictine Church & Monastery
    Костьол Бенедиктинів і монастир
7   Bus Station No 4
    Автобусний вокзал 4

8   TsUM Department Store
    ЦУМ
9   Ivan Franko Opera & Ballet Theatre
    Івана Франка театр опери та балету
10 Ukrainian Drama Theatre
    Український театр драми
11 Church of Maria Snizhnoi
    Костьол Марії Сніжної
12 Marionette Theatre
    Марйонетковий театер
14 House of Seasons
    Дім всіх сезонів
15 Armenian Cathedral
    Вірменьський собор
17 Transfiguration Church
    Преображенська церква
18 Outdoor Arts & Crafts Market
    Відкритий базар по продажу виробів
    мистецтва та художнього
20 Teatralna Kasa
    Театральна каса
21 National Museum
    Національний музей
22 Apteka Museum
    Аптека-музей
24 Dominican Church & Monastery/
    Museum of Historic Religions
    Костьол та монастир
    Домініканв/Музей історії релігії
25 King's Arsenal
    Королівский арсенал
26 Gunpowder Tower and Café
    Порохова башта та кафе
27 St Mary Carmelite Monastery/
    Exhibition Hall
    Монастир Кармеліток
    Св. Марії/виставкова галя
28 Uspensky Church with Three Saints
    Chapel & Kornyakt Bell Tower
    Успеньська церква і каплиця Трьох
    Святителі і вежа Корнякта
29 History Museum
    Історичний музей
30 History Museum
    Історичний музей
31 Museum of Ethnography, Arts & Crafts
    Музей етнографії та художнього
    промислу
32 Town Hall
    Ратуша
34 History Museum
    Історичний музей
35 Jesuit Church
    Костьол Єзуїтів
36 Air Ukraine Office
    Бюро Української Авіалінії

continued next page

continued from previous page

37	Museum of Ethnography, Arts & Crafts Музей етнографії, художнього промислу та мистецтва
39	Taras Shevchenko Statue Пам'ятник Тарасові Шевченку
40	Ploshcha Pidkovy Площа Підкови
43	Town Arsenal & Museum of Old Arms Міський арсенал та музей старовинної зброї
44	Boyim Chapel Боїмська каплиця
45	Roman Catholic Cathedral Католицький собор
48	University Унверситет
49	Ivan Franko Monument Пам'ятник Івана Франка
51	Bernadine Church & Monastery Церква і монастир Бернадинів
52	Halitsky Market Галицький ринок (базар)
55	Pototsky Palace Палата Потоцького
56	Bus Ticket & Information Office Продажу автобусних квитків та інформації
57	OVIR – Visa Office ОВІР - Бюро віз
58	Philharmonia Філармонія
60	Picture Gallery Картинна галерія
61	Main Post Office Головна пошта
63	St George's Cathedral Собор Св. Юра
66	St Nicholas Church Церква Св. Миколи
67	Museum of Old Ukrainian Culture Музей давнього Українського мистецтва

Ukraine in 1990, and with many dissident movements centred in Lviv, the stage was set for Ukrainian independence the following year.

Orientation

Lviv's main street is the park-like, 600-metre-long prospekt Svobody (Freedom), running north from ploshcha Mitskevycha to the Ivan Franko Opera & Ballet Theatre. Directly east are the narrow, old-quarter streets centred around ploshcha Rynok, the former historic market square. Westward, 19th-century streets lead out to Ivan Franko Park. Most of what you'll want is within this roughly 1.25-sq-km area, overlooked from the north-east by Castle Hill (Zamkova Hora) where Lviv was founded.

Information

Tourist Office The service bureau (☎ 72 67 51, 79 84 65; fax 74 21 82) at the Hotel Zhorzh is open from 10 am to 6 pm Monday to Friday. It is one of the few in the country that seems to live up to its name. It is a branch office of the State Committee of Ukraine for Tourism. For US$1 they sell an excellent city

map showing all public transport. There's another, less helpful, tourist bureau in the Hotel Dnistr, open the same hours. Both can arrange expensive group excursions (about US$15 an hour) and car rentals (US$6 to US$8 an hour around town, by the km outside of town – you can get a cheaper rate bargaining with a private taxi driver to chauffeur you around for the day).

Money Almost every hotel has a money exchange office where you can change hard currency into kupons. There's a Western Union and Xchange Points office (☎ 72 08 14; fax 72 08 14) upstairs in the main post office which will exchange travellers' cheques, give cash advances on major credit cards (into US dollars or kupons), and receive money wired from outside the country. They're open Monday to Saturday from 10 am to 6 pm, Sunday from 10 am to 2 pm. In the lobby of the Hotel Zhorzh is a small exchange office of the UKR Exim Bank which will exchange travellers' cheques. It's open from 9.30 am to 6 pm Monday to Saturday, to 3 pm Sunday. Not far from the Hotel Zhorzh at vulitsya

UKRAINE

Kopernika 4 is the National Bank of Ukraine which supposedly will soon begin to cash travellers' cheques. It's open from 8 am to 8 pm Monday to Saturday, to 3 pm on weekends. It's better to exchange money at the beginning of the day as supplies of kupons may run out towards the day's end.

Post & Telecommunications The main post office is at vulitsya Slovatskoho 1. It is open from 6 am to 8 pm Monday to Friday, 8 am to 6 pm on Saturday, 8 am to 2 pm on Sunday. Post international letters in the box marked 'za kordon'. The central telephone office is around the corner from the main post office at vulitsya Doroshenka 39. The phones are open 24 hours, while telegraph and fax services are available from 8 am to 10 pm. You can't, as of yet, use your international calling cards at the telephone office, so the best idea is to politely ask the receptionist at the Grand Hotel or Hotel Zhorzh to connect you to an international operator. There are U-tel cardphones in the lobby of the main post office. All public telephones use tokens called (zhetony) which can be purchased at most kiosks.

Lviv's telephone code is 0322.

Foreign Consulate The Polish Consulate (☎ 72 39 49) is at vulitsya Ivan Franko 10.

Bookshops There are a few good bookshops in a row along the first block of vulitsya Teatralna directly north of ploshcha Mitskevycha.

Film & Photocopy There's a Kodak store at vulitsya Hnatyuka 13 (open from 10 am to 8 pm), just east of ploshcha Hryhorenta, opposite the Air Ukraine office. Another photo shop is at vulitsya Kopernika 11 next to the Pototsky Palace, and one more at vulitsya Teatralna opposite the Roman Catholic Cathedral. Across the street from vulitsya Kopernika 11 you can make photocopies.

Prospekt Svobody
This wide boulevard, affectionately known as the 'Planta' by older locals, acts as a sort

of central promenade, park and gathering place. Its northern end is occupied by the voluptuous 1897-1900 Ivan Franko **Opera & Ballet Theatre**, which was nearly blown up by an undetonated bomb set by the retreating Nazis in WW II. Most Saturdays at 6 pm you can take a tour of the gilded interior of the theatre, but it's better to view it during a performance. In front of the theatre is a recessed flower bed where once stood a massive Lenin statue. The statue's foundations were supposedly composed of tombstones robbed from a Ukrainian cemetery. The 1904 palace at prospekt Svobody 20, now housing the **National Museum**, was once the Lenin Museum. The grand interior is almost completely occupied by a colossal central staircase. Upstairs are displays of 15th to 19th-century Ukrainian icons as well as the Ukrainian section of the Lviv Picture Gallery, comprised mostly of 19th and early 20th-century works from Western Ukraine. Downstairs are temporary galleries displaying works by various local artists. Each exhibit requires a separate ticket. The museum is open daily from 10 am to 6 pm except Thursday and Friday.

Stroll south down the tree-lined boulevard and see the timeless dramatics of Lviv's urban life – old men swarming around chess sets, groups of pensioners engrossed in conversation, young couples nestled on their benches. In the middle of the prospekt is a statue of Ukraine's national poet, Taras Shevchenko, one hand outstretched and never without flowers at his feet. This is the historic site for Ukrainian nationalist gatherings, and even when there aren't speeches going on there are usually excited groups partaking in political discussions or, in the evenings, tight packs of people singing national folk songs well into the night. At prospekt Svobody 15, on the corner of vulitsya Hnatyuka is the **Museum of Ethnography, Arts & Crafts**, with a seated Statue of Liberty atop its parapet. The sumptuous interior (open daily from 10 am to 6 pm, closed Monday and Tuesday) features an excellent collection of farm culture and folk art from Western Ukraine, including embroidery, ethnic dress, woodcarvings, ceramics and *pysanky* (painted eggs). Prospekt Svobody terminates in the south at **ploshcha Mitskevycha**, a busy intersection with a tall column topped with a statue of Polish poet Adam Mickiewicz. A bubbling Baroque fish fountain sits between Shevchenko and Mickiewicz.

Ploshcha Rynok

The old market square was the hub of Lviv life from the 14th to 19th centuries and today is the best preserved urban square in Ukraine. It's a wide square plaza with the large 19th-century **town hall**, rebuilt with a neo-Renaissance tower after a fire destroyed the original building, at its centre. There are public bathrooms near its northern corner. The buildings around its perimeter date from the 16th to 18th centuries and their highly individual stone carvings, many in a decayed state, are worth a close look. Traditionally, any building with more than three windows overlooking the square was heavily taxed, thus the uniformity, broken by only a few of the obviously wealthier citizens. Off each corner stand fountains with sculptures depicting Greek gods, all executed by the same sculptor in 1793. In Western Europe, this square would be filled with tourists, café tables and sunshades, but what you'll probably see are groups of children playing alongside the steady stream of locals chasing trams.

Lviv History Museum Nos 4 and 6 in the north-east corner of ploshcha Rynok, and No 24 in the south-west corner, house the Lviv History Museum. Nos 4 and 6 have 16th-century Renaissance façades and 17th-century carvings. No 4, the 'Black Stone House', built for an Italian merchant in 1588 89, features St Martin on a horse, and along with Nos 2 and 3 to the left, makes an impressive strip of Renaissance façades; it was closed for renovations in 1994. No 6 was built for and named after the Greek merchant Kornyakt. There is an interesting sculptural row, with knights and dolphins lining the

rooftop cornice. Special permission in the 16th century was needed to commission six windows, rather than the obligatory maximum of three. It was built on the site of three former Gothic houses. The interior vaulting in the gift shop directly to the left as you enter has original vaulting from this time. The lovely inner courtyard with a three-tiered gallery is completely Italian Renaissance; a small café serving coffee and tea is in one corner. The ground floor has mostly 20th-century exhibits; upstairs (which requires a separate ticket) is the former palace, with one room having a 200-year-old parquet floor made of 14 different kinds of wood. The displays are of 16th to 18th-century furnishings. It was here that on 22 December 1686 the treaty was signed between Poland and Russia that partitioned Ukraine. No 24 also has 16th- century origins with intriguing stone heads on the façade and an unique sculptural ensemble on its upper corner featuring Christ being baptised by John, a dove hovering above them. Inside exhibits on three floors cover Lviv history from prehistory up to the 18th century with some good Cossack displays. All three museum buildings are open from 10 am to 6 pm daily except Wednesday.

Other Buildings No 10, with cannon and cannonballs on its lower corner and a faceless Roman legionnaire looming high above the parapet, owes its grandiose 18th-century appearance to the Polish Lubomirsky family, its former owners. It houses the impressive furniture and porcelain sections of Lviv's **Museum of Ethnography, Arts & Crafts**, each room representing a different era. In the lobby are two interesting wooden sleighs, one a griffin, the other a swan. The museum is open from 10 am to 6 pm daily except Monday and Tuesday. The lion carving at No 14 is a symbol of Venice, whose consul lived here in the 17th century. But the lions carved on No 28, a beautiful Renaissance façade on the mostly 16th-century western side of the square, are symbols of Lviv. On the north side of the square, where the buildings are

UKRAINE

mostly 18th century, spot the human faces wrapped in lions' skins on No 36 (a goldfish shop), and the grinning Asiatic face on No 41. Next door at No 40, the sickly Atlantes holding up a balcony are similar to those at No 3.

Around Ploshcha Rynok

The small grid of attractive streets around ploshcha Rynok comprise the historic old quarter and are well worth a day's stroll, offering far more than just their diminutive charm. The **Roman Catholic Cathedral** opposite the south-western corner of the square is a busy working church dating from 1360-1481 (Lviv's Polish era). Despite changes and chapel additions it has kept its European Gothic feel, notably at the eastern end with its tall, thin buttresses. The western tower, a Lviv landmark, was added later. On the north side of the ornate interior, the west-ernmost chapel near the entrance was built in black, white and pink marble in 1619 by a notoriously ruthless Lviv mayor called Kampian. Its exterior has fine stone carvings of biblical scenes. The 1609-21 **Boyim Chapel** near the south-eastern corner of the cathedral is the burial chapel of a wealthy Hungarian merchant family. Its west entrance façade is covered from top to bottom in Lviv's most magnificent carvings – including SS Peter and Paul at either end of the lower level, and the passions of Christ on the level above. Below the columns are carved lion heads, the city's symbol, and high above, on top of the cupola, is a suffering Christ glaring down below. The interior's carvings are equally lavish, most notably on its sculpted corbelled dome. Above the door are portraits of Georgi Boyim, who had the chapel built, and his son Pawiel. The chapel is open as a museum daily except Sunday and Monday from 10 am to 5.30 pm, and for a small donation, its knowledgeable old curator can tell you all about it in several languages, but sadly not English.

A block west of ploshcha Rynok on the corner of ploshcha Pidkovy and vulitsya Teatralna is the 1610-35 **Jesuit Church**, the earliest of Lviv's monuments to Baroque

architecture. Its façade reflects the transition from Renaissance to Baroque, incorporating features of each style.

Occupying a 16th-century building opposite the north-east corner of the square is the oldest functioning pharmacy in the city. Established in 1735 and known as the Black Eagle, it today houses the **Apteka Museum**. It's open from 9 am to 7 pm weekdays, 10 am to 5 pm weekends. The back rooms are usually open only for reserved groups, but with a little persuasion you may be able to tour the wonderful display of historic pharmaceutical equipment and original furnishings. For a measly price you can buy a tiny bottle of iron-rich, medicinal wine to cure your ills, but beware of temporary tooth discolouration. Ask for 'vino'.

Vulitsya Virmenska & Around Nearby on vulitsya Virmenska 23 is the '**House of Seasons**', owing its name to the allegorical scenes on its façade depicting each season, and to a band of zodiac symbols running above the pilasters. Lviv had a large colony of Armenian artisans and merchants in the 14th and 16th centuries. Farther west at vulitsya Virmenska No 7/9 is the 1363 **Armenian Cathedral** with another entrance off vulitsya Lesi Ukrainky. Off the alley is a small, delicate colonnade, its pavement comprised of well-worn tombstones. On the far wall stands an intricately carved wooden crucifix ensemble. The bell tower with corner turrets was added in 1571. On the corner of vulitsya Lesi Ukrainky and vulitsya Krakivska is the late 17th-century twin-bell towered **Transfiguration Church**, the first church in the city to revert back to Ukrainian Catholic after independence. Its interior is a lofty parade of colours with painted walls and vaults.

Vulitsya Pidvalna & Around A block north-east of ploshcha Rynok, down vulitsya Stavropihiyska, is the large dome of the 1745-64 **Dominican church & monastery**, Lviv's finest bit of Rococo with definite Baroque and classical features. The lofty oval-shaped interior of the church has impressive gold-covered wooden sculptures and leads to the entrance of the monastery, now housing the **Museum of Historic Religions**, open daily except Thursday from 10 am to 6 pm. Its displays are mostly given over to Catholicism and Orthodoxy, with other exhibits covering Judaism and eastern religions. Directly east of the Dominican Church is the arched façade of the 1630 Renaissance former **King's Arsenal**, now housing the city's historical archives. A door to the right of the loggia leads to a narrow garden courtyard. In a small square facing the arsenal is a statue of Ivan Fedorov, the first to utilise the printing press in Ukraine. Sitting in a park directly east of the arsenal and across vulitsya Pidvalna, is the 1554-56 **Gunpowder Tower**, part of the old system of walls and bastions which once ran along vulitsya Pidvalna. Inside, on the ground floor, is a dimly lit café serving strong coffee.

Immediately south is the three-domed **Uspensky Church** (1591-1629), at the corner of vulitsya Ruska and vulitsya Pidvalna, easily distinguished by the 65-metre-tall, triple-tiered **Kornyakt Bell Tower** (1572-78) rising beside it, named after the Greek merchant who funded its construction (see Lviv History Museum earlier). A door to the right of the tower leads into the churchyard and the small three-domed **Three Saints Chapel** (1578-91). Nestled beneath the tower and built into the north side of the church, the chapel completes Lviv's finest piece of Renaissance architecture. It is the historic centre of the city's Orthodox community. Take a close look at the rich stone carving around its 16th to 17th-century wrought-iron door.

Across vulitsya Ruska at vulitsya Pidvalna 7 is a fine Secessionist (early Art Nouveau) building, the former 'Dnister Insurance Building', built in 1905, now housing a medical clinic. Farther south at vulitsya Pidvalna 5 is the 1554-56 **Town Arsenal**, part of the city's original fortification system but rebuilt after being destroyed by Swedish armies in 1704. Inside is the **Museum of Old Arms**, with an impressive

display of cannons and armour, and a wide variety of weaponry from over 30 countries. It's open daily from 10 am to 5 pm except Wednesday. The basement houses a temporary exhibitions gallery.

Occupying the south-eastern section of the old town is the former **Bernardine church & monastery** complex, built in the early 17th-century Mannerist style, now the Ukrainian Catholic Church of St Andrew. Its tower is another Lviv landmark. The dark and ambient interior features rows of ornate, carved wooden altars beneath a long, painted barrel-vaulted nave. In front of the main façade lies a small park with a 1736 Baroque column. A path to the right of the entrance leads around the church to the monastery complex, past a 1761 rotunda-covered well and along the longest section of medieval defensive walls. South of the church, across the street and beyond the flower vendors, is the colourful and hectic **Halitsky Market**, definitely worth a visit.

West of the Old Town

Lviv's main **University Building** (1877-81) is an attractive neoclassical edifice a few busy 19th-century blocks west of prospekt Svobody on vulitsya Universytetska. Across the street sits a massive monument to the Western Ukrainian poet Ivan Franko, fronting the pleasant tree-filled **Ivan Franko Park** stretching uphill towards the Hotel Dnister at its south-western end. West of the park and rising from a small hilltop is the splendid **St George's Cathedral** (Sobor Yura), the historic and sacred centre of the Ukrainian Catholic Church, handed back in 1990 with great pomp and ceremony after 44 years of compulsory Orthodox control. Constructed between 1774 and 1790 in stylised Ukrainian Baroque, the complex includes, amongst a number of 19th-century buildings, an 1865 bell tower and the 1772 Metropolitan's Palace across from the church. Before you enter the realms of its green and gilded interior, note the sculpture of St George the dragon slayer, high above the entrance portal.

North of the Old Town

The small cluster of streets sandwiched between Castle Hill to the north-east and the old town to the south comprise what was once known as the **Old Rus Quarter**. The first settlement to form beneath the castle, it predates the present old town, but soon began to diminish in importance when the city centre was moved to ploshcha Rynok in the 14th century. Although few of the original structures remain, the quiet streets are still peppered with some of the city's oldest and smallest churches, making it worth an afternoon's stroll.

Start from the north-eastern corner of ploshcha Rynok and walk north for three blocks on vulitsya Drukarska to the small, green ploshcha Danyla Halytskoho park, the western end of which is occupied by the Lviv Marionette Theatre. Cross vulitsya Honty and continue; the street becomes vulitsya Vicheva. To your right and through a gateway at Vicheva 2 is the former **Benedictine church & monastery** complex (1596-1627). Closed since communist times, the monastery now houses music students, but the church may soon reopen.

Take an immediate left from the monastery on vulitsya Snizhna. Directly to your right on the corner is a plaque commemorating the house that a young Ivan Franko lived in for a year in 1876-77. Half a block down at vulitsya Snizhna 2 is the **Church of Maria Sniznoi**, a 13th-century Romanesque church rebuilt in the 19th century. The interior, entered around the corner to the left, has a finely painted vaulted ceiling.

Two blocks north on vulitsya Rybna is **ploshcha Stary Rynok**, once the town's central market square, now a low-key, forgotten open space. There's a small, leafy park at its northern half. Just uphill near the north-eastern end of the square is the small, brick and plaster **Church of St John the Baptist**, built in 1334 and rebuilt in the 19th century. Its interiors are original 14th century and around the back is a small museum displaying 12th to 13th-century icons and statuary. It's open from noon to 5 pm daily except Monday. The street leading uphill

from the right of the church will lead to Castle Hill.

Continue north from ploshcha Stary Rynok on vulitsya Pylnykarska for a block to the two green cupolas of the tiny **St Nicholas Church**, standing across the street from another small park. Dating from the 13th century and remodelled in the 16th century, it is the oldest remainder of the Old Rus Quarter. Although the colourful, newly restored paintings give the interior a fresh feel, the cruciform plan with three apses surrounding a central nave is original: an excellent example of early Byzantine architecture.

If your hunger for church interiors is not sated, continue north on vulitsya Bohdana Khmelnytskoho for another five minutes where up some steps and through a gateway on your right lies the **Church of St Onefry**, also founded in the 13th century and acquiring its present appearance in the 17th to 19th centuries. Its interior boasts a fine 19th-century iconostasis. More impressive, however, is the 17th-century wooden iconostasis of the **Church of St Pyatnytsa**. Intricately carved and gilded, it's a masterpiece of Ukrainian Renaissance religious art. The tiny church lies farther north up vulitsya Bohdana Khmelnytskoho, its bulbous silver onion dome rising up on the other side of the railroad tracks.

For a sweeping 360° panorama of the city, head for the **High Castle** (Vysoky Zamok), the 14th-century remains of a stone castle that replaced the earlier 13th-century wooden fort atop Castle Hill. Today it's a well-manicured hillside park with walking paths, fresh air and a few traces of stone walls and foundations. To reach the summit, walk uphill to the right of the Church of St John the Baptist on vulitsya Uzhhorodska toward the 1958 TV tower in the distance. Turn left at the end of the street and continue uphill alongside the park until you reach the park entrance, the Vysoky Zamok restaurant to your far right. Take the tree-lined dirt path which will lead you around the base of the hill until eventually a sharp right will spiral up to the top.

East of the Old Town

Just east and uphill from the old town at Vynnychenka 30 is the former late Renaissance 1644 **St Mary Carmelite Monastery**, now an exhibition hall.

About 2.5 km east of the centre in the huge Shevchenkivsky Hayye Park is Lviv's enjoyable open-air **Museum of Popular Architecture & Life** (Muzey Narodnoyi Arkhitektury i Pobutu), well worth the visit. About 100 old wooden buildings – farmsteads, smithies, windmills, churches, schools – are dotted over 60 hectares, divided into and representing the many ethnographic groups of Western Ukraine including, amongst others, the Hutsuls, Lemkos, and Boikos of the Carpathian highlands. Most of the buildings are authentically decked out with historical everyday objects and folk art, and the old curators are often happy to try to explain things to you. One highlight is the 1763 St Nicholas Church from Kryvky, in the Boyko region south of Lviv.

The museum is at vulitsya Chernecha Hora 1, and it's open daily except Monday from 10 am to 6 pm. To get there take tram No 2 or 7 from the centre, or bus No 7 or 10 from near the end of vulitsya Valova north of the Bernardine monastery, to the 'vulitsya Mechnikova' stop on vulitsya Lychakivska. The easiest route is by tram No 2; from ploshcha Rynok it's five stops heading east. From the vulitsya Mechnikova tram and bus stop you'll see a small wooden sign across the street directing you uphill, north on vulitsya Krupyarska. At the top of this street turn right and follow the signs. The entrance will be to your left, next to the white, seated statue of Shevchenko – it's about a 1.25-km walk.

About 1.5 km south of the outdoor museum on vulitsya Mechnikova is the **Lychakiv Cemetery** (Lychakivska Kladovyshche), one of the most beautiful in Eastern Europe and designated a historic landmark in 1990. Amongst its 40 hectares of tree-lined paths are over 3600 monuments, including those of famous Ukrainians, such as poet Ivan Franko, many of which are topped with impressive sculpture designed by prominent artists. The variety of nationalities represented here is testament to Lviv's historic cultural diversity. Apparently, during periods of occupation, both the Poles and Russians destroyed many Ukrainian grave sites to make way for their own. You may be stopped by a roving ticket salesman on the grounds. To reach the cemetery, stay on tram No 7 one stop past the open air museum stop, to the 'Lychakivska Kladovyshche' tram stop.

South of the Old Town

A block south of ploshcha Mitskevycha, around the corner from the Hotel Zhorzh, runs Lviv's lesser grand boulevard, **prospekt Shevchenka**. This avenue lost its elegance when the city, a few years back, cut down the row of trees which once lined its central pedestrian strip. Nevertheless, it still attracts a decent strolling crowd, with its rows of attractive turn-of-the-century buildings and various shops. At the far southern end to the right is a statue of a seated Mykhailo Hrushevsky, Ukraine's most famous historian and later the country's first president in 1918. Beyond the monument and to the east of the small St Nicholas Church, vulitsya Drahomanova leads to the **Museum of Old Ukrainian Culture** at No 42, 300 metres uphill. Housed in a fanciful 19th-century Polish palace, it later became the residence of the head of the Ukrainian Catholic Church before being turned into a branch of the National Museum. Its main salon occasionally has classical concerts. The exhibits are similar to those of the Ethnographic Museum, but not quite as impressive, although there is an excellent selection of small, carved wooden Carpathian crosses. It's open daily from 11 am to 5 pm except on Friday.

From the top end of prospekt Shevchenka, vulitsya Chaykovskoho runs south-west a few blocks past the Philharmonia toward the **Lviv Picture Gallery** at vulitsya Stefanyka 3. Housed in a former 19th-century palace, this is one of the largest collections of European paintings in the country, with over 1000 on display, and another 5000 in storage.

Upstairs features mainly 17th to 19th-century works, the lower floor covers mostly 20th-century works. Among the best are the Polish, Italian and Flemish sections. It's open daily except Monday from 10 am to 5 pm.

Heading back to ploshcha Mitskevycha, at vulitsya Kopernika 15 is the former 1880 **Pototsky Palace**, designed in the French Renaissance style. It is now a popular venue for weddings and receptions.

Big **Strysky Park**, about 2.5 km south of the centre, was laid out in the 19th century with formal gardens and landscaped woodland. It retains much of its glory in its northern and western quarters, but the rest is ruined by shabby modern buildings. To its north stretches Bohdan Khmelnytsky Culture Park. Bus No 8 or trolleybus No 5 from ploshcha Petrushevycha, a few blocks south of prospekt Shevchenka, run along vulitsya Stryska between the two parks.

Places to Stay

Camping Lvivsky (☎ 72 13 73, 72 14 73), with category B cabins and tent sites, is marked by a sign about 10 km north-east of the centre on the Kiev road near the village of Dublyany. It's open all year and supposedly has room for caravans.

Hotel Lviv (☎ 79 22 70), two blocks north of the Ballet & Opera Theatre at vulitsya 700-richchya Lvova 7, is a tall, bland 1970s structure with Spartan but cheap rooms. It's popular and often overcrowded with groups of young people. Singles/doubles without bath cost up to US$8/13; US$12/20 with bath, payable in kupons. There are a few bargain triples, a bare room with three beds and no bath, for US$10. The concrete *Hotel Dnister* (☎ 72 07 83) at the south-western end of Ivan Franko Park is equally as tall and characterless, but with comfortable rooms overpriced at US$46/62 for singles/doubles, payable in hard currency only.

Two more Soviet-style hotels lurk well outside the centre in bleak suburbs. These are last options. The *Hotel Tourist* (☎ 35 23 91) at vulitsya Konovaltsa 103 has rooms at US$5/9/15 for singles/doubles/triples with bath. Take tram No 2 from prospekt Svoboda to the end of the line. The *Hotel Sputnik* (☎ 64 58 22) at Knyahyni Olhy 116 charges US$20/20/30 for singles/doubles/triples with bath and breakfast. Take tram No 3 from in front of the Halitsky Market to the end of the line.

There are also a few other dirty hotels around the city, that may or may not take foreigners, including the *Hotel Ukrainia* (☎ 72 66 46) at ploshcha Mitskevycha 4, the *Hotel Dnipro* (☎ 74 21 02) at ploshcha Svobody 45, and the *Hotel Kiev* (☎ 74 21 05) at Horodetska 15. At the time of writing none of them officially allowed foreigners, but this may change.

Lviv's top-notch hotel is the central *Grand Hotel* (☎ 76 90 60; fax 72 76 65) at prospekt Svobody 13. It's an elegant, fully restored 1898 Habsburg-era building and is completely up to Western standards with professional staff and superb rooms, but at a high price: US$70/110/140 for singles/doubles/triples with breakfast, payable with hard currency or by credit card only. For US$7 a night parking is provided.

The *Hotel Zhorzh* (pronounced 'George'; ☎ 72 59 52; fax 74 21 92) is equally central at ploshcha Mitskevycha 1 and is the best deal in town. It's another elegant turn-of-the-century building complete with an imposing grand staircase and the feel of faded grandeur. Singles/doubles/triples without bath are US$12/17/26; with bath US$46/56/78, hard currency only. The rooms without bath have a sink and the facilities in the corridor are wholly adequate. All prices include an excellent breakfast. The crowded tram No 1, five stops from the railway station, will deposit you in the centre just before prospekt Svobody, near both hotels. Going back to the railway station take tram No 9 travelling in the opposite direction.

Places to Eat

The chance of getting a decent meal in Lviv has improved in recent years, and should not require the melodramatics often associated with other former Soviet cities. All the hotels mentioned have reliable restaurants, the

Grand Hotel being very good and very expensive (hard currency or credit card only). The *Hotel Zhorzh* restaurant, entered from prospekt Shevchenka, around the corner from the main entrance, is probably the best bet with a good selection and cheap prices in a nice atmosphere.

A number of respectable restaurants are within the centre – eat early as some restaurants run out of food. The *Pid Levom* (beneath the lion) at ploshcha Rynok 20 serves borscht and salads with meat and chicken dishes for about US$4 to US$5 in a large medievalesque hall and downstairs cellar. It's open daily from noon to midnight, and closed from 5 to 6 pm. There is live music after 8 pm.

The *Stari Royal* on vulitsya Stavropihiyska to the right of the Apteka Museum serves a tasty pork cutlet along with traditional borscht and varenyky for under US$4. The cosy interior is either embellished by a live piano or ruined by a blaring speaker. It's open from 10 am to 9 pm daily. A good choice for quick food is the cafeteria-style *Kafe Ratusha*, entered up the steps on the western side of the town hall. It is open Monday to Saturday from 9 am to 8 pm, offering a starch-filled selection of heaped portions for about US$1. Downstairs in the *Kafe Katedralna*, mediocre pizza is served after a long wait.

The *Kafe Bilya Fontana*, open daily from noon to 11 pm, closed 5 to 6 pm, is off the northern end of ploshcha Mitskevycha. It is similar to the Kafe Ratusha but has a more Spartan atmosphere. The *Restoran Lyux* at vulitsya Kopernika 6/7, on the corner of prospekt Svobody, has an elegant upstairs dining area but the food is average. It is open daily from noon to 11 pm, closed 5 to 6 pm. The *Grono* restaurant supposedly serves good Georgian dishes in its small dining room, just south of the Hotel Dnistr at Ryleeva 12. The *Restoran Festival* at vulitsya Sichovykh Striltsiv 12, near the university, used to be the best in town. Its spacious interiors are popular with wedding receptions, and guests are often entertained with cabaret shows. The menu is varied and

the food reasonably priced. It's open daily from noon to 11 pm.

Lviv has loads of cafés serving thick Turkish-style coffee and delicious sweet cakes for a pittance. Two cafés on vulitsya Virmenska just north of ploshcha Rynok are popular hang-outs. The *Kofeyenaya* at No 19 (open daily from 9 am to 8 pm, closed 3 to 4 pm) on the corner of vulitsya Krakivska has excellent cakes, and the *Virmenska Kafe* (open daily from 11 am to 8 pm, closed 2 to 3 pm), at the point where vulitsya Federova dead-ends at Virmenska, serves small sandwiches in a cellar atmosphere. The *Kafe Katedralna* near the corner of vulitsya Katedralna and ploshcha Rynok serves espresso if you get tired of floating grinds. There's a popular café/bar open daily from noon to 10 pm in the ground floor of the old *Gunpowder Tower*. At prospekt Svobody 22 near the opera theatre is the *Kafe Teatralne*, open daily from 9 am to 9 pm, closed 3 to 4 pm. Besides drinks, they serve good shashlyk, soups, and bowls of tiny varenyky. The *Kafe Chervona Kalyna* is a quaint corner café just down from the Philharmonia at vulitsya Chaykovskoho 16, open daily from 8 am to 7 pm, closed 3 to 4 pm and an hour earlier on weekends.

For ice cream, the *Korona* on the corner of prospekt Svobody and vulitsya Doroshenka is very popular as is the *Snihuronka* ice-cream bar on prospekt Shevchenka 22. At prospekt Shevchenka 10 is the *Svitou* candy shop worth a visit just for its regal interior. Ask for a 'Ukrainian Snickers'.

Your raw meat and fibre needs can be met at the *Halitsky Market*, off ploshcha Soborna. It's a heaving mass of colourful market mayhem with piles of fresh fruit, vegetables, nuts and honey; it's open daily during daylight hours. Have your small bills ready. A small store in the back of ploshcha Rynok No 25 sells some Western food products.

Entertainment

A walk through the old town streets at dusk will reveal the hum of local life shuffling to a close. For a perfect evening, combine a leisurely evening stroll down 'the Planta' with a performance at the lavish Opera & Ballet Theatre, where you can be entertained in gilded surroundings for less than US$1.

The Philharmonia performs in their swan-crested building at vulitsya Chaykovskoho 7, off prospekt Shevchenka. The Ukrainian Drama Theatre is immediately east of the opera theatre, and the Marionette Theatre is on the western end of ploshcha Danyla Halytskoho. Folklore shows are often given at various venues, sometimes at the outdoor theatre of the Museum of Popular Architecture.

Music festivals are held throughout the year with May being a busy month. The Teatralna Kasa is the main city ticket office with schedules and advance tickets for all performances at all theatres. It's at prospekt Svobody 37 near the opera theatre, with an easily recognisable blue sign, open daily from 11 am to 7 pm, closed 2 to 4 pm. Tickets for same-day performances usually have to be bought at the individual theatres. During July and August the theatres and ticket office shut down – check listings at the Hotel Zhorzh service bureau during the off season.

Both the Grand Hotel and the Hotel Zhorzh have casinos ready to take your money, and the Hotel Dnistr's hard currency, basement Night Bar can get a bit lively. Most restaurants listed have live music and dancing from around 8 pm until closing time.

Things to Buy

The gift shop Khudozhnyk at prospekt Svobody 2, across the street from the Hotel Zhorzh, has folk art and paintings. There's also a tiny folk art shop in the lobby of the Ethnographic Museum, selling painted wooden eggs. But the best and most enjoyable place to buy folk art and souvenirs is the colourful outdoor arts & crafts market a block east from the top end of prospekt Svobody, between vulitsya Lesi Ukrainky and vulitsya Zamok Kornyakta. Here you can bargain for pottery, ceramics and wood craft, and a wide range of embroidered shirts, blouses and tablecloths. Prices for such items tend to be a bit cheaper in Kiev. There's also a small outdoor crafts market with more wooden boxes and souvenirs at the corner of vulitsya Shpytalna and vulitsya Kulisha a block west of the opera theatre, next to the TsUM department store, which also sells souvenirs. During the summer, a few of the wooden houses in the Museum of Popular Architecture have folk craft, art work, and embroidery for sale. There's an Ukrainsky Suvenir at vulitsya Horodetska 35, but the selection is not so good. The gift shop off the lobby of the History Museum at ploshcha Rynok 6 sells some nice antique trinkets and art work. At the southern end of the Town Arsenal building is a gift shop heavily stocked with religious art and icons. Women can have a stylish wool hat custom-made for them at the shop at ploshcha Rynok 13 or the one at vulitsya Teatralna 10.

Getting There & Away

Lviv is the first major city inside Ukraine for rail or road travellers from southern Poland, 85 km away. The border crossing point by rail is Medyka, 15 km east of Przemysl. On the Ukrainian side, Shehyni is the border point for road travellers. Most people entering Ukraine from Slovakia or Hungary arrive in Lviv after Uzhhorod or Mukacheve.

Air Weekly direct flights with Ukraine International include Lviv to/from Amsterdam, Frankfurt, either London or Manchester, and Moscow. ČSA occasionally runs seasonal flights to/from Prague. All other international flights are via Warsaw on Lot airlines or via Kiev with Air Ukraine. Domestic flights with Air Ukraine fly to/from Kiev and Simferopol daily, as well as to/from Kharkiv, Uzhhorod, Odessa and a few others, but schedules are sporadic. The Air Ukraine and Ukraine International main office (☎ 72 78 18) is at ploshcha Hryhorenka, three blocks west of prospekt Svobody. It's open Monday to Friday from 8 am to 8 pm, Saturday 8 am to 6 pm, closed on Sunday. Lot and CSA airline offices are located at the airport. For air information call ☎ 69 21 12.

Bus Bus transportation is often more frequent to destinations less than four hours away. Besides the main long-distance bus station, located about eight km south of the centre, there are eight smaller bus stations scattered throughout the city which service all outlying destinations within about 75 km from the city centre. For advance purchase of tickets and information, the bus ticket office (☎ 72 19 91) is at vulitsya Voronoho 3, a block south of the Hotel Zhorzh. It's open daily from 7 am to 7 pm, closed for lunch. For all bus info call ☎ 004, until 8 pm.

Train Railways from nine directions converge at Lviv's main 1904 railway station, three km west of the centre. Daily trains run to/from Budapest (12 hours), Bratislava (17 hours), Prague (21 hours), Vienna (22 hours), Belgrade (20 hours), Sofia (29 hours) and Warsaw (13 hours). To other Polish destinations, trains to/from Przemysl (2½ hours) run three times daily; from there you can take trains to other Polish destinations. Moscow trains (28 hours) travel four times daily, and St Petersburg trains (30 hours, via Vilnius) twice daily.

Domestic services include Uzhhorod (seven hours), Chernivtsi (six hours), Ivano-Frankivsk (three hours) and Ternopil (two hours), twice or more a day; Odessa (13 hours), Simferopol (30 hours), Rivne (4½ hours) and Lutsk (four hours), at least daily. The train service to/from Kiev (10-12 hours) runs about seven times a day. For local trains to surrounding towns within the Lviv region, like Sambir, Drohobych, Stry and Chervonohrad, there is daily electric train service. Tickets and information for local electric trains is in the hall to the right of the central hall as you enter the railway station. The central hall has large information boards posting long-distance train times. The info board on the wall to your right as you enter (Prybyttya) has train arrival times at Lviv; the info board to your left as you enter (Vidpravlennya) has train departure times from Lviv. The information booth (good luck) is at the far end, opposite the entrance.

Buying Tickets Tickets can be purchased at the railway station, but the queues, crowds and confusion can be overwhelming and often only produce frustration. For complete ease with no headaches, go to the travel info and ticket office to the far right of the lobby in the Hotel Zhorzh, open daily from 9 am to 6 pm, closed noon to 2 pm. For only a small service fee, foreigners can painlessly purchase tickets in advance and usually on the same day as well: domestic tickets payable in kupons, international tickets in hard currency only. For all train info call ☎ 005 or 74 820 68, 24 hours.

Car & Motorbike Main roads in Western Ukraine are generally busy, narrow, winding and sometimes polluted, but often scenic. From Lviv it's 278 km to Uzhhorod, 152 km to Lutsk, 135 km to Ivano-Frankivsk, 127 km to Ternopil, 278 km to Chernivtsi, and 544 km to Kiev. A good, current, detailed road map is advised. For car rentals see Tourist Office under Information earlier in this chapter.

Getting Around
To/From the Airport The airport is about eight km west of the centre, a 20-minute ride on trolleybus No 9 from a stop in front of the main University Building.

Public Transport The railway station (vokzal) is about three km west of the centre at the end of vulitsya Chernivetska, which runs north-west off vulitsya Horodetska. Tram Nos 1 and 9 go from the tram terminus in front of the railway station to prospekt Svobody and ploshcha Rynok in the centre. To get to the centre from the railway station take tram No 1; to go from the centre back to the station, take tram No 9. Tram No 6 runs from the railway station close to the Hotel Lviv. Trolleybus No 5 from ploshcha Petrushevycha and bus No 18 from the railway station go to the long-distance bus station (avtovokzal) in the far south of the city at vulitsya Stryska 271. Tram and trolleybus tickets (a few cents) can be purchased at most kiosks or on the trams by passing money up to the driver. Taxi cabs congregate outside the main railway station and along prospekt Svobody, usually near the Grand Hotel.

Driving in Lviv is a unique combination of cobbles, potholes, trolleybuses, trams, tram lines, congestion, pollution, and multiple intersections where the only apparent rule is 'first come, first serve'.

ZHOVKVA
ЖОВКВА

An enjoyable day trip from Lviv is a visit to the historical town of Zhovkva, about 32 km north of Lviv. The town's heyday was during the late 17th century when it became an influential cultural and educational centre, as well as the home to a thriving colony of artists and craftspeople whose work had great influence in Western Ukraine.

Ploshcha Vicheva

The town revolves around the sprawling, central ploshcha Vicheva, its southern and eastern sides lined with unkempt 17th to 18th-century buildings. Before you reach the square from the bus station, on your right is the abandoned but impressive walled **Church of St Joseph**, a 1653-55 former Dominican Church. The south side of the square is taken up by the simplistic Renaissance **palace**, originally built as a defensive castle in 1594 and rebuilt 100 years later as a palace. To the left are some walls leading to the small 17th-century **Zvirynetska Gate**, through which Khmelnytsky and his Cossacks supposedly marched when liberating the town from the Poles in 1648. Beyond the gate is the pleasant **Vidpochynku Park** that circles behind the palace and along a narrow branch of the Svyna River. To the right of the palace is the old **town hall** with a clock tower and memorial mound in front commemorating WW II victims. Farther to the right is another **gateway** – across the street from the octagonal bell tower of the impressive and large 1606-23 **Roman Catholic Church** that dominates the western side of the square. Built under the Poles, the locked interior houses some beautiful sculpture and paint-

ings. Note the exterior sculptural band beneath the ridge depicting various symbols and figures. Behind and to the north lies the **Holy Trinity Church** of the Basilian monastery, built in 1612 and distinguished by its unique Byzantine-looking dome rising above a cluster of semicircular apses. The southern Renaissance **gateway tower** was built in the 17th century. A few blocks east, just downhill and north of the square is a 1692-1700 Renaissance **synagogue**, rebuilt with eclectic details after being destroyed in WW II. Next to the synagogue is a small outdoor marketplace.

Getting There & Away

There are about 10 buses a day between Lviv and Zhovkva (45 minutes) leaving from bus station No 4 in Lviv, located next to the Krakivsky market at vulitsya Bazarna 11 (about a 10-minute walk north-west from the opera theatre). Some buses also leave from Lviv's bus station No 2, three km north of town at the end of tram line No 6. Many of the buses go to Chervonohrad, an hour north of Zhovkva.

The bus station in Zhovkva is about 1.5 km east of town. Follow the crowd for the right direction, or ask for the 'Tsentr'. Halfway there, at Lvivska 90, is the beautiful 1720 wooden **Trinity Church**, originally built without nails.

OLESKO
ОЛЕСЬКО

Population: 2500

The French-chateau-style hilltop castle at Olesko, some 70 km east of Lviv, is an excellent stop on the road to/from Kiev or Lutsk, or an easy day trip from Lviv. The 17th to 18th-century castle, built on the site of an earlier 13th-century fortress which was repeatedly destroyed by Tatar attacks during the 15th century, was restored in 1960-75. To get there turn north off the main road where it bends past **Olesko Cathedral** (founded 1625) in the middle of town.

An 18th-century former **Capuchin church & monastery** stands opposite the castle hill, a few hundred metres from town.

The castle houses a **museum** of 15th to 18th century Western Ukrainian and related art plus some archaeological artefacts from the region. It is open from 11 am to 5 pm daily except Monday. Particularly interesting is the 17th and 18th-century portrait gallery, which includes a huge 1692 canvas of the Battle of Vienna against the Turks in 1683. Raduga Publishers' *Lviv* guide has a fairly full account of the works displayed. You may be able to get a guide who speaks English, but most speak only Russian or Ukrainian. There's a café in the castle wall, but it's not likely to be open. A slightly overgrown formal garden spreads around the foot of the castle, with ponds marking the old moat.

The equestrian statue leaping out at drivers a couple of km east of Olesko is dedicated to Civil War cavalrymen. The village of **Pidhirtsi**, about five km to the south-east, has a 17th-century castle rebuilt into a **palace**, which now houses a crumbling sanatorium for elderly patients. A formal garden leads to a grassy field with a Baroque 18th-century **Basilian church** standing amidst geese and cows.

Getting There & Away

About eight daily buses go to/from Brody through Olesko (1½ hours) from Lviv's auto bus station No 2, located about three km north of the centre, at the end of tram line No 6. Olesko is a popular all-day excursion organised by the service bureau in the Hotel Zhorzh, costing about US$18 per person in large groups and about US$120 with a private guide for up to three individuals.

Transcarpathia
Закарпатска област

UZHHOROD
УЖГОРОД
Population: 125,000

Uzhhorod (formerly Ungvar), four km from the Slovak border and 25 km from the Hungarian border, is the southern gateway to the Ukraine section of the Carpathian Mountains, and the main town of the Zakarpatska (Transcarpathian) region of Ukraine, which covers the south side of the mountains. It's a relaxed town with a large Hungarian and Romanian minority giving it a Balkan feel. The old centre is on a refreshingly human scale, with a quiet, old-fashioned air to its streets. The river embankment west of the pedestrian-only ploshcha Teatralna is an enjoyable stroll, dotted with cypress trees and protected from the north winds by the Carpathians. The long autumn is reckoned to be the best season, with the beeches turning and the grape harvest coming in.

History

Uzhhorod has existed since at least 903 AD. Transcarpathia was in Hungary or the Austro-Hungarian Empire from the 10th or 11th century to the end of WW I, apart from periods in the 16th and 17th centuries when parts were subject to Transylvanian and Cossack revolts. One hundred and fifty years after its founding in 1596, the Ukrainian Catholic (or Uniate) Church, combining Orthodox ritual with Roman Catholic doctrine, was established in Uzhhorod. It persuaded the peasants – traditionally Orthodox as a result of the area having been on the fringe of Kievan Rus – to look to Catholic Hungary rather than Protestant Transylvania. As in Lviv, this helped foster a 'Ruthenian' identity in what became a corner of the Habsburg Empire, an identity which still survives in Transcarpathia and neighbouring corners of Slovakia, Hungary and Romania.

At the end of WW I Transcarpathia was included in the new country of Czechoslovakia. Pro-German Hungary took over its southern districts, including Uzhhorod, in November 1938 and the rest in March 1939 after an independent state, Carpatho-Ukraine, had existed for one day. Hungary remained in occupation until spring 1944, when German troops moved in for the final half year before the Red Army conquered the region. At the end of WW II Transcarpathia was incorporated into the USSR as the Zakarpatska region of Ukraine.

UKRAINE

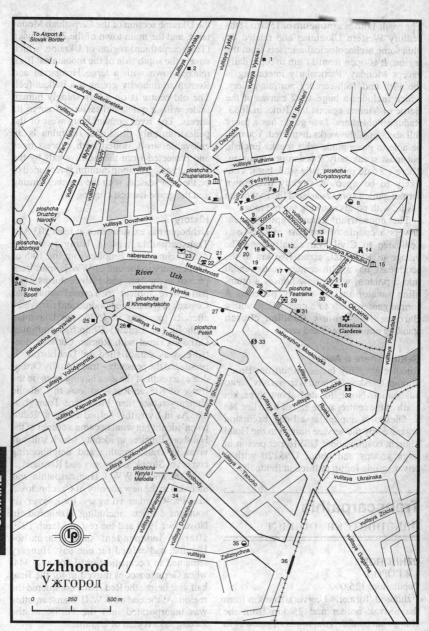

Uzhhorod
Ужгород

0   250   500 m

Orientation & Information

The River Uzh runs east to west across the city. A footbridge crosses it from the city centre which is on the north side. There are road bridges 750 metres to the east and west. The south side of the river, with the main railway station, is less pleasant with loud and busy streets.

The Travel Bureau in the Hotel Zakarpattya sells train tickets and can arrange tours and excursions and perhaps give you some general information. They're open week-

days from 8 am to 6 pm, closing at 4 pm on Fridays.

Most hotels have hard-currency exchange offices, but the exchange office in the Hotel Uzhhorod is supposed to also change travellers' cheques. The Exim Bank at ploshcha Petefi 19 will also exchange your travellers' cheques.

Uzhhorod's telephone code is 03122.

Castle

Uzhhorod Castle, at the end of vulitsya

Kapitulna on the hill in the middle of town, dates in its present form mostly from the 15th and 16th centuries. The massive walls and big corner bastions were built against the Turks. The palace, in the centre of the unkempt but peaceful grounds, houses the **Transcarpathian Museum of Local Lore**, with sections on archaeology and the folk art and dress of the region, which shows great variation between the different ethnic groups. Upstairs there's an exhibit of traditional folk instruments from wooden flutes and violins to the four-metre-long Hutzul mountain horns. It's open from 9 am to 5.30 pm daily except Monday.

Adjacent to the palace lies the partial foundations of a 12th to 13th-century **church**, burned down in 1728 and excavated in 1987.

Popular Architecture & Life Museum

Adjacent to the castle is the excellent Transcarpathian Museum of Popular Architecture & Life, with a couple of dozen old wooden buildings, many decked out with traditional furnishings, costumes and crafts, and staffed by friendly old ladies. It's interesting to compare the products of Transcarpathia's different ethnic groups like the Romanians and Hungarians, and the Boyky and Hutsulky, Ukrainian highlanders from the Carpathians. The Hutzul farmstead almost resembles a fort. The highlight is the wooden **St Michael Church**, moved from neighbouring Mukacheve in 1974. The interior boasts a 200-year-old carved wooden iconostasis and candelabra. The museum is open daily except Tuesday from 10 am to 5 pm.

Cathedral

The twin-towered cathedral on vulitsya Kapitulna, built as part of a Jesuit monastery in the 1640s, became Ukrainian Catholic in the late 18th century and Russian Orthodox after WW II, before recently returning to Ukrainian Catholic. It's Baroque inside, and 1870s classical outside. On the corner just west of the cathedral, vulitsya Dukhovycha 23 and 25 used to house priests.

Other Things to See & Do

The **Transcarpathian Art Museum**, housed in the former Transcarpathian communist headquarters, is a fine 1809 building at ploshcha Zhupanatska 3. Open daily from 10 am to 6 pm except Monday, it harbours a nice collection of historical and contemporary works by little-known Transcarpathian artists.

Down from the castle on vulitsya Ivana Olbrakhta is the pink, turn-of-the-century main **University Building** with the **University Botanical Gardens** farther east down the street. Rather overgrown, the gardens have metasequoia trees from Tibet which were once believed to be extinct.

The red brick **Philharmonia** building at the eastern end of ploshcha Teatralna looks like it dropped out of Moorish Spain. Indeed, it's the former **synagogue** and once home to a large Jewish population wiped out in WW II. The attendant next door may show you inside the beautiful interior if you ask politely. Behind the Philharmonia is a tiny **railway** run by children which putts one km east along the river from May to October.

On the opposite side of the river and east along naberezhna Moskovska, is a splendid little candy-house **Orthodox church** which used to house an atheism museum.

Places to Stay

The *Hotel Zakarpattya* (☎ 9 75 10) is an agreeable effort, with modern, well-kept but overpriced rooms at US$45/70/90 (hard currency only) for singles/doubles/triples with breakfast. The staff is helpful and the hotel is loaded with facilities. It's at ploshcha Kyryla i Mefodia 5, one km south of the city centre, west of the railway station.

The *Hotel Uzhhorod* (☎ 3 50 60) at ploshcha B Khmelnytskoho 2, south of the river about one km west of the centre, is bland and off a busy intersection but with decent rooms, most with balconies, for US$21/37/48 a single/double/triple, hard currency only.

There are two hotels, each about one km uphill north of the centre. The *Hotel Druzhba* (☎ 3 32 32) at vulitsya Vysoka 2 is the nicest but most expensive at US$44/60/69 for singles/doubles/triples. The *Hotel Svitanok* (☎ 3 43 09) at vulitsya Koshytska 30 is friendly with adequate rooms for US$10/20/30, with breakfast in the restaurant across the street included. Most buses going northwest along prospekt Svobody pass the Hotel Uzhhorod, cross the river and then head north up to vulitsya Sobranetska, which is not far from the Druzhba and Svitanok hotels.

Near the large flea market at Avanhard Stadium is the *Hotel Sport* (☎ 4 33 44) at vulitsya Profspilkova 4. Popular with athletes and market vendors, it has decent accommodation for US$5 per person in single/double/triple rooms. Bus No 8 from prospekt Svobody goes nearby.

The *Hotel Koruna* at ploshcha Teatralna 5 was closed for restoration at the time of writing. When it opens again, its location and character will make it the place to stay.

Places to Eat

The Hungarian Hall upstairs in the *Hotel Zakarpattya* is the best hotel restaurant with decent food and usually a dance band or floor show. There's a smaller café in the lobby selling ice cream and quick food.

The restaurant in the *Hotel Koruna* is old and elegant, also with live music and decent meals for about US$4. The *Hotel Druzhba's* restaurant is supposed to be good.

In the centre, the faded dining hall of the *Edelveys* on vulitsya Voloshyna is open until 9 pm. Next to the basement restaurant *Stare Misto* at vulitsya Korzo 9 is a dirt-cheap cafeteria-style eatery. At vulitsya Korzo 16 there's a *pizzeria* open until 7 pm, and the *Zoloty Kluchyk* (golden key) café and candy store is nearby on the corner of vulitsya Korzo and vulitsya Voloshyna. The best café in town is the *Pid Zamkom Expres Kafe* at vulitsya Ivana Olbrakhta 3. Owned by a friendly couple who hope to open a pension down the road, it serves all sorts of drinks and snacks and is open until midnight.

In summer, try 'kokteily' – ice cream and honey shakes – from the ice cream and juice places around the city centre. The market off

ploshcha Koryatovycha sells fresh fruit and vegetables.

Locals say that, unlike the Moldovans, they had the sense not to start uprooting vines during the Gorbachev anti-alcohol drive in the mid 1980s. Troyanda Zakarpatie (a red dessert wine), Beregivske (a riesling) and Serednyanske are three of their best wines.

Entertainment

The Transcarpathian Folk Choir is one of the best of its type. If it happens to be singing on home ground, make an effort to hear it. They (and other troupes) perform at the big, white, modern-looking Transcarpathian Music & Drama Theatre just west of the footbridge. The small theatre in ploshcha Teatralna is the Marionette Theatre and the modern appendage to the left of the Philharmonia sometimes has performances. Most restaurants have live music of one form or another until late.

Things to Buy

There's an interesting bookshop at ploshcha Koryatovycha 1 and a small arts and crafts salon a couple doors down at No 5. There's a corner souvenir shop on vulitsya Voloshyna to the left of the Catholic church. Farther down at vulitsya Voloshyna 18A is a fine art gallery that also sells some embroidery and folk craft; across the street at No 21 is a small antique shop.

The huge bustling flea market near Avanhard Stadium in a park one km west of the centre sells everything from puppy dogs to spare engine parts to rubber boots.

Getting There & Away

Air The airport is on the western side of town, on the road to the Slovak border. There are weekly flights to/from major domestic sites. For international destinations (except once a week to Moscow and Istanbul) you must connect at Kiev (five times weekly). For tickets and information go to the airline office at vulitsya Lva Tolstoho 33 just east of ploshcha Khmelnytskoho. Bus No 4 from the main bus station goes to the airport.

Bus Daily cross-border buses link Uzhhorod with Michalovce and Košice in Slovakia and Miskolc in Hungary, as well as Chop with Nyiregyhaza in Hungary. Uzhhorod's bus station is opposite the railway station at vulitsya Zaliznychna 2. There are five buses a day to/from Mukacheve (45 minutes), and three a day to/from Rakhiv via Khust.

Train Chop, 23 km south of Uzhhorod, is the border town for rail travellers to and from Hungary (border town Zahony) and Slovakia (border town Čierna nad Tisou). Daily trains linking Moscow, Kiev and Lviv with Budapest, Prague, Bratislava, Vienna and Belgrade pass through Chop, but not all of them go through Uzhhorod, since there is an alternative line through Mukacheve. You may have to change trains in Chop or take a bus from Mukacheve if your train doesn't go through Uzhhorod.

There are three or four daily trains to Lviv (seven hours) and Kiev (20-21 hours), and two trains a day to/from Ivano-Frankivsk (10 hours). A long scenic train trip along the southern base of the Carpathians to Chernivtsi through Khust and Rakhiv runs every other day. The train ride over the Carpathians to Lviv is also very scenic.

Advance tickets can be purchased at the Tourist Bureau in the Hotel Zakarpattya, open weekdays from 8 am to 6 pm, closing at 4 pm on Fridays. There's also a train ticket office next to the airline office at vulitsya Lva Tolstoho 33, open daily from 8 am to 7 pm.

Car & Motorbike The road from Košice and Michalovce in Slovakia enters Ukraine about four km west of central Uzhhorod. The old 'Intourist' sign pointing left soon after the border sends you to Lviv. For Uzhhorod centre, go straight on. The road from Debrecen in Hungary crosses the border at Zahony, opposite Chop. Both road borders are extremely busy: try to avoid Fridays and Sundays, the busiest days.

The 250 km from Uzhhorod to Lviv are rural and pretty as you cross the Carpathians, with the road not too steep. Between Uzhhorod and Chernivtsi, the usual route is via Stry and Ivano-Frankivsk (415 km), with the more direct-looking route via Khust and Rakhiv windier and slower but more scenic.

MUKACHEVE
МУКАЧЕВЕ
Population: 90,000

Often the first train stop past the border into Ukraine from Slovakia or Hungary, Mukacheve is the unassuming secondary city of Transcarpathia and the site of the best hilltop castle in the area. First settled in the 9th century by White Croatians, it was subsequently seized and settled by Kievan Rus, Hungarians, Tatars, Transylvanians, Ukrainians, and Hungarians again. Today's population is a true Transcarpathian mix, and Mukacheve reflects this with a lively and unpretentious small-town atmosphere. It merits a stop only if you have a day to spare.

Orientation & Information
The centre revolves around the elongated ploshcha Miru with the railway station about 1.5 km south-west on vulitsya Lenina. Two blocks before you reach ploshcha Miru, off the corner of vulitsya Lenina and vulitsya Moskovska, are the main post office, a bank and the militia. The bus station is about the same distance east of the centre off vulitsya Miru, which is the street extending southeast from ploshcha Miru. Follow vulitsya Miru as it curves left, then take a right on vulitsya Yesenina, across from vulitsya Miru 65, and walk 200 metres to the end. It's off to the left.

Mukacheve's telephone code is 03131.

Town Centre
The eastern end of ploshcha Miru has a 19th-century Roman Catholic church with a fine 15th-century **Gothic chapel** beside it. The western end of ploshcha Miru has the eclectic **Bily Budynok** (white building), a former palace, entirely rebuilt in Mannerist style in the 18th century as the town hall. Halfway along the south side of ploshcha Miru is a gateway that leads to an 18th-century former **palace** surrounded by a park and church, now housing an art academy. Inside is a

small museum dedicated to the famous 19th-century Hungarian artist Munkacsy, a Mukacheve native. A bust of Munkacsy sits in front of the grassy strip that runs down the middle of ploshcha Miru. Off the north side of ploshcha Miru, the pedestrian passazh Pobutu will lead a block north to the thriving **market place** (rynok), another heaving mass of home-grown produce with a large, covered hall.

Palanok Castle

Cresting the top of the 'Zamkova Hora' (Castle Hill), Palanok Castle (open daily from 9 am to 5 pm, closed Monday) was founded in the 14th century, and lived in and expanded upon by each subsequent ruler. The rather unkempt complex includes a series of two main, staggered courtyards with a palace and chapel around the upper one. You're free to wander around the grounds and buildings, which are supposed to be under restoration. Many of them offer panoramic views. Inside one is a **Regional Museum** with historical and ethnographic exhibits. The castle was once home to the famous Hungarian princess Ilona Zrini in the 17th century. In the 19th century it served as an infamous prison. Today there's a large military base at the foot of Castle Hill.

From the north-western end of ploshcha Miru turn left, past the Bily Budynok, and then take the first right on vulitsya Ilona Zrini and head west for about 1.5 km. Bus No 3 will save you the walk.

St Nicholas Monastery

If you have time, continue north-west beyond ploshcha Miru, cross the Latorytsya River, and turn right, walking north-east along the river for one km until you see the green spire of St Nicholas Church and its monastery in the distance. The complex is a serene place with a simple 1804 church, a cluster of small dormitory buildings and a walled garden, all backed by rolling, verdant hills.

Places to Stay & Eat

The *Hotel Zvezda (Zirka)* (☎ 20 08) at ploshcha Miru 20, across from the Bily Budynok, probably won't take foreigners but you can try. Otherwise it's the *Hotel Latorika* (☎ 2 32 01) at vulitsya Dykhovycha 93, back from the street and next to a park about one km north-east from the south-east corner of ploshcha Miru. Single/double rooms cost US$10 per person – hard currency only.

Both hotels have standard restaurants but the best in town is *Slavianska*, just off the south-east end of ploshcha Miru. It's open from 8 am to 9 pm, but closes between 4 and 4.30 pm. *Kafe Viktoria* at ploshcha Miru 13 has cakes and coffee.

Getting There & Away

Plenty of trains pull through with daily services to Lviv, Kiev, Ivano-Frankivsk and Chernivtsi. The trains to Uzhhorod (about two hours) have to go back through Chop, so it's much faster to take the bus. About five daily buses go to Uzhhorod (45 minutes) and to other sites in Transcarpathia, including Khust and Rakhiv.

Ivano-Frankivsk Region
Івано-Франківська область

IVANO-FRANKIVSK
ІВАНО-ФРАНКІВСЬК
Population: 234,000

Lviv's lesser partner in Galicia, Ivano-Frankivsk has traditionally been the cultural and economic capital of the Carpathian region, the hilly lands on the opposite (north-east) side of the mountains from Transcarpathia, although it's not as old as many of the smaller towns nearby. Its centre is a lively mix of open spaces, crowded streets and parks, and there's a teeming market place with a few fine churches mixed in. Due to some nasty military factories on the outskirts, the city was off limits to foreigners a few years ago.

Founded in the mid-17th century on

Ivano-Frankivsk
Івано-Франківськ

0   125   250 m

Cossack trade routes between the southern Danube and Lviv, it quickly fell under Polish rule and then to the Habsburgs a century later. The city was the second capital of the temporary Republic of Western Ukraine, established in Lviv during the war for an independence against Poland in 1919. During WW II the city was a centre for UPA partisans who fought against both the Germans and the Russians. Until 1962, the city was known as Stanyslaviv.

Orientation & Information

The centre lies about one km south of the main train and bus stations. The popular pedestrian section of vulitsya Nezalezhnosti culminates at its western end in ploshcha Vichevy, but lots of activity takes place just to the north around the traditional centre of ploshcha Rynok.

There are no good maps of the city, but you can check at some of the bookshops along vulitsya Nezalezhnosti. The best source of information is the friendly front desk of the Hotel Roxolana. The hotel also organises city tours and six different excursions to the surrounding area, as well as car rentals.

PLACES TO STAY

3 Hotel Roxolana
   Готель Роксоляна
21 Hotel Ukraina
   Гостинниця Україна
29 Hotel/Restaurant Kiev
   Гостинниця Київ
34 Hotel Dnister
   Гостинниця Дністер

PLACES TO EAT

19 Cafés
   Кафе
20 Kafe/Restoran Pegas
   Кафе/Ресторан Пегас
23 Prykarpatsky Korovay Kafe
   Кафе Прикарпатский Коровай
26 Kafe Yuvileyny
   Кафе Ювілейний
28 Restaurant Taystra
   Ресторан Тайстра
30 Kafe Bily Kamin
   Кафе Білий Камінь
31 Kafe & Restoran Svitlitsya
   Кафе& Ресторан Світлиця
32 Kafe Zatyshok
   Кафе Затишок

OTHER

1 Railway Station
   Залізничний вокзал
2 Bus Station
   Автобусний вокзал
4 Church
   Церква
5 Pototsky Palace Complex
   (now hospital)
   Комплекс палацу Потоцького
   (тепер шпиталь)

6 Covered Market
   Закритий ринок
7 Brewery
   Броварня
8 Brewery
   Броварня
9 Flea Market
   Базар
10 Main Outdoor Market
   Центральний ринок
11 Main Outdoor Market
   Центральний ринок
12 Regional Government Building
   Державний обласний будинок
13 Former Armenian Church
   (now Ukrainian Catholic)
   Українська католицька церква
14 Synagogue
   Синагога
15 Regional Museum
   Краєзнавчий музей
16 Parish Church/Museum of Sacred
   Galician Art
   Парафіяльний костел/музей святого
   мистецтва Галиччини
17 Jesuit Collegium
   Колегя Єзуїтів
18 Ukrainian Catholic Cathedral
   Україньський католицький собор
22 Ivan Franko Ukrainian Music & Drama
   Theatre
   Український театр музики
   і драми ім. Івана Франка
24 Ukrainsky Suvenir
   Український сувенір
25 Administration Building (1894)
   Будинок адміністрації
27 Gallery Passazh
   Галерія пасаж
33 Post Office
   Пошта

Both the Roxolana and Ukraina hotels can exchange currency.

Ivano-Frankivsk's phone code is 03422.

City Centre

The traditional heart of the city is **ploshcha Rynok**, surrounded by a hodge-podge mix of colourful buildings with the angular 1929 star-shaped town hall in the centre, built on the site of a former 1695 structure. Today the building houses the **Regional Museum**, featuring the 12th-century sarcophagus of king Yaroslav Osmomsyl, which was excavated from the nearby town of Halych. There are also some ethnographic exhibits. It's open daily from 10 am to 5 pm, closed on Monday. Just east of the square is the former 1742 **Armenian church** with an attractive, undulating Baroque façade and twin, rounded bell towers. The interior ceiling was finely painted when converted to Ukrainian Catholic. A block south is an 1897 **synagogue** built in the typical Eastern European style.

Just west of ploshcha Rynok is the elongated ploshcha Sheptytskoho with two impressive churches at either end. To the south is the Baroque, former **Jesuit church** (1729) which was recently restored and converted into a Ukrainian Catholic Cathedral. Its painted interior is highlighted by a large, gilded iconostasis. Next to the church is the plain 1742 former Jesuit Collegium. At the opposite end of ploshcha Rynok is the 1672 former Roman Catholic parish church, its design reflecting the transition from the Renaissance to the Baroque with rows of stubby buttresses along its sides. The superbly vaulted interior now houses the **Museum of Sacred Galician Art**, open from 11 am to 6 pm daily except Friday and Saturday. Inside are mostly 16th to 19th-century icons and wooden sculpture with English texts on the displays. Directly behind and west of the church is a lively flea market where bustling vendors hawk their sad selection of wares. Farther around the corner, on either side of vulitsya Novhorodska is an abandoned **brewery complex** dating from 1767.

North of ploshcha Rynok is a large outdoor market with plenty of activity and heaps of fresh produce. Just east is an ageing hospital housed in the former **Pototsky Palace** (1622-82) complex, home of a Polish nobleman whose son, Stanisław, the city was originally named after.

Popular, pleasant and reserved for pedestrians along its western side, **vulitsya Nezalezhnosti** (sometimes known by its former name of vulitsya Radyanska) has a number of refined turn-of-the-century buildings as well as a few less inspiring modern additions. It's lined with bookshops and cafés, culminating at its western end with the spacious **ploshcha Vichevy**, another bustling combination of old and new architecture with a pleasing scale. Between vulitsya Nezalezhnosti and ploshcha Rynok there are two city blocks of relaxing parks with plenty of benches.

Places to Stay

The *Hotel Roxolana* (☎ 2 52 21; fax 2 47 69), with only 25 rooms, is one of the nicest in the country. It is professionally run in a fully restored 1907 Secessionist (early Art Nouveau) building at vulitsya Grunvadska 7-9, and is completely up to Western standards of comfort. Rooms with breakfast cost US$75/90 (May-September), US$55/70 (October, April), and US$35/50 (November-March) for singles/doubles, hard currency only, with a 10% discount on weekdays. The hotel is within walking distance from the railway station, and a larger Roxolana II hotel is under construction nearby.

The *Hotel Ukraina* (☎ 43 135) at vulitsya Nezalezhnosti 52 is a standard 1970s construction, but clean and well kept with friendly service. Rooms are US$25/40 for singles/doubles. Next to the hotel is the large Ivan Franko Ukrainian Theatre of Music & Drama. Bus No 2 or 5 from the railway station goes down vulitsya B Lepkoho to the hotel, but it's only about a one-km walk.

The cheapest hotel in town is the *Hotel Dnister* (☎ 2 23 32) at vulitsya Sichovykh Striltsiv 12 on the corner of vulitsya Shevchenka with reasonable singles/doubles/triples for a cheap US$7/12/14, and bathrooms down the hall.

Places to Eat

Restaurants The *Restoran Svitlitsya*, with a traditionally carved wood ceiling, is above the café with the same name. Soup, salad and main course costs about US$2 to US$3. The café/restaurant *Pegas* on vulitsya Furmanova is popular with the more well-to-do locals, serving delicious grilled chicken and beef dishes for about US$4 to US$6. The restaurant *Taystra* on ploshcha Vichevy serves a half-chicken with trimmings for US$2. Downstairs in the cellar is a bar filled with a young crowd, a pool table and beer.

Cafés The pedestrian section of vulitsya Nezalezhnosti is loaded with cafés. *The Prykarpatsky Korovay Kafe* at No 30, at the eastern end, is two adjacent cafés, both serving the same tasty cookies, pastries and drinks – the one on the left is more popular but you can sit down in the one on your right. At the western end of the street, at No 2, is the *Kafe Bily Kamin*, whose white rock interior dishes out bowls of ice cream. The *Kafe Zatyshok* is your standard coffee, vodka and cake outfit at vulitsya Komarova 3, a side street off the middle of vulitsya Nezalezhnosti. Across the street is the more spacious and up-market *Kafe Svitlitsya*.

The south-eastern edge of ploshcha Rynok has a row of three cafés, the *Kafe Zavyvanets* on the corner, followed by the *Kafe Zoloty Pochatok*, and the *Kafe Play*. All have the same sweets and drinks but the Kafe Play serves tasty pizzas.

Hotels The *Hotel Roxolana* restaurant has excellent Ukrainian dishes but it's pricey and only hard currency is accepted. The *Hotel Ukraina* does respectable meals in its restaurant and the *Hotel Dnister* has a small kafe on the ground floor that serves light food and drinks.

Things to Buy
There's a pretty good selection of folk art and embroidery at the Ukrainsky Suvenir on the corner of vulitsya Komarova and vulitsya Hrushevskoho.

Getting There & Away
Air A small airport, about 10 km south of the centre at vulitsya Daduhin 264A, has weekly flights to Lviv, Kiev and other major domestic locations on Air Ukraine, who also has a seasonal weekly service direct from New York to Ivano-Frankivsk. Ukraine International provides summer weekly connections to/from Manchester. The Air Ukraine and Ukraine International offices (☎ 31 068) are at vulitsya Sichovykh Striltsiv 15. Bus No 1 or 1A from the railway station goes to the airport in about 25 minutes. Other flights from Eastern Europe are at times directed here rather than to Lviv due to a better running of the Ivano-Frankivsk airport.

Bus The bus station is directly east of the railway station with several daily buses to

Lviv, Kolomyya, Kosiv, Chernivtsi and Ternopil.

Train There are five daily trains to/from Lviv (three to four hours), three or four to/from Chernivtsi (three to four hours), and two a day to/from Kiev (13-14 hours). There are also daily services to/from Uzhhorod (10 hours), Odessa (21 hours), Moscow (15 hours), Sofia (27 hours), Brest (15 hours) and St Petersburg (36 hours).

Frequent electric train services go out to surrounding destinations including Kolomyya, Rohatyn, Nadvirna and Rakhiv.

KOLOMYYA
КОЛОМИЯ
Population: 70,000

About 65 km south of Ivano-Frankivsk on the Prut River, Kolomyya is a pleasant small town and an enjoyable stopover between Ivano-Frankivsk and Chernivtsi if you have time to spare. Dating from the 13th century, Kolomyya was an important station on the salt-trade routes between Galicia and the Black Sea. The city was frequently devastated by Tatar raids.

At the base of low mountains, Kolomyya is the traditional centre of the Hutzuls, regional ethnic Ukrainians from the Carpathian Mountains who are known for their traditional folk crafts.

Orientation & Information
The centre of the town, with its marketplace, shops and cafés lies around the busy and colourful ploshcha Vidrodzhennya, with prospekt Hrushevskoho and the old town hall to its south. The two main commercial streets, vulitsya Teatralna and vulitsya Vidrodzhennya, fan out north from ploshcha Vidrodzhennya on either side of the statue of Shevchenko.

Kolomyya's telephone code is 03433.

Museum of Hutzul Folk Art
The highlight of the town is the Museum of Hutzul Folk Art, on vulitsya Teatralna about 500 metres north of ploshcha Vidrodzhennya, open daily except Friday from 10

UKRAINE

am to 6 pm. Established in 1935, the museum has over 15,000 items in 20 exhibition halls ranging from carved wooden tools, boxes and furniture to traditional folk-embroidered dress and ceramic tableware. The ground floor has mostly 18th to 19th-century displays with the upper floor containing contemporary work: happy creations carrying on the Hutzul traditions.

Carpathian State National Park

About 55 km south-west of Kolomyya lies the country's largest national park, with some of the highest peaks in the Ukrainian Carpathians and lots of Alpine vegetation.

The principal village in the park is Vorokhta (Ворохта), but you're more likely to find accommodation in either Yaremcha (Яремча) to the north, or Yasinya (Ясіня) to the south – two mountain resort towns on either side of Vorokhta near the entrances to the park. Yaremcha is larger with more facilities.

Rakhiv (Рахів), about 55 km to the south-west, lies on the opposite side of the park from Kolomyya with bus service to the park from either town. There's also a train line connecting Kolomyya and Rakhiv which runs daily through the park, stopping at Yaremcha, Vorokhta and Yasinya along the way. The village of Dora, about three km north of Yaremcha just as you enter the park, has an impressive 17th-century wooden Hutzul church. There's good hiking around Yaremcha.

The Hotel Roxolana in Ivano-Frankivsk arranges summer time and occasional off-season excursions to Yaremcha (about US$30 per person for a large group), usually with a stopover in the village of Manyava for a visit to the 17th-century Skyt Manyavsky Monastery.

The Carpathian State National Park straddles the border between the Ivano-Frankivsk and Zakarpatska oblasts with parts of the park in either region.

Places to Stay

The only hotel in town is the Intourist-style but friendly *Hotel Prykarpattya* (☎ 2 78 80) at prospekt Hrushevskoho 82, right across the street from the bus station. Rooms cost US$4/7/10 for singles/doubles/triples. The hotel has a decent restaurant and exchange office.

Getting There & Away

Bus At least five daily buses go to/from Ivano-Frankivsk, with a few less to/from Chernivtsi. At least three daily buses go to/from Kosiv. Buying tickets can get hectic with kasa No 1 for Lviv and Chernivtsi. You can also push your way on a bus and pay the driver on board. The bus station is one km west of the centre down vulitsya Hrushevskoho.

Train Kolomyya is the halfway point on the Ivano-Frankivsk to Chernivtsi line with trains stopping en route three or four times a day. There are also about five daily electric trains servicing Ivano-Frankivsk. About three daily trains to/from Lviv as well as one to/from Odessa pass through Kolomyya. The railway station is about two km north-east of the centre on vulitsya Sichovykh Striltsiv. Overcrowded city bus No 12 runs between the railway station and the bus station, travelling through the centre.

KOSIV
КОСІВ
Population: 9000

Kosiv was always known as a centre for folk craft production. Rooted firmly in its traditions, the town was a bastion of Ukrainian identity during the years of Polish occupation and is the home of the Hutsul Technical Art Institute. Despite its fine mountain location and several museums, travellers usually come to Kosiv only for one reason: the Saturday morning **craft market**. Craftspeople roll their carts down from the hills in the early morning to sell their variety of folk art and handicrafts, ranging from embroidery to hand-carved wooden boxes – perfect souvenirs. The market is officially open on Saturdays from 6 am to 2 pm, but by 8 am it's already in full gear, so get there early.

If you don't have your own transport (it's

a 2½-hour drive from Ivano-Frankivsk) you'll have to take the earliest possible bus to Kosiv from Ivano-Frankivsk or Kolomyya. During the summer and occasionally in the off season the Hotel Roxolana in Ivano-Frankivsk has weekly all-day excursions including lunch, but they're a bit pricey; it's cheaper (about US$30 per person) if you can join a larger group of 10 or more people.

Volyn & Rivne Regions
Волинська та Рівнеська області

LUTSK
ЛУЦЬК
Population: 216,000
Lutsk, the chief city of the Volyn region, is preferable to Rivne, 67 km down the road, as a stop between Brest and Lviv or Kiev. It's smaller, quieter, better looking and it has a genuinely historic area. Probably founded about 1000 AD by Volodymyr of Kiev, it became part of the Galician-Volynian Principality when Kievan Rus broke up. Taken over by Lithuania in the 14th century, it grew in trade importance despite occasional Tatar attacks. It passed to Poland in 1569, Russia in 1795, and between WW I and WW II was back under Poland.

Orientation & Information
The most interesting parts of town are south of Teatralna ploshcha, which is at the western end of the main street, prospekt Voli. The traffic-free section of vulitsya Lesi Ukrainky is the city's main pedestrian artery, lined with shops, restaurants and cafés. It leads southwest from Teatralna ploshcha across busy vulitsya Kovelska, a former moat, down into the old town in a bend of the Styr River, from where parkland stretches east along the northern bank of the river.

There's an exchange office and a small tourist bureau in the Hotel Ukraina, but its services are limited.

Lutsk's telephone code is 03322.

Castle
Known as Lubart's Castle after the Lithuanian prince who had it built in the 14th century, this is the centrepiece of the old town. Its 13-metre-high brick walls atop earth ramparts are surmounted by three tall towers. You enter through the massive brick crenulated **Vizdova Tower** at the western corner. Inside to the far right is the similarly massive **Stiroka Tower** and to the far left, near a small temple-like building, is the wood-roofed **Vladycha Tower**, once used to store gunpowder and ammunition. Near the Vladycha Tower is a stairway leading up to the elevated wooden walkway along the far wall with views down over the patchwork of gardens below. In the courtyard, the remains of the 12th-century **Church of St John the Divine** (Ioanna Bohoslova), around which the castle was built, are being lazily excavated. On the southern side of the courtyard, against the wall, there's an **art museum** with a small selection of 17th to 20th-century European paintings as well as a temporary gallery. The castle is open daily except Monday from 10 am to 6 pm.

Old Town
The old town is a higgledy-piggledy quarter of wooden cottages and pretty gardens. It is dotted with monastic buildings from Lutsk's Polish period, and has more of a sprawling village feel than that of a dense urban core. The most imposing building is the **Jesuits' complex** on vulitsya Kafedralna, just west of the castle. The stately façade of their church was originally built in 1610 but it was reconstructed in the 1780s. Its interior, resembling the inside of a massive Easter egg, is now under restoration after years of being used as a museum. Opposite is an odd triple-arched 1536 **bell tower**. The austere, main Jesuit monastery building behind the church – also early 17th century – became a prison in the 19th century.

UKRAINE

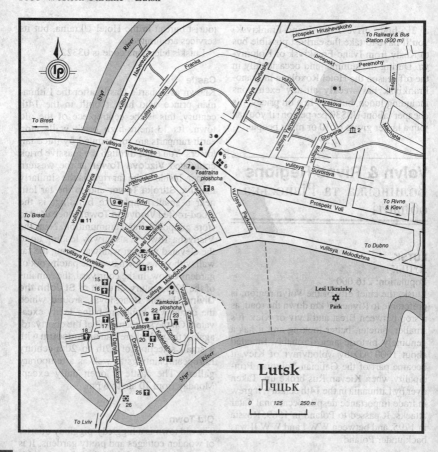

Lutsk
Лчцьк

Between the church and the castle is the wide-open cobbled **Zamkova ploshcha**, a perfect spot for an outdoor café, but for now you'll have to settle for the small water pump halfway down on the left (north) side. There should be a glass hanging on the fence nearby. Down vulitsya Kafedralna to the south is the plain, 17th-century **Birgittine monastery**, converted into a prison in 1846; it's now Lutsk's music academy. Across the street is a tiny park and **memorial** to Pasha Saveleva, a WW II partisan burnt alive in the prison yard by the Nazis. Stroll around the base of the castle on cottage-lined vulitsya

Zamkova for nice views up to the formidable walls.

The 18th-century **Trinity Church** on the east side of Teatralna ploshcha, once part of a Catholic monastery, is now Orthodox with a painted interior and continually wafting incense. Services are usually at 6 pm.

Farther south from the castle, towards the end of vulitsya Drahomanova, is the former **Dominican monastery**, originally built of wood in 1390. It was reconstructed in stone 300 years later. In 1847 the monastery became a military hospital and today it's an Orthodox seminary. A block west at vulitsya

PLACES TO STAY

4   Hotel Ukraina
     Гостинниця Україна
11   Hotel Svityaz
     Гостинниця Світязь

PLACES TO EAT

10   Kafe Expres
     Кафе Експрес
12   Kafe Stary Zamok
     Кафе Старий Замок

OTHER

1   Eternal Glory Memorial Complex
     Меморальний комплекс Вічної слави
2   Volyn Regional Museum
     Волинський краєзнавчий музей
3   Bus Ticket Office
     Бюро автобусних квитків
5   Train & Airline Ticket Office
     Каса продажу залізничних та авіаційних
     квитків
6   Lutsk Department Store
     Універмаг Луцьк
7   Shevchenko Theatre & Lesia
     Ukrainka Monument
     Театр імені Т. Г. Шевченка та
     пам'ятник Лесі Українці
8   Trinity Church
     Церква Св. Трійці

9   Theatre Lyalok
     Театр Ляльок
13   Former Trinitarian Monastery
     (18th century)
     Колишній монастир Св. Трійці
14   Central Market
     Центральний ринок
15   Planetarium
     Планетарій
16   Vasilian Monastery (17th century)
     Монастир Василианов
17   Intercession Church
     (14th to 17th century)
     Покровська церква
18   Lutheran Church
     Лютеранська церква
19   Bell Tower
     Дзвіниця
20   Jesuit Church
     Костьол Єзуїтів
21   Jesuit Monastery
     Монастир Єзуїтів
22   Monastery (16th to 18th century)
     Монастир
23   Castle
     Замок
24   Brigittine Monastery
     Монастир Бригідок
25   Dominican Monastery
     Домініканський монастир
26   Synagogue
     Синагога

Danyla Halytskoho 33 is a former 14th-century **synagogue**, restored after being partially destroyed in WW II. East of vulitsya Danyla Halytskoho are a few alleys and small streets where children, chickens and geese wander past cottages and gardens to the grassy river's edge.

Other Things to See & Do

Pleasant, tree-covered **Lesi Ukrainky Park** stretches along the river east of the castle and market. A funfair, playground and so on lurk amid the greenery.

The **Eternal Glory Memorial Complex** on vulitsya Nekrasova is a small park commemorating Volynian WW II heroes and victims. The names of 107 villages destroyed by the Nazis are engraved on a wall beside other statistics – 165,339 Volynians tortured and executed, 47,960 lost in prison camps – and a verse which translates as 'These are not just numbers, but ashes and blood; these are not just numbers, but anguish and cries'.

The **Volyn Regional Museum** with a large classical entrance is nearby at vulitsya Shopena 20, open daily from 10 am to 6 pm except Monday. Upstairs are a number of interesting historical and ethnographic exhibits.

Places to Stay

The *Hotel Ukraina* (☎ 4 33 51) at vulitsya Slovatskoho 2, opposite Teatralna ploshcha, is nothing too special, but it has pleasant service and relatively large rooms and beds for US$6/10/12 a single/double/triple.

UKRAINE

The *Hotel Svityaz* (☎ 4 41 72) at vulitsya Naberezhna 4, just west of the centre, has a friendly staff that will brag about their sauna. Rooms are the same price as at the Hotel Ukraina, but with breakfast included.

Places to Eat

The restaurant in the *Hotel Ukraina* is a lively place, with decent meals – around US$2 to US$3 for three courses and a beer – and a reasonable band at night. The upstairs restaurant at the *Hotel Svityaz* is more down to earth, and also has good cheap food and a comfortable bar downstairs that sells beer on tap and plays polka music.

For daytime bites on vulitsya Lesi Ukrainky, try the *Kafe Stary Zamok (Old Castle)* in a basement on the corner of vulitsya Medvedeva, or the *Kafe Expres*, up the street to the north. The Stary Zamok serves good soups, salads, coffee, main dishes like stuffed peppers, and desserts like baked apples. It has counter service and nothing costs more than US$1. The Expres, with similar prices, has omelette and potato pancakes as well as the standard meatballs and so on. Both are open from noon to 8 or 9 pm, with an hour's break in mid-afternoon. The fare is freshest soon after opening time. At vulitsya Lesi Ukrainky 40 is the *Pelmenna*, a small dive which shells out little platefuls of vareniky for US$0.25.

The Central Market is a sure thing for colourful, fruit-filled chaos, a block away on the corner of vulitsya Zamkova and vulitsya Molodizhna.

Getting There & Away

Lutsk has a small airport in the village of Krupa, about 10 km south-east of the centre, with some rare flights to major domestic destinations. There are three to four buses a day to/from Lviv (four hours), six a day to/from Rivne (1½ hours) and to all surrounding destinations. Trains go daily to/from Lviv, Rivne, Kiev, Moscow, St Petersburg and Minsk.

The air and train ticket and information office is at vulitsya Striletska 2, just north of Teatralna ploshcha. The bus ticket and infor-

mation office is a block farther north on the opposite side of the street at No 23. Same day bus and train tickets usually have to be bought at the station.

Getting Around

The central area is eminently walkable. Bus No 8 and trolleybus Nos 4 and 7 from the railway station, about two km north-east of the centre, go to Teatralna ploshcha. You can walk the distance in about 20 minutes.

There are two bus stations in the city. The main bus station is on the other side of the tracks a bit farther east of the railway station. Trolleybus No 5 or 6 from there takes you to Teatralna ploshcha.

RIVNE

РІВНЕ

Population: 250,000

Rivne dates back to at least the 13th century. In the 18th and 19th centuries, though officially in Russia at the time, it was the 'capital' of what was virtually the private kingdom of the Polish Lubomirsky family, which had its own army. Their palace was burnt down in 1927. During WW II the Germans used the city as their administrative capital in Ukraine, and it was thoroughly destroyed as a result of fierce fighting. Today it's a city of little interest and aesthetic value but may serve as a stopover on the way to some smaller historical towns nearby.

Rivne's telephone code is 0362.

City Centre

The city centre, east of the Ustie River which cuts through Rivne from south to north, has a lot of pleasant parkland along both banks of the river. Its main street is vulitsya Soborna, running roughly east-west, with **maydan Nezalezhnosti**, halfway down, as the main square. A promenade occupies the northern half of the square behind the Teatr Ukraina. The pretty 1895 **Resurrection Cathedral** (formerly the atheism museum) at vulitsya Soborna 39, off the southern end of the square, has seven small golden onion domes and five cupolas. Farther west down vulitsya Soborna is the large neoclassical

Music & Drama Theatre, recessed from the street in front of a wide plaza.

At vulitsya Drahomanov 19, south from maydan Nezalezhnosti, down vulitsya 16 Lypnya and then right, there's the **Regional Ethnographic Museum** housed in a former gymnasium built in 1839, open daily except Monday. The **Victims of Fascism monument**, a few km west of the centre on Belaya vulitsya, is on the site of a concentration camp where the Nazis killed about 80,000 people. Bus Nos 2 and 4 and trolleybus No 1 from vulitsya Soborna go there.

Places to Stay & Eat

The *Hotel Mir* (☎ 22 13 35), is central, off the north-eastern end of maydan Nezalezhnosti, at vulitsya Mitskevycha 32. It's the best place in town, with a decent ground-floor café and a restaurant where live bands play at night. Rooms cost US$7/10 a single/double.

Right next to the bus station at vulitsya Kyivska 36 is the *Hotel Tourist* (☎ 6 74 13). The staff aren't accommodating and it's nowhere near as nice as the Hotel Mir, but its rooms are available for about the same price.

Between the railway station and the Hotel Mir at prospekt Mira 10 is the *Restoran Rivne*, with coffee and sweets on the 1st floor, a bar on the 2nd, and a lively restaurant on the 3rd with loud music and decent food.

Getting There & Away

The airport, seven km from the centre on the Lviv road, may have weekly flights to/from most major domestic destinations, if the fuel shortage hasn't closed things down.

There are frequent bus services to all outlying towns and larger cities, including six daily buses to Lutsk (1½ hours), Ostroh (1½ hours) and Ternopil (four hours via Kremenets).

Rivne is also on some major long-distance north-south train lines. There are around three trains daily to/from Kiev (7½ hours), Lviv (four to six hours) and St Petersburg (20-23 hours). Daily train services include Odessa (16 hours), Simferopol (22 hours), Ivano-Frankivsk (nine hours), Riga (21 hours), Chernivtsi (11 hours) and Minsk (10 hours).

Getting Around

Bus No 9 runs between the railway station and the airport, via the Hotel Mir and the central section of vulitsya Soborna. You can walk from the railway station to the Hotel Mir and maydan Nezalezhnosti by simply walking south-east down prospekt Mira for about one km.

The bus station is about two km east from maydan Nezalezhnosti on vulitsya Soborna which becomes vulitsya Kyivsky. Trolleybus No 3 or bus No 7 run the three stops between.

OSTROH
ОСТРОГ

Some 46 km south from Rivne, the small town of Ostroh is one of the oldest settlements in Ukraine, dating from 1100. The town's main claim to fame is its cultural and educational heyday in the 16th century when a Greek/Latin/Slavic collegium and printing centre was established here to rival the Polish/Roman establishments in the West. Today it's an innocuous little town, but it does have an impressive, although small, fortress complex along with two excellent museums. Nearby is the fortified monastery of Mezhyrich and the surrounding countryside is pleasant rolling hills, which can make for a relaxed day trip or stopover if you're heading south from Rivne.

Ostroh's telephone code is 03654.

Fortress

Known as the 'Zamkova Hora' (Castle Hill), the present 14th to 19th-century fortress complex was built on the hilltop site of an older 11th to 12th-century settlement. It's entered from a park through a 1905 gate tower. The gracious 15th-century **Bohayevayenska Church**, rebuilt in the lofty Ukrainian Byzantine style 300 years later, dominates the peaceful grounds. In the south-eastern corner is a squat 1386 medieval tower remodelled with Renaissance features in the 15th century, including the heavy band of crenulation around the top. The opposite corner of the complex is occupied by a small 16th-century **palace**, rebuilt in the 19th century, which has formidable buttresses spilling over the hillside below. Inside is the regional **Ethnographic & Historic Museum**, open from 9 am to 4.30 pm, closed from 11 am to 1 pm and on Mondays. The surly guards that occupy the shack behind the church will let you in, even if they don't make you feel comfortable. Inside, on three levels (enter the lower level first), is a surprisingly good variety of displays documenting the town's rich history, including a model of the town as it looked 900 years ago.

Town

Very little is left of the formidable fortification system that once surrounded the town. Across the park, west of the fortress, is the 15th-century **Uspensky Church**. Formerly part of a Dominican monastery, it was rebuilt in the 19th century in neoclassical style. A block north, the 15th to 16th-century **Lutsk Gate Tower**, up some steps from near the corner of vulitsya Lutska and vulitsya Nezalezhnosti, is now the **History of Books & Printing Museum**, open daily except Monday from 9 am to 4.30 pm, closed between noon and 2 pm. Among many lavish old books is a tiny old Slavonic alphabet book from 1578 and a copy of the famous 1581 'Ostroh Bible', the first Bible to be printed in the old Slavic language by Ivan Federov, as well as the 17th-century 'Ostrov Chronicles', a history book of Volyn and Galicia between the 16th and 17th centuries. A block east on vulitsya Tatarska is the crumbling 15th-century **Tatar Bastion**.

Mezhyrich

Roughly four km south of Ostroh on the road to Kremenets is the pretty village of Mezhyrich with the impressive and formidable **Holy Trinity Monastery Fortress**. The complex, off the main road and behind a duck pond, is surrounded by walls with four octagonal towers. The inner church has Gothic detailing with Byzantine domes and dates from the 15th century. The two adjacent monastic wings with their four pointed towers and Renaissance portals are 200 years older. The complex now houses an Orthodox Seminary with lots of friendly, long-haired students fixing things up who would be eager to show you around. The inside of the church has some important old icons and moving frescoes with deep colours; the iconostasis is carved wood from the 18th century.

Places to Stay & Eat

There's one hotel in town, the *Hotel Viliya* (☎ 5 82 60) at vulitsya Nezalezhnosti 5 with rooms for US$5/10 a single/double. Inside is the spartan *Kafe Zatychok*. A better bet for drinks is the tiny *Kafe Hrot* across the street, and for food the *Restoran Ostroh* a block east.

Getting There & Away

The nearest railway station is 14 km north, so take one of the at least six daily buses to/from Rivne, 1½ hours away. There are also a few daily buses to/from Ternopil, Kremenets, Shepetivka, Izyaslav and Dubno.

Getting Around

The main street is vulitsya Nezalezhnosti, which runs from the small bus station two km east to the centre; connecting buses are rare, but the walk is not bad. The fortress is in a park a block south of the centre, uphill off vulitsya Akademichna.

To get to Mezhyvich walk down vulitsya Na Kremenets, the main road running off the centre of vulitsya Nezalezhnosti (across from the Lutsk Tower) and leading south out of town towards Kremenets. It's four km away with rare bus connections but like George you could easily catch a ride there on a horse cart and a ride back on a tractor.

UKRAINE

Ternopil Region
Тернопільська област

KREMENETS
КРЕМЕНЕЦЬ

Population: 25,000

Kremenets, located beside a picturesque and narrow wooded valley, is one of the nicest small towns in Ukraine, with a lot of history. Its proximity to the Pochayiv Monastery makes it a pleasant and relaxing stopover or a day trip from Ternopil.

Ever since a stone castle was built in the 12th century, high up on a hill overlooking the town, there have been fights over who controls it. It was the site of a fierce battle in 1226 when a Tatar attack was repulsed by Slavic warriors in 1240. After a long period of Polish rule, it was stormed and taken by Cossack forces in 1648. When Poland regained control they recruited the Jesuits to build a cathedral and collegium in the town below. In 1795 the town became part of Russia, developing in the late 19th century when the railroad arrived.

Town
The main road through town is vulitsya Shevchenko. The bulk of the old town is uphill and a block to the west around the former 1731-43 **Jesuit Cathedral**, which was converted into the Kremenets Lyceum in 1805. It is now being restored back into a church. A beautiful and worn stone balustrade leads up to the fine Baroque façade with a courtyard beside the central dome around the back. The former **Jesuit collegium** complex is a block south along vulitsya Drahomanova, on the corner of vulitsya Slovatskoho. Uphill on vulitsya Slovatskoho is the **Slovatsky library**, the former house of the Polish poet Juliusz Słowacki. Across the street are peaceful 1806 botanical gardens which stretch up from the collegium.

Still farther up vulitsya Slovatskoho and along your first left (south) a quaint street winds to the top of a stadium and wooden ski jump in the distance.

Just downhill and directly across the main vulitsya Shevchenko from the Jesuit Cathedral is **St Nicholas Cathedral** (1636). The fancy blue and white Baroque façade along the street is actually the gateway bell tower, through which you enter into a narrow courtyard and the church beyond.

Two blocks south at vulitsya Shevchenko 30 is a **Polish Catholic church**. The stone gateway leads around the back to a small wooden church leaning with old age.

Just under one km north of the centre along vulitsya Shevchenko towards the bus station is the excellent **Kremenets Regional Museum**, open from 9 am to 5 pm daily except Wednesday. Inside are lots of displays covering the town's history from the Cossack and Polish battles to the Nazi massacre in the village of Shpykolisy (six km south of Kremenets) on 14 July 1943. According to Ukrainian documents, about 300 men, women and children were killed and over 240 houses burned as a reprisal for partisan attacks nearby.

Next to the museum is the 1760 **Bohoyavlensky Monastery**. For a while it was a school, now it's once again an Orthodox convent. The exquisite blue and white bell tower and gateway are a fine example of late 19th-century Ukrainian Baroque. Still farther south and across the street is the oldest church in town, the 16th-century toy-like, painted, wooden **Church of the Faithful Christ**.

Pyatnytske Cemetery
Known as the **Kozatske Kladovyshche** (Cossack cemetery), this cemetery, on a small hill overlooking the Bohoyavlensky Monastery, is the grave site of Kozaks who died in 1646 liberating the town from the Poles. About 100 small, weathered stone crosses are scattered about, a few with faint old Slavonic inscriptions still visible. Walking north (towards the bus station) from the centre, take the first right off vulitsya Shevchenko past the town market. Bear left when the road forks and it will be on your

UKRAINE

left-hand side after about a 10-minute walk uphill to the north-east.

Castle

Slightly marred by the presence of a TV antenna, the hilltop fortress offers panoramic views over the town and the surrounding picturesque countryside. On a clear day you can see the sparkle of the distant Pochayiv Monastery on a hilltop 25 km to the southwest. The castle was first constructed in the 12th century and its wooden fortifications were replaced by stone 150 years later. Today there is only a ring of walls and a gate tower with a plaque commemorating the words of Tatar Khan Batu when he realised his attack on the castle in 1240 was bound for defeat.

To get to the castle take one of the roads leading up the hillside and follow it uphill well south of the castle before you turn sharp left (north). There are smaller, steeper paths that are quicker. If you get confused ask someone for 'fzamok'.

Places to Stay & Eat

There's one shabby hotel in town that may or may not take you. George had to get his passport stamped by the passport office on vulitsya Ulasa Samuchka, around the corner from the Polish Catholic church before they'd take him. If you're allowed, the *Hotel Kyiv* (☎ 2 23 72) at vulitsya Shevchenko 57 has rooms for US$4 per person but the bathrooms down the hall are disgusting. It's best to get into town early and work things out.

Across the street from the hotel at vulitsya Shevchenko 39 is a stylish little café. The *Bufet Khvylynka*, upstairs in the kafe Ikva building at vulitsya Shevchenko 75, serves heaped plates for less than a dollar. The more established *Kremenets Restoran* is across the street and south of the morning fruit and vegetable market, which is behind a small green gate at vulitsya Shevchenko 59.

Getting There & Away

Kremenets is off the beaten path, but it's on a main north-south road with all buses going south from Lutsk or Rivne to Ternopil passing through. Even the Moscow-Istanbul bus somehow stumbles through.

There are about 10 daily buses to/from Ternopil (1½ hours), six a day to/from Rivne (2½ hours) and seven daily to/from Pochayiv (30 minutes), with one bus a day to Lutsk, Lviv, Kiev and Ivano-Frankivsk.

As it's at the end of an infrequently used train line, there are few passenger trains coming in.

Getting Around

The bus station is about 2.5 km north of the centre on vulitsya Shevchenko. There are bus stops along the way, and any bus going in that direction from the bus station will take you there. Many people hitch rides. The railway station is still a few km farther north on vulitsya Shevchenko.

POCHAYIV

ПОЧАЇВ

The monastery in Pochayiv (Pochayivska Lavra), 25 km south-west of Kremenets and 75 km north of Ternopil, is the second-largest Orthodox pilgrimage monastery complex in Ukraine after the Caves Monastery in Kiev. It was supposedly founded by monks who escaped the monastery in Kiev after a Tatar raid in 1240. The 1597 Mother of God icon is thought to have miraculous powers and is attributed with having saved the monastery from a Turkish attack in 1675. In 1730 control of the monastery switched to the Ukrainian Catholics, then Russian Orthodox in 1831, before being recently switched over to the Ukrainian Orthodox Church.

The site is sacred to all devout Ukrainians and is flooded with pilgrims during religious festivals, most notably during the Feast of the Assumption on August 28, and the Feast of St Job on September 10. It's a peaceful place evoking the strange mixture of mystery and ambience associated with holy sites. Numerous pilgrims mumble, pray, and camp out. Most are tiny old ladies dressed in black with rucksacks and walking sticks. Most buildings are closed during the day, except for special excursions. Services begin daily

UKRAINE

Ukrainian people

Ukrainian people

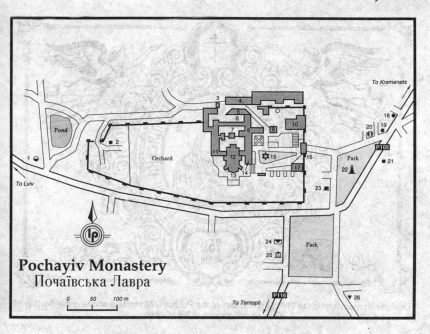

Pochayiv Monastery
Почаївська Лавра

To Kremenets

To Lviv

To Ternopil

Pond

Orchard

Park

Park

P105

P116

0   50   100 m

PLACES TO STAY

4   Former Seminary
      Building
      Бувший будинок
      семинарі

2   Pochayiv Monastery
      Hotel
      Готель Свято-Успенської
      Почаївської Лаври

21   Hotel Pochayiv
      Гостинниця Почаїв

5   Bathrooms
      Лазнички

6   Refectory Courtyard
      Трапезна

7   Inner Chapel
      Внуршня каплиця

PLACES TO EAT

8   Monks' Cells
      Келії монахів

23   Bar, Café, Restaurant
      & Ice-Cream Parlour
      Бар, Кафе, Перекуска
      та Морожене

9   Bell Tower
      Дзвінниця

10   Holy Trinity Cathedral
      Собор Пресвятої Троїци

26   Restaurant
      Ресторан

11   Troyitska Church
      Троїцька церква

12   Uspensky Cathedral
      Успенський собор

OTHER

13   View Terrace
      Вид з тераси

1   Bus Station
      Автобусний вокзал

14   Gift Shop
      Магазин подарунків

3   Rear Gate
      Задня брама

15   Well Garden
      Сад з студнею

16   Main Entrance Gate
      Головний вхід

17   Bishop's Palace
      Єпископський палац

18   Market
      Ринок

19   Seminary Building
      Будинок семінарії

20   Bank
      Банк

22   Bohdan Khmelnytsky
      Statue
      Пам'ятник Богдану
      Хмельницькому

24   Post Office
      Пошта

25   Regional Museum
      Районовий музей

UKRAINE

Design commemorating the 750th anniversary of the Pochayiv Monastery showing the 'Mother of God' and 'Footprint of Mary' icons

at 5 pm and visitors are free to wander into the main churches at this time.

Pochayiv's telephone code is 03546.

Uspensky Cathedral

The main Uspensky Cathedral (1771-83) is an overwhelming Baroque affair. Its interior, able to hold over 6000 people, is one endless expression of Orthodox iconography. Have a good look around – nearly every surface is lavishly and masterfully painted and gilded with saints and patriarchs. The side aisles have interesting oculi which look up into the upper galleries. Several relics and icons – including the famed 'footprint of Mary'– and 'healing waters' (on the right-hand side of the central nave) attract lines of faithful. Wave after wave of old and young line up to kiss the imprint and gulp a cup of water poured by a bored looking priest. The relics of St Job and the miraculous icon of the Mother of God are at the far end of the right-hand aisle. Monk dormitories stretch out north from the cathedral.

Holy Trinity Cathedral

Built over 100 years earlier, the simple Holy Trinity Cathedral (1649), with a golden dome is smaller and has a different atmosphere. The interior is dark and evocative with massive pillars and thick vaults beneath a deep cupola. Where the Uspensky Cathedral attempts to portray the splendour of God, the Holy Trinity Cathedral evokes the mystery of the Orthodox divinity. Note the large candelabra.

Bell Tower

Directly west of the Holy Trinity Cathedral is the 65-metre-tall Baroque bell tower, built in 1861-71. Sneak in with a tour group or a monk and climb to the top for the view and a look at the massive 100-year-old bell, weighing 11 tons and almost three metres in diameter. The central knocker itself weighs over 315 kg.

Monastery Grounds

The monastery grounds are extremely peaceful and reflective. The main garden area has plenty of benches and trees with a spigot that offers cool refreshing water. Just south of the entrance gate is the 1825 **Bishop's Palace**. The terrace in front of the Uspensky Cathedral dishes out expansive views over the sprawling farming village and surrounding countryside.

Regional Museum

There's a regional museum off the west side of the park, just past the post office, which was closed at the time of writing.

Places to Stay & Eat

The *Hotel Pochayiv* is not 'officially' open to foreigners but you can try. Otherwise you can stay for US$2 per night in the *Pochayiv Monastery Hotel*, run by a few nuns, at the far western end of the monastery complex; it's often occupied by visiting priests. They offer communal rooms with six to seven beds. There are two rooms for men downstairs and rooms for women upstairs. But there are some drawbacks: the hotel is closed daily during services, which are usually from 4 to 10 pm, and on Sundays until 11 pm. No place in the tiny village stays open that late so you'll either have to loiter within the cathedral, following the throngs from one shrine to another amidst the sacred theatrics, or hang out around the grounds. It may get cold so dress accordingly. Also, you may be awakened between 5 and 6 am by non-obligatory morning prayer, which is conducted in front of the icon hanging in the corner of each room. Don't choose the bed beneath the icon. All in all It's an unique experience.

Often the nuns will give you a delicious meal, but if you stay in the hotel, you're entitled to a hot and tasty afternoon feed at the monastery's refectory. The small street branching south just outside the monastery has a row of establishments – a bar, a café, a small restaurant and an ice-cream parlour. Off the south side of the park is a restaurant that may be closed. A tiny market around the corner from the seminary building east of the monastery can offer fruit.

Getting There & Away

The small bus station is just west of the monastery grounds, not far from the monastery hotel. There are at least seven daily buses to/from Kremenets (40 minutes), four daily to/from Ternopil (two hours), six daily to Brody (from where you can transfer to Rivne or Lutsk), and one daily to Lviv. Often tickets are only sold shortly before the bus arrives and the station closes in the late evening.

TERNOPIL
ТЕРНОПІЛЬ

Population: 230,000

Dating from 1549, and founded on the site of an earlier 14th-century fortress, Ternopil was always a historic crossroads. Despite being destroyed many times throughout its history, taking an especially heavy toll in WW II, a few nice churches and a small but pleasant centre still remain. Ternopil is a good stopover, and a strategic base for exploring some of the smaller historic towns nearby.

Orientation & Information

Vulitsya Hetmana Sahayoachnoha is Ternopil's pedestrian artery running east-west, connecting the Hotel Ternopil and maydan Voli, a park to the west, with bulvar T Shevchenko to the east near the main railway station. Vulitsya Ruska is the city's main thoroughfare and runs parallel with vulitsya Hetmana Sahayoachnoha 200 metres to the south.

The main source of tourist information is the front desk of the Hotel Ternopil, used to catering to tour groups. The main post and telephone office is 200 metres west of the main railway station straight down vulitsya Zaliznychna on the corner with vulitsya Kopernika, in front of a small narrow park.

The Hotel Ternopil can change money as

will the bank on the north side of maydan Voli in front of the hotel.

Ternopil's telephone code is 0352.

City Centre

The **Dominican church & monastery** off the north-east corner of maydan Voli is the city's finest silhouette. Built in the mid-18th century, its twin towers rise from a Baroque façade. Halfway down vulitsya Hetmana Sahayoachnoha, opposite a fountain, vulitsya Valova leads south through a vaulted gateway onto vulitsya Ruska and the **Rizdva Khrystovoho Church**. Recent reconstruction has altered the original 17th-century appearance. The small interior is an explosion of gilded colour.

Bulvar Taras Shevchenko, the town's leafy showpiece and popular hang-out is a nice venue for a stroll, with landscaping and fountains. At its northern end is the neoclassical **Shevchenko Theatre** where, amidst a sculptural ensemble of worker and peasant revelry on the pediment, is the familiar 'face behind the moustache'.

Behind the Hotel Ternopil is a bit of parkland on the lakeside with views across the water to bland post-war development and more parkland beyond. South-west of the Hotel Ternopil, near the water's edge, is the small 450-year-old **Zavyzhenska Church**, the city's oldest church entirely reconstructed after being shut for over 45 years. It is referred to as the 'Church on the Pond', as it's supposedly where Khmelnytsky prayed with his gang of Cossacks before his infamous battle against the Polish king Casimir II near Zboriv in 1649, 35 km north-west of Ternopil.

Regional Museum

The Regional Museum on vulitsya Zatserkovna, housed in an ugly modern building, is one of the best in the country. Skip the stuffed animals on the ground floor and go to the upper two floors which are full of impressive historic and ethnographic displays along with the usual section on WW II. It's open daily from 10 am to 5.45 pm, closed Monday and Wednesday. To get there, walk south 100 metres from the Rizdva Khrystoroho Church on the corner of vulitsya Ruska and vulitsya Zatserkovna.

Places to Stay & Eat

The *Hotel Ternopil* (☎ 2 42 63) at vulitsya Zamkova 14, on the west side of maydan Voli, is friendly and central with comfortable rooms costing US$12/20 a single/double. An exchange office and small gift stand are in the lobby. To the right of the hotel entrance is the fairly elegant hotel restaurant with good full meals of Ukrainian and standard fare for about US$3 to US$4.

On the opposite side of the lake, one km west of the centre, is the tall *Hotel Halychyna* (☎ 3 53 94) at vulitsya Zaozerna 3, which is similar in service and price, but is in a worse location.

The ageing and elegant *Hotel Ukraina* on the north-east corner of bulvar Shevchenko isn't open to foreigners, but its faded restaurant will serve anyone.

Around the east end of vulitsya Hetmana Sahayoachnoha, before bulvar Shevchenko, are a number of cafés. The pricey but delightful café/restaurant *Uropa* has tables and chairs out in the street – rare in Ukraine. Across the street the *Kafe Muza* sells plastic bowls of ice cream with fruit topping.' Around the corner to your right on bulvar Shevchenko is the *Kafe Pyrizhkova*, a typical cafeteria-style eatery serving hot plates of vareniky, soup and salad.

Getting There & Away

Air The Ternopil airport is 10 km east of the centre on the main road to Khmelnytsky with weekly flights to domestic locations when fuel is available. For Air Ukraine information call ☎ 2 36 47.

Bus The destinations reached by bus from Ternopil are: Kremenets (seven a day), Ivano-Frankivsk (five), Pochayiv (three), Kamyanets-Podilsky (three), Chernivtsi (four), Chortkiv (four) and Buchach (three). The bus station is about one km south of the centre; trolleybus No 9 or bus No 20 go to the centre.

Train Almost all east-west trains between Eastern Europe and Kiev pass through Ternopil. About eight daily trains go to/from Lviv (three hours), about four to/from Kiev (nine hours), and five to/from Moscow (30 hours). There's one train a day to/from Odessa (13 hours), Simferopol (17 hours), Kharkiv (11 hours), Chernivtsi (four to five hours), Prague (25 hours), and Warsaw (every other day – 27 hours). From the railway station, which is more organised and cleaner than most, walk west on vulitsya Zaliznychna for two blocks until you get to bulvar Shevchenko and the centre of town.

BEREZHANY
БЕРЕЖАНИ

Population: 50,000

Berezhany is a picturesque small town with a provincial atmosphere in the heartland of Western Ukraine. It is 52 km west of Ternopil and lies beside the Zoloma River, surrounded by rolling hills. Dating from the 14th century, the town played a major role in the Polish-Ukrainian wars, its fortified castle being the centre of power in the region.

Berezhany's telephone code is 03548.

Castle
From the bus station cross the street and walk due west for about 300 metres. The 1554 castle, designed and built by Italian masons is in a wooded park on your right. The nicest part of the surrounding walls is the south-eastern, rounded bastion with a row of blind arcading. Within the grassy compound are the ruins of the palace, in the south-eastern corner, but the real gem is the abandoned **Troyitsky Church** built in 1554. The exterior still has beautiful stone carvings but much more impressive is the interior ornamentation in the two domed side chapel mausoleums. The one on the right has two crumbling black marble altars and a ceiling covered with sculptured carvings. The level of detail is comparable to the Boyim chapel in Lviv, but it's in a sad state of disrepair.

Other Things to See
Continue west from the castle into the central ploshcha Rynok, which is the heart of the town. The 1811 town hall in the centre houses the **Municipal Museum**, open daily from 10 am to 5 pm, closed Wednesday. It has a nice model of the castle among its displays. Off the courtyard is a small **Book Museum**. Dominating the western side of the square near the Shevchenko statue is the large, Baroque **Trinity Catholic Church**, built in 1768 with twin dome-capped bell towers. Behind it, two blocks to the west, is a small stone **Armenian church**, abandoned and locked. A block uphill and south of the square is the 1600 Gothic **Rizdva Bohorodytsi Church** and 1741 bell tower, now housing a primary school.

The 17th-century **St Nicholas Church** and former Benedictine monastery is one km north of the centre. The communists made it into a prison, which became notorious. Today it is a prison for juveniles. Farther north are two small lakes in a fertile valley.

Places to Eat
On a south corner of ploshcha Rynok is the *restaurant Halychanka*. On the opposite side of the square is a tea café and the *Zolota Lipa* restaurant. Just east and back from the square is an outdoor market.

Getting There & Away
Buses run to/from Lviv (2½ hours; five to six daily), Ternopil (1½ hours; about 10 daily) and Ivano-Frankivsk (2½ hours; three daily). The bus station is about one km east of the centre.

CHORTKIV
ЧОРТКІВ

Population: 55,000

Chortkiv, along the Seret River 76 km south of Ternopil, is a bustling town with an active and colourful market centre. It dates from 1522 and was a border point under Turkish, Polish and Austrian rule with plenty of Cossack and peasant uprisings in between. In 1919, during the Ukrainian revolution, the town was the site of a crucial counter attack by Ukrainian forces against the Polish army.

Chortkiv's telephone code is 03552.

UKRAINE

Things to See

The compact centre is highlighted by the tall, brick, pseudo-Gothic 18th-century **Polish Catholic church** on the corner of vulitsya Shevchenka and vulitsya Mitskevycha. Its stately appearance is dominated by an eclectic bell tower and the interior has a series of attractive stone columns. A tiny cluster of streets and alleys spills down to the 19th-century **market hall** to the east which occupies two levels with a barn-like corner clock tower. Busy vulitsya Rynok, a broad street to the south, leads to another outdoor market place.

North of the centre, vulitsya Lomonosova leads across the Seret River where your second right branches off past an Orthodox church to the 1610 remains of the private **castle/residence** of the Potosky family. Within the walls is the unlikely site of a shabby fuel depot, supposedly to be moved elsewhere. Continuing north for about one km on Lomonosova will lead to the railway station. En route is the 1717 **Voznesenska (Ascension) Church**, its original wooden exterior better than its remodelled interior.

Two blocks south-east of the centre, the new, wooden **Uspensky Church** and bell tower were rebuilt in the likeness of a former 1635 church previously on the site. The **Regional Museum**, closed on Wednesdays, is a block west on vulitsya Zelena and is not one of the best.

Places to Stay & Eat

The *Sputnyk Hotel* (☎ 2 13 72) at vulitsya Shevchenka 34, off the large open square just south of the centre, can put you up in a dirty little room for about US$2 per person, with bathrooms down the hall. The *Vareniky* eatery at vulitsya Mitskevicha 8, between the Polish Catholic church and the market hall, serves platefuls of hot, tasty but starchy food for a pittance. The upstairs *Dnister* restaurant on vulitsya Shevchenka, just south of the Polish Catholic church, is a bit more upmarket. Fresh fruit and vegies can easily be bought on the upper floor of the market hall or from the outdoor market just a block south off vulitsya Rynok.

Getting There & Away

More buses ply through town than trains, but unfortunately the bus station is a 20-minute, two-km walk uphill south from the centre. From the bus station, rather than following the main exhaust-filled road down into town, cut across the road and make your way downhill, passing an old Jewish graveyard along the way. The former **synagogue** is on vulitsya Shevchenka on the way into town. Any bus continuing past the bus station is going to stop in the centre.

About five buses a day go to Ternopil, Chernivtsi and Ivano-Frankivsk (via Buchach).

The sleepy railway station is on the northern side of town, across the river and at the far end of vulitsya Lomonosova. One train a day runs to Chernivtsi, Odessa and Simferopol. Three trains a day run to Ternopil. You can get your hair cut while waiting for the train.

BUCHACH
БУЧАЧ
Population: 15,000

Strung out along a narrow wooded valley straddling the Strypa River 70 km south of Ternopil and 30 km west of Chortkiv, the pretty town of Buchach dates from 1397. It has been controlled at different times through its history by Ukrainians, Poles, Tatars and Turks. It's an effort to get to, but it provides a pleasant glimpse into small-town Ukraine. You are sure to be the only tourist passing through.

Buchach's telephone code is 03544.

Things to See

The centre of the town is the small square around the 18th-century **town hall**, one of the most extravagant pieces of civil architecture of its day. Created by the same architect who designed St George Cathedral in Lviv, it's a highly ornate box with a stylised Baroque tower rising 35 metres from its midst. On the square, just down from the Shevchenko statue, is a small gallery and **Ethnographic Museum**. A block west of the square is the 1763 **Uspensky Catholic**

Church, a formidable structure behind a gateway and stone wall. The first street to the right of the church eventually leads up to the ruins of a 14th to 16th-century **castle**, overlooking the river and town below.

Vulitsya Mitskevycha heads south from the town hall, across the river and up to the 1753-70 **Basilian monastery** complex. The main church is simple Baroque with tall bell towers seen from afar. Up a hill and a flight of steps on the opposite, northern, side of the town hall is the 1610 wooden **Mykolayivska Church**, the oldest building in town.

North-west of the town hall on vulitsya Halytska is the *Zamok Restoran*. East of the town hall is a small café on a corner and to the right of the museum. You'll pass the market on the right just before you reach the town hall from the bus station.

Getting There & Around

There are about four daily buses to Ivano-Frankivsk and Ternopil. There are also two buses a day to Chernivtsi (via Chortkiv). The bus station is about two km outside the centre. From the bus station, turn left (south) and walk downhill past the train tracks, following the road as it turns right and over the river, becoming vulitsya Halytska. Continue west for another km to the centre and town hall.

Chernivtsi Region
Чернівецка область

CHERNIVTSI
ЧЕРНІВЦІ
Population: 263,000

Chernivtsi (formerly Czernowitz), like most of Western Ukraine, wasn't drawn into the Russian sphere until WW II. It has a Central European appearance as a result of it having been for 140 years an outpost of the Habsburg Empire. Its mixed history has bestowed upon it a wide variety of architectural styles, from Byzantine to Baroque, and the elegant streets of its old quarter are lined with grand façades. Before WW II, the city was cosmopolitan with large Jewish, Armenian and German minorities – an atmosphere that remains to some degree today, giving the place a more southern and relaxed feel than most Ukrainian cities. It's definitely worth a visit. It is pedestrian friendly and best seen on foot.

History

Chernivtsi was the chief city of Bukovina (Beech Tree Land), the northernmost part of old Moldavia. In the 12th century it was a southern fortress outpost of the Galician-Volynian Principality. Later, in the 15th century, it was fought over by Lithuania and the Ottoman Turks who were vying for control of Moldavia. The Turks eventually succeeded and Moldavia became an Ottoman vassal. Bukovina was then part of the Habsburg Empire, from 1775 to the end of WW I, after which it was tossed into an enlarged Romania. In 1940, as a result of the Molotov/Ribbentrop carve-up of Eastern Europe the previous year, northern Bukovina including Chernivtsi was taken over by the USSR. Southern Bukovina remains part of Romania.

Orientation & Information

Chernivtsi is on the Prut River, but the centre is a good three km south of the river. The old core surrounds Tsentralna ploshcha, the city's main hub with most everything you'll want to see within easy walking distance. The main post office is at vulitsya Khydyakova 6, a block north of Tsentralna ploshcha. The telephones are a block south at vulitsya Universytetska. You'll probably have better luck making any long-distance phone call from the lobby of the Hotel Cheremosh.

The Hotel Cheremosh also has a currency exchange office, and there's a bank on the south-east corner of Tsentralna ploshcha at No 3. There will probably be both an UKR and EximBank open in Chernivtsi before you arrive that will change travellers' cheques, but until then the only place that seems able to do this is the PromInvest Bank at vulitsya Holovna 205, just north of the bus

UKRAINE

Chernivtsi

Чернівці

0   0.5   1 km

PLACES TO STAY

11	Hotel Verkhovyna Гостинниця Верховина
27	Hotel Kiev Гостинниця Київ
35	Hotel Bukovina Гостинниця Буковина
36	Hotel Turist Гостинниця Турист
37	Hotel Cheremosh Гостинниця Черемош

PLACES TO EAT

16	Teatralny Kafe/Bar Театральне кафе/бар
18	Bakery Пекарня
19	Kafe Nadia Кафе Надія
20	Kafe/Bar Haleya Кафе/бар Галея
21	Restoran Dnister Ресторан Дністер
22	Restoran Chernivchanka Ресторан Чернівчанка
24	Kafe/Restoran Maestro Кафе/ресторан Маестро
26	Café Кафе

OTHER

1	Railway Station & Hotel Vokzal Залізничний вокзал та гостинниця Вокзал
2	University (former Metropolitan Palace) Університет
3	Parasvevya Church Церква Св. Параскеви
4	Old Market Hall Старий ринок
5	Philharmonia Філармонія
6	Polish Catholic Church Польский католицький костьол
7	Main Post Office Головна пошта
8	St Nicholas Church Церква Св. Миколи
9	St Nicholas Cathedral Собор Св. Миколи
10	Uspenska Ukrainian Catholic Church Успенська Українсько-католицка церква
12	Telephones Телефони
13	Main Regional Museum Головний краєзнавчий музей
14	Teatralna ploshcha Театральна площа
15	Music & Drama Theatre Театр музики та драми
17	City Hall Міська ратуша
23	Khudozhny Salon Shop Магазин Художній Салон
25	Armenian Cathedral, Organ & Concert Hall Вірменський собор, орг ан та концертна заля
28	Regional Museum Краєзнавчий музей
29	Red Army Monument Пам'ятник Червоній Армії
30	Orthodox Cathedral Православний собор
31	Market Ринок
32	Church Церква
33	Botanical Gardens Ботанічний сад
34	Litny Theatre Літній театр

station. The entrance is on the far left of the building (open Monday to Friday from 9.30 am to 1 pm).

For tourist information, check the facilities at the Hotel Cheremosh.

Chernivtsi's telephone code is 03722.

City Centre

Tree-lined **vulitsya O Kobylyanska**, named after the 19th to 20th-century writer and civil activist Olha Kobylyanska, with its many cafés, restaurants and shops, is the city's main pedestrian venue. Many of the Habsburg façades are completely vine-covered, giving the street an attractive and aged look. Peak into a number of courtyards (Nos 22, 23, 27), and a different, very Ottoman world opens up before you with wooden balconies and covered staircases. A branch of the

Regional Museum is at No 28, open from 9 am to 5 pm, closed Wednesday. A block farther south-east in the midst of a small park is an 1844 **Orthodox Cathedral** with three large cupolas and twin bell towers. The interior is undergoing major restoration, being turned from a museum back into a functioning church. Across vulitsya Holovna and curving west are two park-like blocks, leading to the busy ploshcha Soborna.

A block east of vulitsya O Kobylyanska is the former **Armenian Cathedral** (1869-75), its design based on ancient Armenian architecture featuring beautiful masonry detailing. Note the interesting flying buttressing off the side apses. Its meticulously painted interior has excellent acoustics, housing an Organ & Concert Hall since 1922.

UKRAINE

The northern end of vulitsya O Kobylyanska and vulitsya Holovna converge at the bustling Tsentralna ploshcha, the historic town centre, surrounded by attractive 19th-century buildings. The 1847 **City Hall** stands on the southern side. Across vulitsya Ivana Franka at Tsentralna ploshcha 10 is the main **Regional Museum** (open daily from 9 am to 5 pm except Monday). It is housed in a turn-of-the-century Art Nouveau building with a unique central staircase. Inside are 20th-century paintings and embroidery-rich ethnographic displays, with the top floor dedicated to the work of native artists.

North on vulitsya Holovna from Tsentralna ploshcha are two churches, the first is a **Polish Catholic church**, and a block north on a narrow corner is the **Parasvevya Church**. A block west in the centre of ploshcha Filharmonyi is an attractive **old market hall**, a bustling hive of buying, selling and yelling. Next to the market is a small green plot of land where old ladies sell flowers. West of the Polish Catholic church is the **Philharmonia** building, attractive but closed for renovation.

West of vulitsya Ivana Franka are a number of interesting smaller streets surrounding the sunk-in **Teatralna ploshcha**, a perfect place to relax with plenty of seating, roses, and nice views. At the western end of the square is the turn-of-the-century **Music & Drama Theatre**, a gift from the Habsburgs. It was designed in the De Stijl style by the same Viennese architects who designed the Opera House in Odessa.

Chernivtsi University

The architectural complex housing the former palatial residence of the Metropolitans of Bukovina is now the Chernivtsi University. It's a fantastic brick ensemble with pseudo-Byzantine, pseudo-Moorish and pseudo-Teutonic-looking palaces surrounding a small landscaped court. Designed in 1864-82 by Hlavka, the Czech architect who created the Armenian Cathedral on the other side of the city, it was heavily damaged and looted in WW II, and subsequently restored as the University. It's not a long walk, about 1.5 km north-west of the centre, but you can catch any trolleybus heading down vulitsya Universytetska.

Immediately to your left as you enter the gateway is the **Seminarska Church** and the former theological seminary, with an attractive arcaded garden courtyard. The church, with its elongated central cupola, is now used for concerts and ceremonies. The interior is strikingly ornamented in Byzantine fashion. On the opposite side of the complex is the main **University Building**, its central clock tower composed of a unique, staggering cluster of forms rising up to a central cupola. The building straight ahead as you first enter is the former main **palace** residence of the Metropolitans. It now houses the administration offices and is well worth a wander around. Two remarkable staircases are located in the far back corners. Walk up the one in the left corner and ask someone if you can see the '**Marmurovy Zal**', a fantastic salon surrounded by rows of two-tiered arcades with an intricately painted wooden ceiling. The 'Krasny Zal', where the rectors convene, also has an intricate wood-panelled ceiling. A small park lies behind the University complex.

Other Things to See

On vulitsya Ruska, about 1.5 km east of Tsentralna ploshcha past the Uspenksa Ukrainian Catholic Church halfway down, is **St Nicholas Cathedral**. With four twisted cupolas that make you think you're looking at an Escher painting, it's a 1930s copy of a 14th-century royal church in Curtea de Arges, Romania. The interior is another dark and mysterious Orthodox experience, this time with Assyrian-looking arches and interior columns with carved capitals. The small, wooden **St Nicholas Church** (1607) once stood a little way around the corner on vulitsya Sahaidachnoho. It was the oldest church in the city until a fire burned it down a few years ago. Slow reconstruction is taking place, giving you a chance to see some skilled axe-wielders perform their art. A few blocks farther east on vulitsya Ruska, the first left after a bridge is vulitsya Zelena which leads to a few interesting old cemeteries which are divided into nationalities. The huge Jewish cemetery, on the left about 750 metres down, has an old synagogue at its entrance and hundreds of carved and faded tombstones. At the far end of vulitsya Zelena and to your right, about 1.5 km past the cemetery, is the small 1783 wooden **Uspenska Church**.

Trolleybus No 4, which runs east down vulitsya Ruska from Tsentralna ploshcha, goes past St Nicholas Cathedral before eventually coming to a dead end at the open-air **folk architecture museum** (Muzey Arkhitekturi), which is open from 10 am to 6 pm daily, closed Monday. It's across the street from the trolley roundabout and camping ground. On site are two old windmills with wooden gears, a 220-year-old wooden church, and a few old cottages spread out over a sloping grassy meadow.

Park Kalinina, south of the centre, is a big plot of trees, benches and paths, popular for strolling. There are botanical gardens at its south-western edge, which are entered from vulitsya Federovycha, halfway along the park's edge.

Places to Stay

Camping Turbaza-Chernivtsi (☎ 2 50 37) is a nice camping ground with some landscaping and lots of trees. It's open from May 15 to October 1. They've got two and three-person bungalows for US$4 per person plus plenty of room to pitch your tent. There's even room for your car, plus a randomly open café on the premises. Reception is open from 9 am to 5 pm, so call ahead of time if you're arriving later. Trolleybus No 4 from Tsentralna ploshcha ends at the camping ground, which is across the street from the open-air folk architecture museum, slightly hidden by the trees. A trail through the trees near the camping ground leads to the attractive Paraskeve Yuriya church just to the east.

Hotel Turist (☎ 4 89 97) at vulitsya Chervonoarmiyska 184 is a typically ugly 1970s creation with the concrete already crumbling. The rooms are average and cost US$5/10 for a single/double.

The *Hotel Kiev* (☎ 2 24 88) at vulitsya Holovna 46 has the best location, smack in the centre, with a bit of faded charm but is in need of refurbishing. The rooms are decent but the service could be better. Rooms cost US$13/18 for a single/double with bath.

The *Hotel Verkhovyna* (☎ 2 27 23), off the north-eastern corner of Tsentralna ploshcha, and the *Hotel Bukovina* (☎ 3 86 15) at vulitsya Holovna 141, near the southern end of Park Kalinina, both insisted that they don't accept foreigners, but you can still try. They'll probably refer you to the Hotel Cheremosh.

The *Hotel Cheremosh* (☎ 4 87 77), in the unpleasant southern suburbs about 3.5 km outside the centre at vulitsya Komarova 13a, is one of the best of the former Intourist hotels in the country. It is modern and comfortable with excellent service and lots of amenities. Prices are a steep US$51/76 for a single/double, with an extra dollar for breakfast, payable only in hard currency. Trolleybus No 6 runs past the hotel from the central ploshcha Soborna.

There's also the *Hotel Vokzal* (☎ 9 24 70) in the railway station; the entrance is to the right at vulitsya Yuri Gagarina 38. With the barest minimum in comfort, service and facilities, singles/doubles/triples/quads run to about US$3 per person with the bathroom in the corridor.

Places to Eat

Each hotel, except for the Hotel Vokzal, has a restaurant. The *Cheremosh* also has a smaller café, quieter than the main restaurant which features live music nightly. The restaurant in the *Hotel Kiev* is semi-elegant and relaxing for lunch or an early dinner before the band starts up. The food is good and inexpensive.

The best restaurant in town is the tastefully decorated *Kafe/Restoran Maestro*, next to the Armenian Cathedral at vulitsya Ukrainska 30. The selection and quality of food is excellent and the service very polite. Try their borscht and pork cutlet for about US$4. The corner *Kafe Nadia* at vulitsya Ivana Franka 1 is the sort of relaxing, low-key

UKRAINE

place you always hope to find, with friendly service and a steaming samovar. They have a tasty three-course fixed menu for about US$3.

Along vulitsya O Kobylyanska are a few restaurants and cafés. At the northern end, No 4 is a bakery with fresh and hot sweet rolls. The *Kafe/Bar Haleya* serves good coffee and light food in a lively atmosphere. Across the street the *Restoran Dnister* on the corner looks to be a decent establishment. Farther down the *Restoran Chernivchanka* at No 22 has meat and potato dishes and live music some nights.

Entertainment

For classical entertainment see what's playing at the concert hall in the Armenian Cathedral on vulitsya Ukrainska, or in the Music & Drama Theatre on Teatralna ploshcha. The Philharmonia looks to be closed for renovation for some time. The outdoor Litny Theatre in Kalinina Park hosts a wide variety of performances during the summer.

Things to Buy

Khudozhny Salon, opposite the café with outdoor tables at vulitsya O Kobylyanska 22, is a good craft shop with attractive textiles. There's often an outdoor market around the kinateatr on the corner of vulitsya Universitetska and vulitsya Zamkovetska.

Getting There & Away

Air There are a limited number of domestic flights from the small airport south-east of the centre at vulitsya Chkalov 30 (☎ 4 32 21). They fly to Uzhhorod, Odessa, Lviv and Kiev. For flight information consult the former Air Ukraine office (☎ 006) at vulitsya Holovna 128.

Bus The bus station is at vulitsya Holovna 219, about four km south-east of the centre. At least two buses a day run between Chernivtsi and all the major West Ukrainian cities. Four to six daily buses run to/from Ivano-Frankivsk (2½ hours) and Ternopil three hours via Chortkiv), and at least eight daily run to/from Kamyanets-Podilsky (two hours), including the ones which go to Khmelnytsky.

Train The railway station is north and downhill from the centre (about 1.5 km) on smoggy vulitsya Yuri Gagarina. Chernivtsi is close to the rail border at Vadul-Siret (Romania). All trains heading to other Ukrainian destinations to the east, north-east or south-east pass, at least briefly, through Moldova. If you're going through to a Ukrainian destination, a Moldova visa isn't needed (see To/From Moldova under Land in the Ukraine Getting There & Away chapter).

There are two trains a day to/from Sofia (23 hours) and Moscow (27-31 hours), and at least four trains a day to/from Kiev (11-13 hours), stopping at Vinnytsya or Khmelnytsky along the way. Two to three daily trains run to/from Lviv (five hours), stopping in Ivano-Frankivsk (three to four hours). Daily trains also service Bucharest (11 hours), Chisinau (11-12 hours), Odessa (16 hours) and St Petersburg (40 hours). The only trains that stop in Kamyanets-Podilsky (two to three hours) are the trains going to Khmelnytsky, once or twice daily. To Kamyanets-Podilsky, the bus runs more frequently.

Getting Around

The trolleybuses are unbelievably crowded with lots of pushing and shoving. It's not often a pleasant experience and it's no time to be timid. Trolleybus No 3 runs along vulitsya Holovna between the bus station and the centre, continuing to the railway station. From the railway station it's a 15-minute walk to the centre, or you can hop on trolleybus No 3 or 5.

KHOTYN
ХОТИН
Population: 11,000

About 75 km from Chernivtsi, halfway along the road to Kamyanets-Podilsky, lies the small town of Khotyn, near the banks of the great Dnister River. The large, picturesque fortress whose massive walls loom high above the smooth water is well worth the stop if you have the time.

Khotyn Fortress

Originally built out of wood in the 12th century, it was rebuilt and strengthened over the years and replaced by stone in the 15th century. Its strategic location was critical in ensuring trade routes along the Dnister River, thus making it a well sought-after prize. First an outpost of the Galician-Volynian Principality, it was under the control of the Cossacks before the Poles took it over in the 15th century, only to be kicked out by the Turks the following century. The Russians finally took it over and partially destroyed it in the 19th century. Its greatest battle took place in 1621 when a unified Slav army, including a large Cossack contingency, defeated and thwarted a major Turkish invasion.

There usually aren't many people around, save for a few old cow herders and fishers near the river, so you can simply walk right over the elevated wooden bridge and begin exploring. Within the walls are a keep, a chapel, four towers (two round, two square), several ruined walls which once formed part of a commandant's palace, and some underground cellars. Many of the rooms in the keep look out over the Dnister River. The chapel has fantastic acoustics, carved tracery windows, and an attractive vaulted porch overlooking the courtyard. While walking around the grounds, watch out for holes that drop down to the cellars. Two staircases provide safer access. Take a stroll around the base of the walls and along the river to truly appreciate how impregnable the fortress was. Note the interesting brick pattern on the outside of the walls facing the hills opposite the river.

Getting There & Around

Since very few trains stop in Khotyn, you'll probably be arriving by bus. The fortress is about four km north of the bus station on the opposite side of town, on the riverbank. You can walk (about 45 minutes), hitchhike, or get lucky and hop aboard an infrequent public bus. From the bus station turn right and walk north down vulitsya Shevchenko, through the shabby market square and beyond, following the occasional sign that says 'Fortetsya'. Turn right after the road curves and head towards a statue in the distance. Walk past the statue, through the first set of walls and through to the other side for a spectacular view down across a grassy hillside towards the fortress, perched above the river. Uphill from the fortress is a beautiful 200-year-old blue domed **church**, with a small *restaurant/café* in between (don't expect it to be open).

There are at least five or six buses per day running between Chernivtsi and Kamyanets-Podilsky that stop in Khotyn, making it a feasible stopover for a few hours en route, if you leave very early. There seems to be no hotel in town, but a few tents were seen on the large grassy hillside behind the fortress.

Khmelnytsky Region
Хмельницька область

KAMYANETS-PODILSKY
КАМ'ЯНЕЦЬ-ПОДІЛЬСЬКИЙ

Population: 108,000

The old town of Kamyanets-Podilsky, 85 km north-east of Chernivtsi on the Khmelnytsky road, has stood since at least the 11th century on a sheer-walled rock 'island' carved out of the steppe by a sharp loop in the Smotrych River. The south-western bridge, which for centuries was the only link between the old town and the 'mainland', is guarded by a highly picturesque castle. In 1977, the old town was designated an architectural and historical reserve, with slow restoration taking place ever since. The combination of historic architecture and dramatic landscape is well worth a stop on your way to or from Chernivtsi.

UKRAINE

History

In the mid-11th century, Kamyanets-Podilsky was an important Kievan Rus

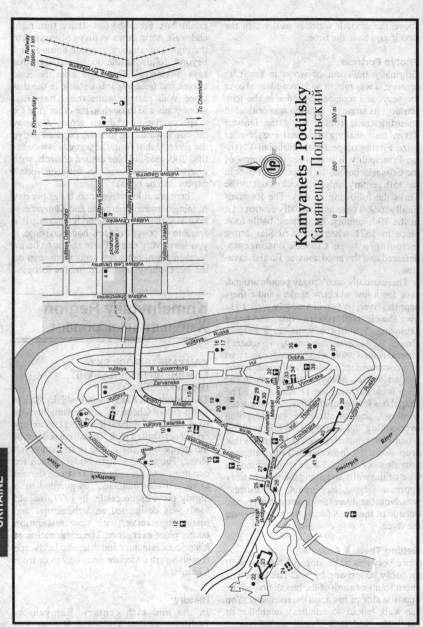

PLACES TO STAY

3 Hotel Smotrych
  Гостинниця Смотрич
4 Hotel Ukraina
  Гостинниця Україна

PLACES TO EAT

17 Restoran Stara Fortetsya
   Ресторан Стара Фортеця
26 Kafe Pid Bramoyu
   Каварня Під Брамою

OTHER

1 Bus Station
  Автобусний вокзал
2 Market
  Ринок
5 Brewery (Ruins)
  Пивзавод (руїни)
6 Vitryana Gate & Furriers' Tower
  Вітряна Брама та Кушнірська Вежа
7 Turkish Walls
  Турецькі стіни
8 First Commercial Bank Building
  Будинок Першого комерсійного банку
9 Church of SS Peter & Paul
  Петропавлівська церква
10 Building of First Russian Gymnasium
   Будинок першої Російської гимназії
11 Polish Gate
   Польска брама
12 Church of St George
   Церква Св. Юря
13 Franciscan Monastery
   Монастир Францисканів
14 Cathedral of SS Peter & Paul
   Кафедральний петропавлівський
   костьол
15 Restored Merchant Houses
   Відреставровані купецькі будинки
16 Black Tower
   Чорна вежа
18 Former Ukrainian & Polish Market Square
   Майдан колишнього Українсько
   Польського ринку
19 Town Hall with History Museum (now
   Ukrainian-Polish Magistry Building)
   Ратуша (Будинок
   Українсько-Польського магістрату)

20 Armenian Well
   Вірменський колодязь
21 Dominican Convent
   Монастир Домініканок
22 New Castle
   Новий замок
23 Castle
   Замок
24 Church of the Exhaltation of the Cross
   Хрестовоздвиженська церква
25 City Gate
   Міська Брама
27 Armenian Bastion
   Вірменський бастіон
28 Trinitarian Catholic Church
   Тринітарський костьол
29 Dominican Monastery & Church
   Домініканський монастир та костьол
30 Noblemen's Assembly Building
   Будинок дворянського зібрання
31 Orthodox Church Seminary Building
   (now the Picture Gallery)
   Будинок Православної Семинарії
   церква (тепер картинна галерея)
32 Church of St John the Baptist
   Церква Св. Іоанахрестителя
   (фундамент)
33 House of Armenian Clergymen
   Дім Вірменських священників
34 Armenian Church of St Nicholas & Bell
   Tower
   Миколаївська вірменська
   церква та дзвінниця
35 Slyusarska Tower
   Вежа Слюсарська
36 Kushnirska Tower
   Вежа Кушнірська
37 18th-century Armenian Houses
   Вірменські доми з XVIII
   століття
38 Church of the Annunciation
   Благовіщенська церква
39 Fortress Barracks
   Казарми фортеці
40 Southern Defensive Walls
   Південна оборонна брама та стіни
41 Ruska Gate
   Російська брама
42 Church of the Intercession
   Покровська церква

UKRAINE

settlement, on the main trade routes from Kiev south into the Balkans. Controlled by the Galician-Volynian Principality from the 12th to the 14th centuries, it briefly fell into Lithuanian hands before the Poles took it over in 1430. As it was a key southern border post of Poland for over two centuries, it was subjected to numerous attacks by Tatars, Moldavians and Ottoman Turks. It fell to a Turkish siege in 1672. In 1699 it was returned to Poland, but only after its churches had been looted. It then fell to the Russians in 1793, who used the castle as a prison for Ukrainian nationalists in the 19th century. It became the temporary capital of the brief Ukrainian National Republic in 1919. During WW II the Germans used the old town as an isolated 'ghetto', where an estimated 85,000 people died. During intensive fighting and air raids, 70% of the buildings in the old town were destroyed, giving parts of the area today, where once tightly packed buildings stood, a vacant feel.

Orientation & Information

The fortified old town is literally a rock island lassoed by a tight loop of the Smotrych River, accessed by two main bridges. One bridge to the west leads to the castle, and to the east another bridge leads to the 'new town', a Soviet-style street grid where you'll find the hotels and the majority of the population. Central vulitsya Koriatovychiv runs for about two km east-west through the new town, from the bus station in the far east, to the old town in the far west. A nice row of wooded parkland east of the river lies between the old and new towns. The railway station is about one km north of the bus station on vulitsya Pryvokzalna.

There's often a city historian working in the Cathedral of SS Peter & Paul who can arrange a private tour of the old town and castle, including a climb up the 145 steps to the top of the minaret. The narrow, illustrated *Kamyanets-Podilsky, State Historical and Architectural Preserve* guide by Kiev Mistetsvo Publishers is informative if you can find it. Try at the small information table in the Cathedral of SS Peter & Paul.

Kamyanets-Podilsky's telephone code is 03849.

Old Town

The main settlers of the old town were Ukrainians, Poles, Armenians and Jews. Each traditionally occupied a different quarter, yet all intermixed and feuded with each other and their persistent southern invaders, the Turks. This diversity was wiped out in WW II, but the legacy remains. In the town's heyday there were over 30 different churches, but today only 13 (in various degrees) survive.

Churches & Other Buildings In the centre of the old town you'll find the 16th-century **Dominican monastery & church** with its tall, ornately moulded bell tower. It was founded in the 14th century but remodelled and expanded in Baroque style in the 18th century. It was recently gutted by fire after long years of restoration. The upper spire of the bell tower was completely destroyed. North of the monastery is a park-like area, which was once the Ukrainian and Polish market square. Its vacant feeling is the result of the destruction of two major blocks of merchant houses in WW II.

In the centre of the park is the former **town hall**, or the Ukrainian-Polish Magistry building. Constructed in the mid-14th century with an exterior stone staircase, it's the oldest preserved town hall in Ukraine, although the clock tower was added in the 18th century. It now houses a small **history museum** which is dedicated mostly to WW II, with a few interesting historic photos. You may notice a photo showing a large and grand cathedral rising on the other side of the river where the present ploshcha Soborna lies. It was completely destroyed by Soviet authorities in the 1930s. Beside the town hall is an enclosed 1638 **Armenian Well**, supposedly to be converted into a café.

The 1580 **Cathedral of SS Peter & Paul** (Petropavlovska) is off what was the northwestern corner of the market square. It is entered by passing through a **Triumphal Gate**, which was erected in 1781 in honour of a visit by Polish King Stanislas II Augustus (the Latin inscription above the arch commemorates the event). The Turks used the cathedral as a mosque in the late 17th century, adding a 36.5-metre-high **minaret**, which the Poles topped with a golden Virgin Mary statue when they won the town back again. The attractive and solemn interior is a museum, which is sometimes used for concerts. To the left as you enter, you can see a staircase with Arabic inscriptions. On the grounds next to the church is a box-like stone **bell tower** adjacent to a small former refectory. South-west of the cathedral lie two other Roman Catholic churches, a **Franciscan monastery** and a **Dominican Convent** – both small, abandoned and in bad shape.

Armenian Quarter South of the Dominican monastery & church is the long and narrow former **Armenian market square**. Founded in the 14th century, the square has seen many architectural transformations, its northern side presently occupied by the long façade of the 1857 **Noblemen's Assembly building**. At the far eastern end is a small **picture gallery** (open from 10 am to 5 pm), housed in a former Orthodox Seminary building. Behind it are the foundations of the 15th-century **Church of St John the Baptist**, which was destroyed, along with another nearby 16th-century church, by the Soviet regime in the 1930s. Across the street is a former Armenian clergyman's house, south of which, down vulitsya Virmenska, lies the heart of the historic Armenian Quarter.

The Armenian **Church of St Nicholas** was built in the 15th century only to be destroyed in 1672 by invading Turks. Beside the reconstructed defensive bell tower are the only remains of the church, a beautiful three-arched fragment of the gallery and some foundation ruins behind it. Further south is the small **Church of the Annunciation**, built around the ruined altar of an older Armenian cathedral (13th century) that was also destroyed by the Turks. Wander through the rough cobbled and dirt back streets of the Armenian quarter. The layers of terraced cottages huddled among remnants of stone walls wind down to the river giving the area a very oriental feel. Vulitsya Dobha is especially attractive with 18th-century Armenian houses halfway down on the left.

Gates, Towers & Other Buildings Down vulitsya Tatarska and north of the Cathedral of SS Peter & Paul is the smaller stone **Church of SS Peter & Paul** (1580). Its interior has fragments of 16th-century frescoes. Beyond, at the northern edge of the old town, is the 16th-century **Windy (Vitryanye) Gate**, where Peter the Great's hat blew off in 1711. Connected to it is the seven-storeyed stone **Kushnir (Furriers') Tower**, a defensive structure funded by artisans who lived nearby. From the grassy spot just to the east of the tower you can look down upon the ruins of the old **brewery building** and across at the sheer cliffs dropping down to the river. From the tower, Staropochtovy uzviz turns south-west and descends steeply into the ravine, past a stretch of 17th-century **Turkish Walls** and down to the **Polish Gate**. This gate was named after the historic Polish section of the city, which was on the other side of the river around the hill dominated by the five-cupola 19th-century Orthodox **Church of St George**. Just before the Polish Gate is a stone stairway built in the 19th century that leads back up to the old town.

Both the Polish Gate and the **Ruska Gate**, on the opposite side of the isthmus, where the Ruthenian (Ukrainian) quarter was centred, were built in the 16th to 17th centuries to guard the two most vulnerable entrances into the old town. Both gates were ingeniously fashioned with dike mechanisms which could alter the flow of the Smotrych River and flood the entrances – an engineering feat for the time. The Ruska Gate, with its covered interior walkway, is almost a small fortress in itself. It is along a tiny dirt road which runs through a patchwork of cottages below a row of partially ruined **southern defensive walls**. Further perimeter fortifications on the south-eastern edge of the old town include the **Slyusarka** and **Kushnirska towers**. On the eastern

UKRAINE

edge, the 1583 **Black Tower** stands next to the former **synagogue** with a crenulated roof line, now a restaurant.

Castle

The western end of the Armenian market square funnels past the 18th-century **Trinitarian Catholic church**. It has a well-proportioned pilastered façade fronted by a sculpture-laden front entry porch. Beyond, the road dips past further fortifications on the northern side of vulitsya Zamkova, the 16th-century **Armenian Bastion** and main **City Gate**. Anyone wishing to enter the fortified city to trade or conduct business not only had to pass through these defenses but first had to initially pass the massive castle guarding the western side of the 11th-century **Turkish Bridge**, named after the Turks who rebuilt and fortified it in the 17th century.

The castle/fortress was originally built of wood in the 10th to 13th centuries, then redesigned and rebuilt in stone by Italian military engineers in the 16th century. Today it's in the shape of a polygon, with nine towers of all shapes and sizes, as well as dungeons, turrets and galleries. It's open from 8.30 am to 5 pm daily except Friday, when it closes an hour earlier. Most of the towers were used to store gunpowder and ammunition, and you can climb in, up and even beneath several of them. The **New East Tower** (1544) to your right as you enter houses a well and wooden winch that stretches 40 metres down through the cliff below. The **Papska** or **Kamalyuk Tower** (1503-17) to the far left as you enter is the tallest tower and was used as a prison. A plaque commemorates the folk hero Ustym Kamalyuk, who was imprisoned here on three separate occasions between 1817 and 1823. Inside is a small exhibit. On the right side (north) of the elongated, grassy courtyard are two buildings which house an **Ethnographic Museum**, with excellent displays of not only traditional folk craft and costumes, but a wide range of archaeological finds excavated in the castle and vicinity. Behind the castle to the west is the '**new castle**', a series of earth ramparts and stone

walls built in the 17th century for further defence and for positioning cannons on. There are some cellars beneath them. A climb to the top and a walk around the castle offer nice views.

Karvasary

The small quarter of wood houses to the south of the castle at the river's edge was named after the eastern term 'caravanserai', a resting spot along a trade route where caravans could stop and spend the night. In the centre of the Karvasary quarter is the 17th-century wooden **Church of the Exaltation of the Cross** and bell tower, a fine example of Podilian (Podilia was a historic province of south-western Ukraine) wood architecture, built with a stone foundation to protect against flood waters. To reach the church take the narrow staircase that branches off the southern side of the Turkish Bridge and follow it along the road.

Places to Stay & Eat

There are two hotels on opposite sides of ploshcha Soborna in the new town, halfway between the bus station and the old town. The *Hotel Ukraina* (☎ 3 91 48) at vulitsya Lesi Ukrainky 32 is the cheapest at US$3 per person in single/double/triple rooms without bath, but the shared bathrooms are hard to stomach. It's probably worth it to pay extra at the *Hotel Smotrych* (☎ 3 87 00) at vulitsya Soborna 4, where nicer rooms with bath cost US$8 for singles or doubles.

Both hotels have decent restaurants with live music after about 8 pm. The one in the Hotel Smotrych is the more popular. There's also the *Restoran Stara Fortetsya* housed in the former synagogue in the old town off vulitsya Lyuxemburg next to the Black Tower. Just before you cross the Turkish Bridge on the south side in the old town is the *Kafe Pid Bramoyu*. Set inside part of the bridge fortifications, they serve coffee, beer and light food.

Getting There & Away

Bus Between Chernivtsi and Kamyanets-Podilsky there are a lot more buses than trains. At least eight daily buses run to/from Khmelnytsky (three hours) and Chernivtsi (two hours), with about four or five of the Chernivtsi buses stopping at Khotyn (one hour) on the way. There are also daily buses to Vinnytsya, Zhytomyr, Ternopil and Kiev.

Train Kamyanets-Podilsky is on the line between Chernivtsi and Khmelnytsky, with trains usually continuing on past Khmelnytsky to Kiev (12 hours), Rivne or Lviv. There are daily trains to each.

Getting Around
Bus No 9 runs from the bus station to the new town and ploshcha Soborna, but it's not a long walk to the hotels (about 15 minutes). From ploshcha Soborna bus No 5 runs to the old town, but again it's a short walk. From the railway station, bus No 1 runs through the new town and into the old town.

KHMELNYTSKY
ХМЕЛЬНИЦЬКИЙ
Population: 253,000

Khmelnytsky (formerly known as Prokuriv) on the Southern Buh River, was founded as a military outpost in the late 15th century. It was repeatedly pillaged by Tatars in the 16th century before becoming privately owned by various noblemen. It burned to the ground in 1822 and suffered heavily during WW II.

Things to See
There's not much to see. The outskirts are drab and boring, but the centre is not unpleasant. **Vulitsya Proskurivska**, stretching north-west from Shevchenko Park to vulitsya Soborna, is the main drag with shops and cafés. **Shevchenko Park** itself, between vulitsya Proskurivska and vulitsya Teatralna, is a pleasant place with an outdoor café behind the cinema. South-west of the park is the spacious ploshcha Svobody with the neoclassical Regional Government building in the centre and the **Regional Museum** just south. A huge, dramatic and lunging statue of Khmelnytsky is around the corner in front of the Philharmonia, just down from the Hotel Tsentrala.

Places to Stay & Eat
The oldish *Hotel Tsentrala* (☎ 6 47 23), off the south side of ploshcha Svobody at vulitsya Yuri Gagarina 5, has a decent restaurant and rooms for US$4/8 a single/double. North-east, between ploshcha Svobody and Shevchenko Park, is the *Hotel Eneyida* (☎ 8 12 42) at vulitsya Teatralna 8. It is newer with cleaner rooms for US$5/9/11 a single/double/triple. Across from Shevchenko Park, at vulitsya Proskurivska 44, the *Hotel Zhovtnevyi* (☎ 6 46 69) has a restaurant and may or may not take foreigners, depending on who's at the reception.

Getting There & Away
Bus There are about eight daily buses to Chernivtsi passing through Kamyanets-Podilsky, with as many going to Ivano-Frankivsk, Zhytomyr and Vinnytsya.

Train There are at least eight daily trains to/from Lviv (five hours), five or six to/from Kiev (seven hours via Vinnytsya), and at least one a day to Chernivtsi (nine hours), Uzhhorod (12 hours), Simferopol (24 hours) and Odessa (nine hours).

Getting Around
Trolleybus No 2 or 10 from the centre will drop you off at a large roundabout about 300 metres west of the bus station. The railway station is about 1.5 km west of the centre, down vulitsya Proskurivska.

MEDZHYBIZH
МЕДЖИБІЖ

The large, photogenic fortress at the village of Medzhybizh near the Trebukhovka River is worth a short detour for motorists, and can be seen by bus as a stopover between Khmelnytsky and Vinnytsya.

Built in the 14th to 16th centuries on the site of an ancient settlement, it passed through Lithuanian, Cossack, Turkish and Polish hands before being taken over by Russia in 1793. It's open from 9 am to 6 pm, closed Monday. Within the grounds lies a small steep-roofed 1586 **church**, and occupying the far eastern end are the ruins of the

UKRAINE

former 16th-century **palace** with a beautiful Renaissance parapet lining the top of the walls. To the left of the entrance is a small **history & ethnographic museum** housed in the former soldier barracks. The surrounding village has some picturesque small streets lined with colourful cottages.

Getting There & Away
The turn-off is north of the highway, 84 km from Vinnytsya or 32 km from Khmelnytsky. Only about four of the 10 or so buses going between the two cities stops at Medzhybizh, but the others can, if you request, drop you off on the main road only about two km away. Likewise, you can flag a bus down when leaving or, from Medzhybizh, catch a more frequent bus to Letychiv, halfway between Khmelnytsky and Vinnytsya on the main road, where you can then catch another bus to either destination.

Southern Ukraine
Південна Україна

For hundreds of years Southern Ukraine, bordering the lands of the Ukrainian Cossacks and those of the Crimean Tatars, resembled a 'wild-west' no-man's land. Military outposts, and settlements of renegades and runaway peasants, sprang up along the banks of the Dnipro. After Russia's victory in the Russo-Ottoman War of 1768-75, Catherine II deemed the Ukrainian 'buffer zone' unnecessary and ordered the disbandment and destruction of the quasi-independent Cossack Hetmanate State (which, incidentally, was crucial to her victory over the Ottomans). With the Cossacks and Tatars defeated, much of the land was distributed among Russian, Serbian and German colonists, and the doors opened for massive Russian expansion, which led to the annexation of not only southern Ukraine, but Crimea as well. Hit hard by the famine of 1932-33, large rural populations were wiped out.

The landscape of southern Ukraine is predominantly rich, fertile steppe, sucking nutrients from its many estuaries and rivers. About 100 km east of Kherson is the Askaniya Nova Reserve, 33,000 hectares of virgin steppe land populated with feral animals whose ancestors were brought to the site by a German settler in 1828.

ODESSA
ОДЕСА

Population: 1.1 million

Odessa, the Black Sea's gateway to Ukraine, is a potent brew of diverse ingredients yielding a strange southern magic. It is the country's biggest commercial Black Sea port, a hectic industrial city with polluted seas, yet it is also an enticing holiday centre where people flock to laze on beaches and stroll through leafy streets. Odessa is a crossroads of cultures, languages and trade, and a leading centre of capitalist and black-market activity. Past associations make it dear to both Russian and Ukrainian hearts: Pushkin lived here in exile during the 1820s and it was home to writer and film director Dovzhenko; the city also conjures up historical reminders of Russian campaigns against the Turks and the 1905 revolution.

The Dnister estuary is 40 km south-west of Odessa, and the Dnipro estuary 60 km to the east. Inland from this coast are several *limany*, estuaries now cut off from the sea, with mud which supposedly has curative powers drawing thousands to Odessa's sanatoria. May to September are the best months, with maximum temperatures averaging between 20°C and 27°C. In winter the sea may freeze for a few days, but ships still get through.

History

The site of Odessa, useful as both port and fort, was controlled from 1526 to 1789 by the Ottoman Turks. During its expansionist campaign in the 18th century, Russia took this coastal region and constructed, with slave labor, a new port at Odessa, rebuilding the town and naming it after the ancient Greek colony Odessos, thought to be nearby but later identified in modern Bulgaria.

Armand-Emmanuel du Plessis, Duc de Richelieu, a nobleman who had fled to

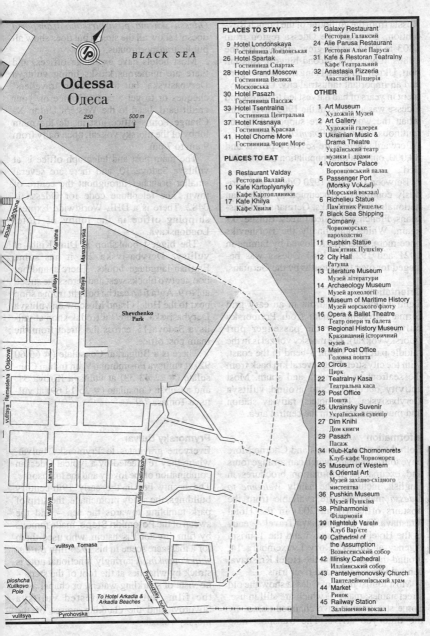

BLACK SEA

Odessa
Одеса

0   250   500 m

Solisk Kanatna

vulitsya Kanatna

vulitsya Marazlyevska

vulitsya Remeslena (Osipova)

Shevchenko Park

vulitsya Kanatna

vulitsya Belinskoho

vulitsya Tomasa

ploshcha Kulikovo Pole

Frantsuzsky Bulvar

vulitsya Pyrohovska

To Hotel Arkadia & Arkadia Beaches

PLACES TO STAY
9 Hotel Londonskaya
  Гостинниця Лондонська
26 Hotel Spartak
  Гостинниця Спартак
28 Hotel Grand Moscow
  Гостинниця Велика Московська
30 Hotel Pasazh
  Гостинниця Пассаж
33 Hotel Tsentralna
  Гостинниця Центральна
37 Hotel Krasnaya
  Гостинниця Красная
41 Hotel Chorne More
  Гостинниця Чорне Море

PLACES TO EAT
8 Restaurant Valday
  Ресторан Валдай
10 Kafe Kartoplyanyku
  Кафе Картопляники
17 Kafe Khilya
  Кафе Хвиля

21 Galaxy Restaurant
  Ресторан Галаксий
24 Alie Parusa Restaurant
  Ресторан Алые Паруса
31 Kafe & Restoran Teatralny
  Кафе Театральний
32 Anastasia Pizzeria
  Анастасия Піщерія

OTHER
1 Art Museum
  Художній Музей
2 Art Gallery
  Художній галерея
3 Ukrainian Music & Drama Theatre
  Український театр музики і драми
4 Vorontsov Palace
  Воронцовський палац
5 Passenger Port (Morsky Vokzal)
  (Морський вокзал)
6 Richelieu Statue
  Пам'ятник Рішельє
7 Black Sea Shipping Company
  Чорноморське пароходство
11 Pushkin Statue
  Пам'ятник Пушкіну
12 City Hall
  Ратуша
13 Literature Museum
  Музей літератури
14 Archaeology Museum
  Музей археології
15 Museum of Maritime History
  Музей морського флоту
16 Opera & Ballet Theatre
  Театр опери та балета
18 Regional History Museum
  Краззнавчий історичний музей
19 Main Post Office
  Головна пошта
20 Circus
  Цирк
22 Teatralny Kasa
  Театральна каса
23 Post Office
  Пошта
25 Ukrainsky Suvenir
  Український сувенір
27 Dim Knihi
  Дом книги
29 Pasazh
  Пасаж
34 Klub-Kafe Chornomorets
  Клуб-кафе Чорноморец
35 Museum of Western & Oriental Art
  Музей західно-східного мистецтва
36 Pushkin Museum
  Музей Пушкіна
38 Philharmonia
  Філармонія
39 Nightclub Varete
  Клуб Вар'єте
40 Cathedral of the Assumption
  Вознесенський собор
42 Illinsky Cathedral
  Іллійнський собор
43 Panteleymonovsky Church
  Пантелеймонівський храм
44 Market
  Ринок
45 Railway Station
  Залізничний вокзал

Russia from the guillotine of the French Revolution, governed the Odessa region from 1803 to 1814 and it grew quickly. By the 1880s it was the second-biggest Russian port, Ukrainian grain being the main export, and an important industrial city. Unemployment in years of bad harvest led to unrest and Odessa was a hotbed of the 1905 revolution, when the workers were supported by the mutinous battleship *Potemkin Tavrichesky*. Afterwards there were severe reprisals and 80,000, out of a total population of 600,000, fled.

Between 1917 and 1920 Odessa was variously controlled or occupied by Ukrainian nationalists, Bolsheviks, Germans and Austrians, French and Allied forces, Bolsheviks again, Whites and finally the Bolsheviks once more. This was followed by famine in 1921 and 1922. In 1941 Odessa was besieged for over two months by the Germans.

Orientation

Central Odessa is laid out in an easy grid format, stretching south from Prymorsky bulvar overlooking the passenger port (morsky vokzal). The morsky vokzal is in the middle part of a 35-km S-bend in the coast, with the city stretching several km back from the seafront to the north and south. Most activity occurs on and around vulitsya Derybasivska. The hotels, railway station and museums are all in the central area.

Information

Both the hotels Krasnaya and Chorne More have tourist bureaus which can arrange tours and excursions. Information brochures in English, including the handy *Welcome to Odessa* magazine, are available from the upstairs office (room 202) in the Hotel Krasnaya. The Londonskaya Travel Agency in the Hotel Londonskaya and the Tourism Agency at vulitsya Rozy Lyuxemburg 14, around the corner from the Hotel Krasnaya, can help arrange sea and river trips.

Most tourist maps of Odessa show the old street names, many of which are still in use. Some streets may have changed names by the time you arrive. The transport map *Odessa skhema pasazhirskoho transporta* doesn't show all the streets but does show all public transport routes.

Most hotels have exchange offices, and there are numerous kiosks lining vulitsya Derybasivska, but to exchange travellers' cheques or to get a cash advance on your credit card, head to the Western Union X-Change Points office just inside the main lobby of the morsky vokzal, open daily from 9 am to 7 pm.

The main post and telegraph office is at vulitsya Sadova 10, and there are several smaller branches throughout the centre of town. The telephone code for Odessa is 0482. There is a DHL Worldwide Express shipping office in the lobby of Hotel Londonskaya.

The biggest bookshop is Dim Knihi at vulitsya Derybasivska 27; it has some English-language books. There's another booster two blocks west and across the street, at No 9. Agfa film can be bought from a shop next to the Hotel Grand Moscow on vulitsya Derybasivska. There's a Kodak shop at vulitsya Sadova 13, across the street from the main post office.

There is a Bulgarian Consulate (☎ 66 60 92) at vulitsya Posmitnoho 9, an Indian Consulate (☎ 22 43 33) at vulitsya Kirova 31, and a Cuban Consulate (☎ 25 14 69) at vulitsya Tomasa 7/9.

Prymorsky Bulvar

Everyone gravitates to Prymorsky bulvar, where they're greeted by a typical Odessan combination of the lovely and the loathsome. The beauty lies in the early 19th-century buildings, the shady promenade, the strip of park tumbling towards the sea – and the sweep of the **Potemkin Steps**, made famous by film director Eisenstein, who used them for a massacre scene in his 1925 film *Battleship Potemkin*. A jarringly functional note is struck by what lies at the foot of the steps – no vista of sparkling waters, or chapel as in the film, but truck-infested vulitsya Suvorova and the clanking noises of the morsky vokzal.

The 193 steps, built between 1837 and 1841, descend from a statue of the Duc de Richelieu in a Roman toga about halfway along the boulevard. They're best seen from below, where they look higher than they are, thanks to a gradual narrowing from the bottom (where they're 21 metres wide) to the top (13 metres wide). An enclosed escalator runs up beside them for those whose legs won't work.

A block inland from the Richelieu statue is ploshcha Potemkyntsev, with a statue of the 1905 mutineers. At the eastern end of Prymorsky bulvar, a Pushkin statue and a British cannon from the Crimean War stand before the pink-and-white colonnaded **Odessa City Hall**, originally the Stock Exchange and later housing the Regional Soviet Headquarters. Set in the façade in two low niches are the two financial symbols of the city, Mercury, god of trade, to the right, and to the left Fortuna, goddess of fate. Several of the city's fine museums lie just to the south.

At the western end of Prymorsky bulvar, past the bust of Valentyn Hrushko, an Ukrainian cosmonaut hero, is the sombre **Palace of Vorontsov**. The residence of a former governor of the city, it was built in 1826 in a heavy classical style with surprising Arabic detailing on the interior and is the site where, in 1917, the first local workers' deputies met and organised. Today the palace houses a children's music and dance academy. The terrace behind the palace offers brilliant views over Odessa's bustling port. There is a footbridge to the left, supposedly built at the request of a communist official to make it easier for his mother to visit him, which leads to a park and the pleasing pedestrian-only extension of the promenade.

City Centre

The blocks south of Prymorsky bulvar are tree-lined and low-rise, and at their liveliest and most intriguing on warm summer evenings. On vulitsya Lanzheronovska (Lastochkina), facing down vulitsya Rishelevska (Lenina), proudly sits the elaborate and famous **Opera & Ballet Theatre**. It was designed in the 1880s by Viennese architects Felner & Gelmer in the Habsburg Baroque of the day, with a number of Italian Renaissance features thrown in to liven up the ensemble. A block south is Odessa's main commercial street, vulitsya Derybasivska (Deribasovskaya in Russian), named after a Frenchman, De Ribas, who led the capture of Odessa from the Turks in 1789. It's a popular place to take a stroll, and you'll find lots of eager capitalists staffing tiny kiosks which sell all sorts of flashy items. Two pleasant tree-filled parks lie at its western end, including ploshcha Soborna (Cathedral Square) on the corner of vulitsya Preobrazhenska (Sovietskoy Armii), named after a large cathedral which stood on the site before it was torn down by the Soviet regime in the 1930s. Stroll through the **Pasazh**, a lavishly ornate shopping mall built in the late 1800s which boasts rows of baroque sculptures. Enter at vulitsya Derybasivska 33 and follow the arcade around the corner to the exit on vulitsya Preobrazhenska.

At vulitsya Preobrazhenska (Sovietskoy Armii) 70 is the **Cathedral of the Assumption**, an impressive blue-and-white ensemble of five swooping domes and a very tall bell tower rising over the entrance.

There are two fine churches on the southeast side of the city centre, near the railway station. Five very bulbous silver domes and a pointed bell tower rise from the neo-Byzantine **Pantelyemonovsky Church**, the interior of which is under restoration. Just down Pushkinska is the blue **Illinsky Cathedral** (1886), very richly adorned beneath a large central dome.

Museums & Galleries

Odessa has an excellent collection of museums, mostly of an agreeably moderate size and all housed in sumptuous former palaces, worth a visit for their architecture alone. One of the most interesting is the **Archaeology Museum**, at vulitsya Lanzheronovska (Lastochkina) 4 on the corner of Pushkinska vulitsya, open daily from 10 am to 5 pm, closed on Monday. Established in 1875, it was the first museum of its kind

UKRAINE

in the former Russian Empire. Sadly there are no English-language labels on the displays. It houses archaeological finds from the Black Sea region predominantly, including a replica statue of a Slavic pagan god. The highlight is the Gold Room (Zolota Kladova), which has jewellery and coins from early Black Sea civilisations, including the first Slavic coins of St Volodomyr (10th century AD) with the *tryzub* symbol on them. The prize item is a simple 14th-century BC gold vase from the Crete Mycenaean civilisation. It's in a room downstairs, off the second Kievan Rus room before the Egyptian Room, and often only open by request. If they won't open it for you, tag along with a group.

Across the road is the **Museum of Maritime History**, at vulitsya Lanzheronovska 6, covering the history of shipbuilding and navigation with lots of models and naval paraphernalia. The museum is open daily, except Thursday, from 10 am to 6 pm. There is a small antique shop and café inside. At vulitsya Lanzheronovska 2, the **Literature Museum** focuses on the literary history of the city, with excellent exhibits on the lives and works of Pushkin, Gogol, Chekhov, Tolstoy, Gorky, Shevchenko, Franko and Dovzhenko. It's open daily from 10 am to 6 pm, except Monday.

At vulitsya Pushkinska 13, near the Hotel Krasnaya, is a small **Pushkin Museum**. On the opposite corner of the Hotel Krasnaya,

The Tryzub

It doesn't take the visitor to Ukraine long to notice a ubiquitous symbol stamped on everything from flags and buildings to cars, trains, money, telephone tokens and all kinds of official documents. The *tryzub*, тризуб (in English, 'three-toothed' or 'trident'), is Ukraine's national symbol, and its history can be traced back 1000 years. Some of the first Slavic coins (now displayed in Odessa's archaeological museum), which date from the reign of Prince Volodymyr in Kiev (980-1015), depict the tryzub, as do other archaeological finds from this time, including tombs of the nobility and fragments from portals.

The exact origins of the symbol are unknown, but there are several theories. Some historians believe it to be derived from the classic mythological symbol of Neptune's trident spear. The most widely accepted theory, however, claims the design of the tryzub is based on the Cyrillic letters В, Я and О, which represent the three most celebrated rulers of ancient Kievan Rus – Prince Volodymyr, King Yaroslav and Queen Olha. Variations on this theory suggest the design is patterned on the word *volya*, воля, meaning 'freedom'; or simply derived from the letter В and its mirror image, an acronym for Volodymyr Velyky (Volodymyr the Great), the Slav ruler who converted Kievan Rus to Christianity in 988.

Throughout Ukrainian history the tryzub has been used to symbolise Ukrainian identity and sovereignty. When Ukraine declared its independence from the Russian empire in 1917, the fledgling government was quick to adopt the mark as its national emblem. Forbidden under the Soviet regime, the 'nationalist' symbol was again adopted during the 1980s by the Ukrainian independence movement, Rukh. After the break-up of the USSR and the coming of independence in 1991, the Ukrainian Parliament officially readopted the tryzub, set against a heraldic shield, as the country's coat of arms. The tryzub often appears on the Ukrainian flag, centred between its bands of blue and gold – the blue representing the sky, the gold representing wheat. ■

and designed by the same Italian architect as the hotel, is the building which houses the **Odessa Philharmonia**. It was originally a Stock Exchange built in the late 1800s to replace the smaller one on Prymorsky bulvar.

The **Museum of Western & Oriental Art**, housed in a gilded palace at Pushkinska 9, is open daily, except Wednesday, from 11 am to 4.30 pm. Upstairs there are 14 rooms full of works by European masters such as Hals, Caravaggio and Canaletto. On the ground floor is the smaller exhibit of Oriental crafts and paintings. Russian and Ukrainian art are well covered in the **Art Museum** at vulitsya Korolenko 5A, open daily, except Thursday, from 10 am to 5 pm. Its maze of over 15 rooms on two floors has treasures which run from 15th-century icons onwards and includes works by Levitsky, Ayvazovsky and Repin. The main hall, No 6, has a beautiful inlaid floor and intricate plasterwork.

The **Regional History Museum** at vulitsya Khalturyna 5 is open from 10 am to 5 pm daily, closed on Monday. Inside is a fascinating assortment of displays covering all aspects of the city's history, including old maps, photos, furniture, and household objects.

Catacombs

The sandstone on which Odessa stands is riddled with about 1000 km of tunnels, quarried out for building in the 19th century. They have been used by smugglers, revolutionaries and others who needed somewhere to hide, notably WW II partisans. They have not been used for burials, however. There are many entrances, but don't wander in without a reliable guide; it's easy to get lost. One network of tunnels in Nerubayske village on the north-west edge of Odessa, which sheltered a group of partisans in WW II, has been turned into the **Museum of Partisan Glory**, open daily from 9 am to 1 pm and 2 to 7.30 pm. Visitors are given a guided tour in Russian or Ukrainian. Inside are relics of the partisan occupation – and of an apparently failed German attack.

The very infrequent bus No 87 from the stop at the end of prospekt Myra, near the market, stops right outside these catacombs. Ask the driver for *katakombi*. Alternatively, taking a taxi (US$6) would be much easier. If you have your own vehicle, head along the Kiev road, then two km after the ring road (Obezdna doroha) turn right at the 'Muzey Partizanskaya Slava' sign, then right again about two km later, at the 'Memorial Katakombi' sign. Organised tours, available from the tourist bureaus in the hotels Krasnaya and Chorne More, remove most of the sense of adventure.

Beaches & Ferries

Odessa's beaches are unbelievably crowded in summer, and the water is none too clean, but they're still fun to visit – not least for the sight of thousands of pale citizens squeezing happily into spaces fit for a few hundred at most. They queue with smiles for showers and drinks, pay money for two sq metres of deck-chair space and pose beside stuffed tigers lugged to the beach by opportunist photographers.

Odessa has northern beaches and southern beaches. Luzanovka in the north, about six km across the bay from the morsky vokzal, is very busy and has a fun fair, an open-air disco and so on. The southern beaches are

Taras Schevchenko, Ukraine's foremost poet

UKRAINE

often less crowded and more picturesque, with rocky headlands breaking up the coastline, and parkland stretching back up from the beach. In order, going from the centre of Odessa they are: Lanzheron (three km out), Otrada, Delfin, Arkadia, Chayka, Kurortny, Zoloty Plyazh (Zolotoy Bereg in Russian, and sometimes called Bolshoy Fontan) and Chernomorka, which is about 18 km out. The Arkadia area is the most popular and has plenty of restaurants and activities. Zoloty Plyazh and Chernomorka are two of the best beaches.

Trams, buses or trolleybuses go within walking distance of all the beaches, but ferries from the morsky vokzal are more fun. From May to September they run from about 8 am to 8 pm. Luzanovka boats leave every 20 to 30 minutes, while southbound boats go to Arkadia every 20 minutes (a 45-minute trip), Zoloty Plyazh every 40 minutes (one hour 15 minutes) and Chernomorka about hourly (one hour 45 minutes). Most stop at Lanzheron, and Chayka if they go that far. Tickets are cheap and the ferries are usually motor vessels *(katery)* or more expensive hydrofoils. The piers and ticket offices are down to the left from the big main jetty at the morsky vokzal.

Places to Stay

Camping Delfin (☎ 55 52 50) is about 10 km north of the city centre, near Luzanovka beach, at doroha Kotovsky 307, on the western side of the busy thoroughfare. Two-person cabins (category B), a bit bigger than usual, but with pretty disgusting toilets, are US$7 per person. Larger three to five-person bungalows without bath are US$5 per person. To pitch your tent costs US$3 per person. The camp site has its own restaurant with reasonable food and service, plus a grilled-chicken bar which is open only erratically. It also has a little private beach across the road, which gets a bit less crowded than the public beach next door. Drivers from the city centre should follow vulitsya Suvorova westward, then turn north along vulitsya Moskovska, which becomes doroha Kotovsky. Bus Nos 130, 160 and 170 from

Hretsky (Martynovskoho) ploshcha stop at a busy intersection about 300 metres north of Delfin (ask the driver to stop at 'camping Delfin' – they may let you out in front), but the best way to get there is by ferry (from the morsky vokzal) to Luzanovka pier, which is half a km south of the camp site.

For the cheapest accommodation look for old women at the railway station holding small signs with the word *kimnaty* (rooms). Make sure you work out the price (usually about US$5 per person) and the location before you commit. A location way outside the city centre may be difficult to reach and involve travelling on crowded trolleybuses. Odessa is blessed with a number of centrally located, deliciously low-rise 19th-century hotels with grand staircases, wide corridors and big rooms, although some of them are falling apart due to neglect.

For the cheapest of these head to one of four decrepit but charming hotels around the western end of vulitsya Derybasivska, all right in the city centre. The best is probably the *Hotel Tsentralna* (☎ 26 84 06) at vulitsya Preobrazhenska 40, with singles/doubles for US$30/50 and triples without bath for US$40. A block north-west, at No 34, is the *Hotel Pasazh* (☎ 22 48 49), above the ornate shopping arcade, with rooms costing US$30/35/38 for singles/doubles/triples; the triples have a sink but no toilet. Around the corner, at vulitsya Derybasivska 29, is the *Hotel Grand Moscow* (☎ 22 40 16) with rooms the same price and standard as at the Hotel Pasazh. The most run-down, though undergoing slow restoration, is the *Hotel Spartak* (☎ 26 89 24) at vulitsya Derybasivska 25, with singles/doubles for US$24/40 and triples for US$50.

The *Hotel Krasnaya* (☎ 25 85 20), at vulitsya Pushkinska 15 on the corner of vulitsya Rozy Lyuxemburg, is also extremely grand, with the front door flanked by big, half-naked classical figures. Unfortunately it is also overpriced at US$92/124 for single/double rooms. Trolleybus Nos 4 and 10 and bus Nos 109 and 155 head south to the railway station and north to the morsky vokzal, stopping one block east of the hotel.

The *Hotel Londonskaya* (☎ 25 53 70), at Prymorsky bulvar 11, is a fully restored old gem with a beautiful courtyard and a ridiculously high price tag. Rooms cost US$142/152 for a single/double. Marshrutnoe taxi No 170, from the park in front of the railway station, runs up vulitsya Ekaterynynska (Karla Marxa) to ploshcha Potemkyntsev, just round the corner from the hotel.

The typical Intourist-style outfit, *Hotel Chorne More* (☎ 24 20 28) on vulitsya Rishelevska (Lenina), is in decent shape for a 1970s concrete box. It's only five minutes walk from the railway station, but rooms are overpriced at US$60/70 for a single/double.

About six km south-east of the city centre, near Arkadia beach, is the *Hotel Arkadia* (☎ 63 75 27) at vulitsya Henuezska (Genuezskaya) 24, with singles/doubles for US$15/25. The *Hotel Viktoria* (☎ 61 89 03), next door to the Hotel Arkadia, is nicer but far more expensive at US$45/104 for a single/double. Trolleybus Nos 5 and 9, and tram No 5, from ploshcha Hretsky (Martynovskoho) in the city centre, or bus No 129 from the airport or railway station, will get you to ploshcha Shevchenko (with the tall obelisk) for the Arkadia hotels. From the city centre, you can also take a ferry from the morsky vokzal to Arkadia pier. Take tram No 5 or trolleybus Nos 5 or 13 from the pier for two stops to get to the hotels.

In the morsky vokzal itself, the *Hotel Gloria* (☎ 22 84 49) has clean new single or double rooms for US$80.

Places to Eat

The restaurant in the *Hotel Krasnaya* serves reasonably priced meals (US$6 to US$9) and a nice selection of zakusky (appetisers). Next to the Krasnaya's restaurant is the semi-ritzy café/bar *Bristol*, a good place to relax over a drink. The restaurant in the *Hotel Londonskaya* is excellent but only accepts hard currency and is very expensive.

The *Galaxy Restaurant* at vulitsya Preobrazhenska 23 has decor which tries to convince you you're in outer space. The food is good, with a diverse menu in English featuring galactic dishes such as 'space cocoon' and 'barbecue in trance'. Full meals cost US$8 to US$10.

The *Restaurant Valday* on ploshcha Potemkyntsev is up-market, with excellent service and good fish dishes for around US$7.

Less pretentious is the restaurant *Alie Parusa*, on the corner of vulitsya Derybasivska and vulitsya Ekaterynynska (Karla Marxa), which has a variety of chicken and meat dishes for about US$6.

Around the city centre are a number of small, cheap cafeteria-style eateries where strange salads and plates heaped with tasty meat-and-potato dishes cost no more than US$2, but try to get there by 7 pm as they tend to run out of food. The best is the friendly *Kafe Kartoplyanyky* just off ploshcha Potemkyntsev, at vulitsya Ekaterynynska 2, serving delicious meat, potato and vegetable stews in clay pots, as well as salads, stuffed varenyky, and coffee and cakes. It's open from 9 am to 9 pm. Up the street, at vulitsya Ekaterynynska 12, is the *Kafe Khvelya*, which has pizzas, salads, potatoes and meat. The *Kafe Spartak* next to the hotel of the same name is a relaxed café with light food but lots of drinks. On vulitsya Preobrazhenska two doors down from the Hotel Pasazh is the *Kafe Teatralny*, and next door, the *Restoran Teatralny*, both serving the same sort meat-and-potato dishes. The café has good cakes and is cheaper, but the restaurant has a larger selection to choose from. The best pizza in town is nearby at vulitsya Preobrazhenska 38 in the *Anastasia Pizzeria*. For US$1 to US$2 you can have a fresh hot mini-pizza, including vegetarian options.

On the opposite side of vulitsya Derybasivska from the Hotel Grand Moscow is the *Bilosnizhka* (White Snow), a sit down ice-cream place. There's a shop selling sweets at vulitsya Derybasivska 29, and the *Sladky Dom* (Sweet House), which serves Turkish cakes, is nearby at vulitsya Khalturyna 13. On the corner of vulitsya Derybasivska and vulitsya Preobrazhenska is a grocery shop which sells bottled water and some Western food products. The central market is on vulitsya Privozna at the south-eastern end of prospekt Myra.

Entertainment

For advance tickets and information for most theatre performances, head to the *teatralny kasa* at vulitsya Preobrazhenska 28, which is open from 10 am to 5 pm daily. Tickets are ridiculously cheap. Try to see a performance at the impressive Opera & Ballet Theatre. Its interior is decorated in lavish Louis XVI style, and its ceiling is painted with Shakespearean scenes. For same-day performances buy your tickets from the *kasa* (ticket office) on the western side of the theatre. For classical music, check out the regional Philharmonia at vulitsya Pushkinska 17, on the corner of vulitsya Rozy Lyuxemburg. The Ukrainian Music and Drama Theatre is at vulitsya Pastera 15. The Circus is at vulitsya Podbelsky 25. In

Odessa woman

summer Odessa receives visits from a steady flow of theatre companies, musicians and other performers. Sometimes touring fashion parades (look for the words *maniken gruppa*) from Kiev or Moscow hold shows.

Next to the Philharmonia is the popular nightclub/theatre Varete, entered from vulitsya Rozy Lyuxemburg, which usually has a few live rock-and-roll bands and a late-night disco. Adjacent is an up-market and uptight nightclub/casino. There's also another casino ready to take your money at the Hotel Londonskaya. Most restaurants flaunt some form of evening entertainment, often an annoyingly loud band. The floor show in the Hotel Krasnaya restaurant is usually colourful, lively and varied. You need to have dinner to see it. The Hotel Chorne More also has a floor show. The small Klub-Kafe Chornomorets on the corner of vulitsya Derybasivska and vulitsya Pushkinska has jazz bands occasionally. During the summer months there is usually a popular open-air disco in the courtyard of the Dvorets Moryakov on Prymorsky bulvar, two doors from the Hotel Londonskaya.

Things to Buy

The Odessa *tolkuchka* or *tolchak* (both meaning 'crush' or 'push'), held on the western edge of the city on Saturday and Sunday, is one of the country's biggest flea markets – a wonderland of every kind of imitation-Western junk imaginable. The site is just south of Ovidiopilska doroha, shortly before the ring road. To get there by public transport, take tram No 4 travelling southwest along vulitsya Uspenska (Chicherina) to the Zastava-II stop at the end of the line, then take bus No 160.

In town you'll find a good range of Ukrainian pottery, textiles and folk craft in Ukrainsky Suvenir at vulitsya Derybasivska 16. The city park on the northern side of vulitsya Derybasivska, at its western end, has a casual craft market with vendors selling a wide variety of items. At vulitsya Hretska (Karla Libnekhta) 20 is a small ceramic shop which sells interesting pieces. There is some-

UKRAINE

times an interesting book market off ploshcha Hretsky (Martynovskoho).

Getting There & Away

Air Odessa is linked by flights to Kiev (Air Ukraine), Vienna (Austrian Airlines, twice weekly) and Moscow (Aeroflot, three times a week). For most other destinations a change in Kiev is necessary. For information and tickets check with the travel bureau (☎ 25 85 20) in the Hotel Krasnaya. For Air Ukraine and Ukraine International Airlines information call ☎ 25 93 67.

Bus Odessa's long-distance bus station (avtovokzal) is at vulitsya Dzerzhinskoho 58, about three km west of the railway station. Tram No 5 travels between the two.

Train At least two trains daily run to/from Kiev (12 hours), Moscow (23 to 29 hours), Kharkiv (16 hours) and Chisinau (five to seven hours). Daily service also includes Lviv (15 hours), Simferopol (13 hours), Zaporizhzhya (five hours), Izmayil (eight hours), Chernivtsi (12½ hours, in summer only), St Petersburg (29 hours) and Rostov (27 hours). There are trains every other day to/from Warsaw (27 hours) and Minsk (26 hours).

Many trains heading to western Ukraine pass through Moldova; however a visa for Moldova isn't needed if you're going straight through to a Ukrainian destination (see To/From Moldova in the Land section of Ukraine Getting There & Away).

For full information and hassle-free purchasing of tickets, don't waste your time at the station, but go straight to the Travel Bureau (☎ 25 85 20) in the Hotel Krasnaya, open daily from 9 am to 5 pm, closed between 1 and 2 pm. The railway station is on ploshcha Pryvokzalna at the southern end of vulitsya Pushkinska.

Electric trains fan out from the city to surrounding towns within the Odessa oblast. Tickets can be bought in front of the platform from kasa Nos 32 and 33, and timetables are posted there also. There are eight trains daily to Bilhorod-Dnistrovsky (2½ hours), as well

as trains to Rozdilna, Berezivka and Illichivsk.

Car & Motorbike The roads from Chisinau (180 km) and Kiev (490 km) are mostly straight and in good condition. The Odessa-Crimea road runs via Mykolayiv and Kherson.

Boat Odessa is the home port of the Black Sea Shipping Company (Chernomorsky morsky Parokhodstvo), which operates scheduled passenger and vehicle services all over the Mediterranean. It plies the routes to Istanbul and Piraeus (Greece), so it's possible to enter or leave the country by sea through Odessa, even with a car. See the Ukraine Getting There & Away section for details. Prices have drastically increased recently, making a voyage an expensive outing. The one-way fare to Istanbul is about US$100; and to Piraeus about US$200 for the cheapest possible ticket, but the prices are about one-third less in the low season. Boats sail at least weekly in summer and usually twice a month during winter. The same company runs year-round passenger and vehicle ferries connecting Odessa with nine other Black Sea ports, including Yalta and Sochi, but at the time of writing most of these services were temporarily suspended due to lack of business and because of fuel shortages.

For information head to the company's main office (☎ 25 35 39) at ploshcha Potemkyntsev 1, at the top of the Potemkin Steps. Some of the travel agencies mentioned in the information section can book your trip. Odessa is also a terminus for the Dnipro River hydrofoils and passenger boats (see the Ukraine Getting Around section).

All these services dock at Odessa's passenger port (morsky vokzal) on vulitsya Suvorova. Timetables and ticket offices can be found inside the terminal building.

Getting Around

To/From the Airport The airport is about 12 km south-west of the city centre, off Ovidiopilska doroha. Bus No 129 and marshrutnoe taxi No 156 go to/from the railway station, and bus No 101 runs to/from ploshcha Hretsky (Martynovskoho) in the city centre, but a taxi is much more reliable.

Local Transport Odessa has a comprehensive (but confusing) public transport network. Ploshcha Hretsky (Martynovskoho) and the circular roundabout in front of the railway station are the main downtown terminuses and central taxi stands.

A daunting and crowded variety of buses, trams, trolleybuses and marshrutnoe taxis can take you to the centre from the railway station (a 20-minute walk). Marshrutnoe taxi No 170 goes right up vulitsya Ekaterynynska (Karla Marxa) into the centre. Bus Nos 137 and 146 pass the railway station on the way to ploshcha Hretsky. Bus Nos 155 and 109, and trolleybus Nos 4 and 10, go up vulitsya Pushkinska before curving around to vulitsya Suvorova past the morsky vokzal and the foot of the Potemkin Steps. Tram Nos 2, 3 and 12 depart from west of the railway station and run down vulitsya Preobrazhenska to the city centre. A block east of the railway station, trolleybus Nos 5 and 9 leave for ploshcha Hretsky .

The regular passenger ferries fanning out to Odessa's beaches and suburbs are described in Beaches & Ferries earlier in the Odessa section.

BILHOROD-DNISTROVSKY
БІЛГОРОД-ДНІСТРОВСЬКИЙ
Population: 59,000

The White City on the Dnister, 55 km from Odessa on the west side of the Dnister estuary, is an ordinary industrial port town but has an impressive fortress on the banks of the river, comprised mostly of a large system of walls and bastions. First settled by Greeks, then Romans, the site was then subsequently controlled by Cossacks, Tatars, Russians and Romanians. With frequent electric train services to/from Odessa, it's an easy day trip.

Orientation
From the railway station walk straight down vulitsya Vokzalna, past the bus station and along the park to your right. Take the first street on the right after the park, vulitsya Dzerzhinskoho, which, after about 1.5 km, will take you to the fortress, bearing right towards the end. Halfway there you'll pass the main market.

The Fortress
Sometimes referred to as Akerman Fortress and dating back to the 13th century, this place was founded by Stefan II of Moldavia on a strategic spur of land overlooking the Dnister estuary. It was built on the site of the ancient Greek colony of Tyras, which existed from the 6th to 1st centuries BC. There are some scattered ruins opposite the entrance into the fortress, open daily from 9 am to 5 pm.

The fortress is one of the largest in Ukraine; its walls stretch nearly two km and its moat, once filled by an artificial tributary of the river, is six metres deep. The large and unkempt grounds inside the walls are separated into two main sections by a tall internal wall with two gateways. In the first section, which was home to the merchants and craftspeople, stands a single broken minaret, formerly part of a Tatar mosque. At the far end of the second sector, home to the soldiers and leaders, is the stout citadel overlooking the river, with four towers at each corner and a small inner courtyard. You can walk along most of the walls, accessed by several stairways, for views of the complex.

There is a display of the artefacts excavated from Tyras and the fortress at the **Regional Museum** at vulitsya Pushkina 19, open daily from 10 am to 6 pm, closed Monday. Especially impressive are the highly intricate Greek figurines. If walking *towards* the fortress from the railway station, turn right between vulitsya Dzerzhinskoho Nos 11 and 13 into vulitsya Lenina. Turn right at the park, then take the first left into vulitsya Pushkina – it's about three blocks down on your right, with a cannon out the front.

Getting There & Away
There are eight electric trains daily between

A: Lutsk, Ukraine
B: Lviv, Ukraine
C: Feodosia, Crimea

D: Lutsk, Ukraine
E: Kamyanets-Podilsky, Ukraine

JOHN NOBLE

GEORGE WESELY

GEORGE WESELY

Top: St Andrew's Church, Kiev
Bottom: Kremenets, Ukraine
Right: Swallow's Nest, Crimea

Odessa and Bilhorod-Dnistrovsky (2½ hours). The trains between Odessa and Izmayil stop in Bilhorod-Dnistrovsky on the way. There's also a bus service to Odessa and Izmayil as well as to some outlying towns.

IZMAYIL
IЗМАЇЛ
Population: 95,000

The Danube River port of Izmayil, 80 km from the Black Sea, provides a rarely used back door into the country. It is a pleasant enough city but is not really worth making a special trip to see. The telephone code for Izmayil is 04841.

City Centre

The main artery of the city is the north-south prospekt Suvorova. From the railway station take bus No 10 to the stop marked 'Tsentr', next to the **Regional Museum** on the corner of prospekt Suvorova and vulitsya Pushkina, with two cannons in front. There is a sort of extended park pleasantly running down the middle of prospekt Suvorova. South from the regional museum it leads to the large blue and white Pokorovsky Cathedral. Further south of the church is the equestrian statue of Suvorov, the war hero who helped take the city from the Turks during the Russian-Turkish War in 1790. Prospekt Suvorova continues south with more parks and, eventually, past the WWII boat monument and on to the passenger port at vulitsya Komnata 34. Seasonal boats up and down the Danube as well as to Black Sea destinations leave from here (see the Ukraine Getting There & Away section).

Things to See & Do

There used to be a **Turkish fort** about two km west of the city centre, overlooking and guarding the Danube – but today you'll need a good imagination, as there's close to nothing left. It's near the Hotel Dunaye, a typical 1970s Intourist structure on the western side of town. Just past the hotel a track leads to the **Mala Mechet** (small mosque) – a remnant of the mosque's

minaret is the only substantial trace of the fort. Further along are two dilapidated churches. Bus No 3 runs the length of vulitsya Kutuzova (a few blocks west of prospekt Suvorova) to the Hotel Dunaye and the fortress, but is somewhat infrequent.

A fun way to while away a few hours is to take a **hydrofoil ride** east along the last tiny leg of the Danube to the small towns of Kilia (50 minutes) and Vylkove (two hours) before it spills into the Black Sea. About four boats a day run in summer, with two a day in winter.

Places to Stay & Eat

The only hotel in town is the *Hotel Dunaye* which was closed when we visited. To get there follow the directions to the Turkish fort. Most of the snack kiosks and places to eat are clustered around the regional museum and the central bus stop on prospekt Suvorova.

Getting There & Away

There are two trains daily to/from Odessa – one at night and one during the day, taking eight hours and stopping in Bilhorod-Dnistrovsky on the way. Two buses daily travel to/from Bilhorod-Dnistrovsky as well as to a number of small outlying towns.

Izmayil is also the home port of the Ukrainian Danube Shipping Company, which runs trips up and down the Danube as far as Passau and Vienna, and to other ports in the Black Sea, including Odessa, Varna and Istanbul – so it's possible or enter and exit the county through Izmayil. At the time of writing, due to the war in former Yugoslavia the company had temporarily suspended passenger boat traffic through Belgrade, thus limiting the potential of this back door into Ukraine. Their office (☎ 90 210) is at prospekt Suvorova 2, or visit the office of Transkruyz (☎ 90 959, or 23 064) upstairs at the morsky vokzal at vulitsya Komnata 34, at the southern end of vulitsya Suvorova. For more information see the Ukraine Getting There & Away section.

UKRAINE

Crimea
Крим

Hanging off mainland Ukraine into the Black Sea, the Crimean peninsula is a golden prize that has always been difficult to control. A land bridge merging East and West, it was fought over for hundreds of years by numerous nations, but it was Russia that eventually wielded the firmest fist. Today, although officially part of Ukraine, the language you'll hear is Russian. After expelling ethnic Tatars, Stalin sent Russians in droves, and today's population of 2.7 million is 63% Russian, 25% Ukrainian, and only 9% Tatar. Crimea even follows Moscow's time, one hour later than Kiev's.

Russia first made the peninsula a favourite rest-and-recreation spot when the imperial family built a summer pad at Livadia in the 1860s. Millions now follow in their footsteps each year for warmth and beauty, sea and mountain air. The Yalta area is the main magnet, with its varied string of resorts and historic sites along a narrow coastal strip, behind which soar the highest mountains between the Caucasus and the Carpathians. But for a more complete picture, visit the old Tatar capital of Bakhchysaray, or some of the more unpretentious and rarely visited places such as Yevpatoria and Feodosia. Air and rail travellers arrive at the inland town of Simferopol, transferring by road to/from Yalta.

HISTORY

Greeks set up colonies on Crimea's coast at roughly the same time as the Scythians arrived from the east, during the 8th to 6th centuries BC. They coexisted for many centuries. The Scythians, squeezed out of 'mainland' Ukraine by the Sarmatians, were confined to Crimea from about the 2nd century BC until their state disappeared in the 3rd or 4th century AD. Panticapaeum, a Greek city at Crimea's eastern tip, ruled the Bosporan kingdom which held sway round

the Sea of Azov and over much of Crimea till at least the 4th century AD. Latterly it became subject to the Romans, who brought Christianity. Another Greek settlement, Chersonesus near Sevastopol (Khersones to Russians and Kherson to Ukrainians) became the seat of a bishop and, until the 13th century, an outpost of the Byzantine Empire. But most of Crimea fell to new arrivals from the East, such as the Khazar empire (descended from the Karaim) of the 7th to 9th centuries, the tribal Polovtsy in the 11th century and, in 1243, the Tatars, Crimean descendants of the Golden Horde.

From another direction came the Venetians and Genoese, rivals for eastern Mediterranean and Black Sea trade. The Genoese held a number of trading towns and forts along the Crimean coast until the late 15th century. The decaying Golden Horde spun off a number of smaller khanates of which the Crimean one, founded in 1443 and ruled from Bakhchysaray, lasted longest. It controlled Crimea itself, plus some areas immediately to the north and around the Sea of Azov. It became a vassal of the expanding Turkish Empire in 1475 and was a severe thorn in Russia and Ukraine's side, frequently raiding Cossack border towns and even attacking Moscow in the 1550s. The Russian Empire eventually annexed the pen-

insula in 1783 following successes against the Turks. The takeover prompted an exodus of Crimean Tatars, as the Crimean descendants of the Tatars (now with an admixture of Greek, Turkish and other blood) are known, to the Ottoman Empire. Russians, Ukrainians, as well as some Bulgarians and Germans resettled the peninsula.

The blunder-strewn Crimean War of 1854-56 was a classic clash of imperial ambitions. Russia wanted to take over the decaying Turkish Empire, while Britain and France wanted to stop this. So when in 1853 Russia occupied some Turkish provinces north of the Danube, the British and French assembled a big force at Varna, in what's now Bulgaria, to defend Istanbul. The Russians withdrew, but the allies were now committed to a fight, so together with the Turks they decided to invade Crimea. They took Sevastopol, Russia's main Black Sea port, in September 1855 after a year's siege.

The charge of the British Light Cavalry Brigade at Russian artillery resulted from misunderstood commands at the battle of Balaklava (October 1854), one of two Russian attempts to break the siege (the other was at Inkerman in November). Each side lost an estimated 250,000 in the war – many of those on the allied side dying from disease, bad hospitals and poor supplies, to which Florence Nightingale drew attention. After the war, Russian warships were banned from the Black Sea for 15 years, severely curtailing Russian expansion in the region.

In the civil war that followed the Russian Revolution, Crimea was one of the last White bastions, holding out till November 1920. In WW II it suffered a three-year German occupation and lost nearly half its population. Stalin then deported the remaining Crimean Tatars, about 250,000, for alleged collaboration with the Germans – mainly to Uzbekistan, where at least a third died en route. In the last few years an estimated quarter of the million or so Tatars in Uzbekistan have moved back to Crimea. In 1954 Khrushchev transferred legislative control of Crimea to Ukraine.

Since Ukrainian independence, many political complications have arisen. The Russian majority in Crimea has been anxious for more autonomy, even possible reunification with Russia. This sentiment is especially strong in Sevastopol where the controversial Black Sea Fleet sits rusting in the harbour. In

February 1992, the status of Crimea was changed from an autonomous republic to the official Republic of Crimea, with local leadership even drawing up a new constitution essentially claiming complete independence, which in turn drew threats of an economic blockade from Kiev. Tensions grew until heated negotiations resulted in Crimea remaining within the Ukraine but under a great degree of autonomy. In an act of defiance the Crimean authorities aligned the Crimean time zone with Moscow's (one hour ahead of Ukraine), although Crimea is 1500 km to the south of the Russian capital. The latest president of Crimea, Yuri Meshkov, a solid pro-Russia politician, is making sure this issue stays at the forefront, constantly bickering with his superiors in Kiev, who, incidentally, control all water coming into the peninsula. Moscow's stance: wait and see what happens.

GEOGRAPHY & CLIMATE
Crimea is linked to the mainland only by the Perekop Isthmus in the north-west. In the north-east, the Arabatskaya Strelka, a 110-km long sandspit, almost encloses the very shallow Sivash Lagoon, which is crossed by the main road and railway from the north. Northern and central Crimea are level, dry steppe. The forested Crimean Mountains begin south of Simferopol, reaching 1000 to 1500 metres before plummeting away to the narrow coastal resort strip. July and August are the warmest months on the south coast, with daily highs around 26°C. The temperature usually reaches 17°C or 18°C between May and October. In winter, it's rarely more than a degree or two below freezing.

BOOKS
The South Coast of the Crimea (Raduga Publishers) in English is a bit dated but covers the Greater Yalta area quite well. *Trekking in Russia & Central Asia* by Frith Maier (published by Cordee, Leicester, England; The Mountaineers, Seattle, USA; and Douglas & McIntyre, Vancouver, Canada) includes a 14-page chapter detailing walks, treks and climbs in Crimea. Keep

your eye out for *Peshchernye Goroda Kryma* (Cave Cities of the Crimea), a booklet that documents eight possible hiking and camping routes geared around exploring some of the historic cave cities with excellent trail maps and diagrams. It's helpful even if you can't read its Russian text. It's put out by the Kiev-based firm Krok and you can order one by phoning ☎ (044) 213 94 09 or 213 93 91. We found a copy at the kiosk in the Simferopol railway station, but you can also look in Yalta.

BEACHES
Crimean beaches are rarely sandy and nearly always jam-packed in summer. The water isn't warm and is often dirty around the cities. Ask about the water's cleanliness if you feel like a dip. Many beaches are either privately owned by sanatoria or hotels, or are pay-beaches, which are usually divided by unsightly concrete barriers into smaller zones, sadly ruining a long swathe of beach.

SANATORIA & HOLIDAY HOMES
The Crimean coasts – especially the southern one with its healthy mix of sea and mountain air – are littered with sanatoria and rest and holiday homes run by a number of organisations for their members. Many, such as the Livadia Palace and the Dnipro Sanatorium near Cape Ai-Todor, are in former palaces surrounded by superb parks, converted to a new use after Lenin's 1920 decree 'On the Use of the Crimea for the Medical Treatment of the Working People'. Others are big and imposing purpose-built structures like the Druzhba International Trade Union Boarding House (Mezhdunarodny Pansionat Druzhba) between Livadia and Cape Ai-Todor. Since independence, many sanatoria sit empty and neglected, no longer affordable and no longer being filled with the groups of Soviet workers on organised holidays. Often there's no problem wandering around the grounds of one of these places – if stopped at the gate, just say *'turist'*.

GETTING THERE & AWAY
Because of Crimea's former role as the top

holiday spot in the USSR, several major cities in Ukraine, Russia and Belarus have numerous daily direct trains to the region via Simferopol. Air traffic from Kiev, Moscow and St Petersburg also brings visitors in to Simferopol (see Getting There & Away in Simferopol). It's also possible to arrive in Crimea by boat to Yalta via Odessa (see Getting There & Away in Yalta).

GETTING AROUND
Most visitors to Crimea arrive in Simferopol. From there, buses and electric trains branch out to most destinations throughout the peninsula. Yalta is serviced by frequent trolleybuses from the Simferopol railway station (2½ hours). For details on getting to/from specific sites, see the relevant sections.

SIMFEROPOL
СІМФЕРОПОЛЬ
Population: 358,000
Simferopol is the crossroads of Crimea where the northern plains end and the southern mountains start. It's worth an overnight stop if you're interested in history, and makes a good base from which to explore other regions of Crimea, such as Bakhchysaray. Founded in the 18th century beside the 15th-century Crimean Tatar town of Ak-Mechet (White Mosque), it was the last Russian stop before the front line during the Crimean War, and a giant hospital for the wounded. Long ago the Scythian town of Neapolis, whose site can be visited, stood here. In summer, take an evening stroll around the pleasant low-rise, park-dotted centre: vehicles are banned from some streets, a holiday atmosphere washes up from the coast, and sailors come in from the Crimean naval bases. Make sure to set your watch one hour ahead when entering Crimea.

Orientation & Information
The centre of town, with most of the cafés and shops, is around vulitsya Karla Marxa, vulitsya Pushkina and vulitsya Horkoho, with much of this area pedestrian zones. The railway station is at the north-western end of vulitsya Karla Marxa, two km from the centre. There's a tourist bureau in the Hotel Ukraina (☎ 27 46 71) and another one at vulitsya Leytenanta Shmidta 9 (☎ 27 42 46), but neither offers much except expensive group tours of things better seen on your own. Various maps of the city and Crimea can be bought at most kiosks, including the one in the railway station, and in the bookshops along the pedestrian section of vulitsya Pushkina. Pick up a good map of Yalta before you depart.

Simferopol's telephone area code is 0652.

City Centre
The **Crimean Regional Museum** on the corner of vulitsya Pushkina and vulitsya Hoholya takes you through Crimean history. Check out the 'Skifskoe Gosudarstvo' cabinet on the 1st floor, which has a map of Neapolis and gold Scythian body adornments. Upstairs covers the Crimean War with maps, tombstones, weaponry and a series of English lithographs. The museum is open from 9 am to 5 pm daily, closed Tuesday. A block north-west on vulitsya Hoholya is the impressive **Three Saints Church** with its five onion domes. A small **Art Museum** (open daily from 10 am to 4.30 pm, closed Monday) lies between the city centre and the railway station at vulitsya Lybknekhta 35.

Just east of the city centre the recently restored **Church of SS Peter & Paul**, with its swooping dome and bell tower, is now open after 60 years of closure. Nearby is the **Holy Trinity Cathedral**, also restored with a nice iconostasis. A bit further east up quaint vulitsya Kurchatova is a restored **mosque** in a small colourful neighbourhood recently repopulated by returning Crimean Tatars.

A pleasant and strollable park strip follows the winding Salhir River north-east of the centre.

Neapolis
Neapolis was probably the capital of the late Scythian state in Crimea from the 3rd century BC to the 3rd or 4th century AD. Its

UKRAINE

To Zaporizhzhya & Odessa

To Yevpatoria & Simferopol Airport

vulitsya Kechkemetska

ploshcha Moskovska

vulitsya Sadova

vulitsya Kyivska

shosse Yevpatoriyske

vulitsya Kym

vulitsya Gagarina

Salhir River

Simferopol
Сімферополь

0   0.5   1 km

To Feodosia

ploshcha Kuybysheva

prospekt Pobedy

bulvar Lenina

bulvar Lenina

vulitsya Tolstoho

5

vulitsya Pavlenko

vulitsya Karla Marxa

vulitsya Rozy Lyuxemburg

4

vulitsya Kirova

vulitsya Mayorskoho

vulitsya Toistoho

vulitsya Adzhynyoshka

vulitsya Zhukovskoho

6

7

8

Ploshcha Radyanska

9

vulitsya Leytenanta Shmida

Salhir River

vulitsya Horkoho

vulitsya Pushkina

vulitsya Karla Marxa

18

17

16

15

19

20

vulitsya Samokisha

prospekt Kirova

vulitsya Horkoho

12

13

21

25

22

24

23

10

Vorovskoho

11

26

vulitsya Obezna

ploshcha Lenina

vulitsya Prolitarska

vulitsya Kurchatova

vulitsya Lenina

To Alushta & Yalta

ploshcha Radyansky Konstytutsy

vulitsya Chekhova

28

27

vulitsya Krylova

vulitsya Chervonoarmiyska

29

vulitsya Kozlova

vulitsya Sevastopolska

vulitsya Subkhi

To Bakhchysaray Sevastopol & Zavodskoe Airport

	PLACES TO STAY			10	Central Bus Station
					Центральний автобусний вокзал
6	Hotel Ukraina			13	TsUM Department Store
	Гостинниця Україна				ЦУМ
11	Hotel Moskva			15	Circus
	Гостинниця Москва				Цирк
26	Hotel Sportivnaya			16	Bookshop
	Гостинниця Спортівная				Книгарня
				17	Horkoho Theatre
	PLACES TO EAT				Театр ім. Горького
				18	Biblioteka
12	Pizza Kafe				Бібліотека
	Піцца кафе			19	Three Saints Church
14	Row of Cafes				Церква Трьох Святих
	Кафе			20	Crimean Regional Museum
					Кримский краєзнавчий музей
	OTHER			21	Ukrainian Music & Drama Theatre
					Український театр музики
1	Trolleybus terminal for Alushta & Yalta				та драми
	Тролеейбусна станція до Алушта			22	Church of SS Peter & Paul
	та Ялта				Петропавлівська церква
2	Railway Station			23	Mosque
	Залізничний вокзал				Мечеть
3	Small Bus Station			24	Svayatotroiska Cathedral
	Мала автобусна стація				Святотроїцька катедра
4	Art Museum			25	Former House of Soviets
	Художній музей				Бувший дім Советів
5	Market			27	Central Market
	Ринок				Центральний ринок
7	Post & Telephone Office			28	Train & Airline Ticket Office
	Пошта та телефон				Каса продажу залізничних та
8	Russian Drama Theatre				авіаційних квитків
	Руский театр драми			29	Neapolis
9	Simferopol Cinema				Скіфський неаполь
	Кіно Симферополь				

site is 20 hectares of hilltop two km east of the town centre, between vulitsya Vorovskoho and vulitsya Chervonoarmiyska (Krasnoarmeyskaya). There's really not much to see except for some scattered excavations, mounds, humps and an untidy stone reconstruction of a **royal mausoleum** dating from the 2nd century BC to the 1st century AD. Bus No 4 from the railway station runs through the city centre to the site.

Places to Stay

The cheapest and bleakest is the *Hotel Sportivnaya* (☎ 25 83 81), 1.5 km south-west of the city centre at vulitsya H Adzhymoshka (Zhelyabova) 50, poorly reached by public transport (take bus A to 'Hostinitsa Sportyvnaya'), but a walkable distance from the centre. Adequate rooms cost US$10/ 20/30 a single/double/triple.

The *Hotel Moskva* (☎ 23 20 12) at vulitsya Kyivska (Kievskaya) 2, off ploshcha Radyansky Konstytutsy (Sovietskoy Konstitutsii) is newer and less run-down, and although it's two km east of the centre, it's near the central bus station. Rooms cost US$15/30 a single/double. Take trolleybus No 1, 2 or 6 from the railway station, or No 4 from the city centre, and get off at the avtovokzal (bus station).

Hotel Ukraina (☎ 27 55 73) at vulitsya Rozy Lyuxemburg 9 is attractive and central

UKRAINE

with well-worn singles/doubles/triples for US$21/36/50; but it's a bit overpriced given the fact that the bathrooms are in the corridor. Trolleybus Nos 5 and 2 from the railway station stop in front of it ('Hostinitsa Ukraina' stop), and Nos 1, 4 and 6 stop nearby ('Ploshcha Lenina').

Places to Eat

The restaurant at the back of the *Hotel Ukraina* had been closed for renovation, but may be reopened. The best places to get food at the *Hotel Moskva* are the small bufety on the 3rd and 5th floors, where they cook you up a meal on the spot. The *Hotel Sportivnaya* has a small café.

At the southern end of vulitsya Horkoho there is a row of four places where you can grab a bite. The *Russkie Bayny* to the left of the circus serves tasty hot bliny dripping with honey and butter. Next door, the *Desert* is a spacious smoke-free café serving ice cream and sweets. Upstairs is the *Restoran Astoryya*. Finally, on the corner of vulitsya Horkoho and prospekt Kirova, there is the *Kafe Bistro* which serves up plates of varenyky, meatballs, noodles and soups for about US$1. Just north of the TsUM department store on prospekt Kirova is the popular *Pizza Kafe*, and farther down at Kirova 25 there is a shop that sells lots of Western food products.

Getting There & Away

Air Simferopol has two airports. Zavodskoe Airport handles a few occasional shorter flights to places like Poltava and Kherson, but Simferopol Airport (also known as Tsentralny), on the northern side of the city, is the main one. There are daily flights to/from Moscow (two hours) and St Petersburg (three hours) on Aeroflot, to/from Kiev (1½ hours) and occasionally Odessa (one hour) on Air Ukraine in summer, and reduced services in winter. The Air Ukraine office (☎ 27 21 16) is at vulitsya Sevastopolska (Sevastopolskaya) 22.

Bus & Trolleybus Apart from Yevpatoria, Sevastopol and Bakhchysaray (served by

electric trains), other sites in Crimea such as Yalta, Alushta, Feodosia, Sudak and Kerch are better reached from Simferopol by trolleybus or bus services.

To/From Yalta & Alushta There are no direct trains going to the Yalta area, so from Simferopol you'll have to take the world's longest trolleybus line, which crosses a 748-metre-high mountain pass on its 85-km journey. The service is cheap (less than US$1) and unbelievably frequent, departing from the trolleybus terminal immediately to the right of the railway station. Trolleybus No 52 to Yalta (2½ hours) and No 51 to Alushta (1½ hours) run every 20 minutes from 5.35 am to 11 pm, the Alushta service ending at 9 pm. (A taxi can take you to Yalta an hour faster for about US$25.) Trolleybus No 55 runs between Simferopol Airport and Yalta every 20 minutes from dawn to dusk, stopping at Alushta on the way.

To/From Other Places Most buses depart from the main bus station at vulitsya Kyivska (Kievskaya) 4 near the Hotel Moskva, but some buses also depart from the small bus station next to the railway station in front of the Yalta/Alushta trolleybus terminal, including those for Sudak. There also two other smaller stations, the Zapadnaya station, south of the city centre (take trolleybus No 5 from the railway station), and the Vostochnaya station, north of the city centre (trolleybus Nos 3 and 13 from the railway station). All tickets are bought at the stations.

Train Simferopol is Crimea's main railway junction. There are four trains daily to/from Moscow (21 to 26 hours) via Kharkiv and Zaporizhzhya and two trains a day to/from Kiev (14 to 15 hours). There are also daily services to/from Lviv (30 hours), Odessa (13 hours), Kerch (seven hours), Riga (21 hours), Minsk (29 hours) and St Petersburg (35 hours). There are seasonal services to/from Rostov-on-Don (14 to 15 hours) and even Siberia. Tickets can usually be bought at the station, but it may be easier to buy them in advance at the ticket office (☎ 27 33 16) at vulitsya Sevastopolska 22.

There are also three lines of efficient electric railway on the Crimean peninsula, with trains running to/from Yevpatoria (two hours), Bakhchysaray (40 minutes) and Sevastopol (two hours), and Dzhankoy (three hours), each about seven times a day. The ticket and information booths are at the *prymiski kasy (prigorodny kassy)* outside and south of the main hall at the railway station.

Car & Motorbike The main road from the north divides four ways at Simferopol – for Yevpatoria, Sevastopol, Alushta and Kerch. The main road to Yalta is excellent and picturesque, winding down through the Crimean Mountains, then running above the coast from Alushta, with side roads descending to the coastal towns and villages. But the most scenic, though slightly longer, drive to Yalta is south-west towards Sevastopol, then south-east past Bakhchysaray toward Tankovoe and Kuybysheve (Kuyebishevo), and then onward. The descent into Yalta is spectacular.

Getting Around
The railway station is a chief terminus for buses and trolleybuses. Some stop in the large forecourt, others on the road. Trolleybus No 9 runs between the station and the main airport; No 11 between the station and Zavodskoe Airport, stopping in the centre at ploshcha Lenina on the way; No 5 between the railway station, ploshcha Radyanska (Sovietskaya), ploshcha Lenina and the central market. Trolleybus Nos 1, 2 and 6 all run from the railway station through the city centre to the central bus station.

YEVPATORIA
ЄВПАТОРІЯ
Population: 115,000
Off the usual beaten track for Western tourists, Yevpatoria, like Feodosia, is an ancient city holding a delightful array of relics reflecting the rich and diverse cultures involved in Crimean history. Its fine coastal site includes an old town and a pleasant

waterfront area making it an enjoyable and easy day trip from Simferopol, 78 km to the south-east. Don't get too discouraged by the bleak industrial surroundings as you approach the city.

On the northern rim of Kalamytsky Bay, Yevpatoria was first settled by Greeks in the 6th to 5th centuries BC as the town of Kirkinitida. Later inhabited by immigrant Slavs in the 10th to 12th centuries, it was renamed Hezlev by the Turks who fortified it and turned it into a major slave-trading market in the 15th century. When the city fell to Russian control in 1783, it was renamed Yevpatoria.

Orientation
The old town spreads out west from the small Yevpatoria Bay and is bordered on the north by vulitsya Internatsyonalna (Internatsionalnaya) and to the west by vulitsya Lva Tolstoho. The commercial centre lies along vulitsya Revolyutsy which runs east to the waterfront from ploshcha Teatralna (Teatralnaya). The train and bus stations are about 1.5 km north-west of the city centre. Good city maps can be bought from some kiosks – try the one at the railway station.

Yevpatoria's telephone area code is 06569.

Old Town
Although the surrounding walls have long gone and the wooden houses have been replaced by small stone ones, the twisted layout of the old town has more or less survived intact, harbouring a run-down and lively atmosphere. Most of the streets are low-scale residential with children playing and old people gossiping. Take a good look around – the most interesting things are behind the fenced courtyards where laundry lines hang and tiny gardens grow.

On and around the eastern half of vulitsya Matveeva are a few interesting pieces of historic architecture. At vulitsya Matveeva 68, recessed from the street, is a set of 18th-century **kenassas**, prayer houses of the historic Karaite Jewish sect (for more information on kenassas see Chufut-Kale in the

Yevpatoria
Євпаторія

0   250   500 m

YEVPATORIA BAY

ploshcha Prymorska

ploshcha Moryakov

ploshcha Teatralna

KALAMYTSKY BAY

To Hotel Yevpatoria (500 m)

Bakhchysaray section). Beyond a formal gateway a walkway lined with Hebrew-carved plaques leads to a beautiful arcaded courtyard where the kenassas are located, both built in the first half of the 19th century. If they are closed for renovation, persuade a worker to let you in for a quick look. Farther down vulitsya Matveeva, No 53 is an 18th-century **Karaite house** with a lovely porch supported by carved wooden columns in its courtyard. It's still a private home.

On the next corner is an abandoned stone **synagogue** rising from a huddle of houses below. A block further and down on vulitsya Chervonoarmiyska (Krasnoarmeyskaya) are two 15th to 18th-century Turkish **hamams** (bathhouses), both in states of disrepair. The one at No 26 is behind a stone wall and inaccessible, but at No 20 you can peek through the barred windows. A green gate to the left leads around to the boiler room and the ventilation holes in the small domes on the roof.

Through a gateway and in a courtyard at vulitsya Internatsyonalna 44 is a stone **Armenian church** now barred shut, but a group of civilians is supposed to have hidden inside during the German occupation.

PLACES TO STAY		OTHER		13	Hotel Borybazh Building (1915)
17	Hotel Krim Гостинниця Крим	1	Train Station Залізничний вокзал		Готель Будинок Борибажа
25	Hotel Ukraina Гостинниця Україна	2	Bus Station Автобусний вокзал	14	St Nicholas Cathedral Собор Св. Миколи
26	Hotel Skazka Гостинниця Сказка	3	Kenassas Комплекс Кенасий	16	Dzhuma-Dzhami Mosque
27	Hotel Yuzhnaya Гостинниця Южная	4	Karaite House Караїмський дім		Мечеть Джума-Джамі
		5	Synagogue Синагога	20	Hrecheska Church Греческа церква
PLACES TO EAT		6	Turkish Hamam Турецький гамам	21	Morsky Vokzal (Sea Port)
11	Zemnoy Ray Кафе/Бар Земний Рай	7	Armenian Church Вірменська церква		Морський вокзал
12	Safryn Restaurant Ресторан Сафрин	8	Tekye-Dervishey Hermitage & Shukulay-Yefendy Mosque	23	Pushkina Theatre Театр Пушкіна
15	Pizzeria/Bar Піццерія/Бар		Текіє Дервішей монастир та мечет Шукулай-Єфенді	24	Central Department Store Центральний універмаг
18	Restoran Urodnyka Ресторан Уродника	9	Turkish Hamams Турецький гамам	28	Regional Museum Краєзнавчий музей
19	Kafe Novynka Кафе Новинка	10	Post & Telephone Office Пошта і телефон	29	Children's Resort & Sanatorium
22	Kafe Belochka Кафе Белочка				Детский клинический санаторий

At the corner of vulitsya Internatsyonalna and vulitsya Karaeva is the 14th-century **Tekye-Dervishey hermitage**, distinguished by the broken minaret of the **Shukulay-Yefendy Mosque**, much of it in a semi-ruined state. Walk through the corner gate and some workers will gladly show you around and perhaps even let you climb up the narrow minaret, accessed through a low opening in the eastern wall of the roofless mosque. Inside the adjacent hermitage building, where the religious men lived, narrow cells line each side of the square, vaulted space.

At the end of vulitsya Karaeva **St Nicholas Cathedral** sits opposite the waterfront. It was built in 1893, 10 years after the 100th anniversary of Russia's control of Crimea. Its central dome is surrounded by 16 narrow arched windows and supported by eight buttressing chapels, with a bell tower rising above the entrance.

A block south-west is the 1552 **Dzhuma-Dzhami Mosque**, the 77th of 81 mosques designed in a traditional Turkish style by the famous architect Khodzhy Synan, and by far the largest mosque in Crimea. Its two tall minarets were restored in 1976 as well as the twin mihrabs (prayer niches) on either side of the entrance, which has a carved Arabic inscription above it indicating the year the mosque was constructed. To the left of the entrance are two ornate marble tombs of Turkish generals killed during the Crimean War. Stick around in the afternoon and you'll hear the Muslim call to prayer immediately followed by the Orthodox tolling of the bells from a block away. Both houses of worship are, ironically, roughly based on the same building, the Hagia Sophia Cathedral in Istanbul.

Further south-west along the waterfront is the **Hrecheska Church**, built of golden sandstone in traditional Slavic Orthodox style. The **regional museum** is south-west of the old town on the corner of vulitsya

Duvanovska (Duvanovskaya; formerly Sverdlova) and vulitsya Kirova, housed in a small 1910 Ottoman-style palace. There's a good display of Greek and Tatar artefacts along with lots of WW II paraphernalia. It's open daily from 10 am to 5 pm, closed Wednesday.

Contrasting with the narrow and curving streets of the old town is classic Soviet planning to the south-west – a large and monotonous grid of streets with dull parks and dozens of even duller sanatoria – absolutely nothing of interest save the nice beach that lines the long southern seaside strip.

Places to Stay

Standard accommodation is limited, but most people stay in the mass of sanatoria south-west of the old town. The *Hotel Ukraina* (☎ 3 02 90) at prospekt Lenina 42/19, on the corner of vulitsya Frunze, is the best bet. It's an attractive old hotel with decent singles/doubles/triples for US$6/10/15. The rooms have baths and there are showers down the hall. If you can't find anyone downstairs go to the reception upstairs. To get there from the railway station take tram No 3 down vulitsya Frunze for three stops.

The tall and ugly *Hotel Yevpatoria* (☎ 5 14 18) is farther away from the old town and has two separate buildings; the first is three blocks west of the Hotel Ukraina on the corner of prospekt Lenina and prospekt Pobedy, and the other is two blocks south at vulitsya Moskovska (Moskovskaya) 29. Rooms cost about US$10 per person. To get there walk from the Hotel Ukraina or take tram No 1 west down prospekt Lenina.

The *Hotel Krym* (☎ 10 559) at vulitsya Revolyutsy 46 is small and in an excellent location but is only open from mid-May to the end of October, and is usually filled with groups of noisy kids, but it's still worth a try. They charge US$8 per person in a single/double/triple room; the bathroom is down the corridor. To get there from ploshcha Teatralna, walk or take tram No 1 north-east.

South of the Hotel Ukraina there are two

other hotels: the *Skazka* at vulitsya Pushkina 40 and the *Yuzhnaya* at vulitsya Kirova 50.

Places to Eat

The *Hotel Ukraina* has a pleasant restaurant, but it only has a limited selection. There's also a bar off the lobby and a small 2nd-floor buffet. Probably the nicest restaurant in town is the *Safryn*, opposite St Nicholas Cathedral, at vulitsya Karaeva 2, which serves borscht, a meat dish with salad and a drink for about US$4. The lively *Restoran Urodnyka*, in the old post office at vulitsya Revolyutsy 50, is similar. Both are open until 11 pm. Across the street from Urodnyka is the *Kafe Novynka*, serving cakes and coffee. In a park, just up from the regional museum, is the *Kafe Belochka*, a plain cafeteria dishing out tasty platefuls of hot and starchy food for less than US$1. There's a *pizzeria* and bar on the corner opposite the cathedral. On the other side of the cathedral, around the corner from the Safryn, is the seedy but likeable downstairs café/bar *Zemnoy Ray*, where you can sit in a private booth and draw the curtain. At the far eastern end of the train-station platform is a place that sells quick, hot plates of varenyky.

Getting There & Away

There are eight electric trains daily travelling between Simferopol and Yevpatoria, about every two hours from around 5.40 am to 8.30 pm, taking roughly 2½ hours. There's also a daily train to Kiev and Moscow, but it has to go through Simferopol, which has trains going to all destinations. If the daily train does not suit you, you're better off catching any train to Simferopol and changing there.

During summer there are a few sporadic boats to Odessa overnight and even up the Dnipro to Kiev (two days). For information check at the passenger port (morsky vokzal) at the southern end of the waterfront at ploshcha Moryakov 1.

Getting Around

Three tram lines run through the city. Tram No 3 runs from the railway station south and then east to ploshcha Teatralna; No 1 runs from the west of town through ploshcha Teatralna and along the waterfront to the old town; and No 2, less useful, runs from ploshcha Teatralna south and west through the sanatoria zone.

If you're just visiting for the day you can walk from the railway station to the old town in about 20 minutes – turn left down vulitsya Internatsyonalna, then right down vulitsya Lva Tolstoho and then left into vulitsya Volodarskoho. Or you can take tram No 3 to ploshcha Teatralna and then walk or take tram No 1 to the waterfront.

BAKHCHYSARAY
БАХЧИСАРАЙ

Population: 20,000

The small town of Bakhchysaray, 33 km south-west of Simferopol, and the abandoned cave cities in its surrounding limestone hills, bring you face to face with the Tatar era and other remnants of Crimea's past. From the 15th century until 1783, Bakhchysaray (Turkish for 'garden palace') was the seat of the Crimean khans, the last westward bastion of the descendants of Jenghiz Khan's hordes. From 1475, these Crimean Tatars were vassals of the Ottoman Empire; and as the embodiment of both the terrible Tatar hordes and the 'depraved infidel' Turks, they are the cruel bogeymen of many a Slavic fairy tale.

Before WW II Bakhchysaray had 36 mosques and a mainly Crimean Tatar population. After being hauled off to Uzbekistan by Stalin, the Tatars have been slowly returning to their homeland since the late 1980s, many settling in and around their historic capital.

Bakhchysaray's telephone code is 06554.

Khans' Palace

The Tatar rulers' palace (Khansky Palats), sometimes referred to as the Khan Serai, was built primarily by Russian and Ukrainian slaves in the 16th century under the direction of Persian, Ottoman and Italian master builders. It has been rebuilt several times since, but still resembles its pre-Russian state. It's

at vulitsya Richkov 129 in the older, eastern part of town, and is easily recognisable by the tall minarets of its main mosque. It's open daily from 9 am to 5 pm; closed Tuesday, Wednesday and the last day of the month. You can wander around the serene grounds freely, but to visit the palace and the museum you need to purchase a ticket at the kasa to the left as you enter.

Inside the main **mosque** (no ticket necessary), which dates from 1740, there is a nice wooden *minbar* (pulpit) and carved mihrabs (prayer niches facing Mecca). The khans' private prayer room, with an original carved wooden ceiling, is upstairs to the right. The carved wooden balcony *(mafil)* was for women only.

Past the mosque is the khans' **cemetery** (no ticket necessary) where, among finely carved tombstones, there are two octagonal rotunda tombs *(dyurbe)*, miniature mausoleums for the khans.

Opposite the mosque are the main palace and museum complex – a series of courtyards and Ottoman-style buildings where the indoor and outdoor spaces blend together. In front of you as you enter is the finely carved **Ambassadors' Gate**, also called the Portal Aleviza, after its Italian creator Alevisio Novi. In the inner courtyard is the white marble **Fountain of Tears** (Fontan Slez), said to have been made by a captive Persian, Omer, for the last Crimean khan, Giri, who was so ruthless that people said he had a lump of wool for a heart. Eventually Giri fell in love with a captive Polish girl in his harem who, when she died, caused him to weep, proving he had a heart after all. He ordered Omer to make a rock weep too, to perpetuate his grief. Also in the courtyard are the Holy Paradise Fountain, the Fountain of Life and the Lullaby Fountain.

In the back garden behind the palace is the **harem**, three rooms decorated with cushioned seats and carpets, and with prettily painted walls and stained-glass windows.

The north wing of the palace houses the extensive and fascinating **historical museum**. Its 12 rooms contain a variety of exhibits covering Tatar culture and the life of

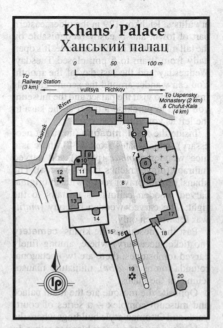

Khans' Palace
Ханський палац

0   50   100 m

To Railway Station (3 km)

vulitsya Richkov

To Uspensky Monastery (2 km) & Chufut-Kale (4 km)

Churuk River

1	Historical Museum
	Головні виставки кімнати
2	Entrance Gateway
	Вхід
3	Ticket Kasa
	Каса
4	Mosque
	Мечеть
5	Khans' Cemetery
	Ханський цвинтар
6	Mausoleums
	Гробівниці Ханоб
7	Entrance to the Cemetery
	Вхід на цвинтар
8	Main Grounds
	Головний грунт
9	Entrance to Khans' Palace & Museum
	Вхід до Ханського Палацу та музею
10	Ambassador's Gate
	Амбасадорська брама
11	Courtyard & Fountain of Tears
	Гаремний город і Фонтан Сліз
12	Palace Gardens
	Сади палацу
13	Harem/Summer House
	Гаремовий/Літній дім
14	Tower
	Башта
15	Bathrooms
16	Alexander I Fountain
	Фонтан Александра I
17	Former Stables
	Бувші стайні
18	Gateway
	Брама
19	WW II Park
	Парк Великої Вітчизняної війни
20	Tower
	Башта

the khans, including textiles, furnishings, glassware, documents and old photos. Catherine the Great supposedly spent the night in one of these rooms.

Uspensky Monastery

Not far to the east of the palace the main road changes its name to vulitsya Lyuxemburg. About a km down this road is the small **Mosque of Tokhtala-Dzhama** with a 16-sided minaret. Another km along this road, past small cottages on the right and sheer rock walls on the left, is the hamlet of **Starosele**. From here, just past the bus stop and small car park, a track branches up to the right to the deserted Uspensky Monastery (and Chufut-Kale beyond), five minutes' walk away. The monastery – probably founded by Byzantine monks in the 8th or 9th century – is a series of shallow caves carved out of a rock face. Some of the caves served as churches, others as cells. There are steps and then a little path leading up to them.

At the top of the steps, an upper path to the left leads along the cliff and to 86 **stone steps** cut out of the rock which climb to the top of the outcrop and provide excellent views of the canyon. Across the canyon there are more trails and some smaller caves – good for hiking.

Chufut-Kale
ЧУФУТ-КАЛЕ

The biggest and most accessible of several cave cities in the limestone hills of southwest Crimea is on top of a long bluff, two km down the track past the Uspensky Monastery, then up the steep hillside to the left. Chufut-Kale dates from somewhere between the 6th and 12th centuries. Early on, it was probably inhabited by Christians, who built a church which was later rebuilt as a mosque. Around 1400, Tokhtamysh, the last powerful ruler of the Golden Horde, used it as a refuge after his empire was smashed by Timur in the 1390s. In the 17th century Crimean khans imprisoned eminent Poles, Russians and Ukrainians here. The last regular inhabitants, who had left by the mid-19th century, were the Karaites, a dissident Jewish sect founded in Baghdad in 770 AD who spread to Egypt, Syria and the northern Black Sea. The name Chufut-Kale (Jews' Castle) comes from them.

You'll probably enter by the 14th-century South Gate, leading to a Swiss-cheese composition of carved-out rooms and steps. Over to the right on the clifftop are two kenassas in a walled courtyard. One, with Hebrew inscriptions, is from the 18th century; the other, with a beautifully carved stone porch, is from the 14th century. Beyond the kenassas are a series of foundations and low stone walls. A stone path farther beyond leads to the lovely little Muslim mausoleum of Dzhanike-Khanym, daughter of Tokhtamysh. The delicate stone carvings around the portal are exquisite. Beyond the mausoleum, the cliff drops dramatically and there is an expansive view over the next valley. Further along, the stone path leads through an archway, which was part of an impressive system of defensive walls from the 10th to 14th centuries. To the left after the archway a path leads to two burial chambers next to the cliff's edge. About two km farther east of Chufut-Kale is another smaller cave city called **Tepe-Kermen**.

Places to Stay

There is a small hotel past the Khans' Palace on the eastern outskirts of town (ask for the *turistsky baza* Prival) but you can visit the Khans' Palace, Uspensky Monastery and Chufut-Kale as a day trip from Simferopol. It is also possible to camp near Chufut-Kale;

water is available from a fountain at the chapel next to the Uspensky Monastery. Bring your own food and supplies from Simferopol.

Getting There & Away

There are seven electric trains daily between Simferopol and Sevastopol, stopping in Bakhchysaray (40 minutes from Simferopol) on the way. The first train leaves Simferopol at 5.47 am, the last train from Bakhchysaray back to Simferopol is at 10.25 pm. There are also a few buses daily between Bakhchysaray and Simferopol, but the electric train is the more frequent and faster.

Guided tours of Bakhchysaray can be arranged from Yalta (see Information in the Yalta section), but it's cheaper on your own.

Getting Around

Bakhchysaray's railway station is about three km west of the Khans' Palace, and the bus station is 1.5 km north-east of the railway station. From the railway station, bus Nos 1 and 2 go through the old town to the Khans' Palace, and No 2 continues on to Starosele, stopping at the base of the track leading to the Uspensky Monastery and Chufut-Kale. Bus No 4 goes between the bus and railway stations.

You could walk the entire way; it's about 45 minutes from the railway station to the Khans' Palace, and a little over an hour from there to Chufut-Kale. To get to the palace, walk about 300 metres east of the railway station to the large intersection, and from there continue straight ahead (third road from left).

If you're in a hurry, take a taxi from the railway station to the Khan's Palace for about US$2. Bring your own food and supplies from Simferopol because Bakhchysaray is meagre on facilities.

MANHUP-KALE
МАНГУП-КАЛЕ

Manhup-Kale, about 22 km south of Bakhchysaray, is another famous and fascinating cave city. It's less accessible but still possible as a long day trip from Simferopol, especially

UKRAINE

easy if you have your own vehicle. Manhup-Kale dates from the 6th century and, like Chufut-Kale, it was settled by various peoples – pagan to Christian to Tatar to Karaite – and finally abandoned in the 15th century. Manhup-Kale is more spread out than Chufut-Kale.

It's possible to camp in the area; unfortunately people camping in the caves in the past have been very destructive, leaving litter and vandalising the walls. There's an official camping ground, *Turistsky Stoyanky Manhup*, above the small cluster of cottages and up the hillside on the opposite side of the track which leads to the caves.

The booklet *Peshchernye Goroda Kryma* (Cave Cities of the Crimea – see the Books section earlier in this chapter) is useful when visiting Manhup-Kale and other cave sites.

Exploring the Caves

From the southern end of Zalesnoe walk about one km until you see on your left four rock peaks rising in a row out of wooded ravines. They're actually four fingers of land stretching out from the same long ridge. Turn off the road toward the small hamlet at the base of the ridge. On the farthest fingertip east you'll see small holes and some cave openings – that's where the biggest concentration of caves is. The other three fingers have only a few scattered walls. The best way up is between the first two fingers; a trail leads up to your right just as you approach the small group of cottages. At the top of the ridge follow the trail to the farthest finger of land until you see a large stone gateway and long wall. Beyond is where the mass of carved-out chambers and caves lie. Explore especially along the far eastern edge of the cliff, many chambers having windows looking out over the vast vista. The most impressive is the final cave room carved out of the very tip of the cliff with stairs leading down the west side to a burial chamber with tiny cells.

Getting There & Away

The closest village to Manhup-Kale is Zalesnoe, about three km away, reached from the Bakhchysaray bus station by two useless daily buses, one too early to catch if you're coming from Simferopol (5.10 am), the other too late to make it worthwhile (4.25 pm). The easiest way to reach the village is by taxi from the Bakhchysaray railway station, costing about US$6 for the 20-km ride. One railway station past Bakhchysaray is a tiny village called Syren, 10 km north of Zalesnoe, from where you could possibly hitchhike the rest of the way.

From Zalesnoe back to Bakhchysaray, there's usually a daily bus leaving Zalesnoe at around 4.55 pm from the tiny bus stop (taking 30 minutes). From Bakhchysaray there are numerous trains back to Simferopol until around 10.25 pm. If you miss the last bus from Zolesnoe, you'll have to hitchhike to Bakhchysaray or Syren to get back to the train tracks.

YALTA
ЯЛТА
Population: 90,000

First mentioned in the 12th century as the Polovtsian (the Polovtsy were a nomadic tribe from the steppe) city of Dzhalita, it later became known as Healita under the control of the Genoese in the 14th century. After a 15th-century earthquake it was repopulated by Greeks, Armenians and Tatars, with frequent Cossack attacks from the north. In the late 18th century Crimea came under Russian control, and Yalta became the Empire's classiest Black Sea resort when Tsar Alexander II made nearby Livadia a summer residence. Before the revolution the coast was peppered with aristocratic estates, and artistic figures such as Tolstoy, Chekhov and Rachmaninov spent much time here. After the revolution the palaces became sanatoria for the workers, but once again new generations of high and mighty soon established themselves, building lavish dachas and continuing the area's tradition as the exclusive hideaway of the rich and powerful.

The setting is spectacular, a narrow cypress-strewn strip between the Crimean Mountains and the Black Sea, reminiscent in different ways of Cornwall, the Costa del

Sol, Windermere and the French Riviera. Shielded from north winds, temperatures only just dip below freezing in winter and are several degrees warmer than Kiev and Moscow in summer. People bathe from June to October – by which time they can usually look up to snow on the peaks above.

Orientation
Yalta lies between the gently curving shore of Yalta Bay (Yaltinsky Zaliv) and Yuzhnoberezhnoe shose, the highway which forms a winding ring road round the edge of town, a km or two up from the bay. The main bus station is 1.5 km north of the city centre just before the ring road. The commercial centre is around and back from the mouth of the little Bystra (Bystraya) River; the area where visitors tend to congregate is the waterfront promenade, naberezhna Lenina, which stretches west from the Bystra River to the Vodopadna (Volopadnaya) River on the east side of town.

Information
Tourist Office The tourist bureau in the Hotel Yalta, at vulitsya Drazhynskoho 50 east of the city centre, is one of the best in the country, and can arrange expensive tours including spectacular helicopter rides and cave excursions. Prices for excursions with private guides are around US$63 per person if you're with a small group of two or three, and about US$10 per person if you have a large group of 20 to 30 people. You can rent a car for about US$53 per day, or US$16 per hour with a driver. The tourist bureau is open from 8 am to 8 pm daily and gets crowded in summer.

Money To exchange travellers' cheques go to the Bank Ukrainy at naberezhna Lenina 3, open weekdays from 8.30 am to 5 pm, but closed between 1 and 2 pm. The bank in the Hotel Yalta will also exchange travellers' cheques. There are exchange kiosks along the waterfront ready to take your hard currency.

Post & Telecommunications The main post office is on ploshcha Lenina. Yalta's telephone area code is 0654.

Books & Maps The bookstall in the Hotel Yalta has guides and other books in English, and the bookshop on vulitsya Ruzvelta usually stocks maps of the town and Crimea. Try to buy the green detailed Yalta map showing all the streets.

Around the Waterfront
Everyone gravitates to **naberezhna Lenina**, the vehicle-free waterfront promenade with its jetties, palms, pebbly beaches, snack bars, photographers, gardens and art markets. The naberezhna stretches south-west to **Prymorsky Park**, where there's a monument inscribed with part of Lenin's Crimea decree. Some of Yalta's main beaches are in front of Prymorsky Park. The pleasant, shady streets north-west of the naberezhna, such as the mostly pedestrian vulitsya Chekhova, have lots of big, old wooden houses. At the western end of the naberezhna, before the Hotel Oreanda, vulitsya Pushkinska (Pushkinskaya) is a pretty promenade stretching west along the small Vodopadna River past stately sanatoria and grand mansions. The **Artists' Union Exhibition Hall** at vulitsya Hoholya 1, straddling the Vodopadna River, has some good exhibitions. An informal art market often sets up in the garden behind naberezhna Lenina just east of here.

The boarding point for the **chair lift** which swings above the rooftops to Darsan, a temple-like lookout up the hill, is behind the Kafe Sochi building. The 10-minute ride costs a few cents each way, and the chair lift operates from 9 am to 5 pm daily, till later in summer.

The **Alexandr Nevsky Cathedral** off vulitsya Sadova (Sadovaya) is a beautifully composed piece of neo-Byzantine architecture built at the turn of the century with fantastic detailing.

East of the centre is the lone gold-pointed bell tower of the former Church of St John, offering great views when it's not locked. Stretching farther east along the coast towards the Hotel Yalta is another series of

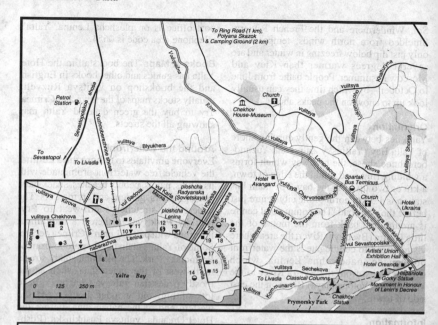

PLACES TO STAY

2   Hotel Palas
    Гостинниця Палац
9   Hotel Tavrida
    Гостинниця Таврида
15 Hotel Yuzhnaya
    Гостинниця Южная
19 Hotel Krim
    Гостинниця Крим

PLACES TO EAT

4   Restoran Slavyansky
    Ресторан Слав'янський
5   Crimean Wines
    Кримські вина
10 Kafe Russky Chay, Kafe Morozhenoe &
    Kafe Vanda
    Кафе Русский Чай, Кафе
    Мороженое та Кафе Ванда
11 Restoran Gurman
    Ресторан Гурман
16 Kafe Syren
    Кафе Сирена
18 Kafe Pelemy
    Кафе Пелеми

20 Kafe Krim
    Кафе Крим

OTHER

1   Chekhov Theatre
    Театр ім. Чехова
3   Summer Stage
    Літний театр
6   Piers 6,7, & 8
    Причаил No 6 - 7 та 8
7   Chair Lift
    Ліфт
8   Alexander Nevsky Cathedral
    Катедра Александра Невського
12 Bank Ukraini
    Банк України
13 Post Office
    Пошта
14 Passanger Port
    Морський вокзал
17 Bookshop
    Книгарня
21 Bus Terminus
    Автобусний кінцевий
22 Central Market
    Центральний ринок

UKRAINE

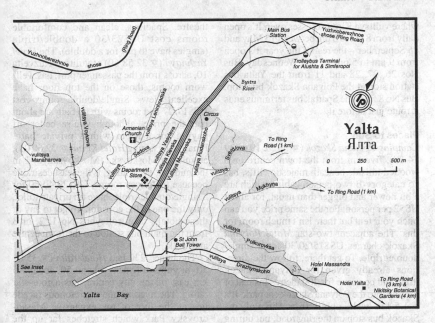

Yalta
Ялта

0   250   500 m

subdivided beaches. There is a festive and busy **market** just off the small park north of the Hotel Krym in the city centre.

Way up the hill off vulitsya Zahorodna (Zahorodnaya) is the **Armenian church** built in traditional Armenian style. Concerts are often performed inside.

Chekhov House-Museum

Chekhov spent much of his last five years, 1899 to 1904, in Yalta after contracting tuberculosis, and had his own dacha built at vulitsya Kirova 112, which was then outside the town. In Yalta he wrote *The Cherry Orchard* and *Three Sisters* and met Tolstoy. Chaliapin and Rachmaninov played the piano which is still in the house.

The garden, house and an exhibition hall, with innumerable editions of Chekhov's works and memorabilia such as his medical kit, pens and gardening gloves, form the Chekhov House-Museum, open from 10 am to 5 pm daily except Monday, Tuesday and the last day of the month. The ticket office is in the exhibition hall across the garden from the house-museum. Make sure you ask for an English text from one of the friendly attendants to take around with you. Bus No 8 from the Spartak bus terminus to the 'Dom-Muzey A P Chekhova' stop will take you there. Trolleybus No 1 from ploshcha Radyanska (Sovietskaya) will drop you a few blocks downhill to the south; the walk through the attractive neighbourhood is enjoyable.

Polyana Skazok

Yalta's Polyana Skazok (Fairy-Tale Glade) is full of characters from Ukrainian and Russian children's stories cast in iron, concrete and wood. The work is clever and the setting, amid fresh air and pine trees, is beautiful. You might recognise the three bears, Winnie the Pooh and Mowgli.

Polyana Skazok is five km from the centre of town, before the camping ground – about three-quarters of a km up from the Polyana Skazok bus stop on Yuzhnoberezhnoe shose where vulitsya Kirova crosses over. It's open daily from 8 am to 8 pm between 15 May and 15 September – the rest of the year it's open from 9 am to 5 pm, closed Wednesday. Bus Nos 26, 27, 28 and 11 from the Yalta bus station stop at the Polyana Skazok bus stop. Bus No 8 from the Spartak bus terminus ends it route just before it.

Places to Stay

Camping Polyana Skazok (☎ 39 52 19 or 39 74 39), five km from the town centre on a wooded hillside beneath majestic cliffs, has 15 category-B two-person cabins which are a bit newer and bigger than usual, for about US$2 per person. For the same price you can pitch your tent but there isn't much room for this. The adjacent two-star *Motel Polyana Skazok* charges US$15/20/30 for a single/double/triple. To get there, follow the directions already given for Polyana Skazok itself, but continue for 200 metres instead of turning into the Polyana Skazok car park. It's a 1.5-km walk uphill from the Polyana Skazok bus stop on the ring road, but during summer, the camping ground sometimes runs a morning and evening shuttle into town.

There's a good variety of hotels in Yalta, but many of them fill up quickly because, aside from the Hotel Yalta, most are small. During summer, make reservations if you can. Ask about the water supply when checking in because it may not be available at all hours.

If you're desperate, there's the *Hotel Avangard* (☎ 32 87 77) at vulitsya Pyrohova 24, 1.5 km west of the town centre. The rooms aren't very clean, but they're bearable, and the cheapest at US$9/10 a single/double, though the water supply is questionable. Trolleybus No 1 from the Yalta bus station or town centre drops you off a block away at the 'Pyonerska' stop.

There are three older hotels in the town centre which provide quaint and cheap lodging. The best of these is the *Hotel Palas* (☎ 32 43 80) at vulitsya Chekhova 8, with four tiers of columns on its façade, located on a pretty block behind the summer stage theatre. Spacious, clean and comfortable rooms cost US$23/30 a double/triple (singles have to pay for a double). The *Hotel Yuzhnaya* (☎ 32 58 60) at vulitsya Ruzvelta 10, across from the passenger port, has well-worn rooms; those on the top floor have excellent views. Single/double rooms cost US$17/27 and rooms with no bath are about half the price, although you're better off paying for a room with a private bath. Finally, the ageing *Hotel Krym* (☎ 32 60 01), at vulitsya Moskovska (Moskovskaya) 1 in the midst of everything, is the least desirable because the pricey rooms, US$20/40/60 for a single/double/triple, have no private toilet, only the one in the corridor. To get to any of these hotels, take trolleybus No 1, 2, or 3 from the main bus station to the town centre and walk.

The huge 2230-bed *Hotel Yalta* (☎ 35 01 50) at vulitsya Drazhynskoho 50, about 1.5 km east of the city centre, has a four-star rating. The massive and monotonous façade lies at the foot of the expansive Masandrovsky Park which stretches far up the hillside. It's modern and clean, and each room has a balcony and view. Within the large complex are restaurants, a bank, concert hall, tennis court, pool and a lift to the Hotel's own beach which boasts summertime cafés, disco and boats. There's also an excellent information bureau off the lobby (see Information). Rooms cost US$21/30 a single/double; triple rooms cost US$15 per person. Bus No 34 from the central market stops just below the hotel, but the walk from the centre of town is pleasant.

The most expensive and poshest is the four-star *Hotel Oreanda* (☎ 32 81 66; fax 32 83 36) at Naberezhna Lenina 35/2. It was built in 1895 and its renovated interior is spacious. Rooms are expensive at US$70/90/135 a single/double/triple, hard currency only. The hotel boasts a tennis court, small swimming pool, sauna and a private beach just across the promenade. There's no direct bus but it's not a long walk from the town centre, or take a taxi from the main bus station.

You can also try the *Hotel Massandra*

(☎ 32 78 00) at vulitsya Drazhynskoho 48, just west of the Hotel Yalta, but it was closed for renovation when we visited, as was the impressive *Hotel Tavrida* (☎ 32 77 84) behind the Kafe Sochi building. The *Hotel Ukraina*, at the south-western end of vulitsya Chekhova, is another grand mansion unfortunately closed and awaiting future restoration.

Places to Eat

Hotel Restaurants The main restaurant in the *Hotel Oreanda* has good service and food. A full meal costs about US$5 to US$8. Choose between the early session (quicker and quieter with tour groups) or the late session (slower and noisier with a rock band). The hotel's 'express café' sadly doesn't live up to its name.

The *Hotel Yalta* has a plethora of restaurants, cafés and bars, although they may not all be open; ask at the front desk. The giant Volga express bar downstairs is reliable for tea and coffee, cakes, eggs, cheese, buterbrody, vodka and brandy.

The restaurant at the *Hotel Palas* looks good, and is a bit quieter than the rest. The tacky restaurant *Cruise*, next door and attached to the Hotel, has a decent variety on its menu.

Other Restaurants One of the most popular places in town is the *Restoran Gurman*, at the back of the Kafe Sochi on naberezhna Lenina. The menu is in English, with meat-based main courses and seafood and vegetarian options among the starters. Open from noon to 2 am, a full meal costs about US$6 a head; bring your own alcohol. To the left of the Kafe Sochi building is the *Restoran Vanda*, attached to the Kafe Vanda, which may be worth a try.

Another good bet is the 'Captain's Table' in the *Hispaniola*, an ex-movie galleon beached opposite the Hotel Oreanda, open only in the summer. You get a room to yourselves and a fish-based meal including fish pies for about US$15, or pizza for less. Book at Hotel Oreanda's reception. *Restoran*

Slavyansky on the naberezhna serves typical shashlyk and coffee and cakes.

Next to the Hotel Krym is the *Restoran Venice*, which has no Italian food, but does have traditional shashlyk and potatoes for about US$4.

For a hot plate of fresh varenyky and bread for less than US$1, head to the *Kafe Pelemy*, open until 6 pm, on the corner opposite the small bus terminus. Similar but with more variety is the cafeteria-style *Kafe Krym* next to the Hotel Krym, serving a full meal with carrot salad, mashed potatoes, meatballs and soup for about US$1. It's open from 8 am to 7 pm. The *Kafe Syren* at vulitsya Ruzvelta 4 near the Hotel Yuzhnaya is similar to the Kafe Krym, but not as good.

Cafés & Bars The Kafe Sochi building on naberezhna Lenina houses a variety of places serving coffee and ice cream. On the left side are the *Kafe Russky Chay*, which serves tea and cakes, the *Kafe Morozhenoe* serving ice cream, and the *Kafe Vanda*, serving light food as well as drinks. Before the Kafe Sochi is the *Kafe Yalos*, recessed off the promenade with umbrellas and tables. Farther down the promenade in front of the piers is the *Crimean Wines* shop which has a pleasant smoke-free café inside to the right.

The hard-currency bar at the *Hotel Yalta* is livelier than the one at the *Oreanda*. There are usually open-air pivnoy (beer) bars in the park on the eastern side of the Tavrida Hotel and in Prymorsky Park in summer.

The ground floor of the Casino Diana, about halfway down naberezhna Lenina to the left of the Kafe Sochi building, has a shop (hastronom) selling food, bottled water, and sweets. At vulitsya Morska (Morskaya) 3, off naberezhna Lenina, is the Aypetry hard-currency shop selling lots of Western food products.

Entertainment

The rock band in the Hotel Oreanda restaurant keeps the dance floor filled and the atmosphere's usually pretty celebratory. Some Hotel Yalta restaurants also have music and dancing – as do the Vanda and

UKRAINE

Vostok restaurants in the Kafe Sochi building. The Restoran Sochi itself is a licensed open-air disco with – surprise, surprise – rather surly door attendants. Down in the Hotel Yalta's basement, there's sometimes a skimpy-costume variety show. Prymorsky Park has a couple of summertime video cafés and some nights there's an alcohol-free disco in the open-air Kurzal, a sort of plaza-like area at the far south-western end of the park. The hotels Yalta and Oreanda often put on entertaining folk evenings and there are balalaika shows most nights during the high season. For details ask at the information bureau in the Hotel Yalta.

The two main performance venues in town are the Chekhov Theatre and the Summer Stage (Letnyaya Estrada), both near naberezhna Lenina. The Crimean Symphony Orchestra plays at the Chekhov Theatre, mainly in autumn, winter and spring.

Things to Buy
Khudozhestvenny Salon on naberezhna Lenina next to the Crimean Wines shop sells decent-looking pottery and wooden boxes.

Wine Much of this coast has been covered in vines for 150 years; and at Massandra, which has famous cellars, wine-making started in 1785. Among the best are the sweet dessert wines such as the white muscat, and the red Kamin Alushta red is also good. The Crimean Wines shop on naberezhna Lenina in front of the piers sells Crimean wine cheaper than hotels do, but you can find it for even less in some food shops. The information bureau in the Hotel Yalta arranges tasting trips to a rather dismal wine-tasting centre near Alupka (see the Around Yalta section).

Getting There & Away
Bus & Trolleybus See the Simferopol section for information on transport to/from Simferopol to Yalta. The trolleybuses to/from Simferopol leave from beside the main Yalta bus station on Moskovska (Moskovskaya) vulitsya. There are usually four buses a day to/from Sevastopol (2½ hours) and

two buses a day to/from Bakhchysaray (three hours). Daily buses to/from Sudak (four hours) and Feodosia (six hours) also run although sometimes not in winter.

Car & Motorbike Non-Yalta residents are not supposed to drive through the town centre in summer, so motorists heading for the Hotel Oreanda and other central hotels should officially continue along the highway to the Livadia turn-off, then descend by vulitsya Blyukhera (first left off the Livadia road). There *are* occasional police checks on town-centre traffic.

Boat The Black Sea Shipping Company (Chornomorsky Morsky Parokhodstvo) operates a few passenger and car services between Yalta, Odessa (12 hours overnight) and other ports in the Black and Mediterranean seas each summer, including a regular service to Istanbul. From April to September or October, Morpasflot (the former Soviet Shipping Ministry) hydrofoils also run and are a bit quicker than the ships, with fares similar to a place in a cheaper ship cabin. The recent fuel shortage and political upheavals have dramatically reduced the frequency of trips and has raised prices. For information, check at the passenger port (morskoy vokzal) at the end of vulitsya Ruzvelta, or better yet, at the Hotel Yalta tourist bureau. You may want to book a ticket in advance if you can. See Ukraine – Getting There & Away and Getting Around for more info.

Getting Around
Buses and trolleybuses run around town, along the coast and into the hills. The Yalta bus and trolleybus stations are between vulitsya Moskovska and vulitsya Kievska, about 1.5 km back from the waterfront. Many town routes stop at ploshcha Radyanska (Sovietskaya) or at the bus terminus in front of the small park next to the central market. A few buses also depart from the Spartak terminus (next to the Spartak cinema) about three-quarters of a km west of the Hotel Oreanda, where vulitsya Marshaka and vulitsya Pushkinska (Pushkinskaya)

join. There are useful taxi ranks at Spartak, outside the Hotel Krym in the town centre, and at the main bus station.

AROUND YALTA
ДОВКОЛИШНІЙ РАЙОНИЙ ЯЛТИ

The coastal strip east and west of Yalta is full of palaces, parks, resorts and beauty spots which make great day trips. A good network of buses, trolleybuses and small ferries called *katery* forms a transport alternative to group excursions, taxis and rental cars. Buses and trolleybuses mostly leave from Yalta's main bus and trolleybus stations. There are signs posted at each platform with the times and destinations. Tickets are usually bought from the driver. Katery, which only run from about May to October, depart from piers 6, 7 and 8 on naberezhna Lenina – buy tickets from the kasy on the lower tier of the promenade. Timetables are posted here and at the destinations.

The Nikitsky Botanical Gardens and Hurzuf are both on the same kater route while Swallow's Nest, Alupka and Miskhor are all on another. Swallow's Nest and Alupka Palace are both close to the No 27 bus route. The roads along this coast are a real maze, with sometimes three or four of them running parallel at different levels. If you keep climbing far enough you'll always reach the Yalta-Sevastopol highway.

The tourist bureau in the Hotel Yalta can arrange guided excursions to most destinations around Yalta.

Alushta
Алушта

Yalta's poorer sibling is 40 km north-east, with less of interest to see and do. From the roundabout beside the avtovokzal (main bus station), where the Simferopol-Yalta road touches north-west Alushta, vulitsya Horkoho runs down to the harbour about one km away. Bus Nos 2 and 4 run down vulitsya Horkoho between the main bus station and a bus stop at the end of the street just up from the passenger port.

West from the harbour is an area of parks

and paths leading towards the Rabochy Uholok (Workers' Corner) where the sanatoria are concentrated. East of the harbour is the promenade, with a few small subdivided beaches and a larger non-paying half-sand, half-rock beach at the far end. A park stretches out beyond the beach. At vulitsya 15 Aprelya, up behind the post office, a 6th-century **Byzantine tower** and wall still stand.

Hotel Alushta (☎ 3 05 52) at vulitsya Oktyabrska 50, the tall unsightly building next to the main bus station, will give you a single/double room for US$10/13. There's a restaurant connected to the hotel. Behind Alushta the Simferopol road passes between Mt Chatyrdag (1527 metres) to the west, and Mt Demerdzhi (1239 metres) and Mt Severnaya Demerdzhi to the east. Mt Demerdzhi has some spectacular rock pillars.

Getting There & Away Between Yalta and Alushta (one hour) the frequent trolleybus Nos 52 (Yalta-Simferopol railway station) and 55 (Yalta-Simferopol Airport) go through Alushta (every 20 minutes) and – if they'll stop there for you – are quicker than No 53 (Yalta-Alushta – every 20 minutes). No 51 runs between Alushta and the Simferopol railway station. There are two or three seasonal ferries a day from Yalta, taking 2.10 hours one way. Some summertime hydrofoils stop at Alushta en route between Yalta, Novorossiysk and Sochi, but this service is not always operational. Check at the passenger port (morsky vokzal).

Hurzuf
Гурзуф

The winding streets and old wooden houses of Hurzuf, backed by Mt Roman Kosh (1545 metres), are a magnet for artists and writers. The village is about 18 km north-east of Yalta, built around a picturesque little bay with a rocky massif called the Genoese Cliff (Skala Dzhenevez) at its eastern end. The 565-metre hump of Bear Mountain (Gora Medved or Ayudag) looms along the coast to the east, protruding out into the sea. The village once had a substantial Tatar population, but today the tight pack of wooden houses is somewhat marred by ugly development higher up, and the nice long beach is spoiled by concrete walls and elevated piers that subdivide it.

Behind the bathing beaches just west of the town centre are the iron gates of **Hurzufsky Park** which contains a bunch of sanatoria, some friendly red squirrels and busts of artistic figures associated with Crimea. Several of the 19th-century sanatoria in the park are stunning wooden structures with splendid detailing. The main dining hall of the **Hurzufsky Sanatorium**, formerly an elite restaurant, has beautiful ornate wooden vaults. Next to the sanatorium is a former hotel (now housing a military sanatorium) with carved wooden balconies and a sculptural fountain in front. On the opposite side of the same park to the west is the **Pushkin in Crimea Museum**, open daily from 10 am to 5 pm, except Monday and Tuesday. The museum is housed in the dacha of the Duc de Richelieu, former governor of Odessa. The museum has a small but nice selection of exhibits concerning Pushkin and the history of Hurzuf, including some Tatar artefacts.

Stretching east from the old bus station in the centre of town is vulitsya Leningradska, the curving, picturesque main street with overhanging wooden balconies and a few cafés and odd shops. Vulitsya Chekhova runs parallel to the **Chekhov's dacha**, now a museum, at No 22 near the foot of the Genoese Cliff. It's open from May to October, daily except Monday, with a pretty little garden overlooking a small cove.

Artek Pioneer Camp, a vast children's holiday complex, stretches most of the way to Bear Mountain from the east side of the Genoese Cliff. There is an entrance at the eastern end of vulitsya Leningradska, Hurzuf's main street. Just to the right inside the entrance, on the Genoese Cliff, are the remains of a 6th to 15th-century **clifftop fortress** founded by the Byzantines, and rebuilt by the Genoese. Signs say it's dangerous to climb on the crag, but a little path round to the left leads through a rock tunnel to the sea-cliff edge. Beyond the cliff the Artek Camp has a nice swathe of beach.

Getting There & Away Around 10 katery a day make the 50-minute journey from Yalta to Hurzuf, calling at Nikitsky Botanical Gardens along the way. The last one back from Hurzuf departs at around 6.30 pm. More frequent are bus Nos 31 and 31A (express), which depart every 30 to 45 minutes from Yalta bus station.

Nikitsky Botanical Gardens

Even if you're no gardener or botanist, the Nikitsky Botanical Gardens, tumbling down three sq km of hillside to the sea five km east of Yalta, are well worth a visit for their beauty and excellent views. The gardens, founded in 1812, hold 28,000 species and varieties, including 2000 types of rose. Many of the trees and plants adorning the parks and gardens of Crimea originated here.

The gardens, open daily from 8 am to 5 pm (till 8 pm in summer), are divided into four main sections: the Upper Park (Verkhny Park) and Lower Park (Nizhny Park), together called the Arboretum; Prymorsky Park; and Cape Montedor Park (Mys-Montedor Park). The Upper Park has the rose garden, and the best views are from its observation area. Prymorsky Park has delicate subtropical plants.

Getting There & Away By combining modes of transport, you can visit most of the gardens walking downhill all the way. Take bus No 34 – which runs from the bus terminus next to the Yalta central market to the Upper and Lower gates of the Nikitsky Gardens and back 11 times daily – to the Upper Gate, then walk down through the gardens to Nikitsky Botanichesky Sad jetty at the foot of Prymorsky Park, where katery to Yalta or Hurzuf depart 10 times a day. You could add about two km to the start of your walk by beginning at the GNBS bus stop on the Yalta-Alushta highway, where the frequent Hurzuf bus, No 31, stops.

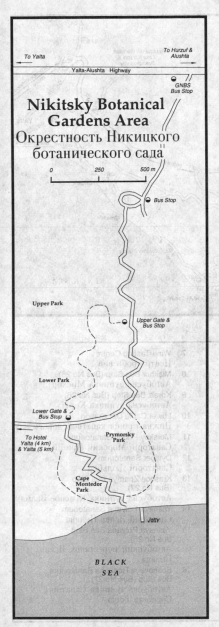

Nikitsky Botanical Gardens Area
Окрестность Никицкого ботанического сада

To Yalta

To Hurzuf & Alushta

Yalta-Alushta Highway

GNBS Bus Stop

0   250   500 m

Bus Stop

Upper Park

Upper Gate & Bus Stop

Lower Park

Lower Gate & Bus Stop

To Hotel Yalta (4 km) & Yalta (5 km)

Prymorsky Park

Cape Montedor Park

Jetty

BLACK SEA

Hrusheva Polyana
Грушева Поляна

Many native animals of the Crimean Mountains – deer, bears, boar and wild sheep – can be seen in enclosures at Hrusheva Polyana (Pear Tree Glade), high above the Nikitsky Gardens, about 11 km from Yalta within the Crimean Game Reserve, one of the only parts of the reserve open to visitors. The road leads up from Massandra on the eastern side of the Yalta ring road. Bus No 33, departing Yalta bus station three times daily (twice in the morning, once in the early evening), goes there.

Uchansu Waterfall, Lake Karagol & Mt Ai-Petri

Bus No 30 takes you within walking distance of two beauty spots in the mountains off the Bakhchysaray road. It departs about four times daily from Yalta bus station (the first bus leaves at 8.05 am, the last at 5.15 pm). From the Vodopad (Waterfall) stop about 11 km out, you can walk to a platform beside the 100-metre Uchansu Waterfall, visible over to the right. From the Karagol stop, three km further up the road, a track leads down to little, forest-ringed Lake Karagol. Both places have decent restaurants.

Past the Karagol bus stop, the road winds spectacularly up to the top of the range 13 km further on, where the 1233-metre summit of Mt Ai-Petri (St Peter) is over to the left. A cable car from a peak north of Ai-Petri carries passengers all the way down to Miskhor, near Alupka, 16 km west of Yalta. According to Yalta bus timetables, bus No 41 goes to Ai-Petri a few times a day, but it's easier to get there with your own transport.

Livadia
Лівадія

It was Livadia, three km west of Yalta, that put the Yalta area on the maps of both Russia and the world – first in 1860 when the imperial family started building here, then in February 1945 when Stalin, Roosevelt and Churchill held their Yalta Conference in the **Livadia Palace**. Built in 1911 as a summer

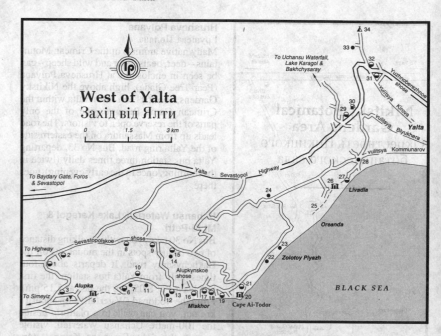

West of Yalta
Захід від Ялти

0 1.5 3 km

To Baydary Gate, Foros & Sevastopol

Yalta – Sevastopol Highway

To Uchansu Waterfall, Lake Karagol & Bakhchysaray

Yuzhnoberezhnoe shose

vulitsya Kirova

vulitsya Blyukhera

Yalta

vulitsya Kommunarov

Livadia

Oreanda

Sevastopolskoe shose

To Highway

Alupkynskoe shose

Alupka

To Simeyiz

Miskhor

Cape Ai-Todor

Zolotoy Plyazh

BLACK SEA

PLACES TO STAY

34 Polyana Skazok Camping Ground & Motel
    Кемпинг і Мотель Поляна Сказок

PLACES TO EAT

4 Restoran Alupka & Kafe Luna
   Ресторан Алупка та Кафе Луна

OTHER

1 Razbylka Bus Stop (Bus No 26)
   Автобусна зупинка Разбилка
2 Pozharka Bus Stop (Bus No 26)
   Автобусна зупинка Пожарка
3 Horsovet Bus Stop (Bus No 26)
   Автобусна зупинка Горсовет
5 Alupka Palace
   Алупкінський дворец
6 Alupka Bus Stop (Bus No 27)
   Автобусна зупинка Алупка

7 Wine-Tasting Centre
   Центр проби вин
8 Miskhor Bus Stop (Bus No 26)
   Автобусна зупинка Мисхор
9 Koreiz Bus Stop (Bus No 26)
   Автобусна зупинка Кореїз
10 Lower Cable Car Station
   Нижня станця канатной дороги
11 Morskoy Priboy Sanatorium
   Санаторій Морский Прибій
12 Dyulber Sanatorium
   Санаторій Дюльбер
13 Krasnoe Znamya Bus Stop
   (Bus No 27)
   Автобусна зупинка Красное Знамя
14 Yasnaya Polyana Sanatorium
   Санаторій Ясная Поляна
15 Yasnaya Polyana Bus Stop
   Bus No 26)
   Автобусний перестанок Ясная
   Поляна
16 Sosnovaya Roshcha Sanatorium
   Bus Stop (Bus No 27)
   Автобусна зупинка Санаторій
   Сосновая Роща

17	Marat Bus Stop (Bus No 27) Автобусна зупинка Марат	26	Livadia Palace Ливадийський дворец
18	Ukraina Sanatorium Bus Stop (Bus No 27) Автобусна зупинка Санаторій Україна	27	Livadia Bus Stop (Bus No 5) Автобусна зупинка Лівадія
19	Dnepr Sanatorium Bus Stop (Bus No 27) Автобусна зупинка Санаторій Днепр	28	Livadia Signpost Дороговказ Лівадія
20	Swallow's Nest Ластівкове гніздо	29	Razv na Bakhchysaray Bus Stop Автобусна зупинка Разв. на Бахчисарай
21	Zhemchuzhyna Bus Stop (Bus No 27) Автобусна зупинка Жемчужина	30	Petrol Station Бензинова станція
22	Druzhba International Boarding House Международний пансионат Дружба	31	Polyana Skazok Stop (Bus No 8) Автобусна зупинка Поляна Сказок
23	Zolotoy Plyazh Sanatorium Санаторія Золотий Пляж	32	Polyana Skazok Bus Stop (Bus Nos 26, 27, 28 & 11) Автобусна зупинка Поляна Сказок
24	Sanatory Zolotoy Plyazh Signpost Дороговказ санаторій Золотий Пляж	33	Polyana Skazok Поляна Сказок
25	Sunny Path Солнечная Тропа		

residence for Nicholas II, it replaced earlier royal dwellings and used much white Crimean granite in the process. It's built in Italian Renaissance style with pretty Florentine and Arabic courtyards. After the revolution, the palace became the first peasants' sanatorium in the country.

The 1945 conference was mainly a matter of the three WW II victors confirming earlier decisions on the carve-up of Europe. The UK and the USA couldn't stop Stalin keeping the eastern third of Poland, conquered by the Red Army, but Poland got part of Germany as compensation. Stalin agreed to allow free elections in Poland, which never happened, and to declare war on Japan, which he did only after the atom bomb had been dropped on Hiroshima. A reproduction of the round table at which they reached these agreements stands in the conference room, along with photos and other memorabilia. Ironically, the most popular exhibits are those recently installed upstairs in a series of rooms dedicated to Tsar Nicholas II and his family. They're full of furnishings and photos of the royal family and their entourage traipsing stylishly around the area.

The palace is open daily, except Wednesday and the last day of the month, from 8 am

to 7.30 pm from June to October, and from 9 am to 4.30 pm the rest of the year. A small church used by the royal family is next to the entrance and kasa.

The palace has a lovely park and gardens, a highlight of which is the 'sunny path' (solnechnaya tropa), running about 1.5 km west from just below the palace to a lookout over Oreanda. Bus No 5 leaves every 40 minutes from the Spartak Bus Terminal in Yalta from about 6.15 am to 9.50 pm (about 20 times a day) and goes to the Livadia stop, five minutes' walk from the palace.

Swallow's Nest
Ласточкіно Гнездо

Swallow's Nest (Lastochkino Gnezdo) is a fairy-tale castle, the glory of a million postcards, perched at the top of a sheer cliff on Cape Ai-Todor, about 10 km west of Yalta. Built in 1912 for Baron Steingel, a German oil magnate, it's now a swish hard-currency Italian restaurant. Meals cost about US$25 to US$30.

Katery to Lastochkino Gnezdo jetty, which is just below the castle, leave Yalta every hour and take 40 minutes. The last boat back departs about 8.50 pm. Alternatively,

UKRAINE

The Swallow's Nest on Cape Ai-Todor

take bus No 27, which leaves hourly from Yalta bus station, to the 'Zhemchuzhyna' bus stop where a road leads down to the jetty and castle – it's about a 10-minute walk.

Swallow's Nest to Alupka
Bus No 27 travels along the road from Swallow's Nest to Alupka. Halfway down at the Krasnoe Znamya stop is the blue and white **Dyulber sanatorium**, a 19th-century mansion designed as an Arabian palace with exquisite stucco work around the windows and doors. Gardens terrace down to Miskhor beach below, ordinary but backed by a pleasant park at its eastern end with views up at dramatic Mt Ai-Petri.

The **wine-tasting centre** used for group tours is between Miskhor and Alupka. The tour includes a boring lecture in Russian and meagre tastings. You'd be better off buying a bottle and heading for the beach or a pleasant park. Between the Dyulber sanatorium and Alupka is the lower station for the cable car (kanatnoye dorohy) up the cliff just north to Mt Ai-Petri.

Alupka Palace
Алупка палац
The most exotic palace-park complex on the whole coast is at Alupka, about 16 km west of Yalta. Designed and built between 1828 and 1846 by English architects for the English-educated Count Mikhail Vorontsov, the immensely rich regional governor, the palace is a bizarre combination of Scottish castle on its landward side, and Arabic fantasy facing the sea. Vorontsov brought serfs from his estates all over Russia to create the palace and the large park above and below it on the hillside.

Six gorgeous Italian-marble lions flank the staircase outside the palace's seaward front. Entry into the landscaped park is free year-round; but the palace's luxuriant interior, now the **Alupkinsky Dvorets-Muzey**, is open daily from 8 am to 9 pm from 1 June to 1 October; from 10 am to 4 pm the rest of the year; and is closed on Monday, Friday and days of high humidity. Highlights of the interior include an 1860 Becker piano, a beautiful sun room and a main dining room with impressive woodwork and a balcony for musicians.

Places to Eat If you want a bite to eat, then walk up to the little town of Alupka above the western entrance of the palace. There's a café, a shop that sells drinks, and a couple of restaurants: the *Restoran Alupka* and *Kafe Kluna*. Kafe Kluna is a cafeteria-style restaurant that serves cheap, heaped portions.

Getting There & Away Seasonal boats from Yalta sail hourly, take just over an hour, and the last one back to Yalta departs at about 8.40 pm. From the top of the steps up from the jetty, head up through the lower park to the palace entrance. Bus No 27 runs hourly from the Yalta bus station, terminating at the Alupka stop, from where you can walk across the park to the palace.

If you're continuing to Simeyiz walk up to the town of Alupka above the western end of the palace. Turn left at the Lenin statue and follow vulitsya Lyuxemburg for about 300 metres until it meets the main road and the

Horsovet bus stop. Bus No 26 (every 45 minutes) goes to Simeyiz, No 39 (three times a day) to Foros, and both go back to the Yalta main bus station.

Simeyiz
Сімеїз

Five km west of Alupka, Simeyiz is one of the coast's smaller, quieter resorts. A few interesting Moorish-looking buildings poke up among the trees above its pebbly beach, with dramatic cliffs providing the backdrop. The sea is clear, and leading up to the bus station behind the beach is an attractive park with cypress and pine trees and an open-air theatre. At the western end of the beach, in front of a rocky hill with Genoese walls, a flight of steps leads up 50-metre-high Diva Rock which juts out into the sea. To the far west is 260-metre Cat Mountain (Gora Koshka), which vaguely resembles a feline animal about to spring. The only place to get something to eat is the *Kafe Simeyiz* up the hill and down a bit from the bus station.

Getting There & Away Only a couple of seasonal ferries a day make the 1½-hour trip to Simeyiz from Yalta, but bus No 26 goes from Yalta bus station every 45 minutes, stopping in Alupka, above the palace, on its way. Express bus No 42 from the Yalta bus station also goes to Simeyiz six times daily. The less frequent bus Nos 43 and 51 from Yalta also stop at Simeyiz. It's about one km, mostly downhill, to the beach from the bus station.

Baydary Gate & Foros Church

The Baydary Gate is a stone arch over the old Yalta-Sevastopol road where it crests the coastal escarpment at 527 metres, 51 km from Yalta, about an hour's drive past Simeyiz. It was built in 1848 to mark the completion of this road, most of which is now superseded by the highway lower down. Turn up from the highway about 45 km west of Yalta at a crossroads where 'Foros' is signposted down the hill and 'Baydarskie Vorota 6.5 km' points up the hill. The crossroads is the nearest bus stop: Bus Nos 28

(five times daily through Simeyiz) and 39 (three times daily) run between Yalta's main bus station and the stop.

The way up is beneath towering rock walls. After four km from the bus stop (two km below the gate) is the picturesque Foros Church, with its nine golden-domes of various sizes, dramatically overlooking the sea from the top of a precipitous crag. The story goes that a runaway horse bearing the daughter of 19th-century tea tycoon Alexandr Kuznetsov suddenly reared up and stopped on this spot, saving her from certain death. Kuznetsov built the church in thanks.

The *Shalash* restaurant beside the Baydary Gate is supposedly good, but don't rely on it being open. Far below the cliffs lies the town of **Foros** is an unattractive modern development. Somewhere in the area is Gorbachev's dacha where he was put under house arrest during the 1991 coup attempt.

SEVASTOPOL
СЕВАСТОПОЛЬ
Population: 375,000

Still officially a closed city, Sevastopol with its ageing and rusty Black Sea Fleet remains a top-secret affair. After independence the ownership of the fleet was a hot topic, with tensions building between Ukraine and Russia. Eventually, after high-ranking negotiations, Ukraine decided to lease the port to Russia and sell off part of their claim to the fleet in lieu of its increasing oil debt to the big bear, easing tensions somewhat, but only temporarily side-stepping an issue which will surely resurface in the future.

Sevastopol was the focus of the Crimean War, besieged and bombarded for 349 days by the British, French and Turks in 1854-55, devastating the city so badly that Mark Twain, when visiting the city a decade later, wrote, 'In whatsoever direction you please, your eye encounters scarcely anything but ruin, ruin, ruin!' Eighty-eight years later the same catastrophe repeated itself when the city fell to the Germans after 250 brutal days of siege in 1942.

Visits usually centre on Istorichesky

bulvar, site of a defensive bastion during the Crimean War. The highlight is the painted panorama of the defence, in the big circular building at the centre of the gun emplacements and redoubts. Around town are many more monuments plus the Vladimirsky Cathedral, the Black Sea Fleet Museum (vulitsya Lenina 11), an art museum (prospekt Nakhimova 9) and a dolphinarium. The Eagle Column on a rock in front of Prymorsky bulvar commemorates Russian ships sunk in the harbour mouth in 1854 to stop enemy ships entering.

Sevastopol's telephone area code is 0692.

Khersones

The ruins of old Greek Chersonesus, on a peninsula three km south-west of Sevastopol, don't feature on most group trips unless you specify ahead of time and,

Figurine of a hussar from the Crimean War

usually, pay a higher price. Founded in 422 BC, Chersonesus went through wars, trade-based prosperity, absorption into the Roman then Byzantine empires, nomad attacks, and capture in 988 AD by Volodymyr of Kiev. In return for marriage to the Byzantine emperor's sister, Volodymyr returned the city to Byzantine control and agreed to be baptised as a Christian on the spot, thus launching what eventually became the Russian Orthodox Church. The town was finally ruined by the Tatars in the late 14th century. Much of what has been excavated is little over knee-high, but there are exceptions – most picturesquely, a row of marble columns from an early Christian church a few metres from the shore. Adjacent is a fine mosaic floor. There's a Khersones Museum on the site as well.

Getting There & Away

The best place to 'legally' organise a tour of Sevastopol is the tourist bureau in the Hotel Yalta. Tours cost about US$200 for three to four people with a private guide all day, or about US$10 per person if you have a large group of 20 to 30 people. Try to join one of the group tours during the summer, usually operating on Wednesday and Thursday.

From Simferopol you could try staying on one of the seven electric trains daily that run to/from Sevastopol in two hours. About 1½ hours into the trip young boyish soldiers in Black Sea Fleet uniforms board the train and check *dokumenty* and, when finding you haven't the proper ones, will escort you off the train at the tiny station of Verkhnesadovaya, three stops before Sevastopol. You'll have to sit there with the others until the next train going back to Simferopol pulls through. Not everyone seems to be checked, though.

Although Lonely Planet does not recommend this, an alternative possibility entails getting off at Syren, one station past Bakhchysaray, and catching a bus or hitchhiking to the village of Ternovka, about 30 km south. From here buses, rarely checked, go into Sevastopol.

SUDAK
СУДАК

Population: 15,000

Sudak, at the base of a shallow bay, is about 125 km north-east of Yalta along the twisted and rocky coastline. It was once one of the main Genoese trading centres on the Great Silk Road; in the 14th and 15th centuries they built an enormous fortress with a series of walls and towers snaking along a massive cliff perched out over the sea. The scenery is spectacular and the fortress is dramatic, but though the beach below is nice, the small town is a boring modern development, offering nothing of interest.

Sudak's telephone area code is 06566.

Genoese Fortress

The fortress (Sudakska Krepost) zigzags up and around a hillside at the western edge of the beach, its silhouette a striking combination of towers and crenulated walls. Of the 18 original towers, only 10 of substantial size have survived, most with their original Italian names. The fortress is open from 9 am to 9 pm between May and October, and from 9 am to 6 pm the rest of the year. You enter a forecourt which leads through the Holovna (Main) Gate between the **Tower of Torcello** to the right, and the **Tower of Di Franco** to the left. Inside, the walls encircle over 30 hectares of desolate sloping terrain with a few overgrown ruins and foundations lying about. On the eastern edge, next to the **Kruhla Tower**, are the foundations of the **Church of the 12 Apostles**. In the upper eastern corner is a single-domed 13th-century **mosque**, probably there before the fortress and perhaps used by a substantial Tatar workforce.

The largest tower on the dramatically sloping south side along the coastline is the 14th-century two-towered **Consul's Tower**; a small castle in itself.

The next tower up, the 14th to 15th-century **Tower of St-George** leads out to a viewpoint and a stepped path on the seaward side of the long crenulated wall that eventually leads to the apex, the remains of the 14th-century **Dozornaya Tower**.

To the west rises 576-metre Mt Perchem, its face dramatically dropping into a sheer cliff. To the far east along the coast is 352-metre Mt Urmani-Ustu, its two peninsular points protruding out into the sea. Below and stretching east is a fairly nice long strip of sandy beach from which the views up to the fortress are stunning.

Places to Stay & Eat

The only reliable place to stay is the white *Hotel Horyzont* (☎ 33 48 82) on vulitsya Turistikoyu, located conveniently near the foot of the fortress. Decent and comfortable rooms, some with views up to the fortress, cost US$10/15/25 a single/double/triple with bath and breakfast. You pay for dinner, a dismal affair, at the reception when you check in. Good luck trying to find food elsewhere. There's a popular pool table on the 2nd floor of the lobby.

From the bus station, north of town, take the bus from the station through town to the fortress. Get off at the second-to-last stop, 'Hostynytsa Horyzont'.

Getting There & Away

More buses go to/from Sudak from Simferopol (2½ hours; five to seven daily), than Yalta (four hours; two daily, which may not run in the winter). Buses also run to/from Feodosia (two hours) about twice daily. In the summer you may be able to catch a boat to/from Sochi or Yalta.

KARA-DAH NATURE RESERVE
КАРА-ДАГ ЗАПОВІДНИК

The road between Sudak and Feodosia is dry, rugged and mountainous with weathered old vineyards on sloping patches of terrain. About halfway along the coast just east of the village of Shchebetovka is the Kara-Dah Nature Reserve, with a number of dramatic rock formations boasting names such as 'The Devil's Finger' and 'The King and the Earth', all situated around Mt Svyataya (575 metres). Hikers are supposedly limited due to its status as a nature reserve. From the northern end of Shchebetovka, walk to the seaside hamlet of **Kurortnoe** about 3.5 km

UKRAINE

away. From here trek north-east about six km through the Kara-Dah reserve, eventually reaching the village of **Planerske** (also known as **Koktebel**). From here you can catch another bus to Feodosia, 35 minutes away.

Bring water, food and a good map, as supplies are rare. There's a *tourist hotel* in Planerske – ask for the 'turistsky baza Prymore'. There's also a *camp site* about seven km east of Planerske on the way to the village of Orzhonykydze along the coast. Twice daily, once in the morning and once in the evening, buses run to/from Sudak and Feodosia (two hours), stopping halfway en route at both Shchebetovka and Planerske along the way.

FEODOSIA
ФЕОДОСІЯ
Population: 87,000

Tucked in a coastal corner of Crimea about 115 km east of Simferopol, the city of Feodosia is a somehow pleasant conglomeration of clanking industry, crooked cottages, elegant old mansions, sandy beaches, good museums, and a number of Genoese stone walls and Armenian churches thrown in.

Founded as far back as 6 BC, the city belonged to the Golden Horde before the Genoese took over, ruling from the 13th to 15th centuries, and turned it into a rich trading post. An Ottoman and Tatar invasion in 1475 transformed it into the largest slave-trading centre on the Black Sea coast. Continually supplied by slaves from frequent Tatar raids, the city, known as Kafa, was referred to by the Slavs as 'the vampire that drinks the blood of Rus'. In 1616 Cossacks raided the city and freed hundreds of slaves. The city remained under Tatar control until the Russians annexed Crimea in 1783. There was always a large merchant population of Armenians in Feodosia, who left behind a number of abandoned Armenian churches throughout the city. Many immigrated in the 14th and 18th centuries but most left during WW II. Today the city is also a big military base so expect to see some soldiers milling about.

Orientation & Information
The city curves around the westernmost shores of the crescent-shaped Feodosia Bay. The city centre lies in the group of streets just west of the waterfront railway station. The old section of town is farther south-east along the curve of the bay behind the port. The bus station is about two km north of the centre.

Feodosia's telephone area code is 06562.

City Centre
There are two fine museums right across the street from each other. The most popular is the **Ayvazovsky Museum** at vulitsya Halereyna (Halereynaya) 2, dedicated to the famous 19th-century Armenian seascape artist who was born, lived and worked in Feodosia. Housed in his former residence, the museum has about 80 of his dramatic paintings whose recurring theme is that of a ship hopelessly caught in a storm. It's open daily from 10 am to 5 pm, but closed Wednesday and the last Thursday of every month.

Opposite is the **Regional Museum** with an excellent archaeology exhibit tracing some of the diverse cultures involved in Crimean history, going back to the 3rd century BC, covering the Greek, Armenian, Tatar and Genoese influence. Exhibits include ceramics, jewellery, glassware, tools, coins and sculpture, including a 9th to 12-century BC pagan statue. Upstairs is mostly dedicated to WW II and has some amusing war propaganda posters. There's also a small ethnographic section where you can learn about the Turkish influence on Crimean culture. The museum is open daily from 10.30 am to 5.30 pm, closed Tuesday.

Just up vulitsya Halereyna on the corner of vulitsya Sverdlova and with a ship on its façade, is a small but impressive **A S Hryna House Museum**, now a contemporary gallery.

North of the city centre, up prospekt Lenina near the corner of vulitsya Revolyutsyonna, is an attractive row of former mansions, now sanatoria. Farther north, past a park, is the **Dacha Stamboly**, an Ottoman-style palace built by a Turkish magnate from Istanbul who owned a tobacco factory in Feodosia and reputedly had his own private harem. During WW II, the mansion was used as Nazi headquarters, and people were executed in the back garden. A sanatorium for alcoholics under the communists, it's currently under restoration and now houses a bank.

Just north of the city centre at vulitsya Karla Marxa 52 is the charming **Kazansky Cathedral**, with an elongated dome. In front of the main bus station is the intricate **Church of St Catherine**, a compact ensemble of domes and arches. Behind the central bus terminus ('Tsentr') is an old **cemetery** with interesting tombstones and two ornate chapels.

Old Town

From the **Tower of Constantine** (1382-1488) in the town centre continue south along vulitsya Horkoho. To your right is the Ottoman-looking 1888 **Ayvazovsky Fountain** erected in honour of the artist. Farther south, within a fenced-in park, is the 14th-century Armenian **Serhiya Church** with exquisitely carved marble tablets embedded in its façade. In front of the church is the lower portion of a bell tower. Next to this is the **Tomb of Ayvazovsky**, with a plaque containing Armenian script. Up vulitsya Timiryazeva is the 1408 Armenian **Church of the Archangels Mykhayla & Havryila** (Michael & Gabriel). Note the tiny figure embedded into the wall to the right of the carved white tablet next to the entrance.

Two blocks east of the Serhiya Church is the 1623 **Mufty-Dzhamy Mosque** with an elegant 12-sided white minaret. In the side garden are a few scattered tombstones (mostly Jewish) from an old cemetery that was destroyed to build a factory outside the centre. The mosque is under reconstruction. Continue east on vulitsya Lenina and turn right on vulitsya Krupskoy and follow it uphill to the partially ruined **Tower of St Giovanni di Scaffa** (1342), and **Tower of St**

Fomi (St Thomas; 1373), both part of the city's Genoese fortification system. There is a nice view over the rooftops of the old town from between the towers.

Citadel

The Citadel was erected on a bluff overlooking the bay as the centre of a formidable defence system built in the 13th century by the Genoese after they took control of the city from the Golden Horde. Vulitsya Karantynna (Karantynnaya) leads to the main entrance. To the right is the **Klymenta Tower**, and around the corner towards the water is the **Krysko Tower**, both mid-14th century with a good section of stone wall in between and beyond.

East of the towers and down a hillside is a fantastic ensemble of small 14th-century Armenian churches. The **Church of St John the Baptist**, between the two other churches, is a classic example of medieval Armenian architecture, with an octagonal cupola rising from and elongated cruciform plan. The **Church of St John the Divine** has a walled entrance courtyard where four column stumps mark the spot of a former bell tower. Toward the sea is the tiny **Chapel of St George**. Sticking up out of the water beyond are rusty fragments of wrecked barges. Turn right past the chapel and continue along the coastline to the water's edge and the sturdy **Dokova Tower**. Further in the distance is a long stretch of original 14th-century defensive walls stretching over the crest of a hill down to the sea, beyond which is an off-limits military zone. Nearby there is another small Armenian church, **St Stephen's**, with fragments of frescoes still visible in the vaulted interior above the entrance and along the rear apse. Half of the 12 apostles with Christ seated to their right are on the left-hand side of the apse; their faces have been scratched out.

Beaches

North of the railway station is a row of sandy beaches, usually swarming with plump roasted bodies during the summer, but empty

UKRAINE

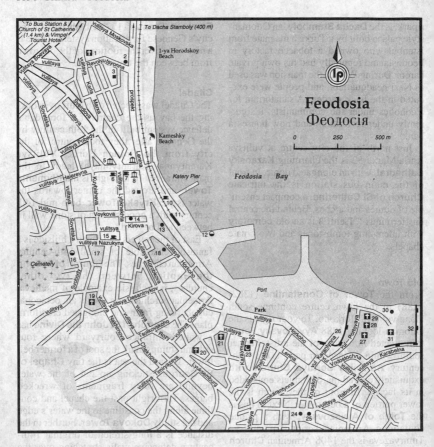

Feodosia
Феодосія

0   250   500 m

Feodosia   Bay

Port

Park

in winter. Kameshky Beach is just past the railway station, followed by 1-ya Horodskoy beach. Head farther north, past the small Bayabuha River and east over the tracks, where the beaches (called 2-ya Horodskoy) are nicer and less crowded. Even farther north, on the other side of a large industrial centre, the beaches are nicest. Bus Nos 2 and 4 from the central bus terminus will save you some walking. In summer the best way to hop from beach to beach is with the small katery (ferries) that shuttle beach-goers around. The katery pier is behind the main railway station.

Places to Stay

Lodging in Feodosia is limited and in summer you should try to make reservations in advance, or at least plan on getting into town early. During the off season there should be no problem. The *Hotel Astoria* (☎ 3 23 25 or 3 23 16) at prospekt Lenina 9 is central and, although slightly run-down, is the best place in town. They charge US$10 per person. The *Hotel Moryak* (☎ 39 33 72 or 39 33 73) is in the old town at vulitsya Lenina 8, next to the mosque. It's a plain institutional-looking hotel popular with groups of school kids. Rooms cost the same

UKRAINE

PLACES TO STAY

3 Hotel Feodosiya
Гостинниця Феодосія
9 Hotel Astoria
Гостинниця Асторія
22 Hotel Moryak
Гостинниця Моряк

PLACES TO EAT

6 Kafe Assol
Кафе Ассоль
7 Kafe Kafa
КафеКафа
10 Kafe Roxolana
Кафе Роксолана
15 Kafe Svyatkoe
Кафе Святкове

OTHER

1 Kazansky Cathedral
Казанський собор
2 Sanatoria Voskhod
Санаторія Восход
4 Ayvazovsky Museum
Картинна галерея Айвазовського
5 A S Hryna House Museum
Дім-музей А. С. Грина
8 Regional Museum
Краєзнавчий музей
11 Train Station
Залізничний вокзал
12 Passenger Port
13 Tower of Constantine
Вежа Константина

14 Train & Airline Ticket Office
Каса продажу залізничних та
авіаційних квитків
16 Central Bus Terminus ('Tsentr')
„Центр" кінцевих автобусів
17 Central Market
Центральний ринок
18 Ayvazovsky Fountain
Айвазівська фонтана
19 Armenian Church
Вірменська церква
20 Armenian Church of the Archangels
Mikhayla & Havryila
Вірменська церква архангелів
Михайла та Гавриїла
21 Serhiya Church & Ayvazovsky's Tomb
Церква Сергія та Айвазіський гріб
23 Mufty-Dzhamy Mosque
Мечеть Муфті-Джами
24 Tower of St Fomi
Вежа Св. Фоми
25 Tower of St Giovanni-di-Scaffa
Вежа Джованні ді Скаффа
26 Geonese Citadel
Генуйська цитадель
27 Church of St John the Divine
Церква Божественного Св. Іоана
28 Church of St John the Baptist
Церква Св. Іоана Хрестителя
29 Chapel of St George
Каплиця Св. Юрія
30 Dokova Tower
Докова вежа
31 St Stephen's Church
Церква Св. Стефана
32 Genoese Walls
Генуйські стіни

UKRAINE

as at the Astoria and the entrance is around the back. Bus A from the central bus terminus goes past the hotel.

The *Hotel Feodosia* (☎ 3 23 55) just north of the centre at vulitsya Kavkorpusa 6 looks nice but was closed when we visited. Way up north, about 3.5 km from the town centre, is the *Vimpel Tourist Hotel* (☎ 7 31 97) next to a nice sandy beach and an ugly factory. They usually only take package tours but you could try it as a last resort. Take bus No 2, 4A, or 13 from the central bus terminus or from the main bus station and get off at

'Prymorske' bus stop. Head to the right toward the rectangular white building north of the industrial complex.

About six km from the centre, where the main road out of the city meets the main road heading east to Kerch, there's a camping ground called *Zolotoy Plyazh*.

Places to Eat

The Hotel Astoria has two restaurants – the *Restaurant Odysseye* to the right of the entrance seems more popular and louder than the quieter *Restoran Astoria* on the left. Both have decent menus.

There are a number of cafés in and around the streets behind the Hotel Astoria, the two best are a block west. The *Kafe Assol* on the corner of vulitsya Lybknekhta and vulitsya Halereyna is cosy and smoke-free, and serves coffee, beer, salads and clay pots full of beef stew (zharkovya). The *Kafe Kafa* across the street has good borscht, meat and potato dishes, and fruit tea. You can sit in one of the private booths.

On the waterfront, near the Tower of Constantine, there is a *café* that serves drinks and sweets. Next to the railway station, the *Kafe Roxolana* serves some food, but most people come to this popular place to drink.

The central market is just east of the central bus terminus.

Getting There & Away
Bus There's no direct train connection to/from Simferopol, so most people take the bus. The main bus station is two km north of the centre. Anywhere from eight to 10 buses a day go to/from Simferopol (2½ hours), but tickets are only sold at the bus station and often just before the bus arrives, causing much confusion and long queues. Sometimes the best strategy is to muscle your way onto the back of the bus and pay the driver later. There are also two buses a day to Sudak (two hours) and at least four a day to Kerch (two hours). There are usually one or two buses a day to/from Yalta (six hours), although this service may not run in winter.

Train Trains roar right along the beach and into the heart of the city. But the long-distance train service is limited with one daily train to Moscow (22 to 26 hours) through Zaporizhzhya and Kharkiv. Trains to Kiev (16 hours) run every other day. Four trains a day travel to Vladislavovka (30 minutes), where you can catch a train to Kerch (two hours).

Train tickets can be purchased at the station or in advance from the ticket office on vulitsya Voykova 5.

Boat During the summer there may be a few passenger boats stopping on their way between Sochi and Yalta or Odessa, but don't count on it. Most of these boats stop at the passenger port (morsky vokzal) just south of the railway station and the katery landing pier.

Getting Around
The central bus terminus ('Tsentr') is on the western edge of the town centre. Most city buses begin, end or stop here. Nos 4, 4B and 2 run between here and the main bus station; No 2 is the most frequent.

The summer katery all arrive and depart from the pier behind the railway station.

STARY KRYM & SURP-KHACH MONASTERY
СТАРИЙ КРИМ ТА СУРП-ХАЧ МОНАСТЕР
On the main road to Simferopol, about 23 km west of Feodosia is the unassuming farming town of Stary Krym. About three km south, hidden in the hills, is the 14th-century stone Armenian Surp-Khach Monastery. Surrounded by dense woods the complex includes original monks' cells, a refectory and a beautiful church with a series of vaulted chambers.

To get there, head west out of town towards Simferopol. Turn left (south) on the last street before leaving the town, about one km west of the bus station. At the T-intersection turn left again and continue up and around into the hills for about three km until you eventually reach the caretakers' hut and a gate. To get out of Stary Krym may be a problem as most buses passing through are already full and don't even stop. George, along with countless desperate others, had to hitchhike. There's a small **museum** in town with artefacts from the monastery as well as the 1314 **Khan Uzbek mosque**, the oldest in the Crimea, rebuilt several times.

KERCH
КЕРЧ
Population: 182,000
At the eastern tip of the Crimean peninsula,

Kerch is an industrial port and military base. Its sights include the ruins of ancient Panticapaeum, a well-known history and archaeology museum, and several old tombs which have yielded much fine ancient Greek art.

There are daily buses to/from Simferopol (about five hours), and trains from the northern Crimean city of Dzhankoy. You can catch a ferry to Russia from Kerch, usually north to Temryuk (83 km), or south to Anapa (96 km).

Eastern Ukraine
Східна Україна

Eastern Ukraine is mostly sprawling steppe, punctuated by swathes of forest and thousands of cultivated fields, and highlighted by stretches of undulating grassland. As the region lies closer to Russia than the rest of Ukraine, the empire had more influence here, and the people were often forced to assimilate with their northern neighbours. Well over 80% of Ukraine's 22% Russian population lives in this eastern area's major cities, many of which are heavy industrial centres, in particular the eastern Donbas coal region centred around Donetsk and Luhansk. Although Ukrainians constitute the majority of the population, the Russian language predominates.

KHARKIV
ХАРКІВ
Population: 1.6 million

Ukraine's second major city is an unpretentious working place, but with a curious history and an active cultural life. Its looks are a surprisingly likeable combination of old and new, narrow and spacious, grey and green. Kharkiv lies only 40 km from the Russian border, but well over half of its population is Ukrainian.

History
Founded in 1654 as a Cossack outpost, it quickly became a major trading centre and crossroads. Kharkiv was one of the first Ukrainian cities to be absorbed into the Russian sphere of influence, supporting Moscow's tsars consistently through Cossack uprisings and campaigns against the Crimean Tatars. It grew into an important fort on the Tatar frontier, and became the administrative and cultural centre of Russian Ukraine in the 1760s. It was the capital of Soviet Ukraine from 1917 to 1934, and was the site of the first wave of repression against Ukrainian nationalists and intelligentsia.

The city was heavily damaged in WW II, and has since become a centre for the manufacturing of machines such as tractors, turbines and engines.

Orientation
Central Kharkiv lies between three main squares. Southernmost, with the River Lopan along its western end, is ploshcha Rozy Lyuxemburg. Upon the slope on Universytetska Hora (University Hill), where Kharkiv began, is ploshcha Radyansky Ukrainy (ploshchad Sovetskoy Ukrainy). From here, vulitsya Sumska (Sumskaya) heads north in the direction of Moscow, past vast ploshcha Svobody. Many street signs are in Russian as well as Ukrainian. We use Ukrainian but give the Russian in parentheses if there's a major difference, or if both names are commonly used.

Information
Knihi on the corner of ploshcha Radyansky Ukrainy and prospekt Moskovsky has maps and a few books in English. Many kiosks also sell city maps, including the one in the railway station. There's a big post and telegraph office at the far eastern extension of ploshcha Rozy Lyuxemburg, at the top of pereulok Armyansky. Most hotels have a currency-exchange booth. There are also

exchange kiosks around ploshcha Radyansky Ukrainy, but there still seems to be nowhere in town to exchange travellers' cheques. A photo store at vulitsya Sumska 22 sells some Western-brand film. There's a small tourist information desk in the lobby of the Hotel National, but its services are limited. Kharkiv's telephone area code is 0572.

Ploshcha Svobody

Huge ploshcha Svobody, almost 750 metres long, is probably the only large square in the world designed as a unit in the Constructivist style, although it was never entirely completed. Planned as an ensemble of Ukraine government buildings when Kharkiv was the republican capital, it was built between 1925 and 1935. The complex was badly damaged during WW II, and largely rebuilt using German POW labour. The late 1920s **House of State Industry** (Hosprom) at the western end was the first Soviet skyscraper – a geometric series of concrete and glass blocks and bridges. Its symmetry is now ruined by the TV pylon on one tower. On the southern side of the square is the **university**, formerly the House of Planning and displaying classic Soviet aesthetics. Both the university and **Hotel Kharkiv** on the opposite side of ploshcha Svobody date from the early 1930s. Lenin still proudly stands in the midst of it all, his hand outstretched across the vast open space. Universytet metro is nearby. The pleasant **Shevchenko Park** and zoological gardens line the southern side of the square, stretching far to the south and providing a popular place for evening strolls.

Vulitsya Universytetska & Around

Vulitsya Universytetska runs south from the western side of ploshcha Radyansky Ukrainy, Kharkiv's original marketplace. In the centre of the square is a large granite sculptural ensemble commemorating Kharkiv's designation as the first capital of Soviet Ukraine on 24 December 1917. Across the square at vulitsya Universytetska 8, entered through a classical gateway, are the 1820s **Bishop's Palace** and the fine 1689

Pokrovska Church (Intercession of the Virgin). The church is an enlarged and more extravagant stone version of Ukraine's typical wooden church architecture, with a bell tower on the western end that was once part of the city's fortification system. It is the oldest building in the city, and its brick detailing is still superb today; further restoration promises to return it to a shining white splendour.

To the right of the church, with tanks from WW I and WW II outside it, is the Bishop's Palace, which now houses the 19th and 20th-century section of the **Kharkiv History Museum** (open from 9 am to 5 pm daily except Tuesday). The upstairs section is devoted to 20th-century warfare, with lots of old photos and weapons; downstairs there are two exhibits, one on historic sacred art, the other on folk art. The pre-industrial part of the History Museum, at vulitsya Universytetska 10, has been closed for restoration.

Farther down the street, the golden-domed 1770s **Uspensky (Assumption) Cathedral** is now a concert hall. Its eclectic 19th-century bell tower (90 metres tall) is a Kharkiv landmark, with neoclassical pediments and detailing capped by a Byzantine dome. It was built to commemorate Russia's victory over Napoleon.

The striking red-and-cream striped brickwork on the 1881-1901 **Blahoveshchensky Cathedral**, across the River Lopan on ploshcha Karla Marxa, was based on Istanbul's Hagia Sophia. The bell tower is a beautifully proportioned Eastern Baroque sugar-candy cane. The cathedral is open for services.

Vulitsya Sumska

Kharkiv's main drag is lively and hectic, lined with an elegant mix of theatres, cafés, stores and restaurants. The pretty **Shevchenko Ukrainian Drama Theatre** at No 9 is across the street from ploshcha Teatralna, and is flanked by the busts of two famous writers, Gogol (who was an ethnic Ukrainian) on the west side, and Pushkin on the east.

Farther north up vulitsya Sumska, across

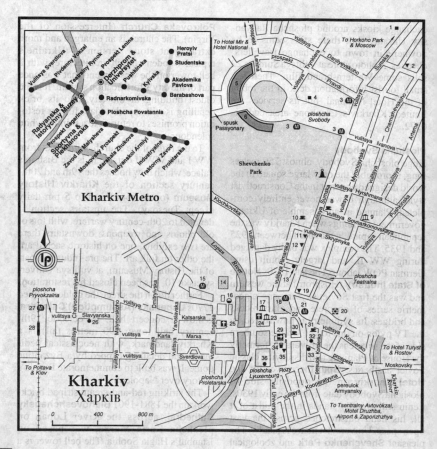

Kharkiv Metro

Kharkiv
Харків

the street from a pleasant tree-filled park, is the large granite **Opera & Ballet Theatre**. The building was designed in the brutalist style, but the interior is softer and more aesthetically pleasing than the harsh exterior would lead you to believe. Vulitsya Sovnarkomovskaya runs along the northern edge of the park, with the city **Art Museum** at No 11, three blocks down. Just before the museum, on the corner of vulitsya Myronosytska, is the former KGB building. A bust of Felyx Yandmundovych, a high-ranking member, sits outside. The Art Museum (open daily from 10 am to 5.30 pm) has a couple of

paintings by Repin, including a version of his famous *Zaporizky Cossacks Writing a Letter to the Turkish Sultan*, as well as impressive 19th-century Ukrainian works and some icons going back to the 16th century.

Still farther north on vulitsya Sumska on the eastern edge of Shevchenko Park, halfway between the opera theatre and ploshcha Svobody, is a tall statue of Shevchenko. Dramatic enough to rival nearby Lenin, the hero-poet is encircled by an ensemble of Cossacks and peasants. About two km north of ploshcha Svobody, vulitsya Sumska runs along **Horkoho Park**, where

PLACES TO STAY

1 Hotel Kievskaya
   Гостинниця Київська
4 Hotel Kharkiv
   Гостинниця Харків

PLACES TO EAT

2 Restoran Dom Chaya
   Ресторан Дом Чая
8 Kafe Kharkivyanka
   Кафе Харків'яанка
10 Opera & Ballet
   Theatre & Cafés
   Театр опери та балету і
   кафе
11 Ukrainsky Varenyky
   Українські вареники
12 Sumska vulitsya eater-
   ies
   Сумска вуліця 17
19 Restoran Teatralny
   Ресторан Театралний
30 Kafe Tsentr
   Кафе Центр
31 Kafe Yunist
   Кафе Юнисть
34 Stare Misto Bar
   Бар Старе Місто
35 Restoran Stare Misto
   Ресторан Старе Місто

OTHER

5 Hosprom Building
   Дім Госпрому
6 University
   Університет
7 Shevchenko Monument
   Пам'ятник Шевченку
9 Art Museum
   Художній музей
13 Shevchenko Ukrainian
   Drama Theatre
   Український театр драми
   імені Шевченка
14 Central Market
   Центральний ринок
16 Bus Station No 2
   Автобусна станція 2
17 History Museum,
   Modern Section
   Історичний музей,
   сучасний відділ
20 Synagogue
   Синагога
22 Ploshcha Radyansky
   Ukrainy
   Площа Радянської України
23 History Museum, Old
   Section
   Історичний музей, старий
   відділ
24 Pokrovska Church
   Покровська церква

25 Blahoveshchensky
   Cathedral
   Благовещенський
   собор
26 Train Ticket Office
   Каса продажу
   залізничних квитків
28 Pivdenny (Southern)
   Railway Station
   Південний вокзал
29 Uspensky Cathedral
   Успенський собор
32 Ukrainsky Suvenir
   Український сувенір
33 Knihi (Bookshop)
   Книги
36 TsUM Department
   Store
   ЦУМ

METRO STATIONS

3 Universytet
   Університет
15 Tsentralny Rinok
   Центральний ринок
18 Istorychny Muzey
   Історичний музей
21 Radyanska
   (Sovetskaya)
   Радянська
27 Pivdenny (Yuzhny)
   Vokzal
   Південний вокзал

WEST TO EAST LINE

Вулиця Свердлова
Vulitsya Sverdlova
Південний Вокзал
Pivdenny Vokzal
Театральний Ринок
Teatralny Rynok
Радянська
Radyanska
Проспект Гагаріна
Prospekt Gagarina
Спортивна
Sportyvna
Завод ім. Малишева
Zavod im. Malysheva
Московський Проспект
Moskovsky Prospekt
Маршала Жукова
Marshala Zhukova

Радянської Армії
Radyanskoi Armiyi
Індустряльна
Industryalna
Тракторний Завод
Traktorny Zavod
Пролетарська
Proletarska

FROM RIVER TO NORTH

Історичний Музей
Istorychny Muzoy
Держпром
Derzhprom
Пушкінська
Pushkinska
Київська
Kyivska
Барабашова
Barabashova

Академіка Павлова
Akademika Pavlova
Студентська
Studentska
Героїв Праці
Heroyiv Pratsi

NORTH TO SOUTH LINE

Проспект Леніна
Prospekt Lenina
Університет
Univoroytot
Раднаркомівська
Radnarkomivska
Площа Повстання
Ploshcha Povstannia
Плеханівська
Plekhanovska

you'll find plenty of tree-lined paths to stroll along, a funfair, a cinema and a summertime chair lift and children's locomotive, as well as hills for wintertime sledding.

Places to Stay

The only hotel in the centre of town is the 1930s *Hotel Kharkiv* (☎ 45 61 25), on the northern side of ploshcha Svobody. Its grand and cavernous interior makes you feel like you're entering an elaborate stage setting. Rooms cost US$50/60/70 a single/double/ triple, hard currency only. Get off at the Universytet metro stop.

North of ploshcha Svobody on prospekt Lenina are two comparable hotels with good service and comfortable rooms. The *Hotel National* (☎ 32 05 08) at prospekt Lenina 21 is smaller and a few blocks closer to town, but more expensive at US$47/74 for a single/double. The *Hotel Mir* (☎ 30 55 43), at prospekt Lenina 27A, is a large white building in a small park with rooms for US$30/50 a single/double. Both hotels accept hard currency only and are reached by trolleybus Nos 8, 18 and 38 from the north-eastern corner of ploshcha Svobody: the third stop down (Hyprostal) for the Hotel National, and the fifth stop (Otkara Yarosha) for the Hotel Mir.

Probably the nicest but most expensive place to stay in town is the *Hotel Kievskaya* (☎ 43 90 31), on vulitsya Sumska next to the Baroque Wedding Palace, three blocks north of ploshcha Svobody. Rooms cost US$60/80 a single/double, hard currency only.

For cheaper accommodation, try the *Hotel Turyst* (☎ 92 10 46) at prospekt Moskovsky 144, about five km south-east of the centre on the road to Rostov, conveniently near the Marshala Zhukova metro stop. It's a typical Soviet-looking hotel with typical Soviet service, but you may be lucky enough to get a nice attendant. Rooms cost US$15/24/35 a single/double/triple.

The two-star *Motel Druzhba* (☎ 52 20 91) at prospekt Gagarina 185, six km south of ploshcha Radyansky Ukrainy, is a decent roadside hotel, but if you don't have a car, getting there involves a long and hellishly crowded ride on trolleybus No 5, 6 or 9, or bus No 10 from the metro stop Prospekt Gagarina. Get off at L'Hovska stop after about 20 minutes. Rooms cost US$14/28 for a single/double, hard currency only.

About 300 metres due east of the railway station, on the corner of vulitsya Karla Marxa and vulitsya Dmytrivska, is the *Hotel Yuzhnaya* – at the time of writing it didn't accept foreigners, but you could ask the staff if this policy has changed.

Places to Eat

Hotels The large restaurant in the *Hotel Mir* serves up standard dishes, with big helpings. A lot of drinking and dancing goes on here, so you'll only get a quiet, relaxed dinner at about 6 pm. The *Hotel National* also has a big restaurant with live music. Both hotels have cafés – the Mir's is on the main lobby floor, and the National's is beneath the northern end of the restaurant. The restaurant at the *Hotel Kharkiv* has a good reputation and a 1930s atmosphere.

Restaurants & Cafés Behind the Uspensky Cathedral, the *Restoran Stare Misto* at vulitsya Kvitki-Osnovyanenko 12 is decorated like a medieval hall and serves a full meal of beefsteak, potatoes, soup and salad for about US$4. The entrance to the restaurant is around the corner from the *Stare Misto Bar*, a popular hang-out serving cakes, snacks and an assortment of drinks. A block away is *Kafe Tsentr* with a good selection of cakes and ice cream. *Kafe Yunist*, off ploshcha Radyansky Ukrainy on pereulok Korolenko, has pre-served plates of tasty hot food for about US$3.

Vulitsya Sumska is a gold mine of eating establishments. At the southern end, on the corner of ploshcha Radyansky Ukrainy, is the *Restoran Teatralny*, with a pleasant atmosphere, friendly service and reasonable food costing about US$4 for a full meal. Upstairs at vulitsya Sumska 21 is the cafeteria-style *Ukrainsky Varenyky* (open until 10 pm), where less than US$2 gets you a plateful of hot varenyky, a bowl of weak borscht with bread, and a bottle of beer. Just south at No 17 is a row of four separate eateries, all open from morning to 9 pm. *Tryl*, on the northern end, has good roast chicken and pizzas; the others deal more in cakes and ice cream.

Kharkiv's most popular cafés are in the basement of the Opera & Ballet Theatre at vulitsya Sumska 25. There are rich cakes, bowls of fruit (with cream if you like) and coffee. Prices are low and the cafés are open in the day and evening – and there's a good pay public toilet. Opposite the entrance to the cafés is a Melodya store which sells some Western food products. Around the corner, off the southern end of the theatre, is *Yekzotyk*, a tea shop with a relaxing corner where you can sit and have a quiet cup of tea; it's open from 10 am to 6 pm daily except Sunday.

Just north of the theatre on the opposite corner is the *Kafe Kharkivyanka* (open until 8 pm), a long interior hallway with numerous counters and tables selling various food and drink.

One of the nicest restaurants in the city is the *Restoran Dom Chaya* (House of Tea), two blocks north of ploshcha Svobody on the north-eastern corner of vulitsya Karazina and vulitsya Myronosytska. It's a bit expensive, but the food and service are good and the atmosphere is pleasant and relaxing. Hopefully, the friendly old doorman who speaks good English will be there to greet you.

Market The vast Central Market, west of the River Lopan at vulitsya Engelsa 33, is a small city in itself. In and around the large covered hall are piles of fresh vegetables you rarely see in restaurants, and in autumn there are the biggest pumpkins you're likely to see anywhere – plus honey, nuts, meat and fish. Behind the market hall is a sea of vendors selling everything from cheap booze and expensive fur hats to used car parts. Tsentralny Rynok metro is close.

Entertainment
Kharkiv's Opera & Ballet Theatre at vulitsya Sumska 25 stages all the classics, as well as

musical concerts. The booking office is open from noon to 7 pm, and tickets are ridiculously cheap. The Uspensky Cathedral often has a variety of concerts; the ticket kiosk is to the right of the bell tower. The Shevchenko Ukrainian Drama Theatre is at vulitsya Sumska 9. Live-music accompaniment is a feature at most restaurants.

Things to Buy
Ukrainsky Suvenir at prospekt Moskovsky 1 sells typical folk souvenirs, including embroidery and wooden trinkets. At vulitsya Universytetska 9 there's a small art gallery and gift shop with interesting work for sale. A bigger art gallery/gift shop is on the eastern side of ploshcha Radyansky Ukrainy at No 26. There's usually a few street vendors near the entrance to the opera theatre. TsUM, at ploshcha Rozy Lyuxemburg 1, is the main department store.

Getting There & Away
Air Air Ukraine has weekly flights to/from Kiev, and occasional flights to other domestic destinations. For information try the information desk at the Hotel National, or call the airport on ☎ 50 53 47.

Bus The main bus station is the Tsentralny Avtovokzal (☎ 21 65 02) at prospekt Gagarina 22, near Prospekt Gagarina metro. There are also three smaller bus stations; bus station No 2, which services the northern city of Sumy, is between Blahoveshchensky Cathedral and the Central Market.

Train Several lines meet at Kharkiv, with numerous trains travelling to/from Moscow daily, taking about 12 or 13 hours. Other services, at least daily, include: Kiev (10 hours), Odessa (20 hours), Rostov-on-Don (12 hours), Simferopol (10 hours), Sochi (22 hours), Tbilisi (31 hours), Zaporizhzhya (4½ hours) and Minsk (17 hours, via Sumy). There are trains to/from Lviv (24 hours) every other day. The main station, known as the Pivdenny (Southern; Yuzhny in Russian) or Pasazhirsky, is about two km west of ploshcha Rozy Lyuxemburg on ploshcha

UKRAINE

Pryvokzalna. Pivdenny Vokzal (Yuzhny Vokzal) metro is adjacent.

To buy tickets, don't bother trying at the main station; go to the nearby ticket office at vulitsya Slavyanska 6. The last (fourth) stairway leads into the office for foreigners (Byuro Mizhnarodnykh Perevezen); it doesn't usually have long queues and it's open daily from 7 am to 5 pm.

Car & Motorbike Kharkiv is where the Moscow-Crimea road meets the Kiev-Caucasus road. Kursk (Russia) is 200 km to the north, Poltava 135 km west, Zaporizhzhya 300 km south and Rostov-on-Don (Russia) 465 km south-east.

Getting Around

To/From the Airport The airport is eight km south of the centre, just off prospekt Gagarina. Trolleybus No 5 from Prospekt Gagarina metro terminates at the airport. Bus No 19T runs north-south through the city down prospekt Lenina, vulitsya Sumska and prospekt Gagarina, terminating at the airport. However, a taxi would be much easier; you can usually find a taxi near one of the city's three squares.

Public Transport Kharkiv is an easily walkable city. It also has an efficient two-line metro, and as in Kiev, you have to buy a plastic token (zheton) before you can take a ride. A third line, running north-south, is under construction, and will have a metro stop conveniently north of ploshcha Svobody at prospekt Lenina, near the Hotel Mir. Trolleybuses and buses are usually unbearably crowded, a daunting challenge.

POLTAVA
ПОЛТАВА
Population: 325,000

The 480 km from Kharkiv to Kiev is classic Ukraine steppe, partially wooded, and sweeping expanses of flat terrain broken only by Poltava, which is set on three hills on the Vorskla River. Here, in 1709, Peter the Great decisively defeated the combined forces of Sweden's Charles XII and the Ukrainian Cossack leader Ivan Mazepa, ending both Sweden's expansionist ambitions and Ukraine's hopes for an independent Cossack state, and paving the way for Russian domination in Ukraine and beyond.

Orientation
The centre of town, about three km north-west from the main railway station, lies along the 1.5-km stretch of vulitsya Zhovtneva between Kruhla ploshcha in the north-west and the maydan Soborna park in the south-east. The middle section of vulitsya Zhovtneva has been turned into a small pedestrian strip. The battle site is about seven km north of the centre. Poltava's telephone area code is 0532.

City Centre
The focal point of the town is the circular plaza/park **Kruhla ploshcha** (round square), often referred to by its former name, Oktyabry Park. Laid out in the early 19th century in an attempt to emulate the grand planning ideals of St Petersburg, it is surrounded by a number of large neoclassical administration buildings, including the central post and telephone office (Zhovtneva 33) and a former meeting hall for noblemen. In the centre of the park is the **Iron Column of Glory**, surrounded by miniature cannons and topped by a golden eagle, erected on the 100th anniversary of Peter the Great's battle.

South-east of Kruhla ploshcha, vulitsya Zhovtneva becomes a pedestrian precinct for a few blocks until it comes to the classical **Hohol Music & Drama Theatre**, recessed off the southern side of the street. Ukrainsky Suvenir is at No 25, and the TsUM department store is at No 28.

Farther down is the leafy Zhovtnevy Park, with the **Poltava Regional Museum** along its south-eastern edge, in front of a 1926 cubist Shevchenko monument. Housed in the former regional government headquarters, the Art-Nouveau building (1903-8) is ornamented with the ceramic crests of each district capital in the Poltava oblast. Inside are historic and ethnographic exhibits; open daily except Wednesday from 10 am to 6 pm.

Continue down vulitsya Zhovtneva for a block and turn left (north-east) on vulitsya Spaska to get to the 1705 **Spaska Church** – a small, squat building set off the street in a park setting. Its simple design is based on the even older wooden church that previously stood on the site. A block farther north on vulitsya Spaska is the 1919 **Poltava Art Museum**, the last building on the left. It has eight rooms, mostly containing 18th to 19th-century European paintings and sculpture, and is open from 10 am to 6 pm; closed on Monday.

Back on vulitsya Zhovtneva, the street heads a block farther south-east to the **bell tower** of the once-beautiful Ukrainian Baroque Uspensky Cathedral, one of the numerous cultural symbols destroyed by the Soviet regime in the early 1930s. The wedding-cake bell tower (1774-81) is all that remains. Inside, to your left as you enter, is a small chapel with an old photograph of the cathedral and bell tower. The famous Kyzykerman Bell, made from captured Turkish cannons in the 18th century, which used to hang in the belfry is now displayed in the Regional Museum.

Beyond the bell tower is maydan Soborna, with a small classical rotunda overlooking the Vorskla River at the far end of the park. To the right of the rotunda is the charmingly reconstructed 19th-century wooden cottage **house museum** of the Poltava poet Ivan Komlyarovsoho; open from 9 am to 5 pm daily except Monday.

Khrestovozdvyzhensky Monastery

About three km north-east of the centre is the Khrestovozdvyzhensky Monastery (Elevation of the Cross) complex, built in the early 18th century in the Ukrainian Baroque style. The main cathedral is the only one still standing in the country with seven cupolas, rather than the usual five. The 45-metre-high bell tower was built about 80 years later in a more heavily ornate Baroque style. You can walk to the monastery in about 30 minutes by heading east on vulitsya Radyanska from Kruhla ploshcha. There's also the infrequent No 10 bus, caught just south-west of the

Regional Museum on vulitsya Lenina, or best of all take a taxi for about US$2.

Battlefield

You may want to hire a taxi (US$2 to US$3) to take you out to the battle site, about seven km north of the centre. It's also reachable by the very rare No 5 bus from the rynok (marketplace) on vulitsya Shevchenko, two blocks south-west of Kruhla ploshcha. If you have your own car, follow vulitsya Zhovtneva north from Kruhla ploshcha and bear right up vulitsya Zinkivska at the end. The battle was fought over a large area around what's now vulitsya Zinkivska. The best starting point is the **Poltava Battle Museum** at Shvedska mohyla 32, by the Peter the Great statue; open from 9.30 am to 5.30 pm daily except Monday. Inside are numerous interesting displays concerning the battle including maps, paintings and military diagrams. Obviously glorifying Peter the Great's tremendous victory, the displays are short on Sweden's viewpoint and there's nothing to document the experiences of the Cossack forces under Hetman Ivan Mazepa.

In front of the museum on a hill is a cross memorial to the Russian troops killed, behind which lies a pretty brick Orthodox church (1895) with some impressive frescoes in the process of being restored inside. Farther down the road is a cross memorial to the 9000 Swedes who died in the battle.

Places to Stay & Eat

The standard *Hotel Turyst* (☎ 2 09 21) at vulitsya Miru 2 is about half a km west of the main railway station, over the bridge and to the right. They seem to only take tour groups, but you can try your luck as an individual traveller. Rooms cost US$6/8 a single/double.

The *Motel Poltava* (☎ 3 00 24) is about four km west of the centre on the Kiev road at Sovnarkomovskaya 1. From the main railway station, trolleybus No 6 (Motel stop) or No 2 (Bozhenko stop) will take you close by, but the hotel is hard to find as it's hidden in a park. Trolleybus No 6 is the better of the two, but a taxi (about US$2) is best. The

UKRAINE

motel's service is good and the rooms are comfortable but overpriced at US$30/40 for a single/double (hard currency only). You can also try the Hotel Kiev (☎ 2 42 86) at vulitsya Sinna, a few block north-west from Kruhla ploshcha off vulitsya Zhovtneva, but it was closed at the time of writing. You could also ask if the management has changed its no-foreigners policy at the *Hotel Teatralny*, off vulitsya Zhovtneva and next to the Hohol Music & Drama Theatre.

The restaurant at the *Motel Poltava* serves good meat dishes and borscht, but the loud music makes the food hard to digest. At the time of writing, the restaurant in the *Hotel Turyst* appeared to have closed. In the centre there's the *Restoran Teatralny* across the street from the Hohol Theatre. The *Lileya*, at the very south-eastern end of vulitsya Zhovtneva to the left of the classical colonnade, has a terraced dining area.

Getting There & Away

There are two railway stations in Poltava; make sure you get off at the main one, known as Poltava-Pivdenna (south). There are about four daily trains to/from Kiev (seven hours) and at least six a day to Kharkiv (three to four hours). Three a day run to/from Odessa (13 hours), two to/from Moscow (20 hours) and one to/from Simferopol (16 hours) and Lviv (21 hours).

Getting Around

From the main railway station, trolleybus Nos 1, 2, 4, 6 and 11 all go to the centre. Trolleybus No 1 runs between the two railway stations.

ZAPORIZHZHYA
ЗАПОРІЖЖЯ
Population: 900,000

Zaporizhzhya (Beyond the Rapids) is one of the smoggiest places on earth – even the midday sun can be blocked out by a thick blanket of grime – which is a pity, because it has an attractive location on the east bank of the Dnipro River and a lot of history. It's at the foot of the 40-km series of rapids which

previously made navigation on the Dnipro near impossible.

Khortytsya Island below the rapids was the *sich* (fortified base) of the famous Zaporizky Cossacks. The rapids are now submerged by the lake behind Zaporizhzhya's Dneproges Hydroelectric Dam, the USSR's first, built to much fanfare between 1927 and 1932. Dneproges made Zaporizhzhya a major Ukrainian industrial centre, and the ageing power plant now pours out the smoke and fumes that choke the city. Unless you're a real Cossack buff, a visit to Zaporizhzhya isn't a must, as there's not a lot to see on the island and the city itself is rather boring with only two hotels, both very expensive. You could arrive in the morning and take a night train out if you don't want to pay for the expensive accommodation.

Orientation & Information

The Kharkiv-Simferopol highway skirts the eastern side of Zaporizhzhya, but signposts barely admit that the city exists. The entire city branches off its one main artery, the 10-km-long prospekt Lenina, with the main Zaporizhzhya-1 railway station at the south-eastern end, and ploshcha Lenina, which overlooks the Dneproges Dam, at the opposite end. The city centre stretches out along the last four or five km of ploshcha Lenina, ending at the dam. Khortytsya Island lies in the Dnipro, parallel and two km south-west of prospekt Lenina.

A big post, telegraph and telephone office is at prospekt Lenina 186. For about US$10 or US$15 an hour, the tourist bureau in the Hotel Zaporizhzhya at prospekt Lenina 135 can arrange a tour around Khortytsya Island or to the west-bank powerhouse of the Dneproges Dam. The hotel's tourist bureau is open from Monday to Friday from 9 am to 4 pm; closed between 1 and 2 pm. Zaporizhzhya's telephone area code is 0612.

Dneproges Dam

You can look down on the 760-metre curve of the Dneproges Dam (Dneprovska Hidro-elektrostantsya) from ploshcha Lenina. A road runs across the top and boats pass by two channels along the east bank. The dam's early promoters didn't emphasise the fact that it was built under US supervision with mainly US equipment. Partly wrecked in WW II, it was rebuilt and a second powerhouse was later added on the east bank, more than doubling the capacity to 1500 MW. Today, the Zaporizhzhya region also has nuclear and thermal power, so Dneproges' capacity is rarely used.

Khortytsya Island

Sometime around 1553-54, the Cossack hero-leader Baida gathered together scattered groups of Cossacks to build a fort on what was then a remote and strategically located island below the Dnipro rapids. Beyond the control of Polish or Russian authority, the famous Zaporizky Sich was the cradle of Ukrainian Cossackdom, the 'free base' where any man, irrespective of social background, could come to join the Cossack brotherhood.

The island has been a reserve since 1965, but it's hard to imagine the Cossack revelry of the past with electrical cables and a massive bridge crossing over to the island, and the dam and industrial facilities in plain view. Nevertheless, you can visit the **Historical Museum of Zaporizky Cossacks**, open from 10 am to 5 pm daily except Monday, which contains interesting exhibits and Cossack artefacts excavated from around the island, including some scattered tombstones near the entrance. The museum is on the island's rocky northern end, about one km past the bus stop and restaurant (see Places to Eat). There are other Cossack haunts here – places like the Sechebny Vorota, the Cossacks' jetty, and the Hadyucha Pechera (Snake Cave). Also here is the Chyorna Skala (Black Rock), where the Kievan King Svyatoslav is said to have been killed by the Pechenegs in 972.

Trolleybus No 2 or 16, travelling westbound from the Hotel Zaporizhzhya, goes to the northern end of Khortytsya. Get off at the Muzey stop, and head right before the road leaves the island again. The trolleybus is infrequent and always so unbelievably crowded that it might be better to take a taxi and spare yourself the ordeal. In summer, there are two-hour cruises around the island, two or three times a day from the mainland jetty at the foot of bulvar Tarasa Shevchenka. Trolleybus No 14 heading west along prospekt Lenina terminates nearby.

There's an **art museum** with some interesting local work just off vulitsya Lenina, about one km down from the Hotel Zaporizhzhya and recessed off the street in a park (ploshcha Mayakovskoho), where there's sometimes a small craft market. The museum is open from 9 am to 4 pm daily; closed on Sunday and Monday.

Zaporizhzhya Oak

West of the Dnipro River in the Verkhnya Khortytsya area is a 600 to 700-year-old oak (dub) from which you can dangle any Cossack legend you choose. Did Bohdan Khmelnytsky address his troops beneath it before they marched against the Poles in 1648? Or was this where the Cossacks wrote their insulting letter to the Turkish sultan immortalised (or just imagined?) in Repin's painting? We may never know, but we can certainly admire the oak's girth of 6.5 metres. You can find the tree down vulitsya Hoholya off vulitsya Istomina, reached by the very rare No 19 bus from ploshcha Lenina, at the far north-western end of prospekt Lenina near the dam.

Places to Stay & Eat

The three-star *Hotel Zaporizhzhya* (☎ 34 12 92) at prospekt Lenina 135 is clean, well staffed and comfortable, with a good restaurant, but it's so overpriced for a town with few attractions that it's surprising it gets any business at all. Rooms go for an exorbitant US$80/90 a single/double, hard currency only. The *Hotel Ukraina* (☎ 34 66 73), a block east at prospekt Lenina 162A (set half a block off the road), is just as expensive, with similar standards, but it's a bit less friendly. You can try the *Hotel Dnipro* (☎ 33 04 45) at prospekt Lenina 202, between the Hotel Zaporizhzhya and the dam, or the *Hotel Teatralny* at Chekistiv 25, off prospekt

Lenina and about two km down from the railway station, but at the time of writing, both hotels stated that they don't accept Westerners.

The *Kafe Vesna* at prospekt Lenina 143, a block down the hill from the Hotel Zaporizhzhya, is a cafeteria-style eatery serving salads, roast chicken and noodles at cheap prices. The *Kafe Paris*, about one km farther down prospekt Lenina on the left-hand corner of vulitsya Stalevarov and opposite ploshcha Mayakovskoho, is a pleasant and popular smoke-free café. The market (rynok) is across the street and a long block north of the Kafe Paris, near the circus.

On Khortytsya Island, near the bus stop for the Cossack Museum, is the *Zaporizka Sich* restaurant, with banquet-style dining.

Getting There & Away

Air Air Ukraine occasionally has flights to/from Kiev. The airline office is at bulvar Tsentralny 3, or ask at the Hotel Zaporizhzhya's tourist bureau.

Bus The bus station (avtovokzal) is towards the south-eastern end of prospekt Lenina at No 22, near the Zaporizhzhya-1 railway station.

Train Zaporizhzhya-1 railway station, at the south-eastern end of prospekt Lenina, has more trains than Zaporizhzhya-2, which is about four km north-west down vulitsya Lenina and north-east on vulitsya Leppika. Services from Zaporizhzhya-1 include around six daily trains to/from Kiev (14 hours), at least four daily to/from Moscow (16-20 hours), two daily to Kharkiv (4½ hours) and Lviv (27 hours), and one a day to/from Odessa (17 hours). There are at least five trains a day to/from Simferopol (five hours).

Boat Zaporizhzhya has two river ports: the richkovy vokzal at the southern end of vulitsya Leppika (about four km down vulitsya Lenina from the Zaporizhzhya-1 railway station, then left into vulitsya Leppika); and Port Lenina, just north of the Dneproges

Dam, where most river boats from Kiev pull in. For information on the seasonal boats to Kiev or Odessa, ask at the helpful tourist bureau in the Hotel Zaporizhzhya.

Getting Around

To/From the Airport The airport is 20-odd km north-east of the centre. Bus No 3 goes from the airport to Zaporizhzhya-1 railway station, and Nos 4 and 8 go to ploshcha Mayakovskoho, about one km north-west of the Hotel Zaporizhzhya on prospekt Lenina.

Trolleybus Trolleybus Nos 3 and 23 travel the whole 10-km length of prospekt Lenina between Zaporizhzhya-1 railway station and ploshcha Lenina, with No 3 crossing the Dneproges Dam. No 8 covers all of prospekt Lenina but for the easternmost km or so. These trolleybuses, the lifelines of the city, are so overcrowded that people are literally hanging out the doors.

DONETSK
ДОНЕЦЬК
Population 1.1 million

About 240 km east of Zaporizhzhya and 280 km south-east of Kharkiv, Donetsk is the 'capital' of the Donbas (Donets Basin) – eastern Ukraine's great mining and industrial belt, whose coal-miners are one of the most powerful labour groups in the country. Donetsk never seems to have the water shortage and sewage problems that plague other Ukrainian cities. But besides a hot shower, there's not much to attract tourists, unless you're interested in seeing a model Soviet city.

Until 1924, Donetsk was called Yuzovka after a Welshman, John Hughes, who set up the first metallurgical plant here in 1872 to exploit the region's coal. Khrushchev began his career here in the 1920s, and Ukrainian President Kuchma was once the director of a rocket factory in nearby Luhansk. Donetsk's telephone area code is 0622.

Things to See & Do
Despite the fact that there are about 50 mines in the city itself, it doesn't really seem too

dirty a place. In fact, the city once won a UNESCO prize for being one of the cleanest industrial centres with a population of over one million. Vulitsya Artema is the 10-km-long main street, with the railway station at the northern end, and the **Opera & Ballet Theatre** in the middle at No 82. The **Art Museum** is just behind it to the east at vulitsya Pushkina 35. A **Regional Museum** is about two km north-east at vulitsya Cheluskintsiv 189A. There's a pleasant stretch of park running north-south with a few large ponds, west of the centre.

Places to Stay & Eat

The *Hotel Donbas* (☎ 93 13 66) at vulitsya Artema 147 is just south of the opera theatre. North of the Shevchenko monument is the *Hotel Ukraina* (☎ 91 19 50) at Artema 88. Not far to the east is the *Hotel Druzhba* (☎ 91 19 87) at vulitsya Universytetska 98. All the hotels have standard restaurants.

Getting There & Away

The airport is north of the centre of town, and Air Ukraine has weekly flights to Kiev. Air Ukraine's office (☎ 58 81 80) is at vulitsya Artema 167.

The 'Donbas' train with sleeping cars goes daily to/from Kharkiv (5½ hours) and Moscow (16½ hours); there's also a daily train to/from Kiev (15 hours), as well as an Odessa train that pulls through Zaporizhzhya. The ticket office is not far from the Hotel Ukraina at vulitsya Universytetska 35.

UKRAINE

BELARUS

Facts about Belarus

Belarus has been described as a flat, dull piece of land straddling the shortest route between Moscow and the Polish border. Flat it is, but dull is a subjective term. Wide stretches of unbroken birch groves, vast, forested marshlands and gently sloping green and black fields may not be exciting but retain a haunting beauty – especially when interspersed with wooden villages which seem frozen in 18th-century isolation. Obviously, this swathe of terrain was of great interest to many people, including the Russians, Poles, Lithuanians, Germans and others who fought savagely over this borderland for centuries. The real victims were the Belarusians, pawns in the destiny of greater powers who cared nothing for their fate. The country suffered grievously in both world wars, WW II taking a quarter of its population and laying waste most of its cities.

Today there's a lot more to see than one would expect from a country not known for its tourist appeal. Minsk is the newly emerging cosmopolitan centre of the Commonwealth of Independent States (CIS) and a shining testament to classical Soviet urban planning. Brest is a lively and hectic border town, Hrodna a cocktail of historical legacies, and Polatsk a sleepy legacy of past glory. The countryside is virtually without tourists and historic towns like Njasvizh make a relaxing day's excursion.

One thing visitors won't be able to avoid are the countless memorials to the Great Patriotic War (the Soviet name for WW II). The propagandist element of some of these memorials almost overshadows the appalling events and wartime suffering they commemorate. This is particularly ironic when you realise that after a quarter of the Belarusian population had died for 'the cause', hundreds of thousands were later purged or sent off to Siberia for alleged 'collaborations' – something to which there are no memorials.

Belarus was probably worse hit by the

1986 Chornobyl disaster than any other region, with 70% of the fallout landing on its territory and around one-fifth of its area seriously affected. By 1990, two million people, 20% of the country's forests and well over 250,000 hectares of agricultural land had been contaminated. The plight of the residents in the worst hit south-eastern areas only gradually became clear with increasing reports of cancer and related diseases, birth deformities and so on. More than 45,000 people were evacuated, but by the spring of 1993 some 70,000 were still waiting. Western authorities have repeated to us, however, that short-term visitors have no reason for concern. For more information on Chornobyl, see the boxed aside in Ukraine Facts for the Visitor.

HISTORY
Arrival of the Slavs
Evidence of human occupation in Belarus goes back to the early Stone Age. Eastern Slavs were certainly here in the 6th to 8th centuries AD during the Slav expansion, and those who settled on the territory of modern Belarus formed a number of principalities including Polatsk (first mentioned in 862), Pinsk, Turov and Minsk. These fell under the general control of Kievan Rus, the Slavic state founded at Kiev in the 9th century, which brought Orthodox Christianity. The

Belarus
Беларусь

economy was based on slash-and-burn agriculture and a certain amount of river trade, particularly on the Dnjapro.

Lithuanian & Polish Control

When Kievan Rus was smashed by the Mongol Tatars in 1240, many Belarusian towns became Tatar vassals. In the 14th century, Belarus was gradually taken over by Lithuania, a growing power on its northwestern border. It was to be 400 years before Belarus came under Russian control, a period in which Belarusians became linguistically and culturally differentiated from the Russians to their east and the Ukrainians to their south. Belarus means 'White Russia', a term of obscure origin said, among other things, to be derived from the people's pale complexion or their white dress.

Lithuania permitted its subject peoples a fair degree of autonomy – even using Belarusian as its own state language during the early years. Even after Lithuania became Roman Catholic following the uniting of its crown with Poland's in 1386, the Belarusian peasantry remained Orthodox. However, they were effectively reduced to serf status by agricultural reforms in the 16th century.

Lithuania sank into a junior role in its partnership with Poland, especially after the two
states' formal union in 1569, and across Lithuanian territory (including Belarus) the
nobility adopted Polish culture and language
and the Catholic religion.

In 1596, the Polish authorities arranged
the Union of Brest, which set up the Uniate
Church (also known as Ukrainian Catholic
or Greek Catholic) and brought much of the
Orthodox Church in Belarus under the
authority of the Vatican. The Uniate Church
insisted on the pope's supremacy and Catholic doctrine but permitted Orthodox forms
of ritual.

For the next two centuries of Polish rule,
Belarus largely stagnated. Trade was controlled by Poles and Jews and most
Belarusians remained peasants. Poland
became steadily weaker, and towards the end
of the 18th century it and its dominions were
carved up between Russia, Prussia and
Austria in the three Partitions of Poland
(1772, 1793 and 1795-96). All of Belarus
was absorbed into Russia.

Tsarist Rule

Under Russian rule a policy of cultural Russification was frequently pursued, and in
1839 the Uniate Church was abolished, with
most Belarusians turning to Orthodoxy. The
Russian rulers and the Orthodox Church
regarded Belarus as 'western Russia' and
tried to obliterate any sense of a separate
Belarusian nationality. Publishing in the
Belarusian language was banned.

The economy slowly developed in the
19th century with the emergence of small
industries such as timber milling, glass-
making and boat-building, the freeing of the
serfs in the 1860s, and the building of railways in the 1880s. However, poverty in the
countryside remained at such a high level
that 1.5 million people emigrated in the 50
years before 1917, mostly to Siberia or the
USA. During the 19th century Belarus was
part of the Pale of Settlement, the area where
Jews in the Russian Empire were required to
settle, and developed a large Jewish population, especially in the towns, where they

made up over half the population. The majority of Belarusians remained on the land –
poor and illiterate – and they were outnumbered in towns by Russians as well as
Jews. Due to their cultural stagnation, their
absence from positions of influence, and
their historical domination by Poles and Russians, any sense among Belarusian-speakers
that they were a distinct nationality was very
slow to emerge.

World Wars & Soviet Rule

During WW I, there was considerable fighting between Russia and Germany, and
consequently much destruction, on Belarusian soil. In 1918, under German occupation,
an independent Belarusian Democratic
Republic was declared, before Polish and
Bolshevik forces took up the cudgels over
Belarus in 1919. The 1921 Treaty of Riga
allotted roughly the western third of modern
Belarus to Poland, which launched a programme of Polonisation that provoked
armed resistance by Belarusians.

The Bolshevik-controlled area, the Belo-
russian Soviet Socialist Republic (SSR),
became a founding member of the USSR in
1922. This small area, centred on Minsk, was
enlarged a few years later with the transfer
from the USSR's Russian Republic of the
eastern Polatsk, Vitsebsk, Orsha, Mahileu
and Homel areas, all with large Belarusian
populations.

The Soviet regime in the 1920s encouraged Belarusian literature and culture, but in
the 1930s, as throughout the USSR, nationalism and the Belarusian language were
discouraged and their proponents persecuted. The 1930s also saw industrialisation,
agricultural collectivisation and purges in
which hundreds of thousands were executed
– most in the Kurapaty Forest, outside
Minsk. When the USSR and Nazi Germany
began WW II by invading opposite sides of
Poland in September 1939, western Belarus
was seized from Poland by the Red Army –
only to find itself on the front line again when
the Nazis turned around and invaded the
USSR in 1941. Belarus was quickly overrun
by the Germans despite a heroic stand by the

Soviet garrison at Brest. The German occupation was savage and partisan resistance widespread until the Red Army drove the Germans out, with massive destruction on both sides, in 1944. There were big battles around Vitsebsk, Barysau and Minsk. Barely a stone was left standing in Minsk. At least one in four of Belarus' population died between 1939 and 1945 – more than two million people – many of them, Jews and others, in 200-plus Nazi concentration camps, many more in Soviet deportations and executions before 1941.

Western Belarus remained in Soviet hands at the end of the war. The first postwar five-year plan succeeded in repairing most of the war damage, and industrialisation began again, with Minsk developing into the industrial hub of the western USSR and Belarus becoming one of the Soviet Union's most prosperous republics. The population balance shifted from the country to the cities and heavy Russian immigration took place to bolster the industrial workforce. The postwar political leadership of Belarus until 1980, drawn largely from local WW II partisans, managed to emphasise Belarusia's nationhood at the same time as it acknowledged its place in the 'Soviet family'.

Protest & Independence

The 1986 Chornobyl disaster in Ukraine hit Belarus even worse than Ukraine itself, with around one-fifth of the country seriously contaminated (see the introduction to this chapter). This was one of the few issues which crystallised political opposition in a country considered to be among the most rigidly communist of the Soviet republics.

In 1988 the Belarusian Popular Front was formed to address the issues raised by the Chornobyl disaster and the declining use of the Belarusian language. The leader of the Popular Front since its inception has been the archaeologist Zjanon Paznjak, who first revealed the existence of enormous mass graves in the Kurapaty Forest. The graves contained the bodies of victims of Soviet executions carried out between 1937 and 1941 – by some estimates as many as 900,000 people. The Popular Front staged some well-attended demonstrations but the communist authorities employed various devices to reduce its representation in the new republican Supreme Soviet (parliament), elected in 1990.

However, in response to the growth of nationalist feeling, on 27 July 1990 the republic issued a declaration of sovereignty

The Coat of Arms of Belarus

Where once the hammer and sickle were displayed, the national emblem of Belarus now appears. The symbol of a silver knight on his rearing horse, sword drawn, dates to medieval times and represents the call to arms in defence of the homeland. This is something Belarusians have become used to through their region's long history. Constantly ruled, and often overrun, by outside powers, it isn't surprising that when Belarus finally achieved independence, it chose for its coat of arms this defiant symbol of self-determination. The six-ended golden cross on the knight's shield is the ancient symbol of Jarillo, the pagan Slavic sun god. The knight is usually displayed against a red background. Red, a symbol of valour and courage, and white, which represents freedom and purity, are the colours of the Belarusian flag. ■

within the USSR. That same year, Belarusian was declared the republic's official language, though with a transition period from Russian of up to 10 years in some institutions. In April 1991, in response to price rises, two one-day general strikes won across-the-board wage increases for Belarusian workers, though not the resignation of the republic's communist-dominated leadership. The leadership abolished a state commission which criticised the inaction of high Belarusian government officials in the wake of Chornobyl.

After many Party and government leaders supported the failed anti-Gorbachev coup in Moscow in August 1991, the Party and Supreme Soviet were forced to backtrack almost immediately and on 25 August issued a declaration of full national independence. The country's name was changed to the Republic of Belarus in September. With no history whatsoever as a politically or economically independent entity, the country of Belarus was one of the oddest products of the disintegration of the USSR.

Post-Independence Politics

Stanislau Shushkevich, a Popular Front-supported physicist who had campaigned to expose official negligence over Chornobyl, was chosen head of the Supreme Soviet – effectively, head of state – replacing the discredited Mikalaj Dzemjantsei, who had failed to oppose the Moscow putsch. The Supreme Soviet as a whole, however, remained dominated by the communist old guard. In December 1991 Belarus became a founding member of the Commonwealth of Independent States (CIS) and the Belarusian capital (Minsk) was named the headquarters of this new grouping.

Shushkevich pursued a centrist line between the old guard and the reformist Popular Front block in the Supreme Soviet. The Communist Party was suspended after the 1991 Moscow coup, but was reinstated in 1993 and gradually reasserted its power. The KGB remained in existence. Economic reform was slow, with the old guard opposing the privatisation of state enterprises or large collective and state-run farms.

With the communists advocating closer ties with Russia and regaining popularity during these economically difficult times, Shushkevich came into increasing conflict with them. Against his will, Belarus signed a CIS collective-security agreement subordinating Belarus' military policy to Russia's, and plans were laid for monetary union with Russia in exchange for a transfer of resources. Finally, Shushkevich was dismissed in January 1994, having lost a Supreme Soviet vote of confidence over corruption charges. He was replaced by a former senior police officer, Mechislau Gryb.

In Belarus' first direct presidential elections, in July 1994, Alexandr Lukashenko, a quirky, non-party former collective-farm director, heavily defeated Vjacheslav

Alexandr Lukashenko, first directly elected president of Belarus, who in a 1995 referendum won the power to dissolve the Supreme Soviet

Kebich, a communist who had served as prime minister since 1990. Lukashenko, who had supported the 1991 anti-Gorbachev coup in Moscow, and led the anti-corruption investigation which unseated Shushkevich, had campaigned on promises to reverse price rises, stop privatisation and corruption, break the Mafia and move closer to Russia. In practice, one of his early moves was to appoint a strongly market-oriented prime minister, Mikhail Chigir, and while he kept some prices in check, he freed others. He kept his word over Russia, however, agreeing a treaty which made the two countries into a 'single economic space' and laid the foundations of a military alliance.

Lukashenko's style of presidency was individualistic and authoritarian and he clashed frequently with the Supreme Soviet. See the Government section for the results of the latest election and referendum.

GEOGRAPHY

Belarus has an area of 207,600 sq km, slightly smaller than the UK or Romania. It borders Russia in the north and east, Latvia and Lithuania in the north-west, Poland in the west and Ukraine in the south.

It's a low-lying country, with the highest hill, Dzjarzhinskaja in the central west, reaching only 345 metres. The terrain consists of low ridges dividing broad, often marshy lowlands with many small lakes. One of the two main upland ridges runs in an arc across the country from the Polish border to the Russian border in the east, passing north of Minsk; the other runs north-west from central Belarus towards Vilnius in Lithuania. In the south are the Pripet Marshes, Europe's largest marsh area, though they have now in large part been drained for agriculture.

Belarus' major river is the Dnjapro, which flows into eastern Belarus from Smolensk in Russia (where it's known as the Dnepr), then turns south to cross into Ukraine (where they call it the Dnipro). Tributaries of the Dnjapro include the Bjarezina, flowing down from central Belarus, and the Pripet, flowing eastward across the south of the country. The

Pripet is joined to the Buh, which forms a short length of the Belarus-Poland border, by the Dnjapro-Buh Canal. Since the Buh flows into the Vistula, which empties into the Baltic Sea, and the Pripet joins the Dnjapro, which flows into the Black Sea, this canal provides a shipping link between the two seas. The north of Belarus is drained by the Dzvina River which flows from Russia to Latvia, while the Nioman flows north through Hrodna into Lithuania.

CLIMATE

Belarus has a continental climate, which becomes marginally more severe as you move from south-west to north-east. Average January temperatures are between -4°C and -8°C, with frosts experienced for seven to eight months of the year. The warmest month is July, when temperatures normally reach 17°C to 19°C. Rainfall is moderate at 500 to 700 mm a year, with June to August the wettest months. There's snow cover continuously from December/January to March/April.

FLORA & FAUNA

Belarus was once completely covered in forest. By the 16th century a majority was removed for farming but great plots have regrown, especially in the south around the Pripet Marshes, where hundreds of species of swamp flora thrive. The forests are a mixture of coniferous and deciduous trees, with conifers such as pine and spruce dominating in the north, and deciduous trees such as oak and beech in the south. Silver birch is the most common everywhere, growing in dense groves that break up the otherwise monotonous landscape.

The Belavezhskaja Pushcha Nature Reserve, north of Brest on the western border with Poland, is Europe's largest piece of surviving primeval mixed forest, with about 1300 sq km of the rich vegetation that once covered most of the continent. Once used as private hunting grounds for Polish and Russian royalty, the forest is now jointly managed by Poland and Belarus, with the vast majority of its land falling within

BELARUS

Belarus. The real success story goes to the European bison (wisent), Europe's largest mammal, whose population was reduced to 40 in captivity in 1945. Thanks to breeding programmes in this park and elsewhere, bison have been returned to the wild in places such as the Caucasus. Now there are several thousand in Europe, with about 1000 in the park alone.

Other significant reserves in Belarus include the Bjarezinski Nature Reserve, south of Polatsk, and the Pripet Nature Reserve, west of Mazyr. The famed Blue Lakes (Blakitnye Ozera), north of the town of Lake Narach off the Vilnius-Polatsk road, are renowned for their natural beauty. See Activities in Belarus Facts for the Visitor for more on these lakes.

Other animal species found in the nature reserves as well as throughout the wooded areas of the country include the elk, deer, boar, wolf, fox, squirrel, marten and hare. Beaver, otter, mink and badger can be found in and around the 20,000 streams and 10,000 small lakes of Belarus, with the largest populations in the isolated southern swamp regions and along the northern marshes of the Dzvina River, near Polatsk. The main fowl populations consist of ducks, grouse, woodcock and partridge.

The primary agricultural crop, besides a variety of grains, is flax. Prior to the harvest season, great fields of the delicate blue flower are a striking sight.

GOVERNMENT
Since 1994 Belarus has had an executive president, chosen in direct popular elections. The president chooses a prime minister, who is responsible for many of the day-to-day affairs of government. The country's parliament is the Supreme Soviet, with which the 1994-elected president, Alexandr Lukashenko, frequently clashed in his first months of office.

Elections to the Supreme Soviet, the first since 1990, were held in 1995, but at the time of writing the outcome was uncertain because in only 20 of the 260 seats did any candidate receive the 50% of the vote required for election. A second round of voting was to be held for the remaining seats, but there were fears that low voter turnout would render the results invalid in many seats, meaning that the Supreme Soviet would not have the two-thirds quorum required for it to function. With such an outcome, it was expected that the old communist-dominated Supreme Soviet would continue in place, at least temporarily.

A referendum held at the same time as the 1995 elections voted strongly in favour of allowing the president to dissolve the Supreme Soviet if it seriously violated the constitution. This, combined with an inconclusive outcome to the Supreme Soviet elections, could give Lukashenko the excuse to introduce direct presidential rule.

The country is divided into six administrative regions centred on the cities of Minsk, Brest, Hrodna, Vitsebsk, Homel and Mahileu.

ECONOMY
Agriculture employs about 21% of the workforce and occupies more than half the land, with livestock (chiefly cattle and pigs) responsible for 60% of agricultural produce, and potatoes, grain, sugar beet and flax the main crops.

Industry employs about 30% of the workforce. Heavy industry is concentrated mainly in Minsk, which produces heavy-duty trucks and tractors. Machine tools, TVs and radios are other products. More important are the mineral and chemical processing industries such as the fertiliser plants at Salihorsk and Hrodna and the oil refineries at Navapolatsk and Mazyr.

The country has few mineral resources and is almost totally dependent on Russia for oil and gas supplies. It is, however, rich in peat, which is used as fuel for power stations and in the manufacture of chemicals.

Despite its relative prosperity in Soviet times Belarus, like other ex-Soviet states, suffered severe economic problems during and after the break-up of the USSR. Problems included falling output, massive inflation (around 2000% in 1993), falling average wages (US$25 a month by 1994), the abandonment of agricultural land because of Chornobyl fallout, and the closure of many enterprises due to lack of fuel and raw materials and declining demand for military equipment. Belarus was hit particularly hard, since the specialised nature of many of its industries made them dependent on raw materials and customers from all over the Soviet Union. For example, although Belarus is a big flax grower, it does not make any machines for cultivating or harvesting flax – all these were imported from other Soviet republics. These economic imperatives have underpinned Belarus' continuing close ties with Russia since independence.

Privatisation and market-style economic reforms were virtually shelved in the early years of independence. However, in 1994, following the election of Alexandr Lukashenko as president and his choice of the market reformer Mikhail Chigir as prime minister, Belarus announced plans for tight government spending controls to limit its budget deficit and to curb inflation. It was hoped this would bring loans from the International Monetary Fund and greater foreign investment. President Lukashenko was reluctant to abandon price controls and centralised control of the economy, which were seen as a barrier to greater international support.

POPULATION & PEOPLE

Belarus has 10.2 million people, with nearly 80% Belarusian, 13% Russian, 4% Ukrainian and about 3% Polish. There was once a huge Polish and Jewish population as well as a substantial German minority – all of whom were either killed or fled during WW II, or were sent off to Siberia in its aftermath. Prior to WW II, 10% of the national population was Jewish and in cities like Minsk, Hrodna and Pinsk, Jews made up between one and two-thirds of the population. A conservative estimate of the overall death toll in the war is put at 2.2 million, with close to another 700,000 'purged' by the Soviet regime before and after the war.

To bolster industry and fill the shortage in the labour force, large Russian immigrations took place during the 1960s, the core of the 1.3 million-strong ethnic Russian minority today.

The overall population density of the country is low (an average of less than 50 persons per sq km), though it is higher around the cities and substantially lower in isolated regions like the Pripet Marshes and the north-western lowlands.

Following WW II, the desperate economic situation forced a mass migration to urban areas, raising the urban population from 20% after 1945 to 65% in 1989. This influx was heavily encouraged during the Soviet regime's push towards industrialisation, and has left in its wake semi-abandoned villages and greatly diminished infrastructure in rural areas.

ARTS & CULTURE

Few cultural artefacts survive from the early Slavic settlements of the 6th to 8th centuries, which were followed by long periods of foreign rule, first by Lithuania and later by

More than half of Belarus is farmland

BELARUS

the Polish and Russian empires. Without control of its own destiny, Belarusian cultural identity was, outside the rural framework, subdued and often suppressed, with only brief periods of revival in the 16th and 19th centuries.

Literature & Drama

Many 12th-century Orthodox hymns and sermons can trace their origins to Belarus. The hero of early Belarusian literary achievement was Francyska Skaryny of Polatsk (after whom Minsk's main street is named). In the early 16th century he became the first person to translate the Bible into the Belarusian language. This, as well as other editions by Skaryny between 1517 and 1525, were some of the first books to be printed in all of Eastern Europe. In the late 16th century, the philosopher and humanist Simon Budny printed a number of works in the Belarusian language, including controversial editions of the day such as *Justification of a Sinner Before God*. The 17th-century Belarusian poet Symeon of Polatsk was the first writer to introduce the Baroque style of literature to Russia.

The 19th century saw the beginning of modern Belarusian literature with works by writers and poets such as Maxim Haradsky, Maxim Bohdanovish, Janka Kupala and Jakub Kolas, all of whom have streets in Minsk named in their honour. Many of these writers had been active in the influential nationalist newspaper *Nasha Niva* (Our Cornfield), which had to be published in Lithuania from 1906 to 1916. Haradsky's novel *Two Souls* (1919) and Kupala's play *The Locals* (1922) are poignant expressions of the repressed state of Belarus after WW I and during the revolution. Kolas is considered by many as the pioneer of classical Belarusian literature.

A brief period of cultural revival in the 1920s and early 1930s saw the rise of many talented poets and prose writers, including Jazep Pushcha and the satirist playwright Kandrat Krapiva. Others included Natalla Arseneva, whose collection of poems *Beneath the Blue Sky* (1927) won wide

acclaim, and Maxim Tank, whose story-like poetry in works such as *Narch* (1937) and *Kalinovsky* (1938) established a much-copied style.

During the subsequent occupation and Soviet rule, most writers either emigrated or were forced to follow the prescribed literary formulas dictated by the Soviet regime. A slight revival occurred in the 1960s with works by Vasyl Bykov and V Karatkevich, who became the inspiration for a younger generation of writers including present-day short-story author Anatol Sys and poet Ales Razanov.

Music

Belarusian folk music is well known; don't miss a performance if you get the opportunity in Minsk (see the Minsk Entertainment section). Modern folk music originated from ritualistic ceremonies – either based on peasant seasonal feasts or, more commonly, on the traditions of church music – hymns and psalms – which became highly developed in Belarus from the 16th century onwards. Classical music in the modern sense only developed in Belarus within the last 100 years, with composers such as Kulikovich Shchehlov and Yevheny Hlebov, who composed the operas *Your Spring* (1963) and *Alpine Ballad* (1967). Minsk has a conservatory of music and a philharmonic society as well as the National Academic Opera & Ballet Theatre, which regularly hosts performances. Both the opera and ballet companies have long-standing reputations.

Architecture

Almost no architectural legacies remain from the early Slavic settlements of the 6th to 8th centuries or the following period of Kievan Rus. The exception is the 10th-century St Sophia Cathedral in Polatsk, which is the oldest surviving building in the country although completely renovated in the 18th century. The tiny Church of SS Boris & Hlib in Hrodna has some small curved stone apses from the 12th century.

Other than this, only a few scattered ruins remain from this distant period.

Polish control in the 17th and 18th centuries brought the Baroque style to Belarus, a style which later filtered to Russia through travelling Belarusian and Ukrainian artisans. Baroque examples include the reconstruction of St Sophia Cathedral in Polatsk, Hrodna's Farny Church and Minsk's Bernadine Convent, all commissioned by the Polish crown.

The classical revival in the late 18th and early 19th centuries is exemplified in the reconstruction of the Governor's Palace in Hrodna.

WW II did a thorough job of destroying centuries of architectural heritage, though some examples still survive. Minsk was essentially rebuilt from scratch and, in this way, is perhaps one of the most complete examples of pure Stalinist classicism. Much of the later postwar construction, however, is characterised by the mundane and sterile housing blocks that cluster on the outskirts of the city.

RELIGION

Belarus, like Ukraine, has always been a crossing point between Latin and Eastern Orthodox Christianity, with the Polish Catholics to the west and the Orthodox Russians to the east. Some 70% of the populace is Eastern Orthodox. In 1990 the Belarusian Orthodox Church was officially established. As a legacy of centuries of Polish rule, 20% of the population is Roman Catholic (about two million), of whom 15% are ethnic Poles. This small group dominates the clergy. Some tension exists between the Polish Catholics, who favour services in the Polish language, and the Belarusian Catholics, who resist the Polonisation of their church. In the early 1990s the Uniate Church was re-established, the majority of its adherents belonging to Belarus' Ukrainian minority. There's also a small Protestant minority, a remnant of a once large German population. The number of Baptist churches has grown to over 200 and there are small pockets of Tatars, who practise Islam, as well as scattered urban Jewish communities, although most of the latter are emigrating.

LANGUAGE

The centralised Soviet system subjected Belarus to a process of Russification, with the result that well over 80% of Belarusian school pupils were taught exclusively in Russian until 1988 and Russian was imposed as the official language of all business and government transactions.

In 1990, shortly before independence, Belarusian was announced as the country's only official language. The government, reacting to popular demand, began to provide the necessary provisions for education to shift emphasis back to Belarusian history and literature. Street names have begun to change and the people are finally being allowed to express pride in their country and language, albeit timidly.

Yet old habits are hard to break and Russian is still the language spoken by the majority of people, especially the urban populations. As closer ties to Russia once again came to the forefront of government policy, a referendum in 1995 voted to give Russian equal status with Belarusian as an official language. Whether or not this will curtail the progress of a 'Belarusian identity' remains to be seen.

Belarusian is an Eastern Slavonic language, related to both Russian and Ukrainian. It's normally written in the Cyrillic alphabet, but there does exist a rarely used Belarusian language in the Roman alphabet.

Belarusian, like Ukrainian but not Russian, has the letter i, pronounced *ee*. It also has the unique letter ў, pronounced like the 'w' in the word 'west'. Transliteration is also different, with й transcribed as *j*, ю as *ju*, я as *ja* and ë as *io*. Г is pronounced and transcribed *h*, as in Ukrainian. The Russian letter o often becomes a in Belarusian – making, for example, Komsomolskaya into Kamsamolskaja, which looks closer to its pronunciation in any case. The Russian Gogolya becomes Hoholja in Belarusian. You'll see an apostrophe used in written

Belarusian to separate a consonant from the syllable that follows it.

To honour the language we use the new form of transliteration described above, however confusing it may seem. Although Russian is understood everywhere, it will be appreciated if you try a little Belarusian.

Belarus
  beh-lah-ROOS
  Беларусь
Hello.
  DOB-ree DZHEN
  Добры джень.
Goodbye.
  DA pah-bah-CHEN-nyah
  Да пабачэньня.

yes
  tahk
  так
no
  nye
  не
Please.
  kah-LEE LAHS-kah
  Калі ласка.
Thank you.
  DZYAH-koo-ee
  Дзякуй.
good
  DOHB-ree
  добры
bad
  DREHN-nee
  дрэнны

Facts for the Visitor

VISAS & EMBASSIES
Visas

All foreigners visiting Belarus will need a visa. Arranging a visa before you arrive will save you complications at the border. (Visas will only be issued at the border if you have the correct documentation, ie a valid passport, a completed visa application form, a passport photo and an official invitation from a person or business in Belarus or hotel confirmation from a travel agency.) Once you enter the country you must be officially registered, a process most hotels will do for a small fee. In Brest, go to the Hotel Intourist; in Minsk, to the Hotel Minsk.

Types of Visa The type of visa you're issued depends on what sort of invitation or confirmation you receive. If you receive an invitation from a private individual in Belarus, then your visa is classified as a visitor's visa. If you receive a hotel confirmation, your visa is classified as a tourist visa. If you receive an invitation from a registered business organisation inside Belarus, your visa is classified as a business visa. All are essentially identical as far as other requirements and costs go. (See Applying for a Visa.)

The maximum duration for visitor's, tourist and business visas is 90 days. For transit visas see the following section.

Transit Visas A good number of people only plan to see Belarus from the window of their train and need only a Belarus transit visa or a valid Russian visa to get them across the country.

Transit visas are valid for 48 hours and can be issued at the Belarusian border for around US$40 – but only if your train ticket proves your destination is beyond the border. Transit visas can also be obtained in advance from a Belarusian embassy or consulate, but you must have, along with the completed application form, a copy of your train ticket proving your destination lies beyond the border.

According to the Belarusian Embassy in the USA, travellers heading to Russia who have a valid Russian visa and a ticket proving their destination is beyond the border do not need a Belarusian transit visa – the Russian visa will suffice. This is supposed to apply for travel to and from Russia – make sure your Russian visa is still valid for your return trip. If you're not on a through train, however, meaning you have to change trains in Belarus, you will have to purchase an official Belarusian transit visa.

There may be a problem when taking certain trains from St Petersburg or Pskov to Warsaw, as some pass through Latvia and Lithuania before crossing a tiny corner of Belarus. On these trains your Russian visa may be taken away from you as you leave Russia and enter Latvia (Russian visas are separate slips of paper). If this happens, even though your Russian visa would still have been valid when you crossed Belarus, you wouldn't have it with you to prove that fact – so you might get hit with the cost of a Belarusian transit visa. Travellers should check up on the route of their train and, if it goes through Latvia or Lithuania, be prepared for any transit visa complications that might result. Also check the latest situation from other travellers, hostels etc.

Applying for a Visa

To apply for a visa you will need a valid passport, a completed visa application form, a passport photo and an official invitation from Belarus or hotel confirmation from a travel agency.

- Passport – the expiration date of your passport should extend for at least a month beyond your departure from Belarus. Don't forget to take photocopies of the personal data and validity pages for your own security backup.
- Visa Application Form – this can be obtained from any Belarusian consulate or embassy (in

person, or by mail or fax). The form consists of a few basic identification questions followed by questions regarding the purpose of your visit, intended destinations, and the name and other details of the inviting persons, organisation or travel agency. It's wise to overestimate your intended length of stay.

- Passport Photo – although only one is necessary, it's a good idea to have a few extra. It's also probably smart not to make radical changes in your appearance between photo time and your arrival in Belarus.

- Official Invitation or Hotel Confirmation – acquiring an invitation is not as difficult as it may seem. If you don't know anyone personally within the country, a travel agency can take care of it for you, or you can contact a hotel inside the country and have them send you a confirmation. Many overseas travel agencies have contacts in Belarus (see Travel Agencies under Belarus Getting There & Away). Your hotel (or homestay) confirmation need not cover the entire duration of your intended stay. If you're receiving a personal invitation *(izveshchenie)* from an individual or business in Belarus, it must be obtained by them from a local passport office (OVIR) of the Ministry of the Interior. In practice, however, not all Belarusian embassies even require an invitation or hotel confirmation – check when you collect your application form. (In Warsaw, George received one for US$60 the same day without any prior invitation or hotel confirmation.)

    For a transit visa, no invitation is necessary, only a copy of your train ticket proving your destination lies beyond the border.

- Fees – the visa processing fee is US$30 for seven-working-day service, US$60 for next-day service, and US$100 for same-day processing. Transit visas cost US$20 for seven-working day service, US$40 for next-day service. Some embassies will issue same-day visas for US$60.

It's possible to apply for a visa in advance by mail if you enclose a self-addressed, stamped envelope along with the requested documents and appropriate payment. The visa is completely contained in the passport; there are no extra papers.

Visa Extensions
According to the Belarusian Embassy in the USA, you cannot extend your transit visa inside Belarus if you decide to stay longer than the alloted 48 hours. In practice, however, this may be possible. Try at the

service bureaus in the Hotel Minsk or Hotel Jubileynaja or at the Belintourist office.

Non-transit visas cannot be extended beyond the 90-day limit; you will need to apply for a new visa.

Belarusian Embassies & Consulates
Unless otherwise specified, details below are for embassies:

Austria
    Erzherzog Karl-Strasse 182, A-1220 Vienna (☎ (0222) 283 58 85; fax (0222) 283 58 86)
Belgium
    Rue Merlo 8A/9, 1180 Brussels UCCLE (☎ (02) 332 38 84; fax (02) 332 38 85)
Bulgaria
    1113 Sofia, ulitsa Kokyche, 20 (☎ (02) 66 17 65; fax (02) 65 28 43)
China
    PO 100600, Beijing, Chao Yand District, Xin Dong Rd, Ta Yuan Office Bldg, 2-10-1 (☎ (01) 532 64 26; fax (01) 532 64 17)
Czech Republic
    Schweigerowa 2, 16000 Prague 6 (☎ & fax (02) 32 20 39)
Estonia
    Tallinn (☎ & fax (3722) 632 00 70)
France
    38 Boulevard Suchet, 75016, Paris (☎ (1) 40 50 10 66; fax (1) 45 25 64 00)
Germany
    Fritz-Schäffer-Strasse 20, 53113 Bonn (☎ (0228) 26 54 57; fax (0228) 26 55 54)
    Consulate: Fritz-Schäffer-Strasse 20, 53113 Bonn ☎ (0228) 26 57 55; fax (0228) 26 58 60)
    Unter den Linden 55-61, 10117 Berlin (☎ (030) 229 29 78; fax (030) 229 24 69); consular dept: (☎ (030) 229 95 94; fax (030) 229 95 19)
Italy
    Via della Giuliana, 113 int 11, Roma 00195 (☎ (06) 397 41 268; fax (06) 372 46 34)
Israel
    2 Kaufman St, 68012 Tel Aviv (☎ (03) 510 22 36; fax (03) 510 22 35)
Latvia
    Embassy: Elizabetes iela 29, Riga 1010 (☎ (22) 32 25 50; fax (22) 32 28 91)
    Consulate: Daugavpils (☎ (254) 37 573; fax (254) 52 945)
Lithuania
    Embassy: Klimo gatvė 8, Vilnius (☎ (22) 26 38 28; fax (22) 26 34 43)
    Consulate: Muitinės gatve 41, Vilnius (☎ (22) 23 06 26)

Netherlands
   Piet Heinstraat 3, 2518 CB Den Haag (☎ (070)
   363 15 66; fax (070) 364 05 55)
Poland
   Embassy: Ulica Atenska 67, 03-978 Warsaw
   (☎ (02) 617 32 12; fax (02) 617 84 41)
   Consulate: Ulica Yackova Dolina 50, 80-251
   Gdansk (☎ (058) 41 00 26; fax (058) 41 40 26)
   Ulica Warshiskeho 4, 15-461 Bialystok (☎ 52 28
   75; fax 52 18 51)
Romania
   Bucharest (☎ (090) 617 01 28)
Russia
   Maroseyka ulitsa 17/6, 101000 Moscow
   (☎ (095) 924 70 31, 924 70 95 for visa enquiries;
   fax (095) 928 64 03)
   Consulate: Armyansky pereulok 6, 101000
   Moscow (☎ (095) 921 65 89)
Switzerland
   39 Neuengasse, 3011 Bern (☎ (031) 311 38 00;
   fax (031) 311 03 22)
UK
   6 Kensington Court, London W8 5DL (☎ (0171)
   937 3288; fax (0171) 361 0005)
Ukraine
   vulitsya Kutuzova 8, 252011 Kiev (☎ (044) 294
   82 12; fax (044) 294 80 06)
USA
   1619 New Hampshire Ave, NW, Washington, DC
   20009 (☎ (202) 986 1606; fax (202) 986 1805)

DOCUMENTS
See Documents in the Ukraine Facts for the
Visitor chapter for documents you may need
(including the identical customs form) other
than your passport and visa.

CUSTOMS
When you arrive (or beforehand, on the
train) you'll be given a small customs declaration form (deklaratsia) to fill out. On the
train they often don't have one in English.
For a description of this customs form and
how to fill it out see Customs in the Ukraine
Facts for the Visitor section. The customs
form is identical for both countries.

For legalities concerning what you can
bring in or take out of the country refer to
Customs in the European Russia Facts for
the Visitor section. At the time of writing,
Belarus was in the process of revamping its
customs laws, which included the same basic
restrictions as Russia. For current information, contact the State Customs Office in

Minsk (☎ (0172) 34 43 55) at vulitsa Khoru-
zhoy 29, or the local customs office (☎ 20 38
22) at vulitsa Ostrovskoho 2A in Minsk.

MONEY
Currency
The official currency is the Belarusian
rouble, which replaced the Russian rouble in
May 1992. It was intended to be a transitional monetary unit, to be used only until the
economy stabilised and the Belarusian Taler
could be issued (a stockpile of these, printed
in Germany, is supposedly still waiting).

Belarusian roubles are better known as
zaichiki or 'rabbits', named after the completely worthless one rouble note that
featured a leaping rabbit. In fact, most of the
smaller bills feature some kind of animal – a
fox, bobcat, elk, squirrel – so one bison
equals four elk, five bobcats one squirrel,
and so on. Of course, all these animals are
worth very little but are nonetheless crucial
to hang on to, not only for souvenirs but
because most people are very adamant about
receiving the exact change – so if you're
short a few foxes you may have to pay with
a Supreme Soviet (the higher bills feature
buildings).

Exchange Rates
Shortly after independence, inflation
reached to the stars and in September 1993
there was a push to bring the Belarusian
currency back into the Russian rouble zone.
So far this hasn't happened due to Russia's
demand that if it takes over the monetary unit
it basically takes over the economy – something the Belarusian parliament opposes.

In November 1994, US$1 could be
exchanged for 7000 Belarusian roubles; a
month later the rate had risen to 8000
roubles. Given inflation, it makes sense to
exchange smaller amounts at a time. Be sure
not to run out of roubles because some services (local transport and food) won't accept
foreign currency.

Changing Money
Travellers should carry the usual credit cards
and travellers' cheques as these are the safest,

but will need to be prepared to cash them regularly as very few shops will accept them. For this reason, it's important to have a substantial amount of cash as well – the most widely accepted being US dollars and Deutschmarks. Make sure the notes are new, as no-one (not even banks) will accept any with tears or markings. Bring a variety of smaller denominations if possible (eg US$5, US$10 or US$20, and a bunch of US$1 bills for quick tips).

Besides all hotels, there are a number of exchange kiosks (with the sign *obmin valjuty*) on the main streets. Exchanging on the black market is illegal, and with the rates not much higher, is not worthwhile.

In Minsk it is possible to exchange travellers' cheques, and to get cash advances (in US dollars or roubles) on your credit card, but outside the capital this is unlikely (see the Money section in Minsk for more information).

Costs
Your major cost will be accommodation (refer to hotel prices in city chapters) but everything else is very cheap. A full meal will rarely cost more than US$6, a night at the opera never more than US$1 (bought at the theatre), and domestic train tickets are also cheap (eg US$3 for the Minsk-Polatsk train). You can pay for all food, entertainment and basic services in roubles, as well as most accommodation (which is much cheaper than paying in US dollars). However, you'll have to pay in hard currency for a train ticket out of the country, which can get fairly expensive (eg US$70 for Minsk-Prague, and US$15 for Brest-Warsaw).

As a foreigner, you will be subject to paying a higher price than locals for things like hotel accomodation and domestic train fares.

WHEN TO GO
There is no high or low season as far as tourism is concerned – it's always low, only slightly higher during the traditional high season in summer. With summer being the warmest but wettest, and with winter a grey

freezer, the best time would probably be late summer or spring simply because of the weather. For more details see the When to Go section in Ukraine Facts for the Visitor.

WHAT TO BRING
See the What to Bring sections in the European Russia and Ukraine Facts for the Visitor chapters for ideas on what to take on a trip to Belarus.

TOURIST OFFICES
There are no tourist information offices in the accepted sense in Belarus, but there are some service bureaus and excursion offices, which may be willing to provide information and sell services. Outside Belarus information is rare and hard to come by. Consult some of the travel agencies listed in the Belarus Getting There & Away section as well as your local embassy (see the list earlier in this chapter).

The main tourist office in Belarus is Belintourist, basically Belarus' version of Intourist (see Tourist Offices in the Minsk chapter for more details). Many hotels have service bureaus, which vary as to what sort of tourist information they provide, but are usually worth a try.

BUSINESS HOURS & HOLIDAYS
Most shops close for an hour in the afternoon, usually between 2 and 3 pm. For the typical business hours of restaurants, banks and museums, see the Business Hours & Holidays section in Ukraine Facts for the Visitor.

Public Holidays
The main public holidays are:

1 January
   New Year's Day
7 January
   Orthodox Christmas Day
8 March
   International Women's Day
15 March
   Constitution Day (1994)
March/April
   Catholic Easter

March/April
Orthodox Easter
1 May
International Labour Day
April/May
Rasounitsa (9th day following Orthodox Easter)
9 May
Victory (1945) Day & Mother's Day
27 July
1990 Independence Day – commemorating the declaration of sovereignty
2 November
Dzyady (Memory Day) – in remembrance of those who died in wars
25 December
Catholic Christmas
31 December
New Year's Eve

POST & TELECOMMUNICATIONS
Post
The post office is called *pashtamt*. Ordinary mail in and out takes about the same time as in Ukraine (see Ukraine Facts for the Visitor).

Sending Mail The best way to mail important items which need to be delivered on time is by using the more reliable Express Mail Service (EMS) that is offered at most main post offices. They advertise a one-week service to over 130 countries.

Receiving Mail The best way to receive mail in Belarus is through a personal contact, but many hotels (especially if you've pre-booked) will hold clearly marked mail for you if you let them know when you're coming. Receiving valuable items by post is risky and you can forget packages altogether. Embassies and consulates won't hold mail for transient travellers, but if you're a UK passport holder (or from a Commonwealth country) you can try asking at the British Council in the Institute of Foreign Languages at vulitsa Zakharava 21(see Embassies & Consulates in the Minsk chapter).

Addresses Addresses are written the same way as in Ukraine, basically in the opposite direction to the West, with the country first and the name last (see Ukraine Facts for the Visitor).

Telephone
Local Calls Local calls in most cities are free due to the lack of coins – great if you can find a phone that works.

Intercity Intercity calls within Belarus are dialled the same way as calls to former USSR countries: dial 8, wait for a new tone, then dial the city code and number. These calls can be made from the main post office or your hotel. Some city telephone codes in Belarus are as follows (numbers with a '2' in parentheses require an extra '2' when dialling five-digit numbers; it is not required if dialling a six-digit number): Babrujsk 02251, Baranavichy 01634, Barysau 01777, Brest 01622, Homel 0232(2), Hrodna 0152(2), Mahileu 022(2), Minsk 0172, Orsha 02161, Pinsk 01653 and Vitsebsk 0212(2).

Most of these phones have a little button that you have to press to initiate the connection when you hear your call being answered. Useful numbers include:

Minsk Information (☎ 09)
CIS & Baltics Information (☎ 053)
International Information (☎ 33 29 84)

International All international phone calls must be made from private phones (not public ones), and these can be found in special long-distance telephone offices called *perehovorny punkt* or calling stations (different from main post and telegraph offices) or at most hotels. To dial any country except the three Baltic states and all other former USSR countries. dial 8, wait for the new tone, then dial 10, the country code, city code and the number. If you can't get through, try placing your call with an international operator by dialling (in Minsk) ☎ 33 29 71.

For all calls within the Baltic states and the former USSR, dial 8, wait for the new tone, then dial the city code and number.

To phone Belarus from any country outside the Baltics and former USSR, dial 7 (Belarus' country code) followed by the city code and number.

Telegram, Telex & Fax
Some hotels provide these services, and you can try even if you're not staying at the hotel. Most long-distance telephone offices (perehovorny punkt) have fax services. In Minsk and most other cities these are separate from the main telegraph and post office. If you wish to place a telegram, ask for *blank mizhnarodnoho telegramma* (international telegram form).

TIME
The entire country is on the same time zone as most of Ukraine, ie GMT/UMC plus two hours. At midnight on the last Sunday in March the country shifts to 'summer time', setting clocks ahead one hour, and on the last Sunday in September sets them back again.

When it's noon in Minsk, it's...

2 am in San Francisco;
5 am in New York and Toronto;
10 am in London;
11 am in Paris, Warsaw, Prague and Budapest;
noon in Kiev, Helsinki, Bucharest, Ankara and Cairo;
1 pm in Moscow and Simferopol;
5 pm in summer Beijing;
6 pm in Ulan Bator and winter Beijing;
7 pm in winter Sydney;
9 pm in summer Sydney and winter Auckland;
11 pm in summer Auckland.

ELECTRICITY, WEIGHTS & MEASURES
The systems are the same as Russia's – see European Russia Facts for the Visitor.

BOOKS
Some of the books mentioned in European Russia Facts for the Visitor deal with the whole former USSR and include portions relating to Belarus.

Hippocrene Books, at 171 Madison Ave, New York, NY 10016 (☎ (718) 454 2366), puts out a *Belarusian-English/English-Belarusian Concise Dictionary* with 6500 entries.

History & Culture
Belorussia: the Making of a Nation by Nicholas Vakar covers history up to the 1950s including the origins of folk traditions. *Belorussia Under Soviet Rule: 1917-57* by Ivan Lubachko covers in detail just what it says.

The Byelorussian Theater & Drama by Vladimir Seduro covers the early and mid-20th century. *A History of Belorusian Literature: from its Origins to the Present Day* by Wilhelm Schmitz does a good job fulfilling its title, and includes some translations of works by Kolas and Kupala.

Belarus: at a Crossroads in History by Jan Zaprudnik is probably the best up-to-date history and commentary on the conditions affecting the newly independent nation.

Out of Fire, edited by Ales Adamovich, Janka Bryl & Vladimir Kolesnik, is a shocking collection of first-hand stories and recollections by witnesses who tell of the brutal atrocities committed against the ordinary citizens of Belarus during WW II.

Guidebooks
Fodor's *Russia & the Baltic Countries* (1993) has brief coverage of Belarus, highlighting Minsk and Brest.

Both *Eastern Europe* (1993) and *Russia* (1994) by Insight Guides have brief chapters covering Belarus; while low on practical information these are high on excellent photography. *Minsk – A Historical Guide* by Guy Picarda (1993) has detailed background historical information as well as plenty of travel information on Minsk, including walking tours of the city and motoring tours of the surrounding region.

The handy little guide in English *Minsk in Your Pocket* is updated annually and should be promptly bought if you find it in any kiosk or hotel lobby newsstand in Minsk. It contains listings of restaurants, hotels, and a bunch of important addresses.

MAPS
Country & Regional Maps
A country map is useful to have before you arrive in Belarus, especially if you'll be

driving, as these are not easy to find once you're there. The best, with accurate road detail, is the series of four maps (1:750,000) covering Ukraine, Belarus, European Russia and the Caucasus, put out by the map company Marco Polo. Maps No 2/3, *Belarus-Russia-Ukraine*, and No 1, *Russia*, cover all of Belarus and beyond.

There's a series of city maps that include detailed topographic information of the greater area surrounding the city in question. These are called *Minsk i Okrestnosti* and *Brest i Okrestnosti*. There's also a series of detailed topographic maps *(topografycheska karta)* (1:200,000) that cover the six different geographic regions of Belarus and show every river, forest, road, contour and village. Though rare and therefore difficult to find, we found some in the small bookshops downstairs in the main Warsaw railway station.

An informative map showing detailed information on levels of radiation contamination throughout the country, with English text, is simply called *Respublika Belarus* and is scantily available. Ask for the *karta z danymi radyjatsynaha zabrudzhannja*.

City Maps
In addition to the city maps mentioned in the previous section, there's a good map of Minsk out called *Minsk – Biznes i Turizm*. Most hotel kiosks in Minsk sell it, and you can also find it at the Warsaw railway station. We also found a decent map of Brest, but at the time of writing, maps of other cities were almost impossible to find.

MEDIA
Newspapers & Magazines
Most daily newspapers are still government-owned, which means freedom of the press is still subjective. The most popular are *Beloruska Niva* (*Belarusian Cornfield*), *Narodnaya Hazeta* (*The People's Newspaper*), and the *Sovetskaya Belorossiya* (*Soviet Belarusia*) – all organs of the Council of Ministers and each with a different party bias. *Dobry Vechar* (*Good Evening*) and

Vecherny Minsk (*Evening Minsk*) have listings of cultural events.

The only English-language newspaper produced in Belarus seems to be the independent monthly *Minsk Economic News*, based in Minsk at vulitsa Kazlova 4A (☎ 33 22 51). Other foreign newspapers are nearly impossible to find – try at the British Council in Minsk.

Belarus is a monthly journal put out by the Union of Writers of Belarus and is comprised of fiction and political essays. The *Holas Radzimy* (*Voice of the Motherland*) is a weekly sent out to Belarusian nationals around the world. *Nabat* is an ecologically-oriented periodical focusing primarily on the effects of Chornobyl. *Maladost* (*Youth*) is a monthly periodical with short stories, essays etc aimed at young people.

Radio & TV
Almost all radio and TV is still owned and controlled by the National Television & Radio Company of Belarus. Radio Minsk, heavy on classical concerts, can usually be picked up from anywhere along the dial on the plastic radio hanging on your hotel room wall. At FM 102.1 is a station with some Western rock and roll, and news from Moscow. FM 104.6 is Radion BA, the first private radio station in the country, with a variety of international programming. FM 108 is Belarus State Radio.

If your hotel TV works, besides the national Belarusian TV channel, you'll probably be able to pick up the Russian and, if you're lucky, perhaps the Polish and Ukrainian national channels as well.

FILM & PHOTOGRAPHY
Film (predominantly only colour print) can be purchased in Minsk at a few select stores (see the Minsk Information section). In general it's a good idea to bring all the film and extra batteries you'll need for the duration of your trip. For further information and photo tips, refer to the Film & Photography sections in the Ukraine and European Russia Facts for the Visitor chapters.

HEALTH

Most of the information given under Health in European Russia Facts for the Visitor also applies to Belarus, including the incidence of tick encephalitis and Lyme disease in rural areas in summer. Diphtheria has been on the increase in Minsk. Travellers should check with their local public health service office for information on current epidemic or health risks in Belarus. Certain immunisations, such as tetanus, typhoid and diphtheria, should be current.

Chornobyl

Western medical and governmental sources we have questioned are unanimous that the risk to short-term visitors from the aftermath of the Chornobyl nuclear disaster is insignificant. The areas to stay away from, at least for long-term exposure, are the south-eastern regions, the most contaminated being the very south-eastern corner of the country. The city of Homel and south of Mahileu were heavily exposed. See the aside on Chornobyl in Ukraine Facts for the Visitor (under Health).

DANGERS & ANNOYANCES

Crime levels in Belarus, though still far below those of the West, are on the rise. As a foreigner you have a slightly higher chance of being targeted – don't flash your money around or put yourself in a vulnerable situation. For further information and advice see the Dangers & Annoyances sections in the Ukraine and European Russia Facts for the Visitor chapters.

WORK

Most foreigners working in Belarus are affiliated with either an embassy, a joint venture, or a university such as the Institute of Foreign Languages at vulitsa Zakharava 21, 220662 Minsk. Transient seasonal workers don't exist.

ACTIVITIES
Outdoor

Nature lovers should visit the Belavezhskaja Pushcha Nature Reserve, north of Brest on the western border with Poland. It's the largest area of ancient forest in Europe and has substantial herds of the once nearly extinct European bison (see the Brest section and Flora & Fauna in Facts about Belarus for more on both the reserve and this beast).

If you have your own vehicle, the region known as the Blue Lakes (Blakitnye Ozera), north of the town of Narach off the Vilnius-Polatsk road, is renowned for its natural beauty, and is a popular camping and hiking area. The two main Blue Lakes are Lake Bolbuk and Lake Hlublja. About 20 km south-east is the country's largest lake, Lake Naroch (80 sq km), which is also a popular outdoor recreational area. With thousands of small lakes and streams totalling more than 90,000 km in length, fishing is obviously a national pastime.

Cultural

The dynamic independent youth organisation Next Stop – New Life, based in Minsk (☎ & fax (0172) 21 81 79), sponsors international festivals and youth exchanges, cultural events and ecological summer camps. Its address is Mayakovskoho 172A, 220028 Minsk, Belarus. See Minsk's Entertainment section for a listing of cultural events and activities.

ACCOMMODATION
Hotels

While accommodation standards in Belarus tend to be lower than those in the West, they are still generally acceptable. Prices and brief descriptions of most hotels are given in city Places to Stay sections. Unless stated otherwise, these prices include rooms with a private bathroom (toilet and shower) and are payable in Belarusian currency.

For descriptions of rooms and check-in procedures see the Accommodation section in Ukraine Facts for the Visitor.

Homestays

Homestays and exchanges are catching on, and more and more travel agencies are organising them. Usually the host family also acts as your personal guide and sort of first-hand information source. Agencies that deal with homestays, usually only in the Minsk area, include:

Gateway Travel
  48 The Boulevard, Strathfield, NSW 2135, Australia (☎ (02) 745 3333; fax (02) 745 3237)
HOFA (Host Families Association)
  St Petersburg, Russia (☎ & fax (812) 275 19 92; e-mail alexei@hofak.stu.spb.su); HOFA also has agents in the USA (☎ (202) 333 9343), UK (☎ (01295) 710 648) and Australia (☎ (03) 725 8555)
Home & Host International
  2445 Park Ave, Minneapolis, MN 55404, USA (☎ (612) 871 0596; fax (612) 871 8853)

FOOD & DRINK
Cuisine
The Belarusians love their mushrooms as much as the Ukrainians love their beets and cabbage, and mushroom gathering is a traditional expeditions in Belarus. Many main dishes utilise the fungus in one way or another – in a rich sauce, in a creamy filling, or else by themselves. *Hrybi v smtane* are baked mushrooms with sour cream, *hribnoy sup* is a mushroom and barley soup, and *kotleta pokrestyansky* is usually a pork cutlet smothered with a mushroom sauce. *Dranniki s miasom* are potato pancakes, usually with flecks of bacon – a tasty mainstay in most restaurants. *Kletsky* are dumplings stuffed with either (surprise) mushrooms, cheese or potatoes. *Mokanka* is a type of salad that has 101 variations, but is worth a try. Most dishes have a nice amount of garlic and occasionally caraway. Various fish dishes are popular as well.

To drink, try Belarusian *kvas*, a popular elixir made of malt, flour, sugar, mint, and fruit. *Belovezhskaja* is a bitter medicinal herbal drink.

Restaurants
Expect a militant doorman whose joy in life is to greet everyone with the harsh demand '*Kakoh?*' (literally, 'What?' as in 'What do you want?'). This is always followed by the demand to relinquish your coat at all costs. The administrator will then seat you at his or her leisure. If you sit near the band you won't be able to taste your food above the din. Beyond these irritating obstacles, getting a meal shouldn't prove too difficult.

ENTERTAINMENT
Most forms of entertainment are staged in Minsk, the cultural capital of the country. The Minsk Ballet is one of the best in Eastern Europe and is not to be missed. Belarusian folk choirs are popular, with a long performing tradition. For listings of cultural events and activities see the Minsk Entertainment section.

THINGS TO BUY
Folk art is the main source of souvenirs, which include carved wooden trinkets, ceramics, and woven textiles. Unique to Belarus are wooden boxes intricately ornamented with geometric patterns composed of multicoloured pieces of straw. For a list of souvenir shops see Things to Buy in the Minsk chapter.

BELARUS

Getting There & Away

Travel into Belarus is unrestricted at all border points, provided you have a valid visa (See Visas & Embassies in Belarus Facts for the Visitor). Land travel in either direction is possible between Belarus and Russia to the east, Lithuania and Latvia to the north, Poland to the west, and Ukraine to the south. Most international flights arrive and depart from Minsk, with a few shorter flights in and out of Brest.

Some information on visa requirements for neighbouring countries is given in the Land section of this chapter; for more details, see the European Russia and Ukraine Getting There & Away chapters.

AIR

Most international flights entering and departing Belarus do so at the Minsk-2 International Airport, about 40 km east of Minsk. A few, shorter, international flights to/from Kiev, Moscow and St Petersburg (flights to Moscow and St Petersburg use both airports) arrive at the smaller and closer Minsk-1 Airport.

European and Middle-Eastern connections with Minsk-2 Airport include Berlin, Beirut, Frankfurt, Larnaka, Moscow, Munich, St Petersburg, Tallinn, Tel Aviv, Vienna, Warsaw and Zürich. All destinations are served at least twice weekly; there are daily Moscow flights, and connections to Warsaw and Frankfurt six days a week.

For a listing of airline offices in Minsk – including Austrian Airlines, SwissAir, SAS, Lufthansa, LOT Polish, Transaero and Belavia (the Belarusian national airline) – see the Minsk Getting There & Away section.

The smaller international airport at Brest is usually limited to shorter international flights to/from Moscow, St Petersburg and Kiev, with an occasional flight to/from Warsaw and Odessa. See also the Air Travel Glossary in European Russia Getting There & Away.

LAND

At the time of writing, according to the Belarusian Embassy in the USA, all major land border crossings into Belarus were unrestricted provided you had a proper visa. Further information is given in city Getting There & Away sections.

The most common bus crossings are the quick four-hour-trip between Vilnius and Minsk, and the seven-hour trip between Minsk and Białystok in Poland. Buses stop at the border for customs and passport controls.

If you're driving your own vehicle, there are about 10 main road routes into Belarus through border stations. To avoid possible complications, drivers should enter by one of these official routes although there are some smaller roads that cross over, especially along the Ukrainian border. For information on driving permits, insurance, safety and other requirements, see Ukraine Getting There & Away. For details on road conditions, fuel availability etc inside the country, see Belarus Getting Around.

International trains cross into Belarus at more than 10 crossing points and from five different countries. About an hour or so before crossing the border by train you'll be given a customs form to fill out (see Facts for the Visitor). When leaving the country, you'll have to provide the original customs document you received when entering. You may have your bags checked by a customs official, usually when leaving the country. The international train ticket you buy in Belarus to leave the country is payable in hard currency only, and costs much more than domestic train tickets.

To/From Latvia

The main road (A215 in Belarus, A6 in Latvia) and rail crossing lies between Polatsk and Daugavpils (four to five hours) along the Dzvina River valley, which is also

At the Border: A Soviet Spoke in the Wheels of Progress

Life has changed very little over the past few years for Stanisław Kudrzycki, a shift supervisor for the Polish National Railway (PKP) and his 19-person crew at Kuznica on what is now the Poland-Belarus border. At the railway station of this desolate town, a 24-hour-a-day operation functions in exactly the same way it did when it was established in 1972 to change the wheel trucks on trains crossing into and out of the Soviet Union.

The Russian rail gauge is 24 cm wider than European gauge (a legacy of tsarist xenophobia) – the reasoning being that foreigners intending to invade by train would first need to capture rolling stock. If the system ever did thwart foreign invaders (it managed to severely impede the progress of Nazi troops, who scrambled to regauge the rail lines to Moscow during WW II), it caused far greater frustration to rail travellers from Europe, who were compelled to change trains at the Polish-Soviet Border.

As one traveller put it, 'The border crossing was the worst part of the trip. It was freezing, we had to go through the nightmare of a Soviet customs clearance before walking half a km hauling our luggage. The experience didn't exactly translate as "welcome to the Soviet Union".' But in the 1960s, as the Soviet authorities began to rely upon tourism as an important source of hard-currency income, they were forced to change the abominable border conditions.

They redesigned their train cars to be little more than flat-bottomed cargo containers with seats, which could be placed upon changeable wheel-truck assemblies. The wheel trucks consist of two axles, four wheels, shock absorbers and a seat upon which the train can be fastened using a 'male/female' connector in a manner similar to a key fitting into a lock. For inbound trains, the European-gauged wheel trucks are removed and rolled out from underneath the cars, and Soviet-gauged wheel trucks are rolled in and attached; the outbound procedure is the reverse.

In 1972 the Soviet Union constructed the changing station at Kuznica and contracted PKP to operate and maintain it (it is and always has been a Polish operation despite the facility's decidedly Soviet appearance). Now, as a train reaches the border, its cars are separated and placed next to hydraulic lift platforms which work in essentially the same manner as giant car jacks. After the wagons are separated, they are hoisted two metres off the ground, the wheel trucks are rolled out from beneath the train, and new wheel trucks rolled in. Once the new wheel trucks have been manually lined up with the lynch point, the wagons are lowered on to the trucks, fastened and reconnected.

It is a complicated, labor-intensive operation. After each car has been lifted, workers walk underneath and attach the wheel trucks to a steel cable which pulls them down the track, where they are stored until the train's return. When the new wheel trucks are rolled in, they must be manually positioned using such crude tools as bent pieces of track as hammers and extra long crowbars to rock the wheel trucks backwards and forwards until the connecting points are aligned.

To one not aware of what is happening (and most Westerners aren't), the procedure can be a harrowing experience with threatening Cold War overtones. Passengers are forbidden to leave the cars during the operation, which often takes place very early in the morning, and spend the turnaround time watching workers scurrying beneath their windows. Armed Polish soldiers patrol the half-mile stretch of the work area, and the eerie silence is broken only by the concussive slamming of wheel trucks being pulled into line and rolled down the track.

Every aspect of the procedure, which takes between 60 and 90 minutes per train, is dangerous. During the winter, when the average temperature falls to -15°C, workers stand exposed for periods of up to two hours and then retreat to an overheated lounge area; illnesses are common. The hydraulic lifts, which are both electrically and manually operated during the procedure, have failed on at least one occasion, sending one of the 50-odd-tonne cars and its passengers crashing to the ground.

Workers say that one woman passenger has been killed, and seven people have lost limbs when they were caught between nine-tonne wheel trucks that were being rolled down the track. Drunken passengers routinely fall out of the cars. And there's always the danger that a conductor will forget to lock the door to prevent entry to a car's toilet, which empties directly on to the tracks. Should a toilet be flushed during the wheel-truck changing procedure, the consequences are unfortunate for any workers who happen to be standing on the tracks beneath the drain output.

Kuznica, five hours east of Warsaw, is a tiny farming town that also happens to have major rail and road border crossings. These are seeing more business than ever. Russians and citizens of other former Soviet republics bring all their worldly possessions to sell in Warsaw's markets, and wait in line at the border for an average of three days to cross into Poland. On their return, having sold their possessions and the car in which they came, they buy a train ticket to Kuznica, where they walk back over the border. They then walk the few miles to Hrodna (Grodno) station, where they can pay for connecting tickets in roubles.

Where Mr Kudrzycki and his crew used to be controlled absolutely by the military – even to the extent that they had to request permission to go to the toilet – they are now very much under their own control. These days, the crew makes it very clear to the guards that they are merely putting up with them.

Even the once-powerful and feared Russian train conductors, who would use any opportunity to excercise their authority, now stand by sheepishly as the workers go about their business. 'They still try to throw their weight around from time to time', says Mr Kudrzycki, 'but now they're just a joke.'

'We used to do our job while the Army stood guard, keeping passengers in the cars, making sure people weren't taking photographs of the facility or sneaking around near the border', one of the workers said. 'Now the Army is "protecting" us from the Russians, trying to keep them out!' The whole crew, having a tea break between train arrivals in their smoke-filled lounge, began to laugh. 'An hour ago, two Russian passengers got sent back over the border', said another. 'They tried to get in with invitations written in outrageous Polish – bad grammar, made-up streets and towns, ridiculous names. It must have been written by a Pole with a great sense of humor.' (While Russians do not need a visa to enter Poland, they must have an invitation from a Polish citizen.)

The crew's tea break ends. The St Petersburg-Warsaw train is pulling in, and we follow Mr Kudrzycki to the 15-metre-high control tower. Standing at his control console, he presses one of several dozen lighted buttons as he speaks. This action has no discernible effect, and a worker's voice blares over a two-way radio speaker: the remote control is not functioning, so he'll do whatever needs to be done manually. 'That's normal', Mr Kudrzycki says, pointing scornfully to the console, which looks like a 1950s comic-strip version of a control panel of the future.

'You hear that radio? It was installed last month', he continues. 'I've been here for four years, everyone else since 1972, and they only installed a radio last month. Before that we would use hand signals, or send messages in a chain: he tells him, that guy tells the other guy, the other guy comes upstairs and tells me...'

There may be a lot of problems, but Mr Kudrzycki is still sure of at least one thing: he's not in danger of being laid off. 'In Portugal', he says almost wistfully, 'they have the wide-gauge rails as well. But there they use a new technology. They have contractable axles on the trains; as they cross the border the axles expand by springs and become wide enough to run on the rails.'

'But', he continues, 'my job's safe. Do you have any idea how expensive that system is?'

Nick Selby

used by some Kaliningrad-Moscow and Bryansk-Riga trains.

Some Westerners may not require a visa for entry into Latvia, and visas are issued at the border for those who do.

To/From Lithuania
Road The main road crossing is on the M12 Minsk-Vilnius road at Kamenny-Loh on the Belarusian side and Medininkai on the Lithuanian side. You're supposedly able to pass

the long lines of trucks and pull right up to the border crossing. Four buses a day run between Vilnius and Minsk (four hours). The Vilnius-Polatsk road (A235) crosses just to the north at the Belarusian town of Katlauka. The Vilnius-Lida road (A234) crosses to the south at the Belarusian town of Benjakoni. The Vilnius-Hrodna road (A232) crosses to the west at the Belarusian town of Dazishki.

Some Westerners may not require a visa for entry into Lithuania; those who do will have visas issued at the border.

Train There are three train lines converging on Vilnius from Belarus. The busiest is the Minsk-Vilnius line (four to five hours, several trains daily) which passes through Maldazechna. The Baranavichy-Vilnius line (five to six hours) is also used by trains from Lviv to Vilnius (15 to 19 hours; via Rivne in Ukraine). The Warsaw-Vilnius line passes through Hrodna (3½ hours). A few electric trains also run between Hrodna and Druskininkai, just inside the Lithuanian border.

To/From Poland

The main train route into Belarus from Poland is the Brest crossing; the Polish border station is the town of Terespol. Dozens of trains pull through each day, including the well-used Warsaw-Minsk-Moscow route. The E30 (M1) road crossing is also here and can be backed up for a few days during the high season, although foreigners are sometimes given special treatment. For advice on taking the train from Brest to Warsaw, see the Brest Getting There & Away section.

The other rail and road crossing is between Hrodna and Białystok, the same crossing used by some of the St Petersburg-Vilnius-Warsaw trains (road 18 in Poland). The Polish border station is Kuźnica Bialostocka. Two buses a day run between Minsk and Bialystok in Poland (seven hours).

To/From Russia

The main northern rail and road (M1/E30) crossing from Minsk to St Petersburg (via Vitsebsk) is the Belarusian border town of Ezjaryshcha and the Russian town of Lobok. The train and main road (M1/E30) between Minsk and Moscow crosses the border between Orsha (Belarus) and Smolensk (Russia), near the Russian town of Krasnoe. Train and road (A141) traffic between Smolensk and Vitsebsk crosses the border just to the north near the Russian town of Rudnya and the Belarusian town of Lezna. Train and road traffic between Homel and Moscow crosses the border 45 km east of Homel, passing through either Bryansk or Orel in Russia.

To/From Ukraine

Ukraine issues 72-hour emergency visas at the border (see Ukraine Facts for the Visitor). For details on major road and rail crossings between Belarus and Ukraine, see Ukraine Getting There & Away.

RIVER

In the south of Belarus, between the cities of Kobryn and Pinsk, the Mukhavets and Pripet rivers are connected by the strategic Dnjapro-Buh Canal – which essentially links the Dnjapro River to the Buh (Bug) River, which, in turn, connects to the Baltic and Black seas. So, in theory, you could start at the Baltic port of Gdańsk in Poland and sail upriver (south) along the Vistula River, switch to the Buh north of Warsaw, change to the Mukhavets at Brest Fortress, flow along the crucial Southern Belarus Canal, connect to the Pripet in the midst of marshes, flow into the Dnjapro (Dnipro) past Chornobyl, through Kiev and then down around the long curve of Ukrainian steppe through several cities before being finally spat out in the Black Sea. Unfortunately, this potentially epic 2000-odd km voyage from sea to sea is not yet readily available to tourists.

TRAVEL AGENCIES & TOURS

Very few travel agencies specialise in trips to Belarus – yet there are a number of agencies which handle travel to the former USSR, including Belarus.

The services provided by most of these travel agencies include arranging airfares to/from Belarus, accommodation, intercity transport, excursions, meals, tour guides etc. They can also arrange your visa if you purchase airline tickets or book a hotel through them. Fully packaged trips are pricey, ranging from US$75 to US$175 per day depending on the services provided (excluding airfares).

Several of the agencies mentioned in the Ukraine and European Russia Getting There & Away chapters can also make arrangements for Belarus. Add to the list Belintourist (☎ (0172) 26 98 40; fax (0172) 23 11 43), at praspekt Masherava 19, Minsk 220078, Belarus – a Belarusian joint-stock company for foreign tourism which can, among other things, assist with visa formalities.

WARNING

The information in this chapter is particularly vulnerable to change: prices for international travel are volatile, routes are introduced and cancelled, schedules change, special deals come and go, and rules and visa requirements are amended. Airlines and governments seem to take a perverse pleasure in making price structures and regulations as complicated as possible. You should check directly with the airline or a travel agent to make sure you understand how a fare (and ticket you may buy) works. In addition, the travel industry is highly competitive and there are many lurks and perks.

The upshot of this is that you should get opinions, quotes and advice from as many airlines and travel agents as possible before you part with your hard-earned cash. The details given in this chapter should be regarded as pointers and are not a substitute for your own careful, up-to-date research.

Getting Around

Travel within Belarus, although not always easy, is completely unrestricted – except (obviously) for the evacuated contaminated zone north of Chornobyl (Chernobyl).

The country is linked by a system of train lines, bus routes and roads, and the cities themselves are navigable by trolleybus, tram, city bus and, in Minsk, a metro.

Belarus, like Ukraine, is experiencing a fuel crisis as it is unable to pay Russia the going rate. Consequently, the frequency and reliability of buses and domestic flights has dropped severely. Services on major intercity train routes are still relatively reliable and frequent but local transport in country areas, while sporadically available, can be unreliable and is often overcrowded.

AIR

Minsk and Brest can handle domestic as well as international flights, though the bulk of all international flights are in and out of Minsk. Domestic flights (along with an occasional flight to Moscow) are also serviced by Homel, Hrodna, Mahileu, Mazyr and Vitsebsk. However, most of these runways are currently unused as domestic flights were one of the first things to be cut following fuel restrictions. Contact the Minsk office of the Belarusian national airline, Belavia (☎ 22 18 82), at vulitsa Karla Marxa 29, for the current status of domestic flights in Belarus.

BUS

The bus system in Belarus is identical to that of Ukraine and Russia. For information on bus services, tickets and strategies for the ride, see the Ukraine Getting Around chapter. Information on the duration and frequency of services to specific bus destinations is given in the Getting There & Away sections for each city concerned. A bus journey from Minsk to Hrodna (six hours) will cost about US$3.

TRAIN

Trains between major cities are frequent, relatively cheap and often a convenient night's journey. For listings of journey durations see the Getting There & Away sections for each city concerned. A typical train ticket between Minsk and Polatsk or Minsk and Brest on a 2nd-class sleeper *(kupe)* costs around US$3 to US$5. Local electric trains are much cheaper. Railway stations are called *zhelznadarazhniy* or *chugunachny vokzal* or just *vokzal* (station). All trains to and from Minsk run on Minsk time.

The train system in Belarus is identical to that of Ukraine and Russia. For information concerning types of trains, accommodation classes, tickets and tips for the journey, see the European Russia and Ukraine Getting Around chapters. The only difference is that in Belarusian, fast trains are called *khutki*, odd dates are called *nyachot* and even dates *chot*.

CAR & MOTORBIKE

With fuel hard to come by, spare parts rare, road conditions rugged, and getting lost inevitable, driving or riding in Belarus is undeniably problematic, but is always an adventure and the best way to really see the country. Make sure you know a bit about general mechanics, and don't take a shiny, new car and expect it to stay that way. For more information on road conditions, rules and regulations, fuel, repairs and motorbikes, see the Getting Around chapters for Ukraine and European Russia.

Car Rental

Cars can be rented in Belarus with or without a driver – but it may be cheaper to bargain with a taxi driver if you just want to go to one destination and back, say, for a day trip. Prices for car rental range from US$8 to US$15 an hour or US$50 to US$300 a day depending on the type of car and whether or not you have a driver. Sometimes the charge is by the km, sometimes by the hour, sometimes by the day – and there are always a few hidden taxes and fees. The reliability and availability of rental cars is sketchy, even if you have reservations. Make sure you read all the fine print of the rental agreement.

See the Minsk Getting There & Away section for details of some car rental agencies.

HITCHING

Hitching is never entirely safe in any country in the world, and we don't recommend it. Nevertheless, hitching is a very common method of getting around in Belarus (see European Russia Getting Around). Travellers who decide to hitch should understand that they are taking a small but potentially serious risk. People who do choose to hitch will be safer if they travel in pairs and let someone know where they are planning to go. Avoid hitching at night. Women should exercise extreme caution and everyone should avoid hitching alone.

LOCAL TRANSPORT

Local transport in Minsk is reasonably effi-

cient, in Brest below average, and in other cities outright pathetic. Few people can afford cars so everybody takes public transport and it often gets quite crowded, but usually not as badly as in Ukraine.

Tickets *(kvitok* or *bilet)* are very cheap. You can buy them at most kiosks around bus stops. Plastic metro tokens *(zhetony)* are sold at the windows downstairs in Minsk's metro stations. Minsk sells monthly passes during the first week of every month for all modes of transport, costing less than US$2. There are ticket inspectors but the fine is very small.

An A sign indicates a bus stop, T a tram stop, Tp a trolleybus stop, and M a metro station.

TOURS

Once you're in the country and you wish to have a tour or excursion arranged for you, contact Belintourist (☎ (0172) 26 98 40; fax (0172) 23 11 43), at prospekt Masherava 19, Minsk. They may be able to arrange something for you. See also the list of foreign travel agencies in the Ukraine and European Russia Getting There & Away chapters.

Minsk
Мінск

Population: 1.7 million

In a land of war memorials, Minsk is the greatest of all testimonies to the horrors of WW II. It's estimated that half the city's people died in WW II – a proportion close to its prewar Jewish population. (This was one of the handful of towns where Tsar Nicholas II had ordered Jews to congregate in 1835.) Virtually every building has been erected since 1944, when Minsk's recapture by the Soviet army left barely a stone standing.

Minsk is probably the single best example of pure Soviet planning on a grand scale. The excess of monumental classicism was supposed to give the impression of worker utopia – and beneath the dreary grey it almost does. The uniformity of the façades is softened by the wide streets and pleasant parks that were built into the scheme.

Over the past 30 years the city has watched its population triple with the pouring in of industry. Before independence, Minsk used to be the industrial powerhouse of the western USSR – a steel and concrete giant towering unexpectedly out of the endless plains. It has an undeniable pride in having survived innumerable disasters – coming back from the dead not just after WW II but after frequent destruction by fire down the centuries, sacking by Crimean Tatars in 1505, ruin by the French in 1812, and damage by the Germans in 1918 and by the Poles in 1919-20.

Today, as the proud capital of independent Belarus and the headquarters of the CIS, Minsk is developing a bustling, cosmopolitan atmosphere. There's definitely a cleaner and brighter feel than in other former Soviet cities where the housing and industrial plants are a generation older. Minsk is rightfully shedding its reputation as one of the worst cities in the former USSR, and it's worth more than a view out the train window on the way to Moscow.

Minsk has temperatures that typically pass 20°C in July but rarely rise above freezing from December to March. See Appendix III for climate chart.

In 1988, excavations near the outlying district of Kurapaty revealed more than 100,000 bodies of victims – men and women – executed in the late 1930s during Stalin's numerous terror purges. Other partly excavated graves nearby bring some estimates up to a staggering 900,000 innocent people murdered between 1937 and 1941. A small booklet in English entitled *Kurapaty*, which is sold at a few kiosks, gives the harrowing and graphic details of this atrocity, only one of many carried out by the Stalin regime before the war.

ORIENTATION

Minsk stretches about 15 km from north to south and east to west, the Brest-Moscow highway crossing it from south-west to north-east. The highway is called praspekt Francyska Skaryny in the centre, and the main focus is the 2.5-km stretch between ploshcha Nezalezhnastsi and ploshcha Peramohi. Vulitsa Lenina, 750 metres north-east of ploshcha Nezalezhnastsi, is one of the main streets intersecting praspekt Francyska Skaryny. To the north, Lenina becomes praspekt Masherava, where you'll find the

Belintourist office. Both the main railway and bus stations are two blocks south-east of ploshcha Nezalezhnastsi, with the metro station (of the same name) on the spot. There's a big ring road *(koltsevaja doroha)* around the city perimeter. The Svislach River twists through the city centre and has some nice parks along its banks.

INFORMATION
Tourist Offices

The main tourist office, Belintourist (☎ 26 98 40; fax 23 11 43) is next door to the Hotel Jubileynaja at praspekt Masherava 19. This is where you can purchase your train tickets as well as organise a city tour or excursion anywhere in the country – that is, if you can get any service. (When we were in Minsk the information personnel were too busy watching TV to respond to our beckoning – old habits are hard to kill.)

Upstairs in the Hotel Belarus is a small office that can arrange tours and the like. You can also try the friendly reception at the Hotel Jubileynaja for questions and help.

Off the far end of the lobby in the Hotel Minsk is a service bureau where the English-speaking staff are friendly and very helpful. You're supposed to register your visa with the authorities within 24 hours of arrival in the country, and this service bureau (as well as other hotels) will gladly do it for you (for a minimal fee). They'll also call other hotels and arrange the cheapest accommodation for you – true top-notch service.

Minskturyst (☎ 23 88 55) on vulitsa Tankavaja, 1.5 km west of the Minsk city centre, is similar in scope to Belintourist but doesn't sell train tickets.

Money

There are exchange offices in every hotel. The one to the rear and left of the lobby in the Hotel Jubileynaja is a branch of Belzneshekanambank and will exchange your travellers' cheques as well as make cash advances on your major credit card; it's open daily from 9 am to 7 pm. The exchange office in the Hotel Kastrychnitskaja (Oktjabrskaja) also makes cash advances on your credit card.

There is a Western Union Office (☎ 27 24 69, 31 34 77), at vulitsa Kujbysheva 75, just north-east of the opera and ballet theatre, which is open on weekdays from 9.30 am to 5 pm. It will exchange travellers' cheques, give cash advances on your credit card and arrange wire transfers from other countries.

Along praspekt Skaryny you'll find hard-currency exchange kiosks such as the one upstairs and to the left in the foyer of No 23. There's also an exchange kiosk off the stairway in the main railway station.

Post & Telecommunications

The central post office (pashtamt) is at the eastern end of ploshcha Nezalezhnastsi at praspekt Francyska Skaryny 10, and is open daily from 8 am to 8 pm (to 5 pm on Sunday). The best option is the Express Mail Service (EMS), which guarantees delivery within seven days to more than 130 countries worldwide.

The Central Telegraph Office (Tsentralny Telegraf), also at praspekt Skaryny 10, is open daily from 7.30 am to 11 pm. You can send telegrams internationally but you can't call internationally outside the CIS. To do this you have to go to the calling station (perehovorny punkt) nearby at vulitsa Valadarskaha 18; it's open daily from 10 am to 9.30 pm, closed from 3 to 4 pm. You can also send faxes here. For more information on making international calls, see Post & Telecommunications in Belarus Facts for the Visitor.

As in Kiev, calls from public phones are free because there are no longer any coins in circulation. The Minsk telephone code is 0172.

Foreign Embassies & Consulates

The following countries are represented in Minsk:

Bulgaria
    Branjavy zavulak 5 (☎ 27 55 02; fax 36 56 61)
China
    vulitsa Berastjanskaja 22 (☎ 76 85 41; fax 76 86 43)
CIS Headquarters
    vulitsa Kirava 17 (☎ 29 35 27; fax 27 23 39)
Czech Republic
    Branjavy zavulak 5A (☎ 36 34 15; fax 36 74 35)

Minsk Metro

Pushkinskaja (future stop)
Maladziozhnaja (future stop)
Frunzenskaja (future stop)
Njamiha
Kupalawskaja/ Kastrychnitskaja
Instituta Kultury
Ploshcha Nezaliezhnasci
Ploshcha Peramohi
Ploshcha Jakuba Kolasa
Akademija Navuk
Park Chaljuskintsau
Maskouskaja
Uschod

Pershamajskaja
Praletarskaja
Traktamyzavod
Partyzanskaja (future stop)
Autazavodskaja (future stop)
Satsyjalistychnaja (future stop)

Minsk
Мінск

0   250   500 m

To Khatyn (60 km)

To Zhdanovichi, Minsk Sea & Zaslavl

To Vilnius

ploshcha Jakuba Kolasa

To Botanical Gardens, Chaljuskintsau Park, Hotel Druzhba (2 km), Minsk-2 Airport, Smolensk & Moscow

Park Janki Kupaly

Horkaha Central Children's Park

praspekt Dzhjarzhinskaja

To Hotel Savetskaja, Motel & Camping Minsky & Brest

To Minsk-1 Airport

ploshcha Pryvakzalnaja

To Vostochny Bus Station (2 km)

BELARUS

PLACES TO STAY

5   Hotel Belarus
    Гасцініца Беларусь
6   Hotel Planeta
    Гасцініца Планета
8   Hotel Jubileynaya
    Гасцініца Юбілейная
41   Hotel Kastrychhitskaja
    Гасцініца Кастрычніцкая
46   Hotel Svislach
    Гасцініца Свіслач
50   Hotel Minsk
    Гасцініца Мінск

PLACES TO EAT

18   Trajetskaje Pradmetse
    Троіцкае прадмесце
19   Karchma Trajetskaja
    Карчма Троіцкая
31   Capriccio & Kafe Svitanak
    Капрычча і Кафэ Світанак
32   Restaran Patsdam
    Рэстаран Патсдам
34   Bar/Restaran Sem Pjatnits
    Бар-рэстаран Сем пятніц
38   Kafe Vyjasna
    Кафэ Вясна
40   Kafe Uzbekistan
    Кафэ Узбекістан
57   Kafe Vjasjolka
    Кафэ Вясёлка

OTHER

1   Kamarowski Rynok Market
    Камароўскі рынак
3   Belarusian State Philharmonia
    Беларуская Дзяржаўная філармонія
4   St Mary Magdeline Church
    Царква св. Мары Магдалены
7   Belintourist Office
    Кантора Белінтурыст
9   Kino Moskva
    Кінатэатр Масква
10   National Academic Opera & Ballet
    Theatre
    Дзяржаўны акадэмічны вялікі
    тэатр оперы і балета
12   St Roha Church
    Царква св. Роха
13   Art Palace
    Палац мастацтва
14   Ploshcha Peramohi & Victory Obelisk
    Плошча Перамогі і манумент Перамогі

15   Institute of Foreign Languages & the
    British Council
    Інстітут замежных моў і кансулат
    Вялікабрытаніі
16   Workers Party Congress House-Museum
    Дом-музей 1 з'езда Расійскай
    сацыял-дэмакратычнай партыі
17   Republican Exhibition Centre
    Рэспубліканскі выставачны цэнтр
20   Restored Area
    Рэстаўрываная зона
23   SS Peter & Paul Church
    Петрапаўлаўская царква
24   Cathedral of St Dukhawski
    Святадухаўскі царква
25   Bernardine Church
    Бернардзінская царква
26   Ploshcha Svabody
    Плошча Свабоды
27   Museum of the Great Patriotic War
    Музей гісторыі Вялікай
    Айчыннай вайны
28   Trade Unions' Culture Palace
    Палац культуры прафсаюзаў
29   Circus
    Дзяржаўны цырк
33   GUM Department Store
    Дзяржаўны універсальны магазін
35   KGB Building
    Будынак КДБ
36   Russian Drama Theatre
    Рускі драматычны тэатр
37   Train Ticket Office
    Чыгуначныя білетныя касы
39   Belarusian State Art Museum
    Дзяржаўны мастацкі музей Беларусі
43   Dinamo Stadium
    Стадыён Дынама
44   Belarus National Museum of History &
    Culture
    Беларускі Дзяржаўны
    краязнаўчы музей
45   Suveniry
    Крама Сувеніры
47   Long-Distance Calling Station
    Міжнародная тэлефонная станцыя
48   Central Post & Telegraph Office
    Глаўпаштамт
49   Teatralnaja Kasa
    Тэатральная каса
51   Polish Catholic Church of St Simon
    Касцёл Сымона і Елены
52   Belarusian Government Building
    Дом ураду Беларусі

continued next page

BELARUS

continued from previous page

53 Music & Comedy Theatre
Тэатр музычнай камедыі

54 Ploshcha Nezalezhnastsi
Плошча Незалежнасці

56 Belarusian State University
Беларускі дзяржаўны універсітэт

58 Main Train Station

59 Yanka Kupala Belarusian National
Theatre

METRO STATIONS

2 Ploshcha Jakuba Kolasa
Плошча Якуба Коласа

11 Ploshcha Peramohi
Плошча Перамогі

21 Njamiha
Няміга

22 Frunzenskaja
Фрунзенская

30 Kupalawskaja/Kastrichnitskaja
Купалаўская Кастрычніцкая

42 Pershamajskaja
Першамайская

55 Ploshcha Nezalezhnastsi
Плошча Незалежнасці

WEST TO EAST LINE

Інстытут Культуры
Institut Kultury
Плошча Незалежнасці
Ploshcha
Nezalezhnastsi
Кастрычніцкая
Kastrychnitskaja
Плошча Перемогі
Ploshcha Peramohi
Плошча Якуба Коласа
Ploshcha Jakuba Kolasa
Акадэмія Навук
Akademija Navuk

Парк Чалюскінцау
Park Chaljuskintsau
Маскоуская
Maskouskaja
Усход
Uskhod

NORTH TO SOUTH LINE

Пушкінская
Pushkinskaja
Маладзёжная
Maladziozhnaja
Фрунзенская
Frunzenskaja

Няміга
Njamiha
Купалауская
Kupalawskaja
Першамайская
Pershamajskaja
Пралетарская
Praletarskaja
Трактарнызавод
Traktarnyzavod
Партызанская
Partyzanskaja
Аутазаводская
Autazavodskaja
Сацыялістычная
Satsyjalistychnaja

France
Hotel Belarus, room 1102 (☎ & fax 34 34 43)
Germany
vulitsa Zakharava 26 (☎ 33 27 14; fax 36 85 52)
India
Hotel Belarus, room 804 (☎ 62 99 70; fax 62 97 99)
Israel
Hotel Belarus, rooms 501-507 (☎ 69 08 06; fax
76 94 09)
Japan
Hotel Kastrychnitskaja (Oktjabrskaja), room 303
(☎ 27 47 18; fax 27 43 19)
Kyrgyzstan
vulitsa Kalvarijaskaja 17/613 (☎ 23 61 82; fax 23
58 22)
Korea (North)
vulitsa Partyzanskaja 83/59 (☎ 45 12 94; fax 25
24 84)
Latvia
Hotel Belarus, room 1907 (☎ 39 16 12; fax 50 67 84)

Lithuania
vulitsa Varvasheni 1/7 (☎ & fax 34 87 88)
Poland
vulitsa Rumjantsava 6 (☎ 33 11 14; fax 36 49 92)
Romania
vulitsa Drozdy 21/2 (☎ & fax 23 83 64)
Russia
vulitsa Staravilenskaja 48 (☎ & fax 50 36 66)
Slovakia
Branjavy zavulak 5A (☎ 36 34 15; fax 36 74 35)
Turkey
vulitsa Kirava 17-402 (☎ 27 13 83; fax 27 27 46)
UK
Karla Marxa 37 (☎ 229 23 03; fax 229 23 06)
Ukraine
vulitsa Kirava 17-306 (☎ 27 23 54; fax 27 28 61)
UN office
vulitsa Kirava, 6th floor (☎ 27 48 76; fax 26 03 40)
USA
vulitsa Staravilenskaja 46 (☎ 34 77 61; fax 34 78 53)

BELARUS

Cultural Centres

There's a small British Council office in the Institute of Foreign Languages at vulitsa Zakharava 21. It's open Tuesday, Thursday and Friday from 10 am to 5 pm, Wednesday from 2 to 7 pm, Saturday from 10 am to 3 pm, and is closed on Sunday and Monday. It has a good supply of English-language books.

Bookshops

The two main bookshops are Tsentralnaya Kniharnya Mahazin (Central Bookshop) at praspekt Skaryny 19, and Svetoch at praspekt Masherava 11.

Film & Photography

The Kodak outlet is in the department store at vulitsa Njamiha 8, a few blocks north-west of ploshcha Nezalezhnastsi. There's also the nearby Dom Fota on vulitsa Mjasnikova 78, and the Fuji outlet in the Central Bookshop at praspekt Skaryny 19.

PRASPEKT FRANCYSKA SKARYNY

Minsk's main street, praspekt Skaryny (formerly Leninsky prospekt) was renamed after the national hero, Francyska Skaryny, who, in the 16th century, was the first printer in Belarus (and one of the first anywhere) to utilise the printing press in the Old Slavic and Belarusian languages. Today the thoroughfare is a huge (it tripled in width when it was rebuilt after WW II) and hectic promenade with long blocks and underground crossings – the local police (called DIA) will issue annoying tickets to those who run across the street on foot. There are two metro stations at either end – Ploshcha Nezalezhnastsi and Ploshcha Peramohi, with the Kupalawskaja/Kastrychnitskaja metro station interchange halfway down. Trolleybus Nos 1, 2 and 18 ply praspekt Skaryny.

The 500-metre-long **ploshcha Nezalezhnastsi** (Independence Square) at the southwestern end of praspekt Skaryny is dominated by the Belarusian government building (behind the Lenin statue) on its northern side, and the equally proletarian Belarusian State University on the south side.

Breaking the theme of Soviet classicism that dominates ploshcha Nezalezhnastsi is the red-brick **Polish Catholic Church of St Simon** (1910), next to the Belarusian government building. Its tall, gabled bell tower and attractive detailing are reminiscent of many brick churches in the former Teutonic north of Poland.

Between ploshcha Nezalezhnastsi and vulitsa Lenina are many of Minsk's main shops and cafés, including the large GUM department store at No 21. An entire block at No 17 is occupied by a yellow neoclassical building with an ominous, temple-like Corinthian portal. This is the still-functioning headquarters of the KGB, its radio antenna at the far end busy intercepting useless messages. On the opposite side of the street is a long narrow park with the bust of Felix Dzerzhynsky, the founder of the KGB's predecessor, the Cheka, and a native of Belarus.

After praspekt Skaryny crosses the Svislach River it reaches **ploshcha Peramohi** (Victory Square), a busy intersection with the tall victory obelisk – the former symbol of Soviet Minsk – rising from its centre beside the eternal flame. It's floodlit at night and there's an underground passage leading to it if you want to look closely at the heroic reliefs around the base.

Just north, at vulitsa Kisjaleva 2, is the apartment building where Lee Harvey Oswald – the future alleged assassin of US President John F Kennedy – lived for a few years in his early 20s. The psychological influence of his short stay is open to interpretation.

MUSEUMS & ART GALLERIES
Belarus National Museum of History & Culture

This museum, a block south on vulitsa Karla Marxa 12, has a cannon near the front entrance and is open from 11 am to 7 pm daily except Wednesday. Inside you can take a journey into the turbulent history of this nation; there are also some interesting ethnographic displays.

Belarusian State Art Museum

Behind a formal, grey classical façade at vulitsa Lenina 20, this museum has 17th to 20th-century paintings, including some by Repin, Levitan and Vrubel as well as an impressive collection of Belarusian art. The *Bulgarian Martyrs* by Makovsky is brilliant and moving. Some crafts and ceramics are usually for sale on the ground floor. The museum is open from 11 am to 7 pm daily except Tuesday.

Museum of the Great Patriotic War

This sobering museum (Great Patriotic War is the Soviet name for WW II) is at praspekt Skaryny 25A, recessed off the street, between vulitsa Lenina and Janki Kupaly, behind the classical-style Trade Unions' Culture Palace. The museum is open daily except Monday from 11 am to 6 pm. The 28 rooms graphically display the horrors of WW II and go a long way towards explaining Belarus' apparent obsession with the Great Patriotic War. Most grisly are the POW displays and photos of partisans being executed. It's ironic to think that all the suffering served only to 'liberate' the people from one reign of terror and deliver them to another, equally oppressive regime.

Republican Exhibition Centre

About 500 metres north of praspekt Skaryny at vulitsa Janki Kupaly 27, this glass box usually has some form of international trade fair going on and may be worth a peek.

Art Palace

Large and modern-looking, the Art Palace is a block north-east of ploshcha Peramohi at vulitsa Kazlova 3, and nearly always features an exhibition of some sort, often of Belarusian art or crafts (closed Monday). There's also a good little information kiosk inside, and a tiny antique store upstairs. The small St Roha Church sits hidden behind the Art Palace.

PARKS & GARDENS

The **Park Janki Kupaly** is a pleasant stretch of greenery bordered on two sides by the snaking Svislach River, and has rowboats for rent on the east side during the summer. On the far bank across the river stands a replica of the small green wooden house where the Russian Social Democratic Workers' Party – Russia's original Marxist party – held its illegal founding congress in 1898. The house bears the sign '133 Ul. Zakharevskaja' – the former address of this location which, in those days, was on the edge of the city. Today its address is vulitsa Kamunistychnaja 31A and the small museum inside is undergoing ideological restoration and should reopen with a somewhat more neutral stance.

East of praspekt Skaryny, across the river and opposite the circus, is the big **Horkaha Central Children's Park**, with plenty of venues for strolling and a funfair.

About three km north-east of ploshcha Peramohi are two pleasant parks – the **Botanical Garden**, open Wednesday to Sunday, and the woodland **Chaljuskintsau Park**, both near the Park Chaljuskintsau metro station.

OLD TOWN

The congested overpass that now carries vulitsa Lenina over vulitsa Njamiha near the Njamiha metro station was the site of Minsk's marketplace in the 12th century, but there's no trace left today. **Ploshcha Svabody** to the south-east became the new city centre in the 16th century. The Baroque, twin-towered Orthodox **Cathedral of St Dukhawski** off the northern end of the square stands defiantly on a small hill overlooking its rather bleak surroundings. It was once part of a Polish Bernardine convent founded in the 17th century along with the former **Bernardine church** next door, which now houses city archives. The former monastery buildings farther to the right (east) have recently been restored and now house a music academy affiliated with the classical-looking conservatory building at the far south-western end of ploshcha Svabody.

Across the vulitsa Lenina overpass sits the attractively restored 17th-century **SS Peter**

& Paul Church, dwarfed by the imposing concrete housing blocks and institutional buildings that surround it.

A small area of housing on the east bank of the Svislach River, immediately north of vulitsa Maxima Bahdanovicha, has been rebuilt in 17th/18th-century style to make a quaint, small-scale, low-rise contrast with the rest of the city – a refreshing stroll off the big, wide and noisy boulevards. There are a few cafés, bars, restaurants and the odd craft/gift shop, to tempt you there. Two blocks north-east is the **National Academic Opera & Ballet Theatre** set in a leafy park.

The nicest small church in the city is about 500 metres north of here near the Hotel Belarus. Attractive little **St Mary Magdeline Church** and chapel was built in 1847 in the ancient Orthodox style, with a pointed octagonal bell tower over the entrance and a single sweeping dome over the cruciform plan.

PLACES TO STAY

The first place to head for is the stately *Hotel Minsk* (☎ 20 01 32) on the far north-eastern side of ploshcha Nezalezhnastsi at praspekt Skaryny 11; it's walking distance from the main railway station. Decent singles/doubles cost US$36/40 – but if this is too expensive, the very helpful service bureau, off a hallway at the rear of the lobby, will book you a room in a cheaper hotel. Off the lobby are a small gift shop, newsstand and bar; the restaurant is upstairs and the bathroom is downstairs.

If the Hotel Minsk is too expensive for your budget, the service bureau there will probably reserve you a room in the *Hotel Svislach* (☎ 20 97 83, 20 42 11) 2½ blocks south-east at vulitsa Kirava 13, on the vulitsa Valadarskaha corner – a faded example of pure Soviet Baroque architecture. Adequate singles/doubles cost US$11/26. There's a toilet in the room, though you have to pay the dezhurnaja about US$0.20 to use the shower in the corridor. The restaurant is around the corner and is entered off vulitsa Kirava.

The service bureau in the Hotel Minsk might also set you up in the less desirable

Hotel Savetskaja (☎ 25 35 29) at vulitsa Sorsa 5. It's about the same price and standard as the Hotel Svislach but about 2.5 km south-west of the centre – four stops on trolleybus No 5 from the north-western end of ploshcha Nezalezhnastsi.

Probably the nicest place in town is the central *Hotel Kastrychnitskaja (Oktjabrskaja)* (☎ 29 39 10) at vulitsa Enhelsa 13, recessed off the street on the corner of vulitsa Kirava, and the favourite of visiting diplomats. Deluxe singles/doubles with refrigerator and working TV cost US$70/80, payable in hard currency or with a major credit card. The hotel boasts a tiny pool and sauna, and there are a small gift shop and an exchange office that will make cash advances on your credit card. The Kupalawskaja/Kastrychnitskaja metro station is two blocks north-west.

The two former Intourist hotels, where most tourists to Minsk once stayed, are large and modern-looking and a few hundred metres apart on praspekt Masherava, about 1.5 km north of praspekt Skaryny. The brighter of the two is the older (1969) but less institutional *Hotel Jubileynaja* (☎ 26 91 71, 26 90 24) at No 19. Rooms are comfortable but on the small side, and overpriced at US$53/63, hard currency only. There's a decent range of coffee shops and bars and an exchange office at the rear of the lobby that exchanges travellers' cheques and makes credit card cash advances. The restaurant is next door and upstairs.

The *Hotel Planeta* (☎ 26 78 53), at praspekt Masherava 31, has rooms slightly cheaper in price and quality – US$50/60 for a single/double, payable in hard currency, travellers' cheques or by credit card. For both hotels, bus Nos 36 and 69 travel between the Hotel Jubileynaja and the bus stop in front of vulitsa Kirava 4, a block north of the main railway station. Trolleybus Nos 21, 39 and 56 leave from in front of the GUM department store (a block south-west of the Kupalawskaja/Kastrychnitskaja metro station) and run straight along vulitsa Lenina and praspekt Masherava to both hotels.

Newer and slightly better than the

Jubileynaja and the Planeta is the towering 23-storey *Hotel Belarus* (☎ 39 17 05) at vulitsa Starazhouskaja 15, farther north and on the other side of the river. Clean singles/doubles cost US$40/60, hard currency only. Tram No 4 from the railway station goes all the way; otherwise, take tram No 3, 4 or 10 from outside the Art Palace on vulitsa Kazlova (two blocks north-east of the Ploshcha Peramohi metro station). Get off at the Teatr Moladzi stop then walk south two blocks past the small St Mary Magdeline Church. Bus No 13 or 39 from ploshcha Peramohi will also take you there.

The *Motel Minsky* and *Camping Minsky* (☎ 99 51 40) are 17 km west of the city centre on the Brest highway (Brestskoe shose; E30/M1) at the 727-km marker, shortly beyond the Ptich Reservoir (Vodokhranilishche Ptich), a favourite local recreation spot. The motel, a popular truck stop, is noisy and tatty with small rooms (US$10/16 a single/double) and a restaurant – but the desk staff are helpful. The camp site is one of the better ones you'll find, with cabins for US$3 per person (with toilet and shower) or US$2 (without facilities). Tent sites cost US$1 per person. Its setting is among pine woods and it has its own restaurant. Getting out there is not easy as buses are infrequent, so unless you have your own transport it may not be worth it. From the bus station there are six buses a day to/from the town of Dzerzhinsk that stop on the highway outside the motel and camp site on the way. A taxi to/from the city should cost about US$5.

Another option is the *Hotel Druzhba* (☎ 66 24 81) at vulitsa Tolbukhina 3, near the Park Chaljuskintsau metro station, where Spartan quad rooms with common bath go for US$5 per person.

The 14-storey *Mezhdunarodnie Turistsky Tsentr Yunost* (Youth International Tourist Centre), (☎ 36 23 97, 37 99 27), is beside the Minsk Sea about 18 km north-west of the centre, near picturesque surroundings. Bus No 125 or 219 goes there from the railway station, or you can take one of the numerous daily electric trains to Maladzechna or Aljakhnovich, get off after about half an hour at the Zelenoe station, and walk east through the forest for about three km.

PLACES TO EAT
Hotels
The big banquet-hall style restaurants in the hotels Belarus, Jubileynaja and Planeta are all comparable, with respectable service, similar menus in broken English, and decent food for about US$5 per person. Any appetiser with mushrooms is incredibly tasty, as are the potato pancakes (dranniki). Try the filet kurechi, a deliciously stuffed piece of chicken available at all three restaurants. Each restaurant also has live music with the same carbon-copy band crooning the same 1970s top 10.

For lighter fare, the *Hotel Jubileynaja* has a decent ground-floor coffee shop and its express bar, also on the ground floor, may have beer. The *Hotel Planeta* has a hard-currency bar on the 2nd floor and a ground-floor express bar with snacks.

On the 5th floor of the *Hotel Minsk* there's an average restaurant with a sweeping view over ploshcha Nezalezhnastsi. The restaurant in the *Hotel Svislach* seems to be where all the dethroned communist big fellows gather and dine.

Restaurants
The *Restaran Patsdam*, at vulitsa Lenina 2, is supposed to have German-style food, but the dishes are typical of most restaurants. The best on the menu is the 'sans sousi', a meat medley with pork, beef and chicken with a crispy garnish (about US$4). The downstairs bar/restaurant *Sem Pjatnits* (Five Fridays), specialising in Polish and Belarusian food, is half a block left (west) of the GUM department store. Full meals cost about US$5 and the spiffy interior usually comes with a small orchestra after 7 pm (there's a tiny cover charge).

The *Kafe Uzbekistan* on vulitsa Kirava around the corner from vulitsa Lenina, is small and popular and serves spicy Central Asian food. Try their home-made bread and ravioli-style 'manty'.

Across the street from the main railway

station, on the vulitsa Kirava corner, is the *Kafe Vjasjolka*. Downstairs is a quiet restaurant serving bifshtek (steak) or kotleta (pork cutlets) with potatoes and soup for about US$3. Upstairs is a cheap cafeteria-style eatery where you can piece together the same sort of fare for about half the price.

There are a number of restaurants and cafés within the tiny cluster of restored buildings between the river and vulitsa Bahdanovicha. The *Karchma Trajetskaja* (Trinity Tavern), at vulitsa Staravilenskaja 4 along the riverfront, has a cosy upstairs dining area and friendly service. The kurina trajetskaja (chicken, potatoes and a mushroom sauce) is the speciality. More popular is the nearby *Trajetskaje Pradmestse*, at Staravilenskaja 10, which is similar to the Karchma but bigger, with two dining areas in wood-beam surroundings. Dranniki s miasom are tasty potato pancakes drenched with bacon. Next door is the café/bar *Marozhanaje* in a red-brick gabled house with a pleasing beer-hall atmosphere.

Cafés

Beside the ones in the restored area, praspekt Skaryny has several cafés. The best is the bustling *Capriccio* at praspekt Skaryny 23, upstairs to the right as you enter. It's a deluxe stand-up eatery selling all sorts of tasty cakes, pastries, small sandwiches, pizzas, stuffed potato and cheese rolls, fruit drinks, beer and real espresso. You have to first pay at the cashier, then give the receipt to the proper counter to receive your food or drink – a thoroughly confusing system. There's a 5000-rouble (about US$0.60) deposit for the espresso cups. The café is actually a joint venture which also operates the grocery store upstairs – one of the best of its kind in the former CIS. Here you can stock up on food – the *skazka* and *kievsky* cakes they sell are delectable. To the left as you enter, directly opposite the entrance to the Capriccio café and up a small flight of stairs past the exchange booth, is the *Kafe Svitanak*, a relaxing place to sit down and enjoy a drink. They sell delicious small pizzas as well as soup.

The *Kafe Vjasna*, at praspekt Skaryny 18

(entered from the left of the small lobby) is an elegant café serving an assortment of light food in a long and narrow dining area.

The *Kafe Berezka*, on the west side of ploshcha Peramohi, is good for a stiff coffee or a shot of vodka, but that's about it.

There's a *Pinguin* ice-cream shop on vulitsa Lenina 3 across the street from the Restaran Patsdam.

Market

The immense Kamarowski Rynok market on vulitsa Very Haruzaj – one very long block north-west of the Ploshcha Jakuba Kolasa metro station – is a mini-city of market mayhem. Inside the cavernous covered hall are hundreds of neat piles of nuts, spices, breads, dried fish, meat carcasses and other produce. Outside, beneath the canopies, it all repeats itself in a more chaotic fashion with a smaller selection but cheaper prices.

ENTERTAINMENT

Minsk has quite a lively cultural life and its Belarusian Ballet is one of the best classical ballet companies in Eastern Europe. Ballets, along with a whole host of operas, are performed at the grand, Soviet-style State Academic Opera & Ballet Theatre, set in a park at vulitsa Paskevic 23. (During the intermission you can count the number of hammers-and-sickles ornamenting the interior.) The Belarusian State Philharmonic Society also has a high reputation – it has folk ensembles as well as a symphony orchestra and is based at praspekt Skaryny 50, next to the Ploshcha Jakuba Kolasa metro station. To buy advance tickets or to find out what's playing, head to the *teatralnaja kasa* (ticket office) at praspekt Skaryny 13; or you can pay more at the service bureau in the Hotel Jubileynaja or at Belintourist. Tickets for performances the same day can be purchased at the theatre an hour before curtain call.

Belarusian folk song and dance shows periodically occur and are well known for their rich traditions – check the listings at the ticket office or ask at the Belintourist office. You could also try asking at the Hotel

Jubileynaja, which often organises shows for its package-tour groups. The Belarusian Musical Autumn in the last 10 days of November is a festival of folk and classical music and dance.

Other theatres include the Yanka Kupala Belarusian National Theatre on vulitsa Enhelsa 7, a block from the Hotel Kastrychnitskaja (Oktjabrskaja). Just down vulitsa Enhelsa at No 20 is the State Puppet Theatre. The State Theatre of Musical Comedy is on vulitsa Mjasnikova 44, west of ploshcha Nezalezhnastsi, and the Russian Drama Theatre is at vulitsa Valadarskaha 5.

Most of the restaurants mentioned earlier – especially the ones at hotels – have music and dancing so you're likely to dine to some form of entertainment.

A few discos do exist. The Randevu at vulitsa Majakouskaha 15 is supposedly popular with art students. The Paradise Club, inside the Kinateatr Maskva at vulitsa Masherava 13, has two floors of lights and late-night dancing. The most popular disco is the Xantia, south-east of the centre at vulitsa Chyrvonaarmejskaja 3. A former officers' club, it's now an expensive car show-room during the day, then at night, patrons can boogie around its polished Fords and Citroëns.

Dinamo Minsk, Belarus' top soccer club, which often appears in European competitions, has a 55,000-capacity stadium at vulitsa Kirava 8. In winter there's cross-country skiing at the Motel Minsky.

THINGS TO BUY

The best gift and souvenir shop is the Suveniry next to the Hotel Svislach at vulitsa Valadarskaha 23, with a good selection of wooden 'straw boxes', ceramics and textiles for cheap prices. At praspekt Skaryny 13, just up the road from the teatralnaja kasa on the corner of Haradski Val, is the Magazin Charaunitsa, with a good selection of porcelain and wooden souvenirs. At Skaryny 19, next to GUM, is the Paulinka gift shop, with a selection of folk souvenirs. The Vyanok bookshop at Handljebaja nabjarezhnaja 46, along the south riverfront of the restored

area, has interesting gifts, art work and antique books. Nearby at vulitsa Maxima Bahdanovicha 21, on the vulitsa Janki Kupaly corner, is a small art gallery with some nice work for sale. The Art Palace has a small antique kiosk upstairs, and there's a selection of ceramics for sale in the lobby of the Belarusian State Art Museum.

GETTING THERE & AWAY

Air

Most international flights use Minsk-2 Airport, about 40 km east of the city off the Moscow highway. A few domestic and shorter international flights – including those to Kiev, St Petersburg and Moscow (flights to Moscow and St Petersburg use both airports) – use Minsk-1 Airport, at the end of vulitsa Chkalava, about three km south of ploshcha Nezalezhnastsi. See Belarus Getting There & Away for more information on international flights to/from Minsk.

Airline offices include: Austrian Airlines/SwissAir/SAS (☎ 76 89 70/1) at praspekt Masherava 19; Lufthansa (☎ 97 37 45, 97 30 59) at the Minsk-2 Airport; LOT Polish (☎ 26 66 28) at praspekt Masherava 7, and Transaero (☎ 26 92 33) at Masherava 19. The Belarusian national airline, Belavia, has two offices: one for international flights (☎ 25 02 31) at vulitsa Chkalava 38; the other for flights to CIS destinations (☎ 22 18 82) at vulitsa Karla Marxa 29. For international flight information call (☎ 25 02 31), for Minsk-2 Airport information call (☎ 97 31 20).

Bus

Minsk has two bus stations. The central long-distance bus station (tsentralny avtovokzal) is at vulitsa Babrujskaja 12, about 200 metres east of the railway station. There are two buses a day to Białystok in Poland (seven hours) and nine to Hrodna (six hours). Other daily buses include Brest (seven hours, odd days only), Kaliningrad (Russia, 12 hours), and Riga (Latvia, 10½ hours). Three cities in Lithuania are serviced daily: Kaunas (5½ hours), Klaipéda (eight hours) and Vilnius (four hours, four times daily). Six buses daily service the town of Navahrudak

(3½ hours) stopping at Mir (two to 2½ hours) along the way. Two buses daily go to the town of Kletsk, stopping at Njasvizh (2½ to three hours) on the way.

The Vostochny (eastern) bus station is about three km south-east of the centre. Bus No 8 travels between the two bus stations. Daily buses from Vostochny bus station include those to Homel (seven hours), Vitsebsk (6½ hours), Pinsk (eight hours), Polatsk (seven hours) and Warsaw (11 hours). There are also eight buses daily to Mahileu/Mogilev (four hours).

Train

The upper floor of the main railway station is where international and long-distance train times are displayed and tickets sold; the ground floor has information and tickets for local electric trains.

Minsk is on the main Moscow-Warsaw-Berlin line, and there are around nine trains daily to Moscow (11 to 12 hours), between two and four to Warsaw (nine to 12 hours), and one to Berlin (19 hours). Most Moscow trains stop at Smolensk on the way (usually four hours).

At least two trains a day go to St Petersburg (16 hours, via Vitsebsk), Vilnius (3½ hours), Kaliningrad (13 hours) and Kiev (13 hours). Other international cities served by at least one train daily include Lviv (Ukraine, 17 hours), Riga (9½ hours), Tallinn (Estonia, 17½ hours), Prague (25 hours), Paris (31 hours) and Brussels. Every other day (dropping to twice weekly in winter) there are trains to Chisinau (27 hours), Odessa (27 hours), and Simferopol (31 hours), all three passing through Kiev.

Domestic trains include about eight a day to Brest (four to five hours), some of which continue on to Warsaw. Three or four trains a day go to Hrodna (six to eight hours), two or three a day to Polatsk (seven to eight hours), six a day to Homel (five hours), and at least four a day to Vitsebsk (five to six hours), including those to St Petersburg.

Local commuter trains include about seven a day to Baranavichy and about 15 a day to Maladzechna. Times are posted on the wall on the ground floor of the main railway station; the times in red are for weekends only, those in black for weekdays.

Outside, to the left of the main hall, is the underground passage leading to the platforms, with a sign above listing the departing trains.

Buying Tickets Tickets for local electric trains are easily bought from the *kasy* on the ground floor of the railway station.

For long-distance or international tickets, head to the ticket office in the Belintourist office (☎ 26 98 40; fax 23 11 43) at praspekt Masherava 19, next door to the Hotel Jubileynaja; it's open daily from 8 am to 8 pm. Domestic train tickets can be purchased with roubles, including (for the time being) tickets to Russia, Ukraine, and other CIS states except the Baltic states. International tickets, including those to the Baltic states and Poland, must be purchased with hard currency. This office sells most advance train tickets but for a few same-day tickets they may send you to the ticket office on praspekt Skaryny 18, between vulitsa Lenina and Kamsamolskaja. It's open daily, except Sunday, from 9 am to 6 pm (closed between 1 and 2 pm). There's also a more hectic ticket office, across the street from the railway station, which sells only same-day tickets. The most hectic of all are the ticket windows upstairs in the station itself.

Car & Motorbike

The Brestskoe shose, the road from Minsk to Brest (E30/M1), is one of the best in the country – an excellent dual carriageway all the way. Minsk to Smolensk has a few narrow, slow stretches, though patches of forest alleviate its tedium.

Car rental agencies in Minsk include Avis (☎ 34 78 80; fax 38 16 13) upstairs at the Hotel Belarus, vulitsa Starazhouskaja 15, and Eurocar (☎ 26 90 62; fax 23 87 16) at praspekt Masherava 11, upstairs in the Belintourist building next to the Hotel Jubileynaja. Both have offices at the Minsk-2 Airport as well. The Hotel Jubileynaja can also arrange rental cars (with drivers), which are hired by the hour.

GETTING AROUND
To/From the Airport

The taxi drivers who lurk around Minsk-2 Airport are vultures who all want about US$35 to US$50 for the 40-minute ride into the city. You can try to bargain them down (speak Russian if you can) or else wait for one of the infrequent buses (every one to two hours) that take you for the same ride for less than US$1.

Bus & Trolleybus

Buses and trolleybuses serve those parts of the city not covered by the metro system. Trolleybus Nos 1, 2 and 18 ply praspekt Skaryny between ploshcha Nezalezhnastsi and ploshcha Peramohi.

Buses, trolleybuses and trams operate from 5.30 am to 1 am.

Metro

Minsk has two handy metro lines, intersecting at the midpoint of praspekt Skaryny. Ploshcha Nezalezhnastsi metro station has one entrance at the railway station, with that metro line following praspekt Skaryny across the city, stopping in the middle and at ploshcha Peramohi. Plastic tokens called zhetony can be bought downstairs at all stations from the attendant. Purchase a handful (they're very cheap) so you won't be bothered later.

Note that a few metro stations may still have their old names up – ones to look out for are Ploshcha Nezalezhnastsi, which may be marked as Ploshcha Lenina; Ploshcha Peramohi, which may be marked as Ploshcha Pobedy; and Kupalawskaja, which may be marked as Oktjabrskaja.

The metro operates from 6 am to 12.30 am.

AROUND MINSK
ВАКОЛ МІНСКА
Minsk Sea & Zaslavl
Мінскае Мора і Заслаўе

If you have an extra day, there are two sights of interest just outside the city. About 12 km north-west of the centre, just below where the Svislach River meets the 25-square km lake known as the Minsk Sea (Minskoe More), is the small town of Zhdanovichi. Just north of the town is a pleasant pine forest with walking paths that lead to picnic shelters and tables beside the Svislach River. Just east is the dam that forms the Minsk Sea. On the other side of the river from the picnic shelters are more pine forests and trails leading north along the lake shore.

In the small town of Zaslavl, 13 km beyond Zhdanovichi and a km or so west of the Maladzechna road, a rectangular medieval rampart from the 10th century surrounds the 17th century **Transfiguration Church** (Spaso-Preobrazhenskaja), identifiable by its red-roofed white tower. It used to be a museum, but has been renovated and is now operating as a church again. There's not much else to see except a bunch of neglected wooden cottages around the base of the ramparts and another church off the town's main square to the south – but no-one seems to mind if you wander around.

Getting There & Away Praspekt Masherava, which leads north-west from central Minsk, passes beneath the ring road shortly before entering Zhdanovichi. But the easiest way to get to both places is to take one of the frequent electric trains heading to either Maladzechna or Aljakhnovich from the main railway station – between the two there are about 20 a day. Tickets and schedules are on the ground floor of the main railway station. For Zhdanovichi get off after about 20 minutes at the Zhdanovichi station, the stop after the Masyukovshchina station. One stop farther will bring you right to the Minsk Sea. For Zaslavl, stay on for another 20 minutes or so and get off at the Belarus station right in Zaslavl; you'll see the Transfiguration Church on the other side of the tracks to the east, with a cluster of wooden cottages in between. It's the fifth stop after Zhdanovichi, just before the Zelenoe station.

Khatyn
Хатынь

The hamlet of Khatyn, 60 km north of Minsk, was burned to the ground with all its inhabitants in a 1943 Nazi reprisal. The site is now a memorial centred around a sculpture modelled on the only survivor, Yuzif Kaminsky. Also here are the Graveyard of Villages, commemorating 185 other Belarusian villages annihilated by the Germans; the Trees of Life (actually concrete posts) commemorating a further 433 villages that were destroyed but rebuilt; and a Memory Wall listing the Nazi concentration camps in Belarus and some of their victims.

Khatyn is about five km east of the Minsk-Vitsebsk road. The turn-off is about 15 km north of Lohoysk, opposite the village of Kazyny. There's no reliable public transport out there, but a taxi will cost between US$20 and US$25 for the return journey. Belintourist or the Hotel Jubileynaja can rent out cars with drivers for US$10 to US$15 an hour, or else you can rent a car through one of the agencies listed in the Minsk Getting There & Away section. Organised trips through Belintourist run during the summer, and cost about US$10 per person if you latch onto a big group.

Don't confuse Khatyn with the Katyn Forest near Smolensk, where the NKVD (the predecessor of the KGB) murdered thousands of 'enemies of the people' and Polish officers in the 1930s and 1940. Can it be coincidence that when, in the 1960s, the Soviet authorities chose a site to commemorate the Nazis' victims, they picked one whose name might muddle the truth of the Soviet atrocities?

Kurhan Slavy
Курган Славы

At the turn-off for Minsk-2 Airport near the town of Sloboda, about 22 km from central Minsk, is a 35-metre-high mound with an enormous bent fork sticking out of the top. Yes, it's a war memorial. The 'fork' is four giant bayonets and the mound is Kurhan Slavy (Mound of Glory). This time the killers, not the killed, are glorified: Kurhan Slavy commemorates a big Soviet victory here in 1944, when a large German force was surrounded and about 70,000 killed.

Mir
Мір

About 85 km south-west of Minsk and eight km north off the Minsk-Brest road is the small town of Mir where, overlooking a pond, sits a fine 16th-century castle. Built predominantly of stone and red brick, it's a walled complex with five formidable towers surrounding a courtyard and keep. The impressive exterior detailing was intended to be aesthetic as well as defensive. The complex was the personal fortress of the Radziwill family – a Polish noble family who ruled a part of Belarus around this town and who built another palace and fortress ensemble in nearby Njasvizh. Today the castle is under restoration; it may be completed (along with a museum) by the time you arrive. North of town the Usha River flows into the Nioman River through pretty forests with a few small lakes and marshes.

Getting There & Away From the central bus station in Minsk there are about six or seven buses a day heading to the town of Navahrudak (Novogrudok in Russian), stopping in Mir shortly after they turn off the main highway, just over two hours into the trip. Navahrudak itself, about 45 km farther north-west, was once the ancient capital of the Polish-Lithuanian state and is said to have some interesting castle ruins. (See directions for Njasvizh for an alternative way of getting to Mir.)

Njasvizh
Нясвіж

Njasvizh, 120 km from Minsk, is one of the oldest sites in the country and dates from the 13th century. It reached its zenith in the mid-16th century while owned by the mighty Radziwill magnates, who had the town designed and rebuilt with the most advanced system of fortification known to the day. Over the centuries, war, fire and neglect diminished the town's status and today it's a random mix of painted wooden cottages and bland housing, but with enough fine pieces of 16th-century architecture scattered about to happily occupy you for a few hours.

BELARUS

Things to See Walk south-east (to your right) down vulitsa Savetskaja from the bus station. On your right after about five minutes is the 16th-century **town hall**, in the middle of the main square, one of the oldest of its kind surviving in the country. It's shabby and faded but interesting in its design. Off the western corner of the square near the Hotel Njasvizh is the swooping gable of an 18th-century **artisan house**, now housing a library.

Continue south-east down vulitsa Savetskaja. The first street to the right (south) after the main square, vulitsa Chkalava, leads past some wooden cottages straight to the former **Benedictine monastery**, now a pedagogical institute with student dormitories in the former monks' quarters to the right of the courtyard. Only the tower is original late 16th century.

Back on vulitsa Savetskaja, a block farther south-east the street changes name to Slutskaja Gulvar and leads to the 16th-century **Slutsk Gate**, redone in Baroque two centuries later. Once part of a series of fortifications, it still sits at the main entrance into town from the Slutsk road. Across the Zamkayaja Pond to the north the fortress palace rises from the water and wooded embankment.

On the way to the palace you'll pass the impressive **Farny Polish Roman Catholic Church**. Large and sombre, it was built between 1584 and 1593 in early Baroque style and features a splendidly proportioned façade. The building facing it is a former **printing house** where, in the late 16th century, the philosopher Simon Budny printed some controversial works in the Belarusian language (see Literature in the Facts about Belarus chapter for details). Budny's statue stands in front of the printing house.

Just beyond the Farny Church is the striking red-brick arcaded **Castle Gate Tower**. Built in the 16th century, it was part of a wall and gateway controlling the passage between the palace and the town.

The lakes surrounding the town are a popular spot for summertime rowboats. During the long winter months the frozen water can be crowded with young hockey enthusiasts or deserted except for a lone ice fisherman.

Beyond the Farny Church a causeway leads to the 16th-century **Radziwill Palace Fortress** designed by the Italian architect Bernardoni (who was also responsible for the Farny Church). The Bolshevik army marched in and looted the palace in November 1917. Today the complex houses a sanatorium for up to 200 patients with cardiac and neurological disorders.

Farther north of the fortress is **Azerna Park**, laid out in 1878 and in need of a gardener or two. It's still an enjoyable stroll, especially along the water's edge.

Places to Stay & Eat The Hotel Njasvizh (☎ 5 53 67), off the main square on vulitsa Belaruskaja 9, is a friendly place with a sleepy restaurant. Simple and decent rooms cost US$5/7 for a single/double. Near the artisan house on the main square is the *Kafe Teremok* with sweets, drinks and ice cream.

Getting There & Away Buses to Kletsk, about 16 km south of Njasvizh, stop at Njasvizh along the way. Unfortunately, there are only one or two buses a day from the central bus station in Minsk. Alternatively, take one of the six to eight daily electric trains to Baranavichy (tickets and schedules on the ground floor of the main Minsk railway station) and get off at the Haradzeja stop, about two hours (12 stops) from Minsk. This station is between Mir, 15 km to the north, and Njasvizh, 15 km to the south. At least eight buses a day make the 30-minute trip to Njasvizh. Buses leave from in front of the Haradzeja railway station; tickets are bought from the small window in the station. Check the train times back to Minsk (scribbled next to the ticket window) before hopping on a crowded bus to Njasvizh. There are also two buses daily running between Njasvizh and Mir, stopping in Haradzeja en route.

Elsewhere in Belarus
Па Беларусі

Outside Minsk and Brest, the rest of the country sees relatively few tourists. The majority of cities suffered great destruction in WWII, both architecturally and culturally as many of the multiethnic communities were killed or driven out. Yet much still remains to entice the traveller off the beaten path. In cities such as Hrodna and Polatsk many historic vestiges remain, and many of the small villages are still lost somewhere in the 18th century. The countryside is serene with great swathes of forest, clusters of lakes and miles of streams, drawing many campers and hikers from the cities.

With a bit of patience and fortitude, the rest of Belarus is accessible by both train and bus. Inevitably, it will be the people that leave the most lasting impression.

BREST
БРЕСТ
Population: 270,000
One of the busiest road and rail border points in Eastern Europe, Brest lies less than 200 km from Warsaw and 346 km from Minsk. Like all border towns there's a hustle-and-bustle atmosphere, with Belarusians swarming over the border on quick buying forays to supply their kiosks. If you have a spare day it's worth stopping to walk around town and to take in Brest Fortress – a uniquely melodramatic example of that bizarre architectural genre, the aged Soviet war memorial. Requiring more time is the Belavezhskaja Pushcha Nature Reserve, 40 km north. One of the former USSR's biggest commodity markets, known as the Varshavsky Rynok (Warsaw Market), sets up somewhere on Brest's north-western outskirts on weekends. Many of the goods on sale – which range from cosmetics and condoms to guns and computers – are brought in, often illegally, by Poles, who go home, equally illegally, with gold.

History
First mentioned in 1017 and originally known as Bereste, Brest was sacked by the Tatars in 1241. The Uniate Church was set up here in 1596 at the Union of Brest. The Treaty of Brest-Litovsk, negotiated here in March 1918, bought time for the new Soviet government in Russia by surrendering Poland, the Baltic states and most of Ukraine and Belarus to German control. Brest was well inside Poland from 1919 to 1939 but when the Soviet Union and Nazi Germany carved up Poland in September 1939, the town found itself on their frontier. It was therefore the front line when Germany attacked the USSR on 22 June 1941. The two regiments in its fortress held out for a month – a heroic defence for which Brest was named one of the former Soviet Union's 11 'Hero Cities' of WW II – a name it is still proud of.

Orientation & Information
Central Brest, about two km square, fans out south-east from the main railway station to the Mukhavets River. Vulitsa Savetskaja is the main drag and has several pedestrian sections. Brest Fortress lies at the confluence of the Buh and Mukhavets rivers, about two km south-west of the centre down vulitsa Maskouskaja.

If you're heading straight for Minsk by road from the international border point, south of the Mukhavets, the E30 (M1) road crosses the river and bypasses the centre to the south on vulitsa Maskouskaja. The Brest telephone code is 01622.

Churches
From the railway station, cross the footbridge that leads over the train tracks towards the town and head down vulitsa Savetskaja. On the corner of vulitsa Mitskevicha is the attractively detailed 200-year-old **St Nikolaiv**

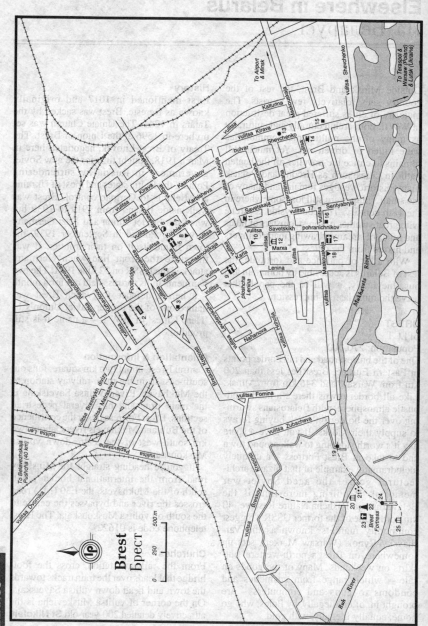

Brest
Брест

0   250   500 m

BELARUS

Church, with traditional Orthodox aesthetics – a pointed bell tower over the entrance and a large central cupola surrounded by a cluster of four lesser domes. A block farther east is the central bus station and circular **market hall**, surrounded on the outside by vendors hawking their cheap wares. Turn right (west) on Pushkinskaja and you'll reach ploshcha Lenina, where a statue of Lenin points east towards Moscow – but, ironically, appears more to be pointing across the street to the 1882 **St Christopher's Polish Catholic Church**.

Next to the Hotel Intourist on vulitsa Maskouskaja is the gold and white 17th-century **St Simon Orthodox Cathedral** with a richly gilded interior – it's the only bright spot in otherwise grey surroundings.

Museums

Three blocks west of vulitsa Savetskaja on the corner of vulitsa Karla Marxa and vulitsa Budyennaha is the **Regional Museum**, which has recently been moved into an attractive former mansion with two cannons sitting out front. It should be open by the time you arrive.

Across the bridge outside the Kholmskie Gate at the Brest Fortress and a short distance to the right (west) is the **Bereste Archaeological Museum**. The main exhibit is part of the artisans' quarter of 13th-century Brest, which has been excavated and preserved under a protective roof. Around the central pit are a number of small, interesting exhibits. The museum is open Wednesday to Sunday from 9 am to 5 pm.

Brest Fortress

Between 1838 and 1842 the entire town of Brest was moved east to make way for a massive fort (Brestskaja krepost) around the confluence of the Buh and Mukhavets rivers. The fort was ruined in the fighting of 1941 and its remains have been turned into a grandiose memorial to its defenders. It's at the western end of vulitsa Maskouskaja; the rare bus No 17 travels between here and the Hotel Intourist, but the walk's not far.

At the main entrance, recorded explosions and gunfire echo from a large, star-shaped opening in a huge concrete mass on top of the old brick outer wall. Also heard is the scratchy 1941 Russian radio broadcast informing of the German attack. Inside, the enormous central monument comes into view – a stone soldier's head projecting from a massive rock, entitled 'Valour'. In front of this are memorial slabs to the defenders around which mournful music plays. Nearby is a tall, slender, metallic obelisk. The back side of the rock has some carved scenes featuring soldiers.

Just as you step on to the island, to your right are the brick ruins of the **White Palace**, where the 1918 Treaty of Brest-Litovsk negotiations were held. You can walk down into the foundations. Farther to the right is the **Defence of Brest Fortress Museum**, which is open Wednesday to Sunday from 9.30 am to 6 pm. Its extensive and dramatic exhibits try hard to glorify the 'heroism' of the defenders.

Behind the Valour rock is the partly ruined shell of the **Nikolaivsky Church**, the oldest church in the city, which dates from when the town centre occupied the fortress site. Once part of a large monastery before being turned into a soldier's garrison club, it was gutted during the 1941 siege. Peek inside at the lovely colonnaded altar.

To the south is the **Kholmskie Gate**; its bricks are decorated with crenulated turrets and its outer face is riddled with hundreds of bullet and shrapnel holes.

Belavezhskaja Pushcha Nature Reserve

About 1300 sq km of primeval European forest survives in the Belavezhskaja Pushcha reserve, which stretches north from the town of Kamjanjuky, about 40 km north of Brest. A small part of it is in Poland, which administers it jointly with Belarus. Some 55 mammal species including elk, deer, lynx, boar, wild horse, wolf, badger, ermine, marten, otter, mink and beaver live here, but it's most celebrated for its 1000 or so European bison – a species which was near extinction in the 1920s before individual animals from Germany and Sweden were brought together here.

There's a **nature museum** and enclosures where you can view bison, deer, boar and other animals. Only a few buses a day go from Brest central bus station to Kamjanjuky, the main town just inside the reserve. To visit the reserve in your own vehicle without a guide you may need a police permit, depending on current regulations. The Hotel Intourist service bureau in Brest can get this for you for the same day if you ask first thing in the morning. The service bureau also sometimes arranges group excursions during the summer, but you may not see much more than the museum and enclosures.

Places to Stay

The *Hotel Intourist* (☎ 5 20 82/3) at vulitsa Maskouskaja 15 is a typical 1970s creation, but well staffed and comfortable. Rooms cost a high US$30/50/75 for singles/doubles/triples, hard currency only. Better value for money is the friendly *Hotel Belarus* (☎ 5 25 66) about a km east along the road at vulitsa Shevchenko 6. Similar, though slightly more run-down singles/doubles cost US$15/30; a deluxe double is US$58. Both hotels can be reached by bus No 6 or trolleybus No 2 or 3 from the railway station. For the Hotel Intourist get off at the Intourist stop; for the Belarus get off at the Maskouskaja stop.

There are also two cheap, seedy hotels near the railway station. The *Hotel Buh* (☎ 5 64 17) at vulitsa Lenina 2, near the vulitsa Ordzhonikidze corner, is the better of the two, with a small restaurant off the lobby and rooms for US$5/12/14 a single double/triple (the triples share a common bath). The *Hotel Maladzyezhnaja* (☎ 6 10 76), two blocks east at vulitsa Kamsamolskaja 6, has triples with common bath for US$6 a person.

Places to Eat

The *Hotel Intourist* has a lively banquet hall with tasty bifshtek and potatoes, and mushroom-stuffed egg appetisers; a full meal costs US$4 to US$5. The band is seemingly the most popular in town. The Hotel Belarus also has a decent restaurant and a tiny *bufetin* (snack bar) in room 304. Nearby, on the corner of vulitsa Maskouskaja and vulitsa Shevchenko, is the *Kafe Bulbjanaja*, a cafeteria-style eatery where a plate scooped high with potatoes and meatballs, along with a limp salad and soup, will cost about a dollar. *Kafe Krez*, on vulitsa Savetskaja 63, just south of vulitsa Hoholja, is an up-market hang-out with German beer on tap and savoury mini-pizzas.

The *Restoran Brest*, on the corner of vulitsa Savetskaja and vulitsa Pushkinskaja, has a menu which boasts beef stroganoff, omelettes and bean soup. The large upstairs dining hall is supposedly open until 5 am.

The best place in town is the *Restoran Indija* on the corner of vulitsa Karla Marxa and vulitsa Hoholja. It's run by an Indian family, and the food is outstanding. Prices are in US dollars, but you can pay in roubles at a poor exchange rate; a full meal costs around US$8 to US$12. The chicken curry and home-made bread are excellent.

Across the street from the St Simon Cathedral on vulitsa Maskouskaja, near the Hotel Intourist, is a *Pinguin* ice-cream shop.

Getting There & Away

Air The airport is about 15 km east of the centre, off the Minsk road. There are occasional flights to places like Moscow, Kiev, Warsaw and St Petersburg. Try the Hotel Intourist's service bureau for flight information.

Bus The central bus station is in the centre of town, next to the market. If you're heading to Hrodna, you may consider a bus because the only train takes the longest possible route via Baranavichy. Head for the ticket office on vulitsa Shevchenko for tickets and information.

Train Brest is an important border crossing on the well-used Warsaw-Minsk-Moscow line. There are at least eight trains a day to Warsaw (four to five hours) and about the same number to Moscow (12 to 15 hours), stopping at Minsk (four to five hours) and Smolensk (Russia) on the way. There are three or four trains daily to Kiev (10 to 15 hours). Other daily trains go to Prague (16 hours), Berlin (12 hours), St Petersburg (23 hours), Kaliningrad (20 hours), Sevastopol (Ukraine, 21 hours), Chernivtsi (Ukraine, 21 hours), Paris (25 hours) and Brussels. There are trains every other day to Odessa (16 hours) and Tallinn (four hours).

Domestic trains, besides those to Minsk, include two a day to Pinsk (three to four hours) and Vitsebsk (13 hours), and one a day to Hrodna (12 hours).

For all trains leaving Brest for Poland, you have to go through customs at the station. This entails filling out another customs form (deklaratsia) as well as producing the original deklaratsia you filled out upon entering the country. This takes some time, so get to the station at least an hour early. International tickets are purchased with hard currency only from the *mezhdunarodnie kassi* (international ticket windows) in the Intourist Hall at the station. There's always a long and frantic line, and sometimes they sell only tickets for travel the same day. It can be frustrating. It's perhaps a better idea to stop in Brest on the way into Belarus and take a train straight through from, say, Minsk, when leaving the country.

If you're buying a ticket to Warsaw, avoid the cheaper electric trains that connect Brest with Warsaw and make many stops en route. These trains are crowded with literally hundreds of 'prospectors' crossing the border to buy and sell cigarettes and booze. The madness trying to get through customs is harrowing. Buy a ticket for one of the main

BELARUS

train lines like Moscow-Warsaw, or Moscow-Prague, that don't stop at the border towns. It's a bit more expensive, but it will save your sanity.

For all domestic trains (say, to Minsk, Pinsk or Polatsk), tickets can be purchased without difficulty (for roubles), in the smaller building, across the tracks and over the pedestrian bridge from the main hall, with the sign *passazhirsky pavilon* (passenger train terminal). Domestic bus and train tickets and information can also be obtained from the ticket offices on bulvar Shevchenko, just up from vulitsa Maskouskaja.

HRODNA
ГРОДНА
Population: 277,000
Hrodna, 282 km west of Minsk, is probably the most picturesque city in all of Belarus simply because it survived the war better than anywhere else and has more historic buildings intact to prove it. Settled since ancient times, it was an important town under the Polatsk princedom and became a crucial outpost on the fringes of Kievan Rus.

Absorbed by Lithuania in the late 14th century, Hrodna fast became a major defensive fort and trading centre. Control quickly shifted to the Polish crown, which built an extensive palace and added several churches to bolster its presence.

After Poland was carved up in 1772, the city went to Russia before being taken by Napoleon on his march to Moscow in 1812. Overrun in WW I, the city was one of the first (after Brest) to be besieged by the invading Germans in 1941. Unlike Brest, it fell easily, suffering far less damage than it did when the Soviet forces came back through at the end of WW II. In the process, the once multi-ethnic population, including a large Jewish contingency, was wiped out. Today it's an industrial and cultural centre and, with its proximity to both Lithuania (42 km) and Poland (24 km), has a bit of a cosmopolitan atmosphere.

The Hrodna telephone code is 0152 for six-digit numbers and 01522 for five-digit numbers.

Orientation
The centre is about two km south-west of the railway station and occupies an elevated portion of land overlooking a shallow bend in the Nioman River to the south. The focus is along the commercial, pedestrian-only vulitsa Savetskaja and the spacious ploshcha Savetskaja at its southern end. Vulitsa Azhyeshka stretches from the railway station to the centre. At No 23, near the railway station, is the attractive 1904-5 Pokrovsky Cathedral, a red and white candy house with blue and gold domes. The bus station is a km south of the railway station down vulitsa Chyrvonaarmejskaja, and a km east of the centre down vulitsa Karla Marxa.

Vulitsa Savetskaja
Vulitsa Savetskaja is a favourite strolling venue – a pleasing strip of cobblestones with curious shops and cafés behind pastel façades. The southern end spills into the wide and elongated **ploshcha Savetskaja**, which in turn ends in an extended, tree-filled park.

The attractive red-brick building at the far northern end of ploshcha Savetskaja, just west of the Farny Cathedral, has a plaque commemorating the first meeting of the Hrodna communists, who gathered there in 1918.

Churches
At the north-eastern corner of ploshcha Savetskaja is the proud and pointy Baroque **Farny Cathedral**, built during Polish rule in the 18th century. Inside is a row of ornate altars leading to a huge main altarpiece constructed of multiple columns interspersed with sculpted saints. Another church once stood to the west on the opposite side of the square. It was damaged in WW II and later razed by the Soviet regime; fragmented foundation ruins mark the spot.

Off the far southern end of ploshcha Savetskaja is the **Bernardine church & monastery**. Built predominantly in Renaissance style in the 16th century, the bell tower was redone with a defiant Baroque flair 250 years later, and again after damage in WW II.

Heading west along vulitsa Novo Zamko-

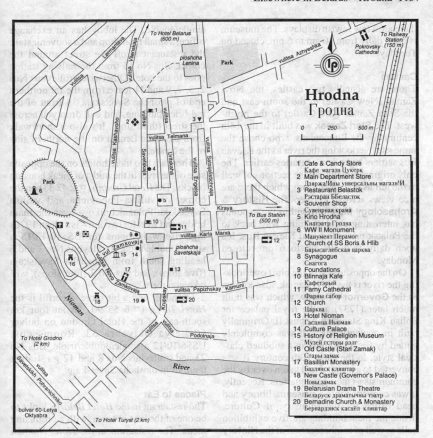

Hrodna
Гродна

0   250   500 m

1 Cafe & Candy Store
 Кафе магазн Цукерк
2 Main Department Store
 Дзяржа!Ины унверсальны магазн!И
3 Restaurant Belastok
 Рэстаран ББеласток
4 Souvenir Shop
 Сувенрная крама
5 Kino Hrodna
 Кнатэатр Гродна
6 WW II Monument
 Манумент Перамог
7 Church of SS Boris & Hlib
 Барысаглебская царква
8 Synagogue
 Снагога
9 Foundations
10 Blinnaja Kafe
 Кафетэрый
11 Farny Cathedral
 Фарны сабор
12 Church
 Царква
13 Hotel Nioman
 Гасцнца Ньюман
14 Culture Palace
15 History of Religion Museum
 Музей гсторы рэлг
16 Old Castle (Stari Zamak)
 Стары замак
17 Basilian Monastery
 Базлянск кляштар
18 New Castle (Governor's Palace)
 Новы замак
19 Belarusian Drama Theatre
 Беларуск драматычны тэатр
20 Bernadine Church & Monastery
 Бернардзнск касцёл кляштар

vaja takes you past the small 16th-century **Basilian monastery** with its dark central dome and simple bell towers. The entrance into the courtyard is around the back.

Just before the castle, take the small road leading down to the right near the river, and you'll find the **Church of SS Boris & Hlib**, a small, unassuming wooden church on a hillside. The two stone curved apses at the rear of the church date from the 12th century, making it the second-oldest surviving structure in the country after St Sophia Cathedral in Polatsk.

Back on vulitsa Novo Zamkovaja, and a

bit farther north, you'll see a dilapidated and abandoned 19th-century **synagogue**, the largest still standing in Belarus.

History of Religion Museum

A short walk west along vulitsa Zamkovaja from the north-western side of ploshcha Savetskaja will lead you to this museum at No 16, housed in a recently renovated 18th-century palace with the crest of Hrodna over the portal. Entered from the courtyard, it has some interesting etchings and artefacts showing predominantly Polish Catholic and Russian Orthodox church influences, though there are a few Jewish displays. The museum is open daily from 10 am to 6 pm, closed on Tuesday.

Castles

There are actually two castles, the Novi Zamak (New Castle) to the south-east and the Stari Zamak (Old Castle) to the north-west. The **Stari Zamak** was built in the 14th century by the Lithuanians, who chose the same site overlooking the river as the Kievan Rus settlers had a few centuries earlier. The only original remains are the sections of wall to the left as you enter, from which there are nice views across the river. The **History & Archaeology Museum** within the grounds has interesting exhibits going way back to the Polatsk princedom and Kievan Rus. It's open daily from 10 am to 6 pm, closed Monday.

On the opposite side of the bluff overlooking the river is the Novi Zamak, also known as the **Governor's Palace**, which was built much later (1737) as the royal palace for Polish King Stanislav August II. Originally built in opulent rococo, it was completely gutted by fire and rebuilt in a subdued classical style. In the early 20th century it was converted to a hospital and taken over by the communists as their headquarters. Recently, it was converted into a museum, library and head office for the Ministry of Culture. Inside the main building are five exhibition halls as well as another section of the **History & Archaeology Museum**, open daily from 10 am to 6 pm, closed Monday.

Places to Stay

The *Hotel Nioman* (☎ 44 17 53) at vulitsa Krupskay 8, off ploshcha Savetskaja, has worn but passable rooms for US$4/8/12 a single/double/triple. All rooms have a sink but the bathroom is down the hall. Only a few larger, five-person rooms (US$15 per person) have a private bath.

Much nicer is the *Hotel Belarus* (☎ 44 16 74) at vulitsa Kalinovskoho 1/2, on the vulitsa Norkoho corner about two km north of ploshcha Savetskaja. The staff is friendly, and the rooms are comfortable at US$7/12 a

single/double. The lobby has an exchange office, a small food shop and a souvenir stall; the restaurant is off the street around the corner. Bus No 15 from the railway station goes to the hotel. Otherwise, trolleybus Nos 2, 3, 7, 9 and 11 leave from the far northern end of ploshcha Savetskaja, in front of the red-brick building, and will drop you across the street (third stop). It's also a short walk from ploshcha Lenina on the northern side of the centre.

There are two more hotels on the opposite side of the river in the midst of bleak housing blocks. The *Hotel Grodno* (☎ 2 42 33) on the corner of vulitsa Popovicha and vulitsa Savetskikh Pohranichniko – over the main bridge and west for two km – is a clean 1970s high-rise with rooms for US$10/13/15 a single/double/triple. Trolleybus Nos 1 and 6 heading south from ploshcha Savetskaja (five stops), and bus No 3 (four stops), will take you there.

Friendlier and a bit more cheerful is the *Hotel Turyst* (☎ 6 55 90), about four km south-east of the Hotel Grodno on bulvar 60-Letya Oktyabra 63. Rooms cost US$6/10/12 a single/double/triple. Bus No 23 and trolleybus Nos 8 and 12 go straight there from ploshcha Savetskaja.

Places to Eat

The restaurant in the *Hotel Belarus* looks to be one of the best in town, with a promising menu. The restaurant in the *Hotel Nioman* does a fair cutlet with soup and potatoes for US$2. The *Hotel Turyst* has a small TV snack bar off the lobby as well as a popular and seemingly proficient restaurant upstairs. The *Hotel Grodno* has a casino next to its restaurant, just in case you get the urge.

The *Restaran Belastok* at the northern end of vulitsa Enhelsa may be worth a try. On vulitsa Savetskaja 5, just north of the ploshcha, is the small stand-up *Blinnaja Kafe* (open 8 am to 3 pm and 4 to 8 pm) which does delicious bliny z miasom or bliny z cerem (pancakes with meat or cheese) for a fraction of a dollar. At the far opposite end of vulitsa Savetskaja, at No 31 – downstairs and to your right – is a café and candy store (open until 9 pm) where you can alternate between shots of vodka, sips of coffee and bites of chocolate. If you have to wait for a late-night train, the *Kafe Zpalet*, upstairs at vulitsa Azhyeshka 30 (across from the Pokrovsky Cathedral), is open until 11 pm and serves a varied selection of drinks and snacks.

Getting There & Away

Train There are three or four trains a day to Minsk (six to eight hours), including a convenient night train; two a day to Polatsk (seven to eight hours); and one a day each to Brest (12 hours) and Vitsebsk (12 hours).

Hrodna lies on the main St Petersburg-Warsaw line. Four trains cross the border to Warsaw each day (six hours) stopping in Białystok along the way. At least two trains a day go to St Petersburg (21 hours), some stopping in Vilnius (three to four hours) along the way and some continuing through Minsk and Vitsebsk before heading directly to Russia. Two trains a day run to Moscow (21 hours) and one a day to Berlin (17 hours).

Electric trains run to a number of outlying towns, including Lida (three hours, twice daily) and Baranavichy (six hours, four times daily), which lies halfway along the Minsk-Brest line. Electric trains also go to Druskininkai in Lithuania (about 1½ hours).

Bus There are daily buses to Minsk (six hours, nine per day) as well as to a number of other destinations.

Getting Around

From the railway station, head left (west) down vulitsa Azhyeshka past the Pokrovsky Cathedral and on for 1.5 km, crossing a stream and vulitsa Satsijalistichnaja just before you reach the northern end of vulitsa Savetskaja. Bus No 3 will take you straight to ploshcha Savetskaja, but the walk is pleasant.

From the bus station, cross the railway tracks and head west down the congested vulitsa Karla Marxa for 1.5 km until it reaches ploshcha Savetskaja. Any trolleybus or bus going down Karla Marxa will take you

there. Bus No 18 runs between the railway and bus stations.

Ploshcha Savetskaja is the central stop for almost all city buses and trolleybuses, and taxis congregate along its western side.

POLATSK
ПОЛАЦК

Population: 125,000

Polatsk, 261 km north of Minsk, is a sleepy riverfront town with a rich history, and is a possible stopover en route to the Baltic states.

Polatsk goes way back to the Varangians in the 6th century. The princedom of Polatsk, first mentioned in 862, was one of the earliest Slav settlements and arguably the birthplace of modern Belarus. Just out of striking range of the Mongol hordes that sacked Kiev in 1240, it was absorbed by the Kingdom of Lithuania and later by Poland, which introduced the Catholic Church and reduced the citizens to serfs under powerful Polish and German landowners. Polatsk prospered as a river port but was continually flung back and forth between the feuding Muscovy tsars and Polish crown, being reduced to rubble more than once. Battles between Napoleonic and tsarist forces were waged here in 1812. The spark of nationalist fervour that arose out of Polatsk in the late 19th century ended with WW I and was sealed with the Soviet takeover shortly after.

Orientation

The centre lies one km south of the railway and bus stations along the east-west praspekt Karla Marxa, which has ploshcha Svabody at its western end, but the most interesting area is along vulitsa Lenina, parallel and one street closer to the Dzvina River from praspekt Karla Marxa.

Things to See

From the railway station, cross the street and walk straight (south) down vulitsa Hoholja for about 15 minutes until it stops at ploshcha Francyska Skaryny, which has a large, elevated statue of Skaryny. The Hotel Dzvina is on your right, its entrance behind a row of columns. The stretch of praspekt Karla Marxa running west from ploshcha Francyska Skaryny for about a km to ploshcha Svabody is the main thoroughfare and has a tree-lined pedestrian lane down the middle.

Ploshcha Svabody is a wide and sombre piece of Soviet planning. The small tombstone in the middle commemorates the spot where a tall monument to the French-Russian war of 1812 once stood. Farther west, where some trees now stand, used to be the large Baroque Nikolaivsky Cathedral, but that was destroyed by the communists in 1964 and replaced by the dismal WW II monument you see there now. To the north lies a large, faded concert hall with oversized Corinthian columns, and beyond are some nicely painted wooden cottages.

Where praspekt Karla Marxa terminates at ploshcha Svabody, vulitsa Krizhovaja leads south, and a block downhill is the 18th-century domed **Bohajavlensky Cathedral**, a working Orthodox church. To the right (west) is the fascinating **Muzey Belarushka Knihadrukavanni** (Belarusian Museum of Historical Books & Printing), which is open Tuesday to Saturday from 10 am to 5 pm and closed Sunday and Monday. From the Bohajavlensky Cathedral turn right (west) down vulitsa Lenina – which runs parallel with the Dzvina River – one of the oldest streets in town and lined with a few charming wooden cottages. At No 11, about 500 metres down, is the small, brick **Regional Historic Museum**, housed in a former Lutheran church from the late 18th century. The museum (open daily except Monday from 10 am to 5 pm) has two floors of interesting historical displays, including numerous artefacts from Polatsk's rich history and some old photos of Nikolaivsky Cathedral before it was destroyed.

St Sophia Cathedral

Farther down vulitsa Lenina is the finely moulded façade of **St Sophia Cathedral**, its twin Baroque bell towers rising high over the Dzvina River. It's the oldest surviving monument of architecture in Belarus and one of two original 11th-century Kievan Rus ca-

thedrals (the other is in Novgorod) which were modelled and named after the St Sophia Cathedral in Kiev. The original 11th-century appearance, however, has long gone. Damaged by fire in the 15th century, it was turned into a military headquarters until the Poles, in the 18th century, reconstructed it – inside and out – as a Baroque Catholic cathedral. The interior is a museum (open daily from 10 am to 5 pm, closed Thursday) with a model inside showing the original Kievan Rus Byzantine appearance. Original 11th-century foundations can be can seen in the vaulted basement along with a number of historic displays. Inside one of the east chapels is a bit of original fresco work. Concerts are regularly given inside the cathedral – ask at the ticket table. There are fine views of a stretch of the Dzvina River from in front of the cathedral.

Places to Stay & Eat

The one hotel in town is the *Hotel Dzvina* (☎ 4 22 35), a stately piece of Soviet Baroque on praspekt Karla Marxa 13, at the north-western corner of ploshcha Francyska Skaryny. Adequate singles/doubles/triples cost US$8/11/12. The restaurant, entered off praspekt Karla Marxa around the corner, serves a decent meal in a semi-elegant atmosphere.

Across ploshcha Skaryny, on the opposite corner of vulitsa Hoholja, is the *Kafe Knatstva* – a typical cafeteria-style eatery where you can get a plate of hot potatoes and meatballs with a salad for about a dollar. There are a few cafés along praspekt Karla Marxa, and the central market is a block south of the railway station.

Getting There & Away

The modern-looking building next to (east of) the older railway station building seems to sell more train tickets, including all the long-distance domestic and international tickets. There's a left-luggage office *(kamera khranennja)* downstairs. The bus station is 100 metres east of the railway station.

Two to three trains a day run to Minsk (seven to eight hours). Polatsk is on an alternative Kaliningrad-Moscow line (most Kaliningrad-Moscow trains go via Vilnius and Minsk) with one or two trains a day to Kaliningrad (20 hours) via Daugavpils in Lithuania (four to five hours), and one or two to Moscow (13 hours) via Vitsebsk (two hours) and Smolensk (five hours). There are four trains a week to Riga (11 to 13 hours), also via Daugavpils. Two trains weekly run to Warsaw (16 to 19 hours, via Minsk). Every other day there's a train to Simferopol (29 hours) stopping in Mahileu (Mogilev; six hours) and Homel (11 hours) en route.

Local electric trains connect Polatsk and Vitsebsk (two hours) about eight times daily.

VITSEBSK
ВІЦЕБСК

Population: 356,000

Vitsebsk, 277 km north of Minsk, once boasted over 30 churches and was a cosmopolitan and cultural centre. WW II and the Soviet legacy took care of all that, replacing what it destroyed with Stalinist planning and industrial might. Yet an air of elegance still lingers in parts of the old town, and it's a lively enough place to warrant a stopover on the way to or from Moscow or St Petersburg, if you have time to spare.

Vitsebsk, like Polatsk, has a rich history going way back to the 6th-century Varangian explorers from Scandinavia who began to settle at strategic river junctions on their migration south. Part of the Polatsk principedom, Vitsebsk was also pulled into the sphere of Kievan Rus, then fell under the Lithuanian and Polish umbrella before being finally pinched by Moscow. Its location at a crossroads and close to a border (only 45 km from Russia) helped promote the city's cultural flair, and it became a haunt for many artists including Kandinsky, Malevich and Chagall (who was born there in 1887).

The Vitsebsk telephone code is 0212.

Orientation

The remnants of the old town lie along a ridge near the confluence of the Dzvina and Luchosa rivers about two km north-east of the railway station. Heading due east from the station is the main thoroughfare, vulitsa Kirava (with a tree-lined pedestrian strip), which becomes vulitsa Zamkovaja after it crosses the river, and vulitsa Frunze after it crosses vulitsa Lenina, the main north-south thoroughfare.

Things to See

From the railway station, bus No 3, 4 or 5 will drop you (after two stops) at the intersection of vulitsa Zamkovaja and vulitsa Lenina, just north of the old town. However, it's a short and pleasant 1.5-km walk from the railway station heading east along vulitsa Kirava and crossing high above the Dzvina River, from where there's a nice view of the old town occupying a low hill to the northeast.

At the intersection, turn left onto vulitsa Lenina. Immediately on the right at No 2 is the **City Art Museum**, which contains temporary exhibitions as well as 18th to 20th-century European works. Continue past the museum to the old **town hall**, distinguished by its clock tower. Across busy vulitsa Lenina is an elevated walkway leading to the modern opera and ballet theatre. Across the street from the old town hall is a building with an outside wall painted with a panorama of spire-filled, historic Vitsebsk. Of the 30-odd churches in the city, those that survived the Soviet purges of the 1930s were then toppled in WW II.

To the left (west) of the town hall and heading north is vulitsa Suvarova, the main street of the old town. Vulitsa Suvarova eventually leads to a pleasant park, but if you turn left halfway there (opposite the Hotel Oridan), into vulitsa Savetskaja, you'll reach a smaller park with a monument to the French-Russian war of 1812. Beyond the memorial graves, a view opens up over the valley. The elegant former palace you see to the left is the still-functioning KGB headquarters.

There are plans to set up a Chagall Museum in the house where the artist was born – ask at the City Art Museum or at the Hotel Oridan.

Places to Stay & Eat

The *Hotel Vitsebsk* (☎ 37 28 35), at vulitsa Zamkovaja 21, is a standard high-rise post-Soviet hotel. It's a km east of the railway station on the other side of the main bridge spanning the Dzvina River. Standard rooms cost US$8/15/35 for a single/double/triple, and there is a restaurant. Much more intimate and expensive is the *Hotel Oridan* (☎ 36 24 56), at vulitsa Savetskaja 21/17 in the old town. Singles/doubles cost US$42/74, and off the lobby is a restaurant.

Getting There & Away

Vitsebsk is on one of the major railway lines heading south from St Petersburg into Ukraine. At least four trains a day run from Vitsebsk to Minsk (five to six hours) and St Petersburg (10 to 13 hours). Two or three trains run to Kiev (16 hours) and there are daily trains to Lviv (25 hours) and Odessa (26 hours). Two trains daily cross the border into Smolensk (three to four hours), one continuing on to Moscow (10 to 11 hours). Four trains a week run to Riga (13 hours) and one a day to Kaliningrad (22 hours), all via Daugavpils in Lithuania (six to seven hours). Trains to Warsaw (14 to 17 hours) run twice a week.

Domestic trains other than those to Minsk include at least two to Brest (13 hours), Hrodna (12 hours), Mahileu/Mogilev (three hours) and Homel (seven to eight hours). Local electric trains connect Polatsk and Vitsebsk (two hours) about eight times daily.

This glossary is a list of words commonly used in Russia (R), Ukraine (U) and Belarus (B).

aeroport – airport
aerovokzal – air terminal in city
apteka – pharmacy
avtobus – bus
avtomat – automatic ticket machine
avtovokzal – bus station

babushka – grandmother
banya – bathhouse
benzin – petrol
bilet – ticket
biznesmen, biznesmenka – literally businessman/woman but often means a small time operator on the fringe of the law
boyar – high-ranking noble
bufet – snack bar, usually in a hotel, selling cheap cold meals, boiled eggs, salads, bread, pastries etc
bulochnaya – bakery
bulvar – boulevard
buterbrod – open sandwich

dacha – country cottage, summer house
datsan – Buddhist monastery
deklaratsia – customs declaration
detdom – orphanage
detsky – child's, children's
Detsky Mir – Children's World, name for many department stores
dezhurnaya – hotel floor lady
dolina – valley
dom – house
dorogoy – expensive
duma – parliament
dvorets kultury – literally culture palace; a meeting, social, entertainment education center, usually for a group like railway workers, chumra etc

elektrichka – suburban train; see also prigorodny poezd
etazh – floor (storey)

finift – multilayered glazed or painted miniatures on metal from 18th and 19th century Rostov Veliky
firmenny poezd – 'name train', usually the best train on its route

GAI (Gosudarstvennaya Avtomobilnaya Inspektsia) – State Automobile Inspectorate, traffic police
gastronom (R) – grocery or specialty food shop
gazeta – newspaper
glasnost – 'openness', the free expression aspect of the Gorbachev reforms
glavpochtamt – main post office
gril-bar – grill bar, often limited to roast chicken
gora – mountain
gorod – city, town
gostinitsa (R) – hotel
Gulag (Glavny Upravlenie Lagerey) – Main Administration for Camps; the Soviet network of concentration camps
GUM (Gosudarstvenny Universmag) – State Department Store

hastronom (U) – grocery or specialty food shop; see also gastronom
hostelnitsa (U) – hotel; see also gostinitsa

ikra – caviar
inostranets – foreigner
Intourist – the old Soviet State Committee for Tourism, now hived off, split up and in competition with hundreds of other travel agencies
istochnik – mineral spring
izba – traditional single-storey wooden cottage
izveshchenie – notification

kafe – cafe
kamera khranenia – left luggage office
kanal – canal
kassa – ticket office, cashier, desk
kater – small ferry

Glossary

This glossary is a list of words commonly used in Russia (R), Ukraine (U) and Belarus (B).

aeroport – airport
aerovokzal – air terminal in city
apteka – pharmacy
avtobus – bus
avtomat – automatic ticket machine
avtovokzal – bus station

babushka – grandmother
banya – bathhouse
benzin – petrol
bilet – ticket
biznesmen, biznesmenka – literally, businessman/woman, but often means a small-time operator on the fringe of the law
boyar – high-ranking noble
bufet – snack bar, usually in a hotel, selling cheap cold meats, boiled eggs, salads, bread, pastries etc
bulochnaya – bakery
bulvar – boulevard
buterbrod – open sandwich

dacha – country cottage, summer house
datsan – Buddhist monastery
deklaratsia – customs declaration
dendrariy – arboretum
detsky – child's, children's
Detsky Mir – Children's World, name for many department stores
dezhurnaya – hotel floor lady
dolina – valley
dom – house
dorogoy – expensive
duma – parliament
dvorets kultury – literally 'culture palace'; a meeting, social, entertainment, education centre, usually for a group like railway workers, children etc

elektrichka – suburban train, see also *prigorodnyy poezd*
etazh – floor (storey)

finift – multilayered glazed or painted miniatures on metal from 18th and 19th century Rostov-Veliky
firmennyy poezd – 'name train', usually the best train on its route

GAI (Gosudarstvennaya Avtomobilnaya Inspektsia) – State Automobile Inspectorate (traffic police)
gastronom (R) – grocery or speciality food shop
gazeta – newspaper
glasnost – 'openness'; the free-expression aspect of the Gorbachev reforms
glavpochtamt – main post office
gril-bar – grill bar, often limited to roast chicken
gora – mountain
gorod – city, town
gostinitsa (R) – hotel
Gulag (Glavny Upravlenie Lagerey) – Main Administration for Camps; the Soviet network of concentration camps
GUM (Gosudarstvenny Univermag) – State Department Store

hastronom (U) – grocery or speciality food shop, see also *gastronom*
hostinitsa (U) – hotel, see also *gostinitsa*

ikra – caviar
inostranets – foreigner
Intourist – the old Soviet State Committee for Tourism, now hived off, split up and in competition with hundreds of other travel agencies
istochnik – mineral spring
izba – traditional single-storey wooden cottage
izveshchenie – notification

kafe – café
kamera khranenia – left-luggage office
kanal – canal
kassa – ticket office, cashier's desk
kater – small ferry

Kazak – Cossack
kemping – camp site, often with small cabins as well as tent sites
khleb – bread
kholm – hill
kipyatok – boiled water
kladbishche – cemetery
klyuch – key
kniga – book
kolkhoz – collective farm
koltsevaya doroga – ring road
kombinat – complex of factories
Komsomol – Communist Youth League
kopek – kopeck; the smallest, almost worthless, unit of Russian currency
komplex – set meal
kray – territory
krazha – theft
kreml – kremlin, a town's fortified stronghold
kruglosutochno – round the clock
krugovoy – round trip
kulak – Stalinist name for a wealthier peasant
kvartira – flat, apartment
kvitantsia – receipt

lavra – senior monastery
lednik – glacier
les – forest

Mafia – anyone who has anything to do with crime, from genuine gangsters to victims of their protection rackets; also applied to anyone who's successful at anything (no-one believes they could have done it legally)
magazin – shop
magizdat – Soviet-era underground music publishing, see also *samizdat*
manezh – riding school
marka – postage stamp or brand, trade mark
marshrut – route
marshrutnoe taxi – minibus that runs along a fixed route
mashina – car
matryoshka – set of painted wooden dolls within dolls
mavzoley – mausoleum
mestnoe vremya – local time
mesto – place, seat

mezhdugorodnyy – intercity
mezhdugorodnyy telefonnyy punkt – long-distance telephone office
mezhdunarodnyy – international
militsia – police
mineralnaya voda – mineral water
more – sea
morskoy vokzal (R), **morsky vokzal** (U) – sea terminal
Moskovskoe vremya – Moscow time
most – bridge
muzey – museum
muzhskoy – men's (toilet)

naberezhnaya – embankment
nomenklatura – literally, 'list of nominees'; the old Communist Party and government elite
novyy – new

obed – lunch
oblast – region
obmen valyuty – currency exchange
okrug – district
ostanovka – bus stop
ostrov – island
ozero – lake

passazhirskiy poezd – intercity stopping train
perestroika – 'restructuring'; Mikhail Gorbachev's attempt to revive the Soviet economy
pereryv – break (when shops, ticket offices, restaurants etc close for an hour or so during the day; this always happens just as you arrive)
pereulok – lane
peshchera – cave
plan goroda – city map
ploshcha (B, U), **ploshchad** (R) – square
pochtamt – post office
poezd – train
poliklinika – medical centre
polyana – glade, clearing
posolstvo – embassy
praspekt (B) – avenue; see also *prospekt*
predvaritelnaya kassa – advance-booking office
prichal – landing, pier

priglashenie – invitation
prigorodnyy poezd – suburban train, see also *elektrichka*
prodazha – sale
proezd – passage
prokat – rental
prospekt (R, U) – avenue; see also *praspekt*
provodnik, provodnitsa – carriage attendant on a train

rabochy den – working day (Monday to Friday)
rayon – district
rechnoy vokzal – river terminal
reka – river
remont – closed for repairs (a sign you'll see all too often)
restoran – restaurant
rubl – rouble; 100 kopecks (see *kopek*)
ruchnoy – handmade
rynok – market

samizdat – Soviet-era underground publishing, see *magizdat*
samolyot – aeroplane
samovar – urn with an inner tube filled with hot charcoal used for heating water for tea
sanitarnyy den – literally 'sanitary day'; the monthly day on which a shop, museum, restaurant, hotel dining room etc shuts down for cleaning
schyot – bill
schyotchik – taxi meter
selo – village
sever – north
shosse – highway
Shvedsky stol – literally, Swedish table; smorgasbord cafeteria
skhema transporta – transport map
skoryy poezd – literally, fast train; a long-distance train
sobor – cathedral
Sodruzhestvo Nezavisimykh Gosudarstv (SNG) – Commonwealth of Independent States (CIS)
soviet – council
sovkhoz – state-owned business for large-scale farming of single crops by paid staff
spravka – certificate
spusk – descent, slope

Sputnik – former youth-travel arm of Komsomol; now just one of the bigger tourism agencies
staryy – old
stolovaya – canteen, cafeteria
sutok – period of 24 hours
suvenir – souvenir

taiga – northern pine, fir, spruce and larch forest
talon – bus ticket, coupon
taxi – taxi
taxofon – pay telephone
teatr – theatre
telegramma – telegram
tovarishch – comrade
traktir – tavern
tramvay – tram
troyka – vehicle drawn by three horses
tserkov – church
tsirk – circus
TsUM (Tsentralny Univermag) – name of department store
tualet – toilet
tuda i obratno – 'there and back', return ticket
turbaza, turistskaya baza (R), **turistsky baza** (U) – tourist camp
turistska stoyanka (U) – camping ground

ulitsa (R) – street; see also *vulitsa*, *vulitsya*
univermag, universalnyy magazin – department store
uzhin – dinner

valyuta – foreign currency
vanna – bath
vareniki (R), **varenyky** (U) – Ukrainian dumplings, with a variety of possible fillings
vkhid (U), **vkhod** (R) – way in, entrance
voda – water
vodnyy vokzal – ferry terminal
vokzal – station
vorovstvo – theft
vostok – east
vulitsa (B), **vulitsya** (U) – street; see also *ulitsa*
vykhid (U), **vykhod** (R) – way out, exit
vykhodnoy den – day off (Saturday, Sunday and holidays)

yantar – amber
yezhednevno – every day
yug – south
yurt – nomad's portable, round tent-house made of felt or skins stretched over a collapsible frame of wood slats

zakaz – reservation
zakaznoe – registration (mail)
zakuski (R), **zakusky** (U) – appetisers
zal – hall, room

zaliv – gulf, bay
zapad – west
zapovednik – (nature) reserve
zavtrak – breakfast
zheleznodorozhnye biletnye kassy – railway ticket office
zheleznodorozhnyy vokzal – railway station
zhenskiy – women's (toilet)
zheton – token (for metro etc)
zona otdykha – leisure area

Appendix I – The Cyrillic Alphabet

Letter	Russian Transliteration	Ukrainian Transliteration	Belarusian Transliteration
А, а	*A, a*	*A, a*	*A, a*
Б, б	*B, b*	*B, b*	*B, b*
В, в	*V, v*	*V, v*	*V,v*
Г, г	*G, g*	*H,h*	*H,h*
Д, д	*D, d*	*D, d*	*D, d*
Е, е	*E, e**	*E, e*	*Je, je*
Ё, ё**	*Yo, yo*	–	*Jo, jo*
Ж, ж	*Zh, zh*	*Zh, zh*	*Zh, zh*
З, з	*Z, z*	*Z, z*	*Z, z*
И, и	*I, i*	*Y, y*	–
Й, й	*Y, y*	*Y, y*	*J, j*
К, к	*K, k*	*K, k*	*K, k*
Л, л	*L, l*	*L, l*	*L, l*
М, м	*M, m*	*M, m*	*M, m*
Н, н	*N, n*	*N, n*	*N, n*
О, о	*O, o*	*O, o*	*O, o*
П, п	*P, p*	*P, p*	*P, p*
Р, р	*R, r*	*R, r*	*R, r*
С, с	*S, s*	*S, s*	*S, s*
Т, т	*T, t*	*T, t*	*T, t*
У, у	*U, u*	*U, u*	*U, u*
Ў, ў	–	–	*W, w*
Ф, ф	*F, f*	*F, f*	*F, f*
Х, х	*Kh, kh*	*Kh, kh*	*Kh, kh*
Ц, ц	*Ts, ts*	*Ts, ts*	*Ts, ts*
Ч, ч	*Ch, ch*	*Ch, ch*	*Ch, ch*
Ш, ш	*Sh, sh*	*Sh, sh*	*Sh, sh*
Щ, щ	*Shch, shch*	*Shch, shch*	–
ъ	(no symbol)	–	–
Ы, ы	*Y, y*	–	*Y, y*
ь	(no symbol)	(no symbol)	(no symbol)
Э, э	*E, e*	–	*E,e*
Ю, ю	*Yu, yu*	*Yu, yu*	*Ju, ju*
Я, я	*Ya, ya*	*Ya, ya*	*Ja, ja*
Є, є	–	*Ye, ye*	–
I, і	–	*I, i*	*I,i*
Ї, ї	–	*Yi, yi*	–

Russian Pronunciation	Ukrainian Pronunciation	Belarusian Pronunciation
like the 'a' in 'father' (if in a stressed syllable)	like the 'a' in 'father'	like the 'a' in 'father'
like the 'a' in 'about' (if in an unstressed syllable)		
like the 'b' in 'but'	like the 'b' in 'but'	like the 'b' in 'but'
like the 'v' in 'van'	like the 'v' in 'van'	like the 'v' in 'van'
like the 'g' in 'god'	like the 'h' in 'hello'	like the 'h' in 'hello'
like the 'd' in 'dog'	like the 'd' in 'dog'	like the 'd' in 'dog'
like the 'ye' in 'yet' (If in a stressed syllable)	like the 'e' in 'end'	like the 'ye' in 'yet'
like the 'yi' in 'yin' (if in an unstressed syllable)		
like the 'yo' in 'yore'	–	like the 'yo' in 'yore'
like the 's' in 'measure'	like the 's' in 'measure'	like the 's' in 'measure'
like the 'z' in 'zoo'	like the 'z' in 'zoo'	like the 'z' in 'zoo'
like the 'ee' in 'meet'	like the 'ee' in 'meet'	–
like the 'y' in 'boy'	like the 'y' in 'boy'	like the 'y' in 'boy'
like the 'k' in 'kind'	like the 'k' in 'kind'	like the 'k' in 'kind'
like the 'l' in 'lamp'	like the 'l' in 'lamp'	like the 'l' in 'lamp'
like the 'm' in 'mad'	like the 'm' in 'mad'	like the 'm' in 'mad'
like the 'n' in 'not'	like the 'n' in 'not'	like the 'n' in 'not'
like the 'o' in 'more' (if in a stressed syllable)	like the 'o' in 'more'	like the 'o' in 'more'
like the 'a' in 'hard' (if in an unstressed syllable)		
like the 'p' in 'pig'	like the 'p' in 'pig'	like the 'p' in 'pig'
like the 'r' in 'rub' (but rolled)	like the 'r' in 'rub' (but rolled)	like the 'r' in 'rub' (but rolled)
like the 's' in 'sing'	like the 's' in 'sing'	like the 's' in 'sing'
like the 't' in 'ten'	like the 't' in 'ten'	like the 't' in 'ten'
like the 'oo' in 'fool'	like the 'oo' in 'fool'	like the 'oo' in 'fool'
–	–	like the 'w' in 'untoward'
like the 'f' in 'fan'	like the 'f' in 'fan'	like the 'f' in 'fan'
like the 'ch' in 'Bach'	like the 'ch' in 'Bach'	like the 'ch' in 'Bach'
like the 'ts' in 'bits'	like the 'ts' in 'bits'	like the 'ts' in 'bits'
like the 'ch' in 'chin'	like the 'ch' in 'chin'	like the 'ch' in 'chin'
like the 'sh' in 'shop'	like the 'sh' in 'shop'	like the 'sh' in 'shop'
like the 'sh ch' in 'fresh chips'	like the 'sh ch' in 'fresh chips'	–
('hard sign'; see text)	–	–
like the 'i' in 'ill'	–	like the 'i' in 'ill'
('soft sign'; see text)	('soft sign'; see text)	('soft sign'; see text)
like the 'e' in 'end'	–	like the 'e' in 'end'
like the 'u' in 'use'	like the 'u' in 'use'	like the 'u' in 'use'
like the 'ya' in 'yard' (if in a stressed syllable)	like the 'ya' in 'yard'	like the 'ya' in 'yard'
like the 'ye' in 'yearn' (if in an unstressed syllable)		
–	like the 'ye' in 'yet'	–
–	like the 'i' in 'ill'	like the 'i' in 'ill'
–	like the 'yi' in 'yin'	–

Using the Chart

Russian, Ukrainian and Belarusian all use the Cyrillic alphabet, each with a slightly different combination of letters. The chart shows, for each of the three languages, the transliterations (Roman-letter equivalents) used in this book, and pronunciations. English words used as illustrations have British pronunciations.

Ukrainian and Belarusian use an apostrophe ' to separate a consonant from the vowel that follows it. Thus the word reads as if by syllable.

Exceptions we make to the general transliteration rules are as follows:

* The Russian ending -ия and the Ukrainian and Belarusian ending -ія are transliterated -ia.
* кс is transliterated x.
* The ending -ье is transliterated -ie.
* The ending -ьи is transliterated -yi for Russian.
* The endings -ый and -ий *in names* are transliterated -y. In writing a few words this book bows to common English usages that are at variance with our systems – thus Tchaikovsky, Gorbachev, Kiev, nyet and soviet, not Chaykovsky, Gorbachyov, Kyiv, net or sovet.

* The Cyrillic letter Е, е is transliterated *Ye, ye* when at the beginning of a word in Russian
** The Cyrillic letter Ё, ё is often printed without dots in Russian

Appendix II – Alternative Place Names

The lists show some variants you may come across for place names used in this book. The following abbreviations are used:

(B) Belarusian
(E) English
(G) German
(L) Lithuanian
(K) Kazakh
(M) Mongolian
(R) Russian
(S) Soviet name
(U) Ukrainian

RUSSIA

Black Sea – Chyornoe More (R)
Dnepr (River) – Dnipro (U), Dnjapro (B)
Izhevsk – Ustinov (S)
Kaliningrad – Königsberg (G)
Kurshskaya kosa – Courland Spit (E), Kuršiu nerija or Neringa (L), Kurische Nehrung (G)
Lake Ladoga – Ladozhskoe ozero (R)
Lake Onega – Onezhskoe ozero (R)
Lake Peipus – Chudskoe ozero (R)
Nizhny Novgorod – Gorky (S)
Rybinsk – Andropov (S)
St Petersburg – Sankt-Peterburg (R), Leningrad (S)
Sakha (republic) – Yakutia (S)
Samara – Kuybyshev (S)
Sergiev Posad – Zagorsk (S)
Svetlogorsk – Rauschen (G)
Tver – Kalinin (S)
Vladikavkaz – Ordzhonikidze (S)
White Sea – Beloe More (R)
Yekaterinburg – Sverdlovsk (S)
Zelenogradsk – Cranz (G)
Zemlya Frantsa-Iosifa – Franz Josef Land (E)

UKRAINE

Bilhorod-Dnistrovsky – Belgorod-Dnestrovsky (R)
Chernihiv – Chernigov (R)
Chernivtsi – Chernovtsy (R)
Chornobyl – Chernobyl (R)
Dnipro (River) – Dnepr (R), Dnjapro (B)
Dnipropetrovsk – Dnepropetrovsk (R)
Hluchiv – Glukhov (R)
Ivano-Frankivsk – Ivano-Frankovsk (R)
Izmayil – Izmail (R)
Kamyanets-Podilski – Kamenets-Podilsky (R)
Kharkiv – Kharkov (R)
Khmelnytsky – Khmelnitsky (R)
Kiev – Kyiv (U)
Kirovohrad – Kirovograd (R)
Krivy Rih – Krivoy Rog (R)
Luhansk – Lugansk (R), Voroshilovgrad (S)
Lviv – Lvov (R)
Mariupol – Zhdanov (S)
Mukacheve – Mukachevo (R)
Ostroh – Ostrog (R)
Pochaiv – Pochaev (R)
Rivne – Rovno (R)
Ternopil – Ternopol (R)
Uzhhorod – Uzhgorod (R)
Vinnytsya – Vinnitsa (R)
Zaporizhzhya – Zaporozhie (R)
Zhytomyr – Zhitomir (R)

BELARUS

Belarus – Belorussia (S)
Baranavichy – Baranovichi (R)
Dnjapro (River) – Dnepr (R), Dnipro (U)
Ezjaryshcha – Yezerishche (R)
Homel – Gomel (R)
Horodeja – Gorodeya (R)
Hrodna – Grodno (R)
Mahileu – Mogilyov (R)
Malaryta – Malorita (R)
Maldzechna – Molodechno (R)
Mazyr – Mozir (R)
Navahrudak – Novogrudok (R)
Polatsk – Polotsk (R)
Vitsebsk – Vitebsk (R)

AUSTRIA

Vienna – Vena (R)

1171

CHINA
Beijing – Pekin (R)
Harbin – Kharbin (R)
Manzhouli – Manchzhuria (R)
Shenyang – Shenyan (R)
Ürümqi – Urumchi (R)

CZECH REPUBLIC
Prague – Praga (R)

FINLAND
Helsinki – Khelsinki (R)

GERMANY
Hannover – Gannover (R)

GREECE
Athens – Afiny (R)

HUNGARY
Budapest – Budapesht (R)
Debrecen – Debretsen (R)
Zahony – Zakhon (R)

KAZAKHSTAN
Aktau – Shevchenko (S), Aqtau (K)
Aqmola – Tselinograd (S/R)
Aktyubinsk – Aqtöbe (K)
Almaty – Alma-Ata (R/S)
Atyrau – Gurev (R/S)
Karaganda – Qaraghandy (K)
Kustanay – Qostanay (K)
Petropavlovsk – Petropavl (K)
Semey – Semipalatinsk (R)

KYRGYZSTAN
Bishkek – Frunze (S)

LITHUANIA
Vilnius – Vilnyus (R)

MOLDOVA
Chisinau – Kishinyov (R)

MONGOLIA
Darkhan – Darhan (M)
Sukhe-Bator – Suhbaatar (M)
Ulan Bator – Ulaan Baatar (M)

NORTH KOREA
Pyongyang – Pkhyonyan (R)

POLAND
Białystok – Belostok (R)
Braniewo – Branevo (R)
Elblag – Elblong (R)
Gdynia – Gdynya (R)
Krakow – Krakov (R)
Kuźnica Bialostocka – Kuznitsa (R)
Olsztyn – Olshtyn (R)
Przemysl – Pshemysl (R)
Warsaw – Varshava (R)

SLOVAKIA
Čierna-nad-Tisou – Chierna-nad-Tissoy (R)
Košice – Koshitse (R)

TURKMENISTAN
Ashghabat – Ashkhabad (R)
Turkmenbashi – Krasnovodsk (S/R)

Appendix III – Climate Charts

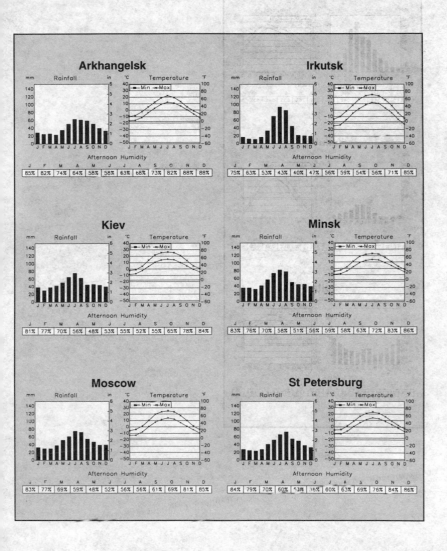

Arkhangelsk

Rainfall (mm / in) · **Temperature** (°C / °F) — Min, Max

Afternoon Humidity

J	F	M	A	M	J	J	A	S	O	N	D
85%	82%	74%	64%	58%	58%	63%	68%	73%	82%	88%	88%

Irkutsk

Rainfall (mm / in) · **Temperature** (°C / °F) — Min, Max

Afternoon Humidity

J	F	M	A	M	J	J	A	S	O	N	D
75%	63%	53%	43%	40%	47%	56%	59%	54%	56%	71%	85%

Kiev

Rainfall (mm / in) · **Temperature** (°C / °F) — Min, Max

Afternoon Humidity

J	F	M	A	M	J	J	A	S	O	N	D
81%	77%	70%	56%	48%	53%	55%	52%	55%	65%	78%	84%

Minsk

Rainfall (mm / in) · **Temperature** (°C / °F) — Min, Max

Afternoon Humidity

J	F	M	A	M	J	J	A	S	O	N	D
83%	76%	70%	58%	51%	56%	59%	58%	63%	72%	83%	86%

Moscow

Rainfall (mm / in) · **Temperature** (°C / °F) — Min, Max

Afternoon Humidity

J	F	M	A	M	J	J	A	S	O	N	D
83%	77%	69%	59%	48%	52%	56%	56%	61%	69%	81%	85%

St Petersburg

Rainfall (mm / in) · **Temperature** (°C / °F) — Min, Max

Afternoon Humidity

J	F	M	A	M	J	J	A	S	O	N	D
84%	79%	70%	60%	51%	56%	60%	63%	69%	76%	84%	86%

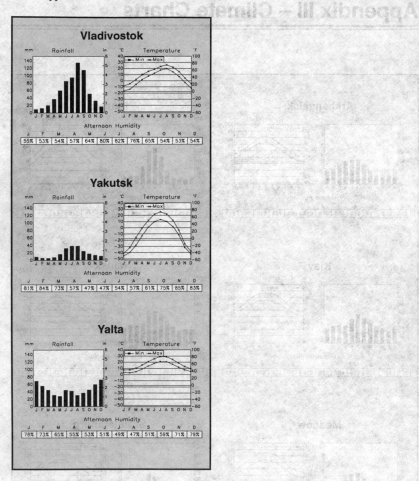

Vladivostok

Rainfall

Temperature

Afternoon Humidity

J	F	M	A	M	J	J	A	S	O	N	D
55%	53%	54%	57%	64%	80%	82%	76%	65%	54%	53%	54%

Yakutsk

Rainfall

Temperature

Afternoon Humidity

J	F	M	A	M	J	J	A	S	O	N	D
81%	84%	73%	57%	47%	47%	54%	57%	61%	75%	85%	83%

Yalta

Rainfall

Temperature

Afternoon Humidity

J	F	M	A	M	J	J	A	S	O	N	D
78%	73%	65%	55%	53%	51%	49%	47%	51%	59%	71%	79%

Index

TEXT

Map references are in **bold** type

ACKNOWLEDGMENTS

Lines on page 574 from *The Gulag Archipelago* by Aleksandr Solzhenitsyn, translated from the Russian by Thomas P Whitney and Harry Willetts. The English translation © Harper & Row, Publishers, Inc. 1973, 1974, 1975, 1978. ©The Russian Social Fund. Reproduced by permission of The Harvill Press.

THANKS

Thanks to those travellers who took the time and trouble to write to us about their experiences in the former USSR. Writers (apologies if we've misspelt your name) to whom thanks must go include:

Stephen Abraham (UK), Tord Akerbaek (N), Benet Allen (UK), Thomas Anderson (USA), Mrs A Andrews (Aus), Jose Azkarrage (Sp), Frank Baard (SA), Jim Barrows (USA), Adam Bartlett, Adam Bedkowski (UK), Paul Bello (USA), Geoff Bennett (UK), Roger Beund (CH), Cas Bijlholt (Nl), Ian Birbeck (UK), Hans Bjorkman (S), Arnold Blades (Aus), William Blatt (USA), Daniel M Bleed (USA), Luke Bosman (UK), David Bowers (Aus), Steve Bradley (NZ), Birgit Brauer (USA), Ruth Brown (USA), Mike Burkett (UK), Christopher Camponovo (USA), Juliet Chamberlain (UK), Joanne Chamberlin (USA), John & Kim Chesarek (USA), Polly Chilchik (UK), Mary Chrestenson (USA), Neil Clarksen (UK), Cynthia Connolly (USA), Timothy Coonen (C), Tom Coupe (UK), Kevin Crawford (UK), Dr Michel Dagonneau (F), Joe David (USA), Adam Davies (UK), Cait Davis (UK), Jane Davis (USA), Olivia D de Cartaret (UK), Dr Krzysztof Debnicki (Pl), Betty Dechert (USA), Benedicte B Denizet (USA), Christine Diefenbacher (D), Lloyd Donaldson (Aus), Maud Edjdeholt (S), Bob Egan (USA), Eli S Eisenhard (USA), Jo Eliot (USA), Carolyn Ellis (USA), Derek Emson (UK), Ferdinand Fellinger (A), Roel Forceville (B), Mary Fox (UK), Tom Freeman (Aus), Nickolaus Frey (USA), Eric Frykman (USA), Tom Garcia (USA), Piotr Gasyrski (Pl), Paul Geldhof (B), Liam Guitar (Aus), Luek Haas (F), Lucy Harris (UK), Eric Haws (USA), Todd Hedrick (USA), Arjan Heere (Nl), Paul Henderson & Marjorie Dawson (UK), Regina Henry (USA), Marianne Herrscher (D), Gabriele Holtschmidt (D), Philip Hopkins (Aus), Kelsey Hoppe (USA), Wendy Hughes (UK), Fiona Husheer (UK), Nikolai Ivanov (Rus), Laurel Jacobson (USA), Laurie Jensen (UK), Ronny Johannessen (N), Helen Jones (UK), M Kedzierski (UK), C Kerby

(N), Wendy Kertzman (USA), Antonina Kisliakov (Aus), Christoph Knorre (D), Shepard Kopp (USA), Pavel Koutsenko (T), S Lee (UK), Ernst Lennartz (D), Fiona MacGillivray, Calum MacLeod, Glenn Mair (Aus), N H K Mallett (UK), Karel Martens (Nl), Anna Maspero (I), Katarzuna Mazurkiewicz (Pl), John McClure (USA), Christina McElroy (USA), Elizabeth McLaughlin (Aus), Claus Michelfelder (D), Steve Miles (UK), Tara Miller (Aus), Paul & Susan Mitchell (USA), Georges Moneyron (F), Sara S Moore (USA), Roger Morgan (UK), Ana Mulder (Nl), John Nobles (UK), Siobahn O'Hegarty (Irl), Christoph Oelke (D), Gary Ogden (UK), Leonardo Pagliarin (I), Jan Passoff, Felix Patton (Aus), Pier Paolo Piciucco (I), Wendy Pilmer (UK), David Pinder (UK), John Porter (Aus), Nancy Shari Pretzer (USA), Brooke Ratliff (USA), Christopher Rea (Aus), Anne-Sophie Redisch (N), Keith Richmond (UK), Guy Russell (UK), Ilmar Saar (USA), Andrew Sandor (USA), Luis Santiago (B), Robert Schwartz (USA), Thomas Schweiger (A), E B Seemann (UK), Anatoli Semenov (Rus), Erik Slavenas (Aus), Raphael Smith (USA), Gerald Sorg (D), Carole Spiers (UK), Gretchen Stanton (F), Alexander Statiev (Rus), John Steedman (UK), Steven Steinbrecher (USA), Itzy Stone (Aus), Ann-Sofie Svensson (S), Bob Swacker (USA), Rob Taylor (UK), Mark Thompson (UK), Alexander Tourkov (Rus), Julle Tuuliainen (Fin), Heleen van der Beek (B), Wim van Ginkel (Nl), David Vanes (UK), Satish Vangal (Ind), Hans Verboom (Nl), Steve Vojtecky (USA), George Von der Muhll (USA), Till von Feilitzsch (D), Alex von Furstenberg (USA), Leisel Wagner (H), Steven Wakefield (UK), C Walker (NZ), Michael Walker (USA), Marianne Wilkens (Nl), Andrew Wiseman (UK), Torsten Wolf, Rashit Yahin (Rus), Athol Yates (Aus), Helmut Zettl (A), Lloyd Zinverferth, Adam Sebire & Kate Glover (Aus), Geoff Cox (UK), Jane Hepburn (UK), L Akal (Russ), Marion Rimmer & L Bowers (Aus), Mike & Sherry DiBari (USA), Paul Hubers (USA), Rob Taylor (UK), Thomas Whitcroft (USA), John McMahon (UK), Niklas Becker (D), Stephen Kenmar (Aus)

A – Austria, Aus – Australia, B – Belgium, CH – Switzerland, D – Germany, F – France, Fin– Finland, H – Hungary, I – Italy, Ind – India, Irl – Ireland, N – Norway, NZ – New Zealand, Pl –Poland, Rus – Russia, SA – South Africa, SL – Sri Lanka, Sp – Spain, S – Sweden, T – Taiwan, UK – United Kingdom, USA – United States of America

Update – August 1996

Petty crime and zealous officials bent on fining foreigners for minor infringements continue to be the major dangers for travellers. Watch out for more commonplace hazards such as bad driving and poor roads, and a tendency to overcharge foreigners. Russia is undergoing a spate of gangster-style crime which can be very violent but is not targetted at tourists.

GETTING THERE & AWAY
Aeroflot no longer has direct flights from Australia, but some Qantas, Thai Air and British Airways flights from Sydney connect with Aeroflot in Singapore, Bangkok and Kuala Lumpur.

RUSSIA
The Russian economy remains a basket case. Production is down by 50%, investment by 66% and living standards by 28%. There is no money to pay state pensions, 37 million people subsist below the poverty line and the death toll from organised crime is higher than Russian losses in Afghanistan.

International economists blame either lack of aid from the developed world (which was promised but arrived about four years too late) or the sell-off of the huge state industries, which produced a climate where corruption could flourish. Corruption has led to an utter lack of trust and a lack of forward planning. Despite all this, France and Germany are pressing for Russia to be admitted to the Group of Seven (which would become the Group of Eight), comprising the richest industrial nations, and Boris Yeltsin hosted a Group of Seven meeting in Moscow just before the Russian presidential election.

As was widely expected, the election became a contest between Yeltsin and Communist Party leader Gennady Zyuganov. Zyuganov attracted voters nostalgic for the stability and security of the Communist past – and lamenting the loss of superpower status. Yeltsin campaigned on his ability to control the country and to beat organised

Dear traveller
Prices go up, good places go bad, bad places go bankrupt...and every guidebook is inevitably out-dated in places. Fortunately, many travellers write to us about their experiences, telling us when things have changed. If we reprint a book between editions, we try to include the best of this information in an Update section. We also make travellers' tips immediately available on our award-winning World Wide Web Internet site (http://www.lonelyplanet.com) and in a free quarterly newsletter, *Planet Talk*.

Although much of this information has not been verified by our own first-hand research, we believe it can be very useful. We cannot vouch for its accuracy, however, so bear in mind that it could be wrong.

We really enjoy hearing from people out on the road, and apart from guaranteeing that others will benefit from your good and bad experiences, we're prepared to bribe you with an offer of a free book for sending us substantial useful information.

I hope you do find this book useful – and that you let us know when it isn't. Thank you to everyone who has written.

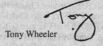

Tony Wheeler

crime, neither of which had been notable successes for him.

The wild card in the electoral pack, however, was former general Alexander Lebed, who scored so well in the first round of voting that Yeltsin promptly appointed him national security adviser. With Lebed's supporters on side, Yeltsin went on to win the second round by a comfortable margin despite the fact that he disappeared from public view during the last week of the campaign. Even on the eve of his inauguration in August, more than a month later, the president had hardly been seen in public since before the election and the state of his health was a close secret. Yeltsin had two heart attacks during 1995, but aides denied rumours that his heart problems had resurfaced or that he had suffered a mild stroke and said instead that he was extremely tired after the rigorous election campaign.

Visas

Responsibility for the issuance of triple and multiple-entry visas has been shifted to the ministry of foreign affairs from OVIR. According to an article in the *St Petersburg Press*, this means that foreigners who want visas of this kind will have to buy them at a Russian consulate in their home country. The article said that while the cost of such visas varies from consulate to consulate, the average cost is about US$350.

The effect of such changes to the average traveller in Russia will be slight (the changes target resident business people). However, the article suggests that these changes are in retaliation for restrictions on Russians in foreign countries, and given that it's unlikely that major countries will change their visa policies, travellers can expect more restrictions in Russia.

St Petersburg

Part of St Petersburg's Metro closed in late 1995 after damage caused by water leaking from an underground river. A section of the Kirovsko-Vyborgskaya line between Lesnaya and Ploshchad Muzhestva remained closed at last report, although free buses were connecting the two stations.

Chechnya

The Chechen war continues. In May 1996, in the lead-up to the Russian presidential election, a meeting between Boris Yeltsin and the Chechen rebel leader Zelimkhan Yandarbiev resulted in a shaky ceasefire, but this did not hold for long. Russian forces resumed attacks on villages in the south of Chechnya shortly after Yeltsin's re-election on 3 July, and in early August a group of rebel fighters came down from the mountains and took control of much of the capital, Grozny. The Russians replied with air attacks, shelling and fighting in the streets, and the rebels were not expected to hold the territory they had won for long. Much of Grozny was damaged and many buildings destroyed.

Yandarbiev had taken over as leader of the rebels after Jokar Dudaev was reportedly killed during a Russian rocket attack in April 1996. In July, however, a rebel field commander, Salman Raduev, whom the Russians claimed to have killed in March, appeared to Chechen and foreign TV camera crews and claimed that the reports of Dudaev's death were as inaccurate as those of his own demise. There has been no confirmation of reports – or should that be rumours? – that Dudaev is alive and recovering from his wounds in Turkey.

UKRAINE

The 10th anniversary of the Chernobyl nuclear disaster was observed in April 1996. There were several conferences, high-minded speeches and much public concern for the victims, old, new and future. There has been a big increase in death rates in surrounding areas, caused by the radiation levels. The problem is not going away and could get worse for a long time to come. Scientific debate still rages about what actually happened before and during the explosion in the reactor. Until that is known, the safety of similar reactors still in use must be in doubt. Experts say that the roof of the Chernobyl reactor's concrete 'tomb' is in danger of collapse and there is still nuclear fuel inside.

Meanwhile, the deserted farmlands near the reactor are being gradually taken over by people too worried about their next meal to care about the grave risk from the radiation levels.

BELARUS

In mid-1996 Belarusian president Alexander Lukashenko stepped up the level of confrontation with his many opponents by demanding that the Supreme Soviet extend his term in office by two years. The country's opposition predicted that, should Lukashenko be thwarted in his bid for increased powers, he would be prepared to declare a state of emergency and override the constitution. Two senior figures from the opposition Belarusian Popular Front, party leader Zenon Poznyak and press secretary Sergei Naumchik, sought political asylum while on a visit to the USA. Earlier in the year, after Lukashenko called for close cooperation with Russia, nationalist protesters took to the streets; police arrested hundreds of them, as well as journalists and opposition politicians.

TRAVELLERS' TIPS & COMMENTS

It is possible to receive money from the US via Western Union, 9MPI Bank 1/3 Bldg 2, Tikhdinskaya St Moscow – contact American Express in the US.

Larissa & Will McCabe

If you are in St Petersburg, try hailing down a private car and get them to take you up to the seat on the Gulf of Finland. It's an amazing sight in winter to see the sea frozen for as far as you can see. There is a small hovercraft which can take you further out to the more precarious spots where fishermen drill holes in the ice.

Adrian Brooks

When travelling on the Trans-Siberian, the No 9 train from Irkutsk to Moscow is more modern and in better condition than trains from Vladivostok to Irkutsk. Travellers' cheques are virtually impossible to cash in Irkutsk. Apparently the only place is the Central Bank, however I didn't try there.

American Express in St Petersburg is now in the Grand Hotel Europe and this is the only place I found in Russia which did not charge commission to change its own travellers' cheques.

Malcolm Miller

In Volgograd, the sign proclaiming the triumph of Lenin's ideas no longer exists. The exchange office indicated as No 15 on the map has moved onto the 2nd floor of the Central Department Store. Some new exchange offices were opened recently: one on ulitsa Gagarina (just where the first letter in the word Gagarina is put); the second on ulitsa Mira (2nd floor, Bank of Constructions, found near Fine Arts Museum); and the third on prospekt Lenina, just opposite No 32 (2nd floor in the shop 'Flowers').

Vladimir Mylnikov

In Irkutsk, it is impossible to buy a 3rd-class train ticket. Every other town I tried to I could, even in Moscow with effort. I took 3rd-class (*platskartnyy*) trains across Russia most of the time. I found all the Russians I met extremely hospitable and I felt completely safe and comfortable in my surroundings.

Heather Fenton

In Belarus, the lowest denomination note now in circulation is 100 Belarusian roubles (one bison). The exchange rate in April 1996 was 13,000 Belarusian roubles to US$1 ... Minsk telephone numbers have an extra '2' added as a prefix ... The DIA ('mili' to the locals) will demand US$20 to US$50 to return a passport given them for inspection. Either pretend you've not got it on you or show it carefully to them – validity and visa pages open – keeping a firm grip.

Vincent Guiry

INTERNET INFO

For the latest travel information check out Lonely Planet's award-winning web site, which contains updates, recent travellers' letters and a useful bulletin board:

http://www.lonelyplanet.com

The *St Petersburg Times* (formerly the *St Petersburg Press*) is an on-line newspaper in English which gives a good insight into life in that city and major news from the country. There are also some interesting classifieds, including accommodation:

http://www.spb.su/times/index.html

ACKNOWLEDGMENTS

The information in this Update was compiled from various sources, including author Nick Selby. Thanks to all the readers who wrote in to tell us about their experiences.

LONELY PLANET JOURNEYS

JOURNEYS is a unique collection of travellers' tales – published by the company that understands travel better than anyone else. It is a series for anyone who has ever experienced – or dreamed of – the magical moment when they encountered a strange culture or saw a place for the first time. They are tales to read while you're planning a trip, while you're on the road or while you're in an armchair, in front of a fire.

JOURNEYS books will catch the spirit of a place, illuminate a culture, recount a crazy adventure, or introduce a fascinating way of life. They will always entertain, and always enrich the experience of travel.

ISLANDS IN THE CLOUDS
Travels in the Highlands of New Guinea
Isabella Tree

This is the fascinating account of a journey to the remote and beautiful Highlands of Papua New Guinea and Irian Jaya. The author travels with a PNG Highlander who introduces her to his intriguing and complex world. *Islands in the Clouds* is a thoughtful, moving book, full of insights into a region that is rarely noticed by the rest of the world.

'One of the most accomplished travel writers to appear on the horizon for many years . . . the dialogue is brilliant' – Eric Newby

LOST JAPAN
Alex Kerr

Lost Japan draws on the author's personal experiences of Japan over a period of 30 years. Alex Kerr takes his readers on a backstage tour: friendships with Kabuki actors, buying and selling art, studying calligraphy, exploring rarely visited temples and shrines . . . The Japanese edition of this book was awarded the 1994 Shincho Gakugei Literature Prize for the best work of non-fiction.

'This deeply personal witness to Japan's wilful loss of its traditional culture is at the same time an immensely valuable evaluation of just what that culture was'
– Donald Richie of the Japan Times

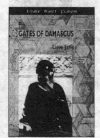

THE GATES OF DAMASCUS
Lieve Joris
Translated by Sam Garrett

This best-selling book is a beautifully drawn portrait of day-to-day life in modern Syria. Through her intimate contact with local people, Lieve Joris draws us into the fascinating world that lies behind the gates of Damascus.

'A brilliant book . . . Not since Naguib Mahfouz has the everyday life of the modern Arab world been so intimately described' – William Dalrymple

SEAN & DAVID'S LONG DRIVE
Sean Condon

Sean and David are young townies who have rarely strayed beyond city limits. One day, for no good reason, they set out to discover their homeland, and what follows is a wildly entertaining adventure that covers half of Australia. Sean Condon has written a hilarious, offbeat road book that mixes sharp insights with deadpan humour and outright lies.

'Funny, pithy, kitsch and surreal . . . This book will do for Australia what Chernobyl did for Kiev, but hey you'll laugh as the stereotypes go boom' – Andrew Tuck, Time Out

LONELY PLANET TRAVEL ATLASES

Lonely Planet has long been famous for the number and quality of its guidebook maps. Now we've gone one step further and in conjunction with Steinhart Katzir Publishers produced a handy companion series: Lonely Planet travel atlases – maps of a country produced in book form.

Unlike other maps, which look good but lead travellers astray, our travel atlases have been researched on the road by Lonely Planet's experienced team of writers. All details are carefully checked to ensure the atlas corresponds with the equivalent Lonely Planet guidebook.

The handy atlas format means no holes, wrinkles, torn sections or constant folding and unfolding. These atlases can survive long periods on the road, unlike cumbersome fold-out maps. The comprehensive index ensures easy reference.

- full-colour throughout
- maps researched and checked by Lonely Planet authors
- place names correspond with Lonely Planet guidebooks
  – no confusing spelling differences
- legend and travelling information in English, French, German, Japanese and Spanish
- size: 230 x 160 mm

Available now:
Thailand; India & Bangladesh; Vietnam;
Zimbabwe, Botswana & Namibia

Coming soon:
Chile; Egypt; Israel; Laos; Turkey

LONELY PLANET TV SERIES & VIDEOS

Lonely Planet travel guides have been brought to life on television screens around the world. Like our guides, the programmes are based on the joy of independent travel, and look honestly at some of the most exciting, picturesque and frustrating places in the world. Each show is presented by one of three travellers from Australia, England or the USA and combines an innovative mixture of video, Super-8 film, atmospheric soundscapes and original music.

Videos of each episode – containing additional footage not shown on television – are available from good book and video shops, but the availability of individual videos varies with regional screening schedules.

Video destinations include: Alaska; Australia (Southeast); Brazil; Ecuador & the Galápagos Islands; Indonesia; Israel & the Sinai Desert; Japan; La Ruta Maya (Yucatán, Guatemala & Belize); Morocco; North India (Varanasi to the Himalaya); Pacific Islands; Vietnam; Zimbabwe, Botswana & Namibia.

Coming soon: The Arctic (Norway & Finland); Baja California; Chile & Easter Island; China (Southeast); Costa Rica; East Africa (Tanzania & Zanzibar); Great Barrier Reef (Australia); Jamaica; Papua New Guinea; the Rockies (USA); Syria & Jordan; Turkey.

The Lonely Planet TV series is produced by:
Pilot Productions
Duke of Sussex Studios
44 Uxbridge St
London W8 7TG UK

Lonely Planet videos are distributed by:
IVN Communications Inc
2246 Camino Ramon
California 94583, USA

107 Power Road, Chiswick
London W4 5PL UK

Music from the TV series is available on CD & cassette.
For ordering information contact your nearest Lonely Planet office.

PLANET TALK

Lonely Planet's FREE quarterly newsletter

We love hearing from you and think you'd like to hear from us.

When...is the right time to see reindeer in Finland?
Where...can you hear the best palm-wine music in Ghana?
How...do you get from Asunción to Areguá by steam train?
What...is the best way to see India?

For the answer to these and many other questions read PLANET TALK.

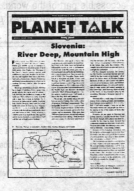

Every issue is packed with up-to-date travel news and advice including:

• a letter from Lonely Planet co-founders Tony and Maureen Wheeler
• go behind the scenes on the road with a Lonely Planet author
• feature article on an important and topical travel issue
• a selection of recent letters from travellers
• details on forthcoming Lonely Planet promotions
• complete list of Lonely Planet products

To join our mailing list contact any Lonely Planet office.

Also available: Lonely Planet T-shirts. 100% heavyweight cotton.

LONELY PLANET ONLINE

Get the latest travel information before you leave or while you're on the road

Whether you've just begun planning your next trip, or you're chasing down specific info on currency regulations or visa requirements, check out the Lonely Planet World Wide Web site for up-to-the-minute travel information.

As well as travel profiles of your favourite destinations (including interactive maps and full-colour photos), you'll find current reports from our army of researchers and other travellers, updates on health and visas, travel advisories, and the ecological and political issues you need to be aware of as you travel.

There's an online travellers' forum (the Thorn Tree) where you can share your experiences of life on the road, meet travel companions and ask other travellers for their recommendations and advice. We also have plenty of links to other Web sites useful to independent travellers.

With tens of thousands of visitors a month, the Lonely Planet Web site is one of the most popular on the Internet and has won a number of awards including GNN's Best of the Net travel award.

http://www.lonelyplanet.com

LONELY PLANET PRODUCTS

Lonely Planet is known worldwide for publishing practical, reliable and no-nonsense travel information in our guides and on our web site. The Lonely Planet list covers just about every accessible part of the world. Currently there are eight series: *travel guides*, *shoestring guides*, *walking guides*, *city guides*, *phrasebooks*, *audio packs*, *travel atlases* and *Journeys* – a unique collection of travellers' tales.

EUROPE

Austria • Baltic States & Kaliningrad • Baltic States phrasebook • Britain • Central Europe on a shoestring • Central Europe phrasebook • Czech & Slovak Republics • Denmark • Dublin city guide • Eastern Europe on a shoestring • Eastern Europe phrasebook • Finland • France • Greece • Greek phrasebook • Hungary • Iceland, Greenland & the Faroe Islands • Ireland • Italy • Mediterranean Europe on a shoestring • Mediterranean Europe phrasebook • Paris city guide • Poland • Prague city guide • Russia, Ukraine & Belarus • Russian phrasebook • Scandinavian & Baltic Europe on a shoestring • Scandinavian Europe phrasebook • Slovenia • St Petersburg city guide • Switzerland • Trekking in Greece • Trekking in Spain • Ukranian phrasebook • Vienna city guide • Walking in Switzerland • Western Europe on a shoestring • Western Europe phrasebook

NORTH AMERICA

Alaska • Backpacking in Alaska • Baja California • California & Nevada • Canada • Hawaii • Honolulu city guide • Los Angeles city guide • Mexico • New England • Pacific Northwest USA • Rocky Mountain States • San Francisco city guide • Southwest USA • USA phrasebook

CENTRAL AMERICA & THE CARIBBEAN

Central America on a shoestring • Costa Rica • Eastern Caribbean • Guatemala, Belize & Yucatán: La Ruta Maya • Jamaica

SOUTH AMERICA

Argentina, Uruguay & Paraguay • Bolivia • Brazil • Brazilian phrasebook • Buenos Aires city guide • Chile & Easter Island • Colombia • Ecuador & the Galápagos Islands • Latin American Spanish phrasebook • Peru • Quechua phrasebook • Rio de Janeiro city guide • South America on a shoestring • Trekking in the Patagonian Andes • Venezuela

AFRICA

Arabic (Moroccan) phrasebook • Africa on a shoestring • Cape Town city guide • Central Africa • East Africa • Egypt & the Sudan • Ethiopian (Amharic) phrasebook • Kenya • Morocco • North Africa • South Africa, Lesotho & Swaziland • Swahili phrasebook • Trekking in East Africa • West Africa • Zimbabwe, Botswana & Namibia • Zimbabwe, Botswana & Namibia travel atlas

ALSO AVAILABLE:

Travel with Children • Traveller's Tales

MAIL ORDER

Lonely Planet products are distributed worldwide. They are also available by mail order from Lonely Planet, so if you have difficulty finding a title please write to us. North American and South American residents should write to Embarcadero West, 155 Filbert St, Suite 251, Oakland CA 94607, USA; European and African residents should write to 10 Barley Mow Passage, Chiswick, London W4 4PH; and residents of other countries to PO Box 617, Hawthorn, Victoria 3122, Australia.

NORTH-EAST ASIA

Beijing city guide • Cantonese phrasebook • China • Hong Kong, Macau & Canton • Hong Kong city guide • Japan • Japanese phrasebook • Japanese audio pack • Korea • Korean phrasebook • Mandarin phrasebook • Mongolia • Mongolian phrasebook • North-East Asia on a shoestring • Seoul city guide • Taiwan • Tibet • Tibet phrasebook • Tokyo city guide

MIDDLE EAST & CENTRAL ASIA

Arab Gulf States • Arabic (Egyptian) phrasebook • Central Asia • Iran • Israel • Jordan & Syria • Middle East • Turkey • Turkish phrasebook • Trekking in Turkey • Yemen

Travel Literature: The Gates of Damascus

ISLANDS OF THE INDIAN OCEAN

Madagascar & Comoros • Maldives & Islands of the East Indian Ocean • Mauritius, Réunion & Seychelles

INDIAN SUBCONTINENT

Bengali phrasebook • Bangladesh • Delhi city guide • Hindi/Urdu phrasebook • India • India & Bangladesh travel atlas• Indian Himalaya• Karakoram Highway • Nepal • Nepali phrasebook • Pakistan • Sri Lanka • Sri Lanka phrasebook • Trekking in the Indian Himalaya • Trekking in the Nepal Himalaya

SOUTH-EAST ASIA

Bali & Lombok • Bangkok city guide • Burmese phrasebook • Cambodia • Ho Chi Minh city guide • Indonesia • Indonesian phrasebook • Indonesian audio pack • Jakarta city guide • Java • Laos • Lao phrasebook • Malaysia, Singapore & Brunei • Myanmar (Burma) • Philippines • Pilipino phrasebook • Singapore city guide • South-East Asia on a shoestring • Thailand • Thailand travel atlas • Thai phrasebook • Thai audio pack • Thai Hill Tribes phrasebook • Vietnam • Vietnamese phrasebook • Vietnam travel atlas

AUSTRALIA & THE PACIFIC

Australia • Australian phrasebook • Bushwalking in Australia• Bushwalking in Papua New Guinea • Fiji • Fijian phrasebook • Islands of Australia's Great Barrier Reef • Melbourne city guide • Micronesia • New Caledonia • New South Wales & the ACT • New Zealand • Northern Territory• Outback Australia • Papua New Guinea • Papua New Guinea phrasebook • Queensland • Rarotonga & the Cook Islands • Samoa • Solomon Islands • South Australia • Sydney city guide • Tahiti & French Polynesia • Tasmania • Tonga • Tramping in New Zealand • Vanuatu • Victoria • Western Australia

Travel Literature: Islands in the Clouds • Sean & David's Long Drive

THE LONELY PLANET STORY

Lonely Planet published its first book in 1973 in response to the numerous 'How did you do it?' questions Maureen and Tony Wheeler were asked after driving, bussing, hitching, sailing and railing their way from England to Australia.

Written at a kitchen table and hand collated, trimmed and stapled, *Across Asia on the Cheap* became an instant local bestseller, inspiring thoughts of another book.

Eighteen months in South-East Asia resulted in their second guide, *South-East Asia on a shoestring*, which they put together in a backstreet Chinese hotel in Singapore in 1975. The 'yellow bible', as it quickly became known to backpackers around the world, soon became *the* guide to the region. It has sold well over half a million copies and is now in its 8th edition, still retaining its familiar yellow cover.

Today there are over 180 titles, including travel guides, walking guides, language kits & phrasebooks, travel atlases and travel literature. The company is one of the largest travel publishers in the world. Although Lonely Planet initially specialised in guides to Asia, we now cover most regions of the world, including the Pacific, North America, South America, Africa, the Middle East and Europe.

The emphasis continues to be on travel for independent travellers. Tony and Maureen still travel for several months of each year and play an active part in the writing, updating and quality control of Lonely Planet's guides.

They have been joined by over 70 authors and 170 staff at our offices in Melbourne (Australia), Oakland (USA), London (UK) and Paris (France). Travellers themselves also make a valuable contribution to the guides through the feedback we receive in thousands of letters each year.

The people at Lonely Planet strongly believe that travellers can make a positive contribution to the countries they visit, both through their appreciation of the countries' culture, wildlife and natural features, and through the money they spend. In addition, the company makes a direct contribution to the countries and regions it covers. Since 1986 a percentage of the income from each book has been donated to ventures such as famine relief in Africa; aid projects in India; agricultural projects in Central America; Greenpeace's efforts to halt French nuclear testing in the Pacific; and Amnesty International.

'I hope we send the people out with the right attitude about travel. You realise when you travel that there are so many different perspectives about the world, so we hope these books will make people more interested in what they see. These are guidebooks, but you can't really guide people. All you can do is point them in the right direction.'
— Tony Wheeler

LONELY PLANET PUBLICATIONS

Australia
PO Box 617, Hawthorn 3122, Victoria
tel: (03) 9819 1877 fax: (03) 9819 6459
e-mail: talk2us@lonelyplanet.com.au

USA
Embarcadero West, 155 Filbert St, Suite 251,
Oakland, CA 94607
tel: (510) 893 8555 TOLL FREE: 800 275-8555
fax: (510) 893 8563
e-mail: info@lonelyplanet.com

UK
10 Barley Mow Passage, Chiswick,
London W4 4PH
tel: (0181) 742 3161 fax: (0181) 742 2772
e-mail: 100413.3551@compuserve.com

France:
71 bis rue du Cardinal Lemoine, 75005 Paris
tel: 1 44 32 06 20 fax: 1 46 34 72 55
e-mail: 100560.415@compuserve.com

World Wide Web: http://www.lonelyplanet.com